$\mathcal{P}$resented to

$\mathcal{R}$ichard $\mathcal{V}$oke

on the occasion of your

Confirmation

by

The Bishop of Edmonton

on 14th September 2003

at All Saints' Church
Child's Hill

† Peter Edmonton

The INSIGHT Bible

The
INS?GHT
Bible

NEW INTERNATIONAL VERSION

NOTES BY PHILIP YANCEY AND TIM STAFFORD

Hodder & Stoughton
LONDON SYDNEY AUCKLAND

The Insight Bible, New International Version

Originally published in the U.S.A. under
the title of
THE STUDENT BIBLE
Copyright © 1986, 1992 by Zondervan Publishing House

Book Introductions, Insights, Highlights, A Line-up of Rulers, Outline of Old
Testament History, Subject Guide, 3-Track Reading Plan, More Track 1
Courses, Overview of Old Testament and New Testament, Where to Find It,
Glossary of Non-biblical People and Places, Why The Insight Bible, copyright
© 1986, 1992 by Zondervan Publishing House. All rights reserved. Used by
permission of Zondervan Publishing House.

European edition published under
special arrangements with
Zondervan Publishing House
Grand Rapids, Michigan, U.S.A.

You will be pleased to know that a portion of the purchase price of your new
NIV Bible has been allocated to the International Bible Society to help spread
the Gospel of Jesus Christ around the world.

British Library Cataloguing in Publication Data is available for this title

*This publication is not included under licences issued by the Copyright Licensing Agency.
Typeset by Auto-Graphics Inc., Pomona, CA 91768. Printed in Great Britain for Hodder &
Stoughton Ltd, Mill Road, Dunton Green, Sevenoaks, Kent, by Richard Clay Ltd, St Ives plc.*

■ CONTENTS

■ THE BOOKS OF THE OLD TESTAMENT

■ THE BOOKS OF THE NEW TESTAMENT

■ ALPHABETICAL ORDER OF BOOKS OF THE BIBLE

The books of the New Testament are indicated by *italics*.

Acts	943	Isaiah	585	Nehemiah	415
Amos	776			Numbers	114
		James	1072		
1 Chronicles	348	Jeremiah	642	Obadiah	784
2 Chronicles	375	Job	437		
Colossians	1033	Joel	771	*1 Peter*	1077
1 Corinthians	992	*John*	917	*2 Peter*	1083
2 Corinthians	1006	*1 John*	1087	*Philemon*	1057
		2 John	1092	*Philippians*	1028
Daniel	746	*3 John*	1094	Proverbs	542
Deuteronomy	149	Jonah	787	Psalms	467
		Joshua	182		
Ecclesiastes	570	*Jude*	1095	*Revelation*	1097
Ephesians	1022	Judges	205	*Romans*	976
Esther	429			Ruth	227
Exodus	50	1 Kings	294		
Ezekiel	703	2 Kings	321	1 Samuel	231
Ezra	404			2 Samuel	260
		Lamentations	696	Song of Songs	579
Galatians	1016	Leviticus	87		
Genesis	3	*Luke*	885	*1 Thessalonians*	1037
				2 Thessalonians	1041
Habakkuk	801	Malachi	821	*1 Timothy*	1044
Haggai	809	*Mark*	863	*2 Timothy*	1050
Hebrews	1059	*Matthew*	831	*Titus*	1054
Hosea	761	Micah	790		
				Zechariah	812
		Nahum	797	Zephaniah	805

■ ACKNOWLEDGMENTS

■ *The Insight Bible* is a carefully anglicised and totally redesigned edition of the *The Student Bible*, the United States' bestselling study Bible. It was conceived by Philip Yancey, the General Editor, to help ordinary people to enjoy regular and beneficial Bible reading. Philip Yancey divides his time between free-lance writing and his responsibilities as Editor at Large for *Christianity Today.* He has written ten books, including *Where is God When It Hurts* and *Disappointment with God.*

■ Tim Stafford wrote many of the notes for the *The Student Bible*, especially in the Old Testament portions. He too divides his time between free-lance writing and editorial responsibilities at *Christianity Today.* His books include *Knowing the Face of God and As Our Years Increase.*

■ In 1992 *The Student Bible*, partly in response to letters from the public, was revised, existing material updated and new features added, including 400 new Highlights and a greatly expanded Subject Guide. This edition has a "parallel passages" feature under many of the sectional headings in Matthew, Mark, Luke, and John, sending you to other places where the same event or teaching is recorded. Note also the Glossary of Non-biblical People and Places at the back of the Bible, where you will find a brief description of names used in Introductions, Insights, and Highlights.

■ The new title for the anglicised edition, *The Insight Bible*, was chosen, partly as a result of a competition, by the Hodder team as it gives an indication of the Bible's aims and draws attention to one of the Bible's special features. Our thanks go to all those who entered the competition and particularly to the winners Gilbert Hart of Stoke on Trent and Jill Black from Ilford, Essex.

■ The design of the Bible and its jacket was carried out by Tony Cantale, with helpful input from Professor Donald Wiseman on behalf of the Committee on Bible Translation.

■ WHY THE INSIGHT BIBLE?

The Bible is the most important book ever written—a gift to us from God himself. Styles and tastes change, but people all through history have recognised the Bible's uniqueness. They have treated it with special reverence.

Yet, strangely, even people who value the Bible often fail to read it. Most Britons believe the Bible to be from God. But Gallup polls reveal that only a small percentage of them can name basic biblical facts, such as four of the Ten Commandments. Their Bibles sit somewhere on a shelf or coffee table, impressive to look at, but unread.

Christians we meet mention repeatedly their guilt about not reading the Bible

consistently. They believe in the Bible. They expect to find help there. But they do not read the Bible nearly as often as they think they should.

Troubled by this reality, we began work on *The Insight Bible*. Our aim: to produce an edition of the New International Version of the Bible that ordinary people could—and would—read on a regular, sustained basis. We used modern research techniques to try to find an answer to the question, "What keeps you from reading the Bible?" We discovered three main reasons. In developing this edition of the Bible, we worked hard to address those three reasons.

■ "I GET DISCOURAGED"

Simple discouragement was the most common reason we heard for not reading the Bible. Many of the people we surveyed had tried to read the Bible regularly, but such experiments usually ended in failure.

The Bible is a big book—about 1,000 pages long. People who plan to read through the whole Bible starting with Genesis often get bogged down somewhere around Numbers or Deuteronomy. Fatigue sets in.

Other people never even start a reading plan. With busy schedules and limited confidence, they feel sure they'll fail at such a project. Instead, they occasionally turn to familiar passages from the Gospel of John or the Psalms. They wouldn't know where to start venturing out into unfamiliar books.

We spent much time and research trying to find an answer to the discouragement problem. The result: the 3-TRACK READING PLAN, which recognises that people approach the Bible at different levels. All three "tracks" suggest reading one chapter a day—just 5 or 10 minutes, for most readers.

the most fundamental parts of the Bible. Pages x–xi present two-week selections on Jesus and Paul, and a two-week sampling of the Old Testament. Pages xiv–xv list a variety of further options, depending on your personal interests. Just a few hours' investment can yield a solid introduction into the best of books.

TRACK 2 represents the next level of commitment. It takes six months, reading about one chapter a day. In Track 2 you will read at least one chapter from every book in the Bible. When you finish, you will have read the best-known, most-quoted, easiest-to-understand portions of the Bible. (The Zondervan book *A Guided Tour of the Bible* offers a more detailed overview of the Bible based on Track 2.)

TRACK 3 includes every word of the Bible. Reading about one chapter a day, you devote three years to reading the entire Bible.

We believe the 3-Track Reading Plan offers a handy, realistic method for approaching the Bible. It builds in several levels of success to combat the discouragement that afflicts Bible readers. A complete description of the 3-track plan follows on the next pages. In addition, the How to Read section in the Introduction to each book of the Bible describes how the 3-track plan fits into that book.

TRACK 1 requires a commitment of two weeks at a time, reading one chapter a day. By following it, a reader can encounter some of

■ "I CAN'T UNDERSTAND IT"

Many readers grow up with very little exposure to the Bible. They may never have heard of Goliath or Abraham. Often they ask, "What is the point of reading about spears and chariots and village wells and leprosy?"

Because it was written several thousand years ago, the Bible presents a culture gap: it mentions hard-to-pronounce names and refers to many outdated customs. For most readers, the Bible is the most ancient book in their library.

Most of us need some coaching on how to jump the 2,000-year gap back to when the Bible was written. *The Insight Bible* addresses this problem with hundreds of additional notes scattered throughout the book.

INTRODUCTION: Each of the 66 books of the Bible is preceded by an Introduction that gives crucial background to the book and tells why it was written. By reading the Introduction, you'll gain a sense of how one particular book is different from, and yet fits together with, every other book in the Bible. In addition, you'll get clues to the book's contemporary relevance.

INSIGHTS: Throughout *The Insight Bible*, you'll find short articles marked "Insight". Written in the style of a modern magazine article, Insights include important background information right in the Bible, near the passage they shed light on. They condense the material that, in our judgment, will most help you understand and find meaning in the Bible. At the end of each Insight, LIFE QUESTIONS help relate the passage to practical life situations.

HIGHLIGHTS: Much shorter notes, called "Highlights", appear frequently in *The Insight Bible*. These explain confusing verses, point out interesting facts, and, in effect, highlight something in the passage that might get overlooked. They're designed to catch your attention and draw you to read the Bible more closely.

■ "I CAN'T FIND IT"

"I spend a lot of time just flipping through the Bible, looking for something," we were told again and again. Many Bible readers are searching for help on specific issues—but they don't know where to find it.

Everybody has heard of something in the Bible: The Ten Commandments, the Golden Rule, the story of Daniel in the lions' den. But how do you know where to look for them? The Bible is too large just to flip through on a random search.

To aid in such a search, *The Insight Bible* contains a SUBJECT GUIDE at the back of the book. The Guide concentrates on major passages, not single verses. Whether you are looking for information about a familiar passage or searching for help with a crucial life question, the Subject Guide should eliminate the "I can't find it" problem.

We hope these notes will help you learn some of the basic facts about the background and message of each book in the Bible. *The Insight Bible* does not, of course, take the place

of a Bible commentary or concordance. It is primarily a *reading* Bible. We believe that the habit of regular Bible reading is the best way for ordinary Christians to become familiar with the full breadth of God's Word.

In publishing *The Insight Bible*, we are not trying to add to the Bible or to enliven it. The Bible speaks for itself. It is the most powerful book ever written, and it needs no help. We, its readers, are the ones who need help, and *The Insight Bible* merely offers practical aids for the average reader. A good measure of our success will be whether this book helps you to read the Bible for yourself. That, after all, is our ultimate goal.

Philip Yancey and Tim Stafford

■ 3-TRACK PLAN FOR READING THE BIBLE

Of all the reasons people mention for not reading the Bible, simple discouragement ranks highest. The Bible's length alone, about 1,000 pages, is imposing. More like a self-contained library than a book, it includes 66 different books, by several dozen authors. Little wonder people get confused and discouraged.

The following 3-Track Reading Plan helps break the Bible into more manageable portions. If you're new to the Bible, begin with Track 1, then proceed to Track 2, and finally—if you're ambitious—tackle Track 3. Your understanding

and appreciation for the Bible should gradually increase.

All three tracks share one thing in common: they each assign usually one chapter a day. Reading an average Bible chapter should take only 5–10 minutes.

The 3-track plan for each book is included within the Introduction to the book (see, for example, "How to Read Genesis", page 4). You can record your progress by checking off the boxes here, or within each individual book.

■ TRACK 1: INTRODUCTION TO THE BIBLE
■ TIME COMMITMENT: TWO WEEKS
■ GOAL: TO SURVEY BASIC BIBLICAL FOUNDATIONS

Track 1 is a place to begin reading the Bible. Three two-week reading courses take you quickly into passages of the Bible every Christian should know. These were selected with two concerns in mind: first, they are frequently quoted or referred to. Second, they are relatively easy to read and

understand. Track 1 is a taster, designed to whet your appetite for more.

If you like Track 1, but feel unready to tackle Track 2, you can find more Track 1 courses on pages xiv–xv.

1. TWO WEEKS ON THE LIFE AND TEACHINGS OF JESUS

- ☐ Day 1 LUKE 1 Preparing for Jesus' arrival
- ☐ Day 2 LUKE 2 The story of Jesus' birth
- ☐ Day 3 MARK 1 The beginning of Jesus' ministry
- ☐ Day 4 MARK 9 A day in the life of Jesus
- ☐ Day 5 MATTHEW 5 The Sermon on the Mount
- ☐ Day 6 MATTHEW 6 The Sermon on the Mount
- ☐ Day 7 LUKE 15 Parables of Jesus

- ☐ Day 8 JOHN 3 A conversation with Jesus
- ☐ Day 9 JOHN 14 Jesus' final instructions
- ☐ Day 10 JOHN 17 Jesus' prayer for his disciples
- ☐ Day 11 MATTHEW 26 Betrayal and arrest
- ☐ Day 12 MATTHEW 27 Jesus' execution on a cross
- ☐ Day 13 JOHN 20 Resurrection
- ☐ Day 14 LUKE 24 Jesus' appearance after resurrection

2. TWO WEEKS ON THE LIFE AND TEACHINGS OF PAUL

- ☐ Day 1 ACTS 9 The conversion of Saul
- ☐ Day 2 ACTS 16 Paul's Macedonian call and a jail-break
- ☐ Day 3 ACTS 17 Scenes from Paul's missionary journey
- ☐ Day 4 ACTS 26 Paul tells his life story to a king
- ☐ Day 5 ACTS 27 Shipwreck on the way to Rome
- ☐ Day 6 ACTS 28 Paul's arrival in Rome
- ☐ Day 7 ROMANS 3 Paul's theology in a nutshell

- ☐ Day 8 ROMANS 7 Struggle with sin
- ☐ Day 9 ROMANS 8 Life in the Spirit
- ☐ Day 10 1 CORINTHIANS 13 Paul's description of love
- ☐ Day 11 1 CORINTHIANS 15 Thoughts on the after-life
- ☐ Day 12 GALATIANS 5 Freedom in Christ
- ☐ Day 13 EPHESIANS 3 Paul's summary of his mission
- ☐ Day 14 PHILIPPIANS 2 Imitating Christ

3. TWO WEEKS ON THE OLD TESTAMENT

- ☐ Day 1 GENESIS 1 The story of creation
- ☐ Day 2 GENESIS 3 The origin of sin
- ☐ Day 3 GENESIS 22 Abraham and Isaac
- ☐ Day 4 EXODUS 3 Moses' encounter with God
- ☐ Day 5 EXODUS 20 The gift of the Ten Commandments
- ☐ Day 6 1 SAMUEL 17 David and Goliath
- ☐ Day 7 2 SAMUEL 11 David and Bathsheba
- ☐ Day 8 2 SAMUEL 12 Nathan's rebuke of the king
- ☐ Day 9 1 KINGS 18 Elijah and the prophets of Baal
- ☐ Day 10 JOB 38 God's answer to Job
- ☐ Day 11 PSALM 51 A classic confession
- ☐ Day 12 ISAIAH 40 Words of comfort from God
- ☐ Day 13 DANIEL 6 Daniel and the lions
- ☐ Day 14. AMOS 4 A prophet's stern warning

■ TRACK 2: EVERY BOOK IN THE BIBLE

■ TIME COMMITMENT: SIX MONTHS
■ GOAL: TO GAIN AN OVERVIEW OF THE ENTIRE BIBLE

Track 2 includes 186 of the 1,189 chapters in the Bible. Many well-known parts of the Bible are not represented, and from some books (Leviticus, for example), you will read only a single chapter. These 186 chapters have been selected because they are understandable to the average reader without commentary. Taken together, they provide a good foundation of Bible understanding.

If you miss a few days, don't worry. Just resume reading when you can, about a chapter a day. In 180 days' total, you will get an overview that includes something from every book in the Bible.

Track 2 recommends reading the Introduction to each book. You may also find it helpful to read the Insights that appear next to the assigned chapters.

GENESIS ☐ 1 ☐ 2 ☐ 3 ☐ 4 ☐ 7 ☐ 8 ☐ 15 ☐ 19 ☐ 22 ☐ 27 ☐ 28 ☐ 37 ☐ 41 ☐ 45
EXODUS ☐ 3 ☐ 10–11 ☐ 14 ☐ 20 ☐ 32
LEVITICUS ☐ 26
NUMBERS ☐ 11 ☐ 14
DEUTERONOMY ☐ 4 ☐ 8 ☐ 28
JOSHUA ☐ 2 ☐ 6 ☐ 7 ☐ 24
JUDGES ☐ 6 ☐ 7 ☐ 16
RUTH ☐ 1
1 SAMUEL ☐ 3 ☐ 16 ☐ 17 ☐ 20
2 SAMUEL ☐ 6 ☐ 11 ☐ 12
1 KINGS ☐ 3 ☐ 8 ☐ 17 ☐ 18
2 KINGS ☐ 5 ☐ 17 ☐ 22
1 CHRONICLES ☐ 17
2 CHRONICLES ☐ 20 ☐ 30 ☐ 32
EZRA ☐ 3
NEHEMIAH ☐ 2 ☐ 8
ESTHER ☐ 4
JOB ☐ 1–2 ☐ 38 ☐ 42
PSALMS ☐ 19 ☐ 23 ☐ 27 ☐ 51 ☐ 84 ☐ 103 ☐ 139
PROVERBS ☐ 4 ☐ 10 ☐ The proverbs listed in "Verbal Dynamite" (page 556)
ECCLESIASTES ☐ 3
SONG OF SONGS ☐ 2
ISAIAH ☐ 6 ☐ 25 ☐ 40 ☐ 52 ☐ 53 ☐ 55
JEREMIAH ☐ 2 ☐ 15 ☐ 31 ☐ 38
LAMENTATIONS ☐ 3

EZEKIEL ☐ 1 ☐ 2–3 ☐ 4 ☐ 37
DANIEL ☐ 1 ☐ 3 ☐ 5 ☐ 6
HOSEA ☐ 2–3 ☐ 11
JOEL ☐ 2
AMOS ☐ 4
OBADIAH ☐ Obadiah
JONAH ☐ 3–4
MICAH ☐ 6
NAHUM ☐ 1
HABAKKUK ☐ 1
ZEPHANIAH ☐ 3
HAGGAI ☐ 1
ZECHARIAH ☐ 8
MALACHI ☐ 3
MATTHEW ☐ 5 ☐ 6 ☐ 13 ☐ 19 ☐ 26 ☐ 27 ☐ 28
MARK ☐ 1 ☐ 2 ☐ 3 ☐ 4 ☐ 5 ☐ 6 ☐ 7 ☐ 8 ☐ 9 ☐ 10 ☐ 11 ☐ 12 ☐ 13 ☐ 14 ☐ 15–16
LUKE ☐ 1 ☐ 2 ☐ 10 ☐ 12 ☐ 15 ☐ 16 ☐ 18 ☐ 24
JOHN ☐ 3 ☐ 6 ☐ 10 ☐ 14 ☐ 15 ☐ 16 ☐ 17 ☐ 20
ACTS ☐ 1 ☐ 2 ☐ 5 ☐ 9 ☐ 16 ☐ 17 ☐ 26 ☐ 27 ☐ 28
ROMANS ☐ 3 ☐ 7 ☐ 8 ☐ 12
1 CORINTHIANS ☐ 13 ☐ 15
2 CORINTHIANS ☐ 4 ☐ 12
GALATIANS ☐ 3
EPHESIANS ☐ 2 ☐ 3
PHILIPPIANS ☐ 2
COLOSSIANS ☐ 1
1 THESSALONIANS ☐ 3–4
2 THESSALONIANS ☐ 2
1 TIMOTHY ☐ 1
2 TIMOTHY ☐ 2
TITUS ☐ 2
PHILEMON ☐ Philemon
HEBREWS ☐ 2 ☐ 11 ☐ 12
JAMES ☐ 1
1 PETER ☐ 1
2 PETER ☐ 1
1 JOHN ☐ 3
2 and 3 JOHN ☐ 2, 3 John
JUDE ☐ Jude
REVELATION ☐ 1 ☐ 12 ☐ 21

■ TRACK 3: EVERY WORD OF THE BIBLE
■ TIME COMMITMENT: THREE YEARS
■ GOAL: TO READ ALL THE WAY THROUGH THE BIBLE WITH UNDERSTANDING

Track 3 takes you completely through the Bible, reading every word. Other Bible-reading plans allot only a year for this project, requiring that at least 3 chapters be read each day. But many readers find such a pace to be unrealistic and discouraging. For this reason, Track 3 assigns usually only one chapter a day. (Some short chapters have been combined, so occasionally you will read two brief chapters in a day.) In all, the reading plan works out evenly to a three-year total.

The Track 3 plan alternates between the Old Testament and New Testament. This mixing provides variety and reduces the fatigue that may set in from reading long sections of the Old Testament.

GENESIS ☐1 ☐2 ☐3 ☐4 ☐5 ☐6 ☐7 ☐8
☐9 ☐10–11 ☐12 ☐13 ☐14 ☐15 ☐16
☐17 ☐18 ☐19 ☐20 ☐21 ☐22 ☐23
☐24 ☐25 ☐26 ☐27 ☐28 ☐29 ☐30
☐31 ☐32 ☐33 ☐34 ☐35 ☐36 ☐37
☐38 ☐39 ☐40 ☐41 ☐42 ☐43 ☐44
☐45 ☐46 ☐47 ☐48 ☐49 ☐50
MATTHEW 1–9 ☐1 ☐2 ☐3 ☐4 ☐5 ☐6 ☐7
☐8 ☐9
EXODUS ☐1 ☐2 ☐3 ☐4 ☐5 ☐6 ☐7 ☐8
☐9 ☐10–11 ☐12 ☐13 ☐14 ☐15 ☐16
☐17 ☐18 ☐19 ☐20 ☐21 ☐22 ☐23
☐24 ☐25 ☐26 ☐27 ☐28 ☐29 ☐30
☐31 ☐32 ☐33 ☐34 ☐35 ☐36 ☐37
☐38 ☐39 ☐40
MATTHEW 10–20 ☐10 ☐11 ☐12 ☐13 ☐14
☐15 ☐16 ☐17 ☐18 ☐19 ☐20
LEVITICUS 1–14 ☐1 ☐2 ☐3 ☐4 ☐5 ☐6
☐7 ☐8 ☐9 ☐10 ☐11–12 ☐13 ☐14
MATTHEW 21–28 ☐21 ☐22 ☐23 ☐24 ☐25
☐26 ☐27 ☐28
LEVITICUS 15–27 ☐15 ☐16 ☐17 ☐18 ☐19
☐20 ☐21 ☐22 ☐23 ☐24 ☐25 ☐26
☐27
MARK 1–8 ☐1 ☐2 ☐3 ☐4 ☐5 ☐6 ☐7
☐8
NUMBERS ☐1–2 ☐3 ☐4 ☐5 ☐6 ☐7 ☐8
☐9 ☐10 ☐11 ☐12 ☐13 ☐14 ☐15
☐16 ☐17 ☐18 ☐19 ☐20 ☐21 ☐22
☐23 ☐24 ☐25 ☐26 ☐27 ☐28 ☐29
☐30 ☐31 ☐32 ☐33 ☐34 ☐35 ☐36
MARK 9–16 ☐9 ☐10 ☐11 ☐12 ☐13 ☐14
☐15–16
DEUTERONOMY 1–17 ☐1 ☐2 ☐3 ☐4 ☐5
☐6 ☐7 ☐8 ☐9 ☐10 ☐11 ☐12 ☐13
☐14 ☐15 ☐16 ☐17
LUKE 1–8 ☐1 ☐2 ☐3 ☐4 ☐5 ☐6 ☐7 ☐8
DEUTERONOMY 18–34 ☐18 ☐19 ☐20 ☐21
☐22 ☐23 ☐24 ☐25 ☐26 ☐27 ☐28
☐29 ☐30 ☐31 ☐32 ☐33 ☐34
LUKE 9–16 ☐9 ☐10 ☐11 ☐12 ☐13 ☐14
☐15 ☐16
JOSHUA ☐1 ☐2 ☐3 ☐4 ☐5 ☐6 ☐7 ☐8
☐9 ☐10 ☐11 ☐12–13 ☐14–15 ☐16–17
☐18 ☐19 ☐20 ☐21 ☐22 ☐23 ☐24

LUKE 17–24 ☐17 ☐18 ☐19 ☐20 ☐21 ☐22
☐23 ☐24
JUDGES ☐1 ☐2 ☐3 ☐4 ☐5 ☐6 ☐7 ☐8
☐9 ☐10 ☐11 ☐12 ☐13 ☐14 ☐15
☐16 ☐17 ☐18 ☐19 ☐20 ☐21
JOHN 1–7 ☐1 ☐2 ☐3 ☐4 ☐5 ☐6 ☐7
RUTH ☐1 ☐2 ☐3 ☐4
1 SAMUEL 1–15 ☐1 ☐2 ☐3 ☐4 ☐5 ☐6
☐7 ☐8 ☐9 ☐10 ☐11 ☐12 ☐13 ☐14
☐15
JOHN 8–14 ☐8 ☐9 ☐10 ☐11 ☐12 ☐13
☐14
1 SAMUEL 16–31 ☐16 ☐17 ☐18 ☐19 ☐20
☐21 ☐22 ☐23 ☐24 ☐25 ☐26 ☐27
☐28 ☐29 ☐30 ☐31
JOHN 15–21 ☐15 ☐16 ☐17 ☐18 ☐19
☐20 ☐21
2 SAMUEL ☐1 ☐2 ☐3 ☐4 ☐5 ☐6 ☐7
☐8 ☐9 ☐10 ☐11 ☐12 ☐13 ☐14 ☐15
☐16 ☐17 ☐18 ☐19 ☐20 ☐21 ☐22
☐23 ☐24
ACTS 1–7 ☐1 ☐2 ☐3 ☐4 ☐5 ☐6 ☐7
1 KINGS 1–11 ☐1 ☐2 ☐3 ☐4–5 ☐6 ☐7
☐8 ☐9 ☐10 ☐11
ACTS 8–14 ☐8 ☐9 ☐10 ☐11 ☐12 ☐13
☐14
1 KINGS 12–22 ☐12 ☐13 ☐14 ☐15 ☐16
☐17 ☐18 ☐19 ☐20 ☐21 ☐22
ACTS 15–21 ☐15 ☐16 ☐17 ☐18 ☐19 ☐20
☐21
2 KINGS ☐1 ☐2 ☐3 ☐4 ☐5 ☐6 ☐7 ☐8
☐9 ☐10 ☐11 ☐12 ☐13 ☐14 ☐15
☐16 ☐17 ☐18 ☐19 ☐20 ☐21 ☐22
☐23 ☐24 ☐25
ACTS 22–28 ☐22 ☐23 ☐24 ☐25 ☐26 ☐27
☐28
1 CHRONICLES 1–14 ☐1–9 ☐10 ☐11 ☐12
☐13 ☐14
ROMANS 1–8 ☐1 ☐2 ☐3 ☐4 ☐5 ☐6 ☐7
☐8
1 CHRONICLES 15–29 ☐15 ☐16 ☐17 ☐18
☐19 ☐20 ☐21 ☐22 ☐23–27 ☐28 ☐29
ROMANS 9–16 ☐9 ☐10 ☐11 ☐12–13 ☐14
☐15–16
2 CHRONICLES 1–18 ☐1 ☐2 ☐3 ☐4 ☐5
☐6 ☐7 ☐8 ☐9 ☐10 ☐11 ☐12 ☐13
☐14 ☐15 ☐16–17 ☐18
1 CORINTHIANS 1–9 ☐1 ☐2 ☐3 ☐4–5 ☐6
☐7 ☐8–9
2 CHRONICLES 19–36 ☐19 ☐20 ☐21 ☐22
☐23 ☐24 ☐25 ☐26–27 ☐28 ☐29 ☐30
☐31 ☐32 ☐33 ☐34 ☐35 ☐36
1 CORINTHIANS 10–16 ☐10 ☐11 ☐12 ☐13
☐14 ☐15 ☐16
EZRA ☐1–2 ☐3 ☐4 ☐5 ☐6 ☐7 ☐8 ☐9
☐10
NEHEMIAH ☐1 ☐2–3 ☐4 ☐5 ☐6 ☐7 ☐8
☐9 ☐10 ☐11 ☐12 ☐13
2 CORINTHIANS ☐1 ☐2–3 ☐4 ☐5 ☐6 ☐7
☐8–9 ☐10 ☐11 ☐12–13

ESTHER □1 □2 □3 □4 □5 □6–7 □8
□9–10
JOB 1–21 □1 □2 □3 □4 □5 □6 □7 □8
□9 □10 □11 □12 □13 □14 □15
□16 □17 □18 □19 □20 □21
GALATIANS □1 □2 □3 □4 □5–6
JOB 22–42 □22 □23 □24 □25–26 □27
□28 □29 □30 □31 □32 □33 □34
□35 □36 □37 □38 □39 □40 □41
□42
EPHESIANS □1 □2 □3 □4 □5 □6
PSALMS 1–40 □1–2 □3–4 □5 □6 □7 □8
□9 □10 □11–12 □13–14 □15–16 □17
□18 □19 □20–21 □22 □23–24 □25
□26 □27 □28–29 □30 □31 □32 □33
□34 □35 □36 □37 □38 □39 □40
PHILIPPIANS □1 □2 □3 □4
PSALMS 41–80 □41 □42–43 □44 □45
□46–47 □48 □49 □50 □51 □52
□53–54 □55 □56 □57 □58 □59
□60–61 □62 □63–64 □65 □66 □67
□68 □69 □70 □71 □72 □73 □74
□75 □76 □77 □78 □79 □80
COLOSSIANS □1 □2 □3 □4
PSALMS 81–121 □81 □82 □83 □84 □85
□86 □87 □88 □89 □90 □91 □92–93
□94 □95 □96 □97 □98–99 □100–101
□102 □103 □104 □105 □106 □107
□108 □109 □110–111 □112 □113
□114 □115 □116–117 □118 □119:1–48
□119:49–96 □119:97–144 □119:145–176
□120–121
1 THESSALONIANS □1–2 □3–4 □5
2 THESSALONIANS □1–2 □3
PSALMS 122–150 □122–123 □124–125
□126–128 □129–130 □131–132
□133–134 □135 □135 □137–138 □139
□140 □141–142 □143 □144 □145
□146 □147 □148 □149–150
PROVERBS □1 □2 □3 □4 □5 □6 □7
□8 □9 □10 □11 □12 □13 □14 □15
□16 □17 □18 □19 □20 □21 □22
□23 □24 □25 □26 □27 □28 □29
□30 □31
1 TIMOTHY □1–2 □3–4 □5 □6
ECCLESIASTES □1 □2 □3 □4 □5 □6
□7 □8 □9 □10 □11 □12
SONG OF SONGS □1 □2 □3 □4 □5 □6
□7 □8
2 TIMOTHY □1 □2 □3 □4
ISAIAH 1–36 □1 □2 □3 □4–5 □6 □7 □8
□9 □10 □11 □12 □13 □14 □15
□16 □17 □18 □19–20 □21 □22 □23
□24 □25 □26 □27 □28 □29 □30
□31 □32 □33 □34 □35 □36

TITUS □1 □2–3
ISAIAH 37–66 □37 □38–39 □40 □41 □42
□43 □44 □45 □46 □47 □48 □49
□50 □51 □52 □53 □54 □55 □56
□57 □58 □59 □60 □61 □62 □63
□64 □65 □66
PHILEMON □Philemon
JEREMIAH 1–26 □1 □2 □3 □4 □5 □6
□7 □8 □9 □10 □11 □12 □13 □14
□15 □16 □17 □18 □19 □20 □21
□22 □23 □24 □25 □26
HEBREWS 1–7 □1 □2 □3–4 □5–6 □7
JEREMIAH 27–52 □27 □28 □29 □30 □31
□32 □33 □34 □35 □36 □37 □38
□39 □40 □41 □42 □43 □44–45 □46
□47 □48 □49 □50 □51 □52
HEBREWS 8–13 □8 □9 □10 □11 □12
□13
LAMENTATIONS □1 □2 □3 □4 □5
EZEKIEL 1–24 □1 □2–3 □4 □5 □6 □7
□8 □9 □10 □11 □12 □13 □14 □15
□16 □17 □18 □19 □20 □21 □22
□23 □24
JAMES □1 □2 □3–4 □5
EZEKIEL 25–48 □25 □26 □27 □28 □29
□30 □31 □32 □33 □34 □35 □36
□37 □38 □39 □40 □41 □42 □43
□44 □45 □46 □47 □48
1 PETER □1 □2 □3 □4–5
DANIEL □1 □2 □3 □4 □5 □6 □7 □8
□9 □10 □11 □12
2 PETER □1 □2 □3
HOSEA □1 □2–3 □4 □5 □6–7 □8 □9
□10 □11–12 □13–14
1 JOHN □1–2 □3 □4 □5
JOEL □1 □2 □3
AMOS □1 □2 □3 □4 □5 □6 □7 □8
□9
OBADIAH □Obadiah
JONAH □1–2 □3–4
2 and 3 JOHN □2 John, 3 John
MICAH □1 □2 □3 □4 □5 □6 □7
NAHUM □1 □2 □3
JUDE □Jude
HABAKKUK □1 □2 □3
ZEPHANIAH □1 □2 □3
REVELATION 1–7 □1 □2 □3 □4–5 □6 □7
HAGGAI □1 □2
REVELATION 8–14 □8 □9 □10–11 □12
□13 □14
ZECHARIAH □1 □2–3 □4–5 □6 □7 □8
□9 □10 □11 □12–13 □14
MALACHI □1 □2 □3–4
REVELATION □15–22 □15–16 □17 □18
□19 □20 □21 □22

■ MORE TRACK 1 COURSES

■ TWO WEEKS ON BECOMING A CHRISTIAN

☐ Day 1 GENESIS 3 The first sin creates a need
☐ Day 2 ISAIAH 52 Salvation prophesied
☐ Day 3 ISAIAH 53 The role of the suffering servant
☐ Day 4 LUKE 15 Three stories about God's love
☐ Day 5 JOHN 3 Jesus explains "born again"
☐ Day 6 JOHN 10 The good shepherd
☐ Day 7 ACTS 8 Conversions spread outside the Jews

☐ Day 8 ACTS 26 Paul testifies of his conversion before a king
☐ Day 9 ROMANS 3 God's provision for sin
☐ Day 10 ROMANS 5 Peace with God
☐ Day 11 GALATIANS 3 Salvation unavailable by obeying the law
☐ Day 12 EPHESIANS 2 New life in Christ
☐ Day 13 1 PETER 1 Future rewards of salvation
☐ Day 14 2 PETER 1 Making your salvation sure

■ TWO WEEKS ON PRAYERS OF THE BIBLE

☐ Day 1 GENESIS 18 Abraham's plea for Sodom
☐ Day 2 EXODUS 15 Moses' song to the Lord
☐ Day 3 EXODUS 33 Moses meets with God
☐ Day 4 2 SAMUEL 7 David's response to God's promises
☐ Day 5 1 KINGS 8 Solomon's dedication of the temple
☐ Day 6 2 CHRONICLES 20 Jehoshaphat prays for victory
☐ Day 7 EZRA 9 Ezra's prayer for the people's sins

☐ Day 8 PSALM 22 A cry to God for help
☐ Day 9 PSALM 104 A prayer of praise
☐ Day 10 DANIEL 9 Daniel's prayer for the salvation of Jerusalem
☐ Day 11 HABAKKUK 3 A prophet's prayer of acceptance
☐ Day 12 MATTHEW 6 The Lord's prayer
☐ Day 13 JOHN 17 Jesus' prayer for his disciples
☐ Day 14 COLOSSIANS 1 Paul's prayer of thanksgiving

■ TWO WEEKS ON THE HOLY SPIRIT

☐ Day 1 JUDGES 14 The Spirit gives Samson strength
☐ Day 2 1 SAMUEL 10 King Saul's experience
☐ Day 3 MATTHEW 3:1–4:10 Role in Jesus' baptism and temptation
☐ Day 4 JOHN 14 Jesus promises the Spirit
☐ Day 5 JOHN 16 The work of the Spirit
☐ Day 6 ACTS 2 The Spirit comes at Pentecost
☐ Day 7 ACTS 10 The Spirit guides Peter to accept Gentiles

☐ Day 8 ROMANS 8 Christians' victory in the Spirit
☐ Day 9 1 CORINTHIANS 2 Wisdom from the Spirit
☐ Day 10 1 CORINTHIANS 12 Gifts of the Spirit
☐ Day 11 1 CORINTHIANS 14 Gifts of tongues and prophecy
☐ Day 12 GALATIANS 5 Life in the Spirit
☐ Day 13 EPHESIANS 4 Unity and gifts
☐ Day 14 1 JOHN 4 Signs of the Spirit

■ TWO WEEKS ON WOMEN OF THE BIBLE

☐ Day 1 GENESIS 2 Eve, the first woman
☐ Day 2 GENESIS 18 Sarah laughs at God's promise
☐ Day 3 GENESIS 24 Rebekah's marriage to Isaac
☐ Day 4 Genesis 27 Rebekah, the manipulative mother
☐ Day 5 JUDGES 4 Deborah's leadership frees her people
☐ Day 6 RUTH 1 Ruth and Naomi's deep friendship
☐ Day 7 1 SAMUEL 1 Hannah prays for a son
☐ Day 8 1 KINGS 17 A poor widow and the prophet Elijah

☐ Day 9 1 KINGS 21 Jezebel, an emblem of wickedness
☐ Day 10 ESTHER 2 Esther is chosen as queen
☐ Day 11 ESTHER 4 Esther's courage at the risk of death
☐ Day 12 LUKE 1 Mary and Elizabeth receive great news
☐ Day 13 LUKE 2 Mary gives birth to Jesus
☐ Day 14 JOHN 11 Mary and Martha and their brother's death

■ TWO WEEKS ON MEN OF THE OLD TESTAMENT

☐ Day 1 JUDGES 6 God calls Gideon to rescue his people
☐ Day 2 JUDGES 7 Gideon conquers his fears—and his enemies
☐ Day 3 1 SAMUEL 3 God calls young Samuel
☐ Day 4 1 KINGS 3 Solomon is given wisdom
☐ Day 5 1 KINGS 19 Elijah runs for his life
☐ Day 6 2 KINGS 5 Elisha heals a powerful foreign general
☐ Day 7 ISAIAH 6 God calls the prophet Isaiah
☐ Day 8 2 KINGS 18 King Hezekiah under military siege
☐ Day 9 2 KINGS 19 Isaiah speaks God's word to King Hezekiah
☐ Day 10 2 CHRONICLES 34 Josiah sets his nation back on course
☐ Day 11 NEHEMIAH 2 Nehemiah courageously begins rebuilding a wall
☐ Day 12 JEREMIAH 38 Jeremiah, in prison, refuses to change his message
☐ Day 13 DANIEL 1 Daniel risks his life in captivity
☐ Day 14 DANIEL 5 Daniel's word to a royal orgy

■ TWO WEEKS ON SOCIAL JUSTICE

☐ Day 1 EXODUS 3 God hears the cries of the slaves
☐ Day 2 LEVITICUS 25 The Year of Jubilee, a time of economic revolution
☐ Day 3 RUTH 2 A poor woman finds help
☐ Day 4 1 KINGS 21 Elijah speaks to a land-grabbing, murderous king
☐ Day 5 NEHEMIAH 5 Nehemiah demands justice for the poor
☐ Day 6 ISAIAH 5 Warning to fun-loving materialists
☐ Day 7 ISAIAH 58 Worship that God appreciates
☐ Day 8 JEREMIAH 34 Freedom for slaves
☐ Day 9 AMOS 2 Sins against God by his own people
☐ Day 10 AMOS 6 Warning to the complacent
☐ Day 11 MICAH 6 What the Lord requires
☐ Day 12 LUKE 3 John the Baptist tells how to prepare for Jesus
☐ Day 13 MATTHEW 6 Jesus speaks on material things
☐ Day 14 JAMES 2 How to treat the rich and the poor

■ TWO WEEKS ON GOD AND NATURE

☐ Day 1 GENESIS 1 God creates the earth
☐ Day 2 GENESIS 2 God creates human beings
☐ Day 3 PROVERBS 8 Wisdom's view of creation
☐ Day 4 GENESIS 7 God preserves the species
☐ Day 5 JOB 38 The greatness of nature
☐ Day 6 JOB 39 The wildness of nature
☐ Day 7 JOB 40 God's mastery of nature
☐ Day 8 PSALM 8 Praise for the Creator
☐ Day 9 PSALM 98 Nature joins in the praise
☐ Day 10 PSALM 104 God sustains the earth
☐ Day 11 ISAIAH 40 The ruler of all creation
☐ Day 12 ROMANS 8 The "groanings" of our present state
☐ Day 13 ISAIAH 65 Preview of a restored earth
☐ Day 14 REVELATION 22 The end of history

■ FURTHER TWO-WEEK COURSES FOR PERSONAL STUDY

Two weeks on Abraham, Isaac, and Jacob:
    GENESIS 12, 13, 15, 17, 18, 19, 22, 24, 27, 28, 29, 31, 32, 33
Two weeks on Moses and the exodus: EXODUS 2, 3, 4, 7, 12, 14, 16, 19, 32; NUMBERS 14; DEUTERONOMY 1, 2, 4, 31
Two weeks on David: 1 SAMUEL 16, 17, 18, 20, 21, 22, 24; 2 SAMUEL 6, 7, 11, 12, 13, 15, 18

■ OVERVIEW: THE OLD TESTAMENT

THE FIVE BOOKS
The first five books of the Bible tell the origins of the Jewish race and culture.

■ GENESIS: The book of beginnings describes creation, the first rebellions against God, and God's choosing of Abraham and his offspring.

■ EXODUS: God rescued the Israelites from slavery in Egypt and led them to the Desert of Sinai. There, he gave Moses the laws to govern the new nation.

■ LEVITICUS: God set up laws for the Israelites, mostly regarding holiness and worship.

■ NUMBERS: Because of their rebellion and disobedience, the Israelites had to wander in a wilderness for 40 years before entering the promised land.

■ DEUTERONOMY: Just before his death, Moses made three emotional farewell speeches, recapping history and warning the Israelites against further mistakes.

HISTORY BOOKS
The next 12 books continue the history of the Israelites: they moved into the land of Canaan and established a kingdom that lasted almost 500 years.

■ JOSHUA: After Moses' death, Joshua commanded the armies that conquered much of the territory in the promised land.

■ JUDGES: The new nation fell into a series of dismal failures. God raised up leaders called "judges".

■ RUTH: This story of love and loyalty between two widows shines out brightly in an otherwise dark period.

■ 1 SAMUEL: Samuel became a transition leader between the time of the judges and that of the kings. He appointed Israel's first king, Saul. After his own failure, Saul tried violently to prevent God's king-elect David from taking the throne.

■ 2 SAMUEL: David, a man after God's own heart, brought the nation together. But after committing adultery and murder, he was haunted by family and national crises.

■ 1 KINGS: Solomon succeeded David, with mixed success. At his death, a civil war tore apart the nation. Successive kings were mostly bad, and the prophet Elijah had dramatic confrontations with King Ahab.

■ 2 KINGS: This book continues the record of the rulers of the divided kingdom. None of the northern kings

followed God consistently, and so Israel was finally destroyed by an invader. The South, Judah, lasted much longer, but finally Babylon conquered Judah and deported its citizens.

■ 1 CHRONICLES: The book opens with the most complete genealogical record in the Bible, then adds many incidents from the life of David (often the same as those in 2 Samuel).

■ 2 CHRONICLES: Often paralleling the books of Kings, this book records the history of the rulers of Judah, emphasising the good kings.

■ EZRA: After being held captive in Babylon for decades, the Jews were allowed to return to their homeland. Ezra, a priest, emerged from one of the first waves of refugees.

■ NEHEMIAH: Nehemiah returned from the Babylonian captivity after the temple had been rebuilt. He concentrated on restoring the protective wall around Jerusalem and joined Ezra in leading a religious revival.

■ ESTHER: This story is set among captive Jews in Persia. A courageous Jewish queen foiled a plan to exterminate her people.

BOOKS OF POETRY
Almost one-third of the Old Testament was originally written in poetry. These books concentrate on questions about pain, God, life, and love.

■ JOB: The best man of his day suffers the greatest personal tragedy. The entire book deals with the question, "Why?"

■ PSALMS: These prayers and hymns cover the full range of human emotion; together, they represent a personal

journal of how to relate to God. Some were also used in public worship services.

■ PROVERBS: The proverbs offer advice on every imaginable area of life. The style of wise living described here leads to a fulfilled life.

■ ECCLESIASTES: A life without God, "under the sun", leads to meaninglessness and despair, says the Teacher in a strikingly modern book.

■ SONG OF SONGS: This beautiful poem celebrates romantic and physical love.

BOOKS OF THE PROPHETS

During the years when kings ruled Israel and Judah, God spoke through prophets. Though some prophets did predict future events, their primary role was to call God's people back to him.

■ ISAIAH: The most eloquent of the prophets, Isaiah analysed the failures of all the nations around him and pointed to a future Messiah who would bring peace.

■ JEREMIAH: Jeremiah led an emotionally tortured life, yet held to his stern message. He spoke to Judah in the last decades before Babylon destroyed the nation.

■ LAMENTATIONS: All Jeremiah's warnings about Jerusalem came true, and Lamentations records five poems of sorrow for the fallen city.

■ EZEKIEL: Ezekiel spoke to the Jews who were captive in Babylon. He often used dramatic stories and "enacted parables" to make his points.

■ DANIEL: A captive in Babylon, Daniel rose to the office of prime minister. Despite intense political pressure, he lived a model life of integrity and left highly symbolic prophecies about the future.

■ HOSEA: By marrying a loose-living wife, Hosea lived out his message: that Israel had committed spiritual adultery against God.

■ JOEL: Beginning with a recent catastrophe in Judah (a locust plague), Joel foretold God's judgment on Judah.

■ AMOS: A country boy, Amos preached to Israel at the height of its prosperity. His grim warnings focused on materialism.

■ OBADIAH: Obadiah warned Edom, a nation bordering Judah.

■ JONAH: Jonah reluctantly went to Nineveh and found Israel's enemies responsive to God's message.

■ MICAH: Micah exposed corruption in every level of society, but closed with a promise of forgiveness and restoration.

■ NAHUM: Long after Jonah had stirred Nineveh to repentance, Nahum foretold the mighty city's total destruction.

■ HABAKKUK: Habakkuk addressed his book to God, not people. In a frank dialogue with God, he discussed problems of suffering and justice.

■ ZEPHANIAH: Zephaniah focused on the coming day of the Lord, which would purge Judah, resulting in a remnant used to bless the entire world.

■ HAGGAI: After returning from the Babylonian captivity, the Jews began rebuilding the temple of God. But before long they set aside that task to work on their own homes. Haggai reminded them to put God first.

■ ZECHARIAH: Writing around the same time as Haggai, Zechariah also urged the Jews to work on the temple. He used a more uplifting approach, describing how the temple would point to the coming Messiah.

■ MALACHI: The last Old Testament prophet, Malachi faced a nation that had grown indifferent. He sought to stir them from apathy.

■ OVERVIEW: THE NEW TESTAMENT

HISTORY BOOKS

The word *gospel* means "good news". Almost half of the New Testament consists of four accounts of the life of Jesus and the good news he brought to earth. Each of these four books, or Gospels, has a different focus and a different audience; taken together, they give a complete picture of Jesus' life and teaching. About a third of their pages are devoted to the events of his last week on earth, including the crucifixion and resurrection. ACTS continues the history into the period after Jesus left earth.

■ MATTHEW: Written to a Jewish audience, this Gospel links the Old and New Testaments. It presents Jesus as the Messiah and King promised in the Old Testament. Matthew emphasises Jesus' authority and power.

■ MARK: Mark probably had pragmatic Roman readers in mind. His Gospel stresses action and gives a straightforward, blow-by-blow account of Jesus' work on earth.

■ LUKE: A doctor, Luke was also a fine writer. His Gospel provides many details of human interest,

especially in Jesus' treatment of the poor and needy. A joyful tone characterises Luke's book.
■ JOHN: John has a different, more reflective style than the other Gospels. Its author selected seven signs that pointed to Jesus as the Son of God and wove together

everything else to emphasise that point.
■ ACTS: Acts relates what happened to Jesus' followers after he left them. Peter and Paul soon emerged as leaders of the rapidly spreading church.

THE LETTERS

The young church was nourished by apostles who set down their beliefs and messages in a series of letters. The first 13 such letters (ROMANS to PHILEMON) were written by the apostle Paul, who led the advance of Christianity to non-Jewish people.

■ PAUL'S LETTERS

■ ROMANS: Written for a sophisticated audience, Romans sets forth theology in a logical, organised form.
■ 1 CORINTHIANS: A very practical book, 1 Corinthians takes up the problems of a tumultuous church in Corinth: marriage, factions, immorality, public worship, and lawsuits.
■ 2 CORINTHIANS: Paul wrote this follow-up letter to defend himself against a rebellion led by certain false apostles.
■ GALATIANS: A short version of the message of Romans, this book addresses legalism. It shows how Christ came to bring freedom, not bondage to a set of laws.
■ EPHESIANS: Although written in jail, this letter is Paul's most optimistic and encouraging. It tells of the advantages a believer has in Christ.
■ PHILIPPIANS: The church at Philippi ranked among Paul's favourites. This friendly letter stresses that joy can be found in any situation.
■ COLOSSIANS: Written to oppose certain cults,

Colossians tells how faith in Christ is complete. Nothing needs to be added to what Christ did.
■ 1 THESSALONIANS: Composed early in Paul's ministry, this letter gives a capsular history of one church, as well as Paul's direct advice about specific problems.
■ 2 THESSALONIANS: Stronger in tone than his first letter to the Thessalonians, the sequel goes over the same topics, especially the church's questions about Christ's second coming.
■ 1 TIMOTHY: As Paul neared the end of his life, he chose young men such as Timothy to carry on his work. His two letters to Timothy form a leadership manual for a young pastor.
■ 2 TIMOTHY: Written just before Paul's death, 2 Timothy offers Paul's final words to his young assistant.
■ TITUS: Titus was left in Crete, a notoriously difficult place to nurture a church. Paul's letter gave practical advice on how to go about it.
■ PHILEMON: Paul urged Philemon, owner of runaway slave Onesimus, to forgive his slave and accept him as a brother in Christ.

■ OTHER LETTERS

■ HEBREWS: No one knows who wrote Hebrews, but it probably first went to Christians in danger of slipping back into Judaism. It interprets the Old Testament, explaining many Jewish practices as symbols that prepared the way for Christ.
■ JAMES: James, a man of action, emphasised the right kind of behaviour for a believer. Someone who calls himself or herself a Christian ought to act like it, James believed, and his letter spells out the specifics.
■ 1 PETER: Early Christians often met violent opposition, and Peter's letter comforted and encouraged Christians who were being persecuted for their faith.
■ 2 PETER: In contrast to Peter's first letter, this one focused on problems that sprang up from the inside. It warns against false teachers.

■ 1 JOHN: John could fill simple words—*light, love, life*—with deep meaning, and in this letter, he elegantly explains basic truths about the Christian life.
■ 2 JOHN: Warning against false teachers, John counselled churches on how to respond to them.
■ 3 JOHN: Balancing 2 John, this companion letter mentions the need to be hospitable to true teachers.
■ JUDE: Jude gave a brief but fiery exposé of heretics.
■ REVELATION: A book of visions and symbols, Revelation is the only New Testament book that concentrates on prophecy. It completes the story, begun in Genesis, of the cosmic battle between good and evil being waged on earth. It ends with a picture of a new heaven and new earth.

■ PREFACE

■ The New International Version is a completely new translation of the Holy Bible made by over a hundred scholars working directly from the best available Hebrew, Aramaic and Greek texts. It had its beginning in 1965 when, after several years of exploratory study by committees from the Christian Reformed Church and the National Association of Evangelicals, a group of scholars met at Palos Heights, Illinois, and concurred in the need for a new translation of the Bible in contemporary English. This group, though not made up of official church representatives, was transdenominational. Its conclusion was endorsed by a large number of leaders from many denominations who met in Chicago in 1966.

Responsibility for the new version was delegated by the Palos Heights group to a self-governing body of fifteen, the Committee on Bible Translation, composed for the most part of biblical scholars from colleges, universities and seminaries. In 1967 the New York Bible Society (now the International Bible Society) generously undertook the financial sponsorship of the project — a sponsorship that made it possible to enlist the help of many distinguished scholars. The fact that participants from the United States, Great Britain, Canada, Australia and New Zealand worked together gave the project its international scope. That they were from many denominations — including Anglican, Assemblies of God, Baptist, Brethren, Christian Reformed, Church of Christ, Evangelical Free, Lutheran, Mennonite, Methodist, Nazarene, Presbyterian, Wesleyan and other churches — helped to safeguard the translation from sectarian bias.

■ How it was made helps to give the New International Version its distinctiveness. The translation of each book was assigned to a team of scholars. Next, one of the Intermediate Editorial Committees revised the initial translation, with constant reference to the Hebrew, Aramaic or Greek. Their work then went to one of the General Editorial Committees, which checked it in detail and made another thorough revision. This revision in turn was carefully reviewed by the Committee on Bible Translation, which made further changes and then released the final version for publication. In this way the entire Bible underwent three revisions, during each of which the translation was examined for its faithfulness to the original languages and for its English style.

All this involved many thousands of hours of research and discussion regarding the meaning of the texts and the precise way of putting them into English. It may well be that no other translation has been made by a more thorough process of review and revision from committee to committee than this one.

■ From the beginning of the project, the Committee on Bible Translation held to certain goals for the New International Version: that it would be an accurate translation and one that would have clarity and literary quality and so prove suitable for public and private reading, teaching, preaching, memorising and liturgical use. The Committee also sought to preserve some measure of continuity with the long tradition of translating the Scriptures into English.

In working towards these goals, the translators were united in their commitment to the authority and infallibility of the Bible as God's Word in written form. They believe that it contains the divine answer to the deepest needs of humanity, that it sheds unique light on our path in a dark world, and that it sets forth the way to our eternal well-being.

The first concern of the translators has been the accuracy of the translation and its fidelity to the thought of the biblical writers. They have weighed the significance of the lexical and grammatical details of the Hebrew, Aramaic and Greek texts. At the same time, they have striven for more than a word-for-word translation. Because thought patterns and syntax differ from language to language, faithful communication of the meaning of the writers of the Bible demands frequent modifications in sentence structure and constant regard for the contextual meanings of words.

A sensitive feeling for style does not always accompany scholarship. Accordingly the Committee on Bible Translation submitted the developing version to a number of stylistic consultants. Two of them read every book of both Old and New Testaments twice — once before and once after the last major revision — and made invaluable suggestions. Samples of the translation were tested for clarity and ease of reading by various kinds of people — young and old, highly educated and less well educated, ministers and laymen.

Concern for clear and natural English — that the New International Version should be idiomatic but not idiosyncratic, contemporary but not dated — motivated the translators and consultants. At the same time, they tried to reflect the differing styles of the biblical writers. In view of the international use of English, the translators sought to avoid obvious Americanisms on the one hand and obvious Anglicisms on the other. A British edition reflects the comparatively few differences of significant idiom and of spelling.

As for the traditional pronouns "thou", "thee" and "thine" in reference to the Deity, the translators judged that to use these archaisms (along with old verb forms such as "doest", "wouldest" and "hadst") would violate accuracy in translation. Neither Hebrew, Aramaic nor Greek uses special pronouns for the persons of the Godhead. A present-day translation is not enhanced by forms that in the time of the King James Version were used in everyday speech, whether referring to God or man.

■ For the Old Testament the standard Hebrew text, the Masoretic Text as published in the latest editions of *Biblia Hebraica*, was used throughout. The Dead Sea Scrolls contain material bearing on an earlier stage of the Hebrew text. They were consulted, as were the Samaritan Pentateuch and the ancient scribal traditions relating to textual changes. Sometimes a variant Hebrew reading in the margin of the Masoretic Text was followed instead of the text itself. Such instances, being variants within the Masoretic tradition, are not specified by footnotes. In rare cases, words in the consonantal text were divided differently from the way they appear in the Masoretic Text. Footnotes indicate this. The translators also consulted the more important early versions—the Septuagint; Aquila, Symmachus and Theodotion; the Vulgate; the Syriac Peshitta; the Targums; and for the Psalms the *Juxta Hebraica* of Jerome. Readings from these versions were occasionally followed where the Masoretic Text seemed doubtful and where accepted principles of textual criticism showed that one or more of these textual witnesses appeared to provide the correct reading. Such instances are footnoted. Sometimes vowel letters and vowel signs did not, in the judgment of the translators, represent the correct vowels for the original consonantal text. Accordingly some words were read with a different set of vowels. These instances are usually not indicated by footnotes.

The Greek text used in translating the New Testament was an eclectic one. No other piece of ancient literature has such an abundance of manuscript witnesses as does the New Testament. Where existing manuscripts differ, the translators made their choice of readings according to accepted principles of New Testament textual criticism. Footnotes call attention to places where there was uncertainty about what the original text was. The best current printed texts of the Greek New Testament were used.

■ There is a sense in which the work of translation is never wholly finished. This applies to all great literature and uniquely so to the Bible. In 1973 the New Testament in the New International Version was published. Since then, suggestions for corrections and revisions have been received from various sources. The Committee on Bible Translation carefully considered the suggestions and adopted a number of them. These were incorporated in the first printing of the entire Bible in 1978. Additional revisions were made by the Committee on Bible Translation in 1983 and appear in printings after that date.

As in other ancient documents, the precise meaning of the biblical texts is sometimes uncertain. This is more often the case with the Hebrew and Aramaic texts than with the Greek text. Although archaeological and linguistic discoveries in this century aid in understanding difficult passages, some uncertainties remain. The more significant of these have been called to the reader's attention in the footnotes.

In regard to the divine name *YHWH*, commonly referred to as the *Tetragrammaton*, the translators adopted the device used in most English versions of rendering that name as "LORD" in capital letters to distinguish it from *Adonai*, another Hebrew word rendered "Lord", for which small letters are used. Wherever the two names stand together in the Old Testament as a compound name of God, they are rendered "Sovereign LORD".

Because for most readers today the phrases "the LORD of hosts" and "God of hosts" have little meaning, this version renders them "the LORD Almighty" and "God Almighty". These renderings convey the sense of the Hebrew, namely, "he who is sovereign over all the 'hosts' (powers) in heaven and on earth, especially over the 'hosts' (armies) of Israel." For readers unacquainted with Hebrew this does not make clear the distinction between *Sabaoth* ("hosts" or "Almighty") and *Shaddai* (which can also be translated "Almighty"), but the latter occurs infrequently and is always footnoted. When *Adonai* and *YHWH Sabaoth* occur together, they are rendered "the Lord, the LORD Almighty".

As for other proper nouns, the familiar spellings of the Authorised Version are generally retained. Names traditionally spelled with "ch", except where it is final, are usually spelled in this translation with "k" or "c", since the biblical languages do not have the sound that "ch" frequently indicates in English—for example, in *chant*. For well-known names such as Zechariah, however, the traditional spelling has been retained. Variation in the spelling of names in the original languages has usually not been indicated. Where a person or place has two or more different names in the Hebrew, Aramaic or Greek texts, the more familiar one has generally been used, with footnotes where needed.

To achieve clarity the translators sometimes supplied words not in the original texts but required by the context. If there was uncertainty about such material, it is enclosed in brackets. Also for the sake of clarity or style, nouns, including some proper nouns, are sometimes substituted for pronouns, and vice versa. And though the Hebrew writers often shifted back and forth between first, second and third personal pronouns without change of antecedent, this translation often makes them uniform, in accordance with English style and without the use of footnotes.

■ Poetical passages are printed as poetry, that is, with indentation of lines and with separate stanzas. These are generally designed to reflect the structure of Hebrew poetry. This poetry is normally characterised by parallelism in balanced lines. Most of the poetry in the Bible is in the Old Testament, and scholars differ regarding the scansion of Hebrew lines. The translators determined the stanza divisions for the most part by analysis of the subject matter. The stanzas therefore serve as poetic paragraphs.

As an aid to the reader, sectional headings are inserted in most of the books. They are not to be regarded as part of the NIV text, are not for oral reading, and are not intended to dictate the interpretation of the sections they head.

■ The footnotes in this version are of several kinds, most of which need no explanation. Those giving alternative translations begin with "Or" and generally introduce the alternative with the last word preceding it in the text, except when it is a single-word alternative; in poetry quoted in a footnote a slant mark indicates a line division. Footnotes introduced by "Or" do not have uniform significance. In some cases two possible translations were considered to have about equal validity. In other cases, though the translators were convinced that the translation in the text was correct, they judged that another interpretation was possible and of sufficient importance to be represented in a footnote.

In the New Testament, footnotes that refer to uncertainty regarding the original text are introduced by "Some manuscripts" or similar expressions. In the Old Testament, evidence for the reading chosen is given first and evidence for the alternative is added after a semicolon (for example: Septuagint; Hebrew *father*). In such notes the term "Hebrew" refers to the Masoretic Text.

It should be noted that minerals, flora and fauna, architectural details, articles of clothing and jewellery, musical instruments and other articles cannot always be identified with precision. Also measures of capacity in the biblical period are particularly uncertain (see the table of weights and measures following the text).

■ Like all translations of the Bible, made as they are by imperfect man, this one undoubtedly falls short of its goals. Yet we are grateful to God for the extent to which he has enabled us to realise these goals and for the strength he has given us and our colleagues to complete our task. We offer this version of the Bible to him in whose name and for whose glory it has been made. We pray that it will lead many into a better understanding of the Holy Scriptures and a fuller knowledge of Jesus Christ the incarnate Word, of whom the Scriptures so faithfully testify.

THE COMMITTEE ON BIBLE TRANSLATION

June 1978
(Revised August 1983)

Names of the translators and editors may be secured from the International Bible Society, 1820 Jet Stream Drive, Colorado Springs, CO 80921-3696 USA.

THE OLD TESTAMENT

GENESIS

INTRODUCTION

■ GOD AT WORK

EVERYTHING – LITERALLY EVERYTHING – BEGINS HERE

AND GOD BLESSED THE SEVENTH DAY AND MADE IT HOLY, BECAUSE ON IT HE RESTED
FROM ALL THE WORK OF CREATING THAT HE HAD DONE. ■ 2:3

The Bible begins with words that have become
famous, "In the beginning God created". God, like
an artist, fashioned a universe. How can we grasp
the grandeur of this?

Michelangelo, perhaps the greatest artist
in history, may help us to understand. He
painted Rome's famous Sistine Chapel to retell
Genesis' story of creation. His experience
proves one thing: creativity is work.

■ AN EXHAUSTING EFFORT
Michelangelo had 6,000 square feet of ceiling to
cover – the size of four average house roofs.
Anyone who has painted a ceiling with a paint
roller has caught a hint of the physical difficulty of
such a task. But Michelangelo's plan called for
300 separate, detailed portraits of men and
women. For more than three years the 5' 4" artist
devoted all his labours to the exhausting strain of
painting the vast overhead space with his tiny
brushes.

Sometimes he painted standing on a
huge scaffold, a paintbrush high over his head.
Sometimes he sat, his nose inches from the
ceiling. Sometimes he painted while lying on his
back. His back, shoulders, neck, and arms
cramped painfully.

In the long days of summer, he had light
to paint 17 hours a day, taking food and a
chamber pot with him on to the 60-foot scaffold.
For 30 days at a stretch he slept in his clothes,
not even taking off his boots. Paint dribbled into
his eyes so that he could barely see. Freezing in
the winter, sweating in the summer, he painted
until at last the ceiling looked like a ceiling no
more. He had transformed it into the creation
drama, with creatures so real they seemed to
breathe. Never before or since have paint and
plaster been so changed.

■ THE MIRACLE OF LIFE
But, as Michelangelo knew very well, his work was
a poor, dim image of what God had created. Over
the plaster vault of the Sistine Chapel rose the

immense dome of God's sky, breathtaking in its
simple beauty. Mountains, seas, the
continents – all these, and much more, are the
creative work of God, the Master Artist.

God's world, so much bigger and more
beautiful than Michelangelo's masterpiece, is the
product of incomparably greater energy. As
author Eugene Peterson has written, "The Bible
begins with the announcement, 'In the beginning
God created', not 'sat majestic in the heavens'
and not 'was filled with beauty and love'. He
created. He did something". In the beginning,
God went to work.

Genesis focuses attention on this
creative, hardworking God. The word *God*
appears 30 times in the 31 verses of chapter 1.
He grabs our attention in action. Genesis is an
account of his deeds, ringing splendidly with the
magnificent effort of creation.

■ MENDING BROKEN PIECES
Genesis also talks about the work of
humankind – but the tone changes abruptly. God
had barely finished creating the universe when
human rebellion marred it, like a delinquent
spraying graffiti on the Sistine Chapel. Chapters
3–11 of Genesis portray a series of disasters:
Adam and Eve's rebellion, Cain's calculated
murder of his brother, the worldwide wickedness
leading to the great flood, and human arrogance
at Babel.

God immediately began to mend the
pieces his creatures had broken. He narrowed
his scope from the whole universe to a single
man – not a king or wealthy landowner, but a
childless nomad, Abraham. Abraham, Sarah,
Isaac, Rebekah, Jacob, Rachel, Joseph – the
upward thrust from chapter 12 onwards came
through God's work in these startlingly human
individuals. They were far from perfect, yet God
picked them up where they were and carried
them forward. He promised them great things.
He moved through them to restore his art. His
creative activity did not stop on the seventh day.

■ GENESIS AND REVELATION

Many people read the Old Testament as though it portrayed the "bad old days" before Jesus. But that's not an accurate picture. Actually, the first three chapters of Genesis are linked to the last book of the Bible, Revelation. They are like brackets of perfection around the sadness of life marred by sin, death, suffering, and hatred. In Genesis we learn that life didn't start out that way. In Revelation we find out it won't end that way either. But the Old and New Testaments take place between those brackets. Through Abraham, through Moses, ultimately in Jesus, God is hard at work to make things right.

■ HOW TO READ GENESIS

Genesis is one of the most enjoyable Old Testament books, full of memorable stories of people and events. It is a crucial book to know, for the rest of the Bible often refers back to it.

Genesis tells the story of many beginnings – the beginning of the universe, the beginning of sin, and perhaps most importantly, the beginning of God's work to restore a sinful humanity.

The book breaks into two major sections. The first 11 chapters take a broad view. They give the origins of human society, including the familiar stories of Adam and Eve, Cain and Abel, Noah's ark, and the tower of Babel. Here, a few words carry great significance. You need to read slowly and reflectively, because events for centuries to come will hark back to what happens in a single line. For instance, Adam and Eve's sin, because it was the *first* sin, became an emblem of disobedience against God.

Beginning at chapter 12, Genesis tells a different kind of story – that of a single family. The pace of the story slows to develop the personalities of Abraham, Isaac, Jacob, and Joseph. These fathers and sons are full of human faults and oddities. Do you recognise any of their traits in people you know?

Seeing their fully human personalities, try to understand what God's plans were for them as individuals – and through them, for the restoration of a whole world marred by sin.

■ 3-TRACK READING PLAN

For an explanation and complete listing of the 3-track reading plan, turn to page x.

■ TRACK 1:
Two-Week Courses on the Bible
The Track 1 reading programme on the Old Testament includes three chapters from Genesis. See page x for a complete listing of this course.

■ TRACK 2:
An Overview of Genesis in 14 Days
☐ Day 1. Read the Introduction to Genesis and chapter 1, the story of creation.
☐ Day 2. Read chapter 2, the story of Adam and Eve.
☐ Day 3. Read chapter 3, where sin enters a perfect world.
☐ Day 4. Read chapter 4, the story of Cain and Abel.
☐ Day 5. Read chapter 7,

the story of Noah and the great flood.
☐ Day 6. Read chapter 8, the end of the great flood.
☐ Day 7. Read chapter 15, God's covenant with Abraham.
☐ Day 8. Read chapter 19, the destruction of Sodom and Gomorrah.
☐ Day 9. Read chapter 22, God's testing of Abraham.
☐ Day 10. Read chapter 27, in which Jacob cheats his brother Esau.
☐ Day 11. Read chapter 28, when Jacob, fleeing Esau, dreams about God.
☐ Day 12. Read chapter 37, the story of Joseph sold into slavery.
☐ Day 13. Read chapter 41, in which Joseph is raised to the highest position in Egypt.
☐ Day 14. Read chapter 45,

in which Joseph reveals his identity to his brothers.
Now turn to page xi for your next Track 2 reading project.

■ TRACK 3:
All of Genesis in 49 Days
After you have read through Genesis, turn to pages xii–xiii for your next Track 3 reading project.

☐ 1	☐ 2	☐ 3	☐ 4
☐ 5	☐ 6	☐ 7	☐ 8
☐ 9	☐ 10–11		☐ 12
☐ 13	☐ 14	☐ 15	☐ 16
☐ 17	☐ 18	☐ 19	☐ 20
☐ 21	☐ 22	☐ 23	☐ 24
☐ 25	☐ 26	☐ 27	☐ 28
☐ 29	☐ 30	☐ 31	☐ 32
☐ 33	☐ 34	☐ 35	☐ 36
☐ 37	☐ 38	☐ 39	☐ 40
☐ 41	☐ 42	☐ 43	☐ 44
☐ 45	☐ 46	☐ 47	☐ 48
☐ 49	☐ 50		

■ The Beginning

1 In the beginning God created the heavens and the earth. ²Now the earth was[a] formless and empty, darkness was over the surface of the deep, and the Spirit of God was hovering over the waters.

³And God said, "Let there be light," and there was light. ⁴God saw that the light was good, and he separated the light from the darkness. ⁵God called the light "day", and the darkness he called "night". And there was evening, and there was morning—the first day.

⁶And God said, "Let there be an expanse between the waters to separate water from water." ⁷So God made the expanse and separated the water under the expanse from the water above it. And it was so. ⁸God called the expanse "sky". And there was evening, and there was morning—the second day.

⁹And God said, "Let the water under the sky be gathered to one place, and let dry ground appear." And it was so. ¹⁰God called the dry ground "land", and the gathered waters he called "seas". And God saw that it was good.

¹¹Then God said, "Let the land produce vegetation: seed-bearing plants and trees on the land that bear fruit with seed in it, according to their various kinds." And it was so. ¹²The land produced vegetation: plants bearing seed according to their kinds and trees bearing fruit with seed in it according to their kinds. And God saw that it was good. ¹³And there was evening, and there was morning—the third day.

¹⁴And God said, "Let there be lights in the expanse of the sky to separate the day from the night, and let them serve as signs to mark seasons and days and years, ¹⁵and let them be lights in the expanse of the sky to give light on the earth." And it was so. ¹⁶God made two great lights—the greater light to govern the day and the lesser light to govern the night. He also made the stars. ¹⁷God set them in the expanse of the sky to give light on the earth, ¹⁸to govern the day and the night, and to separate light from darkness. And God saw that it was good. ¹⁹And there was evening, and there was morning—the fourth day.

²⁰And God said, "Let the water teem with living creatures, and let birds fly above the earth across the expanse of the sky." ²¹So God created the great creatures of the sea and every living and moving thing with which the water teems, according to their kinds, and every winged bird according to its kind. And God saw that it was good. ²²God blessed them and said, "Be fruitful and increase in number and fill the water in the seas, and let the birds increase on the earth." ²³And there was evening, and there was morning—the fifth day.

²⁴And God said, "Let the land produce living creatures according to their kinds: livestock, creatures that move along the ground, and wild animals, each according to its kind." And it was so. ²⁵God made the wild animals according to their kinds, the livestock according to their kinds, and all the creatures that move along the ground according to their kinds. And God saw that it was good.

²⁶Then God said, "Let us make man in our image, in our likeness, and let them rule over the fish of the sea and the birds of the air, over the livestock, over all the earth,[b] and over all the creatures that move along the ground."

²⁷So God created man
in his own image,
in the image of God
he created him;
male and female
he created them.

²⁸God blessed them and said to them, "Be fruitful and increase in number; fill the earth and subdue it. Rule over the fish of the sea and the birds of the air and over every living creature that moves on the ground." ²⁹Then God said, "I give you every seed-bearing plant on the face of the whole earth and every tree that has fruit with seed in it. They will be yours for food. ³⁰And to all the beasts of the earth and all the birds of the air and all the creatures that move on the ground—everything that has the breath of life in it—I give every green plant for food." And it was so.

³¹God saw all that he had made, and it was very good. And there was evening, and there was morning—the sixth day.

1:31 ■ GOD TAKES TIME
Why did God take "six days" to create? Why not make it all instantaneously—as he certainly could have done? Genesis introduces God's normal way of working: through a process. Work that begins with a word may take time to complete. Similarly, Israel was freed from slavery overnight, but required forty years to reach the promised land. Christians are born anew in an instant, and, in a process that lasts a lifetime, God makes them new. The new heaven and new earth have been a long time coming, but God is in the *process* of making all things new.

---

2 Thus the heavens and the earth were completed in all their vast array.

²By the seventh day God had finished the work he had been doing; so on the seventh day he rested[a] from all his work. ³And God blessed the seventh day and made it holy, because on it he rested from all the work of creating that he had done.

■ Adam and Eve

⁴This is the account of the heavens and the earth when they were created.

When the LORD God made the earth and the heavens—⁵and no shrub of the field had yet appeared on the earth[b] and no plant of the field had yet sprung up, for the LORD God had not sent rain on the earth[b]

---

and there was no man to work the ground, [6]but streams[c] came up from the earth and watered the whole surface of the ground—[7]the LORD God formed the man[d] from the dust of the ground and breathed into his nostrils the breath of life, and the man became a living being.

[8]Now the LORD God had planted a garden in the east, in Eden; and there he put the man he had formed. [9]And the LORD God made all kinds of trees grow out of the ground—trees that were pleasing to the eye and good for food. In the middle of the garden were the tree of life and the tree of the knowledge of good and evil.

[10]A river watering the garden flowed from Eden; from there it was separated into four headwaters. [11]The name of the first is the Pishon; it winds through the entire land of Havilah, where there is gold. [12](The gold of that land is good; aromatic resin[e] and onyx are also there.) [13]The name of the second river is the Gihon; it winds through the entire land of Cush.[f] [14]The name of the third river is the Tigris; it runs along the east side of Asshur. And the fourth river is the Euphrates.

[15]The LORD God took the man and put him in the Garden of Eden to work it and take care of it. [16]And the LORD God commanded the man, "You are free to eat from any tree in the garden; [17]but you must not eat from the tree of the knowledge of good and evil, for when you eat of it you will surely die."

[18]The LORD God said, "It is not good for the man to be alone. I will make a helper suitable for him."

[19]Now the LORD God had formed out of the ground all the beasts of the field and all the birds of the air. He brought them to the man to see what he would name them; and whatever the man called each living creature, that was its name. [20]So the man gave names to all the livestock, the birds of the air and all the beasts of the field.

But for Adam[g] no suitable helper was found. [21]So the LORD God caused the man to fall into a deep sleep; and while he was sleeping, he took one of the man's ribs[b] and closed up the place with flesh. [22]Then the LORD God made a woman from the rib[i] he had taken out of the man, and he brought her to the man.

[23]The man said,

"This is now bone of my bones
  and flesh of my flesh;

■ HOW THE WORLD BEGAN
ABOVE ALL ELSE, GENESIS SAYS THIS: GOD DID IT

INSIGHT

IN THE BEGINNING GOD CREATED THE HEAVENS AND THE EARTH. ■ 1:1

The headline in one of the national newspapers on Friday, 24 April 1992 ran *"So this is how it all began."* The news had just broken that C.O.B.E., a spacecraft launched by the American space agency N.A.S.A., had discovered huge ripples in matter at the very edge of the cosmos. Here at last, they believed, was unquestionable evidence for the Big Bang theory, here was the *"fingerprint of Creation itself"*.

Hailed as the *"Holy Grail of cosmology"*, the reporters picked up on the religious implications of the discovery and asked theologians and clergy for their comment. Perhaps surprisingly, very little concern was shown, God and the Christian faith were not thought to be threatened.

■ THE MAIN POINT
This would not always have been the case, controversy over Darwin's Theory of Evolution still rages in some parts of the world. For centuries, scientific discoveries have thrown confusion over the first three chapters of the Bible. People have even gone to court or lost their jobs over such issues. Important as these are, it is unfortunate that the debate over process diverts attention from the main truth Genesis teaches.

Above everything else, it proclaims this: God did it. We are not here by accident, nor are we here merely to please ourselves. We owe our very existence to God. Every helium atom, every spiral galaxy, every living creature exists because God wants it to. Genesis 1–3 is the artist's signature on the painting, saying, "This is mine."

■ GOD MADE US GOOD
Genesis 1–3 pays humanity its highest compliment. After making all the glories of the world, God topped his work with man and woman. He put them in charge. Unlike the animals, they were like him, "in his image". "Very good," he said to himself when he had finished. With humans he stopped, satisfied.

Nobody, including God, has been satisfied with human beings since then. We were made good, but we disobeyed God right from the beginning. We've been suffering the consequences ever since. Genesis helps us to understand why the universe is so flagrantly lovely, and yet so tragic. It is lovely because God made it. But it is tragic because he entrusted it to us—and we failed.

□ LIFE QUESTIONS:
People say they can see God reflected in stars, forests, sunsets. What about people? How can you see God's artistry in them?

[c]6 Or mist   [d]7 The Hebrew for *man* (*adam*) sounds like and may be related to the Hebrew for *ground* (*adamah*); it is also the name *Adam* (see Gen. 2:20).
[e]12 Or *good; pearls*   [f]13 Possibly south-east Mesopotamia   [g]20 Or *the man*   [b]21 Or *took part of the man's side*   [i]22 Or *part*

she shall be called 'woman',[j]
for she was taken out of man."

2:23-25 ■ THE FIRST MARRIAGE
Adam joyfully recognised that he and Eve belonged together. As verse 24 suggests, this suitability is the basis for all marriages. This passage was quoted by Jesus (Matthew 19:5; Mark 10:7-8) and Paul (1 Corinthians 6:16; Ephesians 5:31) in their comments on sex and marriage.

24For this reason a man will leave his father and mother and be united to his wife, and they will become one flesh. 25The man and his wife were both naked, and they felt no shame.

■ The Fall of Man

3 Now the serpent was more crafty than any of the wild animals the LORD God had made. He said to the woman, "Did God really say, 'You must not eat from any tree in the garden'?"
2The woman said to the serpent, "We may eat fruit from the trees in the garden, 3but God did say, 'You must not eat fruit from the tree that is in the middle of the garden, and you must not touch it, or you will die.'"
4"You will not surely die," the serpent said to the woman. 5"For God knows that when you eat of it your eyes will be opened, and you will be like God, knowing good and evil."
6When the woman saw that the fruit of the tree was good for food and pleasing to the eye, and also desirable for gaining wisdom, she took some and ate it. She also gave some to her husband, who was with her, and he ate it. 7Then the eyes of both of them were opened, and they realised that they were naked; so they sewed fig leaves together and made coverings for themselves.

3:7 ■ SIN AND SHAME
When Adam and Eve disobeyed God, they immediately became ashamed of their bodies and wanted to hide. Ever since, sinful human beings have been "hiding" from each other and from God.
   God asked Adam and Eve three questions, typical of the questions he puts to anyone "in hiding": 1) Where are you? (And why are you hiding from me?) 2) Who told you that you were naked? (And why did you believe somebody else, not me?) 3) What is this you have done? (And are you ready to take responsibility for it?)

8Then the man and his wife heard the sound of the LORD God as he was walking in the garden in the cool of the day, and they hid from the LORD God among the trees of the garden. 9But the LORD God called to the man, "Where are you?"
10He answered, "I heard you in the garden, and I was afraid because I was naked; so I hid."
11And he said, "Who told you that you were naked? Have you eaten from the tree from which I commanded you not to eat?"
12The man said, "The woman you put here with me—she gave me some fruit from the tree, and I ate it."
13Then the LORD God said to the woman, "What is this you have done?"
The woman said, "The serpent deceived me, and I ate."
14So the LORD God said to the serpent, "Because you have done this,

"Cursed are you above all the livestock
    and all the wild animals!
You will crawl on your belly
    and you will eat dust
    all the days of your life.
15And I will put enmity
    between you and the woman,
    and between your offspring[a] and hers;
he will crush[b] your head,
    and you will strike his heel."

16To the woman he said,

"I will greatly increase your pains in
    childbearing;
    with pain you will give birth to children.
Your desire will be for your husband,
    and he will rule over you."

17To Adam he said, "Because you listened to your wife and ate from the tree about which I commanded you, 'You must not eat of it,'

"Cursed is the ground because of you;
    through painful toil you will eat of it
    all the days of your life.
18It will produce thorns and thistles for you,
    and you will eat the plants of the field.
19By the sweat of your brow
    you will eat your food
until you return to the ground,
    since from it you were taken;
for dust you are
    and to dust you will return."

20Adam[c] named his wife Eve,[d] because she would become the mother of all the living.
21The LORD God made garments of skin for Adam and his wife and clothed them. 22And the LORD God said, "The man has now become like one of us, knowing good and evil. He must not be allowed to reach out his hand and take also from the tree of life and eat, and live for ever." 23So the LORD God banished him from the Garden of Eden to work the ground from which he had been taken. 24After he drove the man out, he placed on the east side[e] of the Garden of Eden cherubim and a flaming sword flashing back and forth to guard the way to the tree of life.

■ Cain and Abel

4 Adam[a] lay with his wife Eve, and she became pregnant and gave birth to Cain.[b] She said, "With the help of the LORD I have brought forth[c] a man." 2Later she gave birth to his brother Abel.
Now Abel kept flocks, and Cain worked the soil.

j23 The Hebrew for woman sounds like the Hebrew for man.   a15 Or seed   b15 Or strike   c20 Or The man   d20 Eve probably means living.
e24 Or placed in front   a1 Or The man   b1 Cain sounds like the Hebrew for brought forth or acquired.   c1 Or have acquired

³In the course of time Cain brought some of the fruits of the soil as an offering to the LORD. ⁴But Abel brought fat portions from some of the firstborn of his flock. The LORD looked with favour on Abel and his offering, ⁵but on Cain and his offering he did not look with favour. So Cain was very angry, and his face was downcast.

4:4 ■ IMPROPER OFFERINGS

Why God preferred Abel's offering to Cain's is uncertain; later in the Old Testament both animal and agricultural offerings were accepted by God. Quite possibly, Cain's attitude was a problem. Cain certainly became instantly angry with God when things did not go his way.

⁶Then the LORD said to Cain, "Why are you angry? Why is your face downcast? ⁷If you do what is right, will you not be accepted? But if you do not do what is right, sin is crouching at your door; it desires to have you, but you must master it."

⁸Now Cain said to his brother Abel, "Let's go out to the field."ᵈ And while they were in the field, Cain attacked his brother Abel and killed him.

⁹Then the LORD said to Cain, "Where is your brother Abel?"

"I don't know," he replied. "Am I my brother's keeper?"

¹⁰The LORD said, "What have you done? Listen! Your brother's blood cries out to me from the ground. ¹¹Now you are under a curse and driven from the ground, which opened its mouth to receive your brother's blood from your hand. ¹²When you work the ground, it will no longer yield its crops for you. You will be a restless wanderer on the earth."

¹³Cain said to the LORD, "My punishment is more than I can bear. ¹⁴Today you are driving me from the land, and I will be hidden from your presence; I will be a restless wanderer on the earth, and whoever finds me will kill me."

¹⁵But the LORD said to him, "Not so;ᵉ if anyone kills Cain, he will suffer vengeance seven times over." Then the LORD put a mark on Cain so that no-one who found him would kill him. ¹⁶So Cain went out from the LORD's presence and lived in the land of Nod,ᶠ east of Eden.

¹⁷Cain lay with his wife, and she became pregnant and gave birth to Enoch. Cain was then building a city, and he named it after his son Enoch. ¹⁸To Enoch was born Irad, and Irad was the father of Mehujael, and Mehujael was the father of Methushael, and Methushael was the father of Lamech.

¹⁹Lamech married two women, one named Adah and the other Zillah. ²⁰Adah gave birth to Jabal; he was the father of those who live in tents and raise livestock. ²¹His brother's name was Jubal; he was the father of all who play the harp and flute. ²²Zillah also had a son, Tubal-Cain, who forged all kinds of tools out ofᵍ bronze and iron. Tubal-Cain's sister was Naamah.

²³Lamech said to his wives,

"Adah and Zillah, listen to me;

wives of Lamech, hear my words.
I have killedᵇ a man for wounding me,
    a young man for injuring me.
²⁴If Cain is avenged seven times,
    then Lamech seventy-seven times."

²⁵Adam lay with his wife again, and she gave birth to a son and named him Seth,ⁱ saying, "God has granted me another child in place of Abel, since Cain killed him." ²⁶Seth also had a son, and he named him Enosh.

At that time men began to call onʲ the name of the LORD.

■ From Adam to Noah

5 This is the written account of Adam's line.

When God created man, he made him in the likeness of God. ²He created them male and female and blessed them. And when they were created, he called them "man".ᵃ

³When Adam had lived 130 years, he had a son in his own likeness, in his own image; and he named him Seth. ⁴After Seth was born, Adam lived 800 years and had other sons and daughters. ⁵Altogether, Adam lived 930 years, and then he died.

⁶When Seth had lived 105 years, he became the fatherᵇ of Enosh. ⁷And after he became the father of Enosh, Seth lived 807 years and had other sons and daughters. ⁸Altogether, Seth lived 912 years, and then he died.

⁹When Enosh had lived 90 years, he became the father of Kenan. ¹⁰And after he became the father of Kenan, Enosh lived 815 years and had other sons and daughters. ¹¹Altogether, Enosh lived 905 years, and then he died.

¹²When Kenan had lived 70 years, he became the father of Mahalalel. ¹³And after he became the father of Mahalalel, Kenan lived 840 years and had other sons and daughters. ¹⁴Altogether, Kenan lived 910 years, and then he died.

¹⁵When Mahalalel had lived 65 years, he became the father of Jared. ¹⁶And after he became the father of Jared, Mahalalel lived 830 years and had other sons and daughters. ¹⁷Altogether, Mahalalel lived 895 years, and then he died.

¹⁸When Jared had lived 162 years, he became the father of Enoch. ¹⁹And after he became the father of Enoch, Jared lived 800 years and had other sons and daughters. ²⁰Altogether, Jared lived 962 years, and then he died.

²¹When Enoch had lived 65 years, he became the father of Methuselah. ²²And after he became the father of Methuselah, Enoch walked with God 300 years and had other sons and daughters. ²³Altogether, Enoch lived 365 years. ²⁴Enoch walked with God; then he was no more, because God took him away.

²⁵When Methuselah had lived 187 years, he became the father of Lamech. ²⁶And after he became the father of Lamech, Methuselah lived 782 years and had other sons and daughters. ²⁷Altogether, Methuselah lived 969 years, and then he died.

²⁸When Lamech had lived 182 years, he had a son.

ᵈ8 Samaritan Pentateuch, Septuagint, Vulgate and Syriac; Masoretic Text does not have "Let's go out to the field."   ᵉ15 Septuagint, Vulgate and Syriac; Hebrew Very well   ᶠ16 Nod means wandering (see verses 12 and 14).   ᵍ22 Or who instructed all who work in   ᵇ23 Or I will kill   ⁱ25 Seth probably means granted.   ʲ26 Or to proclaim   ᵃ2 Hebrew adam   ᵇ6 Father may mean ancestor; also in verses 7–26.

²⁹He named him Noah*c* and said, "He will comfort us in the labour and painful toil of our hands caused by the ground the LORD has cursed." ³⁰After Noah was born, Lamech lived 595 years and had other sons and daughters. ³¹Altogether, Lamech lived 777 years, and then he died.

5:24 ■ THE MAN WHO DID NOT DIE

All but one of the brief biographies in chapter 5 end with the words, "And then he died". We know very little about the exception, Enoch, except that he walked with God. Enoch did not die; he "was no more, because God took him away". Based on this evidence, Hebrews 11:5–6 commends Enoch as a man of faith, since "without faith it is impossible to please God".

³²After Noah was 500 years old, he became the father of Shem, Ham and Japheth.

■ The Flood

6 When men began to increase in number on the earth and daughters were born to them, ²the sons of God saw that the daughters of men were beautiful, and they married any of them they chose. ³Then the LORD said, "My Spirit will not contend with*a* man for ever, for he is mortal;*b* his days will be a hundred and twenty years."

6:2 ■ THE SONS OF GOD

This mysterious description may refer to the "sons of Seth", the line of God's people from Adam to Noah, or it may refer to angels, often called "sons of God" in the Old Testament. However you interpret it, the point is that evil behaviour increased in the world, a fact that led to punishment by a flood.

⁴The Nephilim were on the earth in those days—and also afterwards—when the sons of God went to the daughters of men and had children by them. They were the heroes of old, men of renown.

⁵The LORD saw how great man's wickedness on the earth had become, and that every inclination of the thoughts of his heart was only evil all the time. ⁶The LORD was grieved that he had made man on the earth, and his heart was filled with pain. ⁷So the LORD said, "I will wipe mankind, whom I have created, from the face of the earth—men and animals, and creatures that move along the ground, and birds of the air—for I am grieved that I have made them." ⁸But Noah found favour in the eyes of the LORD.

⁹This is the account of Noah.

Noah was a righteous man, blameless among the people of his time, and he walked with God. ¹⁰Noah had three sons: Shem, Ham and Japheth. ¹¹Now the earth was corrupt in God's sight and was full of violence. ¹²God saw how corrupt the earth had become, for all the people on earth had corrupted their ways. ¹³So God said to Noah, "I am

going to put an end to all people, for the earth is filled with violence because of them. I am surely going to destroy both them and the earth. ¹⁴So make yourself an ark of cypress*c* wood; make rooms in it and coat it with pitch inside and out. ¹⁵This is how you are to build it: The ark is to be 450 feet long, 75 feet wide and 45 feet high.*d* ¹⁶Make a roof for it and finish*e* the ark to within 18 inches*f* of the top. Put a door in the side of the ark and make lower, middle and upper decks. ¹⁷I am going to bring floodwaters on the earth to destroy all life under the heavens, every creature that has the breath of life in it. Everything on earth will perish. ¹⁸But I will establish my covenant with you, and you will enter the ark—you and your sons and your wife and your sons' wives with you. ¹⁹You are to bring into the ark two of all living creatures, male and female, to keep them alive with you. ²⁰Two of every kind of bird, of every kind of animal and of every kind of creature that moves along the ground will come to you to be kept alive. ²¹You are to take every kind of food that is to be eaten and store it away as food for you and for them."

²²Noah did everything just as God commanded him.

7 The LORD then said to Noah, "Go into the ark, you and your whole family, because I have found you righteous in this generation. ²Take with you seven*a* of every kind of clean animal, a male and its mate, and two of every kind of unclean animal, a male and its mate, ³and also seven of every kind of bird, male and female, to keep their various kinds alive throughout the earth. ⁴Seven days from now I will send rain on the earth for forty days and forty nights, and I will wipe from the face of the earth every living creature I have made."

⁵And Noah did all that the LORD commanded him.

⁶Noah was six hundred years old when the floodwaters came on the earth. ⁷And Noah and his sons and his wife and his sons' wives entered the ark to escape the waters of the flood. ⁸Pairs of clean and unclean animals, of birds and of all creatures that move along the ground, ⁹male and female, came to Noah and entered the ark, as God had commanded Noah. ¹⁰And after the seven days the floodwaters came on the earth.

¹¹In the six hundredth year of Noah's life, on the seventeenth day of the second month—on that day all the springs of the great deep burst forth, and the floodgates of the heavens were opened. ¹²And rain fell on the earth for forty days and forty nights.

¹³On that very day Noah and his sons, Shem, Ham and Japheth, together with his wife and the wives of his three sons, entered the ark. ¹⁴They had with them every wild animal according to its kind, all livestock according to their kinds, every creature that moves along the ground according to its kind and every bird according to its kind, everything with wings. ¹⁵Pairs of all creatures that have the breath of life in them came to Noah and entered the ark. ¹⁶The animals going in were male and female of every living thing, as God had commanded Noah. Then the LORD shut him in.

¹⁷For forty days the flood kept coming on the

---

*c*29 *Noah* sounds like the Hebrew for *comfort.*   *a*3 Or *My spirit will not remain in* uncertain.   *d*15 Hebrew *300 cubits long, 50 cubits wide and 30 cubits high* (about 140 metres long, 23 metres wide and 13.6 metres high)   *e*16 Or *Make an opening for light by finishing*   *f*16 Hebrew *a cubit* (about 0.5 metre)   *a*2 Or *seven pairs;* also in verse 3   *b*3 Or *corrupt*   *c*14 The meaning of the Hebrew for this word is earth, and as the waters increased they lifted the ark high above the earth. [18]The waters rose and increased greatly on the earth, and the ark floated on the surface of the water. [19]They rose greatly on the earth, and all the high mountains under the entire heavens were covered. [20]The waters rose and covered the mountains to a depth of more than twenty feet.[b, c] [21]Every living thing that moved on the earth perished—birds, livestock, wild animals, all the creatures that swarm over the earth, and all mankind. [22]Everything on dry land that had the breath of life in its nostrils died. [23]Every living thing on the face of the earth was wiped out; men and animals and the creatures that move along the ground and the birds of the air were wiped from the earth. Only Noah was left, and those with him in the ark.

[24]The waters flooded the earth for a hundred and fifty days.

8 But God remembered Noah and all the wild animals and the livestock that were with him in the ark, and he sent a wind over the earth, and the waters receded. [2]Now the springs of the deep and the floodgates of the heavens had been closed, and the rain had stopped falling from the sky. [3]The water receded steadily from the earth. At the end of the hundred and fifty days the water had gone down, [4]and on the seventeenth day of the seventh month the ark came to rest on the mountains of Ararat. [5]The waters continued to recede until the tenth month, and on the first day of the tenth month the tops of the mountains became visible.

[6]After forty days Noah opened the window he had made in the ark [7]and sent out a raven, and it kept flying back and forth until the water had dried up from the earth. [8]Then he sent out a dove to see if the water had receded from the surface of the ground. [9]But the dove could find no place to set its feet because there was water over all the surface of the earth; so it returned to Noah in the ark. He reached out his hand and took the dove and brought it back to himself in the ark. [10]He waited seven more days and again sent out the dove from the ark. [11]When the dove returned to him in the evening, there in its beak was a freshly plucked olive leaf! Then Noah knew that the water had receded from the earth.

8:11 ■ PEACE SYMBOL

The dove with an olive branch stands as a symbol for peace, and the origin of that symbol traces back to this account of restored peace between God and his creation. The olive leaf carried by the dove told Noah that lower altitudes (where olives grow) were above water and had sprouted new life.

---

[12]He waited seven more days and sent the dove out again, but this time it did not return to him.

[13]By the first day of the first month of Noah's six hundred and first year, the water had dried up from the earth. Noah then removed the covering from the ark and saw that the surface of the ground was dry. [14]By the twenty-seventh day of the second month the earth was completely dry.

[15]Then God said to Noah, [16]"Come out of the ark, you and your wife and your sons and their wives. [17]Bring out every kind of living creature that is with you—the birds, the animals, and all the creatures that move along the ground—so they can multiply on the earth and be fruitful and increase in number upon it."

[18]So Noah came out, together with his sons and his wife and his sons' wives. [19]All the animals and all the creatures that move along the ground and all the birds—everything that moves on the earth—came out of the ark, one kind after another.

[20]Then Noah built an altar to the LORD and, taking some of all the clean animals and clean birds, he sacrificed burnt offerings on it. [21]The LORD smelled the pleasing aroma and said in his heart: "Never again will I curse the ground because of man, even though[a] every inclination of his heart is evil from childhood. And never again will I destroy all living creatures, as I have done.

[22]"As long as the earth endures,
   seedtime and harvest,
   cold and heat,
   summer and winter,
   day and night
   will never cease."

■ God's Covenant With Noah

9 Then God blessed Noah and his sons, saying to them, "Be fruitful and increase in number and fill the earth. [2]The fear and dread of you will fall upon all the beasts of the earth and all the birds of the air, upon every creature that moves along the ground, and upon all the fish of the sea; they are given into your hands. [3]Everything that lives and moves will be food for you. Just as I gave you the green plants, I now give you everything.

[4]"But you must not eat meat that has its lifeblood still in it. [5]And for your lifeblood I will surely demand an accounting. I will demand an accounting from every animal. And from each man, too, I will demand an accounting for the life of his fellow man.

[6]"Whoever sheds the blood of man,
   by man shall his blood be shed;
  for in the image of God
   has God made man.

[7]As for you, be fruitful and increase in number; multiply on the earth and increase upon it."

[8]Then God said to Noah and to his sons with him: [9]"I now establish my covenant with you and with your descendants after you [10]and with every living creature that was with you—the birds, the livestock and all the wild animals, all those that came out of the ark with you—every living creature on earth. [11]I establish my covenant with you: Never again will all life be cut off by the waters of a flood; never again will there be a flood to destroy the earth."

[12]And God said, "This is the sign of the covenant I am making between me and you and every living creature with you, a covenant for all generations to come: [13]I have set my rainbow in the clouds, and it will be the sign of the covenant between me and the earth. [14]Whenever I bring clouds over the earth and

---

[b]20 Hebrew *fifteen cubits* (about 6.9 metres)   [c]20 Or *rose more than twenty feet, and the mountains were covered*   [a]21 Or *man, for*

the rainbow appears in the clouds, [15]I will remember my covenant between me and you and all living creatures of every kind. Never again will the waters become a flood to destroy all life. [16]Whenever the rainbow appears in the clouds, I will see it and remember the everlasting covenant between God and all living creatures of every kind on the earth."

9:4 ■ REVERENCE FOR LIFE
In the Garden of Eden God had provided plants for humanity's food. Here, for the first time, he gave permission to add meat to their diet. Although an animal was not to be eaten with "its lifeblood still in it". Kosher dietary requirements kept by Orthodox Jews today derive partly from this statement. Leviticus 17:10–14 gives more detail.

The intent, many commentators believe, was to remind God's people to reverence life, including animal life. This passage makes clear, however, that human life has a special significance. Ironically, capital punishment derives its legitimacy from this. Murderers who destroy human life actually attack the image of God. Therefore God demands an accounting.

9:12 ■ THE REASON FOR RAINBOWS
Throughout the Bible, God makes covenant agreements with the people he loves. This first recorded covenant was marked by an appropriate symbol – the rainbow. While later covenants applied specifically to the Israelites, this one extended – and still extends – to every living creature.

[17]So God said to Noah, "This is the sign of the covenant I have established between me and all life on the earth."

■ The Sons of Noah
[18]The sons of Noah who came out of the ark were Shem, Ham and Japheth. (Ham was the father of Canaan.) [19]These were the three sons of Noah, and from them came the people who were scattered over the earth.

[20]Noah, a man of the soil, proceeded[a] to plant a vineyard. [21]When he drank some of its wine, he became drunk and lay uncovered inside his tent. [22]Ham, the father of Canaan, saw his father's nakedness and told his two brothers outside. [23]But Shem and Japheth took a garment and laid it across their shoulders; then they walked in backwards and covered their father's nakedness. Their faces were turned the other way so that they would not see their father's nakedness.

[24]When Noah awoke from his wine and found out what his youngest son had done to him, [25]he said,

"Cursed be Canaan!
    The lowest of slaves
will he be to his brothers."

[26]He also said,

"Blessed be the LORD, the God of Shem!
    May Canaan be the slave of Shem.[b]
[27]May God extend the territory of Japheth;[c]
    may Japheth live in the tents of Shem,
    and may Canaan be his[d] slave."

[28]After the flood Noah lived 350 years. [29]Altogether, Noah lived 950 years, and then he died.

■ The Table of Nations
10 This is the account of Shem, Ham and Japheth, Noah's sons, who themselves had sons after the flood.

☐ The Japhethites
[2]The sons[a] of Japheth:
    Gomer, Magog, Madai, Javan, Tubal, Meshech and Tiras.
[3]The sons of Gomer:
    Ashkenaz, Riphath and Togarmah.
[4]The sons of Javan:
    Elishah, Tarshish, the Kittim and the Rodanim.[b] [5](From these the maritime peoples spread out into their territories by their clans within their nations, each with its own language.)

☐ The Hamites
[6]The sons of Ham:
    Cush, Mizraim,[c] Put and Canaan.
[7]The sons of Cush:
    Seba, Havilah, Sabtah, Raamah and Sabteca.
The sons of Raamah:
    Sheba and Dedan.

[8]Cush was the father[d] of Nimrod, who grew to be a mighty warrior on the earth. [9]He was a mighty hunter before the LORD; that is why it is said, "Like Nimrod, a mighty hunter before the LORD." [10]The first centres of his kingdom were Babylon, Erech, Akkad and Calneh, in[e] Shinar.[f] [11]From that land he went to Assyria, where he built Nineveh, Rehoboth Ir,[g] Calah [12]and Resen, which is between Nineveh and Calah; that is the great city.

[13]Mizraim was the father of
    the Ludites, Anamites, Lehabites, Naphtuhites, [14]Pathrusites, Casluhites (from whom the Philistines came) and Caphtorites.
[15]Canaan was the father of
    Sidon his firstborn,[b] and of the Hittites,
[16]Jebusites, Amorites, Girgashites, [17]Hivites, Arkites, Sinites, [18]Arvadites, Zemarites and Hamathites.

Later the Canaanite clans scattered [19]and the borders of Canaan reached from Sidon towards Gerar as far as Gaza, and then towards Sodom, Gomorrah, Admah and Zeboiim, as far as Lasha.

[20]These are the sons of Ham by their clans and languages, in their territories and nations.

a20 Or soil, was the first   b26 Or be his slave   c27 Japheth sounds like the Hebrew for extend.   d27 Or their   a2 Sons may mean descendants or successors or nations; also in verses 3, 4, 6, 7, 20–23, 29 and 31.   b4 Some manuscripts of the Masoretic Text and Samaritan Pentateuch (see also Septuagint and 1 Chron. 1.7), most manuscripts of the Masoretic Text Dodanim   c6 That is, Egypt; also in verse 13   d8 Father may mean ancestor or predecessor or founder; also in verses 13, 15, 24 and 26.   e10 Or Erech and Akkad–all of them in   f10 That is, Babylonia   g11 Or Nineveh with its city squares   b15 Or of the Sidonians, the foremost

☐ The Semites

21Sons were also born to Shem, whose older brother was[i] Japheth; Shem was the ancestor of all the sons of Eber.

22The sons of Shem:
Elam, Asshur, Arphaxad, Lud and Aram.
23The sons of Aram:
Uz, Hul, Gether and Meshech.[j]
24Arphaxad was the father of[k] Shelah,
and Shelah the father of Eber.
25Two sons were born to Eber:
One was named Peleg,[l] because in his time the earth was divided; his brother was named Joktan.
26Joktan was the father of
Almodad, Sheleph, Hazarmaveth, Jerah, 27Hadoram, Uzal, Diklah, 28Obal, Abimael, Sheba, 29Ophir, Havilah and Jobab. All these were sons of Joktan.

30The region where they lived stretched from Mesha towards Sephar, in the eastern hill country.
31These are the sons of Shem by their clans and languages, in their territories and nations.

32These are the clans of Noah's sons, according to their lines of descent, within their nations. From these the nations spread out over the earth after the flood.

■ The Tower of Babel

11 Now the whole world had one language and a common speech. 2As men moved eastward,[a] they found a plain in Shinar[b] and settled there.

3They said to each other, "Come, let's make bricks and bake them thoroughly." They used brick instead of stone, and bitumen for mortar. 4Then they said, "Come, let us build ourselves a city, with a tower that reaches to the heavens, so that we may make a name for ourselves and not be scattered over the face of the whole earth."

5But the LORD came down to see the city and the tower that the men were building. 6The LORD said, "If as one people speaking the same language they have begun to do this, then nothing they plan to do will be impossible for them. 7Come, let us go down and confuse their language so they will not understand each other."

11:6 ■ HUMAN AMBITION
People are ambitious — they want to succeed. Genesis portrays humans as being so ambitious that they try to compete with, rather than serve, God. This was Adam and Eve's sin (3:5,22), and at Babel people were at it again, in a citywide effort. God frustrated their plans by confusing their language.

8So the LORD scattered them from there over all the earth, and they stopped building the city. 9That is why it was called Babel[c] — because there the LORD confused the language of the whole world. From there the LORD scattered them over the face of the whole earth.

■ From Shem to Abram
10This is the account of Shem.

Two years after the flood, when Shem was 100 years old, he became the father[d] of Arphaxad. 11And after he became the father of Arphaxad, Shem lived 500 years and had other sons and daughters.

12When Arphaxad had lived 35 years, he became the father of Shelah. 13And after he became the father of Shelah, Arphaxad lived 403 years and had other sons and daughters.[e]

14When Shelah had lived 30 years, he became the father of Eber. 15And after he became the father of Eber, Shelah lived 403 years and had other sons and daughters.

16When Eber had lived 34 years, he became the father of Peleg. 17And after he became the father of Peleg, Eber lived 430 years and had other sons and daughters.

18When Peleg had lived 30 years, he became the father of Reu. 19And after he became the father of Reu, Peleg lived 209 years and had other sons and daughters.

20When Reu had lived 32 years, he became the father of Serug. 21And after he became the father of Serug, Reu lived 207 years and had other sons and daughters.

22When Serug had lived 30 years, he became the father of Nahor. 23And after he became the father of Nahor, Serug lived 200 years and had other sons and daughters.

24When Nahor had lived 29 years, he became the father of Terah. 25And after he became the father of Terah, Nahor lived 119 years and had other sons and daughters.

26After Terah had lived 70 years, he became the father of Abram, Nahor and Haran.

27This is the account of Terah.

Terah became the father of Abram, Nahor and Haran. And Haran became the father of Lot. 28While his father Terah was still alive, Haran died in Ur of the Chaldeans, in the land of his birth. 29Abram and Nahor both married. The name of Abram's wife was Sarai, and the name of Nahor's wife was Milcah; she was the daughter of Haran, the father of both Milcah and Iscah. 30Now Sarai was barren; she had no children.

31Terah took his son Abram, his grandson Lot son of Haran, and his daughter-in-law Sarai, the wife of his son Abram, and together they set out from Ur of the Chaldeans to go to Canaan. But when they came to Haran, they settled there.

32Terah lived 205 years, and he died in Haran.

i21 Or Shem, the older brother of   j23 See Septuagint and 1 Chron. 1:17; Hebrew Mash.   k24 Hebrew; Septuagint father of Cainan, and Cainan was the father of   l25 Peleg means division.   a2 Or from the east; or in the east   b2 That is, Babylonia   c9 That is, Babylon; Babel sounds like the Hebrew for confused.   d10 Father may mean ancestor; also in verses 11–25.   e12,13 Hebrew; Septuagint (see also Luke 3:35, 36 and note at Gen. 10:24) 35 years, he became the father of Cainan. 13And after he became the father of Cainan, Arphaxad lived 430 years and had other sons and daughters, and then he died. When Cainan had lived 130 years, he became the father of Shelah. And after he became the father of Shelah, Cainan lived 330 years and had other sons and daughters

■ The Call of Abram

12 The LORD had said to Abram, "Leave your country, your people and your father's household and go to the land I will show you.

2"I will make you into a great nation
     and I will bless you;
I will make your name great,
     and you will be a blessing.
3I will bless those who bless you,
     and whoever curses you I will curse;
and all peoples on earth
     will be blessed through you."

4So Abram left, as the LORD had told him; and Lot went with him. Abram was seventy-five years old when he set out from Haran. 5He took his wife Sarai, his nephew Lot, all the possessions they had accumulated and the people they had acquired in Haran, and they set out for the land of Canaan, and they arrived there.

6Abram travelled through the land as far as the site of the great tree of Moreh at Shechem. At that time the Canaanites were in the land. 7The LORD appeared to Abram and said, "To your offspring*a* I will give this land." So he built an altar there to the LORD, who had appeared to him.

8From there he went on towards the hills east of Bethel and pitched his tent, with Bethel on the west and Ai on the east. There he built an altar to the LORD and called on the name of the LORD. 9Then Abram set out and continued towards the Negev.

■ Abram in Egypt

10Now there was a famine in the land, and Abram went down to Egypt to live there for a while because the famine was severe. 11As he was about to enter Egypt, he said to his wife Sarai, "I know what a

---

■ ABRAHAM
GOD BEGINS TO REBUILD

INSIGHT

I WILL MAKE YOU INTO A GREAT NATION AND I WILL BLESS YOU . . . . AND ALL PEOPLES ON EARTH WILL BE BLESSED THROUGH YOU. ■ 12:2–3

After scanning centuries, Genesis changes dramatically at chapter 12. Leaving the big picture of world history, it settles on one lonely individual – not a great king or a wealthy landowner, but a childless nomad, Abraham.

At God's call, Abraham had uprooted himself from civilisation and begun wandering in the wilderness. With a few changes (cattle substituted for sheep, covered wagons for tents), you could make a cowboy film about his life. Moving his flocks from place to place, fighting skirmishes and pitched battles with hostile local people, Abraham had to be tough to survive. But this hardly made him unique; lots of tough nomads wandered around the Middle East. What made this particular wanderer so important?

■ GOD'S NEW WAY OF WORKING
Abraham was important, first of all, simply because God chose him. Shortly after the destruction caused by the great flood, God picked Abraham as the foundation of a new humanity. On several remarkable occasions God spoke directly to him, promising to make his family great in the land he roamed. The promises were hard to believe: Abraham's wife was barren, Abraham was getting too old to have children, he owned no land and had no prospect of any. Nonetheless, God asked Abraham to trust him.

The second reason why Abraham matters follows from the first: when God spoke to him, Abraham listened. He was far from perfect. Sometimes he strayed from the path God put him on, lying and trying to make the promises work out in his own way. Yet in the decisive moments of life, he listened to God and obeyed. He was willing to sacrifice anything for God – even his only son. God put his mark on Abraham, the mark of circumcision. His descendants were to be for ever known as "God's people".

■ UNCENSORED TRUTH
The life of Abraham is a fascinating story, true to life, full of bad moments as well as good. He was hardly a theologian; a more comprehensive understanding of God would have to wait for Moses. But Abraham's faith is the root of Judaism and, thus, of Christianity. In his encounters with God we get raw, uncensored truth, not religion invented by a philosopher but religion as it really happens when God meets man.

No wonder the New Testament cites Abraham more than 80 times, and Paul tells Christians they are the true descendants of Abraham (Galatians 3:6–9). Abraham's life began to unfold the story of God's long-term plans. Two thousand years later, Abraham's descendant Jesus came to fulfil the promises made to Abraham and his descendants.

☐ LIFE QUESTIONS:
God asked Abraham to leave his home and family and go to a far-off foreign country. If you were in his place, how would you have responded? Has God ever asked anything hard or risky of you?

---

a 7 Or seed

beautiful woman you are. [12]When the Egyptians see you, they will say, 'This is his wife.' Then they will kill me but will let you live. [13]Say you are my sister, so that I will be treated well for your sake and my life will be spared because of you."

12:13 ■ ABRAHAM'S HALF-TRUTH

"A lie is an attempt to deceive", according to one definition, and by that standard Abraham was lying when he claimed Sarai was his sister. Yet he was telling half the truth, for she was his half sister (20:12). Abraham pulled this same trick years later and got caught again (chapter 20). On both occasions he had feared for his life, a situation in which half-truths are particularly appealing.

[14]When Abram came to Egypt, the Egyptians saw that she was a very beautiful woman. [15]And when Pharaoh's officials saw her, they praised her to Pharaoh, and she was taken into his palace. [16]He treated Abram well for her sake, and Abram acquired sheep and cattle, male and female donkeys, menservants and maidservants, and camels.

[17]But the LORD inflicted serious diseases on Pharaoh and his household because of Abram's wife Sarai. [18]So Pharaoh summoned Abram. "What have you done to me?" he said. "Why didn't you tell me she was your wife? [19]Why did you say, 'She is my sister,' so that I took her to be my wife? Now then, here is your wife. Take her and go!" [20]Then Pharaoh gave orders about Abram to his men, and they sent him on his way, with his wife and everything he had.

■ Abram and Lot Separate

13 So Abram went up from Egypt to the Negev, with his wife and everything he had, and Lot went with him. [2]Abram had become very wealthy in livestock and in silver and gold.

[3]From the Negev he went from place to place until he came to Bethel, to the place between Bethel and Ai where his tent had been earlier [4]and where he had first built an altar. There Abram called on the name of the LORD.

13:3 ■ ON THE ROAD

The main trade route through Canaan passed north to south through Shechem, Bethel, Hebron, and Beersheba. As Abraham and his children travelled, they naturally stopped in those places. These place-names crop up again and again in the story of God's work.

[5]Now Lot, who was moving about with Abram, also had flocks and herds and tents. [6]But the land could not support them while they stayed together, for their possessions were so great that they were not able to stay together. [7]And quarrelling arose between Abram's herdsmen and the herdsmen of Lot. The Canaanites and Perizzites were also living in the land at that time.

[8]So Abram said to Lot, "Let's not have any quarrelling between you and me, or between your herdsmen and mine, for we are brothers. [9]Is not the whole land before you? Let's part company. If you go to the left, I'll go to the right; if you go to the right, I'll go to the left."

[10]Lot looked up and saw that the whole plain of the Jordan was well watered, like the garden of the LORD, like the land of Egypt, towards Zoar. (This was before the LORD destroyed Sodom and Gomorrah.) [11]So Lot chose for himself the whole plain of the Jordan and set out towards the east. The two men parted company: [12]Abram lived in the land of Canaan, while Lot lived among the cities of the plain and pitched his tents near Sodom. [13]Now the men of Sodom were wicked and were sinning greatly against the LORD.

[14]The LORD said to Abram after Lot had parted from him, "Lift up your eyes from where you are and look north and south, east and west. [15]All the land that you see I will give to you and your offspring[a] for ever. [16]I will make your offspring like the dust of the earth, so that if anyone could count the dust, then your offspring could be counted. [17]Go, walk through the length and breadth of the land, for I am giving it to you."

[18]So Abram moved his tents and went to live near the great trees of Mamre at Hebron, where he built an altar to the LORD.

■ Abram Rescues Lot

14 At this time Amraphel king of Shinar,[a] Arioch king of Ellasar, Kedorlaomer king of Elam and Tidal king of Goiim [2]went to war against Bera king of Sodom, Birsha king of Gomorrah, Shinab king of Admah, Shemeber king of Zeboiim, and the king of Bela (that is, Zoar). [3]All these latter kings joined forces in the Valley of Siddim (the Salt Sea[b]). [4]For twelve years they had been subject to Kedorlaomer, but in the thirteenth year they rebelled.

[5]In the fourteenth year, Kedorlaomer and the kings allied with him went out and defeated the Rephaites in Ashteroth Karnaim, the Zuzites in Ham, the Emites in Shaveh Kiriathaim [6]and the Horites in the hill country of Seir, as far as El Paran near the desert. [7]Then they turned back and went to En Mishpat (that is, Kadesh), and they conquered the whole territory of the Amalekites, as well as the Amorites who were living in Hazezon Tamar.

[8]Then the king of Sodom, the king of Gomorrah, the king of Admah, the king of Zeboiim and the king of Bela (that is, Zoar) marched out and drew up their battle lines in the Valley of Siddim [9]against Kedorlaomer king of Elam, Tidal king of Goiim, Amraphel king of Shinar and Arioch king of Ellasar—four kings against five. [10]Now the Valley of Siddim was full of tar pits, and when the kings of Sodom and Gomorrah fled, some of the men fell into them and the rest fled to the hills. [11]The four kings seized all the goods of Sodom and Gomorrah and all their food; then they went away. [12]They also carried off Abram's nephew Lot and his possessions, since he was living in Sodom.

[13]One who had escaped came and reported this to Abram the Hebrew. Now Abram was living near the great trees of Mamre the Amorite, a brother[c] of Eshcol and Aner, all of whom were allied with

Abram. [14]When Abram heard that his relative had been taken captive, he called out the 318 trained men born in his household and went in pursuit as far as Dan. [15]During the night Abram divided his men to attack them and he routed them, pursuing them as far as Hobah, north of Damascus. [16]He recovered all the goods and brought back his relative Lot and his possessions, together with the women and the other people.

[17]After Abram returned from defeating Kedorlaomer and the kings allied with him, the king of Sodom came out to meet him in the Valley of Shaveh (that is, the King's Valley).

[18]Then Melchizedek king of Salem[d] brought out bread and wine. He was priest of God Most High, [19]and he blessed Abram, saying,

"Blessed be Abram by God Most High,
    Creator[e] of heaven and earth.
[20]And blessed be[f] God Most High,
    who delivered your enemies into your hand."

Then Abram gave him a tenth of everything.

14:20 ■ MYSTERY MAN

Melchizedek appeared to Abraham without warning, received tremendous honour, and then disappeared. Yet hundreds of years later he earned a mention in Psalm 110, and hundreds of years after that in Hebrews 7:11–17. Melchizedek remains a mysterious figure, but he does set an important precedent for the Messiah: the same man can serve as both priest and king. (Jewish priests came from one tribe, and kings from another, different tribe.) Though Melchizedek did not have the proper family lineage, his spiritual power impressed Abraham, the father of Judaism.

[21]The king of Sodom said to Abram, "Give me the people and keep the goods for yourself."

[22]But Abram said to the king of Sodom, "I have raised my hand to the LORD, God Most High, Creator of heaven and earth, and have taken an oath [23]that I will accept nothing belonging to you, not even a thread or the thong of a sandal, so that you will never be able to say, 'I made Abram rich.' [24]I will accept nothing but what my men have eaten and the share that belongs to the men who went with me — to Aner, Eshcol and Mamre. Let them have their share."

■ God's Covenant With Abram

15 After this, the word of the LORD came to Abram in a vision:

"Do not be afraid, Abram.
    I am your shield,[a]
    your very great reward."[b]

[2]But Abram said, "O Sovereign LORD, what can you give me since I remain childless and the one who will inherit[c] my estate is Eliezer of Damascus?" [3]And Abram said, "You have given me no children; so a servant in my household will be my heir."

[4]Then the word of the LORD came to him: "This man will not be your heir, but a son coming from your own body will be your heir." [5]He took him outside and said, "Look up at the heavens and count the stars — if indeed you can count them." Then he said to him, "So shall your offspring be."

[6]Abram believed the LORD, and he credited it to him as righteousness.

15:6 ■ WHAT GOD LOOKS FOR

God accepted Abraham not because he led a perfect life but because of his responsiveness to God's promises. This verse was quoted three times in the New Testament to demonstrate that salvation by faith was nothing new (Romans 4:3; Galatians 3:6; James 2:23). Even in the Old Testament, God looked for faith, not moral perfection.

[7]He also said to him, "I am the LORD, who brought you out of Ur of the Chaldeans to give you this land to take possession of it."

[8]But Abram said, "O Sovereign LORD, how can I know that I shall gain possession of it?"

[9]So the LORD said to him, "Bring me a heifer, a goat and a ram, each three years old, along with a dove and a young pigeon."

[10]Abram brought all these to him, cut them in two and arranged the halves opposite each other; the birds, however, he did not cut in half. [11]Then birds of prey came down on the carcasses, but Abram drove them away.

[12]As the sun was setting, Abram fell into a deep sleep, and a thick and dreadful darkness came over him. [13]Then the LORD said to him, "Know for certain that your descendants will be strangers in a country not their own, and they will be enslaved and ill-treated four hundred years. [14]But I will punish the nation they serve as slaves, and afterwards they will come out with great possessions. [15]You, however, will go to your fathers in peace and be buried at a good old age. [16]In the fourth generation your descendants will come back here, for the sin of the Amorites has not yet reached its full measure."

[17]When the sun had set and darkness had fallen, a smoking brazier with a blazing torch appeared and passed between the pieces. [18]On that day the LORD made a covenant with Abram and said, "To your descendants I give this land, from the river[d] of Egypt to the great river, the Euphrates — [19]the land of the Kenites, Kenizzites, Kadmonites, [20]Hittites, Perizzites, Rephaites, [21]Amorites, Canaanites, Girgashites and Jebusites."

■ Hagar and Ishmael

16 Now Sarai, Abram's wife, had borne him no children. But she had an Egyptian maidservant named Hagar; [2]so she said to Abram, "The LORD has kept me from having children. Go, sleep with my maidservant; perhaps I can build a family through her."

Abram agreed to what Sarai said. [3]So after Abram had been living in Canaan ten years, Sarai his wife took her Egyptian maidservant Hagar and gave her

d 18 That is, Jerusalem   e 19 Or Possessor; also in verse 22   f 20 Or And praise be to   a 1 Or sovereign   b 1 Or shield; / your reward will be very great   c 2 The meaning of the Hebrew for this phrase is uncertain.   d 18 Or Wadi to her husband to be his wife. ⁴He slept with Hagar, and she conceived.

When she knew she was pregnant, she began to despise her mistress. ⁵Then Sarai said to Abram, "You are responsible for the wrong I am suffering. I put my servant in your arms, and now that she knows she is pregnant, she despises me. May the LORD judge between you and me."

16:2 ■ A SUBSTITUTE WIFE

According to custom, a man could sleep with a servant and include her children in his household. Abraham was trying to get the children he and his wife longed for and to "help God out" in fulfilling his promise of a son. Abraham's way was not God's way, however, and Abraham's attempt led to considerable jealousy and sorrow. The same practice also led to trouble for Jacob's family (chapter 30).

⁶"Your servant is in your hands," Abram said. "Do with her whatever you think best." Then Sarai ill-treated Hagar; so she fled from her.

⁷The angel of the LORD found Hagar near a spring in the desert; it was the spring that is beside the road to Shur. ⁸And he said, "Hagar, servant of Sarai, where have you come from, and where are you going?"

"I'm running away from my mistress Sarai," she answered.

⁹Then the angel of the LORD told her, "Go back to your mistress and submit to her." ¹⁰The angel added, "I will so increase your descendants that they will be too numerous to count."

¹¹The angel of the LORD also said to her:

"You are now with child
    and you will have a son.
You shall name him Ishmael,ᵃ
    for the LORD has heard of your misery.
¹²He will be a wild donkey of a man;
    his hand will be against everyone
    and everyone's hand against him,
and he will live in hostility
    towardsᵇ all his brothers."

¹³She gave this name to the LORD who spoke to her: "You are the God who sees me," for she said, "I have now seenᶜ the One who sees me." ¹⁴That is why the well was called Beer Lahai Roi;ᵈ it is still there, between Kadesh and Bered.

¹⁵So Hagar bore Abram a son, and Abram gave the name Ishmael to the son she had borne. ¹⁶Abram was eighty-six years old when Hagar bore him Ishmael.

■ The Covenant of Circumcision

17 When Abram was ninety-nine years old, the LORD appeared to him and said, "I am God Almighty;ᵃ walk before me and be blameless. ²I will confirm my covenant between me and you and will greatly increase your numbers."

³Abram fell face down, and God said to him, ⁴"As for me, this is my covenant with you: You will be the father of many nations. ⁵No longer will you be called Abram;ᵇ your name will be Abraham,ᶜ for I have made you a father of many nations. ⁶I will make you very fruitful; I will make nations of you, and kings will come from you. ⁷I will establish my covenant as an everlasting covenant between me and you and your descendants after you for the generations to come, to be your God and the God of your descendants after you. ⁸The whole land of Canaan, where you are now an alien, I will give as an everlasting possession to you and your descendants after you; and I will be their God."

⁹Then God said to Abraham, "As for you, you must keep my covenant, you and your descendants after you for the generations to come. ¹⁰This is my covenant with you and your descendants after you, the covenant you are to keep: Every male among you shall be circumcised. ¹¹You are to undergo circumcision, and it will be the sign of the covenant between me and you. ¹²For the generations to come every male among you who is eight days old must be circumcised, including those born in your household or bought with money from a foreigner—those who are not your offspring. ¹³Whether born in your household or bought with your money, they must be circumcised. My covenant in your flesh is to be an everlasting covenant. ¹⁴Any uncircumcised male, who has not been circumcised in the flesh, will be cut off from his people; he has broken my covenant."

¹⁵God also said to Abraham, "As for Sarai your wife, you are no longer to call her Sarai; her name will be Sarah. ¹⁶I will bless her and will surely give you a son by her. I will bless her so that she will be the mother of nations; kings of peoples will come from her."

¹⁷Abraham fell face down; he laughed and said to himself, "Will a son be born to a man a hundred years old? Will Sarah bear a child at the age of ninety?" ¹⁸And Abraham said to God, "If only Ishmael might live under your blessing!"

17:17 ■ LAUGHING AT GOD

Abraham was a man of faith, but his faith was less than 100 per cent. Here, nearing the age of 100, he laughed heartily at God's promise that he would father a son, and he demonstrated his lack of belief by suggesting that God accept Ishmael as an adequate substitute. Some time later Sarah, his wife, shared in the "joke" (18:12).

¹⁹Then God said, "Yes, but your wife Sarah will bear you a son, and you will call him Isaac.ᵈ I will establish my covenant with him as an everlasting covenant for his descendants after him. ²⁰And as for Ishmael, I have heard you: I will surely bless him; I will make him fruitful and will greatly increase his numbers. He will be the father of twelve rulers, and I will make him into a great nation. ²¹But my covenant I will establish with Isaac, whom Sarah will bear to you by this time next year." ²²When he had finished speaking with Abraham, God went up from him.

²³On that very day Abraham took his son Ishmael and all those born in his household or bought with

---

ᵃ11 Ishmael means God hears.   ᵇ12 Or live to the east / of   ᶜ13 Or seen the back of   ᵈ14 Beer Lahai Roi means well of the Living One who sees
me.   ᵃ1 Hebrew El-Shaddai   ᵇ5 Abram means exalted father.   ᶜ5 Abraham means father of many.   ᵈ19 Isaac means he laughs.

his money, every male in his household, and circumcised them, as God told him. 24Abraham was ninety-nine years old when he was circumcised, 25and his son Ishmael was thirteen; 26Abraham and his son Ishmael were both circumcised on that same day. 27And every male in Abraham's household, including those born in his household or bought from a foreigner, was circumcised with him.

■ The Three Visitors

18 The LORD appeared to Abraham near the great trees of Mamre while he was sitting at the entrance to his tent in the heat of the day. 2Abraham looked up and saw three men standing nearby. When he saw them, he hurried from the entrance of his tent to meet them and bowed low to the ground. 3He said, "If I have found favour in your eyes, my lord,ᵃ do not pass your servant by. 4Let a little water be brought, and then you may all wash your feet and rest under this tree. 5Let me get you something to eat, so you can be refreshed and then go on your way—now that you have come to your servant."

"Very well," they answered, "do as you say."

6So Abraham hurried into the tent to Sarah. "Quick," he said, "get three seahsᵇ of fine flour and knead it and bake some bread."

7Then he ran to the herd and selected a choice, tender calf and gave it to a servant, who hurried to prepare it. 8He then brought some curds and milk and the calf that had been prepared, and set these before them. While they ate, he stood near them under a tree.

9"Where is your wife Sarah?" they asked him.

"There, in the tent," he said.

10Then the LORDᶜ said, "I will surely return to you about this time next year, and Sarah your wife will have a son."

Now Sarah was listening at the entrance to the tent, which was behind him. 11Abraham and Sarah were already old and well advanced in years, and Sarah was past the age of childbearing. 12So Sarah laughed to herself as she thought, "After I am worn out and my masterᵈ is old, will I now have this pleasure?"

13Then the LORD said to Abraham, "Why did Sarah laugh and say, 'Will I really have a child, now that I am old?' 14Is anything too hard for the LORD? I will return to you at the appointed time next year and Sarah will have a son."

15Sarah was afraid, so she lied and said, "I did not laugh."

But he said, "Yes, you did laugh."

■ Abraham Pleads for Sodom

16When the men got up to leave, they looked down towards Sodom, and Abraham walked along with them to see them on their way. 17Then the LORD said, "Shall I hide from Abraham what I am about to do? 18Abraham will surely become a great and powerful nation, and all nations on earth will be blessed through him. 19For I have chosen him, so that he will direct his children and his household after him to keep the way of the LORD by doing what

is right and just, so that the LORD will bring about for Abraham what he has promised him."

18:18 ■ THE GOSPEL TO ABRAHAM
God predicted here (and in several other places) that all nations on earth would be blessed through Abraham. About two thousand years later the apostle Paul, seeing in this a prediction of God reaching out through Jews to non-Jews with the message of Christianity, wrote that God had "announced the gospel in advance to Abraham" (Galatians 3:8).

20Then the LORD said, "The outcry against Sodom and Gomorrah is so great and their sin so grievous 21that I will go down and see if what they have done is as bad as the outcry that has reached me. If not, I will know."

22The men turned away and went towards Sodom, but Abraham remained standing before the LORD.ᵉ 23Then Abraham approached him and said: "Will you sweep away the righteous with the wicked? 24What if there are fifty righteous people in the city? Will you really sweep it away and not spareᶠ the place for the sake of the fifty righteous people in it? 25Far be it from you to do such a thing—to kill the righteous with the wicked, treating the righteous and the wicked alike. Far be it from you! Will not the Judgeᵍ of all the earth do right?"

26The LORD said, "If I find fifty righteous people in the city of Sodom, I will spare the whole place for their sake."

27Then Abraham spoke up again: "Now that I have been so bold as to speak to the Lord, though I am nothing but dust and ashes, 28what if the number of the righteous is five less than fifty? Will you destroy the whole city because of five people?"

"If I find forty-five there," he said, "I will not destroy it."

29Once again he spoke to him, "What if only forty are found there?"

He said, "For the sake of forty, I will not do it."

30Then he said, "May the Lord not be angry, but let me speak. What if only thirty can be found there?"

He answered, "I will not do it if I find thirty there."

31Abraham said, "Now that I have been so bold as to speak to the Lord, what if only twenty can be found there?"

He said, "For the sake of twenty, I will not destroy it."

32Then he said, "May the Lord not be angry, but let me speak just once more. What if only ten can be found there?"

He answered, "For the sake of ten, I will not destroy it."

33When the LORD had finished speaking with Abraham, he left, and Abraham returned home.

■ Sodom and Gomorrah Destroyed

19 The two angels arrived at Sodom in the evening, and Lot was sitting in the gateway of the city. When he saw them, he got up to meet them and bowed down with his face to the ground. 2"My

ᵃ3 Or O Lord   ᵇ6 That is, probably about 39 pints (about 22 litres)   ᶜ10 Hebrew Then he   ᵈ12 Or husband   ᵉ22 Masoretic Text; an ancient Hebrew scribal tradition but the LORD remained standing before Abraham   ᶠ24 Or forgive; also in verse 26   ᵍ25 Or Ruler lords," he said, "please turn aside to your servant's house. You can wash your feet and spend the night and then go on your way early in the morning."

"No," they answered, "we will spend the night in the square."

19:1 ■ A MAN OF SUBSTANCE
The angels found Lot in the gateway to Sodom — a fact loaded with significance. Traditionally, city fathers gathered in the gateway to make important decisions. Lot's presence suggests that he had become "one of them" during his time in Sodom, which may explain why he struggled against leaving.

3But he insisted so strongly that they did go with him and entered his house. He prepared a meal for them, baking bread without yeast, and they ate. 4Before they had gone to bed, all the men from every part of the city of Sodom — both young and old — surrounded the house. 5They called to Lot, "Where are the men who came to you tonight? Bring them out to us so that we can have sex with them."

6Lot went outside to meet them and shut the door behind him 7and said, "No, my friends. Don't do this wicked thing. 8Look, I have two daughters who have never slept with a man. Let me bring them out to you, and you can do what you like with them. But don't do anything to these men, for they have come under the protection of my roof."

9"Get out of our way," they replied. And they said, "This fellow came here as an alien, and now he wants to play the judge! We'll treat you worse than them." They kept bringing pressure on Lot and moved forward to break down the door.

10But the men inside reached out and pulled Lot back into the house and shut the door. 11Then they struck the men who were at the door of the house, young and old, with blindness so that they could not find the door.

12The two men said to Lot, "Do you have anyone

■ A CATASTROPHE SENT FROM GOD
SODOM: A CITY THAT EARNED DESTRUCTION

INSIGHT

"DO YOU HAVE ANYONE ELSE HERE — SONS-IN-LAW, SONS OR DAUGHTERS, OR ANYONE ELSE IN THE CITY WHO BELONGS TO YOU? GET THEM OUT OF HERE, BECAUSE WE ARE GOING TO DESTROY THIS PLACE." ■ 19:12–13

Should a catastrophe be read as a punishment from God? Do floods, famines, earthquakes come because God is angry? The Bible's answer is, "Sometimes, and sometimes not." In Genesis, several catastrophes seemed to "just happen" — they were not a punishment or a warning, though God used them to advance his plans. These included several famines such as the one that brought Joseph to power (chapter 41), a war (chapter 14), a rape (chapter 34).

But a few catastrophes God took full credit for — like the one at Sodom and Gomorrah. As usual, the Bible shows little or no interest in telling us the scientific facts about the destruction. Was it a volcanic eruption, like the Philippines' Mount Pinatubo, for instance?

The Bible doesn't say, and the area, now apparently at the bottom of the Dead Sea, cannot easily be investigated. The Bible stresses not how it happened, but why.

■ GANG RAPE
Sodom was a wretched place. The whole town saw the coming of strangers as a chance for homosexual gang rape. Sexual violence was not the town's only problem. Ezekiel 16:49 says that Sodom was "arrogant, overfed and unconcerned; they did not help the poor and needy." God would have let the city stand if Abraham could have located just ten righteous people. Apparently, ten such people did not exist. God's great patience finally ran out.

Years earlier, Abraham had refused to accept even a well-earned reward from the government of Sodom (14:21–24). He wanted nothing to do with such a society. But Lot had chosen the path of prosperity, the easy and successful life on the fertile plain near Sodom.

Lot had become a somebody there, a civic heavy who made important decisions in the city gateway. He was so entangled with life in Sodom that he hesitated to leave until it was nearly too late. When Sodom went up in smoke, his hard-earned importance disappeared too. The shock was too great for him. Unable to start again, he ended up in a cave, too drunk to know that his two daughters were having sex with him. He is the perfect example of a man who, excessively tangled in a corrupt system, cannot bear to leave it behind.

Jesus did not let his followers think of Sodom simply as "those terrible people". He warned them that God would be even harder on those who saw Jesus' miracles, but ignored them (Matthew 11:24). God's patience has a limit.

□ LIFE QUESTIONS:
Are any catastrophes of our time punishments from God? How would you know?

else here — sons-in-law, sons or daughters, or anyone else in the city who belongs to you? Get them
out of here, ¹³because we are going to destroy this
place. The outcry to the LORD against its people is so
great that he has sent us to destroy it."

¹⁴So Lot went out and spoke to his sons-in-law,
who were pledged to marry*ᵃ his daughters. He
said, "Hurry and get out of this place, because the
LORD is about to destroy the city!" But his sons-in-
law thought he was joking.

¹⁵With the coming of dawn, the angels urged Lot,
saying, "Hurry! Take your wife and your two daughters who are here, or you will be swept away when
the city is punished."

¹⁶When he hesitated, the men grasped his hand
and the hands of his wife and of his two daughters
and led them safely out of the city, for the LORD was
merciful to them. ¹⁷As soon as they had brought
them out, one of them said, "Flee for your lives!
Don't look back, and don't stop anywhere in the
plain! Flee to the mountains or you will be swept
away!"

¹⁸But Lot said to them, "No, my lords,ᵇ please!
¹⁹Yourᶜ servant has found favour in yourᶜ eyes,
and youᶜ have shown great kindness to me in sparing my life. But I can't flee to the mountains; this
disaster will overtake me, and I'll die. ²⁰Look, here
is a town near enough to run to, and it is small. Let
me flee to it — it is very small, isn't it? Then my life
will be spared."

²¹He said to him, "Very well, I will grant this request too; I will not overthrow the town you speak
of. ²²But flee there quickly, because I cannot do anything until you reach it." (That is why the town was
called Zoar.ᵈ)

²³By the time Lot reached Zoar, the sun had risen
over the land. ²⁴Then the LORD rained down burning
sulphur on Sodom and Gomorrah — from the LORD
out of the heavens. ²⁵Thus he overthrew those cities
and the entire plain, including all those living in the
cities — and also the vegetation in the land. ²⁶But
Lot's wife looked back, and she became a pillar of
salt.

19:26 ■ DON'T LOOK BACK
Lot and his family found it hard to leave their
adopted home of Sodom, despite its immorality.
Angel messengers warned them to hurry, not even
stopping to look back. When Lot's wife disobeyed,
she turned into a pillar of salt — perhaps caught in
volcanic explosions that engulfed Sodom. For this
she became a symbol of indecision. Jesus urged
his followers to remember her example when their
time of trouble came (Luke 17:32).

²⁷Early the next morning Abraham got up and returned to the place where he had stood before the
LORD. ²⁸He looked down towards Sodom and Gomorrah, towards all the land of the plain, and he saw
dense smoke rising from the land, like smoke from
a furnace.

²⁹So when God destroyed the cities of the plain,
he remembered Abraham, and he brought Lot out of

the catastrophe that overthrew the cities where Lot
had lived.

■ Lot and His Daughters
³⁰Lot and his two daughters left Zoar and settled
in the mountains, for he was afraid to stay in Zoar.
He and his two daughters lived in a cave. ³¹One day
the older daughter said to the younger, "Our father
is old, and there is no man around here to lie with
us, as is the custom all over the earth. ³²Let's get our
father to drink wine and then lie with him and preserve our family line through our father."

³³That night they got their father to drink wine,
and the older daughter went in and lay with him. He
was not aware of it when she lay down or when she
got up.

³⁴The next day the older daughter said to the
younger, "Last night I lay with my father. Let's get
him to drink wine again tonight, and you go in and
lie with him so we can preserve our family line
through our father." ³⁵So they got their father to
drink wine that night also, and the younger daughter
went and lay with him. Again he was not aware of
it when she lay down or when she got up.

³⁶So both of Lot's daughtersᶜ became pregnant by
their father. ³⁷The older daughter had a son, and she
named him Moab;ᵉ he is the father of the Moabites
of today. ³⁸The younger daughter also had a son, and
she named him Ben-Ammi;ᶠ he is the father of the
Ammonites of today.

19:37 ■ FAMILY QUARRELS
Lot's determination to enjoy life in Sodom ended
tragically here, in drunken incest. The resulting
sons founded the family-nations of Moab and
Ammon, which for centuries fought with their
distant relatives in Israel and tempted them to sin.

■ Abraham and Abimelech
20 Now Abraham moved on from there into the
region of the Negev and lived between Kadesh and Shur. For a while he stayed in Gerar, ²and
there Abraham said of his wife Sarah, "She is my sister." Then Abimelech king of Gerar sent for Sarah
and took her.

³But God came to Abimelech in a dream one
night and said to him, "You are as good as dead because of the woman you have taken; she is a married
woman."

⁴Now Abimelech had not gone near her, so he
said, "Lord, will you destroy an innocent nation?
⁵Did he not say to me, 'She is my sister,' and didn't
she also say, 'He is my brother'? I have done this with
a clear conscience and clean hands."

⁶Then God said to him in the dream, "Yes, I know
you did this with a clear conscience, and so I have
kept you from sinning against me. That is why I did
not let you touch her. ⁷Now return the man's wife,
for he is a prophet, and he will pray for you and you
will live. But if you do not return her, you may be
sure that you and all yours will die."

⁸Early the next morning Abimelech summoned
all his officials, and when he told them all that had

ᵃ14 Or were married to   ᵇ18 Or No, Lord; or No, my lord   ᶜ19 The Hebrew is singular.   ᵈ22 Zoar means small.   ᵉ37 Moab sounds like the
Hebrew for from father.   ᶠ38 Ben-Ammi means son of my people.

happened, they were very much afraid. ⁹Then Abimelech called Abraham in and said, "What have you done to us? How have I wronged you that you have brought such great guilt upon me and my kingdom? You have done things to me that should not be done." ¹⁰And Abimelech asked Abraham, "What was your reason for doing this?"

¹¹Abraham replied, "I said to myself, 'There is surely no fear of God in this place, and they will kill me because of my wife.' ¹²Besides, she really is my sister, the daughter of my father though not of my mother; and she became my wife. ¹³And when God caused me to wander from my father's household, I said to her, 'This is how you can show your love to me: Everywhere we go, say of me, "He is my brother."' "

¹⁴Then Abimelech brought sheep and cattle and male and female slaves and gave them to Abraham, and he returned Sarah his wife to him. ¹⁵And Abimelech said, "My land is before you; live wherever you like."

¹⁶To Sarah he said, "I am giving your brother a thousand shekels^a of silver. This is to cover the offence against you before all who are with you; you are completely vindicated."

¹⁷Then Abraham prayed to God, and God healed Abimelech, his wife and his slave girls so they could have children again, ¹⁸for the LORD had closed up every womb in Abimelech's household because of Abraham's wife Sarah.

■ The Birth of Isaac

21 Now the LORD was gracious to Sarah as he had said, and the LORD did for Sarah what he had promised. ²Sarah became pregnant and bore a son to Abraham in his old age, at the very time God had promised him. ³Abraham gave the name Isaac^a to the son Sarah bore him. ⁴When his son Isaac was eight days old, Abraham circumcised him, as God commanded him. ⁵Abraham was a hundred years old when his son Isaac was born to him.

⁶Sarah said, "God has brought me laughter, and everyone who hears about this will laugh with me." ⁷And she added, "Who would have said to Abraham that Sarah would nurse children? Yet I have borne him a son in his old age."

■ Hagar and Ishmael Sent Away

⁸The child grew and was weaned, and on the day Isaac was weaned Abraham held a great feast. ⁹But Sarah saw that the son whom Hagar the Egyptian had borne to Abraham was mocking, ¹⁰and she said to Abraham, "Get rid of that slave woman and her son, for that slave woman's son will never share in the inheritance with my son Isaac."

¹¹The matter distressed Abraham greatly because it concerned his son. ¹²But God said to him, "Do not be so distressed about the boy and your maidservant. Listen to whatever Sarah tells you, because it is through Isaac that your offspring^b will be reckoned. ¹³I will make the son of the maidservant into a nation also, because he is your offspring."

¹⁴Early the next morning Abraham took some food and a skin of water and gave them to Hagar. He set them on her shoulders and then sent her off with the boy. She went on her way and wandered in the desert of Beersheba.

¹⁵When the water in the skin was gone, she put the boy under one of the bushes. ¹⁶Then she went off and sat down nearby, about a bow-shot away, for she thought, "I cannot watch the boy die." And as she sat there nearby, she^c began to sob.

¹⁷God heard the boy crying, and the angel of God called to Hagar from heaven and said to her, "What is the matter, Hagar? Do not be afraid; God has heard the boy crying as he lies there. ¹⁸Lift the boy up and take him by the hand, for I will make him into a great nation."

¹⁹Then God opened her eyes and she saw a well of water. So she went and filled the skin with water and gave the boy a drink. ²⁰God was with the boy as he grew up. He lived in the desert and became an archer. ²¹While he was living in the Desert of Paran, his mother got a wife for him from Egypt.

■ The Treaty at Beersheba

²²At that time Abimelech and Phicol the commander of his forces said to Abraham, "God is with you in everything you do. ²³Now swear to me here before God that you will not deal falsely with me or my children or my descendants. Show to me and the country where you are living as an alien the same kindness that I have shown to you."

²⁴Abraham said, "I swear it."

²⁵Then Abraham complained to Abimelech about a well of water that Abimelech's servants had seized. ²⁶But Abimelech said, "I don't know who has done this. You did not tell me, and I heard about it only today."

²⁷So Abraham brought sheep and cattle and gave them to Abimelech, and the two men made a treaty. ²⁸Abraham set apart seven ewe lambs from the flock, ²⁹and Abimelech asked Abraham, "What is the meaning of these seven ewe lambs you have set apart by themselves?"

³⁰He replied, "Accept these seven lambs from my hand as a witness that I dug this well."

³¹So that place was called Beersheba,^d because the two men swore an oath there.

³²After the treaty had been made at Beersheba, Abimelech and Phicol the commander of his forces returned to the land of the Philistines. ³³Abraham planted a tamarisk tree in Beersheba, and there he called upon the name of the LORD, the Eternal God. ³⁴And Abraham stayed in the land of the Philistines for a long time.

■ Abraham Tested

22 Some time later God tested Abraham. He said to him, "Abraham!"

"Here I am," he replied.

²Then God said, "Take your son, your only son, Isaac, whom you love, and go to the region of Moriah. Sacrifice him there as a burnt offering on one of the mountains I will tell you about."

³Early the next morning Abraham got up and saddled his donkey. He took with him two of his servants and his son Isaac. When he had cut enough

^a16 That is, about 25 pounds (about 11.5 kilograms)   ^a3 Isaac means he laughs.   ^b12 Or seed   ^c16 Hebrew; Septuagint the child
^d31 Beersheba can mean well of seven or well of the oath.

wood for the burnt offering, he set out for the place God had told him about. ⁴On the third day Abraham looked up and saw the place in the distance. ⁵He said to his servants, "Stay here with the donkey while I and the boy go over there. We will worship and then we will come back to you."

⁶Abraham took the wood for the burnt offering and placed it on his son Isaac, and he himself carried the fire and the knife. As the two of them went on together, ⁷Isaac spoke up and said to his father Abraham, "Father?"

"Yes, my son?" Abraham replied.

"The fire and wood are here," Isaac said, "but where is the lamb for the burnt offering?"

⁸Abraham answered, "God himself will provide the lamb for the burnt offering, my son." And the two of them went on together.

⁹When they reached the place God had told him about, Abraham built an altar there and arranged the wood on it. He bound his son Isaac and laid him on the altar, on top of the wood. ¹⁰Then he reached out his hand and took the knife to slay his son. ¹¹But the angel of the LORD called out to him from heaven, "Abraham! Abraham!"

"Here I am," he replied.

¹²"Do not lay a hand on the boy," he said. "Do not do anything to him. Now I know that you fear God,

because you have not withheld from me your son, your only son."

¹³Abraham looked up and there in a thicket he saw a ram*ᵃ* caught by its horns. He went over and took the ram and sacrificed it as a burnt offering instead of his son. ¹⁴So Abraham called that place The LORD Will Provide. And to this day it is said, "On the mountain of the LORD it will be provided."

¹⁵The angel of the LORD called to Abraham from heaven a second time ¹⁶and said, "I swear by myself, declares the LORD, that because you have done this and have not withheld your son, your only son, ¹⁷I will surely bless you and make your descendants as numerous as the stars in the sky and as the sand on the seashore. Your descendants will take possession of the cities of their enemies, ¹⁸and through your offspring*ᵇ* all nations on earth will be blessed, because you have obeyed me."

¹⁹Then Abraham returned to his servants, and they set off together for Beersheba. And Abraham stayed in Beersheba.

■ Nahor's Sons

²⁰Some time later Abraham was told, "Milcah is also a mother; she has borne sons to your brother Nahor: ²¹Uz the firstborn, Buz his brother, Kemuel (the father of Aram), ²²Kesed, Hazo, Pildash, Jidlaph

■ PROMISES, PROMISES
GOD PROMISED TO GIVE ABRAHAM ALL THAT HE LONGED FOR . . . AND MORE

INSIGHT

"THROUGH YOUR OFFSPRING ALL NATIONS ON EARTH WILL BE BLESSED, BECAUSE YOU HAVE OBEYED ME."
■ 22:18

Human beings haven't changed much in 4,000 years. The longing for children and the desire for land still surge up with surprising emotional power.

Consider the estimated 15 per cent of couples in this country who are childless. For most of them, this brings deep anguish. Or think about the people who work double shifts, sacrificing their free time in order to own a home rather than rent one.

Abraham would have understood. When God wanted his attention, he promised him land and more sons than he could count. To a Babylonian emigrant, 75 years old and childless, owning nothing but his tents and animals, the promises sounded wonderful. In fact, they sounded impossible. Yet, because God himself was making the promise, Abraham "believed the LORD, and he credited it to him as righteousness" (15:6).

For the God who had created the heavens and the earth, making good the promises ought to have been a cinch. But God did not make it easy for Abraham. Not until

25 years later, when Abraham was 100, did the promise of a son come true. Then, incredibly, God told Abraham to make a human sacrifice of his little boy. It was really asking too much.

Astonishingly, Abraham followed God's orders. And God gave him back his son.

■ FAR FROM FULFILLED
When Abraham died, God's promises were far from fully realised. Abraham had only that one son to cling to. His only land was a burial plot. He still lived in a tent: his only permanent structures were altars erected to worship the God who had made all those promises.

God, having promised him everything a man of that time could want, apparently wanted Abraham to think even bigger thoughts. He had slipped some words in along with the promises of offspring and land: "All peoples on earth will be blessed through you" (12:3). God wanted to bless not just Abraham, but the whole world. Thousands of years later, in the time of Jesus, the full meaning of those words became clear (see Galatians 3:6–9,16–18).

□ LIFE QUESTIONS:
What kind of promises does God make today? What longings does he fulfil?

ᵃ13 Many manuscripts of the Masoretic Text, Samaritan Pentateuch, Septuagint and Syriac; most manuscripts of the Masoretic Text *a ram behind ⌐him⌐*
ᵇ18 Or *seed*

and Bethuel." [23]Bethuel became the father of Rebekah. Milcah bore these eight sons to Abraham's brother Nahor. [24]His concubine, whose name was Reumah, also had sons: Tebah, Gaham, Tahash and Maacah.

■ The Death of Sarah

23 Sarah lived to be a hundred and twenty-seven years old. [2]She died at Kiriath Arba (that is, Hebron) in the land of Canaan, and Abraham went to mourn for Sarah and to weep over her.

[3]Then Abraham rose from beside his dead wife and spoke to the Hittites.[a] He said, [4]"I am an alien and a stranger among you. Sell me some property for a burial site here so that I can bury my dead."

[5]The Hittites replied to Abraham, [6]"Sir, listen to us. You are a mighty prince among us. Bury your dead in the choicest of our tombs. None of us will refuse you his tomb for burying your dead."

[7]Then Abraham rose and bowed down before the people of the land, the Hittites. [8]He said to them, "If you are willing to let me bury my dead, then listen to me and intercede with Ephron son of Zohar on my behalf [9]so that he will sell me the cave of Machpelah, which belongs to him and is at the end of his field. Ask him to sell it to me for the full price as a burial site among you."

[10]Ephron the Hittite was sitting among his people and he replied to Abraham in the hearing of all the Hittites who had come to the gate of his city. [11]"No, my lord," he said. "Listen to me; I give[b] you the field, and I give[b] you the cave that is in it. I give[b] it to you in the presence of my people. Bury your dead."

[12]Again Abraham bowed down before the people of the land [13]and he said to Ephron in their hearing, "Listen to me, if you will. I will pay the price of the field. Accept it from me so that I can bury my dead there."

[14]Ephron answered Abraham, [15]"Listen to me, my lord; the land is worth four hundred shekels[c] of silver, but what is that between me and you? Bury your dead."

23:15 ■ LET'S MAKE A DEAL

This may be the oldest recorded business deal. The elaborate politeness sounds very much like bargaining in the Middle East today. Underneath the smooth words, shrewd negotiating is going on. The Hittites were probably reluctant to allow Abraham, an alien, to own property of any kind lest he gain a legal foothold in their country. Abraham zeroed in on Ephron, who stood to gain financially from the sale.

[16]Abraham agreed to Ephron's terms and weighed out for him the price he had named in the hearing of the Hittites: four hundred shekels of silver, according to the weight current among the merchants. [17]So Ephron's field in Machpelah near Mamre — both the field and the cave in it, and all the trees within the borders of the field — was legally made over [18]to Abraham as his property in the presence of all the Hittites who had come to the gate of the city. [19]Afterwards Abraham buried his wife Sarah in the cave in the field of Machpelah near Mamre (which is at Hebron) in the land of Canaan. [20]So the field and the cave in it were legally made over to Abraham by the Hittites as a burial site.

■ Isaac and Rebekah

24 Abraham was now old and well advanced in years, and the LORD had blessed him in every way. [2]He said to the chief[a] servant in his household, the one in charge of all that he had, "Put your hand under my thigh. [3]I want you to swear by the LORD, the God of heaven and the God of earth, that you will not get a wife for my son from the daughters of the Canaanites, among whom I am living, [4]but will go to my country and my own relatives and get a wife for my son Isaac."

24:3 ■ MARRYING FOREIGNERS

From this earliest period of Israelite history, there was an emphasis on not marrying foreigners. The reason had to do with religion, not race — in many cases foreigners were distant relatives. When foreigners were willing to worship Israel's God, they were welcomed (see the book of Ruth, for example).

[5]The servant asked him, "What if the woman is unwilling to come back with me to this land? Shall I then take your son back to the country you came from?"

[6]"Make sure that you do not take my son back there," Abraham said. [7]"The LORD, the God of heaven, who brought me out of my father's household and my native land and who spoke to me and promised me on oath, saying, 'To your offspring[b] I will give this land' — he will send his angel before you so that you can get a wife for my son from there. [8]If the woman is unwilling to come back with you, then you will be released from this oath of mine. Only do not take my son back there." [9]So the servant put his hand under the thigh of his master Abraham and swore an oath to him concerning this matter.

[10]Then the servant took ten of his master's camels and left, taking with him all kinds of good things from his master. He set out for Aram Naharaim[c] and made his way to the town of Nahor. [11]He made the camels kneel down near the well outside the town; it was towards evening, the time the women go out to draw water.

[12]Then he prayed, "O LORD, God of my master Abraham, give me success today, and show kindness to my master Abraham. [13]See, I am standing beside this spring, and the daughters of the townspeople are coming out to draw water. [14]May it be that when I say to a girl, 'Please let down your jar that I may have a drink,' and she says, 'Drink, and I'll water your camels too' — let her be the one you have chosen for your servant Isaac. By this I will know that you have shown kindness to my master."

[15]Before he had finished praying, Rebekah came out with her jar on her shoulder. She was the

---

[a]3 Or the sons of Heth; also in verses 5, 7, 10, 16, 18 and 20   [b]11 Or sell   [c]15 That is, about 10 pounds (about 4.5 kilograms)   [a]2 Or oldest
[b]7 Or seed   [c]10 That is, North-west Mesopotamia

daughter of Bethuel son of Milcah, who was the wife of Abraham's brother Nahor. [16]The girl was very beautiful, a virgin; no man had ever lain with her. She went down to the spring, filled her jar and came up again.

[17]The servant hurried to meet her and said, "Please give me a little water from your jar."

[18]"Drink, my lord," she said, and quickly lowered the jar to her hands and gave him a drink.

[19]After she had given him a drink, she said, "I'll draw water for your camels too, until they have finished drinking." [20]So she quickly emptied her jar into the trough, ran back to the well to draw more water, and drew enough for all his camels. [21]Without saying a word, the man watched her closely to learn whether or not the LORD had made his journey successful.

[22]When the camels had finished drinking, the man took out a gold nose ring weighing a beka[d] and two gold bracelets weighing ten shekels.[e] [23]Then he asked, "Whose daughter are you? Please tell me, is there room in your father's house for us to spend the night?"

[24]She answered him, "I am the daughter of Bethuel, the son that Milcah bore to Nahor." [25]And she added, "We have plenty of straw and fodder, as well as room for you to spend the night."

[26]Then the man bowed down and worshipped the LORD, [27]saying, "Praise be to the LORD, the God of my master Abraham, who has not abandoned his kindness and faithfulness to my master. As for me, the LORD has led me on the journey to the house of my master's relatives."

[28]The girl ran and told her mother's household about these things. [29]Now Rebekah had a brother named Laban, and he hurried out to the man at the spring. [30]As soon as he had seen the nose ring, and the bracelets on his sister's arms, and had heard Rebekah tell what the man said to her, he went out to the man and found him standing by the camels near the spring. [31]"Come, you who are blessed by the LORD," he said. "Why are you standing out here? I have prepared the house and a place for the camels."

[32]So the man went to the house, and the camels were unloaded. Straw and fodder were brought for the camels, and water for him and his men to wash their feet. [33]Then food was set before him, but he said, "I will not eat until I have told you what I have to say."

"Then tell us," ⌊Laban⌋ said.

[34]So he said, "I am Abraham's servant. [35]The LORD has blessed my master abundantly, and he has become wealthy. He has given him sheep and cattle, silver and gold, menservants and maidservants, and camels and donkeys. [36]My master's wife Sarah has borne him a son in her[f] old age, and he has given him everything he owns. [37]And my master made me swear an oath, and said, 'You must not get a wife for my son from the daughters of the Canaanites, in whose land I live, [38]but go to my father's family and to my own clan, and get a wife for my son.'

[39]"Then I asked my master, 'What if the woman will not come back with me?'

[40]"He replied, 'The LORD, before whom I have walked, will send his angel with you and make your journey a success, so that you can get a wife for my son from my own clan and from my father's family. [41]Then, when you go to my clan, you will be released from my oath even if they refuse to give her to you—you will be released from my oath.'

[42]"When I came to the spring today, I said, 'O LORD, God of my master Abraham, if you will, please grant success to the journey on which I have come. [43]See, I am standing beside this spring; if a maiden comes out to draw water and I say to her, "Please let me drink a little water from your jar," [44]and if she says to me, "Drink, and I'll draw water for your camels too," let her be the one the LORD has chosen for my master's son.'

[45]"Before I finished praying in my heart, Rebekah came out, with her jar on her shoulder. She went down to the spring and drew water, and I said to her, 'Please give me a drink.'

[46]"She quickly lowered her jar from her shoulder and said, 'Drink, and I'll water your camels too.' So I drank, and she watered the camels also.

[47]"I asked her, 'Whose daughter are you?'

"She said, 'The daughter of Bethuel son of Nahor, whom Milcah bore to him.'

"Then I put the ring in her nose and the bracelets on her arms, [48]and I bowed down and worshipped the LORD. I praised the LORD, the God of my master Abraham, who had led me on the right road to get the granddaughter of my master's brother for his son. [49]Now if you will show kindness and faithfulness to my master, tell me; and if not, tell me, so I may know which way to turn."

[50]Laban and Bethuel answered, "This is from the LORD; we can say nothing to you one way or the other. [51]Here is Rebekah; take her and go, and let her become the wife of your master's son, as the LORD has directed."

[52]When Abraham's servant heard what they said, he bowed down to the ground before the LORD. [53]Then the servant brought out gold and silver jewellery and articles of clothing and gave them to Rebekah; he also gave costly gifts to her brother and to her mother. [54]Then he and the men who were with him ate and drank and spent the night there.

When they got up the next morning, he said, "Send me on my way to my master."

[55]But her brother and her mother replied, "Let the girl remain with us ten days or so; then you[g] may go."

[56]But he said to them, "Do not detain me, now that the LORD has granted success to my journey. Send me on my way so I may go to my master."

[57]Then they said, "Let's call the girl and ask her about it." [58]So they called Rebekah and asked her, "Will you go with this man?"

"I will go," she said.

[59]So they sent their sister Rebekah on her way, along with her nurse and Abraham's servant and his men. [60]And they blessed Rebekah and said to her,

"Our sister, may you increase
  to thousands upon thousands;
may your offspring possess
  the gates of their enemies."

[61]Then Rebekah and her maids got ready and

d 22 That is, about ⅕ ounce (about 6 grams)   e 22 That is, about 4 ounces (about 115 grams)   f 36 Or his   g 55 Or she mounted their camels and went back with the man. So the servant took Rebekah and left.

⁶²Now Isaac had come from Beer Lahai Roi, for he was living in the Negev. ⁶³He went out to the field one evening to meditate,ᵇ and as he looked up, he saw camels approaching. ⁶⁴Rebekah also looked up and saw Isaac. She got down from her camel ⁶⁵and asked the servant, "Who is that man in the field coming to meet us?"

"He is my master," the servant answered. So she took her veil and covered herself.

⁶⁶Then the servant told Isaac all he had done. ⁶⁷Isaac brought her into the tent of his mother Sarah, and he married Rebekah. So she became his wife, and he loved her; and Isaac was comforted after his mother's death.

■ The Death of Abraham

25 Abraham tookᵃ another wife, whose name was Keturah. ²She bore him Zimran, Jokshan, Medan, Midian, Ishbak and Shuah. ³Jokshan was the father of Sheba and Dedan; the descendants of Dedan were the Asshurites, the Letushites and the Leummites. ⁴The sons of Midian were Ephah, Epher, Hanoch, Abida and Eldaah. All these were descendants of Keturah.

⁵Abraham left everything he owned to Isaac. ⁶But while he was still living, he gave gifts to the sons of his concubines and sent them away from his son Isaac to the land of the east.

⁷Altogether, Abraham lived a hundred and seventy-five years. ⁸Then Abraham breathed his last and died at a good old age, an old man and full of years; and he was gathered to his people. ⁹His sons Isaac and Ishmael buried him in the cave of Machpelah near Mamre, in the field of Ephron son of Zohar the Hittite, ¹⁰the field Abraham had bought from the Hittites.ᵇ There Abraham was buried with his wife Sarah. ¹¹After Abraham's death, God blessed his son Isaac, who then lived near Beer Lahai Roi.

■ Ishmael's Sons

¹²This is the account of Abraham's son Ishmael, whom Sarah's maidservant, Hagar the Egyptian, bore to Abraham.

¹³These are the names of the sons of Ishmael, listed in the order of their birth: Nebaioth the firstborn of Ishmael, Kedar, Adbeel, Mibsam, ¹⁴Mishma, Dumah, Massa, ¹⁵Hadad, Tema, Jetur, Naphish and Kedemah. ¹⁶These were the sons of Ishmael, and these are the names of the twelve tribal rulers according to their settlements and camps. ¹⁷Altogether, Ishmael lived a hundred and thirty-seven years. He breathed his last and died, and he was gathered to his people. ¹⁸His descendants settled in the area from Havilah to Shur, near the border of Egypt, as you go towards Asshur. And they lived in hostility towardsᶜ all their brothers.

■ Jacob and Esau

¹⁹This is the account of Abraham's son Isaac.

Abraham became the father of Isaac, ²⁰and Isaac was forty years old when he married Rebekah daughter of Bethuel the Aramean from Paddan Aramᵈ and sister of Laban the Aramean.

²¹Isaac prayed to the LORD on behalf of his wife, because she was barren. The LORD answered his prayer, and his wife Rebekah became pregnant. ²²The babies jostled each other within her, and she said, "Why is this happening to me?" So she went to enquire of the LORD.

²³The LORD said to her,

"Two nations are in your womb,
    and two peoples from within you will be
        separated;
one people will be stronger than the other,
    and the older will serve the younger."

²⁴When the time came for her to give birth, there were twin boys in her womb. ²⁵The first to come out was red, and his whole body was like a hairy garment; so they named him Esau.ᵉ ²⁶After this, his brother came out, with his hand grasping Esau's heel; so he was named Jacob.ᶠ Isaac was sixty years old when Rebekah gave birth to them.

²⁷The boys grew up, and Esau became a skilful hunter, a man of the open country, while Jacob was a quiet man, staying among the tents. ²⁸Isaac, who had a taste for wild game, loved Esau, but Rebekah loved Jacob.

²⁹Once when Jacob was cooking some stew, Esau came in from the open country, famished. ³⁰He said to Jacob, "Quick, let me have some of that red stew! I'm famished!" (That is why he was also called Edom.ᵍ)

³¹Jacob replied, "First sell me your birthright."

³²"Look, I am about to die," Esau said. "What good is the birthright to me?"

³³But Jacob said, "Swear to me first." So he swore an oath to him, selling his birthright to Jacob.

25:33 ■ NO SYMPATHY FOR ESAU

Esau's birthright, which he sold for a meal, was his inheritance as the firstborn son. He stood to be head of a large extended family and its property. Though his brother Jacob took advantage of him, the Bible spares Esau little sympathy for his role as victim: he "despised his birthright" (verse 34) by letting his hunger overwhelm his concern for things of lasting value. Because of this, he was later labelled "godless" (Hebrews 12:16).

³⁴Then Jacob gave Esau some bread and some lentil stew. He ate and drank, and then got up and left. So Esau despised his birthright.

■ Isaac and Abimelech

26 Now there was a famine in the land—besides the earlier famine of Abraham's time—and Isaac went to Abimelech king of the Philistines in Gerar. ²The LORD appeared to Isaac and said, "Do not go down to Egypt; live in the land where I tell you to live. ³Stay in this land for a while, and I will be with you and will bless you. For to you and your

---

ᵇ63 The meaning of the Hebrew for this word is uncertain.   ᵃ1 Or had taken   ᵇ10 Or the sons of Heth   ᶜ18 Or lived to the east of   ᵈ20 That is,
North-west Mesopotamia   ᵉ25 Esau may mean hairy; he was also called Edom, which means red.   ᶠ26 Jacob means he grasps the heel (figuratively,
he deceives).   ᵍ30 Edom means red.

descendants I will give all these lands and will confirm the oath I swore to your father Abraham. ⁴I will make your descendants as numerous as the stars in the sky and will give them all these lands, and through your offspring*a* all nations on earth will be blessed, ⁵because Abraham obeyed me and kept my requirements, my commands, my decrees and my laws." ⁶So Isaac stayed in Gerar.

⁷When the men of that place asked him about his wife, he said, "She is my sister," because he was afraid to say, "She is my wife." He thought, "The men of this place might kill me on account of Rebekah, because she is beautiful."

⁸When Isaac had been there a long time, Abimelech king of the Philistines looked down from a window and saw Isaac caressing his wife Rebekah. ⁹So Abimelech summoned Isaac and said, "She is really your wife! Why did you say, 'She is my sister'?"

Isaac answered him, "Because I thought I might lose my life on account of her."

¹⁰Then Abimelech said, "What is this you have done to us? One of the men might well have slept with your wife, and you would have brought guilt upon us."

¹¹So Abimelech gave orders to all the people: "Anyone who molests this man or his wife shall surely be put to death."

¹²Isaac planted crops in that land and the same year reaped a hundredfold, because the LORD blessed him. ¹³The man became rich, and his wealth continued to grow until he became very wealthy. ¹⁴He had so many flocks and herds and servants that the Philistines envied him. ¹⁵So all the wells that his father's servants had dug in the time of his father Abraham, the Philistines stopped up, filling them with earth.

¹⁶Then Abimelech said to Isaac, "Move away from us; you have become too powerful for us."

¹⁷So Isaac moved away from there and encamped in the Valley of Gerar and settled there. ¹⁸Isaac reopened the wells that had been dug in the time of his father Abraham, which the Philistines had stopped up after Abraham died, and he gave them the same names his father had given them.

¹⁹Isaac's servants dug in the valley and discovered a well of fresh water there. ²⁰But the herdsmen of Gerar quarrelled with Isaac's herdsmen and said, "The water is ours!" So he named the well Esek,*b* because they disputed with him. ²¹Then they dug another well, but they quarrelled over that one also; so he named it Sitnah.*c* ²²He moved on from there and dug another well, and no-one quarrelled over it. He named it Rehoboth,*d* saying, "Now the LORD has given us room and we will flourish in the land."

²³From there he went up to Beersheba. ²⁴That night the LORD appeared to him and said, "I am the God of your father Abraham. Do not be afraid, for I am with you; I will bless you and will increase the number of your descendants for the sake of my servant Abraham."

²⁵Isaac built an altar there and called on the name of the LORD. There he pitched his tent, and there his servants dug a well.

²⁶Meanwhile, Abimelech had come to him from Gerar, with Ahuzzath his personal adviser and Phicol the commander of his forces. ²⁷Isaac asked them, "Why have you come to me, since you were hostile to me and sent me away?"

²⁸They answered, "We saw clearly that the LORD was with you; so we said, 'There ought to be a sworn agreement between us'—between us and you. Let us make a treaty with you ²⁹that you will do us no harm, just as we did not molest you but always treated you well and sent you away in peace. And now you are blessed by the LORD."

³⁰Isaac then made a feast for them, and they ate and drank. ³¹Early the next morning the men swore an oath to each other. Then Isaac sent them on their way, and they left him in peace.

³²That day Isaac's servants came and told him about the well they had dug. They said, "We've found water!" ³³He called it Shibah,*e* and to this day the name of the town has been Beersheba.*f*

³⁴When Esau was forty years old, he married Judith daughter of Beeri the Hittite, and also Basemath daughter of Elon the Hittite. ³⁵They were a source of grief to Isaac and Rebekah.

■ Jacob Gets Isaac's Blessing

27 When Isaac was old and his eyes were so weak that he could no longer see, he called for Esau his older son and said to him, "My son."

"Here I am," he answered.

²Isaac said, "I am now an old man and don't know the day of my death. ³Now then, get your weapons—your quiver and bow—and go out to the open country to hunt some wild game for me. ⁴Prepare me the kind of tasty food I like and bring it to me to eat, so that I may give you my blessing before I die."

⁵Now Rebekah was listening as Isaac spoke to his son Esau. When Esau left for the open country to hunt game and bring it back, ⁶Rebekah said to her son Jacob, "Look, I overheard your father say to your brother Esau, ⁷'Bring me some game and prepare me some tasty food to eat, so that I may give you my blessing in the presence of the LORD before I die.' ⁸Now, my son, listen carefully and do what I tell you: ⁹Go out to the flock and bring me two choice young goats, so that I can prepare some tasty food for your father, just the way he likes it. ¹⁰Then take it to your father to eat, so that he may give you his blessing before he dies."

¹¹Jacob said to Rebekah his mother, "But my brother Esau is a hairy man, and I'm a man with smooth skin. ¹²What if my father touches me? I would appear to be tricking him and would bring down a curse on myself rather than a blessing."

¹³His mother said to him, "My son, let the curse fall on me. Just do what I say; go and get them for me."

¹⁴So he went and got them and brought them to his mother, and she prepared some tasty food, just the way his father liked it. ¹⁵Then Rebekah took the best clothes of Esau her older son, which she had in the house, and put them on her younger son Jacob. ¹⁶She also covered his hands and the smooth part of his neck with the goatskins. ¹⁷Then she handed to her son Jacob the tasty food and the bread she had made.

18He went to his father and said, "My father."

"Yes, my son," he answered. "Who is it?"

19Jacob said to his father, "I am Esau your first-born. I have done as you told me. Please sit up and eat some of my game so that you may give me your blessing."

20Isaac asked his son, "How did you find it so quickly, my son?"

"The LORD your God gave me success," he replied.

21Then Isaac said to Jacob, "Come near so I can touch you, my son, to know whether you really are my son Esau or not."

22Jacob went close to his father Isaac, who touched him and said, "The voice is the voice of Jacob, but the hands are the hands of Esau." 23He did not recognise him, for his hands were hairy like those of his brother Esau; so he blessed him. 24"Are you really my son Esau?" he asked.

"I am," he replied.

25Then he said, "My son, bring me some of your game to eat, so that I may give you my blessing."

Jacob brought it to him and he ate; and he brought some wine and he drank. 26Then his father Isaac said to him, "Come here, my son, and kiss me."

27So he went to him and kissed him. When Isaac caught the smell of his clothes, he blessed him and said,

"Ah, the smell of my son
    is like the smell of a field
    that the LORD has blessed.

27:27 ■ SENSE OF SMELL

An old man, Isaac had lost his eyesight and apparently much of his sense of touch. He could still smell though, and thought he recognised his son by the scent of his clothes. In an age before deodorants and frequent laundering, people had distinctive scents.

28May God give you of heaven's dew
    and of earth's richness—
    an abundance of grain and new wine.
29May nations serve you
    and peoples bow down to you.
Be lord over your brothers,
    and may the sons of your mother bow down
        to you.
May those who curse you be cursed
    and those who bless you be blessed."

30After Isaac finished blessing him and Jacob had scarcely left his father's presence, his brother Esau came in from hunting. 31He too prepared some tasty food and brought it to his father. Then he said to him, "My father, sit up and eat some of my game, so that you may give me your blessing."

32His father Isaac asked him, "Who are you?"

"I am your son," he answered, "your firstborn, Esau."

33Isaac trembled violently and said, "Who was it, then, that hunted game and brought it to me? I ate it just before you came and I blessed him—and indeed he will be blessed!"

34When Esau heard his father's words, he burst out with a loud and bitter cry and said to his father, "Bless me—me too, my father!"

35But he said, "Your brother came deceitfully and took your blessing."

36Esau said, "Isn't he rightly named Jacob?a He has deceived me these two times: He took my birthright, and now he's taken my blessing!" Then he asked, "Haven't you reserved any blessing for me?"

37Isaac answered Esau, "I have made him lord over you and have made all his relatives his servants, and I have sustained him with grain and new wine. So what can I possibly do for you, my son?"

38Esau said to his father, "Do you have only one blessing, my father? Bless me too, my father!" Then Esau wept aloud.

39His father Isaac answered him,

"Your dwelling will be
    away from the earth's richness,
    away from the dew of heaven above.
40You will live by the sword
    and you will serve your brother.
But when you grow restless,
    you will throw his yoke
    from off your neck."

■ Jacob Flees to Laban

41Esau held a grudge against Jacob because of the blessing his father had given him. He said to himself, "The days of mourning for my father are near; then I will kill my brother Jacob."

42When Rebekah was told what her older son Esau had said, she sent for her younger son Jacob and said to him, "Your brother Esau is consoling himself with the thought of killing you. 43Now then, my son, do what I say: Flee at once to my brother Laban in Haran. 44Stay with him for a while until your brother's fury subsides. 45When your brother is no longer angry with you and forgets what you did to him, I'll send word for you to come back from there. Why should I lose both of you in one day?"

46Then Rebekah said to Isaac, "I'm disgusted with living because of these Hittite women. If Jacob takes a wife from among the women of this land, from Hittite women like these, my life will not be worth living."

28 So Isaac called for Jacob and blesseda him and commanded him: "Do not marry a Canaanite woman. 2Go at once to Paddan Aram,b to the house of your mother's father Bethuel. Take a wife for yourself there, from among the daughters of Laban, your mother's brother. 3May God Almightyc bless you and make you fruitful and increase your numbers until you become a community of peoples. 4May he give you and your descendants the blessing given to Abraham, so that you may take possession of the land where you now live as an alien, the land God gave to Abraham." 5Then Isaac sent Jacob on his way, and he went to Paddan Aram, to Laban son of Bethuel the Aramean, the brother of Rebekah, who was the mother of Jacob and Esau.

6Now Esau learned that Isaac had blessed Jacob and had sent him to Paddan Aram to take a wife from

a36 Jacob means he grasps the heel (figuratively, he deceives).   a1 Or greeted   b2 That is, North-west Mesopotamia; also in verses 5, 6 and 7
c3 Hebrew El-Shaddai

there, and that when he blessed him he commanded him, "Do not marry a Canaanite woman," [7]and that Jacob had obeyed his father and mother and had gone to Paddan Aram. [8]Esau then realised how displeasing the Canaanite women were to his father Isaac; [9]so he went to Ishmael and married Mahalath, the sister of Nebaioth and daughter of Ishmael son of Abraham, in addition to the wives he already had.

■ Jacob's Dream at Bethel

[10]Jacob left Beersheba and set out for Haran. [11]When he reached a certain place, he stopped for

INSIGHT

■ CON MAN IN GOD'S FAMILY?
THE BIBLE DOESN'T COVER UP JACOB'S SCHEMING

"HE HAS DECEIVED ME THESE TWO TIMES: HE TOOK MY BIRTHRIGHT, AND NOW HE'S TAKEN MY BLESSING!"
■ 27:36

Ask people why they don't go to church, and you'll often hear this answer: "There are too many hypocrites." It may be an excuse, but there's a troubling reality behind it. How can a religion with such high standards include so many people with such low standards?

Jacob's life poses the same question. The Bible does not mince words in describing his grasping, con-man character. He took advantage of his twin brother's impulsiveness to switch places with him in the family will (25:29–34). Later, seeing that his father Isaac still favoured Esau, Jacob (with his mother) tricked the old man into blessing him in place of his brother. (A father's blessing was not merely symbolic. It had a permanent significance, like a swearing-in ceremony.)

■ THE TRICKS BACKFIRE
Dressed in Esau's clothes and some fresh goatskins, Jacob flatly lied to his father and took the Lord's name in vain. Isaac, trusting his sense of smell over his sense of hearing, fell for it (27:1–40). Yet the trick backfired. Jacob had to run for his life, and he spent 20 years in exile with his uncle. Uncle Laban gave Jacob a dose of his own medicine, planting an unwanted sister in his wedding bed and repeatedly changing his wages as head shepherd.

You might think Jacob would learn that tricks aren't nice. Yet Jacob didn't noticeably improve his ways. He made a poor husband, neglecting one of his wives and creating rivalry. He favoured two sons, so that the neglected ones grew jealous to the point of murder. He certainly doesn't seem like choice material for a religious leader.

■ GOD MAKES THE CHOICE
But God chose Jacob. He was always making those kinds of choices, sometimes with no apparent reason at all. Often he went against the time-honoured practice of letting the firstborn son be number one, as he did in choosing number-two sons Abel, Jacob and Ephraim. In fact, an inspired prophecy marked Jacob as God's choice before he was even born — before he had done a single thing to merit the choice.

So God's choice did not necessarily depend on how a person behaved. God chose the one that he wanted — it was as simple as that.

Is this fair? That's what the apostle Paul asked in Romans 9. He concluded that we have no right to find fault with God's choices, knowing as little as we do compared to his infinite understanding. And while we may never understand God's choices, we should note that all the "rejected" brothers of Genesis — Cain, Canaan, Ishmael, Reuben, Esau and Manasseh — were treated more than fairly. Their offspring multiplied into nations under God's protection.

■ NO-ONE EXCLUDED
For his chosen people, God had a much greater honour. Good or bad, they would be made a channel of blessing for the whole world. He told Abraham, right from the beginning, "All peoples on earth will be blessed through you" (12:3). By selecting a few, God planned to extend his blessings to all. And that is how it worked out: Abraham's small, fault-ridden family grew into a sizeable, fault-ridden nation that brought forth, in the fullness of time, a faultless Jesus.

No wonder Paul wrote that we have no business questioning the wisdom of God. We may not see why he chose people like Jacob. But unquestionably, those choices worked for good — and the whole world became eligible to join the "chosen people". As Paul wrote, "You are all sons of God through faith in Christ Jesus. . . . There is neither Jew nor Greek, slave nor free, male nor female, for you are all one in Christ Jesus. If you belong to Christ, then you are Abraham's seed" (Galatians 3:26–29). God has a habit of choosing flawed people to achieve great good. Who can say what he is doing with the hypocrites of our day?

□ LIFE QUESTIONS:
Why do you think God chooses imperfect people like Jacob? Why did he choose you?

the night because the sun had set. Taking one of the stones there, he put it under his head and lay down to sleep. [12]He had a dream in which he saw a stairway[d] resting on the earth, with its top reaching to heaven, and the angels of God were ascending and descending on it. [13]There above it[e] stood the LORD, and he said: "I am the LORD, the God of your father Abraham and the God of Isaac. I will give you and your descendants the land on which you are lying. [14]Your descendants will be like the dust of the earth, and you will spread out to the west and to the east, to the north and to the south. All peoples on earth will be blessed through you and your offspring. [15]I am with you and will watch over you wherever you go, and I will bring you back to this land. I will not leave you until I have done what I have promised you."

28:12 ■ A STAIRWAY TO HEAVEN

God's grace: this is what Jacob found while travelling alone in the desert. Through his own greedy scheming he had won the family birthright and then, ironically, had had to run away from the family. Yet God came to him full of promises, not the reproaches he deserved. Jacob had not looked for God, but God had looked for him. Jacob's vision of a stairway to heaven looked forward to Jesus, who is himself the bridge between heaven and earth (John 1:51).

[16]When Jacob awoke from his sleep, he thought, "Surely the LORD is in this place, and I was not aware of it." [17]He was afraid and said, "How awesome is this place! This is none other than the house of God; this is the gate of heaven."

[18]Early the next morning Jacob took the stone he had placed under his head and set it up as a pillar and poured oil on top of it. [19]He called that place Bethel,[f] though the city used to be called Luz. [20]Then Jacob made a vow, saying, "If God will be with me and will watch over me on this journey I am taking and will give me food to eat and clothes to wear [21]so that I return safely to my father's house, then the LORD[g] will be my God [22]and[b] this stone that I have set up as a pillar will be God's house, and of all that you give me I will give you a tenth."

■ Jacob Arrives in Paddan Aram

29 Then Jacob continued on his journey and came to the land of the eastern peoples. [2]There he saw a well in the field, with three flocks of sheep lying near it because the flocks were watered from that well. The stone over the mouth of the well was large. [3]When all the flocks were gathered there, the shepherds would roll the stone away from the well's mouth and water the sheep. Then they would return the stone to its place over the mouth of the well.

[4]Jacob asked the shepherds, "My brothers, where are you from?"

"We're from Haran," they replied.

[5]He said to them, "Do you know Laban, Nahor's grandson?"

"Yes, we know him," they answered.

[6]Then Jacob asked them, "Is he well?"

"Yes, he is," they said, "and here comes his daughter Rachel with the sheep."

[7]"Look," he said, "the sun is still high; it is not time for the flocks to be gathered. Water the sheep and take them back to pasture."

[8]"We can't," they replied, "until all the flocks are gathered and the stone has been rolled away from the mouth of the well. Then we will water the sheep."

[9]While he was still talking with them, Rachel came with her father's sheep, for she was a shepherdess. [10]When Jacob saw Rachel daughter of Laban, his mother's brother, and Laban's sheep, he went over and rolled the stone away from the mouth of the well and watered his uncle's sheep. [11]Then Jacob kissed Rachel and began to weep aloud. [12]He had told Rachel that he was a relative of her father and a son of Rebekah. So she ran and told her father.

[13]As soon as Laban heard the news about Jacob, his sister's son, he hurried to meet him. He embraced him and kissed him and brought him to his home, and there Jacob told him all these things. [14]Then Laban said to him, "You are my own flesh and blood."

■ Jacob Marries Leah and Rachel

After Jacob had stayed with him for a whole month, [15]Laban said to him, "Just because you are a relative of mine, should you work for me for nothing? Tell me what your wages should be."

[16]Now Laban had two daughters; the name of the older was Leah, and the name of the younger was Rachel. [17]Leah had weak[a] eyes, but Rachel was lovely in form, and beautiful. [18]Jacob was in love with Rachel and said, "I'll work for you seven years in return for your younger daughter Rachel."

[19]Laban said, "It's better that I give her to you than to some other man. Stay here with me." [20]So Jacob served seven years to get Rachel, but they seemed like only a few days to him because of his love for her.

[21]Then Jacob said to Laban, "Give me my wife. My time is completed, and I want to lie with her."

[22]So Laban brought together all the people of the place and gave a feast. [23]But when evening came, he took his daughter Leah and gave her to Jacob, and Jacob lay with her. [24]And Laban gave his servant girl Zilpah to his daughter as her maidservant.

[25]When morning came, there was Leah! So Jacob said to Laban, "What is this you have done to me? I served you for Rachel, didn't I? Why have you deceived me?"

[26]Laban replied, "It is not our custom here to give the younger daughter in marriage before the older one. [27]Finish this daughter's bridal week; then we will give you the younger one also, in return for another seven years of work."

[28]And Jacob did so. He finished the week with Leah, and then Laban gave him his daughter Rachel to be his wife. [29]Laban gave his servant girl Bilhah to his daughter Rachel as her maidservant. [30]Jacob lay with Rachel also, and he loved Rachel more than Leah. And he worked for Laban another seven years.

■ THE WOMEN OF GENESIS
DESPITE THEIR LOW STATUS, THEY WERE ANYONE'S EQUAL   INSIGHT

THE MAN SAID, "THIS IS NOW BONE OF MY BONES AND FLESH OF MY FLESH; SHE SHALL BE CALLED 'WOMAN', FOR SHE WAS TAKEN OUT OF MAN." ■ 2:23

PARTNER SOUGHT for vast creative endeavour. Global plans. Unlimited compensation. Immediate responsibilities include maintenance of large property, care and authority over all kinds of creatures — flying, walking, creeping, crawling. Object: teamwork and companionship. Female only. Contact Adam.
No woman after Eve got such an opportunity. After sin came into the picture, the original idea of marriage got twisted. " 'To love and to cherish' became 'to desire and to dominate' ", as author Derek Kidner put it. Throughout the Old Testament you catch only glimpses of the original spontaneous joy with which man greeted woman and regarded her as a partner. Granted, the people of God had a higher view of women than did their pagan neighbours. Still, women had value chiefly as seconds to men, whose children they bore, whose desires they fulfilled.
Yet the women of Genesis were no pushovers. They had strong characters, minds of their own. They exerted all the influence they were allowed, and more.

■ THE JOKE WAS ON HER
Sarah, Abraham's partner, was caught laughing at God's astonishing promise (18:12–15). She thought she knew better than to expect babies at the age of 90. She later had the grace to admit the joke was on her (21:6). Though the New Testament commends her as an ideal submissive wife (1 Peter 3:5–6), she certainly expressed her views strongly to Abraham. Twice she had her rival Hagar driven out of their home and into the desert.
Hagar, though only a servant girl, showed backbone too. After her first expulsion from Abraham and Sarah's home she met God himself, who comforted her and sent her back to Abraham with promises of a great future. Later she showed strength of character by bringing up her son alone in the desert.

■ A SCHEME THAT BACKFIRED
Rebekah shows up in chapter 24 as a young girl drawing water for a stranger's camels. By the next day you know that she has a mind of her own — and enough courage to set off with a stranger for marriage in unknown territory. Her husband Isaac loved her, and so did her

son Jacob. From her, it seems, Jacob got his strong, scheming personality. She initiated the plan to instal him in family leadership, against the custom of firstborn sons — and against his father's will. Sadly for Rebekah, her scheme partly backfired, and she never saw Jacob again.
Rachel and Leah, sisters, fought for years over Jacob. Rachel had the looks, as well as a monopoly on her husband's love. Jacob neglected Leah, whom he hadn't wanted to marry in the first place. But to make up for that slight, God gave Leah children — four sons in a row. Rachel took each one like a fist to the face, which is probably what Leah intended. After a while, Jacob seemed to be just a tool in the struggle for dominance between two sisters, especially when Leah coolly informed him that she had hired his services for the night (30:16).
Who won? It's hard to say. Rachel held the love of Jacob to the end, her two sons most favoured by him though last in line. But Leah's sons gained prominence of their own, especially Judah, who became the ancestor of kings — and Jesus. Leah would have enjoyed knowing that she, not Rachel, was great-great-great-grandmother to the King of kings.

■ HARDLY DELICATE VIOLETS
In short, the women in Genesis were not delicate violets, but tough, pioneer women. One cannot approve of everything they did, by a long chalk. But their toughness and courage demolish any theory that women are, by nature, weak. They used every advantage they had, fairly or unfairly — and did it skilfully. For instance, Rachel displayed classic "chutzpah" in standing up to her father as he searched for some idols she had stolen. She sweetly claimed that she couldn't stand up because she was having her period. In truth, she was sitting on the goods, knowing perfectly well even Laban lacked the nerve to try moving a woman in that condition (31:25–35).
They were a match for their men: in courage, in character, in independence, in determination. In that culture they were second-class citizens. But in real life these women were, as God intended, the equal of anybody.

□ LIFE QUESTIONS:
Creative people often find ways to transcend the limits put on them. What do you feel hemmed in by? How can you achieve God's will despite obstacles?

■ Jacob's Children

31When the LORD saw that Leah was not loved, he opened her womb, but Rachel was barren. 32Leah became pregnant and gave birth to a son. She named him Reuben,*b* for she said, "It is because the LORD has seen my misery. Surely my husband will love me now."

29:25 ■ JACOB MEETS HIS MATCH

When Jacob ran into Laban, one cheat met another. Just as Jacob had taken advantage of his brother by playing on his love for food (25:33), Laban cheated Jacob by playing on his love for Rachel. Additional ironies: Jacob learned his deceit from his mother, Laban's sister. And eventually it was Laban's daughter Rachel who enabled Jacob to escape her father's cheating grasp.

29:30 ■ PLAYING FAVOURITES

Throughout his life, Jacob's favouritism would cause problems in his family. He must have learned the habit from his own parents (see 25:28). Here, he favours one wife over the other. Later, he spoiled his son Joseph with favours, making his other sons so jealous they wanted to kill Joseph (see 37:4,18).

33She conceived again, and when she gave birth to a son she said, "Because the LORD heard that I am not loved, he gave me this one too." So she named him Simeon.*c*

34Again she conceived, and when she gave birth to a son she said, "Now at last my husband will become attached to me, because I have borne him three sons." So he was named Levi.*d*

35She conceived again, and when she gave birth to a son she said, "This time I will praise the LORD." So she named him Judah.*e* Then she stopped having children.

30 When Rachel saw that she was not bearing Jacob any children, she became jealous of her sister. So she said to Jacob, "Give me children, or I'll die!"

2Jacob became angry with her and said, "Am I in the place of God, who has kept you from having children?"

3Then she said, "Here is Bilhah, my maidservant. Sleep with her so that she can bear children for me and that through her I too can build a family."

4So she gave him her servant Bilhah as a wife. Jacob slept with her, 5and she became pregnant and bore him a son. 6Then Rachel said, "God has vindicated me; he has listened to my plea and given me a son." Because of this she named him Dan.*a*

7Rachel's servant Bilhah conceived again and bore Jacob a second son. 8Then Rachel said, "I have had a great struggle with my sister, and I have won." So she named him Naphtali.*b*

9When Leah saw that she had stopped having

children, she took her maidservant Zilpah and gave her to Jacob as a wife. 10Leah's servant Zilpah bore Jacob a son. 11Then Leah said, "What good fortune!"*c* So she named him Gad.*d*

12Leah's servant Zilpah bore Jacob a second son. 13Then Leah said, "How happy I am! The women will call me happy." So she named him Asher.*e*

14During wheat harvest, Reuben went out into the fields and found some mandrake plants, which he brought to his mother Leah. Rachel said to Leah, "Please give me some of your son's mandrakes."

15But she said to her, "Wasn't it enough that you took away my husband? Will you take my son's mandrakes too?"

"Very well," Rachel said, "he can sleep with you tonight in return for your son's mandrakes."

16So when Jacob came in from the fields that evening, Leah went out to meet him. "You must sleep with me," she said. "I have hired you with my son's mandrakes." So he slept with her that night.

17God listened to Leah, and she became pregnant and bore Jacob a fifth son. 18Then Leah said, "God has rewarded me for giving my maidservant to my husband." So she named him Issachar.*f*

19Leah conceived again and bore Jacob a sixth son. 20Then Leah said, "God has presented me with a precious gift. This time my husband will treat me with honour, because I have borne him six sons." So she named him Zebulun.*g*

21Some time later she gave birth to a daughter and named her Dinah.

22Then God remembered Rachel; he listened to her and opened her womb. 23She became pregnant and gave birth to a son and said, "God has taken away my disgrace." 24She named him Joseph,*b* and said, "May the LORD add to me another son."

■ Jacob's Flocks Increase

25After Rachel gave birth to Joseph, Jacob said to Laban, "Send me on my way so that I can go back to my own homeland. 26Give me my wives and children, for whom I have served you, and I will be on my way. You know how much work I've done for you."

27But Laban said to him, "If I have found favour in your eyes, please stay. I have learned by divination that*i* the LORD has blessed me because of you." 28He added, "Name your wages, and I will pay them."

29Jacob said to him, "You know how I have worked for you and how your livestock has fared under my care. 30The little you had before I came has increased greatly, and the LORD has blessed you wherever I have been. But now, when may I do something for my own household?"

31"What shall I give you?" he asked.

"Don't give me anything," Jacob replied. "But if you will do this one thing for me, I will go on tending your flocks and watching over them: 32Let me go through all your flocks today and remove from them every speckled or spotted sheep, every dark-coloured lamb and every spotted or speckled goat. They will be my wages. 33And my honesty will

---

b 32 Reuben sounds like the Hebrew for *he has seen my misery*; the name means *see, a son.*   *c 33 Simeon* probably means *one who hears.*   *d 34 Levi* sounds like and may be derived from the Hebrew for *attached.*   *e 35 Judah* sounds like and may be derived from the Hebrew for *praise.*   *a 6 Dan* here means *he has vindicated.*   *b 8 Naphtali* means *my struggle.*   *c 11* Or *"A troop is coming!"*   *d 11 Gad* can mean *good fortune* or *a troop.*   *e 13 Asher* means *happy.*   *f 18 Issachar* sounds like the Hebrew for *reward.*   *g 20 Zebulun* probably means *honour.*   *b 24 Joseph* means *may he add.*   *i 27* Or possibly *have become rich and* testify for me in the future, whenever you check on the wages you have paid me. Any goat in my possession that is not speckled or spotted, or any lamb that is not dark-coloured, will be considered stolen."

34"Agreed," said Laban. "Let it be as you have said." 35That same day he removed all the male goats that were streaked or spotted, and all the speckled or spotted female goats (all that had white on them) and all the dark-coloured lambs, and he placed them in the care of his sons. 36Then he put a three-day journey between himself and Jacob, while Jacob continued to tend the rest of Laban's flocks.

37Jacob, however, took fresh-cut branches from poplar, almond and plane trees and made white stripes on them by peeling the bark and exposing the white inner wood of the branches. 38Then he placed the peeled branches in all the watering troughs, so that they would be directly in front of the flocks when they came to drink. When the flocks were in heat and came to drink, 39they mated in front of the branches. And they bore young that were streaked or speckled or spotted. 40Jacob set apart the young of the flock by themselves, but made the rest face the streaked and dark-coloured animals that belonged to Laban. Thus he made separate flocks for himself and did not put them with Laban's animals. 41Whenever the stronger females were in heat, Jacob would place the branches in the troughs in front of the animals so that they would mate near the branches, 42but if the animals were weak, he would not place them there. So the weak animals went to Laban and the strong ones to Jacob. 43In this way the man grew exceedingly prosperous and came to own large flocks, and maidservants and menservants, and camels and donkeys.

■ Jacob Flees From Laban

31 Jacob heard that Laban's sons were saying, "Jacob has taken everything our father owned and has gained all this wealth from what belonged to our father." 2And Jacob noticed that Laban's attitude towards him was not what it had been.

3Then the LORD said to Jacob, "Go back to the land of your fathers and to your relatives, and I will be with you."

4So Jacob sent word to Rachel and Leah to come out to the fields where his flocks were. 5He said to them, "I see that your father's attitude towards me is not what it was before, but the God of my father has been with me. 6You know that I've worked for your father with all my strength, 7yet your father has

cheated me by changing my wages ten times. However, God has not allowed him to harm me. 8If he said, 'The speckled ones will be your wages,' then all the flocks gave birth to speckled young; and if he said, 'The streaked ones will be your wages,' then all the flocks bore streaked young. 9So God has taken away your father's livestock and has given them to me.

10"In the breeding season I once had a dream in which I looked up and saw that the male goats mating with the flock were streaked, speckled or spotted. 11The angel of God said to me in the dream, 'Jacob.' I answered, 'Here I am.' 12And he said, 'Look up and see that all the male goats mating with the flock are streaked, speckled or spotted, for I have seen all that Laban has been doing to you. 13I am the God of Bethel, where you anointed a pillar and where you made a vow to me. Now leave this land at once and go back to your native land.' "

14Then Rachel and Leah replied, "Do we still have any share in the inheritance of our father's estate? 15Does he not regard us as foreigners? Not only has he sold us, but he has used up what was paid for us. 16Surely all the wealth that God took away from our father belongs to us and our children. So do whatever God has told you."

17Then Jacob put his children and his wives on camels, 18and he drove all his livestock ahead of him, along with all the goods he had accumulated in Paddan Aram,[a] to go to his father Isaac in the land of Canaan.

19When Laban had gone to shear his sheep, Rachel stole her father's household gods. 20Moreover, Jacob deceived Laban the Aramean by not telling him he was running away. 21So he fled with all he had, and crossing the River,[b] he headed for the hill country of Gilead.

■ Laban Pursues Jacob

22On the third day Laban was told that Jacob had fled. 23Taking his relatives with him, he pursued Jacob for seven days and caught up with him in the hill country of Gilead. 24Then God came to Laban the Aramean in a dream at night and said to him, "Be careful not to say anything to Jacob, either good or bad."

25Jacob had pitched his tent in the hill country of Gilead when Laban overtook him, and Laban and his relatives camped there too. 26Then Laban said to Jacob, "What have you done? You've deceived me, and you've carried off my daughters like captives in war. 27Why did you run off secretly and deceive me? Why didn't you tell me, so that I could send you away with joy and singing to the music of tambourines and harps? 28You didn't even let me kiss my grandchildren and my daughters good-bye. You have done a foolish thing. 29I have the power to harm you; but last night the God of your father said to me, 'Be careful not to say anything to Jacob, either good or bad.' 30Now you have gone off because you longed to return to your father's house. But why did you steal my gods?"

31Jacob answered Laban, "I was afraid, because I thought you would take your daughters away from me by force. 32But if you find anyone who has your

a 18 That is, North-west Mesopotamia   *b 21* That is, the Euphrates gods, he shall not live. In the presence of our relatives, see for yourself whether there is anything of yours here with me; and if so, take it." Now Jacob did not know that Rachel had stolen the gods.

33So Laban went into Jacob's tent and into Leah's tent and into the tent of the two maidservants, but he found nothing. After he came out of Leah's tent, he entered Rachel's tent. 34Now Rachel had taken the household gods and put them inside her camel's saddle and was sitting on them. Laban searched through everything in the tent but found nothing.

35Rachel said to her father, "Don't be angry, my lord, that I cannot stand up in your presence; I'm having my period." So he searched but could not find the household gods.

31:35 ■ HOUSEHOLD GODS

The "gods" Rachel had stolen from her father (verse 19) were small idols or "charms" supposed to protect the family from harm. They may also have served as something like a title deed for the family inheritance. Such idols continued to water down Israel's commitment to God for many generations to come.

36Jacob was angry and took Laban to task. "What is my crime?" he asked Laban. "What sin have I committed that you hunt me down? 37Now that you have searched through all my goods, what have you found that belongs to your household? Put it here in front of your relatives and mine, and let them judge between the two of us.

38"I have been with you for twenty years now. Your sheep and goats have not miscarried, nor have I eaten rams from your flocks. 39I did not bring you animals torn by wild beasts; I bore the loss myself. And you demanded payment from me for whatever was stolen by day or night. 40This was my situation: The heat consumed me in the daytime and the cold at night, and sleep fled from my eyes. 41It was like this for the twenty years I was in your household. I worked for you fourteen years for your two daughters and six years for your flocks, and you changed my wages ten times. 42If the God of my father, the God of Abraham and the Fear of Isaac, had not been with me, you would surely have sent me away empty-handed. But God has seen my hardship and the toil of my hands, and last night he rebuked you."

43Laban answered Jacob, "The women are my daughters, the children are my children, and the flocks are my flocks. All you see is mine. Yet what can I do today about these daughters of mine, or about the children they have borne? 44Come now, let's make a covenant, you and I, and let it serve as a witness between us."

45So Jacob took a stone and set it up as a pillar. 46He said to his relatives, "Gather some stones." So they took stones and piled them in a heap, and they ate there by the heap. 47Laban called it Jegar Sahadutha,c and Jacob called it Galeed.d

48Laban said, "This heap is a witness between you and me today." That is why it was called Galeed. 49It was also called Mizpah,e because he said, "May the

LORD keep watch between you and me when we are away from each other. 50If you ill-treat my daughters or if you take any wives besides my daughters, even though no-one is with us, remember that God is a witness between you and me."

51Laban also said to Jacob, "Here is this heap, and here is this pillar I have set up between you and me. 52This heap is a witness, and this pillar is a witness, that I will not go past this heap to your side to harm you and that you will not go past this heap and pillar to my side to harm me. 53May the God of Abraham and the God of Nahor, the God of their father, judge between us."

So Jacob took an oath in the name of the Fear of his father Isaac. 54He offered a sacrifice there in the hill country and invited his relatives to a meal. After they had eaten, they spent the night there.

55Early the next morning Laban kissed his grandchildren and his daughters and blessed them. Then he left and returned home.

■ Jacob Prepares to Meet Esau

32 Jacob also went on his way, and the angels of God met him. 2When Jacob saw them, he said, "This is the camp of God!" So he named that place Mahanaim.a

3Jacob sent messengers ahead of him to his brother Esau in the land of Seir, the country of Edom. 4He instructed them: "This is what you are to say to my master Esau: 'Your servant Jacob says, I have been staying with Laban and have remained there till now. 5I have cattle and donkeys, sheep and goats, menservants and maidservants. Now I am sending this message to my lord, that I may find favour in your eyes.' "

6When the messengers returned to Jacob, they said, "We went to your brother Esau, and now he is coming to meet you, and four hundred men are with him."

7In great fear and distress Jacob divided the people who were with him into two groups,b and the flocks and herds and camels as well. 8He thought, "If Esau comes and attacks one group,c the groupc that is left may escape."

9Then Jacob prayed, "O God of my father Abraham, God of my father Isaac, O LORD, who said to me, 'Go back to your country and your relatives, and I will make you prosper,' 10I am unworthy of all the kindness and faithfulness you have shown your servant. I had only my staff when I crossed this Jordan, but now I have become two groups. 11Save me, I pray, from the hand of my brother Esau, for I am afraid he will come and attack me, and also the mothers with their children. 12But you have said, 'I will surely make you prosper and will make your descendants like the sand of the sea, which cannot be counted.' "

13He spent the night there, and from what he had with him he selected a gift for his brother Esau: 14two hundred female goats and twenty male goats, two hundred ewes and twenty rams, 15thirty female camels with their young, forty cows and ten bulls, and twenty female donkeys and ten male donkeys. 16He put them in the care of his servants, each herd

c47 The Aramaic *Jegar Sahadutha* means *witness heap.*   d47 The Hebrew *Galeed* means *witness heap.*   e49 *Mizpah* means *watchtower.*
a2 *Mahanaim* means *two camps.*   b7 Or *camps;* also in verse 10   c8 Or *camp*

by itself, and said to his servants, "Go ahead of me, and keep some space between the herds."

17He instructed the one in the lead: "When my brother Esau meets you and asks, 'To whom do you belong, and where are you going, and who owns all these animals in front of you?' 18then you are to say, 'They belong to your servant Jacob. They are a gift sent to my lord Esau, and he is coming behind us.' "

19He also instructed the second, the third and all the others who followed the herds: "You are to say the same thing to Esau when you meet him. 20And be sure to say, 'Your servant Jacob is coming behind us.' " For he thought, "I will pacify him with these gifts I am sending on ahead; later, when I see him, perhaps he will receive me." 21So Jacob's gifts went on ahead of him, but he himself spent the night in the camp.

■ Jacob Wrestles With God

22That night Jacob got up and took his two wives, his two maidservants and his eleven sons and crossed the ford of the Jabbok. 23After he had sent them across the stream, he sent over all his possessions. 24So Jacob was left alone, and a man wrestled with him till daybreak. 25When the man saw that he could not overpower him, he touched the socket of Jacob's hip so that his hip was wrenched as he wrestled with the man. 26Then the man said, "Let me go, for it is daybreak."

But Jacob replied, "I will not let you go unless you bless me."

> **32:24 ■ WRESTLING WITH GOD**
> This night-time encounter, as strange as any in the Bible, sounds somewhat similar to Jacob's previous on-the-road encounter with God (28:12) in a dream. But this time God left Jacob evidence of his physical presence – a limp.

27The man asked him, "What is your name?"

"Jacob," he answered.

28Then the man said, "Your name will no longer be Jacob, but Israel,d because you have struggled with God and with men and have overcome."

29Jacob said, "Please tell me your name."

But he replied, "Why do you ask my name?" Then he blessed him there.

30So Jacob called the place Peniel,e saying, "It is because I saw God face to face, and yet my life was spared."

31The sun rose above him as he passed Peniel,f and he was limping because of his hip. 32Therefore to this day the Israelites do not eat the tendon attached to the socket of the hip, because the socket of Jacob's hip was touched near the tendon.

■ Jacob Meets Esau

33 Jacob looked up and there was Esau, coming with his four hundred men; so he divided the children among Leah, Rachel and the two maidservants. 2He put the maidservants and their children in front, Leah and her children next, and Rachel

and Joseph in the rear. 3He himself went on ahead and bowed down to the ground seven times as he approached his brother.

4But Esau ran to meet Jacob and embraced him; he threw his arms around his neck and kissed him. And they wept. 5Then Esau looked up and saw the women and children. "Who are these with you?" he asked.

Jacob answered, "They are the children God has graciously given your servant."

6Then the maidservants and their children approached and bowed down. 7Next, Leah and her children came and bowed down. Last of all came Joseph and Rachel, and they too bowed down.

8Esau asked, "What do you mean by all these droves I met?"

"To find favour in your eyes, my lord," he said.

9But Esau said, "I already have plenty, my brother. Keep what you have for yourself."

10"No, please!" said Jacob. "If I have found favour in your eyes, accept this gift from me. For to see your face is like seeing the face of God, now that you have received me favourably. 11Please accept the present that was brought to you, for God has been gracious to me and I have all I need." And because Jacob insisted, Esau accepted it.

12Then Esau said, "Let us be on our way; I'll accompany you."

13But Jacob said to him, "My lord knows that the children are tender and that I must care for the ewes and cows that are nursing their young. If they are driven hard just one day, all the animals will die. 14So let my lord go on ahead of his servant, while I move along slowly at the pace of the droves before me and that of the children, until I come to my lord in Seir."

15Esau said, "Then let me leave some of my men with you."

"But why do that?" Jacob asked. "Just let me find favour in the eyes of my lord."

> **33:15 ■ SURFACE RECONCILIATION**
> On the surface, Jacob and Esau had been reconciled. Underneath the niceties, however, mistrust continued, at least on Jacob's part. He did not want Esau to accompany him on his way, nor did he wish Esau to leave some of his men for "protection". He let his brother think he was on his way to Seir (verse 14), but turned north to Succoth as soon as Esau was out of sight.

16So that day Esau started on his way back to Seir. 17Jacob, however, went to Succoth, where he built a place for himself and made shelters for his livestock. That is why the place is called Succoth.a

18After Jacob came from Paddan Aram,b he arrived safely at thec city of Shechem in Canaan and camped within sight of the city. 19For a hundred pieces of silver,d he bought from the sons of Hamor, the father of Shechem, the plot of ground where he pitched his tent. 20There he set up an altar and called it El Elohe Israel.e

---

d28 Israel means he struggles with God.   e30 Peniel means face of God.   f31 Hebrew Penuel, a variant of Peniel   a17 Succoth means shelters.
b18 That is, North-west Mesopotamia   c18 Or arrived at Shalem, a   d19 Hebrew hundred kesitahs; a kesitah was a unit of money of unknown weight
and value.   e20 El Elohe Israel can mean God, the God of Israel or mighty is the God of Israel.

■ Dinah and the Shechemites

34 Now Dinah, the daughter Leah had borne to Jacob, went out to visit the women of the land. ²When Shechem son of Hamor the Hivite, the ruler of that area, saw her, he took her and raped her. ³His heart was drawn to Dinah daughter of Jacob, and he loved the girl and spoke tenderly to her. ⁴And Shechem said to his father Hamor, "Get me this girl as my wife."

⁵When Jacob heard that his daughter Dinah had been defiled, his sons were in the fields with his livestock; so he kept quiet about it until they came home.

⁶Then Shechem's father Hamor went out to talk with Jacob. ⁷Now Jacob's sons had come in from the fields as soon as they heard what had happened. They were filled with grief and fury, because Shechem had done a disgraceful thing in[a] Israel by lying with Jacob's daughter—a thing that should not be done.

⁸But Hamor said to them, "My son Shechem has his heart set on your daughter. Please give her to him as his wife. ⁹Intermarry with us; give us your daughters and take our daughters for yourselves. ¹⁰You can settle among us; the land is open to you. Live in it, trade[b] in it, and acquire property in it."

¹¹Then Shechem said to Dinah's father and brothers, "Let me find favour in your eyes, and I will give you whatever you ask. ¹²Make the price for the bride and the gift I am to bring as great as you like, and I'll pay whatever you ask me. Only give me the girl as my wife."

¹³Because their sister Dinah had been defiled, Jacob's sons replied deceitfully as they spoke to Shechem and his father Hamor. ¹⁴They said to them, "We can't do such a thing; we can't give our sister to a man who is not circumcised. That would be a disgrace to us. ¹⁵We will give our consent to you on one condition only: that you become like us by circumcising all your males. ¹⁶Then we will give you our daughters and take your daughters for ourselves. We'll settle among you and become one people with you. ¹⁷But if you will not agree to be circumcised, we'll take our sister[c] and go."

¹⁸Their proposal seemed good to Hamor and his son Shechem. ¹⁹The young man, who was the most honoured of all his father's household, lost no time in doing what they said, because he was delighted with Jacob's daughter. ²⁰So Hamor and his son Shechem went to the gate of their city to speak to their fellow townsmen. ²¹"These men are friendly towards us," they said. "Let them live in our land and trade in it; the land has plenty of room for them. We can marry their daughters and they can marry ours. ²²But the men will consent to live with us as one people only on the condition that our males be circumcised, as they themselves are. ²³Won't their livestock, their property and all their other animals become ours? So let us give our consent to them, and they will settle among us."

²⁴All the men who went out of the city gate agreed with Hamor and his son Shechem, and every male in the city was circumcised.

²⁵Three days later, while all of them were still in pain, two of Jacob's sons, Simeon and Levi, Dinah's brothers, took their swords and attacked the unsuspecting city, killing every male. ²⁶They put Hamor and his son Shechem to the sword and took Dinah from Shechem's house and left. ²⁷The sons of Jacob came upon the dead bodies and looted the city where[d] their sister had been defiled. ²⁸They seized their flocks and herds and donkeys and everything else of theirs in the city and out in the fields. ²⁹They carried off all their wealth and all their women and children, taking as plunder everything in the houses.

³⁰Then Jacob said to Simeon and Levi, "You have brought trouble on me by making me a stench to the Canaanites and Perizzites, the people living in this land. We are few in number, and if they join forces against me and attack me, I and my household will be destroyed."

³¹But they replied, "Should he have treated our sister like a prostitute?"

■ Jacob Returns to Bethel

35 Then God said to Jacob, "Go up to Bethel and settle there, and build an altar there to God, who appeared to you when you were fleeing from your brother Esau."

²So Jacob said to his household and to all who were with him, "Get rid of the foreign gods you have with you, and purify yourselves and change your clothes. ³Then come, let us go up to Bethel, where I will build an altar to God, who answered me in the day of my distress and who has been with me wherever I have gone." ⁴So they gave Jacob all the foreign gods they had and the rings in their ears, and Jacob buried them under the oak at Shechem. ⁵Then they set out, and the terror of God fell upon the towns all around them so that no-one pursued them.

⁶Jacob and all the people with him came to Luz (that is, Bethel) in the land of Canaan. ⁷There he built an altar, and he called the place El Bethel,[a] because it was there that God revealed himself to him when he was fleeing from his brother.

⁸Now Deborah, Rebekah's nurse, died and was buried under the oak below Bethel. So it was named Allon Bacuth.[b]

⁹After Jacob returned from Paddan Aram,[c] God appeared to him again and blessed him. ¹⁰God said to him, "Your name is Jacob,[d] but you will no longer be called Jacob; your name will be Israel."[e] So he named him Israel.

¹¹And God said to him, "I am God Almighty;[f] be fruitful and increase in number. A nation and a community of nations will come from you, and kings will come from your body. ¹²The land I gave to Abraham and Isaac I also give to you, and I will give this land to your descendants after you." ¹³Then God went up from him at the place where he had talked with him.

¹⁴Jacob set up a stone pillar at the place where God had talked with him, and he poured out a drink offering on it; he also poured oil on it. ¹⁵Jacob called the place where God had talked with him Bethel.[g]

■ The Deaths of Rachel and Isaac

¹⁶Then they moved on from Bethel. While they were still some distance from Ephrath, Rachel began

---

a 7 Or *against*   *b* 10 Or *move about freely; also in verse 21*   *c* 17 Hebrew *daughter*   *d* 27 Or *because*   *a* 7 *El Bethel* means *God of Bethel.*
b 8 *Allon Bacuth* means *oak of weeping.*   *c* 9 That is, North-west Mesopotamia; also in verse 26   *d* 10 *Jacob* means *he grasps the heel* (figuratively, *he deceives*).   *e* 10 *Israel* means *he struggles with God.*   *f* 11 Hebrew *El-Shaddai*   *g* 15 *Bethel* means *house of God.*

to give birth and had great difficulty. [17]And as she was having great difficulty in childbirth, the midwife said to her, "Don't be afraid, for you have another son." [18]As she breathed her last—for she was dying—she named her son Ben-Oni.[b] But his father named him Benjamin.[i]

[19]So Rachel died and was buried on the way to Ephrath (that is, Bethlehem). [20]Over her tomb Jacob set up a pillar, and to this day that pillar marks Rachel's tomb.

[21]Israel moved on again and pitched his tent beyond Migdal Eder. [22]While Israel was living in that region, Reuben went in and slept with his father's concubine Bilhah, and Israel heard of it.

35:22 ■ A SIN THAT LIES SLEEPING

This passage offers no indication that what Reuben did was wrong, let alone subject to punishment. Yet his deed was not forgotten. Decades later, when Jacob called his sons in for a final blessing, he brought up this sin (49:4) and predicted that leadership would pass from Reuben, the firstborn.

Jacob had twelve sons:

[23]The sons of Leah:
    Reuben the firstborn of Jacob,
    Simeon, Levi, Judah, Issachar and Zebulun.
[24]The sons of Rachel:
    Joseph and Benjamin.
[25]The sons of Rachel's maidservant Bilhah:
    Dan and Naphtali.
[26]The sons of Leah's maidservant Zilpah:
    Gad and Asher.

These were the sons of Jacob, who were born to him in Paddan Aram.

[27]Jacob came home to his father Isaac in Mamre, near Kiriath Arba (that is, Hebron), where Abraham and Isaac had stayed. [28]Isaac lived a hundred and eighty years. [29]Then he breathed his last and died and was gathered to his people, old and full of years. And his sons Esau and Jacob buried him.

■ Esau's Descendants

36

This is the account of Esau (that is, Edom).

[2]Esau took his wives from the women of Canaan: Adah daughter of Elon the Hittite, and Oholibamah daughter of Anah and granddaughter of Zibeon the Hivite—[3]also Basemath daughter of Ishmael and sister of Nebaioth.

[4]Adah bore Eliphaz to Esau, Basemath bore Reuel, [5]and Oholibamah bore Jeush, Jalam and Korah. These were the sons of Esau, who were born to him in Canaan.

[6]Esau took his wives and sons and daughters and all the members of his household, as well as his livestock and all his other animals and all the goods he had acquired in Canaan, and moved to a land some distance from his brother Jacob. [7]Their possessions were too great for them to remain together; the land where they were staying could not support them both because of their livestock. [8]So Esau (that is, Edom) settled in the hill country of Seir.

[9]This is the account of Esau the father of the Edomites in the hill country of Seir.

[10]These are the names of Esau's sons:
    Eliphaz, the son of Esau's wife Adah, and
    Reuel, the son of Esau's wife Basemath.
[11]The sons of Eliphaz:
    Teman, Omar, Zepho, Gatam and Kenaz.
[12]Esau's son Eliphaz also had a concubine named Timna, who bore him Amalek. These were grandsons of Esau's wife Adah.
[13]The sons of Reuel:
    Nahath, Zerah, Shammah and Mizzah. These were grandsons of Esau's wife Basemath.
[14]The sons of Esau's wife Oholibamah daughter of Anah and granddaughter of Zibeon, whom she bore to Esau:
    Jeush, Jalam and Korah.

[15]These were the chiefs among Esau's descendants:
    The sons of Eliphaz the firstborn of Esau:
    Chiefs Teman, Omar, Zepho, Kenaz, [16]Korah,[a] Gatam and Amalek. These were the chiefs descended from Eliphaz in Edom; they were grandsons of Adah.
[17]The sons of Esau's son Reuel:
    Chiefs Nahath, Zerah, Shammah and Mizzah. These were the chiefs descended from Reuel in Edom; they were grandsons of Esau's wife Basemath.
[18]The sons of Esau's wife Oholibamah:
    Chiefs Jeush, Jalam and Korah. These were the chiefs descended from Esau's wife Oholibamah daughter of Anah.
[19]These were the sons of Esau (that is, Edom), and these were their chiefs.

[20]These were the sons of Seir the Horite, who were living in the region:
    Lotan, Shobal, Zibeon, Anah, [21]Dishon, Ezer and Dishan. These sons of Seir in Edom were Horite chiefs.
[22]The sons of Lotan:
    Hori and Homam.[b] Timna was Lotan's sister.
[23]The sons of Shobal:
    Alvan, Manahath, Ebal, Shepho and Onam.
[24]The sons of Zibeon:
    Aiah and Anah. This is the Anah who discovered the hot springs[c] in the desert while he was grazing the donkeys of his father Zibeon.
[25]The children of Anah:
    Dishon and Oholibamah daughter of Anah.
[26]The sons of Dishon:[d]
    Hemdan, Eshban, Ithran and Keran.
[27]The sons of Ezer:
    Bilhan, Zaavan and Akan.
[28]The sons of Dishan:
    Uz and Aran.
[29]These were the Horite chiefs:

---

[b]18 Ben-Oni means son of my trouble.   [i]18 Benjamin means son of my right hand.   [a]16 Masoretic Text; Samaritan Pentateuch (see also Gen. 36:11 and 1 Chron. 1:36) does not have Korah.   [b]22 Hebrew Hemam, a variant of Homam (see 1 Chron. 1:39)   [c]24 Vulgate; Syriac discovered water; the meaning of the Hebrew for this word is uncertain.   [d]26 Hebrew Dishan, a variant of Dishon

Lotan, Shobal, Zibeon, Anah, 30Dishon, Ezer and Dishan. These were the Horite chiefs, according to their divisions, in the land of Seir.

■ The Rulers of Edom
31These were the kings who reigned in Edom before any Israelite king reigned:e
32Bela son of Beor became king of Edom. His city was named Dinhabah.
33When Bela died, Jobab son of Zerah from Bozrah succeeded him as king.
34When Jobab died, Husham from the land of the Temanites succeeded him as king.
35When Husham died, Hadad son of Bedad, who defeated Midian in the country of Moab, succeeded him as king. His city was named Avith.
36When Hadad died, Samlah from Masrekah succeeded him as king.
37When Samlah died, Shaul from Rehoboth on the riverf succeeded him as king.
38When Shaul died, Baal-Hanan son of Acbor succeeded him as king.
39When Baal-Hanan son of Acbor died, Hadadg succeeded him as king. His city was named Pau, and his wife's name was Mehetabel daughter of Matred, the daughter of Me-Zahab.

40These were the chiefs descended from Esau, by name, according to their clans and regions:
Timna, Alvah, Jetheth, 41Oholibamah, Elah, Pinon, 42Kenaz, Teman, Mibzar, 43Magdiel and Iram. These were the chiefs of Edom, according to their settlements in the land they occupied.

This was Esau the father of the Edomites.

■ Joseph's Dreams

37 Jacob lived in the land where his father had stayed, the land of Canaan.

2This is the account of Jacob.

Joseph, a young man of seventeen, was tending the flocks with his brothers, the sons of Bilhah and the sons of Zilpah, his father's wives, and he brought their father a bad report about them.

3Now Israel loved Joseph more than any of his other sons, because he had been born to him in his old age; and he made a richly ornamenteda robe for him. 4When his brothers saw that their father loved him more than any of them, they hated him and could not speak a kind word to him.

5Joseph had a dream, and when he told it to his brothers, they hated him all the more. 6He said to them, "Listen to this dream I had: 7We were binding sheaves of corn out in the field when suddenly my sheaf rose and stood upright, while your sheaves gathered round mine and bowed down to it."

8His brothers said to him, "Do you intend to reign over us? Will you actually rule us?" And they hated him all the more because of his dream and what he had said.

9Then he had another dream, and he told it to his brothers. "Listen," he said, "I had another dream, and

this time the sun and moon and eleven stars were bowing down to me."

37:8 ■ BIG MOUTH
God revealed Joseph's future by way of two dreams. Foolishly, Joseph told everything to his brothers, who hated him all the more. The spoiled, naive Joseph we meet here is a different character from the careful, prudent leader who would emerge from prison years later to lead Egypt.

10When he told his father as well as his brothers, his father rebuked him and said, "What is this dream you had? Will your mother and I and your brothers actually come and bow down to the ground before you?" 11His brothers were jealous of him, but his father kept the matter in mind.

■ Joseph Sold by His Brothers
12Now his brothers had gone to graze their father's flocks near Shechem, 13and Israel said to Joseph, "As you know, your brothers are grazing the flocks near Shechem. Come, I am going to send you to them."
"Very well," he replied.
14So he said to him, "Go and see if all is well with your brothers and with the flocks, and bring word back to me." Then he sent him off from the Valley of Hebron.
When Joseph arrived at Shechem, 15a man found him wandering around in the fields and asked him, "What are you looking for?"
16He replied, "I'm looking for my brothers. Can you tell me where they are grazing their flocks?"
17"They have moved on from here," the man answered. "I heard them say, 'Let's go to Dothan.' "
So Joseph went after his brothers and found them near Dothan. 18But they saw him in the distance, and before he reached them, they plotted to kill him.
19"Here comes that dreamer!" they said to each other. 20"Come now, let's kill him and throw him into one of these cisterns and say that a ferocious animal devoured him. Then we'll see what comes of his dreams."
21When Reuben heard this, he tried to rescue him from their hands. "Let's not take his life," he said. 22"Don't shed any blood. Throw him into this cistern here in the desert, but don't lay a hand on him." Reuben said this to rescue him from them and take him back to his father.
23So when Joseph came to his brothers, they stripped him of his robe—the richly ornamented robe he was wearing—24and they took him and threw him into the cistern. Now the cistern was empty; there was no water in it.
25As they sat down to eat their meal, they looked up and saw a caravan of Ishmaelites coming from Gilead. Their camels were loaded with spices, balm and myrrh, and they were on their way to take them down to Egypt.
26Judah said to his brothers, "What will we gain if we kill our brother and cover up his blood?

---

e31 Or before an Israelite king reigned over them   f37 Possibly the Euphrates
Syriac (see also 1 Chron. 1:50); most manuscripts of the Masoretic Text Hadar
verses 23 and 32.

g39 Many manuscripts of the Masoretic Text, Samaritan Pentateuch and
a3 The meaning of the Hebrew for richly ornamented is uncertain; also in

²⁷Come, let's sell him to the Ishmaelites and not lay our hands on him; after all, he is our brother, our own flesh and blood." His brothers agreed.

²⁸So when the Midianite merchants came by, his brothers pulled Joseph up out of the cistern and sold him for twenty shekels*b* of silver to the Ishmaelites, who took him to Egypt.

²⁹When Reuben returned to the cistern and saw that Joseph was not there, he tore his clothes. ³⁰He went back to his brothers and said, "The boy isn't there! Where can I turn now?"

³¹Then they got Joseph's robe, slaughtered a goat and dipped the robe in the blood. ³²They took the ornamented robe back to their father and said, "We found this. Examine it to see whether it is your son's robe."

³³He recognised it and said, "It is my son's robe! Some ferocious animal has devoured him. Joseph has surely been torn to pieces."

³⁴Then Jacob tore his clothes, put on sackcloth and mourned for his son many days. ³⁵All his sons and daughters came to comfort him, but he refused to be comforted. "No," he said, "in mourning will I go down to the grave*c* to my son." So his father wept for him.

³⁶Meanwhile, the Midianites*d* sold Joseph in Egypt to Potiphar, one of Pharaoh's officials, the captain of the guard.

■ Judah and Tamar

38 At that time, Judah left his brothers and went down to stay with a man of Adullam named Hirah. ²There Judah met the daughter of a Canaanite man named Shua. He married her and lay with her; ³she became pregnant and gave birth to a son, who was named Er. ⁴She conceived again and gave birth to a son and named him Onan. ⁵She gave birth to still another son and named him Shelah. It was at Kezib that she gave birth to him.

⁶Judah got a wife for Er, his firstborn, and her name was Tamar. ⁷But Er, Judah's firstborn, was wicked in the LORD's sight; so the LORD put him to death.

⁸Then Judah said to Onan, "Lie with your brother's wife and fulfil your duty to her as a brother-in-law to produce offspring for your brother." ⁹But Onan knew that the offspring would not be his; so whenever he lay with his brother's wife, he spilled his semen on the ground to keep from producing offspring for his brother. ¹⁰What he did was wicked in the LORD's sight; so he put him to death also.

¹¹Judah then said to his daughter-in-law Tamar, "Live as a widow in your father's house until my son Shelah grows up." For he thought, "He may die too, just like his brothers." So Tamar went to live in her father's house.

¹²After a long time Judah's wife, the daughter of Shua, died. When Judah had recovered from his grief, he went up to Timnah, to the men who were shearing his sheep, and his friend Hirah the Adullamite went with him.

¹³When Tamar was told, "Your father-in-law is on his way to Timnah to shear his sheep," ¹⁴she took off her widow's clothes, covered herself with a veil to disguise herself, and then sat down at the entrance to Enaim, which is on the road to Timnah. For she saw that, though Shelah had now grown up, she had not been given to him as his wife.

38:8 ■ A BROTHER'S DUTY

Having children was so important in Old Testament times that if a man died childless, his brother was required to sleep with his widow in order to produce a family for him. (The regulations are found in Deuteronomy 25:5–10.) Onan's sin was a deliberate refusal to treat his brother's widow fairly by giving her children. Family quarrels had split Jacob and Esau and had sent Jacob's son Joseph into slavery; now the next generation was carrying on in the same way.

---

¹⁵When Judah saw her, he thought she was a prostitute, for she had covered her face. ¹⁶Not realising that she was his daughter-in-law, he went over to her by the roadside and said, "Come now, let me sleep with you."

"And what will you give me to sleep with you?" she asked.

¹⁷"I'll send you a young goat from my flock," he said.

"Will you give me something as a pledge until you send it?" she asked.

¹⁸He said, "What pledge should I give you?"

"Your seal and its cord, and the staff in your hand," she answered. So he gave them to her and slept with her, and she became pregnant by him. ¹⁹After she left, she took off her veil and put on her widow's clothes again.

²⁰Meanwhile Judah sent the young goat by his friend the Adullamite in order to get his pledge back from the woman, but he did not find her. ²¹He asked the men who lived there, "Where is the shrine-prostitute who was beside the road at Enaim?"

"There hasn't been any shrine-prostitute here," they said.

²²So he went back to Judah and said, "I didn't find her. Besides, the men who lived there said, 'There hasn't been any shrine-prostitute here.' "

²³Then Judah said, "Let her keep what she has, or we will become a laughing-stock. After all, I did send her this young goat, but you didn't find her."

²⁴About three months later Judah was told, "Your daughter-in-law Tamar is guilty of prostitution, and as a result she is now pregnant."

Judah said, "Bring her out and have her burned to death!"

²⁵As she was being brought out, she sent a message to her father-in-law. "I am pregnant by the man who owns these," she said. And she added, "See if you recognise whose seal and cord and staff these are."

²⁶Judah recognised them and said, "She is more righteous than I, since I wouldn't give her to my son Shelah." And he did not sleep with her again.

²⁷When the time came for her to give birth, there were twin boys in her womb. ²⁸As she was giving birth, one of them put out his hand; so the midwife

---

b 28 That is, about 8 ounces (about 0.2 kilogram)   *c 35* Hebrew *Sheol*   *d 36* Samaritan Pentateuch, Septuagint, Vulgate and Syriac (see also verse 28); Masoretic Text *Medanites* took a scarlet thread and tied it on his wrist and said, "This one came out first." 29But when he drew back his hand, his brother came out, and she said, "So this is how you have broken out!" And he was named Perez.*a* 30Then his brother, who had the scarlet thread on his wrist, came out and he was given the name Zerah.*b*

■ Joseph and Potiphar's Wife

39 Now Joseph had been taken down to Egypt. Potiphar, an Egyptian who was one of Pharaoh's officials, the captain of the guard, bought him from the Ishmaelites who had taken him there.

2The LORD was with Joseph and he prospered, and he lived in the house of his Egyptian master. 3When his master saw that the LORD was with him and that the LORD gave him success in everything he did, 4Joseph found favour in his eyes and became his attendant. Potiphar put him in charge of his household, and he entrusted to his care everything he owned. 5From the time he put him in charge of his household and of all that he owned, the LORD blessed the household of the Egyptian because of Joseph. The blessing of the LORD was on everything Potiphar had, both in the house and in the field. 6So he left in Joseph's care everything he had; with Joseph in charge, he did not concern himself with anything except the food he ate.

Now Joseph was well-built and handsome, 7and after a while his master's wife took notice of Joseph and said, "Come to bed with me!"

8But he refused. "With me in charge," he told her, "my master does not concern himself with anything in the house; everything he owns he has entrusted to my care. 9No-one is greater in this house than I am. My master has withheld nothing from me except you, because you are his wife. How then could I do such a wicked thing and sin against God?" 10And though she spoke to Joseph day after day, he refused to go to bed with her or even to be with her.

11One day he went into the house to attend to his duties, and none of the household servants was inside. 12She caught him by his cloak and said, "Come

---

■ **FAMILY BATTLES**
THE CLOSER THEY ARE, THE HARDER THEY FIGHT

INSIGHT

"HERE COMES THAT DREAMER!" THEY SAID TO EACH OTHER. "COME NOW, LET'S KILL HIM." ■ 37:19–20

Joseph and his brothers fought bitterly – almost to the death. Nobody, it seems, can fight like brothers and sisters. Their very closeness seems to rub salt into their wounds.

Sibling rivalry and family quarrels always make for a good read or even a good TV plot. JR, Bobby and Gary, sons of Miss Ellie and Jock Ewing, became household names because of their fighting over Ewing Oil.

Shakespeare himself made use of this theme in the tragedy, *King Lear*. Goneril, Regan and Cordelia are the king's daughters – they are not close. Cordelia doesn't trust her sisters and they are jealous of her youth and the place she holds in her father's heart.

"Tell me, my daughters . . . which of you shall we say doth love us most?", Lear asks. The competition begins and in the scene that follows, Cordelia loses her father's favour and their separation begins. Goneril and Regan are left to fight it out for the kingdom and for Edmund's favour, jealous now of each other.

These two sisters turn against their father and Cordelia and in true tragic style all four come to a sad end. The three sisters are never reconciled although, mercifully, Lear and Cordelia are as we can see from Lear's famous speech:

We two alone will sing like the birds i' th' cage;

When thou dost ask me blessing, I'll kneel down
And ask of thee forgiveness; so we'll live
And pray, and sing, and tell of old tales, and laugh . . .

■ A FATHER'S FAVOURITE
Joseph's story is the last of the brotherly battles of Genesis. Cain and Abel, Isaac and Ishmael, Jacob and Esau all quarrelled. Joseph set his 11 brothers against him by telling his dream of their bowing down to him. He was his father's favourite and perhaps flaunted it. So when his brothers got a chance, they paid him back. They sold him as a slave to travelling merchants, who took him to Egypt. Never expecting to see him again, they made up a story that he had been killed by wild animals.

God had other plans. In Egypt, he gave Joseph the interpretation to several dreams. It was a ticket to prominence. Egyptians of that day were fascinated by dreams: archaeologists have uncovered lengthy textbooks on dream interpretation. Joseph soon found himself at the top of Pharaoh's government.

But success was not enough. The Bible story goes on from there, for God wanted forgiveness within the family. A famine forced Joseph's brothers out of Palestine; they came to Egypt looking for food. Kneeling before Joseph – so Egyptian by now that they did not recognise him – they begged for the right to buy food.

---

a 29 Perez means breaking out.   *b* 30 Zerah can mean scarlet or brightness.

to bed with me!" But he left his cloak in her hand and ran out of the house.

13When she saw that he had left his cloak in her hand and had run out of the house, 14she called her household servants. "Look," she said to them, "this Hebrew has been brought to us to make sport of us! He came in here to sleep with me, but I screamed. 15When he heard me scream for help, he left his cloak beside me and ran out of the house."

16She kept his cloak beside her until his master came home. 17Then she told him this story: "That Hebrew slave you brought us came to me to make sport of me. 18But as soon as I screamed for help, he left his cloak beside me and ran out of the house."

19When his master heard the story his wife told him, saying, "This is how your slave treated me," he burned with anger. 20Joseph's master took him and put him in prison, the place where the king's prisoners were confined.

But while Joseph was there in the prison, 21the LORD was with him; he showed him kindness and granted him favour in the eyes of the prison warder.

22So the warder put Joseph in charge of all those held in the prison, and he was made responsible for all that was done there. 23The warder paid no attention to anything under Joseph's care, because the LORD was with Joseph and gave him success in whatever he did.

■ The Cupbearer and the Baker

40 Some time later, the cupbearer and the baker of the king of Egypt offended their master, the king of Egypt. 2Pharaoh was angry with his two officials, the chief cupbearer and the chief baker, 3and put them in custody in the house of the captain of the guard, in the same prison where Joseph was confined. 4The captain of the guard assigned them to Joseph, and he attended them.

After they had been in custody for some time, 5each of the two men — the cupbearer and the baker of the king of Egypt, who were being held in prison — had a dream the same night, and each dream had a meaning of its own.

6When Joseph came to them the next morning,

■ A STRANGE STRUGGLE

So began one of the strangest struggles of the Bible. Joseph could have made up with his brothers on the spot, welcoming them with open arms. Or he could have taken revenge, putting them to death. He did neither. He began a series of elaborate tests, demanding things from them, playing tricks on them, accusing them. For nearly two years he played these games. They brought confusion and fear to his brothers — and an admission of guilt.

Twenty years had not erased the brothers' memory of Joseph. The moment their troubles began, their guilt surfaced. "They said to one another, 'Surely we are being punished because of our brother. We saw how distressed he was when he pleaded with us for his life, but we would not listen' " (42:21). For Joseph, the drama brought tremendous emotional strain. Five times Genesis records that he broke into tears, once weeping so loudly that people in the next room heard him.

Joseph felt the strain of forgiveness. He wanted to be reconciled with his brothers, whom he loved, but it was not easy. And until they had been pushed to the point of admitting and accepting their guilt, reconciliation could not occur. Their sins had planted deep-rooted bitterness, and only an emotionally wrenching struggle could pull it out.

■ SEEDS OF BITTERNESS

In this sense Joseph's story is the story of God and his people — the struggle to root out the sin that began in Genesis 3. Victory over sin does not happen automatically or easily. Ultimately, it demanded the death of God's Son.

Joseph's story points towards Jesus — a man God sent to save his people, one who was hated and betrayed by them just as Joseph was. But God's will to save conquers all. As Joseph told his brothers, "You intended to harm me, but God intended it for good to accomplish . . . the saving of many lives" (50:20).

■ THE BIRTH OF A NATION

Joseph closes one chapter in the story of Israel. The children of Abraham were transformed from a chain of individuals to a nation. God did not choose Joseph over his brothers, as he did Abraham over Lot, Isaac over Ishmael, Jacob over Esau. The brothers' reconciliation opened the way for them to become one family of 12 tribes — a single nation.

But the story leads on. Prosperous and numerous though the 12 were to become, they still had no land. And so Genesis ends happily, but on a note of suspense: When will Joseph's bones go back to the land God promised? When will God's promises be fulfilled?

□ LIFE QUESTIONS:

Have you ever fought hard with a person close to you, and then experienced reconciliation? What process did you go through?

he saw that they were dejected. ⁷So he asked Pharaoh's officials who were in custody with him in his master's house, "Why are your faces so sad today?"

40:2 ■ IMPORTANT OFFICIALS

When Joseph was thrown into prison on a false charge, his future seemed to vanish. Yet in prison he came into contact with men who would eventually help raise him to the highest post in the nation. The "chief baker" and "chief cupbearer" were important officials in Pharaoh's court.

⁸"We both had dreams," they answered, "but there is no-one to interpret them."

Then Joseph said to them, "Do not interpretations belong to God? Tell me your dreams."

⁹So the chief cupbearer told Joseph his dream. He said to him, "In my dream I saw a vine in front of me, ¹⁰and on the vine were three branches. As soon as it budded, it blossomed, and its clusters ripened into grapes. ¹¹Pharaoh's cup was in my hand, and I took the grapes, squeezed them into Pharaoh's cup and put the cup in his hand."

¹²"This is what it means," Joseph said to him. "The three branches are three days. ¹³Within three days Pharaoh will lift up your head and restore you to your position, and you will put Pharaoh's cup in his hand, just as you used to do when you were his cupbearer. ¹⁴But when all goes well with you, remember me and show me kindness; mention me to Pharaoh and get me out of this prison. ¹⁵For I was forcibly carried off from the land of the Hebrews, and even here I have done nothing to deserve being put in a dungeon."

¹⁶When the chief baker saw that Joseph had given a favourable interpretation, he said to Joseph, "I too had a dream: On my head were three baskets of bread.ᵃ ¹⁷In the top basket were all kinds of baked goods for Pharaoh, but the birds were eating them out of the basket on my head."

¹⁸"This is what it means," Joseph said. "The three baskets are three days. ¹⁹Within three days Pharaoh will lift off your head and hang you on a tree.ᵇ And the birds will eat away your flesh."

²⁰Now the third day was Pharaoh's birthday, and he gave a feast for all his officials. He lifted up the heads of the chief cupbearer and the chief baker in the presence of his officials: ²¹He restored the chief cupbearer to his position, so that he once again put the cup into Pharaoh's hand, ²²but he hangedᶜ the chief baker, just as Joseph had said to them in his interpretation.

²³The chief cupbearer, however, did not remember Joseph; he forgot him.

■ Pharaoh's Dreams

41 When two full years had passed, Pharaoh had a dream: He was standing by the Nile, ²when out of the river there came up seven cows, sleek and fat, and they grazed among the reeds. ³After them, seven other cows, ugly and gaunt, came up out of the Nile and stood beside those on the riverbank.

⁴And the cows that were ugly and gaunt ate up the seven sleek, fat cows. Then Pharaoh woke up.

40:23 ■ A FORGOTTEN MAN

Joseph had carefully prepared the way for his release from prison (verses 14–15). Everything worked according to plan except for one detail: the chief cupbearer forgot all about Joseph. Humanly speaking, Joseph was a forgotten man, stuck in prison with no hope of ever getting out. God alone remembered his existence.

⁵He fell asleep again and had a second dream: Seven ears of corn, healthy and good, were growing on a single stalk. ⁶After them, seven other ears of corn sprouted—thin and scorched by the east wind. ⁷The thin ears of corn swallowed up the seven healthy, full ears. Then Pharaoh woke up; it had been a dream.

⁸In the morning his mind was troubled, so he sent for all the magicians and wise men of Egypt. Pharaoh told them his dreams, but no-one could interpret them for him.

⁹Then the chief cupbearer said to Pharaoh, "Today I am reminded of my shortcomings. ¹⁰Pharaoh was once angry with his servants, and he imprisoned me and the chief baker in the house of the captain of the guard. ¹¹Each of us had a dream the same night, and each dream had a meaning of its own. ¹²Now a young Hebrew was there with us, a servant of the captain of the guard. We told him our dreams, and he interpreted them for us, giving each man the interpretation of his dream. ¹³And things turned out exactly as he interpreted them to us: I was restored to my position, and the other man was hanged."ᵃ

¹⁴So Pharaoh sent for Joseph, and he was quickly brought from the dungeon. When he had shaved and changed his clothes, he came before Pharaoh.

¹⁵Pharaoh said to Joseph, "I had a dream, and no-one can interpret it. But I have heard it said of you that when you hear a dream you can interpret it."

¹⁶"I cannot do it," Joseph replied to Pharaoh, "but God will give Pharaoh the answer he desires."

¹⁷Then Pharaoh said to Joseph, "In my dream I was standing on the bank of the Nile, ¹⁸when out of the river there came up seven cows, fat and sleek, and they grazed among the reeds. ¹⁹After them, seven other cows came up—scrawny and very ugly and lean. I had never seen such ugly cows in all the land of Egypt. ²⁰The lean, ugly cows ate up the seven fat cows that came up first. ²¹But even after they ate them, no-one could tell that they had done so; they looked just as ugly as before. Then I woke up.

²²"In my dreams I also saw seven ears of corn, full and good, growing on a single stalk. ²³After them, seven other ears sprouted—withered and thin and scorched by the east wind. ²⁴The thin ears of corn swallowed up the seven good ears. I told this to the magicians, but none could explain it to me."

²⁵Then Joseph said to Pharaoh, "The dreams of Pharaoh are one and the same. God has revealed to Pharaoh what he is about to do. ²⁶The seven good cows are seven years, and the seven good ears of

ᵃ 16 Or three wicker baskets   ᵇ 19 Or and impale you on a pole   ᶜ 22 Or impaled   ᵃ 13 Or impaled corn are seven years; it is one and the same dream. [27]The seven lean, ugly cows that came up afterwards are seven years, and so are the seven worthless ears of corn scorched by the east wind: They are seven years of famine.

[28]"It is just as I said to Pharaoh: God has shown Pharaoh what he is about to do. [29]Seven years of great abundance are coming throughout the land of Egypt, [30]but seven years of famine will follow them. Then all the abundance in Egypt will be forgotten, and the famine will ravage the land. [31]The abundance in the land will not be remembered, because the famine that follows it will be so severe. [32]The reason the dream was given to Pharaoh in two forms is that the matter has been firmly decided by God, and God will do it soon.

[33]"And now let Pharaoh look for a discerning and wise man and put him in charge of the land of Egypt. [34]Let Pharaoh appoint commissioners over the land to take a fifth of the harvest of Egypt during the seven years of abundance. [35]They should collect all the food of these good years that are coming and store up the grain under the authority of Pharaoh, to be kept in the cities for food. [36]This food should be held in reserve for the country, to be used during the seven years of famine that will come upon Egypt, so that the country may not be ruined by the famine."

[37]The plan seemed good to Pharaoh and to all his officials. [38]So Pharaoh asked them, "Can we find anyone like this man, one in whom is the spirit of God?"[b]

[39]Then Pharaoh said to Joseph, "Since God has made all this known to you, there is no-one so discerning and wise as you. [40]You shall be in charge of my palace, and all my people are to submit to your orders. Only with respect to the throne will I be greater than you."

■ Joseph in Charge of Egypt

[41]So Pharaoh said to Joseph, "I hereby put you in charge of the whole land of Egypt." [42]Then Pharaoh took his signet ring from his finger and put it on Joseph's finger. He dressed him in robes of fine linen and put a gold chain around his neck. [43]He had him ride in a chariot as his second-in-command,[c] and men shouted before him, "Make way!"[d] Thus he put him in charge of the whole land of Egypt.

[44]Then Pharaoh said to Joseph, "I am Pharaoh, but without your word no-one will lift hand or foot in all Egypt." [45]Pharaoh gave Joseph the name Zaphenath-Paneah and gave him Asenath daughter of Potiphera, priest of On,[e] to be his wife. And Joseph went throughout the land of Egypt.

[46]Joseph was thirty years old when he entered the service of Pharaoh king of Egypt. And Joseph went out from Pharaoh's presence and travelled throughout Egypt. [47]During the seven years of abundance the land produced plentifully. [48]Joseph collected all the food produced in those seven years of abundance in Egypt and stored it in the cities. In each city he put the food grown in the fields surrounding it. [49]Joseph stored up huge quantities of grain, like the sand of the sea; it was so much that he stopped keeping records because it was beyond measure.

[50]Before the years of famine came, two sons were born to Joseph by Asenath daughter of Potiphera, priest of On. [51]Joseph named his firstborn Manasseh[f] and said, "It is because God has made me forget all my trouble and all my father's household." [52]The second son he named Ephraim[g] and said, "It is because God has made me fruitful in the land of my suffering."

41:45 ■ ERASING JOSEPH'S PAST

Proud Egyptians did not care for Hebrews. In order that Joseph's ethnic past be erased as quickly as possible, Pharaoh gave Joseph an Egyptian name and married him into a prominent Egyptian family. Joseph gave his own sons Hebrew names, however, a practice that suggests he maintained his own identity.

[53]The seven years of abundance in Egypt came to an end, [54]and the seven years of famine began, just as Joseph had said. There was famine in all the other lands, but in the whole land of Egypt there was food. [55]When all Egypt began to feel the famine, the people cried to Pharaoh for food. Then Pharaoh told all the Egyptians, "Go to Joseph and do what he tells you."

[56]When the famine had spread over the whole country, Joseph opened the storehouses and sold grain to the Egyptians, for the famine was severe throughout Egypt. [57]And all the countries came to Egypt to buy grain from Joseph, because the famine was severe in all the world.

41:56 ■ AN UNUSUAL FAMINE

Famine is common in the Middle East. There are records of two Egyptian famines so severe that starving people killed and ate each other. But it was rare for famine to affect both Egypt and Palestine at the same time, for they depended on totally different sources of water—Egypt on the Nile and Palestine on local rainfall.

■ Joseph's Brothers Go to Egypt

42 When Jacob learned that there was grain in Egypt, he said to his sons, "Why do you just keep looking at each other?" [2]He continued, "I have heard that there is grain in Egypt. Go down there and buy some for us, so that we may live and not die."

[3]Then ten of Joseph's brothers went down to buy grain from Egypt. [4]But Jacob did not send Benjamin, Joseph's brother, with the others, because he was afraid that harm might come to him. [5]So Israel's sons were among those who went to buy grain, for the famine was in the land of Canaan also.

[6]Now Joseph was the governor of the land, the one who sold grain to all its people. So when Joseph's brothers arrived, they bowed down to him with their faces to the ground. [7]As soon as Joseph saw his brothers, he recognised them, but he

---

[b]38 Or of the gods   [c]43 Or in the chariot of his second-in-command; or in his second chariot   [d]43 Or Bow down   [e]45 That is, Heliopolis; also in verse 50   [f]51 Manasseh sounds like and may be derived from the Hebrew for forget.   [g]52 Ephraim sounds like the Hebrew for twice fruitful.

pretended to be a stranger and spoke harshly to them. "Where do you come from?" he asked.

"From the land of Canaan," they replied, "to buy food."

8Although Joseph recognised his brothers, they did not recognise him. 9Then he remembered his dreams about them and said to them, "You are spies! You have come to see where our land is unprotected."

10"No, my lord," they answered. "Your servants have come to buy food. 11We are all the sons of one man. Your servants are honest men, not spies."

12"No!" he said to them. "You have come to see where our land is unprotected."

13But they replied, "Your servants were twelve brothers, the sons of one man, who lives in the land of Canaan. The youngest is now with our father, and one is no more."

14Joseph said to them, "It is just as I told you: You are spies! 15And this is how you will be tested: As surely as Pharaoh lives, you will not leave this place unless your youngest brother comes here. 16Send one of your number to get your brother; the rest of you will be kept in prison, so that your words may be tested to see if you are telling the truth. If you are not, then as surely as Pharaoh lives, you are spies!" 17And he put them all in custody for three days.

18On the third day, Joseph said to them, "Do this and you will live, for I fear God: 19If you are honest men, let one of your brothers stay here in prison, while the rest of you go and take grain back for your starving households. 20But you must bring your youngest brother to me, so that your words may be verified and that you may not die." This they proceeded to do.

21They said to one another, "Surely we are being punished because of our brother. We saw how distressed he was when he pleaded with us for his life, but we would not listen; that's why this distress has come upon us."

22Reuben replied, "Didn't I tell you not to sin against the boy? But you wouldn't listen! Now we must give an accounting for his blood." 23They did not realise that Joseph could understand them, since he was using an interpreter.

24He turned away from them and began to weep, but then turned back and spoke to them again. He had Simeon taken from them and bound before their eyes.

42:24 ■ JOSEPH IN TEARS

Five times Genesis records Joseph weeping as he dealt with his brothers (43:30; 45:2,14–15; 50:17). They had sold him into slavery, and all those years had not erased his hurt and anger. Yet he loved his brothers, and wanted to be reconciled. He felt his conflicting emotions intensely: love versus anger, forgiveness versus bitterness.

25Joseph gave orders to fill their bags with grain, to put each man's silver back in his sack, and to give them provisions for their journey. After this was done for them, 26they loaded their grain on their donkeys and left.

27At the place where they stopped for the night one of them opened his sack to get feed for his donkey, and he saw his silver in the mouth of his sack. 28"My silver has been returned," he said to his brothers. "Here it is in my sack."

Their hearts sank and they turned to each other trembling and said, "What is this that God has done to us?"

29When they came to their father Jacob in the land of Canaan, they told him all that had happened to them. They said, 30"The man who is lord over the land spoke harshly to us and treated us as though we were spying on the land. 31But we said to him, 'We are honest men; we are not spies. 32We were twelve brothers, sons of one father. One is no more, and the youngest is now with our father in Canaan.'

33"Then the man who is lord over the land said to us, 'This is how I will know whether you are honest men: Leave one of your brothers here with me, and take food for your starving households and go. 34But bring your youngest brother to me so I will know that you are not spies but honest men. Then I will give your brother back to you, and you can trade*a* in the land.' "

35As they were emptying their sacks, there in each man's sack was his pouch of silver! When they and their father saw the money pouches, they were frightened. 36Their father Jacob said to them, "You have deprived me of my children. Joseph is no more and Simeon is no more, and now you want to take Benjamin. Everything is against me!"

37Then Reuben said to his father, "You may put both of my sons to death if I do not bring him back to you. Entrust him to my care, and I will bring him back."

38But Jacob said, "My son will not go down there with you; his brother is dead and he is the only one left. If harm comes to him on the journey you are taking, you will bring my grey head down to the grave*b* in sorrow."

■ The Second Journey to Egypt

43 Now the famine was still severe in the land. 2So when they had eaten all the grain they had brought from Egypt, their father said to them, "Go back and buy us a little more food."

3But Judah said to him, "The man warned us solemnly, 'You will not see my face again unless your brother is with you.' 4If you will send our brother along with us, we will go down and buy food for you. 5But if you will not send him, we will not go down, because the man said to us, 'You will not see my face again unless your brother is with you.' "

6Israel asked, "Why did you bring this trouble on me by telling the man you had another brother?"

7They replied, "The man questioned us closely about ourselves and our family. 'Is your father still living?' he asked us. 'Do you have another brother?' We simply answered his questions. How were we to know he would say, 'Bring your brother down here'?"

8Then Judah said to Israel his father, "Send the boy along with me and we will go at once, so that

a 34 Or move about freely　b 38 Hebrew Sheol

we and you and our children may live and not die. 9I myself will guarantee his safety; you can hold me personally responsible for him. If I do not bring him back to you and set him here before you, I will bear the blame before you all my life. 10As it is, if we had not delayed, we could have gone and returned twice."

11Then their father Israel said to them, "If it must be, then do this: Put some of the best products of the land in your bags and take them down to the man as a gift — a little balm and a little honey, some spices and myrrh, some pistachio nuts and almonds. 12Take double the amount of silver with you, for you must return the silver that was put back into the mouths of your sacks. Perhaps it was a mistake. 13Take your brother also and go back to the man at once. 14And may God Almighty*a* grant you mercy before the man so that he will let your other brother and Benjamin come back with you. As for me, if I am bereaved, I am bereaved."

43:11 ■ THE PERFECT GIFT

What kind of gift can you send to a man who has everything? Egypt was among the richest and most sophisticated countries in the world, and Israel (Jacob), a desert nomad. He wisely chose simple gifts of local produce — things that might not be available in Egypt.

15So the men took the gifts and double the amount of silver, and Benjamin also. They hurried down to Egypt and presented themselves to Joseph. 16When Joseph saw Benjamin with them, he said to the steward of his house, "Take these men to my house, slaughter an animal and prepare dinner; they are to eat with me at noon."

17The man did as Joseph told him and took the men to Joseph's house. 18Now the men were frightened when they were taken to his house. They thought, "We were brought here because of the silver that was put back into our sacks the first time. He wants to attack us and overpower us and seize us as slaves and take our donkeys."

19So they went up to Joseph's steward and spoke to him at the entrance to the house. 20"Please, sir," they said, "we came down here the first time to buy food. 21But at the place where we stopped for the night we opened our sacks and each of us found his silver — the exact weight — in the mouth of his sack. So we have brought it back with us. 22We have also brought additional silver with us to buy food. We don't know who put our silver in our sacks."

23"It's all right," he said. "Don't be afraid. Your God, the God of your father, has given you treasure in your sacks; I received your silver." Then he brought Simeon out to them.

24The steward took the men into Joseph's house, gave them water to wash their feet and provided fodder for their donkeys. 25They prepared their gifts for Joseph's arrival at noon, because they had heard that they were to eat there.

26When Joseph came home, they presented to him the gifts they had brought into the house, and they bowed down before him to the ground. 27He asked them how they were, and then he said, "How is your aged father you told me about? Is he still living?"

28They replied, "Your servant our father is still alive and well." And they bowed low to pay him honour.

29As he looked about and saw his brother Benjamin, his own mother's son, he asked, "Is this your youngest brother, the one you told me about?" And he said, "God be gracious to you, my son." 30Deeply moved at the sight of his brother, Joseph hurried out and looked for a place to weep. He went into his private room and wept there.

31After he had washed his face, he came out and, controlling himself, said, "Serve the food."

32They served him by himself, the brothers by themselves, and the Egyptians who ate with him by themselves, because Egyptians could not eat with Hebrews, for that is detestable to Egyptians. 33The men had been seated before him in the order of their ages, from the firstborn to the youngest; and they looked at each other in astonishment. 34When portions were served to them from Joseph's table, Benjamin's portion was five times as much as anyone else's. So they feasted and drank freely with him.

43:32 ■ PREJUDICE

Despite his high rank, Joseph still fell victim to Egyptian prejudice: they would not eat at the same table with a Hebrew. Chapter 46 (verses 33–34) adds that Egyptians detested shepherds — and Hebrews herded sheep.

■ A Silver Cup in a Sack

44 Now Joseph gave these instructions to the steward of his house: "Fill the men's sacks with as much food as they can carry, and put each man's silver in the mouth of his sack. 2Then put my cup, the silver one, in the mouth of the youngest one's sack, along with the silver for his grain." And he did as Joseph said.

3As morning dawned, the men were sent on their way with their donkeys. 4They had not gone far from the city when Joseph said to his steward, "Go after those men at once, and when you catch up with them, say to them, 'Why have you repaid good with evil? 5Isn't this the cup my master drinks from and also uses for divination? This is a wicked thing you have done.'"

6When he caught up with them, he repeated these words to them. 7But they said to him, "Why does my lord say such things? Far be it from your servants to do anything like that! 8We even brought back to you from the land of Canaan the silver we found inside the mouths of our sacks. So why would we steal silver or gold from your master's house? 9If any of your servants is found to have it, he will die; and the rest of us will become my lord's slaves."

10"Very well, then," he said, "let it be as you say. Whoever is found to have it will become my slave; the rest of you will be free from blame."

a 14 Hebrew El-Shaddai

11Each of them quickly lowered his sack to the ground and opened it. 12Then the steward proceeded to search, beginning with the oldest and ending with the youngest. And the cup was found in Benjamin's sack. 13At this, they tore their clothes. Then they all loaded their donkeys and returned to the city.

14Joseph was still in the house when Judah and his brothers came in, and they threw themselves to the ground before him. 15Joseph said to them, "What is this you have done? Don't you know that a man like me can find things out by divination?"

16"What can we say to my lord?" Judah replied. "What can we say? How can we prove our innocence? God has uncovered your servants' guilt. We are now my lord's slaves — we ourselves and the one who was found to have the cup."

17But Joseph said, "Far be it from me to do such a thing! Only the man who was found to have the cup will become my slave. The rest of you, go back to your father in peace."

18Then Judah went up to him and said: "Please, my lord, let your servant speak a word to my lord. Do not be angry with your servant, though you are equal to Pharaoh himself. 19My lord asked his servants, 'Do you have a father or a brother?' 20And we answered, 'We have an aged father, and there is a young son born to him in his old age. His brother is dead, and he is the only one of his mother's sons left, and his father loves him.'

21"Then you said to your servants, 'Bring him down to me so I can see him for myself.' 22And we said to my lord, 'The boy cannot leave his father; if he leaves him, his father will die.' 23But you told your servants, 'Unless your youngest brother comes down with you, you will not see my face again.' 24When we went back to your servant my father, we told him what my lord had said.

25"Then our father said, 'Go back and buy a little more food.' 26But we said, 'We cannot go down. Only if our youngest brother is with us will we go. We cannot see the man's face unless our youngest brother is with us.'

27"Your servant my father said to us, 'You know that my wife bore me two sons. 28One of them went away from me, and I said, "He has surely been torn to pieces." And I have not seen him since. 29If you take this one from me too and harm comes to him, you will bring my grey head down to the gravea in misery.'

30"So now, if the boy is not with us when I go back to your servant my father and if my father, whose life is closely bound up with the boy's life, 31sees that the boy isn't there, he will die. Your servants will bring the grey head of our father down to the grave in sorrow. 32Your servant guaranteed the boy's safety to my father. I said, 'If I do not bring him back to you, I will bear the blame before you, my father, all my life!'

33"Now then, please let your servant remain here as my lord's slave in place of the boy, and let the boy return with his brothers. 34How can I go back to my father if the boy is not with me? No! Do not let me see the misery that would come upon my father."

■ Joseph Makes Himself Known

45

Then Joseph could no longer control himself before all his attendants, and he cried out, "Make everyone leave my presence!" So there was no-one with Joseph when he made himself known to his brothers. 2And he wept so loudly that the Egyptians heard him, and Pharaoh's household heard about it.

45:2 ■ WEEPING AND TERROR
This is one of the Bible's most intensely emotional scenes: it shows Joseph weeping so loudly that people in the next room heard him, and Joseph's brothers were left speechless with terror and guilt. Though the moment ended with embraces and kissing (verses 14–15), years later the brothers were still afraid of revenge (50:15).

3Joseph said to his brothers, "I am Joseph! Is my father still living?" But his brothers were not able to answer him, because they were terrified at his presence.

4Then Joseph said to his brothers, "Come close to me." When they had done so, he said, "I am your brother Joseph, the one you sold into Egypt! 5And now, do not be distressed and do not be angry with yourselves for selling me here, because it was to save lives that God sent me ahead of you. 6For two years now there has been famine in the land, and for the next five years there will not be ploughing and reaping. 7But God sent me ahead of you to preserve for you a remnant on earth and to save your lives by a great deliverance.a

8"So then, it was not you who sent me here, but God. He made me father to Pharaoh, lord of his entire household and ruler of all Egypt. 9Now hurry back to my father and say to him, 'This is what your son Joseph says: God has made me lord of all Egypt. Come down to me; don't delay. 10You shall live in the region of Goshen and be near me — you, your children and grandchildren, your flocks and herds, and all you have. 11I will provide for you there, because five years of famine are still to come. Otherwise you and your household and all who belong to you will become destitute.'

12"You can see for yourselves, and so can my brother Benjamin, that it is really I who am speaking to you. 13Tell my father about all the honour accorded me in Egypt and about everything you have seen. And bring my father down here quickly."

14Then he threw his arms around his brother Benjamin and wept, and Benjamin embraced him, weeping. 15And he kissed all his brothers and wept over them. Afterwards his brothers talked with him.

16When the news reached Pharaoh's palace that Joseph's brothers had come, Pharaoh and all his officials were pleased. 17Pharaoh said to Joseph, "Tell your brothers, 'Do this: Load your animals and return to the land of Canaan, 18and bring your father and your families back to me. I will give you the best of the land of Egypt and you can enjoy the fat of the land.'

19"You are also directed to tell them, 'Do this:

---

a 29 Hebrew Sheol; also in verse 31   a 7 Or save you as a great band of survivors

Take some carts from Egypt for your children and your wives, and get your father and come. [20]Never mind about your belongings, because the best of all Egypt will be yours.' "

[21]So the sons of Israel did this. Joseph gave them carts, as Pharaoh had commanded, and he also gave them provisions for their journey. [22]To each of them he gave new clothing, but to Benjamin he gave three hundred shekels[b] of silver and five sets of clothes. [23]And this is what he sent to his father: ten donkeys loaded with the best things of Egypt, and ten female donkeys loaded with grain and bread and other provisions for his journey. [24]Then he sent his brothers away, and as they were leaving he said to them, "Don't quarrel on the way!"

[25]So they went up out of Egypt and came to their father Jacob in the land of Canaan. [26]They told him, "Joseph is still alive! In fact, he is ruler of all Egypt." Jacob was stunned; he did not believe them. [27]But when they told him everything Joseph had said to them, and when he saw the carts Joseph had sent to carry him back, the spirit of their father Jacob revived. [28]And Israel said, "I'm convinced! My son Joseph is still alive. I will go and see him before I die."

■ Jacob Goes to Egypt

46 So Israel set out with all that was his, and when he reached Beersheba, he offered sacrifices to the God of his father Isaac.

[2]And God spoke to Israel in a vision at night and said, "Jacob! Jacob!"

"Here I am," he replied.

[3]"I am God, the God of your father," he said. "Do not be afraid to go down to Egypt, for I will make you into a great nation there. [4]I will go down to Egypt with you, and I will surely bring you back again. And Joseph's own hand will close your eyes."

[5]Then Jacob left Beersheba, and Israel's sons took their father Jacob and their children and their wives in the carts that Pharaoh had sent to transport him. [6]They also took with them their livestock and the possessions they had acquired in Canaan, and Jacob and all his offspring went to Egypt. [7]He took with him to Egypt his sons and grandsons and his daughters and granddaughters—all his offspring.

[8]These are the names of the sons of Israel (Jacob and his descendants) who went to Egypt:

Reuben the firstborn of Jacob.
[9]The sons of Reuben:
Hanoch, Pallu, Hezron and Carmi.
[10]The sons of Simeon:
Jemuel, Jamin, Ohad, Jakin, Zohar and Shaul the son of a Canaanite woman.
[11]The sons of Levi:
Gershon, Kohath and Merari.
[12]The sons of Judah:
Er, Onan, Shelah, Perez and Zerah (but Er and Onan had died in the land of Canaan).
The sons of Perez:
Hezron and Hamul.
[13]The sons of Issachar:
Tola, Puah,[a] Jashub[b] and Shimron.

[14]The sons of Zebulun:
Sered, Elon and Jahleel.
[15]These were the sons Leah bore to Jacob in Paddan Aram,[c] besides his daughter Dinah. These sons and daughters of his were thirty-three in all.

[16]The sons of Gad:
Zephon,[d] Haggi, Shuni, Ezbon, Eri, Arodi and Areli.
[17]The sons of Asher:
Imnah, Ishvah, Ishvi and Beriah.
Their sister was Serah.
The sons of Beriah:
Heber and Malkiel.
[18]These were the children born to Jacob by Zilpah, whom Laban had given to his daughter Leah—sixteen in all.

[19]The sons of Jacob's wife Rachel:
Joseph and Benjamin. [20]In Egypt, Manasseh and Ephraim were born to Joseph by Asenath daughter of Potiphera, priest of On.[e]
[21]The sons of Benjamin:
Bela, Beker, Ashbel, Gera, Naaman, Ehi, Rosh, Muppim, Huppim and Ard.
[22]These were the sons of Rachel who were born to Jacob—fourteen in all.

[23]The son of Dan:
Hushim.
[24]The sons of Naphtali:
Jahziel, Guni, Jezer and Shillem.
[25]These were the sons born to Jacob by Bilhah, whom Laban had given to his daughter Rachel—seven in all.

[26]All those who went to Egypt with Jacob—those who were his direct descendants, not counting his sons' wives—numbered sixty-six persons. [27]With the two sons[f] who had been born to Joseph in Egypt, the members of Jacob's family, which went to Egypt, were seventy[g] in all.

[28]Now Jacob sent Judah ahead of him to Joseph to get directions to Goshen. When they arrived in the region of Goshen, [29]Joseph had his chariot made ready and went to Goshen to meet his father Israel. As soon as Joseph appeared before him, he threw his arms around his father[h] and wept for a long time.

[30]Israel said to Joseph, "Now I am ready to die, since I have seen for myself that you are still alive."

[31]Then Joseph said to his brothers and to his father's household, "I will go up and speak to Pharaoh and will say to him, 'My brothers and my father's household, who were living in the land of Canaan, have come to me. [32]The men are shepherds; they tend livestock, and they have brought along their flocks and herds and everything they own.' [33]When Pharaoh calls you in and asks, 'What is your occupation?' [34]you should answer, 'Your servants have tended livestock from our boyhood on, just as our fathers did.' Then you will be allowed to settle in the region of Goshen, for all shepherds are detestable to the Egyptians."

---

[b] 22 That is, about 7½ pounds (about 3.5 kilograms)   [a] 13 Samaritan Pentateuch and Syriac (see also 1 Chron. 7:1); Masoretic Text *Puvah*
[b] 13 Samaritan Pentateuch and some Septuagint manuscripts (see also Num. 26:24 and 1 Chron. 7:1); Masoretic Text *Job*   [c] 15 That is, North-west Mesopotamia   [d] 16 Samaritan Pentateuch and Septuagint (see also Num. 26:15); Masoretic Text *Ziphion*   [e] 20 That is, Heliopolis   [f] 27 Hebrew; Septuagint *the nine children*   [g] 27 Hebrew (see also Exodus 1:5 and footnote); Septuagint (see also Acts 7:14) *seventy-five*   [h] 29 Hebrew *around him*

47 Joseph went and told Pharaoh, "My father and brothers, with their flocks and herds and everything they own, have come from the land of Canaan and are now in Goshen." [2]He chose five of his brothers and presented them before Pharaoh.

[3]Pharaoh asked the brothers, "What is your occupation?"

"Your servants are shepherds," they replied to Pharaoh, "just as our fathers were." [4]They also said to him, "We have come to live here awhile, because the famine is severe in Canaan and your servants' flocks have no pasture. So now, please let your servants settle in Goshen."

[5]Pharaoh said to Joseph, "Your father and your brothers have come to you, [6]and the land of Egypt is before you; settle your father and your brothers in the best part of the land. Let them live in Goshen. And if you know of any among them with special ability, put them in charge of my own livestock."

[7]Then Joseph brought his father Jacob and presented him before Pharaoh. After Jacob blessed[a] Pharaoh, [8]Pharaoh asked him, "How old are you?"

[9]And Jacob said to Pharaoh, "The years of my pilgrimage are a hundred and thirty. My years have been few and difficult, and they do not equal the years of the pilgrimage of my fathers." [10]Then Jacob blessed[b] Pharaoh and went out from his presence.

[11]So Joseph settled his father and his brothers in Egypt and gave them property in the best part of the land, the district of Rameses, as Pharaoh directed. [12]Joseph also provided his father and his brothers and all his father's household with food, according to the number of their children.

■ Joseph and the Famine

[13]There was no food, however, in the whole region because the famine was severe; both Egypt and Canaan wasted away because of the famine. [14]Joseph collected all the money that was to be found in Egypt and Canaan in payment for the grain they were buying, and he brought it to Pharaoh's palace. [15]When the money of the people of Egypt and Canaan was gone, all Egypt came to Joseph and said, "Give us food. Why should we die before your eyes? Our money is used up."

[16]"Then bring your livestock," said Joseph. "I will sell you food in exchange for your livestock, since your money is gone." [17]So they brought their livestock to Joseph, and he gave them food in exchange for their horses, their sheep and goats, their cattle and donkeys. And he brought them through that year with food in exchange for all their livestock.

[18]When that year was over, they came to him the following year and said, "We cannot hide from our lord the fact that since our money is gone and our livestock belongs to you, there is nothing left for our lord except our bodies and our land. [19]Why should we perish before your eyes—we and our land as well? Buy us and our land in exchange for food, and we with our land will be in bondage to Pharaoh. Give us seed so that we may live and not die, and that the land may not become desolate."

[20]So Joseph bought all the land in Egypt for Pharaoh. The Egyptians, one and all, sold their fields, because the famine was too severe for them. The land became Pharaoh's, [21]and Joseph reduced the people to servitude,[c] from one end of Egypt to the other. [22]However, he did not buy the land of the priests, because they received a regular allotment from Pharaoh and had food enough from the allotment Pharaoh gave them. That is why they did not sell their land.

[23]Joseph said to the people, "Now that I have bought you and your land today for Pharaoh, here is seed for you so you can plant the ground. [24]But when the crop comes in, give a fifth of it to Pharaoh. The other four-fifths you may keep as seed for the fields and as food for yourselves and your households and your children."

[25]"You have saved our lives," they said. "May we find favour in the eyes of our lord; we will be in bondage to Pharaoh."

[26]So Joseph established it as a law concerning land in Egypt—still in force today—that a fifth of the produce belongs to Pharaoh. It was only the land of the priests that did not become Pharaoh's.

[27]Now the Israelites settled in Egypt in the region of Goshen. They acquired property there and were fruitful and increased greatly in number.

[28]Jacob lived in Egypt seventeen years, and the years of his life were a hundred and forty-seven. [29]When the time drew near for Israel to die, he called for his son Joseph and said to him, "If I have found favour in your eyes, put your hand under my thigh and promise that you will show me kindness and faithfulness. Do not bury me in Egypt, [30]but when I rest with my fathers, carry me out of Egypt and bury me where they are buried."

"I will do as you say," he said.

[31]"Swear to me," he said. Then Joseph swore to him, and Israel worshipped as he leaned on the top of his staff.[d]

■ Manasseh and Ephraim

48 Some time later Joseph was told, "Your father is ill." So he took his two sons Manasseh and Ephraim along with him. [2]When Jacob was told, "Your son Joseph has come to you," Israel rallied his strength and sat up on the bed.

[3]Jacob said to Joseph, "God Almighty[a] appeared to me at Luz in the land of Canaan, and there he blessed me [4]and said to me, 'I am going to make you fruitful and will increase your numbers. I will make you a community of peoples, and I will give this land as an everlasting possession to your descendants after you.'

[5]"Now then, your two sons born to you in Egypt before I came to you here will be reckoned as mine; Ephraim and Manasseh will be mine, just as Reuben and Simeon are mine. [6]Any children born to you after them will be yours; in the territory they inherit they will be reckoned under the names of their brothers. [7]As I was returning from Paddan,[b] to my sorrow Rachel died in the land of Canaan while we were still on the way, a little distance from Ephrath. So I buried her there beside the road to Ephrath" (that is, Bethlehem).

[8]When Israel saw the sons of Joseph, he asked, "Who are these?"

---

a 7 Or greeted   b 10 Or said farewell to   c 21 Samaritan Pentateuch and Septuagint (see also Vulgate); Masoretic Text and he moved the people into the cities   d 31 Or Israel bowed down at the head of his bed   a 3 Hebrew El-Shaddai   b 7 That is, North-west Mesopotamia

9"They are the sons God has given me here," Joseph said to his father.

Then Israel said, "Bring them to me so that I may bless them."

10Now Israel's eyes were failing because of old age, and he could hardly see. So Joseph brought his sons close to him, and his father kissed them and embraced them.

11Israel said to Joseph, "I never expected to see your face again, and now God has allowed me to see your children too."

12Then Joseph removed them from Israel's knees and bowed down with his face to the ground. 13And Joseph took both of them, Ephraim on his right towards Israel's left hand and Manasseh on his left towards Israel's right hand, and brought them close to him. 14But Israel reached out his right hand and put it on Ephraim's head, though he was the younger, and crossing his arms, he put his left hand on Manasseh's head, even though Manasseh was the firstborn.

48:14 ■ THE YOUNGER BROTHER
Jacob gave his firstborn blessings to the younger of Joseph's boys, just as had been done for Isaac over Ishmael, for Jacob over Esau, and for Joseph over Reuben. In adopting both Manasseh and Ephraim as his own sons, Jacob was also giving Joseph's family a double share in the inheritance — these two grandsons would each receive a full share along with Jacob's other 11 sons. The "12 tribes" of Israel were the offspring of Jacob's sons; substituting Manasseh and Ephraim for Joseph made a total of 13.

15Then he blessed Joseph and said,

"May the God before whom my fathers
    Abraham and Isaac walked,
the God who has been my shepherd
    all my life to this day,
16the Angel who has delivered me from all harm
    — may he bless these boys.
May they be called by my name
    and the names of my fathers Abraham and
        Isaac,
and may they increase greatly
    upon the earth."

17When Joseph saw his father placing his right hand on Ephraim's head he was displeased; so he took hold of his father's hand to move it from Ephraim's head to Manasseh's head. 18Joseph said to him, "No, my father, this one is the firstborn; put your right hand on his head."

19But his father refused and said, "I know, my son, I know. He too will become a people, and he too will become great. Nevertheless, his younger brother will be greater than he, and his descendants will become a group of nations." 20He blessed them that day and said,

"In your*c* name will Israel pronounce this
    blessing:

'May God make you like Ephraim and
    Manasseh.'"

So he put Ephraim ahead of Manasseh.

21Then Israel said to Joseph, "I am about to die, but God will be with you*d* and take you*d* back to the land of your*d* fathers. 22And to you, as one who is over your brothers, I give the ridge of land*e* I took from the Amorites with my sword and my bow."

■ Jacob Blesses His Sons

49 Then Jacob called for his sons and said: "Gather round so that I can tell you what will happen to you in days to come.

2"Assemble and listen, sons of Jacob;
    listen to your father Israel.

3"Reuben, you are my firstborn,
    my might, the first sign of my strength,
    excelling in honour, excelling in power.
4Turbulent as the waters, you will no longer
        excel,
for you went up onto your father's bed,
    onto my couch and defiled it.

5"Simeon and Levi are brothers —
    their swords*a* are weapons of violence.
6Let me not enter their council,
    let me not join their assembly,
for they have killed men in their anger
    and hamstrung oxen as they pleased.
7Cursed be their anger, so fierce,
    and their fury, so cruel!
I will scatter them in Jacob
    and disperse them in Israel.

8"Judah,*b* your brothers will praise you;
    your hand will be on the neck of your
        enemies;
    your father's sons will bow down to you.
9You are a lion's cub, O Judah;
    you return from the prey, my son.
Like a lion he crouches and lies down,
    like a lioness — who dares to rouse him?
10The sceptre will not depart from Judah,
    nor the ruler's staff from between his feet,
until he comes to whom it belongs*c*
    and the obedience of the nations is his.
11He will tether his donkey to a vine,
    his colt to the choicest branch;
he will wash his garments in wine,
    his robes in the blood of grapes.
12His eyes will be darker than wine,
    his teeth whiter than milk.*d*

13"Zebulun will live by the seashore
    and become a haven for ships;
his border will extend towards Sidon.

14"Issachar is a scrawny*e* donkey
    lying down between two saddlebags.*f*
15When he sees how good is his resting place
    and how pleasant is his land,
he will bend his shoulder to the burden
    and submit to forced labour.

---

*c20 The Hebrew is singular.   d21 The Hebrew is plural.   e22 Or And to you I give one portion more than to your brothers — the portion
a5 The meaning of the Hebrew for this word is uncertain.   b8 Judah sounds like and may be derived from the Hebrew for praise.   c10 Or until Shiloh
comes; or until he comes to whom tribute belongs   d12 Or will be dull from wine, / his teeth white from milk   e14 Or strong   f14 Or campfires*

16"Dan *g* will provide justice for his people
    as one of the tribes of Israel.
17Dan will be a serpent by the roadside,
    a viper along the path,
  that bites the horse's heels
    so that its rider tumbles backwards.

18"I look for your deliverance, O LORD.

19"Gad*b* will be attacked by a band of raiders,
    but he will attack them at their heels.

20"Asher's food will be rich;
    he will provide delicacies fit for a king.

21"Naphtali is a doe set free
    that bears beautiful fawns.*i*

22"Joseph is a fruitful vine,
    a fruitful vine near a spring,
    whose branches climb over a wall.*j*
23With bitterness archers attacked him;
    they shot at him with hostility.
24But his bow remained steady,
    his strong arms stayed*k* supple,
  because of the hand of the Mighty One of
    Jacob,
  because of the Shepherd, the Rock of Israel,
25because of your father's God, who helps you,
    because of the Almighty,*l* who blesses you
  with blessings of the heavens above,
    blessings of the deep that lies below,
    blessings of the breast and womb.
26Your father's blessings are greater
    than the blessings of the ancient mountains,
    than*m* the bounty of the age-old hills.
  Let all these rest on the head of Joseph,
    on the brow of the prince among*n* his
      brothers.

27"Benjamin is a ravenous wolf;
    in the morning he devours the prey,
    in the evening he divides the plunder."

28All these are the twelve tribes of Israel, and this
is what their father said to them when he blessed
them, giving each the blessing appropriate to him.

■ The Death of Jacob
    29Then he gave them these instructions: "I am
about to be gathered to my people. Bury me with my
fathers in the cave in the field of Ephron the Hittite,
30the cave in the field of Machpelah, near Mamre in
Canaan, which Abraham bought as a burial place
from Ephron the Hittite, along with the field.
31There Abraham and his wife Sarah were buried,
there Isaac and his wife Rebekah were buried, and
there I buried Leah. 32The field and the cave in it
were bought from the Hittites."*o*
    33When Jacob had finished giving instructions to
his sons, he drew his feet up into the bed, breathed
his last and was gathered to his people.

50 Joseph threw himself upon his father and
wept over him and kissed him. 2Then Joseph
directed the physicians in his service to embalm his
father Israel. So the physicians embalmed him, 3tak-
ing a full forty days, for that was the time required

for embalming. And the Egyptians mourned for him
seventy days.

50:3 ■ AN EGYPTIAN FUNERAL
Joseph's political importance is underlined by this
elaborate mummification procedure for his father.
Jacob's mourning period was only two days
shorter than that given for a pharaoh. All the court
dignitaries went along for the funeral, a substantial
journey (verse 7).

    4When the days of mourning had passed, Joseph
said to Pharaoh's court, "If I have found favour in
your eyes, speak to Pharaoh for me. Tell him, 5'My
father made me swear an oath and said, "I am about
to die; bury me in the tomb I dug for myself in the
land of Canaan." Now let me go up and bury my
father; then I will return.' "
    6Pharaoh said, "Go up and bury your father, as he
made you swear to do."
    7So Joseph went up to bury his father. All Phar-
aoh's officials accompanied him — the dignitaries of
his court and all the dignitaries of Egypt — 8besides
all the members of Joseph's household and his
brothers and those belonging to his father's household. Only their children and their flocks and
herds were left in Goshen. 9Chariots and horsemen*a* also went up with him. It was a very large
company.
    10When they reached the threshing-floor of Atad,
near the Jordan, they lamented loudly and bitterly;
and there Joseph observed a seven-day period of
mourning for his father. 11When the Canaanites who
lived there saw the mourning at the threshing-floor
of Atad, they said, "The Egyptians are holding a solemn ceremony of mourning." That is why that place
near the Jordan is called Abel Mizraim.*b*
    12So Jacob's sons did as he had commanded them:
13They carried him to the land of Canaan and buried
him in the cave in the field of Machpelah, near
Mamre, which Abraham had bought as a burial place
from Ephron the Hittite, along with the field. 14After
burying his father, Joseph returned to Egypt, together with his brothers and all the others who had
gone with him to bury his father.

■ Joseph Reassures His Brothers
    15When Joseph's brothers saw that their father
was dead, they said, "What if Joseph holds a grudge
against us and pays us back for all the wrongs we did
to him?" 16So they sent word to Joseph, saying,
"Your father left these instructions before he died:
17'This is what you are to say to Joseph: I ask you to
forgive your brothers the sins and the wrongs they
committed in treating you so badly.' Now please forgive the sins of the servants of the God of your
father." When their message came to him, Joseph
wept.
    18His brothers then came and threw themselves
down before him. "We are your slaves," they said.

---

g 16 Dan here means *he provides justice*.   *b* 19 Gad can mean *attack* and *band of raiders*.   *i* 21 Or *free; / he utters beautiful words*   *j* 22 Or *Joseph is a wild colt, / a wild colt near a spring, / a wild donkey on a terraced hill*   *k* 23,24 Or *archers will attack . . . will shoot . . . will remain . . . will stay*
l 25 Hebrew *Shaddai*   *m* 26 Or *of my progenitors, / as great as*   *n* 26 Or *the one separated from*   *o* 32 Or *the sons of Heth*   *a* 9 Or *charioteers*
b 11 Abel Mizraim means *mourning of the Egyptians*.

[19]But Joseph said to them, "Don't be afraid. Am I in the place of God? [20]You intended to harm me, but God intended it for good to accomplish what is now being done, the saving of many lives. [21]So then, don't be afraid. I will provide for you and your children." And he reassured them and spoke kindly to them.

50:19 ■ YOU INTENDED EVIL

Joseph's summation of his experience might apply to many human situations: you intended evil, but God intended good. Joseph's trust that God can bring good out of bad intentions enabled him finally to forgive his brothers, leaving judgment to God.

■ The Death of Joseph

[22]Joseph stayed in Egypt, along with all his father's family. He lived a hundred and ten years [23]and saw the third generation of Ephraim's children. Also the children of Makir son of Manasseh were placed at birth on Joseph's knees.[c]

[24]Then Joseph said to his brothers, "I am about to die. But God will surely come to your aid and take you up out of this land to the land he promised on oath to Abraham, Isaac and Jacob." [25]And Joseph made the sons of Israel swear an oath and said, "God will surely come to your aid, and then you must carry my bones up from this place."

[26]So Joseph died at the age of a hundred and ten. And after they embalmed him, he was placed in a coffin in Egypt.

EXODUS

■ FREE AT LAST

THE SLAVES IN EGYPT GET A LIBERATOR

THE LORD SAID, "I HAVE INDEED SEEN THE MISERY OF MY PEOPLE IN EGYPT. I HAVE HEARD THEM CRYING OUT BECAUSE OF THEIR SLAVE DRIVERS, AND I AM CONCERNED ABOUT THEIR SUFFERING." ■ 3:7

Nothing stirs a nation's blood like a liberator. The United States remembers two especially: Washington and Lincoln. George Washington led the original fight for independence. A century later Abraham Lincoln set three million people free. For those slaves, Lincoln was a true liberator.

Other places, too, have liberators. India called a scrawny little man named Gandhi "Mahatma" (or "the great one") for leading his people to freedom. Modern Poles honour Lech Walesa. For the Israelites, one liberator named Moses accomplished what all these did — and more.

The Bible devotes one-eighth of its pages to the story of Moses' time (a bulk of material two-thirds the length of the entire New Testament). And when Jesus came as the great Liberator who set all humanity free, the New Testament reached back to Moses for a comparison (Hebrews 3:1–6).

■ BONDAGE IN EGYPT

The time was ripe for a liberator. Genesis closed with Jacob's family of 70 moving to Egypt. But in the opening scene of Exodus, 350 years later, hundreds of thousands of their descendants were toiling on Pharaoh's huge construction projects — not as guests but as slaves.

One particularly ruthless pharaoh ordered the murder of all male Israelite babies, unwittingly setting the stage for one of the great ironies of history. Moses' parents hid him in a watertight basket among the grasses of a swamp. There, the tiny baby caught the eye of the pharaoh's daughter. The very edict intended to destroy the Israelites led to their deliverance.

Adopted into the palace, Moses benefited from a superb classical education. His Egyptian upbringing was balanced by Israelite nurture: in another striking irony, the pharaoh's daughter paid Moses' own mother to nurse him. The son of slaves, yet brought up in the seat of power, Moses prepared for his eventual goal of forging a nation out of a rag-tag band of captives.

His career had to wait, though, for a period of humbling in the desert. Moses fled Egypt as a brash, self-confident man who liked to take matters into his own hands. Forty years later he reluctantly returned, with little besides a stick and a donkey.

■ FREE AT LAST

The Israelites had endured nearly four centuries of oppression — twice as long as the history of America as a nation — before liberation. So far as we know, during those years they received no direct communication from heaven. Surely God must have seemed silent.

Moses faced a formidable challenge. Somehow he had to earn the trust of the slaves and inspire hope in them so that they could indeed throw off their chains. He had to prove that God had not forgotten them. When the time was right, God unleashed a spectacle of might and power that brought a cruel pharaoh to his knees — and convinced the Israelites that God really did care for them.

God used Moses in remarkable ways. He was the first person recorded in the Bible to work miracles. He met God in intimate ways granted to no other human. He had a hand in the authorship of a good portion of the Old Testament. But in Jewish history he earned a place primarily as a liberator. He led the march from slavery to freedom, from Egypt to the promised land.

◼ HOW TO READ EXODUS

Exodus divides neatly into two parts. The first 20 chapters, on the Israelites' flight from Egypt, read like an exciting novel. Movies based on the action here have strained Hollywood special-effects crews. Everything else in the Old Testament flows out of the events of the exodus – these 20 chapters simply cannot be missed.

As you read Exodus, look for important lessons that apply to your life. For example, study the life of Moses, one of a handful of truly great leaders in history. Chapter 18 shows Moses learning an important leadership principle, and chapters 32–35 include encounters and conversations with God that have no equal in the Bible.

Exodus contains much material about the nature of God. Search for each place where God makes an appearance. Exodus shows a greater proportion of miracles – direct supernatural acts of God – than any part of the Bible except the Gospels. Why were these miracles performed? Can you see a pattern? What should the Israelites have learned from them? Did they?

The last 20 chapters mainly consist of laws and regulations, given at Mount Sinai, to govern the life of the nation. Read them to note the concerns and priorities important to God as he designs an entire culture.

The instructions are usually clustered in groups, encompassing every area of life:

1. Moral rules, such as the Ten Commandments
2. Civil and social rules, much like a criminal code
3. Religious and ceremonial rules for the Israelites.

See "A National Law Library", page 106, for more information on these laws.

The religious rituals with their many sacrifices and feasts seem strange to modern westerners, but they were not at all unusual then. Also, they prepared the way for a Redeemer who was greater than Moses: Jesus Christ. You will need study books and commentaries to find all the symbols that apply to Jesus' life, as shown, for example, in the Passover. Fortunately, the Bible includes a brief but powerful commentary in Hebrews (see especially Hebrews 7–10). This book should be read alongside Exodus and the three books that follow.

◼ 3-TRACK READING PLAN

For an explanation and complete listing of the 3-track reading plan, turn to page x.

◼ TRACK 1:
Two-Week Courses on the Bible
The Track 1 reading programme on the Old Testament includes two chapters from Exodus. See page x for a complete listing of this course.

◼ TRACK 2:
An Overview of Exodus in 5 Days
☐ Day 1. Read the Introduction to Exodus and then chapter 3, God's call of Moses.
☐ Day 2. Read chapter 10 and the very brief chapter 11; they record three of the ten plagues against Egypt.
☐ Day 3. Read chapter 14, which contains the exciting story of crossing the Red Sea.
☐ Day 4. Read the Ten Commandments as recorded in chapter 20. (If you have time, chapter 19 gives the dramatic setting for these laws.)
☐ Day 5. Read chapter 32. It records the most striking example of what was to become a characteristic of the Israelites: mass rebellion. Now turn to page xi for your next Track 2 reading project.

◼ TRACK 3:
All of Exodus in 39 Days
After you have read through Exodus, turn to pages xii–xiii for your next Track 3 reading project.

☐ 1	☐ 2	☐ 3	☐ 4
☐ 5	☐ 6	☐ 7	☐ 8
☐ 9	☐ 10-11		☐ 12
☐ 13	☐ 14	☐ 15	☐ 16
☐ 17	☐ 18	☐ 19	☐ 20
☐ 21	☐ 22	☐ 23	☐ 24
☐ 25	☐ 26	☐ 27	☐ 28
☐ 29	☐ 30	☐ 31	☐ 32
☐ 33	☐ 34	☐ 35	☐ 36
☐ 37	☐ 38	☐ 39	☐ 40

■ The Israelites Oppressed

1 These are the names of the sons of Israel who went to Egypt with Jacob, each with his family: [2]Reuben, Simeon, Levi and Judah; [3]Issachar, Zebulun and Benjamin; [4]Dan and Naphtali; Gad and Asher. [5]The descendants of Jacob numbered seventy[a] in all; Joseph was already in Egypt.

[6]Now Joseph and all his brothers and all that generation died, [7]but the Israelites were fruitful and multiplied greatly and became exceedingly numerous, so that the land was filled with them.

[8]Then a new king, who did not know about Joseph, came to power in Egypt. [9]"Look," he said to his people, "the Israelites have become much too numerous for us. [10]Come, we must deal shrewdly with them or they will become even more numerous and, if war breaks out, will join our enemies, fight against us and leave the country."

[11]So they put slave masters over them to oppress them with forced labour, and they built Pithom and Rameses as store cities for Pharaoh. [12]But the more they were oppressed, the more they multiplied and spread; so the Egyptians came to dread the Israelites [13]and worked them ruthlessly. [14]They made their lives bitter with hard labour in brick and mortar and with all kinds of work in the fields; in all their hard labour the Egyptians used them ruthlessly.

[15]The king of Egypt said to the Hebrew midwives, whose names were Shiphrah and Puah, [16]"When you help the Hebrew women in childbirth and observe them on the delivery stool, if it is a boy, kill him; but if it is a girl, let her live." [17]The midwives, however, feared God and did not do what the king of Egypt had told them to do; they let the boys live. [18]Then the king of Egypt summoned the midwives and asked them, "Why have you done this? Why have you let the boys live?"

1:16 ■ NEW TYRANT IN TOWN

Dictators often take out their wrath on a helpless minority: witness Hitler and the Jews or Saddam Hussein and the Kurds. At first pharaohs welcomed their Hebrew guests, and God used the peace and quiet of Egypt, far from the squabbling tribes of Canaan, to "grow" the people of Israel. But now the Israelites' very size and strength threatened the new pharaoh, who ruthlessly clamped down on them.

[19]The midwives answered Pharaoh, "Hebrew women are not like Egyptian women; they are vigorous and give birth before the midwives arrive."

[20]So God was kind to the midwives and the people increased and became even more numerous. [21]And because the midwives feared God, he gave them families of their own.

[22]Then Pharaoh gave this order to all his people: "Every boy that is born[b] you must throw into the Nile, but let every girl live."

■ The Birth of Moses

2 Now a man of the house of Levi married a Levite woman, [2]and she became pregnant and gave birth to a son. When she saw that he was a fine child, she hid him for three months. [3]But when she could hide him no longer, she got a papyrus basket for him and coated it with tar and pitch. Then she placed the child in it and put it among the reeds along the bank of the Nile. [4]His sister stood at a distance to see what would happen to him.

[5]Then Pharaoh's daughter went down to the Nile to bathe, and her attendants were walking along the river bank. She saw the basket among the reeds and sent her slave girl to get it. [6]She opened it and saw the baby. He was crying, and she felt sorry for him. "This is one of the Hebrew babies," she said.

[7]Then his sister asked Pharaoh's daughter, "Shall I go and get one of the Hebrew women to nurse the baby for you?"

[8]"Yes, go," she answered. And the girl went and got the baby's mother. [9]Pharaoh's daughter said to her, "Take this baby and nurse him for me, and I will pay you." So the woman took the baby and nursed him. [10]When the child grew older, she took him to Pharaoh's daughter and he became her son. She named him Moses,[a] saying, "I drew him out of the water."

2:10 ■ SELECTIVE HISTORY

Exodus illustrates how selective the Bible's history is. The first chapter, for example, skips over the name of the Egyptian pharaoh (leaving a riddle for scholars to argue over ever since), and yet identifies by name two Hebrew midwives (1:15). After compressing three-and-a-half centuries into a few verses, Exodus devotes chapters 3–40 to the events of a single year. In contrast to Genesis' large cast of characters, Exodus focuses on one main character, Moses.

■ Moses Flees to Midian

[11]One day, after Moses had grown up, he went out to where his own people were and watched them at their hard labour. He saw an Egyptian beating a Hebrew, one of his own people. [12]Glancing this way and that and seeing no-one, he killed the Egyptian and hid him in the sand. [13]The next day he went out and saw two Hebrews fighting. He asked the one in the wrong, "Why are you hitting your fellow Hebrew?"

[14]The man said, "Who made you ruler and judge over us? Are you thinking of killing me as you killed the Egyptian?" Then Moses was afraid and thought, "What I did must have become known."

[15]When Pharaoh heard of this, he tried to kill Moses, but Moses fled from Pharaoh and went to live in Midian, where he sat down by a well. [16]Now a priest of Midian had seven daughters, and they came to draw water and fill the troughs to water their father's flock. [17]Some shepherds came along and drove them away, but Moses got up and came to their rescue and watered their flock.

[18]When the girls returned to Reuel their father,

a 5 Masoretic Text (see also Gen. 46:27); Dead Sea Scrolls and Septuagint (see also Acts 7:14 and note at Gen. 46:27) *seventy-five*　　*b 22* Masoretic Text; Samaritan Pentateuch, Septuagint and Targums *born to the Hebrews*　　*a 10 Moses* sounds like the Hebrew for *draw out.*

he asked them, "Why have you returned so early today?"

¹⁹They answered, "An Egyptian rescued us from the shepherds. He even drew water for us and watered the flock."

²⁰"And where is he?" he asked his daughters. "Why did you leave him? Invite him to have something to eat."

²¹Moses agreed to stay with the man, who gave his daughter Zipporah to Moses in marriage. ²²Zipporah gave birth to a son, and Moses named him Gershom,ᵇ saying, "I have become an alien in a foreign land."

²³During that long period, the king of Egypt died. The Israelites groaned in their slavery and cried out, and their cry for help because of their slavery went up to God. ²⁴God heard their groaning and he remembered his covenant with Abraham, with Isaac and with Jacob. ²⁵So God looked on the Israelites and was concerned about them.

■ Moses and the Burning Bush

3 Now Moses was tending the flock of Jethro his father-in-law, the priest of Midian, and he led the flock to the far side of the desert and came to Horeb, the mountain of God. ²There the angel of the LORD appeared to him in flames of fire from within a bush. Moses saw that though the bush was on fire it did not burn up. ³So Moses thought, "I will go over and see this strange sight—why the bush does not burn up."

⁴When the LORD saw that he had gone over to look, God called to him from within the bush, "Moses! Moses!"

And Moses said, "Here I am."

⁵"Do not come any closer," God said. "Take off your sandals, for the place where you are standing is holy ground." ⁶Then he said, "I am the God of your father, the God of Abraham, the God of Isaac and the God of Jacob." At this, Moses hid his face, because he was afraid to look at God.

⁷The LORD said, "I have indeed seen the misery of my people in Egypt. I have heard them crying out because of their slave drivers, and I am concerned about their suffering. ⁸So I have come down to rescue them from the hand of the Egyptians and to bring them up out of that land into a good and spacious land, a land flowing with milk and honey—the home of the Canaanites, Hittites, Amorites, Perizzites, Hivites and Jebusites. ⁹And now the cry of the Israelites has reached me, and I have seen the way the Egyptians are oppressing them. ¹⁰So now, go. I am sending you to Pharaoh to bring my people the Israelites out of Egypt."

¹¹But Moses said to God, "Who am I, that I should go to Pharaoh and bring the Israelites out of Egypt?"

¹²And God said, "I will be with you. And this will be the sign to you that it is I who have sent you: When you have brought the people out of Egypt, youᵃ will worship God on this mountain."

¹³Moses said to God, "Suppose I go to the Israelites and say to them, 'The God of your fathers has sent me to you,' and they ask me, 'What is his name?' Then what shall I tell them?"

¹⁴God said to Moses, "I AM WHO I AM.ᵇ This is what

you are to say to the Israelites: 'I AM has sent me to you.'"

3:11 ■ WHO, ME?
Moses had big doubts about his ability to lead. He resisted God, bringing up his unworthiness (here) and lack of authority (verse 13), his fear of the people's distrust (4:1), his speech difficulties (4:10), and his sheer cowardice (4:13). The remainder of Exodus should give people with similar self-doubts great hope, for it traces Moses' personal development from this fumbling start to his emergence as one of history's most decisive and powerful leaders.

¹⁵God also said to Moses, "Say to the Israelites, 'The LORD,ᶜ the God of your fathers—the God of Abraham, the God of Isaac and the God of Jacob—has sent me to you.' This is my name for ever, the name by which I am to be remembered from generation to generation.

¹⁶"Go, assemble the elders of Israel and say to them, 'The LORD, the God of your fathers—the God of Abraham, Isaac and Jacob—appeared to me and said: I have watched over you and have seen what has been done to you in Egypt. ¹⁷And I have promised to bring you up out of your misery in Egypt into the land of the Canaanites, Hittites, Amorites, Perizzites, Hivites and Jebusites—a land flowing with milk and honey.'

¹⁸"The elders of Israel will listen to you. Then you and the elders are to go to the king of Egypt and say to him, 'The LORD, the God of the Hebrews, has met with us. Let us take a three-day journey into the desert to offer sacrifices to the LORD our God.' ¹⁹But I know that the king of Egypt will not let you go unless a mighty hand compels him. ²⁰So I will stretch out my hand and strike the Egyptians with all the wonders that I will perform among them. After that, he will let you go.

²¹"And I will make the Egyptians favourably disposed towards this people, so that when you leave you will not go empty-handed. ²²Every woman is to ask her neighbour and any woman living in her house for articles of silver and gold and for clothing, which you will put on your sons and daughters. And so you will plunder the Egyptians."

■ Signs for Moses

4 Moses answered, "What if they do not believe me or listen to me and say, 'The LORD did not appear to you'?"

²Then the LORD said to him, "What is that in your hand?"

"A staff," he replied.

³The LORD said, "Throw it on the ground."

Moses threw it on the ground and it became a snake, and he ran from it. ⁴Then the LORD said to him, "Reach out your hand and take it by the tail." So Moses reached out and took hold of the snake and it turned back into a staff in his hand. ⁵"This," said the LORD, "is so that they may believe that the LORD, the God of their fathers—the God of Abraham, the

God of Isaac and the God of Jacob—has appeared to you."

6Then the LORD said, "Put your hand inside your cloak." So Moses put his hand into his cloak, and when he took it out, it was leprous,a like snow.

7"Now put it back into your cloak," he said. So Moses put his hand back into his cloak, and when he took it out, it was restored, like the rest of his flesh.

8Then the LORD said, "If they do not believe you or pay attention to the first miraculous sign, they may believe the second. 9But if they do not believe these two signs or listen to you, take some water from the Nile and pour it on the dry ground. The water you take from the river will become blood on the ground."

10Moses said to the LORD, "O Lord, I have never been eloquent, neither in the past nor since you have spoken to your servant. I am slow of speech and tongue."

11The LORD said to him, "Who gave man his mouth? Who makes him deaf or mute? Who gives him sight or makes him blind? Is it not I, the LORD? 12Now go; I will help you speak and will teach you what to say."

13But Moses said, "O Lord, please send someone else to do it."

14Then the LORD's anger burned against Moses and he said, "What about your brother, Aaron the Levite? I know he can speak well. He is already on his way to meet you, and his heart will be glad when he sees you. 15You shall speak to him and put words in his mouth; I will help both of you speak and will teach you what to do. 16He will speak to the people for you, and it will be as if he were your mouth and as if you were God to him. 17But take this staff in your hand so that you can perform miraculous signs with it."

■ Moses Returns to Egypt

18Then Moses went back to Jethro his father-in-law and said to him, "Let me go back to my own people in Egypt to see if any of them are still alive." Jethro said, "Go, and I wish you well."

19Now the LORD had said to Moses in Midian, "Go back to Egypt, for all the men who wanted to kill you are dead." 20So Moses took his wife and sons, put them on a donkey and started back to Egypt. And he took the staff of God in his hand.

21The LORD said to Moses, "When you return to Egypt, see that you perform before Pharaoh all the wonders I have given you the power to do. But I will harden his heart so that he will not let the people go. 22Then say to Pharaoh, 'This is what the LORD says: Israel is my firstborn son, 23and I told you, "Let my son go, so that he may worship me." But you refused to let him go; so I will kill your firstborn son.' "

24At a lodging place on the way, the LORD met ⌞Moses⌟b and was about to kill him. 25But Zipporah took a flint knife, cut off her son's foreskin and touched ⌞Moses'⌟ feet with it.c "Surely you are a bridegroom of blood to me," she said. 26So the LORD let him alone. (At that time she said "bridegroom of blood", referring to circumcision.)

27The LORD said to Aaron, "Go into the desert to meet Moses." So he met Moses at the mountain of God and kissed him. 28Then Moses told Aaron everything the LORD had sent him to say, and also about all the miraculous signs he had commanded him to perform.

29Moses and Aaron brought together all the elders of the Israelites, 30and Aaron told them everything the LORD had said to Moses. He also performed the signs before the people, 31and they believed. And when they heard that the LORD was concerned about them and had seen their misery, they bowed down and worshipped.

■ Bricks Without Straw

5 Afterwards Moses and Aaron went to Pharaoh and said, "This is what the LORD, the God of Israel, says: 'Let my people go, so that they may hold a festival to me in the desert.' "

2Pharaoh said, "Who is the LORD, that I should obey him and let Israel go? I do not know the LORD and I will not let Israel go."

3Then they said, "The God of the Hebrews has met with us. Now let us take a three-day journey into the desert to offer sacrifices to the LORD our God, or he may strike us with plagues or with the sword."

4But the king of Egypt said, "Moses and Aaron, why are you taking the people away from their labour? Get back to your work!" 5Then Pharaoh said, "Look, the people of the land are now numerous, and you are stopping them from working."

6That same day Pharaoh gave this order to the slave drivers and foremen in charge of the people: 7"You are no longer to supply the people with straw for making bricks; let them go and gather their own straw. 8But require them to make the same number of bricks as before; don't reduce the quota. They are lazy; that is why they are crying out, 'Let us go and sacrifice to our God.' 9Make the work harder for the men so that they keep working and pay no attention to lies."

10Then the slave drivers and the foremen went out and said to the people, "This is what Pharaoh says: 'I will not give you any more straw. 11Go and get your own straw wherever you can find it, but your work will not be reduced at all.' " 12So the people scattered all over Egypt to gather stubble to use for straw. 13The slave drivers kept pressing them, saying, "Complete the work required of you for each day, just as when you had straw." 14The Israelite foremen appointed by Pharaoh's slave drivers were beaten and were asked, "Why didn't you meet your quota of bricks yesterday or today, as before?"

5:10 ■ THREE KINDS OF BRICK
Archaeologists digging up settlements from ancient Egypt have unearthed three kinds of sun-dried brick—some made of good straw, some containing mere roots and bits of straw, and some with no straw—confirming this account of slave labour.

15Then the Israelite foremen went and appealed to Pharaoh: "Why have you treated your servants

---

a6 The Hebrew word was used for various diseases affecting the skin—not necessarily leprosy.   b24 Or ⌞Moses' son⌟; Hebrew him   c25 Or and drew near ⌞Moses'⌟ feet this way? [16]Your servants are given no straw, yet we are told, 'Make bricks!' Your servants are being beaten, but the fault is with your own people."

[17]Pharaoh said, "Lazy, that's what you are—lazy! That is why you keep saying, 'Let us go and sacrifice to the LORD.' [18]Now get to work. You will not be given any straw, yet you must produce your full quota of bricks."

[19]The Israelite foremen realised they were in trouble when they were told, "You are not to reduce the number of bricks required of you for each day." [20]When they left Pharaoh, they found Moses and Aaron waiting to meet them, [21]and they said, "May the LORD look upon you and judge you! You have made us a stench to Pharaoh and his officials and have put a sword in their hand to kill us."

■ God Promises Deliverance

[22]Moses returned to the LORD and said, "O Lord, why have you brought trouble upon this people? Is this why you sent me? [23]Ever since I went to Pharaoh to speak in your name, he has brought trouble upon this people, and you have not rescued your people at all."

6 Then the LORD said to Moses, "Now you will see what I will do to Pharaoh: Because of my mighty hand he will let them go; because of my mighty hand he will drive them out of his country."

[2]God also said to Moses, "I am the LORD. [3]I appeared to Abraham, to Isaac and to Jacob as God Almighty,[a] but by my name the LORD[b] I did not make myself known to them.[c] [4]I also established my covenant with them to give them the land of Canaan, where they lived as aliens. [5]Moreover, I have heard the groaning of the Israelites, whom the Egyptians are enslaving, and I have remembered my covenant.

[6]"Therefore, say to the Israelites: 'I am the LORD, and I will bring you out from under the yoke of the Egyptians. I will free you from being slaves to them, and I will redeem you with an outstretched arm and with mighty acts of judgment. [7]I will take you as my own people, and I will be your God. Then you will know that I am the LORD your God, who brought you out from under the yoke of the Egyptians. [8]And I will bring you to the land I swore with uplifted hand to give to Abraham, to Isaac and to Jacob. I will give it to you as a possession. I am the LORD.' "

[9]Moses reported this to the Israelites, but they did not listen to him because of their discouragement and cruel bondage.

[10]Then the LORD said to Moses, [11]"Go, tell Pharaoh king of Egypt to let the Israelites go out of his country."

[12]But Moses said to the LORD, "If the Israelites will not listen to me, why would Pharaoh listen to me, since I speak with faltering lips?"[d]

■ Family Record of Moses and Aaron

[13]Now the LORD spoke to Moses and Aaron about the Israelites and Pharaoh king of Egypt, and he commanded them to bring the Israelites out of Egypt.

[14]These were the heads of their families:[e]

The sons of Reuben the firstborn son of Israel were Hanoch and Pallu, Hezron and Carmi. These were the clans of Reuben.

6:9 ■ OPPRESSED BY EGYPT

With Egypt at the peak of its power, Pharaoh used slaves to build massive monuments, enforcing his rule with an army of renowned charioteers and bowmen. Egyptian hieroglyphics pictured the word for *foreigner* as a bound man with blood flowing from a wound in his head; the Israelites felt the full weight of such oppression. For a while, the increasing cruelty of Egyptian taskmasters turned the Israelites against Moses and his campaign to free them. But this oppression also made them anxious to leave.

[15]The sons of Simeon were Jemuel, Jamin, Ohad, Jakin, Zohar and Shaul the son of a Canaanite woman. These were the clans of Simeon.

[16]These were the names of the sons of Levi according to their records: Gershon, Kohath and Merari. Levi lived 137 years.

[17]The sons of Gershon, by clans, were Libni and Shimei.

[18]The sons of Kohath were Amram, Izhar, Hebron and Uzziel. Kohath lived 133 years.

[19]The sons of Merari were Mahli and Mushi. These were the clans of Levi according to their records.

[20]Amram married his father's sister Jochebed, who bore him Aaron and Moses. Amram lived 137 years.

[21]The sons of Izhar were Korah, Nepheg and Zicri.

[22]The sons of Uzziel were Mishael, Elzaphan and Sithri.

[23]Aaron married Elisheba, daughter of Amminadab and sister of Nahshon, and she bore him Nadab and Abihu, Eleazar and Ithamar.

[24]The sons of Korah were Assir, Elkanah and Abiasaph. These were the Korahite clans.

[25]Eleazar son of Aaron married one of the daughters of Putiel, and she bore him Phinehas.

These were the heads of the Levite families, clan by clan.

[26]It was this same Aaron and Moses to whom the LORD said, "Bring the Israelites out of Egypt by their divisions." [27]They were the ones who spoke to Pharaoh king of Egypt about bringing the Israelites out of Egypt. It was the same Moses and Aaron.

■ Aaron to Speak for Moses

[28]Now when the LORD spoke to Moses in Egypt, [29]he said to him, "I am the LORD. Tell Pharaoh king of Egypt everything I tell you."

[30]But Moses said to the LORD, "Since I speak with faltering lips, why would Pharaoh listen to me?"

7 Then the LORD said to Moses, "See, I have made you like God to Pharaoh, and your brother Aaron will be your prophet. [2]You are to say

---

[a]3 Hebrew *El-Shaddai*   [b]3 See note at Exodus 3:15.   [c]3 Or *Almighty, and by my name the LORD did I not let myself be known to them?*
[d]12 Hebrew *I am uncircumcised of lips;* also in verse 30   [e]14 The Hebrew for *families* here and in verse 25 refers to units larger than clans.

everything I command you, and your brother Aaron is to tell Pharaoh to let the Israelites go out of his country. ³But I will harden Pharaoh's heart, and though I multiply my miraculous signs and wonders in Egypt, ⁴he will not listen to you. Then I will lay my hand on Egypt and with mighty acts of judgment I will bring out my divisions, my people the Israelites. ⁵And the Egyptians will know that I am the LORD when I stretch out my hand against Egypt and bring the Israelites out of it."

⁶Moses and Aaron did just as the LORD commanded them. ⁷Moses was eighty years old and Aaron eighty-three when they spoke to Pharaoh.

■ Aaron's Staff Becomes a Snake

⁸The LORD said to Moses and Aaron, ⁹"When Pharaoh says to you, 'Perform a miracle,' then say to Aaron, 'Take your staff and throw it down before Pharaoh,' and it will become a snake."

¹⁰So Moses and Aaron went to Pharaoh and did just as the LORD commanded. Aaron threw his staff down in front of Pharaoh and his officials, and it became a snake. ¹¹Pharaoh then summoned the wise men and sorcerers, and the Egyptian magicians also did the same things by their secret arts: ¹²Each one threw down his staff and it became a snake. But Aaron's staff swallowed up their staffs. ¹³Yet Pharaoh's heart became hard and he would not listen to them, just as the LORD had said.

■ The Plague of Blood

¹⁴Then the LORD said to Moses, "Pharaoh's heart is unyielding; he refuses to let the people go. ¹⁵Go to Pharaoh in the morning as he goes out to the

■ DAY OF THE LOCUSTS
THE TEN PLAGUES PROVED A POINT FOR BOTH JEWS AND EGYPTIANS

INSIGHT

"AND THE EGYPTIANS WILL KNOW THAT I AM THE LORD WHEN I STRETCH OUT MY HAND AGAINST EGYPT AND BRING THE ISRAELITES OUT OF IT." ■ 7:5

Locusts, or grasshoppers, normally live a solitary life, hopping from stalk to stalk and placidly munching on leaves and flowers. Then something happens – whether in response to climate, food supply or crowded conditions – that triggers a change. The locusts become restless, turn an ominous pink colour, and begin to seek other locusts.

They become a plague. Great clattering hordes of them, millions strong, blacken the sky, shutting out sunlight. Groups of them fall to the ground like cluster bombs and disperse to destroy every sign of vegetation. Pesticide spraying may kill a few million, but the migratory swarm will barely notice such losses.

A single swarm crossing the Red Sea was once measured at 15 miles wide, three miles deep and 100 miles long. Upon landing, the locusts consumed crops, leather, fences and even tool handles, leaving behind total devastation over 2,000 square miles.

■ WHY THE TEN PLAGUES?
Exodus (7–12) depicts ten cataclysmic plagues on Egypt – including a locust swarm – in brief but graphic detail. The Bible does not concern itself with the question of how these natural phenomena occurred; it merely affirms that something supernatural took place. The miracles were an unprecedented display of God's power.

A nation was about to be born, and the Israelites' uprooting from Egypt called for such power. They had, after all, lived for centuries in Egypt. It would take a strong incentive indeed to motivate a massive, abrupt departure. And Egypt would not easily let thousands of valuable slaves walk away free.

■ TWO REPUTATIONS AT STAKE
The ten plagues convincingly established Moses' authority. He had hesitated to accept a leadership role, doubting whether the other Israelites would trust him (4:1). But Moses' dramatic confrontations with Pharaoh dispelled all doubts. He and he alone could lead them to freedom.

Someone else's credibility was also at stake: that of God himself. In Egypt, religion centred around idolatry, with scores of gods – including even snakes and dung beetles – held up as objects of worship. Against that background, the plagues appear as God's open warfare against the false gods of Egypt. He said as much: "I will bring judgment on all the gods of Egypt" (12:12).

Exodus asserts more than a dozen times that the plagues were given so that Israel and Egypt would know the power of Israel's God. Evidently they worked. Egyptians became so convinced of God's power that they let thousands of slaves leave, with the wealth of Egypt showered upon them as farewell presents. The Israelites were so convinced that they left their home and history and marched out behind a single man towards a desert and a new life.

☐ LIFE QUESTIONS:
Do you know of any modern countries that treat minorities cruelly, like the Egyptians treated the Israelites? What would make such a government change its ways?

water. Wait on the bank of the Nile to meet him, and take in your hand the staff that was changed into a snake. [16]Then say to him, 'The LORD, the God of the Hebrews, has sent me to say to you: Let my people go, so that they may worship me in the desert. But until now you have not listened. [17]This is what the LORD says: By this you will know that I am the LORD: With the staff that is in my hand I will strike the water of the Nile, and it will be changed into blood. [18]The fish in the Nile will die, and the river will stink; the Egyptians will not be able to drink its water.' "

[19]The LORD said to Moses, "Tell Aaron, 'Take your staff and stretch out your hand over the waters of Egypt — over the streams and canals, over the ponds and all the reservoirs' — and they will turn to blood. Blood will be everywhere in Egypt, even in the wooden buckets and stone jars."

[20]Moses and Aaron did just as the LORD had commanded. He raised his staff in the presence of Pharaoh and his officials and struck the water of the Nile, and all the water was changed into blood. [21]The fish in the Nile died, and the river smelled so bad that the Egyptians could not drink its water. Blood was everywhere in Egypt.

[22]But the Egyptian magicians did the same things by their secret arts, and Pharaoh's heart became hard; he would not listen to Moses and Aaron, just as the LORD had said. [23]Instead, he turned and went into his palace, and did not take even this to heart. [24]And all the Egyptians dug along the Nile to get drinking water, because they could not drink the water of the river.

■ The Plague of Frogs

[25]Seven days passed after the LORD struck the Nile. **8** [1]Then the LORD said to Moses, "Go to Pharaoh and say to him, 'This is what the LORD says: Let my people go, so that they may worship me. [2]If you refuse to let them go, I will plague your whole country with frogs. [3]The Nile will teem with frogs. They will come up into your palace and your bedroom and onto your bed, into the houses of your officials and on your people, and into your ovens and kneading troughs. [4]The frogs will go up on you and your people and all your officials.' "

[5]Then the LORD said to Moses, "Tell Aaron, 'Stretch out your hand with your staff over the streams and canals and ponds, and make frogs come up on the land of Egypt.' "

[6]So Aaron stretched out his hand over the waters of Egypt, and the frogs came up and covered the land. [7]But the magicians did the same things by their secret arts; they also made frogs come up on the land of Egypt.

[8]Pharaoh summoned Moses and Aaron and said, "Pray to the LORD to take the frogs away from me and my people, and I will let your people go to offer sacrifices to the LORD."

[9]Moses said to Pharaoh, "I leave to you the honour of setting the time for me to pray for you and your officials and your people that you and your houses may be rid of the frogs, except for those that remain in the Nile."

[10]"Tomorrow," Pharaoh said.

Moses replied, "It will be as you say, so that you

may know there is no-one like the LORD our God. [11]The frogs will leave you and your houses, your officials and your people; they will remain only in the Nile."

[12]After Moses and Aaron left Pharaoh, Moses cried out to the LORD about the frogs he had brought on Pharaoh. [13]And the LORD did what Moses asked. The frogs died in the houses, in the courtyards and in the fields. [14]They were piled into heaps, and the land reeked of them. [15]But when Pharaoh saw that there was relief, he hardened his heart and would not listen to Moses and Aaron, just as the LORD had said.

8:15 ■ PHARAOH'S HARD HEART

The Bible describes Pharaoh's stubbornness in three ways. Sometimes, as here, it says Pharaoh "hardened his heart", sometimes, God "hardened his heart" (10:1), and also, "Pharaoh's heart became hard" (7:13). This is consistent with the Old Testament view: all of history was an act of God. Beyond that, the writers did not normally make clear distinctions on questions of who caused what.

■ The Plague of Gnats

[16]Then the LORD said to Moses, "Tell Aaron, 'Stretch out your staff and strike the dust of the ground,' and throughout the land of Egypt the dust will become gnats." [17]They did this, and when Aaron stretched out his hand with the staff and struck the dust of the ground, gnats came upon men and animals. All the dust throughout the land of Egypt became gnats. [18]But when the magicians tried to produce gnats by their secret arts, they could not. And the gnats were on men and animals.

[19]The magicians said to Pharaoh, "This is the finger of God." But Pharaoh's heart was hard and he would not listen, just as the LORD had said.

■ The Plague of Flies

[20]Then the LORD said to Moses, "Get up early in the morning and confront Pharaoh as he goes to the water and say to him, 'This is what the LORD says: Let my people go, so that they may worship me. [21]If you do not let my people go, I will send swarms of flies on you and your officials, on your people and into your houses. The houses of the Egyptians will be full of flies, and even the ground where they are.

[22]" 'But on that day I will deal differently with the land of Goshen, where my people live; no swarms of flies will be there, so that you will know that I, the LORD, am in this land. [23]I will make a distinction[a] between my people and your people. This miraculous sign will occur tomorrow.' "

[24]And the LORD did this. Dense swarms of flies poured into Pharaoh's palace and into the houses of his officials, and throughout Egypt the land was ruined by the flies.

[25]Then Pharaoh summoned Moses and Aaron and said, "Go, sacrifice to your God here in the land."

[26]But Moses said, "That would not be right. The sacrifices we offer the LORD our God would be

a 23 Septuagint and Vulgate; Hebrew *will put a deliverance* detestable to the Egyptians. And if we offer sacrifices that are detestable in their eyes, will they not stone us? 27We must take a three-day journey into the desert to offer sacrifices to the LORD our God, as he commands us."

8:27 ■ ORIENTAL BARGAINING

Those who have lived in the Middle East recognise in Moses' encounters with Pharaoh an example of high-level Oriental bargaining. As the pressure increased, Pharaoh kept raising his offers: from allowing sacrifices within Egypt (verse 25), to permitting sacrifices nearby in the desert (verse 28), to letting only the adult males go (10:11), to releasing all people but no flocks (10:24). Finally, with the tenth and final plague Pharaoh agreed to all Moses' demands (12:32).

28Pharaoh said, "I will let you go to offer sacrifices to the LORD your God in the desert, but you must not go very far. Now pray for me."

29Moses answered, "As soon as I leave you, I will pray to the LORD, and tomorrow the flies will leave Pharaoh and his officials and his people. Only be sure that Pharaoh does not act deceitfully again by not letting the people go to offer sacrifices to the LORD."

30Then Moses left Pharaoh and prayed to the LORD, 31and the LORD did what Moses asked: The flies left Pharaoh and his officials and his people; not a fly remained. 32But this time also Pharaoh hardened his heart and would not let the people go.

■ The Plague on Livestock

9 Then the LORD said to Moses, "Go to Pharaoh and say to him, 'This is what the LORD, the God of the Hebrews, says: "Let my people go, so that they may worship me." 2If you refuse to let them go and continue to hold them back, 3the hand of the LORD will bring a terrible plague on your livestock in the field—on your horses and donkeys and camels and on your cattle and sheep and goats. 4But the LORD will make a distinction between the livestock of Israel and that of Egypt, so that no animal belonging to the Israelites will die.' "

5The LORD set a time and said, "Tomorrow the LORD will do this in the land." 6And the next day the LORD did it: All the livestock of the Egyptians died, but not one animal belonging to the Israelites died. 7Pharaoh sent men to investigate and found that not even one of the animals of the Israelites had died. Yet his heart was unyielding and he would not let the people go.

■ The Plague of Boils

8Then the LORD said to Moses and Aaron, "Take handfuls of soot from a furnace and have Moses toss it into the air in the presence of Pharaoh. 9It will become fine dust over the whole land of Egypt, and festering boils will break out on men and animals throughout the land."

10So they took soot from a furnace and stood before Pharaoh. Moses tossed it into the air, and festering boils broke out on men and animals. 11The magicians could not stand before Moses because of the boils that were on them and on all the Egyptians. 12But the LORD hardened Pharaoh's heart and he would not listen to Moses and Aaron, just as the LORD had said to Moses.

9:7 ■ "SMART" PLAGUES

Like "smart bombs", targeted precisely, most of the plagues affected the Egyptians but not the Israelites—a miracle in itself. This fact should have convinced Pharaoh that he was contending against supernatural force, not just the caprice of nature. But it took ten plagues in all to persuade him to allow his main supply of cheap labour to walk away, and even then he had second thoughts and chased after them (14:5).

■ The Plague of Hail

13Then the LORD said to Moses, "Get up early in the morning, confront Pharaoh and say to him, 'This is what the LORD, the God of the Hebrews, says: Let my people go, so that they may worship me, 14or this time I will send the full force of my plagues against you and against your officials and your people, so you may know that there is no-one like me in all the earth. 15For by now I could have stretched out my hand and struck you and your people with a plague that would have wiped you off the earth. 16But I have raised you up[a] for this very purpose, that I might show you my power and that my name might be proclaimed in all the earth. 17You still set yourself against my people and will not let them go. 18Therefore, at this time tomorrow I will send the worst hailstorm that has ever fallen on Egypt, from the day it was founded till now. 19Give an order now to bring your livestock and everything you have in the field to a place of shelter, because the hail will fall on every man and animal that has not been brought in and is still out in the field, and they will die.' "

20Those officials of Pharaoh who feared the word of the LORD hurried to bring their slaves and their livestock inside. 21But those who ignored the word of the LORD left their slaves and livestock in the field.

22Then the LORD said to Moses, "Stretch out your hand towards the sky so that hail will fall all over Egypt—on men and animals and on everything growing in the fields of Egypt." 23When Moses stretched out his staff towards the sky, the LORD sent thunder and hail, and lightning flashed down to the ground. So the LORD rained hail on the land of Egypt; 24hail fell and lightning flashed back and forth. It was the worst storm in all the land of Egypt since it had become a nation. 25Throughout Egypt hail struck everything in the fields—both men and animals; it beat down everything growing in the fields and stripped every tree. 26The only place it did not hail was the land of Goshen, where the Israelites were.

27Then Pharaoh summoned Moses and Aaron. "This time I have sinned," he said to them. "The LORD is in the right, and I and my people are in the wrong. 28Pray to the LORD, for we have had enough thunder

a 16 Or have spared you

and hail. I will let you go; you don't have to stay any longer."

²⁹Moses replied, "When I have gone out of the city, I will spread out my hands in prayer to the LORD. The thunder will stop and there will be no more hail, so you may know that the earth is the LORD's. ³⁰But I know that you and your officials still do not fear the LORD God."

³¹(The flax and barley were destroyed, since the barley was in the ear and the flax was in bloom. ³²The wheat and spelt, however, were not destroyed, because they ripen later.)

³³Then Moses left Pharaoh and went out of the city. He spread out his hands towards the LORD; the thunder and hail stopped, and the rain no longer poured down on the land. ³⁴When Pharaoh saw that the rain and hail and thunder had stopped, he sinned again: He and his officials hardened their hearts. ³⁵So Pharaoh's heart was hard and he would not let the Israelites go, just as the LORD had said through Moses.

■ The Plague of Locusts

10 Then the LORD said to Moses, "Go to Pharaoh, for I have hardened his heart and the hearts of his officials so that I may perform these miraculous signs of mine among them ²that you may tell your children and grandchildren how I dealt harshly with the Egyptians and how I performed my signs among them, and that you may know that I am the LORD."

³So Moses and Aaron went to Pharaoh and said to him, "This is what the LORD, the God of the Hebrews, says: 'How long will you refuse to humble yourself before me? Let my people go, so that they may worship me. ⁴If you refuse to let them go, I will bring locusts into your country tomorrow. ⁵They will cover the face of the ground so that it cannot be seen. They will devour what little you have left after the hail, including every tree that is growing in your fields. ⁶They will fill your houses and those of all your officials and all the Egyptians — something neither your fathers nor your forefathers have ever seen from the day they settled in this land till now.' " Then Moses turned and left Pharaoh.

⁷Pharaoh's officials said to him, "How long will this man be a snare to us? Let the people go, so that they may worship the LORD their God. Do you not yet realise that Egypt is ruined?"

⁸Then Moses and Aaron were brought back to Pharaoh. "Go, worship the LORD your God," he said. "But just who will be going?"

⁹Moses answered, "We will go with our young and old, with our sons and daughters, and with our flocks and herds, because we are to celebrate a festival to the LORD."

¹⁰Pharaoh said, "The LORD be with you — if I let you go, along with your women and children! Clearly you are bent on evil.ᵃ ¹¹No! Let only the men go; and worship the LORD, since that's what you have been asking for." Then Moses and Aaron were driven out of Pharaoh's presence.

¹²And the LORD said to Moses, "Stretch out your hand over Egypt so that locusts will swarm over the land and devour everything growing in the fields, everything left by the hail."

¹³So Moses stretched out his staff over Egypt, and the LORD made an east wind blow across the land all that day and all that night. By morning the wind had brought the locusts; ¹⁴they invaded all Egypt and settled down in every area of the country in great numbers. Never before had there been such a plague of locusts, nor will there ever be again. ¹⁵They covered all the ground until it was black. They devoured all that was left after the hail — everything growing in the fields and the fruit on the trees. Nothing green remained on tree or plant in all the land of Egypt.

¹⁶Pharaoh quickly summoned Moses and Aaron and said, "I have sinned against the LORD your God and against you. ¹⁷Now forgive my sin once more and pray to the LORD your God to take this deadly plague away from me."

¹⁸Moses then left Pharaoh and prayed to the LORD. ¹⁹And the LORD changed the wind to a very strong west wind, which caught up the locusts and carried them into the Red Sea.ᵇ Not a locust was left anywhere in Egypt. ²⁰But the LORD hardened Pharaoh's heart, and he would not let the Israelites go.

■ The Plague of Darkness

²¹Then the LORD said to Moses, "Stretch out your hand towards the sky so that darkness will spread over Egypt — darkness that can be felt." ²²So Moses stretched out his hand towards the sky, and total darkness covered all Egypt for three days. ²³No-one could see anyone else or leave his place for three days. Yet all the Israelites had light in the places where they lived.

10:21 ■ ATTACK ON FALSE GODS
God used ten plagues as a form of warfare against the gods of Egypt (12:12). Some scholars see in each individual punishment an attack against a specific Egyptian idol. Thus they believe the plague on the Nile River opposed the Egyptians' river god, the plague of flies flouted worship of the sacred fly, the plague of darkness attacked the sun-god Ra, and the plague on livestock countered the sacred bull.

---

²⁴Then Pharaoh summoned Moses and said, "Go, worship the LORD. Even your women and children may go with you; only leave your flocks and herds behind."

²⁵But Moses said, "You must allow us to have sacrifices and burnt offerings to present to the LORD our God. ²⁶Our livestock too must go with us; not a hoof is to be left behind. We have to use some of them in worshipping the LORD our God, and until we get there we will not know what we are to use to worship the LORD."

²⁷But the LORD hardened Pharaoh's heart, and he was not willing to let them go. ²⁸Pharaoh said to Moses, "Get out of my sight! Make sure you do not appear before me again! The day you see my face you will die."

ᵃ10 Or Be careful, trouble is in store for you!   ᵇ19 Hebrew Yam Suph; that is, Sea of Reeds

²⁹"Just as you say," Moses replied, "I will never appear before you again."

■ The Plague on the Firstborn

11 Now the LORD said to Moses, "I will bring one more plague on Pharaoh and on Egypt. After that, he will let you go from here, and when he does, he will drive you out completely. ²Tell the people that men and women alike are to ask their neighbours for articles of silver and gold." ³(The LORD made the Egyptians favourably disposed towards the people, and Moses himself was highly regarded in Egypt by Pharaoh's officials and by the people.)

⁴So Moses said, "This is what the LORD says: 'About midnight I will go throughout Egypt. ⁵Every firstborn son in Egypt will die, from the firstborn son of Pharaoh, who sits on the throne, to the firstborn son of the slave girl, who is at her hand mill, and all the firstborn of the cattle as well. ⁶There will be loud wailing throughout Egypt—worse than there has

INSIGHT

■ INDEPENDENCE DAY
AN UNUSUAL STYLE OF CELEBRATING FREEDOM

"THERE WILL BE LOUD WAILING THROUGHOUT EGYPT—WORSE THAN THERE HAS EVER BEEN OR EVER WILL BE AGAIN." ■ 11:6

The United States celebrates July 4 like no other day. The parades, the picnics and the fireworks boisterously express national pride. Everyone is proud to be an American and to have played a part in the creation of their nation.

■ A DIFFERENT MOOD FOR THE JEWS
This style of celebration—noisy and flag-waving and proud—captures something of the original spirit that led a young nation to declare independence. A similar spirit surges up in France on Bastille Day and in many other nations on their birthdays. But these celebrations bear a striking *dissimilarity* to the Jewish independence day, a day called Passover.

The Jews trace their cultural birthday back to a dark, foreboding night—the Israelites' last in Egypt (Exodus 12). There are no blaring bands nor balloons nor fireworks to commemorate this event. Everything takes place inside a home, with a family or cluster of families gathered around a table. Participants taste morsels of food, pausing before each portion to hear Old Testament accounts of the history they are reliving. Their independence day resembles a worship service, not a party.

■ A WORK OF GOD ALONE
More than anything else, the Jewish independence day expresses this one fact: God did it. No Israelite armies stood against the mighty Egyptians. Freedom came in the blackest night while Israelite families huddled around the Passover table, their bags packed, waiting for deliverance.

When God's time came, the Egyptian captors not only released the Israelites, but begged them to go and showered them with gold and riches. The Jews remember that event with humility and praise; there is no room for pride. Later, when Pharaoh changed his mind

and set his chariots loose upon the fleeing tribes, God came through again. Israelites stood trembling like cowards, already second-guessing their freedom. But God destroyed the great Egyptian army.

For the children of Israel, independence from Egypt meant dependence on God. In fact, God came back to this event throughout the Bible as a way of describing himself: "I am the LORD your God, who brought you out of Egypt."

The pattern of dependence was to continue all through Exodus. When the wilderness wanderers ran out of water, God provided some. When food supplies failed, God provided some. When raiders attacked, God provided help. Independence day merely set the tone for a national history that was an active movement of God.

■ PASSOVER'S NEW MEANING
Much later, Passover night would take on an even broader significance. During one particular Passover feast, as thousands of Jews were bringing their choice lambs to Jerusalem, one man was selected as the Passover Lamb for all humanity (1 Corinthians 5:7). The words "When I see the blood, I will pass over you" (12:13) came to convey a whole new meaning.

Today, though Jewish people still celebrate Passover, most Christians do not. Rather, that ceremony has been incorporated into a new one called the Eucharist, or the Lord's Supper, with Christ representing the Passover lamb. Although much of the ceremony's content has changed, one thing has not. The Lord's Supper, too, memorialises a time of pain and of bloodshed, a time of freedom and deliverance. It, too, was God's act alone. He gets the credit.

□ LIFE QUESTIONS:
Does your church's celebration of the Eucharist, or Lord's Supper, resemble the Jewish Passover described here? How are they similar or different?

ever been or ever will be again. 7But among the Is-raelites not a dog will bark at any man or animal.' Then you will know that the LORD makes a distinction between Egypt and Israel. 8All these officials of yours will come to me, bowing down before me and saying, 'Go, you and all the people who follow you!' After that I will leave." Then Moses, hot with anger, left Pharaoh.

9The LORD had said to Moses, "Pharaoh will refuse to listen to you—so that my wonders may be multiplied in Egypt." 10Moses and Aaron performed all these wonders before Pharaoh, but the LORD hardened Pharaoh's heart, and he would not let the Israelites go out of his country.

■ The Passover

12 The LORD said to Moses and Aaron in Egypt, 2"This month is to be for you the first month, the first month of your year. 3Tell the whole community of Israel that on the tenth day of this month each man is to take a lamb*a* for his family, one for each household. 4If any household is too small for a whole lamb, they must share one with their nearest neighbour, having taken into account the number of people there are. You are to determine the amount of lamb needed in accordance with what each person will eat. 5The animals you choose must be year-old males without defect, and you may take them from the sheep or the goats. 6Take care of them until the fourteenth day of the month, when all the people of the community of Israel must slaughter them at twilight. 7Then they are to take some of the blood and put it on the sides and tops of the door-frames of the houses where they eat the lambs. 8That same night they are to eat the meat roasted over the fire, along with bitter herbs, and bread made without yeast. 9Do not eat the meat raw or cooked in water, but roast it over the fire—head, legs and inner parts. 10Do not leave any of it till morning; if some is left till morning, you must burn it. 11This is how you are to eat it: with your cloak tucked into your belt, your sandals on your feet and your staff in your hand. Eat it in haste; it is the LORD's Passover.

12:11 ■ FAST FOOD
God's instructions for the Passover stress the need for haste. Roasting over fire cooks meat faster than boiling, and (unlike frying or baking) requires no pan or oven. Likewise, bread without yeast doesn't need time to rise. The emphasis on speed indicated to the Israelites how terrible this plague would be, and how swiftly they had to flee from Egypt.

12"On that same night I will pass through Egypt and strike down every firstborn—both men and animals—and I will bring judgment on all the gods of Egypt. I am the LORD. 13The blood will be a sign for you on the houses where you are; and when I see the blood, I will pass over you. No destructive plague will touch you when I strike Egypt.

14"This is a day you are to commemorate; for the

generations to come you shall celebrate it as a festival to the LORD—a lasting ordinance. 15For seven days you are to eat bread made without yeast. On the first day remove the yeast from your houses, for whoever eats anything with yeast in it from the first day until the seventh must be cut off from Israel. 16On the first day hold a sacred assembly, and another one on the seventh day. Do no work at all on these days, except to prepare food for everyone to eat—that is all you may do.

17"Celebrate the Feast of Unleavened Bread, because it was on this very day that I brought your divisions out of Egypt. Celebrate this day as a lasting ordinance for the generations to come. 18In the first month you are to eat bread made without yeast, from the evening of the fourteenth day until the evening of the twenty-first day. 19For seven days no yeast is to be found in your houses. And whoever eats anything with yeast in it must be cut off from the community of Israel, whether he is an alien or native-born. 20Eat nothing made with yeast. Wherever you live, you must eat unleavened bread."

21Then Moses summoned all the elders of Israel and said to them, "Go at once and select the animals for your families and slaughter the Passover lamb. 22Take a bunch of hyssop, dip it into the blood in the basin and put some of the blood on the top and on both sides of the door-frame. Not one of you shall go out of the door of his house until morning. 23When the LORD goes through the land to strike down the Egyptians, he will see the blood on the top and sides of the door-frame and will pass over that doorway, and he will not permit the destroyer to enter your houses and strike you down.

24"Obey these instructions as a lasting ordinance for you and your descendants. 25When you enter the land that the LORD will give you as he promised, observe this ceremony. 26And when your children ask you, 'What does this ceremony mean to you?' 27then tell them, 'It is the Passover sacrifice to the LORD, who passed over the houses of the Israelites in Egypt and spared our homes when he struck down the Egyptians.' " Then the people bowed down and worshipped. 28The Israelites did just what the LORD commanded Moses and Aaron.

29At midnight the LORD struck down all the firstborn in Egypt, from the firstborn of Pharaoh, who sat on the throne, to the firstborn of the prisoner, who was in the dungeon, and the firstborn of all the livestock as well. 30Pharaoh and all his officials and all the Egyptians got up during the night, and there was loud wailing in Egypt, for there was not a house without someone dead.

■ The Exodus

31During the night Pharaoh summoned Moses and Aaron and said, "Up! Leave my people, you and the Israelites! Go, worship the LORD as you have requested. 32Take your flocks and herds, as you have said, and go. And also bless me."

33The Egyptians urged the people to hurry and leave the country. "For otherwise," they said, "we will all die!" 34So the people took their dough before the yeast was added, and carried it on their shoulders in kneading troughs wrapped in clothing. 35The

a3 The Hebrew word can mean lamb or kid; also in verse 4.

Israelites did as Moses instructed and asked the Egyptians for articles of silver and gold and for clothing. 36The LORD had made the Egyptians favourably disposed towards the people, and they gave them what they asked for; so they plundered the Egyptians.

37The Israelites journeyed from Rameses to Succoth. There were about six hundred thousand men on foot, besides women and children. 38Many other people went up with them, as well as large droves of livestock, both flocks and herds. 39With the dough they had brought from Egypt, they baked cakes of unleavened bread. The dough was without yeast because they had been driven out of Egypt and did not have time to prepare food for themselves.

40Now the length of time the Israelite people lived in Egypt*b* was 430 years. 41At the end of the 430 years, to the very day, all the LORD's divisions left Egypt. 42Because the LORD kept vigil that night to bring them out of Egypt, on this night all the Israelites are to keep vigil to honour the LORD for the generations to come.

■ Passover Restrictions

43The LORD said to Moses and Aaron, "These are the regulations for the Passover:

"No foreigner is to eat of it. 44Any slave you have bought may eat of it after you have circumcised him, 45but a temporary resident and a hired worker may not eat of it.

46"It must be eaten inside one house; take none of the meat outside the house. Do not break any of the bones. 47The whole community of Israel must celebrate it.

48"An alien living among you who wants to celebrate the LORD's Passover must have all the males in his household circumcised; then he may take part like one born in the land. No uncircumcised male may eat of it. 49The same law applies to the native-born and to the alien living among you."

50All the Israelites did just what the LORD had commanded Moses and Aaron. 51And on that very day the LORD brought the Israelites out of Egypt by their divisions.

■ Consecration of the Firstborn

13 The LORD said to Moses, 2"Consecrate to me every firstborn male. The first offspring of every womb among the Israelites belongs to me, whether man or animal."

13:1 ■ THE FIRSTBORN PRINCIPLE

At the time of the Passover and the exodus from Egypt, God introduced an important principle: every firstborn male, including animals, was to be dedicated to him. Later, the Levites were established as a symbolic firstborn for all the people, with very precise accounting (Numbers 3:40–51).

3Then Moses said to the people, "Commemorate this day, the day you came out of Egypt, out of the land of slavery, because the LORD brought you out

of it with a mighty hand. Eat nothing containing yeast. 4Today, in the month of Abib, you are leaving. 5When the LORD brings you into the land of the Canaanites, Hittites, Amorites, Hivites and Jebusites — the land he swore to your forefathers to give you, a land flowing with milk and honey — you are to observe this ceremony in this month: 6For seven days eat bread made without yeast and on the seventh day hold a festival to the LORD. 7Eat unleavened bread during those seven days; nothing with yeast in it is to be seen among you, nor shall any yeast be seen anywhere within your borders. 8On that day tell your son, 'I do this because of what the LORD did for me when I came out of Egypt.' 9This observance will be for you like a sign on your hand and a reminder on your forehead that the law of the LORD is to be on your lips. For the LORD brought you out of Egypt with his mighty hand. 10You must keep this ordinance at the appointed time year after year.

11"After the LORD brings you into the land of the Canaanites and gives it to you, as he promised on oath to you and your forefathers, 12you are to give over to the LORD the first offspring of every womb. All the firstborn males of your livestock belong to the LORD. 13Redeem with a lamb every firstborn donkey, but if you do not redeem it, break its neck. Redeem every firstborn among your sons.

14"In days to come when your son asks you, 'What does this mean?' say to him, 'With a mighty hand the LORD brought us out of Egypt, out of the land of slavery. 15When Pharaoh stubbornly refused to let us go, the LORD killed every firstborn in Egypt, both man and animal. This is why I sacrifice to the LORD the first male offspring of every womb and redeem each of my firstborn sons.' 16And it will be like a sign on your hand and a symbol on your forehead that the LORD brought us out of Egypt with his mighty hand."

■ Crossing the Sea

17When Pharaoh let the people go, God did not lead them on the road through the Philistine country, though that was shorter. For God said, "If they face war, they might change their minds and return to Egypt." 18So God led the people around by the desert road towards the Red Sea.*a* The Israelites went up out of Egypt armed for battle.

19Moses took the bones of Joseph with him because Joseph had made the sons of Israel swear an oath. He had said, "God will surely come to your aid, and then you must carry my bones up with you from this place."*b*

20After leaving Succoth they camped at Etham on the edge of the desert. 21By day the LORD went ahead of them in a pillar of cloud to guide them on their way and by night in a pillar of fire to give them light, so that they could travel by day or night. 22Neither the pillar of cloud by day nor the pillar of fire by night left its place in front of the people.

14 Then the LORD said to Moses, 2"Tell the Israelites to turn back and camp near Pi Hahiroth, between Migdol and the sea. They are to camp by the sea, directly opposite Baal Zephon. 3Pharaoh will think, 'The Israelites are wandering around the land in confusion, hemmed in by the desert.' 4And I will harden Pharaoh's heart, and he will pursue

---

b40 Masoretic Text; Samaritan Pentateuch and Septuagint *Egypt and Canaan*   *a18* Hebrew *Yam Suph*; that is, Sea of Reeds   *b19* See Gen. 50:25.

them. But I will gain glory for myself through Pharaoh and all his army, and the Egyptians will know that I am the LORD." So the Israelites did this.

⁵When the king of Egypt was told that the people had fled, Pharaoh and his officials changed their minds about them and said, "What have we done? We have let the Israelites go and have lost their services!" ⁶So he had his chariot made ready and took his army with him. ⁷He took six hundred of the best chariots, along with all the other chariots of Egypt, with officers over all of them. ⁸The LORD hardened the heart of Pharaoh king of Egypt, so that he pursued the Israelites, who were marching out boldly. ⁹The Egyptians — all Pharaoh's horses and chariots, horsemen*ᵃ* and troops — pursued the Israelites and overtook them as they camped by the sea near Pi Hahiroth, opposite Baal Zephon.

¹⁰As Pharaoh approached, the Israelites looked up, and there were the Egyptians, marching after them. They were terrified and cried out to the LORD. ¹¹They said to Moses, "Was it because there were no graves in Egypt that you brought us to the desert to die? What have you done to us by bringing us out of Egypt? ¹²Didn't we say to you in Egypt, 'Leave us alone; let us serve the Egyptians'? It would have been better for us to serve the Egyptians than to die in the desert!"

¹³Moses answered the people, "Do not be afraid. Stand firm and you will see the deliverance the LORD will bring you today. The Egyptians you see today you will never see again. ¹⁴The LORD will fight for you; you need only to be still."

¹⁵Then the LORD said to Moses, "Why are you crying out to me? Tell the Israelites to move on. ¹⁶Raise your staff and stretch out your hand over the sea to divide the water so that the Israelites can go through the sea on dry ground. ¹⁷I will harden the hearts of the Egyptians so that they will go in after them. And I will gain glory through Pharaoh and all his army, through his chariots and his horsemen. ¹⁸The Egyptians will know that I am the LORD when I gain glory through Pharaoh, his chariots and his horsemen."

¹⁹Then the angel of God, who had been travelling in front of Israel's army, withdrew and went behind them. The pillar of cloud also moved from in front and stood behind them, ²⁰coming between the armies of Egypt and Israel. Throughout the night the cloud brought darkness to the one side and light to the other; so neither went near the other all night long.

²¹Then Moses stretched out his hand over the sea, and all that night the LORD drove the sea back with a strong east wind and turned it into dry land. The waters were divided, ²²and the Israelites went through the sea on dry ground, with a wall of water on their right and on their left.

²³The Egyptians pursued them, and all Pharaoh's horses and chariots and horsemen followed them into the sea. ²⁴During the last watch of the night the LORD looked down from the pillar of fire and cloud at the Egyptian army and threw it into confusion. ²⁵He made the wheels of their chariots come off*ᵇ* so that they had difficulty driving. And the Egyptians said, "Let's get away from the Israelites! The LORD is fighting for them against Egypt."

²⁶Then the LORD said to Moses, "Stretch out your hand over the sea so that the waters may flow back over the Egyptians and their chariots and horsemen." ²⁷Moses stretched out his hand over the sea, and at daybreak the sea went back to its place. The Egyptians were fleeing towards*ᶜ* it, and the LORD swept them into the sea. ²⁸The water flowed back and covered the chariots and horsemen — the entire army of Pharaoh that had followed the Israelites into the sea. Not one of them survived.

14:21 ■ FINAL ESCAPE
Hemmed in by mountains, the sea, and the Egyptian army, the Israelites seemed doomed until God opened a highway through the sea. This miracle closed an important chapter in the Israelites' history. Never again would the powerful Egyptian empire rule over them; most of their future enemies swept in from the north and east.

²⁹But the Israelites went through the sea on dry ground, with a wall of water on their right and on their left. ³⁰That day the LORD saved Israel from the hands of the Egyptians, and Israel saw the Egyptians lying dead on the shore. ³¹And when the Israelites saw the great power the LORD displayed against the Egyptians, the people feared the LORD and put their trust in him and in Moses his servant.

■ The Song of Moses and Miriam

15 Then Moses and the Israelites sang this song to the LORD:

"I will sing to the LORD,
   for he is highly exalted.
The horse and its rider
   he has hurled into the sea.

15:1 ■ A STORY FOR ALL TIME
Moses' song celebrates the event from which this book gets its name: "the exodus" from Egypt, when a band of slaves escaped from the most powerful civilisation on earth. The psalmists never tired of celebrating that event in song (see, for example, Psalms 78 and 105), and the prophets later harked back to the days of the exodus to stir the conscience of their nation. The Israelites' liberation gave inspiration to the slaves of the American South, who often commemorated the exodus in their spirituals.

²The LORD is my strength and my song;
   he has become my salvation.
He is my God, and I will praise him,
   my father's God, and I will exalt him.
³The LORD is a warrior;
   the LORD is his name.
⁴Pharaoh's chariots and his army
   he has hurled into the sea.
The best of Pharaoh's officers
   are drowned in the Red Sea.*ᵃ*
⁵The deep waters have covered them;

ᵃ9 Or charioteers; also in verses 17, 18, 23, 26 and 28   ᵇ25 Or He jammed the wheels of their chariots (see Samaritan Pentateuch, Septuagint and Syriac)
ᶜ27 Or from   ᵃ4 Hebrew Yam Suph; that is, Sea of Reeds; also in verse 22

they sank to the depths like a stone.

6"Your right hand, O LORD,
     was majestic in power.
Your right hand, O LORD,
     shattered the enemy.
7In the greatness of your majesty
     you threw down those who opposed you.
You unleashed your burning anger;
     it consumed them like stubble.
8By the blast of your nostrils
     the waters piled up.
The surging waters stood firm like a wall;
     the deep waters congealed in the heart of
         the sea.

9"The enemy boasted,
     'I will pursue, I will overtake them.
I will divide the spoils;
     I will gorge myself on them.
I will draw my sword
     and my hand will destroy them.'
10But you blew with your breath,
     and the sea covered them.
They sank like lead
     in the mighty waters.

11"Who among the gods is like you, O LORD?
     Who is like you—
         majestic in holiness,
         awesome in glory,
         working wonders?
12You stretched out your right hand
     and the earth swallowed them.

13"In your unfailing love you will lead
     the people you have redeemed.
In your strength you will guide them
     to your holy dwelling.
14The nations will hear and tremble;
     anguish will grip the people of Philistia.
15The chiefs of Edom will be terrified,
     the leaders of Moab will be seized with
         trembling,
     the people*b* of Canaan will melt away;
16   terror and dread will fall upon them.
By the power of your arm
     they will be as still as a stone—
until your people pass by, O LORD,
     until the people you bought*c* pass by.
17You will bring them in and plant them
     on the mountain of your inheritance—
the place, O LORD, you made for your dwelling,
     the sanctuary, O Lord, your hands
         established.
18The LORD will reign
     for ever and ever."

19When Pharaoh's horses, chariots and horsemen*d* went into the sea, the LORD brought the
waters of the sea back over them, but the Israelites
walked through the sea on dry ground. 20Then Miriam the prophetess, Aaron's sister, took a tambourine in her hand, and all the women followed her,
with tambourines and dancing. 21Miriam sang to
them:

     "Sing to the LORD,

for he is highly exalted.
The horse and its rider
     he has hurled into the sea."

■ The Waters of Marah and Elim
     22Then Moses led Israel from the Red Sea and they
went into the Desert of Shur. For three days they
travelled in the desert without finding water.
23When they came to Marah, they could not drink
its water because it was bitter. (That is why the
place is called Marah.*e*) 24So the people grumbled
against Moses, saying, "What are we to drink?"
     25Then Moses cried out to the LORD, and the LORD
showed him a piece of wood. He threw it into the
water, and the water became sweet.
     There the LORD made a decree and a law for them,
and there he tested them. 26He said, "If you listen
carefully to the voice of the LORD your God and do
what is right in his eyes, if you pay attention to his
commands and keep all his decrees, I will not bring
on you any of the diseases I brought on the Egyptians, for I am the LORD, who heals you."
     27Then they came to Elim, where there were
twelve springs and seventy palm trees, and they
camped there near the water.

■ Manna and Quail
16 The whole Israelite community set out from
     Elim and came to the Desert of Sin, which is
between Elim and Sinai, on the fifteenth day of the
second month after they had come out of Egypt. 2In
the desert the whole community grumbled against
Moses and Aaron. 3The Israelites said to them, "If
only we had died by the LORD's hand in Egypt! There
we sat round pots of meat and ate all the food we
wanted, but you have brought us out into this desert
to starve this entire assembly to death."
     4Then the LORD said to Moses, "I will rain down
bread from heaven for you. The people are to go out
each day and gather enough for that day. In this way
I will test them and see whether they will follow my
instructions. 5On the sixth day they are to prepare
what they bring in, and that is to be twice as much
as they gather on the other days."
     6So Moses and Aaron said to all the Israelites, "In
the evening you will know that it was the LORD who
brought you out of Egypt, 7and in the morning you
will see the glory of the LORD, because he has heard
your grumbling against him. Who are we, that you
should grumble against us?" 8Moses also said, "You
will know that it was the LORD when he gives you
meat to eat in the evening and all the bread you want
in the morning, because he has heard your grumbling against him. Who are we? You are not grumbling against us, but against the LORD."
     9Then Moses told Aaron, "Say to the entire Israel-
ite community, 'Come before the LORD, for he has
heard your grumbling.' "
     10While Aaron was speaking to the whole Israelite
community, they looked towards the desert, and
there was the glory of the LORD appearing in the
cloud.
     11The LORD said to Moses, 12"I have heard the
grumbling of the Israelites. Tell them, 'At twilight
you will eat meat, and in the morning you will be

b 15 Or *rulers*   *c 16* Or *created*   *d 19* Or *charioteers*   *e 23* Marah means *bitter.*

filled with bread. Then you will know that I am the LORD your God.' "

16:12 ■ FOOD SUPPLY

The word *manna* means literally, "What is it?", recalling the Israelites' first reaction to it (verse 15). Manna is a clear example of the Israelites' enforced dependence on God; they had to rely on him every day for 40 years, just to survive. God's provision of manna made greed impossible: it could not be hoarded and was distributed with precise equity (verses 17–21).

Quail, referred to here and in Numbers 11, still migrate across the Sinai peninsula, flying in great flocks between Europe and Arabia. Exhausted by their long flight, they roost on the ground or in low bushes at night, making capture easy.

¹³That evening quail came and covered the camp, and in the morning there was a layer of dew around the camp. ¹⁴When the dew was gone, thin flakes like frost on the ground appeared on the desert floor. ¹⁵When the Israelites saw it, they said to each other, "What is it?" For they did not know what it was.

Moses said to them, "It is the bread the LORD has given you to eat. ¹⁶This is what the LORD has commanded: 'Each one is to gather as much as he needs. Take an omer*ᵃ* for each person you have in your tent.' "

¹⁷The Israelites did as they were told; some gathered much, some little. ¹⁸And when they measured it by the omer, he who gathered much did not have too much, and he who gathered little did not have too little. Each one gathered as much as he needed.

¹⁹Then Moses said to them, "No-one is to keep any of it until morning."

²⁰However, some of them paid no attention to Moses; they kept part of it until morning, but it was full of maggots and began to smell. So Moses was angry with them.

²¹Each morning everyone gathered as much as he needed, and when the sun grew hot, it melted away. ²²On the sixth day, they gathered twice as much — two omers*ᵇ* for each person — and the leaders of the community came and reported this to Moses. ²³He said to them, "This is what the LORD commanded: 'Tomorrow is to be a day of rest, a holy Sabbath to the LORD. So bake what you want to bake and boil what you want to boil. Save whatever is left and keep it until morning.' "

²⁴So they saved it until morning, as Moses commanded, and it did not stink or get maggots in it. ²⁵"Eat it today," Moses said, "because today is a Sabbath to the LORD. You will not find any of it on the ground today. ²⁶Six days you are to gather it, but on the seventh day, the Sabbath, there will be not be any."

²⁷Nevertheless, some of the people went out on the seventh day to gather it, but they found none. ²⁸Then the LORD said to Moses, "How long will you*ᶜ* refuse to keep my commands and my instructions? ²⁹Bear in mind that the LORD has given you the Sabbath; that is why on the sixth day he gives you bread for two days. Everyone is to stay where he is on the

seventh day; no-one is to go out." ³⁰So the people rested on the seventh day.

³¹The people of Israel called the bread manna.*ᵈ* It was white like coriander seed and tasted like wafers made with honey. ³²Moses said, "This is what the LORD has commanded: 'Take an omer of manna and keep it for the generations to come, so they can see the bread I gave you to eat in the desert when I brought you out of Egypt.' "

³³So Moses said to Aaron, "Take a jar and put an omer of manna in it. Then place it before the LORD to be kept for the generations to come."

³⁴As the LORD commanded Moses, Aaron put the manna in front of the Testimony, that it might be kept. ³⁵The Israelites ate manna for forty years, until they came to a land that was settled; they ate manna until they reached the border of Canaan.

³⁶(An omer is one tenth of an ephah.)

■ Water From the Rock

17 The whole Israelite community set out from the Desert of Sin, travelling from place to place as the LORD commanded. They camped at Rephidim, but there was no water for the people to drink. ²So they quarrelled with Moses and said, "Give us water to drink."

Moses replied, "Why do you quarrel with me? Why do you put the LORD to the test?"

17:1 ■ CHANGE OF SCENERY

Unlike the Sahara and Saudi Arabian deserts, the Sinai peninsula is no dry, sandy wasteland. A high plateau in the north gives way to a broad belt of sandstone and sand, and then a tumbled mass of mountains (some reaching 9,000 feet) in the south. Herbs and acacia trees grow, and widely scattered springs permit some farming, although the Sinai cannot support a large population. Moses' 40-year stint as a shepherd here would have taught him much about wilderness survival.

³But the people were thirsty for water there, and they grumbled against Moses. They said, "Why did you bring us up out of Egypt to make us and our children and livestock die of thirst?"

⁴Then Moses cried out to the LORD, "What am I to do with these people? They are almost ready to stone me."

⁵The LORD answered Moses, "Walk on ahead of the people. Take with you some of the elders of Israel and take in your hand the staff with which you struck the Nile, and go. ⁶I will stand there before you by the rock at Horeb. Strike the rock, and water will come out of it for the people to drink." So Moses did this in the sight of the elders of Israel. ⁷And he called the place Massah*ᵃ* and Meribah*ᵇ* because the Israelites quarrelled and because they tested the LORD saying, "Is the LORD among us or not?"

■ The Amalekites Defeated

⁸The Amalekites came and attacked the Israelites at Rephidim. ⁹Moses said to Joshua, "Choose some of our men and go out to fight the Amalekites.

ᵃ 16 That is, probably about 4 pints (about 2 litres); also in verses 18, 32, 33 and 36   *ᵇ 22* That is, probably about 7½ pints (about 4.5 litres)   *ᶜ 28* The Hebrew is plural.   *ᵈ 31* Manna means *What is it?* (see verse 15).   *ᵃ 7* Massah means *testing.*   *ᵇ 7* Meribah means *quarrelling.*

Tomorrow I will stand on top of the hill with the staff of God in my hands."

10So Joshua fought the Amalekites as Moses had ordered, and Moses, Aaron and Hur went to the top of the hill. 11As long as Moses held up his hands, the Israelites were winning, but whenever he lowered his hands, the Amalekites were winning. 12When Moses' hands grew tired, they took a stone and put it under him and he sat on it. Aaron and Hur held his hands up—one on one side, one on the other—so that his hands remained steady till sunset. 13So Joshua overcame the Amalekite army with the sword.

14Then the LORD said to Moses, "Write this on a scroll as something to be remembered and make sure that Joshua hears it, because I will completely blot out the memory of Amalek from under heaven."

17:14 ■ FIRST WRITING

Civilisation mastered the skill of writing at least as early as 3400 B.C., when a society near present-day Iraq introduced it, but this is the Bible's first mention of the practice. Moses' training in Egypt would have included writing on "paper" made from pulpy reeds of the papyrus plant. A basket fashioned out of such reeds had helped save Moses' life as an infant (2:3).

15Moses built an altar and called it The LORD is my Banner. 16He said, "For hands were lifted up to the throne of the LORD. Thec LORD will be at war against the Amalekites from generation to generation."

■ Jethro Visits Moses

18 Now Jethro, the priest of Midian and father-in-law of Moses, heard of everything God had done for Moses and for his people Israel, and how the LORD had brought Israel out of Egypt.

2After Moses had sent away his wife Zipporah, his father-in-law Jethro received her 3and her two sons. One son was named Gershom,a for Moses said, "I have become an alien in a foreign land"; 4and the other was named Eliezer,b for he said, "My father's God was my helper; he saved me from the sword of Pharaoh."

5Jethro, Moses' father-in-law, together with Moses' sons and wife, came to him in the desert, where he was camped near the mountain of God. 6Jethro had sent word to him, "I, your father-in-law Jethro, am coming to you with your wife and her two sons."

7So Moses went out to meet his father-in-law and bowed down and kissed him. They greeted each other and then went into the tent. 8Moses told his father-in-law about everything the LORD had done to Pharaoh and the Egyptians for Israel's sake and about all the hardships they had met along the way and how the LORD had saved them.

9Jethro was delighted to hear about all the good things the LORD had done for Israel in rescuing them from the hand of the Egyptians. 10He said, "Praise be

to the LORD, who rescued you from the hand of the Egyptians and of Pharaoh, and who rescued the people from the hand of the Egyptians. 11Now I know that the LORD is greater than all other gods, for he did this to those who had treated Israel arrogantly." 12Then Jethro, Moses' father-in-law, brought a burnt offering and other sacrifices to God, and Aaron came with all the elders of Israel to eat bread with Moses' father-in-law in the presence of God.

13The next day Moses took his seat to serve as judge for the people, and they stood round him from morning till evening. 14When his father-in-law saw all that Moses was doing for the people, he said, "What is this you are doing for the people? Why do you alone sit as judge, while all these people stand round you from morning till evening?"

15Moses answered him, "Because the people come to me to seek God's will. 16Whenever they have a dispute, it is brought to me, and I decide between the parties and inform them of God's decrees and laws."

17Moses' father-in-law replied, "What you are doing is not good. 18You and these people who come to you will only wear yourselves out. The work is too heavy for you; you cannot handle it alone. 19Listen now to me and I will give you some advice, and may God be with you. You must be the people's representative before God and bring their disputes to him. 20Teach them the decrees and laws, and show them the way to live and the duties they are to perform. 21But select capable men from all the people—men who fear God, trustworthy men who hate dishonest gain—and appoint them as officials over thousands, hundreds, fifties and tens. 22Have them serve as judges for the people at all times, but have them bring every difficult case to you; the simple cases they can decide themselves. That will make your load lighter, because they will share it with you. 23If you do this and God so commands, you will be able to stand the strain, and all these people will go home satisfied."

24Moses listened to his father-in-law and did everything he said. 25He chose capable men from all Israel and made them leaders of the people, officials over thousands, hundreds, fifties and tens. 26They served as judges for the people at all times. The difficult cases they brought to Moses, but the simple ones they decided themselves.

27Then Moses sent his father-in-law on his way, and Jethro returned to his own country.

■ At Mount Sinai

19 In the third month after the Israelites left Egypt—on the very day—they came to the Desert of Sinai. 2After they set out from Rephidim, they entered the Desert of Sinai, and Israel camped there in the desert in front of the mountain.

3Then Moses went up to God, and the LORD called to him from the mountain and said, "This is what you are to say to the house of Jacob and what you are to tell the people of Israel: 4'You yourselves have seen what I did to Egypt, and how I carried you on eagles' wings and brought you to myself. 5Now if you obey

---

c 16 Or "Because a hand was against the throne of the LORD, the   a 3 Gershom sounds like the Hebrew for an alien there.
b 4 Eliezer means my God is helper.

me fully and keep my covenant, then out of all nations you will be my treasured possession. Although the whole earth is mine, ⁶you*a* will be for me a kingdom of priests and a holy nation.' These are the words you are to speak to the Israelites."

19:5 ■ BOOK OF THE COVENANT

The word *covenant* appears throughout the next portion of Exodus. Chapter 19 gives the dramatic setting, and chapters 20–23 contain the actual covenant, a treaty between God and the Israelites. Chapter 24 shows the covenant being confirmed. Another word for covenant is *testament*, and, in fact, the rest of the Old *Testament* builds on what took place in these six chapters. Centuries later, biblical writers would dust off the old word *covenant* and apply it to Jesus Christ (as in 1 Corinthians 11:25). He fulfilled and completed the reconciliation with God begun at Sinai.

---

⁷So Moses went back and summoned the elders of the people and set before them all the words the LORD had commanded him to speak. ⁸The people all responded together, "We will do everything the LORD has said." So Moses brought their answer back to the LORD.

⁹The LORD said to Moses, "I am going to come to you in a dense cloud, so that the people will hear me speaking with you and will always put their trust in you." Then Moses told the LORD what the people had said.

¹⁰And the LORD said to Moses, "Go to the people and consecrate them today and tomorrow. Make them wash their clothes ¹¹and be ready by the third day, because on that day the LORD will come down on Mount Sinai in the sight of all the people. ¹²Put limits for the people around the mountain and tell them, 'Be careful that you do not go up the mountain or touch the foot of it. Whoever touches the mountain shall surely be put to death. ¹³He shall surely be stoned or shot with arrows; not a hand is to be laid on him. Whether man or animal, he shall not be permitted to live.' Only when the ram's horn sounds a long blast may they go up to the mountain."

¹⁴After Moses had gone down the mountain to the people, he consecrated them, and they washed their clothes. ¹⁵Then he said to the people, "Prepare yourselves for the third day. Abstain from sexual relations."

¹⁶On the morning of the third day there was thunder and lightning, with a thick cloud over the mountain, and a very loud trumpet blast. Everyone in the camp trembled. ¹⁷Then Moses led the people out of the camp to meet with God, and they stood at the foot of the mountain. ¹⁸Mount Sinai was covered with smoke, because the LORD descended on it in fire. The smoke billowed up from it like smoke from a furnace, the whole mountain*b* trembled violently, ¹⁹and the sound of the trumpet grew louder and louder. Then Moses spoke and the voice of God answered him.*c*

²⁰The LORD descended to the top of Mount Sinai and called Moses to the top of the mountain. So Moses went up ²¹and the LORD said to him, "Go down and warn the people so they do not force their way through to see the LORD and many of them perish. ²²Even the priests, who approach the LORD, must consecrate themselves, or the LORD will break out against them."

²³Moses said to the LORD, "The people cannot come up Mount Sinai, because you yourself warned us, 'Put limits around the mountain and set it apart as holy.' "

²⁴The LORD replied, "Go down and bring Aaron up with you. But the priests and the people must not force their way through to come up to the LORD, or he will break out against them."

²⁵So Moses went down to the people and told them.

■ The Ten Commandments

20 And God spoke all these words:

²"I am the LORD your God, who brought you out of Egypt, out of the land of slavery.

³"You shall have no other gods before*a* me.

⁴"You shall not make for yourself an idol in the form of anything in heaven above or on the earth beneath or in the waters below. ⁵You shall not bow down to them or worship them; for I, the LORD your God, am a jealous God, punishing the children for the sin of the fathers to the third and fourth generation of those who hate me, ⁶but showing love to a thousand ⌐generations⌐ of those who love me and keep my commandments.

⁷"You shall not misuse the name of the LORD your God, for the LORD will not hold anyone guiltless who misuses his name.

⁸"Remember the Sabbath day by keeping it holy. ⁹Six days you shall labour and do all your work, ¹⁰but the seventh day is a Sabbath to the LORD your God. On it you shall not do any work, neither you, nor your son or daughter, nor your manservant or maidservant, nor your animals, nor the alien within your gates. ¹¹For in six days the LORD made the heavens and the earth, the sea, and all that is in them, but he rested on the seventh day. Therefore the LORD blessed the Sabbath day and made it holy.

¹²"Honour your father and your mother, so that you may live long in the land the LORD your God is giving you.

¹³"You shall not murder.

¹⁴"You shall not commit adultery.

¹⁵"You shall not steal.

¹⁶"You shall not give false testimony against your neighbour.

¹⁷"You shall not covet your neighbour's house. You shall not covet your neighbour's wife, or his manservant or maidservant, his ox or donkey, or anything that belongs to your neighbour."

a 5,6 Or *possession, for the whole earth is mine.* 6*You*   *b 18* Most Hebrew manuscripts; a few Hebrew manuscripts and Septuagint *all the people*
c 19 Or *and God answered him with thunder*   *a 3* Or *besides*

18When the people saw the thunder and lightning and heard the trumpet and saw the mountain in smoke, they trembled with fear. They stayed at a distance 19and said to Moses, "Speak to us yourself and we will listen. But do not have God speak to us or we will die."

20Moses said to the people, "Do not be afraid. God has come to test you, so that the fear of God will be with you to keep you from sinning."

21The people remained at a distance, while Moses approached the thick darkness where God was.

■ Idols and Altars

22Then the LORD said to Moses, "Tell the Israelites this: 'You have seen for yourselves that I have spoken to you from heaven: 23Do not make any gods to be alongside me; do not make for yourselves gods of silver or gods of gold.

24" 'Make an altar of earth for me and sacrifice on it your burnt offerings and fellowship offerings,*b* your sheep and goats and your cattle. Wherever I cause my name to be honoured, I will come to you and bless you. 25If you make an altar of stones for me, do not build it with dressed stones, for you will defile it if you use a tool on it. 26And do not go up to my altar on steps, lest your nakedness be exposed on it.'

20:1-17 ■ LONG-LASTING LAWS

The Ten Commandments given here and in Deuteronomy 5 form a central core of morality, a major advance from other legal codes of the day. The phrase "Judaeo-Christian ethics", heard often in U.S. courtrooms and legislative chambers, refers to the broad moral principles derived from laws outlined here and in the next three books.

■ THE COVENANT
WHAT DIFFERENCE DOES A STONE TABLET MAKE?

INSIGHT

"NOW IF YOU OBEY ME FULLY AND KEEP MY COVENANT, THEN OUT OF ALL NATIONS YOU WILL BE MY TREASURED POSSESSION." ■ 19:5

Many scholars call the next few chapters the most pivotal section of the Old Testament. The Israelites, called before a trembling and smoking mountain by loud trumpet blasts, were about to receive something unique in all history: a stone document to be deposited in the most valuable piece of furniture in the nation, the ark of the covenant. What made a stone tablet so valuable? The "covenant" it summarised was sacred, signed by the hand of God himself.

And yet someone who simply turned to Exodus and started reading the contents of the covenant might have trouble understanding all the fuss. The covenant begins with the familiar Ten Commandments. It proceeds from there to rules on cursing parents and knocking out teeth, oddly mixed in with rules on interest rates and cooking young goats in their mothers' milk. What is so special, after all, about the laws and instructions described here?

Since we don't normally communicate on stone tablets today, the question "What made a stone tablet so valuable?" might better be rephrased, "What makes a piece of paper valuable?" Seen in that light, our society, like the Israelites', stakes an awful lot on certain pieces of paper. Take just three examples: an ancient charter, a birth certificate and a marriage certificate.

■ MAGNA CARTA

In January 1215, the King of England, King John, signed the famous Magna Carta. Similar in aim to the American Constitution, this was a charter securing the political and personal liberties of the English people. Designed to secure justice, it was a revolutionary document in its time. Amongst others, it states that no subject was to be punished without fair trial; punishment was to be proportionate to the offence; justice was not to be bought by or denied to anyone; additional taxation by the King was not allowed without Parliament's consent.

The Government of this country and its legal system have developed considerably since then, and the Magna Carta is now something only read about in history textbooks. The principles of justice and fair government, however, have been absorbed and built upon.

For Israel, the covenant was much more than a great charter. Details of the law came out in three main places: here at Sinai (Exodus and Leviticus), during the wilderness wanderings (Numbers), and on the plains of Moab (Deuteronomy). The complete legal code, far longer than either the Magna Carta or the American Constitution, extended from the grand sweep of national policy to petty disputes of living together. God was shaping an entire culture for a group of homeless pilgrims. In all, 613 separate commands ordered their political, social, and spiritual lives.

b 24 Traditionally peace offerings

21

"These are the laws you are to set before them:

■ Hebrew Servants

2"If you buy a Hebrew servant, he is to serve you for six years. But in the seventh year, he shall go free, without paying anything. 3If he comes alone, he is to go free alone; but if he has a wife when he comes, she is to go with him. 4If his master gives him a wife and she bears him sons or daughters, the woman and her children shall belong to her master, and only the man shall go free.

5"But if the servant declares, 'I love my master and my wife and children and do not want to go free,' 6then his master must take him before the judges.*a* He shall take him to the door or the door-post and pierce his ear with an awl. Then he will be his servant for life.

7"If a man sells his daughter as a servant, she is not to go free as menservants do. 8If she does not please the master who has selected her for himself,*b* he must let her be redeemed. He has no right to sell her to foreigners, because he has broken faith with her. 9If he selects her for his son, he must grant her the rights of a daughter. 10If he marries another woman, he must not deprive the first one of her food, clothing and marital rights. 11If he does not provide her with these three things, she is to go free, without any payment of money.

■ Personal Injuries

12"Anyone who strikes a man and kills him shall surely be put to death. 13However, if he does not do it intentionally, but God lets it happen, he is to flee to a place I will designate. 14But if a man schemes and kills another man deliberately, take him away from my altar and put him to death.

15"Anyone who attacks*c* his father or his mother must be put to death.

16"Anyone who kidnaps another and either sells him or still has him when he is caught must be put to death.

Other nations were haunted by the unpredictability of their gods. Who could tell what would anger or please them? But because of the covenant, Israelites knew exactly what God required and where they stood before him. They had a basis for trust and security as a nation.

■ BIRTH CERTIFICATE
This piece of paper, with its fancy script, sits in a file drawer 99 per cent of the time. But when you need it, you really need it. It can prove that a young-looking person deserves a driver's licence or that an older person qualifies for State benefits. It establishes your rights as a citizen. A birth certificate is valuable indeed.

For Israel, the covenant established its birth as a nation. God said that he had chosen the children of Israel as a treasured possession (19:5–6). He wanted a nation unlike any other, a model society centred around a commitment to him. He needed a pure people, kept separate.

The next few books of the Bible spell out the obligations, but also the rewards, of being God's chosen people, his "family". If they obeyed, the Israelites would live free from diseases, their crops would grow bountifully, their women would give birth to many children, their armies would prove victorious — in short, they would enjoy unprecedented national wealth and security (23:20–28). The covenant defined those benefits — all part of being born as the children of God.

■ MARRIAGE CERTIFICATE
Marriage is far more than a piece of paper, surely. It involves love and trust, sexuality, the thousand details involved in two people sharing life together. But in the eyes of the law, marriage requires a piece of paper. The document makes formal and legal the most intimate, personal relationship human beings ever have.

Later, the prophets Hosea, Jeremiah, and Ezekiel would poignantly compare the covenant to marriage. They pointed out that Israel's treatment of God amounted to adultery, and they called the nation back to its original covenant. The laws listed in numbing detail are merely the formal expression of a love relationship between God and his people.

Pieces of paper define the boundaries of a relationship, but in no way can they express it adequately. You cannot get an adequate picture of life in the United States by reading the Constitution's dry prose, nor can you understand the mystery of marriage by studying a certificate in a county archive. In the same way, the laws and rules in the Book of the Covenant surely do not present a complete picture of life in a nation bound to God. But the covenant, and the context in which it came, show much about what God desired from his followers.

□ LIFE QUESTIONS:
Do you own any valuable papers that express a kind of "covenant"? If you drew up a covenant between yourself and God, what would it say?

---

a 6 Or before God   *b* 8 Or master so that he does not choose her   *c* 15 Or kills

17"Anyone who curses his father or mother must be put to death.

18"If men quarrel and one hits the other with a stone or with his fist[d] and he does not die but is confined to bed, 19the one who struck the blow will not be held responsible if the other gets up and walks around outside with his staff; however, he must pay the injured man for the loss of his time and see that he is completely healed.

20"If a man beats his male or female slave with a rod and the slave dies as a direct result, he must be punished, 21but he is not to be punished if the slave gets up after a day or two, since the slave is his property.

22"If men who are fighting hit a pregnant woman and she gives birth prematurely[e] but there is no serious injury, the offender must be fined whatever the woman's husband demands and the court allows. 23But if there is serious injury, you are to take life for life, 24eye for eye, tooth for tooth, hand for hand, foot for foot, 25burn for burn, wound for wound, bruise for bruise.

26"If a man hits a manservant or maidservant in the eye and destroys it, he must let the servant go free to compensate for the eye. 27And if he knocks out the tooth of a manservant or maidservant, he must let the servant go free to compensate for the tooth.

28"If a bull gores a man or a woman to death, the bull must be stoned to death, and its meat must not be eaten. But the owner of the bull will not be held responsible. 29If, however, the bull has had the habit of goring and the owner has been warned but has not kept it penned up and it kills a man or woman, the bull must be stoned and the owner also must be put to death. 30However, if payment is demanded of him, he may redeem his life by paying whatever is demanded. 31This law also applies if the bull gores a son or a daughter. 32If the bull gores a male or female slave, the owner must pay thirty shekels[f] of silver to the master of the slave, and the bull must be stoned.

33"If a man uncovers a pit or digs one and fails to cover it and an ox or a donkey falls into it, 34the owner of the pit must pay for the loss; he must pay its owner, and the dead animal will be his.

35"If a man's bull injures the bull of another and it dies, they are to sell the live one and divide both the money and the dead animal equally. 36However,

if it was known that the bull had the habit of goring, yet the owner did not keep it penned up, the owner must pay, animal for animal, and the dead animal will be his.

■ Protection of Property

22 "If a man steals an ox or a sheep and slaughters it or sells it, he must pay back five head of cattle for the ox and four sheep for the sheep.

2"If a thief is caught breaking in and is struck so that he dies, the defender is not guilty of bloodshed; 3but if it happens[a] after sunrise, he is guilty of bloodshed.

"A thief must certainly make restitution, but if he has nothing, he must be sold to pay for his theft.

4"If the stolen animal is found alive in his possession—whether ox or donkey or sheep—he must pay back double.

5"If a man grazes his livestock in a field or vineyard and lets them stray and they graze in another man's field, he must make restitution from the best of his own field or vineyard.

6"If a fire breaks out and spreads into thornbushes so that it burns shocks of grain or standing corn or the whole field, the one who started the fire must make restitution.

7"If a man gives his neighbour silver or goods for safekeeping and they are stolen from the neighbour's house, the thief, if he is caught, must pay back double. 8But if the thief is not found, the owner of the house must appear before the judges[b] to determine whether he has laid his hands on the other man's property. 9In all cases of illegal possession of an ox, a donkey, a sheep, a garment, or any other lost property about which somebody says, 'This is mine,' both parties are to bring their cases before the judges. The one whom the judges declare[c] guilty must pay back double to his neighbour.

10"If a man gives a donkey, an ox, a sheep or any other animal to his neighbour for safekeeping and it dies or is injured or is taken away while no-one is looking, 11the issue between them will be settled by the taking of an oath before the LORD that the neighbour did not lay his hands on the other person's property. The owner is to accept this, and no restitution is required. 12But if the animal was stolen from the neighbour, he must make restitution to the owner. 13If it was torn to pieces by a wild animal, he shall bring in the remains as evidence and he will not be required to pay for the torn animal.

14"If a man borrows an animal from his neighbour and it is injured or dies while the owner is not

d 18 Or with a tool   e 22 Or she has a miscarriage   f 32 That is, about 12 ounces (about 0.3 kilogram)   a 3 Or if he strikes him   b 8 Or before God; also in verse 9   c 9 Or whom God declares present, he must make restitution. ¹⁵But if the owner is with the animal, the borrower will not have to pay. If the animal was hired, the money paid for the hire covers the loss.

■ Social Responsibility

¹⁶"If a man seduces a virgin who is not pledged to be married and sleeps with her, he must pay the bride-price, and she shall be his wife. ¹⁷If her father absolutely refuses to give her to him, he must still pay the bride-price for virgins.

¹⁸"Do not allow a sorceress to live.

¹⁹"Anyone who has sexual relations with an animal must be put to death.

²⁰"Whoever sacrifices to any god other than the LORD must be destroyed.ᵈ

²¹"Do not ill-treat an alien or oppress him, for you were aliens in Egypt.

²²"Do not take advantage of a widow or an orphan. ²³If you do and they cry out to me, I will certainly hear their cry. ²⁴My anger will be aroused, and I will kill you with the sword; your wives will become widows and your children fatherless.

²⁵"If you lend money to one of my people among you who is needy, do not be like a money-lender; charge him no interest.ᵉ ²⁶If you take your neighbour's cloak as a pledge, return it to him by sunset, ²⁷because his cloak is the only covering he has for his body. What else will he sleep in? When he cries out to me, I will hear, for I am compassionate.

²⁸"Do not blaspheme Godᶠ or curse the ruler of your people.

²⁹"Do not hold back offerings from your granaries or your vats.ᵍ

"You must give me the firstborn of your sons. ³⁰Do the same with your cattle and your sheep. Let them stay with their mothers for seven days, but give them to me on the eighth day.

³¹"You are to be my holy people. So do not eat the meat of an animal torn by wild beasts; throw it to the dogs.

■ Laws of Justice and Mercy

23 "Do not spread false reports. Do not help a wicked man by being a malicious witness.

²"Do not follow the crowd in doing wrong. When you give testimony in a lawsuit, do not pervert justice by siding with the crowd, ³and do not show favouritism to a poor man in his lawsuit.

⁴"If you come across your enemy's ox or donkey wandering off, be sure to take it back to him. ⁵If you see the donkey of someone who hates you fallen down under its load, do not leave it there; be sure you help him with it.

⁶"Do not deny justice to your poor people in their lawsuits. ⁷Have nothing to do with a false charge and do not put an innocent or honest person to death, for I will not acquit the guilty.

⁸"Do not accept a bribe, for a bribe blinds those who see and twists the words of the righteous.

⁹"Do not oppress an alien; you yourselves know how it feels to be aliens, because you were aliens in Egypt.

■ Sabbath Laws

¹⁰"For six years you are to sow your fields and harvest the crops, ¹¹but during the seventh year let the land lie unploughed and unused. Then the poor among your people may get food from it, and the wild animals may eat what they leave. Do the same with your vineyard and your olive grove.

¹²"Six days do your work, but on the seventh day do not work, so that your ox and your donkey may rest and the slave born in your household, and the alien as well, may be refreshed.

¹³"Be careful to do everything I have said to you. Do not invoke the names of other gods; do not let them be heard on your lips.

■ The Three Annual Festivals

¹⁴"Three times a year you are to celebrate a festival to me.

¹⁵"Celebrate the Feast of Unleavened Bread; for seven days eat bread made without yeast, as I commanded you. Do this at the appointed time in the month of Abib, for in that month you came out of Egypt.

"No-one is to appear before me empty-handed.

¹⁶"Celebrate the Feast of Harvest with the firstfruits of the crops you sow in your field.

"Celebrate the Feast of Ingathering at the end of the year, when you gather in your crops from the field.

¹⁷"Three times a year all the men are to appear before the Sovereign LORD.

¹⁸"Do not offer the blood of a sacrifice to me along with anything containing yeast.

"The fat of my festival offerings must not be kept until morning.

¹⁹"Bring the best of the firstfruits of your soil to the house of the LORD your God.

"Do not cook a young goat in its mother's milk.

■ God's Angel to Prepare the Way

²⁰"See, I am sending an angel ahead of you to guard you along the way and to bring you to the place I have prepared. ²¹Pay attention to him and listen to what he says. Do not rebel against him; he will not forgive your rebellion, since my Name is in him. ²²If you listen carefully to what he says and do all that I say, I will be an enemy to your enemies and will oppose those who oppose you. ²³My angel will go ahead of you and bring you into the land of the Amorites, Hittites, Perizzites, Canaanites, Hivites and Jebusites, and I will wipe them out. ²⁴Do not bow down before their gods or worship them or follow their practices. You must demolish them and break their sacred stones to pieces. ²⁵Worship the LORD your God, and his blessing will be on your food and water. I will take away sickness from among you, ²⁶and none will miscarry or be barren in your land. I will give you a full life span.

²⁷"I will send my terror ahead of you and throw into confusion every nation you encounter. I will make all your enemies turn their backs and run. ²⁸I will send the hornet ahead of you to drive the Hivites, Canaanites and Hittites out of your way. ²⁹But I will not drive them out in a single year, because the land would become desolate and the wild animals

---

ᵈ20 The Hebrew term refers to the irrevocable giving over of things or persons to the LORD, often by totally destroying them.   ᵉ25 Or excessive interest
ᶠ28 Or Do not revile the judges   ᵍ29 The meaning of the Hebrew for this phrase is uncertain.

too numerous for you. 30Little by little I will drive them out before you, until you have increased enough to take possession of the land.

31"I will establish your borders from the Red Sea*a* to the Sea of the Philistines,*b* and from the desert to the River.*c* I will hand over to you the people who live in the land and you will drive them out before you. 32Do not make a covenant with them or with their gods. 33Do not let them live in your land, or they will cause you to sin against me, because the worship of their gods will certainly be a snare to you."

■ The Covenant Confirmed

24 Then he said to Moses, "Come up to the LORD, you and Aaron, Nadab and Abihu, and seventy of the elders of Israel. You are to worship at a distance, 2but Moses alone is to approach the LORD; the others must not come near. And the people may not come up with him."

3When Moses went and told the people all the LORD's words and laws, they responded with one voice, "Everything the LORD has said we will do." 4Moses then wrote down everything the LORD had said.

He got up early the next morning and built an altar at the foot of the mountain and set up twelve stone pillars representing the twelve tribes of Israel. 5Then he sent young Israelite men, and they offered burnt offerings and sacrificed young bulls as fellowship offerings*a* to the LORD. 6Moses took half of the blood and put it in bowls, and the other half he sprinkled on the altar. 7Then he took the Book of the Covenant and read it to the people. They responded, "We will do everything the LORD has said; we will obey."

8Moses then took the blood, sprinkled it on the people and said, "This is the blood of the covenant that the LORD has made with you in accordance with all these words."

24:8 ■ COVENANT BLOOD
This chapter depicts one of the most important transactions in Israel's history. Since Aaron and his sons had not yet been named or consecrated, Moses served as priest for the dramatic personal encounter with God. A unique sacrifice formally set Israel apart as the people of God and laid the foundation for all the sacrifices to follow.

The New Testament applies the very phraseology from this solemn ceremony to the new covenant made possible by Christ's sacrifice. The phrase "blood of the covenant" appears six times in the New Testament, in each case referring to the death of Christ. Jesus himself used the phrase at the Last Supper (Matthew 26:28), and it became a part of the ceremony of the Lord's Supper.

9Moses and Aaron, Nadab and Abihu, and the seventy elders of Israel went up 10and saw the God of Israel. Under his feet was something like a pavement made of sapphire,*b* clear as the sky itself. 11But God did not raise his hand against these leaders of the Israelites; they saw God, and they ate and drank.

12The LORD said to Moses, "Come up to me on the mountain and stay here, and I will give you the tablets of stone, with the law and commands I have written for their instruction."

13Then Moses set out with Joshua his assistant, and Moses went up on the mountain of God. 14He said to the elders, "Wait here for us until we come back to you. Aaron and Hur are with you, and anyone involved in a dispute can go to them."

15When Moses went up on the mountain, the cloud covered it, 16and the glory of the LORD settled on Mount Sinai. For six days the cloud covered the mountain, and on the seventh day the LORD called to Moses from within the cloud. 17To the Israelites the glory of the LORD looked like a consuming fire on top of the mountain. 18Then Moses entered the cloud as he went up on the mountain. And he stayed on the mountain forty days and forty nights.

■ Offerings for the Tabernacle

25 The LORD said to Moses, 2"Tell the Israelites to bring me an offering. You are to receive the offering for me from each man whose heart prompts him to give. 3These are the offerings you are to receive from them: gold, silver and bronze; 4blue, purple and scarlet yarn and fine linen; goat hair; 5ram skins dyed red and hides of sea cows;*a* acacia wood; 6olive oil for the light; spices for the anointing oil and for the fragrant incense; 7and onyx stones and other gems to be mounted on the ephod and breastpiece.

8"Then have them make a sanctuary for me, and I will dwell among them. 9Make this tabernacle and all its furnishings exactly like the pattern I will show you.

25:8 ■ THE SKILLS OF CIVILISATION
The children of Jacob, or Israel, had arrived in Egypt as a band of nomads. But 400 years in an advanced culture permitted them time to master the arts and trades of civilisation. Crafting the sacred objects of the tabernacle put all these learned skills to use. In addition, God gave specific abilities to some key workmen (see 31:1–6).

■ The Ark
10"Have them make a chest of acacia wood — two and a half cubits long, a cubit and a half wide, and a cubit and a half high.*b* 11Overlay it with pure gold, both inside and out, and make a gold moulding around it. 12Cast four gold rings for it and fasten them to its four feet, with two rings on one side and two rings on the other. 13Then make poles of acacia wood and overlay them with gold. 14Insert the poles into the rings on the sides of the chest to carry it. 15The poles are to remain in the rings of this ark; they are not to be removed. 16Then put in the ark the Testimony, which I will give you.

---

a31 Hebrew *Yam Suph*; that is, Sea of Reeds   *b31* That is, the Mediterranean   *c31* That is, the Euphrates   *a5* Traditionally *peace offerings*
b10 Or *lapis lazuli*   *a5* That is, large aquatic mammals   *b10* That is, about 3¾ feet (about 1.1 metres) long and 2¼ feet (about 0.7 metre) wide and high

¹⁷"Make an atonement cover*c* of pure gold—two and a half cubits long and a cubit and a half wide.*d* ¹⁸And make two cherubim out of hammered gold at the ends of the cover. ¹⁹Make one cherub on one end and the second cherub on the other; make the cherubim of one piece with the cover, at the two ends. ²⁰The cherubim are to have their wings spread upwards, overshadowing the cover with them. The cherubim are to face each other, looking towards the cover. ²¹Place the cover on top of the ark and put in the ark the Testimony, which I will give you. ²²There, above the cover between the two cherubim that are over the ark of the Testimony, I will meet with you and give you all my commands for the Israelites.

■ The Table

²³"Make a table of acacia wood—two cubits long, a cubit wide and a cubit and a half high.*e* ²⁴Overlay it with pure gold and make a gold moulding around it. ²⁵Also make around it a rim a handbreadth*f* wide and put a gold moulding on the rim. ²⁶Make four gold rings for the table and fasten them to the four corners, where the four legs are. ²⁷The rings are to be close to the rim to hold the poles used in carrying the table. ²⁸Make the poles of acacia wood, overlay them with gold and carry the table with them. ²⁹And make its plates and dishes of pure gold, as well as its pitchers and bowls for the pouring out of offerings. ³⁰Put the bread of the Presence on this table to be before me at all times.

■ WHEN GOD WAS OBVIOUS
FEW ATHEISTS, BUT MANY REBELS

INSIGHT

TO THE ISRAELITES THE GLORY OF THE LORD LOOKED LIKE A CONSUMING FIRE ON TOP OF THE MOUNTAIN. ■ 24:17

Why doesn't God intervene more? Why doesn't he directly feed the hungry, heal all the sick and stop all wars? If God really exists, at least why doesn't he make himself more obvious?

People who ask such questions often assume that if God ever did spectacularly reveal himself, all doubts would vanish. Everyone would line up to believe in him.

■ ASTONISHING REACTIONS
Exodus tells of a time when God made himself perfectly obvious. The plagues on Egypt revealed his mighty power. An enormous miracle at the Red Sea provided sensational deliverance. A recurring miracle supplied food for the Israelites every morning. And, if questions about God's existence arose, doubters needed only to look to the ever-present glory cloud or pillar of fire. It must have been hard to be an atheist in those days.

Yet every instance of God's faithfulness seemed to summon up astonishing human *un*faithfulness. The same Israelites who had watched God crush a pharaoh quaked at the first sign of Egyptian chariots. Three days after a miraculous escape across the Red Sea they were grumbling to Moses and God about water supplies.

A month or so later, when hunger pangs began to gnaw at them, they bitterly complained, "If only we had died by the LORD's hand in Egypt! There we sat round pots of meat and ate all the food we wanted, but you have brought us out into this desert to starve this entire assembly to death" (16:3). God responded with a provision of manna (that would continue for 40 years) and quail, but the Israelites were soon complaining about the water supplies again.

■ THE GREAT REBELLION
Exodus 32 shows the Israelites at their worst. People who had eaten manna for breakfast, who had just solemnly agreed to keep every word of the covenant, who were at that moment standing beside a mountain stormy with the Lord's presence—those very people proceeded to melt down their gold jewellery and flagrantly flout the first commandment.

"Stiff-necked," God called the Israelites as he burned in anger against them. Only Moses' eloquent appeal saved their lives.

The history of the Israelites should nail a coffin lid on the notion that impressive displays of God's power will guarantee faith. (Jesus would later say, "If they do not listen to Moses and the Prophets, they will not be convinced even if someone rises from the dead," Luke 16:31.) People who had everyday proof of God demonstrated only one thing: the monotonous consistency of human nature.

The offenders would pay for their acts by wandering for 40 years in a desolate wilderness while a new, untainted generation grew up to replace them. But a pattern was beginning to emerge: if the Israelites failed God in the shadow of Mount Sinai, how would they possibly withstand the seduction of new cultures in the promised land? The next generation, too, would fail God, as would all their descendants. The old covenant, as Paul would so convincingly argue in the book of Galatians, succeeded mainly by proving undeniably the need for a new one.

□ LIFE QUESTIONS:
Do you ever have doubts about God's existence? What would it take to completely convince you?

---

c 17 Traditionally *a mercy seat*   *d 17* That is, about 3¾ feet (about 1.1 metres) long and 2¼ feet (about 0.7 metre) wide   *e 23* That is, about 3 feet (about 0.9 metre) long and 1½ feet (about 0.5 metre) wide and 2¼ feet (about 0.7 metre) high   *f 25* That is, about 3 inches (about 8 centimetres)

The Lampstand

31"Make a lampstand of pure gold and hammer it out, base and shaft; its flowerlike cups, buds and blossoms shall be of one piece with it. 32Six branches are to extend from the sides of the lampstand — three on one side and three on the other. 33Three cups shaped like almond flowers with buds and blossoms are to be on one branch, three on the next branch, and the same for all six branches extending from the lampstand. 34And on the lampstand there are to be four cups shaped like almond flowers with buds and blossoms. 35One bud shall be under the first pair of branches extending from the lampstand, a second bud under the second pair, and a third bud under the third pair — six branches in all. 36The buds and branches shall all be of one piece with the lampstand, hammered out of pure gold.

37"Then make its seven lamps and set them up on it so that they light the space in front of it. 38Its wick trimmers and trays are to be of pure gold. 39A talent*g* of pure gold is to be used for the lampstand and all these accessories. 40See that you make them according to the pattern shown you on the mountain.

The Tabernacle

26 "Make the tabernacle with ten curtains of finely twisted linen and blue, purple and scarlet yarn, with cherubim worked into them by a skilled craftsman. 2All the curtains are to be the same size — twenty-eight cubits long and four cubits wide.*a* 3Join five of the curtains together, and do the same with the other five. 4Make loops of blue material along the edge of the end curtain in one set, and do the same with the end curtain in the other set. 5Make fifty loops on one curtain and fifty loops on the end curtain of the other set, with the loops opposite each other. 6Then make fifty gold clasps and use them to fasten the curtains together so that the tabernacle is a unit.

7"Make curtains of goat hair for the tent over the tabernacle — eleven altogether. 8All eleven curtains are to be the same size — thirty cubits long and four cubits wide.*b* 9Join five of the curtains together into one set and the other six into another set. Fold the sixth curtain double at the front of the tent. 10Make fifty loops along the edge of the end curtain in one set and also along the edge of the end curtain in the other set. 11Then make fifty bronze clasps and put them in the loops to fasten the tent together as a unit. 12As for the additional length of the tent curtains, the half curtain that is left over is to hang down at the rear of the tabernacle. 13The tent curtains will be a cubit*c* longer on both sides; what is left will hang over the sides of the tabernacle so as to cover it. 14Make for the tent a covering of ram skins dyed red, and over that a covering of hides of sea cows.*d*

15"Make upright frames of acacia wood for the tabernacle. 16Each frame is to be ten cubits long and a cubit and a half wide,*e* 17with two projections set parallel to each other. Make all the frames of the tabernacle in this way. 18Make twenty frames for the south side of the tabernacle 19and make forty silver bases to go under them — two bases for each frame, one under each projection. 20For the other side, the north side of the tabernacle, make twenty frames 21and forty silver bases — two under each frame. 22Make six frames for the far end, that is, the west end of the tabernacle, 23and make two frames for the corners at the far end. 24At these two corners they must be double from the bottom all the way to the top, and fitted into a single ring; both shall be like that. 25So there will be eight frames and sixteen silver bases — two under each frame.

26"Also make crossbars of acacia wood: five for the frames on one side of the tabernacle, 27five for those on the other side, and five for the frames on the west, at the far end of the tabernacle. 28The centre crossbar is to extend from end to end at the middle of the frames. 29Overlay the frames with gold and make gold rings to hold the crossbars. Also overlay the crossbars with gold.

30"Set up the tabernacle according to the plan shown you on the mountain.

31"Make a curtain of blue, purple and scarlet yarn and finely twisted linen, with cherubim worked into it by a skilled craftsman. 32Hang it with gold hooks on four posts of acacia wood overlaid with gold and standing on four silver bases. 33Hang the curtain from the clasps and place the ark of the Testimony behind the curtain. The curtain will separate the Holy Place from the Most Holy Place. 34Put the atonement cover on the ark of the Testimony in the Most Holy Place. 35Place the table outside the curtain on the north side of the tabernacle and put the lampstand opposite it on the south side.

26:33 ■ A TORN CURTAIN

The thick curtain described here separated the Holy Place from the Most Holy Place. Anyone who ventured beyond that curtain would die. The New Testament, however, records that at Jesus' crucifixion the curtain tore in two, from top to bottom. The tearing symbolised what Christ had accomplished: he broke down the separation between God and humanity (Matthew 27:51; Hebrews 10:20).

36"For the entrance to the tent make a curtain of blue, purple and scarlet yarn and finely twisted linen — the work of an embroiderer. 37Make gold hooks for this curtain and five posts of acacia wood overlaid with gold. And cast five bronze bases for them.

The Altar of Burnt Offering

27 "Build an altar of acacia wood, three cubits*a* high; it is to be square, five cubits long and five cubits wide.*b* 2Make a horn at each of the four corners, so that the horns and the altar are of one piece, and overlay the altar with bronze. 3Make all its utensils of bronze — its pots to remove the ashes, and its shovels, sprinkling bowls, meat forks and firepans. 4Make a grating for it, a bronze network, and make a bronze ring at each of the four corners of the

---

g 39 That is, about 75 pounds (about 34 kilograms)   *a 2* That is, about 42 feet (about 13 metres) long and 6 feet (about 1.8 metres) wide   *b 8* That is, about 45 feet (about 13.5 metres) long and 6 feet (about 1.8 metres) wide   *c 13* That is, about 1½ feet (about 0.5 metre)   *d 14* That is, large aquatic mammals   *e 16* That is, about 15 feet (about 4.5 metres) long and 2¼ feet (about 0.7 metre) wide   *a 1* That is, about 4½ feet (about 1.4 metres) *b 1* That is, about 7½ feet (about 2.3 metres) long and wide network. 5Put it under the ledge of the altar so that it is halfway up the altar. 6Make poles of acacia wood for the altar and overlay them with bronze. 7The poles are to be inserted into the rings so they will be on two sides of the altar when it is carried. 8Make the altar hollow, out of boards. It is to be made just as you were shown on the mountain.

The Courtyard

9"Make a courtyard for the tabernacle. The south side shall be a hundred cubits^c long and is to have curtains of finely twisted linen, 10with twenty posts and twenty bronze bases and with silver hooks and bands on the posts. 11The north side shall also be a hundred cubits long and is to have curtains, with twenty posts and twenty bronze bases and with silver hooks and bands on the posts.

12"The west end of the courtyard shall be fifty cubits^d wide and have curtains, with ten posts and ten bases. 13On the east end, towards the sunrise, the courtyard shall also be fifty cubits wide. 14Curtains fifteen cubits^e long are to be on one side of the entrance, with three posts and three bases, 15and curtains fifteen cubits long are to be on the other side, with three posts and three bases.

16"For the entrance to the courtyard, provide a curtain twenty cubits^f long, of blue, purple and scarlet yarn and finely twisted linen — the work of an embroiderer — with four posts and four bases. 17All the posts around the courtyard are to have silver bands and hooks, and bronze bases. 18The courtyard shall be a hundred cubits long and fifty cubits wide,^{g} with curtains of finely twisted linen five cubits^b high, and with bronze bases. 19All the other articles used in the service of the tabernacle, whatever their function, including all the tent pegs for it and those for the courtyard, are to be of bronze.

Oil for the Lampstand

20"Command the Israelites to bring you clear oil of pressed olives for the light so that the lamps may be kept burning. 21In the Tent of Meeting, outside the curtain that is in front of the Testimony, Aaron and his sons are to keep the lamps burning before the LORD from evening till morning. This is to be a lasting ordinance among the Israelites for the generations to come.

The Priestly Garments

28 "Have Aaron your brother brought to you from among the Israelites, with his sons Nadab and Abihu, Eleazar and Ithamar, so that they may serve me as priests. 2Make sacred garments for your brother Aaron, to give him dignity and honour. 3Tell all the skilled men to whom I have given wisdom in such matters that they are to make garments for Aaron, for his consecration, so that he may serve me as priest. 4These are the garments they are to make: a breastpiece, an ephod, a robe, a woven tunic, a turban and a sash. They are to make these sacred garments for your brother Aaron and his sons, so that they may serve me as priests. 5Make them use

gold, and blue, purple and scarlet yarn, and fine linen.

The Ephod

6"Make the ephod of gold, and of blue, purple and scarlet yarn, and of finely twisted linen — the work of a skilled craftsman. 7It is to have two shoulder pieces attached to two of its corners, so that it can be fastened. 8Its skilfully woven waistband is to be like it — of one piece with the ephod and made with gold, and with blue, purple and scarlet yarn, and with finely twisted linen.

9"Take two onyx stones and engrave on them the names of the sons of Israel 10in the order of their birth — six names on one stone and the remaining six on the other. 11Engrave the names of the sons of Israel on the two stones the way a gem cutter engraves a seal. Then mount the stones in gold filigree settings 12and fasten them on the shoulder pieces of the ephod as memorial stones for the sons of Israel. Aaron is to bear the names on his shoulders as a memorial before the LORD. 13Make gold filigree settings 14and two braided chains of pure gold, like a rope, and attach the chains to the settings.

The Breastpiece

15"Fashion a breastpiece for making decisions — the work of a skilled craftsman. Make it like the ephod: of gold, and of blue, purple and scarlet yarn, and of finely twisted linen. 16It is to be square — a span^a long and a span wide — and folded double. 17Then mount four rows of precious stones on it. In the first row there shall be a ruby, a topaz and a beryl; 18in the second row a turquoise, a sapphire^b and an emerald; 19in the third row a jacinth, an agate and an amethyst; 20in the fourth row a chrysolite, an onyx and a jasper.^{c} Mount them in gold filigree settings. 21There are to be twelve stones, one for each of the names of the sons of Israel, each engraved like a seal with the name of one of the twelve tribes.

22"For the breastpiece make braided chains of pure gold, like a rope. 23Make two gold rings for it and fasten them to two corners of the breastpiece. 24Fasten the two gold chains to the rings at the corners of the breastpiece, 25and the other ends of the chains to the two settings, attaching them to the shoulder pieces of the ephod at the front. 26Make two gold rings and attach them to the other two corners of the breastpiece on the inside edge next to the ephod. 27Make two more gold rings and attach them to the bottom of the shoulder pieces on the front of the ephod, close to the seam just above the waistband of the ephod. 28The rings of the breastpiece are to be tied to the rings of the ephod with blue cord, connecting it to the waistband, so that the breastpiece will not swing out from the ephod.

29"Whenever Aaron enters the Holy Place, he will bear the names of the sons of Israel over his heart on the breastpiece of decision as a continuing memorial before the LORD. 30Also put the Urim and the Thummim in the breastpiece, so they may be over Aaron's heart whenever he enters the presence of the LORD. Thus Aaron will always bear the means of

---

^{c}9 That is, about 150 feet (about 46 metres); also in verse 11 ^{d}12 That is, about 75 feet (about 23 metres); also in verse 13 ^{e}14 That is, about 22½ feet (about 6.9 metres); also in verse 15 ^{f}16 That is, about 30 feet (about 9 metres) ^{g}18 That is, about 150 feet (about 46 metres) long and 75 feet (about 23 metres) wide ^{b}18 That is, about 7½ feet (about 2.3 metres) ^{a}16 That is, about 9 inches (about 23 centimetres) ^{b}18 Or lapis lazuli ^{c}20 The precise identification of some of these precious stones is uncertain.

making decisions for the Israelites over his heart before the LORD.

■ Other Priestly Garments

31"Make the robe of the ephod entirely of blue cloth, 32with an opening for the head in its centre. There shall be a woven edge like a collar*d* around this opening, so that it will not tear. 33Make pomegranates of blue, purple and scarlet yarn around the hem of the robe, with gold bells between them. 34The gold bells and the pomegranates are to alternate around the hem of the robe. 35Aaron must wear it when he ministers. The sound of the bells will be heard when he enters the Holy Place before the LORD and when he comes out, so that he will not die.

36"Make a plate of pure gold and engrave on it as on a seal: HOLY TO THE LORD. 37Fasten a blue cord to it to attach it to the turban; it is to be on the front of the turban. 38It will be on Aaron's forehead, and he will bear the guilt involved in the sacred gifts the Israelites consecrate, whatever their gifts may be. It will be on Aaron's forehead continually so that they will be acceptable to the LORD.

39"Weave the tunic of fine linen and make the turban of fine linen. The sash is to be the work of an embroiderer. 40Make tunics, sashes and headbands for Aaron's sons, to give them dignity and honour. 41After you put these clothes on your brother Aaron and his sons, anoint and ordain them. Consecrate them so they may serve me as priests.

42"Make linen undergarments as a covering for the body, reaching from the waist to the thigh. 43Aaron and his sons must wear them whenever they enter the Tent of Meeting or approach the altar to minister in the Holy Place, so that they will not incur guilt and die.

"This is to be a lasting ordinance for Aaron and his descendants.

■ Consecration of the Priests

29 "This is what you are to do to consecrate them, so that they may serve me as priests: Take a young bull and two rams without defect. 2And from fine wheat flour, without yeast, make bread, and cakes mixed with oil, and wafers spread with oil. 3Put them in a basket and present them in it—along with the bull and the two rams. 4Then bring Aaron and his sons to the entrance to the Tent of Meeting and wash them with water. 5Take the garments and dress Aaron with the tunic, the robe of the ephod, the ephod itself and the breastpiece. Fasten the ephod on him by its skilfully woven waistband. 6Put the turban on his head and attach the sacred diadem to the turban. 7Take the anointing oil and anoint him by pouring it on his head. 8Bring his sons and dress them in tunics 9and put headbands on them. Then tie sashes on Aaron and his sons.*a* The priesthood is theirs by a lasting ordinance. In this way you shall ordain Aaron and his sons.

10"Bring the bull to the front of the Tent of Meeting, and Aaron and his sons shall lay their hands on its head. 11Slaughter it in the LORD's presence at the entrance to the Tent of Meeting. 12Take some of the bull's blood and put it on the horns of the altar with your finger, and pour out the rest of it at the base

of the altar. 13Then take all the fat around the inner parts, the covering of the liver, and both kidneys with the fat on them, and burn them on the altar. 14But burn the bull's flesh and its hide and its offal outside the camp. It is a sin offering.

15"Take one of the rams, and Aaron and his sons shall lay their hands on its head. 16Slaughter it and take the blood and sprinkle it against the altar on all sides. 17Cut the ram into pieces and wash the inner parts and the legs, putting them with the head and the other pieces. 18Then burn the entire ram on the altar. It is a burnt offering to the LORD, a pleasing aroma, an offering made to the LORD by fire.

19"Take the other ram, and Aaron and his sons shall lay their hands on its head. 20Slaughter it, take some of its blood and put it on the lobes of the right ears of Aaron and his sons, on the thumbs of their right hands, and on the big toes of their right feet. Then sprinkle blood against the altar on all sides. 21And take some of the blood on the altar and some of the anointing oil and sprinkle it on Aaron and his garments and on his sons and their garments. Then he and his sons and their garments will be consecrated.

29:20 ■ THE WHOLE BODY
As part of their purification, the priests daubed blood on their ears (which hear God's laws), their hands (which do his will), and their toes (which were prepared to follow in his steps).

22"Take from this ram the fat, the fat tail, the fat around the inner parts, the covering of the liver, both kidneys with the fat on them, and the right thigh. (This is the ram for the ordination.) 23From the basket of bread made without yeast, which is before the LORD, take a loaf, and a cake made with oil, and a wafer. 24Put all these in the hands of Aaron and his sons and wave them before the LORD as a wave offering. 25Then take them from their hands and burn them on the altar along with the burnt offering for a pleasing aroma to the LORD, an offering made to the LORD by fire. 26After you take the breast of the ram for Aaron's ordination, wave it before the LORD as a wave offering, and it will be your share.

27"Consecrate those parts of the ordination ram that belong to Aaron and his sons: the breast that was waved and the thigh that was presented. 28This is always to be the regular share from the Israelites for Aaron and his sons. It is the contribution the Israelites are to make to the LORD from their fellowship offerings.*b*

29"Aaron's sacred garments will belong to his descendants so that they can be anointed and ordained in them. 30The son who succeeds him as priest and comes to the Tent of Meeting to minister in the Holy Place is to wear them seven days.

31"Take the ram for the ordination and cook the meat in a sacred place. 32At the entrance to the Tent of Meeting, Aaron and his sons are to eat the meat of the ram and the bread that is in the basket. 33They are to eat these offerings by which atonement was made for their ordination and consecration. But no-

---

*d 32 The meaning of the Hebrew for this word is uncertain.   *a 9 Hebrew; Septuagint *on them*   *b 28 Traditionally *peace offerings* one else may eat them, because they are sacred. [34]And if any of the meat of the ordination ram or any bread is left over till morning, burn it up. It must not be eaten, because it is sacred.

[35]"Do for Aaron and his sons everything I have commanded you, taking seven days to ordain them. [36]Sacrifice a bull each day as a sin offering to make atonement. Purify the altar by making atonement for it, and anoint it to consecrate it. [37]For seven days make atonement for the altar and consecrate it. Then the altar will be most holy, and whatever touches it will be holy.

[38]"This is what you are to offer on the altar regularly each day: two lambs a year old. [39]Offer one in the morning and the other at twilight. [40]With the first lamb offer a tenth of an ephah[c] of fine flour mixed with a quarter of a hin[d] of oil from pressed olives, and a quarter of a hin of wine as a drink offering. [41]Sacrifice the other lamb at twilight with the same grain offering and its drink offering as in the morning — a pleasing aroma, an offering made to the LORD by fire.

[42]"For the generations to come this burnt offering is to be made regularly at the entrance to the Tent of Meeting before the LORD. There I will meet you and speak to you; [43]there also I will meet with the Israelites, and the place will be consecrated by my glory.

[44]"So I will consecrate the Tent of Meeting and the altar and will consecrate Aaron and his sons to serve me as priests. [45]Then I will dwell among the Israelites and be their God. [46]They will know that I am the LORD their God, who brought them out of Egypt so that I might dwell among them. I am the LORD their God.

■ The Altar of Incense

30 "Make an altar of acacia wood for burning incense. [2]It is to be square, a cubit long and a cubit wide, and two cubits high[a] — its horns of one piece with it. [3]Overlay the top and all the sides and the horns with pure gold, and make a gold moulding around it. [4]Make two gold rings for the altar below the moulding — two on opposite sides — to hold the poles used to carry it. [5]Make the poles of acacia wood and overlay them with gold. [6]Put the altar in front of the curtain that is before the ark of the Testimony — before the atonement cover that is over the Testimony — where I will meet with you.

[7]"Aaron must burn fragrant incense on the altar every morning when he tends the lamps. [8]He must burn incense again when he lights the lamps at twilight so that incense will burn regularly before the LORD for the generations to come. [9]Do not offer on this altar any other incense or any burnt offering or grain offering, and do not pour a drink offering on it. [10]Once a year Aaron shall make atonement on its horns. This annual atonement must be made with the blood of the atoning sin offering for the generations to come. It is most holy to the LORD."

■ Atonement Money

[11]Then the LORD said to Moses, [12]"When you take a census of the Israelites to count them, each one

must pay the LORD a ransom for his life at the time he is counted. Then no plague will come on them when you number them. [13]Each one who crosses over to those already counted is to give a half shekel,[b] according to the sanctuary shekel, which weighs twenty gerahs. This half shekel is an offering to the LORD. [14]All who cross over, those twenty years old or more, are to give an offering to the LORD. [15]The rich are not to give more than a half shekel and the poor are not to give less when you make the offering to the LORD to atone for your lives. [16]Receive the atonement money from the Israelites and use it for the service of the Tent of Meeting. It will be a memorial for the Israelites before the LORD, making atonement for your lives."

30:10 ■ JEWISH HOLY DAYS
Orthodox Jews still faithfully honour the Day of Atonement described here, the holy day of Yom Kippur. But the New Testament book of Hebrews reinterprets this period of time as a copy, or shadow, of the real thing to come in Jesus Christ. What a high priest accomplished, through elaborate ceremony, once a year on the Day of Atonement, Christ did once for all (Hebrews 8–9). As a consequence, all of us — not just a purified priest — can confidently "enter the Most Holy Place".

■ Basin for Washing

[17]Then the LORD said to Moses, [18]"Make a bronze basin, with its bronze stand, for washing. Place it between the Tent of Meeting and the altar, and put water in it. [19]Aaron and his sons are to wash their hands and feet with water from it. [20]Whenever they enter the Tent of Meeting, they shall wash with water so that they will not die. Also, when they approach the altar to minister by presenting an offering made to the LORD by fire, [21]they shall wash their hands and feet so that they will not die. This is to be a lasting ordinance for Aaron and his descendants for the generations to come."

■ Anointing Oil

[22]Then the LORD said to Moses, [23]"Take the following fine spices: 500 shekels[c] of liquid myrrh, half as much (that is, 250 shekels) of fragrant cinnamon, 250 shekels of fragrant cane, [24]500 shekels of cassia — all according to the sanctuary shekel — and a hin[d] of olive oil. [25]Make these into a sacred anointing oil, a fragrant blend, the work of a perfumer. It will be the sacred anointing oil. [26]Then use it to anoint the Tent of Meeting, the ark of the Testimony, [27]the table and all its articles, the lampstand and its accessories, the altar of incense, [28]the altar of burnt offering and all its utensils, and the basin with its stand. [29]You shall consecrate them so they will be most holy, and whatever touches them will be holy.

[30]"Anoint Aaron and his sons and consecrate them so they may serve me as priests. [31]Say to the Israelites, 'This is to be my sacred anointing oil for

---

c40 That is, probably about 4 pints (about 2 litres)   d40 That is, probably about 1½ pints (about 1 litre)   a2 That is, about 1½ feet (about 0.5 metre) long and wide and about 3 feet (about 0.9 metre) high   b13 That is, about ⅕ ounce (about 6 grams); also in verse 15   c23 That is, about 12½ pounds (about 6 kilograms)   d24 That is, probably about 6½ pints (about 4 litres) the generations to come. ³²Do not pour it on men's bodies and do not make any oil with the same formula. It is sacred, and you are to consider it sacred. ³³Whoever makes perfume like it and whoever puts it on anyone other than a priest must be cut off from his people.' "

■ Incense

³⁴Then the LORD said to Moses, "Take fragrant spices—gum resin, onycha and galbanum—and pure frankincense, all in equal amounts, ³⁵and make a fragrant blend of incense, the work of a perfumer. It is to be salted and pure and sacred. ³⁶Grind some of it to powder and place it in front of the Testimony in the Tent of Meeting, where I will meet with you. It shall be most holy to you. ³⁷Do not make any incense with this formula for yourselves; consider it holy to the LORD. ³⁸Whoever makes any like it to enjoy its fragrance must be cut off from his people."

■ Bezalel and Oholiab

31 Then the LORD said to Moses, ²"See I have chosen Bezalel son of Uri, the son of Hur, of the tribe of Judah, ³and I have filled him with the Spirit of God, with skill, ability and knowledge in all kinds of crafts—⁴to make artistic designs for work in gold, silver and bronze, ⁵to cut and set stones, to work in wood, and to engage in all kinds of craftsmanship. ⁶Moreover, I have appointed Oholiab son of Ahisamach, of the tribe of Dan, to help him. Also I have given skill to all the craftsmen to make everything I have commanded you: ⁷the Tent of Meeting, the ark of the Testimony with the atonement cover on it, and all the other furnishings of the tent—⁸the table and its articles, the pure gold lampstand and all its accessories, the altar of incense, ⁹the altar of burnt offering and all its utensils, the basin with its stand—¹⁰and also the woven garments, both the sacred garments for Aaron the priest and the garments for his sons when they serve as priests, ¹¹and the anointing oil and fragrant incense for the Holy Place. They are to make them just as I commanded you."

■ The Sabbath

¹²Then the LORD said to Moses, ¹³"Say to the Israelites, 'You must observe my Sabbaths. This will be a sign between me and you for the generations to come, so that you may know that I am the LORD, who makes you holy.ᵃ

¹⁴"'Observe the Sabbath, because it is holy to you. Anyone who desecrates it must be put to death; whoever does any work on that day must be cut off from his people. ¹⁵For six days, work is to be done, but the seventh day is a Sabbath of rest, holy to the LORD. Whoever does any work on the Sabbath day must be put to death. ¹⁶The Israelites are to observe the Sabbath, celebrating it for the generations to come as a lasting covenant. ¹⁷It will be a sign between me and the Israelites for ever, for in six days the LORD made the heavens and the earth, and on the seventh day he abstained from work and rested.' "

¹⁸When the LORD finished speaking to Moses on Mount Sinai, he gave him the two tablets of the Testimony, the tablets of stone inscribed by the finger of God.

■ The Golden Calf

32 When the people saw that Moses was so long in coming down from the mountain, they gathered round Aaron and said, "Come, make us godsᵃ who will go before us. As for this fellow Moses who brought us up out of Egypt, we don't know what has happened to him."

²Aaron answered them, "Take off the gold ear-rings that your wives, your sons and your daughters are wearing, and bring them to me." ³So all the people took off their ear-rings and brought them to Aaron. ⁴He took what they handed him and made it into an idol cast in the shape of a calf, fashioning it with a tool. Then they said, "These are your gods,ᵇ O Israel, who brought you up out of Egypt."

32:4 ■ RECENT DISCOVERY

Not until 1990 did archaeologists unearth the first golden calf in Palestine, and, to their surprise, it stood only a few inches tall. Contrary to popular depictions in films and historical books, Aaron's solid gold calf too may have been very small, but elevated on a pedestal for visual emphasis. Undoubtedly the Israelites knew of the bull-god Apis, one of Egypt's important gods.

Moses stayed on Mount Sinai for nearly six weeks (24:18), which helps explain the Israelites' panicky behaviour. Had Moses died or run away? Would he ever come back? Nevertheless, by flagrantly breaking the second commandment they failed their first test under the new covenant with God.

⁵When Aaron saw this, he built an altar in front of the calf and announced, "Tomorrow there will be a festival to the LORD." ⁶So the next day the people rose early and sacrificed burnt offerings and presented fellowship offerings.ᶜ Afterwards they sat down to eat and drink and got up to indulge in revelry.

⁷Then the LORD said to Moses, "Go down, because your people, whom you brought up out of Egypt, have become corrupt. ⁸They have been quick to turn away from what I commanded them and have made themselves an idol cast in the shape of a calf. They have bowed down to it and sacrificed to it and have said, 'These are your gods, O Israel, who brought you up out of Egypt.'

⁹"I have seen these people," the LORD said to Moses, "and they are a stiff-necked people. ¹⁰Now leave me alone so that my anger may burn against them and that I may destroy them. Then I will make you into a great nation."

¹¹But Moses sought the favour of the LORD his God. "O LORD," he said, "why should your anger burn against your people, whom you brought out of Egypt with great power and a mighty hand? ¹²Why should the Egyptians say, 'It was with evil intent that he brought them out, to kill them in the mountains and to wipe them off the face of the earth'? Turn from your fierce anger; relent and do not bring disaster on your people. ¹³Remember your servants Abraham, Isaac and Israel, to whom you swore by

---

ᵃ13 Or who sanctifies you; or who sets you apart as holy   ᵃ1 Or a god; also in verses 23 and 31   ᵇ4 Or This is your god; also in verse 8
ᶜ6 Traditionally peace offerings

your own self: 'I will make your descendants as numerous as the stars in the sky and I will give your descendants all this land I promised them, and it will be their inheritance for ever.' " ¹⁴Then the LORD relented and did not bring on his people the disaster he had threatened.

¹⁵Moses turned and went down the mountain with the two tablets of the Testimony in his hands. They were inscribed on both sides, front and back. ¹⁶The tablets were the work of God; the writing was the writing of God, engraved on the tablets.

¹⁷When Joshua heard the noise of the people shouting, he said to Moses, "There is the sound of war in the camp."

¹⁸Moses replied:

"It is not the sound of victory,
   it is not the sound of defeat;
   it is the sound of singing that I hear."

¹⁹When Moses approached the camp and saw the calf and the dancing, his anger burned and he threw the tablets out of his hands, breaking them to pieces at the foot of the mountain. ²⁰And he took the calf they had made and burned it in the fire; then he ground it to powder, scattered it on the water and made the Israelites drink it.

²¹He said to Aaron, "What did these people do to you, that you led them into such great sin?"

²²"Do not be angry, my lord," Aaron answered. "You know how prone these people are to evil. ²³They said to me, 'Make us gods who will go before us. As for this fellow Moses who brought us up out of Egypt, we don't know what has happened to him.' ²⁴So I told them, 'Whoever has any gold jewellery, take it off.' Then they gave me the gold, and I threw it into the fire, and out came this calf!"

²⁵Moses saw that the people were running wild and that Aaron had let them get out of control and so become a laughing-stock to their enemies. ²⁶So he stood at the entrance to the camp and said, "Whoever is for the LORD, come to me." And all the Levites rallied to him.

²⁷Then he said to them, "This is what the LORD, the God of Israel, says: 'Each man strap a sword to his side. Go back and forth through the camp from one end to the other, each killing his brother and friend and neighbour.' " ²⁸The Levites did as Moses commanded, and that day about three thousand of the people died. ²⁹Then Moses said, "You have been set apart to the LORD today, for you were against your own sons and brothers, and he has blessed you this day."

³⁰The next day Moses said to the people, "You have committed a great sin. But now I will go up to the LORD; perhaps I can make atonement for your sin."

³¹So Moses went back to the LORD and said, "Oh, what a great sin these people have committed! They have made themselves gods of gold. ³²But now, please forgive their sin—but if not, then blot me out of the book you have written."

³³The LORD replied to Moses, "Whoever has sinned against me I will blot out of my book. ³⁴Now go, lead the people to the place I spoke of, and my angel will go before you. However, when the time comes for me to punish, I will punish them for their sin."

³⁵And the LORD struck the people with a plague because of what they did with the calf Aaron had made.

33 Then the LORD said to Moses, "Leave this place, you and the people you brought up out of Egypt, and go up to the land I promised on oath to Abraham, Isaac and Jacob, saying, 'I will give it to your descendants.' ²I will send an angel before you and drive out the Canaanites, Amorites, Hittites, Perizzites, Hivites and Jebusites. ³Go up to the land flowing with milk and honey. But I will not go with you, because you are a stiff-necked people and I might destroy you on the way."

33:3 ■ WHY THE ISRAELITES?
This remarkable scene shows Moses pleading with God not to abandon the Israelites, his chosen people. Eventually, God did agree to lead them on (verse 17). Why were the children of Israel chosen? Why not some other race? When the Bible touches on the question at all, it gives no comprehensive answer. Usually, the reply boils down to something like this, "I will have mercy on whom I will have mercy" (verse 19). God reserves the right to choose whomever he wants. But Exodus makes one thing clear. Israelites were not chosen because of their bravery or impressiveness or even faithfulness. Their selection was an act of God's pure grace; no-one else can take the credit.

⁴When the people heard these distressing words, they began to mourn and no-one put on any ornaments. ⁵For the LORD had said to Moses, "Tell the Israelites, 'You are a stiff-necked people. If I were to go with you even for a moment, I might destroy you. Now take off your ornaments and I will decide what to do with you.' " ⁶So the Israelites stripped off their ornaments at Mount Horeb.

■ The Tent of Meeting

⁷Now Moses used to take a tent and pitch it outside the camp some distance away, calling it the "tent of meeting". Anyone enquiring of the LORD would go to the tent of meeting outside the camp. ⁸And whenever Moses went out to the tent, all the people rose and stood at the entrances to their tents, watching Moses until he entered the tent. ⁹As Moses went into the tent, the pillar of cloud would come down and stay at the entrance, while the LORD spoke with Moses. ¹⁰Whenever the people saw the pillar of cloud standing at the entrance to the tent, they all stood and worshipped, each at the entrance to his tent. ¹¹The LORD would speak to Moses face to face, as a man speaks with his friend. Then Moses would return to the camp, but his young assistant Joshua son of Nun did not leave the tent.

■ Moses and the Glory of the LORD

¹²Moses said to the LORD, "You have been telling me, 'Lead these people,' but you have not let me know whom you will send with me. You have said,

'I know you by name and you have found favour with me.' 13If you are pleased with me, teach me your ways so I may know you and continue to find favour with you. Remember that this nation is your people."

14The LORD replied, "My Presence will go with you, and I will give you rest."

15Then Moses said to him, "If your Presence does not go with us, do not send us up from here. 16How will anyone know that you are pleased with me and with your people unless you go with us? What else will distinguish me and your people from all the other people on the face of the earth?"

17And the LORD said to Moses, "I will do the very thing you have asked, because I am pleased with you and I know you by name."

18Then Moses said, "Now show me your glory."

19And the LORD said, "I will cause all my goodness to pass in front of you, and I will proclaim my name, the LORD, in your presence. I will have mercy on whom I will have mercy, and I will have compassion on whom I will have compassion. 20But," he said, "you cannot see my face, for no-one may see me and live."

21Then the LORD said, "There is a place near me where you may stand on a rock. 22When my glory passes by, I will put you in a cleft in the rock and cover you with my hand until I have passed by. 23Then I will remove my hand and you will see my back; but my face must not be seen."

■ The New Stone Tablets

34 The LORD said to Moses, "Chisel out two stone tablets like the first ones, and I will write on them the words that were on the first tablets, which you broke. 2Be ready in the morning, and then come up on Mount Sinai. Present yourself to me there on top of the mountain. 3No-one is to come with you or be seen anywhere on the mountain; not even the flocks and herds may graze in front of the mountain."

4So Moses chiselled out two stone tablets like the first ones and went up Mount Sinai early in the morning, as the LORD had commanded him; and he carried the two stone tablets in his hands. 5Then the LORD came down in the cloud and stood there with him and proclaimed his name, the LORD. 6And he passed in front of Moses, proclaiming, "The LORD, the LORD, the compassionate and gracious God, slow

---

34:6-7 ■ DESCRIPTION OF GOD
The self-description of God found in these two verses became for the Jews a profound summary of God's nature. The Old Testament quotes or alludes to this passage more than any other.

---

to anger, abounding in love and faithfulness, 7maintaining love to thousands, and forgiving wickedness, rebellion and sin. Yet he does not leave the guilty unpunished; he punishes the children and their children for the sin of the fathers to the third and fourth generation."

8Moses bowed to the ground at once and

worshipped. 9"O Lord, if I have found favour in your eyes," he said, "then let the Lord go with us. Although this is a stiff-necked people, forgive our wickedness and our sin, and take us as your inheritance."

10Then the LORD said: "I am making a covenant with you. Before all your people I will do wonders never before done in any nation in all the world. The people you live among will see how awesome is the work that I, the LORD, will do for you. 11Obey what I command you today. I will drive out before you the Amorites, Canaanites, Hittites, Perizzites, Hivites and Jebusites. 12Be careful not to make a treaty with those who live in the land where you are going, or they will be a snare among you. 13Break down their altars, smash their sacred stones and cut down their Asherah poles.a 14Do not worship any other god, for the LORD, whose name is Jealous, is a jealous God.

15"Be careful not to make a treaty with those who live in the land; for when they prostitute themselves to their gods and sacrifice to them, they will invite you and you will eat their sacrifices. 16And when you choose some of their daughters as wives for your sons and those daughters prostitute themselves to their gods, they will lead your sons to do the same.

17"Do not make cast idols.

18"Celebrate the Feast of Unleavened Bread. For seven days eat bread made without yeast, as I commanded you. Do this at the appointed time in the month of Abib, for in that month you came out of Egypt.

19"The first offspring of every womb belongs to me, including all the firstborn males of your livestock, whether from herd or flock. 20Redeem the firstborn donkey with a lamb, but if you do not redeem it, break its neck. Redeem all your firstborn sons.

"No-one is to appear before me empty-handed.

21"Six days you shall labour, but on the seventh day you shall rest; even during the ploughing season and harvest you must rest.

22"Celebrate the Feast of Weeks with the firstfruits of the wheat harvest, and the Feast of Ingathering at the turn of the year.b 23Three times a year all your men are to appear before the Sovereign LORD, the God of Israel. 24I will drive out nations before you and enlarge your territory, and no-one will covet your land when you go up three times each year to appear before the LORD your God.

25"Do not offer the blood of a sacrifice to me along with anything containing yeast, and do not let any of the sacrifice from the Passover Feast remain until morning.

26"Bring the best of the firstfruits of your soil to the house of the LORD your God.

"Do not cook a young goat in its mother's milk."

27Then the LORD said to Moses, "Write down these words, for in accordance with these words I have made a covenant with you and with Israel." 28Moses was there with the LORD forty days and forty nights without eating bread or drinking water. And he wrote on the tablets the words of the covenant — the Ten Commandments.

---

a 13 That is, symbols of the goddess Asherah   b 22 That is, in the autumn

■ The Radiant Face of Moses

29When Moses came down from Mount Sinai with the two tablets of the Testimony in his hands, he was not aware that his face was radiant because he had spoken with the LORD. 30When Aaron and all the Israelites saw Moses, his face was radiant, and they were afraid to come near him. 31But Moses called to them; so Aaron and all the leaders of the community came back to him, and he spoke to them. 32Afterwards all the Israelites came near him, and he gave them all the commands the LORD had given him on Mount Sinai.

33When Moses finished speaking to them, he put a veil over his face. 34But whenever he entered the LORD's presence to speak with him, he removed the veil until he came out. And when he came out and told the Israelites what he had been commanded, 35they saw that his face was radiant. Then Moses would put the veil back over his face until he went in to speak with the LORD.

■ Sabbath Regulations

35 Moses assembled the whole Israelite community and said to them, "These are the things the LORD has commanded you to do: 2For six days, work is to be done, but the seventh day shall be your holy day, a Sabbath of rest to the LORD. Whoever does any work on it must be put to death. 3Do not light a fire in any of your dwellings on the Sabbath day."

■ Materials for the Tabernacle

4Moses said to the whole Israelite community, "This is what the LORD has commanded: 5From what you have, take an offering for the LORD. Everyone who is willing is to bring to the LORD an offering of gold, silver and bronze; 6blue, purple and scarlet yarn and fine linen; goat hair; 7ram skins dyed red and hides of sea cows;*a* acacia wood; 8olive oil for the light; spices for the anointing oil and for the fragrant incense; 9and onyx stones and other gems to be mounted on the ephod and breastpiece.

10"All who are skilled among you are to come and make everything the LORD has commanded: 11the tabernacle with its tent and its covering, clasps, frames, crossbars, posts and bases; 12the ark with its poles and the atonement cover and the curtain that shields it; 13the table with its poles and all its articles and the bread of the Presence; 14the lampstand that is for light with its accessories, lamps and oil for the light; 15the altar of incense with its poles, the anointing oil and the fragrant incense; the curtain for the doorway at the entrance to the tabernacle; 16the altar of burnt offering with its bronze grating, its poles and all its utensils; the bronze basin with its stand; 17the curtains of the courtyard with its posts and bases, and the curtain for the entrance to the courtyard; 18the tent pegs for the tabernacle and for the courtyard, and their ropes; 19the woven garments worn for ministering in the sanctuary—both the sacred garments for Aaron the priest and the garments for his sons when they serve as priests."

20Then the whole Israelite community withdrew from Moses' presence, 21and everyone who was willing and whose heart moved him came and brought an offering to the LORD for the work on the Tent of Meeting, for all its service, and for the sacred garments. 22All who were willing, men and women alike, came and brought gold jewellery of all kinds: brooches, ear-rings, rings and ornaments. They all presented their gold as a wave offering to the LORD. 23Everyone who had blue, purple or scarlet yarn or fine linen, or goat hair, ram skins dyed red or hides of sea cows brought them. 24Those presenting an offering of silver or bronze brought it as an offering to the LORD, and everyone who had acacia wood for any part of the work brought it. 25Every skilled woman spun with her hands and brought what she had spun—blue, purple or scarlet yarn or fine linen. 26And all the women who were willing and had the skill spun the goat hair. 27The leaders brought onyx stones and other gems to be mounted on the ephod and breastpiece. 28They also brought spices and olive oil for the light and for the anointing oil and for the fragrant incense. 29All the Israelite men and women who were willing brought to the LORD freewill offerings for all the work the LORD through Moses had commanded them to do.

■ Bezalel and Oholiab

30Then Moses said to the Israelites, "See, the LORD has chosen Bezalel son of Uri, the son of Hur, of the tribe of Judah, 31and he has filled him with the Spirit of God, with skill, ability and knowledge in all kinds of crafts—32to make artistic designs for work in gold, silver and bronze, 33to cut and set stones, to work in wood and to engage in all kinds of artistic craftsmanship. 34And he has given both him and Oholiab son of Ahisamach, of the tribe of Dan, the ability to teach others. 35He has filled them with skill to do all kinds of work as craftsmen, designers, embroiderers in blue, purple and scarlet yarn and fine linen, and weavers—all of them master craftsmen

36 and designers. 1So Bezalel, Oholiab and every skilled person to whom the LORD has given skill and ability to know how to carry out all the work of constructing the sanctuary are to do the work just as the LORD has commanded."

2Then Moses summoned Bezalel and Oholiab and every skilled person to whom the LORD had given ability and who was willing to come and do the work. 3They received from Moses all the offerings the Israelites had brought to carry out the work of constructing the sanctuary. And the people continued to bring freewill offerings morning after morning. 4So all the skilled craftsmen who were doing all the work on the sanctuary left their work 5and said to Moses, "The people are bringing more than enough for doing the work the LORD commanded to be done."

6Then Moses gave an order and they sent this word throughout the camp: "No man or woman is to make anything else as an offering for the sanctuary." And so the people were restrained from bringing more, 7because what they already had was more than enough to do all the work.

■ The Tabernacle

8All the skilled men among the workmen made the tabernacle with ten curtains of finely twisted

a 7 That is, large aquatic mammals; also in verse 23

linen and blue, purple and scarlet yarn, with cherubim worked into them by a skilled craftsman. 9All the curtains were the same size—twenty-eight cubits long and four cubits wide.*a* 10They joined five of the curtains together and did the same with the other five. 11Then they made loops of blue material along the edge of the end curtain in one set, and the same was done with the end curtain in the other set. 12They also made fifty loops on one curtain and fifty loops on the end curtain of the other set, with the loops opposite each other. 13Then they made fifty gold clasps and used them to fasten the two sets of curtains together so that the tabernacle was a unit.

14They made curtains of goat hair for the tent over the tabernacle—eleven altogether. 15All eleven curtains were the same size—thirty cubits long and four cubits wide.*b* 16They joined five of the curtains into one set and the other six into another set. 17Then they made fifty loops along the edge of the end curtain in one set and also along the

---

■ A PORTABLE CATHEDRAL
AN UNLIKELY SIGHT IN THE DESERT

INSIGHT

AND EVERYONE WHO WAS WILLING AND WHOSE HEART MOVED HIM CAME AND BROUGHT AN OFFERING TO THE LORD FOR THE WORK ON THE TENT OF MEETING. ■ 35:21

In A.D. 1144 a great building began to take shape in a village in north-west France. Enthusiasm for the project soon spread across the entire country, and volunteer workers streamed to the site. Working together, the people managed to construct one of the most beautiful buildings in the world, the magnificent cathedral at Chartres.

Fifty years later, after a terrible fire, the villagers of France rebuilt their cathedral from scratch. Today, tourists throng to marvel at what was splendidly fashioned to the glory of God so long ago.

■ INSPIRED BUILDERS
A work of art took shape in similar fashion thousands of years earlier than Chartres, and the last chapters of Exodus provide a wealth of details. In a hostile desert landscape, a tribe of just-liberated slaves built something of exquisite beauty: a portable cathedral, or tabernacle.

God directed the project personally, specially endowing the craftsmen with skill (31:1–6) and elaborating right down to the colour choice of woven yarns, the precise length of curtains and wooden frames and the design of gold filigree. The people of Israel joined together in a flurry of activity, carefully following God's pattern. A tonne of gold went into the project, as well as nearly four tonnes of silver and stockpiles of precious gems and rare woods.

■ GOD MOVES IN
After describing the tabernacle construction in great detail, the Bible devotes just five verses, the last five in Exodus, to its culmination. In a matter-of-fact tone, those sentences record a remarkable event.

Throughout the book of Exodus God had been progressively revealing himself to Moses: once in a burning bush, once in a mysterious appearance beside a rock, once on a trembling mountain, and often in a cloud-covered Tent of Meeting. God's presence caused such fear and awe that the people of Israel begged that he not speak to them directly (20:19). When Moses had come down from Mount Sinai after meeting with God, he glowed as if radioactive, and everyone was too frightened to go near him (34:30).

Yet, on the day the tabernacle was completed, this same God moved in. His glory filled the new tabernacle. God took up residence with his people.

■ A VISIBLE REMINDER
From then on, whenever the Israelites marched or camped, their portable cathedral stayed in the exact centre of the camp, with their tents and personal belongings radiating out from the Most Holy Place and ark of the covenant. The tabernacle gave them a visible reminder of God's central place. Each day priests performed functions of sacrifice and worship there.

The story of the tabernacle, which takes up one-third of Exodus, reveals much about the character of God. He can never be taken lightly—the rituals here and in the next three books show that God must be approached with care and reverence. He cannot be experienced directly, in his fulness, by ordinary people; a holy God is simply too overwhelming. Even Moses, Exodus says, could not look on God's face and live (33:20).

And yet, amazingly, that same God who seemed so distant came near. Despite the huge gulf separating God and humanity—a gulf that all the rules on holiness and purification only hint at—God allowed personal access to himself. He made himself available.

□ LIFE QUESTIONS:
Where does God "live" now?

---

a 9 That is, about 42 feet (about 13 metres) long and 6 feet (about 1.8 metres) wide
1.8 metres) wide

b 15 That is, about 45 feet (about 13.5 metres) long and 6 feet (about edge of the end curtain in the other set. [18]They made fifty bronze clasps to fasten the tent together as a unit. [19]Then they made for the tent a covering of ram skins dyed red, and over that a covering of hides of sea cows.[c]

36:5 ■ ENTHUSIASTIC GIVERS

Some commentators estimate that descriptions of the tabernacle make up the largest single subject covered in the Bible. When the time came for construction, the Israelites pitched in with such enthusiasm that they had to be restrained from bringing more offerings. Those who could not afford material gifts donated their time and labour.

[20]They made upright frames of acacia wood for the tabernacle. [21]Each frame was ten cubits long and a cubit and a half wide,[d] [22]with two projections set parallel to each other. They made all the frames of the tabernacle in this way. [23]They made twenty frames for the south side of the tabernacle [24]and made forty silver bases to go under them—two bases for each frame, one under each projection. [25]For the other side, the north side of the tabernacle, they made twenty frames [26]and forty silver bases—two under each frame. [27]They made six frames for the far end, that is, the west end of the tabernacle, [28]and two frames were made for the corners of the tabernacle at the far end. [29]At these two corners the frames were double from the bottom all the way to the top and fitted into a single ring; both were made alike. [30]So there were eight frames and sixteen silver bases—two under each frame.

[31]They also made crossbars of acacia wood: five for the frames on one side of the tabernacle, [32]five for those on the other side, and five for the frames on the west, at the far end of the tabernacle. [33]They made the centre crossbar so that it extended from end to end at the middle of the frames. [34]They overlaid the frames with gold and made gold rings to hold the crossbars. They also overlaid the crossbars with gold.

[35]They made the curtain of blue, purple and scarlet yarn and finely twisted linen, with cherubim worked into it by a skilled craftsman. [36]They made four posts of acacia wood for it and overlaid them with gold. They made gold hooks for them and cast their four silver bases. [37]For the entrance to the tent they made a curtain of blue, purple and scarlet yarn and finely twisted linen—the work of an embroiderer; [38]and they made five posts with hooks for them. They overlaid the tops of the posts and their bands with gold and made their five bases of bronze.

■ The Ark

37 Bezalel made the ark of acacia wood—two and a half cubits long, a cubit and a half wide, and a cubit and a half high.[a] [2]He overlaid it with pure gold, both inside and out, and made a gold moulding around it. [3]He cast four gold rings for it and fastened them to its four feet, with two rings on one side and two rings on the other. [4]Then he made

poles of acacia wood and overlaid them with gold. [5]And he inserted the poles into the rings on the sides of the ark to carry it.

37:1 ■ SACRED FURNITURE

In contrast to the elaborate worship sites of the pagans, the Hebrews' tabernacle was sparsely furnished and decorated. Obviously God did not need a place to live. Rather, the furnishings mentioned in this passage—only six pieces—had a specific purpose in showing the proper way for human beings to approach God.

[6]He made the atonement cover of pure gold—two and a half cubits long and a cubit and a half wide.[b] [7]Then he made two cherubim out of hammered gold at the ends of the cover. [8]He made one cherub on one end and the second cherub on the other; at the two ends he made them of one piece with the cover. [9]The cherubim had their wings spread upwards, overshadowing the cover with them. The cherubim faced each other, looking towards the cover.

■ The Table

[10]They[c] made the table of acacia wood—two cubits long, a cubit wide, and a cubit and a half high.[d] [11]Then they overlaid it with pure gold and made a gold moulding around it. [12]They also made around it a rim a handbreadth[e] wide and put a gold moulding on the rim. [13]They cast four gold rings for the table and fastened them to the four corners, where the four legs were. [14]The rings were put close to the rim to hold the poles used in carrying the table. [15]The poles for carrying the table were made of acacia wood and were overlaid with gold. [16]And they made from pure gold the articles for the table—its plates and dishes and bowls and its pitchers for the pouring out of drink offerings.

■ The Lampstand

[17]They made the lampstand of pure gold and hammered it out, base and shaft; its flowerlike cups, buds and blossoms were of one piece with it. [18]Six branches extended from the sides of the lampstand—three on one side and three on the other. [19]Three cups shaped like almond flowers with buds and blossoms were on one branch, three on the next branch and the same for all six branches extending from the lampstand. [20]And on the lampstand were four cups shaped like almond flowers with buds and blossoms. [21]One bud was under the first pair of branches extending from the lampstand, a second bud under the second pair, and a third bud under the third pair—six branches in all. [22]The buds and the branches were all of one piece with the lampstand, hammered out of pure gold.

[23]They made its seven lamps, as well as its wick trimmers and trays, of pure gold. [24]They made the lampstand and all its accessories from one talent[f] of pure gold.

c19 That is, large aquatic mammals   d21 That is, about 15 feet (about 4.5 metres) long and 2¼ feet (about 0.7 metre) wide   a1 That is, about 3¾ feet (about 1.1 metres) long and 2¼ feet (about 0.7 metre) wide and high   b6 That is, about 3¾ feet (about 1.1 metres) long and 2¼ feet (about 0.7 metre) wide
c10 Or He; also in verses 11–29   d10 That is, about 3 feet (about 0.9 metre) long, 1½ feet (about 0.5 metre) wide, and 2¼ feet (about 0.7 metre) high
e12 That is, about 3 inches (about 8 centimetres)   f24 That is, about 75 pounds (about 34 kilograms)

The Altar of Incense

25They made the altar of incense out of acacia wood. It was square, a cubit long and a cubit wide, and two cubits high*g*—its horns of one piece with it. 26They overlaid the top and all the sides and the horns with pure gold, and made a gold moulding around it. 27They made two gold rings below the moulding—two on opposite sides—to hold the poles used to carry it. 28They made the poles of acacia wood and overlaid them with gold.

29They also made the sacred anointing oil and the pure, fragrant incense—the work of a perfumer.

The Altar of Burnt Offering

38 They*a* built the altar of burnt offering of acacia wood, three cubits*b* high; it was square, five cubits long and five cubits wide.*c* 2They made a horn at each of the four corners, so that the horns and the altar were of one piece, and they overlaid the altar with bronze. 3They made all its utensils of bronze—its pots, shovels, sprinkling bowls, meat forks and firepans. 4They made a grating for the altar, a bronze network, to be under its ledge, halfway up the altar. 5They cast bronze rings to hold the poles for the four corners of the bronze grating. 6They made the poles of acacia wood and overlaid them with bronze. 7They inserted the poles into the rings so they would be on the sides of the altar for carrying it. They made it hollow, out of boards.

Basin for Washing

8They made the bronze basin and its bronze stand from the mirrors of the women who served at the entrance to the Tent of Meeting.

The Courtyard

9Next they made the courtyard. The south side was a hundred cubits*d* long and had curtains of finely twisted linen, 10with twenty posts and twenty bronze bases, and with silver hooks and bands on the posts. 11The north side was also a hundred cubits long and had twenty posts and twenty bronze bases, with silver hooks and bands on the posts.

38:9 ■ TABERNACLE LAYOUT

Unlike a church or synagogue, neither the tabernacle nor temple functioned as a gathering place for public meetings. Worshippers entered a large, open courtyard area to present their offerings and sacrifices. After receiving the offerings, the priests approached the Holy Place, which contained some of the sacred furniture. Only the high priest could go further, into the Most Holy Place where the ark of the covenant stayed, and he did so only once a year, on the Day of Atonement.

12The west end was fifty cubits*e* wide and had curtains, with ten posts and ten bases, with silver hooks and bands on the posts. 13The east end,

towards the sunrise, was also fifty cubits wide. 14Curtains fifteen cubits*f* long were on one side of the entrance, with three posts and three bases, 15and curtains fifteen cubits long were on the other side of the entrance to the courtyard, with three posts and three bases. 16All the curtains around the courtyard were of finely twisted linen. 17The bases for the posts were bronze. The hooks and bands on the posts were silver, and their tops were overlaid with silver; so all the posts of the courtyard had silver bands.

18The curtain for the entrance to the courtyard was of blue, purple and scarlet yarn and finely twisted linen—the work of an embroiderer. It was twenty cubits*g* long and, like the curtains of the courtyard, five cubits*b* high, 19with four posts and four bronze bases. Their hooks and bands were silver, and their tops were overlaid with silver. 20All the tent pegs of the tabernacle and of the surrounding courtyard were bronze.

The Materials Used

21These are the amounts of the materials used for the tabernacle, the tabernacle of the Testimony, which were recorded at Moses' command by the Levites under the direction of Ithamar son of Aaron, the priest. 22(Bezalel son of Uri, the son of Hur, of the tribe of Judah, made everything the LORD commanded Moses; 23with him was Oholiab son of Ahisamach, of the tribe of Dan—a craftsman and designer, and an embroiderer in blue, purple and scarlet yarn and fine linen.) 24The total amount of the gold from the wave offering used for all the work on the sanctuary was 29 talents and 730 shekels,*i* according to the sanctuary shekel.

25The silver obtained from those of the community who were counted in the census was 100 talents and 1,775 shekels,*j* according to the sanctuary shekel—26one beka per person, that is, half a shekel,*k* according to the sanctuary shekel, from everyone who had crossed over to those counted, twenty years old or more, a total of 603,550 men. 27The 100 talents*l* of silver were used to cast the bases for the sanctuary and for the curtain—100 bases from the 100 talents, one talent for each base. 28They used the 1,775 shekels*m* to make the hooks for the posts, to overlay the tops of the posts, and to make their bands.

29The bronze from the wave offering was 70 talents and 2,400 shekels.*n* 30They used it to make the bases for the entrance to the Tent of Meeting, the bronze altar with its bronze grating and all its utensils, 31the bases for the surrounding courtyard and those for its entrance and all the tent pegs for the tabernacle and those for the surrounding courtyard.

The Priestly Garments

39 From the blue, purple and scarlet yarn they made woven garments for ministering in the sanctuary. They also made sacred garments for Aaron, as the LORD commanded Moses.

---

g 25 That is, about 1½ feet (about 0.5 metre) long and wide, and about 3 feet (about 0.9 metre) high   *a 1* Or *He;* also in verses 2–9   *b 1* That is, about 4½ feet (about 1.4 metres)   *c 1* That is, about 7½ feet (about 2.3 metres) long and wide   *d 9* That is, about 150 feet (about 46 metres)   *e 12* That is, about 75 feet (about 23 metres)   *f 14* That is, about 22½ feet (about 6.9 metres)   *g 18* That is, about 30 feet (about 9 metres)   *b 18* That is, about 7½ feet (about 2.3 metres)   *i 24* The weight of the gold was about one ton (about 1 metric ton).   *j 25* The weight of the silver was about 3⅓ tons (about 3.4 metric tons).   *k 26* That is, about ⅕ ounce (about 6 grams)   *l 27* That is, about 3⅓ tons (about 3.4 metric tons)   *m 28* That is, about 45 pounds (about 20 kilograms)   *n 29* The weight of the bronze was about 2⅓ tons (about 2.4 metric tons).

■ **The Ephod**

2They*a* made the ephod of gold, and of blue, purple and scarlet yarn, and of finely twisted linen. 3They hammered out thin sheets of gold and cut strands to be worked into the blue, purple and scarlet yarn and fine linen — the work of a skilled craftsman. 4They made shoulder pieces for the ephod, which were attached to two of its corners, so that it could be fastened. 5Its skilfully woven waistband was like it — of one piece with the ephod and made with gold, and with blue, purple and scarlet yarn, and with finely twisted linen, as the LORD commanded Moses.

6They mounted the onyx stones in gold filigree settings and engraved them like a seal with the names of the sons of Israel. 7Then they fastened them on the shoulder pieces of the ephod as memorial stones for the sons of Israel, as the LORD commanded Moses.

■ **The Breastpiece**

8They fashioned the breastpiece — the work of a skilled craftsman. They made it like the ephod: of gold, and of blue, purple and scarlet yarn, and of finely twisted linen. 9It was square — a span*b* long and a span wide — and folded double. 10Then they mounted four rows of precious stones on it. In the first row there was a ruby, a topaz and a beryl; 11in the second row a turquoise, a sapphire*c* and an emerald; 12in the third row a jacinth, an agate and an amethyst; 13in the fourth row a chrysolite, an onyx and a jasper.*d* They were mounted in gold filigree settings. 14There were twelve stones, one for each of the names of the sons of Israel, each engraved like a seal with the name of one of the twelve tribes.

15For the breastpiece they made braided chains of pure gold, like a rope. 16They made two gold filigree settings and two gold rings, and fastened the rings to two of the corners of the breastpiece. 17They fastened the two gold chains to the rings at the corners of the breastpiece, 18and the other ends of the chains to the two settings, attaching them to the shoulder pieces of the ephod at the front. 19They made two gold rings and attached them to the other two corners of the breastpiece on the inside edge next to the ephod. 20Then they made two more gold rings and attached them to the bottom of the shoulder pieces on the front of the ephod, close to the seam just above the waistband of the ephod. 21They tied the rings of the breastpiece to the rings of the ephod with blue cord, connecting it to the waistband so that the breastpiece would not swing out from the ephod — as the LORD commanded Moses.

■ **Other Priestly Garments**

22They made the robe of the ephod entirely of blue cloth — the work of a weaver — 23with an opening in the centre of the robe like the opening of a collar,*e* and a band around this opening, so that it would not tear. 24They made pomegranates of blue, purple and scarlet yarn and finely twisted linen

around the hem of the robe. 25And they made bells of pure gold and attached them around the hem between the pomegranates. 26The bells and pomegranates alternated around the hem of the robe to be worn for ministering, as the LORD commanded Moses.

27For Aaron and his sons, they made tunics of fine linen — the work of a weaver — 28and the turban of fine linen, the linen headbands and the undergarments of finely twisted linen. 29The sash was of finely twisted linen and blue, purple and scarlet yarn — the work of an embroiderer — as the LORD commanded Moses.

30They made the plate, the sacred diadem, out of pure gold and engraved on it, like an inscription on a seal: HOLY TO THE LORD. 31Then they fastened a blue cord to it to attach it to the turban, as the LORD commanded Moses.

■ **Moses Inspects the Tabernacle**

32So all the work on the tabernacle, the Tent of Meeting, was completed. The Israelites did every-

---

39:32 ■ FOLLOWING ORDERS

The last few chapters of Exodus repeat almost verbatim what has gone before; they simply record that the Israelites followed all of God's prior instructions for building the tabernacle. The phrase "as the LORD commanded" resonates like a drumbeat through this section. A people not known for following orders took the tabernacle project very seriously. It became for them not just a symbol, but the actual reality of God living in their midst. The tabernacle was the focal point of worship for 300 years, until the temple was built. Later, the apostle Paul used this imagery when he called believers God's "temple", or dwelling-place.

---

thing just as the LORD commanded Moses. 33Then they brought the tabernacle to Moses: the tent and all its furnishings, its clasps, frames, crossbars, posts and bases; 34the covering of ram skins dyed red, the covering of hides of sea cows*f* and the shielding curtain; 35the ark of the Testimony with its poles and the atonement cover; 36the table with all its articles and the bread of the Presence; 37the pure gold lampstand with its row of lamps and all its accessories, and the oil for the light; 38the gold altar, the anointing oil, the fragrant incense, and the curtain for the entrance to the tent; 39the bronze altar with its bronze grating, its poles and all its utensils; the basin with its stand; 40the curtains of the courtyard with its posts and bases, and the curtain for the entrance to the courtyard; the ropes and tent pegs for the courtyard; all the furnishings for the tabernacle, the Tent of Meeting; 41and the woven garments worn for ministering in the sanctuary, both the sacred garments for Aaron the priest and the garments for his sons when serving as priests.

42The Israelites had done all the work just as the LORD had commanded Moses. 43Moses inspected the work and saw that they had done it just as the LORD had commanded. So Moses blessed them.

---

a2 Or *He*; also in verses 7, 8 and 22 of these precious stones is uncertain. *b9* That is, about 9 inches (about 23 centimetres) *c11* Or *lapis lazuli* *d13* The precise identification of some *e23* The meaning of the Hebrew for this word is uncertain. *f34* That is, large aquatic mammals

■ Setting Up the Tabernacle

40 Then the LORD said to Moses: [2]"Set up the tabernacle, the Tent of Meeting, on the first day of the first month. [3]Place the ark of the Testimony in it and shield the ark with the curtain. [4]Bring in the table and set out what belongs on it. Then bring in the lampstand and set up its lamps. [5]Place the gold altar of incense in front of the ark of the Testimony and put the curtain at the entrance to the tabernacle.

[6]"Place the altar of burnt offering in front of the entrance to the tabernacle, the Tent of Meeting; [7]place the basin between the Tent of Meeting and the altar and put water in it. [8]Set up the courtyard around it and put the curtain at the entrance to the courtyard.

[9]"Take the anointing oil and anoint the tabernacle and everything in it; consecrate it and all its furnishings, and it will be holy. [10]Then anoint the altar of burnt offering and all its utensils; consecrate the altar, and it will be most holy. [11]Anoint the basin and its stand and consecrate them.

[12]"Bring Aaron and his sons to the entrance to the Tent of Meeting and wash them with water. [13]Then dress Aaron in the sacred garments, anoint him and consecrate him so that he may serve me as priest. [14]Bring his sons and dress them in tunics. [15]Anoint them just as you anointed their father, so that they may serve me as priests. Their anointing will be to a priesthood that will continue for all generations to come." [16]Moses did everything just as the LORD commanded him.

[17]So the tabernacle was set up on the first day of the first month in the second year. [18]When Moses set up the tabernacle, he put the bases in place, erected the frames, inserted the crossbars and set up the posts. [19]Then he spread the tent over the tabernacle and put the covering over the tent, as the LORD commanded him.

[20]He took the Testimony and placed it in the ark, attached the poles to the ark and put the atonement cover over it. [21]Then he brought the ark into the tabernacle and hung the shielding curtain and shielded the ark of the Testimony, as the LORD commanded him.

[22]Moses placed the table in the Tent of Meeting on the north side of the tabernacle outside the curtain [23]and set out the bread on it before the LORD, as the LORD commanded him.

[24]He placed the lampstand in the Tent of Meeting opposite the table on the south side of the tabernacle [25]and set up the lamps before the LORD, as the LORD commanded him.

[26]Moses placed the gold altar in the Tent of Meeting in front of the curtain [27]and burned fragrant incense on it, as the LORD commanded him. [28]Then he put up the curtain at the entrance to the tabernacle.

[29]He set the altar of burnt offering near the entrance to the tabernacle, the Tent of Meeting, and offered on it burnt offerings and grain offerings, as the LORD commanded him.

[30]He placed the basin between the Tent of Meeting and the altar and put water in it for washing, [31]and Moses and Aaron and his sons used it to wash their hands and feet. [32]They washed whenever they entered the Tent of Meeting or approached the altar, as the LORD commanded Moses.

[33]Then Moses set up the courtyard around the tabernacle and altar and put up the curtain at the entrance to the courtyard. And so Moses finished the work.

■ The Glory of the LORD

[34]Then the cloud covered the Tent of Meeting, and the glory of the LORD filled the tabernacle. [35]Moses could not enter the Tent of Meeting because the cloud had settled upon it, and the glory of the LORD filled the tabernacle.

[36]In all the travels of the Israelites, whenever the cloud lifted from above the tabernacle, they would set out; [37]but if the cloud did not lift, they did not set out—until the day it lifted. [38]So the cloud of the LORD was over the tabernacle by day, and fire was in the cloud by night, in the sight of all the house of Israel during all their travels.

LEVITICUS

INTRODUCTION

■ LIVING WITH FIRE
DANGEROUS MATERIAL MORE POWERFUL THAN THE ATOM

I WILL PUT MY DWELLING-PLACE AMONG YOU, AND I WILL NOT ABHOR YOU. I WILL WALK
AMONG YOU AND BE YOUR GOD, AND YOU WILL BE MY PEOPLE. ■ 26:11–12

Leviticus seems very strange to the modern world.
Unlike most of the Bible, it has few personalities
and stories, and no poetry. Instead, it is crammed
full of detailed rules and procedures.

Its painstaking ritual is, however,
strikingly similar to the procedures used when
handling radioactive material. The specialised
clothing, the concern for purification, the precise
handling of crucial materials – both nuclear
workers and Old Testament priests share these.
This similarity gives an important clue to
understanding Leviticus.

■ CLEANING UP A NUCLEAR SPILL
On motorways right across the United Kingdom
you can see them. Huge great lorries with those
black and yellow signs that look just like 3-armed
fans or propellers. These are warning signs telling
other drivers to keep their distance at all times
because the load is radioactive.

If an accident occurs, and a leak or
spillage develops, the area must be sealed off
and then cleansed through laborious scrubbing
with soap and water. Carefully trained workers in
protective clothing dispose of the dirty water in
a specially protected toxic waste area. Anyone
contaminated must also be "cleansed" from the
exposure. In extreme cases, she or he must stay
away from other people for months.

These rigid rules grew out of hard
experience. For decades no-one knew the
dangers of radioactivity. Workers who used
radioactive materials to hand-paint the first
"glow in the dark" watches licked their
paintbrushes to get a fine tip; their supervisors
said they would gain sex appeal. Instead, they
got cancer. The introduction of nuclear weapons
and nuclear power plants increased the amount
of radioactive material being handled. Gradually
scientists realised: if you are going to use the
atom, you must adopt procedures to fit its
power.

■ THE INTIMATE PRESENCE OF GOD
Leviticus reads something like a training manual
for atomic plant workers or transporters of nuclear
waste. Its "dangerous material", however, is more
powerful than the atom. Leviticus gives exhaustive
detail on how to live with God.

A pamphlet on "how to survive a nuclear
accident" may be dull if read on holiday, but it's
gripping if read in a vibrating nuclear reactor.
Similarly, Leviticus is dull if you do not realise the
wonderful news behind it: a powerful God, the
Creator of the universe, has entered the life of a
small and insignificant tribe. The Israelites could
not merely fit this God into their lives. They
needed to restructure their lives – food, sex,
economics – to fit with his. It was essential not
just for priests, but for everyone.

Ignoring the operations manual could be
deadly. It was for Aaron's two sons (chapter 10).

■ FREE FROM CONTAMINATION
Today, because of Jesus Christ, we don't live in
the world of Leviticus. Jesus' perfect self-sacrifice
made the daily sacrifice of animals unnecessary.
He replaced the high priest as our representative
before God. Jesus cleanses the real source of
contamination, our sinful nature. Leviticus was
meant to teach people some basic truths about
God, and when their lessons were complete, they
could go on to bigger and better things. (The New
Testament book of Hebrews spells out this
graduation.)

Yet we need to be reminded of the
principles Leviticus taught. It tells us that God
was then, as he is today, "a consuming fire"
(Hebrews 12:29). He has taught us how to live
with that fire, not because we deserved to know,
but because he wanted our company. We dare
not treat him lightly.

■ HOW TO READ LEVITICUS

Many well-intentioned readers, determined to read the Bible from beginning to end, get bogged down in Leviticus. It's a law-book, a procedural manual for getting along with a holy and powerful God. Sheer detail can bore you, especially if you miss the point behind it.

When you read the Bible, careful attention to detail is usually a key to understanding. In Leviticus, however, you will get more from looking at the big picture than from studying the details. Some laws we simply don't understand. But Leviticus as a whole shows what kind of people God wanted the Israelites to be. As you read, keep your mind on the big picture. Pay special attention to the explanatory notes. Try to imagine how these laws affected everyday life. Keep asking yourself: how would these laws make the Israelites different from other people – and why were those differences important to God?

■ 3-TRACK READING PLAN

For an explanation and complete listing of the 3-track reading plan, turn to page x.

■ TRACK 1:
Two-Week Courses on the Bible
See page x for information on these courses.

■ TRACK 2:
An Overview of Leviticus in 1 Day
□ Day 1. Read the Introduction to Leviticus and chapter 26, which summarises the purpose of God's laws. Scan through the sectional headings of the book to get an idea of what subjects it covers.
Now turn to page xi for your next Track 2 reading project.

■ TRACK 3:
All of Leviticus in 26 Days

After you have read through Leviticus, turn to pages xii–xiii for your next Track 3 reading project.

□ 1   □ 2   □ 3   □ 4
□ 5   □ 6   □ 7   □ 8
□ 9   □ 10   □ 11–12
□ 13   □ 14   □ 15   □ 16
□ 17   □ 18   □ 19   □ 20
□ 21   □ 22   □ 23   □ 24
□ 25   □ 26   □ 27

■ The Burnt Offering

1 The LORD called to Moses and spoke to him from the Tent of Meeting. He said, ²"Speak to the Israelites and say to them: 'When any of you brings an offering to the LORD, bring as your offering an animal from either the herd or the flock.

³" 'If the offering is a burnt offering from the herd, he is to offer a male without defect. He must present it at the entrance to the Tent of Meeting so that it*a* will be acceptable to the LORD. ⁴He is to lay his hand on the head of the burnt offering, and it will be accepted on his behalf to make atonement for him. ⁵He is to slaughter the young bull before the LORD, and then Aaron's sons the priests shall bring the blood and sprinkle it against the altar on all sides at the entrance to the Tent of Meeting. ⁶He is to skin the burnt offering and cut it into pieces. ⁷The sons of Aaron the priest are to put fire on the altar and arrange wood on the fire. ⁸Then Aaron's sons the priests shall arrange the pieces, including the head and the fat, on the burning wood that is on the altar. ⁹He is to wash the inner parts and the legs with water, and the priest is to burn all of it on the altar. It is a burnt offering, an offering made by fire, an aroma pleasing to the LORD.

¹⁰" 'If the offering is a burnt offering from the flock, from either the sheep or the goats, he is to offer a male without defect. ¹¹He is to slaughter it at the north side of the altar before the LORD, and Aaron's sons the priests shall sprinkle its blood against the altar on all sides. ¹²He is to cut it into pieces, and the priest shall arrange them, including the head and the fat, on the burning wood that is on the altar. ¹³He is to wash the inner parts and the legs with water, and the priest is to bring all of it and burn it on the altar. It is a burnt offering, an offering made by fire, an aroma pleasing to the LORD.

1:9 ■ ORIGINAL HOLOCAUST

The word "holocaust", which simply means "burnt whole", derives from the Israelite practice of offering up the entire animal, including legs, head, and inner parts. Later the word stood for a great devastation, especially by fire. After World War II, Jews began referring to Hitler's mass destruction of their race in gas chambers and ovens as "The Holocaust".

¹⁴" 'If the offering to the LORD is a burnt offering of birds, he is to offer a dove or a young pigeon. ¹⁵The priest shall bring it to the altar, wring off the head and burn it on the altar; its blood shall be drained out on the side of the altar. ¹⁶He is to remove the crop with its contents*b* and throw it to the east side of the altar, where the ashes are. ¹⁷He shall tear it open by the wings, not severing it completely, and then the priest shall burn it on the wood that is on the fire on the altar. It is a burnt offering, an offering made by fire, an aroma pleasing to the LORD.

■ The Grain Offering

2 "When someone brings a grain offering to the LORD, his offering is to be of fine flour. He is to pour oil on it, put incense on it ²and take it to Aaron's sons the priests. The priest shall take a handful of the fine flour and oil, together with all the incense, and burn this as a memorial portion on the

*a*3 Or he   *b*16 Or *crop and the feathers*; the meaning of the Hebrew for this word is uncertain.

altar, an offering made by fire, an aroma pleasing to the LORD. ³The rest of the grain offering belongs to Aaron and his sons; it is a most holy part of the offerings made to the LORD by fire.

⁴" 'If you bring a grain offering baked in an oven, it is to consist of fine flour: cakes made without yeast and mixed with oil, or*ᵃ* wafers made without yeast and spread with oil. ⁵If your grain offering is prepared on a griddle, it is to be made of fine flour mixed with oil, and without yeast. ⁶Crumble it and pour oil on it; it is a grain offering. ⁷If your grain offering is cooked in a pan, it is to be made of fine flour and oil. ⁸Bring the grain offering made of these things to the LORD; present it to the priest, who shall take it to the altar. ⁹He shall take out the memorial portion from the grain offering and burn it on the altar as an offering made by fire, an aroma pleasing to the LORD. ¹⁰The rest of the grain offering belongs to Aaron and his sons; it is a most holy part of the offerings made to the LORD by fire.

¹¹" 'Every grain offering you bring to the LORD must be made without yeast, for you are not to burn any yeast or honey in an offering made to the LORD by fire. ¹²You may bring them to the LORD as an offering of the firstfruits, but they are not to be offered on the altar as a pleasing aroma. ¹³Season all your grain offerings with salt. Do not leave the salt of the covenant of your God out of your grain offerings; add salt to all your offerings.

¹⁴" 'If you bring a grain offering of firstfruits to the LORD, offer crushed heads of new grain roasted in the fire. ¹⁵Put oil and incense on it; it is a grain offering. ¹⁶The priest shall burn the memorial portion of the crushed grain and the oil, together with all the incense, as an offering made to the LORD by fire.

■ The Fellowship Offering

3 " 'If someone's offering is a fellowship offering,*ᵃ* and he offers an animal from the herd, whether male or female, he is to present before the LORD an animal without defect. ²He is to lay his hand on the head of his offering and slaughter it at the entrance to the Tent of Meeting. Then Aaron's sons the priests shall sprinkle the blood against the altar on all sides. ³From the fellowship offering he is to bring a sacrifice made to the LORD by fire: all the fat that covers the inner parts or is connected to them, ⁴both kidneys with the fat on them near the loins, and the covering of the liver, which he will remove with the kidneys. ⁵Then Aaron's sons are to burn it on the altar on top of the burnt offering that is on the burning wood, as an offering made by fire, an aroma pleasing to the LORD.

⁶" 'If he offers an animal from the flock as a fellowship offering to the LORD, he is to offer a male or female without defect. ⁷If he offers a lamb, he is to present it before the LORD. ⁸He is to lay his hand on the head of his offering and slaughter it in front of the Tent of Meeting. Then Aaron's sons shall sprinkle its blood against the altar on all sides. ⁹From the fellowship offering he is to bring a sacrifice made to the LORD by fire: its fat, the entire fat tail cut off close to the backbone, all the fat that covers the inner parts or is connected to them, ¹⁰both kidneys with the fat on them near the loins, and the covering of the liver,

which he will remove with the kidneys. ¹¹The priest shall burn them on the altar as food, an offering made to the LORD by fire.

¹²" 'If his offering is a goat, he is to present it before the LORD. ¹³He is to lay his hand on its head and slaughter it in front of the Tent of Meeting. Then Aaron's sons shall sprinkle its blood against the altar on all sides. ¹⁴From what he offers he is to make this offering to the LORD by fire: all the fat that covers the inner parts or is connected to them, ¹⁵both kidneys with the fat on them near the loins, and the covering of the liver, which he will remove with the kidneys. ¹⁶The priest shall burn them on the altar as food, an offering made by fire, a pleasing aroma. All the fat is the LORD's.

¹⁷" 'This is a lasting ordinance for the generations to come, wherever you live: You must not eat any fat or any blood.' "

■ The Sin Offering

4 The LORD said to Moses, ²"Say to the Israelites: 'When anyone sins unintentionally and does what is forbidden in any of the LORD's commands—

³" 'If the anointed priest sins, bringing guilt on the people, he must bring to the LORD a young bull without defect as a sin offering for the sin he has committed. ⁴He is to present the bull at the entrance to the Tent of Meeting before the LORD. He is to lay his hand on its head and slaughter it before the LORD. ⁵Then the anointed priest shall take some of the bull's blood and carry it into the Tent of Meeting. ⁶He is to dip his finger into the blood and sprinkle some of it seven times before the LORD, in front of the curtain of the sanctuary. ⁷The priest shall then put some of the blood on the horns of the altar of fragrant incense that is before the LORD in the Tent of Meeting. The rest of the bull's blood he shall pour out at the base of the altar of burnt offering at the entrance to the Tent of Meeting. ⁸He shall remove all the fat from the bull of the sin offering—the fat that covers the inner parts or is connected to them, ⁹both kidneys with the fat on them near the loins, and the covering of the liver, which he will remove with the kidneys— ¹⁰just as the fat is removed from the ox*ᵃ* sacrificed as a fellowship offering.*ᵇ* Then the priest shall burn them on the altar of burnt offering. ¹¹But the hide of the bull and all its flesh, as well as the head and legs, the inner parts and offal— ¹²that is, all the rest of the bull—he must take outside the camp to a place ceremonially clean, where the ashes are thrown, and burn it in a wood fire on the ash heap.

4:3 ■ THE ONE FOR THE MANY
For his sin, a priest had to sacrifice one bull—the same sacrifice required for a sin by the whole community (verses 13–14). The two sins were, in a sense, equal, for the high priest represented the whole community before God. The belief that a single purified individual can stand up for a nation prepared the way for Jesus, whose sinless obedience stands before God in our place.

ᵃ4 Or and   *ᵃ1* Traditionally *peace offering*; also in verses 3, 6 and 9 *peace offering*; also in verses 26, 31 and 35   *ᵃ10* The Hebrew word can include both male and female.   *ᵇ10* Traditionally

13" 'If the whole Israelite community sins unintentionally and does what is forbidden in any of the LORD's commands, even though the community is unaware of the matter, they are guilty. 14When they become aware of the sin they committed, the assembly must bring a young bull as a sin offering and present it before the Tent of Meeting. 15The elders of the community are to lay their hands on the bull's head before the LORD, and the bull shall be slaughtered before the LORD. 16Then the anointed priest is to take some of the bull's blood into the Tent of Meeting. 17He shall dip his finger into the blood and sprinkle it before the LORD seven times in front of the curtain. 18He is to put some of the blood on the horns of the altar that is before the LORD in the Tent of Meeting. The rest of the blood he shall pour out at the base of the altar of burnt offering at the entrance to the Tent of Meeting. 19He shall remove all the fat from it and burn it on the altar, 20and do with this bull just as he did with the bull for the sin offering. In this way the priest will make atonement for them, and they will be forgiven. 21Then he shall take the bull outside the camp and burn it as he burned the first bull. This is the sin offering for the community.

4:13 ■ IGNORANCE ISN'T BLISS

"I didn't know the speed limit had dropped to 30, officer. How can you give me a ticket?" Under the law, ignorance provides no excuse. This chapter and the next cover many instances of unintentional sin. Although held accountable for such wrongdoing, the Israelites could overcome their guilt by offering the prescribed sacrifices.

22" 'When a leader sins unintentionally and does what is forbidden in any of the commands of the LORD his God, he is guilty. 23When he is made aware of the sin he committed, he must bring as his offering a male goat without defect. 24He is to lay his hand on the goat's head and slaughter it at the place where the burnt offering is slaughtered before the LORD. It is a sin offering. 25Then the priest shall take some of the blood of the sin offering with his finger and put it on the horns of the altar of burnt offering and pour out the rest of the blood at the base of the altar. 26He shall burn all the fat on the altar as he burned the fat of the fellowship offering. In this way the priest will make atonement for the man's sin, and he will be forgiven.

27" 'If a member of the community sins unintentionally and does what is forbidden in any of the LORD's commands, he is guilty. 28When he is made aware of the sin he committed, he must bring as his offering for the sin he committed a female goat without defect. 29He is to lay his hand on the head of the sin offering and slaughter it at the place of the burnt offering. 30Then the priest is to take some of the blood with his finger and put it on the horns of the altar of burnt offering and pour out the rest of the blood at the base of the altar. 31He shall remove all the fat, just as the fat is removed from the fellowship offering, and the priest shall burn it on the altar as

an aroma pleasing to the LORD. In this way the priest will make atonement for him, and he will be forgiven.

32" 'If he brings a lamb as his sin offering, he is to bring a female without defect. 33He is to lay his hand on its head and slaughter it for a sin offering at the place where the burnt offering is slaughtered. 34Then the priest shall take some of the blood of the sin offering with his finger and put it on the horns of the altar of burnt offering and pour out the rest of the blood at the base of the altar. 35He shall remove all the fat, just as the fat is removed from the lamb of the fellowship offering, and the priest shall burn it on the altar on top of the offerings made to the LORD by fire. In this way the priest will make atonement for him for the sin he has committed, and he will be forgiven.

5 " 'If a person sins because he does not speak up when he hears a public charge to testify regarding something he has seen or learned about, he will be held responsible.

2" 'Or if a person touches anything ceremonially unclean—whether the carcasses of unclean wild animals or of unclean livestock or of unclean creatures that move along the ground—even though he is unaware of it, he has become unclean and is guilty.

3" 'Or if he touches human uncleanness—anything that would make him unclean—even though he is unaware of it, when he learns of it he will be guilty.

4" 'Or if a person thoughtlessly takes an oath to do anything, whether good or evil—in any matter one might carelessly swear about—even though he is unaware of it, in any case when he learns of it he will be guilty.

5" 'When anyone is guilty in any of these ways, he must confess in what way he has sinned 6and, as a penalty for the sin he has committed, he must bring to the LORD a female lamb or goat from the flock as a sin offering; and the priest shall make atonement for him for his sin.

7" 'If he cannot afford a lamb, he is to bring two doves or two young pigeons to the LORD as a penalty for his sin—one for a sin offering and the other for a burnt offering. 8He is to bring them to the priest, who shall first offer the one for the sin offering. He is to wring its head from its neck, not severing it completely, 9and is to sprinkle some of the blood of the sin offering against the side of the altar; the rest of the blood must be drained out at the base of the altar. It is a sin offering. 10The priest shall then offer the other as a burnt offering in the prescribed way and make atonement for him for the sin he has committed, and he will be forgiven.

11" 'If, however, he cannot afford two doves or two young pigeons, he is to bring as an offering for his sin a tenth of an ephah*a* of fine flour for a sin offering. He must not put oil or incense on it, because it is a sin offering. 12He is to bring it to the priest, who shall take a handful of it as a memorial portion and burn it on the altar on top of the offerings made to the LORD by fire. It is a sin offering. 13In this way the priest will make atonement for him for any of these sins he has committed, and he will be

a 11 That is, probably about 4 pints (about 2 litres)

forgiven. The rest of the offering will belong to the priest, as in the case of the grain offering.' "

■ The Guilt Offering

¹⁴The LORD said to Moses: ¹⁵"When a person commits a violation and sins unintentionally in regard to any of the LORD's holy things, he is to bring to the LORD as a penalty a ram from the flock, one without defect and of the proper value in silver, according to the sanctuary shekel.^b It is a guilt offering. ¹⁶He must make restitution for what he has failed to do in regard to the holy things, add a fifth of the value to that and give it all to the priest, who will make atonement for him with the ram as a guilt offering, and he will be forgiven.

¹⁷"If a person sins and does what is forbidden in any of the LORD's commands, even though he does not know it, he is guilty and will be held responsible. ¹⁸He is to bring to the priest as a guilt offering a ram from the flock, one without defect and of the proper value. In this way the priest will make atonement for him for the wrong he has committed unintentionally, and he will be forgiven. ¹⁹It is a guilt offering; he has been guilty of^c wrongdoing against the LORD."

6 The LORD said to Moses: ²"If anyone sins and is unfaithful to the LORD by deceiving his neighbour about something entrusted to him or left in his care or stolen, or if he cheats him, ³or if he finds lost property and lies about it, or if he swears falsely, or

■ THE REASON FOR SACRIFICE
JUSTICE: SOMEONE HAS TO PAY

IN THIS WAY THE PRIEST WILL MAKE ATONEMENT FOR HIM FOR THE SIN HE HAS COMMITTED, AND HE WILL BE FORGIVEN. ■ 4:35

When you commit a crime, you don't get off in court just by saying "Sorry, I'll try not to do it again." Justice requires that you pay for what you did.

The Israelites, therefore, could not just march into God's presence to fellowship with him. They had to bring sacrifices to pay, or "atone," for their inadequacies.

These sacrifices cost dearly. To subsistence farmers, a bull or goat represented a sizeable contribution. Very poor people could give less — a pair of doves, or some flour. But, in all cases, a person would feel the cost, cost in terms of something he had worked for, something grown on his own farm.

■ UP IN SMOKE
A good portion of the national economy went up in smoke each year: hundreds of animals and a lot of manpower to gather wood, keep the fire lit and offer sacrifices. Since the Tent of Meeting stood at the centre of the camp, the smell of the two-a-day sacrifices always hung over the Israelites. They rarely could afford meat, but every day they smelled the aroma of the barbecue dedicated to God.

Offerings fell into three broad types. The guilt and sin offerings were usually offered first: they cleansed people from sin. Then came the burnt offerings, in which whole animals were burnt to ashes. Made at least twice a day, these sacrifices evidently expressed complete dedication to God. The final sacrifice was the fellowship offering, essentially a family meal shared in the presence of God. (The grain offerings were usually given together with one of the other offerings.)

The sequence of the offerings — forgiveness of sins, then total dedication, then fellowship — shows that their goal was fellowship with God. To reach that goal, forgiveness of sin and complete dedication to God were necessary.

Leviticus, however, does not explain this underlying philosophy: it reads more like an instruction manual on how to make sacrifices exactly the way God wanted. The exactness helped produce a proper attitude. You couldn't approach God carelessly. You had to be very careful to do just what he said, to obey him in every detail.

■ CAN AN ANIMAL REALLY PAY?
The whole scene — with its concern for blood, priests, ritual — is strange to modern people. Just how can killing a goat make things right between God and people? Is the sacrifice of an animal really enough to "pay for" our mistakes? We may forget that throughout history, people have intuitively felt that sacrifice was needed to satisfy God. Many religions around the world still sacrifice today.

For us these sacrifices seem outmoded primarily because one great sacrifice — that of God's own Son — outdid them all. The animal sacrifices were not enough, ultimately, to pay for human sin. They prepared the way for a sacrifice that was.

The cost of an animal was substantial, but the true cost, even for us, is infinitely greater. Yet we don't have to pay the cost. Jesus paid it all.

□ LIFE QUESTIONS:
Do you think of God as requiring sacrifice? How does the picture of God in Leviticus fit with your ideas about God?

---

^b 15 That is, about ⅖ ounce (about 11.5 grams)   ^c 19 Or has made full expiation for his

if he commits any such sin that people may do — ⁴when he thus sins and becomes guilty, he must return what he has stolen or taken by extortion, or what was entrusted to him, or the lost property he found, ⁵or whatever it was he swore falsely about. He must make restitution in full, add a fifth of the value to it and give it all to the owner on the day he presents his guilt offering. ⁶And as a penalty he must bring to the priest, that is, to the LORD, his guilt offering, a ram from the flock, one without defect and of the proper value. ⁷In this way the priest will make atonement for him before the LORD, and he will be forgiven for any of these things he did that made him guilty."

6:5 ■ DOUBLE JEOPARDY

An Israelite who committed a crime against another person (such as stealing) had two parties to reckon with. First, the offender had to make full restitution, along with a 20 per cent penalty, to the person cheated. Second, he or she had to bring a special offering to God. A crime against another person also counted as a sin against God.

■ The Burnt Offering

⁸The LORD said to Moses: ⁹"Give Aaron and his sons this command: 'These are the regulations for the burnt offering: The burnt offering is to remain on the altar hearth throughout the night, till morning, and the fire must be kept burning on the altar. ¹⁰The priest shall then put on his linen clothes, with linen undergarments next to his body, and shall remove the ashes of the burnt offering that the fire has consumed on the altar and place them beside the altar. ¹¹Then he is to take off these clothes and put on others, and carry the ashes outside the camp to a place that is ceremonially clean. ¹²The fire on the altar must be kept burning; it must not go out. Every morning the priest is to add firewood and arrange the burnt offering on the fire and burn the fat of the fellowship offerings*a* on it. ¹³The fire must be kept burning on the altar continuously; it must not go out.

■ The Grain Offering

¹⁴" 'These are the regulations for the grain offering: Aaron's sons are to bring it before the LORD, in front of the altar. ¹⁵The priest is to take a handful of fine flour and oil, together with all the incense on the grain offering, and burn the memorial portion on the altar as an aroma pleasing to the LORD. ¹⁶Aaron and his sons shall eat the rest of it, but it is to be eaten without yeast in a holy place; they are to eat it in the courtyard of the Tent of Meeting. ¹⁷It must not be baked with yeast; I have given it as their share of the offerings made to me by fire. Like the sin offering and the guilt offering, it is most holy. ¹⁸Any male descendant of Aaron may eat it. It is his regular share of the offerings made to the LORD by fire for the generations to come. Whatever touches it will become holy.' "*b*

¹⁹The LORD also said to Moses, ²⁰"This is the offering Aaron and his sons are to bring to the LORD on the day he*c* is anointed: a tenth of an ephah*d* of fine flour as a regular grain offering, half of it in the morning and half in the evening. ²¹Prepare it with oil on a griddle; bring it well-mixed and present the grain offering broken*e* in pieces as an aroma pleasing to the LORD. ²²The son who is to succeed him as anointed priest shall prepare it. It is the LORD's regular share and is to be burned completely. ²³Every grain offering of a priest shall be burned completely; it must not be eaten."

■ The Sin Offering

²⁴The LORD said to Moses, ²⁵"Say to Aaron and his sons: 'These are the regulations for the sin offering: The sin offering is to be slaughtered before the LORD in the place where the burnt offering is slaughtered; it is most holy. ²⁶The priest who offers it shall eat it; it is to be eaten in a holy place, in the courtyard of the Tent of Meeting. ²⁷Whatever touches any of the flesh will become holy, and if any of the blood is spattered on a garment, you must wash it in a holy place. ²⁸The clay pot that the meat is cooked in must be broken; but if it is cooked in a bronze pot, the pot is to be scoured and rinsed with water. ²⁹Any male in a priest's family may eat it; it is most holy. ³⁰But any sin offering whose blood is brought into the Tent of Meeting to make atonement in the Holy Place must not be eaten; it must be burned.

■ The Guilt Offering

7 " 'These are the regulations for the guilt offering, which is most holy: ²The guilt offering is to be slaughtered in the place where the burnt offering is slaughtered, and its blood is to be sprinkled against the altar on all sides. ³All its fat shall be offered: the fat tail and the fat that covers the inner parts, ⁴both kidneys with the fat on them near the loins, and the covering of the liver, which is to be removed with the kidneys. ⁵The priest shall burn them on the altar as an offering made to the LORD by fire. It is a guilt offering. ⁶Any male in a priest's family may eat it, but it must be eaten in a holy place; it is most holy.

⁷" 'The same law applies to both the sin offering and the guilt offering: They belong to the priest who makes atonement with them. ⁸The priest who offers a burnt offering for anyone may keep its hide for himself. ⁹Every grain offering baked in an oven or cooked in a pan or on a griddle belongs to the priest who offers it, ¹⁰and every grain offering, whether mixed with oil or dry, belongs equally to all the sons of Aaron.

■ The Fellowship Offering

¹¹" 'These are the regulations for the fellowship offering*a* a person may present to the LORD:

¹²" 'If he offers it as an expression of thankfulness, then along with this thank-offering he is to offer cakes of bread made without yeast and mixed with oil, wafers made without yeast and spread with oil, and cakes of fine flour well-kneaded and mixed with oil. ¹³Along with his fellowship offering of thanksgiving he is to present an offering with cakes of bread made with yeast. ¹⁴He is to bring one of each kind as an offering, a contribution to the LORD; it

---

a12 Traditionally peace offerings   *b18 Or Whoever touches them must be holy; similarly in verse 27*   *c20 Or each*   *d20 That is, probably about 4 pints (about 2 litres)*   *e21 The meaning of the Hebrew for this word is uncertain.*   *a11 Traditionally peace offering; also in verses 13–37* belongs to the priest who sprinkles the blood of the fellowship offerings. [15]The meat of his fellowship offering of thanksgiving must be eaten on the day it is offered; he must leave none of it till morning.

[16]" 'If, however, his offering is the result of a vow or is a freewill offering, the sacrifice shall be eaten on the day he offers it, but anything left over may be eaten on the next day. [17]Any meat of the sacrifice left over till the third day must be burned up. [18]If any meat of the fellowship offering is eaten on the third day, it will not be accepted. It will not be credited to the one who offered it, for it is impure; the person who eats any of it will be held responsible.

[19]" 'Meat that touches anything ceremonially unclean must not be eaten; it must be burned up. As for other meat, anyone ceremonially clean may eat it. [20]But if anyone who is unclean eats any meat of the fellowship offering belonging to the LORD, that person must be cut off from his people. [21]If anyone touches something unclean — whether human uncleanness or an unclean animal or any unclean, detestable thing — and then eats any of the meat of the fellowship offering belonging to the LORD, that person must be cut off from his people.' "

■ Eating Fat and Blood Forbidden

[22]The LORD said to Moses, [23]"Say to the Israelites: 'Do not eat any of the fat of cattle, sheep or goats. [24]The fat of an animal found dead or torn by wild animals may be used for any other purpose, but you must not eat it. [25]Anyone who eats the fat of an animal from which an offering by fire may be[b] made to the LORD must be cut off from his people. [26]And wherever you live, you must not eat the blood of any bird or animal. [27]If anyone eats blood, that person must be cut off from his people.' "

■ The Priests' Share

[28]The LORD said to Moses, [29]"Say to the Israelites: 'Anyone who brings a fellowship offering to the LORD is to bring part of it as his sacrifice to the LORD. [30]With his own hands he is to bring the offering made to the LORD by fire; he is to bring the fat, together with the breast, and wave the breast before the LORD as a wave offering. [31]The priest shall burn the fat on the altar, but the breast belongs to Aaron and his sons. [32]You are to give the right thigh of your fellowship offerings to the priest as a contribution. [33]The son of Aaron who offers the blood and the fat of the fellowship offering shall have the right thigh as his share. [34]From the fellowship offerings of the Israelites, I have taken the breast that is waved and the thigh that is presented and have given them to Aaron the priest and his sons as their regular share from the Israelites.' "

[35]This is the portion of the offerings made to the LORD by fire that were allotted to Aaron and his sons on the day they were presented to serve the LORD as priests. [36]On the day they were anointed, the LORD commanded that the Israelites give this to them as their regular share for the generations to come.

[37]These, then, are the regulations for the burnt offering, the grain offering, the sin offering, the guilt offering, the ordination offering and the fellowship offering, [38]which the LORD gave Moses on Mount Sinai on the day he commanded the Israelites to bring their offerings to the LORD, in the Desert of Sinai.

7:34 ■ PRIESTLY PRIVILEGES

Priests enjoyed certain privileges, such as exemption from military duty and the right to keep portions of the offerings as food. Yet the priests were not "holier than thou". They had to offer regular sacrifices for their own sins as well as for the sins of the people (9:7–12). The New Testament book of Hebrews uses this fact to emphasise Christ's superiority: sinless, he offered a perfect, once-for-all sacrifice for the sake of others.

■ The Ordination of Aaron and His Sons

8 The LORD said to Moses, [2]"Bring Aaron and his sons, their garments, the anointing oil, the bull for the sin offering, the two rams and the basket containing bread made without yeast, [3]and gather the entire assembly at the entrance to the Tent of Meeting." [4]Moses did as the LORD commanded him, and the assembly gathered at the entrance to the Tent of Meeting.

8:2 ■ THE FIRST HIGH PRIEST

God had set apart the tribe of Levi to perform religious duties for the entire nation. In this scene Moses' brother Aaron assumed the new office of high priest. The impressive public ceremony lasted eight days in all and culminated in a dramatic display of God's approval (9:24). From then on, the priesthood remained in Aaron's family.

---

[5]Moses said to the assembly, "This is what the LORD has commanded to be done." [6]Then Moses brought Aaron and his sons forward and washed them with water. [7]He put the tunic on Aaron, tied the sash around him, clothed him with the robe and put the ephod on him. He also tied the ephod to him by its skilfully woven waistband; so it was fastened on him. [8]He placed the breastpiece on him and put the Urim and Thummim in the breastpiece. [9]Then he placed the turban on Aaron's head and set the gold plate, the sacred diadem, on the front of it, as the LORD commanded Moses.

[10]Then Moses took the anointing oil and anointed the tabernacle and everything in it, and so consecrated them. [11]He sprinkled some of the oil on the altar seven times, anointing the altar and all its utensils and the basin with its stand, to consecrate them. [12]He poured some of the anointing oil on Aaron's head and anointed him to consecrate him. [13]Then he brought Aaron's sons forward, put tunics on them, tied sashes around them and put headbands on them, as the LORD commanded Moses.

[14]He then presented the bull for the sin offering, and Aaron and his sons laid their hands on its head.

[b] 25 Or fire is

15Moses slaughtered the bull and took some of the blood, and with his finger he put it on all the horns of the altar to purify the altar. He poured out the rest of the blood at the base of the altar. So he consecrated it to make atonement for it. 16Moses also took all the fat around the inner parts, the covering of the liver, and both kidneys and their fat, and burned it on the altar. 17But the bull with its hide and its flesh and its offal he burned up outside the camp, as the LORD commanded Moses.

18He then presented the ram for the burnt offering, and Aaron and his sons laid their hands on its head. 19Then Moses slaughtered the ram and sprinkled the blood against the altar on all sides. 20He cut the ram into pieces and burned the head, the pieces and the fat. 21He washed the inner parts and the legs with water and burned the whole ram on the altar as a burnt offering, a pleasing aroma, an offering made to the LORD by fire, as the LORD commanded Moses.

22He then presented the other ram, the ram for the ordination, and Aaron and his sons laid their hands on its head. 23Moses slaughtered the ram and took some of its blood and put it on the lobe of Aaron's right ear, on the thumb of his right hand and on the big toe of his right foot. 24Moses also brought Aaron's sons forward and put some of the blood on the lobes of their right ears, on the thumbs of their right hands and on the big toes of their right feet. Then he sprinkled blood against the altar on all sides. 25He took the fat, the fat tail, all the fat around the inner parts, the covering of the liver, both kidneys and their fat and the right thigh. 26Then from the basket of bread made without yeast, which was before the LORD, he took a cake of bread, and one made with oil, and a wafer; he put these on the fat portions and on the right thigh. 27He put all these in the hands of Aaron and his sons and waved them before the LORD as a wave offering. 28Then Moses took them from their hands and burned them on the altar on top of the burnt offering as an ordination offering, a pleasing aroma, an offering made to the LORD by fire. 29He also took the breast — Moses' share of the ordination ram — and waved it before the LORD as a wave offering, as the LORD commanded Moses.

30Then Moses took some of the anointing oil and some of the blood from the altar and sprinkled them on Aaron and his garments and on his sons and their garments. So he consecrated Aaron and his garments and his sons and their garments.

31Moses then said to Aaron and his sons, "Cook the meat at the entrance to the Tent of Meeting and eat it there with the bread from the basket of ordination offerings, as I commanded, saying,a 'Aaron and his sons are to eat it.' 32Then burn up the rest of the meat and the bread. 33Do not leave the entrance to the Tent of Meeting for seven days, until the days of your ordination are completed, for your ordination will last seven days. 34What has been done today was commanded by the LORD to make atonement for you. 35You must stay at the entrance to the Tent of Meeting day and night for seven days and do what the LORD requires, so that you will not die; for that is what I have been commanded." 36So Aaron and his

sons did everything the LORD commanded through Moses.

■ The Priests Begin Their Ministry

9 On the eighth day Moses summoned Aaron and his sons and the elders of Israel. 2He said to Aaron, "Take a bull calf for your sin offering and a ram for your burnt offering, both without defect, and present them before the LORD. 3Then say to the Israelites: 'Take a male goat for a sin offering, a calf and a lamb — both a year old and without defect — for a burnt offering, 4and an oxa and a ram for a fellowship offeringb to sacrifice before the LORD, together with a grain offering mixed with oil. For today the LORD will appear to you.' "

5They took the things Moses commanded to the front of the Tent of Meeting, and the entire assembly came near and stood before the LORD. 6Then Moses said, "This is what the LORD has commanded you to do, so that the glory of the LORD may appear to you." 7Moses said to Aaron, "Come to the altar and sacrifice your sin offering and your burnt offering and make atonement for yourself and the people; sacrifice the offering that is for the people and make atonement for them, as the LORD has commanded."

8So Aaron came to the altar and slaughtered the calf as a sin offering for himself. 9His sons brought the blood to him, and he dipped his finger into the blood and put it on the horns of the altar; the rest of the blood he poured out at the base of the altar. 10On the altar he burned the fat, the kidneys and the covering of the liver from the sin offering, as the LORD commanded Moses; 11the flesh and the hide he burned up outside the camp.

12Then he slaughtered the burnt offering. His sons handed him the blood, and he sprinkled it against the altar on all sides. 13They handed him the burnt offering piece by piece, including the head, and he burned them on the altar. 14He washed the inner parts and the legs and burned them on top of the burnt offering on the altar.

15Aaron then brought the offering that was for the people. He took the goat for the people's sin offering and slaughtered it and offered it for a sin offering as he did with the first one.

16He brought the burnt offering and offered it in the prescribed way. 17He also brought the grain offering, took a handful of it and burned it on the altar in addition to the morning's burnt offering.

18He slaughtered the ox and the ram as the fellowship offering for the people. His sons handed him the blood, and he sprinkled it against the altar on all sides. 19But the fat portions of the ox and the ram — the fat tail, the layer of fat, the kidneys and the covering of the liver — 20these they laid on the breasts, and then Aaron burned the fat on the altar. 21Aaron waved the breasts and the right thigh before the LORD as a wave offering, as Moses commanded.

22Then Aaron lifted his hands towards the people and blessed them. And having sacrificed the sin offering, the burnt offering and the fellowship offering, he stepped down.

23Moses and Aaron then went into the Tent of Meeting. When they came out, they blessed the people; and the glory of the LORD appeared to all the

a31 Or I was commanded: a4 The Hebrew word can include both male and female; also in verses 18 and 19. b4 Traditionally peace offering; also in verses 18 and 22 people. ²⁴Fire came out from the presence of the LORD and consumed the burnt offering and the fat portions on the altar. And when all the people saw it, they shouted for joy and fell face down.

9:23 ■ THE GLORY OF THE LORD
Israelites were familiar with the brilliant glory of the Lord, but they had seen it only from a distance, on Mount Sinai. Even from that distance it had frightened them (Exodus 19:16–22). Now this glory had come to the Tent of Meeting itself, in the camp's centre. They were indeed "close to God".

■ The Death of Nadab and Abihu

10 Aaron's sons Nadab and Abihu took their censers, put fire in them and added incense; and they offered unauthorised fire before the LORD, contrary to his command. ²So fire came out from the presence of the LORD and consumed them, and they died before the LORD. ³Moses then said to Aaron, "This is what the LORD spoke of when he said:

" 'Among those who approach me
    I will show myself holy;
in the sight of all the people
    I will be honoured.' "

Aaron remained silent.

10:2 ■ FATAL ERROR
At first Aaron and his sons did everything according to God's instructions, and God honoured them (8:36; 9:24). But in very short order some of the first official priests got careless about following God's explicit orders. The severe punishment sent out a strong message to other priests: they were there to carry out God's plan, not their own.

⁴Moses summoned Mishael and Elzaphan, sons of Aaron's uncle Uzziel, and said to them, "Come here; carry your cousins outside the camp, away from the front of the sanctuary." ⁵So they came and carried them, still in their tunics, outside the camp, as Moses ordered.
⁶Then Moses said to Aaron and his sons Eleazar and Ithamar, "Do not let your hair become unkempt,^a and do not tear your clothes, or you will die and the LORD will be angry with the whole community. But your relatives, all the house of Israel, may mourn for those the LORD has destroyed by fire. ⁷Do not leave the entrance to the Tent of Meeting or you will die, because the LORD's anointing oil is on you." So they did as Moses said.
⁸Then the LORD said to Aaron, ⁹"You and your sons are not to drink wine or other fermented drink whenever you go into the Tent of Meeting, or you will die. This is a lasting ordinance for the generations to come. ¹⁰You must distinguish between the holy and the common, between the unclean and the

clean, ¹¹and you must teach the Israelites all the decrees the LORD has given them through Moses."
¹²Moses said to Aaron and his remaining sons, Eleazar and Ithamar, "Take the grain offering left over from the offerings made to the LORD by fire and eat it prepared without yeast beside the altar, for it is most holy. ¹³Eat it in a holy place, because it is your share and your sons' share of the offerings made to the LORD by fire; for so I have been commanded. ¹⁴But you and your sons and your daughters may eat the breast that was waved and the thigh that was presented. Eat them in a ceremonially clean place; they have been given to you and your children as your share of the Israelites' fellowship offerings.^b ¹⁵The thigh that was presented and the breast that was waved must be brought with the fat portions of the offerings made by fire, to be waved before the LORD as a wave offering. This will be the regular share for you and your children, as the LORD has commanded."
¹⁶When Moses enquired about the goat of the sin offering and found that it had been burned up, he was angry with Eleazar and Ithamar, Aaron's remaining sons, and asked, ¹⁷"Why didn't you eat the sin offering in the sanctuary area? It is most holy; it was given to you to take away the guilt of the community by making atonement for them before the LORD. ¹⁸Since its blood was not taken into the Holy Place, you should have eaten the goat in the sanctuary area, as I commanded."
¹⁹Aaron replied to Moses, "Today they sacrificed their sin offering and their burnt offering before the LORD, but such things as this have happened to me. Would the LORD have been pleased if I had eaten the sin offering today?" ²⁰When Moses heard this, he was satisfied.

■ Clean and Unclean Food

11 The LORD said to Moses and Aaron, ²"Say to the Israelites: 'Of all the animals that live on land, these are the ones you may eat: ³You may eat any animal that has a split hoof completely divided and that chews the cud.
⁴" 'There are some that only chew the cud or only have a split hoof, but you must not eat them. The camel, though it chews the cud, does not have a split hoof; it is ceremonially unclean for you. ⁵The coney,^a though it chews the cud, does not have a split hoof; it is unclean for you. ⁶The rabbit, though it chews the cud, does not have a split hoof; it is unclean for you. ⁷And the pig, though it has a split hoof completely divided, does not chew the cud; it is unclean for you. ⁸You must not eat their meat or touch their carcasses; they are unclean for you.
⁹" 'Of all the creatures living in the water of the seas and the streams, you may eat any that have fins and scales. ¹⁰But all creatures in the seas or streams that do not have fins and scales — whether among all the swarming things or among all the other living creatures in the water — you are to detest. ¹¹And since you are to detest them, you must not eat their meat and you must detest their carcasses. ¹²Anything living in the water that does not have fins and scales is to be detestable to you.
¹³" 'These are the birds you are to detest and not

---

^a6 Or *Do not uncover your heads*   ^b14 Traditionally *peace offerings*   ^a5 That is, the hyrax or rock badger

eat because they are detestable: the eagle, the vulture, the black vulture, [14]the red kite, any kind of black kite, [15]any kind of raven, [16]the horned owl, the screech owl, the gull, any kind of hawk, [17]the little owl, the cormorant, the great owl, [18]the white owl, the desert owl, the osprey, [19]the stork, any kind of heron, the hoopoe and the bat.[b]

[20]" 'All flying insects that walk on all fours are to be detestable to you. [21]There are, however, some winged creatures that walk on all fours that you may eat: those that have jointed legs for hopping on the ground. [22]Of these you may eat any kind of locust, katydid, cricket or grasshopper. [23]But all other winged creatures that have four legs you are to detest.

[24]" 'You will make yourselves unclean by these; whoever touches their carcasses will be unclean till evening. [25]Whoever picks up one of their carcasses must wash his clothes, and he will be unclean till evening.

[26]" 'Every animal that has a split hoof not completely divided or that does not chew the cud is unclean for you; whoever touches ⌊the carcass of⌋ any of them will be unclean. [27]Of all the animals that walk on all fours, those that walk on their paws are unclean for you; whoever touches their carcasses will be unclean till evening. [28]Anyone who picks up their carcasses must wash his clothes, and he will be unclean till evening. They are unclean for you.

[29]" 'Of the animals that move about on the ground, these are unclean for you: the weasel, the rat, any kind of great lizard, [30]the gecko, the monitor lizard, the wall lizard, the skink and the chameleon. [31]Of all those that move along the ground, these are unclean for you. Whoever touches them when they are dead will be unclean till evening. [32]When one of them dies and falls on something, that article, whatever its use, will be unclean, whether it is made of wood, cloth, hide or sackcloth. Put it in water; it will be unclean till evening, and then it will be clean. [33]If one of them falls into a clay pot, everything in it will be unclean, and you must break the pot. [34]Any food that could be eaten but has water on it from such a pot is unclean, and any liquid that could be drunk from it is unclean. [35]Anything that one of their carcasses falls on becomes unclean; an oven or cooking pot must be broken up. They are unclean, and you are to regard them as unclean. [36]A spring, however, or a cistern for collecting water remains clean, but anyone who touches one of these carcasses is unclean. [37]If a carcass falls on any seeds that are to be planted, they remain clean. [38]But if water has been put on the seed and a carcass falls on it, it is unclean for you.

[39]" 'If an animal that you are allowed to eat dies, anyone who touches the carcass will be unclean till evening. [40]Anyone who eats some of the carcass must wash his clothes, and he will be unclean till evening. Anyone who picks up the carcass must wash his clothes, and he will be unclean till evening.

[41]" 'Every creature that moves about on the ground is detestable; it is not to be eaten. [42]You are not to eat any creature that moves about on the ground, whether it moves on its belly or walks on all fours or on many feet; it is detestable. [43]Do not defile yourselves by any of these creatures. Do not make yourselves unclean by means of them or be made unclean by them. [44]I am the LORD your God; consecrate yourselves and be holy, because I am holy. Do not make yourselves unclean by any creature that moves about on the ground. [45]I am the LORD who brought you up out of Egypt to be your God; therefore be holy, because I am holy.

[46]" 'These are the regulations concerning animals, birds, every living thing that moves in the water and every creature that moves about on the ground. [47]You must distinguish between the unclean and the clean, between living creatures that may be eaten and those that may not be eaten.' "

11:47 ■ OF RAVENS AND RABBITS
Scholars have long puzzled over the seemingly arbitrary division between "clean" and "unclean" foods. Why permit the eating of certain fish but not shrimp, and cows but not pigs? "An Invisible Danger", page 98, discusses some of the theories that have been proposed. Probably the best explanation is that God was indeed being arbitrary, in order to form a nation different from any other (see 20:26). In Acts 10 God shows that there is nothing intrinsically wrong with the animals labelled "unclean" in Leviticus.

■ Purification After Childbirth

12 The LORD said to Moses, [2]"Say to the Israelites: 'A woman who becomes pregnant and gives birth to a son will be ceremonially unclean for seven days, just as she is unclean during her monthly period. [3]On the eighth day the boy is to be circumcised. [4]Then the woman must wait thirty-three days to be purified from her bleeding. She must not touch anything sacred or go to the sanctuary until the days of her purification are over. [5]If she gives birth to a daughter, for two weeks the woman will be unclean, as during her period. Then she must wait sixty-six days to be purified from her bleeding.

[6]" 'When the days of her purification for a son or daughter are over, she is to bring to the priest at the entrance to the Tent of Meeting a year-old lamb for a burnt offering and a young pigeon or a dove for a sin offering. [7]He shall offer them before the LORD to make atonement for her, and then she will be ceremonially clean from her flow of blood.

" 'These are the regulations for the woman who gives birth to a boy or a girl. [8]If she cannot afford a lamb, she is to bring two doves or two young pigeons, one for a burnt offering and the other for a sin offering. In this way the priest will make atonement for her, and she will be clean.' "

12:8 ■ FOR POOR PEOPLE
This alternative offering enabled poor women to live up to their duty to God. Mary offered such a sacrifice after Jesus' birth (see Luke 2:24) — an indication that Jesus' family was not well-off.

---

[b] 19 The precise identification of some of the birds, insects and animals in this chapter is uncertain.

■ Regulations About Infectious Skin Diseases

13 The LORD said to Moses and Aaron, [2]"When anyone has a swelling or a rash or a bright spot on his skin that may become an infectious skin disease,[a] he must be brought to Aaron the priest or to one of his sons[b] who is a priest. [3]The priest is to examine the sore on his skin, and if the hair in the sore has turned white and the sore appears to be more than skin deep,[c] it is an infectious skin disease. When the priest examines him, he shall pronounce him ceremonially unclean. [4]If the spot on his skin is white but does not appear to be more than skin deep and the hair in it has not turned white, the priest is to put the infected person in isolation for seven days. [5]On the seventh day the priest is to examine him, and if he sees that the sore is unchanged and has not spread in the skin, he is to keep him in isolation another seven days. [6]On the seventh day the priest is to examine him again, and if the sore has faded and has not spread in the skin, the priest shall pronounce him clean; it is only a rash. The man must wash his clothes, and he will be clean. [7]But if the rash does spread in his skin after he has shown himself to the priest to be pronounced clean, he must appear before the priest again. [8]The priest is to examine him, and if the rash has spread in the skin, he shall pronounce him unclean; it is an infectious disease.

[9]"When anyone has an infectious skin disease, he must be brought to the priest. [10]The priest is to examine him, and if there is a white swelling in the skin that has turned the hair white and if there is raw flesh in the swelling, [11]it is a chronic skin disease and the priest shall pronounce him unclean. He is not to put him in isolation, because he is already unclean.

[12]"If the disease breaks out all over his skin and, so far as the priest can see, it covers all the skin of the infected person from head to foot, [13]the priest is to examine him, and if the disease has covered his whole body, he shall pronounce that person clean. Since it has all turned white, he is clean. [14]But whenever raw flesh appears on him, he will be unclean. [15]When the priest sees the raw flesh, he shall pronounce him unclean. The raw flesh is unclean; he has an infectious disease. [16]Should the raw flesh change and turn white, he must go to the priest. [17]The priest is to examine him, and if the sores have turned white, the priest shall pronounce the infected person clean; then he will be clean.

13:17 ■ MISIDENTIFICATION
Victims of leprosy, or Hansen's disease, have endured untold suffering because earlier versions of the Bible translated as "leprosy" the Hebrew word for "infectious skin disease" mentioned in this chapter. The symptoms described here have little to do with leprosy, a disease of the nerves — not skin — which is barely contagious.

---

[18]"When someone has a boil on his skin and it heals, [19]and in the place where the boil was, a white swelling or reddish-white spot appears, he must present himself to the priest. [20]The priest is to examine it, and if it appears to be more than skin deep and the hair in it has turned white, the priest shall pronounce him unclean. It is an infectious skin disease that has broken out where the boil was. [21]But if, when the priest examines it, there is no white hair in it and it is not more than skin deep and has faded, then the priest is to put him in isolation for seven days. [22]If it is spreading in the skin, the priest shall pronounce him unclean; it is infectious. [23]But if the spot is unchanged and has not spread, it is only a scar from the boil, and the priest shall pronounce him clean.

[24]"When someone has a burn on his skin and a reddish-white or white spot appears in the raw flesh of the burn, [25]the priest is to examine the spot, and if the hair in it has turned white, and it appears to be more than skin deep, it is an infectious disease that has broken out in the burn. The priest shall pronounce him unclean; it is an infectious skin disease. [26]But if the priest examines it and there is no white hair in the spot and if it is not more than skin deep and has faded, then the priest is to put him in isolation for seven days. [27]On the seventh day the priest is to examine him, and if it is spreading in the skin, the priest shall pronounce him unclean; it is an infectious skin disease. [28]If, however, the spot is unchanged and has not spread in the skin but has faded, it is a swelling from the burn, and the priest shall pronounce him clean; it is only a scar from the burn.

[29]"If a man or woman has a sore on the head or on the chin, [30]the priest is to examine the sore, and if it appears to be more than skin deep and the hair in it is yellow and thin, the priest shall pronounce that person unclean; it is an itch, an infectious disease of the head or chin. [31]But if, when the priest examines this kind of sore, it does not seem to be more than skin deep and there is no black hair in it, then the priest is to put the infected person in isolation for seven days. [32]On the seventh day the priest is to examine the sore, and if the itch has not spread and there is no yellow hair in it and it does not appear to be more than skin deep, [33]he must be shaved except for the diseased area, and the priest is to keep him in isolation another seven days. [34]On the seventh day the priest is to examine the itch, and if it has not spread in the skin and appears to be no more than skin deep, the priest shall pronounce him clean. He must wash his clothes, and he will be clean. [35]But if the itch does spread in the skin after he is pronounced clean, [36]the priest is to examine him, and if the itch has spread in the skin, the priest does not need to look for yellow hair; the person is unclean. [37]If, however, in his judgment it is unchanged and black hair has grown in it, the itch is healed. He is clean, and the priest shall pronounce him clean.

[38]"When a man or woman has white spots on the skin, [39]the priest is to examine them, and if the spots are dull white, it is a harmless rash that has broken out on the skin; that person is clean.

[40]"When a man has lost his hair and is bald, he is clean. [41]If he has lost his hair from the front of his scalp and has a bald forehead, he is clean. [42]But if he has a reddish-white sore on his bald head or forehead, it is an infectious disease breaking out on his head or forehead. [43]The priest is to examine him,

---

[a]2 Traditionally *leprosy*; the Hebrew word was used for various diseases affecting the skin—not necessarily leprosy; also elsewhere in this chapter.
[b]2 Or *descendants*   [c]3 Or *be lower than the rest of the skin*; also elsewhere in this chapter

and if the swollen sore on his head or forehead is reddish-white like an infectious skin disease, [44]the man is diseased and is unclean. The priest shall pronounce him unclean because of the sore on his head.

[45]"The person with such an infectious disease must wear torn clothes, let his hair be unkempt,[d] cover the lower part of his face and cry out, 'Unclean! Unclean!' [46]As long as he has the infection he remains unclean. He must live alone; he must live outside the camp.

■ Regulations About Mildew

[47]"If any clothing is contaminated with mildew — any woollen or linen clothing, [48]any woven or knitted material of linen or wool, any leather or anything made of leather — [49]and if the contamination in the clothing, or leather, or woven or knitted material, or any leather article, is greenish or reddish, it is a spreading mildew and must be shown to the priest. [50]The priest is to examine the mildew and isolate the affected article for seven days. [51]On the seventh day he is to examine it, and if the mildew has spread in the clothing, or the woven or knitted material, or

the leather, whatever its use, it is a destructive mildew; the article is unclean. [52]He must burn up the clothing, or the woven or knitted material of wool or linen, or any leather article that has the contamination in it, because the mildew is destructive; the article must be burned up.

[53]"But if, when the priest examines it, the mildew has not spread in the clothing, or the woven or knitted material, or the leather article, [54]he shall order that the contaminated article be washed. Then he is to isolate it for another seven days. [55]After the affected article has been washed, the priest is to examine it, and if the mildew has not changed its appearance, even though it has not spread, it is unclean. Burn it with fire, whether the mildew has affected one side or the other. [56]If, when the priest examines it, the mildew has faded after the article has been washed, he is to tear the contaminated part out of the clothing, or the leather, or the woven or knitted material. [57]But if it reappears in the clothing, or in the woven or knitted material, or in the leather article, it is spreading, and whatever has the mildew must be burned with fire. [58]The clothing, or the woven or

■ AN INVISIBLE DANGER
TAKING PRECAUTIONS: LIKE A SURGEON PREPARING TO OPERATE

INSIGHT

YOU MUST DISTINGUISH BETWEEN THE UNCLEAN AND THE CLEAN. ■ 11:47

For many years surgery remained a desperate last resort for the hopelessly ill. Surgeons knew nothing about germs. Without washing, they would put on operating clothes, usually an old coat caked with blood and pus from numerous operations. They would pick up the scalpel, wiped clean with an old rag after the last operation, and go to work. Half of those operated on died.

One pioneer after another stumbled on the correct sterile techniques. But each was scorned and humiliated by fellow doctors. Professor Ignaz Semmelweis, for one, discovered that making doctors wash their hands could dramatically cut the death rate in maternity wards. Yet his colleagues opposed Semmelweis strenuously, and though he argued for handwashing throughout his life, he died without seeing his ideas take hold.

■ WHY SO SLOW?
Why were doctors so slow to adopt sterile techniques? The answer is simple: germs had not yet been discovered. Doctors could not see — and reformers like Semmelweis could not give them — any reason why washing hands should make a difference.

Then Louis Pasteur discovered microorganisms under his microscope. Sterile

procedures began to make sense: they made war on germs. Even so, each reform, from rubber gloves to gauze masks, was accepted only grudgingly and with considerable opposition. It was as though doctors had a hard time remembering that something invisible could be so devastating. Fifty years of constant education and reform were necessary before "sterile technique" became a routine part of surgery, and germs became "real" to most medical minds.

■ WHY ALL THE RULES?
As germs are to a surgeon, "uncleanness" is to Leviticus. Chapters 11–15 describe elaborate precautions — what animals to avoid and how to treat "unclean" skin disease, mildewed clothing or walls and bodily emissions.

Scholars point out that many clean and unclean rules have good health habits behind them, such as the rule to quarantine a person with an infectious disease or the rule against eating pork (which carries many parasites).

Others say that dietary laws were meant to keep the Israelites apart from their neighbours. Pigs were prominent in Canaanite worship; therefore the Israelites were not to eat pigs. A different dietary standard would keep the two groups from mixing socially, for a meal was always part of Middle Eastern hospitality.

Still other scholars suggest that the uncleanness rules simply fit into what knitted material, or any leather article that has been washed and is rid of the mildew, must be washed again, and it will be clean."

⁵⁹These are the regulations concerning contamination by mildew in woollen or linen clothing, woven or knitted material, or any leather article, for pronouncing them clean or unclean.

■ Cleansing From Infectious Skin Diseases

14 The LORD said to Moses, ²"These are the regulations for the diseased person at the time of his ceremonial cleansing, when he is brought to the priest: ³The priest is to go outside the camp and examine him. If the person has been healed of his infectious skin disease,ᵃ ⁴the priest shall order that two live clean birds and some cedar wood, scarlet yarn and hyssop be brought for the one to be cleansed. ⁵Then the priest shall order that one of the birds be killed over fresh water in a clay pot. ⁶He is then to take the live bird and dip it, together with the cedar wood, the scarlet yarn and the hyssop, into the blood of the bird that was killed over the fresh water. ⁷Seven times he shall sprinkle the one to be cleansed of the infectious disease and pronounce him clean. Then he is to release the live bird in the open fields.

14:7 ■ A BIRD SET FREE
It is difficult to assign definite symbolic meaning to all the details in this ceremony for the cleansing of skin diseases. Many scholars suggest that the bird that was killed represented purification by sacrifice, while the bird set free represented new liberty after a long quarantine. When Jesus healed a man with leprosy (Matthew 8:4), he told him to follow these instructions.

⁸"The person to be cleansed must wash his clothes, shave off all his hair and bathe with water; then he will be ceremonially clean. After this he may come into the camp, but he must stay outside his tent for seven days. ⁹On the seventh day he must shave off all his hair; he must shave his head, his beard, his eyebrows and the rest of his hair. He must

Israelites intuitively thought proper. God was reinforcing a natural sense of repulsion towards creeping insects, scavenger birds, bodily emissions and skin diseases.

■ THE HABIT OF CAREFULNESS
All these explanations have merit, but the underlying basis of clean and unclean was religious. Being unclean was not dangerous or wrong. In fact, you could hardly avoid it. Practically everyone became "unclean" from time to time. But you could not worship God in the Tent of Meeting while you were unclean, nor bring anything unclean into the presence of God. His holiness would destroy it — and you (Leviticus 15:31).

So Leviticus trains God's people to watch their lives as carefully as surgeons watch their sterile techniques. They must develop the habit of carefulness, even about something they cannot see or feel. They must think about preparing themselves for God, not just do whatever "feels right".

It was not a question of how they felt about God, any more than a surgeon's concern is how he "feels" about germs. Clear, absolute standards laid out what could be acceptable to a God who is perfectly clean, absolute, unchanging. Just as surgeons had to struggle to take germs seriously, so God's people must learn to "purify themselves" for God.

■ TOUCHING THE UNCLEAN
The uncleanness rules of Leviticus are outmoded because of Jesus' declaration that all things are clean (Mark 7:19; see also Acts 10:9–16). But the lessons behind these rules remain valid. God still may not be approached carelessly. Each person must examine his or her life, to be certain that God's purity is not violated.

Until Jesus' day, the slow spread of uncleanness seemed irreversible. You could avoid it, but you could not get rid of it. Contact with anything unclean made you unclean yourself. Naturally, certain diseases, notably leprosy, were twice cursed: they were both dangerous and unclean. You kept away from leprosy, absolutely.

Then Jesus touched a man with leprosy, and he became clean. Jesus touched a woman suffering from internal bleeding, and she was healed. For the first time, cleanness rather than uncleanness spread. The rules of Leviticus tell how to avoid uncleanness. Contact with Jesus, however, changes the unclean to clean.

□ LIFE QUESTIONS:
Suppose sin were visible — small green spots that break out on the skin. Do you think it would help people to take sin more seriously?

ᵃ3 Traditionally *leprosy*; the Hebrew word was used for various diseases affecting the skin—not necessarily leprosy; also elsewhere in this chapter.

wash his clothes and bathe himself with water, and he will be clean.

¹⁰"On the eighth day he must bring two male lambs and one ewe lamb a year old, each without defect, along with three-tenths of an ephah*b* of fine flour mixed with oil for a grain offering, and one log*c* of oil. ¹¹The priest who pronounces him clean shall present both the one to be cleansed and his offerings before the LORD at the entrance to the Tent of Meeting.

¹²"Then the priest is to take one of the male lambs and offer it as a guilt offering, along with the log of oil; he shall wave them before the LORD as a wave offering. ¹³He is to slaughter the lamb in the holy place where the sin offering and the burnt offering are slaughtered. Like the sin offering, the guilt offering belongs to the priest; it is most holy. ¹⁴The priest is to take some of the blood of the guilt offering and put it on the lobe of the right ear of the one to be cleansed, on the thumb of his right hand and on the big toe of his right foot. ¹⁵The priest shall then take some of the log of oil, pour it in the palm of his own left hand, ¹⁶dip his right forefinger into the oil in his palm, and with his finger sprinkle some of it before the LORD seven times. ¹⁷The priest is to put some of the oil remaining in his palm on the lobe of the right ear of the one to be cleansed, on the thumb of his right hand and on the big toe of his right foot, on top of the blood of the guilt offering. ¹⁸The rest of the oil in his palm the priest shall put on the head of the one to be cleansed and make atonement for him before the LORD.

¹⁹"Then the priest is to sacrifice the sin offering and make atonement for the one to be cleansed from his uncleanness. After that, the priest shall slaughter the burnt offering ²⁰and offer it on the altar, together with the grain offering, and make atonement for him, and he will be clean.

²¹"If, however, he is poor and cannot afford these, he must take one male lamb as a guilt offering to be waved to make atonement for him, together with a tenth of an ephah*d* of fine flour mixed with oil for a grain offering, a log of oil, ²²and two doves or two young pigeons, which he can afford, one for a sin offering and the other for a burnt offering.

²³"On the eighth day he must bring them for his cleansing to the priest at the entrance to the Tent of Meeting, before the LORD. ²⁴The priest is to take the lamb for the guilt offering, together with the log of oil, and wave them before the LORD as a wave offering. ²⁵He shall slaughter the lamb for the guilt offering and take some of its blood and put it on the lobe of the right ear of the one to be cleansed, on the thumb of his right hand and on the big toe of his right foot. ²⁶The priest is to pour some of the oil into the palm of his own left hand, ²⁷and with his right forefinger sprinkle some of the oil from his palm seven times before the LORD. ²⁸Some of the oil in his palm he is to put on the same places he put the blood of the guilt offering—on the lobe of the right ear of the one to be cleansed, on the thumb of his right hand and on the big toe of his right foot. ²⁹The rest of the oil in his palm the priest shall put on the head of the one to be cleansed, to make atonement for him before the LORD. ³⁰Then he shall sacrifice the

doves or the young pigeons, which the person can afford, ³¹one*e* as a sin offering and the other as a burnt offering, together with the grain offering. In this way the priest will make atonement before the LORD on behalf of the one to be cleansed."

³²These are the regulations for anyone who has an infectious skin disease and who cannot afford the regular offerings for his cleansing.

■ Cleansing From Mildew

³³The LORD said to Moses and Aaron, ³⁴"When you enter the land of Canaan, which I am giving you as your possession, and I put a spreading mildew in a house in that land, ³⁵the owner of the house must go and tell the priest, 'I have seen something that looks like mildew in my house.' ³⁶The priest is to order the house to be emptied before he goes in to examine the mildew, so that nothing in the house will be pronounced unclean. After this the priest is to go in and inspect the house. ³⁷He is to examine the mildew on the walls, and if it has greenish or reddish depressions that appear to be deeper than the surface of the wall, ³⁸the priest shall go out of the doorway of the house and close it up for seven days. ³⁹On the seventh day the priest shall return to inspect the house. If the mildew has spread on the walls, ⁴⁰he is to order that the contaminated stones be torn out and thrown into an unclean place outside the town. ⁴¹He must have all the inside walls of the house scraped and the material that is scraped off dumped into an unclean place outside the town. ⁴²Then they are to take other stones to replace these and take new clay and plaster the house.

⁴³"If the mildew reappears in the house after the stones have been torn out and the house scraped and plastered, ⁴⁴the priest is to go and examine it and, if the mildew has spread in the house, it is a destructive mildew; the house is unclean. ⁴⁵It must be torn down—its stones, timbers and all the plaster—and taken out of the town to an unclean place.

⁴⁶"Anyone who goes into the house while it is closed up will be unclean till evening. ⁴⁷Anyone who sleeps or eats in the house must wash his clothes.

⁴⁸"But if the priest comes to examine it and the mildew has not spread after the house has been plastered, he shall pronounce the house clean, because the mildew is gone. ⁴⁹To purify the house he is to take two birds and some cedar wood, scarlet yarn and hyssop. ⁵⁰He shall kill one of the birds over fresh water in a clay pot. ⁵¹Then he is to take the cedar wood, the hyssop, the scarlet yarn and the live bird, dip them into the blood of the dead bird and the fresh water, and sprinkle the house seven times. ⁵²He shall purify the house with the bird's blood, the fresh water, the live bird, the cedar wood, the hyssop and the scarlet yarn. ⁵³Then he is to release the live bird in the open fields outside the town. In this way he will make atonement for the house, and it will be clean."

⁵⁴These are the regulations for any infectious skin disease, for an itch, ⁵⁵for mildew in clothing or in a house, ⁵⁶and for a swelling, a rash or a bright spot, ⁵⁷to determine when something is clean or unclean.

---

b 10 That is, probably about 11½ pints (about 6.5 litres) *c 10* That is, probably about ½ pint (about 0.3 litre); also in verses 12, 15, 21 and 24 *d 21* That is, probably about 4 pints (about 2 litres) *e 31* Septuagint and Syriac; Hebrew ³¹*such as the person can afford, one*

These are the regulations for infectious skin diseases and mildew.

■ Discharges Causing Uncleanness

15 The LORD said to Moses and Aaron, [2]"Speak to the Israelites and say to them: 'When any man has a bodily discharge, the discharge is unclean. [3]Whether it continues flowing from his body or is blocked, it will make him unclean. This is how his discharge will bring about uncleanness:

15:2 ■ SEX RULES

Some of the rules regarding sex and bodily discharges mystify modern readers, but the Israelites took for granted that God had dominion over the most private aspects of their lives. The Bible does not provide a detailed rationale for these regulations. Some relate to health and hygiene: following the rules would help the Israelites avoid the venereal diseases that plagued their neighbours. Also, pagan religions commonly employed temple prostitutes, and God clearly intended for the Israelites to keep worship and sex separate.

[4]"'Any bed the man with a discharge lies on will be unclean, and anything he sits on will be unclean. [5]Anyone who touches his bed must wash his clothes and bathe with water, and he will be unclean till evening. [6]Whoever sits on anything that the man with a discharge sat on must wash his clothes and bathe with water, and he will be unclean till evening. [7]"'Whoever touches the man who has a discharge must wash his clothes and bathe with water, and he will be unclean till evening.

[8]"'If the man with the discharge spits on someone who is clean, that person must wash his clothes and bathe with water, and he will be unclean till evening.

[9]"'Everything the man sits on when riding will be unclean, [10]and whoever touches any of the things that were under him will be unclean till evening; whoever picks up those things must wash his clothes and bathe with water, and he will be unclean till evening.

[11]"'Anyone the man with a discharge touches without rinsing his hands with water must wash his clothes and bathe with water, and he will be unclean till evening.

[12]"'A clay pot that the man touches must be broken, and any wooden article is to be rinsed with water.

[13]"'When a man is cleansed from his discharge, he is to count off seven days for his ceremonial cleansing; he must wash his clothes and bathe himself with fresh water, and he will be clean. [14]On the eighth day he must take two doves or two young pigeons and come before the LORD to the entrance to the Tent of Meeting and give them to the priest. [15]The priest is to sacrifice them, the one for a sin offering and the other for a burnt offering. In this way he will make atonement before the LORD for the man because of his discharge.

[16]"'When a man has an emission of semen, he must bathe his whole body with water, and he will be unclean till evening. [17]Any clothing or leather that has semen on it must be washed with water, and it will be unclean till evening. [18]When a man lies with a woman and there is an emission of semen, both must bathe with water, and they will be unclean till evening.

[19]"'When a woman has her regular flow of blood, the impurity of her monthly period will last seven days, and anyone who touches her will be unclean till evening.

[20]"'Anything she lies on during her period will be unclean, and anything she sits on will be unclean. [21]Whoever touches her bed must wash his clothes and bathe with water, and he will be unclean till evening. [22]Whoever touches anything she sits on must wash his clothes and bathe with water, and he will be unclean till evening. [23]Whether it is the bed or anything she was sitting on, when anyone touches it, he will be unclean till evening.

[24]"'If a man lies with her and her monthly flow touches him, he will be unclean for seven days; any bed he lies on will be unclean.

[25]"'When a woman has a discharge of blood for many days at a time other than her monthly period or has a discharge that continues beyond her period, she will be unclean as long as she has the discharge, just as in the days of her period. [26]Any bed she lies on while her discharge continues will be unclean, as is her bed during her monthly period, and anything she sits on will be unclean, as during her period. [27]Whoever touches them will be unclean; he must wash his clothes and bathe with water, and he will be unclean till evening.

[28]"'When she is cleansed from her discharge, she must count off seven days, and after that she will be ceremonially clean. [29]On the eighth day she must take two doves or two young pigeons and bring them to the priest at the entrance to the Tent of Meeting. [30]The priest is to sacrifice one for a sin offering and the other for a burnt offering. In this way he will make atonement for her before the LORD for the uncleanness of her discharge.

[31]"'You must keep the Israelites separate from things that make them unclean, so they will not die in their uncleanness for defiling my dwelling-place,[a] which is among them.' "

[32]These are the regulations for a man with a discharge, for anyone made unclean by an emission of semen, [33]for a woman in her monthly period, for a man or a woman with a discharge, and for a man who lies with a woman who is ceremonially unclean.

■ The Day of Atonement

16 The LORD spoke to Moses after the death of the two sons of Aaron who died when they approached the LORD. [2]The LORD said to Moses: "Tell your brother Aaron not to come whenever he chooses into the Most Holy Place behind the curtain in front of the atonement cover on the ark, or else he will die, because I appear in the cloud over the atonement cover.

[3]"This is how Aaron is to enter the sanctuary area: with a young bull for a sin offering and a ram for a

[a] 31 Or my tabernacle

burnt offering. [4]He is to put on the sacred linen tunic, with linen undergarments next to his body; he is to tie the linen sash around him and put on the linen turban. These are sacred garments; so he must bathe himself with water before he puts them on. [5]From the Israelite community he is to take two male goats for a sin offering and a ram for a burnt offering.

[6]"Aaron is to offer the bull for his own sin offering to make atonement for himself and his household. [7]Then he is to take the two goats and present them before the LORD at the entrance to the Tent of Meeting. [8]He is to cast lots for the two goats—one lot for the LORD and the other for the scapegoat.[a] [9]Aaron shall bring the goat whose lot falls to the LORD and sacrifice it for a sin offering. [10]But the goat chosen by lot as the scapegoat shall be presented alive before the LORD to be used for making atonement by sending it into the desert as a scapegoat.

[11]"Aaron shall bring the bull for his own sin offering to make atonement for himself and his household, and he is to slaughter the bull for his own sin offering. [12]He is to take a censer full of burning coals from the altar before the LORD and two handfuls of finely ground fragrant incense and take them behind the curtain. [13]He is to put the incense on the fire before the LORD, and the smoke of the incense will conceal the atonement cover above the Testimony, so that he will not die. [14]He is to take some of the bull's blood and with his finger sprinkle it on the front of the atonement cover; then he shall sprinkle some of it with his finger seven times before the atonement cover.

[15]"He shall then slaughter the goat for the sin offering for the people and take its blood behind the curtain and do with it as he did with the bull's blood: He shall sprinkle it on the atonement cover and in front of it. [16]In this way he will make atonement for the Most Holy Place because of the uncleanness and rebellion of the Israelites, whatever their sins have been. He is to do the same for the Tent of Meeting, which is among them in the midst of their uncleanness. [17]No-one is to be in the Tent of Meeting from the time Aaron goes in to make atonement in the Most Holy Place until he comes out, having made atonement for himself, his household and the whole community of Israel.

[18]"Then he shall come out to the altar that is before the LORD and make atonement for it. He shall take some of the bull's blood and some of the goat's blood and put it on all the horns of the altar. [19]He shall sprinkle some of the blood on it with his finger seven times to cleanse it and consecrate it from the uncleanness of the Israelites.

[20]"When Aaron has finished making atonement for the Most Holy Place, the Tent of Meeting and the altar, he shall bring forward the live goat. [21]He is to lay both hands on the head of the live goat and confess over it all the wickedness and rebellion of the Israelites—all their sins—and put them on the goat's head. He shall send the goat away into the desert in the care of a man appointed for the task. [22]The goat will carry on itself all their sins to a solitary place; and the man shall release it in the desert.

[23]"Then Aaron is to go into the Tent of Meeting and take off the linen garments he put on before he entered the Most Holy Place, and he is to leave them there. [24]He shall bathe himself with water in a holy place and put on his regular garments. Then he shall come out and sacrifice the burnt offering for himself and the burnt offering for the people, to make atonement for himself and for the people. [25]He shall also burn the fat of the sin offering on the altar.

16:20 ■ SCAPEGOAT

The English word *scapegoat* (escape goat) was formed to capture the essence of this crucial ceremony in which a goat symbolically carried all the sins of Israel into the desert. Today the word is applied to anyone who takes the blame for something other people did.

[26]"The man who releases the goat as a scapegoat must wash his clothes and bathe himself with water; afterwards he may come into the camp. [27]The bull and the goat for the sin offerings, whose blood was brought into the Most Holy Place to make atonement, must be taken outside the camp; their hides, flesh and offal are to be burned up. [28]The man who burns them must wash his clothes and bathe himself with water; afterwards he may come into the camp.

[29]"This is to be a lasting ordinance for you: On the tenth day of the seventh month you must deny yourselves[b] and not do any work—whether native-born or an alien living among you—[30]because on this day atonement will be made for you, to cleanse you. Then, before the LORD, you will be clean from all your sins. [31]It is a sabbath of rest, and you must deny yourselves; it is a lasting ordinance. [32]The priest who is anointed and ordained to succeed his father as high priest is to make atonement. He is to put on the sacred linen garments [33]and make atonement for the Most Holy Place, for the Tent of Meeting and the altar, and for the priests and all the people of the community.

[34]"This is to be a lasting ordinance for you: Atonement is to be made once a year for all the sins of the Israelites."

And it was done, as the LORD commanded Moses.

■ Eating Blood Forbidden

17 The LORD said to Moses, [2]"Speak to Aaron and his sons and to all the Israelites and say to them: 'This is what the LORD has commanded: [3]Any Israelite who sacrifices an ox,[a] a lamb or a goat in the camp or outside of it [4]instead of bringing it to the entrance to the Tent of Meeting to present it as an offering to the LORD in front of the tabernacle of the LORD—that man shall be considered guilty of bloodshed; he has shed blood and must be cut off from his people. [5]This is so that the Israelites will bring to the LORD the sacrifices they are now making in the open fields. They must bring them to the priest, that is, to the LORD, at the entrance to the Tent of Meeting and sacrifice them as fellowship offerings.[b] [6]The priest is to sprinkle the blood against the altar of the LORD at the entrance to the Tent of Meeting and burn the fat as an aroma pleasing to the

---

[a]8 That is, the goat of removal; Hebrew *azazel*; also in verses 10 and 26 male and female.   [b]5 Traditionally *peace offerings*   [b]29 Or *must fast*; also in verse 31   [a]3 The Hebrew word can include both

LORD. 7They must no longer offer any of their sacrifices to the goat idols*c* to whom they prostitute themselves. This is to be a lasting ordinance for them and for the generations to come.'

8"Say to them: 'Any Israelite or any alien living among them who offers a burnt offering or sacrifice 9and does not bring it to the entrance to the Tent of Meeting to sacrifice it to the LORD—that man must be cut off from his people.

10" 'Any Israelite or any alien living among them who eats any blood—I will set my face against that person who eats blood and will cut him off from his people. 11For the life of a creature is in the blood, and I have given it to you to make atonement for yourselves on the altar; it is the blood that makes atonement for one's life. 12Therefore I say to the Israelites, "None of you may eat blood, nor may an alien living among you eat blood."

17:10 ■ KOSHER

To this day many Jews avoid meat unless it has been carefully drained of blood. Blood, which represented the life of living creatures, was to make atonement for, or to "cover up", sins. Thus Jesus' blood, signifying his death, has special significance to Christians. It is the blood of the ultimate sacrifice for sin.

The first Christians debated how much of the law should be required of non-Jews who became Christians (Acts 15). Of the four requirements they settled on, two were "kosher".

13" 'Any Israelite or any alien living among you who hunts any animal or bird that may be eaten must drain out the blood and cover it with earth, 14because the life of every creature is its blood. That is why I have said to the Israelites, "You must not eat the blood of any creature, because the life of every creature is its blood; anyone who eats it must be cut off."

15" 'Anyone, whether native-born or alien, who eats anything found dead or torn by wild animals must wash his clothes and bathe with water, and he will be ceremonially unclean till evening; then he will be clean. 16But if he does not wash his clothes and bathe himself, he will be held responsible.' "

■ Unlawful Sexual Relations

18 The LORD said to Moses, 2"Speak to the Israelites and say to them: 'I am the LORD your God. 3You must not do as they do in Egypt, where you used to live, and you must not do as they do in the land of Canaan, where I am bringing you. Do not follow their practices. 4You must obey my laws and be careful to follow my decrees. I am the LORD your God. 5Keep my decrees and laws, for the man who obeys them will live by them. I am the LORD.

6" 'No-one is to approach any close relative to have sexual relations. I am the LORD.

7" 'Do not dishonour your father by having sexual relations with your mother. She is your mother; do not have relations with her.

8" 'Do not have sexual relations with your father's wife; that would dishonour your father.

9" 'Do not have sexual relations with your sister, either your father's daughter or your mother's daughter, whether she was born in the same home or elsewhere.

10" 'Do not have sexual relations with your son's daughter or your daughter's daughter; that would dishonour you.

11" 'Do not have sexual relations with the daughter of your father's wife, born to your father; she is your sister.

12" 'Do not have sexual relations with your father's sister; she is your father's close relative.

13" 'Do not have sexual relations with your mother's sister, because she is your mother's close relative.

14" 'Do not dishonour your father's brother by approaching his wife to have sexual relations; she is your aunt.

15" 'Do not have sexual relations with your daughter-in-law. She is your son's wife; do not have relations with her.

16" 'Do not have sexual relations with your brother's wife; that would dishonour your brother.

17" 'Do not have sexual relations with both a woman and her daughter. Do not have sexual relations with either her son's daughter or her daughter's daughter; they are her close relatives. That is wickedness.

18" 'Do not take your wife's sister as a rival wife and have sexual relations with her while your wife is living.

19" 'Do not approach a woman to have sexual relations during the uncleanness of her monthly period.

20" 'Do not have sexual relations with your neighbour's wife and defile yourself with her.

21" 'Do not give any of your children to be sacrificed*a* to Molech, for you must not profane the name of your God. I am the LORD.

18:21 ■ CHILD SACRIFICE AND SEX

This warning against child sacrifice (repeated and expanded in 20:1–5) seems out of place in the middle of a chapter on rules about sex. Yet, for the Israelites, there was a connection. Their neighbours, who sacrificed their children as a part of their religion, also practised temple prostitution as a way of worship. To them, sex was a way to get in touch with their gods. God's warnings against various sexual practices begin and end with warnings to behave differently from these neighbours (verses 3,24).

22" 'Do not lie with a man as one lies with a woman; that is detestable.

23" 'Do not have sexual relations with an animal and defile yourself with it. A woman must not present herself to an animal to have sexual relations with it; that is a perversion.

24" 'Do not defile yourselves in any of these ways, because this is how the nations that I am going to drive out before you became defiled. 25Even the land was defiled; so I punished it for its sin, and the land vomited out its inhabitants. ²⁶But you must keep my decrees and my laws. The native-born and the aliens living among you must not do any of these detestable things, ²⁷for all these things were done by the people who lived in the land before you, and the land became defiled. ²⁸And if you defile the land, it will vomit you out as it vomited out the nations that were before you.

²⁹" 'Everyone who does any of these detestable things—such persons must be cut off from their people. ³⁰Keep my requirements and do not follow any of the detestable customs that were practised before you came and do not defile yourselves with them. I am the LORD your God.' "

■ Various Laws

19 The LORD said to Moses, ²"Speak to the entire assembly of Israel and say to them: 'Be holy because I, the LORD your God, am holy.

³" 'Each of you must respect his mother and father, and you must observe my Sabbaths. I am the LORD your God.

⁴" 'Do not turn to idols or make gods of cast metal for yourselves. I am the LORD your God.

⁵" 'When you sacrifice a fellowship offering^a to the LORD, sacrifice it in such a way that it will be accepted on your behalf. ⁶It shall be eaten on the day you sacrifice it or on the next day; anything left over until the third day must be burned up. ⁷If any of it is eaten on the third day, it is impure and will not be accepted. ⁸Whoever eats it will be held responsible because he has desecrated what is holy to the LORD; that person must be cut off from his people.

⁹" 'When you reap the harvest of your land, do not reap to the very edges of your field or gather the gleanings of your harvest. ¹⁰Do not go over your vineyard a second time or pick up the grapes that have fallen. Leave them for the poor and the alien. I am the LORD your God.

19:9 ■ A FORM OF WELFARE

God's law was persistently concerned with the welfare of the poor. Everyday farming was to be done in such a way that poor and foreign people could fend for themselves. The reasons for such care are given: we are to imitate the holy character of God (verse 2), who cares for the poor, and to love our neighbour as ourselves (verse 18).

¹¹" 'Do not steal.

" 'Do not lie.

" 'Do not deceive one another.

¹²" 'Do not swear falsely by my name and so profane the name of your God. I am the LORD.

¹³" 'Do not defraud your neighbour or rob him.

" 'Do not hold back the wages of a hired man overnight.

¹⁴" 'Do not curse the deaf or put a stumbling-block in front of the blind, but fear your God. I am the LORD.

¹⁵" 'Do not pervert justice; do not show partiality to the poor or favouritism to the great, but judge your neighbour fairly.

¹⁶" 'Do not go about spreading slander among your people.

" 'Do not do anything that endangers your neighbour's life. I am the LORD.

¹⁷" 'Do not hate your brother in your heart. Rebuke your neighbour frankly so that you will not share in his guilt.

¹⁸" 'Do not seek revenge or bear a grudge against one of your people, but love your neighbour as yourself. I am the LORD.

¹⁹" 'Keep my decrees.

" 'Do not mate different kinds of animals.

" 'Do not plant your field with two kinds of seed.

" 'Do not wear clothing woven of two kinds of material.

²⁰" 'If a man sleeps with a woman who is a slave girl promised to another man but who has not been ransomed or given her freedom, there must be due punishment. Yet they are not to be put to death, because she had not been freed. ²¹The man, however, must bring a ram to the entrance to the Tent of Meeting for a guilt offering to the LORD. ²²With the ram of the guilt offering the priest is to make atonement for him before the LORD for the sin he has committed, and his sin will be forgiven.

²³" 'When you enter the land and plant any kind of fruit tree, regard its fruit as forbidden.^b For three years you are to consider it forbidden;^b it must not be eaten. ²⁴In the fourth year all its fruit will be holy, an offering of praise to the LORD. ²⁵But in the fifth year you may eat its fruit. In this way your harvest will be increased. I am the LORD your God.

²⁶" 'Do not eat any meat with the blood still in it.

" 'Do not practise divination or sorcery.

²⁷" 'Do not cut the hair at the sides of your head or clip off the edges of your beard.

²⁸" 'Do not cut your bodies for the dead or put tattoo marks on yourselves. I am the LORD.

²⁹" 'Do not degrade your daughter by making her a prostitute, or the land will turn to prostitution and be filled with wickedness.

³⁰" 'Observe my Sabbaths and have reverence for my sanctuary. I am the LORD.

³¹" 'Do not turn to mediums or seek out spiritists, for you will be defiled by them. I am the LORD your God.

³²" 'Rise in the presence of the aged, show respect for the elderly and revere your God. I am the LORD.

³³" 'When an alien lives with you in your land, do not ill-treat him. ³⁴The alien living with you must be treated as one of your native-born. Love him as yourself, for you were aliens in Egypt. I am the LORD your God.

³⁵" 'Do not use dishonest standards when measuring length, weight or quantity. ³⁶Use honest scales and honest weights, an honest ephah^c and an honest hin.^d I am the LORD your God, who brought you out of Egypt.

³⁷" 'Keep all my decrees and all my laws and follow them. I am the LORD.' "

---

^a5 Traditionally *peace offering*   ^b23 Hebrew *uncircumcised*   ^c36 An ephah was a dry measure.   ^d36 A hin was a liquid measure.

■ Punishments for Sin

20 The LORD said to Moses, [2]"Say to the Israelites: 'Any Israelite or any alien living in Israel who gives[a] any of his children to Molech must be put to death. The people of the community are to stone him. [3]I will set my face against that man and I will cut him off from his people; for by giving his children to Molech, he has defiled my sanctuary and profaned my holy name. [4]If the people of the community close their eyes when that man gives one of his children to Molech and they fail to put him to death, [5]I will set my face against that man and his family and will cut off from their people both him and all who follow him in prostituting themselves to Molech.

[6]" 'I will set my face against the person who turns to mediums and spiritists to prostitute himself by following them, and I will cut him off from his people.

[7]" 'Consecrate yourselves and be holy, because I am the LORD your God. [8]Keep my decrees and follow them. I am the LORD, who makes you holy.[b]

20:7-8 ■ THE BOTTOM LINE

These verses, along with verse 26, sum up the underlying reason for many of the laws outlined in Leviticus: God wanted the Israelites to be different. The New Testament makes clear that some of these regulations — eating forbidden animals, touching unclean persons — do not apply for all time. But at this moment, as God's people entered their new land, God wanted them to stand out from the nations around them (verses 22–24). Sadly, before long the Israelites were mimicking almost all of the practices of their pagan neighbours.

---

[9]" 'If anyone curses his father or mother, he must be put to death. He has cursed his father or his mother, and his blood will be on his own head.

[10]" 'If a man commits adultery with another man's wife — with the wife of his neighbour — both the adulterer and the adulteress must be put to death.

[11]" 'If a man sleeps with his father's wife, he has dishonoured his father. Both the man and the woman must be put to death; their blood will be on their own heads.

[12]" 'If a man sleeps with his daughter-in-law, both of them must be put to death. What they have done is a perversion; their blood will be on their own heads.

[13]" 'If a man lies with a man as one lies with a woman, both of them have done what is detestable. They must be put to death; their blood will be on their own heads.

[14]" 'If a man marries both a woman and her mother, it is wicked. Both he and they must be burned in the fire, so that no wickedness will be among you.

[15]" 'If a man has sexual relations with an animal, he must be put to death, and you must kill the animal.

[16]" 'If a woman approaches an animal to have sexual relations with it, kill both the woman and the animal. They must be put to death; their blood will be on their own heads.

[17]" 'If a man marries his sister, the daughter of either his father or his mother, and they have sexual relations, it is a disgrace. They must be cut off before the eyes of their people. He has dishonoured his sister and will be held responsible.

[18]" 'If a man lies with a woman during her monthly period and has sexual relations with her, he has exposed the source of her flow, and she has also uncovered it. Both of them must be cut off from their people.

[19]" 'Do not have sexual relations with the sister of either your mother or your father, for that would dishonour a close relative; both of you would be held responsible.

[20]" 'If a man sleeps with his aunt, he has dishonoured his uncle. They will be held responsible; they will die childless.

[21]" 'If a man marries his brother's wife, it is an act of impurity; he has dishonoured his brother. They will be childless.

[22]" 'Keep all my decrees and laws and follow them, so that the land where I am bringing you to live may not vomit you out. [23]You must not live according to the customs of the nations I am going to drive out before you. Because they did all these things, I abhorred them. [24]But I said to you, "You will possess their land; I will give it to you as an inheritance, a land flowing with milk and honey." I am the LORD your God, who has set you apart from the nations.

[25]" 'You must therefore make a distinction between clean and unclean animals and between unclean and clean birds. Do not defile yourselves by any animal or bird or anything that moves along the ground — those which I have set apart as unclean for you. [26]You are to be holy to me[c] because I, the LORD, am holy, and I have set you apart from the nations to be my own.

[27]" 'A man or woman who is a medium or spiritist among you must be put to death. You are to stone them; their blood will be on their own heads.' "

■ Rules for Priests

21 The LORD said to Moses, "Speak to the priests, the sons of Aaron, and say to them: 'A priest must not make himself ceremonially unclean for any of his people who die, [2]except for a close relative, such as his mother or father, his son or daughter, his brother, [3]or an unmarried sister who is dependent on him since she has no husband — for her he may make himself unclean. [4]He must not make himself unclean for people related to him by marriage,[a] and so defile himself.

[5]" 'Priests must not shave their heads or shave off the edges of their beards or cut their bodies. [6]They must be holy to their God and must not profane the name of their God. Because they present the offerings made to the LORD by fire, the food of their God, they are to be holy.

[7]" 'They must not marry women defiled by prostitution or divorced from their husbands, because priests are holy to their God. [8]Regard them as holy,

---

[a]2 Or sacrifices; also in verses 3 and 4   [b]8 Or who sanctifies you; or who sets you apart as holy   [c]26 Or be my holy ones   [a]4 Or unclean as a leader among his people

because they offer up the food of your God. Consider them holy, because I the LORD am holy—I who make you holy.*b*

9" 'If a priest's daughter defiles herself by becoming a prostitute, she disgraces her father; she must be burned in the fire.

10" 'The high priest, the one among his brothers who has had the anointing oil poured on his head and who has been ordained to wear the priestly garments, must not let his hair become unkempt*c* or tear his clothes. 11He must not enter a place where there is a dead body. He must not make himself unclean, even for his father or mother, 12nor leave the sanctuary of his God or desecrate it, because he has been dedicated by the anointing oil of his God. I am the LORD.

13" 'The woman he marries must be a virgin. 14He must not marry a widow, a divorced woman, or a

■ A NATIONAL LAW LIBRARY
SETTING ISRAEL APART FROM ITS NEIGHBOURS

INSIGHT

YOU ARE TO BE HOLY TO ME BECAUSE I, THE LORD, AM HOLY, AND I HAVE SET YOU APART FROM THE NATIONS TO BE MY OWN. ■ 20:26

The law of the land is complex and lengthy. Lawyers have to study for years to qualify and then they may specialise in only one particular area - civil law or divorce law for example. No one person can know even a fraction of all there is to know about the law.

If the Old Testament laws recorded in Leviticus (and Exodus, Numbers and Deuteronomy) seem dull and long-winded, keep them in perspective. These—just over 600 in all—were the entire set of laws for a nation, as far as we know. Their most striking feature, to a lawyer, is brevity and simplicity. You don't have to be a lawyer to understand them.

The laws are listed in no particular order. A law against witchcraft is followed by a law against improper haircuts, which is followed by a law against tattoos, which in turn is followed by a law against making your daughter into a prostitute. This mixing reveals an important feature of Old Testament thinking. Life is not analysed in separate components, but seen as a whole.

For the Israelites, separation of church and state did not exist. Every aspect of life—politics, family life, diet, economics—concerned God. Even the Ten Commandments (in Exodus 20) show this, for they include laws regarding our relationship to both God and our neighbour. The two cannot be separated.

■ REMARKABLE FEATURES
In comparison with laws from other countries at that time, the Old Testament made a considerable advance. (Indeed, these laws have greatly influenced laws for our day.) Some of the remarkable features:

● *People were more important than property.* For instance, there was never a death penalty for a crime against someone's property. Also, slaves were treated as human beings, not property. This was not true of many other legal codes of that time.

● *There was no class system.* In many ancient countries, a noble was treated far differently from a commoner. Not so in Israel: everybody stood on the same level before the law. Even a foreigner had clearly defined rights.

● *The punishment fitted the crime.* No "cruel and unusual punishment" was allowed. "Eye for eye" (Leviticus 24:20) ensured that no privileged character was "let off" for a crime, while at the same time it limited revenge.

● *Sexuality mattered.* In most countries, the law cared little whether you slept with your neighbour's wife. In Israel, sexual immorality got stern treatment.

● *The poor and weak had protection.* Specific provisions protected their rights from the powerful and wealthy. "Welfare" offered them a way to stay alive, such as the right to "glean the fields". In 19:9,13–14,32–33, God gave protection to various groups that could not defend themselves.

● *Attitudes, as well as actions, mattered.* For instance, Leviticus 19:18 contains the famous law to "love your neighbour as yourself". Living up to the letter of the law was not enough. The law aimed to develop loving relationships.

■ DESIGNED TO BE DIFFERENT
While we do not understand the reasons for some of the laws (many may have been designed simply to keep the Israelites "different" from their pagan neighbours), their overall impact is clear. These rules were intended to form a nation of compassionate, consistent, fair-minded people. They insisted that each person act positively and lovingly towards his or her neighbour—and particularly towards those in need. The reason? God lived with them. Since he is both just and merciful, his people must be too.

□ LIFE QUESTIONS:
Everybody has a code to live by. Does your personal rule book show as much concern for the poor and defenceless as Leviticus'?

b 8 Or who sanctify you; or who set you apart as holy   *c* 10 Or not uncover his head woman defiled by prostitution, but only a virgin from his own people, 15so that he will not defile his offspring among his people. I am the LORD, who makes him holy.' "*d*

16The LORD said to Moses, 17"Say to Aaron: 'For the generations to come none of your descendants who has a defect may come near to offer the food of his God. 18No man who has any defect may come near: no man who is blind or lame, disfigured or deformed; 19no man with a crippled foot or hand, 20or who is hunchbacked or dwarfed, or who has any eye defect, or who has festering or running sores or damaged testicles. 21No descendant of Aaron the priest who has any defect is to come near to present the offerings made to the LORD by fire. He has a defect; he must not come near to offer the food of his God. 22He may eat the most holy food of his God, as well as the holy food; 23yet because of his defect, he must not go near the curtain or approach the altar, and so desecrate my sanctuary. I am the LORD, who makes them holy.' "*e*

24So Moses told this to Aaron and his sons and to all the Israelites.

22 The LORD said to Moses, 2"Tell Aaron and his sons to treat with respect the sacred offerings the Israelites consecrate to me, so that they will not profane my holy name. I am the LORD.

3"Say to them: 'For the generations to come, if any of your descendants is ceremonially unclean and yet comes near the sacred offerings that the Israelites consecrate to the LORD, that person must be cut off from my presence. I am the LORD.

4" 'If a descendant of Aaron has an infectious skin disease*a* or a bodily discharge, he may not eat the sacred offerings until he is cleansed. He will also be unclean if he touches something defiled by a corpse or by anyone who has an emission of semen, 5or if he touches any crawling thing that makes him unclean, or any person who makes him unclean, whatever the uncleanness may be. 6The one who touches any such thing will be unclean till evening. He must not eat any of the sacred offerings unless he has bathed himself with water. 7When the sun goes down, he will be clean, and after that he may eat the sacred offerings, for they are his food. 8He must not eat anything found dead or torn by wild animals, and so become unclean through it. I am the LORD.

9" 'The priests are to keep my requirements so that they do not become guilty and die for treating them with contempt. I am the LORD, who makes them holy.*b*

10" 'No-one outside a priest's family may eat the sacred offering, nor may the guest of a priest or his hired worker eat it. 11But if a priest buys a slave with money, or if a slave is born in his household, that slave may eat his food. 12If a priest's daughter marries anyone other than a priest, she may not eat any of the sacred contributions. 13But if a priest's daughter becomes a widow or is divorced, yet has no children, and she returns to live in her father's house as in her youth, she may eat of her father's food. No unauthorised person, however, may eat any of it.

14" 'If anyone eats a sacred offering by mistake, he must make restitution to the priest for the offering and add a fifth of the value to it. 15The priests must not desecrate the sacred offerings the Israelites present to the LORD 16by allowing them to eat the sacred offerings and so bring upon them guilt requiring payment. I am the LORD, who makes them holy.' "

■ Unacceptable Sacrifices

17The LORD said to Moses, 18"Speak to Aaron and his sons and to all the Israelites and say to them: 'If any of you — either an Israelite or an alien living in Israel — presents a gift for a burnt offering to the LORD, either to fulfil a vow or as a freewill offering, 19you must present a male without defect from the cattle, sheep or goats in order that it may be accepted on your behalf. 20Do not bring anything with a defect, because it will not be accepted on your behalf. 21When anyone brings from the herd or flock a fellowship offering*c* to the LORD to fulfil a special vow or as a freewill offering, it must be without defect or blemish to be acceptable. 22Do not offer to the LORD the blind, the injured or the maimed, or anything with warts or festering or running sores. Do not place any of these on the altar as an offering made to the LORD by fire. 23You may, however, present as a freewill offering an ox*d* or a sheep that is deformed or stunted, but it will not be accepted in fulfilment of a vow. 24You must not offer to the LORD an animal whose testicles are bruised, crushed, torn or cut. You must not do this in your own land, 25and you must not accept such animals from the hand of a foreigner and offer them as the food of your God. They will not be accepted on your behalf, because they are deformed and have defects.' "

22:19 ■ THE VERY BEST FOR GOD

For the Israelite farmers, a farm animal represented a considerable contribution. It would have been tempting to cull their weakest animals. Instead, they were commanded to give their very best. Similarly, at every harvest they were to bring their very first grain to the Lord (23:10). These practices reminded them again and again of God's place in their lives.

26The LORD said to Moses, 27"When a calf, a lamb or a goat is born, it is to remain with its mother for seven days. From the eighth day on, it will be acceptable as an offering made to the LORD by fire. 28Do not slaughter a cow or a sheep and its young on the same day.

29"When you sacrifice a thank-offering to the LORD, sacrifice it in such a way that it will be accepted on your behalf. 30It must be eaten that same day; leave none of it till morning. I am the LORD.

31"Keep my commands and follow them. I am the LORD. 32Do not profane my holy name. I must be acknowledged as holy by the Israelites. I am the LORD, who makes*e* you holy*f* 33and who brought you out of Egypt to be your God. I am the LORD."

d15 Or who sanctifies him; or who sets him apart as holy   e23 Or who sanctifies them; or who sets them apart as holy   a4 Traditionally leprosy; the Hebrew word was used for various diseases affecting the skin — not necessarily leprosy.   b9 Or who sanctifies them; or who sets them apart as holy; also in verse 16   c21 Traditionally peace offering   d23 The Hebrew word can include both male and female.   e32 Or made   f32 Or who sanctifies you; or who sets you apart as holy

23 The LORD said to Moses, [2]"Speak to the Israelites and say to them: 'These are my appointed feasts, the appointed feasts of the LORD, which you are to proclaim as sacred assemblies.

The Sabbath

[3]" 'There are six days when you may work, but the seventh day is a Sabbath of rest, a day of sacred assembly. You are not to do any work; wherever you live, it is a Sabbath to the LORD.

The Passover and Unleavened Bread

[4]" 'These are the LORD's appointed feasts, the sacred assemblies you are to proclaim at their appointed times: [5]The LORD's Passover begins at twilight on the fourteenth day of the first month. [6]On the fifteenth day of that month the LORD's Feast of Unleavened Bread begins; for seven days you must eat bread made without yeast. [7]On the first day hold a sacred assembly and do no regular work. [8]For seven days present an offering made to the LORD by fire. And on the seventh day hold a sacred assembly and do no regular work.' "

Firstfruits

[9]The LORD said to Moses, [10]"Speak to the Israelites and say to them: 'When you enter the land I am going to give you and you reap its harvest, bring to the priest a sheaf of the first grain you harvest. [11]He is to wave the sheaf before the LORD so it will be accepted on your behalf; the priest is to wave it on the day after the Sabbath. [12]On the day you wave the sheaf, you must sacrifice as a burnt offering to the LORD a lamb a year old without defect, [13]together with its grain offering of two-tenths of an ephah[a] of fine flour mixed with oil — an offering made to the LORD by fire, a pleasing aroma — and its drink offering of a quarter of a hin[b] of wine. [14]You must not eat any bread, or roasted or new grain, until the very day you bring this offering to your God. This is to be a lasting ordinance for the generations to come, wherever you live.

Feast of Weeks

[15]" 'From the day after the Sabbath, the day you brought the sheaf of the wave offering, count off seven full weeks. [16]Count off fifty days up to the day after the seventh Sabbath, and then present an offering of new grain to the LORD. [17]From wherever you live, bring two loaves made of two-tenths of an ephah of fine flour, baked with yeast, as a wave offering of firstfruits to the LORD. [18]Present with this bread seven male lambs, each a year old and without defect, one young bull and two rams. They will be a burnt offering to the LORD, together with their grain offerings and drink offerings — an offering made by fire, an aroma pleasing to the LORD. [19]Then sacrifice one male goat for a sin offering and two lambs, each a year old, for a fellowship offering.[c] [20]The priest is to wave the two lambs before the LORD as a wave offering, together with the bread of the firstfruits. They are a sacred offering to the LORD for the priest. [21]On that same day you are to proclaim a sacred assembly and do no regular work.

This is to be a lasting ordinance for the generations to come, wherever you live.

[22]" 'When you reap the harvest of your land, do not reap to the very edges of your field or gather the gleanings of your harvest. Leave them for the poor and the alien. I am the LORD your God.' "

Feast of Trumpets

[23]The LORD said to Moses, [24]"Say to the Israelites: 'On the first day of the seventh month you are to have a day of rest, a sacred assembly commemorated with trumpet blasts. [25]Do no regular work, but present an offering made to the LORD by fire.' "

Day of Atonement

[26]The LORD said to Moses, [27]"The tenth day of this seventh month is the Day of Atonement. Hold a sacred assembly and deny yourselves,[d] and present an offering made to the LORD by fire. [28]Do no work on that day, because it is the Day of Atonement, when atonement is made for you before the LORD your God. [29]Anyone who does not deny himself on that day must be cut off from his people. [30]I will destroy from among his people anyone who does any work on that day. [31]You shall do no work at all. This is to be a lasting ordinance for the generations to come, wherever you live. [32]It is a sabbath of rest for you, and you must deny yourselves. From the evening of the ninth day of the month until the following evening you are to observe your sabbath."

Feast of Tabernacles

[33]The LORD said to Moses, [34]"Say to the Israelites: 'On the fifteenth day of the seventh month the LORD's Feast of Tabernacles begins, and it lasts for seven days. [35]The first day is a sacred assembly; do no regular work. [36]For seven days present offerings made to the LORD by fire, and on the eighth day hold a sacred assembly and present an offering made to the LORD by fire. It is the closing assembly; do no regular work.

[37](" 'These are the LORD's appointed feasts, which you are to proclaim as sacred assemblies for bringing offerings made to the LORD by fire — the burnt offerings and grain offerings, sacrifices and drink offerings required for each day. [38]These offerings are in addition to those for the LORD's Sabbaths and[e] in addition to your gifts and whatever you have vowed and all the freewill offerings you give to the LORD.)

[39]" 'So beginning with the fifteenth day of the seventh month, after you have gathered the crops of the land, celebrate the festival to the LORD for seven days; the first day is a day of rest, and the eighth day also is a day of rest. [40]On the first day you are to take choice fruit from the trees, and palm fronds, leafy branches and poplars, and rejoice before the LORD your God for seven days. [41]Celebrate this as a festival to the LORD for seven days each year. This is to be a lasting ordinance for the generations to come; celebrate it in the seventh month. [42]Live in booths for seven days: All native-born Israelites are to live in booths [43]so that your descendants will know that I made the Israelites live in booths when I brought them out of Egypt. I am the LORD your God.' "

---

a 13 That is, probably about 7½ pints (about 4.5 litres); also in verse 17   *b 13* That is, probably about 1½ pints (about 1 litre)   *c 19* Traditionally *peace offering*   *d 27* Or *and fast*; also in verses 29 and 32   *e 38* Or *These feasts are in addition to the LORD's Sabbaths, and these offerings are*

⁴⁴So Moses announced to the Israelites the appointed feasts of the LORD.

■ Oil and Bread Set Before the LORD

24 The LORD said to Moses, ²"Command the Israelites to bring you clear oil of pressed olives for the light so that the lamps may be kept burning continually. ³Outside the curtain of the Testimony in the Tent of Meeting, Aaron is to tend the lamps before the LORD from evening till morning,

continually. This is to be a lasting ordinance for the generations to come. ⁴The lamps on the pure gold lampstand before the LORD must be tended continually.

⁵"Take fine flour and bake twelve loaves of bread, using two-tenths of an ephah*ᵃ* for each loaf. ⁶Set them in two rows, six in each row, on the table of pure gold before the LORD. ⁷Along each row put some pure incense as a memorial portion to represent the bread and to be an offering made to the LORD by fire. ⁸This bread is to be set out before the LORD regularly, Sabbath after Sabbath, on behalf of the Israelites, as a lasting covenant. ⁹It belongs to Aaron and his sons, who are to eat it in a holy place, because it is a most holy part of their regular share of the offerings made to the LORD by fire."

■ IN CELEBRATION OF GOD
JEWISH HOLIDAYS FOCUSED ON ONE THING

INSIGHT

REJOICE BEFORE THE LORD YOUR GOD FOR SEVEN DAYS. ■ 23:40

Anthropologists studying remote tribes routinely describe their feast days, for these show the people's common values. What would stand out to an anthropologist studying the United Kingdom? Undoubtedly he or she would notice that our celebration of Christmas and New Year or Hogmanay, of birthdays and Guy Fawkes night emphasise family, food and the giving of presents – the more the better.

What about the Israelites? Leviticus describes five feasts, all focusing on God. Each was marked by special sacrifices to God and a sacred assembly in the Tent of Meeting where God had "pitched his tent". Rather than giving gifts to each other, the Israelites gave gifts to God.

Sometimes they rejoiced: during the Feast of Tabernacles everyone camped out to "rejoice before the LORD" for a solid week (23:40). On other occasions, such as the Day of Atonement, they were sober and solemn (chapter 16, 23:26–32). But always their orientation was God-directed.

■ **GOD OVER MONEY**
Nobody worked on Israelite feast days, but their "days off" had a different motive than ours. An Israelite farmer never got a paid holiday. In fact, a holiday could cost him – it might fall on a day perfect for harvesting. But God took priority over work. The weekly Sabbath day reinforced the same idea. You had to stop working to worship.

God mattered more than wealth. This fundamental belief showed itself even more in the sabbath year and in the Year of Jubilee (chapter 25). Every seventh year, people did

not farm at all. They lived off whatever the land produced by itself, and dedicated themselves to God. This would be like our closing all businesses and factories for a year.

After 49 years – seven sabbath years – the Year of Jubilee came. This time, people went for two years in a row without planting. All land bought or sold during the previous 49 years went back to its original family ownership. Since the land had originally been equally distributed, this meant that no family would ever become either totally destitute or overwhelmingly rich. Any Israelites who had sold themselves as slaves would also be freed in that year.

■ **PROSPERITY CAME FROM GOD**
Hard work and the resulting abundance were never scorned in Israel. But prosperity always came ultimately from God, not from hard work or clever dealings alone. The feasts and Sabbaths, set aside as special days, helped people remember and praise the God who had given them so much.

So far as we know, no Year of Jubilee was ever actually practised. Some of the feasts were forgotten for long periods of time. But such failure is not surprising. After all, think what we have done to the holy day of Christmas! The feast days described in Leviticus give us a good idea of what God wanted Israel to be. Sadly, reality did not often match the ideal.

□ **LIFE QUESTIONS:**
If someone examined the way you spend your holidays and weekends, what would he or she conclude about your priorities?

---

*ᵃ*5 That is, probably about 7½ pints (about 4.5 litres)

■ A Blasphemer Stoned

¹⁰Now the son of an Israelite mother and an Egyptian father went out among the Israelites, and a fight broke out in the camp between him and an Israelite. ¹¹The son of the Israelite woman blasphemed the Name with a curse; so they brought him to Moses. (His mother's name was Shelomith, the daughter of Dibri the Danite.) ¹²They put him in custody until the will of the LORD should be made clear to them.

¹³Then the LORD said to Moses: ¹⁴"Take the blasphemer outside the camp. All those who heard him are to lay their hands on his head, and the entire assembly is to stone him. ¹⁵Say to the Israelites: 'If anyone curses his God, he will be held responsible; ¹⁶anyone who blasphemes the name of the LORD must be put to death. The entire assembly must stone him. Whether an alien or native-born, when he blasphemes the Name, he must be put to death.

¹⁷" 'If anyone takes the life of a human being, he must be put to death. ¹⁸Anyone who takes the life of someone's animal must make restitution—life for life. ¹⁹If anyone injures his neighbour, whatever he has done must be done to him: ²⁰fracture for fracture, eye for eye, tooth for tooth. As he has injured the other, so he is to be injured. ²¹Whoever kills an animal must make restitution, but whoever kills a man must be put to death. ²²You are to have the same law for the alien and the native-born. I am the LORD your God.' "

24:20 ■ AN EYE FOR AN EYE

Jesus, speaking of this law in Matthew 5:38, told his followers not to resist evil people. Apparently people had been taking "eye for eye" as a basis for private vengeance—as some do today. The law's original intent, however, was to set a standard for punishment in court. It limited vengeance and made certain that both rich and poor, native and foreigner, would pay the same price for their crimes.

---

²³Then Moses spoke to the Israelites, and they took the blasphemer outside the camp and stoned him. The Israelites did as the LORD commanded Moses.

■ The Sabbath Year

25 The LORD said to Moses on Mount Sinai, ²"Speak to the Israelites and say to them: 'When you enter the land I am going to give you, the land itself must observe a sabbath to the LORD. ³For six years sow your fields, and for six years prune your vineyards and gather their crops. ⁴But in the seventh year the land is to have a sabbath of rest, a sabbath to the LORD. Do not sow your fields or prune your vineyards. ⁵Do not reap what grows of itself or harvest the grapes of your untended vines. The land is to have a year of rest. ⁶Whatever the land yields during the sabbath year will be food for you—for yourself, your manservant and maidservant, and the hired worker and temporary resident who live among you, ⁷as well as for your livestock and the wild animals in your land. Whatever the land produces may be eaten.

■ The Year of Jubilee

⁸" 'Count off seven sabbaths of years—seven times seven years—so that the seven sabbaths of years amount to a period of forty-nine years. ⁹Then have the trumpet sounded everywhere on the tenth day of the seventh month; on the Day of Atonement sound the trumpet throughout your land. ¹⁰Consecrate the fiftieth year and proclaim liberty throughout the land to all its inhabitants. It shall be a jubilee for you; each one of you is to return to his family property and each to his own clan. ¹¹The fiftieth year shall be a jubilee for you; do not sow and do not reap what grows of itself or harvest the untended vines. ¹²For it is a jubilee and is to be holy for you; eat only what is taken directly from the fields.

¹³" 'In this Year of Jubilee everyone is to return to his own property.

¹⁴" 'If you sell land to one of your countrymen or buy any from him, do not take advantage of each other. ¹⁵You are to buy from your countryman on the basis of the number of years since the Jubilee. And he is to sell to you on the basis of the number of years left for harvesting crops. ¹⁶When the years are many, you are to increase the price, and when the years are few, you are to decrease the price, because what he is really selling you is the number of crops. ¹⁷Do not take advantage of each other, but fear your God. I am the LORD your God.

¹⁸" 'Follow my decrees and be careful to obey my laws, and you will live safely in the land. ¹⁹Then the land will yield its fruit, and you will eat your fill and live there in safety. ²⁰You may ask, "What will we eat in the seventh year if we do not plant or harvest our crops?" ²¹I will send you such a blessing in the sixth year that the land will yield enough for three years. ²²While you plant during the eighth year, you will eat from the old crop and will continue to eat from it until the harvest of the ninth year comes in.

²³" 'The land must not be sold permanently, because the land is mine and you are but aliens and my tenants. ²⁴Throughout the country that you hold as a possession, you must provide for the redemption of the land.

²⁵" 'If one of your countrymen becomes poor and sells some of his property, his nearest relative is to come and redeem what his countryman has sold. ²⁶If, however, a man has no-one to redeem it for him but he himself prospers and acquires sufficient means to redeem it, ²⁷he is to determine the value for the years since he sold it and refund the balance to the man to whom he sold it; he can then go back to his own property. ²⁸But if he does not acquire the means to repay him, what he sold will remain in the possession of the buyer until the Year of Jubilee. It will be returned in the Jubilee, and he can then go back to his property.

²⁹" 'If a man sells a house in a walled city, he retains the right of redemption a full year after its sale. During that time he may redeem it. ³⁰If it is not redeemed before a full year has passed, the house in the walled city shall belong permanently to the buyer and his descendants. It is not to be returned

in the Jubilee. [31]But houses in villages without walls round them are to be considered as open country. They can be redeemed, and they are to be returned in the Jubilee.

[32]"The Levites always have the right to redeem their houses in the Levitical towns, which they possess. [33]So the property of the Levites is redeemable—that is, a house sold in any town they hold—and is to be returned in the Jubilee, because the houses in the towns of the Levites are their property among the Israelites. [34]But the pasture-land belonging to their towns must not be sold; it is their permanent possession.

[35]"If one of your countrymen becomes poor and is unable to support himself among you, help him as you would an alien or a temporary resident, so that he can continue to live among you. [36]Do not take interest of any kind[a] from him, but fear your God, so that your countryman may continue to live among you. [37]You must not lend him money at interest or sell him food at a profit. [38]I am the LORD your God, who brought you out of Egypt to give you the land of Canaan and to be your God.

[39]"If one of your countrymen becomes poor among you and sells himself to you, do not make him work as a slave. [40]He is to be treated as a hired worker or a temporary resident among you; he is to work for you until the Year of Jubilee. [41]Then he and his children are to be released, and he will go back to his own clan and to the property of his forefathers. [42]Because the Israelites are my servants, whom I brought out of Egypt, they must not be sold as slaves. [43]Do not rule over them ruthlessly, but fear your God.

[44]"Your male and female slaves are to come from the nations around you; from them you may buy slaves. [45]You may also buy some of the temporary residents living among you and members of their clans born in your country, and they will become your property. [46]You can will them to your children as inherited property and can make them slaves for life, but you must not rule over your fellow Israelites ruthlessly.

[47]"If an alien or a temporary resident among you becomes rich and one of your countrymen becomes poor and sells himself to the alien living among you or to a member of the alien's clan, [48]he retains the right of redemption after he has sold himself. One of his relatives may redeem him: [49]An uncle or a cousin or any blood-relative in his clan may redeem him. Or if he prospers, he may redeem himself. [50]He and his buyer are to count the time from the year he sold himself up to the Year of Jubilee. The price for his release is to be based on the rate paid to a hired man for that number of years. [51]If many years remain, he must pay for his redemption a larger share of the price paid for him. [52]If only a few years remain until the Year of Jubilee, he is to compute that and pay for his redemption accordingly. [53]He is to be treated as a man hired from year to year; you must see to it that his owner does not rule over him ruthlessly.

[54]"Even if he is not redeemed in any of these ways, he and his children are to be released in the Year of Jubilee, [55]for the Israelites belong to me as servants. They are my servants, whom I brought out of Egypt. I am the LORD your God.

■ Reward for Obedience

26 "Do not make idols or set up an image or a sacred stone for yourselves, and do not place a carved stone in your land to bow down before it. I am the LORD your God.

[2]"Observe my Sabbaths and have reverence for my sanctuary. I am the LORD.

[3]"If you follow my decrees and are careful to obey my commands, [4]I will send you rain in its season, and the ground will yield its crops and the trees of the field their fruit. [5]Your threshing will continue until grape harvest and the grape harvest will continue until planting, and you will eat all the food you want and live in safety in your land.

[6]"I will grant peace in the land, and you will lie down and no-one will make you afraid. I will remove savage beasts from the land, and the sword will not pass through your country. [7]You will pursue your enemies, and they will fall by the sword before you. [8]Five of you will chase a hundred, and a hundred of you will chase ten thousand, and your enemies will fall by the sword before you.

[9]"I will look on you with favour and make you fruitful and increase your numbers, and I will keep my covenant with you. [10]You will still be eating last year's harvest when you will have to move it out to make room for the new. [11]I will put my dwelling-place[a] among you, and I will not abhor you. [12]I will walk among you and be your God, and you will be my people. [13]I am the LORD your God, who brought you out of Egypt so that you would no longer be slaves to the Egyptians; I broke the bars of your yoke and enabled you to walk with heads held high.

■ Punishment for Disobedience

[14]"But if you will not listen to me and carry out all these commands, [15]and if you reject my decrees and abhor my laws and fail to carry out all my commands and so violate my covenant, [16]then I will do this to you: I will bring upon you sudden terror, wasting diseases and fever that will destroy your sight and drain away your life. You will plant seed in vain, because your enemies will eat it. [17]I will set my face against you so that you will be defeated by your enemies; those who hate you will rule over you, and you will flee even when no-one is pursuing you.

[18]"If after all this you will not listen to me, I will punish you for your sins seven times over. [19]I will break down your stubborn pride and make the sky above you like iron and the ground beneath you like

---

[a] 36 Or take excessive interest; similarly in verse 37   [a] 11 Or my tabernacle

bronze. 20Your strength will be spent in vain, because your soil will not yield its crops, nor will the trees of the land yield their fruit.

21" 'If you remain hostile towards me and refuse to listen to me, I will multiply your afflictions seven times over, as your sins deserve. 22I will send wild animals against you, and they will rob you of your children, destroy your cattle and make you so few in number that your roads will be deserted.

23" 'If in spite of these things you do not accept my correction but continue to be hostile towards me, 24I myself will be hostile towards you and will afflict you for your sins seven times over. 25And I will bring the sword upon you to avenge the breaking of the covenant. When you withdraw into your cities, I will send a plague among you, and you will be given into enemy hands. 26When I cut off your supply of bread, ten women will be able to bake your bread in one oven, and they will dole out the bread by weight. You will eat, but you will not be satisfied.

27" 'If in spite of this you still do not listen to me but continue to be hostile towards me, 28then in my anger I will be hostile towards you, and I myself will punish you for your sins seven times over. 29You will eat the flesh of your sons and the flesh of your daughters. 30I will destroy your high places, cut down your incense altars and pile your dead bodies on the lifeless forms of your idols, and I will abhor you. 31I will turn your cities into ruins and lay waste your sanctuaries, and I will take no delight in the pleasing aroma of your offerings. 32I will lay waste the land, so that your enemies who live there will be appalled. 33I will scatter you among the nations and will draw out my sword and pursue you. Your land will be laid waste, and your cities will lie in ruins. 34Then the land will enjoy its sabbath years all the time that it lies desolate and you are in the country of your enemies; then the land will rest and enjoy its sabbaths. 35All the time that it lies desolate, the land will have the rest it did not have during the sabbaths you lived in it.

26:34 ■ REVENGE OF THE LAND

There is little evidence that the Israelites ever followed the rules on sabbath years and Jubilee. Nevertheless, as ominously foretold here, the land eventually did get its rest. For 70 years the Babylonians held the Israelites hostage, far away from their homeland. And the land had rest.

36" 'As for those of you who are left, I will make their hearts so fearful in the lands of their enemies that the sound of a wind-blown leaf will put them to flight. They will run as though fleeing from the sword, and they will fall, even though no-one is pursuing them. 37They will stumble over one another as though fleeing from the sword, even though no-one is pursuing them. So you will not be able to stand before your enemies. 38You will perish among the nations; the land of your enemies will devour you. 39Those of you who are left will waste away in the lands of their enemies because of their sins; also because of their fathers' sins they will waste away.

40" 'But if they will confess their sins and the sins of their fathers—their treachery against me and their hostility towards me, 41which made me hostile towards them so that I sent them into the land of their enemies—then when their uncircumcised hearts are humbled and they pay for their sin, 42I will remember my covenant with Jacob and my covenant with Isaac and my covenant with Abraham, and I will remember the land. 43For the land will be deserted by them and will enjoy its sabbaths while it lies desolate without them. They will pay for their sins because they rejected my laws and abhorred my decrees. 44Yet in spite of this, when they are in the land of their enemies, I will not reject them or abhor them so as to destroy them completely, breaking my covenant with them. I am the LORD their God. 45But for their sake I will remember the covenant with their ancestors whom I brought out of Egypt in the sight of the nations to be their God. I am the LORD.' "

26:41 ■ UNCIRCUMCISED HEARTS

Circumcision was the ritual that made a man into a Jew, so to speak. But this reference to uncircumcised hearts shows that, right from the beginning, the inward attitude, as well as the physical operation, was crucial. Six hundred years later Jeremiah accused the Israelites of being uncircumcised in heart (Jeremiah 9:26); another 600 years after him Stephen made the same complaint (Acts 7:51). On this basis Paul wrote, "A man is not a Jew if he is only one outwardly . . . No, a man is a Jew if he is one inwardly; and circumcision is a circumcision of the heart, by the Spirit" (Romans 2:28–29). Leviticus offered more than a legal system; these laws appealed to a person's relationship with God.

46These are the decrees, the laws and the regulations that the LORD established on Mount Sinai between himself and the Israelites through Moses.

■ Redeeming What Is the LORD's

27 The LORD said to Moses, 2"Speak to the Israelites and say to them: 'If anyone makes a special vow to dedicate persons to the LORD by giving equivalent values, 3set the value of a male between the ages of twenty and sixty at fifty shekels^a of silver, according to the sanctuary shekel;^b 4and if it is a female, set her value at thirty shekels.^c 5If it is a person between the ages of five and twenty, set the value of a male at twenty shekels^d and of a female at ten shekels.^e 6If it is a person between one month and five years, set the value of a male at five shekels^f of silver and that of a female at three shekels^g of silver. 7If it is a person sixty years old or more, set the value of a male at fifteen shekels^b and of a female at ten shekels. 8If anyone making the vow is too poor to pay the specified amount, he is to

a3 That is, about 1¼ pounds (about 0.6 kilogram); also in verse 16   b3 That is, about ⅔ ounce (about 11.5 grams); also in verse 25   c4 That is, about 12 ounces (about 0.3 kilogram)   d5 That is, about 8 ounces (about 0.2 kilogram)   e5 That is, about 4 ounces (about 115 grams); also in verse 7   f6 That is, about 2 ounces (about 55 grams)   g6 That is, about 1¼ ounces (about 35 grams)   b7 That is, about 6 ounces (about 170 grams) present the person to the priest, who will set the value for him according to what the man making the vow can afford.

9" 'If what he vowed is an animal that is acceptable as an offering to the LORD, such an animal given to the LORD becomes holy. 10He must not exchange it or substitute a good one for a bad one, or a bad one for a good one; if he should substitute one animal for another, both it and the substitute become holy. 11If what he vowed is a ceremonially unclean animal — one that is not acceptable as an offering to the LORD — the animal must be presented to the priest, 12who will judge its quality as good or bad. Whatever value the priest then sets, that is what it will be. 13If the owner wishes to redeem the animal, he must add a fifth to its value.

14" 'If a man dedicates his house as something holy to the LORD, the priest will judge its quality as good or bad. Whatever value the priest then sets, so it will remain. 15If the man who dedicates his house redeems it, he must add a fifth to its value, and the house will again become his.

16" 'If a man dedicates to the LORD part of his family land, its value is to be set according to the amount of seed required for it — fifty shekels of silver to a homer[i] of barley seed. 17If he dedicates his field during the Year of Jubilee, the value that has been set remains. 18But if he dedicates his field after the Jubilee, the priest will determine the value according to the number of years that remain until the next Year of Jubilee, and its set value will be reduced. 19If the man who dedicates the field wishes to redeem it, he must add a fifth to its value, and the field will again become his. 20If, however, he does not redeem the field, or if he has sold it to someone else, it can never be redeemed. 21When the field is released in the Jubilee, it will become holy, like a field devoted to the LORD; it will become the property of the priests.[j]

22" 'If a man dedicates to the LORD a field he has bought, which is not part of his family land, 23the priest will determine its value up to the Year of Jubilee, and the man must pay its value on that day as something holy to the LORD. 24In the Year of Jubilee the field will revert to the person from whom he bought it, the one whose land it was. 25Every value is to be set according to the sanctuary shekel, twenty gerahs to the shekel.

26" 'No-one, however, may dedicate the firstborn of an animal, since the firstborn already belongs to the LORD; whether an ox[k] or a sheep, it is the LORD's. 27If it is one of the unclean animals, he may buy it back at its set value, adding a fifth of the value to it. If he does not redeem it, it is to be sold at its set value.

28" 'But nothing that a man owns and devotes[l] to the LORD — whether man or animal or family land — may be sold or redeemed; everything so devoted is most holy to the LORD.

29" 'No person devoted to destruction[m] may be ransomed; he must be put to death.

30" 'A tithe of everything from the land, whether grain from the soil or fruit from the trees, belongs to the LORD; it is holy to the LORD. 31If a man redeems any of his tithe, he must add a fifth of the value to it. 32The entire tithe of the herd and flock — every tenth animal that passes under the shepherd's rod — will be holy to the LORD. 33He must not pick out the good from the bad or make any substitution. If he does make a substitution, both the animal and its substitute become holy and cannot be redeemed.' "

34These are the commands the LORD gave Moses on Mount Sinai for the Israelites.

---

i 16 That is, probably about 6 bushels (about 220 litres)   j 21 Or priest   k 26 The Hebrew word can include both male and female.   l 28 The Hebrew
term refers to the irrevocable giving over of things or persons to the LORD,   m 29 The Hebrew term refers to the irrevocable giving over of things or persons
to the LORD, often by totally destroying them.

NUMBERS

INTRODUCTION

■ FORTY YEARS OF MISERY

A JOYOUS ADVENTURE COMES TO A TRAGIC END

NOW THE PEOPLE COMPLAINED ABOUT THEIR HARDSHIPS IN THE HEARING OF THE LORD, AND WHEN HE HEARD THEM HIS ANGER WAS AROUSED. ■ 11:1

As Numbers opens, the Israelites are gearing up for a great adventure. Free at last from the chains of slavery, they are heading for the promised land. Yet the book that begins with a bang ends with a whimper. Weeks, months, and then years in a hostile desert have seemed to erode the spirit of adventure. The Israelites act like people who have lost their moorings. In relentless detail, Numbers records a whole sequence of grumblings and rebellions.

■ FORTY-YEAR DETOUR

Stomachs complained first, as the Israelites began to long for the spices of Egypt. Soon, the great mob of people simply fell to pieces. At least ten times they lashed out in despair or rose up in open rebellion. They plotted against their leaders and denounced God. Revolt spread to the priests, to the top military scouts, to Moses' family, and finally to Moses himself.

The original Hebrew title of this book was not "Numbers" but rather "In the desert", and this cryptic phrase expresses a little of the Israelites' futility. Surrounded by hostile nations, they had to march under the scorching sun in a desert plagued by snakes, scorpions, and drought. Even today, visitors to the Sinai Desert marvel that an entire nation wandered that ground for so long.

A march through the desert should have taken about two weeks. Instead, it took almost 40 years. Numbers spans the years of wandering and ends where the trek began: at the very spot (Kadesh) where the Israelites' faith had failed. Of the many thousands who left Egypt, only two adults, Joshua and Caleb, would make it into the promised land.

■ A DIFFERENT KIND OF HISTORY

Most ancient histories sound very different from this book. They tell of heroic exploits by mighty warriors and unblemished leaders. With an almost numbing monotony, Numbers presents a far more realistic picture. It shows the early symptoms, the full progression, and the tragic end of grumbling and unbelief.

The Israelites lost faith not only in themselves, but in their God. Because of that, a whole generation of them lies buried in the peninsula known as Sinai.

References to the "desert wanderings" crop up again and again in the Bible. The period of rebellion left an indelible mark on the Jewish people. Exactly what went wrong? The book of Numbers is given to tell us. The apostle Paul points out that these failures "happened to them as examples and were written down as warnings for us, on whom the fulfilment of the ages has come. So, if you think you are standing firm, be careful that you don't fall!" (1 Corinthians 10:11–12).

■ HOW TO READ NUMBERS

People who read straight through Numbers very often come away confused or discouraged. The book begins with a long description of a census and proceeds into lists of laws and rituals. These were the official records of a nation, and each word had great significance for the Israelites. (Imagine how our Yellow Pages or Electoral Rolls would appear to people 3,000 years from now.)

Yet, unlike Leviticus, Numbers does not consist mainly of these long descriptions. Rather, it focuses on stories, with laws and rituals sprinkled in at various points. The stories are exciting, and some, such as the story of Balaam, are quite remarkable.

The action in Numbers takes place in three different settings: (1) Chapters 1–14 begin in the same place Exodus ended: at the foot of Mount Sinai. (2) Chapters 15–19 cover a period of 37 years, the time of the desert wanderings. Moses' summary in chapter 33 lists 42 stops in the desert, but Numbers details very few of them. (3) Chapters 20–36 concern a whole new generation of Israelites, who were making final preparations before the invasion.

As you read Numbers, it will help to have a major theme in mind, such as grumbling and rebellion. Work through the book, looking at examples of this problem. Major outbreaks occur in chapters 11, 12, 13, 14, 16, 20, and 21 – at least ten incidents in all. Notice the cause of each rebellion, and also God's response. Can you see parallels to the Israelites' experience in your own life?

Numbers also offers insight into the leadership of Moses by showing his response to each crisis. One illustration of his prominence: over 80 times the book says that "the LORD said to Moses". Look for the qualities, both positive and negative, that made him an effective leader.

Other parts of the Bible often refer to Numbers. Some of the historical psalms, such as Psalms 78, 105, and 136, recast these events in poetry.

■ 3-TRACK READING PLAN

For an explanation and complete listing of the 3-track reading plan, turn to page x.

■ TRACK 1:
Two-Week Courses on the Bible
See page x for information on these courses.

■ TRACK 2:
An Overview of Numbers in 2 Days
☐ Day 1. Read the Introduction to Numbers and

then chapter 11, which shows a typical Israelite response to hardship.
☐ Day 2. Read chapter 14, the hinge chapter of Numbers. Now turn to page xi for your next Track 2 reading project.

■ TRACK 3:
All of Numbers in 35 Days
After you have read through

Numbers, turn to pages xii–xiii for your next Track 3 reading project.

☐ 1–2 ☐ 3   ☐ 4   ☐ 5
☐ 6   ☐ 7   ☐ 8   ☐ 9
☐ 10   ☐ 11   ☐ 12   ☐ 13
☐ 14   ☐ 15   ☐ 16   ☐ 17
☐ 18   ☐ 19   ☐ 20   ☐ 21
☐ 22   ☐ 23   ☐ 24   ☐ 25
☐ 26   ☐ 27   ☐ 28   ☐ 29
☐ 30   ☐ 31   ☐ 32   ☐ 33
☐ 34   ☐ 35   ☐ 36

■ The Census

1 The LORD spoke to Moses in the Tent of Meeting in the Desert of Sinai on the first day of the second month of the second year after the Israelites came out of Egypt. He said: 2"Take a census of the whole Israelite community by their clans and families, listing every man by name, one by one. 3You and Aaron are to number by their divisions all the men in Israel twenty years old or more who are able to serve in the army. 4One man from each tribe, each the head of his family, is to help you. 5These are the names of the men who are to assist you:

from Reuben, Elizur son of Shedeur;
6from Simeon, Shelumiel son of Zurishaddai;
7from Judah, Nahshon son of Amminadab;
8from Issachar, Nethanel son of Zuar;
9from Zebulun, Eliab son of Helon;
10from the sons of Joseph:
    from Ephraim, Elishama son of Ammihud;
    from Manasseh, Gamaliel son of Pedahzur;
11from Benjamin, Abidan son of Gideoni;
12from Dan, Ahiezer son of Ammishaddai;
13from Asher, Pagiel son of Ocran;
14from Gad, Eliasaph son of Deuel;
15from Naphtali, Ahira son of Enan."

16These were the men appointed from the community, the leaders of their ancestral tribes. They were the heads of the clans of Israel.

17Moses and Aaron took these men whose names had been given, 18and they called the whole community together on the first day of the second month. The people indicated their ancestry by their clans and families, and the men twenty years old or more were listed by name, one by one, 19as the LORD commanded Moses. And so he counted them in the Desert of Sinai:

20From the descendants of Reuben the firstborn son of Israel:
    All the men twenty years old or more who were able to serve in the army were listed by name, one by one, according to the records of their clans and families. 21The number from the tribe of Reuben was 46,500.

22From the descendants of Simeon:
    All the men twenty years old or more who were able to serve in the army were counted and listed by name, one by one, according to the records of their clans and families. 23The number from the tribe of Simeon was 59,300.

24From the descendants of Gad:
    All the men twenty years old or more who were able to serve in the army were listed by name, according to the records of their clans and families. 25The number from the tribe of Gad was 45,650.

26From the descendants of Judah:
    All the men twenty years old or more who were able to serve in the army were listed by name, according to the records of their clans and families. 27The number from the tribe of Judah was 74,600.

28From the descendants of Issachar:
All the men twenty years old or more who
were able to serve in the army were listed by
name, according to the records of their clans
and families. 29The number from the tribe of
Issachar was 54,400.

30From the descendants of Zebulun:
All the men twenty years old or more who
were able to serve in the army were listed by
name, according to the records of their clans
and families. 31The number from the tribe of
Zebulun was 57,400.

32From the sons of Joseph:
From the descendants of Ephraim:
All the men twenty years old or more who
were able to serve in the army were listed by
name, according to the records of their clans
and families. 33The number from the tribe of
Ephraim was 40,500.

1:32 ■ TWO FOR ONE

Although Joseph was only one of the twelve
brothers who formed the tribes of Israel, his father
Israel (Jacob) had adopted Joseph's two sons,
Ephraim and Manasseh, as his own (see Genesis
48:5–6). Thus Joseph got a double share of the
family inheritance, and there are really thirteen
tribes of Israel.

The tribe of Levi were often treated separately,
however, because of their special role in worship.
This census, for example, taken primarily to
prepare a roster for military purposes, excluded
the tribe of Levi. As caretakers of God's
tabernacle, Levites were ineligible for military
service.

34From the descendants of Manasseh:
All the men twenty years old or more who
were able to serve in the army were listed by
name, according to the records of their clans
and families. 35The number from the tribe of
Manasseh was 32,200.

36From the descendants of Benjamin:
All the men twenty years old or more who
were able to serve in the army were listed by
name, according to the records of their clans
and families. 37The number from the tribe of
Benjamin was 35,400.

38From the descendants of Dan:
All the men twenty years old or more who
were able to serve in the army were listed by
name, according to the records of their clans
and families. 39The number from the tribe of
Dan was 62,700.

40From the descendants of Asher:
All the men twenty years old or more who
were able to serve in the army were listed by
name, according to the records of their clans
and families. 41The number from the tribe of
Asher was 41,500.

42From the descendants of Naphtali:
All the men twenty years old or more who
were able to serve in the army were listed by
name, according to the records of their clans
and families. 43The number from the tribe of
Naphtali was 53,400.

44These were the men counted by Moses and
Aaron and the twelve leaders of Israel, each one representing his family. 45All the Israelites twenty years
old or more who were able to serve in Israel's army
were counted according to their families. 46The total number was 603,550.

47The families of the tribe of Levi, however, were
not counted along with the others. 48The LORD had
said to Moses: 49"You must not count the tribe of
Levi or include them in the census of the other Israelites. 50Instead, appoint the Levites to be in
charge of the tabernacle of the Testimony—over all
its furnishings and everything belonging to it. They
are to carry the tabernacle and all its furnishings;
they are to take care of it and encamp round it.
51Whenever the tabernacle is to move, the Levites
are to take it down, and whenever the tabernacle is
to be set up, the Levites shall do it. Anyone else who
goes near it shall be put to death. 52The Israelites are
to set up their tents by divisions, each man in his
own camp under his own standard. 53The Levites,
however, are to set up their tents round the tabernacle of the Testimony so that wrath will not fall on
the Israelite community. The Levites are to be responsible for the care of the tabernacle of the Testimony."

54The Israelites did all this just as the LORD commanded Moses.

■ The Arrangement of the Tribal Camps

2 The LORD said to Moses and Aaron: 2"The Israelites are to camp round the Tent of Meeting
some distance from it, each man under his standard
with the banners of his family."

2:2 ■ A PLACE FOR EVERYONE

The Israelites did not wander through the desert
as an undisciplined mob. On the contrary, each
tribe had an assigned place to camp. At the
centre of their camp was the Tent of Meeting (the
tabernacle)—a visual reminder, each time they
pitched their tents, of what should be at the
centre of their lives.

3On the east, towards the sunrise, the divisions of the camp of Judah are to encamp under
their standard. The leader of the people of Judah is Nahshon son of Amminadab. 4His division numbers 74,600.

5The tribe of Issachar will camp next to
them. The leader of the people of Issachar is
Nethanel son of Zuar. 6His division numbers
54,400.

7The tribe of Zebulun will be next. The
leader of the people of Zebulun is Eliab son of
Helon. 8His division numbers 57,400.

9All the men assigned to the camp of Judah, according to their divisions, number 186,400. They will set out first.

10On the south will be the divisions of the camp of Reuben under their standard. The leader of the people of Reuben is Elizur son of Shedeur. 11His division numbers 46,500. 12The tribe of Simeon will camp next to them. The leader of the people of Simeon is Shelumiel son of Zurishaddai. 13His division numbers 59,300. 14The tribe of Gad will be next. The leader of the people of Gad is Eliasaph son of Deuel.*a* 15His division numbers 45,650. 16All the men assigned to the camp of Reuben, according to their divisions, number 151,450. They will set out second.

17Then the Tent of Meeting and the camp of the Levites will set out in the middle of the camps. They will set out in the same order as they encamp, each in his own place under his standard.

18On the west will be the divisions of the camp of Ephraim under their standard. The leader of the people of Ephraim is Elishama son of Ammihud. 19His division numbers 40,500. 20The tribe of Manasseh will be next to them. The leader of the people of Manasseh is Gamaliel son of Pedahzur. 21His division numbers 32,200. 22The tribe of Benjamin will be next. The leader of the people of Benjamin is Abidan son of Gideoni. 23His division numbers 35,400. 24All the men assigned to the camp of Ephraim, according to their divisions, number 108,100. They will set out third.

25On the north will be the divisions of the camp of Dan, under their standard. The leader of the people of Dan is Ahiezer son of Ammishaddai. 26His division numbers 62,700. 27The tribe of Asher will camp next to them. The leader of the people of Asher is Pagiel son of Ocran. 28His division numbers 41,500. 29The tribe of Naphtali will be next. The leader of the people of Naphtali is Ahira son of Enan. 30His division numbers 53,400. 31All the men assigned to the camp of Dan number 157,600. They will set out last, under their standards.

32These are the Israelites, counted according to their families. All those in the camps, by their divisions, number 603,550. 33The Levites, however, were not counted along with the other Israelites, as the LORD commanded Moses.

34So the Israelites did everything the LORD commanded Moses; that is the way they encamped under their standards, and that is the way they set out, each with his clan and family.

■ The Levites

3 This is the account of the family of Aaron and Moses at the time the LORD talked with Moses on Mount Sinai.

2:32 ■ HOW MANY ISRAELITES?
Debate has raged among scholars about the vast numbers of Israelites reported in the censuses of Numbers. Could two-and-a-half million people (counting women and children) have left Egypt in one day and then survived for 40 years in a desolate desert? Those who defend the large numbers point out that climatic conditions might have been very different in those days when, for example, Egypt was the granary of the world. (Also, the Bible gives many indications of God's miraculous supply of food and water.) Opposing scholars note that the Hebrews had different means of counting, and that the word translated "thousand" could have other meanings, resulting in much smaller figures. Regardless, both positions admit to a very large band of people wandering around a desert for a very long time.

2The names of the sons of Aaron were Nadab the firstborn and Abihu, Eleazar and Ithamar. 3Those were the names of Aaron's sons, the anointed priests, who were ordained to serve as priests. 4Nadab and Abihu, however, fell dead before the LORD when they made an offering with unauthorised fire before him in the Desert of Sinai. They had no sons; so only Eleazar and Ithamar served as priests during the lifetime of their father Aaron.

5The LORD said to Moses, 6"Bring the tribe of Levi and present them to Aaron the priest to assist him. 7They are to perform duties for him and for the whole community at the Tent of Meeting by doing the work of the tabernacle. 8They are to take care of all the furnishings of the Tent of Meeting, fulfilling the obligations of the Israelites by doing the work of the tabernacle. 9Give the Levites to Aaron and his sons; they are the Israelites who are to be given wholly to him.*a* 10Appoint Aaron and his sons to serve as priests; anyone else who approaches the sanctuary must be put to death."

11The LORD also said to Moses, 12"I have taken the Levites from among the Israelites in place of the first male offspring of every Israelite woman. The Levites are mine, 13for all the firstborn are mine. When I struck down all the firstborn in Egypt, I set apart for myself every firstborn in Israel, whether man or animal. They are to be mine. I am the LORD."

14The LORD said to Moses in the Desert of Sinai, 15"Count the Levites by their families and clans. Count every male a month old or more." 16So Moses counted them, as he was commanded by the word of the LORD.

17These were the names of the sons of Levi:
    Gershon, Kohath and Merari.
18These were the names of the Gershonite clans:
    Libni and Shimei.
19The Kohathite clans:
    Amram, Izhar, Hebron and Uzziel.

a 14 Many manuscripts of the Masoretic Text, Samaritan Pentateuch and Vulgate (see also Num. 1:14); most manuscripts of the Masoretic Text *Reuel*
a 9 Most manuscripts of the Masoretic Text; some manuscripts of the Masoretic Text, Samaritan Pentateuch and Septuagint (see also Num. 8:16) *to me*

²⁰The Merarite clans:
Mahli and Mushi.
These were the Levite clans, according to their families.

²¹To Gershon belonged the clans of the Libnites and Shimeites; these were the Gershonite clans. ²²The number of all the males a month old or more who were counted was 7,500. ²³The Gershonite clans were to camp on the west, behind the tabernacle. ²⁴The leader of the families of the Gershonites was Eliasaph son of Lael. ²⁵At the Tent of Meeting the Gershonites were responsible for the care of the tabernacle and tent, its coverings, the curtain at the entrance to the Tent of Meeting, ²⁶the curtains of the courtyard, the curtain at the entrance to the courtyard surrounding the tabernacle and altar, and the ropes—and everything related to their use.

²⁷To Kohath belonged the clans of the Amramites, Izharites, Hebronites and Uzzielites; these were the Kohathite clans. ²⁸The number of all the males a month old or more was 8,600.ᵇ The Kohathites were responsible for the care of the sanctuary. ²⁹The Kohathite clans were to camp on the south side of the tabernacle. ³⁰The leader of the families of the Kohathite clans was Elizaphan son of Uzziel. ³¹They were responsible for the care of the ark, the table, the lampstand, the altars, the articles of the sanctuary used in ministering, the curtain, and everything related to their use. ³²The chief leader of the Levites was Eleazar son of Aaron, the priest. He was appointed over those who were responsible for the care of the sanctuary.

³³To Merari belonged the clans of the Mahlites and the Mushites; these were the Merarite clans. ³⁴The number of all the males a month old or more who were counted was 6,200. ³⁵The leader of the families of the Merarite clans was Zuriel son of Abihail; they were to camp on the north side of the tabernacle. ³⁶The Merarites were appointed to take care of the frames of the tabernacle, its crossbars, posts, bases, all its equipment, and everything related to their use, ³⁷as well as the posts of the surrounding courtyard with their bases, tent pegs and ropes.

³⁸Moses and Aaron and his sons were to camp to the east of the tabernacle, towards the sunrise, in front of the Tent of Meeting. They were responsible for the care of the sanctuary on behalf of the Israelites. Anyone else who approached the sanctuary was to be put to death.

³⁹The total number of Levites counted at the LORD's command by Moses and Aaron according to their clans, including every male a month old or more, was 22,000.

⁴⁰The LORD said to Moses, "Count all the firstborn Israelite males who are a month old or more and make a list of their names. ⁴¹Take the Levites for me in place of all the firstborn of the Israelites, and the livestock of the Levites in place of all the firstborn of the livestock of the Israelites. I am the LORD."

⁴²So Moses counted all the firstborn of the Israelites, as the LORD commanded him. ⁴³The total number of firstborn males a month old or more, listed by name, was 22,273.

⁴⁴The LORD also said to Moses, ⁴⁵"Take the Levites in place of all the firstborn of Israel, and the livestock of the Levites in place of their livestock. The Levites are to be mine. I am the LORD. ⁴⁶To redeem the 273 firstborn Israelites who exceed the number of the Levites, ⁴⁷collect five shekelsᶜ for each one, according to the sanctuary shekel, which weighs twenty gerahs. ⁴⁸Give the money for the redemption of the additional Israelites to Aaron and his sons."

3:44 ■ DESIGNATED FIRSTBORN

At the first Passover (Exodus 13:2) God established the firstborn principle, which held that every firstborn male, human or animal, must be dedicated to him. Here, in careful accounting, the Levites are accepted as "designated firstborn" offerings to God. Just as there is a tradition whereby the oldest son follows his father into the family business and may even be called David Jr after his father (David Snr), so here a whole tribe is named to take the place of firstborn members from every family.

⁴⁹So Moses collected the redemption money from those who exceeded the number redeemed by the Levites. ⁵⁰From the firstborn of the Israelites he collected silver weighing 1,365 shekels,ᵈ according to the sanctuary shekel. ⁵¹Moses gave the redemption money to Aaron and his sons, as he was commanded by the word of the LORD.

■ The Kohathites

4 The LORD said to Moses and Aaron: ²"Take a census of the Kohathite branch of the Levites by their clans and families. ³Count all the men from thirty to fifty years of age who come to serve in the work in the Tent of Meeting.

⁴"This is the work of the Kohathites in the Tent of Meeting: the care of the most holy things. ⁵When the camp is to move, Aaron and his sons are to go in and take down the shielding curtain and cover the ark of the Testimony with it. ⁶Then they are to cover this with hides of sea cows,ᵃ spread a cloth of solid blue over that and put the poles in place.

⁷"Over the table of the Presence they are to spread a blue cloth and put on it the plates, dishes and bowls, and the jars for drink offerings; the bread that is continually there is to remain on it. ⁸Over these they are to spread a scarlet cloth, cover that with hides of sea cows and put its poles in place.

⁹"They are to take a blue cloth and cover the lampstand that is for light, together with its lamps, its wick trimmers and trays, and all its jars for the oil used to supply it. ¹⁰Then they are to wrap it and all its accessories in a covering of hides of sea cows and put it on a carrying frame.

ᵇ28 Hebrew; some Septuagint manuscripts 8,300   ᶜ47 That is, about 2 ounces (about 55 grams)   ᵈ50 That is, about 35 pounds (about 15.5 kilograms)
ᵃ6 That is, large aquatic mammals; also elsewhere in this chapter

11"Over the gold altar they are to spread a blue cloth and cover that with hides of sea cows and put its poles in place.

12"They are to take all the articles used for ministering in the sanctuary, wrap them in a blue cloth, cover that with hides of sea cows and put them on a carrying frame.

13"They are to remove the ashes from the bronze altar and spread a purple cloth over it. 14Then they are to place on it all the utensils used for ministering at the altar, including the firepans, meat forks, shovels and sprinkling bowls. Over it they are to spread a covering of hides of sea cows and put its poles in place.

15"After Aaron and his sons have finished covering the holy furnishings and all the holy articles, and when the camp is ready to move, the Kohathites are to come to do the carrying. But they must not touch the holy things or they will die. The Kohathites are to carry those things that are in the Tent of Meeting.

4:15 ■ TOUCH AND DIE

The precise instructions for moving the holy things reflected the awe and respect that were due to God alone. Years later, King David's men flagrantly ignored these instructions and one man, Uzzah, died as a result (see "Why Did Uzzah Die?" page 361). Earlier in Numbers, two of Aaron's sons had died while trying out their own version of worship, ignoring God's directions (3:4, also Leviticus 10:1–5). In the Bible, these drastic punishments tend to occur as God's people enter a new phase of their history (see Joshua 7; 2 Samuel 6:7; Acts 5:1–11). There is no compromising God's holiness.

16"Eleazar son of Aaron, the priest, is to have charge of the oil for the light, the fragrant incense, the regular grain offering and the anointing oil. He is to be in charge of the entire tabernacle and everything in it, including its holy furnishings and articles."

17The LORD said to Moses and Aaron, 18"See that the Kohathite tribal clans are not cut off from the Levites. 19So that they may live and not die when they come near the most holy things, do this for them: Aaron and his sons are to go into the sanctuary and assign to each man his work and what he is to carry. 20But the Kohathites must not go in to look at the holy things, even for a moment, or they will die."

■ The Gershonites

21The LORD said to Moses, 22"Take a census also of the Gershonites by their families and clans. 23Count all the men from thirty to fifty years of age who come to serve in the work at the Tent of Meeting.

24"This is the service of the Gershonite clans as they work and carry burdens: 25They are to carry the curtains of the tabernacle, the Tent of Meeting, its covering and the outer covering of hides of sea cows, the curtains for the entrance to the Tent of

Meeting, 26the curtains of the courtyard surrounding the tabernacle and altar, the curtain for the entrance, the ropes and all the equipment used in its service. The Gershonites are to do all that needs to be done with these things. 27All their service, whether carrying or doing other work, is to be done under the direction of Aaron and his sons. You shall assign to them as their responsibility all they are to carry. 28This is the service of the Gershonite clans at the Tent of Meeting. Their duties are to be under the direction of Ithamar son of Aaron, the priest.

■ The Merarites

29"Count the Merarites by their clans and families. 30Count all the men from thirty to fifty years of age who come to serve in the work at the Tent of Meeting. 31This is their duty as they perform service at the Tent of Meeting: to carry the frames of the tabernacle, its crossbars, posts and bases, 32as well as the posts of the surrounding courtyard with their bases, tent pegs, ropes, all their equipment and everything related to their use. Assign to each man the specific things he is to carry. 33This is the service of the Merarite clans as they work at the Tent of Meeting under the direction of Ithamar son of Aaron, the priest."

■ The Numbering of the Levite Clans

34Moses, Aaron and the leaders of the community counted the Kohathites by their clans and families. 35All the men from thirty to fifty years of age who came to serve in the work in the Tent of Meeting, 36counted by clans, were 2,750. 37This was the total of all those in the Kohathite clans who served in the Tent of Meeting. Moses and Aaron counted them according to the LORD's command through Moses.

38The Gershonites were counted by their clans and families. 39All the men from thirty to fifty years of age who came to serve in the work at the Tent of Meeting, 40counted by their clans and families, were 2,630. 41This was the total of those in the Gershonite clans who served at the Tent of Meeting. Moses and Aaron counted them according to the LORD's command.

42The Merarites were counted by their clans and families. 43All the men from thirty to fifty years of age who came to serve in the work at the Tent of Meeting, 44counted by their clans, were 3,200. 45This was the total of those in the Merarite clans. Moses and Aaron counted them according to the LORD's command through Moses.

46So Moses, Aaron and the leaders of Israel counted all the Levites by their clans and families. 47All the men from thirty to fifty years of age who came to do the work of serving and carrying the Tent of Meeting 48numbered 8,580. 49At the LORD's command through Moses, each was assigned his work and told what to carry.

Thus they were counted, as the LORD commanded Moses.

■ The Purity of the Camp

5 The LORD said to Moses, 2"Command the Israelites to send away from the camp anyone who has an infectious skin disease*a* or a discharge of any

---

a 2 Traditionally *leprosy*; the Hebrew word was used for various diseases affecting the skin—not necessarily leprosy.

kind, or who is ceremonially unclean because of a dead body. ³Send away male and female alike; send them outside the camp so that they will not defile their camp, where I dwell among them." ⁴The Israelites did this; they sent them outside the camp. They did just as the LORD had instructed Moses.

■ Restitution for Wrongs

⁵The LORD said to Moses, ⁶"Say to the Israelites: 'When a man or woman wrongs another in any wayᵇ and so is unfaithful to the LORD, that person is guilty ⁷and must confess the sin he has committed. He must make full restitution for his wrong, add one fifth to it and give it all to the person he has wronged. ⁸But if that person has no close relative to whom restitution can be made for the wrong, the restitution belongs to the LORD and must be given to the priest, along with the ram with which atonement is made for him. ⁹All the sacred contributions the Israelites bring to a priest will belong to him. ¹⁰Each man's sacred gifts are his own, but what he gives to the priest will belong to the priest.' "

■ The Test for an Unfaithful Wife

¹¹Then the LORD said to Moses, ¹²"Speak to the Israelites and say to them: 'If a man's wife goes astray and is unfaithful to him ¹³by sleeping with another man, and this is hidden from her husband and her impurity is undetected (since there is no witness against her and she has not been caught in the act), ¹⁴and if feelings of jealousy come over her husband and he suspects his wife and she is impure — or if he is jealous and suspects her even though she is not impure — ¹⁵then he is to take his wife to the priest. He must also take an offering of a tenth of an ephahᶜ of barley flour on her behalf. He must not pour oil on it or put incense on it, because it is a grain offering for jealousy, a reminder offering to draw attention to guilt.

¹⁶" 'The priest shall bring her and make her stand before the LORD. ¹⁷Then he shall take some holy water in a clay jar and put some dust from the tabernacle floor into the water. ¹⁸After the priest has made the woman stand before the LORD, he shall loosen her hair and place in her hands the reminder offering, the grain offering for jealousy, while he himself holds the bitter water that brings a curse. ¹⁹Then the priest shall put the woman under oath and say to her, "If no other man has slept with you and you have not gone astray and become impure while married to your husband, may this bitter water that brings a curse not harm you. ²⁰But if you have gone astray while married to your husband and you have defiled yourself by sleeping with a man other than your husband" — ²¹here the priest is to put the woman under this curse of the oath — "may the LORD cause your people to curse and denounce you when he causes your thigh to waste away and your abdomen to swell.ᵈ ²²May this water that brings a curse enter your body so that your abdomen swells and your thigh wastes away."ᵉ

" 'Then the woman is to say, "Amen. So be it."

²³" 'The priest is to write these curses on a scroll and then wash them off into the bitter water. ²⁴He

shall make the woman drink the bitter water that brings a curse, and this water will enter her and cause bitter suffering. ²⁵The priest is to take from her hands the grain offering for jealousy, wave it before the LORD and bring it to the altar. ²⁶The priest is then to take a handful of the grain offering as a memorial offering and burn it on the altar; after that, he is to make the woman drink the water. ²⁷If she has defiled herself and been unfaithful to her husband, then when she is made to drink the water that brings a curse, it will go into her and cause bitter suffering; her abdomen will swell and her thigh waste away,ᶠ and she will become accursed among her people. ²⁸If, however, the woman has not defiled herself and is free from impurity, she will be cleared of guilt and will be able to have children.

5:16 ■ TEST FOR ADULTERY

The strange test for adultery described here resembles other "trials by ordeal" common then in the Middle East. Presumably, either the emotional reactions of the guilty woman would give her away physiologically (much as a lie detector may), or God would reveal true results through the outcome of the ordeal. The public trial may have helped to clear the reputation of wives who had been falsely accused by their husbands. There is no biblical record of the procedure actually being used, and the trial described is the only one like it in the Bible.

²⁹" 'This, then, is the law of jealousy when a woman goes astray and defiles herself while married to her husband, ³⁰or when feelings of jealousy come over a man because he suspects his wife. The priest is to make her stand before the LORD and is to apply this entire law to her. ³¹The husband will be innocent of any wrongdoing, but the woman will bear the consequences of her sin.' "

■ The Nazirite

6 The LORD said to Moses, ²"Speak to the Israelites and say to them: 'If a man or woman wants to make a special vow, a vow of separation to the LORD as a Nazirite, ³he must abstain from wine and other fermented drink and must not drink vinegar made from wine or from other fermented drink. He must not drink grape juice or eat grapes or raisins. ⁴As long as he is a Nazirite, he must not eat anything that comes from the grapevine, not even the seeds or skins.

⁵" 'During the entire period of his vow of separation no razor may be used on his head. He must be holy until the period of his separation to the LORD is over; he must let the hair of his head grow long. ⁶Throughout the period of his separation to the LORD he must not go near a dead body. ⁷Even if his own father or mother or brother or sister dies, he must not make himself ceremonially unclean on account of them, because the symbol of his separation to God is on his head. ⁸Throughout the period of his separation he is consecrated to the LORD.

9" 'If someone dies suddenly in his presence, thus defiling the hair he has dedicated, he must shave his head on the day of his cleansing — the seventh day. 10Then on the eighth day he must bring two doves or two young pigeons to the priest at the entrance to the Tent of Meeting. 11The priest is to offer one as a sin offering and the other as a burnt offering to make atonement for him because he sinned by being in the presence of the dead body. That same day he is to consecrate his head. 12He must dedicate himself to the LORD for the period of his separation and must bring a year-old male lamb as a guilt offering. The previous days do not count, because he became defiled during his separation.

6:6 ■ TYPES OF UNCLEANNESS

In its emphasis on purity, Numbers lists three types of unclean persons: victims of certain diseases, people with "a discharge of any kind" (including sexual ones), and those in contact with dead bodies. Besides offering obvious health benefits, these rules served to draw a sharp contrast between the Israelites and those who practised other religions: Egyptians who virtually worshipped the dead, and Phoenicians and others who made sex an important part of religious rites.

An unclean person went into a period of quarantine (5:1–4). When Miriam got leprosy, she was kept away from camp for seven days (12:15). Soldiers, too, went through the same cleansing ritual if they had killed anyone or touched anyone who had died (31:19).

13" 'Now this is the law for the Nazirite when the period of his separation is over. He is to be brought to the entrance to the Tent of Meeting. 14There he is to present his offerings to the LORD: a year-old male lamb without defect for a burnt offering, a year-old ewe lamb without defect for a sin offering, a ram without defect for a fellowship offering,*a* 15together with their grain offerings and drink offerings, and a basket of bread made without yeast — cakes made of fine flour mixed with oil, and wafers spread with oil.

16" 'The priest is to present them before the LORD and make the sin offering and the burnt offering. 17He is to present the basket of unleavened bread and is to sacrifice the ram as a fellowship offering to the LORD, together with its grain offering and drink offering.

18" 'Then at the entrance to the Tent of Meeting, the Nazirite must shave off the hair that he dedicated. He is to take the hair and put it in the fire that is under the sacrifice of the fellowship offering.

19" 'After the Nazirite has shaved off the hair of his dedication, the priest is to place in his hands a boiled shoulder of the ram, and a cake and a wafer from the basket, both made without yeast. 20The priest shall then wave them before the LORD as a wave offering; they are holy and belong to the priest, together with the breast that was waved and the thigh that was presented. After that, the Nazirite may drink wine.

21" 'This is the law of the Nazirite who vows his offering to the LORD in accordance with his separation, in addition to whatever else he can afford. He must fulfil the vow he has made, according to the law of the Nazirite.' "

6:18 ■ WELL-KNOWN NAZIRITES

Samson and John the Baptist are two of the most famous Nazirites in the Bible. The apostle Paul took a Nazirite vow in Jerusalem (Acts 21:21–29) to demonstrate his conformity to Jewish law.

■ The Priestly Blessing

22The LORD said to Moses, 23"Tell Aaron and his sons, 'This is how you are to bless the Israelites. Say to them:

24" ' "The LORD bless you
and keep you;
25the LORD make his face shine upon you
and be gracious to you;
26the LORD turn his face towards you
and give you peace." '

27"So they will put my name on the Israelites, and I will bless them."

■ Offerings at the Dedication of the Tabernacle

7 When Moses finished setting up the tabernacle, he anointed it and consecrated it and all its furnishings. He also anointed and consecrated the altar and all its utensils. 2Then the leaders of Israel, the heads of families who were the tribal leaders in charge of those who were counted, made offerings. 3They brought as their gifts before the LORD six covered carts and twelve oxen — an ox from each leader and a cart from every two. These they presented before the tabernacle.

4The LORD said to Moses, 5"Accept these from them, that they may be used in the work at the Tent of Meeting. Give them to the Levites as each man's work requires."

6So Moses took the carts and oxen and gave them to the Levites. 7He gave two carts and four oxen to the Gershonites, as their work required, 8and he gave four carts and eight oxen to the Merarites, as their work required. They were all under the direction of Ithamar son of Aaron, the priest. 9But Moses did not give any to the Kohathites, because they were to carry on their shoulders the holy things, for which they were responsible.

10When the altar was anointed, the leaders brought their offerings for its dedication and presented them before the altar. 11For the LORD had said to Moses, "Each day one leader is to bring his offering for the dedication of the altar."

12The one who brought his offering on the first day was Nahshon son of Amminadab of the tribe of Judah. 13His offering was one silver plate weighing a hundred and thirty shekels,*a* and one silver sprinkling bowl weighing seventy shekels,*b* both according to the sanctuary shekel, each filled with fine flour mixed with oil as a grain

a 14 Traditionally peace offering; also in verses 17 and 18   a 13 That is, about 3¼ pounds (about 1.5 kilograms); also elsewhere in this chapter
b 13 That is, about 1¾ pounds (about 0.8 kilogram); also elsewhere in this chapter

offering; [14]one gold dish weighing ten shekels,[c] filled with incense; [15]one young bull, one ram and one male lamb a year old, for a burnt offering; [16]one male goat for a sin offering; [17]and two oxen, five rams, five male goats and five male lambs a year old, to be sacrificed as a fellowship offering.[d] This was the offering of Nahshon son of Amminadab.

[18]On the second day Nethanel son of Zuar, the leader of Issachar, brought his offering. [19]The offering he brought was one silver plate weighing a hundred and thirty shekels, and one silver sprinkling bowl weighing seventy shekels, both according to the sanctuary shekel, each filled with fine flour mixed with oil as a grain offering; [20]one gold dish weighing ten shekels, filled with incense; [21]one young bull, one ram and one male lamb a year old, for a burnt offering; [22]one male goat for a sin offering; [23]and two oxen, five rams, five male goats and five male lambs a year old, to be sacrificed as a fellowship offering. This was the offering of Nethanel son of Zuar.

[24]On the third day, Eliab son of Helon, the leader of the people of Zebulun, brought his offering. [25]His offering was one silver plate weighing a hundred and thirty shekels, and one silver sprinkling bowl weighing seventy shekels, both according to the sanctuary shekel, each filled with fine flour mixed with oil as a grain offering; [26]one gold dish weighing ten shekels, filled with incense; [27]one young bull, one ram and one male lamb a year old, for a burnt offering; [28]one male goat for a sin offering; [29]and two oxen, five rams, five male goats and five male lambs a year old, to be sacrificed as a fellowship offering. This was the offering of Eliab son of Helon.

[30]On the fourth day Elizur son of Shedeur, the leader of the people of Reuben, brought his offering. [31]His offering was one silver plate weighing a hundred and thirty shekels, and one silver sprinkling bowl weighing seventy shekels, both according to the sanctuary shekel, each filled with fine flour mixed with oil as a grain offering; [32]one gold dish weighing ten shekels, filled with incense; [33]one young bull, one ram and one male lamb a year old, for a burnt offering; [34]one male goat for a sin offering; [35]and two oxen, five rams, five male goats and five male lambs a year old, to be sacrificed as a fellowship offering. This was the offering of Elizur son of Shedeur.

[36]On the fifth day Shelumiel son of Zurishaddai, the leader of the people of Simeon, brought his offering. [37]His offering was one silver plate weighing a hundred and thirty shekels, and one silver sprinkling bowl weighing seventy shekels, both according to the sanctuary shekel, each filled with fine flour mixed with oil as a grain offering; [38]one gold dish weighing ten shekels, filled with incense; [39]one young bull, one ram and one male lamb a year old, for a burnt offering;

[40]one male goat for a sin offering; [41]and two oxen, five rams, five male goats and five male lambs a year old, to be sacrificed as a fellowship offering. This was the offering of Shelumiel son of Zurishaddai.

[42]On the sixth day Eliasaph son of Deuel, the leader of the people of Gad, brought his offering. [43]His offering was one silver plate weighing a hundred and thirty shekels, and one silver sprinkling bowl weighing seventy shekels, both according to the sanctuary shekel, each filled with fine flour mixed with oil as a grain offering; [44]one gold dish weighing ten shekels, filled with incense; [45]one young bull, one ram and one male lamb a year old, for a burnt offering; [46]one male goat for a sin offering; [47]and two oxen, five rams, five male goats and five male lambs a year old, to be sacrificed as a fellowship offering. This was the offering of Eliasaph son of Deuel.

[48]On the seventh day Elishama son of Ammihud, the leader of the people of Ephraim, brought his offering. [49]His offering was one silver plate weighing a hundred and thirty shekels, and one silver sprinkling bowl weighing seventy shekels, both according to the sanctuary shekel, each filled with fine flour mixed with oil as a grain offering; [50]one gold dish weighing ten shekels, filled with incense; [51]one young bull, one ram and one male lamb a year old, for a burnt offering; [52]one male goat for a sin offering; [53]and two oxen, five rams, five male goats and five male lambs a year old, to be sacrificed as a fellowship offering. This was the offering of Elishama son of Ammihud.

[54]On the eighth day Gamaliel son of Pedahzur, the leader of the people of Manasseh, brought his offering. [55]His offering was one silver plate weighing a hundred and thirty shekels, and one silver sprinkling bowl weighing seventy shekels, both according to the sanctuary shekel, each filled with fine flour mixed with oil as a grain offering; [56]one gold dish weighing ten shekels, filled with incense; [57]one young bull, one ram and one male lamb a year old, for a burnt offering; [58]one male goat for a sin offering; [59]and two oxen, five rams, five male goats and five male lambs a year old, to be sacrificed as a fellowship offering. This was the offering of Gamaliel son of Pedahzur.

[60]On the ninth day Abidan son of Gideoni, the leader of the people of Benjamin, brought his offering. [61]His offering was one silver plate weighing a hundred and thirty shekels, and one silver sprinkling bowl weighing seventy shekels, both according to the sanctuary shekel, each filled with fine flour mixed with oil as a grain offering; [62]one gold dish weighing ten shekels, filled with incense; [63]one young bull, one ram and one male lamb a year old, for a burnt offering; [64]one male goat for a sin offering; [65]and two

---

[c] 14 That is, about 4 ounces (about 115 grams); also elsewhere in this chapter   [d] 17 Traditionally *peace offering*; also elsewhere in this chapter

oxen, five rams, five male goats and five male lambs a year old, to be sacrificed as a fellowship offering. This was the offering of Abidan son of Gideoni.

7:55 ■ GOLD AND SILVER DISHES
The plates and bowls used in Israelite worship have a history of their own. Some of these originals, perhaps all, were lost during the dark years of the judges. David produced more, which his son Solomon installed in the temple (2 Chronicles 5:1); all were taken as captured goods when the Babylonians destroyed Jerusalem (2 Kings 25:15). At last they were returned to Jerusalem when the Persian king Cyrus let the Jews return (Ezra 1:9–10).

66On the tenth day Ahiezer son of Ammishaddai, the leader of the people of Dan, brought his offering. 67His offering was one silver plate weighing a hundred and thirty shekels, and one silver sprinkling bowl weighing seventy shekels, both according to the sanctuary shekel, each filled with fine flour mixed with oil as a grain offering; 68one gold dish weighing ten shekels, filled with incense; 69one young bull, one ram and one male lamb a year old, for a burnt offering; 70one male goat for a sin offering; 71and two oxen, five rams, five male goats and five male lambs a year old, to be sacrificed as a fellowship offering. This was the offering of Ahiezer son of Ammishaddai.

72On the eleventh day Pagiel son of Ocran, the leader of the people of Asher, brought his offering. 73His offering was one silver plate weighing a hundred and thirty shekels, and one silver sprinkling bowl weighing seventy shekels, both according to the sanctuary shekel, each filled with fine flour mixed with oil as a grain offering; 74one gold dish weighing ten shekels, filled with incense; 75one young bull, one ram and one male lamb a year old, for a burnt offering; 76one male goat for a sin offering; 77and two oxen, five rams, five male goats and five male lambs a year old, to be sacrificed as a fellowship offering. This was the offering of Pagiel son of Ocran.

78On the twelfth day Ahira son of Enan, the leader of the people of Naphtali, brought his offering. 79His offering was one silver plate weighing a hundred and thirty shekels, and one silver sprinkling bowl weighing seventy shekels, both according to the sanctuary shekel, each filled with fine flour mixed with oil as a grain offering; 80one gold dish weighing ten shekels, filled with incense; 81one young bull, one ram and one male lamb a year old, for a burnt offering; 82one male goat for a sin offering; 83and two oxen, five rams, five male goats and five male lambs a year old, to be sacrificed as a fellowship offering. This was the offering of Ahira son of Enan.

84These were the offerings of the Israelite leaders for the dedication of the altar when it was anointed: twelve silver plates, twelve silver sprinkling bowls and twelve gold dishes. 85Each silver plate weighed a hundred and thirty shekels, and each sprinkling bowl seventy shekels. Altogether, the silver dishes weighed two thousand four hundred shekels,e according to the sanctuary shekel. 86The twelve gold dishes filled with incense weighed ten shekels each, according to the sanctuary shekel. Altogether, the gold dishes weighed a hundred and twenty shekels.f 87The total number of animals for the burnt offering came to twelve young bulls, twelve rams and twelve male lambs a year old, together with their grain offering. Twelve male goats were used for the sin offering. 88The total number of animals for the sacrifice of the fellowship offering came to twenty-four oxen, sixty rams, sixty male goats and sixty male lambs a year old. These were the offerings for the dedication of the altar after it was anointed.

89When Moses entered the Tent of Meeting to speak with the LORD, he heard the voice speaking to him from between the two cherubim above the atonement cover on the ark of the Testimony. And he spoke with him.

■ Setting Up the Lamps

8 The LORD said to Moses, 2"Speak to Aaron and say to him, 'When you set up the seven lamps, they are to light the area in front of the lampstand.'"

8:1 ■ THE LORD TO MOSES
Numbers emphasises time and again – over 150 times – that God spoke directly to Moses, and through him to the people of Israel. When Moses' leadership was challenged, God insisted that his communication with Moses was unique (12:6–8).

3Aaron did so; he set up the lamps so that they faced forward on the lampstand, just as the LORD commanded Moses. 4This is how the lampstand was made: It was made of hammered gold – from its base to its blossoms. The lampstand was made exactly like the pattern the LORD had shown Moses.

■ The Setting Apart of the Levites

5The LORD said to Moses: 6"Take the Levites from among the other Israelites and make them ceremonially clean. 7To purify them, do this: Sprinkle the water of cleansing on them; then make them shave their whole bodies and wash their clothes, and so purify themselves. 8Make them take a young bull with its grain offering of fine flour mixed with oil; then you are to take a second young bull for a sin offering. 9Bring the Levites to the front of the Tent of Meeting and assemble the whole Israelite community. 10You are to bring the Levites before the LORD, and the Israelites are to lay their hands on them. 11Aaron is to present the Levites before the LORD as a wave offering from the Israelites, so that they may be ready to do the work of the LORD.

12"After the Levites lay their hands on the heads of the bulls, use the one for a sin offering to the LORD

e85 That is, about 61 pounds (about 28 kilograms)   f86 That is, about 3 pounds (about 1.4 kilograms) and the other for a burnt offering, to make atonement for the Levites. [13]Make the Levites stand in front of Aaron and his sons and then present them as a wave offering to the LORD. [14]In this way you are to set the Levites apart from the other Israelites, and the Levites will be mine.

[15]"After you have purified the Levites and presented them as a wave offering, they are to come to do their work at the Tent of Meeting. [16]They are the Israelites who are to be given wholly to me. I have taken them as my own in place of the firstborn, the first male offspring from every Israelite woman. [17]Every firstborn male in Israel, whether man or animal, is mine. When I struck down all the firstborn in Egypt, I set them apart for myself. [18]And I have taken the Levites in place of all the firstborn sons in Israel. [19]Of all the Israelites, I have given the Levites as gifts to Aaron and his sons to do the work at the Tent of Meeting on behalf of the Israelites and to make atonement for them so that no plague will strike the Israelites when they go near the sanctuary."

[20]Moses, Aaron and the whole Israelite community did with the Levites just as the LORD commanded Moses. [21]The Levites purified themselves and washed their clothes. Then Aaron presented them as a wave offering before the LORD and made atonement for them to purify them. [22]After that, the Levites came to do their work at the Tent of Meeting under the supervision of Aaron and his sons. They did with the Levites just as the LORD commanded Moses.

[23]The LORD said to Moses, [24]"This applies to the Levites: Men twenty-five years old or more shall come to take part in the work at the Tent of Meeting, [25]but at the age of fifty, they must retire from their regular service and work no longer. [26]They may assist their brothers in performing their duties at the Tent of Meeting, but they themselves must not do the work. This, then, is how you are to assign the responsibilities of the Levites."

■ The Passover

9 The LORD spoke to Moses in the Desert of Sinai in the first month of the second year after they came out of Egypt. He said, [2]"Make the Israelites

---

■ NATIONAL REMINDERS
BUILT-IN OBJECT LESSONS FOR THE ISRAELITES

INSIGHT

AARON IS TO PRESENT THE LEVITES BEFORE THE LORD AS A WAVE OFFERING FROM THE ISRAELITES, SO THAT THEY MAY BE READY TO DO THE WORK OF THE LORD. ■ 8:11

Although parts of Numbers may seem strange to a modern reader, it clearly expresses two of the Israelites' chief values: purity and holiness. They had to become pure before they could approach God. And they were called to demonstrate God's holiness before other nations. The need for purity and holiness was reflected in what the Israelites ate and wore, and how they acted each day.

■ VISUAL REMINDERS
God set aside certain groups of people as a visual reminder of purity and holiness. The Levites, who somewhat parallel the full-time clergy of our day, took care of formal religious duties (chapters 3, 4, 8). One of their clans packed up the holy objects for moving, while other clans carried the tabernacle curtains and covers and structural parts.

Numbers describes a second group: the Nazirites (chapter 6). These ordinary laypeople dedicated themselves to an extra regimen of purity. They drank no wine and let their hair grow long. Much as the Amish people do today, they stood out from the majority in their dress and style.

Holiness was not left to special groups, though. Every Israelite participated in the daily offerings, sacrifices, and occasional festivals. When a family brought a whole bull and saw it skinned, butchered, and then burned on the altar, they were forced to reflect. Sin was serious, and a great gulf appeared between them and God. In some way, either through story, ritual or visual symbol, Numbers expresses that separateness on almost every page. In approaching God, the Israelites had to use great care.

■ BRIDGING THE GULF
The style of life described in this book differs from our own era of casual dress, informal worship, and talk of "friendship" with God. Later, the New Testament would spell out a God who is our Father, who can be approached at any time, who is interested in the personal details of our individual lives. But Numbers serves as an important background to that kind of relationship. It shows graphically just how great was the gulf between people and God, and helps us fully appreciate all that Jesus Christ did in providing a way across that gulf.

□ LIFE QUESTIONS:
Words like *holiness* and *purity* are not heard in many churches today. Do you think we take God for granted and approach him too casually?

celebrate the Passover at the appointed time. ³Celebrate it at the appointed time, at twilight on the fourteenth day of this month, in accordance with all its rules and regulations."

⁴So Moses told the Israelites to celebrate the Passover, ⁵and they did so in the Desert of Sinai at twilight on the fourteenth day of the first month. The Israelites did everything just as the LORD commanded Moses.

⁶But some of them could not celebrate the Passover on that day because they were ceremonially unclean on account of a dead body. So they came to Moses and Aaron that same day ⁷and said to Moses, "We have become unclean because of a dead body, but why should we be kept from presenting the LORD's offering with the other Israelites at the appointed time?"

⁸Moses answered them, "Wait until I find out what the LORD commands concerning you."

⁹Then the LORD said to Moses, ¹⁰"Tell the Israelites: 'When any of you or your descendants are unclean because of a dead body or are away on a journey, they may still celebrate the LORD's Passover. ¹¹They are to celebrate it on the fourteenth day of the second month at twilight. They are to eat the lamb, together with unleavened bread and bitter herbs. ¹²They must not leave any of it till morning or break any of its bones. When they celebrate the Passover, they must follow all the regulations. ¹³But if a man who is ceremonially clean and not on a journey fails to celebrate the Passover, that person must be cut off from his people because he did not present the LORD's offering at the appointed time. That man will bear the consequences of his sin.

¹⁴" 'An alien living among you who wants to celebrate the LORD's Passover must do so in accordance with its rules and regulations. You must have the same regulations for the alien and the native-born.' "

■ The Cloud Above the Tabernacle

¹⁵On the day the tabernacle, the Tent of the Testimony, was set up, the cloud covered it. From evening till morning the cloud above the tabernacle looked like fire. ¹⁶That is how it continued to be; the cloud covered it, and at night it looked like fire. ¹⁷Whenever the cloud lifted from above the Tent, the Israelites set out; wherever the cloud settled, the Israelites encamped. ¹⁸At the LORD's command the Israelites set out, and at his command they encamped. As long as the cloud stayed over the tabernacle, they remained in camp. ¹⁹When the cloud remained over the tabernacle a long time, the Israelites obeyed the LORD's order and did not set out. ²⁰Sometimes the cloud was over the tabernacle only a few days; at the LORD's command they would encamp, and then at his command they would set out. ²¹Sometimes the cloud stayed only from evening till morning, and when it lifted in the morning, they set out. Whether by day or by night, whenever the cloud lifted, they set out. ²²Whether the cloud stayed over the tabernacle for two days or a month or a year, the Israelites would remain in camp and not set out; but when it lifted, they would set out. ²³At the LORD's command they encamped, and at the LORD's command they set out. They obeyed the

LORD's order, in accordance with his command through Moses.

■ The Silver Trumpets

10 The LORD said to Moses: ²"Make two trumpets of hammered silver, and use them for calling the community together and for having the camps set out. ³When both are sounded, the whole community is to assemble before you at the entrance to the Tent of Meeting. ⁴If only one is sounded, the leaders—the heads of the clans of Israel—are to assemble before you. ⁵When a trumpet blast is sounded, the tribes camping on the east are to set out. ⁶At the sounding of a second blast, the camps on the south are to set out. The blast will be the signal for setting out. ⁷To gather the assembly, blow the trumpets, but not with the same signal.

⁸"The sons of Aaron, the priests, are to blow the trumpets. This is to be a lasting ordinance for you and the generations to come. ⁹When you go into battle in your own land against an enemy who is oppressing you, sound a blast on the trumpets. Then you will be remembered by the LORD your God and rescued from your enemies. ¹⁰Also at your times of rejoicing—your appointed feasts and New Moon festivals—you are to sound the trumpets over your burnt offerings and fellowship offerings,ᵃ and they will be a memorial for you before your God. I am the LORD your God."

■ The Israelites Leave Sinai

¹¹On the twentieth day of the second month of the second year, the cloud lifted from above the tabernacle of the Testimony. ¹²Then the Israelites set out from the Desert of Sinai and travelled from place to place until the cloud came to rest in the Desert of Paran. ¹³They set out, this first time, at the LORD's command through Moses.

¹⁴The divisions of the camp of Judah went first, under their standard. Nahshon son of Amminadab was in command. ¹⁵Nethanel son of Zuar was over the division of the tribe of Issachar, ¹⁶and Eliab son of Helon was over the division of the tribe of Zebulun. ¹⁷Then the tabernacle was taken down, and the Gershonites and Merarites, who carried it, set out.

¹⁸The divisions of the camp of Reuben went next, under their standard. Elizur son of Shedeur was in command. ¹⁹Shelumiel son of Zurishaddai was over the division of the tribe of Simeon, ²⁰and Eliasaph son of Deuel was over the division of the tribe of Gad. ²¹Then the Kohathites set out, carrying the holy things. The tabernacle was to be set up before they arrived.

²²The divisions of the camp of Ephraim went next, under their standard. Elishama son of

ᵃ 10 Traditionally *peace offerings*

Ammihud was in command. 23Gamaliel son of Pedahzur was over the division of the tribe of Manasseh, 24and Abidan son of Gideoni was over the division of the tribe of Benjamin.

25Finally, as the rear guard for all the units, the divisions of the camp of Dan set out, under their standard. Ahiezer son of Ammishaddai was in command. 26Pagiel son of Ocran was over the division of the tribe of Asher, 27and Ahira son of Enan was over the division of the tribe of Naphtali. 28This was the order of march for the Israelite divisions as they set out.

29Now Moses said to Hobab son of Reuel the Midianite, Moses' father-in-law, "We are setting out for the place about which the LORD said, 'I will give it to you.' Come with us and we will treat you well, for the LORD has promised good things to Israel."

30He answered, "No, I will not go; I am going back to my own land and my own people."

31But Moses said, "Please do not leave us. You know where we should camp in the desert, and you can be our eyes. 32If you come with us, we will share with you whatever good things the LORD gives us."

33So they set out from the mountain of the LORD and travelled for three days. The ark of the covenant of the LORD went before them during those three days to find them a place to rest. 34The cloud of the LORD was over them by day when they set out from the camp.

35Whenever the ark set out, Moses said,

"Rise up, O LORD!
  May your enemies be scattered;
  may your foes flee before you."

36Whenever it came to rest, he said,

"Return, O LORD,
  to the countless thousands of Israel."

10:36 ■ FAMOUS PRAYERS

Moses' prayer is still repeated in Jewish services when the scroll of the law is removed from its container. Another prayer from Numbers, the blessing of 6:24–26, is quoted both in Jewish and Christian services. In ancient thought, a person's name stood for his character, including all his virtues and powers, and the benediction in 6:27 showed God "putting his name on" the Israelites.

■ Fire From the LORD

11 Now the people complained about their hardships in the hearing of the LORD, and when he heard them his anger was aroused. Then fire from the LORD burned among them and consumed some of the outskirts of the camp. 2When the people cried out to Moses, he prayed to the LORD and the fire died down. 3So that place was called Taberah,a because fire from the LORD had burned among them.

■ Quail From the LORD

4The rabble with them began to crave other food, and again the Israelites started wailing and said, "If only we had meat to eat! 5We remember the fish we ate in Egypt at no cost — also the cucumbers, melons, leeks, onions and garlic. 6But now we have lost our appetite; we never see anything but this manna!"

7The manna was like coriander seed and looked like resin. 8The people went around gathering it, and then ground it in a hand mill or crushed it in a mortar. They cooked it in a pot or made it into cakes. And it tasted like something made with olive oil. 9When the dew settled on the camp at night, the manna also came down.

10Moses heard the people of every family wailing, each at the entrance to his tent. The LORD became exceedingly angry, and Moses was troubled. 11He asked the LORD, "Why have you brought this trouble on your servant? What have I done to displease you that you put the burden of all these people on me? 12Did I conceive all these people? Did I give them birth? Why do you tell me to carry them in my arms, as a nurse carries an infant, to the land you promised on oath to their forefathers? 13Where can I get meat for all these people? They keep wailing to me, 'Give us meat to eat!' 14I cannot carry all these people by myself; the burden is too heavy for me. 15If this is how you are going to treat me, put me to death right now — if I have found favour in your eyes — and do not let me face my own ruin."

16The LORD said to Moses: "Bring me seventy of Israel's elders who are known to you as leaders and officials among the people. Make them come to the Tent of Meeting, that they may stand there with you. 17I will come down and speak with you there, and I will take of the Spirit that is on you and put the Spirit on them. They will help you carry the burden of the people so that you will not have to carry it alone.

18"Tell the people: 'Consecrate yourselves in preparation for tomorrow, when you will eat meat. The LORD heard you when you wailed, "If only we had meat to eat! We were better off in Egypt!" Now the LORD will give you meat, and you will eat it. 19You will not eat it for just one day, or two days, or five, ten or twenty days, 20but for a whole month — until it comes out of your nostrils and you loathe it — because you have rejected the LORD, who is among you, and have wailed before him, saying, "Why did we ever leave Egypt?" ' "

21But Moses said, "Here I am among six hundred thousand men on foot, and you say, 'I will give them meat to eat for a whole month!' 22Would they have enough if flocks and herds were slaughtered for them? Would they have enough if all the fish in the sea were caught for them?"

23The LORD answered Moses, "Is the LORD's arm too short? You will now see whether or not what I say will come true for you."

24So Moses went out and told the people what the LORD had said. He brought together seventy of their elders and made them stand round the Tent. 25Then the LORD came down in the cloud and spoke with him, and he took of the Spirit that was on him and put the Spirit on the seventy elders. When the Spirit rested on them, they prophesied, but they did not do so again.b

26However, two men, whose names were Eldad

a3 Taberah means burning.   b25 Or prophesied and continued to do so and Medad, had remained in the camp. They were listed among the elders, but did not go out to the Tent. Yet the Spirit also rested on them, and they prophesied in the camp. 27A young man ran and told Moses, "Eldad and Medad are prophesying in the camp."

28Joshua son of Nun, who had been Moses' assistant since youth, spoke up and said, "Moses, my lord, stop them!"

29But Moses replied, "Are you jealous for my sake? I wish that all the LORD's people were prophets and

that the LORD would put his Spirit on them!" 30Then Moses and the elders of Israel returned to the camp.

31Now a wind went out from the LORD and drove quail in from the sea. It brought them*c* down all around the camp to about three feet*d* above the ground, as far as a day's walk in any direction. 32All that day and night and all the next day the people went out and gathered quail. No-one gathered less than ten homers.*e* Then they spread them out all around the camp. 33But while the meat was still between their teeth and before it could be consumed, the anger of the LORD burned against the people, and he struck them with a severe plague. 34Therefore the place was named Kibroth Hattaavah,*f* because there they buried the people who had craved other food.

35From Kibroth Hattaavah the people travelled to Hazeroth and stayed there.

■ Miriam and Aaron Oppose Moses

12 Miriam and Aaron began to talk against Moses because of his Cushite wife, for he had married a Cushite. 2"Has the LORD spoken only through Moses?" they asked. "Hasn't he also spoken through us?" And the LORD heard this.

3(Now Moses was a very humble man, more humble than anyone else on the face of the earth.)

4At once the LORD said to Moses, Aaron and Miriam, "Come out to the Tent of Meeting, all three of you." So the three of them came out. 5Then the LORD came down in a pillar of cloud; he stood at the entrance to the Tent and summoned Aaron and Miriam. When both of them stepped forward, 6he said, "Listen to my words:

"When a prophet of the LORD is among you,
    I reveal myself to him in visions,
    I speak to him in dreams.
7But this is not true of my servant Moses;
    he is faithful in all my house.
8With him I speak face to face,
    clearly and not in riddles;
    he sees the form of the LORD.
Why then were you not afraid
    to speak against my servant Moses?"

9The anger of the LORD burned against them, and he left them.

10When the cloud lifted from above the Tent, there stood Miriam — leprous,*a* like snow. Aaron turned towards her and saw that she had leprosy; 11and he said to Moses, "Please, my lord, do not hold against us the sin we have so foolishly committed. 12Do not let her be like a stillborn infant coming from its mother's womb with its flesh half eaten away."

13So Moses cried out to the LORD, "O God, please heal her!"

14The LORD replied to Moses, "If her father had spat in her face, would she not have been in disgrace for seven days? Confine her outside the camp for seven days; after that she can be brought back." 15So Miriam was confined outside the camp for seven days, and the people did not move on till she was brought back.

16After that, the people left Hazeroth and encamped in the Desert of Paran.

■ Exploring Canaan

13 The LORD said to Moses, 2"Send some men to explore the land of Canaan, which I am giving to the Israelites. From each ancestral tribe send one of its leaders."

3So at the LORD's command Moses sent them out from the Desert of Paran. All of them were leaders of the Israelites. 4These are their names:

    from the tribe of Reuben, Shammua son of
        Zaccur;
    5from the tribe of Simeon, Shaphat son of Hori;
    6from the tribe of Judah, Caleb son of Jephunneh;
    7from the tribe of Issachar, Igal son of Joseph;
    8from the tribe of Ephraim, Hoshea son of
        Nun;
    9from the tribe of Benjamin, Palti son of Raphu;
    10from the tribe of Zebulun, Gaddiel son of
        Sodi;

---

c31 Or *They flew*   *d31* Hebrew *two cubits* (about 0.9 metre)   *e32* That is, probably about 60 bushels (about 2.2 kilolitres)   *f34* *Kibroth Hattaavah* means *graves of craving*.   *a10* The Hebrew word was used for various diseases affecting the skin — not necessarily leprosy.

11from the tribe of Manasseh (a tribe of Joseph), Gaddi son of Susi;
12from the tribe of Dan, Ammiel son of Gemalli;
13from the tribe of Asher, Sethur son of Michael;
14from the tribe of Naphtali, Nahbi son of Vophsi;
15from the tribe of Gad, Geuel son of Maki.

16These are the names of the men Moses sent to explore the land. (Moses gave Hoshea son of Nun the name Joshua.)

17When Moses sent them to explore Canaan, he said, "Go up through the Negev and on into the hill country. 18See what the land is like and whether the people who live there are strong or weak, few or many. 19What kind of land do they live in? Is it good or bad? What kind of towns do they live in? Are they unwalled or fortified? 20How is the soil? Is it fertile or poor? Are there trees on it or not? Do your best to bring back some of the fruit of the land." (It was the season for the first ripe grapes.)

21So they went up and explored the land from the Desert of Zin as far as Rehob, towards Lebo*a* Hamath. 22They went up through the Negev and came to Hebron, where Ahiman, Sheshai and Talmai, the descendants of Anak, lived. (Hebron had been built seven years before Zoan in Egypt.) 23When they reached the Valley of Eshcol,*b* they cut off a branch bearing a single cluster of grapes. Two of them carried it on a pole between them, along with some pomegranates and figs. 24That place was called the Valley of Eshcol because of the cluster of grapes the Israelites cut off there. 25At the end of forty days they returned from exploring the land.

■ Report on the Exploration
26They came back to Moses and Aaron and the whole Israelite community at Kadesh in the Desert of Paran. There they reported to them and to the whole assembly and showed them the fruit of the land. 27They gave Moses this account: "We went into the land to which you sent us, and it does flow with milk and honey! Here is its fruit. 28But the people who live there are powerful, and the cities are fortified and very large. We even saw descendants of Anak there. 29The Amalekites live in the Negev; the Hittites, Jebusites and Amorites live in the hill country; and the Canaanites live near the sea and along the Jordan."

30Then Caleb silenced the people before Moses and said, "We should go up and take possession of the land, for we can certainly do it."

31But the men who had gone up with him said, "We can't attack those people; they are stronger than we are." 32And they spread among the Israelites a bad report about the land they had explored. They said, "The land we explored devours those living in it. All the people we saw there are of great size. 33We saw the Nephilim there (the descendants of Anak come from the Nephilim). We seemed like grasshoppers in our own eyes, and we looked the same to them."

■ The People Rebel

14 That night all the people of the community raised their voices and wept aloud. 2All the Israelites grumbled against Moses and Aaron, and the whole assembly said to them, "If only we had died in Egypt! Or in this desert! 3Why is the LORD bringing us to this land only to let us fall by the sword? Our wives and children will be taken as plunder. Wouldn't it be better for us to go back to Egypt?" 4And they said to each other, "We should choose a leader and go back to Egypt."

14:1 ■ THE WORST REBELLION
Chapter 14 records the tragic watershed of Numbers. Despite numerous proofs of God's power on their behalf, the Israelites cowered at the spies' report from Canaan. Fear led to open rebellion, and the nation plotted mutiny against Moses. At the very border of the promised land, theirs for the taking, they lost faith and turned away. In the face of such rebellion, God decided to wait for a whole new generation of Israelites; the original slaves would not cross into the promised land. All of them over the age of 20 – except for Caleb and Joshua – were destined to fall as carcasses in the desert.

5Then Moses and Aaron fell face down in front of the whole Israelite assembly gathered there. 6Joshua son of Nun and Caleb son of Jephunneh, who were among those who had explored the land, tore their clothes 7and said to the entire Israelite assembly, "The land we passed through and explored is exceedingly good. 8If the LORD is pleased with us, he will lead us into that land, a land flowing with milk and honey, and will give it to us. 9Only do not rebel against the LORD. And do not be afraid of the people of the land, because we will swallow them up. Their protection is gone, but the LORD is with us. Do not be afraid of them."

10But the whole assembly talked about stoning them. Then the glory of the LORD appeared at the Tent of Meeting to all the Israelites. 11The LORD said to Moses, "How long will these people treat me with contempt? How long will they refuse to believe in me, in spite of all the miraculous signs I have performed among them? 12I will strike them down with a plague and destroy them, but I will make you into a nation greater and stronger than they."

13Moses said to the LORD, "Then the Egyptians will hear about it! By your power you brought these people up from among them. 14And they will tell the inhabitants of this land about it. They have already heard that you, O LORD, are with these people and that you, O LORD, have been seen face to face, that your cloud stays over them, and that you go before them in a pillar of cloud by day and a pillar of fire by night. 15If you put these people to death all at one time, the nations who have heard this report about you will say, 16'The LORD was not able to bring these people into the land he promised them on oath; so he slaughtered them in the desert.' 17"Now may the Lord's strength be displayed, just

a 21 Or towards the entrance to   *b* 23 Eshcol means cluster; also in verse 24.

as you have declared: 18'The LORD is slow to anger, abounding in love and forgiving sin and rebellion. Yet he does not leave the guilty unpunished; he punishes the children for the sin of the fathers to the third and fourth generation.' 19In accordance with your great love, forgive the sin of these people, just as you have pardoned them from the time they left Egypt until now."

20The LORD replied, "I have forgiven them, as you asked. 21Nevertheless, as surely as I live and as surely as the glory of the LORD fills the whole earth, 22not one of the men who saw my glory and the miraculous signs I performed in Egypt and in the desert but who disobeyed me and tested me ten times — 23not one of them will ever see the land I promised on oath to their forefathers. No-one who has treated me with contempt will ever see it. 24But because my servant Caleb has a different spirit and follows me wholeheartedly, I will bring him into the land he went to, and his descendants will inherit it. 25Since the Amalekites and Canaanites are living in the valleys, turn back tomorrow and set out towards the desert along the route to the Red Sea."*a*

26The LORD said to Moses and Aaron: 27"How long will this wicked community grumble against me? I have heard the complaints of these grumbling Israelites. 28So tell them, 'As surely as I live, declares the LORD, I will do to you the very things I heard you say: 29In this desert your bodies will fall — every one of you twenty years old or more who was counted in the census and who has grumbled against me. 30Not one of you will enter the land I swore with uplifted hand to make your home, except Caleb son of Jephunneh and Joshua son of Nun. 31As for your children that you said would be taken as plunder, I will bring them in to enjoy the land you have rejected. 32But you — your bodies will fall in this desert. 33Your children will be shepherds here for forty years, suffering for your unfaithfulness, until the last of your bodies lies in the desert. 34For forty years — one year for each of the forty days you explored the land — you will suffer for your sins and know what it is like to have me against you.' 35I, the LORD, have spoken, and I will surely do these things to this whole wicked community, which has banded together against me. They will meet their end in this desert; here they will die."

36So the men Moses had sent to explore the land, who returned and made the whole community grumble against him by spreading a bad report about it — 37these men responsible for spreading the bad report about the land were struck down and died of a plague before the LORD. 38Of the men who went to explore the land, only Joshua son of Nun and Caleb son of Jephunneh survived.

39When Moses reported this to all the Israelites, they mourned bitterly. 40Early the next morning they went up towards the high hill country. "We have sinned," they said. "We will go up to the place the LORD promised."

41But Moses said, "Why are you disobeying the LORD's command? This will not succeed! 42Do not go up, because the LORD is not with you. You will be defeated by your enemies, 43for the Amalekites and Canaanites will face you there. Because you have turned away from the LORD, he will not be with you and you will fall by the sword."

14:39 ■ IMPERFECT TIMING
When the Israelites heard how God would punish them for disobeying, they suddenly found the courage to go up and fight. God sought obedience, though, not courage, and obedience meant following directions immediately. Though Moses warned the Israelites that their courage came too late, and that God would not support them, they went anyway — and were soundly beaten.

44Nevertheless, in their presumption they went up towards the high hill country, though neither Moses nor the ark of the LORD's covenant moved from the camp. 45Then the Amalekites and Canaanites who lived in that hill country came down and attacked them and beat them down all the way to Hormah.

■ Supplementary Offerings

15 The LORD said to Moses, 2"Speak to the Israelites and say to them: 'After you enter the land I am giving you as a home 3and you present to the LORD offerings made by fire, from the herd or the flock, as an aroma pleasing to the LORD — whether burnt offerings or sacrifices, for special vows or freewill offerings or festival offerings — 4then the one who brings his offering shall present to the LORD a grain offering of a tenth of an ephah*a* of fine flour mixed with a quarter of a hin*b* of oil. 5With each lamb for the burnt offering or the sacrifice, prepare a quarter of a hin of wine as a drink offering.

6" 'With a ram prepare a grain offering of two-tenths of an ephah*c* of fine flour mixed with a third of a hin*d* of oil, 7and a third of a hin of wine as a drink offering. Offer it as an aroma pleasing to the LORD.

8" 'When you prepare a young bull as a burnt offering or sacrifice, for a special vow or a fellowship offering*e* to the LORD, 9bring with the bull a grain offering of three-tenths of an ephah*f* of fine flour mixed with half a hin*g* of oil. 10Also bring half a hin of wine as a drink offering. It will be an offering made by fire, an aroma pleasing to the LORD. 11Each bull or ram, each lamb or young goat, is to be prepared in this manner. 12Do this for each one, for as many as you prepare.

13" 'Everyone who is native-born must do these things in this way when he brings an offering made by fire as an aroma pleasing to the LORD. 14For the generations to come, whenever an alien or anyone else living among you presents an offering made by fire as an aroma pleasing to the LORD, he must do exactly as you do. 15The community is to have the same rules for you and for the alien living among you; this is a lasting ordinance for the generations to come. You and the alien shall be the same before the

---

a25 Hebrew *Yam Suph;* that is, Sea of Reeds   *a4* That is, probably about 4 pints (about 2 litres)   *b4* That is, probably about 1½ pints (about 1 litre); also in verse 5   *c6* That is, probably about 7½ pints (about 4.5 litres)   *d6* That is, probably about 2¼ pints (about 1.2 litres); also in verse 7   *e8* Traditionally *peace offering*   *f9* That is, probably about 11½ pints (about 6.5 litres)   *g9* That is, probably about 3 pints (about 2 litres); also in verse 10

LORD: ¹⁶The same laws and regulations will apply both to you and to the alien living among you.' "

¹⁷The LORD said to Moses, ¹⁸"Speak to the Israelites and say to them: 'When you enter the land to which I am taking you ¹⁹and you eat the food of the land, present a portion as an offering to the LORD. ²⁰Present a cake from the first of your ground meal and present it as an offering from the threshing-floor. ²¹Throughout the generations to come you are to give this offering to the LORD from the first of your ground meal.

■ Offerings for Unintentional Sins

²²" 'Now if you unintentionally fail to keep any of these commands the LORD gave Moses—²³any of the LORD's commands to you through him, from the day the LORD gave them and continuing through the generations to come—²⁴and if this is done unintentionally without the community being aware of it, then the whole community is to offer a young bull for a burnt offering as an aroma pleasing to the LORD, along with its prescribed grain offering and drink offering, and a male goat for a sin offering. ²⁵The priest is to make atonement for the whole Israelite community, and they will be forgiven, for it was not intentional and they have brought to the LORD for their wrong an offering made by fire and a sin offering. ²⁶The whole Israelite community and the aliens living among them will be forgiven, because all the people were involved in the unintentional wrong.

²⁷" 'But if just one person sins unintentionally, he must bring a year-old female goat for a sin offering. ²⁸The priest is to make atonement before the LORD for the one who erred by sinning unintentionally, and when atonement has been made for him, he will be forgiven. ²⁹One and the same law applies to everyone who sins unintentionally, whether he is a native-born Israelite or an alien.

³⁰" 'But anyone who sins defiantly, whether native-born or alien, blasphemes the LORD, and that person must be cut off from his people. ³¹Because he has despised the LORD's word and broken his commands, that person must surely be cut off; his guilt remains on him.' "

■ The Sabbath-Breaker Put to Death

³²While the Israelites were in the desert, a man was found gathering wood on the Sabbath day. ³³Those who found him gathering wood brought him to Moses and Aaron and the whole assembly, ³⁴and they kept him in custody, because it was not clear what should be done to him. ³⁵Then the LORD said to Moses, "The man must die. The whole assembly must stone him outside the camp." ³⁶So the assembly took him outside the camp and stoned him to death, as the LORD commanded Moses.

■ Tassels on Garments

³⁷The LORD said to Moses, ³⁸"Speak to the Israelites and say to them: 'Throughout the generations to come you are to make tassels on the corners of your garments, with a blue cord on each tassel. ³⁹You will have these tassels to look at and so you will remember all the commands of the LORD, that you may obey them and not prostitute yourselves by going after the lusts of your own hearts and eyes. ⁴⁰Then you will remember to obey all my commands and will be consecrated to your God. ⁴¹I am the LORD your God, who brought you out of Egypt to be your God. I am the LORD your God.' "

15:38 ■ A SAFEGUARD AGAINST LUST

The Israelites had large reminders of God—such as the pillar of fire—and small ones: they wore tassels and blue cords on the corners of clothing to remind them of the Lord's commands. God specifically mentions this practice as a safeguard against lust—a reminder impossible to avoid for one tempted to adultery.

■ Korah, Dathan and Abiram

16 Korah son of Izhar, the son of Kohath, the son of Levi, and certain Reubenites—Dathan and Abiram, sons of Eliab, and On son of Peleth—became insolent^a ²and rose up against Moses. With them were 250 Israelite men, well-known community leaders who had been appointed members of the council. ³They came as a group to oppose Moses and Aaron and said to them, "You have gone too far! The whole community is holy, every one of them, and the LORD is with them. Why then do you set yourselves above the LORD's assembly?"

16:3 ■ OPEN REVOLT

Two hundred and fifty well-known council members, led by Korah, Dathan, and Abiram, rebelled against Moses' leadership. They apparently wanted more people recognised as priests. But in a dramatic test, Moses showed that he was the leader God had chosen.

This rebellion and a second one immediately afterwards (verse 41) are the only two major events that the Bible mentions during the Israelites' 37 years of wandering in the desert. Deuteronomy, however (2:7; 8:4; 29:5–6), indicates that the people were well cared for.

⁴When Moses heard this, he fell face down. ⁵Then he said to Korah and all his followers: "In the morning the LORD will show who belongs to him and who is holy, and he will make that person come near him. The man he chooses he will cause to come near him. ⁶You, Korah, and all your followers are to do this: Take censers ⁷and tomorrow put fire and incense in them before the LORD. The man the LORD chooses will be the one who is holy. You Levites have gone too far!"

⁸Moses also said to Korah, "Now listen, you Levites! ⁹Isn't it enough for you that the God of Israel has separated you from the rest of the Israelite community and brought you near himself to do the work at the LORD's tabernacle and to stand before the community and minister to them? ¹⁰He has brought you and all your fellow Levites near himself, but now you are trying to get the priesthood too. ¹¹It is against

^a1 Or Peleth—took ¸men¸

the LORD that you and all your followers have banded together. Who is Aaron that you should grumble against him?"

¹²Then Moses summoned Dathan and Abiram, the sons of Eliab. But they said, "We will not come! ¹³Isn't it enough that you have brought us up out of a land flowing with milk and honey to kill us in the desert? And now you also want to lord it over us? ¹⁴Moreover, you haven't brought us into a land flowing with milk and honey or given us an inheritance of fields and vineyards. Will you gouge out the eyes of*b* these men? No, we will not come!"

¹⁵Then Moses became very angry and said to the LORD, "Do not accept their offering. I have not taken so much as a donkey from them, nor have I wronged any of them."

¹⁶Moses said to Korah, "You and all your followers are to appear before the LORD tomorrow—you and they and Aaron. ¹⁷Each man is to take his censer and put incense in it—250 censers in all—and present it before the LORD. You and Aaron are to present your censers also." ¹⁸So each man took his censer, put fire and incense in it, and stood with Moses and Aaron at the entrance to the Tent of Meeting. ¹⁹When Korah had gathered all his followers in opposition to them at the entrance to the Tent of Meeting, the glory of the LORD appeared to the entire assembly. ²⁰The LORD said to Moses and Aaron, ²¹"Separate yourselves from this assembly so that I can put an end to them at once."

²²But Moses and Aaron fell face down and cried out, "O God, God of the spirits of all mankind, will you be angry with the entire assembly when only one man sins?"

²³Then the LORD said to Moses, ²⁴"Say to the assembly, 'Move away from the tents of Korah, Dathan and Abiram.' "

²⁵Moses got up and went to Dathan and Abiram, and the elders of Israel followed him. ²⁶He warned the assembly, "Move back from the tents of these wicked men! Do not touch anything belonging to them, or you will be swept away because of all their sins." ²⁷So they moved away from the tents of Korah, Dathan and Abiram. Dathan and Abiram had come out and were standing with their wives, children and little ones at the entrances to their tents.

²⁸Then Moses said, "This is how you will know that the LORD has sent me to do all these things and that it was not my idea: ²⁹If these men die a natural death and experience only what usually happens to men, then the LORD has not sent me. ³⁰But if the LORD brings about something totally new, and the earth opens its mouth and swallows them, with everything that belongs to them, and they go down alive into the grave,*c* then you will know that these men have treated the LORD with contempt."

³¹As soon as he finished saying all this, the ground under them split apart ³²and the earth opened its mouth and swallowed them, with their households and all Korah's men and all their possessions. ³³They went down alive into the grave, with everything they owned; the earth closed over them, and they perished and were gone from the community. ³⁴At their cries, all the Israelites around them fled, shouting, "The earth is going to swallow us too!"

³⁵And fire came out from the LORD and consumed the 250 men who were offering the incense.

³⁶The LORD said to Moses, ³⁷"Tell Eleazar son of Aaron, the priest, to take the censers out of the smouldering remains and scatter the coals some distance away, for the censers are holy—³⁸the censers of the men who sinned at the cost of their lives. Hammer the censers into sheets to overlay the altar, for they were presented before the LORD and have become holy. Let them be a sign to the Israelites."

³⁹So Eleazar the priest collected the bronze censers brought by those who had been burned up, and he had them hammered out to overlay the altar, ⁴⁰as the LORD directed him through Moses. This was to remind the Israelites that no-one except a descendant of Aaron should come to burn incense before the LORD, or he would become like Korah and his followers.

⁴¹The next day the whole Israelite community grumbled against Moses and Aaron. "You have killed the LORD's people," they said.

⁴²But when the assembly gathered in opposition to Moses and Aaron and turned towards the Tent of Meeting, suddenly the cloud covered it and the glory of the LORD appeared. ⁴³Then Moses and Aaron went to the front of the Tent of Meeting, ⁴⁴and the LORD said to Moses, ⁴⁵"Get away from this assembly so that I can put an end to them at once." And they fell face down.

⁴⁶Then Moses said to Aaron, "Take your censer and put incense in it, along with fire from the altar, and hurry to the assembly to make atonement for them. Wrath has come out from the LORD; the plague has started." ⁴⁷So Aaron did as Moses said, and ran into the midst of the assembly. The plague had already started among the people, but Aaron offered the incense and made atonement for them. ⁴⁸He stood between the living and the dead, and the plague stopped. ⁴⁹But 14,700 people died from the plague, in addition to those who had died because of Korah. ⁵⁰Then Aaron returned to Moses at the entrance to the Tent of Meeting, for the plague had stopped.

■ The Budding of Aaron's Staff

17 The LORD said to Moses, ²"Speak to the Israelites and get twelve staffs from them, one from the leader of each of their ancestral tribes. Write the name of each man on his staff. ³On the staff of Levi write Aaron's name, for there must be one staff for the head of each ancestral tribe. ⁴Place them in the Tent of Meeting in front of the Testimony, where I meet with you. ⁵The staff belonging to the man I choose will sprout, and I will rid myself of this constant grumbling against you by the Israelites."

⁶So Moses spoke to the Israelites, and their leaders gave him twelve staffs, one for the leader of each of their ancestral tribes, and Aaron's staff was among them. ⁷Moses placed the staffs before the LORD in the Tent of the Testimony.

⁸The next day Moses entered the Tent of the Testimony and saw that Aaron's staff, which represented the house of Levi, had not only sprouted but had budded, blossomed and produced almonds. ⁹Then Moses brought out all the staffs from the

b 14 Or you make slaves of; or you deceive   c 30 Hebrew Sheol; also in verse 33

LORD's presence to all the Israelites. They looked at them, and each man took his own staff.

¹⁰The LORD said to Moses, "Put back Aaron's staff in front of the Testimony, to be kept as a sign to the rebellious. This will put an end to their grumbling against me, so that they will not die." ¹¹Moses did just as the LORD commanded him.

17:10 ■ WHAT'S IN THE ARK

The ark of the covenant was the holiest sign of God's presence. In or near it were placed a few highly significant mementos of the journey to the promised land: the stone tablets of the Law of Moses (Exodus 25:16), a jar of the miraculous manna (Exodus 16:33–34), and Aaron's sprouted staff. As a visible proof that God had chosen Aaron to be priest, the miraculous staff could help deter future rebellions.

---

¹²The Israelites said to Moses, "We shall die! We are lost, we are all lost! ¹³Anyone who even comes near the tabernacle of the LORD will die. Are we all going to die?"

■ Duties of Priests and Levites

18 The LORD said to Aaron, "You, your sons and your father's family are to bear the responsibility for offences against the sanctuary, and you and your sons alone are to bear the responsibility for offences against the priesthood. ²Bring your fellow Levites from your ancestral tribe to join you and assist you when you and your sons minister before the Tent of the Testimony. ³They are to be responsible to you and are to perform all the duties of the Tent, but they must not go near the furnishings of the sanctuary or the altar, or both they and you will die. ⁴They are to join you and be responsible for the care of the Tent of Meeting—all the work at the Tent—and no-one else may come near where you are.

⁵"You are to be responsible for the care of the sanctuary and the altar, so that wrath will not fall on the Israelites again. ⁶I myself have selected your fellow Levites from among the Israelites as a gift to you, dedicated to the LORD to do the work at the Tent of Meeting. ⁷But only you and your sons may serve as priests in connection with everything at the altar and inside the curtain. I am giving you the service of the priesthood as a gift. Anyone else who comes near the sanctuary must be put to death."

■ Offerings for Priests and Levites

⁸Then the LORD said to Aaron, "I myself have put you in charge of the offerings presented to me; all the holy offerings the Israelites give me I give to you and your sons as your portion and regular share. ⁹You are to have the part of the most holy offerings that is kept from the fire. From all the gifts they bring me as most holy offerings, whether grain or sin or guilt offerings, that part belongs to you and your sons. ¹⁰Eat it as something most holy; every male shall eat it. You must regard it as holy.

¹¹"This also is yours: whatever is set aside from the gifts of all the wave offerings of the Israelites. I give this to you and your sons and daughters as your regular share. Everyone in your household who is ceremonially clean may eat it.

¹²"I give you all the finest olive oil and all the finest new wine and grain they give to the LORD as the firstfruits of their harvest. ¹³All the land's firstfruits that they bring to the LORD will be yours. Everyone in your household who is ceremonially clean may eat it.

¹⁴"Everything in Israel that is devoted[a] to the LORD is yours. ¹⁵The first offspring of every womb, both man and animal, that is offered to the LORD is yours. But you must redeem every firstborn son and every firstborn male of unclean animals. ¹⁶When they are a month old, you must redeem them at the redemption price set at five shekels[b] of silver, according to the sanctuary shekel, which weighs twenty gerahs.

¹⁷"But you must not redeem the firstborn of an ox, a sheep or a goat; they are holy. Sprinkle their blood on the altar and burn their fat as an offering made by fire, an aroma pleasing to the LORD. ¹⁸Their meat is to be yours, just as the breast of the wave offering and the right thigh are yours. ¹⁹Whatever is set aside from the holy offerings the Israelites present to the LORD I give to you and your sons and daughters as your regular share. It is an everlasting covenant of salt before the LORD for both you and your offspring."

²⁰The LORD said to Aaron, "You will have no inheritance in their land, nor will you have any share among them; I am your share and your inheritance among the Israelites.

18:20 ■ NO LAND FOR LEVITES

The tribe of Levites were granted special privileges, but in contrast to the wealthy priestly caste of, say, Egypt, they received no land. God himself was their share and inheritance. For food, they relied largely on offerings from other tribes. Thus the physical survival of "full-time ministers" depended on how faithful the other Israelites were.

---

²¹"I give to the Levites all the tithes in Israel as their inheritance in return for the work they do while serving at the Tent of Meeting. ²²From now on the Israelites must not go near the Tent of Meeting, or they will bear the consequences of their sin and will die. ²³It is the Levites who are to do the work at the Tent of Meeting and bear the responsibility for offences against it. This is a lasting ordinance for the generations to come. They will receive no inheritance among the Israelites. ²⁴Instead, I give to the Levites as their inheritance the tithes that the Israelites present as an offering to the LORD. That is why I said concerning them: 'They will have no inheritance among the Israelites.' "

²⁵The LORD said to Moses, ²⁶"Speak to the Levites and say to them: 'When you receive from the Israelites the tithe I give you as your inheritance, you must present a tenth of that tithe as the LORD's offering. ²⁷Your offering will be reckoned to you as grain

---

a 14 The Hebrew term refers to the irrevocable giving over of things or persons to the LORD.   *b 16* That is, about 2 ounces (about 55 grams) from the threshing-floor or juice from the wine-press. 28In this way you also will present an offering to the LORD from all the tithes you receive from the Israelites. From these tithes you must give the LORD's portion to Aaron the priest. 29You must present as the LORD's portion the best and holiest part of every-thing given to you.'

30"Say to the Levites: 'When you present the best part, it will be reckoned to you as the product of the threshing-floor or the winepress. 31You and your households may eat the rest of it anywhere, for it is your wages for your work at the Tent of Meeting. 32By presenting the best part of it you will not be guilty in this matter; then you will not defile the holy offerings of the Israelites, and you will not die.' "

■ The Water of Cleansing

19 The LORD said to Moses and Aaron: 2"This is a requirement of the law that the LORD has commanded: Tell the Israelites to bring you a red heifer without defect or blemish and that has never been under a yoke. 3Give it to Eleazar the priest; it is to be taken outside the camp and slaughtered in his presence. 4Then Eleazar the priest is to take some of its blood on his finger and sprinkle it seven times towards the front of the Tent of Meeting. 5While he watches, the heifer is to be burned—its hide, flesh, blood and offal. 6The priest is to take some cedar wood, hyssop and scarlet wool and throw them onto the burning heifer. 7After that, the priest must wash his clothes and bathe himself with water. He may then come into the camp, but he will be ceremonially unclean till evening. 8The man who burns it must also wash his clothes and bathe with water, and he too will be unclean till evening.

9"A man who is clean shall gather up the ashes of the heifer and put them in a ceremonially clean place outside the camp. They shall be kept by the Israelite community for use in the water of cleans-ing; it is for purification from sin. 10The man who gathers up the ashes of the heifer must also wash his clothes, and he too will be unclean till evening. This will be a lasting ordinance both for the Israelites and for the aliens living among them.

11"Whoever touches the dead body of anyone will be unclean for seven days. 12He must purify himself with the water on the third day and on the seventh day; then he will be clean. But if he does not purify himself on the third and seventh days, he will not be clean. 13Whoever touches the dead body of anyone and fails to purify himself defiles the LORD's tabernacle. That person must be cut off from Israel. Because the water of cleansing has not been sprin-kled on him, he is unclean; his uncleanness remains on him.

14"This is the law that applies when a person dies in a tent: Anyone who enters the tent and anyone who is in it will be unclean for seven days, 15and every open container without a lid fastened on it will be unclean.

16"Anyone out in the open who touches someone who has been killed with a sword or someone who has died a natural death, or anyone who touches a human bone or a grave, will be unclean for seven days.

17"For the unclean person, put some ashes from the burned purification offering into a jar and pour fresh water over them. 18Then a man who is ceremo-nially clean is to take some hyssop, dip it in the water and sprinkle the tent and all the furnishings and the people who were there. He must also sprinkle any-one who has touched a human bone or a grave or someone who has been killed or someone who has died a natural death. 19The man who is clean is to sprinkle the unclean person on the third and sev-enth days, and on the seventh day he is to purify him. The person being cleansed must wash his clothes and bathe with water, and that evening he will be clean. 20But if a person who is unclean does not pu-rify himself, he must be cut off from the community, because he has defiled the sanctuary of the LORD. The water of cleansing has not been sprinkled on him, and he is unclean. 21This is a lasting ordinance for them.

"The man who sprinkles the water of cleansing must also wash his clothes, and anyone who touches the water of cleansing will be unclean till evening. 22Anything that an unclean person touches becomes unclean, and anyone who touches it becomes un-clean till evening."

■ Water From the Rock

20 In the first month the whole Israelite com-munity arrived at the Desert of Zin, and they stayed at Kadesh. There Miriam died and was buried.

2Now there was no water for the community, and the people gathered in opposition to Moses and Aaron. 3They quarrelled with Moses and said, "If only we had died when our brothers fell dead before the LORD! 4Why did you bring the LORD's community into this desert, that we and our livestock should die here? 5Why did you bring us up out of Egypt to this terrible place? It has no grain or figs, grapevines or pomegranates. And there is no water to drink!"

6Moses and Aaron went from the assembly to the entrance to the Tent of Meeting and fell face down, and the glory of the LORD appeared to them. 7The LORD said to Moses, 8"Take the staff, and you and your brother Aaron gather the assembly together. Speak to that rock before their eyes and it will pour out its water. You will bring water out of the rock for the community so that they and their livestock can drink."

9So Moses took the staff from the LORD's presence, just as he commanded him. 10He and Aaron gathered the assembly together in front of the rock and Moses said to them, "Listen, you rebels, must we bring you water out of this rock?" 11Then Moses raised his arm and struck the rock twice with his staff. Water gushed out, and the community and their livestock drank.

12But the LORD said to Moses and Aaron, "Because you did not trust in me enough to honour me as holy in the sight of the Israelites, you will not bring this community into the land I give them."

13These were the waters of Meribah,a where the Israelites quarrelled with the LORD and where he showed himself holy among them.

a 13 Meribah means quarrelling.

■ Edom Denies Israel Passage

14Moses sent messengers from Kadesh to the king of Edom, saying:

20:12 ■ MOSES' SIN

After so many displays of loyalty and courage, Moses faltered. Numbers does not specify exactly what Moses did that upset God. Was it striking the rock rather than speaking to it as God commanded? Regardless, Moses lashed out angrily against the Israelites and was faulted for his lack of trust in God. In Deuteronomy, God describes the sin as "breaking faith" with him and tells Moses that he "did not uphold my holiness among the Israelites" (32:51).

The scene at Meribah brought a tragic end to a great man's career: Moses, footsore and weary, was told he too would die in the desert, before the Israelites crossed into the promised land. Deuteronomy 3:23–27 adds a postscript: Moses pleaded with God to reverse the punishment, and, when that failed, he threw the blame back on the Israelites.

"This is what your brother Israel says: You know about all the hardships that have come upon us. 15Our forefathers went down into Egypt, and we lived there many years. The Egyptians ill-treated us and our fathers, 16but when we cried out to the LORD, he heard our cry and sent an angel and brought us out of Egypt.

"Now we are here at Kadesh, a town on the edge of your territory. 17Please let us pass through your country. We will not go through any field or vineyard, or drink water from any well. We will travel along the king's highway and not turn to the right or to the left until we have passed through your territory."

18But Edom answered:

"You may not pass through here; if you try, we will march out and attack you with the sword."

19The Israelites replied:

"We will go along the main road, and if we or our livestock drink any of your water, we will pay for it. We only want to pass through on foot — nothing else."

20Again they answered:

"You may not pass through."

Then Edom came out against them with a large and powerful army. 21Since Edom refused to let them go through their territory, Israel turned away from them.

■ The Death of Aaron

22The whole Israelite community set out from Kadesh and came to Mount Hor. 23At Mount Hor, near the border of Edom, the LORD said to Moses and Aaron, 24"Aaron will be gathered to his people. He

will not enter the land I give the Israelites, because both of you rebelled against my command at the waters of Meribah. 25Call Aaron and his son Eleazar and take them up Mount Hor. 26Remove Aaron's garments and put them on his son Eleazar, for Aaron will be gathered to his people; he will die there."

20:21 ■ BLOOD FEUD

Israel asked politely for the right to pass through Edom, offering to pay for water rights. Since the Edomites were distant relatives, descendants of Jacob's brother Esau, Israel expected a favourable response. Instead, Edom's refusal meant a long, hard detour. Moses warned the Israelites not to hate the Edomites, their kin (Deuteronomy 23:7–8). But for the rest of biblical history, there were wars and hatred between the two nations.

27Moses did as the LORD commanded: They went up Mount Hor in the sight of the whole community. 28Moses removed Aaron's garments and put them on his son Eleazar. And Aaron died there on top of the mountain. Then Moses and Eleazar came down from the mountain, 29and when the whole community learned that Aaron had died, the entire house of Israel mourned for him thirty days.

■ Arad Destroyed

21 When the Canaanite king of Arad, who lived in the Negev, heard that Israel was coming along the road to Atharim, he attacked the Israelites and captured some of them. 2Then Israel made this vow to the LORD: "If you will deliver these people into our hands, we will totally destroy[a] their cities." 3The LORD listened to Israel's plea and gave the Canaanites over to them. They completely destroyed them and their towns; so the place was named Hormah.[b]

■ The Bronze Snake

4They travelled from Mount Hor along the route to the Red Sea,[c] to go round Edom. But the people grew impatient on the way; 5they spoke against God and against Moses, and said, "Why have you brought us up out of Egypt to die in the desert? There is no bread! There is no water! And we detest this miserable food!"

6Then the LORD sent venomous snakes among them; they bit the people and many Israelites died. 7The people came to Moses and said, "We sinned when we spoke against the LORD and against you. Pray that the LORD will take the snakes away from us." So Moses prayed for the people.

8The LORD said to Moses, "Make a snake and put it up on a pole; anyone who is bitten can look at it and live." 9So Moses made a bronze snake and put it up on a pole. Then when anyone was bitten by a snake and looked at the bronze snake, he lived.

■ The Journey to Moab

10The Israelites moved on and camped at Oboth. 11Then they set out from Oboth and camped in Iye Abarim, in the desert that faces Moab towards the

a2 The Hebrew term refers to the irrevocable giving over of things or persons to the LORD, often by totally destroying them; also in verse 3.　　b3 Hormah means destruction.　　c4 Hebrew Yam Suph; that is, Sea of Reeds sunrise. [12]From there they moved on and camped in the Zered Valley. [13]They set out from there and camped alongside the Arnon, which is in the desert extending into Amorite territory. The Arnon is the border of Moab, between Moab and the Amorites.

21:9 ■ BRONZE SNAKE

Jesus chose this incident as one of the examples from Old Testament history that illustrates his own person and work (John 3:14). Through the snake and through Jesus, God provided a way of escape that required only faith from the people. In typical style, the Israelites corrupted the meaning by keeping the bronze snake as an idol to worship. Centuries later, King Hezekiah destroyed this image (2 Kings 18:4).

[14]That is why the Book of the Wars of the LORD says:

"... Waheb in Suphah[d] and the ravines,
    the Arnon [15]and[e] the slopes of the ravines
that lead to the site of Ar
    and lie along the border of Moab."

21:14 ■ OUT OF PRINT

This quotation comes from a book no longer in existence. The Bible makes many mentions of such vanished books. Joshua 10:13 and 2 Samuel 1:18, for example, name the Book of Jashar. There are references to the works of various prophets or seers (Gad, Ahijah, Shemaiah) and many references to royal annals such as the book of the kings of Israel (1 Chronicles 9:1). Israel must have had a sizeable library.

[16]From there they continued on to Beer, the well where the LORD said to Moses, "Gather the people together and I will give them water."
[17]Then Israel sang this song:

"Spring up, O well!
    Sing about it,
[18]about the well that the princes dug,
    that the nobles of the people sank—
    the nobles with sceptres and staffs."

Then they went from the desert to Mattanah, [19]from Mattanah to Nahaliel, from Nahaliel to Bamoth, [20]and from Bamoth to the valley in Moab where the top of Pisgah overlooks the wasteland.

■ Defeat of Sihon and Og
[21]Israel sent messengers to say to Sihon king of the Amorites:

[22]"Let us pass through your country. We will not turn aside into any field or vineyard, or drink water from any well. We will travel along the king's highway until we have passed through your territory."

[23]But Sihon would not let Israel pass through his territory. He mustered his entire army and marched out into the desert against Israel. When he reached Jahaz, he fought with Israel. [24]Israel, however, put

him to the sword and took over his land from the Arnon to the Jabbok, but only as far as the Ammonites, because their border was fortified. [25]Israel captured all the cities of the Amorites and occupied them, including Heshbon and all its surrounding settlements. [26]Heshbon was the city of Sihon king of the Amorites, who had fought against the former king of Moab and had taken from him all his land as far as the Arnon.
[27]That is why the poets say:

"Come to Heshbon and let it be rebuilt;
    let Sihon's city be restored.

[28]"Fire went out from Heshbon,
    a blaze from the city of Sihon.
It consumed Ar of Moab,
    the citizens of Arnon's heights.
[29]Woe to you, O Moab!
    You are destroyed, O people of Chemosh!
He has given up his sons as fugitives
    and his daughters as captives
to Sihon king of the Amorites.

[30]"But we have overthrown them;
    Heshbon is destroyed all the way to Dibon.
We have demolished them as far as Nophah,
    which extends to Medeba."

[31]So Israel settled in the land of the Amorites. [32]After Moses had sent spies to Jazer, the Israelites captured its surrounding settlements and drove out the Amorites who were there. [33]Then they turned and went up along the road towards Bashan, and Og king of Bashan and his whole army marched out to meet them in battle at Edrei.
[34]The LORD said to Moses, "Do not be afraid of him, for I have handed him over to you, with his whole army and his land. Do to him what you did to Sihon king of the Amorites, who reigned in Heshbon."
[35]So they struck him down, together with his sons and his whole army, leaving them no survivors. And they took possession of his land.

■ Balak Summons Balaam

22 Then the Israelites travelled to the plains of Moab and camped along the Jordan across from Jericho.[a]
[2]Now Balak son of Zippor saw all that Israel had done to the Amorites, [3]and Moab was terrified because there were so many people. Indeed, Moab was filled with dread because of the Israelites.
[4]The Moabites said to the elders of Midian, "This horde is going to lick up everything around us, as an ox licks up the grass of the field."
So Balak son of Zippor, who was king of Moab at that time, [5]sent messengers to summon Balaam son of Beor, who was at Pethor, near the River,[b] in his native land. Balak said:

"A people has come out of Egypt; they cover the face of the land and have settled next to me. [6]Now come and put a curse on these people, because they are too powerful for me. Perhaps then I will be able to defeat them and drive them out of the country. For I know that those

---

[d]14 The meaning of the Hebrew for this phrase is uncertain.   [e]14,15 Or "I have been given from Suphah and the ravines / of the Arnon [15]to
[a]1 Hebrew Jordan of Jericho; possibly an ancient name for the Jordan River   [b]5 That is, the Euphrates

you bless are blessed, and those you curse are cursed."

7The elders of Moab and Midian left, taking with them the fee for divination. When they came to Balaam, they told him what Balak had said.

8"Spend the night here," Balaam said to them, "and I will bring you back the answer the LORD gives me." So the Moabite princes stayed with him.

9God came to Balaam and asked, "Who are these men with you?"

10Balaam said to God, "Balak son of Zippor, king of Moab, sent me this message: 11'A people that has come out of Egypt covers the face of the land. Now come and put a curse on them for me. Perhaps then I will be able to fight them and drive them away.'"

12But God said to Balaam, "Do not go with them. You must not put a curse on those people, because they are blessed."

13The next morning Balaam got up and said to Balak's princes, "Go back to your own country, for the LORD has refused to let me go with you."

14So the Moabite princes returned to Balak and said, "Balaam refused to come with us."

15Then Balak sent other princes, more numerous and more distinguished than the first. 16They came to Balaam and said:

"This is what Balak son of Zippor says: Do not let anything keep you from coming to me, 17because I will reward you handsomely and do whatever you say. Come and put a curse on these people for me."

18But Balaam answered them, "Even if Balak gave me his palace filled with silver and gold, I could not do anything great or small to go beyond the command of the LORD my God. 19Now stay here tonight as the others did, and I will find out what else the LORD will tell me."

20That night God came to Balaam and said, "Since these men have come to summon you, go with them, but do only what I tell you."

■ Balaam's Donkey

21Balaam got up in the morning, saddled his donkey and went with the princes of Moab. 22But God was very angry when he went, and the angel of the LORD stood in the road to oppose him. Balaam was riding on his donkey, and his two servants were with him. 23When the donkey saw the angel of the LORD standing in the road with a drawn sword in his hand, she turned off the road into a field. Balaam beat her to get her back on the road.

24Then the angel of the LORD stood in a narrow path between two vineyards, with walls on both sides. 25When the donkey saw the angel of the LORD, she pressed close to the wall, crushing Balaam's foot against it. So he beat her again.

26Then the angel of the LORD moved on ahead and stood in a narrow place where there was no room to turn, either to the right or to the left. 27When the donkey saw the angel of the LORD, she lay down under Balaam, and he was angry and beat her with his staff. 28Then the LORD opened the donkey's mouth, and she said to Balaam, "What have I done to you to make you beat me these three times?"

29Balaam answered the donkey, "You have made a fool of me! If I had a sword in my hand, I would kill you right now."

30The donkey said to Balaam, "Am I not your own donkey, which you have always ridden, to this day? Have I been in the habit of doing this to you?"

"No," he said.

31Then the LORD opened Balaam's eyes, and he saw the angel of the LORD standing in the road with his sword drawn. So he bowed low and fell face down.

32The angel of the LORD asked him, "Why have you beaten your donkey these three times? I have come here to oppose you because your path is a reckless one before me.c 33The donkey saw me and turned away from me these three times. If she had not turned away, I would certainly have killed you by now, but I would have spared her."

34Balaam said to the angel of the LORD, "I have sinned. I did not realise you were standing in the road to oppose me. Now if you are displeased, I will go back."

35The angel of the LORD said to Balaam, "Go with the men, but speak only what I tell you." So Balaam went with the princes of Balak.

36When Balak heard that Balaam was coming, he went out to meet him at the Moabite town on the Arnon border, at the edge of his territory. 37Balak said to Balaam, "Did I not send you an urgent summons? Why didn't you come to me? Am I really not able to reward you?"

38"Well, I have come to you now," Balaam replied. "But can I say just anything? I must speak only what God puts in my mouth."

39Then Balaam went with Balak to Kiriath Huzoth. 40Balak sacrificed cattle and sheep, and gave some to Balaam and the princes who were with him. 41The next morning Balak took Balaam up to Bamoth Baal, and from there he saw part of the people.

■ Balaam's First Oracle

23 Balaam said, "Build me seven altars here, and prepare seven bulls and seven rams for me." 2Balak did as Balaam said, and the two of them offered a bull and a ram on each altar.

3Then Balaam said to Balak, "Stay here beside your offering while I go aside. Perhaps the LORD will come to meet with me. Whatever he reveals to me I will tell you." Then he went off to a barren height.

4God met with him, and Balaam said, "I have prepared seven altars, and on each altar I have offered a bull and a ram."

5The LORD put a message in Balaam's mouth and said, "Go back to Balak and give him this message."

6So he went back to him and found him standing beside his offering, with all the princes of Moab. 7Then Balaam uttered his oracle:

"Balak brought me from Aram,
    the king of Moab from the eastern
        mountains.
'Come,' he said, 'curse Jacob for me;
    come, denounce Israel.'

c 32 The meaning of the Hebrew for this clause is uncertain.

⁸How can I curse
    those whom God has not cursed?
How can I denounce
    those whom the LORD has not denounced?
⁹From the rocky peaks I see them,
    from the heights I view them.
I see people who live apart
    and do not consider themselves one of the
        nations.
¹⁰Who can count the dust of Jacob
    or number the fourth part of Israel?
Let me die the death of the righteous,
    and may my end be like theirs!"

¹¹Balak said to Balaam, "What have you done to
me? I brought you to curse my enemies, but you
have done nothing but bless them!"

¹²He answered, "Must I not speak what the LORD
puts in my mouth?"

■ Balaam's Second Oracle
¹³Then Balak said to him, "Come with me to an-
other place where you can see them; you will see
only a part but not all of them. And from there, curse
them for me." ¹⁴So he took him to the field of Zophim on the top of Pisgah, and there he built seven
altars and offered a bull and a ram on each altar.
¹⁵Balaam said to Balak, "Stay here beside your
offering while I meet with him over there."
¹⁶The LORD met with Balaam and put a message
in his mouth and said, "Go back to Balak and give
him this message."

■ WHOSE SIDE IS BALAAM ON? INSIGHT
A RELUCTANT PROPHET, A TALKING DONKEY, AND A FURIOUS KING

BALAK SAID TO BALAAM, "WHAT HAVE
YOU DONE TO ME? I BROUGHT YOU TO
CURSE MY ENEMIES, BUT YOU HAVE
DONE NOTHING BUT BLESS THEM!"
■ 23:11

Numbers 22–24 contains one of the most
bizarre stories in the entire Bible. It features a
donkey speaking fluent Hebrew and showing
more insight than a prophet. One man is at the
centre of the story, the mysterious character
named Balaam.
    Balaam was evidently a professional
magician of a nomadic clan somewhat like the
gypsies. He had an impressive reputation:
nearby kings alarmed by the Israelites hired him
to work magic and get the gods on their side.

■ PROPHET FOR HIRE
Numbers gives enough detail to paint a
colourful, dramatic story, but even so, Balaam is
cloaked in a fog of mystery. Clearly, God chose
to speak through him: he communicated directly
to Balaam seven times. Just as clearly, Balaam
proved a reluctant prophet, subject to ambition
and a handsome bribe. Even his own donkey
rebuked him, in the only biblical account of an
animal speaking. An angel gave not Balaam, but
the donkey, high praise.
    Balaam appeared at a solemn occasion
designed to curse the Israelites, but instead he
pronounced blessings on them and curses on
their enemies. He gave four stirring messages,
far different in content from what his employer
wanted to hear.
    "How can I curse those whom God
has not cursed?" Balaam asked (23:8). His
magnificent prophecies shine out from scenes of
comic irony. Balaam grew bolder and bolder,
changing from a sorcerer into a prophet with
backbone.

■ PROPHET OR TRAITOR?
Numbers 22–24 presents Balaam as an
apparent convert. Tragically, the changes in
him were only temporary. Balaam next appears
in Numbers 31:8, the slain victim of an Israelite
raid. Outright condemnations in 2 Peter 2:15,
Jude 11 and Revelation 2:14 indicate that
Balaam quickly returned to his treacherous
ways. Having failed to manipulate the Israelites'
God for his purposes, he resorted to
manipulating the Israelites themselves. He
convinced other nations to seduce them with
sex and the worship of false gods. His actions
led to the deaths of 24,000 people (25:9).
    Some have called Balaam the Judas of
the Old Testament, and certain parallels do
emerge. Both men came close enough to truth
to appear sincere and faithful. For a time, both
seemed to serve the true God. But, motivated
by ambition and greed, they renounced God
and turned against him, with catastrophic
results.

■ PART OF A BIGGER BATTLE
Seven books of the Bible refer to Balaam. The
importance given to his story implies that it
was a key event in the Israelites' relationship to
pagan cultures. The Israelites were about to
enter a land where magic and sorcery were
used as national weapons. In a stroke of irony,
God selected a spokesman who was both
magician and pagan. Through him God
rebuked those nations and their false gods.

☐ LIFE QUESTIONS:
Have you ever been used by God despite your
own reluctance?

¹⁷So he went to him and found him standing beside his offering, with the princes of Moab. Balak asked him, "What did the LORD say?"
¹⁸Then he uttered his oracle:

"Arise, Balak, and listen;
    hear me, son of Zippor.
¹⁹God is not a man, that he should lie,
    nor a son of man, that he should change his mind.
Does he speak and then not act?
Does he promise and not fulfil?
²⁰I have received a command to bless;
    he has blessed, and I cannot change it.

²¹"No misfortune is seen in Jacob,
    no misery observed in Israel.ᵃ
The LORD their God is with them;
    the shout of the King is among them.
²²God brought them out of Egypt;
    they have the strength of a wild ox.
²³There is no sorcery against Jacob,
    no divination against Israel.
It will now be said of Jacob
    and of Israel, 'See what God has done!'
²⁴The people rise like a lioness;
    they rouse themselves like a lion
that does not rest till he devours his prey
    and drinks the blood of his victims."

²⁵Then Balak said to Balaam, "Neither curse them at all nor bless them at all!"
²⁶Balaam answered, "Did I not tell you I must do whatever the LORD says?"

■ Balaam's Third Oracle
²⁷Then Balak said to Balaam, "Come, let me take you to another place. Perhaps it will please God to let you curse them for me from there." ²⁸And Balak took Balaam to the top of Peor, overlooking the wasteland.
²⁹Balaam said, "Build me seven altars here, and prepare seven bulls and seven rams for me." ³⁰Balak did as Balaam had said, and offered a bull and a ram on each altar.

24 Now when Balaam saw that it pleased the LORD to bless Israel, he did not resort to sorcery as at other times, but turned his face towards the desert. ²When Balaam looked out and saw Israel encamped tribe by tribe, the Spirit of God came upon him ³and he uttered his oracle:

"The oracle of Balaam son of Beor,
    the oracle of one whose eye sees clearly,
⁴the oracle of one who hears the words of God,
    who sees a vision from the Almighty,ᵃ
who falls prostrate, and whose eyes are
    opened:

⁵"How beautiful are your tents, O Jacob,
    your dwelling-places, O Israel!

⁶"Like valleys they spread out,
    like gardens beside a river,
like aloes planted by the LORD,
    like cedars beside the waters.

⁷Water will flow from their buckets;
    their seed will have abundant water.

"Their king will be greater than Agag;
    their kingdom will be exalted.

⁸"God brought them out of Egypt;
    they have the strength of a wild ox.
They devour hostile nations
    and break their bones in pieces;
    with their arrows they pierce them.
⁹Like a lion they crouch and lie down,
    like a lioness—who dares to rouse them?

"May those who bless you be blessed
    and those who curse you be cursed!"

¹⁰Then Balak's anger burned against Balaam. He struck his hands together and said to him, "I summoned you to curse my enemies, but you have blessed them these three times. ¹¹Now leave at once and go home! I said I would reward you handsomely, but the LORD has kept you from being rewarded."
¹²Balaam answered Balak, "Did I not tell the messengers you sent me, ¹³'Even if Balak gave me his palace filled with silver and gold, I could not do anything of my own accord, good or bad, to go beyond the command of the LORD—and I must say only what the LORD says'? ¹⁴Now I am going back to my people, but come, let me warn you of what this people will do to your people in days to come."

■ Balaam's Fourth Oracle
¹⁵Then he uttered his oracle:

"The oracle of Balaam son of Beor,
    the oracle of one whose eye sees clearly,
¹⁶the oracle of one who hears the words of God,
    who has knowledge from the Most High,
who sees a vision from the Almighty,
    who falls prostrate, and whose eyes are
        opened:

¹⁷"I see him, but not now;
    I behold him, but not near.
A star will come out of Jacob;
    a sceptre will rise out of Israel.
He will crush the foreheads of Moab,
    the skullsᵇ ofᶜ all the sons of Sheth.ᵈ
¹⁸Edom will be conquered;
    Seir, his enemy, will be conquered,
    but Israel will grow strong.
¹⁹A ruler will come out of Jacob
    and destroy the survivors of the city."

24:17 ■ BALAAM'S PROPHECY
This prediction delivered by Balaam came true during the reign of King David, who crushed the nations of Moab and Edom (2 Samuel 8:2,14).

■ Balaam's Final Oracles
²⁰Then Balaam saw Amalek and uttered his oracle:

"Amalek was first among the nations,

ᵃ21 Or He has not looked on Jacob's offences / or on the wrongs found in Israel. (see also Jer. 48:45); the meaning of the word in the Masoretic Text is uncertain.   ᵃ4 Hebrew Shaddai; also in verse 16   ᵇ17 Samaritan Pentateuch   ᶜ17 Or possibly Moab, / batter   ᵈ17 Or all the noisy boasters but he will come to ruin at last."

21Then he saw the Kenites and uttered his oracle:

"Your dwelling-place is secure,
    your nest is set in a rock;
22yet you Kenites will be destroyed
    when Asshur takes you captive."

23Then he uttered his oracle:

"Ah, who can live when God does this?e
24   Ships will come from the shores of Kittim;
    they will subdue Asshur and Eber,
        but they too will come to ruin."

25Then Balaam got up and returned home and Balak went his own way.

■ Moab Seduces Israel

25 While Israel was staying in Shittim, the men began to indulge in sexual immorality with Moabite women, 2who invited them to the sacrifices to their gods. The people ate and bowed down before these gods. 3So Israel joined in worshipping the Baal of Peor. And the LORD's anger burned against them.

25:1 ■ SEXUAL SEDUCTION
Militarily, Israel was doing well. Their enemies were terrified (22:3), and the man summoned to put a curse on Israel had instead spoken God's blessing (24:8–9). But the Israelites were vulnerable to sexual temptation. Moabite women offered sexual favours, then invited the foreigners to local religious services. (Numbers 31:16 reports that Balaam suggested the tactic.) It is an old method of subverting God's people, and it still works.

4The LORD said to Moses, "Take all the leaders of these people, kill them and expose them in broad daylight before the LORD, so that the LORD's fierce anger may turn away from Israel."

5So Moses said to Israel's judges, "Each of you must put to death those of your men who have joined in worshipping the Baal of Peor."

6Then an Israelite man brought to his family a Midianite woman right before the eyes of Moses and the whole assembly of Israel while they were weeping at the entrance to the Tent of Meeting. 7When Phinehas son of Eleazar, the son of Aaron, the priest, saw this, he left the assembly, took a spear in his hand 8and followed the Israelite into the tent. He drove the spear through both of them—through the Israelite and into the woman's body. Then the plague against the Israelites was stopped; 9but those who died in the plague numbered 24,000.

10The LORD said to Moses, 11"Phinehas son of Eleazar, the son of Aaron, the priest, has turned my anger away from the Israelites; for he was as zealous as I am for my honour among them, so that in my zeal I did not put an end to them. 12Therefore tell him I am making my covenant of peace with him. 13He and his descendants will have a covenant of a lasting priesthood, because he was zealous for the honour of his God and made atonement for the Israelites."

14The name of the Israelite who was killed with the Midianite woman was Zimri son of Salu, the leader of a Simeonite family. 15And the name of the Midianite woman who was put to death was Cozbi daughter of Zur, a tribal chief of a Midianite family.

16The LORD said to Moses, 17"Treat the Midianites as enemies and kill them, 18because they treated you as enemies when they deceived you in the affair of Peor and their sister Cozbi, the daughter of a Midianite leader, the woman who was killed when the plague came as a result of Peor."

■ The Second Census

26 After the plague the LORD said to Moses and Eleazar son of Aaron, the priest, 2"Take a census of the whole Israelite community by families— all those twenty years old or more who are able to serve in the army of Israel." 3So on the plains of Moab by the Jordan across from Jericho,a Moses and Eleazar the priest spoke with them and said, 4"Take a census of men twenty years old or more, as the LORD commanded Moses."

These were the Israelites who came out of Egypt:

5The descendants of Reuben, the firstborn son of Israel, were:
    through Hanoch, the Hanochite clan;
    through Pallu, the Palluite clan;
    6through Hezron, the Hezronite clan;
    through Carmi, the Carmite clan.
7These were the clans of Reuben; those numbered were 43,730.

8The son of Pallu was Eliab, 9and the sons of Eliab were Nemuel, Dathan and Abiram. The same Dathan and Abiram were the community officials who rebelled against Moses and Aaron and were among Korah's followers when they rebelled against the LORD. 10The earth opened its mouth and swallowed them along with Korah, whose followers died when the fire devoured the 250 men. And they served as a warning sign. 11The line of Korah, however, did not die out.

12The descendants of Simeon by their clans were:
    through Nemuel, the Nemuelite clan;
    through Jamin, the Jaminite clan;
    through Jakin, the Jakinite clan;
    13through Zerah, the Zerahite clan;
    through Shaul, the Shaulite clan.
14These were the clans of Simeon; there were 22,200 men.

15The descendants of Gad by their clans were:
    through Zephon, the Zephonite clan;
    through Haggi, the Haggite clan;
    through Shuni, the Shunite clan;
    16through Ozni, the Oznite clan;
    through Eri, the Erite clan;
    17through Arodi,b the Arodite clan;
    through Areli, the Arelite clan.
18These were the clans of Gad; those numbered were 40,500.

19Er and Onan were sons of Judah, but they died in Canaan. 20The descendants of Judah by their clans were:

---

e23 Masoretic Text; with a different word division of the Hebrew A people will gather from the north.   a3 Hebrew Jordan of Jericho; possibly an ancient name for the Jordan River; also in verse 63   b17 Samaritan Pentateuch and Syriac (see also Gen. 46:16); Masoretic Text Arod

through Shelah, the Shelanite clan;
through Perez, the Perezite clan;
through Zerah, the Zerahite clan.
21 The descendants of Perez were:
through Hezron, the Hezronite clan;
through Hamul, the Hamulite clan.
22 These were the clans of Judah; those numbered
were 76,500.

23 The descendants of Issachar by their clans were:
through Tola, the Tolaite clan;
through Puah, the Puite[c] clan;
24 through Jashub, the Jashubite clan;
through Shimron, the Shimronite clan.
25 These were the clans of Issachar; those numbered
were 64,300.

26 The descendants of Zebulun by their clans were:
through Sered, the Seredite clan;
through Elon, the Elonite clan;
through Jahleel, the Jahleelite clan.
27 These were the clans of Zebulun; those numbered
were 60,500.

28 The descendants of Joseph by their clans through
Manasseh and Ephraim were:

29 The descendants of Manasseh:
through Makir, the Makirite clan (Makir was
the father of Gilead);
through Gilead, the Gileadite clan.
30 These were the descendants of Gilead:
through Iezer, the Iezerite clan;
through Helek, the Helekite clan;
31 through Asriel, the Asrielite clan;
through Shechem, the Shechemite clan;
32 through Shemida, the Shemidaite clan;
through Hepher, the Hepherite clan.
33 (Zelophehad son of Hepher had no sons; he
had only daughters, whose names were Mahlah, Noah, Hoglah, Milcah and Tirzah.)
34 These were the clans of Manasseh; those numbered were 52,700.

35 These were the descendants of Ephraim by their
clans:
through Shuthelah, the Shuthelahite clan;
through Beker, the Bekerite clan;
through Tahan, the Tahanite clan.
36 These were the descendants of Shuthelah:
through Eran, the Eranite clan.
37 These were the clans of Ephraim; those numbered
were 32,500.

These were the descendants of Joseph by their clans.

38 The descendants of Benjamin by their clans were:
through Bela, the Belaite clan;
through Ashbel, the Ashbelite clan;
through Ahiram, the Ahiramite clan;
39 through Shupham,[d] the Shuphamite clan;
through Hupham, the Huphamite clan.
40 The descendants of Bela through Ard and Naaman were:
through Ard,[e] the Ardite clan;
through Naaman, the Naamite clan.

41 These were the clans of Benjamin; those numbered were 45,600.

42 These were the descendants of Dan by their clans:
through Shuham, the Shuhamite clan.
These were the clans of Dan: 43 All of them were Shuhamite clans; and those numbered were 64,400.

44 The descendants of Asher by their clans were:
through Imnah, the Imnite clan;
through Ishvi, the Ishvite clan;
through Beriah, the Beriite clan;
45 and through the descendants of Beriah:
through Heber, the Heberite clan;
through Malkiel, the Malkielite clan.
46 (Asher had a daughter named Serah.)
47 These were the clans of Asher; those numbered
were 53,400.

48 The descendants of Naphtali by their clans were:
through Jahzeel, the Jahzeelite clan;
through Guni, the Gunite clan;
49 through Jezer, the Jezerite clan;
through Shillem, the Shillemite clan.
50 These were the clans of Naphtali; those numbered
were 45,400.

51 The total number of the men of Israel was
601,730.

26:51 ■ RECOUNT

The two censuses in Numbers (chapter 1 and
here) stand like book-ends, marking the hopeful
beginning and tragic end of the vast numbers of
Israelites heading towards freedom. After 40 years,
the totals were nearly the same – 600,000 men –
but only two of the original pilgrims would cross
the Jordan River. The nation renewed itself like a
human body, which looks the same but replaces
all its cells every few years.

52 The LORD said to Moses, 53 "The land is to be
allotted to them as an inheritance based on the number of names. 54 To a larger group give a larger inheritance, and to a smaller group a smaller one; each
is to receive its inheritance according to the number
of those listed. 55 Be sure that the land is distributed
by lot. What each group inherits will be according
to the names for its ancestral tribe. 56 Each inheritance is to be distributed by lot among the larger and
smaller groups."

57 These were the Levites who were counted by
their clans:
through Gershon, the Gershonite clan;
through Kohath, the Kohathite clan;
through Merari, the Merarite clan.
58 These also were Levite clans:
the Libnite clan,
the Hebronite clan,
the Mahlite clan,
the Mushite clan,
the Korahite clan.

c 23 Samaritan Pentateuch, Septuagint, Vulgate and Syriac (see also 1 Chron. 7:1); Masoretic Text through Puvah, the Punite   d 39 A few manuscripts of
the Masoretic Text, Samaritan Pentateuch, Vulgate and Syriac (see also Septuagint); most manuscripts of the Masoretic Text Shephupham   e 40 Samaritan
Pentateuch and Vulgate (see also Septuagint); Masoretic Text does not have through Ard,

(Kohath was the forefather of Amram; [59]the name of Amram's wife was Jochebed, a descendant of Levi, who was born to the Levites*f* in Egypt. To Amram she bore Aaron, Moses and their sister Miriam. [60]Aaron was the father of Nadab and Abihu, Eleazar and Ithamar. [61]But Nadab and Abihu died when they made an offering before the LORD with unauthorised fire.)

[62]All the male Levites a month old or more numbered 23,000. They were not counted along with the other Israelites because they received no inheritance among them.

[63]These are the ones counted by Moses and Eleazar the priest when they counted the Israelites on the plains of Moab by the Jordan across from Jericho. [64]Not one of them was among those counted by Moses and Aaron the priest when they counted the Israelites in the Desert of Sinai. [65]For the LORD had told those Israelites they would surely die in the desert, and not one of them was left except Caleb son of Jephunneh and Joshua son of Nun.

■ Zelophehad's Daughters

27 The daughters of Zelophehad son of Hepher, the son of Gilead, the son of Makir, the son of Manasseh, belonged to the clans of Manasseh son of Joseph. The names of the daughters were Mahlah, Noah, Hoglah, Milcah and Tirzah. They approached [2]the entrance to the Tent of Meeting and stood before Moses, Eleazar the priest, the leaders and the whole assembly, and said, [3]"Our father died in the desert. He was not among Korah's followers, who banded together against the LORD, but he died for his own sin and left no sons. [4]Why should our father's name disappear from his clan because he had no son? Give us property among our father's relatives."

[5]So Moses brought their case before the LORD [6]and the LORD said to him, [7]"What Zelophehad's daughters are saying is right. You must certainly give them property as an inheritance among their father's relatives and give their father's inheritance over to them.

[8]"Say to the Israelites, 'If a man dies and leaves no son, give his inheritance over to his daughter. [9]If he has no daughter, give his inheritance to his brothers. [10]If he has no brothers, give his inheritance to his father's brothers. [11]If his father had no brothers, give his inheritance to the nearest relative in his clan, that he may possess it. This is to be a legal requirement for the Israelites, as the LORD commanded Moses.' "

■ Joshua to Succeed Moses

[12]Then the LORD said to Moses, "Go up this mountain in the Abarim Range and see the land I have given the Israelites. [13]After you have seen it, you too will be gathered to your people, as your brother Aaron was, [14]for when the community rebelled at the waters in the Desert of Zin, both of you disobeyed my command to honour me as holy before their eyes." (These were the waters of Meribah Kadesh, in the Desert of Zin.)

[15]Moses said to the LORD, [16]"May the LORD, the God of the spirits of all mankind, appoint a man over this community [17]to go out and come in before them, one who will lead them out and bring them in, so that the LORD's people will not be like sheep without a shepherd."

27:14 ■ MOSES STAYED OUT

Because Moses had disobeyed God (the scene is described in 20:1–13), he was not allowed to enter the promised land. In this account he seems to accept his punishment without complaint, quietly turning over his leadership to Joshua. But in his great final speech, recorded in Deuteronomy, he bitterly raised the topic three times (Deuteronomy 1:37, 3:23–27, 4:21–24). The punishment was not for ever; Moses did "get in" hundreds of years after his death, in the company of Jesus (Mark 9:4).

---

[18]So the LORD said to Moses, "Take Joshua son of Nun, a man in whom is the spirit,*a* and lay your hand on him. [19]Make him stand before Eleazar the priest and the entire assembly and commission him in their presence. [20]Give him some of your authority so that the whole Israelite community will obey him. [21]He is to stand before Eleazar the priest, who will obtain decisions for him by enquiring of the Urim before the LORD. At his command he and the entire community of the Israelites will go out, and at his command they will come in."

[22]Moses did as the LORD commanded him. He took Joshua and made him stand before Eleazar the priest and the whole assembly. [23]Then he laid his hands on him and commissioned him, as the LORD instructed through Moses.

■ Daily Offerings

28 The LORD said to Moses, [2]"Give this command to the Israelites and say to them: 'See that you present to me at the appointed time the food for my offerings made by fire, as an aroma pleasing to me.' [3]Say to them: 'This is the offering made by fire that you are to present to the LORD: two lambs a year old without defect, as a regular burnt offering each day. [4]Prepare one lamb in the morning and the other at twilight, [5]together with a grain offering of a tenth of an ephah*a* of fine flour mixed with a quarter of a hin*b* of oil from pressed olives. [6]This is the regular burnt offering instituted at Mount Sinai as a pleasing aroma, an offering made to the LORD by fire. [7]The accompanying drink offering is to be a quarter of a hin of fermented drink with each lamb. Pour out the drink offering to the LORD at the sanctuary. [8]Prepare the second lamb at twilight, along with the same kind of grain offering and drink offering that you prepare in the morning. This is an offering made by fire, an aroma pleasing to the LORD.

---

*f*59 Or *Jochebed, a daughter of Levi, who was born to Levi* and 29   *b*5 That is, probably about 1½ pints (about 1 litre); also in verses 7 and 14   *a*18 Or *Spirit*   *a*5 That is, probably about 4 pints (about 2 litres); also in verses 13, 21

■ Sabbath Offerings

9" 'On the Sabbath day, make an offering of two lambs a year old without defect, together with its drink offering and a grain offering of two-tenths of an ephah[c] of fine flour mixed with oil. [10]This is the burnt offering for every Sabbath, in addition to the regular burnt offering and its drink offering.

■ Monthly Offerings

11" 'On the first of every month, present to the LORD a burnt offering of two young bulls, one ram and seven male lambs a year old, all without defect. [12]With each bull there is to be a grain offering of three-tenths of an ephah[d] of fine flour mixed with oil; with the ram, a grain offering of two-tenths of an ephah of fine flour mixed with oil; [13]and with each lamb, a grain offering of a tenth of an ephah of fine flour mixed with oil. This is for a burnt offering, a pleasing aroma, an offering made to the LORD by fire. [14]With each bull there is to be a drink offering of half a hin[e] of wine; with the ram, a third of a hin;[f] and with each lamb, a quarter of a hin. This is the monthly burnt offering to be made at each new moon during the year. [15]Besides the regular burnt offering with its drink offering, one male goat is to be presented to the LORD as a sin offering.

■ The Passover

16" 'On the fourteenth day of the first month the LORD's Passover is to be held. [17]On the fifteenth day of this month there is to be a festival; for seven days eat bread made without yeast. [18]On the first day hold a sacred assembly and do no regular work. [19]Present to the LORD an offering made by fire, a burnt offering of two young bulls, one ram and seven male lambs a year old, all without defect. [20]With each bull prepare a grain offering of three-tenths of an ephah of fine flour mixed with oil; with the ram, two-tenths; [21]and with each of the seven lambs, one-tenth. [22]Include one male goat as a sin offering to make atonement for you. [23]Prepare these in addition to the regular morning burnt offering. [24]In this way prepare the food for the offering made by fire every day for seven days as an aroma pleasing to the LORD; it is to be prepared in addition to the regular burnt offering and its drink offering. [25]On the seventh day hold a sacred assembly and do no regular work.

■ Feast of Weeks

26" 'On the day of firstfruits, when you present to the LORD an offering of new grain during the Feast of Weeks, hold a sacred assembly and do no regular work. [27]Present a burnt offering of two young bulls, one ram and seven male lambs a year old as an aroma pleasing to the LORD. [28]With each bull there is to be a grain offering of three-tenths of an ephah of fine flour mixed with oil; with the ram, two-tenths; [29]and with each of the seven lambs, one-tenth. [30]Include one male goat to make atonement for you. [31]Prepare these together with their drink offerings, in addition to the regular burnt offering and its grain offering. Be sure the animals are without defect.

■ Feast of Trumpets

29 " 'On the first day of the seventh month hold a sacred assembly and do no regular work. It is a day for you to sound the trumpets. [2]As an aroma pleasing to the LORD, prepare a burnt offering of one young bull, one ram and seven male lambs a year old, all without defect. [3]With the bull prepare a grain offering of three-tenths of an ephah[a] of fine flour mixed with oil; with the ram, two-tenths;[b] [4]and with each of the seven lambs, one-tenth.[c] [5]Include one male goat as a sin offering to make atonement for you. [6]These are in addition to the monthly and daily burnt offerings with their grain offerings and drink offerings as specified. They are offerings made to the LORD by fire—a pleasing aroma.

29:1 ■ INTERRUPTIONS TO THE STORY

Numbers periodically interrupts its history with lists of rules or rituals, such as in this section, chapters 28–30. Usually, they relate to what appears just before or afterwards. The instructions here were not new, but God saw a need to review them just as the nation was about to enter the promised land.

■ Day of Atonement

7" 'On the tenth day of this seventh month hold a sacred assembly. You must deny yourselves[d] and do no work. [8]Present as an aroma pleasing to the LORD a burnt offering of one young bull, one ram and seven male lambs a year old, all without defect. [9]With the bull prepare a grain offering of three-tenths of an ephah of fine flour mixed with oil; with the ram, two-tenths; [10]and with each of the seven lambs, one-tenth. [11]Include one male goat as a sin offering, in addition to the sin offering for atonement and the regular burnt offering with its grain offering, and their drink offerings.

■ Feast of Tabernacles

12" 'On the fifteenth day of the seventh month, hold a sacred assembly and do no regular work. Celebrate a festival to the LORD for seven days. [13]Present an offering made by fire as an aroma pleasing to the LORD, a burnt offering of thirteen young bulls, two rams and fourteen male lambs a year old, all without defect. [14]With each of the thirteen bulls prepare a grain offering of three-tenths of an ephah of fine flour mixed with oil; with each of the two rams, two-tenths; [15]and with each of the fourteen lambs, one-tenth. [16]Include one male goat as a sin offering, in addition to the regular burnt offering with its grain offering and drink offering.

17" 'On the second day prepare twelve young bulls, two rams and fourteen male lambs a year old, all without defect. [18]With the bulls, rams and lambs, prepare their grain offerings and drink offerings according to the number specified. [19]Include one male goat as a sin offering, in addition to the regular burnt offering with its grain offering, and their drink offerings.

---

[c]9 That is, probably about 7½ pints (about 4.5 litres); also in verses 12, 20 and 28   [d]12 That is, probably about 11½ pints (about 6.5 litres); also in verses 20 and 28   [e]14 That is, probably about 3 pints (about 2 litres)   [f]14 That is, probably about 2¼ pints (about 1.2 litres)   [a]3 That is, probably about 11½ pints (about 6.5 litres); also in verses 9 and 14   [b]3 That is, probably about 7½ pints (about 4.5 litres); also in verses 9 and 14   [c]4 That is, probably about 4 pints (about 2 litres); also in verses 10 and 15   [d]7 Or must fast

20" 'On the third day prepare eleven bulls, two rams and fourteen male lambs a year old, all without defect. 21With the bulls, rams and lambs, prepare their grain offerings and drink offerings according to the number specified. 22Include one male goat as a sin offering, in addition to the regular burnt offering with its grain offering and drink offering.

23" 'On the fourth day prepare ten bulls, two rams and fourteen male lambs a year old, all without defect. 24With the bulls, rams and lambs, prepare their grain offerings and drink offerings according to the number specified. 25Include one male goat as a sin offering, in addition to the regular burnt offering with its grain offering and drink offering.

26" 'On the fifth day prepare nine bulls, two rams and fourteen male lambs a year old, all without defect. 27With the bulls, rams and lambs, prepare their grain offerings and drink offerings according to the number specified. 28Include one male goat as a sin offering, in addition to the regular burnt offering with its grain offering and drink offering.

29" 'On the sixth day prepare eight bulls, two rams and fourteen male lambs a year old, all without defect. 30With the bulls, rams and lambs, prepare their grain offerings and drink offerings according to the number specified. 31Include one male goat as a sin offering, in addition to the regular burnt offering with its grain offering and drink offering.

32" 'On the seventh day prepare seven bulls, two rams and fourteen male lambs a year old, all without defect. 33With the bulls, rams and lambs, prepare their grain offerings and drink offerings according to the number specified. 34Include one male goat as a sin offering, in addition to the regular burnt offering with its grain offering and drink offering.

35" 'On the eighth day hold an assembly and do no regular work. 36Present an offering made by fire as an aroma pleasing to the LORD, a burnt offering of one bull, one ram and seven male lambs a year old, all without defect. 37With the bull, the ram and the lambs, prepare their grain offerings and drink offerings according to the number specified. 38Include one male goat as a sin offering, in addition to the regular burnt offering with its grain offering and drink offering.

39" 'In addition to what you vow and your freewill offerings, prepare these for the LORD at your appointed feasts: your burnt offerings, grain offerings, drink offerings and fellowship offerings.' "e

40Moses told the Israelites all that the LORD commanded him.

■ Vows

30 Moses said to the heads of the tribes of Israel: "This is what the LORD commands: 2When a man makes a vow to the LORD or takes an oath to bind himself by a pledge, he must not break his word but must do everything he said.

3"When a young woman still living in her father's house makes a vow to the LORD or binds herself by a pledge 4and her father hears about her vow or pledge but says nothing to her, then all her vows and every pledge by which she bound herself will stand. 5But if her father forbids her when he hears about it, none of her vows or the pledges by which she

bound herself will stand; the LORD will release her because her father has forbidden her.

6"If she marries after she makes a vow or after her lips utter a rash promise by which she binds herself 7and her husband hears about it but says nothing to her, then her vows or the pledges by which she bound herself will stand. 8But if her husband forbids her when he hears about it, he nullifies the vow that binds her or the rash promise by which she binds herself, and the LORD will release her.

9"Any vow or obligation taken by a widow or divorced woman will be binding on her.

10"If a woman living with her husband makes a vow or binds herself by a pledge under oath 11and her husband hears about it but says nothing to her and does not forbid her, then all her vows or the pledges by which she bound herself will stand. 12But if her husband nullifies them when he hears about them, then none of the vows or pledges that came from her lips will stand. Her husband has nullified them, and the LORD will release her. 13Her husband may confirm or nullify any vow she makes or any sworn pledge to deny herself. 14But if her husband says nothing to her about it from day to day, then he confirms all her vows or the pledges binding on her. He confirms them by saying nothing to her when he hears about them. 15If, however, he nullifies them some time after he hears about them, then he is responsible for her guilt."

16These are the regulations the LORD gave Moses concerning relationships between a man and his wife, and between a father and his young daughter still living in his house.

■ Vengeance on the Midianites

31 The LORD said to Moses, 2"Take vengeance on the Midianites for the Israelites. After that, you will be gathered to your people."

3So Moses said to the people, "Arm some of your men to go to war against the Midianites and to carry out the LORD's vengeance on them. 4Send into battle a thousand men from each of the tribes of Israel." 5So twelve thousand men armed for battle, a thousand from each tribe, were supplied from the clans of Israel. 6Moses sent them into battle, a thousand from each tribe, along with Phinehas son of Eleazar, the priest, who took with him articles from the sanctuary and the trumpets for signalling.

7They fought against Midian, as the LORD commanded Moses, and killed every man. 8Among their victims were Evi, Rekem, Zur, Hur and Reba—the five kings of Midian. They also killed Balaam son of Beor with the sword. 9The Israelites captured the Midianite women and children and took all the Midianite herds, flocks and goods as plunder. 10They burned all the towns where the Midianites had settled, as well as all their camps. 11They took all the plunder and spoils, including the people and animals, 12and brought the captives, spoils and plunder to Moses and Eleazar the priest and the Israelite assembly at their camp on the plains of Moab, by the Jordan across from Jericho.a

13Moses, Eleazar the priest and all the leaders of the community went to meet them outside the camp. 14Moses was angry with the officers of the

e 39 Traditionally peace offerings   a 12 Hebrew Jordan of Jericho; possibly an ancient name for the Jordan River army—the commanders of thousands and commanders of hundreds—who returned from the battle.

15"Have you allowed all the women to live?" he asked them. 16"They were the ones who followed Balaam's advice and were the means of turning the Israelites away from the LORD in what happened at Peor, so that a plague struck the LORD's people. 17Now kill all the boys. And kill every woman who has slept with a man, 18but save for yourselves every girl who has never slept with a man.

19"All of you who have killed anyone or touched anyone who was killed must stay outside the camp seven days. On the third and seventh days you must purify yourselves and your captives. 20Purify every garment as well as everything made of leather, goat hair or wood."

31:19 ■ ACTS OF WAR

Many readers struggle with the harsh warfare policies God demanded of the Israelites. Numbers 35:34 summarises one basic reason why policies were so strict: so that the land itself, set apart by God, would not become defiled (see "Is a War Ever Holy?" page 192). Even so, this passage shows that killing was not taken lightly—even war heroes had to go through the process of purification.

21Then Eleazar the priest said to the soldiers who had gone into battle, "This is the requirement of the law that the LORD gave Moses: 22Gold, silver, bronze, iron, tin, lead 23and anything else that can withstand fire must be put through the fire, and then it will be clean. But it must also be purified with the water of cleansing. And whatever cannot withstand fire must be put through that water. 24On the seventh day wash your clothes and you will be clean. Then you may come into the camp."

■ Dividing the Spoils

25The LORD said to Moses, 26"You and Eleazar the priest and the family heads of the community are to count all the people and animals that were captured. 27Divide the spoils between the soldiers who took part in the battle and the rest of the community. 28From the soldiers who fought in the battle, set apart as tribute for the LORD one out of every five hundred, whether persons, cattle, donkeys, sheep or goats. 29Take this tribute from their half share and give it to Eleazar the priest as the LORD's part. 30From the Israelites' half, select one out of every fifty, whether persons, cattle, donkeys, sheep, goats or other animals. Give them to the Levites, who are responsible for the care of the LORD's tabernacle." 31So Moses and Eleazar the priest did as the LORD commanded Moses.

32The plunder remaining from the spoils that the soldiers took was 675,000 sheep, 3372,000 cattle, 3461,000 donkeys 35and 32,000 women who had never slept with a man.

36The half share of those who fought in the battle was:

337,500 sheep, 37of which the tribute for the LORD was 675;
3836,000 cattle, of which the tribute for the LORD was 72;
3930,500 donkeys, of which the tribute for the LORD was 61;
4016,000 people, of which the tribute for the LORD was 32.

41Moses gave the tribute to Eleazar the priest as the LORD's part, as the LORD commanded Moses.

42The half belonging to the Israelites, which Moses set apart from that of the fighting men—43the community's half—was 337,500 sheep, 4436,000 cattle, 4530,500 donkeys 46and 16,000 people. 47From the Israelites' half, Moses selected one out of every fifty persons and animals, as the LORD commanded him, and gave them to the Levites, who were responsible for the care of the LORD's tabernacle.

48Then the officers who were over the units of the army—the commanders of thousands and commanders of hundreds—went to Moses 49and said to him, "Your servants have counted the soldiers under our command, and not one is missing. 50So we have brought as an offering to the LORD the gold articles each of us acquired—armlets, bracelets, signet rings, ear-rings and necklaces—to make atonement for ourselves before the LORD."

51Moses and Eleazar the priest accepted from them the gold—all the handcrafted articles. 52All the gold from the commanders of thousands and commanders of hundreds that Moses and Eleazar presented as a gift to the LORD weighed 16,750 shekels.b 53Each soldier had taken plunder for himself. 54Moses and Eleazar the priest accepted the gold from the commanders of thousands and commanders of hundreds and brought it into the Tent of Meeting as a memorial for the Israelites before the LORD.

■ The Transjordan Tribes

32 The Reubenites and Gadites, who had very large herds and flocks, saw that the lands of Jazer and Gilead were suitable for livestock. 2So they came to Moses and Eleazar the priest and to the leaders of the community, and said, 3"Ataroth, Dibon, Jazer, Nimrah, Heshbon, Elealeh, Sebam, Nebo and Beon—4the land the LORD subdued before the people of Israel—are suitable for livestock, and your servants have livestock. 5If we have found favour in your eyes," they said, "let this land be given to your servants as our possession. Do not make us cross the Jordan."

6Moses said to the Gadites and Reubenites, "Shall your countrymen go to war while you sit here? 7Why do you discourage the Israelites from going over into the land the LORD has given them? 8This is what your fathers did when I sent them from Kadesh Barnea to look over the land. 9After they went up to the Valley of Eshcol and viewed the land, they discouraged the Israelites from entering the land the LORD had given them. 10The LORD's anger was aroused that day and he swore this oath: 11'Because they have not followed me wholeheartedly, not one of the men twenty years old or more who came up

b 52 That is, about 420 pounds (about 190 kilograms)

out of Egypt will see the land I promised on oath to Abraham, Isaac and Jacob — 12not one except Caleb son of Jephunneh the Kenizzite and Joshua son of Nun, for they followed the LORD wholeheartedly.' 13The LORD's anger burned against Israel and he made them wander in the desert for forty years, until the whole generation of those who had done evil in his sight was gone.

14"And here you are, a brood of sinners, standing in the place of your fathers and making the LORD even more angry with Israel. 15If you turn away from following him, he will again leave all this people in the desert, and you will be the cause of their destruction."

16Then they came up to him and said, "We would like to build pens here for our livestock and cities for our women and children. 17But we are ready to arm ourselves and go ahead of the Israelites until we have brought them to their place. Meanwhile our women and children will live in fortified cities, for protection from the inhabitants of the land. 18We will not return to our homes until every Israelite has received his inheritance. 19We will not receive any inheritance with them on the other side of the Jordan, because our inheritance has come to us on the east side of the Jordan."

20Then Moses said to them, "If you will do this — if you will arm yourselves before the LORD for battle, 21and if all of you will go armed over the Jordan before the LORD until he has driven his enemies out before him — 22then when the land is subdued before the LORD, you may return and be free from your obligation to the LORD and to Israel. And this land will be your possession before the LORD.

32:22 ■ TROUBLE AHEAD

According to Joshua 22:1–6, the two and a half tribes did keep their promise to fight with the others. The land they chose was appealing, with park-like scenery, wide pastures, and lush forests. However, their settlement proved troublesome. With no natural borders, the land was open to enemy attack and easy infiltration.

23"But if you fail to do this, you will be sinning against the LORD; and you may be sure that your sin will find you out. 24Build cities for your women and children, and pens for your flocks, but do what you have promised."

25The Gadites and Reubenites said to Moses, "We your servants will do as our lord commands. 26Our children and wives, our flocks and herds will remain here in the cities of Gilead. 27But your servants, every man armed for battle, will cross over to fight before the LORD, just as our lord says."

28Then Moses gave orders about them to Eleazar the priest and Joshua son of Nun and to the family heads of the Israelite tribes. 29He said to them, "If the Gadites and Reubenites, every man armed for battle, cross over the Jordan with you before the LORD, then when the land is subdued before you, give them the land of Gilead as their possession. 30But if they do

not cross over with you armed, they must accept their possession with you in Canaan."

31The Gadites and Reubenites answered, "Your servants will do what the LORD has said. 32We will cross over before the LORD into Canaan armed, but the property we inherit will be on this side of the Jordan."

33Then Moses gave to the Gadites, the Reubenites and the half-tribe of Manasseh son of Joseph the kingdom of Sihon king of the Amorites and the kingdom of Og king of Bashan — the whole land with its cities and the territory around them.

34The Gadites built up Dibon, Ataroth, Aroer, 35Atroth Shophan, Jazer, Jogbehah, 36Beth Nimrah and Beth Haran as fortified cities, and built pens for their flocks. 37And the Reubenites rebuilt Heshbon, Elealeh and Kiriathaim, 38as well as Nebo and Baal Meon (these names were changed) and Sibmah. They gave names to the cities they rebuilt.

39The descendants of Makir son of Manasseh went to Gilead, captured it and drove out the Amorites who were there. 40So Moses gave Gilead to the Makirites, the descendants of Manasseh, and they settled there. 41Jair, a descendant of Manasseh, captured their settlements and called them Havvoth Jair.*a* 42And Nobah captured Kenath and its surrounding settlements and called it Nobah after himself.

■ Stages in Israel's Journey

33 Here are the stages in the journey of the Israelites when they came out of Egypt by divisions under the leadership of Moses and Aaron. 2At the LORD's command Moses recorded the stages in their journey. This is their journey by stages:

3The Israelites set out from Rameses on the fifteenth day of the first month, the day after the Passover. They marched out boldly in full view of all the Egyptians, 4who were burying all their firstborn, whom the LORD had struck down among them; for the LORD had brought judgment on their gods.

5The Israelites left Rameses and camped at Succoth.

6They left Succoth and camped at Etham, on the edge of the desert.

7They left Etham, turned back to Pi Hahiroth, to the east of Baal Zephon, and camped near Migdol.

8They left Pi Hahiroth*a* and passed through the sea into the desert, and when they had travelled for three days in the Desert of Etham, they camped at Marah.

9They left Marah and went to Elim, where there were twelve springs and seventy palm trees, and they camped there.

10They left Elim and camped by the Red Sea.*b*

11They left the Red Sea and camped in the Desert of Sin.

12They left the Desert of Sin and camped at Dophkah.

13They left Dophkah and camped at Alush.

14They left Alush and camped at Rephidim,

where there was no water for the people to drink.

¹⁵They left Rephidim and camped in the Desert of Sinai.

¹⁶They left the Desert of Sinai and camped at Kibroth Hattaavah.

¹⁷They left Kibroth Hattaavah and camped at Hazeroth.

¹⁸They left Hazeroth and camped at Rithmah.

¹⁹They left Rithmah and camped at Rimmon Perez.

²⁰They left Rimmon Perez and camped at Libnah.

²¹They left Libnah and camped at Rissah.

²²They left Rissah and camped at Kehelathah.

²³They left Kehelathah and camped at Mount Shepher.

²⁴They left Mount Shepher and camped at Haradah.

²⁵They left Haradah and camped at Makheloth.

²⁶They left Makheloth and camped at Tahath.

²⁷They left Tahath and camped at Terah.

²⁸They left Terah and camped at Mithcah.

²⁹They left Mithcah and camped at Hashmonah.

³⁰They left Hashmonah and camped at Moseroth.

³¹They left Moseroth and camped at Bene Jaakan.

³²They left Bene Jaakan and camped at Hor Haggidgad.

³³They left Hor Haggidgad and camped at Jotbathah.

³⁴They left Jotbathah and camped at Abronah.

³⁵They left Abronah and camped at Ezion Geber.

³⁶They left Ezion Geber and camped at Kadesh, in the Desert of Zin.

³⁷They left Kadesh and camped at Mount Hor, on the border of Edom. ³⁸At the LORD's command Aaron the priest went up Mount Hor, where he died on the first day of the fifth month of the fortieth year after the Israelites came out of Egypt. ³⁹Aaron was a hundred and twenty-three years old when he died on Mount Hor.

⁴⁰The Canaanite king of Arad, who lived in the Negev of Canaan, heard that the Israelites were coming.

⁴¹They left Mount Hor and camped at Zalmonah.

⁴²They left Zalmonah and camped at Punon.

⁴³They left Punon and camped at Oboth.

⁴⁴They left Oboth and camped at Iye Abarim, on the border of Moab.

⁴⁵They left Iyim*c* and camped at Dibon Gad.

⁴⁶They left Dibon Gad and camped at Almon Diblathaim.

⁴⁷They left Almon Diblathaim and camped in the mountains of Abarim, near Nebo.

⁴⁸They left the mountains of Abarim and camped on the plains of Moab by the Jordan across from Jericho.*d* ⁴⁹There on the plains of Moab they camped along the Jordan from Beth Jeshimoth to Abel Shittim.

⁵⁰On the plains of Moab by the Jordan across from Jericho the LORD said to Moses, ⁵¹"Speak to the Israelites and say to them: 'When you cross the Jordan into Canaan, ⁵²drive out all the inhabitants of the land before you. Destroy all their carved images and their cast idols, and demolish all their high places. ⁵³Take possession of the land and settle in it, for I have given you the land to possess. ⁵⁴Distribute the land by lot, according to your clans. To a larger group give a larger inheritance, and to a smaller group a smaller one. Whatever falls to them by lot will be theirs. Distribute it according to your ancestral tribes.

⁵⁵" 'But if you do not drive out the inhabitants of the land, those you allow to remain will become barbs in your eyes and thorns in your sides. They will give you trouble in the land where you will live. ⁵⁶And then I will do to you what I plan to do to them.' "

33:50-56 ■ FINAL WARNINGS

Just before the dramatic crossing into the promised land, God gave a clear statement of his priorities and a warning of what would happen if the Israelites failed to obey. His words would one day come back to haunt them, for they failed to carry out fully any of his orders.

■ Boundaries of Canaan

34 The LORD said to Moses, ²"Command the Israelites and say to them: 'When you enter Canaan, the land that will be allotted to you as an inheritance will have these boundaries:

³" 'Your southern side will include some of the Desert of Zin along the border of Edom. On the east, your southern boundary will start from the end of the Salt Sea,*a* ⁴cross south of Scorpion*b* Pass, continue on to Zin and go south of Kadesh Barnea. Then it will go to Hazar Addar and over to Azmon, ⁵where it will turn, join the Wadi of Egypt and end at the Sea.*c*

⁶" 'Your western boundary will be the coast of the Great Sea. This will be your boundary on the west.

⁷" 'For your northern boundary, run a line from the Great Sea to Mount Hor ⁸and from Mount Hor to Lebo*d* Hamath. Then the boundary will go to Zedad, ⁹continue to Ziphron and end at Hazar Enan. This will be your boundary on the north.

¹⁰" 'For your eastern boundary, run a line from Hazar Enan to Shepham. ¹¹The boundary will go down from Shepham to Riblah on the east side of Ain and continue along the slopes east of the Sea of Kinnereth.*e* ¹²Then the boundary will go down along the Jordan and end at the Salt Sea.

---

c45 That is, Iye Abarim   *d48* Hebrew *Jordan of Jericho*; possibly an ancient name for the Jordan River; also in verse 50   *a3* That is, the Dead Sea; also in verse 12   *b4* Hebrew *Akrabbim*   *c5* That is, the Mediterranean; also in verses 6 and 7   *d8* Or *to the entrance to*   *e11* That is, Galilee

" 'This will be your land, with its boundaries on every side.' "

¹³Moses commanded the Israelites: "Assign this land by lot as an inheritance. The LORD has ordered that it be given to the nine and a half tribes, ¹⁴because the families of the tribe of Reuben, the tribe of Gad and the half-tribe of Manasseh have received their inheritance. ¹⁵These two and a half tribes have received their inheritance on the east side of the Jordan of Jericho,*f* towards the sunrise."

¹⁶The LORD said to Moses, ¹⁷"These are the names of the men who are to assign the land for you as an inheritance: Eleazar the priest and Joshua son of Nun. ¹⁸And appoint one leader from each tribe to help assign the land. ¹⁹These are their names:

Caleb son of Jephunneh,
  from the tribe of Judah;
²⁰Shemuel son of Ammihud,
  from the tribe of Simeon;
²¹Elidad son of Kislon,
  from the tribe of Benjamin;
²²Bukki son of Jogli,
  the leader from the tribe of Dan;
²³Hanniel son of Ephod,
  the leader from the tribe of Manasseh son of Joseph;
²⁴Kemuel son of Shiphtan,
  the leader from the tribe of Ephraim son of Joseph;
²⁵Elizaphan son of Parnach,
  the leader from the tribe of Zebulun;
²⁶Paltiel son of Azzan,
  the leader from the tribe of Issachar;
²⁷Ahihud son of Shelomi,
  the leader from the tribe of Asher;
²⁸Pedahel son of Ammihud,
  the leader from the tribe of Naphtali."

²⁹These are the men the LORD commanded to assign the inheritance to the Israelites in the land of Canaan.

■ Towns for the Levites

35 On the plains of Moab by the Jordan across from Jericho,*a* the LORD said to Moses, ²"Command the Israelites to give the Levites towns to live in from the inheritance the Israelites will possess. And give them pasture-lands around the towns. ³Then they will have towns to live in and pasture-lands for their cattle, flocks and all their other livestock.

⁴"The pasture-lands around the towns that you give the Levites will extend out fifteen hundred feet*b* from the town wall. ⁵Outside the town, measure three thousand feet*c* on the east side, three thousand on the south side, three thousand on the west and three thousand on the north, with the town in the centre. They will have this area as pasture-land for the towns.

■ Cities of Refuge

⁶"Six of the towns you give the Levites will be cities of refuge, to which a person who has killed someone may flee. In addition, give them forty-two other towns. ⁷In all you must give the Levites forty-eight towns, together with their pasture-lands. ⁸The towns you give the Levites from the land the Israelites possess are to be given in proportion to the inheritance of each tribe: Take many towns from a tribe that has many, but few from one that has few."

35:6 ■ CONTROLLING BLOOD FEUDS
Even today some nomadic tribes still follow the principles of blood feuds. If a person is responsible, even accidentally, for another's death, a relative of the victim can in turn kill either the murderer or, as a substitute, one of the murderer's relatives. The cities of refuge put a control on this practice, making allowance for "involuntary manslaughter". The assembly judged whether the killing was accidental or intentional (verse 24).

---

⁹Then the LORD said to Moses: ¹⁰"Speak to the Israelites and say to them: 'When you cross the Jordan into Canaan, ¹¹select some towns to be your cities of refuge, to which a person who has killed someone accidentally may flee. ¹²They will be places of refuge from the avenger, so that a person accused of murder may not die before he stands trial before the assembly. ¹³These six towns you give will be your cities of refuge. ¹⁴Give three on this side of the Jordan and three in Canaan as cities of refuge. ¹⁵These six towns will be a place of refuge for Israelites, aliens and any other people living among them, so that anyone who has killed another accidentally can flee there.

¹⁶" 'If a man strikes someone with an iron object so that he dies, he is a murderer; the murderer shall be put to death. ¹⁷Or if anyone has a stone in his hand that could kill, and he strikes someone so that he dies, he is a murderer; the murderer shall be put to death. ¹⁸Or if anyone has a wooden object in his hand that could kill, and he hits someone so that he dies, he is a murderer; the murderer shall be put to death. ¹⁹The avenger of blood shall put the murderer to death; when he meets him, he shall put him to death. ²⁰If anyone with malice aforethought pushes another or throws something at him intentionally so that he dies ²¹or if in hostility he hits him with his fist so that he dies, that person shall be put to death; he is a murderer. The avenger of blood shall put the murderer to death when he meets him.

²²" 'But if without hostility someone suddenly pushes another or throws something at him unintentionally ²³or, without seeing him, drops a stone on him that could kill him, and he dies, then since he was not his enemy and he did not intend to harm him, ²⁴the assembly must judge between him and the avenger of blood according to these regulations. ²⁵The assembly must protect the one accused of murder from the avenger of blood and send him back to the city of refuge to which he fled. He must stay there until the death of the high priest, who was anointed with holy oil.

²⁶" 'But if the accused ever goes outside the limits of the city of refuge to which he has fled ²⁷and the avenger of blood finds him outside the city, the

---

*f*15 *Jordan of Jericho* was possibly an ancient name for the Jordan River
*b*4 Hebrew *a thousand cubits* (about 450 metres)   *c*5 Hebrew *two thousand cubits* (about 900 metres)
*a*1 Hebrew *Jordan of Jericho*; possibly an ancient name for the Jordan River

avenger of blood may kill the accused without being guilty of murder. 28The accused must stay in his city of refuge until the death of the high priest; only after the death of the high priest may he return to his own property.

29" 'These are to be legal requirements for you throughout the generations to come, wherever you live.

30" 'Anyone who kills a person is to be put to death as a murderer only on the testimony of witnesses. But no-one is to be put to death on the testimony of only one witness.

31" 'Do not accept a ransom for the life of a murderer, who deserves to die. He must surely be put to death.

32" 'Do not accept a ransom for anyone who has fled to a city of refuge and so allow him to go back and live on his own land before the death of the high priest.

33" 'Do not pollute the land where you are. Bloodshed pollutes the land, and atonement cannot be made for the land on which blood has been shed, except by the blood of the one who shed it. 34Do not defile the land where you live and where I dwell, for I, the LORD, dwell among the Israelites.' "

■ Inheritance of Zelophehad's Daughters

36 The family heads of the clan of Gilead son of Makir, the son of Manasseh, who were from the clans of the descendants of Joseph, came and spoke before Moses and the leaders, the heads of the Israelite families. 2They said, "When the LORD commanded my lord to give the land as an inheritance to the Israelites by lot, he ordered you to give the inheritance of our brother Zelophehad to his daughters. 3Now suppose they marry men from other Israelite tribes; then their inheritance will be taken from our ancestral inheritance and added to that of the tribe they marry into. And so part of the inheritance allotted to us will be taken away. 4When the Year of Jubilee for the Israelites comes, their inheritance will be added to that of the tribe into which they marry, and their property will be taken from the tribal inheritance of our forefathers."

5Then at the LORD's command Moses gave this order to the Israelites: "What the tribe of the descendants of Joseph is saying is right. 6This is what the LORD commands for Zelophehad's daughters: They may marry anyone they please as long as they marry within the tribal clan of their father. 7No inheritance in Israel is to pass from tribe to tribe, for every Israelite shall keep the tribal land inherited from his forefathers. 8Every daughter who inherits land in any Israelite tribe must marry someone in her father's tribal clan, so that every Israelite will possess the inheritance of his fathers. 9No inheritance may pass from tribe to tribe, for each Israelite tribe is to keep the land it inherits."

10So Zelophehad's daughters did as the LORD commanded Moses. 11Zelophehad's daughters—Mahlah, Tirzah, Hoglah, Milcah and Noah—married their cousins on their father's side. 12They married within the clans of the descendants of Manasseh son of Joseph, and their inheritance remained in their father's clan and tribe.

13These are the commands and regulations the LORD gave through Moses to the Israelites on the plains of Moab by the Jordan across from Jericho.[a]

a 13 Hebrew Jordan of Jericho; possibly an ancient name for the Jordan River

DEUTERONOMY

■ A PERSONAL PLEA

MOSES' LAST CHANCE WITH THE PEOPLE HE LOVED

BUT IF FROM THERE YOU SEEK THE LORD YOUR GOD, YOU WILL FIND HIM IF YOU LOOK
FOR HIM WITH ALL YOUR HEART AND WITH ALL YOUR SOUL. ■ 4:29

Politicians get this advice: "When you deliver a speech, make it seem as if you're having a personal talk in a small room with each one of your listeners". No-one took that advice better than Franklin Delano Roosevelt – unless, perhaps, you consider Moses' speeches in Deuteronomy.

When Roosevelt became President of the United States in 1932, he faced a national crisis greater than any since the Civil War. Fifteen million people were unemployed in the Great Depression (a 25 per cent unemployment rate), and two million of those wandered around the country, homeless, searching for work and food. War in Europe was not far away.

■ FIRESIDE CHATS

To combat the mood of despair, Roosevelt turned to a powerful new communications weapon: radio. The very first week of his presidency he gave his first "fireside chat" from a homely setting in the White House, and a series of such chats helped him pull the nation through its hard times.

Warm and personal in tone, the book of Deuteronomy resembles just such a fireside chat, delivered by the great leader Moses to his people, the Israelites. He, too, led a nation through dangerous times, and at the end of his life he had many parting words. This book is Moses' State of the Union address, personal diary, and tearful swan song all combined into one.

■ POISED ON THE EDGE

For their length and emotional power, these speeches have no equal in the Bible. Moses passionately went over and over the same ground, occasionally lashing out, but more often showing the anguish and love of a doting parent. An undercurrent of sadness runs through the speeches: Moses knew he would not join in the triumph of entering Canaan. God had revealed that Moses would die before then.

In Exodus, Moses was marked by a quick temper and a reluctance to speak. His humility and eloquence as seen in Deuteronomy show how far he had come in 40 years.

Deep in his soul, Moses felt that the entire history of the Israelites depended on what happened next. Poised on the banks of the Jordan River, they were about to enter the promised land and face the most crucial test of their lives. How would they react to the new land? Would they keep their covenant with God or reject it for the more immediate pleasures around them?

Desert-bred, the Israelites knew little about the seductions of other cultures: the sensuality, the exotic religions, the glittering wealth. They had spent their lives in near-isolation, sheltered from civilisation. Now they were marching into a land full of enticements.

■ THREE SPEECHES

Moses' first great speech, in chapters 1–3, reviewed God's dealings with Israel. Moses recalled Israel's history through his own eyes, mentioning such details as the irrigation system in Egypt, the abrupt departure, the fearsome desert with its snakes and scorpions, and the amazing miracles of God. He filled the account with personal reflections, like an ageing father telling his children what to remember after he is gone.

The longest speech, chapters 4–26, went over the moral and civil code the Israelites had agreed to keep. Even here, a personal tone came through. Moses did not list laws as in a textbook; he discussed and amplified and preached them. Along with the laws, he included reminders, object lessons, personal outbursts.

In chapters 27–33 Moses gave a final summing up, a farewell charge from an old man facing certain death. As clearly as he could, he presented the choices facing the Israelites. He would not be with them as they chose their future. They were on their own; they held their destiny in their own hands.

■ HOW TO READ DEUTERONOMY

Early in this century archaeologists began turning up samples of Near Eastern treaties. These "suzerainty treaties" set down in official form the relationship between a powerful king (suzerain) and the people he ruled over. Such treaties shed new light on the book of Deuteronomy, which seems to follow very closely the pattern of such a treaty. Typically, a treaty with a powerful king consisted of the following elements:

1. *A preamble identifying the parties of the treaty,* such as a king and a small cluster of tribes who want his protection.

2. *A capsular history describing previous relations between the two parties.*

3. *Rules defining each party's obligations.* The king may swear to defend some tribes with his armies in return for allegiance, taxes, and a percentage of produce.

4. *Witnesses to the treaties,* including, in many cases, a list of gods.

5. *Curses and blessings specifying what will take place if one of the parties breaks the treaty.* The king may promise the people prosperity and peace if they keep the terms, but invasion, deportation, or death if they break them.

Read Deuteronomy as an example of a treaty between a king and his people. *Treaty* is another word for the one we have been using — *covenant* — to describe the formal agreement between God and the Israelites. With a little work, you can identify various portions of Deuteronomy that parallel the five elements above.

Chapters 1–11 and 27–34 contain the best summary of Moses' speeches to the Israelites. He holds back no emotion as he retells the story of his life. Almost all the action he describes repeats what we've heard before (see Exodus 12–20; 32–34; Numbers 11 – 17; 20–24), but Deuteronomy provides a much more personal account.

Unlike other ancient books, the Bible gives major emphasis to "nobodies" – poor people, aliens, widows, orphans, the sick. Many of the laws relating to them repeat laws from the three preceding books. But Deuteronomy gives hidden insights into why God has such special concern for nobodies and why the Israelites should also. It also gives intriguing ideas on how such concern can be translated into actual political and economic policies. As you go through the book, mark each passage that relates to such people.

The New Testament quotes Deuteronomy more often than any other Old Testament book. Twenty-one of the 27 New Testament books allude to Deuteronomy; some scholars count 90 different citations. Jesus himself drew from it during his temptation (Matthew 4).

■ 3-TRACK READING PLAN

For an explanation and complete listing of the 3-track reading plan, turn to page x.

■ TRACK 1:
Two-Week Courses on the Bible
See page x for information on these courses.

■ TRACK 2:
An Overview of Deuteronomy in 3 Days
☐ Day 1. Read the Introduction to Deuteronomy and then chapter 4, part of Moses' first emotional speech.

☐ Day 2. Read chapter 8; here, Moses reveals his fears about how success may have a harmful effect on the Israelites.
☐ Day 3. Read chapter 28, which, in vivid, shocking language, sets out before the Israelites the choice between obedience and disobedience. Now turn to page xi for your next Track 2 reading project.

■ TRACK 3:
All of Deuteronomy in 34 Days
After you have read through Deuteronomy, turn to pages xii–xiii for your next Track 3 reading project.

☐ 1	☐ 2	☐ 3	☐ 4
☐ 5	☐ 6	☐ 7	☐ 8
☐ 9	☐ 10	☐ 11	☐ 12
☐ 13	☐ 14	☐ 15	☐ 16
☐ 17	☐ 18	☐ 19	☐ 20
☐ 21	☐ 22	☐ 23	☐ 24
☐ 25	☐ 26	☐ 27	☐ 28
☐ 29	☐ 30	☐ 31	☐ 32
☐ 33	☐ 34		

■ The Command to Leave Horeb

1 These are the words Moses spoke to all Israel in the desert east of the Jordan — that is, in the Arabah — opposite Suph, between Paran and Tophel, Laban, Hazeroth and Dizahab. [2](It takes eleven days to go from Horeb to Kadesh Barnea by the Mount Seir road.)

[3]In the fortieth year, on the first day of the eleventh month, Moses proclaimed to the Israelites all that the LORD had commanded him concerning them. [4]This was after he had defeated Sihon king of the Amorites, who reigned in Heshbon, and at Edrei had defeated Og king of Bashan, who reigned in Ashtaroth.

[5]East of the Jordan in the territory of Moab, Moses began to expound this law, saying:

[6]The LORD our God said to us at Horeb, "You have stayed long enough at this mountain. [7]Break camp and advance into the hill country of the Amorites; go to all the neighbouring peoples in the Arabah, in the mountains, in the western foothills, in the Negev and along the coast, to the land of the Canaanites and to Lebanon, as far as the great river, the Euphrates. [8]See, I have given you this land. Go in and take possession of the land that the LORD swore he would give to your fathers — to Abraham, Isaac and Jacob — and to their descendants after them."

■ The Appointment of Leaders

[9]At that time I said to you, "You are too heavy a burden for me to carry alone. [10]The LORD your God has increased your numbers so that today you are as many as the stars in the sky. [11]May the LORD, the God of your fathers, increase you a thousand times and bless you as he has promised! [12]But how can I bear your problems and your burdens and your disputes all by myself? [13]Choose some wise, understanding and respected men from each of your tribes, and I will set them over you."

[14]You answered me, "What you propose to do is good."

[15]So I took the leading men of your tribes, wise and respected men, and appointed them to have authority over you — as commanders of thousands, of hundreds, of fifties and of tens and as tribal officials. [16]And I charged your judges at that time: Hear the disputes between your brothers and judge fairly, whether the case is between brother Israelites or between one of them and an alien. [17]Do not show partiality in judging; hear both small and great alike. Do not be afraid of any man, for judgment belongs to God. Bring me any case too hard for you, and I will hear it. [18]And at that time I told you everything you were to do.

■ Spies Sent Out

[19]Then, as the LORD our God commanded us, we set out from Horeb and went towards the hill country of the Amorites through all that vast and dreadful desert that you have seen, and so we reached Kadesh Barnea. [20]Then I said to you, "You have reached the hill country of the Amorites, which the LORD our God is giving us. [21]See, the LORD your God has given you the land. Go up and take possession of it as the LORD, the God of your fathers, told you. Do not be afraid; do not be discouraged."

[22]Then all of you came to me and said, "Let us send men ahead to spy out the land for us and bring back a report about the route we are to take and the towns we will come to."

[23]The idea seemed good to me; so I selected twelve of you, one man from each tribe. [24]They left and went up into the hill country, and came to the Valley of Eshcol and explored it. [25]Taking with them some of the fruit of the land, they brought it down to us and reported, "It is a good land that the LORD our God is giving us."

■ Rebellion Against the LORD

[26]But you were unwilling to go up; you rebelled against the command of the LORD your God. [27]You grumbled in your tents and said, "The LORD hates us; so he brought us out of Egypt to deliver us into the hands of the Amorites to destroy us. [28]Where can we go? Our brothers have made us lose heart. They say, 'The people are stronger and taller than we are; the cities are large, with walls up to the sky. We even saw the Anakites there.'"

[29]Then I said to you, "Do not be terrified; do not be afraid of them. [30]The LORD your God, who is going before you, will fight for you, as he did for you in Egypt, before your very eyes, [31]and in the desert. There you saw how the LORD your God carried you, as a father carries his son, all the way you went until you reached this place."

[32]In spite of this, you did not trust in the LORD your God, [33]who went ahead of you on your journey, in fire by night and in a cloud by day, to search out places for you to camp and to show you the way you should go.

[34]When the LORD heard what you said, he was angry and solemnly swore: [35]"Not a man of this evil generation shall see the good land I swore to give your forefathers, [36]except Caleb son of Jephunneh. He will see it, and I will give him and his descendants the land he set his feet on, because he followed the LORD wholeheartedly."

[37]Because of you the LORD became angry with me also and said, "You shall not enter it, either. [38]But your assistant, Joshua son of Nun, will enter it. Encourage him, because he will lead Israel to inherit it. [39]And the little ones that you said would be taken captive, your children who do not yet know good from bad — they will enter the land. I will give it to them and they will take possession of it. [40]But as for you, turn round and set out towards the desert along the route to the Red Sea."[a]

1:37 ■ DISTRIBUTING BLAME
God forbade Moses to enter the promised land because of the incident reported in Numbers 20. In his farewell speech, Moses could not resist expressing his own resentment at the Israelites' part in provoking his punishment. In this verse and in 3:26 and 4:21, he turned the blame back on his countrymen.

---

a 40 Hebrew *Yam Suph*; that is, Sea of Reeds

⁴¹Then you replied, "We have sinned against the LORD. We will go up and fight, as the LORD our God commanded us." So every one of you put on his weapons, thinking it easy to go up into the hill country.

⁴²But the LORD said to me, "Tell them, 'Do not go up and fight, because I will not be with you. You will be defeated by your enemies.' "

⁴³So I told you, but you would not listen. You rebelled against the LORD's command and in your arrogance you marched up into the hill country. ⁴⁴The Amorites who lived in those hills came out against you; they chased you like a swarm of bees and beat you down from Seir all the way to Hormah. ⁴⁵You came back and wept before the LORD, but he paid no attention to your weeping and turned a deaf ear to you. ⁴⁶And so you stayed in Kadesh many days—all the time you spent there.

■ Wanderings in the Desert

2 Then we turned back and set out towards the desert along the route to the Red Sea,ᵃ as the LORD had directed me. For a long time we made our way around the hill country of Seir.

²Then the LORD said to me, ³"You have made your way around this hill country long enough; now turn north. ⁴Give the people these orders: 'You are about to pass through the territory of your brothers the descendants of Esau, who live in Seir. They will be afraid of you, but be very careful. ⁵Do not provoke them to war, for I will not give you any of their land, not even enough to put your foot on. I have given Esau the hill country of Seir as his own. ⁶You are to pay them in silver for the food you eat and the water you drink.' "

⁷The LORD your God has blessed you in all the work of your hands. He has watched over your journey through this vast desert. These forty years the LORD your God has been with you, and you have not lacked anything.

⁸So we went on past our brothers the descendants of Esau, who live in Seir. We turned from the Arabah road, which comes up from Elath and Ezion Geber, and travelled along the desert road of Moab.

⁹Then the LORD said to me, "Do not harass the Moabites or provoke them to war, for I will not give you any part of their land. I have given Ar to the descendants of Lot as a possession."

¹⁰(The Emites used to live there—a people strong and numerous, and as tall as the Anakites. ¹¹Like the Anakites, they too were considered Rephaites, but the Moabites called them Emites. ¹²Horites used to live in Seir, but the descendants of Esau drove them out. They destroyed the Horites from before them and settled in their place, just as Israel did in the land the LORD gave them as their possession.)

¹³And the LORD said, "Now get up and cross the Zered Valley." So we crossed the valley.

¹⁴Thirty-eight years passed from the time we left Kadesh Barnea until we crossed the Zered Valley. By then, that entire generation of fighting men had perished from the camp, as the LORD had sworn to them. ¹⁵The LORD's hand was against them until he had completely eliminated them from the camp.

¹⁶Now when the last of these fighting men among the people had died, ¹⁷the LORD said to me, ¹⁸"Today you are to pass by the region of Moab at Ar. ¹⁹When you come to the Ammonites, do not harass them or provoke them to war, for I will not give you possession of any land belonging to the Ammonites. I have given it as a possession to the descendants of Lot."

2:14 ■ CHILDREN OF THE DESERT

As he reviewed the Israelites' history, Moses recalled with bitterness the series of rebellions leading to the 40-year punishment in "that vast and dreadful desert" (1:19). Actually, of course, the people listening to him had been mere children when the decisive rebellions occurred (1:39); their parents were the ones forbidden to enter the promised land. Except for Joshua, Caleb, and Moses' own family, all those listening to Moses had grown up in the desert.

²⁰(That too was considered a land of the Rephaites, who used to live there; but the Ammonites called them Zamzummites. ²¹They were a people strong and numerous, and as tall as the Anakites. The LORD destroyed them from before the Ammonites, who drove them out and settled in their place. ²²The LORD had done the same for the descendants of Esau, who lived in Seir, when he destroyed the Horites from before them. They drove them out and have lived in their place to this day. ²³And as for the Avvites who lived in villages as far as Gaza, the Caphtorites coming out from Caphtorᵇ destroyed them and settled in their place.)

■ Defeat of Sihon King of Heshbon

²⁴"Set out now and cross the Arnon Gorge. See, I have given into your hand Sihon the Amorite, king of Heshbon, and his country. Begin to take possession of it and engage him in battle. ²⁵This very day I will begin to put the terror and fear of you on all the nations under heaven. They will hear reports of you and will tremble and be in anguish because of you."

²⁶From the desert of Kedemoth I sent messengers to Sihon king of Heshbon offering peace and saying, ²⁷"Let us pass through your country. We will stay on the main road; we will not turn aside to the right or to the left. ²⁸Sell us food to eat and water to drink for their price in silver. Only let us pass through on foot— ²⁹as the descendants of Esau, who live in Seir, and the Moabites, who live in Ar, did for us—until we cross the Jordan into the land the LORD our God is giving us." ³⁰But Sihon king of Heshbon refused to let us pass through. For the LORD your God had made his spirit stubborn and his heart obstinate in order to give him into your hands, as he has now done.

³¹The LORD said to me, "See, I have begun to deliver Sihon and his country over to you. Now begin to conquer and possess his land."

³²When Sihon and all his army came out to meet us in battle at Jahaz, ³³the LORD our God delivered him over to us and we struck him down, together with his sons and his whole army. ³⁴At that time we

took all his towns and completely destroyed[c] them — men, women and children. We left no survivors. [35]But the livestock and the plunder from the towns we had captured we carried off for ourselves. [36]From Aroer on the rim of the Arnon Gorge, and from the town in the gorge, even as far as Gilead, not one town was too strong for us. The LORD our God gave us all of them. [37]But in accordance with the command of the LORD our God, you did not encroach on any of the land of the Ammonites, neither the land along the course of the Jabbok nor that around the towns in the hills.

■ Defeat of Og King of Bashan

3 Next we turned and went up along the road towards Bashan, and Og king of Bashan with his whole army marched out to meet us in battle at Edrei. [2]The LORD said to me, "Do not be afraid of him, for I have handed him over to you with his whole army and his land. Do to him what you did to Sihon king of the Amorites, who reigned in Heshbon."

[3]So the LORD our God also gave into our hands Og king of Bashan and all his army. We struck them down, leaving no survivors. [4]At that time we took all his cities. There was not one of the sixty cities that we did not take from them — the whole region of Argob, Og's kingdom in Bashan. [5]All these cities were fortified with high walls and with gates and bars, and there were also a great many unwalled villages. [6]We completely destroyed[a] them, as we had done with Sihon king of Heshbon, destroying[a] every city — men, women and children. [7]But all the livestock and the plunder from their cities we carried off for ourselves.

[8]So at that time we took from these two kings of the Amorites the territory east of the Jordan, from the Arnon Gorge as far as Mount Hermon. [9](Hermon is called Sirion by the Sidonians; the Amorites call it Senir.) [10]We took all the towns on the plateau, and all Gilead, and all Bashan as far as Salecah and Edrei, towns of Og's kingdom in Bashan. [11](Only Og king of Bashan was left of the remnant of the Rephaites. His bed[b] was made of iron and was more than thirteen feet long and six feet wide.[c] It is still in Rabbah of the Ammonites.)

■ Division of the Land

[12]Of the land that we took over at that time, I gave the Reubenites and the Gadites the territory north of Aroer by the Arnon Gorge, including half the hill country of Gilead, together with its towns. [13]The rest of Gilead and also all of Bashan, the kingdom of Og, I gave to the half-tribe of Manasseh. (The whole region of Argob in Bashan used to be known as a land of the Rephaites. [14]Jair, a descendant of Manasseh, took the whole region of Argob as far as the border of the Geshurites and the Maacathites; it was named after him, so that to this day Bashan is called Havvoth Jair.[d]) [15]And I gave Gilead to Makir. [16]But to the Reubenites and the Gadites I gave the territory extending from Gilead down to the Arnon Gorge (the middle of the gorge being the border) and out to the Jabbok River, which is the border of the Ammonites. [17]Its western border was the Jordan in the Arabah,

from Kinnereth to the Sea of the Arabah (the Salt Sea[e]), below the slopes of Pisgah.

[18]I commanded you at that time: "The LORD your God has given you this land to take possession of it. But all your able-bodied men, armed for battle, must cross over ahead of your brother Israelites. [19]However, your wives, your children and your livestock (I know you have much livestock) may stay in the towns I have given you, [20]until the LORD gives rest to your brothers as he has to you, and they too have taken over the land that the LORD your God is giving them, across the Jordan. After that, each of you may go back to the possession I have given you."

■ Moses Forbidden to Cross the Jordan

[21]At that time I commanded Joshua: "You have seen with your own eyes all that the LORD your God has done to these two kings. The LORD will do the same to all the kingdoms over there where you are going. [22]Do not be afraid of them; the LORD your God himself will fight for you."

[23]At that time I pleaded with the LORD: [24]"O Sovereign LORD, you have begun to show to your servant your greatness and your strong hand. For what god is there in heaven or on earth who can do the deeds and mighty works you do? [25]Let me go over and see the good land beyond the Jordan — that fine hill country and Lebanon."

[26]But because of you the LORD was angry with me and would not listen to me. "That is enough," the LORD said. "Do not speak to me any more about this matter. [27]Go up to the top of Pisgah and look west and north and south and east. Look at the land with your own eyes, since you are not going to cross this Jordan. [28]But commission Joshua, and encourage and strengthen him, for he will lead this people across and will cause them to inherit the land that you will see." [29]So we stayed in the valley near Beth Peor.

■ Obedience Commanded

4 Hear now, O Israel, the decrees and laws I am about to teach you. Follow them so that you may live and may go in and take possession of the land that the LORD, the God of your fathers, is giving you. [2]Do not add to what I command you and do not subtract from it, but keep the commands of the LORD your God that I give you.

> **4:2 ■ DO NOT ADD**
> People usually remember that they are not supposed to "drop" one of God's commands, but it is more subtly tempting to add commands. Religious people of Jesus' time, for example, invented elaborate rules on how far you could walk on the Sabbath. Such "legalism" may seem holy, but goes against God's directions.

[3]You saw with your own eyes what the LORD did at Baal Peor. The LORD your God destroyed from among you everyone who followed the Baal of Peor,

---

[c]34 The Hebrew term refers to the irrevocable giving over of things or persons to the LORD, often by totally destroying them.   [a]6 The Hebrew term refers to the irrevocable giving over of things or persons to the LORD, often by totally destroying them.   [b]11 Or sarcophagus   [c]11 Hebrew nine cubits long and four cubits wide (about 4 metres long and 1.8 metres wide)   [d]14 Or called the settlements of Jair   [e]17 That is, the Dead Sea

4but all of you who held fast to the LORD your God are still alive today.

5See, I have taught you decrees and laws as the LORD my God commanded me, so that you may follow them in the land you are entering to take possession of it. 6Observe them carefully, for this will show your wisdom and understanding to the nations, who will hear about all these decrees and say, "Surely this great nation is a wise and understanding people." 7What other nation is so great as to have their gods near them the way the LORD our God is near us whenever we pray to him? 8And what other nation is so great as to have such righteous decrees and laws as this body of laws I am setting before you today?

4:6 ■ OLD TESTAMENT EVANGELISM

As he explained various laws to the Israelites, Moses often appealed to their unique calling as a nation. God had chosen them as a "kingdom of priests" and a "treasured possession". This passage describes yet another benefit to keeping the law: what today we would call evangelism. The purity of the Israelites would serve as an example to the nations around them, who would thus be attracted to the true God.

9Only be careful, and watch yourselves closely so that you do not forget the things your eyes have seen or let them slip from your heart as long as you live. Teach them to your children and to their children after them. 10Remember the day you stood before the LORD your God at Horeb, when he said to me, "Assemble the people before me to hear my words so that they may learn to revere me as long as they live in the land and may teach them to their children." 11You came near and stood at the foot of the mountain while it blazed with fire to the very heavens, with black clouds and deep darkness. 12Then the LORD spoke to you out of the fire. You heard the sound of words but saw no form; there was only a voice. 13He declared to you his covenant, the Ten Commandments, which he commanded you to follow and then wrote them on two stone tablets. 14And the LORD directed me at that time to teach you the decrees and laws you are to follow in the land that you are crossing the Jordan to possess.

■ Idolatry Forbidden

15You saw no form of any kind the day the LORD spoke to you at Horeb out of the fire. Therefore watch yourselves very carefully, 16so that you do not become corrupt and make for yourselves an idol, an image of any shape, whether formed like a man or a woman, 17or like any animal on earth or any bird that flies in the air, 18or like any creature that moves along the ground or any fish in the waters below. 19And when you look up to the sky and see the sun, the moon and the stars—all the heavenly array—do not be enticed into bowing down to them and worshipping things the LORD your God has apportioned to all the nations under heaven. 20But as for you, the LORD took you and brought you out of the iron-smelting furnace, out of Egypt, to be the people of his inheritance, as you now are.

21The LORD was angry with me because of you, and he solemnly swore that I would not cross the Jordan and enter the good land the LORD your God is giving you as your inheritance. 22I will die in this land; I will not cross the Jordan; but you are about to cross over and take possession of that good land. 23Be careful not to forget the covenant of the LORD your God that he made with you; do not make for yourselves an idol in the form of anything the LORD your God has forbidden. 24For the LORD your God is a consuming fire, a jealous God.

25After you have had children and grandchildren and have lived in the land a long time—if you then become corrupt and make any kind of idol, doing evil in the eyes of the LORD your God and provoking him to anger, 26I call heaven and earth as witnesses against you this day that you will quickly perish from the land that you are crossing the Jordan to possess. You will not live there long but will certainly be destroyed. 27The LORD will scatter you among the peoples, and only a few of you will survive among the nations to which the LORD will drive you. 28There you will worship man-made gods of wood and stone, which cannot see or hear or eat or smell. 29But if from there you seek the LORD your God, you will find him if you look for him with all your heart and with all your soul. 30When you are in distress and all these things have happened to you, then in later days you will return to the LORD your God and obey him. 31For the LORD your God is a merciful God; he will not abandon or destroy you or forget the covenant with your forefathers, which he confirmed to them by oath.

■ The LORD Is God

32Ask now about the former days, long before your time, from the day God created man on the earth; ask from one end of the heavens to the other. Has anything so great as this ever happened, or has anything like it ever been heard of? 33Has any other people heard the voice of God*a* speaking out of fire, as you have, and lived? 34Has any god ever tried to take for himself one nation out of another nation, by testings, by miraculous signs and wonders, by war, by a mighty hand and an outstretched arm, or by great and awesome deeds, like all the things the LORD your God did for you in Egypt before your very eyes?

35You were shown these things so that you might know that the LORD is God; besides him there is no other. 36From heaven he made you hear his voice to discipline you. On earth he showed you his great fire, and you heard his words from out of the fire. 37Because he loved your forefathers and chose their descendants after them, he brought you out of Egypt by his Presence and his great strength, 38to drive out before you nations greater and stronger than you and to bring you into their land to give it to you for your inheritance, as it is today.

39Acknowledge and take to heart this day that the LORD is God in heaven above and on the earth below. There is no other. 40Keep his decrees and commands, which I am giving you today, so that it may

a 33 Or of a god

go well with you and your children after you and that you may live long in the land the LORD your God gives you for all time.

4:35 ■ EXPERIENCE TEACHES

Chapter 4 follows a typical pattern in Deuteronomy: Moses begins with the Israelites' experience and then shows how the laws of the covenant relate directly to that experience. In this chapter, he vividly reminds them of their own encounters with God, especially at Mount Sinai. How did God reveal himself to them? "You saw no form of any kind", Moses concludes (verse 15); therefore, idols made with human hands would insult and devalue such a God. Then he describes the unique privilege the Israelites have: to know personally the God who created the universe.

■ Cities of Refuge

⁴¹Then Moses set aside three cities east of the Jordan, ⁴²to which anyone who had killed a person could flee if he had unintentionally killed his neighbour without malice aforethought. He could flee into one of these cities and save his life. ⁴³The cities were these: Bezer in the desert plateau, for the Reubenites; Ramoth in Gilead, for the Gadites; and Golan in Bashan, for the Manassites.

■ Introduction to the Law

⁴⁴This is the law Moses set before the Israelites. ⁴⁵These are the stipulations, decrees and laws Moses gave them when they came out of Egypt ⁴⁶and were in the valley near Beth Peor east of the Jordan, in the land of Sihon king of the Amorites, who reigned in Heshbon and was defeated by Moses and the Israelites as they came out of Egypt. ⁴⁷They took possession of his land and the land of Og king of Bashan, the two Amorite kings east of the Jordan. ⁴⁸This land extended from Aroer on the rim of the Arnon Gorge to Mount Siyon*b* (that is, Hermon), ⁴⁹and included all the Arabah east of the Jordan, as far as the Sea of the Arabah,*c* below the slopes of Pisgah.

■ The Ten Commandments

5 Moses summoned all Israel and said:
Hear, O Israel, the decrees and the laws I declare in your hearing today. Learn them and be sure to follow them. ²The LORD our God made a covenant with us at Horeb. ³It was not with our fathers that the LORD made this covenant, but with us, with all of us who are alive here today. ⁴The LORD spoke to you face to face out of the fire on the mountain. ⁵(At that time I stood between the LORD and you to declare to you the word of the LORD, because you were afraid of the fire and did not go up the mountain.) And he said:

⁶"I am the LORD your God, who brought you out of Egypt, out of the land of slavery.
⁷"You shall have no other gods before*a* me.
⁸"You shall not make for yourself an idol in the form of anything in heaven above or on the earth beneath or in the waters below.

⁹You shall not bow down to them or worship them; for I, the LORD your God, am a jealous God, punishing the children for the sin of the fathers to the third and fourth generation of those who hate me, ¹⁰but showing love to a thousand ⌐generations⌐ of those who love me and keep my commandments.

¹¹"You shall not misuse the name of the LORD your God, for the LORD will not hold anyone guiltless who misuses his name.

¹²"Observe the Sabbath day by keeping it holy, as the LORD your God has commanded you. ¹³Six days you shall labour and do all your work, ¹⁴but the seventh day is a Sabbath to the LORD your God. On it you shall not do any work, neither you, nor your son or daughter, nor your manservant or maidservant, nor your ox, your donkey or any of your animals, nor the alien within your gates, so that your manservant and maidservant may rest, as you do. ¹⁵Remember that you were slaves in Egypt and that the LORD your God brought you out of there with a mighty hand and an outstretched arm. Therefore the LORD your God has commanded you to observe the Sabbath day.

¹⁶"Honour your father and your mother, as the LORD your God has commanded you, so that you may live long and that it may go well with you in the land the LORD your God is giving you.

¹⁷"You shall not murder.
¹⁸"You shall not commit adultery.
¹⁹"You shall not steal.
²⁰"You shall not give false testimony against your neighbour.
²¹"You shall not covet your neighbour's wife. You shall not set your desire on your neighbour's house or land, his manservant or maidservant, his ox or donkey, or anything that belongs to your neighbour."

²²These are the commandments the LORD proclaimed in a loud voice to your whole assembly there on the mountain from out of the fire, the cloud and the deep darkness; and he added nothing more. Then he wrote them on two stone tablets and gave them to me.

²³When you heard the voice out of the darkness, while the mountain was ablaze with fire, all the leading men of your tribes and your elders came to me. ²⁴And you said, "The LORD our God has shown us his glory and his majesty, and we have heard his voice from the fire. Today we have seen that a man can live even if God speaks with him. ²⁵But now, why should we die? This great fire will consume us, and we will die if we hear the voice of the LORD our God any longer. ²⁶For what mortal man has ever heard the voice of the living God speaking out of fire, as we have, and survived? ²⁷Go near and listen to all that the LORD our God says. Then tell us whatever the LORD our God tells you. We will listen and obey."

²⁸The LORD heard you when you spoke to me and

---

b 48 Hebrew; Syriac (see also Deut. 3:9) *Sirion*   *c 49* That is, the Dead Sea   *a 7 Or besides* the LORD said to me, "I have heard what this people said to you. Everything they said was good. ²⁹Oh, that their hearts would be inclined to fear me and keep all my commands always, so that it might go well with them and their children for ever!

³⁰"Go, tell them to return to their tents. ³¹But you stay here with me so that I may give you all the commands, decrees and laws that you are to teach them to follow in the land I am giving them to possess."

³²So be careful to do what the LORD your God has commanded you; do not turn aside to the right or to the left. ³³Walk in all the way that the LORD your God has commanded you, so that you may live and prosper and prolong your days in the land that you will possess.

■ Love the LORD Your God

6 These are the commands, decrees and laws the LORD your God directed me to teach you to observe in the land that you are crossing the Jordan to possess, ²so that you, your children and their children after them may fear the LORD your God as long as you live by keeping all his decrees and commands that I give you, and so that you may enjoy long life. ³Hear, O Israel, and be careful to obey so that it may go well with you and that you may increase greatly in a land flowing with milk and honey, just as the LORD, the God of your fathers, promised you.

⁴Hear, O Israel: The LORD our God, the LORD is one.*ᵃ* ⁵Love the LORD your God with all your heart and with all your soul and with all your strength. ⁶These commandments that I give you today are to be upon your hearts. ⁷Impress them on your children. Talk about them when you sit at home and when you walk along the road, when you lie down and when you get up. ⁸Tie them as symbols on your hands and bind them on your foreheads. ⁹Write them on the door-frames of your houses and on your gates.

6:4 ■ MOST QUOTED VERSES
These six verses (4–9) may well be the most quoted portion in the entire Bible. Known as the *Shema,* they are recited every morning and every evening by orthodox Jews – and have been for hundreds of years. They graphically emphasise the importance of God's laws to the Israelites.

---

¹⁰When the LORD your God brings you into the land he swore to your fathers, to Abraham, Isaac and Jacob, to give you — a land with large, flourishing cities you did not build, ¹¹houses filled with all kinds of good things you did not provide, wells you did not dig, and vineyards and olive groves you did not plant — then when you eat and are satisfied, ¹²be careful that you do not forget the LORD, who brought you out of Egypt, out of the land of slavery.

¹³Fear the LORD your God, serve him only and take your oaths in his name. ¹⁴Do not follow other gods, the gods of the peoples around you; ¹⁵for the LORD your God, who is among you, is a jealous God and his anger will burn against you, and he will destroy you from the face of the land. ¹⁶Do not test the LORD your God as you did at Massah. ¹⁷Be sure to keep the commands of the LORD your God and the stipulations and decrees he has given you. ¹⁸Do what is right and good in the LORD's sight, so that it may go well with you and you may go in and take over the good land that the LORD promised on oath to your forefathers, ¹⁹thrusting out all your enemies before you, as the LORD said.

²⁰In the future, when your son asks you, "What is the meaning of the stipulations, decrees and laws the LORD our God has commanded you?" ²¹tell him: "We were slaves of Pharaoh in Egypt, but the LORD brought us out of Egypt with a mighty hand. ²²Before our eyes the LORD sent miraculous signs and wonders — great and terrible — upon Egypt and Pharaoh and his whole household. ²³But he brought us out from there to bring us in and give us the land that he promised on oath to our forefathers. ²⁴The LORD commanded us to obey all these decrees and to fear the LORD our God, so that we might always prosper and be kept alive, as is the case today. ²⁵And if we are careful to obey all this law before the LORD our God, as he has commanded us, that will be our righteousness."

■ Driving Out the Nations

7 When the LORD your God brings you into the land you are entering to possess and drives out before you many nations — the Hittites, Girgashites, Amorites, Canaanites, Perizzites, Hivites and Jebusites, seven nations larger and stronger than you — ²and when the LORD your God has delivered them over to you and you have defeated them, then you must destroy them totally.*ᵃ* Make no treaty with them, and show them no mercy. ³Do not intermarry with them. Do not give your daughters to their sons or take their daughters for your sons, ⁴for they will turn your sons away from following me to serve other gods, and the LORD's anger will burn against you and will quickly destroy you. ⁵This is what you are to do to them: Break down their altars, smash their sacred stones, cut down their Asherah poles*ᵇ* and burn their idols in the fire. ⁶For you are a people holy to the LORD your God. The LORD your God has chosen you out of all the peoples on the face of the earth to be his people, his treasured possession.

⁷The LORD did not set his affection on you and choose you because you were more numerous than other peoples, for you were the fewest of all peoples. ⁸But it was because the LORD loved you and kept the oath he swore to your forefathers that he brought you out with a mighty hand and redeemed you from the land of slavery, from the power of Pharaoh king of Egypt. ⁹Know therefore that the LORD your God is God; he is the faithful God, keeping his covenant of love to a thousand generations of those who love him and keep his commands. ¹⁰But

those who hate him he will repay to their face
    by destruction;
he will not be slow to repay to their face
    those who hate him.

ᵃ4 Or The LORD our God is one LORD; or The LORD is our God, the LORD is one; or The LORD is our God, the LORD alone   ᵃ2 The Hebrew term refers to the irrevocable giving over of things or persons to the LORD, often by totally destroying them; also in verse 26.   ᵇ5 That is, symbols of the goddess Asherah; here and elsewhere in Deuteronomy

11Therefore, take care to follow the commands, decrees and laws I give you today.

7:7 ■ WHY THE ISRAELITES?
Deuteronomy makes clear that God chose Israel out of pure grace. He did not select them for their impressiveness (this verse), their goodness (9:5), or their faithfulness (9:24). Rather, he chose them because he loved them, and he had made absolute promises to their ancestors. Deuteronomy promises the new land to the Israelites 69 times.

12If you pay attention to these laws and are careful to follow them, then the LORD your God will keep his covenant of love with you, as he swore to your forefathers. 13He will love you and bless you and increase your numbers. He will bless the fruit of your womb, the crops of your land—your grain, new wine and oil—the calves of your herds and the lambs of your flocks in the land that he swore to your forefathers to give you. 14You will be blessed more than any other people; none of your men or women will be childless, nor any of your livestock without young. 15The LORD will keep you free from every disease. He will not inflict on you the horrible diseases you knew in Egypt, but he will inflict them on all who hate you. 16You must destroy all the peoples the LORD your God gives over to you. Do not look on them with pity and do not serve their gods, for that will be a snare to you.

17You may say to yourselves, "These nations are stronger than we are. How can we drive them out?" 18But do not be afraid of them; remember well what the LORD your God did to Pharaoh and to all Egypt. 19You saw with your own eyes the great trials, the miraculous signs and wonders, the mighty hand and outstretched arm, with which the LORD your God brought you out. The LORD your God will do the same to all the peoples you now fear. 20Moreover, the LORD your God will send the hornet among them until even the survivors who hide from you have perished. 21Do not be terrified by them, for the LORD your God, who is among you, is a great and awesome God. 22The LORD your God will drive out those nations before you, little by little. You will not be allowed to eliminate them all at once, or the wild animals will multiply around you. 23But the LORD your God will deliver them over to you, throwing them into great confusion until they are destroyed. 24He will give their kings into your hand, and you will wipe out their names from under heaven. No-one will be able to stand up against you; you will destroy them. 25The images of their gods you are to burn in the fire. Do not covet the silver and gold on them, and do not take it for yourselves, or you will be ensnared by it, for it is detestable to the LORD your God. 26Do not bring a detestable thing into your house or you, like it, will be set apart for destruction. Utterly abhor and detest it, for it is set apart for destruction.

■ Do Not Forget the LORD

8 Be careful to follow every command I am giving you today, so that you may live and increase and may enter and possess the land that the LORD promised on oath to your forefathers. 2Remember how the LORD your God led you all the way in the desert these forty years, to humble you and to test you in order to know what was in your heart, whether or not you would keep his commands. 3He humbled you, causing you to hunger and then feeding you with manna, which neither you nor your fathers had known, to teach you that man does not live on bread alone but on every word that comes from the mouth of the LORD. 4Your clothes did not wear out and your feet did not swell during these forty years. 5Know then in your heart that as a man disciplines his son, so the LORD your God disciplines you.

8:3 ■ WORDS FOR THE DEVIL
When tempted by Satan (Luke 4:1–13), Jesus responded with three separate quotations from Deuteronomy: this verse, and Deuteronomy 6:13,16. In the desert, Israelites had learned that God would provide all they needed. Jesus, also in the desert, quoted Scripture to forcefully remind Satan of that lesson.

6Observe the commands of the LORD your God, walking in his ways and revering him. 7For the LORD your God is bringing you into a good land—a land with streams and pools of water, with springs flowing in the valleys and hills; 8a land with wheat and barley, vines and fig-trees, pomegranates, olive oil and honey; 9a land where bread will not be scarce and you will lack nothing; a land where the rocks are iron and you can dig copper out of the hills.

10When you have eaten and are satisfied, praise the LORD your God for the good land he has given you. 11Be careful that you do not forget the LORD your God, failing to observe his commands, his laws and his decrees that I am giving you this day. 12Otherwise, when you eat and are satisfied, when you build fine houses and settle down, 13and when your herds and flocks grow large and your silver and gold increase and all you have is multiplied, 14then your heart will become proud and you will forget the LORD your God, who brought you out of Egypt, out of the land of slavery. 15He led you through the vast and dreadful desert, that thirsty and waterless land, with its venomous snakes and scorpions. He brought you water out of hard rock. 16He gave you manna to eat in the desert, something your fathers had never known, to humble and to test you so that in the end it might go well with you. 17You may say to yourself, "My power and the strength of my hands have produced this wealth for me." 18But remember the LORD your God, for it is he who gives you the ability to produce wealth, and so confirms his covenant, which he swore to your forefathers, as it is today.

19If you ever forget the LORD your God and follow other gods and worship and bow down to them, I testify against you today that you will surely be destroyed. ²⁰Like the nations the LORD destroyed before you, so you will be destroyed for not obeying the LORD your God.

■ Not Because of Israel's Righteousness

9 Hear, O Israel. You are now about to cross the Jordan to go in and dispossess nations greater and stronger than you, with large cities that have walls up to the sky. ²The people are strong and tall — Anakites! You know about them and have heard it said: "Who can stand up against the Anakites?" ³But be assured today that the LORD your God is the one who goes across ahead of you like a devouring fire. He will destroy them; he will subdue them before you. And you will drive them out and annihilate them quickly, as the LORD has promised you.

⁴After the LORD your God has driven them out before you, do not say to yourself, "The LORD has brought me here to take possession of this land because of my righteousness." No, it is on account of the wickedness of these nations that the LORD is going to drive them out before you. ⁵It is not because of your righteousness or your integrity that you are going in to take possession of their land; but on account of the wickedness of these nations, the LORD your God will drive them out before you, to accomplish what he swore to your fathers, to Abraham, Isaac and Jacob. ⁶Understand, then, that it is not because of your righteousness that the LORD your God is giving you this good land to possess, for you are a stiff-necked people.

9:4 ■ REASONS FOR WARFARE

Commands for the Israelites to utterly destroy other nations have caused modern readers of the Old Testament much concern. This passage reveals that God was acting not because of the Israelites' superior moral character, but because of the inhabitants' own wickedness. Chapter 20:16–18 gives yet another rationale for the wars: to keep Israel free from contamination by other nations. The Israelites never followed these commands completely, and their nation was ultimately weakened and destroyed precisely because of such contamination. (See "Is a War Ever Holy?" page 192, for further details.)

■ HEALTHIER, WEALTHIER AND WISER
DO ONLY GOOD THINGS HAPPEN TO GOOD PEOPLE?

INSIGHT

WHEN YOUR HERDS AND FLOCKS GROW LARGE AND YOUR SILVER AND GOLD INCREASE AND ALL YOU HAVE IS MULTIPLIED, THEN YOUR HEART WILL BECOME PROUD AND YOU WILL FORGET THE LORD YOUR GOD, WHO BROUGHT YOU OUT OF EGYPT, OUT OF THE LAND OF SLAVERY. ■ 8:13–14

Do Christians have car accidents? Do they get cancer? Are they ever fired from their jobs? The answer to all three questions is, of course, yes. But that answer causes big problems for some new Christians. Doesn't the Bible promise that God will look out for and protect his followers? How can such bad things occur?

People puzzled by such questions often refer to Old Testament books where God clearly promised success and protection to the Israelites. In Deuteronomy, Moses spelled out God's promises in complete detail. Israelite wives would have many babies. All the crops — grain, grapes, olive trees — would produce bountifully. Cattle and sheep would multiply. And Moses even included this extraordinary promise: "The LORD will keep you free from every disease" (7:15).

■ A SPECIAL ARRANGEMENT
For the Israelites to receive these benefits, God asked only one thing in return: follow the covenant agreement first set forth in the book of Exodus. Deuteronomy repeats much of the covenant and affirms, "It was not with our fathers that the LORD made this covenant, but with us, with all of us who are alive here today" (5:3).

God had a unique relationship with the band of refugees who had been roaming the Sinai for 40 years (10:15; 14:2). Moses, for one, could not seem to get over the arrangement. "Ask from one end of the heavens to the other," he said. "Has anything so great as this ever happened, or has anything like it ever been heard of? Has any god ever tried to take for himself one nation out of another nation . . . like . . . the LORD your God did for you in Egypt before your very eyes?" (4:32,34).

Moses promised that good things would come the Israelites' way if they merely held up their end of the covenant. If, he said — underscoring that small but very crucial word. Threads of doubt and anxiety run all through the book. Will the Israelites stick to the terms of the covenant? Will they obey?

■ DANGERS OF SUCCESS
Moses seemed to fear the coming prosperity even more than the rigours of the desert, and he voiced those fears in chapter 8. In the promised land, a lush country of streams and fruit trees and valuable resources, the Israelites might forget God and begin to take credit for

■ The Golden Calf

7Remember this and never forget how you provoked the LORD your God to anger in the desert. From the day you left Egypt until you arrived here, you have been rebellious against the LORD. 8At Horeb you aroused the LORD's wrath so that he was angry enough to destroy you. 9When I went up on the mountain to receive the tablets of stone, the tablets of the covenant that the LORD had made with you, I stayed on the mountain forty days and forty nights; I ate no bread and drank no water. 10The LORD gave me two stone tablets inscribed by the finger of God. On them were all the commandments the LORD proclaimed to you on the mountain out of the fire, on the day of the assembly.

11At the end of the forty days and forty nights, the LORD gave me the two stone tablets, the tablets of the covenant. 12Then the LORD told me, "Go down from here at once, because your people whom you brought out of Egypt have become corrupt. They have turned away quickly from what I commanded them and have made a cast idol for themselves."

13And the LORD said to me, "I have seen this people, and they are a stiff-necked people indeed! 14Let me alone, so that I may destroy them and blot out their name from under heaven. And I will make you into a nation stronger and more numerous than they."

15So I turned and went down from the mountain while it was ablaze with fire. And the two tablets of the covenant were in my hands.ᵃ 16When I looked, I saw that you had sinned against the LORD your God; you had made for yourselves an idol cast in the shape of a calf. You had turned aside quickly from the way that the LORD had commanded you. 17So I took the two tablets and threw them out of my hands, breaking them to pieces before your eyes.

18Then once again I fell prostrate before the LORD for forty days and forty nights; I ate no bread and drank no water, because of all the sin you had committed, doing what was evil in the LORD's sight and so provoking him to anger. 19I feared the anger and wrath of the LORD, for he was angry enough with you to destroy you. But again the LORD listened to me. 20And the LORD was angry enough with Aaron to destroy him, but at that time I prayed for Aaron too. 21Also I took that sinful thing of yours, the calf you had made, and burned it in the fire. Then I crushed it and ground it to powder as fine as dust and threw

their own success. That, at least, was the danger, and the reason Moses kept urging, "Remember!" Remember the days of slavery in Egypt, and God's acts in liberating you. Remember the trials of the vast and desolate desert, and God's faithfulness there. Remember your special calling as a treasured possession of God. Do not forget, as a prosperous nation, what you learned as refugees in the Sinai.

God predicted bluntly, "When I have brought them into the land flowing with milk and honey, the land I promised on oath to their forefathers, and when they eat their fill and thrive, they will turn to other gods and worship them, rejecting me and breaking my covenant" (31:20).

As the books following Deuteronomy record, all that God and Moses feared came true. The covenant was irreparably broken. Ultimately, the Israelites received not wealth and happiness but slavery and suffering.

■ A MESSAGE FOR US TODAY

The promises of Deuteronomy were given to a particular people, the Israelites, in a special covenant relationship — a covenant that God prophesied would be broken. The formula was simple: "Do good, get rewarded; do evil, get punished." But Christians of today cannot simply turn to those flagrant promises of wealth and prosperity and apply them directly. Rather, we must look at this book in light of the new covenant introduced by Jesus Christ and spelled out in the New Testament.

When Jesus came, he promised certain rewards for Christians, but he also predicted poverty, rejection and even persecution. Rewards on this earth cannot be reduced to such a simple "Do good, get rewarded; do evil, get punished" formula. (See Hebrews 11 and "What Is True Faith?" page 1068.) Jesus' disciples proved faithful to him, and yet most of them lived through poverty and persecution and died martyrs' deaths. For them, full rewards had to wait until heaven.

Deuteronomy may offer a clue as to why God does not exempt his followers from every bad thing in life. Ironically, prosperity and health may make it harder to depend on God. Moses' fears came true: the Israelites proved least faithful to God after they moved into the prosperity of the promised land. In the desert, at least, they had been forced to lean on God just for daily survival. But after a very short time in Canaan, they forgot about him. There is a grave danger in finally getting what you want.

□ LIFE QUESTIONS:

When do you think most about God: when things are going well or when you are in trouble?

ᵃ 15 Or And I had the two tablets of the covenant with me, one in each hand the dust into a stream that flowed down the mountain.

22You also made the LORD angry at Taberah, at Massah and at Kibroth Hattaavah.

23And when the LORD sent you out from Kadesh Barnea, he said, "Go up and take possession of the land I have given you." But you rebelled against the command of the LORD your God. You did not trust him or obey him. 24You have been rebellious against the LORD ever since I have known you.

25I lay prostrate before the LORD those forty days and forty nights because the LORD had said he would destroy you. 26I prayed to the LORD and said, "O Sovereign LORD, do not destroy your people, your own inheritance that you redeemed by your great power and brought out of Egypt with a mighty hand. 27Remember your servants Abraham, Isaac and Jacob. Overlook the stubbornness of this people, their wickedness and their sin. 28Otherwise, the country from which you brought us will say, 'Because the LORD was not able to take them into the land he had promised them, and because he hated them, he brought them out to put them to death in the desert.' 29But they are your people, your inheritance that you brought out by your great power and your outstretched arm."

■ Tablets Like the First Ones

10 At that time the LORD said to me, "Chisel out two stone tablets like the first ones and come up to me on the mountain. Also make a wooden chest.a 2I will write on the tablets the words that were on the first tablets, which you broke. Then you are to put them in the chest."

3So I made the ark out of acacia wood and chiselled out two stone tablets like the first ones, and I went up on the mountain with the two tablets in my hands. 4The LORD wrote on these tablets what he had written before, the Ten Commandments he had proclaimed to you on the mountain, out of the fire, on the day of the assembly. And the LORD gave them to me. 5Then I came back down the mountain and put the tablets in the ark I had made, as the LORD commanded me, and they are there now.

6(The Israelites travelled from the wells of the Jaakanites to Moserah. There Aaron died and was buried, and Eleazar his son succeeded him as priest. 7From there they travelled to Gudgodah and on to Jotbathah, a land with streams of water. 8At that time the LORD set apart the tribe of Levi to carry the ark of the covenant of the LORD, to stand before the LORD to minister and to pronounce blessings in his name, as they still do today. 9That is why the Levites have no share or inheritance among their brothers; the LORD is their inheritance, as the LORD your God told them.)

10Now I had stayed on the mountain forty days and nights, as I did the first time, and the LORD listened to me at this time also. It was not his will to destroy you. 11"Go," the LORD said to me, "and lead the people on their way, so that they may enter and possess the land that I swore to their fathers to give them."

■ Fear the LORD

12And now, O Israel, what does the LORD your God ask of you but to fear the LORD your God, to walk in all his ways, to love him, to serve the LORD your God with all your heart and with all your soul, 13and to observe the LORD's commands and decrees that I am giving you today for your own good?

10:12 ■ MORE THAN A FEELING

Twelve times Deuteronomy says that we are to love God. In fact, Jesus was quoting Deuteronomy 6:5 when he gave the most important commandment as "Love the Lord your God with all your heart" (Mark 12:30). How can we love when we don't feel loving? In the Bible, love is more than a feeling; it is a decision to serve another person's interest. Only through God's help can this decision be made with "all your heart".

14To the LORD your God belong the heavens, even the highest heavens, the earth and everything in it. 15Yet the LORD set his affection on your forefathers and loved them, and he chose you, their descendants, above all the nations, as it is today. 16Circumcise your hearts, therefore, and do not be stiff-necked any longer. 17For the LORD your God is God of gods and Lord of lords, the great God, mighty and awesome, who shows no partiality and accepts no bribes. 18He defends the cause of the fatherless and the widow, and loves the alien, giving him food and clothing. 19And you are to love those who are aliens, for you yourselves were aliens in Egypt. 20Fear the LORD your God and serve him. Hold fast to him and take your oaths in his name. 21He is your praise; he is your God, who performed for you those great and awesome wonders you saw with your own eyes. 22Your forefathers who went down into Egypt were seventy in all, and now the LORD your God has made you as numerous as the stars in the sky.

■ Love and Obey the LORD

11 Love the LORD your God and keep his requirements, his decrees, his laws and his commands always. 2Remember today that your children were not the ones who saw and experienced the discipline of the LORD your God: his majesty, his mighty hand, his outstretched arm; 3the signs he performed and the things he did in the heart of Egypt, both to Pharaoh king of Egypt and to his whole country; 4what he did to the Egyptian army, to its horses and chariots, how he overwhelmed them with the waters of the Red Seaa as they were pursuing you, and how the LORD brought lasting ruin on them. 5It was not your children who saw what he did for you in the desert until you arrived at this place, 6and what he did to Dathan and Abiram, sons of Eliab the Reubenite, when the earth opened its mouth right in the middle of all Israel and swallowed them up with their households, their tents and every living thing that belonged to them. 7But it was your own eyes that saw all these great things the LORD has done.

8Observe therefore all the commands I am giving

---

a1 That is, an ark   a4 Hebrew Yam Suph; that is, Sea of Reeds you today, so that you may have the strength to go in and take over the land that you are crossing the Jordan to possess, 9and so that you may live long in the land that the LORD swore to your forefathers to give to them and their descendants, a land flowing with milk and honey. 10The land you are entering to take over is not like the land of Egypt, from which you have come, where you planted your seed and irrigated it by foot as in a vegetable garden. 11But the land you are crossing the Jordan to take possession of is a land of mountains and valleys that drinks rain from heaven. 12It is a land the LORD your God cares for; the eyes of the LORD your God are continually on it from the beginning of the year to its end.

13So if you faithfully obey the commands I am giving you today—to love the LORD your God and to serve him with all your heart and with all your soul—14then I will send rain on your land in its season, both autumn and spring rains, so that you may gather in your grain, new wine and oil. 15I will provide grass in the fields for your cattle, and you will eat and be satisfied.

16Be careful, or you will be enticed to turn away and worship other gods and bow down to them. 17Then the LORD's anger will burn against you, and he will shut the heavens so that it will not rain and the ground will yield no produce, and you will soon perish from the good land the LORD is giving you. 18Fix these words of mine in your hearts and minds; tie them as symbols on your hands and bind them on your foreheads. 19Teach them to your children, talking about them when you sit at home and when you walk along the road, when you lie down and when you get up. 20Write them on the door-frames of your houses and on your gates, 21so that your days and the days of your children may be many in the land that the LORD swore to give your forefathers, as many as the days that the heavens are above the earth.

11:18 ■ LAWS ON THE HEAD

Many commentators, both Jewish and Christian, read these sentences figuratively. But strict Jews take them literally. They wear handwritten portions of the Old Testament (including Deuteronomy 6:4–9 and 11:18–20) in a small box strapped to their foreheads, and they also mount them in a box beside the door to their homes. The boxes are called "phylacteries". Jesus referred to the practice (Matthew 23:5), commenting that it could become a showy way of expressing spiritual pride.

22If you carefully observe all these commands I am giving you to follow—to love the LORD your God, to walk in all his ways and to hold fast to him—23then the LORD will drive out all these nations before you, and you will dispossess nations larger and stronger than you. 24Every place where you set your foot will be yours: Your territory will extend from the desert to Lebanon, and from the Euphrates River to the western sea.b 25No man will be able to stand against you. The LORD your God, as he promised you,

will put the terror and fear of you on the whole land, wherever you go.

26See, I am setting before you today a blessing and a curse—27the blessing if you obey the commands of the LORD your God that I am giving you today; 28the curse if you disobey the commands of the LORD your God and turn from the way that I command you today by following other gods, which you have not known. 29When the LORD your God has brought you into the land you are entering to possess, you are to proclaim on Mount Gerizim the blessings, and on Mount Ebal the curses. 30As you know, these mountains are across the Jordan, west of the road,c towards the setting sun, near the great trees of Moreh, in the territory of those Canaanites living in the Arabah in the vicinity of Gilgal. 31You are about to cross the Jordan to enter and take possession of the land the LORD your God is giving you. When you have taken it over and are living there, 32be sure that you obey all the decrees and laws I am setting before you today.

■ The One Place of Worship

12 These are the decrees and laws you must be careful to follow in the land that the LORD, the God of your fathers, has given you to possess—as long as you live in the land. 2Destroy completely all the places on the high mountains and on the hills and under every spreading tree where the nations you are dispossessing worship their gods. 3Break down their altars, smash their sacred stones and burn their Asherah poles in the fire; cut down the idols of their gods and wipe out their names from those places.

12:2 ■ HISTORIC DISCOVERY

The Israelites did not fully follow these instructions on destroying the "high places", which were centres of idol worship. But hundreds of years after this scene with Moses, a dramatic event took place. In the midst of a temple renovation, workers came across an old scroll containing the Book of the Law. Discovery of the book had an electrifying effect on the nation. When King Josiah heard it read, he wept and tore his robes, then called for all the elders to hear the words. The event ushered in a sweeping spiritual revival that included a campaign against idolatry and the "high places". Many scholars believe Deuteronomy was the book that stirred a kingdom (see 2 Kings 22–23 for the full account).

4You must not worship the LORD your God in their way. 5But you are to seek the place the LORD your God will choose from among all your tribes to put his Name there for his dwelling. To that place you must go; 6there bring your burnt offerings and sacrifices, your tithes and special gifts, what you have vowed to give and your freewill offerings, and the firstborn of your herds and flocks. 7There, in the presence of the LORD your God, you and your families shall eat and shall rejoice in everything you have

b24 That is, the Mediterranean   c30 Or Jordan, westward

put your hand to, because the LORD your God has blessed you.

⁸You are not to do as we do here today, everyone as he sees fit, ⁹since you have not yet reached the resting place and the inheritance the LORD your God is giving you. ¹⁰But you will cross the Jordan and settle in the land the LORD your God is giving you as an inheritance, and he will give you rest from all your enemies around you so that you will live in safety. ¹¹Then to the place the LORD your God will choose as a dwelling for his Name—there you are to bring everything I command you: your burnt offerings and sacrifices, your tithes and special gifts, and all the choice possessions you have vowed to the LORD. ¹²And there rejoice before the LORD your God, you, your sons and daughters, your menservants and maidservants, and the Levites from your towns, who have no allotment or inheritance of their own. ¹³Be careful not to sacrifice your burnt offerings anywhere you please. ¹⁴Offer them only at the place the LORD will choose in one of your tribes, and there observe everything I command you.

¹⁵Nevertheless, you may slaughter your animals in any of your towns and eat as much of the meat as you want, as if it were gazelle or deer, according to the blessing the LORD your God gives you. Both the ceremonially unclean and the clean may eat it. ¹⁶But you must not eat the blood; pour it out on the ground like water. ¹⁷You must not eat in your own towns the tithe of your grain and new wine and oil, or the firstborn of your herds and flocks, or whatever you have vowed to give, or your freewill offerings or special gifts. ¹⁸Instead, you are to eat them in the presence of the LORD your God at the place the LORD your God will choose—you, your sons and daughters, your menservants and maidservants, and the Levites from your towns—and you are to rejoice before the LORD your God in everything you put your hand to. ¹⁹Be careful not to neglect the Levites as long as you live in your land.

²⁰When the LORD your God has enlarged your territory as he promised you, and you crave meat and say, "I would like some meat," then you may eat as much of it as you want. ²¹If the place where the LORD your God chooses to put his Name is too far away from you, you may slaughter animals from the herds and flocks the LORD has given you, as I have commanded you, and in your own towns you may eat as much of them as you want. ²²Eat them as you would gazelle or deer. Both the ceremonially unclean and the clean may eat. ²³But be sure you do not eat the blood, because the blood is the life, and you must not eat the life with the meat. ²⁴You must not eat the blood; pour it out on the ground like water. ²⁵Do not eat it, so that it may go well with you and your children after you, because you will be doing what is right in the eyes of the LORD.

²⁶But take your consecrated things and whatever you have vowed to give, and go to the place the LORD will choose. ²⁷Present your burnt offerings on the altar of the LORD your God, both the meat and the blood. The blood of your sacrifices must be poured beside the altar of the LORD your God, but you may eat the meat. ²⁸Be careful to obey all these regulations I am giving you, so that it may always go well

with you and your children after you, because you will be doing what is good and right in the eyes of the LORD your God.

²⁹The LORD your God will cut off before you the nations you are about to invade and dispossess. But when you have driven them out and settled in their land, ³⁰and after they have been destroyed before you, be careful not to be ensnared by enquiring about their gods, saying, "How do these nations serve their gods? We will do the same." ³¹You must not worship the LORD your God in their way, because in worshipping their gods, they do all kinds of detestable things the LORD hates. They even burn their sons and daughters in the fire as sacrifices to their gods.

³²See that you do all I command you; do not add to it or take away from it.

■ Worshipping Other Gods

13 If a prophet, or one who foretells by dreams, appears among you and announces to you a miraculous sign or wonder, ²and if the sign or wonder of which he has spoken takes place, and he says, "Let us follow other gods" (gods you have not known) "and let us worship them," ³you must not listen to the words of that prophet or dreamer. The LORD your God is testing you to find out whether you love him with all your heart and with all your soul. ⁴It is the LORD your God you must follow, and him you must revere. Keep his commands and obey him; serve him and hold fast to him. ⁵That prophet or dreamer must be put to death, because he preached rebellion against the LORD your God, who brought you out of Egypt and redeemed you from the land of slavery; he has tried to turn you from the way the LORD your God commanded you to follow. You must purge the evil from among you.

13:1 ■ TESTING PROPHETS

Lots of people—cult members as well as Christians—claim that God has spoken to them. How do you evaluate those claims? Deuteronomy offers two tests. First, a prediction made in God's name must in fact come true (18:21–22). The second test, given here, matters just as much. If a prediction does come true, but the prophet tries to lead people to worship some other god, that prophet should be rejected.

⁶If your very own brother, or your son or daughter, or the wife you love, or your closest friend secretly entices you, saying, "Let us go and worship other gods" (gods that neither you nor your fathers have known, ⁷gods of the peoples around you, whether near or far, from one end of the land to the other), ⁸do not yield to him or listen to him. Show him no pity. Do not spare him or shield him. ⁹You must certainly put him to death. Your hand must be the first in putting him to death, and then the hands of all the people. ¹⁰Stone him to death, because he tried to turn you away from the LORD your God, who brought you out of Egypt, out of the land of slavery.

¹¹Then all Israel will hear and be afraid, and no-one among you will do such an evil thing again.

¹²If you hear it said about one of the towns the LORD your God is giving you to live in ¹³that wicked men have arisen among you and have led the people of their town astray, saying, "Let us go and worship other gods" (gods you have not known), ¹⁴then you must enquire, probe and investigate it thoroughly. And if it is true and it has been proved that this detestable thing has been done among you, ¹⁵you must certainly put to the sword all who live in that town.

Destroy it completely,ᵃ both its people and its livestock. ¹⁶Gather all the plunder of the town into the middle of the public square and completely burn the town and all its plunder as a whole burnt offering to the LORD your God. It is to remain a ruin for ever, never to be rebuilt. ¹⁷None of those condemned thingsᵃ shall be found in your hands, so that the LORD will turn from his fierce anger; he will show you mercy, have compassion on you, and increase your numbers, as he promised on oath to your forefathers, ¹⁸because you obey the LORD your God,

■ WHO NEEDS LAWS?
LOVE MAKES THE DIFFERENCE IN THIS RULE BOOK

INSIGHT

BE CAREFUL TO OBEY ALL THESE REGULATIONS I AM GIVING YOU, SO THAT IT MAY ALWAYS GO WELL WITH YOU AND YOUR CHILDREN AFTER YOU, BECAUSE YOU WILL BE DOING WHAT IS GOOD AND RIGHT IN THE EYES OF THE LORD YOUR GOD. ■ 12:28

Deuteronomy repeats verbatim many of the laws given in Exodus, Leviticus and Numbers. Yet it is far from a rule book. A different spirit pervades it: the spirit of love. The rules in Deuteronomy read more like a guide on "How to Have a Successful Family" than, say, a car maintenance manual. To keep up a car you need only follow the rules. To maintain a close personal relationship you need more – you need love.

■ WHAT MAKES DEUTERONOMY DIFFERENT
Deuteronomy focuses on motives: *why* people should obey laws. The preceding three books barely mentioned the love of God for his people, but Deuteronomy again and again refers to it (see 4:37; 7:7–8; 10:15; 23:5). The author portrays God as a father with his children, as a mother who gives them life, as an eagle hovering over its young.

In return, God asks for obedience based on love, not on a sense of duty. At least 15 times in the book Moses tells the Israelites to love God and cling to him. God wants not just an outward conformity, but an obedience that comes from the heart. (Later, in summing up the Old Testament, Jesus quoted the first and greatest commandment from Deuteronomy: "Love the Lord your God with all your heart and with all your soul and with all your mind" [Matthew 22:37; Deuteronomy 6:5].)

■ RESTATING THE NEGATIVES
Deuteronomy also hints at why laws are needed in the first place. Moses stated the principle directly, "The LORD commanded us to obey all these decrees and to fear the LORD our God, so that we might always prosper and be kept alive,

as is the case today" (6:24). In other words, the laws were given for the Israelites' own good.

Most of the Ten Commandments were given in a negative form, "You shall not". But each of these negative statements protects a privileged relationship between two people or a person and God. For example, "Do not murder" could be restated, "Human life is sacred and has enormous worth. Respect such life as the image of God, and defend it." Other commandments protect marriage, private property, honesty and the day set aside to worship God.

■ NEVER FORGET
Moses could not have emphasised the laws more strongly. "These commandments that I give you today are to be upon your hearts," he said. "Impress them on your children. Talk about them when you sit at home and when you walk along the road, when you lie down and when you get up" (6:6–7).

Moses wanted to make sure the Israelites would not possibly forget the laws. He instructed the priests to gather the whole nation together to hear them read aloud every seven years (31:9–13). Any king of Israel was required, as one of his first acts, to write out the laws by hand (17:18–19).

One last visual reminder served to impress the laws on the Israelites' minds. The priests wrote them in bold letters on stones covered with plaster. As the tribes marched across the Jordan River into the new land, they passed between the writing-covered stones (27:1–8).

No-one in Israel could plead ignorance of what God required of them – his rules were carved in stone. As history would prove, obeying the rules was another matter.

□ LIFE QUESTIONS:
Read over the Ten Commandments in Deuteronomy 5. How do they help us? What "rights" are they protecting?

ᵃ 15,17 The Hebrew term refers to the irrevocable giving over of things or persons to the LORD, often by totally destroying them.

keeping all his commands that I am giving you today and doing what is right in his eyes.

■ Clean and Unclean Food

14 You are the children of the LORD your God. Do not cut yourselves or shave the front of your heads for the dead, ²for you are a people holy to the LORD your God. Out of all the peoples on the face of the earth, the LORD has chosen you to be his treasured possession.

³Do not eat any detestable thing. ⁴These are the animals you may eat: the ox, the sheep, the goat, ⁵the deer, the gazelle, the roe deer, the wild goat, the ibex, the antelope and the mountain sheep.*ᵃ* ⁶You may eat any animal that has a split hoof divided in two and that chews the cud. ⁷However, of those that chew the cud or that have a split hoof completely divided you may not eat the camel, the rabbit or the coney.*ᵇ* Although they chew the cud, they do not have a split hoof; they are ceremonially unclean for you. ⁸The pig is also unclean; although it has a split hoof, it does not chew the cud. You are not to eat their meat or touch their carcasses.

⁹Of all the creatures living in the water, you may eat any that has fins and scales. ¹⁰But anything that does not have fins and scales you may not eat; for you it is unclean.

¹¹You may eat any clean bird. ¹²But these you may not eat: the eagle, the vulture, the black vulture, ¹³the red kite, the black kite, any kind of falcon, ¹⁴any kind of raven, ¹⁵the horned owl, the screech owl, the gull, any kind of hawk, ¹⁶the little owl, the great owl, the white owl, ¹⁷the desert owl, the osprey, the cormorant, ¹⁸the stork, any kind of heron, the hoopoe and the bat.

¹⁹All flying insects that swarm are unclean to you; do not eat them. ²⁰But any winged creature that is clean you may eat.

²¹Do not eat anything you find already dead. You may give it to an alien living in any of your towns, and he may eat it, or you may sell it to a foreigner. But you are a people holy to the LORD your God.

Do not cook a young goat in its mother's milk.

■ Tithes

²²Be sure to set aside a tenth of all that your fields produce each year. ²³Eat the tithe of your grain, new wine and oil, and the firstborn of your herds and flocks in the presence of the LORD your God at the place he will choose as a dwelling for his Name, so that you may learn to revere the LORD your God always. ²⁴But if that place is too distant and you have been blessed by the LORD your God and cannot carry your tithe (because the place where the LORD will choose to put his Name is so far away), ²⁵then exchange your tithe for silver, and take the silver with you and go to the place the LORD your God will choose. ²⁶Use the silver to buy whatever you like: cattle, sheep, wine or other fermented drink, or anything you wish. Then you and your household shall eat there in the presence of the LORD your God and rejoice. ²⁷And do not neglect the Levites living in your towns, for they have no allotment or inheritance of their own.

²⁸At the end of every three years, bring all the tithes of that year's produce and store it in your towns, ²⁹so that the Levites (who have no allotment or inheritance of their own) and the aliens, the fatherless and the widows who live in your towns may come and eat and be satisfied, and so that the LORD your God may bless you in all the work of your hands.

14:28–29 ■ TITHE TO THE POOR
Each year the Israelites presented a tithe of produce as an offering to God. Every third year the tithe would be distributed to needy people. God accepted the gifts to these people as an offering to himself. The principle behind this practice was later powerfully expressed in a parable by Jesus (Matthew 25:31–46), who said, "I tell you the truth, whatever you did for one of the least of these brothers of mine, you did for me."

■ The Year for Cancelling Debts

15 At the end of every seven years you must cancel debts. ²This is how it is to be done: Every creditor shall cancel the loan he has made to his fellow Israelite. He shall not require payment from his fellow Israelite or brother, because the LORD's time for cancelling debts has been proclaimed. ³You may require payment from a foreigner, but you must cancel any debt your brother owes you. ⁴However, there should be no poor among you, for in the land the LORD your God is giving you to possess as your inheritance, he will richly bless you, ⁵if only you fully obey the LORD your God and are careful to follow all these commands I am giving you today. ⁶For the LORD your God will bless you as he has promised, and you will lend to many nations but will borrow from none. You will rule over many nations but none will rule over you.

⁷If there is a poor man among your brothers in any of the towns of the land that the LORD your God is giving you, do not be hard-hearted or tight-fisted towards your poor brother. ⁸Rather be open-handed and freely lend him whatever he needs. ⁹Be careful not to harbour this wicked thought: "The seventh year, the year for cancelling debts, is near," so that you do not show ill will towards your needy brother and give him nothing. He may then appeal to the LORD against you, and you will be found guilty of sin. ¹⁰Give generously to him and do so without a grudging heart; then because of this the LORD your God will bless you in all your work and in everything you put your hand to. ¹¹There will always be poor people in the land. Therefore I command you to be open-handed towards your brothers and towards the poor and needy in your land.

■ Freeing Servants

¹²If a fellow Hebrew, a man or woman, sells himself to you and serves you six years, in the seventh year you must let him go free. ¹³And when you release him, do not send him away empty-handed. ¹⁴Supply him liberally from your flock, your threshing-floor and your winepress. Give to him as

---

ᵃ5 The precise identification of some of the birds and animals in this chapter is uncertain.   *ᵇ7 That is, the hyrax or rock badger* the LORD your God has blessed you. [15]Remember that you were slaves in Egypt and the LORD your God redeemed you. That is why I give you this command today.

15:11 ■ ANY POOR PEOPLE?

At first glance, this verse seems to contradict verse 4, which says there should be no poor people in Israel. Moses knew the difference between what *should* happen and what *will* happen. God's blessings in the promised land ought to have eliminated poverty — if the Israelites had obeyed completely. But since some people always fall short, poverty remains a problem. (Jesus confirmed this in a passing remark in Matthew 26:11.) As a result, in our time as in Moses', generosity is essential.

[16]But if your servant says to you, "I do not want to leave you," because he loves you and your family and is well off with you, [17]then take an awl and push it through his ear lobe into the door, and he will become your servant for life. Do the same for your maidservant.

[18]Do not consider it a hardship to set your servant free, because his service to you these six years has been worth twice as much as that of a hired hand. And the LORD your God will bless you in everything you do.

■ The Firstborn Animals

[19]Set apart for the LORD your God every firstborn male of your herds and flocks. Do not put the firstborn of your oxen to work, and do not shear the firstborn of your sheep. [20]Each year you and your family are to eat them in the presence of the LORD your God at the place he will choose. [21]If an animal has a defect, is lame or blind, or has any serious flaw, you must not sacrifice it to the LORD your God. [22]You are to eat it in your own towns. Both the ceremonially unclean and the clean may eat it, as if it were gazelle or deer. [23]But you must not eat the blood; pour it out on the ground like water.

■ Passover

16 Observe the month of Abib and celebrate the Passover of the LORD your God, because in the month of Abib he brought you out of Egypt by night. [2]Sacrifice as the Passover to the LORD your God an animal from your flock or herd at the place the LORD will choose as a dwelling for his Name. [3]Do not eat it with bread made with yeast, but for seven days eat unleavened bread, the bread of affliction, because you left Egypt in haste — so that all the days of your life you may remember the time of your departure from Egypt. [4]Let no yeast be found in your possession in all your land for seven days. Do not let any of the meat you sacrifice on the evening of the first day remain until morning.

[5]You must not sacrifice the Passover in any town the LORD your God gives you [6]except in the place he will choose as a dwelling for his Name. There you must sacrifice the Passover in the evening, when the sun goes down, on the anniversary[a] of your departure from Egypt. [7]Roast it and eat it at the place the LORD your God will choose. Then in the morning return to your tents. [8]For six days eat unleavened bread and on the seventh day hold an assembly to the LORD your God and do no work.

■ Feast of Weeks

[9]Count off seven weeks from the time you begin to put the sickle to the standing corn. [10]Then celebrate the Feast of Weeks to the LORD your God by giving a freewill offering in proportion to the blessings the LORD your God has given you. [11]And rejoice before the LORD your God at the place he will choose as a dwelling for his Name — you, your sons and daughters, your menservants and maidservants, the Levites in your towns, and the aliens, the fatherless and the widows living among you. [12]Remember that you were slaves in Egypt, and follow carefully these decrees.

■ Feast of Tabernacles

[13]Celebrate the Feast of Tabernacles for seven days after you have gathered the produce of your threshing-floor and your winepress. [14]Be joyful at your Feast — you, your sons and daughters, your menservants and maidservants, and the Levites, the aliens, the fatherless and the widows who live in your towns. [15]For seven days celebrate the Feast to the LORD your God at the place the LORD will choose. For the LORD your God will bless you in all your harvest and in all the work of your hands, and your joy will be complete.

[16]Three times a year all your men must appear before the LORD your God at the place he will choose: at the Feast of Unleavened Bread, the Feast of Weeks and the Feast of Tabernacles. No man should appear before the LORD empty-handed: [17]Each of you must bring a gift in proportion to the way the LORD your God has blessed you.

■ Judges

[18]Appoint judges and officials for each of your tribes in every town the LORD your God is giving you, and they shall judge the people fairly. [19]Do not pervert justice or show partiality. Do not accept a bribe, for a bribe blinds the eyes of the wise and twists the words of the righteous. [20]Follow justice and justice alone, so that you may live and possess the land the LORD your God is giving you.

■ Worshipping Other Gods

[21]Do not set up any wooden Asherah pole[b] beside the altar you build to the LORD your God, [22]and do not erect a sacred stone, for these the LORD your God hates.

17 Do not sacrifice to the LORD your God an ox or a sheep that has any defect or flaw in it, for that would be detestable to him.

[2]If a man or woman living among you in one of the towns the LORD gives you is found doing evil in the eyes of the LORD your God in violation of his covenant, [3]and contrary to my command has worshipped other gods, bowing down to them or to the sun or the moon or the stars of the sky, [4]and this has

---

[a]6 Or down, at the time of day   [b]21 Or Do not plant any tree dedicated to Asherah

been brought to your attention, then you must investigate it thoroughly. If it is true and it has been proved that this detestable thing has been done in Israel, [5]take the man or woman who has done this evil deed to your city gate and stone that person to death. [6]On the testimony of two or three witnesses a man shall be put to death, but no-one shall be put to death on the testimony of only one witness. [7]The hands of the witnesses must be the first in putting him to death, and then the hands of all the people. You must purge the evil from among you.

Law Courts

[8]If cases come before your courts that are too difficult for you to judge — whether bloodshed, lawsuits or assaults — take them to the place the LORD your God will choose. [9]Go to the priests, who are Levites, and to the judge who is in office at that time. Enquire of them and they will give you the verdict. [10]You must act according to the decisions they give you at the place the LORD will choose. Be careful to do everything they direct you to do. [11]Act according to the law they teach you and the decisions they give you. Do not turn aside from what they tell you, to the right or to the left. [12]The man who shows contempt for the judge or for the priest who stands ministering there to the LORD your God must be put to death. You must purge the evil from Israel. [13]All the people will hear and be afraid, and will not be contemptuous again.

The King

[14]When you enter the land the LORD your God is giving you and have taken possession of it and settled in it, and you say, "Let us set a king over us like all the nations around us," [15]be sure to appoint over you the king the LORD your God chooses. He must be from among your own brothers. Do not place a foreigner over you, one who is not a brother Israelite. [16]The king, moreover, must not acquire great numbers of horses for himself or make the people return to Egypt to get more of them, for the LORD has told you, "You are not to go back that way again." [17]He must not take many wives, or his heart will be led astray. He must not accumulate large amounts of silver and gold.

17:15 ■ PRESCRIPTION FOR A KING
Until now, the Bible has not mentioned the possibility of an Israelite king. But here, long before the nation actually got a king, God lays down his prescription for a good one. The list of qualities hardly fits the normal image of a king — or the kind of person the Israelites' descendants usually got.

[18]When he takes the throne of his kingdom, he is to write for himself on a scroll a copy of this law, taken from that of the priests, who are Levites. [19]It is to be with him, and he is to read it all the days of his life so that he may learn to revere the LORD his God and follow carefully all the words of this law and these decrees [20]and not consider himself better

than his brothers and turn from the law to the right or to the left. Then he and his descendants will reign a long time over his kingdom in Israel.

Offerings for Priests and Levites

18 The priests, who are Levites — indeed the whole tribe of Levi — are to have no allotment or inheritance with Israel. They shall live on the offerings made to the LORD by fire, for that is their inheritance. [2]They shall have no inheritance among their brothers; the LORD is their inheritance, as he promised them.

[3]This is the share due to the priests from the people who sacrifice a bull or a sheep: the shoulder, the jowls and the inner parts. [4]You are to give them the firstfruits of your grain, new wine and oil, and the first wool from the shearing of your sheep, [5]for the LORD your God has chosen them and their descendants out of all your tribes to stand and minister in the LORD's name always.

[6]If a Levite moves from one of your towns anywhere in Israel where he is living, and comes in all earnestness to the place the LORD will choose, [7]he may minister in the name of the LORD his God like all his fellow Levites who serve there in the presence of the LORD. [8]He is to share equally in their benefits even though he has received money from the sale of family possessions.

Detestable Practices

[9]When you enter the land the LORD your God is giving you, do not learn to imitate the detestable ways of the nations there. [10]Let no-one be found among you who sacrifices his son or daughter in[a] the fire, who practises divination or sorcery, interprets omens, engages in witchcraft, [11]or casts spells, or who is a medium or spiritist or who consults the dead. [12]Anyone who does these things is detestable to the LORD, and because of these detestable practices the LORD your God will drive out those nations before you. [13]You must be blameless before the LORD your God.

18:9 ■ "DETESTABLE WAYS"
This brief paragraph gives a preview of some of the "detestable ways" the Israelites would encounter in the promised land. Child sacrifice was a common part of worship in Canaan. God had already stated that the Israelites' invasion was a form of punishment on the Canaanites for these kinds of practices (9:4).

The Prophet

[14]The nations you will dispossess listen to those who practise sorcery or divination. But as for you, the LORD your God has not permitted you to do so. [15]The LORD your God will raise up for you a prophet like me from among your own brothers. You must listen to him. [16]For this is what you asked of the LORD your God at Horeb on the day of the assembly when you said, "Let us not hear the voice of the LORD our God nor see this great fire any more, or we will die." [17]The LORD said to me: "What they say is good. [18]I

---
[a] 10 Or who makes his son or daughter pass through

will raise up for them a prophet like you from among their brothers; I will put my words in his mouth, and he will tell them everything I command him. ¹⁹If anyone does not listen to my words that the prophet speaks in my name, I myself will call him to account. ²⁰But a prophet who presumes to speak in my name anything I have not commanded him to say, or a prophet who speaks in the name of other gods, must be put to death."

²¹You may say to yourselves, "How can we know when a message has not been spoken by the LORD?" ²²If what a prophet proclaims in the name of the LORD does not take place or come true, that is a message the LORD has not spoken. That prophet has spoken presumptuously. Do not be afraid of him.

■ Cities of Refuge

19 When the LORD your God has destroyed the nations whose land he is giving you, and when you have driven them out and settled in their towns and houses, ²then set aside for yourselves three cities centrally located in the land the LORD your God is giving you to possess. ³Build roads to them and divide into three parts the land the LORD your God is giving you as an inheritance, so that anyone who kills a man may flee there.

⁴This is the rule concerning the man who kills another and flees there to save his life—one who kills his neighbour unintentionally, without malice aforethought. ⁵For instance, a man may go into the forest with his neighbour to cut wood, and as he swings his axe to fell a tree, the head may fly off and hit his neighbour and kill him. That man may flee to one of these cities and save his life. ⁶Otherwise, the avenger of blood might pursue him in a rage, overtake him if the distance is too great, and kill him even though he is not deserving of death, since he did it to his neighbour without malice aforethought. ⁷This is why I command you to set aside for yourselves three cities.

⁸If the LORD your God enlarges your territory, as he promised on oath to your forefathers, and gives you the whole land he promised them, ⁹because you carefully follow all these laws I command you today—to love the LORD your God and to walk always in his ways—then you are to set aside three more cities. ¹⁰Do this so that innocent blood will not be shed in your land, which the LORD your God is giving you as your inheritance, and so that you will not be guilty of bloodshed.

¹¹But if a man hates his neighbour and lies in wait for him, assaults and kills him, and then flees to one of these cities, ¹²the elders of his town shall send for him, bring him back from the city, and hand him over to the avenger of blood to die. ¹³Show him no pity. You must purge from Israel the guilt of shedding innocent blood, so that it may go well with you.

¹⁴Do not move your neighbour's boundary stone set up by your predecessors in the inheritance you receive in the land the LORD your God is giving you to possess.

■ Witnesses

¹⁵One witness is not enough to convict a man accused of any crime or offence he may have committed. A matter must be established by the testimony of two or three witnesses.

¹⁶If a malicious witness takes the stand to accuse a man of a crime, ¹⁷the two men involved in the dispute must stand in the presence of the LORD before the priests and the judges who are in office at the time. ¹⁸The judges must make a thorough investigation, and if the witness proves to be a liar, giving false testimony against his brother, ¹⁹then do to him as he intended to do to his brother. You must purge the evil from among you. ²⁰The rest of the people will hear of this and be afraid, and never again will such an evil thing be done among you. ²¹Show no pity: life for life, eye for eye, tooth for tooth, hand for hand, foot for foot.

■ Going to War

20 When you go to war against your enemies and see horses and chariots and an army greater than yours, do not be afraid of them, because the LORD your God, who brought you up out of Egypt, will be with you. ²When you are about to go into battle, the priest shall come forward and address the army. ³He shall say: "Hear, O Israel, today you are going into battle against your enemies. Do not be faint-hearted or afraid; do not be terrified or give way to panic before them. ⁴For the LORD your God is the one who goes with you to fight for you against your enemies to give you victory."

⁵The officers shall say to the army: "Has anyone built a new house and not dedicated it? Let him go home, or he may die in battle and someone else may dedicate it. ⁶Has anyone planted a vineyard and not begun to enjoy it? Let him go home, or he may die in battle and someone else enjoy it. ⁷Has anyone become pledged to a woman and not married her? Let him go home, or he may die in battle and someone else marry her." ⁸Then the officers shall add, "Is any man afraid or faint-hearted? Let him go home so that his brothers will not become disheartened too." ⁹When the officers have finished speaking to the army, they shall appoint commanders over it.

20:5 ■ UNCOMMON MILITARY RULES
The Israelites gained a reputation as fierce and bloody fighters. Yet Moses' instructions in this chapter defied normal military practice. Soldiers with new homes, new vineyards, and new fiancées—or even just plain scared soldiers—got exemptions from fighting. And before attacking any city, the army was to make a peace offer.

---

¹⁰When you march up to attack a city, make its people an offer of peace. ¹¹If they accept and open their gates, all the people in it shall be subject to forced labour and shall work for you. ¹²If they refuse to make peace and they engage you in battle, lay siege to that city. ¹³When the LORD your God delivers it into your hand, put to the sword all the men in it. ¹⁴As for the women, the children, the livestock and everything else in the city, you may take these as plunder for yourselves. And you may use the plunder the LORD your God gives you from your enemies.

¹⁵This is how you are to treat all the cities that are at a distance from you and do not belong to the nations nearby.

¹⁶However, in the cities of the nations the LORD your God is giving you as an inheritance, do not leave alive anything that breathes. ¹⁷Completely destroy*a* them—the Hittites, Amorites, Canaanites, Perizzites, Hivites and Jebusites—as the LORD your God has commanded you. ¹⁸Otherwise, they will teach you to follow all the detestable things they do in worshipping their gods, and you will sin against the LORD your God.

¹⁹When you lay siege to a city for a long time, fighting against it to capture it, do not destroy its trees by putting an axe to them, because you can eat their fruit. Do not cut them down. Are the trees of the field people, that you should besiege them?*b* ²⁰However, you may cut down trees that you know are not fruit trees and use them to build siege works until the city at war with you falls.

■ Atonement for an Unsolved Murder

21 If a man is found slain, lying in a field in the land the LORD your God is giving you to possess, and it is not known who killed him, ²your elders and judges shall go out and measure the distance from the body to the neighbouring towns. ³Then the elders of the town nearest the body shall take a heifer that has never been worked and has never worn a yoke ⁴and lead her down to a valley that has not been ploughed or planted and where there is a flowing stream. There in the valley they are to break the heifer's neck. ⁵The priests, the sons of Levi, shall step forward, for the LORD your God has chosen them to minister and to pronounce blessings in the name of the LORD and to decide all cases of dispute and assault. ⁶Then all the elders of the town nearest the body shall wash their hands over the heifer whose neck was broken in the valley, ⁷and they shall declare: "Our hands did not shed this blood, nor did our eyes see it done. ⁸Accept this atonement for your people Israel, whom you have redeemed, O LORD, and do not hold your people guilty of the blood of an innocent man." And the bloodshed will be atoned for. ⁹So you will purge from yourselves the guilt of shedding innocent blood, since you have done what is right in the eyes of the LORD.

■ Marrying a Captive Woman

¹⁰When you go to war against your enemies and the LORD your God delivers them into your hands and you take captives, ¹¹if you notice among the captives a beautiful woman and are attracted to her, you may take her as your wife. ¹²Bring her into your home and make her shave her head, trim her nails ¹³and put aside the clothes she was wearing when captured. After she has lived in your house and mourned her father and mother for a full month, then you may go to her and be her husband and she shall be your wife. ¹⁴If you are not pleased with her, let her go wherever she wishes. You must not sell her or treat her as a slave, since you have dishonoured her.

■ The Right of the Firstborn

¹⁵If a man has two wives, and he loves one but not the other, and both bear him sons but the firstborn is the son of the wife he does not love, ¹⁶when he wills his property to his sons, he must not give the rights of the firstborn to the son of the wife he loves in preference to his actual firstborn, the son of the wife he does not love. ¹⁷He must acknowledge the son of his unloved wife as the firstborn by giving him a double share of all he has. That son is the first sign of his father's strength. The right of the firstborn belongs to him.

■ A Rebellious Son

¹⁸If a man has a stubborn and rebellious son who does not obey his father and mother and will not listen to them when they discipline him, ¹⁹his father and mother shall take hold of him and bring him to the elders at the gate of his town. ²⁰They shall say to the elders, "This son of ours is stubborn and rebellious. He will not obey us. He is a profligate and a drunkard." ²¹Then all the men of his town shall stone him to death. You must purge the evil from among you. All Israel will hear of it and be afraid.

■ Various Laws

²²If a man guilty of a capital offence is put to death and his body is hung on a tree, ²³you must not leave his body on the tree overnight. Be sure to bury him that same day, because anyone who is hung on a tree is under God's curse. You must not desecrate the land the LORD your God is giving you as an inheritance.

22 If you see your brother's ox or sheep straying, do not ignore it but be sure to take it back to him. ²If the brother does not live near you or if you do not know who he is, take it home with you and keep it until he comes looking for it. Then give it back to him. ³Do the same if you find your brother's donkey or his cloak or anything he loses. Do not ignore it.

22:1 ■ RESPECT FOR NATURE
The laws in Deuteronomy demonstrate God's concern that nature be treated with respect. In his instructions on war, Moses ordered those who laid siege to a city to choose carefully which trees to cut down (20:19). God's concern for the weak and helpless extended into the animal kingdom, for the law protected oxen, donkeys, and even birds (22:1–7).

---

⁴If you see your brother's donkey or his ox fallen on the road, do not ignore it. Help him to get it to its feet.

⁵A woman must not wear men's clothing, nor a man wear women's clothing, for the LORD your God detests anyone who does this.

⁶If you come across a bird's nest beside the road, either in a tree or on the ground, and the mother is sitting on the young or on the eggs, do not take the mother with the young. ⁷You may take the young,

---

a 17 The Hebrew term refers to the irrevocable giving over of things or persons to the LORD, often by totally destroying them.   b 19 Or down to use in the siege, for the fruit trees are for the benefit of man.

but be sure to let the mother go, so that it may go well with you and you may have a long life.

⁸When you build a new house, make a parapet around your roof so that you may not bring the guilt of bloodshed on your house if someone falls from the roof.

⁹Do not plant two kinds of seed in your vineyard; if you do, not only the crops you plant but also the fruit of the vineyard will be defiled.ᵃ

¹⁰Do not plough with an ox and a donkey yoked together.

¹¹Do not wear clothes of wool and linen woven together.

¹²Make tassels on the four corners of the cloak you wear.

■ Marriage Violations

¹³If a man takes a wife and, after lying with her, dislikes her ¹⁴and slanders her and gives her a bad name, saying, "I married this woman, but when I approached her, I did not find proof of her virginity," ¹⁵then the girl's father and mother shall bring proof that she was a virgin to the town elders at the gate. ¹⁶The girl's father will say to the elders, "I gave my daughter in marriage to this man, but he dislikes her. ¹⁷Now he has slandered her and said, 'I did not find your daughter to be a virgin.' But here is the proof of my daughter's virginity." Then her parents shall display the cloth before the elders of the town, ¹⁸and the elders shall take the man and punish him. ¹⁹They shall fine him a hundred shekels of silverᵇ and give them to the girl's father, because this man has given an Israelite virgin a bad name. She shall continue to be his wife; he must not divorce her as long as he lives.

²⁰If, however, the charge is true and no proof of the girl's virginity can be found, ²¹she shall be brought to the door of her father's house and there the men of her town shall stone her to death. She has done a disgraceful thing in Israel by being promiscuous while still in her father's house. You must purge the evil from among you.

²²If a man is found sleeping with another man's wife, both the man who slept with her and the woman must die. You must purge the evil from Israel.

²³If a man happens to meet in a town a virgin pledged to be married and he sleeps with her, ²⁴you shall take both of them to the gate of that town and stone them to death—the girl because she was in a town and did not scream for help, and the man because he violated another man's wife. You must purge the evil from among you.

²⁵But if out in the country a man happens to meet a girl pledged to be married and rapes her, only the man who has done this shall die. ²⁶Do nothing to the girl; she has committed no sin deserving death. This case is like that of someone who attacks and murders his neighbour, ²⁷for the man found the girl out in the country, and though the betrothed girl screamed, there was no-one to rescue her.

²⁸If a man happens to meet a virgin who is not pledged to be married and rapes her and they are discovered, ²⁹he shall pay the girl's father fifty shekels of silver.ᶜ He must marry the girl, for he has

violated her. He can never divorce her as long as he lives.

³⁰A man is not to marry his father's wife; he must not dishonour his father's bed.

■ Exclusion From the Assembly

23 No-one who has been emasculated by crushing or cutting may enter the assembly of the LORD.

²No-one born of a forbidden marriageᵃ nor any of his descendants may enter the assembly of the LORD, even down to the tenth generation.

³No Ammonite or Moabite or any of his descendants may enter the assembly of the LORD, even down to the tenth generation. ⁴For they did not come to meet you with bread and water on your way when you came out of Egypt, and they hired Balaam son of Beor from Pethor in Aram Naharaimᵇ to pronounce a curse on you. ⁵However, the LORD your God would not listen to Balaam but turned the curse into a blessing for you, because the LORD your God loves you. ⁶Do not seek a treaty of friendship with them as long as you live.

⁷Do not abhor an Edomite, for he is your brother. Do not abhor an Egyptian, because you lived as an alien in his country. ⁸The third generation of children born to them may enter the assembly of the LORD.

■ Uncleanness in the Camp

⁹When you are encamped against your enemies, keep away from everything impure. ¹⁰If one of your men is unclean because of a nocturnal emission, he is to go outside the camp and stay there. ¹¹But as evening approaches he is to wash himself, and at sunset he may return to the camp.

¹²Designate a place outside the camp where you can go to relieve yourself. ¹³As part of your equipment have something to dig with, and when you relieve yourself, dig a hole and cover up your excrement. ¹⁴For the LORD your God moves about in your camp to protect you and to deliver your enemies to you. Your camp must be holy, so that he will not see among you anything indecent and turn away from you.

■ Miscellaneous Laws

¹⁵If a slave has taken refuge with you, do not hand him over to his master. ¹⁶Let him live among you wherever he likes and in whatever town he chooses. Do not oppress him.

¹⁷No Israelite man or woman is to become a shrine-prostitute. ¹⁸You must not bring the earnings of a female prostitute or of a male prostituteᶜ into the house of the LORD your God to pay any vow, because the LORD your God detests them both.

¹⁹Do not charge your brother interest, whether on money or food or anything else that may earn interest. ²⁰You may charge a foreigner interest, but not a brother Israelite, so that the LORD your God may bless you in everything you put your hand to in the land you are entering to possess.

²¹If you make a vow to the LORD your God, do not be slow to pay it, for the LORD your God will certainly demand it of you and you will be guilty of sin.

ᵃ 9 Or be forfeited to the sanctuary   ᵇ 19 That is, about 2½ pounds (about 1 kilogram)   ᶜ 29 That is, about 1¼ pounds (about 0.6 kilogram)
ᵃ 2 Or one of illegitimate birth   ᵇ 4 That is, North-west Mesopotamia   ᶜ 18 Hebrew of a dog

22But if you refrain from making a vow, you will not be guilty. 23Whatever your lips utter you must be sure to do, because you made your vow freely to the LORD your God with your own mouth.

24If you enter your neighbour's vineyard, you may eat all the grapes you want, but do not put any in your basket. 25If you enter your neighbour's cornfield, you may pick the ears with your hands, but you must not put a sickle to his standing corn.

24 If a man marries a woman who becomes displeasing to him because he finds something indecent about her, and he writes her a certificate of divorce, gives it to her and sends her from his house, 2and if after she leaves his house she becomes the wife of another man, 3and her second husband dislikes her and writes her a certificate of divorce, gives it to her and sends her from his house, or if he dies, 4then her first husband, who divorced her, is not allowed to marry her again after she has been defiled. That would be detestable in the eyes of the LORD. Do not bring sin upon the land the LORD your God is giving you as an inheritance.

5If a man has recently married, he must not be sent to war or have any other duty laid on him. For one year he is to be free to stay at home and bring happiness to the wife he has married.

6Do not take a pair of millstones—not even the upper one—as security for a debt, because that would be taking a man's livelihood as security.

24:6 ■ RESPECT PEOPLE, NOT MONEY

Old Testament laws contained many provisions to protect people from exploitation. Israelites could not charge each other interest for loans (Exodus 22:25). And Deuteronomy set limits on the "collateral", or pledge, that secured a loan. Here, the lender could not accept a millstone, for that would threaten the debtor's livelihood. Verses 10–13 show further safeguards. The debtor was allowed to keep everything necessary for living. And the lender could not even enter the debtor's house to get his pledge.

7If a man is caught kidnapping one of his brother Israelites and treats him as a slave or sells him, the kidnapper must die. You must purge the evil from among you.

8In cases of leprousa diseases be very careful to do exactly as the priests, who are Levites, instruct you. You must follow carefully what I have commanded them. 9Remember what the LORD your God did to Miriam along the way after you came out of Egypt.

10When you make a loan of any kind to your neighbour, do not go into his house to get what he is offering as a pledge. 11Stay outside and let the man to whom you are making the loan bring the pledge out to you. 12If the man is poor, do not go to sleep with his pledge in your possession. 13Return his cloak to him by sunset so that he may sleep in it. Then he will thank you, and it will be regarded as a righteous act in the sight of the LORD your God.

14Do not take advantage of a hired man who is poor and needy, whether he is a brother Israelite or an alien living in one of your towns. 15Pay him his wages each day before sunset, because he is poor and is counting on it. Otherwise he may cry to the LORD against you, and you will be guilty of sin.

16Fathers shall not be put to death for their children, nor children put to death for their fathers; each is to die for his own sin.

17Do not deprive the alien or the fatherless of justice, or take the cloak of the widow as a pledge. 18Remember that you were slaves in Egypt and the LORD your God redeemed you from there. That is why I command you to do this.

19When you are harvesting in your field and you overlook a sheaf, do not go back to get it. Leave it for the alien, the fatherless and the widow, so that the LORD your God may bless you in all the work of your hands. 20When you beat the olives from your trees, do not go over the branches a second time. Leave what remains for the alien, the fatherless and the widow. 21When you harvest the grapes in your vineyard, do not go over the vines again. Leave what remains for the alien, the fatherless and the widow. 22Remember that you were slaves in Egypt. That is why I command you to do this.

24:19 ■ DON'T FORGET THE POOR

Chapter 24 contains some of the regulations expressly designed to protect the poor. One, called gleaning, is still practised today in a modern form. Certain religious organisations in America contract with farmers to harvest their "wasted" or abandoned crops in order to feed the poor. God's laws built a concern for the poor into the Israelites' daily routine.

25 When men have a dispute, they are to take it to court and the judges will decide the case, acquitting the innocent and condemning the guilty. 2If the guilty man deserves to be beaten, the judge shall make him lie down and have him flogged in his presence with the number of lashes his crime deserves, 3but he must not give him more than forty lashes. If he is flogged more than that, your brother will be degraded in your eyes.

4Do not muzzle an ox while it is treading out the grain.

5If brothers are living together and one of them dies without a son, his widow must not marry outside the family. Her husband's brother shall take her and marry her and fulfil the duty of a brother-in-law to her. 6The first son she bears shall carry on the name of the dead brother so that his name will not be blotted out from Israel.

7However, if a man does not want to marry his brother's wife, she shall go to the elders at the town gate and say, "My husband's brother refuses to carry on his brother's name in Israel. He will not fulfil the duty of a brother-in-law to me." 8Then the elders of his town shall summon him and talk to him. If he persists in saying, "I do not want to marry her," 9his brother's widow shall go up to him in the presence

a8 The Hebrew word was used for various diseases affecting the skin—not necessarily leprosy.

of the elders, take off one of his sandals, spit in his face and say, "This is what is done to the man who will not build up his brother's family line." ¹⁰That man's line shall be known in Israel as The Family of the Unsandalled.

¹¹If two men are fighting and the wife of one of them comes to rescue her husband from his assailant, and she reaches out and seizes him by his private parts, ¹²you shall cut off her hand. Show her no pity.

¹³Do not have two differing weights in your bag—one heavy, one light. ¹⁴Do not have two differing measures in your house—one large, one small. ¹⁵You must have accurate and honest weights and measures, so that you may live long in the land the LORD your God is giving you. ¹⁶For the LORD your God detests anyone who does these things, anyone who deals dishonestly.

¹⁷Remember what the Amalekites did to you along the way when you came out of Egypt. ¹⁸When you were weary and worn out, they met you on your journey and cut off all who were lagging behind; they had no fear of God. ¹⁹When the LORD your God gives you rest from all the enemies around you in the land he is giving you to possess as an inheritance, you shall blot out the memory of Amalek from under heaven. Do not forget!

■ Firstfruits and Tithes

26 When you have entered the land that the LORD your God is giving you as an inheritance and have taken possession of it and settled in it, ²take some of the firstfruits of all that you produce from the soil of the land that the LORD your God is giving you and put them in a basket. Then go to the place that the LORD your God will choose as a dwelling for his Name ³and say to the priest in office at the time, "I declare today to the LORD your God that I have come to the land that the LORD swore to our forefathers to give us." ⁴The priest shall take the basket from your hands and set it down in front of the altar of the LORD your God. ⁵Then you shall declare before the LORD your God: "My father was a wandering Aramean, and he went down into Egypt with a few people and lived there and became a great nation, powerful and numerous. ⁶But the Egyptians ill-treated us and made us suffer, putting us to hard labour. ⁷Then we cried out to the LORD, the God of our fathers, and the LORD heard our voice and saw our misery, toil and oppression. ⁸So the LORD brought us out of Egypt with a mighty hand and an outstretched arm, with great terror and with miraculous signs and wonders. ⁹He brought us to this place and gave us this land, a land flowing with milk and honey; ¹⁰and now I bring the firstfruits of the soil that you, O LORD, have given me." Place the basket before the LORD your God and bow down before him. ¹¹And you and the Levites and the aliens among you shall rejoice in all the good things the LORD your God has given to you and your household.

¹²When you have finished setting aside a tenth of all your produce in the third year, the year of the tithe, you shall give it to the Levite, the alien, the fatherless and the widow, so that they may eat in your towns and be satisfied. ¹³Then say to the LORD

your God: "I have removed from my house the sacred portion and have given it to the Levite, the alien, the fatherless and the widow, according to all you commanded. I have not turned aside from your commands nor have I forgotten any of them. ¹⁴I have not eaten any of the sacred portion while I was in mourning, nor have I removed any of it while I was unclean, nor have I offered any of it to the dead. I have obeyed the LORD my God; I have done everything you commanded me. ¹⁵Look down from heaven, your holy dwelling-place, and bless your people Israel and the land you have given us as you promised on oath to our forefathers, a land flowing with milk and honey."

■ Follow the LORD's Commands

¹⁶The LORD your God commands you this day to follow these decrees and laws; carefully observe them with all your heart and with all your soul. ¹⁷You have declared this day that the LORD is your God and that you will walk in his ways, that you will keep his decrees, commands and laws, and that you will obey him. ¹⁸And the LORD has declared this day that you are his people, his treasured possession as he promised, and that you are to keep all his commands. ¹⁹He has declared that he will set you in praise, fame and honour high above all the nations he has made and that you will be a people holy to the LORD your God, as he promised.

26:16 ■ LAW OF THE HEART
The Old Testament gives many rules and regulations. Deuteronomy makes clear, however, that the law was meant to penetrate a person's heart. Unless the law becomes part of a person's inner attitudes, it will probably make no difference.

■ The Altar on Mount Ebal

27 Moses and the elders of Israel commanded the people: "Keep all these commands that I give you today. ²When you have crossed the Jordan into the land the LORD your God is giving you, set up some large stones and coat them with plaster. ³Write on them all the words of this law when you have crossed over to enter the land the LORD your God is giving you, a land flowing with milk and honey, just as the LORD, the God of your fathers, promised you. ⁴And when you have crossed the Jordan, set up these stones on Mount Ebal, as I command you today, and coat them with plaster. ⁵Build there an altar to the LORD your God, an altar of stones. Do not use any iron tool upon them. ⁶Build the altar of the LORD your God with stones from the field and offer burnt offerings on it to the LORD your God. ⁷Sacrifice fellowship offerings* there, eating them and rejoicing in the presence of the LORD your God. ⁸And you shall write very clearly all the words of this law on these stones you have set up."

■ Curses From Mount Ebal

⁹Then Moses and the priests, who are Levites, said to all Israel, "Be silent, O Israel, and listen! You have now become the people of the LORD your God.

---

a 7 Traditionally peace offerings

¹⁰Obey the LORD your God and follow his commands and decrees that I give you today."

¹¹On the same day Moses commanded the people:

¹²When you have crossed the Jordan, these tribes shall stand on Mount Gerizim to bless the people: Simeon, Levi, Judah, Issachar, Joseph and Benjamin. ¹³And these tribes shall stand on Mount Ebal to pronounce curses: Reuben, Gad, Asher, Zebulun, Dan and Naphtali.

27:12 ■ A TASK FOR JOSHUA

Joshua carried out Moses' instructions for these blessings and curses, as recorded in Joshua 8:31–35. Mount Ebal had special significance for the Israelites, who believed that Abraham first worshipped God near here after receiving the original promise of the land (Genesis 15).

¹⁴The Levites shall recite to all the people of Israel in a loud voice:

¹⁵"Cursed is the man who carves an image or casts an idol—a thing detestable to the LORD, the work of the craftsman's hands—and sets it up in secret."

Then all the people shall say,

"Amen!"

¹⁶"Cursed is the man who dishonours his father or his mother."

Then all the people shall say,

"Amen!"

¹⁷"Cursed is the man who moves his neighbour's boundary stone."

Then all the people shall say,

"Amen!"

¹⁸"Cursed is the man who leads the blind astray on the road."

Then all the people shall say,

"Amen!"

¹⁹"Cursed is the man who withholds justice from the alien, the fatherless or the widow."

Then all the people shall say,

"Amen!"

²⁰"Cursed is the man who sleeps with his father's wife, for he dishonours his father's bed."

Then all the people shall say,

"Amen!"

²¹"Cursed is the man who has sexual relations with any animal."

Then all the people shall say,

"Amen!"

²²"Cursed is the man who sleeps with his sister, the daughter of his father or the daughter of his mother."

Then all the people shall say,

"Amen!"

²³"Cursed is the man who sleeps with his mother-in-law."

Then all the people shall say,

"Amen!"

²⁴"Cursed is the man who kills his neighbour secretly."

Then all the people shall say,

"Amen!"

²⁵"Cursed is the man who accepts a bribe to kill an innocent person."

Then all the people shall say,

"Amen!"

²⁶"Cursed is the man who does not uphold the words of this law by carrying them out."

Then all the people shall say,

"Amen!"

■ Blessings for Obedience

28 If you fully obey the LORD your God and carefully follow all his commands that I give you today, the LORD your God will set you high above all the nations on earth. ²All these blessings will come upon you and accompany you if you obey the LORD your God:

³You will be blessed in the city and blessed in the country.

⁴The fruit of your womb will be blessed, and the crops of your land and the young of your livestock—the calves of your herds and the lambs of your flocks.

⁵Your basket and your kneading trough will be blessed.

⁶You will be blessed when you come in and blessed when you go out.

⁷The LORD will grant that the enemies who rise up against you will be defeated before you. They will come at you from one direction but flee from you in seven.

⁸The LORD will send a blessing on your barns and on everything you put your hand to. The LORD your God will bless you in the land he is giving you.

⁹The LORD will establish you as his holy people, as he promised you on oath, if you keep the commands of the LORD your God and walk in his ways. ¹⁰Then all the peoples on earth will see that you are called by the name of the LORD, and they will fear you. ¹¹The LORD will grant you abundant prosperity—in the fruit of your womb, the young of your livestock and the crops of your ground—in the land he swore to your forefathers to give you.

¹²The LORD will open the heavens, the storehouse of his bounty, to send rain on your land in season and to bless all the work of your hands. You will lend to many nations but will borrow from none. ¹³The LORD will make you the head, not the tail. If you pay attention to the commands of the LORD your God that I give you this day and carefully follow them, you will always be at the top, never at the bottom. ¹⁴Do not turn aside from any of the commands I give you today, to the right or to the left, following other gods and serving them.

■ Curses for Disobedience

¹⁵However, if you do not obey the LORD your God and do not carefully follow all his commands and decrees I am giving you today, all these curses will come upon you and overtake you:

¹⁶You will be cursed in the city and cursed in the country.

17Your basket and your kneading trough will be cursed.

18The fruit of your womb will be cursed, and the crops of your land, and the calves of your herds and the lambs of your flocks.

19You will be cursed when you come in and cursed when you go out.

20The LORD will send on you curses, confusion and rebuke in everything you put your hand to, until you are destroyed and come to sudden ruin because of the evil you have done in forsaking him.*a* 21The LORD will plague you with diseases until he has destroyed you from the land you are entering to possess. 22The LORD will strike you with wasting disease, with fever and inflammation, with scorching heat and drought, with blight and mildew, which will plague you until you perish. 23The sky over your head will be bronze, the ground beneath you iron. 24The LORD will turn the rain of your country into dust and powder; it will come down from the skies until you are destroyed.

25The LORD will cause you to be defeated before your enemies. You will come at them from one direction but flee from them in seven, and you will become a thing of horror to all the kingdoms on earth. 26Your carcasses will be food for all the birds of the air and the beasts of the earth, and there will be no-one to frighten them away. 27The LORD will afflict you with the boils of Egypt and with tumours, festering sores and the itch, from which you cannot be cured. 28The LORD will afflict you with madness, blindness and confusion of mind. 29At midday you will grope about like a blind man in the dark. You will be unsuccessful in everything you do; day after day you will be oppressed and robbed, with no-one to rescue you.

30You will be pledged to be married to a woman, but another will take her and ravish her. You will build a house, but you will not live in it. You will plant a vineyard, but you will not even begin to enjoy its fruit. 31Your ox will be slaughtered before your eyes, but you will eat none of it. Your donkey will be forcibly taken from you and will not be returned. Your sheep will be given to your enemies, and no-one will rescue them. 32Your sons and daughters will be given to another nation, and you will wear out your eyes watching for them day after day, powerless to lift a hand. 33A people that you do not know will eat what your land and labour produce, and you will have nothing but cruel oppression all your days. 34The sights you see will drive you mad. 35The LORD will afflict your knees and legs with painful boils that cannot be cured, spreading from the soles of your feet to the top of your head.

36The LORD will drive you and the king you set over you to a nation unknown to you or your fathers. There you will worship other gods, gods of wood and stone. 37You will become a thing of horror and an object of scorn and ridicule to all the nations where the LORD will drive you.

38You will sow much seed in the field but you will harvest little, because locusts will devour it. 39You will plant vineyards and cultivate them but you will not drink the wine or gather the grapes, because worms will eat them. 40You will have olive trees throughout your country but you will not use the oil, because the olives will drop off. 41You will have sons and daughters but you will not keep them, because they will go into captivity. 42Swarms of locusts will take over all your trees and the crops of your land.

28:36-37 ■ SCATTERED ABROAD

Moses warned that if the Israelites failed to obey God's law, they would be uprooted from the new land and scattered all over the earth. At least three times in history this kind of dispersion of Jews (called Diaspora) took place on a massive scale. Assyria, Babylon, and finally the Roman empire invaded the homeland of the Jews and scattered them far abroad.

43The alien who lives among you will rise above you higher and higher, but you will sink lower and lower. 44He will lend to you, but you will not lend to him. He will be the head, but you will be the tail.

45All these curses will come upon you. They will pursue you and overtake you until you are destroyed, because you did not obey the LORD your God and observe the commands and decrees he gave you. 46They will be a sign and a wonder to you and your descendants for ever. 47Because you did not serve the LORD your God joyfully and gladly in the time of prosperity, 48therefore in hunger and thirst, in nakedness and dire poverty, you will serve the enemies the LORD sends against you. He will put an iron yoke on your neck until he has destroyed you.

49The LORD will bring a nation against you from far away, from the ends of the earth, like an eagle swooping down, a nation whose language you will not understand, 50a fierce-looking nation without respect for the old or pity for the young. 51They will devour the young of your livestock and the crops of your land until you are destroyed. They will leave you no grain, new wine or oil, nor any calves of your herds or lambs of your flocks until you are ruined. 52They will lay siege to all the cities throughout your land until the high fortified walls in which you trust fall down. They will besiege all the cities throughout the land the LORD your God is giving you.

53Because of the suffering that your enemy will inflict on you during the siege, you will eat the fruit of the womb, the flesh of the sons and daughters the LORD your God has given you. 54Even the most gentle and sensitive man among you will have no compassion on his own brother or the wife he loves or his surviving children, 55and he will not give to one of them any of the flesh of his children that he is eating. It will be all he has left because of the suffering that your enemy will inflict on you during the

a 20 Hebrew me

siege of all your cities. ⁵⁶The most gentle and sensitive woman among you—so sensitive and gentle that she would not venture to touch the ground with the sole of her foot—will begrudge the husband she loves and her own son or daughter ⁵⁷the afterbirth from her womb and the children she bears. For she intends to eat them secretly during the siege and in the distress that your enemy will inflict on you in your cities.

⁵⁸If you do not carefully follow all the words of this law, which are written in this book, and do not revere this glorious and awesome name—the LORD your God—⁵⁹the LORD will send fearful plagues on you and your descendants, harsh and prolonged disasters, and severe and lingering illnesses. ⁶⁰He will bring upon you all the diseases of Egypt that you dreaded, and they will cling to you. ⁶¹The LORD will also bring on you every kind of sickness and disaster not recorded in this Book of the Law, until you are destroyed. ⁶²You who were as numerous as the stars in the sky will be left but few in number, because you did not obey the LORD your God. ⁶³Just as it

pleased the LORD to make you prosper and increase in number, so it will please him to ruin and destroy you. You will be uprooted from the land you are entering to possess.

⁶⁴Then the LORD will scatter you among all nations, from one end of the earth to the other. There you will worship other gods—gods of wood and stone, which neither you nor your fathers have known. ⁶⁵Among those nations you will find no repose, no resting place for the sole of your foot. There the LORD will give you an anxious mind, eyes weary with longing, and a despairing heart. ⁶⁶You will live in constant suspense, filled with dread both night and day, never sure of your life. ⁶⁷In the morning you will say, "If only it were evening!" and in the evening, "If only it were morning!"—because of the terror that will fill your hearts and the sights that your eyes will see. ⁶⁸The LORD will send you back in ships to Egypt on a journey I said you should never make again. There you will offer yourselves for sale to your enemies as male and female slaves, but no-one will buy you.

■ A SCENT OF DOOM
ALL WERE JUBILANT, EXCEPT ONE MAN

INSIGHT

BECAUSE YOU DID NOT SERVE THE LORD YOUR GOD JOYFULLY AND GLADLY IN THE TIME OF PROSPERITY, THEREFORE IN HUNGER AND THIRST, IN NAKEDNESS AND DIRE POVERTY, YOU WILL SERVE THE ENEMIES THE LORD SENDS AGAINST YOU. ■ 28:47–48

Old habits die hard. Deuteronomy underlines that lesson, and the story of a Wild West legend shows that people have not changed much. In 1901 Bill Miner got out of San Quentin Prison, where he had served 33 years in all. It was his third stint, and both times previously he had barely sniffed free air before landing in jail again.
    Miner tried various odd jobs, but most work seemed degrading and boring to a former stagecoach robber. The old restlessness returned. One afternoon, in a Seattle theatre, he watched the movie *The Great Train Robbery,* and discovered a new career, or at least a new twist on an old one. The Gentleman Bandit, at age 60, became The Grey Fox. He went on to mastermind six train robberies, and probably more, until the Mounties tracked him down in British Columbia.

■ A HINT OF DOOM
Three separate times Bill Miner had a chance for a new start. The last chance, he had entered a new city, in a new century, with no-one around to remind him of his reputation. Yet inevitably he went back to the familiar ways of crime. His life had the scent of doom about it.

The last chapters of Deuteronomy show the Israelites facing a situation much like that met by Bill Miner or any prisoner who emerges into freedom after many years. Four decades in the Desert of Sinai had served as a kind of imprisonment, or probation period. And then the long-awaited day of freedom arrived.

■ TWENTIETH CENTURY PRISONERS
It isn't only those repeat offenders like Bill Miner who live trapped into a lifestyle that they cannot escape from. In the affluent and free West there are many, stars of stage and screen, people in the public eye, who have everything going for them but who become prisoners of their own habits. Whether they are addicted to drugs, alcohol or food, they become tangled in a downward spiral of dependency, cure, dependency, and then cure once again, if it isn't too late. Some manage to break free, some succumb and some carry on despite it.
    Everyone in the Israelite camp was jubilant—all but one man, Moses. He could see past the joy. When he spoke to the crowd, he spoke with an air of doom. He knew his people too well to think that geography would change their old ways.

■ MOSES PULLS OUT THE STOPS
For 40 years Moses had led the cranky assortment of tribes. He had listened to their grumbling, endured their gossip and

■ Renewal of the Covenant

29 These are the terms of the covenant the LORD commanded Moses to make with the Israelites in Moab, in addition to the covenant he had made with them at Horeb.

²Moses summoned all the Israelites and said to them:

Your eyes have seen all that the LORD did in Egypt to Pharaoh, to all his officials and to all his land. ³With your own eyes you saw those great trials, those miraculous signs and great wonders. ⁴But to this day the LORD has not given you a mind that understands or eyes that see or ears that hear. ⁵During the forty years that I led you through the desert, your clothes did not wear out, nor did the sandals on your feet. ⁶You ate no bread and drank no wine or other fermented drink. I did this so that you might know that I am the LORD your God.

⁷When you reached this place, Sihon king of Heshbon and Og king of Bashan came out to fight against us, but we defeated them. ⁸We took their

land and gave it as an inheritance to the Reubenites, the Gadites and the half-tribe of Manasseh.

29:5–6 ■ MIRACLES IN THE DESERT
The Sinai peninsula was a harsh place, and the Bible records the Israelites' problems with food and water supplies. But, as these two verses show, God cared for his people there, giving them daily food and drink and even making sure their clothes did not wear out.

---

⁹Carefully follow the terms of this covenant, so that you may prosper in everything you do. ¹⁰All of you are standing today in the presence of the LORD your God — your leaders and chief men, your elders and officials, and all the other men of Israel, ¹¹together with your children and your wives, and the aliens living in your camps who chop your wood and carry your water. ¹²You are standing here in order to enter into a covenant with the LORD your God, a covenant the LORD is making with you this day and

---

survived their insurrections. Now he had one last chance to warn them not to repeat their ways.

You cannot read the last chapters of Deuteronomy without detecting a doleful sense of fatalism in Moses' words. The Israelites' settling down into a life of quiet obedience was about as likely as Bill Miner's becoming a banker. They had failed far too often; they were doomed to fail again.

Moses pulled out all the stops. He orchestrated a dramatic object lesson that would live in their memories for ever. It actually took place after Moses' death, as recorded in Joshua 8:30–35. Representatives from all the tribes climbed two mountains, with a narrow valley in between. These designated speakers shouted out curses and blessings on the Israelites (see 11:26–32; 27–28). As they entered the new land, their ears rang with the dissonance of wonderful blessings and horrific curses.

■ FUTURE TERRORS
Moses starkly summarised the future of the Jewish race. They would, he said, have "an anxious mind, eyes weary with longing, and a despairing heart. You will live in constant suspense, filled with dread both night and day, never sure of your life. In the morning you will say, 'If only it were evening!' and in the evening, 'If only it were morning!' — because of the terror that will fill your hearts and the sights that your eyes will see" (28:65–67). His descriptions of

their future are unmatched for their horror.

Just in case the Israelites didn't get the message, Moses taught them a song given to him by God (chapter 32). It became a kind of national anthem, memorised by everyone and sung as they marched into Canaan. But the song is like no other national anthem. It has virtually no words of encouragement or hope, only doom.

Moses knew that even the promised land would not change his people's ingrained habits of disobeying God. They would fail in the promised land, just as they had failed in the desert. He concluded his farewell speech to the people with these words, "They are not just idle words for you — they are your life" (32:47). And then on that same day he ascended a mountain to die. He had been forbidden by God to cross into Canaan because of his own disobedience.

This sad final scene may have made the strongest impression of all. No-one could get away with rebellion against God — not even Moses, "whom the LORD knew face to face" (34:10).

□ LIFE QUESTIONS:
Why do you think the Bible includes accounts of big failures like this? Have you ever experienced a repeated failure: a sin or problem that keeps returning, no matter what you do?

sealing with an oath, [13]to confirm you this day as his people, that he may be your God as he promised you and as he swore to your fathers, Abraham, Isaac and Jacob. [14]I am making this covenant, with its oath, not only with you [15]who are standing here with us today in the presence of the LORD our God but also with those who are not here today.

[16]You yourselves know how we lived in Egypt and how we passed through the countries on the way here. [17]You saw among them their detestable images and idols of wood and stone, of silver and gold. [18]Make sure there is no man or woman, clan or tribe among you today whose heart turns away from the LORD our God to go and worship the gods of those nations; make sure there is no root among you that produces such bitter poison.

[19]When such a person hears the words of this oath, he invokes a blessing on himself and therefore thinks, "I will be safe, even though I persist in going my own way." This will bring disaster on the watered land as well as the dry.[a] [20]The LORD will never be willing to forgive him; his wrath and zeal will burn against that man. All the curses written in this book will fall upon him, and the LORD will blot out his name from under heaven. [21]The LORD will single him out from all the tribes of Israel for disaster, according to all the curses of the covenant written in this Book of the Law.

[22]Your children who follow you in later generations and foreigners who come from distant lands will see the calamities that have fallen on the land and the diseases with which the LORD has afflicted it. [23]The whole land will be a burning waste of salt and sulphur—nothing planted, nothing sprouting, no vegetation growing on it. It will be like the destruction of Sodom and Gomorrah, Admah and Zeboiim, which the LORD overthrew in fierce anger. [24]All the nations will ask: "Why has the LORD done this to this land? Why this fierce, burning anger?"

[25]And the answer will be: "It is because this people abandoned the covenant of the LORD, the God of their fathers, the covenant he made with them when he brought them out of Egypt. [26]They went off and worshipped other gods and bowed down to them, gods they did not know, gods he had not given them. [27]Therefore the LORD's anger burned against this land, so that he brought on it all the curses written in this book. [28]In furious anger and in great wrath the LORD uprooted them from their land and thrust them into another land, as it is now."

[29]The secret things belong to the LORD our God, but the things revealed belong to us and to our children for ever, that we may follow all the words of this law.

29:29 ■ GOD'S SECRETS

"I don't understand why God is doing this," people say. But God hasn't told us everything. Our finite minds could not possibly grasp some things, and other information is simply unnecessary or unhelpful for us to know. What God has told us (in his law, for instance) he intends for us to obey.

■ Prosperity After Turning to the LORD

30 When all these blessings and curses I have set before you come upon you and you take them to heart wherever the LORD your God disperses you among the nations, [2]and when you and your children return to the LORD your God and obey him with all your heart and with all your soul according to everything I command you today, [3]then the LORD your God will restore your fortunes[a] and have compassion on you and gather you again from all the nations where he scattered you. [4]Even if you have been banished to the most distant land under the heavens, from there the LORD your God will gather you and bring you back. [5]He will bring you to the land that belonged to your fathers, and you will take possession of it. He will make you more prosperous and numerous than your fathers. [6]The LORD your God will circumcise your hearts and the hearts of your descendants, so that you may love him with all your heart and with all your soul, and live. [7]The LORD your God will put all these curses on your enemies who hate and persecute you. [8]You will again obey the LORD and follow all his commands I am giving you today. [9]Then the LORD your God will make you most prosperous in all the work of your hands and in the fruit of your womb, the young of your livestock and the crops of your land. The LORD will again delight in you and make you prosperous, just as he delighted in your fathers, [10]if you obey the LORD your God and keep his commands and decrees that are written in this Book of the Law and turn to the LORD your God with all your heart and with all your soul.

■ The Offer of Life or Death

[11]Now what I am commanding you today is not too difficult for you or beyond your reach. [12]It is not up in heaven, so that you have to ask, "Who will ascend into heaven to get it and proclaim it to us so that we may obey it?" [13]Nor is it beyond the sea, so that you have to ask, "Who will cross the sea to get it and proclaim it to us so that we may obey it?" [14]No, the word is very near you; it is in your mouth and in your heart so that you may obey it.

30:14 ■ KEEP IT SIMPLE

Sometimes people make a relationship with God sound impossibly difficult. Moses emphasises its simplicity. You don't have to swim oceans or ascend into heaven; you just have to understand, believe, and obey the word God has given. In a famous New Testament passage, the apostle Paul applied this lesson to confessing faith in Jesus Christ (Romans 10:6–10).

---

[15]See, I set before you today life and prosperity, death and destruction. [16]For I command you today to love the LORD your God, to walk in his ways, and to keep his commands, decrees and laws; then you will live and increase, and the LORD your God will bless you in the land you are entering to possess. [17]But if your heart turns away and you are not obedient, and if you are drawn away to bow down

---

a 19 Or way, in order to add drunkenness to thirst."   a 3 Or will bring you back from captivity to other gods and worship them, ¹⁸I declare to you this day that you will certainly be destroyed. You will not live long in the land you are crossing the Jordan to enter and possess.

¹⁹This day I call heaven and earth as witnesses against you that I have set before you life and death, blessings and curses. Now choose life, so that you and your children may live ²⁰and that you may love the LORD your God, listen to his voice, and hold fast to him. For the LORD is your life, and he will give you many years in the land he swore to give to your fathers, Abraham, Isaac and Jacob.

Joshua to Succeed Moses

31 Then Moses went out and spoke these words to all Israel: ²"I am now a hundred and twenty years old and I am no longer able to lead you. The LORD has said to me, 'You shall not cross the Jordan.' ³The LORD your God himself will cross over ahead of you. He will destroy these nations before you, and you will take possession of their land. Joshua also will cross over ahead of you, as the LORD said. ⁴And the LORD will do to them what he did to Sihon and Og, the kings of the Amorites, whom he destroyed along with their land. ⁵The LORD will deliver them to you, and you must do to them all that I have commanded you. ⁶Be strong and courageous. Do not be afraid or terrified because of them, for the LORD your God goes with you; he will never leave you nor forsake you."

⁷Then Moses summoned Joshua and said to him in the presence of all Israel, "Be strong and courageous, for you must go with this people into the land that the LORD swore to their forefathers to give them, and you must divide it among them as their inheritance. ⁸The LORD himself goes before you and will be with you; he will never leave you nor forsake you. Do not be afraid; do not be discouraged."

The Reading of the Law

⁹So Moses wrote down this law and gave it to the priests, the sons of Levi, who carried the ark of the covenant of the LORD, and to all the elders of Israel. ¹⁰Then Moses commanded them: "At the end of every seven years, in the year for cancelling debts, during the Feast of Tabernacles, ¹¹when all Israel comes to appear before the LORD your God at the place he will choose, you shall read this law before them in their hearing. ¹²Assemble the people—men, women and children, and the aliens living in your towns—so that they can listen and learn to fear the LORD your God and follow carefully all the words of this law. ¹³Their children, who do not know this law, must hear it and learn to fear the LORD your God as long as you live in the land you are crossing the Jordan to possess."

Israel's Rebellion Predicted

¹⁴The LORD said to Moses, "Now the day of your death is near. Call Joshua and present yourselves at the Tent of Meeting, where I will commission him." So Moses and Joshua came and presented themselves at the Tent of Meeting.

¹⁵Then the LORD appeared at the Tent in a pillar of cloud, and the cloud stood over the entrance to the Tent. ¹⁶And the LORD said to Moses: "You are going to rest with your fathers, and these people will soon prostitute themselves to the foreign gods of the land they are entering. They will forsake me and break the covenant I made with them. ¹⁷On that day I will become angry with them and forsake them; I will hide my face from them, and they will be destroyed. Many disasters and difficulties will come upon them, and on that day they will ask, 'Have not these disasters come upon us because our God is not with us?' ¹⁸And I will certainly hide my face on that day because of all their wickedness in turning to other gods.

¹⁹"Now write down for yourselves this song and teach it to the Israelites and make them sing it, so that it may be a witness for me against them. ²⁰When I have brought them into the land flowing with milk and honey, the land I promised on oath to their forefathers, and when they eat their fill and thrive, they will turn to other gods and worship them, rejecting me and breaking my covenant. ²¹And when many disasters and difficulties come upon them, this song will testify against them, because it will not be forgotten by their descendants. I know what they are disposed to do, even before I bring them into the land I promised them on oath." ²²So Moses wrote down this song that day and taught it to the Israelites.

²³The LORD gave this command to Joshua son of Nun: "Be strong and courageous, for you will bring the Israelites into the land I promised them on oath, and I myself will be with you."

²⁴After Moses finished writing in a book the words of this law from beginning to end, ²⁵he gave this command to the Levites who carried the ark of the covenant of the LORD: ²⁶"Take this Book of the Law and place it beside the ark of the covenant of the LORD your God. There it will remain as a witness against you. ²⁷For I know how rebellious and stiffnecked you are. If you have been rebellious against the LORD while I am still alive and with you, how much more will you rebel after I die! ²⁸Assemble before me all the elders of your tribes and all your officials, so that I can speak these words in their hearing and call heaven and earth to testify against them. ²⁹For I know that after my death you are sure to become utterly corrupt and to turn from the way I have commanded you. In days to come, disaster will fall upon you because you will do evil in the sight of the LORD and provoke him to anger by what your hands have made."

The Song of Moses

³⁰And Moses recited the words of this song from beginning to end in the hearing of the whole assembly of Israel:

32 Listen, O heavens, and I will speak;
　　hear, O earth, the words of my mouth.
²Let my teaching fall like rain
　　and my words descend like dew,
like showers on new grass,
　　like abundant rain on tender plants.

³I will proclaim the name of the LORD.
　　Oh, praise the greatness of our God!

⁴He is the Rock, his works are perfect,
  and all his ways are just.
A faithful God who does no wrong,
  upright and just is he.

⁵They have acted corruptly towards him;
  to their shame they are no longer his
  children,
  but a warped and crooked generation.ᵃ
⁶Is this the way you repay the LORD,
  O foolish and unwise people?
Is he not your Father, your Creator,ᵇ
  who made you and formed you?

⁷Remember the days of old;
  consider the generations long past.
Ask your father and he will tell you,
  your elders, and they will explain to you.
⁸When the Most High gave the nations their
  inheritance,
  when he divided all mankind,
he set up boundaries for the peoples
  according to the number of the sons of
  Israel.ᶜ
⁹For the LORD's portion is his people,
  Jacob his allotted inheritance.

¹⁰In a desert land he found him,
  in a barren and howling waste.
He shielded him and cared for him;
  he guarded him as the apple of his eye,
¹¹like an eagle that stirs up its nest
  and hovers over its young,
that spreads its wings to catch them
  and carries them on its pinions.
¹²The LORD alone led him;
  no foreign god was with him.

32:11 ■ MIXED EMOTIONS

The tender words of the song in this chapter
express God's true love for Israel. And yet the
song contains words of dreadful realism as well.
God knew the Israelites would fail him, and this
song would "testify against them" when they
turned away from him (31:21). Indeed, the apostle
Paul quoted from this in his agonising account of
Jewish rejection of Jesus (Romans 10:19).

¹³He made him ride on the heights of the land
  and fed him with the fruit of the fields.
He nourished him with honey from the rock,
  and with oil from the flinty crag,
¹⁴with curds and milk from herd and flock
  and with fattened lambs and goats,
with choice rams of Bashan
  and the finest grains of wheat.
You drank the foaming blood of the grape.

¹⁵Jeshurunᵈ grew fat and kicked;
  filled with food, he became heavy and sleek.
He abandoned the God who made him
  and rejected the Rock his Saviour.
¹⁶They made him jealous with their foreign gods
  and angered him with their detestable idols.

¹⁷They sacrificed to demons, which are not
  God—
  gods they had not known,
  gods that recently appeared,
  gods your fathers did not fear.
¹⁸You deserted the Rock, who fathered you;
  you forgot the God who gave you birth.

¹⁹The LORD saw this and rejected them
  because he was angered by his sons and
  daughters.
²⁰"I will hide my face from them," he said,
  "and see what their end will be;
for they are a perverse generation,
  children who are unfaithful.
²¹They made me jealous by what is no god
  and angered me with their worthless idols.
I will make them envious by those who are not
  a people;
I will make them angry by a nation that has
  no understanding.
²²For a fire has been kindled by my wrath,
  one that burns to the realm of deathᵉ
  below.
It will devour the earth and its harvests
  and set on fire the foundations of the
  mountains.

²³"I will heap calamities upon them
  and expend my arrows against them.
²⁴I will send wasting famine against them,
  consuming pestilence and deadly plague;
I will send against them the fangs of wild
  beasts,
  the venom of vipers that glide in the dust.
²⁵In the street the sword will make them
  childless;
  in their homes terror will reign.
Young men and young women will perish,
  infants and grey-haired men.
²⁶I said I would scatter them
  and blot out their memory from mankind,
²⁷but I dreaded the taunt of the enemy,
  lest the adversary misunderstand
and say, 'Our hand has triumphed;
  the LORD has not done all this.' "

²⁸They are a nation without sense,
  there is no discernment in them.
²⁹If only they were wise and would understand
  this
  and discern what their end will be!
³⁰How could one man chase a thousand,
  or two put ten thousand to flight,
unless their Rock had sold them,
  unless the LORD had given them up?
³¹For their rock is not like our Rock,
  as even our enemies concede.
³²Their vine comes from the vine of Sodom
  and from the fields of Gomorrah.
Their grapes are filled with poison,
  and their clusters with bitterness.
³³Their wine is the venom of serpents,
  the deadly poison of cobras.

³⁴"Have I not kept this in reserve
  and sealed it in my vaults?

ᵃ5 Or *Corrupt are they and not his children, / a generation warped and twisted to their shame*   ᵇ6 Or *Father, who bought you*   ᶜ8 Masoretic Text;
Dead Sea Scrolls (see also Septuagint) *sons of God*   ᵈ15 *Jeshurun* means *the upright one, that is, Israel.*   ᵉ22 Hebrew *to Sheol*

³⁵It is mine to avenge; I will repay.
  In due time their foot will slip;
  their day of disaster is near
  and their doom rushes upon them."

³⁶The LORD will judge his people
  and have compassion on his servants
when he sees their strength is gone
  and no-one is left, slave or free.
³⁷He will say: "Now where are their gods,
  the rock they took refuge in,
³⁸the gods who ate the fat of their sacrifices
  and drank the wine of their drink offerings?
Let them rise up to help you!
Let them give you shelter!

³⁹"See now that I myself am He!
  There is no god besides me.
I put to death and I bring to life,
  I have wounded and I will heal,
  and no-one can deliver out of my hand.
⁴⁰I lift my hand to heaven and declare:
  As surely as I live for ever,
⁴¹when I sharpen my flashing sword
  and my hand grasps it in judgment,
I will take vengeance on my adversaries
  and repay those who hate me.
⁴²I will make my arrows drunk with blood,
  while my sword devours flesh:
the blood of the slain and the captives,
  the heads of the enemy leaders."

⁴³Rejoice, O nations, with his people,ᶠ·ᵍ
  for he will avenge the blood of his servants;
he will take vengeance on his enemies
  and make atonement for his land and people.

⁴⁴Moses came with Joshuaᵇ son of Nun and
spoke all the words of this song in the hearing of the
people. ⁴⁵When Moses finished reciting all these
words to all Israel, ⁴⁶he said to them, "Take to heart
all the words I have solemnly declared to you this
day, so that you may command your children to
obey carefully all the words of this law. ⁴⁷They are
not just idle words for you—they are your life. By
them you will live long in the land you are crossing
the Jordan to possess."

■ Moses to Die on Mount Nebo
    ⁴⁸On that same day the LORD told Moses, ⁴⁹"Go up
into the Abarim Range to Mount Nebo in Moab,
across from Jericho, and view Canaan, the land I am
giving the Israelites as their own possession. ⁵⁰There
on the mountain that you have climbed you will die

and be gathered to your people, just as your brother
Aaron died on Mount Hor and was gathered to his
people. ⁵¹This is because both of you broke faith
with me in the presence of the Israelites at the
waters of Meribah Kadesh in the Desert of Zin and
because you did not uphold my holiness among the
Israelites. ⁵²Therefore, you will see the land only
from a distance; you will not enter the land I am
giving to the people of Israel."

■ Moses Blesses the Tribes
33 This is the blessing that Moses the man of
      God pronounced on the Israelites before his
death. ²He said:

"The LORD came from Sinai
  and dawned over them from Seir;
  he shone forth from Mount Paran.
He came withᵃ myriads of holy ones
  from the south, from his mountain slopes.ᵇ
³Surely it is you who love the people;
  all the holy ones are in your hand.
At your feet they all bow down,
  and from you receive instruction,
⁴the law that Moses gave us,
  the possession of the assembly of Jacob.
⁵He was king over Jeshurunᶜ
  when the leaders of the people assembled,
  along with the tribes of Israel.

⁶"Let Reuben live and not die,
  norᵈ his men be few."

⁷And this he said about Judah:

"Hear, O LORD, the cry of Judah;
  bring him to his people.
With his own hands he defends his cause.
  Oh, be his help against his foes!"

⁸About Levi he said:

"Your Thummim and Urim belong
  to the man you favoured.
You tested him at Massah;
  you contended with him at the waters of
    Meribah.
⁹He said of his father and mother,
  'I have no regard for them.'
He did not recognise his brothers
  or acknowledge his own children,
but he watched over your word
  and guarded your covenant.

ᶠ43 Or Make his people rejoice, O nations   ᵍ43 Masoretic Text; Dead Sea Scrolls (see also Septuagint) people, / and let all the angels worship him /
ᵇ44 Hebrew Hoshea, a variant of Joshua   ᵃ2 Or from   ᵇ2 The meaning of the Hebrew for this phrase is uncertain.   ᶜ5 Jeshurun means the upright
one, that is, Israel; also in verse 26.   ᵈ6 Or but let

10He teaches your precepts to Jacob
  and your law to Israel.
He offers incense before you
  and whole burnt offerings on your altar.
11Bless all his skills, O LORD,
  and be pleased with the work of his hands.
Smite the loins of those who rise up against
    him;
  strike his foes till they rise no more."

12About Benjamin he said:

"Let the beloved of the LORD rest secure in him,
  for he shields him all day long,
  and the one the LORD loves rests between his
    shoulders."

13About Joseph he said:

"May the LORD bless his land
  with the precious dew from heaven above
  and with the deep waters that lie below;
14with the best the sun brings forth
  and the finest the moon can yield;
15with the choicest gifts of the ancient mountains
  and the fruitfulness of the everlasting hills;
16with the best gifts of the earth and its fulness
  and the favour of him who dwelt in the
    burning bush.
Let all these rest on the head of Joseph,
  on the brow of the prince amonge his
    brothers.
17In majesty he is like a firstborn bull;
  his horns are the horns of a wild ox.
With them he will gore the nations,
  even those at the ends of the earth.
Such are the ten thousands of Ephraim;
  such are the thousands of Manasseh."

18About Zebulun he said:

"Rejoice, Zebulun, in your going out,
  and you, Issachar, in your tents.
19They will summon peoples to the mountain
  and there offer sacrifices of righteousness;
they will feast on the abundance of the seas,
  on the treasures hidden in the sand."

20About Gad he said:

"Blessed is he who enlarges Gad's domain!
Gad lives there like a lion,
  tearing at arm or head.
21He chose the best land for himself;
  the leader's portion was kept for him.
When the heads of the people assembled,
  he carried out the LORD's righteous will,
  and his judgments concerning Israel."

22About Dan he said:

"Dan is a lion's cub,
  springing out of Bashan."

23About Naphtali he said:

"Naphtali is abounding with the favour of the
    LORD
  and is full of his blessing;
he will inherit southward to the lake."

24About Asher he said:

"Most blessed of sons is Asher;
  let him be favoured by his brothers,
  and let him bathe his feet in oil.
25The bolts of your gates will be iron and bronze,
  and your strength will equal your days.

26"There is no-one like the God of Jeshurun,
  who rides on the heavens to help you
  and on the clouds in his majesty.
27The eternal God is your refuge,
  and underneath are the everlasting arms.
He will drive out your enemy before you,
  saying, 'Destroy him!'
28So Israel will live in safety alone;
  Jacob's spring is secure
in a land of grain and new wine,
  where the heavens drop dew.
29Blessed are you, O Israel!
  Who is like you,
  a people saved by the LORD?
He is your shield and helper
  and your glorious sword.
Your enemies will cower before you,
  and you will trample down their high
    places."f

■ The Death of Moses

34 Then Moses climbed Mount Nebo from the
plains of Moab to the top of Pisgah, across
from Jericho. There the LORD showed him the whole
land—from Gilead to Dan, 2all of Naphtali, the territory of Ephraim and Manasseh, all the land of Judah
as far as the western sea,a 3the Negev and the whole
region from the Valley of Jericho, the City of Palms,
as far as Zoar. 4Then the LORD said to him, "This is
the land I promised on oath to Abraham, Isaac and
Jacob when I said, 'I will give it to your descendants.'
I have let you see it with your eyes, but you will not
cross over into it."

5And Moses the servant of the LORD died there in
Moab, as the LORD had said. 6He buried himb in
Moab, in the valley opposite Beth Peor, but to this
day no-one knows where his grave is. 7Moses was a
hundred and twenty years old when he died, yet his
eyes were not weak nor his strength gone. 8The Israelites grieved for Moses in the plains of Moab
thirty days, until the time of weeping and mourning
was over.

34:5 ■ MOSES GETS A PREVIEW
To his great disappointment, Moses could not
lead his people into the new land, for reasons
mentioned in 32:48—52. But God allowed him a
final look over all the promised land. And, in a very
unexpected way, Moses did realise his dream of
setting foot in the promised land. Over a thousand
years later, he returned and appeared with the
prophet Elijah and with Jesus on the Mount of
Transfiguration (Matthew 17; Mark 9; Luke 9).

9Now Joshua son of Nun was filled with the
spiritc of wisdom because Moses had laid his hands

e16 Or of the one separated from   f29 Or will tread upon their bodies   a2 That is, the Mediterranean   b6 Or He was buried   c9 Or Spirit on him. So the Israelites listened to him and did what the LORD had commanded Moses.

¹⁰Since then, no prophet has risen in Israel like Moses, whom the LORD knew face to face, ¹¹who did all those miraculous signs and wonders the LORD sent him to do in Egypt—to Pharaoh and to all his officials and to his whole land. ¹²For no-one has ever shown the mighty power or performed the awesome deeds that Moses did in the sight of all Israel.

JOSHUA

INTRODUCTION

■ THE DIFFERENCE 40 YEARS CAN MAKE

THEY FACED OVERWHELMING ODDS WITH RENEWED HOPE

"DO NOT BE TERRIFIED; DO NOT BE DISCOURAGED, FOR THE LORD YOUR GOD WILL BE WITH YOU WHEREVER YOU GO." ■ 1:9

On the surface, not much had changed in 40 years. The band of refugees amassing beside the Jordan River greatly resembled a similar horde from four decades before. They had panicked once. Would they again?

The Israelites still faced overwhelming odds. They had no chariots or even horses. They had only primitive arms, an untested new leader, and long-delayed marching orders from God.

■ A NEW SPIRIT, A NEW LEADER

Yet, in another sense, everything had changed. Older Israelites with fearful, slave mentalities had died off in the desert – all the older generation except Joshua and Caleb, two legendary warriors. The new generation had decided to trust God, no matter what. In stark contrast to the spies in Numbers (13:31–33), Joshua's scouts brought back this report, "The LORD has surely given the whole land into our hands; all the people are melting in fear because of us" (2:24).

The book of Joshua contains not a word about rebellion against a leader or grumbling against God. It is a good news book, a welcome relief from the discouraging tone of Numbers and the fatalism of Deuteronomy. What a difference 40 years had made!

As newly appointed leader of the Israelites, Joshua took on two main tasks. First, he was to direct a military campaign to take control of the land God had promised. Then, he would parcel out the conquered land among all the tribes.

■ LEARNING TO FOLLOW INSTRUCTIONS

Once inside Canaan, the Israelites followed God's instructions precisely, even when doing so must have strained their faith to new limits. The residents of Jericho had shut themselves behind stone walls, awaiting the onslaught of the feared Israelites. But how did the Israelites spend first week in Canaan? They built a stone monument to God, performed circumcision rituals, and held a Passover celebration. No conquering army had ever behaved in such a manner.

Everything in Joshua seems handpicked to strike home the point that God was really in charge. Covering a period of approximately seven years, Joshua's 24 chapters devote only a few sentences to some extensive military campaigns (see chapters 10–11). But key events, such as the fall of Jericho, get detailed coverage, emphasising the fact that the Israelites succeeded when they relied on God, not on military might. The few negative stories (such as the battle of Ai and the trick of the Gibeonites) show what happened when the Israelites did not seek God's will.

■ A BOOK OF HOPE

The Bible does not relate history for its own sake. Rather, it presents practical and spiritual lessons. Fortunately, Joshua's lessons are overwhelmingly positive ones. Guided by God, the nation of Israel met with unprecedented success. In fact, the book concludes that, "Not one of all the LORD'S good promises to the house of Israel failed; every one was fulfilled" (21:45).

The book of Joshua gives a fresh breeze of hope. Writers of hymns and spirituals have often gone back to it to try to recapture the spirit of success that swept over God's people during those first few years in the new land. It can work: people can follow God. Joshua shows how.

■ HOW TO READ JOSHUA

Phrases in the first two paragraphs of Joshua hint at the tone to follow. "I will never leave you nor forsake you", God promised. "I will give you every place where you set your foot." "Be careful to obey all the law my servant Moses gave you . . . that you may be successful wherever you go."

Often the Israelites offer examples of what *not* to do. Already the books of Exodus, Numbers, and Deuteronomy have given negative examples, and the historical books to follow will describe further failures in lurid detail. But the Old Testament does offer a few bright spots of hope, the book of Joshua being one of the brightest.

(The "good news" character of Joshua causes some people to compare it to the New Testament books of Ephesians and Philippians, which share its success-and-triumph tone. You may want to read one of those New Testament books alongside Joshua.)

Fast-paced battle action appears in chapters 1–11, "the book of war". The latter chapters, "the book of distribution", mostly concern the parcelling out of the land.

You can casually read about the military campaigns of Joshua, but to truly appreciate them you must study a map or Bible atlas. Joshua is a very geographical book. Place names appear in every chapter, describing the military progress and also the division of the land among the tribes of Israel.

As you read Joshua, keep two major themes in mind: Joshua's leadership and God's direct involvement in history. Study Joshua's life as an example of leadership. What were the reasons behind his few failures, such as those recorded in chapters 7 and 9? You may also want to refer to the background passages on his life in Exodus (17,24,32,33) and Numbers (11,13,26). What lesson did Joshua learn at each of these key moments?

■ 3-TRACK READING PLAN

For an explanation and complete listing of the 3-track reading plan, turn to page x.

■ TRACK 1:
Two-Week Courses on the Bible
See page x for information on these courses.

■ TRACK 2:
An Overview of Joshua in 4 Days
□ Day 1. Read the Introduction to Joshua and then chapter 2, the story of Rahab and the spies.
□ Day 2. Read the story of

Jericho in chapter 6; the Israelites practised very unorthodox military tactics, but learned to rely on God.
□ Day 3. Success at Jericho immediately preceded a great failure; read about it in chapter 7.
□ Day 4. Read chapter 24, part of Joshua's stirring farewell speech to the nation he led so well.
Now turn to page xi for your next Track 2 reading project.

■ TRACK 3:
All of Joshua in 21 Days
After you have read through Joshua, turn to pages xii–xiii for your next Track 3 reading project.

□ 1   □ 2   □ 3   □ 4
□ 5   □ 6   □ 7   □ 8
□ 9   □ 10   □ 11
□ 12–13   □ 14–15
□ 16–17   □ 18 □ 19
□ 20 □ 21 □ 22 □ 23
□ 24

■ The LORD Commands Joshua

1 After the death of Moses the servant of the LORD, the LORD said to Joshua son of Nun, Moses' assistant: ²"Moses my servant is dead. Now then, you and all these people, get ready to cross the Jordan River into the land I am about to give to them—to the Israelites. ³I will give you every place where you set your foot, as I promised Moses. ⁴Your territory will extend from the desert to Lebanon, and from the great river, the Euphrates—all the Hittite country—to the Great Sea*ᵃ* on the west. ⁵No-one will be able to stand up against you all the days of your life. As I was with Moses, so I will be with you; I will never leave you nor forsake you.

⁶"Be strong and courageous, because you will lead these people to inherit the land I swore to their forefathers to give them. ⁷Be strong and very courageous. Be careful to obey all the law my servant Moses gave you; do not turn from it to the right or to the left, that you may be successful wherever you

go. ⁸Do not let this Book of the Law depart from your mouth; meditate on it day and night, so that you may be careful to do everything written in it. Then you will be prosperous and successful. ⁹Have I not commanded you? Be strong and courageous. Do not be terrified; do not be discouraged, for the LORD your God will be with you wherever you go."

> **1:8 ■ SECRET OF SUCCESS**
> Three times in this short speech God urged Joshua to "be strong and courageous". Joshua must have quaked at the prospect of taking over from a great man like Moses. But God promised him the resources he needed: God's own presence (verse 5) and the Book of the Law, which Joshua was to lean on every day.

¹⁰So Joshua ordered the officers of the people: ¹¹"Go through the camp and tell the people, 'Get

ᵃ4 That is, the Mediterranean

your supplies ready. Three days from now you will cross the Jordan here to go in and take possession of the land the LORD your God is giving you for your own.' "

12But to the Reubenites, the Gadites and the half-tribe of Manasseh, Joshua said, 13"Remember the command that Moses the servant of the LORD gave you: 'The LORD your God is giving you rest and has granted you this land.' 14Your wives, your children and your livestock may stay in the land that Moses gave you east of the Jordan, but all your fighting men, fully armed, must cross over ahead of your brothers. You are to help your brothers 15until the LORD gives them rest, as he has done for you, and until they too have taken possession of the land that the LORD your God is giving them. After that, you may go back and occupy your own land, which Moses the servant of the LORD gave you east of the Jordan towards the sunrise."

16Then they answered Joshua, "Whatever you have commanded us we will do, and wherever you send us we will go. 17Just as we fully obeyed Moses, so we will obey you. Only may the LORD your God be with you as he was with Moses. 18Whoever rebels against your word and does not obey your words, whatever you may command them, will be put to death. Only be strong and courageous!"

■ Rahab and the Spies

2 Then Joshua son of Nun secretly sent two spies from Shittim. "Go, look over the land," he said, "especially Jericho." So they went and entered the house of a prostitute*a* named Rahab and stayed there.

2The king of Jericho was told, "Look! Some of the Israelites have come here tonight to spy out the land." 3So the king of Jericho sent this message to Rahab: "Bring out the men who came to you and entered your house, because they have come to spy out the whole land."

4But the woman had taken the two men and hidden them. She said, "Yes, the men came to me, but I did not know where they had come from. 5At dusk, when it was time to close the city gate, the men left. I don't know which way they went. Go after them quickly. You may catch up with them." 6(But she had taken them up to the roof and hidden them under the stalks of flax she had laid out on the roof.) 7So the men set out in pursuit of the spies on the road that leads to the fords of the Jordan, and as soon as the pursuers had gone out, the gate was shut.

8Before the spies lay down for the night, she went up on the roof 9and said to them, "I know that the LORD has given this land to you and that a great fear of you has fallen on us, so that all who live in this country are melting in fear because of you. 10We have heard how the LORD dried up the water of the Red Sea*b* for you when you came out of Egypt, and what you did to Sihon and Og, the two kings of the Amorites east of the Jordan, whom you completely destroyed.*c* 11When we heard of it, our hearts sank*d* and everyone's courage failed because of you, for the LORD your God is God in heaven above and on the earth below. 12Now then, please swear to me by the LORD that you will show kindness to my

family, because I have shown kindness to you. Give me a sure sign 13that you will spare the lives of my father and mother, my brothers and sisters, and all who belong to them, and that you will save us from death."

14"Our lives for your lives!" the men assured her. "If you don't tell what we are doing, we will treat you kindly and faithfully when the LORD gives us the land."

15So she let them down by a rope through the window, for the house she lived in was part of the city wall. 16Now she had said to them, "Go to the hills so that the pursuers will not find you. Hide yourselves there three days until they return, and then go on your way."

17The men said to her, "This oath you made us swear will not be binding on us 18unless, when we enter the land, you have tied this scarlet cord in the window through which you let us down, and unless you have brought your father and mother, your brothers and all your family into your house. 19If anyone goes outside your house into the street, his blood will be on his own head; we will not be responsible. As for anyone who is in the house with you, his blood will be on our head if a hand is laid on him. 20But if you tell what we are doing, we will be released from the oath you made us swear."

21"Agreed," she replied. "Let it be as you say." So she sent them away and they departed. And she tied the scarlet cord in the window.

22When they left, they went into the hills and stayed there three days, until the pursuers had searched all along the road and returned without finding them. 23Then the two men started back. They went down out of the hills, forded the river and came to Joshua son of Nun and told him everything that had happened to them. 24They said to Joshua, "The LORD has surely given the whole land into our hands; all the people are melting in fear because of us."

■ Crossing the Jordan

3 Early in the morning Joshua and all the Israelites set out from Shittim and went to the Jordan, where they camped before crossing over. 2After three days the officers went throughout the camp, 3giving orders to the people: "When you see the ark of the covenant of the LORD your God, and the priests, who are Levites, carrying it, you are to move out from your positions and follow it. 4Then you will know which way to go, since you have never been this way before. But keep a distance of about a

thousand yards*a* between you and the ark; do not go near it."

5Joshua told the people, "Consecrate yourselves, for tomorrow the LORD will do amazing things among you."

6Joshua said to the priests, "Take up the ark of the covenant and pass on ahead of the people." So they took it up and went ahead of them.

7And the LORD said to Joshua, "Today I will begin to exalt you in the eyes of all Israel, so that they may know that I am with you as I was with Moses. 8Tell the priests who carry the ark of the covenant: 'When you reach the edge of the Jordan's waters, go and stand in the river.'"

9Joshua said to the Israelites, "Come here and listen to the words of the LORD your God. 10This is how you will know that the living God is among you and that he will certainly drive out before you the Canaanites, Hittites, Hivites, Perizzites, Girgashites, Amorites and Jebusites. 11See, the ark of the covenant of the Lord of all the earth will go into the Jordan ahead of you. 12Now then, choose twelve men from the tribes of Israel, one from each tribe. 13And as soon as the priests who carry the ark of the LORD — the Lord of all the earth — set foot in the Jordan, its waters flowing downstream will be cut off and stand up in a heap."

14So when the people broke camp to cross the Jordan, the priests carrying the ark of the covenant went ahead of them. 15Now the Jordan is in flood all during harvest. Yet as soon as the priests who carried the ark reached the Jordan and their feet touched the water's edge, 16the water from upstream stopped flowing. It piled up in a heap a great distance away, at a town called Adam in the vicinity of Zarethan, while the water flowing down to the Sea of the Arabah (the Salt Sea*b*) was completely cut off. So the people crossed over opposite Jericho. 17The priests who carried the ark of the covenant of the LORD stood firm on dry ground in the middle of the Jordan, while all Israel passed by until the whole nation had completed the crossing on dry ground.

3:16 ■ STOPPING THE JORDAN RIVER
A 1927 earthquake caused the 40-foot clay banks of the Jordan River to collapse, totally damming the Jordan for 21 hours. Whatever means God used to allow the Israelites to cross, this miracle in Joshua achieved a similar result during the river's swollen flood stage. The miracle echoed the crossing of the Red Sea 40 years before, helping to establish Joshua as a worthy successor to Moses. Joshua and the Israelites crossed at a location very close to where Jesus was later baptised.

4 When the whole nation had finished crossing the Jordan, the LORD said to Joshua, 2"Choose twelve men from among the people, one from each tribe, 3and tell them to take up twelve stones from the middle of the Jordan from right where the priests stood and to carry them over with you and put them down at the place where you stay tonight."

4So Joshua called together the twelve men he had appointed from the Israelites, one from each tribe, 5and said to them, "Go over before the ark of the LORD your God into the middle of the Jordan. Each of you is to take up a stone on his shoulder, according to the number of the tribes of the Israelites, 6to serve as a sign among you. In the future, when your children ask you, 'What do these stones mean?' 7tell them that the flow of the Jordan was cut off before the ark of the covenant of the LORD. When it crossed the Jordan, the waters of the Jordan were cut off. These stones are to be a memorial to the people of Israel for ever."

8So the Israelites did as Joshua commanded them. They took twelve stones from the middle of the Jordan, according to the number of the tribes of the Israelites, as the LORD had told Joshua; and they carried them over with them to their camp, where they put them down. 9Joshua set up the twelve stones that had been*a* in the middle of the Jordan at the spot where the priests who carried the ark of the covenant had stood. And they are there to this day.

10Now the priests who carried the ark remained standing in the middle of the Jordan until everything the LORD had commanded Joshua was done by the people, just as Moses had directed Joshua. The people hurried over, 11and as soon as all of them had crossed, the ark of the LORD and the priests came to the other side while the people watched. 12The men of Reuben, Gad and the half-tribe of Manasseh crossed over, armed, in front of the Israelites, as Moses had directed them. 13About forty thousand armed for battle crossed over before the LORD to the plains of Jericho for war.

14That day the LORD exalted Joshua in the sight of all Israel; and they revered him all the days of his life, just as they had revered Moses.

15Then the LORD said to Joshua, 16"Command the priests carrying the ark of the Testimony to come up out of the Jordan."

17So Joshua commanded the priests, "Come up out of the Jordan."

18And the priests came up out of the river carrying the ark of the covenant of the LORD. No sooner had they set their feet on the dry ground than the waters of the Jordan returned to their place and ran in flood as before.

19On the tenth day of the first month the people went up from the Jordan and camped at Gilgal on the eastern border of Jericho. 20And Joshua set up at Gilgal the twelve stones they had taken out of the Jordan. 21He said to the Israelites, "In the future when your descendants ask their fathers, 'What do these stones mean?' 22tell them, 'Israel crossed the Jordan on dry ground.' 23For the LORD your God dried up the Jordan before you until you had crossed over. The LORD your God did to the Jordan just what he had done to the Red Sea*b* when he dried it up before us until we had crossed over. 24He did this so that all the peoples of the earth might know that the hand of the LORD is powerful and so that you might always fear the LORD your God."

---

*a*4 Hebrew *about two thousand cubits* (about 900 metres)   *b*16 That is, the Dead Sea   *a*9 Or *Joshua also set up twelve stones*   *b*23 Hebrew *Yam Suph*; that is, Sea of Reeds

■ Circumcision at Gilgal

5 Now when all the Amorite kings west of the Jordan and all the Canaanite kings along the coast heard how the LORD had dried up the Jordan before the Israelites until we had crossed over, their hearts sank[a] and they no longer had the courage to face the Israelites.

2At that time the LORD said to Joshua, "Make flint knives and circumcise the Israelites again." 3So Joshua made flint knives and circumcised the Israelites at Gibeath Haaraloth.[b]

4Now this is why he did so: All those who came out of Egypt — all the men of military age — died in the desert on the way after leaving Egypt. 5All the people that came out had been circumcised, but all the people born in the desert during the journey from Egypt had not. 6The Israelites had moved about in the desert forty years until all the men who were of military age when they left Egypt had died, since they had not obeyed the LORD. For the LORD had sworn to them that they would not see the land that he had solemnly promised their fathers to give us, a land flowing with milk and honey. 7So he raised up their sons in their place, and these were the ones Joshua circumcised. They were still uncircumcised because they had not been circumcised on the way. 8And after the whole nation had been circumcised, they remained where they were in camp until they were healed.

9Then the LORD said to Joshua, "Today I have rolled away the reproach of Egypt from you." So the place has been called Gilgal[c] to this day.

10On the evening of the fourteenth day of the month, while camped at Gilgal on the plains of Jericho, the Israelites celebrated the Passover. 11The day after the Passover, that very day, they ate some of the produce of the land: unleavened bread and roasted grain. 12The manna stopped the day after[d] they ate this food from the land; there was no longer any manna for the Israelites, but that year they ate of the produce of Canaan.

5:12 ■ NO MORE FREE LUNCH

For 40 years God had provided manna, a miraculous food that appeared like dew on the ground every night. In the desert, manna had been necessary for survival. In Palestine, however, the free food stopped. Israelites would be able to grow or gather adequate food for themselves.

■ The Fall of Jericho

13Now when Joshua was near Jericho, he looked up and saw a man standing in front of him with a drawn sword in his hand. Joshua went up to him and asked, "Are you for us or for our enemies?"

14"Neither," he replied, "but as commander of the army of the LORD I have now come." Then Joshua fell face down to the ground in reverence, and asked him, "What message does my Lord[e] have for his servant?"

15The commander of the LORD's army replied,

"Take off your sandals, for the place where you are standing is holy." And Joshua did so.

6 Now Jericho was tightly shut up because of the Israelites. No-one went out and no-one came in.

2Then the LORD said to Joshua, "See, I have delivered Jericho into your hands, along with its king and its fighting men. 3March around the city once with all the armed men. Do this for six days. 4Make seven priests carry trumpets of rams' horns in front of the ark. On the seventh day, march around the city seven times, with the priests blowing the trumpets. 5When you hear them sound a long blast on the trumpets, make all the people give a loud shout; then the wall of the city will collapse and the people will go up, every man straight in."

6So Joshua son of Nun called the priests and said to them, "Take up the ark of the covenant of the LORD and make seven priests carry trumpets in front of it." 7And he ordered the people, "Advance! March around the city, with the armed guard going ahead of the ark of the LORD."

8When Joshua had spoken to the people, the seven priests carrying the seven trumpets before the LORD went forward, blowing their trumpets, and the ark of the LORD's covenant followed them. 9The armed guard marched ahead of the priests who blew the trumpets, and the rear guard followed the ark. All this time the trumpets were sounding. 10But Joshua had commanded the people, "Do not give a war cry, do not raise your voices, do not say a word until the day I tell you to shout. Then shout!" 11So he had the ark of the LORD carried around the city, circling it once. Then the people returned to camp and spent the night there.

12Joshua got up early the next morning and the priests took up the ark of the LORD. 13The seven priests carrying the seven trumpets went forward, marching before the ark of the LORD and blowing the trumpets. The armed men went ahead of them and the rear guard followed the ark of the LORD, while the trumpets kept sounding. 14So on the second day they marched around the city once and returned to the camp. They did this for six days.

15On the seventh day, they got up at daybreak and marched around the city seven times in the same manner, except that on that day they circled the city seven times. 16The seventh time around, when the priests sounded the trumpet blast, Joshua commanded the people, "Shout! For the LORD has given you the city! 17The city and all that is in it are to be devoted[a] to the LORD. Only Rahab the prostitute[b] and all who are with her in her house shall be spared, because she hid the spies we sent. 18But keep away from the devoted things, so that you will not bring about your own destruction by taking any of them. Otherwise you will make the camp of Israel liable to destruction and bring trouble on it. 19All the silver and gold and the articles of bronze and iron are sacred to the LORD and must go into his treasury."

20When the trumpets sounded, the people shouted, and at the sound of the trumpet, when the people gave a loud shout, the wall collapsed; so every man charged straight in, and they took the city. 21They devoted the city to the LORD and

---

a 1 Hebrew *melted*   *b 3* *Gibeath Haaraloth* means *hill of foreskins.*   *c 9* *Gilgal* sounds like the Hebrew for *roll.*   *d 12* Or *the day*   *e 14* Or *lord*
a 17 The Hebrew term refers to the irrevocable giving over of things or persons to the LORD, often by totally destroying them; also in verses 18 and 21.
b 17 Or possibly *innkeeper*; also in verses 22 and 25

destroyed with the sword every living thing in it—men and women, young and old, cattle, sheep and donkeys.

22Joshua said to the two men who had spied out the land, "Go into the prostitute's house and bring her out and all who belong to her, in accordance with your oath to her." 23So the young men who had done the spying went in and brought out Rahab, her father and mother and brothers and all who belonged to her. They brought out her entire family and put them in a place outside the camp of Israel.

24Then they burned the whole city and everything in it, but they put the silver and gold and the articles of bronze and iron into the treasury of the LORD's house. 25But Joshua spared Rahab the prostitute, with her family and all who belonged to her, because she hid the men Joshua had sent as spies to Jericho—and she lives among the Israelites to this day.

26At that time Joshua pronounced this solemn oath: "Cursed before the LORD is the man who undertakes to rebuild this city, Jericho:

"At the cost of his firstborn son
    will he lay its foundations;
at the cost of his youngest
    will he set up its gates."

27So the LORD was with Joshua, and his fame spread throughout the land.

6:26 ■ CURSED CITY
Joshua's curse was fulfilled literally when a man attempted to rebuild the city of Jericho in the days of King Ahab (see 1 Kings 16:34).

■ Achan's Sin

7 But the Israelites acted unfaithfully in regard to the devoted things;a Achan son of Carmi, the son of Zimri,b the son of Zerah, of the tribe of Judah, took some of them. So the LORD's anger burned against Israel.

2Now Joshua sent men from Jericho to Ai, which is near Beth Aven to the east of Bethel, and told them, "Go up and spy out the region." So the men went up and spied out Ai.

3When they returned to Joshua, they said, "Not all the people will have to go up against Ai. Send two or three thousand men to take it and do not weary all the people, for only a few men are there." 4So about three thousand men went up; but they were routed by the men of Ai, 5who killed about thirty-six of them. They chased the Israelites from the city gate as far as the stone quarriesc and struck them down on the slopes. At this the hearts of the people melted and became like water.

6Then Joshua tore his clothes and fell face down to the ground before the ark of the LORD, remaining there till evening. The elders of Israel did the same, and sprinkled dust on their heads. 7And Joshua said, "Ah, Sovereign LORD, why did you ever bring this people across the Jordan to deliver us into the hands of the Amorites to destroy us? If only we had been

content to stay on the other side of the Jordan! 8O Lord, what can I say, now that Israel has been routed by its enemies? 9The Canaanites and the other people of the country will hear about this and they will surround us and wipe out our name from the earth. What then will you do for your own great name?"

7:7 ■ A CRISIS OF CONFIDENCE
Ai stood near the original location where God had promised the land to Abraham hundreds of years before (Genesis 12:8). Military defeat here, coming so quickly after a great victory at Jericho, caused even Joshua to tremble. Without God's protection, the Israelites were militarily vulnerable—trapped without possibility of escape across the flooding Jordan River.

The trouble at Ai came because of a single man who had greedily disobeyed God's battle commands. His punishment was drastic. Evidently the fledgling nation (like the fledgling church of Acts 5:1–10) needed a strong lesson in the consequences of taking God's word lightly.

10The LORD said to Joshua, "Stand up! What are you doing down on your face? 11Israel has sinned; they have violated my covenant, which I commanded them to keep. They have taken some of the devoted things; they have stolen, they have lied, they have put them with their own possessions. 12That is why the Israelites cannot stand against their enemies; they turn their backs and run because they have been made liable to destruction. I will not be with you any more unless you destroy whatever among you is devoted to destruction.

13"Go, consecrate the people. Tell them, 'Consecrate yourselves in preparation for tomorrow; for this is what the LORD, the God of Israel, says: That which is devoted is among you, O Israel. You cannot stand against your enemies until you remove it.

14"'In the morning, present yourselves tribe by tribe. The tribe that the LORD takes shall come forward clan by clan; the clan that the LORD takes shall come forward family by family; and the family that the LORD takes shall come forward man by man. 15He who is caught with the devoted things shall be destroyed by fire, along with all that belongs to him. He has violated the covenant of the LORD and has done a disgraceful thing in Israel!'"

16Early the next morning Joshua had Israel come forward by tribes, and Judah was taken. 17The clans of Judah came forward, and he took the Zerahites. He had the clan of the Zerahites come forward by families, and Zimri was taken. 18Joshua had his family come forward man by man, and Achan son of Carmi, the son of Zimri, the son of Zerah, of the tribe of Judah, was taken.

19Then Joshua said to Achan, "My son, give glory to the LORD,d the God of Israel, and give him the praise.e Tell me what you have done; do not hide it from me."

20Achan replied, "It is true! I have sinned against the LORD, the God of Israel. This is what I have done:

---

a1 The Hebrew term refers to the irrevocable giving over of things or persons to the LORD, often by totally destroying them; also in verses 11, 12, 13 and 15.   b1 See Septuagint and 1 Chron. 2:6; Hebrew Zabdi; also in verses 17 and 18.   c5 Or as far as Shebarim   d19 A solemn charge to tell the truth   e19 Or and confess to him

21When I saw in the plunder a beautiful robe from Babylonia,ᶠ two hundred shekelsᵍ of silver and a wedge of gold weighing fifty shekels,ᵇ I coveted them and took them. They are hidden in the ground inside my tent, with the silver underneath."

22So Joshua sent messengers, and they ran to the tent, and there it was, hidden in his tent, with the silver underneath. 23They took the things from the tent, brought them to Joshua and all the Israelites and spread them out before the LORD.

24Then Joshua, together with all Israel, took Achan son of Zerah, the silver, the robe, the gold wedge, his sons and daughters, his cattle, donkeys and sheep, his tent and all that he had, to the Valley of Achor. 25Joshua said, "Why have you brought this trouble on us? The LORD will bring trouble on you today."

Then all Israel stoned him, and after they had stoned the rest, they burned them. 26Over Achan they heaped up a large pile of rocks, which remains to this day. Then the LORD turned from his fierce anger. Therefore that place has been called the Valley of Achorⁱ ever since.

■ Ai Destroyed

8 Then the LORD said to Joshua, "Do not be afraid; do not be discouraged. Take the whole army with you, and go up and attack Ai. For I have delivered into your hands the king of Ai, his people, his city and his land. 2You shall do to Ai and its king as you did to Jericho and its king, except that you may carry off their plunder and livestock for yourselves. Set an ambush behind the city."

3So Joshua and the whole army moved out to attack Ai. He chose thirty thousand of his best fighting men and sent them out at night 4with these orders: "Listen carefully. You are to set an ambush behind the city. Don't go very far from it. All of you be on the alert. 5I and all those with me will advance on the city, and when the men come out against us, as they did before, we will flee from them. 6They will pursue us until we have lured them away from the city, for they will say, 'They are running away from us as they did before.' So when we flee from them, 7you are to rise up from ambush and take the city. The LORD your God will give it into your hand. 8When you have taken the city, set it on fire. Do what the LORD has commanded. See to it; you have my orders."

9Then Joshua sent them off, and they went to the place of ambush and lay in wait between Bethel and Ai, to the west of Ai—but Joshua spent that night with the people.

10Early the next morning Joshua mustered his men, and he and the leaders of Israel marched before them to Ai. 11The entire force that was with him marched up and approached the city and arrived in front of it. They set up camp north of Ai, with the valley between them and the city. 12Joshua had taken about five thousand men and set them in ambush between Bethel and Ai, to the west of the city. 13They had the soldiers take up their positions—all those in the camp to the north of the city and the

ambush to the west of it. That night Joshua went into the valley.

14When the king of Ai saw this, he and all the men of the city hurried out early in the morning to meet Israel in battle at a certain place overlooking the Arabah. But he did not know that an ambush had been set against him behind the city. 15Joshua and all Israel let themselves be driven back before them, and they fled towards the desert. 16All the men of Ai were called to pursue them, and they pursued Joshua and were lured away from the city. 17Not a man remained in Ai or Bethel who did not go after Israel. They left the city open and went in pursuit of Israel.

18Then the LORD said to Joshua, "Hold out towards Ai the javelin that is in your hand, for into your hand I will deliver the city." So Joshua held out his javelin towards Ai. 19As soon as he did this, the men in the ambush rose quickly from their position and rushed forward. They entered the city and captured it and quickly set it on fire.

20The men of Ai looked back and saw the smoke of the city rising against the sky, but they had no chance to escape in any direction, for the Israelites who had been fleeing towards the desert had turned back against their pursuers. 21For when Joshua and all Israel saw that the ambush had taken the city and that smoke was going up from the city, they turned round and attacked the men of Ai. 22The men of the ambush also came out of the city against them, so that they were caught in the middle, with Israelites on both sides. Israel cut them down, leaving them neither survivors nor fugitives. 23But they took the king of Ai alive and brought him to Joshua.

24When Israel had finished killing all the men of Ai in the fields and in the desert where they had chased them, and when every one of them had been put to the sword, all the Israelites returned to Ai and killed those who were in it. 25Twelve thousand men and women fell that day—all the people of Ai. 26For Joshua did not draw back the hand that held out his javelin until he had destroyedª all who lived in Ai. 27But Israel did carry off for themselves the livestock and plunder of this city, as the LORD had instructed Joshua.

28So Joshua burned Ai and made it a permanent heap of ruins, a desolate place to this day. 29He hung the king of Ai on a tree and left him there until evening. At sunset, Joshua ordered them to take his body from the tree and throw it down at the entrance of the city gate. And they raised a large pile of rocks over it, which remains to this day.

■ The Covenant Renewed at Mount Ebal

30Then Joshua built on Mount Ebal an altar to the LORD, the God of Israel, 31as Moses the servant of the LORD had commanded the Israelites. He built it according to what is written in the Book of the Law of Moses—an altar of uncut stones, on which no iron tool had been used. On it they offered to the LORD burnt offerings and sacrificed fellowship offerings.ᵇ 32There, in the presence of the Israelites, Joshua copied on stones the law of Moses, which he had written. 33All Israel, aliens and citizens alike, with

ſ21 Hebrew Shinar   ᵍ21 That is, about 5 pounds (about 2.3 kilograms)   ᵇ21 That is, about 1¼ pounds (about 0.6 kilogram)   ⁱ26 Achor means trouble.   ª26 The Hebrew term refers to the irrevocable giving over of things or persons to the LORD, often by totally destroying them.   ᵇ31 Traditionally peace offerings their elders, officials and judges, were standing on both sides of the ark of the covenant of the LORD, facing those who carried it—the priests, who were Levites. Half of the people stood in front of Mount Gerizim and half of them in front of Mount Ebal, as Moses the servant of the LORD had formerly commanded when he gave instructions to bless the people of Israel.

8:30 ■ BLESSINGS AND CURSES

The scene in this section, which describes the carrying out of Moses' instructions in Deuteronomy 27–28, was a profoundly symbolic event in the history of the Israelites. It elaborately portrayed what would happen if they obeyed the covenant, and if they disobeyed. The two mountains, Ebal and Gerizim, formed a natural amphitheatre ideal for such a public ceremony. From their peaks much of the promised land could be seen. (Mount Gerizim eventually became the seat of worship for the Samaritans, which helps explain Jesus' conversation in John 4.)

34Afterwards, Joshua read all the words of the law—the blessings and the curses—just as it is written in the Book of the Law. 35There was not a word of all that Moses had commanded that Joshua did not read to the whole assembly of Israel, including the women and children, and the aliens who lived among them.

■ The Gibeonite Deception

9 Now when all the kings west of the Jordan heard about these things—those in the hill country, in the western foothills, and along the entire coast of the Great Sea*a* as far as Lebanon (the kings of the Hittites, Amorites, Canaanites, Perizzites, Hivites and Jebusites)—2they came together to make war against Joshua and Israel.

9:2 ■ WAR STRATEGY

Joshua used expert military strategy against Israel's many enemies in Canaan. His assignment as one of the original spies had given Joshua valuable knowledge of the topography of the land. Israelite armies entered the middle of Canaan, splitting the country in two and intersecting strategic trade routes. His "flying column" formations, night marches, ambush tactics rather than long sieges, and destruction of key cities showed awareness of advanced military techniques.

3However, when the people of Gibeon heard what Joshua had done to Jericho and Ai, 4they resorted to a ruse: They went as a delegation whose donkeys were loaded*b* with worn-out sacks and old wineskins, cracked and mended. 5The men put worn and patched sandals on their feet and wore old clothes. All the bread of their food supply was dry and mouldy. 6Then they went to Joshua in the camp at Gilgal and said to him and the men of Israel, "We

have come from a distant country; make a treaty with us."

7The men of Israel said to the Hivites, "But perhaps you live near us. How then can we make a treaty with you?"

8"We are your servants," they said to Joshua.

But Joshua asked, "Who are you and where do you come from?"

9They answered: "Your servants have come from a very distant country because of the fame of the LORD your God. For we have heard reports of him: all that he did in Egypt, 10and all that he did to the two kings of the Amorites east of the Jordan—Sihon king of Heshbon, and Og king of Bashan, who reigned in Ashtaroth. 11And our elders and all those living in our country said to us, 'Take provisions for your journey; go and meet them and say to them, "We are your servants; make a treaty with us."' 12This bread of ours was warm when we packed it at home on the day we left to come to you. But now see how dry and mouldy it is. 13And these wineskins that we filled were new, but see how cracked they are. And our clothes and sandals are worn out by the very long journey."

14The men of Israel sampled their provisions but did not enquire of the LORD. 15Then Joshua made a treaty of peace with them to let them live, and the leaders of the assembly ratified it by oath.

9:14 ■ TRICKED!

The Gibeonites saved themselves by performing an elaborate deception on the Israelite soldiers, acting as if they had come from far away. The Israelites tried to check their story, but neglected the most important test of all: they "did not enquire of the LORD". Throughout Joshua, God shows that he is in charge and that following him is the only way to victory.

The Gibeonites' trick saved their lives, but they were forced to become servants. Some of them later converted to Judaism. The book of Nehemiah includes Gibeonites (sometimes called Hivites) among those who helped rebuild the walls of Jerusalem. And at least one of King David's "mighty men" was a Gibeonite. (See also the incident recorded in 2 Samuel 21:1–14.) Even so, the Gibeonites often caused trouble for Israel.

16Three days after they made the treaty with the Gibeonites, the Israelites heard that they were neighbours, living near them. 17So the Israelites set out and on the third day came to their cities: Gibeon, Kephirah, Beeroth and Kiriath Jearim. 18But the Israelites did not attack them, because the leaders of the assembly had sworn an oath to them by the LORD, the God of Israel.

The whole assembly grumbled against the leaders, 19but all the leaders answered, "We have given them our oath by the LORD, the God of Israel, and we cannot touch them now. 20This is what we will do to them: We will let them live, so that wrath will not fall on us for breaking the oath we swore to them." 21They continued, "Let them live, but let them be

a1 That is, the Mediterranean   *b4* Most Hebrew manuscripts; some Hebrew manuscripts, Vulgate and Syriac (see also Septuagint) *They prepared provisions and loaded their donkeys* woodcutters and water-carriers for the entire community." So the leaders' promise to them was kept. 22Then Joshua summoned the Gibeonites and said, "Why did you deceive us by saying, 'We live a long way from you,' while actually you live near us? 23You are now under a curse: You will never cease to serve as woodcutters and water-carriers for the house of my God."

24They answered Joshua, "Your servants were clearly told how the LORD your God had commanded his servant Moses to give you the whole land and to wipe out all its inhabitants from before you. So we feared for our lives because of you, and that is why we did this. 25We are now in your hands. Do to us whatever seems good and right to you."

26So Joshua saved them from the Israelites, and they did not kill them. 27That day he made the Gibeonites woodcutters and water-carriers for the community and for the altar of the LORD at the place the LORD would choose. And that is what they are to this day.

■ The Sun Stands Still

10 Now Adoni-Zedek king of Jerusalem heard that Joshua had taken Ai and totally destroyed*a* it, doing to Ai and its king as he had done to Jericho and its king, and that the people of Gibeon had made a treaty of peace with Israel and were living near them. 2He and his people were very much alarmed at this, because Gibeon was an important city, like one of the royal cities; it was larger than Ai, and all its men were good fighters. 3So Adoni-Zedek king of Jerusalem appealed to Hoham king of Hebron, Piram king of Jarmuth, Japhia king of Lachish and Debir king of Eglon. 4"Come up and help me attack Gibeon," he said, "because it has made peace with Joshua and the Israelites."

5Then the five kings of the Amorites — the kings of Jerusalem, Hebron, Jarmuth, Lachish and Eglon — joined forces. They moved up with all their troops and took up positions against Gibeon and attacked it.

6The Gibeonites then sent word to Joshua in the camp at Gilgal: "Do not abandon your servants. Come up to us quickly and save us! Help us, because all the Amorite kings from the hill country have joined forces against us."

7So Joshua marched up from Gilgal with his entire army, including all the best fighting men. 8The LORD said to Joshua, "Do not be afraid of them; I have given them into your hand. Not one of them will be able to withstand you."

9After an all-night march from Gilgal, Joshua took them by surprise. 10The LORD threw them into confusion before Israel, who defeated them in a great victory at Gibeon. Israel pursued them along the road going up to Beth Horon and cut them down all the way to Azekah and Makkedah. 11As they fled before Israel on the road down from Beth Horon to Azekah, the LORD hurled large hailstones down on them from the sky, and more of them died from the hailstones than were killed by the swords of the Israelites.

12On the day the LORD gave the Amorites over to Israel, Joshua said to the LORD in the presence of Israel:

"O sun, stand still over Gibeon,
    O moon, over the Valley of Aijalon."
13So the sun stood still,
    and the moon stopped,
    till the nation avenged itself on*b* its
        enemies,

as it is written in the Book of Jashar.

The sun stopped in the middle of the sky and delayed going down about a full day. 14There has never been a day like it before or since, a day when the LORD listened to a man. Surely the LORD was fighting for Israel!

15Then Joshua returned with all Israel to the camp at Gilgal.

■ Five Amorite Kings Killed

16Now the five kings had fled and hidden in the cave at Makkedah. 17When Joshua was told that the five kings had been found hiding in the cave at Makkedah, 18he said, "Roll large rocks up to the mouth of the cave, and post some men there to guard it. 19But don't stop! Pursue your enemies, attack them from the rear and don't let them reach their cities, for the LORD your God has given them into your hand."

20So Joshua and the Israelites destroyed them completely — almost to a man — but the few who were left reached their fortified cities. 21The whole army then returned safely to Joshua in the camp at Makkedah, and no-one uttered a word against the Israelites.

22Joshua said, "Open the mouth of the cave and bring those five kings out to me." 23So they brought the five kings out of the cave — the kings of Jerusalem, Hebron, Jarmuth, Lachish and Eglon. 24When they had brought these kings to Joshua, he summoned all the men of Israel and said to the army commanders who had come with him, "Come here and put your feet on the necks of these kings." So they came forward and placed their feet on their necks.

10:24 ■ ACT OF HUMILIATION
This act — stepping on a neck — was the ultimate way to humiliate a king. It expressed utter, enforced submission. Egyptian and Assyrian sculptures frequently portrayed this custom.

25Joshua said to them, "Do not be afraid; do not be discouraged. Be strong and courageous. This is what the LORD will do to all the enemies you are going to fight." 26Then Joshua struck and killed the kings and hung them on five trees, and they were left hanging on the trees until evening.

27At sunset Joshua gave the order and they took them down from the trees and threw them into the cave where they had been hiding. At the mouth of the cave they placed large rocks, which are there to this day.

28That day Joshua took Makkedah. He put the city

a 1 The Hebrew term refers to the irrevocable giving over of things or persons to the LORD, often by totally destroying them; also in verses 28, 35, 37, 39 and 40.   *b 13* Or *nation triumphed over* and its king to the sword and totally destroyed everyone in it. He left no survivors. And he did to the king of Makkedah as he had done to the king of Jericho.

■ Southern Cities Conquered

²⁹Then Joshua and all Israel with him moved on from Makkedah to Libnah and attacked it. ³⁰The LORD also gave that city and its king into Israel's hand. The city and everyone in it Joshua put to the sword. He left no survivors there. And he did to its king as he had done to the king of Jericho.

³¹Then Joshua and all Israel with him moved on from Libnah to Lachish; he took up positions against it and attacked it. ³²The LORD handed Lachish over to Israel, and Joshua took it on the second day. The city and everyone in it he put to the sword, just as he had done to Libnah. ³³Meanwhile, Horam king of Gezer had come up to help Lachish, but Joshua defeated him and his army — until no survivors were left.

³⁴Then Joshua and all Israel with him moved on from Lachish to Eglon; they took up positions against it and attacked it. ³⁵They captured it that same day and put it to the sword and totally destroyed everyone in it, just as they had done to Lachish.

³⁶Then Joshua and all Israel with him went up from Eglon to Hebron and attacked it. ³⁷They took the city and put it to the sword, together with its king, its villages and everyone in it. They left no survivors. Just as at Eglon, they totally destroyed it and everyone in it.

³⁸Then Joshua and all Israel with him turned round and attacked Debir. ³⁹They took the city, its king and its villages, and put them to the sword. Everyone in it they totally destroyed. They left no survivors. They did to Debir and its king as they had done to Libnah and its king and to Hebron.

⁴⁰So Joshua subdued the whole region, including the hill country, the Negev, the western foothills and the mountain slopes, together with all their kings. He left no survivors. He totally destroyed all who breathed, just as the LORD, the God of Israel, had commanded. ⁴¹Joshua subdued them from Kadesh Barnea to Gaza and from the whole region of Goshen to Gibeon. ⁴²All these kings and their lands Joshua conquered in one campaign, because the LORD, the God of Israel, fought for Israel.

⁴³Then Joshua returned with all Israel to the camp at Gilgal.

■ Northern Kings Defeated

11 When Jabin king of Hazor heard of this, he sent word to Jobab king of Madon, to the kings of Shimron and Acshaph, ²and to the northern kings who were in the mountains, in the Arabah south of Kinnereth, in the western foothills and in Naphoth Dorᵃ on the west; ³to the Canaanites in the east and west; to the Amorites, Hittites, Perizzites and Jebusites in the hill country; and to the Hivites below Hermon in the region of Mizpah. ⁴They came out with all their troops and a large number of horses and chariots — a huge army, as numerous

as the sand on the seashore. ⁵All these kings joined forces and made camp together at the Waters of Merom, to fight against Israel.

⁶The LORD said to Joshua, "Do not be afraid of them, because by this time tomorrow I will hand all of them over to Israel, slain. You are to hamstring their horses and burn their chariots."

⁷So Joshua and his whole army came against them suddenly at the Waters of Merom and attacked them, ⁸and the LORD gave them into the hand of Israel. They defeated them and pursued them all the way to Greater Sidon, to Misrephoth Maim, and to the Valley of Mizpah on the east, until no survivors were left. ⁹Joshua did to them as the LORD had directed: He hamstrung their horses and burned their chariots.

11:9 ■ ADVANCED WEAPONRY

If a guerrilla band in Central America captured an F-16 fighter, what could they do with it? Probably nothing, unless they had trained pilots. The Israelites faced a similar situation. War-horses and chariots were advanced weapons of war that the Israelites would not master for hundreds of years. Joshua probably crippled the captured horses to ensure that they would not fall into enemy hands again. Militarily and economically, the Israelites were up against people more sophisticated than themselves.

¹⁰At that time Joshua turned back and captured Hazor and put its king to the sword. (Hazor had been the head of all these kingdoms.) ¹¹Everyone in it they put to the sword. They totally destroyedᵇ them, not sparing anything that breathed, and he burned up Hazor itself.

¹²Joshua took all these royal cities and their kings and put them to the sword. He totally destroyed them, as Moses the servant of the LORD had commanded. ¹³Yet Israel did not burn any of the cities built on their mounds — except Hazor, which Joshua burned. ¹⁴The Israelites carried off for themselves all the plunder and livestock of these cities, but all the people they put to the sword until they completely destroyed them, not sparing anyone that breathed. ¹⁵As the LORD commanded his servant Moses, so Moses commanded Joshua, and Joshua did it; he left nothing undone of all that the LORD commanded Moses.

¹⁶So Joshua took this entire land: the hill country, all the Negev, the whole region of Goshen, the western foothills, the Arabah and the mountains of Israel with their foothills, ¹⁷from Mount Halak, which rises towards Seir, to Baal Gad in the Valley of Lebanon below Mount Hermon. He captured all their kings and struck them down, putting them to death. ¹⁸Joshua waged war against all these kings for a long time. ¹⁹Except for the Hivites living in Gibeon, not one city made a treaty of peace with the Israelites, who took them all in battle. ²⁰For it was the LORD himself who hardened their hearts to wage war against Israel, so that he might destroy them totally,

---

ᵃ2 Or in the heights of Dor   ᵇ11 The Hebrew term refers to the irrevocable giving over of things or persons to the LORD, often by totally destroying them; also in verses 12, 20 and 21.

exterminating them without mercy, as the LORD had commanded Moses.

²¹At that time Joshua went and destroyed the Anakites from the hill country: from Hebron, Debir and Anab, from all the hill country of Judah, and from all the hill country of Israel. Joshua totally destroyed them and their towns. ²²No Anakites were left in Israelite territory; only in Gaza, Gath and Ashdod did any survive. ²³So Joshua took the entire land, just as the LORD had directed Moses, and he gave it as an inheritance to Israel according to their tribal divisions.

Then the land had rest from war.

■ List of Defeated Kings

12 These are the kings of the land whom the Israelites had defeated and whose territory they took over east of the Jordan, from the Arnon Gorge to Mount Hermon, including all the eastern side of the Arabah:

²Sihon king of the Amorites,
who reigned in Heshbon. He ruled from Aroer on the rim of the Arnon Gorge—from the middle of the gorge—to the Jabbok River, which is the border of the Ammonites. This included half of Gilead. ³He also ruled over the eastern

---

■ IS A WAR EVER HOLY?
WHY DID GOD ORDER A RUTHLESS MILITARY CAMPAIGN?

INSIGHT

THE LORD SAID TO JOSHUA, "DO NOT BE AFRAID OF THEM, BECAUSE BY THIS TIME TOMORROW I WILL HAND ALL OF THEM OVER TO ISRAEL, SLAIN." ■ 11:6

Holy war. Ironically, the term applies to the most vicious, bloody wars. And often, far too often, Christians have been at the heart of such holy wars.

There is something irrational and even repulsive about a holy war. It harnesses all the best energies of religion for one of the ugliest acts of human nature. And yet anyone who reads the Bible cannot ignore the holy wars in the Old Testament.

Whole books have been written about the problem, and no brief article can begin to cover the issues. But modern readers need some background to help understand why a fierce holy war is presented in such a good light.

■ A LAND PROMISED TO THE ISRAELITES
The Israelites' fighting style fitted the harsh pattern of warfare in that day. Contemporary Egyptian and Assyrian reports boasted of mass executions, torture and the systematic razing of cities. But God's involvement raises unique questions. He personally ordered the destruction of seven Canaanite nations, with no survivors. Why?

The Old Testament makes clear that the Canaanites were not being uprooted on a sudden whim. God had promised the land to the Israelites over 400 years before Joshua. He had called one man, Abraham, to found a nation of chosen people. He repeated those promises often (Genesis 12:1–3; 15:5–18; 17:2–8; 26:3,23–24; 28:13–14) and finally called the Israelites out of Egypt to take over the promised land. Almost from the beginning Canaan was a vital part of God's plan.

■ DELAYED PUNISHMENT
Israel's inheritance, however, meant kicking out the Canaanites. How could innocent people simply be pushed aside, or killed? In answer to this question, the Bible makes it clear that the Canaanites were *not* "innocent". Through their long history of sin, they had forfeited their right to the land.

Four hundred years before Joshua, God had told Abraham that his descendants would not occupy the land until the sin of its inhabitants had "reached its full measure" (Genesis 15:16). Later, just days before the onset of Joshua's campaign, Moses stated, "It is not because of your righteousness or your integrity that you are going in to take possession of their land; but on account of the wickedness of these nations, the LORD your God will drive them out before you" (Deuteronomy 9:5).

Historians have uncovered plenty of evidence of this wickedness. Canaanite temples featured prostitutes, orgies, and human sacrifice. Relics and plaques of exaggerated sex organs hint at the morality that characterised Canaan.

Canaanite gods, such as Baal and his wife Anath, delighted in butchery and sadism. Archaeologists have found great numbers of jars containing the tiny bones of children sacrificed to Baal. Families seeking good luck in a new home practised "foundation sacrifice". They would kill one of their children and seal the body in the mortar of the wall. In many ways, Canaan had become like Sodom and Gomorrah.

The Bible records that God has patience with decadent societies for a time, but judgment inevitably follows. For Sodom and Gomorrah it took the form of fire and brimstone. For Canaan it came through Joshua's conquering armies. Later, God let his own chosen people be ravaged by invaders, as

Arabah from the Sea of Kinnereth[a] to the Sea of the Arabah (the Salt Sea[b]), to Beth Jeshimoth, and then southward below the slopes of Pisgah.

4And the territory of Og king of Bashan, one of the last of the Rephaites, who reigned in Ashtaroth and Edrei. 5He ruled over Mount Hermon, Salecah, all of Bashan to the border of the people of Geshur and Maacah, and half of Gilead to the border of Sihon king of Heshbon.

6Moses, the servant of the LORD, and the Israelites conquered them. And Moses the servant of the LORD gave their land to the Reubenites, the Gadites and the half-tribe of Manasseh to be their possession.

7These are the kings of the land that Joshua and the Israelites conquered on the west side of the Jordan, from Baal Gad in the Valley of Lebanon to Mount Halak, which rises towards Seir (their lands Joshua gave as an inheritance to the tribes of Israel according to their tribal divisions—8the hill country, the western foothills, the Arabah, the mountain slopes, the desert and the Negev—the lands of the

---

punishment for their sins. The judgment pronounced on Canaan seems severe, but no more severe than what was later inflicted on Israel itself.

■ THE CONTAMINATION PROBLEM
The Israelites could not simply settle down as new neighbours among existing Canaanite cities. From the time when the tribes had made a golden calf while Moses was receiving the Ten Commandments (Exodus 32), Israelites had shown a fatal weakness to infection from outside. They seemed particularly susceptible to sins of sex and idolatry, Canaan's national specialties.

Israel's later history offers negative proof of why God commanded the utter destruction of Canaanites. The damning phrase in Joshua, "the Israelites did not drive out the people", hints at trouble to come, and the very next book, Judges, tells of the devastating results. The Israelites fell to one of their lowest levels because they had not fulfilled the original mission of cleansing the land of impure elements.

■ A STRUGGLE BEYOND NATIONS
Looking back at this period of time, we tend to see the battles of Joshua as national or racial struggles: the Israelites versus the people of Canaan. But the Bible presents the warfare as a wider struggle: one between those who followed God and those who opposed him.

When God judged groups, as he judged the world in Noah's day or as he judged Sodom and Gomorrah, those few who remained faithful to him found a way of escape. And in Joshua one bright story shines out: the story of Rahab, a non-Israelite. A typical Canaanite who worked as a professional prostitute, she nevertheless learned to fear and then trust the God of Israel. She escaped the fall of Jericho. Furthermore,

she went on to marry a leading Israelite and become one of the ancestors of the Messiah himself, Jesus.

Rahab claimed that others in her city of Jericho had quaked in fear for 40 years, waiting for the judgment of the God of Israel (2:9–11). Yet only she took the further step of seeking help. If others in Canaan had repented and turned to God, they might well have escaped punishment, as Rahab did.

■ HOLY WARS TODAY
One fact about "holy war" is very clear. We cannot argue from a war specifically commanded by God in Joshua to any national situation today. In the Old Testament, God was dealing primarily with one particular nation, the Israelites, for a stated purpose. When the Messiah finally emerged out of that nation, everything changed.

Jesus' followers all lived in the same territory captured by Joshua, the "promised land". But four times, in his very last words, Jesus commanded his disciples to go out, away from Jerusalem, into all the world. Go, he told them, not as conquering armies but rather as bearers of the good news that applies to all people, all races, all nations.

Anyone who looks to the book of Joshua for a rationalisation of a holy war must also look ahead to Jesus. Although on a holy crusade, he did not choose violent means. In fact, he chose suffering and death. Nothing in the New Testament gives consolation to a religious warrior.

(For a longer discussion of this topic, see *The Goodness of God,* by John Wenham.)

□ LIFE QUESTIONS:
What arguments have you heard Christians use for or against wars?

---

a 3 That is, Galilee   *b 3* That is, the Dead Sea

Hittites, Amorites, Canaanites, Perizzites, Hivites and Jebusites):

11:23 ■ TWO ACCOUNTS OF WARFARE

Judges 1 summarises the incidents recorded in Joshua, but from a different point of view. Joshua presents the campaign as highly successful; Judges shows that many military goals were never achieved. One possible explanation: Joshua presented the wars as a series of raids on territory and did not include the "mopping up" and settlement process. Judges shows that, after they divided up the land, the Israelites proved far less successful in the second phase of conquest.

9the king of Jericho	one
the king of Ai (near Bethel)	one
10the king of Jerusalem	one
the king of Hebron	one
11the king of Jarmuth	one
the king of Lachish	one
12the king of Eglon	one
the king of Gezer	one
13the king of Debir	one
the king of Geder	one
14the king of Hormah	one
the king of Arad	one
15the king of Libnah	one
the king of Adullam	one
16the king of Makkedah	one
the king of Bethel	one
17the king of Tappuah	one
the king of Hepher	one
18the king of Aphek	one
the king of Lasharon	one
19the king of Madon	one
the king of Hazor	one
20the king of Shimron Meron	one
the king of Acshaph	one
21the king of Taanach	one
the king of Megiddo	one
22the king of Kedesh	one
the king of Jokneam in Carmel	one
23the king of Dor (in Naphoth Dor*c*)	one
the king of Goyim in Gilgal	one
24the king of Tirzah	one

thirty-one kings in all.

■ Land Still to Be Taken

13 When Joshua was old and well advanced in years, the LORD said to him, "You are very old, and there are still very large areas of land to be taken over.

2"This is the land that remains: all the regions of the Philistines and Geshurites: 3from the Shihor River on the east of Egypt to the territory of Ekron on the north, all of it counted as Canaanite (the territory of the five Philistine rulers in Gaza, Ashdod, Ashkelon, Gath and Ekron — that of the Avvites); 4from the south, all the land of the Canaanites, from Arah of the Sidonians as far as Aphek, the region of the Amorites, 5the area of the Gebalites;*a* and all Lebanon to the east, from Baal Gad below Mount Hermon to Lebo*b* Hamath.

6"As for all the inhabitants of the mountain regions from Lebanon to Misrephoth Maim, that is, all the Sidonians, I myself will drive them out before the Israelites. Be sure to allocate this land to Israel for an inheritance, as I have instructed you, 7and divide it as an inheritance among the nine tribes and half of the tribe of Manasseh."

13:1 ■ DIVIDING UP THE LAND

Chapter 13 introduces an abrupt transition. The rest of Joshua relates what happened five to seven years after the crossing of the Jordan. Chapters 13–22 give a kind of land-title record for the new nation. Genesis 48–49 and Deuteronomy 33 provide background material. For example, Reuben's tribe forfeited the right to first choice because of a sexual sin, and Simeon and Levi lost their rights because of their violent past.

■ Division of the Land East of the Jordan

8The other half of Manasseh,*c* the Reubenites and the Gadites had received the inheritance that Moses had given them east of the Jordan, as he, the servant of the LORD, had assigned it to them.

9It extended from Aroer on the rim of the Arnon Gorge, and from the town in the middle of the gorge, and included the whole plateau of Medeba as far as Dibon, 10and all the towns of Sihon king of the Amorites, who ruled in Heshbon, out to the border of the Ammonites. 11It also included Gilead, the territory of the people of Geshur and Maacah, all of Mount Hermon and all Bashan as far as Salecah — 12that is, the whole kingdom of Og in Bashan, who had reigned in Ashtaroth and Edrei and had survived as one of the last of the Rephaites. Moses had defeated them and taken over their land. 13But the Israelites did not drive out the people of Geshur and Maacah, so they continue to live among the Israelites to this day.

14But to the tribe of Levi he gave no inheritance, since the offerings made by fire to the LORD, the God of Israel, are their inheritance, as he promised them.

15This is what Moses had given to the tribe of Reuben, clan by clan:

16The territory from Aroer on the rim of the Arnon Gorge, and from the town in the middle of the gorge, and the whole plateau past Medeba 17to Heshbon and all its towns on the plateau, including Dibon, Bamoth Baal, Beth Baal Meon, 18Jahaz, Kedemoth, Mephaath, 19Kiriathaim, Sibmah, Zereth Shahar on the hill in the valley, 20Beth Peor, the slopes of Pisgah, and Beth Jeshimoth 21 — all the towns on the plateau and the entire realm of Sihon king of the Amorites, who ruled at Heshbon. Moses had defeated him and the Midianite chiefs, Evi, Rekem, Zur, Hur and Reba—princes allied with Sihon—who lived in that country. ²²In addition to those slain in battle, the Israelites had put to the sword Balaam son of Beor, who practised divination. ²³The boundary of the Reubenites was the bank of the Jordan. These towns and their villages were the inheritance of the Reubenites, clan by clan.

²⁴This is what Moses had given to the tribe of Gad, clan by clan:

²⁵The territory of Jazer, all the towns of Gilead and half the Ammonite country as far as Aroer, near Rabbah; ²⁶and from Heshbon to Ramath Mizpah and Betonim, and from Mahanaim to the territory of Debir; ²⁷and in the valley, Beth Haram, Beth Nimrah, Succoth and Zaphon with the rest of the realm of Sihon king of Heshbon (the east side of the Jordan, the territory up to the end of the Sea of Kinnereth*ᵈ*). ²⁸These towns and their villages were the inheritance of the Gadites, clan by clan.

²⁹This is what Moses had given to the half-tribe of Manasseh, that is, to half the family of the descendants of Manasseh, clan by clan:

³⁰The territory extending from Mahanaim and including all of Bashan, the entire realm of Og king of Bashan—all the settlements of Jair in Bashan, sixty towns, ³¹half of Gilead, and Ashtaroth and Edrei (the royal cities of Og in Bashan). This was for the descendants of Makir son of Manasseh—for half of the sons of Makir, clan by clan.

³²This is the inheritance Moses had given when he was in the plains of Moab across the Jordan east of Jericho. ³³But to the tribe of Levi, Moses had given no inheritance; the LORD, the God of Israel, is their inheritance, as he promised them.

■ Division of the Land West of the Jordan

14 Now these are the areas the Israelites received as an inheritance in the land of Canaan, which Eleazar the priest, Joshua son of Nun and the heads of the tribal clans of Israel allotted to them. ²Their inheritances were assigned by lot to the nine-and-a-half tribes, as the LORD had commanded through Moses. ³Moses had granted the two-and-a-half tribes their inheritance east of the Jordan but had not granted the Levites an inheritance among the rest, ⁴for the sons of Joseph had become two tribes—Manasseh and Ephraim. The Levites received no share of the land but only towns to live in, with pasture-lands for their flocks and herds. ⁵So the Israelites divided the land, just as the LORD had commanded Moses.

■ Hebron Given to Caleb

⁶Now the men of Judah approached Joshua at Gilgal, and Caleb son of Jephunneh the Kenizzite said to him, "You know what the LORD said to Moses the man of God at Kadesh Barnea about you and me. ⁷I was forty years old when Moses the servant of the LORD sent me from Kadesh Barnea to explore the land. And I brought him back a report according to my convictions, ⁸but my brothers who went up with me made the hearts of the people sink.*ᵃ* I, however, followed the LORD my God wholeheartedly. ⁹So on that day Moses swore to me, 'The land on which your feet have walked will be your inheritance and that of your children for ever, because you have followed the LORD my God wholeheartedly.'*ᵇ*

¹⁰"Now then, just as the LORD promised, he has kept me alive for forty-five years since the time he said this to Moses, while Israel moved about in the desert. So here I am today, eighty-five years old! ¹¹I am still as strong today as the day Moses sent me out; I'm just as vigorous to go out to battle now as I was then. ¹²Now give me this hill country that the LORD promised me that day. You yourself heard then that the Anakites were there and their cities were large and fortified, but, the LORD helping me, I will drive them out just as he said."

14:10 ■ SEVEN-YEAR FIGHT
Just how long did the capture of Palestine take? The book of Joshua doesn't say, but a little arithmetic shows that the fighting had been going on for about seven years. Caleb was 40 when Moses first sent him to explore the land (verse 7). Israel spent 38 years in the desert after that (Deuteronomy 2:14), making Caleb 78 when they finally invaded. Since he had now reached 85, the last seven years of Caleb's life must have been spent fighting. He was one of the two oldest Israelites; all others of his generation had died in the desert.

¹³Then Joshua blessed Caleb son of Jephunneh and gave him Hebron as his inheritance. ¹⁴So Hebron has belonged to Caleb son of Jephunneh the Kenizzite ever since, because he followed the LORD, the God of Israel, wholeheartedly. ¹⁵(Hebron used to be called Kiriath Arba after Arba, who was the greatest man among the Anakites.)

Then the land had rest from war.

■ Allotment for Judah

15 The allotment for the tribe of Judah, clan by clan, extended down to the territory of Edom, to the Desert of Zin in the extreme south. ²Their southern boundary started from the bay at the southern end of the Salt Sea,*ᵃ* ³crossed south of Scorpion*ᵇ* Pass, continued on to Zin and went over to the south of Kadesh Barnea. Then it ran past Hezron up to Addar and curved around to Karka. ⁴It then passed along to Azmon and joined the Wadi of Egypt, ending at the sea. This is their*ᶜ* southern boundary.

⁵The eastern boundary is the Salt Sea as far as the mouth of the Jordan.

The northern boundary started from the bay of the sea at the mouth of the Jordan, ⁶went up to Beth Hoglah and continued north of Beth Arabah to the Stone of Bohan son of Reuben.

ᵈ27 That is, Galilee   *ᵃ8* Hebrew *melt*   *ᵇ9* Deut. 1:36   *ᵃ2* That is, the Dead Sea; also in verse 5   *ᵇ3* Hebrew *Akrabbim*   *ᶜ4* Hebrew *your*

7The boundary then went up to Debir from the Valley of Achor and turned north to Gilgal, which faces the Pass of Adummim south of the gorge. It continued along to the waters of En Shemesh and came out at En Rogel. 8Then it ran up the Valley of Ben Hinnom along the southern slope of the Jebusite city (that is, Jerusalem). From there it climbed to the top of the hill west of the Hinnom Valley at the northern end of the Valley of Rephaim. 9From the hilltop the boundary headed towards the spring of the waters of Nephtoah, came out at the towns of Mount Ephron and went down towards Baalah (that is, Kiriath Jearim). 10Then it curved westward from Baalah to Mount Seir, ran along the northern slope of Mount Jearim (that is, Kesalon), continued down to Beth Shemesh and crossed to Timnah. 11It went to the northern slope of Ekron, turned towards Shikkeron, passed along to Mount Baalah and reached Jabneel. The boundary ended at the sea.

12The western boundary is the coastline of the Great Sea.*d*

These are the boundaries around the people of Judah by their clans.

13In accordance with the LORD's command to him, Joshua gave to Caleb son of Jephunneh a portion in Judah — Kiriath Arba, that is, Hebron. (Arba was the forefather of Anak.) 14From Hebron Caleb drove out the three Anakites — Sheshai, Ahiman and Talmai — descendants of Anak. 15From there he marched against the people living in Debir (formerly called Kiriath Sepher). 16And Caleb said, "I will give my daughter Acsah in marriage to the man who attacks and captures Kiriath Sepher." 17Othniel son of Kenaz, Caleb's brother, took it; so Caleb gave his daughter Acsah to him in marriage.

18One day when she came to Othniel, she urged him*e* to ask her father for a field. When she got off her donkey, Caleb asked her, "What can I do for you?"

19She replied, "Do me a special favour. Since you have given me land in the Negev, give me also springs of water." So Caleb gave her the upper and lower springs.

20This is the inheritance of the tribe of Judah, clan by clan:

21The southernmost towns of the tribe of Judah in the Negev towards the boundary of Edom were:
Kabzeel, Eder, Jagur, 22Kinah, Dimonah, Adadah, 23Kedesh, Hazor, Ithnan, 24Ziph, Telem, Bealoth, 25Hazor Hadattah, Kerioth Hezron (that is, Hazor), 26Amam, Shema, Moladah, 27Hazar Gaddah, Heshmon, Beth Pelet, 28Hazar Shual, Beersheba, Biziothiah, 29Baalah, Iim, Ezem, 30Eltolad, Kesil, Hormah, 31Ziklag, Madmannah, Sansannah, 32Lebaoth, Shilhim, Ain and Rimmon — a total of twenty-nine towns and their villages.

33In the western foothills:
Eshtaol, Zorah, Ashnah, 34Zanoah, En Gannim, Tappuah, Enam, 35Jarmuth, Adullam,

Socoh, Azekah, 36Shaaraim, Adithaim and Gederah (or Gederothaim)*f* — fourteen towns and their villages.

37Zenan, Hadashah, Migdal Gad, 38Dilean, Mizpah, Joktheel, 39Lachish, Bozkath, Eglon, 40Cabbon, Lahmas, Kitlish, 41Gederoth, Beth Dagon, Naamah and Makkedah — sixteen towns and their villages.

42Libnah, Ether, Ashan, 43Iphtah, Ashnah, Nezib, 44Keilah, Aczib and Mareshah — nine towns and their villages.

45Ekron, with its surrounding settlements and villages; 46west of Ekron, all that were in the vicinity of Ashdod, together with their villages; 47Ashdod, its surrounding settlements and villages; and Gaza, its settlements and villages, as far as the Wadi of Egypt and the coastline of the Great Sea.

48In the hill country:
Shamir, Jattir, Socoh, 49Dannah, Kiriath Sannah (that is, Debir), 50Anab, Eshtemoh, Anim, 51Goshen, Holon and Giloh — eleven towns and their villages.

52Arab, Dumah, Eshan, 53Janim, Beth Tappuah, Aphekah, 54Humtah, Kiriath Arba (that is, Hebron) and Zior — nine towns and their villages.

55Maon, Carmel, Ziph, Juttah, 56Jezreel, Jokdeam, Zanoah, 57Kain, Gibeah and Timnah — ten towns and their villages.

58Halhul, Beth Zur, Gedor, 59Maarath, Beth Anoth and Eltekon — six towns and their villages.

60Kiriath Baal (that is, Kiriath Jearim) and Rabbah — two towns and their villages.

61In the desert:
Beth Arabah, Middin, Secacah, 62Nibshan, the City of Salt and En Gedi — six towns and their villages.

63Judah could not dislodge the Jebusites, who were living in Jerusalem; to this day the Jebusites live there with the people of Judah.

15:63 ■ HINTS OF FAILURE
In several key places (13:2–7; 16:10; 23:4) and in Judges 1, the Bible indicates that pockets of Canaanites remained in the land. The Israelites "could not dislodge" them, or did not "drive them out". The unconquered tribes became thorns in Israel's side.

■ Allotment for Ephraim and Manasseh

16 The allotment for Joseph began at the Jordan of Jericho,*a* east of the waters of Jericho, and went up from there through the desert into the hill country of Bethel. 2It went on from Bethel (that is, Luz),*b* crossed over to the territory of the Arkites in Ataroth, 3descended westward to the territory of the Japhletites as far as the region of Lower Beth Horon and on to Gezer, ending at the sea.

d 12 That is, the Mediterranean; also in verse 47   e 18 Hebrew and some Septuagint manuscripts; other Septuagint manuscripts (see also note at Judges 1:14) Othniel, he urged her   f 36 Or Gederah and Gederothaim   a 1 Jordan of Jericho was possibly an ancient name for the Jordan River.   b 2 Septuagint; Hebrew Bethel to Luz

4So Manasseh and Ephraim, the descendants of Joseph, received their inheritance.

5This was the territory of Ephraim, clan by clan:
    The boundary of their inheritance went from Ataroth Addar in the east to Upper Beth Horon 6and continued to the sea. From Micmethath on the north it curved eastward to Taanath Shiloh, passing by it to Janoah on the east. 7Then it went down from Janoah to Ataroth and Naarah, touched Jericho and came out at the Jordan. 8From Tappuah the border went west to the Kanah Ravine and ended at the sea. This was the inheritance of the tribe of the Ephraimites, clan by clan. 9It also included all the towns and their villages that were set aside for the Ephraimites within the inheritance of the Manassites.

10They did not dislodge the Canaanites living in Gezer; to this day the Canaanites live among the people of Ephraim but are required to do forced labour.

17 This was the allotment for the tribe of Manasseh as Joseph's firstborn, that is, for Makir, Manasseh's firstborn. Makir was the ancestor of the Gileadites, who had received Gilead and Bashan because the Makirites were great soldiers. 2So this allotment was for the rest of the people of Manasseh — the clans of Abiezer, Helek, Asriel, Shechem, Hepher and Shemida. These are the other male descendants of Manasseh son of Joseph by their clans.

3Now Zelophehad son of Hepher, the son of Gilead, the son of Makir, the son of Manasseh, had no sons but only daughters, whose names were Mahlah, Noah, Hoglah, Milcah and Tirzah. 4They went to Eleazar the priest, Joshua son of Nun, and the leaders and said, "The LORD commanded Moses to give us an inheritance among our brothers." So Joshua gave them an inheritance along with the brothers of their father, according to the LORD's command. 5Manasseh's share consisted of ten tracts of land besides Gilead and Bashan east of the Jordan, 6because the daughters of the tribe of Manasseh received an inheritance among the sons. The land of Gilead belonged to the rest of the descendants of Manasseh.

17:4 ■ DAUGHTERS' RIGHTS
See Numbers 27:1–11 and Numbers 36 for the historical context to these women's appeal.

7The territory of Manasseh extended from Asher to Micmethath east of Shechem. The boundary ran southward from there to include the people living at En Tappuah. 8(Manasseh had the land of Tappuah, but Tappuah itself, on the boundary of Manasseh, belonged to the Ephraimites.) 9Then the boundary continued south to the Kanah Ravine. There were towns belonging to Ephraim lying among the towns of Manasseh, but the boundary of Manasseh was the northern side of the ravine and ended at the sea. 10On the south the land belonged to Ephraim, on the north to Manasseh. The territory

of Manasseh reached the sea and bordered Asher on the north and Issachar on the east.

11Within Issachar and Asher, Manasseh also had Beth Shan, Ibleam and the people of Dor, Endor, Taanach and Megiddo, together with their surrounding settlements (the third in the list is Naphoth*a*).

12Yet the Manassites were not able to occupy these towns, for the Canaanites were determined to live in that region. 13However, when the Israelites grew stronger, they subjected the Canaanites to forced labour but did not drive them out completely.

14The people of Joseph said to Joshua, "Why have you given us only one allotment and one portion for an inheritance? We are a numerous people and the LORD has blessed us abundantly."

15"If you are so numerous," Joshua answered, "and if the hill country of Ephraim is too small for you, go up into the forest and clear land for yourselves there in the land of the Perizzites and Rephaites."

16The people of Joseph replied, "The hill country is not enough for us, and all the Canaanites who live in the plain have iron chariots, both those in Beth Shan and its settlements and those in the Valley of Jezreel."

17But Joshua said to the house of Joseph — to Ephraim and Manasseh — "You are numerous and very powerful. You will have not only one allotment 18but the forested hill country as well. Clear it, and its farthest limits will be yours; though the Canaanites have iron chariots and though they are strong, you can drive them out."

■ Division of the Rest of the Land

18 The whole assembly of the Israelites gathered at Shiloh and set up the Tent of Meeting there. The country was brought under their control, 2but there were still seven Israelite tribes who had not yet received their inheritance.

3So Joshua said to the Israelites: "How long will you wait before you begin to take possession of the land that the LORD, the God of your fathers, has given you? 4Appoint three men from each tribe. I will send them out to make a survey of the land and to write a description of it, according to the inheritance of each. Then they will return to me. 5You are to divide the land into seven parts. Judah is to remain in its territory on the south and the house of Joseph in its territory on the north. 6After you have written descriptions of the seven parts of the land, bring them here to me and I will cast lots for you in the presence of the LORD our God. 7The Levites, however, do not get a portion among you, because the priestly service of the LORD is their inheritance. And Gad, Reuben and the half-tribe of Manasseh have already received their inheritance on the east side of the Jordan. Moses the servant of the LORD gave it to them."

8As the men started on their way to map out the land, Joshua instructed them, "Go and make a survey of the land and write a description of it. Then return to me, and I will cast lots for you here at Shiloh in the presence of the LORD." 9So the men left and went through the land. They wrote its description on a scroll, town by town, in seven parts, and returned to

a 11 That is, Naphoth Dor

Joshua in the camp at Shiloh. [10]Joshua then cast lots for them in Shiloh in the presence of the LORD, and there he distributed the land to the Israelites according to their tribal divisions.

18:3 ■ MISSING AN OPPORTUNITY

Such verses as 17:13 and 18:3 imply that the Israelites could have driven out the Canaanites, but chose not to. They were using the Canaanites for forced labour and demanding tribute from them — perhaps they learned to rely too comfortably on these services. Also, some tribes balked at campaigns simply because of fear (17:16).

■ Allotment for Benjamin

[11]The lot came up for the tribe of Benjamin, clan by clan. Their allotted territory lay between the tribes of Judah and Joseph:

[12]On the north side their boundary began at the Jordan, passed the northern slope of Jericho and headed west into the hill country, coming out at the desert of Beth Aven. [13]From there it crossed to the south slope of Luz (that is, Bethel) and went down to Ataroth Addar on the hill south of Lower Beth Horon.

[14]From the hill facing Beth Horon on the south the boundary turned south along the western side and came out at Kiriath Baal (that is, Kiriath Jearim), a town of the people of Judah. This was the western side.

[15]The southern side began at the outskirts of Kiriath Jearim on the west, and the boundary came out at the spring of the waters of Nephtoah. [16]The boundary went down to the foot of the hill facing the Valley of Ben Hinnom, north of the Valley of Rephaim. It continued down the Hinnom Valley along the southern slope of the Jebusite city and so to En Rogel. [17]It then curved north, went to En Shemesh, continued to Geliloth, which faces the Pass of Adummim, and ran down to the Stone of Bohan son of Reuben. [18]It continued to the northern slope of Beth Arabah[a] and on down into the Arabah. [19]It then went to the northern slope of Beth Hoglah and came out at the northern bay of the Salt Sea,[b] at the mouth of the Jordan in the south. This was the southern boundary.

[20]The Jordan formed the boundary on the eastern side.

These were the boundaries that marked out the inheritance of the clans of Benjamin on all sides.

[21]The tribe of Benjamin, clan by clan, had the following cities:

Jericho, Beth Hoglah, Emek Keziz, [22]Beth Arabah, Zemaraim, Bethel, [23]Avvim, Parah, Ophrah, [24]Kephar Ammoni, Ophni and Geba — twelve towns and their villages.

[25]Gibeon, Ramah, Beeroth, [26]Mizpah, Kephirah, Mozah, [27]Rekem, Irpeel, Taralah, [28]Zelah, Haeleph, the Jebusite city (that is, Jerusalem), Gibeah and Kiriath — fourteen towns and their villages.

This was the inheritance of Benjamin for its clans.

■ Allotment for Simeon

19 The second lot came out for the tribe of Simeon, clan by clan. Their inheritance lay within the territory of Judah. [2]It included:

Beersheba (or Sheba),[a] Moladah, [3]Hazar Shual, Balah, Ezem, [4]Eltolad, Bethul, Hormah, [5]Ziklag, Beth Marcaboth, Hazar Susah, [6]Beth Lebaoth and Sharuhen — thirteen towns and their villages;

[7]Ain, Rimmon, Ether and Ashan — four towns and their villages — [8]and all the villages around these towns as far as Baalath Beer (Ramah in the Negev).

This was the inheritance of the tribe of the Simeonites, clan by clan. [9]The inheritance of the Simeonites was taken from the share of Judah, because Judah's portion was more than they needed. So the Simeonites received their inheritance within the territory of Judah.

■ Allotment for Zebulun

[10]The third lot came up for Zebulun, clan by clan:

The boundary of their inheritance went as far as Sarid. [11]Going west it ran to Maralah, touched Dabbesheth, and extended to the ravine near Jokneam. [12]It turned east from Sarid towards the sunrise to the territory of Kisloth Tabor and went on to Daberath and up to Japhia. [13]Then it continued eastward to Gath Hepher and Eth Kazin; it came out at Rimmon and turned towards Neah. [14]There the boundary went round on the north to Hannathon and ended at the Valley of Iphtah El. [15]Included were Kattath, Nahalal, Shimron, Idalah and Bethlehem. There were twelve towns and their villages.

[16]These towns and their villages were the inheritance of Zebulun, clan by clan.

■ Allotment for Issachar

[17]The fourth lot came out for Issachar, clan by clan. [18]Their territory included:

Jezreel, Kesulloth, Shunem, [19]Hapharaim, Shion, Anaharath, [20]Rabbith, Kishion, Ebez, [21]Remeth, En Gannim, En Haddah and Beth Pazzez. [22]The boundary touched Tabor, Shahazumah and Beth Shemesh, and ended at the Jordan. There were sixteen towns and their villages.

[23]These towns and their villages were the inheritance of the tribe of Issachar, clan by clan.

■ Allotment for Asher

[24]The fifth lot came out for the tribe of Asher, clan by clan. [25]Their territory included:

Helkath, Hali, Beten, Acshaph, [26]Allammelech, Amad and Mishal. On the west the boundary touched Carmel and Shihor Libnath. [27]It then turned east towards Beth Dagon, touched Zebulun and the Valley of Iphtah El, and went north to Beth Emek and Neiel, passing Cabul on

---

[a] 18 Septuagint; Hebrew *slope facing the Arabah*   [b] 19 That is, the Dead Sea   [a] 2 Or *Beersheba, Sheba*; 1 Chron. 4:28 does not have *Sheba*.

the left. [28]It went to Abdon,[b] Rehob, Hammon and Kanah, as far as Greater Sidon. [29]The boundary then turned back towards Ramah and went to the fortified city of Tyre, turned towards Hosah and came out at the sea in the region of Aczib, [30]Ummah, Aphek and Rehob. There were twenty-two towns and their villages.

[31]These towns and their villages were the inheritance of the tribe of Asher, clan by clan.

■ Allotment for Naphtali

[32]The sixth lot came out for Naphtali, clan by clan: [33]Their boundary went from Heleph and the large tree in Zaanannim, passing Adami Nekeb and Jabneel to Lakkum and ending at the Jordan. [34]The boundary ran west through Aznoth Tabor and came out at Hukkok. It touched Zebulun on the south, Asher on the west and the Jordan[c] on the east. [35]The fortified cities were Ziddim, Zer, Hammath, Rakkath, Kinnereth, [36]Adamah, Ramah, Hazor, [37]Kedesh, Edrei, En Hazor, [38]Iron, Migdal El, Horem, Beth Anath and Beth Shemesh. There were nineteen towns and their villages.

[39]These towns and their villages were the inheritance of the tribe of Naphtali, clan by clan.

■ Allotment for Dan

[40]The seventh lot came out for the tribe of Dan, clan by clan. [41]The territory of their inheritance included:

Zorah, Eshtaol, Ir Shemesh, [42]Shaalabbin, Aijalon, Ithlah, [43]Elon, Timnah, Ekron, [44]Eltekeh, Gibbethon, Baalath, [45]Jehud, Bene Berak, Gath Rimmon, [46]Me Jarkon and Rakkon, with the area facing Joppa.

[47](But the Danites had difficulty taking possession of their territory, so they went up and attacked Leshem, took it, put it to the sword and occupied it. They settled in Leshem and named it Dan after their forefather.)

[48]These towns and their villages were the inheritance of the tribe of Dan, clan by clan.

■ Allotment for Joshua

[49]When they had finished dividing the land into its allotted portions, the Israelites gave Joshua son of Nun an inheritance among them, [50]as the LORD had commanded. They gave him the town he asked for — Timnath Serah[d] in the hill country of Ephraim. And he built up the town and settled there.

[51]These are the territories that Eleazar the priest, Joshua son of Nun and the heads of the tribal clans of Israel assigned by lot at Shiloh in the presence of the LORD at the entrance to the Tent of Meeting. And so they finished dividing the land.

■ Cities of Refuge

20 Then the LORD said to Joshua: [2]"Tell the Israelites to designate the cities of refuge, as I instructed you through Moses, [3]so that anyone who kills a person accidentally and unintentionally may flee there and find protection from the avenger of blood.

[4]"When he flees to one of these cities, he is to stand in the entrance of the city gate and state his case before the elders of that city. Then they are to admit him into their city and give him a place to live with them. [5]If the avenger of blood pursues him, they must not surrender the one accused, because he killed his neighbour unintentionally and without malice aforethought. [6]He is to stay in that city until he has stood trial before the assembly and until the death of the high priest who is serving at that time. Then he may go back to his own home in the town from which he fled."

20:2 ■ CITIES OF REFUGE

The cities of refuge were designed to aid a person who caused an accidental death or "involuntary manslaughter". They provided a sanctuary from revenge. They did not, however, shelter a person who had committed a premeditated, intentional murder. (See Numbers 35:6 and Deuteronomy 4:41–43; 19:1–21.)

[7]So they set apart Kedesh in Galilee in the hill country of Naphtali, Shechem in the hill country of Ephraim, and Kiriath Arba (that is, Hebron) in the hill country of Judah. [8]On the east side of the Jordan of Jericho[a] they designated Bezer in the desert on the plateau in the tribe of Reuben, Ramoth in Gilead in the tribe of Gad, and Golan in Bashan in the tribe of Manasseh. [9]Any of the Israelites or any alien living among them who killed someone accidentally could flee to these designated cities and not be killed by the avenger of blood prior to standing trial before the assembly.

■ Towns for the Levites

21 Now the family heads of the Levites approached Eleazar the priest, Joshua son of Nun, and the heads of the other tribal families of Israel [2]at Shiloh in Canaan and said to them, "The LORD commanded through Moses that you give us towns to live in, with pasture-lands for our livestock." [3]So, as the LORD had commanded, the Israelites gave the Levites the following towns and pasture-lands out of their own inheritance:

[4]The first lot came out for the Kohathites, clan by clan. The Levites who were descendants of Aaron the priest were allotted thirteen towns from the tribes of Judah, Simeon and Benjamin. [5]The rest of Kohath's descendants were allotted ten towns from the clans of the tribes of Ephraim, Dan and half of Manasseh.

[6]The descendants of Gershon were allotted thirteen towns from the clans of the tribes of Issachar, Asher, Naphtali and the half-tribe of Manasseh in Bashan.

[7]The descendants of Merari, clan by clan, received twelve towns from the tribes of Reuben, Gad and Zebulun.

[8]So the Israelites allotted to the Levites these towns and their pasture-lands, as the LORD had commanded through Moses.

[b]28 Some Hebrew manuscripts (see also Joshua 21:30); most Hebrew manuscripts Ebron   [c]34 Septuagint; Hebrew west, and Judah, the Jordan,   [d]50 Also known as Timnath Heres (see Judges 2:9)   [a]8 Jordan of Jericho was possibly an ancient name for the Jordan River.

9From the tribes of Judah and Simeon they allotted the following towns by name 10(these towns were assigned to the descendants of Aaron who were from the Kohathite clans of the Levites, because the first lot fell to them):

21:8 ■ TOWNS FOR THE LEVITES
As part of their calling to serve God, the Levites were given no land in Canaan. Rather, they received 48 towns scattered in the other tribes' lands — four towns from each tribe. This forced them to depend not on their inheritance of the land, but on God (see Numbers 18:20). It dispersed the priests among all the people and enabled them to instruct the tribes in the law and to lead worship.

11They gave them Kiriath Arba (that is, Hebron), with its surrounding pasture-land, in the hill country of Judah. (Arba was the forefather of Anak.) 12But the fields and villages around the city they had given to Caleb son of Jephunneh as his possession.

13So to the descendants of Aaron the priest they gave Hebron (a city of refuge for one accused of murder), Libnah, 14Jattir, Eshtemoa, 15Holon, Debir, 16Ain, Juttah and Beth Shemesh, together with their pasture-lands — nine towns from these two tribes.

17And from the tribe of Benjamin they gave them Gibeon, Geba, 18Anathoth and Almon, together with their pasture-lands — four towns.

19All the towns for the priests, the descendants of Aaron, were thirteen, together with their pasture-lands.

20The rest of the Kohathite clans of the Levites were allotted towns from the tribe of Ephraim:
21In the hill country of Ephraim they were given Shechem (a city of refuge for one accused of murder) and Gezer, 22Kibzaim and Beth Horon, together with their pasture-lands — four towns.
23Also from the tribe of Dan they received Eltekeh, Gibbethon, 24Aijalon and Gath Rimmon, together with their pasture-lands — four towns.
25From half the tribe of Manasseh they received Taanach and Gath Rimmon, together with their pasture-lands — two towns.
26All these ten towns and their pasture-lands were given to the rest of the Kohathite clans.

27The Levite clans of the Gershonites were given:
from the half-tribe of Manasseh,
Golan in Bashan (a city of refuge for one accused of murder) and Be Eshtarah, together with their pasture-lands — two towns;
28from the tribe of Issachar,
Kishion, Daberath, 29Jarmuth and En Gannim, together with their pasture-lands — four towns;
30from the tribe of Asher,
Mishal, Abdon, 31Helkath and Rehob, together with their pasture-lands — four towns;
32from the tribe of Naphtali,

Kedesh in Galilee (a city of refuge for one accused of murder), Hammoth Dor and Kartan, together with their pasture-lands — three towns.
33All the towns of the Gershonite clans were thirteen, together with their pasture-lands.

34The Merarite clans (the rest of the Levites) were given:
from the tribe of Zebulun,
Jokneam, Kartah, 35Dimnah and Nahalal, together with their pasture-lands — four towns;
36from the tribe of Reuben,
Bezer, Jahaz, 37Kedemoth and Mephaath, together with their pasture-lands — four towns;
38from the tribe of Gad,
Ramoth in Gilead (a city of refuge for one accused of murder), Mahanaim, 39Heshbon and Jazer, together with their pasture-lands — four towns in all.
40All the towns allotted to the Merarite clans, who were the rest of the Levites, were twelve.
41The towns of the Levites in the territory held by the Israelites were forty-eight in all, together with their pasture-lands. 42Each of these towns had pasture-lands surrounding it; this was true for all these towns.

43So the LORD gave Israel all the land he had sworn to give their forefathers, and they took possession of it and settled there. 44The LORD gave them rest on every side, just as he had sworn to their forefathers. Not one of their enemies withstood them; the LORD handed all their enemies over to them. 45Not one of all the LORD's good promises to the house of Israel failed; every one was fulfilled.

■ Eastern Tribes Return Home

22 Then Joshua summoned the Reubenites, the Gadites and the half-tribe of Manasseh 2and said to them, "You have done all that Moses the servant of the LORD commanded, and you have obeyed me in everything I commanded. 3For a long time now — to this very day — you have not deserted your brothers but have carried out the mission the LORD your God gave you. 4Now that the LORD your God has given your brothers rest as he promised, return to your homes in the land that Moses the servant of the LORD gave you on the other side of the Jordan. 5But be very careful to keep the commandment and the law that Moses the servant of the LORD gave you: to love the LORD your God, to walk in all his ways, to obey his commands, to hold fast to him and to serve him with all your heart and all your soul."

6Then Joshua blessed them and sent them away, and they went to their homes. 7(To the half-tribe of Manasseh Moses had given land in Bashan, and to the other half of the tribe Joshua gave land on the west side of the Jordan with their brothers.) When Joshua sent them home, he blessed them, 8saying, "Return to your homes with your great wealth — with large herds of livestock, with silver, gold, bronze and iron, and a great quantity of clothing — and divide with your brothers the plunder from your enemies."

9So the Reubenites, the Gadites and the half-tribe of Manasseh left the Israelites at Shiloh in Canaan to return to Gilead, their own land, which they had acquired in accordance with the command of the LORD through Moses.

¹⁰When they came to Geliloth near the Jordan in the land of Canaan, the Reubenites, the Gadites and the half-tribe of Manasseh built an imposing altar there by the Jordan. ¹¹And when the Israelites heard that they had built the altar on the border of Canaan at Geliloth near the Jordan on the Israelite side, ¹²the whole assembly of Israel gathered at Shiloh to go to war against them.

22:10 ■ EXPLOSIVE QUARREL

Chapter 22 records a misunderstanding that could have led to civil war. Several Israelite tribes built a large altar. This inflamed the other tribes. Weren't the builders grossly violating God's law by erecting an altar, a function only priests should perform? Were these tribes so soon abandoning the rules of worship Moses and Joshua had laid down? Or, perhaps, they had provocatively built their altar on the western side of the Jordan River to stake a claim to others' land? The western tribes soon learned the truth: the easterners had built not an altar, but a monument to commemorate their national unity with the western tribes. A civil war was averted after some heated exchanges. The incident reveals the intensity of religious feeling in the new nation.

¹³So the Israelites sent Phinehas son of Eleazar, the priest, to the land of Gilead—to Reuben, Gad and the half-tribe of Manasseh. ¹⁴With him they sent ten of the chief men, one for each of the tribes of Israel, each the head of a family division among the Israelite clans.

¹⁵When they went to Gilead—to Reuben, Gad and the half-tribe of Manasseh—they said to them: ¹⁶"The whole assembly of the LORD says: 'How could you break faith with the God of Israel like this? How could you turn away from the LORD and build yourselves an altar in rebellion against him now? ¹⁷Was not the sin of Peor enough for us? Up to this very day we have not cleansed ourselves from that sin, even though a plague fell on the community of the LORD! ¹⁸And are you now turning away from the LORD?

" 'If you rebel against the LORD today, tomorrow he will be angry with the whole community of Israel. ¹⁹If the land you possess is defiled, come over to the LORD's land, where the LORD's tabernacle stands, and share the land with us. But do not rebel against the LORD or against us by building an altar for yourselves, other than the altar of the LORD our God. ²⁰When Achan son of Zerah acted unfaithfully regarding the devoted things,ᵃ did not wrath come upon the whole community of Israel? He was not the only one who died for his sin.' "

²¹Then Reuben, Gad and the half-tribe of Manasseh replied to the heads of the clans of Israel: ²²"The Mighty One, God, the LORD! The Mighty One, God, the LORD! He knows! And let Israel know! If this has been in rebellion or disobedience to the LORD, do not spare us this day. ²³If we have built our own altar

to turn away from the LORD and to offer burnt offerings and grain offerings, or to sacrifice fellowship offeringsᵇ on it, may the LORD himself call us to account.

²⁴"No! We did it for fear that some day your descendants might say to ours, 'What do you have to do with the LORD, the God of Israel? ²⁵The LORD has made the Jordan a boundary between us and you—you Reubenites and Gadites! You have no share in the LORD.' So your descendants might cause ours to stop fearing the LORD.

²⁶"That is why we said, 'Let us get ready and build an altar—but not for burnt offerings or sacrifices.' ²⁷On the contrary, it is to be a witness between us and you and the generations that follow, that we will worship the LORD at his sanctuary with our burnt offerings, sacrifices and fellowship offerings. Then in the future your descendants will not be able to say to ours, 'You have no share in the LORD.'

²⁸"And we said, 'If they ever say this to us, or to our descendants, we will answer: Look at the replica of the LORD's altar, which our fathers built, not for burnt offerings and sacrifices, but as a witness between us and you.'

²⁹"Far be it from us to rebel against the LORD and turn away from him today by building an altar for burnt offerings, grain offerings and sacrifices, other than the altar of the LORD our God that stands before his tabernacle."

³⁰When Phinehas the priest and the leaders of the community—the heads of the clans of the Israelites—heard what Reuben, Gad and Manasseh had to say, they were pleased. ³¹And Phinehas son of Eleazar, the priest, said to Reuben, Gad and Manasseh, "Today we know that the LORD is with us, because you have not acted unfaithfully towards the LORD in this matter. Now you have rescued the Israelites from the LORD's hand."

³²Then Phinehas son of Eleazar, the priest, and the leaders returned to Canaan from their meeting with the Reubenites and Gadites in Gilead and reported to the Israelites. ³³They were glad to hear the report and praised God. And they talked no more about going to war against them to devastate the country where the Reubenites and the Gadites lived.

³⁴And the Reubenites and the Gadites gave the altar this name: A Witness Between Us that the LORD is God.

■ Joshua's Farewell to the Leaders

23 After a long time had passed and the LORD had given Israel rest from all their enemies around them, Joshua, by then old and well advanced in years, ²summoned all Israel—their elders, leaders, judges and officials—and said to them: "I am old and well advanced in years. ³You yourselves have seen everything the LORD your God has done to all these nations for your sake; it was the LORD your God who fought for you. ⁴Remember how I have allotted as an inheritance for your tribes all the land of the nations that remain—the nations I conquered—between the Jordan and the Great Seaᵃ in the west. ⁵The LORD your God himself will drive them out of your way. He will push them out before you, and

---

ᵃ20 The Hebrew term refers to the irrevocable giving over of things or persons to the LORD, often by totally destroying them.   ᵇ23 Traditionally *peace offerings*; also in verse 27   ᵃ4 That is, the Mediterranean you will take possession of their land, as the LORD your God promised you.

6"Be very strong; be careful to obey all that is written in the Book of the Law of Moses, without turning aside to the right or to the left. 7Do not associate with these nations that remain among you; do not invoke the names of their gods or swear by them. You must not serve them or bow down to them. 8But you are to hold fast to the LORD your God, as you have until now.

9"The LORD has driven out before you great and powerful nations; to this day no-one has been able to withstand you. 10One of you routs a thousand, because the LORD your God fights for you, just as he promised. 11So be very careful to love the LORD your God.

12"But if you turn away and ally yourselves with the survivors of these nations that remain among you and if you intermarry with them and associate with them, 13then you may be sure that the LORD your God will no longer drive out these nations before you. Instead, they will become snares and traps for you, whips on your backs and thorns in your eyes, until you perish from this good land, which the LORD your God has given you.

14"Now I am about to go the way of all the earth. You know with all your heart and soul that not one of all the good promises the LORD your God gave you has failed. Every promise has been fulfilled; not one has failed. 15But just as every good promise of the LORD your God has come true, so the LORD will bring on you all the evil he has threatened, until he has destroyed you from this good land he has given you. 16If you violate the covenant of the LORD your God, which he commanded you, and go and serve other gods and bow down to them, the LORD's anger will burn against you, and you will quickly perish from the good land he has given you."

■ The Covenant Renewed at Shechem

24 Then Joshua assembled all the tribes of Israel at Shechem. He summoned the elders, leaders, judges and officials of Israel, and they presented themselves before God.

2Joshua said to all the people, "This is what the LORD, the God of Israel, says: 'Long ago your forefathers, including Terah the father of Abraham and Nahor, lived beyond the River[a] and worshipped other gods. 3But I took your father Abraham from the land beyond the River and led him throughout Canaan and gave him many descendants. I gave him Isaac, 4and to Isaac I gave Jacob and Esau. I assigned the hill country of Seir to Esau, but Jacob and his sons went down to Egypt.

5" 'Then I sent Moses and Aaron, and I afflicted the Egyptians by what I did there, and I brought you out. 6When I brought your fathers out of Egypt, you came to the sea, and the Egyptians pursued them with chariots and horsemen[b] as far as the Red Sea.[c] 7But they cried to the LORD for help, and he put darkness between you and the Egyptians; he brought the sea over them and covered them. You saw with your own eyes what I did to the Egyptians. Then you lived in the desert for a long time.

8" 'I brought you to the land of the Amorites who lived east of the Jordan. They fought against you, but I gave them into your hands. I destroyed them from before you, and you took possession of their land. 9When Balak son of Zippor, the king of Moab, prepared to fight against Israel, he sent for Balaam son of Beor to put a curse on you. 10But I would not listen to Balaam, so he blessed you again and again, and I delivered you out of his hand.

11" 'Then you crossed the Jordan and came to Jericho. The citizens of Jericho fought against you, as did also the Amorites, Perizzites, Canaanites, Hittites, Girgashites, Hivites and Jebusites, but I gave them into your hands. 12I sent the hornet ahead of you, which drove them out before you—also the two Amorite kings. You did not do it with your own sword and bow. 13So I gave you a land on which you did not toil and cities you did not build; and you live in them and eat from vineyards and olive groves that you did not plant.'

14"Now fear the LORD and serve him with all faithfulness. Throw away the gods your forefathers worshipped beyond the River and in Egypt, and serve the LORD. 15But if serving the LORD seems undesirable to you, then choose for yourselves this day whom you will serve, whether the gods your forefathers served beyond the River, or the gods of the Amorites, in whose land you are living. But as for me and my household, we will serve the LORD."

16Then the people answered, "Far be it from us to forsake the LORD to serve other gods! 17It was the LORD our God himself who brought us and our fathers up out of Egypt, from that land of slavery, and performed those great signs before our eyes. He protected us on our entire journey and among all the nations through which we travelled. 18And the LORD drove out before us all the nations, including the

---

a2 That is, the Euphrates; also in verses 3, 14 and 15   *b6 Or charioteers*   *c6 Hebrew Yam Suph; that is, Sea of Reeds*

■ FILLING MOSES' SHOES
JOSHUA COULD FOLLOW ORDERS AS WELL AS GIVE THEM

INSIGHT

ISRAEL SERVED THE LORD THROUGHOUT THE LIFETIME OF JOSHUA. ■ 24:31

Like all the Israelites, Joshua began his life in humble surroundings. He was born a slave in Egypt and followed Moses across the Red Sea to freedom. He first appears in the Bible as a military commander. Soon after escaping from Egypt, the Israelites confronted a new enemy, and Moses turned to Joshua to lead their very first battle (Exodus 17:9–15).

A month later, when Moses climbed craggy Mount Sinai to meet with God, Joshua was at his side. He first reported to Moses the strange sounds coming from the camp, sounds that turned out to be the Israelites' great spiritual rebellion (Exodus 32:17). Joshua rose to become Moses' trusted number-two man, an aide who served him at almost every major crisis. Moses changed his name from Hoshea, which meant "help" or "salvation", to Joshua, meaning "The LORD saves". (The Greek form of Joshua is *Jesus*.)

■ BECOMING NUMBER ONE
On the verge of entering Canaan, Moses turned to Joshua again, choosing him as one of 12 spies sent to collect information about the land. Ten came back frightened, with predictions of doom. Only Joshua and Caleb had faith that God would keep his promises to the Israelites despite the military odds.

Joshua learned about the hazards of leadership from that spying trip: on his return, thousands of angry Israelites called for his public stoning (Numbers 14). But he stood firm, and God rewarded him. Of all the Israelites who left Egypt, only he and Caleb were allowed to enter the promised land – not even Moses had that honour. As Moses' death neared, God and Moses made Joshua their uncontested choice for a new leader for Israel. It was time for number two to become number one.

Joshua made a remarkably smooth transition into leadership. In fact, Joshua's life had many parallels to that of Moses. The miracle of crossing the Jordan River poignantly replayed Moses' crossing of the Red Sea. Moses encountered God directly at the burning bush; Joshua met God's special representative, the "commander of the army of the LORD", and likewise took off his shoes at the meeting (5:13–15).

Both Moses and Joshua wrote the law onto stones: Moses creating a permanent record for Israel, and Joshua erecting a monument for the nation to pass by on the way into the new land (8:32). Both leaders pleaded with God on behalf of their people. And both ended their terms with stirring speeches that reviewed history and challenged the people towards a critical choice.

■ WELL-ROUNDED LEADER
Moses, who grew up in the courts of Pharaoh, obviously received a better education than Joshua. He showed a philosophical bent. Joshua, on the other hand, was action-oriented and pragmatic, a perfect military man. He had the rare combination of knowing how to follow orders as well as how to give them.

The Bible, never guilty of glossing over its heroes' flaws, reveals some of Joshua's mistakes. In one incident in the desert, he was rash (Numbers 11:26–30). During the first battle of Ai and the treaty negotiations with the Gibeonites, he acted impulsively, without first seeking God's advice. And, faced with his first major defeat at Ai, he uncharacteristically dissolved in fright, earning God's stern rebuke: "Stand up! What are you doing down on your face?" (7:6–12).

Apart from these few incidents, Joshua's life was marked by unusual faith and obedience. Joshua never let the press of military action interfere with worship and the renewal of the covenant. When he divided up the land (an immense bureaucratic burden that takes up the last half of this book), he did so with wisdom and fairness, selecting his own portion only after all others had chosen.

The Bible records this simple legacy: "Israel served the LORD throughout the lifetime of Joshua" (24:31). History would show how rarely that occurred in the life of a troublesome nation.

□ LIFE QUESTIONS:
Often when a popular leader – a pastor, a politician, a teacher – retires from office, something slips. What made Joshua such an effective replacement?

Amorites, who lived in the land. We too will serve the LORD, because he is our God."

19 Joshua said to the people, "You are not able to serve the LORD. He is a holy God; he is a jealous God. He will not forgive your rebellion and your sins. 20 If you forsake the LORD and serve foreign gods, he will turn and bring disaster on you and make an end of you, after he has been good to you."

21 But the people said to Joshua, "No! We will serve the LORD."

22 Then Joshua said, "You are witnesses against yourselves that you have chosen to serve the LORD." "Yes, we are witnesses," they replied.

23 "Now then," said Joshua, "throw away the foreign gods that are among you and yield your hearts to the LORD, the God of Israel."

24 And the people said to Joshua, "We will serve the LORD our God and obey him."

24:26 ■ MONUMENTS

The Israelites established at least seven memorials to remind future generations of what God had done for them. (Other stone monuments are described in chapters 4,7,8,10,22.) Even if people forgot their debt to God, the land would speak its own story.

25 On that day Joshua made a covenant for the people, and there at Shechem he drew up for them decrees and laws. 26 And Joshua recorded these things in the Book of the Law of God. Then he took a large stone and set it up there under the oak near the holy place of the LORD.

27 "See!" he said to all the people. "This stone will be a witness against us. It has heard all the words the LORD has said to us. It will be a witness against you if you are untrue to your God."

■ Buried in the Promised Land

28 Then Joshua sent the people away, each to his own inheritance.

29 After these things, Joshua son of Nun, the servant of the LORD, died at the age of a hundred and ten. 30 And they buried him in the land of his inheritance, at Timnath Serah^d in the hill country of Ephraim, north of Mount Gaash.

31 Israel served the LORD throughout the lifetime of Joshua and of the elders who outlived him and who had experienced everything the LORD had done for Israel.

32 And Joseph's bones, which the Israelites had brought up from Egypt, were buried at Shechem in the tract of land that Jacob bought for a hundred pieces of silver^e from the sons of Hamor, the father of Shechem. This became the inheritance of Joseph's descendants.

33 And Eleazar son of Aaron died and was buried at Gibeah, which had been allotted to his son Phinehas in the hill country of Ephraim.

^{d} 30 Also known as Timnath Heres (see Judges 2:9) ^{e} 32 Hebrew hundred kesitahs; a kesitah was a unit of money of unknown weight and value.

JUDGES

■ FREEDOM FIGHTERS

THESE "JUDGES" TOOK UP ARMS TO DEFEND THEIR HOMELAND

WHENEVER THE LORD RAISED UP A JUDGE FOR THEM, HE WAS WITH THE JUDGE AND
SAVED THEM OUT OF THE HANDS OF THEIR ENEMIES AS LONG AS THE JUDGE LIVED.
■ 2:18

The "judges" of this book might be called guerrillas
or freedom fighters today. These men (and one
woman) were renowned not for court cases, but
for their military campaigns against foreign
invaders. Like all military leaders, they sometimes
settled disputes; but the book of Judges, however,
is preoccupied not with legal matters, but with the
excitement of fighting for freedom.

Israel's judges certainly did not stick to
"the rules of proper warfare". Judge Ehud
tricked his opponent into a private conference;
behind closed doors he pulled out a knife and
plunged it into the enemy king's belly (3:12–30).
Judge Gideon won a surprise victory in the
middle of the night. His small band so confused
the occupying army with noise and lights that
the enemy soldiers stabbed each other and fled
in the darkness (chapter 7). Samson never led
an army; his battle tricks have been compared
to the pranks of an overgrown juvenile
delinquent (chapters 14–16).

Most of the time the Israelites hid in the
hills while their enemies, with superior weapons,
controlled the plains. (Chariots, like tanks, were
devastating in level country, but almost useless
in muddy or rugged terrain.) Outnumbered, the
Israelites relied on ambushes and sneak attacks.
They knew every gully, for they were fighting for
their homeland. Strategy made up for lack of
strength.

■ UGLIEST STORIES OF THE BIBLE

As a book about early Jewish military heroes,
Judges inspires and fascinates. But you can't
make the whole book fit that description. If you
read strictly looking for heroes, you'd have to
ignore half of Judges – and you would miss its
most important point about God's work with
Israel.

For one thing, Judges' "heroes" were
badly flawed. Samson was pitifully vulnerable to
his lust for women. Gideon won a battle, then
led the nation into idolatry. Jephthah, a former

outlaw, apparently knew very little about the God
he was supposed to serve.

Add to this the "non-heroic" material:
Abimelech, Gideon's son, who slaughtered 70
half-brothers so he could be named king;
Jephthah and Gideon, who massacred fellow
Israelites who had failed to support them; and
the sad characters of the last five chapters of
Judges. These contain some of the ugliest
stories in the Bible – tales of homosexual
assault, idolatry, civil war, thievery, rape, and
murder. The book of Judges runs downhill, from
bad to worse. You may end up wondering what
such material is doing in the Bible.

Every picture has shadows; every thriller
or suspense novel has chapters that look truly
dark. In the story of God and his people, Judges
is that kind of chapter. Heroes appear
sporadically, but humanity remains terribly
unheroic.

■ ENTHUSIASM FADES

God wanted better things for his people than he
got in Judges. He had rescued Israel from slavery
in Egypt. He had given them a rich land and
presented them with a grand system of worship
and government centring on him. He would be no
distant God in the heavens – he would live with
them.

But after some initial enthusiasm, the
Israelites didn't continue the way God had
pointed. Instead, they learned to live with the
sophisticated people they found as their
neighbours – people whose faults included
worshipping idols through sex orgies and child
sacrifice.

The Israelites held the mountains, but the
foreign-held valleys, cutting through the land,
separated the tribes. Soon each group of
isolated Israelites began operating independently.
The next generation lost its sense of national
identity. The people worshipped the idol Baal
alongside the Lord. Though descended from

12 brothers, they spent more time fighting each other than the foreign oppressors. They violated virtually every moral standard. The last verse of Judges sums it up: "everyone did as he saw fit". What they saw fit, wasn't.

■ THE SECRET OF THEIR SURVIVAL

The foreign invasions were no accident, Judges says: they came from God just as surely as the heroic rescuers did. A pattern developed. God allowed suffering as a consequence of the Israelites' disobedience. When things grew really terrible, their attention would turn back to God. He would respond by sending a judge to rescue them. But soon they would fail again. This pattern repeated itself time and again. The Israelites always forgot their need for God, and the dreary cycle ground on.

The secret of Israel's survival was not, then, military heroes or guerrilla tactics. It was the persistent, unwearied love of God himself. Though they forgot him, he did not forget them. He gave innumerable new beginnings. Again and again he sent "judges" to rescue them. He would not let them go. God is the real hero of Judges.

■ HOW TO READ JUDGES

You can read Judges as a collection of heroic stories, the most famous of which are Gideon's and Samson's. But together the tales tell a less heroic story.

Read Judges, therefore, on two levels at once. On one level focus on the new beginning God repeatedly offered by sending a judge to rescue Israel. These are character stories with great fascination. You can gain a great deal by studying the strengths and weaknesses of the individual judges.

On another level, read of the deterioration of a nation that quickly forgot what God had done for it. This will help you understand why, in the next stage of Israel's history, God gave the Israelites a king. For background on this change of government, read "The First King", page 314. Another interesting study is the book of Ruth, a lovely story from the time of Judges that shows a softer, more hopeful side.

■ 3-TRACK READING PLAN

For an explanation and complete listing of the 3-track reading plan, turn to page x.

■ TRACK 1:
Two-Week Courses on the Bible
See page x for information on these courses.

■ TRACK 2:
An Overview of Judges in 3 Days
☐ Day 1. Read the Introduction to Judges and chapter 6, in which God calls Gideon to lead a guerrilla army.
☐ Day 2. Read chapter 7, Gideon's victory in battle.
☐ Day 3. Read chapter 16, the story of Samson and Delilah, and Samson's death. Now turn to page xi for your next Track 2 reading project.

■ TRACK 3:
All of Judges in 21 Days
After you have read through Judges, turn to pages xii–xiii for your next Track 3 reading project.

☐ 1	☐ 2	☐ 3	☐ 4
☐ 5	☐ 6	☐ 7	☐ 8
☐ 9	☐ 10	☐ 11	☐ 12
☐ 13	☐ 14	☐ 15	☐ 16
☐ 17	☐ 18	☐ 19	☐ 20
☐ 21			

■ Israel Fights the Remaining Canaanites

1 After the death of Joshua, the Israelites asked the LORD, "Who will be the first to go up and fight for us against the Canaanites?"

²The LORD answered, "Judah is to go; I have given the land into their hands."

³Then the men of Judah said to the Simeonites their brothers, "Come up with us into the territory allotted to us, to fight against the Canaanites. We in turn will go with you into yours." So the Simeonites went with them.

⁴When Judah attacked, the LORD gave the Canaanites and Perizzites into their hands and they struck down ten thousand men at Bezek. ⁵It was there that they found Adoni-Bezek and fought against him, putting to rout the Canaanites and Perizzites. ⁶Adoni-Bezek fled, but they chased him and caught him, and cut off his thumbs and big toes.

⁷Then Adoni-Bezek said, "Seventy kings with their thumbs and big toes cut off have picked up scraps under my table. Now God has paid me back for what I did to them." They brought him to Jerusalem, and he died there.

1:7 ■ THUMBS AND BIG TOES

A person lacking thumbs and big toes could not grip a weapon or run quickly. So cutting off those appendages guaranteed that a captured enemy would never fight again.

---

⁸The men of Judah attacked Jerusalem also and took it. They put the city to the sword and set it on fire.

⁹After that, the men of Judah went down to fight

against the Canaanites living in the hill country, the Negev and the western foothills. ¹⁰They advanced against the Canaanites living in Hebron (formerly called Kiriath Arba) and defeated Sheshai, Ahiman and Talmai.

¹¹From there they advanced against the people living in Debir (formerly called Kiriath Sepher). ¹²And Caleb said, "I will give my daughter Acsah in marriage to the man who attacks and captures Kiriath Sepher." ¹³Othniel son of Kenaz, Caleb's younger brother, took it; so Caleb gave his daughter Acsah to him in marriage.

¹⁴One day when she came to Othniel, she urged him[a] to ask her father for a field. When she got off her donkey, Caleb asked her, "What can I do for you?"

¹⁵She replied, "Do me a special favour. Since you have given me land in the Negev, give me also springs of water." Then Caleb gave her the upper and lower springs.

¹⁶The descendants of Moses' father-in-law, the Kenite, went up from the City of Palms[b] with the men of Judah to live among the people of the Desert of Judah in the Negev near Arad.

¹⁷Then the men of Judah went with the Simeonites their brothers and attacked the Canaanites living in Zephath, and they totally destroyed[c] the city. Therefore it was called Hormah.[d] ¹⁸The men of Judah also took[e] Gaza, Ashkelon and Ekron—each city with its territory.

¹⁹The LORD was with the men of Judah. They took possession of the hill country, but they were unable to drive the people from the plains, because they had iron chariots. ²⁰As Moses had promised, Hebron was given to Caleb, who drove from it the three sons of Anak. ²¹The Benjamites, however, failed to dislodge the Jebusites, who were living in Jerusalem; to this day the Jebusites live there with the Benjamites.

1:19 ■ MILITARY SETBACKS

Why did the Israelites fail to take all the territory allotted to them? One reason was stubborn military opposition. The Israelites had never developed the sophistication to use chariots, the equivalent of modern-day tanks. Israel controlled the hills where chariots were unwieldy, but could not win the plains. The Israelites also failed to conquer Jerusalem (verse 21); its mountainous setting made that city almost impregnable.

²²Now the house of Joseph attacked Bethel, and the LORD was with them. ²³When they sent men to spy out Bethel (formerly called Luz), ²⁴the spies saw a man coming out of the city and they said to him, "Show us how to get into the city and we will see that you are treated well." ²⁵So he showed them, and they put the city to the sword but spared the man and his whole family. ²⁶He then went to the land of the Hittites, where he built a city and called it Luz, which is its name to this day.

²⁷But Manasseh did not drive out the people of Beth Shan or Taanach or Dor or Ibleam or Megiddo and their surrounding settlements, for the Canaanites were determined to live in that land. ²⁸When Israel became strong, they pressed the Canaanites into forced labour, but never drove them out completely. ²⁹Nor did Ephraim drive out the Canaanites living in Gezer, but the Canaanites continued to live there among them. ³⁰Neither did Zebulun drive out the Canaanites living in Kitron or Nahalol, who remained among them; but they did subject them to forced labour. ³¹Nor did Asher drive out those living in Acco or Sidon or Ahlab or Aczib or Helbah or Aphek or Rehob, ³²and because of this the people of Asher lived among the Canaanite inhabitants of the land. ³³Neither did Naphtali drive out those living in Beth Shemesh or Beth Anath; but the Naphtalites too lived among the Canaanite inhabitants of the land, and those living in Beth Shemesh and Beth Anath became forced labourers for them. ³⁴The Amorites confined the Danites to the hill country, not allowing them to come down into the plain. ³⁵And the Amorites were determined also to hold out in Mount Heres, Aijalon and Shaalbim, but when the power of the house of Joseph increased, they too were pressed into forced labour. ³⁶The boundary of the Amorites was from Scorpion[f] Pass to Sela and beyond.

■ The Angel of the LORD at Bokim

2 The angel of the LORD went up from Gilgal to Bokim and said, "I brought you up out of Egypt and led you into the land that I swore to give to your forefathers. I said, 'I will never break my covenant with you, ²and you shall not make a covenant with the people of this land, but you shall break down their altars.' Yet you have disobeyed me. Why have you done this? ³Now therefore I tell you that I will not drive them out before you; they will be ⌊thorns⌋ in your sides and their gods will be a snare to you."

⁴When the angel of the LORD had spoken these things to all the Israelites, the people wept aloud, ⁵and they called that place Bokim.[a] There they offered sacrifices to the LORD.

■ Disobedience and Defeat

⁶After Joshua had dismissed the Israelites, they went to take possession of the land, each to his own inheritance. ⁷The people served the LORD throughout the lifetime of Joshua and of the elders who outlived him and who had seen all the great things the LORD had done for Israel.

⁸Joshua son of Nun, the servant of the LORD, died at the age of a hundred and ten. ⁹And they buried him in the land of his inheritance, at Timnath Heres[b] in the hill country of Ephraim, north of Mount Gaash.

¹⁰After that whole generation had been gathered to their fathers, another generation grew up, who knew neither the LORD nor what he had done for Israel. ¹¹Then the Israelites did evil in the eyes of the LORD and served the Baals. ¹²They forsook the LORD, the God of their fathers, who had brought them out of Egypt. They followed and worshipped various

gods of the peoples around them. They provoked the LORD to anger ¹³because they forsook him and served Baal and the Ashtoreths. ¹⁴In his anger against Israel the LORD handed them over to raiders who plundered them. He sold them to their enemies all around, whom they were no longer able to resist. ¹⁵Whenever Israel went out to fight, the hand of the LORD was against them to defeat them, just as he had sworn to them. They were in great distress.

2:13 ■ FERTILITY GODS

Israel's neighbours worshipped Baal and Ashtoreth, male and female gods of fertility. Followers practised ritual sex at the shrines, believing that sex with sacred prostitutes led to good crops and many children. Sometimes, too, worshippers sacrificed their children to the gods. The Israelites' attraction to these foreign religions continued for most of their history as a nation.

¹⁶Then the LORD raised up judges,ᶜ who saved them out of the hands of these raiders. ¹⁷Yet they would not listen to their judges but prostituted themselves to other gods and worshipped them. Unlike their fathers, they quickly turned from the way in which their fathers had walked, the way of obedience to the LORD's commands. ¹⁸Whenever the LORD raised up a judge for them, he was with the judge and saved them out of the hands of their enemies as long as the judge lived; for the LORD had compassion on them as they groaned under those who oppressed and afflicted them. ¹⁹But when the judge died, the people returned to ways even more corrupt than those of their fathers, following other gods and serving and worshipping them. They refused to give up their evil practices and stubborn ways.

²⁰Therefore the LORD was very angry with Israel and said, "Because this nation has violated the covenant that I laid down for their forefathers and has not listened to me, ²¹I will no longer drive out before them any of the nations Joshua left when he died. ²²I will use them to test Israel and see whether they will keep the way of the LORD and walk in it as their forefathers did." ²³The LORD had allowed those nations to remain; he did not drive them out at once by giving them into the hands of Joshua.

3 These are the nations the LORD left to test all those Israelites who had not experienced any of the wars in Canaan ²(he did this only to teach warfare to the descendants of the Israelites who had not had previous battle experience): ³the five rulers of the Philistines, all the Canaanites, the Sidonians, and the Hivites living in the Lebanon mountains from Mount Baal Hermon to Leboᵃ Hamath. ⁴They were left to test the Israelites to see whether they would obey the LORD's commands, which he had given their forefathers through Moses. ⁵The Israelites lived among the Canaanites, Hittites, Amorites, Perizzites, Hivites and Jebusites. ⁶They took their daughters in marriage and gave their own daughters to their sons, and served their gods.

3:6 ■ INTERMARRIAGE

This passage shows why the Old Testament opposed mixed marriages, which were common in the period of the judges. Ethnic differences were not the main issue. In fact, during the period of the judges Ruth, a non-Jew, married into a Jewish family with full acceptance (see the book of Ruth). But Ruth had accepted the God of Israel. When mixed marriages meant mixed religions, they diluted faith in God.

■ Othniel

⁷The Israelites did evil in the eyes of the LORD; they forgot the LORD their God and served the Baals and the Asherahs. ⁸The anger of the LORD burned against Israel so that he sold them into the hands of Cushan-Rishathaim king of Aram Naharaim,ᵇ to whom the Israelites were subject for eight years. ⁹But when they cried out to the LORD, he raised up for them a deliverer, Othniel son of Kenaz, Caleb's younger brother, who saved them. ¹⁰The Spirit of the LORD came upon him, so that he became Israel's judgeᶜ and went to war. The LORD gave Cushan-Rishathaim king of Aram into the hands of Othniel, who overpowered him. ¹¹So the land had peace for forty years, until Othniel son of Kenaz died.

■ Ehud

¹²Once again the Israelites did evil in the eyes of the LORD, and because they did this evil the LORD gave Eglon king of Moab power over Israel. ¹³Getting the Ammonites and Amalekites to join him, Eglon came and attacked Israel, and they took possession of the City of Palms.ᵈ ¹⁴The Israelites were subject to Eglon king of Moab for eighteen years.

¹⁵Again the Israelites cried out to the LORD, and he gave them a deliverer—Ehud, a left-handed man, the son of Gera the Benjamite. The Israelites sent him with tribute to Eglon king of Moab. ¹⁶Now Ehud had made a double-edged sword about a foot and a halfᵉ long, which he strapped to his right thigh under his clothing. ¹⁷He presented the tribute to Eglon king of Moab, who was a very fat man. ¹⁸After Ehud had presented the tribute, he sent on their way the men who had carried it. ¹⁹At the idolsᶠ near Gilgal he himself turned back and said, "I have a secret message for you, O king."

The king said, "Quiet!" And all his attendants left him.

²⁰Ehud then approached him while he was sitting alone in the upper room of his summer palaceᵍ and said, "I have a message from God for you." As the king rose from his seat, ²¹Ehud reached with his left hand, drew the sword from his right thigh and plunged it into the king's belly. ²²Even the handle sank in after the blade, which came out of his back. Ehud did not pull the sword out, and the fat closed in over it. ²³Then Ehud went out to the porch;ᵇ he shut the doors of the upper room behind him and locked them.

²⁴After he had gone, the servants came and found

ᶜ16 Or leaders; similarly in verses 17–19   ᵃ3 Or to the entrance to   ᵇ8 That is, North-west Mesopotamia   ᶜ10 Or leader   ᵈ13 That is, Jericho   ᵉ16 Hebrew a cubit (about 0.5 metre)   ᶠ19 Or the stone quarries; also in verse 26   ᵍ20 The meaning of the Hebrew for this phrase is uncertain.   ᵇ23 The meaning of the Hebrew for this word is uncertain.

the doors of the upper room locked. They said, "He must be relieving himself in the inner room of the house." 25They waited to the point of embarrassment, but when he did not open the doors of the room, they took a key and unlocked them. There they saw their lord fallen to the floor, dead. 26While they waited, Ehud got away. He passed by the idols and escaped to Seirah. 27When he arrived there, he blew a trumpet in the hill country of Ephraim, and the Israelites went down with him from the hills, with him leading them.

28"Follow me," he ordered, "for the LORD has given Moab, your enemy, into your hands." So they followed him down and, taking possession of the fords of the Jordan that led to Moab, they allowed no-one to cross over. 29At that time they struck down about ten thousand Moabites, all vigorous and strong; not a man escaped. 30That day Moab was made subject to Israel, and the land had peace for eighty years.

■ Shamgar

31After Ehud came Shamgar son of Anath, who struck down six hundred Philistines with an oxgoad. He too saved Israel.

■ Deborah

4 After Ehud died, the Israelites once again did evil in the eyes of the LORD. 2So the LORD sold them into the hands of Jabin, a king of Canaan, who reigned in Hazor. The commander of his army was Sisera, who lived in Harosheth Haggoyim. 3Because he had nine hundred iron chariots and had cruelly oppressed the Israelites for twenty years, they cried to the LORD for help.

4Deborah, a prophetess, the wife of Lappidoth, was leading*a* Israel at that time. 5She held court under the Palm of Deborah between Ramah and Bethel in the hill country of Ephraim, and the Israelites came to her to have their disputes decided. 6She sent for Barak son of Abinoam from Kedesh in Naphtali and said to him, "The LORD, the God of Israel, commands you: 'Go, take with you ten thousand men of Naphtali and Zebulun and lead the way to Mount Tabor. 7I will lure Sisera, the commander of Jabin's army, with his chariots and his troops to the Kishon River and give him into your hands.' "

8Barak said to her, "If you go with me, I will go; but if you don't go with me, I won't go."

9"Very well," Deborah said, "I will go with you. But because of the way you are going about this,*b* the honour will not be yours, for the LORD will hand Sisera over to a woman." So Deborah went with Barak to Kedesh, 10where he summoned Zebulun and Naphtali. Ten thousand men followed him, and Deborah also went with him.

11Now Heber the Kenite had left the other Kenites, the descendants of Hobab, Moses' brother-in-law,*c* and pitched his tent by the great tree in Zaanannim near Kedesh.

12When they told Sisera that Barak son of Abinoam had gone up to Mount Tabor, 13Sisera gathered together his nine hundred iron chariots and all the men with him, from Harosheth Haggoyim to the Kishon River.

14Then Deborah said to Barak, "Go! This is the day the LORD has given Sisera into your hands. Has not the LORD gone ahead of you?" So Barak went down Mount Tabor, followed by ten thousand men. 15At Barak's advance, the LORD routed Sisera and all his chariots and army by the sword, and Sisera abandoned his chariot and fled on foot. 16But Barak pursued the chariots and army as far as Harosheth Haggoyim. All the troops of Sisera fell by the sword; not a man was left.

4:9 ■ HONOUR TO A WOMAN
The only woman leader in Judges, Deborah had won unquestioned respect. She sent for Barak to lead the army, but he was unwilling to go into battle without her. Deborah predicted that the real hero of the battle would be a woman.

17Sisera, however, fled on foot to the tent of Jael, the wife of Heber the Kenite, because there were friendly relations between Jabin king of Hazor and the clan of Heber the Kenite.

18Jael went out to meet Sisera and said to him, "Come, my lord, come right in. Don't be afraid." So he entered her tent, and she put a covering over him.

19"I'm thirsty," he said. "Please give me some water." She opened a skin of milk, gave him a drink, and covered him up.

20"Stand in the doorway of the tent," he told her. "If someone comes by and asks you, 'Is anyone here?' say 'No.' "

21But Jael, Heber's wife, picked up a tent peg and a hammer and went quietly to him while he lay fast asleep, exhausted. She drove the peg through his temple into the ground, and he died.

22Barak came by in pursuit of Sisera, and Jael went out to meet him. "Come," she said, "I will show you the man you're looking for." So he went in with her, and there lay Sisera with the tent peg through his temple—dead.

23On that day God subdued Jabin, the Canaanite king, before the Israelites. 24And the hand of the Israelites grew stronger and stronger against Jabin, the Canaanite king, until they destroyed him.

■ The Song of Deborah

5 On that day Deborah and Barak son of Abinoam sang this song:

2"When the princes in Israel take the lead,
    when the people willingly offer themselves—
    praise the LORD!

3"Hear this, you kings! Listen, you rulers!
    I will sing to*a* the LORD, I will sing;
    I will make music to*b* the LORD, the God of
    Israel.

4"O LORD, when you went out from Seir,
    when you marched from the land of Edom,
the earth shook, the heavens poured,
    the clouds poured down water.

a4 Traditionally *judging*   *b9* Or *But on the expedition you are undertaking*   *c11* Or *father-in-law*   *a3* Or *of*   *b3* Or *I with song I will praise*

⁵The mountains quaked before the LORD, the
    One of Sinai,
  before the LORD, the God of Israel.

⁶"In the days of Shamgar son of Anath,
    in the days of Jael, the roads were
    abandoned;
  travellers took to winding paths.
⁷Village lifeᶜ in Israel ceased,
    ceased until I,ᵈ Deborah, arose,
    arose a mother in Israel.
⁸When they chose new gods,
    war came to the city gates,
  and not a shield or spear was seen
    among forty thousand in Israel.
⁹My heart is with Israel's princes,
    with the willing volunteers among the
    people.
  Praise the LORD!

¹⁰"You who ride on white donkeys,
    sitting on your saddle blankets,
    and you who walk along the road,
  consider ¹¹the voice of the singersᵉ at the
    watering places.
  They recite the righteous acts of the LORD,
    the righteous acts of his warriorsᶠ in Israel.

  "Then the people of the LORD
    went down to the city gates.
¹²'Wake up, wake up, Deborah!
    Wake up, wake up, break out in song!
  Arise, O Barak!
    Take captive your captives, O son of
    Abinoam.'

¹³"Then the men who were left
    came down to the nobles;
  the people of the LORD
    came to me with the mighty.
¹⁴Some came from Ephraim, whose roots were in
    Amalek;
  Benjamin was with the people who followed
    you.
  From Makir captains came down,
    from Zebulun those who bear a commander's
    staff.
¹⁵The princes of Issachar were with Deborah;
    yes, Issachar was with Barak,
    rushing after him into the valley.
  In the districts of Reuben
    there was much searching of heart.
¹⁶Why did you stay among the campfiresᵍ
    to hear the whistling for the flocks?
  In the districts of Reuben
    there was much searching of heart.
¹⁷Gilead stayed beyond the Jordan.
    And Dan, why did he linger by the ships?
  Asher remained on the coast
    and stayed in his coves.
¹⁸The people of Zebulun risked their very lives;
    so did Naphtali on the heights of the field.

¹⁹"Kings came, they fought;
    the kings of Canaan fought
  at Taanach by the waters of Megiddo,
    but they carried off no silver, no plunder.

²⁰From the heavens the stars fought,
    from their courses they fought against Sisera.
²¹The river Kishon swept them away,
    the age-old river, the river Kishon.
  March on, my soul; be strong!
²²Then thundered the horses' hoofs—
    galloping, galloping go his mighty steeds.
²³'Curse Meroz,' said the angel of the LORD.
    'Curse its people bitterly,
  because they did not come to help the LORD,
    to help the LORD against the mighty.'

²⁴"Most blessed of women be Jael,
    the wife of Heber the Kenite,
    most blessed of tent-dwelling women.
²⁵He asked for water, and she gave him milk;
    in a bowl fit for nobles she brought him
    curdled milk.
²⁶Her hand reached for the tent peg,
    her right hand for the workman's hammer.
  She struck Sisera, she crushed his head,
    she shattered and pierced his temple.
²⁷At her feet he sank,
    he fell; there he lay.
  At her feet he sank, he fell;
    where he sank, there he fell—dead.

²⁸"Through the window peered Sisera's mother;
    behind the lattice she cried out,
  'Why is his chariot so long in coming?
    Why is the clatter of his chariots delayed?'
²⁹The wisest of her ladies answer her;
    indeed, she keeps saying to herself,
³⁰'Are they not finding and dividing the spoils:
    a girl or two for each man,
  colourful garments as plunder for Sisera,
    colourful garments embroidered,
  highly embroidered garments for my neck—
  all this as plunder?'

³¹"So may all your enemies perish, O LORD!
    But may they who love you be like the sun
    when it rises in its strength."

  Then the land had peace for forty years.

■ Gideon

6 Again the Israelites did evil in the eyes of the
  LORD, and for seven years he gave them into the
hands of the Midianites. ²Because the power of Midian was so oppressive, the Israelites prepared shelters for themselves in mountain clefts, caves and
strongholds. ³Whenever the Israelites planted their
crops, the Midianites, Amalekites and other eastern
peoples invaded the country. ⁴They camped on the
land and ruined the crops all the way to Gaza and
did not spare a living thing for Israel, neither sheep
nor cattle nor donkeys. ⁵They came up with their
livestock and their tents like swarms of locusts. It
was impossible to count the men and their camels;
they invaded the land to ravage it. ⁶Midian so impoverished the Israelites that they cried out to the LORD
for help.
  ⁷When the Israelites cried to the LORD because of
Midian, ⁸he sent them a prophet, who said, "This is
what the LORD, the God of Israel, says: I brought you

up out of Egypt, out of the land of slavery. 9I snatched you from the power of Egypt and from the hand of all your oppressors. I drove them from before you and gave them their land. 10I said to you, 'I am the LORD your God; do not worship the gods of the Amorites, in whose land you live.' But you have not listened to me."

6:5 ■ CAMEL POWER

This is the earliest mention in the Bible of camels used for military purposes. Midianite marauders let the Israelites raise their crops, then swept in and took everything when the crops were ripe. With no effective defence, the Israelites hid out in caves and other remote spots.

11The angel of the LORD came and sat down under the oak in Ophrah that belonged to Joash the Abiezrite, where his son Gideon was threshing wheat in a winepress to keep it from the Midianites. 12When the angel of the LORD appeared to Gideon, he said, "The LORD is with you, mighty warrior."

13"But sir," Gideon replied, "if the LORD is with us, why has all this happened to us? Where are all his wonders that our fathers told us about when they said, 'Did not the LORD bring us up out of Egypt?' But now the LORD has abandoned us and put us into the hand of Midian."

14The LORD turned to him and said, "Go in the strength you have and save Israel out of Midian's hand. Am I not sending you?"

15"But Lord,"a Gideon asked, "how can I save Israel? My clan is the weakest in Manasseh, and I am the least in my family."

16The LORD answered, "I will be with you, and you will strike down all the Midianites together."

17Gideon replied, "If now I have found favour in your eyes, give me a sign that it is really you talking to me. 18Please do not go away until I come back and bring my offering and set it before you."

And the LORD said, "I will wait until you return."

19Gideon went in, prepared a young goat, and from an ephahb of flour he made bread without yeast. Putting the meat in a basket and its broth in a pot, he brought them out and offered them to him under the oak.

20The angel of God said to him, "Take the meat and the unleavened bread, place them on this rock, and pour out the broth." And Gideon did so. 21With the tip of the staff that was in his hand, the angel of the LORD touched the meat and the unleavened bread. Fire flared from the rock, consuming the meat and the bread. And the angel of the LORD disappeared. 22When Gideon realised that it was the angel of the LORD, he exclaimed, "Ah, Sovereign LORD! I have seen the angel of the LORD face to face!"

23But the LORD said to him, "Peace! Do not be afraid. You are not going to die."

24So Gideon built an altar to the LORD there and called it The LORD is Peace. To this day it stands in Ophrah of the Abiezrites.

25That same night the LORD said to him, "Take the second bull from your father's herd, the one seven years old.c Tear down your father's altar to Baal and cut down the Asherah poled beside it. 26Then build a proper kinde altar to the LORD your God on the top of this height. Using the wood of the Asherah pole that you cut down, offer the secondf bull as a burnt offering."

27So Gideon took ten of his servants and did as the LORD told him. But because he was afraid of his family and the men of the town, he did it at night rather than in the daytime.

28In the morning when the men of the town got up, there was Baal's altar, demolished, with the Asherah pole beside it cut down and the second bull sacrificed on the newly-built altar!

29They asked each other, "Who did this?"

When they carefully investigated, they were told, "Gideon son of Joash did it."

30The men of the town demanded of Joash, "Bring out your son. He must die, because he has broken down Baal's altar and cut down the Asherah pole beside it."

31But Joash replied to the hostile crowd around him, "Are you going to plead Baal's cause? Are you trying to save him? Whoever fights for him shall be put to death by morning! If Baal really is a god, he can defend himself when someone breaks down his altar." 32So that day they called Gideon "Jerub-Baal,g" saying, "Let Baal contend with him," because he broke down Baal's altar.

6:30 ■ TOPSY-TURVY

Israel had turned God's commands upside down. According to Deuteronomy 13:6–10, those who worshipped idols should be stoned. But here Israelites were ready to execute Gideon for destroying their idols.

33Now all the Midianites, Amalekites and other eastern peoples joined forces and crossed over the Jordan and camped in the Valley of Jezreel. 34Then the Spirit of the LORD came upon Gideon, and he blew a trumpet, summoning the Abiezrites to follow him. 35He sent messengers throughout Manasseh, calling them to arms, and also into Asher, Zebulun and Naphtali, so that they too went up to meet them.

36Gideon said to God, "If you will save Israel by my hand as you have promised— 37look, I will place a wool fleece on the threshing-floor. If there is dew only on the fleece and all the ground is dry, then I will know that you will save Israel by my hand, as you said." 38And that is what happened. Gideon rose early the next day; he squeezed the fleece and wrung out the dew—a bowlful of water.

39Then Gideon said to God, "Do not be angry with me. Let me make just one more request. Allow me one more test with the fleece. This time make the fleece dry and the ground covered with dew." 40That night God did so. Only the fleece was dry; all the ground was covered with dew.

---

a 15 Or sir   b 19 That is, probably about ⅗ bushel (about 22 litres)   c 25 Or Take a full-grown, mature bull from your father's herd   d 25 That is, a symbol of the goddess Asherah; here and elsewhere in Judges   e 26 Or build with layers of stone an   f 26 Or full-grown; also in verse 28   g 32 Jerub-Baal means let Baal contend.

■ Gideon Defeats the Midianites

7 Early in the morning, Jerub-Baal (that is, Gideon) and all his men camped at the spring of Harod. The camp of Midian was north of them in the valley near the hill of Moreh. ²The LORD said to Gideon, "You have too many men for me to deliver Midian into their hands. In order that Israel may not boast against me that her own strength has saved her, ³announce now to the people, 'Anyone who trembles with fear may turn back and leave Mount Gilead.' " So twenty-two thousand men left, while ten thousand remained.

⁴But the LORD said to Gideon, "There are still too many men. Take them down to the water, and I will sift them out for you there. If I say, 'This one shall go with you,' he shall go; but if I say, 'This one shall not go with you,' he shall not go."

⁵So Gideon took the men down to the water. There the LORD told him, "Separate those who lap the water with their tongues like a dog from those who kneel down to drink." ⁶Three hundred men lapped with their hands to their mouths. All the rest got down on their knees to drink.

⁷The LORD said to Gideon, "With the three hundred men that lapped I will save you and give the Midianites into your hands. Let all the other men go, each to his own place." ⁸So Gideon sent the rest of the Israelites to their tents but kept the three hundred, who took over the provisions and trumpets of the others.

Now the camp of Midian lay below him in the valley. ⁹During that night the LORD said to Gideon, "Get up, go down against the camp, because I am going to give it into your hands. ¹⁰If you are afraid to

INSIGHT

■ UNLIKELY LEADERS
GOD DREW OUT GIDEON'S HIDDEN POTENTIAL

THE LORD SAID TO HIM, "PEACE! DO NOT BE AFRAID. YOU ARE NOT GOING TO DIE." ■ 6:23

Gideon made an unlikely fighter – hesitant and fearful. We first meet him as he furtively threshed wheat in a winepress. To thresh wheat openly was to invite the occupying Midianite army to confiscate it. The Midianites dominated Israel so thoroughly that Israelites could rarely harvest crops; some lived in caves.

Gideon was not planning any heroics until the angel of the Lord came to him with a battle commission. "Who, me?" Gideon seemed to ask, trembling.

In view of the facts, his doubts were justified. His family and village worshipped Baal, not the Lord. He himself was subject to paralysing fears, even on the eve of battle. Gideon kept demanding miraculous proof that God really was with him – and one miracle was not enough.

At the same time, God seemed to make Gideon's job more formidable. He reduced his army from 32,000 to a pitiful 300. If an army so outnumbered were to win, that would prove beyond a doubt that God was in charge.

God knew Gideon's potential and patiently brought Gideon to the point of courage. He encouraged him, directed him, transformed him. Overnight Gideon became a strong and decisive general. He used noise and lights for scare tactics, enabling his small band to scatter the enemy. Thorough mopping-up operations followed. The little army devastated the scattered Midianites, and Gideon, triumphant, brought in an era of freedom. Perhaps no-one was as surprised as he.

■ CAST-OFF MATERIAL
The selection of Gideon shows a pattern. At a time when women were regarded as second-class citizens (see 9:54; 19:24), God chose Deborah to lead. Jephthah, another judge, had been a social outcast, the leader of a gang of outlaws, before God chose him to lead.

And the pattern is found not only in Judges. Throughout the Bible, God used cast-off material. Israel was not chosen because of its great size or sophistication. (In fact, archaeologists report a drop in the culture of a city after the Israelites captured it.) God did not seek the most capable people, nor the most naturally "good". He chose a small, weak slave tribe, uncultured, with a short memory for his kindness to them. Time and again the Israelites proved themselves faulty. So did their leaders. With this unlikely material God did great things so the world could see that the glory was his and his alone.

Paul took up this theme when he wrote, over a thousand years later, "Brothers, think of what you were when you were called. Not many of you were wise by human standards; not many were influential; not many were of noble birth. But God chose the foolish things of the world to shame the wise; God chose the weak things of the world to shame the strong. . . . Therefore, as it is written: 'Let him who boasts boast in the Lord' " (1 Corinthians 1:26–31).

☐ LIFE QUESTIONS:
Do you picture yourself as a leader? Why or why not? What would God have to change to make you a leader?

attack, go down to the camp with your servant Purah[11]and listen to what they are saying. Afterwards, you will be encouraged to attack the camp." So he and Purah his servant went down to the outposts of the camp. [12]The Midianites, the Amalekites and all the other eastern peoples had settled in the valley, thick as locusts. Their camels could no more be counted than the sand on the seashore.

6:37 ■ PUTTING OUT A FLEECE

How much proof of God's will does one person need? Though the angel of the Lord had assured Gideon of success, he took fright and wanted to double-check, then triple-check, by asking for miracles. In some circles today, "putting out a fleece" has come to mean asking God to do something unusual to confirm his guidance. However, Gideon's action seems more like a lack of faith than a model of seeking God's guidance.

---

[13]Gideon arrived just as a man was telling a friend his dream. "I had a dream," he was saying. "A round loaf of barley bread came tumbling into the Midianite camp. It struck the tent with such force that the tent overturned and collapsed."

[14]His friend responded, "This can be nothing other than the sword of Gideon son of Joash, the Israelite. God has given the Midianites and the whole camp into his hands."

[15]When Gideon heard the dream and its interpretation, he worshipped God. He returned to the camp of Israel and called out, "Get up! The LORD has given the Midianite camp into your hands." [16]Dividing the three hundred men into three companies, he placed trumpets and empty jars in the hands of all of them, with torches inside.

[17]"Watch me," he told them. "Follow my lead. When I get to the edge of the camp, do exactly as I do. [18]When I and all who are with me blow our trumpets, then from all around the camp blow yours and shout, 'For the LORD and for Gideon.' "

[19]Gideon and the hundred men with him reached the edge of the camp at the beginning of the middle watch, just after they had changed the guard. They blew their trumpets and broke the jars that were in their hands. [20]The three companies blew the trumpets and smashed the jars. Grasping the torches in their left hands and holding in their right hands the trumpets they were to blow, they shouted, "A sword for the LORD and for Gideon!" [21]While each man held his position around the camp, all the Midianites ran, crying out as they fled.

[22]When the three hundred trumpets sounded, the LORD caused the men throughout the camp to turn on each other with their swords. The army fled to Beth Shittah towards Zererah as far as the border of Abel Meholah near Tabbath. [23]Israelites from Naphtali, Asher and all Manasseh were called out, and they pursued the Midianites. [24]Gideon sent messengers throughout the hill country of Ephraim, saying, "Come down against the Midianites and seize the waters of the Jordan ahead of them as far as Beth Barah."

So all the men of Ephraim were called out and they took the waters of the Jordan as far as Beth Barah. [25]They also captured two of the Midianite leaders, Oreb and Zeeb. They killed Oreb at the rock of Oreb, and Zeeb at the winepress of Zeeb. They pursued the Midianites and brought the heads of Oreb and Zeeb to Gideon, who was by the Jordan.

■ Zebah and Zalmunna

8 Now the Ephraimites asked Gideon, "Why have you treated us like this? Why didn't you call us when you went to fight Midian?" And they criticised him sharply.

[2]But he answered them, "What have I accomplished compared to you? Aren't the gleanings of Ephraim's grapes better than the full grape harvest of Abiezer? [3]God gave Oreb and Zeeb, the Midianite leaders, into your hands. What was I able to do compared to you?" At this, their resentment against him subsided.

[4]Gideon and his three hundred men, exhausted yet keeping up the pursuit, came to the Jordan and crossed it. [5]He said to the men of Succoth, "Give my troops some bread; they are worn out, and I am still pursuing Zebah and Zalmunna, the kings of Midian."

[6]But the officials of Succoth said, "Do you already have the hands of Zebah and Zalmunna in your possession? Why should we give bread to your troops?"

[7]Then Gideon replied, "Just for that, when the LORD has given Zebah and Zalmunna into my hand, I will tear your flesh with desert thorns and briers."

[8]From there he went up to Peniel[a] and made the same request of them, but they answered as the men of Succoth had. [9]So he said to the men of Peniel, "When I return in triumph, I will tear down this tower."

[10]Now Zebah and Zalmunna were in Karkor with a force of about fifteen thousand men, all that were left of the armies of the eastern peoples; a hundred and twenty thousand swordsmen had fallen. [11]Gideon went up by the route of the nomads east of Nobah and Jogbehah and fell upon the unsuspecting army. [12]Zebah and Zalmunna, the two kings of Midian, fled, but he pursued them and captured them, routing their entire army.

[13]Gideon son of Joash then returned from the battle by the Pass of Heres. [14]He caught a young man of Succoth and questioned him, and the young man wrote down for him the names of the seventy-seven officials of Succoth, the elders of the town. [15]Then Gideon came and said to the men of Succoth, "Here are Zebah and Zalmunna, about whom you taunted me by saying, 'Do you already have the hands of Zebah and Zalmunna in your possession? Why should we give bread to your exhausted men?' " [16]He took the elders of the town and taught the men of Succoth a lesson by punishing them with desert thorns and briers. [17]He also pulled down the tower of Peniel and killed the men of the town.

[18]Then he asked Zebah and Zalmunna, "What kind of men did you kill at Tabor?"

"Men like you," they answered, "each one with the bearing of a prince."

[19]Gideon replied, "Those were my brothers, the sons of my own mother. As surely as the LORD lives,

---

[a]8 Hebrew Penuel, a variant of Peniel; also in verses 9 and 17

if you had spared their lives, I would not kill you." ²⁰Turning to Jether, his oldest son, he said, "Kill them!" But Jether did not draw his sword, because he was only a boy and was afraid.

8:14 ■ EARLY LITERACY
Some scholars argue that much of the Old Testament was handed down by word of mouth and only written at a much later time. This brief mention of a young man's ability to write suggests that literacy was widespread even at this early date – and thus that the Old Testament books could have been written soon after the events they describe.

²¹Zebah and Zalmunna said, "Come, do it yourself. 'As is the man, so is his strength.'" So Gideon stepped forward and killed them, and took the ornaments off their camels' necks.

■ Gideon's Ephod
²²The Israelites said to Gideon, "Rule over us – you, your son and your grandson – because you have saved us out of the hand of Midian."
²³But Gideon told them, "I will not rule over you, nor will my son rule over you. The LORD will rule over you." ²⁴And he said, "I do have one request, that each of you give me an ear-ring from your share of the plunder." (It was the custom of the Ishmaelites to wear gold ear-rings.)

8:23 ■ NO KING
Unlike most nations of this time, Israel had no king. Gideon, declining an opportunity to rule, explains why: God alone must rule. Generations later, when Israel insisted on royal leadership, Samuel interpreted the move as a rejection of God (1 Samuel 10:19).
Even after Israel gained a king, the king's power had limits; rulers answered to God, the ultimate ruler. That was a novel idea in an era when people worshipped kings as gods.

²⁵They answered, "We'll be glad to give them." So they spread out a garment, and each man threw a ring from his plunder onto it. ²⁶The weight of the gold rings he asked for came to seventeen hundred shekels,ᵇ not counting the ornaments, the pendants and the purple garments worn by the kings of Midian or the chains that were on their camels' necks. ²⁷Gideon made the gold into an ephod, which he placed in Ophrah, his town. All Israel prostituted themselves by worshipping it there, and it became a snare to Gideon and his family.

■ Gideon's Death
²⁸Thus Midian was subdued before the Israelites and did not raise its head again. During Gideon's lifetime, the land enjoyed peace for forty years.
²⁹Jerub-Baal son of Joash went back home to live. ³⁰He had seventy sons of his own, for he had many wives. ³¹His concubine, who lived in Shechem, also

bore him a son, whom he named Abimelech. ³²Gideon son of Joash died at a good old age and was buried in the tomb of his father Joash in Ophrah of the Abiezrites.
³³No sooner had Gideon died than the Israelites again prostituted themselves to the Baals. They set up Baal-Berith as their god and ³⁴did not remember the LORD their God, who had rescued them from the hands of all their enemies on every side. ³⁵They also failed to show kindness to the family of Jerub-Baal (that is, Gideon) for all the good things he had done for them.

■ Abimelech
9 Abimelech son of Jerub-Baal went to his mother's brothers in Shechem and said to them and to all his mother's clan, ²"Ask all the citizens of Shechem, 'Which is better for you: to have all seventy of Jerub-Baal's sons rule over you, or just one man?' Remember, I am your flesh and blood."
³When the brothers repeated all this to the citizens of Shechem, they were inclined to follow Abimelech, for they said, "He is our brother." ⁴They gave him seventy shekelsᵃ of silver from the temple of Baal-Berith, and Abimelech used it to hire reckless adventurers, who became his followers. ⁵He went to his father's home in Ophrah and on one stone murdered his seventy brothers, the sons of Jerub-Baal. But Jotham, the youngest son of Jerub-Baal, escaped by hiding. ⁶Then all the citizens of Shechem and Beth Millo gathered beside the great tree at the pillar in Shechem to crown Abimelech king.
⁷When Jotham was told about this, he climbed up on the top of Mount Gerizim and shouted to them, "Listen to me, citizens of Shechem, so that God may listen to you. ⁸One day the trees went out to anoint a king for themselves. They said to the olive tree, 'Be our king.'
⁹"But the olive tree answered, 'Should I give up my oil, by which both gods and men are honoured, to hold sway over the trees?'
¹⁰"Next, the trees said to the fig-tree, 'Come and be our king.'
¹¹"But the fig-tree replied, 'Should I give up my fruit, so good and sweet, to hold sway over the trees?'
¹²"Then the trees said to the vine, 'Come and be our king.'
¹³"But the vine answered, 'Should I give up my wine, which cheers both gods and men, to hold sway over the trees?'
¹⁴"Finally all the trees said to the thornbush, 'Come and be our king.'
¹⁵"The thornbush said to the trees, 'If you really want to anoint me king over you, come and take refuge in my shade; but if not, then let fire come out of the thornbush and consume the cedars of Lebanon!'
¹⁶"Now if you have acted honourably and in good faith when you made Abimelech king, and if you have been fair to Jerub-Baal and his family, and if you have treated him as he deserves – ¹⁷and to think that my father fought for you, risked his life to rescue you from the hand of Midian ¹⁸(but today you have revolted against my father's family, murdered his

ᵇ26 That is, about 43 pounds (about 19.5 kilograms)   ᵃ4 That is, about 1¾ pounds (about 0.8 kilogram) seventy sons on a single stone, and made Abimelech, the son of his slave girl, king over the citizens of Shechem because he is your brother) — [19]if then you have acted honourably and in good faith towards Jerub-Baal and his family today, may Abimelech be your joy, and may you be his, too! [20]But if you have not, let fire come out from Abimelech and consume you, citizens of Shechem and Beth Millo, and let fire come out from you, citizens of Shechem and Beth Millo, and consume Abimelech!"

[21]Then Jotham fled, escaping to Beer, and he lived there because he was afraid of his brother Abimelech.

[22]After Abimelech had governed Israel for three years, [23]God sent an evil spirit between Abimelech and the citizens of Shechem, who acted treacherously against Abimelech. [24]God did this in order that the crime against Jerub-Baal's seventy sons, the shedding of their blood, might be avenged on their brother Abimelech and on the citizens of Shechem, who had helped him murder his brothers. [25]In opposition to him these citizens of Shechem set men on the hilltops to ambush and rob everyone who passed by, and this was reported to Abimelech.

9:23 ■ EVIL SPIRIT

The "evil spirit" God sent was not necessarily a supernatural being. "Spirit" means literally "wind" or "breath" in the Bible, and this comment might be translated, "God sent an ill wind." Perhaps an attitude of bitterness or distrust grew up between Abimelech and the people of Shechem. Characteristically, the Bible attributes this development to God, though human causes were probably involved as well.

[26]Now Gaal son of Ebed moved with his brothers into Shechem, and its citizens put their confidence in him. [27]After they had gone out into the fields and gathered the grapes and trodden them, they held a festival in the temple of their god. While they were eating and drinking, they cursed Abimelech. [28]Then Gaal son of Ebed said, "Who is Abimelech, and who is Shechem, that we should be subject to him? Isn't he Jerub-Baal's son, and isn't Zebul his deputy? Serve the men of Hamor, Shechem's father! Why should we serve Abimelech? [29]If only this people were under my command! Then I would get rid of him. I would say to Abimelech, 'Call out your whole army!'"[b] [30]When Zebul the governor of the city heard what Gaal son of Ebed said, he was very angry. [31]Under cover he sent messengers to Abimelech, saying, "Gaal son of Ebed and his brothers have come to Shechem and are stirring up the city against you. [32]Now then, during the night you and your men should come and lie in wait in the fields. [33]In the morning at sunrise, advance against the city. When Gaal and his men come out against you, do whatever your hand finds to do."

[34]So Abimelech and all his troops set out by night and took up concealed positions near Shechem in four companies. [35]Now Gaal son of Ebed had gone out and was standing at the entrance to the city gate just as Abimelech and his soldiers came out from their hiding-place.

[36]When Gaal saw them, he said to Zebul, "Look, people are coming down from the tops of the mountains!"

Zebul replied, "You mistake the shadows of the mountains for men."

[37]But Gaal spoke up again: "Look, people are coming down from the centre of the land, and a company is coming from the direction of the soothsayers' tree."

[38]Then Zebul said to him, "Where is your big talk now, you who said, 'Who is Abimelech that we should be subject to him?' Aren't these the men you ridiculed? Go out and fight them!"

[39]So Gaal led out[c] the citizens of Shechem and fought Abimelech. [40]Abimelech chased him, and many fell wounded in the flight — all the way to the entrance to the gate. [41]Abimelech stayed in Arumah, and Zebul drove Gaal and his brothers out of Shechem.

[42]The next day the people of Shechem went out to the fields, and this was reported to Abimelech. [43]So he took his men, divided them into three companies and set an ambush in the fields. When he saw the people coming out of the city, he rose to attack them. [44]Abimelech and the companies with him rushed forward to a position at the entrance to the city gate. Then two companies rushed upon those in the fields and struck them down. [45]All that day Abimelech pressed his attack against the city until he had captured it and killed its people. Then he destroyed the city and scattered salt over it.

[46]On hearing this, the citizens in the tower of Shechem went into the stronghold of the temple of El-Berith. [47]When Abimelech heard that they had assembled there, [48]he and all his men went up Mount Zalmon. He took an axe and cut off some branches, which he lifted to his shoulders. He ordered the men with him, "Quick! Do what you have seen me do!" [49]So all the men cut branches and followed Abimelech. They piled them against the stronghold and set it on fire over the people inside. So all the people in the tower of Shechem, about a thousand men and women, also died.

[50]Next Abimelech went to Thebez and besieged it and captured it. [51]Inside the city, however, was a strong tower, to which all the men and women — all the people of the city — fled. They locked themselves in and climbed up on the tower roof. [52]Abimelech went to the tower and stormed it. But as he approached the entrance to the tower to set it on fire, [53]a woman dropped an upper millstone on his head and cracked his skull.

[54]Hurriedly he called to his armour-bearer, "Draw your sword and kill me, so that they can't say, 'A woman killed him.'" So his servant ran him through, and he died. [55]When the Israelites saw that Abimelech was dead, they went home.

[56]Thus God repaid the wickedness that Abimelech had done to his father by murdering his seventy brothers. [57]God also made the men of Shechem pay for all their wickedness. The curse of Jotham son of Jerub-Baal came on them.

[b] 29 Septuagint; Hebrew him." Then he said to Abimelech, "Call out your whole army!"   [c] 39 Or Gaal went out in the sight of

■ Tola

10 After the time of Abimelech a man of Issachar, Tola son of Puah, the son of Dodo, rose to save Israel. He lived in Shamir, in the hill country of Ephraim. ²He led*ᵃ* Israel for twenty-three years; then he died, and was buried in Shamir.

9:54 ■ SEXIST ATTITUDES

Abimelech preferred dying immediately to having it said that a woman killed him. Sexist attitudes clearly prevailed in the time of the judges, but nevertheless women made their marks, both good and bad. Here and in the story of Jael (4:21), women used domestic implements to kill dangerous men. (Grinding grain with millstones and setting up tents with pegs were traditionally considered "women's work".) Deborah, a judge and general, and Delilah, who seduced Samson, used their wits for good and evil, respectively.

■ Jair

³He was followed by Jair of Gilead, who led Israel for twenty-two years. ⁴He had thirty sons, who rode thirty donkeys. They controlled thirty towns in Gilead, which to this day are called Havvoth Jair.*ᵇ* ⁵When Jair died, he was buried in Kamon.

■ Jephthah

⁶Again the Israelites did evil in the eyes of the LORD. They served the Baals and the Ashtoreths, and the gods of Aram, the gods of Sidon, the gods of Moab, the gods of the Ammonites and the gods of the Philistines. And because the Israelites forsook the LORD and no longer served him, ⁷he became angry with them. He sold them into the hands of the Philistines and the Ammonites, ⁸who that year shattered and crushed them. For eighteen years they oppressed all the Israelites on the east side of the Jordan in Gilead, the land of the Amorites. ⁹The Ammonites also crossed the Jordan to fight against Judah, Benjamin and the house of Ephraim; and Israel was in great distress. ¹⁰Then the Israelites cried out to the LORD, "We have sinned against you, forsaking our God and serving the Baals."

¹¹The LORD replied, "When the Egyptians, the Amorites, the Ammonites, the Philistines, ¹²the Sidonians, the Amalekites and the Maonites*ᶜ* oppressed you and you cried to me for help, did I not save you from their hands? ¹³But you have forsaken me and served other gods, so I will no longer save you. ¹⁴Go and cry out to the gods you have chosen. Let them save you when you are in trouble!"

¹⁵But the Israelites said to the LORD, "We have sinned. Do with us whatever you think best, but please rescue us now." ¹⁶Then they got rid of the foreign gods among them and served the LORD. And he could bear Israel's misery no longer.

¹⁷When the Ammonites were called to arms and camped in Gilead, the Israelites assembled and camped at Mizpah. ¹⁸The leaders of the people of Gilead said to each other, "Whoever will launch the attack against the Ammonites will be the head of all those living in Gilead."

11 Jephthah the Gileadite was a mighty warrior. His father was Gilead; his mother was a prostitute. ²Gilead's wife also bore him sons, and when they were grown up, they drove Jephthah away. "You are not going to get any inheritance in our family," they said, "because you are the son of another woman." ³So Jephthah fled from his brothers and settled in the land of Tob, where a group of adventurers gathered around him and followed him.

⁴Some time later, when the Ammonites made war on Israel, ⁵the elders of Gilead went to get Jephthah from the land of Tob. ⁶"Come," they said, "be our commander, so we can fight the Ammonites."

11:6 ■ A MAN LIKE DAVID

Jephthah, like King David to come, was an outlaw who gained leadership experience at the head of a small band of adventurers. Israel turned to him when they needed military leadership, as they later would turn to David. Yet Jephthah's reputation never equalled David's, and the reason must have had something to do with his lack of wisdom. His rash vow to God (verse 31) and his harsh answer to a complaint (12:3) each had destructive results.

---

⁷Jephthah said to them, "Didn't you hate me and drive me from my father's house? Why do you come to me now, when you're in trouble?"

⁸The elders of Gilead said to him, "Nevertheless, we are turning to you now; come with us to fight the Ammonites, and you will be our head over all who live in Gilead."

⁹Jephthah answered, "Suppose you take me back to fight the Ammonites and the LORD gives them to me—will I really be your head?"

¹⁰The elders of Gilead replied, "The LORD is our witness; we will certainly do as you say." ¹¹So Jephthah went with the elders of Gilead, and the people made him head and commander over them. And he repeated all his words before the LORD in Mizpah.

¹²Then Jephthah sent messengers to the Ammonite king with the question: "What do you have against us that you have attacked our country?"

¹³The king of the Ammonites answered Jephthah's messengers, "When Israel came up out of Egypt, they took away my land from the Arnon to the Jabbok, all the way to the Jordan. Now give it back peaceably."

¹⁴Jephthah sent back messengers to the Ammonite king, ¹⁵saying:

"This is what Jephthah says: Israel did not take the land of Moab or the land of the Ammonites. ¹⁶But when they came up out of Egypt, Israel went through the desert to the Red Sea*ᵃ* and on to Kadesh. ¹⁷Then Israel sent messengers to the king of Edom, saying, 'Give us permission to go through your country,' but the king of Edom would not listen. They sent also to the king of Moab, and he refused. So Israel stayed at Kadesh.

¹⁸"Next they travelled through the desert, skirted the lands of Edom and Moab, passed along the eastern side of the country of Moab,

---

ᵃ2 Traditionally *judged*; also in verse 3   *ᵇ4* Or *called the settlements of Jair*   *ᶜ12* Hebrew; some Septuagint manuscripts *Midianites*   *ᵃ16* Hebrew *Yam Suph*; that is, Sea of Reeds and camped on the other side of the Arnon. They did not enter the territory of Moab, for the Arnon was its border.

19"Then Israel sent messengers to Sihon king of the Amorites, who ruled in Heshbon, and said to him, 'Let us pass through your country to our own place.' 20Sihon, however, did not trust Israel*b* to pass through his territory. He mustered all his men and encamped at Jahaz and fought with Israel.

21"Then the LORD, the God of Israel, gave Sihon and all his men into Israel's hands, and they defeated them. Israel took over all the land of the Amorites who lived in that country, 22capturing all of it from the Arnon to the Jabbok and from the desert to the Jordan.

23"Now since the LORD, the God of Israel, has driven the Amorites out before his people Israel, what right have you to take it over? 24Will you not take what your god Chemosh gives you? Likewise, whatever the LORD our God has given us, we will possess. 25Are you better than Balak son of Zippor, king of Moab? Did he ever quarrel with Israel or fight with them? 26For three hundred years Israel occupied Heshbon, Aroer, the surrounding settlements and all the towns along the Arnon. Why didn't you retake them during that time? 27I have not wronged you, but you are doing me wrong by waging war against me. Let the LORD, the Judge,*c* decide the dispute this day between the Israelites and the Ammonites."

28The king of Ammon, however, paid no attention to the message Jephthah sent him.

29Then the Spirit of the LORD came upon Jephthah. He crossed Gilead and Manasseh, passed through Mizpah of Gilead, and from there he advanced against the Ammonites. 30And Jephthah made a vow to the LORD: "If you give the Ammonites into my hands, 31whatever comes out of the door of my house to meet me when I return in triumph from the Ammonites will be the LORD's, and I will sacrifice it as a burnt offering."

32Then Jephthah went over to fight the Ammonites, and the LORD gave them into his hands. 33He devastated twenty towns from Aroer to the vicinity of Minnith, as far as Abel Keramim. Thus Israel subdued Ammon.

34When Jephthah returned to his home in Mizpah, who should come out to meet him but his daughter, dancing to the sound of tambourines! She was an only child. Except for her he had neither son nor daughter. 35When he saw her, he tore his clothes and cried, "Oh! My daughter! You have made me miserable and wretched, because I have made a vow to the LORD that I cannot break." 36"My father," she replied, "you have given your word to the LORD. Do to me just as you promised, now that the LORD has avenged you of your enemies, the Ammonites. 37But grant me this one request," she said. "Give me two months to roam the hills and weep with my friends, because I will never marry."

38"You may go," he said. And he let her go for two months. She and the girls went into the hills and wept because she would never marry. 39After the two months, she returned to her father and he did to her as he had vowed. And she was a virgin.

From this comes the Israelite custom 40that each year the young women of Israel go out for four days to commemorate the daughter of Jephthah the Gileadite.

■ Jephthah and Ephraim

12 The men of Ephraim called out their forces, crossed over to Zaphon and said to Jephthah, "Why did you go to fight the Ammonites without calling us to go with you? We're going to burn down your house over your head."

2Jephthah answered, "I and my people were engaged in a great struggle with the Ammonites, and although I called, you didn't save me out of their hands. 3When I saw that you wouldn't help, I took my life in my hands and crossed over to fight the Ammonites, and the LORD gave me the victory over them. Now why have you come up today to fight me?"

4Jephthah then called together the men of Gilead and fought against Ephraim. The Gileadites struck them down because the Ephraimites had said, "You Gileadites are renegades from Ephraim and Manasseh." 5The Gileadites captured the fords of the Jordan leading to Ephraim, and whenever a survivor of Ephraim said, "Let me cross over," the men of Gilead asked him, "Are you an Ephraimite?" If he replied, "No," 6they said, "All right, say 'Shibboleth'." If he said, "Sibboleth", because he could not pronounce the word correctly, they seized him and killed him at the fords of the Jordan. Forty-two thousand Ephraimites were killed at that time.

7Jephthah led*a* Israel for six years. Then Jephthah the Gileadite died, and was buried in a town in Gilead.

■ Ibzan, Elon and Abdon

8After him, Ibzan of Bethlehem led Israel. 9He had thirty sons and thirty daughters. He gave his daughters away in marriage to those outside his clan, and for his sons he brought in thirty young women as wives from outside his clan. Ibzan led Israel for seven years. 10Then Ibzan died, and was buried in Bethlehem.

11After him, Elon the Zebulunite led Israel for ten years. 12Then Elon died, and was buried in Aijalon in the land of Zebulun.

b 20 Or however, would not make an agreement for Israel   c 27 Or Ruler   a 7 Traditionally judged; also in verses 8–14

13After him, Abdon son of Hillel, from Pirathon, led Israel. 14He had forty sons and thirty grandsons, who rode on seventy donkeys. He led Israel for eight years. 15Then Abdon son of Hillel died, and was buried at Pirathon in Ephraim, in the hill country of the Amalekites.

■ The Birth of Samson

13 Again the Israelites did evil in the eyes of the LORD, so the LORD delivered them into the hands of the Philistines for forty years.

2A certain man of Zorah, named Manoah, from the clan of the Danites, had a wife who was sterile and remained childless. 3The angel of the LORD appeared to her and said, "You are sterile and childless, but you are going to conceive and have a son. 4Now see to it that you drink no wine or other fermented drink and that you do not eat anything unclean, 5because you will conceive and give birth to a son. No razor may be used on his head, because the boy is to be a Nazirite, set apart to God from birth, and he will begin the deliverance of Israel from the hands of the Philistines."

6Then the woman went to her husband and told him, "A man of God came to me. He looked like an angel of God, very awesome. I didn't ask him where he came from, and he didn't tell me his name. 7But he said to me, 'You will conceive and give birth to a son. Now then, drink no wine or other fermented drink and do not eat anything unclean, because the boy will be a Nazirite of God from birth until the day of his death.' "

8Then Manoah prayed to the LORD: "O Lord, I beg you, let the man of God you sent to us come again to teach us how to bring up the boy who is to be born."

9God heard Manoah, and the angel of God came again to the woman while she was out in the field; but her husband Manoah was not with her. 10The woman hurried to tell her husband, "He's here! The man who appeared to me the other day!"

11Manoah got up and followed his wife. When he came to the man, he said, "Are you the one who talked to my wife?"

"I am," he said.

12So Manoah asked him, "When your words are fulfilled, what is to be the rule for the boy's life and work?"

13The angel of the LORD answered, "Your wife must do all that I have told her. 14She must not eat anything that comes from the grapevine, nor drink any wine or other fermented drink nor eat anything unclean. She must do everything I have commanded her."

15Manoah said to the angel of the LORD, "We would like you to stay until we prepare a young goat for you."

16The angel of the LORD replied, "Even though you detain me, I will not eat any of your food. But if you prepare a burnt offering, offer it to the LORD." (Manoah did not realise that it was the angel of the LORD.)

17Then Manoah enquired of the angel of the LORD, "What is your name, so that we may honour you when your word comes true?"

18He replied, "Why do you ask my name? It is beyond understanding."[a] 19Then Manoah took a young goat, together with the grain offering, and sacrificed it on a rock to the LORD. And the LORD did an amazing thing while Manoah and his wife watched: 20As the flame blazed up from the altar towards heaven, the angel of the LORD ascended in the flame. Seeing this, Manoah and his wife fell with their faces to the ground. 21When the angel of the LORD did not show himself again to Manoah and his wife, Manoah realised that it was the angel of the LORD.

22"We are doomed to die!" he said to his wife. "We have seen God!"

23But his wife answered, "If the LORD had meant to kill us, he would not have accepted a burnt offering and grain offering from our hands, nor shown us all these things or now told us this."

24The woman gave birth to a boy and named him Samson. He grew and the LORD blessed him, 25and the Spirit of the LORD began to stir him while he was in Mahaneh Dan, between Zorah and Eshtaol.

■ Samson's Marriage

14 Samson went down to Timnah and saw there a young Philistine woman. 2When he returned, he said to his father and mother, "I have seen a Philistine woman in Timnah; now get her for me as my wife."

14:1 ■ THE FIRST SIGN OF TROUBLE
Timnah was only four miles across the valley from Samson's home town. Apparently, the Philistines and Israelites moved freely back and forth, and not all Israelites opposed the Philistines (see 15:11). Samson, making the short stroll, was attracted to a young Philistine woman. His lack of concern for differences of religion and his lack of submission to his parents were bad omens.

3His father and mother replied, "Isn't there an acceptable woman among your relatives or among all our people? Must you go to the uncircumcised Philistines to get a wife?"

But Samson said to his father, "Get her for me. She's the right one for me." 4(His parents did not know that this was from the LORD, who was seeking an occasion to confront the Philistines; for at that time they were ruling over Israel.) 5Samson went down to Timnah together with his father and mother. As they approached the vineyards of Timnah, suddenly a young lion came roaring towards him. 6The Spirit of the LORD came upon him in power so that he tore the lion apart with his bare hands as he might have torn a young goat. But he told neither his father nor his mother what he had done. 7Then he went down and talked with the woman, and he liked her.

8Some time later, when he went back to marry her, he turned aside to look at the lion's carcass. In it was a swarm of bees and some honey, 9which he scooped out with his hands and ate as he went along. When he rejoined his parents, he gave them some,

a 18 Or is wonderful

and they too ate it. But he did not tell them that he had taken the honey from the lion's carcass.

¹⁰Now his father went down to see the woman. And Samson made a feast there, as was customary for bridegrooms. ¹¹When he appeared, he was given thirty companions.

¹²"Let me tell you a riddle," Samson said to them. "If you can give me the answer within the seven days of the feast, I will give you thirty linen garments and thirty sets of clothes. ¹³If you can't tell me the answer, you must give me thirty linen garments and thirty sets of clothes."

"Tell us your riddle," they said. "Let's hear it."

¹⁴He replied,

"Out of the eater, something to eat;
    out of the strong, something sweet."

For three days they could not give the answer.

¹⁵On the fourth*ᵃ* day, they said to Samson's wife, "Coax your husband into explaining the riddle for us, or we will burn you and your father's household to death. Did you invite us here to rob us?"

¹⁶Then Samson's wife threw herself on him, sobbing, "You hate me! You don't really love me. You've given my people a riddle, but you haven't told me the answer."

"I haven't even explained it to my father or mother," he replied, "so why should I explain it to you?" ¹⁷She cried the whole seven days of the feast. So on the seventh day he finally told her, because she continued to press him. She in turn explained the riddle to her people.

¹⁸Before sunset on the seventh day the men of the town said to him,

"What is sweeter than honey?
    What is stronger than a lion?"

Samson said to them,

"If you had not ploughed with my heifer,
    you would not have solved my riddle."

¹⁹Then the Spirit of the LORD came upon him in power. He went down to Ashkelon, struck down thirty of their men, stripped them of their

■ SAMSON: A WEAKNESS FOR WOMEN
THE STRONGEST MAN OF HIS GENERATION NEVER LIVED UP TO HIS PROMISE

INSIGHT

"I HAVE SEEN A PHILISTINE WOMAN . . . NOW GET HER FOR ME AS MY WIFE."
■ 14:2

Samson, the strongest man of his generation, was tragically unable to control his lust. When he saw an attractive woman, he wanted her. He first fell for a young woman he saw in a Philistine village just across the valley from his home. His parents tried to dissuade him, since her religion and culture were unacceptable, but he would not listen. Desire was his only rule. The marriage ended in a matter of days and resulted in dozens of deaths.

The famous Delilah was at least the third woman who dallied with Samson, according to Judges. She, like his first love, was a Philistine living near his home. Where thousands of men had failed to overcome Samson, a wheedling woman succeeded. Thanks to her, he was captured, blinded, and set to work pushing a grinding machine. His final triumph was ironically fitting: blind and bound, brought out like a freak for a shouting crowd's amusement, he destroyed himself while wreaking vengeance on the crowd. At his death, as throughout his life, it was hard to say who suffered most from Samson's hot temper: the Philistines or Samson.

■ NEEDED: A LEADER
When you think of what God meant Samson to be, his life appears particularly tragic. Israel desperately needed a strong, confident leader, for the Philistines were moving in as masters,

and many Israelites were willing to let them do so. God intended Samson for great things. Of all the judges, only Samson was announced by an angel before he was born (13:3). He was assigned to that special class of people known as Nazirites (described in Numbers 6), whose lives were specially devoted to God. Nazirites never drank wine, went near a dead body or cut their hair.

Samson never lived up to his promise. Rule 3 was probably the only part of the Nazirite vow he kept – it required little self-discipline to let hair grow.

Despite all of Samson's weaknesses, God used him. He is mentioned in the Bible "Hall of Fame" (Hebrews 11:32) as a hero of faith together with Gideon, Barak and Jephthah, all from Judges. Barely conscious of what it meant to live for God, and given to fits of lust and temper, Samson still had great physical strength, which came supernaturally from God. With it, he pushed back the Philistines – more by accident than by intention – and kept Israel intact.

Samson seems like a train whose engineer has fallen out of the engine, an oversized accident smashing into everything it meets. But for God, there are no accidents. He used the tragedy of Samson's life for good.

□ LIFE QUESTIONS:
Which might best be said of you: "Oh, what he/she might have been!" or "He/she made the best of his/her abilities"?

ᵃ 15 Some Septuagint manuscripts and Syriac; Hebrew *seventh* belongings and gave their clothes to those who had explained the riddle. Burning with anger, he went up to his father's house. 20And Samson's wife was given to the friend who had attended him at his wedding.

■ Samson's Vengeance on the Philistines

15 Later on, at the time of wheat harvest, Samson took a young goat and went to visit his wife. He said, "I'm going to my wife's room." But her father would not let him go in.

2"I was so sure you thoroughly hated her," he said, "that I gave her to your friend. Isn't her younger sister more attractive? Take her instead."

3Samson said to them, "This time I have a right to get even with the Philistines; I will really harm them." 4So he went out and caught three hundred foxes and tied them tail to tail in pairs. He then fastened a torch to every pair of tails, 5lit the torches and let the foxes loose in the standing corn of the Philistines. He burned up the shocks and standing corn, together with the vineyards and olive groves.

6When the Philistines asked, "Who did this?" they were told, "Samson, the Timnite's son-in-law, because his wife was given to his friend."

So the Philistines went up and burned her and her father to death. 7Samson said to them, "Since you've acted like this, I won't stop until I get my revenge on you." 8He attacked them viciously and slaughtered many of them. Then he went down and stayed in a cave in the rock of Etam.

9The Philistines went up and camped in Judah, spreading out near Lehi. 10The men of Judah asked, "Why have you come to fight us?"

"We have come to take Samson prisoner," they answered, "to do to him as he did to us."

11Then three thousand men from Judah went down to the cave in the rock of Etam and said to Samson, "Don't you realise that the Philistines are rulers over us? What have you done to us?"

He answered, "I merely did to them what they did to me."

12They said to him, "We've come to tie you up and hand you over to the Philistines."

Samson said, "Swear to me that you won't kill me yourselves."

13"Agreed," they answered. "We will only tie you up and hand you over to them. We will not kill you." So they bound him with two new ropes and led him up from the rock. 14As he approached Lehi, the Philistines came towards him shouting. The Spirit of the LORD came upon him in power. The ropes on his arms became like charred flax, and the bindings dropped from his hands. 15Finding a fresh jaw-bone of a donkey, he grabbed it and struck down a thousand men.

16Then Samson said,

"With a donkey's jaw-bone
   I have made donkeys of them.*a*
With a donkey's jaw-bone
   I have killed a thousand men."

17When he finished speaking, he threw away the jaw-bone; and the place was called Ramath Lehi.*b*

18Because he was very thirsty, he cried out to the LORD, "You have given your servant this great victory. Must I now die of thirst and fall into the hands of the uncircumcised?" 19Then God opened up the hollow place in Lehi, and water came out of it. When Samson drank, his strength returned and he revived. So the spring was called En Hakkore,*c* and it is still there in Lehi.

15:14 ■ THE SPIRIT AND SAMSON
Four times (see also 13:25; 14:6,19) Judges comments that "the Spirit of the LORD" came on Samson. The same comment is made of other judges, though less frequently. But the Spirit only gave Samson great strength, as far as we can see; fruit of the Spirit like love and self-control seem lacking from his life.

20Samson led*d* Israel for twenty years in the days of the Philistines.

■ Samson and Delilah

16 One day Samson went to Gaza, where he saw a prostitute. He went in to spend the night with her. 2The people of Gaza were told, "Samson is here!" So they surrounded the place and lay in wait for him all night at the city gate. They made no move during the night, saying, "At dawn we'll kill him."

3But Samson lay there only until the middle of the night. Then he got up and took hold of the doors of the city gate, together with the two posts, and tore them loose, bar and all. He lifted them to his shoulders and carried them to the top of the hill that faces Hebron.

4Some time later, he fell in love with a woman in the Valley of Sorek whose name was Delilah. 5The rulers of the Philistines went to her and said, "See if you can lure him into showing you the secret of his great strength and how we can overpower him so that we may tie him up and subdue him. Each one of us will give you eleven hundred shekels*a* of silver."

6So Delilah said to Samson, "Tell me the secret of your great strength and how you can be tied up and subdued."

7Samson answered her, "If anyone ties me with seven fresh thongs*b* that have not been dried, I'll become as weak as any other man."

8Then the rulers of the Philistines brought her seven fresh thongs that had not been dried, and she tied him with them. 9With men hidden in the room, she called to him, "Samson, the Philistines are upon you!" But he snapped the thongs as easily as a piece of string snaps when it comes close to a flame. So the secret of his strength was not discovered.

10Then Delilah said to Samson, "You have made a fool of me; you lied to me. Come now, tell me how you can be tied."

11He said, "If anyone ties me securely with new ropes that have never been used, I'll become as weak as any other man."

12So Delilah took new ropes and tied him with them. Then, with men hidden in the room, she called to him, "Samson, the Philistines are upon

---

a 16 Or made a heap or two; the Hebrew for donkey sounds like the Hebrew for heap.   *b 17 Ramath Lehi means jaw-bone hill.*   *c 19 En Hakkore means caller's spring.*   *d 20 Traditionally judged*   *a 5 That is, about 28 pounds (about 13 kilograms)*   *b 7 Or bow-strings; also in verses 8 and 9* you!" But he snapped the ropes off his arms as if they were threads.

13Delilah then said to Samson, "Until now, you have been making a fool of me and lying to me. Tell me how you can be tied."

He replied, "If you weave the seven braids of my head into the fabric ⌊on the loom⌋ and tighten it with the pin, I'll become as weak as any other man." So while he was sleeping, Delilah took the seven braids of his head, wove them into the fabric 14andᶜ tightened it with the pin.

Again she called to him, "Samson, the Philistines are upon you!" He awoke from his sleep and pulled up the pin and the loom, with the fabric.

15Then she said to him, "How can you say, 'I love you,' when you won't confide in me? This is the third time you have made a fool of me and haven't told me the secret of your great strength." 16With such nagging she prodded him day after day until he was tired to death.

17So he told her everything. "No razor has ever been used on my head," he said, "because I have been a Nazirite set apart to God since birth. If my head were shaved, my strength would leave me, and I would become as weak as any other man."

18When Delilah saw that he had told her everything, she sent word to the rulers of the Philistines, "Come back once more; he has told me everything." So the rulers of the Philistines returned with the silver in their hands. 19Having put him to sleep on her lap, she called a man to shave off the seven braids of his hair, and so began to subdue him.ᵈ And his strength left him.

20Then she called, "Samson, the Philistines are upon you!"

He awoke from his sleep and thought, "I'll go out as before and shake myself free." But he did not know that the LORD had left him.

21Then the Philistines seized him, gouged out his eyes and took him down to Gaza. Binding him with bronze shackles, they set him to grinding in the prison. 22But the hair on his head began to grow again after it had been shaved.

■ The Death of Samson

23Now the rulers of the Philistines assembled to offer a great sacrifice to Dagon their god and to celebrate, saying, "Our god has delivered Samson, our enemy, into our hands."

24When the people saw him, they praised their god, saying,

"Our god has delivered our enemy
   into our hands,
the one who laid waste our land
   and multiplied our slain."

25While they were in high spirits, they shouted, "Bring out Samson to entertain us." So they called Samson out of the prison, and he performed for them.

When they stood him among the pillars, 26Samson said to the servant who held his hand, "Put me where I can feel the pillars that support the temple,

so that I may lean against them." 27Now the temple was crowded with men and women; all the rulers of the Philistines were there, and on the roof were about three thousand men and women watching Samson perform. 28Then Samson prayed to the LORD, "O Sovereign LORD, remember me. O God, please strengthen me just once more, and let me with one blow get revenge on the Philistines for my two eyes." 29Then Samson reached towards the two central pillars on which the temple stood. Bracing himself against them, his right hand on the one and his left hand on the other, 30Samson said, "Let me die with the Philistines!" Then he pushed with all his might, and down came the temple on the rulers and all the people in it. Thus he killed many more when he died than while he lived.

> **16:30 ■ BRING THE HOUSE DOWN**
> Archaeologists have excavated temples from Samson's period. Typically, wooden pillars were set close together to support a roof, which sometimes included a covered area for spectators. Quite possibly this structure was already creaking under the weight of 3,000 people, who would have crowded to one side to see Samson perform. Samson managed to push the pillars off their stone bases, and the roof collapsed.

31Then his brothers and his father's whole family went down to get him. They brought him back and buried him between Zorah and Eshtaol in the tomb of Manoah his father. He had ledᵉ Israel for twenty years.

■ Micah's Idols

17 Now a man named Micah from the hill country of Ephraim 2said to his mother, "The eleven hundred shekelsᵃ of silver that were taken from you and about which I heard you utter a curse—I have that silver with me; I took it."

Then his mother said, "The LORD bless you, my son!"

3When he returned the eleven hundred shekels of silver to his mother, she said, "I solemnly consecrate my silver to the LORD for my son to make a carved image and a cast idol. I will give it back to you."

4So he returned the silver to his mother, and she took two hundred shekelsᵇ of silver and gave them to a silversmith, who made them into the image and the idol. And they were put in Micah's house.

5Now this man Micah had a shrine, and he made an ephod and some idols and installed one of his sons as his priest. 6In those days Israel had no king; everyone did as he saw fit.

7A young Levite from Bethlehem in Judah, who had been living within the clan of Judah, 8left that town in search of some other place to stay. On his wayᶜ he came to Micah's house in the hill country of Ephraim.

9Micah asked him, "Where are you from?"

"I'm a Levite from Bethlehem in Judah," he said, "and I'm looking for a place to stay."

ᶜ13,14 Some Septuagint manuscripts; Hebrew "⌊I can⌋ if you weave the seven braids of my head into the fabric ⌊on the loom⌋." 14So she   ᵈ19 Hebrew; some Septuagint manuscripts and he began to weaken   ᵉ31 Traditionally judged   ᵃ2 That is, about 28 pounds (about 13 kilograms)   ᵇ4 That is, about 5 pounds (about 2.3 kilograms)   ᶜ8 Or To carry on his profession

17:6 ■ A STATE OF ANARCHY

Four times the final chapters of Judges mention that there was "no king". Twice Judges adds that "everyone did as he saw fit". This editorial remark was probably made later, after the monarchy had begun under Saul and David; a king unified the nation. Some problems of this period are evident in verse 5: idolatry and the installation of a priest who did not come from the priestly family. The story that follows shows one group of Israelites raiding another, as though they were enemies, not relatives.

¹⁰Then Micah said to him, "Live with me and be my father and priest, and I'll give you ten shekels*d* of silver a year, your clothes and your food." ¹¹So the Levite agreed to live with him, and the young man was to him like one of his sons. ¹²Then Micah installed the Levite, and the young man became his priest and lived in his house. ¹³And Micah said, "Now I know that the LORD will be good to me, since this Levite has become my priest."

■ Danites Settle in Laish

18 In those days Israel had no king.
And in those days the tribe of the Danites was seeking a place of their own where they might settle, because they had not yet come into an inheritance among the tribes of Israel. ²So the Danites sent five warriors from Zorah and Eshtaol to spy out the land and explore it. These men represented all their clans. They told them, "Go, explore the land."

The men entered the hill country of Ephraim and came to the house of Micah, where they spent the night. ³When they were near Micah's house, they recognised the voice of the young Levite; so they turned in there and asked him, "Who brought you here? What are you doing in this place? Why are you here?"

■ HANGING BY A THREAD
THEFT, RAPE, MURDER, IDOLATRY: ISRAEL WAS DESTROYING ITSELF

INSIGHT

IN THOSE DAYS ISRAEL HAD NO KING; EVERYONE DID AS HE SAW FIT. ■ 17:6

A time comes when you can no longer blame your problems on other people. In the comic strip character Pogo's immortal words, "We have met the enemy, and he is us."

So it is at the end of Judges. The camera zooms in for a close-up, focusing on internal violence. Foreign enemies are no longer in view: the enemy is Israel itself.

They make ugly portraits, these last five chapters. Pointless and violent, they begin with a son stealing from his mother and end with parents agreeing to let their daughters be kidnapped. In between are homosexual and heterosexual gang rape, murder, idolatry, armed robbery, mass slaughter. No enemy does all this: Israelites do it to each other. Clearly, the exalted nation of Israel, God's chosen people, has lost all sense of direction.

■ WHO CAN RESCUE THEM NOW?
The first 16 chapters of Judges tell of repeated enemy invasions that moved Israel to call out to God. Hearing his people, God would send a freedom fighter to save them.

In the last five chapters, by contrast, God sends no freedom fighters. No military leader could rescue them from themselves. These chapters instead repeat the solemn words: "In those days Israel had no king; everyone did as he saw fit."

"Everyone did as he saw fit" may not sound very negative in our time, which places high value on individualism and personal freedom. But God prizes something more: unity. He wants his people united in love for him and each other. God's law had bound his people to a common worship in the tabernacle and to a common standard of caring for each other. For this the Israelites substituted do-as-you-please religion and a fractured society, where each family or group fought for its own rights alone. The result? These chapters tell the dismal story.

■ ISRAEL'S WORST ENEMY
By the end of Judges, Israelites are reduced to fighting themselves. They have adopted their enemies' customs. They worship idols. They are sexually immoral. They lack respect for parents. They cannot remember the pattern of life God had set out. It is hard to say, by the end of Judges, why God should save Israel from their enemies. It is hard to say whether Israelites are the least bit different from their enemies. Israel has become, in fact, its own worst enemy.

Only one glimmer of hope appears: the Israelites' shock at the Benjamites' gang rape. They can still get together to punish such outrages, and they still consult the Lord about them. But they are a far cry from the hopeful people Joshua led into the promised land.

☐ LIFE QUESTIONS:
Do your troubles come more from your circumstances or from your own internal weaknesses? What kind of help do you need from God?

d 10 That is, about 4 ounces (about 115 grams)

⁴He told them what Micah had done for him, and said, "He has hired me and I am his priest."

⁵Then they said to him, "Please enquire of God to learn whether our journey will be successful."

⁶The priest answered them, "Go in peace. Your journey has the LORD's approval."

⁷So the five men left and came to Laish, where they saw that the people were living in safety, like the Sidonians, unsuspecting and secure. And since their land lacked nothing, they were prosperous.ᵃ Also, they lived a long way from the Sidonians and had no relationship with anyone else.ᵇ

⁸When they returned to Zorah and Eshtaol, their brothers asked them, "How did you find things?"

⁹They answered, "Come on, let's attack them! We have seen that the land is very good. Aren't you going to do something? Don't hesitate to go there and take it over. ¹⁰When you get there, you will find an unsuspecting people and a spacious land that God has put into your hands, a land that lacks nothing whatever."

¹¹Then six hundred men from the clan of the Danites, armed for battle, set out from Zorah and Eshtaol. ¹²On their way they set up camp near Kiriath Jearim in Judah. This is why the place west of Kiriath Jearim is called Mahaneh Danᶜ to this day. ¹³From there they went on to the hill country of Ephraim and came to Micah's house.

¹⁴Then the five men who had spied out the land of Laish said to their brothers, "Do you know that one of these houses has an ephod, other household gods, a carved image and a cast idol? Now you know what to do." ¹⁵So they turned in there and went to the house of the young Levite at Micah's place and greeted him. ¹⁶The six hundred Danites, armed for battle, stood at the entrance to the gate. ¹⁷The five men who had spied out the land went inside and took the carved image, the ephod, the other household gods and the cast idol while the priest and the six hundred armed men stood at the entrance to the gate.

¹⁸When these men went into Micah's house and took the carved image, the ephod, the other household gods and the cast idol, the priest said to them, "What are you doing?"

¹⁹They answered him, "Be quiet! Don't say a word. Come with us, and be our father and priest. Isn't it better that you serve a tribe and clan in Israel as priest rather than just one man's household?" ²⁰Then the priest was glad. He took the ephod, the other household gods and the carved image and went along with the people. ²¹Putting their little children, their livestock and their possessions in front of them, they turned away and left.

²²When they had gone some distance from Micah's house, the men who lived near Micah were called together and overtook the Danites. ²³As they shouted after them, the Danites turned and said to Micah, "What's the matter with you that you called out your men to fight?"

²⁴He replied, "You took the gods I made, and my priest, and went away. What else do I have? How can you ask, 'What's the matter with you?'"

²⁵The Danites answered, "Don't argue with us, or some hot-tempered men will attack you, and you

and your family will lose your lives." ²⁶So the Danites went their way, and Micah, seeing that they were too strong for him, turned round and went back home.

18:24 ■ SAD COMMENTARY
Micah's outraged cry offers a sad commentary on the state of Israel. Even though his stolen gods were obviously unable to protect themselves, let alone him, Micah knew no other refuge. Anarchy ruled, as did idolatry.

²⁷Then they took what Micah had made, and his priest, and went on to Laish, against a peaceful and unsuspecting people. They attacked them with the sword and burned down their city. ²⁸There was no-one to rescue them because they lived a long way from Sidon and had no relationship with anyone else. The city was in a valley near Beth Rehob.

The Danites rebuilt the city and settled there. ²⁹They named it Dan after their forefather Dan, who was born to Israel — though the city used to be called Laish. ³⁰There the Danites set up for themselves the idols, and Jonathan son of Gershom, the son of Moses,ᵈ and his sons were priests for the tribe of Dan until the time of the captivity of the land. ³¹They continued to use the idols Micah had made, all the time the house of God was in Shiloh.

■ A Levite and His Concubine

19 In those days Israel had no king.

Now a Levite who lived in a remote area in the hill country of Ephraim took a concubine from Bethlehem in Judah. ²But she was unfaithful to him. She left him and went back to her father's house in Bethlehem, Judah. After she had been there for four months, ³her husband went to her to persuade her to return. He had with him his servant and two donkeys. She took him into her father's house, and when her father saw him, he gladly welcomed him. ⁴His father-in-law, the girl's father, prevailed upon him to stay; so he remained with him three days, eating and drinking, and sleeping there.

⁵On the fourth day they got up early and he prepared to leave, but the girl's father said to his son-in-law, "Refresh yourself with something to eat; then you can go." ⁶So the two of them sat down to eat and drink together. Afterwards the girl's father said, "Please stay tonight and enjoy yourself." ⁷And when the man got up to go, his father-in-law persuaded him, so he stayed there that night. ⁸On the morning of the fifth day, when he rose to go, the girl's father said, "Refresh yourself. Wait till afternoon!" So the two of them ate together.

⁹Then when the man, with his concubine and his servant, got up to leave, his father-in-law, the girl's father, said, "Now look, it's almost evening. Spend the night here; the day is nearly over. Stay and enjoy yourself. Early tomorrow morning you can get up and be on your way home." ¹⁰But, unwilling to stay another night, the man left and went towards Jebus (that is, Jerusalem), with his two saddled donkeys and his concubine.

ᵃ7 The meaning of the Hebrew for this clause is uncertain.   ᵇ7 Hebrew; some Septuagint manuscripts *with the Arameans*   ᶜ12 *Mahaneh Dan* means *Dan's camp.*   ᵈ30 An ancient Hebrew scribal tradition, some Septuagint manuscripts and Vulgate; Masoretic Text *Manasseh*

11When they were near Jebus and the day was almost gone, the servant said to his master, "Come, let's stop at this city of the Jebusites and spend the night."

12His master replied, "No. We won't go into an alien city, whose people are not Israelites. We will go on to Gibeah." 13He added, "Come, let's try to reach Gibeah or Ramah and spend the night in one of those places." 14So they went on, and the sun set as they neared Gibeah in Benjamin. 15There they stopped to spend the night. They went and sat in the city square, but no-one took them into his home for the night.

19:15 ■ A BREACH OF HOSPITALITY

In the ancient Middle East, people took hospitality very seriously. When the Levite sat down in the city square of an Israelite city, he expected the townspeople (his relatives) to offer him a place to stay. But only an old man from his home area offered the Levite lodging – the locals were inhospitable, an ominous sign.

The old man obviously took hospitality seriously. Unfortunately, he took women much less seriously. In fact, he urged the hostile mob to rape his daughter and his guest's concubine as a substitute for the guest himself. His response was nearly identical to Lot's on the eve of Sodom's destruction (Genesis 19:6–8). The story suggests that Israel had become as bad as Sodom.

16That evening an old man from the hill country of Ephraim, who was living in Gibeah (the men of the place were Benjamites), came in from his work in the fields. 17When he looked and saw the traveller in the city square, the old man asked, "Where are you going? Where did you come from?"

18He answered, "We are on our way from Bethlehem in Judah to a remote area in the hill country of Ephraim where I live. I have been to Bethlehem in Judah and now I am going to the house of the LORD. No-one has taken me into his house. 19We have both straw and fodder for our donkeys and bread and wine for ourselves your servants — me, your maidservant, and the young man with us. We don't need anything."

20"You are welcome at my house," the old man said. "Let me supply whatever you need. Only don't spend the night in the square." 21So he took him into his house and fed his donkeys. After they had washed their feet, they had something to eat and drink.

22While they were enjoying themselves, some of the wicked men of the city surrounded the house. Pounding on the door, they shouted to the old man who owned the house, "Bring out the man who came to your house so we can have sex with him."

23The owner of the house went outside and said to them, "No, my friends, don't be so vile. Since this man is my guest, don't do this disgraceful thing. 24Look, here is my virgin daughter, and his concubine. I will bring them out to you now, and you can

use them and do to them whatever you wish. But to this man, don't do such a disgraceful thing."

25But the men would not listen to him. So the man took his concubine and sent her outside to them, and they raped her and abused her throughout the night, and at dawn they let her go. 26At daybreak the woman went back to the house where her master was staying, fell down at the door and lay there until daylight.

27When her master got up in the morning and opened the door of the house and stepped out to continue on his way, there lay his concubine, fallen in the doorway of the house, with her hands on the threshold. 28He said to her, "Get up; let's go." But there was no answer. Then the man put her on his donkey and set out for home.

29When he reached home, he took a knife and cut up his concubine, limb by limb, into twelve parts and sent them into all the areas of Israel. 30Everyone who saw it said, "Such a thing has never been seen or done, not since the day the Israelites came up out of Egypt. Think about it! Consider it! Tell us what to do!"

■ Israelites Fight the Benjamites

20 Then all the Israelites from Dan to Beersheba and from the land of Gilead came out as one man and assembled before the LORD in Mizpah. 2The leaders of all the people of the tribes of Israel took their places in the assembly of the people of God, four hundred thousand soldiers armed with swords. 3(The Benjamites heard that the Israelites had gone up to Mizpah.) Then the Israelites said, "Tell us how this awful thing happened."

4So the Levite, the husband of the murdered woman, said, "I and my concubine came to Gibeah in Benjamin to spend the night. 5During the night the men of Gibeah came after me and surrounded the house, intending to kill me. They raped my concubine, and she died. 6I took my concubine, cut her into pieces and sent one piece to each region of Israel's inheritance, because they committed this lewd and disgraceful act in Israel. 7Now, all you Israelites, speak up and give your verdict."

8All the people rose as one man, saying, "None of us will go home. No, not one of us will return to his house. 9But now this is what we'll do to Gibeah: We'll go up against it as the lot directs. 10We'll take ten men out of every hundred from all the tribes of Israel, and a hundred from a thousand, and a thousand from ten thousand, to get provisions for the army. Then, when the army arrives at Gibeah[a] in Benjamin, it can give them what they deserve for all this vileness done in Israel." 11So all the men of Israel got together and united as one man against the city.

12The tribes of Israel sent men throughout the tribe of Benjamin, saying, "What about this awful crime that was committed among you? 13Now surrender those wicked men of Gibeah so that we may put them to death and purge the evil from Israel." But the Benjamites would not listen to their fellow Israelites. 14From their towns they came together at Gibeah to fight against the Israelites. 15At once the Benjamites mobilised twenty-six thousand swordsmen from their towns, in addition to seven hundred chosen men from those living in Gibeah. 16Among all these soldiers there were seven hundred chosen men who were left-handed, each of whom could sling a stone at a hair and not miss.

17Israel, apart from Benjamin, mustered four hundred thousand swordsmen, all of them fighting men. 18The Israelites went up to Bethel[b] and enquired of God. They said, "Who of us shall go first to fight against the Benjamites?"

The LORD replied, "Judah shall go first."

19The next morning the Israelites got up and pitched camp near Gibeah. 20The men of Israel went out to fight the Benjamites and took up battle positions against them at Gibeah. 21The Benjamites came out of Gibeah and cut down twenty-two thousand Israelites on the battlefield that day. 22But the men of Israel encouraged one another and again took up their positions where they had stationed themselves the first day. 23The Israelites went up and wept before the LORD until evening, and they enquired of the LORD. They said, "Shall we go up again to battle against the Benjamites, our brothers?"

The LORD answered, "Go up against them."

24Then the Israelites drew near to Benjamin the second day. 25This time, when the Benjamites came out from Gibeah to oppose them, they cut down another eighteen thousand Israelites, all of them armed with swords.

26Then the Israelites, all the people, went up to Bethel, and there they sat weeping before the LORD. They fasted that day until evening and presented burnt offerings and fellowship offerings[c] to the LORD. 27And the Israelites enquired of the LORD. (In those days the ark of the covenant of God was there, 28with Phinehas son of Eleazar, the son of Aaron, ministering before it.) They asked, "Shall we go up again to battle with Benjamin our brother, or not?"

The LORD responded, "Go, for tomorrow I will give them into your hands."

29Then Israel set an ambush around Gibeah. 30They went up against the Benjamites on the third day and took up positions against Gibeah as they had done before. 31The Benjamites came out to meet them and were drawn away from the city. They began to inflict casualties on the Israelites as before, so that about thirty men fell in the open field and on the roads—the one leading to Bethel and the other to Gibeah.

32While the Benjamites were saying, "We are defeating them as before," the Israelites were saying, "Let's retreat and draw them away from the city to the roads."

33All the men of Israel moved from their places and took up positions at Baal Tamar, and the Israelite ambush charged out of its place on the west[d] of Gibeah.[e] 34Then ten thousand of Israel's finest men made a frontal attack on Gibeah. The fighting was so heavy that the Benjamites did not realise how near disaster was. 35The LORD defeated Benjamin before Israel, and on that day the Israelites struck down 25,100 Benjamites, all armed with swords. 36Then the Benjamites saw that they were beaten.

Now the men of Israel had given way before Benjamin, because they relied on the ambush they had set near Gibeah. 37The men who had been in ambush made a sudden dash into Gibeah, spread out and put the whole city to the sword. 38The men of Israel had arranged with the ambush that they should send up a great cloud of smoke from the city, 39and then the men of Israel would turn in the battle.

The Benjamites had begun to inflict casualties on the men of Israel (about thirty), and they said, "We are defeating them as in the first battle." 40But when the column of smoke began to rise from the city, the Benjamites turned and saw the smoke of the whole city going up into the sky. 41Then the men of Israel turned on them, and the men of Benjamin were terrified, because they realised that disaster had come upon them. 42So they fled before the Israelites in the direction of the desert, but they could not escape the battle. And the men of Israel who came out of the towns cut them down there. 43They surrounded the Benjamites, chased them and easily[f] overran them in the vicinity of Gibeah on the east. 44Eighteen thousand Benjamites fell, all of them valiant fighters. 45As they turned and fled towards the desert to the rock of Rimmon, the Israelites cut down five thousand men along the roads. They kept pressing after the Benjamites as far as Gidom and struck down two thousand more.

46On that day twenty-five thousand Benjamite swordsmen fell, all of them valiant fighters. 47But six hundred men turned and fled into the desert to the rock of Rimmon, where they stayed for four months. 48The men of Israel went back to Benjamin and put all the towns to the sword, including the animals and everything else they found. All the towns they came across they set on fire.

■ Wives for the Benjamites

21 The men of Israel had taken an oath at Mizpah: "Not one of us will give his daughter in marriage to a Benjamite."

2The people went to Bethel,[a] where they sat before God until evening, raising their voices and weeping bitterly. 3"O LORD, the God of Israel," they cried, "why has this happened to Israel? Why should one tribe be missing from Israel today?"

4Early the next day the people built an altar and presented burnt offerings and fellowship offerings.[b]

5Then the Israelites asked, "Who from all the tribes of Israel has failed to assemble before the LORD?" For they had taken a solemn oath that anyone who failed to assemble before the LORD at Mizpah should certainly be put to death.

6Now the Israelites grieved for their brothers, the Benjamites. "Today one tribe is cut off from Israel," they said. 7"How can we provide wives for those who are left, since we have taken an oath by the LORD not to give them any of our daughters in marriage?" 8Then they asked, "Which one of the tribes of Israel failed to assemble before the LORD at Mizpah?" They discovered that no-one from Jabesh Gilead had come to the camp for the assembly. 9For when they counted the people, they found that none of the people of Jabesh Gilead were there.

10So the assembly sent twelve thousand fighting

b 18 Or *to the house of God*; also in verse 26   *b* 26 Traditionally *peace offerings* Hebrew for this word is uncertain.   *e* 33 Hebrew *Geba*, a variant of *Gibeah*   *f* 43 The meaning of the Hebrew for this word is uncertain.   *a* 2 Or *to the house of God*   *b* 4 Traditionally *peace offerings*   *d* 33 Some Septuagint manuscripts and Vulgate; the meaning of the men with instructions to go to Jabesh Gilead and put to the sword those living there, including the women and children. [11]"This is what you are to do," they said. "Kill every male and every woman who is not a virgin." [12]They found among the people living in Jabesh Gilead four hundred young women who had never slept with a man, and they took them to the camp at Shiloh in Canaan.

[13]Then the whole assembly sent an offer of peace to the Benjamites at the rock of Rimmon. [14]So the Benjamites returned at that time and were given the women of Jabesh Gilead who had been spared. But there were not enough for all of them.

[15]The people grieved for Benjamin, because the LORD had made a gap in the tribes of Israel. [16]And the elders of the assembly said, "With the women of Benjamin destroyed, how shall we provide wives for the men who are left? [17]The Benjamite survivors must have heirs," they said, "so that a tribe of Israel will not be wiped out. [18]We can't give them our daughters as wives, since we Israelites have taken this oath: 'Cursed be anyone who gives a wife to a Benjamite.' [19]But look, there is the annual festival of the LORD in Shiloh, to the north of Bethel, and east of the road that goes from Bethel to Shechem, and to the south of Lebonah."

[20]So they instructed the Benjamites, saying, "Go and hide in the vineyards [21]and watch. When the girls of Shiloh come out to join in the dancing, then rush from the vineyards and each of you seize a wife from the girls of Shiloh and go to the land of Benjamin. [22]When their fathers or brothers complain to us, we will say to them, 'Do us a kindness by helping them, because we did not get wives for them during the war, and you are innocent, since you did not give your daughters to them.' "

[23]So that is what the Benjamites did. While the girls were dancing, each man caught one and carried her off to be his wife. Then they returned to their inheritance and rebuilt the towns and settled in them.

[24]At that time the Israelites left that place and went home to their tribes and clans, each to his own inheritance.

[25]In those days Israel had no king; everyone did as he saw fit.

RUTH

INTRODUCTION

■ A RARE BOND OF LOVE

RUTH AND NAOMI LOST EVERYTHING, EXCEPT THEIR CARE FOR EACH OTHER

"WHERE YOU GO I WILL GO, AND WHERE YOU STAY I WILL STAY. YOUR PEOPLE WILL BE MY PEOPLE AND YOUR GOD MY GOD. . . . MAY THE LORD DEAL WITH ME, BE IT EVER SO SEVERELY, IF ANYTHING BUT DEATH SEPARATES YOU AND ME." ■ 1:16–17

Ruth and Naomi were unlikely friends: a generation apart, one young and strong, the other past middle age. Stranger still, one was the other's mother-in-law and came from a completely different ethnic and religious background. Who would have put them together?

They had lost everything when their husbands died. With no man to rely on, their lives were at risk in those rough times. No-one else would come to their defence: they had only each other.

■ THE WOMAN'S INITIATIVE

The book of Ruth is not "two women against the world". Rather, it shows the women taking initiative to find, by God's help, a man who would care for them.

A woman's initiative rarely gets so direct as in Ruth. At her mother-in-law's direction Ruth located where Boaz, a relative, was camping out. She waited until dark, then crept to his feet and lay down. When Boaz woke and found her, he didn't have to be told what was on her mind. She wanted him for a husband. Flattered, he didn't let another sun set before making the legal arrangements for marriage.

Society the way God had designed it encouraged men like Boaz to help the needy. For instance, by Old Testament law a farmer had to leave some of his grain behind so that poor people like Ruth could harvest it. And, also by law, a helpless widow had to be taken into the home of her husband's family. This was the law by which Boaz claimed Ruth (4:1–12).

■ GOD'S INVISIBLE PRESENCE

Behind the eloquent story of Ruth looms an invisible helper – God. He didn't intervene in the events, so far as the story tells. But nobody in Ruth doubted that life proceeded under God's direction. It was the Lord by whom Ruth swore when declaring her love to Naomi (1:17), and the Lord whom Naomi credited for bringing Ruth to Boaz's field (2:20). God's law brought Boaz and Ruth into marriage. Finally, the Lord gave them a son, in whom mother, father, and "grandmother" found deep satisfaction.

The last verses of Ruth show, furthermore, that God's plan extended beyond Ruth and Naomi's personal problems. Ruth was a member of the despised Moabites – enemies of Israel. Yet God not only accepted her into his family, but also used her to produce Israel's greatest king. Ruth's great-grandson turned out to be David. To anyone who thought that God's love was for Israelites only, Ruth's life made a striking contradiction.

■ HOW TO READ RUTH

Ruth, brief enough to read in 15 minutes, is a delight. The German poet Goethe called it "the loveliest complete work on a small scale". But because Ruth's author didn't hammer his points home, it is possible to overlook his deeper meaning. As you read, concentrate on the loving bond between Ruth and Naomi. This love, which thrived in suffering, is the root of the book. It offers hope for other people in hard circumstances.

The author of Ruth assumed that readers understood the cultural and historical background of Ruth's time. You may read up on it: Deuteronomy 25:5–10 describes the background on marriage for a widow with a member of her husband's family, the "kinsman-redeemer". Leviticus 25:23–28 gives background on a poor person's property. The Introduction to Judges offers historical perspective, for the book of Judges is an overview of the brutal times Ruth lived in.

■ 3-TRACK READING PLAN

For an explanation and complete listing of the 3-track reading plan, turn to page x.

■ TRACK 1:
Two-Week Courses on the Bible
See page x for information on these courses.

■ TRACK 2:
An Overview of Ruth in 1 Day

☐ Day 1. Read the Introduction to Ruth and chapter 1, which describes an unusual friendship developing under the unkindest of conditions.
Now turn to page xi for your next Track 2 reading project.

■ TRACK 3:
All of Ruth in 4 Days
After you have read through Ruth, turn to pages xii–xiii for your next Track 3 reading project.

☐ 1   ☐ 2   ☐ 3   ☐ 4

■ Naomi and Ruth

1 In the days when the judges ruled,*a* there was a famine in the land, and a man from Bethlehem in Judah, together with his wife and two sons, went to live for a while in the country of Moab. ²The man's name was Elimelech, his wife's name Naomi, and the names of his two sons were Mahlon and Kilion. They were Ephrathites from Bethlehem, Judah. And they went to Moab and lived there.

³Now Elimelech, Naomi's husband, died, and she was left with her two sons. ⁴They married Moabite women, one named Orpah and the other Ruth. After they had lived there about ten years, ⁵both Mahlon and Kilion also died, and Naomi was left without her two sons and her husband.

⁶When she heard in Moab that the LORD had come to the aid of his people by providing food for them, Naomi and her daughters-in-law prepared to return home from there. ⁷With her two daughters-in-law she left the place where she had been living and set out on the road that would take them back to the land of Judah.

⁸Then Naomi said to her two daughters-in-law, "Go back, each of you, to your mother's home. May the LORD show kindness to you, as you have shown to your dead and to me. ⁹May the LORD grant that each of you will find rest in the home of another husband."

Then she kissed them and they wept aloud ¹⁰and said to her, "We will go back with you to your people."

¹¹But Naomi said, "Return home, my daughters. Why would you come with me? Am I going to have any more sons, who could become your husbands? ¹²Return home, my daughters; I am too old to have another husband. Even if I thought there was still hope for me—even if I had a husband tonight and then gave birth to sons—¹³would you wait until they grew up? Would you remain unmarried for them? No, my daughters. It is more bitter for me than for you, because the LORD's hand has gone out against me!"

¹⁴At this they wept again. Then Orpah kissed her mother-in-law good-bye, but Ruth clung to her.

¹⁵"Look," said Naomi, "your sister-in-law is going back to her people and her gods. Go back with her."

¹⁶But Ruth replied, "Don't urge me to leave you or to turn back from you. Where you go I will go, and where you stay I will stay. Your people will be my people and your God my God. ¹⁷Where you die I will die, and there I will be buried. May the LORD deal with me, be it ever so severely, if anything but death separates you and me." ¹⁸When Naomi realised that Ruth was determined to go with her, she stopped urging her.

¹⁹So the two women went on until they came to Bethlehem. When they arrived in Bethlehem, the whole town was stirred because of them, and the women exclaimed, "Can this be Naomi?"

²⁰"Don't call me Naomi,"*b* she told them. "Call me Mara,*c* because the Almighty*d* has made my life very bitter. ²¹I went away full, but the LORD has brought me back empty. Why call me Naomi? The LORD has afflicted*e* me; the Almighty has brought misfortune upon me."

²²So Naomi returned from Moab accompanied by Ruth the Moabitess, her daughter-in-law, arriving in Bethlehem as the barley harvest was beginning.

1:22 ■ THE WORST OF TIMES

The author stresses that Ruth was a Moabitess, a fact that would have greatly impressed the original readers. Moab and Israel were bitter enemies, and Ruth took a risk by emigrating to a land that might treat her as a despised foreigner. This story of family love and loyalty took place during the time of the judges, when murder, immorality, and general anarchy prevailed.

■ Ruth Meets Boaz

2 Now Naomi had a relative on her husband's side, from the clan of Elimelech, a man of standing, whose name was Boaz.

²And Ruth the Moabitess said to Naomi, "Let me go to the fields and pick up the leftover grain behind anyone in whose eyes I find favour."

Naomi said to her, "Go ahead, my daughter." ³So she went out and began to glean in the fields behind the harvesters. As it turned out, she found herself working in a field belonging to Boaz, who was from the clan of Elimelech.

⁴Just then Boaz arrived from Bethlehem and greeted the harvesters, "The LORD be with you!"

"The LORD bless you!" they called back.

⁵Boaz asked the foreman of his harvesters, "Whose young woman is that?"

⁶The foreman replied, "She is the Moabitess who came back from Moab with Naomi. ⁷She said, 'Please

a 1 Traditionally judged has testified against   *b 20 Naomi means pleasant; also in verse 21.*   *c 20 Mara means bitter.*   *d 20 Hebrew Shaddai; also in verse 21*   *e 21 Or* let me glean and gather among the sheaves behind the harvesters.' She went into the field and has worked steadily from morning till now, except for a short rest in the shelter."

2:3 ■ CARING FOR THE POOR

In the Old Testament God used several welfare programmes to help poor people. One, reflected in this passage, was the command to leave some of the harvest in the field for the poor to gather. Poor people didn't beg for handouts, but worked for what they got. (Leviticus 19:9–10 and Deuteronomy 24:19–22 give the directions.)

Gleaning was humiliating and sometimes dangerous work. Ruth, a single woman and a foreigner, showed courage by working in the fields, and her diligence soon attracted the foreman's attention.

⁸So Boaz said to Ruth, "My daughter, listen to me. Don't go and glean in another field and don't go away from here. Stay here with my servant girls. ⁹Watch the field where the men are harvesting, and follow along after the girls. I have told the men not to touch you. And whenever you are thirsty, go and get a drink from the water jars the men have filled."

¹⁰At this, she bowed down with her face to the ground. She exclaimed, "Why have I found such favour in your eyes that you notice me—a foreigner?"

¹¹Boaz replied, "I've been told all about what you have done for your mother-in-law since the death of your husband—how you left your father and mother and your homeland and came to live with a people you did not know before. ¹²May the LORD repay you for what you have done. May you be richly rewarded by the LORD, the God of Israel, under whose wings you have come to take refuge."

¹³"May I continue to find favour in your eyes, my lord," she said. "You have given me comfort and have spoken kindly to your servant—though I do not have the standing of one of your servant girls."

¹⁴At mealtime Boaz said to her, "Come over here. Have some bread and dip it in the wine vinegar."

When they sat down with the harvesters, he offered her some roasted grain. She ate all she wanted and had some left over. ¹⁵As she got up to glean, Boaz gave orders to his men, "Even if she gathers among the sheaves, don't embarrass her. ¹⁶Rather, pull out some stalks for her from the bundles and leave them for her to pick up, and don't rebuke her."

¹⁷So Ruth gleaned in the field until evening. Then she threshed the barley she had gathered, and it amounted to about an ephah.ᵃ ¹⁸She carried it back to town, and her mother-in-law saw how much she had gathered. Ruth also brought out and gave her what she had left over after she had eaten enough.

¹⁹Her mother-in-law asked her, "Where did you glean today? Where did you work? Blessed be the man who took notice of you!"

Then Ruth told her mother-in-law about the one at whose place she had been working. "The name of the man I worked with today is Boaz," she said.

²⁰"The LORD bless him!" Naomi said to her daughter-in-law. "He has not stopped showing his kindness to the living and the dead." She added, "That man is our close relative; he is one of our kinsman-redeemers."

²¹Then Ruth the Moabitess said, "He even said to me, 'Stay with my workers until they finish harvesting all my grain.' "

²²Naomi said to Ruth her daughter-in-law, "It will be good for you, my daughter, to go with his girls, because in someone else's field you might be harmed."

²³So Ruth stayed close to the servant girls of Boaz to glean until the barley and wheat harvests were finished. And she lived with her mother-in-law.

■ Ruth and Boaz at the Threshing-Floor

3 One day Naomi her mother-in-law said to her, "My daughter, should I not try to find a homeᵃ for you, where you will be well provided for? ²Is not Boaz, with whose servant girls you have been, a kinsman of ours? Tonight he will be winnowing barley on the threshing-floor. ³Wash and perfume yourself, and put on your best clothes. Then go down to the threshing-floor, but don't let him know you are there until he has finished eating and drinking. ⁴When he lies down, note the place where he is lying. Then go and uncover his feet and lie down. He will tell you what to do."

⁵"I will do whatever you say," Ruth answered. ⁶So she went down to the threshing-floor and did everything her mother-in-law told her to do.

⁷When Boaz had finished eating and drinking and was in good spirits, he went over to lie down at the far end of the grain pile. Ruth approached quietly, uncovered his feet and lay down. ⁸In the middle of the night something startled the man, and he turned and discovered a woman lying at his feet.

⁹"Who are you?" he asked.

"I am your servant Ruth," she said. "Spread the corner of your garment over me, since you are a kinsman-redeemer."

¹⁰"The LORD bless you, my daughter," he replied. "This kindness is greater than that which you showed earlier: You have not run after the younger men, whether rich or poor. ¹¹And now, my daughter, don't be afraid. I will do for you all you ask. All my fellow townsmen know that you are a woman of noble character. ¹²Although it is true that I am near of kin, there is a kinsman-redeemer nearer than I. ¹³Stay here for the night, and in the morning if he wants to redeem, good; let him redeem. But if he is not willing, as surely as the LORD lives I will do it. Lie here until morning."

¹⁴So she lay at his feet until morning, but got up before anyone could be recognised; and he said, "Don't let it be known that a woman came to the threshing-floor."

¹⁵He also said, "Bring me the shawl you are wearing and hold it out." When she did so, he poured into it six measures of barley and put it on her. Then heᵇ went back to town.

¹⁶When Ruth came to her mother-in-law, Naomi asked, "How did it go, my daughter?"

Then she told her everything Boaz had done for her ¹⁷and added, "He gave me these six measures of

ᵃ17 That is, probably about ⅗ bushel (about 22 litres) manuscripts, Vulgate and Syriac she　　ᵃ1 Hebrew find rest (see Ruth 1:9)　　ᵇ15 Most Hebrew manuscripts; many Hebrew barley, saying, 'Don't go back to your mother-in-law empty-handed.' "

¹⁸Then Naomi said, "Wait, my daughter, until you find out what happens. For the man will not rest until the matter is settled today."

■ Boaz Marries Ruth

4 Meanwhile Boaz went up to the town gate and sat there. When the kinsman-redeemer he had mentioned came along, Boaz said, "Come over here, my friend, and sit down." So he went over and sat down.

4:1 ■ EXPENSIVE BRIDE

In order to marry Ruth, Boaz had to go through a complicated legal procedure at the town gate, a public gathering place. The laws were designed to keep property in the family and to protect family members who might have suffered financial or other setbacks. As a distant relative, Boaz could purchase, or "redeem", Naomi's family property, but only after a closer relative, the "kinsman-redeemer", had declined. Along with the property, Boaz acquired marriage rights to Ruth, Naomi's relative.

---

²Boaz took ten of the elders of the town and said, "Sit here," and they did so. ³Then he said to the kinsman-redeemer, "Naomi, who has come back from Moab, is selling the piece of land that belonged to our brother Elimelech. ⁴I thought I should bring the matter to your attention and suggest that you buy it in the presence of these seated here and in the presence of the elders of my people. If you will redeem it, do so. But if you*a* will not, tell me, so I will know. For no-one has the right to do it except you, and I am next in line."

"I will redeem it," he said.

⁵Then Boaz said, "On the day you buy the land from Naomi and from Ruth the Moabitess, you acquire*b* the dead man's widow, in order to maintain the name of the dead with his property."

⁶At this, the kinsman-redeemer said, "Then I cannot redeem it because I might endanger my own estate. You redeem it yourself. I cannot do it."

⁷(Now in earlier times in Israel, for the redemp-

tion and transfer of property to become final, one party took off his sandal and gave it to the other. This was the method of legalising transactions in Israel.)

⁸So the kinsman-redeemer said to Boaz, "Buy it yourself." And he removed his sandal.

⁹Then Boaz announced to the elders and all the people, "Today you are witnesses that I have bought from Naomi all the property of Elimelech, Kilion and Mahlon. ¹⁰I have also acquired Ruth the Moabitess, Mahlon's widow, as my wife, in order to maintain the name of the dead with his property, so that his name will not disappear from among his family or from the town records. Today you are witnesses!"

¹¹Then the elders and all those at the gate said, "We are witnesses. May the LORD make the woman who is coming into your home like Rachel and Leah, who together built up the house of Israel. May you have standing in Ephrathah and be famous in Bethlehem. ¹²Through the offspring the LORD gives you by this young woman, may your family be like that of Perez, whom Tamar bore to Judah."

■ The Genealogy of David

¹³So Boaz took Ruth and she became his wife. Then he went to her, and the LORD enabled her to conceive, and she gave birth to a son. ¹⁴The women said to Naomi: "Praise be to the LORD, who this day has not left you without a kinsman-redeemer. May he become famous throughout Israel! ¹⁵He will renew your life and sustain you in your old age. For your daughter-in-law, who loves you and who is better to you than seven sons, has given him birth."

¹⁶Then Naomi took the child, laid him in her lap and cared for him. ¹⁷The women living there said, "Naomi has a son." And they named him Obed. He was the father of Jesse, the father of David.

¹⁸This, then, is the family line of Perez:

Perez was the father of Hezron,
¹⁹Hezron the father of Ram,
    Ram the father of Amminadab,
²⁰Amminadab the father of Nahshon,
    Nahshon the father of Salmon,*c*
²¹Salmon the father of Boaz,
    Boaz the father of Obed,
²²Obed the father of Jesse,
    and Jesse the father of David.

---

a4 Many Hebrew manuscripts, Septuagint, Vulgate and Syriac; most Hebrew manuscripts *he*   *b5* Hebrew; Vulgate and Syriac *Naomi, you acquire Ruth the Moabitess,*   *c20* A few Hebrew manuscripts, some Septuagint manuscripts and Vulgate (see also verse 21 and Septuagint of 1 Chron. 2:11); most Hebrew manuscripts *Salma*

1 SAMUEL

■ WHAT LEADERSHIP REQUIRES

ISRAEL, FIGHTING FOR SURVIVAL, NEEDED A LEADER

IT IS NOT BY STRENGTH THAT ONE PREVAILS; THOSE WHO OPPOSE THE LORD WILL BE SHATTERED. ■ 2:9–10

No country, no organisation, no family is great without great leadership. But how do you get it? Israel was forced to ask that question during a critical, do-or-die period. Three men rose to the highest power: Samuel, Saul, and David. All were attractive, powerful figures who commanded admiration and respect. Two, David and Samuel, made very successful leaders. The other, Saul, had a promising beginning but ended as a failure.

■ FIGHTING FOR SURVIVAL

Israel was fighting for survival. The Philistines had migrated to the region about the same time Israel had escaped from Egypt. Now, from their cities near the Mediterranean coast, they were gradually pushing deeper into the mountains of Israel. They had superior weapons – chariots, in particular. Though less populous than Israel, they were apparently better organised.

Israel had neither central administration nor a regular army. A loose confederation of 12 tribes, Israelites called on each other for help only in emergencies. Occasional inspired leaders – "judges" – took charge of military defence when necessary. The nation had worked that way for well over 100 years, and the tribes seemed too independent to change. But the Philistines were pressing them. A crisis of leadership – a crisis testing the very existence of Israel – was building.

■ WHY BEGIN WITH HANNAH?

Surprisingly, 1 Samuel opens not with a battle or even with the leadership crisis, but with a very private family problem. Two bitterly jealous wives had a long-standing quarrel, one taunting the other because of her infertility. Hannah, the childless woman, turned to God in desperation, praying and promising to dedicate a son to him. The result was a little boy named Samuel.

Hannah kept her vow to God, and Samuel grew into one of the greatest leaders Israel had ever known. He had a triple role: he served as a prophet who could discern God's

will, as a priest who led Israel to worship, and as a military leader. He chose, under God's direction, Israel's first two kings. Samuel's strong personality undergirds the entire book of 1 Samuel, even though he officially retired at the end of chapter 15.

Why begin 1 Samuel with Hannah? Hannah's struggles are Israel's, in miniature. Her frustration forced her to look to God, and as a result her son Samuel served in the tabernacle instead of following in his father's footsteps as a farmer. Hannah's story shows that from bitter pain may come great promise, if that pain leads you to God. The Israelites, who were going to experience a great many more troubles in their history, needed Hannah's example.

■ GOD CHOOSES HIS OWN LEADERS

Hannah's story also reminds us that God's leaders don't necessarily come through the regular channels. Ordinarily, Eli's corrupt sons would have carried on the national leadership. But God wanted no part of them. Instead, he blessed a woman who had turned to him in her troubles, and he blessed her son as long as that son trusted in him for help. God chose a leader to suit himself, a leader who listened to him. "The LORD declares . . . 'Those who honour me I will honour, but those who despise me will be disdained' " (2:30).

Samuel never forgot that lesson. He anointed Saul as the first king, and then, when Saul failed to honour God, stripped him of his authority. Passing over many impressive men, Samuel chose David, a young shepherd, to replace Saul. Under David, Israel would be transformed into a wealthy, secure kingdom. Was this because David had such natural leadership qualities? First Samuel suggests a different perspective: David succeeded because God chose him for the job, and because David persistently turned to God for his direction. The best leadership, ultimately, belongs to God.

■ HOW TO READ 1 SAMUEL

Some of the stories of 1 Samuel — David and Goliath, for instance — are justly famous as great adventures. But you should read for more than excitement. Look for insights into the character required for leadership. Samuel and David were great leaders. Saul, on the other hand, was a miserable failure.

These men led Israel during a crucial, bloody period. Israel had been dominated by a foreign power and, partly because of this, was changing its government to a monarchy. This change in governmental institutions, together with tribal tensions, forms the background for the book. A good commentary can help explain this, but you can get much of it for yourself by asking, as you read, three questions: What are the most important national problems facing Israel? What kind of leadership is needed? How do these three leaders (and numerous smaller figures) respond to these needs?

■ 3-TRACK READING PLAN

For an explanation and complete listing of the 3-track reading plan, turn to page x.

■ TRACK 1:
Two-Week Courses on the Bible
The Track 1 reading programme includes one chapter from 1 Samuel. See page x for a complete listing of this course.

■ TRACK 2:
An Overview of 1 Samuel in 4 Days
□ Day 1. Read the Introduction to 1 Samuel and chapter 3, God's call of Samuel when he was very young.
□ Day 2. Read chapter 16 to see how God chose David, and why.
□ Day 3. Read chapter 17 for the exciting story of David's victory over Goliath, noting the qualities David showed.
□ Day 4. Read chapter 20 for a glimpse of a model friendship between David and Jonathan.
Now turn to page xi for your next Track 2 reading project.

■ TRACK 3:
All of 1 Samuel in 31 Days
After you have read through 1 Samuel, turn to pages xii–xiii for your next Track 3 reading project.

□ 1   □ 2   □ 3   □ 4
□ 5   □ 6   □ 7   □ 8
□ 9   □ 10   □ 11   □ 12
□ 13   □ 14   □ 15   □ 16
□ 17   □ 18   □ 19   □ 20
□ 21   □ 22   □ 23   □ 24
□ 25   □ 26   □ 27   □ 28
□ 29   □ 30   □ 31

■ The Birth of Samuel

1 There was a certain man from Ramathaim, a Zuphite*a* from the hill country of Ephraim, whose name was Elkanah son of Jeroham, the son of Elihu, the son of Tohu, the son of Zuph, an Ephraimite. ²He had two wives; one was called Hannah and the other Peninnah. Peninnah had children, but Hannah had none.

³Year after year this man went up from his town to worship and sacrifice to the LORD Almighty at Shiloh, where Hophni and Phinehas, the two sons of Eli, were priests of the LORD. ⁴Whenever the day came for Elkanah to sacrifice, he would give portions of the meat to his wife Peninnah and to all her sons and daughters. ⁵But to Hannah he gave a double portion because he loved her, and the LORD had closed her womb. ⁶And because the LORD had closed her womb, her rival kept provoking her in order to irritate her. ⁷This went on year after year. Whenever Hannah went up to the house of the LORD, her rival provoked her till she wept and would not eat. ⁸Elkanah her husband would say to her, "Hannah, why are you weeping? Why don't you eat? Why are you downhearted? Don't I mean more to you than ten sons?"

⁹Once when they had finished eating and drinking in Shiloh, Hannah stood up. Now Eli the priest was sitting on a chair by the doorpost of the LORD's temple.*b* ¹⁰In bitterness of soul Hannah wept much and prayed to the LORD. ¹¹And she made a vow, saying, "O LORD Almighty, if you will only look upon your servant's misery and remember me, and not forget your servant but give her a son, then I will give him to the LORD for all the days of his life, and no razor will ever be used on his head."

¹²As she kept on praying to the LORD, Eli observed her mouth. ¹³Hannah was praying in her heart, and her lips were moving but her voice was not heard. Eli thought she was drunk ¹⁴and said to her, "How long will you keep on getting drunk? Get rid of your wine."

1:13 ■ SAD, NOT DRUNK

Eli's mistaken assumption suggests that people sometimes came to the tabernacle drunk. Perhaps in these troubled times drunkenness was more common than heartfelt prayer. Hannah prayed with great anguish because she had no children. She is one of several barren women in the Bible whom God helped; others include Sarah (Genesis 11:30), Rebekah (Genesis 25:21), Rachel (Genesis 29:31), and Elizabeth (Luke 1:7).

¹⁵"Not so, my lord," Hannah replied, "I am a woman who is deeply troubled. I have not been drinking wine or beer; I was pouring out my soul to the LORD. ¹⁶Do not take your servant for a wicked woman; I have been praying here out of my great anguish and grief."

a 1 Or from Ramathaim Zuphim   *b 9 That is, tabernacle*

¹⁷Eli answered, "Go in peace, and may the God of Israel grant you what you have asked of him."
¹⁸She said, "May your servant find favour in your eyes." Then she went her way and ate something, and her face was no longer downcast.
¹⁹Early the next morning they arose and worshipped before the LORD and then went back to their home at Ramah. Elkanah lay with Hannah his wife, and the LORD remembered her. ²⁰So in the course of time Hannah conceived and gave birth to a son. She named him Samuel,ᶜ saying, "Because I asked the LORD for him."

■ Hannah Dedicates Samuel

²¹When the man Elkanah went up with all his family to offer the annual sacrifice to the LORD and to fulfil his vow, ²²Hannah did not go. She said to her husband, "After the boy is weaned, I will take him and present him before the LORD, and he will live there always."
²³"Do what seems best to you," Elkanah her husband told her. "Stay here until you have weaned him; only may the LORD make good hisᵈ word." So the woman stayed at home and nursed her son until she had weaned him.
²⁴After he was weaned, she took the boy with her, young as he was, along with a three-year-old bull,ᵉ an ephahᶠ of flour and a skin of wine, and brought him to the house of the LORD at Shiloh. ²⁵When they had slaughtered the bull, they brought the boy to Eli, ²⁶and she said to him, "As surely as you live, my lord, I am the woman who stood here beside you praying to the LORD. ²⁷I prayed for this child, and the LORD has granted me what I asked of him. ²⁸So now I give him to the LORD. For his whole life he shall be given over to the LORD." And he worshipped the LORD there.

■ Hannah's Prayer

2 Then Hannah prayed and said:

"My heart rejoices in the LORD;
    in the LORD my hornᵃ is lifted high.
My mouth boasts over my enemies,
    for I delight in your deliverance.

²"There is no-one holyᵇ like the LORD;
    there is no-one besides you;
    there is no Rock like our God.

³"Do not keep talking so proudly
    or let your mouth speak such arrogance,
for the LORD is a God who knows,
    and by him deeds are weighed.

⁴"The bows of the warriors are broken,
    but those who stumbled are armed with
        strength.
⁵Those who were full hire themselves out for
        food,
    but those who were hungry hunger no more.
She who was barren has borne seven children,
    but she who has had many sons pines away.

⁶"The LORD brings death and makes alive;
    he brings down to the graveᶜ and raises up.

⁷The LORD sends poverty and wealth;
    he humbles and he exalts.
⁸He raises the poor from the dust
    and lifts the needy from the ash heap;
he seats them with princes
    and has them inherit a throne of honour.

"For the foundations of the earth are the LORD's;
    upon them he has set the world.
⁹He will guard the feet of his saints,
    but the wicked will be silenced in darkness.

"It is not by strength that one prevails;
¹⁰   those who oppose the LORD will be shattered.
He will thunder against them from heaven;
    the LORD will judge the ends of the earth.

"He will give strength to his king
    and exalt the horn of his anointed."

¹¹Then Elkanah went home to Ramah, but the boy ministered before the LORD under Eli the priest.

■ Eli's Wicked Sons

¹²Eli's sons were wicked men; they had no regard for the LORD. ¹³Now it was the practice of the priests with the people that whenever anyone offered a sacrifice and while the meat was being boiled, the servant of the priest would come with a three-pronged fork in his hand. ¹⁴He would plunge it into the pan or kettle or cauldron or pot, and the priest would take for himself whatever the fork brought up. This is how they treated all the Israelites who came to Shiloh. ¹⁵But even before the fat was burned, the servant of the priest would come and say to the man who was sacrificing, "Give the priest some meat to roast; he won't accept boiled meat from you, but only raw."
¹⁶If the man said to him, "Let the fat be burned up first, and then take whatever you want," the servant would then answer, "No, hand it over now; if you don't, I'll take it by force."
¹⁷This sin of the young men was very great in the LORD's sight, for theyᵈ were treating the LORD's offering with contempt.
¹⁸But Samuel was ministering before the LORD — a boy wearing a linen ephod. ¹⁹Each year his mother made him a little robe and took it to him when she went up with her husband to offer the annual sacrifice. ²⁰Eli would bless Elkanah and his wife, saying, "May the LORD give you children by this woman to take the place of the one she prayed for and gave to the LORD." Then they would go home. ²¹And the LORD was gracious to Hannah; she conceived and gave birth to three sons and two daughters. Meanwhile, the boy Samuel grew up in the presence of the LORD.
²²Now Eli, who was very old, heard about everything his sons were doing to all Israel and how they slept with the women who served at the entrance to the Tent of Meeting. ²³So he said to them, "Why do you do such things? I hear from all the people about these wicked deeds of yours. ²⁴No, my sons; it is not a good report that I hear spreading among the LORD's

ᶜ20 Samuel sounds like the Hebrew for heard of God.   ᵈ23 Masoretic Text; Dead Sea Scrolls, Septuagint and Syriac your   ᵉ24 Dead Sea Scrolls, Septuagint and Syriac; Masoretic Text with three bulls   ᶠ24 That is, probably about ⅗ bushel (about 22 litres)   ᵃ1 Horn here symbolises strength; also in verse 10.   ᵇ2 Or no Holy One   ᶜ6 Hebrew Sheol   ᵈ17 Or men people. ²⁵If a man sins against another man, God^e may mediate for him; but if a man sins against the LORD, who will intercede for him?" His sons, however, did not listen to their father's rebuke, for it was the LORD's will to put them to death.

2:25 ■ GOD IN CHARGE

Eli's sons disobeyed, the Bible says, because God wanted to put them to death. Does this mean that God took away their free choice? To Old Testament writers this "contradiction" seemed less troubling than to us. To them every event occurred only because, ultimately, God let it. Within his overall control people acted freely. In this case, Eli's sons were free to obey or disobey. The author wants us to know, however, that their disobedience was not beyond God's power: he planned to judge their evil activities.

²⁶And the boy Samuel continued to grow in stature and in favour with the LORD and with men.

■ Prophecy Against the House of Eli

²⁷Now a man of God came to Eli and said to him, "This is what the LORD says: 'Did I not clearly reveal myself to your father's house when they were in Egypt under Pharaoh? ²⁸I chose your father out of all the tribes of Israel to be my priest, to go up to my altar, to burn incense, and to wear an ephod in my presence. I also gave your father's house all the offerings made with fire by the Israelites. ²⁹Why do you^f scorn my sacrifice and offering that I prescribed for my dwelling? Why do you honour your sons more than me by fattening yourselves on the choice parts of every offering made by my people Israel?'

³⁰"Therefore the LORD, the God of Israel, declares: 'I promised that your house and your father's house would minister before me for ever.' But now the LORD declares: 'Far be it from me! Those who honour me I will honour, but those who despise me will be disdained. ³¹The time is coming when I will cut short your strength and the strength of your father's house, so that there will not be an old man in your family line ³²and you will see distress in my dwelling. Although good will be done to Israel, in your family line there will never be an old man. ³³Every one of you that I do not cut off from my altar will be spared only to blind your eyes with tears and to grieve your heart, and all your descendants will die in the prime of life. ³⁴" 'And what happens to your two sons, Hophni and Phinehas, will be a sign to you — they will both die on the same day. ³⁵I will raise up for myself a faithful priest, who will do according to what is in my heart and mind. I will firmly establish his house, and he will minister before my anointed one always. ³⁶Then everyone left in your family line will come and bow down before him for a piece of silver and a crust of bread and plead, "Appoint me to some priestly office so that I can have food to eat." ' "

■ The LORD Calls Samuel

3 The boy Samuel ministered before the LORD under Eli. In those days the word of the LORD was rare; there were not many visions.

2:30 ■ BAD NEWS FOR ELI

The film "Chariots of Fire" commemorated this verse. "Those who honour me I will honour," read a note slipped to Eric Liddell just before he ran in the Olympic sprints. The race that followed rewarded Liddell's public honouring of God.

But for Eli, the pronouncement came as bad news. He was held responsible for his sons' disgraceful behaviour in the tabernacle. Eli rebuked them, but "failed to restrain them" (3:13). As the priest in charge of the tabernacle, it was his job to stop any abuse there.

²One night Eli, whose eyes were becoming so weak that he could barely see, was lying down in his usual place. ³The lamp of God had not yet gone out, and Samuel was lying down in the temple^a of the LORD, where the ark of God was. ⁴Then the LORD called Samuel.

Samuel answered, "Here I am." ⁵And he ran to Eli and said, "Here I am; you called me."

But Eli said, "I did not call; go back and lie down." So he went and lay down.

⁶Again the LORD called, "Samuel!" And Samuel got up and went to Eli and said, "Here I am; you called me."

"My son," Eli said, "I did not call; go back and lie down."

⁷Now Samuel did not yet know the LORD: The word of the LORD had not yet been revealed to him.

⁸The LORD called Samuel a third time, and Samuel got up and went to Eli and said, "Here I am; you called me."

Then Eli realised that the LORD was calling the boy. ⁹So Eli told Samuel, "Go and lie down, and if he calls you, say, 'Speak, LORD, for your servant is listening.' " So Samuel went and lay down in his place.

¹⁰The LORD came and stood there, calling as at the other times, "Samuel! Samuel!"

Then Samuel said, "Speak, for your servant is listening."

3:10 ■ STILL A BOY

While still a boy, Samuel heard God speak. He delivered God's message even though it rebuked Eli, the man who had raised him from childhood. This was one indication that Samuel was a genuine prophet, for false prophets usually delivered only good news. Samuel's message agreed with the prophecy given earlier by a man of God (2:27–36), confirming that God had indeed spoken to him.

¹¹And the LORD said to Samuel: "See, I am about to do something in Israel that will make the ears of everyone who hears of it tingle. ¹²At that time I will carry out against Eli everything I spoke against his

family—from beginning to end. ¹³For I told him that I would judge his family for ever because of the sin he knew about; his sons made themselves contemptible,*ᵇ* and he failed to restrain them. ¹⁴Therefore, I swore to the house of Eli, 'The guilt of Eli's house will never be atoned for by sacrifice or offering.' "

¹⁵Samuel lay down until morning and then opened the doors of the house of the LORD. He was afraid to tell Eli the vision, ¹⁶but Eli called him and said, "Samuel, my son."

Samuel answered, "Here I am."

¹⁷"What was it he said to you?" Eli asked. "Do not hide it from me. May God deal with you, be it ever so severely, if you hide from me anything he told you." ¹⁸So Samuel told him everything, hiding nothing from him. Then Eli said, "He is the LORD; let him do what is good in his eyes."

¹⁹The LORD was with Samuel as he grew up, and he let none of his words fall to the ground. ²⁰And all Israel from Dan to Beersheba recognised that Samuel was attested as a prophet of the LORD. ²¹The LORD continued to appear at Shiloh, and there he revealed himself to Samuel through his word.

4 And Samuel's word came to all Israel.

■ The Philistines Capture the Ark

Now the Israelites went out to fight against the Philistines. The Israelites camped at Ebenezer, and the Philistines at Aphek. ²The Philistines deployed their forces to meet Israel, and as the battle spread, Israel was defeated by the Philistines, who killed about four thousand of them on the battlefield. ³When the soldiers returned to camp, the elders of Israel asked, "Why did the LORD bring defeat upon us today before the Philistines? Let us bring the ark of the LORD's covenant from Shiloh, so that it*ᵃ* may go with us and save us from the hand of our enemies."

⁴So the people sent men to Shiloh, and they brought back the ark of the covenant of the LORD Almighty, who is enthroned between the cherubim. And Eli's two sons, Hophni and Phinehas, were there with the ark of the covenant of God.

⁵When the ark of the LORD's covenant came into the camp, all Israel raised such a great shout that the ground shook. ⁶Hearing the uproar, the Philistines asked, "What's all this shouting in the Hebrew camp?"

When they learned that the ark of the LORD had come into the camp, ⁷the Philistines were afraid. "A god has come into the camp," they said. "We're in trouble! Nothing like this has happened before. ⁸Woe to us! Who will deliver us from the hand of these mighty gods? They are the gods who struck the Egyptians with all kinds of plagues in the desert. ⁹Be strong, Philistines! Be men, or you will be subject to the Hebrews, as they have been to you. Be men, and fight!"

¹⁰So the Philistines fought, and the Israelites were defeated and every man fled to his tent. The slaughter was very great; Israel lost thirty thousand foot soldiers. ¹¹The ark of God was captured, and Eli's two sons, Hophni and Phinehas, died.

■ Death of Eli

¹²That same day a Benjamite ran from the battle line and went to Shiloh, his clothes torn and dust on his head. ¹³When he arrived, there was Eli sitting on his chair by the side of the road, watching, because his heart feared for the ark of God. When the man entered the town and told what had happened, the whole town sent up a cry.

> **4:12 ■ THE END OF SHILOH**
> The Philistine victory may have led to Shiloh's capture, for the next time we encounter Eli's family, they have moved as a group to Nob. Several Bible passages mention Shiloh's destruction as a punishment for sin: Jeremiah 7:12,14; 26:6,9; Psalm 78:60. If Shiloh did fall at this time, its capture must have added greatly to Israel's general sense of despair, for the city was an important site for worship.

¹⁴Eli heard the outcry and asked, "What is the meaning of this uproar?"

The man hurried over to Eli, ¹⁵who was ninety-eight years old and whose eyes were set so that he could not see. ¹⁶He told Eli, "I have just come from the battle line; I fled from it this very day."

Eli asked, "What happened, my son?"

¹⁷The man who brought the news replied, "Israel fled before the Philistines, and the army has suffered heavy losses. Also your two sons, Hophni and Phinehas, are dead, and the ark of God has been captured."

¹⁸When he mentioned the ark of God, Eli fell backwards off his chair by the side of the gate. His neck was broken and he died, for he was an old man and heavy. He had led*ᵇ* Israel for forty years.

¹⁹His daughter-in-law, the wife of Phinehas, was pregnant and near the time of delivery. When she heard the news that the ark of God had been captured and that her father-in-law and her husband were dead, she went into labour and gave birth, but was overcome by her labour pains. ²⁰As she was dying, the women attending her said, "Don't despair; you have given birth to a son." But she did not respond or pay any attention.

²¹She named the boy Ichabod,*ᶜ* saying, "The glory has departed from Israel"—because of the capture of the ark of God and the deaths of her father-in-law and her husband. ²²She said, "The glory has departed from Israel, for the ark of God has been captured."

■ The Ark in Ashdod and Ekron

5 After the Philistines had captured the ark of God, they took it from Ebenezer to Ashdod. ²Then they carried the ark into Dagon's temple and set it beside Dagon. ³When the people of Ashdod rose early the next day, there was Dagon, fallen on his face on the ground before the ark of the LORD! They took Dagon and put him back in his place. ⁴But the following morning when they rose, there was Dagon, fallen on his face on the ground before the ark of the LORD! His head and hands had been broken off and were lying on the threshold; only his body

---

*ᵇ*13 Masoretic Text; an ancient Hebrew scribal tradition and Septuagint *sons blasphemed God*   *ᵃ*3 Or *he*   *ᵇ*18 Traditionally *judged*   *ᶜ*21 *Ichabod* means *no glory*.

remained. 5That is why to this day neither the priests of Dagon nor any others who enter Dagon's temple at Ashdod step on the threshold.

6The LORD's hand was heavy upon the people of Ashdod and its vicinity; he brought devastation upon them and afflicted them with tumours.*a* 7When the men of Ashdod saw what was happening, they said, "The ark of the god of Israel must not stay here with us, because his hand is heavy upon us and upon Dagon our god." 8So they called together all the rulers of the Philistines and asked them, "What shall we do with the ark of the god of Israel?"

They answered, "Have the ark of the god of Israel moved to Gath." So they moved the ark of the God of Israel.

9But after they had moved it, the LORD's hand was against that city, throwing it into a great panic. He afflicted the people of the city, both young and old, with an outbreak of tumours.*b* 10So they sent the ark of God to Ekron.

As the ark of God was entering Ekron, the people of Ekron cried out, "They have brought the ark of the god of Israel round to us to kill us and our people." 11So they called together all the rulers of the Philistines and said, "Send the ark of the god of Israel away; let it go back to its own place, or it*c* will kill us and our people." For death had filled the city with panic; God's hand was very heavy upon it. 12Those who did not die were afflicted with tumours, and the outcry of the city went up to heaven.

■ The Ark Returned to Israel

6 When the ark of the LORD had been in Philistine territory for seven months, 2the Philistines called for the priests and the diviners and said, "What shall we do with the ark of the LORD? Tell us how we should send it back to its place."

3They answered, "If you return the ark of the god of Israel, do not send it away empty, but by all means send a guilt offering to him. Then you will be healed, and you will know why his hand has not been lifted from you."

4The Philistines asked, "What guilt offering should we send to him?"

They replied, "Five gold tumours and five gold rats, according to the number of the Philistine rulers, because the same plague has struck both you and your rulers. 5Make models of the tumours and of the rats that are destroying the country, and pay honour to Israel's god. Perhaps he will lift his hand from you and your gods and your land. 6Why do you harden your hearts as the Egyptians and Pharaoh did? When he*a* treated them harshly, did they not send the Israelites out so that they could go on their way?

7"Now then, get a new cart ready, with two cows that have calved and have never been yoked. Hitch the cows to the cart, but take their calves away and pen them up. 8Take the ark of the LORD and put it on the cart, and in a chest beside it put the gold objects you are sending back to him as a guilt offering. Send it on its way, 9but keep watching it. If it goes up to its own territory, towards Beth Shemesh, then the LORD has brought this great disaster on us. But

if it does not, then we shall know that it was not his hand that struck us and that it happened to us by chance."

6:5 ■ MAGIC

The Philistine strategy shows traditional magical thinking, still common in some occult or voodoo rites. By sending gold models of the tumours and rats out of the country, the Philistines hoped to send the originals out of the country too. This is similar to the voodoo practice of sticking pins into wax models of your enemies.

The Israelites, instead of looking for a magical technique, appealed to the overwhelming power of a personal God, who could not be manipulated with magic.

10So they did this. They took two such cows and hitched them to the cart and penned up their calves. 11They placed the ark of the LORD on the cart and along with it the chest containing the gold rats and the models of the tumours. 12Then the cows went straight up towards Beth Shemesh, keeping on the road and lowing all the way; they did not turn to the right or to the left. The rulers of the Philistines followed them as far as the border of Beth Shemesh.

13Now the people of Beth Shemesh were harvesting their wheat in the valley, and when they looked up and saw the ark, they rejoiced at the sight. 14The cart came to the field of Joshua of Beth Shemesh, and there it stopped beside a large rock. The people chopped up the wood of the cart and sacrificed the cows as a burnt offering to the LORD. 15The Levites took down the ark of the LORD, together with the chest containing the gold objects, and placed them on the large rock. On that day the people of Beth Shemesh offered burnt offerings and made sacrifices to the LORD. 16The five rulers of the Philistines saw all this and then returned that same day to Ekron.

17These are the gold tumours the Philistines sent as a guilt offering to the LORD — one each for Ashdod, Gaza, Ashkelon, Gath and Ekron. 18And the number of the gold rats was according to the number of Philistine towns belonging to the five rulers — the fortified towns with their country villages. The large rock, on which*b* they set the ark of the LORD, is a witness to this day in the field of Joshua of Beth Shemesh.

19But God struck down some of the men of Beth Shemesh, putting seventy*c* of them to death because they had looked into the ark of the LORD. The people mourned because of the heavy blow the LORD had dealt them, 20and the men of Beth Shemesh asked, "Who can stand in the presence of the LORD, this holy God? To whom will the ark go up from here?"

21Then they sent messengers to the people of Kiriath Jearim, saying, "The Philistines have returned the ark of the LORD. Come down and take it up to your place." 1So the men of Kiriath Jearim came

7 and took up the ark of the LORD. They took it to

---

a 6 Hebrew; Septuagint and Vulgate *tumours. And rats appeared in their land, and death and destruction were throughout the city*   *b 9* Or *with tumours in the groin* (see Septuagint)   *c 11* Or *he*   *a 6* That is, God   *b 18* A few Hebrew manuscripts (see also Septuagint); most Hebrew manuscripts *villages as far as Greater Abel, where*   *c 19* A few Hebrew manuscripts; most Hebrew manuscripts and Septuagint *50,070*

Abinadab's house on the hill and consecrated Eleazar his son to guard the ark of the LORD.

■ Samuel Subdues the Philistines at Mizpah

2It was a long time, twenty years in all, that the ark remained at Kiriath Jearim, and all the people of Israel mourned and sought after the LORD. 3And Samuel said to the whole house of Israel, "If you are returning to the LORD with all your hearts, then rid yourselves of the foreign gods and the Ashtoreths and commit yourselves to the LORD and serve him only, and he will deliver you out of the hand of the Philistines." 4So the Israelites put away their Baals and Ashtoreths, and served the LORD only.

5Then Samuel said, "Assemble all Israel at Mizpah and I will intercede with the LORD for you." 6When they had assembled at Mizpah, they drew water and poured it out before the LORD. On that day they fasted and there they confessed, "We have sinned against the LORD." And Samuel was leader*a* of Israel at Mizpah.

7When the Philistines heard that Israel had assembled at Mizpah, the rulers of the Philistines came up to attack them. And when the Israelites heard of it, they were afraid because of the Philistines. 8They said to Samuel, "Do not stop crying out to the LORD our God for us, that he may rescue us from the hand of the Philistines." 9Then Samuel took a suckling lamb and offered it up as a whole burnt offering to the LORD. He cried out to the LORD on Israel's behalf, and the LORD answered him.

10While Samuel was sacrificing the burnt offering, the Philistines drew near to engage Israel in battle. But that day the LORD thundered with loud thunder against the Philistines and threw them into such a panic that they were routed before the Israelites. 11The men of Israel rushed out of Mizpah and pursued the Philistines, slaughtering them along the way to a point below Beth Car.

12Then Samuel took a stone and set it up between Mizpah and Shen. He named it Ebenezer,*b* saying, "Thus far has the LORD helped us." 13So the Philistines were subdued and did not invade Israelite territory again.

Throughout Samuel's lifetime, the hand of the LORD was against the Philistines. 14The towns from Ekron to Gath that the Philistines had captured from Israel were restored to her, and Israel delivered the neighbouring territory from the power of the Philistines. And there was peace between Israel and the Amorites.

15Samuel continued as judge over Israel all the days of his life. 16From year to year he went on a circuit from Bethel to Gilgal to Mizpah, judging Israel in all those places. 17But he always went back to Ramah, where his home was, and there he also judged Israel. And he built an altar there to the LORD.

■ Israel Asks for a King

8 When Samuel grew old, he appointed his sons as judges for Israel. 2The name of his firstborn was Joel and the name of his second was Abijah, and they served at Beersheba. 3But his sons did not walk

in his ways. They turned aside after dishonest gain and accepted bribes and perverted justice.

4So all the elders of Israel gathered together and came to Samuel at Ramah. 5They said to him, "You are old, and your sons do not walk in your ways; now appoint a king to lead*a* us, such as all the other nations have."

8:5 ■ WHY NOT A KING?
Considering the disorganised state of the Israelite nation, their request for a new form of government – a monarchy – seems understandable. A king would centralise power, making the nation more efficient in defending itself. However, both Samuel and God opposed the idea, particularly because of the Israelites' motive: they wanted "a king to lead us, such as all the other nations have". Israel was supposed to be different from the other nations. Whatever the form of their government, they were to trust in God as their leader.

6But when they said, "Give us a king to lead us," this displeased Samuel; so he prayed to the LORD. 7And the LORD told him: "Listen to all that the people are saying to you; it is not you they have rejected, but they have rejected me as their king. 8As they have done from the day I brought them up out of Egypt until this day, forsaking me and serving other gods, so they are doing to you. 9Now listen to them; but warn them solemnly and let them know what the king who will reign over them will do."

10Samuel told all the words of the LORD to the people who were asking him for a king. 11He said, "This is what the king who will reign over you will do: He will take your sons and make them serve with his chariots and horses, and they will run in front of his chariots. 12Some he will assign to be commanders of thousands and commanders of fifties, and others to plough his ground and reap his harvest, and still others to make weapons of war and equipment for his chariots. 13He will take your daughters to be perfumers and cooks and bakers. 14He will take the best of your fields and vineyards and olive groves and give them to his attendants. 15He will take a tenth of your grain and of your vintage and give it to his officials and attendants. 16Your menservants and maidservants and the best of your cattle*b* and donkeys he will take for his own use. 17He will take a tenth of your flocks, and you yourselves will become his slaves. 18When that day comes, you will cry out for relief from the king you have chosen, and the LORD will not answer you in that day."

19But the people refused to listen to Samuel. "No!" they said. "We want a king over us. 20Then we shall be like all the other nations, with a king to lead us and to go out before us and fight our battles."

21When Samuel heard all that the people said, he repeated it before the LORD. 22The LORD answered, "Listen to them and give them a king."

Then Samuel said to the men of Israel, "Everyone is to go back to his town."

a 6 Traditionally *judge*   *b 12 Ebenezer* means *stone of help.*   *a 5* Traditionally *judge*; also in verses 6 and 20   *b 16* Septuagint; Hebrew *young men*

■ Samuel Anoints Saul

9 There was a Benjamite, a man of standing, whose name was Kish son of Abiel, the son of Zeror, the son of Becorath, the son of Aphiah of Benjamin. ²He had a son named Saul, an impressive young man without equal among the Israelites—a head taller than any of the others.

³Now the donkeys belonging to Saul's father Kish were lost, and Kish said to his son Saul, "Take one of the servants with you and go and look for the donkeys." ⁴So he passed through the hill country of Ephraim and through the area around Shalisha, but they did not find them. They went on into the district of Shaalim, but the donkeys were not there. Then he passed through the territory of Benjamin, but they did not find them.

9:3 ■ A DONKEY HUNT

Saul, hunting for donkeys, certainly was not looking for a chance to become king. He was so politically unaware that he didn't even know about the great man Samuel. Similarly, Samuel was a small boy when God called him (chapter 3), and David was anointed king while tending sheep (16:11–13). The leaders God appoints are not necessarily those seeking power.

---

⁵When they reached the district of Zuph, Saul said to the servant who was with him, "Come, let's go back, or my father will stop thinking about the donkeys and start worrying about us."

⁶But the servant replied, "Look, in this town there is a man of God; he is highly respected, and everything he says comes true. Let's go there now. Perhaps he will tell us what way to take."

⁷Saul said to his servant, "If we go, what can we give the man? The food in our sacks is gone. We have no gift to take to the man of God. What do we have?"

⁸The servant answered him again. "Look," he said, "I have a quarter of a shekel[a] of silver. I will give it to the man of God so that he will tell us what way to take." ⁹(Formerly in Israel, if a man went to enquire of God, he would say, "Come, let us go to the seer," because the prophet of today used to be called a seer.)

¹⁰"Good," Saul said to his servant. "Come, let's go." So they set out for the town where the man of God was.

¹¹As they were going up the hill to the town, they met some girls coming out to draw water, and they asked them, "Is the seer here?"

¹²"He is," they answered. "He's ahead of you. Hurry now; he has just come to our town today, for the people have a sacrifice at the high place. ¹³As soon as you enter the town, you will find him before he goes up to the high place to eat. The people will not begin eating until he comes, because he must bless the sacrifice; afterwards, those who are invited will eat. Go up now; you should find him about this time."

¹⁴They went up to the town, and as they were entering it, there was Samuel, coming towards them on his way up to the high place.

¹⁵Now the day before Saul came, the LORD had revealed this to Samuel: ¹⁶"About this time tomorrow I will send you a man from the land of Benjamin. Anoint him leader over my people Israel; he will deliver my people from the hand of the Philistines. I have looked upon my people, for their cry has reached me."

¹⁷When Samuel caught sight of Saul, the LORD said to him, "This is the man I spoke to you about; he will govern my people."

¹⁸Saul approached Samuel in the gateway and asked, "Would you please tell me where the seer's house is?"

¹⁹"I am the seer," Samuel replied. "Go up ahead of me to the high place, for today you are to eat with me, and in the morning I will let you go and will tell you all that is in your heart. ²⁰As for the donkeys you lost three days ago, do not worry about them; they have been found. And to whom is all the desire of Israel turned, if not to you and all your father's family?"

²¹Saul answered, "But am I not a Benjamite, from the smallest tribe of Israel, and is not my clan the least of all the clans of the tribe of Benjamin? Why do you say such a thing to me?"

²²Then Samuel brought Saul and his servant into the hall and seated them at the head of those who were invited—about thirty in number. ²³Samuel said to the cook, "Bring the piece of meat I gave you, the one I told you to lay aside."

²⁴So the cook took up the leg with what was on it and set it in front of Saul. Samuel said, "Here is what has been kept for you. Eat, because it was set aside for you for this occasion, from the time I said, 'I have invited guests.' " And Saul dined with Samuel that day.

²⁵After they came down from the high place to the town, Samuel talked with Saul on the roof of his house. ²⁶They rose about daybreak and Samuel called to Saul on the roof, "Get ready, and I will send you on your way." When Saul got ready, he and Samuel went outside together. ²⁷As they were going down to the edge of the town, Samuel said to Saul, "Tell the servant to go on ahead of us—and the servant did so—"but you stay here awhile, so that I may give you a message from God."

10 Then Samuel took a flask of oil and poured it on Saul's head and kissed him, saying, "Has not the LORD anointed you leader over his inheritance?[a] ²When you leave me today, you will meet two men near Rachel's tomb, at Zelzah on the border of Benjamin. They will say to you, 'The donkeys you set out to look for have been found. And now your father has stopped thinking about them and is worried about you. He is asking, "What shall I do about my son?" '

³"Then you will go on from there until you reach the great tree of Tabor. Three men going up to God at Bethel will meet you there. One will be carrying three young goats, another three loaves of bread, and another a skin of wine. ⁴They will greet you and offer you two loaves of bread, which you will accept from them.

⁵"After that you will go to Gibeah of God, where there is a Philistine outpost. As you approach the

---

a8 That is, about ¹⁄₁₀ ounce (about 3 grams)   *a1 Hebrew; Septuagint and Vulgate over his people Israel? You will reign over the LORD's people and save them from the power of their enemies round about. And this will be a sign to you that the LORD has anointed you leader over his inheritance:*

town, you will meet a procession of prophets coming down from the high place with lyres, tambourines, flutes and harps being played before them, and they will be prophesying. 6The Spirit of the LORD will come upon you in power, and you will prophesy with them; and you will be changed into a different person. 7Once these signs are fulfilled, do whatever your hand finds to do, for God is with you.

10:5 ■ MUSICAL PROPHETS
This is one of the earliest references to prophets in the Bible. Under the kings, prophets became much more significant, possibly because they so often spoke out against the kings. The description of the prophets' musical procession is intriguing, though we can only guess what exactly they were doing. Unquestionably, the Spirit's powerful effect on Saul made a startling change in him (verse 11).

8"Go down ahead of me to Gilgal. I will surely come down to you to sacrifice burnt offerings and fellowship offerings,b but you must wait seven days until I come to you and tell you what you are to do."

■ Saul Made King
9As Saul turned to leave Samuel, God changed Saul's heart, and all these signs were fulfilled that day. 10When they arrived at Gibeah, a procession of prophets met him; the Spirit of God came upon him in power, and he joined in their prophesying. 11When all those who had formerly known him saw him prophesying with the prophets, they asked each other, "What is this that has happened to the son of Kish? Is Saul also among the prophets?"
12A man who lived there answered, "And who is their father?" So it became a saying: "Is Saul also among the prophets?" 13After Saul stopped prophesying, he went to the high place.
14Now Saul's uncle asked him and his servant, "Where have you been?"
"Looking for the donkeys," he said. "But when we saw they were not to be found, we went to Samuel."
15Saul's uncle said, "Tell me what Samuel said to you."
16Saul replied, "He assured us that the donkeys had been found." But he did not tell his uncle what Samuel had said about the kingship.
17Samuel summoned the people of Israel to the LORD at Mizpah 18and said to them, "This is what the LORD, the God of Israel, says: 'I brought Israel up out of Egypt, and I delivered you from the power of Egypt and all the kingdoms that oppressed you.' 19But you have now rejected your God, who saves you out of all your calamities and distresses. And you have said, 'No, set a king over us.' So now present yourselves before the LORD by your tribes and clans."
20When Samuel brought all the tribes of Israel near, the tribe of Benjamin was chosen. 21Then he brought forward the tribe of Benjamin, clan by clan, and Matri's clan was chosen. Finally Saul son of Kish was chosen. But when they looked for him, he was

not to be found. 22So they enquired further of the LORD, "Has the man come here yet?"
And the LORD said, "Yes, he has hidden himself among the baggage."
23They ran and brought him out, and as he stood among the people he was a head taller than any of the others. 24Samuel said to all the people, "Do you see the man the LORD has chosen? There is no-one like him among all the people."
Then the people shouted, "Long live the king!"
25Samuel explained to the people the regulations of the kingship. He wrote them down on a scroll and deposited it before the LORD. Then Samuel dismissed the people, each to his own home.

10:25 ■ LIMITS ON THE KING
Though Samuel reluctantly designated Saul as the first king, he insisted on safeguards. Much as the power of the Queen to govern in the United Kingdom is defined and limited by Parliament, particularly the House of Commons, so Saul's kingship was defined and limited by certain rules, which Samuel wrote down and placed in the tabernacle as a permanent record.

26Saul also went to his home in Gibeah, accompanied by valiant men whose hearts God had touched. 27But some troublemakers said, "How can this fellow save us?" They despised him and brought him no gifts. But Saul kept silent.

■ Saul Rescues the City of Jabesh

11 Nahash the Ammonite went up and besieged Jabesh Gilead. And all the men of Jabesh said to him, "Make a treaty with us, and we will be subject to you."
2But Nahash the Ammonite replied, "I will make a treaty with you only on the condition that I gouge out the right eye of every one of you and so bring disgrace on all Israel."
3The elders of Jabesh said to him, "Give us seven days so that we can send messengers throughout Israel; if no-one comes to rescue us, we will surrender to you."
4When the messengers came to Gibeah of Saul and reported these terms to the people, they all wept aloud. 5Just then Saul was returning from the fields, behind his oxen, and he asked, "What is wrong with the people? Why are they weeping?" Then they repeated to him what the men of Jabesh had said.
6When Saul heard their words, the Spirit of God came upon him in power, and he burned with anger. 7He took a pair of oxen, cut them into pieces, and sent the pieces by messengers throughout Israel, proclaiming, "This is what will be done to the oxen of anyone who does not follow Saul and Samuel." Then the terror of the LORD fell on the people, and they turned out as one man. 8When Saul mustered them at Bezek, the men of Israel numbered three hundred thousand and the men of Judah thirty thousand.
9They told the messengers who had come, "Say to

b8 Traditionally *peace offerings*

the men of Jabesh Gilead, 'By the time the sun is hot tomorrow, you will be delivered.' " When the messengers went and reported this to the men of Jabesh, they were elated. [10]They said to the Ammonites, "Tomorrow we will surrender to you, and you can do to us whatever seems good to you."

[11]The next day Saul separated his men into three divisions; during the last watch of the night they broke into the camp of the Ammonites and slaughtered them until the heat of the day. Those who survived were scattered, so that no two of them were left together.

■ Saul Confirmed as King

[12]The people then said to Samuel, "Who was it that asked, 'Shall Saul reign over us?' Bring these men to us and we will put them to death."

[13]But Saul said, "No-one shall be put to death today, for this day the LORD has rescued Israel."

[14]Then Samuel said to the people, "Come, let us go to Gilgal and there reaffirm the kingship." [15]So all the people went to Gilgal and confirmed Saul as king in the presence of the LORD. There they sacrificed fellowship offerings[a] before the LORD, and Saul and all the Israelites held a great celebration.

■ Samuel's Farewell Speech

12 Samuel said to all Israel, "I have listened to everything you said to me and have set a king over you. [2]Now you have a king as your leader. As for me, I am old and grey, and my sons are here with you. I have been your leader from my youth until this day. [3]Here I stand. Testify against me in the presence of the LORD and his anointed. Whose ox have I taken? Whose donkey have I taken? Whom have I cheated? Whom have I oppressed? From whose hand have I accepted a bribe to make me shut my eyes? If I have done any of these, I will make it right."

[4]"You have not cheated or oppressed us," they replied. "You have not taken anything from anyone's hand."

12:4 ■ ACCUSE ME!
Unlike some political and religious leaders who get caught in financial scandals, Samuel considered himself publicly accountable. He began his farewell speech by offering an opportunity for anyone to stand up and testify that he, Samuel, had been dishonest or had taken advantage of his leadership position. Before going on, he asked those present to witness aloud to his honesty.

[5]Samuel said to them, "The LORD is witness against you, and also his anointed is witness this day, that you have not found anything in my hand."

"He is witness," they said.

[6]Then Samuel said to the people, "It is the LORD who appointed Moses and Aaron and brought your forefathers up out of Egypt. [7]Now then, stand here, because I am going to confront you with evidence before the LORD as to all the righteous acts performed by the LORD for you and your fathers.

[8]"After Jacob entered Egypt, they cried to the LORD for help, and the LORD sent Moses and Aaron, who brought your forefathers out of Egypt and settled them in this place.

[9]"But they forgot the LORD their God; so he sold them into the hands of Sisera, the commander of the army of Hazor, and into the hands of the Philistines and the king of Moab, who fought against them. [10]They cried out to the LORD and said, 'We have sinned; we have forsaken the LORD and served the Baals and the Ashtoreths. But now deliver us from the hands of our enemies, and we will serve you.' [11]Then the LORD sent Jerub-Baal,[a] Barak,[b] Jephthah and Samuel,[c] and he delivered you from the hands of your enemies on every side, so that you lived securely.

[12]"But when you saw that Nahash king of the Ammonites was moving against you, you said to me, 'No, we want a king to rule over us' — even though the LORD your God was your king. [13]Now here is the king you have chosen, the one you asked for; see, the LORD has set a king over you. [14]If you fear the LORD and serve and obey him and do not rebel against his commands, and if both you and the king who reigns over you follow the LORD your God — good! [15]But if you do not obey the LORD, and if you rebel against his commands, his hand will be against you, as it was against your fathers.

[16]"Now then, stand still and see this great thing the LORD is about to do before your eyes! [17]Is it not wheat harvest now? I will call upon the LORD to send thunder and rain. And you will realise what an evil thing you did in the eyes of the LORD when you asked for a king."

[18]Then Samuel called upon the LORD, and that same day the LORD sent thunder and rain. So all the people stood in awe of the LORD and of Samuel.

[19]The people all said to Samuel, "Pray to the LORD your God for your servants so that we will not die, for we have added to all our other sins the evil of asking for a king."

[20]"Do not be afraid," Samuel replied. "You have done all this evil; yet do not turn away from the LORD, but serve the LORD with all your heart. [21]Do not turn away after useless idols. They can do you no good, nor can they rescue you, because they are useless. [22]For the sake of his great name the LORD will not reject his people, because the LORD was pleased to make you his own. [23]As for me, far be it from me that I should sin against the LORD by failing to pray for you. And I will teach you the way that is good and right. [24]But be sure to fear the LORD and serve him faithfully with all your heart; consider what great things he has done for you. [25]Yet if you persist in doing evil, both you and your king will be swept away."

■ Samuel Rebukes Saul

13 Saul was ˻thirty˼[a] years old when he became king, and he reigned over Israel for ˻forty-˼[b] two years.

[2]Saul[c] chose three thousand men from Israel; two thousand were with him at Michmash and in the hill country of Bethel, and a thousand were with

---

[a]15 Traditionally *peace offerings*   [a]11 Also called *Gideon*   [b]11 Some Septuagint manuscripts and Syriac; Hebrew *Bedan*   [c]11 Hebrew; some Septuagint manuscripts and Syriac *Samson*   [a]1 A few late manuscripts of the Septuagint; Hebrew does not have *thirty*.   [b]1 See the round number in Acts 13:21; Hebrew does not have *forty-*.   [c]1,2 Or *and when he had reigned over Israel for two years*, [2]he

THE FIRST KING
EVERY OTHER NATION HAD ONE – WHY NOT ISRAEL?

INSIGHT

IF BOTH YOU AND THE KING WHO REIGNS OVER YOU FOLLOW THE LORD YOUR GOD – GOOD! BUT IF YOU DO NOT OBEY THE LORD, . . . HIS HAND WILL BE AGAINST YOU. ■ 12:14–15

Making a single nation out of a dozen tribes was not easy. Unity came hard for Israel; it also came hard for the United States. U.S. history may shed light on 1 Samuel's story.

Most people think that George Washington was the first President of the United States, but that honour actually belongs to Samuel Huntington. He never achieved fame because the states he presided over weren't united. They had no Constitution, only Articles of Confederation that made them 13 independent nations loosely linked together.

■ CONGRESS UNDER SIEGE
Two years after Huntington took office, on 21 June 1783, 500 unpaid federal soldiers laid siege to Congress in Philadelphia, breaking windows and shouting threats because Congress, which was supposed to pay them, had no money. The jealously independent states had given them none. Driven out of town by the soldiers, Congress became nomadic, meeting in Princeton, Annapolis, Trenton and New York City. That same June, George Washington wrote, "It is yet to be decided whether the Revolution must ultimately be considered a blessing or a curse."

Troubles continued. In Shays' Rebellion, 1,500 hostile farmers surrounded courtrooms, refusing to let courts meet. The army should have quickly dispersed them, but the national army consisted of only 700 men. Shays' Rebellion made obvious the need for a stronger central government. The next year a constitutional convention met in Philadelphia to work out the document that still unifies Americans. Washington was elected President.

■ WHY ISRAEL NEEDED A KING
The 12 tribes of Israel, like the 13 states, were a nation in name only. They had no central government at all. Since conquering Palestine, they had worked together only during emergencies, when inspired "judges" – military heroes like Gideon, Deborah, and Samson – came forward to lead them into battle.

In Samuel's time, though, the Philistines' military threat wouldn't go away. Israel needed superior leadership, but Samuel was an old man. His sons made unappealing successors. What could be done? Looking around them, the tribes noticed that virtually every other country had a king. A king offered two advantages: first, he provided central government; second, since his sons would normally succeed a king, the nation did not have a crisis of leadership every time its leader got old. So the leaders of Israel asked Samuel to appoint a king (8:4–5).

■ AGAINST GOD'S WILL
The idea seems to have been popular with everyone except Samuel and God. Samuel may have been displeased that he and his sons were being rejected. God had a deeper objection: Israel was rejecting his leadership. God told Samuel to warn the elders that a king would oppress his own citizens. Samuel warned of conscription, of high taxation, of the king's power to make people into slaves (8:10–18).

Was God against a king? Some scholars see the monarchy as a marvellous example of God's using a choice made against his will. God counselled Israel against the very institution that ultimately produced King David, and through him Jesus, King of kings.

Others suggest that God only opposed the motive behind the request. (Deuteronomy 17:14–20 had assumed that the Israelites would eventually want and get a king.) The key is the phrase the elders used: "Then we will be like all the other nations" (8:20). God did not want them to be like all the other nations.

■ THE KING WAS A SERVANT
Yet God gave in to their request, bad motives and all. He not only allowed the Israelites a king, he picked out their man. He accepted the monarchy on condition that Israel still consider the Lord as its ultimate ruler (12:14).

Apparently, Israel's king didn't answer to a parliament or court system, but he did answer to God. In short, the first king, Saul, was rejected because he disobeyed God. God rebuked and punished his replacement, David. Most nations' kings held absolute power. In Israel only God was absolute, and the king was his servant.

□ LIFE QUESTIONS:
Have you ever seen God take a bad request made with bad motives and use it for his own purposes?

Jonathan at Gibeah in Benjamin. The rest of the men he sent back to their homes.

3Jonathan attacked the Philistine outpost at Geba, and the Philistines heard about it. Then Saul had the trumpet blown throughout the land and said, "Let the Hebrews hear!" 4So all Israel heard the news: "Saul has attacked the Philistine outpost, and now Israel has become an offence to the Philistines." And the people were summoned to join Saul at Gilgal.

5The Philistines assembled to fight Israel, with three thousand*d* chariots, six thousand charioteers, and soldiers as numerous as the sand on the seashore. They went up and camped at Michmash, east of Beth Aven. 6When the men of Israel saw that their situation was critical and that their army was hard pressed, they hid in caves and thickets, among the rocks, and in pits and cisterns. 7Some Hebrews even crossed the Jordan to the land of Gad and Gilead.

Saul remained at Gilgal, and all the troops with him were quaking with fear. 8He waited for seven days, the time set by Samuel; but Samuel did not come to Gilgal, and Saul's men began to scatter. 9So he said, "Bring me the burnt offering and the fellowship offerings."*e* And Saul offered up the burnt offering. 10Just as he finished making the offering, Samuel arrived, and Saul went out to greet him.

11"What have you done?" asked Samuel.

Saul replied, "When I saw that the men were scattering, and that you did not come at the set time, and that the Philistines were assembling at Michmash, 12I thought, 'Now the Philistines will come down against me at Gilgal, and I have not sought the LORD's favour.' So I felt compelled to offer the burnt offering."

13"You acted foolishly," Samuel said. "You have not kept the command the LORD your God gave you; if you had, he would have established your kingdom over Israel for all time. 14But now your kingdom will not endure; the LORD has sought out a man after his own heart and appointed him leader of his people, because you have not kept the LORD's command."

15Then Samuel left Gilgal*f* and went up to Gibeah in Benjamin, and Saul counted the men who were with him. They numbered about six hundred.

■ Israel Without Weapons

16Saul and his son Jonathan and the men with them were staying in Gibeah*g* of Benjamin, while the Philistines camped at Michmash. 17Raiding parties went out from the Philistine camp in three detachments. One turned towards Ophrah in the vicinity of Shual, 18another towards Beth Horon, and the third towards the borderland overlooking the Valley of Zeboim facing the desert.

19Not a blacksmith could be found in the whole land of Israel, because the Philistines had said, "Otherwise the Hebrews will make swords or spears!" 20So all Israel went down to the Philistines to have their ploughshares, mattocks, axes and sickles*b* sharpened. 21The price was two thirds of a shekel*i* for sharpening ploughshares and mattocks, and a third of a shekel*j* for sharpening forks and axes and for repointing goads.

22So on the day of the battle not a soldier with Saul and Jonathan had a sword or spear in his hand; only Saul and his son Jonathan had them.

13:19 ■ MILITARY DOMINANCE
Samuel's leadership had kept the Philistines from occupying Israel (see 7:13). However, nobody could question the Philistines' military dominance. They had outposts in several central Israelite towns (10:5; 13:3) and, most important, kept a monopoly on iron weapons by outlawing local blacksmiths. Only the royal family of Israel possessed a sword or a spear (verse 22), presumably weapons that had been smuggled in and hidden.

■ Jonathan Attacks the Philistines

23Now a detachment of Philistines had gone out to the pass at Michmash. **14** 1One day Jonathan son of Saul said to the young man bearing his armour, "Come, let's go over to the Philistine outpost on the other side." But he did not tell his father.

2Saul was staying on the outskirts of Gibeah under a pomegranate tree in Migron. With him were about six hundred men, 3among whom was Ahijah, who was wearing an ephod. He was a son of Ichabod's brother Ahitub son of Phinehas, the son of Eli, the LORD's priest in Shiloh. No-one was aware that Jonathan had left.

4On each side of the pass that Jonathan intended to cross to reach the Philistine outpost was a cliff; one was called Bozez, and the other Seneh. 5One cliff stood to the north towards Michmash, the other to the south towards Geba.

6Jonathan said to his young armour-bearer, "Come, let's go over to the outpost of those uncircumcised fellows. Perhaps the LORD will act on our behalf. Nothing can hinder the LORD from saving, whether by many or by few."

7"Do all that you have in mind," his armour-bearer said. "Go ahead; I am with you heart and soul."

8Jonathan said, "Come, then; we will cross over towards the men and let them see us. 9If they say to us, 'Wait there until we come to you,' we will stay where we are and not go up to them. 10But if they say, 'Come up to us,' we will climb up, because that will be our sign that the LORD has given them into our hands."

11So both of them showed themselves to the Philistine outpost. "Look!" said the Philistines. "The Hebrews are crawling out of the holes they were hiding in." 12The men of the outpost shouted to Jonathan and his armour-bearer, "Come up to us and we'll teach you a lesson."

So Jonathan said to his armour-bearer, "Climb up after me; the LORD has given them into the hand of Israel."

13Jonathan climbed up, using his hands and feet, with his armour-bearer right behind him. The Philistines fell before Jonathan, and his armour-bearer followed and killed behind him. 14In that first attack

---

d 5 Some Septuagint manuscripts and Syriac; Hebrew *thirty thousand*   *e* 9 Traditionally *peace offerings*   *f* 15 Hebrew; Septuagint *Gilgal and went his way; the rest of the people went after Saul to meet the army, and they went out of Gilgal*   *g* 16 Two Hebrew manuscripts; most Hebrew manuscripts *Geba,* a variant of *Gibeah*   *b* 20 Septuagint; Hebrew *ploughshares*   *i* 21 Hebrew *pim*; that is, about ¼ ounce (about 8 grams)   *j* 21 That is, about ⅛ ounce (about 4 grams)

Jonathan and his armour-bearer killed some twenty men in an area of about half an acre.*a*

■ Israel Routs the Philistines

15Then panic struck the whole army—those in the camp and field, and those in the outposts and raiding parties—and the ground shook. It was a panic sent by God.*b*
16Saul's lookouts at Gibeah in Benjamin saw the army melting away in all directions. 17Then Saul said to the men who were with him, "Muster the forces and see who has left us." When they did, it was Jonathan and his armour-bearer who were not there.
18Saul said to Ahijah, "Bring the ark of God." (At that time it was with the Israelites.)*c* 19While Saul was talking to the priest, the tumult in the Philistine camp increased more and more. So Saul said to the priest, "Withdraw your hand."
20Then Saul and all his men assembled and went to the battle. They found the Philistines in total confusion, striking each other with their swords. 21Those Hebrews who had previously been with the Philistines and had gone up with them to their camp went over to the Israelites who were with Saul and Jonathan. 22When all the Israelites who had hidden in the hill country of Ephraim heard that the Philistines were on the run, they joined the battle in hot pursuit. 23So the LORD rescued Israel that day, and the battle moved on beyond Beth Aven.

■ Jonathan Eats Honey

24Now the men of Israel were in distress that day, because Saul had bound the people under an oath, saying, "Cursed be any man who eats food before evening comes, before I have avenged myself on my enemies!" So none of the troops tasted food.

14:24 ■ INFLATED EGO
Saul's problems surface here in two ways. First, he impulsively pronounced a curse (a very solemn vow) without thinking it through. This rash vow made his hungry army less effective, and led to trouble for his own son. Second, Saul apparently saw the battle as a personal vendetta in which *he* was avenging himself on *his* enemies. A wiser leader would have understood that God's honour and the security of his people were the issues.

25The entire army*d* entered the woods, and there was honey on the ground. 26When they went into the woods, they saw the honey oozing out, yet no-one put his hand to his mouth, because they feared the oath. 27But Jonathan had not heard that his father had bound the people with the oath, so he reached out the end of the staff that was in his hand and dipped it into the honeycomb. He raised his hand to his mouth, and his eyes brightened.*e* 28Then one of the soldiers told him, "Your father bound the army under a strict oath, saying, 'Cursed be any man who eats food today!' That is why the men are faint."
29Jonathan said, "My father has made trouble for the country. See how my eyes brightened*f* when I tasted a little of this honey. 30How much better it would have been if the men had eaten today some of the plunder they took from their enemies. Would not the slaughter of the Philistines have been even greater?"
31That day, after the Israelites had struck down the Philistines from Michmash to Aijalon, they were exhausted. 32They pounced on the plunder and, taking sheep, cattle and calves, they butchered them on the ground and ate them, together with the blood. 33Then someone said to Saul, "Look, the men are sinning against the LORD by eating meat that has blood in it."
"You have broken faith," he said. "Roll a large stone over here at once." 34Then he said, "Go out among the men and tell them, 'Each of you bring me your cattle and sheep, and slaughter them here and eat them. Do not sin against the LORD by eating meat with blood still in it.' "
So everyone brought his ox that night and slaughtered it there. 35Then Saul built an altar to the LORD; it was the first time he had done this.
36Saul said, "Let us go down after the Philistines by night and plunder them till dawn, and let us not leave one of them alive."
"Do whatever seems best to you," they replied.
But the priest said, "Let us enquire of God here."
37So Saul asked God, "Shall I go down after the Philistines? Will you give them into Israel's hand?" But God did not answer him that day.
38Saul therefore said, "Come here, all you who are leaders of the army, and let us find out what sin has been committed today. 39As surely as the LORD who rescues Israel lives, even if it lies with my son Jonathan, he must die." But not one of the men said a word.
40Saul then said to all the Israelites, "You stand over there; I and Jonathan my son will stand over here."
"Do what seems best to you," the men replied.
41Then Saul prayed to the LORD, the God of Israel, "Give me the right answer."*g* And Jonathan and Saul were taken by lot, and the men were cleared. 42Saul said, "Cast the lot between me and Jonathan my son." And Jonathan was taken.
43Then Saul said to Jonathan, "Tell me what you have done."
So Jonathan told him, "I merely tasted a little honey with the end of my staff. And now must I die?"
44Saul said, "May God deal with me, be it ever so severely, if you do not die, Jonathan."
45But the men said to Saul, "Should Jonathan die—he who has brought about this great deliverance in Israel? Never! As surely as the LORD lives, not a hair of his head shall fall to the ground, for he did this today with God's help." So the men rescued Jonathan, and he was not put to death.
46Then Saul stopped pursuing the Philistines, and they withdrew to their own land.
47After Saul had assumed rule over Israel, he fought against their enemies on every side: Moab, the Ammonites, Edom, the kings*b* of Zobah, and the

---

*a*14 Hebrew *half a yoke;* a "yoke" was the land ploughed by a yoke of oxen in one day.   *b*15 Or *a terrible panic*   *c*18 Hebrew; Septuagint *"Bring the ephod." (At that time he wore the ephod before the Israelites.)*   *d*25 Or *Now all the people of the land*   *e*27 Or *his strength was renewed*   *f*29 Or *my strength was renewed*   *g*41 Hebrew; Septuagint *"Why have you not answered your servant today? If the fault is in me or my son Jonathan, respond with Urim, but if the men of Israel are at fault, respond with Thummim."*   *b*47 Masoretic Text; Dead Sea Scrolls and Septuagint *king*

Philistines. Wherever he turned, he inflicted punishment on them.[i] [48]He fought valiantly and defeated the Amalekites, delivering Israel from the hands of those who had plundered them.

■ Saul's Family

[49]Saul's sons were Jonathan, Ishvi and Malki-Shua. The name of his older daughter was Merab, and that of the younger was Michal. [50]His wife's name was Ahinoam daughter of Ahimaaz. The name of the commander of Saul's army was Abner son of Ner, and Ner was Saul's uncle. [51]Saul's father Kish and Abner's father Ner were sons of Abiel.

[52]All the days of Saul there was bitter war with the Philistines, and whenever Saul saw a mighty or brave man, he took him into his service.

■ The LORD Rejects Saul as King

15 Samuel said to Saul, "I am the one the LORD sent to anoint you king over his people Israel; so listen now to the message from the LORD. [2]This is what the LORD Almighty says: 'I will punish the Amalekites for what they did to Israel when they waylaid them as they came up from Egypt. [3]Now go, attack the Amalekites and totally destroy[a] everything that belongs to them. Do not spare them; put to death men and women, children and infants, cattle and sheep, camels and donkeys.' "

> ### 15:2 ■ OLD ENEMIES
> The Israelites had first encountered the Amalekites, a semi-nomadic group of pitiless raiders, on their way out of Egypt. Due to the Amalekites' unprovoked attack, Moses had declared that God wanted Amalek wiped out (Exodus 17:8–16; Deuteronomy 25:17–19). The hostility continued. Typically, the Amalekites would sweep into unprotected towns and villages on the edge of the southern desert, killing and looting, leaving the survivors without food. Though Samuel's order to Saul is hard to understand, knowing the Amalekites' reputation makes it easier to sympathise with. For a more general explanation of holy war, see "Is a War Ever Holy?" page 192.

[4]So Saul summoned the men and mustered them at Telaim — two hundred thousand foot soldiers and ten thousand men from Judah. [5]Saul went to the city of Amalek and set an ambush in the ravine. [6]Then he said to the Kenites, "Go away, leave the Amalekites so that I do not destroy you along with them; for you showed kindness to all the Israelites when they came up out of Egypt." So the Kenites moved away from the Amalekites.

[7]Then Saul attacked the Amalekites all the way from Havilah to Shur, to the east of Egypt. [8]He took Agag king of the Amalekites alive, and all his people he totally destroyed with the sword. [9]But Saul and the army spared Agag and the best of the sheep and cattle, the fat calves[b] and lambs — everything that was good. These they were unwilling to destroy completely, but everything that was despised and weak they totally destroyed.

[10]Then the word of the LORD came to Samuel: [11]"I am grieved that I have made Saul king, because he has turned away from me and has not carried out my instructions." Samuel was troubled, and he cried out to the LORD all that night.

[12]Early in the morning Samuel got up and went to meet Saul, but he was told, "Saul has gone to Carmel. There he has set up a monument in his own honour and has turned and gone on down to Gilgal."

[13]When Samuel reached him, Saul said, "The LORD bless you! I have carried out the LORD's instructions."

[14]But Samuel said, "What then is this bleating of sheep in my ears? What is this lowing of cattle that I hear?"

[15]Saul answered, "The soldiers brought them from the Amalekites; they spared the best of the sheep and cattle to sacrifice to the LORD your God, but we totally destroyed the rest."

[16]"Stop!" Samuel said to Saul. "Let me tell you what the LORD said to me last night."

"Tell me," Saul replied.

[17]Samuel said, "Although you were once small in your own eyes, did you not become the head of the tribes of Israel? The LORD anointed you king over Israel. [18]And he sent you on a mission, saying, 'Go and completely destroy those wicked people, the Amalekites; make war on them until you have wiped them out.' [19]Why did you not obey the LORD? Why did you pounce on the plunder and do evil in the eyes of the LORD?"

[20]"But I did obey the LORD," Saul said. "I went on the mission the LORD assigned me. I completely destroyed the Amalekites and brought back Agag their king. [21]The soldiers took sheep and cattle from the plunder, the best of what was devoted to God, in order to sacrifice them to the LORD your God at Gilgal."

[22]But Samuel replied:

"Does the LORD delight in burnt offerings and sacrifices
    as much as in obeying the voice of the LORD?
To obey is better than sacrifice,
    and to heed is better than the fat of rams.
[23]For rebellion is like the sin of divination,
    and arrogance like the evil of idolatry.
Because you have rejected the word of the LORD,
    he has rejected you as king."

[24]Then Saul said to Samuel, "I have sinned. I violated the LORD's command and your instructions. I was afraid of the people and so I gave in to them. [25]Now I beg you, forgive my sin and come back with me, so that I may worship the LORD."

[26]But Samuel said to him, "I will not go back with you. You have rejected the word of the LORD, and the LORD has rejected you as king over Israel!"

[27]As Samuel turned to leave, Saul caught hold of the hem of his robe, and it tore. [28]Samuel said to him, "The LORD has torn the kingdom of Israel from you today and has given it to one of your neighbours — to one better than you. [29]He who is the Glory of

i 47 Hebrew; Septuagint *he was victorious* them; also in verses 8, 9, 15, 18, 20 and 21.   a 3 The Hebrew term refers to the irrevocable giving of things or persons to the LORD, often by totally destroying   b 9 Or *the grown bulls*; the meaning of the Hebrew for this phrase is uncertain.

Israel does not lie or change his mind; for he is not a man, that he should change his mind."

30Saul replied, "I have sinned. But please honour me before the elders of my people and before Israel; come back with me, so that I may worship the LORD your God." 31So Samuel went back with Saul, and Saul worshipped the LORD.

32Then Samuel said, "Bring me Agag king of the Amalekites."

Agag came to him confidently,c thinking, "Surely the bitterness of death is past."

33But Samuel said,

"As your sword has made women childless,
    so will your mother be childless among
    women."

And Samuel put Agag to death before the LORD at Gilgal.

WHY SAUL WAS REJECTED
A LEADER WHO FAILED UNDER PRESSURE

INSIGHT

"BECAUSE YOU HAVE REJECTED THE WORD OF THE LORD, HE HAS REJECTED YOU AS KING." ■ 15:23

Saul had everything going for him. Tall and handsome, he struck people with his appearance. God chose him as the first king in the history of Israel. Soon after he was secretly anointed, God's Spirit came on him – an encounter with God that affected his entire personality.

Almost immediately Saul led a successful rescue operation, saving the people of a besieged city from mutilation. He was then publicly crowned king, even though he himself didn't campaign for the office. (In fact, he hid during the selection.) He wisely refrained from allowing his opponents to be punished. Instead, he united all 12 tribes behind him, even though he himself came from a small, minority tribe.

Saul chose the best young men to serve in his army. One of them, David, was not only a skilled general, but also a loyal follower who would never oppose Saul – even when he had good reason. David married Saul's daughter, and Saul's oldest son, Jonathan, became David's best friend. This should have cemented an alliance, sealing Saul's success.

■ DETERIORATION UNDER PRESSURE
Yet Saul's life went tragically wrong. The first sign of trouble, as 1 Samuel tells the story, came not long after he became king. While preparing for a campaign against the Philistines, Saul grew impatient. Samuel, scheduled to lead in the proper spiritual preparation for battle, was seven days late. Saul's men began to desert, and Saul decided he could wait no longer. He himself began to make the religious sacrifices that Samuel, as priest, was supposed to make. Just then Samuel arrived. He berated Saul (13:13–14). Saul's hastiness, insignificant though it may seem, showed an inner weakness: his willingness to compromise God's directions under pressure.

The battle came soon afterwards, and Israel won miraculously. But in the victory Saul acted sometimes indecisively, sometimes rashly.

He could not decide to attack. Then he made a boastful vow that disrupted the Israelite army, allowing the Philistines to escape.

■ ATTEMPTED MURDER
Sometime later Saul compromised again in a high-pressure situation, not following the precise instructions God had given for a military campaign (15:3). Again, Samuel caught him in the act. This time he accused Saul of rebelling against God. Samuel's words must have rung in Saul's head the rest of his life: "Because you have rejected the word of the LORD, he has rejected you as king" (15:23).

Without God's and Samuel's support, Saul lost his sense of confidence. An evil spirit began to torment him. Instead of building an alliance with David, Saul drove David away, causing him to run for his life in the desert. Eventually fear reduced Saul to a quivering, helpless jellyfish, incapable of leadership. In that condition he and his army lost an historic battle to the Philistines, allowing them to regain control. In the battle, both Saul and Jonathan were killed.

■ WHY SAUL FAILED
The book of 1 Samuel doesn't psychoanalyse Saul; it merely reports what happened. The facts do point to a moral, though. Saul had begun with all the opportunity in the world. He only lacked, it seems, a strong compulsion to obey God no matter what. Under pressure he bent the rules. He lost God's backing. He grew fearful, rash, and jealous.

Saul's poor leadership left Israel worse off than at the beginning. The kingdom David inherited from Saul was again under Philistine military domination, and it was divided between north and south. Saul shows the unique tragedy of a poor leader. He fails not just himself. Inevitably he drags others down with him.

□ LIFE QUESTIONS:
When you are put in the role of leader, how do you respond to pressure? Are Saul's weaknesses your weaknesses?

c32 Or him trembling, yet

34Then Samuel left for Ramah, but Saul went up to his home in Gibeah of Saul. 35Until the day Samuel died, he did not go to see Saul again, though Samuel mourned for him. And the LORD was grieved that he had made Saul king over Israel.

Samuel Anoints David

16 The LORD said to Samuel, "How long will you mourn for Saul, since I have rejected him as king over Israel? Fill your horn with oil and be on your way; I am sending you to Jesse of Bethlehem. I have chosen one of his sons to be king."

2But Samuel said, "How can I go? Saul will hear about it and kill me."

The LORD said, "Take a heifer with you and say, 'I have come to sacrifice to the LORD.' 3Invite Jesse to the sacrifice, and I will show you what to do. You are to anoint for me the one I indicate."

4Samuel did what the LORD said. When he arrived at Bethlehem, the elders of the town trembled when they met him. They asked, "Do you come in peace?"

5Samuel replied, "Yes, in peace; I have come to sacrifice to the LORD. Consecrate yourselves and come to the sacrifice with me." Then he consecrated Jesse and his sons and invited them to the sacrifice.

6When they arrived, Samuel saw Eliab and thought, "Surely the LORD's anointed stands here before the LORD."

7But the LORD said to Samuel, "Do not consider his appearance or his height, for I have rejected him. The LORD does not look at the things man looks at. Man looks at the outward appearance, but the LORD looks at the heart."

16:7 ■ WHAT GOD VALUES
What qualified David to be king? Apparently he did not make an overpowering first impression, but God valued hidden qualities far more. Throughout his life David would demonstrate that he loved and trusted God with all his heart, as the law in Deuteronomy 6:4–6 demanded.

8Then Jesse called Abinadab and made him pass in front of Samuel. But Samuel said, "The LORD has not chosen this one either." 9Jesse then made Shammah pass by, but Samuel said, "Nor has the LORD chosen this one." 10Jesse made seven of his sons pass before Samuel, but Samuel said to him, "The LORD has not chosen these." 11So he asked Jesse, "Are these all the sons you have?"

"There is still the youngest," Jesse answered, "but he is tending the sheep."

Samuel said, "Send for him; we will not sit downa until he arrives."

12So he sent and had him brought in. He was ruddy, with a fine appearance and handsome features.

Then the LORD said, "Rise and anoint him; he is the one."

13So Samuel took the horn of oil and anointed him in the presence of his brothers, and from that day on the Spirit of the LORD came upon David in power. Samuel then went to Ramah.

David in Saul's Service

14Now the Spirit of the LORD had departed from Saul, and an evilb spirit from the LORD tormented him.

15Saul's attendants said to him, "See, an evil spirit from God is tormenting you. 16Let our lord command his servants here to search for someone who can play the harp. He will play when the evil spirit from God comes upon you, and you will feel better."

17So Saul said to his attendants, "Find someone who plays well and bring him to me."

18One of the servants answered, "I have seen a son of Jesse of Bethlehem who knows how to play the harp. He is a brave man and a warrior. He speaks well and is a fine-looking man. And the LORD is with him."

19Then Saul sent messengers to Jesse and said, "Send me your son David, who is with the sheep." 20So Jesse took a donkey loaded with bread, a skin of wine and a young goat and sent them with his son David to Saul.

21David came to Saul and entered his service. Saul liked him very much, and David became one of his armour-bearers. 22Then Saul sent word to Jesse, saying, "Allow David to remain in my service, for I am pleased with him."

23Whenever the spirit from God came upon Saul, David would take his harp and play. Then relief would come to Saul; he would feel better, and the evil spirit would leave him.

David and Goliath

17 Now the Philistines gathered their forces for war and assembled at Socoh in Judah. They pitched camp at Ephes Dammim, between Socoh and Azekah. 2Saul and the Israelites assembled and camped in the Valley of Elah and drew up their battle line to meet the Philistines. 3The Philistines occupied one hill and the Israelites another, with the valley between them.

17:4 ■ EVERYONE WATCHED GOLIATH
Wars in ancient times were sometimes decided by "representative combat": champions from each side would fight, and the results of their combat would determine the battle's result. People believed the outcome of the fight was controlled by the warriors' gods more than by the two sides' military strength.

Saul lacked confidence in God's support. His terror demoralised the Israelite army. David, by contrast, was as confident in his God as Goliath was scornful of God's people.

4A champion named Goliath, who was from Gath, came out of the Philistine camp. He was over nine feeta tall. 5He had a bronze helmet on his head and wore a coat of scale armour of bronze weighing five thousand shekels;b 6on his legs he wore bronze greaves, and a bronze javelin was slung on his back. 7His spear shaft was like a weaver's rod, and its iron point weighed six hundred shekels.c His shield-bearer went ahead of him.

8Goliath stood and shouted to the ranks of Israel,

---

a 11 Some Septuagint manuscripts; Hebrew not gather round   b 14 Or injurious; also in verses 15, 16 and 23   a 4 Hebrew was six cubits and a span
(about 3 metres)   b 5 That is, about 125 pounds (about 57 kilograms)   c 7 That is, about 15 pounds (about 7 kilograms)

"Why do you come out and line up for battle? Am I not a Philistine, and are you not the servants of Saul? Choose a man and have him come down to me. [9]If he is able to fight and kill me, we will become your subjects; but if I overcome him and kill him, you will become our subjects and serve us." [10]Then the Philistine said, "This day I defy the ranks of Israel! Give me a man and let us fight each other." [11]On hearing the Philistine's words, Saul and all the Israelites were dismayed and terrified.

[12]Now David was the son of an Ephrathite named Jesse, who was from Bethlehem in Judah. Jesse had eight sons, and in Saul's time he was old and well advanced in years. [13]Jesse's three oldest sons had followed Saul to the war: The firstborn was Eliab; the second, Abinadab; and the third, Shammah. [14]David was the youngest. The three oldest followed Saul, [15]but David went back and forth from Saul to tend his father's sheep at Bethlehem.

[16]For forty days the Philistine came forward every morning and evening and took his stand.

[17]Now Jesse said to his son David, "Take this ephah[d] of roasted grain and these ten loaves of bread for your brothers and hurry to their camp. [18]Take along these ten cheeses to the commander of their unit.[e] See how your brothers are and bring back some assurance[f] from them. [19]They are with Saul and all the men of Israel in the Valley of Elah, fighting against the Philistines."

[20]Early in the morning David left the flock with a shepherd, loaded up and set out, as Jesse had directed. He reached the camp as the army was going out to its battle positions, shouting the war cry. [21]Israel and the Philistines were drawing up their lines facing each other. [22]David left his things with the keeper of supplies, ran to the battle lines and greeted his brothers. [23]As he was talking with them, Goliath, the Philistine champion from Gath, stepped out from his lines and shouted his usual defiance, and David heard it. [24]When the Israelites saw the man, they all ran from him in great fear.

[25]Now the Israelites had been saying, "Do you see how this man keeps coming out? He comes out to defy Israel. The king will give great wealth to the man who kills him. He will also give him his daughter in marriage and will exempt his father's family from taxes in Israel."

[26]David asked the men standing near him, "What will be done for the man who kills this Philistine and removes this disgrace from Israel? Who is this uncircumcised Philistine that he should defy the armies of the living God?"

[27]They repeated to him what they had been saying and told him, "This is what will be done for the man who kills him."

[28]When Eliab, David's oldest brother, heard him speaking with the men, he burned with anger at him and asked, "Why have you come down here? And with whom did you leave those few sheep in the desert? I know how conceited you are and how wicked your heart is; you came down only to watch the battle."

[29]"Now what have I done?" said David. "Can't I even speak?" [30]He then turned away to someone else and brought up the same matter, and the men

answered him as before. [31]What David said was overheard and reported to Saul, and Saul sent for him.

[32]David said to Saul, "Let no-one lose heart on account of this Philistine; your servant will go and fight him."

[33]Saul replied, "You are not able to go out against this Philistine and fight him; you are only a boy, and he has been a fighting man from his youth."

[34]But David said to Saul, "Your servant has been keeping his father's sheep. When a lion or a bear came and carried off a sheep from the flock, [35]I went after it, struck it and rescued the sheep from its mouth. When it turned on me, I seized it by its hair, struck it and killed it. [36]Your servant has killed both the lion and the bear; this uncircumcised Philistine will be like one of them, because he has defied the armies of the living God. [37]The LORD who delivered me from the paw of the lion and the paw of the bear will deliver me from the hand of this Philistine."

Saul said to David, "Go, and the LORD be with you."

[38]Then Saul dressed David in his own tunic. He put a coat of armour on him and a bronze helmet on his head. [39]David fastened on his sword over the tunic and tried walking around, because he was not used to them.

"I cannot go in these," he said to Saul, "because I am not used to them." So he took them off. [40]Then he took his staff in his hand, chose five smooth stones from the stream, put them in the pouch of his shepherd's bag and, with his sling in his hand, approached the Philistine.

17:40 ■ DEADLY ROCKS

The "five smooth stones" that David took from the stream were each probably bigger than a cricket ball. Someone skilled with a sling could hurl them at close to 100 miles per hour.

[41]Meanwhile, the Philistine, with his shield-bearer in front of him, kept coming closer to David. [42]He looked David over and saw that he was only a boy, ruddy and handsome, and he despised him. [43]He said to David, "Am I a dog, that you come at me with sticks?" And the Philistine cursed David by his gods. [44]"Come here," he said, "and I'll give your flesh to the birds of the air and the beasts of the field!"

[45]David said to the Philistine, "You come against me with sword and spear and javelin, but I come against you in the name of the LORD Almighty, the God of the armies of Israel, whom you have defied. [46]This day the LORD will hand you over to me, and I'll strike you down and cut off your head. Today I will give the carcasses of the Philistine army to the birds of the air and the beasts of the earth, and the whole world will know that there is a God in Israel. [47]All those gathered here will know that it is not by sword or spear that the LORD saves; for the battle is the LORD's, and he will give all of you into our hands."

[48]As the Philistine moved closer to attack him, David ran quickly towards the battle line to meet him. [49]Reaching into his bag and taking out a stone,

d 17 That is, probably about ⅗ bushel (about 22 litres)   e 18 Hebrew thousand   f 18 Or some token; or some pledge of spoils he slung it and struck the Philistine on the forehead. The stone sank into his forehead, and he fell face down on the ground.

50So David triumphed over the Philistine with a sling and a stone; without a sword in his hand he struck down the Philistine and killed him.

51David ran and stood over him. He took hold of the Philistine's sword and drew it from the scabbard. After he killed him, he cut off his head with the sword.

When the Philistines saw that their hero was dead, they turned and ran. 52Then the men of Israel and Judah surged forward with a shout and pursued the Philistines to the entrance of Gath*g* and to the gates of Ekron. Their dead were strewn along the Shaaraim road to Gath and Ekron. 53When the Israelites returned from chasing the Philistines, they plundered their camp. 54David took the Philistine's head and brought it to Jerusalem, and he put the Philistine's weapons in his own tent.

55As Saul watched David going out to meet the Philistine, he said to Abner, commander of the army, "Abner, whose son is that young man?"

Abner replied, "As surely as you live, O king, I don't know."

56The king said, "Find out whose son this young man is."

57As soon as David returned from killing the Philistine, Abner took him and brought him before Saul, with David still holding the Philistine's head.

58"Whose son are you, young man?" Saul asked him.

David said, "I am the son of your servant Jesse of Bethlehem."

■ Saul's Jealousy of David

18 After David had finished talking with Saul, Jonathan became one in spirit with David, and he loved him as himself. 2From that day Saul kept David with him and did not let him return to his father's house. 3And Jonathan made a covenant with David because he loved him as himself. 4Jonathan took off the robe he was wearing and gave it to David, along with his tunic, and even his sword, his bow and his belt.

5Whatever Saul sent him to do, David did it so successfully*a* that Saul gave him a high rank in the army. This pleased all the people, and Saul's officers as well.

6When the men were returning home after David had killed the Philistine, the women came out from all the towns of Israel to meet King Saul with singing and dancing, with joyful songs and with tambourines and lutes. 7As they danced, they sang:

"Saul has slain his thousands,
    and David his tens of thousands."

8Saul was very angry; this refrain galled him. "They have credited David with tens of thousands," he thought, "but me with only thousands. What more can he get but the kingdom?" 9And from that time on Saul kept a jealous eye on David.

10The next day an evil*b* spirit from God came forcefully upon Saul. He was prophesying in his house, while David was playing the harp, as he usually did. Saul had a spear in his hand 11and he hurled it, saying to himself, "I'll pin David to the wall." But David eluded him twice.

12Saul was afraid of David, because the LORD was with David but had left Saul. 13So he sent David away from him and gave him command over a thousand men, and David led the troops in their campaigns. 14In everything he did he had great success,*c* because the LORD was with him. 15When Saul saw how successful*d* he was, he was afraid of him. 16But all Israel and Judah loved David, because he led them in their campaigns.

17Saul said to David, "Here is my older daughter Merab. I will give her to you in marriage; only serve me bravely and fight the battles of the LORD." For Saul said to himself, "I will not raise a hand against him. Let the Philistines do that!"

18But David said to Saul, "Who am I, and what is my family or my father's clan in Israel, that I should become the king's son-in-law?" 19So*e* when the time came for Merab, Saul's daughter, to be given to David, she was given in marriage to Adriel of Meholah.

20Now Saul's daughter Michal was in love with David, and when they told Saul about it, he was pleased. 21"I will give her to him," he thought, "so that she may be a snare to him and so that the hand of the Philistines may be against him." So Saul said to David, "Now you have a second opportunity to become my son-in-law."

22Then Saul ordered his attendants: "Speak to David privately and say, 'Look, the king is pleased with you, and his attendants all like you; now become his son-in-law.'"

23They repeated these words to David. But David said, "Do you think it is a small matter to become the king's son-in-law? I'm only a poor man and little known."

24When Saul's servants told him what David had said, 25Saul replied, "Say to David, 'The king wants no other price for the bride than a hundred Philistine foreskins, to take revenge on his enemies.'" Saul's plan was to have David fall by the hands of the Philistines.

26When the attendants told David these things, he was pleased to become the king's son-in-law. So before the allotted time elapsed, 27David and his men went out and killed two hundred Philistines. He brought their foreskins and presented the full number to the king so that he might become the king's son-in-law. Then Saul gave him his daughter Michal in marriage.

18:27 ■ "SCALPS"
This bloody prize, something like the scalps that native Americans and white settlers collected in battles, proved that David's battle claims were not exaggerated. Foreskins would come from Philistines, since other tribes of the area, like Israel, practised circumcision.

28When Saul realised that the LORD was with David and that his daughter Michal loved David,

g52 Some Septuagint manuscripts; Hebrew *a valley*   *a5* Or *wisely*   *b10* Or *injurious*   *c14* Or *he was very wise*   *d15* Or *wise*
e19 Or *However,*

²⁹Saul became still more afraid of him, and he remained his enemy for the rest of his days.

³⁰The Philistine commanders continued to go out to battle, and as often as they did, David met with more success* than the rest of Saul's officers, and his name became well known.

■ Saul Tries to Kill David

19 Saul told his son Jonathan and all the attendants to kill David. But Jonathan was very fond of David ²and warned him, "My father Saul is looking for a chance to kill you. Be on your guard tomorrow morning; go into hiding and stay there. ³I will go out and stand with my father in the field where you are. I'll speak to him about you and will tell you what I find out."

⁴Jonathan spoke well of David to Saul his father and said to him, "Let not the king do wrong to his servant David; he has not wronged you, and what he has done has benefited you greatly. ⁵He took his life in his hands when he killed the Philistine. The LORD won a great victory for all Israel, and you saw it and were glad. Why then would you do wrong to an innocent man like David by killing him for no reason?"

⁶Saul listened to Jonathan and took this oath: "As surely as the LORD lives, David will not be put to death."

⁷So Jonathan called David and told him the whole conversation. He brought him to Saul, and David was with Saul as before.

⁸Once more war broke out, and David went out and fought the Philistines. He struck them with such force that they fled before him.

⁹But an evil* spirit from the LORD came upon Saul as he was sitting in his house with his spear in his hand. While David was playing the harp, ¹⁰Saul tried to pin him to the wall with his spear, but David eluded him as Saul drove the spear into the wall. That night David made good his escape.

¹¹Saul sent men to David's house to watch it and to kill him in the morning. But Michal, David's wife, warned him, "If you don't run for your life tonight, tomorrow you'll be killed." ¹²So Michal let David down through a window, and he fled and escaped. ¹³Then Michal took an idol* and laid it on the bed, covering it with a garment and putting some goats' hair at the head.

¹⁴When Saul sent the men to capture David, Michal said, "He is ill."

¹⁵Then Saul sent the men back to see David and told them, "Bring him up to me in his bed so that I may kill him." ¹⁶But when the men entered, there was the idol in the bed, and at the head was some goats' hair.

¹⁷Saul said to Michal, "Why did you deceive me like this and send my enemy away so that he escaped?"

Michal told him, "He said to me, 'Let me get away. Why should I kill you?' "

¹⁸When David had fled and made his escape, he went to Samuel at Ramah and told him all that Saul had done to him. Then he and Samuel went to Naioth and stayed there. ¹⁹Word came to Saul: "David is in Naioth at Ramah"; ²⁰so he sent men to capture him. But when they saw a group of prophets

prophesying, with Samuel standing there as their leader, the Spirit of God came upon Saul's men and they also prophesied. ²¹Saul was told about it, and he sent more men, and they prophesied too. Saul sent men a third time, and they also prophesied. ²²Finally, he himself left for Ramah and went to the great cistern at Secu. And he asked, "Where are Samuel and David?"

"Over in Naioth at Ramah," they said.

²³So Saul went to Naioth at Ramah. But the Spirit of God came even upon him, and he walked along prophesying until he came to Naioth. ²⁴He stripped off his robes and also prophesied in Samuel's presence. He lay that way all that day and night. This is why people say, "Is Saul also among the prophets?"

19:23 ■ OUT OF CONTROL
Prophets are usually pictured as sombre figures. First Samuel reveals a different side: prophecy accompanying ecstatic worship. Saul had met a musical band of such prophets soon after he was anointed king (10:5–11). Now that he was planning evil, however, meeting the Spirit of God made him utterly lose control.

■ David and Jonathan

20 Then David fled from Naioth at Ramah and went to Jonathan and asked, "What have I done? What is my crime? How have I wronged your father, that he is trying to take my life?"

²"Never!" Jonathan replied. "You are not going to die! Look, my father doesn't do anything, great or small, without confiding in me. Why should he hide this from me? It's not so!"

³But David took an oath and said, "Your father knows very well that I have found favour in your eyes, and he has said to himself, 'Jonathan must not know this or he will be grieved.' Yet as surely as the LORD lives and as you live, there is only a step between me and death."

⁴Jonathan said to David, "Whatever you want me to do, I'll do for you."

⁵So David said, "Look, tomorrow is the New Moon festival, and I am supposed to dine with the king; but let me go and hide in the field until the evening of the day after tomorrow. ⁶If your father misses me at all, tell him, 'David earnestly asked my permission to hurry to Bethlehem, his home town, because an annual sacrifice is being made there for his whole clan.' ⁷If he says, 'Very well,' then your servant is safe. But if he loses his temper, you can be sure that he is determined to harm me. ⁸As for you, show kindness to your servant, for you have brought him into a covenant with you before the LORD. If I am guilty, then kill me yourself! Why hand me over to your father?"

⁹"Never!" Jonathan said. "If I had the least inkling that my father was determined to harm you, wouldn't I tell you?"

¹⁰David asked, "Who will tell me if your father answers you harshly?"

¹¹"Come," Jonathan said, "let's go out into the field." So they went there together.

¹²Then Jonathan said to David: "By the LORD, the

God of Israel, I will surely sound out my father by this time the day after tomorrow! If he is favourably disposed towards you, will I not send you word and let you know? ¹³But if my father is inclined to harm you, may the LORD deal with me, be it ever so severely, if I do not let you know and send you away safely. May the LORD be with you as he has been with my father. ¹⁴But show me unfailing kindness like that of the LORD as long as I live, so that I may not be killed, ¹⁵and do not ever cut off your kindness from my family — not even when the LORD has cut off every one of David's enemies from the face of the earth."

¹⁶So Jonathan made a covenant with the house of David, saying, "May the LORD call David's enemies to account." ¹⁷And Jonathan made David reaffirm his oath out of love for him, because he loved him as he loved himself.

¹⁸Then Jonathan said to David: "Tomorrow is the New Moon festival. You will be missed, because your seat will be empty. ¹⁹The day after tomorrow, towards evening, go to the place where you hid when this trouble began, and wait by the stone Ezel. ²⁰I will shoot three arrows to the side of it, as though I were shooting at a target. ²¹Then I will send a boy and say, 'Go, find the arrows.' If I say to him, 'Look, the arrows are on this side of you; bring them here,' then come, because, as surely as the LORD lives, you are safe; there is no danger. ²²But if I say to the boy, 'Look, the arrows are beyond you,' then you must go, because the LORD has sent you away. ²³And about the matter you and I discussed — remember, the LORD is witness between you and me for ever."

²⁴So David hid in the field, and when the New Moon festival came, the king sat down to eat. ²⁵He sat in his customary place by the wall, opposite Jonathan,ᵃ and Abner sat next to Saul, but David's place was empty. ²⁶Saul said nothing that day, for he thought, "Something must have happened to David to make him ceremonially unclean — surely he is unclean." ²⁷But the next day, the second day of the month, David's place was empty again. Then Saul said to his son Jonathan, "Why hasn't the son of Jesse come to the meal, either yesterday or today?"

²⁸Jonathan answered, "David earnestly asked me for permission to go to Bethlehem. ²⁹He said, 'Let me go, because our family is observing a sacrifice in the town and my brother has ordered me to be there. If I have found favour in your eyes, let me go to see my brothers.' That is why he has not come to the king's table."

³⁰Saul's anger flared up at Jonathan and he said to him, "You son of a perverse and rebellious woman! Don't I know that you have sided with the son of Jesse to your own shame and to the shame of the mother who bore you? ³¹As long as the son of Jesse lives on this earth, neither you nor your kingdom will be established. Now send and bring him to me, for he must die!"

³²"Why should he be put to death? What has he done?" Jonathan asked his father. ³³But Saul hurled his spear at him to kill him. Then Jonathan knew that his father intended to kill David.

³⁴Jonathan got up from the table in fierce anger; on that second day of the month he did not eat, because he was grieved at his father's shameful treatment of David.

³⁵In the morning Jonathan went out to the field for his meeting with David. He had a small boy with him, ³⁶and he said to the boy, "Run and find the arrows I shoot." As the boy ran, he shot an arrow beyond him. ³⁷When the boy came to the place where Jonathan's arrow had fallen, Jonathan called out after him, "Isn't the arrow beyond you?" ³⁸Then he shouted, "Hurry! Go quickly! Don't stop!" The boy picked up the arrow and returned to his master. ³⁹(The boy knew nothing of all this; only Jonathan and David knew.) ⁴⁰Then Jonathan gave his weapons to the boy and said, "Go, carry them back to town."

⁴¹After the boy had gone, David got up from the south side ˻of the stone˼ and bowed down before Jonathan three times, with his face to the ground. Then they kissed each other and wept together — but David wept the most.

⁴²Jonathan said to David, "Go in peace, for we have sworn friendship with each other in the name of the LORD, saying, 'The LORD is witness between you and me, and between your descendants and my descendants for ever.' " Then David left, and Jonathan went back to the town.

■ David at Nob

21 David went to Nob, to Ahimelech the priest. Ahimelech trembled when he met him, and asked, "Why are you alone? Why is no-one with you?"

²David answered Ahimelech the priest, "The king charged me with a certain matter and said to me, 'No-one is to know anything about your mission and your instructions.' As for my men, I have told them to meet me at a certain place. ³Now then, what have you to hand? Give me five loaves of bread, or whatever you can find."

⁴But the priest answered David, "I don't have any ordinary bread to hand; however, there is some consecrated bread here — provided the men have kept themselves from women."

21:4 ■ DISOBEYING THE LAW
David was desperate when he reached Nob. He did not even have food. He lied about his situation. Then he ate consecrated bread that was supposed to be reserved for the priests. (A thousand years later Jesus raised the issue of the consecrated bread, suggesting that keeping the ritual laws mattered less than David's survival [Matthew 12:3–4].)
David later admitted that he had been wrong to go to Nob and endanger the priests. Saul, suspicious of their involvement, slaughtered them (22:17–18).

⁵David replied, "Indeed women have been kept from us, as usual wheneverᵃ I set out. The men's thingsᵇ are holy even on missions that are not holy.

ᵃ25 Septuagint; Hebrew *wall. Jonathan arose*   ᵃ5 Or *from us in the past few days since*   ᵇ5 Or *bodies*

How much more so today!" 6So the priest gave him the consecrated bread, since there was no bread there except the bread of the Presence that had been removed from before the LORD and replaced by hot bread on the day it was taken away.

7Now one of Saul's servants was there that day, detained before the LORD; he was Doeg the Edomite, Saul's head shepherd.

8David asked Ahimelech, "Don't you have a spear or sword here? I haven't brought my sword or any other weapon, because the king's business was urgent."

9The priest replied, "The sword of Goliath the Philistine, whom you killed in the Valley of Elah, is here; it is wrapped in a cloth behind the ephod. If you want it, take it; there is no sword here but that one."

David said, "There is none like it; give it to me."

■ David at Gath

10That day David fled from Saul and went to Achish king of Gath. 11But the servants of Achish said to him, "Isn't this David, the king of the land? Isn't he the one they sing about in their dances:

" 'Saul has slain his thousands,
    and David his tens of thousands'?"

12David took these words to heart and was very much afraid of Achish king of Gath. 13So he feigned insanity in their presence; and while he was in their hands he acted like a madman, making marks on the doors of the gate and letting saliva run down his beard.

14Achish said to his servants, "Look at the man! He is insane! Why bring him to me? 15Am I so short of madmen that you have to bring this fellow here to carry on like this in front of me? Must this man come into my house?"

■ David at Adullam and Mizpah

22 David left Gath and escaped to the cave of Adullam. When his brothers and his father's household heard about it, they went down to him there. 2All those who were in distress or in debt or discontented gathered round him, and he became their leader. About four hundred men were with him.

3From there David went to Mizpah in Moab and said to the king of Moab, "Would you let my father and mother come and stay with you until I learn what God will do for me?" 4So he left them with the king of Moab, and they stayed with him as long as David was in the stronghold.

5But the prophet Gad said to David, "Do not stay in the stronghold. Go into the land of Judah." So David left and went to the forest of Hereth.

■ Saul Kills the Priests of Nob

6Now Saul heard that David and his men had been discovered. And Saul, spear in hand, was seated under the tamarisk tree on the hill at Gibeah, with all his officials standing round him. 7Saul said to them, "Listen, men of Benjamin! Will the son of Jesse give all of you fields and vineyards? Will he make all of you commanders of thousands and commanders of hundreds? 8Is that why you have all conspired against me? No-one tells me when my son makes a covenant with the son of Jesse. None of you is concerned about me or tells me that my son has incited my servant to lie in wait for me, as he does today."

9But Doeg the Edomite, who was standing with Saul's officials, said, "I saw the son of Jesse come to Ahimelech son of Ahitub at Nob. 10Ahimelech enquired of the LORD for him; he also gave him provisions and the sword of Goliath the Philistine."

11Then the king sent for the priest Ahimelech son of Ahitub and his father's whole family, who were the priests at Nob, and they all came to the king. 12Saul said, "Listen now, son of Ahitub."

"Yes, my lord," he answered.

13Saul said to him, "Why have you conspired against me, you and the son of Jesse, giving him bread and a sword and enquiring of God for him, so that he has rebelled against me and lies in wait for me, as he does today?"

14Ahimelech answered the king, "Who of all your servants is as loyal as David, the king's son-in-law, captain of your bodyguard and highly respected in your household? 15Was that day the first time I enquired of God for him? Of course not! Let not the king accuse your servant or any of his father's family, for your servant knows nothing at all about this whole affair."

16But the king said, "You shall surely die, Ahimelech, you and your father's whole family."

17Then the king ordered the guards at his side: "Turn and kill the priests of the LORD, because they too have sided with David. They knew he was fleeing, yet they did not tell me."

But the king's officials were not willing to raise a hand to strike the priests of the LORD.

18The king then ordered Doeg, "You turn and strike down the priests." So Doeg the Edomite turned and struck them down. That day he killed eighty-five men who wore the linen ephod. 19He also put to the sword Nob, the town of the priests, with its men and women, its children and infants, and its cattle, donkeys and sheep.

20But Abiathar, son of Ahimelech son of Ahitub, escaped and fled to join David. 21He told David that Saul had killed the priests of the LORD. 22Then David said to Abiathar: "That day, when Doeg the Edomite was there, I knew he would be sure to tell Saul. I am responsible for the death of your father's whole family. 23Stay with me; don't be afraid; the man who is seeking your life is seeking mine also. You will be safe with me."

22:3 ■ LONG-LOST RELATIVES
Afraid that Saul would hold his family hostage, David took his parents to the neighbouring kingdom of Moab for safekeeping. Why Moab? Possibly because he had distant relatives there. His great-grandmother, Ruth, had come from Moab.

■ David Saves Keilah

23 When David was told, "Look, the Philistines are fighting against Keilah and are looting the threshing-floors," ²he enquired of the LORD, saying, "Shall I go and attack these Philistines?"

The LORD answered him, "Go, attack the Philistines and save Keilah."

22:20 ■ A TRAUMATIC CAREER

Abiathar was the sole survivor of Saul's slaughter of the priests – a foolish massacre that must have alienated a great many of Saul's potential supporters. The slaughter partly fulfilled God's prediction in 2:31–36 that Eli's family would suffer and be cut off from the high priest's office.

Having survived that day's trauma, Abiathar became a priest for David and his men (23:6,9; 30:7–8). When David became king, he named Abiathar one of two high priests. Later Abiathar, having backed a rebellious faction against Solomon, was dismissed and exiled. The prediction made in Eli's day came fully true (1 Kings 2:26–27).

---

³But David's men said to him, "Here in Judah we are afraid. How much more, then, if we go to Keilah against the Philistine forces!"

⁴Once again David enquired of the LORD, and the LORD answered him, "Go down to Keilah, for I am going to give the Philistines into your hand." ⁵So David and his men went to Keilah, fought the Philistines and carried off their livestock. He inflicted heavy losses on the Philistines and saved the people of Keilah. ⁶(Now Abiathar son of Ahimelech had brought the ephod down with him when he fled to David at Keilah.)

■ Saul Pursues David

⁷Saul was told that David had gone to Keilah, and he said, "God has handed him over to me, for David has imprisoned himself by entering a town with gates and bars." ⁸And Saul called up all his forces for battle, to go down to Keilah to besiege David and his men.

⁹When David learned that Saul was plotting against him, he said to Abiathar the priest, "Bring the ephod." ¹⁰David said, "O LORD, God of Israel, your servant has heard definitely that Saul plans to come to Keilah and destroy the town on account of me. ¹¹Will the citizens of Keilah surrender me to him? Will Saul come down, as your servant has heard? O LORD, God of Israel, tell your servant."

And the LORD said, "He will."

¹²Again David asked, "Will the citizens of Keilah surrender me and my men to Saul?"

And the LORD said, "They will."

¹³So David and his men, about six hundred in number, left Keilah and kept moving from place to place. When Saul was told that David had escaped from Keilah, he did not go there.

¹⁴David stayed in the desert strongholds and in the hills of the Desert of Ziph. Day after day Saul searched for him, but God did not give David into his hands.

¹⁵While David was at Horesh in the Desert of Ziph, he learned that Saul had come out to take his life. ¹⁶And Saul's son Jonathan went to David at Horesh and helped him to find strength in God. ¹⁷"Don't be afraid," he said. "My father Saul will not lay a hand on you. You shall be king over Israel, and I will be second to you. Even my father Saul knows this." ¹⁸The two of them made a covenant before the LORD. Then Jonathan went home, but David remained at Horesh.

23:16 ■ FINAL FAREWELL

This last, secret meeting between Jonathan and David reveals the essence of their friendship. They had grown to love each other despite Saul's (Jonathan's father's) hatred for David. Now, when David was desperate, Jonathan sought him out and "helped him find strength in God". Jonathan expected to become David's right-hand man when David became king, but Jonathan's death soon put an end to that dream (see 31:2).

---

¹⁹The Ziphites went up to Saul at Gibeah and said, "Is not David hiding among us in the strongholds at Horesh, on the hill of Hakilah, south of Jeshimon? ²⁰Now, O king, come down whenever it pleases you to do so, and we will be responsible for handing him over to the king."

²¹Saul replied, "The LORD bless you for your concern for me. ²²Go and make further preparation. Find out where David usually goes and who has seen him there. They tell me he is very crafty. ²³Find out about all the hiding-places he uses and come back to me with definite information.ᵃ Then I will go with you; if he is in the area, I will track him down among all the clans of Judah."

²⁴So they set out and went to Ziph ahead of Saul. Now David and his men were in the Desert of Maon, in the Arabah south of Jeshimon. ²⁵Saul and his men began the search, and when David was told about it, he went down to the rock and stayed in the Desert of Maon. When Saul heard this, he went into the Desert of Maon in pursuit of David.

²⁶Saul was going along one side of the mountain, and David and his men were on the other side, hurrying to get away from Saul. As Saul and his forces were closing in on David and his men to capture them, ²⁷a messenger came to Saul, saying, "Come quickly! The Philistines are raiding the land." ²⁸Then Saul broke off his pursuit of David and went to meet the Philistines. That is why they call this place Sela Hammahlekoth.ᵇ ²⁹And David went up from there and lived in the strongholds of En Gedi.

■ David Spares Saul's Life

24 After Saul returned from pursuing the Philistines, he was told, "David is in the Desert of En Gedi." ²So Saul took three thousand chosen men from all Israel and set out to look for David and his men near the Crags of the Wild Goats.

³He came to the sheep pens along the way; a cave

ᵃ 23 Or me at Nacon   ᵇ 28 Sela Hammahlekoth means rock of parting.

was there, and Saul went in to relieve himself. David and his men were far back in the cave. [4]The men said, "This is the day the LORD spoke of when he said[a] to you, 'I will give your enemy into your hands for you to deal with as you wish.' " Then David crept up unnoticed and cut off a corner of Saul's robe.

[5]Afterwards, David was conscience-stricken for having cut off a corner of his robe. [6]He said to his men, "The LORD forbid that I should do such a thing to my master, the LORD's anointed, or lift my hand against him; for he is the anointed of the LORD." [7]With these words David rebuked his men and did not allow them to attack Saul. And Saul left the cave and went his way.

24:5 ■ DAVID'S BAD CONSCIENCE

David's conscience troubled him after he cut off part of Saul's robe. Why? Possibly because, to people of that day, a man looked ridiculous with his clothes cut short. See 2 Samuel 10:4–5 for a case where cutting a garment was a deliberate insult that led to war.

[8]Then David went out of the cave and called out to Saul, "My lord the king!" When Saul looked behind him, David bowed down and prostrated himself with his face to the ground. [9]He said to Saul, "Why do you listen when men say, 'David is bent on harming you'? [10]This day you have seen with your own eyes how the LORD gave you into my hands in the cave. Some urged me to kill you, but I spared you; I said, 'I will not lift my hand against my master, because he is the LORD's anointed.' [11]See, my father, look at this piece of your robe in my hand! I cut off the corner of your robe but did not kill you. Now understand and recognise that I am not guilty of wrongdoing or rebellion. I have not wronged you, but you are hunting me down to take my life. [12]May the LORD judge between you and me. And may the LORD avenge the wrongs you have done to me, but my hand will not touch you. [13]As the old saying goes, 'From evildoers come evil deeds,' so my hand will not touch you.

[14]"Against whom has the king of Israel come out? Whom are you pursuing? A dead dog? A flea? [15]May the LORD be our judge and decide between us. May he consider my cause and uphold it; may he vindicate me by delivering me from your hand."

[16]When David finished saying this, Saul asked, "Is that your voice, David my son?" And he wept aloud. [17]"You are more righteous than I," he said. "You have treated me well, but I have treated you badly. [18]You have just now told me of the good you did to me; the LORD gave me into your hands, but you did not kill me. [19]When a man finds his enemy, does he let him get away unharmed? May the LORD reward you well for the way you treated me today. [20]I know that you will surely be king and that the kingdom of Israel will be established in your hands. [21]Now swear to me by the LORD that you will not cut off my descendants or wipe out my name from my father's family."

[22]So David gave his oath to Saul. Then Saul returned home, but David and his men went up to the stronghold.

24:21 ■ THE SURVIVAL OF A FAMILY

Slaughtering the rival's entire family was normal practice when one would-be king triumphed over another. Such action tended to lessen the probability that the rival family would compete for the throne again. Jonathan, David's closest friend, is asking David not to follow that course when he becomes king. Because of their relationship, David let Jonathan's son Mephibosheth live (2 Samuel 9).

■ David, Nabal and Abigail

25 Now Samuel died, and all Israel assembled and mourned for him; and they buried him at his home in Ramah.

Then David moved down into the Desert of Maon.[a] [2]A certain man in Maon, who had property there at Carmel, was very wealthy. He had a thousand goats and three thousand sheep, which he was shearing in Carmel. [3]His name was Nabal and his wife's name was Abigail. She was an intelligent and beautiful woman, but her husband, a Calebite, was surly and mean in his dealings.

[4]While David was in the desert, he heard that Nabal was shearing sheep. [5]So he sent ten young men and said to them, "Go up to Nabal at Carmel and greet him in my name. [6]Say to him: 'Long life to you! Good health to you and your household! And good health to all that is yours!

[7]"'Now I hear that it is sheep-shearing time. When your shepherds were with us, we did not ill-treat them, and the whole time they were at Carmel nothing of theirs was missing. [8]Ask your own servants and they will tell you. Therefore be favourable towards my young men, since we come at a festive time. Please give your servants and your son David whatever you can find for them.' "

[9]When David's men arrived, they gave Nabal this message in David's name. Then they waited.

[10]Nabal answered David's servants, "Who is this David? Who is this son of Jesse? Many servants are breaking away from their masters these days. [11]Why should I take my bread and water, and the meat I have slaughtered for my shearers, and give it to men coming from who knows where?"

[12]David's men turned round and went back. When they arrived, they reported every word. [13]David said to his men, "Put on your swords!" So they put on their swords, and David put on his. About four hundred men went up with David, while two hundred stayed with the supplies.

[14]One of the servants told Nabal's wife Abigail: "David sent messengers from the desert to give our master his greetings, but he hurled insults at them. [15]Yet these men were very good to us. They did not ill-treat us, and the whole time we were out in the fields near them nothing was missing. [16]Night and day they were a wall around us all the time we were

a 4 Or "Today the LORD is saying   *a* 1 Some Septuagint manuscripts; Hebrew *Paran* herding our sheep near them. [17]Now think it over and see what you can do, because disaster is hanging over our master and his whole household. He is such a wicked man that no-one can talk to him."

[18]Abigail lost no time. She took two hundred loaves of bread, two skins of wine, five dressed sheep, five seahs[b] of roasted grain, a hundred cakes of raisins and two hundred cakes of pressed figs, and loaded them on donkeys. [19]Then she told her servants, "Go on ahead; I'll follow you." But she did not tell her husband Nabal.

[20]As she came riding her donkey into a mountain ravine, there were David and his men descending towards her, and she met them. [21]David had just said, "It's been useless—all my watching over this fellow's property in the desert so that nothing of his was missing. He has paid me back evil for good. [22]May God deal with David,[c] be it ever so severely,

■ A SENSE OF GOD'S TIMING
TWO LEADERS LOCKED IN A DEATH STRUGGLE—WITH ONE REFUSING TO FIGHT

INSIGHT

"I HAVE NOT WRONGED YOU, BUT YOU ARE HUNTING ME DOWN TO TAKE MY LIFE. MAY THE LORD JUDGE BETWEEN YOU AND ME." ■ 24:11–12

In the winter of 1777, America had two armies. One lived in comfortable homes in Philadelphia. The other had a camp in the snow in the hills to the north-west, at a place called Valley Forge. One showed impeccable discipline. The other tried desperately to keep its untrained recruits from deserting. One was supplied by ship with every luxury. The other fought frostbite because its soldiers had no boots.

In summary, one army had everything it could want to weather a cold winter and a war, while the other hung by a thread. Who could have thought, seeing the two, that within three years the army with nothing would defeat the army with everything?

The impoverished American army could never go head-on against the crack British forces. But it could always outwait them. George Washington's army had the support of the American people, while the British army, for all its strength, was far from home. The British had to win decisively, putting an end to the rebellion. The Americans merely had to survive and outlast them.

Washington was a military genius not at battle tactics, but at a more fundamental necessity: encouraging his men to fight on. A quarter of them died of cold and disease that bitter winter at Valley Forge. Only his personal strength held the miserable army together. That was the key to victory.

■ TWO KINGS IN ISRAEL
David and his followers lived in a similar situation. Saul was the right and proper king, living in luxury. David had been secretly anointed as his replacement, but he lived in the desert, scrabbling to survive. Saul had a professional army, David a small band composed of family members and an assortment of outlaws.

Twice Saul accidentally fell into David's hands, but David refused to kill him. He felt that would violate God's will. He would not use his sword to become king. He fought not to win but to survive.

Survival was not easy. You can read between the lines of chapters 21–31 and see a great drama unfolding. Saul is clearly deteriorating. Can David hold on long enough to outlast him?

At first David ran from one place to another, alone and completely vulnerable. Then, when 400 outlaws gathered around him, the local people turned him in twice (23:19; 26:1). Perhaps they feared that Saul would slaughter them the way he had the Nob priests (22:6–23).

David survived and managed to keep his army intact. He even built popular support by providing military protection to his neighbours. But eventually he saw that his position was impossible. "One of these days I will be destroyed by the hand of Saul," he said (27:1). He left Israel and became, with his army, a hired soldier for one of the Philistine kings.

Sooner or later David's double-agent act would have been found out. In fact, when the Philistines planned a major military effort against Israel, David barely escaped having to fight his own people.

■ TIME ON HIS SIDE
Throughout his desert period, David's position was desperate. David had one precious asset only: God had promised he would be king. David believed this promise even when his situation looked very bad. He would wait for God's timing.

A sense of timing, people say, is essential to leadership. You must know when to act boldly and when to wait patiently; when to bend and when to stand firm. David had that critical sense of timing because he trusted God's control of events.

☐ LIFE QUESTIONS:
What makes you impatient? What can you learn about patience from David's life?

---

b 18 That is, probably about a bushel (about 37 litres)   c 22 Some Septuagint manuscripts; Hebrew with David's enemies

if by morning I leave alive one male of all who belong to him!"

²³When Abigail saw David, she quickly got off her donkey and bowed down before David with her face to the ground. ²⁴She fell at his feet and said: "My lord, let the blame be on me alone. Please let your servant speak to you; hear what your servant has to say. ²⁵May my lord pay no attention to that wicked man Nabal. He is just like his name — his name is Fool, and folly goes with him. But as for me, your servant, I did not see the men my master sent.

25:25 ■ COOL HEAD

One person with a cool head can defuse an extremely dangerous situation. David had lost his temper over the careless words of a fool — Nabal's name, literally translated — and was ready to kill. Fortunately for him, Nabal's wife Abigail used her utmost diplomacy to convince David to restrain his anger. David quickly recognised she was right, and praised God for sending her. Later, he married her (verse 39).

---

²⁶"Now since the LORD has kept you, my master, from bloodshed and from avenging yourself with your own hands, as surely as the LORD lives and as you live, may your enemies and all who intend to harm my master be like Nabal. ²⁷And let this gift, which your servant has brought to my master, be given to the men who follow you. ²⁸Please forgive your servant's offence, for the LORD will certainly make a lasting dynasty for my master, because he fights the LORD's battles. Let no wrongdoing be found in you as long as you live. ²⁹Even though someone is pursuing you to take your life, the life of my master will be bound securely in the bundle of the living by the LORD your God. But the lives of your enemies he will hurl away as from the pocket of a sling. ³⁰When the LORD has done for my master every good thing he promised concerning him and has appointed him leader over Israel, ³¹my master will not have on his conscience the staggering burden of needless bloodshed or of having avenged himself. And when the LORD has brought my master success, remember your servant."

³²David said to Abigail, "Praise be to the LORD, the God of Israel, who has sent you today to meet me. ³³May you be blessed for your good judgment and for keeping me from bloodshed this day and from avenging myself with my own hands. ³⁴Otherwise, as surely as the LORD, the God of Israel, lives, who has kept me from harming you, if you had not come quickly to meet me, not one male belonging to Nabal would have been left alive by daybreak."

³⁵Then David accepted from her hand what she had brought to him and said, "Go home in peace. I have heard your words and granted your request."

³⁶When Abigail went to Nabal, he was in the house holding a banquet like that of a king. So she told him nothing until daybreak. ³⁷Then in the morning, when Nabal was sober, his wife told him all these things, and his heart failed him and he became like a stone.

³⁸About ten days later, the LORD struck Nabal and he died.

³⁹When David heard that Nabal was dead, he said, "Praise be to the LORD, who has upheld my cause against Nabal for treating me with contempt. He has kept his servant from doing wrong and has brought Nabal's wrongdoing down on his own head." Then David sent word to Abigail, asking her to become his wife. ⁴⁰His servants went to Carmel and said to Abigail, "David has sent us to you to take you to become his wife."

⁴¹She bowed down with her face to the ground and said, "Here is your maidservant, ready to serve you and wash the feet of my master's servants." ⁴²Abigail quickly got on a donkey and, attended by her five maids, went with David's messengers and became his wife. ⁴³David had also married Ahinoam of Jezreel, and they both were his wives. ⁴⁴But Saul had given his daughter Michal, David's wife, to Paltiel*ᵈ* son of Laish, who was from Gallim.

■ David Again Spares Saul's Life

26 The Ziphites went to Saul at Gibeah and said, "Is not David hiding on the hill of Hakilah, which faces Jeshimon?"

²So Saul went down to the Desert of Ziph, with his three thousand chosen men of Israel, to search there for David. ³Saul made his camp beside the road on the hill of Hakilah facing Jeshimon, but David stayed in the desert. When he saw that Saul had followed him there, ⁴he sent out scouts and learned that Saul had definitely arrived.ᵃ

⁵Then David set out and went to the place where Saul had camped. He saw where Saul and Abner son of Ner, the commander of the army, had lain down. Saul was lying inside the camp, with the army encamped around him.

⁶David then asked Ahimelech the Hittite and Abishai son of Zeruiah, Joab's brother, "Who will go down into the camp with me to Saul?"

"I'll go with you," said Abishai.

⁷So David and Abishai went to the army by night, and there was Saul, lying asleep inside the camp with his spear stuck in the ground near his head. Abner and the soldiers were lying round him.

⁸Abishai said to David, "Today God has given your enemy into your hands. Now let me pin him to the ground with one thrust of my spear; I won't strike him twice."

⁹But David said to Abishai, "Don't destroy him! Who can lay a hand on the LORD's anointed and be guiltless? ¹⁰As surely as the LORD lives," he said, "the LORD himself will strike him; either his time will come and he will die, or he will go into battle and perish. ¹¹But the LORD forbid that I should lay a hand on the LORD's anointed. Now get the spear and water jug that are near his head, and let's go."

¹²So David took the spear and water jug near Saul's head, and they left. No-one saw or knew about it, nor did anyone wake up. They were all sleeping, because the LORD had put them into a deep sleep.

¹³Then David crossed over to the other side and stood on top of the hill some distance away; there was a wide space between them. ¹⁴He called out to

---

ᵈ44 Hebrew *Palti*, a variant of *Paltiel*   ᵃ4 Or *had come to Nacon* the army and to Abner son of Ner, "Aren't you going to answer me, Abner?"

Abner replied, "Who are you who calls to the king?"

[15]David said, "You're a man, aren't you? And who is like you in Israel? Why didn't you guard your lord the king? Someone came to destroy your lord the king. [16]What you have done is not good. As surely as the LORD lives, you and your men deserve to die, because you did not guard your master, the LORD's anointed. Look around you. Where are the king's spear and water jug that were near his head?"

[17]Saul recognised David's voice and said, "Is that your voice, David my son?"

David replied, "Yes it is, my lord the king." [18]And he added, "Why is my lord pursuing his servant? What have I done, and what wrong am I guilty of? [19]Now let my lord the king listen to his servant's words. If the LORD has incited you against me, then may he accept an offering. If, however, men have done it, may they be cursed before the LORD! They have now driven me from my share in the LORD's inheritance and have said, 'Go, serve other gods.' [20]Now do not let my blood fall to the ground far from the presence of the LORD. The king of Israel has come out to look for a flea — as one hunts a partridge in the mountains."

[21]Then Saul said, "I have sinned. Come back, David my son. Because you considered my life precious today, I will not try to harm you again. Surely I have acted like a fool and have erred greatly."

[22]"Here is the king's spear," David answered. "Let one of your young men come over and get it. [23]The LORD rewards every man for his righteousness and faithfulness. The LORD gave you into my hands today, but I would not lay a hand on the LORD's anointed. [24]As surely as I valued your life today, so may the LORD value my life and deliver me from all trouble."

[25]Then Saul said to David, "May you be blessed, my son David; you will do great things and surely triumph."

So David went on his way, and Saul returned home.

■ David Among the Philistines

27 But David thought to himself, "One of these days I shall be destroyed by the hand of Saul. The best thing I can do is to escape to the land of the Philistines. Then Saul will give up searching for me anywhere in Israel, and I will slip out of his hand."

[2]So David and the six hundred men with him left and went over to Achish son of Maoch king of Gath. [3]David and his men settled in Gath with Achish. Each man had his family with him, and David had his two wives: Ahinoam of Jezreel and Abigail of Carmel, the widow of Nabal. [4]When Saul was told that David had fled to Gath, he no longer searched for him.

[5]Then David said to Achish, "If I have found favour in your eyes, let a place be assigned to me in one of the country towns, that I may live there. Why should your servant live in the royal city with you?"

[6]So on that day Achish gave him Ziklag, and it has belonged to the kings of Judah ever since. [7]David lived in Philistine territory for a year and four months.

[8]Now David and his men went up and raided the Geshurites, the Girzites and the Amalekites. (From ancient times these peoples had lived in the land extending to Shur and Egypt.) [9]Whenever David attacked an area, he did not leave a man or woman alive, but took sheep and cattle, donkeys and camels, and clothes. Then he returned to Achish.

27:8 ■ DAVID'S DOUBLE GAME

The Philistines accepted David because they thought he would fight against his own people. Had they known that he retained his Israelite loyalty, they would never have trusted him. So David had to pretend that he was raiding the Israelites, while actually he raided Israel's nomadic enemies. To keep his game secret, he took no prisoners, for it might be noticed that none of them were Israelites.

[10]When Achish asked, "Where did you go raiding today?" David would say, "Against the Negev of Judah" or "Against the Negev of Jerahmeel" or "Against the Negev of the Kenites." [11]He did not leave a man or woman alive to be brought to Gath, for he thought, "They might inform on us and say, 'This is what David did.'" And such was his practice as long as he lived in Philistine territory. [12]Achish trusted David and said to himself, "He has become so odious to his people, the Israelites, that he will be my servant for ever."

■ Saul and the Witch of Endor

28 In those days the Philistines gathered their forces to fight against Israel. Achish said to David, "You must understand that you and your men will accompany me in the army."

[2]David said, "Then you will see for yourself what your servant can do."

Achish replied, "Very well, I will make you my bodyguard for life."

[3]Now Samuel was dead, and all Israel had mourned for him and buried him in his own town of Ramah. Saul had expelled the mediums and spiritists from the land.

[4]The Philistines assembled and came and set up camp at Shunem, while Saul gathered all the Israelites and set up camp at Gilboa. [5]When Saul saw the Philistine army, he was afraid; terror filled his heart. [6]He enquired of the LORD, but the LORD did not answer him by dreams or Urim or prophets. [7]Saul then said to his attendants, "Find me a woman who is a medium, so that I may go and enquire of her."

"There is one in Endor," they said.

[8]So Saul disguised himself, putting on other clothes, and at night he and two men went to the woman. "Consult a spirit for me," he said, "and bring up for me the one I name."

[9]But the woman said to him, "Surely you know what Saul has done. He has cut off the mediums and spiritists from the land. Why have you set a trap for my life to bring about my death?"

¹⁰Saul swore to her by the LORD, "As surely as the LORD lives, you will not be punished for this."

28:4 ■ BATTLE STRATEGY

For their massive assault from Shunem, the Philistines tried a new tactic. They had fought previous battles in the mountains, rough terrain where their chariots were next to useless. Now they chose strategically important level ground that Israel had to defend. The Valley of Jezreel is the only part of Palestine where you can go from west to east without crossing mountains. A Philistine victory here would cut Israel in half.

---

¹¹Then the woman asked, "Whom shall I bring up for you?"

"Bring up Samuel," he said.

¹²When the woman saw Samuel, she cried out at the top of her voice and said to Saul, "Why have you deceived me? You are Saul!"

28:12 ■ THE WITCH OF ENDOR

Consulting a medium or spiritist was forbidden (Leviticus 20:6,27; Deuteronomy 18:10–12), as Saul knew well. Earlier, he had banned mediums in the kingdom. But through his disobedience Saul had lost contact with God, and was desperate to know the future. Whether Samuel actually appeared or whether the woman faked it, the results were the same: Saul left more fearful than when he came.

---

¹³The king said to her, "Don't be afraid. What do you see?"

The woman said, "I see a spirit*a* coming up out of the ground."

¹⁴"What does he look like?" he asked.

"An old man wearing a robe is coming up," she said.

Then Saul knew it was Samuel, and he bowed down and prostrated himself with his face to the ground.

¹⁵Samuel said to Saul, "Why have you disturbed me by bringing me up?"

"I am in great distress," Saul said. "The Philistines are fighting against me, and God has turned away from me. He no longer answers me, either by prophets or by dreams. So I have called on you to tell me what to do."

¹⁶Samuel said, "Why do you consult me, now that the LORD has turned away from you and become your enemy? ¹⁷The LORD has done what he predicted through me. The LORD has torn the kingdom out of your hands and given it to one of your neighbours—to David. ¹⁸Because you did not obey the LORD or carry out his fierce wrath against the Amalekites, the LORD has done this to you today. ¹⁹The LORD will hand over both Israel and you to the Philistines, and tomorrow you and your sons will be with me. The LORD will also hand over the army of Israel to the Philistines."

²⁰Immediately Saul fell full length on the ground,

a 13 Or see spirits; or see gods

filled with fear because of Samuel's words. His strength was gone, for he had eaten nothing all that day and night.

²¹When the woman came to Saul and saw that he was greatly shaken, she said, "Look, your maidservant has obeyed you. I took my life in my hands and did what you told me to do. ²²Now please listen to your servant and let me give you some food so that you may eat and have the strength to go on your way."

²³He refused and said, "I will not eat."

But his men joined the woman in urging him, and he listened to them. He got up from the ground and sat on the couch.

²⁴The woman had a fattened calf at the house, which she slaughtered at once. She took some flour, kneaded it and baked bread without yeast. ²⁵Then she set it before Saul and his men, and they ate. That same night they got up and left.

■ Achish Sends David Back to Ziklag

29 The Philistines gathered all their forces at Aphek, and Israel camped by the spring in Jezreel. ²As the Philistine rulers marched with their units of hundreds and thousands, David and his men were marching at the rear with Achish. ³The commanders of the Philistines asked, "What about these Hebrews?"

Achish replied, "Is this not David, who was an officer of Saul king of Israel? He has already been with me for over a year, and from the day he left Saul until now, I have found no fault in him."

⁴But the Philistine commanders were angry with him and said, "Send the man back, that he may return to the place you assigned him. He must not go up with us into battle, or he will turn against us during the fighting. How better could he regain his master's favour than by taking the heads of our own men? ⁵Isn't this the David they sang about in their dances:

" 'Saul has slain his thousands,
    and David his tens of thousands'?"

⁶So Achish called David and said to him, "As surely as the LORD lives, you have been reliable, and I would be pleased to have you serve with me in the army. From the day you came to me until now, I have found no fault in you, but the rulers don't approve of you. ⁷Turn back and go in peace; do nothing to displease the Philistine rulers."

⁸"But what have I done?" asked David. "What have you found against your servant from the day I came to you until now? Why can't I go and fight against the enemies of my lord the king?"

⁹Achish answered, "I know that you have been as pleasing in my eyes as an angel of God; nevertheless, the Philistine commanders have said, 'He must not go up with us into battle.' ¹⁰Now get up early, along with your master's servants who have come with you, and leave in the morning as soon as it is light."

¹¹So David and his men got up early in the morning to go back to the land of the Philistines, and the Philistines went up to Jezreel.

■ David Destroys the Amalekites

30 David and his men reached Ziklag on the third day. Now the Amalekites had raided the Negev and Ziklag. They had attacked Ziklag and burned it, [2]and had taken captive the women and all who were in it, both young and old. They killed none of them, but carried them off as they went on their way.

29:8 ■ FAKING IT

For the sake of survival, David had become a mercenary in the Philistine army. But he had not yet fought against his own people, and it is doubtful that he would have done so. Now, dismissed from service because he wasn't trusted in the forthcoming battle, David acted distressed. Was he genuinely upset? It's quite possible that he had hoped to turn the tables against the Philistines by attacking them from behind their own lines. The Philistine commanders made a shrewd move in sending him away.

---

[3]When David and his men came to Ziklag, they found it destroyed by fire and their wives and sons and daughters taken captive. [4]So David and his men wept aloud until they had no strength left to weep. [5]David's two wives had been captured — Ahinoam of Jezreel and Abigail, the widow of Nabal of Carmel. [6]David was greatly distressed because the men were talking of stoning him; each one was bitter in spirit because of his sons and daughters. But David found strength in the LORD his God.

[7]Then David said to Abiathar the priest, the son of Ahimelech, "Bring me the ephod." Abiathar brought it to him, [8]and David enquired of the LORD, "Shall I pursue this raiding party? Will I overtake them?"

"Pursue them," he answered. "You will certainly overtake them and succeed in the rescue."

[9]David and the six hundred men with him came to the Besor Ravine, where some stayed behind, [10]for two hundred men were too exhausted to cross the ravine. But David and four hundred men continued the pursuit.

[11]They found an Egyptian in a field and brought him to David. They gave him water to drink and food to eat — [12]part of a cake of pressed figs and two cakes of raisins. He ate and was revived, for he had not eaten any food or drunk any water for three days and three nights.

[13]David asked him, "To whom do you belong, and where do you come from?"

He said, "I am an Egyptian, the slave of an Amalekite. My master abandoned me when I became ill three days ago. [14]We raided the Negev of the Kerethites and the territory belonging to Judah and the Negev of Caleb. And we burned Ziklag."

[15]David asked him, "Can you lead me down to this raiding party?"

He answered, "Swear to me before God that you will not kill me or hand me over to my master, and I will take you down to them."

[16]He led David down, and there they were, scattered over the countryside, eating, drinking and revelling because of the great amount of plunder they had taken from the land of the Philistines and from Judah. [17]David fought them from dusk until the evening of the next day, and none of them got away, except four hundred young men who rode off on camels and fled. [18]David recovered everything the Amalekites had taken, including his two wives. [19]Nothing was missing: young or old, boy or girl, plunder or anything else they had taken. David brought everything back. [20]He took all the flocks and herds, and his men drove them ahead of the other livestock, saying, "This is David's plunder."

[21]Then David came to the two hundred men who had been too exhausted to follow him and who were left behind at the Besor Ravine. They came out to meet David and the people with him. As David and his men approached, he greeted them. [22]But all the evil men and troublemakers among David's followers said, "Because they did not go out with us, we will not share with them the plunder we recovered. However, each man may take his wife and children and go."

[23]David replied, "No, my brothers, you must not do that with what the LORD has given us. He has protected us and handed over to us the forces that came against us. [24]Who will listen to what you say? The share of the man who stayed with the supplies is to be the same as that of him who went down to the battle. All shall share alike." [25]David made this a statute and ordinance for Israel from that day to this.

[26]When David arrived in Ziklag, he sent some of the plunder to the elders of Judah, who were his friends, saying, "Here is a present for you from the plunder of the LORD's enemies."

[27]He sent it to those who were in Bethel, Ramoth Negev and Jattir; [28]to those in Aroer, Siphmoth, Eshtemoa [29]and Racal; to those in the towns of the Jerahmeelites and the Kenites; [30]to those in Hormah, Bor Ashan, Athach [31]and Hebron; and to those in all the other places where David and his men had roamed.

■ Saul Takes His Life

31 Now the Philistines fought against Israel; the Israelites fled before them, and many fell slain on Mount Gilboa. [2]The Philistines pressed hard after Saul and his sons, and they killed his sons Jonathan, Abinadab and Malki-Shua. [3]The fighting grew fierce around Saul, and when the archers overtook him, they wounded him critically.

[4]Saul said to his armour-bearer, "Draw your sword and run me through, or these uncircumcised fellows will come and run me through and abuse me."

But the armour-bearer was terrified and would not do it; so Saul took his own sword and fell on it. [5]When the armour-bearer saw that Saul was dead, he too fell on his sword and died with him. [6]So Saul and his three sons and his armour-bearer and all his men died together that same day.

[7]When the Israelites along the valley and those across the Jordan saw that the Israelite army had fled and that Saul and his sons had died, they abandoned

their towns and fled. And the Philistines came and occupied them.

31:11 ■ LOYAL FRIENDS IN DEATH

Saul's first military action as king had been the rescue of Jabesh Gilead (chapter 11). Through all these years its citizens had not forgotten. When they heard of the disgraceful display of Saul's and his sons' bodies, they undertook a dangerous night mission to steal the bodies and give them proper burial.

8The next day, when the Philistines came to strip the dead, they found Saul and his three sons fallen on Mount Gilboa. 9They cut off his head and stripped off his armour, and they sent messengers throughout the land of the Philistines to proclaim the news in the temple of their idols and among their people. 10They put his armour in the temple of the Ashtoreths and fastened his body to the wall of Beth Shan.

11When the people of Jabesh Gilead heard of what the Philistines had done to Saul, 12all their valiant men journeyed through the night to Beth Shan. They took down the bodies of Saul and his sons from the wall of Beth Shan and went to Jabesh, where they burned them. 13Then they took their bones and buried them under a tamarisk tree at Jabesh, and they fasted seven days.

A LINE-UP OF RULERS

The two-part book of Kings can be confusing.
First, there's one nation to keep track of, then
two, then one again. In all, 39 rulers are profiled.
Little wonder it takes a biblical scholar to keep all
the details straight.

The following list of 38 kings and one queen
should help clarify the history of Israel in the North
and Judah in the South. As you come across
the name of a ruler in one of the history books or
in a book of the prophets, simply refer to the
description below for a brief summary of life during
the time of that ruler or prophet.

■ UNITED KINGDOM

SAUL
DAVID
SOLOMON
These first three kings of Israel each ruled
approximately 40 years, and so, for 120 years,
Israel was one nation. The books of Samuel and
Chronicles, together with 1 Kings, describe their
reigns in great detail. Later, Jews would look back
on this time as the Golden Age of Israel.

In all, the kingdoms of Israel and Judah were
united for 120 years and divided for just over 200
years. Then Israel disappeared and Judah lasted
alone for another 135 years. After that, no
independent Jewish nation existed until the 20th
century.

The time-line running through the middle of
these pages places the major prophets in the
appropriate time period, along with the rulers of
their era. Prophets whose names appear in
shaded panels spoke to Israel; those listed in
white panels spoke to Judah. (Dating of some
rulers is inexact because of overlapping reigns.)

■ ISRAEL

JEROBOAM I (22 Years)
He was handpicked by God to lead a reform, but this first king of the Northern Kingdom proved to be one of Israel's worst. For years afterwards, evil kings were described as "walking in the ways of Jeroboam". It was he who firmly established the breakaway nation of Israel, uniting 10 rebel tribes. To prevent his people from worshipping in Jerusalem (now enemy territory), he built a new capital city and set up the notorious "high places" as alternative worship sites. The high places and calf worship plagued Israel throughout its entire history. First Kings records that God decided to abandon Israel during the reign of Jeroboam, the Northern Kingdom's very first ruler. (1 Kings 11:26–15:25; 2 Chronicles 10:2–13:20)

NADAB (2 Years)
Jeroboam's son followed the errors of his father in every way, and his reign merits only eight verses. Israel's first dynasty ended abruptly when Nadab fell victim to a murder plot launched by Baasha. (1 Kings 15:25–32)

BAASHA (24 Years)
After gaining the throne in a violent manner, Baasha lasted for 24 years. He showed no inclination to reverse the evil practices begun by Jeroboam. The prophet Jehu predicted his death. (1 Kings 15:33–16:7; 2 Chronicles 16)

■ DIVIDED KINGDOM

■ JUDAH

REHOBOAM (17 Years)
Judah's first king had a chequered career. Sometimes he obeyed God and listened to the prophets; sometimes he did not. At first, the Jewish religion gained strength when all priests and Levites came over to Judah. But, before long, idolatry found its way into Judah as well as into Israel, and Judah suffered humiliating punishment from the armies of Egypt. Thus Judah's first king set an unfortunate pattern for his successors. (1 Kings 11:43–14:31; 2 Chronicles 10–12)

ABIJAH
(3 Years)
War with Israel in the North dragged on throughout Abijah's three-year reign. The two splinter nations were still adjusting to each other's independence. Abijah offered no improvement on his father Rehoboam's immoral ways. (1 Kings 15:1–8; 2 Chronicles 13:1–14:1)

ASA (41 Years)
Asa and his son Jehoshaphat were the only kings mentioned in 1 Kings who did "what was right in the eyes of the Lord". Second Chronicles gives a much fuller account of Asa's 41 years. He began religious reforms that turned into a kind of wildfire revival. He drove heathen cults out of the land—even removing his own grandmother as queen mother because of her idolatry. Asa also welcomed to Judah many refugees from Israel. Backsliding later in his reign, he got bogged down in foreign wars, making an alliance with neighbouring Aram to hold Israel at bay. (1 Kings 15:9–24; 2 Chronicles 14–16)

■ ISRAEL

ELAH (2 Years)
The Bible records only one incident from Elah's reign: his chariot commander staged a military coup while Elah was off getting drunk. Elah was killed, with all other descendants of his father, Baasha. Israel's second dynasty, therefore, lasted 26 years, and another family took the throne. (1 Kings 16:8–14)

ZIMRI (7 Days)
Evidently, mutinous chariot commander Zimri acted without his army's support. The army revolted against him, and his "reign" ended seven days after it had begun, in a suicidal fire in his palace. (1 Kings 16:15–20)

OMRI (12 Years)
Secular historians rate Omri as one of Israel's most powerful and capable political rulers. In fact, Assyrian records call Israel "the land of Omri". He outlasted a rival to the throne, expanded Israel's lands, and founded the city of Samaria, which would remain Israel's capital for 150 years. But he gets scant mention in the Bible; it dismisses him for sinning "more than all those before him". (1 Kings 16:21–28)

AHAB (22 Years)
In a competition for all-time worst king of Israel, Ahab would win hands down. He married the notorious Jezebel, a pagan priestess who promptly installed Baal worship as Israel's official religion. First Kings departs from its usually brief style to give a detailed treatment of Ahab's life and the great spiritual crisis then. During that time, Elijah appeared on the scene to represent the true God against Queen Jezebel's religion. God gave Ahab plenty of opportunities to reform. Ahab humbled himself at least once, postponing disaster, but a nasty incident over Naboth's vineyard sealed his fate. Politically, Ahab forged a successful alliance with Israel's neighbour, Judah, and the divided kingdoms lived at peace for the first time since Jeroboam. Ultimately, however, his evil practices would spread into Judah. (1 Kings 16:29–22:40; 2 Chronicles 18)

AHAZIAH (2 Years)
Like his father, Ahab, and mother, Jezebel, Ahaziah continued to worship Baal and to fight against Elijah. He was no match. His reign lasted only part of two years, and the descriptions of him reveal a weak, vengeful ruler (1 Kings 22:40–2 King 1:18)

ELIJAH

■ JUDAH

JEHOSHAPHAT (25 Years)
Judah enjoyed the rare blessing of one good king after another. Jehoshaphat continued the spirit of Asa's rule, and found ways to further it. He sent out princes to teach from the Book of the Law in the cities of Judah and established courts of justice throughout the country. With a large army and well-fortified cities, he attained a level of peace and prosperity rare in Judah's history. His one serious mistake was in linking himself to Israel's wicked king Ahab through marriage and military alliance. (1 Kings 22:41–50; 2 Chronicles 17–20)

JEHORAM (8 Years)
After 60 good years under Asa and Jehoshaphat, Judah experienced a terrible regression under Jehoram. He began by killing his brothers and then marrying Athaliah, daughter of Israel's Ahab and Jezebel. She promptly led him into Baal worship. Elijah, who mostly prophesied to Israel, sent Judah's king Jehoram a letter predicting the severe bowel disease that would lead to his death. Second Chronicles reports that "he passed away, to no-one's regret". (2 Kings 8:16–24; 2 Chronicles 21)

JORAM (12 Years)

Although an improvement over his father and mother (Ahab and Jezebel), Joram ultimately failed to do what was right. He modified some of the worship of Baal, and at times had a respectful relationship with the prophet Elishah. But Joram lived in treacherous times. The nation of Aram was attacking from the east, and God had set in motion an internal plot, led by Jehu, against Ahab's heirs. Finally, Joram fell victim to Jehu's arrow, ending the evil dynasty founded by Omri. (2 Kings 3:1–9:26)

JEHU (28 Years)

Not to be confused with the prophet of the same name, this Jehu was a fast-driving, impetuous military man. He began a holy mission to purge Ahab's influence out of Israel and Judah, but considerably overstepped his bounds. He killed Joram, had Jezebel thrown from a window, and slew 70 princes, piling their heads in two heaps by a gate. Then he slew all the priests and prophets of Baal and tricked the worshippers of Baal into a trap that led to a mass slaughter. Unfortunately, Jehu's zeal for violence did not translate into zeal for justice. His actions tore Israel apart for generations, and he did little to attend to the nation's spiritual health. Israel also began to lose political strength. (2 Kings 9–10)

JEHOAHAZ (17 Years)

After all his father Jehu had done to exterminate Baal worship, Jehoahaz immediately reinstated it. He ruled for 17 years, marked by a series of embarrassing military defeats at the hands of neighbouring Aram. He did turn to God in desperation at least once, and Israel gained a reprieve. (2 Kings 13:1–9)

SHA

AHAZIAH (1 Year)

In effect Ahaziah served as a mere puppet representative of the notorious queen Athaliah, daughter of Ahab and Jezebel. He fell victim to the bloody purge of Jehu. (2 Kings 8:25–29; 22:1–9)

ATHALIAH (7 Years)

Queen Athaliah first corrupted her husband Jehoram and dominated her son Ahaziah. Then, after Ahaziah's death, she killed off her infant grandchildren to remove rivals to the throne. She ruled Judah for seven years, leading the kingdom into a dark time of Baal worship and evil. Providentially, however, one heir escaped her reach. The young Joash, hidden away by his mother, emerged at the age of seven to lead a popular revolt against Athaliah. Athaliah, the only woman to rule either of the two kingdoms, was the last of Ahab's family to die. She had come within one baby of wiping out King David's royal line. (2 Kings 11; 2 Chronicles 22:10–23:21)

JOASH (40 Years)

He swept into power at the crest of a revolt against his wicked grandmother Athaliah. And as long as Joash followed the advice of Jehoiada the priest, he did well. Most notably, he organised massive projects to repair the temple. After Jehoiada died, however, Joash allowed idolatry to prosper once more. He strayed so far from the ideals of his youth that he ordered the prophet Zechariah to be stoned—the same Zechariah whose father, Johoiada, had saved his life. Punishment came swiftly, at the hands of a plundering army. Finally, Joash's own servants turned against him and avenged Zechariah's murder. (2 Kings 12; 2 Chronicles 24)

■ ISRAEL

JEHOASH (16 Years)
Although Jehoash did not break the evil pattern of Israel's kings, he showed some bright spots. He honoured the prophet Elisha, and God allowed him to recover much of the territory that Aram had taken from Israel. (Note that Judah also had a king named Joash, the shortened version of Jehoash.)
(2 Kings 13:10–14: 16)

JEROBOAM II (41 Years)
It seems that God gave Israel one last chance under King Jeroboam II. This king ruled a strong and prosperous nation. The Bible gives scant mention of his reign, but it lasted for 41 years, during which Israel recovered nearly all of its former territory. The prophet Jonah lived then, possibly assisting the king in his frontier defence against Assyria. In addition, Amos and Hosea were active, railing against the terrible social and religious corruption of those affluent times. In a remarkable turn of events, Israel survived as a nation for only a few decades after this stable period. (2 Kings 14:23–29)

PEKAH (20 Years)
Pekah turned to international intrigue and conspiracy. He attempted to dethrone the king of Judah in the South. But Judah bought help from Assyria, which promptly invaded Israel for the second time. After occupying all major cities in Israel except the capital Samaria, Assyria began deporting thousands of conquered Israelites to other lands.
(2 Kings 15:27–31)

JONAH

■ JUDAH

AMAZIAH (29 Years)
Second Kings concludes that Amaziah "did what was right in the eyes of the Lord, but not as his father David had done". Yet the author comments on Amaziah's failures. He began his rule by executing those who had killed his father. Then he ignored a prophet's advice and attacked Edom, bringing back idols from there. Flushed with military success, he launched a foolhardy campaign against Israel. The trouncing that resulted discredited his leadership, and he spent his last 12 years in exile.
(2 Kings 14:1–22; 2 Chronicles 25)

AZARIAH (52 Years)
Called Uzziah in Chronicles, this king reigned for some 50 years, the longest of Judah's kings. As a young man, he took advice from a prophet named Zechariah. He built up the army of Judah and worked on its agriculture and water supplies. Until Azariah, Judah had been a struggling kingdom, with enemy fortifications just five miles from Jerusalem. Under him, the nation achieved true strength. Even so, Azariah gets a short review in the Bible because of his spiritual failings. He did not remove the high places, and he violated the Law of Moses by taking on the work of priests himself. (2 Kings 15:1–17; 2 Chronicles 26)

■ Assyrian invasion

ZECHARIAH & SHALLUM (7 Months)
After Jeroboam II, the nation splintered into rival factions. The first king (Zechariah) ruled for six months, the second (Shallum) only one month. Both died violently. (2 Kings 15:8–16)

MENAHEM (10 Years)
Menahem lasted for ten turbulent years. He gained the throne by murder, and his reign showed a similar ruthlessness. The first of Assyria's three invasions—Israel's "World War I" see introduction to 2 Kings—occurred during Menahem's years, and he frantically tried to buy off the invaders. (2 Kings 15:14–22)

PEKAHIAH (2 Years)
Israel was quickly sliding towards anarchy and extermination. Pekahiah survived for only two years before a military coup overthrew him. (2 Kings 15:23–26)

HOSHEA (9 Years)
The Bible judges Hoshea as less wicked than some of his predecessors. Nevertheless, Israel's death was certain. Hoshea angered Assyria by turning south to Egypt for aid. The Assyrians attacked, and after a terrible three-year siege, the last stronghold, Samaria, fell to the conquerors. Assyria deported the vast majority of Israel's population, who became the "ten lost tribes of Israel". (2 Kings 17)

■ JUDAH

HEZEKIAH (29 Years)
King Hezekiah gets full treatment in both Kings and Chronicles. The first book stresses the political side of his reign while the second reports on his religious reforms. Both were impressive; Hezekiah was one of the best and most important kings of Judah. He immediately stopped idolatry by re-opening and cleansing the temple and calling for a period of national repentance. He resurrected the Passover celebration, and worship in Israel reached a peak that had not been seen since the time of David and Solomon. In all this, he listened carefully to advice from the prophet Isaiah. Yet Hezekiah hardly lived in a peaceful era. He faced imminent danger from Assyria and barely survived an invasion and siege. God honoured his faithfulness with a miraculous military intervention. In an unprecedented act, he also added 15 years to Hezekiah's life. (2 Kings 18–20; 2 Chronicles 29–32; Isaiah 36–39)

AMOS

HOSEA

MICAH

ISAIAH

JOTHAM (16 Years)
After serving as Azariah's proxy king for 15 years (while Azariah was quarantined with leprosy), Jotham took over and continued the practices of his father. He expanded Judah's economic and military strength, but did not pursue religious reforms as fully as he should have done. (2 Kings 15:32–38; 2 Chronicles 27)

AHAZ (16 Years)
At the very moment Ahaz was being crowned, armies from the North led by King Pekah of Israel were marching into Judah. Ahaz ignored the prophet Isaiah's advice to put his trust in God rather than military alliances. Turning to the mighty empire of Assyria, he purchased aid with treasures from the temple and the king's palace. The strategy worked temporarily: Israel's armies withdrew to defend themselves. But Ahaz opened the doors for later Assyrian invasions of Judah itself. Worse, he made copies of foreign gods and set them up in Jerusalem. Under him, religion in Judah took a precipitous drop. He went so far as to sacrifice his sons in the fire, following the detestable ways of foreign nations. (2 Kings 16; 2 Chronicles 28)

■ JUDAH

MANASSEH (55 Years)
Whatever good Hezekiah had accomplished in
his exemplary reign, his son Manasseh undid
in 55 years of the worst rule in Judah's history.
He reversed Hezekiah's reforms, bringing in
all forms of idolatry, including the occult and
witchcraft. He killed off prophets, erected idols
in God's temple, and sacrificed his own sons
on the altar of a heathen god. The Assyrian
empire took Manasseh prisoner, leading him
away with a hook through his nose. Later he
repented, but great damage had been done.
After Manasseh, God pronounced a final
judgement on the future of Judah. (2 Kings
21:1–18; 2 Chronicles 33:1–20)

ISAIAH (cont.)

MICAH (cont.)

660	650	640	630	620

AMON
(2 Years)
Amon merely
continued
the practices
of his father.
He died at
the hands of
his servants.
(2 Kings
21:19–26;
2 Chronicles
33:21–25)

JOSIAH (31 Years)
Judah's slide to destruction was interrupted
by the amazing rule of its all-time best king.
Josiah came to the throne at the age of eight,
but received good counsel from the high
priests. In 31 years he carried out the most
extensive religious reforms Judah had ever
seen. He removed and destroyed the altars,
idols, and symbols of ungodly worship from
the temple, and destroyed pagan centres
throughout the land. In a thrilling sequence of
events, he oversaw the rediscovery of the Law
of Moses and acted immediately on what it
taught. No king equals Josiah for his sincere
and devout practices. He even extended his
reforms into the decimated regions of Israel in
the North.

Josiah had a time of military peace, for
during his reign the Assyrian empire was
disintegrating. But he unwisely thrust himself
into international politics by marching against
Egypt. (The prophet Jeremiah had urged
against the Egyptian campaign.) Judah would
never recover from this fatal mistake, for
Josiah died suddenly in battle. His death
shocked the nation. After Josiah's death,
Egypt installed a puppet king, and no-one
after him had the ability to rally Judah's
religious or political strength. (2 Kings
22:1–23:30; 2 Chronicles 34–35)

NAHUM

ZEPHANIAH

JEREMIAH

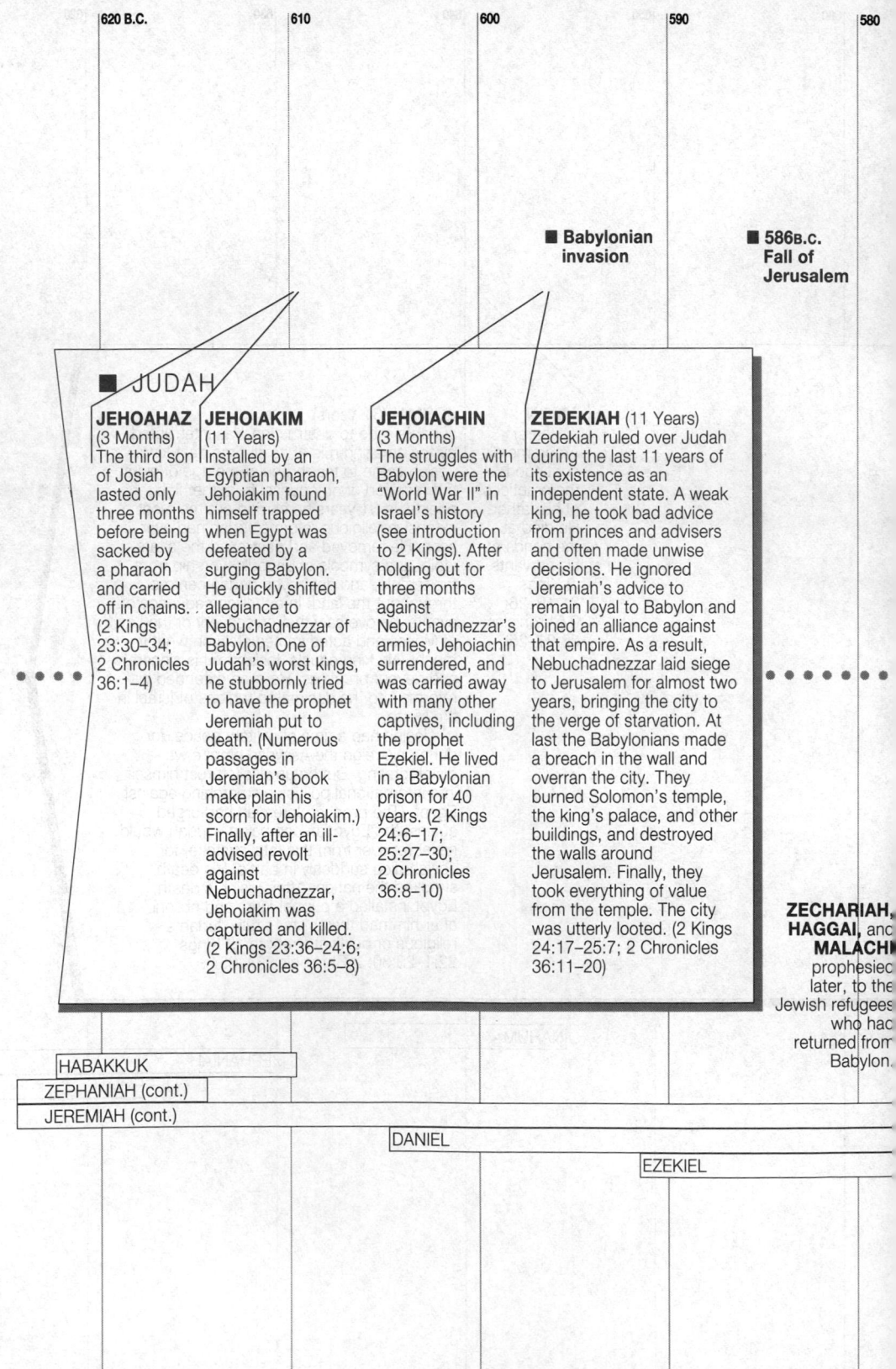

620 B.C.	610	600	590	580

■ Babylonian
invasion

■ 586B.C.
Fall of
Jerusalem

■ JUDAH

JEHOAHAZ
(3 Months)
The third son
of Josiah
lasted only
three months
before being
sacked by
a pharaoh
and carried
off in chains.
(2 Kings
23:30–34;
2 Chronicles
36:1–4)

JEHOIAKIM
(11 Years)
Installed by an
Egyptian pharaoh,
Jehoiakim found
himself trapped
when Egypt was
defeated by a
surging Babylon.
He quickly shifted
allegiance to
Nebuchadnezzar of
Babylon. One of
Judah's worst kings,
he stubbornly tried
to have the prophet
Jeremiah put to
death. (Numerous
passages in
Jeremiah's book
make plain his
scorn for Jehoiakim.)
Finally, after an ill-
advised revolt
against
Nebuchadnezzar,
Jehoiakim was
captured and killed.
(2 Kings 23:36–24:6;
2 Chronicles 36:5–8)

JEHOIACHIN
(3 Months)
The struggles with
Babylon were the
"World War II" in
Israel's history
(see introduction
to 2 Kings). After
holding out for
three months
against
Nebuchadnezzar's
armies, Jehoiachin
surrendered, and
was carried away
with many other
captives, including
the prophet
Ezekiel. He lived
in a Babylonian
prison for 40
years. (2 Kings
24:6–17;
25:27–30;
2 Chronicles
36:8–10)

ZEDEKIAH (11 Years)
Zedekiah ruled over Judah
during the last 11 years of
its existence as an
independent state. A weak
king, he took bad advice
from princes and advisers
and often made unwise
decisions. He ignored
Jeremiah's advice to
remain loyal to Babylon and
joined an alliance against
that empire. As a result,
Nebuchadnezzar laid siege
to Jerusalem for almost two
years, bringing the city to
the verge of starvation. At
last the Babylonians made
a breach in the wall and
overran the city. They
burned Solomon's temple,
the king's palace, and other
buildings, and destroyed
the walls around
Jerusalem. Finally, they
took everything of value
from the temple. The city
was utterly looted. (2 Kings
24:17–25:7; 2 Chronicles
36:11–20)

**ZECHARIAH,
HAGGAI,** and
MALACHI
prophesied
later, to the
Jewish refugees
who had
returned from
Babylon.

HABAKKUK

ZEPHANIAH (cont.)

JEREMIAH (cont.)

DANIEL

EZEKIEL

2 SAMUEL

INTRODUCTION

■ THE LIFE OF KING DAVID

FROM HERDING SHEEP TO RULING A NATION

"I TOOK YOU FROM THE PASTURE AND FROM FOLLOWING THE FLOCK TO BE RULER OVER MY PEOPLE ISRAEL." ■ 7:8

The Bible is filled with strong personalities, but none shines brighter than David. His life was a whirlwind, from which striking images flash. We see him playing his harp, writing poems, fighting battles, faking insanity, dancing jubilantly in praise of God. We watch his tear-streaked face when he learns of his closest friend's death. We see him on his rooftop, gazing down lustfully on Bathsheba's bath. We see Nathan point his finger at him, accusing him of adultery and murder. We hear David's guilty, anguished voice crying to God for the life of his infant child. We see David's bowed head as he stumbles out of Jerusalem, pursued by his murderous son.

David survived the crises of a dozen lives. Somehow he always bounced back. Somehow he maintained a passionate trust in God. First and Second Samuel don't paint him as a flawless character, nor as a perfect model of strength and courage. David had striking weaknesses. Yet he appeals to us as he did to the Israelites: he was completely, passionately alive. Whatever he did, right or wrong, he did with his whole heart. In his love for God, he held nothing back.

■ HEALING THE WOUNDS OF WAR

While 1 Samuel tells of David's youth and his long exile, 2 Samuel focuses on David as king, leading, uniting, inspiring his people. His time in the desert was over. Different qualities of leadership were required in a king.

David inherited a country in tatters. His fellow southerners recognised him as the new king. But Saul's son, backed by a powerful general, launched a civil war for the throne. Ugly infighting followed: intrigue, murder, and treachery.

Even after David's rivals were eliminated, peace was uneasy. Unless David could heal the wounds of war, resentment might smoulder in the hearts of the northerners. David's decisive action showed wisdom and firmness. He justly punished murderers who expected his gratitude.

He showed respect for his enemies by mourning their deaths. From his first day in office David behaved as the king of all the people, not just his loyal followers. The northern tribes soon came over to him, submitting to his leadership (5:1–3).

David's next move was to capture Jerusalem. People said it couldn't be done; mountainous Jerusalem was impregnable. David did it, and made Jerusalem his new political and religious capital. Located on the border between north and south, Jerusalem symbolised a new national unity based on trust in God.

That was just the beginning. David led the unified tribes to do what they had barely dreamed of: they defeated the dreaded Philistines once and for all. Almost overnight the tiny, threatened nation of Israel became safe. Secure borders encouraged expanded trade, and Israel boomed. (David's son Solomon reaped most of the wealth from this.) Naturally, David's popularity increased.

■ A MURDERER AND AN ADULTERER

But David's reign held ironic tragedies, too. Second Samuel makes no effort to hide them. David could lead a nation but not his own children. His ineffective parenting nearly destroyed all that he had done, when his heartless son Absalom led a rebellion. Second Samuel portrays David without touching up his blemishes: he was a murderer and an adulterer and a leader capable of cruelty.

Nevertheless, he was Israel's greatest king. Even at his lowest points, his great strength of character showed. He was never vengeful with his enemies. He took full responsibility for his mistakes. He managed to remember that he had started out as a mere shepherd. He held power only by the grace of God — and he believed that God had every right to take that power away.

Through his love for God and his sense of astonished gratefulness for what God had done for him, David became a living embodiment of the Israel God wanted. Like all truly great leaders, he made his country thrive not just by what he did, but by who he was.

■ HOW TO READ 2 SAMUEL

Second Samuel continues, without a break, the story begun in 1 Samuel – the two were originally one book. The difference is that David, who once sought only to survive, now seeks to unify a badly divided country. His greater responsibilities put extra stress on his leadership qualities. You can study his life with leadership in mind. You can also study chapters 11–20 to see the cancerous

effects of a leader's private sins and poor family leadership.

Chapters 21–24 seem to be an appendix, bringing in other important events and facts of David's reign. Much of 2 Samuel's story is also told in 1 Chronicles 11–21, often word for word the same.

■ 3-TRACK READING PLAN

For an explanation and complete listing of the 3-track reading plan, turn to page x.

■ TRACK 1:
Two-Week Courses on the Bible
The Track 1 reading programme on the Old Testament includes two chapters from 2 Samuel. See page x for a complete listing of this course.

■ TRACK 2:
An Overview of 2 Samuel in 3 Days
☐ Day 1. Read the

Introduction to 2 Samuel and chapter 6, in which the ark of the covenant was brought to Jerusalem and David danced before the Lord.
☐ Day 2. Read chapter 11, in which David's adultery with Bathsheba led to murder.
☐ Day 3. Read chapter 12 for the dramatic account of the prophet Nathan coming to confront David.
Now turn to page xi for your next Track 2 reading project.

■ TRACK 3:
All of 2 Samuel in 24 Days
After you have read through 2 Samuel, turn to pages xii–xiii for your next Track 3 reading project.

☐ 1　☐ 2　☐ 3　☐ 4
☐ 5　☐ 6　☐ 7　☐ 8
☐ 9　☐ 10　☐ 11　☐ 12
☐ 13　☐ 14　☐ 15　☐ 16
☐ 17　☐ 18　☐ 19　☐ 20
☐ 21　☐ 22　☐ 23　☐ 24

■ David Hears of Saul's Death

1 After the death of Saul, David returned from defeating the Amalekites and stayed in Ziklag two days. ²On the third day a man arrived from Saul's camp, with his clothes torn and with dust on his head. When he came to David, he fell to the ground to pay him honour.

³"Where have you come from?" David asked him.

He answered, "I have escaped from the Israelite camp."

⁴"What happened?" David asked. "Tell me."

He said, "The men fled from the battle. Many of them fell and died. And Saul and his son Jonathan are dead."

⁵Then David said to the young man who brought him the report, "How do you know that Saul and his son Jonathan are dead?"

⁶"I happened to be on Mount Gilboa," the young man said, "and there was Saul, leaning on his spear, with the chariots and riders almost upon him. ⁷When he turned round and saw me, he called out to me, and I said, 'What can I do?'

⁸"He asked me, 'Who are you?'

" 'An Amalekite,' I answered.

⁹"Then he said to me, 'Stand over me and kill me! I am in the throes of death, but I'm still alive.'

¹⁰"So I stood over him and killed him, because I knew that after he had fallen he could not survive. And I took the crown that was on his head and the band on his arm and have brought them here to my lord."

¹¹Then David and all the men with him took hold of their clothes and tore them. ¹²They mourned and wept and fasted till evening for Saul and his son Jonathan, and for the army of the LORD and the house of Israel, because they had fallen by the sword.

¹³David said to the young man who brought him the report, "Where are you from?"

"I am the son of an alien, an Amalekite," he answered.

¹⁴David asked him, "Why were you not afraid to lift your hand to destroy the LORD's anointed?"

¹⁵Then David called one of his men and said, "Go, strike him down!" So he struck him down, and he died. ¹⁶For David had said to him, "Your blood be on your own head. Your own mouth testified against you when you said, 'I killed the LORD's anointed.' "

■ David's Lament for Saul and Jonathan

¹⁷David took up this lament concerning Saul and his son Jonathan, ¹⁸and ordered that the men of Judah be taught this lament of the bow (it is written in the Book of Jashar):

¹⁹"Your glory, O Israel, lies slain on your
　　heights.
　How the mighty have fallen!

²⁰"Tell it not in Gath,
　　proclaim it not in the streets of
　　　Ashkelon,
　lest the daughters of the Philistines be
　　glad,

lest the daughters of the uncircumcised
rejoice.

21"O mountains of Gilboa,
may you have neither dew nor rain,
nor fields that yield offerings ⌊of grain⌋.
For there the shield of the mighty was
defiled,
the shield of Saul—no longer rubbed
with oil.
22From the blood of the slain,
from the flesh of the mighty,
the bow of Jonathan did not turn back,
the sword of Saul did not return
unsatisfied.

23"Saul and Jonathan—
in life they were loved and gracious,
and in death they were not parted.
They were swifter than eagles,
they were stronger than lions.

24"O daughters of Israel,
weep for Saul,
who clothed you in scarlet and finery,
who adorned your garments with
ornaments of gold.

25"How the mighty have fallen in battle!
Jonathan lies slain on your heights.
26I grieve for you, Jonathan my brother;
you were very dear to me.
Your love for me was wonderful,
more wonderful than that of women.

27"How the mighty have fallen!
The weapons of war have perished!"

■ David Anointed King Over Judah

2 In the course of time, David enquired of the
LORD. "Shall I go up to one of the towns of Judah?" he asked.
The LORD said, "Go up."
David asked, "Where shall I go?"
"To Hebron," the LORD answered.
2So David went up there with his two wives, Ahinoam of Jezreel and Abigail, the widow of Nabal of
Carmel. 3David also took the men who were with
him, each with his family, and they settled in Hebron
and its towns. 4Then the men of Judah came to Hebron and there they anointed David king over the
house of Judah.
When David was told that it was the men of Jabesh
Gilead who had buried Saul, 5he sent messengers to
the men of Jabesh Gilead to say to them, "The LORD
bless you for showing this kindness to Saul your master by burying him. 6May the LORD now show you
kindness and faithfulness, and I too will show you
the same favour because you have done this. 7Now
then, be strong and brave, for Saul your master is
dead, and the house of Judah has anointed me king
over them."

■ War Between the Houses of David and Saul

8Meanwhile, Abner son of Ner, the commander of
Saul's army, had taken Ish-Bosheth son of Saul and
brought him over to Mahanaim. 9He made him king

over Gilead, Ashuri[a] and Jezreel, and also over Ephraim, Benjamin and all Israel.

2:5 ■ POTENTIAL RIVALS

For their own security, dictators try to eliminate all
competitors. In the ancient world, rulers did the
same: a new king customarily killed the former
king's relatives, since they were potential rivals.
Not David! He executed the man who claimed to
have killed his old enemy King Saul (1:14–15), he
sang a painful lament over Saul's and Jonathan's
deaths, and he blessed the people of Jabesh
Gilead for their kindness in giving Saul a decent
burial. David never abandoned his love for Saul's
family.

10Ish-Bosheth son of Saul was forty years old
when he became king over Israel, and he reigned
two years. The house of Judah, however, followed
David. 11The length of time David was king in Hebron over the house of Judah was seven years and
six months.
12Abner son of Ner, together with the men of Ish-
Bosheth son of Saul, left Mahanaim and went to Gibeon. 13Joab son of Zeruiah and David's men went out
and met them at the pool of Gibeon. One group sat
down on one side of the pool and one group on the
other side.
14Then Abner said to Joab, "Let's have some of the
young men get up and fight hand to hand in front
of us."
"All right, let them do it," Joab said.
15So they stood up and were counted off—twelve
men for Benjamin and Ish-Bosheth son of Saul, and
twelve for David. 16Then each man grabbed his opponent by the head and thrust his dagger into his
opponent's side, and they fell down together. So that
place in Gibeon was called Helkath Hazzurim.[b]
17The battle that day was very fierce, and Abner
and the men of Israel were defeated by David's men.
18The three sons of Zeruiah were there: Joab, Abishai and Asahel. Now Asahel was as fleet-footed as a
wild gazelle. 19He chased Abner, turning neither to
the right nor to the left as he pursued him. 20Abner
looked behind him and asked, "Is that you, Asahel?"
"It is," he answered.
21Then Abner said to him, "Turn aside to the right
or to the left; take on one of the young men and strip
him of his weapons." But Asahel would not stop
chasing him.
22Again Abner warned Asahel, "Stop chasing me!
Why should I strike you down? How could I look
your brother Joab in the face?"
23But Asahel refused to give up the pursuit; so Abner thrust the butt of his spear into Asahel's stomach, and the spear came out through his back. He fell
there and died on the spot. And every man stopped
when he came to the place where Asahel had fallen
and died.
24But Joab and Abishai pursued Abner, and as the
sun was setting, they came to the hill of Ammah,
near Giah on the way to the wasteland of Gibeon.
25Then the men of Benjamin rallied behind Abner.

a 9 Or Asher   b 16 Helkath Hazzurim means field of daggers or field of hostilities.

They formed themselves into a group and took their stand on top of a hill.

26Abner called out to Joab, "Must the sword devour for ever? Don't you realise that this will end in bitterness? How long before you order your men to stop pursuing their brothers?"

27Joab answered, "As surely as God lives, if you had not spoken, the men would have continued the pursuit of their brothers until morning."*c*

28So Joab blew the trumpet, and all the men came to a halt; they no longer pursued Israel, nor did they fight any more.

29All that night Abner and his men marched through the Arabah. They crossed the Jordan, continued through the whole Bithron*d* and came to Mahanaim.

30Then Joab returned from pursuing Abner and assembled all his men. Besides Asahel, nineteen of David's men were found missing. 31But David's men had killed 360 Benjamites who were with Abner. 32They took Asahel and buried him in his father's tomb at Bethlehem. Then Joab and his men marched all night and arrived at Hebron by daybreak.

3 The war between the house of Saul and the house of David lasted a long time. David grew stronger and stronger, while the house of Saul grew weaker and weaker.

2Sons were born to David in Hebron:

His firstborn was Amnon the son of Ahinoam of Jezreel;

3his second, Kileab the son of Abigail the widow of Nabal of Carmel;

the third, Absalom the son of Maacah daughter of Talmai king of Geshur;

4the fourth, Adonijah the son of Haggith;

the fifth, Shephatiah the son of Abital;

5and the sixth, Ithream the son of David's wife Eglah.

These were born to David in Hebron.

■ Abner Goes Over to David

6During the war between the house of Saul and the house of David, Abner had been strengthening his own position in the house of Saul. 7Now Saul had had a concubine named Rizpah daughter of Aiah. And Ish-Bosheth said to Abner, "Why did you sleep with my father's concubine?"

8Abner was very angry because of what Ish-Bosheth said and he answered, "Am I a dog's head — on Judah's side? This very day I am loyal to the house of your father Saul and to his family and friends. I haven't handed you over to David. Yet now you accuse me of an offence involving this woman! 9May God deal with Abner, be it ever so severely, if I do not do for David what the LORD promised him on oath 10and transfer the kingdom from the house of Saul and establish David's throne over Israel and Judah from Dan to Beersheba." 11Ish-Bosheth did not dare to say another word to Abner, because he was afraid of him.

12Then Abner sent messengers on his behalf to say to David, "Whose land is it? Make an agreement with me, and I will help you bring all Israel over to you."

13"Good," said David. "I will make an agreement with you. But I demand one thing of you: Do not come into my presence unless you bring Michal daughter of Saul when you come to see me." 14Then David sent messengers to Ish-Bosheth son of Saul, demanding, "Give me my wife Michal, whom I betrothed to myself for the price of a hundred Philistine foreskins."

3:7 ■ WOMEN IN POLITICS

In David's time, women were political symbols. Abner's sleeping with Saul's concubine would have suggested that he had his eyes on becoming king himself. Later, when Absalom drove his father David out of Jerusalem, he slept with David's concubines in public, demonstrating to all eyes that he had taken over from his father (16:22).

David sometimes may have married for political benefit. One wife, Absalom's mother (verse 3), was a princess from a neighbouring country; the marriage undoubtedly promoted good foreign relations. David's request that Michal be returned to him (though she had remarried, verses 14–16) made political sense: an alliance with Saul's daughter would tie Saul's family to the palace.

15So Ish-Bosheth gave orders and had her taken away from her husband Paltiel son of Laish. 16Her husband, however, went with her, weeping behind her all the way to Bahurim. Then Abner said to him, "Go back home!" So he went back.

17Abner conferred with the elders of Israel and said, "For some time you have wanted to make David your king. 18Now do it! For the LORD promised David, 'By my servant David I will rescue my people Israel from the hand of the Philistines and from the hand of all their enemies.' "

19Abner also spoke to the Benjamites in person. Then he went to Hebron to tell David everything that Israel and the whole house of Benjamin wanted to do. 20When Abner, who had twenty men with him, came to David at Hebron, David prepared a feast for him and his men. 21Then Abner said to David, "Let me go at once and assemble all Israel for my lord the king, so that they may make a compact with you, and that you may rule over all that your heart desires." So David sent Abner away, and he went in peace.

■ Joab Murders Abner

22Just then David's men and Joab returned from a raid and brought with them a great deal of plunder. But Abner was no longer with David in Hebron, because David had sent him away, and he had gone in peace. 23When Joab and all the soldiers with him arrived, he was told that Abner son of Ner had come to the king and that the king had sent him away and that he had gone in peace.

24So Joab went to the king and said, "What have you done? Look, Abner came to you. Why did you let him go? Now he is gone! 25You know Abner son of Ner; he came to deceive you and observe your movements and find out everything you are doing."

c27 Or spoken this morning, the men would not have taken up the pursuit of their brothers; or spoken, the men would have given up the pursuit of their brothers by morning　d29 Or morning; or ravine; the meaning of the Hebrew for this word is uncertain.

26Joab then left David and sent messengers after Abner, and they brought him back from the well of Sirah. But David did not know it. 27Now when Abner returned to Hebron, Joab took him aside into the gateway, as though to speak with him privately. And there, to avenge the blood of his brother Asahel, Joab stabbed him in the stomach, and he died.

28Later, when David heard about this, he said, "I and my kingdom are for ever innocent before the LORD concerning the blood of Abner son of Ner. 29May his blood fall upon the head of Joab and upon all his father's house! May Joab's house never be without someone who has a running sore or leprosy*a* or who leans on a crutch or who falls by the sword or who lacks food."

30(Joab and his brother Abishai murdered Abner because he had killed their brother Asahel in the battle of Gibeon.)

3:30 ■ EASY ON JOAB

Leadership is never easy, and David had to make some hard decisions. First he made peace with Abner, a former enemy. Then, when Abner was tricked and murdered by Joab, David decided not to punish Joab or remove his power even though this action had directly undermined David's policy of bringing harmony to a divided land. Why not? Perhaps he needed Joab's abilities, and feared what Joab might do if alienated. Many years later, when David lay dying, he instructed Solomon to punish Joab for the crime (1 Kings 2:5–6).

31Then David said to Joab and all the people with him, "Tear your clothes and put on sackcloth and walk in mourning in front of Abner." King David himself walked behind the bier. 32They buried Abner in Hebron, and the king wept aloud at Abner's tomb. All the people wept also.

33The king sang this lament for Abner:

"Should Abner have died as the lawless die?
34   Your hands were not bound,
        your feet were not fettered.
You fell as one falls before wicked men."

And all the people wept over him again.

35Then they all came and urged David to eat something while it was still day; but David took an oath, saying, "May God deal with me, be it ever so severely, if I taste bread or anything else before the sun sets!"

36All the people took note and were pleased; indeed, everything the king did pleased them. 37So on that day all the people and all Israel knew that the king had no part in the murder of Abner son of Ner.

38Then the king said to his men, "Do you not realise that a prince and a great man has fallen in Israel this day? 39And today, though I am the anointed king, I am weak, and these sons of Zeruiah are too strong for me. May the LORD repay the evildoer according to his evil deeds!"

■ Ish-Bosheth Murdered

4 When Ish-Bosheth son of Saul heard that Abner had died in Hebron, he lost courage, and all Israel became alarmed. 2Now Saul's son had two men who were leaders of raiding bands. One was named Baanah and the other Recab; they were sons of Rimmon the Beerothite from the tribe of Benjamin — Beeroth is considered part of Benjamin, 3because the people of Beeroth fled to Gittaim and have lived there as aliens to this day.

4(Jonathan son of Saul had a son who was lame in both feet. He was five years old when the news about Saul and Jonathan came from Jezreel. His nurse picked him up and fled, but as she hurried to leave, he fell and became crippled. His name was Mephibosheth.)

5Now Recab and Baanah, the sons of Rimmon the Beerothite, set out for the house of Ish-Bosheth, and they arrived there in the heat of the day while he was taking his noonday rest. 6They went into the inner part of the house as if to get some wheat, and they stabbed him in the stomach. Then Recab and his brother Baanah slipped away.

7They had gone into the house while he was lying on the bed in his bedroom. After they stabbed and killed him, they cut off his head. Taking it with them, they travelled all night by way of the Arabah. 8They brought the head of Ish-Bosheth to David at Hebron and said to the king, "Here is the head of Ish-Bosheth son of Saul, your enemy, who tried to take your life. This day the LORD has avenged my lord the king against Saul and his offspring."

9David answered Recab and his brother Baanah, the sons of Rimmon the Beerothite, "As surely as the LORD lives, who has delivered me out of all trouble, 10when a man told me, 'Saul is dead,' and thought he was bringing good news, I seized him and put him to death in Ziklag. That was the reward I gave him for his news! 11How much more — when wicked men have killed an innocent man in his own house and on his own bed — should I not now demand his blood from your hand and rid the earth of you!"

12So David gave an order to his men, and they killed them. They cut off their hands and feet and hung the bodies by the pool in Hebron. But they took the head of Ish-Bosheth and buried it in Abner's tomb at Hebron.

■ David Becomes King Over Israel

5 All the tribes of Israel came to David at Hebron and said, "We are your own flesh and blood. 2In the past, while Saul was king over us, you were the one who led Israel on their military campaigns. And the LORD said to you, 'You shall shepherd my people Israel, and you shall become their ruler.'"

3When all the elders of Israel had come to King David at Hebron, the king made a compact with them at Hebron before the LORD, and they anointed David king over Israel.

4David was thirty years old when he became king, and he reigned for forty years. 5In Hebron he reigned over Judah for seven years and six months, and in Jerusalem he reigned over all Israel and Judah for thirty-three years.

---

a 29 The Hebrew word was used for various diseases affecting the skin — not necessarily leprosy.

■ David Conquers Jerusalem

⁶The king and his men marched to Jerusalem to attack the Jebusites, who lived there. The Jebusites said to David, "You will not get in here; even the blind and the lame can ward you off." They thought, "David cannot get in here." ⁷Nevertheless, David captured the fortress of Zion, the City of David.

5:6 ■ CHOOSING A CAPITAL

In trying to unify the northern and southern tribes, David wanted a capital that offended neither side. He found it in Jerusalem, on the border between North and South and belonging to neither. Its choice can be compared to the U.S. capital, Washington, D.C., a compromise between North and South.

---

⁸On that day, David said, "Anyone who conquers the Jebusites will have to use the water shaft[a] to reach those 'lame and blind' who are David's enemies."[b] That is why they say, "The 'blind and lame' will not enter the palace."

⁹David then took up residence in the fortress and called it the City of David. He built up the area around it, from the supporting terraces[c] inward. ¹⁰And he became more and more powerful, because the LORD God Almighty was with him.

¹¹Now Hiram king of Tyre sent messengers to David, along with cedar logs and carpenters and stonemasons, and they built a palace for David. ¹²And David knew that the LORD had established him as king over Israel and had exalted his kingdom for the sake of his people Israel.

¹³After he left Hebron, David took more concubines and wives in Jerusalem, and more sons and daughters were born to him. ¹⁴These are the names of the children born to him there: Shammua, Shobab, Nathan, Solomon, ¹⁵Ibhar, Elishua, Nepheg, Japhia, ¹⁶Elishama, Eliada and Eliphelet.

■ David Defeats the Philistines

¹⁷When the Philistines heard that David had been anointed king over Israel, they went up in full force to search for him, but David heard about it and went down to the stronghold. ¹⁸Now the Philistines had come and spread out in the Valley of Rephaim; ¹⁹so David enquired of the LORD, "Shall I go and attack the Philistines? Will you hand them over to me?"

The LORD answered him, "Go, for I will surely hand the Philistines over to you."

²⁰So David went to Baal Perazim, and there he defeated them. He said, "As waters break out, the LORD has broken out against my enemies before me." So that place was called Baal Perazim.[d] ²¹The Philistines abandoned their idols there, and David and his men carried them off.

²²Once more the Philistines came up and spread out in the Valley of Rephaim; ²³so David enquired of the LORD, and he answered, "Do not go straight up, but circle round behind them and attack them in front of the balsam trees. ²⁴As soon as you hear the sound of marching in the tops of the balsam trees, move quickly, because that will mean the LORD has gone out in front of you to strike the Philistine army." ²⁵So David did as the LORD commanded him, and he struck down the Philistines all the way from Gibeon[e] to Gezer.

5:19 ■ SEEKING GUIDANCE

Most ancient kings sought signs from God. David went well beyond that practice, regularly asking God for guidance about military and governmental decisions. David's faith wasn't impersonal; he had a close, practical, and deep relationship with God.

■ The Ark Brought to Jerusalem

6 David again brought together out of Israel chosen men, thirty thousand in all. ²He and all his men set out from Baalah of Judah[a] to bring up from there the ark of God, which is called by the Name,[b] the name of the LORD Almighty, who is enthroned between the cherubim that are on the ark. ³They set the ark of God on a new cart and brought it from the house of Abinadab, which was on the hill. Uzzah and Ahio, sons of Abinadab, were guiding the new cart ⁴with the ark of God on it,[c] and Ahio was walking in front of it. ⁵David and the whole house of Israel were celebrating with all their might before the LORD, with songs[d] and with harps, lyres, tambourines, sistrums and cymbals.

⁶When they came to the threshing-floor of Nacon, Uzzah reached out and took hold of the ark of God, because the oxen stumbled. ⁷The LORD's anger burned against Uzzah because of his irreverent act; therefore God struck him down and he died there beside the ark of God.

⁸Then David was angry because the LORD's wrath had broken out against Uzzah, and to this day that place is called Perez Uzzah.[e]

⁹David was afraid of the LORD that day and said, "How can the ark of the LORD ever come to me?" ¹⁰He was not willing to take the ark of the LORD to be with him in the City of David. Instead, he took it aside to the house of Obed-Edom the Gittite. ¹¹The ark of the LORD remained in the house of Obed-Edom the Gittite for three months, and the LORD blessed him and his entire household.

¹²Now King David was told, "The LORD has blessed the household of Obed-Edom and everything he has, because of the ark of God." So David went down and brought up the ark of God from the house of Obed-Edom to the City of David with rejoicing. ¹³When those who were carrying the ark of the LORD had taken six steps, he sacrificed a bull and a fattened calf. ¹⁴David, wearing a linen ephod, danced before the LORD with all his might, ¹⁵while he and the entire house of Israel brought up the ark of the LORD with shouts and the sound of trumpets.

¹⁶As the ark of the LORD was entering the City of David, Michal daughter of Saul watched from a window. And when she saw King David leaping and

---

a 8 Or use scaling hooks   b 8 Or are hated by David   c 9 Or the Millo   d 20 Baal Perazim means the lord who breaks out.   e 25 Septuagint (see also 1 Chron. 14:16); Hebrew Geba   a 2 That is, Kiriath Jearim; Hebrew Baale Judah, a variant of Baalah of Judah   b 2 Hebrew; Septuagint and Vulgate do not have the Name.   c 3,4 Dead Sea Scrolls and some Septuagint manuscripts; Masoretic Text cart 4and they brought it with the ark of God from the house of Abinadab, which was on the hill   d 5 See Dead Sea Scrolls, and 1 Chron. 13:8; Masoretic Text celebrating before the LORD with all kinds of instruments made of pine.   e 8 Perez Uzzah means the outbreak against Uzzah.

dancing before the LORD, she despised him in her heart.

¹⁷They brought the ark of the LORD and set it in its place inside the tent that David had pitched for it, and David sacrificed burnt offerings and fellowship offerings/ before the LORD. ¹⁸After he had finished sacrificing the burnt offerings and fellowship offerings, he blessed the people in the name of the LORD Almighty. ¹⁹Then he gave a loaf of bread, a cake of dates and a cake of raisins to each person in the whole crowd of Israelites, both men and women. And all the people went to their homes.

²⁰When David returned home to bless his household, Michal daughter of Saul came out to meet him and said, "How the king of Israel has distinguished himself today, disrobing in the sight of the slave girls of his servants as any vulgar fellow would."

²¹David said to Michal, "It was before the LORD, who chose me rather than your father or anyone from his house when he appointed me ruler over the LORD's people Israel—I will celebrate before the LORD. ²²I will become even more undignified than this, and I will be humiliated in my own eyes. But by these slave girls you spoke of, I will be held in honour."

²³And Michal daughter of Saul had no children to the day of her death.

■ God's Promise to David

7 After the king was settled in his palace and the LORD had given him rest from all his enemies around him, ²he said to Nathan the prophet, "Here I am, living in a palace of cedar, while the ark of God remains in a tent."

³Nathan replied to the king, "Whatever you have in mind, go ahead and do it, for the LORD is with you."

⁴That night the word of the LORD came to Nathan, saying:

⁵"Go and tell my servant David, 'This is what the LORD says: Are you the one to build me a house to dwell in? ⁶I have not dwelt in a house from the day I brought the Israelites up out of Egypt to this day. I have been moving from place to place with a tent as my dwelling. ⁷Wherever I have moved with all the Israelites, did I ever say to any of their rulers whom I commanded to shepherd my people Israel, "Why have you not built me a house of cedar?" '

⁸"Now then, tell my servant David, 'This is what the LORD Almighty says: I took you from the pasture and from following the flock to be ruler over my people Israel. ⁹I have been with you wherever you have gone, and I have cut off all your enemies from before you. Now I will make your name great, like the names of the greatest men of the earth. ¹⁰And I will provide a place for my people Israel and will plant them so that they can have a home of their own and no longer be disturbed. Wicked people shall not oppress them any more, as they did at the beginning ¹¹and have done ever since the time I appointed leaders*ᵃ* over my people Israel. I will also give you rest from all your enemies.

" 'The LORD declares to you that the LORD himself will establish a house for you: ¹²When your days are over and you rest with your fathers, I will raise up your offspring to succeed you, who will come from your own body, and I will establish his kingdom. ¹³He is the one who will build a house for my Name, and I will establish the throne of his kingdom for ever. ¹⁴I will be his father, and he shall be my son. When he does wrong, I will punish him with the rod of men, with floggings inflicted by men. ¹⁵But my love will never be taken away from him, as I took it away from Saul, whom I removed from before you. ¹⁶Your house and your kingdom shall endure for ever before me;ᵇ your throne shall be established for ever.' "

7:16 ■ GOD'S GREAT PROMISE

The Lord's promise to "establish David's throne for ever" suggested that Israel would never lack the leadership they needed. This promise was one of a series of covenants between God and his people—with Abraham (Genesis 12), with Moses at Sinai (Exodus 20), and now with David. The New Testament sees this promise fulfilled in Jesus, a son of David, and King of kings for ever (Luke 1:32–33).

¹⁷Nathan reported to David all the words of this entire revelation.

■ David's Prayer

¹⁸Then King David went in and sat before the LORD, and he said:

"Who am I, O Sovereign LORD, and what is my family, that you have brought me this far? ¹⁹And as if this were not enough in your sight, O Sovereign LORD, you have also spoken about the future of the house of your servant. Is this your usual way of dealing with man, O Sovereign LORD?

²⁰"What more can David say to you? For you know your servant, O Sovereign LORD. ²¹For the sake of your word and according to your will, you have done this great thing and made it known to your servant.

²²"How great you are, O Sovereign LORD! There is no-one like you, and there is no God but you, as we have heard with our own ears. ²³And who is like your people Israel—the one nation on earth that God went out to redeem as a people for himself, and to make a name for himself, and to perform great and awesome wonders by driving out nations and their gods from before your people, whom you redeemed from Egypt?ᶜ ²⁴You have established your people Israel as your very own for ever, and you, O LORD, have become their God.

²⁵"And now, LORD God, keep for ever the promise you have made concerning your servant and his house. Do as you promised, ²⁶so that your name will be great for ever. Then men

---

*f*17 Traditionally *peace offerings*; also in verse 18   *a*11 Traditionally *judges*   *b*16 Some Hebrew manuscripts and Septuagint; most Hebrew manuscripts *you*   *c*23 See Septuagint and 1 Chron. 17:21; Hebrew *wonders for your land and before your people, whom you redeemed from Egypt, from the nations and their gods.*

will say, 'The LORD Almighty is God over Israel!' And the house of your servant David will be established before you.

27"O LORD Almighty, God of Israel, you have revealed this to your servant, saying, 'I will build a house for you.' So your servant has found courage to offer you this prayer. 28O Sovereign LORD, you are God! Your words are trustworthy, and you have promised these good things to your servant. 29Now be pleased to bless the house of your servant, that it may continue for ever in your sight; for you, O Sovereign LORD, have spoken, and with your blessing the house of your servant will be blessed for ever."

■ David's Victories

8 In the course of time, David defeated the Philistines and subdued them, and he took Metheg Ammah from the control of the Philistines.

2David also defeated the Moabites. He made them lie down on the ground and measured them off with a length of cord. Every two lengths of them were put to death, and the third length was allowed to live. So the Moabites became subject to David and brought tribute.

3Moreover, David fought Hadadezer son of Rehob, king of Zobah, when he went to restore his control along the Euphrates River. 4David captured a thousand of his chariots, seven thousand charioteers[a] and twenty thousand foot soldiers. He hamstrung all but a hundred of the chariot horses.

8:4 ■ NOT READY FOR CHARIOTS

Chariots were as great an innovation in weaponry as were guns centuries later. However, chariots required trained charioteers. Since David hamstrung all but 100 chariot horses, he may have lacked such trained personnel. Israel could defend the mountains, where chariots were of little use, but they were not ready to take on big armies on the surrounding plains.

5When the Arameans of Damascus came to help Hadadezer king of Zobah, David struck down twenty-two thousand of them. 6He put garrisons in the Aramean kingdom of Damascus, and the Arameans became subject to him and brought tribute. The LORD gave David victory wherever he went.

7David took the gold shields that belonged to the officers of Hadadezer and brought them to Jerusalem. 8From Tebah[b] and Berothai, towns that belonged to Hadadezer, King David took a great quantity of bronze.

9When Tou[c] king of Hamath heard that David had defeated the entire army of Hadadezer, 10he sent his son Joram[d] to King David to greet him and congratulate him on his victory in battle over Hadadezer, who had been at war with Tou. Joram brought with him articles of silver and gold and bronze.

11King David dedicated these articles to the LORD, as he had done with the silver and gold from all the

nations he had subdued: 12Edom[e] and Moab, the Ammonites and the Philistines, and Amalek. He also dedicated the plunder taken from Hadadezer son of Rehob, king of Zobah.

13And David became famous after he returned from striking down eighteen thousand Edomites[f] in the Valley of Salt.

14He put garrisons throughout Edom, and all the Edomites became subject to David. The LORD gave David victory wherever he went.

■ David's Officials

15David reigned over all Israel, doing what was just and right for all his people. 16Joab son of Zeruiah was over the army; Jehoshaphat son of Ahilud was recorder; 17Zadok son of Ahitub and Ahimelech son of Abiathar were priests; Seraiah was secretary; 18Benaiah son of Jehoiada was over the Kerethites and Pelethites; and David's sons were royal advisers.[g]

■ David and Mephibosheth

9 David asked, "Is there anyone still left of the house of Saul to whom I can show kindness for Jonathan's sake?"

2Now there was a servant of Saul's household named Ziba. They called him to appear before David, and the king said to him, "Are you Ziba?"

"Your servant," he replied.

3The king asked, "Is there no-one still left of the house of Saul to whom I can show God's kindness?"

Ziba answered the king, "There is still a son of Jonathan; he is crippled in both feet."

4"Where is he?" the king asked.

Ziba answered, "He is at the house of Makir son of Ammiel in Lo Debar."

5So King David had him brought from Lo Debar, from the house of Makir son of Ammiel.

6When Mephibosheth son of Jonathan, the son of Saul, came to David, he bowed down to pay him honour.

David said, "Mephibosheth!"

"Your servant," he replied.

9:7 ■ SAUL'S LAME GRANDSON

Although Saul had been David's worst enemy, David consistently showed kindness and generosity to his family. In other kingdoms of that day, Mephibosheth would have been killed. David sought him out, restored his land, and welcomed him as a permanent guest at the royal table – a considerable honour. Later, when Mephibosheth suspiciously failed to join David in fleeing from Absalom's insurrection, David gave him the benefit of the doubt (19:24–30).

7"Don't be afraid," David said to him, "for I will surely show you kindness for the sake of your father Jonathan. I will restore to you all the land that belonged to your grandfather Saul, and you will always eat at my table."

8Mephibosheth bowed down and said, "What is

---

a4 Septuagint (see also Dead Sea Scrolls and 1 Chron. 18:4); Masoretic Text *captured seventeen hundred of his charioteers*   *b8* See some Septuagint manuscripts (see also 1 Chron. 18:8); Hebrew *Betah.*   *c9* Hebrew *Toi,* a variant of *Tou;* also in verse 10   *d10* A variant of *Hadoram*   *e12* Some Hebrew manuscripts, Septuagint and Syriac (see also 1 Chron. 18:11); most Hebrew manuscripts *Aram*   *f13* A few Hebrew manuscripts, Septuagint and Syriac (see also 1 Chron. 18:12); most Hebrew manuscripts *Aram* (that is, Arameans)   *g18* Or *were priests* your servant, that you should notice a dead dog like me?"

9Then the king summoned Ziba, Saul's servant, and said to him, "I have given your master's grandson everything that belonged to Saul and his family. 10You and your sons and your servants are to farm the land for him and bring in the crops, so that your master's grandson may be provided for. And Mephibosheth, grandson of your master, will always eat at my table." (Now Ziba had fifteen sons and twenty servants.)

11Then Ziba said to the king, "Your servant will do whatever my lord the king commands his servant to do." So Mephibosheth ate at David's*a* table like one of the king's sons.

12Mephibosheth had a young son named Mica, and all the members of Ziba's household were servants of Mephibosheth. 13And Mephibosheth lived in Jerusalem, because he always ate at the king's table, and he was crippled in both feet.

■ David Defeats the Ammonites

10 In the course of time, the king of the Ammonites died, and his son Hanun succeeded him as king. 2David thought, "I will show kindness to Hanun son of Nahash, just as his father showed kindness to me." So David sent a delegation to express his sympathy to Hanun concerning his father.

When David's men came to the land of the Ammonites, 3the Ammonite nobles said to Hanun their lord, "Do you think David is honouring your father by sending men to you to express sympathy? Hasn't David sent them to you to explore the city and spy it out and overthrow it?" 4So Hanun seized David's men, shaved off half of each man's beard, cut off their garments in the middle at the buttocks, and sent them away.

5When David was told about this, he sent messengers to meet the men, for they were greatly humiliated. The king said, "Stay at Jericho till your beards have grown, and then come back."

6When the Ammonites realised that they had become an offence to David's nostrils, they hired twenty thousand Aramean foot soldiers from Beth Rehob and Zobah, as well as the king of Maacah with a thousand men, and also twelve thousand men from Tob.

7On hearing this, David sent Joab out with the entire army of fighting men. 8The Ammonites came out and drew up in battle formation at the entrance to their city gate, while the Arameans of Zobah and Rehob and the men of Tob and Maacah were by themselves in the open country.

9Joab saw that there were battle lines in front of him and behind him; so he selected some of the best troops in Israel and deployed them against the Arameans. 10He put the rest of the men under the command of Abishai his brother and deployed them against the Ammonites. 11Joab said, "If the Arameans are too strong for me, then you are to come to my rescue; but if the Ammonites are too strong for you, then I will come to rescue you. 12Be strong and let us fight bravely for our people and the cities of our God. The LORD will do what is good in his sight."

13Then Joab and the troops with him advanced to fight the Arameans, and they fled before him. 14When the Ammonites saw that the Arameans were fleeing, they fled before Abishai and went inside the city. So Joab returned from fighting the Ammonites and came to Jerusalem.

15After the Arameans saw that they had been routed by Israel, they regrouped. 16Hadadezer had Arameans brought from beyond the River;*a* they went to Helam, with Shobach the commander of Hadadezer's army leading them.

17When David was told of this, he gathered all Israel, crossed the Jordan and went to Helam. The Arameans formed their battle lines to meet David and fought against him. 18But they fled before Israel, and David killed seven hundred of their charioteers and forty thousand of their foot soldiers.*b* He also struck down Shobach the commander of their army, and he died there. 19When all the kings who were vassals of Hadadezer saw that they had been defeated by Israel, they made peace with the Israelites and became subject to them.

So the Arameans were afraid to help the Ammonites any more.

■ David and Bathsheba

11 In the spring, at the time when kings go off to war, David sent Joab out with the king's men and the whole Israelite army. They destroyed the Ammonites and besieged Rabbah. But David remained in Jerusalem.

2One evening David got up from his bed and walked around on the roof of the palace. From the roof he saw a woman bathing. The woman was very beautiful, 3and David sent someone to find out about her. The man said, "Isn't this Bathsheba, the daughter of Eliam and the wife of Uriah the Hittite?" 4Then David sent messengers to get her. She came to him, and he slept with her. (She had purified herself from her uncleanness.) Then*a* she went back home. 5The woman conceived and sent word to David, saying, "I am pregnant."

6So David sent this word to Joab: "Send me Uriah the Hittite." And Joab sent him to David. 7When Uriah came to him, David asked him how Joab was, how the soldiers were and how the war was going. 8Then David said to Uriah, "Go down to your house and wash your feet." So Uriah left the palace, and a gift from the king was sent after him. 9But Uriah slept at the entrance to the palace with all his master's servants and did not go down to his house.

10When David was told, "Uriah did not go home," he asked him, "Haven't you just come from a distance? Why didn't you go home?"

11Uriah said to David, "The ark and Israel and Judah are staying in tents, and my master Joab and my lord's men are camped in the open fields. How could I go to my house to eat and drink and lie with my wife? As surely as you live, I will not do such a thing!"

12Then David said to him, "Stay here one more day, and tomorrow I will send you back." So Uriah remained in Jerusalem that day and the next. 13At David's invitation, he ate and drank with him, and David made him drunk. But in the evening Uriah went out to sleep on his mat among his master's servants; he did not go home.

---

a11 Septuagint; Hebrew *my*   *a16* That is, the Euphrates   *b18* Some Septuagint manuscripts (see also 1 Chron. 19:18); Hebrew *horsemen*   *a4* Or *with her. When she purified herself from her uncleanness,*

14In the morning David wrote a letter to Joab and sent it with Uriah. 15In it he wrote, "Put Uriah in the front line where the fighting is fiercest. Then withdraw from him so that he will be struck down and die."

11:11 ■ A MILITARY HERO
Israelite soldiers had no sexual relations while they were preparing for battle. (See, for instance, 1 Samuel 21:5.) Uriah refused to sleep with Bathsheba because he remembered duty before pleasure. He is mentioned (in 23:39) as one of the Thirty, a group of leading warriors under David.

16So while Joab had the city under siege, he put Uriah at a place where he knew the strongest defenders were. 17When the men of the city came out and fought against Joab, some of the men in David's army fell; moreover, Uriah the Hittite died.

18Joab sent David a full account of the battle. 19He instructed the messenger: "When you have finished giving the king this account of the battle, 20the king's anger may flare up, and he may ask you, 'Why did you get so close to the city to fight? Didn't you know they would shoot arrows from the wall? 21Who killed Abimelech son of Jerub-Besheth?b Didn't a woman throw an upper millstone on him from the wall, so that he died in Thebez? Why did you get so close to the wall?' If he asks you this, then say to him, 'Also, your servant Uriah the Hittite is dead.' "

22The messenger set out, and when he arrived he told David everything Joab had sent him to say. 23The messenger said to David, "The men overpowered us and came out against us in the open, but we drove them back to the entrance to the city gate. 24Then the archers shot arrows at your servants from the wall, and some of the king's men died. Moreover, your servant Uriah the Hittite is dead."

25David told the messenger, "Say this to Joab: 'Don't let this upset you; the sword devours one as well as another. Press the attack against the city and destroy it.' Say this to encourage Joab."

26When Uriah's wife heard that her husband was dead, she mourned for him. 27After the time of mourning was over, David had her brought to his house, and she became his wife and bore him a son. But the thing David had done displeased the LORD.

■ Nathan Rebukes David

12 The LORD sent Nathan to David. When he came to him, he said, "There were two men in a certain town, one rich and the other poor. 2The rich man had a very large number of sheep and cattle, 3but the poor man had nothing except one little ewe lamb that he had bought. He raised it, and it grew up with him and his children. It shared his food, drank from his cup and even slept in his arms. It was like a daughter to him.

4"Now a traveller came to the rich man, but the rich man refrained from taking one of his own sheep or cattle to prepare a meal for the traveller who had come to him. Instead, he took the ewe lamb that belonged to the poor man and prepared it for the one who had come to him."

5David burned with anger against the man and said to Nathan, "As surely as the LORD lives, the man who did this deserves to die! 6He must pay for that lamb four times over, because he did such a thing and had no pity."

7Then Nathan said to David, "You are the man! This is what the LORD, the God of Israel, says: 'I anointed you king over Israel, and I delivered you from the hand of Saul. 8I gave you your master's house to you, and your master's wives into your arms. I gave you the house of Israel and Judah. And if all this had been too little, I would have given you even more. 9Why did you despise the word of the LORD by doing what is evil in his eyes? You struck down Uriah the Hittite with the sword and took his wife to be your own. You killed him with the sword of the Ammonites. 10Now, therefore, the sword shall never depart from your house, because you despised me and took the wife of Uriah the Hittite to be your own.'

11"This is what the LORD says: 'Out of your own household I am going to bring calamity upon you. Before your very eyes I will take your wives and give them to one who is close to you, and he will lie with your wives in broad daylight. 12You did it in secret, but I will do this thing in broad daylight before all Israel.' "

13Then David said to Nathan, "I have sinned against the LORD."

Nathan replied, "The LORD has taken away your sin. You are not going to die. 14But because by doing this you have made the enemies of the LORD show utter contempt,a the son born to you will die."

12:13 ■ DAVID'S FINEST MOMENT
David, who possessed absolute power, could have had Nathan killed for his daring public confrontation. Or, he could have laughed him off and thrown him out of the palace. But David knew Nathan spoke for God, and in what may have been the greatest moment of his life, he admitted, "I have sinned against the LORD." David revealed what made him a man after God's own heart; though he was king, he humbled himself before the King of kings.

15After Nathan had gone home, the LORD struck the child that Uriah's wife had borne to David, and he became ill. 16David pleaded with God for the child. He fasted and went into his house and spent the nights lying on the ground. 17The elders of his household stood beside him to get him up from the ground, but he refused, and he would not eat any food with them.

18On the seventh day the child died. David's servants were afraid to tell him that the child was dead, for they thought, "While the child was still living, we spoke to David but he would not listen to us. How can we tell him the child is dead? He may do something desperate."

---

b 21 Also known as *Jerub-Baal* (that is, Gideon)   a 14 Masoretic Text; an ancient Hebrew scribal tradition *this you have shown utter contempt for the LORD*

¹⁹David noticed that his servants were whispering among themselves and he realised that the child was dead. "Is the child dead?" he asked.

"Yes," they replied, "he is dead."

²⁰Then David got up from the ground. After he had washed, put on lotions and changed his clothes, he went into the house of the LORD and worshipped. Then he went to his own house, and at his request they served him food, and he ate.

²¹His servants asked him, "Why are you acting in this way? While the child was alive, you fasted and wept, but now that the child is dead, you get up and eat!"

²²He answered, "While the child was still alive, I fasted and wept. I thought, 'Who knows? The LORD may be gracious to me and let the child live.' ²³But now that he is dead, why should I fast? Can I bring him back again? I will go to him, but he will not return to me."

²⁴Then David comforted his wife Bathsheba, and he went to her and lay with her. She gave birth to a son, and they named him Solomon. The LORD loved him; ²⁵and because the LORD loved him, he sent word through Nathan the prophet to name him Jedidiah.^b

²⁶Meanwhile Joab fought against Rabbah of the Ammonites and captured the royal citadel. ²⁷Joab then sent messengers to David, saying, "I have fought against Rabbah and taken its water supply. ²⁸Now muster the rest of the troops and besiege the city and capture it. Otherwise I shall take the city, and it will be named after me."

²⁹So David mustered the entire army and went to Rabbah, and attacked and captured it. ³⁰He took the

---

■ ADULTERY AND MURDER
THE KING COULD DO AS HE PLEASED – OR SO HE THOUGHT

INSIGHT

DAVID BURNED WITH ANGER AGAINST THE MAN AND SAID TO NATHAN, "AS SURELY AS THE LORD LIVES, THE MAN WHO DID THIS DESERVES TO DIE!" . . . THEN NATHAN SAID TO DAVID, "YOU ARE THE MAN!" ■ 12:5,7

An ancient and enduring tradition teaches that the people on top make the rules – they don't have to live by them. Lots of leaders in history have followed this course, taking the women they wanted, the money they wanted, the privileges they wanted.

Nobody, therefore, challenged David's right to sleep with another man's wife. David saw Bathsheba, lusted for her, and sent for her: as far as we know neither his servants nor Bathsheba lodged a protest. Only when she got pregnant did a problem arise. Then David, who had had no thought of marrying Bathsheba, found himself in a jam. He called her husband, Uriah, home on leave from the army, hoping that Uriah would sleep with his wife and later be unable to prove the child belonged to another father.

Uriah's single-minded devotion to duty spoiled David's plan. David rewarded Uriah with murder. Again, not a word of protest was filed: what the king wanted the king got, no questions asked. The murder of Uriah took other good men with him, but David showed no regrets. He was at his worst: cold as iron, arrogant in his power.

After a mourning period, Bathsheba came into his house and he married her. A good many people must have known what had happened – the servants knew, at any rate – but the Bible doesn't report that any of them weredispleased. It only says, "The thing David had done displeased the LORD" (11:27).

■ WHO WILL CHALLENGE THE KING?
Who would have the courage – or the authority – to challenge the king? In most nations, no-one. But Israel had this distinction: its ultimate king was not David, but God. And God had his spokesmen, the prophets. He sent Nathan to David.

Nathan cleverly captivated David with a heart-rending story about a rich man who had abused his power. He offered the case to David, the highest judge in Israel. David knew exactly how to judge such a case: the man deserved death! When he said so, Nathan turned David's own judgment around: "You are the man!"

In this dramatic scene David's greatness showed itself. He could easily have had Nathan killed. Or he could have laughed and shown him out of the palace. Instead, "David said to Nathan, 'I have sinned against the LORD' " (12:13). David recognised that God was the true king of Israel.

Nathan's confrontation with David set the standard for centuries of conflict between kings and prophets. Time and again an Old Testament prophet went to the palace – sometimes risking his life – and told the king that God would punish him for what he was doing. The kings, rich and powerful by birth, did not have to listen. In fact, they rarely did so. David was a great king partly because he did not act with the normal pride of a king. When confronted with the truth, he repented.

□ LIFE QUESTIONS:
What determines your choices? Your own desires? Or your understanding of God's will? Think of some recent decisions you have made and apply this question to them.

---

^b 25 Jedidiah means loved by the LORD.

crown from the head of their king^c — its weight was a talent^d of gold, and it was set with precious stones — and it was placed on David's head. He took a great quantity of plunder from the city ^{31}and brought out the people who were there, consigning them to labour with saws and with iron picks and axes, and he made them work at brickmaking.^{e} He did this to all the Ammonite towns. Then David and his entire army returned to Jerusalem.

■ Amnon and Tamar

13 In the course of time, Amnon son of David fell in love with Tamar, the beautiful sister of Absalom son of David.

^{2}Amnon became frustrated to the point of illness on account of his sister Tamar, for she was a virgin, and it seemed impossible for him to do anything to her.

^{3}Now Amnon had a friend named Jonadab son of Shimeah, David's brother. Jonadab was a very shrewd man. ^{4}He asked Amnon, "Why do you, the king's son, look so haggard morning after morning? Won't you tell me?"

Amnon said to him, "I'm in love with Tamar, my brother Absalom's sister."

^{5}"Go to bed and pretend to be ill," Jonadab said. "When your father comes to see you, say to him, 'I would like my sister Tamar to come and give me something to eat. Let her prepare the food in my sight so that I may watch her and then eat it from her hand.' "

^{6}So Amnon lay down and pretended to be ill. When the king came to see him, Amnon said to him, "I would like my sister Tamar to come and make some special bread in my sight, so that I may eat from her hand."

^{7}David sent word to Tamar at the palace: "Go to the house of your brother Amnon and prepare some food for him." ^{8}So Tamar went to the house of her brother Amnon, who was lying down. She took some dough, kneaded it, made the bread in his sight and baked it. ^{9}Then she took the pan and served him the bread, but he refused to eat.

"Send everyone out of here," Amnon said. So everyone left him. ^{10}Then Amnon said to Tamar, "Bring the food here into my bedroom so that I may eat from your hand." And Tamar took the bread she had prepared and brought it to her brother Amnon in his bedroom. ^{11}But when she took it to him to eat, he grabbed her and said, "Come to bed with me, my sister."

^{12}"Don't, my brother!" she said to him. "Don't force me. Such a thing should not be done in Israel! Don't do this wicked thing. ^{13}What about me? Where could I get rid of my disgrace? And what about you? You would be like one of the wicked fools in Israel. Please speak to the king; he will not keep me from being married to you." ^{14}But he refused to listen to her, and since he was stronger than she, he raped her.

^{15}Then Amnon hated her with intense hatred. In fact, he hated her more than he had loved her. Amnon said to her, "Get up and get out!"

^{16}"No!" she said to him. "Sending me away would

be a greater wrong than what you have already done to me."

But he refused to listen to her. ^{17}He called his personal servant and said, "Get this woman out of here and bolt the door after her." ^{18}So his servant put her out and bolted the door after her. She was wearing a richly ornamented^a robe, for this was the kind of garment the virgin daughters of the king wore. ^{19}Tamar put ashes on her head and tore the ornamented robe she was wearing. She put her hand on her head and went away, weeping aloud as she went.

^{20}Her brother Absalom said to her, "Has that Amnon, your brother, been with you? Be quiet now, my sister; he is your brother. Don't take this thing to heart." And Tamar lived in her brother Absalom's house, a desolate woman.

^{21}When King David heard all this, he was furious. ^{22}Absalom never said a word to Amnon, either good or bad; he hated Amnon because he had disgraced his sister Tamar.

■ Absalom Kills Amnon

^{23}Two years later, when Absalom's sheepshearers were at Baal Hazor near the border of Ephraim, he invited all the king's sons to come there. ^{24}Absalom went to the king and said, "Your servant has had shearers come. Will the king and his officials please join me?"

^{25}"No, my son," the king replied. "All of us should not go; we would only be a burden to you." Although Absalom urged him, he still refused to go, but gave him his blessing.

^{26}Then Absalom said, "If not, please let my brother Amnon come with us."

The king asked him, "Why should he go with you?" ^{27}But Absalom urged him, so he sent with him Amnon and the rest of the king's sons.

^{28}Absalom ordered his men, "Listen! When Amnon is in high spirits from drinking wine and I say to you, 'Strike Amnon down,' then kill him. Don't be afraid. Have not I given you this order? Be strong and brave." ^{29}So Absalom's men did to Amnon what Absalom had ordered. Then all the king's sons got up, mounted their mules and fled.

13:29 ■ VICIOUS CHILDREN
What went wrong with David's children? Amnon raped his sister Tamar. Absalom killed Amnon in revenge. Ultimately Absalom plotted a coup against his father, driving David from Jerusalem. All through these events — rape, murder, rebellion — David failed to discipline his children. According to the law they deserved severe punishment, but David let them off with hardly a word. Perhaps his own guilt over Bathsheba had undercut his sense of moral authority.

^{30}While they were on their way, the report came to David: "Absalom has struck down all the king's sons; not one of them is left." ^{31}The king stood up, tore his clothes and lay down on the ground; and all his servants stood by with their clothes torn.

^{32}But Jonadab son of Shimeah, David's brother,

^{c}*30 Or of Milcom* (that is, Molech) ^{d}*30* That is, about 75 pounds (about 34 kilograms) ^{e}*31* The meaning of the Hebrew for this clause is uncertain.
^{a}*18* The meaning of the Hebrew for this phrase is uncertain; also in verse 19.

said, "My lord should not think that they killed all the princes; only Amnon is dead. This has been Absalom's expressed intention ever since the day that Amnon raped his sister Tamar. 33My lord the king should not be concerned about the report that all the king's sons are dead. Only Amnon is dead."

34Meanwhile, Absalom had fled.

Now the man standing watch looked up and saw many people on the road west of him, coming down the side of the hill. The watchman went and told the king, "I see men in the direction of Horonaim, on the side of the hill."b

35Jonadab said to the king, "See, the king's sons are here; it has happened just as your servant said."

36As he finished speaking, the king's sons came in, wailing loudly. The king, too, and all his servants wept very bitterly.

37Absalom fled and went to Talmai son of Ammihud, the king of Geshur. But King David mourned for his son every day.

38After Absalom fled and went to Geshur, he stayed there for three years. 39And the spirit of the kingc longed to go to Absalom, for he was consoled concerning Amnon's death.

13:38 ■ A REFUGE WITH HIS FAMILY
Absalom ran to Geshur, a neighbouring kingdom, probably because his mother was a daughter of Geshur's king. He could be assured of safety there.

■ Absalom Returns to Jerusalem

14 Joab son of Zeruiah knew that the king's heart longed for Absalom. 2So Joab sent someone to Tekoa and had a wise woman brought from there. He said to her, "Pretend you are in mourning. Dress in mourning clothes, and don't use any cosmetic lotions. Act like a woman who has spent many days grieving for the dead. 3Then go to the king and speak these words to him." And Joab put the words in her mouth.

4When the woman from Tekoa wenta to the king, she fell with her face to the ground to pay him honour, and she said, "Help me, O king!"

5The king asked her, "What is troubling you?"

She said, "I am indeed a widow; my husband is dead. 6I your servant had two sons. They got into a fight with each other in the field, and no-one was there to separate them. One struck the other and killed him. 7Now the whole clan has risen up against your servant; they say, 'Hand over the one who struck his brother down, so that we may put him to death for the life of his brother whom he killed; then we will get rid of the heir as well.' They would put out the only burning coal I have left, leaving my husband neither name nor descendant on the face of the earth."

8The king said to the woman, "Go home, and I will issue an order on your behalf."

9But the woman from Tekoa said to him, "My lord the king, let the blame rest on me and on my father's family, and let the king and his throne be without guilt."

10The king replied, "If anyone says anything to you, bring him to me, and he will not bother you again."

11She said, "Then let the king invoke the LORD his God to prevent the avenger of blood from adding to the destruction, so that my son shall not be destroyed."

"As surely as the LORD lives," he said, "not one hair of your son's head will fall to the ground."

12Then the woman said, "Let your servant speak a word to my lord the king."

"Speak," he replied.

13The woman said, "Why then have you devised a thing like this against the people of God? When the king says this, does he not convict himself, for the king has not brought back his banished son? 14Like water spilled on the ground, which cannot be recovered, so we must die. But God does not take away life; instead, he devises ways so that a banished person may not remain estranged from him.

15"And now I have come to say this to my lord the king because the people have made me afraid. Your servant thought, 'I will speak to the king; perhaps he will do what his servant asks. 16Perhaps the king will agree to deliver his servant from the hand of the man who is trying to cut off both me and my son from the inheritance God gave us.'

17"And now your servant says, 'May the word of my lord the king bring me rest, for my lord the king is like an angel of God in discerning good and evil. May the LORD your God be with you.'"

18Then the king said to the woman, "Do not keep from me the answer to what I am going to ask you."

"Let my lord the king speak," the woman said.

19The king asked, "Isn't the hand of Joab with you in all this?"

The woman answered, "As surely as you live, my lord the king, no-one can turn to the right or to the left from anything my lord the king says. Yes, it was your servant Joab who instructed me to do this and who put all these words into the mouth of your servant. 20Your servant Joab did this to change the present situation. My lord has wisdom like that of an angel of God — he knows everything that happens in the land."

21The king said to Joab, "Very well, I will do it. Go, bring back the young man Absalom."

22Joab fell with his face to the ground to pay him honour, and he blessed the king. Joab said, "Today your servant knows that he has found favour in your eyes, my lord the king, because the king has granted his servant's request."

23Then Joab went to Geshur and brought Absalom back to Jerusalem. 24But the king said, "He must go to his own house; he must not see my face." So Absalom went to his own house and did not see the face of the king.

25In all Israel there was not a man so highly praised for his handsome appearance as Absalom. From the top of his head to the sole of his foot there was no blemish in him. 26Whenever he cut the hair of his head — he used to cut his hair from time to time when it became too heavy for him — he would

---

b34 Septuagint; Hebrew does not have this sentence.　c39 Dead Sea Scrolls and some Septuagint manuscripts; Masoretic Text But ьthe spirit of, David the king　a4 Many Hebrew manuscripts, Septuagint, Vulgate and Syriac; most Hebrew manuscripts spoke weigh it, and its weight was two hundred shekels[b] by the royal standard.

27Three sons and a daughter were born to Absalom. The daughter's name was Tamar, and she became a beautiful woman.

28Absalom lived for two years in Jerusalem without seeing the king's face. 29Then Absalom sent for Joab in order to send him to the king, but Joab refused to come to him. So he sent a second time, but he refused to come. 30Then he said to his servants, "Look, Joab's field is next to mine, and he has barley there. Go and set it on fire." So Absalom's servants set the field on fire.

31Then Joab did go to Absalom's house and he said to him, "Why have your servants set my field on fire?"

32Absalom said to Joab, "Look, I sent word to you and said, 'Come here so that I can send you to the king to ask, "Why have I come from Geshur? It would be better for me if I were still there!" ' Now then, I want to see the king's face, and if I am guilty of anything, let him put me to death."

33So Joab went to the king and told him this. Then the king summoned Absalom, and he came in and bowed down with his face to the ground before the king. And the king kissed Absalom.

■ Absalom's Conspiracy

15 In the course of time, Absalom provided himself with a chariot and horses and with fifty men to run ahead of him. 2He would get up early and stand by the side of the road leading to the city gate. Whenever anyone came with a complaint to be placed before the king for a decision, Absalom would call out to him, "What town are you from?" He would answer, "Your servant is from one of the tribes of Israel." 3Then Absalom would say to him, "Look, your claims are valid and proper, but there is no representative of the king to hear you." 4And Absalom would add, "If only I were appointed judge in the land! Then everyone who has a complaint or case could come to me and I would see that he receives justice."

5Also, whenever anyone approached him to bow down before him, Absalom would reach out his hand, take hold of him and kiss him. 6Absalom behaved in this way towards all the Israelites who came to the king asking for justice, and so he stole the hearts of the men of Israel.

7At the end of four[a] years, Absalom said to the king, "Let me go to Hebron and fulfil a vow I made to the LORD. 8While your servant was living at Geshur in Aram, I made this vow: 'If the LORD takes me back to Jerusalem, I will worship the LORD in Hebron.' "[b]

9The king said to him, "Go in peace." So he went to Hebron.

10Then Absalom sent secret messengers throughout the tribes of Israel to say, "As soon as you hear the sound of the trumpets, then say, 'Absalom is king in Hebron.' " 11Two hundred men from Jerusalem had accompanied Absalom. They had been invited as guests and went quite innocently, knowing nothing about the matter. 12While Absalom was offering sacrifices, he also sent for Ahithophel the Gilonite,

David's counsellor, to come from Giloh, his home town. And so the conspiracy gained strength, and Absalom's following kept on increasing.

■ David Flees

13A messenger came and told David, "The hearts of the men of Israel are with Absalom."

14Then David said to all his officials who were with him in Jerusalem, "Come! We must flee, or none of us will escape from Absalom. We must leave immediately, or he will move quickly to overtake us and bring ruin upon us and put the city to the sword."

15The king's officials answered him, "Your servants are ready to do whatever our lord the king chooses."

16The king set out, with his entire household following him; but he left ten concubines to take care of the palace. 17So the king set out, with all the people following him, and they halted at a place some distance away. 18All his men marched past him, along with all the Kerethites and Pelethites; and all the six hundred Gittites who had accompanied him from Gath marched before the king.

15:18 ■ MERCENARIES
David's army included more than just loyal Israelites; he had added mercenaries (hired soldiers). The Gittites came from the Philistine city of Gath. David had probably recruited them during his stay there (1 Samuel 27:2), and they had loyally followed him ever since.

19The king said to Ittai the Gittite, "Why should you come along with us? Go back and stay with King Absalom. You are a foreigner, an exile from your homeland. 20You came only yesterday. And today shall I make you wander about with us, when I do not know where I am going? Go back, and take your countrymen. May kindness and faithfulness be with you."

21But Ittai replied to the king, "As surely as the LORD lives, and as my lord the king lives, wherever my lord the king may be, whether it means life or death, there will your servant be."

22David said to Ittai, "Go ahead, march on." So Ittai the Gittite marched on with all his men and the families that were with him.

23The whole countryside wept aloud as all the people passed by. The king also crossed the Kidron Valley, and all the people moved on towards the desert.

24Zadok was there, too, and all the Levites who were with him were carrying the ark of the covenant of God. They set down the ark of God, and Abiathar offered sacrifices[c] until all the people had finished leaving the city.

25Then the king said to Zadok, "Take the ark of God back into the city. If I find favour in the LORD's eyes, he will bring me back and let me see it and his dwelling-place again. 26But if he says, 'I am not pleased with you,' then I am ready; let him do to me whatever seems good to him."

---

b26 That is, about 5 pounds (about 2.3 kilograms)   a7 Some Septuagint manuscripts, Syriac and Josephus; Hebrew forty   b8 Some Septuagint manuscripts; Hebrew does not have in Hebron.   c24 Or Abiathar went up

27The king also said to Zadok the priest, "Aren't you a seer? Go back to the city in peace, with your son Ahimaaz and Jonathan son of Abiathar. You and Abiathar take your two sons with you. 28I will wait at the fords in the desert until word comes from you to inform me." 29So Zadok and Abiathar took the ark of God back to Jerusalem and stayed there.

30But David continued up the Mount of Olives, weeping as he went; his head was covered and he was barefoot. All the people with him covered their heads too and were weeping as they went up. 31Now David had been told, "Ahithophel is among the conspirators with Absalom." So David prayed, "O LORD, turn Ahithophel's counsel into foolishness."

32When David arrived at the summit, where people used to worship God, Hushai the Arkite was there to meet him, his robe torn and dust on his head. 33David said to him, "If you go with me, you will be a burden to me. 34But if you return to the city and say to Absalom, 'I will be your servant, O king; I was your father's servant in the past, but now I will be your servant,' then you can help me by frustrating Ahithophel's advice. 35Won't the priests Zadok and Abiathar be there with you? Tell them anything you hear in the king's palace. 36Their two sons, Ahimaaz son of Zadok and Jonathan son of Abiathar, are there with them. Send them to me with anything you hear."

37So David's friend Hushai arrived at Jerusalem as Absalom was entering the city.

■ David and Ziba

16 When David had gone a short distance beyond the summit, there was Ziba, the steward of Mephibosheth, waiting to meet him. He had a string of donkeys saddled and loaded with two hundred loaves of bread, a hundred cakes of raisins, a hundred cakes of figs and a skin of wine.

2The king asked Ziba, "Why have you brought these?"

Ziba answered, "The donkeys are for the king's household to ride on, the bread and fruit are for the men to eat, and the wine is to refresh those who become exhausted in the desert."

3The king then asked, "Where is your master's grandson?"

Ziba said to him, "He is staying in Jerusalem, because he thinks, 'Today the house of Israel will give me back my grandfather's kingdom.' "

4Then the king said to Ziba, "All that belonged to Mephibosheth is now yours."

"I humbly bow," Ziba said. "May I find favour in your eyes, my lord the king."

■ Shimei Curses David

5As King David approached Bahurim, a man from the same clan as Saul's family came out from there. His name was Shimei son of Gera, and he cursed as he came out. 6He pelted David and all the king's officials with stones, though all the troops and the special guard were on David's right and left. 7As he cursed, Shimei said, "Get out, get out, you man of blood, you scoundrel! 8The LORD has repaid you for all the blood you shed in the household of Saul, in whose place you have reigned. The LORD has handed the kingdom over to your son Absalom. You have come to ruin because you are a man of blood!"

9Then Abishai son of Zeruiah said to the king, "Why should this dead dog curse my lord the king? Let me go over and cut off his head."

10But the king said, "What do you and I have in common, you sons of Zeruiah? If he is cursing because the LORD said to him, 'Curse David,' who can ask, 'Why do you do this?' "

11David then said to Abishai and all his officials, "My son, who is of my own flesh, is trying to take my life. How much more, then, this Benjamite! Leave him alone; let him curse, for the LORD has told him to. 12It may be that the LORD will see my distress and repay me with good for the cursing I am receiving today."

13So David and his men continued along the road while Shimei was going along the hillside opposite him, cursing as he went and throwing stones at him and showering him with dirt. 14The king and all the people with him arrived at their destination exhausted. And there he refreshed himself.

■ The Advice of Hushai and Ahithophel

15Meanwhile, Absalom and all the men of Israel came to Jerusalem, and Ahithophel was with him. 16Then Hushai the Arkite, David's friend, went to Absalom and said to him, "Long live the king! Long live the king!"

17Absalom asked Hushai, "Is this the love you show your friend? Why didn't you go with your friend?"

18Hushai said to Absalom, "No, the one chosen by the LORD, by these people and by all the men of Israel – his I will be, and I will remain with him. 19Furthermore, whom should I serve? Should I not serve the son? Just as I served your father, so I will serve you."

20Absalom said to Ahithophel, "Give us your advice. What should we do?"

21Ahithophel answered, "Lie with your father's concubines whom he left to take care of the palace. Then all Israel will hear that you have made yourself an offence to your father's nostrils, and the hands of everyone with you will be strengthened." 22So they pitched a tent for Absalom on the roof, and he lay with his father's concubines in the sight of all Israel.

16:22 ■ NO WAY BACK
Absalom publicly slept with his father's concubines for political reasons. It made clear his claim to the throne (see 3:6 for a similar case) and was extremely offensive to David. Israelites who had held back their allegiance, thinking that father and son would reconcile their differences, knew now that the breach was permanent. They had to take sides.

23Now in those days the advice Ahithophel gave was like that of one who enquires of God. That was how both David and Absalom regarded all of Ahithophel's advice.

17 Ahithophel said to Absalom, "I would[a] choose twelve thousand men and set out tonight in pursuit of David. [2]I would[b] attack him while he is weary and weak. I would[b] strike him with terror, and then all the people with him will flee. I would[b] strike down only the king [3]and bring all the people back to you. The death of the man you seek will mean the return of all; all the people will be unharmed." [4]This plan seemed good to Absalom and to all the elders of Israel.

[5]But Absalom said, "Summon also Hushai the Arkite, so that we can hear what he has to say." [6]When Hushai came to him, Absalom said, "Ahithophel has given this advice. Should we do what he says? If not, give us your opinion."

[7]Hushai replied to Absalom, "The advice Ahithophel has given is not good this time. [8]You know your father and his men; they are fighters, and as fierce as a wild bear robbed of her cubs. Besides, your father is an experienced fighter; he will not spend the night with the troops. [9]Even now, he is hidden in a cave or some other place. If he should attack your troops first,[c] whoever hears about it will say, 'There has been a slaughter among the troops who follow Absalom.' [10]Then even the bravest soldier, whose heart is like the heart of a lion, will melt with fear, for all Israel knows that your father is a fighter and that those with him are brave.

[11]"So I advise you: Let all Israel, from Dan to Beersheba — as numerous as the sand on the seashore — be gathered to you, with you yourself leading them into battle. [12]Then we will attack him wherever he may be found, and we will fall on him as dew settles on the ground. Neither he nor any of his men will be left alive. [13]If he withdraws into a city, then all Israel will bring ropes to that city, and we will drag it down to the valley until not even a piece of it can be found."

17:11 ■ FLATTERING ADVICE

Hushai, one of David's top advisers, slipped into Absalom's camp pretending to have deserted David. He deliberately gave bad advice, cleverly phrasing it to flatter Absalom. Hushai suggested that if Absalom delayed his pursuit of David, Absalom (who had never fought in battle) could gather a gigantic army to lead. Absalom fell for it, and the delay gave David enough time to consolidate his support.

[14]Absalom and all the men of Israel said, "The advice of Hushai the Arkite is better than that of Ahithophel." For the LORD had determined to frustrate the good advice of Ahithophel in order to bring disaster on Absalom.

[15]Hushai told Zadok and Abiathar, the priests, "Ahithophel has advised Absalom and the elders of Israel to do such and such, but I have advised them to do so and so. [16]Now send a message immediately and tell David, 'Do not spend the night at the fords in the desert; cross over without fail, or the king and all the people with him will be swallowed up.' "

[17]Jonathan and Ahimaaz were staying at En Rogel. A servant girl was to go and inform them, and they were to go and tell King David, for they could not risk being seen entering the city. [18]But a young man saw them and told Absalom. So the two of them left quickly and went to the house of a man in Bahurim. He had a well in his courtyard, and they climbed down into it. [19]His wife took a covering and spread it out over the opening of the well and scattered grain over it. No-one knew anything about it.

[20]When Absalom's men came to the woman at the house, they asked, "Where are Ahimaaz and Jonathan?"

The woman answered them, "They crossed over the brook."[d] The men searched but found no-one, so they returned to Jerusalem.

[21]After the men had gone, the two climbed out of the well and went to inform King David. They said to him, "Set out and cross the river at once; Ahithophel has advised such and such against you." [22]So David and all the people with him set out and crossed the Jordan. By daybreak, no-one was left who had not crossed the Jordan.

[23]When Ahithophel saw that his advice had not been followed, he saddled his donkey and set out for his house in his home town. He put his house in order and then hanged himself. So he died and was buried in his father's tomb.

[24]David went to Mahanaim, and Absalom crossed the Jordan with all the men of Israel. [25]Absalom had appointed Amasa over the army in place of Joab. Amasa was the son of a man named Jether,[e] an Israelite[f] who had married Abigail,[g] the daughter of Nahash and sister of Zeruiah, the mother of Joab. [26]The Israelites and Absalom camped in the land of Gilead.

[27]When David came to Mahanaim, Shobi son of Nahash from Rabbah of the Ammonites, and Makir son of Ammiel from Lo Debar, and Barzillai the Gileadite from Rogelim [28]brought bedding and bowls and articles of pottery. They also brought wheat and barley, flour and roasted grain, beans and lentils,[b] [29]honey and curds, sheep, and cheese from cows' milk for David and his people to eat. For they said, "The people have become hungry and tired and thirsty in the desert."

■ Absalom's Death

18 David mustered the men who were with him and appointed over them commanders of thousands and commanders of hundreds. [2]David sent the troops out — a third under the command of Joab, a third under Joab's brother Abishai son of Zeruiah, and a third under Ittai the Gittite. The king told the troops, "I myself will surely march out with you."

[3]But the men said, "You must not go out; if we are forced to flee, they won't care about us. Even if half of us die, they won't care; but you are worth ten thousand of us.[a] It would be better now for you to give us support from the city."

[4]The king answered, "I will do whatever seems best to you."

a 1 Or *Let me*   *b 2* Or *will*   *c 9* Or *When some of the men fall at the first attack*   *d 20* Or *"They passed by the sheep pen towards the water."*
e 25 Hebrew *Ithra*, a variant of *Jether*   *f 25* Hebrew and some Septuagint manuscripts; other Septuagint manuscripts (see also 1 Chron. 2:17) *Ishmaelite* or *Jezreelite*   *g 25* Hebrew *Abigal*, a variant of *Abigail*   *b 28* Most Septuagint manuscripts and Syriac; Hebrew *lentils, and roasted grain*   *a 3* Two Hebrew manuscripts, some Septuagint manuscripts and Vulgate; most Hebrew manuscripts *care; for now there are ten thousand like us*

So the king stood beside the gate while all the men marched out in units of hundreds and of thousands. ⁵The king commanded Joab, Abishai and Ittai, "Be gentle with the young man Absalom for my sake." And all the troops heard the king giving orders concerning Absalom to each of the commanders.

⁶The army marched into the field to fight Israel, and the battle took place in the forest of Ephraim. ⁷There the army of Israel was defeated by David's men, and the casualties that day were great — twenty thousand men. ⁸The battle spread out over the whole countryside, and the forest claimed more lives that day than the sword.

⁹Now Absalom happened to meet David's men. He was riding his mule, and as the mule went under the thick branches of a large oak, Absalom's head got caught in the tree. He was left hanging in mid-air, while the mule he was riding kept on going.

¹⁰When one of the men saw this, he told Joab, "I have just seen Absalom hanging in an oak tree."

¹¹Joab said to the man who had told him this, "What! You saw him? Why didn't you strike him to the ground right there? Then I would have had to give you ten shekels[b] of silver and a warrior's belt."

¹²But the man replied, "Even if a thousand shekels[c] were weighed out into my hands, I would not lift my hand against the king's son. In our hearing the king commanded you and Abishai and Ittai, 'Protect the young man Absalom for my sake.'[d] ¹³And if I had put my life in jeopardy[e] — and nothing is hidden from the king — you would have kept your distance from me."

¹⁴Joab said, "I am not going to wait like this for you." So he took three javelins in his hand and plunged them into Absalom's heart while Absalom was still alive in the oak tree. ¹⁵And ten of Joab's armour-bearers surrounded Absalom, struck him and killed him.

¹⁶Then Joab sounded the trumpet, and the troops stopped pursuing Israel, for Joab halted them. ¹⁷They took Absalom, threw him into a big pit in the forest and piled up a large heap of rocks over him. Meanwhile, all the Israelites fled to their homes. ¹⁸During his life-time Absalom had taken a pillar and erected it in the King's Valley as a monument to himself, for he thought, "I have no son to carry on the memory of my name." He named the pillar after himself, and it is called Absalom's Monument to this day.

■ David Mourns

¹⁹Now Ahimaaz son of Zadok said, "Let me run and take the news to the king that the LORD has delivered him from the hand of his enemies."

²⁰"You are not the one to take the news today," Joab told him. "You may take the news another time, but you must not do so today, because the king's son is dead."

²¹Then Joab said to a Cushite, "Go, tell the king what you have seen." The Cushite bowed down before Joab and ran off.

²²Ahimaaz son of Zadok again said to Joab, "Come what may, please let me run behind the Cushite."

But Joab replied, "My son, why do you want to go? You don't have any news that will bring you a reward."

²³He said, "Come what may, I want to run."

So Joab said, "Run!" Then Ahimaaz ran by way of the plain[f] and outran the Cushite.

²⁴While David was sitting between the inner and outer gates, the watchman went up to the roof of the gateway by the wall. As he looked out, he saw a man running alone. ²⁵The watchman called out to the king and reported it.

The king said, "If he is alone, he must have good news." And the man came closer and closer.

²⁶Then the watchman saw another man running, and he called down to the gatekeeper, "Look, another man running alone!"

The king said, "He must be bringing good news, too."

²⁷The watchman said, "It seems to me that the first one runs like Ahimaaz son of Zadok."

"He's a good man," the king said. "He comes with good news."

²⁸Then Ahimaaz called out to the king, "All is well!" He bowed down before the king with his face to the ground and said, "Praise be to the LORD your God! He has delivered up the men who lifted their hands against my lord the king."

²⁹The king asked, "Is the young man Absalom safe?"

Ahimaaz answered, "I saw great confusion just as Joab was about to send the king's servant and me, your servant, but I don't know what it was."

³⁰The king said, "Stand aside and wait here." So he stepped aside and stood there.

³¹Then the Cushite arrived and said, "My lord the king, hear the good news! The LORD has delivered you today from all who rose up against you."

³²The king asked the Cushite, "Is the young man Absalom safe?"

The Cushite replied, "May the enemies of my lord the king and all who rise up to harm you be like that young man."

³³The king was shaken. He went up to the room over the gateway and wept. As he went, he said: "O my son Absalom! My son, my son Absalom! If only I had died instead of you — O Absalom, my son, my son!"

18:33 ■ ABSALOM, ABSALOM!
David's cry is one of the most poignant in all literature. Yet here again, David's love for his children collided with his effectiveness as a leader. He wept so excessively over Absalom that it demoralised the troops who had just risked their necks for the king (19:3).

19 Joab was told, "The king is weeping and mourning for Absalom." ²And for the whole army the victory that day was turned into mourning, because on that day the troops heard it said, "The king is grieving for his son." ³The men stole into the city that day as men steal in who are ashamed when they flee from battle. ⁴The king covered his face and

b 11 That is, about 4 ounces (about 115 grams)   c 12 That is, about 25 pounds (about 11 kilograms)   d 12 A few Hebrew manuscripts, Septuagint, Vulgate and Syriac; most Hebrew manuscripts may be translated Absalom, whoever you may be.   e 13 Or Otherwise, if I had acted treacherously towards him   f 23 That is, the plain of the Jordan

■ SIN AS A CANCER
FIRST DAVID, THEN HIS FAMILY, THEN A NATION

INSIGHT

"O MY SON ABSALOM! MY SON, MY SON ABSALOM! IF ONLY I HAD DIED INSTEAD OF YOU – O ABSALOM, MY SON, MY SON!" ■ 18:33

Sins: many people think of them as parking tickets. If you get too many, the police may track you down or clamp your car. However, one or two here and there won't make a big difference.

The Bible views sins more as cancer cells. One or two here and there do make a difference – often the difference between life and death. Because cancer cells grow, multiply and take over, major surgery may be needed to save your life.

2 Samuel 11–20 reads like a history of a spreading cancer. In the beginning, David was on top of the world – and so was Israel. The civil war was over, the land was at peace and Israel was entering unprecedented prosperity. God had promised to ensure David's descendants a continuous reign for ever. What more could David hope for? The rest of life appeared as one long celebration.

■ THE CANCER GROWS
That celebration never began. One night David caught a glimpse of Bathsheba's beautiful, naked body and impulsively sent for her. The cover-up required a murder. Nobody could deny it was an ugly business: even David admitted it when Nathan confronted him. However, it was soon over. He repented. He married Bathsheba. He did not intend to fall to that temptation again.

But the consequences of the sin were far from over. Unknown to David, cancer was growing in his own household. David's oldest son Amnon had an eye for women too. He tricked his half sister Tamar into his bedroom, then raped her. Afterwards, filled with disgust, he threw her out.

David was furious. But, maybe because he felt his own sin had robbed him of moral authority, he did nothing to punish his son. According to the law (Leviticus 18:9,29), Amnon deserved exile, but he got off free. David apparently wanted the matter forgotten.

■ A COLD-BLOODED CHARACTER
It merely disappeared from view. Absalom waited two full years to avenge his sister's rape. Then he murdered Amnon in cold blood. Again David was long on regret, short on punishment. He wept over Amnon's death but perhaps recognised his own responsibility for it. After

three years David let Absalom return to Jerusalem unpunished; two years later, when Absalom angrily demanded either a murder trial or full acceptance back into the palace (14:32), David kissed and made up completely.

Again the cancer disappeared from view. But it was not gone; it grew. Now an arrogant Absalom started a programme of public relations designed to make him look better than his aging father. At the end of four years, having become quite popular, he set his coup in motion. Taken completely by surprise, David was driven out of Jerusalem, into the desert.

The shock seemed to awaken David. Though dazed and weeping as he left the city, he had enough sense to make some clever plans. When the battle came at last, David's army won, and Absalom was captured and killed.

■ WEEPING FOR HIS SON
For David the king, Absalom's defeat was a great triumph. For David the father, it was a horrible tragedy. The worst thing that can happen to a father had happened to him. His own son had tried to kill him, and in trying, had been killed. David could not stop weeping over his son's death until Joab, his general, warned him that he was insulting the troops who had fought for him.

David pulled himself together. Piece by piece, he put his kingdom back in order. He sent conciliatory words to the rebellious leaders of his own tribe. He rewarded his supporters. He took no revenge on any rebel faction, but showed remarkable fairness. A second rebellion broke out but was soon put down. The cancer seemed finally to have run its course.

Yet it had not. David had no more trouble with rebellion in his lifetime, but after his death Solomon killed a brother who he thought was scheming to take the throne (1 Kings 2:25). After Solomon's reign, the old tribal tensions rose again, and the North and the South, which David had so carefully knit together, split for good (1 Kings 12). Such may be the consequences when a leader sins. His cancer not only poisons him; it grows to affect all those he leads – and it undermines his work.

□ LIFE QUESTIONS:
Many people will, at some point, see their well-run lives disintegrate. What enables someone to pick up the pieces, as David did?

cried aloud, "O my son Absalom! O Absalom, my son, my son!"

5Then Joab went into the house to the king and said, "Today you have humiliated all your men, who have just saved your life and the lives of your sons and daughters and the lives of your wives and concubines. 6You love those who hate you and hate those who love you. You have made it clear today that the commanders and their men mean nothing to you. I see that you would be pleased if Absalom were alive today and all of us were dead. 7Now go out and encourage your men. I swear by the LORD that if you don't go out, not a man will be left with you by nightfall. This will be worse for you than all the calamities that have come upon you from your youth till now."

8So the king got up and took his seat in the gateway. When the men were told, "The king is sitting in the gateway," they all came before him.

■ David Returns to Jerusalem

Meanwhile, the Israelites had fled to their homes. 9Throughout the tribes of Israel, the people were all arguing with each other, saying, "The king delivered us from the hand of our enemies; he is the one who rescued us from the hand of the Philistines. But now he has fled the country because of Absalom; 10and Absalom, whom we anointed to rule over us, has died in battle. So why do you say nothing about bringing the king back?"

11King David sent this message to Zadok and Abiathar, the priests: "Ask the elders of Judah, 'Why should you be the last to bring the king back to his palace, since what is being said throughout Israel has reached the king at his quarters? 12You are my brothers, my own flesh and blood. So why should you be the last to bring back the king?' 13And say to Amasa, 'Are you not my own flesh and blood? May God deal with me, be it ever so severely, if from now on you are not the commander of my army in place of Joab.' "

14He won over the hearts of all the men of Judah as though they were one man. They sent word to the king, "Return, you and all your men." 15Then the king returned and went as far as the Jordan.

Now the men of Judah had come to Gilgal to go out and meet the king and bring him across the Jordan. 16Shimei son of Gera, the Benjamite from Bahurim, hurried down with the men of Judah to meet King David. 17With him were a thousand Benjamites, along with Ziba, the steward of Saul's household, and his fifteen sons and twenty servants. They rushed to the Jordan, where the king was. 18They crossed at the ford to take the king's household over and to do whatever he wished.

When Shimei son of Gera crossed the Jordan, he fell prostrate before the king 19and said to him, "May my lord not hold me guilty. Do not remember how your servant did wrong on the day my lord the king left Jerusalem. May the king put it out of his mind. 20For I your servant know that I have sinned, but today I have come here as the first of the whole house of Joseph to come down and meet my lord the king."

21Then Abishai son of Zeruiah said, "Shouldn't Shimei be put to death for this? He cursed the LORD's anointed."

22David replied, "What do you and I have in common, you sons of Zeruiah? This day you have become my adversaries! Should anyone be put to death in Israel today? Do I not know that today I am king over Israel?" 23So the king said to Shimei, "You shall not die." And the king promised him on oath.

24Mephibosheth, Saul's grandson, also went down to meet the king. He had not taken care of his feet or trimmed his moustache or washed his clothes from the day the king left until the day he returned safely. 25When he came from Jerusalem to meet the king, the king asked him, "Why didn't you go with me, Mephibosheth?"

26He said, "My lord the king, since I your servant am lame, I said, 'I will have my donkey saddled and will ride on it, so that I can go with the king.' But Ziba my servant betrayed me. 27And he has slandered your servant to my lord the king. My lord the king is like an angel of God; so do whatever pleases you. 28All my grandfather's descendants deserved nothing but death from my lord the king, but you gave your servant a place among those who eat at your table. So what right do I have to make any more appeals to the king?"

29The king said to him, "Why say more? I order you and Ziba to divide the fields."

19:29 ■ THE "TRAITOR'S" STORY

Mephibosheth's servant Ziba had told David that Mephibosheth was a traitor with dreams that he, as Saul's grandson, would be made king (16:1–4). Hearing this, David had given Ziba all of Mephibosheth's property.

Now we hear Mephibosheth's side of the story. He claimed that Ziba had betrayed him, presumably by taking his donkey so he, a cripple, could not follow David. More convincing than his words was his appearance. He had not washed himself or trimmed his moustache. He looked as though he had been mourning, not grooming himself for the throne.

Did David believe him? Perhaps not completely. He ordered Ziba to give back half, but not all, the property.

30Mephibosheth said to the king, "Let him take everything, now that my lord the king has arrived home safely."

31Barzillai the Gileadite also came down from Rogelim to cross the Jordan with the king and to send him on his way from there. 32Now Barzillai was a very old man, eighty years of age. He had provided for the king during his stay in Mahanaim, for he was a very wealthy man. 33The king said to Barzillai, "Cross over with me and stay with me in Jerusalem, and I will provide for you."

34But Barzillai answered the king, "How many more years shall I live, that I should go up to Jerusalem with the king? 35I am now eighty years old. Can I tell the difference between what is good and what is not? Can your servant taste what he eats and drinks? Can I still hear the voices of men and women singers? Why should your servant be an added burden to my lord the king? [36]Your servant will cross over the Jordan with the king for a short distance, but why should the king reward me in this way? [37]Let your servant return, that I may die in my own town near the tomb of my father and mother. But here is your servant Kimham. Let him cross over with my lord the king. Do for him whatever pleases you."

[38]The king said, "Kimham shall cross over with me, and I will do for him whatever pleases you. And anything you desire from me I will do for you."

[39]So all the people crossed the Jordan, and then the king crossed over. The king kissed Barzillai and gave him his blessing, and Barzillai returned to his home.

[40]When the king crossed over to Gilgal, Kimham crossed with him. All the troops of Judah and half the troops of Israel had taken the king over.

[41]Soon all the men of Israel were coming to the king and saying to him, "Why did our brothers, the men of Judah, steal the king away and bring him and his household across the Jordan, together with all his men?"

[42]All the men of Judah answered the men of Israel, "We did this because the king is closely related to us. Why are you angry about it? Have we eaten any of the king's provisions? Have we taken anything for ourselves?"

[43]Then the men of Israel answered the men of Judah, "We have ten shares in the king; and besides, we have a greater claim on David than you have. So why do you treat us with contempt? Were we not the first to speak of bringing back our king?"

But the men of Judah responded even more harshly than the men of Israel.

■ Sheba Rebels Against David

20 Now a troublemaker named Sheba son of Bicri, a Benjamite, happened to be there. He sounded the trumpet and shouted,

"We have no share in David,
    no part in Jesse's son!
Every man to his tent, O Israel!"

[2]So all the men of Israel deserted David to follow Sheba son of Bicri. But the men of Judah stayed by their king all the way from the Jordan to Jerusalem.

20:2 ■ NORTH VERSUS SOUTH
Ethnic tension crackled between North ("Israel") and South ("Judah"). Saul came from the tribe of Benjamin in the north; David was a southerner. David worked hard to heal these divisions, but this rebellion shows that many in the north remained dissatisfied. David and his son Solomon managed to keep the two regions together, but after Solomon's death they broke apart for good.

---

[3]When David returned to his palace in Jerusalem, he took the ten concubines he had left to take care of the palace and put them in a house under guard.

He provided for them, but did not lie with them. They were kept in confinement till the day of their death, living as widows.

[4]Then the king said to Amasa, "Summon the men of Judah to come to me within three days, and be here yourself." [5]But when Amasa went to summon Judah, he took longer than the time the king had set for him.

[6]David said to Abishai, "Now Sheba son of Bicri will do us more harm than Absalom did. Take your master's men and pursue him, or he will find fortified cities and escape from us." [7]So Joab's men and the Kerethites and Pelethites and all the mighty warriors went out under the command of Abishai. They marched out from Jerusalem to pursue Sheba son of Bicri.

[8]While they were at the great rock in Gibeon, Amasa came to meet them. Joab was wearing his military tunic, and strapped over it at his waist was a belt with a dagger in its sheath. As he stepped forward, it dropped out of its sheath.

[9]Joab said to Amasa, "How are you, my brother?" Then Joab took Amasa by the beard with his right hand to kiss him. [10]Amasa was not on his guard against the dagger in Joab's hand, and Joab plunged it into his belly, and his intestines spilled out on the ground. Without being stabbed again, Amasa died. Then Joab and his brother Abishai pursued Sheba son of Bicri.

[11]One of Joab's men stood beside Amasa and said, "Whoever favours Joab, and whoever is for David, let him follow Joab!" [12]Amasa lay wallowing in his blood in the middle of the road, and the man saw that all the troops came to a halt there. When he realised that everyone who came up to Amasa stopped, he dragged him from the road into a field and threw a garment over him. [13]After Amasa had been removed from the road, all the men went on with Joab to pursue Sheba son of Bicri.

[14]Sheba passed through all the tribes of Israel to Abel Beth Maacah[a] and through the entire region of the Berites, who gathered together and followed him. [15]All the troops with Joab came and besieged Sheba in Abel Beth Maacah. They built a siege ramp up to the city, and it stood against the outer fortifications. While they were battering the wall to bring it down, [16]a wise woman called from the city, "Listen! Listen! Tell Joab to come here so that I can speak to him." [17]He went towards her, and she asked, "Are you Joab?"

"I am," he answered.

She said, "Listen to what your servant has to say."

"I'm listening," he said.

[18]She continued, "Long ago they used to say, 'Get your answer at Abel,' and that settled it. [19]We are the peaceful and faithful in Israel. You are trying to destroy a city that is a mother in Israel. Why do you want to swallow up the LORD's inheritance?"

[20]"Far be it from me!" Joab replied, "Far be it from me to swallow up or destroy! [21]That is not the case. A man named Sheba son of Bicri, from the hill country of Ephraim, has lifted up his hand against the king, against David. Hand over this one man, and I'll withdraw from the city."

[a]14 Or Abel, even Beth Maacah; also in verse 15

The woman said to Joab, "His head will be thrown to you from the wall."

22Then the woman went to all the people with her wise advice, and they cut off the head of Sheba son of Bicri and threw it to Joab. So he sounded the trumpet, and his men dispersed from the city, each returning to his home. And Joab went back to the king in Jerusalem.

23Joab was over Israel's entire army; Benaiah son of Jehoiada was over the Kerethites and Pelethites; 24Adoniram*b* was in charge of forced labour; Jehoshaphat son of Ahilud was recorder; 25Sheva was secretary; Zadok and Abiathar were priests; 26and Ira the Jairite was David's priest.

■ The Gibeonites Avenged

21 During the reign of David, there was a famine for three successive years; so David sought the face of the LORD. The LORD said, "It is on account of Saul and his blood-stained house; it is because he put the Gibeonites to death."

2The king summoned the Gibeonites and spoke to them. (Now the Gibeonites were not a part of Israel but were survivors of the Amorites; the Israelites had sworn to ˻spare˼ them, but Saul in his zeal for Israel and Judah had tried to annihilate them.) 3David asked the Gibeonites, "What shall I do for you? How shall I make amends so that you will bless the LORD's inheritance?"

4The Gibeonites answered him, "We have no right to demand silver or gold from Saul or his family, nor do we have the right to put anyone in Israel to death."

"What do you want me to do for you?" David asked.

5They answered the king, "As for the man who destroyed us and plotted against us so that we have been decimated and have no place anywhere in Israel, 6let seven of his male descendants be given to us to be killed and exposed before the LORD at Gibeah of Saul — the LORD's chosen one."

So the king said, "I will give them to you."

21:6 ■ NEEDLESS DEATHS
Is there any excuse for David's agreeing to the execution of Saul's descendants? Perhaps. One must remember that David had certain legal responsibilities as king of Israel. Having offered compensation to the Gibeonites for their mistreatment under Saul, he may have been under legal obligation to co-operate with their demand for blood. In Old Testament times, a family was considered responsible for the crimes of any individual in his family. By modern standards, however, these executions seem needless and cruel.

7The king spared Mephibosheth son of Jonathan, the son of Saul, because of the oath before the LORD between David and Jonathan son of Saul. 8But the king took Armoni and Mephibosheth, the two sons of Aiah's daughter Rizpah, whom she had borne to Saul, together with the five sons of Saul's daughter Merab,*a* whom she had borne to Adriel son of Barzillai the Meholathite. 9He handed them over to the Gibeonites, who killed and exposed them on a hill before the LORD. All seven of them fell together; they were put to death during the first days of harvest, just as the barley harvest was beginning.

10Rizpah daughter of Aiah took sackcloth and spread it out for herself on a rock. From the beginning of the harvest till the rain poured down from the heavens on the bodies, she did not let the birds of the air touch them by day or the wild animals by night. 11When David was told what Aiah's daughter Rizpah, Saul's concubine, had done, 12he went and took the bones of Saul and his son Jonathan from the citizens of Jabesh Gilead. (They had taken them secretly from the public square at Beth Shan, where the Philistines had hung them after they struck Saul down on Gilboa.) 13David brought the bones of Saul and his son Jonathan from there, and the bones of those who had been killed and exposed were gathered up.

14They buried the bones of Saul and his son Jonathan in the tomb of Saul's father Kish, at Zela in Benjamin, and did everything the king commanded. After that, God answered prayer on behalf of the land.

■ Wars Against the Philistines

15Once again there was a battle between the Philistines and Israel. David went down with his men to fight against the Philistines, and he became exhausted. 16And Ishbi-Benob, one of the descendants of Rapha, whose bronze spearhead weighed three hundred shekels*b* and who was armed with a new ˻sword˼, said he would kill David. 17But Abishai son of Zeruiah came to David's rescue; he struck the Philistine down and killed him. Then David's men swore to him, saying, "Never again will you go out with us to battle, so that the lamp of Israel will not be extinguished."

18In the course of time, there was another battle with the Philistines, at Gob. At that time Sibbecai the Hushathite killed Saph, one of the descendants of Rapha.

19In another battle with the Philistines at Gob, Elhanan son of Jaare-Oregim*c* the Bethlehemite killed Goliath*d* the Gittite, who had a spear with a shaft like a weaver's rod.

20In still another battle, which took place at Gath, there was a huge man with six fingers on each hand and six toes on each foot — twenty-four in all. He also was descended from Rapha. 21When he taunted Israel, Jonathan son of Shimeah, David's brother, killed him.

22These four were descendants of Rapha in Gath, and they fell at the hands of David and his men.

■ David's Song of Praise

22 David sang to the LORD the words of this song when the LORD delivered him from the hand of all his enemies and from the hand of Saul. 2He said:

---

b 24 Some Septuagint manuscripts (see also 1 Kings 4:6 and 5:14); Hebrew *Adoram* Syriac (see also 1 Samuel 18:19); most Hebrew and Septuagint manuscripts *Michal* *a 8* Two Hebrew manuscripts, some Septuagint manuscripts and Syriac; most Hebrew and Septuagint manuscripts *Michal*   *b 16* That is, about 7½ pounds (about 3.5 kilograms)   *c 19* Or *son of Jair the weaver*   *d 19* Hebrew and Septuagint; 1 Chron. 20:5 *son of Jair killed Lahmi the brother of Goliath*

"The LORD is my rock, my fortress and my
    deliverer;
3 my God is my rock, in whom I take refuge,
    my shield and the horn[a] of my salvation.
He is my stronghold, my refuge and my
    saviour—
    from violent men you save me.
4I call to the LORD, who is worthy of praise,
    and I am saved from my enemies.

22:1 ■ DAVID'S PSALMS

This song of praise was included in the book of
Psalms as Psalm 18. Many psalms are credited to
David, and some have titles suggesting the events
that inspired them. You can read these as a
spiritual and emotional commentary on key events
in David's life:

Psalm 3. When he fled from his son Absalom
(2 Samuel 15:13)
Psalm 18. When the Lord delivered him from his
enemies and Saul (1 Samuel 19–31)
Psalm 51. After Nathan confronted David over
Bathsheba (2 Samuel 12)
Psalm 52. When Doeg turned in the high priest for
helping David (1 Samuel 22:9–10)
Psalm 54. When the Ziphites told Saul that David
was hiding in their territory (1 Samuel 23:19–20;
26:1–25)
Psalm 56. When the Philistines seized David in
Gath (1 Samuel 21:10–15)
Psalm 57. When David fled from Saul into the
cave (1 Samuel 22:1–2)
Psalm 59. When Saul sent men to watch David's
house in order to kill him (1 Samuel 19:11)
Psalm 60. After an important battle
Psalm 63. When he was in the Desert of Judah
Psalm 142. When he was in the cave, hiding from
Saul

5"The waves of death swirled about me;
    the torrents of destruction overwhelmed me.
6The cords of the grave[b] coiled around me;
    the snares of death confronted me.
7In my distress I called to the LORD;
    I called out to my God.
From his temple he heard my voice;
    my cry came to his ears.
8"The earth trembled and quaked,
    the foundations of the heavens[c] shook;
    they trembled because he was angry.
9Smoke rose from his nostrils;
    consuming fire came from his mouth,
    burning coals blazed out of it.
10He parted the heavens and came down;
    dark clouds were under his feet.
11He mounted the cherubim and flew;
    he soared[d] on the wings of the wind.
12He made darkness his canopy around him—
    the dark[e] rain clouds of the sky.
13Out of the brightness of his presence
    bolts of lightning blazed forth.

14The LORD thundered from heaven;
    the voice of the Most High resounded.
15He shot arrows and scattered ⌊the enemies⌋,
    bolts of lightning and routed them.
16The valleys of the sea were exposed
    and the foundations of the earth laid bare
at the rebuke of the LORD,
    at the blast of breath from his nostrils.

17"He reached down from on high and took hold
    of me;
    he drew me out of deep waters.
18He rescued me from my powerful enemy,
    from my foes, who were too strong for me.
19They confronted me in the day of my disaster,
    but the LORD was my support.
20He brought me out into a spacious place;
    he rescued me because he delighted in me.

21"The LORD has dealt with me according to my
    righteousness;
    according to the cleanness of my hands he
    has rewarded me.
22For I have kept the ways of the LORD;
    I have not done evil by turning from my
    God.
23All his laws are before me;
    I have not turned away from his decrees.
24I have been blameless before him
    and have kept myself from sin.
25The LORD has rewarded me according to my
    righteousness,
    according to my cleanness[f] in his sight.

26"To the faithful you show yourself faithful,
    to the blameless you show yourself
    blameless,
27to the pure you show yourself pure,
    but to the crooked you show yourself
    shrewd.
28You save the humble,
    but your eyes are on the haughty to bring
    them low.
29You are my lamp, O LORD;
    the LORD turns my darkness into light.
30With your help I can advance against a troop;[g]
    with my God I can scale a wall.

31"As for God, his way is perfect;
    the word of the LORD is flawless.
He is a shield
    for all who take refuge in him.
32For who is God besides the LORD?
    And who is the Rock except our God?
33It is God who arms me with strength[b]
    and makes my way perfect.
34He makes my feet like the feet of a deer;
    he enables me to stand on the heights.
35He trains my hands for battle;
    my arms can bend a bow of bronze.
36You give me your shield of victory;
    you stoop down to make me great.
37You broaden the path beneath me,
    so that my ankles do not turn over.

a3 Horn here symbolises strength.   b6 Hebrew Sheol   c8 Hebrew; Vulgate and Syriac (see also Psalm 18:7) mountains   d11 Many Hebrew
manuscripts (see also Psalm 18:10); most Hebrew manuscripts appeared   e12 Septuagint and Vulgate (see also Psalm 18:11); Hebrew massed
f25 Hebrew; Septuagint and Vulgate (see also Psalm 18:24) to the cleanness of my hands   g30 Or can run through a barricade   b33 Dead Sea Scrolls,
some Septuagint manuscripts, Vulgate and Syriac (see also Psalm 18:32); Masoretic Text who is my strong refuge

38"I pursued my enemies and crushed them;
  I did not turn back till they were destroyed.
39I crushed them completely, and they could not
    rise;
  they fell beneath my feet.
40You armed me with strength for battle;
  you made my adversaries bow at my feet.
41You made my enemies turn their backs in
    flight,
  and I destroyed my foes.
42They cried for help, but there was no-one to
    save them—
  to the LORD, but he did not answer.
43I beat them as fine as the dust of the earth;
  I pounded and trampled them like mud in
    the streets.

44"You have delivered me from the attacks of my
    people;
  you have preserved me as the head of
    nations.
  People I did not know are subject to me,
45 and foreigners come cringing to me;
  as soon as they hear me, they obey me.
46They all lose heart;
  they come trembling*i* from their
    strongholds.

47"The LORD lives! Praise be to my Rock!
  Exalted be God, the Rock, my Saviour!
48He is the God who avenges me,
  who puts the nations under me,
49 who sets me free from my enemies.
  You exalted me above my foes;
  from violent men you rescued me.
50Therefore I will praise you, O LORD, among the
    nations;
  I will sing praises to your name.
51He gives his king great victories;
  he shows unfailing kindness to his anointed,
  to David and his descendants for ever."

■ The Last Words of David

23 These are the last words of David:

  "The oracle of David son of Jesse,
    the oracle of the man exalted by the Most
      High,
  the man anointed by the God of Jacob,
    Israel's singer of songs:*a*

23:1 ■ FINAL WORDS

People hold on to a loved one's last words, for
they sometimes sum up his or her life. This,
David's final poem, shows David's deep concern
to be a king who pleases God. He insists that a
leader in tune with God will always be a blessing
to God's people, and recalls God's promise that
his descendants will always rule. A memorial to
David's "mighty men" follows this psalm,
honouring those who fought alongside him with
unusual courage. Uriah the Hittite, whom David
had murdered, makes the list. The vindictive Joab
does not.

2"The Spirit of the LORD spoke through me;
  his word was on my tongue.
3The God of Israel spoke,
  the Rock of Israel said to me:
  'When one rules over men in righteousness,
    when he rules in the fear of God,
4he is like the light of morning at sunrise
  on a cloudless morning,
  like the brightness after rain
  that brings the grass from the earth.'

5"Is not my house right with God?
  Has he not made with me an everlasting
    covenant,
  arranged and secured in every part?
  Will he not bring to fruition my salvation
    and grant me my every desire?
6But evil men are all to be cast aside like thorns,
  which are not gathered with the hand.
7Whoever touches thorns
  uses a tool of iron or the shaft of a spear;
  they are burned up where they lie."

■ David's Mighty Men

8These are the names of David's mighty men:
  Josheb-Basshebeth,*b* a Tahkemonite,*c* was chief
of the Three; he raised his spear against eight hundred men, whom he killed*d* in one encounter.

9Next to him was Eleazar son of Dodai the Ahohite. As one of the three mighty men, he was with
David when they taunted the Philistines gathered ˻at
Pas Dammim˼*e* for battle. Then the men of Israel
retreated, 10but he stood his ground and struck
down the Philistines till his hand grew tired and
froze to the sword. The LORD brought about a great
victory that day. The troops returned to Eleazar, but
only to strip the dead.

11Next to him was Shammah son of Agee the Hararite. When the Philistines banded together at a place
where there was a field full of lentils, Israel's troops
fled from them. 12But Shammah took his stand in the
middle of the field. He defended it and struck the
Philistines down, and the LORD brought about a great
victory.

13During harvest time, three of the thirty chief
men came down to David at the cave of Adullam,
while a band of Philistines was encamped in the Valley of Rephaim. 14At that time David was in the
stronghold, and the Philistine garrison was at Bethlehem. 15David longed for water and said, "Oh, that
someone would get me a drink of water from the
well near the gate of Bethlehem!" 16So the three
mighty men broke through the Philistine lines, drew
water from the well near the gate of Bethlehem and
carried it back to David. But he refused to drink it;
instead, he poured it out before the LORD. 17"Far be
it from me, O LORD, to do this!" he said. "Is it not the
blood of men who went at the risk of their lives?"
And David would not drink it.

Such were the exploits of the three mighty men.
18Abishai the brother of Joab son of Zeruiah was

---

i46 Some Septuagint manuscripts and Vulgate (see also Psalm 18:45); Masoretic Text *they arm themselves.*   *a1* Or *Israel's beloved singer*   *b8* Hebrew;
some Septuagint manuscripts suggest *Ish-Bosheth,* that is, *Esh-Baal* (see also 1 Chron. 11:11 *Jashobeam*).   *c8* Probably a variant of *Hacmonite* (see
1 Chron. 11:11)   *d8* Some Septuagint manuscripts (see also 1 Chron. 11:11); Hebrew and other Septuagint manuscripts *Three; it was Adino the Eznite who
killed eight hundred men*   *e9* See 1 Chron. 11:13; Hebrew *gathered there.*

chief of the Three.*f* He raised his spear against three hundred men, whom he killed, and so he became as famous as the Three. ¹⁹Was he not held in greater honour than the Three? He became their commander, even though he was not included among them.

²⁰Benaiah son of Jehoiada was a valiant fighter from Kabzeel, who performed great exploits. He struck down two of Moab's best men. He also went down into a pit on a snowy day and killed a lion. ²¹And he struck down a huge Egyptian. Although the Egyptian had a spear in his hand, Benaiah went against him with a club. He snatched the spear from the Egyptian's hand and killed him with his own spear. ²²Such were the exploits of Benaiah son of Jehoiada; he too was as famous as the three mighty men. ²³He was held in greater honour than any of the Thirty, but he was not included among the Three. And David put him in charge of his bodyguard.

²⁴Among the Thirty were:
  Asahel the brother of Joab,
  Elhanan son of Dodo from Bethlehem,
²⁵Shammah the Harodite,
  Elika the Harodite,
²⁶Helez the Paltite,
  Ira son of Ikkesh from Tekoa,
²⁷Abiezer from Anathoth,
  Mebunnai*g* the Hushathite,
²⁸Zalmon the Ahohite,
  Maharai the Netophathite,
²⁹Heled*b* son of Baanah the Netophathite,
  Ithai son of Ribai from Gibeah in Benjamin,
³⁰Benaiah the Pirathonite,
  Hiddai*i* from the ravines of Gaash,
³¹Abi-Albon the Arbathite,
  Azmaveth the Barhumite,
³²Eliahba the Shaalbonite,
  the sons of Jashen,
  Jonathan ³³son of*j* Shammah the Hararite,
  Ahiam son of Sharar*k* the Hararite,
³⁴Eliphelet son of Ahasbai the Maacathite,
  Eliam son of Ahithophel the Gilonite,
³⁵Hezro the Carmelite,
  Paarai the Arbite,
³⁶Igal son of Nathan from Zobah,
  the son of Hagri,*l*
³⁷Zelek the Ammonite,
  Naharai the Beerothite, the armour-bearer of Joab son of Zeruiah,
³⁸Ira the Ithrite,
  Gareb the Ithrite
³⁹and Uriah the Hittite.
There were thirty-seven in all.

■ David Counts the Fighting Men

24 Again the anger of the LORD burned against Israel, and he incited David against them, saying, "Go and take a census of Israel and Judah."

²So the king said to Joab and the army commanders*a* with him, "Go throughout the tribes of Israel from Dan to Beersheba and enrol the fighting men, so that I may know how many there are."

24:1 ■ SATAN OR THE LORD?
In a parallel account, 1 Chronicles 21:1 says that Satan incited David to take a census. Who was it—Satan or the Lord? One explanation is that both are true. The Lord, as the ultimate power, allowed the census, and as is typical in the Old Testament, he gets full credit here. The Chronicles version is more concerned about being precise: because the census was clearly evil (David confessed it as a sin, verse 10), Satan was more directly responsible. As is so often true of evil, people (and Satan) meant it for evil, but God used it for his own purposes.

³But Joab replied to the king, "May the LORD your God multiply the troops a hundred times over, and may the eyes of my lord the king see it. But why does my lord the king want to do such a thing?"

⁴The king's word, however, overruled Joab and the army commanders; so they left the presence of the king to enrol the fighting men of Israel.

⁵After crossing the Jordan, they camped near Aroer, south of the town in the gorge, and then went through Gad and on to Jazer. ⁶They went to Gilead and the region of Tahtim Hodshi, and on to Dan Jaan and around towards Sidon. ⁷Then they went towards the fortress of Tyre and all the towns of the Hivites and Canaanites. Finally, they went on to Beersheba in the Negev of Judah.

⁸After they had gone through the entire land, they came back to Jerusalem at the end of nine months and twenty days.

⁹Joab reported the number of the fighting men to the king: In Israel there were eight hundred thousand able-bodied men who could handle a sword, and in Judah five hundred thousand.

¹⁰David was conscience-stricken after he had counted the fighting men, and he said to the LORD, "I have sinned greatly in what I have done. Now, O LORD, I beg you, take away the guilt of your servant. I have done a very foolish thing."

¹¹Before David got up the next morning, the word of the LORD had come to Gad the prophet, David's seer: ¹²"Go and tell David, 'This is what the LORD says: I am giving you three options. Choose one of them for me to carry out against you.'"

¹³So Gad went to David and said to him, "Shall there come upon you three*b* years of famine in your land? Or three months of fleeing from your enemies while they pursue you? Or three days of plague in your land? Now then, think it over and decide how I should answer the one who sent me."

¹⁴David said to Gad, "I am in deep distress. Let us fall into the hands of the LORD, for his mercy is great; but do not let me fall into the hands of men."

¹⁵So the LORD sent a plague on Israel from that morning until the end of the time designated, and seventy thousand of the people from Dan to

*f*18 Most Hebrew manuscripts (see also 1 Chron. 11:20); two Hebrew manuscripts and Syriac *Thirty*   *g*27 Hebrew; some Septuagint manuscripts (see also 1 Chron. 11:29) *Sibbecai*   *b*29 Some Hebrew manuscripts and Vulgate (see also 1 Chron. 11:30); most Hebrew manuscripts *Heleb*   *i*30 Hebrew; some Septuagint manuscripts (see also 1 Chron. 11:32) *Hurai*   *j*33 Some Septuagint manuscripts (see also 1 Chron. 11:34); Hebrew does not have *son of.*
*k*33 Hebrew; some Septuagint manuscripts (see also 1 Chron. 11:35) *Sacar*   *l*36 Some Septuagint manuscripts (see also 1 Chron. 11:38); Hebrew *Haggadi*   *a*2 Septuagint (see also verse 4 and 1 Chron. 21:2); Hebrew *Joab the army commander*   *b*13 Septuagint (see also 1 Chron. 21:12); Hebrew *seven*

Beersheba died. [16]When the angel stretched out his hand to destroy Jerusalem, the LORD was grieved because of the calamity and said to the angel who was afflicting the people, "Enough! Withdraw your hand." The angel of the LORD was then at the threshing-floor of Araunah the Jebusite.

[17]When David saw the angel who was striking down the people, he said to the LORD, "I am the one who has sinned and done wrong. These are but sheep. What have they done? Let your hand fall upon me and my family."

■ David Builds an Altar

[18]On that day Gad went to David and said to him, "Go up and build an altar to the LORD on the threshing-floor of Araunah the Jebusite." [19]So David went up, as the LORD had commanded through Gad. [20]When Araunah looked and saw the king and his men coming towards him, he went out and bowed down before the king with his face to the ground. [21]Araunah said, "Why has my lord the king come to his servant?"

"To buy your threshing-floor," David answered, "so that I can build an altar to the LORD, that the plague on the people may be stopped."

[22]Araunah said to David, "Let my lord the king take whatever pleases him and offer it up. Here are oxen for the burnt offering, and here are threshing-sledges and ox yokes for the wood. [23]O king, Araunah gives all this to the king." Araunah also said to him, "May the LORD your God accept you."

[24]But the king replied to Araunah, "No, I insist on paying you for it. I will not sacrifice to the LORD my God burnt offerings that cost me nothing."

24:24 ■ THE COST OF TRUE WORSHIP

David's response is timeless: he sees that worship which costs you nothing is not true worship at all. It is typical of David that even after falling into sin, he was not blinded to spiritual concerns. Feeling guilty already, he might have thought "one more compromise" would make no difference. Instead he stuck to his principle.

So David bought the threshing-floor and the oxen and paid fifty shekels[c] of silver for them. [25]David built an altar to the LORD there and sacrificed burnt offerings and fellowship offerings.[d] Then the LORD answered prayer on behalf of the land, and the plague on Israel was stopped.

[c]24 That is, about 1¼ pounds (about 0.6 kilogram)   [d]25 Traditionally peace offerings

1 KINGS

■ THE MAN WHO HAD EVERYTHING

THE RICHEST, WISEST, MOST SUCCESSFUL PERSON OF HIS TIME

"IF YOU OR YOUR SONS TURN AWAY FROM ME AND DO NOT OBSERVE THE COMMANDS AND DECREES I HAVE GIVEN YOU AND GO OFF TO SERVE OTHER GODS AND WORSHIP THEM, THEN I WILL CUT OFF ISRAEL FROM THE LAND I HAVE GIVEN THEM AND WILL REJECT THIS TEMPLE I HAVE CONSECRATED FOR MY NAME." ■ 9:6–7

The first half of 1 Kings describes a man who got life handed to him on a silver platter. The son of King David and Queen Bathsheba, young Solomon grew up in the royal palace. At the outset, he astounded others with his talent for songwriting and natural history. He composed 1,005 songs and spun off 3,000 proverbs (a sampling of which were collected in the biblical book of Proverbs).

Solomon became king of Israel and received from God the special gift of wisdom. He was called the wisest man in the world, and kings and queens travelled hundreds of miles to meet him. They went away dazzled by the genius of Israel's king and by the prosperity of his nation.

■ THE BEST YEARS EVER

Israel reached its Golden Age under King Solomon, a time for ever remembered with nostalgia by Jews. Almost all the promised land lay in Israel's hands, and the nation was at peace. Literature and culture flourished. Of the people, the Bible records simply that "they ate, they drank and they were happy" (4:20). "The king made silver as common in Jerusalem as stones" (10:27).

Of all Solomon's accomplishments, one stands out above the others. He built the temple of God, the finest building in the world of that day. Almost 200,000 men laboured for seven years to complete it.

Despite the successes of Solomon's reign, however, later in his life the fortunes of the king took a turn for the worse. His fall eventually brought the kingdom crashing down around him, and the second half of 1 Kings describes the grim process of dismemberment.

■ WHAT WENT WRONG?

How did it happen? How could the liveliest, wealthiest, most contented nation of its day slide so disastrously in one generation?

As 1 Kings tells it, Solomon seemed unable to control his excesses. Reared in a palace, he loved luxury. When Israel launched its first maritime expeditions, he used them to gather such exotica as gold, ivory, apes, peacocks, and silver. He plated the floor of the temple with gold, wastefully gilded over fine cedar and precious ivory, and fashioned militarily useless shields out of gold. First Kings describes the seven-year construction of the temple in elaborate detail. But then it pointedly notes that the construction of Solomon's palace – twice the temple's size – took 13 years (7:1).

Solomon showed similar extravagance in his love life. First, he married the daughter of the Egyptian pharaoh (perhaps indicating that he was relying on military alliances, not on God, for the defence of his country). Then, disobeying God's specific orders, he married the princesses of Moab, Ammon, Edom, Sidon, and other nations. Seven hundred wives in all, and 300 concubines! The entire complexion of the court changed. It became un-Jewish, foreign. To please his wives, Solomon took a final, terrible step: he built altars to all their gods. The one who had built the Israelites' greatest monument to God had fallen to worshipping idols.

■ RUMBLINGS OF DISCONTENT IN THE LAND

To pay for the building projects, Solomon instituted Israel's first national taxation system. He drafted workers for employment and kept them as virtual slaves. When bills mounted, he went so far as to cede certain northern towns in the promised land to another king (9:10–14). Resentment opened up between Israel's North and South.

But the gulf separating Israel from God was even more dangerous. Previously, the people of Israel had looked to God as their leader. Now, however, the focus shifted from

God in heaven to the king in Jerusalem. Solomon had even made himself the unofficial religious leader of the country, and when he slid badly, the nation soon followed.

Solomon started out with every advantage of wealth, power, and wisdom. But 1 Kings gives this tragic conclusion: "So Solomon did evil in the eyes of the LORD; he did not follow the LORD completely, as David his father had done" (11:6).

Solomon seemed obsessed with a desire to outdo anyone who had ever lived. Along the way, he failed to make God the centre of his life. He achieved lasting fame in history, but as a negative example. Jesus Christ himself rendered the final verdict on Solomon and his striving for glory when he pointed to a lily growing wild in the field. "Not even Solomon in all his splendour," he said, "was dressed like one of these" (Matthew 6:29).

■ HOW TO READ 1 KINGS

First and Second Kings were originally one book: the same Hebrew scroll contained both. Hebrew, having no vowels, is a very compact language, and when the book of Kings was translated into the wordier Greek and Latin, more space was needed. Translators arbitrarily split Kings. The two books, however, should be read as one.

First Kings divides neatly almost in half, with mostly good news in the first half. It tells of Israel's Golden Age, when King Solomon brought peace and prosperity to the nation. But he also sowed the seed for the calamities to follow. Chapter 12 marks the beginning of a civil war that ruptured Israel into two nations: Israel in the North and Judah in the South. The rest of Kings describes, ruler by ruler, the reigns of 19 kings in the North and 19 kings and one queen in the South.

Another book, 2 Chronicles, covers the exact same historical period as the book of Kings. In some cases, 2 Chronicles adds more detail, so if a story interests you, read the parallel account there. These books of history form the background for 17 other books of the Bible: the Prophets. Famous prophets such as

Isaiah, Jeremiah, Hosea, and Amos preached during the time of Kings.

Keeping 39 rulers straight can seem hopeless, especially since the book jumps back and forth between two countries. Remember: Israel was the Northern Kingdom, with its capital in Samaria. Its kings were all unfaithful to God. Judah was the Southern Kingdom, with its capital in Jerusalem. Almost half of its rulers remained somewhat faithful to God; the others proved disobedient.

On pages 260–268, you will find a line-up of all the rulers, tracing the rise and fall of both the Northern and Southern Kingdoms. Use this handy reference as you read the history. You may find it helpful to underline the various rulers' names, using different coloured marker pens (for example, red for Judah and blue for Israel). Add a star by those kings cited as doing "what was right in the eyes of the LORD". First Kings mentions two such kings: Asa and Jehoshaphat. By marking the kings and queen with some visual scheme, you can quickly refer back to them when you read references to them in the books of the prophets.

■ 3-TRACK READING PLAN

For an explanation and complete listing of the 3-track reading plan, turn to page x.

■ TRACK 1:
Two-Week Courses on the Bible
The Track 1 reading programme on the Old Testament includes one chapter from 1 Kings. See page x for a complete listing of this course.

■ TRACK 2:
An Overview of 1 Kings in 4 Days
□ Day 1. Read the Introduction to 1 Kings and

then chapter 3, where Solomon asks for wisdom.
□ Day 2. Israel reaches a high point at this ceremony: read chapter 8 through to 9:9.
□ Day 3. Elijah is one of the Bible's most dramatic and colourful characters. The third day, read about him in chapter 17.
□ Day 4. Read chapter 18, in which Elijah takes on the prophets of Baal.
Now turn to page xi for your

next Track 2 reading project.

■ TRACK 3:
All of 1 Kings in 21 Days
After you have read through 1 Kings, turn to pages xii–xiii for your next Track 3 reading project.

□ 1　□ 2　□ 3　□ 4–5
□ 6　□ 7　□ 8　□ 9
□ 10　□ 11　□ 12　□ 13
□ 14　□ 15　□ 16　□ 17
□ 18　□ 19　□ 20　□ 21
□ 22

■ Adonijah Sets Himself Up as King

1 When King David was old and well advanced in years, he could not keep warm even when they put covers over him. ²So his servants said to him, "Let us look for a young virgin to attend the king and take care of him. She can lie beside him so that our lord the king may keep warm."

³Then they searched throughout Israel for a beautiful girl and found Abishag, a Shunammite, and brought her to the king. ⁴The girl was very beautiful; she took care of the king and waited on him, but the king had no intimate relations with her.

⁵Now Adonijah, whose mother was Haggith, put himself forward and said, "I will be king." So he got chariots and horses*a* ready, with fifty men to run ahead of him. ⁶(His father had never interfered with him by asking, "Why do you behave as you do?" He was also very handsome and was born next after Absalom.)

⁷Adonijah conferred with Joab son of Zeruiah and with Abiathar the priest, and they gave him their support. ⁸But Zadok the priest, Benaiah son of Jehoiada, Nathan the prophet, Shimei and Rei*b* and David's special guard did not join Adonijah.

⁹Adonijah then sacrificed sheep, cattle and fattened calves at the Stone of Zoheleth near En Rogel. He invited all his brothers, the king's sons, and all the men of Judah who were royal officials, ¹⁰but he did not invite Nathan the prophet or Benaiah or the special guard or his brother Solomon.

¹¹Then Nathan asked Bathsheba, Solomon's mother, "Have you not heard that Adonijah, the son of Haggith, has become king without our lord David's knowing it? ¹²Now then, let me advise you how you can save your own life and the life of your son Solomon. ¹³Go in to King David and say to him, 'My lord the king, did you not swear to me your servant: "Surely Solomon your son shall be king after me, and he will sit on my throne"? Why then has Adonijah become king?' ¹⁴While you are still there talking to the king, I will come in and confirm what you have said."

¹⁵So Bathsheba went to see the aged king in his room, where Abishag the Shunammite was attending him. ¹⁶Bathsheba bowed low and knelt before the king.

"What is it you want?" the king asked.

¹⁷She said to him, "My lord, you yourself swore to me your servant by the LORD your God: 'Solomon your son shall become king after me, and he will sit on my throne.' ¹⁸But now Adonijah has become king, and you, my lord the king, do not know about it. ¹⁹He has sacrificed great numbers of cattle, fattened calves, and sheep, and has invited all the king's sons, Abiathar the priest and Joab the commander of the army, but he has not invited Solomon your servant. ²⁰My lord the king, the eyes of all Israel are on you, to learn from you who will sit on the throne of my lord the king after him. ²¹Otherwise, as soon as my lord the king is laid to rest with his fathers, I and my son Solomon will be treated as criminals."

²²While she was still speaking with the king, Nathan the prophet arrived. ²³And they told the king, "Nathan the prophet is here." So he went before the king and bowed with his face to the ground.

²⁴Nathan said, "Have you, my lord the king, declared that Adonijah shall be king after you, and that he will sit on your throne? ²⁵Today he has gone down and sacrificed great numbers of cattle, fattened calves, and sheep. He has invited all the king's sons, the commanders of the army and Abiathar the priest. At this very moment they are eating and drinking with him and saying, 'Long live King Adonijah!' ²⁶But me your servant, and Zadok the priest, and Benaiah son of Jehoiada, and your servant Solomon he did not invite. ²⁷Is this something my lord the king has done without letting his servants know who should sit on the throne of my lord the king after him?"

■ David Makes Solomon King

²⁸Then King David said, "Call in Bathsheba." So she came into the king's presence and stood before him.

²⁹The king then took an oath: "As surely as the LORD lives, who has delivered me out of every trouble, ³⁰I will surely carry out today what I swore to you by the LORD, the God of Israel: Solomon your son shall be king after me, and he will sit on my throne in my place."

³¹Then Bathsheba bowed low with her face to the ground and, kneeling before the king, said, "May my lord King David live for ever!"

³²King David said, "Call in Zadok the priest, Nathan the prophet and Benaiah son of Jehoiada." When they came before the king, ³³he said to them: "Take your lord's servants with you and set Solomon my son on my own mule and take him down to Gihon. ³⁴There shall Zadok the priest and Nathan the prophet anoint him king over Israel. Blow the trumpet and shout, 'Long live King Solomon!' ³⁵Then you are to go up with him, and he is to come and sit on my throne and reign in my place. I have appointed him ruler over Israel and Judah."

³⁶Benaiah son of Jehoiada answered the king, "Amen! May the LORD, the God of my lord the king, so declare it. ³⁷As the LORD was with my lord the king, so may he be with Solomon to make his throne even greater than the throne of my lord King David!"

³⁸So Zadok the priest, Nathan the prophet, Benaiah son of Jehoiada, the Kerethites and the Pelethites went down and put Solomon on King David's mule and escorted him to Gihon. ³⁹Zadok the priest took the horn of oil from the sacred tent and anointed Solomon. Then they sounded the trumpet and all the people shouted, "Long live King Solomon!" ⁴⁰And all the people went up after him, playing flutes and rejoicing greatly, so that the ground shook with the sound.

⁴¹Adonijah and all the guests who were with him heard it as they were finishing their feast. On hearing the sound of the trumpet, Joab asked, "What's the meaning of all the noise in the city?"

⁴²Even as he was speaking, Jonathan son of Abiathar the priest arrived. Adonijah said, "Come in. A worthy man like you must be bringing good news."

⁴³"Not at all!" Jonathan answered. "Our lord King David has made Solomon king. ⁴⁴The king has sent with him Zadok the priest, Nathan the prophet, Benaiah son of Jehoiada, the Kerethites and the

a 5 Or charioteers   b 8 Or and his friends

Pelethites, and they have put him on the king's mule, 45and Zadok the priest and Nathan the prophet have anointed him king at Gihon. From there they have gone up cheering, and the city resounds with it. That's the noise you hear. 46Moreover, Solomon has taken his seat on the royal throne. 47Also, the royal officials have come to congratulate our lord King David, saying, 'May your God make Solomon's name more famous than yours and his throne greater than yours!' And the king bowed in worship on his bed 48and said, 'Praise be to the LORD, the God of Israel, who has allowed my eyes to see a successor on my throne today.' "

49At this, all Adonijah's guests rose in alarm and dispersed. 50But Adonijah, in fear of Solomon, went and took hold of the horns of the altar. 51Then Solomon was told, "Adonijah is afraid of King Solomon and is clinging to the horns of the altar. He says, 'Let King Solomon swear to me today that he will not put his servant to death with the sword.' "

52Solomon replied, "If he shows himself to be a worthy man, not a hair of his head will fall to the ground; but if evil is found in him, he will die." 53Then King Solomon sent men, and they brought him down from the altar. And Adonijah came and bowed down to King Solomon, and Solomon said, "Go to your home."

■ David's Charge to Solomon

2 When the time drew near for David to die, he gave a charge to Solomon his son.

2"I am about to go the way of all the earth," he said. "So be strong, show yourself a man, 3and observe what the LORD your God requires: Walk in his ways, and keep his decrees and commands, his laws and requirements, as written in the Law of Moses, so that you may prosper in all you do and wherever you go, 4and that the LORD may keep his promise to me: 'If your descendants watch how they live, and if they walk faithfully before me with all their heart and soul, you will never fail to have a man on the throne of Israel.'

5"Now you yourself know what Joab son of Zeruiah did to me—what he did to the two commanders of Israel's armies, Abner son of Ner and Amasa son of Jether. He killed them, shedding their blood in peacetime as if in battle, and with that blood stained the belt round his waist and the sandals on his feet. 6Deal with him according to your wisdom, but do not let his grey head go down to the grave*a* in peace.

2:5 ■ PAYING BACK JOAB
For the background to David's comments about Joab, see 2 Samuel 3:17–30; 20:4–11.

7"But show kindness to the sons of Barzillai of Gilead and let them be among those who eat at your table. They stood by me when I fled from your brother Absalom.

8"And remember, you have with you Shimei son of Gera, the Benjamite from Bahurim, who called down bitter curses on me the day I went to

Mahanaim. When he came down to meet me at the Jordan, I swore to him by the LORD: 'I will not put you to death by the sword.' 9But now, do not consider him innocent. You are a man of wisdom; you will know what to do to him. Bring his grey head down to the grave in blood."

10Then David rested with his fathers and was buried in the City of David. 11He had reigned for forty years over Israel—seven years in Hebron and thirty-three in Jerusalem. 12So Solomon sat on the throne of his father David, and his rule was firmly established.

■ Solomon's Throne Established

13Now Adonijah, the son of Haggith, went to Bathsheba, Solomon's mother. Bathsheba asked him, "Do you come peacefully?"

He answered, "Yes, peacefully." 14Then he added, "I have something to say to you."

"You may say it," she replied.

15"As you know," he said, "the kingdom was mine. All Israel looked to me as their king. But things changed, and the kingdom has gone to my brother; for it has come to him from the LORD. 16Now I have one request to make of you. Do not refuse me."

"You may make it," she said.

17So he continued, "Please ask King Solomon—he will not refuse you—to give me Abishag the Shunammite as my wife."

2:17 ■ AFTER MORE THAN A WIFE?
Solomon had a rather harsh response (verse 23) to Adonijah's request to marry King David's companion. But asking for her may have been Adonijah's veiled attempt to regain the throne lost to Solomon. In the ancient Middle East, a person who married any of the late king's wives or concubines publicly claimed the rights of the former king (see 2 Samuel 12:8 and 16:21–22 for examples). Adonijah might have been cunningly hatching another conspiracy; Solomon, at least, seemed to think so.

18"Very well," Bathsheba replied, "I will speak to the king for you."

19When Bathsheba went to King Solomon to speak to him for Adonijah, the king stood up to meet her, bowed down to her and sat down on his throne. He had a throne brought for the king's mother, and she sat down at his right hand.

20"I have one small request to make of you," she said. "Do not refuse me."

The king replied, "Make it, my mother; I will not refuse you."

21So she said, "Let Abishag the Shunammite be given in marriage to your brother Adonijah."

22King Solomon answered his mother, "Why do you request Abishag the Shunammite for Adonijah? You might as well request the kingdom for him—after all, he is my older brother—yes, for him and for Abiathar the priest and Joab son of Zeruiah!"

23Then King Solomon swore by the LORD: "May God deal with me, be it ever so severely, if Adonijah

a6 Hebrew Sheol; also in verse 9

does not pay with his life for this request! ²⁴And now, as surely as the LORD lives — he who has established me securely on the throne of my father David and has founded a dynasty for me as he promised — Adonijah shall be put to death today!" ²⁵So King Solomon gave orders to Benaiah son of Jehoiada, and he struck down Adonijah and he died.

²⁶To Abiathar the priest the king said, "Go back to your fields in Anathoth. You deserve to die, but I will not put you to death now, because you carried the ark of the Sovereign LORD before my father David and shared all my father's hardships." ²⁷So Solomon removed Abiathar from the priesthood of the LORD, fulfilling the word the LORD had spoken at Shiloh about the house of Eli.

²⁸When the news reached Joab, who had conspired with Adonijah though not with Absalom, he fled to the tent of the LORD and took hold of the horns of the altar. ²⁹King Solomon was told that Joab had fled to the tent of the LORD and was beside the altar. Then Solomon ordered Benaiah son of Jehoiada, "Go, strike him down!"

³⁰So Benaiah entered the tent of the LORD and said to Joab, "The king says, 'Come out!' "

But he answered, "No, I will die here."

Benaiah reported to the king, "This is how Joab answered me."

³¹Then the king commanded Benaiah, "Do as he says. Strike him down and bury him, and so clear me and my father's house of the guilt of the innocent blood that Joab shed. ³²The LORD will repay him for the blood he shed, because without the knowledge of my father David he attacked two men and killed them with the sword. Both of them — Abner son of Ner, commander of Israel's army, and Amasa son of Jether, commander of Judah's army — were better men and more upright than he. ³³May the guilt of their blood rest on the head of Joab and his descendants for ever. But on David and his descendants, his house and his throne, may there be the LORD's peace for ever."

³⁴So Benaiah son of Jehoiada went up and struck down Joab and killed him, and he was buried on his own land[b] in the desert. ³⁵The king put Benaiah son of Jehoiada over the army in Joab's position and replaced Abiathar with Zadok the priest.

³⁶Then the king sent for Shimei and said to him, "Build yourself a house in Jerusalem and live there, but do not go anywhere else. ³⁷The day you leave and cross the Kidron Valley, you can be sure you will die; your blood will be on your own head."

³⁸Shimei answered the king, "What you say is good. Your servant will do as my lord the king has said." And Shimei stayed in Jerusalem for a long time.

³⁹But three years later, two of Shimei's slaves ran off to Achish son of Maacah, king of Gath, and Shimei was told, "Your slaves are in Gath." ⁴⁰At this, he saddled his donkey and went to Achish at Gath in search of his slaves. So Shimei went away and brought the slaves back from Gath.

⁴¹When Solomon was told that Shimei had gone from Jerusalem to Gath and had returned, ⁴²the king summoned Shimei and said to him, "Did I not make you swear by the LORD and warn you, 'On the day you leave to go anywhere else, you can be sure you

will die'? At that time you said to me, 'What you say is good. I will obey.' ⁴³Why then did you not keep your oath to the LORD and obey the command I gave you?"

⁴⁴The king also said to Shimei, "You know in your heart all the wrong you did to my father David. Now the LORD will repay you for your wrongdoing. ⁴⁵But King Solomon will be blessed, and David's throne will remain secure before the LORD for ever."

⁴⁶Then the king gave the order to Benaiah son of Jehoiada, and he went out and struck Shimei down and killed him.

The kingdom was now firmly established in Solomon's hands.

2:46 ■ WISE YET RUTHLESS

Chapters 2 and 3 show conflicting personality traits in Solomon. In the power struggles of chapter 2 he proved more ruthless than his father David had ever been. This tendency stirred up resentment among the northern tribes of Israel and eventually led to civil war. But chapter 3 shows Solomon could also be faithful, wise, and even humble. Tragically, he gave in to his darker side more and more as his reign wore on.

■ Solomon Asks for Wisdom

3 Solomon made an alliance with Pharaoh king of Egypt and married his daughter. He brought her to the City of David until he finished building his palace and the temple of the LORD, and the wall around Jerusalem. ²The people, however, were still sacrificing at the high places, because a temple had not yet been built for the Name of the LORD. ³Solomon showed his love for the LORD by walking according to the statutes of his father David, except that he offered sacrifices and burned incense on the high places.

⁴The king went to Gibeon to offer sacrifices, for that was the most important high place, and Solomon offered a thousand burnt offerings on that altar. ⁵At Gibeon the LORD appeared to Solomon during the night in a dream, and God said, "Ask for whatever you want me to give you."

⁶Solomon answered, "You have shown great kindness to your servant, my father David, because he was faithful to you and righteous and upright in heart. You have continued this great kindness to him and have given him a son to sit on his throne this very day.

⁷"Now, O LORD my God, you have made your servant king in place of my father David. But I am only a little child and do not know how to carry out my duties. ⁸Your servant is here among the people you have chosen, a great people, too numerous to count or number. ⁹So give your servant a discerning heart to govern your people and to distinguish between right and wrong. For who is able to govern this great people of yours?"

¹⁰The Lord was pleased that Solomon had asked for this. ¹¹So God said to him, "Since you have asked for this and not for long life or wealth for yourself, nor have asked for the death of your enemies but for

^b 34 Or buried in his tomb

discernment in administering justice, 12I will do what you have asked. I will give you a wise and discerning heart, so that there will never have been anyone like you, nor will there ever be. 13Moreover, I will give you what you have not asked for — both riches and honour — so that in your lifetime you will have no equal among kings. 14And if you walk in my ways and obey my statutes and commands as David your father did, I will give you a long life." 15Then Solomon awoke — and he realised it had been a dream.

He returned to Jerusalem, stood before the ark of the Lord's covenant and sacrificed burnt offerings and fellowship offerings.*a* Then he gave a feast for all his court.

■ A Wise Ruling

16Now two prostitutes came to the king and stood before him. 17One of them said, "My lord, this woman and I live in the same house. I had a baby while she was there with me. 18The third day after my child was born, this woman also had a baby. We were alone; there was no-one in the house but the two of us.

19"During the night this woman's son died because she lay on him. 20So she got up in the middle of the night and took my son from my side while I your servant was asleep. She put him by her breast and put her dead son by my breast. 21The next morning, I got up to nurse my son — and he was dead! But when I looked at him closely in the morning light, I saw that it wasn't the son I had borne."

22The other woman said, "No! The living one is my son; the dead one is yours."

But the first one insisted, "No! The dead one is yours; the living one is mine." And so they argued before the king.

23The king said, "This one says, 'My son is alive and your son is dead,' while that one says, 'No! Your son is dead and mine is alive.' "

24Then the king said, "Bring me a sword." So they brought a sword for the king. 25He then gave an order: "Cut the living child in two and give half to one and half to the other."

26The woman whose son was alive was filled with compassion for her son and said to the king, "Please, my lord, give her the living baby! Don't kill him!"

But the other said, "Neither I nor you shall have him. Cut him in two!"

27Then the king gave his ruling: "Give the living baby to the first woman. Do not kill him; she is his mother."

28When all Israel heard the verdict the king had given, they held the king in awe, because they saw that he had wisdom from God to administer justice.

■ Solomon's Officials and Governors

4 So King Solomon ruled over all Israel. 2And these were his chief officials:

Azariah son of Zadok — the priest;
3Elihoreph and Ahijah, sons of Shisha — secretaries;
Jehoshaphat son of Ahilud — recorder;
4Benaiah son of Jehoiada — commander-in-chief;
Zadok and Abiathar — priests;
5Azariah son of Nathan — in charge of the district officers;
Zabud son of Nathan — a priest and personal adviser to the king;
6Ahishar — in charge of the palace;
Adoniram son of Abda — in charge of forced labour.

7Solomon also had twelve district governors over all Israel, who supplied provisions for the king and the royal household. Each one had to provide supplies for one month in the year. 8These are their names:

Ben-Hur — in the hill country of Ephraim;
9Ben-Deker — in Makaz, Shaalbim, Beth Shemesh and Elon Bethhanan;
10Ben-Hesed — in Arubboth (Socoh and all the land of Hepher were his);
11Ben-Abinadab — in Naphoth Dor*a* (he was married to Taphath daughter of Solomon);
12Baana son of Ahilud — in Taanach and Megiddo, and in all of Beth Shan next to Zarethan below Jezreel, from Beth Shan to Abel Meholah across to Jokmeam;
13Ben-Geber — in Ramoth Gilead (the settlements of Jair son of Manasseh in Gilead were his, as well as the district of Argob in Bashan and its sixty large walled cities with bronze gate bars);
14Ahinadab son of Iddo — in Mahanaim;
15Ahimaaz — in Naphtali (he had married Basemath daughter of Solomon);
16Baana son of Hushai — in Asher and in Aloth;
17Jehoshaphat son of Paruah — in Issachar;
18Shimei son of Ela — in Benjamin;
19Geber son of Uri — in Gilead (the country of Sihon king of the Amorites and the country of Og king of Bashan). He was the only governor over the district.

■ Solomon's Daily Provisions

20The people of Judah and Israel were as numerous as the sand on the seashore; they ate, they drank and they were happy. 21And Solomon ruled over all the kingdoms from the River*b* to the land of the Philistines, as far as the border of Egypt. These countries brought tribute and were Solomon's subjects all his life.

22Solomon's daily provisions were thirty cors*c* of fine flour and sixty cors*d* of meal, 23ten head of stall-fed cattle, twenty of pasture-fed cattle and a hundred sheep and goats, as well as deer, gazelles,

---

a 15 Traditionally *peace offerings*   *a 11* Or *in the heights of Dor*   *b 21* That is, the Euphrates; also in verse 24   *c 22* That is, probably about
180 bushels (about 6.6 kilolitres)   *d 22* That is, probably about 365 bushels (about 13.2 kilolitres)

roebucks and choice fowl. ²⁴For he ruled over all the kingdoms west of the River, from Tiphsah to Gaza, and had peace on all sides. ²⁵During Solomon's lifetime Judah and Israel, from Dan to Beersheba, lived in safety, each man under his own vine and fig-tree.

4:21 ■ HOW LARGE WAS ISRAEL?

Under the reigns of David and Solomon, Israel stretched from the border of Egypt to the border of Babylonia. It was approximately three times the size of the modern nation of Israel, encompassing land that now belongs to Jordan, Syria, and Lebanon.

²⁶Solomon had four*ᵉ* thousand stalls for chariot horses, and twelve thousand horses.*ᶠ*

²⁷The district officers, each in his month, supplied provisions for King Solomon and all who came to the king's table. They saw to it that nothing was lacking. ²⁸They also brought to the proper place their quotas of barley and straw for the chariot horses and the other horses.

■ Solomon's Wisdom

²⁹God gave Solomon wisdom and very great insight, and a breadth of understanding as measureless as the sand on the seashore. ³⁰Solomon's wisdom was greater than the wisdom of all the men of the East, and greater than all the wisdom of Egypt. ³¹He was wiser than any other man, including Ethan the Ezrahite — wiser than Heman, Calcol and Darda, the sons of Mahol. And his fame spread to all the surrounding nations. ³²He spoke three thousand proverbs and his songs numbered a thousand and five. ³³He described plant life, from the cedar of Lebanon to the hyssop that grows out of walls. He also taught about animals and birds, reptiles and fish. ³⁴Men of all nations came to listen to Solomon's wisdom, sent by all the kings of the world, who had heard of his wisdom.

■ Preparations for Building the Temple

5 When Hiram king of Tyre heard that Solomon had been anointed king to succeed his father David, he sent his envoys to Solomon, because he had always been on friendly terms with David. ²Solomon sent back this message to Hiram:

³"You know that because of the wars waged against my father David from all sides, he could not build a temple for the Name of the LORD his God until the LORD put his enemies under his feet. ⁴But now the LORD my God has given me rest on every side, and there is no adversary or disaster. ⁵I intend, therefore, to build a temple for the Name of the LORD my God, as the LORD told my father David, when he said, 'Your son whom I will put on the throne in your place will build the temple for my Name.'

⁶"So give orders that cedars of Lebanon be cut for me. My men will work with yours, and I will pay you for your men whatever wages you set. You know that we have no-one so skilled in felling timber as the Sidonians."

⁷When Hiram heard Solomon's message, he was greatly pleased and said, "Praise be to the LORD today, for he has given David a wise son to rule over this great nation."

⁸So Hiram sent word to Solomon:

"I have received the message you sent me and will do all you want in providing the cedar and pine logs. ⁹My men will haul them down from Lebanon to the sea, and I will float them in rafts by sea to the place you specify. There I will separate them and you can take them away. And you are to grant my wish by providing food for my royal household."

¹⁰In this way Hiram kept Solomon supplied with all the cedar and pine logs he wanted, ¹¹and Solomon gave Hiram twenty thousand cors*ᵃ* of wheat as food for his household, in addition to twenty thousand baths*ᵇ,ᶜ* of pressed olive oil. Solomon continued to do this for Hiram year after year. ¹²The LORD gave Solomon wisdom, just as he had promised him. There were peaceful relations between Hiram and Solomon, and the two of them made a treaty.

¹³King Solomon conscripted labourers from all Israel — thirty thousand men. ¹⁴He sent them off to Lebanon in shifts of ten thousand a month, so that they spent one month in Lebanon and two months at home. Adoniram was in charge of the forced labour. ¹⁵Solomon had seventy thousand carriers and eighty thousand stonecutters in the hills, ¹⁶as well as thirty-three hundred*ᵈ* foremen who supervised the project and directed the workmen. ¹⁷At the king's command they removed from the quarry large blocks of quality stone to provide a foundation of dressed stone for the temple. ¹⁸The craftsmen of Solomon and Hiram and the men of Gebal*ᵉ* cut and prepared the timber and stone for the building of the temple.

■ Solomon Builds the Temple

6 In the four hundred and eightieth*ᵃ* year after the Israelites had come out of Egypt, in the fourth year of Solomon's reign over Israel, in the month of Ziv, the second month, he began to build the temple of the LORD.

²The temple that King Solomon built for the LORD was sixty cubits long, twenty wide and thirty high.*ᵇ* ³The portico at the front of the main hall of the temple extended the width of the temple, that is twenty cubits,*ᶜ* and projected ten cubits*ᵈ* from the front of the temple. ⁴He made narrow clerestory windows in the temple. ⁵Against the walls of the main hall and inner sanctuary he built a structure around the building, in which there were side rooms. ⁶The lowest floor was five cubits*ᵉ* wide, the middle floor six cubits*ᶠ* and the third floor seven.*ᵍ* He made offset

ᵉ26 Some Septuagint manuscripts (see also 2 Chron. 9:25); Hebrew *forty*   *ᶠ26* Or *charioteers*   *ᵃ11* That is, probably about 121,000 bushels (about 4,400 kilolitres)   *ᵇ11* Septuagint (see also 2 Chron. 2:10); Hebrew *twenty cors*   *ᶜ11* That is, about 97,000 gallons (about 440 kilolitres)   *ᵈ16* Hebrew; some Septuagint manuscripts (see also 2 Chron. 2:2, 18) *thirty-six hundred*   *ᵉ18* That is, Byblos   *ᵃ1* Hebrew; Septuagint *four hundred and fortieth*   *ᵇ2* That is, about 90 feet (about 27 metres) long and 30 feet (about 9 metres) wide and 45 feet (about 13.5 metres) high   *ᶜ3* That is, about 30 feet (about 9 metres)   *ᵈ3* That is, about 15 feet (about 4.5 metres)   *ᵉ6* That is, about 7½ feet (about 2.3 metres); also in verses 10 and 24   *ᶠ6* That is, about 9 feet (about 2.7 metres)   *ᵍ6* That is, about 10½ feet (about 3.2 metres) ledges around the outside of the temple so that nothing would be inserted into the temple walls.

[7]In building the temple, only blocks dressed at the quarry were used, and no hammer, chisel or any other iron tool was heard at the temple site while it was being built.

[8]The entrance to the lowest[b] floor was on the south side of the temple; a stairway led up to the middle level and from there to the third. [9]So he built the temple and completed it, roofing it with beams and cedar planks. [10]And he built the side rooms all along the temple. The height of each was five cubits, and they were attached to the temple by beams of cedar.

[11]The word of the LORD came to Solomon: [12]"As for this temple you are building, if you follow my decrees, carry out my regulations and keep all my commands and obey them, I will fulfil through you the promise I gave to David your father. [13]And I will live among the Israelites and will not abandon my people Israel."

[14]So Solomon built the temple and completed it. [15]He lined its interior walls with cedar boards, panelling them from the floor of the temple to the ceiling, and covered the floor of the temple with planks of pine. [16]He partitioned off twenty cubits[i] at the rear of the temple with cedar boards from floor to ceiling to form within the temple an inner sanctuary, the Most Holy Place. [17]The main hall in front of this room was forty cubits[j] long. [18]The inside of the temple was cedar, carved with gourds and open flowers. Everything was cedar; no stone was to be seen.

[19]He prepared the inner sanctuary within the temple to set the ark of the covenant of the LORD there. [20]The inner sanctuary was twenty cubits long, twenty wide and twenty high.[k] He overlaid the inside with pure gold, and he also overlaid the altar of cedar. [21]Solomon covered the inside of the temple with pure gold, and he extended gold chains across the front of the inner sanctuary, which was overlaid with gold. [22]So he overlaid the whole interior with gold. He also overlaid with gold the altar that belonged to the inner sanctuary.

[23]In the inner sanctuary he made a pair of cherubim of olive wood, each ten cubits[l] high. [24]One wing of the first cherub was five cubits long, and the other wing five cubits – ten cubits from wing tip to wing tip. [25]The second cherub also measured ten cubits, for the two cherubim were identical in size and shape. [26]The height of each cherub was ten cubits. [27]He placed the cherubim inside the innermost room of the temple, with their wings spread out. The wing of one cherub touched one wall, while the wing of the other touched the other wall, and their wings touched each other in the middle of the room. [28]He overlaid the cherubim with gold.

[29]On the walls all round the temple, in both the inner and outer rooms, he carved cherubim, palm trees and open flowers. [30]He also covered the floors of both the inner and outer rooms of the temple with gold.

[31]For the entrance of the inner sanctuary he made doors of olive wood with five-sided jambs. [32]And on the two olive wood doors he carved cherubim, palm trees and open flowers, and overlaid the cherubim and palm trees with beaten gold. [33]In the same way he made four-sided jambs of olive wood for the entrance to the main hall. [34]He also made two pine doors, each having two leaves that turned in sockets. [35]He carved cherubim, palm trees and open flowers on them and overlaid them with gold hammered evenly over the carvings.

[36]And he built the inner courtyard of three courses of dressed stone and one course of trimmed cedar beams.

[37]The foundation of the temple of the LORD was laid in the fourth year, in the month of Ziv. [38]In the eleventh year in the month of Bul, the eighth month, the temple was finished in all its details according to its specifications. He had spent seven years building it.

■ Solomon Builds His Palace

7 It took Solomon thirteen years, however, to complete the construction of his palace. [2]He built the Palace of the Forest of Lebanon a hundred cubits long, fifty wide and thirty high,[a] with four rows of cedar columns supporting trimmed cedar beams. [3]It was roofed with cedar above the beams that rested on the columns – forty-five beams, fifteen to a row. [4]Its windows were placed high in sets of three, facing each other. [5]All the doorways had rectangular frames; they were in the front part in sets of three, facing each other.[b]

6He made a colonnade fifty cubits long and thirty wide.c In front of it was a portico, and in front of that were pillars and an overhanging roof.

7He built the throne hall, the Hall of Justice, where he was to judge, and he covered it with cedar from floor to ceiling.d 8And the palace in which he was to live, set farther back, was similar in design. Solomon also made a palace like this hall for Pharaoh's daughter, whom he had married.

9All these structures, from the outside to the great courtyard and from foundation to eaves, were made of blocks of high-grade stone cut to size and trimmed with a saw on their inner and outer faces. 10The foundations were laid with large stones of good quality, some measuring ten cubitse and some eight.f 11Above were high-grade stones, cut to size, and cedar beams. 12The great courtyard was surrounded by a wall of three courses of dressed stone and one course of trimmed cedar beams, as was the inner courtyard of the temple of the LORD with its portico.

■ The Temple's Furnishings

13King Solomon sent to Tyre and brought Huram,g 14whose mother was a widow from the tribe of Naphtali and whose father was a man of Tyre and a craftsman in bronze. Huram was highly skilled and experienced in all kinds of bronze work. He came to King Solomon and did all the work assigned to him.

15He cast two bronze pillars, each eighteen cubits high and twelve cubits round,h by line. 16He also made two capitals of cast bronze to set on the tops of the pillars; each capital was five cubitsi high. 17A network of interwoven chains festooned the capitals on top of the pillars, seven for each capital. 18He made pomegranates in two rowsj encircling each network to decorate the capitals on top of the pillars.k He did the same for each capital. 19The capitals on top of the pillars in the portico were in the shape of lilies, four cubitsl high. 20On the capitals of both pillars, above the bowl-shaped part next to the network, were the two hundred pomegranates in rows all around. 21He erected the pillars at the portico of the temple. The pillar to the south he named Jakinm and the one to the north Boaz.n 22The capitals on top were in the shape of lilies. And so the work on the pillars was completed.

23He made the Sea of cast metal, circular in shape, measuring ten cubitso from rim to rim and five cubits high. It took a line of thirty cubitsp to measure round it. 24Below the rim, gourds encircled it — ten to a cubit. The gourds were cast in two rows in one piece with the Sea.

25The Sea stood on twelve bulls, three facing north, three facing west, three facing south and three facing east. The Sea rested on top of them, and their hindquarters were towards the centre. 26It was a handbreadthq in thickness, and its rim was like the rim of a cup, like a lily blossom. It held two thousand baths.r

27He also made ten movable stands of bronze; each was four cubits long, four wide and three high.s 28This is how the stands were made: They had side panels attached to uprights. 29On the panels between the uprights were lions, bulls and cherubim — and on the uprights as well. Above and below the lions and bulls were wreaths of hammered work. 30Each stand had four bronze wheels with bronze axles, and each had a basin resting on four supports, cast with wreaths on each side. 31On the inside of the stand there was an opening that had a circular frame one cubitt deep. This opening was round, and with its basework it measured a cubit and a half.u Around its opening there was engraving. The panels of the stands were square, not round. 32The four wheels were under the panels, and the axles of the wheels were attached to the stand. The diameter of each wheel was a cubit and a half. 33The wheels were made like chariot wheels; the axles, rims, spokes and hubs were all of cast metal.

34Each stand had four handles, one on each corner, projecting from the stand. 35At the top of the stand there was a circular band half a cubitv deep. The supports and panels were attached to the top of the stand. 36He engraved cherubim, lions and palm trees on the surfaces of the supports and on the panels, in every available space, with wreaths all around. 37This is the way he made the ten stands. They were all cast in the same moulds and were identical in size and shape.

38He then made ten bronze basins, each holding forty bathsw and measuring four cubits across, one basin to go on each of the ten stands. 39He placed five of the stands on the south side of the temple and five on the north. He placed the Sea on the south side, at the south-east corner of the temple. 40He also made the basins and shovels and sprinkling bowls.

So Huram finished all the work he had undertaken for King Solomon in the temple of the LORD:

41the two pillars;
the two bowl-shaped capitals on top of the pillars;
the two sets of network decorating the two bowl-shaped capitals on top of the pillars;
42the four hundred pomegranates for the two sets of network (two rows of pomegranates for each network, decorating the bowl-shaped capitals on top of the pillars);
43the ten stands with their ten basins;
44the Sea and the twelve bulls under it;
45the pots, shovels and sprinkling bowls.

All these objects that Huram made for King Solomon for the temple of the LORD were of burnished bronze. 46The king had them cast in clay moulds in the plain of the Jordan between Succoth and

---

c 6 That is, about 75 feet (about 23 metres) long and 45 feet (about 13.5 metres) wide   d 7 Vulgate and Syriac; Hebrew floor   e 10 That is, about 15 feet (about 4.5 metres)   f 10 That is, about 12 feet (about 3.7 metres)   g 13 Hebrew Hiram, a variant of Huram; also in verses 40 and 45   h 15 That is, about 27 feet (about 8.2 metres) high and 18 feet (about 5.5 metres) round   i 16 That is, about 7½ feet (about 2.3 metres); also in verse 23   j 18 Two Hebrew manuscripts and Septuagint; most Hebrew manuscripts made the pillars, and there were two rows   k 18 Many Hebrew manuscripts and Syriac; most Hebrew manuscripts pomegranates   l 19 That is, about 6 feet (about 1.8 metres); also in verse 38   m 21 Jakin probably means he establishes. n 21 Boaz probably means in him is strength.   o 23 That is, about 15 feet (about 4.5 metres)   p 23 That is, about 45 feet (about 13.7 metres) q 26 That is, about 3 inches (about 8 centimetres)   r 26 That is, probably about 9,700 gallons (about 44 kilolitres); the Septuagint does not have this sentence.   s 27 That is, about 6 feet (about 1.8 metres) long and wide and about 4½ feet (about 1.4 metres) high   t 31 That is, about 1½ feet (about 0.5 metre)   u 31 That is, about 2¼ feet (about 0.7 metre); also in verse 32   v 35 That is, about ¾ foot (about 0.2 metre)   w 38 That is, about 195 gallons (about 880 litres)

Zarethan. 47Solomon left all these things unweighed, because there were so many; the weight of the bronze was not determined.

48Solomon also made all the furnishings that were in the LORD's temple:

the golden altar;
the golden table on which was the bread of the Presence;
49the lampstands of pure gold (five on the right and five on the left, in front of the inner sanctuary);
the gold floral work and lamps and tongs;
50the pure gold dishes, wick trimmers, sprinkling bowls, dishes and censers;
and the gold sockets for the doors of the innermost room, the Most Holy Place, and also for the doors of the main hall of the temple.

51When all the work King Solomon had done for the temple of the LORD was finished, he brought in the things his father David had dedicated—the silver and gold and the furnishings—and he placed them in the treasuries of the LORD's temple.

■ The Ark Brought to the Temple

8 Then King Solomon summoned into his presence at Jerusalem the elders of Israel, all the heads of the tribes and the chiefs of the Israelite families, to bring up the ark of the LORD's covenant from Zion, the City of David. 2All the men of Israel came together to King Solomon at the time of the festival in the month of Ethanim, the seventh month.

3When all the elders of Israel had arrived, the priests took up the ark, 4and they brought up the ark of the LORD and the Tent of Meeting and all the sacred furnishings in it. The priests and Levites carried them up, 5and King Solomon and the entire assembly of Israel that had gathered about him were before the ark, sacrificing so many sheep and cattle that they could not be recorded or counted.

6The priests then brought the ark of the LORD's covenant to its place in the inner sanctuary of the temple, the Most Holy Place, and put it beneath the wings of the cherubim. 7The cherubim spread their wings over the place of the ark and overshadowed the ark and its carrying poles. 8These poles were so long that their ends could be seen from the Holy Place in front of the inner sanctuary, but not from outside the Holy Place; and they are still there today. 9There was nothing in the ark except the two stone tablets that Moses had placed in it at Horeb, where the LORD made a covenant with the Israelites after they came out of Egypt.

10When the priests withdrew from the Holy Place, the cloud filled the temple of the LORD. 11And the priests could not perform their service because of the cloud, for the glory of the LORD filled his temple.

12Then Solomon said, "The LORD has said that he would dwell in a dark cloud; 13I have indeed built a magnificent temple for you, a place for you to dwell for ever."

14While the whole assembly of Israel was standing there, the king turned round and blessed them. 15Then he said:

"Praise be to the LORD, the God of Israel, who with his own hand has fulfilled what he promised with his own mouth to my father David. For he said, 16'Since the day I brought my people Israel out of Egypt, I have not chosen a city in any tribe of Israel to have a temple built for my Name to be there, but I have chosen David to rule my people Israel.'

8:11 ■ OFF-LIMITS FOR PEOPLE
Much of the temple stayed off-limits to the general public; only priests went in. Not even priests ventured into the Most Holy Place, except on very special occasions. Solomon had not intended the building for humans—he wanted a place suitable for God to dwell. And on the memorable day described here, the awesome glory of the Lord did indeed fill the temple.

17"My father David had it in his heart to build a temple for the Name of the LORD, the God of Israel. 18But the LORD said to my father David, 'Because it was in your heart to build a temple for my Name, you did well to have this in your heart. 19Nevertheless, you are not the one to build the temple, but your son, who is your own flesh and blood—he is the one who will build the temple for my Name.'

20"The LORD has kept the promise he made: I have succeeded David my father and now I sit on the throne of Israel, just as the LORD promised, and I have built the temple for the Name of the LORD, the God of Israel. 21I have provided a place there for the ark, in which is the covenant of the LORD that he made with our fathers when he brought them out of Egypt."

■ Solomon's Prayer of Dedication

22Then Solomon stood before the altar of the LORD in front of the whole assembly of Israel, spread out his hands towards heaven 23and said:

"O LORD, God of Israel, there is no God like you in heaven above or on earth below—you who keep your covenant of love with your servants who continue wholeheartedly in your way. 24You have kept your promise to your servant David my father; with your mouth you have promised and with your hand you have fulfilled it—as it is today.

25"Now LORD, God of Israel, keep for your servant David my father the promises you made to him when you said, 'You shall never fail to have a man to sit before me on the throne of Israel, if only your sons are careful in all they do to walk before me as you have done.' 26And now, O God of Israel, let your word that you promised your servant David my father come true.

27"But will God really dwell on earth? The heavens, even the highest heaven, cannot contain you. How much less this temple I have built! 28Yet give attention to your servant's prayer and his plea for mercy, O LORD my God.

Hear the cry and the prayer that your servant is praying in your presence this day. ²⁹May your eyes be open towards this temple night and day, this place of which you said, 'My Name shall be there,' so that you will hear the prayer your servant prays towards this place. ³⁰Hear the supplication of your servant and of your people Israel when they pray towards this place. Hear from heaven, your dwelling-place, and when you hear, forgive.

8:27 ■ WHERE GOD DWELLS

King Solomon was at his most eloquent in the great speech and prayer of chapter 8. He made it clear that the Lord of the universe could not fully dwell in a building. Nevertheless, God's presence, or his "Name", would indeed live there. For that reason, Solomon began the practice of praying towards Jerusalem, a practice still followed by many Jews today (verse 29).

³¹"When a man wrongs his neighbour and is required to take an oath and he comes and swears the oath before your altar in this temple, ³²then hear from heaven and act. Judge between your servants, condemning the guilty and bringing down on his own head what he has done. Declare the innocent not guilty, and so establish his innocence.

³³"When your people Israel have been defeated by an enemy because they have sinned against you, and when they turn back to you and confess your name, praying and making supplication to you in this temple, ³⁴then hear from heaven and forgive the sin of your people Israel and bring them back to the land you gave to their fathers.

³⁵"When the heavens are shut up and there is no rain because your people have sinned against you, and when they pray towards this place and confess your name and turn from their sin because you have afflicted them, ³⁶then hear from heaven and forgive the sin of your servants, your people Israel. Teach them the right way to live, and send rain on the land you gave your people for an inheritance.

³⁷"When famine or plague comes to the land, or blight or mildew, locusts or grasshoppers, or when an enemy besieges them in any of their cities, whatever disaster or disease may come, ³⁸and when a prayer or plea is made by any of your people Israel — each one aware of the afflictions of his own heart, and spreading out his hands towards this temple — ³⁹then hear from heaven, your dwelling-place. Forgive and act; deal with each man according to all he does, since you know his heart (for you alone know the hearts of all men), ⁴⁰so that they will fear you all the time they live in the land you gave our fathers.

⁴¹"As for the foreigner who does not belong to your people Israel but has come from a distant land because of your name — ⁴²for men

will hear of your great name and your mighty hand and your outstretched arm — when he comes and prays towards this temple, ⁴³then hear from heaven, your dwelling-place, and do whatever the foreigner asks of you, so that all the peoples of the earth may know your name and fear you, as do your own people Israel, and may know that this house I have built bears your Name.

⁴⁴"When your people go to war against their enemies, wherever you send them, and when they pray to the LORD towards the city you have chosen and the temple I have built for your Name, ⁴⁵then hear from heaven their prayer and their plea, and uphold their cause.

⁴⁶"When they sin against you — for there is no-one who does not sin — and you become angry with them and give them over to the enemy, who takes them captive to his own land, far away or near; ⁴⁷and if they have a change of heart in the land where they are held captive, and repent and plead with you in the land of their conquerors and say, 'We have sinned, we have done wrong, we have acted wickedly'; ⁴⁸and if they turn back to you with all their heart and soul in the land of their enemies who took them captive, and pray to you towards the land you gave their fathers, towards the city you have chosen and the temple I have built for your Name; ⁴⁹then from heaven, your dwelling-place, hear their prayer and their plea, and uphold their cause. ⁵⁰And forgive your people, who have sinned against you; forgive all the offences they have committed against you, and cause their conquerors to show them mercy; ⁵¹for they are your people and your inheritance, whom you brought out of Egypt, out of that iron-smelting furnace.

⁵²"May your eyes be open to your servant's plea and to the plea of your people Israel, and may you listen to them whenever they cry out to you. ⁵³For you singled them out from all the nations of the world to be your own inheritance, just as you declared through your servant Moses when you, O Sovereign LORD, brought our fathers out of Egypt."

⁵⁴When Solomon had finished all these prayers and supplications to the LORD, he rose from before the altar of the LORD, where he had been kneeling with his hands spread out towards heaven. ⁵⁵He stood and blessed the whole assembly of Israel in a loud voice, saying:

⁵⁶"Praise be to the LORD, who has given rest to his people Israel just as he promised. Not one word has failed of all the good promises he gave through his servant Moses. ⁵⁷May the LORD our God be with us as he was with our fathers; may he never leave us nor forsake us. ⁵⁸May he turn our hearts to him, to walk in all his ways and to keep the commands, decrees and regulations he gave our fathers. ⁵⁹And may these words of mine, which I have prayed before the LORD, be near to the LORD our God day and night, that he may uphold the cause of his

servant and the cause of his people Israel according to each day's need, [60]so that all the peoples of the earth may know that the LORD is God and that there is no other. [61]But your hearts must be fully committed to the LORD our God, to live by his decrees and obey his commands, as at this time."

■ The Dedication of the Temple

[62]Then the king and all Israel with him offered sacrifices before the LORD. [63]Solomon offered a sacrifice of fellowship offerings[a] to the LORD: twenty-two thousand cattle and a hundred and twenty thousand sheep and goats. So the king and all the Israelites dedicated the temple of the LORD.

[64]On that same day the king consecrated the middle part of the courtyard in front of the temple of the LORD, and there he offered burnt offerings, grain offerings and the fat of the fellowship offerings, because the bronze altar before the LORD was too small to hold the burnt offerings, the grain offerings and the fat of the fellowship offerings.

[65]So Solomon observed the festival at that time, and all Israel with him — a vast assembly, people from Lebo[b] Hamath to the Wadi of Egypt. They celebrated it before the LORD our God for seven days and seven days more, fourteen days in all. [66]On the following day he sent the people away. They blessed the king and then went home, joyful and glad in heart for all the good things the LORD had done for his servant David and his people Israel.

■ The LORD Appears to Solomon

9 When Solomon had finished building the temple of the LORD and the royal palace, and had achieved all he had desired to do, [2]the LORD appeared to him a second time, as he had appeared to him at Gibeon. [3]The LORD said to him:

"I have heard the prayer and plea you have made before me; I have consecrated this temple, which you have built, by putting my Name there for ever. My eyes and my heart will always be there.

[4]"As for you, if you walk before me in integrity of heart and uprightness, as David your father did, and do all I command and observe my decrees and laws, [5]I will establish your royal throne over Israel for ever, as I promised David your father when I said, 'You shall never fail to have a man on the throne of Israel.'

[6]"But if you[a] or your sons turn away from me and do not observe the commands and decrees I have given you[a] and go off to serve other gods and worship them, [7]then I will cut off Israel from the land I have given them and will reject this temple I have consecrated for my Name. Israel will then become a byword and an object of ridicule among all peoples. [8]And though this temple is now imposing, all who pass by will be appalled and will scoff and say, 'Why has the LORD done such a thing to this land and to this temple?' [9]People will answer, 'Because they have forsaken the LORD their

God, who brought their fathers out of Egypt, and have embraced other gods, worshipping and serving them — that is why the LORD brought all this disaster on them.' "

■ Solomon's Other Activities

[10]At the end of twenty years, during which Solomon built these two buildings — the temple of the LORD and the royal palace — [11]King Solomon gave twenty towns in Galilee to Hiram king of Tyre, because Hiram had supplied him with all the cedar and pine and gold he wanted. [12]But when Hiram went from Tyre to see the towns that Solomon had given him, he was not pleased with them. [13]"What kind of towns are these you have given me, my brother?" he asked. And he called them the Land of Cabul,[b] a name they have to this day. [14]Now Hiram had sent to the king 120 talents[c] of gold.

> **9:13 ■ GOOD-FOR-NOTHING TOWNS**
> Solomon gave away part of God's promised land to a foreigner, an act that may have stirred up the resentment of northern tribes against the South. King Hiram, unimpressed with the 20 Galilean towns Solomon gave him as payment for services, called them "Cabul" (good-for-nothing). Interestingly, Jesus chose this very area as the early focal point of his ministry on earth.

[15]Here is the account of the forced labour King Solomon conscripted to build the LORD's temple, his own palace, the supporting terraces,[d] the wall of Jerusalem, and Hazor, Megiddo and Gezer. [16](Pharaoh king of Egypt had attacked and captured Gezer. He had set it on fire. He killed its Canaanite inhabitants and then gave it as a wedding gift to his daughter, Solomon's wife. [17]And Solomon rebuilt Gezer.) He built up Lower Beth Horon, [18]Baalath, and Tadmor[e] in the desert, within his land, [19]as well as all his store cities and the towns for his chariots and for his horses[f] — whatever he desired to build in Jerusalem, in Lebanon and throughout all the territory he ruled.

[20]All the people left from the Amorites, Hittites, Perizzites, Hivites and Jebusites (these peoples were not Israelites), [21]that is, their descendants remaining in the land, whom the Israelites could not exterminate[g] — these Solomon conscripted for his slave labour force, as it is to this day. [22]But Solomon did not make slaves of any of the Israelites; they were his fighting men, his government officials, his officers, his captains, and the commanders of his chariots and charioteers. [23]They were also the chief officials in charge of Solomon's projects — 550 officials supervising the men who did the work.

[24]After Pharaoh's daughter had come up from the City of David to the palace Solomon had built for her, he constructed the supporting terraces.

[25]Three times a year Solomon sacrificed burnt offerings and fellowship offerings[b] on the altar he had built for the LORD, burning incense before the LORD

a 63 Traditionally *peace offerings*; also in verse 64   b 65 Or *from the entrance to*   a 6 The Hebrew is plural.   b 13 *Cabul* sounds like the Hebrew for *good-for-nothing*.   c 14 That is, about 4 tons (about 4 metric tons)   d 15 Or *the Millo*; also in verse 24   e 18 The Hebrew may also be read *Tamar*.   f 19 Or *charioteers*   g 21 The Hebrew term refers to the irrevocable giving over of things or persons to the LORD, often by totally destroying them.   b 25 Traditionally *peace offerings* along with them, and so fulfilled the temple obligations.

²⁶King Solomon also built ships at Ezion Geber, which is near Elath in Edom, on the shore of the Red Sea.ⁱ ²⁷And Hiram sent his men — sailors who knew the sea — to serve in the fleet with Solomon's men. ²⁸They sailed to Ophir and brought back 420 talentsʲ of gold, which they delivered to King Solomon.

■ The Queen of Sheba Visits Solomon

10 When the queen of Sheba heard about the fame of Solomon and his relation to the name of the LORD, she came to test him with hard questions. ²Arriving at Jerusalem with a very great caravan — with camels carrying spices, large quantities of gold, and precious stones — she came to Solomon and talked with him about all that she had on her mind. ³Solomon answered all her questions; nothing was too hard for the king to explain to her. ⁴When the queen of Sheba saw all the wisdom of Solomon and the palace he had built, ⁵the food on his table, the seating of his officials, the attending servants in their robes, his cupbearers, and the burnt offerings he made atᵃ the temple of the LORD, she was overwhelmed.

⁶She said to the king, "The report I heard in my own country about your achievements and your wisdom is true. ⁷But I did not believe these things until I came and saw with my own eyes. Indeed, not even half was told me; in wisdom and wealth you have far exceeded the report I heard. ⁸How happy your men must be! How happy your officials, who continually stand before you and hear your wisdom! ⁹Praise be to the LORD your God, who has delighted in you and placed you on the throne of Israel. Because of the LORD's eternal love for Israel, he has made you king, to maintain justice and righteousness."

¹⁰And she gave the king 120 talentsᵇ of gold, large quantities of spices, and precious stones. Never again were so many spices brought in as those the queen of Sheba gave to King Solomon.

¹¹(Hiram's ships brought gold from Ophir; and from there they brought great cargoes of almugwoodᶜ and precious stones. ¹²The king used the almug-wood to make supports for the temple of the LORD and for the royal palace, and to make harps and lyres for the musicians. So much almug-wood has never been imported or seen since that day.)

¹³King Solomon gave the queen of Sheba all she desired and asked for, besides what he had given her out of his royal bounty. Then she left and returned with her retinue to her own country.

■ Solomon's Splendour

¹⁴The weight of the gold that Solomon received yearly was 666 talents,ᵈ ¹⁵not including the revenues from merchants and traders and from all the Arabian kings and the governors of the land.

¹⁶King Solomon made two hundred large shields of hammered gold; six hundred bekasᵉ of gold went into each shield. ¹⁷He also made three

hundred small shields of hammered gold, with three minasᶠ of gold in each shield. The king put them in the Palace of the Forest of Lebanon.

10:14 ■ A KING OF EXCESS
This passage (10:14–29) graphically illustrates how far Solomon had strayed from God's ideal. The book of Deuteronomy cites Moses' forthright warnings about what kind of king should rule over Israel (Deuteronomy 17:14–20). Solomon defied those warnings by acquiring huge numbers of horses, getting involved in foreign trade, taking many wives, and accumulating silver and gold.

¹⁸Then the king made a great throne inlaid with ivory and overlaid with fine gold. ¹⁹The throne had six steps, and its back had a rounded top. On both sides of the seat were armrests, with a lion standing beside each of them. ²⁰Twelve lions stood on the six steps, one at either end of each step. Nothing like it had ever been made for any other kingdom. ²¹All King Solomon's goblets were gold, and all the household articles in the Palace of the Forest of Lebanon were pure gold. Nothing was made of silver, because silver was considered of little value in Solomon's days. ²²The king had a fleet of trading shipsᵍ at sea along with the ships of Hiram. Once every three years it returned carrying gold, silver and ivory, and apes and baboons.

²³King Solomon was greater in riches and wisdom than all the other kings of the earth. ²⁴The whole world sought audience with Solomon to hear the wisdom God had put in his heart. ²⁵Year after year, everyone who came brought a gift — articles of silver and gold, robes, weapons and spices, and horses and mules.

²⁶Solomon accumulated chariots and horses; he had fourteen hundred chariots and twelve thousand horses,ᵇ which he kept in the chariot cities and also with him in Jerusalem. ²⁷The king made silver as common in Jerusalem as stones, and cedar as plentiful as sycamore-fig trees in the foothills. ²⁸Solomon's horses were imported from Egyptⁱ and from Kueʲ — the royal merchants purchased them from Kue.ʲ ²⁹They imported a chariot from Egypt for six hundred shekelsᵏ of silver, and a horse for a hundred and fifty.ˡ They also exported them to all the kings of the Hittites and of the Arameans.

■ Solomon's Wives

11 King Solomon, however, loved many foreign women besides Pharaoh's daughter — Moabites, Ammonites, Edomites, Sidonians and Hittites. ²They were from nations about which the LORD had told the Israelites, "You must not intermarry with them, because they will surely turn your hearts after their gods." Nevertheless, Solomon held fast to them in love. ³He had seven hundred wives of royal birth and three hundred concubines, and his wives led him astray. ⁴As Solomon grew old, his wives turned his heart after other gods, and his heart was not fully

---

ⁱ26 Hebrew *Yam Suph*; that is, Sea of Reeds   ʲ28 That is, about 14 tons (about 14.5 metric tons)   ᵃ5 Or *the ascent by which he went up to*
ᵇ10 That is, about 4 tons (about 4 metric tons)   ᶜ11 Probably a variant of *algum-wood*; also in verse 12   ᵈ14 That is, about 22½ tons (about 23 metric
tons)   ᵉ16 That is, about 7½ pounds (about 3.5 kilograms)   ᶠ17 That is, about 3¾ pounds (about 1.7 kilograms)   ᵍ22 Hebrew *of ships of Tarshish*
ᵇ26 Or *charioteers*   ⁱ28 Or possibly *Muzur*, a region in Cilicia; also in verse 29   ʲ28 Probably *Cilicia*   ᵏ29 That is, about 15 pounds (about
7 kilograms)   ˡ29 That is, about 3¾ pounds (about 1.7 kilograms)

devoted to the LORD his God, as the heart of David his father had been. 5He followed Ashtoreth the goddess of the Sidonians, and Molech*a* the detestable god of the Ammonites. 6So Solomon did evil in the eyes of the LORD; he did not follow the LORD completely, as David his father had done.

11:3 ■ SO MANY WOMEN

Solomon's 700 wives were foreigners who worshipped other gods and had different standards of right and wrong. He probably married them as part of treaty arrangements with surrounding nations; a royal marriage was supposed to cement a bond between peoples. These marriages violated God's law (Deuteronomy 7:3–4; 17:17) and ultimately led Solomon away from God. Because of his wives' religions, he built shrines and encouraged pagan worship in Jerusalem itself.

7On a hill east of Jerusalem, Solomon built a high place for Chemosh the detestable god of Moab, and for Molech the detestable god of the Ammonites. 8He did the same for all his foreign wives, who burned incense and offered sacrifices to their gods.

9The LORD became angry with Solomon because his heart had turned away from the LORD, the God of Israel, who had appeared to him twice. 10Although he had forbidden Solomon to follow other gods, Solomon did not keep the LORD's command. 11So the LORD said to Solomon, "Since this is your attitude and you have not kept my covenant and my decrees, which I commanded you, I will most certainly tear the kingdom away from you and give it to one of your subordinates. 12Nevertheless, for the sake of David your father, I will not do it during your lifetime. I will tear it out of the hand of your son. 13Yet I will not tear the whole kingdom from him, but will give him one tribe for the sake of David my servant and for the sake of Jerusalem, which I have chosen."

■ Solomon's Adversaries

14Then the LORD raised up against Solomon an adversary, Hadad the Edomite, from the royal line of Edom. 15Earlier when David was fighting with Edom, Joab the commander of the army, who had gone up to bury the dead, had struck down all the men in Edom. 16Joab and all the Israelites stayed there for six months, until they had destroyed all the men in Edom. 17But Hadad, still only a boy, fled to Egypt with some Edomite officials who had served his father. 18They set out from Midian and went to Paran. Then taking men from Paran with them, they went to Egypt, to Pharaoh king of Egypt, who gave Hadad a house and land and provided him with food.

19Pharaoh was so pleased with Hadad that he gave him a sister of his own wife, Queen Tahpenes, in marriage. 20The sister of Tahpenes bore him a son named Genubath, whom Tahpenes brought up in the royal palace. There Genubath lived with Pharaoh's own children.

21While he was in Egypt, Hadad heard that David rested with his fathers and that Joab the commander of the army was also dead. Then Hadad said to Pharaoh, "Let me go, so that I may return to my own country."

22"What have you lacked here that you want to go back to your own country?" Pharaoh asked.

"Nothing," Hadad replied, "but do let me go!"

23And God raised up against Solomon another adversary, Rezon son of Eliada, who had fled from his master, Hadadezer king of Zobah. 24He gathered men around him and became the leader of a band of rebels when David destroyed the forces*b* ₎of Zobah₎; the rebels went to Damascus, where they settled and took control. 25Rezon was Israel's adversary as long as Solomon lived, adding to the trouble caused by Hadad. So Rezon ruled in Aram and was hostile towards Israel.

■ Jeroboam Rebels Against Solomon

26Also, Jeroboam son of Nebat rebelled against the king. He was one of Solomon's officials, an Ephraimite from Zeredah, and his mother was a widow named Zeruah.

27Here is the account of how he rebelled against the king: Solomon had built the supporting terraces*c* and had filled in the gap in the wall of the city of David his father. 28Now Jeroboam was a man of standing, and when Solomon saw how well the young man did his work, he put him in charge of the whole labour force of the house of Joseph.

29About that time Jeroboam was going out of Jerusalem, and Ahijah the prophet of Shiloh met him on the way, wearing a new cloak. The two of them were alone out in the country, 30and Ahijah took hold of the new cloak he was wearing and tore it into twelve pieces. 31Then he said to Jeroboam, "Take ten pieces for yourself, for this is what the LORD, the God of Israel, says: 'See, I am going to tear the kingdom out of Solomon's hand and give you ten tribes. 32But for the sake of my servant David and the city of Jerusalem, which I have chosen out of all the tribes of Israel, he will have one tribe. 33I will do this because they have*d* forsaken me and worshipped Ashtoreth the goddess of the Sidonians, Chemosh the god of the Moabites, and Molech the god of the Ammonites, and have not walked in my ways, nor done what is right in my eyes, nor kept my statutes and laws as David, Solomon's father, did.

34" 'But I will not take the whole kingdom out of Solomon's hand; I have made him ruler all the days of his life for the sake of David my servant, whom I chose and who observed my commands and statutes. 35I will take the kingdom from his son's hands and give you ten tribes. 36I will give one tribe to his son so that David my servant may always have a lamp before me in Jerusalem, the city where I chose to put my Name. 37However, as for you, I will take you, and you will rule over all that your heart desires; you will be king over Israel. 38If you do whatever I command you and walk in my ways and do what is right in my eyes by keeping my statutes and commands, as David my servant did, I will be with you. I will build you a dynasty as enduring as the one I built for David and will give Israel to you. 39I will humble

*a*5 Hebrew *Milcom*; also in verse 33   *b*24 Hebrew *destroyed them*   *c*27 Or *the Millo*   *d*33 Hebrew; Septuagint, Vulgate and Syriac *because he has*

David's descendants because of this, but not for ever.' "

⁴⁰Solomon tried to kill Jeroboam, but Jeroboam fled to Egypt, to Shishak the king, and stayed there until Solomon's death.

■ Solomon's Death

⁴¹As for the other events of Solomon's reign—all he did and the wisdom he displayed—are they not written in the book of the annals of Solomon? ⁴²Solomon reigned in Jerusalem over all Israel for forty years. ⁴³Then he rested with his fathers and was buried in the city of David his father. And Rehoboam his son succeeded him as king.

11:41 ■ USING OTHER SOURCES

The author makes liberal use of other historical records, most of which have not survived. This verse refers to "the book of the annals of Solomon". Elsewhere, 1 Kings relies on accounts of the kings of Judah (22:45) or of Israel (15:31). In all, the two books of Kings make 34 references to other sources.

■ Israel Rebels Against Rehoboam

12 Rehoboam went to Shechem, for all the Israelites had gone there to make him king. ²When Jeroboam son of Nebat heard this (he was still in Egypt, where he had fled from King Solomon), he returned from^a Egypt. ³So they sent for Jeroboam, and he and the whole assembly of Israel went to Rehoboam and said to him: ⁴"Your father put a heavy yoke on us, but now lighten the harsh labour and the heavy yoke he put on us, and we will serve you."

⁵Rehoboam answered, "Go away for three days and then come back to me." So the people went away.

⁶Then King Rehoboam consulted the elders who had served his father Solomon during his lifetime. "How would you advise me to answer these people?" he asked.

⁷They replied, "If today you will be a servant to these people and serve them and give them a favourable answer, they will always be your servants."

⁸But Rehoboam rejected the advice the elders gave him and consulted the young men who had grown up with him and were serving him. ⁹He asked them, "What is your advice? How should we answer these people who say to me, 'Lighten the yoke your father put on us'?"

¹⁰The young men who had grown up with him replied, "Tell these people who have said to you, 'Your father put a heavy yoke on us, but make our yoke lighter'—tell them, 'My little finger is thicker than my father's waist. ¹¹My father laid on you a heavy yoke; I will make it even heavier. My father scourged you with whips; I will scourge you with scorpions.' "

¹²Three days later Jeroboam and all the people returned to Rehoboam, as the king had said, "Come back to me in three days." ¹³The king answered the people harshly. Rejecting the advice given him by the elders, ¹⁴he followed the advice of the young men and said, "My father made your yoke heavy; I will make it even heavier. My father scourged you with whips; I will scourge you with scorpions." ¹⁵So the king did not listen to the people, for this turn of events was from the LORD, to fulfil the word the LORD had spoken to Jeroboam son of Nebat through Ahijah the Shilonite.

¹⁶When all Israel saw that the king refused to listen to them, they answered the king:

"What share do we have in David,
    what part in Jesse's son?
To your tents, O Israel!
    Look after your own house, O David!"

So the Israelites went home. ¹⁷But as for the Israelites who were living in the towns of Judah, Rehoboam still ruled over them.

¹⁸King Rehoboam sent out Adoniram,^b who was in charge of forced labour, but all Israel stoned him to death. King Rehoboam, however, managed to get into his chariot and escape to Jerusalem. ¹⁹So Israel has been in rebellion against the house of David to this day.

²⁰When all the Israelites heard that Jeroboam had returned, they sent and called him to the assembly and made him king over all Israel. Only the tribe of Judah remained loyal to the house of David.

²¹When Rehoboam arrived in Jerusalem, he mustered the whole house of Judah and the tribe of Benjamin—a hundred and eighty thousand fighting men—to make war against the house of Israel and to regain the kingdom for Rehoboam son of Solomon.

²²But this word of God came to Shemaiah the man of God: ²³"Say to Rehoboam son of Solomon king of Judah, to the whole house of Judah and Benjamin, and to the rest of the people, ²⁴'This is what the LORD says: Do not go up to fight against your brothers, the Israelites. Go home, every one of you, for this is my doing.' " So they obeyed the word of the LORD and went home again, as the LORD had ordered.

■ Golden Calves at Bethel and Dan

²⁵Then Jeroboam fortified Shechem in the hill country of Ephraim and lived there. From there he went out and built up Peniel.^c

²⁶Jeroboam thought to himself, "The kingdom is now likely to revert to the house of David. ²⁷If these people go up to offer sacrifices at the temple of the LORD in Jerusalem, they will again give their allegiance to their lord, Rehoboam king of Judah. They will kill me and return to King Rehoboam."

²⁸After seeking advice, the king made two golden calves. He said to the people, "It is too much for you to go up to Jerusalem. Here are your gods, O Israel, who brought you up out of Egypt." ²⁹One he set up in Bethel, and the other in Dan. ³⁰And this thing became a sin; the people went even as far as Dan to worship the one there.

³¹Jeroboam built shrines on high places and appointed priests from all sorts of people, even though they were not Levites. ³²He instituted a festival on the fifteenth day of the eighth month, like the festival held in Judah, and offered sacrifices on the altar.

---

^a2 Or he remained in
Peniel   ^b18 Some Septuagint manuscripts and Syriac (see also 1 Kings 4:6 and 5:14); Hebrew Adoram   ^c25 Hebrew Penuel, a variant of

This he did in Bethel, sacrificing to the calves he had made. And at Bethel he also installed priests at the high places he had made. 33On the fifteenth day of the eighth month, a month of his own choosing, he offered sacrifices on the altar he had built at Bethel. So he instituted the festival for the Israelites and went up to the altar to make offerings.

The Man of God From Judah

13 By the word of the LORD a man of God came from Judah to Bethel, as Jeroboam was standing by the altar to make an offering. 2He cried out against the altar by the word of the LORD: "O altar, altar! This is what the LORD says: 'A son named Josiah will be born to the house of David. On you he will sacrifice the priests of the high places who now make offerings here, and human bones will be burned on you.'" 3That same day the man of God gave a sign: "This is the sign the LORD has declared: The altar will be split apart and the ashes on it will be poured out."

4When King Jeroboam heard what the man of God cried out against the altar at Bethel, he stretched out his hand from the altar and said, "Seize him!" But the hand he stretched out towards the man shrivelled up, so that he could not pull it back. 5Also, the altar was split apart and its ashes poured out according to the sign given by the man of God by the word of the LORD.

6Then the king said to the man of God, "Intercede with the LORD your God and pray for me that my hand may be restored." So the man of God interceded with the LORD, and the king's hand was restored and became as it was before.

7The king said to the man of God, "Come home with me and have something to eat, and I will give you a gift."

13:7 ■ STANDING UP TO THE KING
Afraid that temple worship in Jerusalem would lure his northern supporters back to the South, Jeroboam lifted a page from Israel's past (Exodus 32:1–4) and put up two golden calves for worship (see 12:32). An anonymous man of God prophesied against this idol worship in the strongest terms.

Jeroboam's offer of a gift to the prophet reflects the kings' tendencies to keep "court prophets", paid to tell the kings what they wanted to hear. The anonymous man of God would have nothing to do with Jeroboam's hospitality. He had come to protest against Jeroboam's new religion, and would not be bought.

8But the man of God answered the king, "Even if you were to give me half your possessions, I would not go with you, nor would I eat bread or drink water here. 9For I was commanded by the word of the LORD: 'You must not eat bread or drink water or return by the way you came.'" 10So he took another road and did not return by the way he had come to Bethel.

11Now there was a certain old prophet living in Bethel, whose sons came and told him all that the man of God had done there that day. They also told their father what he had said to the king. 12Their father asked them, "Which way did he go?" And his sons showed him which road the man of God from Judah had taken. 13So he said to his sons, "Saddle the donkey for me." And when they had saddled the donkey for him, he mounted it 14and rode after the man of God. He found him sitting under an oak tree and asked, "Are you the man of God who came from Judah?"

"I am," he replied.

15So the prophet said to him, "Come home with me and eat."

16The man of God said, "I cannot turn back and go with you, nor can I eat bread or drink water with you in this place. 17I have been told by the word of the LORD: 'You must not eat bread or drink water there or return by the way you came.'"

18The old prophet answered, "I too am a prophet, as you are. And an angel said to me by the word of the LORD: 'Bring him back with you to your house so that he may eat bread and drink water.'" (But he was lying to him.) 19So the man of God returned with him and ate and drank in his house.

20While they were sitting at the table, the word of the LORD came to the old prophet who had brought him back. 21He cried out to the man of God who had come from Judah, "This is what the LORD says: 'You have defied the word of the LORD and have not kept the command the LORD your God gave you. 22You came back and ate bread and drank water in the place where he told you not to eat or drink. Therefore your body will not be buried in the tomb of your fathers.'"

23When the man of God had finished eating and drinking, the prophet who had brought him back saddled his donkey for him. 24As he went on his way, a lion met him on the road and killed him, and his body was thrown down on the road, with both the donkey and the lion standing beside it. 25Some people who passed by saw the body thrown down there, with the lion standing beside the body, and they went and reported it in the city where the old prophet lived.

26When the prophet who had brought him back from his journey heard of it, he said, "It is the man of God who defied the word of the LORD. The LORD has given him over to the lion, which has mauled him and killed him, as the word of the LORD had warned him."

27The prophet said to his sons, "Saddle the donkey for me," and they did so. 28Then he went out and found the body thrown down on the road, with the donkey and the lion standing beside it. The lion had neither eaten the body nor mauled the donkey. 29So the prophet picked up the body of the man of God, laid it on the donkey, and brought it back to his own city to mourn for him and bury him. 30Then he laid the body in his own tomb, and they mourned over him and said, "Oh, my brother!"

31After burying him, he said to his sons, "When I die, bury me in the grave where the man of God is buried; lay my bones beside his bones. 32For the message he declared by the word of the LORD against the altar in Bethel and against all the shrines on the high places in the towns of Samaria will certainly come true."

33Even after this, Jeroboam did not change his evil ways, but once more appointed priests for the high places from all sorts of people. Anyone who wanted to become a priest he consecrated for the high places. 34This was the sin of the house of Jeroboam that led to its downfall and to its destruction from the face of the earth.

■ Ahijah's Prophecy Against Jeroboam

14 At that time Abijah son of Jeroboam became ill, 2and Jeroboam said to his wife, "Go, disguise yourself, so that you won't be recognised as the wife of Jeroboam. Then go to Shiloh. Ahijah the prophet is there — the one who told me I would be king over this people. 3Take ten loaves of bread with you, some cakes and a jar of honey, and go to him. He will tell you what will happen to the boy." 4So Jeroboam's wife did what he said and went to Ahijah's house in Shiloh.

Now Ahijah could not see; his sight was gone because of his age. 5But the LORD had told Ahijah, "Jeroboam's wife is coming to ask you about her son, for he is ill, and you are to give her such and such an answer. When she arrives, she will pretend to be someone else."

6So when Ahijah heard the sound of her footsteps at the door, he said, "Come in, wife of Jeroboam. Why this pretence? I have been sent to you with bad news. 7Go, tell Jeroboam that this is what the LORD, the God of Israel, says: 'I raised you up from among the people and made you a leader over my people Israel. 8I tore the kingdom away from the house of David and gave it to you, but you have not been like my servant David, who kept my commands and followed me with all his heart, doing only what was right in my eyes. 9You have done more evil than all who lived before you. You have made for yourself other gods, idols made of metal; you have provoked me to anger and thrust me behind your back.

10" 'Because of this, I am going to bring disaster on the house of Jeroboam. I will cut off from Jeroboam every last male in Israel — slave or free. I will burn up the house of Jeroboam as one burns dung, until it is all gone. 11Dogs will eat those belonging to Jeroboam who die in the city, and the birds of the air will feed on those who die in the country. The LORD has spoken!'

12"As for you, go back home. When you set foot in your city, the boy will die. 13All Israel will mourn for him and bury him. He is the only one belonging to Jeroboam who will be buried, because he is the only one in the house of Jeroboam in whom the LORD, the God of Israel, has found anything good.

14"The LORD will raise up for himself a king over Israel who will cut off the family of Jeroboam. This is the day! What? Yes, even now.a 15And the LORD will strike Israel, so that it will be like a reed swaying in the water. He will uproot Israel from this good land that he gave to their forefathers and scatter them beyond the River,b because they provoked the LORD to anger by making Asherah poles.c 16And he will give Israel up because of the sins Jeroboam has committed and has caused Israel to commit."

17Then Jeroboam's wife got up and left and went to Tirzah. As soon as she stepped over the threshold of the house, the boy died. 18They buried him, and all Israel mourned for him, as the LORD had said through his servant the prophet Ahijah.

19The other events of Jeroboam's reign, his wars and how he ruled, are written in the book of the annals of the kings of Israel. 20He reigned for twenty-two years and then rested with his fathers. And Nadab his son succeeded him as king.

■ Rehoboam King of Judah

21Rehoboam son of Solomon was king in Judah. He was forty-one years old when he became king, and he reigned for seventeen years in Jerusalem, the city the LORD had chosen out of all the tribes of Israel in which to put his Name. His mother's name was Naamah; she was an Ammonite.

22Judah did evil in the eyes of the LORD. By the sins they committed they stirred up his jealous anger more than their fathers had done. 23They also set up for themselves high places, sacred stones and Asherah poles on every high hill and under every spreading tree. 24There were even male shrine-prostitutes in the land; the people engaged in all the detestable practices of the nations the LORD had driven out before the Israelites.

14:23 ■ NOTORIOUS ASHERAH POLES
Introduced in the reign of Rehoboam, Asherah poles became a regular feature of Judah's landscape for hundreds of years. They were dedicated to a mother-goddess and often erected alongside altars on the high places devoted to God. They came to represent Judah's slide into idolatry. When judging the failures of various kings, the authors often comment, "the high places, however, were not removed".

25In the fifth year of King Rehoboam, Shishak king of Egypt attacked Jerusalem. 26He carried off the treasures of the temple of the LORD and the treasures of the royal palace. He took everything, including all the gold shields Solomon had made. 27So King Rehoboam made bronze shields to replace them and assigned these to the commanders of the guard on duty at the entrance to the royal palace. 28Whenever the king went to the LORD's temple, the guards bore the shields, and afterwards they returned them to the guardroom.

29As for the other events of Rehoboam's reign, and all he did, are they not written in the book of the annals of the kings of Judah? 30There was continual warfare between Rehoboam and Jeroboam. 31And Rehoboam rested with his fathers and was buried with them in the City of David. His mother's name was Naamah; she was an Ammonite. And Abijahd his son succeeded him as king.

---

a 14 The meaning of the Hebrew for this sentence is uncertain.   b 15 That is, the Euphrates   c 15 That is, symbols of the goddess Asherah; here and elsewhere in 1 Kings   d 31 Some Hebrew manuscripts and Septuagint (see also 2 Chron. 12:16); most Hebrew manuscripts Abijam

■ Abijah King of Judah

15 In the eighteenth year of the reign of Jeroboam son of Nebat, Abijah[a] became king of Judah, ²and he reigned in Jerusalem for three years.

His mother's name was Maacah daughter of Abishalom.[b]
³He committed all the sins his father had done before him; his heart was not fully devoted to the

---

■ THE NATION SPLITS APART
A REBELLION LEADS TO CIVIL WAR

INSIGHT

THERE WAS CONTINUAL WARFARE.
■ 14:30

Chapter 12 of 1 Kings marks a decisive turning point in the nation of Israel. For 120 years Saul, David and Solomon had consolidated power, expanded borders and built a strong government. But immediately after Solomon's death everything began to unravel. Simmering hostility in the North boiled over at last, and the northern tribes seceded to form their own nation.

■ TWO NATIONS OUT OF ONE
Ten tribes joined together under Jeroboam to form a nation in the North called Israel. Only two tribes, Judah and Benjamin, remained loyal to Solomon's heir in Jerusalem. These southerners took on the name Judah and made Jerusalem, home of the temple, their capital. From that time forward, the united nation of Israel ceased to exist.

The northern rebellion brought a terrible civil war to Israel, a war that dragged on for 50 years. Despite a peace treaty, war kept breaking out.

The book of Kings records the histories of both nations. Action shifts back and forth between Israel in the North and Judah in the South. The effect resembles an account of America during the Civil War years, first describing events in the North and then shifting to what was simultaneously taking place in the South.

This book does not attempt to give a full history of both nations. Rather, it focuses on their kings and queens. As guardian of the covenant with God, the king or queen came to symbolise the spiritual health of the nation. As that monarch went, so went the nation. There is a summary of each ruler and usually a one-sentence rating of his or her reign. He or she either ruled like David, who "had done what was right in the eyes of the LORD", or like the northern king Jeroboam, who "caused Israel to commit" sin.

■ THE NORTH: A PERPETUAL SLIDE DOWNWARDS
Ironically, the northern tribes seceded as part of a reform movement, to correct some of the excesses of Solomon's reign. But starting with

the first king, Jeroboam, no king of Israel did what was right in God's eyes. The book of Kings condemns all the northern kings.

Northern kings brought idolatry into their religion and corruption into their politics. They adopted all the oppressive ways that had sparked off the original rebellion: harsh taxation, repression of prophets, abuse of power. Of 19 northern kings, eight either were murdered or committed suicide. One king, Zimri, lasted only seven days.

The worst rulers, King Ahab and Queen Jezebel, introduced the terrible practice of Baal worship (see "Why All the Fuss about Idols?" page 340). Israel hit its spiritual low point, and Ahab replaced Jeroboam as a symbol of evil. Kings to follow were called "Ahabs" much as a ruthless tyrant today is compared with Hitler. Israel's future destruction became certain; after Ahab and Jezebel, the nation was merely marking time.

■ THE SOUTH: A SURPRISING TWIST
While Israel — which began as a reform movement — slid towards disaster, the two tribes in the South, Judah, proved more faithful to God. They produced at least a handful of good kings. Even when other nations took advantage of Judah's weakness and plundered Jerusalem, the nation still held together.

Idolatry plagued Judah also, but not to the same extent as in the North. The temple remained a powerful symbol of worship of the true God. And every few generations a sincere, committed king arose to sweep away his predecessors' dangerous practices. The authors pointedly note that these good kings usually outlived the bad rulers.

Within 250 years the Northern Kingdom, Israel, was obliterated. Judah survived another 135 years before likewise falling to foreign invaders. In a sense, their fate was sealed from the time of the original secession. The prophet Isaiah would remember the schism as the worst disaster that had befallen his people (Isaiah 7:17).

□ LIFE QUESTIONS:
Have you seen rebellion lead to "civil war" in families? Churches? Schools? When you don't like what the leaders are doing, are there alternatives to outright rebellion?

---

[a]1 Some Hebrew manuscripts and Septuagint (see also 2 Chron. 12:16); most Hebrew manuscripts *Abijam*; also in verses 7 and 8   [b]2 A variant of *Absalom*; also in verse 10

LORD his God, as the heart of David his forefather had been. ⁴Nevertheless, for David's sake the LORD his God gave him a lamp in Jerusalem by raising up a son to succeed him and by making Jerusalem strong. ⁵For David had done what was right in the eyes of the LORD and had not failed to keep any of the LORD's commands all the days of his life—except in the case of Uriah the Hittite.

⁶There was war between Rehoboam*c* and Jeroboam throughout ⌊Abijah's⌋ lifetime. ⁷As for the other events of Abijah's reign, and all he did, are they not written in the book of the annals of the kings of Judah? There was war between Abijah and Jeroboam. ⁸And Abijah rested with his fathers and was buried in the City of David. And Asa his son succeeded him as king.

■ Asa King of Judah

⁹In the twentieth year of Jeroboam king of Israel, Asa became king of Judah, ¹⁰and he reigned in Jerusalem for forty-one years. His grandmother's name was Maacah daughter of Abishalom.

¹¹Asa did what was right in the eyes of the LORD, as his father David had done. ¹²He expelled the male shrine-prostitutes from the land and got rid of all the idols his fathers had made. ¹³He even deposed his grandmother Maacah from her position as queen mother, because she had made a repulsive Asherah pole. Asa cut the pole down and burned it in the Kidron Valley. ¹⁴Although he did not remove the high places, Asa's heart was fully committed to the LORD all his life. ¹⁵He brought into the temple of the LORD the silver and gold and the articles that he and his father had dedicated.

¹⁶There was war between Asa and Baasha king of Israel throughout their reigns. ¹⁷Baasha king of Israel went up against Judah and fortified Ramah to prevent anyone from leaving or entering the territory of Asa king of Judah.

¹⁸Asa then took all the silver and gold that was left in the treasuries of the LORD's temple and of his own palace. He entrusted it to his officials and sent them to Ben-Hadad son of Tabrimmon, the son of Hezion, the king of Aram, who was ruling in Damascus. ¹⁹"Let there be a treaty between me and you," he said, "as there was between my father and your father. See, I am sending you a gift of silver and gold. Now break your treaty with Baasha king of Israel so that he will withdraw from me."

²⁰Ben-Hadad agreed with King Asa and sent the commanders of his forces against the towns of Israel. He conquered Ijon, Dan, Abel Beth Maacah and all Kinnereth in addition to Naphtali. ²¹When Baasha heard this, he stopped building Ramah and withdrew to Tirzah. ²²Then King Asa issued an order to all Judah—no-one was exempt—and they carried away from Ramah the stones and timber Baasha had been using there. With them King Asa built up Geba in Benjamin, and also Mizpah.

²³As for all the other events of Asa's reign, all his achievements, all he did and the cities he built, are they not written in the book of the annals of the kings of Judah? In his old age, however, his feet became diseased. ²⁴Then Asa rested with his fathers

and was buried with them in the city of his father David. And Jehoshaphat his son succeeded him as king.

■ Nadab King of Israel

²⁵Nadab son of Jeroboam became king of Israel in the second year of Asa king of Judah, and he reigned over Israel for two years. ²⁶He did evil in the eyes of the LORD, walking in the ways of his father and in his sin, which he had caused Israel to commit.

²⁷Baasha son of Ahijah of the house of Issachar plotted against him, and he struck him down at Gibbethon, a Philistine town, while Nadab and all Israel were besieging it. ²⁸Baasha killed Nadab in the third year of Asa king of Judah and succeeded him as king.

²⁹As soon as he began to reign, he killed Jeroboam's whole family. He did not leave Jeroboam anyone that breathed, but destroyed them all, according to the word of the LORD given through his servant Ahijah the Shilonite—³⁰because of the sins Jeroboam had committed and had caused Israel to commit, and because he provoked the LORD, the God of Israel, to anger.

³¹As for the other events of Nadab's reign, and all he did, are they not written in the book of the annals of the kings of Israel? ³²There was war between Asa and Baasha king of Israel throughout their reigns.

■ Baasha King of Israel

³³In the third year of Asa king of Judah, Baasha son of Ahijah became king of all Israel in Tirzah, and he reigned for twenty-four years. ³⁴He did evil in the eyes of the LORD, walking in the ways of Jeroboam and in his sin, which he had caused Israel to commit.

16 Then the word of the LORD came to Jehu son of Hanani against Baasha: ²"I lifted you up from the dust and made you leader of my people Israel, but you walked in the ways of Jeroboam and caused my people Israel to sin and to provoke me to anger by their sins. ³So I am about to consume Baasha and his house, and I will make your house like that of Jeroboam son of Nebat. ⁴Dogs will eat those belonging to Baasha who die in the city, and the birds of the air will feed on those who die in the country."

⁵As for the other events of Baasha's reign, what he did and his achievements, are they not written in the book of the annals of the kings of Israel? ⁶Baasha rested with his fathers and was buried in Tirzah. And Elah his son succeeded him as king.

⁷Moreover, the word of the LORD came through the prophet Jehu son of Hanani to Baasha and his house, because of all the evil he had done in the eyes of the LORD, provoking him to anger by the things he did, and becoming like the house of Jeroboam—and also because he destroyed it.

■ Elah King of Israel

⁸In the twenty-sixth year of Asa king of Judah, Elah son of Baasha became king of Israel, and he reigned in Tirzah for two years. ⁹Zimri, one of his officials, who had command of half his chariots, plotted against him. Elah was in Tirzah at the time, getting drunk in the home of Arza, the man in charge of the palace at Tirzah. ¹⁰Zimri

---

c 6 Most Hebrew manuscripts; some Hebrew manuscripts and Syriac *Abijam* (that is, Abijah) came in, struck him down and killed him in the twenty-seventh year of Asa king of Judah. Then he succeeded him as king.

[11]As soon as he began to reign and was seated on the throne, he killed off Baasha's whole family. He did not spare a single male, whether relative or friend. [12]So Zimri destroyed the whole family of Baasha, in accordance with the word of the LORD spoken against Baasha through the prophet Jehu—[13]because of all the sins Baasha and his son Elah had committed and had caused Israel to commit, so that they provoked the LORD, the God of Israel, to anger by their worthless idols.

[14]As for the other events of Elah's reign, and all he did, are they not written in the book of the annals of the kings of Israel?

■ Zimri King of Israel

[15]In the twenty-seventh year of Asa king of Judah, Zimri reigned in Tirzah for seven days. The army was encamped near Gibbethon, a Philistine town. [16]When the Israelites in the camp heard that Zimri had plotted against the king and murdered him, they proclaimed Omri, the commander of the army, king over Israel that very day there in the camp. [17]Then Omri and all the Israelites with him withdrew from Gibbethon and laid siege to Tirzah. [18]When Zimri saw that the city was taken, he went into the citadel of the royal palace and set the palace on fire around him. So he died, [19]because of the sins he had committed, doing evil in the eyes of the LORD and walking in the ways of Jeroboam and in the sin he had committed and had caused Israel to commit.

[20]As for the other events of Zimri's reign, and the rebellion he carried out, are they not written in the book of the annals of the kings of Israel?

■ Omri King of Israel

[21]Then the people of Israel were split into two factions; half supported Tibni son of Ginath for king, and the other half supported Omri. [22]But Omri's followers proved stronger than those of Tibni son of Ginath. So Tibni died and Omri became king.

16:21 ■ A STRONG, WEAK KING
King Omri gets a grand total of eight verses in 1 Kings, even though secular historians regard him as one of Israel's most powerful kings. After his firm rule, Israel was called Omriland in Assyrian records. He built the capital city of Samaria in a location that guarded all routes north and south. Yet he also started the religious heresies that led to his nation's extinction. Politically shrewd, he married off his son to a neighbouring king's daughter (Jezebel). The book of Kings, however, is concerned with the rulers' spiritual health, and Omri scored very poorly.

[23]In the thirty-first year of Asa king of Judah, Omri became king of Israel, and he reigned for twelve years, six of them in Tirzah. [24]He bought the hill of Samaria from Shemer for two talents[a] of silver and built a city on the hill, calling it Samaria, after Shemer, the name of the former owner of the hill.

[25]But Omri did evil in the eyes of the LORD and sinned more than all those before him. [26]He walked in all the ways of Jeroboam son of Nebat and in his sin, which he had caused Israel to commit, so that they provoked the LORD, the God of Israel, to anger by their worthless idols.

[27]As for the other events of Omri's reign, what he did and the things he achieved, are they not written in the book of the annals of the kings of Israel? [28]Omri rested with his fathers and was buried in Samaria. And Ahab his son succeeded him as king.

■ Ahab Becomes King of Israel

[29]In the thirty-eighth year of Asa king of Judah, Ahab son of Omri became king of Israel, and he reigned in Samaria over Israel for twenty-two years. [30]Ahab son of Omri did more evil in the eyes of the LORD than any of those before him. [31]He not only considered it trivial to commit the sins of Jeroboam son of Nebat, but he also married Jezebel daughter of Ethbaal king of the Sidonians, and began to serve Baal and worship him. [32]He set up an altar for Baal in the temple of Baal that he built in Samaria. [33]Ahab also made an Asherah pole and did more to provoke the LORD, the God of Israel, to anger than did all the kings of Israel before him.

[34]In Ahab's time, Hiel of Bethel rebuilt Jericho. He laid its foundations at the cost of his firstborn son Abiram, and he set up its gates at the cost of his youngest son Segub, in accordance with the word of the LORD spoken by Joshua son of Nun.

16:34 ■ A CURSE FROM JOSHUA
Joshua 6:26 records the solemn pronouncement of what would happen to anyone who attempted to rebuild Jericho. The curse had tragic consequences for Hiel.

■ Elijah Fed by Ravens

17 Now Elijah the Tishbite, from Tishbe[a] in Gilead, said to Ahab, "As the LORD, the God of Israel, lives, whom I serve, there will be neither dew nor rain in the next few years except at my word."

[2]Then the word of the LORD came to Elijah: [3]"Leave here, turn eastward and hide in the Kerith Ravine, east of the Jordan. [4]You will drink from the brook, and I have ordered the ravens to feed you there."

[5]So he did what the LORD had told him. He went to the Kerith Ravine, east of the Jordan, and stayed there. [6]The ravens brought him bread and meat in the morning and bread and meat in the evening, and he drank from the brook.

■ The Widow at Zarephath

[7]Some time later the brook dried up because there had been no rain in the land. [8]Then the word of the LORD came to him: [9]"Go at once to Zarephath of Sidon and stay there. I have commanded a widow in that place to supply you with food." [10]So he went

a 24 That is, about 150 pounds (about 70 kilograms)   a 1 Or Tishbite, of the settlers to Zarephath. When he came to the town gate, a widow was there gathering sticks. He called to her and asked, "Would you bring me a little water in a jar so I may have a drink?" ¹¹As she was going to get it, he called, "And bring me, please, a piece of bread."

¹²"As surely as the LORD your God lives," she replied, "I don't have any bread—only a handful of flour in a jar and a little oil in a jug. I am gathering a few sticks to take home and make a meal for myself and my son, that we may eat it—and die."

17:12 ■ DOWN TO THE LAST MEAL
Elijah's unusual sources of food demanded the utmost faith in God. First, he was fed by ravens. Then, when his water supply gave out, God ordered Elijah to a very unlikely place: the home of a famished, poverty-stricken widow. The widow, not even an Israelite, lived in Jezebel's home territory, a dangerous place for a hunted prophet. Yet the widow at Zarephath showed enough faith in the prophet and his God to use up her last meagre resources. The result proved her faith was well-founded. Jesus referred to this story as an example of God's reaching out to Gentiles (Luke 4:25–26).

---

¹³Elijah said to her, "Don't be afraid. Go home and do as you have said. But first make a small cake of bread for me from what you have and bring it to me, and then make something for yourself and your son. ¹⁴For this is what the LORD, the God of Israel, says: 'The jar of flour will not be used up and the jug of oil will not run dry until the day the LORD gives rain on the land.' "

¹⁵She went away and did as Elijah had told her. So there was food every day for Elijah and for the woman and her family. ¹⁶For the jar of flour was not used up and the jug of oil did not run dry, in keeping with the word of the LORD spoken by Elijah.

¹⁷Some time later the son of the woman who owned the house became ill. He grew worse and worse, and finally stopped breathing. ¹⁸She said to Elijah, "What do you have against me, man of God? Did you come to remind me of my sin and kill my son?"

¹⁹"Give me your son," Elijah replied. He took him from her arms, carried him to the upper room where he was staying, and laid him on his bed. ²⁰Then he cried out to the LORD, "O LORD my God, have you brought tragedy also upon this widow I am staying with, by causing her son to die?" ²¹Then he stretched himself out on the boy three times and cried to the LORD, "O LORD my God, let this boy's life return to him!"

²²The LORD heard Elijah's cry, and the boy's life returned to him, and he lived. ²³Elijah picked up the child and carried him down from the room into the house. He gave him to his mother and said, "Look, your son is alive!"

²⁴Then the woman said to Elijah, "Now I know that you are a man of God and that the word of the LORD from your mouth is the truth."

■ Elijah and Obadiah

18 After a long time, in the third year, the word of the LORD came to Elijah: "Go and present yourself to Ahab, and I will send rain on the land." ²So Elijah went to present himself to Ahab.

Now the famine was severe in Samaria, ³and Ahab had summoned Obadiah, who was in charge of his palace. (Obadiah was a devout believer in the LORD. ⁴While Jezebel was killing off the LORD's prophets, Obadiah had taken a hundred prophets and hidden them in two caves, fifty in each, and had supplied them with food and water.) ⁵Ahab had said to Obadiah, "Go through the land to all the springs and valleys. Maybe we can find some grass to keep the horses and mules alive so we will not have to kill any of our animals." ⁶So they divided the land they were to cover, Ahab going in one direction and Obadiah in another.

⁷As Obadiah was walking along, Elijah met him. Obadiah recognised him, bowed down to the ground, and said, "Is it really you, my lord Elijah?"

⁸"Yes," he replied. "Go tell your master, 'Elijah is here.' "

⁹"What have I done wrong," asked Obadiah, "that you are handing your servant over to Ahab to be put to death? ¹⁰As surely as the LORD your God lives, there is not a nation or kingdom where my master has not sent someone to look for you. And whenever a nation or kingdom claimed you were not there, he made them swear they could not find you. ¹¹But now you tell me to go to my master and say, 'Elijah is here.' ¹²I don't know where the Spirit of the LORD may carry you when I leave you. If I go and tell Ahab and he doesn't find you, he will kill me. Yet I your servant have worshipped the LORD since my youth. ¹³Haven't you heard, my lord, what I did while Jezebel was killing the prophets of the LORD? I hid a hundred of the LORD's prophets in two caves, fifty in each, and supplied them with food and water. ¹⁴And now you tell me to go to my master and say, 'Elijah is here.' He will kill me!"

¹⁵Elijah said, "As the LORD Almighty lives, whom I serve, I will surely present myself to Ahab today."

■ Elijah on Mount Carmel

¹⁶So Obadiah went to meet Ahab and told him, and Ahab went to meet Elijah. ¹⁷When he saw Elijah, he said to him, "Is that you, you troubler of Israel?"

¹⁸"I have not made trouble for Israel," Elijah replied. "But you and your father's family have. You have abandoned the LORD's commands and have followed the Baals. ¹⁹Now summon the people from all over Israel to meet me on Mount Carmel. And bring the four hundred and fifty prophets of Baal and the four hundred prophets of Asherah, who eat at Jezebel's table."

²⁰So Ahab sent word throughout all Israel and assembled the prophets on Mount Carmel. ²¹Elijah went before the people and said, "How long will you waver between two opinions? If the LORD is God, follow him; but if Baal is God, follow him." But the people said nothing.

²²Then Elijah said to them, "I am the only one of the LORD's prophets left, but Baal has four hundred and fifty prophets. ²³Get two bulls for us. Let them

choose one for themselves, and let them cut it into pieces and put it on the wood but not set fire to it. I will prepare the other bull and put it on the wood but not set fire to it. ²⁴Then you call on the name of your god, and I will call on the name of the LORD. The god who answers by fire—he is God."

Then all the people said, "What you say is good."

²⁵Elijah said to the prophets of Baal, "Choose one of the bulls and prepare it first, since there are so many of you. Call on the name of your god, but do not light the fire." ²⁶So they took the bull given them and prepared it.

Then they called on the name of Baal from morning till noon. "O Baal, answer us!" they shouted. But

■ THE CONTEST
ONE LONE PROPHET AGAINST A THOUSAND PRIESTS

INSIGHT

ELIJAH WENT BEFORE THE PEOPLE AND SAID, "HOW LONG WILL YOU WAVER BETWEEN TWO OPINIONS? IF THE LORD IS GOD, FOLLOW HIM; BUT IF BAAL IS GOD, FOLLOW HIM." ■ 18:21

Few scenes in the Bible are more dramatic than this one. The forces of evil and the forces of good collided head on. In books like J.R. Tolkien's *Lord of the Rings* or movies such as *Star Wars*, mythmakers dream up cosmic confrontations. But the incident in 1 Kings 18 is no myth. On that day, a bedraggled desert prophet single-handedly took on a king and nearly a thousand powerful priests.

Elijah had made a grand entrance three years before. Like a wild, startling apparition, he came out of nowhere to stalk the terraced streets of affluent Samaria. Clothed in black camel's hair, he made a striking contrast to the priests of Baal in their white linen robes and high-pointed hats. He had a simple, unpopular message of doom: "There will be neither dew nor rain in the next few years except at my word" (17:1). It was a direct affront to followers of Baal, who believed their god could control the weather.

Having delivered his message, Elijah disappeared. For three years he was the most wanted fugitive in Israel, for he alone had the power to bring rain. And then, in the scene reported in chapter 18, the prophet Elijah returned to Samaria.

■ ELIJAH'S CONTEST
Israel was at a crossroads. Other kings had introduced idolatry into Israelite religion, but King Ahab and the notorious Queen Jezebel were going much further. They wanted to wipe out all worship of the true God.

The prophet Elijah proved a worthy adversary. His very name meant "The LORD is my God". He proposed a showdown, the ultimate contest to prove who was the true God. 1 Kings presents the scene in full colour, complete with the priests' desperate contortions and Elijah's mocking, taunting commentary. In the final analysis, it was no contest at all. God unleashed a spectacular display of raw power.

Elijah was one of the most colourful of all Israel's prophets. He suffered from bouts of depression and self-doubt, but during times of crisis he showed amazing courage. The Mount Carmel showdown was merely one sign of the high drama going on. Elijah lived during one of the greatest outbreaks of miracles in biblical history. God was sounding a final warning to Israel.

■ ISRAEL'S REAL HEROES
The author of the book of Kings started out to record the history of God's anointed leaders. But as the rulers and then priests grow more and more corrupt, this book trains the spotlight on prophets like Elijah. They emerge as Israel's real heroes.

The prophets were not, to Israel, merely preachers or poets. They were channels of God's power, through word and deed. They served on the front line of the struggle between good and evil. Over time, the prophets' significance overtook and even surpassed that of the kings. Kings came and went, but the message of the prophets endured.

■ VOICES IN THE DESERT
Whether they served in the government or wandered in occasionally from the desert, the true prophets remained accountable only to God. They decried other, "false", prophets, employed by the king, who generally told the king whatever he wished to hear.

Not all prophets left written messages (Elijah and Elisha, for example, did not). But those prophetic writings that did survive form 17 books of the Old Testament, most of them stemming from the time period described in 1 and 2 Kings.

The prophets told of a God who worked in history to accomplish his will in the world. Sometimes he seemed silent. Sometimes he worked slowly and mysteriously. But occasionally God did step in directly, spectacularly, with a display of power. And when he did, a prophet was usually right in the middle of things—like Elijah on Mount Carmel.

□ LIFE QUESTIONS:
Who serves the role of "prophet" today?

there was no response; no-one answered. And they danced around the altar they had made.

²⁷At noon Elijah began to taunt them. "Shout louder!" he said. "Surely he is a god! Perhaps he is deep in thought, or busy, or travelling. Maybe he is sleeping and must be awakened." ²⁸So they shouted louder and slashed themselves with swords and spears, as was their custom, until their blood flowed. ²⁹Midday passed, and they continued their frantic prophesying until the time for the evening sacrifice. But there was no response, no-one answered, no-one paid attention.

³⁰Then Elijah said to all the people, "Come here to me." They came to him, and he repaired the altar of the LORD, which was in ruins. ³¹Elijah took twelve stones, one for each of the tribes descended from Jacob, to whom the word of the LORD had come, saying, "Your name shall be Israel." ³²With the stones he built an altar in the name of the LORD, and he dug a trench round it large enough to hold two seahs*a* of seed. ³³He arranged the wood, cut the bull into pieces and laid it on the wood. Then he said to them, "Fill four large jars with water and pour it on the offering and on the wood."

18:33 ■ ELIJAH RUBS IT IN

Elijah designed the contest to expose Baal, the alleged god of weather, who was often depicted carrying a thunderbolt. Elijah doused his own altar with 12 large jars of water — a precious commodity after three years of drought — before calling on God. Fire from heaven burned up the sacrifice, the wood, the stones, the soil, and even licked up the water in the trench.

³⁴"Do it again," he said, and they did it again.

"Do it a third time," he ordered, and they did it the third time. ³⁵The water ran down around the altar and even filled the trench.

³⁶At the time of sacrifice, the prophet Elijah stepped forward and prayed: "O LORD, God of Abraham, Isaac and Israel, let it be known today that you are God in Israel and that I am your servant and have done all these things at your command. ³⁷Answer me, O LORD, answer me, so these people will know that you, O LORD, are God, and that you are turning their hearts back again."

³⁸Then the fire of the LORD fell and burned up the sacrifice, the wood, the stones and the soil, and also licked up the water in the trench.

³⁹When all the people saw this, they fell prostrate and cried, "The LORD—he is God! The LORD—he is God!"

⁴⁰Then Elijah commanded them, "Seize the prophets of Baal. Don't let anyone get away!" They seized them, and Elijah had them brought down to the Kishon Valley and slaughtered there.

⁴¹And Elijah said to Ahab, "Go, eat and drink, for there is the sound of a heavy rain." ⁴²So Ahab went off to eat and drink, but Elijah climbed to the top of Carmel, bent down to the ground and put his face between his knees.

⁴³"Go and look towards the sea," he told his servant. And he went up and looked.

"There is nothing there," he said.

Seven times Elijah said, "Go back."

⁴⁴The seventh time the servant reported, "A cloud as small as a man's hand is rising from the sea."

So Elijah said, "Go and tell Ahab, 'Hitch up your chariot and go down before the rain stops you.'"

⁴⁵Meanwhile, the sky grew black with clouds, the wind rose, a heavy rain came on and Ahab rode off to Jezreel. ⁴⁶The power of the LORD came upon Elijah and, tucking his cloak into his belt, he ran ahead of Ahab all the way to Jezreel.

■ Elijah Flees to Horeb

19 Now Ahab told Jezebel everything Elijah had done and how he had killed all the prophets with the sword. ²So Jezebel sent a messenger to Elijah to say, "May the gods deal with me, be it ever so severely, if by this time tomorrow I do not make your life like that of one of them."

³Elijah was afraid*a* and ran for his life. When he came to Beersheba in Judah, he left his servant there, ⁴while he himself went a day's journey into the desert. He came to a broom tree, sat down under it and prayed that he might die. "I have had enough, LORD," he said. "Take my life; I am no better than my ancestors." ⁵Then he lay down under the tree and fell asleep.

All at once an angel touched him and said, "Get

19:3 ■ WICKED QUEEN JEZEBEL

Queen Jezebel's reputation was such that Elijah ran from her in fear even after God had triumphantly displayed his power on Mount Carmel. The Roman historian Josephus records her family history. Her father, who had served as high priest in a pagan temple in Tyre, murdered the king and ruled there for 32 years. His reign was characterised by murderous idolatries and a reckless contempt for human rights.

Jezebel followed in her father's footsteps. Married to Ahab as part of a political alliance, she installed 950 prophets of Baal and ordered the wholesale slaughter of any prophets of God who opposed her. Ahab fell under her sway. Alone, he could be brave, chivalrous, and even conscientious. But his weakness and Jezebel's influence led him to become the most wicked king of Israel.

up and eat." ⁶He looked around, and there by his head was a cake of bread baked over hot coals, and a jar of water. He ate and drank and then lay down again.

⁷The angel of the LORD came back a second time and touched him and said, "Get up and eat, for the journey is too much for you." ⁸So he got up and ate and drank. Strengthened by that food, he travelled for forty days and forty nights until he reached Horeb, the mountain of God. ⁹There he went into a cave and spent the night.

---

a 32 That is, probably about 26 pints (about 15 litres)   *a 3 Or Elijah saw*

The LORD Appears to Elijah

And the word of the LORD came to him: "What are you doing here, Elijah?"

¹⁰He replied, "I have been very zealous for the LORD God Almighty. The Israelites have rejected your covenant, broken down your altars, and put your prophets to death with the sword. I am the only one left, and now they are trying to kill me too."

¹¹The LORD said, "Go out and stand on the mountain in the presence of the LORD, for the LORD is about to pass by."

Then a great and powerful wind tore the mountains apart and shattered the rocks before the LORD, but the LORD was not in the wind. After the wind there was an earthquake, but the LORD was not in the earthquake. ¹²After the earthquake came a fire, but the LORD was not in the fire. And after the fire came a gentle whisper. ¹³When Elijah heard it, he pulled his cloak over his face and went out and stood at the mouth of the cave.

Then a voice said to him, "What are you doing here, Elijah?"

¹⁴He replied, "I have been very zealous for the LORD God Almighty. The Israelites have rejected your covenant, broken down your altars, and put your prophets to death with the sword. I am the only one left, and now they are trying to kill me too."

¹⁵The LORD said to him, "Go back the way you came, and go to the Desert of Damascus. When you get there, anoint Hazael king over Aram. ¹⁶Also, anoint Jehu son of Nimshi king over Israel, and anoint Elisha son of Shaphat from Abel Meholah to succeed you as prophet. ¹⁷Jehu will put to death any who escape the sword of Hazael, and Elisha will put to death any who escape the sword of Jehu. ¹⁸Yet I reserve seven thousand in Israel—all whose knees have not bowed down to Baal and all whose mouths have not kissed him."

The Call of Elisha

¹⁹So Elijah went from there and found Elisha son of Shaphat. He was ploughing with twelve yoke of oxen, and he himself was driving the twelfth pair. Elijah went up to him and threw his cloak around him. ²⁰Elisha then left his oxen and ran after Elijah. "Let me kiss my father and mother good-bye," he said, "and then I will come with you."

"Go back," Elijah replied. "What have I done to you?"

²¹So Elisha left him and went back. He took his yoke of oxen and slaughtered them. He burned the ploughing equipment to cook the meat and gave it to the people, and they ate. Then he set out to follow Elijah and became his attendant.

Ben-Hadad Attacks Samaria

20 Now Ben-Hadad king of Aram mustered his entire army. Accompanied by thirty-two kings with their horses and chariots, he went up and besieged Samaria and attacked it. ²He sent messengers into the city to Ahab king of Israel, saying, "This is what Ben-Hadad says: ³'Your silver and gold are mine, and the best of your wives and children are mine.' "

⁴The king of Israel answered, "Just as you say, my lord the king. I and all I have are yours."

⁵The messengers came again and said, "This is what Ben-Hadad says: 'I sent to demand your silver and gold, your wives and your children. ⁶But about this time tomorrow I am going to send my officials to search your palace and the houses of your officials. They will seize everything you value and carry it away.' "

⁷The king of Israel summoned all the elders of the land and said to them, "See how this man is looking for trouble! When he sent for my wives and my children, my silver and my gold, I did not refuse him."

⁸The elders and the people all answered, "Don't listen to him or agree to his demands."

⁹So he replied to Ben-Hadad's messengers, "Tell my lord the king, 'Your servant will do all you demanded the first time, but this demand I cannot meet.' " They left and took the answer back to Ben-Hadad.

¹⁰Then Ben-Hadad sent another message to Ahab: "May the gods deal with me, be it ever so severely, if enough dust remains in Samaria to give each of my men a handful."

¹¹The king of Israel answered, "Tell him: 'One who puts on his armour should not boast like one who takes it off.' "

¹²Ben-Hadad heard this message while he and the kings were drinking in their tents,ᵃ and he ordered his men: "Prepare to attack." So they prepared to attack the city.

Ahab Defeats Ben-Hadad

¹³Meanwhile a prophet came to Ahab king of Israel and announced, "This is what the LORD says: 'Do you see this vast army? I will give it into your hand today, and then you will know that I am the LORD.' "

¹⁴"But who will do this?" asked Ahab.

The prophet replied, "This is what the LORD says: 'The young officers of the provincial commanders will do it.' "

"And who will start the battle?" he asked.

The prophet answered, "You will."

¹⁵So Ahab summoned the young officers of the provincial commanders, 232 men. Then he assembled the rest of the Israelites, 7,000 in all. ¹⁶They set out at noon while Ben-Hadad and the 32 kings allied with him were in their tents getting drunk. ¹⁷The young officers of the provincial commanders went out first.

Now Ben-Hadad had dispatched scouts, who reported, "Men are advancing from Samaria."

¹⁸He said, "If they have come out for peace, take them alive; if they have come out for war, take them alive."

¹⁹The young officers of the provincial commanders marched out of the city with the army behind them ²⁰and each one struck down his opponent. At that, the Arameans fled, with the Israelites in pursuit. But Ben-Hadad king of Aram escaped on horseback with some of his horsemen. ²¹The king of Israel advanced and overpowered the horses and chariots and inflicted heavy losses on the Arameans.

²²Afterwards, the prophet came to the king of Israel and said, "Strengthen your position and see

---

ᵃ 12 Or *in Succoth*; also in verse 16

what must be done, because next spring the king of Aram will attack you again."

²³Meanwhile, the officials of the king of Aram advised him, "Their gods are gods of the hills. That is why they were too strong for us. But if we fight them on the plains, surely we will be stronger than they. ²⁴Do this: Remove all the kings from their commands and replace them with other officers. ²⁵You must also raise an army like the one you lost—horse for horse and chariot for chariot—so we can fight Israel on the plains. Then surely we will be stronger than they." He agreed with them and acted accordingly.

²⁶The next spring Ben-Hadad mustered the Arameans and went up to Aphek to fight against Israel. ²⁷When the Israelites were also mustered and given provisions, they marched out to meet them. The Israelites camped opposite them like two small flocks of goats, while the Arameans covered the countryside.

²⁸The man of God came up and told the king of Israel, "This is what the LORD says: 'Because the Arameans think the LORD is a god of the hills and not a god of the valleys, I will deliver this vast army into your hands, and you will know that I am the LORD.'"

²⁹For seven days they camped opposite each other, and on the seventh day the battle was joined. The Israelites inflicted a hundred thousand casualties on the Aramean foot soldiers in one day. ³⁰The rest of them escaped to the city of Aphek, where the wall collapsed on twenty-seven thousand of them. And Ben-Hadad fled to the city and hid in an inner room.

³¹His officials said to him, "Look, we have heard that the kings of the house of Israel are merciful. Let us go to the king of Israel with sackcloth round our waists and ropes round our heads. Perhaps he will spare your life."

³²Wearing sackcloth round their waists and ropes round their heads, they went to the king of Israel and said, "Your servant Ben-Hadad says: 'Please let me live.'"

The king answered, "Is he still alive? He is my brother."

³³The men took this as a good sign and were quick to pick up his word. "Yes, your brother Ben-Hadad!" they said.

"Go and get him," the king said. When Ben-Hadad came out, Ahab had him come up into his chariot.

³⁴"I will return the cities my father took from your father," Ben-Hadad offered. "You may set up your own market areas in Damascus, as my father did in Samaria."

˻Ahab said,˼ "On the basis of a treaty I will set you free." So he made a treaty with him, and let him go.

■ A Prophet Condemns Ahab

³⁵By the word of the LORD one of the sons of the prophets said to his companion, "Strike me with your weapon," but the man refused.

³⁶So the prophet said, "Because you have not obeyed the LORD, as soon as you leave me a lion will kill you." And after the man went away, a lion found him and killed him.

³⁷The prophet found another man and said,

"Strike me, please." So the man struck him and wounded him. ³⁸Then the prophet went and stood by the road waiting for the king. He disguised himself with his headband down over his eyes. ³⁹As the king passed by, the prophet called out to him, "Your servant went into the thick of the battle, and someone came to me with a captive and said, 'Guard this man. If he is missing, it will be your life for his life, or you must pay a talent ᵇ of silver.' ⁴⁰While your servant was busy here and there, the man disappeared."

"That is your sentence," the king of Israel said. "You have pronounced it yourself."

⁴¹Then the prophet quickly removed the headband from his eyes, and the king of Israel recognised him as one of the prophets. ⁴²He said to the king, "This is what the LORD says: 'You have set free a man I had determined should die.ᶜ Therefore it is your life for his life, your people for his people.'" ⁴³Sullen and angry, the king of Israel went to his palace in Samaria.

■ Naboth's Vineyard

21 Some time later there was an incident involving a vineyard belonging to Naboth the Jezreelite. The vineyard was in Jezreel, close to the palace of Ahab king of Samaria. ²Ahab said to Naboth, "Let me have your vineyard to use for a vegetable garden, since it is close to my palace. In exchange I will give you a better vineyard or, if you prefer, I will pay you whatever it is worth."

21:1 ■ A STOLEN VINEYARD

The incident of Naboth's vineyard shows the selective way in which Old Testament authors wove history together. In one sense, the theft was a minor incident in King Ahab's reign. Yet 1 Kings devotes more space to it than to the entire reigns of some kings. It showed the king's abuse of power and disrespect for God's covenant. Every Israelite had the right to possess a piece of the promised land—not even a king could legally usurp that right. In fact, selling the land would break a law God had given Moses (Leviticus 25:23–31). Ahab's greed and Jezebel's intrigue led to murder and ultimately spelled doom for the kingdom.

---

³But Naboth replied, "The LORD forbid that I should give you the inheritance of my fathers."

⁴So Ahab went home, sullen and angry because Naboth the Jezreelite had said, "I will not give you the inheritance of my fathers." He lay on his bed sulking and refused to eat.

⁵His wife Jezebel came in and asked him, "Why are you so sullen? Why won't you eat?"

⁶He answered her, "Because I said to Naboth the Jezreelite, 'Sell me your vineyard; or if you prefer, I will give you another vineyard in its place.' But he said, 'I will not give you my vineyard.'"

⁷Jezebel his wife said, "Is this how you act as king over Israel? Get up and eat! Cheer up. I'll get you the vineyard of Naboth the Jezreelite."

ᵇ39 That is, about 75 pounds (about 34 kilograms)   ᶜ42 The Hebrew term refers to the irrevocable giving over of things or persons to the LORD, often by totally destroying them.

8So she wrote letters in Ahab's name, placed his seal on them, and sent them to the elders and nobles who lived in Naboth's city with him. 9In those letters she wrote:

"Proclaim a day of fasting and seat Naboth in a prominent place among the people. 10But seat two scoundrels opposite him and have them testify that he has cursed both God and the king. Then take him out and stone him to death."

11So the elders and nobles who lived in Naboth's city did as Jezebel directed in the letters she had written to them. 12They proclaimed a fast and seated Naboth in a prominent place among the people. 13Then two scoundrels came and sat opposite him and brought charges against Naboth before the people, saying, "Naboth has cursed both God and the king." So they took him outside the city and stoned him to death. 14Then they sent word to Jezebel: "Naboth has been stoned and is dead."

15As soon as Jezebel heard that Naboth had been stoned to death, she said to Ahab, "Get up and take possession of the vineyard of Naboth the Jezreelite that he refused to sell you. He is no longer alive, but dead." 16When Ahab heard that Naboth was dead, he got up and went down to take possession of Naboth's vineyard.

17Then the word of the LORD came to Elijah the Tishbite: 18"Go down to meet Ahab king of Israel, who rules in Samaria. He is now in Naboth's vineyard, where he has gone to take possession of it. 19Say to him, 'This is what the LORD says: Have you not murdered a man and seized his property?' Then say to him, 'This is what the LORD says: In the place where dogs licked up Naboth's blood, dogs will lick up your blood — yes, yours!' "

20Ahab said to Elijah, "So you have found me, my enemy!"

"I have found you," he answered, "because you have sold yourself to do evil in the eyes of the LORD. 21'I am going to bring disaster on you. I will consume your descendants and cut off from Ahab every last male in Israel — slave or free. 22I will make your house like that of Jeroboam son of Nebat and that of Baasha son of Ahijah, because you have provoked me to anger and have caused Israel to sin.'

23"And also concerning Jezebel the LORD says: 'Dogs will devour Jezebel by the wall of*a* Jezreel.'

24"Dogs will eat those belonging to Ahab who die in the city, and the birds of the air will feed on those who die in the country."

25(There was never a man like Ahab, who sold himself to do evil in the eyes of the LORD, urged on by Jezebel his wife. 26He behaved in the vilest manner by going after idols, like the Amorites the LORD drove out before Israel.)

27When Ahab heard these words, he tore his clothes, put on sackcloth and fasted. He lay in sackcloth and went around meekly.

28Then the word of the LORD came to Elijah the Tishbite: 29"Have you noticed how Ahab has humbled himself before me? Because he has humbled himself, I will not bring this disaster in his day, but I will bring it on his house in the days of his son."

■ Micaiah Prophesies Against Ahab

22 For three years there was no war between Aram and Israel. 2But in the third year Jehoshaphat king of Judah went down to see the king of Israel. 3The king of Israel had said to his officials, "Don't you know that Ramoth Gilead belongs to us and yet we are doing nothing to retake it from the king of Aram?"

4So he asked Jehoshaphat, "Will you go with me to fight against Ramoth Gilead?"

Jehoshaphat replied to the king of Israel, "I am as you are, my people as your people, my horses as

---

22:4 ■ UNHOLY ALLIANCE

After years of warfare, peace was finally arranged between Israel and Judah. Ironically, it joined Israel's worst king, Ahab, with one of Judah's best, King Jehoshaphat. The unholy alliance with Ahab led to a fateful battle against Aram that almost cost Jehoshaphat his life (verses 29–33). Judah's king spurned later offers of co-operation (verse 49), but his son married King Ahab's daughter. This unwise marriage exposed Judah to the evil practices of the North and ultimately led to a royal bloodbath.

---

your horses." 5But Jehoshaphat also said to the king of Israel, "First seek the counsel of the LORD."

6So the king of Israel brought together the prophets — about four hundred men — and asked them, "Shall I go to war against Ramoth Gilead, or shall I refrain?"

"Go," they answered, "for the Lord will give it into the king's hand."

7But Jehoshaphat asked, "Is there not a prophet of the LORD here whom we can enquire of?"

8The king of Israel answered Jehoshaphat, "There is still one man through whom we can enquire of the LORD, but I hate him because he never prophesies anything good about me, but always bad. He is Micaiah son of Imlah."

"The king should not say that," Jehoshaphat replied.

9So the king of Israel called one of his officials and said, "Bring Micaiah son of Imlah at once."

10Dressed in their royal robes, the king of Israel and Jehoshaphat king of Judah were sitting on their thrones at the threshing-floor by the entrance of the gate of Samaria, with all the prophets prophesying before them. 11Now Zedekiah son of Kenaanah had made iron horns and he declared, "This is what the LORD says: 'With these you will gore the Arameans until they are destroyed.' "

12All the other prophets were prophesying the same thing. "Attack Ramoth Gilead and be victorious," they said, "for the LORD will give it into the king's hand."

13The messenger who had gone to summon Micaiah said to him, "Look, as one man the other prophets are predicting success for the king. Let your word agree with theirs, and speak favourably."

14But Micaiah said, "As surely as the LORD lives, I can tell him only what the LORD tells me."

---

a23 Most Hebrew manuscripts; a few Hebrew manuscripts, Vulgate and Syriac (see also 2 Kings 9:26) *the plot of ground at*

¹⁵When he arrived, the king asked him, "Micaiah, shall we go to war against Ramoth Gilead, or shall I refrain?"

"Attack and be victorious," he answered, "for the LORD will give it into the king's hand."

¹⁶The king said to him, "How many times must I make you swear to tell me nothing but the truth in the name of the LORD?"

¹⁷Then Micaiah answered, "I saw all Israel scattered on the hills like sheep without a shepherd, and the LORD said, 'These people have no master. Let each one go home in peace.' "

¹⁸The king of Israel said to Jehoshaphat, "Didn't I tell you that he never prophesies anything good about me, but only bad?"

¹⁹Micaiah continued, "Therefore hear the word of the LORD: I saw the LORD sitting on his throne with all the host of heaven standing round him on his right and on his left. ²⁰And the LORD said, 'Who will entice Ahab into attacking Ramoth Gilead and going to his death there?'

"One suggested this, and another that. ²¹Finally, a spirit came forward, stood before the LORD and said, 'I will entice him.'

²²" 'By what means?' the LORD asked.

" 'I will go out and be a lying spirit in the mouths of all his prophets,' he said.

" 'You will succeed in enticing him,' said the LORD. 'Go and do it.'

²³"So now the LORD has put a lying spirit in the mouths of all these prophets of yours. The LORD has decreed disaster for you."

²⁴Then Zedekiah son of Kenaanah went up and slapped Micaiah in the face. "Which way did the spirit from*a* the LORD go when he went from me to speak to you?" he asked.

²⁵Micaiah replied, "You will find out on the day you go to hide in an inner room."

²⁶The king of Israel then ordered, "Take Micaiah and send him back to Amon the ruler of the city and to Joash the king's son ²⁷and say, 'This is what the king says: Put this fellow in prison and give him nothing but bread and water until I return safely.' "

²⁸Micaiah declared, "If you ever return safely, the LORD has not spoken through me." Then he added, "Mark my words, all you people!"

■ Ahab Killed at Ramoth Gilead

²⁹So the king of Israel and Jehoshaphat king of Judah went up to Ramoth Gilead. ³⁰The king of Israel said to Jehoshaphat, "I will enter the battle in disguise, but you wear your royal robes." So the king of Israel disguised himself and went into battle.

³¹Now the king of Aram had ordered his thirty-two chariot commanders, "Do not fight with anyone, small or great, except the king of Israel." ³²When the chariot commanders saw Jehoshaphat, they thought, "Surely this is the king of Israel." So they turned to attack him, but when Jehoshaphat cried out, ³³the chariot commanders saw that he was not the king of Israel and stopped pursuing him.

³⁴But someone drew his bow at random and hit the king of Israel between the sections of his armour. The king told his chariot driver, "Wheel round and get me out of the fighting. I've been wounded." ³⁵All day long the battle raged, and the king was propped up in his chariot facing the Arameans. The blood from his wound ran onto the floor of the chariot, and that evening he died. ³⁶As the sun was setting, a cry spread through the army: "Every man to his town; everyone to his land!"

³⁷So the king died and was brought to Samaria, and they buried him there. ³⁸They washed the chariot at a pool in Samaria (where the prostitutes bathed),*b* and the dogs licked up his blood, as the word of the LORD had declared.

³⁹As for the other events of Ahab's reign, including all he did, the palace he built and inlaid with ivory, and the cities he fortified, are they not written in the book of the annals of the kings of Israel? ⁴⁰Ahab rested with his fathers. And Ahaziah his son succeeded him as king.

■ Jehoshaphat King of Judah

⁴¹Jehoshaphat son of Asa became king of Judah in the fourth year of Ahab king of Israel. ⁴²Jehoshaphat was thirty-five years old when he became king, and he reigned in Jerusalem for twenty-five years. His mother's name was Azubah daughter of Shilhi. ⁴³In everything he walked in the ways of his father Asa and did not stray from them; he did what was right in the eyes of the LORD. The high places, however, were not removed, and the people continued to offer sacrifices and burn incense there. ⁴⁴Jehoshaphat was also at peace with the king of Israel.

⁴⁵As for the other events of Jehoshaphat's reign, the things he achieved and his military exploits, are they not written in the book of the annals of the kings of Judah? ⁴⁶He rid the land of the rest of the male shrine-prostitutes who remained there even after the reign of his father Asa. ⁴⁷There was then no king in Edom; a deputy ruled.

⁴⁸Now Jehoshaphat built a fleet of trading ships*c* to go to Ophir for gold, but they never set sail — they were wrecked at Ezion Geber. ⁴⁹At that time Ahaziah son of Ahab said to Jehoshaphat, "Let my men sail with your men," but Jehoshaphat refused.

⁵⁰Then Jehoshaphat rested with his fathers and was buried with them in the city of David his father. And Jehoram his son succeeded him.

■ Ahaziah King of Israel

⁵¹Ahaziah son of Ahab became king of Israel in Samaria in the seventeenth year of Jehoshaphat king of Judah, and he reigned over Israel for two years. ⁵²He did evil in the eyes of the LORD, because he walked in the ways of his father and mother and in the ways of Jeroboam son of Nebat, who caused Israel to sin. ⁵³He served and worshipped Baal and provoked the LORD, the God of Israel, to anger, just as his father had done.

---

a 24 Or Spirit of　　*b 38 Or Samaria and cleaned the weapons*　　*c 48 Hebrew of ships of Tarshish*

2 KINGS

■ THE GREAT WARS OF ISRAEL
THE PROMISED LAND TURNS INTO A BLOODY BATTLEFIELD

SO THE LORD SAID, "I WILL REMOVE JUDAH ALSO FROM MY PRESENCE AS I REMOVED ISRAEL, AND I WILL REJECT JERUSALEM, THE CITY I CHOSE, AND THIS TEMPLE, ABOUT WHICH I SAID, 'THERE SHALL MY NAME BE.' " ■ 23:27

The book of 2 Kings tells of dark days in the promised land. First, the Northern Kingdom, Israel, fell to outside invaders. Then Judah, the Southern Kingdom, was conquered. To appreciate what those two events meant in Jewish history, consider our century's two great wars.

In 1918 the bloodiest war of all time came to an end. The entire planet had chosen sides. In all, nine million soldiers died. Survivors thought nothing could ever again match The Great War's ferocity and destruction. "The war to end all wars", they called it.

Yet, in a mere 20 years, a man named Adolf Hitler brought war again. In World War II, global violence stretched from London in the West to Japan in the East. The war finally closed with a blinding mushroom cloud, an ominous portent for the future.

■ TWO LARGE BLOTS IN HISTORY
No matter what else happens, the 20th century has been permanently stained by those two large blots: World War I and World War II. Everything else — art, literature, advances in science and medicine — fades into the background.

As 2 Kings tells it, something very similar occurred in the biblical nation of Israel. Two large blots spread across the land: successive invasions by foreign giants. In the long, turbulent history of the Jews, these two invasions stand out as the Great Wars, overshadowing nearly everything else.

■ ISRAEL FALLS FIRST
The kingdom had already split into two — 1 Kings tells that story. Its sequel, 2 Kings, describes ever-increasing tragedy.

From the very first chapters you can sense the pending crisis in the North. Not one northern king followed the ways of God. National politics slipped into an endless cycle of intrigue and bloody revolt. Meanwhile, Elijah and Elisha intensified their attacks on the kings, and

miracles broke out with unusual frequency.

Assyria's campaigns — the "World War I" in Israel's history — are reported in 2 Kings 15–18. Other records of the period tell of vicious fighting. Samaria, Israel's capital, made one final heroic stand against a two-year siege. Finally, the starving survivors surrendered, and the people of Israel were carried away into captivity.

Only two Israelite tribes remained in the promised land, holding out in the tiny Southern Kingdom of Judah. Ultimately, King Sennacherib of Assyria turned against Judah also, penetrating all the way to the gates of Jerusalem. Contemporary accounts record that he levelled 46 walled cities and carried away 200,150 people, young and old, together with all their horses, mules, cattle, and possessions. He scornfully dismissed King Hezekiah as "a bird in a cage".

■ A BRIEF COMEBACK
Could the tiny nation of Judah survive such an onslaught? Somehow the "caged bird" (Hezekiah) made a remarkable comeback, and Judah did survive for another 135 years. Still, Judah did not learn from the dramatic object lesson of Israel's destruction in the North. Most of the kings who followed Hezekiah failed dismally to obey God. Another foreign invader, Babylon, finally levelled Jerusalem in the "World War II" of that era.

The book of Kings ends with a bleak picture: refugees picking through the rubble of Jerusalem, and the Israelites enslaved by foreign powers. The temple itself, God's house, lay in ruins, its treasures carted off to Babylon. When the dust settled around 600 B.C., the Israelites were scattered across the earth, not to be reunited as an independent nation for 25 centuries.

All along, prophets had given eloquent warnings of what would happen to a nation that turned its back on God. But nothing makes a bigger impact than the object lesson of history itself. Ever since, Jews have looked back on their history and seen two indelible stains. Those were the dark days of Assyria and Babylon, when everything came apart.

■ HOW TO READ 2 KINGS

The first eight chapters of 2 Kings, full of excitement and adventure, read easily. They focus on the last days of the prophet Elijah and on the long life of his successor Elisha. But beginning with chapter 9, the book can become very confusing. It switches back and forth between two histories: that of Israel in the North and Judah in the South.

Israel was strong initially, with 10 of the 12 tribes united there. But it proved less faithful to God and was ultimately destroyed by Assyria. Chapters 18–25 cover the period after the Assyrian invasion, when only Judah existed.

Use the sectional headings in this Bible for orientation: they clearly mark whether a king or queen ruled over Judah or Israel. Also, a line-up of all the rulers appears on pages 260–268, giving an overview of the history of each country.

One important reason for studying the books of Kings and Chronicles is that they give historical background on the prophets. Elijah and Elisha appeared at a crucial turning point in the history of the Northern Kingdom, just as Ahab was changing the official religion from worship of God to worship of Baal. Other prophets, who wrote books of the Bible, were also active during this time.

Amos and Hosea concentrated their work in the Northern Kingdom of Israel. The following prophets lived and preached in the Southern Kingdom of Judah: Obadiah, Joel, Isaiah, Micah, Nahum, Zephaniah, Jeremiah, and Habakkuk. More prophets came later, when the Israelites were still captive in Babylon or after they had returned to their homeland. The How to Read section of each book of the prophets gives a brief summary of when and where each author worked (see An Overview of the Bible, pages xvi–xix, for a list of the books of the prophets).

Second Kings, like its companion books, makes brief and sweeping judgments of each king or queen. As you read, look for what pleased God and what displeased him. The 39 rulers comprise a fine study of leadership of all kinds, from the inspiring to the degenerate.

■ 3-TRACK READING PLAN

For an explanation and complete listing of the 3-track reading plan, turn to page x.

■ TRACK 1:
Two-Week Courses on the Bible
See page x for information on these courses.

■ TRACK 2:
An Overview of 2 Kings in 3 Days
☐ Day 1. Read the Introduction to 2 Kings and then chapter 5 on Elisha's miracle of healing an enemy from Aram.

☐ Day 2. Read chapter 17, which gives a final summary of the decline and utter devastation of the Northern Kingdom of Israel.
☐ Day 3. One of the high points in 2 Kings occurred during the reign of the boy-king Josiah. Read about the beginning of his reforms in chapter 22 and the first three verses of chapter 23.
Now turn to page xi for your next Track 2 reading project.

■ TRACK 3:
All of 2 Kings in 25 Days
After you have read through 2 Kings, turn to pages xii–xiii for your next Track 3 reading project.

☐ 1   ☐ 2   ☐ 3   ☐ 4
☐ 5   ☐ 6   ☐ 7   ☐ 8
☐ 9   ☐ 10 ☐ 11 ☐ 12
☐ 13 ☐ 14 ☐ 15 ☐ 16
☐ 17 ☐ 18 ☐ 19 ☐ 20
☐ 21 ☐ 22 ☐ 23 ☐ 24
☐ 25

■ The LORD's Judgment on Ahaziah

1 After Ahab's death, Moab rebelled against Israel. ²Now Ahaziah had fallen through the lattice of his upper room in Samaria and injured himself. So he sent messengers, saying to them, "Go and consult Baal-Zebub, the god of Ekron, to see if I will recover from this injury."

³But the angel of the LORD said to Elijah the Tishbite, "Go up and meet the messengers of the king of Samaria and ask them, 'Is it because there is no God in Israel that you are going off to consult Baal-Zebub, the god of Ekron?' ⁴Therefore this is what the LORD says: 'You will not leave the bed you are lying on. You will certainly die!' " So Elijah went.

⁵When the messengers returned to the king, he asked them, "Why have you come back?"

⁶"A man came to meet us," they replied. "And he said to us, 'Go back to the king who sent you and tell him, "This is what the LORD says: Is it because there is no God in Israel that you are sending men to consult Baal-Zebub, the god of Ekron? Therefore you will not leave the bed you are lying on. You will certainly die!" ' "

⁷The king asked them, "What kind of man was it who came to meet you and told you this?"

⁸They replied, "He was a man with a garment of hair and with a leather belt round his waist."

The king said, "That was Elijah the Tishbite."

⁹Then he sent to Elijah a captain with his company of fifty men. The captain went up to Elijah, who was sitting on the top of a hill, and said to him, "Man of God, the king says, 'Come down!' "

¹⁰Elijah answered the captain, "If I am a man of God, may fire come down from heaven and consume you and your fifty men!" Then the fire fell from heaven and consumed the captain and his men.

¹¹At this the king sent to Elijah another captain with his fifty men. The captain said to him, "Man of God, this is what the king says, 'Come down at once!' "

¹²"If I am a man of God," Elijah replied, "may fire come down from heaven and consume you and your fifty men!" Then the fire of God fell from heaven and consumed him and his fifty men.

¹³So the king sent a third captain with his fifty men. This third captain went up and fell on his knees before Elijah. "Man of God," he begged, "please have respect for my life and the lives of these fifty men, your servants! ¹⁴See, fire has fallen from heaven and consumed the first two captains and all their men. But now have respect for my life!"

¹⁵The angel of the LORD said to Elijah, "Go down with him; do not be afraid of him." So Elijah got up and went down with him to the king.

¹⁶He told the king, "This is what the LORD says: Is it because there is no God in Israel for you to consult that you have sent messengers to consult Baal-Zebub, the god of Ekron? Because you have done this, you will never leave the bed you are lying on. You will certainly die!" ¹⁷So he died, according to the word of the LORD that Elijah had spoken.

Because Ahaziah had no son, Joram*a* succeeded him as king in the second year of Jehoram son of Jehoshaphat king of Judah. ¹⁸As for all the other events of Ahaziah's reign, and what he did, are they not written in the book of the annals of the kings of Israel?

■ Elijah Taken Up to Heaven

2 When the LORD was about to take Elijah up to heaven in a whirlwind, Elijah and Elisha were on their way from Gilgal. ²Elijah said to Elisha, "Stay here; the LORD has sent me to Bethel."

But Elisha said, "As surely as the LORD lives and as you live, I will not leave you." So they went down to Bethel.

³The company of the prophets at Bethel came out to Elisha and asked, "Do you know that the LORD is going to take your master from you today?"

"Yes, I know," Elisha replied, "but do not speak of it."

⁴Then Elijah said to him, "Stay here, Elisha; the LORD has sent me to Jericho."

And he replied, "As surely as the LORD lives and as you live, I will not leave you." So they went to Jericho.

⁵The company of the prophets at Jericho went up to Elisha and asked him, "Do you know that the LORD is going to take your master from you today?"

"Yes, I know," he replied, "but do not speak of it."

⁶Then Elijah said to him, "Stay here; the LORD has sent me to the Jordan."

And he replied, "As surely as the LORD lives and as you live, I will not leave you." So the two of them walked on.

⁷Fifty men of the company of the prophets went and stood at a distance, facing the place where Elijah and Elisha had stopped at the Jordan. ⁸Elijah took his cloak, rolled it up and struck the water with it. The water divided to the right and to the left, and the two of them crossed over on dry ground.

⁹When they had crossed, Elijah said to Elisha, "Tell me, what can I do for you before I am taken from you?"

"Let me inherit a double portion of your spirit," Elisha replied.

¹⁰"You have asked a difficult thing," Elijah said, "yet if you see me when I am taken from you, it will be yours—otherwise not."

¹¹As they were walking along and talking together, suddenly a chariot of fire and horses of fire appeared and separated the two of them, and Elijah went up to heaven in a whirlwind. ¹²Elisha saw this and cried out, "My father! My father! The chariots and horsemen of Israel!" And Elisha saw him no more. Then he took hold of his own clothes and tore them apart.

2:12 ■ AN OBSCURE COMPLIMENT
Elisha's last words to Elijah were obviously a compliment, but what did they mean? Most probably they referred to Elijah's power, indicating he was worth more to the nation of Israel than a company of chariots and horsemen. Interestingly, a king of Israel said these exact words to Elisha himself as he lay dying (13:14).

---

a 17 Hebrew Jehoram, a variant of Joram

13He picked up the cloak that had fallen from Elijah and went back and stood on the bank of the Jordan. 14Then he took the cloak that had fallen from him and struck the water with it. "Where now is the LORD, the God of Elijah?" he asked. When he struck the water, it divided to the right and to the left, and he crossed over.

15The company of the prophets from Jericho, who were watching, said, "The spirit of Elijah is resting on Elisha." And they went to meet him and bowed to the ground before him. 16"Look," they said, "we your servants have fifty able men. Let them go and look for your master. Perhaps the Spirit of the LORD has picked him up and set him down on some mountain or in some valley."

"No," Elisha replied, "do not send them."

INSIGHT

■ REPLACING A LEGEND
WHO COULD FOLLOW THE GREAT ELIJAH?

WHEN THEY HAD CROSSED, ELIJAH SAID TO ELISHA, "TELL ME, WHAT CAN I DO FOR YOU BEFORE I AM TAKEN FROM YOU?" "LET ME INHERIT A DOUBLE PORTION OF YOUR SPIRIT," ELISHA REPLIED. ■ 2:9

When a prophet like Elijah leaves the scene, who will dare to take his place? As time came to choose a successor, Elijah looked to someone out of a different mould. He settled on his most faithful companion, a farmer named Elisha.

■ SIMILAR NAMES BUT DIFFERENT STYLES
The slight variance in the two men's names expresses their difference in style. Elijah, whose name meant "The LORD is my God", fought a king and the priests of Baal in dramatic confrontations of power. He lived apart from the people and preached judgment and the need for repentance.

Elisha ("God is salvation") shifted the emphasis. He lived among people, preferring the poor and outcast, and stressed life, hope and God's grace. All social classes had access to Elisha, from lowly widows to foreign kings. His colourful life included work as a spy, a miracle worker, an adviser to the king, a leader of a school of prophets and an anointer of revolutionaries.

Elisha travelled widely, and his bald head and wooden walking staff became his trademarks. News of his miracles spread, making him a famous national figure for 50 years. As Elisha lay on his deathbed, the distraught king of Israel knelt beside him, asking for one last word of advice.

■ SERVING THE PEOPLE AND THE KINGDOM
Elisha's exploits fall roughly into two categories, and the Bible seems to group them that way. One set of stories concerns people with evident needs. Elisha showed a deep sensitivity for the suffering and distressed, and sometimes helped them in miraculous ways: providing food, healing diseases, even raising a young boy from the dead. He dealt far more gently with the poor and downtrodden than with kings and generals.

Another group of stories relates to the nation. Israel was reeling from the corruption brought in during King Ahab's reign (see page 262). Politically, Israel was at the mercy of the neighbouring state of Aram (the area known today as Syria), which launched periodic raids across the border.

Sometimes Elisha helped out Israel's army, using his special insight to detect bands of raiders. Twice, miracles he predicted allowed Israel's army to break out of an impossible situation and rout the enemy. Yet he refused to become a "court prophet" serving the king's whims. On at least one occasion, he blatantly insulted a king of Israel (3:13–14). Another time, he anointed a general to overthrow the king in an outright revolution.

■ A DYING BREED
Incidents from Elisha's life – the healing of Naaman, the chariots of fire, the widow's oil – have become among the most familiar of Old Testament stories. In a sense, Elijah and Elisha represent the last of a breed. Prophets who followed them relied less on spectacular displays and more on the power of verbal messages from God.

Elijah and Elisha used both words and dramatic events to convey their message. Everyone knew their power, especially the kings who sometimes sought them out for advice and other times tried to kill them. In a great irony, the kings and political leaders – who thought themselves the centre of history at the time – all faded away. Meanwhile the stories and words of Israel's prophets live on, expressing a message as forceful today as ever.

□ LIFE QUESTIONS:
Elijah and Elisha show how God uses quite different personalities to get his message across. From the description above, which of the two prophets do you more closely identify with?

17But they persisted until he was too ashamed to refuse. So he said, "Send them." And they sent fifty men, who searched for three days but did not find him. 18When they returned to Elisha, who was staying in Jericho, he said to them, "Didn't I tell you not to go?"

■ Healing of the Water

19The men of the city said to Elisha, "Look, our lord, this town is well situated, as you can see, but the water is bad and the land is unproductive."

20"Bring me a new bowl," he said, "and put salt in it." So they brought it to him.

21Then he went out to the spring and threw the salt into it, saying, "This is what the LORD says: 'I have healed this water. Never again will it cause death or make the land unproductive.' " 22And the water has remained wholesome to this day, according to the word Elisha had spoken.

■ Elisha Is Jeered

23From there Elisha went up to Bethel. As he was walking along the road, some youths came out of the town and jeered at him. "Go on up, you baldhead!" they said. "Go on up, you baldhead!" 24He turned round, looked at them and called down a curse on them in the name of the LORD. Then two bears came out of the woods and mauled forty-two of the youths. 25And he went on to Mount Carmel and from there returned to Samaria.

2:23 ■ BACKGROUND ON THE BEARS
At first reading, the brief account in these three verses is very troubling. A prophet calling on bears to maul children? But, in this instance, historical background and a precise translation help cast the event in a different light. Bethel was a hotbed of Baal worship, and its residents were engaged in a life-and-death struggle with the true prophets of God. When the youths called out, "Go on up, you baldhead!" they were probably referring to what had just happened to the prophet Elijah—they were calling for Elisha to vanish into the sky, or in other words, to die. Furthermore, the word translated *youths* usually refers to young people in their late teens. In actuality, a large gang of teenagers was threatening a prophet's life. Elisha cursed them, but there is no indication he actually called for a bear attack.

■ Moab Revolts

3 Jorama son of Ahab became king of Israel in Samaria in the eighteenth year of Jehoshaphat king of Judah, and he reigned for twelve years. 2He did evil in the eyes of the LORD, but not as his father and mother had done. He got rid of the sacred stone of Baal that his father had made. 3Nevertheless he clung to the sins of Jeroboam son of Nebat, which he had caused Israel to commit; he did not turn away from them.

4Now Mesha king of Moab raised sheep, and he had to supply the king of Israel with a hundred thousand lambs and with the wool of a hundred thousand rams. 5But after Ahab died, the king of Moab rebelled against the king of Israel. 6So at that time King Joram set out from Samaria and mobilised all Israel. 7He also sent this message to Jehoshaphat king of Judah: "The king of Moab has rebelled against me. Will you go with me to fight against Moab?"

"I will go with you," he replied. "I am as you are, my people as your people, my horses as your horses."

8"By what route shall we attack?" he asked.

"Through the Desert of Edom," he answered.

9So the king of Israel set out with the king of Judah and the king of Edom. After a roundabout march of seven days, the army had no more water for themselves or for the animals with them.

10"What!" exclaimed the king of Israel. "Has the LORD called us three kings together only to hand us over to Moab?"

11But Jehoshaphat asked, "Is there no prophet of the LORD here, that we may enquire of the LORD through him?"

An officer of the king of Israel answered, "Elisha son of Shaphat is here. He used to pour water on the hands of Elijah."b

12Jehoshaphat said, "The word of the LORD is with him." So the king of Israel and Jehoshaphat and the king of Edom went down to him.

13Elisha said to the king of Israel, "What do we have to do with each other? Go to the prophets of your father and the prophets of your mother."

"No," the king of Israel answered, "because it was the LORD who called us three kings together to hand us over to Moab."

14Elisha said, "As surely as the LORD Almighty lives, whom I serve, if I did not have respect for the presence of Jehoshaphat king of Judah, I would not look at you or even notice you. 15But now bring me a harpist."

While the harpist was playing, the hand of the LORD came upon Elisha 16and he said, "This is what the LORD says: Make this valley full of ditches. 17For this is what the LORD says: You will see neither wind nor rain, yet this valley will be filled with water, and you, your cattle and your other animals will drink. 18This is an easy thing in the eyes of the LORD; he will also hand Moab over to you. 19You will overthrow every fortified city and every major town. You will cut down every good tree, stop up all the springs, and ruin every good field with stones."

20The next morning, about the time for offering the sacrifice, there it was—water flowing from the direction of Edom! And the land was filled with water.

21Now all the Moabites had heard that the kings had come to fight against them; so every man, young and old, who could bear arms was called up and stationed on the border. 22When they got up early in the morning, the sun was shining on the water. To the Moabites across the way, the water looked red—like blood. 23"That's blood!" they said. "Those kings must have fought and slaughtered each other. Now to the plunder, Moab!"

24But when the Moabites came to the camp of Israel, the Israelites rose up and fought them until they fled. And the Israelites invaded the land and slaughtered the Moabites. 25They destroyed the

a 1 Hebrew *Jehoram*, a variant of *Joram*; also in verse 6   b 11 That is, he was Elijah's personal servant.

towns, and each man threw a stone on every good field until it was covered. They stopped up all the springs and cut down every good tree. Only Kir Hareseth was left with its stones in place, but men armed with slings surrounded it and attacked it as well.

26When the king of Moab saw that the battle had gone against him, he took with him seven hundred swordsmen to break through to the king of Edom, but they failed. 27Then he took his firstborn son, who was to succeed him as king, and offered him as a sacrifice on the city wall. The fury against Israel was great; they withdrew and returned to their own land.

■ The Widow's Oil

4 The wife of a man from the company of the prophets cried out to Elisha, "Your servant my husband is dead, and you know that he revered the LORD. But now his creditor is coming to take my two boys as his slaves."

2Elisha replied to her, "How can I help you? Tell me, what do you have in your house?"

"Your servant has nothing there at all," she said, "except a little oil."

3Elisha said, "Go round and ask all your neighbours for empty jars. Don't ask for just a few. 4Then go inside and shut the door behind you and your sons. Pour oil into all the jars, and as each is filled, put it to one side."

5She left him and afterwards shut the door behind her and her sons. They brought the jars to her and she kept pouring. 6When all the jars were full, she said to her son, "Bring me another one."

But he replied, "There is not a jar left." Then the oil stopped flowing.

7She went and told the man of God, and he said, "Go, sell the oil and pay your debts. You and your sons can live on what is left."

■ The Shunammite's Son Restored to Life

8One day Elisha went to Shunem. And a well-to-do woman was there, who urged him to stay for a meal. So whenever he came by, he stopped there to eat. 9She said to her husband, "I know that this man who often comes our way is a holy man of God. 10Let's make a small room on the roof and put in it a bed and a table, a chair and a lamp for him. Then he can stay there whenever he comes to us."

11One day when Elisha came, he went up to his room and lay down there. 12He said to his servant Gehazi, "Call the Shunammite." So he called her, and she stood before him. 13Elisha said to him, "Tell her, 'You have gone to all this trouble for us. Now what can be done for you? Can we speak on your behalf to the king or the commander of the army?' "

She replied, "I have a home among my own people."

14"What can be done for her?" Elisha asked.

Gehazi said, "Well, she has no son and her husband is old."

15Then Elisha said, "Call her." So he called her, and she stood in the doorway. 16"About this time next year," Elisha said, "you will hold a son in your arms."

"No, my lord," she objected. "Don't mislead your servant, O man of God!"

4:8 ■ ELISHA'S MIRACLES

Elisha had asked for a double portion of Elijah's spirit (2:9), and the Bible pointedly records about twice as many miracles performed by Elisha. Many of these miracles, especially those in chapter 4, have great similarities to the miracles Jesus himself would later perform; they show God caring for the needs of ordinary people. Although Elisha was very famous in his own time, his name appears only once outside the book of Kings (Luke 4:27). In contrast, Elijah is often mentioned, and John the Baptist is frequently compared to him.

17But the woman became pregnant, and the next year about that same time she gave birth to a son, just as Elisha had told her.

18The child grew, and one day he went out to his father, who was with the reapers. 19"My head! My head!" he said to his father.

His father told a servant, "Carry him to his mother." 20After the servant had lifted him up and carried him to his mother, the boy sat on her lap until noon, and then he died. 21She went up and laid him on the bed of the man of God, then shut the door and went out.

22She called her husband and said, "Please send me one of the servants and a donkey so I can go to the man of God quickly and return."

23"Why go to him today?" he asked. "It's not the New Moon or the Sabbath."

"It's all right," she said.

24She saddled the donkey and said to her servant, "Lead on; don't slow down for me unless I tell you." 25So she set out and came to the man of God at Mount Carmel.

When he saw her in the distance, the man of God said to his servant Gehazi, "Look! There's the Shunammite! 26Run to meet her and ask her, 'Are you all right? Is your husband all right? Is your child all right?' "

"Everything is all right," she said.

27When she reached the man of God at the mountain, she took hold of his feet. Gehazi came over to push her away, but the man of God said, "Leave her alone! She is in bitter distress, but the LORD has hidden it from me and has not told me why."

28"Did I ask you for a son, my lord?" she said. "Didn't I tell you, 'Don't raise my hopes'?"

29Elisha said to Gehazi, "Tuck your cloak into your belt, take my staff in your hand and run. If you meet anyone, do not greet him, and if anyone greets you, do not answer. Lay my staff on the boy's face."

30But the child's mother said, "As surely as the LORD lives and as you live, I will not leave you." So he got up and followed her.

31Gehazi went on ahead and laid the staff on the boy's face, but there was no sound or response. So Gehazi went back to meet Elisha and told him, "The boy has not awakened."

32When Elisha reached the house, there was the boy lying dead on his couch. 33He went in, shut the door on the two of them and prayed to the LORD. 34Then he got on the bed and lay upon the boy, mouth to mouth, eyes to eyes, hands to hands. As he stretched himself out upon him, the boy's body grew warm. 35Elisha turned away and walked back and forth in the room and then got onto the bed and stretched out upon him once more. The boy sneezed seven times and opened his eyes.

36Elisha summoned Gehazi and said, "Call the Shunammite." And he did. When she came, he said, "Take your son." 37She came in, fell at his feet and bowed to the ground. Then she took her son and went out.

■ Death in the Pot

38Elisha returned to Gilgal and there was a famine in that region. While the company of the prophets was meeting with him, he said to his servant, "Put on the large pot and cook some stew for these men."

39One of them went out into the fields to gather herbs and found a wild vine. He gathered some of its gourds and filled the fold of his cloak. When he returned, he cut them up into the pot of stew, though no-one knew what they were. 40The stew was poured out for the men, but as they began to eat it, they cried out, "O man of God, there is death in the pot!" And they could not eat it.

41Elisha said, "Get some flour." He put it into the pot and said, "Serve it to the people to eat." And there was nothing harmful in the pot.

■ Feeding of a Hundred

42A man came from Baal Shalishah, bringing the man of God twenty loaves of barley bread baked from the first ripe corn, along with some ears of new corn. "Give it to the people to eat," Elisha said.

43"How can I set this before a hundred men?" his servant asked.

But Elisha answered, "Give it to the people to eat. For this is what the LORD says: 'They will eat and have some left over.' " 44Then he set it before them, and they ate and had some left over, according to the word of the LORD.

■ Naaman Healed of Leprosy

5 Now Naaman was commander of the army of the king of Aram. He was a great man in the sight of his master and highly regarded, because through him the LORD had given victory to Aram. He was a valiant soldier, but he had leprosy.[a]

2Now bands from Aram had gone out and had taken captive a young girl from Israel, and she served Naaman's wife. 3She said to her mistress, "If only my master would see the prophet who is in Samaria! He would cure him of his leprosy."

4Naaman went to his master and told him what the girl from Israel had said. 5"By all means, go," the king of Aram replied. "I will send a letter to the king of Israel." So Naaman left, taking with him ten talents[b] of silver, six thousand shekels[c] of gold and ten sets of clothing. 6The letter that he took to the king of Israel read: "With this letter I am sending my servant Naaman to you so that you may cure him of his leprosy."

5:3 ■ A CAPTIVE'S COMPASSION
She had been captured in a raid, taken to a foreign country, and made a slave. Yet instead of bitterness, she showed compassion towards her master. She wanted him healed, and she believed her God would do it. God used this girl's tragedy to heal and convert her enemy — a wonderful example of love reaching out.

7As soon as the king of Israel read the letter, he tore his robes and said, "Am I God? Can I kill and bring back to life? Why does this fellow send someone to me to be cured of his leprosy? See how he is trying to pick a quarrel with me!"

8When Elisha the man of God heard that the king of Israel had torn his robes, he sent him this message: "Why have you torn your robes? Make the man come to me and he will know that there is a prophet in Israel." 9So Naaman went with his horses and chariots and stopped at the door of Elisha's house. 10Elisha sent a messenger to say to him, "Go, wash yourself seven times in the Jordan, and your flesh will be restored and you will be cleansed."

5:10 ■ HARDER ON THE RICH
Elisha's treatment of the general Naaman here, and of the king of Israel elsewhere, contrasts sharply with his mild manner among the poor and oppressed. Elisha's prescribed cure obviously offended Naaman's pride. And Elisha pointedly refused to accept payment from the wealthy general, who was used to paying his way. In this incident, and in another (8:7–15), Elisha was serving the kingdom of Aram, an enemy of Israel.

11But Naaman went away angry and said, "I thought that he would surely come out to me and stand and call on the name of the LORD his God, wave his hand over the spot and cure me of my leprosy. 12Are not Abana and Pharpar, the rivers of Damascus, better than any of the waters of Israel? Couldn't I wash in them and be cleansed?" So he turned and went off in a rage.

13Naaman's servants went to him and said, "My father, if the prophet had told you to do some great thing, would you not have done it? How much more, then, when he tells you, 'Wash and be cleansed'?" 14So he went down and dipped himself in the Jordan seven times, as the man of God had told him, and his flesh was restored and became clean like that of a young boy.

15Then Naaman and all his attendants went back to the man of God. He stood before him and said, "Now I know that there is no God in all the world except in Israel. Please accept now a gift from your servant."

16The prophet answered, "As surely as the LORD lives, whom I serve, I will not accept a thing." And even though Naaman urged him, he refused.

a 1 The Hebrew word was used for various diseases affecting the skin — not necessarily leprosy; also in verses 3, 6, 7, 11 and 27.   b 5 That is, about 750 pounds (about 340 kilograms)   c 5 That is, about 150 pounds (about 70 kilograms)

17"If you will not," said Naaman, "please let me, your servant, be given as much earth as a pair of mules can carry, for your servant will never again make burnt offerings and sacrifices to any other god but the LORD. 18But may the LORD forgive your servant for this one thing: When my master enters the temple of Rimmon to bow down and he is leaning on my arm and I bow there also — when I bow down in the temple of Rimmon, may the LORD forgive your servant for this."

19"Go in peace," Elisha said.

After Naaman had travelled some distance, 20Gehazi, the servant of Elisha the man of God, said to himself, "My master was too easy on Naaman, this Aramean, by not accepting from him what he brought. As surely as the LORD lives, I will run after him and get something from him."

21So Gehazi hurried after Naaman. When Naaman saw him running towards him, he got down from the chariot to meet him. "Is everything all right?" he asked.

22"Everything is all right," Gehazi answered. "My master sent me to say, 'Two young men from the company of the prophets have just come to me from the hill country of Ephraim. Please give them a talent*d* of silver and two sets of clothing.'"

23"By all means, take two talents," said Naaman. He urged Gehazi to accept them, and then tied up the two talents of silver in two bags, with two sets of clothing. He gave them to two of his servants, and they carried them ahead of Gehazi. 24When Gehazi came to the hill, he took the things from the servants and put them away in the house. He sent the men away and they left. 25Then he went in and stood before his master Elisha.

"Where have you been, Gehazi?" Elisha asked.

"Your servant didn't go anywhere," Gehazi answered.

26But Elisha said to him, "Was not my spirit with you when the man got down from his chariot to meet you? Is this the time to take money, or to accept clothes, olive groves, vineyards, flocks, herds, or menservants and maidservants? 27Naaman's leprosy will cling to you and to your descendants for ever." Then Gehazi went from Elisha's presence and he was leprous, as white as snow.

■ An Axe-Head Floats

6 The company of the prophets said to Elisha, "Look, the place where we meet with you is too small for us. 2Let us go to the Jordan, where each of us can get a pole; and let us build a place there for us to live."

And he said, "Go."

3Then one of them said, "Won't you please come with your servants?"

"I will," Elisha replied. 4And he went with them.

They went to the Jordan and began to cut down trees. 5As one of them was cutting down a tree, the iron axe-head fell into the water. "Oh, my lord," he cried out, "it was borrowed!"

6The man of God asked, "Where did it fall?" When he showed him the place, Elisha cut a stick and threw it there, and made the iron float. 7"Lift it out,"

he said. Then the man reached out his hand and took it.

■ Elisha Traps Blinded Arameans

8Now the king of Aram was at war with Israel. After conferring with his officers, he said, "I will set up my camp in such and such a place."

9The man of God sent word to the king of Israel: "Beware of passing that place, because the Arameans are going down there." 10So the king of Israel checked on the place indicated by the man of God. Time and again Elisha warned the king, so that he was on his guard in such places.

11This enraged the king of Aram. He summoned his officers and demanded of them, "Will you not tell me which of us is on the side of the king of Israel?"

12"None of us, my lord the king," said one of his officers, "but Elisha, the prophet who is in Israel, tells the king of Israel the very words you speak in your bedroom."

13"Go, find out where he is," the king ordered, "so that I can send men and capture him." The report came back: "He is in Dothan." 14Then he sent horses and chariots and a strong force there. They went by night and surrounded the city.

15When the servant of the man of God got up and went out early the next morning, an army with horses and chariots had surrounded the city. "Oh, my lord, what shall we do?" the servant asked.

16"Don't be afraid," the prophet answered. "Those who are with us are more than those who are with them."

17And Elisha prayed, "O LORD, open his eyes so that he may see." Then the LORD opened the servant's eyes, and he looked and saw the hills full of horses and chariots of fire all round Elisha.

6:17 ■ CHARIOTS OF FIRE

Surrounded by an army, Elisha's servant cried, "What shall we do?" But when Elisha prayed, the servant could suddenly see that God's forces, invisible to everyone else, far outnumbered the enemy. The story offers a rare glimpse of the "invisible world" of supernatural forces. God has resources to help that we cannot see.

18As the enemy came down towards him, Elisha prayed to the LORD, "Strike these people with blindness." So he struck them with blindness, as Elisha had asked.

19Elisha told them, "This is not the road and this is not the city. Follow me, and I will lead you to the man you are looking for." And he led them to Samaria.

20After they entered the city, Elisha said, "LORD, open the eyes of these men so that they can see." Then the LORD opened their eyes and they looked, and there they were, inside Samaria.

21When the king of Israel saw them, he asked Elisha, "Shall I kill them, my father? Shall I kill them?"

22"Do not kill them," he answered. "Would you kill men you have captured with your own sword or bow? Set food and water before them so that they

d 22 That is, about 75 pounds (about 34 kilograms)

may eat and drink and then go back to their master." 23So he prepared a great feast for them, and after they had finished eating and drinking, he sent them away, and they returned to their master. So the bands from Aram stopped raiding Israel's territory.

■ Famine in Besieged Samaria

24Some time later, Ben-Hadad king of Aram mobilised his entire army and marched up and laid siege to Samaria. 25There was a great famine in the city; the siege lasted so long that a donkey's head sold for eighty shekels*a* of silver, and a quarter of a cab*b* of seed pods*c* for five shekels.*d*

26As the king of Israel was passing by on the wall, a woman cried to him, "Help me, my lord the king!"

27The king replied, "If the LORD does not help you, where can I get help for you? From the threshing-floor? From the winepress?" 28Then he asked her, "What's the matter?"

She answered, "This woman said to me, 'Give up your son so that we may eat him today, and tomorrow we'll eat my son.' 29So we cooked my son and ate him. The next day I said to her, 'Give up your son so that we may eat him,' but she had hidden him."

30When the king heard the woman's words, he tore his robes. As he went along the wall, the people looked, and there, underneath, he had sackcloth on his body. 31He said, "May God deal with me, be it ever so severely, if the head of Elisha son of Shaphat remains on his shoulders today!"

6:31 ■ THE PROPHET AND POLITICS
Elisha's long career spanned the reigns of six kings and included some dramatic ups and downs with them. On occasion Elisha insulted a king outright (3:14). But, as this chapter shows, he could also be an invaluable military resource, serving as a virtual spy. At Elisha's deathbed, the reigning king of Israel knelt beside him, weeping (13:14).

32Now Elisha was sitting in his house, and the elders were sitting with him. The king sent a messenger ahead, but before he arrived, Elisha said to the elders, "Don't you see how this murderer is sending someone to cut off my head? Look, when the messenger comes, shut the door and hold it shut against him. Is not the sound of his master's footsteps behind him?"

33While he was still talking to them, the messenger came down to him. And ⌊the king⌋ said, "This disaster is from the LORD. Why should I wait for the LORD any longer?"

7 Elisha said, "Hear the word of the LORD. This is what the LORD says: About this time tomorrow, a seah*a* of flour will sell for a shekel*b* and two seahs*c* of barley for a shekel at the gate of Samaria."

2The officer on whose arm the king was leaning said to the man of God, "Look, even if the LORD should open the floodgates of the heavens, could this happen?"

"You will see it with your own eyes," answered Elisha, "but you will not eat any of it!"

■ The Siege Lifted

3Now there were four men with leprosy*d* at the entrance of the city gate. They said to each other, "Why stay here until we die? 4If we say, 'We'll go into the city'—the famine is there, and we will die. And if we stay here, we will die. So let's go over to the camp of the Arameans and surrender. If they spare us, we live; if they kill us, then we die."

5At dusk they got up and went to the camp of the Arameans. When they reached the edge of the camp, not a man was there, 6for the Lord had caused the Arameans to hear the sound of chariots and horses and a great army, so that they said to one another, "Look, the king of Israel has hired the Hittite and Egyptian kings to attack us!" 7So they got up and fled in the dusk and abandoned their tents and their horses and donkeys. They left the camp as it was and ran for their lives.

8The men who had leprosy reached the edge of the camp and entered one of the tents. They ate and drank, and carried away silver, gold and clothes, and went off and hid them. They returned and entered another tent and took some things from it and hid them also.

9Then they said to each other, "We're not doing right. This is a day of good news and we are keeping it to ourselves. If we wait until daylight, punishment will overtake us. Let's go at once and report this to the royal palace."

10So they went and called out to the city gate-keepers and told them, "We went into the Aramean camp and not a man was there—not a sound of anyone—only tethered horses and donkeys, and the tents left just as they were." 11The gatekeepers shouted the news, and it was reported within the palace.

12The king got up in the night and said to his officers, "I will tell you what the Arameans have done to us. They know we are starving; so they have left the camp to hide in the countryside, thinking, 'They will surely come out, and then we will take them alive and get into the city.'"

13One of his officers answered, "Make some men take five of the horses that are left in the city. Their plight will be like that of all the Israelites left here—yes, they will only be like all these Israelites who are doomed. So let us send them to find out what happened."

14So they selected two chariots with their horses, and the king sent them after the Aramean army. He commanded the drivers, "Go and find out what has happened." 15They followed them as far as the Jordan, and they found the whole road strewn with the clothing and equipment the Arameans had thrown away in their headlong flight. So the messengers returned and reported to the king. 16Then the people went out and plundered the camp of the Arameans. So a seah of flour sold for a shekel, and two seahs of barley sold for a shekel, as the LORD had said.

17Now the king had put the officer on whose arm

---

a 25 That is, about 2 pounds (about 1 kilogram)   *b 25* That is, probably about ½ pint (about 0.3 litre)   *c 25* Or *of dove's dung*   *d 25* That is, about 2 ounces (about 55 grams)   *a 1* That is, probably about 13 pints (about 7.3 litres); also in verses 16 and 18   *b 1* That is, about ⅖ ounce (about 11 grams); also in verses 16 and 18   *c 1* That is, probably about 13 quarts (about 15 litres); also in verses 16 and 18   *d 3* The Hebrew word is used for various diseases affecting the skin—not necessarily leprosy; also in verse 8.

he leaned in charge of the gate, and the people trampled him in the gateway, and he died, just as the man of God had foretold when the king came down to his house. ¹⁸It happened as the man of God had said to the king: "About this time tomorrow, a seah of flour will sell for a shekel and two seahs of barley for a shekel at the gate of Samaria."

¹⁹The officer had said to the man of God, "Look, even if the LORD should open the floodgates of the heavens, could this happen?" The man of God had replied, "You will see it with your own eyes, but you will not eat any of it!" ²⁰And that is exactly what happened to him, for the people trampled him in the gateway, and he died.

■ The Shunammite's Land Restored

8 Now Elisha had said to the woman whose son he had restored to life, "Go away with your family and stay wherever you can, because the LORD has decreed a famine in the land that will last seven years." ²The woman proceeded to do as the man of God said. She and her family went away and stayed in the land of the Philistines for seven years.

³At the end of the seven years she came back from the land of the Philistines and went to the king to beg for her house and land. ⁴The king was talking to Gehazi, the servant of the man of God, and had said, "Tell me about all the great things Elisha has done." ⁵Just as Gehazi was telling the king how Elisha had restored the dead to life, the woman whose son Elisha had brought back to life came to beg the king for her house and land.

Gehazi said, "This is the woman, my lord the king, and this is her son whom Elisha restored to life." ⁶The king asked the woman about it, and she told him.

Then he assigned an official to her case and said to him, "Give back everything that belonged to her, including all the income from her land from the day she left the country until now."

■ Hazael Murders Ben-Hadad

⁷Elisha went to Damascus, and Ben-Hadad king of Aram was ill. When the king was told, "The man of God has come all the way up here," ⁸he said to Hazael, "Take a gift with you and go to meet the man of God. Consult the LORD through him; ask him, 'Will I recover from this illness?' "

⁹Hazael went to meet Elisha, taking with him as a gift forty camel-loads of all the finest wares of Damascus. He went in and stood before him, and said, "Your son Ben-Hadad king of Aram has sent me to ask, 'Will I recover from this illness?' "

¹⁰Elisha answered, "Go and say to him, 'You will certainly recover'; but* the LORD has revealed to me that he will in fact die." ¹¹He stared at him with a fixed gaze until Hazael felt ashamed. Then the man of God began to weep.

¹²"Why is my lord weeping?" asked Hazael.

"Because I know the harm you will do to the Israelites," he answered. "You will set fire to their fortified places, kill their young men with the sword, dash their little children to the ground, and rip open their pregnant women."

¹³Hazael said, "How could your servant, a mere dog, accomplish such a feat?"

"The LORD has shown me that you will become king of Aram," answered Elisha.

¹⁴Then Hazael left Elisha and returned to his master. When Ben-Hadad asked, "What did Elisha say to you?" Hazael replied, "He told me that you would certainly recover." ¹⁵But the next day he took a thick cloth, soaked it in water and spread it over the king's face, so that he died. Then Hazael succeeded him as king.

■ Jehoram King of Judah

¹⁶In the fifth year of Joram son of Ahab king of Israel, when Jehoshaphat was king of Judah, Jehoram son of Jehoshaphat began his reign as king of Judah. ¹⁷He was thirty-two years old when he became king, and he reigned in Jerusalem for eight years. ¹⁸He walked in the ways of the kings of Israel, as the house of Ahab had done, for he married a daughter of Ahab. He did evil in the eyes of the LORD. ¹⁹Nevertheless, for the sake of his servant David, the LORD was not willing to destroy Judah. He had promised to maintain a lamp for David and his descendants for ever.

8:16 ■ TWO KINGS, ONE NAME
It's difficult enough to keep 39 rulers straight. When two of them from neighbouring countries have the same name, the plot thickens. Joram, a son of Ahab, ruled Israel at the same time as Jehoram (sometimes spelled Joram also) took over Judah's throne. Both were wicked. Jehoram's marriage to Ahab's daughter ushered in a terrible period in Judah's history. (2 Chronicles 21 gives much more detail on this king.) In addition, both Judah and Israel had a king named Ahaziah.

---

²⁰In the time of Jehoram, Edom rebelled against Judah and set up its own king. ²¹So Jehoram*ᵇ* went to Zair with all his chariots. The Edomites surrounded him and his chariot commanders, but he rose up and broke through by night; his army, however, fled back home. ²²To this day Edom has been in rebellion against Judah. Libnah revolted at the same time.

²³As for the other events of Jehoram's reign, and all he did, are they not written in the book of the annals of the kings of Judah? ²⁴Jehoram rested with his fathers and was buried with them in the City of David. And Ahaziah his son succeeded him as king.

■ Ahaziah King of Judah

²⁵In the twelfth year of Joram son of Ahab king of Israel, Ahaziah son of Jehoram king of Judah began to reign. ²⁶Ahaziah was twenty-two years old when he became king, and he reigned in Jerusalem for one year. His mother's name was Athaliah, a granddaughter of Omri king of Israel. ²⁷He walked in the ways of the house of Ahab and did evil in the eyes of the LORD, as the house of Ahab had done, for he was related by marriage to Ahab's family.

²⁸Ahaziah went with Joram son of Ahab to war against Hazael king of Aram at Ramoth Gilead. The

---

a 10 The Hebrew may also be read *Go and say, 'You will certainly not recover,' for.*   *b 21* Hebrew *Joram,* a variant of *Jehoram;* also in verses 23 and 24

Arameans wounded Joram; 29so King Joram returned to Jezreel to recover from the wounds the Arameans had inflicted on him at Ramoth*c* in his battle with Hazael king of Aram.

8:27 ■ POLITICAL MARRIAGES

Ahab shrewdly arranged marriages to cement alliances with Israel's neighbours. His wife Jezebel, for example, hailed from Phoenicia, which thus became an ally of Israel. Ahab also married off his daughter to the king of Judah, bringing peace to the two warring neighbours. Later, when Jehu revolted and slaughtered all of Ahab's family members, he aroused the ire of those allies and threw Israel's foreign policy into disarray.

Then Ahaziah son of Jehoram king of Judah went down to Jezreel to see Joram son of Ahab, because he had been wounded.

■ Jehu Anointed King of Israel

9 The prophet Elisha summoned a man from the company of the prophets and said to him, "Tuck your cloak into your belt, take this flask of oil with you and go to Ramoth Gilead. 2When you get there, look for Jehu son of Jehoshaphat, the son of Nimshi. Go to him, get him away from his companions and take him into an inner room. 3Then take the flask and pour the oil on his head and declare, 'This is what the LORD says: I anoint you king over Israel.' Then open the door and run; don't delay!"

4So the young man, the prophet, went to Ramoth Gilead. 5When he arrived, he found the army officers sitting together. "I have a message for you, commander," he said.

"For which of us?" asked Jehu.

"For you, commander," he replied.

6Jehu got up and went into the house. Then the prophet poured the oil on Jehu's head and declared, "This is what the LORD, the God of Israel, says: 'I anoint you king over the LORD's people Israel. 7You are to destroy the house of Ahab your master, and I will avenge the blood of my servants the prophets and the blood of all the LORD's servants shed by Jezebel. 8The whole house of Ahab will perish. I will cut off from Ahab every last male in Israel—slave or free. 9I will make the house of Ahab like the house of Jeroboam son of Nebat and like the house of Baasha son of Ahijah. 10As for Jezebel, dogs will devour her on the plot of ground at Jezreel, and no-one will bury her.' " Then he opened the door and ran.

11When Jehu went out to his fellow officers, one of them asked him, "Is everything all right? Why did this madman come to you?"

"You know the man and the sort of things he says," Jehu replied.

12"That's not true!" they said. "Tell us."

Jehu said, "Here is what he told me: 'This is what the LORD says: I anoint you king over Israel.' "

13They hurried and took their cloaks and spread them under him on the bare steps. Then they blew the trumpet and shouted, "Jehu is king!"

■ Jehu Kills Joram and Ahaziah

14So Jehu son of Jehoshaphat, the son of Nimshi, conspired against Joram. (Now Joram and all Israel had been defending Ramoth Gilead against Hazael king of Aram, 15but King Joram*a* had returned to Jezreel to recover from the wounds the Arameans had inflicted on him in the battle with Hazael king of Aram.) Jehu said, "If this is the way you feel, don't let anyone slip out of the city to go and tell the news in Jezreel." 16Then he got into his chariot and rode to Jezreel, because Joram was resting there and Ahaziah king of Judah had gone down to see him.

17When the lookout standing on the tower in Jezreel saw Jehu's troops approaching, he called out, "I see some troops coming."

"Get a horseman," Joram ordered. "Send him to meet them and ask, 'Do you come in peace?' "

18The horseman rode off to meet Jehu and said, "This is what the king says: 'Do you come in peace?' "

"What do you have to do with peace?" Jehu replied. "Fall in behind me."

The lookout reported, "The messenger has reached them, but he isn't coming back."

19So the king sent out a second horseman. When he came to them he said, "This is what the king says: 'Do you come in peace?' "

Jehu replied, "What do you have to do with peace? Fall in behind me."

20The lookout reported, "He has reached them, but he isn't coming back either. The driving is like that of Jehu son of Nimshi—he drives like a madman."

21"Hitch up my chariot," Joram ordered. And when it was hitched up, Joram king of Israel and Ahaziah king of Judah rode out, each in his own chariot, to meet Jehu. They met him at the plot of ground that had belonged to Naboth the Jezreelite. 22When Joram saw Jehu he asked, "Have you come in peace, Jehu?"

"How can there be peace," Jehu replied, "as long as all the idolatry and witchcraft of your mother Jezebel abound?"

23Joram turned about and fled, calling out to Ahaziah, "Treachery, Ahaziah!"

24Then Jehu drew his bow and shot Joram between the shoulders. The arrow pierced his heart and he slumped down in his chariot. 25Jehu said to Bidkar, his chariot officer, "Pick him up and throw him on the field that belonged to Naboth the Jezreelite. Remember how you and I were riding together in chariots behind Ahab his father when the LORD made this prophecy about him: 26'Yesterday I saw the blood of Naboth and the blood of his sons, declares the LORD, and I will surely make you pay for it on this plot of ground, declares the LORD.'*b* Now then, pick him up and throw him on that plot, in accordance with the word of the LORD."

27When Ahaziah king of Judah saw what had happened, he fled up the road to Beth Haggan.*c* Jehu chased him, shouting, "Kill him too!" They wounded him in his chariot on the way up to Gur near Ibleam, but he escaped to Megiddo and died there. 28His servants took him by chariot to Jerusalem and buried him with his fathers in his tomb in the City of David.

---

c 29 Hebrew *Ramah*, a variant of *Ramoth*   *a 15* Hebrew *Jehoram*, a variant of *Joram*; also in verses 17 and 21–24   *b 26* See 1 Kings 21:19.
c 27 Or *fled by way of the garden house*

²⁹(In the eleventh year of Joram son of Ahab, Ahaziah had become king of Judah.)

■ Jezebel Killed

³⁰Then Jehu went to Jezreel. When Jezebel heard about it, she painted her eyes, arranged her hair and looked out of a window. ³¹As Jehu entered the gate, she asked, "Have you come in peace, Zimri, you murderer of your master?"*d*

9:30 ■ DYING JEERS

Jezebel died as she had lived, cutting a memorable figure. She didn't beg for mercy; like a Hollywood vamp she dressed up for the showdown and waited at the window to taunt the man who had come to deal with her. A woman who inspired no loyalty, she was tossed out of the window by her own servants. And as Elijah had prophesied (1 Kings 21:23), the town curs devoured her body.

---

³²He looked up at the window and called out, "Who is on my side? Who?" Two or three eunuchs looked down at him. ³³"Throw her down!" Jehu said. So they threw her down, and some of her blood spattered the wall and the horses as they trampled her underfoot.

³⁴Jehu went in and ate and drank. "Take care of that cursed woman," he said, "and bury her, for she was a king's daughter." ³⁵But when they went out to bury her, they found nothing except her skull, her feet and her hands. ³⁶They went back and told Jehu, who said, "This is the word of the LORD that he spoke through his servant Elijah the Tishbite: On the plot of ground at Jezreel dogs will devour Jezebel's flesh.*e* ³⁷Jezebel's body will be like refuse on the ground in the plot at Jezreel, so that no-one will be able to say, 'This is Jezebel.' "

■ Ahab's Family Killed

10 Now there were in Samaria seventy sons of the house of Ahab. So Jehu wrote letters and sent them to Samaria: to the officials of Jezreel,*a* to the elders and to the guardians of Ahab's children. He said, ²"As soon as this letter reaches you, since your master's sons are with you and you have chariots and horses, a fortified city and weapons, ³choose the best and most worthy of your master's sons and set him on his father's throne. Then fight for your master's house."

⁴But they were terrified and said, "If two kings could not resist him, how can we?"

⁵So the palace administrator, the city governor, the elders and the guardians sent this message to Jehu: "We are your servants and we will do anything you say. We will not appoint anyone as king; you do whatever you think best."

⁶Then Jehu wrote them a second letter, saying, "If you are on my side and will obey me, take the heads of your master's sons and come to me in Jezreel by this time tomorrow."

Now the royal princes, seventy of them, were with the leading men of the city, who were bringing

them up. ⁷When the letter arrived, these men took the princes and slaughtered all seventy of them. They put their heads in baskets and sent them to Jehu in Jezreel. ⁸When the messenger arrived, he told Jehu, "They have brought the heads of the princes."

Then Jehu ordered, "Put them in two piles at the entrance of the city gate until morning."

⁹The next morning Jehu went out. He stood before all the people and said, "You are innocent. It was I who conspired against my master and killed him, but who killed all these? ¹⁰Know then, that not a word the LORD has spoken against the house of Ahab will fail. The LORD has done what he promised through his servant Elijah." ¹¹So Jehu killed everyone in Jezreel who remained of the house of Ahab, as well as all his chief men, his close friends and his priests, leaving him no survivor.

¹²Jehu then set out and went towards Samaria. At Beth Eked of the Shepherds, ¹³he met some relatives of Ahaziah king of Judah and asked, "Who are you?"

They said, "We are relatives of Ahaziah, and we have come down to greet the families of the king and of the queen mother."

¹⁴"Take them alive!" he ordered. So they took them alive and slaughtered them by the well of Beth Eked—forty-two men. He left no survivor.

10:14 ■ JEHU'S SLAUGHTERS

Jehu's bold attacks against the princes of Judah had serious consequences. To protect Israel against revenge from Judah and its friends, Jehu had to pay Assyria tribute. In fact, he is the only king of Israel whose picture has survived. A carving on an archaeological relic, the Black Obelisk, shows him paying tribute to Assyria. Although God had chosen Jehu to purge Israel, the Bible makes clear that his violence went far beyond his original assignment. God himself condemns Jehu in Hosea 1:4.

---

¹⁵After he left there, he came upon Jehonadab son of Recab, who was on his way to meet him. Jehu greeted him and said, "Are you in accord with me, as I am with you?"

"I am," Jehonadab answered.

"If so," said Jehu, "give me your hand." So he did, and Jehu helped him up into the chariot. ¹⁶Jehu said, "Come with me and see my zeal for the LORD." Then he made him ride in his chariot.

¹⁷When Jehu came to Samaria, he killed all who were left there of Ahab's family; he destroyed them, according to the word of the LORD spoken to Elijah.

■ Ministers of Baal Killed

¹⁸Then Jehu brought all the people together and said to them, "Ahab served Baal a little; Jehu will serve him much. ¹⁹Now summon all the prophets of Baal, all his ministers and all his priests. See that no-one is missing, because I am going to hold a great sacrifice for Baal. Anyone who fails to come will no longer live." But Jehu was acting deceptively in order to destroy the ministers of Baal.

---

d 31 Or "Did Zimri have peace, who murdered his master?"   *e 36 See 1 Kings 21:23.*   *a 1 Hebrew; some Septuagint manuscripts and Vulgate of the city*

20Jehu said, "Call an assembly in honour of Baal." So they proclaimed it. 21Then he sent word throughout Israel, and all the ministers of Baal came; not one stayed away. They crowded into the temple of Baal until it was full from one end to the other. 22And Jehu said to the keeper of the wardrobe, "Bring robes for all the ministers of Baal." So he brought out robes for them.

23Then Jehu and Jehonadab son of Recab went into the temple of Baal. Jehu said to the ministers of Baal, "Look around and see that no servants of the LORD are here with you—only ministers of Baal." 24So they went in to make sacrifices and burnt offerings. Now Jehu had posted eighty men outside with this warning: "If one of you lets any of the men I am placing in your hands escape, it will be your life for his life."

25As soon as Jehu had finished making the burnt offering, he ordered the guards and officers: "Go in and kill them; let no-one escape." So they cut them down with the sword. The guards and officers threw the bodies out and then entered the inner shrine of the temple of Baal. 26They brought the sacred stone out of the temple of Baal and burned it. 27They demolished the sacred stone of Baal and tore down the temple of Baal, and people have used it for a latrine to this day.

28So Jehu destroyed Baal worship in Israel. 29However, he did not turn away from the sins of Jeroboam son of Nebat, which he had caused Israel to commit—the worship of the golden calves at Bethel and Dan.

30The LORD said to Jehu, "Because you have done well in accomplishing what is right in my eyes and have done to the house of Ahab all I had in mind to do, your descendants will sit on the throne of Israel to the fourth generation." 31Yet Jehu was not careful to keep the law of the LORD, the God of Israel, with all his heart. He did not turn away from the sins of Jeroboam, which he had caused Israel to commit.

32In those days the LORD began to reduce the size of Israel. Hazael overpowered the Israelites throughout their territory 33east of the Jordan in all the land of Gilead (the region of Gad, Reuben and Manasseh), from Aroer by the Arnon Gorge through Gilead to Bashan.

34As for the other events of Jehu's reign, all he did, and all his achievements, are they not written in the book of the annals of the kings of Israel? 35Jehu rested with his fathers and was buried in Samaria. And Jehoahaz his son succeeded him as king. 36The time that Jehu reigned over Israel in Samaria was twenty-eight years.

■ Athaliah and Joash

11 When Athaliah the mother of Ahaziah saw that her son was dead, she proceeded to destroy the whole royal family. 2But Jehosheba, the daughter of King Jehoram*a* and sister of Ahaziah, took Joash son of Ahaziah and stole him away from among the royal princes, who were about to be murdered. She put him and his nurse in a bedroom to hide him from Athaliah; so he was not killed. 3He remained hidden with his nurse at the temple of the LORD for six years while Athaliah ruled the land.

4In the seventh year Jehoiada sent for the commanders of units of a hundred, the Carites and the guards and had them brought to him at the temple of the LORD. He made a covenant with them and put them under oath at the temple of the LORD. Then he showed them the king's son. 5He commanded them, saying, "This is what you are to do: You who are in the three companies that are going on duty on the Sabbath—a third of you guarding the royal palace, 6a third at the Sur Gate, and a third at the gate behind the guard, who take turns guarding the temple—7and you who are in the other two companies that normally go off Sabbath duty are all to guard the temple for the king. 8Station yourselves round the king, each man with his weapon in his hand. Anyone who approaches your ranks*b* must be put to death. Stay close to the king wherever he goes."

11:2 ■ PRESERVING THE ROYAL LINE
Queen Athaliah came within one baby of wiping out the royal line descending from King David. The prophets predicted that Jesus the Messiah would come from David's line, so in a sense the entire future of God's plan rested with the family's success in hiding Joash and returning him to the throne.

9The commanders of units of a hundred did just as Jehoiada the priest ordered. Each one took his men—those who were going on duty on the Sabbath and those who were going off duty—and came to Jehoiada the priest. 10Then he gave the commanders the spears and shields that had belonged to King David and that were in the temple of the LORD. 11The guards, each with his weapon in his hand, stationed themselves round the king—near the altar and the temple, from the south side to the north side of the temple.

12Jehoiada brought out the king's son and put the crown on him; he presented him with a copy of the covenant and proclaimed him king. They anointed him, and the people clapped their hands and shouted, "Long live the king!"

13When Athaliah heard the noise made by the guards and the people, she went to the people at the temple of the LORD. 14She looked and there was the king, standing by the pillar, as the custom was. The officers and the trumpeters were beside the king, and all the people of the land were rejoicing and blowing trumpets. Then Athaliah tore her robes and called out, "Treason! Treason!"

15Jehoiada the priest ordered the commanders of units of a hundred, who were in charge of the troops: "Bring her out between the ranks*c* and put to the sword anyone who follows her." For the priest had said, "She must not be put to death in the temple of the LORD." 16So they seized her as she reached the place where the horses enter the palace grounds, and there she was put to death.

17Jehoiada then made a covenant between the LORD and the king and people that they would be the LORD's people. He also made a covenant between the king and the people. 18All the people of the land

a 2 Hebrew Joram, a variant of Jehoram   *b 8 Or approaches the precincts*   *c 15 Or out from the precincts* went to the temple of Baal and tore it down. They smashed the altars and idols to pieces and killed Mattan the priest of Baal in front of the altars.

Then Jehoiada the priest posted guards at the temple of the LORD. [19]He took with him the commanders of hundreds, the Carites, the guards and all the people of the land, and together they brought the king down from the temple of the LORD and went into the palace, entering by way of the gate of the guards. The king then took his place on the royal throne, [20]and all the people of the land rejoiced. And the city was quiet, because Athaliah had been slain with the sword at the palace.

[21]Joash[d] was seven years old when he began his reign.

■ Joash Repairs the Temple

12 In the seventh year of Jehu, Joash[a] became king, and he reigned in Jerusalem for forty years. His mother's name was Zibiah; she was from Beersheba. [2]Joash did what was right in the eyes of the LORD all the years Jehoiada the priest instructed him. [3]The high places, however, were not removed; the people continued to offer sacrifices and burn incense there.

[4]Joash said to the priests, "Collect all the money that is brought as sacred offerings to the temple of the LORD—the money collected in the census, the money received from personal vows and the money brought voluntarily to the temple. [5]Let every priest receive the money from one of the treasurers, and let it be used to repair whatever damage is found in the temple."

[6]But by the twenty-third year of King Joash the priests still had not repaired the temple. [7]Therefore King Joash summoned Jehoiada the priest and the other priests and asked them, "Why aren't you repairing the damage done to the temple? Take no more money from your treasurers, but hand it over for repairing the temple." [8]The priests agreed that they would not collect any more money from the people and that they would not repair the temple themselves.

[9]Jehoiada the priest took a chest and bored a hole in its lid. He placed it beside the altar, on the right side as one enters the temple of the LORD. The priests who guarded the entrance put into the chest all the money that was brought to the temple of the LORD. [10]Whenever they saw that there was a large amount of money in the chest, the royal secretary and the high priest came, counted the money that had been brought into the temple of the LORD and put it into bags. [11]When the amount had been determined, they gave the money to the men appointed to supervise the work on the temple. With it they paid those who worked on the temple of the LORD—the carpenters and builders, [12]the masons and stonecutters. They purchased timber and dressed stone for the repair of the temple of the LORD, and met all the other expenses of restoring the temple.

[13]The money brought into the temple was not spent for making silver basins, wick trimmers, sprinkling bowls, trumpets or any other articles of gold or silver for the temple of the LORD; [14]it was paid to the workmen, who used it to repair the temple. [15]They did not require an accounting from those to whom they gave the money to pay the workers, because they acted with complete honesty. [16]The money from the guilt offerings and sin offerings was not brought into the temple of the LORD; it belonged to the priests.

[17]About this time Hazael king of Aram went up and attacked Gath and captured it. Then he turned to attack Jerusalem. [18]But Joash king of Judah took all the sacred objects dedicated by his fathers—Jehoshaphat, Jehoram and Ahaziah, the kings of Judah—and the gifts he himself had dedicated and all the gold found in the treasuries of the temple of the LORD and of the royal palace, and he sent them to Hazael king of Aram, who then withdrew from Jerusalem.

[19]As for the other events of the reign of Joash, and all he did, are they not written in the book of the annals of the kings of Judah? [20]His officials conspired against him and assassinated him at Beth Millo, on the road down to Silla. [21]The officials who murdered him were Jozabad son of Shimeath and Jehozabad son of Shomer. He died and was buried with his fathers in the City of David. And Amaziah his son succeeded him as king.

■ Jehoahaz King of Israel

13 In the twenty-third year of Joash son of Ahaziah king of Judah, Jehoahaz son of Jehu became king of Israel in Samaria, and he reigned for seventeen years. [2]He did evil in the eyes of the LORD by following the sins of Jeroboam son of Nebat, which he had caused Israel to commit, and he did not turn away from them. [3]So the LORD's anger burned against Israel, and for a long time he kept them under the power of Hazael king of Aram and Ben-Hadad his son.

[4]Then Jehoahaz sought the LORD's favour, and the LORD listened to him, for he saw how severely the king of Aram was oppressing Israel. [5]The LORD provided a deliverer for Israel, and they escaped from the power of Aram. So the Israelites lived in their own homes as they had before. [6]But they did not turn away from the sins of the house of Jeroboam, which he had caused Israel to commit; they continued in them. Also, the Asherah pole[a] remained standing in Samaria.

13:4 ■ ABOUT TURN

Like so many kings of Israel, Jehoahaz started out doing "evil in the eyes of the LORD". *Unlike* so many kings of Israel, he repented. God, never eager to punish and always willing to relent, accepted his change of heart. Unfortunately, Jehoahaz's repentance didn't rub off. The Israelites continued their idol worship, in direct disobedience of God's command.

[7]Nothing had been left of the army of Jehoahaz except fifty horsemen, ten chariots and ten thousand foot soldiers, for the king of Aram had destroyed the rest and made them like the dust at threshing time.

---

*d21 Hebrew *Jehoash*, a variant of *Joash*   *a1 Hebrew *Jehoash*, a variant of *Joash*; also in verses 2, 4, 6, 7 and 18   *a6 That is, a symbol of the goddess Asherah; here and elsewhere in 2 Kings

[8]As for the other events of the reign of Jehoahaz, all he did and his achievements, are they not written in the book of the annals of the kings of Israel? [9]Jehoahaz rested with his fathers and was buried in Samaria. And Jehoash[b] his son succeeded him as king.

■ Jehoash King of Israel

[10]In the thirty-seventh year of Joash king of Judah, Jehoash son of Jehoahaz became king of Israel in Samaria, and he reigned for sixteen years. [11]He did evil in the eyes of the LORD and did not turn away from any of the sins of Jeroboam son of Nebat, which he had caused Israel to commit; he continued in them. [12]As for the other events of the reign of Jehoash, all he did and his achievements, including his war against Amaziah king of Judah, are they not written in the book of the annals of the kings of Israel? [13]Jehoash rested with his fathers, and Jeroboam succeeded him on the throne. Jehoash was buried in Samaria with the kings of Israel.

[14]Now Elisha was suffering from the illness from which he died. Jehoash king of Israel went down to see him and wept over him. "My father! My father!" he cried. "The chariots and horsemen of Israel!"

[15]Elisha said, "Get a bow and some arrows," and he did so. [16]"Take the bow in your hands," he said to the king of Israel. When he had taken it, Elisha put his hands on the king's hands.

[17]"Open the east window," he said, and he opened it. "Shoot!" Elisha said, and he shot. "The LORD's arrow of victory, the arrow of victory over Aram!" Elisha declared. "You will completely destroy the Arameans at Aphek."

[18]Then he said, "Take the arrows," and the king took them. Elisha told him, "Strike the ground." He struck it three times and stopped. [19]The man of God was angry with him and said, "You should have struck the ground five or six times; then you would have defeated Aram and completely destroyed it. But now you will defeat it only three times."

[20]Elisha died and was buried.

Now Moabite raiders used to enter the country every spring. [21]Once while some Israelites were burying a man, suddenly they saw a band of raiders; so they threw the man's body into Elisha's tomb. When the body touched Elisha's bones, the man came to life and stood up on his feet.

13:20 ■ TROUBLESOME NEIGHBOURS

Moab and Aram (Syria) often make an appearance in the book of Kings. They are small kingdoms much like Judah and Israel. Sometimes they fought against Israel or Judah, and sometimes they joined together in alliances to oppose a larger threat. On the world scene, constant threats came from Egypt and Assyria. Assyria cut a huge swath through history before its empire declined. Later, Babylon became the giant of the region.

---

[22]Hazael king of Aram oppressed Israel throughout the reign of Jehoahaz. [23]But the LORD was gracious to them and had compassion and showed concern for them because of his covenant with Abraham, Isaac and Jacob. To this day he has been unwilling to destroy them or banish them from his presence.

[24]Hazael king of Aram died, and Ben-Hadad his son succeeded him as king. [25]Then Jehoash son of Jehoahaz recaptured from Ben-Hadad son of Hazael the towns he had taken in battle from his father Jehoahaz. Three times Jehoash defeated him, and so he recovered the Israelite towns.

■ Amaziah King of Judah

14 In the second year of Jehoash[a] son of Jehoahaz king of Israel, Amaziah son of Joash king of Judah began to reign. [2]He was twenty-five years old when he became king, and he reigned in Jerusalem for twenty-nine years. His mother's name was Jehoaddin; she was from Jerusalem. [3]He did what was right in the eyes of the LORD, but not as his father David had done. In everything he followed the example of his father Joash. [4]The high places, however, were not removed; the people continued to offer sacrifices and burn incense there.

[5]After the kingdom was firmly in his grasp, he executed the officials who had murdered his father the king. [6]Yet he did not put the sons of the assassins to death, in accordance with what is written in the Book of the Law of Moses where the LORD commanded: "Fathers shall not be put to death for their children, nor children put to death for their fathers; each is to die for his own sins."[b]

[7]He was the one who defeated ten thousand Edomites in the Valley of Salt and captured Sela in battle, calling it Joktheel, the name it has to this day.

[8]Then Amaziah sent messengers to Jehoash son of Jehoahaz, the son of Jehu, king of Israel, with the challenge: "Come, meet me face to face."

[9]But Jehoash king of Israel replied to Amaziah king of Judah: "A thistle in Lebanon sent a message to a cedar in Lebanon, 'Give your daughter to my son in marriage.' Then a wild beast in Lebanon came along and trampled the thistle underfoot. [10]You have indeed defeated Edom and now you are arrogant. Glory in your victory, but stay at home! Why ask for trouble and cause your own downfall and that of Judah also?"

[11]Amaziah, however, would not listen, so Jehoash king of Israel attacked. He and Amaziah king of Judah faced each other at Beth Shemesh in Judah. [12]Judah was routed by Israel, and every man fled to his home. [13]Jehoash king of Israel captured Amaziah king of Judah, the son of Joash, the son of Ahaziah, at Beth Shemesh. Then Jehoash went to Jerusalem and broke down the wall of Jerusalem from the Ephraim Gate to the Corner Gate—a section about six hundred feet long.[c] [14]He took all the gold and silver and all the articles found in the temple of the LORD and in the treasuries of the royal palace. He also took hostages and returned to Samaria.

[15]As for the other events of the reign of Jehoash, what he did and his achievements, including his war against Amaziah king of Judah, are they not written in the book of the annals of the kings of Israel? [16]Jehoash rested with his fathers and was buried

in Samaria with the kings of Israel. And Jeroboam his son succeeded him as king.

[17]Amaziah son of Joash king of Judah lived for fifteen years after the death of Jehoash son of Jehoahaz king of Israel. [18]As for the other events of Amaziah's reign, are they not written in the book of the annals of the kings of Judah?

[19]They conspired against him in Jerusalem, and he fled to Lachish, but they sent men after him to Lachish and killed him there. [20]He was brought back by horse and was buried in Jerusalem with his fathers, in the City of David.

[21]Then all the people of Judah took Azariah,[d] who was sixteen years old, and made him king in place of his father Amaziah. [22]He was the one who rebuilt Elath and restored it to Judah after Amaziah rested with his fathers.

■ Jeroboam II King of Israel

[23]In the fifteenth year of Amaziah son of Joash king of Judah, Jeroboam son of Jehoash king of Israel became king in Samaria, and he reigned for forty-one years. [24]He did evil in the eyes of the LORD and did not turn away from any of the sins of Jeroboam son of Nebat, which he had caused Israel to commit. [25]He was the one who restored the boundaries of Israel from Lebo[e] Hamath to the Sea of the Arabah,[f] in accordance with the word of the LORD, the God of Israel, spoken through his servant Jonah son of Amittai, the prophet from Gath Hepher.

14:23 ■ UNFAIR CREDIT?
Secular historians report that Omri and Jeroboam were the strongest kings of Israel. Under them, the nation gained new heights of power and prestige. But consistently the book of Kings gives little notice to political strength. It judges kings on the basis of spirituality, and thus both Omri and Jeroboam II are dismissed in a few paragraphs.

The wealthy-but-corrupt state of the nation during this time can be seen in the books by Amos and Hosea, both of whom prophesied in the beautiful city of Samaria. (Jonah also lived then — verse 25 — but he prophesied in Nineveh, the capital city of Assyria.) Israel scoffed at these prophets' words of doom, but within 30 years all their dire predictions had come true.

---

[26]The LORD had seen how bitterly everyone in Israel, whether slave or free, was suffering; there was no-one to help them. [27]And since the LORD had not said he would blot out the name of Israel from under heaven, he saved them by the hand of Jeroboam son of Jehoash.

[28]As for the other events of Jeroboam's reign, all he did, and his military achievements, including how he recovered for Israel both Damascus and Hamath, which had belonged to Yaudi,[g] are they not written in the book of the annals of the kings of Israel? [29]Jeroboam rested with his fathers, the kings of Israel. And Zechariah his son succeeded him as king.

■ Azariah King of Judah

15 In the twenty-seventh year of Jeroboam king of Israel, Azariah son of Amaziah king of Judah began to reign. [2]He was sixteen years old when he became king, and he reigned in Jerusalem for fifty-two years. His mother's name was Jecoliah; she was from Jerusalem. [3]He did what was right in the eyes of the LORD, just as his father Amaziah had done. [4]The high places, however, were not removed; the people continued to offer sacrifices and burn incense there.

[5]The LORD afflicted the king with leprosy[a] until the day he died, and he lived in a separate house.[b] Jotham the king's son had charge of the palace and governed the people of the land.

[6]As for the other events of Azariah's reign, and all he did, are they not written in the book of the annals of the kings of Judah? [7]Azariah rested with his fathers and was buried near them in the City of David. And Jotham his son succeeded him as king.

■ Zechariah King of Israel

[8]In the thirty-eighth year of Azariah king of Judah, Zechariah son of Jeroboam became king of Israel in Samaria, and he reigned for six months. [9]He did evil in the eyes of the LORD, as his fathers had done. He did not turn away from the sins of Jeroboam son of Nebat, which he had caused Israel to commit.

[10]Shallum son of Jabesh conspired against Zechariah. He attacked him in front of the people,[c] assassinated him and succeeded him as king. [11]The other events of Zechariah's reign are written in the book of the annals of the kings of Israel. [12]So the word of the LORD spoken to Jehu was fulfilled: "Your descendants will sit on the throne of Israel to the fourth generation."[d]

■ Shallum King of Israel

[13]Shallum son of Jabesh became king in the thirty-ninth year of Uzziah king of Judah, and he reigned in Samaria for one month. [14]Then Menahem son of Gadi went from Tirzah up to Samaria. He attacked Shallum son of Jabesh in Samaria, assassinated him and succeeded him as king.

[15]The other events of Shallum's reign, and the conspiracy he led, are written in the book of the annals of the kings of Israel.

[16]At that time Menahem, starting out from Tirzah, attacked Tiphsah and everyone in the city and its vicinity, because they refused to open their gates. He sacked Tiphsah and ripped open all the pregnant women.

■ Menahem King of Israel

[17]In the thirty-ninth year of Azariah king of Judah, Menahem son of Gadi became king of Israel, and he reigned in Samaria for ten years. [18]He did evil in the eyes of the LORD. During his entire reign he did not turn away from the sins of Jeroboam son of Nebat, which he had caused Israel to commit.

[19]Then Pul[e] king of Assyria invaded the land, and Menahem gave him a thousand talents[f] of silver to gain his support and strengthen his own hold on the kingdom. [20]Menahem exacted this money from

---

[d]21 Also called *Uzziah*   [e]25 Or *from the entrance to*   [f]25 That is, the Dead Sea   [g]28 Or *Judah*   [a]5 The Hebrew word was used for various diseases affecting the skin – not necessarily leprosy.   [b]5 Or *in a house where he was relieved of responsibility*   [c]10 Hebrew; some Septuagint manuscripts *in Ibleam*   [d]12 2 Kings 10:30   [e]19 Also called *Tiglath-Pileser*   [f]19 That is, about 34 tons (about 34 metric tons)

Israel. Every wealthy man had to contribute fifty shekels*g* of silver to be given to the king of Assyria. So the king of Assyria withdrew and stayed in the land no longer.

²¹As for the other events of Menahem's reign, and all he did, are they not written in the book of the annals of the kings of Israel? ²²Menahem rested with his fathers. And Pekahiah his son succeeded him as king.

■ Pekahiah King of Israel

²³In the fiftieth year of Azariah king of Judah, Pekahiah son of Menahem became king of Israel in Samaria, and he reigned for two years. ²⁴Pekahiah did evil in the eyes of the LORD. He did not turn away from the sins of Jeroboam son of Nebat, which he had caused Israel to commit. ²⁵One of his chief officers, Pekah son of Remaliah, conspired against him. Taking fifty men of Gilead with him, he assassinated Pekahiah, along with Argob and Arieh, in the citadel of the royal palace at Samaria. So Pekah killed Pekahiah and succeeded him as king.

²⁶The other events of Pekahiah's reign, and all he did, are written in the book of the annals of the kings of Israel.

■ Pekah King of Israel

²⁷In the fifty-second year of Azariah king of Judah, Pekah son of Remaliah became king of Israel in Samaria, and he reigned for twenty years. ²⁸He did evil in the eyes of the LORD. He did not turn away from the sins of Jeroboam son of Nebat, which he had caused Israel to commit.

²⁹In the time of Pekah king of Israel, Tiglath-Pileser king of Assyria came and took Ijon, Abel Beth Maacah, Janoah, Kedesh and Hazor. He took Gilead and Galilee, including all the land of Naphtali, and deported the people to Assyria. ³⁰Then Hoshea son of Elah conspired against Pekah son of Remaliah. He attacked and assassinated him, and then succeeded him as king in the twentieth year of Jotham son of Uzziah.

³¹As for the other events of Pekah's reign, and all he did, are they not written in the book of the annals of the kings of Israel?

■ Jotham King of Judah

³²In the second year of Pekah son of Remaliah king of Israel, Jotham son of Uzziah king of Judah began to reign. ³³He was twenty-five years old when he became king, and he reigned in Jerusalem for sixteen years. His mother's name was Jerusha daughter of Zadok. ³⁴He did what was right in the eyes of the LORD, just as his father Uzziah had done. ³⁵The high places, however, were not removed; the people continued to offer sacrifices and burn incense there. Jotham rebuilt the Upper Gate of the temple of the LORD.

³⁶As for the other events of Jotham's reign, and what he did, are they not written in the book of the annals of the kings of Judah? ³⁷(In those days the LORD began to send Rezin king of Aram and Pekah son of Remaliah against Judah.) ³⁸Jotham rested with his fathers and was buried with them in the City

of David, the city of his father. And Ahaz his son succeeded him as king.

■ Ahaz King of Judah

16 In the seventeenth year of Pekah son of Remaliah, Ahaz son of Jotham king of Judah began to reign. ²Ahaz was twenty years old when he became king, and he reigned in Jerusalem for sixteen years. Unlike David his father, he did not do what was right in the eyes of the LORD his God. ³He walked in the ways of the kings of Israel and even sacrificed his son in*a* the fire, following the detestable ways of the nations the LORD had driven out before the Israelites. ⁴He offered sacrifices and burned incense at the high places, on the hilltops and under every spreading tree.

16:1 ■ AHAZ'S FATEFUL DECISIONS

King Ahaz figured large in the histories of Israel and Judah. When Israel threatened his kingdom of Judah, he purchased military aid from Assyria. In response, Assyria obliterated Israel and made Judah a virtual puppet. Worse, Ahaz copied the pagan religions of his conquered territories, even to the extent of sacrificing his son in the fire.

⁵Then Rezin king of Aram and Pekah son of Remaliah king of Israel marched up to fight against Jerusalem and besieged Ahaz, but they could not overpower him. ⁶At that time, Rezin king of Aram recovered Elath for Aram by driving out the men of Judah. Edomites then moved into Elath and have lived there to this day.

⁷Ahaz sent messengers to say to Tiglath-Pileser king of Assyria, "I am your servant and vassal. Come up and save me out of the hand of the king of Aram and of the king of Israel who are attacking me." ⁸And Ahaz took the silver and gold found in the temple of the LORD and in the treasuries of the royal palace and sent it as a gift to the king of Assyria. ⁹The king of Assyria complied by attacking Damascus and capturing it. He deported its inhabitants to Kir and put Rezin to death.

¹⁰Then King Ahaz went to Damascus to meet Tiglath-Pileser king of Assyria. He saw an altar in Damascus and sent to Uriah the priest a sketch of the altar, with detailed plans for its construction. ¹¹So Uriah the priest built an altar in accordance with all the plans that King Ahaz had sent from Damascus and finished it before King Ahaz returned. ¹²When the king came back from Damascus and saw the altar, he approached it and presented offerings*b* on it. ¹³He offered up his burnt offering and grain offering, poured out his drink offering, and sprinkled the blood of his fellowship offerings*c* on the altar. ¹⁴The bronze altar that stood before the LORD he brought from the front of the temple — from between the new altar and the temple of the LORD — and put it on the north side of the new altar. ¹⁵King Ahaz then gave these orders to Uriah the priest: "On the large new altar, offer the morning burnt offering and the evening grain offering, the king's burnt offering and his grain offering, and the

g 20 That is, about 1¼ pounds (about 0.6 kilogram)   *a 3* Or *even made his son pass through*   *b 12* Or *and went up*   *c 13* Traditionally *peace offerings* burnt offering of all the people of the land, and their grain offering and their drink offering. Sprinkle on the altar all the blood of the burnt offerings and sacrifices. But I will use the bronze altar for seeking guidance." [16]And Uriah the priest did just as King Ahaz had ordered.

[17]King Ahaz took away the side panels and removed the basins from the movable stands. He removed the Sea from the bronze bulls that supported it and set it on a stone base. [18]He took away the Sabbath canopy[d] that had been built at the temple and removed the royal entrance outside the temple of the LORD, in deference to the king of Assyria.

[19]As for the other events of the reign of Ahaz, and what he did, are they not written in the book of the annals of the kings of Judah? [20]Ahaz rested with his fathers and was buried with them in the City of David. And Hezekiah his son succeeded him as king.

■ Hoshea Last King of Israel

17 In the twelfth year of Ahaz king of Judah, Hoshea son of Elah became king of Israel in Samaria, and he reigned for nine years. [2]He did evil in the eyes of the LORD, but not like the kings of Israel who preceded him.

[3]Shalmaneser king of Assyria came up to attack Hoshea, who had been Shalmaneser's vassal and had paid him tribute. [4]But the king of Assyria discovered that Hoshea was a traitor, for he had sent envoys to So[a] king of Egypt, and he no longer paid tribute to the king of Assyria, as he had done year by year. Therefore Shalmaneser seized him and put him in prison. [5]The king of Assyria invaded the entire land, marched against Samaria and laid siege to it for three years. [6]In the ninth year of Hoshea, the king of Assyria captured Samaria and deported the Israelites to Assyria. He settled them in Halah, in Gozan on the Habor River and in the towns of the Medes.

■ Israel Exiled Because of Sin

[7]All this took place because the Israelites had sinned against the LORD their God, who had brought them up out of Egypt from under the power of Pharaoh king of Egypt. They worshipped other gods [8]and followed the practices of the nations the LORD had driven out before them, as well as the practices that the kings of Israel had introduced. [9]The Israelites secretly did things against the LORD their God that were not right. From watchtower to fortified city they built themselves high places in all their towns. [10]They set up sacred stones and Asherah poles on every high hill and under every spreading tree. [11]At every high place they burned incense, as the nations whom the LORD had driven out before them had done. They did wicked things that provoked the LORD to anger. [12]They worshipped idols, though the LORD had said, "You shall not do this."[b] [13]The LORD warned Israel and Judah through all his prophets and seers: "Turn from your evil ways. Observe my commands and decrees, in accordance with the entire Law that I commanded your fathers to obey and that I delivered to you through my servants the prophets."

[14]But they would not listen and were as stiff-necked as their fathers, who did not trust in the LORD

their God. [15]They rejected his decrees and the covenant he had made with their fathers and the warnings he had given them. They followed worthless idols and themselves became worthless. They imitated the nations around them although the LORD had ordered them, "Do not do as they do," and they did the things the LORD had forbidden them to do.

[16]They forsook all the commands of the LORD their God and made for themselves two idols cast in the shape of calves, and an Asherah pole. They bowed down to all the starry hosts, and they worshipped Baal. [17]They sacrificed their sons and daughters in[c] the fire. They practised divination and sorcery and sold themselves to do evil in the eyes of the LORD, provoking him to anger.

17:17 ■ A HIGHER STANDARD

To the casual eye, it seemed unfair. God let the Assyrians, a much more cruel people, conquer Israel and take the whole nation into exile. Why? Israel was judged by a higher standard, on the basis of the great advantages God had given them. As Jesus would say hundreds of years later, "From the one who has been entrusted with much, much more will be asked" (Luke 12:48).

A hair-raising list of Israel's sins (verses 7–23) shows why they deserved judgment: they adopted their neighbours' fertility religion, even offering their own children as human sacrifices. Assyria lacked Israel's advantages, but they would be judged too – which explains why the powerful nation of Assyria no longer exists.

[18]So the LORD was very angry with Israel and removed them from his presence. Only the tribe of Judah was left, [19]and even Judah did not keep the commands of the LORD their God. They followed the practices Israel had introduced. [20]Therefore the LORD rejected all the people of Israel; he afflicted them and gave them into the hands of plunderers, until he thrust them from his presence.

[21]When he tore Israel away from the house of David, they made Jeroboam son of Nebat their king. Jeroboam enticed Israel away from following the LORD and caused them to commit a great sin. [22]The Israelites persisted in all the sins of Jeroboam and did not turn away from them [23]until the LORD removed them from his presence, as he had warned through all his servants the prophets. So the people of Israel were taken from their homeland into exile in Assyria, and they are still there.

■ Samaria Resettled

[24]The king of Assyria brought people from Babylon, Cuthah, Avva, Hamath and Sepharvaim and settled them in the towns of Samaria to replace the Israelites. They took over Samaria and lived in its towns. [25]When they first lived there, they did not worship the LORD; so he sent lions among them and they killed some of the people. [26]It was reported to the king of Assyria: "The people you deported and resettled in the towns of Samaria do not know what the god of that country requires. He has sent lions

d 18 Or the dais of his throne (see Septuagint)   a 4 Or to Sais, to the; So is possibly an abbreviation for Osorkon.   b 12 Exodus 20:4, 5   c 17 Or They
made their sons and daughters pass through

among them, which are killing them off, because the people do not know what he requires."

27Then the king of Assyria gave this order: "Make one of the priests you took captive from Samaria go back to live there and teach the people what the god of the land requires." 28So one of the priests who had been exiled from Samaria came to live in Bethel and taught them how to worship the LORD.

29Nevertheless, each national group made its own gods in the several towns where they settled, and set them up in the shrines the people of Samaria had made at the high places. 30The men from Babylon made Succoth Benoth, the men from Cuthah made Nergal, and the men from Hamath made Ashima; 31the Avvites made Nibhaz and Tartak, and the Sepharvites burned their children in the fire as sacrifices to Adrammelech and Anammelech, the gods of Sepharvaim. 32They worshipped the LORD, but they also appointed all sorts of their own people to officiate for them as priests in the shrines at the high places. 33They worshipped the LORD, but they also served their own gods in accordance with the customs of the nations from which they had been brought.

34To this day they persist in their former practices. They neither worship the LORD nor adhere to the decrees and ordinances, the laws and commands that the LORD gave the descendants of Jacob, whom he named Israel. 35When the LORD made a covenant with the Israelites, he commanded them: "Do not worship any other gods or bow down to them, serve them or sacrifice to them. 36But the LORD, who brought you up out of Egypt with mighty power and outstretched arm, is the one you must worship. To him you shall bow down and to him offer sacrifices. 37You must always be careful to keep the decrees and ordinances, the laws and commands he wrote for you. Do not worship other gods. 38Do not forget the covenant I have made with you, and do not worship other gods. 39Rather, worship the LORD your God; it is he who will deliver you from the hand of all your enemies." 40They would not listen, however, but persisted in their former practices. 41Even while these people were worshipping the LORD, they were serving their idols. To this day their children and grandchildren continue to do as their fathers did.

■ Hezekiah King of Judah

18 In the third year of Hoshea son of Elah king of Israel, Hezekiah son of Ahaz king of Judah began to reign. 2He was twenty-five years old when he became king, and he reigned in Jerusalem for twenty-nine years. His mother's name was Abijah[a] daughter of Zechariah. 3He did what was right in the eyes of the LORD, just as his father David had done. 4He removed the high places, smashed the sacred stones and cut down the Asherah poles. He broke into pieces the bronze snake Moses had made, for up to that time the Israelites had been burning incense to it. (It was called[b] Nehushtan.[c])

5Hezekiah trusted in the LORD, the God of Israel. There was no-one like him among all the kings of Judah, either before him or after him. 6He held fast to the LORD and did not cease to follow him; he kept the commands the LORD had given Moses. 7And the LORD was with him; he was successful in whatever he undertook. He rebelled against the king of Assyria and did not serve him. 8From watchtower to fortified city, he defeated the Philistines, as far as Gaza and its territory.

9In King Hezekiah's fourth year, which was the seventh year of Hoshea son of Elah king of Israel, Shalmaneser king of Assyria marched against Samaria and laid siege to it. 10At the end of three years the Assyrians took it. So Samaria was captured in Hezekiah's sixth year, which was the ninth year of Hoshea king of Israel. 11The king of Assyria deported Israel to Assyria and settled them in Halah, in Gozan on the Habor River, and in towns of the Medes. 12This happened because they had not obeyed the LORD their God, but had violated his covenant—all that Moses the servant of the LORD commanded. They neither listened to the commands nor carried them out.

13In the fourteenth year of King Hezekiah's reign, Sennacherib king of Assyria attacked all the fortified cities of Judah and captured them. 14So Hezekiah king of Judah sent this message to the king of Assyria at Lachish: "I have done wrong. Withdraw from me, and I will pay whatever you demand of me." The king of Assyria exacted from Hezekiah king of Judah three hundred talents[d] of silver and thirty talents[e] of gold. 15So Hezekiah gave him all the silver that was found in the temple of the LORD and in the treasuries of the royal palace.

16At this time Hezekiah king of Judah stripped off the gold with which he had covered the doors and doorposts of the temple of the LORD, and gave it to the king of Assyria.

■ Sennacherib Threatens Jerusalem

17The king of Assyria sent his supreme commander, his chief officer and his field commander with a large army, from Lachish to King Hezekiah at Jerusalem. They came up to Jerusalem and stopped at the aqueduct of the Upper Pool, on the road to the Washerman's Field. 18They called for the king; and

a2 Hebrew Abi, a variant of Abijah   b4 Or He called it   c4 Nohushtan sounds like the Hebrew for bronze and snake and unclean thing.
d14 That is, about 10 tons (about 10 metric tons)   e14 That is, about 1 ton (about 1 metric ton)

Eliakim son of Hilkiah the palace administrator, Shebna the secretary, and Joah son of Asaph the recorder went out to them.

18:16 ■ KING OF CONTRADICTIONS

Overall, Hezekiah made a good king, trusting in God. But his life contained a mixture of wisdom and folly, vice and virtue. On the good side, Hezekiah "trusted in the LORD" (verse 5), cleansed Judah from idol worship, and won independence from the powerful nations around. When he prayed for healing, he was granted an unprecedented extension of his life (20:1–11).

On the bad side, Hezekiah foolishly tried to bribe the Assyrians with gold stripped from the temple. Later, when representatives from Babylon came (20:13), he boastfully showed them all his treasures. And when the prophet Isaiah warned that Babylon would come back to take those treasures and more, Hezekiah blithely contented himself that there would be "peace and security in my lifetime" (20:19).

¹⁹The field commander said to them, "Tell Hezekiah:

" 'This is what the great king, the king of Assyria, says: On what are you basing this confidence of yours? ²⁰You say you have strategy and military strength—but you speak only empty words. On whom are you depending, that you rebel against me? ²¹Look now, you are depending on Egypt, that splintered reed of a staff, which pierces a man's hand and wounds him if he leans on it! Such is Pharaoh king of Egypt to all who depend on him. ²²And if you say to me, "We are depending on the LORD our God"—isn't he the one whose high places and altars Hezekiah removed, saying to Judah and Jerusalem, "You must worship before this altar in Jerusalem"?

²³" 'Come now, make a bargain with my master, the king of Assyria: I will give you two thousand horses—if you can put riders on them! ²⁴How can you repulse one officer of the least of my master's officials, even though you are depending on Egypt for chariots and horsemen?ƒ ²⁵Furthermore, have I come to attack and destroy this place without word from the LORD? The LORD himself told me to march against this country and destroy it.' "

²⁶Then Eliakim son of Hilkiah, and Shebna and

■ WHY ALL THE FUSS ABOUT IDOLS?
THE STRANGE PRACTICE THAT LED TO A KINGDOM'S FALL

INSIGHT

THEY FOLLOWED WORTHLESS IDOLS AND THEMSELVES BECAME WORTHLESS.
■ 17:15

You cannot read very far into the Old Testament without encountering idols, for idolatry ranks as perhaps the most common topic in the Bible. A nagging question haunts these pages: Why did the Israelites keep deserting the God who had delivered them from Egypt for the sake of carved tree trunks and bronze statues? What was the big attraction?

Idolatry seems especially strange to us in modern times. Today, idols may show up as exotic props in a movie, but does anyone truly believe in them any more? Why do they merit so much attention in the Old Testament?

■ RESPONSES TO IDOLS TODAY

Actually, idols still thrive in such places as Africa and Asia, and their effect on the people there sheds light on Old Testament idolatry. In India, for example, each city and village has its own favourite god—over 1,000 different gods are worshipped. Portable idols stand on street corners of the major cities.

For devout Hindus, idolatry adds a dimension of magic to life. Hindus believe the gods control all events, including such disasters

as monsoons, floods, diseases and traffic accidents. These powerful gods must be kept happy at all costs.

But what pleases a god depends on the god's character, and gods can be fearsome and violent. Some Indians worship idols in the form of a snake; others worship the smallpox goddess. The largest city in India, Calcutta, has adopted the murderous goddess Kali, who wears a garland of gruesome heads around her waist. Devotion to such gods can easily lead to a paralysing fear. If Kali isn't kept happy, her followers believe, she will cruelly punish them.

Other Hindus, less devout, take a different approach. They treat their gods almost as good-luck charms. A taxi driver mounts a tiny statue of a monkey god on the dashboard of his car, occasionally draping it with flowers for decoration. If you ask, he'll say he prays to the god for safety—but you know about the traffic in India, he adds with a laugh.

■ A GOOD-LUCK CHARM OR AN EVIL CULT

Idolatry had similar effects on the ancient Israelites. Some Israelites took the same spirit as the Indian taxi driver: Maybe an idol will help you out, maybe not, but why not play along?

ƒ24 Or charioteers

Joah said to the field commander, "Please speak to your servants in Aramaic, since we understand it. Don't speak to us in Hebrew in the hearing of the people on the wall."

27But the commander replied, "Was it only to your master and you that my master sent me to say these things, and not to the men sitting on the wall — who, like you, will have to eat their own filth and drink their own urine?"

28Then the commander stood and called out in Hebrew: "Hear the word of the great king, the king of Assyria! 29This is what the king says: Do not let Hezekiah deceive you. He cannot deliver you from my hand. 30Do not let Hezekiah persuade you to trust in the LORD when he says, 'The LORD will surely deliver us; this city will not be given into the hand of the king of Assyria.'

31"Do not listen to Hezekiah. This is what the king of Assyria says: Make peace with me and come out to me. Then every one of you will eat from his own vine and fig-tree and drink water from his own cistern, 32until I come and take you to a land like your own, a land of grain and new wine, a land of bread and vineyards, a land of olive trees and honey. Choose life and not death!

"Do not listen to Hezekiah, for he is misleading you when he says, 'The LORD will deliver us.' 33Has the god of any nation ever delivered his land from the hand of the king of Assyria? 34Where are the gods of Hamath and Arpad? Where are the gods of Sepharvaim, Hena and Ivvah? Have they rescued Samaria from my hand? 35Who of all the gods of these countries has been able to save his land from me? How then can the LORD deliver Jerusalem from my hand?"

36But the people remained silent and said nothing in reply, because the king had commanded, "Do not answer him."

37Then Eliakim son of Hilkiah the palace administrator, Shebna the secretary and Joah son of Asaph the recorder went to Hezekiah, with their clothes torn, and told him what the field commander had said.

■ Jerusalem's Deliverance Foretold

19 When King Hezekiah heard this, he tore his clothes and put on sackcloth and went into the temple of the LORD. 2He sent Eliakim the palace administrator, Shebna the secretary and the leading priests, all wearing sackcloth, to the prophet Isaiah son of Amoz. 3They told him, "This is what Hezekiah says: This day is a day of distress and rebuke and disgrace, as when children come to the point of

---

They drifted carelessly from god to god, adopting the religion of whatever group seemed to be having the most success with its agriculture or armies.

No attitude could be further from that demanded by the true God. He had chosen the Israelites as a kingdom of priests, a treasured possession set apart for him. As Lord of the universe, he wanted not a casual faith, but total allegiance. He was not a good-luck charm.

Far too often, however, idols in Israel took on a more sinister form, resembling the evil goddess of Calcutta. Legends about Baal, for example, celebrated his drunkenness and debauchery. Followers worshipped him by having sex in the temple with prostitutes or even by sacrificing a human baby.

Worshipping Baal meant a complete rejection of God's special relationship with the Israelites — a crime very much like adultery, as the prophets often pointed out. Baal worship could not possibly co-exist with the worship of God.

■ WHAT WAS THE APPEAL?

Why did Baal and the other idols prove so appealing to the Israelites? Like peasants gawping at big-city life, the Israelites moved from 40 years of wilderness wanderings into a land of cities and more advanced technology. They had been landless nomads and shepherds. When they settled down to a new occupation of farming, they looked to a Canaanite god, Baal, as a possible means of guaranteeing good crops. In other words, they sought a shortcut through magic.

Similarly, when a mighty army threatened their borders, they smuggled in a few of that army's favourite idols, hedging their bets in case their own religion did not bring them military success. Idols became a phantom source of power, an alternative place to invest faith and hope.

Idolatry made such inroads into Israel and Judah that God had to tear apart both kingdoms in order to root it out. 2 Kings clearly blames idolatry as the chief sin leading to both nations' collapse. History records that the punishment ultimately worked. After the Assyrian and Babylonian invasions, never again did the Israelites dabble in idolatry.

□ LIFE QUESTIONS:

Idolatry need not involve images of wood or stone; it's possible to worship such things as money, another person or fame. What are some "idols" you might be tempted to worship?

birth and there is no strength to deliver them. [4]It may be that the LORD your God will hear all the words of the field commander, whom his master, the king of Assyria, has sent to ridicule the living God, and that he will rebuke him for the words the LORD your God has heard. Therefore pray for the remnant that still survives."

[5]When King Hezekiah's officials came to Isaiah, [6]Isaiah said to them, "Tell your master, 'This is what the LORD says: Do not be afraid of what you have heard—those words with which the underlings of the king of Assyria have blasphemed me. [7]Listen! I am going to put such a spirit in him that when he hears a certain report, he will return to his own country, and there I will have him cut down with the sword.' "

[8]When the field commander heard that the king of Assyria had left Lachish, he withdrew and found the king fighting against Libnah.

[9]Now Sennacherib received a report that Tirhakah, the Cushite[a] king ⌊of Egypt⌋, was marching out to fight against him. So he again sent messengers to Hezekiah with this word: [10]"Say to Hezekiah king of Judah: Do not let the god you depend on deceive you when he says, 'Jerusalem will not be handed over to the king of Assyria.' [11]Surely you have heard what the kings of Assyria have done to all the countries, destroying them completely. And will you be delivered? [12]Did the gods of the nations that were destroyed by my forefathers deliver them: the gods of Gozan, Haran, Rezeph and the people of Eden who were in Tel Assar? [13]Where is the king of Hamath, the king of Arpad, the king of the city of Sepharvaim, or of Hena or Ivvah?"

■ Hezekiah's Prayer

[14]Hezekiah received the letter from the messengers and read it. Then he went up to the temple of the LORD and spread it out before the LORD. [15]And Hezekiah prayed to the LORD: "O LORD, God of Israel, enthroned between the cherubim, you alone are God over all the kingdoms of the earth. You have made heaven and earth. [16]Give ear, O LORD, and hear; open your eyes, O LORD, and see; listen to the words Sennacherib has sent to insult the living God.

[17]"It is true, O LORD, that the Assyrian kings have laid waste these nations and their lands. [18]They have thrown their gods into the fire and destroyed them, for they were not gods but only wood and stone, fashioned by men's hands. [19]Now, O LORD our God, deliver us from his hand, so that all kingdoms on earth may know that you alone, O LORD, are God."

■ Isaiah Prophesies Sennacherib's Fall

[20]Then Isaiah son of Amoz sent a message to Hezekiah: "This is what the LORD, the God of Israel, says: I have heard your prayer concerning Sennacherib king of Assyria. [21]This is the word that the LORD has spoken against him:

" 'The Virgin Daughter of Zion
　despises you and mocks you.
The Daughter of Jerusalem
　tosses her head as you flee.
[22]Who is it you have insulted and blasphemed?

Against whom have you raised your voice
and lifted your eyes in pride?
Against the Holy One of Israel!
[23]By your messengers
　you have heaped insults on the Lord.
And you have said,
　"With my many chariots
I have ascended the heights of the mountains,
　the utmost heights of Lebanon.
I have cut down its tallest cedars,
　the choicest of its pines.
I have reached its remotest parts,
　the finest of its forests.
[24]I have dug wells in foreign lands
　and drunk the water there.
With the soles of my feet
　I have dried up all the streams of Egypt."

[25]" 'Have you not heard?
Long ago I ordained it.
In days of old I planned it;
　now I have brought it to pass,
that you have turned fortified cities
　into piles of stone.
[26]Their people, drained of power,
　are dismayed and put to shame.
They are like plants in the field,
　like tender green shoots,
like grass sprouting on the roof,
　scorched before it grows up.

[27]" 'But I know where you stay
　and when you come and go
　and how you rage against me.
[28]Because you rage against me
　and your insolence has reached my ears,
I will put my hook in your nose
　and my bit in your mouth,
and I will make you return
　by the way you came.'

[29]"This will be the sign for you, O Hezekiah:

This year you will eat what grows by itself,
　and the second year what springs from that.
But in the third year sow and reap,
　plant vineyards and eat their fruit.
[30]Once more a remnant of the house of Judah
　will take root below and bear fruit above.
[31]For out of Jerusalem will come a remnant,
　and out of Mount Zion a band of survivors.

The zeal of the LORD Almighty will accomplish this.

[32]"Therefore this is what the LORD says concerning the king of Assyria:

"He will not enter this city
　or shoot an arrow here.
He will not come before it with shield
　or build a siege ramp against it.
[33]By the way that he came he will return;
　he will not enter this city,
　　　　　　　　declares the LORD.
[34]I will defend this city and save it,
　for my sake and for the sake of David my
　　servant."

[35]That night the angel of the LORD went out and

put to death a hundred and eighty-five thousand men in the Assyrian camp. When the people got up the next morning—there were all the dead bodies! ³⁶So Sennacherib king of Assyria broke camp and withdrew. He returned to Nineveh and stayed there.

19:31 ■ DELIVERANCE FOR JERUSALEM
Jerusalem appeared to be a doomed city during the dark days of Assyria's siege. But two things happened to fulfil this prophecy. First, a great plague struck the Assyrians (verse 35), a plague also recorded by the historian Herodotus. Later, the murder of Assyria's leader brought internal chaos to that country, cancelling out the Assyrian threat. The miraculous deliverance convinced some Israelites that Jerusalem, God's city, was indestructible — a belief that would later be proven false.

---

³⁷One day, while he was worshipping in the temple of his god Nisroch, his sons Adrammelech and Sharezer cut him down with the sword, and they escaped to the land of Ararat. And Esarhaddon his son succeeded him as king.

■ Hezekiah's Illness

20 In those days Hezekiah became ill and was at the point of death. The prophet Isaiah son of Amoz went to him and said, "This is what the LORD says: Put your house in order, because you are going to die; you will not recover."

²Hezekiah turned his face to the wall and prayed to the LORD, ³"Remember, O LORD, how I have walked before you faithfully and with wholehearted devotion and have done what is good in your eyes." And Hezekiah wept bitterly.

⁴Before Isaiah had left the middle court, the word of the LORD came to him: ⁵"Go back and tell Hezekiah, the leader of my people, 'This is what the LORD, the God of your father David, says: I have heard your prayer and seen your tears; I will heal you. On the third day from now you will go up to the temple of the LORD. ⁶I will add fifteen years to your life. And I will deliver you and this city from the hand of the king of Assyria. I will defend this city for my sake and for the sake of my servant David.' "

⁷Then Isaiah said, "Prepare a poultice of figs." They did so and applied it to the boil, and he recovered.

⁸Hezekiah had asked Isaiah, "What will be the sign that the LORD will heal me and that I will go up to the temple of the LORD on the third day from now?"

⁹Isaiah answered, "This is the LORD's sign to you that the LORD will do what he has promised: Shall the shadow go forward ten steps, or shall it go back ten steps?"

¹⁰"It is a simple matter for the shadow to go forward ten steps," said Hezekiah. "Rather, have it go back ten steps."

¹¹Then the prophet Isaiah called upon the LORD, and the LORD made the shadow go back the ten steps it had gone down on the stairway of Ahaz.

■ Envoys From Babylon

¹²At that time Merodach-Baladan son of Baladan king of Babylon sent Hezekiah letters and a gift, because he had heard of Hezekiah's illness. ¹³Hezekiah received the messengers and showed them all that was in his storehouses—the silver, the gold, the spices and the fine oil—his armoury and everything found among his treasures. There was nothing in his palace or in all his kingdom that Hezekiah did not show them.

¹⁴Then Isaiah the prophet went to King Hezekiah and asked, "What did those men say, and where did they come from?"

"From a distant land," Hezekiah replied. "They came from Babylon."

¹⁵The prophet asked, "What did they see in your palace?"

"They saw everything in my palace," Hezekiah said. "There is nothing among my treasures that I did not show them."

¹⁶Then Isaiah said to Hezekiah, "Hear the word of the LORD: ¹⁷The time will surely come when everything in your palace, and all that your fathers have stored up until this day, will be carried off to Babylon. Nothing will be left, says the LORD. ¹⁸And some of your descendants, your own flesh and blood, that will be born to you, will be taken away, and they will become eunuchs in the palace of the king of Babylon."

¹⁹"The word of the LORD you have spoken is good," Hezekiah replied. For he thought, "Will there not be peace and security in my lifetime?"

²⁰As for the other events of Hezekiah's reign, all his achievements and how he made the pool and the tunnel by which he brought water into the city, are they not written in the book of the annals of the kings of Judah? ²¹Hezekiah rested with his fathers. And Manasseh his son succeeded him as king.

20:20 ■ A LIFE-LINE TUNNEL
The tunnel, one of Hezekiah's major accomplishments, can still be seen in modern Jerusalem. In ancient days, Jerusalem had no source of water within its walls, making it vulnerable to an extended siege. Hezekiah undertook a tremendous engineering feat to bring water from a spring to a reservoir inside Jerusalem. In the late 1800s some boys swimming in the pool of Siloam happened upon a carved record, dating from Hezekiah's time, of how the tunnel had been dug. The marks of pickaxes are still clearly visible.

■ Manasseh King of Judah

21 Manasseh was twelve years old when he became king, and he reigned in Jerusalem for fifty-five years. His mother's name was Hephzibah. ²He did evil in the eyes of the LORD, following the detestable practices of the nations the LORD had driven out before the Israelites. ³He rebuilt the high places his father Hezekiah had destroyed; he also erected altars to Baal and made an Asherah pole, as Ahab king of Israel had done. He bowed down to all the starry hosts and worshipped them. ⁴He built altars in the temple of the LORD, of which the LORD had said, "In Jerusalem I will put my Name." ⁵In both courts of the temple of the LORD, he built altars to all the starry hosts. ⁶He sacrificed his own son in*ᵃ* the fire, practised sorcery and divination, and consulted mediums and spiritists. He did much evil in the eyes of the LORD, provoking him to anger.

⁷He took the carved Asherah pole he had made and put it in the temple, of which the LORD had said to David and to his son Solomon, "In this temple and in Jerusalem, which I have chosen out of all the tribes of Israel, I will put my Name for ever. ⁸I will not again make the feet of the Israelites wander from the land I gave their forefathers, if only they will be careful to do everything I commanded them and will keep the whole Law that my servant Moses gave them." ⁹But the people did not listen. Manasseh led them astray, so that they did more evil than the nations the LORD had destroyed before the Israelites.

¹⁰The LORD said through his servants the prophets: ¹¹"Manasseh king of Judah has committed these detestable sins. He has done more evil than the Amorites who preceded him and has led Judah into sin with his idols. ¹²Therefore this is what the LORD, the God of Israel, says: I am going to bring such disaster on Jerusalem and Judah that the ears of everyone who hears of it will tingle. ¹³I will stretch out over Jerusalem the measuring line used against Samaria and the plumb-line used against the house of Ahab. I will wipe out Jerusalem as one wipes out a dish, wiping it and turning it upside-down. ¹⁴I will forsake the remnant of my inheritance and hand them over to their enemies. They will be looted and plundered by all their foes, ¹⁵because they have done evil in my eyes and have provoked me to anger from the day their forefathers came out of Egypt until this day."

¹⁶Moreover, Manasseh also shed so much innocent blood that he filled Jerusalem from end to end—besides the sin that he had caused Judah to commit, so that they did evil in the eyes of the LORD.

¹⁷As for the other events of Manasseh's reign, and all he did, including the sin he committed, are they not written in the book of the annals of the kings of Judah? ¹⁸Manasseh rested with his fathers and was buried in his palace garden, the garden of Uzza. And Amon his son succeeded him as king.

■ Amon King of Judah

¹⁹Amon was twenty-two years old when he became king, and he reigned in Jerusalem for two years. His mother's name was Meshullemeth daughter of Haruz; she was from Jotbah. ²⁰He did evil in the eyes of the LORD, as his father Manasseh had done. ²¹He walked in all the ways of his father; he worshipped the idols his father had worshipped, and bowed down to them. ²²He forsook the LORD, the God of his fathers, and did not walk in the way of the LORD.

²³Amon's officials conspired against him and assassinated the king in his palace. ²⁴Then the people of the land killed all who had plotted against King Amon, and they made Josiah his son king in his place.

²⁵As for the other events of Amon's reign, and what he did, are they not written in the book of the

annals of the kings of Judah? ²⁶He was buried in his grave in the garden of Uzza. And Josiah his son succeeded him as king.

■ The Book of the Law Found

22 Josiah was eight years old when he became king, and he reigned in Jerusalem for thirty-one years. His mother's name was Jedidah daughter of Adaiah; she was from Bozkath. ²He did what was right in the eyes of the LORD and walked in all the ways of his father David, not turning aside to the right or to the left.

³In the eighteenth year of his reign, King Josiah sent the secretary, Shaphan son of Azaliah, the son of Meshullam, to the temple of the LORD. He said: ⁴"Go up to Hilkiah the high priest and make him get ready the money that has been brought into the temple of the LORD, which the doorkeepers have collected from the people. ⁵Make them entrust it to the men appointed to supervise the work on the temple. And make these men pay the workers who repair the temple of the LORD— ⁶the carpenters, the builders and the masons. Also make them purchase timber and dressed stone to repair the temple. ⁷But they need not account for the money entrusted to them, because they are acting faithfully."

⁸Hilkiah the high priest said to Shaphan the secretary, "I have found the Book of the Law in the temple of the LORD." He gave it to Shaphan, who read it. ⁹Then Shaphan the secretary went to the king and reported to him: "Your officials have paid out the money that was in the temple of the LORD and have entrusted it to the workers and supervisors at the temple." ¹⁰Then Shaphan the secretary informed the king, "Hilkiah the priest has given me a book." And Shaphan read from it in the presence of the king.

¹¹When the king heard the words of the Book of the Law, he tore his robes. ¹²He gave these orders to Hilkiah the priest, Ahikam son of Shaphan, Acbor son of Micaiah, Shaphan the secretary and Asaiah the king's attendant: ¹³"Go and enquire of the LORD for me and for the people and for all Judah about what is written in this book that has been found. Great is the LORD's anger that burns against us because our fathers have not obeyed the words of this book; they have not acted in accordance with all that is written there concerning us."

22:11 ■ DRAMATIC DISCOVERY
Most scholars believe that the Book of the Law referred to was Deuteronomy—or at least a portion of that book. The find, confirmed by a prophetess, resulted in the most thoroughgoing religious reform Judah had ever seen.

¹⁴Hilkiah the priest, Ahikam, Acbor, Shaphan and Asaiah went to speak to the prophetess Huldah, who was the wife of Shallum son of Tikvah, the son of Harhas, keeper of the wardrobe. She lived in Jerusalem, in the Second District. ¹⁵She said to them, "This is what the LORD, the God of Israel, says: Tell the man who sent you to me, ¹⁶'This is what the LORD says: I am going to bring

---

ᵃ 6 Or He made his own son pass through

disaster on this place and its people, according to everything written in the book the king of Judah has read. [17]Because they have forsaken me and burned incense to other gods and provoked me to anger by all the idols their hands have made,[a] my anger will burn against this place and will not be quenched.' [18]Tell the king of Judah, who sent you to enquire of the LORD, 'This is what the LORD, the God of Israel, says concerning the words you heard: [19]Because your heart was responsive and you humbled yourself before the LORD when you heard what I have spoken against this place and its people, that they would become accursed and laid waste, and because you tore your robes and wept in my presence, I have heard you, declares the LORD. [20]Therefore I will gather you to your fathers, and you will be buried in peace. Your eyes will not see all the disaster I am going to bring on this place.' "

So they took her answer back to the king.

■ Josiah Renews the Covenant

23 Then the king called together all the elders of Judah and Jerusalem. [2]He went up to the temple of the LORD with the men of Judah, the people of Jerusalem, the priests and the prophets — all the people from the least to the greatest. He read in their hearing all the words of the Book of the Covenant, which had been found in the temple of the LORD. [3]The king stood by the pillar and renewed the covenant in the presence of the LORD — to follow the LORD and keep his commands, regulations and decrees with all his heart and all his soul, thus confirming the words of the covenant written in this book. Then all the people pledged themselves to the covenant.

[4]The king ordered Hilkiah the high priest, the priests next in rank and the doorkeepers to remove from the temple of the LORD all the articles made for Baal and Asherah and all the starry hosts. He burned them outside Jerusalem in the fields of the Kidron Valley and took the ashes to Bethel. [5]He did away with the pagan priests appointed by the kings of Judah to burn incense on the high places of the towns of Judah and on those around Jerusalem — those who burned incense to Baal, to the sun and moon, to the constellations and to all the starry hosts. [6]He took the Asherah pole from the temple of the LORD to the Kidron Valley outside Jerusalem and burned it there. He ground it to powder and scattered the dust over the graves of the common people. [7]He also tore down the quarters of the male shrine-prostitutes, which were in the temple of the LORD and where women did weaving for Asherah.

[8]Josiah brought all the priests from the towns of Judah and desecrated the high places, from Geba to Beersheba, where the priests had burned incense. He broke down the shrines[a] at the gates — at the entrance to the Gate of Joshua, the city governor, which is on the left of the city gate. [9]Although the priests of the high places did not serve at the altar of the LORD in Jerusalem, they ate unleavened bread with their fellow priests.

[10]He desecrated Topheth, which was in the Valley of Ben Hinnom, so no-one could use it to sacrifice his son or daughter in[b] the fire to Molech. [11]He removed from the entrance to the temple of the LORD the horses that the kings of Judah had dedicated to the sun. They were in the court near the room of an official named Nathan-Melech. Josiah then burned the chariots dedicated to the sun.

[12]He pulled down the altars the kings of Judah had erected on the roof near the upper room of Ahaz, and the altars Manasseh had built in the two courts of the temple of the LORD. He removed them from there, smashed them to pieces and threw the rubble into the Kidron Valley. [13]The king also desecrated the high places that were east of Jerusalem on the south of the Hill of Corruption — the ones Solomon king of Israel had built for Ashtoreth the vile goddess of the Sidonians, for Chemosh the vile god of Moab, and for Molech[c] the detestable god of the people of Ammon. [14]Josiah smashed the sacred stones and cut down the Asherah poles and covered the sites with human bones.

[15]Even the altar at Bethel, the high place made by Jeroboam son of Nebat, who had caused Israel to sin — even that altar and high place he demolished. He burned the high place and ground it to powder, and burned the Asherah pole also. [16]Then Josiah looked around, and when he saw the tombs that were there on the hillside, he had the bones removed from them and burned on the altar to defile it, in accordance with the word of the LORD proclaimed by the man of God who foretold these things.

[17]The king asked, "What is that tombstone I see?"

The men of the city said, "It marks the tomb of the man of God who came from Judah and pronounced against the altar of Bethel the very things you have done to it."

[18]"Leave it alone," he said. "Don't let anyone disturb his bones." So they spared his bones and those of the prophet who had come from Samaria.

[19]Just as he had done at Bethel, Josiah removed and defiled all the shrines at the high places that the kings of Israel had built in the towns of Samaria that had provoked the LORD to anger. [20]Josiah slaughtered all the priests of those high places on the altars and burned human bones on them. Then he went back to Jerusalem.

[21]The king gave this order to all the people: "Celebrate the Passover to the LORD your God, as it is written in this Book of the Covenant." [22]Not since the days of the judges who led Israel, nor throughout the days of the kings of Israel and the kings of Judah, had any such Passover been observed. [23]But in the eighteenth year of King Josiah, this Passover was celebrated to the LORD in Jerusalem.

[24]Furthermore, Josiah got rid of the mediums and spiritists, the household gods, the idols and all the other detestable things seen in Judah and Jerusalem. This he did to fulfil the requirements of the law written in the book that Hilkiah the priest had discovered in the temple of the LORD. [25]Neither before nor after Josiah was there a king like him who turned to the LORD as he did — with all his heart and with all his soul and with all his strength, in accordance with all the Law of Moses.

[26]Nevertheless, the LORD did not turn away from the heat of his fierce anger, which burned against

---

a 17 Or by everything they have done   a 8 Or high places   b 10 Or to make his son or daughter pass through   c 13 Hebrew Milcom

Judah because of all that Manasseh had done to provoke him to anger. ²⁷So the LORD said, "I will remove Judah also from my presence as I removed Israel, and I will reject Jerusalem, the city I chose, and this temple, about which I said, 'There shall my Name be.'*d*"

23:26 ■ TOO LITTLE TOO LATE
Josiah became king when he was only eight, and at the age of 26 he led a dramatic reform movement. Yet for all that this wise king accomplished, the Lord still determined to punish Judah, as this verse tells us. Evil had become so deeply ingrained that the best efforts of one good king could not root it out. In fact, as soon as Josiah died, Judah reverted to their previous form.

---

²⁸As for the other events of Josiah's reign, and all he did, are they not written in the book of the annals of the kings of Judah?
²⁹While Josiah was king, Pharaoh Neco king of Egypt went up to the Euphrates River to help the king of Assyria. King Josiah marched out to meet him in battle, but Neco faced him and killed him at Megiddo. ³⁰Josiah's servants brought his body in a chariot from Megiddo to Jerusalem and buried him in his own tomb. And the people of the land took Jehoahaz son of Josiah and anointed him and made him king in place of his father.

■ Jehoahaz King of Judah
³¹Jehoahaz was twenty-three years old when he became king, and he reigned in Jerusalem for three months. His mother's name was Hamutal daughter of Jeremiah; she was from Libnah. ³²He did evil in the eyes of the LORD, just as his fathers had done. ³³Pharaoh Neco put him in chains at Riblah in the land of Hamath*e* so that he might not reign in Jerusalem, and he imposed on Judah a levy of a hundred talents*f* of silver and a talent*g* of gold. ³⁴Pharaoh Neco made Eliakim son of Josiah king in place of his father Josiah and changed Eliakim's name to Jehoiakim. But he took Jehoahaz and carried him off to Egypt, and there he died. ³⁵Jehoiakim paid Pharaoh Neco the silver and gold he demanded. In order to do so, he taxed the land and exacted the silver and gold from the people of the land according to their assessments.

■ Jehoiakim King of Judah
³⁶Jehoiakim was twenty-five years old when he became king, and he reigned in Jerusalem for eleven years. His mother's name was Zebidah daughter of Pedaiah; she was from Rumah. ³⁷And he did evil in the eyes of the LORD, just as his fathers had done.
24 During Jehoiakim's reign, Nebuchadnezzar king of Babylon invaded the land, and Jehoiakim became his vassal for three years. But then he changed his mind and rebelled against Nebuchadnezzar. ²The LORD sent Babylonian,*a* Aramean, Moabite and Ammonite raiders against him. He sent them to destroy Judah, in accordance with the word of the LORD proclaimed by his servants the prophets.

³Surely these things happened to Judah according to the LORD's command, in order to remove them from his presence because of the sins of Manasseh and all he had done, ⁴including the shedding of innocent blood. For he had filled Jerusalem with innocent blood, and the LORD was not willing to forgive.

24:1 ■ JEREMIAH'S INFLUENCE
The last two chapters, which closely parallel material in Jeremiah 52, reveal the influence of that prophet on the book of Kings. Some scholars have concluded that he wrote this historical record.

---

⁵As for the other events of Jehoiakim's reign, and all he did, are they not written in the book of the annals of the kings of Judah? ⁶Jehoiakim rested with his fathers. And Jehoiachin his son succeeded him as king.
⁷The king of Egypt did not march out from his own country again, because the king of Babylon had taken all his territory, from the Wadi of Egypt to the Euphrates River.

■ Jehoiachin King of Judah
⁸Jehoiachin was eighteen years old when he became king, and he reigned in Jerusalem for three months. His mother's name was Nehushta daughter of Elnathan; she was from Jerusalem. ⁹He did evil in the eyes of the LORD, just as his father had done.
¹⁰At that time the officers of Nebuchadnezzar king of Babylon advanced on Jerusalem and laid siege to it, ¹¹and Nebuchadnezzar himself came up to the city while his officers were besieging it. ¹²Jehoiachin king of Judah, his mother, his attendants, his nobles and his officials all surrendered to him.
In the eighth year of the reign of the king of Babylon, he took Jehoiachin prisoner. ¹³As the LORD had declared, Nebuchadnezzar removed all the treasures from the temple of the LORD and from the royal palace, and took away all the gold articles that Solomon king of Israel had made for the temple of the LORD. ¹⁴He carried into exile all Jerusalem: all the officers and fighting men, and all the craftsmen and artisans—a total of ten thousand. Only the poorest people of the land were left.
¹⁵Nebuchadnezzar took Jehoiachin captive to Babylon. He also took from Jerusalem to Babylon the king's mother, his wives, his officials and the leading men of the land. ¹⁶The king of Babylon also deported to Babylon the entire force of seven thousand fighting men, strong and fit for war, and a thousand craftsmen and artisans. ¹⁷He made Mattaniah, Jehoiachin's uncle, king in his place and changed his name to Zedekiah.

■ Zedekiah King of Judah
¹⁸Zedekiah was twenty-one years old when he became king, and he reigned in Jerusalem for eleven years. His mother's name was Hamutal daughter of Jeremiah; she was from Libnah. ¹⁹He did evil in the eyes of the LORD, just as Jehoiakim had done. ²⁰It was because of the LORD's anger that all this happened to

---

d27 1 Kings 8:29   *e33* Hebrew; Septuagint (see also 2 Chron. 36:3) *Neco at Riblah in Hamath removed him*   *f33* That is, about 3½ tons (about
3.4 metric tons)   *g33* That is, about 75 pounds (about 34 kilograms)   *a2* Or *Chaldean*

Jerusalem and Judah, and in the end he thrust them from his presence.

■ The Fall of Jerusalem

Now Zedekiah rebelled against the king of Babylon.

25 So in the ninth year of Zedekiah's reign, on the tenth day of the tenth month, Nebuchadnezzar king of Babylon marched against Jerusalem with his whole army. He encamped outside the city and built siege works all around it. ²The city was kept under siege until the eleventh year of King Zedekiah. ³By the ninth day of the ₍fourth₎[a] month the famine in the city had become so severe that there was no food for the people to eat. ⁴Then the city wall was broken through, and the whole army fled at night through the gate between the two walls near the king's garden, though the Babylonians[b] were surrounding the city. They fled towards the Arabah,[c] ⁵but the Babylonian[d] army pursued the king and overtook him in the plains of Jericho. All his soldiers were separated from him and scattered, ⁶and he was captured. He was taken to the king of Babylon at Riblah, where sentence was pronounced on him. ⁷They killed the sons of Zedekiah before his eyes. Then they put out his eyes, bound him with bronze shackles and took him to Babylon.

⁸On the seventh day of the fifth month, in the nineteenth year of Nebuchadnezzar king of Babylon, Nebuzaradan commander of the imperial guard, an official of the king of Babylon, came to Jerusalem. ⁹He set fire to the temple of the LORD, the royal palace and all the houses of Jerusalem. Every important building he burned down. ¹⁰The whole Babylonian army, under the commander of the imperial guard, broke down the walls around Jerusalem. ¹¹Nebuzaradan the commander of the guard carried into exile the people who remained in the city, along with the rest of the populace and those who had gone over to the king of Babylon. ¹²But the commander left behind some of the poorest people of the land to work the vineyards and fields.

¹³The Babylonians broke up the bronze pillars, the movable stands and the bronze Sea that were at the temple of the LORD and they carried the bronze to Babylon. ¹⁴They also took away the pots, shovels, wick trimmers, dishes and all the bronze articles used in the temple service. ¹⁵The commander of the imperial guard took away the censers and sprinkling bowls — all that were made of pure gold or silver.

¹⁶The bronze from the two pillars, the Sea and the movable stands, which Solomon had made for the temple of the LORD, was more than could be weighed. ¹⁷Each pillar was twenty-seven feet[e] high. The bronze capital on top of one pillar was four and a half feet[f] high and was decorated with a network and pomegranates of bronze all around. The other pillar, with its network, was similar.

¹⁸The commander of the guard took as prisoners Seraiah the chief priest, Zephaniah the priest next in rank and the three doorkeepers. ¹⁹Of those still in the city, he took the officer in charge of the fighting men and five royal advisers. He also took the secretary who was chief officer in charge of conscripting the people of the land and sixty of his men who were found in the city. ²⁰Nebuzaradan the commander took them all and brought them to the king of Babylon at Riblah. ²¹There at Riblah, in the land of Hamath, the king had them executed.

So Judah went into captivity, away from her land.

²²Nebuchadnezzar king of Babylon appointed Gedaliah son of Ahikam, the son of Shaphan, to be over

> **25:24 ■ A KINGDOM DISAPPEARS**
> Judah's final rebellion against mighty Babylon failed, resulting in an 18-month siege and the destruction of Jerusalem. Survivors were taken away in what became known as the "Babylonian captivity", a tragic moment in Jewish history. God spelled out the reasons for this disaster in 2 Kings 21:10–16.

the people he had left behind in Judah. ²³When all the army officers and their men heard that the king of Babylon had appointed Gedaliah as governor, they came to Gedaliah at Mizpah—Ishmael son of Nethaniah, Johanan son of Kareah, Seraiah son of Tanhumeth the Netophathite, Jaazaniah the son of the Maacathite, and their men. ²⁴Gedaliah took an oath to reassure them and their men. "Do not be afraid of the Babylonian officials," he said. "Settle down in the land and serve the king of Babylon, and it will go well with you."

²⁵In the seventh month, however, Ishmael son of Nethaniah, the son of Elishama, who was of royal blood, came with ten men and assassinated Gedaliah and also the men of Judah and the Babylonians who were with him at Mizpah. ²⁶At this, all the people from the least to the greatest, together with the army officers, fled to Egypt for fear of the Babylonians.

■ Jehoiachin Released

²⁷In the thirty-seventh year of the exile of Jehoiachin king of Judah, in the year Evil-Merodach[g] became king of Babylon, he released Jehoiachin from prison on the twenty-seventh day of the twelfth month. ²⁸He spoke kindly to him and gave him a seat of honour higher than those of the other kings who were with him in Babylon. ²⁹So Jehoiachin put aside his prison clothes and for the rest of his life ate regularly at the king's table. ³⁰Day by day the king gave Jehoiachin a regular allowance as long as he lived.

*a*3 See Jer. 52:6.   *b* Or *Chaldeans*; also in verses 13, 25 and 26   *c*4 Or *the Jordan Valley*   *d*5 Or *Chaldean*; also in verses 10 and 24
*e*17 Hebrew *eighteen cubits* (about 8.2 metres)   *f*17 Hebrew *three cubits* (about 1.4 metres)   *g*27 Also called *Amel-Marduk*

1 CHRONICLES

■ A FAMILY RECORD

THESE FACTS REMINDED ISRAELITES OF THEIR PLACE IN GOD'S PLAN

"AND WHO IS LIKE YOUR PEOPLE ISRAEL – THE ONE NATION ON EARTH WHOSE GOD WENT OUT TO REDEEM A PEOPLE FOR HIMSELF?" ■ 17:21

In Victorian times, many British families prized a huge black family Bible. Often the only book in the house, it served for more than reading. It was also the family memory bank. Every important event – a marriage, a birth, a death – was recorded on its flyleaves. The Bible was passed down from generation to generation, and through it, a family kept track of its past.

The book of 1 Chronicles is something like that – a record of Israel's family history, and particularly of David, Israel's greatest king. In fact, at first glance, 1 Chronicles looks like a rehash of David's life as told in 2 Samuel and 1 Kings. Some of the most dramatic episodes in David's life – his clash with Goliath, his sin with Bathsheba – don't make it into this account. But David's organisation of the temple is told in great detail, and long lists and genealogies fill over half the book.

Because of that, few people read 1 Chronicles. Most of us are more interested in personalities than in institutions and genealogies.

■ DAVID'S LASTING IMPACT

First Chronicles, however, is far more interested in David's lasting accomplishments than in his ups

and downs as an individual. The nation he led was more than a collection of inspired individuals. It was founded on God's unshakeable promises to the children of Abraham. He had promised to be with them. He had promised to provide leadership. He had promised to make them a blessing to the world. These promises took shape in enduring institutions – the temple and the monarchy, most notably.

■ WHY A LIST OF NAMES?

The first nine chapters of 1 Chronicles trace the genealogy of Israel back to Adam. The author brings together more family records than you'll find anywhere else in the Bible. These records helped the Israelites remember their position as members in God's chosen family. God had given them unique ways to follow and worship him. First Chronicles reminded the Israelites – as it reminds us – of how different their family was meant to be.

■ HOW TO READ 1 CHRONICLES

Few will enjoy reading 1 Chronicles' many lists and genealogies straight through. You should approach them more like a puzzle. Don't get lost in the hundreds of names. Instead, try to understand how the different parts of 1 Chronicles fit together. For each section ask, "Why was this included? What did it mean to the original audience – to the Israelites who had returned from exile in Babylon? How did it encourage them as they made a new beginning?"

First Chronicles divides cleanly into two parts. The first nine chapters are mainly lists of names. In these, the Israelites read their family tree and discovered their heritage. David's story, chapters 10–29, focuses on the legacy he left behind for future generations – especially the temple. David, a founding father of Israel, transformed the nation in a way that lasted hundreds of years.

■ 3-TRACK READING PLAN

For an explanation and complete listing of the 3-track reading plan, turn to page x.

■ TRACK 1:
Two-Week Courses on the
Bible
See page x for information on
these courses.

■ TRACK 2:
An Overview of 1 Chronicles in
1 Day
☐ Day 1. Read the
Introduction to 1 Chronicles

and chapter 17, which
describes God's promise to
David and David's prayerful
response.
Now turn to page xi for your
next Track 2 reading project.

■ TRACK 3:
All of 1 Chronicles in 17 Days
You should only skim chapters
1–9 and 23–27, which contain

lists and genealogies. After
you have skimmed and read
1 Chronicles, turn to pages
xii–xiii for your next Track 3
reading project.

☐ 1–9 ☐ 10 ☐ 11 ☐ 12
☐ 13 ☐ 14 ☐ 15 ☐ 16
☐ 17 ☐ 18 ☐ 19 ☐ 20
☐ 21 ☐ 22 ☐ 23–27
☐ 28 ☐ 29

■ Historical Records From Adam to Abraham

☐ To Noah's Sons

1 Adam, Seth, Enosh, ²Kenan, Mahalalel, Jared, ³Enoch, Methuselah, Lamech, Noah.

⁴The sons of Noah:ᵃ
Shem, Ham and Japheth.

☐ The Japhethites
⁵The sonsᵇ of Japheth:
Gomer, Magog, Madai, Javan, Tubal, Meshech and Tiras.
⁶The sons of Gomer:
Ashkenaz, Riphathᶜ and Togarmah.
⁷The sons of Javan:
Elishah, Tarshish, the Kittim and the Rodanim.

☐ The Hamites
⁸The sons of Ham:
Cush, Mizraim,ᵈ Put and Canaan.
⁹The sons of Cush:
Seba, Havilah, Sabta, Raamah and Sabteca.
The sons of Raamah:
Sheba and Dedan.
¹⁰Cush was the fatherᵉ of
Nimrod, who grew to be a mighty warrior on earth.
¹¹Mizraim was the father of
the Ludites, Anamites, Lehabites, Naphtuhites, ¹²Pathrusites, Casluhites (from whom the Philistines came) and Caphtorites.
¹³Canaan was the father of
Sidon his firstborn,ᶠ and of the Hittites, ¹⁴Jebusites, Amorites, Girgashites, ¹⁵Hivites, Arkites, Sinites, ¹⁶Arvadites, Zemarites and Hamathites.

☐ The Semites
¹⁷The sons of Shem:
Elam, Asshur, Arphaxad, Lud and Aram.
The sons of Aram:ᵍ
Uz, Hul, Gether and Meshech.

¹⁸Arphaxad was the father of Shelah, and Shelah the father of Eber.
¹⁹Two sons were born to Eber:
One was named Peleg,ᵇ because in his time the earth was divided; his brother was named Joktan.
²⁰Joktan was the father of
Almodad, Sheleph, Hazarmaveth, Jerah, ²¹Hadoram, Uzal, Diklah, ²²Obal,ⁱ Abimael, Sheba, ²³Ophir, Havilah and Jobab. All these were sons of Joktan.

²⁴Shem, Arphaxad,ʲ Shelah,
²⁵Eber, Peleg, Reu,
²⁶Serug, Nahor, Terah
²⁷and Abram (that is, Abraham).

■ The Family of Abraham
²⁸The sons of Abraham:
Isaac and Ishmael.

1:28 ■ COMPRESSED HISTORY
The books of 1 and 2 Chronicles, focusing on the kings of the recent past, do not pretend to give a complete history of the Israelites. But by recording individuals' names all the way back to Adam, the books point out that God has kept his hand on this line of people from the very beginning. The Gospels complete the list begun here: Matthew traces Jesus' lineage back to Abraham, and Luke traces it back to Adam.

☐ Descendants of Hagar
²⁹These were their descendants:
Nebaioth the firstborn of Ishmael, Kedar, Adbeel, Mibsam, ³⁰Mishma, Dumah, Massa, Hadad, Tema, ³¹Jetur, Naphish and Kedemah. These were the sons of Ishmael.

☐ Descendants of Keturah
³²The sons born to Keturah, Abraham's concubine:

ᵃ4 Septuagint; Hebrew does not have *The sons of Noah:*   ᵇ5 *Sons* may mean *descendants* or *successors* or *nations*; also in verses 6–10, 17 and 20.   ᶜ6 Many Hebrew manuscripts and Vulgate (see also Septuagint and Gen. 10:3); most Hebrew manuscripts *Diphath*   ᵈ8 That is, Egypt; also in verse 11   ᵉ10 *Father* may mean *ancestor* or *predecessor* or *founder*; also in verses 11, 13, 18 and 20.   ᶠ13 Or *of the Sidonians, the foremost*   ᵍ17 One Hebrew manuscript and some Septuagint manuscripts (see also Gen. 10:23); most Hebrew manuscripts do not have this line.   ᵇ19 *Peleg* means *division*.   ⁱ22 Some Hebrew manuscripts and Syriac (see also Gen. 10:28); most Hebrew manuscripts *Ebal*   ʲ24 Hebrew; some Septuagint manuscripts *Arphaxad, Cainan* (see also note at Gen. 11:10)

Zimran, Jokshan, Medan, Midian, Ishbak and Shuah.
The sons of Jokshan:
Sheba and Dedan.
33The sons of Midian:
Ephah, Epher, Hanoch, Abida and Eldaah.
All these were descendants of Keturah.

□ Descendants of Sarah
34Abraham was the father of Isaac.
The sons of Isaac:
Esau and Israel.

■ Esau's Sons
35The sons of Esau:
Eliphaz, Reuel, Jeush, Jalam and Korah.
36The sons of Eliphaz:
Teman, Omar, Zepho,*k* Gatam and Kenaz;
by Timna: Amalek.*l*
37The sons of Reuel:
Nahath, Zerah, Shammah and Mizzah.

□ The People of Seir in Edom
38The sons of Seir:
Lotan, Shobal, Zibeon, Anah, Dishon, Ezer and Dishan.
39The sons of Lotan:
Hori and Homam. Timna was Lotan's sister.
40The sons of Shobal:
Alvan,*m* Manahath, Ebal, Shepho and Onam.
The sons of Zibeon:
Aiah and Anah.
41The son of Anah:
Dishon.
The sons of Dishon:
Hemdan,*n* Eshban, Ithran and Keran.
42The sons of Ezer:
Bilhan, Zaavan and Akan.*o*
The sons of Dishan:*p*
Uz and Aran.

□ The Rulers of Edom
43These were the kings who reigned in Edom before any Israelite king reigned:*q*
Bela son of Beor, whose city was named Dinhabah.
44When Bela died, Jobab son of Zerah from Bozrah succeeded him as king.
45When Jobab died, Husham from the land of the Temanites succeeded him as king.
46When Husham died, Hadad son of Bedad, who defeated Midian in the country of Moab, succeeded him as king. His city was named Avith.
47When Hadad died, Samlah from Masrekah succeeded him as king.
48When Samlah died, Shaul from Rehoboth on the river*r* succeeded him as king.
49When Shaul died, Baal-Hanan son of Acbor succeeded him as king.
50When Baal-Hanan died, Hadad succeeded him

as king. His city was named Pau,*s* and his wife's name was Mehetabel daughter of Matred, the daughter of Me-Zahab. 51Hadad also died.

The chiefs of Edom were:
Timna, Alvah, Jetheth, 52Oholibamah, Elah, Pinon, 53Kenaz, Teman, Mibzar, 54Magdiel and Iram. These were the chiefs of Edom.

■ Israel's Sons
2 These were the sons of Israel:
Reuben, Simeon, Levi, Judah, Issachar, Zebulun, 2Dan, Joseph, Benjamin, Naphtali, Gad and Asher.

■ Judah

□ To Hezron's Sons
3The sons of Judah:
Er, Onan and Shelah. These three were born to him by a Canaanite woman, the daughter of Shua. Er, Judah's firstborn, was wicked in the LORD's sight; so the LORD put him to death. 4Tamar, Judah's daughter-in-law, bore him Perez and Zerah. Judah had five sons in all.

5The sons of Perez:
Hezron and Hamul.
6The sons of Zerah:
Zimri, Ethan, Heman, Calcol and Darda*a* — five in all.
7The son of Carmi:
Achar,*b* who brought trouble on Israel by violating the ban on taking devoted things.*c*
8The son of Ethan:
Azariah.
9The sons born to Hezron were:
Jerahmeel, Ram and Caleb.*d*

□ From Ram Son of Hezron
10Ram was the father of
Amminadab, and Amminadab the father of Nahshon, the leader of the people of Judah. 11Nahshon was the father of Salmon,*e* Salmon the father of Boaz, 12Boaz the father of Obed and Obed the father of Jesse.
13Jesse was the father of
Eliab his firstborn; the second son was Abinadab, the third Shimea, 14the fourth Nethanel, the fifth Raddai, 15the sixth Ozem and the seventh David. 16Their sisters were Zeruiah and Abigail. Zeruiah's three sons were Abishai, Joab and Asahel. 17Abigail was the mother of Amasa, whose father was Jether the Ishmaelite.

□ Caleb Son of Hezron
18Caleb son of Hezron had children by his wife Azubah (and by Jerioth). These were her sons: Jesher, Shobab and Ardon. 19When

k 36 Many Hebrew manuscripts, some Septuagint manuscripts and Syriac (see also Gen. 36:11); most Hebrew manuscripts *Zephi*　*l 36* Some Septuagint manuscripts (see also Gen. 36:12); Hebrew *Gatam, Kenaz, Timna and Amalek*　*m 40* Many Hebrew manuscripts and some Septuagint manuscripts (see also Gen. 36:23); most Hebrew manuscripts *Alian*　*n 41* Many Hebrew manuscripts and some Septuagint manuscripts (see also Gen. 36:26); most Hebrew manuscripts *Hamran*　*o 42* Many Hebrew and Septuagint manuscripts (see also Gen. 36:27); most Hebrew manuscripts *Zaavan, Jaakan*　*p 42* Hebrew *Dishon*, a variant of *Dishan*　*q 43* Or *before an Israelite king reigned over them*　*r 48* Possibly the Euphrates　*s 50* Many Hebrew manuscripts, some Septuagint manuscripts, Vulgate and Syriac (see also Gen. 36:39); most Hebrew manuscripts *Pai*　*a 6* Many Hebrew manuscripts, some Septuagint manuscripts and Syriac (see also 1 Kings 4:31); most Hebrew manuscripts *Dara*　*b 7* *Achar* means *trouble*; *Achar* is called *Achan* in Joshua. *c 7* The Hebrew term refers to the irrevocable giving over of things or persons to the LORD, often by totally destroying them.　*d 9* Hebrew *Kelubai*, a variant of *Caleb*　*e 11* Septuagint (see also Ruth 4:21); Hebrew *Salma*

Azubah died, Caleb married Ephrath, who bore him Hur. [20]Hur was the father of Uri, and Uri the father of Bezalel.

[21]Later, Hezron lay with the daughter of Makir the father of Gilead (he had married her when he was sixty years old), and she bore him Segub. [22]Segub was the father of Jair, who controlled twenty-three towns in Gilead. [23](But Geshur and Aram captured Havvoth Jair,[f] as well as Kenath with its surrounding settlements—sixty towns.) All these were descendants of Makir the father of Gilead.

[24]After Hezron died in Caleb Ephrathah, Abijah the wife of Hezron bore him Ashhur the father[g] of Tekoa.

□ Jerahmeel Son of Hezron

[25]The sons of Jerahmeel the firstborn of Hezron:
Ram his firstborn, Bunah, Oren, Ozem and[b] Ahijah. [26]Jerahmeel had another wife, whose name was Atarah; she was the mother of Onam.

[27]The sons of Ram the firstborn of Jerahmeel:
Maaz, Jamin and Eker.

[28]The sons of Onam:
Shammai and Jada.
The sons of Shammai:
Nadab and Abishur.

[29]Abishur's wife was named Abihail, who bore him Ahban and Molid.

[30]The sons of Nadab:
Seled and Appaim. Seled died without children.

[31]The son of Appaim:
Ishi, who was the father of Sheshan.
Sheshan was the father of Ahlai.

[32]The sons of Jada, Shammai's brother:
Jether and Jonathan. Jether died without children.

[33]The sons of Jonathan:
Peleth and Zaza.
These were the descendants of Jerahmeel.

[34]Sheshan had no sons—only daughters.
He had an Egyptian servant named Jarha. [35]Sheshan gave his daughter in marriage to his servant Jarha, and she bore him Attai.

[36]Attai was the father of Nathan,
Nathan the father of Zabad,

[37]Zabad the father of Ephlal,
Ephlal the father of Obed,

[38]Obed the father of Jehu,
Jehu the father of Azariah,

[39]Azariah the father of Helez,
Helez the father of Eleasah,

[40]Eleasah the father of Sismai,
Sismai the father of Shallum,

[41]Shallum the father of Jekamiah, and Jekamiah the father of Elishama.

□ The Clans of Caleb

[42]The sons of Caleb the brother of Jerahmeel:
Mesha his firstborn, who was the father of Ziph, and his son Mareshah,[i] who was the father of Hebron.

[43]The sons of Hebron:
Korah, Tappuah, Rekem and Shema. [44]Shema was the father of Raham, and Raham the father of Jorkeam. Rekem was the father of Shammai. [45]The son of Shammai was Maon, and Maon was the father of Beth Zur.

[46]Caleb's concubine Ephah was the mother of Haran, Moza and Gazez. Haran was the father of Gazez.

[47]The sons of Jahdai:
Regem, Jotham, Geshan, Pelet, Ephah and Shaaph.

[48]Caleb's concubine Maacah was the mother of Sheber and Tirhanah. [49]She also gave birth to Shaaph the father of Madmannah and to Sheva the father of Macbenah and Gibea. Caleb's daughter was Acsah. [50]These were the descendants of Caleb.

The sons of Hur the firstborn of Ephrathah:
Shobal the father of Kiriath Jearim, [51]Salma the father of Bethlehem, and Hareph the father of Beth Gader.

[52]The descendants of Shobal the father of Kiriath Jearim were:
Haroeh, half the Manahathites, [53]and the clans of Kiriath Jearim: the Ithrites, Puthites, Shumathites and Mishraites. From these descended the Zorathites and Eshtaolites.

[54]The descendants of Salma:
Bethlehem, the Netophathites, Atroth Beth Joab, half the Manahathites, the Zorites, [55]and the clans of scribes[j] who lived at Jabez: the Tirathites, Shimeathites and Sucathites. These are the Kenites who came from Hammath, the father of the house of Recab.[k]

□ The Sons of David

3 These were the sons of David born to him in Hebron:
The firstborn was Amnon the son of Ahinoam of Jezreel;
the second, Daniel the son of Abigail of Carmel;
[2]the third, Absalom the son of Maacah daughter of Talmai king of Geshur;
the fourth, Adonijah the son of Haggith;
[3]the fifth, Shephatiah the son of Abital;
and the sixth, Ithream, by his wife Eglah.
[4]These six were born to David in Hebron, where he reigned for seven years and six months.
David reigned in Jerusalem for thirty-three years, [5]and these were the children born to him there:
Shammua,[a] Shobab, Nathan and Solomon. These four were by Bathsheba[b] daughter of Ammiel. [6]There were also Ibhar, Elishua,[c] Eliphelet, [7]Nogah, Nepheg, Japhia, [8]Elishama, Eliada and Eliphelet—nine in all. [9]All these were the sons of David, besides his sons by his concubines. And Tamar was their sister.

[f]23 Or captured the settlements of Jair   [g]24 Father may mean civic leader or military leader; also in verses 42, 45, 49–52 and possibly elsewhere.
[b]25 Or Oren and Ozem, by   [i]42 The meaning of the Hebrew for this phrase is uncertain.   [j]55 Or of the Sopherites   [k]55 Or father of Beth Recab
[a]5 Hebrew Shimea, a variant of Shammua   [b]5 One Hebrew manuscript and Vulgate (see also Septuagint and 2 Sam. 11:3); most Hebrew manuscripts Bathshua   [c]6 Two Hebrew manuscripts (see also 2 Sam. 5:15 and 1 Chron. 14:5); most Hebrew manuscripts Elishama

☐ The Kings of Judah

¹⁰Solomon's son was Rehoboam,
Abijah his son,
Asa his son,
Jehoshaphat his son,

3:5 ■ WHY THE CLEAN UP?

Names like Bathsheba, Absalom, and Tamar all bring to mind unsavoury scenes from David's life (see 2 Samuel 11–18). The author certainly would have known about these stories, but chose to omit them. Writing to dispirited refugees, he wanted to inspire them with a model of what the nation could become, not remind them of how it had failed in the past.

¹¹Jehoram*d* his son,
Ahaziah his son,
Joash his son,
¹²Amaziah his son,
Azariah his son,
Jotham his son,
¹³Ahaz his son,
Hezekiah his son,
Manasseh his son,
¹⁴Amon his son,
Josiah his son.
¹⁵The sons of Josiah:
Johanan the firstborn,
Jehoiakim the second son,
Zedekiah the third,
Shallum the fourth.
¹⁶The successors of Jehoiakim:
Jehoiachin*e* his son,
and Zedekiah.

☐ The Royal Line After the Exile

¹⁷The descendants of Jehoiachin the captive:
Shealtiel his son, ¹⁸Malkiram, Pedaiah, She-nazzar, Jekamiah, Hoshama and Nedabiah.
¹⁹The sons of Pedaiah:
Zerubbabel and Shimei.
The sons of Zerubbabel:
Meshullam and Hananiah.
Shelomith was their sister.
²⁰There were also five others:
Hashubah, Ohel, Berekiah, Hasadiah and Jushab-Hesed.
²¹The descendants of Hananiah:
Pelatiah and Jeshaiah, and the sons of Re-phaiah, of Arnan, of Obadiah and of Sheca-niah.
²²The descendants of Shecaniah:
Shemaiah and his sons:
Hattush, Igal, Bariah, Neariah and Shaphat — six in all.
²³The sons of Neariah:
Elioenai, Hizkiah and Azrikam — three in all.
²⁴The sons of Elioenai:
Hodaviah, Eliashib, Pelaiah, Akkub, Johanan, Delaiah and Anani — seven in all.

☐ Other Clans of Judah

4 The descendants of Judah:
Perez, Hezron, Carmi, Hur and Shobal.
²Reaiah son of Shobal was the father of Jahath, and Jahath the father of Ahumai and Lahad. These were the clans of the Zorathites.

3:17 ■ THE ROYAL LINE

Chronicles was written to people who no longer had a king. However, as this section reminds us, they still knew the royal line. God's promise to provide them with kingly leadership for ever still held. They could expect a son of David to become king again someday. This is one reason why the New Testament takes the trouble to show that Jesus was descended from David. *He* was that King.

³These were the sons*a* of Etam:
Jezreel, Ishma and Idbash. Their sister was named Hazzelelponi. ⁴Penuel was the father of Gedor, and Ezer the father of Hushah.
These were the descendants of Hur, the first-born of Ephrathah and father*b* of Bethlehem.
⁵Ashhur the father of Tekoa had two wives, He-lah and Naarah.
⁶Naarah bore him Ahuzzam, Hepher, Temeni and Haahashtari. These were the descendants of Naarah.
⁷The sons of Helah:
Zereth, Zohar, Ethnan, ⁸and Koz, who was the father of Anub and Hazzobebah and of the clans of Aharhel son of Harum.

⁹Jabez was more honourable than his brothers. His mother had named him Jabez,*c* saying, "I gave birth to him in pain." ¹⁰Jabez cried out to the God of Israel, "Oh, that you would bless me and enlarge my territory! Let your hand be with me, and keep me from harm so that I will be free from pain." And God granted his request.

¹¹Kelub, Shuhah's brother, was the father of Mehir, who was the father of Eshton. ¹²Esh-ton was the father of Beth Rapha, Paseah and Tehinnah the father of Ir Nahash.*d* These were the men of Recah.

¹³The sons of Kenaz:
Othniel and Seraiah.
The sons of Othniel:
Hathath and Meonothai.*e* ¹⁴Meonothai was the father of Ophrah.
Seraiah was the father of Joab,
the father of Ge Harashim.*f* It was called this because its people were craftsmen.
¹⁵The sons of Caleb son of Jephunneh:
Iru, Elah and Naam.
The son of Elah:
Kenaz.
¹⁶The sons of Jehallelel:
Ziph, Ziphah, Tiria and Asarel.
¹⁷The sons of Ezrah:

d 11 Hebrew *Joram*, a variant of *Jehoram*   *e 16* Hebrew *Jeconiah*, a variant of *Jehoiachin*; also in verse 17   *a 3* Some Septuagint manuscripts (see also Vulgate); Hebrew *father*   *b 4* *Father* may mean *civic leader* or *military leader*; also in verses 12, 14, 17, 18 and possibly elsewhere.   *c 9* *Jabez* sounds like the Hebrew for *pain*.   *d 12* Or *of the city of Nahash*   *e 13* Some Septuagint manuscripts and Vulgate; Hebrew does not have *and Meonothai*. *f 14* *Ge Harashim* means *valley of craftsmen*.

Jether, Mered, Epher and Jalon. One of Mered's wives gave birth to Miriam, Shammai and Ishbah the father of Eshtemoa. [18](His Judean wife gave birth to Jered the father of Gedor, Heber the father of Soco, and Jekuthiel the father of Zanoah.) These were the children of Pharaoh's daughter Bithiah, whom Mered had married.

[19]The sons of Hodiah's wife, the sister of Naham: the father of Keilah the Garmite, and Eshtemoa the Maacathite.

[20]The sons of Shimon:

Amnon, Rinnah, Ben-Hanan and Tilon.

The descendants of Ishi:

Zoheth and Ben-Zoheth.

[21]The sons of Shelah son of Judah:

Er the father of Lecah, Laadah the father of Mareshah and the clans of the linen workers at Beth Ashbea, [22]Jokim, the men of Cozeba, and Joash and Saraph, who ruled in Moab and Jashubi Lehem. (These records are from ancient times.) [23]They were the potters who lived at Netaim and Gederah; they stayed there and worked for the king.

■ Simeon

[24]The descendants of Simeon:

Nemuel, Jamin, Jarib, Zerah and Shaul;

[25]Shallum was Shaul's son, Mibsam his son and Mishma his son.

[26]The descendants of Mishma:

Hammuel his son, Zaccur his son and Shimei his son.

[27]Shimei had sixteen sons and six daughters, but his brothers did not have many children; so their entire clan did not become as numerous as the people of Judah. [28]They lived in Beersheba, Moladah, Hazar Shual, [29]Bilhah, Ezem, Tolad, [30]Bethuel, Hormah, Ziklag, [31]Beth Marcaboth, Hazar Susim, Beth Biri and Shaaraim. These were their towns until the reign of David. [32]Their surrounding villages were Etam, Ain, Rimmon, Token and Ashan—five towns—[33]and all the villages around these towns as far as Baalath. [g] These were their settlements. And they kept a genealogical record.

[34]Meshobab, Jamlech, Joshah son of Amaziah, [35]Joel, Jehu son of Joshibiah, the son of Seraiah, the son of Asiel, [36]also Elioenai, Jaakobah, Jeshohaiah, Asaiah, Adiel, Jesimiel, Benaiah, [37]and Ziza son of Shiphi, the son of Allon, the son of Jedaiah, the son of Shimri, the son of Shemaiah.

[38]The men listed above by name were leaders of their clans. Their families increased greatly, [39]and they went to the outskirts of Gedor to the east of the valley in search of pasture for their flocks. [40]They found rich, good pasture, and the land was spacious, peaceful and quiet. Some Hamites had lived there formerly.

[41]The men whose names were listed came in the days of Hezekiah king of Judah. They attacked the Hamites in their dwellings and also the Meunites who were there and completely destroyed[b] them, as is evident to this day. Then they settled in their place, because there was pasture for their flocks. [42]And five hundred of these Simeonites, led by Pelatiah, Neariah, Rephaiah and Uzziel, the sons of Ishi, invaded the hill country of Seir. [43]They killed the remaining Amalekites who had escaped, and they have lived there to this day.

■ Reuben

5 The sons of Reuben the firstborn of Israel (he was the firstborn, but when he defiled his father's marriage bed, his rights as firstborn were given to the sons of Joseph son of Israel; so he could not be listed in the genealogical record in accordance with his birthright, [2]and though Judah was the strongest of his brothers and a ruler came from him, the rights of the firstborn belonged to Joseph)— [3]the sons of Reuben the firstborn of Israel:

Hanoch, Pallu, Hezron and Carmi.

[4]The descendants of Joel:

Shemaiah his son, Gog his son,

Shimei his son, [5]Micah his son,

Reaiah his son, Baal his son,

[6]and Beerah his son, whom Tiglath-Pileser[a] king of Assyria took into exile. Beerah was a leader of the Reubenites.

[7]Their relatives by clans, listed according to their genealogical records:

Jeiel the chief, Zechariah, [8]and Bela son of Azaz, the son of Shema, the son of Joel. They settled in the area from Aroer to Nebo and Baal Meon. [9]To the east they occupied the land up to the edge of the desert that extends to the Euphrates River, because their livestock had increased in Gilead.

[10]During Saul's reign they waged war against the Hagrites, who were defeated at their hands; they occupied the dwellings of the Hagrites throughout the entire region east of Gilead.

■ Gad

[11]The Gadites lived next to them in Bashan, as far as Salecah:

[12]Joel was the chief, Shapham the second, then Janai and Shaphat, in Bashan.

[13]Their relatives, by families, were:

Michael, Meshullam, Sheba, Jorai, Jacan, Zia and Eber—seven in all.

[14]These were the sons of Abihail son of Huri, the son of Jaroah, the son of Gilead, the son of Michael, the son of Jeshishai, the son of Jahdo, the son of Buz.

[15]Ahi son of Abdiel, the son of Guni, was head of their family.

[16]The Gadites lived in Gilead, in Bashan and its outlying villages, and on all the pasture-lands of Sharon as far as they extended.

[17]All these were entered in the genealogical records during the reigns of Jotham king of Judah and Jeroboam king of Israel.

[18]The Reubenites, the Gadites and the half-tribe of Manasseh had 44,760 men ready for military service—able-bodied men who could handle shield and sword, who could use a bow, and who were

---

g 33 Some Septuagint manuscripts (see also Joshua 19:8); Hebrew Baal the LORD, often by totally destroying them.   *b 41 The Hebrew term refers to the irrevocable giving over of things or persons to* *a 6 Hebrew Tilnath-Pilneser, a variant of Tiglath-Pileser, also in verse 26* trained for battle. [19]They waged war against the Hagrites, Jetur, Naphish and Nodab. [20]They were helped in fighting them, and God handed the Hagrites and all their allies over to them, because they cried out to him during the battle. He answered their prayers, because they trusted in him. [21]They seized the livestock of the Hagrites—fifty thousand camels, two hundred and fifty thousand sheep and two thousand donkeys. They also took one hundred thousand people captive, [22]and many others fell slain, because the battle was God's. And they occupied the land until the exile.

■ The Half-Tribe of Manasseh

[23]The people of the half-tribe of Manasseh were numerous; they settled in the land from Bashan to Baal Hermon, that is, to Senir (Mount Hermon).

[24]These were the heads of their families: Epher, Ishi, Eliel, Azriel, Jeremiah, Hodaviah and Jahdiel. They were brave warriors, famous men, and heads of their families. [25]But they were unfaithful to the God of their fathers and prostituted themselves to the gods of the peoples of the land, whom God had destroyed before them. [26]So the God of Israel stirred up the spirit of Pul king of Assyria (that is, Tiglath-Pileser king of Assyria), who took the Reubenites, the Gadites and the half-tribe of Manasseh into exile. He took them to Halah, Habor, Hara and the river of Gozan, where they are to this day.

■ Levi

6 The sons of Levi:
Gershon, Kohath and Merari.
[2]The sons of Kohath:
Amram, Izhar, Hebron and Uzziel.
[3]The children of Amram:
Aaron, Moses and Miriam.
The sons of Aaron:
Nadab, Abihu, Eleazar and Ithamar.
[4]Eleazar was the father of Phinehas,
Phinehas the father of Abishua,
[5]Abishua the father of Bukki,
Bukki the father of Uzzi,
[6]Uzzi the father of Zerahiah,
Zerahiah the father of Meraioth,
[7]Meraioth the father of Amariah,
Amariah the father of Ahitub,
[8]Ahitub the father of Zadok,
Zadok the father of Ahimaaz,
[9]Ahimaaz the father of Azariah,
Azariah the father of Johanan,
[10]Johanan the father of Azariah (it was he who served as priest in the temple Solomon built in Jerusalem),
[11]Azariah the father of Amariah,
Amariah the father of Ahitub,
[12]Ahitub the father of Zadok,
Zadok the father of Shallum,
[13]Shallum the father of Hilkiah,
Hilkiah the father of Azariah,
[14]Azariah the father of Seraiah,
and Seraiah the father of Jehozadak.
[15]Jehozadak was deported when the LORD sent

Judah and Jerusalem into exile by the hand of Nebuchadnezzar.

6:1 ■ KEY PEOPLE
First Chronicles 1–9 form the Bible's most complete genealogical record. These chapters emphasise the two tribes most crucial to God's plans: Judahites, the tribe that David and all the later kings of Judah came from, and Levites, who had responsibility to lead Israel in worship.

It's possible that the Levite priest named Ezra wrote the two books of Chronicles, for they date from his time period. Jewish refugees had returned from exile in Babylon, and leaders like Ezra were trying to inspire the exiles to re-establish their proud nation and rebuild the temple.

[16]The sons of Levi:
Gershon,[a] Kohath and Merari.
[17]These are the names of the sons of Gershon:
Libni and Shimei.
[18]The sons of Kohath:
Amram, Izhar, Hebron and Uzziel.
[19]The sons of Merari:
Mahli and Mushi.
These are the clans of the Levites listed according to their fathers:
[20]Of Gershon:
Libni his son, Jehath his son,
Zimmah his son, [21]Joah his son,
Iddo his son, Zerah his son
and Jeatherai his son.
[22]The descendants of Kohath:
Amminadab his son, Korah his son,
Assir his son, [23]Elkanah his son,
Ebiasaph his son, Assir his son,
[24]Tahath his son, Uriel his son,
Uzziah his son and Shaul his son.
[25]The descendants of Elkanah:
Amasai, Ahimoth,
[26]Elkanah his son,[b] Zophai his son,
Nahath his son, [27]Eliab his son,
Jeroham his son, Elkanah his son
and Samuel his son.[c]
[28]The sons of Samuel:
Joel[d] the firstborn
and Abijah the second son.
[29]The descendants of Merari:
Mahli, Libni his son,
Shimei his son, Uzzah his son,
[30]Shimea his son, Haggiah his son
and Asaiah his son.

□ The Temple Musicians

[31]These are the men David put in charge of the music in the house of the LORD after the ark came to rest there. [32]They ministered with music before the tabernacle, the Tent of Meeting, until Solomon built the temple of the LORD in Jerusalem. They performed their duties according to the regulations laid down for them.

---

[a] 16 Hebrew *Gershom*, a variant of *Gershon*; also in verses 17, 20, 43, 62 and 71   [b] 26 Some Hebrew manuscripts, Septuagint and Syriac; most Hebrew manuscripts *Ahimoth* 26*and Elkanah. The sons of Elkanah:*   [c] 27 Some Septuagint manuscripts (see also 1 Sam. 1:19, 20 and 1 Chron. 6:33, 34); Hebrew does not have *and Samuel his son.*   [d] 28 Some Septuagint manuscripts and Syriac (see also 1 Sam. 8:2 and 1 Chron. 6:33); Hebrew does not have *Joel.*

³³Here are the men who served, together with their sons:

From the Kohathites:

Heman, the musician,
the son of Joel, the son of Samuel,

6:31 ■ AND NOW, THE CHOIR …

The author of 1 Chronicles had a special fondness for musicians. Several times he mentions David's role in establishing guilds of musicians for temple worship, and here he even records their ancestry.

---

³⁴the son of Elkanah, the son of Jeroham,
the son of Eliel, the son of Toah,
³⁵the son of Zuph, the son of Elkanah,
the son of Mahath, the son of Amasai,
³⁶the son of Elkanah, the son of Joel,
the son of Azariah, the son of Zephaniah,
³⁷the son of Tahath, the son of Assir,
the son of Ebiasaph, the son of Korah,
³⁸the son of Izhar, the son of Kohath,
the son of Levi, the son of Israel;
³⁹and Heman's associate Asaph, who served at his
right hand:

Asaph son of Berekiah, the son of Shimea,
⁴⁰the son of Michael, the son of Baaseiah,ᵉ
the son of Malkijah, ⁴¹the son of Ethni,
the son of Zerah, the son of Adaiah,
⁴²the son of Ethan, the son of Zimmah,
the son of Shimei, ⁴³the son of Jahath,
the son of Gershon, the son of Levi;
⁴⁴and from their associates, the Merarites, at his
left hand:

Ethan son of Kishi, the son of Abdi,
the son of Malluch, ⁴⁵the son of Hashabiah,
the son of Amaziah, the son of Hilkiah,
⁴⁶the son of Amzi, the son of Bani,
the son of Shemer, ⁴⁷the son of Mahli,
the son of Mushi, the son of Merari,
the son of Levi.

⁴⁸Their fellow Levites were assigned to all the other duties of the tabernacle, the house of God. ⁴⁹But Aaron and his descendants were the ones who presented offerings on the altar of burnt offering and on the altar of incense in connection with all that was done in the Most Holy Place, making atonement for Israel, in accordance with all that Moses the servant of God had commanded.

⁵⁰These were the descendants of Aaron:

Eleazar his son, Phinehas his son,
Abishua his son, ⁵¹Bukki his son,
Uzzi his son, Zerahiah his son,
⁵²Meraioth his son, Amariah his son,
Ahitub his son, ⁵³Zadok his son
and Ahimaaz his son.

⁵⁴These were the locations of their settlements allotted as their territory (they were assigned to the descendants of Aaron who were from the Kohathite clan, because the first lot was for them):

⁵⁵They were given Hebron in Judah with its surrounding pasture-lands. ⁵⁶But the fields and villages around the city were given to Caleb son of Jephunneh.

⁵⁷So the descendants of Aaron were given Hebron (a city of refuge), and Libnah,ᶠ Jattir, Eshtemoa, ⁵⁸Hilen, Debir, ⁵⁹Ashan, Juttahᵍ and Beth Shemesh, together with their pasture-lands. ⁶⁰And from the tribe of Benjamin they were given Gibeon,ᵇ Geba, Alemeth and Anathoth, together with their pasture-lands.

These towns, which were distributed among the Kohathite clans, were thirteen in all.

⁶¹The rest of Kohath's descendants were allotted ten towns from the clans of half the tribe of Manasseh.

⁶²The descendants of Gershon, clan by clan, were allotted thirteen towns from the tribes of Issachar, Asher and Naphtali, and from the part of the tribe of Manasseh that is in Bashan.

⁶³The descendants of Merari, clan by clan, were allotted twelve towns from the tribes of Reuben, Gad and Zebulun.

⁶⁴So the Israelites gave the Levites these towns and their pasture-lands. ⁶⁵From the tribes of Judah, Simeon and Benjamin they allotted the previously named towns.

⁶⁶Some of the Kohathite clans were given as their territory towns from the tribe of Ephraim.

⁶⁷In the hill country of Ephraim they were given Shechem (a city of refuge), and Gezer,ⁱ ⁶⁸Jokmeam, Beth Horon, ⁶⁹Aijalon and Gath Rimmon, together with their pasture-lands. ⁷⁰And from half the tribe of Manasseh the Israelites gave Aner and Bileam, together with their pasture-lands, to the rest of the Kohathite clans.

⁷¹The Gershonites received the following:

From the clan of the half-tribe of Manasseh
they received Golan in Bashan and also Ashtaroth, together with their pasture-lands;
⁷²from the tribe of Issachar
they received Kedesh, Daberath, ⁷³Ramoth and Anem, together with their pasture-lands;
⁷⁴from the tribe of Asher
they received Mashal, Abdon, ⁷⁵Hukok and Rehob, together with their pasture-lands;
⁷⁶and from the tribe of Naphtali
they received Kedesh in Galilee, Hammon and Kiriathaim, together with their pasture-lands.

⁷⁷The Merarites (the rest of the Levites) received the following:

From the tribe of Zebulun
they received Jokneam, Kartah,ʲ Rimmono and Tabor, together with their pasture-lands;
⁷⁸from the tribe of Reuben across the Jordan east of Jericho
they received Bezer in the desert, Jahzah, ⁷⁹Kedemoth and Mephaath, together with their pasture-lands;
⁸⁰and from the tribe of Gad
they received Ramoth in Gilead, Mahanaim,

ᵉ40 Most Hebrew manuscripts; some Hebrew manuscripts, one Septuagint manuscript and Syriac *Maaseiah*   ᶠ57 See Joshua 21:13; Hebrew *given the cities of refuge: Hebron, Libnah.*   ᵍ59 Syriac (see also Septuagint and Joshua 21:16); Hebrew does not have *Juttah.*   ᵇ60 See Joshua 21:17; Hebrew does not have *Gibeon.*   ⁱ67 See Joshua 21:21; Hebrew *given the cities of refuge: Shechem, Gezer.*   ʲ77 See Septuagint and Joshua 21:34; Hebrew does not have *Jokneam, Kartah.*

⁸¹Heshbon and Jazer, together with their pasture-lands.

■ Issachar

7 The sons of Issachar:
Tola, Puah, Jashub and Shimron—four in all.
²The sons of Tola:
Uzzi, Rephaiah, Jeriel, Jahmai, Ibsam and Samuel—heads of their families. During the reign of David, the descendants of Tola listed as fighting men in their genealogy numbered 22,600.
³The son of Uzzi:
Izrahiah.
The sons of Izrahiah:
Michael, Obadiah, Joel and Isshiah. All five of them were chiefs. ⁴According to their family genealogy, they had 36,000 men ready for battle, for they had many wives and children. ⁵The relatives who were fighting men belonging to all the clans of Issachar, as listed in their genealogy, were 87,000 in all.

■ Benjamin
⁶Three sons of Benjamin:
Bela, Beker and Jediael.
⁷The sons of Bela:
Ezbon, Uzzi, Uzziel, Jerimoth and Iri, heads of families—five in all. Their genealogical record listed 22,034 fighting men.
⁸The sons of Beker:
Zemirah, Joash, Eliezer, Elioenai, Omri, Jeremoth, Abijah, Anathoth and Alemeth. All these were the sons of Beker. ⁹Their genealogical record listed the heads of families and 20,200 fighting men.
¹⁰The son of Jediael:
Bilhan.
The sons of Bilhan:
Jeush, Benjamin, Ehud, Kenaanah, Zethan, Tarshish and Ahishahar. ¹¹All these sons of Jediael were heads of families. There were 17,200 fighting men ready to go out to war.
¹²The Shuppites and Huppites were the descendants of Ir, and the Hushites the descendants of Aher.

■ Naphtali
¹³The sons of Naphtali:
Jahziel, Guni, Jezer and Shillem^a—the descendants of Bilhah.

■ Manasseh
¹⁴The descendants of Manasseh:
Asriel was his descendant through his Aramean concubine. She gave birth to Makir the father of Gilead. ¹⁵Makir took a wife from among the Huppites and Shuppites. His sister's name was Maacah.
Another descendant was named Zelophehad, who had only daughters.
¹⁶Makir's wife Maacah gave birth to a son and named him Peresh. His brother was named Sheresh, and his sons were Ulam and Rakem.
¹⁷The son of Ulam:
Bedan.

These were the sons of Gilead son of Makir, the son of Manasseh. ¹⁸His sister Hammoleketh gave birth to Ishhod, Abiezer and Mahlah.
¹⁹The sons of Shemida were:
Ahian, Shechem, Likhi and Aniam.

7:14 ■ JOSEPH'S HEIRS
Joseph, Jacob's son, by rights deserved to have one of the "twelve tribes of Israel" named after him. Instead, Joseph passed that honour to his own sons Ephraim and Manasseh, whose offspring settled one of the largest tracts of land in Palestine and then competed with each other for prestige and influence. Their mention here is significant, for these tribes lived in the Northern Kingdom of Israel; wounds had healed, and the southern leaders in Jerusalem were now beginning to welcome back their estranged relatives.

■ Ephraim
²⁰The descendants of Ephraim:
Shuthelah, Bered his son,
Tahath his son, Eleadah his son,
Tahath his son, ²¹Zabad his son
and Shuthelah his son.
Ezer and Elead were killed by the native-born men of Gath, when they went down to seize their livestock. ²²Their father Ephraim mourned for them many days, and his relatives came to comfort him. ²³Then he lay with his wife again, and she became pregnant and gave birth to a son. He named him Beriah,^b because there had been misfortune in his family. ²⁴His daughter was Sheerah, who built Lower and Upper Beth Horon as well as Uzzen Sheerah.
²⁵Rephah was his son, Resheph his son,^c
Telah his son, Tahan his son,
²⁶Ladan his son, Ammihud his son,
Elishama his son, ²⁷Nun his son
and Joshua his son.
²⁸Their lands and settlements included Bethel and its surrounding villages, Naaran to the east, Gezer and its villages to the west, and Shechem and its villages all the way to Ayyah and its villages. ²⁹Along the borders of Manasseh were Beth Shan, Taanach, Megiddo and Dor, together with their villages. The descendants of Joseph son of Israel lived in these towns.

■ Asher
³⁰The sons of Asher:
Imnah, Ishvah, Ishvi and Beriah. Their sister was Serah.
³¹The sons of Beriah:
Heber and Malkiel, who was the father of Birzaith.
³²Heber was the father of Japhlet, Shomer and Hotham and of their sister Shua.
³³The sons of Japhlet:
Pasach, Bimhal and Ashvath.
These were Japhlet's sons.

^a 13 Some Hebrew and Septuagint manuscripts (see also Gen. 46:24 and Num. 26:49); most Hebrew manuscripts *Shallum*   ^b 23 *Beriah* sounds like the Hebrew for *misfortune*.   ^c 25 Some Septuagint manuscripts; Hebrew does not have *his son*.

34The sons of Shomer:
Ahi, Rohgah,*d* Hubbah and Aram.
35The sons of his brother Helem:
Zophah, Imna, Shelesh and Amal.
36The sons of Zophah:
Suah, Harnepher, Shual, Beri, Imrah, 37Bezer,
Hod, Shamma, Shilshah, Ithran*e* and Beera.
38The sons of Jether:
Jephunneh, Pispah and Ara.
39The sons of Ulla:
Arah, Hanniel and Rizia.
40All these were descendants of Asher — heads of
families, choice men, brave warriors and outstanding leaders. The number of men ready for battle, as
listed in their genealogy, was 26,000.

■ The Genealogy of Saul the Benjamite

8 Benjamin was the father of Bela his firstborn,
Ashbel the second son, Aharah the third,
2Nohah the fourth and Rapha the fifth.

8:1 ■ DYNASTY REJECTED
Saul, Israel's first king, came from the tribe of
Benjamin. Normally a royal dynasty would have
followed him, descending from that same tribe.
After Saul's dismal performance, however, God
turned instead to the tribe of Judah and selected
David, who became one of the ancestors of Jesus
the Messiah.

3The sons of Bela were:
Addar, Gera, Abihud,*a* 4Abishua, Naaman,
Ahoah, 5Gera, Shephuphan and Huram.
6These were the descendants of Ehud, who
were heads of families of those living in Geba
and were deported to Manahath:
7Naaman, Ahijah and Gera, who deported
them and who was the father of Uzza and Ahi-
hud.

8Sons were born to Shaharaim in Moab after he
had divorced his wives Hushim and Baara.
9By his wife Hodesh he had Jobab, Zibia, Mesha, Malcam, 10Jeuz, Sakia and Mirmah. These
were his sons, heads of families. 11By Hushim
he had Abitub and Elpaal.
12The sons of Elpaal:
Eber, Misham, Shemed (who built Ono and
Lod with its surrounding villages), 13and Beriah and Shema, who were heads of families
of those living in Aijalon and who drove out
the inhabitants of Gath.
14Ahio, Shashak, Jeremoth, 15Zebadiah, Arad,
Eder, 16Michael, Ishpah and Joha were the
sons of Beriah.
17Zebadiah, Meshullam, Hizki, Heber, 18Ishmerai,
Izliah and Jobab were the sons of Elpaal.
19Jakim, Zicri, Zabdi, 20Elienai, Zillethai, Eliel,
21Adaiah, Beraiah and Shimrath were the sons
of Shimei.
22Ishpan, Eber, Eliel, 23Abdon, Zicri, Hanan,
24Hananiah, Elam, Anthothijah, 25Iphdeiah
and Penuel were the sons of Shashak.

26Shamsherai, Shehariah, Athaliah, 27Jaareshiah,
Elijah and Zicri were the sons of Jeroham.
28All these were heads of families, chiefs as listed
in their genealogy, and they lived in Jerusalem.

29Jeiel*b* the father*c* of Gibeon lived in Gibeon.
His wife's name was Maacah, 30and his firstborn son was Abdon, followed by Zur, Kish,
Baal, Ner,*d* Nadab, 31Gedor, Ahio, Zeker
32and Mikloth, who was the father of Shimeah. They too lived near their relatives in
Jerusalem.
33Ner was the father of Kish, Kish the father of
Saul, and Saul the father of Jonathan, Malki-
Shua, Abinadab and Esh-Baal.*e*
34The son of Jonathan:
Merib-Baal,*f* who was the father of Micah.
35The sons of Micah:
Pithon, Melech, Tarea and Ahaz.
36Ahaz was the father of Jehoaddah, Jehoaddah
was the father of Alemeth, Azmaveth and
Zimri, and Zimri was the father of Moza.
37Moza was the father of Binea; Raphah was
his son, Eleasah his son and Azel his son.
38Azel had six sons, and these were their names:
Azrikam, Bokeru, Ishmael, Sheariah, Obadiah
and Hanan. All these were the sons of Azel.
39The sons of his brother Eshek:
Ulam his firstborn, Jeush the second son and
Eliphelet the third. 40The sons of Ulam were
brave warriors who could handle the bow.
They had many sons and grandsons — 150 in
all.
All these were the descendants of Benjamin.

9 All Israel was listed in the genealogies in the
book of the kings of Israel.

■ The People in Jerusalem
The people of Judah were taken captive to Babylon because of their unfaithfulness. 2Now the first

---

9:1 ■ THE SOURCE OF GENEALOGIES
The author of 1 Chronicles acknowledges that he
relied on older documents for his information. In
1 and 2 Chronicles (originally one book)
approximately 14 sources are named. During the
Israelites' exile in Babylon, historical records had
been lost and family information forgotten (see
Ezra 2:59). First Chronicles condenses the most
important of the genealogical information. It was
meant to help the Israelites re-establish their
identity as God's people.

---

to resettle on their own property in their own towns
were some Israelites, priests, Levites and temple servants.
3Those from Judah, from Benjamin, and from Ephraim and Manasseh who lived in Jerusalem were:
4Uthai son of Ammihud, the son of Omri, the son
of Imri, the son of Bani, a descendant of Perez
son of Judah.
5Of the Shilonites:

---

d 34 Or *of his brother Shomer: Rohgah*   *e 37* Possibly a variant of *Jether*   *a 3* Or *Gera the father of Ehud*   *b 29* Some Septuagint manuscripts (see
also 1 Chron. 9:35); Hebrew does not have *Jeiel.*   *c 29* *Father* may mean *civic leader* or *military leader.*   *d 30* Some Septuagint manuscripts (see also
1 Chron. 9:36); Hebrew does not have *Ner.*   *e 33* Also known as *Ish-Bosheth*   *f 34* Also known as *Mephibosheth*

Asaiah the firstborn and his sons.

6Of the Zerahites:

Jeuel.

The people from Judah numbered 690.

7Of the Benjamites:

Sallu son of Meshullam, the son of Hodaviah, the son of Hassenuah;

8Ibneiah son of Jeroham; Elah son of Uzzi, the son of Micri; and Meshullam son of Shephatiah, the son of Reuel, the son of Ibnijah.

9The people from Benjamin, as listed in their genealogy, numbered 956. All these men were heads of their families.

10Of the priests:

Jedaiah; Jehoiarib; Jakin;

11Azariah son of Hilkiah, the son of Meshullam, the son of Zadok, the son of Meraioth, the son of Ahitub, the official in charge of the house of God;

12Adaiah son of Jeroham, the son of Pashhur, the son of Malkijah; and Maasai son of Adiel, the son of Jahzerah, the son of Meshullam, the son of Meshillemith, the son of Immer.

13The priests, who were heads of families, numbered 1,760. They were able men, responsible for ministering in the house of God.

14Of the Levites:

Shemaiah son of Hasshub, the son of Azrikam, the son of Hashabiah, a Merarite; 15Bakbakkar, Heresh, Galal and Mattaniah son of Mica, the son of Zicri, the son of Asaph; 16Obadiah son of Shemaiah, the son of Galal, the son of Jeduthun; and Berekiah son of Asa, the son of Elkanah, who lived in the villages of the Netophathites.

17The gatekeepers:

Shallum, Akkub, Talmon, Ahiman and their brothers, Shallum their chief 18being stationed at the King's Gate on the east, up to the present time. These were the gatekeepers belonging to the camp of the Levites. 19Shallum son of Kore, the son of Ebiasaph, the son of Korah, and his fellow gatekeepers from his family (the Korahites) were responsible for guarding the thresholds of the Tent*a* just as their fathers had been responsible for guarding the entrance to the dwelling of the LORD. 20In earlier times Phinehas son of Eleazar was in charge of the gatekeepers, and the LORD was with him. 21Zechariah son of Meshelemiah was the gatekeeper at the entrance to the Tent of Meeting.

9:2–34 ■ AFTER THE EXILE

While most of 1 Chronicles deals with the time of David, this short section (2–34) jumps ahead 500 years to the time when a small portion of Israel had returned from exile. (See the books of Ezra, Nehemiah, Haggai, and Zechariah for more information about these returned exiles.)

22Altogether, those chosen to be gatekeepers at the thresholds numbered 212. They were registered by genealogy in their villages. The gatekeepers had been assigned to their positions of trust by David and Samuel the seer. 23They and their descendants were in charge of guarding the gates of the house of the LORD—the house called the Tent. 24The gatekeepers were on the four sides: east, west, north and south. 25Their brothers in their villages had to come from time to time and share their duties for seven-day periods. 26But the four principal gatekeepers, who were Levites, were entrusted with the responsibility for the rooms and treasuries in the house of God. 27They would spend the night stationed round the house of God, because they had to guard it; and they had charge of the key for opening it each morning.

28Some of them were in charge of the articles used in the temple service; they counted them when they were brought in and when they were taken out. 29Others were assigned to take care of the furnishings and all the other articles of the sanctuary, as well as the flour and wine, and the oil, incense and spices. 30But some of the priests took care of mixing the spices. 31A Levite named Mattithiah, the firstborn son of Shallum the Korahite, was entrusted with the responsibility for baking the offering bread. 32Some of their Kohathite brothers were in charge of preparing for every Sabbath the bread set out on the table.

33Those who were musicians, heads of Levite families, stayed in the rooms of the temple and were exempt from other duties because they were responsible for the work day and night. 34All these were heads of Levite families, chiefs as listed in their genealogy, and they lived in Jerusalem.

■ The Genealogy of Saul

35Jeiel the father*b* of Gibeon lived in Gibeon.

His wife's name was Maacah, 36and his firstborn son was Abdon, followed by Zur, Kish, Baal, Ner, Nadab, 37Gedor, Ahio, Zechariah and Mikloth. 38Mikloth was the father of Shimeam. They too lived near their relatives in Jerusalem.

39Ner was the father of Kish, Kish the father of Saul, and Saul the father of Jonathan, Malki-Shua, Abinadab and Esh-Baal.*c*

40The son of Jonathan:

Merib-Baal,*d* who was the father of Micah.

41The sons of Micah:

Pithon, Melech, Tahrea and Ahaz.*e*

42Ahaz was the father of Jadah, Jadah*f* was the father of Alemeth, Azmaveth and Zimri, and Zimri was the father of Moza. 43Moza was the father of Binea; Rephaiah was his son, Eleasah his son and Azel his son.

44Azel had six sons, and these were their names: Azrikam, Bokeru, Ishmael, Sheariah, Obadiah and Hanan. These were the sons of Azel.

■ Saul Takes His Life

10 Now the Philistines fought against Israel; the Israelites fled before them, and many fell slain on Mount Gilboa. 2The Philistines pressed hard after

---

a 19 That is, the temple; also in verses 21 and 23   *b 35 Father may mean civic leader or military leader.*   *c 39 Also known as Ish-Bosheth*   *d 40 Also known as Mephibosheth*   *e 41 Vulgate and Syriac (see also Septuagint and 1 Chron. 8:35); Hebrew does not have and Ahaz.*   *f 42 Some Hebrew manuscripts and Septuagint (see also 1 Chron. 8:36); most Hebrew manuscripts Jarah, Jarah*

Saul and his sons, and they killed his sons Jonathan, Abinadab and Malki-Shua. [3]The fighting grew fierce around Saul, and when the archers overtook him, they wounded him.

[4]Saul said to his armour-bearer, "Draw your sword and run me through, or these uncircumcised fellows will come and abuse me."

But his armour-bearer was terrified and would not do it; so Saul took his own sword and fell on it. [5]When the armour-bearer saw that Saul was dead, he too fell on his sword and died. [6]So Saul and his three sons died, and all his house died together.

[7]When all the Israelites in the valley saw that the army had fled and that Saul and his sons had died, they abandoned their towns and fled. And the Philistines came and occupied them.

[8]The next day, when the Philistines came to strip the dead, they found Saul and his sons fallen on Mount Gilboa. [9]They stripped him and took his head and his armour, and sent messengers throughout the land of the Philistines to proclaim the news among their idols and their people. [10]They put his armour in the temple of their gods and hung up his head in the temple of Dagon.

[11]When all the inhabitants of Jabesh Gilead heard of everything the Philistines had done to Saul, [12]all their valiant men went and took the bodies of Saul and his sons and brought them to Jabesh. Then they buried their bones under the great tree in Jabesh, and they fasted seven days.

[13]Saul died because he was unfaithful to the LORD; he did not keep the word of the LORD, and even consulted a medium for guidance, [14]and did not enquire of the LORD. So the LORD put him to death and turned the kingdom over to David son of Jesse.

10:13 ■ MORAL OF THE STORY

First Chronicles covers much the same history as 1 Samuel, but with a distinctive approach. First Samuel gives more details about Saul's failures, while 1 Chronicles primarily concerns itself with drawing moral lessons from them. For example, 1 Samuel 28 tells the background to Saul's consulting a medium; 1 Chronicles merely alludes to it (most original readers would know the story well) and connects that act of disobedience to Saul's death.

■ David Becomes King Over Israel

11 All Israel came together to David at Hebron and said, "We are your own flesh and blood. [2]In the past, even while Saul was king, you were the one who led Israel on their military campaigns. And the LORD your God said to you, 'You will shepherd my people Israel, and you will become their ruler.'"

[3]When all the elders of Israel had come to King David at Hebron, he made a compact with them at Hebron before the LORD, and they anointed David king over Israel, as the LORD had promised through Samuel.

■ David Conquers Jerusalem

[4]David and all the Israelites marched to Jerusalem (that is, Jebus). The Jebusites who lived there [5]said to David, "You will not get in here." Nevertheless, David captured the fortress of Zion, the City of David.

[6]David had said, "Whoever leads the attack on the Jebusites will become commander-in-chief." Joab son of Zeruiah went up first, and so he received the command.

[7]David then took up residence in the fortress, and so it was called the City of David. [8]He built up the city around it, from the supporting terraces[a] to the surrounding wall, while Joab restored the rest of the city. [9]And David became more and more powerful, because the LORD Almighty was with him.

■ David's Mighty Men

[10]These were the chiefs of David's mighty men — they, together with all Israel, gave his kingship strong support to extend it over the whole land, as the LORD had promised — [11]this is the list of David's mighty men:

Jashobeam,[b] a Hacmonite, was chief of the officers;[c] he raised his spear against three hundred men, whom he killed in one encounter.

[12]Next to him was Eleazar son of Dodai the Ahohite, one of the three mighty men. [13]He was with David at Pas Dammim when the Philistines gathered there for battle. At a place where there was a field full of barley, the troops fled from the Philistines. [14]But they took their stand in the middle of the field. They defended it and struck the Philistines down, and the LORD brought about a great victory.

[15]Three of the thirty chiefs came down to David to the rock at the cave of Adullam, while a band of Philistines was encamped in the Valley of Rephaim. [16]At that time David was in the stronghold, and the Philistine garrison was at Bethlehem. [17]David longed for water and said, "Oh, that someone would get me a drink of water from the well near the gate of Bethlehem!" [18]So the Three broke through the Philistine lines, drew water from the well near the gate of Bethlehem and carried it back to David. But he refused to drink it; instead, he poured it out before the LORD. [19]"God forbid that I should do this!" he said. "Should I drink the blood of these men who went at the risk of their lives?" Because they risked their lives to bring it back, David would not drink it.

Such were the exploits of the three mighty men.

[20]Abishai the brother of Joab was chief of the Three. He raised his spear against three hundred men, whom he killed, and so he became as famous as the Three. [21]He was doubly honoured above the Three and became their commander, even though he was not included among them.

[22]Benaiah son of Jehoiada was a valiant fighter from Kabzeel, who performed great exploits. He struck down two of Moab's best men. He also went down into a pit on a snowy day and killed a lion. [23]And he struck down an Egyptian who was seven and a half feet[d] tall. Although the Egyptian had a spear like a weaver's rod in his hand, Benaiah went against him with a club. He snatched the spear from the Egyptian's hand and killed him with his own

---

a 8 Or *the Millo*   *b 11* Possibly a variant of *Jashob-Baal*   *c 11* Or *Thirty*; some Septuagint manuscripts *Three* (see also 2 Sam. 23:8)   *d 23* Hebrew *five cubits* (about 2.3 metres) spear. 24Such were the exploits of Benaiah son of Jehoiada; he too was as famous as the three mighty men. 25He was held in greater honour than any of the Thirty, but he was not included among the Three. And David put him in charge of his bodyguard.

26The mighty men were:
Asahel the brother of Joab,
Elhanan son of Dodo from Bethlehem,
27Shammoth the Harorite,
Helez the Pelonite,
28Ira son of Ikkesh from Tekoa,
Abiezer from Anathoth,
29Sibbecai the Hushathite,
Ilai the Ahohite,
30Maharai the Netophathite,
Heled son of Baanah the Netophathite,
31Ithai son of Ribai from Gibeah in Benjamin,
Benaiah the Pirathonite,
32Hurai from the ravines of Gaash,
Abiel the Arbathite,
33Azmaveth the Baharumite,
Eliahba the Shaalbonite,
34the sons of Hashem the Gizonite,
Jonathan son of Shagee the Hararite,
35Ahiam son of Sacar the Hararite,
Eliphal son of Ur,
36Hepher the Mekerathite,
Ahijah the Pelonite,
37Hezro the Carmelite,
Naarai son of Ezbai,
38Joel the brother of Nathan,
Mibhar son of Hagri,
39Zelek the Ammonite,
Naharai the Berothite, the armour-bearer of Joab son of Zeruiah,
40Ira the Ithrite,
Gareb the Ithrite,
41Uriah the Hittite,
Zabad son of Ahlai,
42Adina son of Shiza the Reubenite, who was chief of the Reubenites, and the thirty with him,
43Hanan son of Maacah,
Joshaphat the Mithnite,
44Uzzia the Ashterathite,
Shama and Jeiel the sons of Hotham the Aroerite,
45Jediael son of Shimri,
his brother Joha the Tizite,
46Eliel the Mahavite,
Jeribai and Joshaviah the sons of Elnaam,
Ithmah the Moabite,
47Eliel, Obed and Jaasiel the Mezobaite.

■ Warriors Join David

12 These were the men who came to David at Ziklag, while he was banished from the presence of Saul son of Kish (they were among the warriors who helped him in battle; 2they were armed with bows and were able to shoot arrows or to sling stones right-handed or left-handed; they were kinsmen of Saul from the tribe of Benjamin):

3Ahiezer their chief and Joash the sons of

Shemaah the Gibeathite; Jeziel and Pelet the sons of Azmaveth; Beracah, Jehu the Anathothite, 4and Ishmaiah the Gibeonite, a mighty man among the Thirty, who was a leader of the Thirty; Jeremiah, Jahaziel, Johanan, Jozabad the Gederathite, 5Eluzai, Jerimoth, Bealiah, Shemariah and Shephatiah the Haruphite; 6Elkanah, Isshiah, Azarel, Joezer and Jashobeam the Korahites; 7and Joelah and Zebadiah the sons of Jeroham from Gedor.

12:2 ■ ACCENT ON UNITY
Chronicles bends over backwards to emphasise the need for unity of "all Israel", an important theme for a nation riven by tribalism and civil war. Here the author points out that even Saul's own kinsmen joined David's revolt. Later in the chapter (verses 23–38) he takes pains to mention compatriots from every tribe of Israel.

8Some Gadites defected to David at his stronghold in the desert. They were brave warriors, ready for battle and able to handle the shield and spear. Their faces were the faces of lions, and they were as swift as gazelles in the mountains.
9Ezer was the chief,
Obadiah the second in command, Eliab the third,
10Mishmannah the fourth, Jeremiah the fifth,
11Attai the sixth, Eliel the seventh,
12Johanan the eighth, Elzabad the ninth,
13Jeremiah the tenth and Macbannai the eleventh.
14These Gadites were army commanders; the least was a match for a hundred, and the greatest for a thousand. 15It was they who crossed the Jordan in the first month when it was overflowing all its banks, and they put to flight everyone living in the valleys, to the east and to the west.

16Other Benjamites and some men from Judah also came to David in his stronghold. 17David went out to meet them and said to them, "If you have come to me in peace, to help me, I am ready to have you unite with me. But if you have come to betray me to my enemies when my hands are free from violence, may the God of our fathers see it and judge you."

18Then the Spirit came upon Amasai, chief of the Thirty, and he said:

"We are yours, O David!
We are with you, O son of Jesse!
Success, success to you,
and success to those who help you,
for your God will help you."

So David received them and made them leaders of his raiding bands.

19Some of the men of Manasseh defected to David when he went with the Philistines to fight against Saul. (He and his men did not help the Philistines because, after consultation, their rulers sent him away. They said, "It will cost us our heads if he deserts to his master Saul.") 20When David went to

Ziklag, these were the men of Manasseh who defected to him: Adnah, Jozabad, Jediael, Michael, Jozabad, Elihu and Zillethai, leaders of units of a thousand in Manasseh. ²¹They helped David against raiding bands, for all of them were brave warriors, and they were commanders in his army. ²²Day after day men came to help David, until he had a great army, like the army of God.ᵃ

■ Others Join David at Hebron

²³These are the numbers of the men armed for battle who came to David at Hebron to turn Saul's kingdom over to him, as the LORD had said:
²⁴men of Judah, carrying shield and spear — 6,800 armed for battle;
²⁵men of Simeon, warriors ready for battle — 7,100;
²⁶men of Levi — 4,600, ²⁷including Jehoiada, leader of the family of Aaron with 3,700 men, ²⁸and Zadok, a brave young warrior, with 22 officers from his family;
²⁹men of Benjamin, Saul's kinsmen — 3,000, most of whom had remained loyal to Saul's house until then;
³⁰men of Ephraim, brave warriors, famous in their own clans — 20,800;
³¹men of half the tribe of Manasseh, designated by name to come and make David king — 18,000;
³²men of Issachar, who understood the times and knew what Israel should do — 200 chiefs, with all their relatives under their command;
³³men of Zebulun, experienced soldiers prepared for battle with every type of weapon, to help David with undivided loyalty — 50,000;
³⁴men of Naphtali — 1,000 officers, together with 37,000 men carrying shields and spears;
³⁵men of Dan, ready for battle — 28,600;
³⁶men of Asher, experienced soldiers prepared for battle — 40,000;
³⁷and from east of the Jordan, men of Reuben, Gad, and the half-tribe of Manasseh, armed with every type of weapon — 120,000.

³⁸All these were fighting men who volunteered to serve in the ranks. They came to Hebron fully determined to make David king over all Israel. All the rest of the Israelites were also of one mind to make David king. ³⁹The men spent three days there with David, eating and drinking, for their families had supplied provisions for them. ⁴⁰Also, their neighbours from as far away as Issachar, Zebulun and Naphtali came bringing food on donkeys, camels, mules and oxen. There were plentiful supplies of flour, fig cakes, raisin cakes, wine, oil, cattle and sheep, for there was joy in Israel.

■ Bringing Back the Ark

13 David conferred with each of his officers, the commanders of thousands and commanders of hundreds. ²He then said to the whole assembly of Israel, "If it seems good to you and if it is the will of the LORD our God, let us send word far and wide to the rest of our brothers throughout the territories of Israel, and also to the priests and Levites who are

with them in their towns and pasture-lands, to come and join us. ³Let us bring the ark of our God back to us, for we did not enquire ofᵃ itᵇ during the reign of Saul." ⁴The whole assembly agreed to do this, because it seemed right to all the people.

⁵So David assembled all the Israelites, from the Shihor River in Egypt to Leboᶜ Hamath, to bring the ark of God from Kiriath Jearim. ⁶David and all the Israelites with him went to Baalah of Judah (Kiriath Jearim) to bring up from there the ark of God the LORD, who is enthroned between the cherubim — the ark that is called by the Name.

⁷They moved the ark of God from Abinadab's house on a new cart, with Uzzah and Ahio guiding it. ⁸David and all the Israelites were celebrating with all their might before God, with songs and with harps, lyres, tambourines, cymbals and trumpets.

⁹When they came to the threshing-floor of Kidon, Uzzah reached out his hand to steady the ark, because the oxen stumbled. ¹⁰The LORD's anger burned against Uzzah, and he struck him down because he had put his hand on the ark. So he died there before God.

13:9 ■ WHY DID UZZAH DIE?

People who read of Uzzah's death in 2 Samuel 6:6–7 have often puzzled over why he died for trying to keep God's ark from tipping over. In 1 Chronicles the reason is clearer. David explained (15:13) that the Lord had been angry at them for moving the ark in a way disobedient to God's law.

Numbers 4:14–15 and Exodus 37:5 specify that Levites were to carry the ark with poles — and never touch it, on pain of death. Uzzah and his brother, non-Levites, were carrying it on an ox cart — the same vehicle the Philistines had used (1 Samuel 6:7). When the oxen stumbled and Uzzah stepped in to catch the ark, that was the final straw. Uzzah's death resulted from prolonged (though possibly well-intentioned) disobedience to God's direction. God had told them how to honour the ark, a sign of his presence. Their sloppiness revealed a lack of concern for God's honour.

---

¹¹Then David was angry because the LORD's wrath had broken out against Uzzah, and to this day that place is called Perez Uzzah.ᵈ

¹²David was afraid of God that day and asked, "How can I ever bring the ark of God to me?" ¹³He did not take the ark to be with him in the City of David. Instead, he took it aside to the house of Obed-Edom the Gittite. ¹⁴The ark of God remained with the family of Obed-Edom in his house for three months, and the LORD blessed his household and everything he had.

■ David's House and Family

14 Now Hiram king of Tyre sent messengers to David, along with cedar logs, stonemasons and carpenters to build a palace for him. ²And David knew that the LORD had established him as king over

Israel and that his kingdom had been highly exalted for the sake of his people Israel.

3In Jerusalem David took more wives and became the father of more sons and daughters. 4These are the names of the children born to him there: Shammua, Shobab, Nathan, Solomon, 5Ibhar, Elishua, Elpelet, 6Nogah, Nepheg, Japhia, 7Elishama, Beeliada*a* and Eliphelet.

■ David Defeats the Philistines

8When the Philistines heard that David had been anointed king over all Israel, they went up in full force to search for him, but David heard about it and went out to meet them. 9Now the Philistines had come and raided the Valley of Rephaim; 10so David enquired of God: "Shall I go and attack the Philistines? Will you hand them over to me?"

The LORD answered him, "Go, I will hand them over to you."

11So David and his men went up to Baal Perazim, and there he defeated them. He said, "As waters break out, God has broken out against my enemies by my hand." So that place was called Baal Perazim.*b* 12The Philistines had abandoned their gods there, and David gave orders to burn them in the fire.

13Once more the Philistines raided the valley; 14so David enquired of God again, and God answered him, "Do not go straight up, but circle round them and attack them in front of the balsam trees. 15As soon as you hear the sound of marching in the tops of the balsam trees, move out to battle, because that will mean God has gone out in front of you to strike the Philistine army." 16So David did as God commanded him, and they struck down the Philistine army, all the way from Gibeon to Gezer.

17So David's fame spread throughout every land, and the LORD made all the nations fear him.

■ The Ark Brought to Jerusalem

15 After David had constructed buildings for himself in the City of David, he prepared a place for the ark of God and pitched a tent for it. 2Then David said, "No-one but the Levites may carry the ark of God, because the LORD chose them to carry the ark of the LORD and to minister before him for ever."

3David assembled all Israel in Jerusalem to bring up the ark of the LORD to the place he had prepared for it. 4He called together the descendants of Aaron and the Levites:

5From the descendants of Kohath,
 Uriel the leader and 120 relatives;
6from the descendants of Merari,
 Asaiah the leader and 220 relatives;
7from the descendants of Gershon,*a*
 Joel the leader and 130 relatives;
8from the descendants of Elizaphan,
 Shemaiah the leader and 200 relatives;
9from the descendants of Hebron,
 Eliel the leader and 80 relatives;
10from the descendants of Uzziel,
 Amminadab the leader and 112 relatives.

11Then David summoned Zadok and Abiathar the priests, and Uriel, Asaiah, Joel, Shemaiah, Eliel and Amminadab the Levites. 12He said to them, "You are the heads of the Levitical families; you and your fellow Levites are to consecrate yourselves and bring up the ark of the LORD, the God of Israel, to the place I have prepared for it. 13It was because you, the Levites, did not bring it up the first time that the LORD our God broke out in anger against us. We did not enquire of him about how to do it in the prescribed way." 14So the priests and Levites consecrated themselves in order to bring up the ark of the LORD, the God of Israel. 15And the Levites carried the ark of God with the poles on their shoulders, as Moses had commanded in accordance with the word of the LORD.

16David told the leaders of the Levites to appoint their brothers as singers to sing joyful songs, accompanied by musical instruments: lyres, harps and cymbals.

17So the Levites appointed Heman son of Joel; from his brothers, Asaph son of Berekiah; and from their brothers the Merarites, Ethan son of Kushaiah; 18and with them their brothers next in rank: Zechariah,*b* Jaaziel, Shemiramoth, Jehiel, Unni, Eliab, Benaiah, Maaseiah, Mattithiah, Eliphelehu, Mikneiah, Obed-Edom and Jeiel,*c* the gatekeepers.

19The musicians Heman, Asaph and Ethan were to sound the bronze cymbals; 20Zechariah, Aziel, Shemiramoth, Jehiel, Unni, Eliab, Maaseiah and Benaiah were to play the lyres according to *alamoth,d* 21and Mattithiah, Eliphelehu, Mikneiah, Obed-Edom, Jeiel and Azaziah were to play the harps, directing according to *sheminith.e* 22Kenaniah the head Levite was in charge of the singing; that was his responsibility because he was skilful at it.

23Berekiah and Elkanah were to be doorkeepers for the ark. 24Shebaniah, Joshaphat, Nethanel, Amasai, Zechariah, Benaiah and Eliezer the priests were to blow trumpets before the ark of God. Obed-Edom and Jehiah were also to be doorkeepers for the ark.

25So David and the elders of Israel and the commanders of units of a thousand went to bring up the ark of the covenant of the LORD from the house of Obed-Edom, with rejoicing. 26Because God had helped the Levites who were carrying the ark of the covenant of the LORD, seven bulls and seven rams were sacrificed. 27Now David was clothed in a robe of fine linen, as were all the Levites who were carrying the ark, and as were the singers, and Kenaniah, who was in charge of the singing of the choirs. David also wore a linen ephod. [28]So all Israel brought up the ark of the covenant of the LORD with shouts, with the sounding of rams' horns and trumpets, and of cymbals, and the playing of lyres and harps.

[29]As the ark of the covenant of the LORD was entering the City of David, Michal daughter of Saul watched from a window. And when she saw King David dancing and celebrating, she despised him in her heart.

16 They brought the ark of God and set it inside the tent that David had pitched for it, and they presented burnt offerings and fellowship offerings[a] before God. [2]After David had finished sacrificing the burnt offerings and fellowship offerings, he blessed the people in the name of the LORD. [3]Then he gave a loaf of bread, a cake of dates and a cake of raisins to each Israelite man and woman.

[4]He appointed some of the Levites to minister before the ark of the LORD, to make petition, to give thanks, and to praise the LORD, the God of Israel: [5]Asaph was the chief, Zechariah second, then Jeiel, Shemiramoth, Jehiel, Mattithiah, Eliab, Benaiah, Obed-Edom and Jeiel. They were to play the lyres and harps, Asaph was to sound the cymbals, [6]and Benaiah and Jahaziel the priests were to blow the trumpets regularly before the ark of the covenant of God.

■ David's Psalm of Thanks

[7]That day David first committed to Asaph and his associates this psalm of thanks to the LORD:

[8]Give thanks to the LORD, call on his name;
     make known among the nations what he has
        done.
[9]Sing to him, sing praise to him;
     tell of all his wonderful acts.
[10]Glory in his holy name;
     let the hearts of those who seek the LORD
        rejoice.
[11]Look to the LORD and his strength;
     seek his face always.
[12]Remember the wonders he has done,
     his miracles, and the judgments he
        pronounced,
[13]O descendants of Israel his servant,
     O sons of Jacob, his chosen ones.

[14]He is the LORD our God;
     his judgments are in all the earth.
[15]He remembers[b] his covenant for ever,
     the word he commanded, for a thousand
        generations,
[16]the covenant he made with Abraham,
     the oath he swore to Isaac.
[17]He confirmed it to Jacob as a decree,
     to Israel as an everlasting covenant:
[18]"To you I will give the land of Canaan
     as the portion you will inherit."

[19]When they were but few in number,
     few indeed, and strangers in it,
[20]they[c] wandered from nation to nation,
     from one kingdom to another.
[21]He allowed no man to oppress them;

for their sake he rebuked kings:
[22]"Do not touch my anointed ones;
     do my prophets no harm."

[23]Sing to the LORD, all the earth;
     proclaim his salvation day after day.
[24]Declare his glory among the nations,
     his marvellous deeds among all peoples.
[25]For great is the LORD and most worthy of
        praise;
     he is to be feared above all gods.
[26]For all the gods of the nations are idols,
     but the LORD made the heavens.
[27]Splendour and majesty are before him;
     strength and joy in his dwelling-place.
[28]Ascribe to the LORD, O families of nations,
     ascribe to the LORD glory and strength,
[29] ascribe to the LORD the glory due to his
        name.
Bring an offering and come before him;
     worship the LORD in the splendour of his[d]
        holiness.
[30]Tremble before him, all the earth!
     The world is firmly established; it cannot be
        moved.
[31]Let the heavens rejoice, let the earth be glad;
     let them say among the nations, "The LORD
        reigns!"
[32]Let the sea resound, and all that is in it;
     let the fields be jubilant, and everything in
        them!
[33]Then the trees of the forest will sing,
     they will sing for joy before the LORD,
     for he comes to judge the earth.

[34]Give thanks to the LORD, for he is good;
     his love endures for ever.
[35]Cry out, "Save us, O God our Saviour;
     gather us and deliver us from the nations,
     that we may give thanks to your holy name,
     that we may glory in your praise."
[36]Praise be to the LORD, the God of Israel,
     from everlasting to everlasting.

Then all the people said "Amen" and "Praise the LORD."

[37]David left Asaph and his associates before the ark of the covenant of the LORD to minister there regularly, according to each day's requirements. [38]He also left Obed-Edom and his sixty-eight associates to minister with them. Obed-Edom son of Jeduthun, and also Hosah, were gatekeepers.

[39]David left Zadok the priest and his fellow priests before the tabernacle of the LORD at the high place in Gibeon [40]to present burnt offerings to the LORD on the altar of burnt offering regularly, morning and evening, in accordance with everything written in the Law of the LORD, which he had given Israel. [41]With them were Heman and Jeduthun and the rest of those chosen and designated by name to give thanks to the LORD, "for his love endures for ever." [42]Heman and Jeduthun were responsible for the sounding of the trumpets and cymbals and for the playing of the other instruments for sacred song. The sons of Jeduthun were stationed at the gate.

---

[a]1 Traditionally *peace offerings*; also in verse 2   [b]15 Some Septuagint manuscripts (see also Psalm 105:8); Hebrew *Remember*   [c]18–20 One Hebrew manuscript, Septuagint and Vulgate (see also Psalm 105:12); most Hebrew manuscripts *inherit, / 19though you are but few in number, / few indeed, and strangers in it." / 20They*   [d]29 Or *LORD with the splendour of*

43Then all the people left, each for his own home, and David returned home to bless his family.

16:39 ■ TWO TABERNACLES

For a number of years, Israel had two tabernacles. David had constructed a new tent for the ark of the covenant when it came to Jerusalem. Yet the old tent, dating from Moses' time, still stood at Gibeon, five miles away. Sacrifices were offered at both locations. When the temple was built under David's son Solomon, worship was centralised at Jerusalem.

■ God's Promise to David

17 After David was settled in his palace, he said to Nathan the prophet, "Here I am, living in a palace of cedar, while the ark of the covenant of the LORD is under a tent."

2Nathan replied to David, "Whatever you have in mind, do it, for God is with you."

3That night the word of God came to Nathan, saying:

4"Go and tell my servant David, 'This is what the LORD says: You are not the one to build me a house to dwell in. 5I have not dwelt in a house from the day I brought Israel up out of Egypt to this day. I have moved from one tent site to another, from one dwelling-place to another. 6Wherever I have moved with all the Israelites, did I ever say to any of their leaders*a* whom I commanded to shepherd my people, "Why have you not built me a house of cedar?" '

7"Now then, tell my servant David, 'This is what the LORD Almighty says: I took you from the pasture and from following the flock, to be ruler over my people Israel. 8I have been with you wherever you have gone, and I have cut off all your enemies from before you. Now I will make your name like the names of the greatest men of the earth. 9And I will provide a place for my people Israel and will plant them so that they can have a home of their own and no longer be disturbed. Wicked people will not oppress them any more, as they did at the beginning 10and have done ever since the time I appointed leaders over my people Israel. I will also subdue all your enemies.

" 'I declare to you that the LORD will build a house for you: 11When your days are over and you go to be with your fathers, I will raise up your offspring to succeed you, one of your own sons, and I will establish his kingdom. 12He is the one who will build a house for me, and I will establish his throne for ever. 13I will be his father, and he will be my son. I will never take my love away from him, as I took it away from your predecessor. 14I will set him over my house and my kingdom for ever; his throne will be established for ever.' "

15Nathan reported to David all the words of this entire revelation.

a 6 Traditionally judges; also in verse 10

■ David's Prayer

16Then King David went in and sat before the LORD, and he said:

"Who am I, O LORD God, and what is my family, that you have brought me this far? 17And as if this were not enough in your sight, O God, you have spoken about the future of the house of your servant. You have looked on me as though I were the most exalted of men, O LORD God.

17:16 ■ RARE TRAIT

King David possessed in abundance that rarest of qualities in a powerful ruler: humility. Ever mindful of his modest background, he credited God's grace, not his own merit, for his success. David could have taken offence at Nathan's message; after all, God was rejecting his offer to build a temple. Instead, David accepted the news with meekness and thanksgiving.

18"What more can David say to you for honouring your servant? For you know your servant, 19O LORD. For the sake of your servant and according to your will, you have done this great thing and made known all these great promises.

20"There is no-one like you, O LORD, and there is no God but you, as we have heard with our own ears. 21And who is like your people Israel—the one nation on earth whose God went out to redeem a people for himself, and to make a name for yourself, and to perform great and awesome wonders by driving out nations from before your people, whom you redeemed from Egypt? 22You made your people Israel your very own for ever, and you, O LORD, have become their God.

23"And now, LORD, let the promise you have made concerning your servant and his house be established for ever. Do as you promised, 24so that it will be established and that your name will be great for ever. Then men will say, 'The LORD Almighty, the God over Israel, is Israel's God!' And the house of your servant David will be established before you.

25"You, my God, have revealed to your servant that you will build a house for him. So your servant has found courage to pray to you. 26O LORD, you are God! You have promised these good things to your servant. 27Now you have been pleased to bless the house of your servant, that it may continue for ever in your sight; for you, O LORD, have blessed it, and it will be blessed for ever."

■ David's Victories

18 In the course of time, David defeated the Philistines and subdued them, and he took Gath and its surrounding villages from the control of the Philistines.

2David also defeated the Moabites, and they became subject to him and brought tribute.

3Moreover, David fought Hadadezer king of Zobah, as far as Hamath, when he went to establish his control along the Euphrates River. 4David captured a thousand of his chariots, seven thousand charioteers and twenty thousand foot soldiers. He hamstrung all but a hundred of the chariot horses.

5When the Arameans of Damascus came to help Hadadezer king of Zobah, David struck down twenty-two thousand of them. 6He put garrisons in the Aramean kingdom of Damascus, and the Arameans became subject to him and brought tribute. The LORD gave David victory everywhere he went.

7David took the gold shields carried by the officers of Hadadezer and brought them to Jerusalem. 8From Tebah*a* and Cun, towns that belonged to Hadadezer, David took a great quantity of bronze, which Solomon used to make the bronze Sea, the pillars and various bronze articles.

9When Tou king of Hamath heard that David had defeated the entire army of Hadadezer king of Zobah, 10he sent his son Hadoram to King David to greet him and congratulate him on his victory in battle over Hadadezer, who had been at war with Tou. Hadoram brought all kinds of articles of gold and silver and bronze.

11King David dedicated these articles to the LORD, as he had done with the silver and gold he had taken from all these nations: Edom and Moab, the Ammonites and the Philistines, and Amalek.

12Abishai son of Zeruiah struck down eighteen thousand Edomites in the Valley of Salt. 13He put garrisons in Edom, and all the Edomites became subject to David. The LORD gave David victory everywhere he went.

■ David's Officials

14David reigned over all Israel, doing what was just and right for all his people. 15Joab son of Zeruiah was over the army; Jehoshaphat son of Ahilud was recorder; 16Zadok son of Ahitub and Ahimelech*b* son of Abiathar were priests; Shavsha was secretary; 17Benaiah son of Jehoiada was over the Kerethites and Pelethites; and David's sons were chief officials at the king's side.

■ HOPE IN A TIME OF SORROW
A PEOPLE STARTING AGAIN NEED TO KNOW GOD'S PROMISES

INSIGHT

"WHO AM I, O LORD GOD, AND WHAT IS MY FAMILY, THAT YOU HAVE BROUGHT ME THIS FAR?" ■ 17:16

First Chronicles was written for Israelites living centuries after David. In those years Israel had gone through tremendous sorrow. None of the kings who followed David had matched him. Israel had deteriorated until God let Babylon capture and destroy Jerusalem, carrying its population into exile.

After half a century as captives, a small proportion of the Israelites returned to their former home. They had lost, in those beaten-down years, their own sense of identity. They were no longer self-governing. They had no king to follow in David's footsteps. Their relatives were scattered all over the Middle East. Chronicles was written to help them get in touch with what Israel had once been and could become again.

After devoting nine chapters to genealogies, 1 Chronicles tells the story of the life of David. In keeping with its goal of encouragement, Chronicles leaves out stories of David's personal sin and failure. Nor does it tell of David's life before he became king. Instead it concentrates on the accomplishments David left behind for future generations.

■ THE IMPORTANCE OF WORSHIP
David emphasised worship as the foundation of Israel. As soon as he conquered Jerusalem, he brought the ark of the covenant there. He made preparations to build the temple and organised the priests and Levites to serve there. He established large bands of musicians to praise God. In response, God promised that a line of leaders would descend from him (17:10–14).

David's days were the high point of Israelite history: prosperous, secure, and, above all, devoted to God. How could the returned exiles recapture that grandeur? What resources could they use to begin again? First Chronicles emphasises a legacy they still possessed. They had Jerusalem, and they had a new temple built on the site of the old one. They had the priests and Levites, so essential to proper worship. In short, they had the resources necessary to rise again, to be God's people in God's land.

Most important, they had God. They could find strength in worshipping him, as David always had. God had made them great before; he could make them great again, and provide a new leader in David's line. A sorrowful people could start again on the old foundations — foundations that depended on an unchanging God and his unchanging choice of them.

□ LIFE QUESTIONS:
If you were to suffer great personal and material loss, as the Israelites did, what would you cling to?

a 8 Hebrew *Tibhath*, a variant of *Tebah*   *b 16* Some Hebrew manuscripts, Vulgate and Syriac (see also 2 Sam. 8:17); most Hebrew manuscripts *Abimelech*

■ The Battle Against the Ammonites

19 In the course of time, Nahash king of the Ammonites died, and his son succeeded him as king. ²David thought, "I will show kindness to Hanun son of Nahash, because his father showed kindness to me." So David sent a delegation to express his sympathy to Hanun concerning his father.

When David's men came to Hanun in the land of the Ammonites to express sympathy to him, ³the Ammonite nobles said to Hanun, "Do you think David is honouring your father by sending men to you to express sympathy? Haven't his men come to you to explore and spy out the country and overthrow it?" ⁴So Hanun seized David's men, shaved them, cut off their garments in the middle at the buttocks, and sent them away.

19:4 ■ COMEDY OF ERRORS

Wars start for the oddest of reasons. One modern war in Central America erupted after a poorly refereed soccer match. In this instance the king of Ammon misjudged the motives of a funeral delegation, and David felt obliged to respond to an insult that today seems more humorous than humiliating. The resulting war crushed one of Israel's most annoying enemies, the Ammonites, offspring of the incestuous relations between Lot and his daughter (Genesis 19).

⁵When someone came and told David about the men, he sent messengers to meet them, for they were greatly humiliated. The king said, "Stay at Jericho till your beards have grown, and then come back."

⁶When the Ammonites realised that they had become an offence to David's nostrils, Hanun and the Ammonites sent a thousand talents*ᵃ* of silver to hire chariots and charioteers from Aram Naharaim,*ᵇ* Aram Maacah and Zobah. ⁷They hired thirty-two thousand chariots and charioteers, as well as the king of Maacah with his troops, who came and camped near Medeba, while the Ammonites were mustered from their towns and moved out for battle.

⁸On hearing this, David sent Joab out with the entire army of fighting men. ⁹The Ammonites came out and drew up in battle formation at the entrance to their city, while the kings who had come were by themselves in the open country.

¹⁰Joab saw that there were battle lines in front of him and behind him; so he selected some of the best troops in Israel and deployed them against the Arameans. ¹¹He put the rest of the men under the command of Abishai his brother, and they were deployed against the Ammonites. ¹²Joab said, "If the Arameans are too strong for me, then you are to rescue me; but if the Ammonites are too strong for you, then I will rescue you. ¹³Be strong and let us fight bravely for our people and the cities of our God. The LORD will do what is good in his sight."

¹⁴Then Joab and the troops with him advanced to fight the Arameans, and they fled before him. ¹⁵When the Ammonites saw that the Arameans were fleeing, they too fled before his brother Abishai and went inside the city. So Joab went back to Jerusalem.

¹⁶After the Arameans saw that they had been routed by Israel, they sent messengers and had Arameans brought from beyond the River,*ᶜ* with Shophach the commander of Hadadezer's army leading them.

¹⁷When David was told of this, he gathered all Israel and crossed the Jordan; he advanced against them and formed his battle lines opposite them. David formed his lines to meet the Arameans in battle, and they fought against him. ¹⁸But they fled before Israel, and David killed seven thousand of their charioteers and forty thousand of their foot soldiers. He also killed Shophach the commander of their army.

¹⁹When the vassals of Hadadezer saw that they had been defeated by Israel, they made peace with David and became subject to him.

So the Arameans were not willing to help the Ammonites any more.

■ The Capture of Rabbah

20 In the spring, at the time when kings go off to war, Joab led out the armed forces. He laid waste the land of the Ammonites and went to Rabbah and besieged it, but David remained in Jerusalem. Joab attacked Rabbah and left it in ruins. ²David took the crown from the head of their king*ᵃ* — its weight was found to be a talent*ᵇ* of gold, and it was set with precious stones — and it was placed on David's head. He took a great quantity of plunder from the city ³and brought out the people who were there, consigning them to labour with saws and with iron picks and axes. David did this to all the Ammonite towns. Then David and his entire army returned to Jerusalem.

■ War With the Philistines

⁴In the course of time, war broke out with the Philistines, at Gezer. At that time Sibbecai the Hushathite killed Sippai, one of the descendants of the Rephaites, and the Philistines were subjugated.

⁵In another battle with the Philistines, Elhanan son of Jair killed Lahmi the brother of Goliath the Gittite, who had a spear with a shaft like a weaver's rod.

⁶In still another battle, which took place at Gath, there was a huge man with six fingers on each hand and six toes on each foot — twenty-four in all. He also was descended from Rapha. ⁷When he taunted Israel, Jonathan son of Shimea, David's brother, killed him.

⁸These were descendants of Rapha in Gath, and they fell at the hands of David and his men.

■ David Numbers the Fighting Men

21 Satan rose up against Israel and incited David to take a census of Israel. ²So David said to Joab and the commanders of the troops, "Go and count the Israelites from Beersheba to Dan. Then report back to me so that I may know how many there are."

³But Joab replied, "May the LORD multiply his troops a hundred times over. My lord the king, are they not all my lord's subjects? Why does my lord

---

ᵃ6 That is, about 34 tons (about 34 metric tons)   *ᵇ6* That is, North-west Mesopotamia   *ᶜ16* That is, the Euphrates   *ᵃ2* Or *of Milcom*, that is, Molech   *ᵇ2* That is, about 75 pounds (about 34 kilograms) want to do this? Why should he bring guilt on Israel?"

4The king's word, however, overruled Joab; so Joab left and went throughout Israel and then came back to Jerusalem. 5Joab reported the number of the fighting men to David: In all Israel there were one million one hundred thousand men who could handle a sword, including four hundred and seventy thousand in Judah.

6But Joab did not include Levi and Benjamin in the numbering, because the king's command was repulsive to him. 7This command was also evil in the sight of God; so he punished Israel.

21:7 ■ ACT OF PRIDE

Taking a census was not in itself immoral – God commanded it in the book of Numbers (chapters 1,26). This census, however, came out of David's desire to survey his kingdom, now at peace, in order to glory in its size and its potential military strength. God wanted him to continue relying on divine help and guidance, not on national pride. Even Joab, a top general, sensed the grievous mistake (verse 3). For more details, see "Satan or the Lord?" page 292.

8Then David said to God, "I have sinned greatly by doing this. Now, I beg you, take away the guilt of your servant. I have done a very foolish thing."

9The LORD said to Gad, David's seer, 10"Go and tell David, 'This is what the LORD says: I am giving you three options. Choose one of them for me to carry out against you.'"

11So Gad went to David and said to him, "This is what the LORD says: 'Take your choice: 12three years of famine, three months of being swept away[a] before your enemies, with their swords overtaking you, or three days of the sword of the LORD—days of plague in the land, with the angel of the LORD ravaging every part of Israel.' Now then, decide how I should answer the one who sent me."

13David said to Gad, "I am in deep distress. Let me fall into the hands of the LORD, for his mercy is very great; but do not let me fall into the hands of men."

14So the LORD sent a plague on Israel, and seventy thousand men of Israel fell dead. 15And God sent an angel to destroy Jerusalem. But as the angel was doing so, the LORD saw it and was grieved because of the calamity and said to the angel who was destroying the people, "Enough! Withdraw your hand." The angel of the LORD was then standing at the threshing-floor of Araunah[b] the Jebusite.

16David looked up and saw the angel of the LORD standing between heaven and earth, with a drawn sword in his hand extended over Jerusalem. Then David and the elders, clothed in sackcloth, fell face down.

17David said to God, "Was it not I who ordered the fighting men to be counted? I am the one who has sinned and done wrong. These are but sheep. What have they done? O LORD my God, let your hand fall upon me and my family, but do not let this plague remain on your people."

18Then the angel of the LORD ordered Gad to tell David to go up and build an altar to the LORD on the threshing-floor of Araunah the Jebusite. 19So David went up in obedience to the word that Gad had spoken in the name of the LORD.

20While Araunah was threshing wheat, he turned and saw the angel; his four sons who were with him hid themselves. 21Then David approached, and when Araunah looked and saw him, he left the threshing-floor and bowed down before David with his face to the ground.

22David said to him, "Let me have the site of your threshing-floor so that I can build an altar to the LORD, that the plague on the people may be stopped. Sell it to me at the full price."

23Araunah said to David, "Take it! Let my lord the king do whatever pleases him. Look, I will give the oxen for the burnt offerings, the threshing-sledges for the wood, and the wheat for the grain offering. I will give all this."

24But King David replied to Araunah, "No, I insist on paying the full price. I will not take for the LORD what is yours, or sacrifice a burnt offering that costs me nothing."

25So David paid Araunah six hundred shekels[c] of gold for the site. 26David built an altar to the LORD there and sacrificed burnt offerings and fellowship offerings.[d] He called on the LORD, and the LORD answered him with fire from heaven on the altar of burnt offering.

27Then the LORD spoke to the angel, and he put his sword back into its sheath. 28At that time, when David saw that the LORD had answered him on the threshing-floor of Araunah the Jebusite, he offered sacrifices there. 29The tabernacle of the LORD, which Moses had made in the desert, and the altar of burnt offering were at that time on the high place at Gibeon. 30But David could not go before it to enquire of God, because he was afraid of the sword of the angel of the LORD.

22 Then David said, "The house of the LORD God is to be here, and also the altar of burnt offering for Israel."

■ Preparations for the Temple

2So David gave orders to assemble the aliens living in Israel, and from among them he appointed stonecutters to prepare dressed stone for building the house of God. 3He provided a large amount of iron to make nails for the doors of the gateways and for the fittings, and more bronze than could be weighed. 4He also provided more cedar logs than could be counted, for the Sidonians and Tyrians had brought large numbers of them to David.

5David said, "My son Solomon is young and inexperienced, and the house to be built for the LORD should be of great magnificence and fame and splendour in the sight of all the nations. Therefore I will make preparations for it." So David made extensive preparations before his death.

6Then he called for his son Solomon and charged him to build a house for the LORD, the God of Israel. 7David said to Solomon: "My son, I had it in my heart to build a house for the Name of the LORD my God. 8But this word of the LORD came to me: 'You have

a 12 Hebrew; Septuagint and Vulgate (see also 2 Sam. 24:13) of fleeing   b 15 Hebrew Ornan, a variant of Araunah; also in verses 18–28   c 25 That is, about 15 pounds (about 7 kilograms)   d 26 Traditionally peace offerings shed much blood and have fought many wars. You are not to build a house for my Name, because you have shed much blood on the earth in my sight. ⁹But you will have a son who will be a man of peace and rest, and I will give him rest from all his enemies on every side. His name will be Solomon,ᵃ and I will grant Israel peace and quiet during his reign. ¹⁰He is the one who will build a house for my Name. He will be my son, and I will be his father. And I will establish the throne of his kingdom over Israel for ever.'

22:8 ■ A MAN OF BLOOD

David explained to Solomon that the Lord had not allowed him to build the temple because of his life of bloodshed. This does not suggest that David had been wrong to lead Israel in battle. God had directed him to conduct at least some of the wars. Nonetheless, war and bloodshed, even when necessary, fall short of God's ideal. He wanted the temple built by a man of peace.

¹¹"Now, my son, the LORD be with you, and may you have success and build the house of the LORD your God, as he said you would. ¹²May the LORD give you discretion and understanding when he puts you in command over Israel, so that you may keep the law of the LORD your God. ¹³Then you will have success if you are careful to observe the decrees and laws that the LORD gave to Moses for Israel. Be strong and courageous. Do not be afraid or discouraged.

¹⁴"I have taken great pains to provide for the temple of the LORD a hundred thousand talentsᵇ of gold, a million talentsᶜ of silver, quantities of bronze and iron too great to be weighed, and wood and stone. And you may add to them. ¹⁵You have many workmen: stonecutters, masons and carpenters, as well as men skilled in every kind of work ¹⁶in gold and silver, bronze and iron—craftsmen beyond number. Now begin the work, and the LORD be with you."

¹⁷Then David ordered all the leaders of Israel to help his son Solomon. ¹⁸He said to them, "Is not the LORD your God with you? And has he not granted you rest on every side? For he has handed the inhabitants of the land over to me, and the land is subject to the LORD and to his people. ¹⁹Now devote your heart and soul to seeking the LORD your God. Begin to build the sanctuary of the LORD God, so that you may bring the ark of the covenant of the LORD and the sacred articles belonging to God into the temple that will be built for the Name of the LORD."

■ The Levites

23 When David was old and full of years, he made his son Solomon king over Israel.

²He also gathered together all the leaders of Israel, as well as the priests and Levites. ³The Levites thirty years old or more were counted, and the total number of men was thirty-eight thousand. ⁴David said, "Of these, twenty-four thousand are to supervise the work of the temple of the LORD and six thousand are to be officials and judges. ⁵Four thousand are to be gatekeepers and four thousand are to praise the LORD with the musical instruments I have provided for that purpose."

⁶David divided the Levites into groups corresponding to the sons of Levi: Gershon, Kohath and Merari.

23:6 ■ KEEPING THE TEMPLE

Ever since the time of Moses, the Levites had been in charge of carrying and caring for the tabernacle—the portable tent where God was worshipped. But now that the ark had been placed permanently in Jerusalem, and a temple was to be built, the Levites needed new duties and organisation. Chapters 23–26 describe those duties in detail.

■ Gershonites

⁷Belonging to the Gershonites:
Ladan and Shimei.
⁸The sons of Ladan:
Jehiel the first, Zetham and Joel—three in all.
⁹The sons of Shimei:
Shelomoth, Haziel and Haran—three in all.
These were the heads of the families of Ladan.
¹⁰And the sons of Shimei:
Jahath, Ziza,ᵃ Jeush and Beriah.
These were the sons of Shimei—four in all.
¹¹Jahath was the first and Ziza the second, but Jeush and Beriah did not have many sons; so they were counted as one family with one assignment.

■ Kohathites

¹²The sons of Kohath:
Amram, Izhar, Hebron and Uzziel—four in all.
¹³The sons of Amram:
Aaron and Moses.
Aaron was set apart, he and his descendants for ever, to consecrate the most holy things, to offer sacrifices before the LORD, to minister before him and to pronounce blessings in his name for ever. ¹⁴The sons of Moses the man of God were counted as part of the tribe of Levi.
¹⁵The sons of Moses:
Gershom and Eliezer.
¹⁶The descendants of Gershom:
Shubael was the first.
¹⁷The descendants of Eliezer:
Rehabiah was the first.
Eliezer had no other sons, but the sons of Rehabiah were very numerous.
¹⁸The sons of Izhar:
Shelomith was the first.
¹⁹The sons of Hebron:
Jeriah the first, Amariah the second, Jahaziel the third and Jekameam the fourth.
²⁰The sons of Uzziel:
Micah the first and Isshiah the second.

ᵃ9 *Solomon* sounds like and may be derived from the Hebrew for *peace.*   ᵇ14 That is, about 3,395 tons (about 3,450 metric tons)   ᶜ14 That is, about 33,950 tons (about 34,500 metric tons)   ᵃ10 One Hebrew manuscript, Septuagint and Vulgate (see also verse 11); most Hebrew manuscripts *Zina*

■ Merarites

21The sons of Merari:
 Mahli and Mushi.
 The sons of Mahli:
 Eleazar and Kish.
22Eleazar died without having sons: he had only daughters. Their cousins, the sons of Kish, married them.
23The sons of Mushi:
 Mahli, Eder and Jerimoth—three in all.

24These were the descendants of Levi by their families—the heads of families as they were registered under their names and counted individually, that is, the workers twenty years old or more who served in the temple of the LORD. 25For David had said, "Since the LORD, the God of Israel, has granted rest to his people and has come to dwell in Jerusalem for ever, 26the Levites no longer need to carry the tabernacle or any of the articles used in its service." 27According to the last instructions of David, the Levites were counted from those twenty years old or more.

28The duty of the Levites was to help Aaron's descendants in the service of the temple of the LORD: to be in charge of the courtyards, the side rooms, the purification of all sacred things and the performance of other duties at the house of God. 29They were in charge of the bread set out on the table, the flour for the grain offerings, the unleavened wafers, the baking and the mixing, and all measurements of quantity and size. 30They were also to stand every morning to thank and praise the LORD. They were to do the same in the evening 31and whenever burnt offerings were presented to the LORD on Sabbaths and at New Moon festivals and at appointed feasts. They were to serve before the LORD regularly in the proper number and in the way prescribed for them.

23:29 ■ LITTLE PEOPLE

The best way to get volunteers is to guarantee them adequate credit, and 1 Chronicles leaves no volunteer in nation-building overlooked. After focusing on King David for several chapters, the book turns attention to those who performed menial tasks: bailiffs, bureaucrats, bread-bakers, weight-checkers, custodians, accountants, musicians, guards, a recording secretary.

32And so the Levites carried out their responsibilities for the Tent of Meeting, for the Holy Place and, under their brothers the descendants of Aaron, for the service of the temple of the LORD.

■ The Divisions of Priests

24 These were the divisions of the sons of Aaron:

The sons of Aaron were Nadab, Abihu, Eleazar and Ithamar. 2But Nadab and Abihu died before their father did, and they had no sons; so Eleazar and Ithamar served as the priests. 3With the help of Zadok a descendant of Eleazar and Ahimelech a descendant of Ithamar, David separated them into divisions for their appointed order of ministering. 4A larger number of leaders were found among Eleazar's descendants than among Ithamar's, and they were divided accordingly: sixteen heads of families from Eleazar's descendants and eight heads of families from Ithamar's descendants. 5They divided them impartially by drawing lots, for there were officials of the sanctuary and officials of God among the descendants of both Eleazar and Ithamar.

6The scribe Shemaiah son of Nethanel, a Levite, recorded their names in the presence of the king and of the officials: Zadok the priest, Ahimelech son of Abiathar and the heads of families of the priests and of the Levites—one family being taken from Eleazar and then one from Ithamar.

7The first lot fell to Jehoiarib,
 the second to Jedaiah,
8the third to Harim,
 the fourth to Seorim,
9the fifth to Malkijah,
 the sixth to Mijamin,
10the seventh to Hakkoz,
 the eighth to Abijah,
11the ninth to Jeshua,
 the tenth to Shecaniah,
12the eleventh to Eliashib,
 the twelfth to Jakim,
13the thirteenth to Huppah,
 the fourteenth to Jeshebeab,
14the fifteenth to Bilgah,
 the sixteenth to Immer,
15the seventeenth to Hezir,
 the eighteenth to Happizzez,
16the nineteenth to Pethahiah,
 the twentieth to Jehezkel,
17the twenty-first to Jakin,
 the twenty-second to Gamul,
18the twenty-third to Delaiah
 and the twenty-fourth to Maaziah.

19This was their appointed order of ministering when they entered the temple of the LORD, according to the regulations prescribed for them by their forefather Aaron, as the LORD, the God of Israel, had commanded him.

■ The Rest of the Levites

20As for the rest of the descendants of Levi:
 from the sons of Amram: Shubael;
 from the sons of Shubael: Jehdeiah.
21As for Rehabiah, from his sons:
 Isshiah was the first.
22From the Izharites: Shelomoth;
 from the sons of Shelomoth: Jahath.
23The sons of Hebron: Jeriah the first,a Amariah the second, Jahaziel the third and Jekameam the fourth.
24The son of Uzziel: Micah;
 from the sons of Micah: Shamir.
25The brother of Micah: Isshiah;
 from the sons of Isshiah: Zechariah.
26The sons of Merari: Mahli and Mushi.
 The son of Jaaziah: Beno.
27The sons of Merari:
 from Jaaziah: Beno, Shoham, Zaccur and Ibri.
28From Mahli: Eleazar, who had no sons.

a23 Two Hebrew manuscripts and some Septuagint manuscripts (see also 1 Chron. 23:19); most Hebrew manuscripts The sons of Jeriah:

²⁹From Kish: the son of Kish: Jerahmeel.

³⁰And the sons of Mushi: Mahli, Eder and Jerimoth.

These were the Levites, according to their families. ³¹They also cast lots, just as their brothers the descendants of Aaron did, in the presence of King David and of Zadok, Ahimelech, and the heads of families of the priests and of the Levites. The families of the oldest brother were treated the same as those of the youngest.

■ The Singers

25 David, together with the commanders of the army, set apart some of the sons of Asaph, Heman and Jeduthun for the ministry of prophesying, accompanied by harps, lyres and cymbals. Here is the list of the men who performed this service:

25:1 ■ CHURCH AND STATE
Israel, a theocracy ruled by God through a king, had no "separation of church and state". David even consulted with his military commanders for such decisions as appointing prophets and musicians for worship.

²From the sons of Asaph:
Zaccur, Joseph, Nethaniah and Asarelah. The sons of Asaph were under the supervision of Asaph, who prophesied under the king's supervision.
³As for Jeduthun, from his sons:
Gedaliah, Zeri, Jeshaiah, Shimei,ᵃ Hashabiah and Mattithiah, six in all, under the supervision of their father Jeduthun, who prophesied, using the harp in thanking and praising the LORD.
⁴As for Heman, from his sons:
Bukkiah, Mattaniah, Uzziel, Shubael and Jerimoth; Hananiah, Hanani, Eliathah, Giddalti and Romamti-Ezer; Joshbekashah, Mallothi, Hothir and Mahazioth. ⁵All these were sons of Heman the king's seer. They were given to him through the promises of God to exalt him.ᵇ God gave Heman fourteen sons and three daughters.

⁶All these men were under the supervision of their fathers for the music of the temple of the LORD, with cymbals, lyres and harps, for the ministry at the house of God. Asaph, Jeduthun and Heman were under the supervision of the king. ⁷Along with their relatives—all of them trained and skilled in music for the LORD—they numbered 288. ⁸Young and old alike, teacher as well as student, cast lots for their duties.

⁹The first lot, which was for Asaph, fell to Joseph,
his sons and relatives,ᶜ   12ᵈ
the second to Gedaliah,
he and his relatives and sons,   12
¹⁰the third to Zaccur,

his sons and relatives,   12
¹¹the fourth to Izri,ᵉ
his sons and relatives,   12
¹²the fifth to Nethaniah,
his sons and relatives,   12
¹³the sixth to Bukkiah,
his sons and relatives,   12
¹⁴the seventh to Jesarelah,ᶠ
his sons and relatives,   12
¹⁵the eighth to Jeshaiah,
his sons and relatives,   12
¹⁶the ninth to Mattaniah,
his sons and relatives,   12
¹⁷the tenth to Shimei,
his sons and relatives,   12
¹⁸the eleventh to Azarel,ᵍ
his sons and relatives,   12
¹⁹the twelfth to Hashabiah,
his sons and relatives,   12
²⁰the thirteenth to Shubael,
his sons and relatives,   12
²¹the fourteenth to Mattithiah,
his sons and relatives,   12
²²the fifteenth to Jerimoth,
his sons and relatives,   12
²³the sixteenth to Hananiah,
his sons and relatives,   12
²⁴the seventeenth to Joshbekashah,
his sons and relatives,   12
²⁵the eighteenth to Hanani,
his sons and relatives,   12
²⁶the nineteenth to Mallothi,
his sons and relatives,   12
²⁷the twentieth to Eliathah,
his sons and relatives,   12
²⁸the twenty-first to Hothir,
his sons and relatives,   12
²⁹the twenty-second to Giddalti,
his sons and relatives,   12
³⁰the twenty-third to Mahazioth,
his sons and relatives,   12
³¹the twenty-fourth to Romamti-Ezer,
his sons and relatives.   12

■ The Gatekeepers

26 The divisions of the gatekeepers:

From the Korahites: Meshelemiah son of Kore, one of the sons of Asaph. ²Meshelemiah had sons:
Zechariah the firstborn,
Jediael the second,
Zebadiah the third,
Jathniel the fourth,
³Elam the fifth,
Jehohanan the sixth
and Eliehoenai the seventh.
⁴Obed-Edom also had sons:
Shemaiah the firstborn,
Jehozabad the second,
Joah the third,
Sacar the fourth,
Nethanel the fifth,
⁵Ammiel the sixth,

ᵃ3 One Hebrew manuscript and some Septuagint manuscripts (see also verse 17); most Hebrew manuscripts do not have *Shimei*.   ᵇ5 Hebrew *exalt the horn*   ᶜ9 See Septuagint; Hebrew does not have *his sons and relatives*.   ᵈ9 See the total in verse 7; Hebrew does not have *twelve*.   ᵉ11 A variant of *Zeri*   ᶠ14 A variant of *Asarelah*   ᵍ18 A variant of *Uzziel*

Issachar the seventh and Peullethai the eighth. (For God had blessed Obed-Edom.)

[6]His son Shemaiah also had sons, who were leaders in their father's family because they were very capable men. [7]The sons of Shemaiah: Othni, Rephael, Obed and Elzabad; his relatives Elihu and Semakiah were also able men. [8]All these were descendants of Obed-Edom; they and their sons and their relatives were capable men with the strength to do the work—descendants of Obed-Edom, 62 in all. [9]Meshelemiah had sons and relatives, who were able men—18 in all.

[10]Hosah the Merarite had sons: Shimri the first (although he was not the firstborn, his father had appointed him the first), [11]Hilkiah the second, Tabaliah the third and Zechariah the fourth. The sons and relatives of Hosah were 13 in all.

[12]These divisions of the gatekeepers, through their chief men, had duties for ministering in the temple of the LORD, just as their relatives had. [13]Lots were cast for each gate, according to their families, young and old alike.

26:12 ■ MAJOR ENTERPRISE

To assist in worship, David appointed 4,000 gatekeepers, or temple guards, and 4,000 musicians (23:3–4). The numbers give some indication of the importance attached to worship in national life. David was preparing his nation for the day when his son Solomon would build the temple.

---

[14]The lot for the East Gate fell to Shelemiah.[a] Then lots were cast for his son Zechariah, a wise counsellor, and the lot for the North Gate fell to him. [15]The lot for the South Gate fell to Obed-Edom, and the lot for the storehouse fell to his sons. [16]The lots for the West Gate and the Shalleketh Gate on the upper road fell to Shuppim and Hosah.

Guard was alongside guard: [17]There were six Levites a day on the east, four a day on the north, four a day on the south and two at a time at the storehouse. [18]As for the court to the west, there were four at the road and two at the court itself.

[19]These were the divisions of the gatekeepers who were descendants of Korah and Merari.

■ The Treasurers and Other Officials

[20]Their fellow Levites were[b] in charge of the treasuries of the house of God and the treasuries for the dedicated things.

[21]The descendants of Ladan, who were Gershonites through Ladan and who were heads of families belonging to Ladan the Gershonite, were Jehieli, [22]the sons of Jehieli, Zetham and his brother Joel. They were in charge of the treasuries of the temple of the LORD.

[23]From the Amramites, the Izharites, the Hebronites and the Uzzielites:

[24]Shubael, a descendant of Gershom son of Moses, was the officer in charge of the treasuries. [25]His relatives through Eliezer: Rehabiah his son, Jeshaiah his son, Joram his son, Zicri his son and Shelomith his son. [26]Shelomith and his relatives were in charge of all the treasuries for the things dedicated by King David, by the heads of families who were the commanders of thousands and commanders of hundreds, and by the other army commanders. [27]Some of the plunder taken in battle they dedicated for the repair of the temple of the LORD. [28]And everything dedicated by Samuel the seer and by Saul son of Kish, Abner son of Ner and Joab son of Zeruiah, and all the other dedicated things were in the care of Shelomith and his relatives.

[29]From the Izharites: Kenaniah and his sons were assigned duties away from the temple, as officials and judges over Israel.

[30]From the Hebronites: Hashabiah and his relatives—seventeen hundred able men—were responsible in Israel west of the Jordan for all the work of the LORD and for the king's service. [31]As for the Hebronites, Jeriah was their chief according to the genealogical records of their families. In the fortieth year of David's reign a search was made in the records, and capable men among the Hebronites were found at Jazer in Gilead. [32]Jeriah had two thousand seven hundred relatives, who were able men and heads of families, and King David put them in charge of the Reubenites, the Gadites and the half-tribe of Manasseh for every matter pertaining to God and for the affairs of the king.

■ Army Divisions

27 This is the list of the Israelites—heads of families, commanders of thousands and commanders of hundreds, and their officers, who served the king in all that concerned the army divisions that were on duty month by month throughout the year. Each division consisted of 24,000 men.

[2]In charge of the first division, for the first month, was Jashobeam son of Zabdiel. There were 24,000 men in his division. [3]He was a descendant of Perez and chief of all the army officers for the first month. [4]In charge of the division for the second month was Dodai the Ahohite; Mikloth was the leader of his division. There were 24,000 men in his division. [5]The third army commander, for the third month, was Benaiah son of Jehoiada the priest. He was chief and there were 24,000 men in his division. [6]This was the Benaiah who was a mighty man among the Thirty and was over the Thirty. His son Ammizabad was in charge of his division. [7]The fourth, for the fourth month, was Asahel the brother of Joab; his son Zebadiah was his successor. There were 24,000 men in his division. [8]The fifth, for the fifth month, was the commander

Shamhuth the Izrahite. There were 24,000 men in his division.
⁹The sixth, for the sixth month, was Ira the son of Ikkesh the Tekoite. There were 24,000 men in his division.
¹⁰The seventh, for the seventh month, was Helez the Pelonite, an Ephraimite. There were 24,000 men in his division.
¹¹The eighth, for the eighth month, was Sibbecai the Hushathite, a Zerahite. There were 24,000 men in his division.
¹²The ninth, for the ninth month, was Abiezer the Anathothite, a Benjamite. There were 24,000 men in his division.
¹³The tenth, for the tenth month, was Maharai the Netophathite, a Zerahite. There were 24,000 men in his division.
¹⁴The eleventh, for the eleventh month, was Benaiah the Pirathonite, an Ephraimite. There were 24,000 men in his division.
¹⁵The twelfth, for the twelfth month, was Heldai the Netophathite, from the family of Othniel. There were 24,000 men in his division.

■ Officers of the Tribes
¹⁶The officers over the tribes of Israel:

over the Reubenites: Eliezer son of Zicri;
over the Simeonites: Shephatiah son of Maacah;
¹⁷over Levi: Hashabiah son of Kemuel;
over Aaron: Zadok;
¹⁸over Judah: Elihu, a brother of David;
over Issachar: Omri son of Michael;
¹⁹over Zebulun: Ishmaiah son of Obadiah;
over Naphtali: Jerimoth son of Azriel;
²⁰over the Ephraimites: Hoshea son of Azaziah;
over half the tribe of Manasseh: Joel son of Pedaiah;
²¹over the half-tribe of Manasseh in Gilead: Iddo son of Zechariah;
over Benjamin: Jaasiel son of Abner;
²²over Dan: Azarel son of Jeroham.
These were the officers over the tribes of Israel.

²³David did not take the number of the men twenty years old or less, because the LORD had promised to make Israel as numerous as the stars in the sky. ²⁴Joab son of Zeruiah began to count the men but did not finish. Wrath came on Israel on account of this numbering, and the number was not entered in the book*a* of the annals of King David.

■ The King's Overseers
²⁵Azmaveth son of Adiel was in charge of the royal storehouses.
Jonathan son of Uzziah was in charge of the storehouses in the outlying districts, in the towns, the villages and the watchtowers.
²⁶Ezri son of Kelub was in charge of the field workers who farmed the land.
²⁷Shimei the Ramathite was in charge of the vineyards.
Zabdi the Shiphmite was in charge of the produce of the vineyards for the wine vats.
²⁸Baal-Hanan the Gederite was in charge of the olive and sycamore-fig trees in the western foothills.

Joash was in charge of the supplies of olive oil.
²⁹Shitrai the Sharonite was in charge of the herds grazing in Sharon.
Shaphat son of Adlai was in charge of the herds in the valleys.
³⁰Obil the Ishmaelite was in charge of the camels.
Jehdeiah the Meronothite was in charge of the donkeys.
³¹Jaziz the Hagrite was in charge of the flocks.
All these were the officials in charge of King David's property.

³²Jonathan, David's uncle, was a counsellor, a man of insight and a scribe. Jehiel son of Hacmoni took care of the king's sons.
³³Ahithophel was the king's counsellor.
Hushai the Arkite was the king's friend. ³⁴Ahithophel was succeeded by Jehoiada son of Benaiah and by Abiathar.
Joab was the commander of the royal army.

■ David's Plans for the Temple
28 David summoned all the officials of Israel to assemble at Jerusalem: the officers over the tribes, the commanders of the divisions in the service of the king, the commanders of thousands and commanders of hundreds, and the officials in charge of all the property and livestock belonging to the king and his sons, together with the palace officials, the mighty men and all the brave warriors.
²King David rose to his feet and said: "Listen to me, my brothers and my people. I had it in my heart to build a house as a place of rest for the ark of the covenant of the LORD, for the footstool of our God, and I made plans to build it. ³But God said to me, 'You are not to build a house for my Name, because you are a warrior and have shed blood.'
⁴"Yet the LORD, the God of Israel, chose me from my whole family to be king over Israel for ever. He chose Judah as leader, and from the house of Judah he chose my family, and from my father's sons he was pleased to make me king over all Israel. ⁵Of all my sons — and the LORD has given me many — he has chosen my son Solomon to sit on the throne of the kingdom of the LORD over Israel. ⁶He said to me, 'Solomon your son is the one who will build my house and my courts, for I have chosen him to be my son, and I will be his father. ⁷I will establish his kingdom for ever if he is unswerving in carrying out my commands and laws, as is being done at this time.'
⁸"So now I charge you in the sight of all Israel and of the assembly of the LORD, and in the hearing of our God: Be careful to follow all the commands of the LORD your God, that you may possess this good land and pass it on as an inheritance to your descendants for ever.
⁹"And you, my son Solomon, acknowledge the God of your father, and serve him with wholehearted devotion and with a willing mind, for the LORD searches every heart and understands every motive behind the thoughts. If you seek him, he will be found by you; but if you forsake him, he will reject you for ever. ¹⁰Consider now, for the LORD has chosen you to build a temple as a sanctuary. Be strong and do the work."

a24 Septuagint; Hebrew *number*

11Then David gave his son Solomon the plans for the portico of the temple, its buildings, its storerooms, its upper parts, its inner rooms and the place of atonement. 12He gave him the plans of all that the Spirit had put in his mind for the courts of the temple of the LORD and all the surrounding rooms, for the treasuries of the temple of God and for the treasuries for the dedicated things. 13He gave him instructions for the divisions of the priests and Levites, and for all the work of serving in the temple of the LORD, as well as for all the articles to be used in its service. 14He designated the weight of gold for all the gold articles to be used in various kinds of service, and the weight of silver for all the silver articles to be used in various kinds of service: 15the weight of gold for the gold lampstands and their lamps, with the weight for each lampstand and its lamps; and the weight of silver for each silver lampstand and its lamps, according to the use of each lampstand; 16the weight of gold for each table for consecrated bread; the weight of silver for the silver tables; 17the weight of pure gold for the forks, sprinkling bowls and pitchers; the weight of gold for each gold dish; the weight of silver for each silver dish; 18and the weight of the refined gold for the altar of incense. He also gave him the plan for the chariot, that is, the cherubim of gold that spread their wings and shelter the ark of the covenant of the LORD.

28:9 ■ CONDITIONAL PROMISE

God's promise to David of unending descendants on the throne was so important to Israel that it was reported, in different forms, several times. (See chapter 17, for instance.) Sometimes it read as though God would bless a line of successful kings regardless of their behaviour. Here, though, David explained that God's favour would depend on Solomon's devotion to God.

19"All this," David said, "I have in writing from the hand of the LORD upon me, and he gave me understanding in all the details of the plan."

20David also said to Solomon his son, "Be strong and courageous, and do the work. Do not be afraid or discouraged, for the LORD God, my God, is with you. He will not fail you or forsake you until all the work for the service of the temple of the LORD is finished. 21The divisions of the priests and Levites are ready for all the work on the temple of God, and every willing man skilled in any craft will help you in all the work. The officials and all the people will obey your every command."

■ Gifts for Building the Temple

29 Then King David said to the whole assembly: "My son Solomon, the one whom God has chosen, is young and inexperienced. The task is great, because this palatial structure is not for man but for the LORD God. 2With all my resources I have provided for the temple of my God—gold for the gold work, silver for the silver, bronze for the

bronze, iron for the iron and wood for the wood, as well as onyx for the settings, turquoise,a stones of various colours, and all kinds of fine stone and marble—all of these in large quantities. 3Besides, in my devotion to the temple of my God I now give my personal treasures of gold and silver for the temple of my God, over and above everything I have provided for this holy temple: 4three thousand talentsb of gold (gold of Ophir) and seven thousand talentsc of refined silver, for the overlaying of the walls of the buildings, 5for the gold work and the silver work, and for all the work to be done by the craftsmen. Now, who is willing to consecrate himself today to the LORD?"

6Then the leaders of families, the officers of the tribes of Israel, the commanders of thousands and commanders of hundreds, and the officials in charge of the king's work gave willingly. 7They gave towards the work on the temple of God five thousand talentsd and ten thousand daricse of gold, ten thousand talents f of silver, eighteen thousand talentsg of bronze and a hundred thousand talentsh of iron. 8Any who had precious stones gave them to the treasury of the temple of the LORD in the custody of Jehiel the Gershonite. 9The people rejoiced at the willing response of their leaders, for they had given freely and wholeheartedly to the LORD. David the king also rejoiced greatly.

■ David's Prayer

10David praised the LORD in the presence of the whole assembly, saying,

"Praise be to you, O LORD,
    God of our father Israel,
    from everlasting to everlasting.
11Yours, O LORD, is the greatness and the power
    and the glory and the majesty and the splendour,
    for everything in heaven and earth is yours.
Yours, O LORD, is the kingdom;
    you are exalted as head over all.
12Wealth and honour come from you;
    you are the ruler of all things.
In your hands are strength and power
    to exalt and give strength to all.
13Now, our God, we give you thanks,
    and praise your glorious name.

29:10 ■ DAVID'S GREAT PRAYER

David's prayer at the beginning of temple construction shows why he was a man after God's own heart. Despite all his achievements, he was deeply humble. He wanted glory to go to God, not himself. This passage would have reminded the original readers of Chronicles, back from exile and without a king, that David's greatest concern was for the temple, where his people could worship and serve God. They, his descendants, did not need a king to carry on David's deepest concerns.

---

a2 The meaning of the Hebrew for this word is uncertain.   b4 That is, about 100 tons (about 100 metric tons)   c4 That is, about 240 tons (about 240 metric tons)   d7 That is, about 170 tons (about 170 metric tons)   e7 That is, about 185 pounds (about 84 kilograms)   f7 That is, about 340 tons (about 345 metric tons)   g7 That is, about 610 tons (about 620 metric tons)   h7 That is, about 3,400 tons (about 3,450 metric tons)

14"But who am I, and who are my people, that we should be able to give as generously as this? Everything comes from you, and we have given you only what comes from your hand. 15We are aliens and strangers in your sight, as were all our forefathers. Our days on earth are like a shadow, without hope. 16O LORD our God, as for all this abundance that we have provided for building you a temple for your Holy Name, it comes from your hand, and all of it belongs to you. 17I know, my God, that you test the heart and are pleased with integrity. All these things have I given willingly and with honest intent. And now I have seen with joy how willingly your people who are here have given to you. 18O LORD, God of our fathers Abraham, Isaac and Israel, keep this desire in the hearts of your people for ever, and keep their hearts loyal to you. 19And give my son Solomon the wholehearted devotion to keep your commands, requirements and decrees and to do everything to build the palatial structure for which I have provided."

20Then David said to the whole assembly, "Praise the LORD your God." So they all praised the LORD, the God of their fathers; they bowed low and fell prostrate before the LORD and the king.

■ Solomon Acknowledged as King

21The next day they made sacrifices to the LORD and presented burnt offerings to him: a thousand bulls, a thousand rams and a thousand male lambs, together with their drink offerings, and other sacrifices in abundance for all Israel. 22They ate and drank with great joy in the presence of the LORD that day.

Then they acknowledged Solomon son of David as king a second time, anointing him before the LORD to be ruler and Zadok to be priest. 23So Solomon sat on the throne of the LORD as king in place of his father David. He prospered and all Israel obeyed him. 24All the officers and mighty men, as well as all of King David's sons, pledged their submission to King Solomon.

25The LORD highly exalted Solomon in the sight of all Israel and bestowed on him royal splendour such as no king over Israel ever had before.

29:24 ■ A SECOND CORONATION
Assuming that his readers were familiar with the family quarrels told of in 1 Kings 1, the author refers to this coronation as the "second time" (verse 22). The first coronation happened when David learned that Solomon's older brother had been conspiring to become king. David immediately called for a private coronation (1 Kings 1:32–40). Only later did this public ceremony occur, when the rebellious brother swore his loyalty. Typically, 1 Chronicles leaves out the nasty politics and emphasises the positive result.

■ The Death of David

26David son of Jesse was king over all Israel. 27He ruled over Israel for forty years—seven in Hebron and thirty-three in Jerusalem. 28He died at a good old age, having enjoyed long life, wealth and honour. His son Solomon succeeded him as king.

29As for the events of King David's reign, from beginning to end, they are written in the records of Samuel the seer, the records of Nathan the prophet and the records of Gad the seer, 30together with the details of his reign and power, and the circumstances that surrounded him and Israel and the kingdoms of all the other lands.

2 CHRONICLES

INTRODUCTION

■ A TIME FOR HOPE
RESTORING PRIDE TO A GROUP OF REFUGEES

"IF MY PEOPLE, WHO ARE CALLED BY MY NAME, WILL HUMBLE THEMSELVES AND PRAY
AND SEEK MY FACE AND TURN FROM THEIR WICKED WAYS, THEN WILL I HEAR FROM
HEAVEN AND WILL FORGIVE THEIR SIN AND WILL HEAL THEIR LAND." ■ 7:14

In the early 1960s, a wave of feeling known as
"black pride" swept across America. It started
when black leaders realised that far more than
legal rights had been repressed for 200 years.
Everything about the black culture, from hair
texture to history, had taken a back seat to that of
the white majority.

A similar surge of feeling swept the UK in
the early 1990s. Black UK citizens were no
longer repressed or discriminated against but
many of them felt "rootless". Generations of
black people had been born in the UK and had
little experience or knowledge of their African
identity and culture.

A people without knowledge of its history
is like a tree without roots they said — it dies.
They had been "fitting in" for years, but no more.
They began to search back into ancient history,
to Nubia, Ethiopia and Ancient Egypt for roots.

■ NEED FOR A PEP TALK
There was a time when the Israelites, too,
desperately needed a new look at the past. Their
ancestors had also been torn from home, beaten,
and dragged off in chains to serve as slaves in a
foreign country. In Babylon, a new generation grew
up knowing little of the Israelite past: the covenant
with God, the promised line of kings, the
magnificent temple in Jerusalem.
When captive Israelites were finally allowed to
return home, they found a pile of rubble. In Israel's
Golden Age, people had travelled thousands of
miles to view the majesty of Jerusalem and its
temple. But to the refugees' horror, not one stone
of the temple remained standing. The carved
beams had all been hacked to pieces, the gold
and ivory stripped away, and the furniture
auctioned off or destroyed.

Outside the capital, whole villages had
disappeared. Vital religious customs had gone
uncelebrated for 70 years. Jewish culture was in
danger of leaking away.

The book of Chronicles was written to
those refugees who returned. For that dispirited
group of people, the author recounted the glory
days of Israel. He wanted to restore pride in the
Israelite past and bring hope to their future.

■ HISTORY IN A NEW LIGHT
Chronicles (both 1 and 2) thus retells history,
starting right at the very beginning, with Adam.
Most of the characters are familiar, but Chronicles
tells old stories in a new light. Its author isn't just
reciting facts. He is delivering a word of bright
hope, a pep talk, to just-freed refugees.

Some accuse Chronicles of being a
"whitewashed" history, especially in comparison
to the Bible's other history books. True, the
book barely mentions the Israelites' great
failures — it says nothing of David's or Solomon's
mistakes, for instance. Presumably, the refugees
had heard plenty about the dark side of their
nation's recent past: the books of Samuel and
Kings, which ruthlessly exposed those failures,
had been around for years.

Similarly, Chronicles ignores the chaotic
Northern Kingdom of Israel, and the civil war
Judah waged against it. Nothing remained of the
ten scattered tribes of the North, and the book
wastes little space on them. Instead, Chronicles
reaches higher, seeking to restore pride in the
original ideals of the nation.

■ A DISTANT HOPE
The good kings of Judah, eight in all, dominate
the story: over two-thirds of 2 Chronicles is
devoted to their reigns. Chronicles focuses on
God's special relationship with the Israelites,
recalling the covenant that had brought about their
Golden Age. It reviews the religious reforms led by
each king, and, above all, highlights the temple,
the house where God's presence came to rest. If
God had lived among them in the past, couldn't
he do so again?

■ HOW TO READ 2 CHRONICLES

You will recognise many of the stories in 2 Chronicles – about half of it closely follows other Bible passages. The author freely admits he has relied on the books of Moses, Samuel, and Kings. He also quotes from Judges, Jeremiah, Psalms, Isaiah, and Lamentations, as well as many books that have been lost to history.

But 2 Chronicles does not merely repeat. It weaves together stories and facts for a specific purpose: a Jewish philosophy of history. Chronicles sheds new light on that history by highlighting rare moments of peace and prosperity. Worship of the true God had made Israel strong. As you read, notice how 2 Chronicles underlines that fact by stressing the temple and the priests.

For comparison, you may want to read companion passages in the book of Kings (for a list, see "A Line-up of Rulers", pages 260–268). Read side by side, the two accounts clearly reveal the distinct purpose behind the book of Chronicles.

Look past all the names and events for the few kings who did right. (See "The Great Reformers", pages 388–389.) What made them successful? What lessons about faith can we learn from them?

■ 3-TRACK READING PLAN

For an explanation and complete listing of the 3-track reading plan, turn to page x.

■ TRACK 1:
Two-Week Courses on the Bible
See page x for information on these courses.

■ TRACK 2:
An Overview of 2 Chronicles in 3 Days
□ Day 1. Read the Introduction to 2 Chronicles and then chapter 20. It tells of a high point when King Jehoshaphat brought the whole nation together in prayer.
□ Day 2. Hezekiah had an eventful life, with soaring highs and deep lows. Read about a national high point in chapter 30.
□ Day 3. Hezekiah lived in treacherous times. Read of his close scrape with disaster in chapter 32.
Now turn to page xi for your next Track 2 reading project.

■ TRACK 3:
All of 2 Chronicles in 34 Days
After you have read through 2 Chronicles, turn to pages xii–xiii for your next Track 3 reading project.

□ 1	□ 2	□ 3	□ 4
□ 5	□ 6	□ 7	□ 8
□ 9	□ 10	□ 11	□ 12
□ 13	□ 14	□ 15	
□ 16–17		□ 18	□ 19
□ 20	□ 21	□ 22	□ 23
□ 24	□ 25	□ 26–27	
□ 28	□ 29	□ 30	□ 31
□ 32	□ 33	□ 34	□ 35
□ 36			

■ Solomon Asks for Wisdom

1 Solomon son of David established himself firmly over his kingdom, for the LORD his God was with him and made him exceedingly great.

²Then Solomon spoke to all Israel – to the commanders of thousands and commanders of hundreds, to the judges and to all the leaders in Israel, the heads of families – ³and Solomon and the whole assembly went to the high place at Gibeon, for God's Tent of Meeting was there, which Moses the LORD's servant had made in the desert. ⁴Now David had brought up the ark of God from Kiriath Jearim to the place he had prepared for it, because he had pitched a tent for it in Jerusalem. ⁵But the bronze altar that Bezalel son of Uri, the son of Hur, had made was in Gibeon in front of the tabernacle of the LORD; so Solomon and the assembly enquired of him there. ⁶Solomon went up to the bronze altar before the LORD in the Tent of Meeting and offered a thousand burnt offerings on it.

⁷That night God appeared to Solomon and said to him, "Ask for whatever you want me to give you."

⁸Solomon answered God, "You have shown great kindness to David my father and have made me king in his place. ⁹Now, LORD God, let your promise to my father David be confirmed, for you have made me king over a people who are as numerous as the dust of the earth. ¹⁰Give me wisdom and knowledge, that I may lead this people, for who is able to govern this great people of yours?"

¹¹God said to Solomon, "Since this is your heart's desire and you have not asked for wealth, riches or honour, nor for the death of your enemies, and since you have not asked for a long life but for wisdom and knowledge to govern my people over whom I have made you king, ¹²therefore wisdom and knowledge will be given you. And I will also give you wealth, riches and honour, such as no king who was before you ever had and none after you will have."

¹³Then Solomon went to Jerusalem from the high place at Gibeon, from before the Tent of Meeting. And he reigned over Israel.

¹⁴Solomon accumulated chariots and horses; he had fourteen hundred chariots and twelve thousand horses,ᵃ which he kept in the chariot cities and also with him in Jerusalem. ¹⁵The king made silver and gold as common in Jerusalem as stones, and cedar as plentiful as sycamore-fig trees in the foothills.

ᵃ 14 Or charioteers

16Solomon's horses were imported from Egypt*b* and from Kue*c*—the royal merchants purchased them from Kue. 17They imported a chariot from Egypt for six hundred shekels*d* of silver, and a horse for a hundred and fifty.*e* They also exported them to all the kings of the Hittites and of the Arameans.

■ Preparations for Building the Temple

2 Solomon gave orders to build a temple for the Name of the LORD and a royal palace for himself. 2He conscripted seventy thousand men as carriers and eighty thousand as stonecutters in the hills and thirty-six hundred as foremen over them.

2:2 ■ SOLOMON'S FORCED LABOUR
King Solomon drafted labourers for his construction projects much like an army drafts soldiers. His policy of forced labour sowed dissension in the kingdom, especially among resentful northern tribes. In keeping with its morale-building purpose, 2 Chronicles has little bad to say about Solomon. The author mentions Solomon's wealth (1:14; 9:22–25) without comment, although such excess defied the rules for kings (Deuteronomy 17:15–17). Chronicles also omits reference to Solomon's palace, which Kings had pointedly described as exceeding even the temple in its splendour.

3Solomon sent this message to Hiram*a* king of Tyre:

"Send me cedar logs as you did for my father David when you sent him cedar to build a palace to live in. 4Now I am about to build a temple for the Name of the LORD my God and to dedicate it to him for burning fragrant incense before him, for setting out the consecrated bread regularly, and for making burnt offerings every morning and evening and on Sabbaths and New Moons and at the appointed feasts of the LORD our God. This is a lasting ordinance for Israel.

5"The temple I am going to build will be great, because our God is greater than all other gods. 6But who is able to build a temple for him, since the heavens, even the highest heavens, cannot contain him? Who then am I to build a temple for him, except as a place to burn sacrifices before him?

7"Send me, therefore, a man skilled to work in gold and silver, bronze and iron, and in purple, crimson and blue yarn, and experienced in the art of engraving, to work in Judah and Jerusalem with my skilled craftsmen, whom my father David provided.

8"Send me also cedar, pine and algum*b* logs from Lebanon, for I know that your men are skilled in cutting timber there. My men shall work with yours 9to provide me with plenty of timber, because the temple I build must be large and magnificent. 10I will give your

servants, the woodsmen who cut the timber, twenty thousand cors*c* of ground wheat, twenty thousand cors of barley, twenty thousand baths*d* of wine and twenty thousand baths of olive oil."

11Hiram king of Tyre replied by letter to Solomon:

"Because the LORD loves his people, he has made you their king."

12And Hiram added:

"Praise be to the LORD, the God of Israel, who made heaven and earth! He has given King David a wise son, endowed with intelligence and discernment, who will build a temple for the LORD and a palace for himself.

13"I am sending you Huram-Abi, a man of great skill, 14whose mother was from Dan and whose father was from Tyre. He is trained to work in gold and silver, bronze and iron, stone and wood, and with purple and blue and crimson yarn and fine linen. He is experienced in all kinds of engraving and can execute any design given to him. He will work with your craftsmen and with those of my lord, David your father.

15"Now let my lord send his servants the wheat and barley and the olive oil and wine he promised, 16and we will cut all the logs from Lebanon that you need and will float them in rafts by sea down to Joppa. You can then take them up to Jerusalem."

17Solomon took a census of all the aliens who were in Israel, after the census his father David had taken; and they were found to be 153,600. 18He assigned 70,000 of them to be carriers and 80,000 to be stonecutters in the hills, with 3,600 foremen over them to keep the people working.

■ Solomon Builds the Temple

3 Then Solomon began to build the temple of the LORD in Jerusalem on Mount Moriah, where the LORD had appeared to his father David. It was on the threshing-floor of Araunah*a* the Jebusite, the place provided by David. 2He began building on the second day of the second month in the fourth year of his reign.

3The foundation Solomon laid for building the temple of God was sixty cubits long and twenty cubits wide*b* (using the cubit of the old standard). 4The portico at the front of the temple was twenty cubits*c* long across the width of the building and twenty cubits*d* high.

He overlaid the inside with pure gold. 5He panelled the main hall with pine and covered it with fine gold and decorated it with palm tree and chain designs. 6He adorned the temple with precious stones. And the gold he used was gold of Parvaim. 7He overlaid the ceiling beams, door-frames, walls and doors of the temple with gold, and he carved cherubim on the walls.

8He built the Most Holy Place, its length corresponding to the width of the temple—twenty cubits

---

b 16 Or possibly *Muzur,* a region in Cilicia; also in verse 17   *c 16* Probably Cilicia   *d 17* That is, about 15 pounds (about 7 kilograms)   *e 17* That is, about 3¾ pounds (about 1.7 kilograms)   *a 3* Hebrew *Huram,* a variant of *Hiram;* also in verses 11 and 12   *b 8* Probably a variant of *almug;* possibly juniper   *c 10* That is, probably about 120,000 bushels (about 4,400 kilolitres)   *d 10* That is, probably about 95,000 gallons (about 440 kilolitres)   *a 1* Hebrew *Ornan,* a variant of *Araunah*   *b 3* That is, about 90 feet (about 27 metres) long and 30 feet (about 9 metres) wide   *c 4* That is, about 30 feet (about 9 metres); also in verses 8, 11 and 13   *d 4* Some Septuagint and Syriac manuscripts; Hebrew *and a hundred and twenty* long and twenty cubits wide. He overlaid the inside with six hundred talents[e] of fine gold. [9]The gold nails weighed fifty shekels.[f] He also overlaid the upper parts with gold.

[10]In the Most Holy Place he made a pair of sculptured cherubim and overlaid them with gold. [11]The total wing-span of the cherubim was twenty cubits. One wing of the first cherub was five cubits[g] long and touched the temple wall, while its other wing, also five cubits long, touched the wing of the other cherub. [12]Similarly one wing of the second cherub was five cubits long and touched the other temple wall, and its other wing, also five cubits long, touched the wing of the first cherub. [13]The wings of these cherubim extended twenty cubits. They stood on their feet, facing the main hall.[b]

[14]He made the curtain of blue, purple and crimson yarn and fine linen, with cherubim worked into it.

3:14 ■ A TEMPORARY SEPARATION

Just as it had in the tabernacle, a curtain in the temple separated the Holy Place and Most Holy Place. The curtain symbolised the distance between God and people. Even priests were forbidden to go beyond that curtain into the presence of God, except on the Day of Atonement. When Jesus died on the cross, this temple curtain miraculously ripped in two. That event also had symbolic meaning: Christ had opened up the way to God (Hebrews 9:7–12).

[15]In the front of the temple he made two pillars, which ⌐together⌐ were thirty-five cubits[i] long, each with a capital on top measuring five cubits. [16]He made interwoven chains[j] and put them on top of the pillars. He also made a hundred pomegranates and attached them to the chains. [17]He erected the pillars in the front of the temple, one to the south and one to the north. The one to the south he named Jakin[k] and the one to the north Boaz.[l]

■ The Temple's Furnishings

4 He made a bronze altar twenty cubits long, twenty cubits wide and ten cubits high.[a] [2]He made the Sea of cast metal, circular in shape, measuring ten cubits from rim to rim and five cubits[b] high. It took a line of thirty cubits[c] to measure round it. [3]Below the rim, figures of bulls encircled it—ten to a cubit.[d] The bulls were cast in two rows in one piece with the Sea.

[4]The Sea stood on twelve bulls, three facing north, three facing west, three facing south and three facing east. The Sea rested on top of them, and their hindquarters were towards the centre. [5]It was a handbreadth[e] in thickness, and its rim was like the rim of a cup, like a lily blossom. It held three thousand baths.[f]

[6]He then made ten basins for washing and placed five on the south side and five on the north. In them the things to be used for the burnt offerings were rinsed, but the Sea was to be used by the priests for washing.

[7]He made ten gold lampstands according to the specifications for them and placed them in the temple, five on the south side and five on the north.

[8]He made ten tables and placed them in the temple, five on the south side and five on the north. He also made a hundred gold sprinkling bowls.

[9]He made the courtyard of the priests, and the large court and the doors for the court, and overlaid the doors with bronze. [10]He placed the Sea on the south side, at the south-east corner.

[11]He also made the pots and shovels and sprinkling bowls.

So Huram finished the work he had undertaken for King Solomon in the temple of God:

[12]the two pillars;
the two bowl-shaped capitals on top of the pillars;
the two sets of network decorating the two bowl-shaped capitals on top of the pillars;
[13]the four hundred pomegranates for the two sets of network (two rows of pomegranates for each network, decorating the bowl-shaped capitals on top of the pillars);
[14]the stands with their basins;
[15]the Sea and the twelve bulls under it;
[16]the pots, shovels, meat forks and all related articles.

All the objects that Huram-Abi made for King Solomon for the temple of the LORD were of polished bronze. [17]The king had them cast in clay moulds in the plain of the Jordan between Succoth and Zarethan.[g] [18]All these things that Solomon made amounted to so much that the weight of the bronze was not determined.

[19]Solomon also made all the furnishings that were in God's temple:

the golden altar;
the tables on which was the bread of the Presence;
[20]the lampstands of pure gold with their lamps, to burn in front of the inner sanctuary as prescribed;
[21]the gold floral work and lamps and tongs (they were solid gold);
[22]the pure gold wick trimmers, sprinkling bowls, dishes and censers; and the gold doors of the temple: the inner doors to the Most Holy Place and the doors of the main hall.

5 When all the work Solomon had done for the temple of the LORD was finished, he brought in the things his father David had dedicated—the silver and gold and all the furnishings—and he placed them in the treasuries of God's temple.

■ The Ark Brought to the Temple

[2]Then Solomon summoned to Jerusalem the elders of Israel, all the heads of the tribes and the chiefs

e8 That is, about 20 tons (about 21 metric tons)   f9 That is, about 1¼ pounds (about 0.6 kilogram)   g11 That is, about 7½ feet (about 2.3 metres); also in verse 15   b13 Or facing inward   i15 That is, about 52 feet (about 16 metres)   j16 Or possibly made chains in the inner sanctuary; the meaning of the Hebrew for this phrase is uncertain.   k17 Jakin probably means he establishes.   l17 Boaz probably means in him is strength.   a1 That is, about 30 feet (about 9 metres) long and wide, and about 15 feet (about 4.5 metres) high   b2 That is, about 7½ feet (about 2.3 metres)   c2 That is, about 45 feet (about 13.5 metres)   d3 That is, about 1½ feet (about 0.5 metre)   e5 That is, about 3 inches (about 8 centimetres)   f5 That is, about 14,500 gallons (about 66 kilolitres)   g17 Hebrew Zeredatha, a variant of Zarethan of the Israelite families, to bring up the ark of the LORD's covenant from Zion, the City of David. ³And all the men of Israel came together to the king at the time of the festival in the seventh month.

⁴When all the elders of Israel had arrived, the Levites took up the ark, ⁵and they brought up the ark and the Tent of Meeting and all the sacred furnishings in it. The priests, who were Levites, carried them up; ⁶and King Solomon and the entire assembly of Israel that had gathered about him were before the ark, sacrificing so many sheep and cattle that they could not be recorded or counted.

⁷The priests then brought the ark of the LORD's covenant to its place in the inner sanctuary of the temple, the Most Holy Place, and put it beneath the wings of the cherubim. ⁸The cherubim spread their wings over the place of the ark and covered the ark and its carrying poles. ⁹These poles were so long that their ends, extending from the ark, could be seen from in front of the inner sanctuary, but not from outside the Holy Place; and they are still there today. ¹⁰There was nothing in the ark except the two tablets that Moses had placed in it at Horeb, where the LORD made a covenant with the Israelites after they came out of Egypt.

5:10 ■ PROOF OF THE COVENANT
Until the invasion by Babylon, the Israelites possessed a visible reminder of God's treaty, or "covenant", with them. It stayed in the most sacred piece of furniture in Israel, the ark. But the ark was lost during the Babylonian captivity – and has never been found.

¹¹The priests then withdrew from the Holy Place. All the priests who were there had consecrated themselves, regardless of their divisions. ¹²All the Levites who were musicians – Asaph, Heman, Jeduthun and their sons and relatives – stood on the east side of the altar, dressed in fine linen and playing cymbals, harps and lyres. They were accompanied by 120 priests sounding trumpets. ¹³The trumpeters and singers joined in unison, as with one voice, to give praise and thanks to the LORD. Accompanied by trumpets, cymbals and other instruments, they raised their voices in praise to the LORD and sang:

"He is good;
    his love endures for ever."

Then the temple of the LORD was filled with a cloud, ¹⁴and the priests could not perform their service because of the cloud, for the glory of the LORD filled the temple of God.

6 Then Solomon said, "The LORD has said that he would dwell in a dark cloud; ²I have built a magnificent temple for you, a place for you to dwell for ever."

³While the whole assembly of Israel was standing there, the king turned round and blessed them. ⁴Then he said:

"Praise be to the LORD, the God of Israel, who with his hands has fulfilled what he promised with his mouth to my father David. For he said,

⁵'Since the day I brought my people out of Egypt, I have not chosen a city in any tribe of Israel to have a temple built for my Name to be there, nor have I chosen anyone to be the leader over my people Israel. ⁶But now I have chosen Jerusalem for my Name to be there, and I have chosen David to rule my people Israel.'

⁷"My father David had it in his heart to build a temple for the Name of the LORD, the God of Israel. ⁸But the LORD said to my father David, 'Because it was in your heart to build a temple for my Name, you did well to have this in your heart. ⁹Nevertheless, you are not the one to build the temple, but your son, who is your own flesh and blood – he is the one who will build the temple for my Name.'

¹⁰"The LORD has kept the promise he made. I have succeeded David my father and now I sit on the throne of Israel, just as the LORD promised, and I have built the temple for the Name of the LORD, the God of Israel. ¹¹There I have placed the ark, in which is the covenant of the LORD that he made with the people of Israel."

■ Solomon's Prayer of Dedication

¹²Then Solomon stood before the altar of the LORD in front of the whole assembly of Israel and spread out his hands. ¹³Now he had made a bronze platform, five cubits*ᵃ* long, five cubits wide and three cubits*ᵇ* high, and had placed it in the centre of the outer court. He stood on the platform and then knelt down before the whole assembly of Israel and spread out his hands towards heaven. ¹⁴He said:

"O LORD, God of Israel, there is no God like you in heaven or on earth – you who keep your covenant of love with your servants who continue wholeheartedly in your way. ¹⁵You have kept your promise to your servant David my father; with your mouth you have promised and with your hand you have fulfilled it – as it is today.

6:14 ■ SOLOMON'S PEAK
This chapter records Solomon's high point as a leader and hints at his lost potential. Thanks to David's conquests, Israel was at peace, and prosperous. Solomon's splendid prayer reveals the depth of his wisdom and spiritual sensitivity. But from this point on, Solomon, potentially the greatest of all Israel's rulers, slid towards selfishness and overindulgence. His failings led the nation into immorality and eventual civil war.

¹⁶"Now LORD, God of Israel, keep for your servant David my father the promises you made to him when you said, 'You shall never fail to have a man to sit before me on the throne of Israel, if only your sons are careful in all they do to walk before me according to my law, as you have done.' ¹⁷And now, O LORD, God of Israel, let your word that you promised your servant David come true.

¹⁸"But will God really dwell on earth with

a 13 That is, about 7½ feet (about 2.3 metres)   *b 13* That is, about 4½ feet (about 1.4 metres) men? The heavens, even the highest heavens, cannot contain you. How much less this temple that I have built! ¹⁹Yet give attention to your servant's prayer and his plea for mercy, O LORD my God. Hear the cry and the prayer that your servant is praying in your presence. ²⁰May your eyes be open towards this temple day and night, this place of which you said you would put your Name there. May you hear the prayer your servant prays towards this place. ²¹Hear the supplications of your servant and of your people Israel when they pray towards this place. Hear from heaven, your dwelling-place; and when you hear, forgive.

²²"When a man wrongs his neighbour and is required to take an oath and he comes and swears the oath before your altar in this temple, ²³then hear from heaven and act. Judge between your servants, repaying the guilty by bringing down on his own head what he has done. Declare the innocent not guilty and so establish his innocence.

²⁴"When your people Israel have been defeated by an enemy because they have sinned against you and when they turn back and confess your name, praying and making supplication before you in this temple, ²⁵then hear from heaven and forgive the sin of your people Israel and bring them back to the land you gave to them and their fathers.

²⁶"When the heavens are shut up and there is no rain because your people have sinned against you, and when they pray towards this place and confess your name and turn from their sin because you have afflicted them, ²⁷then hear from heaven and forgive the sin of your servants, your people Israel. Teach them the right way to live, and send rain on the land that you gave your people for an inheritance.

²⁸"When famine or plague comes to the land, or blight or mildew, locusts or grasshoppers, or when enemies besiege them in any of their cities, whatever disaster or disease may come, ²⁹and when a prayer or plea is made by any of your people Israel — each one aware of his afflictions and pains, and spreading out his hands towards this temple — ³⁰then hear from heaven, your dwelling-place. Forgive, and deal with each man according to all he does, since you know his heart (for you alone know the hearts of men), ³¹so that they will fear you and walk in your ways all the time they live in the land that you gave our fathers.

³²"As for the foreigner who does not belong to your people Israel but has come from a distant land because of your great name and your mighty hand and your outstretched arm — when he comes and prays towards this temple, ³³then hear from heaven, your dwelling-place, and do whatever the foreigner asks of you, so that all the peoples of the earth may know your name and fear you, as do your own people Israel, and may know that this house that I have built bears your Name.

³⁴"When your people go to war against their enemies, wherever you send them, and when they pray to you towards this city you have chosen and towards the temple I have built for your Name, ³⁵then hear from heaven their prayer and their plea, and uphold their cause.

³⁶"When they sin against you — for there is no-one who does not sin — and you become angry with them and give them over to the enemy, who takes them captive to a land far away or near; ³⁷and if they have a change of heart in the land where they are held captive, and repent and plead with you in the land of their captivity and say, 'We have sinned, we have done wrong and acted wickedly'; ³⁸and if they turn back to you with all their heart and soul in the land of their captivity where they were taken, and pray towards the land that you gave their fathers, towards the city you have chosen and towards the temple that I have built for your Name; ³⁹then from heaven, your dwelling-place, hear their prayer and their pleas, and uphold their cause. And forgive your people, who have sinned against you.

⁴⁰"Now, my God, may your eyes be open and your ears attentive to the prayers offered in this place.

⁴¹"Now arise, O LORD God, and come to
      your resting place,
    you and the ark of your might.
May your priests, O LORD God, be clothed
      with salvation,
    may your saints rejoice in your
      goodness.
⁴²O LORD God, do not reject your anointed
      one.
    Remember the great love promised to
      David your servant."

■ The Dedication of the Temple

7 When Solomon finished praying, fire came down from heaven and consumed the burnt offering and the sacrifices, and the glory of the LORD filled the temple. ²The priests could not enter the temple of the LORD because the glory of the LORD filled it. ³When all the Israelites saw the fire coming down and the glory of the LORD above the temple, they knelt on the pavement with their faces to the ground, and they worshipped and gave thanks to the LORD, saying,

"He is good;
    his love endures for ever."

7:1 ■ A HIGH-WATER MARK
Solomon's prayer in chapter 6 and God's response in chapter 7 marked a high point in Israel's existence as a nation. United, the Israelites gathered before the gleaming new temple. They saw fire come down from heaven and the glory of the Lord fill the temple. Later, when this building was destroyed, Ezra led a drive to build a new temple. But the dramatic scene of God's glory coming down was never duplicated.

4Then the king and all the people offered sacrifices before the LORD. 5And King Solomon offered a sacrifice of twenty-two thousand head of cattle and a hundred and twenty thousand sheep and goats. So the king and all the people dedicated the temple of God. 6The priests took their positions, as did the Levites with the LORD's musical instruments, which King David had made for praising the LORD and which were used when he gave thanks, saying, "His love endures for ever." Opposite the Levites, the priests blew their trumpets, and all the Israelites were standing.

7Solomon consecrated the middle part of the courtyard in front of the temple of the LORD, and there he offered burnt offerings and the fat of the fellowship offerings,a because the bronze altar he had made could not hold the burnt offerings, the grain offerings and the fat portions.

8So Solomon observed the festival at that time for seven days, and all Israel with him — a vast assembly, people from Lebob Hamath to the Wadi of Egypt. 9On the eighth day they held an assembly, for they had celebrated the dedication of the altar for seven days and the festival for seven days more. 10On the twenty-third day of the seventh month he sent the people to their homes, joyful and glad in heart for the good things the LORD had done for David and Solomon and for his people Israel.

■ The LORD Appears to Solomon

11When Solomon had finished the temple of the LORD and the royal palace, and had succeeded in carrying out all he had in mind to do in the temple of the LORD and in his own palace, 12the LORD appeared to him at night and said:

"I have heard your prayer and have chosen this place for myself as a temple for sacrifices.

13"When I shut up the heavens so that there is no rain, or command locusts to devour the land or send a plague among my people, 14if my people, who are called by my name, will humble themselves and pray and seek my face and turn from their wicked ways, then will I hear from heaven and will forgive their sin and will heal their land. 15Now my eyes will be open and my ears attentive to the prayers offered in this place. 16I have chosen and consecrated this temple so that my Name may be there for ever. My eyes and my heart will always be there.

17"As for you, if you walk before me as David your father did, and do all I command, and observe my decrees and laws, 18I will establish your royal throne, as I covenanted with David your father when I said, 'You shall never fail to have a man to rule over Israel.'

19"But if youc turn away and forsake the decrees and commands I have given youc and go off to serve other gods and worship them, 20then I will uproot Israel from my land, which I have given them, and will reject this temple which I have consecrated for my Name. I will make it a byword and an object of ridicule among all peoples. 21And though this temple is now so imposing, all who pass by will be

appalled and say, 'Why has the LORD done such a thing to this land and to this temple?' 22People will answer, 'Because they have forsaken the LORD, the God of their fathers, who brought them out of Egypt, and have embraced other gods, worshipping and serving them — that is why he brought all this disaster on them.' "

■ Solomon's Other Activities

8 At the end of twenty years, during which Solomon built the temple of the LORD and his own palace, 2Solomon rebuilt the villages that Hirama had given him, and settled Israelites in them. 3Solomon then went to Hamath Zobah and captured it. 4He also built up Tadmor in the desert and all the store cities he had built in Hamath. 5He rebuilt Upper Beth Horon and Lower Beth Horon as fortified cities, with walls and with gates and bars, 6as well as Baalath and all his store cities, and all the cities for his chariots and for his horsesb — whatever he desired to build in Jerusalem, in Lebanon and throughout all the territory that he ruled.

7All the people left from the Hittites, Amorites, Perizzites, Hivites and Jebusites (these peoples were not Israelites), 8that is, their descendants remaining in the land, whom the Israelites had not destroyed — these Solomon conscripted for his slave labour force, as it is to this day. 9But Solomon did not make slaves of the Israelites for his work; they were his fighting men, commanders of his captains, and commanders of his chariots and charioteers. 10They were also King Solomon's chief officials — two hundred and fifty officials supervising the men.

11Solomon brought Pharaoh's daughter up from the City of David to the palace he had built for her, for he said, "My wife must not live in the palace of David king of Israel, because the places the ark of the LORD has entered are holy."

> **8:11 ■ INCONSISTENT ETHICS**
> Solomon scrupulously kept Pharaoh's daughter, a Gentile foreigner, apart from the Israelite sacred places. Yet as the book of Kings shows, he eventually allowed his foreign wives to bring in their own idols, which had a disastrous effect on Israel.

12On the altar of the LORD that he had built in front of the portico, Solomon sacrificed burnt offerings to the LORD, 13according to the daily requirement for offerings commanded by Moses for Sabbaths, New Moons and the three annual feasts — the Feast of Unleavened Bread, the Feast of Weeks and the Feast of Tabernacles. 14In keeping with the ordinance of his father David, he appointed the divisions of the priests for their duties and the Levites to lead the praise and to assist the priests according to each day's requirement. He also appointed the gatekeepers by divisions for the various gates, because this was what David the man of God had ordered. 15They did not deviate from the king's commands to the priests or to the Levites in any matter, including that of the treasuries.

a7 Traditionally peace offerings   b8 Or from the entrance to   c19 The Hebrew is plural.   a2 Hebrew Huram, a variant of Hiram; also in verse 18
b6 Or charioteers

16All Solomon's work was carried out, from the day the foundation of the temple of the LORD was laid until its completion. So the temple of the LORD was finished.

17Then Solomon went to Ezion Geber and Elath on the coast of Edom. 18And Hiram sent him ships commanded by his own officers, men who knew the sea. These, with Solomon's men, sailed to Ophir and brought back four hundred and fifty talents*c* of gold, which they delivered to King Solomon.

■ The Queen of Sheba Visits Solomon

9 When the queen of Sheba heard of Solomon's fame, she came to Jerusalem to test him with hard questions. Arriving with a very great caravan — with camels carrying spices, large quantities of gold, and precious stones — she came to Solomon and talked with him about all she had on her mind. 2Solomon answered all her questions; nothing was too hard for him to explain to her. 3When the queen of Sheba saw the wisdom of Solomon, as well as the palace he had built, 4the food on his table, the seating of his officials, the attending servants in their robes, the cupbearers in their robes and the burnt offerings he made at*a* the temple of the LORD, she was overwhelmed.

5She said to the king, "The report I heard in my own country about your achievements and your wisdom is true. 6But I did not believe what they said until I came and saw with my own eyes. Indeed, not even half the greatness of your wisdom was told me; you have far exceeded the report I heard. 7How happy your men must be! How happy your officials, who continually stand before you and hear your wisdom! 8Praise be to the LORD your God, who has delighted in you and placed you on his throne as king to rule for the LORD your God. Because of the love of your God for Israel and his desire to uphold them for ever, he has made you king over them, to maintain justice and righteousness."

9Then she gave the king 120 talents*b* of gold, large quantities of spices, and precious stones. There had never been such spices as those the queen of Sheba gave to King Solomon.

10(The men of Hiram and the men of Solomon brought gold from Ophir; they also brought algumwood*c* and precious stones. 11The king used the algum-wood to make steps for the temple of the LORD and for the royal palace, and to make harps and lyres for the musicians. Nothing like them had ever been seen in Judah.)

12King Solomon gave the queen of Sheba all she desired and asked for; he gave her more than she had brought to him. Then she left and returned with her retinue to her own country.

■ Solomon's Splendour

13The weight of the gold that Solomon received yearly was 666 talents,*d* 14not including the revenues brought in by merchants and traders. Also all the kings of Arabia and the governors of the land brought gold and silver to Solomon.

15King Solomon made two hundred large shields of hammered gold; six hundred bekas*e* of hammered gold went into each shield. 16He also made three hundred small shields of hammered gold, with three hundred bekas*f* of gold in each shield. The king put them in the Palace of the Forest of Lebanon.

9:12 ■ AN UNFOUNDED RUMOUR

The Queen of Sheba has mistakenly gone down in legend as one of Solomon's lovers. The king had 700 wives and 300 concubines, but the Queen of Sheba was not among them.

The queen's personal visit from hundreds of miles away shows Jerusalem's reputation as the sumptuous showpiece of the Middle East. She was probably on a high-level diplomatic mission. Solomon's kingdom represented a huge threat to her land, which previously had held a trade monopoly over the land route through Israel.

Solomon financed his building projects through iron and copper-smelting industries. He traded these products to Arabia and Africa for gold, silver, ivory, and exotic animals. Evidently, he and the queen reached an agreement.

17Then the king made a great throne inlaid with ivory and overlaid with pure gold. 18The throne had six steps, and a footstool of gold was attached to it. On both sides of the seat were armrests, with a lion standing beside each of them. 19Twelve lions stood on the six steps, one at either end of each step. Nothing like it had ever been made for any other kingdom. 20All King Solomon's goblets were gold, and all the household articles in the Palace of the Forest of Lebanon were pure gold. Nothing was made of silver, because silver was considered of little value in Solomon's day. 21The king had a fleet of trading ships*g* manned by Hiram's*b* men. Once every three years it returned, carrying gold, silver and ivory, and apes and baboons.

22King Solomon was greater in riches and wisdom than all the other kings of the earth. 23All the kings of the earth sought audience with Solomon to hear the wisdom God had put in his heart. 24Year after year, everyone who came brought a gift — articles of silver and gold, and robes, weapons and spices, and horses and mules.

25Solomon had four thousand stalls for horses and chariots, and twelve thousand horses,*i* which he kept in the chariot cities and also with him in Jerusalem. 26He ruled over all the kings from the River*j* to the land of the Philistines, as far as the border of Egypt. 27The king made silver as common in Jerusalem as stones, and cedar as plentiful as sycamore-fig trees in the foothills. 28Solomon's horses were imported from Egypt*k* and from all other countries.

■ Solomon's Death

29As for the other events of Solomon's reign, from beginning to end, are they not written in the records of Nathan the prophet, in the prophecy of Ahijah the Shilonite and in the visions of Iddo the seer concerning Jeroboam son of Nebat? 30Solomon reigned in

---

c 18 That is, about 17 tons (about 16 metric tons)   *a 4* Or *the ascent by which he went up to*   *b 9* That is, about 4 tons (about 4 metric tons)
c 10 Probably a variant of *almug-wood*   *d 13* That is, about 23 tons (about 23 metric tons)   *e 15* That is, about 7½ pounds (about 3.5 kilograms)
f 16 That is, about 3¾ pounds (about 1.7 kilograms)   *g 21* Hebrew *of ships that could go to Tarshish*   *b 21* Hebrew *Huram*, a variant of *Hiram*
i 25 Or *charioteers*   *j 26* That is, the Euphrates   *k 28* Or possibly *Muzur*, a region in Cilicia

Jerusalem over all Israel for forty years. 31Then he rested with his fathers and was buried in the city of David his father. And Rehoboam his son succeeded him as king.

■ Israel Rebels Against Rehoboam

10 Rehoboam went to Shechem, for all the Israelites had gone there to make him king. 2When Jeroboam son of Nebat heard this (he was in Egypt, where he had fled from King Solomon), he returned from Egypt. 3So they sent for Jeroboam, and he and all Israel went to Rehoboam and said to him: 4"Your father put a heavy yoke on us, but now lighten the harsh labour and the heavy yoke he put on us, and we will serve you."

5Rehoboam answered, "Come back to me in three days." So the people went away.

6Then King Rehoboam consulted the elders who had served his father Solomon during his lifetime. "How would you advise me to answer these people?" he asked.

7They replied, "If you will be kind to these people and please them and give them a favourable answer, they will always be your servants."

8But Rehoboam rejected the advice the elders gave him and consulted the young men who had grown up with him and were serving him. 9He asked them, "What is your advice? How should we answer these people who say to me, 'Lighten the yoke your father put on us'?"

10The young men who had grown up with him replied, "Tell the people who have said to you, 'Your father put a heavy yoke on us, but make our yoke lighter'—tell them, 'My little finger is thicker than my father's waist. 11My father laid on you a heavy yoke; I will make it even heavier. My father scourged you with whips; I will scourge you with scorpions.' "

12Three days later Jeroboam and all the people returned to Rehoboam, as the king had said, "Come back to me in three days." 13The king answered them harshly. Rejecting the advice of the elders, 14he followed the advice of the young men and said, "My father made your yoke heavy; I will make it even heavier. My father scourged you with whips; I will scourge you with scorpions." 15So the king did not listen to the people, for this turn of events was from God, to fulfil the word that the LORD had spoken to Jeroboam son of Nebat through Ahijah the Shilonite.

16When all Israel saw that the king refused to listen to them, they answered the king:

"What share do we have in David,
    what part in Jesse's son?
To your tents, O Israel!
Look after your own house, O David!"

So all the Israelites went home. 17But as for the Israelites who were living in the towns of Judah, Rehoboam still ruled over them.

18King Rehoboam sent out Adoniram,*a* who was in charge of forced labour, but the Israelites stoned him to death. King Rehoboam, however, managed to get into his chariot and escape to Jerusalem. 19So Israel has been in rebellion against the house of David to this day.

a 18 Hebrew Hadoram, a variant of Adoniram

11 When Rehoboam arrived in Jerusalem, he mustered the house of Judah and Benjamin—a hundred and eighty thousand fighting men—to make war against Israel and to regain the kingdom for Rehoboam.

10:19 ■ UNIFIED FRONT
Second Chronicles pays little attention to the rebellion of the ten northern tribes against the two tribes in Judah. As the book of Kings shows, the two kingdoms existed side by side, and the North, Israel, often achieved more power than the South. But Chronicles, written to survivors in the South, virtually ignores the history of the North. In fact, in several places it uses the word *Israel* to refer to the South, Judah.

2But this word of the LORD came to Shemaiah the man of God: 3"Say to Rehoboam son of Solomon king of Judah and to all the Israelites in Judah and Benjamin, 4'This is what the LORD says: Do not go up to fight against your brothers. Go home, every one of you, for this is my doing.' " So they obeyed the words of the LORD and turned back from marching against Jeroboam.

■ Rehoboam Fortifies Judah

5Rehoboam lived in Jerusalem and built up towns for defence in Judah: 6Bethlehem, Etam, Tekoa, 7Beth Zur, Soco, Adullam, 8Gath, Mareshah, Ziph, 9Adoraim, Lachish, Azekah, 10Zorah, Aijalon and Hebron. These were fortified cities in Judah and Benjamin. 11He strengthened their defences and put commanders in them, with supplies of food, olive oil and wine. 12He put shields and spears in all the cities, and made them very strong. So Judah and Benjamin were his.

13The priests and Levites from all their districts throughout Israel sided with him. 14The Levites even abandoned their pasture-lands and property, and came to Judah and Jerusalem because Jeroboam and his sons had rejected them as priests of the LORD. 15And he appointed his own priests for the high places and for the goat and calf idols he had made. 16Those from every tribe of Israel who set their hearts on seeking the LORD, the God of Israel, followed the Levites to Jerusalem to offer sacrifices to the LORD, the God of their fathers. 17They strengthened the kingdom of Judah and supported Rehoboam son of Solomon for three years, walking in the ways of David and Solomon during this time.

■ Rehoboam's Family

18Rehoboam married Mahalath, who was the daughter of David's son Jerimoth and of Abihail, the daughter of Jesse's son Eliab. 19She bore him sons: Jeush, Shemariah and Zaham. 20Then he married Maacah daughter of Absalom, who bore him Abijah, Attai, Ziza and Shelomith. 21Rehoboam loved Maacah daughter of Absalom more than any of his other wives and concubines. In all he had eighteen wives and sixty concubines, twenty-eight sons and sixty daughters.

²²Rehoboam appointed Abijah son of Maacah to be the chief prince among his brothers, in order to make him king. ²³He acted wisely, dispersing some of his sons throughout the districts of Judah and Benjamin, and to all the fortified cities. He gave them abundant provisions and took many wives for them.

■ Shishak Attacks Jerusalem

12 After Rehoboam's position as king was established and he had become strong, he and all Israel*a* with him abandoned the law of the LORD. ²Because they had been unfaithful to the LORD, Shishak king of Egypt attacked Jerusalem in the fifth year of King Rehoboam. ³With twelve hundred chariots and sixty thousand horsemen and the innumerable troops of Libyans, Sukkites and Cushites*b* that came with him from Egypt, ⁴he captured the fortified cities of Judah and came as far as Jerusalem.

⁵Then the prophet Shemaiah came to Rehoboam and to the leaders of Judah who had assembled in Jerusalem for fear of Shishak, and he said to them, "This is what the LORD says: 'You have abandoned me; therefore I now abandon you to Shishak.' "

⁶The leaders of Israel and the king humbled themselves and said, "The LORD is just."

⁷When the LORD saw that they had humbled themselves, this word of the LORD came to Shemaiah: "Since they have humbled themselves, I will not destroy them but will soon give them deliverance. My wrath will not be poured out on Jerusalem through Shishak. ⁸They will, however, become subject to him, so that they may learn the difference between serving me and serving the kings of other lands."

⁹When Shishak king of Egypt attacked Jerusalem, he carried off the treasures of the temple of the LORD and the treasures of the royal palace. He took everything, including the gold shields that Solomon had made. ¹⁰So King Rehoboam made bronze shields to replace them and assigned these to the commanders of the guard on duty at the entrance to the royal palace. ¹¹Whenever the king went to the LORD's temple, the guards went with him, bearing the shields, and afterwards they returned them to the guardroom.

¹²Because Rehoboam humbled himself, the LORD's anger turned from him, and he was not totally destroyed. Indeed, there was some good in Judah.

¹³King Rehoboam established himself firmly in Jerusalem and continued as king. He was forty-one years old when he became king, and he reigned for seventeen years in Jerusalem, the city the LORD had chosen out of all the tribes of Israel in which to put his Name. His mother's name was Naamah; she was an Ammonite. ¹⁴He did evil because he had not set his heart on seeking the LORD.

¹⁵As for the events of Rehoboam's reign, from beginning to end, are they not written in the records of Shemaiah the prophet and of Iddo the seer that deal with genealogies? There was continual warfare between Rehoboam and Jeroboam. ¹⁶Rehoboam rested with his fathers and was buried in the City of David. And Abijah his son succeeded him as king.

■ Abijah King of Judah

13 In the eighteenth year of the reign of Jeroboam, Abijah became king of Judah, ²and he reigned in Jerusalem for three years. His mother's name was Maacah,*a* a daughter*b* of Uriel of Gibeah.

There was war between Abijah and Jeroboam. ³Abijah went into battle with a force of four hundred thousand able fighting men, and Jeroboam drew up a battle line against him with eight hundred thousand able troops.

⁴Abijah stood on Mount Zemaraim, in the hill country of Ephraim, and said, "Jeroboam and all Israel, listen to me! ⁵Don't you know that the LORD, the God of Israel, has given the kingship of Israel to David and his descendants for ever by a covenant of salt? ⁶Yet Jeroboam son of Nebat, an official of Solomon son of David, rebelled against his master. ⁷Some worthless scoundrels gathered around him and opposed Rehoboam son of Solomon when he was young and indecisive and not strong enough to resist them.

13:4 ■ A BRIGHTER OUTLOOK
Typically, Chronicles paints a rosy picture of Judah's kings. The account of Abijah in Kings, for example, tells nothing of this speech and dismisses his reign as wicked (1 Kings 15:1–8).

---

⁸"And now you plan to resist the kingdom of the LORD, which is in the hands of David's descendants. You are indeed a vast army and have with you the golden calves that Jeroboam made to be your gods. ⁹But didn't you drive out the priests of the LORD, the sons of Aaron, and the Levites, and make priests of your own as the peoples of other lands do? Whoever comes to consecrate himself with a young bull and seven rams may become a priest of what are not gods.

¹⁰"As for us, the LORD is our God, and we have not forsaken him. The priests who serve the LORD are sons of Aaron, and the Levites assist them. ¹¹Every morning and evening they present burnt offerings and fragrant incense to the LORD. They set out the bread on the ceremonially clean table and light the lamps on the gold lampstand every evening. We are observing the requirements of the LORD our God. But you have forsaken him. ¹²God is with us; he is our leader. His priests with their trumpets will sound the battle cry against you. Men of Israel, do not fight against the LORD, the God of your fathers, for you will not succeed."

¹³Now Jeroboam had sent troops round to the rear, so that while he was in front of Judah the ambush was behind them. ¹⁴Judah turned and saw that they were being attacked at both front and rear. Then they cried out to the LORD. The priests blew their trumpets ¹⁵and the men of Judah raised the battle cry. At the sound of their battle cry, God routed Jeroboam and all Israel before Abijah and Judah. ¹⁶The Israelites fled before Judah, and God delivered them into their hands. ¹⁷Abijah and his men inflicted heavy losses on them, so that there were five hundred thousand casualties among Israel's able

---

a1 That is, Judah, as frequently in 2 Chronicles 2 Chron. 11:20 and 1 Kings 15:2); Hebrew *Micaiah*   *b3* That is, people from the upper Nile region   *b2* Or *granddaughter*   *a2* Most Septuagint manuscripts and Syriac (see also men. 18The men of Israel were subdued on that occasion, and the men of Judah were victorious because they relied on the LORD, the God of their fathers.

19Abijah pursued Jeroboam and took from him the towns of Bethel, Jeshanah and Ephron, with their surrounding villages. 20Jeroboam did not regain power during the time of Abijah. And the LORD struck him down and he died.

21But Abijah grew in strength. He married fourteen wives and had twenty-two sons and sixteen daughters.

22The other events of Abijah's reign, what he did and what he said, are written in the annotations of the prophet Iddo.

14 And Abijah rested with his fathers and was buried in the City of David. Asa his son succeeded him as king, and in his days the country was at peace for ten years.

■ Asa King of Judah

2Asa did what was good and right in the eyes of the LORD his God. 3He removed the foreign altars and the high places, smashed the sacred stones and cut down the Asherah poles.a 4He commanded Judah to seek the LORD, the God of their fathers, and to obey his laws and commands. 5He removed the high places and incense altars in every town in Judah, and the kingdom was at peace under him. 6He built up the fortified cities of Judah, since the land was at peace. No-one was at war with him during those years, for the LORD gave him rest.

7"Let us build up these towns," he said to Judah, "and put walls round them, with towers, gates and bars. The land is still ours, because we have sought the LORD our God; we sought him and he has given us rest on every side." So they built and prospered.

8Asa had an army of three hundred thousand men from Judah, equipped with large shields and with spears, and two hundred and eighty thousand from Benjamin, armed with small shields and with bows. All these were brave fighting men.

9Zerah the Cushite marched out against them with a vast armyb and three hundred chariots, and came as far as Mareshah. 10Asa went out to meet him, and they took up battle positions in the Valley of Zephathah near Mareshah.

11Then Asa called to the LORD his God and said, "LORD, there is no-one like you to help the powerless against the mighty. Help us, O LORD our God, for we rely on you, and in your name we have come against this vast army. O LORD, you are our God; do not let man prevail against you."

12The LORD struck down the Cushites before Asa and Judah. The Cushites fled, 13and Asa and his army pursued them as far as Gerar. Such a great number of Cushites fell that they could not recover; they were crushed before the LORD and his forces. The men of Judah carried off a large amount of plunder. 14They destroyed all the villages around Gerar, for the terror of the LORD had fallen upon them. They plundered all these villages, since there was much booty there. 15They also attacked the camps of the herdsmen and carried off droves of sheep and goats and camels. Then they returned to Jerusalem.

■ Asa's Reform

15 The Spirit of God came upon Azariah son of Oded. 2He went out to meet Asa and said to him, "Listen to me, Asa and all Judah and Benjamin. The LORD is with you when you are with him. If you seek him, he will be found by you, but if you forsake him, he will forsake you. 3For a long time Israel was without the true God, without a priest to teach and without the law. 4But in their distress they turned to the LORD, the God of Israel, and sought him, and he was found by them. 5In those days it was not safe to travel about, for all the inhabitants of the lands were in great turmoil. 6One nation was being crushed by another and one city by another, because God was troubling them with every kind of distress. 7But as for you, be strong and do not give up, for your work will be rewarded."

8When Asa heard these words and the prophecy of Azariah son ofa Oded the prophet, he took courage. He removed the detestable idols from the whole land of Judah and Benjamin and from the towns he had captured in the hills of Ephraim. He repaired the altar of the LORD that was in front of the portico of the LORD's temple.

9Then he assembled all Judah and Benjamin and the people from Ephraim, Manasseh and Simeon who had settled among them, for large numbers had come over to him from Israel when they saw that the LORD his God was with him.

15:9 ■ NORTHERN VISITORS

For the first 50 years after Jeroboam's rebellion, Israel and Judah fought a civil war. Judah was badly outnumbered, but had one great rallying point: God's temple in the city of Jerusalem. Many of the kings of Israel had built idols on "high places" as alternative worship sites to discourage their citizens from making the pilgrimage to Jerusalem. But when a southern king such as Asa launched a religious revival, members of the northern tribes would sometimes come over to Jerusalem.

10They assembled at Jerusalem in the third month of the fifteenth year of Asa's reign. 11At that time they sacrificed to the LORD seven hundred head of cattle and seven thousand sheep and goats from the plunder they had brought back. 12They entered into a covenant to seek the LORD, the God of their fathers, with all their heart and soul. 13All who would not seek the LORD, the God of Israel, were to be put to death, whether small or great, man or woman. 14They took an oath to the LORD with loud acclamation, with shouting and with trumpets and horns. 15All Judah rejoiced about the oath because they had sworn it wholeheartedly. They sought God eagerly, and he was found by them. So the LORD gave them rest on every side.

16King Asa also deposed his grandmother Maacah from her position as queen mother, because she had made a repulsive Asherah pole. Asa cut the pole down, broke it up and burned it in the Kidron Valley. 17Although he did not remove the high places from

---

a3 That is, symbols of the goddess Asherah; here and elsewhere in 2 Chronicles   b9 Hebrew with an army of a thousand thousands or with an army of
thousands upon thousands   a8 Vulgate and Syriac (see also Septuagint and verse 1); Hebrew does not have Azariah son of.

Israel, Asa's heart was fully committed ⌊to the LORD⌋ all his life. 18He brought into the temple of God the silver and gold and the articles that he and his father had dedicated.

19There was no more war until the thirty-fifth year of Asa's reign.

■ Asa's Last Years

16 In the thirty-sixth year of Asa's reign Baasha king of Israel went up against Judah and fortified Ramah to prevent anyone from leaving or entering the territory of Asa king of Judah.

2Asa then took the silver and gold out of the treasuries of the LORD's temple and of his own palace and sent it to Ben-Hadad king of Aram, who was ruling in Damascus. 3"Let there be a treaty between me and you," he said, "as there was between my father and your father. See, I am sending you silver and gold. Now break your treaty with Baasha king of Israel so that he will withdraw from me."

4Ben-Hadad agreed with King Asa and sent the commanders of his forces against the towns of Israel. They conquered Ijon, Dan, Abel Maim*a* and all the store cities of Naphtali. 5When Baasha heard this, he stopped building Ramah and abandoned his work. 6Then King Asa brought all the men of Judah, and they carried away from Ramah the stones and timber Baasha had been using. With them he built up Geba and Mizpah.

7At that time Hanani the seer came to Asa king of Judah and said to him: "Because you relied on the king of Aram and not on the LORD your God, the army of the king of Aram has escaped from your hand. 8Were not the Cushites*b* and Libyans a mighty army with great numbers of chariots and horsemen*c*? Yet when you relied on the LORD, he delivered them into your hand. 9For the eyes of the LORD range throughout the earth to strengthen those whose hearts are fully committed to him. You have done a foolish thing, and from now on you will be at war."

10Asa was angry with the seer because of this; he was so enraged that he put him in prison. At the same time Asa brutally oppressed some of the people.

11The events of Asa's reign, from beginning to end, are written in the book of the kings of Judah and Israel. 12In the thirty-ninth year of his reign Asa was afflicted with a disease in his feet. Though his disease was severe, even in his illness he did not seek help from the LORD, but only from the physicians. 13Then in the forty-first year of his reign Asa died and rested with his fathers. 14They buried him in the tomb that he had cut out for himself in the City of David. They laid him on a bier covered with spices and various blended perfumes, and they made a huge fire in his honour.

■ Jehoshaphat King of Judah

17 Jehoshaphat his son succeeded him as king and strengthened himself against Israel. 2He stationed troops in all the fortified cities of Judah and put garrisons in Judah and in the towns of Ephraim that his father Asa had captured.

3The LORD was with Jehoshaphat because in his early years he walked in the ways that his father David had followed. He did not consult the Baals 4but sought the God of his father and followed his commands rather than the practices of Israel. 5The LORD established the kingdom under his control; and all Judah brought gifts to Jehoshaphat, so that he had great wealth and honour. 6His heart was devoted to the ways of the LORD; furthermore, he removed the high places and the Asherah poles from Judah.

16:12 ■ BAD MEDICAL ADVICE
King Asa suffered from a serious foot disease, which some scholars think was dropsy. The Bible criticises his consultations with physicians because in those days "physicians" were pagan healers who used rituals that conflicted with the law of God.

7In the third year of his reign he sent his officials Ben-Hail, Obadiah, Zechariah, Nethanel and Micaiah to teach in the towns of Judah. 8With them were certain Levites—Shemaiah, Nethaniah, Zebadiah, Asahel, Shemiramoth, Jehonathan, Adonijah, Tobijah and Tob-Adonijah—and the priests Elishama and Jehoram. 9They taught throughout Judah, taking with them the Book of the Law of the LORD; they went round to all the towns of Judah and taught the people.

10The fear of the LORD fell on all the kingdoms of the lands surrounding Judah, so that they did not make war with Jehoshaphat. 11Some Philistines brought Jehoshaphat gifts and silver as tribute, and the Arabs brought him flocks: seven thousand seven hundred rams and seven thousand seven hundred goats.

12Jehoshaphat became more and more powerful; he built forts and store cities in Judah 13and had large supplies in the towns of Judah. He also kept experienced fighting men in Jerusalem. 14Their enrolment by families was as follows:

From Judah, commanders of units of 1,000:
Adnah the commander, with 300,000 fighting men;
15next, Jehohanan the commander, with 280,000;
16next, Amasiah son of Zicri, who volunteered himself for the service of the LORD, with 200,000.
17From Benjamin:
Eliada, a valiant soldier, with 200,000 men armed with bows and shields;
18next, Jehozabad, with 180,000 men armed for battle.

19These were the men who served the king, besides those he stationed in the fortified cities throughout Judah.

■ Micaiah Prophesies Against Ahab

18 Now Jehoshaphat had great wealth and honour, and he allied himself with Ahab by marriage. 2Some years later he went down to visit Ahab in Samaria. Ahab slaughtered many sheep and cattle

for him and the people with him and urged him to attack Ramoth Gilead. ³Ahab king of Israel asked Jehoshaphat king of Judah, "Will you go with me against Ramoth Gilead?"

Jehoshaphat replied, "I am as you are, and my people as your people; we will join you in the war." ⁴But Jehoshaphat also said to the king of Israel, "First seek the counsel of the LORD."

⁵So the king of Israel brought together the prophets — four hundred men — and asked them, "Shall we go to war against Ramoth Gilead, or shall I refrain?"

"Go," they answered, "for God will give it into the king's hand."

⁶But Jehoshaphat asked, "Is there not a prophet of the LORD here whom we can enquire of?"

18:6 ■ A TRUE OR FALSE PROPHET?

Looking back from a modern perspective, it is difficult to imagine the confusion that surrounded ancient prophets. Which ones were true prophets and which were false? In this case, 400 prophets all insisted God said one thing; only one bold man contradicted them. King Jehoshaphat sensed a falseness in the 400 and insisted on listening to the true prophet. Yet, unaccountably, he failed to heed Micaiah's warning. The decision nearly cost him his life. See Deuteronomy 18:17–22 for advice on distinguishing true prophets from false.

⁷The king of Israel answered Jehoshaphat, "There is still one man through whom we can enquire of the LORD, but I hate him because he never prophesies anything good about me, but always bad. He is Micaiah son of Imlah."

"The king should not say that," Jehoshaphat replied.

⁸So the king of Israel called one of his officials and said, "Bring Micaiah son of Imlah at once."

⁹Dressed in their royal robes, the king of Israel and Jehoshaphat king of Judah were sitting on their thrones at the threshing-floor by the entrance to the gate of Samaria, with all the prophets prophesying before them. ¹⁰Now Zedekiah son of Kenaanah had made iron horns, and he declared, "This is what the LORD says: 'With these you will gore the Arameans until they are destroyed.' "

¹¹All the other prophets were prophesying the same thing. "Attack Ramoth Gilead and be victorious," they said, "for the LORD will give it into the king's hand."

¹²The messenger who had gone to summon Micaiah said to him, "Look, as one man the other prophets are predicting success for the king. Let your word agree with theirs, and speak favourably."

¹³But Micaiah said, "As surely as the LORD lives, I can tell him only what my God says."

¹⁴When he arrived, the king asked him, "Micaiah, shall we go to war against Ramoth Gilead, or shall I refrain?"

"Attack and be victorious," he answered, "for they will be given into your hand."

¹⁵The king said to him, "How many times must I

make you swear to tell me nothing but the truth in the name of the LORD?"

¹⁶Then Micaiah answered, "I saw all Israel scattered on the hills like sheep without a shepherd, and the LORD said, 'These people have no master. Let each one go home in peace.' "

¹⁷The king of Israel said to Jehoshaphat, "Didn't I tell you that he never prophesies anything good about me, but only bad?"

¹⁸Micaiah continued, "Therefore hear the word of the LORD: I saw the LORD sitting on his throne with all the host of heaven standing on his right and on his left. ¹⁹And the LORD said, 'Who will entice Ahab king of Israel into attacking Ramoth Gilead and going to his death there?'

"One suggested this, and another that. ²⁰Finally, a spirit came forward, stood before the LORD and said, 'I will entice him.'

" 'By what means?' the LORD asked.

²¹" 'I will go and be a lying spirit in the mouths of all his prophets,' he said.

" 'You will succeed in enticing him,' said the LORD. 'Go and do it.'

²²"So now the LORD has put a lying spirit in the mouths of these prophets of yours. The LORD has decreed disaster for you."

²³Then Zedekiah son of Kenaanah went up and slapped Micaiah in the face. "Which way did the spirit from ᵃ the LORD go when he went from me to speak to you?" he asked.

²⁴Micaiah replied, "You will find out on the day you go to hide in an inner room."

²⁵The king of Israel then ordered, "Take Micaiah and send him back to Amon the ruler of the city and to Joash the king's son, ²⁶and say, 'This is what the king says: Put this fellow in prison and give him nothing but bread and water until I return safely.' "

²⁷Micaiah declared, "If you ever return safely, the LORD has not spoken through me." Then he added, "Mark my words, all you people!"

■ Ahab Killed at Ramoth Gilead

²⁸So the king of Israel and Jehoshaphat king of Judah went up to Ramoth Gilead. ²⁹The king of Israel said to Jehoshaphat, "I will enter the battle in disguise, but you wear your royal robes." So the king of Israel disguised himself and went into battle.

³⁰Now the king of Aram had ordered his chariot commanders, "Do not fight with anyone, small or great, except the king of Israel." ³¹When the chariot commanders saw Jehoshaphat, they thought, "This is the king of Israel." So they turned to attack him, but Jehoshaphat cried out, and the LORD helped him. God drew them away from him, ³²for when the chariot commanders saw that he was not the king of Israel, they stopped pursuing him.

³³But someone drew his bow at random and hit the king of Israel between the sections of his armour. The king told the chariot driver, "Wheel around and get me out of the fighting. I've been wounded." ³⁴All day long the battle raged, and the king of Israel propped himself up in his chariot facing the Arameans until evening. Then at sunset he died.

ᵃ23 Or Spirit of

19 When Jehoshaphat king of Judah returned safely to his palace in Jerusalem, ²Jehu the seer, the son of Hanani, went out to meet him and said to the king, "Should you help the wicked and love*ᵃ* those who hate the LORD? Because of this, the wrath of the LORD is upon you. ³There is, however, some good in you, for you have rid the land of the Asherah poles and have set your heart on seeking God."

■ Jehoshaphat Appoints Judges

⁴Jehoshaphat lived in Jerusalem, and he went out again among the people from Beersheba to the hill country of Ephraim and turned them back to the LORD, the God of their fathers. ⁵He appointed judges in the land, in each of the fortified cities of Judah. ⁶He told them, "Consider carefully what you do, because you are not judging for man but for the LORD, who is with you whenever you give a verdict. ⁷Now let the fear of the LORD be upon you. Judge carefully, for with the LORD our God there is no injustice or partiality or bribery."

⁸In Jerusalem also, Jehoshaphat appointed some of the Levites, priests and heads of Israelite families to administer the law of the LORD and to settle disputes. And they lived in Jerusalem. ⁹He gave them these orders: "You must serve faithfully and wholeheartedly in the fear of the LORD. ¹⁰In every case that comes before you from your fellow countrymen who live in the cities — whether bloodshed or other concerns of the law, commands, decrees or ordinances — you are to warn them not to sin against the LORD; otherwise his wrath will come on you and your brothers. Do this, and you will not sin.

¹¹"Amariah the chief priest will be over you in any matter concerning the LORD, and Zebadiah son of Ishmael, the leader of the tribe of Judah, will be over you in any matter concerning the king, and the Levites will serve as officials before you. Act with courage, and may the LORD be with those who do well."

■ Jehoshaphat Defeats Moab and Ammon

20 After this, the Moabites and Ammonites with some of the Meunites*ᵃ* came to make war on Jehoshaphat.

²Some men came and told Jehoshaphat, "A vast army is coming against you from Edom,*ᵇ* from the other side of the Sea.*ᶜ* It is already in Hazezon Tamar" (that is, En Gedi). ³Alarmed, Jehoshaphat resolved to enquire of the LORD, and he proclaimed a

---

■ THE GREAT REFORMERS
PROFILES IN COURAGE: THE HEROIC KINGS OF JUDAH

INSIGHT

"THE LORD IS WITH YOU WHEN YOU ARE WITH HIM. IF YOU SEEK HIM, HE WILL BE FOUND BY YOU, BUT IF YOU FORSAKE HIM, HE WILL FORSAKE YOU." ■ 15:2

Corrie ten Boom was 52 years old and unwell when she was captured and imprisoned by the Nazis for her part in the anti-Nazi underground in Holland.

Corrie and her sister Betsie suffered much hardship in prison: separation from each other for the first time in 53 years; the death of their beloved father; illness and deprivation; hard labour and punishments such as solitary confinement. Despite their conditions, the fleas, the squalor and the inhumanity of the Nazi system, Corrie and Betsie courageously managed to stand firm and continued to use their time for God. The bestselling book *The Hiding Place* tells Corrie's story.

■ COURAGE IN JUDAH
The book of 2 Chronicles can be seen as a kind of "profiles in courage" for the nation of Judah. The vast majority of kings failed the courage test. But a few exceptions did stand out, and 2 Chronicles dwells on them.

This book records a form of courage similar to that of people like Corrie. Judah was drifting further and further away from the worship of the true God. It took great courage to fight against that trend and call for a return to the law of Moses. Therefore these kings excelled not so much because of military or political strength, but because of their faithfulness to God. All the great reformers described here took over in difficult times. They helped stop, at least temporarily, their nation's tragic slide away from God.

■ ASA: CLEANING UP THE LAND (CHAPTERS 14–16)
Asa inherited a country full of crime and anarchy. He led a wildfire revival, with the whole nation uniting behind him in a huge celebration in Jerusalem. Yet Asa became cocky in his later years: he jailed a prophet of God and lived out his last days plagued by war and by disease. He did much good, but fell short of the kind of courage that endures a national crisis.

■ JEHOSHAPHAT: THE ORGANISER (CHAPTERS 17–20)
Where Asa inspired the nation, Jehoshaphat organised it. He had an outstanding domestic policy: he educated his citizens in the Book of the Law and built up a national court system and large army. Curiously, Jehoshaphat's wise judgment failed to carry over into foreign policy, for he made foolish alliances with neighbouring Israel's very worst king, Ahab.

ᵃ2 Or *and make alliances with* Septuagint and Vulgate *Aram*   *ᵃ1* Some Septuagint manuscripts; Hebrew *Ammonites*   *ᵇ2* One Hebrew manuscript; most Hebrew manuscripts, *ᶜ2* That is, the Dead Sea fast for all Judah. 4The people of Judah came together to seek help from the LORD; indeed, they came from every town in Judah to seek him.

5Then Jehoshaphat stood up in the assembly of Judah and Jerusalem at the temple of the LORD in the front of the new courtyard 6and said:

"O LORD, God of our fathers, are you not the God who is in heaven? You rule over all the kingdoms of the nations. Power and might are in your hand, and no-one can withstand you. 7O our God, did you not drive out the inhabitants of this land before your people Israel and give it for ever to the descendants of Abraham your friend? 8They have lived in it and have built in it a sanctuary for your Name, saying, 9'If calamity comes upon us, whether the sword of judgment, or plague or famine, we will stand in your presence before this temple that bears your Name and will cry out to you in our distress, and you will hear us and save us.'

10"But now here are men from Ammon, Moab and Mount Seir, whose territory you would not allow Israel to invade when they came from Egypt; so they turned away from them and did not destroy them. 11See how they are repaying us by coming to drive us out of the possession you gave us as an inheritance. 12O our God, will you not judge them? For we have no power to face this vast army that is attacking us. We do not know what to do, but our eyes are upon you."

20:6 ■ A MODEL PRAYER

Second Chronicles contains two great prayers: Solomon's in chapter 6 and King Jehoshaphat's here. Commentators often point to this as a model prayer. Jehoshaphat began with adoration of God, reminded him of his promises, set forth a problem, and asked for help. Confident, Jehoshaphat thanked God for the answer even before it came.

13All the men of Judah, with their wives and children and little ones, stood there before the LORD.

14Then the Spirit of the LORD came upon Jahaziel son of Zechariah, the son of Benaiah, the son of Jeiel, the son of Mattaniah, a Levite and descendant of Asaph, as he stood in the assembly.

15He said: "Listen, King Jehoshaphat and all who live in Judah and Jerusalem! This is what the LORD

■ JOASH: REFURBISHING THE TEMPLE (CHAPTERS 23–24)

Joash stepped onto the throne as a boy of seven. He reigned for 40 years and accomplished much that was good. 2 Chronicles focuses mainly on his repairs to the temple, which he tried to restore to former glory.

■ JEHOIADA: STRENGTH BEHIND THE THRONE (CHAPTERS 23–24)

King Joash hardly deserves a compliment without the mention of a priest named Jehoiada. He hid the boy Joash from a murderous queen and led the dramatic revolt against her. When he died at a very old age, the nation gave him the extraordinary honour of a burial place alongside kings. After Jehoiada's death, everything went downhill. The boy king who had shown such promise murdered Jehoiada's son, a deed that went down as one of the great crimes of Israelite history. It became clear that the real strength of the kingdom had come from the old priest, not the young king.

■ HEZEKIAH: A DAY TO REMEMBER (CHAPTERS 29–32)

2 Chronicles gives more space to the reign of Hezekiah than to that of any other reformer. He sponsored a great religious festival, an idea that first met with scorn and ridicule. But the nation did come together in a remarkable scene of happiness and unity. "There was great joy in Jerusalem," the Bible says, "for since the days of Solomon son of David king of Israel there had been nothing like this in Jerusalem" (30:26).

■ JOSIAH: THE COMPLETE REFORMER (CHAPTERS 34–35)

Josiah was perhaps the most reform-conscious of all Judah's kings. When the Book of the Law (probably Deuteronomy) was discovered, Josiah realised just how far his kingdom had strayed from God's ideal. He tore his robes and wept, and led Judah back towards God. A foolish military campaign brought about Josiah's death and ruined the chances for permanent change in Judah. Known as "the good king Josiah", he was mourned by the whole nation. The prophet Jeremiah composed songs, or laments, in his memory.

□ LIFE QUESTIONS:

These kings demonstrate that one person's faith can affect a great many others. Think of strong leaders you know very well. What makes them effective at inspiring and motivating others?

says to you: 'Do not be afraid or discouraged because of this vast army. For the battle is not yours, but God's. ¹⁶Tomorrow march down against them. They will be climbing up by the Pass of Ziz, and you will find them at the end of the gorge in the Desert of Jeruel. ¹⁷You will not have to fight this battle. Take up your positions; stand firm and see the deliverance the LORD will give you, O Judah and Jerusalem. Do not be afraid; do not be discouraged. Go out to face them tomorrow, and the LORD will be with you.' "

¹⁸Jehoshaphat bowed with his face to the ground, and all the people of Judah and Jerusalem fell down in worship before the LORD. ¹⁹Then some Levites from the Kohathites and Korahites stood up and praised the LORD, the God of Israel, with a very loud voice.

²⁰Early in the morning they left for the Desert of Tekoa. As they set out, Jehoshaphat stood and said, "Listen to me, Judah and people of Jerusalem! Have faith in the LORD your God and you will be upheld; have faith in his prophets and you will be successful." ²¹After consulting the people, Jehoshaphat appointed men to sing to the LORD and to praise him for the splendour of his^d holiness as they went out at the head of the army, saying:

"Give thanks to the LORD,
    for his love endures for ever."

²²As they began to sing and praise, the LORD set ambushes against the men of Ammon and Moab and Mount Seir who were invading Judah, and they were defeated. ²³The men of Ammon and Moab rose up against the men from Mount Seir to destroy and annihilate them. After they finished slaughtering the men from Seir, they helped to destroy one another.

²⁴When the men of Judah came to the place that overlooks the desert and looked towards the vast army, they saw only dead bodies lying on the ground; no-one had escaped. ²⁵So Jehoshaphat and his men went to carry off their plunder, and they found among them a great amount of equipment and clothing^e and also articles of value—more than they could take away. There was so much plunder that it took three days to collect it. ²⁶On the fourth day they assembled in the Valley of Beracah, where they praised the LORD. This is why it is called the Valley of Beracah^f to this day.

²⁷Then, led by Jehoshaphat, all the men of Judah and Jerusalem returned joyfully to Jerusalem, for the LORD had given them cause to rejoice over their enemies. ²⁸They entered Jerusalem and went to the temple of the LORD with harps and lutes and trumpets.

²⁹The fear of God came upon all the kingdoms of the countries when they heard how the LORD had fought against the enemies of Israel. ³⁰And the kingdom of Jehoshaphat was at peace, for his God had given him rest on every side.

■ The End of Jehoshaphat's Reign

³¹So Jehoshaphat reigned over Judah. He was thirty-five years old when he became king of Judah, and he reigned in Jerusalem for twenty-five years. His mother's name was Azubah daughter of Shilhi.

³²He walked in the ways of his father Asa and did not stray from them; he did what was right in the eyes of the LORD. ³³The high places, however, were not removed, and the people still had not set their hearts on the God of their fathers.

³⁴The other events of Jehoshaphat's reign, from beginning to end, are written in the annals of Jehu son of Hanani, which are recorded in the book of the kings of Israel.

³⁵Later, Jehoshaphat king of Judah made an alliance with Ahaziah king of Israel, who was guilty of wickedness. ³⁶He agreed with him to construct a fleet of trading ships.^g After these were built at Ezion Geber, ³⁷Eliezer son of Dodavahu of Mareshah prophesied against Jehoshaphat, saying, "Because you have made an alliance with Ahaziah, the LORD will destroy what you have made." The ships were wrecked and were not able to set sail to trade.^b

21 Then Jehoshaphat rested with his fathers and was buried with them in the City of David. And Jehoram his son succeeded him as king. ²Jehoram's brothers, the sons of Jehoshaphat, were Azariah, Jehiel, Zechariah, Azariahu, Michael and Shephatiah. All these were sons of Jehoshaphat king of Israel.^a ³Their father had given them many gifts of silver and gold and articles of value, as well as fortified cities in Judah, but he had given the kingdom to Jehoram because he was his firstborn son.

■ Jehoram King of Judah

⁴When Jehoram established himself firmly over his father's kingdom, he put all his brothers to the sword along with some of the princes of Israel. ⁵Jehoram was thirty-two years old when he became king, and he reigned in Jerusalem for eight years. ⁶He walked in the ways of the kings of Israel, as the house of Ahab had done, for he married a daughter of Ahab. He did evil in the eyes of the LORD. ⁷Nevertheless, because of the covenant the LORD had made with David, the LORD was not willing to destroy the house of David. He had promised to maintain a lamp for him and his descendants for ever.

21:4 ■ MARRIED DESPOTS
After the benign reign of Jehoshaphat, Judah got one of its worst kings ever, Jehoram. His marriage to Athaliah, daughter of a despised pagan king, undoubtedly stirred up revolt. To eliminate rivals, Jehoram promptly killed off his brothers, along with the "princes of Israel" (possibly leaders of the revolt). Later, Athaliah would become Judah's only reigning queen—and commit even greater atrocities (22:10).

⁸In the time of Jehoram, Edom rebelled against Judah and set up its own king. ⁹So Jehoram went there with his officers and all his chariots. The Edomites surrounded him and his chariot commanders, but he rose up and broke through by night. ¹⁰To this day Edom has been in rebellion against Judah.

Libnah revolted at the same time, because Jehoram had forsaken the LORD, the God of his fathers. ¹¹He had also built high places on the hills of Judah

^d21 Or him with the splendour of   ^e25 Some Hebrew manuscripts and Vulgate; most Hebrew manuscripts corpses   ^f26 Beracah means praise.
^g36 Hebrew of ships that could go to Tarshish   ^b37 Hebrew sail for Tarshish   ^a2 That is, Judah, as frequently in 2 Chronicles

and had caused the people of Jerusalem to prostitute themselves and had led Judah astray.

¹²Jehoram received a letter from Elijah the prophet, which said:

"This is what the LORD, the God of your father David, says: 'You have not walked in the ways of your father Jehoshaphat or of Asa king of Judah. ¹³But you have walked in the ways of the kings of Israel, and you have led Judah and the people of Jerusalem to prostitute themselves, just as the house of Ahab did. You have also murdered your own brothers, members of your father's house, men who were better than you. ¹⁴So now the LORD is about to strike your people, your sons, your wives and everything that is yours, with a heavy blow. ¹⁵You yourself will be very ill with a lingering disease of the bowels, until the disease causes your bowels to come out.' "

¹⁶The LORD aroused against Jehoram the hostility of the Philistines and of the Arabs who lived near the Cushites. ¹⁷They attacked Judah, invaded it and carried off all the goods found in the king's palace, together with his sons and wives. Not a son was left to him except Ahaziah,*ᵇ* the youngest.

¹⁸After all this, the LORD afflicted Jehoram with an incurable disease of the bowels. ¹⁹In the course of time, at the end of the second year, his bowels came out because of the disease, and he died in great pain. His people made no fire in his honour, as they had for his fathers.

²⁰Jehoram was thirty-two years old when he became king, and he reigned in Jerusalem for eight years. He passed away, to no-one's regret, and was buried in the City of David, but not in the tombs of the kings.

Ahaziah King of Judah

22 The people of Jerusalem made Ahaziah, Jehoram's youngest son, king in his place, since the raiders, who came with the Arabs into the camp, had killed all the older sons. So Ahaziah son of Jehoram king of Judah began to reign.

²Ahaziah was twenty-two*ᵃ* years old when he became king, and he reigned in Jerusalem for one year. His mother's name was Athaliah, a granddaughter of Omri.

³He too walked in the ways of the house of Ahab, for his mother encouraged him in doing wrong. ⁴He did evil in the eyes of the LORD, as the house of Ahab had done, for after his father's death they became his advisers, to his undoing. ⁵He also followed their counsel when he went with Joram*ᵇ* son of Ahab king of Israel to war against Hazael king of Aram at Ramoth Gilead. The Arameans wounded Joram; ⁶so he returned to Jezreel to recover from the wounds they had inflicted on him at Ramoth*ᶜ* in his battle with Hazael king of Aram.

Then Ahaziah*ᵈ* son of Jehoram king of Judah went down to Jezreel to see Joram son of Ahab because he had been wounded.

⁷Through Ahaziah's visit to Joram, God brought about Ahaziah's downfall. When Ahaziah arrived, he went out with Joram to meet Jehu son of Nimshi, whom the LORD had anointed to destroy the house of Ahab. ⁸While Jehu was executing judgment on the house of Ahab, he found the princes of Judah and the sons of Ahaziah's relatives, who had been attending Ahaziah, and he killed them. ⁹He then went in search of Ahaziah, and his men captured him while he was hiding in Samaria. He was brought to Jehu and put to death. They buried him, for they said, "He was a son of Jehoshaphat, who sought the LORD with all his heart." So there was no-one in the house of Ahaziah powerful enough to retain the kingdom.

Athaliah and Joash

¹⁰When Athaliah the mother of Ahaziah saw that her son was dead, she proceeded to destroy the whole royal family of the house of Judah. ¹¹But Jehosheba,*ᵉ* the daughter of King Jehoram, took Joash son of Ahaziah and stole him away from among the royal princes who were about to be murdered and put him and his nurse in a bedroom. Because Jehosheba,*ᵉ* the daughter of King Jehoram and wife of the priest Jehoiada, was Ahaziah's sister, she hid the child from Athaliah so that she could not kill him. ¹²He remained hidden with them at the temple of God for six years while Athaliah ruled the land.

23 In the seventh year Jehoiada showed his strength. He made a covenant with the commanders of units of a hundred: Azariah son of Jeroham, Ishmael son of Jehohanan, Azariah son of Obed, Maaseiah son of Adaiah, and Elishaphat son of Zicri. ²They went throughout Judah and gathered the Levites and the heads of Israelite families from all the towns. When they came to Jerusalem, ³the whole assembly made a covenant with the king at the temple of God.

Jehoiada said to them, "The king's son shall reign, as the LORD promised concerning the descendants of David. ⁴Now this is what you are to do: A third of you priests and Levites who are going on duty on the Sabbath are to keep watch at the doors, ⁵a third of you at the royal palace and a third at the Foundation Gate, and all the other men are to be in the courtyards of the temple of the LORD. ⁶No-one is to enter the temple of the LORD except the priests and Levites on duty; they may enter because they are consecrated, but all the other men are to guard what the LORD has assigned to them.*ᵃ* ⁷The Levites are to station themselves round the king, each man with his weapons in his hand. Anyone who enters the temple must be put to death. Stay close to the king wherever he goes."

23:7 ■ THE PRIESTS TAKE UP ARMS
Athaliah, daughter of Jezebel, introduced Baal worship to Judah and very nearly destroyed the entire royal line of David. Conditions in Judah got so bad that a priest, Jehoiada, took the extraordinary step of arming the Levites for a palace coup. They placed the rightful heir, Joash, on the throne.

ᵇ17 Hebrew *Jehoahaz*, a variant of *Ahaziah*   *ᵃ2* Some Septuagint manuscripts and Syriac (see also 2 Kings 8:26); Hebrew *forty-two*   *ᵇ5* Hebrew *Jehoram*, a variant of *Joram*; also in verses 6 and 7   *ᶜ6* Hebrew *Ramah*, a variant of *Ramoth*   *ᵈ6* Some Hebrew manuscripts, Septuagint, Vulgate and Syriac (see also 2 Kings 8:29); most Hebrew manuscripts *Azariah*   *ᵉ11* Hebrew *Jehoshabeath*, a variant of *Jehosheba*   *ᵃ6* Or *to observe the LORD's command ˌnot to enterˌ*

8The Levites and all the men of Judah did just as Jehoiada the priest ordered. Each one took his men—those who were going on duty on the Sabbath and those who were going off duty—for Jehoiada the priest had not released any of the divisions. 9Then he gave the commanders of units of a hundred the spears and the large and small shields that had belonged to King David and that were in the temple of God. 10He stationed all the men, each with his weapon in his hand, round the king—near the altar and the temple, from the south side to the north side of the temple.

11Jehoiada and his sons brought out the king's son and put the crown on him; they presented him with a copy of the covenant and proclaimed him king. They anointed him and shouted, "Long live the king!"

12When Athaliah heard the noise of the people running and cheering the king, she went to them at the temple of the LORD. 13She looked, and there was the king, standing by his pillar at the entrance. The officers and the trumpeters were beside the king, and all the people of the land were rejoicing and blowing trumpets, and singers with musical instruments were leading the praises. Then Athaliah tore her robes and shouted, "Treason! Treason!"

14Jehoiada the priest sent out the commanders of units of a hundred, who were in charge of the troops, and said to them: "Bring her out between the ranks[b] and put to the sword anyone who follows her." For the priest had said, "Do not put her to death at the temple of the LORD." 15So they seized her as she reached the entrance of the Horse Gate on the palace grounds, and there they put her to death.

16Jehoiada then made a covenant that he and the people and the king[c] would be the LORD's people. 17All the people went to the temple of Baal and tore it down. They smashed the altars and idols and killed Mattan the priest of Baal in front of the altars.

18Then Jehoiada placed the oversight of the temple of the LORD in the hands of the priests, who were Levites, to whom David had made assignments in the temple, to present the burnt offerings of the LORD as written in the Law of Moses, with rejoicing and singing, as David had ordered. 19He also stationed doorkeepers at the gates of the LORD's temple so that no-one who was in any way unclean might enter.

20He took with him the commanders of hundreds, the nobles, the rulers of the people and all the people of the land and brought the king down from the temple of the LORD. They went into the palace through the Upper Gate and seated the king on the royal throne, 21and all the people of the land rejoiced. And the city was quiet, because Athaliah had been slain with the sword.

■ Joash Repairs the Temple

24 Joash was seven years old when he became king, and he reigned in Jerusalem for forty years. His mother's name was Zibiah; she was from Beersheba. 2Joash did what was right in the eyes of the LORD all the years of Jehoiada the priest. 3Jehoiada chose two wives for him, and he had sons and daughters.

4Some time later Joash decided to restore the temple of the LORD. 5He called together the priests and Levites and said to them, "Go to the towns of Judah and collect the money due annually from all Israel, to repair the temple of your God. Do it now." But the Levites did not act at once.

6Therefore the king summoned Jehoiada the chief priest and said to him, "Why haven't you required the Levites to bring in from Judah and Jerusalem the tax imposed by Moses the servant of the LORD and by the assembly of Israel for the Tent of the Testimony?"

7Now the sons of that wicked woman Athaliah had broken into the temple of God and had used even its sacred objects for the Baals.

8At the king's command, a chest was made and placed outside, at the gate of the temple of the LORD. 9A proclamation was then issued in Judah and Jerusalem that they should bring to the LORD the tax that Moses the servant of God had required of Israel in the desert. 10All the officials and all the people brought their contributions gladly, dropping them into the chest until it was full. 11Whenever the chest was brought in by the Levites to the king's officials and they saw that there was a large amount of money, the royal secretary and the officer of the chief priest would come and empty the chest and carry it back to its place. They did this regularly and collected a great amount of money. 12The king and Jehoiada gave it to the men who carried out the work required for the temple of the LORD. They hired masons and carpenters to restore the LORD's temple, and also workers in iron and bronze to repair the temple.

13The men in charge of the work were diligent, and the repairs progressed under them. They rebuilt the temple of God according to its original design and reinforced it. 14When they had finished, they brought the rest of the money to the king and Jehoiada, and with it were made articles for the LORD's temple: articles for the service and for the burnt offerings, and also dishes and other objects of gold and silver. As long as Jehoiada lived, burnt offerings were presented continually in the temple of the LORD.

15Now Jehoiada was old and full of years, and he died at the age of a hundred and thirty. 16He was buried with the kings in the City of David, because of the good he had done in Israel for God and his temple.

■ The Wickedness of Joash

17After the death of Jehoiada, the officials of Judah came and paid homage to the king, and he listened to them. 18They abandoned the temple of the LORD, the God of their fathers, and worshipped Asherah poles and idols. Because of their guilt, God's anger came upon Judah and Jerusalem. 19Although the LORD sent prophets to the people to bring them back to him, and though they testified against them, they would not listen.

20Then the Spirit of God came upon Zechariah son of Jehoiada the priest. He stood before the people and said, "This is what God says: 'Why do you disobey the LORD's commands? You will not prosper. Because you have forsaken the LORD, he has forsaken you.'"

b 14 Or out from the precincts   c 16 Or covenant between the LORD and the people and the king that they (see 2 Kings 11:17)

²¹But they plotted against him, and by order of the king they stoned him to death in the courtyard of the LORD's temple. ²²King Joash did not remember the kindness Zechariah's father Jehoiada had shown him but killed his son, who said as he lay dying, "May the LORD see this and call you to account."

24:21 ■ AN INFAMOUS MURDER

Joash showed promise in his early years as king. But, like many other kings, he could not tolerate the damning words of one of God's prophets. The murder carried out on his order brought in enemy armies, inspired a conspiracy against Joash, and destroyed his reputation for ever. Jesus may have been speaking of this incident when he alluded to a murder hundreds of years later (Luke 11:51; Matthew 23:35).

²³At the turn of the year,ᵃ the army of Aram marched against Joash; it invaded Judah and Jerusalem and killed all the leaders of the people. They sent all the plunder to their king in Damascus. ²⁴Although the Aramean army had come with only a few men, the LORD delivered into their hands a much larger army. Because Judah had forsaken the LORD, the God of their fathers, judgment was executed on Joash. ²⁵When the Arameans withdrew, they left Joash severely wounded. His officials conspired against him for murdering the son of Jehoiada the priest, and they killed him in his bed. So he died and was buried in the City of David, but not in the tombs of the kings.

²⁶Those who conspired against him were Zabad,ᵇ son of Shimeath an Ammonite woman, and Jehozabad, son of Shimrithᶜ a Moabite woman. ²⁷The account of his sons, the many prophecies about him, and the record of the restoration of the temple of God are written in the annotations on the book of the kings. And Amaziah his son succeeded him as king.

■ Amaziah King of Judah

25 Amaziah was twenty-five years old when he became king, and he reigned in Jerusalem for twenty-nine years. His mother's name was Jehoaddin;ᵃ she was from Jerusalem. ²He did what was right in the eyes of the LORD, but not wholeheartedly. ³After the kingdom was firmly in his control, he executed the officials who had murdered his father the king. ⁴Yet he did not put their sons to death, but acted in accordance with what is written in the Law, in the Book of Moses, where the LORD commanded: "Fathers shall not be put to death for their children, nor children put to death for their fathers; each is to die for his own sins."ᵇ

⁵Amaziah called the people of Judah together and assigned them according to their families to commanders of thousands and commanders of hundreds for all Judah and Benjamin. He then mustered those twenty years old or more and found that there were three hundred thousand men ready for military service, able to handle the spear and shield. ⁶He also

hired a hundred thousand fighting men from Israel for a hundred talentsᶜ of silver.

⁷But a man of God came to him and said, "O king, these troops from Israel must not march with you, for the LORD is not with Israel—not with any of the people of Ephraim. ⁸Even if you go and fight courageously in battle, God will overthrow you before the enemy, for God has the power to help or to overthrow."

⁹Amaziah asked the man of God, "But what about the hundred talents I paid for these Israelite troops?"

The man of God replied, "The LORD can give you much more than that."

¹⁰So Amaziah dismissed the troops who had come to him from Ephraim and sent them home. They were furious with Judah and left for home in a great rage.

¹¹Amaziah then marshalled his strength and led his army to the Valley of Salt, where he killed ten thousand men of Seir. ¹²The army of Judah also captured ten thousand men alive, took them to the top of a cliff and threw them down so that all were dashed to pieces.

¹³Meanwhile the troops that Amaziah had sent back and had not allowed to take part in the war raided Judean towns from Samaria to Beth Horon. They killed three thousand people and carried off great quantities of plunder.

¹⁴When Amaziah returned from slaughtering the Edomites, he brought back the gods of the people of Seir. He set them up as his own gods, bowed down to them and burned sacrifices to them. ¹⁵The anger of the LORD burned against Amaziah, and he sent a prophet to him, who said, "Why do you consult this people's gods, which could not save their own people from your hand?"

¹⁶While he was still speaking, the king said to him, "Have we appointed you an adviser to the king? Stop! Why be struck down?"

So the prophet stopped but said, "I know that God has determined to destroy you, because you have done this and have not listened to my counsel."

¹⁷After Amaziah king of Judah consulted his advisers, he sent this challenge to Jehoashᵈ son of Jehoahaz, the son of Jehu, king of Israel: "Come, meet me face to face."

¹⁸But Jehoash king of Israel replied to Amaziah king of Judah, "A thistle in Lebanon sent a message to a cedar in Lebanon, 'Give your daughter to my son in marriage.' Then a wild beast in Lebanon came along and trampled the thistle underfoot. ¹⁹You say to yourself that you have defeated Edom, and now you are arrogant and proud. But stay at home! Why ask for trouble and cause your own downfall and that of Judah also?"

²⁰Amaziah, however, would not listen, for God so worked that he might hand them over to Jehoash, because they sought the gods of Edom. ²¹So Jehoash king of Israel attacked. He and Amaziah king of Judah faced each other at Beth Shemesh in Judah. ²²Judah was routed by Israel, and every man fled to his home. ²³Jehoash king of Israel captured Amaziah king of Judah, the son of Joash, the son of Ahaziah,ᵉ at Beth Shemesh. Then Jehoash brought him to

ᵃ23 Probably in the spring   ᵇ26 A variant of Jozabad   ᶜ26 A variant of Shomer   ᵃ1 Hebrew Jehoaddan, a variant of Jehoaddin   ᵇ4 Deut. 24:16
ᶜ6 That is, about 3⅓ tons (about 3.4 metric tons); also in verse 9   ᵈ17 Hebrew Joash, a variant of Jehoash; also in verses 18, 21, 23 and 25
ᵉ23 Hebrew Jehoahaz, a variant of Ahaziah

Jerusalem and broke down the wall of Jerusalem from the Ephraim Gate to the Corner Gate — a section about six hundred feet *f* long. ²⁴He took all the gold and silver and all the articles found in the temple of God that had been in the care of Obed-Edom, together with the palace treasures and the hostages, and returned to Samaria.

²⁵Amaziah son of Joash king of Judah lived for fifteen years after the death of Jehoash son of Jehoahaz king of Israel. ²⁶As for the other events of Amaziah's reign, from beginning to end, are they not written in the book of the kings of Judah and Israel? ²⁷From the time that Amaziah turned away from following the LORD, they conspired against him in Jerusalem and he fled to Lachish, but they sent men after him to Lachish and killed him there. ²⁸He was brought back by horse and was buried with his fathers in the City of Judah.

■ Uzziah King of Judah

26 Then all the people of Judah took Uzziah,*a* who was sixteen years old, and made him king in place of his father Amaziah. ²He was the one who rebuilt Elath and restored it to Judah after Amaziah rested with his fathers.

³Uzziah was sixteen years old when he became king, and he reigned in Jerusalem for fifty-two years. His mother's name was Jecoliah; she was from Jerusalem. ⁴He did what was right in the eyes of the LORD, just as his father Amaziah had done. ⁵He sought God during the days of Zechariah, who instructed him in the fear*b* of God. As long as he sought the LORD, God gave him success.

⁶He went to war against the Philistines and broke down the walls of Gath, Jabneh and Ashdod. He then rebuilt towns near Ashdod and elsewhere among the Philistines. ⁷God helped him against the Philistines and against the Arabs who lived in Gur Baal and against the Meunites. ⁸The Ammonites brought tribute to Uzziah, and his fame spread as far as the border of Egypt, because he had become very powerful.

⁹Uzziah built towers in Jerusalem at the Corner Gate, at the Valley Gate and at the angle of the wall, and he fortified them. ¹⁰He also built towers in the desert and dug many cisterns, because he had much livestock in the foothills and in the plain. He had people working his fields and vineyards in the hills and in the fertile lands, for he loved the soil.

¹¹Uzziah had a well-trained army, ready to go out by divisions according to their numbers as mustered by Jeiel the secretary and Maaseiah the officer under the direction of Hananiah, one of the royal officials. ¹²The total number of family leaders over the fighting men was 2,600. ¹³Under their command was an army of 307,500 men trained for war, a powerful force to support the king against his enemies. ¹⁴Uzziah provided shields, spears, helmets, coats of armour, bows and slingstones for the entire army. ¹⁵In Jerusalem he made machines designed by skilful men for use on the towers and on the corner defences to shoot arrows and hurl large stones. His fame spread far and wide, for he was greatly helped until he became powerful.

¹⁶But after Uzziah became powerful, his pride led to his downfall. He was unfaithful to the LORD his God, and entered the temple of the LORD to burn incense on the altar of incense. ¹⁷Azariah the priest with eighty other courageous priests of the LORD followed him in. ¹⁸They confronted him and said, "It is not right for you, Uzziah, to burn incense to the LORD. That is for the priests, the descendants of Aaron, who have been consecrated to burn incense. Leave the sanctuary, for you have been unfaithful; and you will not be honoured by the LORD God."

26:16 ■ A KING'S PRIDE
Archaeological discoveries have verified the prosperity of Judah during Uzziah's reign. However, like many of Judah's kings, he fell victim to the sin of pride. He usurped the role of the priests and suffered ever after from a contagious skin disease.

¹⁹Uzziah, who had a censer in his hand ready to burn incense, became angry. While he was raging at the priests in their presence before the incense altar in the LORD's temple, leprosy*c* broke out on his forehead. ²⁰When Azariah the chief priest and all the other priests looked at him, they saw that he had leprosy on his forehead, so they hurried him out. Indeed, he himself was eager to leave, because the LORD had afflicted him.

²¹King Uzziah had leprosy until the day he died. He lived in a separate house*d* — leprous, and excluded from the temple of the LORD. Jotham his son had charge of the palace and governed the people of the land.

²²The other events of Uzziah's reign, from beginning to end, are recorded by the prophet Isaiah son of Amoz. ²³Uzziah rested with his fathers and was buried near them in a field for burial that belonged to the kings, for people said, "He had leprosy." And Jotham his son succeeded him as king.

■ Jotham King of Judah

27 Jotham was twenty-five years old when he became king, and he reigned in Jerusalem for sixteen years. His mother's name was Jerusha daughter of Zadok. ²He did what was right in the eyes of the LORD, just as his father Uzziah had done, but unlike him he did not enter the temple of the LORD. The people, however, continued their corrupt practices. ³Jotham rebuilt the Upper Gate of the temple of the LORD and did extensive work on the wall at the hill of Ophel. ⁴He built towns in the Judean hills and forts and towers in the wooded areas.

⁵Jotham made war on the king of the Ammonites and conquered them. That year the Ammonites paid him a hundred talents*a* of silver, ten thousand cors*b* of wheat and ten thousand cors of barley. The Ammonites brought him the same amount also in the second and third years.

⁶Jotham grew powerful because he walked steadfastly before the LORD his God.

⁷The other events in Jotham's reign, including all

---

f23 Hebrew four hundred cubits (about 180 metres)   a1 Also called Azariah   b5 Many Hebrew manuscripts, Septuagint and Syriac; other Hebrew manuscripts vision   c19 The Hebrew word was used for various diseases affecting the skin — not necessarily leprosy; also in verses 20, 21 and 23. d21 Or in a house where he was relieved of responsibilities   a5 That is, about 3⅓ tons (about 3.4 metric tons)   b5 That is, probably about 60,500 bushels (about 2,200 kilolitres) his wars and the other things he did, are written in the book of the kings of Israel and Judah. [8]He was twenty-five years old when he became king, and he reigned in Jerusalem for sixteen years. [9]Jotham rested with his fathers and was buried in the City of David. And Ahaz his son succeeded him as king.

■ Ahaz King of Judah

28 Ahaz was twenty years old when he became king, and he reigned in Jerusalem for sixteen years. Unlike David his father, he did not do what was right in the eyes of the LORD. [2]He walked in the ways of the kings of Israel and also made cast idols for worshipping the Baals. [3]He burned sacrifices in the Valley of Ben Hinnom and sacrificed his sons in the fire, following the detestable ways of the nations that the LORD had driven out before the Israelites. [4]He offered sacrifices and burned incense at the high places, on the hilltops and under every spreading tree.

[5]Therefore the LORD his God handed him over to the king of Aram. The Arameans defeated him and took many of his people as prisoners and brought them to Damascus.

He was also given into the hands of the king of Israel, who inflicted heavy casualties on him. [6]In one day Pekah son of Remaliah killed a hundred and twenty thousand soldiers in Judah—because Judah had forsaken the LORD, the God of their fathers. [7]Zicri, an Ephraimite warrior, killed Maaseiah the king's son, Azrikam the officer in charge of the palace, and Elkanah, second to the king. [8]The Israelites took captive from their kinsmen two hundred thousand wives, sons and daughters. They also took a great deal of plunder, which they carried back to Samaria.

[9]But a prophet of the LORD named Oded was there, and he went out to meet the army when it returned to Samaria. He said to them, "Because the LORD, the God of your fathers, was angry with Judah, he gave them into your hand. But you have slaughtered them in a rage that reaches to heaven. [10]And now you intend to make the men and women of Judah and Jerusalem your slaves. But aren't you also guilty of sins against the LORD your God? [11]Now listen to me! Send back your fellow countrymen that you have taken as prisoners, for the LORD's fierce anger rests on you."

[12]Then some of the leaders in Ephraim—Azariah son of Jehohanan, Berekiah son of Meshillemoth, Jehizkiah son of Shallum, and Amasa son of Hadlai—confronted those who were arriving from the war. [13]"You must not bring those prisoners here," they said, "or we will be guilty before the LORD. Do you intend to add to our sin and guilt? For our guilt is already great, and his fierce anger rests on Israel."

[14]So the soldiers gave up the prisoners and plunder in the presence of the officials and all the assembly. [15]The men designated by name took the prisoners, and from the plunder they clothed all who were naked. They provided them with clothes and sandals, food and drink, and healing balm. All those who were weak they put on donkeys. So they took them back to their fellow countrymen at Jericho, the City of Palms, and returned to Samaria.

[16]At that time King Ahaz sent to the king[a] of Assyria for help. [17]The Edomites had again come and attacked Judah and carried away prisoners, [18]while the Philistines had raided towns in the foothills and in the Negev of Judah. They captured and occupied Beth Shemesh, Aijalon and Gederoth, as well as Soco, Timnah and Gimzo, with their surrounding villages. [19]The LORD had humbled Judah because of Ahaz king of Israel,[b] for he had promoted wickedness in Judah and had been most unfaithful to the LORD. [20]Tiglath-Pileser[c] king of Assyria came to him, but gave him trouble instead of help. [21]Ahaz took some of the things from the temple of the LORD and from the royal palace and from the princes and presented them to the king of Assyria, but that did not help him.

28:9 ■ LIMITS OF A JUST WAR

Advocates of a "just war" theory sometimes cite the fascinating story in this chapter. God sanctioned Israel's attack on Judah, but the invaders from the North went too far. They slaughtered many civilians and carried away others as captives. A prophet rebuked Israel's army for their crimes committed "in a rage that reaches to heaven". The Israelites had fought a war with a just end—carrying out God's punishment—but used cruel and unjust means in waging it.

The prophet convinced the Israelites to give up plunder and prisoners and make restitution. They fed the prisoners from Judah, gave them clothes, sandals, and medicine, and put them on donkeys to return home. This scene is one of the few in 2 Chronicles that shows the Northern Kingdom in a favourable light.

[22]In his time of trouble King Ahaz became even more unfaithful to the LORD. [23]He offered sacrifices to the gods of Damascus, who had defeated him; for he thought, "Since the gods of the kings of Aram have helped them, I will sacrifice to them so that they will help me." But they were his downfall and the downfall of all Israel.

[24]Ahaz gathered together the furnishings from the temple of God and took them away.[d] He shut the doors of the LORD's temple and set up altars at every street corner in Jerusalem. [25]In every town in Judah he built high places to burn sacrifices to other gods and provoked the LORD, the God of his fathers, to anger.

[26]The other events of his reign and all his ways, from beginning to end, are written in the book of the kings of Judah and Israel. [27]Ahaz rested with his fathers and was buried in the city of Jerusalem, but he was not placed in the tombs of the kings of Israel. And Hezekiah his son succeeded him as king.

■ Hezekiah Purifies the Temple

29 Hezekiah was twenty-five years old when he became king, and he reigned in Jerusalem for twenty-nine years. His mother's name was Abijah daughter of Zechariah. [2]He did what was right in the eyes of the LORD, just as his father David had done.

[a]16 One Hebrew manuscript, Septuagint and Vulgate (see also 2 Kings 16:7); most Hebrew manuscripts *kings* 2 Chronicles   [c]20 Hebrew *Tilgath-Pilneser*, a variant of *Tiglath-Pileser*   [b]19 That is, Judah, as frequently in   [d]24 Or *and cut them up*

³In the first month of the first year of his reign, he opened the doors of the temple of the LORD and repaired them. ⁴He brought in the priests and the Levites, assembled them in the square on the east side ⁵and said, "Listen to me, Levites! Consecrate yourselves now and consecrate the temple of the LORD, the God of your fathers. Remove all defilement from the sanctuary. ⁶Our fathers were unfaithful; they did evil in the eyes of the LORD our God and forsook him. They turned their faces away from the LORD's dwelling-place and turned their backs on him. ⁷They also shut the doors of the portico and put out the lamps. They did not burn incense or present any burnt offerings at the sanctuary to the God of Israel. ⁸Therefore, the anger of the LORD has fallen on Judah and Jerusalem; he has made them an object of dread and horror and scorn, as you can see with your own eyes. ⁹This is why our fathers have fallen by the sword and why our sons and daughters and our wives are in captivity. ¹⁰Now I intend to make a covenant with the LORD, the God of Israel, so that his fierce anger will turn away from us. ¹¹My sons, do not be negligent now, for the LORD has chosen you to stand before him and serve him, to minister before him and to burn incense."

¹²Then these Levites set to work:
from the Kohathites,
  Mahath son of Amasai and Joel son of Azariah;
from the Merarites,
  Kish son of Abdi and Azariah son of Jehallelel;
from the Gershonites,
  Joah son of Zimmah and Eden son of Joah;
¹³from the descendants of Elizaphan,
  Shimri and Jeiel;
from the descendants of Asaph,
  Zechariah and Mattaniah;
¹⁴from the descendants of Heman,
  Jehiel and Shimei;
from the descendants of Jeduthun,
  Shemaiah and Uzziel.

¹⁵When they had assembled their brothers and consecrated themselves, they went in to purify the temple of the LORD, as the king had ordered, following the word of the LORD. ¹⁶The priests went into the sanctuary of the LORD to purify it. They brought out to the courtyard of the LORD's temple everything unclean that they found in the temple of the LORD. The Levites took it and carried it out to the Kidron Valley. ¹⁷They began the consecration on the first day of the first month, and by the eighth day of the month they reached the portico of the LORD. For eight more days they consecrated the temple of the LORD itself, finishing in the sixteenth day of the first month.

¹⁸Then they went in to King Hezekiah and reported: "We have purified the entire temple of the LORD, the altar of burnt offering with all its utensils, and the table for setting out the consecrated bread, with all its articles. ¹⁹We have prepared and consecrated all the articles that King Ahaz removed in his unfaithfulness while he was king. They are now in front of the LORD's altar."

²⁰Early the next morning King Hezekiah gathered the city officials together and went up to the temple of the LORD. ²¹They brought seven bulls, seven rams, seven male lambs and seven male goats as a sin offering for the kingdom, for the sanctuary and for Judah. The king commanded the priests, the descendants of Aaron, to offer these on the altar of the LORD. ²²So they slaughtered the bulls, and the priests took the blood and sprinkled it on the altar; next they slaughtered the rams and sprinkled their blood on the altar; then they slaughtered the lambs and sprinkled their blood on the altar. ²³The goats for the sin offering were brought before the king and the assembly, and they laid their hands on them. ²⁴The priests then slaughtered the goats and presented their blood on the altar for a sin offering to atone for all Israel, because the king had ordered the burnt offering and the sin offering for all Israel.

²⁵He stationed the Levites in the temple of the LORD with cymbals, harps and lyres in the way prescribed by David and Gad the king's seer and Nathan the prophet; this was commanded by the LORD through his prophets. ²⁶So the Levites stood ready with David's instruments, and the priests with their trumpets.

²⁷Hezekiah gave the order to sacrifice the burnt offering on the altar. As the offering began, singing to the LORD began also, accompanied by trumpets and the instruments of David king of Israel. ²⁸The whole assembly bowed in worship, while the singers sang and the trumpeters played. All this continued until the sacrifice of the burnt offering was completed.

²⁹When the offerings were finished, the king and everyone present with him knelt down and worshipped. ³⁰King Hezekiah and his officials ordered the Levites to praise the LORD with the words of David and of Asaph the seer. So they sang praises with gladness and bowed their heads and worshipped.

³¹Then Hezekiah said, "You have now dedicated yourselves to the LORD. Come and bring sacrifices and thank-offerings to the temple of the LORD." So the assembly brought sacrifices and thank-offerings, and all whose hearts were willing brought burnt offerings.

³²The number of burnt offerings the assembly brought was seventy bulls, a hundred rams and two hundred male lambs — all of them for burnt offerings to the LORD. ³³The animals consecrated as sacrifices amounted to six hundred bulls and three thousand sheep and goats. ³⁴The priests, however, were too few to skin all the burnt offerings; so their kinsmen the Levites helped them until the task was finished and until other priests had been consecrated, for the Levites had been more conscientious in consecrating themselves than the priests had been. ³⁵There were burnt offerings in abundance, together with the fat of the fellowship offerings[a] and the drink offerings that accompanied the burnt offerings.

So the service of the temple of the LORD was re-established. ³⁶Hezekiah and all the people rejoiced at what God had brought about for his people, because it was done so quickly.

_a 35_ Traditionally _peace offerings_

■ Hezekiah Celebrates the Passover

30 Hezekiah sent word to all Israel and Judah and also wrote letters to Ephraim and Manasseh, inviting them to come to the temple of the LORD in Jerusalem and celebrate the Passover to the LORD, the God of Israel. ²The king and his officials and the whole assembly in Jerusalem decided to celebrate the Passover in the second month. ³They had not been able to celebrate it at the regular time because not enough priests had consecrated themselves and the people had not assembled in Jerusalem. ⁴The plan seemed right both to the king and to the whole assembly. ⁵They decided to send a proclamation throughout Israel, from Beersheba to Dan, calling the people to come to Jerusalem and celebrate the Passover to the LORD, the God of Israel. It had not been celebrated in large numbers according to what was written.

30:1 ■ DELAYED PASSOVER
By moving the Passover date back one month, Hezekiah allowed extra time for priests to prepare and for pilgrims to make travel plans. Pointedly, Hezekiah invited tribes from the ravaged Northern Kingdom. For the first time in 200 years, the entire nation celebrated a religious festival together.

⁶At the king's command, couriers went throughout Israel and Judah with letters from the king and from his officials, which read:

"People of Israel, return to the LORD, the God of Abraham, Isaac and Israel, that he may return to you who are left, who have escaped from the hand of the kings of Assyria. ⁷Do not be like your fathers and brothers, who were unfaithful to the LORD, the God of their fathers, so that he made them an object of horror, as you see. ⁸Do not be stiff-necked, as your fathers were; submit to the LORD. Come to the sanctuary, which he has consecrated for ever. Serve the LORD your God, so that his fierce anger will turn away from you. ⁹If you return to the LORD, then your brothers and your children will be shown compassion by their captors and will come back to this land, for the LORD your God is gracious and compassionate. He will not turn his face from you if you return to him."

¹⁰The couriers went from town to town in Ephraim and Manasseh, as far as Zebulun, but the people scorned and ridiculed them. ¹¹Nevertheless, some men of Asher, Manasseh and Zebulun humbled themselves and went to Jerusalem. ¹²Also in Judah the hand of God was on the people to give them unity of mind to carry out what the king and his officials had ordered, following the word of the LORD.

¹³A very large crowd of people assembled in Jerusalem to celebrate the Feast of Unleavened Bread in the second month. ¹⁴They removed the altars in Jerusalem and cleared away the incense altars and threw them into the Kidron Valley.

¹⁵They slaughtered the Passover lamb on the fourteenth day of the second month. The priests and the Levites were ashamed and consecrated themselves and brought burnt offerings to the temple of the LORD. ¹⁶Then they took up their regular positions as prescribed in the Law of Moses the man of God. The priests sprinkled the blood handed to them by the Levites. ¹⁷Since many in the crowd had not consecrated themselves, the Levites had to kill the Passover lambs for all those who were not ceremonially clean and could not consecrate ⌊their lambs⌋ to the LORD. ¹⁸Although most of the many people who came from Ephraim, Manasseh, Issachar and Zebulun had not purified themselves, yet they ate the Passover, contrary to what was written. But Hezekiah prayed for them, saying, "May the LORD, who is good, pardon everyone ¹⁹who sets his heart on seeking God — the LORD, the God of his fathers — even if he is not clean according to the rules of the sanctuary." ²⁰And the LORD heard Hezekiah and healed the people.

²¹The Israelites who were present in Jerusalem celebrated the Feast of Unleavened Bread for seven days with great rejoicing, while the Levites and priests sang to the LORD every day, accompanied by the LORD's instruments of praise.ᵃ

²²Hezekiah spoke encouragingly to all the Levites, who showed good understanding of the service of the LORD. For the seven days they ate their assigned portion and offered fellowship offeringsᵇ and praised the LORD, the God of their fathers.

²³The whole assembly then agreed to celebrate the festival seven more days; so for another seven days they celebrated joyfully. ²⁴Hezekiah king of Judah provided a thousand bulls and seven thousand sheep and goats for the assembly, and the officials provided them with a thousand bulls and ten thousand sheep and goats. A great number of priests consecrated themselves. ²⁵The entire assembly of Judah rejoiced, along with the priests and Levites and all who had assembled from Israel, including the aliens who had come from Israel and those who lived in Judah. ²⁶There was great joy in Jerusalem, for since the days of Solomon son of David king of Israel there had been nothing like this in Jerusalem. ²⁷The priests and the Levites stood to bless the people, and God heard them, for their prayer reached heaven, his holy dwelling-place.

31 When all this had ended, the Israelites who were there went out to the towns of Judah, smashed the sacred stones and cut down the Asherah poles. They destroyed the high places and the altars throughout Judah and Benjamin and in Ephraim and Manasseh. After they had destroyed all of them, the Israelites returned to their own towns and to their own property.

■ Contributions for Worship

²Hezekiah assigned the priests and Levites to divisions — each of them according to their duties as priests or Levites — to offer burnt offerings and fellowship offerings,ᵃ to minister, to give thanks and to sing praises at the gates of the LORD's dwelling. ³The king contributed from his own possessions for the morning and evening burnt offerings and for the burnt offerings on the Sabbaths, New Moons and appointed feasts as written in the Law of the LORD. ⁴He

ᵃ21 Or priests praised the LORD every day with resounding instruments belonging to the LORD.   ᵇ22 Traditionally peace offerings   ᵃ2 Traditionally peace offerings ordered the people living in Jerusalem to give the portion due to the priests and Levites so that they could devote themselves to the Law of the LORD. 5As soon as the order went out, the Israelites generously gave the firstfruits of their grain, new wine, oil and honey and all that the fields produced. They brought a great amount, a tithe of everything. 6The men of Israel and Judah who lived in the towns of Judah also brought a tithe of their herds and flocks and a tithe of the holy things dedicated to the LORD their God, and they piled them in heaps. 7They began doing this in the third month and finished in the seventh month. 8When Hezekiah and his officials came and saw the heaps, they praised the LORD and blessed his people Israel.

9Hezekiah asked the priests and Levites about the heaps; 10and Azariah the chief priest, from the family of Zadok, answered, "Since the people began to bring their contributions to the temple of the LORD, we have had enough to eat and plenty to spare, because the LORD has blessed his people, and this great amount is left over."

11Hezekiah gave orders to prepare storerooms in the temple of the LORD, and this was done. 12Then they faithfully brought in the contributions, tithes and dedicated gifts. Conaniah, a Levite, was in charge of these things, and his brother Shimei was next in rank. 13Jehiel, Azaziah, Nahath, Asahel, Jerimoth, Jozabad, Eliel, Ismakiah, Mahath and Benaiah were supervisors under Conaniah and Shimei his brother, by appointment of King Hezekiah and Azariah the official in charge of the temple of God.

14Kore son of Imnah the Levite, keeper of the East Gate, was in charge of the freewill offerings given to God, distributing the contributions made to the LORD and also the consecrated gifts. 15Eden, Miniamin, Jeshua, Shemaiah, Amariah and Shecaniah assisted him faithfully in the towns of the priests, distributing to their fellow priests according to their divisions, old and young alike.

16In addition, they distributed to the males three years old or more whose names were in the genealogical records—all who would enter the temple of the LORD to perform the daily duties of their various tasks, according to their responsibilities and their divisions. 17And they distributed to the priests enrolled by their families in the genealogical records and likewise to the Levites twenty years old or more, according to their responsibilities and their divisions. 18They included all the little ones, the wives, and the sons and daughters of the whole community listed in these genealogical records. For they were faithful in consecrating themselves.

19As for the priests, the descendants of Aaron, who lived on the farm lands around their towns or in any other towns, men were designated by name to distribute portions to every male among them and to all who were recorded in the genealogies of the Levites.

20This is what Hezekiah did throughout Judah, doing what was good and right and faithful before the LORD his God. 21In everything that he undertook in the service of God's temple and in obedience to the law and the commands, he sought his God and worked wholeheartedly. And so he prospered.

■ Sennacherib Threatens Jerusalem

32 After all that Hezekiah had so faithfully done, Sennacherib king of Assyria came and invaded Judah. He laid siege to the fortified cities, thinking to conquer them for himself. 2When Hezekiah saw that Sennacherib had come and that he intended to make war on Jerusalem, 3he consulted with his officials and military staff about blocking off the water from the springs outside the city, and they helped him. 4A large force of men assembled, and they blocked all the springs and the stream that flowed through the land. "Why should the kings*a* of Assyria come and find plenty of water?" they said. 5Then he worked hard repairing all the broken sections of the wall and building towers on it. He built another wall outside that one and reinforced the supporting terraces*b* of the City of David. He also made large numbers of weapons and shields.

6He appointed military officers over the people and assembled them before him in the square at the city gate and encouraged them with these words: 7"Be strong and courageous. Do not be afraid or discouraged because of the king of Assyria and the vast army with him, for there is a greater power with us than with him. 8With him is only the arm of flesh, but with us is the LORD our God to help us and to fight our battles." And the people gained confidence from what Hezekiah the king of Judah said.

9Later, when Sennacherib king of Assyria and all his forces were laying siege to Lachish, he sent his officers to Jerusalem with this message for Hezekiah king of Judah and for all the people of Judah who were there:

10"This is what Sennacherib king of Assyria says: On what are you basing your confidence, that you remain in Jerusalem under siege? 11When Hezekiah says, 'The LORD our God will save us from the hand of the king of Assyria,' he is misleading you, to let you die of hunger and thirst. 12Did not Hezekiah himself remove this god's high places and altars, saying to Judah and Jerusalem, 'You must worship before one altar and burn sacrifices on it'?

13"Do you not know what I and my fathers have done to all the peoples of the other lands? Were the gods of those nations ever able to deliver their land from my hand? 14Who of all the gods of these nations that my fathers destroyed has been able to save his people from me? How then can your god deliver you from my hand? 15Now do not let Hezekiah deceive you and mislead you like this. Do not believe him, for no god of any nation or kingdom has been able to deliver his people from my hand or the hand of my fathers. How much less will your god deliver you from my hand!"

16Sennacherib's officers spoke further against the LORD God and against his servant Hezekiah. 17The king also wrote letters insulting the LORD, the God of Israel, and saying this against him: "Just as the gods of the peoples of the other lands did not rescue their people from my hand, so the god of Hezekiah will

a4 Hebrew; Septuagint and Syriac *king*   *b5* Or the Millo not rescue his people from my hand." 18Then they called out in Hebrew to the people of Jerusalem who were on the wall, to terrify them and make them afraid in order to capture the city. 19They spoke about the God of Jerusalem as they did about the gods of the other peoples of the world — the work of men's hands.

20King Hezekiah and the prophet Isaiah son of Amoz cried out in prayer to heaven about this. 21And the LORD sent an angel, who annihilated all the fighting men and the leaders and officers in the camp of the Assyrian king. So he withdrew to his own land in disgrace. And when he went into the temple of his god, some of his sons cut him down with the sword.

22So the LORD saved Hezekiah and the people of Jerusalem from the hand of Sennacherib king of Assyria and from the hand of all others. He took care of them*c* on every side. 23Many brought offerings to Jerusalem for the LORD and valuable gifts for Hezekiah king of Judah. From then on he was highly regarded by all the nations.

32:1–21 ■ INVASION
Sennacherib's campaign is well-documented, for he kept scrupulous records of his military ventures. Invading Palestine in 701 B.C., his armies captured 46 cities in Judah and then laid siege to Jerusalem. The Bible includes three different accounts of this major event: here, in 2 Kings 18, and in Isaiah 36.

■ LESSONS FROM THE BATTLEFIELD INSIGHT
WHAT MADE JUDAH WIN SOME WARS AND LOSE OTHERS?

DO NOT BE AFRAID OR DISCOURAGED BECAUSE OF THE KING OF ASSYRIA AND THE VAST ARMY WITH HIM, FOR THERE IS A GREATER POWER WITH US THAN WITH HIM. ■ 32:7

No king of Judah had a wholly peaceful reign. As a result, much of the action in 2 Chronicles takes place on a battlefield. And, in a nutshell, here is the book's philosophy of war: "Humble yourself and rely totally on God – regardless of the odds against you. If you rely on your own military might or that of powerful neighbours, you will lose."

■ LISTENING TO THE PROPHETS
Chapter 12, for example, tells of a grave crisis facing Judah's very first king. Five years into Rehoboam's reign, a huge military machine from Egypt rolled in with chariots and battering rams. Surrounded, Rehoboam wanted a word of hope from a prophet. Instead, he got a rebuke: "This is what the LORD says, 'You have abandoned me; therefore, I now abandon you to Shishak' " (12:5).

God was using the armies of Egypt to punish Judah for its errors. This first invasion set a pattern: whenever an immoral king corrupted the nation, God sent an invading army as punishment.

Often the kings of Judah ignored their prophets' hard advice. But in this first case, King Rehoboam repented and humbled himself, saving his country from even greater devastation.

■ A WRONG WAY AND A RIGHT WAY
Few kings had the faith to believe in God alone at moments of great peril. Even the best of them reached into the royal treasury and purchased help from neighbouring nations. When they did, Judah usually ended up weaker than before. But 2 Chronicles concentrates on the good moments, when kings turned to God.

King Jehoshaphat was a textbook example of the proper response. He called the entire nation together in a giant prayer meeting (20:4–28). When the time came for battle, he sent a choir in front of his army to sing praises to God. Judah's enemies all turned on each other and Jehoshaphat's armies marched home victorious.

■ HEZEKIAH'S FAITH
Perhaps the greatest single example of a king following his prophet's advice occurred during the reign of Hezekiah. The Bible reports the incident in three places: 2 Chronicles 32, 2 Kings 18–19 and Isaiah 36–37. At the time, Judah's situation looked hopeless. Mighty Assyria had taken 27 cities and villages in Judah and was now laying siege to Jerusalem.

Hezekiah showed his true moral strength by joining together with the prophet Isaiah to humble himself in prayer. God granted a miracle that drove off the Assyrian army.

2 Chronicles stressed incidents like these as a lesson to its first readers, who had inherited a land in ruins. Looking back over their history, they could see what had gone wrong: the nation had forgotten to rely on God. To rebuild their nation they would have to re-learn the simple faith that had brought them victory in the past.

□ LIFE QUESTIONS:
What does it mean to trust God completely today?

---

*c*22 Hebrew; Septuagint and Vulgate *He gave them rest*

■ Hezekiah's Pride, Success and Death

24In those days Hezekiah became ill and was at the point of death. He prayed to the LORD, who answered him and gave him a miraculous sign. 25But Hezekiah's heart was proud and he did not respond to the kindness shown him; therefore the LORD's wrath was on him and on Judah and Jerusalem. 26Then Hezekiah repented of the pride of his heart, as did the people of Jerusalem; therefore the LORD's wrath did not come upon them during the days of Hezekiah.

27Hezekiah had very great riches and honour, and he made treasuries for his silver and gold and for his precious stones, spices, shields and all kinds of valuables. 28He also made buildings to store the harvest of grain, new wine and oil; and he made stalls for various kinds of cattle, and pens for the flocks. 29He built villages and acquired great numbers of flocks and herds, for God had given him very great riches. 30It was Hezekiah who blocked the upper outlet of the Gihon spring and channelled the water down to the west side of the City of David. He succeeded in everything he undertook. 31But when envoys were sent by the rulers of Babylon to ask him about the miraculous sign that had occurred in the land, God left him to test him and to know everything that was in his heart.

32The other events of Hezekiah's reign and his acts of devotion are written in the vision of the prophet Isaiah son of Amoz in the book of the kings of Judah and Israel. 33Hezekiah rested with his fathers and was buried on the hill where the tombs of David's descendants are. All Judah and the people of Jerusalem honoured him when he died. And Manasseh his son succeeded him as king.

■ Manasseh King of Judah

33 Manasseh was twelve years old when he became king, and he reigned in Jerusalem for fifty-five years. 2He did evil in the eyes of the LORD, following the detestable practices of the nations the LORD had driven out before the Israelites. 3He rebuilt the high places his father Hezekiah had demolished; he also erected altars to the Baals and made Asherah poles. He bowed down to all the starry hosts and worshipped them. 4He built altars in the temple of the LORD, of which the LORD had said, "My Name will remain in Jerusalem for ever." 5In both courts of the temple of the LORD, he built altars to all the starry hosts. 6He sacrificed his sons in*a* the fire in the Valley of Ben Hinnom, practised sorcery, divination and witchcraft, and consulted mediums and spiritists. He did much evil in the eyes of the LORD, provoking him to anger.

7He took the carved image he had made and put it in God's temple, of which God had said to David and to his son Solomon, "In this temple and in Jerusalem, which I have chosen out of all the tribes of Israel, I will put my Name for ever. 8I will not again make the feet of the Israelites leave the land I assigned to your forefathers, if only they will be careful to do everything that I commanded them concerning all the laws, decrees and ordinances given through Moses." 9But Manasseh led Judah and the people of Jerusalem astray, so that they did more

evil than the nations the LORD had destroyed before the Israelites.

10The LORD spoke to Manasseh and his people, but they paid no attention. 11So the LORD brought against them the army commanders of the king of Assyria, who took Manasseh prisoner, put a hook in his nose, bound him with bronze shackles and took him to Babylon. 12In his distress he sought the favour of the LORD his God and humbled himself greatly before the God of his fathers. 13And when he prayed to him, the LORD was moved by his entreaty and listened to his plea; so he brought him back to Jerusalem and to his kingdom. Then Manasseh knew that the LORD is God.

33:13 ■ A TARDY CHANGE OF MIND
Unlike the other history books, Chronicles records great moments of faith, even when they have no lasting consequences for the nation as a whole. Second Chronicles characteristically adds a new perspective on the reign of Manasseh, one of Judah's worst kings. While acknowledging his weaknesses, it adds this account of his amazing turnaround late in life. This brief episode gave an object lesson to the nation on what happens when even a wicked king repents.

14Afterwards he rebuilt the outer wall of the City of David, west of the Gihon spring in the valley, as far as the entrance of the Fish Gate and encircling the hill of Ophel; he also made it much higher. He stationed military commanders in all the fortified cities in Judah.

15He got rid of the foreign gods and removed the image from the temple of the LORD, as well as all the altars he had built on the temple hill and in Jerusalem; and he threw them out of the city. 16Then he restored the altar of the LORD and sacrificed fellowship offerings*b* and thank-offerings on it, and told Judah to serve the LORD, the God of Israel. 17The people, however, continued to sacrifice at the high places, but only to the LORD their God.

18The other events of Manasseh's reign, including his prayer to his God and the words the seers spoke to him in the name of the LORD, the God of Israel, are written in the annals of the kings of Israel.*c* 19His prayer and how God was moved by his entreaty, as well as all his sins and unfaithfulness, and the sites where he built high places and set up Asherah poles and idols before he humbled himself — all are written in the records of the seers.*d* 20Manasseh rested with his fathers and was buried in his palace. And Amon his son succeeded him as king.

■ Amon King of Judah

21Amon was twenty-two years old when he became king, and he reigned in Jerusalem for two years. 22He did evil in the eyes of the LORD, as his father Manasseh had done. Amon worshipped and offered sacrifices to all the idols Manasseh had made. 23But unlike his father Manasseh, he did not humble himself before the LORD; Amon increased his guilt. 24Amon's officials conspired against him and

a 6 Or He made his sons pass through   b 16 Traditionally peace offerings   c 18 That is, Judah, as frequently in 2 Chronicles   d 19 One Hebrew
manuscript and Septuagint; most Hebrew manuscripts of Hozai

assassinated him in his palace. [25]Then the people of the land killed all who had plotted against King Amon, and they made Josiah his son king in his place.

■ Josiah's Reforms

34 Josiah was eight years old when he became king, and he reigned in Jerusalem for thirty-one years. [2]He did what was right in the eyes of the LORD and walked in the ways of his father David, not turning aside to the right or to the left.

[3]In the eighth year of his reign, while he was still young, he began to seek the God of his father David. In his twelfth year he began to purge Judah and Jerusalem of high places, Asherah poles, carved idols and cast images. [4]Under his direction the altars of the Baals were torn down; he cut to pieces the incense altars that were above them, and smashed the Asherah poles, the idols and the images. These he broke to pieces and scattered over the graves of those who had sacrificed to them. [5]He burned the bones of the priests on their altars, and so he purged Judah and Jerusalem. [6]In the towns of Manasseh, Ephraim and Simeon, as far as Naphtali, and in the ruins around them, [7]he tore down the altars and the Asherah poles and crushed the idols to powder and cut to pieces all the incense altars throughout Israel. Then he went back to Jerusalem.

[8]In the eighteenth year of Josiah's reign, to purify the land and the temple, he sent Shaphan son of Azaliah and Maaseiah the ruler of the city, with Joah son of Joahaz, the recorder, to repair the temple of the LORD his God.

[9]They went to Hilkiah the high priest and gave him the money that had been brought into the temple of God, which the Levites who were the doorkeepers had collected from the people of Manasseh, Ephraim and the entire remnant of Israel and from all the people of Judah and Benjamin and the inhabitants of Jerusalem. [10]Then they entrusted it to the men appointed to supervise the work on the LORD's temple. These men paid the workers who repaired and restored the temple. [11]They also gave money to the carpenters and builders to purchase dressed stone, and timber for joists and beams for the buildings that the kings of Judah had allowed to fall into ruin.

[12]The men did the work faithfully. Over them to direct them were Jahath and Obadiah, Levites descended from Merari, and Zechariah and Meshullam, descended from Kohath. The Levites — all who were skilled in playing musical instruments — [13]had charge of the labourers and supervised all the workers from job to job. Some of the Levites were secretaries, scribes and doorkeepers.

■ The Book of the Law Found

[14]While they were bringing out the money that had been taken into the temple of the LORD, Hilkiah the priest found the Book of the Law of the LORD that had been given through Moses. [15]Hilkiah said to Shaphan the secretary, "I have found the Book of the Law in the temple of the LORD." He gave it to Shaphan.

[16]Then Shaphan took the book to the king and reported to him: "Your officials are doing everything that has been committed to them. [17]They have paid out the money that was in the temple of the LORD and have entrusted it to the supervisors and workers." [18]Then Shaphan the secretary informed the king, "Hilkiah the priest has given me a book." And Shaphan read from it in the presence of the king.

[19]When the king heard the words of the Law, he tore his robes. [20]He gave these orders to Hilkiah, Ahikam son of Shaphan, Abdon son of Micah,[a] Shaphan the secretary and Asaiah the king's attendant: [21]"Go and enquire of the LORD for me and for the remnant in Israel and Judah about what is written in this book that has been found. Great is the LORD's anger that is poured out on us because our fathers have not kept the word of the LORD; they have not acted in accordance with all that is written in this book."

[22]Hilkiah and those the king had sent with him[b] went to speak to the prophetess Huldah, who was the wife of Shallum son of Tokhath,[c] the son of Hasrah,[d] keeper of the wardrobe. She lived in Jerusalem, in the Second District.

[23]She said to them, "This is what the LORD, the God of Israel, says: Tell the man who sent you to me, [24]'This is what the LORD says: I am going to bring disaster on this place and its people — all the curses written in the book that has been read in the presence of the king of Judah. [25]Because they have forsaken me and burned incense to other gods and provoked me to anger by all that their hands have made,[e] my anger will be poured out on this place and will not be quenched.' [26]Tell the king of Judah, who sent you to enquire of the LORD, 'This is what the LORD, the God of Israel, says concerning the words you heard: [27]Because your heart was responsive and you humbled yourself before God when you heard what he spoke against this place and its people, and because you humbled yourself before me and tore your robes and wept in my presence, I have heard you, declares the LORD. [28]Now I will gather you to your fathers, and you will be buried in peace. Your eyes will not see all the disaster I am going to bring on this place and on those who live here.'"

So they took her answer back to the king.

[29]Then the king called together all the elders of Judah and Jerusalem. [30]He went up to the temple of the LORD with the men of Judah, the people of Jerusalem, the priests and the Levites — all the people from the least to the greatest. He read in their hearing all the words of the Book of the Covenant, which had been found in the temple of the LORD. [31]The king stood by his pillar and renewed the covenant in the presence of the LORD — to follow the LORD and keep his commands, regulations and decrees with all his heart and all his soul, and to obey the words of the covenant written in this book.

[32]Then he made everyone in Jerusalem and Benjamin pledge themselves to it; the people of Jerusalem did this in accordance with the covenant of God, the God of their fathers.

[33]Josiah removed all the detestable idols from all the territory belonging to the Israelites, and he made all who were present in Israel serve the LORD their

[a]20 Also called Acbor son of Micaiah   [b]22 One Hebrew manuscript, Vulgate and Syriac; most Hebrew manuscripts do not have had sent with him.
[c]22 Also called Tikvah   [d]22 Also called Harhas   [e]25 Or by everything they have done

God. As long as he lived, they did not fail to follow the LORD, the God of their fathers.

■ Josiah Celebrates the Passover

35 Josiah celebrated the Passover to the LORD in Jerusalem, and the Passover lamb was slaughtered on the fourteenth day of the first month. [2]He appointed the priests to their duties and encouraged them in the service of the LORD's temple. [3]He said to the Levites, who instructed all Israel and who had been consecrated to the LORD: "Put the sacred ark in the temple that Solomon son of David king of Israel built. It is not to be carried about on your shoulders. Now serve the LORD your God and his people Israel. [4]Prepare yourselves by families in your divisions, according to the directions written by David king of Israel and by his son Solomon.

[5]"Stand in the holy place with a group of Levites for each sub-division of the families of your fellow countrymen, the lay people. [6]Slaughter the Passover lambs, consecrate yourselves and prepare ⌊the lambs⌋ for your fellow countrymen, doing what the LORD commanded through Moses."

[7]Josiah provided for all the lay people who were there a total of thirty thousand sheep and goats for the Passover offerings, and also three thousand cattle—all from the king's own possessions.

[8]His officials also contributed voluntarily to the people and the priests and Levites. Hilkiah, Zechariah and Jehiel, the administrators of God's temple, gave the priests two thousand six hundred Passover offerings and three hundred cattle. [9]Also Conaniah along with Shemaiah and Nethanel, his brothers, and Hashabiah, Jeiel and Jozabad, the leaders of the Levites, provided five thousand Passover offerings and five hundred head of cattle for the Levites.

[10]The service was arranged and the priests stood in their places with the Levites in their divisions as the king had ordered. [11]The Passover lambs were slaughtered, and the priests sprinkled the blood handed to them, while the Levites skinned the animals. [12]They set aside the burnt offerings to give them to the sub-divisions of the families of the people to offer to the LORD, as is written in the Book of Moses. They did the same with the cattle. [13]They roasted the Passover animals over the fire as prescribed, and boiled the holy offerings in pots, cauldrons and pans and served them quickly to all the people. [14]After this, they made preparations for themselves and for the priests, because the priests, the descendants of Aaron, were sacrificing the burnt offerings and the fat portions until nightfall. So the Levites made preparations for themselves and for the Aaronic priests.

[15]The musicians, the descendants of Asaph, were in the places prescribed by David, Asaph, Heman and Jeduthun the king's seer. The gatekeepers at each gate did not need to leave their posts, because their fellow Levites made the preparations for them.

[16]So at that time the entire service of the LORD was carried out for the celebration of the Passover and the offering of burnt offerings on the altar of the LORD, as King Josiah had ordered. [17]The Israelites who were present celebrated the Passover at that time and observed the Feast of Unleavened Bread for seven days. [18]The Passover had not been observed like this in Israel since the days of the prophet Samuel; and none of the kings of Israel had ever celebrated such a Passover as did Josiah, with the priests, the Levites and all Judah and Israel who were there with the people of Jerusalem. [19]This Passover was celebrated in the eighteenth year of Josiah's reign.

■ The Death of Josiah

[20]After all this, when Josiah had set the temple in order, Neco king of Egypt went up to fight at Carchemish on the Euphrates, and Josiah marched out to meet him in battle. [21]But Neco sent messengers to him saying, "What quarrel is there between you and me, O king of Judah? It is not you I am attacking at this time, but the house with which I am at war. God has told me to hurry; so stop opposing God, who is with me, or he will destroy you."

[22]Josiah, however, would not turn away from him, but disguised himself to engage him in battle. He would not listen to what Neco had said at God's command but went to fight him on the plain of Megiddo.

> **35:22 ■ A BLOODY BATTLEFIELD**
> Some historians estimate that the valley of Megiddo has seen more fighting and bloodshed than any other spot on earth. Sitting astride the chief north-south trade route in Canaan, it has great strategic significance. The book of Revelation records that the last battle of the age, Armageddon, will take place here (Revelation 16:16).

[23]Archers shot King Josiah, and he told his officers, "Take me away; I am badly wounded." [24]So they took him out of his chariot, put him in the other chariot he had and brought him to Jerusalem, where he died. He was buried in the tombs of his fathers, and all Judah and Jerusalem mourned for him.

[25]Jeremiah composed laments for Josiah, and to this day all the men and women singers commemorate Josiah in the laments. These became a tradition in Israel and are written in the Laments.

[26]The other events of Josiah's reign and his acts of devotion, according to what is written in the Law of the LORD—[27]all the events, from beginning to end, are written in the book of the kings of Israel and 36 Judah. [1]And the people of the land took Jehoahaz son of Josiah and made him king in Jerusalem in place of his father.

■ Jehoahaz King of Judah

[2]Jehoahaz[a] was twenty-three years old when he became king, and he reigned in Jerusalem for three months. [3]The king of Egypt dethroned him in Jerusalem and imposed on Judah a levy of a hundred talents[b] of silver and a talent[c] of gold. [4]The king of Egypt made Eliakim, a brother of Jehoahaz, king over Judah and Jerusalem and changed Eliakim's name to Jehoiakim. But Neco took Eliakim's brother Jehoahaz and carried him off to Egypt.

---

[a]2 Hebrew *Joahaz*, a variant of *Jehoahaz*; also in verse 4   [b]3 That is, about 3⅓ tons (about 3.4 metric tons)   [c]3 That is, about 75 pounds (about 34 kilograms)

Jehoiakim King of Judah

⁵Jehoiakim was twenty-five years old when he became king, and he reigned in Jerusalem for eleven years. He did evil in the eyes of the LORD his God. ⁶Nebuchadnezzar king of Babylon attacked him and bound him with bronze shackles to take him to Babylon. ⁷Nebuchadnezzar also took to Babylon articles from the temple of the LORD and put them in his temple*d* there.

⁸The other events of Jehoiakim's reign, the detestable things he did and all that was found against him, are written in the book of the kings of Israel and Judah. And Jehoiachin his son succeeded him as king.

Jehoiachin King of Judah

⁹Jehoiachin was eighteen*e* years old when he became king, and he reigned in Jerusalem for three months and ten days. He did evil in the eyes of the LORD. ¹⁰In the spring, King Nebuchadnezzar sent for him and brought him to Babylon, together with articles of value from the temple of the LORD, and he made Jehoiachin's uncle,*f* Zedekiah, king over Judah and Jerusalem.

Zedekiah King of Judah

¹¹Zedekiah was twenty-one years old when he became king, and he reigned in Jerusalem for eleven years. ¹²He did evil in the eyes of the LORD his God and did not humble himself before Jeremiah the prophet, who spoke the word of the LORD. ¹³He also rebelled against King Nebuchadnezzar, who had made him take an oath in God's name. He became stiff-necked and hardened his heart and would not turn to the LORD, the God of Israel. ¹⁴Furthermore, all the leaders of the priests and the people became more and more unfaithful, following all the detestable practices of the nations and defiling the temple of the LORD, which he had consecrated in Jerusalem.

The Fall of Jerusalem

¹⁵The LORD, the God of their fathers, sent word to them through his messengers again and again, because he had pity on his people and on his dwelling-place. ¹⁶But they mocked God's messengers, despised his words and scoffed at his prophets until the wrath of the LORD was aroused against his people

and there was no remedy. ¹⁷He brought up against them the king of the Babylonians,*g* who killed their young men with the sword in the sanctuary, and spared neither young man nor young woman, old man or aged. God handed all of them over to Nebuchadnezzar. ¹⁸He carried to Babylon all the articles from the temple of God, both large and small, and the treasures of the LORD's temple and the treasures of the king and his officials. ¹⁹They set fire to God's temple and broke down the wall of Jerusalem; they burned all the palaces and destroyed everything of value there.

²⁰He carried into exile to Babylon the remnant who escaped from the sword, and they became servants to him and his sons until the kingdom of Persia came to power. ²¹The land enjoyed its sabbath rests; all the time of its desolation it rested, until the seventy years were completed in fulfilment of the word of the LORD spoken by Jeremiah.

36:19 ■ BETWEEN THE TEMPLES
For about 70 years the Jews had no temple. The first local synagogues probably developed during this time, as gathering places where Jews could hear readings from the Old Testament and offer prayers. The last few verses of Chronicles hint that a more hopeful time is coming when the temple will be rebuilt. These verses are repeated at the beginning of Ezra. Most scholars believe Chronicles, Ezra, and Nehemiah were originally connected in one book.

---

²²In the first year of Cyrus king of Persia, in order to fulfil the word of the LORD spoken by Jeremiah, the LORD moved the heart of Cyrus king of Persia to make a proclamation throughout his realm and to put it in writing:

²³"This is what Cyrus king of Persia says:

" 'The LORD, the God of heaven, has given me all the kingdoms of the earth and he has appointed me to build a temple for him at Jerusalem in Judah. Anyone of his people among you — may the LORD his God be with him, and let him go up.' "

---

d 7 Or *palace*   *e* 9 One Hebrew manuscript, some Septuagint manuscripts and Syriac (see also 2 Kings 24:8); most Hebrew manuscripts *eight*
f 10 Hebrew *brother*, that is, relative (see 2 Kings 24:17)   *g* 17 Or *Chaldeans*

EZRA

■ BEGINNING AGAIN

FOR THE EXILES FROM BABYLON, NEWS ALMOST TOO GOOD TO BE TRUE

MANY OF THE OLDER PRIESTS AND LEVITES AND FAMILY HEADS, WHO HAD SEEN THE
FORMER TEMPLE, WEPT ALOUD . . . WHILE MANY OTHERS SHOUTED FOR JOY. ■ 3:12

Ezra begins with exiles returning to a ruined
city – a brush-covered ghost town burned and
pillaged nearly 50 years before by an overpowering
Babylonian army. Would Jerusalem now have a
new beginning?

Psalm 126 captures the returning exiles'
feelings: "We were like men who dreamed. Our
mouths were filled with laughter, our tongues
with songs of joy". The Persian empire had
conquered mighty Babylon and, under the
emperor Cyrus, offered all Jews a chance to
return to their land. It was too good to believe.

■ A NEW START WITH GOD

One poet in exile had written, "If I forget you,
O Jerusalem, may my right hand forget its skill"
(Psalm 137:5). These returned exiles were the
minority who, decades afterwards, had not
forgotten. They treasured their spiritual heritage
more than the houses and businesses they had
built in Babylon. They wanted to live and worship
in the place God had given his people. Any
sacrifice was worth this opportunity. Their first
impulse when they arrived was to rebuild the
temple, God's home.

The tolerant Persians (whose official
policy was to encourage the local religion in
every area they governed) had even brought out
the silver and gold temple articles, carefully
preserved in a Babylonian temple as though
waiting on God's timing. When the returned
exiles laid the foundation to the new temple, the
sound of their shouting (and noisy weeping)
could be heard from far away (3:13). The temple,
after all, was the place where they would meet
God. It symbolised a new start with him.

■ THE PROBLEMS OF BEGINNING AGAIN

God had opened the way, but the exiles needed
determination to follow it. The book of Ezra divides
into three parts, each one dealing with an obstacle
that arose. The first part tells how, immediately
after the return of the exiles, their neighbours in
the surrounding countryside became hostile. After

their deceptive offer of "help" was turned down,
these neighbours began a campaign of opposition.
They managed to stop further progress on the
temple.

The temple lay in ruins for nearly 20
more years, until the prophets Haggai and
Zechariah (whose messages are recorded in the
books named after them) again stirred up
interest in building. This "second push" is
described in chapters 5 and 6. When opposition
arose this time, the Jews managed to push
through – again with the assistance of a Persian
king.

Another problem preoccupies the final
four chapters. Ezra, the man after whom this
book is named, actually arrived in Jerusalem
during this period, 80 years after the first party.
The temple had by then been up for half a
century. But the "new beginning" stood in severe
jeopardy again. The Jews had begun to mingle
(and compromise their faith) with the hostile
people around them. Ezra's leadership, which
came from deep biblical faith and genuine
sorrow over sin, forced a radical, painful
solution.

■ EZRA LEADS UP TO JESUS

The book of Ezra introduces an entirely new
period in Israel's history – a period in which they
became more like a church than a nation.
Israelites before the exile had given much of their
energy to fighting enemy armies. Now they
focused on fighting sin and spiritual compromise.

The minority who returned could build a
temple only with the permission of a foreign
government in Persia. They had lost political
independence, yet they clung to their religion,
especially to the Old Testament Scriptures and
temple worship. They feared repeating the
mistakes that had sent them into exile. True,
they did flirt with spiritual compromise. Yet when
God's prophets spoke, people responded.

As those who had chosen a ruined
Jerusalem over a prosperous Babylon, the

returned Jews looked to God instead of to government for help. Still they dreamed, more than ever, of the powerful Messiah the prophets promised. This dream, and their strong

determination to obey the law of God, continued right up until the time of Jesus, about 450 years after Ezra's last words.

■ HOW TO READ EZRA

The book of Ezra describes several highly emotional events. Yet it reads like a historical report, citing official documents, letters, and lists written over an 80-year span. You are often left to imagine for yourself the feelings of the returning exiles. The book can, therefore, seem confusing and dry unless you take time to imagine how the scenes must have looked and to reflect on how people must have felt.

The three distinct periods Ezra deals with all have the same theme: a new beginning for God's people. In each situation God gave opportunity and the outside world threatened it. God's people drifted back and forth in their

response. Carefully take note of the "messages" from both God and the world, and how the Israelites responded. Examine Ezra's model, as an unwavering man of the law as well as of deep personal faith.

To understand how Ezra fits into Israel's long-term pattern of response to God and the world, read some historical background. Articles on "Ezra", "Haggai" or "Israel, History of" in a Bible dictionary may offer the best summary. The short book of Haggai zeroes in on the crucial months described in Ezra 5:1–2 and makes a valuable companion to any study of Ezra.

■ 3-TRACK READING PLAN

For an explanation and complete listing of the 3-track reading plan, turn to page x.

■ TRACK 1:
Two-Week Courses on the Bible
See page x for information on these courses.

■ TRACK 2:
An Overview of Ezra in 1 Day
☐ Day 1. Read the

Introduction to Ezra and chapter 3 for the emotional story of how the returned exiles laid the foundation for the new temple.
Now turn to page xi for your next Track 2 reading project.

■ TRACK 3:
All of Ezra in 9 Days
After you have read through Ezra, turn to pages xii–xiii for your next Track 3 reading project.

☐ 1–2 ☐ 3   ☐ 4   ☐ 5
☐ 6   ☐ 7   ☐ 8   ☐ 9
☐ 10

■ Cyrus Helps the Exiles to Return

1 In the first year of Cyrus king of Persia, in order to fulfil the word of the LORD spoken by Jeremiah, the LORD moved the heart of Cyrus king of Persia to make a proclamation throughout his realm and to put it in writing:

2"This is what Cyrus king of Persia says:

" 'The LORD, the God of heaven, has given me all the kingdoms of the earth and he has appointed me to build a temple for him at Jerusalem in Judah. 3Anyone of his people among you — may his God be with him, and let him go up to Jerusalem in Judah and build the temple of the LORD, the God of Israel, the God who is in Jerusalem. 4And the people of any place where survivors may now be living are to provide him with silver and gold, with goods and livestock, and with freewill offerings for the temple of God in Jerusalem.' "

5Then the family heads of Judah and Benjamin, and the priests and Levites — everyone whose heart God had moved — prepared to go up and build the house of the LORD in Jerusalem. 6All their neighbours assisted them with articles of silver and gold, with goods and livestock, and with valuable gifts, in addition to all the freewill offerings. 7Moreover, King

Cyrus brought out the articles belonging to the temple of the LORD, which Nebuchadnezzar had carried away from Jerusalem and had placed in the temple of his god.*a* 8Cyrus king of Persia had them brought by Mithredath the treasurer, who counted them out to Sheshbazzar the prince of Judah.

1:2 ■ PREDICTION FULFILLED
The fulfilled prophecy was probably Jeremiah 29:10, God's promise to bring Israel back to Jerusalem after 70 years. Additionally, Isaiah 44:28 and 45:1,13 had named Cyrus of Persia as God's agent to see Jerusalem and the temple rebuilt. This is not evidence that Cyrus worshipped Israel's God. He had a policy of religious toleration and contributed to the rebuilding of several nations' temples.

9This was the inventory:

gold dishes	30
silver dishes	1,000
silver pans*b*	29
10gold bowls	30
matching silver bowls	410
other articles	1,000

a 7 Or *gods*   *b 9* The meaning of the Hebrew for this word is uncertain.

11In all, there were 5,400 articles of gold and of silver. Sheshbazzar brought all these along when the exiles came up from Babylon to Jerusalem.

■ The List of the Exiles Who Returned

2 Now these are the people of the province who came up from the captivity of the exiles, whom Nebuchadnezzar king of Babylon had taken captive to Babylon (they returned to Jerusalem and Judah,

2:1 ■ A PEOPLE PRESERVED

Lists of names, whether in the Bible or the telephone book, make dull reading. But the way these names are grouped reveals God's care for the people of Israel. They had not lost track of their Israelite identity during two generations in Babylon. They knew their family record, and they could place themselves according to Israelite families, Israelite towns, and Israelite religious duties in the temple. Like the temple articles, carefully stored in readiness (1:7), these were a people preserved to serve God again.

each to his own town, 2in company with Zerubbabel, Jeshua, Nehemiah, Seraiah, Reelaiah, Mordecai, Bilshan, Mispar, Bigvai, Rehum and Baanah):

The list of the men of the people of Israel:

3the descendants of Parosh	2,172
4of Shephatiah	372
5of Arah	775
6of Pahath-Moab (through the line of Jeshua and Joab)	2,812
7of Elam	1,254
8of Zattu	945
9of Zaccai	760
10of Bani	642
11of Bebai	623
12of Azgad	1,222
13of Adonikam	666
14of Bigvai	2,056
15of Adin	454
16of Ater (through Hezekiah)	98
17of Bezai	323
18of Jorah	112
19of Hashum	223
20of Gibbar	95
21the men of Bethlehem	123
22of Netophah	56
23of Anathoth	128
24of Azmaveth	42
25of Kiriath Jearim,a Kephirah and Beeroth	743
26of Ramah and Geba	621
27of Michmash	122
28of Bethel and Ai	223
29of Nebo	52
30of Magbish	156
31of the other Elam	1,254
32of Harim	320
33of Lod, Hadid and Ono	725
34of Jericho	345
35of Senaah	3,630

36The priests:

the descendants of Jedaiah (through the family of Jeshua)	973
37of Immer	1,052
38of Pashhur	1,247
39of Harim	1,017

40The Levites:

the descendants of Jeshua and Kadmiel (through the line of Hodaviah)	74

41The singers:

the descendants of Asaph	128

42The gatekeepers of the temple:

the descendants of Shallum, Ater, Talmon, Akkub, Hatita and Shobai	139

43The temple servants:

the descendants of
Ziha, Hasupha, Tabbaoth,
44Keros, Siaha, Padon,
45Lebanah, Hagabah, Akkub,
46Hagab, Shalmai, Hanan,
47Giddel, Gahar, Reaiah,
48Rezin, Nekoda, Gazzam,
49Uzza, Paseah, Besai,
50Asnah, Meunim, Nephussim,
51Bakbuk, Hakupha, Harhur,
52Bazluth, Mehida, Harsha,
53Barkos, Sisera, Temah,
54Neziah and Hatipha

55The descendants of the servants of Solomon:

the descendants of
Sotai, Hassophereth, Peruda,
56Jaala, Darkon, Giddel,
57Shephatiah, Hattil,
Pokereth-Hazzebaim and Ami

58The temple servants and the descendants of the servants of Solomon	392

59The following came up from the towns of Tel Melah, Tel Harsha, Kerub, Addon and Immer, but they could not show that their families were descended from Israel:

60The descendants of Delaiah, Tobiah and Nekoda	652

61And from among the priests:

The descendants of Hobaiah, Hakkoz and Barzillai (a man who had married a daughter of Barzillai the Gileadite and was called by that name).

62These searched for their family records, but they could not find them and so were excluded from the priesthood as unclean. 63The governor ordered them not to eat any of the most sacred food until there was a priest ministering with the Urim and Thummim.

64The whole company numbered 42,360, 65besides their 7,337 menservants and

a25 See Septuagint (see also Neh. 7:29); Hebrew Kiriath Arim.

maidservants; and they also had 200 men and women singers. 66They had 736 horses, 245 mules, 67435 camels and 6,720 donkeys.

68When they arrived at the house of the LORD in Jerusalem, some of the heads of the families gave freewill offerings towards the rebuilding of the house of God on its site. 69According to their ability they gave to the treasury for this work 61,000 drachmas*b* of gold, 5,000 minas*c* of silver and 100 priestly garments.

70The priests, the Levites, the singers, the gatekeepers and the temple servants settled in their own towns, along with some of the other people, and the rest of the Israelites settled in their towns.

■ Rebuilding the Altar

3 When the seventh month came and the Israelites had settled in their towns, the people assembled as one man in Jerusalem. 2Then Jeshua son of Jozadak and his fellow priests and Zerubbabel son of Shealtiel and his associates began to build the altar of the God of Israel to sacrifice burnt offerings on it, in accordance with what is written in the Law of Moses the man of God. 3Despite their fear of the peoples around them, they built the altar on its foundation and sacrificed burnt offerings on it to the LORD, both the morning and evening sacrifices. 4Then in accordance with what is written, they celebrated the Feast of Tabernacles with the required number of burnt offerings prescribed for each day. 5After that, they presented the regular burnt offerings, the New Moon sacrifices and the sacrifices for all the appointed sacred feasts of the LORD, as well as those brought as freewill offerings to the LORD. 6On the first day of the seventh month they began to offer burnt offerings to the LORD, though the foundation of the LORD's temple had not yet been laid.

■ Rebuilding the Temple

7Then they gave money to the masons and carpenters, and gave food and drink and oil to the people of Sidon and Tyre, so that they would bring cedar logs by sea from Lebanon to Joppa, as authorised by Cyrus king of Persia.

8In the second month of the second year after their arrival at the house of God in Jerusalem, Zerubbabel son of Shealtiel, Jeshua son of Jozadak and the rest of their brothers (the priests and the Levites and all who had returned from the captivity to Jerusalem) began the work, appointing Levites twenty years of age and older to supervise the building of the house of the LORD. 9Jeshua and his sons and brothers and Kadmiel and his sons (descendants of Hodaviah*a*) and the sons of Henadad and their sons and brothers—all Levites—joined together in supervising those working on the house of God.

10When the builders laid the foundation of the temple of the LORD, the priests in their vestments and with trumpets, and the Levites (the sons of Asaph) with cymbals, took their places to praise the LORD, as prescribed by David king of Israel. 11With praise and thanksgiving they sang to the LORD:

"He is good;
    his love to Israel endures for ever."

And all the people gave a great shout of praise to the LORD, because the foundation of the house of the LORD was laid. 12But many of the older priests and Levites and family heads, who had seen the former temple, wept aloud when they saw the foundation of this temple being laid, while many others shouted for joy. 13No-one could distinguish the sound of the shouts of joy from the sound of weeping, because the people made so much noise. And the sound was heard far away.

■ Opposition to the Rebuilding

4 When the enemies of Judah and Benjamin heard that the exiles were building a temple for the LORD, the God of Israel, 2they came to Zerubbabel and to the heads of the families and said, "Let us help you build because, like you, we seek your God and have been sacrificing to him since the time of Esarhaddon king of Assyria, who brought us here."

3But Zerubbabel, Jeshua and the rest of the heads of the families of Israel answered, "You have no part with us in building a temple to our God. We alone will build it for the LORD, the God of Israel, as King Cyrus, the king of Persia, commanded us."

4Then the peoples around them set out to discourage the people of Judah and make them afraid to go on building.*a* 5They hired counsellors to work against them and frustrate their plans during the entire reign of Cyrus king of Persia and down to the reign of Darius king of Persia.

■ Later Opposition Under Xerxes and Artaxerxes

6At the beginning of the reign of Xerxes,*b* they lodged an accusation against the people of Judah and Jerusalem.

b 69 That is, about 1,100 pounds (about 500 kilograms)   *c* 69 That is, about 2⅖ tons (about 2.9 metric tons)   *a* 9 Hebrew *Yehudah*, probably a variant
of *Hodaviah*   *a* 4 Or *and troubled them as they built*   *b* 6 Hebrew *Ahasuerus*, a variant of Xerxes' Persian name

7And in the days of Artaxerxes king of Persia, Bishlam, Mithredath, Tabeel and the rest of his associates wrote a letter to Artaxerxes. The letter was written in Aramaic script and in the Aramaic language.c d

4:6-23 ■ A FLASH FORWARD

This section is a glance forward in history. The Israelites would continue to feel opposition from their neighbours even long after the temple was successfully completed. The quarrel described here, during Xerxes' and Artaxerxes' reigns, was not over the temple but the defensive wall to be built around Jerusalem – a wall Nehemiah, with Ezra's help, completed years later.

8Rehum the commanding officer and Shimshai the secretary wrote a letter against Jerusalem to Artaxerxes the king as follows:

9Rehum the commanding officer and Shimshai the secretary, together with the rest of their associates—the judges and officials over the men from Tripolis, Persia,e Erech and Babylon, the Elamites of Susa, 10and the other people whom the great and honourable Ashurbanipalf deported and settled in the city of Samaria and elsewhere in Trans-Euphrates.

11(This is a copy of the letter they sent him.)

To King Artaxerxes,

From your servants, the men of Trans-Euphrates:

12The king should know that the Jews who came up to us from you have gone to Jerusalem and are rebuilding that rebellious and wicked city. They are restoring the walls and repairing the foundations.
13Furthermore, the king should know that if this city is built and its walls are restored, no more taxes, tribute or duty will be paid, and the royal revenues will suffer. 14Now since we are under obligation to the palace and it is not proper for us to see the king dishonoured, we are sending this message to inform the king, 15so that a search may be made in the archives of your predecessors. In these records you will find that this city is a rebellious city, troublesome to kings and provinces, a place of rebellion from ancient times. That is why this city was destroyed. 16We inform the king that if this city is built and its walls are restored, you will be left with nothing in Trans-Euphrates.

17The king sent this reply:

To Rehum the commanding officer, Shimshai the secretary and the rest of their associates living in Samaria and elsewhere in Trans-Euphrates:

Greetings.

18The letter you sent us has been read and translated in my presence. 19I issued an order

and a search was made, and it was found that this city has a long history of revolt against kings and has been a place of rebellion and sedition. 20Jerusalem has had powerful kings ruling over the whole of Trans-Euphrates, and taxes, tribute and duty were paid to them. 21Now issue an order to these men to stop work, so that this city will not be rebuilt until I so order. 22Be careful not to neglect this matter. Why let this threat grow, to the detriment of the royal interests?

23As soon as the copy of the letter of King Artaxerxes was read to Rehum and Shimshai the secretary and their associates, they went immediately to the Jews in Jerusalem and compelled them by force to stop.

24Thus the work on the house of God in Jerusalem came to a standstill until the second year of the reign of Darius king of Persia.

■ Tattenai's Letter to Darius

5 Now Haggai the prophet and Zechariah the prophet, a descendant of Iddo, prophesied to the Jews in Judah and Jerusalem in the name of the God of Israel, who was over them. 2Then Zerubbabel son of Shealtiel and Jeshua son of Jozadak set to work to rebuild the house of God in Jerusalem. And the prophets of God were with them, helping them.
3At that time Tattenai, governor of Trans-Euphrates, and Shethar-Bozenai and their associates went to them and asked, "Who authorised you to rebuild this temple and restore this structure?" 4They also asked, "What are the names of the men constructing this building?"a 5But the eye of their God was watching over the elders of the Jews, and they were not stopped until a report could go to Darius and his written reply be received.
6This is a copy of the letter that Tattenai, governor of Trans-Euphrates, and Shethar-Bozenai and their associates, the officials of Trans-Euphrates, sent to King Darius. 7The report they sent him read as follows:

To King Darius:

Cordial greetings.

8The king should know that we went to the district of Judah, to the temple of the great God. The people are building it with large stones and placing the timbers in the walls. The work is being carried on with diligence and is making rapid progress under their direction.
9We questioned the elders and asked them, "Who authorised you to rebuild this temple and restore this structure?" 10We also asked them their names, so that we could write down the names of their leaders for your information.
11This is the answer they gave us:

"We are the servants of the God of heaven and earth, and we are rebuilding the temple that was built many years ago, one that a great king of Israel built and finished. 12But because our fathers angered the God of heaven, he

c7 Or written in Aramaic and translated   d7 The text of Ezra 4:8–6:18 is in Aramaic.   e9 Or officials, magistrates and governors over the men from
f10 Aramaic Osnappar, a variant of Ashurbanipal   a4 See Septuagint; Aramaic 4We told them the names of the men constructing this building.

handed them over to Nebuchadnezzar the Chaldean, king of Babylon, who destroyed this temple and deported the people to Babylon.

13"However, in the first year of Cyrus king of Babylon, King Cyrus issued a decree to rebuild this house of God. 14He even removed from the temple*b* of Babylon the gold and silver articles of the house of God, which Nebuchadnezzar had taken from the temple in Jerusalem and brought to the temple*b* in Babylon.

"Then King Cyrus gave them to a man named Sheshbazzar, whom he had appointed governor, 15and he told him, 'Take these articles and go and deposit them in the temple in Jerusalem. And rebuild the house of God on its site.' 16So this Sheshbazzar came and laid the foundations of the house of God in Jerusalem. From that day to the present it has been under construction but is not yet finished."

17Now if it pleases the king, let a search be made in the royal archives of Babylon to see if King Cyrus did in fact issue a decree to rebuild this house of God in Jerusalem. Then let the king send us his decision in this matter.

■ The Decree of Darius

6 King Darius then issued an order, and they searched in the archives stored in the treasury at Babylon. 2A scroll was found in the citadel of Ecbatana in the province of Media, and this was written on it:

Memorandum:

> **6:2 ■ THE RING OF TRUTH**
> In a made-up legend, there is no need for insignificant, divergent details. All the loose ends tie up neatly. Real life, however, is messier. Ezra records a typical example: a document was searched for in Babylon, but it unexpectedly turned up in remote Ecbatana, where (history records) Cyrus spent the summer of his first year as king. Such details suggest that Ezra is based on accurate and detailed historical sources.

3In the first year of King Cyrus, the king issued a decree concerning the temple of God in Jerusalem:

Let the temple be rebuilt as a place to present sacrifices, and let its foundations be laid. It is to be ninety feet*a* high and ninety feet wide, 4with three courses of large stones and one of timbers. The costs are to be paid by the royal treasury. 5Also, the gold and silver articles of the house of God, which Nebuchadnezzar took from the temple in Jerusalem and brought to Babylon, are to be returned to their places in the temple in Jerusalem; they are to be deposited in the house of God.

6Now then, Tattenai, governor of Trans-Euphrates, and Shethar-Bozenai and you, their fellow officials of that province, stay away from there. 7Do not interfere with the work on this temple of God. Let the governor of the Jews and the Jewish elders rebuild this house of God on its site.

8Moreover, I hereby decree what you are to do for these elders of the Jews in the construction of this house of God:

The expenses of these men are to be fully paid out of the royal treasury, from the revenues of Trans-Euphrates, so that the work will not stop. 9Whatever is needed—young bulls, rams, male lambs for burnt offerings to the God of heaven, and wheat, salt, wine and oil, as requested by the priests in Jerusalem—must be given them daily without fail, 10so that they may offer sacrifices pleasing to the God of heaven and pray for the well-being of the king and his sons.

11Furthermore, I decree that if anyone changes this edict, a beam is to be pulled from his house and he is to be lifted up and impaled on it. And for this crime his house is to be made a pile of rubble. 12May God, who has caused his Name to dwell there, overthrow any king or people who lifts a hand to change this decree or to destroy this temple in Jerusalem.

I Darius have decreed it. Let it be carried out with diligence.

> **6:11 ■ IRONIC OUTCOME**
> Governor Tattenai had written to the central government in order to harass the Jews who sought to rebuild the temple (5:7–17). As it turned out, his strategy backfired. He and his local government were ordered to pay all the Jews' expenses or be impaled on their own roof beams.

■ Completion and Dedication of the Temple

13Then, because of the decree King Darius had sent, Tattenai, governor of Trans-Euphrates, and Shethar-Bozenai and their associates carried it out with diligence. 14So the elders of the Jews continued to build and prosper under the preaching of Haggai the prophet and Zechariah, a descendant of Iddo. They finished building the temple according to the command of the God of Israel and the decrees of Cyrus, Darius and Artaxerxes, kings of Persia. 15The temple was completed on the third day of the month Adar, in the sixth year of the reign of King Darius. 16Then the people of Israel—the priests, the Levites and the rest of the exiles—celebrated the dedication of the house of God with joy. 17For the dedication of this house of God they offered a hundred bulls, two hundred rams, four hundred male lambs and, as a sin offering for all Israel, twelve male goats, one for each of the tribes of Israel. 18And they installed the priests in their divisions and the Levites in their groups for the service of God at Jerusalem, according to what is written in the Book of Moses.

■ The Passover

19On the fourteenth day of the first month, the

b 14 Or palace   *a 3 Aramaic sixty cubits (about 27 metres)* exiles celebrated the Passover. ²⁰The priests and Levites had purified themselves and were all ceremonially clean. The Levites slaughtered the Passover lamb for all the exiles, for their brothers the priests and for themselves. ²¹So the Israelites who had returned from the exile ate it, together with all who had separated themselves from the unclean practices of their Gentile neighbours in order to seek the LORD, the God of Israel. ²²For seven days they celebrated with joy the Feast of Unleavened Bread, because the LORD had filled them with joy by changing the attitude of the king of Assyria, so that he assisted them in the work on the house of God, the God of Israel.

■ Ezra Comes to Jerusalem

7 After these things, during the reign of Artaxerxes king of Persia, Ezra son of Seraiah, the son of Azariah, the son of Hilkiah, ²the son of Shallum, the son of Zadok, the son of Ahitub, ³the son of Amariah, the son of Azariah, the son of Meraioth, ⁴the son of Zerahiah, the son of Uzzi, the son of Bukki, ⁵the son of Abishua, the son of Phinehas, the son of Eleazar, the son of Aaron the chief priest— ⁶this Ezra came up from Babylon. He was a teacher well versed in the Law of Moses, which the LORD, the God of Israel, had given. The king had granted him everything he asked, for the hand of the LORD his God was on him. ⁷Some of the Israelites, including

INSIGHT

■ EZRA, A MAN OF THE HEART
HE APPLIED GOD'S WORD TO HIMSELF BEFORE PREACHING IT TO OTHERS

WHILE EZRA WAS PRAYING AND CONFESSING, WEEPING AND THROWING HIMSELF DOWN BEFORE THE HOUSE OF GOD, A LARGE CROWD OF ISRAELITES — MEN, WOMEN AND CHILDREN — GATHERED ROUND HIM.
■ 10:1

Ezra knew how to get things done. He had the political know-how to win a Persian king's support for the trip back to Jerusalem, the salesmanship to convince Jewish family leaders to go along, and the organisational know-how to mount the long, complicated and dangerous expedition. (There were no Holiday Inns.)

At the same time, Ezra was a priest who depended on God. He set aside days for fasting and prayer. He knew and lived by the Old Testament law, but used it as a path to a profound relationship with God. When he studied Scripture, he applied it to himself before applying it to others (7:10).

■ A STRONG NEGATIVE REACTION
Ezra's party got to Jerusalem 80 years after the first exiles had returned. Yet within four months the Jewish leaders were asking this latecomer for advice on the most sensitive matters.

They told Ezra that Israelites were marrying their idolatrous neighbours. At the news, Ezra completely lost his composure, tore his clothes and sat down stunned (9:3). His grief-filled prayer of repentance inspired a large crowd to join him in bitter weeping. Then and there they resolved to break up the marriages. The women and children were to be sent away. Ezra, a practical man even in his emotional condition, put the machinery into operation and saw it done.

Why did Ezra react so negatively to these marriages? How could he allow children to be sent away from their fathers, families split? Some people see proof that he was racially

oriented, bound to exclude non-Jews from Israel.

But racial purity was not Ezra's worry. Non-Jews like Rahab and Ruth, who converted to Judaism, had long been accepted in Israel. Ezra 6:21 suggests that outsiders who sought the Lord were still welcomed. Ezra's concern was that intermarriage represented a compromised faith that threatened the future existence of Israel.

■ TOSSING AWAY ONE LAST CHANCE
Marriage in those days was more than a personal matter. It created a political and religious alliance between two families. These mixed marriages were tying Israelites to other faiths — for Israel's neighbours worshipped idols, an act God hated. Ezra knew that his God must hold the only place in his people's hearts. They must be a special people with a sense of their unique destiny. The law told them not to intermarry (Exodus 34:15–16; Deuteronomy 7:3–6). (In a related situation Paul instructed Christians not to be "yoked together to unbelievers" [2 Corinthians 6:14], though he told Christians already married to non-Christians not to divorce [1 Corinthians 7:12–16].)

Ezra's prayer shows that petty technicalities of the law were far from his mind. His concerns involved the heart. He saw his people falling into the same pattern of compromise that had led God to give them up to the Babylonians years before. Had they learned nothing from their long exile? They were throwing away one last remarkable chance to start again.

□ LIFE QUESTIONS:
Ezra saw intermarriage as a compromise to people's faith. Do people today make other compromises that have the same impact on their faith?

priests, Levites, singers, gatekeepers and temple servants, also came up to Jerusalem in the seventh year of King Artaxerxes.

⁸Ezra arrived in Jerusalem in the fifth month of the seventh year of the king. ⁹He had begun his journey from Babylon on the first day of the first month, and he arrived in Jerusalem on the first day of the fifth month, for the gracious hand of his God was on him. ¹⁰For Ezra had devoted himself to the study and observance of the Law of the LORD, and to teaching its decrees and laws in Israel.

■ King Artaxerxes' Letter to Ezra

¹¹This is a copy of the letter King Artaxerxes had given to Ezra the priest and teacher, a man learned in matters concerning the commands and decrees of the LORD for Israel:

¹²ᵃArtaxerxes, king of kings,

To Ezra the priest, a teacher of the Law of the God of heaven:

Greetings.

¹³Now I decree that any of the Israelites in my kingdom, including priests and Levites, who wish to go to Jerusalem with you, may go. ¹⁴You are sent by the king and his seven advisers to enquire about Judah and Jerusalem with regard to the Law of your God, which is in your hand. ¹⁵Moreover, you are to take with you the silver and gold that the king and his advisers have freely given to the God of Israel, whose dwelling is in Jerusalem, ¹⁶together with all the silver and gold you may obtain from the province of Babylon, as well as the freewill offerings of the people and priests for the temple of their God in Jerusalem. ¹⁷With this money be sure to buy bulls, rams and male lambs, together with their grain offerings and drink offerings, and sacrifice them on the altar of the temple of your God in Jerusalem. ¹⁸You and your brother Jews may then do whatever seems best with the rest of the silver and gold, in accordance with the will of your God. ¹⁹Deliver to the God of Jerusalem all the articles entrusted to you for worship in the temple of your God. ²⁰And anything else needed for the temple of your God that you may have occasion to supply, you may provide from the royal treasury.

²¹Now I, King Artaxerxes, order all the treasurers of Trans-Euphrates to provide with diligence whatever Ezra the priest, a teacher of the Law of the God of heaven, may ask of you — ²²up to a hundred talentsᵇ of silver, a hundred corsᶜ of wheat, a hundred bathsᵈ of wine, a hundred bathsᵈ of olive oil, and salt without limit. ²³Whatever the God of heaven has prescribed, let it be done with diligence for the temple of the God of heaven. Why should there be wrath against the realm of the king and of his sons? ²⁴You are also to know that you have no authority to impose taxes, tribute or duty on any of the priests, Levites, singers, gatekeepers,

temple servants or other workers at this house of God.

²⁵And you, Ezra, in accordance with the wisdom of your God, which you possess, appoint magistrates and judges to administer justice to all the people of Trans-Euphrates — all who know the laws of your God. And you are to teach any who do not know them. ²⁶Whoever does not obey the law of your God and the law of the king must surely be punished by death, banishment, confiscation of property, or imprisonment.

²⁷Praise be to the LORD, the God of our fathers, who has put it into the king's heart to bring honour to the house of the LORD in Jerusalem in this way ²⁸and who has extended his good favour to me before the king and his advisers and all the king's powerful officials. Because the hand of the LORD my God was on me, I took courage and gathered leading men from Israel to go up with me.

■ List of the Family Heads Returning With Ezra

8 These are the family heads and those registered with them who came up with me from Babylon during the reign of King Artaxerxes:

²of the descendants of Phinehas, Gershom;
of the descendants of Ithamar, Daniel;
of the descendants of David, Hattush ³of the descendants of Shecaniah;

of the descendants of Parosh, Zechariah, and with him were registered 150 men;
⁴of the descendants of Pahath-Moab, Eliehoenai son of Zerahiah, and with him 200 men;
⁵of the descendants of Zattu,ᵃ Shecaniah son of Jahaziel, and with him 300 men;
⁶of the descendants of Adin, Ebed son of Jonathan, and with him 50 men;
⁷of the descendants of Elam, Jeshaiah son of Athaliah, and with him 70 men;
⁸of the descendants of Shephatiah, Zebadiah son of Michael, and with him 80 men;
⁹of the descendants of Joab, Obadiah son of Jehiel, and with him 218 men;
¹⁰of the descendants of Bani,ᵇ Shelomith son of Josiphiah, and with him 160 men;
¹¹of the descendants of Bebai, Zechariah son of Bebai, and with him 28 men;
¹²of the descendants of Azgad, Johanan son of Hakkatan, and with him 110 men;
¹³of the descendants of Adonikam, the last ones, whose names were Eliphelet, Jeuel and Shemaiah, and with them 60 men;
¹⁴of the descendants of Bigvai, Uthai and Zaccur, and with them 70 men.

■ The Return to Jerusalem

¹⁵I assembled them at the canal that flows towards Ahava, and we camped there three days. When I checked among the people and the priests, I found no Levites there. ¹⁶So I summoned Eliezer, Ariel, Shemaiah, Elnathan, Jarib, Elnathan, Nathan, Zechariah and Meshullam, who were leaders, and

ᵃ12 The text of Ezra 7:12–26 is in Aramaic.   ᵇ22 That is, about 3⅓ tons (about 3.4 metric tons)   ᶜ22 That is, probably about 600 bushels (about 22 kilolitres)   ᵈ22 That is, probably about 500 gallons (about 2.2 kilolitres)   ᵃ5 Some Septuagint manuscripts (also 1 Esdras 8:32); Hebrew does not have Zattu.   ᵇ10 Some Septuagint manuscripts (also 1 Esdras 8:36); Hebrew does not have Bani.

Joiarib and Elnathan, who were men of learning, [17]and I sent them to Iddo, the leader in Casiphia. I told them what to say to Iddo and his kinsmen, the temple servants in Casiphia, so that they might bring attendants to us for the house of our God. [18]Because the gracious hand of our God was on us, they brought us Sherebiah, a capable man, from the descendants of Mahli son of Levi, the son of Israel, and Sherebiah's sons and brothers, 18 men; [19]and Hashabiah, together with Jeshaiah from the descendants of Merari, and his brothers and nephews, 20 men. [20]They also brought 220 of the temple servants — a body that David and the officials had established to assist the Levites. All were registered by name.

[21]There, by the Ahava Canal, I proclaimed a fast, so that we might humble ourselves before our God and ask him for a safe journey for us and our children, with all our possessions. [22]I was ashamed to ask the king for soldiers and horsemen to protect us from enemies on the road, because we had told the king, "The gracious hand of our God is on everyone who looks to him, but his great anger is against all who forsake him." [23]So we fasted and petitioned our God about this, and he answered our prayer.

8:22 ■ RISK OF FAITH

Like gold shipments in the old Wild West, Ezra's consignment of treasure made for a dangerous journey through lawless Palestine. A military escort would surely have helped. But, having told the king that God would protect the settlers, Ezra was ashamed to ask for help that would seem to contradict his statement. His faith on the line, he determined to rely on prayer rather than soldiers.

[24]Then I set apart twelve of the leading priests, together with Sherebiah, Hashabiah and ten of their brothers, [25]and I weighed out to them the offering of silver and gold and the articles that the king, his advisers, his officials and all Israel present there had donated for the house of our God. [26]I weighed out to them 650 talents[c] of silver, silver articles weighing 100 talents,[d] 100 talents[d] of gold, [27]20 bowls of gold valued at 1,000 darics,[e] and two fine articles of polished bronze, as precious as gold.

[28]I said to them, "You as well as these articles are consecrated to the LORD. The silver and gold are a freewill offering to the LORD, the God of your fathers. [29]Guard them carefully until you weigh them out in the chambers of the house of the LORD in Jerusalem before the leading priests and the Levites and the family heads of Israel." [30]Then the priests and Levites received the silver and gold and sacred articles that had been weighed out to be taken to the house of our God in Jerusalem.

[31]On the twelfth day of the first month we set out from the Ahava Canal to go to Jerusalem. The hand of our God was on us, and he protected us from enemies and bandits along the way. [32]So we arrived in Jerusalem, where we rested three days.

[33]On the fourth day, in the house of our God, we weighed out the silver and gold and the sacred articles into the hands of Meremoth son of Uriah, the priest. Eleazar son of Phinehas was with him, and so were the Levites Jozabad son of Jeshua and Noadiah son of Binnui. [34]Everything was accounted for by number and weight, and the entire weight was recorded at that time.

[35]Then the exiles who had returned from captivity sacrificed burnt offerings to the God of Israel: twelve bulls for all Israel, ninety-six rams, seventy-seven male lambs and, as a sin offering, twelve male goats. All this was a burnt offering to the LORD. [36]They also delivered the king's orders to the royal satraps and to the governors of Trans-Euphrates who then gave assistance to the people and to the house of God.

■ Ezra's Prayer About Intermarriage

9 After these things had been done, the leaders came to me and said, "The people of Israel, including the priests and the Levites, have not kept themselves separate from the neighbouring peoples with their detestable practices, like those of the Canaanites, Hittites, Perizzites, Jebusites, Ammonites, Moabites, Egyptians and Amorites. [2]They have taken some of their daughters as wives for themselves and their sons, and have mingled the holy race with the peoples around them. And the leaders and officials have led the way in this unfaithfulness."

[3]When I heard this, I tore my tunic and cloak, pulled hair from my head and beard and sat down appalled. [4]Then everyone who trembled at the words of the God of Israel gathered round me because of this unfaithfulness of the exiles. And I sat there appalled until the evening sacrifice.

[5]Then, at the evening sacrifice, I rose from my self-abasement, with my tunic and cloak torn, and fell on my knees with my hands spread out to the LORD my God [6]and prayed:

"O my God, I am too ashamed and disgraced to lift up my face to you, my God, because our sins are higher than our heads and our guilt has reached to the heavens. [7]From the days of our forefathers until now, our guilt has been great. Because of our sins, we and our kings and our priests have been subjected to the sword and captivity, to pillage and humiliation at the hand of foreign kings, as it is today.

[8]"But now, for a brief moment, the LORD our God has been gracious in leaving us a remnant and giving us a firm place in his sanctuary, and so our God gives light to our eyes and a little relief in our bondage. [9]Though we are slaves, our God has not deserted us in our bondage. He has shown us kindness in the sight of the kings of Persia: He has granted us new life to rebuild the house of our God and repair its ruins, and he has given us a wall of protection in Judah and Jerusalem.

[10]"But now, O our God, what can we say after this? For we have disregarded the commands [11]you gave through your servants the prophets when you said: 'The land you are entering to possess is a land polluted by the corruption of its peoples. By their detestable

---

[c]26 That is, about 22 tons (about 22 metric tons)   [d]26 That is, about 3⅓ tons (about 3.4 metric tons)   [e]27 That is, about 19 pounds (about 8.5 kilograms)

practices they have filled it with their impurity from one end to the other. 12Therefore, do not give your daughters in marriage to their sons or take their daughters for your sons. Do not seek a treaty of friendship with them at any time, that you may be strong and eat the good things of the land and leave it to your children as an everlasting inheritance.'

13"What has happened to us is a result of our evil deeds and our great guilt, and yet, our God, you have punished us less than our sins have deserved and have given us a remnant like this. 14Shall we again break your commands and intermarry with the peoples who commit such detestable practices? Would you not be angry enough with us to destroy us, leaving us no remnant or survivor? 15O LORD, God of Israel, you are righteous! We are left this day as a remnant. Here we are before you in our guilt, though because of it not one of us can stand in your presence."

■ The People's Confession of Sin

10 While Ezra was praying and confessing, weeping and throwing himself down before the house of God, a large crowd of Israelites — men, women and children — gathered round him. They too wept bitterly. 2Then Shecaniah son of Jehiel, one of the descendants of Elam, said to Ezra, "We have been unfaithful to our God by marrying foreign women from the peoples around us. But in spite of this, there is still hope for Israel. 3Now let us make a covenant before our God to send away all these women and their children, in accordance with the counsel of my lord and of those who fear the commands of our God. Let it be done according to the Law. 4Rise up; this matter is in your hands. We will support you, so take courage and do it."

10:1 ■ UNPRECEDENTED RESPONSE
Ezra's grief over Israel's spiritual compromise was similar to that of many prophets. But the people's response to Ezra was unprecedented. Pre-exile prophets like Amos or Jeremiah never saw such heartfelt repentance. Evidently the exile really had purified Israel.

5So Ezra rose up and put the leading priests and Levites and all Israel under oath to do what had been suggested. And they took the oath. 6Then Ezra withdrew from before the house of God and went to the room of Jehohanan son of Eliashib. While he was there, he ate no food and drank no water, because he continued to mourn over the unfaithfulness of the exiles.

7A proclamation was then issued throughout Judah and Jerusalem for all the exiles to assemble in Jerusalem. 8Anyone who failed to appear within three days would forfeit all his property, in accordance with the decision of the officials and elders, and would himself be expelled from the assembly of the exiles.

9Within the three days, all the men of Judah and Benjamin had gathered in Jerusalem. And on the twentieth day of the ninth month, all the people were sitting in the square before the house of God, greatly distressed by the occasion and because of the rain. 10Then Ezra the priest stood up and said to them, "You have been unfaithful; you have married foreign women, adding to Israel's guilt. 11Now make confession to the LORD, the God of your fathers, and do his will. Separate yourselves from the peoples around you and from your foreign wives."

12The whole assembly responded with a loud voice: "You are right! We must do as you say. 13But there are many people here and it is the rainy season; so we cannot stand outside. Besides, this matter cannot be taken care of in a day or two, because we have sinned greatly in this thing. 14Let our officials act for the whole assembly. Then let everyone in our towns who has married a foreign woman come at a set time, along with the elders and judges of each town, until the fierce anger of our God in this matter is turned away from us." 15Only Jonathan son of Asahel and Jahzeiah son of Tikvah, supported by Meshullam and Shabbethai the Levite, opposed this.

16So the exiles did as was proposed. Ezra the priest selected men who were family heads, one from each family division, and all of them designated by name. On the first day of the tenth month they sat down to investigate the cases, 17and by the first day of the first month they finished dealing with all the men who had married foreign women.

10:17 ■ CORRUPT LEADERS
The problem Ezra had evidently expected to solve in a day (verse 13) took, in fact, two months to sort out. Intermarriage must have been more widespread than he realised. The list of those involved shows that the priests and Levites, who were the religious leaders, had a higher proportion of intermarriage than the rest of the people.

■ Those Guilty of Intermarriage

18Among the descendants of the priests, the following had married foreign women:

From the descendants of Jeshua son of Jozadak, and his brothers:
Maaseiah, Eliezer, Jarib and Gedaliah. 19(They all gave their hands in pledge to put away their wives, and for their guilt they each presented a ram from the flock as a guilt offering.)

20From the descendants of Immer:
Hanani and Zebadiah.

21From the descendants of Harim:
Maaseiah, Elijah, Shemaiah, Jehiel and Uzziah.

22From the descendants of Pashhur:
Elioenai, Maaseiah, Ishmael, Nethanel, Jozabad and Elasah.

23Among the Levites:

Jozabad, Shimei, Kelaiah (that is Kelita), Pethahiah, Judah and Eliezer.

24From the singers:
Eliashib.
From the gatekeepers:
Shallum, Telem and Uri.

25And among the other Israelites:

From the descendants of Parosh:
Ramiah, Izziah, Malkijah, Mijamin, Eleazar,
Malkijah and Benaiah.
26From the descendants of Elam:
Mattaniah, Zechariah, Jehiel, Abdi, Jeremoth
and Elijah.
27From the descendants of Zattu:
Elioenai, Eliashib, Mattaniah, Jeremoth,
Zabad and Aziza.
28From the descendants of Bebai:
Jehohanan, Hananiah, Zabbai and Athlai.
29From the descendants of Bani:
Meshullam, Malluch, Adaiah, Jashub, Sheal
and Jeremoth.
30From the descendants of Pahath-Moab:

Adna, Kelal, Benaiah, Maaseiah, Mattaniah,
Bezalel, Binnui and Manasseh.
31From the descendants of Harim:
Eliezer, Ishijah, Malkijah, Shemaiah, Shimeon,
32Benjamin, Malluch and Shemariah.
33From the descendants of Hashum:
Mattenai, Mattattah, Zabad, Eliphelet, Jere-
mai, Manasseh and Shimei.
34From the descendants of Bani:
Maadai, Amram, Uel, 35Benaiah, Bedeiah, Kel-
uhi, 36Vaniah, Meremoth, Eliashib, 37Mattan-
iah, Mattenai and Jaasu.
38From the descendants of Binnui:a
Shimei, 39Shelemiah, Nathan, Adaiah, 40Mac-
nadebai, Shashai, Sharai, 41Azarel, Shelemiah,
Shemariah, 42Shallum, Amariah and Joseph.
43From the descendants of Nebo:
Jeiel, Mattithiah, Zabad, Zebina, Jaddai, Joel
and Benaiah.

44All these had married foreign women, and some
of them had children by these wives.b

---

a 37,38 See Septuagint (also 1 Esdras 9:34); Hebrew Jaasu 38and Bani and Binnui,   b 44 Or and they sent them away with their children

NEHEMIAH

■ A MAN OF ACTION

HE SET OUT TO BUILD A WALL, BUT LEFT AN ENDURING LEGACY OF LEADERSHIP

"DON'T BE AFRAID OF THEM. REMEMBER THE LORD, WHO IS GREAT AND AWESOME, AND FIGHT." ■ 4:14

In the book of Nehemiah we peek inside the personal memoirs of a great leader. You can't mistake his style. He was an organiser, a pragmatic leader. That, no doubt, is why he had made his way to a top position in the Persian empire, one of the grandest in the history of the world.

Yet his heart was elsewhere – in Jerusalem, a small, troublesome place far from the centre of power. When he heard of the difficulties his people were experiencing there, he took his career – and probably his life – in his hands and spoke to the king about it. Shortly thereafter he was touring, by night, the broken-down walls of a city he probably had never seen before.

Nearly 100 years had passed since his people had returned to Jerusalem from exile. Though the temple had been rebuilt, the city was barely occupied. More Jews lived in the outlying villages and towns than in the holy city. They mixed with all kinds of foreigners. They were in danger of losing their identity. Why? Partly because the city lacked a wall.

■ WHAT'S IN A WALL?

Compared to many concerns, building a wall may not seem terribly important. But think of it this way – what if the border between Mexico and the United States was wide open, so that anyone could cross and live on either side at will? One thing is certain: the distinction between Mexico and Texas would soon dissolve.

For lack of a wall the Jews were facing assimilation into the culture of their neighbours. In those days a city without a wall was easy pickings for any robber band. Jews, concerned for security, had scattered among other nationalities in small villages outside Jerusalem. There they were intermarrying and gradually losing their own language, culture and – most important – their own religion. A wall would give them a chance to make Jerusalem a truly Jewish city, keeping it safe and controlling who came and went.

■ WAITING FOR A LEADER

What had kept them from doing anything about the broken-down wall for nearly 100 years? One obstacle was local resistance: powerful politicians were determined to keep the Jews down. Perhaps another reason was the lack of a leader like Nehemiah. In his memoirs, which fill most of this book, he shows remarkable qualities of leadership: impassioned speech, prayer, organisation, resolve, trust in God, quick and determined response to problems, unselfishness. Perhaps his years in the Persian court had been preparing him. Organising a difficult building project and handling fierce opposition seemed to come easily to him.

Nehemiah was more than a good business manager. He was a man of God. He did not act without prayer, and he did not pray without acting. His prayers punctuate the book. He recognised God's role in all that happened and never forgot to give him credit. He was not looking for earthly status – if he had been, he would never have left Persia.

■ HOW TO READ NEHEMIAH

Nehemiah's personality is the outstanding quality of the book that bears his name. No other biblical character gives such clear information about how to "practise the presence of God" while carrying a leadership role. As you read, take note of the qualities that made Nehemiah successful as a leader and man of God. You may also wish to contrast his leadership with Ezra's. They worked in tandem but had very different styles. Nehemiah was an activist, Ezra a student; Nehemiah was outspoken, Ezra more withdrawn. Yet both faced similar problems and had similar success – and the two worked smoothly together.

The books of Ezra and Nehemiah both tell how the disgraced and chastened Jews returned from exile to rebuild their country. As history, Nehemiah includes some long lists of different family groups, as well as a detailed description of who built which parts of the Jerusalem wall. Unless you are very familiar with the Old Testament, you should skim these lists mainly to get an understanding of why they were kept. Concentrate more on how the Israelites had been transformed and purified by exile, making them ready to meet new challenges when they returned home.

■ 3-TRACK READING PLAN

For an explanation and complete listing of the 3-track reading plan, turn to page x.

■ TRACK 1:
Two-Week Courses on the Bible
See page x for information on these courses.

■ TRACK 2:
An Overview of Nehemiah in 2 Days
☐ Day 1. Read the

Introduction to Nehemiah and chapter 2, which tells how Nehemiah began his work on the wall.
☐ Day 2. Read chapter 8, showing the power of God's Word read aloud.
Now turn to page xi for your next Track 2 reading project.

■ TRACK 3:
All of Nehemiah in 12 Days
After you have read through Nehemiah, turn to pages xii–xiii for your next Track 3 reading project.

☐ 1   ☐ 2–3 ☐ 4   ☐ 5
☐ 6   ☐ 7   ☐ 8   ☐ 9
☐ 10 ☐ 11 ☐ 12 ☐ 13

■ Nehemiah's Prayer

1 The words of Nehemiah son of Hacaliah:

In the month of Kislev in the twentieth year, while I was in the citadel of Susa, ²Hanani, one of my brothers, came from Judah with some other men, and I questioned them about the Jewish remnant that survived the exile, and also about Jerusalem.

³They said to me, "Those who survived the exile and are back in the province are in great trouble and disgrace. The wall of Jerusalem is broken down, and its gates have been burned with fire."

⁴When I heard these things, I sat down and wept. For some days I mourned and fasted and prayed before the God of heaven. ⁵Then I said:

"O LORD, God of heaven, the great and awesome God, who keeps his covenant of love with those who love him and obey his commands, ⁶let your ear be attentive and your eyes open to hear the prayer your servant is praying before you day and night for your servants, the people of Israel. I confess the sins we Israelites, including myself and my father's house, have committed against you. ⁷We have acted very wickedly towards you. We have not obeyed the commands, decrees and laws you gave your servant Moses.

⁸"Remember the instruction you gave your servant Moses, saying, 'If you are unfaithful, I will scatter you among the nations, ⁹but if you return to me and obey my commands, then even if your exiled people are at the farthest horizon, I will gather them from there and bring them to the place I have chosen as a dwelling for my Name.'

¹⁰"They are your servants and your people, whom you redeemed by your great strength and your mighty hand. ¹¹O Lord, let your ear be attentive to the prayer of this your servant and to the prayer of your servants who delight

in revering your name. Give your servant success today by granting him favour in the presence of this man."

I was cupbearer to the king.

■ Artaxerxes Sends Nehemiah to Jerusalem

2 In the month of Nisan in the twentieth year of King Artaxerxes, when wine was brought for him, I took the wine and gave it to the king. I had not been sad in his presence before; ²so the king asked me, "Why does your face look so sad when you are not ill? This can be nothing but sadness of heart."

I was very much afraid, ³but I said to the king, "May the king live for ever! Why should my face look sad when the city where my fathers are buried lies in ruins, and its gates have been destroyed by fire?"

⁴The king said to me, "What is it you want?"

Then I prayed to the God of heaven, ⁵and I answered the king, "If it pleases the king and if your servant has found favour in his sight, let him send me to the city in Judah where my fathers are buried so that I can rebuild it."

2:4 ■ THE "ARROW PRAYER"
Nehemiah characteristically prayed to God while he went about his duties. He even "shot an arrow" to God, silently asking him for help in the middle of this crucial conversation with the king. He spontaneously inserted prayers as he wrote his memoirs. Some other examples: 1:5–11; 4:4–5; 5:19; 6:9,14; 13:14,22,31.

⁶Then the king, with the queen sitting beside him, asked me, "How long will your journey take, and when will you get back?" It pleased the king to send me; so I set a time.

7I also said to him, "If it pleases the king, may I have letters to the governors of Trans-Euphrates, so that they will provide me safe-conduct until I arrive in Judah? 8And may I have a letter to Asaph, keeper of the king's forest, so he will give me timber to make beams for the gates of the citadel by the temple and for the city wall and for the residence I will occupy?" And because the gracious hand of my God was upon me, the king granted my requests. 9So I went to the governors of Trans-Euphrates and gave them the king's letters. The king had also sent army officers and cavalry with me.

10When Sanballat the Horonite and Tobiah the Ammonite official heard about this, they were very much disturbed that someone had come to promote the welfare of the Israelites.

2:10 ■ POWERFUL OPPONENTS
Both Sanballat and Tobiah were influential local politicians. Sanballat's family governed Samaria and had managed to marry into the high priest's family (see 13:28). Tobiah, an official in Ammon (a small country east of Judah), had family ties and influence among the top Jewish families (see 6:17–19; 13:4–5). There is some evidence that both men were from Jewish backgrounds, though they preferred the political status quo in which Jewish identity was diluted.

■ Nehemiah Inspects Jerusalem's Walls
11I went to Jerusalem, and after staying there three days 12I set out during the night with a few men. I had not told anyone what my God had put in my heart to do for Jerusalem. There were no mounts with me except the one I was riding on.

13By night I went out through the Valley Gate towards the Jackal*a* Well and the Dung Gate, examining the walls of Jerusalem, which had been broken down, and its gates, which had been destroyed by fire. 14Then I moved on towards the Fountain Gate and the King's Pool, but there was not enough room for my mount to get through; 15so I went up the valley by night, examining the wall. Finally, I turned back and re-entered through the Valley Gate. 16The officials did not know where I had gone or what I was doing, because as yet I had said nothing to the Jews or the priests or nobles or officials or any others who would be doing the work.

17Then I said to them, "You see the trouble we are in: Jerusalem lies in ruins, and its gates have been burned with fire. Come, let us rebuild the wall of Jerusalem, and we will no longer be in disgrace." 18I also told them about the gracious hand of my God upon me and what the king had said to me.

They replied, "Let us start rebuilding." So they began this good work.

19But when Sanballat the Horonite, Tobiah the Ammonite official and Geshem the Arab heard about it, they mocked and ridiculed us. "What is this you are doing?" they asked. "Are you rebelling against the king?"

20I answered them by saying, "The God of heaven will give us success. We his servants will start rebuilding, but as for you, you have no share in Jerusalem or any claim or historic right to it."

■ Builders of the Wall
3 Eliashib the high priest and his fellow priests went to work and rebuilt the Sheep Gate. They dedicated it and set its doors in place, building as far as the Tower of the Hundred, which they dedicated, and as far as the Tower of Hananel. 2The men of Jericho built the adjoining section, and Zaccur son of Imri built next to them.

3The Fish Gate was rebuilt by the sons of Hassenaah. They laid its beams and put its doors and bolts and bars in place. 4Meremoth son of Uriah, the son of Hakkoz, repaired the next section. Next to him Meshullam son of Berekiah, the son of Meshezabel, made repairs, and next to him Zadok son of Baana also made repairs. 5The next section was repaired by the men of Tekoa, but their nobles would not put their shoulders to the work under their supervisors.*a*

6The Jeshanah*b* Gate was repaired by Joiada son of Paseah and Meshullam son of Besodeiah. They laid its beams and put its doors and bolts and bars in place. 7Next to them, repairs were made by men from Gibeon and Mizpah — Melatiah of Gibeon and Jadon of Meronoth — places under the authority of the governor of Trans-Euphrates. 8Uzziel son of Harhaiah, one of the goldsmiths, repaired the next section; and Hananiah, one of the perfume-makers, made repairs next to that. They restored*c* Jerusalem as far as the Broad Wall. 9Rephaiah son of Hur, ruler of a half-district of Jerusalem, repaired the next section. 10Adjoining this, Jedaiah son of Harumaph made repairs opposite his house, and Hattush son of Hashabneiah made repairs next to him. 11Malkijah son of Harim and Hasshub son of Pahath-Moab repaired another section and the Tower of the Ovens. 12Shallum son of Hallohesh, ruler of a half-district of Jerusalem, repaired the next section with the help of his daughters.

13The Valley Gate was repaired by Hanun and the residents of Zanoah. They rebuilt it and put its doors and bolts and bars in place. They also repaired five hundred yards*d* of the wall as far as the Dung Gate.

14The Dung Gate was repaired by Malkijah son of Recab, ruler of the district of Beth Hakkerem. He rebuilt it and put its doors and bolts and bars in place.

15The Fountain Gate was repaired by Shallun son of Col-Hozeh, ruler of the district of Mizpah. He rebuilt it, roofing it over and putting its doors and bolts and bars in place. He also repaired the wall of the Pool of Siloam,*e* by the King's Garden, as far as the steps going down from the City of David. 16Beyond him, Nehemiah son of Azbuk, ruler of a half-district of Beth Zur, made repairs up to a point opposite the tombs*f* of David, as far as the artificial pool and the House of the Heroes.

17Next to him, the repairs were made by the Levites under Rehum son of Bani. Beside him, Hashabiah, ruler of half the district of Keilah, carried out

---

a 13 Or Serpent or Fig   *a 5* Or their Lord or the governor   *b 6* Or Old (about 450 metres)   *e 15* Hebrew Shelah, a variant of Shiloah, that is, Siloam   *c 8* Or They left out part of   *d 13* Hebrew a thousand cubits   *f 16* Hebrew; Septuagint, some Vulgate manuscripts and Syriac tomb repairs for his district. [18]Next to him, the repairs were made by their countrymen under Binnui[g] son of Henadad, ruler of the other half-district of Keilah. [19]Next to him, Ezer son of Jeshua, ruler of Mizpah, repaired another section, from a point facing the ascent to the armoury as far as the angle. [20]Next to him, Baruch son of Zabbai zealously repaired another section, from the angle to the entrance of the house of Eliashib the high priest. [21]Next to him, Meremoth son of Uriah, the son of Hakkoz, repaired another section, from the entrance of Eliashib's house to the end of it.

[22]The repairs next to him were made by the priests from the surrounding region. [23]Beyond them, Benjamin and Hasshub made repairs in front of their house; and next to them, Azariah son of Maaseiah, the son of Ananiah, made repairs beside his house. [24]Next to him, Binnui son of Henadad repaired another section, from Azariah's house to the angle and the corner, [25]and Palal son of Uzai worked opposite the angle and the tower projecting from the upper palace near the court of the guard. Next to him, Pedaiah son of Parosh [26]and the temple servants living on the hill of Ophel made repairs up to a point opposite the Water Gate towards the east and the projecting tower. [27]Next to them, the men of Tekoa repaired another section, from the great projecting tower to the wall of Ophel.

[28]Above the Horse Gate, the priests made repairs, each in front of his own house. [29]Next to them, Zadok son of Immer made repairs opposite his house. Next to him, Shemaiah son of Shecaniah, the guard at the East Gate, made repairs. [30]Next to him, Hananiah son of Shelemiah, and Hanun, the sixth son of Zalaph, repaired another section. Next to them, Meshullam son of Berekiah made repairs opposite his living quarters. [31]Next to him, Malkijah, one of the goldsmiths, made repairs as far as the house of the temple servants and the merchants, opposite the Inspection Gate, and as far as the room above the corner; [32]and between the room above the corner and the Sheep Gate the goldsmiths and merchants made repairs.

3:28 ■ LASTING CREDIT
Archaeologists love this chapter for its valuable clues to the design of ancient Jerusalem. Other readers may find these details less inspiring, but they do give evidence of Nehemiah's organisational genius. Somehow he motivated skilled craftsmen to work alongside ordinary labourers, and he even got children to pitch in. For added motivation, he assigned families repair projects just outside their own homes. This chapter, like a brass plaque listing "Important Contributors", assured that they would receive lasting credit for their efforts.

■ Opposition to the Rebuilding

4 When Sanballat heard that we were rebuilding the wall, he became angry and was greatly incensed. He ridiculed the Jews, [2]and in the presence of his associates and the army of Samaria, he said, "What are those feeble Jews doing? Will they restore their wall? Will they offer sacrifices? Will they finish in a day? Can they bring the stones back to life from those heaps of rubble—burned as they are?"

[3]Tobiah the Ammonite, who was at his side, said, "What they are building—if even a fox climbed up on it, he would break down their wall of stones!"

[4]Hear us, O our God, for we are despised. Turn their insults back on their own heads. Give them over as plunder in a land of captivity. [5]Do not cover up their guilt or blot out their sins from your sight, for they have thrown insults in the face of[a] the builders.

[6]So we rebuilt the wall till all of it reached half its height, for the people worked with all their heart.

[7]But when Sanballat, Tobiah, the Arabs, the Ammonites and the men of Ashdod heard that the repairs to Jerusalem's walls had gone ahead and that the gaps were being closed, they were very angry. [8]They all plotted together to come and fight against Jerusalem and stir up trouble against it. [9]But we prayed to our God and posted a guard day and night to meet this threat.

4:9 ■ PRAISE THE LORD AND FIGHT
Nehemiah felt no difficulty combining prayer and action, as this verse shows: "We prayed to our God and posted a guard." Verse 14 gives another unembarrassed combination of spiritual and military tactics: "Remember the Lord . . . and fight."

[10]Meanwhile, the people in Judah said, "The strength of the labourers is giving out, and there is so much rubble that we cannot rebuild the wall."

[11]Also our enemies said, "Before they know it or see us, we will be right there among them and will kill them and put an end to the work."

[12]Then the Jews who lived near them came and told us ten times over, "Wherever you turn, they will attack us."

[13]Therefore I stationed some of the people behind the lowest points of the wall at the exposed places, posting them by families, with their swords, spears and bows. [14]After I looked things over, I stood up and said to the nobles, the officials and the rest of the people, "Don't be afraid of them. Remember the Lord, who is great and awesome, and fight for your brothers, your sons and your daughters, your wives and your homes."

[15]When our enemies heard that we were aware of their plot and that God had frustrated it, we all returned to the wall, each to his own work.

[16]From that day on, half of my men did the work, while the other half were equipped with spears, shields, bows and armour. The officers posted themselves behind all the people of Judah [17]who were building the wall. Those who carried materials did their work with one hand and held a weapon in the other, [18]and each of the builders wore his sword at

his side as he worked. But the man who sounded the trumpet stayed with me.

[19]Then I said to the nobles, the officials and the rest of the people, "The work is extensive and spread out, and we are widely separated from each other along the wall. [20]Wherever you hear the sound of the trumpet, join us there. Our God will fight for us!"

[21]So we continued the work with half the men holding spears, from the first light of dawn till the stars came out. [22]At that time I also said to the people, "Have every man and his helper stay inside Jerusalem at night, so that they can serve us as guards by night and workmen by day." [23]Neither I nor my brothers nor my men nor the guards with me took off our clothes; each had his weapon, even when he went for water.[b]

■ Nehemiah Helps the Poor

5 Now the men and their wives raised a great outcry against their Jewish brothers. [2]Some were saying, "We and our sons and daughters are numerous; in order for us to eat and stay alive, we must get grain."

[3]Others were saying, "We are mortgaging our fields, our vineyards and our homes to get grain during the famine."

[4]Still others were saying, "We have had to borrow money to pay the king's tax on our fields and vineyards. [5]Although we are of the same flesh and blood as our countrymen and though our sons are as good as theirs, yet we have to subject our sons and daughters to slavery. Some of our daughters have already been enslaved, but we are powerless, because our fields and our vineyards belong to others."

[6]When I heard their outcry and these charges, I was very angry. [7]I pondered them in my mind and then accused the nobles and officials. I told them, "You are exacting usury from your own countrymen!" So I called together a large meeting to deal with them [8]and said: "As far as possible, we have bought back our Jewish brothers who were sold to the Gentiles. Now you are selling your brothers, only for them to be sold back to us!" They kept quiet, because they could find nothing to say.

[9]So I continued, "What you are doing is not right. Shouldn't you walk in the fear of our God to avoid the reproach of our Gentile enemies? [10]I and my brothers and my men are also lending the people money and grain. But let the exacting of usury stop! [11]Give back to them immediately their fields, vineyards, olive groves and houses, and also the usury you are charging them—the hundredth part of the money, grain, new wine and oil."

[12]"We will give it back," they said. "And we will not demand anything more from them. We will do as you say."

Then I summoned the priests and made the nobles and officials take an oath to do what they had promised. [13]I also shook out the folds of my robe and said, "In this way may God shake out of his house and possessions every man who does not keep this promise. So may such a man be shaken out and emptied!"

At this the whole assembly said, "Amen," and praised the LORD. And the people did as they had promised.

[14]Moreover, from the twentieth year of King Artaxerxes, when I was appointed to be their governor in the land of Judah, until his thirty-second year—twelve years—neither I nor my brothers ate the food allotted to the governor. [15]But the earlier governors—those preceding me—placed a heavy burden on the people and took forty shekels[a] of silver from them in addition to food and wine. Their assistants also lorded it over the people. But out of reverence for God I did not act like that. [16]Instead, I devoted myself to the work on this wall. All my men were assembled there for the work; we[b] did not acquire any land.

> **5:14 ■ POLITICIAN WITHOUT GREED**
> Nehemiah faced a daunting task similar to that confronting many leaders of developing countries today. The land was devastated, with all wealth concentrated in the hands of a few powerful families. Jews were mortgaging their property and even selling their children into slavery in order to raise money to pay taxes. Nehemiah, who apparently came from wealth, could have profited further from his political position. Instead, he set a sterling example of generosity and self-sacrifice that made a profound impression on his oppressed countrymen.

[17]Furthermore, a hundred and fifty Jews and officials ate at my table, as well as those who came to us from the surrounding nations. [18]Each day one ox, six choice sheep and some poultry were prepared for me, and every ten days an abundant supply of wine of all kinds. In spite of all this, I never demanded the food allotted to the governor, because the demands were heavy on these people.

[19]Remember me with favour, O my God, for all I have done for these people.

■ Further Opposition to the Rebuilding

6 When word came to Sanballat, Tobiah, Geshem the Arab and the rest of our enemies that I had rebuilt the wall and not a gap was left in it—though up to that time I had not set the doors in the gates—[2]Sanballat and Geshem sent me this message: "Come, let us meet together in one of the villages[a] on the plain of Ono."

But they were scheming to harm me; [3]so I sent messengers to them with this reply: "I am carrying on a great project and cannot go down. Why should the work stop while I leave it and go down to you?" [4]Four times they sent me the same message, and each time I gave them the same answer.

[5]Then, the fifth time, Sanballat sent his assistant to me with the same message, and in his hand was an unsealed letter [6]in which was written:

> "It is reported among the nations—and Geshem[b] says it is true—that you and the Jews are plotting to revolt, and therefore you are building the wall. Moreover, according to these reports you are about to become their king

[b]23 The meaning of the Hebrew for this clause is uncertain.   [a]15 That is, about 1 pound (about 0.5 kilogram)   [b]16 Most Hebrew manuscripts; some Hebrew manuscripts, Septuagint, Vulgate and Syriac I   [a]2 Or in Kephirim   [b]6 Hebrew Gashmu, a variant of Geshem

7and have even appointed prophets to make this proclamation about you in Jerusalem: 'There is a king in Judah!' Now this report will get back to the king; so come, let us confer together."

6:5 ■ PSYCHOLOGICAL WARFARE

After fending off ridicule and threats of violence from his enemies (chapter 4), Nehemiah suddenly faced a new scare tactic. The author points out that this accusatory letter came "unsealed", or open to public view. Ordinarily, letters were rolled up, tied, sealed with wax, and delivered in a silk bag to guarantee privacy. Opponents were doubtless trying to intimidate Nehemiah by openly spreading rumours to arouse the suspicion of his Persian overseers. As usual, he was not easily intimidated.

8I sent him this reply: "Nothing like what you are saying is happening; you are just making it up out of your head."

9They were all trying to frighten us, thinking, "Their hands will get too weak for the work, and it will not be completed."

⌊But I prayed,⌋ "Now strengthen my hands."

10One day I went to the house of Shemaiah son of Delaiah, the son of Mehetabel, who was shut in at his home. He said, "Let us meet in the house of God, inside the temple, and let us close the temple doors, because men are coming to kill you—by night they are coming to kill you."

11But I said, "Should a man like me run away? Or should one like me go into the temple to save his life? I will not go!" 12I realised that God had not sent him, but that he had prophesied against me because Tobiah and Sanballat had hired him. 13He had been hired to intimidate me so that I would commit a sin by doing this, and then they would give me a bad name to discredit me.

14Remember Tobiah and Sanballat, O my God, because of what they have done; remember also the prophetess Noadiah and the rest of the prophets who have been trying to intimidate me.

■ The Completion of the Wall

15So the wall was completed on the twenty-fifth of Elul, in fifty-two days. 16When all our enemies heard about this, all the surrounding nations were afraid and lost their self-confidence, because they realised that this work had been done with the help of our God.

17Also, in those days the nobles of Judah were sending many letters to Tobiah, and replies from Tobiah kept coming to them. 18For many in Judah were under oath to him, since he was son-in-law to Shecaniah son of Arah, and his son Jehohanan had married the daughter of Meshullam son of Berekiah. 19Moreover, they kept reporting to me his good deeds and then telling him what I said. And Tobiah sent letters to intimidate me.

a2 Or Hanani, that is,

7 After the wall had been rebuilt and I had set the doors in place, the gatekeepers and the singers and the Levites were appointed. 2I put in charge of Jerusalem my brother Hanani, along witha Hananiah the commander of the citadel, because he was a man of integrity and feared God more than most men do. 3I said to them, "The gates of Jerusalem are not to be opened until the sun is hot. While the gatekeepers are still on duty, make them shut the doors and bar them. Also appoint residents of Jerusalem as guards, some at their posts and some near their own houses."

■ The List of the Exiles Who Returned

4Now the city was large and spacious, but there were few people in it, and the houses had not yet been rebuilt. 5So my God put it into my heart to assemble the nobles, the officials and the common people for registration by families. I found the genealogical record of those who had been the first to return. This is what I found written there:

6These are the people of the province who came up from the captivity of the exiles whom Nebuchadnezzar king of Babylon had taken captive (they returned to Jerusalem and Judah, each to his own town, 7in company with Zerubbabel, Jeshua, Nehemiah, Azariah, Raamiah, Nahamani, Mordecai, Bilshan, Mispereth, Bigvai, Nehum and Baanah):

The list of the men of Israel:

7:6 ■ REMEMBERING OUR PAST

Because their cultural identity was threatened, the Jews in Ezra and Nehemiah kept careful track of their roots. All Jews wanted to trace their family lineage back to Abraham's grandson Israel (Jacob) in order to prove their Jewishness. In addition, descendants of Levi the priest and David the king took great pains to establish their heritage. The process had been vastly complicated by Nebuchadnezzar's burning of Jerusalem, which destroyed many records (see verses 61,64). This list (verses 8–73) almost exactly repeats the one found in Ezra 2.

8the descendants of Parosh	2,172
9of Shephatiah	372
10of Arah	652
11of Pahath-Moab (through the line of Jeshua and Joab)	2,818
12of Elam	1,254
13of Zattu	845
14of Zaccai	760
15of Binnui	648
16of Bebai	628
17of Azgad	2,322
18of Adonikam	667
19of Bigvai	2,067
20of Adin	655
21of Ater (through Hezekiah)	98
22of Hashum	328
23of Bezai	324

²⁴of Hariph   112
²⁵of Gibeon   95

²⁶the men of Bethlehem and Netophah   188
²⁷of Anathoth   128
²⁸of Beth Azmaveth   42
²⁹of Kiriath Jearim, Kephirah and
     Beeroth   743
³⁰of Ramah and Geba   621
³¹of Michmash   122
³²of Bethel and Ai   123
³³of the other Nebo   52
³⁴of the other Elam   1,254
³⁵of Harim   320
³⁶of Jericho   345
³⁷of Lod, Hadid and Ono   721
³⁸of Senaah   3,930

³⁹The priests:

the descendants of Jedaiah (through the
     family of Jeshua)   973
⁴⁰of Immer   1,052
⁴¹of Pashhur   1,247
⁴²of Harim   1,017

⁴³The Levites:

the descendants of Jeshua (through
     Kadmiel through the line of Hodaviah)   74

⁴⁴The singers:

the descendants of Asaph   148

⁴⁵The gatekeepers:

the descendants of
     Shallum, Ater, Talmon, Akkub, Hatita
     and Shobai   138

⁴⁶The temple servants:

the descendants of
     Ziha, Hasupha, Tabbaoth,
⁴⁷Keros, Sia, Padon,
⁴⁸Lebana, Hagaba, Shalmai,
⁴⁹Hanan, Giddel, Gahar,
⁵⁰Reaiah, Rezin, Nekoda,
⁵¹Gazzam, Uzza, Paseah,
⁵²Besai, Meunim, Nephussim,
⁵³Bakbuk, Hakupha, Harhur,
⁵⁴Bazluth, Mehida, Harsha,
⁵⁵Barkos, Sisera, Temah,
⁵⁶Neziah and Hatipha

⁵⁷The descendants of the servants of Solomon:

the descendants of
     Sotai, Sophereth, Perida,
⁵⁸Jaala, Darkon, Giddel,
⁵⁹Shephatiah, Hattil,
     Pokereth-Hazzebaim and Amon

⁶⁰The temple servants and the descendants
     of the servants of Solomon   392

⁶¹The following came up from the towns
of Tel Melah, Tel Harsha, Kerub, Addon and
Immer, but they could not show that their families were descended from Israel:

⁶²the descendants of
     Delaiah, Tobiah and Nekoda   642

⁶³And from among the priests:

the descendants of
     Hobaiah, Hakkoz and Barzillai (a man who
     had married a daughter of Barzillai the
     Gileadite and was called by that name).
⁶⁴These searched for their family records,
but they could not find them and so were excluded from the priesthood as unclean. ⁶⁵The
governor, therefore, ordered them not to eat
any of the most sacred food until there should
be a priest ministering with the Urim and
Thummim.

⁶⁶The whole company numbered 42,360,
⁶⁷besides their 7,337 menservants and maid-
servants; and they also had 245 men and
women singers. ⁶⁸There were 736 horses, 245
mules,^b ⁶⁹435 camels and 6,720 donkeys.

⁷⁰Some of the heads of the families contrib-
uted to the work. The governor gave to the
treasury 1,000 drachmas^c of gold, 50 bowls
and 530 garments for priests. ⁷¹Some of the
heads of the families gave to the treasury for the
work 20,000 drachmas^d of gold and 2,200
minas^e of silver. ⁷²The total given by the rest
of the people was 20,000 drachmas of gold,
2,000 minas^f of silver and 67 garments for
priests.
⁷³The priests, the Levites, the gatekeepers,
the singers and the temple servants, along with
certain of the people and the rest of the Israelites, settled in their own towns.

■ Ezra Reads the Law
When the seventh month came and the Israelites
had settled in their towns, ¹all the people as-
8 sembled as one man in the square before the
Water Gate. They told Ezra the scribe to bring out
the Book of the Law of Moses, which the LORD had
commanded for Israel.

²So on the first day of the seventh month, Ezra the
priest brought the Law before the assembly, which
was made up of men and women and all who were
able to understand. ³He read it aloud from daybreak
till noon as he faced the square before the Water
Gate in the presence of the men, women and others
who could understand. And all the people listened
attentively to the Book of the Law.

⁴Ezra the scribe stood on a high wooden platform
built for the occasion. Beside him on his right stood
Mattithiah, Shema, Anaiah, Uriah, Hilkiah and
Maaseiah; and on his left were Pedaiah, Mishael,
Malkijah, Hashum, Hashbaddanah, Zechariah and
Meshullam.

⁵Ezra opened the book. All the people could see
him because he was standing above them; and as he
opened it, the people all stood up. ⁶Ezra praised the
LORD, the great God; and all the people lifted their

^b68 Some Hebrew manuscripts (see also Ezra 2:66); most Hebrew manuscripts do not have this verse.   ^c70 That is, about 19 pounds (about
8.5 kilograms)   ^d71 That is, about 375 pounds (about 170 kilograms); also in verse 72   ^e71 That is, about 1¼ tons (about 1.3 metric tons)
^f72 That is, about 1 ton (about 1.1 metric tons)

hands and responded, "Amen! Amen!" Then they bowed down and worshipped the LORD with their faces to the ground.

7The Levites—Jeshua, Bani, Sherebiah, Jamin, Akkub, Shabbethai, Hodiah, Maaseiah, Kelita, Azariah, Jozabad, Hanan and Pelaiah—instructed the people in the Law while the people were standing there. 8They read from the Book of the Law of God, making it clear*a* and giving the meaning so that the people could understand what was being read.

9Then Nehemiah the governor, Ezra the priest and scribe, and the Levites who were instructing the people said to them all, "This day is sacred to the LORD your God. Do not mourn or weep." For all the

people had been weeping as they listened to the words of the Law.

8:9 ■ THE JOY OF THE LORD
People sometimes think of the Old Testament as gloomy. Here, however (verses 9–12), Israel's leaders urged the people to stop weeping. Sadness, they said, did not suit a sacred day. As they discovered the next day, the law they mourned over commanded not weeping, but eight days of celebration and camping.

10Nehemiah said, "Go and enjoy choice food and

■ A PEOPLE OF THE BOOK
EZRA STOOD ON A WOODEN PLATFORM, READING FROM A SIMPLE SCROLL

EZRA THE PRIEST BROUGHT THE LAW BEFORE THE ASSEMBLY. . . . HE READ IT ALOUD FROM DAYBREAK TILL NOON.
■ 8:2–3

Picture this: a vast, hushed crowd watching as Ezra ascends a newly-built platform in the square. As he opens the book, they stand up. They praise God, hands lifted high; then they bow down, faces in the dirt. Ezra begins to read. His helpers circulate in the crowd, explaining and interpreting what God's Word says. The people listen attentively. And then a strange sound begins to rise, spreading through the multitude. It is the sound of weeping.

The Law Ezra read was very ancient, but that day marked something new. The Jews were becoming, in a way they had never been before, a people of the book. They were being rebuilt, with material as strong as the stones in their newly-built city wall.

Throughout their history, they had drawn strength from two sources besides the Law. One was the temple, where they worshipped God. It was a magnificently beautiful building in which they met God. The other was their leadership—first Moses, then Joshua, then the judges, and finally David and his offspring, the kings.

■ THE DISAPPOINTING REALITY
But these realities had not saved them from disgrace. The temple? For all its splendour it had become a meaningless symbol to most Jews. They had even put idols in it. God had finally allowed the Babylonians to burn the temple down.

After the exile the Jews had made rebuilding the temple their first priority (see Ezra 1–6). But it was no longer an automatic insurance policy. They could never again see the building as a substitute for real devotion to God.

Their leaders? Not one king, over hundreds of years, had come close to matching God's ideal. Most kings had been scoundrels—descendants of David in name only. After the exile, Israel had no king of its own. The Israelites were under the thumb of a Persian, who was determined to keep all power himself.

■ THE POWER OF THE WORD
They turned to another source of power: the Word of God. The great gathering of chapter 8 stands in contrast to temples and kings. The splendour of jewels and crowns is replaced by a single man on top of a wooden platform, reading from a simple scroll. Yet the words he reads, carefully explained to all, show their power in the way they affect those who hear them. The people are moved to praise God, to weep over their sins, to change their behaviour, and to make renewed promises to God.

From this time on, the Jews were known as the people of the book. They lived under foreign domination, so their political leadership became secondary. Their temple, while important, was never again a guarantee of God's presence. Increasingly they studied God's law and tried to obey it. A new kind of leader emerged, following Ezra—the scribe, a student of Scripture. The nation we see at the end of Nehemiah looks very much like the nation we find, after 400 years of Scriptural silence, when Jesus appears. Israelites found their unique strength neither in government nor in worship rituals, but in reverence for God's written Word.

□ LIFE QUESTIONS:
Can you point to ways in which God's Word has been powerful in your life? How has it changed you?

a 8 Or God, translating it

sweet drinks, and send some to those who have nothing prepared. This day is sacred to our Lord. Do not grieve, for the joy of the LORD is your strength."

[11]The Levites calmed all the people, saying, "Be still, for this is a sacred day. Do not grieve."

[12]Then all the people went away to eat and drink, to send portions of food and to celebrate with great joy, because they now understood the words that had been made known to them.

[13]On the second day of the month, the heads of all the families, along with the priests and the Levites, gathered round Ezra the scribe to give attention to the words of the Law. [14]They found written in the Law, which the LORD had commanded through Moses, that the Israelites were to live in booths during the feast of the seventh month [15]and that they should proclaim this word and spread it throughout their towns and in Jerusalem: "Go out into the hill country and bring back branches from olive and wild olive trees, and from myrtles, palms and shade trees, to make booths"—as it is written.[b]

[16]So the people went out and brought back branches and built themselves booths on their own roofs, in their courtyards, in the courts of the house of God and in the square by the Water Gate and the one by the Gate of Ephraim. [17]The whole company that had returned from exile built booths and lived in them. From the days of Joshua son of Nun until that day, the Israelites had not celebrated it like this. And their joy was very great.

[18]Day after day, from the first day to the last, Ezra read from the Book of the Law of God. They celebrated the feast for seven days, and on the eighth day, in accordance with the regulation, there was an assembly.

■ The Israelites Confess Their Sins

9 On the twenty-fourth day of the same month, the Israelites gathered together, fasting and wearing sackcloth and having dust on their heads. [2]Those of Israelite descent had separated themselves from all foreigners. They stood in their places and confessed their sins and the wickedness of their fathers. [3]They stood where they were and read from the Book of the Law of the LORD their God for a quarter of the day, and spent another quarter in confession and in worshipping the LORD their God. [4]Standing on the stairs were the Levites—Jeshua, Bani, Kadmiel, Shebaniah, Bunni, Sherebiah, Bani and Kenani—who called with loud voices to the LORD their God. [5]And the Levites—Jeshua, Kadmiel, Bani, Hashabneiah, Sherebiah, Hodiah, Shebaniah and Pethahiah—said: "Stand up and praise the LORD your God, who is from everlasting to everlasting."[a]

"Blessed be your glorious name, and may it be exalted above all blessing and praise. [6]You alone are the LORD. You made the heavens, even the highest heavens, and all their starry host, the earth and all that is on it, the seas and all that is in them. You give life to everything, and the multitudes of heaven worship you.

[7]"You are the LORD God, who chose Abram and brought him out of Ur of the Chaldeans and named him Abraham. [8]You found his heart

faithful to you, and you made a covenant with him to give to his descendants the land of the Canaanites, Hittites, Amorites, Perizzites, Jebusites and Girgashites. You have kept your promise because you are righteous.

9:6 ■ STAINED-GLASS PRAYER

In cathedrals of medieval Europe, stained-glass windows served a dual purpose: 1) the artists designed them as aids to the worship of God; and 2) for a non-literate society, scenes depicted in glass made it easier to learn biblical history. Old Testament Jews prohibited all images, but often their prayers served a similar purpose: they expressed worship and reminded the listeners of their providential past. This beautiful example reviews essential lessons from all of human history—an important guide for a people beginning a new life.

[9]"You saw the suffering of our forefathers in Egypt; you heard their cry at the Red Sea.[b] [10]You sent miraculous signs and wonders against Pharaoh, against all his officials and all the people of his land, for you knew how arrogantly the Egyptians treated them. You made a name for yourself, which remains to this day. [11]You divided the sea before them, so that they passed through it on dry ground, but you hurled their pursuers into the depths, like a stone into mighty waters. [12]By day you led them with a pillar of cloud, and by night with a pillar of fire to give them light on the way they were to take.

[13]"You came down on Mount Sinai; you spoke to them from heaven. You gave them regulations and laws that are just and right, and decrees and commands that are good. [14]You made known to them your holy Sabbath and gave them commands, decrees and laws through your servant Moses. [15]In their hunger you gave them bread from heaven and in their thirst you brought them water from the rock; you told them to go in and take possession of the land you had sworn with uplifted hand to give them.

[16]"But they, our forefathers, became arrogant and stiff-necked, and did not obey your commands. [17]They refused to listen and failed to remember the miracles you performed among them. They became stiff-necked and in their rebellion appointed a leader in order to return to their slavery. But you are a forgiving God, gracious and compassionate, slow to anger and abounding in love. Therefore you did not desert them, [18]even when they cast for themselves an image of a calf and said, 'This is your god, who brought you up out of Egypt,' or when they committed awful blasphemies.

[19]"Because of your great compassion you did not abandon them in the desert. By day the pillar of cloud did not cease to guide them on their path, nor the pillar of fire by night to shine

b 15 See Lev. 23:37–40.   a 5 Or God for ever and ever   b 9 Hebrew Yam Suph; that is, Sea of Reeds on the way they were to take. 20You gave your good Spirit to instruct them. You did not withhold your manna from their mouths, and you gave them water for their thirst. 21For forty years you sustained them in the desert; they lacked nothing, their clothes did not wear out nor did their feet become swollen.

22"You gave them kingdoms and nations, allotting to them even the remotest frontiers. They took over the country of Sihon[c] king of Heshbon and the country of Og king of Bashan. 23You made their sons as numerous as the stars in the sky, and you brought them into the land that you told their fathers to enter and possess. 24Their sons went in and took possession of the land. You subdued before them the Canaanites, who lived in the land; you handed the Canaanites over to them, along with their kings and the peoples of the land, to deal with them as they pleased. 25They captured fortified cities and fertile land; they took possession of houses filled with all kinds of good things, wells already dug, vineyards, olive groves and fruit trees in abundance. They ate to the full and were well-nourished; they revelled in your great goodness.

26"But they were disobedient and rebelled against you; they put your law behind their backs. They killed your prophets, who had admonished them in order to turn them back to you; they committed awful blasphemies. 27So you handed them over to their enemies, who oppressed them. But when they were oppressed they cried out to you. From heaven you heard them, and in your great compassion you gave them deliverers, who rescued them from the hand of their enemies.

28"But as soon as they were at rest, they again did what was evil in your sight. Then you abandoned them to the hand of their enemies so that they ruled over them. And when they cried out to you again, you heard from heaven, and in your compassion you delivered them time after time.

29"You warned them to return to your law, but they became arrogant and disobeyed your commands. They sinned against your ordinances, by which a man will live if he obeys them. Stubbornly they turned their backs on you, became stiff-necked and refused to listen. 30For many years you were patient with them. By your Spirit you admonished them through your prophets. Yet they paid no attention, so you handed them over to the neighbouring peoples. 31But in your great mercy you did not put an end to them or abandon them, for you are a gracious and merciful God.

32"Now therefore, O our God, the great, mighty and awesome God, who keeps his covenant of love, do not let all this hardship seem trifling in your eyes—the hardship that has come upon us, upon our kings and leaders, upon our priests and prophets, upon our fathers and all your people, from the days of the kings of Assyria until today. 33In all that has

happened to us, you have been just; you have acted faithfully, while we did wrong. 34Our kings, our leaders, our priests and our fathers did not follow your law; they did not pay attention to your commands or the warnings you gave them. 35Even while they were in their kingdom, enjoying your great goodness to them in the spacious and fertile land you gave them, they did not serve you or turn from their evil ways.

36"But see, we are slaves today, slaves in the land you gave our forefathers so that they could eat its fruit and the other good things it produces. 37Because of our sins, its abundant harvest goes to the kings you have placed over us. They rule over our bodies and our cattle as they please. We are in great distress.

■ The Agreement of the People

38"In view of all this, we are making a binding agreement, putting it in writing, and our leaders, our Levites and our priests are affixing their seals to it."

10 Those who sealed it were:

Nehemiah the governor, the son of Hacaliah.

Zedekiah, 2Seraiah, Azariah, Jeremiah, 3Pashhur, Amariah, Malkijah, 4Hattush, Shebaniah, Malluch, 5Harim, Meremoth, Obadiah, 6Daniel, Ginnethon, Baruch, 7Meshullam, Abijah, Mijamin, 8Maaziah, Bilgai and Shemaiah. These were the priests.

9The Levites:

Jeshua son of Azaniah, Binnui of the sons of Henadad, Kadmiel, 10and their associates: Shebaniah, Hodiah, Kelita, Pelaiah, Hanan, 11Mica, Rehob, Hashabiah, 12Zaccur, Sherebiah, Shebaniah, 13Hodiah, Bani and Beninu.

14The leaders of the people:

Parosh, Pahath-Moab, Elam, Zattu, Bani, 15Bunni, Azgad, Bebai, 16Adonijah, Bigvai, Adin, 17Ater, Hezekiah, Azzur, 18Hodiah, Hashum, Bezai, 19Hariph, Anathoth, Nebai, 20Magpiash, Meshullam, Hezir, 21Meshezabel, Zadok, Jaddua, 22Pelatiah, Hanan, Anaiah, 23Hoshea, Hananiah, Hasshub, 24Hallohesh, Pilha, Shobek, 25Rehum, Hashabnah, Maaseiah, 26Ahiah, Hanan, Anan, 27Malluch, Harim and Baanah.

28"The rest of the people—priests, Levites, gatekeepers, singers, temple servants and all who separated themselves from the neighbouring peoples for the sake of the Law of God, together with their wives and all their sons and daughters who are able to understand—²⁹all these now join their brothers the nobles, and bind themselves with a curse and an oath to follow the Law of God given through Moses the servant of God and to obey carefully all the commands, regulations and decrees of the LORD our Lord.

³⁰"We promise not to give our daughters in marriage to the peoples around us or take their daughters for our sons.

³¹"When the neighbouring peoples bring merchandise or grain to sell on the Sabbath, we will not buy from them on the Sabbath or on any holy day. Every seventh year we will forgo working the land and will cancel all debts.

10:31 ■ A YEAR OF FREEDOM
According to God's law, Jews were supposed to take every seventh day – the Sabbath – off from work. Not only that, but every seventh year was a holiday from farming and a time when all debts were cancelled (see Leviticus 25:1–7; Deuteronomy 15:1–11). But these rules for the seventh year were seldom if ever followed; "business as usual" generally prevailed.

³²"We assume the responsibility for carrying out the commands to give a third of a shekel*a* each year for the service of the house of our God: ³³for the bread set out on the table; for the regular grain offerings and burnt offerings; for the offerings on the Sabbaths, New Moon festivals and appointed feasts; for the holy offerings; for sin offerings to make atonement for Israel; and for all the duties of the house of our God.

³⁴"We—the priests, the Levites and the people—have cast lots to determine when each of our families is to bring to the house of our God at set times each year a contribution of wood to burn on the altar of the LORD our God, as it is written in the Law.

³⁵"We also assume responsibility for bringing to the house of the LORD each year the firstfruits of our crops and of every fruit tree.

³⁶"As it is also written in the Law, we will bring the firstborn of our sons and of our cattle, of our herds and of our flocks to the house of our God, to the priests ministering there.

³⁷"Moreover, we will bring to the storerooms of the house of our God, to the priests, the first of our ground meal, of our grain, offerings, of the fruit of all our trees and of our new wine and oil. And we will bring a tithe of our crops to the Levites, for it is the Levites who collect the tithes in all the towns where we work. ³⁸A priest descended from Aaron is to accompany the Levites when they receive the tithes, and the Levites are to bring a tenth of the tithes up to the house of our God, to the storerooms of the treasury. ³⁹The people of Israel, including the Levites, are to bring their contributions of grain, new wine and oil to the

storerooms where the articles for the sanctuary are kept and where the ministering priests, the gatekeepers and the singers stay.

"We will not neglect the house of our God."

■ The New Residents of Jerusalem

11 Now the leaders of the people settled in Jerusalem, and the rest of the people cast lots to bring one out of every ten to live in Jerusalem, the holy city, while the remaining nine were to stay in their own towns. ²The people commended all the men who volunteered to live in Jerusalem.

11:1 ■ CITY FRIGHT
The 1990 U.S. census revealed that for the first time a majority of Americans lived in cities having more than a million in population. Worldwide, people are flocking to mega-cities such as Tokyo, London, and Mexico City. Not so in Nehemiah's day. The Israelites had learned that big cities like Jerusalem made prime targets for invading armies. In order to repopulate the city, leaders had to resort to a lottery system. (Characteristically, Nehemiah made sure the new settlers were given proper credit.)

³These are the provincial leaders who settled in Jerusalem (now some Israelites, priests, Levites, temple servants and descendants of Solomon's servants lived in the towns of Judah, each on his own property in the various towns, ⁴while other people from both Judah and Benjamin lived in Jerusalem):

From the descendants of Judah:

Athaiah son of Uzziah, the son of Zechariah, the son of Amariah, the son of Shephatiah, the son of Mahalalel, a descendant of Perez; ⁵and Maaseiah son of Baruch, the son of Col-Hozeh, the son of Hazaiah, the son of Adaiah, the son of Joiarib, the son of Zechariah, a descendant of Shelah. ⁶The descendants of Perez who lived in Jerusalem totalled 468 able men.

⁷From the descendants of Benjamin:

Sallu son of Meshullam, the son of Joed, the son of Pedaiah, the son of Kolaiah, the son of Maaseiah, the son of Ithiel, the son of Jeshaiah, ⁸and his followers, Gabbai and Sallai—928 men. ⁹Joel son of Zicri was their chief officer, and Judah son of Hassenuah was over the Second District of the city.

¹⁰From the priests:

Jedaiah; the son of Joiarib; Jakin; ¹¹Seraiah son of Hilkiah, the son of Meshullam, the son of Zadok, the son of Meraioth, the son of Ahitub, supervisor in the house of God, ¹²and their associates, who carried on work for the temple— 822 men; Adaiah son of Jeroham, the son of Pelaliah, the son of Amzi, the son of Zechariah, the son of Pashhur, the son of Malkijah, ¹³and his associates, who were heads of families— 242 men; Amashsai son of Azarel, the son of

a 32 That is, about ⅙ ounce (about 4 grams)

Ahzai, the son of Meshillemoth, the son of Immer, [14]and his*a* associates, who were able men — 128 men. Their chief officer was Zabdiel son of Haggedolim.

[15]From the Levites:

Shemaiah son of Hasshub, the son of Azrikam, the son of Hashabiah, the son of Bunni; [16]Shabbethai and Jozabad, two of the heads of the Levites, who had charge of the outside work of the house of God; [17]Mattaniah son of Mica, the son of Zabdi, the son of Asaph, the director who led in thanksgiving and prayer; Bakbukiah, second among his associates; and Abda son of Shammua, the son of Galal, the son of Jeduthun. [18]The Levites in the holy city totalled 284.

[19]The gatekeepers:

Akkub, Talmon and their associates, who kept watch at the gates — 172 men.

[20]The rest of the Israelites, with the priests and Levites, were in all the towns of Judah, each on his ancestral property.

[21]The temple servants lived on the hill of Ophel, and Ziha and Gishpa were in charge of them.

[22]The chief officer of the Levites in Jerusalem was Uzzi son of Bani, the son of Hashabiah, the son of Mattaniah, the son of Mica. Uzzi was one of Asaph's descendants, who were the singers responsible for the service of the house of God. [23]The singers were under the king's orders, which regulated their daily activity.

[24]Pethahiah son of Meshezabel, one of the descendants of Zerah son of Judah, was the king's agent in all affairs relating to the people.

[25]As for the villages with their fields, some of the people of Judah lived in Kiriath Arba and its surrounding settlements, in Dibon and its settlements, in Jekabzeel and its villages, [26]in Jeshua, in Moladah, in Beth Pelet, [27]in Hazar Shual, in Beersheba and its settlements, [28]in Ziklag, in Meconah and its settlements, [29]in En Rimmon, in Zorah, in Jarmuth, [30]Zanoah, Adullam and their villages, in Lachish and its fields, and in Azekah and its settlements. So they were living all the way from Beersheba to the Valley of Hinnom.

[31]The descendants of the Benjamites from Geba lived in Michmash, Aija, Bethel and its settlements, [32]in Anathoth, Nob and Ananiah, [33]in Hazor, Ramah and Gittaim, [34]in Hadid, Zeboim and Neballat, [35]in Lod and Ono, and in the Valley of the Craftsmen.

[36]Some of the divisions of the Levites of Judah settled in Benjamin.

■ Priests and Levites

12 These were the priests and Levites who returned with Zerubbabel son of Shealtiel and with Jeshua:

Seraiah, Jeremiah, Ezra,
[2]Amariah, Malluch, Hattush,
[3]Shecaniah, Rehum, Meremoth,
[4]Iddo, Ginnethon,*a* Abijah,
[5]Mijamin,*b* Moadiah, Bilgah,

[6]Shemaiah, Joiarib, Jedaiah,
[7]Sallu, Amok, Hilkiah and Jedaiah.
These were the leaders of the priests and their associates in the days of Jeshua.

[8]The Levites were Jeshua, Binnui, Kadmiel, Sherebiah, Judah, and also Mattaniah, who, together with his associates, was in charge of the songs of thanksgiving. [9]Bakbukiah and Unni, their associates, stood opposite them in the services.

[10]Jeshua was the father of Joiakim, Joiakim the father of Eliashib, Eliashib the father of Joiada, [11]Joiada the father of Jonathan, and Jonathan the father of Jaddua.

[12]In the days of Joiakim, these were the heads of the priestly families:
of Seraiah's family, Meraiah;
of Jeremiah's, Hananiah;
[13]of Ezra's, Meshullam;
of Amariah's, Jehohanan;
[14]of Malluch's, Jonathan;
of Shecaniah's,*c* Joseph;
[15]of Harim's, Adna;
of Meremoth's,*d* Helkai;
[16]of Iddo's, Zechariah;
of Ginnethon's, Meshullam;
[17]of Abijah's, Zicri;
of Miniamin's and of Moadiah's, Piltai;
[18]of Bilgah's, Shammua;
of Shemaiah's, Jehonathan;
[19]of Joiarib's, Mattenai;
of Jedaiah's, Uzzi;
[20]of Sallu's, Kallai;
of Amok's, Eber;
[21]of Hilkiah's, Hashabiah;
of Jedaiah's, Nethanel.

[22]The family heads of the Levites in the days of Eliashib, Joiada, Johanan and Jaddua, as well as those of the priests, were recorded in the reign of Darius the Persian. [23]The family heads among the descendants of Levi up to the time of Johanan son of Eliashib were recorded in the book of the annals. [24]And the leaders of the Levites were Hashabiah, Sherebiah, Jeshua son of Kadmiel, and their associates, who stood opposite them to give praise and thanksgiving, one section responding to the other, as prescribed by David the man of God.

[25]Mattaniah, Bakbukiah, Obadiah, Meshullam, Talmon and Akkub were gatekeepers who guarded the storerooms at the gates. [26]They served in the days of Joiakim son of Jeshua, the son of Jozadak, and in the days of Nehemiah the governor and of Ezra the priest and scribe.

■ Dedication of the Wall of Jerusalem

[27]At the dedication of the wall of Jerusalem, the Levites were sought out from where they lived and were brought to Jerusalem to celebrate joyfully the dedication with songs of thanksgiving and with the music of cymbals, harps and lyres. [28]The singers also were brought together from the region around Jerusalem — from the villages of the Netophathites, [29]from Beth Gilgal, and from the area of Geba and Azmaveth, for the singers had built villages for themselves around Jerusalem. [30]When the priests and

---

a 14 Most Septuagint manuscripts; Hebrew *their*   *a 4* Many Hebrew manuscripts and Vulgate (see also Neh. 12:16); most Hebrew manuscripts *Ginnethoi*
b 5 A variant of *Miniamin*   *c 14* Very many Hebrew manuscripts, some Septuagint manuscripts and Syriac (see also Neh. 12:3); most Hebrew manuscripts
Shebaniah's   *d 15* Some Septuagint manuscripts (see also Neh. 12:3); Hebrew *Meraioth's*

Levites had purified themselves ceremonially, they purified the people, the gates and the wall.

12:27 ■ VICTORY PARTY

Ezra, a religious leader, tried for a decade to get the wall rebuilt. Nehemiah, more pragmatic and action-oriented, managed to get the job done in 52 days (6:15). When the huge task was finished, he orchestrated a giant celebration featuring two choirs that circled the wall in opposite directions. Ezra led one of the choirs; Nehemiah, in an act of humility, brought up the rear of the other. When they met in the middle, near the temple area, they held a worship service such as Jerusalem had not seen in more than a century.

31I had the leaders of Judah go up on top*e* of the wall. I also assigned two large choirs to give thanks. One was to proceed on top*f* of the wall to the right, towards the Dung Gate. 32Hoshaiah and half the leaders of Judah followed them, 33along with Azariah, Ezra, Meshullam, 34Judah, Benjamin, Shemaiah, Jeremiah, 35as well as some priests with trumpets, and also Zechariah son of Jonathan, the son of Shemaiah, the son of Mattaniah, the son of Micaiah, the son of Zaccur, the son of Asaph, 36and his associates—Shemaiah, Azarel, Milalai, Gilalai, Maai, Nethanel, Judah and Hanani—with musical instruments ⌊ prescribed by⌋ David the man of God. Ezra the scribe led the procession. 37At the Fountain Gate they continued directly up the steps of the City of David on the ascent to the wall and passed above the house of David to the Water Gate on the east.

38The second choir proceeded in the opposite direction. I followed them on top*g* of the wall, together with half the people—past the Tower of the Ovens to the Broad Wall, 39over the Gate of Ephraim, the Jeshanah*b* Gate, the Fish Gate, the Tower of Hananel and the Tower of the Hundred, as far as the Sheep Gate. At the Gate of the Guard they stopped.

40The two choirs that gave thanks then took their places in the house of God; so did I, together with half the officials, 41as well as the priests—Eliakim, Maaseiah, Miniamin, Micaiah, Elioenai, Zechariah and Hananiah with their trumpets—42and also Maaseiah, Shemaiah, Eleazar, Uzzi, Jehohanan, Malkijah, Elam and Ezer. The choirs sang under the direction of Jezrahiah. 43And on that day they offered great sacrifices, rejoicing because God had given them great joy. The women and children also rejoiced. The sound of rejoicing in Jerusalem could be heard far away.

44At that time men were appointed to be in charge of the storerooms for the contributions, first-fruits and tithes. From the fields around the towns they were to bring into the storerooms the portions required by the Law for the priests and the Levites, for Judah was pleased with the ministering priests and Levites. 45They performed the service of their God and the service of purification, as did also the singers and gatekeepers, according to the commands of David and his son Solomon. 46For long ago, in the days of David and Asaph, there had been directors for the singers and for the songs of praise and thanksgiving to God. 47So in the days of Zerubbabel and of Nehemiah, all Israel contributed the daily portions for the singers and gatekeepers. They also set aside the portion for the other Levites, and the Levites set aside the portion for the descendants of Aaron.

■ Nehemiah's Final Reforms

13 On that day the Book of Moses was read aloud in the hearing of the people and there it was found written that no Ammonite or Moabite should ever be admitted into the assembly of God, 2because they had not met the Israelites with food and water but had hired Balaam to call a curse down on them. (Our God, however, turned the curse into a blessing.) 3When the people heard this law, they excluded from Israel all who were of foreign descent.

4Before this, Eliashib the priest had been put in charge of the storerooms of the house of our God. He was closely associated with Tobiah, 5and he had provided him with a large room formerly used to store the grain offerings and incense and temple articles, and also the tithes of grain, new wine and oil prescribed for the Levites, singers and gatekeepers, as well as the contributions for the priests.

6But while all this was going on, I was not in Jerusalem, for in the thirty-second year of Artaxerxes king of Babylon I had returned to the king. Some time later I asked his permission 7and came back to Jerusalem. Here I learned about the evil thing Eliashib had done in providing Tobiah a room in the courts of the house of God. 8I was greatly displeased and threw all Tobiah's household goods out of the room. 9I gave orders to purify the rooms, and then I put back into them the equipment of the house of God, with the grain offerings and the incense.

10I also learned that the portions assigned to the Levites had not been given to them, and that all the Levites and singers responsible for the service had gone back to their own fields. 11So I rebuked the officials and asked them, "Why is the house of God neglected?" Then I called them together and stationed them at their posts.

12All Judah brought the tithes of grain, new wine and oil into the storerooms. 13I put Shelemiah the priest, Zadok the scribe, and a Levite named Pedaiah in charge of the storerooms and made Hanan son of Zaccur, the son of Mattaniah, their assistant, because these men were considered trustworthy. They were made responsible for distributing the supplies to their brothers.

14Remember me for this, O my God, and do not blot out what I have so faithfully done for the house of my God and its services.

15In those days I saw men in Judah treading winepresses on the Sabbath and bringing in grain and loading it on donkeys, together with wine, grapes, figs and all other kinds of loads. And they were bringing all this into Jerusalem on the Sabbath. Therefore I warned them against selling food on that day.

---

e 31 Or go alongside   *f 31 Or proceed alongside*   *g 38 Or them alongside*   *b 39 Or Old*

¹⁶Men from Tyre who lived in Jerusalem were bringing in fish and all kinds of merchandise and selling them in Jerusalem on the Sabbath to the people of Judah. ¹⁷I rebuked the nobles of Judah and said to them, "What is this wicked thing you are doing—desecrating the Sabbath day? ¹⁸Didn't your forefathers do the same things, so that our God brought all this calamity upon us and upon this city? Now you are stirring up more wrath against Israel by desecrating the Sabbath."

¹⁹When evening shadows fell on the gates of Jerusalem before the Sabbath, I ordered the doors to be shut and not opened until the Sabbath was over. I stationed some of my own men at the gates so that no load could be brought in on the Sabbath day. ²⁰Once or twice the merchants and sellers of all kinds of goods spent the night outside Jerusalem. ²¹But I warned them and said, "Why do you spend the night by the wall? If you do this again, I will lay hands on you." From that time on they no longer came on the Sabbath. ²²Then I commanded the Levites to purify themselves and go and guard the gates in order to keep the Sabbath day holy.

13:19 ■ NEVER-ENDING TASK

Fairy tales end, "and they lived happily ever after", but real life isn't always like that. Pointedly, Nehemiah's book does not close with the triumph of chapter 12, but with a preview of the continuing hassles of leadership. Old problems recurred, new problems sprang up, and Nehemiah tackled both kinds with courage and wisdom.

Remember me for this also, O my God, and show mercy to me according to your great love.

²³Moreover, in those days I saw men of Judah who had married women from Ashdod, Ammon and Moab. ²⁴Half of their children spoke the language of Ashdod or the language of one of the other peoples, and did not know how to speak the language of Judah. ²⁵I rebuked them and called curses down on them. I beat some of the men and pulled out their hair. I made them take an oath in God's name and said: "You are not to give your daughters in marriage to their sons, nor are you to take their daughters in marriage for your sons or for yourselves. ²⁶Was it not because of marriages like these that Solomon king of Israel sinned? Among the many nations there was no king like him. He was loved by his God, and God made him king over all Israel, but even he was led into sin by foreign women. ²⁷Must we hear now that you too are doing all this terrible wickedness and are being unfaithful to our God by marrying foreign women?"

²⁸One of the sons of Joiada son of Eliashib the high priest was son-in-law to Sanballat the Horonite. And I drove him away from me.

²⁹Remember them, O my God, because they defiled the priestly office and the covenant of the priesthood and of the Levites.

³⁰So I purified the priests and the Levites of everything foreign, and assigned them duties, each to his own task. ³¹I also made provision for contributions of wood at designated times, and for the firstfruits.

Remember me with favour, O my God.

ESTHER

INTRODUCTION

■ A PROFILE OF COURAGE

HEROES ACT WHILE OTHERS STAND AND WATCH

"I WILL GO TO THE KING, EVEN THOUGH IT IS AGAINST THE LAW. AND IF I PERISH, I PERISH." ■ 4:16

What makes a hero? Ask one, and you may find a surprising nonchalance: "I'm sure other people would have done exactly the same thing;" they say. "I was just in the right place at the right time."

People become heroes because they take quick action just at the "right time", while others stand watching in horror. The true hero recognises the crisis and moves to meet it. This kind of courage made Esther great — worthy of a book in the Bible.

■ A QUEEN RISKS HER LIFE

By the "accident" of her beauty and the "accident" of the former queen's dismissal, Esther found herself queen of one of the greatest powers of the world. Then, when all seemed smooth, her crucial moment came.

This moment has been echoed many times since. As a successful racial minority in the Persian empire, Esther's people, the Jews, had not melted into their surroundings. Others were jealous of their success and separatism. A vengeful Prime Minister, Haman, made up his mind to destroy them. He issued an edict of government-sponsored genocide.

Would Queen Esther intervene? Doing so would risk her life. And what difference could she make? She was a powerless sex partner to a king who strongly preferred women who never interfered with his wishes. She came only when he called, and he had not called her for a month. And yet she alone, of all the Jews, had access to the king.

Esther's cousin Mordecai reminded her of her unique place: "who knows but that you have come to royal position for such a time as this?" Esther responded with action. Her courageous words are a classic statement of heroism: "I will go to the king, even though it is against the law. And if I perish, I perish" (4:16).

■ COINCIDENCE OR PLAN?

The book of Esther shows, though indirectly, God's heroic concern for the Jews. The story runs on a series of extraordinary coincidences. Esther just "happened" to be chosen as the new queen. The king just "happened" to be unable to sleep, and, when he picked up some reading, just "happened" across an account of a good deed Esther's cousin Mordecai had done. The evil Haman just "happened" along at that crucial moment. These coincidences, together with Esther's courage, tilted terrible events in the Jews' favour.

Were these really mere coincidences? Or was God behind them? The book of Esther doesn't say directly: God is not mentioned even once, and sometimes seems deliberately left out. But believing readers, whether Jews or Christians, can have no doubt. All of life is under God's command. Nothing just happens. These "coincidences" were part of God's plan to save the Jews.

God protected his people because he loved them — because he had chosen them from the beginning. Even their enemies knew the "luck" of the Jews. (See Esther 6:13, for instance.) Esther's story is another chapter in the amazing story of God's perpetual love for the Jews. Though sometimes far from his will, this tiny, often hated minority has survived and thrived down the centuries.

From Haman to Hitler, vindictive leaders have hated the Jews. Yet while no other group has been so hated, no other group has shown the Jews' ability to overcome adversity. Nor can any other ethnic group alive today point to such continuity with their ancestors. They have endured as a unique and great people. How? Esther shows that God's exquisite timing — combined with the courage of individuals who "happened" to be in the right place at the right time — made his chosen people prosper.

■ HOW TO READ ESTHER

Esther makes such suspenseful reading that most people will find it hard to stop. As in a detective story, every detail folds into another. You don't know, from one page to the next, how the drama will turn out.

The essence of Esther lies in its characters. Study Esther, Mordecai, Haman, and King Xerxes. What kind of people were they? What were their ambitions? What were their strengths and weaknesses? What crucial

moment showed the true character of each? What do you learn from them that can help you rise to the challenge when you are "the right person at the right place at the right time"?

Knowing the historical setting for Esther's story can enrich your study. A good commentary or Bible dictionary (under "Esther") will illuminate many of the details that make Esther such a convincing historical document.

■ 3-TRACK READING PLAN

For an explanation and complete listing of the 3-track reading plan, turn to page x.

■ TRACK 1:
Two-Week Courses on the Bible
See page x for information on these courses.

■ TRACK 2:
An Overview of Esther in 1 Day

☐ Day 1. Read the Introduction to Esther and chapter 4, in which Esther learns that her people are in dire straits and decides to take action.
Now turn to page xi for your next Track 2 reading project.

■ TRACK 3:
All of Esther in 8 Days
After you have read through Esther, turn to pages xii–xiii for your next Track 3 reading project.

☐ 1   ☐ 2   ☐ 3   ☐ 4
☐ 5   ☐ 6–7 ☐ 8
☐ 9–10

■ Queen Vashti Deposed

1 This is what happened during the time of Xerxes,*a* the Xerxes who ruled over 127 provinces stretching from India to Cush:*b* 2At that time King Xerxes reigned from his royal throne in the citadel of Susa, 3and in the third year of his reign he gave a banquet for all his nobles and officials. The military leaders of Persia and Media, the princes, and the nobles of the provinces were present.

4For a full 180 days he displayed the vast wealth of his kingdom and the splendour and glory of his majesty. 5When these days were over, the king gave a banquet, lasting seven days, in the enclosed garden of the king's palace, for all the people from the least to the greatest, who were in the citadel of Susa. 6The garden had hangings of white and blue linen, fastened with cords of white linen and purple material to silver rings on marble pillars. There were couches of gold and silver on a mosaic pavement of porphyry, marble, mother-of-pearl and other costly stones. 7Wine was served in goblets of gold, each one different from the other, and the royal wine was abundant, in keeping with the king's liberality. 8By the king's command each guest was allowed to drink in his own way, for the king instructed all the wine stewards to serve each man what he wished.

9Queen Vashti also gave a banquet for the women in the royal palace of King Xerxes.

10On the seventh day, when King Xerxes was in high spirits from wine, he commanded the seven eunuchs who served him—Mehuman, Biztha, Harbona, Bigtha, Abagtha, Zethar and Carcas—11to bring before him Queen Vashti, wearing her royal crown, in order to display her beauty to the people and nobles, for she was lovely to look at. 12But when

the attendants delivered the king's command, Queen Vashti refused to come. Then the king became furious and burned with anger.

1:7 ■ THE INFLUENCE OF WINE

Other historical sources bear out the accuracy of this verse. Greek historian Herodotus wrote that the Persians "are very fond of wine, and drink it in large quantities . . . It is also their general practice to deliberate upon affairs of weight when they are drunk . . . Sometimes, however, they are sober at their first deliberation, but in this case they always reconsider the matter under the influence of wine."

13Since it was customary for the king to consult experts in matters of law and justice, he spoke with the wise men who understood the times 14and were closest to the king—Carshena, Shethar, Admatha, Tarshish, Meres, Marsena and Memucan, the seven nobles of Persia and Media who had special access to the king and were highest in the kingdom.

15"According to law, what must be done to Queen Vashti?" he asked. "She has not obeyed the command of King Xerxes that the eunuchs have taken to her." 16Then Memucan replied in the presence of the king and the nobles, "Queen Vashti has done wrong, not only against the king but also against all the nobles and the peoples of all the provinces of King Xerxes. 17For the queen's conduct will become known to all the women, and so they will despise their husbands and say, 'King Xerxes commanded Queen Vashti to be brought before him, but she would not come.' 18This very day the Persian and Median women of the nobility who have heard

*a*1 Hebrew *Ahasuerus*, a variant of Xerxes' Persian name; here and throughout Esther   *b*1 That is, the upper Nile region about the queen's conduct will respond to all the king's nobles in the same way. There will be no end of disrespect and discord.

19"Therefore, if it pleases the king, let him issue a royal decree and let it be written in the laws of Persia and Media, which cannot be repealed, that Vashti is never again to enter the presence of King Xerxes. Also let the king give her royal position to someone else who is better than she. 20Then when the king's edict is proclaimed throughout all his vast realm, all the women will respect their husbands, from the least to the greatest."

21The king and his nobles were pleased with this advice, so the king did as Memucan proposed. 22He sent dispatches to all parts of the kingdom, to each province in its own script and to each people in its own language, proclaiming in each people's tongue that every man should be ruler over his own household.

Esther Made Queen

2 Later when the anger of King Xerxes had subsided, he remembered Vashti and what she had done and what he had decreed about her. 2Then the king's personal attendants proposed, "Let a search be made for beautiful young virgins for the king. 3Let the king appoint commissioners in every province of his realm to bring all these beautiful girls into the harem at the citadel of Susa. Let them be placed under the care of Hegai, the king's eunuch, who is in charge of the women; and let beauty treatments be given to them. 4Then let the girl who pleases the king be queen instead of Vashti." This advice appealed to the king, and he followed it.

5Now there was in the citadel of Susa a Jew of the tribe of Benjamin, named Mordecai son of Jair, the son of Shimei, the son of Kish, 6who had been carried into exile from Jerusalem by Nebuchadnezzar king of Babylon, among those taken captive with Jehoiachin[a] king of Judah. 7Mordecai had a cousin named Hadassah, whom he had brought up because she had neither father nor mother. This girl, who was also known as Esther, was lovely in form and features, and Mordecai had taken her as his own daughter when her father and mother died.

2:6 ■ THOSE WHO STAYED BEHIND
Ezra and Nehemiah, the books preceding Esther, tell the inspiring story of Jews returning to Jerusalem after years of captivity. Actually, only 50,000 Jews came back to their plundered land, however. Many more — among them Mordecai's family — stayed behind, and some of these prospered. The story of Esther takes place in that foreign setting, ruled by the Persian empire. Modern-day communities of Jews in Iraq and Iran have descended from these ancient exiles.

8When the king's order and edict had been proclaimed, many girls were brought to the citadel of Susa and put under the care of Hegai. Esther also was taken to the king's palace and entrusted to Hegai, who had charge of the harem. 9The girl pleased him and won his favour. Immediately he provided her with her beauty treatments and special food. He assigned to her seven maids selected from the king's palace and moved her and her maids into the best place in the harem.

10Esther had not revealed her nationality and family background, because Mordecai had forbidden her to do so. 11Every day he walked to and fro near the courtyard of the harem to find out how Esther was and what was happening to her.

12Before a girl's turn came to go in to King Xerxes, she had to complete twelve months of beauty treatments prescribed for the women, six months with oil of myrrh and six with perfumes and cosmetics. 13And this is how she would go to the king: Anything she wanted was given to her to take with her from the harem to the king's palace. 14In the evening she would go there and in the morning return to another part of the harem to the care of Shaashgaz, the king's eunuch who was in charge of the concubines. She would not return to the king unless he was pleased with her and summoned her by name.

15When the turn came for Esther (the girl Mordecai had adopted, the daughter of his uncle Abihail) to go to the king, she asked for nothing other than what Hegai, the king's eunuch who was in charge of the harem, suggested. And Esther won the favour of everyone who saw her. 16She was taken to King Xerxes in the royal residence in the tenth month, the month of Tebeth, in the seventh year of his reign.

2:16 ■ AWAY AT WAR
Between Queen Vashti's dismissal (chapter 1) and Esther's acceptance as the new queen, four years passed. Why did Xerxes wait so long? Historians say that during these four years he was away fighting, unsuccessfully trying to conquer Greece. The six-month conference described in chapter 1 was, most probably, a consultation to prepare the invasion.

17Now the king was attracted to Esther more than to any of the other women, and she won his favour and approval more than any of the other virgins. So he set a royal crown on her head and made her queen instead of Vashti. 18And the king gave a great banquet, Esther's banquet, for all his nobles and officials. He proclaimed a holiday throughout the provinces and distributed gifts with royal liberality.

■ Mordecai Uncovers a Conspiracy

19When the virgins were assembled a second time, Mordecai was sitting at the king's gate. 20But Esther had kept secret her family background and nationality just as Mordecai had told her to do, for she continued to follow Mordecai's instructions as she had done when he was bringing her up.

21During the time Mordecai was sitting at the king's gate, Bigthana[b] and Teresh, two of the king's officers who guarded the doorway, became angry and conspired to assassinate King Xerxes. 22But Mordecai found out about the plot and told Queen

---

Esther, who in turn reported it to the king, giving credit to Mordecai. [23]And when the report was investigated and found to be true, the two officials were hanged on a gallows.[c] All this was recorded in the book of the annals in the presence of the king.

■ Haman's Plot to Destroy the Jews

3 After these events, King Xerxes honoured Haman son of Hammedatha, the Agagite, elevating him and giving him a seat of honour higher than that of all the other nobles. [2]All the royal officials at the king's gate knelt down and paid honour to Haman, for the king had commanded this concerning him. But Mordecai would not kneel down or pay him honour.

[3]Then the royal officials at the king's gate asked Mordecai, "Why do you disobey the king's command?" [4]Day after day they spoke to him but he refused to comply. Therefore they told Haman about it to see whether Mordecai's behaviour would be tolerated, for he had told them he was a Jew.

[5]When Haman saw that Mordecai would not kneel down or pay him honour, he was enraged. [6]Yet having learned who Mordecai's people were, he scorned the idea of killing only Mordecai. Instead Haman looked for a way to destroy all Mordecai's people, the Jews, throughout the whole kingdom of Xerxes.

[7]In the twelfth year of King Xerxes, in the first month, the month of Nisan, they cast the *pur* (that is, the lot) in the presence of Haman to select a day and month. And the lot fell on[a] the twelfth month, the month of Adar.

[8]Then Haman said to King Xerxes, "There is a certain people dispersed and scattered among the peoples in all the provinces of your kingdom whose customs are different from those of all other people and who do not obey the king's laws; it is not in the king's best interest to tolerate them. [9]If it pleases the king, let a decree be issued to destroy them, and I will put ten thousand talents[b] of silver into the royal treasury for the men who carry out this business."

[10]So the king took his signet ring from his finger and gave it to Haman son of Hammedatha, the Agagite, the enemy of the Jews. [11]"Keep the money," the king said to Haman, "and do with the people as you please."

[12]Then on the thirteenth day of the first month the royal secretaries were summoned. They wrote out in the script of each province and in the language of each people all Haman's orders to the king's satraps, the governors of the various provinces and the nobles of the various peoples. These were written in the name of King Xerxes himself and sealed with his own ring. [13]Dispatches were sent by couriers to all the king's provinces with the order to destroy, kill and annihilate all the Jews—young and old, women and little children—on a single day, the thirteenth day of the twelfth month, the month of Adar, and to plunder their goods. [14]A copy of the text of the edict was to be issued as law in every province and made known to the people of every nationality so that they would be ready for that day.

[15]Spurred on by the king's command, the couriers went out, and the edict was issued in the citadel of Susa. The king and Haman sat down to drink, but the city of Susa was bewildered.

3:13 ■ PONY EXPRESS

Persia boasted one of the first efficient communication systems. The king kept men and horses stationed a day's journey apart on all major highways. Each messenger rode for a day and relayed the message on to the next station. "Nothing mortal travels so fast as these Persian messengers," wrote the historian Herodotus. Their efficiency made it essential for Mordecai and Esther to overturn the king's edict as soon as possible.

■ Mordecai Persuades Esther to Help

4 When Mordecai learned of all that had been done, he tore his clothes, put on sackcloth and ashes, and went out into the city, wailing loudly and bitterly. [2]But he went only as far as the king's gate, because no-one clothed in sackcloth was allowed to enter it. [3]In every province to which the edict and order of the king came, there was great mourning among the Jews, with fasting, weeping and wailing. Many lay in sackcloth and ashes.

[4]When Esther's maids and eunuchs came and told her about Mordecai, she was in great distress. She sent clothes for him to put on instead of his sackcloth, but he would not accept them. [5]Then Esther summoned Hathach, one of the king's eunuchs assigned to attend her, and ordered him to find out what was troubling Mordecai and why.

[6]So Hathach went out to Mordecai in the open square of the city in front of the king's gate. [7]Mordecai told him everything that had happened to him, including the exact amount of money Haman had promised to pay into the royal treasury for the destruction of the Jews. [8]He also gave him a copy of the text of the edict for their annihilation, which had been published in Susa, to show to Esther and explain it to her, and he told him to urge her to go into the king's presence to beg for mercy and plead with him for her people.

[9]Hathach went back and reported to Esther what Mordecai had said. [10]Then she instructed him to say to Mordecai, [11]"All the king's officials and the people of the royal provinces know that for any man or woman who approaches the king in the inner court without being summoned the king has but one law: that he be put to death. The only exception to this is for the king to extend the gold sceptre to him and spare his life. But thirty days have passed since I was called to go to the king."

[12]When Esther's words were reported to Mordecai, [13]he sent back this answer: "Do not think that because you are in the king's house you alone of all the Jews will escape. [14]For if you remain silent at this time, relief and deliverance for the Jews will arise from another place, but you and your father's family will perish. And who knows but that you have come to royal position for such a time as this?"

[15]Then Esther sent this reply to Mordecai: [16]"Go,

---

[c]23 Or *were hung* (or *impaled*) *on poles*; similarly elsewhere in Esther   [a]7 Septuagint; Hebrew does not have *And the lot fell on.*   [b]9 That is, about 340 tons (about 345 metric tons)

gather together all the Jews who are in Susa, and fast for me. Do not eat or drink for three days, night or day. I and my maids will fast as you do. When this is done, I will go to the king, even though it is against the law. And if I perish, I perish."

4:13 ■ ONE SAFE JEW?
Esther, ensconced in the safety and luxury of the palace, was possibly the only Jew in Persia who had not heard of the extermination plans. It is more than likely that she would have been spared, but, as Mordecai warned, the king might just as easily turn against her. Mordecai had a sophisticated view of God's providence that never lapsed into fatalism. He believed that God would somehow preserve his people; yet he also knew that God might accomplish that goal through the courageous actions of people like himself and Esther.

17So Mordecai went away and carried out all of Esther's instructions.

■ Esther's Request to the King

5 On the third day Esther put on her royal robes and stood in the inner court of the palace, in front of the king's hall. The king was sitting on his royal throne in the hall, facing the entrance. 2When he saw Queen Esther standing in the court, he was pleased with her and held out to her the gold sceptre that was in his hand. So Esther approached and touched the tip of the sceptre.

3Then the king asked, "What is it, Queen Esther? What is your request? Even up to half the kingdom, it will be given you."

4"If it pleases the king," replied Esther, "let the king, together with Haman, come today to a banquet I have prepared for him."

5"Bring Haman at once," the king said, "so that we may do what Esther asks."

So the king and Haman went to the banquet Esther had prepared. 6As they were drinking wine, the king again asked Esther, "Now what is your petition? It will be given you. And what is your request? Even up to half the kingdom, it will be granted."

7Esther replied, "My petition and my request is this: 8If the king regards me with favour and if it pleases the king to grant my petition and fulfil my request, let the king and Haman come tomorrow to the banquet I will prepare for them. Then I will answer the king's question."

■ Haman's Rage Against Mordecai

9Haman went out that day happy and in high spirits. But when he saw Mordecai at the king's gate and observed that he neither rose nor showed fear in his presence, he was filled with rage against Mordecai. 10Nevertheless, Haman restrained himself and went home.

Calling together his friends and Zeresh, his wife, 11Haman boasted to them about his vast wealth, his many sons, and all the ways the king had honoured him and how he had elevated him above the other nobles and officials. 12"And that's not all," Haman added. "I'm the only person Queen Esther invited to accompany the king to the banquet she gave. And she has invited me along with the king tomorrow. 13But all this gives me no satisfaction as long as I see that Jew Mordecai sitting at the king's gate."

14His wife Zeresh and all his friends said to him, "Have a gallows built, seventy-five feet*a* high, and ask the king in the morning to have Mordecai hanged on it. Then go with the king to the dinner and be happy." This suggestion delighted Haman, and he had the gallows built.

■ Mordecai Honoured

6 That night the king could not sleep; so he ordered the book of the chronicles, the record of his reign, to be brought in and read to him. 2It was found recorded there that Mordecai had exposed Bigthana and Teresh, two of the king's officers who guarded the doorway, who had conspired to assassinate King Xerxes.

6:1 ■ XERXES: A WILD MAN
Other historical sources portray Xerxes as a dangerously impulsive king. When a bridge he had ordered built was destroyed in a storm, he commanded that the sea receive 300 lashes, and then had the bridge builders beheaded. When one of his loyal subjects contributed a huge sum towards a military expedition, Xerxes was so enraptured that he returned the money, along with a handsome gift of his own. But when the same man asked Xerxes to let just one of his sons go free from military service, Xerxes, enraged, ordered the son cut into two and the army to march between the pieces.

3"What honour and recognition has Mordecai received for this?" the king asked.

"Nothing has been done for him," his attendants answered.

4The king said, "Who is in the court?" Now Haman had just entered the outer court of the palace to speak to the king about hanging Mordecai on the gallows he had erected for him.

5His attendants answered, "Haman is standing in the court."

"Bring him in," the king ordered.

6When Haman entered, the king asked him, "What should be done for the man the king delights to honour?"

Now Haman thought to himself, "Who is there that the king would rather honour than me?" 7So he answered the king, "For the man the king delights to honour, 8have them bring a royal robe the king has worn and a horse the king has ridden, one with a royal crest placed on its head. 9Then let the robe and horse be entrusted to one of the king's most noble princes. Let them robe the man the king delights to honour, and lead him on the horse through the city streets, proclaiming before him, 'This is what is done for the man the king delights to honour!' "

10"Go at once," the king commanded Haman.

a 14 Hebrew fifty cubits (about 23 metres)

"Get the robe and the horse and do just as you have suggested for Mordecai the Jew, who sits at the king's gate. Do not neglect anything you have recommended."

11So Haman got the robe and the horse. He robed Mordecai, and led him on horseback through the city streets, proclaiming before him, "This is what is done for the man the king delights to honour!"

12Afterwards Mordecai returned to the king's gate. But Haman rushed home, with his head covered, in grief, 13and told Zeresh his wife and all his friends everything that had happened to him.

His advisers and his wife Zeresh said to him, "Since Mordecai, before whom your downfall has started, is of Jewish origin, you cannot stand against him—you will surely come to ruin!" 14While they were still talking with him, the king's eunuchs arrived and hurried Haman away to the banquet Esther had prepared.

■ Haman Hanged

7 So the king and Haman went to dine with Queen Esther, 2and as they were drinking wine on that second day, the king again asked, "Queen Esther, what is your petition? It will be given you. What is your request? Even up to half the kingdom, it will be granted."

7:1 ■ SUBTLE APPROACH

Esther knew well the perils of standing up to autocratic Xerxes: she had got her job because of the king's furious response to a queen's brashness (1:12–2:7). Esther's "banquet plot" shows that she had mastered the wiles necessary to soften the king. She grew increasingly bold and more direct, finally convincing the king to issue another decree, countering the one against the Jews—a rare change of heart for a Persian ruler (8:8).

3Then Queen Esther answered, "If I have found favour with you, O king, and if it pleases your majesty, grant me my life—this is my petition. And spare my people—this is my request. 4For I and my people have been sold for destruction and slaughter and annihilation. If we had merely been sold as male and female slaves, I would have kept quiet, because no such distress would justify disturbing the king."a

5King Xerxes asked Queen Esther, "Who is he? Where is the man who has dared to do such a thing?"

6Esther said, "The adversary and enemy is this vile Haman."

Then Haman was terrified before the king and queen. 7The king got up in a rage, left his wine and went out into the palace garden. But Haman, realising that the king had already decided his fate, stayed behind to beg Queen Esther for his life.

8Just as the king returned from the palace garden to the banquet hall, Haman was falling on the couch where Esther was reclining.

The king exclaimed, "Will he even molest the queen while she is with me in the house?"

As soon as the word left the king's mouth, they covered Haman's face. 9Then Harbona, one of the eunuchs attending the king, said, "A gallows seventy-five feetb high stands by Haman's house. He had it made for Mordecai, who spoke up to help the king."

The king said, "Hang him on it!" 10So they hanged Haman on the gallows he had prepared for Mordecai. Then the king's fury subsided.

■ The King's Edict on Behalf of the Jews

8 That same day King Xerxes gave Queen Esther the estate of Haman, the enemy of the Jews. And Mordecai came into the presence of the king, for Esther had told how he was related to her. 2The king took off his signet ring, which he had reclaimed from Haman, and presented it to Mordecai. And Esther appointed him over Haman's estate.

3Esther again pleaded with the king, falling at his feet and weeping. She begged him to put an end to the evil plan of Haman the Agagite, which he had devised against the Jews. 4Then the king extended the gold sceptre to Esther and she arose and stood before him.

5"If it pleases the king," she said, "and if he regards me with favour and thinks it the right thing to do, and if he is pleased with me, let an order be written overruling the dispatches that Haman son of Hammedatha, the Agagite, devised and wrote to destroy the Jews in all the king's provinces. 6For how can I bear to see disaster fall on my people? How can I bear to see the destruction of my family?"

7King Xerxes replied to Queen Esther and to Mordecai the Jew, "Because Haman attacked the Jews, I have given his estate to Esther, and they have hanged him on the gallows. 8Now write another decree in the king's name on behalf of the Jews as seems best to you, and seal it with the king's signet ring—for no document written in the king's name and sealed with his ring can be revoked."

9At once the royal secretaries were summoned—on the twenty-third day of the third month, the month of Sivan. They wrote out all Mordecai's orders to the Jews, and to the satraps, governors and nobles of the 127 provinces stretching from India to Cush.a These orders were written in the script of each province and the language of each people and also to the Jews in their own script and language. 10Mordecai wrote in the name of King Xerxes, sealed the dispatches with the king's signet ring, and sent them by mounted couriers, who rode fast horses especially bred for the king.

11The king's edict granted the Jews in every city the right to assemble and protect themselves; to destroy, kill and annihilate any armed force of any nationality or province that might attack them and their women and children; and to plunder the property of their enemies. 12The day appointed for the Jews to do this in all the provinces of King Xerxes was the thirteenth day of the twelfth month, the month of Adar. 13A copy of the text of the edict was to be issued as law in every province and made known to the people of every nationality so that the Jews would be ready on that day to avenge themselves on their enemies.

14The couriers, riding the royal horses, raced out,

---

a4 Or quiet, but the compensation our adversary offers cannot be compared with the loss the king would suffer   b9 Hebrew fifty cubits (about 23 metres)
a9 That is, the upper Nile region

spurred on by the king's command. And the edict was also issued in the citadel of Susa.

¹⁵Mordecai left the king's presence wearing royal garments of blue and white, a large crown of gold and a purple robe of fine linen. And the city of Susa held a joyous celebration. ¹⁶For the Jews it was a time of happiness and joy, gladness and honour. ¹⁷In every province and in every city, wherever the edict of the king went, there was joy and gladness among the Jews, with feasting and celebrating. And many people of other nationalities became Jews because fear of the Jews had seized them.

8:16 ■ WHAT ABOUT GOD?

Why is God's name not mentioned in Esther — especially in obvious places like this one? Scholars suggest several answers to this riddle. Some, reading between the lines, suggest that Esther and Mordecai were not outstanding examples of faith. They were even willing to hide Esther's Jewish background. Esther showed no reluctance to be married to a pagan king and become part of his harem. Most critically, she and Mordecai (along with all the other Jews in Esther) had chosen not to return to Jerusalem with the first wave of Jews nearly half a century before. (The story of that return is told in Ezra 1–6.) Those who stayed in Persia presumably cared more about their finances than about God's plans for the Jews to return to Jerusalem from exile. Perhaps because of this, Esther is told as a secular story, to illustrate God's care over even "secularised" Jews.

■ Triumph of the Jews

9 On the thirteenth day of the twelfth month, the month of Adar, the edict commanded by the king was to be carried out. On this day the enemies of the Jews had hoped to overpower them, but now the tables were turned and the Jews got the upper hand over those who hated them. ²The Jews assembled in their cities in all the provinces of King Xerxes to attack those seeking their destruction. No-one could stand against them, because the people of all the other nationalities were afraid of them. ³And all the nobles of the provinces, the satraps, the governors and the king's administrators helped the Jews, because fear of Mordecai had seized them. ⁴Mordecai was prominent in the palace; his reputation spread throughout the provinces, and he became more and more powerful.

⁵The Jews struck down all their enemies with the sword, killing and destroying them, and they did what they pleased to those who hated them. ⁶In the citadel of Susa, the Jews killed and destroyed five hundred men. ⁷They also killed Parshandatha, Dalphon, Aspatha, ⁸Poratha, Adalia, Aridatha, ⁹Parmashta, Arisai, Aridai and Vaizatha, ¹⁰the ten sons of Haman son of Hammedatha, the enemy of the Jews. But they did not lay their hands on the plunder.

¹¹The number of those slain in the citadel of Susa was reported to the king that same day. ¹²The king said to Queen Esther, "The Jews have killed and destroyed five hundred men and the ten sons of Haman

in the citadel of Susa. What have they done in the rest of the king's provinces? Now what is your petition? It will be given you. What is your request? It will also be granted."

¹³"If it pleases the king," Esther answered, "give the Jews in Susa permission to carry out this day's edict tomorrow also, and let Haman's ten sons be hanged on gallows."

¹⁴So the king commanded that this be done. An edict was issued in Susa, and they hanged the ten sons of Haman. ¹⁵The Jews in Susa came together on the fourteenth day of the month of Adar, and they put to death in Susa three hundred men, but they did not lay their hands on the plunder.

¹⁶Meanwhile, the remainder of the Jews who were in the king's provinces also assembled to protect themselves and get relief from their enemies. They killed seventy-five thousand of them but did not lay their hands on the plunder. ¹⁷This happened on the thirteenth day of the month of Adar, and on the fourteenth they rested and made it a day of feasting and joy.

■ Purim Celebrated

¹⁸The Jews in Susa, however, had assembled on the thirteenth and fourteenth, and then on the fifteenth they rested and made it a day of feasting and joy.

¹⁹That is why rural Jews—those living in villages—observe the fourteenth of the month of Adar as a day of joy and feasting, a day for giving presents to each other.

9:19 ■ A DAY TO REMEMBER

Just as Christians retell the Christmas story each December, acting it out in church plays and manger scenes, the Jews commemorate great moments from their history. Jewish families read the book of Esther aloud on the day of Purim. The festival got its name from the casting of lots (like dice) against the Jews (3:7), a gamble that eventually backfired against Haman. The author explains the origin of celebrating Purim on two different days; even today, Jews observe Purim on the 14th everywhere except in Jerusalem, which schedules it on the 15th.

²⁰Mordecai recorded these events, and he sent letters to all the Jews throughout the provinces of King Xerxes, near and far, ²¹to have them celebrate annually the fourteenth and fifteenth days of the month of Adar ²²as the time when the Jews got relief from their enemies, and as the month when their sorrow was turned into joy and their mourning into a day of celebration. He wrote to them to observe the days as days of feasting and joy and giving presents of food to one another and gifts to the poor.

²³So the Jews agreed to continue the celebration they had begun, doing what Mordecai had written to them. ²⁴For Haman son of Hammedatha, the Agagite, the enemy of all the Jews, had plotted against the Jews to destroy them and had cast the *pur* (that

is, the lot) for their ruin and destruction. 25But when the plot came to the king's attention,*a* he issued written orders that the evil scheme Haman had devised against the Jews should come back on to his own head, and that he and his sons should be hanged on the gallows. 26(Therefore these days were called Purim, from the word *pur*.) Because of everything written in this letter and because of what they had seen and what had happened to them, 27the Jews took it upon themselves to establish the custom that they and their descendants and all who join them should without fail observe these two days every year, in the way prescribed and at the time appointed. 28These days should be remembered and observed in every generation by every family, and in every province and in every city. And these days of Purim should never cease to be celebrated by the Jews, nor should the memory of them die out among their descendants.

29So Queen Esther, daughter of Abihail, along with Mordecai the Jew, wrote with full authority to confirm this second letter concerning Purim. 30And Mordecai sent letters to all the Jews in the 127 provinces of the kingdom of Xerxes — words of goodwill and assurance — 31to establish these days of Purim at their designated times, as Mordecai the Jew and Queen Esther had decreed for them, and as they had established for themselves and their descendants in regard to their times of fasting and lamentation.

32Esther's decree confirmed these regulations about Purim, and it was written down in the records.

■ The Greatness of Mordecai

10 King Xerxes imposed tribute throughout the empire, to its distant shores. 2And all his acts of power and might, together with a full account of the greatness of Mordecai to which the king had raised him, are they not written in the book of the annals of the kings of Media and Persia? 3Mordecai the Jew was second in rank to King Xerxes, preeminent among the Jews, and held in high esteem by his many fellow Jews, because he worked for the good of his people and spoke up for the welfare of all the Jews.

10:2 ■ IS ESTHER ACCURATE?

Because of the many coincidences in Esther, some have considered it "just a story", having little or no historical validity. Yet as archaeologists have learned more about ancient Persian history, the details of Esther have proven remarkably reliable. Certainly the book presents itself as history: here the author confidently asserts that readers can check the facts in the historical records. These records are lost — but evidently they were known to the early readers of Esther.

JOB

■ WHEN BAD THINGS HAPPENED TO A GOOD PERSON

NOBODY SUFFERED MORE; NOBODY DESERVED IT LESS

"HAVE YOU CONSIDERED MY SERVANT JOB? THERE IS NO-ONE ON EARTH LIKE HIM; HE IS BLAMELESS AND UPRIGHT, A MAN WHO FEARS GOD AND SHUNS EVIL." ■ 1:8

How could it happen? All at once the world came crashing down on a single innocent man, a man named Job. It was the ultimate in unfairness.

First, raiders stole his belongings and slaughtered his servants. Then fire from the sky burned up his sheep, and a mighty wind destroyed his house and killed his sons and daughters. Finally, Job came down with a horrible, painful disease. *What did I do to deserve such suffering?* he wailed.

■ A COSMIC CONTEST

The book of Job reads like a detective story in which the readers know far more than the central characters. The very first chapter answers Job's main question: he had done nothing to deserve such suffering. We, the readers, know that, but nobody tells Job and his friends.

Unknown to him, Job was involved in a cosmic test, a contest proposed in heaven but staged on earth. In this extreme test of faith, the best man on earth suffered the worst calamities. Satan had claimed that people like Job love God only because of the good things he provides. Remove those good things, Satan challenged, and Job's faith would melt away together with his riches and health.

God's reputation was on the line. Would Job continue to trust him, even while his life was falling apart? This is the crucial question of the book: Would Job turn against God?

Job's wife mocked him, "Are you still holding on to your integrity? Curse God and die!" (2:9). His friends were even more cruel: they argued that Job was being punished, that he fully deserved the tragedies crashing into his life. For his part, Job struggled to do what seemed impossible: to keep on believing in a loving, fair God even though all the evidence pointed against such a God.

■ JOB ON TRIAL

It helps to think of this book as a courtroom drama, full of long, eloquent speeches. For most of the book, Job sits in the defendant's chair listening to his friends' harangues. He knows no airtight refutations; what they say about suffering as punishment seems to make sense. Yet he also knows, deep in his soul, that they are wrong. He does not deserve the treatment he is getting. There has to be some other explanation.

Like all grieving persons, Job went through emotional cycles. He whined, exploded, cajoled, and collapsed into self-pity. He agreed with his friends, then shifted positions and contradicted himself. And occasionally he came up with a statement of brilliant hope.

Mainly, Job asked for one thing: an appearance by the one Person who could explain his miserable fate. He wanted to meet God himself, face to face. Eventually Job got his wish; God did show up in person. And when God finally spoke, no-one — not Job, nor any of his friends — was prepared for what he had to say.

■ WHEN WE FEEL LIKE JOB

Sooner or later we all find ourselves in a position somewhat like Job's. Our world seems to crumble. Nothing makes sense any more. God seems distant and silent.

At such moments of great crisis, each one of us is put on trial. In a sense we become actors in a contest like the one Job went through. This book records every step in that process with unflinching honesty. Job's life stands as an example to every person who must go through great suffering.

■ HOW TO READ JOB

The book of Job is regarded as one of the world's truly great literary masterpieces. It contains some of the finest, most expressive poetry in the Bible. Yet first-time readers of Job can easily get lost because the complete "story line" is found in the first two chapters and the last one. Everything in between consists of a series of speeches.

The sectional headings and the phrases that follow, such as "And Job continued his discourse" and "Then Eliphaz the Temanite replied", serve as markers or signposts throughout the book. Rather than reading large sections of the book, read one entire speech by Job, or a speech by Job and a rebuttal from one of his friends.

It may help if you try to summarise the statement behind each speech in one sentence and write that sentence in the margin (for example, "Job protests that he's innocent"). Speakers of that day impressed their audience more by eloquence than by rigorous logic, so the speeches may seem flowery. The issues Job and his friends address, however, are life-and-death ones.

As you read the speeches of Job's friends, remember that their views do not necessarily reflect God's. The book of Job merely records the friends' viewpoints; it does not endorse them.

■ 3-TRACK READING PLAN

For an explanation and complete listing of the 3-track reading plan, turn to page x.

■ Prologue

1 In the land of Uz there lived a man whose name was Job. This man was blameless and upright; he feared God and shunned evil. ²He had seven sons and three daughters, ³and he owned seven thousand sheep, three thousand camels, five hundred yoke of oxen and five hundred donkeys, and had a large number of servants. He was the greatest man among all the people of the East.

⁴His sons used to take turns holding feasts in their homes, and they would invite their three sisters to eat and drink with them. ⁵When a period of feasting had run its course, Job would send and have them purified. Early in the morning he would sacrifice a burnt offering for each of them, thinking, "Perhaps my children have sinned and cursed God in their hearts." This was Job's regular custom.

■ Job's First Test

⁶One day the angels*a* came to present themselves before the LORD, and Satan*b* also came with them. ⁷The LORD said to Satan, "Where have you come from?"

Satan answered the LORD, "From roaming through the earth and going to and fro in it."

⁸Then the LORD said to Satan, "Have you considered my servant Job? There is no-one on earth like him; he is blameless and upright, a man who fears God and shuns evil."

⁹"Does Job fear God for nothing?" Satan replied. ¹⁰"Have you not put a hedge around him and his household and everything he has? You have blessed the work of his hands, so that his flocks and herds are spread throughout the land. ¹¹But stretch out your hand and strike everything he has, and he will surely curse you to your face."

¹²The LORD said to Satan, "Very well, then, everything he has is in your hands, but on the man himself do not lay a finger."

Then Satan went out from the presence of the LORD.

¹³One day when Job's sons and daughters were feasting and drinking wine at the oldest brother's house, ¹⁴a messenger came to Job and said, "The oxen were ploughing and the donkeys were grazing nearby, ¹⁵and the Sabeans attacked and carried them

*a*6 Hebrew *the sons of God*   *b*6 *Satan* means *accuser*.

off. They put the servants to the sword, and I am the only one who has escaped to tell you!"

[16]While he was still speaking, another messenger came and said, "The fire of God fell from the sky and burned up the sheep and the servants, and I am the only one who has escaped to tell you!"

[17]While he was still speaking, another messenger came and said, "The Chaldeans formed three raiding parties and swept down on your camels and carried them off. They put the servants to the sword, and I am the only one who has escaped to tell you!"

[18]While he was still speaking, yet another messenger came and said, "Your sons and daughters were feasting and drinking wine at the oldest brother's house, [19]when suddenly a mighty wind swept in from the desert and struck the four corners of the house. It collapsed on them and they are dead, and I am the only one who has escaped to tell you!"

[20]At this, Job got up and tore his robe and shaved his head. Then he fell to the ground in worship [21]and said:

> "Naked I came from my mother's womb,
> and naked I shall depart.[c]
> The LORD gave and the LORD has taken away;
> may the name of the LORD be praised."

[22]In all this, Job did not sin by charging God with wrongdoing.

■ Job's Second Test

2 On another day the angels[a] came to present themselves before the LORD, and Satan also came with them to present himself before him. [2]And the LORD said to Satan, "Where have you come from?"

Satan answered the LORD, "From roaming through the earth and going to and fro in it."

[3]Then the LORD said to Satan, "Have you considered my servant Job? There is no-one on earth like him; he is blameless and upright, a man who fears God and shuns evil. And he still maintains his integrity, though you incited me against him to ruin him without any reason."

[4]"Skin for skin!" Satan replied. "A man will give all he has for his own life. [5]But stretch out your hand and strike his flesh and bones, and he will surely curse you to your face."

[6]The LORD said to Satan, "Very well, then, he is in your hands; but you must spare his life."

2:6 ■ THE EXTENT OF SATAN'S POWER

Job's portrayal of Satan echoes the story in Genesis 3: he has supernatural power to oppress people, but is restrained by God. As John Newton said, "Satan can only go to the end of his chain." The Bible records at least one other instance where Satan specifically asked for permission to attack an individual: Luke 22:31–32.

[7]So Satan went out from the presence of the LORD and afflicted Job with painful sores from the soles of his feet to the top of his head. [8]Then Job took a piece of broken pottery and scraped himself with it as he sat among the ashes.

[9]His wife said to him, "Are you still holding on to your integrity? Curse God and die!"

[10]He replied, "You are talking like a foolish[b] woman. Shall we accept good from God, and not trouble?"

In all this, Job did not sin in what he said.

■ Job's Three Friends

[11]When Job's three friends, Eliphaz the Temanite, Bildad the Shuhite and Zophar the Naamathite, heard about all the troubles that had come upon him, they set out from their homes and met together by agreement to go and sympathise with him and comfort him. [12]When they saw him from a distance, they could hardly recognise him; they began to weep aloud, and they tore their robes and sprinkled dust on their heads. [13]Then they sat on the ground with him for seven days and seven nights. No-one said a word to him, because they saw how great his suffering was.

2:13 ■ KEEPING QUIET

The term "Job's comforter" has come to describe how *not* to act around a suffering person. These three friends proved of scant help to Job and were dismissed by God himself in the end. This verse, though, reveals the depth of their feeling for Job: they sat with him for a whole week in shared, silent grief. As it turned out, compassionate silence was the most profound help they imparted to Job — a good lesson to remember for anyone who works with suffering people.

■ Job Speaks

3 After this, Job opened his mouth and cursed the day of his birth. [2]He said:

> [3]"May the day of my birth perish,
> and the night it was said, 'A boy is born!'
> [4]That day — may it turn to darkness;
> may God above not care about it;
> may no light shine upon it.
> [5]May darkness and deep shadow[a] claim it once more;
> may a cloud settle over it;
> may blackness overwhelm its light.
> [6]That night — may thick darkness seize it;
> may it not be included among the days of the year
> nor be entered in any of the months.
> [7]May that night be barren;
> may no shout of joy be heard in it.
> [8]May those who curse days[b] curse that day,
> those who are ready to rouse Leviathan.
> [9]May its morning stars become dark;
> may it wait for daylight in vain
> and not see the first rays of dawn,
> [10]for it did not shut the doors of the womb on me
> to hide trouble from my eyes.
> [11]"Why did I not perish at birth,

---

[c] 21 Or *shall return there*   [a] 1 Hebrew *the sons of God*   [b] 10 The Hebrew word rendered *foolish* denotes moral deficiency.   [a] 5 Or *and the shadow of death*   [b] 8 Or *the sea*

and die as I came from the womb?
12Why were there knees to receive me
　and breasts that I might be nursed?
13For now I would be lying down in peace;
　I would be asleep and at rest
14with kings and counsellors of the earth,
　who built for themselves places now lying in
　　ruins,
15with rulers who had gold,
　who filled their houses with silver.
16Or why was I not hidden in the ground like a
　　stillborn child,
　like an infant who never saw the light of day?
17There the wicked cease from turmoil,
　and there the weary are at rest.
18Captives also enjoy their ease;
　they no longer hear the slave driver's shout.
19The small and the great are there,
　and the slave is freed from his master.

20"Why is light given to those in misery,
　and life to the bitter of soul,
21to those who long for death that does not
　　come,
　who search for it more than for hidden
　　treasure,
22who are filled with gladness
　and rejoice when they reach the grave?
23Why is life given to a man
　whose way is hidden,
　whom God has hedged in?
24For sighing comes to me instead of food;
　my groans pour out like water.
25What I feared has come upon me;
　what I dreaded has happened to me.
26I have no peace, no quietness;
　I have no rest, but only turmoil."

■ Eliphaz

4 Then Eliphaz the Temanite replied:

2"If someone ventures a word with you, will you
　　be impatient?
　But who can keep from speaking?
3Think how you have instructed many,
　how you have strengthened feeble hands.
4Your words have supported those who
　　stumbled;
　you have strengthened faltering knees.
5But now trouble comes to you, and you are
　　discouraged;
　it strikes you, and you are dismayed.
6Should not your piety be your confidence
　and your blameless ways your hope?

7"Consider now: Who, being innocent, has ever
　　perished?
　Where were the upright ever destroyed?
8As I have observed, those who plough evil
　and those who sow trouble reap it.
9At the breath of God they are destroyed;
　at the blast of his anger they perish.
10The lions may roar and growl,
　yet the teeth of the great lions are broken.
11The lion perishes for lack of prey,
　and the cubs of the lioness are scattered.

12"A word was secretly brought to me,
　my ears caught a whisper of it.
13Amid disquieting dreams in the night,
　when deep sleep falls on men,
14fear and trembling seized me
　and made all my bones shake.
15A spirit glided past my face,
　and the hair on my body stood on end.
16It stopped,
　but I could not tell what it was.
　A form stood before my eyes,
　and I heard a hushed voice:
17'Can a mortal be more righteous than God?
　Can a man be more pure than his Maker?

4:13 ■ APPEALING TO A VISION
The book of Job includes parallels to most
modern-day responses to people in pain. To
impress the other listeners with his religious
authority, Eliphaz appealed to a mysterious vision
in which a "spirit" restated Eliphaz's own line of
argument. In the next chapter, he hints that Job
should turn to God for a miracle (5:8–10).

18If God places no trust in his servants,
　if he charges his angels with error,
19how much more those who live in houses of
　　clay,
　whose foundations are in the dust,
　who are crushed more readily than a moth!
20Between dawn and dusk they are broken to
　　pieces;
　unnoticed, they perish for ever.
21Are not the cords of their tent pulled up,
　so that they die without wisdom?'a

5 "Call if you will, but who will answer you?
　To which of the holy ones will you turn?
2Resentment kills a fool,
　and envy slays the simple.
3I myself have seen a fool taking root,
　but suddenly his house was cursed.
4His children are far from safety,
　crushed in court without a defender.
5The hungry consume his harvest,
　taking it even from among thorns,
　and the thirsty pant after his wealth.
6For hardship does not spring from the soil,
　nor does trouble sprout from the ground.
7Yet man is born to trouble
　as surely as sparks fly upward.

8"But if it were I, I would appeal to God;
　I would lay my cause before him.
9He performs wonders that cannot be fathomed,
　miracles that cannot be counted.
10He bestows rain on the earth;
　he sends water upon the countryside.
11The lowly he sets on high,
　and those who mourn are lifted to safety.
12He thwarts the plans of the crafty,
　so that their hands achieve no success.
13He catches the wise in their craftiness,
　and the schemes of the wily are swept away.

a21 Some interpreters end the quotation after verse 17.

14Darkness comes upon them in the daytime;
  at noon they grope as in the night.
15He saves the needy from the sword in their
  mouth;
  he saves them from the clutches of the
  powerful.
16So the poor have hope,
  and injustice shuts its mouth.

17"Blessed is the man whom God corrects;
  so do not despise the discipline of the
  Almighty.[a]

5:17 ■ PAIN AS PUNISHMENT

Job's friends sound so pious and eloquent
that it's easy to accept their words as
all-encompassing truth. Some Christians have
quoted this verse like a proverb, applying it
indiscriminately to instances of suffering. In reality,
Eliphaz was completely wrong in his theory that
God was disciplining Job. God had already held
Job up as a model of goodness (1:9).

18For he wounds, but he also binds up;
  he injures, but his hands also heal.
19From six calamities he will rescue you;
  in seven no harm will befall you.
20In famine he will ransom you from death,
  and in battle from the stroke of the sword.
21You will be protected from the lash of the
  tongue,
  and need not fear when destruction comes.
22You will laugh at destruction and famine,
  and need not fear the beasts of the earth.
23For you will have a covenant with the stones of
  the field,
  and the wild animals will be at peace with
  you.
24You will know that your tent is secure;
  you will take stock of your property and find
  nothing missing.
25You will know that your children will be many,
  and your descendants like the grass of the
  earth.
26You will come to the grave in full vigour,
  like sheaves gathered in season.

27"We have examined this, and it is true.
  So hear it and apply it to yourself."

■ Job

6 Then Job replied:

2"If only my anguish could be weighed
  and all my misery be placed on the scales!
3It would surely outweigh the sand of the seas—
  no wonder my words have been impetuous.
4The arrows of the Almighty are in me,
  my spirit drinks in their poison;
  God's terrors are marshalled against me.
5Does a wild donkey bray when it has grass,
  or an ox bellow when it has fodder?
6Is tasteless food eaten without salt,
  or is there flavour in the white of an egg?[a]

7I refuse to touch it;
  such food makes me ill.

8"Oh, that I might have my request,
  that God would grant what I hope for,
9that God would be willing to crush me,
  to let loose his hand and cut me off!
10Then I would still have this consolation—
  my joy in unrelenting pain—
  that I had not denied the words of the Holy
  One.

6:9 ■ WHY KEEP ON LIVING?

Job steadfastly refused to curse God, but he did
curse the day he was born. In this speech he
asked for a quick death, realising he could not
hold out trusting in God for ever. If he died soon,
at least he would die still believing. His speeches
contain some of the most profound expressions of
pain and despair in all of literature.

11"What strength do I have, that I should still
  hope?
  What prospects, that I should be patient?
12Do I have the strength of stone?
  Is my flesh bronze?
13Do I have any power to help myself,
  now that success has been driven from me?

14"A despairing man should have the devotion of
  his friends,
  even though he forsakes the fear of the
  Almighty.
15But my brothers are as undependable as
  intermittent streams,
  as the streams that overflow
16when darkened by thawing ice
  and swollen with melting snow,
17but that cease to flow in the dry season,
  and in the heat vanish from their channels.
18Caravans turn aside from their routes;
  they go up into the wasteland and perish.
19The caravans of Tema look for water,
  the travelling merchants of Sheba look in
  hope.
20They are distressed, because they had been
  confident;
  they arrive there, only to be disappointed.
21Now you too have proved to be of no help;
  you see something dreadful and are afraid.
22Have I ever said, 'Give something on my behalf,
  pay a ransom for me from your wealth,
23deliver me from the hand of the enemy,
  ransom me from the clutches of the
  ruthless'?

24"Teach me, and I will be quiet;
  show me where I have been wrong.
25How painful are honest words!
  But what do your arguments prove?
26Do you mean to correct what I say,
  and treat the words of a despairing man as
  wind?
27You would even cast lots for the fatherless

and barter away your friend.

28"But now be so kind as to look at me.
　　Would I lie to your face?
29Relent, do not be unjust;
　　reconsider, for my integrity is at stake.*b*
30Is there any wickedness on my lips?
　　Can my mouth not discern malice?

7 "Does not man have hard service on earth?
　　Are not his days like those of a hired man?
2Like a slave longing for the evening shadows,
　　or a hired man waiting eagerly for his wages,

3so I have been allotted months of futility,
　　and nights of misery have been assigned to
　　me.
4When I lie down I think, 'How long before I
　　get up?'
　　The night drags on, and I toss till dawn.
5My body is clothed with worms and scabs,
　　my skin is broken and festering.

6"My days are swifter than a weaver's shuttle,
　　and they come to an end without hope.
7Remember, O God, that my life is but a breath;
　　my eyes will never see happiness again.

■ WHAT NOT TO SAY TO A HURTING PERSON
JOB'S FRIENDS ONLY MADE IT WORSE

"NOW YOU TOO HAVE PROVED TO BE OF NO HELP." ■ 6:21

You are sitting in a hospital room, where the faint smell of antiseptic lingers and the sound of lowered voices rustles all around you. The medical prognosis of your friend is bleak. You've listened to your friend's anger and despair, and a welter of other emotions. Now it's your turn to reply. Everyone in the room waits for your response.

What do you say to a suffering person? The book of Job gives page after page of examples. Job's three friends, finding him in despair, filled the air with high-sounding advice. But unfortunately they offer models of what *not* to say. Their main argument only made Job feel worse, and at the end God dismissed them all with a scowl.

■ WHO WERE JOB'S FRIENDS?
This book gives few details on time and place, but it presents Job as a very wealthy "sheikh" of the Middle East. His three friends, from neighbouring lands, were also prosperous and well-respected. When they first saw Job, they wept aloud and sat with him on the ground, silent, for seven days and nights, overcome with grief (2:13).

After Job finally broke the silence, each friend delivered a flowery speech on Job's dilemma. There are three cycles of speeches in all, with Eliphaz, Bildad and Zophar taking turns, allowing Job to respond to each. Eliphaz, who led off, had strong and noble ideas. Bildad was briefer and slightly less sympathetic. Zophar (who did not speak in the third cycle) showed passion and fire.

The friends seemed to build up in emotional intensity. In the first cycle (chapters 4–14), they showed hope of winning Job over to their point of view. In the second cycle (chapters 15–21), the speeches grew more severe and threatening. And by the time of the concluding speeches (chapters 22–25), Job's friends were making direct accusations against him.

■ A FLAWED THEORY ABOUT SUFFERING
Job's friends believed in a God of love and fairness; their arguments started from that fact. Surely a just God would not allow an *innocent* man to suffer so much, they reasoned. Most of their comments boil down to one simple theory: Job must have committed some great crime for which God was punishing him. All three believed that good people prosper and bad people suffer; therefore, suffering must betray some hidden sin.

"Surely God does not reject a blameless man or strengthen the hands of evildoers," they said to Job (8:20). Repent, they admonished him, and God will forgive and restore you. Their words got this response from Job: "You . . . smear me with lies; you are worthless physicians, all of you!" (13:4). Job also believed in a loving God, but he knew he was innocent.

When God finally made his appearance, he dismissed the three friends in one sentence to Eliphaz, "I am angry with you and your two friends, because you have not spoken of me what is right, as my servant Job has" (42:7).

Although the Bible elsewhere gives examples of suffering that resulted from a person's sin, Job clearly shows that such a theory cannot be applied in every case. (For a related discussion, see "Healthier, Wealthier and Wiser", page 158.) It is not for us to try to reason out the specific cause of a person's suffering; God reserves that knowledge for himself.

□ LIFE QUESTIONS:
What is the most "unfair" thing that has ever happened to you? How did it affect the way you thought about God?

---

b 29 Or my righteousness still stands

[8]The eye that now sees me will see me no
  longer;
    you will look for me, but I will be no more.
[9]As a cloud vanishes and is gone,
    so he who goes down to the grave[a] does
      not return.
[10]He will never come to his house again;
    his place will know him no more.

[11]"Therefore I will not keep silent;
    I will speak out in the anguish of my spirit,
    I will complain in the bitterness of my soul.
[12]Am I the sea, or the monster of the deep,
    that you put me under guard?
[13]When I think my bed will comfort me
    and my couch will ease my complaint,
[14]even then you frighten me with dreams
    and terrify me with visions,
[15]so that I prefer strangling and death,
    rather than this body of mine.
[16]I despise my life; I would not live for ever.
    Let me alone; my days have no meaning.

[17]"What is man that you make so much of him,
    that you give him so much attention,
[18]that you examine him every morning
    and test him every moment?
[19]Will you never look away from me,
    or let me alone even for an instant?
[20]If I have sinned, what have I done to you,
    O watcher of men?
  Why have you made me your target?
    Have I become a burden to you?[b]
[21]Why do you not pardon my offences
    and forgive my sins?
  For I shall soon lie down in the dust;
    you will search for me, but I shall be no
      more."

■ Bildad

8 Then Bildad the Shuhite replied:

[2]"How long will you say such things?
    Your words are a blustering wind.
[3]Does God pervert justice?
    Does the Almighty pervert what is right?
[4]When your children sinned against him,
    he gave them over to the penalty of their sin.
[5]But if you will look to God
    and plead with the Almighty,
[6]if you are pure and upright,
    even now he will rouse himself on your
      behalf
    and restore you to your rightful place.
[7]Your beginnings will seem humble,
    so prosperous will your future be.

[8]"Ask the former generations
    and find out what their fathers learned,
[9]for we were born only yesterday and know
      nothing,
    and our days on earth are but a shadow.
[10]Will they not instruct you and tell you?
    Will they not bring forth words from their
      understanding?
[11]Can papyrus grow tall where there is no marsh?

Can reeds thrive without water?
[12]While still growing and uncut,
    they wither more quickly than grass.

**8:4 ■ A MIXTURE OF TRUE AND
FALSE**
Although God rejected the overall force of their
arguments, Job's three friends said some things
that were totally false and others that were true. In
this case, Bildad appealed to common sense,
("Surely God does not reject a blameless man",
verse 20), implying that Job sinned to deserve his
suffering. But God specifically had called Job
"blameless and upright" (2:3). Elsewhere, a
statement by Eliphaz (5:11–13) is quoted
approvingly in the New Testament (1 Corinthians
3:19).

---

[13]Such is the destiny of all who forget God;
    so perishes the hope of the godless.
[14]What he trusts in is fragile;[a]
    what he relies on is a spider's web.
[15]He leans on his web, but it gives way;
    he clings to it, but it does not hold.
[16]He is like a well-watered plant in the sunshine,
    spreading its shoots over the garden;
[17]it entwines its roots around a pile of rocks
    and looks for a place among the stones.
[18]But when it is torn from its spot,
    that place disowns it and says, 'I never saw
      you.'
[19]Surely its life withers away,
    and[b] from the soil other plants grow.

[20]"Surely God does not reject a blameless man
    or strengthen the hands of evildoers.
[21]He will yet fill your mouth with laughter
    and your lips with shouts of joy.
[22]Your enemies will be clothed in shame,
    and the tents of the wicked will be no
      more."

■ Job

9 Then Job replied:

[2]"Indeed, I know that this is true.
    But how can a mortal be righteous before
      God?
[3]Though one wished to dispute with him,
    he could not answer him one time out of a
      thousand.
[4]His wisdom is profound, his power is vast.
    Who has resisted him and come out
      unscathed?
[5]He moves mountains without their knowing it
    and overturns them in his anger.
[6]He shakes the earth from its place
    and makes its pillars tremble.
[7]He speaks to the sun and it does not shine;
    he seals off the light of the stars.
[8]He alone stretches out the heavens
    and treads on the waves of the sea.
[9]He is the Maker of the Bear and Orion,

---

[a]9 Hebrew Sheol   [b]20 A few manuscripts of the Masoretic Text, an ancient Hebrew scribal tradition and Septuagint; most manuscripts of the Masoretic
Text I have become a burden to myself.   [a]14 The meaning of the Hebrew for this word is uncertain.   [b]19 Or Surely all the joy it has / is that

the Pleiades and the constellations of the
south.
¹⁰He performs wonders that cannot be fathomed,
miracles that cannot be counted.
¹¹When he passes me, I cannot see him;
when he goes by, I cannot perceive him.
¹²If he snatches away, who can stop him?
Who can say to him, 'What are you doing?'
¹³God does not restrain his anger;
even the cohorts of Rahab cowered at his
feet.

9:4 ■ ARMS TOO SHORT

A gospel musical based on the book of Job took
the title "Arms Too Short to Box with God". From
the beginning Job knew he didn't stand a chance
in a dispute with God. Moreover, he wasn't sure
what to dispute — much of the time Job
demonstrated a better grasp of theology than his
friends. (For example, his words in this chapter
bear striking resemblance to what God says at the
end of the book.) But good insights did not relieve
Job's sense of being abandoned by God. His
crisis of faith was more personal than intellectual.

¹⁴"How then can I dispute with him?
How can I find words to argue with him?
¹⁵Though I were innocent, I could not answer
him;
I could only plead with my Judge for mercy.
¹⁶Even if I summoned him and he responded,
I do not believe he would give me a hearing.
¹⁷He would crush me with a storm
and multiply my wounds for no reason.
¹⁸He would not let me regain my breath
but would overwhelm me with misery.
¹⁹If it is a matter of strength, he is mighty!
And if it is a matter of justice, who will
summon him?ᵃ
²⁰Even if I were innocent, my mouth would
condemn me;
if I were blameless, it would pronounce me
guilty.
²¹"Although I am blameless,
I have no concern for myself;
I despise my own life.
²²It is all the same; that is why I say,
'He destroys both the blameless and the
wicked.'
²³When a scourge brings sudden death,
he mocks the despair of the innocent.
²⁴When a land falls into the hands of the wicked,
he blindfolds its judges.
If it is not he, then who is it?
²⁵"My days are swifter than a runner;
they fly away without a glimpse of joy.
²⁶They skim past like boats of papyrus,
like eagles swooping down on their prey.
²⁷If I say, 'I will forget my complaint,
I will change my expression, and smile,'
²⁸I still dread all my sufferings,
for I know you will not hold me innocent.

²⁹Since I am already found guilty,
why should I struggle in vain?
³⁰Even if I washed myself with soapᵇ
and my hands with washing soda,
³¹you would plunge me into a slime pit
so that even my clothes would detest me.
³²"He is not a man like me that I might answer
him,
that we might confront each other in court.
³³If only there were someone to arbitrate
between us,
to lay his hand upon us both,
³⁴someone to remove God's rod from me,
so that his terror would frighten me no
more.
³⁵Then I would speak up without fear of him,
but as it now stands with me, I cannot.

9:33 ■ LOOKING FOR AN ARBITRATOR

Job recognised the enormous gulf between God
and people. He poignantly asked for an arbitrator
"to lay his hand upon us both". A few such
comments of Job, expressing great longing for an
advocate, found their full realisation in Jesus, who
was called the "one mediator between God and
men" (1 Timothy 2:5).

10 "I loathe my very life;
therefore I will give free rein to my
complaint
and speak out in the bitterness of my soul.
²I will say to God: Do not condemn me,
but tell me what charges you have against
me.
³Does it please you to oppress me,
to spurn the work of your hands,
while you smile on the schemes of the
wicked?
⁴Do you have eyes of flesh?
Do you see as a mortal sees?
⁵Are your days like those of a mortal
or your years like those of a man,
⁶that you must search out my faults
and probe after my sin —
⁷though you know that I am not guilty
and that no-one can rescue me from your
hand?
⁸"Your hands shaped me and made me.
Will you now turn and destroy me?
⁹Remember that you moulded me like clay.
Will you now turn me to dust again?
¹⁰Did you not pour me out like milk
and curdle me like cheese,
¹¹clothe me with skin and flesh
and knit me together with bones and sinews?
¹²You gave me life and showed me kindness,
and in your providence watched over my
spirit.
¹³"But this is what you concealed in your heart,
and I know that this was in your mind:

ᵃ 19 See Septuagint; Hebrew me.   ᵇ 30 Or snow

¹⁴If I sinned, you would be watching me
    and would not let my offence go unpunished.

10:8 ■ FOND MEMORIES
Author Joseph Bayly, who watched three of his
sons die in their youth, said, "Don't forget in the
darkness what you've learned in the light." Job
lived by this same principle. Even though he could
not understand God at the moment, he never
belittled the blessings he had already received. In
a fit of anger, a divorcée might say, "Oh, I never
really loved him anyway"; Job never once turned
his back on God in that way.

¹⁵If I am guilty—woe to me!
    Even if I am innocent, I cannot lift my head,
  for I am full of shame
    and drowned in*a* my affliction.
¹⁶If I hold my head high, you stalk me like a lion
    and again display your awesome power
      against me.
¹⁷You bring new witnesses against me
    and increase your anger towards me;
    your forces come against me wave upon
      wave.

¹⁸"Why then did you bring me out of the womb?
    I wish I had died before any eye saw me.
¹⁹If only I had never come into being,
    or had been carried straight from the womb
      to the grave!
²⁰Are not my few days almost over?
    Turn away from me so that I can have a
      moment's joy
²¹before I go to the place of no return,
    to the land of gloom and deep shadow,*b*
²²to the land of deepest night,
    of deep shadow and disorder,
    where even the light is like darkness."

■ Zophar

11

Then Zophar the Naamathite replied:

²"Are all these words to go unanswered?
  Is this talker to be vindicated?
³Will your idle talk reduce men to silence?
  Will no-one rebuke you when you mock?
⁴You say to God, 'My beliefs are flawless
  and I am pure in your sight.'
⁵Oh, how I wish that God would speak,
  that he would open his lips against you
⁶and disclose to you the secrets of wisdom,
  for true wisdom has two sides.
  Know this: God has even forgotten some of
    your sin.

⁷"Can you fathom the mysteries of God?
  Can you probe the limits of the Almighty?
⁸They are higher than the heavens—what can
    you do?
  They are deeper than the depths of the
    grave*a*—what can you know?
⁹Their measure is longer than the earth
  and wider than the sea.

¹⁰"If he comes along and confines you in prison
    and convenes a court, who can oppose him?
¹¹Surely he recognises deceitful men;
    and when he sees evil, does he not take
      note?
¹²But a witless man can no more become wise
    than a wild donkey's colt can be born a
      man.*b*

¹³"Yet if you devote your heart to him
    and stretch out your hands to him,
¹⁴if you put away the sin that is in your hand
    and allow no evil to dwell in your tent,
¹⁵then you will lift up your face without shame;
    you will stand firm and without fear.
¹⁶You will surely forget your trouble,
    recalling it only as waters gone by.
¹⁷Life will be brighter than noonday,
    and darkness will become like morning.
¹⁸You will be secure, because there is hope;
    you will look about you and take your rest in
      safety.
¹⁹You will lie down, with no-one to make you
      afraid,
    and many will court your favour.
²⁰But the eyes of the wicked will fail,
    and escape will elude them;
    their hope will become a dying gasp."

11:14 ■ UNFAIR ACCUSATION
Zophar, the least tactful of the three friends, made
direct accusations against Job, repeating the
common refrain that Job was being punished for
some sin. In a speech recorded in chapter 12,
Job agreed in principle that God rewards the
righteous and punishes the wicked. But in his own
case he knew he was innocent. No matter how
convincing their arguments, he had to protest
against them.

■ Job

12

Then Job replied:

²"Doubtless you are the people,
  and wisdom will die with you!
³But I have a mind as well as you;
  I am not inferior to you.
  Who does not know all these things?

⁴"I have become a laughing-stock to my friends,
    though I called upon God and he
      answered—
    a mere laughing-stock, though righteous and
      blameless!
⁵Men at ease have contempt for misfortune
    as the fate of those whose feet are slipping.
⁶The tents of marauders are undisturbed,
    and those who provoke God are secure—
    those who carry their god in their hands.*a*

⁷"But ask the animals, and they will teach you,
    or the birds of the air, and they will tell you;
⁸or speak to the earth, and it will teach you,
    or let the fish of the sea inform you.

*a*15 Or and aware of   *b*21 Or and the shadow of death; also in verse 22   *a*8 Hebrew *than Sheol*   *b*12 Or *wild donkey can be born tame*
*a*6 Or *secure / in what God's hand brings them*

9Which of all these does not know
  that the hand of the LORD has done this?

12:5 ■ CONTEMPT, NOT SYMPATHY

After his release from a Siberian prison, Alexander Solzhenitsyn gained overnight fame as a novelist. One day he was summoned to the opulent office of an admiring Soviet official. In those comfortable surroundings, the agony of the Soviet prison camps seemed very far away. "It is impossible for a man who is warm to understand one who is cold," he concluded. Job accused his friends – and even God – of the same lack of sympathy. His complaint against God would be answered finally by the Incarnation, when God voluntarily subjected himself to cold, hunger, and every other human misfortune.

10In his hand is the life of every creature
  and the breath of all mankind.
11Does not the ear test words
  as the tongue tastes food?
12Is not wisdom found among the aged?
  Does not long life bring understanding?

13"To God belong wisdom and power;
  counsel and understanding are his.
14What he tears down cannot be rebuilt;
  the man he imprisons cannot be released.
15If he holds back the waters, there is drought;
  if he lets them loose, they devastate the land.
16To him belong strength and victory;
  both deceived and deceiver are his.
17He leads counsellors away stripped
  and makes fools of judges.
18He takes off the shackles put on by kings
  and ties a loincloth*b* round their waist.
19He leads priests away stripped
  and overthrows men long established.
20He silences the lips of trusted advisers
  and takes away the discernment of elders.
21He pours contempt on nobles
  and disarms the mighty.
22He reveals the deep things of darkness
  and brings deep shadows into the light.
23He makes nations great, and destroys them;
  he enlarges nations, and disperses them.
24He deprives the leaders of the earth of their reason;
  he sends them wandering through a trackless waste.
25They grope in darkness with no light;
  he makes them stagger like drunkards.

13 "My eyes have seen all this,
    my ears have heard and understood it.
2What you know, I also know;
  I am not inferior to you.
3But I desire to speak to the Almighty
  and to argue my case with God.
4You, however, smear me with lies;
  you are worthless physicians, all of you!
5If only you would be altogether silent!
  For you, that would be wisdom.

6Hear now my argument;
  listen to the plea of my lips.
7Will you speak wickedly on God's behalf?
  Will you speak deceitfully for him?
8Will you show him partiality?
  Will you argue the case for God?
9Would it turn out well if he examined you?
  Could you deceive him as you might deceive men?
10He would surely rebuke you
  if you secretly showed partiality.
11Would not his splendour terrify you?
  Would not the dread of him fall on you?
12Your maxims are proverbs of ashes;
  your defences are defences of clay.

13"Keep silent and let me speak;
  then let come to me what may.
14Why do I put myself in jeopardy
  and take my life in my hands?
15Though he slay me, yet will I hope in him;
  I will surely*a* defend my ways to his face.
16Indeed, this will turn out for my deliverance,
  for no godless man would dare come before him!
17Listen carefully to my words;
  let your ears take in what I say.
18Now that I have prepared my case,
  I know I will be vindicated.
19Can anyone bring charges against me?
  If so, I will be silent and die.

13:15 ■ A DESPERATE HOPE

This statement more than any other shows the depth of Job's faith, and the reason he succeeded in God's challenge against Satan. He valued his faith in God even above his own life. He asked only for a "day in court", a chance to confront God personally and hear an explanation.

20"Only grant me these two things, O God,
  and then I will not hide from you:
21Withdraw your hand far from me,
  and stop frightening me with your terrors.
22Then summon me and I will answer,
  or let me speak, and you reply.
23How many wrongs and sins have I committed?
  Show me my offence and my sin.
24Why do you hide your face
  and consider me your enemy?
25Will you torment a wind-blown leaf?
  Will you chase after dry chaff?
26For you write down bitter things against me
  and make me inherit the sins of my youth.
27You fasten my feet in shackles;
  you keep close watch on all my paths
  by putting marks on the soles of my feet.

28"So man wastes away like something rotten,
  like a garment eaten by moths.

14 "Man born of woman
    is of few days and full of trouble.
2He springs up like a flower and withers away;
  like a fleeting shadow, he does not endure.

b 18 Or shackles of kings / and ties a belt   *a* 15 Or He will surely slay me; I have no hope – / yet I will

³Do you fix your eye on such a one?
  Will you bring him*ᵃ* before you for
    judgment?
⁴Who can bring what is pure from the impure?
  No-one!
⁵Man's days are determined;
  you have decreed the number of his months
    and have set limits he cannot exceed.
⁶So look away from him and let him alone,
  till he has put in his time like a hired man.

⁷"At least there is hope for a tree:
  If it is cut down, it will sprout again,
    and its new shoots will not fail.
⁸Its roots may grow old in the ground
  and its stump die in the soil,
⁹yet at the scent of water it will bud
  and put forth shoots like a plant.
¹⁰But man dies and is laid low;
  he breathes his last and is no more.
¹¹As water disappears from the sea
  or a river bed becomes parched and dry,
¹²so man lies down and does not rise;
  till the heavens are no more, men will not
    awake
  or be roused from their sleep.

¹³"If only you would hide me in the grave*ᵇ*
  and conceal me till your anger has passed!
  If only you would set me a time
    and then remember me!
¹⁴If a man dies, will he live again?
  All the days of my hard service
  I will wait for my renewal*ᶜ* to come.
¹⁵You will call and I will answer you;
  you will long for the creature your hands
    have made.
¹⁶Surely then you will count my steps
  but not keep track of my sin.
¹⁷My offences will be sealed up in a bag;
  you will cover over my sin.

¹⁸"But as a mountain erodes and crumbles
  and as a rock is moved from its place,
¹⁹as water wears away stones
  and torrents wash away the soil,
  so you destroy man's hope.
²⁰You overpower him once for all, and he is
    gone;
  you change his countenance and send him
    away.
²¹If his sons are honoured, he does not know it;
  if they are brought low, he does not see it.
²²He feels but the pain of his own body
  and mourns only for himself."

■ Eliphaz

15 Then Eliphaz the Temanite replied:

²"Would a wise man answer with empty notions
  or fill his belly with the hot east wind?
³Would he argue with useless words,
  with speeches that have no value?
⁴But you even undermine piety
  and hinder devotion to God.
⁵Your sin prompts your mouth;
  you adopt the tongue of the crafty.

⁶Your own mouth condemns you, not mine;
  your own lips testify against you.

15:4 ■ A SHOCKING LACK OF PIETY
Job minced no words in his complaints against
God. As a result, his friends criticised him for
undermining piety and hindering devotion to God.
Notably, in his summing-up speech God did not
condemn Job's varying moods; instead he
dismissed the pious words of Job's friends.
  Counsellors know that repressed feelings of
anger or disappointment don't just disappear; they
usually fester inside, and grow even more toxic.
Job expressed his feelings openly, much to his
friends' dismay.

---

⁷"Are you the first man ever born?
  Were you brought forth before the hills?
⁸Do you listen in on God's council?
  Do you limit wisdom to yourself?
⁹What do you know that we do not know?
  What insights do you have that we do not
    have?
¹⁰The grey-haired and the aged are on our side,
  men even older than your father.
¹¹Are God's consolations not enough for you,
  words spoken gently to you?
¹²Why has your heart carried you away,
  and why do your eyes flash,
¹³so that you vent your rage against God
  and pour out such words from your mouth?

¹⁴"What is man, that he could be pure,
  or one born of woman, that he could be
    righteous?
¹⁵If God places no trust in his holy ones,
  if even the heavens are not pure in his eyes,
¹⁶how much less man, who is vile and corrupt,
  who drinks up evil like water!

¹⁷"Listen to me and I will explain to you;
  let me tell you what I have seen,
¹⁸what wise men have declared,
  hiding nothing received from their fathers
¹⁹(to whom alone the land was given
  when no alien passed among them):
²⁰All his days the wicked man suffers torment,
  the ruthless through all the years stored up
    for him.
²¹Terrifying sounds fill his ears;
  when all seems well, marauders attack him.
²²He despairs of escaping the darkness;
  he is marked for the sword.
²³He wanders about—food for vultures;*ᵃ*
  he knows the day of darkness is at hand.
²⁴Distress and anguish fill him with terror;
  they overwhelm him, like a king poised to
    attack,
²⁵because he shakes his fist at God
  and vaunts himself against the Almighty,
²⁶defiantly charging against him
  with a thick, strong shield.

²⁷"Though his face is covered with fat

ᵃ3 Septuagint, Vulgate and Syriac; Hebrew me   *ᵇ13 Hebrew Sheol*   *ᶜ14 Or release*   *ᵃ23 Or about, looking for food*

and his waist bulges with flesh,
²⁸he will inhabit ruined towns
and houses where no-one lives,
houses crumbling to rubble.
²⁹He will no longer be rich and his wealth will
not endure,
nor will his possessions spread over the land.
³⁰He will not escape the darkness;
a flame will wither his shoots,
and the breath of God's mouth will carry him
away.
³¹Let him not deceive himself by trusting what is
worthless,
for he will get nothing in return.
³²Before his time he will be paid in full,
and his branches will not flourish.
³³He will be like a vine stripped of its unripe
grapes,
like an olive tree shedding its blossoms.
³⁴For the company of the godless will be barren,
and fire will consume the tents of those who
love bribes.
³⁵They conceive trouble and give birth to evil;
their womb fashions deceit."

■ Job

16   Then Job replied:

²"I have heard many things like these;
miserable comforters are you all!
³Will your long-winded speeches never end?
What ails you that you keep on arguing?
⁴I also could speak like you,
if you were in my place;
I could make fine speeches against you
and shake my head at you.
⁵But my mouth would encourage you;
comfort from my lips would bring you relief.

⁶"Yet if I speak, my pain is not relieved;
and if I refrain, it does not go away.
⁷Surely, O God, you have worn me out;
you have devastated my entire household.
⁸You have bound me—and it has become a
witness;
my gauntness rises up and testifies against
me.
⁹God assails me and tears me in his anger
and gnashes his teeth at me;
my opponent fastens on me his piercing
eyes.
¹⁰Men open their mouths to jeer at me;
they strike my cheek in scorn
and unite together against me.
¹¹God has turned me over to evil men
and thrown me into the clutches of the
wicked.
¹²All was well with me, but he shattered me;
he seized me by the neck and crushed me.
He has made me his target;
¹³   his archers surround me.
Without pity, he pierces my kidneys
and spills my gall on the ground.
¹⁴Again and again he bursts upon me;
he rushes at me like a warrior.

¹⁵"I have sewed sackcloth over my skin
and buried my brow in the dust.

16:9 ■ WHEN GOD SEEMS ANGRY

In his trauma, Job could not help feeling that he
was the object of God's anger. Many people who
undergo great pain feel the same. In Job's case,
however, we know that God was not angry with
him. God had held him up before Satan as "a man
who fears God and shuns evil" (1:8).

---

¹⁶My face is red with weeping,
deep shadows ring my eyes;
¹⁷yet my hands have been free of violence
and my prayer is pure.

¹⁸"O earth, do not cover my blood;
may my cry never be laid to rest!
¹⁹Even now my witness is in heaven;
my advocate is on high.
²⁰My intercessor is my friend^a
as my eyes pour out tears to God;
²¹on behalf of a man he pleads with God
as a man pleads for his friend.

²²"Only a few years will pass
before I go on the journey of no return.

17   ¹My spirit is broken,
my days are cut short,
the grave awaits me.
²Surely mockers surround me;
my eyes must dwell on their hostility.

³"Give me, O God, the pledge you demand.
Who else will put up security for me?
⁴You have closed their minds to understanding;
therefore you will not let them triumph.
⁵If a man denounces his friends for reward,
the eyes of his children will fail.

⁶"God has made me a byword to everyone,
a man in whose face people spit.
⁷My eyes have grown dim with grief;
my whole frame is but a shadow.
⁸Upright men are appalled at this;
the innocent are aroused against the ungodly.
⁹Nevertheless, the righteous will hold to their
ways,
and those with clean hands will grow
stronger.

¹⁰"But come on, all of you, try again!
I will not find a wise man among you.
¹¹My days have passed, my plans are shattered,
and so are the desires of my heart.
¹²These men turn night into day;
in the face of darkness they say, 'Light is
near.'
¹³If the only home I hope for is the grave,^a
if I spread out my bed in darkness,
¹⁴if I say to corruption, 'You are my father,'
and to the worm, 'My mother' or 'My sister',
¹⁵where then is my hope?
Who can see any hope for me?
¹⁶Will it go down to the gates of death?^b
Will we descend together into the dust?"

---

^a20 Or My friends treat me with scorn   ^a13 Hebrew Sheol   ^b16 Hebrew to Sheol

■ Bildad

18
Then Bildad the Shuhite replied:

2"When will you end these speeches?
  Be sensible, and then we can talk.

17:12 ■ A WRONG TIME FOR CHEER
Falsely cheerful advice can actually make a
suffering person even more discouraged. Job's
sentiments here are echoed in a verse from
Proverbs: "Like one who takes away a garment on
a cold day, or like vinegar poured on soda, is one
who sings songs to a heavy heart" (25:20).

3Why are we regarded as cattle
  and considered stupid in your sight?
4You who tear yourself to pieces in your anger,
  is the earth to be abandoned for your sake?
  Or must the rocks be moved from their
    place?

5"The lamp of the wicked is snuffed out;
  the flame of his fire stops burning.
6The light in his tent becomes dark;
  the lamp beside him goes out.
7The vigour of his step is weakened;
  his own schemes throw him down.
8His feet thrust him into a net
  and he wanders into its mesh.
9A trap seizes him by the heel;
  a snare holds him fast.
10A noose is hidden for him on the ground;
  a trap lies in his path.
11Terrors startle him on every side
  and dog his every step.
12Calamity is hungry for him;
  disaster is ready for him when he falls.
13It eats away parts of his skin;
  death's firstborn devours his limbs.
14He is torn from the security of his tent
  and marched off to the king of terrors.
15Fire resides*a* in his tent;
  burning sulphur is scattered over his
    dwelling.
16His roots dry up below
  and his branches wither above.
17The memory of him perishes from the earth;
  he has no name in the land.
18He is driven from light into darkness
  and is banished from the world.
19He has no offspring or descendants among his
    people,
  no survivor where once he lived.
20Men of the west are appalled at his fate;
  men of the east are seized with horror.
21Surely such is the dwelling of an evil man;
  such is the place of one who knows not
    God."

■ Job

19
Then Job replied:

2"How long will you torment me
  and crush me with words?

3Ten times now you have reproached me;
  shamelessly you attack me.

18:13 ■ BATTLE OF WORDS
After Job lashed out at his friends (see 17:10–12),
Bildad retorted in kind, followed by Zophar in
chapter 20. These two speeches, among the
nastiest in the book, show the danger of bitter
argument about anything, including theology.
Friends who were overwhelmed with compassion
when they first visited Job are now seen cruelly
heaping more grief upon him – just to defend their
(faulty) theological point.

4If it is true that I have gone astray,
  my error remains my concern alone.
5If indeed you would exalt yourselves above me
  and use my humiliation against me,
6then know that God has wronged me
  and drawn his net around me.

7"Though I cry, 'I've been wronged!' I get no
    response;
  though I call for help, there is no justice.
8He has blocked my way so that I cannot pass;
  he has shrouded my paths in darkness.
9He has stripped me of my honour
  and removed the crown from my head.
10He tears me down on every side till I am gone;
  he uproots my hope like a tree.
11His anger burns against me;
  he counts me among his enemies.
12His troops advance in force;
  they build a siege ramp against me
  and encamp around my tent.

13"He has alienated my brothers from me;
  my acquaintances are completely estranged
    from me.
14My kinsmen have gone away;
  my friends have forgotten me.
15My guests and my maidservants count me a
    stranger;
  they look upon me as an alien.
16I summon my servant, but he does not answer,
  though I beg him with my own mouth.
17My breath is offensive to my wife;
  I am loathsome to my own brothers.
18Even the little boys scorn me;
  when I appear, they ridicule me.
19All my intimate friends detest me;
  those I love have turned against me.
20I am nothing but skin and bones;
  I have escaped by only the skin of my
    teeth.*a*

21"Have pity on me, my friends, have pity,
  for the hand of God has struck me.
22Why do you pursue me as God does?
  Will you never get enough of my flesh?

23"Oh, that my words were recorded,
  that they were written on a scroll,
24that they were inscribed with an iron tool on*b*
    lead,

---

a 15 Or *Nothing he had remains*   *a* 20 Or *only my gums*   *b* 24 Or *and*

or engraved in rock for ever!
²⁵I know that my Redeemer^c lives,
  and that in the end he will stand upon the
    earth.^d
²⁶And after my skin has been destroyed,
  yet^e in^f my flesh I will see God;
²⁷I myself will see him
  with my own eyes—I, and not another.
  How my heart yearns within me!

²⁸"If you say, 'How we will hound him,
  since the root of the trouble lies in him,'^g

> **19:25 ■ AN OUTBURST OF HOPE**
> In the midst of his deepest agony, Job expressed
> astonishing words of hope. This prophecy
> expands on two other flashes of hope (9:33;
> 16:19–21). Job did not try to hide his despair and
> anguish, but, as this verse shows, the trials never
> crushed all of his hope.

²⁹you should fear the sword yourselves;
  for wrath will bring punishment by the
    sword,
  and then you will know that there is
    judgment."^b

■ Zophar

20 Then Zophar the Naamathite replied:

²"My troubled thoughts prompt me to answer
  because I am greatly disturbed.
³I hear a rebuke that dishonours me,
  and my understanding inspires me to reply.

⁴"Surely you know how it has been from of old,
  ever since man^a was placed on the earth,
⁵that the mirth of the wicked is brief,
  the joy of the godless lasts but a moment.
⁶Though his pride reaches to the heavens
  and his head touches the clouds,
⁷he will perish for ever, like his own dung;
  those who have seen him will say, 'Where is
    he?'
⁸Like a dream he flies away, no more to be
    found,
  banished like a vision of the night.
⁹The eye that saw him will not see him again;
  his place will look on him no more.
¹⁰His children must make amends to the poor;
  his own hands must give back his wealth.
¹¹The youthful vigour that fills his bones
  will lie with him in the dust.

¹²"Though evil is sweet in his mouth
  and he hides it under his tongue,
¹³though he cannot bear to let it go
  and keeps it in his mouth,
¹⁴yet his food will turn sour in his stomach;
  it will become the venom of serpents within
    him.
¹⁵He will spit out the riches he swallowed;
  God will make his stomach vomit them up.
¹⁶He will suck the poison of serpents;

the fangs of an adder will kill him.
¹⁷He will not enjoy the streams,
  the rivers flowing with honey and cream.
¹⁸What he toiled for he must give back uneaten;
  he will not enjoy the profit from his trading.
¹⁹For he has oppressed the poor and left them
    destitute;
  he has seized houses he did not build.

²⁰"Surely he will have no respite from his
    craving;
  he cannot save himself by his treasure.
²¹Nothing is left for him to devour;
  his prosperity will not endure.
²²In the midst of his plenty, distress will overtake
    him;
  the full force of misery will come upon him.
²³When he has filled his belly,
  God will vent his burning anger against him
  and rain down his blows upon him.
²⁴Though he flees from an iron weapon,
  a bronze-tipped arrow pierces him.
²⁵He pulls it out of his back,
  the gleaming point out of his liver.
  Terrors will come over him;
²⁶ total darkness lies in wait for his treasures.
  A fire unfanned will consume him
  and devour what is left in his tent.
²⁷The heavens will expose his guilt;
  the earth will rise up against him.
²⁸A flood will carry off his house,
  rushing waters^b on the day of God's wrath.
²⁹Such is the fate God allots the wicked,
  the heritage appointed for them by God."

■ Job

21 Then Job replied:

²"Listen carefully to my words;
  let this be the consolation you give me.
³Bear with me while I speak,
  and after I have spoken, mock on.

⁴"Is my complaint directed to man?
  Why should I not be impatient?
⁵Look at me and be astonished;
  clap your hand over your mouth.
⁶When I think about this, I am terrified;
  trembling seizes my body.
⁷Why do the wicked live on,
  growing old and increasing in power?
⁸They see their children established around
    them,
  their offspring before their eyes.
⁹Their homes are safe and free from fear;
  the rod of God is not upon them.
¹⁰Their bulls never fail to breed;
  their cows calve and do not miscarry.
¹¹They send forth their children as a flock;
  their little ones dance about.
¹²They sing to the music of tambourine and harp;
  they make merry to the sound of the flute.
¹³They spend their years in prosperity
  and go down to the grave^a in peace.^b
¹⁴Yet they say to God, 'Leave us alone!

---

^c25 Or defender   ^d25 Or upon my grave   ^e26 Or And after I awake, / though this body, has been destroyed, / then   ^f26 Or / apart from
^g28 Many Hebrew manuscripts, Septuagint and Vulgate; most Hebrew manuscripts me   ^b29 Or / that you may come to know the Almighty
^a4 Or Adam   ^b28 Or The possessions in his house will be carried off, / washed away   ^a13 Hebrew Sheol   ^b13 Or in an instant

We have no desire to know your ways.
¹⁵Who is the Almighty, that we should serve him?
What would we gain by praying to him?'
¹⁶But their prosperity is not in their own hands,
so I stand aloof from the counsel of the
wicked.

21:7 ■ WICKED PEOPLE PROSPER

In most of his speeches Job accepted the general
principle that evil people suffer punishment in this
life. But in this speech he began to question that
theory. He cited examples of wicked people who
lived comfortable, successful lives. His meandering
thoughts proved so convincing to him that he
concluded his friends' advice was "nonsense"
(verse 34).

¹⁷"Yet how often is the lamp of the wicked
snuffed out?
How often does calamity come upon them,
the fate God allots in his anger?
¹⁸How often are they like straw before the wind,
like chaff swept away by a gale?
¹⁹⌊It is said,⌋ 'God stores up a man's punishment
for his sons.'
Let him repay the man himself, so that he
will know it!
²⁰Let his own eyes see his destruction;
let him drink of the wrath of the Almighty.ᶜ
²¹For what does he care about the family he
leaves behind
when his allotted months come to an end?

²²"Can anyone teach knowledge to God,
since he judges even the highest?
²³One man dies in full vigour,
completely secure and at ease,
²⁴his bodyᵈ well nourished,
his bones rich with marrow.
²⁵Another man dies in bitterness of soul,
never having enjoyed anything good.
²⁶Side by side they lie in the dust,
and worms cover them both.

²⁷"I know full well what you are thinking,
the schemes by which you would wrong me.
²⁸You say, 'Where now is the great man's house,
the tents where wicked men lived?'
²⁹Have you never questioned those who travel?
Have you paid no regard to their accounts—
³⁰that the evil man is spared from the day of
calamity,
that he is delivered fromᵉ the day of wrath?
³¹Who denounces his conduct to his face?
Who repays him for what he has done?
³²He is carried to the grave,
and watch is kept over his tomb.
³³The soil in the valley is sweet to him;
all men follow after him,
and a countless throng goesᶠ before him.

³⁴"So how can you console me with your
nonsense?
Nothing is left of your answers but
falsehood!"

■ Eliphaz

22

Then Eliphaz the Temanite replied:

²"Can a man be of benefit to God?
Can even a wise man benefit him?
³What pleasure would it give the Almighty if
you were righteous?
What would he gain if your ways were
blameless?

⁴"Is it for your piety that he rebukes you
and brings charges against you?
⁵Is not your wickedness great?
Are not your sins endless?
⁶You demanded security from your brothers for
no reason;
you stripped men of their clothing, leaving
them naked.
⁷You gave no water to the weary
and you withheld food from the hungry,
⁸though you were a powerful man, owning
land—
an honoured man, living on it.
⁹And you sent widows away empty-handed
and broke the strength of the fatherless.
¹⁰That is why snares are all around you,
why sudden peril terrifies you,
¹¹why it is so dark that you cannot see,
and why a flood of water covers you.

22:6 ■ THE ATTACKS GET PERSONAL

Unable to convince Job through philosophising,
Eliphaz shifted to more personal attacks against
Job's behaviour. These arguments were perhaps
the unkindest of all, and Job specifically refuted
each one in his closing speech (chapters 29–31).

¹²"Is not God in the heights of heaven?
And see how lofty are the highest stars!
¹³Yet you say, 'What does God know?
Does he judge through such darkness?
¹⁴Thick clouds veil him, so he does not see us
as he goes about in the vaulted heavens.'
¹⁵Will you keep to the old path
that evil men have trod?
¹⁶They were carried off before their time,
their foundations washed away by a flood.
¹⁷They said to God, 'Leave us alone!
What can the Almighty do to us?'
¹⁸Yet it was he who filled their houses with good
things,
so I stand aloof from the counsel of the
wicked.

¹⁹"The righteous see their ruin and rejoice;
the innocent mock them, saying,
²⁰'Surely our foes are destroyed,
and fire devours their wealth.'

²¹"Submit to God and be at peace with him;
in this way prosperity will come to you.
²²Accept instruction from his mouth
and lay up his words in your heart.
²³If you return to the Almighty, you will be
restored:

ᶜ 17–20 Verses 17 and 18 may be taken as exclamations and 19 and 20 as declarations.   ᵈ 24 The meaning of the Hebrew for this word is uncertain.
ᵉ 30 Or man is reserved for the day of calamity, / that he is brought forth to   ᶠ 33 Or / as a countless throng went

If you remove wickedness far from your tent
24and assign your nuggets to the dust,
    your gold of Ophir to the rocks in the
        ravines,
25then the Almighty will be your gold,
    the choicest silver for you.
26Surely then you will find delight in the
        Almighty
    and will lift up your face to God.
27You will pray to him, and he will hear you,
    and you will fulfil your vows.
28What you decide on will be done,
    and light will shine on your ways.
29When men are brought low and you say, 'Lift
        them up!'
    then he will save the downcast.
30He will deliver even one who is not innocent,
    who will be delivered through the cleanness
        of your hands."

■ Job

23

Then Job replied:

2"Even today my complaint is bitter;
    his hand*a* is heavy in spite of*b* my
        groaning.
3If only I knew where to find him;
    if only I could go to his dwelling!
4I would state my case before him
    and fill my mouth with arguments.
5I would find out what he would answer me,
    and consider what he would say.
6Would he oppose me with great power?
    No, he would not press charges against me.
7There an upright man could present his case
        before him,
    and I would be delivered for ever from my
        judge.

8"But if I go to the east, he is not there;
    if I go to the west, I do not find him.
9When he is at work in the north, I do not see
        him;
    when he turns to the south, I catch no
        glimpse of him.
10But he knows the way that I take;
    when he has tested me, I shall come forth as
        gold.
11My feet have closely followed his steps;
    I have kept to his way without turning aside.
12I have not departed from the commands of his
        lips;
    I have treasured the words of his mouth
        more than my daily bread.

13"But he stands alone, and who can oppose him?
    He does whatever he pleases.
14He carries out his decree against me,
    and many such plans he still has in store.
15That is why I am terrified before him;
    when I think of all this, I fear him.
16God has made my heart faint;
    the Almighty has terrified me.
17Yet I am not silenced by the darkness,
    by the thick darkness that covers my face.

24

"Why does the Almighty not set times for
judgment?
    Why must those who know him look in vain
        for such days?

23:13 ■ UNSTABLE GROUND

Job's friends hammered away at consistent
themes whereas Job, like most people in pain,
found himself shifting back and forth, unsure what
to believe. In the first paragraph of chapter 23, he
is ready to take God on; in the second, he
wonders if he'll ever find God to state his case; in
the third, he trembles to think what might happen
if he actually does locate God!

2Men move boundary stones;
    they pasture flocks they have stolen.
3They drive away the orphan's donkey
    and take the widow's ox in pledge.
4They thrust the needy from the path
    and force all the poor of the land into hiding.
5Like wild donkeys in the desert,
    the poor go about their labour of foraging
        food;
    the wasteland provides food for their
        children.
6They gather fodder in the fields
    and glean in the vineyards of the wicked.
7Lacking clothes, they spend the night naked;
    they have nothing to cover themselves in the
        cold.
8They are drenched by mountain rains
    and hug the rocks for lack of shelter.
9The fatherless child is snatched from the breast;
    the infant of the poor is seized for a debt.
10Lacking clothes, they go about naked;
    they carry the sheaves, but still go hungry.
11They crush olives among the terraces;*a*
    they tread the winepresses, yet suffer thirst.
12The groans of the dying rise from the city,
    and the souls of the wounded cry out for
        help.
    But God charges no-one with wrongdoing.

13"There are those who rebel against the light,
    who do not know its ways
    or stay in its paths.
14When daylight is gone, the murderer rises up
    and kills the poor and needy;
    in the night he steals forth like a thief.
15The eye of the adulterer watches for dusk;
    he thinks, 'No eye will see me,'
    and he keeps his face concealed.
16In the dark, men break into houses,
    but by day they shut themselves in;
    they want nothing to do with the light.
17For all of them, deep darkness is their
        morning;*b*
    they make friends with the terrors of
        darkness.*c*

18"Yet they are foam on the surface of the water;
    their portion of the land is cursed,
    so that no-one goes to the vineyards.

---

*a*2 Septuagint and Syriac; Hebrew / *the hand on me*   *b*2 Or *heavy on me in*
word is uncertain.   *b*17 Or *them, their morning is like the shadow of death*

*a*11 Or *olives between the millstones*; the meaning of the Hebrew for this
*c*17 Or *of the shadow of death*

¹⁹As heat and drought snatch away the melted
    snow,
    so the grave*ᵈ* snatches away those who have
        sinned.
²⁰The womb forgets them,
    the worm feasts on them;
    evil men are no longer remembered
    but are broken like a tree.
²¹They prey on the barren and childless woman,
    and to the widow show no kindness.
²²But God drags away the mighty by his power;
    though they become established, they have
        no assurance of life.
²³He may let them rest in a feeling of security,
    but his eyes are on their ways.
²⁴For a little while they are exalted, and then
        they are gone;
    they are brought low and gathered up like all
        others;
    they are cut off like ears of corn.

²⁵"If this is not so, who can prove me false
    and reduce my words to nothing?"

■ Bildad

25

Then Bildad the Shuhite replied:

²"Dominion and awe belong to God;
    he establishes order in the heights of heaven.
³Can his forces be numbered?
    Upon whom does his light not rise?
⁴How then can a man be righteous before God?
    How can one born of woman be pure?
⁵If even the moon is not bright
    and the stars are not pure in his eyes,
⁶how much less man, who is but a maggot—
    a son of man, who is only a worm!"

25:6 ■ WHERE IS GOD?
In the speech recorded in chapters 23–24, Job
movingly described the feeling of God's absence
at his time of greatest need. God must also seem
absent to the poor, the fatherless, and all those
suffering without relief, he said. Bildad replied with
the shortest speech in the book (chapter 25). He
questioned whether any person ("who is but a
maggot . . . a worm") had the right to challenge
God so boldly.

■ Job

26

Then Job replied:

²"How you have helped the powerless!
    How you have saved the arm that is feeble!
³What advice you have offered to one without
        wisdom!
    And what great insight you have displayed!
⁴Who has helped you utter these words?
    And whose spirit spoke from your mouth?

⁵"The dead are in deep anguish,
    those beneath the waters and all that live in
        them.
⁶Death*ᵃ* is naked before God;

Destruction*ᵇ* lies uncovered.
⁷He spreads out the northern ⌞skies⌟ over empty
        space;
    he suspends the earth over nothing.
⁸He wraps up the waters in his clouds,
    yet the clouds do not burst under their
        weight.
⁹He covers the face of the full moon,
    spreading his clouds over it.
¹⁰He marks out the horizon on the face of the
        waters
    for a boundary between light and darkness.
¹¹The pillars of the heavens quake,
    aghast at his rebuke.
¹²By his power he churned up the sea;
    by his wisdom he cut Rahab to pieces.
¹³By his breath the skies became fair;
    his hand pierced the gliding serpent.
¹⁴And these are but the outer fringe of his works;
    how faint the whisper we hear of him!
    Who then can understand the thunder of his
        power?"

26:14 ■ A FAINT WHISPER OF GOD
The book of Job contains some of the best nature
poetry ever written; it frequently cites nature as
one of the proofs of God's existence. Job himself
never denied God's power. All the wonders of
nature, he said, are "but the outer fringe of his
works", a faint whisper of God. His complaint was
not about power, but about justice. How could a
God so powerful treat him so unfairly?

27

And Job continued his discourse:

²"As surely as God lives, who has denied me
        justice,
    the Almighty, who has made me taste
        bitterness of soul,
³as long as I have life within me,
    the breath of God in my nostrils,
⁴my lips will not speak wickedness,
    and my tongue will utter no deceit.
⁵I will never admit you are in the right;
    till I die, I will not deny my integrity.
⁶I will maintain my righteousness and never let
        go of it;
    my conscience will not reproach me as long
        as I live.

⁷"May my enemies be like the wicked,
    my adversaries like the unjust!
⁸For what hope has the godless when he is cut
        off,
    when God takes away his life?
⁹Does God listen to his cry
    when distress comes upon him?
¹⁰Will he find delight in the Almighty?
    Will he call upon God at all times?

¹¹"I will teach you about the power of God;
    the ways of the Almighty I will not conceal.
¹²You have all seen this yourselves.
    Why then this meaningless talk?

ᵈ 19 Hebrew Sheol   ᵃ 6 Hebrew Sheol   ᵇ 6 Hebrew Abaddon

¹³"Here is the fate God allots to the wicked,
    the heritage a ruthless man receives from the
      Almighty:
¹⁴However many his children, their fate is the
      sword;
    his offspring will never have enough to eat.
¹⁵The plague will bury those who survive him,
    and their widows will not weep for them.
¹⁶Though he heaps up silver like dust
    and clothes like piles of clay,
¹⁷what he lays up the righteous will wear,
    and the innocent will divide his silver.
¹⁸The house he builds is like a moth's cocoon,
    like a hut made by a watchman.
¹⁹He lies down wealthy, but will do so no more;
    when he opens his eyes, all is gone.
²⁰Terrors overtake him like a flood;
    a tempest snatches him away in the night.
²¹The east wind carries him off, and he is gone;
    it sweeps him out of his place.
²²It hurls itself against him without mercy
    as he flees headlong from its power.
²³It claps its hands in derision
    and hisses him out of his place.

28 "There is a mine for silver
       and a place where gold is refined.
²Iron is taken from the earth,
    and copper is smelted from ore.
³Man puts an end to the darkness;
    he searches the farthest recesses
    for ore in the blackest darkness.
⁴Far from where people dwell he cuts a shaft,
    in places forgotten by the foot of man;
    far from men he dangles and sways.
⁵The earth, from which food comes,
    is transformed below as by fire;
⁶sapphires*ᵃ* come from its rocks,
    and its dust contains nuggets of gold.
⁷No bird of prey knows that hidden path,
    no falcon's eye has seen it.
⁸Proud beasts do not set foot on it,
    and no lion prowls there.
⁹Man's hand assaults the flinty rock
    and lays bare the roots of the mountains.
¹⁰He tunnels through the rock;
    his eyes see all its treasures.
¹¹He searches*ᵇ* the sources of the rivers
    and brings hidden things to light.

28:1 ■ A POEM ON WISDOM
In the midst of one of his most beautiful speeches,
Job included a self-contained poem on wisdom. It
uses the analogy of mining precious metals to
make the point that wisdom cannot be found by
any amount of searching (verses 1–19). God alone
knows where it dwells. In the rest of the poem,
Job admitted some things were beyond his
understanding, then lapsed into a reminiscence of
what life was like before his time of trials.

---

¹²"But where can wisdom be found?
    Where does understanding dwell?
¹³Man does not comprehend its worth;

it cannot be found in the land of the living.
¹⁴The deep says, 'It is not in me';
    the sea says, 'It is not with me.'
¹⁵It cannot be bought with the finest gold,
    nor can its price be weighed in silver.
¹⁶It cannot be bought with the gold of Ophir,
    with precious onyx or sapphires.
¹⁷Neither gold nor crystal can compare with it,
    nor can it be had for jewels of gold.
¹⁸Coral and jasper are not worthy of mention;
    the price of wisdom is beyond rubies.
¹⁹The topaz of Cush cannot compare with it;
    it cannot be bought with pure gold.

²⁰"Where then does wisdom come from?
    Where does understanding dwell?
²¹It is hidden from the eyes of every living thing,
    concealed even from the birds of the air.
²²Destruction*ᶜ* and Death say,
    'Only a rumour of it has reached our ears.'
²³God understands the way to it
    and he alone knows where it dwells,
²⁴for he views the ends of the earth
    and sees everything under the heavens.
²⁵When he established the force of the wind
    and measured out the waters,
²⁶when he made a decree for the rain
    and a path for the thunderstorm,
²⁷then he looked at wisdom and appraised it;
    he confirmed it and tested it.
²⁸And he said to man,
    'The fear of the Lord—that is wisdom,
    and to shun evil is understanding.' "

29 Job continued his discourse:

²"How I long for the months gone by,
    for the days when God watched over me,
³when his lamp shone upon my head
    and by his light I walked through darkness!
⁴Oh, for the days when I was in my prime,
    when God's intimate friendship blessed my
      house,
⁵when the Almighty was still with me
    and my children were around me,
⁶when my path was drenched with cream
    and the rock poured out for me streams of
      olive oil.

⁷"When I went to the gate of the city
    and took my seat in the public square,
⁸the young men saw me and stepped aside
    and the old men rose to their feet;
⁹the chief men refrained from speaking
    and covered their mouths with their hands;
¹⁰the voices of the nobles were hushed,
    and their tongues stuck to the roof of their
      mouths.
¹¹Whoever heard me spoke well of me,
    and those who saw me commended me,
¹²because I rescued the poor who cried for help,
    and the fatherless who had none to assist
      him.
¹³The man who was dying blessed me;
    I made the widow's heart sing.
¹⁴I put on righteousness as my clothing;

ᵃ6 Or *lapis lazuli;* also in verse 16   *ᵇ11* Septuagint, Aquila and Vulgate; Hebrew *He dams up*   *ᶜ22* Hebrew *Abaddon*

justice was my robe and my turban.
¹⁵I was eyes to the blind
and feet to the lame.
¹⁶I was a father to the needy;
I took up the case of the stranger.
¹⁷I broke the fangs of the wicked
and snatched the victims from their teeth.

29:11 ■ THE GOOD OLD DAYS
Tenderly, Job reminisces about the "months gone
by" (verse 2), before his trials began. Job could
think of no reason why he might "deserve" such
treatment – the point of the book of Job exactly.
His recollections of life in those days refute his
friends' accusations against him. He had shown
concern for the poor and oppressed – a fact that
must have increased his puzzlement over the
unfair treatment *he* was receiving.

¹⁸"I thought, 'I shall die in my own house,
my days as numerous as the grains of sand.
¹⁹My roots will reach to the water,
and the dew will lie all night on my
branches.
²⁰My glory will remain fresh in me,
the bow ever new in my hand.'
²¹"Men listened to me expectantly,
waiting in silence for my counsel.
²²After I had spoken, they spoke no more;
my words fell gently on their ears.
²³They waited for me as for showers
and drank in my words as the spring rain.
²⁴When I smiled at them, they scarcely believed
it;
the light of my face was precious to them.ᵃ
²⁵I chose the way for them and sat as their chief;
I dwelt as a king among his troops;
I was like one who comforts mourners.

30 "But now they mock me,
men younger than I,
whose fathers I would have disdained
to put with my sheep dogs.
²Of what use was the strength of their hands to
me,
since their vigour had gone from them?
³Haggard from want and hunger,
they roamedᵃ the parched land
in desolate wastelands at night.
⁴In the brush they gathered salt herbs,
and their foodᵇ was the root of the broom
tree.
⁵They were banished from their fellow-men,
shouted at as if they were thieves.
⁶They were forced to live in the dry stream
beds,
among the rocks and in holes in the ground.
⁷They brayed among the bushes
and huddled in the undergrowth.
⁸A base and nameless brood,
they were driven out of the land.

⁹"And now their sons mock me in song;
I have become a byword among them.

¹⁰They detest me and keep their distance;
they do not hesitate to spit in my face.
¹¹Now that God has unstrung my bow and
afflicted me,
they throw off restraint in my presence.
¹²On my right the tribeᶜ attacks;
they lay snares for my feet,
they build their siege ramps against me.
¹³They break up my road;
they succeed in destroying me –
without anyone's helping them.ᵈ
¹⁴They advance as through a gaping breach;
amid the ruins they come rolling in.
¹⁵Terrors overwhelm me;
my dignity is driven away as by the wind,
my safety vanishes like a cloud.

¹⁶"And now my life ebbs away;
days of suffering grip me.
¹⁷Night pierces my bones;
my gnawing pains never rest.
¹⁸In his great power ˻God˼ becomes like clothing
to me;ᵉ
he binds me like the neck of my garment.
¹⁹He throws me into the mud,
and I am reduced to dust and ashes.

²⁰"I cry out to you, O God, but you do not
answer;
I stand up, but you merely look at me.
²¹You turn on me ruthlessly;
with the might of your hand you attack me.
²²You snatch me up and drive me before the
wind;
you toss me about in the storm.
²³I know you will bring me down to death,
to the place appointed for all the living.

²⁴"Surely no-one lays a hand on a broken man
when he cries for help in his distress.
²⁵Have I not wept for those in trouble?
Has not my soul grieved for the poor?
²⁶Yet when I hoped for good, evil came;
when I looked for light, then came darkness.
²⁷The churning inside me never stops;
days of suffering confront me.
²⁸I go about blackened, but not by the sun;
I stand up in the assembly and cry for help.
²⁹I have become a brother of jackals,
a companion of owls.
³⁰My skin grows black and peels;
my body burns with fever.
³¹My harp is tuned to mourning,
and my flute to the sound of wailing.

31 "I made a covenant with my eyes
not to look lustfully at a girl.
²For what is man's lot from God above,
his heritage from the Almighty on high?
³Is it not ruin for the wicked,
disaster for those who do wrong?
⁴Does he not see my ways
and count my every step?

⁵"If I have walked in falsehood
or my foot has hurried after deceit –
⁶let God weigh me in honest scales

ᵃ24 The meaning of the Hebrew for this clause is uncertain.   ᵃ3 Or gnawed   ᵇ4 Or fuel   ᶜ12 The meaning of the Hebrew for this word is uncertain.
ᵈ13 Or me. / 'No-one can help him,' ˻they say˼   ᵉ18 Hebrew; Septuagint ˻God˼ grasps my clothing

and he will know that I am blameless—
⁷if my steps have turned from the path,
    if my heart has been led by my eyes,
    or if my hands have been defiled,
⁸then may others eat what I have sown,
    and may my crops be uprooted.

31:1 ■ BINDING OATHS

This chapter, Job's final line of defence, is written in a form that had legal significance to his hearers. Job was solemnly swearing his innocence in response to a whole series of accusations. He called down curses on himself if he could be proved wrong. The oaths were somewhat like our modern custom of swearing on the Bible "to tell the truth, the whole truth and nothing but the truth". Job's oaths impressed his three friends and effectively ended the debate. Then a new character, Elihu, joined in.

⁹"If my heart has been enticed by a woman,
    or if I have lurked at my neighbour's door,
¹⁰then may my wife grind another man's grain,
    and may other men sleep with her.
¹¹For that would have been shameful,
    a sin to be judged.
¹²It is a fire that burns to Destruction;ᵃ
    it would have uprooted my harvest.

¹³"If I have denied justice to my menservants and
        maidservants
    when they had a grievance against me,
¹⁴what will I do when God confronts me?
    What will I answer when called to account?
¹⁵Did not he who made me in the womb make
        them?
    Did not the same one form us both within
        our mothers?

¹⁶"If I have denied the desires of the poor
    or let the eyes of the widow grow weary,
¹⁷if I have kept my bread to myself,
    not sharing it with the fatherless—
¹⁸but from my youth I reared him as would a
        father,
    and from my birth I guided the widow—
¹⁹if I have seen anyone perishing for lack of
        clothing,
    or a needy man without a garment,
²⁰and his heart did not bless me
    for warming him with the fleece from my
        sheep,
²¹if I have raised my hand against the fatherless,
    knowing that I had influence in court,
²²then let my arm fall from the shoulder,
    let it be broken off at the joint.
²³For I dreaded destruction from God,
    and for fear of his splendour I could not do
        such things.

²⁴"If I have put my trust in gold
    or said to pure gold, 'You are my security,'
²⁵if I have rejoiced over my great wealth,
    the fortune my hands had gained,
²⁶if I have regarded the sun in its radiance

or the moon moving in splendour,
²⁷so that my heart was secretly enticed
    and my hand offered them a kiss of homage,
²⁸then these also would be sins to be judged,
    for I would have been unfaithful to God on
        high.

31:16 ■ A HABIT OF TRUST

This chapter gives insights into Job's life of spiritual discipline. He had developed the habit of obeying God. Now, with all the props knocked out, he still turned to God for strength, even though God seemed utterly absent. It was as if he had a resource bank of trust in God: the trust he had accumulated in more comfortable times helped him survive his time of hardship.

²⁹"If I have rejoiced at my enemy's misfortune
    or gloated over the trouble that came to
        him—
³⁰I have not allowed my mouth to sin
    by invoking a curse against his life—
³¹if the men of my household have never said,
    'Who has not had his fill of Job's meat?'—
³²but no stranger had to spend the night in the
        street,
    for my door was always open to the
        traveller—
³³if I have concealed my sin as men do,ᵇ
    by hiding my guilt in my heart
³⁴because I so feared the crowd
    and so dreaded the contempt of the clans
    that I kept silent and would not go outside—

³⁵("Oh, that I had someone to hear me!
    I sign now my defence—let the Almighty
        answer me;
    let my accuser put his indictment in writing.
³⁶Surely I would wear it on my shoulder,
    I would put it on like a crown.
³⁷I would give him an account of my every step;
    like a prince I would approach him.)—

³⁸"if my land cries out against me
    and all its furrows are wet with tears,
³⁹if I have devoured its yield without payment
    or broken the spirit of its tenants,
⁴⁰then let briers come up instead of wheat
    and weeds instead of barley."

The words of Job are ended.

■ Elihu

32 So these three men stopped answering Job, because he was righteous in his own eyes. ²But Elihu son of Barakel the Buzite, of the family of Ram, became very angry with Job for justifying himself rather than God. ³He was also angry with the three friends, because they had found no way to refute Job, and yet had condemned him.ᵃ ⁴Now Elihu had waited before speaking to Job because they were older than he. ⁵But when he saw that the three men had nothing more to say, his anger was aroused. ⁶So Elihu son of Barakel the Buzite said:

ᵃ12 Hebrew *Abaddon*   ᵇ33 Or *as Adam did*   ᵃ3 *Masoretic Text; an ancient Hebrew scribal tradition* Job, and so had condemned God

"I am young in years,
and you are old;
that is why I was fearful,
not daring to tell you what I know.
7I thought, 'Age should speak;
advanced years should teach wisdom.'
8But it is the spirit[b] in a man,
the breath of the Almighty, that gives him
understanding.
9It is not only the old[c] who are wise,
not only the aged who understand what is
right.

10"Therefore I say: Listen to me;
I too will tell you what I know.
11I waited while you spoke,
I listened to your reasoning;
while you were searching for words,
12 I gave you my full attention.
But not one of you has proved Job wrong;
none of you has answered his arguments.
13Do not say, 'We have found wisdom;
let God refute him, not man.'
14But Job has not marshalled his words against
me,
and I will not answer him with your
arguments.

15"They are dismayed and have no more to say;
words have failed them.

16Must I wait, now that they are silent,
now that they stand there with no reply?
17I too will have my say;
I too will tell what I know.
18For I am full of words,
and the spirit within me compels me;
19inside I am like bottled-up wine,
like new wineskins ready to burst.
20I must speak and find relief;
I must open my lips and reply.
21I will show partiality to no-one,
nor will I flatter any man;
22for if I were skilled in flattery,
my Maker would soon take me away.

33 "But now, Job, listen to my words;
pay attention to everything I say.
2I am about to open my mouth;
my words are on the tip of my tongue.
3My words come from an upright heart;
my lips sincerely speak what I know.
4The Spirit of God has made me;
the breath of the Almighty gives me life.
5Answer me then, if you can;
prepare yourself and confront me.
6I am just like you before God;
I too have been taken from clay.
7No fear of me should alarm you,
nor should my hand be heavy upon you.

■ A SILENT FRIEND DECIDES TO SPEAK UP
ELIHU, OUT OF NOWHERE, PROPOSES NEW IDEAS ABOUT SUFFERING

"NOT ONE OF YOU HAS PROVED JOB
WRONG; NONE OF YOU HAS ANSWERED
HIS ARGUMENTS." ■ 32:12

Up to this point in Job, the action has revolved
around Job and his three friends. The debate
between them, growing ever more heated, finally
breaks off. They have reached a standstill. Job
will not admit to any sin deserving of terrible
punishment, and his three friends will not back
down from their ideas about suffering.

    Suddenly, a new voice is heard. Elihu, a
young man, has been listening in silence all this
time. He can restrain himself no longer. He flares
up, first at Job for being so self-righteous and
then at the three friends for not coming up with
an answer to Job's questions. He refutes all four
of them, turning their own words against them.

■ IS ELIHU RIGHT?
Elihu is shocked at Job's vigorous self-defence.
Surely God cannot be unjust, he insists. Submit
to the pain, even if you don't understand it.
Don't blame God; praise him. God has shown
too much of his wisdom and perfection,
especially in nature, for anyone to doubt him.

    Elihu offers a new explanation for Job's
pain. Perhaps, he suggests, God gave suffering
to Job not as punishment but as a purifying
influence. God can use suffering to improve a
person, if it is received in the right spirit.

    Where did Elihu come from? Who is
he? Are his theories right? Mystery surrounds
the man. His speeches stand alone, and no-
one responds to them. As a result, the book of
Job gives no clue as to whether Elihu
expressed a worthy point of view.

    Some readers believe Elihu forms a
bridge between the flawed theories of Job's
three friends and God's own speech. Perhaps
his speeches prepare the way for God's.
Others see him as repeating the same fine-
sounding, but not-quite-true, advice of Job's
three friends.

    When God does make an entrance, he
dismisses Job's friends and has some mild
criticism for Job. But he ignores Elihu entirely.
Elihu remains a mysterious figure.

□ LIFE QUESTIONS:
Do Elihu's arguments sound familiar? What do
you think of friends who have similar thoughts
about others who suffer?

---

b 8 Or Spirit; also in verse 18   c 9 Or many; or great

8"But you have said in my hearing—
  I heard the very words—
9'I am pure and without sin;
  I am clean and free from guilt.
10Yet God has found fault with me;
  he considers me his enemy.
11He fastens my feet in shackles;
  he keeps close watch on all my paths.'

12"But I tell you, in this you are not right,
  for God is greater than man.
13Why do you complain to him
  that he answers none of man's words?ᵃ
14For God does speak—now one way, now
  another—
  though man may not perceive it.
15In a dream, in a vision of the night,
  when deep sleep falls on men
  as they slumber in their beds,
16he may speak in their ears
  and terrify them with warnings,
17to turn man from wrongdoing
  and keep him from pride,
18to preserve his soul from the pit,ᵇ
  his life from perishing by the sword.ᶜ
19Or a man may be chastened on a bed of pain
  with constant distress in his bones,
20so that his very being finds food repulsive
  and his soul loathes the choicest meal.
21His flesh wastes away to nothing,
  and his bones, once hidden, now stick out.
22His soul draws near to the pit,ᵈ
  and his life to the messengers of death.ᵉ

33:19 ■ KINDER, GENTLER FRIEND

Evidently, Elihu had sat in silence throughout the discussions to this point (in deference to the other speakers' age, as he explains). That fact alone shows his calmer nature: he refused to jump into very heated arguments. Although Elihu introduces some new ideas, he also follows the general line of reasoning—"You're being punished for your sins, Job" (see verses 17–22)—that God corrects in the end.

23"Yet if there is an angel on his side
  as a mediator, one out of a thousand,
  to tell a man what is right for him,
24to be gracious to him and say,
  'Spare him from going down to the pit;ᶠ
  I have found a ransom for him'—
25then his flesh is renewed like a child's;
  it is restored as in the days of his youth.
26He prays to God and finds favour with him,
  he sees God's face and shouts for joy;
  he is restored by God to his righteous state.
27Then he comes to men and says,
  'I have sinned, and perverted what was right,
  but I did not get what I deserved.
28He redeemed my soul from going down to the
  pit,ᵍ
  and I shall live to enjoy the light.'

29"God does all these things to a man—
  twice, even three times—
30to turn back his soul from the pit,ᵇ
  that the light of life may shine on him.

33:30 ■ PAIN AS A WARNING

Elihu did not defend Job as innocent. But his arguments shifted the emphasis of suffering from punishment to warning. Perhaps, he suggested, God allows a man to suffer in order "to turn back his soul from the pit". Primarily, however, Elihu defended God's actions. "It is unthinkable that God would do wrong, that the Almighty would pervert justice" (34:12).

31"Pay attention, Job, and listen to me;
  be silent, and I will speak.
32If you have anything to say, answer me;
  speak up, for I want you to be cleared.
33But if not, then listen to me;
  be silent, and I will teach you wisdom."

34

Then Elihu said:

2"Hear my words, you wise men;
  listen to me, you men of learning.
3For the ear tests words
  as the tongue tastes food.
4Let us discern for ourselves what is right;
  let us learn together what is good.

5"Job says, 'I am innocent,
  but God denies me justice.
6Although I am right,
  I am considered a liar;
  although I am guiltless,
  his arrow inflicts an incurable wound.'
7What man is like Job,
  who drinks scorn like water?
8He keeps company with evildoers;
  he associates with wicked men.
9For he says, 'It profits a man nothing
  when he tries to please God.'

10"So listen to me, you men of understanding.
  Far be it from God to do evil,
  from the Almighty to do wrong.
11He repays a man for what he has done;
  he brings upon him what his conduct
  deserves.
12It is unthinkable that God would do wrong,
  that the Almighty would pervert justice.
13Who appointed him over the earth?
  Who put him in charge of the whole world?
14If it were his intention
  and he withdrew his spiritᵃ and breath,
15all mankind would perish together
  and man would return to the dust.

16"If you have understanding, hear this;
  listen to what I say.
17Can he who hates justice govern?
  Will you condemn the just and mighty One?

ᵃ13 Or that he does not answer for any of his actions   ᵇ18 Or preserve him from the grave   ᶜ18 Or from crossing the River   ᵈ22 Or He draws near
to the grave   ᵉ22 Or to the dead   ᶠ24 Or grave   ᵍ28 Or redeemed me from going down to the grave   ᵇ30 Or turn him back from the grave
ᵃ14 Or Spirit

¹⁸Is he not the One who says to kings, 'You are
worthless,'
and to nobles, 'You are wicked,'
¹⁹who shows no partiality to princes
and does not favour the rich over the poor,
for they are all the work of his hands?
²⁰They die in an instant, in the middle of the
night;
the people are shaken and they pass away;
the mighty are removed without human
hand.

²¹"His eyes are on the ways of men;
he sees their every step.
²²There is no dark place, no deep shadow,
where evildoers can hide.
²³God has no need to examine men further,
that they should come before him for
judgment.
²⁴Without enquiry he shatters the mighty
and sets up others in their place.
²⁵Because he takes note of their deeds,
he overthrows them in the night and they
are crushed.
²⁶He punishes them for their wickedness
where everyone can see them,
²⁷because they turned from following him
and had no regard for any of his ways.
²⁸They caused the cry of the poor to come
before him,
so that he heard the cry of the needy.
²⁹But if he remains silent, who can condemn
him?
If he hides his face, who can see him?
Yet he is over man and nation alike,
³⁰ to keep a godless man from ruling,
from laying snares for the people.

³¹"Suppose a man says to God,
'I am guilty but will offend no more.
³²Teach me what I cannot see;
if I have done wrong, I will not do so again.'
³³Should God then reward you on your terms,
when you refuse to repent?
You must decide, not I;
so tell me what you know.

³⁴"Men of understanding declare,
wise men who hear me say to me,
³⁵'Job speaks without knowledge;
his words lack insight.'
³⁶Oh, that Job might be tested to the utmost
for answering like a wicked man!
³⁷To his sin he adds rebellion;
scornfully he claps his hands among us
and multiplies his words against God."

35 Then Elihu said:

²"Do you think this is just?
You say, 'I shall be cleared by God.'ᵃ
³Yet you ask him, 'What profit is it to me,ᵇ
and what do I gain by not sinning?'

⁴"I would like to reply to you
and to your friends with you.
⁵Look up at the heavens and see;

gaze at the clouds so high above you.
⁶If you sin, how does that affect him?
If your sins are many, what does that do to
him?
⁷If you are righteous, what do you give to him,
or what does he receive from your hand?
⁸Your wickedness affects only a man like
yourself,
and your righteousness only the sons of men.

⁹"Men cry out under a load of oppression;
they plead for relief from the arm of the
powerful.
¹⁰But no-one says, 'Where is God my Maker,
who gives songs in the night,
¹¹who teaches more to us than toᶜ the beasts of
the earth
and makes us wiser thanᵈ the birds of the
air?'
¹²He does not answer when men cry out
because of the arrogance of the wicked.
¹³Indeed, God does not listen to their empty
plea;
the Almighty pays no attention to it.
¹⁴How much less, then, will he listen
when you say that you do not see him,
that your case is before him
and you must wait for him,
¹⁵and further, that his anger never punishes
and he does not take the least notice of
wickedness.ᵉ
¹⁶So Job opens his mouth with empty talk;
without knowledge he multiplies words."

35:14 ■ IS GOD REALLY LISTENING?
Readers differ on how true Elihu's words were.
But in this chapter he seems to say Job had no
right to argue before God or to ask for a personal
appearance. Why should God be concerned about
one man's wickedness or righteousness? he asks
(verse 8). The opening chapters of the book,
however, revealed how much hung on Job's
responses. And ultimately God did step in and
reveal himself. In fact, he made an entrance just
as Elihu was explaining why God would not
appear.

36 Elihu continued:

²"Bear with me a little longer and I will show
you
that there is more to be said on God's behalf.
³I get my knowledge from afar;
I will ascribe justice to my Maker.
⁴Be assured that my words are not false;
one perfect in knowledge is with you.

⁵"God is mighty, but does not despise men;
he is mighty, and firm in his purpose.
⁶He does not keep the wicked alive
but gives the afflicted their rights.
⁷He does not take his eyes off the righteous;
he enthrones them with kings
and exalts them for ever.

ᵃ2 Or *My righteousness is more than God's*   ᵇ3 Or *you*   ᶜ11 Or *teaches us by*   ᵈ11 Or *us wise by*   ᵉ15 Symmachus, Theodotion and Vulgate;
the meaning of the Hebrew for this word is uncertain.

8But if men are bound in chains,
    held fast by cords of affliction,
9he tells them what they have done —
    that they have sinned arrogantly.
10He makes them listen to correction
    and commands them to repent of their evil.
11If they obey and serve him,
    they will spend the rest of their days in
        prosperity
    and their years in contentment.
12But if they do not listen,
    they will perish by the sword[a]
    and die without knowledge.

13"The godless in heart harbour resentment;
    even when he fetters them, they do not cry
        for help.
14They die in their youth,
    among male prostitutes of the shrines.
15But those who suffer he delivers in their
        suffering;
    he speaks to them in their affliction.

16"He is wooing you from the jaws of distress
    to a spacious place free from restriction,
    to the comfort of your table laden with
        choice food.
17But now you are laden with the judgment due
    to the wicked;
    judgment and justice have taken hold of you.
18Be careful that no-one entices you by riches;
    do not let a large bribe turn you aside.
19Would your wealth
    or even all your mighty efforts
    sustain you so you would not be in distress?
20Do not long for the night,
    to drag people away from their homes.[b]
21Beware of turning to evil,
    which you seem to prefer to affliction.

22"God is exalted in his power.
    Who is a teacher like him?
23Who has prescribed his ways for him,
    or said to him, 'You have done wrong'?
24Remember to extol his work,
    which men have praised in song.

■ WHAT JOB TEACHES ABOUT SUFFERING
THE PROBLEM OF PAIN AND THE BOOK OF JOB

INSIGHT

"BUT THOSE WHO SUFFER HE DELIVERS IN THEIR SUFFERING; HE SPEAKS TO THEM IN THEIR AFFLICTION." ■ 36:15

Why me?" Almost everyone asks this question when terrible suffering strikes. A car accident, a diagnosis of cancer, a long-term disease like arthritis — each of these raises intense questions about why God allows pain.

Over the centuries, suffering Christians have gained help and comfort from studying the book of Job. The book gives no compact theory as to why good people suffer. Nevertheless, the following insights into the problem of suffering do come out of the book of Job.

■ PRINCIPLES FROM JOB
1. *Some suffering is caused by Satan.* Chapters 1 and 2 make the important distinction that God did not cause Job's problems. He allowed them, but Satan actually caused the pain.
2. *God is all-powerful and good.* Nowhere does the book of Job suggest that God lacks power or goodness. Some people say that God is weak and powerless to prevent human suffering. Others, called deists, assume he runs the world at a distance, without personal involvement. But in Job, God's power is never questioned; only his fairness. And in his final summation speech, God used splendid illustrations from nature to prove his power.

3. *Suffering doesn't always come as a result of sin.* The Bible supports the general principle that "a man reaps what he sows", even in this life (Galatians 6:7; see Psalms 1:3; 37:25). But other people have no right to apply that *general* principle to a *particular* person. Job's friends tried with all their persuasive power. However, when God rendered the final verdict, he said simply, "You have not spoken of me what is right, as my servant Job has" (42:7). The Old Testament includes other examples of people who suffered through no fault of their own, such as Abel (Genesis 4) and Uriah (2 Samuel 11). And Jesus spoke out against the notion that suffering implies sin (see John 9:1–5 and Luke 13:1–5).

4. *God will reward and punish fairly in a final judgment after death.* Job's friends, together with most Old Testament folk, did not have a clearly formed belief in an afterlife. Therefore, they expected that God's fairness — his approval or disapproval of people — had to be shown in this life. Other parts of the Bible teach that God will reward and punish fairly after death.

5. *God does not condemn doubt and despair.* God did not condemn Job's anguished responses, only his ignorance. Job did not take his pain meekly; he cried out in anguish to God. His strong remarks scandalised his friends (see, for example,

[a] 12 Or *will cross the River*   [b] 20 The meaning of the Hebrew for verses 18–20 is uncertain.

²⁵All mankind has seen it;
  men gaze on it from afar.
²⁶How great is God—beyond our understanding!
  The number of his years is past finding out.

²⁷"He draws up the drops of water,
  which distil as rain to the streams;ᶜ
²⁸the clouds pour down their moisture
  and abundant showers fall on mankind.
²⁹Who can understand how he spreads out the
    clouds,
  how he thunders from his pavilion?
³⁰See how he scatters his lightning about him,
  bathing the depths of the sea.
³¹This is the way he governsᵈ the nations
  and provides food in abundance.
³²He fills his hands with lightning
  and commands it to strike its mark.
³³His thunder announces the coming storm;
  even the cattle make known its approach.ᵉ

37 "At this my heart pounds
      and leaps from its place.
²Listen! Listen to the roar of his voice,

to the rumbling that comes from his mouth.
³He unleashes his lightning beneath the whole
    heaven
  and sends it to the ends of the earth.
⁴After that comes the sound of his roar;
  he thunders with his majestic voice.
 When his voice resounds,
  he holds nothing back.
⁵God's voice thunders in marvellous ways;
  he does great things beyond our
    understanding.
⁶He says to the snow, 'Fall on the earth,'
  and to the rain shower, 'Be a mighty
    downpour.'
⁷So that all men he has made may know his
    work,
  he stops every man from his labour.ᵃ
⁸The animals take cover;
  they remain in their dens.
⁹The tempest comes out from its chamber,
  the cold from the driving winds.
¹⁰The breath of God produces ice,

15:1–16), but not God. Ironically, despite his bitter speeches, Job earned God's praise, while his pious friends were soundly rebuked.

6. *No one person has all the facts about suffering.* Neither Job nor his friends had enough facts. Job concluded God was unfair, treating him like an enemy. His friends maintained that God opposed Job because of his sin. All of them later learned that they had been viewing the situation from a very limited perspective, blind to the real war being waged in heaven.

7. *God is never totally silent.* Elihu made that point convincingly, reminding Job of dreams, visions, past blessings, even the daily works of God in nature (chapter 33). God also appealed to nature as giving evidence of his wisdom and power. Although he may seem silent, some evidence of him can be found. One contemporary author expressed that truth this way, "Remember in the darkness what you have learned in the light."

8. *Well-intentioned advice can sometimes do more harm than good.* Job's friends were classic examples of people who let their pride and sense of being right interfere with their compassion. They repeated pious phrases and argued theology with Job. His response: "If only you would be altogether silent! For you, that would be wisdom" (13:5).

9. *God asks for faith.* God refocused the central issue from the *cause* of Job's suffering to his *response*. Mysteriously, God never gave

an explanation for the problem of suffering. He did not even inform Job of the reason behind it: the contest recorded in chapters 1 and 2. He concentrated instead on Job's response. The real issue at stake was Job's faith—whether he would continue to trust God even when everything went wrong.

10. *Suffering can be used for a higher good.* In Job's case, God used a time of very great pain to win an important, even cosmic, victory over Satan. Looking backwards, but only looking backwards, we can see the "advantage" Job gained by continuing to trust God. Job is often cited as an Old Testament picture of Jesus Christ, who lived a perfectly innocent life but endured great pain and death. The terrible event of Christ's death was also transformed into a great victory.

Thousands of years later, Job's questions have not gone away. People who suffer still find themselves borrowing Job's own words as they cry out against God's seeming lack of concern. But Job affirms that God is not deaf to our cries and is in control of this world no matter how it looks. God did not answer all Job's questions, but his very appearance caused Job's doubts to melt away. Job learned that God cared about him and that God rules the world. It was enough.

☐ LIFE QUESTIONS:
Do these principles from Job match up with what you have heard about suffering from other Christians?

ᶜ 27 Or *distil from the mist as rain*   ᵈ 31 Or *nourishes*   ᵉ 33 Or *announces his coming— / the One zealous against evil*   ᵃ 7 Or / *he fills all men with fear by his power*

and the broad waters become frozen.
¹¹He loads the clouds with moisture;
  he scatters his lightning through them.
¹²At his direction they swirl around
  over the face of the whole earth
  to do whatever he commands them.
¹³He brings the clouds to punish men,
  or to water his earth[b] and show his love.

37:7 ■ THE MESSAGE OF A BLIZZARD

Anyone who has lived in a northern climate can identify with Elihu's comment about a snowstorm. A blizzard "stops every man from his labour", as schools, businesses, and buses shut down. It's a reminder, says Elihu, of God's undeniable power.

¹⁴"Listen to this, Job;
  stop and consider God's wonders.
¹⁵Do you know how God controls the clouds
  and makes his lightning flash?
¹⁶Do you know how the clouds hang poised,
  those wonders of him who is perfect in
    knowledge?
¹⁷You who swelter in your clothes
  when the land lies hushed under the south
    wind,
¹⁸can you join him in spreading out the skies,
  hard as a mirror of cast bronze?

¹⁹"Tell us what we should say to him;
  we cannot draw up our case because of our
    darkness.
²⁰Should he be told that I want to speak?
  Would any man ask to be swallowed up?
²¹Now no-one can look at the sun,
  bright as it is in the skies
  after the wind has swept them clean.
²²Out of the north he comes in golden
    splendour;
  God comes in awesome majesty.
²³The Almighty is beyond our reach and exalted
    in power;
  in his justice and great righteousness, he
    does not oppress.
²⁴Therefore, men revere him,
  for does he not have regard for all the wise
    in heart?"[c]

■ The LORD Speaks

38

Then the LORD answered Job out of the storm. He said:

²"Who is this that darkens my counsel
  with words without knowledge?
³Brace yourself like a man;
  I will question you,
  and you shall answer me.

⁴"Where were you when I laid the earth's
    foundation?
  Tell me, if you understand.
⁵Who marked off its dimensions? Surely you
    know!
  Who stretched a measuring line across it?
⁶On what were its footings set,

or who laid its cornerstone—
⁷while the morning stars sang together
  and all the angels[a] shouted for joy?

⁸"Who shut up the sea behind doors
  when it burst forth from the womb,
⁹when I made the clouds its garment
  and wrapped it in thick darkness,
¹⁰when I fixed limits for it
  and set its doors and bars in place,
¹¹when I said, 'This far you may come and no
    farther;
  here is where your proud waves halt'?

¹²"Have you ever given orders to the morning,
  or shown the dawn its place,
¹³that it might take the earth by the edges
  and shake the wicked out of it?
¹⁴The earth takes shape like clay under a seal;
  its features stand out like those of a garment.
¹⁵The wicked are denied their light,
  and their upraised arm is broken.

¹⁶"Have you journeyed to the springs of the sea
  or walked in the recesses of the deep?
¹⁷Have the gates of death been shown to you?
  Have you seen the gates of the shadow of
    death?[b]
¹⁸Have you comprehended the vast expanses of
    the earth?
  Tell me, if you know all this.

¹⁹"What is the way to the abode of light?
  And where does darkness reside?
²⁰Can you take them to their places?
  Do you know the paths to their dwellings?
²¹Surely you know, for you were already born!
  You have lived so many years!

38:21 ■ GOD PULLS OUT THE STOPS

God is not above using sarcasm, as this barb directed at Job clearly shows. His entire speech stressed the vast difference between a God of all creation and one puny man like Job. "Do you have an arm like God's?" he asked (40:9).

²²"Have you entered the storehouses of the snow
  or seen the storehouses of the hail,
²³which I reserve for times of trouble,
  for days of war and battle?
²⁴What is the way to the place where the
    lightning is dispersed,
  or the place where the east winds are
    scattered over the earth?
²⁵Who cuts a channel for the torrents of rain,
  and a path for the thunderstorm,
²⁶to water a land where no man lives,
  a desert with no-one in it,
²⁷to satisfy a desolate wasteland
  and make it sprout with grass?
²⁸Does the rain have a father?
  Who fathers the drops of dew?
²⁹From whose womb comes the ice?
  Who gives birth to the frost from the
    heavens

^b 13 Or to favour them   ^c 24 Or for he does not have regard for any who think they are wise.   ^a 7 Hebrew the sons of God   ^b 17 Or gates of deep shadows

30when the waters become hard as stone,
  when the surface of the deep is frozen?
31"Can you bind the beautiful^c Pleiades?
  Can you loose the cords of Orion?
32Can you bring forth the constellations in their
    seasons^d
  or lead out the Bear^e with its cubs?
33Do you know the laws of the heavens?
  Can you set up ⌊God's^f⌋ dominion over the
    earth?
34"Can you raise your voice to the clouds
  and cover yourself with a flood of water?
35Do you send the lightning bolts on their way?
  Do they report to you, 'Here we are'?
36Who endowed the heart^g with wisdom
  or gave understanding to the mind?^h
37Who has the wisdom to count the clouds?
  Who can tip over the water jars of the
    heavens
38when the dust becomes hard
  and the clods of earth stick together?

39"Do you hunt the prey for the lioness
  and satisfy the hunger of the lions
40when they crouch down in their dens
  or lie in wait in a thicket?
41Who provides food for the raven
  when its young cry out to God
  and wander about for lack of food?

39 "Do you know when the mountain goats
  give birth?
  Do you watch when the doe bears her fawn?
2Do you count the months till they bear?
  Do you know the time they give birth?
3They crouch down and bring forth their young;
  their labour pains are ended.
4Their young thrive and grow strong in the
    wilds;
  they leave and do not return.

5"Who let the wild donkey go free?
  Who untied his ropes?
6I gave him the wasteland as his home,
  the salt flats as his habitat.
7He laughs at the commotion in the town;
  he does not hear a driver's shout.
8He ranges the hills for his pasture
  and searches for any green thing.

9"Will the wild ox consent to serve you?
  Will he stay by your manger at night?
10Can you hold him to the furrow with a harness?
  Will he till the valleys behind you?
11Will you rely on him for his great strength?
  Will you leave your heavy work to him?
12Can you trust him to bring in your grain
  and gather it to your threshing-floor?

> **39:9 ■ THE WILDNESS OF ANIMALS**
> God seems to take special delight in animals with
> a streak of wildness: mountain goats, lions, wild
> donkeys, hawks, wild oxen. They serve as
> reminders that people are not as fully in control of
> the world as they might think.

13"The wings of the ostrich flap joyfully,
  but they cannot compare with the pinions
    and feathers of the stork.
14She lays her eggs on the ground
  and lets them warm in the sand,
15unmindful that a foot may crush them,
  that some wild animal may trample them.
16She treats her young harshly, as if they were
    not hers;
  she cares not that her labour was in vain,
17for God did not endow her with wisdom
  or give her a share of good sense.
18Yet when she spreads her feathers to run,
  she laughs at horse and rider.

19"Do you give the horse his strength
  or clothe his neck with a flowing mane?
20Do you make him leap like a locust,
  striking terror with his proud snorting?
21He paws fiercely, rejoicing in his strength,
  and charges into the fray.
22He laughs at fear, afraid of nothing;
  he does not shy away from the sword.
23The quiver rattles against his side,
  along with the flashing spear and lance.
24In frenzied excitement he eats up the ground;
  he cannot stand still when the trumpet
    sounds.
25At the blast of the trumpet he snorts, 'Aha!'
  He catches the scent of battle from afar,
  the shout of commanders and the battle cry.

26"Does the hawk take flight by your wisdom
  and spread his wings towards the south?
27Does the eagle soar at your command
  and build his nest on high?
28He dwells on a cliff and stays there at night;
  a rocky crag is his stronghold.
29From there he seeks out his food;
  his eyes detect it from afar.
30His young ones feast on blood,
  and where the slain are, there is he."

40 The LORD said to Job:

2"Will the one who contends with the Almighty
    correct him?
  Let him who accuses God answer him!"

3Then Job answered the LORD:

4"I am unworthy—how can I reply to you?
  I put my hand over my mouth.
5I spoke once, but I have no answer—
  twice, but I will say no more."

6Then the LORD spoke to Job out of the storm:

7"Brace yourself like a man;
  I will question you,
  and you shall answer me.

8"Would you discredit my justice?
  Would you condemn me to justify yourself?
9Do you have an arm like God's,
  and can your voice thunder like his?
10Then adorn yourself with glory and splendour,
  and clothe yourself in honour and majesty.

---

^c 31 Or the twinkling; or the chains of the   ^d 32 Or the morning star in its season   ^e 32 Or out Leo   ^f 33 Or his; or their   ^g 36 The meaning of the
Hebrew for this word is uncertain.   ^h 36 The meaning of the Hebrew for this word is uncertain.

¹¹Unleash the fury of your wrath,
　　look at every proud man and bring him low,
¹²look at every proud man and humble him,
　　crush the wicked where they stand.
¹³Bury them all in the dust together;
　　shroud their faces in the grave.
¹⁴Then I myself will admit to you
　　that your own right hand can save you.

¹⁵"Look at the behemoth,ᵃ
　　which I made along with you
　　and which feeds on grass like an ox.
¹⁶What strength he has in his loins,
　　what power in the muscles of his belly!

¹⁷His tailᵇ sways like a cedar;
　　the sinews of his thighs are close-knit.
¹⁸His bones are tubes of bronze,
　　his limbs like rods of iron.
¹⁹He ranks first among the works of God,
　　yet his Maker can approach him with his
　　　sword.
²⁰The hills bring him their produce,
　　and all the wild animals play nearby.
²¹Under the lotus plant he lies,
　　hidden among the reeds in the marsh.
²²The lotuses conceal him in their shadow;
　　the poplars by the stream surround him.
²³When the river rages, he is not alarmed;

■ GOD SPEAKS TO JOB
AT LAST, JOB GETS WHAT HE DEMANDED

INSIGHT

"WILL THE ONE WHO CONTENDS WITH
THE ALMIGHTY CORRECT HIM? LET HIM
WHO ACCUSES GOD ANSWER HIM!"
■ 40:2

In the span of a few days Job experienced more
tragedy than most people encounter in a
lifetime. He scratched himself with shards of
pottery and mourned the day he was born. He
could not even suffer with dignity; he had to
endure his wife's taunts and his friends'
ramblings. Nothing anyone said helped him.
　　Through it all, Job steadfastly refused to
turn his back on God. He had only one request.
He wanted to hear from God in person. He
wanted an explanation straight from the Source.
　　At last Job got his wish. God answered
Job with a speech often quoted for its majesty
and beauty. In a touch of irony, God made his
entrance just as Elihu was explaining why Job
could not expect a direct answer from him.

■ NOT THE EXPECTED MESSAGE
Job had saved up a long list of questions, but it
was God who asked the questions, not Job.
"Brace yourself like a man," he began. "I will
question you, and you shall answer me."
　　Author Frederick Buechner sums up
what follows: "God doesn't explain. He
explodes. He asks Job who he thinks he is
anyway. He says that to try to explain the kind
of things Job wants explained would be like
trying to explain Einstein to a little-neck clam."
God did not need Job's or anyone else's advice
on how to run the world.
　　God's reply resembled a nature lesson
more than an explanation of the problem of
suffering. He pointed out, one by one, all the
creations that gave him greatest pride. In short,
God asked Job, "Do you want to try running the
universe for a while? Go ahead, try designing an
ostrich, or a mountain goat, or even a
snowflake."

Astonishingly, the question of suffering
itself did not even come up. Yet somehow Job
seemed satisfied – humiliated, actually. "Surely
I spoke of things I did not understand," he
confessed, "things too wonderful for me to
know" (42:3).

■ JOB PASSES THE TEST
Job had endured his terrible sufferings in the
dark. When he needed God most, God had
stayed silent. And that was exactly the point of
the contest begun at the beginning of the
book, back in chapter 1. Satan had promised
God that Job would "surely curse you to your
face". He lost the challenge. Despite everything
that happened, Job did not curse God. He
clung to his belief in a just God, even when
everything in his experience seemed to
contradict it.
　　God had some words of correction for
Job. No-one, not Job and especially not his
friends, had the evidence needed to make
judgments about how he runs the world. But
mainly, God had praise for Job. He called him
"my servant", and, in an ironic twist, told the
three friends to go to Job and ask for his
mercy (42:7–8). Much later, in the book of
Ezekiel (14:14), God included Job in a list of
the finest human examples of righteousness.
　　The book of Job ends on a note of
surprise. Job's friends, who had spouted all
the right pieties and clichés, ask for
forgiveness. Job, who had raged and cried
out, is given twice as much as he ever had
before. "And so he died, old and full of years"
(42:17).

□ LIFE QUESTIONS:
In Job's place, what kind of answer would you
have wanted from God? Does God's reply to
Job surprise you?

ᵃ15 Possibly the hippopotamus or the elephant　　ᵇ17 Possibly trunk

he is secure, though the Jordan should surge
  against his mouth.
24Can anyone capture him by the eyes,c
  or trap him and pierce his nose?

40:15 ■ BEHEMOTH AND LEVIATHAN?

No-one is quite sure what is meant by these two
words, so the English Bible leaves them
untranslated. The behemoth resembles a
hippopotamus or elephant. The leviathan (41:1)
has some features of a crocodile and some of a
dragon. In other places, the Bible refers to the
leviathan as either a whale-like creature (Psalm
104:26) or a serpent or monster of the sea (Isaiah
27:1). God used the leviathan as a symbol of
something powerful and uncontrollable. Job got
the message: if you can't take on one of God's
fearsome creatures, don't attempt to take on God.

41 "Can you pull in the leviathana with a
       fishhook
  or tie down his tongue with a rope?
2Can you put a cord through his nose
  or pierce his jaw with a hook?
3Will he keep begging you for mercy?
  Will he speak to you with gentle words?
4Will he make an agreement with you
  for you to take him as your slave for life?
5Can you make a pet of him like a bird
  or put him on a leash for your girls?
6Will traders barter for him?
  Will they divide him up among the
      merchants?
7Can you fill his hide with harpoons
  or his head with fishing spears?
8If you lay a hand on him,
  you will remember the struggle and never do
      it again!
9Any hope of subduing him is false;
  the mere sight of him is overpowering.
10No-one is fierce enough to rouse him.
  Who then is able to stand against me?
11Who has a claim against me that I must pay?
  Everything under heaven belongs to me.

12"I will not fail to speak of his limbs,
  his strength and his graceful form.
13Who can strip off his outer coat?
  Who would approach him with a bridle?
14Who dares open the doors of his mouth,
  ringed about with his fearsome teeth?
15His back hasb rows of shields
  tightly sealed together;
16each is so close to the next
  that no air can pass between.
17They are joined fast to one another;
  they cling together and cannot be parted.
18His snorting throws out flashes of light;
  his eyes are like the rays of dawn.
19Firebrands stream from his mouth;
  sparks of fire shoot out.
20Smoke pours from his nostrils
  as from a boiling pot over a fire of reeds.
21His breath sets coals ablaze,

and flames dart from his mouth.
22Strength resides in his neck;
  dismay goes before him.
23The folds of his flesh are tightly joined;
  they are firm and immovable.
24His chest is hard as rock,
  hard as a lower millstone.
25When he rises up, the mighty are terrified;
  they retreat before his thrashing.
26The sword that reaches him has no effect,
  nor does the spear or the dart or the javelin.
27Iron he treats like straw
  and bronze like rotten wood.
28Arrows do not make him flee;
  slingstones are like chaff to him.
29A club seems to him but a piece of straw;
  he laughs at the rattling of the lance.
30His undersides are jagged potsherds,
  leaving a trail in the mud like a
      threshing-sledge.
31He makes the depths churn like a boiling
      cauldron
  and stirs up the sea like a pot of ointment.
32Behind him he leaves a glistening wake;
  one would think the deep had white hair.
33Nothing on earth is his equal—
  a creature without fear.
34He looks down on all that are haughty;
  he is king over all that are proud."

■ Job

42 Then Job replied to the LORD:

2"I know that you can do all things;
  no plan of yours can be thwarted.
3 You asked, 'Who is this that obscures my
      counsel without knowledge?'
  Surely I spoke of things I did not understand,
      things too wonderful for me to know.

4 "You said, 'Listen now, and I will speak;
  I will question you,
      and you shall answer me.'
5My ears had heard of you
  but now my eyes have seen you.
6Therefore I despise myself
  and repent in dust and ashes."

42:5 ■ A VISIT FOR ALL TIME

A personal visit from God utterly silenced all Job's
questions about unfairness. Once he saw God, he
had nothing more to say. Few people in history
have had such a direct, visible encounter with
God, but the book of Job foreshadows a time
when God paid a much longer personal visit to
earth. In Jesus, God came not in power and
majesty, but in poverty and pain. Job stands as
the clearest Old Testament example of unfairness:
an upright man who suffered greatly. Jesus stands
as the New Testament example: a perfect man
who suffered even more. Both hint at a happy
ending after all.

---

c24 Or by a water hole   a1 Possibly the crocodile   b15 Or His pride is his

■ Epilogue

7After the LORD had said these things to Job, he said to Eliphaz the Temanite, "I am angry with you and your two friends, because you have not spoken of me what is right, as my servant Job has. 8So now take seven bulls and seven rams and go to my servant Job and sacrifice a burnt offering for yourselves. My servant Job will pray for you, and I will accept his prayer and not deal with you according to your folly. You have not spoken of me what is right, as my servant Job has." 9So Eliphaz the Temanite, Bildad the Shuhite and Zophar the Naamathite did what the LORD told them; and the LORD accepted Job's prayer.

10After Job had prayed for his friends, the LORD made him prosperous again and gave him twice as much as he had before. 11All his brothers and sisters and everyone who had known him before came and ate with him in his house. They comforted and consoled him over all the trouble the LORD had brought upon him, and each one gave him a piece of silver*a* and a gold ring.

12The LORD blessed the latter part of Job's life more than the first. He had fourteen thousand sheep,

42:10 ■ SEEING IN THE DARK

Significantly, Job spoke his contrite words (verse 6) *before* any of his losses had been restored, while still sitting in a pile of ashes, naked and covered with sores. Because he had seen God, he had learned to believe God even in the midst of suffering, with no certainty of relief.

six thousand camels, a thousand yoke of oxen and a thousand donkeys. 13And he also had seven sons and three daughters. 14The first daughter he named Jemimah, the second Keziah and the third Keren-Happuch. 15Nowhere in all the land were there found women as beautiful as Job's daughters, and their father granted them an inheritance along with their brothers.

16After this, Job lived a hundred and forty years; he saw his children and their children to the fourth generation. 17And so he died, old and full of years.

---

a 11 Hebrew *him a kesitah*; a kesitah was a unit of money of unknown weight and value.

PSALMS

■ CRIES FROM THE HEART

SONGS FOR SORROW AS WELL AS JOY

YOU ARE MY HIDING-PLACE; YOU WILL PROTECT ME FROM TROUBLE AND SURROUND ME
WITH SONGS OF DELIVERANCE. ■ 32:7

Here at the very centre of the Bible are songs, rising up like a tune from its heart. They capture the innermost thoughts and prayers of Old Testament people – and they still speak directly to our needs.

For every emotion and mood you can find a psalm to match. The psalms wrestle with the deepest sorrow and ask God the hardest questions about suffering and injustice. Their voice is refreshingly spontaneous. They do not pay flowery compliments to God: they cry out to him, or shout for joy before him.

After you read these poems, you can't think of the Old Testament as dry and rule-bound. Nor is the Old Testament God distant and impersonal. In almost every psalm you find the presence of God, not as a philosophical principle, but as an active, strong, and loving ruler – a God who makes a difference in life.

■ HOW DID THE PSALMS COME TOGETHER?

While almost half of the psalms are credited to David, at least one was written 500 years after his birth. A number of poets and writers contributed, and about a third of the psalms are completely anonymous.

How did the psalms come together? They seem to have been compiled as a hymnbook for use in temple worship. Some psalms were written from an individual's experiences, but were adapted for congregational use. Directions for musicians were added, along with a few verses to widen the psalms' meaning to everybody.

The psalms show tremendous variation, reflecting the many personalities who contributed their poems and prayers over several centuries. Yet readers have found an inner consistency in the whole book, so they can move from one psalm to the next without being particularly aware that one poem is centuries older than another. Some have called the psalms a Bible within the Bible – different books telling a single story.

Others have compared the book of Psalms to a beautiful cathedral built over centuries. Each wing and each window show the individual genius of its designers, yet all the parts are somehow harmonious. This harmony comes not merely from a common sense of style, but from unity of purpose: the whole cathedral is made for the worship of one and the same God. Just so, the psalms reflect, in a hundred moods and experiences, the never-changing reality of a strong and loving God who cares for his people.

■ THE PRESENCE OF REAL ENEMIES

God is not the only reality in the psalms. Equally persistent are enemies who sneer and hurt and plot violence. They, too, appear in nearly every psalm. For the psalmists, faith in God was a struggle against powerful forces that often seemed more real than God.

The psalm writers frequently asked, "Where are you, God? Why don't you help me?" Despite their love for God, they often felt abandoned, misused, betrayed. They found no guarantee of safety in their closeness to God. The joy and praise that saturate these prayers came not from an absence of problems, but from a deep conviction that a great God would overcome them.

Jesus, dying on the cross, twice expressed himself in the words of psalms (22:1 and 31:5), and his disciples, in trying to explain his life, quoted from Psalms more than any other book. They appear to have meditated on the psalms often as they considered the meaning of Jesus' life. In the psalms they could see that even the best men – even David, the great king – suffer agony and feel abandoned.

Living by faith is not easy. It was not for David; it was not for Jesus either. These powerful poems of praise and worship, some of the most beautiful ever written, offer no magical formulas to make troubles go away. Yet, while real-life questions, struggles, and discouragements have a strong voice in these poems, more powerful still is the voice of joy and security in the strength and fortress of Israel: the Lord himself.

■ HOW TO READ PSALMS

The best way to read the psalms is also the most common way: to make these ancient prayers your own and speak them directly to God. So many of the poems catch such deep human feelings that you can't help being moved by them.

But not all the psalms seem attractive. Some sound harsh, self-congratulatory, or boring. You will not find it easy to pray these until you understand them.

And there are so many psalms! This is the longest book in the Bible. To compensate, many people read only selected psalms, skimming over the others. But then they miss the deeper messages found there, including the messages that the New Testament writers saw when they quoted Psalms more than any other Old Testament book. The richest lessons from Psalms may come from particularly difficult poems you must read again and again until you begin to see what the author had in mind.

The original Hebrew of these poems probably used no rhyme or strict rhythm as traditional English poems do. Instead, the psalmists wrote with parallelism, following one thought by a "rhyming" thought or by its opposite. (For more on this, see "Hebrew Poetry", page 549.) Fortunately, this kind of poetry can be translated into almost any language without loss.

Readers may be confused by the psalms' frequent change of voice. In a single poem the psalmist may talk to God, then talk about him, and then return to talking to him, all in rapid succession. This would be strange English prose, but was common in Hebrew poetry.

Because so many of the psalm titles refer to David, you may find it helpful to refer to his life story. It is found in 1 Samuel 16–31, the whole book of 2 Samuel, and the first two chapters of 1 Kings. However, most of the psalms can make perfect sense without reference to any outside information. They merely ask – and reward – time and close attention. Read and re-read them. They grow richer with careful study.

■ 3-TRACK READING PLAN

For an explanation and complete listing of the 3-track reading plan, turn to page x.

■ TRACK 1:
Two-Week Courses on the Bible
The Track 1 reading programme on the Old Testament includes one chapter from Psalms. See page x for a complete listing of this course.

■ TRACK 2:
An Overview of Psalms in 7 Days
☐ Day 1. Read the Introduction to Psalms and Psalm 19: Perfect Harmony.
☐ Day 2. Read Psalm 23: The Shepherd Song.
☐ Day 3. Read Psalm 27: Confidence in Trouble.
☐ Day 4. Read Psalm 51: The Great Confession.
☐ Day 5. Read Psalm 84: The Delight of Worshipping God.
☐ Day 6. Read Psalm 103: God's Benefits.
☐ Day 7. Read Psalm 139: God's Care.

Now turn to page xi for your next Track 2 reading project.

■ TRACK 3:
All of Psalms in Two Two-Month Periods (122 days)
After you have read through Psalms, turn to pages xii–xiii for your next Track 3 reading project.

Part I

☐ 1–2 ☐ 3–4 ☐ 5 ☐ 6
☐ 7 ☐ 8 ☐ 9 ☐ 10
☐ 11–12 ☐ 13–14
☐ 15–16 ☐ 17 ☐ 18
☐ 19 ☐ 20–21 ☐ 22
☐ 23–24 ☐ 25 ☐ 26
☐ 27 ☐ 28–29 ☐ 30
☐ 31 ☐ 32 ☐ 33 ☐ 34
☐ 35 ☐ 36 ☐ 37 ☐ 38
☐ 39 ☐ 40 ☐ 41
☐ 42–43 ☐ 44 ☐ 45
☐ 46–47 ☐ 48 ☐ 49
☐ 50 ☐ 51 ☐ 52
☐ 53–54 ☐ 55 ☐ 56
☐ 57 ☐ 58 ☐ 59

☐ 60–61 ☐ 62
☐ 63–64 ☐ 65 ☐ 66
☐ 67 ☐ 68 ☐ 69 ☐ 70
☐ 71 ☐ 72 ☐ 73 ☐ 74
☐ 75

Part II

☐ 76 ☐ 77 ☐ 78 ☐ 79
☐ 80 ☐ 81 ☐ 82 ☐ 83
☐ 84 ☐ 85 ☐ 86 ☐ 87
☐ 88 ☐ 89 ☐ 90 ☐ 91
☐ 92–93 ☐ 94 ☐ 95
☐ 96 ☐ 97 ☐ 98–99
☐ 100–101 ☐ 102 ☐ 103
☐ 104 ☐ 105 ☐ 106 ☐ 107
☐ 108 ☐ 109 ☐ 110–111
☐ 112–113 ☐ 114 ☐ 115
☐ 116–117 ☐ 118
☐ 119:1–48 ☐ 119:49–96
☐ 119:97–144
☐ 119:145–176
☐ 120–121 ☐ 122–123
☐ 124–125 ☐ 126–128
☐ 129–130 ☐ 131–132
☐ 133–134 ☐ 135 ☐ 136
☐ 137–138 ☐ 139 ☐ 140
☐ 141–142 ☐ 143 ☐ 144
☐ 145 ☐ 146 ☐ 147 ☐ 148
☐ 149–150

BOOK I
☐ Psalms 1–41

■ PSALM 1

¹Blessed is the man
 who does not walk in the counsel of the
  wicked
 or stand in the way of sinners
  or sit in the seat of mockers.
²But his delight is in the law of the LORD,
 and on his law he meditates day and night.
³He is like a tree planted by streams of water,
 which yields its fruit in season
 and whose leaf does not wither.
 Whatever he does prospers.

⁴Not so the wicked!
 They are like chaff
 that the wind blows away.
⁵Therefore the wicked will not stand in the
  judgment,
 nor sinners in the assembly of the righteous.

1:4 ■ BLOWING IN THE WIND
The opposite of "a tree planted by streams" (verse
3) should be a tree withered by drought – and so
it is in Jeremiah 17:5–8, which paints a similar
contrast between good and bad people. This
image of the wicked as "chaff", however, is far
more absolute – for chaff, utterly worthless even
for a fire, disappears in the wind. God's judgment
day is what finally makes the wicked seem like
chaff.

⁶For the LORD watches over the way of the
  righteous,
 but the way of the wicked will perish.

■ PSALM 2

¹Why do the nations conspire*ᵃ*
 and the peoples plot in vain?
²The kings of the earth take their stand
 and the rulers gather together against the
  LORD
 and against his Anointed One.*ᵇ*
³"Let us break their chains," they say,
 "and throw off their fetters."

⁴The One enthroned in heaven laughs;
 the Lord scoffs at them.
⁵Then he rebukes them in his anger
 and terrifies them in his wrath, saying,
⁶"I have installed my King*ᶜ*
 on Zion, my holy hill."

⁷I will proclaim the decree of the LORD:

 He said to me, "You are my Son;*ᵈ*
 today I have become your Father.*ᵉ*
⁸Ask of me,
 and I will make the nations your inheritance,
 the ends of the earth your possession.

⁹You will rule them with an iron sceptre;*ᶠ*
 you will dash them to pieces like pottery."

¹⁰Therefore, you kings, be wise;
 be warned, you rulers of the earth.
¹¹Serve the LORD with fear
 and rejoice with trembling.
¹²Kiss the Son, lest he be angry
 and you be destroyed in your way,
 for his wrath can flare up in a moment.
 Blessed are all who take refuge in him.

2:2 ■ THE MESSIAH IN THE PSALMS
Israelite kings and priests were anointed with oil
when they took office. The "Anointed One"
probably originally meant "king". It came, however,
to stand for more. The Hebrew word is *masiah,*
which became *Messiah* and translated into Greek
as *Christos* or *Christ.* This psalm was understood
in the New Testament as referring to Jesus – for
no Old Testament king ever gained the control of
the nations implied here. You can find quotations
in Acts 4:25–26; 13:33; Hebrews 1:5; 5:5; and
Revelation 2:27; 12:5; and 19:15.

■ PSALM 3
☐ A psalm of David. When he fled from his son Absalom.

¹O LORD, how many are my foes!
 How many rise up against me!
²Many are saying of me,
 "God will not deliver him."   *Selah*ᵃ

³But you are a shield around me, O LORD;
 you bestow glory on me and lift*ᵇ* up my
  head.
⁴To the LORD I cry aloud,
 and he answers me from his holy hill.   *Selah*

⁵I lie down and sleep;
 I wake again, because the LORD sustains me.
⁶I will not fear the tens of thousands
 drawn up against me on every side.

⁷Arise, O LORD!
 Deliver me, O my God!
 Strike all my enemies on the jaw;
 break the teeth of the wicked.

⁸From the LORD comes deliverance.
 May your blessing be on your people.   *Selah*

■ PSALM 4
☐ For the director of music. With stringed instruments.
A psalm of David.

¹Answer me when I call to you,
 O my righteous God.
 Give me relief from my distress;
 be merciful to me and hear my prayer.

²How long, O men, will you turn my glory into
  shame?*ᵃ*

ᵃ1 Hebrew; Septuagint rage   *ᵇ2 Or anointed one*   *ᶜ6 Or king*   *ᵈ7 Or son; also in verse 12*   *ᵉ7 Or have begotten you*   *ᶠ9 Or will break them
with a rod of iron*   *ᵃ2 A word of uncertain meaning, occurring frequently in the Psalms; possibly a musical term*   *ᵇ3 Or LORD, / my Glorious One, who
lifts*   *ᵃ2 Or you dishonour my Glorious One*

How long will you love delusions and seek
  false gods?*b*   *Selah*
3Know that the LORD has set apart the godly for
  himself;
  the LORD will hear when I call to him.

4In your anger do not sin;
  when you are on your beds,
  search your hearts and be silent.   *Selah*
5Offer right sacrifices
  and trust in the LORD.

4:4 ■ ANGRY INSIDE
Is anger sinful? No, though it can certainly *lead* to
sin. This prayer depicts anger springing from
anxiety, which proves especially troublesome on
sleepless nights. The psalm suggests that, rather
than venting your worry in outbursts against
others, you should examine your own heart. Paul
applied this verse to another situation: difficult
personal relationships (Ephesians 4:26).

6Many are asking, "Who can show us any good?"
  Let the light of your face shine upon us,
  O LORD.
7You have filled my heart with greater joy
  than when their grain and new wine abound.
8I will lie down and sleep in peace,
  for you alone, O LORD,
  make me dwell in safety.

■ PSALM 5
☐ For the director of music. For flutes. A psalm of David.

1Give ear to my words, O LORD,
  consider my sighing.
2Listen to my cry for help,
  my King and my God,
  for to you I pray.
3In the morning, O LORD, you hear my voice;
  in the morning I lay my requests before you
  and wait in expectation.

4You are not a God who takes pleasure in evil;
  with you the wicked cannot dwell.
5The arrogant cannot stand in your presence;
  you hate all who do wrong.
6You destroy those who tell lies;
  bloodthirsty and deceitful men
  the LORD abhors.

7But I, by your great mercy,
  will come into your house;
  in reverence will I bow down
  towards your holy temple.
8Lead me, O LORD, in your righteousness
  because of my enemies—
  make straight your way before me.

9Not a word from their mouth can be trusted;
  their heart is filled with destruction.
  Their throat is an open grave;
  with their tongue they speak deceit.
10Declare them guilty, O God!
  Let their intrigues be their downfall.

Banish them for their many sins,
  for they have rebelled against you.

5:9 ■ EVIL EVERYWHERE
Renowned for their beautiful pictures of God's
love, the psalms present equally heartfelt portraits
of evil. They often describe people who deeply
deserve God's punishment. In Romans 3:10–18,
Paul quotes from a number of different psalms like
this one, making his case that evil infects all
people, everywhere.

11But let all who take refuge in you be glad;
  let them ever sing for joy.
  Spread your protection over them,
  that those who love your name may rejoice
  in you.
12For surely, O LORD, you bless the righteous;
  you surround them with your favour as with
  a shield.

■ PSALM 6
☐ For the director of music. With stringed instruments.
According to *sheminith.a* A psalm of David.

1O LORD, do not rebuke me in your anger
  or discipline me in your wrath.
2Be merciful to me, LORD, for I am faint;
  O LORD, heal me, for my bones are in agony.
3My soul is in anguish.
  How long, O LORD, how long?

4Turn, O LORD, and deliver me;
  save me because of your unfailing love.
5No-one remembers you when he is dead.
  Who praises you from his grave?*b*

6I am worn out from groaning;
  all night long I flood my bed with weeping
  and drench my couch with tears.
7My eyes grow weak with sorrow;
  they fail because of all my foes.

8Away from me, all you who do evil,
  for the LORD has heard my weeping.
9The LORD has heard my cry for mercy;
  the LORD accepts my prayer.
10All my enemies will be ashamed and dismayed;
  they will turn back in sudden disgrace.

■ PSALM 7
☐ A *shiggaiona* of David, which he sang to the LORD
concerning Cush, a Benjamite.

1O LORD my God, I take refuge in you;
  save and deliver me from all who pursue me,
2or they will tear me like a lion
  and rip me to pieces with no-one to rescue
  me.

3O LORD my God, if I have done this
  and there is guilt on my hands—
4if I have done evil to him who is at peace with
  me
  or without cause have robbed my foe—

---

*b*2 Or *seek lies*   *a*Title: Probably a musical term   *b*5 Hebrew *Sheol*   *a*Title: Probably a literary or musical term

⁵then let my enemy pursue and overtake me;
    let him trample my life to the ground
    and make me sleep in the dust.   *Selah*

⁶Arise, O LORD, in your anger;
    rise up against the rage of my enemies.
    Awake, my God; decree justice.
⁷Let the assembled peoples gather round you.
    Rule over them from on high;
⁸ let the LORD judge the peoples.
  Judge me, O LORD, according to my
        righteousness,
    according to my integrity, O Most High.
⁹O righteous God,
    who searches minds and hearts,
  bring to an end the violence of the wicked
    and make the righteous secure.

¹⁰My shield*b* is God Most High,
    who saves the upright in heart.
¹¹God is a righteous judge,
    a God who expresses his wrath every day.
¹²If he does not relent,
    he*c* will sharpen his sword;
    he will bend and string his bow.
¹³He has prepared his deadly weapons;
    he makes ready his flaming arrows.

¹⁴He who is pregnant with evil
    and conceives trouble gives birth to
        disillusionment.
¹⁵He who digs a hole and scoops it out
    falls into the pit he has made.
¹⁶The trouble he causes recoils on himself;
    his violence comes down on his own head.

¹⁷I will give thanks to the LORD because of his
        righteousness
    and will sing praise to the name of the LORD
        Most High.

■ PSALM 8
□ For the director of music. According to *gittith.ᵃ* A psalm
of David.

¹O LORD, our Lord,
    how majestic is your name in all the earth!

  You have set your glory
    above the heavens.
²From the lips of children and infants
    you have ordained praise*b*
  because of your enemies,
    to silence the foe and the avenger.

8:2 ■ CHILDREN'S POWER
An almighty God needs no great powers to back
him. He shuts up his enemies through little
children and their spontaneous praise. That is
exactly what happened in Jesus' time (Matthew
21:16).

³When I consider your heavens,
    the work of your fingers,
    the moon and the stars,

which you have set in place,
⁴what is man that you are mindful of him,
    the son of man that you care for him?
⁵You made him a little lower than the heavenly
        beings*c*
    and crowned him with glory and honour.

⁶You made him ruler over the works of your
        hands;
    you put everything under his feet:
⁷all flocks and herds,
    and the beasts of the field,
⁸the birds of the air,
    and the fish of the sea,
    all that swim the paths of the seas.

⁹O LORD, our Lord,
    how majestic is your name in all the earth!

■ PSALM 9ᵃ
□ For the director of music. To ⌊the tune of⌋ "The Death of
the Son". A psalm of David.

¹I will praise you, O LORD, with all my heart;
    I will tell of all your wonders.
²I will be glad and rejoice in you;
    I will sing praise to your name, O Most High.

³My enemies turn back;
    they stumble and perish before you.
⁴For you have upheld my right and my cause;
    you have sat on your throne, judging
        righteously.
⁵You have rebuked the nations and destroyed
        the wicked;
    you have blotted out their name for ever and
        ever.
⁶Endless ruin has overtaken the enemy,
    you have uprooted their cities;
    even the memory of them has perished.

⁷The LORD reigns for ever;
    he has established his throne for judgment.
⁸He will judge the world in righteousness;
    he will govern the peoples with justice.
⁹The LORD is a refuge for the oppressed,
    a stronghold in times of trouble.
¹⁰Those who know your name will trust in you,
    for you, LORD, have never forsaken those who
        seek you.

¹¹Sing praises to the LORD, enthroned in Zion;
    proclaim among the nations what he has
        done.
¹²For he who avenges blood remembers;
    he does not ignore the cry of the afflicted.

¹³O LORD, see how my enemies persecute me!
    Have mercy and lift me up from the gates of
        death,
¹⁴that I may declare your praises
    in the gates of the Daughter of Zion
    and there rejoice in your salvation.
¹⁵The nations have fallen into the pit they have
        dug;
    their feet are caught in the net they have
        hidden.

b 10 Or *sovereign*   *c* 12 Or *If a man does not repent, / God*   *a* Title: Probably a musical term   *b* 2 Or *strength*   *c* 5 Or *than God*   *a* Psalms 9
and 10 may have been originally a single acrostic poem, the stanzas of which begin with the successive letters of the Hebrew alphabet. In the Septuagint they
constitute one psalm.

16The LORD is known by his justice;
the wicked are ensnared by the work of their
hands.   *Higgaion.*[b] *Selah*

17The wicked return to the grave,[c]
all the nations that forget God.
18But the needy will not always be forgotten,
nor the hope of the afflicted ever perish.

19Arise, O LORD, let not man triumph;
let the nations be judged in your presence.
20Strike them with terror, O LORD;
let the nations know they are but men. *Selah*

■ PSALM 10[a]

1Why, O LORD, do you stand far off?
Why do you hide yourself in times of
trouble?

2In his arrogance the wicked man hunts down
the weak,
who are caught in the schemes he devises.
3He boasts of the cravings of his heart;
he blesses the greedy and reviles the LORD.
4In his pride the wicked does not seek him;
in all his thoughts there is no room for God.
5His ways are always prosperous;
he is haughty and your laws are far from
him;
he sneers at all his enemies.
6He says to himself, "Nothing will shake me;
I'll always be happy and never have trouble."
7His mouth is full of curses and lies and threats;
trouble and evil are under his tongue.
8He lies in wait near the villages;
from ambush he murders the innocent,
watching in secret for his victims.
9He lies in wait like a lion in cover;
he lies in wait to catch the helpless;
he catches the helpless and drags them off in
his net.
10His victims are crushed, they collapse;
they fall under his strength.
11He says to himself, "God has forgotten;
he covers his face and never sees."

12Arise, LORD! Lift up your hand, O God.
Do not forget the helpless.
13Why does the wicked man revile God?
Why does he say to himself,
"He won't call me to account"?
14But you, O God, do see trouble and grief;
you consider it to take it in hand.
The victim commits himself to you;
you are the helper of the fatherless.
15Break the arm of the wicked and evil man;
call him to account for his wickedness
that would not be found out.

16The LORD is King for ever and ever;
the nations will perish from his land.
17You hear, O LORD, the desire of the afflicted;
you encourage them, and you listen to their
cry,
18defending the fatherless and the oppressed,

in order that man, who is of the earth, may
terrify no more.

■ PSALM 11
☐ For the director of music. Of David.

1In the LORD I take refuge.
How then can you say to me:
"Flee like a bird to your mountain.
2For look, the wicked bend their bows;
they set their arrows against the strings
to shoot from the shadows
at the upright in heart.
3When the foundations are being destroyed,
what can the righteous do?"[a]

4The LORD is in his holy temple;
the LORD is on his heavenly throne.
He observes the sons of men;
his eyes examine them.
5The LORD examines the righteous,
but the wicked[b] and those who love
violence
his soul hates.
6On the wicked he will rain
fiery coals and burning sulphur;
a scorching wind will be their lot.

7For the LORD is righteous,
he loves justice;
upright men will see his face.

■ PSALM 12
☐ For the director of music. According to *sheminith.*[a]
A psalm of David.

1Help, LORD, for the godly are no more;
the faithful have vanished from among men.
2Everyone lies to his neighbour;
their flattering lips speak with deception.

3May the LORD cut off all flattering lips
and every boastful tongue
4that says, "We will triumph with our tongues;
we own our lips[b] — who is our master?"

12:4 ■ WHO OWNS YOUR LIPS?
Repeatedly the Bible stresses that your talk can
do tremendous good or evil. One key distinction is
suggested here: wicked people use words to build
themselves up over others. They insist that no-one
has the right to tell them what to say.

5"Because of the oppression of the weak
and the groaning of the needy,
I will now arise," says the LORD.
"I will protect them from those who malign
them."
6And the words of the LORD are flawless,
like silver refined in a furnace of clay,
purified seven times.

7O LORD, you will keep us safe
and protect us from such people for ever.

b 16 Or *Meditation*; possibly a musical notation   *c* 17 Hebrew *Sheol*   *a*Psalms 9 and 10 may have been originally a single acrostic poem, the stanzas of
which begin with the successive letters of the Hebrew alphabet. In the Septuagint they constitute one psalm.   *a* 3 Or *what is the Righteous One doing*
b 5 Or *The LORD, the Righteous One, examines the wicked,* /   *a*Title: Probably a musical term   *b* 4 Or / *our lips are our ploughshares*

⁸The wicked freely strut about
  when what is vile is honoured among men.

■ PSALM 13
☐ For the director of music. A psalm of David.

¹How long, O LORD? Will you forget me for
  ever?
  How long will you hide your face from me?
²How long must I wrestle with my thoughts
  and every day have sorrow in my heart?
  How long will my enemy triumph over me?

³Look on me and answer, O LORD my God.
  Give light to my eyes, or I will sleep in
    death;
⁴my enemy will say, "I have overcome him,"
  and my foes will rejoice when I fall.

⁵But I trust in your unfailing love;
  my heart rejoices in your salvation.
⁶I will sing to the LORD,
  for he has been good to me.

■ PSALM 14
☐ For the director of music. Of David.

¹The fool*ᵃ* says in his heart,
  "There is no God."
They are corrupt, their deeds are vile;
  there is no-one who does good.

²The LORD looks down from heaven
  on the sons of men
to see if there are any who understand,
  any who seek God.
³All have turned aside,
  they have together become corrupt;
there is no-one who does good,
  not even one.

14:3 ■ WHO SEEKS GOD?
Though David was called a "man after God's own
heart", he is credited with this chilling assessment
of humankind — including himself. In God's eyes,
nobody — not even David — is good. Paul quoted
this in a crucial New Testament passage, Romans
3:10–12.

⁴Will evildoers never learn —
  those who devour my people as men eat
    bread
  and who do not call on the LORD?
⁵There they are, overwhelmed with dread,
  for God is present in the company of the
    righteous.
⁶You evildoers frustrate the plans of the poor,
  but the LORD is their refuge.

⁷Oh, that salvation for Israel would come out of
  Zion!
When the LORD restores the fortunes of his
  people,
let Jacob rejoice and Israel be glad!

■ PSALM 15
☐ A psalm of David.

¹LORD, who may dwell in your sanctuary?
  Who may live on your holy hill?

²He whose walk is blameless
  and who does what is righteous,
who speaks the truth from his heart
³ and has no slander on his tongue,
who does his neighbour no wrong
  and casts no slur on his fellow-man,
⁴who despises a vile man
  but honours those who fear the LORD,
who keeps his oath
  even when it hurts,
⁵who lends his money without usury
  and does not accept a bribe against the
    innocent.

He who does these things
  will never be shaken.

■ PSALM 16
☐ A *miktam*ᵃ of David.

¹Keep me safe, O God,
  for in you I take refuge.

²I said to the LORD, "You are my Lord;
  apart from you I have no good thing."
³As for the saints who are in the land,
  they are the glorious ones in whom is all my
    delight.*ᵇ*
⁴The sorrows of those will increase
  who run after other gods.
I will not pour out their libations of blood
  or take up their names on my lips.

⁵LORD, you have assigned me my portion and my
    cup;
  you have made my lot secure.
⁶The boundary lines have fallen for me in
    pleasant places;
  surely I have a delightful inheritance.

⁷I will praise the LORD, who counsels me;
  even at night my heart instructs me.
⁸I have set the LORD always before me.
  Because he is at my right hand,
  I shall not be shaken.

⁹Therefore my heart is glad and my tongue
    rejoices;
  my body also will rest secure,
¹⁰because you will not abandon me to the
    grave,*ᶜ*
  nor will you let your Holy One*ᵈ* see decay.
¹¹You have made known*ᵉ* to me the path of life;
  you will fill me with joy in your presence,
  with eternal pleasures at your right hand.

■ PSALM 17
☐ A prayer of David.

¹Hear, O LORD, my righteous plea;
  listen to my cry.

ᵃ1 The Hebrew words rendered *fool* in Psalms denote one who is morally deficient.   *ᵃ*Title: Probably a literary or musical term   *ᵇ3* Or *As for the pagan priests who are in the land / and the nobles in whom all delight, I said:*   *ᶜ10* Hebrew *Sheol*   *ᵈ10* Or *your faithful one*   *ᵉ11* Or *You will make known*

Give ear to my prayer—
    it does not rise from deceitful lips.
²May my vindication come from you;
    may your eyes see what is right.

16:10 ■ RESURRECTION!

In this confident, happy psalm, David rejoices that the life God gives cannot be cancelled by the grave. Generally, the Old Testament offers little insight into life after death, but here David's faith carries him to a deeper understanding. The apostles Peter and Paul understood this psalm as prophesying Jesus' resurrection (see Acts 2:25–28; 13:35–37). Because of Jesus' resurrection, David and all God's people would come to new life in him.

---

³Though you probe my heart and examine me at
        night,
    though you test me, you will find nothing;
    I have resolved that my mouth will not sin.
⁴As for the deeds of men—
    by the word of your lips
I have kept myself
    from the ways of the violent.

⁵My steps have held to your paths;
    my feet have not slipped.

⁶I call on you, O God, for you will answer me;
    give ear to me and hear my prayer.
⁷Show the wonder of your great love,
    you who save by your right hand
    those who take refuge in you from their foes.
⁸Keep me as the apple of your eye;
    hide me in the shadow of your wings
⁹from the wicked who assail me,
    from my mortal enemies who surround me.

¹⁰They close up their callous hearts,
    and their mouths speak with arrogance.
¹¹They have tracked me down, they now
        surround me,
    with eyes alert, to throw me to the ground.
¹²They are like a lion hungry for prey,
    like a great lion crouching in cover.

¹³Rise up, O LORD, confront them, bring them
        down;
    rescue me from the wicked by your sword.
¹⁴O LORD, by your hand save me from such men,
    from men of this world whose reward is in
        this life.

You still the hunger of those you cherish;

■ LIFE AFTER DEATH
WHEN YOU DIE, WILL IT ALL BE OVER?

INSIGHT

YOU WILL NOT ABANDON ME TO THE GRAVE, NOR WILL YOU LET YOUR HOLY ONE SEE DECAY. ■ 16:10

What happens to you after you die? People have always wanted an answer to that, and the psalmists were no different. They lived in an age without effective medicine, in an age when wars were fought hand-to-hand. Dead bodies were a familiar reality. Yet death, however familiar, remained mysterious and frightening to them.

Israelites called the dark and shadowy place where dead people go "Sheol". When you got there, your life seemed thoroughly finished. The psalmists emphatically did not want to go there, and they asked God, when praying for his help, what possible good there might be in death. "Are your wonders known in the place of darkness, or your righteous deeds in the land of oblivion?" (Psalm 88:12). Sheol was the great leveller: it meant the end of plans, of worship, of a relationship with God (Psalms 30:9; 88:5; 146:4). The dead were found there, not the living.

■ GOD'S POWER OVER DEATH

Yet some psalms also hint at a happier view. They hold such a strong view of God's authority that they show—vaguely, but

unmistakably—God's power over the grave. For instance, God is *in* Sheol (Psalm 139:8). He—and only he—can redeem a person from there (49:7–9,15). God will not let his "Holy One" see decay—a claim that both Peter and Paul saw as a clear prediction of Jesus' resurrection from the dead (Psalm 16:10, quoted in Acts 2:27; 13:35).

What did they expect life after death to be like, if God's power redeemed someone from Sheol? You won't find a clearly defined picture of heaven here—only hints. The psalmists' thoughts centre on God's face and his presence. For God is the only unchangeable reality: wherever you are, in life or in death, he will be there. He is the ultimate reward to those who love him.

The expectation of God's face shows through in Psalms 16:8–11; 17:15; 49:15; 73:23–26. But for a clearer perspective on life after death, you must read, in the Old Testament, Isaiah 26:19 and Daniel 12:1–3, and in the New Testament, 2 Corinthians 5:1–10, among many other passages.

□ LIFE QUESTIONS:

Describe what you believe happens after you die. Is this a frightening or an encouraging picture to you?

their sons have plenty,
    and they store up wealth for their children.
¹⁵And I—in righteousness I shall see your face;
    when I awake, I shall be satisfied with seeing
    your likeness.

17:15 ■ THE FACE OF GOD

While the psalms often ask God to provide "refuge" in a time of trouble, they also look forward to "seeing his face"—a goal that is valuable only to someone who deeply loves God. To see God's face is to see and know him personally, deeply, and without the clouds of mystery that so often make faith difficult.

■ PSALM 18

☐ For the director of music. Of David the servant of the LORD. He sang to the LORD the words of this song when the LORD delivered him from the hand of all his enemies and from the hand of Saul. He said:

¹I love you, O LORD, my strength.

²The LORD is my rock, my fortress and my
    deliverer;
    my God is my rock, in whom I take refuge.
    He is my shield and the horn^a of my
      salvation, my stronghold.
³I call to the LORD, who is worthy of praise,
    and I am saved from my enemies.

⁴The cords of death entangled me;
    the torrents of destruction overwhelmed me.
⁵The cords of the grave^b coiled around me;
    the snares of death confronted me.
⁶In my distress I called to the LORD;
    I cried to my God for help.
 From his temple he heard my voice;
    my cry came before him, into his ears.

⁷The earth trembled and quaked,
    and the foundations of the mountains shook;
    they trembled because he was angry.
⁸Smoke rose from his nostrils;
    consuming fire came from his mouth,
    burning coals blazed out of it.
⁹He parted the heavens and came down;
    dark clouds were under his feet.
¹⁰He mounted the cherubim and flew;
    he soared on the wings of the wind.
¹¹He made darkness his covering, his canopy
    around him—
    the dark rain clouds of the sky.
¹²Out of the brightness of his presence clouds
    advanced,
    with hailstones and bolts of lightning.
¹³The LORD thundered from heaven;
    the voice of the Most High resounded.^c
¹⁴He shot his arrows and scattered ⌊the enemies⌋,
    great bolts of lightning and routed them.
¹⁵The valleys of the sea were exposed
    and the foundations of the earth laid bare
 at your rebuke, O LORD,
    at the blast of breath from your nostrils.

¹⁶He reached down from on high and took hold
    of me;
    he drew me out of deep waters.
¹⁷He rescued me from my powerful enemy,
    from my foes, who were too strong for me.
¹⁸They confronted me in the day of my disaster,
    but the LORD was my support.
¹⁹He brought me out into a spacious place;
    he rescued me because he delighted in me.

²⁰The LORD has dealt with me according to my
    righteousness;
    according to the cleanness of my hands he
      has rewarded me.
²¹For I have kept the ways of the LORD;
    I have not done evil by turning from my
      God.
²²All his laws are before me;
    I have not turned away from his decrees.
²³I have been blameless before him
    and have kept myself from sin.
²⁴The LORD has rewarded me according to my
    righteousness,
    according to the cleanness of my hands in
      his sight.

²⁵To the faithful you show yourself faithful,
    to the blameless you show yourself
      blameless,
²⁶to the pure you show yourself pure,
    but to the crooked you show yourself
      shrewd.
²⁷You save the humble
    but bring low those whose eyes are haughty.
²⁸You, O LORD, keep my lamp burning;
    my God turns my darkness into light.
²⁹With your help I can advance against a troop;^d
    with my God I can scale a wall.

³⁰As for God, his way is perfect;
    the word of the LORD is flawless.
 He is a shield
    for all who take refuge in him.
³¹For who is God besides the LORD?
    And who is the Rock except our God?
³²It is God who arms me with strength
    and makes my way perfect.
³³He makes my feet like the feet of a deer;
    he enables me to stand on the heights.
³⁴He trains my hands for battle;
    my arms can bend a bow of bronze.
³⁵You give me your shield of victory,
    and your right hand sustains me;
    you stoop down to make me great.
³⁶You broaden the path beneath me,
    so that my ankles do not turn over.

³⁷I pursued my enemies and overtook them;
    I did not turn back till they were destroyed.
³⁸I crushed them so that they could not rise;
    they fell beneath my feet.
³⁹You armed me with strength for battle;
    you made my adversaries bow at my feet.
⁴⁰You made my enemies turn their backs in
    flight,
    and I destroyed my foes.

---

^a2 *Horn* here symbolises strength.   ^b5 Hebrew *Sheol*   ^c13 Some Hebrew manuscripts and Septuagint (see also 2 Samuel 22:14); most Hebrew manuscripts *resounded, / amid hailstones and bolts of lightning*   ^d29 Or *can run through a barricade*

41They cried for help, but there was no-one to
    save them—
  to the LORD, but he did not answer.
42I beat them as fine as dust borne on the wind;
  I poured them out like mud in the streets.

43You have delivered me from the attacks of the
    people;
  you have made me the head of nations;
  people I did not know are subject to me.
44As soon as they hear me, they obey me;
  foreigners cringe before me.
45They all lose heart;
  they come trembling from their strongholds.

46The LORD lives! Praise be to my Rock!
  Exalted be God my Saviour!
47He is the God who avenges me,
  who subdues nations under me,
48 who saves me from my enemies.
  You exalted me above my foes;
  from violent men you rescued me.
49Therefore I will praise you among the nations,
  O LORD;
  I will sing praises to your name.
50He gives his king great victories;
  he shows unfailing kindness to his anointed,
  to David and his descendants for ever.

18:49 ■ GOING PUBLIC

For the psalmists, praising God was more than a
personal matter between the believer and his God.
They praised God publicly—even in front of
unbelievers—often inviting their audience to join in.
Such public praise anticipated New Testament
evangelism, the spreading of good news to the
entire world. Paul quoted this verse in Romans
15:9 to stress that God had always meant his love
to reach out from the Jews to the rest of
humanity.

■ PSALM 19
☐ For the director of music. A psalm of David.

1The heavens declare the glory of God;
  the skies proclaim the work of his hands.
2Day after day they pour forth speech;
  night after night they display knowledge.
3There is no speech or language
  where their voice is not heard.a
4Their voiceb goes out into all the earth,
  their words to the ends of the world.

  In the heavens he has pitched a tent for the
    sun,
5 which is like a bridegroom coming forth
    from his pavilion,
  like a champion rejoicing to run his course.
6It rises at one end of the heavens
  and makes its circuit to the other;
  nothing is hidden from its heat.

7The law of the LORD is perfect,
  reviving the soul.
  The statutes of the LORD are trustworthy,

  making wise the simple.
8The precepts of the LORD are right,
  giving joy to the heart.
  The commands of the LORD are radiant,
  giving light to the eyes.
9The fear of the LORD is pure,
  enduring for ever.
  The ordinances of the LORD are sure
  and altogether righteous.
10They are more precious than gold,
  than much pure gold;
  they are sweeter than honey,
  than honey from the comb.
11By them is your servant warned;
  in keeping them there is great reward.

19:7 ■ THE NAMES OF GOD

After describing the skies as a reflection of God's
glory in the first six verses, Psalm 19 switches
gears. From the sun, moon, and stars it turns to
consider the beauty of God's law. Reflecting that
change, the poem in Hebrew uses a different,
more personal name for God. The first six verses
refer to God with a general name that anyone, of
any religion, might use—just like our English word
God. But from verse seven on, God is called "the
LORD" (a translation of the Hebrew Yahweh)—the
personal name God revealed to Moses from the
burning bush (Exodus 3:15). The heavens declare
the glory of God, but God's law reveals even
more—his personal voice to his chosen people.
He introduces himself to them by his first name,
as it were.

12Who can discern his errors?
  Forgive my hidden faults.
13Keep your servant also from wilful sins;
  may they not rule over me.
  Then will I be blameless,
  innocent of great transgression.

14May the words of my mouth and the
    meditation of my heart
  be pleasing in your sight,
  O LORD, my Rock and my Redeemer.

■ PSALM 20
☐ For the director of music. A psalm of David.

1May the LORD answer you when you are in
    distress;
  may the name of the God of Jacob protect
    you.
2May he send you help from the sanctuary
  and grant you support from Zion.
3May he remember all your sacrifices
  and accept your burnt offerings.   Selah
4May he give you the desire of your heart
  and make all your plans succeed.
5We will shout for joy when you are victorious
  and will lift up our banners in the name of
    our God.
  May the LORD grant all your requests.

a3 Or They have no speech, there are no words; / no sound is heard from them   b4 Septuagint, Jerome and Syriac; Hebrew line

6Now I know that the LORD saves his anointed;
he answers him from his holy heaven
with the saving power of his right hand.
7Some trust in chariots and some in horses,
but we trust in the name of the LORD our
God.
8They are brought to their knees and fall,
but we rise up and stand firm.
9O LORD, save the king!
Answer[a] us when we call!

■ PSALM 21
☐ For the director of music. A psalm of David.

1O LORD, the king rejoices in your strength.
How great is his joy in the victories you
give!
2You have granted him the desire of his heart
and have not withheld the request of his lips.
Selah
3You welcomed him with rich blessings
and placed a crown of pure gold on his head.
4He asked you for life, and you gave it to him —
length of days, for ever and ever.
5Through the victories you gave, his glory is
great;
you have bestowed on him splendour and
majesty.
6Surely you have granted him eternal blessings
and made him glad with the joy of your
presence.
7For the king trusts in the LORD;
through the unfailing love of the Most High
he will not be shaken.

8Your hand will lay hold on all your enemies;
your right hand will seize your foes.
9At the time of your appearing
you will make them like a fiery furnace.
In his wrath the LORD will swallow them up,
and his fire will consume them.
10You will destroy their descendants from the
earth,
their posterity from mankind.
11Though they plot evil against you
and devise wicked schemes, they cannot
succeed;
12for you will make them turn their backs
when you aim at them with drawn bow.

13Be exalted, O LORD, in your strength;
we will sing and praise your might.

■ PSALM 22
☐ For the director of music. To ˻the tune of˼ "The Doe of the
Morning". A psalm of David.

1My God, my God, why have you forsaken me?
Why are you so far from saving me,
so far from the words of my groaning?
2O my God, I cry out by day, but you do not
answer,
by night, and am not silent.

3Yet you are enthroned as the Holy One;

you are the praise of Israel.[a]
4In you our fathers put their trust;
they trusted and you delivered them.
5They cried to you and were saved;
in you they trusted and were not
disappointed.

6But I am a worm and not a man,
scorned by men and despised by the people.
7All who see me mock me;
they hurl insults, shaking their heads:
8"He trusts in the LORD;
let the LORD rescue him.
Let him deliver him,
since he delights in him."

9Yet you brought me out of the womb;
you made me trust in you
even at my mother's breast.
10From birth I was cast upon you;
from my mother's womb you have been my
God.
11Do not be far from me,
for trouble is near
and there is no-one to help.

12Many bulls surround me;
strong bulls of Bashan encircle me.
13Roaring lions tearing their prey
open their mouths wide against me.
14I am poured out like water,
and all my bones are out of joint.
My heart has turned to wax;
it has melted away within me.
15My strength is dried up like a potsherd,
and my tongue sticks to the roof of my
mouth;
you lay me[b] in the dust of death.
16Dogs have surrounded me;
a band of evil men has encircled me,
they have pierced[c] my hands and my feet.
17I can count all my bones;
people stare and gloat over me.
18They divide my garments among them
and cast lots for my clothing.

19But you, O LORD, be not far off;
O my Strength, come quickly to help me.
20Deliver my life from the sword,
my precious life from the power of the dogs.
21Rescue me from the mouth of the lions;
save[d] me from the horns of the wild oxen.

22I will declare your name to my brothers;
in the congregation I will praise you.
23You who fear the LORD, praise him!
All you descendants of Jacob, honour him!
Revere him, all you descendants of Israel!
24For he has not despised or disdained
the suffering of the afflicted one;
he has not hidden his face from him
but has listened to his cry for help.

25From you comes the theme of my praise in the
great assembly;
before those who fear you[e] will I fulfil my
vows.

---

[a]9 Or save! / O King, answer   [a]3 Or Yet you are holy, / enthroned on the praises of Israel   [b]15 Or / I am laid   [c]16 Some Hebrew manuscripts,
Septuagint and Syriac; most Hebrew manuscripts / like the lion,   [d]21 Or / you have heard   [e]25 Hebrew him

26The poor will eat and be satisfied;
  they who seek the LORD will praise him—
  may your hearts live for ever!
27All the ends of the earth
  will remember and turn to the LORD,
and all the families of the nations
  will bow down before him,
28for dominion belongs to the LORD
  and he rules over the nations.

29All the rich of the earth will feast and worship;
  all who go down to the dust will kneel
    before him—
  those who cannot keep themselves alive.
30Posterity will serve him;
  future generations will be told about the
    Lord.

31They will proclaim his righteousness
  to a people yet unborn—
  for he has done it.

■ PSALM 23
□ A psalm of David.

1The LORD is my shepherd, I shall not be in
    want.
2 He makes me lie down in green pastures,
  he leads me beside quiet waters,
3 he restores my soul.
  He guides me in paths of righteousness
    for his name's sake.
4Even though I walk
  through the valley of the shadow of death,a

■ THE SONG OF THE CROSS
EVEN THE BEST PEOPLE SOMETIMES SUFFER

INSIGHT

THEY DIVIDE MY GARMENTS AMONG
THEM AND CAST LOTS FOR MY
CLOTHING. ■ 22:18

Superficially, the Old Testament can sometimes
read like it's taken from old films. The good
guys are the Israelites, and they fight with the
bad guys from nations around them. The
Israelites have moments when they get off the
track, worshipping idols and acting like their
"bad guy" neighbours. But when they turn back
to God, they invariably win, and win big. The
ending, in story after story, is happy. God *is* on
their side.

Yet, in Psalm 22, and a few other
places, the "good guy" story doesn't fit—at all.
This poem, credited to David, the great king and
man "after God's own heart", tells about
tremendous suffering with no relief from God. It
sounds like a mob scene, a lynching. The "good
guy's" enemies have him. They surround him,
jeering, like a pack of dogs. He is helpless and
exhausted. All he can do is cry out to God.

The psalmist wavers back and forth, first
crying out his misery, then taking stock of God's
wonderful character, then describing his misery
again. The whole poem is a prayer to God.
Although this cry has gone up day and night
(verse 2), God remains silent.

■ WHOSE HUMILIATIONS?
Then, at verse 22, the poem takes a dramatic
turn, switching from grief to jubilation.
Somehow, God has saved the sufferer, who, in
great excitement, tells others about it. He sees
more than his own good fortune: he foresees
this deliverance spilling over into the whole
world. He predicts the story of God's help told
to future generations for ever. God will be
worshipped by the entire world.

A person might read Psalm 22 as an
extravagantly poetic description of David's
troubles. But Jesus and the writers of the New
Testament saw something more in it. When
Jesus was dying on the cross, he had this
psalm on his lips (Matthew 27:46). Afterwards,
when his disciples wanted to explain Jesus' life
and sufferings, they turned to this psalm and
others like it.

In them the disciples saw a pattern
and a foreshadowing. The pattern is
redemptive suffering. If good guys do not
always win, if God seems actually to desert
them—if David himself, the great leader and
true man of God, knew these pains—then
surely no-one is exempt. And this suffering has
a point. After it (and because of it) come
victory and power, and the salvation of the
world. This pattern helped Jesus' followers
appreciate why Jesus, together with his
followers, had to suffer.

■ A FULFILMENT OF PROPHECY
Psalm 22 also helped the New Testament
writers to see Jesus' life as a fulfilment of Old
Testament prophecy. Jews had expected a
Warrior-Messiah, a son of David who, like
David, would lead his people to victory through
battle. In Psalm 22 they saw that David had
left another legacy: victory through suffering.
The Messiah would lead his followers in
suffering. Only Isaiah had put it more clearly, in
his famous "servant" passages (Isaiah 42:1–9;
49:1–7; 50:4–9; 52:13–53:12). Psalm 22
stretches beyond the time of David; Jesus fits
it perfectly.

□ LIFE QUESTIONS:
Have you ever seen good come out of
suffering for your friends or family?

a4 Or through the darkest valley

I will fear no evil,
for you are with me;
your rod and your staff,
they comfort me.

5You prepare a table before me
in the presence of my enemies.
You anoint my head with oil;
my cup overflows.
6Surely goodness and love will follow me
all the days of my life,
and I will dwell in the house of the LORD
for ever.

■ PSALM 24
□ Of David. A psalm.

1The earth is the LORD's, and everything in it,
the world, and all who live in it;
2for he founded it upon the seas
and established it upon the waters.

3Who may ascend the hill of the LORD?
Who may stand in his holy place?
4He who has clean hands and a pure heart,
who does not lift up his soul to an idol
or swear by what is false.a
5He will receive blessing from the LORD
and vindication from God his Saviour.
6Such is the generation of those who seek him,
who seek your face, O God of Jacob.b Selah

7Lift up your heads, O you gates;
be lifted up, you ancient doors,
that the King of glory may come in.
8Who is this King of glory?
The LORD strong and mighty,
the LORD mighty in battle.
9Lift up your heads, O you gates;
lift them up, you ancient doors,
that the King of glory may come in.
10Who is he, this King of glory?
The LORD Almighty—
he is the King of glory. Selah

■ PSALM 25a
□ Of David.

1To you, O LORD, I lift up my soul;
2 in you I trust, O my God.
Do not let me be put to shame,
nor let my enemies triumph over me.
3No-one whose hope is in you
will ever be put to shame,
but they will be put to shame
who are treacherous without excuse.

4Show me your ways, O LORD,
teach me your paths;
5guide me in your truth and teach me,
for you are God my Saviour,
and my hope is in you all day long.
6Remember, O LORD, your great mercy and love,
for they are from of old.

7Remember not the sins of my youth
and my rebellious ways;
according to your love remember me,
for you are good, O LORD.

8Good and upright is the LORD;
therefore he instructs sinners in his ways.
9He guides the humble in what is right
and teaches them his way.
10All the ways of the LORD are loving and faithful
for those who keep the demands of his
covenant.
11For the sake of your name, O LORD,
forgive my iniquity, though it is great.
12Who, then, is the man that fears the LORD?
He will instruct him in the way chosen for
him.
13He will spend his days in prosperity,
and his descendants will inherit the land.
14The LORD confides in those who fear him;
he makes his covenant known to them.
15My eyes are ever on the LORD,
for only he will release my feet from the
snare.

16Turn to me and be gracious to me,
for I am lonely and afflicted.
17The troubles of my heart have multiplied;
free me from my anguish.
18Look upon my affliction and my distress
and take away all my sins.
19See how my enemies have increased
and how fiercely they hate me!
20Guard my life and rescue me;
let me not be put to shame,
for I take refuge in you.
21May integrity and uprightness protect me,
because my hope is in you.

22Redeem Israel, O God,
from all their troubles!

■ PSALM 26
□ Of David.

1Vindicate me, O LORD,
for I have led a blameless life;
I have trusted in the LORD
without wavering.
2Test me, O LORD, and try me,
examine my heart and my mind;
3for your love is ever before me,
and I walk continually in your truth.
4I do not sit with deceitful men,
nor do I consort with hypocrites;
5I abhor the assembly of evildoers
and refuse to sit with the wicked.
6I wash my hands in innocence,
and go about your altar, O LORD,
7proclaiming aloud your praise
and telling of all your wonderful deeds.
8I love the house where you live, O LORD,
the place where your glory dwells.

9Do not take away my soul along with sinners,
my life with bloodthirsty men,

a4 Or swear falsely   b6 Two Hebrew manuscripts and Syriac (see also Septuagint); most Hebrew manuscripts face, Jacob   aThis psalm is an acrostic
poem, the verses of which begin with the successive letters of the Hebrew alphabet.

¹⁰in whose hands are wicked schemes,
whose right hands are full of bribes.
¹¹But I lead a blameless life;
redeem me and be merciful to me.

¹²My feet stand on level ground;
in the great assembly I will praise the LORD.

26:11 ■ SELF-RIGHTEOUS?

This claim to be blameless or righteous – repeated many times in other psalms – should not be stretched too far. Whenever the psalmists examined themselves before God, they acknowledged their deep need for forgiveness (see 19:12; 32:1–5; 130:3; and 143:2).

Here, though, the issue is God's fairness. Knowing little about life after death, the psalmists expected that good people would do better in this life than bad people. They were deeply puzzled when they did not. Didn't God control every event? In calling for justice, they emphasised that they had been more faithful to God than their enemies.

Compared to the people plotting murder and betrayal against him, the psalmist was blameless. In a wholehearted, sincere way he had followed God. He was no hypocrite. He responds like a person swearing in court about his traffic accident: "My driving is blameless." He doesn't mean he never makes a mistake. He means only that he doesn't deserve punishment.

■ PSALM 27
☐ Of David.

¹The LORD is my light and my salvation –
whom shall I fear?
The LORD is the stronghold of my life –
of whom shall I be afraid?
²When evil men advance against me
to devour my flesh,^a
when my enemies and my foes attack me,
they will stumble and fall.
³Though an army besiege me,
my heart will not fear;
though war break out against me,
even then will I be confident.

⁴One thing I ask of the LORD,
this is what I seek:
that I may dwell in the house of the LORD
all the days of my life,
to gaze upon the beauty of the LORD
and to seek him in his temple.
⁵For in the day of trouble
he will keep me safe in his dwelling;
he will hide me in the shelter of his tabernacle
and set me high upon a rock.
⁶Then my head will be exalted
above the enemies who surround me;
at his tabernacle will I sacrifice with shouts of
joy;
I will sing and make music to the LORD.

⁷Hear my voice when I call, O LORD;
be merciful to me and answer me.
⁸My heart says of you, "Seek his^b face!"
Your face, LORD, I will seek.
⁹Do not hide your face from me,
do not turn your servant away in anger;
you have been my helper.
Do not reject me or forsake me,
O God my Saviour.
¹⁰Though my father and mother forsake me,
the LORD will receive me.
¹¹Teach me your way, O LORD;
lead me in a straight path
because of my oppressors.
¹²Do not hand me over to the desire of my foes,
for false witnesses rise up against me,
breathing out violence.

¹³I am still confident of this:
I will see the goodness of the LORD
in the land of the living.
¹⁴Wait for the LORD;
be strong and take heart
and wait for the LORD.

■ PSALM 28
☐ Of David.

¹To you I call, O LORD my Rock;
do not turn a deaf ear to me.
For if you remain silent,
I shall be like those who have gone down to
the pit.
²Hear my cry for mercy
as I call to you for help,
as I lift up my hands
towards your Most Holy Place.

³Do not drag me away with the wicked,
with those who do evil,
who speak cordially with their neighbours
but harbour malice in their hearts.
⁴Repay them for their deeds
and for their evil work;
repay them for what their hands have done
and bring back upon them what they
deserve.
⁵Since they show no regard for the works of the
LORD
and what his hands have done,
he will tear them down
and never build them up again.

⁶Praise be to the LORD,
for he has heard my cry for mercy.
⁷The LORD is my strength and my shield;
my heart trusts in him, and I am helped.
My heart leaps for joy
and I will give thanks to him in song.

⁸The LORD is the strength of his people,
a fortress of salvation for his anointed one.
⁹Save your people and bless your inheritance;
be their shepherd and carry them for ever.

^a2 Or to slander me   ^b8 Or To you, O my heart, he has said, "Seek my

■ PSALM 29

☐ A psalm of David.

[1]Ascribe to the LORD, O mighty ones,
    ascribe to the LORD glory and strength.
[2]Ascribe to the LORD the glory due to his name;
    worship the LORD in the splendour of his[a]
        holiness.

[3]The voice of the LORD is over the waters;
    the God of glory thunders,
    the LORD thunders over the mighty waters.
[4]The voice of the LORD is powerful;
    the voice of the LORD is majestic.
[5]The voice of the LORD breaks the cedars;
    the LORD breaks in pieces the cedars of
        Lebanon.
[6]He makes Lebanon skip like a calf,
    Sirion[b] like a young wild ox.
[7]The voice of the LORD strikes
    with flashes of lightning.
[8]The voice of the LORD shakes the desert;
    the LORD shakes the Desert of Kadesh.
[9]The voice of the LORD twists the oaks[c]
    and strips the forests bare.
    And in his temple all cry, "Glory!"

[10]The LORD sits[d] enthroned over the flood;
    the LORD is enthroned as King for ever.
[11]The LORD gives strength to his people;
    the LORD blesses his people with peace.

■ PSALM 30

☐ A psalm. A song. For the dedication of the temple.[a]
Of David.

[1]I will exalt you, O LORD,
    for you lifted me out of the depths
    and did not let my enemies gloat over me.
[2]O LORD my God, I called to you for help
    and you healed me.
[3]O LORD, you brought me up from the grave;[b]
    you spared me from going down into the pit.

[4]Sing to the LORD, you saints of his;
    praise his holy name.
[5]For his anger lasts only a moment,
    but his favour lasts a lifetime;
weeping may remain for a night,
    but rejoicing comes in the morning.

30:5 ■ ONE-NIGHT GUEST
The Bible never ignores the emotions of the
moment. Here, the psalmist acknowledges the
tough times that come with living as God's child.
But the Bible also insists on a long-range
perspective. Difficulties don't last; God's care
does. This psalm pictures "weeping" as a guest
who comes to stay for just a single night.

---

[6]When I felt secure, I said,
    "I shall never be shaken."
[7]O LORD, when you favoured me,
    you made my mountain[c] stand firm;
    but when you hid your face,

I was dismayed.

[8]To you, O LORD, I called;
    to the Lord I cried for mercy:
[9]"What gain is there in my destruction,[d]
    in my going down into the pit?
Will the dust praise you?
    Will it proclaim your faithfulness?
[10]Hear, O LORD, and be merciful to me;
    O LORD, be my help."

[11]You turned my wailing into dancing;
    you removed my sackcloth and clothed me
        with joy,
[12]that my heart may sing to you and not be
        silent.
    O LORD my God, I will give you thanks for
        ever.

■ PSALM 31

☐ For the director of music. A psalm of David.

[1]In you, O LORD, I have taken refuge;
    let me never be put to shame;
    deliver me in your righteousness.
[2]Turn your ear to me,
    come quickly to my rescue;
    be my rock of refuge,
    a strong fortress to save me.
[3]Since you are my rock and my fortress,
    for the sake of your name lead and guide me.
[4]Free me from the trap that is set for me,
    for you are my refuge.
[5]Into your hands I commit my spirit;
    redeem me, O LORD, the God of truth.

[6]I hate those who cling to worthless idols;
    I trust in the LORD.
[7]I will be glad and rejoice in your love,
    for you saw my affliction
    and knew the anguish of my soul.
[8]You have not handed me over to the enemy
    but have set my feet in a spacious place.

[9]Be merciful to me, O LORD, for I am in distress;
    my eyes grow weak with sorrow,
    my soul and my body with grief.
[10]My life is consumed by anguish
    and my years by groaning;
    my strength fails because of my affliction,[a]
    and my bones grow weak.
[11]Because of all my enemies,
    I am the utter contempt of my neighbours;
    I am a dread to my friends—
    those who see me on the street flee from
        me.
[12]I am forgotten by them as though I were dead;
    I have become like broken pottery.
[13]For I hear the slander of many;
    there is terror on every side;
    they conspire against me
    and plot to take my life.

[14]But I trust in you, O LORD;
    I say, "You are my God."
[15]My times are in your hands;
    deliver me from my enemies

---

a2 Or LORD with the splendour of   *b6* That is, Mount Hermon   *c9* Or LORD makes the deer give birth   *d10* Or sat   *a*Title: Or palace
b3 Hebrew Sheol   *c7* Or hill country   *d9* Or there if I am silenced   *a10* Or guilt

and from those who pursue me.
¹⁶Let your face shine on your servant;
    save me in your unfailing love.
¹⁷Let me not be put to shame, O LORD,
    for I have cried out to you;
but let the wicked be put to shame
    and lie silent in the grave.ᵇ
¹⁸Let their lying lips be silenced,
    for with pride and contempt
    they speak arrogantly against the righteous.

¹⁹How great is your goodness,
    which you have stored up for those who fear
        you,
which you bestow in the sight of men
    on those who take refuge in you.
²⁰In the shelter of your presence you hide them
    from the intrigues of men;
in your dwelling you keep them safe
    from accusing tongues.

²¹Praise be to the LORD,
    for he showed his wonderful love to me
    when I was in a besieged city.
²²In my alarm I said,
    "I am cut off from your sight!"
Yet you heard my cry for mercy
    when I called to you for help.

²³Love the LORD, all his saints!
    The LORD preserves the faithful,
    but the proud he pays back in full.
²⁴Be strong and take heart,
    all you who hope in the LORD.

■ PSALM 32
□ Of David. A *maskil.*ᵃ

¹Blessed is he
    whose transgressions are forgiven,
    whose sins are covered.
²Blessed is the man
    whose sin the LORD does not count against
        him
    and in whose spirit is no deceit.

32:2 ■ THE BENEFITS OF FAITH
Paul quoted this verse in Romans 4:6–8, while
making his case that we do not earn status in
God's eyes: God must credit righteousness on the
basis of faith.

³When I kept silent,
    my bones wasted away
    through my groaning all day long.
⁴For day and night
    your hand was heavy upon me;
my strength was sapped
    as in the heat of summer.   *Selah*
⁵Then I acknowledged my sin to you
    and did not cover up my iniquity.
I said, "I will confess
    my transgressions to the LORD" —
    and you forgave

the guilt of my sin.   *Selah*

⁶Therefore let everyone who is godly pray to
        you
    while you may be found;
surely when the mighty waters rise,
    they will not reach him.
⁷You are my hiding-place;
    you will protect me from trouble
    and surround me with songs of deliverance.
                                        Selah

⁸I will instruct you and teach you in the way
        you should go;
    I will counsel you and watch over you.
⁹Do not be like the horse or the mule,
    which have no understanding
but must be controlled by bit and bridle
    or they will not come to you.
¹⁰Many are the woes of the wicked,
    but the LORD's unfailing love
    surrounds the man who trusts in him.

¹¹Rejoice in the LORD and be glad, you righteous;
    sing, all you who are upright in heart!

■ PSALM 33

¹Sing joyfully to the LORD, you righteous;
    it is fitting for the upright to praise him.
²Praise the LORD with the harp;
    make music to him on the ten-stringed lyre.
³Sing to him a new song;
    play skilfully, and shout for joy.

⁴For the word of the LORD is right and true;
    he is faithful in all he does.
⁵The LORD loves righteousness and justice;
    the earth is full of his unfailing love.

⁶By the word of the LORD were the heavens
        made,
    their starry host by the breath of his mouth.
⁷He gathers the waters of the sea into jars;ᵃ
    he puts the deep into storehouses.
⁸Let all the earth fear the LORD;
    let all the people of the world revere him.
⁹For he spoke, and it came to be;
    he commanded, and it stood firm.
¹⁰The LORD foils the plans of the nations;
    he thwarts the purposes of the peoples.
¹¹But the plans of the LORD stand firm for ever,
    the purposes of his heart through all
        generations.

¹²Blessed is the nation whose God is the LORD,
    the people he chose for his inheritance.
¹³From heaven the LORD looks down
    and sees all mankind;
¹⁴from his dwelling-place he watches
    all who live on earth—
¹⁵he who forms the hearts of all,
    who considers everything they do.
¹⁶No king is saved by the size of his army;
    no warrior escapes by his great strength.
¹⁷A horse is a vain hope for deliverance;
    despite all its great strength it cannot save.

ᵇ 17 Hebrew *Sheol*   ᵃ Title: Probably a literary or musical term   ᵃ 7 Or *sea as into a heap*

¹⁸But the eyes of the LORD are on those who fear
      him,
    on those whose hope is in his unfailing love,
¹⁹to deliver them from death
    and keep them alive in famine.

²⁰We wait in hope for the LORD;
    he is our help and our shield.
²¹In him our hearts rejoice,
    for we trust in his holy name.
²²May your unfailing love rest upon us, O LORD,
    even as we put our hope in you.

■ PSALM 34^a
☐ Of David. When he pretended to be insane before
Abimelech, who drove him away, and he left.

¹I will extol the LORD at all times;
    his praise will always be on my lips.

²My soul will boast in the LORD;
    let the afflicted hear and rejoice.
³Glorify the LORD with me:
    let us exalt his name together.

⁴I sought the LORD, and he answered me;
    he delivered me from all my fears.
⁵Those who look to him are radiant;
    their faces are never covered with shame.
⁶This poor man called, and the LORD heard him;
    he saved him out of all his troubles.
⁷The angel of the LORD encamps around those
        who fear him,
    and he delivers them.

⁸Taste and see that the LORD is good;
    blessed is the man who takes refuge in him.
⁹Fear the LORD, you his saints,
    for those who fear him lack nothing.
¹⁰The lions may grow weak and hungry,

■ LYRICS FOR THE LIVING GOD   INSIGHT
THE PSALMS WERE MEANT TO BE SUNG – AND SHOUTED

SING TO HIM A NEW SONG; PLAY SKILFULLY, AND SHOUT FOR JOY. ■ 33:3

William Booth, believing the 19th-century
English church had become too refined to reach
the cities' poor, took the gospel into the streets.
He organised his workers into a "salvation
army", complete with uniforms and military rank.
    With hecklers and drunks abounding,
the "army" didn't always find preaching easy or
safe. A local builder, Charles William Fry, offered
himself and his three sons as bodyguards. As it
happened all four played brass instruments,
which they carried along to accompany singing.
    Booth's rowdier supporters were soon
dragging along concertinas, bells, hunting horns,
banjos, tambourines and drums to praise the
Lord. Said one leader, "It sounds as if a brass
band's gone out of its mind."
    Salvation Army recruits did not stick to
traditional hymns but invented their own words
for rousing popular tunes. "Here's to Good Old
Whiskey" became "Storm the Forts of
Darkness". Booth had his doubts about this
trend until one night, hearing a beautiful
rendition of "Bless His Name, He Sets Me Free",
he asked about the tune. "Why, Mr. Booth,
that's 'Champagne Charlie Is My Name,' " the
embarrassed singer replied.
    "That settles it," Booth said. "Why
should the devil have all the best tunes?" Soon
400 bands were crashing about England,
playing hit tunes with Christian words.

■ THE BEST MUSIC AVAILABLE
David and his people would have liked that
spirit. Many of the psalms were meant to be

sung, and sung joyfully. Modern church
formality seems far removed from their
frequent command: "Sing for joy! Shout aloud!"
Their instruments included cymbals,
tambourines, trumpets, ram's horns, harps and
lyres. Sometimes dancing erupted. The world,
in the psalmist's imagination, can't contain the
delight God inspires. A *new* song must be
sung. "Shout for joy to the LORD, all the earth,
burst into jubilant song" (98:4).
    1 Chronicles 15:16 and 23:5 report
that David appointed 4,000 professional
musicians to provide their services to the
temple. They offered the best music available,
and the congregation joined in. Nobody knows
exactly what it sounded like, but scholars
doubt it was all soft and soothing. Musicians
improvised. Most of the instruments used
suggest rousing, rhythmic sound.
    Every generation of Christians renews
the discovery of this "new song", sometimes
through the music of their forebears,
sometimes in a form that shocks their solemn
elders. The Salvation Army did, as did the
Jesus Movement in the 60s and Christian rock
music in the 80s and 90s. David would not
have been surprised. He astonished his own
wife with spontaneous dancing (see 1
Chronicles 15:29). When people know God,
they come to life with a jubilant song on their
lips.

☐ LIFE QUESTIONS:
When you sing to God, what kind of emotions
do you hope to feel? What kind of music
contributes to that?

---

^aThis psalm is an acrostic poem, the verses of which begin with the successive letters of the Hebrew alphabet.

but those who seek the LORD lack no good
   thing.

34:9 ■ IS GOD FRIGHTENING?

"Fear of the LORD" is a phrase you find frequently
in the Old Testament. Does it mean that we
should be frightened of God? Apparently not.
"Fear of the LORD" gradually became a standard
phrase for a good relationship with God. A good
relationship begins with a reverent sense that God
is so powerful and righteous that we dare not take
him lightly. But it goes on from awe to a sense of
deep security, as this psalm fully demonstrates.

11Come, my children, listen to me;
   I will teach you the fear of the LORD.
12Whoever of you loves life
   and desires to see many good days,
13keep your tongue from evil
   and your lips from speaking lies.
14Turn from evil and do good;
   seek peace and pursue it.

15The eyes of the LORD are on the righteous
   and his ears are attentive to their cry;
16the face of the LORD is against those who do
     evil,
   to cut off the memory of them from the
     earth.

17The righteous cry out, and the LORD hears
     them;
   he delivers them from all their troubles.
18The LORD is close to the broken-hearted
   and saves those who are crushed in spirit.

19A righteous man may have many troubles,
   but the LORD delivers him from them all;
20he protects all his bones,
   not one of them will be broken.

21Evil will slay the wicked;
   the foes of the righteous will be condemned.
22The LORD redeems his servants;
   no-one will be condemned who takes refuge
     in him.

■ PSALM 35
□ Of David.

1Contend, O LORD, with those who contend with
     me;
   fight against those who fight against me.
2Take up shield and buckler;
   arise and come to my aid.
3Brandish spear and javelin*a*
   against those who pursue me.
   Say to my soul,
     "I am your salvation."

4May those who seek my life
   be disgraced and put to shame;
   may those who plot my ruin
   be turned back in dismay.
5May they be like chaff before the wind,

with the angel of the LORD driving them
     away;
6may their path be dark and slippery,
   with the angel of the LORD pursuing them.
7Since they hid their net for me without cause
   and without cause dug a pit for me,
8may ruin overtake them by surprise—
   may the net they hid entangle them,
   may they fall into the pit, to their ruin.
9Then my soul will rejoice in the LORD
   and delight in his salvation.
10My whole being will exclaim,
   "Who is like you, O LORD?
  You rescue the poor from those too strong for
     them,
   the poor and needy from those who rob
     them."

11Ruthless witnesses come forward;
   they question me on things I know nothing
     about.
12They repay me evil for good
   and leave my soul forlorn.
13Yet when they were ill, I put on sackcloth
   and humbled myself with fasting.
  When my prayers returned to me unanswered,
14 I went about mourning
   as though for my friend or brother.
  I bowed my head in grief
   as though weeping for my mother.
15But when I stumbled, they gathered in glee;
   attackers gathered against me when I was
     unaware.
  They slandered me without ceasing.
16Like the ungodly they maliciously mocked;*b*
   they gnashed their teeth at me.
17O Lord, how long will you look on?
   Rescue my life from their ravages,
   my precious life from these lions.
18I will give you thanks in the great assembly;
   among throngs of people I will praise you.

19Let not those gloat over me
   who are my enemies without cause;
  let not those who hate me without reason
   maliciously wink the eye.
20They do not speak peaceably,
   but devise false accusations
   against those who live quietly in the land.
21They gape at me and say, "Aha! Aha!
   With our own eyes we have seen it."

22O LORD, you have seen this; be not silent.
   Do not be far from me, O Lord.
23Awake, and rise to my defence!
   Contend for me, my God and Lord.
24Vindicate me in your righteousness, O LORD my
     God;
   do not let them gloat over me.
25Do not let them think, "Aha, just what we
     wanted!"
   or say, "We have swallowed him up."

26May all who gloat over my distress
   be put to shame and confusion;
  may all who exalt themselves over me
   be clothed with shame and disgrace.

---

a3 Or *and block the way*   *b16* Septuagint; Hebrew may mean *ungodly circle of mockers.*

27May those who delight in my vindication
  shout for joy and gladness;
may they always say, "The LORD be exalted,
  who delights in the well-being of his
  servant."
28My tongue will speak of your righteousness
  and of your praises all day long.

■ PSALM 36
☐ For the director of music. Of David the servant of the
LORD.

1An oracle is within my heart
  concerning the sinfulness of the wicked:a
There is no fear of God
  before his eyes.
2For in his own eyes he flatters himself
  too much to detect or hate his sin.
3The words of his mouth are wicked and
  deceitful;
  he has ceased to be wise and to do good.
4Even on his bed he plots evil;
  he commits himself to a sinful course
  and does not reject what is wrong.

5Your love, O LORD, reaches to the heavens,
  your faithfulness to the skies.
6Your righteousness is like the mighty
  mountains,
  your justice like the great deep.
O LORD, you preserve both man and beast.
7 How priceless is your unfailing love!
Both high and low among men
  findb refuge in the shadow of your wings.
8They feast in the abundance of your house;
  you give them drink from your river of
  delights.
9For with you is the fountain of life;
  in your light we see light.

36:9 ■ LIGHT MAKES LIGHT
By itself, light is invisible; and yet *everything* is
invisible until light strikes it. So it is with God: we
can't see him, but "in his light" (under his loving
influence) we see and understand his love in all
that surrounds us. God's overwhelming generosity
stands in complete contrast to the self-important
plotting of wicked human beings (verses 1–4).

10Continue your love to those who know you,
  your righteousness to the upright in heart.
11May the foot of the proud not come against me,
  nor the hand of the wicked drive me away.
12See how the evildoers lie fallen—
  thrown down, not able to rise!

■ PSALM 37a
☐ Of David.

1Do not fret because of evil men
  or be envious of those who do wrong;
2for like the grass they will soon wither,
  like green plants they will soon die away.

3Trust in the LORD and do good;
  dwell in the land and enjoy safe pasture.
4Delight yourself in the LORD
  and he will give you the desires of your
  heart.

5Commit your way to the LORD;
  trust in him and he will do this:
6He will make your righteousness shine like the
  dawn,
  the justice of your cause like the noonday
  sun.

7Be still before the LORD and wait patiently for
  him;
  do not fret when men succeed in their ways,
  when they carry out their wicked schemes.

8Refrain from anger and turn from wrath;
  do not fret—it leads only to evil.
9For evil men will be cut off,
  but those who hope in the LORD will inherit
  the land.

10A little while, and the wicked will be no more;
  though you look for them, they will not be
  found.
11But the meek will inherit the land
  and enjoy great peace.

12The wicked plot against the righteous
  and gnash their teeth at them;
13but the Lord laughs at the wicked,
  for he knows their day is coming.

14The wicked draw the sword
  and bend the bow
to bring down the poor and needy,
  to slay those whose ways are upright.
15But their swords will pierce their own hearts,
  and their bows will be broken.

16Better the little that the righteous have
  than the wealth of many wicked;
17for the power of the wicked will be broken,
  but the LORD upholds the righteous.

18The days of the blameless are known to the
  LORD,
  and their inheritance will endure for ever.
19In times of disaster they will not wither;
  in days of famine they will enjoy plenty.

20But the wicked will perish:
  The LORD's enemies will be like the beauty of
  the fields,
  they will vanish—vanish like smoke.

21The wicked borrow and do not repay,
  but the righteous give generously;
22those the LORD blesses will inherit the land,
  but those he curses will be cut off.

23If the LORD delights in a man's way,
  he makes his steps firm;
24though he stumble, he will not fall,
  for the LORD upholds him with his hand.

25I was young and now I am old,
  yet I have never seen the righteous forsaken
  or their children begging bread.

a 1 Or heart: / Sin proceeds from the wicked.   b 7 Or love, O God! / Men find; or love! / Both heavenly beings and men / find   aThis psalm is an
acrostic poem, the stanzas of which begin with the successive letters of the Hebrew alphabet.

26They are always generous and lend freely;
   their children will be blessed.

37:25 ■ NEVER ABANDONED

Is life unfair? Psalm 37 ponders that perplexing
question. Its basic conclusion: the success of
wicked people won't last, while in the long run
people who do right will flourish. The psalmist
adds this observation, based on experience:
through a lifetime of troubles and anxieties, he has
yet to see the righteous abandoned by God and
unable to provide the basics of life for their
children. Their generosity doesn't bankrupt them.

27Turn from evil and do good;
   then you will dwell in the land for ever.
28For the LORD loves the just
   and will not forsake his faithful ones.

   They will be protected for ever,
   but the offspring of the wicked will be cut
      off;
29the righteous will inherit the land
   and dwell in it for ever.

30The mouth of the righteous man utters wisdom,
   and his tongue speaks what is just.
31The law of his God is in his heart;
   his feet do not slip.

32The wicked lie in wait for the righteous,
   seeking their very lives;
33but the LORD will not leave them in their
      power
   or let them be condemned when brought to
      trial.

34Wait for the LORD
   and keep his way.
   He will exalt you to inherit the land;
   when the wicked are cut off, you will see it.

35I have seen a wicked and ruthless man
   flourishing like a green tree in its native soil,
36but he soon passed away and was no more;
   though I looked for him, he could not be
      found.

37Consider the blameless, observe the upright;
   there is a future[b] for the man of peace.
38But all sinners will be destroyed;
   the future[c] of the wicked will be cut off.

39The salvation of the righteous comes from the
      LORD;
   he is their stronghold in time of trouble.
40The LORD helps them and delivers them;
   he delivers them from the wicked and saves
      them,
   because they take refuge in him.

■ PSALM 38
☐ A psalm of David. A petition.

1O LORD, do not rebuke me in your anger
   or discipline me in your wrath.

2For your arrows have pierced me,
   and your hand has come down upon me.
3Because of your wrath there is no health in my
      body;
   my bones have no soundness because of my
      sin.
4My guilt has overwhelmed me
   like a burden too heavy to bear.

5My wounds fester and are loathsome
   because of my sinful folly.
6I am bowed down and brought very low;
   all day long I go about mourning.
7My back is filled with searing pain;
   there is no health in my body.
8I am feeble and utterly crushed;
   I groan in anguish of heart.

9All my longings lie open before you, O Lord:
   my sighing is not hidden from you.
10My heart pounds, my strength fails me;
   even the light has gone from my eyes.
11My friends and companions avoid me because
      of my wounds;
   my neighbours stay far away.
12Those who seek my life set their traps,
   those who would harm me talk of my ruin;
   all day long they plot deception.

13I am like a deaf man, who cannot hear,
   like a mute, who cannot open his mouth;
14I have become like a man who does not hear,
   whose mouth can offer no reply.
15I wait for you, O LORD;
   you will answer, O Lord my God.
16For I said, "Do not let them gloat
   or exalt themselves over me when my foot
      slips."

17For I am about to fall,
   and my pain is ever with me.
18I confess my iniquity;
   I am troubled by my sin.
19Many are those who are my vigorous enemies;
   those who hate me without reason are
      numerous.
20Those who repay my good with evil
   slander me when I pursue what is good.

21O LORD, do not forsake me;
   be not far from me, O my God.
22Come quickly to help me,
   O Lord my Saviour.

■ PSALM 39
☐ For the director of music. For Jeduthun. A psalm of David.

1I said, "I will watch my ways
   and keep my tongue from sin;
   I will put a muzzle on my mouth
   as long as the wicked are in my presence."
2But when I was silent and still,
   not even saying anything good,
   my anguish increased.
3My heart grew hot within me,
   and as I meditated, the fire burned;
   then I spoke with my tongue:

b 37 Or there will be posterity   c 38 Or posterity

4"Show me, O LORD, my life's end
    and the number of my days;
    let me know how fleeting is my life.
5You have made my days a mere handbreadth;
    the span of my years is as nothing before
      you.
    Each man's life is but a breath.   *Selah*
6Man is a mere phantom as he goes to and fro:
    He bustles about, but only in vain;
    he heaps up wealth, not knowing who will
      get it.

7"But now, Lord, what do I look for?
    My hope is in you.
8Save me from all my transgressions;
    do not make me the scorn of fools.
9I was silent; I would not open my mouth,
    for you are the one who has done this.
10Remove your scourge from me;
    I am overcome by the blow of your hand.
11You rebuke and discipline men for their sin;
    you consume their wealth like a moth—
    each man is but a breath.   *Selah*

39:10 ■ WRESTLING WITH GOD
Not all the psalms are happy. Some, such as this
one and Psalms 44 and 88, are intensely sad.
They try to make sense out of suffering, and fail.
They ask God for help and receive none. The
Bible's inclusion of such hopeless cries eloquently
testifies to God's acceptance of human struggles.
These psalms are not the final word on suffering.
They show, however, that wrestling with God has
value even when you fail to find answers.

12"Hear my prayer, O LORD,
    listen to my cry for help;
    be not deaf to my weeping.
    For I dwell with you as an alien,
    a stranger, as all my fathers were.
13Look away from me, that I may rejoice again
    before I depart and am no more."

■ PSALM 40
☐ For the director of music. Of David. A psalm.

1I waited patiently for the LORD;
    he turned to me and heard my cry.
2He lifted me out of the slimy pit,
    out of the mud and mire;
    he set my feet on a rock
    and gave me a firm place to stand.
3He put a new song in my mouth,
    a hymn of praise to our God.
    Many will see and fear
    and put their trust in the LORD.

4Blessed is the man
    who makes the LORD his trust,
    who does not look to the proud,
    to those who turn aside to false gods.*a*
5Many, O LORD my God,
    are the wonders you have done.
    The things you planned for us

no-one can recount to you;
    were I to speak and tell of them,
    they would be too many to declare.

6Sacrifice and offering you did not desire,
    but my ears you have pierced;*b, c*
    burnt offerings and sin offerings
    you did not require.
7Then I said, "Here I am, I have come—
    it is written about me in the scroll.*d*
8I desire to do your will, O my God;
    your law is within my heart."

40:6 ■ A BETTER SACRIFICE
While the Old Testament law prescribed animal
and grain sacrifices to deal with the problem of
sin, Old Testament writers made clear that God
really wanted obedient lives, not ritual
performances. Hebrews 10:5–9 quotes these
verses (6–8) in explaining that Jesus' sacrifice
made all the animal sacrifices obsolete. Only
Jesus' sacrifice has the power to actually forgive
sins and change lives.

9I proclaim righteousness in the great assembly;
    I do not seal my lips,
    as you know, O LORD.
10I do not hide your righteousness in my heart;
    I speak of your faithfulness and salvation.
    I do not conceal your love and your truth
    from the great assembly.
11Do not withhold your mercy from me, O LORD;
    may your love and your truth always protect
      me.
12For troubles without number surround me;
    my sins have overtaken me, and I cannot see.
    They are more than the hairs of my head,
    and my heart fails within me.

13Be pleased, O LORD, to save me;
    O LORD, come quickly to help me.
14May all who seek to take my life
    be put to shame and confusion;
    may all who desire my ruin
    be turned back in disgrace.
15May those who say to me, "Aha! Aha!"
    be appalled at their own shame.
16But may all who seek you
    rejoice and be glad in you;
    may those who love your salvation always say,
    "The LORD be exalted!"

17Yet I am poor and needy;
    may the Lord think of me.
    You are my help and my deliverer;
    O my God, do not delay.

■ PSALM 41
☐ For the director of music. A psalm of David.

1Blessed is he who has regard for the weak;
    the LORD delivers him in times of trouble.
2The LORD will protect him and preserve his life;
    he will bless him in the land

---

a 4 Or *to falsehood*   *b* 6 Hebrew; Septuagint *but a body you have prepared for me* (see also Symmachus and Theodotion)   *c* 6 Or *opened*
d 7 Or *come / with the scroll written for me*

and not surrender him to the desire of his
        foes.
³The LORD will sustain him on his sick-bed
        and restore him from his bed of illness.

41:1 ■ A KEY CHARACTERISTIC

The psalmist was severely ill. Enemies and rivals —
and even a close friend, verse 9 — whispered that
he was dying. What made him so confident that
God would heal him? He knew that God helps
those who show "regard for the weak". Because
he had shown integrity in this, he confidently
expected God to show mercy to him. Jesus
reflected this value when he said, "Blessed are the
merciful, for they will be shown mercy" (Matthew
5:7).

⁴I said, "O LORD, have mercy on me;
        heal me, for I have sinned against you."
⁵My enemies say of me in malice,
        "When will he die and his name perish?"
⁶Whenever one comes to see me,
        he speaks falsely, while his heart gathers
                slander;
        then he goes out and spreads it abroad.

⁷All my enemies whisper together against me;
        they imagine the worst for me, saying,
⁸"A vile disease has beset him;
        he will never get up from the place where
                he lies."
⁹Even my close friend, whom I trusted,
        he who shared my bread,
        has lifted up his heel against me.

¹⁰But you, O LORD, have mercy on me;
        raise me up, that I may repay them.
¹¹I know that you are pleased with me,
        for my enemy does not triumph over me.
¹²In my integrity you uphold me
        and set me in your presence for ever.

¹³Praise be to the LORD, the God of Israel,
        from everlasting to everlasting.
                Amen and Amen.

BOOK II
☐ Psalms 42–72

■ PSALM 42ª
☐ For the director of music. A *maskil*ᵇ of the Sons of
Korah.

¹As the deer pants for streams of water,
        so my soul pants for you, O God.
²My soul thirsts for God, for the living God.
        When can I go and meet with God?
³My tears have been my food
                day and night,
        while men say to me all day long,
        "Where is your God?"
⁴These things I remember

as I pour out my soul:
how I used to go with the multitude,
        leading the procession to the house of God,
with shouts of joy and thanksgiving
        among the festive throng.

⁵Why are you downcast, O my soul?
        Why so disturbed within me?
Put your hope in God,
        for I will yet praise him,
        my Saviour and ⁶my God.

Myᶜ soul is downcast within me;
        therefore I will remember you
from the land of the Jordan,
        the heights of Hermon — from Mount Mizar.
⁷Deep calls to deep
        in the roar of your waterfalls;
all your waves and breakers
        have swept over me.

⁸By day the LORD directs his love,
        at night his song is with me —
        a prayer to the God of my life.

⁹I say to God my Rock,
        "Why have you forgotten me?
Why must I go about mourning,
        oppressed by the enemy?"
¹⁰My bones suffer mortal agony
        as my foes taunt me,
saying to me all day long,
        "Where is your God?"

¹¹Why are you downcast, O my soul?
        Why so disturbed within me?
Put your hope in God,
        for I will yet praise him,
        my Saviour and my God.

■ PSALM 43ª

¹Vindicate me, O God,
        and plead my cause against an ungodly
                nation;
        rescue me from deceitful and wicked men.
²You are God my stronghold.
        Why have you rejected me?
Why must I go about mourning,
        oppressed by the enemy?
³Send forth your light and your truth,
        let them guide me;
let them bring me to your holy mountain,
        to the place where you dwell.
⁴Then will I go to the altar of God,
        to God, my joy and my delight.
I will praise you with the harp,
        O God, my God.

⁵Why are you downcast, O my soul?
        Why so disturbed within me?
Put your hope in God,
        for I will yet praise him,
        my Saviour and my God.

ªIn many Hebrew manuscripts Psalms 42 and 43 constitute one psalm.   ᵇTitle: Probably a literary or musical term   ᶜ5,6 A few Hebrew manuscripts,
Septuagint and Syriac; most Hebrew manuscripts *praise him for his saving help.* / ⁶O my God, my   ᵈIn many Hebrew manuscripts Psalms 42 and 43
constitute one psalm.

■ PSALM 44
☐ For the director of music. Of the Sons of Korah.
A *maskil.ᵃ*

¹We have heard with our ears, O God;
    our fathers have told us
what you did in their days,
    in days long ago.
²With your hand you drove out the nations
    and planted our fathers;
you crushed the peoples
    and made our fathers flourish.
³It was not by their sword that they won the
    land,
    nor did their arm bring them victory;
it was your right hand, your arm,
    and the light of your face, for you loved
    them.

⁴You are my King and my God,
    who decrees*ᵇ* victories for Jacob.
⁵Through you we push back our enemies;
    through your name we trample our foes.
⁶I do not trust in my bow,
    my sword does not bring me victory;
⁷but you give us victory over our enemies,
    you put our adversaries to shame.
⁸In God we make our boast all day long,
    and we will praise your name for ever. *Selah*

⁹But now you have rejected and humbled us;
    you no longer go out with our armies.
¹⁰You made us retreat before the enemy,
    and our adversaries have plundered us.
¹¹You gave us up to be devoured like sheep
    and have scattered us among the nations.
¹²You sold your people for a pittance,
    gaining nothing from their sale.

¹³You have made us a reproach to our
    neighbours,
    the scorn and derision of those around us.
¹⁴You have made us a byword among the nations;
    the peoples shake their heads at us.
¹⁵My disgrace is before me all day long,
    and my face is covered with shame
¹⁶at the taunts of those who reproach and revile
    me,
    because of the enemy, who is bent on
    revenge.

¹⁷All this happened to us,
    though we had not forgotten you
    or been false to your covenant.
¹⁸Our hearts had not turned back;
    our feet had not strayed from your path.
¹⁹But you crushed us and made us a haunt for
    jackals
    and covered us over with deep darkness.

²⁰If we had forgotten the name of our God
    or spread out our hands to a foreign god,
²¹would not God have discovered it,
    since he knows the secrets of the heart?
²²Yet for your sake we face death all day long;
    we are considered as sheep to be
    slaughtered.

²³Awake, O Lord! Why do you sleep?
    Rouse yourself! Do not reject us for ever.

44:22 ■ NO HAPPY ENDING
Not all of the psalms have happy endings. This
one, while beginning with distant memories of
what God did in the past, ends with a poignant
plea for help. Prayers and faith in God have not
produced any results. Is God asleep?
    Yet God works in bigger patterns than we can
see. The apostle Paul, considering the place of
suffering in a Christian's life, quoted this verse to
remind his readers that suffering was nothing new
for believers (Romans 8:36). He asked, "Who shall
separate us from the love of Christ?" His
response: "No-one! Nothing!" He would have loved
to go back in time and tell the suffering psalmist
about all the good things in store for God's
people.

²⁴Why do you hide your face
    and forget our misery and oppression?

²⁵We are brought down to the dust;
    our bodies cling to the ground.
²⁶Rise up and help us;
    redeem us because of your unfailing love.

■ PSALM 45
☐ For the director of music. To ⌊the tune of⌋ "Lilies". Of the
Sons of Korah. A *maskil.ᵃ* A wedding song.

¹My heart is stirred by a noble theme
    as I recite my verses for the king;
    my tongue is the pen of a skilful writer.

²You are the most excellent of men
    and your lips have been anointed with grace,
    since God has blessed you for ever.
³Gird your sword upon your side, O mighty one;
    clothe yourself with splendour and majesty.
⁴In your majesty ride forth victoriously
    on behalf of truth, humility and
    righteousness;
    let your right hand display awesome deeds.
⁵Let your sharp arrows pierce the hearts of the
    king's enemies;
    let the nations fall beneath your feet.
⁶Your throne, O God, will last for ever and ever;
    a sceptre of justice will be the sceptre of
    your kingdom.
⁷You love righteousness and hate wickedness;
    therefore God, your God, has set you above
    your companions
    by anointing you with the oil of joy.
⁸All your robes are fragrant with myrrh and
    aloes and cassia;
    from palaces adorned with ivory
    the music of the strings makes you glad.
⁹Daughters of kings are among your honoured
    women;
    at your right hand is the royal bride in gold
    of Ophir.

ᵃTitle: Probably a literary or musical term   *ᵇ4* Septuagint, Aquila and Syriac; Hebrew *King, O God; / command*   ᵃTitle: Probably a literary or musical
term

¹⁰Listen, O daughter, consider and give ear:
　　Forget your people and your father's house.
¹¹The king is enthralled by your beauty;
　　honour him, for he is your lord.
¹²The Daughter of Tyre will come with a gift,ᵇ
　　men of wealth will seek your favour.

¹³All glorious is the princess within ˌher
　　chamberˌ;
　　her gown is interwoven with gold.
¹⁴In embroidered garments she is led to the king;
　　her virgin companions follow her
　　and are brought to you.
¹⁵They are led in with joy and gladness;
　　they enter the palace of the king.

¹⁶Your sons will take the place of your fathers;
　　you will make them princes throughout the
　　land.

¹⁷I will perpetuate your memory through all
　　generations;
　　therefore the nations will praise you for ever
　　and ever.

■ PSALM 46
☐ For the director of music. Of the Sons of Korah. According
to *alamoth.ᵃ* A song.

¹God is our refuge and strength,
　　an ever-present help in trouble.
²Therefore we will not fear, though the earth
　　give way
　　and the mountains fall into the heart of the
　　sea,
³though its waters roar and foam
　　and the mountains quake with their surging.
　　　　　　　　　　　　　　　　　　Selah

⁴There is a river whose streams make glad the
　　city of God,
　　the holy place where the Most High dwells.
⁵God is within her, she will not fall;
　　God will help her at break of day.
⁶Nations are in uproar, kingdoms fall;
　　he lifts his voice, the earth melts.

⁷The LORD Almighty is with us;
　　the God of Jacob is our fortress.　　*Selah*

■ A WEDDING FIT FOR A KING
WHY SHOULD THIS POEM BE FOUND IN A BOOK OF PRAYERS?

INSIGHT

YOUR THRONE, O GOD, WILL LAST FOR EVER AND EVER. ■ 45:6

In the middle of a book of heartfelt prayers, a wedding poem suddenly appears. Does Psalm 45 belong here? Its "noble theme" (verse 1) is not God's kindness, but the excellence of his majesty the king as he prepares to take a bride. While most of the psalms express an intimacy with God that could have been written yesterday, thrones, sceptres and royal robes make us think of an old Hollywood epic.

To understand why this psalm was included we need to know, first, that the king in biblical times was more than just a symbol. He was the Prime Minister, the Commander-in-Chief of all Armed Forces and the Lord Chief Justice, all rolled into one. An unjust or cowardly king could cost his people their lives. A clever, successful king, on the other hand, could assure them of prosperity.

When the Israelites wished the king well, therefore, they wished themselves well. Seeing their king decked out in finery was like looking at a picture of their own success. And when their king made a happy and fruitful marriage, it assured them of stable leadership for years to come. The king's welfare represented the welfare of God's people.

■ THE PROMISE TO DAVID
David was the first good king Israel had known. God had told David that his "house" would endure for ever (2 Samuel 7:16). This meant that Israel would endure, too. When David's people combined this promise with the other benefits God had promised to Abraham and Moses, they could foresee a great future for their small, poor, war-weary nation.

Yet David's descendants disappointed these hopes. Israel remained a small, hemmed-in nation. Gradually, Israelites began to expect another king who would live up to the Bible's praises and promises. They called him "the Anointed" (for kings and priests took office through an official anointing with oil, like our swearing-in ceremonies). When they read psalms that mentioned the king, they thought of this coming ruler.

As the years went by and Israel's kings failed miserably, Israel's longing grew stronger and stronger. People looked for "the consolation of Israel" (Luke 2:25). The word for "the Anointed" became *Messiah* or (in Greek) *Christ*.

Only when "the Anointed" came — in Jesus — did the extravagant language of Psalm 45:6–7 (together with unusual descriptions in Psalms 2 and 110) make sense. These verses were quoted in Hebrews 1:8–9 to show that the king the Jews had long expected could be no ordinary man. The king turned out to *be* God — as verse 6 had suggested. The poem that seemed to be only about a king's marriage turned out, in the end, to be about God's marriage to humanity.

ᵇ12 Or A Tyrian robe is among the gifts　　　*ᵃTitle: Probably a musical term*

⁸Come and see the works of the LORD,
   the desolations he has brought on the earth.
⁹He makes wars cease to the ends of the earth;
   he breaks the bow and shatters the spear,
   he burns the shields*ᵇ* with fire.
¹⁰"Be still, and know that I am God;
   I will be exalted among the nations,
   I will be exalted in the earth."

¹¹The LORD Almighty is with us;
   the God of Jacob is our fortress.   *Selah*

■ PSALM 47
☐ For the director of music. Of the Sons of Korah. A psalm.

¹Clap your hands, all you nations;
   shout to God with cries of joy.
²How awesome is the LORD Most High,
   the great King over all the earth!
³He subdued nations under us,
   peoples under our feet.
⁴He chose our inheritance for us,
   the pride of Jacob, whom he loved.   *Selah*

⁵God has ascended amid shouts of joy,
   the LORD amid the sounding of trumpets.
⁶Sing praises to God, sing praises;
   sing praises to our King, sing praises.

⁷For God is the King of all the earth;
   sing to him a psalm*ᵃ* of praise.
⁸God reigns over the nations;
   God is seated on his holy throne.
⁹The nobles of the nations assemble
   as the people of the God of Abraham,
   for the kings*ᵇ* of the earth belong to God;
   he is greatly exalted.

47:9 ■ WHO ARE GOD'S PEOPLE?
While the Israelites often thought of themselves as
exclusively God's people, Psalms contains
frequent references to a day when "the nations"
– that is, all ethnic groups – will exultantly praise
God. In this psalm they not only join in, they do so
as "the people of the God of Abraham" – that is,
as insiders included in God's covenant with the
Israelites.

■ PSALM 48
☐ A song. A psalm of the Sons of Korah.

¹Great is the LORD, and most worthy of praise,
   in the city of our God, his holy mountain.
²It is beautiful in its loftiness,
   the joy of the whole earth.
   Like the utmost heights of Zaphon*ᵃ* is Mount
      Zion,
   the*ᵇ* city of the Great King.
³God is in her citadels;
   he has shown himself to be her fortress.

⁴When the kings joined forces,
   when they advanced together,
⁵they saw ⌊her⌋ and were astounded;
   they fled in terror.

⁶Trembling seized them there,
   pain like that of a woman in labour.
⁷You destroyed them like ships of Tarshish
   shattered by an east wind.

⁸As we have heard,
   so have we seen
   in the city of the LORD Almighty,
   in the city of our God:
   God makes her secure for ever.   *Selah*

⁹Within your temple, O God,
   we meditate on your unfailing love.
¹⁰Like your name, O God,
   your praise reaches to the ends of the earth;
   your right hand is filled with righteousness.
¹¹Mount Zion rejoices,
   the villages of Judah are glad
   because of your judgments.

¹²Walk about Zion, go round her,
   count her towers,
¹³consider well her ramparts,
   view her citadels,
   that you may tell of them to the next
      generation.
¹⁴For this God is our God for ever and ever;
   he will be our guide even to the end.

■ PSALM 49
☐ For the director of music. Of the Sons of Korah. A psalm.

¹Hear this, all you peoples;
   listen, all who live in this world,
²both low and high,
   rich and poor alike:
³My mouth will speak words of wisdom;
   the utterance from my heart will give
      understanding.
⁴I will turn my ear to a proverb;
   with the harp I will expound my riddle:

⁵Why should I fear when evil days come,
   when wicked deceivers surround me —
⁶those who trust in their wealth
   and boast of their great riches?
⁷No man can redeem the life of another
   or give to God a ransom for him —
⁸the ransom for a life is costly,
   no payment is ever enough —
⁹that he should live on for ever
   and not see decay.

¹⁰For all can see that wise men die;
   the foolish and the senseless alike perish
   and leave their wealth to others.
¹¹Their tombs will remain their houses*ᵃ* for
      ever,
   their dwellings for endless generations,
   though they had*ᵇ* named lands after
      themselves.

¹²But man, despite his riches, does not endure;
   he is*ᶜ* like the beasts that perish.

¹³This is the fate of those who trust in
      themselves,

---

*ᵇ9 Or chariots   *ᵃ7 Or a maskil (probably a literary or musical term)   *ᵇ9 Or shields   *ᵃ2 Zaphon can refer to a sacred mountain or the direction
north.   *ᵇ2 Or earth, / Mount Zion, on the northern side / of the   *ᵃ11 Septuagint and Syriac; Hebrew In their thoughts their houses will remain
*ᵇ11 Or / for they have   *ᶜ12 Hebrew; Septuagint and Syriac read verse 12 the same as verse 20.

and of their followers, who approve their
  sayings.   *Selah*
[14]Like sheep they are destined for the grave,[d]
  and death will feed on them.
The upright will rule over them in the
  morning;
  their forms will decay in the grave,[d]
  far from their princely mansions.
[15]But God will redeem my life[e] from the grave;
  he will surely take me to himself.   *Selah*

49:15 ■ MONEY CAN'T BUY LIFE

How do you make sense of a world in which bad
people get rich and actually oppress good
people? This psalm ponders this riddle and finds
the answer on the other side of death. Money can
do many things, but it simply cannot buy an
escape from the grave. "No man can redeem the
life of another . . . no payment is ever enough—
that he should live on for ever" (verses 7–9). But
"God will redeem my life from the grave," says
verse 15; "he will surely take me to himself."

---

[16]Do not be overawed when a man grows rich,
  when the splendour of his house increases;
[17]for he will take nothing with him when he dies,
  his splendour will not descend with him.
[18]Though while he lived he counted himself
  blessed—
  and men praise you when you prosper—
[19]he will join the generation of his fathers,
  who will never see the light ˌof lifeˌ.

[20]A man who has riches without understanding
  is like the beasts that perish.

■ PSALM 50
☐ A psalm of Asaph.

[1]The Mighty One, God, the LORD,
  speaks and summons the earth
  from the rising of the sun to the place where
    it sets.
[2]From Zion, perfect in beauty,
  God shines forth.
[3]Our God comes and will not be silent;
  a fire devours before him,
  and around him a tempest rages.
[4]He summons the heavens above,
  and the earth, that he may judge his people:
[5]"Gather to me my consecrated ones,
  who made a covenant with me by sacrifice."
[6]And the heavens proclaim his righteousness,
  for God himself is judge.   *Selah*

[7]"Hear, O my people, and I will speak,
  O Israel, and I will testify against you:
  I am God, your God.
[8]I do not rebuke you for your sacrifices
  or your burnt offerings, which are ever
    before me.
[9]I have no need of a bull from your stall
  or of goats from your pens,
[10]for every animal of the forest is mine,

and the cattle on a thousand hills.
[11]I know every bird in the mountains,
  and the creatures of the field are mine.
[12]If I were hungry I would not tell you,
  for the world is mine, and all that is in it.
[13]Do I eat the flesh of bulls
  or drink the blood of goats?
[14]Sacrifice thank-offerings to God,
  fulfil your vows to the Most High,
[15]and call upon me in the day of trouble;
  I will deliver you, and you will honour me."

50:9 ■ DOES GOD NEED OUR GIFTS?

People often try to bargain with God, thinking that
by their good deeds they can get God to do what
they want. Old Testament people sometimes
viewed their animal sacrifices this way: not as an
act of commitment and fellowship with God, but
as a way to manipulate God into putting his stamp
of approval on their plans. These majestic words
from God scorn such a view. He is rich beyond
their dreams; he has no need of their offerings.
What matters to him is the attitude they take
towards him.

---

[16]But to the wicked, God says:

"What right have you to recite my laws
  or take my covenant on your lips?
[17]You hate my instruction
  and cast my words behind you.
[18]When you see a thief, you join with him;
  you throw in your lot with adulterers.
[19]You use your mouth for evil
  and harness your tongue to deceit.
[20]You speak continually against your brother
  and slander your own mother's son.
[21]These things you have done and I kept silent;
  you thought I was altogether[a] like you.
But I will rebuke you
  and accuse you to your face.

[22]"Consider this, you who forget God,
  or I will tear you to pieces, with none to
    rescue:
[23]He who sacrifices thank-offerings honours me,
  and he prepares the way
  so that I may show him[b] the salvation of
    God."

■ PSALM 51
☐ For the director of music. A psalm of David. When the
prophet Nathan came to him after David had committed
adultery with Bathsheba.

[1]Have mercy on me, O God,
  according to your unfailing love;
  according to your great compassion
  blot out my transgressions.
[2]Wash away all my iniquity
  and cleanse me from my sin.

[3]For I know my transgressions,
  and my sin is always before me.

---

d 14 Hebrew Sheol; also in verse 15   *e 15 Or soul*   *a 21 Or thought the 'I AM' was*   *b 23 Or and to him who considers his way / I will show*

⁴Against you, you only, have I sinned
  and done what is evil in your sight,
so that you are proved right when you speak
  and justified when you judge.
⁵Surely I was sinful at birth,
  sinful from the time my mother conceived
    me.
⁶Surely you desire truth in the inner parts;ᵃ
  you teachᵇ me wisdom in the inmost place.

⁷Cleanse me with hyssop, and I shall be clean;
  wash me, and I shall be whiter than snow.
⁸Let me hear joy and gladness;
  let the bones you have crushed rejoice.
⁹Hide your face from my sins
  and blot out all my iniquity.

¹⁰Create in me a pure heart, O God,
  and renew a steadfast spirit within me.
¹¹Do not cast me from your presence
  or take your Holy Spirit from me.
¹²Restore to me the joy of your salvation
  and grant me a willing spirit, to sustain me.

¹³Then I will teach transgressors your ways,
  and sinners will turn back to you.
¹⁴Save me from bloodguilt, O God,
  the God who saves me,
  and my tongue will sing of your
    righteousness.
¹⁵O Lord, open my lips,

and my mouth will declare your praise.
¹⁶You do not delight in sacrifice, or I would
    bring it;
  you do not take pleasure in burnt offerings.
¹⁷The sacrifices of God areᶜ a broken spirit;
  a broken and contrite heart,
  O God, you will not despise.

¹⁸In your good pleasure make Zion prosper;
  build up the walls of Jerusalem.
¹⁹Then there will be righteous sacrifices,
  whole burnt offerings to delight you;
  then bulls will be offered on your altar.

■ PSALM 52
☐ For the director of music. A maskilᵃ of David. When Doeg
the Edomite had gone to Saul and told him: "David has gone
to the house of Ahimelech."

¹Why do you boast of evil, you mighty man?
  Why do you boast all day long,
  you who are a disgrace in the eyes of God?
²Your tongue plots destruction;
  it is like a sharpened razor,
  you who practise deceit.
³You love evil rather than good,
  falsehood rather than speaking the truth.
                                                    Selah

⁴You love every harmful word,
  O you deceitful tongue!

■ DAVID CAUGHT IN THE ACT
ISRAEL HAD A STRANGE WAY OF REMEMBERING ITS HEROES

INSIGHT

AGAINST YOU, YOU ONLY, HAVE I SINNED
AND DONE WHAT IS EVIL IN YOUR SIGHT.
■ 51:4

David found a place in the hearts of Israelites,
similar to the place Winston Churchill found in
the hearts of those whom he served during the
second world war. Both men led their nations
through dark hours with courage, wisdom, and
deep faith.
     But there are essential differences in the
way they are remembered. Although the British
people decided that Churchill was not needed in
peacetime and failed to re-elect him immediately
after the war, his honour and integrity were
never questioned.
     David's sins however are well-
documented, as you discover by reading Psalm
51 which records David's anguished reaction
when he was caught in sin. The story behind
the psalm is told in 2 Samuel 11 and 12 – a
sordid tale of adultery, intrigue and murder.
David, the greatest king in Israel's history, acted
like the worst.
     David apparently thought nothing of his
crime until the prophet Nathan accused him to
his face. Then, in tears, David confessed – and

this poem was one result. It was recorded
(together with the story of David's deeds) in
the holy Scriptures. It may well have been
used in worship services, as a guide for
others' confession.

■ DAVID'S GREATEST LEGACY
All nations have heroes. Israel may have been
alone in making up heroic literature about its
heroes' failings. In confessing his failures
openly, David was certainly unique among all
leaders of his day. He knew his place before
God, and this humility made him an example
for his people.
     Ultimately Israel remembered David
more for his devotion to God than for his
military achievements. In centuries to come,
Israel looked for a "son of David" to come and
save them. They wanted a truly strong
leader – one humble enough to know that God
must lead the leaders.

☐ LIFE QUESTIONS:
When you fail, what is your response – to
cover up your failure, or to publicise your
confession?

ᵃ6 The meaning of the Hebrew for this phrase is uncertain.   ᵇ6 Or you desired . . . ; / you taught   ᶜ17 Or My sacrifice, O God, is   ᵃTitle: Probably a
literary or musical term

5Surely God will bring you down to everlasting
      ruin:
   He will snatch you up and tear you from
      your tent;
   he will uproot you from the land of the
      living.   *Selah*
6The righteous will see and fear;
   they will laugh at him, saying,
7"Here now is the man
   who did not make God his stronghold
 but trusted in his great wealth
   and grew strong by destroying others!"

8But I am like an olive tree
   flourishing in the house of God;
 I trust in God's unfailing love
   for ever and ever.
9I will praise you for ever for what you have
      done;
   in your name I will hope, for your name is
      good.
   I will praise you in the presence of your
      saints.

■ PSALM 53
□ For the director of music. According to *mahalath.a* A
maskilb of David.

1The fool says in his heart,
   "There is no God."
 They are corrupt, and their ways are vile;
   there is no-one who does good.

2God looks down from heaven
   on the sons of men
 to see if there are any who understand,
   any who seek God.
3Everyone has turned away,
   they have together become corrupt;
 there is no-one who does good,
   not even one.

> **53:3 ■ SOUND FAMILIAR?**
> Psalm 53 is nearly identical to Psalm 14. Scholars
> think the book of Psalms bundled together several
> different collections of hymns; this duplication is
> one reason they believe so.

4Will the evildoers never learn—
   those who devour my people as men eat
      bread
   and who do not call on God?
5There they were, overwhelmed with dread,
   where there was nothing to dread.
 God scattered the bones of those who attacked
      you;
   you put them to shame, for God despised
      them.

6Oh, that salvation for Israel would come out of
      Zion!
   When God restores the fortunes of his
      people,
   let Jacob rejoice and Israel be glad!

■ PSALM 54
□ For the director of music. With stringed instruments. A
maskila of David. When the Ziphites had gone to Saul and
said, "Is not David hiding among us?"

1Save me, O God, by your name;
   vindicate me by your might.
2Hear my prayer, O God;
   listen to the words of my mouth.

3Strangers are attacking me;
   ruthless men seek my life—
   men without regard for God.   *Selah*

4Surely God is my help;
   the Lord is the one who sustains me.

5Let evil recoil on those who slander me;
   in your faithfulness destroy them.

6I will sacrifice a freewill offering to you;
   I will praise your name, O LORD,
   for it is good.
7For he has delivered me from all my troubles,
   and my eyes have looked in triumph on my
      foes.

■ PSALM 55
□ For the director of music. With stringed instruments.
A *maskila* of David.

1Listen to my prayer, O God,
   do not ignore my plea;
2   hear me and answer me.
 My thoughts trouble me and I am distraught
3   at the voice of the enemy,
      at the stares of the wicked;
   for they bring down suffering upon me
      and revile me in their anger.

4My heart is in anguish within me;
   the terrors of death assail me.
5Fear and trembling have beset me;
   horror has overwhelmed me.
6I said, "Oh, that I had the wings of a dove!
   I would fly away and be at rest—
7I would flee far away
   and stay in the desert;   *Selah*
8I would hurry to my place of shelter,
   far from the tempest and storm."

9Confuse the wicked, O Lord, confound their
      speech,
   for I see violence and strife in the city.
10Day and night they prowl about on its walls;
   malice and abuse are within it.
11Destructive forces are at work in the city;
   threats and lies never leave its streets.

12If an enemy were insulting me,
   I could endure it;
 if a foe were raising himself against me,
   I could hide from him.
13But it is you, a man like myself,
   my companion, my close friend,
14with whom I once enjoyed sweet fellowship
   as we walked with the throng at the house of
      God.

---

aTitle: Probably a musical term   bTitle: Probably a literary or musical
musical term   term

aTitle: Probably a literary or musical term   aTitle: Probably a literary or

¹⁵Let death take my enemies by surprise;
    let them go down alive to the grave,^b
    for evil finds lodging among them.

55:14 ■ BETRAYED BY A FRIEND
It is hard enough to deal with enemies, but far harder to face the fact of betrayal by a close friend. Feeling that he can no longer trust anyone, the psalmist turns to God for help. God, he knows, will never betray him.

¹⁶But I call to God,
    and the LORD saves me.
¹⁷Evening, morning and noon
    I cry out in distress,
    and he hears my voice.
¹⁸He ransoms me unharmed
    from the battle waged against me,
    even though many oppose me.
¹⁹God, who is enthroned for ever,
    will hear them and afflict them—   *Selah*
    men who never change their ways
    and have no fear of God.

²⁰My companion attacks his friends;
    he violates his covenant.
²¹His speech is smooth as butter,
    yet war is in his heart;
    his words are more soothing than oil,
    yet they are drawn swords.

²²Cast your cares on the LORD
    and he will sustain you;
    he will never let the righteous fall.
²³But you, O God, will bring down the wicked
    into the pit of corruption;
    bloodthirsty and deceitful men
    will not live out half their days.

But as for me, I trust in you.

■ PSALM 56
□ For the director of music. To ⌊the tune of⌋ "A Dove on Distant Oaks". Of David. A *miktam.*^a When the Philistines had seized him in Gath.

¹Be merciful to me, O God, for men hotly
        pursue me;
    all day long they press their attack.
²My slanderers pursue me all day long;
    many are attacking me in their pride.

³When I am afraid,
    I will trust in you.
⁴In God, whose word I praise,
    in God I trust; I will not be afraid.
    What can mortal man do to me?

⁵All day long they twist my words;
    they are always plotting to harm me.
⁶They conspire, they lurk,
    they watch my steps,
    eager to take my life.

⁷On no account let them escape;

in your anger, O God, bring down the
    nations.
⁸Record my lament;
    list my tears on your scroll^b—
    are they not in your record?

⁹Then my enemies will turn back
    when I call for help.
    By this I will know that God is for me.
¹⁰In God, whose word I praise,
    in the LORD, whose word I praise—
¹¹in God I trust; I will not be afraid.
    What can man do to me?

¹²I am under vows to you, O God;
    I will present my thank-offerings to you.
¹³For you have delivered me^c from death
    and my feet from stumbling,
    that I may walk before God
    in the light of life.^d

■ PSALM 57
□ For the director of music. ⌊To the tune of⌋ "Do Not Destroy". Of David. A *miktam.*^a When he had fled from Saul into the cave.

¹Have mercy on me, O God, have mercy on me,
    for in you my soul takes refuge.
I will take refuge in the shadow of your wings
    until the disaster has passed.

²I cry out to God Most High,
    to God, who fulfils ⌊his purpose⌋ for me.
³He sends from heaven and saves me,
    rebuking those who hotly pursue me;   *Selah*
    God sends his love and his faithfulness.

⁴I am in the midst of lions;
    I lie among ravenous beasts—
    men whose teeth are spears and arrows,
    whose tongues are sharp swords.

⁵Be exalted, O God, above the heavens;
    let your glory be over all the earth.

⁶They spread a net for my feet—
    I was bowed down in distress.
They dug a pit in my path—
    but they have fallen into it themselves. *Selah*

⁷My heart is steadfast, O God,
    my heart is steadfast;
    I will sing and make music.
⁸Awake, my soul!
    Awake, harp and lyre!
    I will awaken the dawn.

⁹I will praise you, O Lord, among the nations;
    I will sing of you among the peoples.
¹⁰For great is your love, reaching to the heavens;
    your faithfulness reaches to the skies.

¹¹Be exalted, O God, above the heavens;
    let your glory be over all the earth.

■ PSALM 58

□ For the director of music. ⌐To the tune of⌐ "Do Not Destroy". Of David. A *miktam.ᵃ*

¹Do you rulers indeed speak justly?
   Do you judge uprightly among men?
²No, in your heart you devise injustice,
   and your hands mete out violence on the
      earth.
³Even from birth the wicked go astray;
   from the womb they are wayward and speak
      lies.
⁴Their venom is like the venom of a snake,
   like that of a cobra that has stopped its ears,
⁵that will not heed the tune of the charmer,
   however skilful the enchanter may be.

⁶Break the teeth in their mouths, O God;
   tear out, O LORD, the fangs of the lions!
⁷Let them vanish like water that flows away;
   when they draw the bow, let their arrows be
      blunted.
⁸Like a slug melting away as it moves along,
   like a stillborn child, may they not see the
      sun.

⁹Before your pots can feel ⌐the heat of⌐ the
      thorns—
   whether they be green or dry—the wicked
      will be swept away.ᵇ
¹⁰The righteous will be glad when they are
      avenged,
   when they bathe their feet in the blood of
      the wicked.
¹¹Then men will say,
   "Surely the righteous still are rewarded;
   surely there is a God who judges the earth."

58:8 ■ ROUGH WORDS

The psalmist's white-hot anger is never more obvious than in these ardent words asking God to punish wicked people. His demand for retribution is a far cry from Jesus' command to love your enemies; no Christian should make this a model of prayer. We ought to remember, though, that the psalmist is asking *God* for justice—not planning how he will bring it about himself. For more on this subject, see "What About Curses?" page 536.

■ PSALM 59

□ For the director of music. ⌐To the tune of⌐ "Do Not Destroy". Of David. A *miktam.ᵃ* When Saul had sent men to watch David's house in order to kill him.

¹Deliver me from my enemies, O God;
   protect me from those who rise up against
      me.
²Deliver me from evildoers
   and save me from bloodthirsty men.

³See how they lie in wait for me!
   Fierce men conspire against me
   for no offence or sin of mine, O LORD.

⁴I have done no wrong, yet they are ready to
      attack me.
   Arise to help me; look on my plight!
⁵O LORD God Almighty, the God of Israel,
   rouse yourself to punish all the nations;
   show no mercy to wicked traitors.   *Selah*

⁶They return at evening,
   snarling like dogs,
   and prowl about the city.
⁷See what they spew from their mouths—
   they spew out swords from their lips,
   and they say, "Who can hear us?"
⁸But you, O LORD, laugh at them;
   you scoff at all those nations.

⁹O my Strength, I watch for you;
   you, O God, are my fortress, ¹⁰my loving
      God.

God will go before me
   and will let me gloat over those who slander
      me.
¹¹But do not kill them, O Lord our shield,ᵇ
   or my people will forget.
In your might make them wander about,
   and bring them down.
¹²For the sins of their mouths,
   for the words of their lips,
   let them be caught in their pride.
For the curses and lies they utter,
¹³   consume them in wrath,
   consume them till they are no more.
Then it will be known to the ends of the earth
   that God rules over Jacob.   *Selah*

¹⁴They return at evening,
   snarling like dogs,
   and prowl about the city.
¹⁵They wander about for food
   and howl if not satisfied.
¹⁶But I will sing of your strength,
   in the morning I will sing of your love;
for you are my fortress,
   my refuge in times of trouble.

¹⁷O my Strength, I sing praise to you;
   you, O God, are my fortress, my loving God.

■ PSALM 60

□ For the director of music. To ⌐the tune of⌐ "The Lily of the Covenant". A *miktamᵃ* of David. For teaching. When he fought Aram Naharaimᵇ and Aram Zobah,ᶜ and when Joab returned and struck down twelve thousand Edomites in the Valley of Salt.

¹You have rejected us, O God, and burst forth
      upon us;
   you have been angry—now restore us!
²You have shaken the land and torn it open;
   mend its fractures, for it is quaking.
³You have shown your people desperate times;
   you have given us wine that makes us
      stagger.

⁴But for those who fear you, you have raised a
      banner

ᵃTitle: Probably a literary or musical term   ᵇ9 The meaning of the Hebrew for this verse is uncertain.   ᵃTitle: Probably a literary or musical term
ᵇ11 Or *sovereign*   ᵃTitle: Probably a literary or musical term   ᵇTitle: That is, Arameans of North-west Mesopotamia   ᶜTitle: That is, Arameans of central Syria

to be unfurled against the bow.   *Selah*

⁵Save us and help us with your right hand,
    that those you love may be delivered.
⁶God has spoken from his sanctuary:
    "In triumph I will parcel out Shechem
    and measure off the Valley of Succoth.
⁷Gilead is mine, and Manasseh is mine;
    Ephraim is my helmet,
    Judah my sceptre.
⁸Moab is my washbasin,
    upon Edom I toss my sandal;
    over Philistia I shout in triumph."

⁹Who will bring me to the fortified city?
    Who will lead me to Edom?
¹⁰Is it not you, O God, you who have rejected us
    and no longer go out with our armies?
¹¹Give us aid against the enemy,
    for the help of man is worthless.
¹²With God we shall gain the victory,
    and he will trample down our enemies.

■ PSALM 61
☐ For the director of music. With stringed instruments.
Of David.

¹Hear my cry, O God;
    listen to my prayer.

²From the ends of the earth I call to you,
    I call as my heart grows faint;
    lead me to the rock that is higher than I.
³For you have been my refuge,
    a strong tower against the foe.

⁴I long to dwell in your tent for ever
    and take refuge in the shelter of your wings.
                                    Selah
⁵For you have heard my vows, O God;
    you have given me the heritage of those who
        fear your name.

⁶Increase the days of the king's life,
    his years for many generations.
⁷May he be enthroned in God's presence for
        ever;
    appoint your love and faithfulness to protect
        him.

⁸Then will I ever sing praise to your name
    and fulfil my vows day after day.

■ PSALM 62
☐ For the director of music. For Jeduthun. A psalm of David.

¹My soul finds rest in God alone;
    my salvation comes from him.
²He alone is my rock and my salvation;
    he is my fortress, I shall never be shaken.

³How long will you assault a man?
    Would all of you throw him down—
    this leaning wall, this tottering fence?
⁴They fully intend to topple him
    from his lofty place;
    they take delight in lies.
With their mouths they bless,

but in their hearts they curse.   *Selah*

⁵Find rest, O my soul, in God alone;
    my hope comes from him.
⁶He alone is my rock and my salvation;
    he is my fortress, I shall not be shaken.
⁷My salvation and my honour depend on God;*a*
    he is my mighty rock, my refuge.
⁸Trust in him at all times, O people;
    pour out your hearts to him,
    for God is our refuge.   *Selah*

62:7 ■ THE HIDEOUT
In the years when David was an outlaw from King
Saul, his hideouts included a "rock" in the desert
(1 Samuel 23:25–28), as well as a "stronghold"
(1 Samuel 22:4). As an experienced fighter, David
knew the value of such defences. He recognised,
however, that he owed his safety to God, his true
rock and fortress.

---

⁹Lowborn men are but a breath,
    the highborn are but a lie;
if weighed on a balance, they are nothing;
    together they are only a breath.
¹⁰Do not trust in extortion
    or take pride in stolen goods;
though your riches increase,
    do not set your heart on them.

¹¹One thing God has spoken,
    two things have I heard:
that you, O God, are strong,
¹²   and that you, O Lord, are loving.
Surely you will reward each person
    according to what he has done.

■ PSALM 63
☐ A psalm of David. When he was in the Desert of Judah.

¹O God, you are my God,
    earnestly I seek you;
my soul thirsts for you,
    my body longs for you,
in a dry and weary land
    where there is no water.

²I have seen you in the sanctuary
    and beheld your power and your glory.
³Because your love is better than life,
    my lips will glorify you.
⁴I will praise you as long as I live,
    and in your name I will lift up my hands.
⁵My soul will be satisfied as with the richest of
        foods;
    with singing lips my mouth will praise you.

⁶On my bed I remember you;
    I think of you through the watches of the
        night.
⁷Because you are my help,
    I sing in the shadow of your wings.
⁸My soul clings to you;
    your right hand upholds me.

a 7 Or / God Most High is my salvation and my honour

9They who seek my life will be destroyed;
　they will go down to the depths of the earth.
10They will be given over to the sword
　and become food for jackals.

11But the king will rejoice in God;
　all who swear by God's name will praise him,
　while the mouths of liars will be silenced.

■ PSALM 64
☐ For the director of music. A psalm of David.

1Hear me, O God, as I voice my complaint;
　protect my life from the threat of the enemy.
2Hide me from the conspiracy of the wicked,
　from that noisy crowd of evildoers.

3They sharpen their tongues like swords
　and aim their words like deadly arrows.
4They shoot from ambush at the innocent man;
　they shoot at him suddenly, without fear.

5They encourage each other in evil plans,
　they talk about hiding their snares;
　they say, "Who will see them?"a
6They plot injustice and say,
　"We have devised a perfect plan!"
　Surely the mind and heart of man are
　　cunning.

7But God will shoot them with arrows;
　suddenly they will be struck down.
8He will turn their own tongues against them
　and bring them to ruin;
　all who see them will shake their heads in
　　scorn.

9All mankind will fear;
　they will proclaim the works of God
　and ponder what he has done.
10Let the righteous rejoice in the LORD
　and take refuge in him;
　let all the upright in heart praise him!

■ PSALM 65
☐ For the director of music. A psalm of David. A song.

1Praise awaitsa you, O God, in Zion;
　to you our vows will be fulfilled.
2O you who hear prayer,
　to you all men will come.
3When we were overwhelmed by sins,
　you forgaveb our transgressions.
4Blessed are those you choose
　and bring near to live in your courts!
We are filled with the good things of your
　　house,
　of your holy temple.

5You answer us with awesome deeds of
　　righteousness,
　O God our Saviour,
　the hope of all the ends of the earth
　and of the farthest seas,
6who formed the mountains by your power,
　having armed yourself with strength,
7who stilled the roaring of the seas,

　the roaring of their waves,
　and the turmoil of the nations.
8Those living far away fear your wonders;
　where morning dawns and evening fades
　you call forth songs of joy.

65:8 ■ GOD REACHES OUT
God's Old Testament people primarily came from
a specially chosen ethnic group. Some outsiders
joined them in their faith (Ruth, for instance), but
the Israelites didn't issue blanket invitations.
Nevertheless, they recognised that God's love
extended to people over the horizon. His care for
the earth, so beautifully described here, called for
a response everywhere, not just in Israel.

9You care for the land and water it;
　you enrich it abundantly.
The streams of God are filled with water
　to provide the people with corn,
　for so you have ordained it.c
10You drench its furrows
　and level its ridges;
　you soften it with showers
　and bless its crops.
11You crown the year with your bounty,
　and your carts overflow with abundance.
12The grasslands of the desert overflow;
　the hills are clothed with gladness.
13The meadows are covered with flocks
　and the valleys are mantled with corn;
　they shout for joy and sing.

■ PSALM 66
☐ For the director of music. A song. A psalm.

1Shout with joy to God, all the earth!
2　Sing the glory of his name;
　make his praise glorious!
3Say to God, "How awesome are your deeds!
　So great is your power
　that your enemies cringe before you.
4All the earth bows down to you;
　they sing praise to you,
　they sing praise to your name."　　　*Selah*

5Come and see what God has done,
　how awesome his works on man's behalf!
6He turned the sea into dry land,
　they passed through the waters on foot—
　come, let us rejoice in him.
7He rules for ever by his power,
　his eyes watch the nations—
　let not the rebellious rise up against him.
　　　　　　　　　　　　　　　　　Selah

8Praise our God, O peoples,
　let the sound of his praise be heard;
9he has preserved our lives
　and kept our feet from slipping.
10For you, O God, tested us;
　you refined us like silver.
11You brought us into prison
　and laid burdens on our backs.

a5 Or us　　a1 Or befits; the meaning of the Hebrew for this word is uncertain.　　b3 Or made atonement for　　c9 Or for that is how you prepare the
land

¹²You let men ride over our heads;
    we went through fire and water,
    but you brought us to a place of abundance.

¹³I will come to your temple with burnt offerings
    and fulfil my vows to you—
¹⁴vows my lips promised and my mouth spoke
    when I was in trouble.
¹⁵I will sacrifice fat animals to you
    and an offering of rams;
    I will offer bulls and goats.   *Selah*

¹⁶Come and listen, all you who fear God;
    let me tell you what he has done for me.
¹⁷I cried out to him with my mouth;
    his praise was on my tongue.
¹⁸If I had cherished sin in my heart,
    the Lord would not have listened;
¹⁹but God has surely listened
    and heard my voice in prayer.
²⁰Praise be to God,
    who has not rejected my prayer
    or withheld his love from me!

■ PSALM 67
□ For the director of music. With stringed instruments.
A psalm. A song.

¹May God be gracious to us and bless us
    and make his face shine upon us,   *Selah*
²that your ways may be known on earth,
    your salvation among all nations.

³May the peoples praise you, O God;
    may all the peoples praise you.
⁴May the nations be glad and sing for joy,
    for you rule the peoples justly
    and guide the nations of the earth.   *Selah*
⁵May the peoples praise you, O God;
    may all the peoples praise you.

⁶Then the land will yield its harvest,
    and God, our God, will bless us.
⁷God will bless us,
    and all the ends of the earth will fear him.

■ PSALM 68
□ For the director of music. Of David. A psalm. A song.

¹May God arise, may his enemies be scattered;
    may his foes flee before him.
²As smoke is blown away by the wind,
    may you blow them away;
    as wax melts before the fire,
    may the wicked perish before God.
³But may the righteous be glad
    and rejoice before God;
    may they be happy and joyful.

⁴Sing to God, sing praise to his name,
    extol him who rides on the clouds*ᵃ*—
    his name is the LORD—
    and rejoice before him.
⁵A father to the fatherless, a defender of widows,
    is God in his holy dwelling.
⁶God sets the lonely in families,*ᵇ*
    he leads forth the prisoners with singing;

but the rebellious live in a sun-scorched
    land.

⁷When you went out before your people,
    O God,
    when you marched through the wasteland,
                                              Selah
⁸the earth shook,
    the heavens poured down rain,
    before God, the One of Sinai,
    before God, the God of Israel.
⁹You gave abundant showers, O God;
    you refreshed your weary inheritance.
¹⁰Your people settled in it,
    and from your bounty, O God, you provided
    for the poor.

¹¹The Lord announced the word,
    and great was the company of those who
    proclaimed it:
¹²"Kings and armies flee in haste;
    in the camps men divide the plunder.
¹³Even while you sleep among the campfires,*ᶜ*
    the wings of ⌐my⌐ dove are sheathed with
    silver,
    its feathers with shining gold."
¹⁴When the Almighty*ᵈ* scattered the kings in the
    land,
    it was like snow fallen on Zalmon.

¹⁵The mountains of Bashan are majestic
    mountains;
    rugged are the mountains of Bashan.
¹⁶Why gaze in envy, O rugged mountains,
    at the mountain where God chooses to reign,
    where the LORD himself will dwell for ever?
¹⁷The chariots of God are tens of thousands
    and thousands of thousands;
    the Lord ⌐has come⌐ from Sinai into his
    sanctuary.
¹⁸When you ascended on high,
    you led captives in your train;
    you received gifts from men,
    even from*ᵉ* the rebellious—
    that you,*ᶠ* O LORD God, might dwell there.

¹⁹Praise be to the Lord, to God our Saviour,
    who daily bears our burdens.   *Selah*
²⁰Our God is a God who saves;
    from the Sovereign LORD comes escape from
    death.

²¹Surely God will crush the heads of his enemies,
    the hairy crowns of those who go on in their
    sins.
²²The Lord says, "I will bring them from Bashan;
    I will bring them from the depths of the sea,
²³that you may plunge your feet in the blood of
    your foes,
    while the tongues of your dogs have their
    share."

²⁴Your procession has come into view, O God,
    the procession of my God and King into the
    sanctuary.
²⁵In front are the singers, after them the
    musicians;

*ᵃ4 Or / prepare the way for him who rides through the deserts   ᵇ6 Or the desolate in a homeland   ᶜ13 Or saddlebags   ᵈ14 Hebrew Shaddai
ᵉ18 Or gifts for men, / even   ᶠ18 Or they*

with them are the maidens playing
   tambourines.
26Praise God in the great congregation;
   praise the LORD in the assembly of Israel.
27There is the little tribe of Benjamin, leading
   them,
   there the great throng of Judah's princes,
   and there the princes of Zebulun and of
   Naphtali.

68:24 ■ THE WAY THEY WORSHIPPED

Many of the psalms were sung in the temple, to
worship God. Exactly how people worshipped,
however, is difficult to know. This verse offers
unmistakable clues to how this psalm was used –
in a procession leading to the temple. It may have
been sung first when David brought the ark – the
sign of God's actual presence – into Jerusalem
(2 Samuel 6; 1 Chronicles 15–16). Or it may have
been used in one of the annual festivals that drew
Israelites from all over to the capital.

28Summon your power, O God;g
   show us your strength, O God, as you have
      done before.
29Because of your temple at Jerusalem
   kings will bring you gifts.
30Rebuke the beast among the reeds,
   the herd of bulls among the calves of the
      nations.
   Humbled, may it bring bars of silver.
   Scatter the nations who delight in war.
31Envoys will come from Egypt;
   Cushb will submit herself to God.

32Sing to God, O kingdoms of the earth,
   sing praise to the Lord,   Selah
33to him who rides the ancient skies above,
   who thunders with mighty voice.
34Proclaim the power of God,
   whose majesty is over Israel,
   whose power is in the skies.
35You are awesome, O God, in your sanctuary;
   the God of Israel gives power and strength to
      his people.

   Praise be to God!

■ PSALM 69
□ For the director of music. To ˌthe tune ofˌ "Lilies".
Of David.

1Save me, O God,
   for the waters have come up to my neck.
2I sink in the miry depths,
   where there is no foothold.
   I have come into the deep waters;
   the floods engulf me.
3I am worn out calling for help;
   my throat is parched.
   My eyes fail,
   looking for my God.
4Those who hate me without reason
   outnumber the hairs of my head;

many are my enemies without cause,
   those who seek to destroy me.
   I am forced to restore
   what I did not steal.

5You know my folly, O God;
   my guilt is not hidden from you.

6May those who hope in you
   not be disgraced because of me,
   O Lord, the LORD Almighty;
   may those who seek you
   not be put to shame because of me,
   O God of Israel.
7For I endure scorn for your sake,
   and shame covers my face.
8I am a stranger to my brothers,
   an alien to my own mother's sons;
9for zeal for your house consumes me,
   and the insults of those who insult you fall
      on me.
10When I weep and fast,
   I must endure scorn;
11when I put on sackcloth,
   people make sport of me.
12Those who sit at the gate mock me,
   and I am the song of the drunkards.

69:9 ■ FORESHADOWING JESUS

Psalm 69 was quoted repeatedly by New
Testament writers, who identify Jesus as the
righteous sufferer. "Zeal for your house consumes
me" was quoted in John 2:17, for instance, when
Jesus drove out the money-changers, and
Romans 15:3 quoted the second half of that
verse, referring to Jesus' self-sacrificial attitude.
   Why did the New Testament writers see Jesus
in this psalm? The psalm was attributed to David,
the great king. Yet it is not David's greatness and
majesty that are described here. Instead, the
psalm is a cry of suffering from a righteous man,
alienated even from his family because of his zeal
for God. It is strange: Israel's greatest hero is
portrayed as a helpless victim because of his faith
in God. Yet Jesus filled this pattern completely. He
did not, however, follow every part of the psalm:
instead of the curses this psalm directs towards
enemies, Jesus prayed that God would forgive the
men murdering him.

13But I pray to you, O LORD,
   in the time of your favour;
   in your great love, O God,
   answer me with your sure salvation.
14Rescue me from the mire,
   do not let me sink;
   deliver me from those who hate me,
   from the deep waters.
15Do not let the floodwaters engulf me
   or the depths swallow me up
   or the pit close its mouth over me.
16Answer me, O LORD, out of the goodness of
      your love;
   in your great mercy turn to me.

g 28 Many Hebrew manuscripts, Septuagint and Syriac; most Hebrew manuscripts Your God has summoned power for you   b 31 That is, the upper Nile
region

¹⁷Do not hide your face from your servant;
    answer me quickly, for I am in trouble.
¹⁸Come near and rescue me;
    redeem me because of my foes.

¹⁹You know how I am scorned, disgraced and
        shamed;
    all my enemies are before you.
²⁰Scorn has broken my heart
    and has left me helpless;
  I looked for sympathy, but there was none,
    for comforters, but I found none.
²¹They put gall in my food
    and gave me vinegar for my thirst.

²²May the table set before them become a snare;
    may it become retribution and*ᵃ* a trap.
²³May their eyes be darkened so that they cannot
        see,
    and their backs be bent for ever.
²⁴Pour out your wrath on them;
    let your fierce anger overtake them.
²⁵May their place be deserted;
    let there be no-one to dwell in their tents.
²⁶For they persecute those you wound
    and talk about the pain of those you hurt.
²⁷Charge them with crime upon crime;
    do not let them share in your salvation.
²⁸May they be blotted out of the book of life
    and not be listed with the righteous.

²⁹I am in pain and distress;
    may your salvation, O God, protect me.

³⁰I will praise God's name in song
    and glorify him with thanksgiving.
³¹This will please the LORD more than an ox,
    more than a bull with its horns and hoofs.
³²The poor will see and be glad —
    you who seek God, may your hearts live!
³³The LORD hears the needy
    and does not despise his captive people.

³⁴Let heaven and earth praise him,
    the seas and all that move in them,
³⁵for God will save Zion
    and rebuild the cities of Judah.
  Then people will settle there and possess it;
³⁶ the children of his servants will inherit it,
    and those who love his name will dwell
        there.

■ PSALM 70
□ For the director of music. Of David. A petition.

¹Hasten, O God, to save me;
    O LORD, come quickly to help me.
²May those who seek my life
    be put to shame and confusion;
  may all who desire my ruin
    be turned back in disgrace.
³May those who say to me, "Aha! Aha!"
    turn back because of their shame.
⁴But may all who seek you
    rejoice and be glad in you;
  may those who love your salvation always say,
    "Let God be exalted!"

ᵃ 22 Or snare / and their fellowship become

⁵Yet I am poor and needy;
    come quickly to me, O God.
  You are my help and my deliverer;
    O LORD, do not delay.

■ PSALM 71

¹In you, O LORD, I have taken refuge;
    let me never be put to shame.
²Rescue me and deliver me in your
        righteousness;
    turn your ear to me and save me.
³Be my rock of refuge,
    to which I can always go;
  give the command to save me,
    for you are my rock and my fortress.
⁴Deliver me, O my God, from the hand of the
        wicked,
    from the grasp of evil and cruel men.

⁵For you have been my hope, O Sovereign LORD,
    my confidence since my youth.
⁶From my birth I have relied on you;
    you brought me forth from my mother's
        womb.
    I will ever praise you.
⁷I have become like a portent to many,
    but you are my strong refuge.
⁸My mouth is filled with your praise,
    declaring your splendour all day long.

⁹Do not cast me away when I am old;
    do not forsake me when my strength is gone.
¹⁰For my enemies speak against me;
    those who wait to kill me conspire together.
¹¹They say, "God has forsaken him;
    pursue him and seize him,
    for no-one will rescue him."
¹²Be not far from me, O God;
    come quickly, O my God, to help me.
¹³May my accusers perish in shame;
    may those who want to harm me
    be covered with scorn and disgrace.

¹⁴But as for me, I shall always have hope;
    I will praise you more and more.
¹⁵My mouth will tell of your righteousness,
    of your salvation all day long,
    though I know not its measure.
¹⁶I will come and proclaim your mighty acts,
        O Sovereign LORD;
    I will proclaim your righteousness, yours
        alone.
¹⁷Since my youth, O God, you have taught me,
    and to this day I declare your marvellous
        deeds.
¹⁸Even when I am old and grey,
    do not forsake me, O God,
    till I declare your power to the next
        generation,
    your might to all who are to come.

¹⁹Your righteousness reaches to the skies, O God,
    you who have done great things.
    Who, O God, is like you?

20Though you have made me see troubles, many
and bitter,

71:18 ■ A VIEW FROM OLD AGE
Older people have a peculiar privilege: the chance
to see God's faithfulness over a lifetime. Their
troubles do not grow smaller as the years go by
(see verses 9–11), but their experiences can
strengthen confidence that God will deliver as he
always has (verses 20–21).

you will restore my life again;
from the depths of the earth
you will again bring me up.
21You will increase my honour
and comfort me once again.

22I will praise you with the harp
for your faithfulness, O my God;
I will sing praise to you with the lyre,
O Holy One of Israel.
23My lips will shout for joy
when I sing praise to you —
I, whom you have redeemed.
24My tongue will tell of your righteous acts
all day long,
for those who wanted to harm me
have been put to shame and confusion.

■ PSALM 72
□ Of Solomon.

1Endow the king with your justice, O God,
the royal son with your righteousness.
2He will*a* judge your people in righteousness,
your afflicted ones with justice.
3The mountains will bring prosperity to the
people,
the hills the fruit of righteousness.
4He will defend the afflicted among the people
and save the children of the needy;
he will crush the oppressor.

5He will endure*b* as long as the sun,
as long as the moon, through all generations.
6He will be like rain falling on a mown field,
like showers watering the earth.
7In his days the righteous will flourish;
prosperity will abound till the moon is no
more.

8He will rule from sea to sea
and from the River*c* to the ends of the
earth.*d*
9The desert tribes will bow before him
and his enemies will lick the dust.
10The kings of Tarshish and of distant shores
will bring tribute to him;
the kings of Sheba and Seba
will present him gifts.
11All kings will bow down to him
and all nations will serve him.

12For he will deliver the needy who cry out,
the afflicted who have no-one to help.

13He will take pity on the weak and the needy
and save the needy from death.
14He will rescue them from oppression and
violence,
for precious is their blood in his sight.

15Long may he live!
May gold from Sheba be given to him.
May people ever pray for him
and bless him all day long.
16Let corn abound throughout the land;
on the tops of the hills may it sway.
Let its fruit flourish like Lebanon;
let it thrive like the grass of the field.
17May his name endure for ever;
may it continue as long as the sun.

All nations will be blessed through him,
and they will call him blessed.

18Praise be to the LORD God, the God of Israel,
who alone does marvellous deeds.
19Praise be to his glorious name for ever;
may the whole earth be filled with his glory.
Amen and Amen.

20This concludes the prayers of David son of
Jesse.

72:20 ■ THE FIVE BOOKS
Psalms was probably made into one big book
from five separate collections. These are divided
up in our Bible as Book I, Book II, and so on,
each book ending with a concluding line of praise.
The contents sometimes overlap: Psalm 14 in
Book I turns up again as Psalm 53 in Book II. Part
of Psalm 40 (Book I) becomes Psalm 70 (Book II),
and parts of Psalms 57 and 60 make up Psalm
108 (Book IV). Other less noticeable differences
stand out between the books. But perhaps the
most eloquent proof that all these psalms were
not originally collected together is found at the
end of Psalm 72, "This concludes the prayers of
David son of Jesse." Since 18 more "psalms of
David" appear in Psalms, it seems very likely that
Psalm 72:20 originally concluded a songbook.
Later, this collection was incorporated into the
book of Psalms.

BOOK III
□ Psalms 73–89

■ PSALM 73
□ A psalm of Asaph.

1Surely God is good to Israel,
to those who are pure in heart.

2But as for me, my feet had almost slipped;
I had nearly lost my foothold.
3For I envied the arrogant
when I saw the prosperity of the wicked.

4They have no struggles;

a2 Or May he; similarly in verses 3–11 and 17   b5 Septuagint; Hebrew You will be feared   c8 That is, the Euphrates   d8 Or the end of the land their bodies are healthy and strong.^a

⁵They are free from the burdens common to
man;
they are not plagued by human ills.

⁶Therefore pride is their necklace;
they clothe themselves with violence.

⁷From their callous hearts comes iniquity;^b
the evil conceits of their minds know no
limits.

⁸They scoff, and speak with malice;
in their arrogance they threaten oppression.

⁹Their mouths lay claim to heaven,
and their tongues take possession of the
earth.

¹⁰Therefore their people turn to them
and drink up waters in abundance.^c

¹¹They say, "How can God know?
Does the Most High have knowledge?"

73:4 ■ SHORT-RUN REWARDS

Some people are deeply disturbed when they see
evil people living without a care. Does a bad life
always make you unhappy? Not in the short run,
according to this description. In fact, the life of the
wicked sometimes looks enviable. Only in the light
of eternity is godly living always more rewarding.

¹²This is what the wicked are like—
always carefree, they increase in wealth.

¹³Surely in vain have I kept my heart pure;
in vain have I washed my hands in
innocence.

¹⁴All day long I have been plagued;
I have been punished every morning.

¹⁵If I had said, "I will speak thus,"
I would have betrayed your children.

¹⁶When I tried to understand all this,
it was oppressive to me

¹⁷till I entered the sanctuary of God;
then I understood their final destiny.

¹⁸Surely you place them on slippery ground;
you cast them down to ruin.

¹⁹How suddenly are they destroyed,
completely swept away by terrors!

²⁰As a dream when one awakes,
so when you arise, O Lord,
you will despise them as fantasies.

²¹When my heart was grieved
and my spirit embittered,

²²I was senseless and ignorant;
I was a brute beast before you.

²³Yet I am always with you;
you hold me by my right hand.

²⁴You guide me with your counsel,
and afterwards you will take me into glory.

²⁵Whom have I in heaven but you?
And earth has nothing I desire besides you.

²⁶My flesh and my heart may fail,
but God is the strength of my heart
and my portion for ever.

²⁷Those who are far from you will perish;
you destroy all who are unfaithful to you.

²⁸But as for me, it is good to be near God.
I have made the Sovereign LORD my refuge;
I will tell of all your deeds.

■ PSALM 74

□ A maskil^a of Asaph.

¹Why have you rejected us for ever, O God?
Why does your anger smoulder against the
sheep of your pasture?

²Remember the people you purchased of old,
the tribe of your inheritance, whom you
redeemed—
Mount Zion, where you dwelt.

³Turn your steps towards these everlasting ruins,
all this destruction the enemy has brought
on the sanctuary.

⁴Your foes roared in the place where you met
with us;
they set up their standards as signs.

⁵They behaved like men wielding axes
to cut through a thicket of trees.

⁶They smashed all the carved panelling
with their axes and hatchets.

⁷They burned your sanctuary to the ground;
they defiled the dwelling-place of your
Name.

⁸They said in their hearts, "We will crush them
completely!"
They burned every place where God was
worshipped in the land.

⁹We are given no miraculous signs;
no prophets are left,
and none of us knows how long this will be.

¹⁰How long will the enemy mock you, O God?
Will the foe revile your name for ever?

¹¹Why do you hold back your hand, your right
hand?
Take it from the folds of your garment and
destroy them!

¹²But you, O God, are my king from of old;
you bring salvation upon the earth.

¹³It was you who split open the sea by your
power;
you broke the heads of the monster in the
waters.

¹⁴It was you who crushed the heads of Leviathan
and gave him as food to the creatures of the
desert.

¹⁵It was you who opened up springs and streams;
you dried up the ever-flowing rivers.

¹⁶The day is yours, and yours also the night;
you established the sun and moon.

¹⁷It was you who set all the boundaries of the
earth;
you made both summer and winter.

¹⁸Remember how the enemy has mocked you,
O LORD,
how foolish people have reviled your name.

^a 4 With a different word division of the Hebrew; Masoretic Text *struggles at their death; / their bodies are healthy*   ^b 7 Syriac (see also Septuagint); Hebrew *Their eyes bulge with fat*   ^c 10 The meaning of the Hebrew for this verse is uncertain.   ^a Title: Probably a literary or musical term

19Do not hand over the life of your dove to wild
beasts;
do not forget the lives of your afflicted
people for ever.
20Have regard for your covenant,
because haunts of violence fill the dark
places of the land.
21Do not let the oppressed retreat in disgrace;
may the poor and needy praise your name.

22Rise up, O God, and defend your cause;
remember how fools mock you all day long.
23Do not ignore the clamour of your adversaries,
the uproar of your enemies, which rises
continually.

■ PSALM 75
☐ For the director of music. ⌞To the tune of⌟ "Do Not
Destroy". A psalm of Asaph. A song.

1We give thanks to you, O God,
we give thanks, for your Name is near;
men tell of your wonderful deeds.

2You say, "I choose the appointed time;
it is I who judge uprightly.
3When the earth and all its people quake,
it is I who hold its pillars firm.   Selah
4To the arrogant I say, 'Boast no more,'
and to the wicked, 'Do not lift up your
horns.
5Do not lift your horns against heaven;
do not speak with outstretched neck.' "

6No-one from the east or the west
or from the desert can exalt a man.
7But it is God who judges:
He brings one down, he exalts another.
8In the hand of the LORD is a cup
full of foaming wine mixed with spices;
he pours it out, and all the wicked of the earth
drink it down to its very dregs.

9As for me, I will declare this for ever;
I will sing praise to the God of Jacob.
10I will cut off the horns of all the wicked,
but the horns of the righteous shall be lifted
up.

■ PSALM 76
☐ For the director of music. With stringed instruments. A
psalm of Asaph. A song.

1In Judah God is known;
his name is great in Israel.
2His tent is in Salem,
his dwelling-place in Zion.
3There he broke the flashing arrows,
the shields and the swords, the weapons of
war.   Selah

4You are resplendent with light,
more majestic than mountains rich with
game.
5Valiant men lie plundered,
they sleep their last sleep;
not one of the warriors

can lift his hands.
6At your rebuke, O God of Jacob,
both horse and chariot lie still.
7You alone are to be feared.
Who can stand before you when you are
angry?
8From heaven you pronounced judgment,
and the land feared and was quiet—
9when you, O God, rose up to judge,
to save all the afflicted of the land.   Selah
10Surely your wrath against men brings you
praise,
and the survivors of your wrath are
restrained.a

11Make vows to the LORD your God and fulfil
them;
let all the neighbouring lands
bring gifts to the One to be feared.
12He breaks the spirit of rulers;
he is feared by the kings of the earth.

■ PSALM 77
☐ For the director of music. For Jeduthun. Of Asaph.
A psalm.

1I cried out to God for help;
I cried out to God to hear me.
2When I was in distress, I sought the Lord;
at night I stretched out untiring hands
and my soul refused to be comforted.

3I remembered you, O God, and I groaned;
I mused, and my spirit grew faint.   Selah

77:3 ■ SLEEPLESS NIGHTS
Sleeplessness afflicts millions, and this psalm
shows that it is nothing new. Anxiety tormented
the psalmist while he lay awake at night. What to
do? He deliberately turned his thoughts to the
past, remembering what God had done for him
and for his people.

4You kept my eyes from closing;
I was too troubled to speak.
5I thought about the former days,
the years of long ago;
6I remembered my songs in the night.
My heart mused and my spirit enquired:

7"Will the Lord reject for ever?
Will he never show his favour again?
8Has his unfailing love vanished for ever?
Has his promise failed for all time?
9Has God forgotten to be merciful?
Has he in anger withheld his compassion?"
Selah

10Then I thought, "To this I will appeal:
the years of the right hand of the Most
High."
11I will remember the deeds of the LORD;
yes, I will remember your miracles of long
ago.
12I will meditate on all your works

a 10 Or Surely the wrath of men brings you praise, / and with the remainder of wrath you arm yourself and consider all your mighty deeds.

¹³Your ways, O God, are holy.
    What god is so great as our God?
¹⁴You are the God who performs miracles;
    you display your power among the peoples.
¹⁵With your mighty arm you redeemed your
        people,
    the descendants of Jacob and Joseph.   *Selah*

¹⁶The waters saw you, O God,
    the waters saw you and writhed;
    the very depths were convulsed.
¹⁷The clouds poured down water,
    the skies resounded with thunder;
    your arrows flashed back and forth.
¹⁸Your thunder was heard in the whirlwind,
    your lightning lit up the world;
    the earth trembled and quaked.
¹⁹Your path led through the sea,
    your way through the mighty waters,
    though your footprints were not seen.

²⁰You led your people like a flock
    by the hand of Moses and Aaron.

■ PSALM 78
☐ A *maskil*[a] of Asaph.

¹O my people, hear my teaching;
    listen to the words of my mouth.
²I will open my mouth in parables,
    I will utter hidden things, things from of
        old —
³what we have heard and known,
    what our fathers have told us.
⁴We will not hide them from their children;
    we will tell the next generation
    the praiseworthy deeds of the LORD,
        his power, and the wonders he has done.
⁵He decreed statutes for Jacob
    and established the law in Israel,
    which he commanded our forefathers
        to teach their children,

■ REMEMBERING BACK
THE PAST CAN GIVE YOU HOPE FOR THE FUTURE

INSIGHT

I WILL REMEMBER THE DEEDS OF THE
LORD. ■ 77:11

Married people make it their business to
remember how love began. Anniversaries recall
their wedding day, year after year. Wedding rings
remind them of their commitment. Wedding
photos capture the moment when "two become
one". In remembering the beginning of their
love, couples often find new hope for the future.
        Forgetting, on the other hand, amounts
to treason. If one person forgets the all-
important anniversary, tears and anger may
follow.

■ AN ANNIVERSARY DAY
The book of Psalms remembers too. When
things get bad, these poems often refer to the
past — particularly to the great events when,
under Moses, the Israelite nation began. God
freed the Israelites from Egyptian slavery, carried
them through the Red Sea, gave them directions
for living and ushered them into the promised
land. This miraculous beginning was as
significant to Jews as the cross is to Christians.
        The Israelites even had an "anniversary
day" — known as Passover — to remember it.
Every spring Passover reminded them of their
escape from Egypt. It's no accident that Easter
often occurs in the same week. Both days
celebrate liberation from slavery.
        The memories weren't all positive. The
Israelites could, in fact, be brutally frank about
their early failings. Even as they remembered
how persistently wonderful God had been, they

also remembered how rebellious, complaining
and forgetful they had been. Yet they had one
great, happy reason to celebrate: God had
kept his promise to love them.

■ HOPE IN A TIME OF DESPAIR
Psalm 77 is a "remembering" poem. It starts
with deep despair. "Will the Lord reject for
ever? Will he never show his favour again? Has
God forgotten to be merciful? Has he in anger
withheld his compassion?" (77:7,9). Imagine a
wife asking such questions about her husband.
        Then thoughts turn, deliberately, to the
past. Remember the turmoil at the banks of
the Red Sea? Could anything be worse? But in
that turbulent water they had seen the Lord's
power: he had led them through to safety. He
would do the same again.
        The historical psalms (77, 78, 105,
106) invite us, together with the Israelites, to
relive history. Like married couples
remembering back, we can recall God's
work — his powerful victories recorded all
through Scripture, his promises and proofs of
love towards his people. And we can refer to
God's history with us as individuals, too. Who
cannot count some blessings, some
undeserved favours? Through such
remembering we are strengthened to face the
future, and to recommit ourselves to trusting
God's care.

☐ LIFE QUESTIONS:
If you were to refer to a single past event for
encouragement, what would it be?

a Title: Probably a literary or musical term

⁶so that the next generation would know them,
    even the children yet to be born,
    and they in turn would tell their children.
⁷Then they would put their trust in God
    and would not forget his deeds
    but would keep his commands.
⁸They would not be like their forefathers—
    a stubborn and rebellious generation,
    whose hearts were not loyal to God,
    whose spirits were not faithful to him.

78:2 ■ SPEAKING IN PARABLES

Matthew saw this verse as foreshadowing Jesus'
teaching style (Matthew 13:35). A "parable" or
"proverb" (the Hebrew word is the same) simply
compares one thing with another. This psalm
compares the present to the past. By going over
the great things God has done—and the great
indifference God's people have often shown—the
psalmist warns against making the same mistakes
again.

⁹The men of Ephraim, though armed with bows,
    turned back on the day of battle;
¹⁰they did not keep God's covenant
    and refused to live by his law.
¹¹They forgot what he had done,
    the wonders he had shown them.
¹²He did miracles in the sight of their fathers
    in the land of Egypt, in the region of Zoan.
¹³He divided the sea and led them through;
    he made the water stand firm like a wall.
¹⁴He guided them with the cloud by day
    and with light from the fire all night.
¹⁵He split the rocks in the desert
    and gave them water as abundant as the seas;
¹⁶he brought streams out of a rocky crag
    and made water flow down like rivers.

¹⁷But they continued to sin against him,
    rebelling in the desert against the Most High.
¹⁸They wilfully put God to the test
    by demanding the food they craved.
¹⁹They spoke against God, saying,
    "Can God spread a table in the desert?
²⁰When he struck the rock, water gushed out,
    and streams flowed abundantly.
But can he also give us food?
    Can he supply meat for his people?"
²¹When the LORD heard them, he was very angry;
    his fire broke out against Jacob,
    and his wrath rose against Israel,
²²for they did not believe in God
    or trust in his deliverance.
²³Yet he gave a command to the skies above
    and opened the doors of the heavens;
²⁴he rained down manna for the people to eat,
    he gave them the grain of heaven.
²⁵Men ate the bread of angels;
    he sent them all the food they could eat.
²⁶He let loose the east wind from the heavens
    and led forth the south wind by his power.

²⁷He rained meat down on them like dust,
    flying birds like sand on the seashore.
²⁸He made them come down inside their camp,
    all around their tents.
²⁹They ate till they had more than enough,
    for he had given them what they craved.
³⁰But before they turned from the food they
    craved,
    even while it was still in their mouths,
³¹God's anger rose against them;
    he put to death the sturdiest among them,
    cutting down the young men of Israel.

³²In spite of all this, they kept on sinning;
    in spite of his wonders, they did not believe.
³³So he ended their days in futility
    and their years in terror.
³⁴Whenever God slew them, they would seek
    him;
    they eagerly turned to him again.
³⁵They remembered that God was their Rock,
    that God Most High was their Redeemer.
³⁶But then they would flatter him with their
    mouths,
    lying to him with their tongues;
³⁷their hearts were not loyal to him,
    they were not faithful to his covenant.
³⁸Yet he was merciful;
    he forgave their iniquities
    and did not destroy them.
Time after time he restrained his anger
    and did not stir up his full wrath.
³⁹He remembered that they were but flesh,
    a passing breeze that does not return.

⁴⁰How often they rebelled against him in the
    desert
    and grieved him in the wasteland!
⁴¹Again and again they put God to the test;
    they vexed the Holy One of Israel.
⁴²They did not remember his power—
    the day he redeemed them from the
    oppressor,
⁴³the day he displayed his miraculous signs in
    Egypt,
    his wonders in the region of Zoan.
⁴⁴He turned their rivers to blood;
    they could not drink from their streams.
⁴⁵He sent swarms of flies that devoured them,
    and frogs that devastated them.
⁴⁶He gave their crops to the grasshopper,
    their produce to the locust.
⁴⁷He destroyed their vines with hail
    and their sycamore-figs with sleet.
⁴⁸He gave over their cattle to the hail,
    their livestock to bolts of lightning.
⁴⁹He unleashed against them his hot anger,
    his wrath, indignation and hostility—
    a band of destroying angels.
⁵⁰He prepared a path for his anger;
    he did not spare them from death
    but gave them over to the plague.
⁵¹He struck down all the firstborn of Egypt,
    the firstfruits of manhood in the tents of
    Ham.

52But he brought his people out like a flock;
  he led them like sheep through the desert.
53He guided them safely, so they were unafraid;
  but the sea engulfed their enemies.
54Thus he brought them to the border of his holy
    land,
  to the hill country his right hand had taken.
55He drove out nations before them
  and allotted their lands to them as an
    inheritance;
  he settled the tribes of Israel in their homes.

56But they put God to the test
  and rebelled against the Most High;
  they did not keep his statutes.
57Like their fathers they were disloyal and
    faithless,
  as unreliable as a faulty bow.
58They angered him with their high places;
  they aroused his jealousy with their idols.
59When God heard them, he was very angry;
  he rejected Israel completely.
60He abandoned the tabernacle of Shiloh,
  the tent he had set up among men.
61He sent ⌊the ark of⌋ his might into captivity,
  his splendour into the hands of the enemy.
62He gave his people over to the sword;
  he was very angry with his inheritance.
63Fire consumed their young men,
  and their maidens had no wedding songs;
64their priests were put to the sword,
  and their widows could not weep.

78:64 ■ THE BAD OLD DAYS
From the time they entered the promised land to
the time when Saul was named their first king,
Israelites had no central government. Instead they
were governed by "judges", colourful volunteer
leaders like Deborah, Gideon, and Samson. Israel
had few nostalgic memories of those days. Psalm
78 portrays them as a time when Israel
abandoned God – and God rejected Israel. These
verses (59–64) draw from the events described in
1 Samuel 4.

65Then the Lord awoke as from sleep,
  as a man wakes from the stupor of wine.
66He beat back his enemies;
  he put them to everlasting shame.
67Then he rejected the tents of Joseph,
  he did not choose the tribe of Ephraim;
68but he chose the tribe of Judah,
  Mount Zion, which he loved.
69He built his sanctuary like the heights,
  like the earth that he established for ever.
70He chose David his servant
  and took him from the sheep pens;
71from tending the sheep he brought him
  to be the shepherd of his people Jacob,
  of Israel his inheritance.
72And David shepherded them with integrity of
    heart;
  with skilful hands he led them.

■ PSALM 79
□ A psalm of Asaph.

1O God, the nations have invaded your
    inheritance;
  they have defiled your holy temple,
  they have reduced Jerusalem to rubble.
2They have given the dead bodies of your
    servants
  as food to the birds of the air,
  the flesh of your saints to the beasts of the
    earth.
3They have poured out blood like water
  all around Jerusalem,
  and there is no-one to bury the dead.
4We are objects of reproach to our neighbours,
  of scorn and derision to those around us.

5How long, O LORD? Will you be angry for ever?
  How long will your jealousy burn like fire?
6Pour out your wrath on the nations
  that do not acknowledge you,
 on the kingdoms
  that do not call on your name;
7for they have devoured Jacob
  and destroyed his homeland.
8Do not hold against us the sins of the fathers;
  may your mercy come quickly to meet us,
  for we are in desperate need.

9Help us, O God our Saviour,
  for the glory of your name;
 deliver us and forgive our sins
  for your name's sake.
10Why should the nations say,
  "Where is their God?"
 Before our eyes, make known among the
    nations
  that you avenge the outpoured blood of your
    servants.
11May the groans of the prisoners come before
    you;
  by the strength of your arm
  preserve those condemned to die.
12Pay back into the laps of our neighbours seven
    times
  the reproach they have hurled at you,
  O Lord.
13Then we your people, the sheep of your
    pasture,
  will praise you for ever;
 from generation to generation
  we will recount your praise.

■ PSALM 80
□ For the director of music. To ⌊the tune of⌋ "The Lilies of the
Covenant". Of Asaph. A psalm.

1Hear us, O Shepherd of Israel,
  you who lead Joseph like a flock;
  you who sit enthroned between the cherubim,
    shine forth
2 before Ephraim, Benjamin and Manasseh.
  Awaken your might;
    come and save us.

³Restore us, O God;
    make your face shine upon us,
    that we may be saved.

⁴O LORD God Almighty,
    how long will your anger smoulder
    against the prayers of your people?
⁵You have fed them with the bread of tears;
    you have made them drink tears by the
      bowlful.
⁶You have made us a source of contention to
      our neighbours,
    and our enemies mock us.

⁷Restore us, O God Almighty;
    make your face shine upon us,
    that we may be saved.

⁸You brought a vine out of Egypt;
    you drove out the nations and planted it.
⁹You cleared the ground for it,
    and it took root and filled the land.
¹⁰The mountains were covered with its shade,
    the mighty cedars with its branches.
¹¹It sent out its boughs to the Sea,ᵃ
    its shoots as far as the River.ᵇ

¹²Why have you broken down its walls
    so that all who pass by pick its grapes?
¹³Boars from the forest ravage it
    and the creatures of the field feed on it.
¹⁴Return to us, O God Almighty!
    Look down from heaven and see!
    Watch over this vine,
¹⁵   the root your right hand has planted,
    the sonᶜ you have raised up for yourself.

80:14 ■ GRAPEVINES

The Old Testament often portrays God's people as a vineyard. Jesus, too, used the image (see Mark 12:1–9; John 15:1–5). Raising grapes was as familiar to Israelites as playing football is to the British. Many sermon illustrations have been made from both.

¹⁶Your vine is cut down, it is burned with fire;
    at your rebuke your people perish.
¹⁷Let your hand rest on the man at your right
      hand,
    the son of man you have raised up for
      yourself.
¹⁸Then we will not turn away from you;
    revive us, and we will call on your name.

¹⁹Restore us, O LORD God Almighty;
    make your face shine upon us,
    that we may be saved.

■ PSALM 81
☐ For the director of music. According to *gittith.*ᵃ Of Asaph.

¹Sing for joy to God our strength;
    shout aloud to the God of Jacob!
²Begin the music, strike the tambourine,
    play the melodious harp and lyre.

³Sound the ram's horn at the New Moon,
    and when the moon is full, on the day of our
      Feast;
⁴this is a decree for Israel,
    an ordinance of the God of Jacob.
⁵He established it as a statute for Joseph
    when he went out against Egypt,
    where we heard a language we did not
      understand.ᵇ

⁶He says, "I removed the burden from their
      shoulders;
    their hands were set free from the basket.
⁷In your distress you called and I rescued you,
    I answered you out of a thundercloud;
    I tested you at the waters of Meribah.   *Selah*

⁸"Hear, O my people, and I will warn you—
    if you would but listen to me, O Israel!
⁹You shall have no foreign god among you;
    you shall not bow down to an alien god.
¹⁰I am the LORD your God,
    who brought you up out of Egypt.
    Open wide your mouth and I will fill it.

¹¹"But my people would not listen to me;
    Israel would not submit to me.
¹²So I gave them over to their stubborn hearts
    to follow their own devices.

¹³"If my people would but listen to me,
    if Israel would follow my ways,
¹⁴how quickly would I subdue their enemies
    and turn my hand against their foes!
¹⁵Those who hate the LORD would cringe before
      him,
    and their punishment would last for ever.
¹⁶But you would be fed with the finest of wheat;
    with honey from the rock I would satisfy
      you."

■ PSALM 82
☐ A psalm of Asaph.

¹God presides in the great assembly;
    he gives judgment among the "gods":

82:1 ■ AMONG "THE GODS"

Human beings like to think of themselves as godlike—able to do whatever they like. Many commentators believe this psalm's snort of disdain is aimed at human judges and "powers that be" who set themselves up as little gods. What will become of their arrogance if they defy God? They will "die like mere men" (verse 7). The grave is a perfect answer to their pretensions.

When Jesus was accused of blasphemy for claiming to be God's Son, he referred his critics to this psalm (John 10:35). If Scripture could apply such lofty terminology to sinful human beings, was it not possible that a perfect man could be God's own Son?

²"How long will youᵃ defend the unjust
    and show partiality to the wicked?   *Selah*

ᵃ11 Probably the Mediterranean   ᵇ11 That is, the Euphrates   ᶜ15 Or *branch*   ᵃTitle: Probably a musical term   ᵇ5 Or / *and we heard a voice we* *had not known*   ᵃ2 The Hebrew is plural.

³Defend the cause of the weak and fatherless;
   maintain the rights of the poor and
      oppressed.
⁴Rescue the weak and needy;
   deliver them from the hand of the wicked.

⁵"They know nothing, they understand nothing.
   They walk about in darkness;
   all the foundations of the earth are shaken.

⁶"I said, 'You are "gods";
   you are all sons of the Most High.'
⁷But you will die like mere men;
   you will fall like every other ruler."

⁸Rise up, O God, judge the earth,
   for all the nations are your inheritance.

■ PSALM 83
☐ A song. A psalm of Asaph.

¹O God, do not keep silent;
   be not quiet, O God, be not still.
²See how your enemies are astir,
   how your foes rear their heads.
³With cunning they conspire against your
      people;
   they plot against those you cherish.
⁴"Come," they say, "let us destroy them as a
      nation,
   that the name of Israel be remembered no
      more."

⁵With one mind they plot together;
   they form an alliance against you—
⁶the tents of Edom and the Ishmaelites,
   of Moab and the Hagrites,
⁷Gebal,ᵃ Ammon and Amalek,
   Philistia, with the people of Tyre.
⁸Even Assyria has joined them
   to lend strength to the descendants of Lot.
                                    Selah

⁹Do to them as you did to Midian,
   as you did to Sisera and Jabin at the river
      Kishon,
¹⁰who perished at Endor
   and became like refuse on the ground.
¹¹Make their nobles like Oreb and Zeeb,
   all their princes like Zebah and Zalmunna,
¹²who said, "Let us take possession
   of the pasture-lands of God."

¹³Make them like tumble-weed, O my God,
   like chaff before the wind.
¹⁴As fire consumes the forest
   or a flame sets the mountains ablaze,
¹⁵so pursue them with your tempest
   and terrify them with your storm.
¹⁶Cover their faces with shame
   so that men will seek your name, O LORD.

¹⁷May they ever be ashamed and dismayed;
   may they perish in disgrace.
¹⁸Let them know that you, whose name is the
      LORD—
   that you alone are the Most High over all the
      earth.

■ PSALM 84
☐ For the director of music. According to gittith.ᵃ Of the
Sons of Korah. A psalm.

¹How lovely is your dwelling-place,
   O LORD Almighty!
²My soul yearns, even faints,
   for the courts of the LORD;
   my heart and my flesh cry out
   for the living God.

³Even the sparrow has found a home,
   and the swallow a nest for herself,
   where she may have her young—
a place near your altar,
   O LORD Almighty, my King and my God.
⁴Blessed are those who dwell in your house;
   they are ever praising you.   Selah

84:4 ■ HOME-COMING
"Home Sweet Home" probably adorns more
plaques than any other motto. Home is a place
where you can lay down your tired body and
bruised ego in safety. Psalm 84 contains the same
idea, but with a dramatic difference. Home is in
God's house, a place that brings comfort right
down into your bones. You'd rather spend one
day near God, praising him, than a thousand days
anywhere else.

⁵Blessed are those whose strength is in you,
   who have set their hearts on pilgrimage.
⁶As they pass through the Valley of Baca,
   they make it a place of springs;
   the autumn rains also cover it with pools.ᵇ
⁷They go from strength to strength,
   till each appears before God in Zion.

⁸Hear my prayer, O LORD God Almighty;
   listen to me, O God of Jacob.   Selah
⁹Look upon our shield,ᶜ O God;
   look with favour on your anointed one.

¹⁰Better is one day in your courts
   than a thousand elsewhere;
I would rather be a doorkeeper in the house of
      my God
   than dwell in the tents of the wicked.
¹¹For the LORD God is a sun and shield;
   the LORD bestows favour and honour;
no good thing does he withhold
   from those whose walk is blameless.

¹²O LORD Almighty,
   blessed is the man who trusts in you.

■ PSALM 85
☐ For the director of music. Of the Sons of Korah. A psalm.

¹You showed favour to your land, O LORD;
   you restored the fortunes of Jacob.
²You forgave the iniquity of your people
   and covered all their sins.   Selah
³You set aside all your wrath
   and turned from your fierce anger.

ᵃ7 That is, Byblos   ᵃTitle: Probably a musical term   ᵇ6 Or blessings   ᶜ9 Or sovereign

⁴Restore us again, O God our Saviour,
   and put away your displeasure towards us.
⁵Will you be angry with us for ever?
   Will you prolong your anger through all
     generations?
⁶Will you not revive us again,
   that your people may rejoice in you?
⁷Show us your unfailing love, O LORD,
   and grant us your salvation.

⁸I will listen to what God the LORD will say;
   he promises peace to his people, his saints—
   but let them not return to folly.
⁹Surely his salvation is near those who fear him,
   that his glory may dwell in our land.

¹⁰Love and faithfulness meet together;
   righteousness and peace kiss each other.
¹¹Faithfulness springs forth from the earth,
   and righteousness looks down from heaven.
¹²The LORD will indeed give what is good,
   and our land will yield its harvest.
¹³Righteousness goes before him
   and prepares the way for his steps.

■ PSALM 86
☐ A prayer of David.

¹Hear, O LORD, and answer me,
   for I am poor and needy.
²Guard my life, for I am devoted to you.
   You are my God; save your servant
   who trusts in you.
³Have mercy on me, O Lord,
   for I call to you all day long.
⁴Bring joy to your servant,
   for to you, O Lord,
   I lift up my soul.

⁵You are forgiving and good, O Lord,
   abounding in love to all who call to you.
⁶Hear my prayer, O LORD;
   listen to my cry for mercy.
⁷In the day of my trouble I will call to you,
   for you will answer me.

⁸Among the gods there is none like you, O Lord;
   no deeds can compare with yours.
⁹All the nations you have made
   will come and worship before you, O Lord;
   they will bring glory to your name.
¹⁰For you are great and do marvellous deeds;
   you alone are God.

¹¹Teach me your way, O LORD,
   and I will walk in your truth;
  give me an undivided heart,
   that I may fear your name.
¹²I will praise you, O Lord my God, with all my
    heart;
   I will glorify your name for ever.
¹³For great is your love towards me;
   you have delivered me from the depths of
    the grave.^a

¹⁴The arrogant are attacking me, O God;
   a band of ruthless men seeks my life—

men without regard for you.
¹⁵But you, O Lord, are a compassionate and
    gracious God,
   slow to anger, abounding in love and
    faithfulness.
¹⁶Turn to me and have mercy on me;
   grant your strength to your servant
   and save the son of your maidservant.^b
¹⁷Give me a sign of your goodness,
   that my enemies may see it and be put to
    shame,
   for you, O LORD, have helped me and
    comforted me.

86:11 ■ HEART SURGERY

David prays for an undivided heart, in order to give all of it to God in his praise. "Heart" in the Bible doesn't refer merely to emotions, but to the whole person. David's prayer means, "Help me aim myself in a single direction!"

■ PSALM 87
☐ Of the Sons of Korah. A psalm. A song.

¹He has set his foundation on the holy
    mountain;
² the LORD loves the gates of Zion
   more than all the dwellings of Jacob.
³Glorious things are said of you,
   O city of God: *Selah*
⁴"I will record Rahab^a and Babylon
   among those who acknowledge me—
  Philistia too, and Tyre, along with Cush^b—
   and will say, 'This^c one was born in Zion.'"

⁵Indeed, of Zion it will be said,
   "This one and that one were born in her,
   and the Most High himself will establish her."
⁶The LORD will write in the register of the
    peoples:
   "This one was born in Zion."   *Selah*
⁷As they make music they will sing,
   "All my fountains are in you."

■ PSALM 88
☐ A song. A psalm of the Sons of Korah. For the director of music. According to *mahalath leannoth.*^a A *maskil*^b of Heman the Ezrahite.

¹O LORD, the God who saves me,
   day and night I cry out before you.
²May my prayer come before you;
   turn your ear to my cry.

³For my soul is full of trouble
   and my life draws near the grave.^c
⁴I am counted among those who go down to the
    pit;
   I am like a man without strength.
⁵I am set apart with the dead,
   like the slain who lie in the grave,
   whom you remember no more,

---

^a13 Hebrew *Sheol*   ^b16 Or *save your faithful son*   ^a4 A poetic name for Egypt / *Philistia, Tyre and Cush, / I will record concerning those who acknowledge me: / 'This*   ^b4 That is, the upper Nile region   ^c4 Or "O Rahab and Babylon, Probably a literary or musical term   ^c3 Hebrew *Sheol*   ^aTitle: Possibly a tune, "The Suffering of Affliction"   ^bTitle:

who are cut off from your care.
⁶You have put me in the lowest pit,
   in the darkest depths.

88:1 ■ BAD FATHER, GOOD CHILDREN

Psalm 88 is the last of 12 psalms ascribed to "the Sons of Korah". Korah, a rebel against Moses' leadership, died in his rebellion (Numbers 16). His children were spared, and many years later David chose their clan to found a temple choir (1 Chronicles 6:31–37). Apparently these psalms were part of a musical collection they used.

⁷Your wrath lies heavily upon me;
   you have overwhelmed me with all your
      waves.   *Selah*
⁸You have taken from me my closest friends
   and have made me repulsive to them.
 I am confined and cannot escape;
⁹ my eyes are dim with grief.

 I call to you, O LORD, every day;
   I spread out my hands to you.
¹⁰Do you show your wonders to the dead?
   Do those who are dead rise up and praise
      you?   *Selah*
¹¹Is your love declared in the grave,
   your faithfulness in Destruction?ᵈ
¹²Are your wonders known in the place of
      darkness,
   or your righteous deeds in the land of
      oblivion?

¹³But I cry to you for help, O LORD;
   in the morning my prayer comes before you.
¹⁴Why, O LORD, do you reject me
   and hide your face from me?

¹⁵From my youth I have been afflicted and close
      to death;
   I have suffered your terrors and am in
      despair.
¹⁶Your wrath has swept over me;
   your terrors have destroyed me.
¹⁷All day long they surround me like a flood;
   they have completely engulfed me.
¹⁸You have taken my companions and loved ones
      from me;
   the darkness is my closest friend.

■ PSALM 89
□ A *maskil*ᵃ of Ethan the Ezrahite.

¹I will sing of the LORD's great love for ever;
   with my mouth I will make your faithfulness
      known through all generations.
²I will declare that your love stands firm for
      ever,
   that you established your faithfulness in
      heaven itself.

³You said, "I have made a covenant with my
      chosen one,
   I have sworn to David my servant,

⁴'I will establish your line for ever
   and make your throne firm through all
      generations.' "   *Selah*

⁵The heavens praise your wonders, O LORD,
   your faithfulness too, in the assembly of the
      holy ones.
⁶For who in the skies above can compare with
      the LORD?
   Who is like the LORD among the heavenly
      beings?
⁷In the council of the holy ones God is greatly
      feared;
   he is more awesome than all who surround
      him.
⁸O LORD God Almighty, who is like you?
   You are mighty, O LORD, and your
      faithfulness surrounds you.

⁹You rule over the surging sea;
   when its waves mount up, you still them.
¹⁰You crushed Rahab like one of the slain;
   with your strong arm you scattered your
      enemies.
¹¹The heavens are yours, and yours also the
      earth;
   you founded the world and all that is in it.
¹²You created the north and the south;
   Tabor and Hermon sing for joy at your name.
¹³Your arm is endued with power;
   your hand is strong, your right hand exalted.

¹⁴Righteousness and justice are the foundation of
      your throne;
   love and faithfulness go before you.
¹⁵Blessed are those who have learned to acclaim
      you,
   who walk in the light of your presence,
      O LORD.
¹⁶They rejoice in your name all day long;
   they exult in your righteousness.
¹⁷For you are their glory and strength,
   and by your favour you exalt our horn.ᵇ
¹⁸Indeed, our shieldᶜ belongs to the LORD,
   our king to the Holy One of Israel.

¹⁹Once you spoke in a vision,
   to your faithful people you said:
 "I have bestowed strength on a warrior;
   I have exalted a young man from among the
      people.
²⁰I have found David my servant;
   with my sacred oil I have anointed him.
²¹My hand will sustain him;
   surely my arm will strengthen him.
²²No enemy will subject him to tribute;
   no wicked man will oppress him.
²³I will crush his foes before him
   and strike down his adversaries.
²⁴My faithful love will be with him,
   and through my name his hornᵈ will be
      exalted.
²⁵I will set his hand over the sea,
   his right hand over the rivers.
²⁶He will call out to me, 'You are my Father,
   my God, the Rock my Saviour.'
²⁷I will also appoint him my firstborn,

ᵈ11 Hebrew *Abaddon*   ᵃTitle: Probably a literary or musical term   ᵇ17 *Horn* here symbolises strong one.   ᶜ18 Or *sovereign*   ᵈ24 *Horn* here
symbolises strength.

the most exalted of the kings of the earth.
²⁸I will maintain my love to him for ever,
   and my covenant with him will never fail.
²⁹I will establish his line for ever,
   his throne as long as the heavens endure.

³⁰"If his sons forsake my law
   and do not follow my statutes,
³¹if they violate my decrees
   and fail to keep my commands,
³²I will punish their sin with the rod,
   their iniquity with flogging;
³³but I will not take my love from him,
   nor will I ever betray my faithfulness.
³⁴I will not violate my covenant
   or alter what my lips have uttered.
³⁵Once for all, I have sworn by my holiness—
   and I will not lie to David—
³⁶that his line will continue for ever
   and his throne endure before me like the
      sun;
³⁷it will be established for ever like the moon,
   the faithful witness in the sky."   *Selah*

³⁸But you have rejected, you have spurned,
   you have been very angry with your
      anointed one.
³⁹You have renounced the covenant with your
      servant
   and have defiled his crown in the dust.
⁴⁰You have broken through all his walls
   and reduced his strongholds to ruins.
⁴¹All who pass by have plundered him;
   he has become the scorn of his neighbours.
⁴²You have exalted the right hand of his foes;
   you have made all his enemies rejoice.
⁴³You have turned back the edge of his sword
   and have not supported him in battle.
⁴⁴You have put an end to his splendour
   and cast his throne to the ground.
⁴⁵You have cut short the days of his youth;
   you have covered him with a mantle of
      shame.   *Selah*

89:45 ■ SHAME FOR EVER?
God, as this psalm notes, had made tremendous
promises to David and to his descendants (see
2 Samuel 7:4–17). But what do you do when
God's promises don't match your experience?
This psalm was probably written after the
Babylonians had deported the young king
Jehoiachin (see here and 2 Kings 24:8,15) and
torn down Jerusalem (see verse 40 and 2 Kings
25:10). It gives no explanation of how God's
promises fit with this humiliation and suffering. But
it offers a model of how to respond, taking the
problem straight to God in the frankest of terms.
Only when Jesus came centuries later did Israel
see God fulfil these promises to honour and love a
"son of David" as his own Son (verses 26–29).

---

⁴⁶How long, O LORD? Will you hide yourself for
      ever?
   How long will your wrath burn like fire?

⁴⁷Remember how fleeting is my life.
   For what futility you have created all men!
⁴⁸What man can live and not see death,
   or save himself from the power of the
      grave?ᵉ   *Selah*
⁴⁹O Lord, where is your former great love,
   which in your faithfulness you swore to
      David?
⁵⁰Remember, Lord, how your servant hasᶠ been
      mocked,
   how I bear in my heart the taunts of all the
      nations,
⁵¹the taunts with which your enemies have
      mocked, O LORD,
   with which they have mocked every step of
      your anointed one.

⁵²Praise be to the LORD for ever!
   Amen and Amen.

BOOK IV
☐ Psalms 90–106

■ **PSALM 90**
☐ A prayer of Moses the man of God.

¹Lord, you have been our dwelling-place
   throughout all generations.
²Before the mountains were born
   or you brought forth the earth and the
      world,
   from everlasting to everlasting you are God.

³You turn men back to dust,
   saying, "Return to dust, O sons of men."
⁴For a thousand years in your sight
   are like a day that has just gone by,
   or like a watch in the night.
⁵You sweep men away in the sleep of death;
   they are like the new grass of the morning—
⁶though in the morning it springs up new,
   by evening it is dry and withered.

⁷We are consumed by your anger
   and terrified by your indignation.
⁸You have set our iniquities before you,
   our secret sins in the light of your presence.
⁹All our days pass away under your wrath;
   we finish our years with a moan.
¹⁰The length of our days is seventy years—
   or eighty, if we have the strength;
   yet their spanᵃ is but trouble and sorrow,
   for they quickly pass, and we fly away.

¹¹Who knows the power of your anger?
   For your wrath is as great as the fear that is
      due to you.
¹²Teach us to number our days aright,
   that we may gain a heart of wisdom.

¹³Relent, O LORD! How long will it be?
   Have compassion on your servants.
¹⁴Satisfy us in the morning with your unfailing
      love,

ᵉ 48 Hebrew *Sheol*   ᶠ 50 Or *your servants have*   ᵃ 10 Or *yet the best of them*

that we may sing for joy and be glad all our
  days.
15Make us glad for as many days as you have
  afflicted us,
  for as many years as we have seen trouble.
16May your deeds be shown to your servants,
  your splendour to their children.

17May the favour*b* of the Lord our God rest
  upon us;
  establish the work of our hands for us—
  yes, establish the work of our hands.

■ PSALM 91

1He who dwells in the shelter of the Most High
  will rest in the shadow of the Almighty.*a*
2I will say*b* of the LORD, "He is my refuge and
  my fortress,
  my God, in whom I trust."

3Surely he will save you from the fowler's snare
  and from the deadly pestilence.
4He will cover you with his feathers,
  and under his wings you will find refuge;
  his faithfulness will be your shield and
  rampart.
5You will not fear the terror of night,
  nor the arrow that flies by day,
6nor the pestilence that stalks in the darkness,
  nor the plague that destroys at midday.
7A thousand may fall at your side,
  ten thousand at your right hand,
  but it will not come near you.
8You will only observe with your eyes
  and see the punishment of the wicked.

9If you make the Most High your dwelling—
  even the LORD, who is my refuge—
10then no harm will befall you,
  no disaster will come near your tent.
11For he will command his angels concerning
  you
  to guard you in all your ways;
12they will lift you up in their hands,
  so that you will not strike your foot against a
  stone.
13You will tread upon the lion and the cobra;
  you will trample the great lion and the
  serpent.

91:12 ■ SATAN AND THE BIBLE
Satan knows Scripture. He quoted this promise to
Jesus when tempting him to spiritual arrogance
(see Matthew 4:6). Jesus recognised that Satan
had twisted its meaning. The magnificent
assurances in this psalm encourage us to *rest* in
God, not *test* him.

14"Because he loves me," says the LORD, "I will
  rescue him;
  I will protect him, for he acknowledges my
  name.
15He will call upon me, and I will answer him;

I will be with him in trouble,
  I will deliver him and honour him.
16With long life will I satisfy him
  and show him my salvation."

■ PSALM 92
☐ A psalm. A song. For the Sabbath day.

1It is good to praise the LORD
  and make music to your name, O Most High,
2to proclaim your love in the morning
  and your faithfulness at night,
3to the music of the ten-stringed lyre
  and the melody of the harp.

4For you make me glad by your deeds, O LORD;
  I sing for joy at the work of your hands.
5How great are your works, O LORD,
  how profound your thoughts!
6The senseless man does not know,
  fools do not understand,
7that though the wicked spring up like grass
  and all evildoers flourish,
  they will be for ever destroyed.

8But you, O LORD, are exalted for ever.

9For surely your enemies, O LORD,
  surely your enemies will perish;
  all evildoers will be scattered.
10You have exalted my horn*a* like that of a wild
  ox;
  fine oils have been poured upon me.
11My eyes have seen the defeat of my adversaries;
  my ears have heard the rout of my wicked
  foes.

12The righteous will flourish like a palm tree,
  they will grow like a cedar of Lebanon;
13planted in the house of the LORD,
  they will flourish in the courts of our God.
14They will still bear fruit in old age,
  they will stay fresh and green,
15proclaiming, "The LORD is upright;
  he is my Rock, and there is no wickedness in
  him."

■ PSALM 93

1The LORD reigns, he is robed in majesty;
  the LORD is robed in majesty
  and is armed with strength.
  The world is firmly established;
  it cannot be moved.
2Your throne was established long ago;
  you are from all eternity.

3The seas have lifted up, O LORD,
  the seas have lifted up their voice;
  the seas have lifted up their pounding waves.
4Mightier than the thunder of the great waters,
  mightier than the breakers of the sea—
  the LORD on high is mighty.

5Your statutes stand firm;
  holiness adorns your house
  for endless days, O LORD.

*b*17 Or beauty   *a*1 Hebrew Shaddai   *b*2 Or He says   *a*10 Horn here symbolises strength.

■ PSALM 94

¹O LORD, the God who avenges,
  O God who avenges, shine forth.
²Rise up, O Judge of the earth;
  pay back to the proud what they deserve.
³How long will the wicked, O LORD,
  how long will the wicked be jubilant?

⁴They pour out arrogant words;
  all the evildoers are full of boasting.
⁵They crush your people, O LORD;
  they oppress your inheritance.
⁶They slay the widow and the alien;
  they murder the fatherless.
⁷They say, "The LORD does not see;
  the God of Jacob pays no heed."

⁸Take heed, you senseless ones among the
    people;
  you fools, when will you become wise?
⁹Does he who implanted the ear not hear?
  Does he who formed the eye not see?
¹⁰Does he who disciplines nations not punish?
  Does he who teaches man lack knowledge?
¹¹The LORD knows the thoughts of man;
  he knows that they are futile.

¹²Blessed is the man you discipline, O LORD,
  the man you teach from your law;
¹³you grant him relief from days of trouble,
  till a pit is dug for the wicked.
¹⁴For the LORD will not reject his people;
  he will never forsake his inheritance.
¹⁵Judgment will again be founded on
    righteousness,
  and all the upright in heart will follow it.

¹⁶Who will rise up for me against the wicked?
  Who will take a stand for me against
    evildoers?
¹⁷Unless the LORD had given me help,
  I would soon have dwelt in the silence of
    death.
¹⁸When I said, "My foot is slipping,"
  your love, O LORD, supported me.
¹⁹When anxiety was great within me,
  your consolation brought joy to my soul.

²⁰Can a corrupt throne be allied with you—
  one that brings on misery by its decrees?
²¹They band together against the righteous
  and condemn the innocent to death.
²²But the LORD has become my fortress,
  and my God the rock in whom I take refuge.
²³He will repay them for their sins
  and destroy them for their wickedness;
  the LORD our God will destroy them.

■ PSALM 95

¹Come, let us sing for joy to the LORD;
  let us shout aloud to the Rock of our
    salvation.
²Let us come before him with thanksgiving
  and extol him with music and song.

³For the LORD is the great God,
  the great King above all gods.
⁴In his hand are the depths of the earth,
  and the mountain peaks belong to him.
⁵The sea is his, for he made it,
  and his hands formed the dry land.

⁶Come, let us bow down in worship,
  let us kneel before the LORD our Maker;
⁷for he is our God
  and we are the people of his pasture,
  the flock under his care.

  Today, if you hear his voice,
⁸   do not harden your hearts as you did at
      Meribah,ᵃ
    as you did that day at Massahᵇ in the desert,
⁹where your fathers tested and tried me,
  though they had seen what I did.
¹⁰For forty years I was angry with that
    generation;
  I said, "They are a people whose hearts go
    astray,
  and they have not known my ways."
¹¹So I declared on oath in my anger,
  "They shall never enter my rest."

95:8 ■ REBELLION

One of Israel's worst memories involved a place
known as Massah and Meribah. There, on their
way to the promised land, the Israelites ran out of
water (Exodus 17:1–7) and rebelled against Moses
and God. Because of their lack of faith, God made
them wander the wilderness for 40 years.

Now, hundreds of years later, Psalm 95 warns
another generation of Israelites not to repeat the
mistake that had made their forebears miss
"God's rest". In the New Testament, Hebrews
4:1–13 argues that "God's rest" means not merely
the promised land of Israel, but a state of peaceful
unity with God. The warning still applies.

■ PSALM 96

¹Sing to the LORD a new song;
  sing to the LORD, all the earth.
²Sing to the LORD, praise his name;
  proclaim his salvation day after day.
³Declare his glory among the nations,
  his marvellous deeds among all peoples.

⁴For great is the LORD and most worthy of
    praise;
  he is to be feared above all gods.
⁵For all the gods of the nations are idols,
  but the LORD made the heavens.
⁶Splendour and majesty are before him;
  strength and glory are in his sanctuary.

⁷Ascribe to the LORD, O families of nations,
  ascribe to the LORD glory and strength.
⁸Ascribe to the LORD the glory due to his name;
  bring an offering and come into his courts.

ᵃ8 Meribah means *quarrelling*.   ᵇ8 Massah means *testing*.

9Worship the LORD in the splendour of his*a*
　　holiness;
　　tremble before him, all the earth.

10Say among the nations, "The LORD reigns."
　　The world is firmly established, it cannot be
　　　moved;
　　he will judge the peoples with equity.
11Let the heavens rejoice, let the earth be glad;
　　let the sea resound, and all that is in it;
12　let the fields be jubilant, and everything in
　　them.
　Then all the trees of the forest will sing for joy;
13　they will sing before the LORD, for he comes,
　　he comes to judge the earth.
　He will judge the world in righteousness
　　and the peoples in his truth.

■ PSALM 97

1The LORD reigns, let the earth be glad;
　　let the distant shores rejoice.

2Clouds and thick darkness surround him;
　　righteousness and justice are the foundation
　　　of his throne.
3Fire goes before him
　　and consumes his foes on every side.
4His lightning lights up the world;
　　the earth sees and trembles.
5The mountains melt like wax before the LORD,
　　before the Lord of all the earth.
6The heavens proclaim his righteousness,
　　and all the peoples see his glory.

7All who worship images are put to shame,
　　those who boast in idols—
　　worship him, all you gods!

8Zion hears and rejoices
　　and the villages of Judah are glad
　　because of your judgments, O LORD.
9For you, O LORD, are the Most High over all the
　　earth;
　　you are exalted far above all gods.

10Let those who love the LORD hate evil,
　　for he guards the lives of his faithful ones
　　and delivers them from the hand of the
　　　wicked.
11Light is shed upon the righteous
　　and joy on the upright in heart.
12Rejoice in the LORD, you who are righteous,
　　and praise his holy name.

■ PSALM 98

□ A psalm.

1Sing to the LORD a new song,
　　for he has done marvellous things;
　his right hand and his holy arm
　　have worked salvation for him.
2The LORD has made his salvation known
　　and revealed his righteousness to the nations.
3He has remembered his love
　　and his faithfulness to the house of Israel;

all the ends of the earth have seen
　　the salvation of our God.

4Shout for joy to the LORD, all the earth,
　　burst into jubilant song with music;
5make music to the LORD with the harp,
　　with the harp and the sound of singing,
6with trumpets and the blast of the ram's horn—
　　shout for joy before the LORD, the King.

7Let the sea resound, and everything in it,
　　the world, and all who live in it.
8Let the rivers clap their hands,
　　let the mountains sing together for joy;
9let them sing before the LORD,
　　for he comes to judge the earth.
　He will judge the world in righteousness
　　and the peoples with equity.

98:8 ■ ECOLOGICAL CHOIR
Seas, rivers, and mountains crown this psalm with
their praise. God's salvation doesn't just affect
human beings. When rebellion against God finally
ends, nature itself will celebrate. Romans 8:18–22
takes up this theme as part of the wonderful
salvation God offers to all people.

■ PSALM 99

1The LORD reigns,
　　let the nations tremble;
　he sits enthroned between the cherubim,
　　let the earth shake.
2Great is the LORD in Zion;
　　he is exalted over all the nations.
3Let them praise your great and awesome
　　　name—
　　he is holy.

4The King is mighty, he loves justice—
　　you have established equity;
　in Jacob you have done
　　what is just and right.
5Exalt the LORD our God
　　and worship at his footstool;
　　he is holy.

6Moses and Aaron were among his priests,
　　Samuel was among those who called on his
　　　name;
　they called on the LORD
　　and he answered them.
7He spoke to them from the pillar of cloud;
　　they kept his statutes and the decrees he
　　　gave them.

8O LORD our God,
　　you answered them;
　you were to Israel*a* a forgiving God,
　　though you punished their misdeeds.*b*
9Exalt the LORD our God
　　and worship at his holy mountain,
　　for the LORD our God is holy.

a9 Or LORD with the splendour of　　*a8* Hebrew them　　*b8* Or / an avenger of the wrongs done to them

■ PSALM 100

☐ A psalm. For giving thanks.

¹Shout for joy to the LORD, all the earth.
² Worship the LORD with gladness;
   come before him with joyful songs.
³Know that the LORD is God.
   It is he who made us, and we are his;*ᵃ*
   we are his people, the sheep of his pasture.

⁴Enter his gates with thanksgiving
   and his courts with praise;
   give thanks to him and praise his name.
⁵For the LORD is good and his love endures for
      ever;
   his faithfulness continues through all
      generations.

■ PSALM 101

☐ Of David. A psalm.

¹I will sing of your love and justice;
   to you, O LORD, I will sing praise.
²I will be careful to lead a blameless life—
   when will you come to me?

I will walk in my house
   with blameless heart.
³I will set before my eyes
   no vile thing.

The deeds of faithless men I hate;
   they shall not cling to me.
⁴Men of perverse heart shall be far from me;
   I will have nothing to do with evil.

⁵Whoever slanders his neighbour in secret,
   him will I put to silence;
whoever has haughty eyes and a proud heart,
   him will I not endure.

⁶My eyes will be on the faithful in the land,
   that they may dwell with me;
he whose walk is blameless
   will minister to me.

⁷No-one who practises deceit
   will dwell in my house;
no-one who speaks falsely
   will stand in my presence.

101:7 ■ THE COMPANY YOU KEEP
Some friends build you up, others tear you down.
That's true for people in influential positions as
well. "Politics makes strange bedfellows", they
say, because a politician must work with people
from various political factions, whether he or she
admires them or not. But here David, the head of
state, pledges to steer clear of all shady alliances.
He wants a clean administration, from the top
down.

⁸Every morning I will put to silence
   all the wicked in the land;
I will cut off every evildoer
   from the city of the LORD.

■ PSALM 102

☐ A prayer of an afflicted man. When he is faint and pours
out his lament before the LORD.

¹Hear my prayer, O LORD;
   let my cry for help come to you.
²Do not hide your face from me
   when I am in distress.
Turn your ear to me;
   when I call, answer me quickly.

³For my days vanish like smoke;
   my bones burn like glowing embers.
⁴My heart is blighted and withered like grass;
   I forget to eat my food.
⁵Because of my loud groaning
   I am reduced to skin and bones.
⁶I am like a desert owl,
   like an owl among the ruins.
⁷I lie awake; I have become
   like a bird alone on a roof.
⁸All day long my enemies taunt me;
   those who rail against me use my name as a
      curse.
⁹For I eat ashes as my food
   and mingle my drink with tears
¹⁰because of your great wrath,
   for you have taken me up and thrown me
      aside.
¹¹My days are like the evening shadow;
   I wither away like grass.

¹²But you, O LORD, sit enthroned for ever;
   your renown endures through all
      generations.
¹³You will arise and have compassion on Zion,
   for it is time to show favour to her;
   the appointed time has come.
¹⁴For her stones are dear to your servants;
   her very dust moves them to pity.
¹⁵The nations will fear the name of the LORD,
   all the kings of the earth will revere your
      glory.
¹⁶For the LORD will rebuild Zion
   and appear in his glory.
¹⁷He will respond to the prayer of the destitute;
   he will not despise their plea.

¹⁸Let this be written for a future generation,
   that a people not yet created may praise the
      LORD:
¹⁹"The LORD looked down from his sanctuary on
      high,
   from heaven he viewed the earth,
²⁰to hear the groans of the prisoners
   and release those condemned to death."
²¹So the name of the LORD will be declared in
      Zion
   and his praise in Jerusalem
²²when the peoples and the kingdoms
   assemble to worship the LORD.

²³In the course of my life*ᵃ* he broke my
      strength;
   he cut short my days.
²⁴So I said:

ᵃ3 Or and not we ourselves   ᵃ23 Or By his power

"Do not take me away, O my God, in the
  midst of my days;
your years go on through all generations.
²⁵In the beginning you laid the foundations of the
  earth,
and the heavens are the work of your hands.
²⁶They will perish, but you remain;
  they will all wear out like a garment.
Like clothing you will change them
  and they will be discarded.
²⁷But you remain the same,
  and your years will never end.
²⁸The children of your servants will live in your
  presence;
  their descendants will be established before
  you."

102:26 ■ OUTLASTING THE UNIVERSE
Is a diamond for ever? Not according to the
psalmist, who predicts that the universe, which
God made, will wear out like old clothes. But God
remains the same for ever — and he will preserve
his people, to whom he is committed far more
than to his universe.

■ PSALM 103
□ Of David.

¹Praise the LORD, O my soul;
  all my inmost being, praise his holy name.
²Praise the LORD, O my soul,
  and forget not all his benefits—
³who forgives all your sins
  and heals all your diseases,
⁴who redeems your life from the pit
  and crowns you with love and compassion,
⁵who satisfies your desires with good things
  so that your youth is renewed like the
  eagle's.

⁶The LORD works righteousness
  and justice for all the oppressed.

⁷He made known his ways to Moses,
  his deeds to the people of Israel:
⁸The LORD is compassionate and gracious,
  slow to anger, abounding in love.
⁹He will not always accuse,
  nor will he harbour his anger for ever;
¹⁰he does not treat us as our sins deserve
  or repay us according to our iniquities.
¹¹For as high as the heavens are above the earth,
  so great is his love for those who fear him;
¹²as far as the east is from the west,
  so far has he removed our transgressions
  from us.
¹³As a father has compassion on his children,
  so the LORD has compassion on those who
  fear him;
¹⁴for he knows how we are formed,
  he remembers that we are dust.
¹⁵As for man, his days are like grass,
  he flourishes like a flower of the field;
¹⁶the wind blows over it and it is gone,

a 4 Or angels

and its place remembers it no more.
¹⁷But from everlasting to everlasting
  the LORD's love is with those who fear him,
  and his righteousness with their children's
  children—
¹⁸with those who keep his covenant
  and remember to obey his precepts.

¹⁹The LORD has established his throne in heaven,
  and his kingdom rules over all.

²⁰Praise the LORD, you his angels,
  you mighty ones who do his bidding,
  who obey his word.
²¹Praise the LORD, all his heavenly hosts,
  you his servants who do his will.
²²Praise the LORD, all his works
  everywhere in his dominion.

Praise the LORD, O my soul.

■ PSALM 104

¹Praise the LORD, O my soul.

O LORD my God, you are very great;
  you are clothed with splendour and majesty.
²He wraps himself in light as with a garment;
  he stretches out the heavens like a tent
³ and lays the beams of his upper chambers on
  their waters.
He makes the clouds his chariot
  and rides on the wings of the wind.
⁴He makes winds his messengers,ᵃ
  flames of fire his servants.

⁵He set the earth on its foundations;
  it can never be moved.
⁶You covered it with the deep as with a
  garment;
  the waters stood above the mountains.
⁷But at your rebuke the waters fled,
  at the sound of your thunder they took to
  flight;
⁸they flowed over the mountains,
  they went down into the valleys,
  to the place you assigned for them.
⁹You set a boundary they cannot cross;
  never again will they cover the earth.

¹⁰He makes springs pour water into the ravines;
  it flows between the mountains.
¹¹They give water to all the beasts of the field;
  the wild donkeys quench their thirst.
¹²The birds of the air nest by the waters;
  they sing among the branches.
¹³He waters the mountains from his upper
  chambers;
  the earth is satisfied by the fruit of his work.
¹⁴He makes grass grow for the cattle,
  and plants for man to cultivate—
  bringing forth food from the earth:
¹⁵wine that gladdens the heart of man,
  oil to make his face shine,
  and bread that sustains his heart.
¹⁶The trees of the LORD are well watered,
  the cedars of Lebanon that he planted.

¹⁷There the birds make their nests;
   the stork has its home in the pine trees.
¹⁸The high mountains belong to the wild goats;
   the crags are a refuge for the conies.^b

¹⁹The moon marks off the seasons,
   and the sun knows when to go down.
²⁰You bring darkness, it becomes night,
   and all the beasts of the forest prowl.
²¹The lions roar for their prey
   and seek their food from God.
²²The sun rises, and they steal away;
   they return and lie down in their dens.
²³Then man goes out to his work,
   to his labour until evening.

²⁴How many are your works, O LORD!
   In wisdom you made them all;
   the earth is full of your creatures.
²⁵There is the sea, vast and spacious,

teeming with creatures beyond number—
   living things both large and small.
²⁶There the ships go to and fro,
   and the leviathan, which you formed to frolic
    there.

104:26 ■ JUST FOR FUN

What good is a leviathan (possibly a whale, but to the land-locked Israelites a frightening sea monster)? Why would God make such a creature? Simply "to frolic". God makes and delights in each creature for its own sake.

²⁷These all look to you
   to give them their food at the proper time.
²⁸When you give it to them,
   they gather it up;
   when you open your hand,

■ ECOLOGY PLUS
CREATION SINGS GOD'S PRAISE

INSIGHT

HOW MANY ARE YOUR WORKS, O LORD!
IN WISDOM YOU MADE THEM ALL.
■ 104:24

In 1962 biologist Rachel Carson published *Silent Spring*, a book tracing the effects of pesticides—DDT in particular. Until then, DDT had been treated like a wonder chemical, sprayed almost at random to kill pests. Carson showed how it worked its way up the food chain, killing larger animals—like songbirds. If no birds were left to sing, we would have an ominously "silent spring".

Until then, *ecology* had been a word known only to specialists. But with Carson's book, ordinary people began to take an interest in what only biologists had known: the delicate balance of nature, in which each creature is intertwined with every other. The ecology movement had begun.

■ THE VALUE IN "USELESS" CREATURES

Ecology was new, but its ideas were old. You could have learned its basic principles from Psalm 104. It shows appreciation for every aspect of nature, even creatures like wild goats, lions and the "leviathan", the crocodile or sea monster. The Israelites, as herders and farmers, had no romantic idealisation of the outdoors. Nobody who herds sheep thinks of them as soft and fluffy pets. But to the poet who wrote Psalm 104, creatures that are of no "use" to anyone still have intrinsic worth—especially to God.

The author saw how the world fits together, everything in its proper sphere. At night wild animals hunt; at daybreak humans go out to work. The rain falls, nourishing crops for people and grass for cattle, but also watering the forest to provide a place for birds to nest.

■ ECOLOGY IS GOD'S WORK

The intertwining of nature is not, for the psalmist, like a complex machine, dangerously sensitive. Things fit together because an intimate, personal God watches over his creation. Animals eat on schedule not just because their habitat contains adequate food, but because God gives them their food "at the proper time". Every breath of life depends on his will. So do the weather, the winds and clouds, the water supply, the very stability of the earth. The psalmist doesn't just marvel over the complexity and beauty of nature; in it he sees the work of God.

When modern people think of ecology, they are preoccupied with the fear of overcrowding and of poisoning the planet with landfills, oil spills, and toxic chemicals. The psalms show no such fear, for overcrowding and pollution were not major problems in that pre-industrial civilisation. Yet interestingly enough, this psalm ends with a wish that God would clean up the earth—cleanse it of sinners, who mar its perfection by their rejection of God's will. The beauty of the earth, made by God, calls out for purity—purity of the heart.

□ LIFE QUESTIONS:

How does nature affect you? How do you affect it?

^b 18 That is, the hyrax or rock badger

they are satisfied with good things.
²⁹When you hide your face,
    they are terrified;
  when you take away their breath,
    they die and return to the dust.
³⁰When you send your Spirit,
    they are created,
  and you renew the face of the earth.

³¹May the glory of the LORD endure for ever;
    may the LORD rejoice in his works—
³²he who looks at the earth, and it trembles,
    who touches the mountains, and they smoke.

³³I will sing to the LORD all my life;
    I will sing praise to my God as long as I live.
³⁴May my meditation be pleasing to him,
    as I rejoice in the LORD.
³⁵But may sinners vanish from the earth
    and the wicked be no more.

Praise the LORD, O my soul.

Praise the LORD.ᶜ

■ PSALM 105

¹Give thanks to the LORD, call on his name;
    make known among the nations what he has
      done.
²Sing to him, sing praise to him;
    tell of all his wonderful acts.
³Glory in his holy name;
    let the hearts of those who seek the LORD
      rejoice.
⁴Look to the LORD and his strength;
    seek his face always.

⁵Remember the wonders he has done,
    his miracles, and the judgments he
      pronounced,
⁶O descendants of Abraham his servant,
    O sons of Jacob, his chosen ones.
⁷He is the LORD our God;
    his judgments are in all the earth.

⁸He remembers his covenant for ever,
    the word he commanded, for a thousand
      generations,
⁹the covenant he made with Abraham,
    the oath he swore to Isaac.
¹⁰He confirmed it to Jacob as a decree,
    to Israel as an everlasting covenant:
¹¹"To you I will give the land of Canaan
    as the portion you will inherit."

¹²When they were but few in number,
    few indeed, and strangers in it,
¹³they wandered from nation to nation,
    from one kingdom to another.
¹⁴He allowed no-one to oppress them;
    for their sake he rebuked kings:
¹⁵"Do not touch my anointed ones;
    do my prophets no harm."

¹⁶He called down famine on the land
    and destroyed all their supplies of food;
¹⁷and he sent a man before them—

Joseph, sold as a slave.
¹⁸They bruised his feet with shackles,
    his neck was put in irons,
¹⁹till what he foretold came to pass,
    till the word of the LORD proved him true.
²⁰The king sent and released him,
    the ruler of peoples set him free.
²¹He made him master of his household,
    ruler over all he possessed,
²²to instruct his princes as he pleased
    and teach his elders wisdom.

²³Then Israel entered Egypt;
    Jacob lived as an alien in the land of Ham.
²⁴The LORD made his people very fruitful;
    he made them too numerous for their foes,
²⁵whose hearts he turned to hate his people,
    to conspire against his servants.
²⁶He sent Moses his servant,
    and Aaron, whom he had chosen.
²⁷They performed his miraculous signs among
      them,
    his wonders in the land of Ham.
²⁸He sent darkness and made the land dark—
    for had they not rebelled against his words?
²⁹He turned their waters into blood,
    causing their fish to die.
³⁰Their land teemed with frogs,
    which went up into the bedrooms of their
      rulers.
³¹He spoke, and there came swarms of flies,
    and gnats throughout their country.
³²He turned their rain into hail,
    with lightning throughout their land;
³³he struck down their vines and fig-trees
    and shattered the trees of their country.
³⁴He spoke, and the locusts came,
    grasshoppers without number;
³⁵they ate up every green thing in their land,
    ate up the produce of their soil.
³⁶Then he struck down all the firstborn in their
      land,
    the firstfruits of all their manhood.

³⁷He brought out Israel, laden with silver and
      gold,
    and from among their tribes no-one faltered.
³⁸Egypt was glad when they left,
    because dread of Israel had fallen on them.
³⁹He spread out a cloud as a covering,
    and a fire to give light at night.
⁴⁰They asked, and he brought them quail
    and satisfied them with the bread of heaven.
⁴¹He opened the rock, and water gushed out;
    like a river it flowed in the desert.

⁴²For he remembered his holy promise
    given to his servant Abraham.
⁴³He brought out his people with rejoicing,
    his chosen ones with shouts of joy;
⁴⁴he gave them the lands of the nations,
    and they fell heir to what others had toiled
      for—
⁴⁵that they might keep his precepts
    and observe his laws.

Praise the LORD.ᵃ

ᶜ35 Hebrew *Hallelu Yah*; in the Septuagint this line stands at the beginning of Psalm 105.   ᵃ45 Hebrew *Hallelu Yah*

■ PSALM 106

¹Praise the LORD.ᵃ

Give thanks to the LORD, for he is good;
  his love endures for ever.
²Who can proclaim the mighty acts of the LORD
  or fully declare his praise?
³Blessed are they who maintain justice,
  who constantly do what is right.
⁴Remember me, O LORD, when you show favour
    to your people,
  come to my aid when you save them,
⁵that I may enjoy the prosperity of your chosen
    ones,
  that I may share in the joy of your nation
  and join your inheritance in giving praise.

⁶We have sinned, even as our fathers did;
  we have done wrong and acted wickedly.
⁷When our fathers were in Egypt,
  they gave no thought to your miracles;
  they did not remember your many kindnesses,
  and they rebelled by the sea, the Red Sea.ᵇ
⁸Yet he saved them for his name's sake,
  to make his mighty power known.
⁹He rebuked the Red Sea, and it dried up;
  he led them through the depths as through a
    desert.
¹⁰He saved them from the hand of the foe;
  from the hand of the enemy he redeemed
    them.
¹¹The waters covered their adversaries;
  not one of them survived.
¹²Then they believed his promises
  and sang his praise.

106:12 ■ THE TURNING POINT

When the Israelites praised God, their thoughts
turned naturally back to the time when God
(through Moses) freed them from slavery and gave
them a country all of their own. In it they saw
God's pure graciousness. They had done nothing
to win their freedom; God had done it all. Similarly,
Christians look back to Jesus' death and
resurrection, which freed them from sin's slavery.

¹³But they soon forgot what he had done
  and did not wait for his counsel.
¹⁴In the desert they gave in to their craving;
  in the wasteland they put God to the test.
¹⁵So he gave them what they asked for,
  but sent a wasting disease upon them.

¹⁶In the camp they grew envious of Moses
  and of Aaron, who was consecrated to the
    LORD.
¹⁷The earth opened up and swallowed Dathan;
  it buried the company of Abiram.
¹⁸Fire blazed among their followers;
  a flame consumed the wicked.

¹⁹At Horeb they made a calf
  and worshipped an idol cast from metal.
²⁰They exchanged their Glory
  for an image of a bull, which eats grass.

²¹They forgot the God who saved them,
  who had done great things in Egypt,
²²miracles in the land of Ham
  and awesome deeds by the Red Sea.
²³So he said he would destroy them—
  had not Moses, his chosen one,
  stood in the breach before him
  to keep his wrath from destroying them.

²⁴Then they despised the pleasant land;
  they did not believe his promise.
²⁵They grumbled in their tents
  and did not obey the LORD.
²⁶So he swore to them with uplifted hand
  that he would make them fall in the desert,
²⁷make their descendants fall among the nations
  and scatter them throughout the lands.

²⁸They yoked themselves to the Baal of Peor
  and ate sacrifices offered to lifeless gods;
²⁹they provoked the LORD to anger by their
    wicked deeds,
  and a plague broke out among them.
³⁰But Phinehas stood up and intervened,
  and the plague was checked.
³¹This was credited to him as righteousness
  for endless generations to come.

³²By the waters of Meribah they angered the
    LORD,
  and trouble came to Moses because of them;
³³for they rebelled against the Spirit of God,
  and rash words came from Moses' lips.ᶜ

³⁴They did not destroy the peoples
  as the LORD had commanded them,
³⁵but they mingled with the nations
  and adopted their customs.
³⁶They worshipped their idols,
  which became a snare to them.
³⁷They sacrificed their sons
  and their daughters to demons.
³⁸They shed innocent blood,
  the blood of their sons and daughters,
  whom they sacrificed to the idols of Canaan,
  and the land was desecrated by their blood.
³⁹They defiled themselves by what they did;
  by their deeds they prostituted themselves.

⁴⁰Therefore the LORD was angry with his people
  and abhorred his inheritance.
⁴¹He handed them over to the nations,
  and their foes ruled over them.
⁴²Their enemies oppressed them
  and subjected them to their power.
⁴³Many times he delivered them,
  but they were bent on rebellion
  and they wasted away in their sin.

⁴⁴But he took note of their distress
  when he heard their cry;
⁴⁵for their sake he remembered his covenant
  and out of his great love he relented.
⁴⁶He caused them to be pitied
  by all who held them captive.

⁴⁷Save us, O LORD our God,
  and gather us from the nations,

ᵃ1 Hebrew *Hallelu Yah*; also in verse 48   ᵇ7 Hebrew *Yam Suph*; that is, Sea of Reeds; also in verses 9 and 22   ᶜ33 Or *against his spirit, / and rash
words came from his lips*

that we may give thanks to your holy name
and glory in your praise.

48Praise be to the LORD, the God of Israel,
from everlasting to everlasting.
Let all the people say, "Amen!"

Praise the LORD.

BOOK V
☐ Psalms 107–150

■ PSALM 107

1Give thanks to the LORD, for he is good;
his love endures for ever.
2Let the redeemed of the LORD say this —
those he redeemed from the hand of the foe,
3those he gathered from the lands,
from east and west, from north and south.*a*

4Some wandered in desert wastelands,
finding no way to a city where they could
settle.
5They were hungry and thirsty,
and their lives ebbed away.
6Then they cried out to the LORD in their
trouble,
and he delivered them from their distress.
7He led them by a straight way
to a city where they could settle.
8Let them give thanks to the LORD for his
unfailing love
and his wonderful deeds for men,
9for he satisfies the thirsty
and fills the hungry with good things.

10Some sat in darkness and the deepest gloom,
prisoners suffering in iron chains,
11for they had rebelled against the words of God
and despised the counsel of the Most High.
12So he subjected them to bitter labour;
they stumbled, and there was no-one to help.
13Then they cried to the LORD in their trouble,
and he saved them from their distress.
14He brought them out of darkness and the
deepest gloom
and broke away their chains.
15Let them give thanks to the LORD for his
unfailing love
and his wonderful deeds for men,
16for he breaks down gates of bronze
and cuts through bars of iron.

17Some became fools through their rebellious
ways
and suffered affliction because of their
iniquities.
18They loathed all food
and drew near the gates of death.
19Then they cried to the LORD in their trouble,
and he saved them from their distress.
20He sent forth his word and healed them;
he rescued them from the grave.
21Let them give thanks to the LORD for his
unfailing love

and his wonderful deeds for men.
22Let them sacrifice thank-offerings
and tell of his works with songs of joy.

23Others went out on the sea in ships;
they were merchants on the mighty waters.
24They saw the works of the LORD,
his wonderful deeds in the deep.
25For he spoke and stirred up a tempest
that lifted high the waves.
26They mounted up to the heavens and went
down to the depths;
in their peril their courage melted away.
27They reeled and staggered like drunken men;
they were at their wits' end.
28Then they cried out to the LORD in their
trouble,
and he brought them out of their distress.
29He stilled the storm to a whisper;
the waves of the sea were hushed.
30They were glad when it grew calm,
and he guided them to their desired haven.
31Let them give thanks to the LORD for his
unfailing love
and his wonderful deeds for men.
32Let them exalt him in the assembly of the
people
and praise him in the council of the elders.

107:27 ■ WORST CASE

No problem is too great for God. This psalm
imagines the worst calamities a Jew could think
of: homelessness and starvation (verses 4–5),
imprisonment (10–12), self-inflicted disease
(17–18), and — the ultimate — imminent shipwreck
(23–27). (Since Israel was land-locked, Jews had
little experience with turbulent seas — and they
dreaded them.) In all these cases, God was able
to rescue those who called for his help.

33He turned rivers into a desert,
flowing springs into thirsty ground,
34and fruitful land into a salt waste,
because of the wickedness of those who
lived there.
35He turned the desert into pools of water
and the parched ground into flowing springs;
36there he brought the hungry to live,
and they founded a city where they could
settle.
37They sowed fields and planted vineyards
that yielded a fruitful harvest;
38he blessed them, and their numbers greatly
increased,
and he did not let their herds diminish.

39Then their numbers decreased, and they were
humbled
by oppression, calamity and sorrow;
40he who pours contempt on nobles
made them wander in a trackless waste.
41But he lifted the needy out of their affliction
and increased their families like flocks.
42The upright see and rejoice,

a 3 Hebrew north and the sea

but all the wicked shut their mouths.

43Whoever is wise, let him heed these things
and consider the great love of the LORD.

■ PSALM 108
□ A song. A psalm of David.

1My heart is steadfast, O God;
I will sing and make music with all my soul.
2Awake, harp and lyre!
I will awaken the dawn.
3I will praise you, O LORD, among the nations;
I will sing of you among the peoples.
4For great is your love, higher than the heavens;
your faithfulness reaches to the skies.
5Be exalted, O God, above the heavens,
and let your glory be over all the earth.

6Save us and help us with your right hand,
that those you love may be delivered.
7God has spoken from his sanctuary:
"In triumph I will parcel out Shechem
and measure off the Valley of Succoth.
8Gilead is mine, Manasseh is mine;
Ephraim is my helmet,
Judah my sceptre.
9Moab is my washbasin,
upon Edom I toss my sandal;
over Philistia I shout in triumph."

10Who will bring me to the fortified city?
Who will lead me to Edom?
11Is it not you, O God, you who have rejected us
and no longer go out with our armies?
12Give us aid against the enemy,
for the help of man is worthless.
13With God we shall gain the victory,
and he will trample down our enemies.

■ PSALM 109
□ For the director of music. Of David. A psalm.

1O God, whom I praise,
do not remain silent,
2for wicked and deceitful men
have opened their mouths against me;
they have spoken against me with lying
tongues.
3With words of hatred they surround me;
they attack me without cause.
4In return for my friendship they accuse me,
but I am a man of prayer.
5They repay me evil for good,
and hatred for my friendship.

6Appoint[a] an evil man[b] to oppose him;
let an accuser[c] stand at his right hand.
7When he is tried, let him be found guilty,
and may his prayers condemn him.
8May his days be few;
may another take his place of leadership.
9May his children be fatherless
and his wife a widow.
10May his children be wandering beggars;

may they be driven[d] from their ruined
homes.
11May a creditor seize all he has;
may strangers plunder the fruits of his
labour.
12May no-one extend kindness to him
or take pity on his fatherless children.
13May his descendants be cut off,
their names blotted out from the next
generation.
14May the iniquity of his fathers be remembered
before the LORD;
may the sin of his mother never be blotted
out.
15May their sins always remain before the LORD,
that he may cut off the memory of them
from the earth.

109:8 ■ THE JUDAS PRINCIPLE
Peter applied this verse to Judas (Acts 1:20). The
New Testament writers saw David's life as the
pattern and foreshadowing of the Messiah, David's
son. The savage betrayal recorded in this poem
shows, as do many psalms, that unexplained
suffering comes to the most devoted of God's
people: first to David, then to Jesus.

16For he never thought of doing a kindness,
but hounded to death the poor
and the needy and the broken-hearted.
17He loved to pronounce a curse—
may it[e] come on him;
he found no pleasure in blessing—
may it be[f] far from him.
18He wore cursing as his garment;
it entered into his body like water,
into his bones like oil.
19May it be like a cloak wrapped about him,
like a belt tied for ever round him.
20May this be the LORD's payment to my accusers,
to those who speak evil of me.

21But you, O Sovereign LORD,
deal well with me for your name's sake;
out of the goodness of your love, deliver me.
22For I am poor and needy,
and my heart is wounded within me.
23I fade away like an evening shadow;
I am shaken off like a locust.
24My knees give way from fasting;
my body is thin and gaunt.
25I am an object of scorn to my accusers;
when they see me, they shake their heads.

26Help me, O LORD my God;
save me in accordance with your love.
27Let them know that it is your hand,
that you, O LORD, have done it.
28They may curse, but you will bless;
when they attack they will be put to shame,
but your servant will rejoice.
29My accusers will be clothed with disgrace
and wrapped in shame as in a cloak.

30With my mouth I will greatly extol the LORD;

a 6 Or They say, "Appoint (with quotation marks at the end of verse 19)   b 6 Or the Evil One   c 6 Or let Satan   d 10 Septuagint; Hebrew sought
e 17 Or curse, / and it has   f 17 Or blessing, / and it is

in the great throng I will praise him.
³¹For he stands at the right hand of the needy
   one,
   to save his life from those who condemn
   him.

■ PSALM 110
☐ Of David. A psalm.

¹The LORD says to my Lord:
   "Sit at my right hand
   until I make your enemies
   a footstool for your feet."

110:1 ■ THE SON OF GOD
Jesus quoted this verse in Mark 12:35–37 to
show that the Messiah would not be merely a
human military leader, as many Jews expected.
Here David refers to the coming King (David's
descendant) as "my Lord". If the Messiah were
strictly his human descendant, David would not
address him so respectfully.

²The LORD will extend your mighty sceptre from
   Zion;
   you will rule in the midst of your enemies.
³Your troops will be willing
   on your day of battle.
Arrayed in holy majesty,
   from the womb of the dawn
   you will receive the dew of your youth.ᵃ

⁴The LORD has sworn
   and will not change his mind:
   "You are a priest for ever,
   in the order of Melchizedek."

⁵The Lord is at your right hand;
   he will crush kings on the day of his wrath.
⁶He will judge nations, heaping up the dead
   and crushing the rulers of the whole earth.
⁷He will drink from a brook beside the way;ᵇ
   therefore he will lift up his head.

■ PSALM 111ᵃ

¹Praise the LORD.ᵇ

I will extol the LORD with all my heart
   in the council of the upright and in the
   assembly.

²Great are the works of the LORD;
   they are pondered by all who delight in
   them.
³Glorious and majestic are his deeds,
   and his righteousness endures for ever.
⁴He has caused his wonders to be remembered;
   the LORD is gracious and compassionate.
⁵He provides food for those who fear him;
   he remembers his covenant for ever.
⁶He has shown his people the power of his
   works,

giving them the lands of other nations.
⁷The works of his hands are faithful and just;
   all his precepts are trustworthy.
⁸They are steadfast for ever and ever,
   done in faithfulness and uprightness.
⁹He provided redemption for his people;
   he ordained his covenant for ever —
   holy and awesome is his name.

¹⁰The fear of the LORD is the beginning of
   wisdom;
   all who follow his precepts have good
   understanding.
   To him belongs eternal praise.

■ PSALM 112ᵃ

¹Praise the LORD.ᵇ

Blessed is the man who fears the LORD,
   who finds great delight in his commands.

²His children will be mighty in the land;
   the generation of the upright will be blessed.
³Wealth and riches are in his house,
   and his righteousness endures for ever.
⁴Even in darkness light dawns for the upright,
   for the gracious and compassionate and
   righteous man.ᶜ
⁵Good will come to him who is generous and
   lends freely,
   who conducts his affairs with justice.
⁶Surely he will never be shaken;
   a righteous man will be remembered for
   ever.
⁷He will have no fear of bad news;
   his heart is steadfast, trusting in the LORD.
⁸His heart is secure, he will have no fear;
   in the end he will look in triumph on his
   foes.
⁹He has scattered abroad his gifts to the poor,
   his righteousness endures for ever;
   his hornᵈ will be lifted high in honour.

¹⁰The wicked man will see and be vexed,
   he will gnash his teeth and waste away;
   the longings of the wicked will come to
   nothing.

■ PSALM 113

¹Praise the LORD.ᵃ

Praise, O servants of the LORD,
   praise the name of the LORD.
²Let the name of the LORD be praised,
   both now and for evermore.
³From the rising of the sun to the place where it
   sets,
   the name of the LORD is to be praised.

⁴The LORD is exalted over all the nations,
   his glory above the heavens.
⁵Who is like the LORD our God,
   the One who sits enthroned on high,

ᵃ3 Or / your young men will come to you like the dew   ᵇ7 Or / The One who grants succession will set him in authority   ᵃThis psalm is an acrostic
poem, the lines of which begin with the successive letters of the Hebrew alphabet.   ᵇ1 Hebrew Hallelu Yah   ᵃThis psalm is an acrostic poem, the lines
of which begin with the successive letters of the Hebrew alphabet.   ᵇ1 Hebrew Hallelu Yah   ᶜ4 Or / for ₎the LORD₎ is gracious and compassionate and
righteous   ᵈ9 Horn here symbolises dignity.   ᵃ1 Hebrew Hallelu Yah; also in verse 9

⁶who stoops down to look
   on the heavens and the earth?

113:1 ■ PSALMS OF THE LAST SUPPER

Psalms 113 to 118 were traditionally sung at the Passover meal – the first two before the meal, the last four after. These were probably the last songs Jesus sang with his disciples before his death (Mark 14:26).

⁷He raises the poor from the dust
   and lifts the needy from the ash heap;
⁸he seats them with princes,
   with the princes of their people.
⁹He settles the barren woman in her home
   as a happy mother of children.

  Praise the LORD.

■ PSALM 114

¹When Israel came out of Egypt,
   the house of Jacob from a people of foreign
    tongue,

■ OUT OF NOWHERE
HE CAME "OUT OF NOWHERE" TO WIN GREAT RESPECT

INSIGHT

"YOU ARE A PRIEST FOR EVER, IN THE ORDER OF MELCHIZEDEK." ■ 110:4

Just about every year at Wimbledon it's the same, a top tennis seed is beaten by an unknown. They may not get through to the next round, but they certainly make a lasting impression on the top player they have just beaten.
    Likewise in athletics, the crowd always love it when the leader has just rounded the last bend and is heading into the last 100 metres, when suddenly someone steams up on the outside, they're neck and neck for a while, the leader can't find any more to give and the other runner, the one he didn't see coming, wins the title.
    In everyday life, heroes also come "out of nowhere". A tragedy strikes, somebody goes under a tube train, no-one responds, then this wierd looking girl in the punk outfit, spiky hair, ripped jeans, the works, goes under the train and keeps the injured person alive until the rescue services arrive. She certainly didn't look like a hero.

■ MYSTERY MAN
The Bible has a kind of "unknown", a shadowy figure who is mentioned only three times, but leaves a great impression. Melchizedek came "out of nowhere" in Genesis 14:18–20 as a priest whom Abraham honoured. Melchizedek never reappeared. But Psalm 110 mentions him in referring to the Messiah, the conquering king whom Israelites expected. And in the New Testament, the book of Hebrews devotes more than a chapter to Melchizedek's significance. Why so? The answer has to do with Israel's longing for great leadership.
    Much as the government of the United Kingdom recognises three branches of government, Israel had three important kinds of leaders: prophets, priests and kings. Prophets told the truth, revealing God's righteousness.

Kings were to put righteousness into effect, as head of the government. Priests were to see that God met his people in worship: they represented God to the people, and the people to God. According to the God-given Israelite constitution, kings and priests always came from different tribes: a priest from the family of Levi and a king from the family of Judah. Ordinarily, a king could not be a priest.

■ TOTAL LEADERSHIP
The Messiah, however, must be a total leader: a perfect king governing justly, a perfect prophet revealing God's truth, a perfect priest bringing God and people together. But how could he be all three, when priests and kings were supposed to come from different families? Wouldn't that violate God's law?
    Psalm 110 suggests (and Hebrews 7 amplifies) the answer. Just as a football player need not necessarily come from the athletic stable, so Melchizedek's example proves that a priest need not necessarily come from the proper family. Melchizedek was not even an Israelite, let alone from the Levite family. He knew nothing about the temple or the Old Testament law, for these came after his time. Yet his spiritual power impressed Abraham. Melchizedek showed the kind of leadership Christ was to bring. He was both a priest and a king.
    Psalm 110's brief praise provides a thread between the Old and New Testaments. It hints that the Messiah would be greater than David, while being David's descendant. And by tracing the Messiah's roots to Melchizedek, it established his credibility as both priest and king.

□ LIFE QUESTIONS:
What are the "proper channels" you expect to see spiritual leadership come from? Has God ever led you through someone outside those channels?

²Judah became God's sanctuary,
  Israel his dominion.

³The sea looked and fled,
  the Jordan turned back;
⁴the mountains skipped like rams,
  the hills like lambs.

⁵Why was it, O sea, that you fled,
  O Jordan, that you turned back,
⁶you mountains, that you skipped like rams,
  you hills, like lambs?

⁷Tremble, O earth, at the presence of the Lord,
  at the presence of the God of Jacob,
⁸who turned the rock into a pool,
  the hard rock into springs of water.

■ PSALM 115

¹Not to us, O Lord, not to us
  but to your name be the glory,
  because of your love and faithfulness.

²Why do the nations say,
  "Where is their God?"
³Our God is in heaven;
  he does whatever pleases him.
⁴But their idols are silver and gold,
  made by the hands of men.
⁵They have mouths, but cannot speak,
  eyes, but they cannot see;
⁶they have ears, but cannot hear,
  noses, but they cannot smell;
⁷they have hands, but cannot feel,
  feet, but they cannot walk;
  nor can they utter a sound with their throats.
⁸Those who make them will be like them,
  and so will all who trust in them.

⁹O house of Israel, trust in the Lord —
  he is their help and shield.
¹⁰O house of Aaron, trust in the Lord —
  he is their help and shield.
¹¹You who fear him, trust in the Lord —
  he is their help and shield.

¹²The Lord remembers us and will bless us:
  He will bless the house of Israel,
  he will bless the house of Aaron,
¹³he will bless those who fear the Lord —
  small and great alike.

¹⁴May the Lord make you increase,
  both you and your children.
¹⁵May you be blessed by the Lord,
  the Maker of heaven and earth.

¹⁶The highest heavens belong to the Lord,
  but the earth he has given to man.
¹⁷It is not the dead who praise the Lord,
  those who go down to silence;
¹⁸it is we who extol the Lord,
  both now and for evermore.

Praise the Lord.ᵃ

■ PSALM 116

¹I love the Lord, for he heard my voice;
  he heard my cry for mercy.
²Because he turned his ear to me,
  I will call on him as long as I live.

³The cords of death entangled me,
  the anguish of the graveᵃ came upon me;
  I was overcome by trouble and sorrow.
⁴Then I called on the name of the Lord:
  "O Lord, save me!"

⁵The Lord is gracious and righteous;
  our God is full of compassion.
⁶The Lord protects the simple-hearted;
  when I was in great need, he saved me.

⁷Be at rest once more, O my soul,
  for the Lord has been good to you.

⁸For you, O Lord, have delivered my soul from
    death,
  my eyes from tears,
  my feet from stumbling,
⁹that I may walk before the Lord
  in the land of the living.
¹⁰I believed; thereforeᵇ I said,
  "I am greatly afflicted."
¹¹And in my dismay I said,
  "All men are liars."

¹²How can I repay the Lord
  for all his goodness to me?
¹³I will lift up the cup of salvation
  and call on the name of the Lord.
¹⁴I will fulfil my vows to the Lord
  in the presence of all his people.

¹⁵Precious in the sight of the Lord
  is the death of his saints.
¹⁶O Lord, truly I am your servant;
  I am your servant, the son of your
    maidservant;ᶜ
  you have freed me from my chains.

116:15 ■ PRECIOUS DEATH

This verse, often read at funerals, in no way
implies that God enjoys the death of his people.
Instead, it means that he carefully watches over
their death, and that it matters deeply to him. The
whole psalm praises God for *saving* from death.
Psalm 72:14 uses a similar phrase in a similar
way: "precious is their blood in his sight".

¹⁷I will sacrifice a thank-offering to you
  and call on the name of the Lord.
¹⁸I will fulfil my vows to the Lord
  in the presence of all his people,
¹⁹in the courts of the house of the Lord —
  in your midst, O Jerusalem.

Praise the Lord.ᵈ

ᵃ 18 Hebrew *Hallelu Yah*   ᵃ 3 Hebrew *Sheol*   ᵇ 10 Or *believed even when*   ᶜ 16 Or *servant, your faithful son*   ᵈ 19 Hebrew *Hallelu Yah*

■ **PSALM 117**

¹Praise the LORD, all you nations;
 extol him, all you peoples.
²For great is his love towards us,
 and the faithfulness of the LORD endures for
  ever.

Praise the LORD.*ᵃ*

■ **PSALM 118**

¹Give thanks to the LORD, for he is good;
 his love endures for ever.

²Let Israel say:
 "His love endures for ever."
³Let the house of Aaron say:
 "His love endures for ever."
⁴Let those who fear the LORD say:
 "His love endures for ever."

⁵In my anguish I cried to the LORD,
 and he answered by setting me free.
⁶The LORD is with me; I will not be afraid.
 What can man do to me?
⁷The LORD is with me; he is my helper.
 I will look in triumph on my enemies.

⁸It is better to take refuge in the LORD
 than to trust in man.
⁹It is better to take refuge in the LORD
 than to trust in princes.

¹⁰All the nations surrounded me,
 but in the name of the LORD I cut them off.
¹¹They surrounded me on every side,
 but in the name of the LORD I cut them off.
¹²They swarmed around me like bees,
 but they died out as quickly as burning
  thorns;
 in the name of the LORD I cut them off.

¹³I was pushed back and about to fall,
 but the LORD helped me.
¹⁴The LORD is my strength and my song;
 he has become my salvation.

¹⁵Shouts of joy and victory
 resound in the tents of the righteous:
 "The LORD's right hand has done mighty things!
¹⁶ The LORD's right hand is lifted high;
 the LORD's right hand has done mighty
  things!"

¹⁷I will not die but live,
 and will proclaim what the LORD has done.
¹⁸The LORD has chastened me severely,
 but he has not given me over to death.

¹⁹Open for me the gates of righteousness;
 I will enter and give thanks to the LORD.
²⁰This is the gate of the LORD
 through which the righteous may enter.
²¹I will give you thanks, for you answered me;
 you have become my salvation.

²²The stone the builders rejected
 has become the capstone;
²³the LORD has done this,

and it is marvellous in our eyes.
²⁴This is the day the LORD has made;
 let us rejoice and be glad in it.

118:22 ■ LAST-PLACE WINNER
God has a habit of reversing people's status. The
poor and needy end up satisfied, while the rich
and arrogant lose their position. As Jesus said,
"many who are first will be last, and many who are
last will be first" (Matthew 19:30). This psalm
expresses the concept with an image: a stone
builders considered unusable ends up holding the
whole building together. Jesus applied it to
himself, and it was quoted by Peter as a prophecy
fulfilled by Jesus' death and resurrection (see
Matthew 21:42; 1 Peter 2:7; and Acts 4:11).

²⁵O LORD, save us;
 O LORD, grant us success.
²⁶Blessed is he who comes in the name of the
  LORD.
 From the house of the LORD we bless you.*ᵃ*
²⁷The LORD is God,
 and he has made his light shine upon us.
 With boughs in hand, join in the festal
  procession
 up*ᵇ* to the horns of the altar.

²⁸You are my God, and I will give thanks;
 you are my God, and I will exalt you.

²⁹Give thanks to the LORD, for he is good;
 his love endures for ever.

■ **PSALM 119**ᵃ

א **Aleph**

¹Blessed are they whose ways are blameless,
 who walk according to the law of the LORD.
²Blessed are they who keep his statutes
 and seek him with all their heart.
³They do nothing wrong;
 they walk in his ways.
⁴You have laid down precepts
 that are to be fully obeyed.
⁵Oh, that my ways were steadfast
 in obeying your decrees!
⁶Then I would not be put to shame
 when I consider all your commands.
⁷I will praise you with an upright heart
 as I learn your righteous laws.
⁸I will obey your decrees;
 do not utterly forsake me.

ב **Beth**

⁹How can a young man keep his way pure?
 By living according to your word.
¹⁰I seek you with all my heart;
 do not let me stray from your commands.
¹¹I have hidden your word in my heart
 that I might not sin against you.
¹²Praise be to you, O LORD;

ᵃ2 Hebrew *Hallelu Yah*   *ᵃ26* The Hebrew is plural.   *ᵇ27* Or *Bind the festal sacrifice with ropes / and take it*   *ᵃ*This psalm is an acrostic poem; the
verses of each stanza begin with the same letter of the Hebrew alphabet.

teach me your decrees.
13With my lips I recount
all the laws that come from your mouth.
14I rejoice in following your statutes
as one rejoices in great riches.
15I meditate on your precepts
and consider your ways.
16I delight in your decrees;
I will not neglect your word.

ג   Gimel

17Do good to your servant, and I will live;
I will obey your word.
18Open my eyes that I may see
wonderful things in your law.
19I am a stranger on earth;
do not hide your commands from me.
20My soul is consumed with longing
for your laws at all times.
21You rebuke the arrogant, who are cursed
and who stray from your commands.
22Remove from me scorn and contempt,
for I keep your statutes.
23Though rulers sit together and slander me,
your servant will meditate on your decrees.
24Your statutes are my delight;
they are my counsellors.

ד   Daleth

25I am laid low in the dust;
preserve my life according to your word.
26I recounted my ways and you answered me;
teach me your decrees.
27Let me understand the teaching of your
precepts;
then I will meditate on your wonders.
28My soul is weary with sorrow;
strengthen me according to your word.
29Keep me from deceitful ways;
be gracious to me through your law.
30I have chosen the way of truth;
I have set my heart on your laws.
31I hold fast to your statutes, O LORD;
do not let me be put to shame.
32I run in the path of your commands,
for you have set my heart free.

ה   He

33Teach me, O LORD, to follow your decrees;
then I will keep them to the end.
34Give me understanding, and I will keep your
law
and obey it with all my heart.
35Direct me in the path of your commands,
for there I find delight.
36Turn my heart towards your statutes
and not towards selfish gain.
37Turn my eyes away from worthless things;
preserve my life according to your word.b
38Fulfil your promise to your servant,
so that you may be feared.

39Take away the disgrace I dread,
for your laws are good.
40How I long for your precepts!
Preserve my life in your righteousness.

ו   Waw

41May your unfailing love come to me, O LORD,
your salvation according to your promise;
42then I will answer the one who taunts me,
for I trust in your word.
43Do not snatch the word of truth from my
mouth,
for I have put my hope in your laws.
44I will always obey your law,
for ever and ever.
45I will walk about in freedom,
for I have sought out your precepts.
46I will speak of your statutes before kings
and will not be put to shame,
47for I delight in your commands
because I love them.
48I lift up my hands toc your commands, which
I love,
and I meditate on your decrees.

ז   Zayin

49Remember your word to your servant,
for you have given me hope.
50My comfort in my suffering is this:
Your promise preserves my life.
51The arrogant mock me without restraint,
but I do not turn from your law.
52I remember your ancient laws, O LORD,
and I find comfort in them.
53Indignation grips me because of the wicked,
who have forsaken your law.
54Your decrees are the theme of my song
wherever I lodge.
55In the night I remember your name, O LORD,
and I will keep your law.
56This has been my practice:
I obey your precepts.

119:55 ■ LYING IN BED

The psalms consider every aspect of life – even the thoughts that come while lying in bed at night. You can easily become obsessed with other people's wrongs against you. But you can also turn your thoughts to God and quiet your anxieties while strengthening your commitment. Other psalms that refer to such night-time thoughts, good and bad, are these: 4:4; 6:6; 16:7; 17:3; 63:6; 77:2; 102:7; and 119:62,148.

ח   Heth

57You are my portion, O LORD;
I have promised to obey your words.
58I have sought your face with all my heart;
be gracious to me according to your
promise.

b 37 Two manuscripts of the Masoretic Text and Dead Sea Scrolls; most manuscripts of the Masoretic Text life in your way   c 48 Or for

⁵⁹I have considered my ways
  and have turned my steps to your statutes.
⁶⁰I will hasten and not delay
  to obey your commands.
⁶¹Though the wicked bind me with ropes,
  I will not forget your law.
⁶²At midnight I rise to give you thanks
  for your righteous laws.
⁶³I am a friend to all who fear you,
  to all who follow your precepts.
⁶⁴The earth is filled with your love, O LORD;
  teach me your decrees.

ত Teth

⁶⁵Do good to your servant
  according to your word, O LORD.
⁶⁶Teach me knowledge and good judgment,
  for I believe in your commands.
⁶⁷Before I was afflicted I went astray,
  but now I obey your word.
⁶⁸You are good, and what you do is good;
  teach me your decrees.
⁶⁹Though the arrogant have smeared me with
  lies,

■ A LOVE POEM TO GOD'S LAW   INSIGHT
HOW COULD SCRIPTURE INSPIRE SUCH POETRY?

I LIFT UP MY HANDS TO YOUR
COMMANDS, WHICH I LOVE. ■ 119:48

For all the hundreds of books written about
William Shakespeare, he remains a mysterious
figure. His "dark lady" prompts endless theories.
He wrote 26 passionate poems to her, yet we
do not even know her name. Numerous books
try to guess it, "proving" that one lady or
another must have been the one.

One thing we do know: she had
captivated Shakespeare. Seldom has love
produced such writhing emotion as his sonnets
express. Helplessly ravished by her
unfashionable "black (brunette) beauty",
Shakespeare longed to forget her, to escape her
evil character. Yet he was uncontrollably drawn.

> My thoughts and my discourse as
> madman's are . . .
> For I have sworn thee fair, and thought
> thee bright,
> Who art as black as hell, as dark as
> night.

But what an oddity to express such
fevered emotion in sonnets! The sonnets require
discipline: precisely 14 lines, an exact rhyming
scheme and iambic pentameter rhythm. How
can a raging storm be reflected in such a small,
still pond? Yet the evidence of the poems is
unmistakable. The discipline gave wild emotion a
backbone.

■ A LOVE POEM TO THE LAW
Psalm 119 contains even greater oddities. As
emotional as Shakespeare's sonnets, this poem
also takes a very systematic form: the acrostic,
where each line of each stanza begins with a
letter from the Hebrew alphabet, A in the first
stanza, B in the second, and so on, through all
22 letters of the Hebrew alphabet.

But the subject is the biggest surprise.
Psalm 119 is a long, passionate love poem
about God's law.

How do you fall in love with law? Most
people admit that rules are necessary, and
appreciate them grudgingly. But no-one writes
love poems extolling the latest Government
white paper.

The word translated "law" doesn't
merely mean rules. It expresses the totality of
God's written instructions. The poet sees life
full of uncertainties, of enemies, of pain. But
God has given a reliable guide for living – like
pavement underfoot after you have been stuck
in mud. Obeying God's law, to the psalmist, is
no slavery – rather it is freedom. "I run in the
path of your commands, for you have set my
heart free" (verse 32).

■ ON THE EDGE OF DEATH
Psalm 119 is not written from an ivory tower.
The poet has apparently been near death
(verse 87), and even as he writes, "the wicked
are waiting to destroy" him (verse 95). But in
this dangerous situation he has learned to
hang on to God's wisdom. The lesson is so
valuable he has become grateful for his
sufferings: "It was good for me to be afflicted
so that I might learn your decrees" (verse 71).

The psalmist simply does not see
God's law as a dusty, rigid rule book. He hears
God's loving voice in it. "The earth is filled with
your love, O LORD; teach me your decrees"
(verse 64). "Your statutes . . . are the joy of my
heart" (verse 111).

God's laws channel God's love into the
poet's life. They protect him from doing wrong,
give him wisdom to understand his situation.
They make new life flow into him. No wonder
he writes with such thankfulness. In God's
word he finds more than direction. He finds
God himself.

□ LIFE QUESTIONS:
Do you ever feel with the psalmist that life has
become frighteningly out of control? How can
God's law help you to regain confidence?

I keep your precepts with all my heart.
70Their hearts are callous and unfeeling,
  but I delight in your law.
71It was good for me to be afflicted
  so that I might learn your decrees.
72The law from your mouth is more precious to
    me
  than thousands of pieces of silver and gold.

' Yodh

73Your hands made me and formed me;
  give me understanding to learn your
    commands.
74May those who fear you rejoice when they see
    me,
  for I have put my hope in your word.
75I know, O LORD, that your laws are righteous,
  and in faithfulness you have afflicted me.
76May your unfailing love be my comfort,
  according to your promise to your servant.
77Let your compassion come to me that I may
    live,
  for your law is my delight.
78May the arrogant be put to shame for wronging
    me without cause;
  but I will meditate on your precepts.
79May those who fear you turn to me,
  those who understand your statutes.
80May my heart be blameless towards your
    decrees,
  that I may not be put to shame.

כ Kaph

81My soul faints with longing for your salvation,
  but I have put my hope in your word.
82My eyes fail, looking for your promise;
  I say, "When will you comfort me?"
83Though I am like a wineskin in the smoke,
  I do not forget your decrees.
84How long must your servant wait?
  When will you punish my persecutors?
85The arrogant dig pitfalls for me,
  contrary to your law.
86All your commands are trustworthy;
  help me, for men persecute me without
    cause.
87They almost wiped me from the earth,
  but I have not forsaken your precepts.
88Preserve my life according to your love,
  and I will obey the statutes of your mouth.

ל Lamedh

89Your word, O LORD, is eternal;
  it stands firm in the heavens.
90Your faithfulness continues through all
    generations;
  you established the earth, and it endures.
91Your laws endure to this day,
  for all things serve you.
92If your law had not been my delight,
  I would have perished in my affliction.
93I will never forget your precepts,
  for by them you have preserved my life.
94Save me, for I am yours;

I have sought out your precepts.
95The wicked are waiting to destroy me,
  but I will ponder your statutes.
96To all perfection I see a limit;
  but your commands are boundless.

119:96 ■ FREE AT LAST
People often wonder if following God's law will
restrict them, but actual experience shows that
God's law liberates — by freeing us from the
destructive impact of sinful behaviour, and by
introducing us to the mind-expanding realm of
God's wisdom. Like the author of Ecclesiastes,
the psalmist had looked around and seen limits to
everything. Only in following God's commands, he
sees, can a person escape this frustrating sense
of boundaries.

מ Mem

97Oh, how I love your law!
  I meditate on it all day long.
98Your commands make me wiser than my
    enemies,
  for they are ever with me.
99I have more insight than all my teachers,
  for I meditate on your statutes.
100I have more understanding than the elders,
  for I obey your precepts.
101I have kept my feet from every evil path
  so that I might obey your word.
102I have not departed from your laws,
  for you yourself have taught me.
103How sweet are your words to my taste,
  sweeter than honey to my mouth!
104I gain understanding from your precepts;
  therefore I hate every wrong path.

נ Nun

105Your word is a lamp to my feet
  and a light for my path.
106I have taken an oath and confirmed it,
  that I will follow your righteous laws.
107I have suffered much;
  preserve my life, O LORD, according to your
    word.
108Accept, O LORD, the willing praise of my
    mouth,
  and teach me your laws.
109Though I constantly take my life in my hands,
  I will not forget your law.
110The wicked have set a snare for me,
  but I have not strayed from your precepts.
111Your statutes are my heritage for ever;
  they are the joy of my heart.
112My heart is set on keeping your decrees
  to the very end.

ס Samekh

113I hate double-minded men,
  but I love your law.
114You are my refuge and my shield;

I have put my hope in your word.
115Away from me, you evildoers,
    that I may keep the commands of my God!
116Sustain me according to your promise, and I
    shall live;
    do not let my hopes be dashed.
117Uphold me, and I shall be delivered;
    I shall always have regard for your decrees.
118You reject all who stray from your decrees,
    for their deceitfulness is in vain.
119All the wicked of the earth you discard like
    dross;
    therefore I love your statutes.
120My flesh trembles in fear of you;
    I stand in awe of your laws.

ע   Ayin

121I have done what is righteous and just;
    do not leave me to my oppressors.
122Ensure your servant's well-being;
    let not the arrogant oppress me.
123My eyes fail, looking for your salvation,
    looking for your righteous promise.
124Deal with your servant according to your love
    and teach me your decrees.
125I am your servant; give me discernment
    that I may understand your statutes.
126It is time for you to act, O LORD;
    your law is being broken.
127Because I love your commands
    more than gold, more than pure gold,
128and because I consider all your precepts right,
    I hate every wrong path.

פ   Pe

129Your statutes are wonderful;
    therefore I obey them.
130The unfolding of your words gives light;
    it gives understanding to the simple.
131I open my mouth and pant,
    longing for your commands.
132Turn to me and have mercy on me,
    as you always do to those who love your
    name.
133Direct my footsteps according to your word;
    let no sin rule over me.
134Redeem me from the oppression of men,
    that I may obey your precepts.
135Make your face shine upon your servant
    and teach me your decrees.
136Streams of tears flow from my eyes,
    for your law is not obeyed.

צ   Tsadhe

137Righteous are you, O LORD,
    and your laws are right.
138The statutes you have laid down are righteous;
    they are fully trustworthy.
139My zeal wears me out,
    for my enemies ignore your words.
140Your promises have been thoroughly tested,
    and your servant loves them.
141Though I am lowly and despised,

I do not forget your precepts.
142Your righteousness is everlasting
    and your law is true.
143Trouble and distress have come upon me,
    but your commands are my delight.
144Your statutes are for ever right;
    give me understanding that I may live.

ק   Qoph

145I call with all my heart; answer me, O LORD,
    and I will obey your decrees.
146I call out to you; save me
    and I will keep your statutes.
147I rise before dawn and cry for help;
    I have put my hope in your word.
148My eyes stay open through the watches of the
    night,
    that I may meditate on your promises.
149Hear my voice in accordance with your love;
    preserve my life, O LORD, according to your
    laws.
150Those who devise wicked schemes are near,
    but they are far from your law.
151Yet you are near, O LORD,
    and all your commands are true.
152Long ago I learned from your statutes
    that you established them to last for ever.

119:151 ■ NEAR AND NEARER
The psalmist doesn't claim that God makes
problem people disappear. He merely points out
that while they are near, so is God. Big problems
gain a different perspective when we remember
the nearness of a bigger God.

ר   Resh

153Look upon my suffering and deliver me,
    for I have not forgotten your law.
154Defend my cause and redeem me;
    preserve my life according to your promise.
155Salvation is far from the wicked,
    for they do not seek out your decrees.
156Your compassion is great, O LORD;
    preserve my life according to your laws.
157Many are the foes who persecute me,
    but I have not turned from your statutes.
158I look on the faithless with loathing,
    for they do not obey your word.
159See how I love your precepts;
    preserve my life, O LORD, according to your
    love.
160All your words are true;
    all your righteous laws are eternal.

ש   Sin and Shin

161Rulers persecute me without cause,
    but my heart trembles at your word.
162I rejoice in your promise
    like one who finds great spoil.
163I hate and abhor falsehood
    but I love your law.

164Seven times a day I praise you
for your righteous laws.
165Great peace have they who love your law,
and nothing can make them stumble.
166I wait for your salvation, O LORD,
and I follow your commands.
167I obey your statutes,
for I love them greatly.
168I obey your precepts and your statutes,
for all my ways are known to you.

ת Taw

169May my cry come before you, O LORD;
give me understanding according to your
word.
170May my supplication come before you;
deliver me according to your promise.
171May my lips overflow with praise,
for you teach me your decrees.
172May my tongue sing of your word,
for all your commands are righteous.
173May your hand be ready to help me,
for I have chosen your precepts.
174I long for your salvation, O LORD,
and your law is my delight.
175Let me live that I may praise you,
and may your laws sustain me.
176I have strayed like a lost sheep.
Seek your servant,
for I have not forgotten your commands.

■ PSALM 120
☐ A song of ascents.

1I call on the LORD in my distress,
and he answers me.
2Save me, O LORD, from lying lips
and from deceitful tongues.

3What will he do to you,
and what more besides, O deceitful tongue?
4He will punish you with a warrior's sharp
arrows,
with burning coals of the broom tree.

5Woe to me that I dwell in Meshech,
that I live among the tents of Kedar!
6Too long have I lived
among those who hate peace.
7I am a man of peace;
but when I speak, they are for war.

■ PSALM 121
☐ A song of ascents.

1I lift up my eyes to the hills—
where does my help come from?
2My help comes from the LORD,
the Maker of heaven and earth.

3He will not let your foot slip—
he who watches over you will not slumber;
4indeed, he who watches over Israel
will neither slumber nor sleep.

5The LORD watches over you—
the LORD is your shade at your right hand;
6the sun will not harm you by day,
nor the moon by night.

7The LORD will keep you from all harm—
he will watch over your life;
8the LORD will watch over your coming and
going
both now and for evermore.

■ PSALM 122
☐ A song of ascents. Of David.

1I rejoiced with those who said to me,
"Let us go to the house of the LORD."
2Our feet are standing
in your gates, O Jerusalem.

3Jerusalem is built like a city
that is closely compacted together.
4That is where the tribes go up,
the tribes of the LORD,
to praise the name of the LORD
according to the statute given to Israel.
5There the thrones for judgment stand,
the thrones of the house of David.

6Pray for the peace of Jerusalem:
"May those who love you be secure.
7May there be peace within your walls
and security within your citadels."
8For the sake of my brothers and friends,
I will say, "Peace be within you."
9For the sake of the house of the LORD our God,
I will seek your prosperity.

■ PSALM 123
☐ A song of ascents.

1I lift up my eyes to you,
to you whose throne is in heaven.
2As the eyes of slaves look to the hand of their
master,
as the eyes of a maid look to the hand of her
mistress,
so our eyes look to the LORD our God,
till he shows us his mercy.

3Have mercy on us, O LORD, have mercy on us,
for we have endured much contempt.
4We have endured much ridicule from the
proud,
much contempt from the arrogant.

■ PSALM 124
☐ A song of ascents. Of David.

1If the LORD had not been on our side—
let Israel say—
2if the LORD had not been on our side
when men attacked us,
3when their anger flared against us,
they would have swallowed us alive;
4the flood would have engulfed us,
the torrent would have swept over us,

⁵the raging waters
  would have swept us away.

⁶Praise be to the LORD,
  who has not let us be torn by their teeth.
⁷We have escaped like a bird
  out of the fowler's snare;
the snare has been broken,
  and we have escaped.
⁸Our help is in the name of the LORD,
  the Maker of heaven and earth.

124:7 ■ DEEPER AND DEEPER

Some trouble is quick – bang and it's over. If you
get caught parked on double yellow lines, for
instance, you pay your fine and that ends the
whole affair. But with other trouble, trying to
escape only gets you more deeply entangled.
Spreading gossip, for instance, may lead you into
all kinds of unexpected consequences as the
gossip spreads. If you try to undo the damage,
you only make it worse.

That's exactly the picture of "the fowler's
snare". The bird that caught its neck in the noose
only tightened the snare's choke-hold by
struggling. The bird could not get out by its own
effort. But this time, says David, the snare has
miraculously broken, and the bird has flown to
safety. When you escape that way, there's only
one person to thank: the Lord.

■ PSALM 125
☐ A song of ascents.

¹Those who trust in the LORD are like Mount
    Zion,
  which cannot be shaken but endures for
    ever.
²As the mountains surround Jerusalem,
  so the LORD surrounds his people
  both now and for evermore.

³The sceptre of the wicked will not remain
  over the land allotted to the righteous,
for then the righteous might use
  their hands to do evil.

⁴Do good, O LORD, to those who are good,
  to those who are upright in heart.
⁵But those who turn to crooked ways
  the LORD will banish with the evildoers.

  Peace be upon Israel.

■ PSALM 126
☐ A song of ascents.

¹When the LORD brought back the captives to*a*
    Zion,
  we were like men who dreamed.*b*
²Our mouths were filled with laughter,
  our tongues with songs of joy.
Then it was said among the nations,
  "The LORD has done great things for them."

³The LORD has done great things for us,
  and we are filled with joy.

⁴Restore our fortunes,*c* O LORD,
  like streams in the Negev.
⁵Those who sow in tears
  will reap with songs of joy.
⁶He who goes out weeping,
  carrying seed to sow,
will return with songs of joy,
  carrying sheaves with him.

■ PSALM 127
☐ A song of ascents. Of Solomon.

¹Unless the LORD builds the house,
  its builders labour in vain.
Unless the LORD watches over the city,
  the watchmen stand guard in vain.
²In vain you rise early
  and stay up late,
toiling for food to eat –
  for he grants sleep to*a* those he loves.

³Sons are a heritage from the LORD,
  children a reward from him.
⁴Like arrows in the hands of a warrior
  are sons born in one's youth.
⁵Blessed is the man
  whose quiver is full of them.
They will not be put to shame
  when they contend with their enemies in the
    gate.

■ PSALM 128
☐ A song of ascents.

¹Blessed are all who fear the LORD,
  who walk in his ways.
²You will eat the fruit of your labour;
  blessings and prosperity will be yours.
³Your wife will be like a fruitful vine
  within your house;
your sons will be like olive shoots
  round your table.
⁴Thus is the man blessed
  who fears the LORD.

⁵May the LORD bless you from Zion
  all the days of your life;
may you see the prosperity of Jerusalem,
⁶   and may you live to see your children's
    children.

  Peace be upon Israel.

■ PSALM 129
☐ A song of ascents.

¹They have greatly oppressed me from my
    youth –
  let Israel say –
²they have greatly oppressed me from my youth,
  but they have not gained the victory over
    me.
³Ploughmen have ploughed my back

---

*a*1 Or LORD restored the fortunes of   *b*1 Or men restored to health   *c*4 Or Bring back our captives   *a*2 Or eat – / for while they sleep he provides
for

and made their furrows long.
⁴But the LORD is righteous;
   he has cut me free from the cords of the
     wicked.

129:3 ■ THE RIGHT WORDS

You can't improve on the vivid images used in great poetry. If someone asks you, "What's it about?" you can only quote the poem. The psalms are full of such unforgettable language. "Ploughmen have ploughed my back and made their furrows long" makes you grit your teeth with the sense of oppression. "May they be like grass on the roof, which withers before it can grow" (verse 6) says it better than any alternative phrase like, "Let their successes amount to nothing."

⁵May all who hate Zion
   be turned back in shame.
⁶May they be like grass on the roof,
   which withers before it can grow;
⁷with it the reaper cannot fill his hands,
   nor the one who gathers fill his arms.
⁸May those who pass by not say,
   "The blessing of the LORD be upon you;
   we bless you in the name of the LORD."

■ PSALM 130
☐ A song of ascents.

¹Out of the depths I cry to you, O LORD;
² O Lord, hear my voice.
 Let your ears be attentive
   to my cry for mercy.

³If you, O LORD, kept a record of sins,
   O Lord, who could stand?
⁴But with you there is forgiveness;
   therefore you are feared.

⁵I wait for the LORD, my soul waits,
   and in his word I put my hope.
⁶My soul waits for the Lord
   more than watchmen wait for the morning,
   more than watchmen wait for the morning.

⁷O Israel, put your hope in the LORD,
   for with the LORD is unfailing love
   and with him is full redemption.
⁸He himself will redeem Israel
   from all their sins.

■ PSALM 131
☐ A song of ascents. Of David.

¹My heart is not proud, O LORD,
   my eyes are not haughty;
 I do not concern myself with great matters
   or things too wonderful for me.
²But I have stilled and quietened my soul;
   like a weaned child with its mother,
   like a weaned child is my soul within me.

³O Israel, put your hope in the LORD
   both now and for evermore.

131:2 ■ A CHILD WITH ITS MOTHER

How trusting is a baby? Not very, some would say, for babies cry violently as soon as they feel the slightest hunger. It is the weaned child, a little older, who has learned to trust its mother, to fret less and simply ask for food instead of wailing. The profound simplicity of this patience is David's model for how he, and all Israel, should wait on the Lord. The apostle Paul comments similarly, "I have learned the secret of being content in any and every situation . . . I can do everything through him who gives me strength" (Philippians 4:12–13).

■ PSALM 132
☐ A song of ascents.

¹O LORD, remember David
   and all the hardships he endured.

²He swore an oath to the LORD
   and made a vow to the Mighty One of Jacob:
³"I will not enter my house
   or go to my bed—
⁴I will allow no sleep to my eyes,
   no slumber to my eyelids,
⁵till I find a place for the LORD,
   a dwelling for the Mighty One of Jacob."

⁶We heard it in Ephrathah,
   we came upon it in the fields of Jaar:ᵃ ᵇ
⁷"Let us go to his dwelling-place;
   let us worship at his footstool—
⁸arise, O LORD, and come to your resting place,
   you and the ark of your might.
⁹May your priests be clothed with righteousness;
   may your saints sing for joy."

¹⁰For the sake of David your servant,
   do not reject your anointed one.

¹¹The LORD swore an oath to David,
   a sure oath that he will not revoke:
"One of your own descendants
   I will place on your throne—
¹²if your sons keep my covenant
   and the statutes I teach them,
then their sons shall sit
   on your throne for ever and ever."

¹³For the LORD has chosen Zion,
   he has desired it for his dwelling:
¹⁴"This is my resting place for ever and ever;
   here I will sit enthroned, for I have desired
     it—
¹⁵I will bless her with abundant provisions;
   her poor will I satisfy with food.
¹⁶I will clothe her priests with salvation,
   and her saints shall ever sing for joy.

¹⁷"Here I will make a hornᶜ grow for David
   and set up a lamp for my anointed one.
¹⁸I will clothe his enemies with shame,

ᵃ6 That is, Kiriath Jearim   *ᵇ6 Or heard of it in Ephrathah, / we found it in the fields of Jaar. (and no quotation marks around verses 7–9)*   *ᶜ17 Horn here symbolises strong one, that is, king.*

but the crown on his head shall be
resplendent."

132:11 ■ PROMISE TO DAVID

God's covenant with David promised that he and
his descendants would always reign over Israel.
For Israel, this promise meant that God would
never let the nation disintegrate, that he would
always provide a leader. Over the centuries, when
Israel chafed under the domination of other
nations, Jews remembered this promise and
looked for a "Messiah" or "anointed one" (a king)
who would provide this leadership. That is why the
New Testament often refers to Jesus as a "son of
David".

■ PSALM 133
☐ A song of ascents. Of David.

¹How good and pleasant it is
  when brothers live together in unity!
²It is like precious oil poured on the head,
  running down on the beard,
running down on Aaron's beard,
  down upon the collar of his robes.
³It is as if the dew of Hermon
  were falling on Mount Zion.
For there the LORD bestows his blessing,
  even life for evermore.

■ PSALM 134
☐ A song of ascents.

¹Praise the LORD, all you servants of the LORD
  who minister by night in the house of the
  LORD.
²Lift up your hands in the sanctuary
  and praise the LORD.

³May the LORD, the Maker of heaven and earth,
  bless you from Zion.

■ PSALM 135

¹Praise the LORD.*a*

Praise the name of the LORD;
  praise him, you servants of the LORD,
²you who minister in the house of the LORD,
  in the courts of the house of our God.

³Praise the LORD, for the LORD is good;
  sing praise to his name, for that is pleasant.
⁴For the LORD has chosen Jacob to be his own,
  Israel to be his treasured possession.

⁵I know that the LORD is great,
  that our Lord is greater than all gods.
⁶The LORD does whatever pleases him,
  in the heavens and on the earth,
  in the seas and all their depths.
⁷He makes clouds rise from the ends of the
    earth;
  he sends lightning with the rain

and brings out the wind from his
  storehouses.

⁸He struck down the firstborn of Egypt,
  the firstborn of men and animals.
⁹He sent his signs and wonders into your midst,
  O Egypt,
  against Pharaoh and all his servants.
¹⁰He struck down many nations
  and killed mighty kings—
¹¹Sihon king of the Amorites,
  Og king of Bashan
  and all the kings of Canaan—
¹²and he gave their land as an inheritance,
  an inheritance to his people Israel.

¹³Your name, O LORD, endures for ever,
  your renown, O LORD, through all
    generations.
¹⁴For the LORD will vindicate his people
  and have compassion on his servants.

¹⁵The idols of the nations are silver and gold,
  made by the hands of men.
¹⁶They have mouths, but cannot speak,
  eyes, but they cannot see;
¹⁷they have ears, but cannot hear,
  nor is there breath in their mouths.
¹⁸Those who make them will be like them,
  and so will all who trust in them.

¹⁹O house of Israel, praise the LORD;
  O house of Aaron, praise the LORD;
²⁰O house of Levi, praise the LORD;
  you who fear him, praise the LORD.
²¹Praise be to the LORD from Zion,
  to him who dwells in Jerusalem.

Praise the LORD.

■ PSALM 136

¹Give thanks to the LORD, for he is good.
    His love endures for ever.
²Give thanks to the God of gods.
    His love endures for ever.
³Give thanks to the Lord of lords:
    His love endures for ever.

⁴to him who alone does great wonders,
    His love endures for ever.
⁵who by his understanding made the heavens,
    His love endures for ever.
⁶who spread out the earth upon the waters,
    His love endures for ever.
⁷who made the great lights—
    His love endures for ever.
⁸the sun to govern the day,
    His love endures for ever.
⁹the moon and stars to govern the night;
    His love endures for ever.

¹⁰to him who struck down the firstborn of Egypt
    His love endures for ever.
¹¹and brought Israel out from among them
    His love endures for ever.
¹²with a mighty hand and outstretched arm;
    His love endures for ever.

*a*1 Hebrew *Hallelu Yah*; also in verses 3 and 21

"Tear it down," they cried,
"tear it down to its foundations!"

[8]O Daughter of Babylon, doomed to destruction,
happy is he who repays you
for what you have done to us—
[9]he who seizes your infants
and dashes them against the rocks.

136:1 ■ CALL AND RESPONSE
Scholars think most of the psalms were used in
temple worship, but they are unsure how they
were sung. This psalm seems like an example of
what is known in African-American music as "call
and response". A leader sings out a story, and the
congregation shouts back a rhythmic refrain.

[13]to him who divided the Red Sea[a] asunder
His love endures for ever.
[14]and brought Israel through the midst of it,
His love endures for ever.
[15]but swept Pharaoh and his army into the Red
Sea;
His love endures for ever.

[16]to him who led his people through the desert,
His love endures for ever.
[17]who struck down great kings,
His love endures for ever.
[18]and killed mighty kings—
His love endures for ever.
[19]Sihon king of the Amorites
His love endures for ever.
[20]and Og king of Bashan—
His love endures for ever.
[21]and gave their land as an inheritance,
His love endures for ever.
[22]an inheritance to his servant Israel;
His love endures for ever.

[23]to the One who remembered us in our low
estate
His love endures for ever.
[24]and freed us from our enemies,
His love endures for ever.
[25]and who gives food to every creature.
His love endures for ever.

[26]Give thanks to the God of heaven.
His love endures for ever.

■ PSALM 137

[1]By the rivers of Babylon we sat and wept
when we remembered Zion.
[2]There on the poplars
we hung our harps,
[3]for there our captors asked us for songs,
our tormentors demanded songs of joy;
they said, "Sing us one of the songs of Zion!"

[4]How can we sing the songs of the LORD
while in a foreign land?
[5]If I forget you, O Jerusalem,
may my right hand forget ⌊its skill⌋.
[6]May my tongue cling to the roof of my mouth
if I do not remember you,
if I do not consider Jerusalem
my highest joy.

[7]Remember, O LORD, what the Edomites did
on the day Jerusalem fell.

■ PSALM 138
□ Of David.

[1]I will praise you, O LORD, with all my heart;
before the "gods" I will sing your praise.
[2]I will bow down towards your holy temple
and will praise your name
for your love and your faithfulness,
for you have exalted above all things
your name and your word.
[3]When I called, you answered me;
you made me bold and stout-hearted.

[4]May all the kings of the earth praise you,
O LORD,
when they hear the words of your mouth.
[5]May they sing of the ways of the LORD,
for the glory of the LORD is great.

[6]Though the LORD is on high, he looks upon the
lowly,
but the proud he knows from afar.
[7]Though I walk in the midst of trouble,
you preserve my life;
you stretch out your hand against the anger of
my foes,
with your right hand you save me.
[8]The LORD will fulfil ⌊his purpose⌋ for me;
your love, O LORD, endures for ever—
do not abandon the works of your hands.

■ PSALM 139
□ For the director of music. Of David. A psalm.

[1]O LORD, you have searched me
and you know me.
[2]You know when I sit and when I rise;
you perceive my thoughts from afar.
[3]You discern my going out and my lying down;
you are familiar with all my ways.
[4]Before a word is on my tongue
you know it completely, O LORD.

[5]You hem me in—behind and before;
you have laid your hand upon me.
[6]Such knowledge is too wonderful for me,
too lofty for me to attain.

[7]Where can I go from your Spirit?
Where can I flee from your presence?
[8]If I go up to the heavens, you are there;
if I make my bed in the depths,[a] you are
there.
[9]If I rise on the wings of the dawn,
if I settle on the far side of the sea,
[10]even there your hand will guide me,
your right hand will hold me fast.

---

a 13 Hebrew Yam Suph; that is, Sea of Reeds; also in verse 15   a 8 Hebrew Sheol

¹¹If I say, "Surely the darkness will hide me
        and the light become night around me,"
¹²even the darkness will not be dark to you;
        the night will shine like the day,
        for darkness is as light to you.

¹³For you created my inmost being;
        you knit me together in my mother's womb.
¹⁴I praise you because I am fearfully and
            wonderfully made;
        your works are wonderful,
        I know that full well.
¹⁵My frame was not hidden from you
        when I was made in the secret place.
    When I was woven together in the depths of
            the earth,
¹⁶   your eyes saw my unformed body.
    All the days ordained for me
        were written in your book
        before one of them came to be.

¹⁷How precious to^b me are your thoughts,
        O God!
    How vast is the sum of them!
¹⁸Were I to count them,
        they would outnumber the grains of sand.

When I awake,
    I am still with you.

139:13 ■ LOVE BEFORE BIRTH

Does life begin at conception, or at birth? This verse doesn't directly answer that question, but it does make clear that God's loving involvement with our lives starts long before birth. Nothing can escape God's concern, according to this psalm — no person, no thought, no place, no time.

---

¹⁹If only you would slay the wicked, O God!
        Away from me, you bloodthirsty men!
²⁰They speak of you with evil intent;
        your adversaries misuse your name.
²¹Do I not hate those who hate you, O LORD,
        and abhor those who rise up against you?
²²I have nothing but hatred for them;
        I count them my enemies.

²³Search me, O God, and know my heart;
        test me and know my anxious thoughts.
²⁴See if there is any offensive way in me,
        and lead me in the way everlasting.

■ WHAT ABOUT CURSES?
BITTER EMOTIONS EXPRESSED IN SORROW

INSIGHT

HAPPY IS HE . . . WHO SEIZES YOUR INFANTS AND DASHES THEM AGAINST THE ROCKS. ■ 137:8–9

The so-called "cursing psalms" come as a shock. Psalm 137 is the most famous example. In a gorgeous lament from exile, the poet crescendoes to wish that God would bless anyone who knocks a Babylonian baby's brains out.

To many people, this wish seems too bitter to belong in the Bible. Aren't Christians supposed to love their enemies and pray for those who persecute them (Matthew 5:44)? Even in the Old Testament, enemies were not to be treated unkindly (Exodus 23:4). How does this outburst fit into God's Word?

■ A CRY FOR JUSTICE

To answer we must go to the courtroom, where more and more judges are allowing the victims of a crime to testify during sentencing. A mother who has lost her child to a murderer may spout wild and even vindictive emotions as she stands to demand the death sentence. Still the court needs to hear her. She alone knows fully what was lost. She alone feels the full outrage of the crime.

The cursing psalms voice such "victim testimony" to God, the judge. They always assume that the punishment they ask for is deserved. For example, Psalm 109 calls down curses on a man who "hounded to death the poor and the needy and the broken-hearted. He loved to pronounce a curse — may it come on him" (109:16–17).

Psalm 137 was written out of similar anguish. As a nation, Babylon had callously murdered, earning punishment. The Bible says that God hears the cries of the innocent. He promises to punish those who have hurt them.

With all his teaching on forgiving enemies, Jesus did not change this idea of justice. He taught that justice will be done by God after death. (See, for instance, Matthew 25:31–46.) But Old Testament Israelites had only vague ideas about life after death. For them, justice had to be done in this life, before their eyes. They asked for it in the cursing psalms.

■ MERCY FOR YOUR ENEMIES

What about mercy? Isn't our duty to forgive our enemies, and love them? How do the cursing psalms fit with that?

Three things must be said. First, while no mercy shows through in the cursing psalms, that doesn't mean the people who wrote them were wholly unmerciful. David,

^b17 Or *concerning*

PSALM 140

☐ For the director of music. A psalm of David.

¹Rescue me, O LORD, from evil men;
  protect me from men of violence,
²who devise evil plans in their hearts
  and stir up war every day.
³They make their tongues as sharp as a serpent's;
  the poison of vipers is on their lips.   *Selah*

⁴Keep me, O LORD, from the hands of the
    wicked;
  protect me from men of violence
  who plan to trip my feet.
⁵Proud men have hidden a snare for me;
  they have spread out the cords of their net
  and have set traps for me along my path.
                                        Selah

⁶O LORD, I say to you, "You are my God."
  Hear, O LORD, my cry for mercy.
⁷O Sovereign LORD, my strong deliverer,
  who shields my head in the day of battle —
⁸do not grant the wicked their desires, O LORD;
  do not let their plans succeed,
  or they will become proud.   *Selah*

⁹Let the heads of those who surround me
  be covered with the trouble their lips have
    caused.
¹⁰Let burning coals fall upon them;
  may they be thrown into the fire,
  into miry pits, never to rise.
¹¹Let slanderers not be established in the land;
  may disaster hunt down men of violence.

¹²I know that the LORD secures justice for the
    poor
  and upholds the cause of the needy.
¹³Surely the righteous will praise your name
  and the upright will live before you.

140:12 ■ JUSTICE FOR THE POOR

In ancient societies (and in most of the world today) poor people lose all status. Nobody of influence will listen to them or take up their cause. In the Bible, though, God emphasises his concern for the poor. He will see that they get just treatment. Naturally he expects his followers to do the same.

---

credited with some of the strongest cursing psalms, showed extraordinary mercy towards Saul, his vengeful enemy. The cursing psalms are unbridled cries of agony. They honestly reflect the way people felt. Their authors' lives sometimes balanced this cry with compassion.

Second, the psalmists wrote before Jesus offered forgiveness to all by dying, as God's Son, in people's place. Even today many people find it difficult to accept Jesus' teaching on forgiving enemies, for it means forgiving rapists, child molesters, mass murderers. We can only forgive them because Jesus paid the price for their crimes. The psalmists lived before that payment.

Third, the cursing psalms prepared the way for forgiveness. You can only be genuinely merciful if you start with a full appreciation of guilt. The judge who carelessly lets a criminal off on a technicality is not showing mercy. Maybe he or she just lacks sympathy for the crime's victim. True mercy comes when victims themselves turn and forgive the people who hurt them, releasing them to liberty.

■ JESUS THE VICTIM

The cursing psalms express the hideousness of violence and injustice. Unless you feel the depth of this, you cannot understand the depth of God's forgiveness, offered freely to anyone who pleads for mercy. God is not merely letting people off on a legal technicality. He hears the cry of their victims, and more: he shares it. In Jesus, God was the victim, beaten, cursed, killed.

The New Testament actually quoted two of the cursing psalms, referring to Judas' betrayal of Jesus. These psalms speak of bitter injustice, and Jesus suffered the ultimate injustice. But the final word comes from Jesus himself: "Father, forgive them, for they do not know what they are doing."

If we follow Jesus' example, we dare not mouth the cursing psalms when we think of our enemies. These psalms are not for us to borrow from, as are other psalms. Yet these cursing psalms remind us of the bitter suffering many experience, and reading them can impel us to fight for justice. Moreover, they remind us to forgive. For God, hearing such cries from the victim, having suffered as they suffer, forgives. So can we.

☐ LIFE QUESTIONS:

What is the worst injustice you have ever experienced? Did you feel some of the anger expressed in the cursing psalms? Were you able to forgive?

■ PSALM 141

☐ A psalm of David.

¹O LORD, I call to you; come quickly to me.
  Hear my voice when I call to you.
²May my prayer be set before you like incense;
  may the lifting up of my hands be like the
  evening sacrifice.

³Set a guard over my mouth, O LORD;
  keep watch over the door of my lips.
⁴Let not my heart be drawn to what is evil,
  to take part in wicked deeds
with men who are evildoers;
  let me not eat of their delicacies.

⁵Let a righteous man*ᵃ* strike me — it is a
  kindness;
  let him rebuke me — it is oil on my head.
My head will not refuse it.

Yet my prayer is ever against the deeds of
  evildoers;
6 their rulers will be thrown down from the
  cliffs,
and the wicked will learn that my words
  were well spoken.
7⌊They will say,⌋ "As one ploughs and breaks up
  the earth,
so our bones have been scattered at the
  mouth of the grave."*ᵇ*

⁸But my eyes are fixed on you, O Sovereign
  LORD;
  in you I take refuge — do not give me over to
  death.
⁹Keep me from the snares they have laid for me,
  from the traps set by evildoers.
¹⁰Let the wicked fall into their own nets,
  while I pass by in safety.

■ PSALM 142

☐ A *maskil*ᵃ of David. When he was in the cave. A prayer.

¹I cry aloud to the LORD;
  I lift up my voice to the LORD for mercy.
²I pour out my complaint before him;
  before him I tell my trouble.

³When my spirit grows faint within me,
  it is you who know my way.
In the path where I walk
  men have hidden a snare for me.
⁴Look to my right and see;
  no-one is concerned for me.
I have no refuge;
  no-one cares for my life.

⁵I cry to you, O LORD;
  I say, "You are my refuge,
  my portion in the land of the living."
⁶Listen to my cry,
  for I am in desperate need;
rescue me from those who pursue me,
  for they are too strong for me.
⁷Set me free from my prison,
  that I may praise your name.

Then the righteous will gather about me
  because of your goodness to me.

■ PSALM 143

☐ A psalm of David.

¹O LORD, hear my prayer,
  listen to my cry for mercy;
in your faithfulness and righteousness
  come to my relief.
²Do not bring your servant into judgment,
  for no-one living is righteous before you.

³The enemy pursues me,
  he crushes me to the ground;
he makes me dwell in darkness
  like those long dead.
⁴So my spirit grows faint within me;
  my heart within me is dismayed.

⁵I remember the days of long ago;
  I meditate on all your works
  and consider what your hands have done.
⁶I spread out my hands to you;
  my soul thirsts for you like a parched land.
                                                   Selah

⁷Answer me quickly, O LORD;
  my spirit fails.
Do not hide your face from me
  or I will be like those who go down to the
  pit.
⁸Let the morning bring me word of your
  unfailing love,
  for I have put my trust in you.
Show me the way I should go,
  for to you I lift up my soul.
⁹Rescue me from my enemies, O LORD,
  for I hide myself in you.
¹⁰Teach me to do your will,
  for you are my God;
may your good Spirit
  lead me on level ground.

¹¹For your name's sake, O LORD, preserve my life;
  in your righteousness, bring me out of
  trouble.
¹²In your unfailing love, silence my enemies;
  destroy all my foes,
  for I am your servant.

■ PSALM 144

☐ Of David.

¹Praise be to the LORD my Rock,
  who trains my hands for war,
  my fingers for battle.
²He is my loving God and my fortress,
  my stronghold and my deliverer,
my shield, in whom I take refuge,
  who subdues peoples*ᵃ* under me.

³O LORD, what is man that you care for him,
  the son of man that you think of him?
⁴Man is like a breath;
  his days are like a fleeting shadow.

*ᵃ5 Or Let the Righteous One   ᵇ7 Hebrew Sheol   ᵃTitle: Probably a literary or musical term   ᵃ2 Many manuscripts of the Masoretic Text, Dead Sea
Scrolls, Aquila, Jerome and Syriac; most manuscripts of the Masoretic Text subdues my people*

⁵Part your heavens, O LORD, and come down;
    touch the mountains, so that they smoke.
⁶Send forth lightning and scatter ⸤the enemies⸥;
    shoot your arrows and rout them.
⁷Reach down your hand from on high;
    deliver me and rescue me
  from the mighty waters,
    from the hands of foreigners
⁸whose mouths are full of lies,
    whose right hands are deceitful.

⁹I will sing a new song to you, O God;
    on the ten-stringed lyre I will make music to
      you,
¹⁰to the One who gives victory to kings,
    who delivers his servant David from the
      deadly sword.

¹¹Deliver me and rescue me
  from the hands of foreigners
  whose mouths are full of lies,
    whose right hands are deceitful.

¹²Then our sons in their youth
    will be like well-nurtured plants,
  and our daughters will be like pillars
    carved to adorn a palace.
¹³Our barns will be filled
    with every kind of provision.
  Our sheep will increase by thousands,
    by tens of thousands in our fields;
¹⁴ our oxen will draw heavy loads.ᵇ
  There will be no breaching of walls,
    no going into captivity,
    no cry of distress in our streets.

¹⁵Blessed are the people of whom this is true;
    blessed are the people whose God is the
      LORD.

■ PSALM 145ᵃ
□ A psalm of praise. Of David.

¹I will exalt you, my God the King;
    I will praise your name for ever and ever.
²Every day I will praise you
    and extol your name for ever and ever.

³Great is the LORD and most worthy of praise;
    his greatness no-one can fathom.
⁴One generation will commend your works to
      another;
    they will tell of your mighty acts.
⁵They will speak of the glorious splendour of
      your majesty,
    and I will meditate on your wonderful
      works.ᵇ
⁶They will tell of the power of your awesome
      works,
    and I will proclaim your great deeds.
⁷They will celebrate your abundant goodness
    and joyfully sing of your righteousness.

⁸The LORD is gracious and compassionate,
    slow to anger and rich in love.
⁹The LORD is good to all;

he has compassion on all he has made.
¹⁰All you have made will praise you, O LORD;
    your saints will extol you.
¹¹They will tell of the glory of your kingdom
    and speak of your might,
¹²so that all men may know of your mighty acts
    and the glorious splendour of your kingdom.
¹³Your kingdom is an everlasting kingdom,
    and your dominion endures through all
      generations.

The LORD is faithful to all his promises
    and loving towards all he has made.ᶜ
¹⁴The LORD upholds all those who fall
    and lifts up all who are bowed down.
¹⁵The eyes of all look to you,
    and you give them their food at the proper
      time.
¹⁶You open your hand
    and satisfy the desires of every living thing.

¹⁷The LORD is righteous in all his ways
    and loving towards all he has made.
¹⁸The LORD is near to all who call on him,
    to all who call on him in truth.
¹⁹He fulfils the desires of those who fear him;
    he hears their cry and saves them.
²⁰The LORD watches over all who love him,
    but all the wicked he will destroy.

²¹My mouth will speak in praise of the LORD.
    Let every creature praise his holy name
      for ever and ever.

■ PSALM 146

¹Praise the LORD.ᵃ

Praise the LORD, O my soul.
² I will praise the LORD all my life;
    I will sing praise to my God as long as I live.

³Do not put your trust in princes,
    in mortal men, who cannot save.
⁴When their spirit departs, they return to the
      ground;
    on that very day their plans come to nothing.

⁵Blessed is he whose help is the God of Jacob,
    whose hope is in the LORD his God,
⁶the Maker of heaven and earth,
    the sea, and everything in them—
    the LORD, who remains faithful for ever.
⁷He upholds the cause of the oppressed
    and gives food to the hungry.
  The LORD sets prisoners free,
⁸ the LORD gives sight to the blind,
    the LORD lifts up those who are bowed down,
    the LORD loves the righteous.
⁹The LORD watches over the alien
    and sustains the fatherless and the widow,
    but he frustrates the ways of the wicked.

¹⁰The LORD reigns for ever,
    your God, O Zion, for all generations.

Praise the LORD.

ᵇ 14 Or our chieftains will be firmly established   ᵃThis psalm is an acrostic poem, the verses of which (including verse 13b) begin with the successive letters
of the Hebrew alphabet.   ᵇ 5 Dead Sea Scrolls and Syriac (see also Septuagint); Masoretic Text On the glorious splendour of your majesty / and on your
wonderful works I will meditate   ᶜ 13 One manuscript of the Masoretic Text, Dead Sea Scrolls and Syriac (see also Septuagint); most manuscripts of the
Masoretic Text do not have the last two lines of verse 13.   ᵃ 1 Hebrew Hallelu Yah; also in verse 10

■ PSALM 147

¹Praise the LORD.ᵃ

How good it is to sing praises to our God,
how pleasant and fitting to praise him!

²The LORD builds up Jerusalem;
he gathers the exiles of Israel.
³He heals the broken-hearted
and binds up their wounds.

⁴He determines the number of the stars
and calls them each by name.
⁵Great is our Lord and mighty in power;
his understanding has no limit.
⁶The LORD sustains the humble
but casts the wicked to the ground.

⁷Sing to the LORD with thanksgiving;
make music to our God on the harp.
⁸He covers the sky with clouds;
he supplies the earth with rain
and makes grass grow on the hills.
⁹He provides food for the cattle
and for the young ravens when they call.

¹⁰His pleasure is not in the strength of the horse,
nor his delight in the legs of a man;
¹¹the LORD delights in those who fear him,
who put their hope in his unfailing love.

147:11 ■ GOD'S GREAT CONCERN
The Lord is a God of strength, as this song amply
demonstrates. But power doesn't delight him
(verse 10). More than anything he loves to be in a
close relationship to people who respond to his
love.

---

¹²Extol the LORD, O Jerusalem;
praise your God, O Zion;
¹³for he strengthens the bars of your gates

and blesses your people within you.
¹⁴He grants peace to your borders
and satisfies you with the finest of wheat.

¹⁵He sends his command to the earth;
his word runs swiftly.
¹⁶He spreads the snow like wool
and scatters the frost like ashes.
¹⁷He hurls down hail like pebbles.
Who can withstand his icy blast?
¹⁸He sends his word and melts them;
he stirs up his breezes, and the waters flow.

¹⁹He has revealed his word to Jacob,
his laws and decrees to Israel.
²⁰He has done this for no other nation;
they do not know his laws.

Praise the LORD.

■ PSALM 148

¹Praise the LORD.ᵃ

Praise the LORD from the heavens,
praise him in the heights above.
²Praise him, all his angels,
praise him, all his heavenly hosts.
³Praise him, sun and moon,
praise him, all you shining stars.
⁴Praise him, you highest heavens
and you waters above the skies.
⁵Let them praise the name of the LORD,
for he commanded and they were created.
⁶He set them in place for ever and ever;
he gave a decree that will never pass away.

⁷Praise the LORD from the earth,
you great sea creatures and all ocean depths,
⁸lightning and hail, snow and clouds,
stormy winds that do his bidding,
⁹you mountains and all hills,
fruit trees and all cedars,

■ SOME NOTABLE PSALMS
A LISTING OF SOME OF THE BEST-LOVED OR BEST-KNOWN PSALMS

INSIGHT

A plea for help in time of trouble: 5, 17, 25, 31, 61
A prayer when near despair: 39, 42, 43, 55, 73, 77, 86, 88, 102, 130
A prayer for forgiveness and help: 6, 32, 38, 51, 143
Rest in God's goodness: 4, 11, 23, 27, 63, 67, 91, 115, 121, 125, 139
Israel's cry of anguish at God's anger: 44, 74, 80, 85
Praise with shouts and singing: 33, 47, 66, 81, 95, 96, 98, 149, 150
Praise for God's personal blessings: 18, 30, 34, 40, 92, 103, 107, 113, 116, 118, 146
Praise for God's blessings to Israel: 68, 77, 100, 108, 124, 126, 129
Praise for God's awesome majesty: 8, 24, 29, 46, 50, 90, 93, 114, 145
Praise for God's law: 19, 119
Songs of war and vindication: 35, 58, 76, 79, 83, 109, 137
The history of God and the people of Israel: 78, 105, 106
Nature: 19, 65, 104, 147, 148
The Messiah: 2, 16, 22, 45, 69, 89, 110, 132
Jerusalem and the temple: 48, 84, 87, 122
The fates of the wicked and the righteous: 1, 15, 37, 49

ᵃ1 Hebrew *Hallelu Yah*; also in verse 20   ᵃ1 Hebrew *Hallelu Yah*; also in verse 14

¹⁰wild animals and all cattle,
  small creatures and flying birds,
¹¹kings of the earth and all nations,
  you princes and all rulers on earth,
¹²young men and maidens,
  old men and children.

¹³Let them praise the name of the LORD,
  for his name alone is exalted;
  his splendour is above the earth and the
  heavens.
¹⁴He has raised up for his people a horn,ᵇ
  the praise of all his saints,
  of Israel, the people close to his heart.

  Praise the LORD.

■ PSALM 149

¹Praise the LORD.ᵃ

Sing to the LORD a new song,
  his praise in the assembly of the saints.

²Let Israel rejoice in their Maker;
  let the people of Zion be glad in their King.
³Let them praise his name with dancing
  and make music to him with tambourine and
  harp.
⁴For the LORD takes delight in his people;
  he crowns the humble with salvation.

⁵Let the saints rejoice in this honour
  and sing for joy on their beds.

⁶May the praise of God be in their mouths
  and a double-edged sword in their hands,
⁷to inflict vengeance on the nations
  and punishment on the peoples,
⁸to bind their kings with fetters,
  their nobles with shackles of iron,
⁹to carry out the sentence written against them.
  This is the glory of all his saints.

  Praise the LORD.

■ PSALM 150

¹Praise the LORD.ᵃ

Praise God in his sanctuary;
  praise him in his mighty heavens.
²Praise him for his acts of power;
  praise him for his surpassing greatness.
³Praise him with the sounding of the trumpet,
  praise him with the harp and lyre,
⁴praise him with tambourine and dancing,
  praise him with the strings and flute,
⁵praise him with the clash of cymbals,
  praise him with resounding cymbals.

⁶Let everything that has breath praise the LORD.

  Praise the LORD.

ᵇ14 *Horn* here symbolises strong one, that is, king.   ᵃ1 Hebrew *Hallelu Yah*; also in verse 9   ᵃ1 Hebrew *Hallelu Yah*; also in verse 6

PROVERBS

■ UNCOMMON SENSE
A MOST DOWN-TO-EARTH BOOK

IF YOU CALL OUT FOR INSIGHT AND CRY ALOUD FOR UNDERSTANDING, AND IF YOU LOOK FOR IT AS FOR SILVER AND SEARCH FOR IT AS FOR HIDDEN TREASURE, THEN YOU WILL UNDERSTAND THE FEAR OF THE LORD AND FIND THE KNOWLEDGE OF GOD.
■ 2:3 – 5

"Sesame Street", the educational TV show, changed a lot of people's ideas about education. It offers a kaleidoscopic mix of gentle fun that seems to have nothing to do with education at all. One episode may start with a band of puppet rock stars – the Beetles – singing an ode entitled "Letter B" (to a tune that sounds surprisingly like the Beatles' "Let It Be"). Then the picture cuts to Big Bird asking Oscar the Grouch to help him write a letter to his uncle – Uncle Bird, whose name just happens to start with the letter *B*. Five minutes later, a cartoon letter *B* is jumping in front of various letter combinations while a voice intones the words spelled out: "B-b-boy", "B-b-bathtub", "B-b-bicycle".

"Sesame Street" showed that teaching youngsters doesn't always mean forcing them to sit down and memorise lists. By watching Big Bird, Cookie Monster, and Oscar the Grouch, children painlessly learn the letter *B* as well as colours, shapes, and a lot more.

The book of Proverbs does for wisdom what "Sesame Street" does for the ABCs. Much of Proverbs reads like a collection of one-liners, moving quickly (and apparently illogically) from one subject to another. A proverb pleases the ear much as "Sesame Street" pleases the eye, using "shortness, sense and salt" to compress life into a handful of memorable words. But just as with the TV programme, Proverbs has an overall objective behind its disorder. If you spend enough time in Proverbs, you will gain a subtle and practical understanding of life.

■ A FATHER'S GUIDANCE
Proverbs is probably the most down-to-earth book in the Bible. Its education prepares you for the street and the market-place, not the schoolroom. (Proverbs 1:20–21 expresses this poetically.) The book offers the warm advice you get by growing up in a good family: practical guidance for successfully making your way in the world. It covers small questions as well as large: talking too much, visiting neighbours too often, being unbearably cheerful too early in the morning.

The first nine chapters, which explain the purpose of Proverbs' wisdom, are spoken from father to son. Fifteen times the fatherly voice says, "My son". Some of the advice seems particularly well suited to young people: warnings against joining gangs, for instance, or urgent cautions against sex outside marriage. But the central message of Proverbs applies to anyone, old or young: "Get wisdom at all costs". It is a plea to strain your mind and your ears searching for the wise way to live.

■ VIRTUE IS NOT ITS ONLY REWARD
Anybody with a brain can find exceptions to Proverbs' generalities. For instance, Proverbs 28:19 proclaims that "he who works his land will have abundant food, but the one who chases fantasies will have his fill of poverty". Yet farmers who work hard go hungry in a drought, and dreamers win a million on the football pools or thousands in a lottery.

Proverbs simply tells how life works most of the time. You can worry about the exceptions after you have learned the rule. Try to live by the exceptions, and you court disaster.

The rule is that the godly, moral, hardworking, and wise will reap many rewards. Those who learn the practical and godly wisdom of Proverbs not only sleep better, they succeed and become able to help their family and friends. Fools and scoffers, though they appear successful, will eventually pay the cost of their lifestyle.

Much of Proverbs' practical advice makes no mention of God, and its concern for success may therefore seem quite secular. But if you take the book as a whole, it becomes obvious that the lifestyle Proverbs teaches depends on a healthy respect for God (1:7) affecting every aspect of life (3:5–7). Proverbs frankly concedes that the wise path will not be chosen by many; it is easier to live carelessly and godlessly. But those who choose to live by Proverbs will get success and safety, and more:

they will get to know God himself. "Then you will understand the fear of the LORD and find the knowledge of God" (2:5).

■ HOW TO READ PROVERBS

People love to quote proverbs. Often they express truth about life in an elegant, witty kernel. You'll find more humour in Proverbs than anywhere else in the Bible.

Yet Proverbs may well be the most abused book in the Bible. People often quote the proverbs as though they were absolute promises from God or rigid rules for living. In fact, few of the proverbs should be read that way. And some proverbs, read alone, would give you a distorted point of view.

To understand Proverbs, you should not hunt through it for proverbs you like. You should study the whole book to get its overall point of view. This takes time, for Proverbs covers dozens of subjects in subtle detail.

Each of the more than 500 proverbs is a tough nut you have to crack before you get the inner flesh. Read Proverbs slowly, but not for too long at one sitting.

Some people like to read a small number of proverbs each day in addition to their regular Bible readings. Others concentrate on memorising proverbs, so they can run them through their heads as they go about the day. Whatever technique you use, keep two things in mind: think carefully about each proverb, and try to put each into the wider context of the teachings of all of Proverbs. To help you see the total picture of Proverbs' teaching on some key subjects, ten Insights scattered throughout Proverbs briefly introduce ten subjects and list relevant proverbs.

The book of Proverbs is divided into two main parts: an introduction in the first nine chapters and the proverbs themselves in the remaining 22 chapters. If you skip the introduction, you won't understand the point of Proverbs as a book. It introduces "Lady Wisdom", and explains what she can do for you.

■ 3-TRACK READING PLAN

For an explanation and complete listing of the 3-track reading plan, turn to page x.

■ TRACK 1:
Two-Week Courses on the Bible
See page x for information on these courses.

■ TRACK 2:
An Overview of Proverbs in 3 Days
□ Day 1. Read the Introduction to Proverbs and chapter 4, which gives an introduction to the importance

of wisdom and the style of life you need to pursue it.
□ Day 2. Read chapter 10, which covers a fairly typical range of subject matter.
□ Day 3. Read all the proverbs listed in "Verbal Dynamite", on page 556. Now turn to page xi for your next Track 2 reading project.

■ TRACK 3:
All of Proverbs in 31 Days

After you have read through Proverbs, turn to pages xii–xiii for your next Track 3 reading project.

□ 1	□ 2	□ 3	□ 4
□ 5	□ 6	□ 7	□ 8
□ 9	□ 10	□ 11	□ 12
□ 13	□ 14	□ 15	□ 16
□ 17	□ 18	□ 19	□ 20
□ 21	□ 22	□ 23	□ 24
□ 25	□ 26	□ 27	□ 28
□ 29	□ 30	□ 31	

■ PROLOGUE: PURPOSE AND THEME

1 The proverbs of Solomon son of David, king of Israel:

²for attaining wisdom and discipline;
for understanding words of insight;
³for acquiring a disciplined and prudent life,
doing what is right and just and fair;
⁴for giving prudence to the simple,
knowledge and discretion to the young—
⁵let the wise listen and add to their learning,
and let the discerning get guidance—
⁶for understanding proverbs and parables,
the sayings and riddles of the wise.

⁷The fear of the LORD is the beginning of knowledge,
but fools*a* despise wisdom and discipline.

■ EXHORTATIONS TO EMBRACE WISDOM

■ Warning Against Enticement
⁸Listen, my son, to your father's instruction
and do not forsake your mother's teaching.
⁹They will be a garland to grace your head
and a chain to adorn your neck.

¹⁰My son, if sinners entice you,
do not give in to them.
¹¹If they say, "Come along with us;
let's lie in wait for someone's blood,
let's waylay some harmless soul;
¹²let's swallow them alive, like the grave,*b*
and whole, like those who go down to the pit;
¹³we will get all sorts of valuable things
and fill our houses with plunder;
¹⁴throw in your lot with us,
and we will share a common purse"—

---

a 7 The Hebrew words rendered *fool* in Proverbs, and often elsewhere in the Old Testament, denote one who is morally deficient.   *b* 12 Hebrew *Sheol*

15my son, do not go along with them,
　do not set foot on their paths;
16for their feet rush into sin,
　they are swift to shed blood.
17How useless to spread a net
　in full view of all the birds!
18These men lie in wait for their own blood;
　they waylay only themselves!
19Such is the end of all who go after ill-gotten
　gain;
　it takes away the lives of those who get it.

■ Warning Against Rejecting Wisdom
20Wisdom calls aloud in the street,
　she raises her voice in the public squares;
21at the head of the noisy streets*c* she cries out,
　in the gateways of the city she makes her
　speech:

22"How long will you simple ones*d* love your
　simple ways?
　How long will mockers delight in mockery
　and fools hate knowledge?
23If you had responded to my rebuke,
　I would have poured out my heart to you
　and made my thoughts known to you.
24But since you rejected me when I called
　and no-one gave heed when I stretched out
　my hand,
25since you ignored all my advice
　and would not accept my rebuke,
26I in turn will laugh at your disaster;
　I will mock when calamity overtakes you—
27when calamity overtakes you like a storm,
　when disaster sweeps over you like a
　whirlwind,
　when distress and trouble overwhelm you.

1:22 ■ THREE PROBLEM PEOPLE

Mockers, fools, the simple: Proverbs keeps using these words to define the "bad characters" we should stay away from. What kind of people are they? The "simple" are the least harmful group: they live without thinking and are too lazy to change. But they, like the others, will end up sorry. "Fools" are smarter but have made a conscious decision to live solely as they choose, independent of God and independent of advice. "Mockers", worst of all, are rebels against God who make their prideful position known to everyone. They mock God, but God will mock them in the end (verse 26).

28"Then they will call to me but I will not
　answer;
　they will look for me but will not find me.
29Since they hated knowledge
　and did not choose to fear the LORD,
30since they would not accept my advice
　and spurned my rebuke,
31they will eat the fruit of their ways
　and be filled with the fruit of their schemes.
32For the waywardness of the simple will kill
　them,

and the complacency of fools will destroy
　them;
33but whoever listens to me will live in safety
　and be at ease, without fear of harm."

■ Moral Benefits of Wisdom
2 My son, if you accept my words
　and store up my commands within you,
2turning your ear to wisdom
　and applying your heart to understanding,
3and if you call out for insight
　and cry aloud for understanding,
4and if you look for it as for silver
　and search for it as for hidden treasure,
5then you will understand the fear of the LORD
　and find the knowledge of God.
6For the LORD gives wisdom,
　and from his mouth come knowledge and
　understanding.
7He holds victory in store for the upright,
　he is a shield to those whose walk is
　blameless,
8for he guards the course of the just
　and protects the way of his faithful ones.

9Then you will understand what is right and just
　and fair—every good path.
10For wisdom will enter your heart,
　and knowledge will be pleasant to your soul.
11Discretion will protect you,
　and understanding will guard you.

12Wisdom will save you from the ways of wicked
　men,
　from men whose words are perverse,
13who leave the straight paths
　to walk in dark ways,
14who delight in doing wrong
　and rejoice in the perverseness of evil,
15whose paths are crooked
　and who are devious in their ways.

16It will save you also from the adulteress,
　from the wayward wife with her seductive
　words,
17who has left the partner of her youth
　and ignored the covenant she made before
　God.*a*
18For her house leads down to death
　and her paths to the spirits of the dead.
19None who go to her return
　or attain the paths of life.

20Thus you will walk in the ways of good men
　and keep to the paths of the righteous.
21For the upright will live in the land,
　and the blameless will remain in it;
22but the wicked will be cut off from the land,
　and the unfaithful will be torn from it.

■ Further Benefits of Wisdom
3 My son, do not forget my teaching,
　but keep my commands in your heart,
2for they will prolong your life many years
　and bring you prosperity.

3Let love and faithfulness never leave you;

c 21 Hebrew; Septuagint / on the tops of the walls　　d 22 The Hebrew word rendered simple in Proverbs generally denotes one without moral direction and inclined to evil.　　a 17 Or covenant of her God

bind them around your neck,
write them on the tablet of your heart.
⁴Then you will win favour and a good name
in the sight of God and man.

⁵Trust in the LORD with all your heart
and lean not on your own understanding;
⁶in all your ways acknowledge him,
and he will make your paths straight.ᵃ

3:6 ■ WALKING WITH GOD
In the original Hebrew, "in all your ways acknowledge him" is more literally "in all your ways *know* him". This fundamental statement of how to relate to God implies more than mere reverence. Nodding in God's direction is not enough: you must know him by living closely with him, relating to him personally in every aspect of your life.

⁷Do not be wise in your own eyes;
fear the LORD and shun evil.
⁸This will bring health to your body
and nourishment to your bones.

⁹Honour the LORD with your wealth,
with the firstfruits of all your crops;
¹⁰then your barns will be filled to overflowing,
and your vats will brim over with new wine.

¹¹My son, do not despise the LORD's discipline
and do not resent his rebuke,
¹²because the LORD disciplines those he loves,
as a fatherᵇ the son he delights in.

¹³Blessed is the man who finds wisdom,
the man who gains understanding,
¹⁴for she is more profitable than silver
and yields better returns than gold.
¹⁵She is more precious than rubies;
nothing you desire can compare with her.
¹⁶Long life is in her right hand;
in her left hand are riches and honour.
¹⁷Her ways are pleasant ways,
and all her paths are peace.
¹⁸She is a tree of life to those who embrace her;
those who lay hold of her will be blessed.

¹⁹By wisdom the LORD laid the earth's
foundations,
by understanding he set the heavens in place;
²⁰by his knowledge the deeps were divided,
and the clouds let drop the dew.

²¹My son, preserve sound judgment and
discernment,
do not let them out of your sight;
²²they will be life for you,
an ornament to grace your neck.
²³Then you will go on your way in safety,
and your foot will not stumble;
²⁴when you lie down, you will not be afraid;
when you lie down, your sleep will be sweet.
²⁵Have no fear of sudden disaster
or of the ruin that overtakes the wicked,
²⁶for the LORD will be your confidence
and will keep your foot from being snared.

²⁷Do not withhold good from those who deserve
it,
when it is in your power to act.
²⁸Do not say to your neighbour,
"Come back later; I'll give it tomorrow"—
when you now have it with you.

²⁹Do not plot harm against your neighbour,
who lives trustfully near you.
³⁰Do not accuse a man for no reason—
when he has done you no harm.

³¹Do not envy a violent man
or choose any of his ways,
³²for the LORD detests a perverse man
but takes the upright into his confidence.

³³The LORD's curse is on the house of the wicked,
but he blesses the home of the righteous.
³⁴He mocks proud mockers
but gives grace to the humble.
³⁵The wise inherit honour,
but fools he holds up to shame.

■ Wisdom Is Supreme

4 Listen, my sons, to a father's instruction;
pay attention and gain understanding.
²I give you sound learning,
so do not forsake my teaching.
³When I was a boy in my father's house,
still tender, and an only child of my mother,
⁴he taught me and said,
"Lay hold of my words with all your heart;
keep my commands and you will live.
⁵Get wisdom, get understanding;
do not forget my words or swerve from
them.
⁶Do not forsake wisdom, and she will protect
you;
love her, and she will watch over you.
⁷Wisdom is supreme; therefore get wisdom.
Though it cost all you have,ᵃ get
understanding.
⁸Esteem her, and she will exalt you;
embrace her, and she will honour you.
⁹She will set a garland of grace on your head
and present you with a crown of splendour."

4:7 ■ A LIFELONG QUEST
A father's advice can easily degenerate into, "Don't do this, don't do that." But the fatherly advice of Proverbs isn't preoccupied with rules. Instead, this father tries to help his son develop a love for the best things in life—just as *his* father did for him. This love for the best—and most of all for wisdom—begins with listening to your father's advice, but it goes beyond taking instructions. The love of wisdom becomes a lifelong quest that may make you wiser than your father.

¹⁰Listen, my son, accept what I say,
and the years of your life will be many.
¹¹I guide you in the way of wisdom
and lead you along straight paths.

ᵃ6 Or *will direct your paths.*   ᵇ12 Hebrew; Septuagint / *and he punishes*   ᵃ7 Or *Whatever else you get*

¹²When you walk, your steps will not be
        hampered;
    when you run, you will not stumble.
¹³Hold on to instruction, do not let it go;
    guard it well, for it is your life.
¹⁴Do not set foot on the path of the wicked
    or walk in the way of evil men.
¹⁵Avoid it, do not travel on it;
    turn from it and go on your way.
¹⁶For they cannot sleep till they do evil;
    they are robbed of slumber till they make
        someone fall.
¹⁷They eat the bread of wickedness
    and drink the wine of violence.

¹⁸The path of the righteous is like the first gleam
        of dawn,
    shining ever brighter till the full light of day.
¹⁹But the way of the wicked is like deep
        darkness;
    they do not know what makes them stumble.

²⁰My son, pay attention to what I say;
    listen closely to my words.
²¹Do not let them out of your sight,
    keep them within your heart;
²²for they are life to those who find them
    and health to a man's whole body.
²³Above all else, guard your heart,
    for it is the wellspring of life.
²⁴Put away perversity from your mouth;
    keep corrupt talk far from your lips.
²⁵Let your eyes look straight ahead,
    fix your gaze directly before you.
²⁶Make level*b* paths for your feet
    and take only ways that are firm.
²⁷Do not swerve to the right or the left;
    keep your foot from evil.

■ Warning Against Adultery

5 My son, pay attention to my wisdom,
    listen well to my words of insight,
²that you may maintain discretion
    and your lips may preserve knowledge.
³For the lips of an adulteress drip honey,
    and her speech is smoother than oil;
⁴but in the end she is bitter as gall,
    sharp as a double-edged sword.
⁵Her feet go down to death;
    her steps lead straight to the grave.*a*
⁶She gives no thought to the way of life;
    her paths are crooked, but she knows it not.

⁷Now then, my sons, listen to me;
    do not turn aside from what I say.
⁸Keep to a path far from her,
    do not go near the door of her house,
⁹lest you give your best strength to others
    and your years to one who is cruel,
¹⁰lest strangers feast on your wealth
    and your toil enrich another man's house.
¹¹At the end of your life you will groan,
    when your flesh and body are spent.
¹²You will say, "How I hated discipline!
    How my heart spurned correction!
¹³I would not obey my teachers

or listen to my instructors.
¹⁴I have come to the brink of utter ruin
    in the midst of the whole assembly."

¹⁵Drink water from your own cistern,
    running water from your own well.
¹⁶Should your springs overflow in the streets,
    your streams of water in the public squares?
¹⁷Let them be yours alone,
    never to be shared with strangers.
¹⁸May your fountain be blessed,
    and may you rejoice in the wife of your
        youth.
¹⁹A loving doe, a graceful deer —
    may her breasts satisfy you always,
    may you ever be captivated by her love.
²⁰Why be captivated, my son, by an adulteress?
    Why embrace the bosom of another man's
        wife?

²¹For a man's ways are in full view of the LORD,
    and he examines all his paths.
²²The evil deeds of a wicked man ensnare him;
    the cords of his sin hold him fast.
²³He will die for lack of discipline,
    led astray by his own great folly.

■ Warnings Against Folly

6 My son, if you have put up security for your
    neighbour,
    if you have struck hands in pledge for
        another,
²if you have been trapped by what you said,
    ensnared by the words of your mouth,
³then do this, my son, to free yourself,
    since you have fallen into your neighbour's
        hands:
Go and humble yourself;
    press your plea with your neighbour!
⁴Allow no sleep to your eyes,
    no slumber to your eyelids.
⁵Free yourself, like a gazelle from the hand of
        the hunter,
    like a bird from the snare of the fowler.

6:1 ■ DANGER IN DEBT
Proverbs warns against "putting up security" for a
neighbour — something like co-signing a loan for a
friend who doesn't otherwise qualify. Proverbs
supports generosity, but not open-ended charity in
which the amount you must give and the timing
are determined by circumstances beyond your
control. Too often it leads to disaster. (See also
11:15; 17:18; 22:26–27.)

⁶Go to the ant, you sluggard;
    consider its ways and be wise!
⁷It has no commander,
    no overseer or ruler,
⁸yet it stores its provisions in summer
    and gathers its food at harvest.

⁹How long will you lie there, you sluggard?
    When will you get up from your sleep?
¹⁰A little sleep, a little slumber,

b 26 Or Consider the   *a 5 Hebrew Sheol*

a little folding of the hands to rest—
11and poverty will come on you like a bandit
and scarcity like an armed man.*

12A scoundrel and villain,
who goes about with a corrupt mouth,
13 who winks with his eye,
signals with his feet
and motions with his fingers,
14 who plots evil with deceit in his heart—
he always stirs up dissension.
15Therefore disaster will overtake him in an
instant;
he will suddenly be destroyed—without
remedy.

16There are six things the LORD hates,
seven that are detestable to him:
17 haughty eyes,
a lying tongue,
hands that shed innocent blood,
18 a heart that devises wicked schemes,
feet that are quick to rush into evil,
19 a false witness who pours out lies
and a man who stirs up dissension among
brothers.

■ Warning Against Adultery
20My son, keep your father's commands
and do not forsake your mother's teaching.
21Bind them upon your heart for ever;
fasten them around your neck.
22When you walk, they will guide you;
when you sleep, they will watch over you;
when you awake, they will speak to you.
23For these commands are a lamp,
this teaching is a light,
and the corrections of discipline
are the way to life,
24keeping you from the immoral woman,
from the smooth tongue of the wayward
wife.
25Do not lust in your heart after her beauty
or let her captivate you with her eyes,
26for the prostitute reduces you to a loaf of
bread,
and the adulteress preys upon your very life.
27Can a man scoop fire into his lap
without his clothes being burned?
28Can a man walk on hot coals
without his feet being scorched?
29So is he who sleeps with another man's wife;
no-one who touches her will go unpunished.

30Men do not despise a thief if he steals
to satisfy his hunger when he is starving.
31Yet if he is caught, he must pay sevenfold,
though it costs him all the wealth of his
house.
32But a man who commits adultery lacks
judgment;
whoever does so destroys himself.
33Blows and disgrace are his lot,
and his shame will never be wiped away;

34for jealousy arouses a husband's fury,
and he will show no mercy when he takes
revenge.
35He will not accept any compensation;
he will refuse the bribe, however great it is.

■ Warning Against the Adulteress
7 My son, keep my words
and store up my commands within you.
2Keep my commands and you will live;
guard my teachings as the apple of your eye.
3Bind them on your fingers;
write them on the tablet of your heart.
4Say to wisdom, "You are my sister,"
and call understanding your kinsman;
5they will keep you from the adulteress,
from the wayward wife with her seductive
words.

7:2 ■ THE APPLE OF YOUR EYE
The "apple of your eye" is an Old English
expression for the eye's centre, or pupil. The
whole body is tuned to protect that pupil from
harm: eyelids reflexively snap shut at the slightest
hint of danger; tear ducts bathe your eye with a
cleansing liquid if any irritant enters; nerve endings
scream "danger" at the slightest pain or pressure.
Proverbs urges you to take as much care of its
teachings as you do of your eye.

6At the window of my house
I looked out through the lattice.
7I saw among the simple,
I noticed among the young men,
a youth who lacked judgment.
8He was going down the street near her corner,
walking along in the direction of her house
9at twilight, as the day was fading,
as the dark of night set in.

10Then out came a woman to meet him,
dressed like a prostitute and with crafty
intent.
11(She is loud and defiant,
her feet never stay at home;
12now in the street, now in the squares,
at every corner she lurks.)
13She took hold of him and kissed him
and with a brazen face she said:

14"I have fellowship offerings* at home;
today I fulfilled my vows.
15So I came out to meet you;
I looked for you and have found you!
16I have covered my bed
with coloured linens from Egypt.
17I have perfumed my bed
with myrrh, aloes and cinnamon.
18Come, let's drink deep of love till morning;
let's enjoy ourselves with love!
19My husband is not at home;
he has gone on a long journey.

*11 Or like a vagrant / and scarcity like a beggar   *14 Traditionally peace offerings

²⁰He took his purse filled with money
and will not be home till full moon."

²¹With persuasive words she led him astray;
she seduced him with her smooth talk.
²²All at once he followed her
like an ox going to the slaughter,
like a deer^b stepping into a noose^c
²³ till an arrow pierces his liver,
like a bird darting into a snare,
little knowing it will cost him his life.

²⁴Now then, my sons, listen to me;
pay attention to what I say.
²⁵Do not let your heart turn to her ways
or stray into her paths.
²⁶Many are the victims she has brought down;
her slain are a mighty throng.
²⁷Her house is a highway to the grave,^d
leading down to the chambers of death.

■ Wisdom's Call

8 Does not wisdom call out?
Does not understanding raise her voice?
²On the heights along the way,
where the paths meet, she takes her stand;
³beside the gates leading into the city,
at the entrances, she cries aloud:
⁴"To you, O men, I call out;
I raise my voice to all mankind.
⁵You who are simple, gain prudence;
you who are foolish, gain understanding.
⁶Listen, for I have worthy things to say;
I open my lips to speak what is right.
⁷My mouth speaks what is true,
for my lips detest wickedness.
⁸All the words of my mouth are just;
none of them is crooked or perverse.
⁹To the discerning all of them are right;
they are faultless to those who have
knowledge.
¹⁰Choose my instruction instead of silver,
knowledge rather than choice gold,
¹¹for wisdom is more precious than rubies,
and nothing you desire can compare with
her.

¹²"I, wisdom, dwell together with prudence;
I possess knowledge and discretion.
¹³To fear the LORD is to hate evil;
I hate pride and arrogance,
evil behaviour and perverse speech.
¹⁴Counsel and sound judgment are mine;
I have understanding and power.
¹⁵By me kings reign
and rulers make laws that are just;
¹⁶by me princes govern,
and all nobles who rule on earth.^a
¹⁷I love those who love me,
and those who seek me find me.
¹⁸With me are riches and honour,
enduring wealth and prosperity.
¹⁹My fruit is better than fine gold;
what I yield surpasses choice silver.

²⁰I walk in the way of righteousness,
along the paths of justice,
²¹bestowing wealth on those who love me
and making their treasuries full.

8:13 ■ THE FEAR OF THE LORD
The phrase "fear of the LORD" doesn't mean fright
or terror. It means "a good relationship with God",
based on reverence and respect for him and his
commands. Here, for instance, the fear of the
Lord means righteous living.

²²"The LORD brought me forth as the first of his
works,^{b, c}
before his deeds of old;
²³I was appointed^d from eternity,
from the beginning, before the world began.
²⁴When there were no oceans, I was given birth,
when there were no springs abounding with
water;
²⁵before the mountains were settled in place,
before the hills, I was given birth,
²⁶before he made the earth or its fields
or any of the dust of the world.
²⁷I was there when he set the heavens in place,
when he marked out the horizon on the face
of the deep,
²⁸when he established the clouds above
and fixed securely the fountains of the deep,
²⁹when he gave the sea its boundary
so that the waters would not overstep his
command,
and when he marked out the foundations of the
earth.
³⁰ Then I was the craftsman at his side.
I was filled with delight day after day,
rejoicing always in his presence,
³¹rejoicing in his whole world
and delighting in mankind.

³²"Now then, my sons, listen to me;
blessed are those who keep my ways.
³³Listen to my instruction and be wise;
do not ignore it.
³⁴Blessed is the man who listens to me,
watching daily at my doors,
waiting at my doorway.
³⁵For whoever finds me finds life
and receives favour from the LORD.
³⁶But whoever fails to find me harms himself;
all who hate me love death."

■ Invitations of Wisdom and of Folly

9 Wisdom has built her house;
she has hewn out its seven pillars.
²She has prepared her meat and mixed her wine;
she has also set her table.
³She has sent out her maids, and she calls
from the highest point of the city.
⁴"Let all who are simple come in here!"

^b22 Syriac (see also Septuagint); Hebrew *fool*   ^c22 The meaning of the Hebrew for this line is uncertain.   ^d27 Hebrew *Sheol*   ^a16 Many Hebrew
manuscripts and Septuagint; most Hebrew manuscripts *and nobles—all righteous rulers*   ^b22 Or *way;* or *dominion*   ^c22 Or *The LORD possessed me at
the beginning of his work;* or *The LORD brought me forth at the beginning of his work*   ^d23 Or *fashioned*

she says to those who lack judgment.
⁵"Come, eat my food
　　and drink the wine I have mixed.
⁶Leave your simple ways and you will live;
　　walk in the way of understanding.

⁷"Whoever corrects a mocker invites insult,
　　whoever rebukes a wicked man incurs abuse.
⁸Do not rebuke a mocker or he will hate you;
　　rebuke a wise man and he will love you.
⁹Instruct a wise man and he will be wiser still;
　　teach a righteous man and he will add to his
　　　learning.

¹⁰"The fear of the LORD is the beginning of
　　wisdom,
　　and knowledge of the Holy One is
　　understanding.
¹¹For through me your days will be many,
　　and years will be added to your life.
¹²If you are wise, your wisdom will reward you;
　　if you are a mocker, you alone will suffer."

¹³The woman Folly is loud;
　　she is undisciplined and without knowledge.
¹⁴She sits at the door of her house,
　　on a seat at the highest point of the city,
¹⁵calling out to those who pass by,
　　who go straight on their way.
¹⁶"Let all who are simple come in here!"
　　she says to those who lack judgment.
¹⁷"Stolen water is sweet;
　　food eaten in secret is delicious!"
¹⁸But little do they know that the dead are there,
　　that her guests are in the depths of the
　　　grave.*ᵃ*

■ PROVERBS OF SOLOMON

10 The proverbs of Solomon:

A wise son brings joy to his father,
　　but a foolish son grief to his mother.

10:1 ■ HEBREW POETRY

"Parallelism" is a technical term for the form of
Hebrew poetry that repeats a thought in slightly
different ways. "Synonymous parallelism" is found
in Proverbs 15:30, "A cheerful look brings joy to
the heart, and good news gives health to the
bones." "Antithetical parallelism", in which a
thought is followed by its opposite, is found in
14:30, "A heart at peace gives life to the body,
but envy rots the bones."

In studying parallelism the trick is to compare
each part with its pair in the other half of the
proverb. For instance, in 14:30 "a heart at peace"
pairs with its opposite, "envy", and "rots the
bones" is the opposite of "gives life to the body".
Sometimes these comparisons bare subtle shades
of meaning.

²Ill-gotten treasures are of no value,
　　but righteousness delivers from death.

³The LORD does not let the righteous go hungry
　　but he thwarts the craving of the wicked.

⁴Lazy hands make a man poor,
　　but diligent hands bring wealth.

⁵He who gathers crops in summer is a wise son,

■ GOD AND "HOW-TO-SUCCEED" INSIGHT
DOES PROVERBS CARE MORE FOR SUCCESS THAN FOR GOD?

THE FEAR OF THE LORD IS THE
BEGINNING OF WISDOM. ■ 9:10

Bookshops are full of "how-to" books, each
promising to teach you how to make a success
of yourself by just following a few simple rules.
Is Proverbs an ancient "how-to" book? It seems,
at first look, more interested in success and
prosperity than in God. Many of the proverbs
can be adopted by those who have no love for
God.

But if you look at Proverbs as a book,
rather than a collection of unrelated fragments,
you will find that its "how-tos" of wise living
can't be separated from God. While some
proverbs observe the hard facts of life – that
bribes are effective, for instance, or that money
does buy friends of a kind – the book never for
a moment endorses success techniques that
involve immorality. More importantly, a deep
sense of people's sin and their utter
dependence on God pervades Proverbs.

Wisdom, that fundamental tool for living, starts
with the fear of God and leads to a knowledge
of him.

The words *LORD* or *God* are actually
mentioned nearly 100 times, so a complete
study of God's place in Proverbs takes you
through virtually the entire book.
*Proverbs on God's relationship to
wisdom*: 1:7; 2:5–9; 8:22–31; 9:10; 22:17–19.
Proverbs on sin: 15:8; 16:6; 20:9;
24:11–12; 28:9,13.
Proverbs on trust in God: 3:5–12;
14:26–27; 16:20; 18:10; 19:21; 21:31;
29:25–26; 30:5–9.
Proverbs on God's blessing:
10:22,27,29; 15:16.
Other proverbs of particular interest:
11:1; 17:3; 19:3; 20:12; 21:3; 28:5.

□ LIFE QUESTIONS:
What are your plans for success? Is God's will
the basis of your plans or an afterthought?

ᵃ 18 Hebrew *Sheol*

but he who sleeps during harvest is a
disgraceful son.

6Blessings crown the head of the righteous,
but violence overwhelms the mouth of the
wicked.*a*

7The memory of the righteous will be a blessing,
but the name of the wicked will rot.

8The wise in heart accept commands,
but a chattering fool comes to ruin.

9The man of integrity walks securely,
but he who takes crooked paths will be
found out.

10He who winks maliciously causes grief,
and a chattering fool comes to ruin.

11The mouth of the righteous is a fountain of life,
but violence overwhelms the mouth of the
wicked.

12Hatred stirs up dissension,
but love covers over all wrongs.

10:12 ■ LOVE IS THE GREATEST

If you think of love as restricted to the New
Testament, Proverbs will surprise you. Here love is
the all-purpose cure, covering all wrongs. It is
worth searching for. It should be expressed
openly.

Some of the proverbs on love are found in the
following passages: 3:3–4; 9:8; 10:12; 14:22;
15:17; 16:6; 17:9; 19:22; 20:6,28; 21:21; 27:5.

13Wisdom is found on the lips of the discerning,

but a rod is for the back of him who lacks
judgment.

14Wise men store up knowledge,
but the mouth of a fool invites ruin.

15The wealth of the rich is their fortified city,
but poverty is the ruin of the poor.

16The wages of the righteous bring them life,
but the income of the wicked brings them
punishment.

17He who heeds discipline shows the way to life,
but whoever ignores correction leads others
astray.

18He who conceals his hatred has lying lips,
and whoever spreads slander is a fool.

19When words are many, sin is not absent,
but he who holds his tongue is wise.

20The tongue of the righteous is choice silver,
but the heart of the wicked is of little value.

21The lips of the righteous nourish many,
but fools die for lack of judgment.

22The blessing of the LORD brings wealth,
and he adds no trouble to it.

23A fool finds pleasure in evil conduct,
but a man of understanding delights in
wisdom.

24What the wicked dreads will overtake him;
what the righteous desire will be granted.

25When the storm has swept by, the wicked are
gone,
but the righteous stand firm for ever.

26As vinegar to the teeth and smoke to the eyes,
so is a sluggard to those who send him.

■ WHAT MAKES PEOPLE POOR?
A CLEAR-EYED VIEW OF WEALTH AND POVERTY

INSIGHT

THE WEALTH OF THE RICH IS THEIR
FORTIFIED CITY, BUT POVERTY IS THE
RUIN OF THE POOR. ■ 10:15

"Poor people are lazy," says one person.
Someone else claims the opposite: "They are
poor because the rich control the system."
People tend to oversimplify when they discuss
wealth and poverty. Curiously, both sides may
quote Proverbs to prove their point.
        You have to read all of Proverbs to get
its subtle view. It says people are poor for
various reasons: because of laziness and
drunkenness, but also because the rich oppress
them. People get rich for various reasons too:
because of hard work, because of the Lord's
blessing, because they cheated.

Proverbs gives an even-handed view of
what money does for people. Wealth brings
benefits, including eager friends, Proverbs
says; but it also brings worries and troubles.
Proverbs strongly urges the rich and powerful
to be generous and fair to poor people. It
remains remarkably clear-eyed about the
tangled causes of poverty and about the
dangers and benefits of wealth.
        Proverbs on money: 10:4,15,22;
11:4,16,28; 13:8,18,22–23; 14:20,23,31;
15:16; 18:23; 19:1,4,17; 20:13; 21:5,17;
22:1–2,4,7,9,16,22–23; 23:5;
28:3,6,8,11,19,20,22,27; 29:7,14; 30:7–9.

□ LIFE QUESTIONS:
Think of the richest and the poorest people
you know. Have stereotypes about wealth and
poverty affected your attitude towards them?

---

*a*6 Or *but the mouth of the wicked conceals violence*; also in verse 11

27The fear of the LORD adds length to life,
  but the years of the wicked are cut short.

28The prospect of the righteous is joy,
  but the hopes of the wicked come to
    nothing.

29The way of the LORD is a refuge for the
    righteous,
  but it is the ruin of those who do evil.

30The righteous will never be uprooted,
  but the wicked will not remain in the land.

31The mouth of the righteous brings forth
    wisdom,
  but a perverse tongue will be cut out.

32The lips of the righteous know what is fitting,
  but the mouth of the wicked only what is
    perverse.

11 The LORD abhors dishonest scales,
     but accurate weights are his delight.

2When pride comes, then comes disgrace,
  but with humility comes wisdom.

3The integrity of the upright guides them,
  but the unfaithful are destroyed by their
    duplicity.

4Wealth is worthless in the day of wrath,
  but righteousness delivers from death.

5The righteousness of the blameless makes a
    straight way for them,
  but the wicked are brought down by their
    own wickedness.

6The righteousness of the upright delivers them,
  but the unfaithful are trapped by evil desires.

7When a wicked man dies, his hope perishes;
  all he expected from his power comes to
    nothing.

8The righteous man is rescued from trouble,
  and it comes on the wicked instead.

9With his mouth the godless destroys his
    neighbour,
  but through knowledge the righteous escape.

10When the righteous prosper, the city rejoices;
  when the wicked perish, there are shouts of
    joy.

11Through the blessing of the upright a city is
    exalted,
  but by the mouth of the wicked it is
    destroyed.

12A man who lacks judgment derides his
    neighbour,
  but a man of understanding holds his tongue.

13A gossip betrays a confidence,
  but a trustworthy man keeps a secret.

14For lack of guidance a nation falls,
  but many advisers make victory sure.

15He who puts up security for another will surely
    suffer,
  but whoever refuses to strike hands in
    pledge is safe.

16A kind-hearted woman gains respect,
  but ruthless men gain only wealth.

17A kind man benefits himself,
  but a cruel man brings trouble on himself.

18The wicked man earns deceptive wages,
  but he who sows righteousness reaps a sure
    reward.

19The truly righteous man attains life,
  but he who pursues evil goes to his death.

20The LORD detests men of perverse heart
  but he delights in those whose ways are
    blameless.

21Be sure of this: The wicked will not go
    unpunished,
  but those who are righteous will go free.

22Like a gold ring in a pig's snout
  is a beautiful woman who shows no
    discretion.

11:22 ■ SKIN-DEEP BEAUTY
Throughout Proverbs, character is what counts.
When not matched by inward beauty, good looks
seem ridiculous, as this saying humorously
suggests.

23The desire of the righteous ends only in good,
  but the hope of the wicked only in wrath.

24One man gives freely, yet gains even more;
  another withholds unduly, but comes to
    poverty.

25A generous man will prosper;
  he who refreshes others will himself be
    refreshed.

26People curse the man who hoards grain,
  but blessing crowns him who is willing to
    sell.

27He who seeks good finds goodwill,
  but evil comes to him who searches for it.

28Whoever trusts in his riches will fall,
  but the righteous will thrive like a green leaf.

29He who brings trouble on his family will inherit
    only wind,
  and the fool will be servant to the wise.

30The fruit of the righteous is a tree of life,
  and he who wins souls is wise.

31If the righteous receive their due on earth,
  how much more the ungodly and the sinner!

12 Whoever loves discipline loves knowledge,
     but he who hates correction is stupid.

2A good man obtains favour from the LORD,
  but the LORD condemns a crafty man.

³A man cannot be established through
  wickedness,
  but the righteous cannot be uprooted.

⁴A wife of noble character is her husband's
  crown,
  but a disgraceful wife is like decay in his
  bones.

⁵The plans of the righteous are just,
  but the advice of the wicked is deceitful.

⁶The words of the wicked lie in wait for blood,
  but the speech of the upright rescues them.

⁷Wicked men are overthrown and are no more,
  but the house of the righteous stands firm.

⁸A man is praised according to his wisdom,
  but men with warped minds are despised.

⁹Better to be a nobody and yet have a servant
  than pretend to be somebody and have no
  food.

¹⁰A righteous man cares for the needs of his
  animal,
  but the kindest acts of the wicked are cruel.

¹¹He who works his land will have abundant
  food,
  but he who chases fantasies lacks judgment.

¹²The wicked desire the plunder of evil men,
  but the root of the righteous flourishes.

¹³An evil man is trapped by his sinful talk,
  but a righteous man escapes trouble.

¹⁴From the fruit of his lips a man is filled with
  good things
  as surely as the work of his hands rewards
  him.

¹⁵The way of a fool seems right to him,
  but a wise man listens to advice.

¹⁶A fool shows his annoyance at once,
  but a prudent man overlooks an insult.

¹⁷A truthful witness gives honest testimony,
  but a false witness tells lies.

12:17 ■ DEEPER MEANINGS

Some proverbs, disarmingly obvious at first
glance, offer deep truth when chewed on. For
instance, verse 17 seems merely to repeat the
obvious. But its underlying meaning is that a
person's character determines his or her actions.
You can reflect at length on what this implies
about why you do what you do.

¹⁸Reckless words pierce like a sword,
  but the tongue of the wise brings healing.

¹⁹Truthful lips endure for ever,
  but a lying tongue lasts only a moment.

²⁰There is deceit in the hearts of those who plot
  evil,
  but joy for those who promote peace.

²¹No harm befalls the righteous,
  but the wicked have their fill of trouble.

²²The LORD detests lying lips,
  but he delights in men who are truthful.

²³A prudent man keeps his knowledge to himself,
  but the heart of fools blurts out folly.

²⁴Diligent hands will rule,
  but laziness ends in slave labour.

²⁵An anxious heart weighs a man down,
  but a kind word cheers him up.

²⁶A righteous man is cautious in friendship,ᵃ
  but the way of the wicked leads them astray.

²⁷The lazy man does not roastᵇ his game,
  but the diligent man prizes his possessions.

²⁸In the way of righteousness there is life;
  along that path is immortality.

13 A wise son heeds his father's instruction,
    but a mocker does not listen to rebuke.

²From the fruit of his lips a man enjoys good
  things,
  but the unfaithful have a craving for violence.

³He who guards his lips guards his life,
  but he who speaks rashly will come to ruin.

⁴The sluggard craves and gets nothing,
  but the desires of the diligent are fully
  satisfied.

⁵The righteous hate what is false,
  but the wicked bring shame and disgrace.

⁶Righteousness guards the man of integrity,
  but wickedness overthrows the sinner.

⁷One man pretends to be rich, yet has nothing;
  another pretends to be poor, yet has great
  wealth.

⁸A man's riches may ransom his life,
  but a poor man hears no threat.

⁹The light of the righteous shines brightly,
  but the lamp of the wicked is snuffed out.

¹⁰Pride only breeds quarrels,
  but wisdom is found in those who take
  advice.

¹¹Dishonest money dwindles away,
  but he who gathers money little by little
  makes it grow.

¹²Hope deferred makes the heart sick,
  but a longing fulfilled is a tree of life.

¹³He who scorns instruction will pay for it,
  but he who respects a command is rewarded.

¹⁴The teaching of the wise is a fountain of life,
  turning a man from the snares of death.

¹⁵Good understanding wins favour,
  but the way of the unfaithful is hard.ᵃ

¹⁶Every prudent man acts out of knowledge,
  but a fool exposes his folly.

ᵃ26 Or man is a guide to his neighbour   ᵇ27 The meaning of the Hebrew for this word is uncertain.   ᵃ15 Or unfaithful does not endure

¹⁷A wicked messenger falls into trouble,
　　but a trustworthy envoy brings healing.

¹⁸He who ignores discipline comes to poverty
　　and shame,
　　but whoever heeds correction is honoured.

¹⁹A longing fulfilled is sweet to the soul,
　　but fools detest turning from evil.

²⁰He who walks with the wise grows wise,
　　but a companion of fools suffers harm.

²¹Misfortune pursues the sinner,
　　but prosperity is the reward of the righteous.

²²A good man leaves an inheritance for his
　　children's children,
　　but a sinner's wealth is stored up for the
　　righteous.

²³A poor man's field may produce abundant food,
　　but injustice sweeps it away.

²⁴He who spares the rod hates his son,
　　but he who loves him is careful to discipline
　　him.

²⁵The righteous eat to their hearts' content,
　　but the stomach of the wicked goes hungry.

14 The wise woman builds her house,
　　but with her own hands the foolish one
　　tears hers down.

²He whose walk is upright fears the LORD,
　　but he whose ways are devious despises him.

³A fool's talk brings a rod to his back,
　　but the lips of the wise protect them.

⁴Where there are no oxen, the manger is empty,
　　but from the strength of an ox comes an
　　abundant harvest.

⁵A truthful witness does not deceive,
　　but a false witness pours out lies.

⁶The mocker seeks wisdom and finds none,
　　but knowledge comes easily to the
　　discerning.

⁷Stay away from a foolish man,
　　for you will not find knowledge on his lips.

⁸The wisdom of the prudent is to give thought
　　to their ways,
　　but the folly of fools is deception.

⁹Fools mock at making amends for sin,
　　but goodwill is found among the upright.

¹⁰Each heart knows its own bitterness,
　　and no-one else can share its joy.

¹¹The house of the wicked will be destroyed,
　　but the tent of the upright will flourish.

¹²There is a way that seems right to a man,
　　but in the end it leads to death.

14:12 ■ BE CAREFUL
Proverbs offers common sense, but doesn't
encourage simply trusting your own sense.
Choices that seem perfectly right may end up
destroying you. That is precisely why people need
to cultivate wisdom: what looks good often isn't.

---

¹³Even in laughter the heart may ache,
　　and joy may end in grief.

■ THE SUPREME GIFT OF WISDOM   INSIGHT
FIRST, LEARN TO LISTEN

HE WHO WALKS WITH THE WISE GROWS
WISE, BUT A COMPANION OF FOOLS
SUFFERS HARM. ■ 13:20

Proverbs judges every thought or action by one
standard: "Is this wise?" The word *wisdom*
brings up pictures of grey-haired old men
muttering obscure philosophic maxims. But that
is almost the opposite of what Proverbs means
by the word. Wisdom is above all practical and
down to earth. Young people as well as old can
and should have it. Wisdom teaches you how to
live. It combines understanding with
discipline — the kind of discipline an athlete
needs in training. It also adds a healthy dose of
good common sense — except that common
sense isn't, and never has been, common.

How do you become a wise person?
You must first begin to listen. Wisdom is freely
available to those who will stop talking and
start paying attention — to God and his Word,
to parents, to wise counsellors. Anybody can
become wise, Proverbs says. Wisdom is not
reserved for a brainy elite. But becoming wise
requires self-discipline to study and humbly
seek wisdom at every opportunity.
　　Proverbs on becoming a wise person:
2:1–6; 9:1–10; 10:1,5,8,14,19,23; 11:2; 12:18;
13:10,20; 14:8; 15:7,31; 16:23; 17:24; 18:15;
19:11,20; 20:1; 21:11,20,30; 23:4;
29:3,8,11,15; 30:5–6.

☐ LIFE QUESTIONS:
Think over the last two years of your life. To
whom do you listen? Who has the greatest
influence on you?

¹⁴The faithless will be fully repaid for their ways,
    and the good man rewarded for his.

¹⁵A simple man believes anything,
    but a prudent man gives thought to his steps.

¹⁶A wise man fears the LORD and shuns evil,
    but a fool is hotheaded and reckless.

¹⁷A quick-tempered man does foolish things,
    and a crafty man is hated.

¹⁸The simple inherit folly,
    but the prudent are crowned with
        knowledge.

¹⁹Evil men will bow down in the presence of the
        good,
    and the wicked at the gates of the righteous.

²⁰The poor are shunned even by their
        neighbours,
    but the rich have many friends.

14:20 ■ LUCKY RICH

Rich people have many friends, whereas the poor
often get ignored. That's the way life is. But,
according to the next proverb (verse 21), life isn't
meant to be "the way it is". Verse 31 goes on to
show God himself closely involved in the way we
treat poor people.

---

²¹He who despises his neighbour sins,
    but blessed is he who is kind to the needy.

²²Do not those who plot evil go astray?
    But those who plan what is good find*a* love
        and faithfulness.

²³All hard work brings a profit,
    but mere talk leads only to poverty.

²⁴The wealth of the wise is their crown,
    but the folly of fools yields folly.

²⁵A truthful witness saves lives,
    but a false witness is deceitful.

²⁶He who fears the LORD has a secure fortress,
    and for his children it will be a refuge.

²⁷The fear of the LORD is a fountain of life,
    turning a man from the snares of death.

²⁸A large population is a king's glory,
    but without subjects a prince is ruined.

²⁹A patient man has great understanding,
    but a quick-tempered man displays folly.

³⁰A heart at peace gives life to the body,
    but envy rots the bones.

³¹He who oppresses the poor shows contempt
        for their Maker,
    but whoever is kind to the needy honours
        God.

³²When calamity comes, the wicked are brought
        down,
    but even in death the righteous have a
        refuge.

³³Wisdom reposes in the heart of the discerning
    and even among fools she lets herself be
        known.*b*

³⁴Righteousness exalts a nation,
    but sin is a disgrace to any people.

³⁵A king delights in a wise servant,
    but a shameful servant incurs his wrath.

15 A gentle answer turns away wrath,
    but a harsh word stirs up anger.

²The tongue of the wise commends knowledge,
    but the mouth of the fool gushes folly.

³The eyes of the LORD are everywhere,
    keeping watch on the wicked and the good.

■ A MATTER OF LIFE AND DEATH   INSIGHT
MORE THAN MERE SURVIVAL

THERE IS A WAY THAT SEEMS RIGHT TO
A MAN, BUT IN THE END IT LEADS TO
DEATH. ■ 14:12

Proverbs frequently talks about life and death.
Wise living, it says, tends to make you live
longer, while foolish living will push you into an
early grave.
    If you take this observation at face value,
you'll have a problem: plenty of people who live
foolishly survive into old age. But the concept of
life and death in Proverbs includes much more
than physical survival. By life, Proverbs means
"real living" full of peace and joy and wisdom.
By death, it means spiritual as well as physical

decay. A person who misses the way of
wisdom may be as good as dead, even though
he or she is still walking around.
    Proverbs on "real living": 3:18,21–22;
4:23; 8:34–36; 10:11,16; 12:28; 13:12;
14:27,30; 15:4,27; 18:21; 19:23; 21:21; 28:16.
    Proverbs on "real dying": 2:16–18;
5:3–6,22–23; 10:21; 14:12,32; 15:10; 19:16;
21:25; 27:20.

☐ LIFE QUESTIONS:
Can you remember a specific experience that
represents, for you, "real living"? How about
"real dying"?

---

a 22 Or *show*   *b* 33 Hebrew; Septuagint and Syriac / *but in the heart of fools she is not known*

⁴The tongue that brings healing is a tree of life,
  but a deceitful tongue crushes the spirit.

⁵A fool spurns his father's discipline,
  but whoever heeds correction shows
    prudence.

⁶The house of the righteous contains great
    treasure,
  but the income of the wicked brings them
    trouble.

⁷The lips of the wise spread knowledge;
  not so the hearts of fools.

⁸The LORD detests the sacrifice of the wicked,
  but the prayer of the upright pleases him.

⁹The LORD detests the way of the wicked
  but he loves those who pursue righteousness.

¹⁰Stern discipline awaits him who leaves the path;
  he who hates correction will die.

¹¹Death and Destruction*a* lie open before the
    LORD—
  how much more the hearts of men!

¹²A mocker resents correction;
  he will not consult the wise.

¹³A happy heart makes the face cheerful,
  but heartache crushes the spirit.

¹⁴The discerning heart seeks knowledge,
  but the mouth of a fool feeds on folly.

¹⁵All the days of the oppressed are wretched,
  but the cheerful heart has a continual feast.

¹⁶Better a little with the fear of the LORD
  than great wealth with turmoil.

¹⁷Better a meal of vegetables where there is love
  than a fattened calf with hatred.

¹⁸A hot-tempered man stirs up dissension,
  but a patient man calms a quarrel.

¹⁹The way of the sluggard is blocked with thorns,
  but the path of the upright is a highway.

²⁰A wise son brings joy to his father,
  but a foolish man despises his mother.

²¹Folly delights a man who lacks judgment,
  but a man of understanding keeps a straight
    course.

²²Plans fail for lack of counsel,
  but with many advisers they succeed.

²³A man finds joy in giving an apt reply—
  and how good is a timely word!

²⁴The path of life leads upward for the wise
  to keep him from going down to the grave.*b*

²⁵The LORD tears down the proud man's house
  but he keeps the widow's boundaries intact.

²⁶The LORD detests the thoughts of the wicked,
  but those of the pure are pleasing to him.

²⁷A greedy man brings trouble to his family,
  but he who hates bribes will live.

²⁸The heart of the righteous weighs its answers,
  but the mouth of the wicked gushes evil.

15:25 ■ POOR AND HELPLESS
In Old Testament society the most helpless person
was the widow. With no-one to protect her, she
could only watch as her late husband's land was
grabbed by bullying neighbours. But a widow was
never completely helpless. The Lord was on her
side. In the final analysis her condition was more
secure than that of her proud, rich neighbour.

²⁹The LORD is far from the wicked
  but he hears the prayer of the righteous.

³⁰A cheerful look brings joy to the heart,
  and good news gives health to the bones.

³¹He who listens to a life-giving rebuke
  will be at home among the wise.

³²He who ignores discipline despises himself,
  but whoever heeds correction gains
    understanding.

³³The fear of the LORD teaches a man wisdom,*c*
  and humility comes before honour.

16 To man belong the plans of the heart,
    but from the LORD comes the reply of the
    tongue.

²All a man's ways seem innocent to him,
  but motives are weighed by the LORD.

³Commit to the LORD whatever you do,
  and your plans will succeed.

⁴The LORD works out everything for his own
    ends—
  even the wicked for a day of disaster.

⁵The LORD detests all the proud of heart.
  Be sure of this: They will not go unpunished.

⁶Through love and faithfulness sin is atoned for;
  through the fear of the LORD a man avoids
    evil.

⁷When a man's ways are pleasing to the LORD,
  he makes even his enemies live at peace with
    him.

⁸Better a little with righteousness
  than much gain with injustice.

⁹In his heart a man plans his course,
  but the LORD determines his steps.

¹⁰The lips of a king speak as an oracle,
  and his mouth should not betray justice.

¹¹Honest scales and balances are from the LORD;
  all the weights in the bag are of his making.

¹²Kings detest wrongdoing,
  for a throne is established through
    righteousness.

¹³Kings take pleasure in honest lips;
  they value a man who speaks the truth.

a 11 Hebrew *Sheol and Abaddon*   *b* 24 Hebrew *Sheol*   *c* 33 Or *Wisdom teaches the fear of the LORD*

¹⁴A king's wrath is a messenger of death,
  but a wise man will appease it.

¹⁵When a king's face brightens, it means life;
  his favour is like a rain cloud in spring.

¹⁶How much better to get wisdom than gold,
  to choose understanding rather than silver!

¹⁷The highway of the upright avoids evil;
  he who guards his way guards his life.

¹⁸Pride goes before destruction,
  a haughty spirit before a fall.

¹⁹Better to be lowly in spirit and among the
    oppressed
  than to share plunder with the proud.

²⁰Whoever gives heed to instruction prospers,
  and blessed is he who trusts in the LORD.

²¹The wise in heart are called discerning,
  and pleasant words promote instruction.ᵃ

²²Understanding is a fountain of life to those who
    have it,
  but folly brings punishment to fools.

²³A wise man's heart guides his mouth,
  and his lips promote instruction.ᵇ

²⁴Pleasant words are a honeycomb,
  sweet to the soul and healing to the bones.

²⁵There is a way that seems right to a man,
  but in the end it leads to death.

²⁶The labourer's appetite works for him;
  his hunger drives him on.

²⁷A scoundrel plots evil,
  and his speech is like a scorching fire.

²⁸A perverse man stirs up dissension,
  and a gossip separates close friends.

²⁹A violent man entices his neighbour
  and leads him down a path that is not good.

³⁰He who winks with his eye is plotting
    perversity;
  he who purses his lips is bent on evil.

³¹Grey hair is a crown of splendour;
  it is attained by a righteous life.

³²Better a patient man than a warrior,
  a man who controls his temper than one
    who takes a city.

³³The lot is cast into the lap,
  but its every decision is from the LORD.

17 Better a dry crust with peace and quiet
  than a house full of feasting,ᵃ with strife.

²A wise servant will rule over a disgraceful son,
  and will share the inheritance as one of the
    brothers.

³The crucible for silver and the furnace for gold,
  but the LORD tests the heart.

⁴A wicked man listens to evil lips;
  a liar pays attention to a malicious tongue.

⁵He who mocks the poor shows contempt for
    their Maker;
  whoever gloats over disaster will not go
    unpunished.

⁶Children's children are a crown to the aged,
  and parents are the pride of their children.

⁷Arrogantᵇ lips are unsuited to a fool—
  how much worse lying lips to a ruler!

⁸A bribe is a charm to the one who gives it;
  wherever he turns, he succeeds.

⁹He who covers over an offence promotes love,
  but whoever repeats the matter separates
    close friends.

■ VERBAL DYNAMITE
EVEN TRUTHFUL WORDS CAN DAMAGE OTHER PEOPLE

INSIGHT

A PERVERSE MAN STIRS UP DISSENSION,
AND A GOSSIP SEPARATES CLOSE
FRIENDS. ■ 16:28

What could be wrong with just talking, as long
as you don't actually lie? Proverbs sees plenty
of danger. Words are dynamite; they can destroy
people. They should be carefully weighed before
they are spoken. Even truthful words can
damage. Yet they can also save a friend from
going wrong. Proverbs speaks strongly about
both the danger of gossip and the good done
when someone justly rebukes his or her friend.
      "The tongue has the power of life and
death," Proverbs 18:21 says, "and those who
love it will eat its fruit." Proverbs teaches the
skill of speaking so as to give life.

   Proverbs on the importance of words:
10:11,20; 12:14; 15:4; 17:10; 18:21; 25:11.
   Proverbs on the wrong way to speak:
6:16–19; 11:9,12–13; 12:18; 13:3; 16:27–28;
18:8,13; 26:23–28; 29:5.
   Proverbs on the right way to speak:
10:14,21,32; 12:25; 15:1,23,28; 16:13,23–24;
17:27–28; 25:12,15; 27:5–6; 28:23.
   Proverbs on the dangers of words:
10:19; 14:23.

□ LIFE QUESTIONS:
Have you said anything recently that you wish
you could take back? What are the most life-
giving words you've spoken lately?

---

¹⁰A rebuke impresses a man of discernment
 more than a hundred lashes a fool.

17:8 ■ BRIBERY WORKS WONDERS!
Proverbs is utterly realistic about the hard facts of
life. One is that bribery works. A complete
education ought to include that fact! But does that
make bribery right? No – just a few verses later
(verse 23), Proverbs condemns bribery.

¹¹An evil man is bent only on rebellion;
 a merciless official will be sent against him.

¹²Better to meet a bear robbed of her cubs
 than a fool in his folly.

¹³If a man pays back evil for good,
 evil will never leave his house.

¹⁴Starting a quarrel is like breaching a dam;
 so drop the matter before a dispute breaks
 out.

¹⁵Acquitting the guilty and condemning the
 innocent –
 the LORD detests them both.

¹⁶Of what use is money in the hand of a fool,
 since he has no desire to get wisdom?

¹⁷A friend loves at all times,
 and a brother is born for adversity.

17:17 ■ HOW TO BE A GOOD FRIEND
The Old Testament puts great emphasis on close
family relationships. Surprisingly, Proverbs rates a
good friend even higher, for he or she "sticks
closer than a brother" (18:24). Fair-weather friends
are common (14:20), and the wrong kind of
companions will bring you trouble. But a true
friend loves you at all times, even when things are
bad.
  Some key proverbs on being a good friend and
neighbour can be found in the following passages:
3:27–28; 11:12; 12:26; 17:9,17; 18:24; 22:24–25;
25:20; 26:18–19; 27:6,9–10,14,17; 28:23; 29:5.

¹⁸A man lacking in judgment strikes hands in
 pledge
 and puts up security for his neighbour.

¹⁹He who loves a quarrel loves sin;
 he who builds a high gate invites destruction.

²⁰A man of perverse heart does not prosper;
 he whose tongue is deceitful falls into
 trouble.

²¹To have a fool for a son brings grief;
 there is no joy for the father of a fool.

²²A cheerful heart is good medicine,
 but a crushed spirit dries up the bones.

²³A wicked man accepts a bribe in secret
 to pervert the course of justice.

²⁴A discerning man keeps wisdom in view,
 but a fool's eyes wander to the ends of the
 earth.

²⁵A foolish son brings grief to his father
 and bitterness to the one who bore him.

²⁶It is not good to punish an innocent man,
 or to flog officials for their integrity.

²⁷A man of knowledge uses words with restraint,
 and a man of understanding is
 even-tempered.

²⁸Even a fool is thought wise if he keeps silent,
 and discerning if he holds his tongue.

18 An unfriendly man pursues selfish ends;
 he defies all sound judgment.

²A fool finds no pleasure in understanding
 but delights in airing his own opinions.

³When wickedness comes, so does contempt,
 and with shame comes disgrace.

⁴The words of a man's mouth are deep waters,
 but the fountain of wisdom is a bubbling
 brook.

⁵It is not good to be partial to the wicked
 or to deprive the innocent of justice.

⁶A fool's lips bring him strife,
 and his mouth invites a beating.

⁷A fool's mouth is his undoing,
 and his lips are a snare to his soul.

⁸The words of a gossip are like choice morsels;
 they go down to a man's inmost parts.

⁹One who is slack in his work
 is brother to one who destroys.

¹⁰The name of the LORD is a strong tower;
 the righteous run to it and are safe.

¹¹The wealth of the rich is their fortified city;
 they imagine it an unscalable wall.

¹²Before his downfall a man's heart is proud,
 but humility comes before honour.

¹³He who answers before listening –
 that is his folly and his shame.

¹⁴A man's spirit sustains him in sickness,
 but a crushed spirit who can bear?

¹⁵The heart of the discerning acquires
 knowledge;
 the ears of the wise seek it out.

¹⁶A gift opens the way for the giver
 and ushers him into the presence of the
 great.

¹⁷The first to present his case seems right,
 till another comes forward and questions
 him.

¹⁸Casting the lot settles disputes
 and keeps strong opponents apart.

¹⁹An offended brother is more unyielding than a
      fortified city,
  and disputes are like the barred gates of a
      citadel.

²⁰From the fruit of his mouth a man's stomach is
      filled;
  with the harvest from his lips he is satisfied.

²¹The tongue has the power of life and death,
  and those who love it will eat its fruit.

²²He who finds a wife finds what is good
  and receives favour from the LORD.

²³A poor man pleads for mercy,
  but a rich man answers harshly.

²⁴A man of many companions may come to ruin,
  but there is a friend who sticks closer than a
      brother.

19 Better a poor man whose walk is
      blameless
  than a fool whose lips are perverse.

²It is not good to have zeal without knowledge,
  nor to be hasty and miss the way.

³A man's own folly ruins his life,
  yet his heart rages against the LORD.

⁴Wealth brings many friends,
  but a poor man's friend deserts him.

⁵A false witness will not go unpunished,
  and he who pours out lies will not go free.

⁶Many curry favour with a ruler,
  and everyone is the friend of a man who
      gives gifts.

⁷A poor man is shunned by all his relatives—
  how much more do his friends avoid him!
Though he pursues them with pleading,
  they are nowhere to be found.ᵃ

⁸He who gets wisdom loves his own soul;
  he who cherishes understanding prospers.

⁹A false witness will not go unpunished,
  and he who pours out lies will perish.

¹⁰It is not fitting for a fool to live in luxury—
  how much worse for a slave to rule over
      princes!

¹¹A man's wisdom gives him patience;
  it is to his glory to overlook an offence.

¹²A king's rage is like the roar of a lion,
  but his favour is like dew on the grass.

¹³A foolish son is his father's ruin,
  and a quarrelsome wife is like a constant
      dripping.

¹⁴Houses and wealth are inherited from parents,
  but a prudent wife is from the LORD.

¹⁵Laziness brings on deep sleep,
  and the shiftless man goes hungry.

¹⁶He who obeys instructions guards his life,

but he who is contemptuous of his ways will
      die.

¹⁷He who is kind to the poor lends to the LORD,
  and he will reward him for what he has
      done.

¹⁸Discipline your son, for in that there is hope;
  do not be a willing party to his death.

¹⁹A hot-tempered man must pay the penalty;
  if you rescue him, you will have to do it
      again.

²⁰Listen to advice and accept instruction,
  and in the end you will be wise.

²¹Many are the plans in a man's heart,
  but it is the LORD's purpose that prevails.

²²What a man desires is unfailing love;ᵇ
  better to be poor than a liar.

²³The fear of the LORD leads to life:
  Then one rests content, untouched by
      trouble.

²⁴The sluggard buries his hand in the dish;
  he will not even bring it back to his mouth!

²⁵Flog a mocker, and the simple will learn
      prudence;
  rebuke a discerning man, and he will gain
      knowledge.

²⁶He who robs his father and drives out his
      mother
  is a son who brings shame and disgrace.

²⁷Stop listening to instruction, my son,
  and you will stray from the words of
      knowledge.

²⁸A corrupt witness mocks at justice,
  and the mouth of the wicked gulps down
      evil.

²⁹Penalties are prepared for mockers,
  and beatings for the backs of fools.

20 Wine is a mocker and beer a brawler;
  whoever is led astray by them is not wise.

²A king's wrath is like the roar of a lion;
  he who angers him forfeits his life.

³It is to a man's honour to avoid strife,
  but every fool is quick to quarrel.

⁴A sluggard does not plough in season;
  so at harvest time he looks but finds nothing.

⁵The purposes of a man's heart are deep waters,
  but a man of understanding draws them out.

⁶Many a man claims to have unfailing love,
  but a faithful man who can find?

⁷The righteous man leads a blameless life;
  blessed are his children after him.

⁸When a king sits on his throne to judge,
  he winnows out all evil with his eyes.

⁹Who can say, "I have kept my heart pure;
  I am clean and without sin"?

ᵃ7 The meaning of the Hebrew for this sentence is uncertain.   ᵇ22 Or A man's greed is his shame

¹⁰Differing weights and differing measures—
the LORD detests them both.

¹¹Even a child is known by his actions,
by whether his conduct is pure and right.

¹²Ears that hear and eyes that see—
the LORD has made them both.

¹³Do not love sleep or you will grow poor;
stay awake and you will have food to spare.

¹⁴"It's no good, it's no good!" says the buyer;
then off he goes and boasts about his
purchase.

¹⁵Gold there is, and rubies in abundance,
but lips that speak knowledge are a rare
jewel.

¹⁶Take the garment of one who puts up security
for a stranger;
hold it in pledge if he does it for a wayward
woman.

¹⁷Food gained by fraud tastes sweet to a man,
but he ends up with a mouth full of gravel.

¹⁸Make plans by seeking advice;
if you wage war, obtain guidance.

¹⁹A gossip betrays a confidence;
so avoid a man who talks too much.

²⁰If a man curses his father or mother,
his lamp will be snuffed out in pitch
darkness.

²¹An inheritance quickly gained at the beginning
will not be blessed at the end.

²²Do not say, "I'll pay you back for this wrong!"
Wait for the LORD, and he will deliver you.

²³The LORD detests differing weights,
and dishonest scales do not please him.

²⁴A man's steps are directed by the LORD.
How then can anyone understand his own
way?

²⁵It is a trap for a man to dedicate something
rashly
and only later to consider his vows.

²⁶A wise king winnows out the wicked;
he drives the threshing wheel over them.

²⁷The lamp of the LORD searches the spirit of a
man;ᵃ
it searches out his inmost being.

²⁸Love and faithfulness keep a king safe;
through love his throne is made secure.

²⁹The glory of young men is their strength,
grey hair the splendour of the old.

³⁰Blows and wounds cleanse away evil,
and beatings purge the inmost being.

21 The king's heart is in the hand of the
LORD;
he directs it like a watercourse wherever he
pleases.

²All a man's ways seem right to him,
but the LORD weighs the heart.

³To do what is right and just
is more acceptable to the LORD than sacrifice.

⁴Haughty eyes and a proud heart,
the lamp of the wicked, are sin!

⁵The plans of the diligent lead to profit
as surely as haste leads to poverty.

⁶A fortune made by a lying tongue
is a fleeting vapour and a deadly snare.ᵃ

⁷The violence of the wicked will drag them
away,
for they refuse to do what is right.

⁸The way of the guilty is devious,
but the conduct of the innocent is upright.

⁹Better to live on a corner of the roof
than share a house with a quarrelsome wife.

¹⁰The wicked man craves evil;
his neighbour gets no mercy from him.

¹¹When a mocker is punished, the simple gain
wisdom;
when a wise man is instructed, he gets
knowledge.

21:11 ■ LEARNING THE EASY WAY
"The simple"—those who live without thinking—
are rarely persuaded to change, because they
don't listen. One lesson may get through to them,
though: seeing a troublemaker—the "mocker"—
get punished. Wise people learn in a much less
painful way. When told something, they pay
attention.

¹²The Righteous Oneᵇ takes note of the house
of the wicked
and brings the wicked to ruin.

¹³If a man shuts his ears to the cry of the poor,
he too will cry out and not be answered.

¹⁴A gift given in secret soothes anger,
and a bribe concealed in the cloak pacifies
great wrath.

¹⁵When justice is done, it brings joy to the
righteous
but terror to evildoers.

¹⁶A man who strays from the path of
understanding
comes to rest in the company of the dead.

¹⁷He who loves pleasure will become poor;
whoever loves wine and oil will never be
rich.

¹⁸The wicked become a ransom for the righteous,
and the unfaithful for the upright.

¹⁹Better to live in a desert
than with a quarrelsome and ill-tempered
wife.

ᵃ27 Or *The spirit of man is the LORD's lamp*
seek death   ᵇ12 Or *The righteous man*   ᵃ6 Some Hebrew manuscripts, Septuagint and Vulgate; most Hebrew manuscripts *vapour for those who*

²⁰In the house of the wise are stores of choice
      food and oil,
   but a foolish man devours all he has.

²¹He who pursues righteousness and love
   finds life, prosperity*c* and honour.

²²A wise man attacks the city of the mighty
   and pulls down the stronghold in which they
      trust.

²³He who guards his mouth and his tongue
   keeps himself from calamity.

²⁴The proud and arrogant man—"Mocker" is his
      name;
   he behaves with overweening pride.

²⁵The sluggard's craving will be the death of him,
   because his hands refuse to work.

²⁶All day long he craves for more,
   but the righteous give without sparing.

²⁷The sacrifice of the wicked is detestable—
   how much more so when brought with evil
      intent!

²⁸A false witness will perish,
   and whoever listens to him will be destroyed
      for ever.*d*

²⁹A wicked man puts up a bold front,
   but an upright man gives thought to his
      ways.

³⁰There is no wisdom, no insight, no plan
   that can succeed against the LORD.

³¹The horse is made ready for the day of battle,
   but victory rests with the LORD.

22 A good name is more desirable than great
      riches;
   to be esteemed is better than silver or gold.

²Rich and poor have this in common:
   The LORD is the Maker of them all.

³A prudent man sees danger and takes refuge,
   but the simple keep going and suffer for it.

⁴Humility and the fear of the LORD
   bring wealth and honour and life.

⁵In the paths of the wicked lie thorns and
      snares,
   but he who guards his soul stays far from
      them.

⁶Train*a* a child in the way he should go,
   and when he is old he will not turn from it.

22:6 ■ GOOD PARENTING

An individual proverb shouldn't be read as either
an invariable rule or a binding promise from God.
Proverbs 10:4 generalises truthfully, "diligent
hands bring wealth", but you would not have to
look too far to find an exception to the rule. Verse
6, a famous proverb, reinforces the importance of
early training in forming a person's lifelong
character. But you can find individuals who,
though well brought up, choose to reject their
training. Proverbs studies life the way it normally
works. The general rule is this: good parents raise
good children.

⁷The rich rule over the poor,
   and the borrower is servant to the lender.

⁸He who sows wickedness reaps trouble,
   and the rod of his fury will be destroyed.

⁹A generous man will himself be blessed,
   for he shares his food with the poor.

■ WHOM SHOULD YOU MARRY?
A GOOD PARTNER CAN MAKE OR BREAK YOUR LIFE

INSIGHT

**BETTER TO LIVE ON A CORNER OF THE
ROOF THAN SHARE A HOUSE WITH A
QUARRELSOME WIFE. ■ 21:9**

In ancient times women were often viewed as
men's property, good for bearing children and
not much more. Proverbs, addressed to young
men approaching the age of marriage, takes a
different view. It holds up marriage as a crucial
choice, to be made with great care.

   A good wife (or husband, we can
assume) will make or break her partner's life.
Her duties lay the foundation for her family's
welfare (14:1; 31:10–31). She shares with her
husband the most significant task of teaching
their children the way of wisdom (1:8–9; 6:20).
Therefore, her character matters far more than
her physical beauty.

   Not that Proverbs ignores the physical
side of love. It urges marriage partners to
rejoice in their love, to be captivated by it
(5:18–19). It warns young people against
sexual sin precisely because this wastes
sexuality on unsatisfying, unloving
relationships. Sex ought to be saved for the
long-lasting, productive joy of marriage.
   Proverbs on sexual sin: 2:16–19;
5:1–23; 6:20–35; 7:6–27; 23:26–28.
   Proverbs on marriage: 5:15–19; 12:4;
14:1; 18:22; 19:13–14; 21:9,19; 27:15–16;
31:10–31.

□ LIFE QUESTIONS:
What do you look for in a mate? How does
your list compare with Proverbs' rating of
attributes such as physical attractiveness?

¹⁰Drive out the mocker, and out goes strife;
  quarrels and insults are ended.

¹¹He who loves a pure heart and whose speech is
    gracious
  will have the king for his friend.

¹²The eyes of the LORD keep watch over
    knowledge,
  but he frustrates the words of the unfaithful.

¹³The sluggard says, "There is a lion outside!"
  or, "I will be murdered in the streets!"

¹⁴The mouth of an adulteress is a deep pit;
  he who is under the LORD's wrath will fall
    into it.

¹⁵Folly is bound up in the heart of a child,
  but the rod of discipline will drive it far from
    him.

¹⁶He who oppresses the poor to increase his
    wealth
  and he who gives gifts to the rich—both
    come to poverty.

■ SAYINGS OF THE WISE

¹⁷Pay attention and listen to the sayings of the
    wise;
  apply your heart to what I teach,
¹⁸for it is pleasing when you keep them in your
    heart
  and have all of them ready on your lips.
¹⁹So that your trust may be in the LORD,
  I teach you today, even you.
²⁰Have I not written thirty*b* sayings for you,
  sayings of counsel and knowledge,
²¹teaching you true and reliable words,
  so that you can give sound answers
    to him who sent you?

²²Do not exploit the poor because they are poor
  and do not crush the needy in court,
²³for the LORD will take up their case
  and will plunder those who plunder them.

²⁴Do not make friends with a hot-tempered man,
  do not associate with one easily angered,
²⁵or you may learn his ways
  and get yourself ensnared.

²⁶Do not be a man who strikes hands in pledge
  or puts up security for debts;
²⁷if you lack the means to pay,
  your very bed will be snatched from under
    you.

²⁸Do not move an ancient boundary stone
  set up by your forefathers.

²⁹Do you see a man skilled in his work?
  He will serve before kings;
  he will not serve before obscure men.

23 When you sit to dine with a ruler,
    note well what*a* is before you,
²and put a knife to your throat
  if you are given to gluttony.
³Do not crave his delicacies,
  for that food is deceptive.

⁴Do not wear yourself out to get rich;
  have the wisdom to show restraint.
⁵Cast but a glance at riches, and they are gone,
  for they will surely sprout wings
  and fly off to the sky like an eagle.

⁶Do not eat the food of a stingy man,
  do not crave his delicacies;
⁷for he is the kind of man
  who is always thinking about the cost.*b*
  "Eat and drink," he says to you,
    but his heart is not with you.
⁸You will vomit up the little you have eaten

■ **HOW TO RAISE CHILDREN** INSIGHT
FAMILY MEMBERS SHOULD BE ALLIES, NOT ADVERSARIES

TRAIN A CHILD IN THE WAY HE SHOULD
GO, AND WHEN HE IS OLD HE WILL NOT
TURN FROM IT. ■ 22:6

"Spare the rod and spoil the child" may be the
most famous of the Bible's proverbs. Proverbs
calls punishment a form of love and says that
parents who won't discipline their children are in
danger of ruining them (29:15). But that much-
quoted maxim is only a small part of what
Proverbs has to offer on the subject of bringing
up children.
      The overwhelming emphasis of Proverbs
is on verbal encouragement and teaching. The
whole book is framed as a father's words to his
son, teaching him those "facts of life" that have
nothing to do with biology. Again and again he

pleads, "Listen, my son". Mother has equally
important words (1:8; 6:20). The parent-child
conversation is a warm one, and Proverbs 17:6
bears out what the whole book implies:
parents and children are not meant to be
adversaries, but allies in life who are proud of
each other.
      Proverbs on parent-child relationships:
3:11–12; 10:1,5; 13:1,24; 14:26; 15:20;
17:6,21; 19:18,26–27; 20:20; 22:6,15;
23:13–16,22–25; 27:11; 29:15,17; 31:28.

□ LIFE QUESTIONS:
In your upbringing, which had the most effect:
punishment and discipline, or verbal instruction
and encouragement?

*b 20 Or not formerly written; not written excellent   a 1 Or who   b 7 Or for as he thinks within himself, / so he is; or for as he puts on a feast, / so he
is*

and will have wasted your compliments.

⁹Do not speak to a fool,
for he will scorn the wisdom of your words.

¹⁰Do not move an ancient boundary stone
or encroach on the fields of the fatherless,
¹¹for their Defender is strong;
he will take up their case against you.

¹²Apply your heart to instruction
and your ears to words of knowledge.

¹³Do not withhold discipline from a child;
if you punish him with the rod, he will not
die.
¹⁴Punish him with the rod
and save his soul from death.ᶜ

¹⁵My son, if your heart is wise,
then my heart will be glad;
¹⁶my inmost being will rejoice
when your lips speak what is right.

¹⁷Do not let your heart envy sinners,
but always be zealous for the fear of the
LORD.
¹⁸There is surely a future hope for you,
and your hope will not be cut off.

¹⁹Listen, my son, and be wise,
and keep your heart on the right path.
²⁰Do not join those who drink too much wine
or gorge themselves on meat,
²¹for drunkards and gluttons become poor,
and drowsiness clothes them in rags.

²²Listen to your father, who gave you life,
and do not despise your mother when she is
old.
²³Buy the truth and do not sell it;
get wisdom, discipline and understanding.
²⁴The father of a righteous man has great joy;
he who has a wise son delights in him.
²⁵May your father and mother be glad;
may she who gave you birth rejoice!

²⁶My son, give me your heart
and let your eyes keep to my ways,
²⁷for a prostitute is a deep pit
and a wayward wife is a narrow well.
²⁸Like a bandit she lies in wait,
and multiplies the unfaithful among men.

²⁹Who has woe? Who has sorrow?
Who has strife? Who has complaints?
Who has needless bruises? Who has
bloodshot eyes?
³⁰Those who linger over wine,
who go to sample bowls of mixed wine.
³¹Do not gaze at wine when it is red,
when it sparkles in the cup,
when it goes down smoothly!
³²In the end it bites like a snake
and poisons like a viper.
³³Your eyes will see strange sights
and your mind imagine confusing things.
³⁴You will be like one sleeping on the high seas,
lying on top of the rigging.
³⁵"They hit me," you will say, "but I'm not hurt!

ᶜ14 Hebrew *Sheol*

They beat me, but I don't feel it!
When will I wake up
so I can find another drink?"

23:35 ■ THE DANGERS OF WINE

Wine was common in biblical times, but its
dangers were recognised. Proverbs contains some
of the Bible's strongest warnings against
overindulgence: 20:1; 21:17; 23:20–21, 30–35;
31:4–7.

24 Do not envy wicked men,
do not desire their company;
²for their hearts plot violence,
and their lips talk about making trouble.

³By wisdom a house is built,
and through understanding it is established;
⁴through knowledge its rooms are filled
with rare and beautiful treasures.

⁵A wise man has great power,
and a man of knowledge increases strength;
⁶for waging war you need guidance,
and for victory many advisers.

⁷Wisdom is too high for a fool;
in the assembly at the gate he has nothing to
say.

⁸He who plots evil
will be known as a schemer.
⁹The schemes of folly are sin,
and men detest a mocker.

¹⁰If you falter in times of trouble,
how small is your strength!

¹¹Rescue those being led away to death;
hold back those staggering towards slaughter.
¹²If you say, "But we knew nothing about this,"
does not he who weighs the heart perceive
it?
Does not he who guards your life know it?
Will he not repay each person according to
what he has done?

¹³Eat honey, my son, for it is good;
honey from the comb is sweet to your taste.
¹⁴Know also that wisdom is sweet to your soul;
if you find it, there is a future hope for you,
and your hope will not be cut off.

¹⁵Do not lie in wait like an outlaw against a
righteous man's house,
do not raid his dwelling-place;
¹⁶for though a righteous man falls seven times, he
rises again,
but the wicked are brought down by
calamity.

¹⁷Do not gloat when your enemy falls;
when he stumbles, do not let your heart
rejoice,
¹⁸or the LORD will see and disapprove
and turn his wrath away from him.

¹⁹Do not fret because of evil men
  or be envious of the wicked,
²⁰for the evil man has no future hope,
  and the lamp of the wicked will be snuffed
  out.

²¹Fear the LORD and the king, my son,
  and do not join with the rebellious,
²²for those two will send sudden destruction
  upon them,
  and who knows what calamities they can
  bring?

■ FURTHER SAYINGS OF THE WISE
  ²³These also are sayings of the wise:

To show partiality in judging is not good:
²⁴Whoever says to the guilty, "You are
          innocent" —
  peoples will curse him and nations denounce
  him.
²⁵But it will go well with those who convict the
  guilty,
  and rich blessing will come upon them.

²⁶An honest answer
  is like a kiss on the lips.

²⁷Finish your outdoor work
  and get your fields ready;
  after that, build your house.

²⁸Do not testify against your neighbour without
          cause,
  or use your lips to deceive.

²⁹Do not say, "I'll do to him as he has done to
  me;
  I'll pay that man back for what he did."

³⁰I went past the field of the sluggard,
  past the vineyard of the man who lacks
  judgment;
³¹thorns had come up everywhere,
  the ground was covered with weeds,

and the stone wall was in ruins.
³²I applied my heart to what I observed
  and learned a lesson from what I saw:
³³A little sleep, a little slumber,
  a little folding of the hands to rest —
³⁴and poverty will come on you like a bandit
  and scarcity like an armed man.ᵃ

■ MORE PROVERBS OF SOLOMON

25 These are more proverbs of Solomon, cop-
    ied by the men of Hezekiah king of Judah:

²It is the glory of God to conceal a matter;
  to search out a matter is the glory of kings.

25:1 ■ GOOD GOVERNMENT
Proverbs lists three kings in its credits: Solomon
(1:1; 10:1), Hezekiah (25:1), and Lemuel (31:1). So,
naturally, it shows concern for what makes good
government. The qualities needed in a king still
apply to governmental heads today. Proverbs
doesn't mention political philosophy or
administrative efficiency. Justice and fairness
matter most.
    Proverbs on good government include the
following: 14:35; 16:10,12–13; 20:26; 22:11;
25:4–5; 29:4,14; 31:3–5.

---

³As the heavens are high and the earth is deep,
  so the hearts of kings are unsearchable.

⁴Remove the dross from the silver,
  and out comes material forᵃ the silversmith;
⁵remove the wicked from the king's presence,
  and his throne will be established through
  righteousness.

⁶Do not exalt yourself in the king's presence,
  and do not claim a place among great men;

■ **THE PROBLEM WITH LAZINESS**
BECOMING A SLUGGARD REQUIRES LITTLE EFFORT

INSIGHT

A LITTLE SLEEP, A LITTLE SLUMBER, A
LITTLE FOLDING OF THE HANDS TO
REST — AND POVERTY WILL COME ON
YOU LIKE A BANDIT. ■ 24:33

The "sluggard" is lazier than a pig on holiday.
His only exercise is turning on his bed; Proverbs
says he is *hinged* to it. Any far-fetched
excuse — "there is a lion in the road!" — will keep
him from going to work. Proverbs laughs at the
sluggard a little, but uses him to teach serious
lessons. You can be like him very easily, for it
doesn't require much: "a little sleep, a little
slumber, a little folding of the hands to rest".
Putting things off, making excuses, sleeping in:

who doesn't sometimes fall victim to these
tendencies?
    The result of such a life? Poverty,
frustration, broken relationships. The sluggard
still wants the luxuries hard work earns, but he
never gets them. "The sluggard's craving will
be the death of him" (21:25).
    Proverbs on laziness: 6:6–11; 10:4,26;
12:24,27; 13:4; 15:19; 19:15,24; 20:4; 21:25;
22:13; 24:30–34; 26:13–16.

☐ LIFE QUESTIONS:
What attributes of a sluggard do you recognise
in yourself? Do you think of these as serious?

ᵃ 34 Or like a vagrant / and scarcity like a beggar   ᵃ 4 Or comes a vessel from

7it is better for him to say to you, "Come up
  here,"
than for him to humiliate you before a
  nobleman.

What you have seen with your eyes
8 do not bring*b* hastily to court,
for what will you do in the end
  if your neighbour puts you to shame?

9If you argue your case with a neighbour,
  do not betray another man's confidence,
10or he who hears it may shame you
  and you will never lose your bad reputation.

11A word aptly spoken
  is like apples of gold in settings of silver.

12Like an ear-ring of gold or an ornament of fine
  gold
  is a wise man's rebuke to a listening ear.

13Like the coolness of snow at harvest time
  is a trustworthy messenger to those who
    send him;
  he refreshes the spirit of his masters.

14Like clouds and wind without rain
  is a man who boasts of gifts he does not give.

15Through patience a ruler can be persuaded,
  and a gentle tongue can break a bone.

16If you find honey, eat just enough—
  too much of it, and you will vomit.
17Seldom set foot in your neighbour's house—
  too much of you, and he will hate you.

18Like a club or a sword or a sharp arrow
  is the man who gives false testimony against
    his neighbour.

19Like a bad tooth or a lame foot
  is reliance on the unfaithful in times of
    trouble.

20Like one who takes away a garment on a cold
    day,
  or like vinegar poured on soda,
  is one who sings songs to a heavy heart.

21If your enemy is hungry, give him food to eat;
  if he is thirsty, give him water to drink.
22In doing this, you will heap burning coals on
    his head,
  and the LORD will reward you.

23As a north wind brings rain,
  so a sly tongue brings angry looks.

24Better to live on a corner of the roof
  than share a house with a quarrelsome wife.

25Like cold water to a weary soul
  is good news from a distant land.

26Like a muddied spring or a polluted well
  is a righteous man who gives way to the
    wicked.

27It is not good to eat too much honey,
  nor is it honourable to seek one's own
    honour.

28Like a city whose walls are broken down
  is a man who lacks self-control.

26 Like snow in summer or rain in harvest,
  honour is not fitting for a fool.

2Like a fluttering sparrow or a darting swallow,
  an undeserved curse does not come to rest.

3A whip for the horse, a halter for the donkey,
  and a rod for the backs of fools!

4Do not answer a fool according to his folly,
  or you will be like him yourself.

5Answer a fool according to his folly,
  or he will be wise in his own eyes.

6Like cutting off one's feet or drinking violence
  is the sending of a message by the hand of a
    fool.

7Like a lame man's legs that hang limp
  is a proverb in the mouth of a fool.

8Like tying a stone in a sling
  is the giving of honour to a fool.

9Like a thornbush in a drunkard's hand
  is a proverb in the mouth of a fool.

10Like an archer who wounds at random
  is he who hires a fool or any passer-by.

11As a dog returns to its vomit,
  so a fool repeats his folly.

12Do you see a man wise in his own eyes?
  There is more hope for a fool than for him.

13The sluggard says, "There is a lion in the road,
  a fierce lion roaming the streets!"

26:13 ■ THE EXCUSES OF A LAZY MAN

At first glance some proverbs, like this one,
appear incomplete and pointless. But this proverb
cleverly pinpoints a lazy man's habit of seeing
dangerous obstacles to every plan and making
incredible excuses. He will not go anywhere (on a
road) or even get out of his house (into the
streets) because his imagination conjures up all
the things that could go wrong.

14As a door turns on its hinges,
  so a sluggard turns on his bed.

15The sluggard buries his hand in the dish;
  he is too lazy to bring it back to his mouth.

16The sluggard is wiser in his own eyes
  than seven men who answer discreetly.

17Like one who seizes a dog by the ears
  is a passer-by who meddles in a quarrel not
    his own.

18Like a madman shooting
  firebrands or deadly arrows
19is a man who deceives his neighbour
  and says, "I was only joking!"

b7, 8 Or nobleman / on whom you had set your eyes. / 8Do not go

20Without wood a fire goes out;
  without gossip a quarrel dies down.

21As charcoal to embers and as wood to fire,
  so is a quarrelsome man for kindling strife.

22The words of a gossip are like choice morsels;
  they go down to a man's inmost parts.

23Like a coating of glaze*a* over earthenware
  are fervent lips with an evil heart.

24A malicious man disguises himself with his lips,
  but in his heart he harbours deceit.

25Though his speech is charming, do not believe
    him,
  for seven abominations fill his heart.

26His malice may be concealed by deception,
  but his wickedness will be exposed in the
    assembly.

27If a man digs a pit, he will fall into it;
  if a man rolls a stone, it will roll back on
    him.

28A lying tongue hates those it hurts,
  and a flattering mouth works ruin.

27 Do not boast about tomorrow,
   for you do not know what a day may
   bring forth.

2Let another praise you, and not your own
    mouth;
  someone else, and not your own lips.

3Stone is heavy and sand a burden,
  but provocation by a fool is heavier than
    both.

4Anger is cruel and fury overwhelming,
  but who can stand before jealousy?

5Better is open rebuke
  than hidden love.

6Wounds from a friend can be trusted,
  but an enemy multiplies kisses.

7He who is full loathes honey,
  but to the hungry even what is bitter tastes
    sweet.

8Like a bird that strays from its nest
  is a man who strays from his home.

9Perfume and incense bring joy to the heart,
  and the pleasantness of one's friend springs
    from his earnest counsel.

10Do not forsake your friend and the friend of
    your father,
  and do not go to your brother's house when
    disaster strikes you —
  better a neighbour nearby than a brother far
    away.

11Be wise, my son, and bring joy to my heart;
  then I can answer anyone who treats me
    with contempt.

12The prudent see danger and take refuge,
  but the simple keep going and suffer for it.

13Take the garment of one who puts up security
    for a stranger;
  hold it in pledge if he does it for a wayward
    woman.

14If a man loudly blesses his neighbour early in
    the morning,
  it will be taken as a curse.

15A quarrelsome wife is like
  a constant dripping on a rainy day;
16restraining her is like restraining the wind
  or grasping oil with the hand.

17As iron sharpens iron,
  so one man sharpens another.

■ THE MAKING OF A FOOL
EVEN A GENIUS CAN BE ONE

INSIGHT

AS A DOG RETURNS TO ITS VOMIT, SO A
FOOL REPEATS HIS FOLLY. ■ 26:11

Fools, in modern English, are people who lack
brains. But the word has a different meaning in
the Bible. Fools may have high IQs. People may
admire their reputation for success. Yet a wise
person views them as a disaster.
    One of the Bible's worst insults is "You
fool!" People become fools by ignoring the
wisdom God offers them, preferring to follow the
crowd or their own conceited opinions. They
may think themselves very clever, but their
cleverness will land them in trouble.

Proverbs aims its sharpest warnings,
not against acting immorally, but against
becoming a fool. If you develop such a
character, no set of rules can keep you out of
trouble. A wise person ought to learn to
recognise a fool from far away, and stay out of
his or her path.
    Poignant proverbs on foolishness: 1:7;
10:8; 12:15–16,23; 14:8–9,16,24; 15:14;
17:10,12,16; 18:2,6; 20:3; 26:3,11; 27:22;
28:26; 29:11.

□ LIFE QUESTIONS:
Do you know anyone whom Proverbs would
call a fool? If so, how should you relate to him
or her?

a 23 With a different word division of the Hebrew; Masoretic Text *of silver dross*

¹⁸He who tends a fig-tree will eat its fruit,
  and he who looks after his master will be
  honoured.

¹⁹As water reflects a face,
  so a man's heart reflects the man.

²⁰Death and Destruction*a* are never satisfied,
  and neither are the eyes of man.

²¹The crucible for silver and the furnace for gold,
  but man is tested by the praise he receives.

²²Though you grind a fool in a mortar,
  grinding him like grain with a pestle,
  you will not remove his folly from him.

²³Be sure you know the condition of your flocks,
  give careful attention to your herds;
²⁴for riches do not endure for ever,
  and a crown is not secure for all generations.
²⁵When the hay is removed and new growth
  appears
  and the grass from the hills is gathered in,
²⁶the lambs will provide you with clothing,
  and the goats with the price of a field.
²⁷You will have plenty of goats' milk
  to feed you and your family
  and to nourish your servant girls.

28 The wicked man flees though no-one
       pursues,
  but the righteous are as bold as a lion.

²When a country is rebellious, it has many
  rulers,
  but a man of understanding and knowledge
  maintains order.

³A ruler*a* who oppresses the poor
  is like a driving rain that leaves no crops.

⁴Those who forsake the law praise the wicked,
  but those who keep the law resist them.

⁵Evil men do not understand justice,
  but those who seek the LORD understand it
  fully.

⁶Better a poor man whose walk is blameless
  than a rich man whose ways are perverse.

⁷He who keeps the law is a discerning son,
  but a companion of gluttons disgraces his
  father.

⁸He who increases his wealth by exorbitant
  interest
  amasses it for another, who will be kind to
  the poor.

⁹If anyone turns a deaf ear to the law,
  even his prayers are detestable.

¹⁰He who leads the upright along an evil path
  will fall into his own trap,
  but the blameless will receive a good
  inheritance.

¹¹A rich man may be wise in his own eyes,
  but a poor man who has discernment sees
  through him.

¹²When the righteous triumph, there is great
  elation;
  but when the wicked rise to power, men go
  into hiding.

¹³He who conceals his sins does not prosper,
  but whoever confesses and renounces them
  finds mercy.

¹⁴Blessed is the man who always fears the LORD,
  but he who hardens his heart falls into
  trouble.

¹⁵Like a roaring lion or a charging bear
  is a wicked man ruling over a helpless
  people.

¹⁶A tyrannical ruler lacks judgment,
  but he who hates ill-gotten gain will enjoy a
  long life.

¹⁷A man tormented by the guilt of murder
  will be a fugitive till death;
  let no-one support him.

¹⁸He whose walk is blameless is kept safe,
  but he whose ways are perverse will
  suddenly fall.

¹⁹He who works his land will have abundant
  food,
  but the one who chases fantasies will have
  his fill of poverty.

²⁰A faithful man will be richly blessed,
  but one eager to get rich will not go
  unpunished.

²¹To show partiality is not good—
  yet a man will do wrong for a piece of bread.

²²A stingy man is eager to get rich
  and is unaware that poverty awaits him.

²³He who rebukes a man will in the end gain
  more favour
  than he who has a flattering tongue.

²⁴He who robs his father or mother
  and says, "It's not wrong"—
  he is partner to him who destroys.

²⁵A greedy man stirs up dissension,
  but he who trusts in the LORD will prosper.

²⁶He who trusts in himself is a fool,
  but he who walks in wisdom is kept safe.

²⁷He who gives to the poor will lack nothing,
  but he who closes his eyes to them receives
  many curses.

²⁸When the wicked rise to power, people go into
  hiding;
  but when the wicked perish, the righteous
  thrive.

29 A man who remains stiff-necked after
       many rebukes
  will suddenly be destroyed—without
  remedy.

²When the righteous thrive, the people rejoice;
  when the wicked rule, the people groan.

a20 Hebrew Sheol and Abaddon   a3 Or A poor man

³A man who loves wisdom brings joy to his
     father,
  but a companion of prostitutes squanders his
     wealth.

⁴By justice a king gives a country stability,
  but one who is greedy for bribes tears it
     down.

⁵Whoever flatters his neighbour
  is spreading a net for his feet.

29:5 ■ DANGEROUS FLATTERY
"Flattery can get you anywhere", some say. But
flattery – the art of making someone feel good by
stretching the truth – can be downright harmful. It
can leave a trusting friend unprepared for troubles
ahead. Instead of flattering, we should warn a
friend about where he or she is heading (see
28:23).

---

⁶An evil man is snared by his own sin,
  but a righteous one can sing and be glad.

⁷The righteous care about justice for the poor,
  but the wicked have no such concern.

⁸Mockers stir up a city,
  but wise men turn away anger.

⁹If a wise man goes to court with a fool,
  the fool rages and scoffs, and there is no
     peace.

¹⁰Bloodthirsty men hate a man of integrity
  and seek to kill the upright.

¹¹A fool gives full vent to his anger,
  but a wise man keeps himself under control.

¹²If a ruler listens to lies,
  all his officials become wicked.

¹³The poor man and the oppressor have this in
     common:
  The LORD gives sight to the eyes of both.

¹⁴If a king judges the poor with fairness,
  his throne will always be secure.

¹⁵The rod of correction imparts wisdom,
  but a child left to himself disgraces his
     mother.

¹⁶When the wicked thrive, so does sin,
  but the righteous will see their downfall.

¹⁷Discipline your son, and he will give you peace;
  he will bring delight to your soul.

¹⁸Where there is no revelation, the people cast
     off restraint;
  but blessed is he who keeps the law.

¹⁹A servant cannot be corrected by mere words;
  though he understands, he will not respond.

²⁰Do you see a man who speaks in haste?
  There is more hope for a fool than for him.

²¹If a man pampers his servant from youth,
  he will bring grief*ᵃ* in the end.

²²An angry man stirs up dissension,
  and a hot-tempered one commits many sins.

²³A man's pride brings him low,
  but a man of lowly spirit gains honour.

²⁴The accomplice of a thief is his own enemy;
  he is put under oath and dare not testify.

²⁵Fear of man will prove to be a snare,
  but whoever trusts in the LORD is kept safe.

²⁶Many seek an audience with a ruler,
  but it is from the LORD that man gets justice.

²⁷The righteous detest the dishonest;
  the wicked detest the upright.

■ SAYINGS OF AGUR

30 The sayings of Agur son of Jakeh – an ora-
     cle:*ᵇ*

  This man declared to Ithiel,
     to Ithiel and to Ucal:*ᵇ*

²"I am the most ignorant of men;
  I do not have a man's understanding.
³I have not learned wisdom,

■ FIVE DANGEROUS RESPONSES INSIGHT
INNER ATTITUDES CAN DESTROY YOU

A WISE MAN KEEPS HIMSELF UNDER
CONTROL. ■ 29:11

Anger will destroy you before it destroys anyone
else. Control your temper! Read Proverbs 14:17;
14:29; 15:18; 19:19; 22:24–25; 29:11; 29:22.
     Pride will lead to your downfall. Humility
is far more rewarding. See Proverbs 3:34; 11:2;
13:10; 16:5,18–19; 18:12; 21:4.
     Jealousy grows like a cancer. Read
Proverbs 14:30; 23:17; 24:1; 27:4.

     Fear of people is unnecessary if you
trust God. See Proverbs 3:25–26; 29:25.
     Conceit is ugly. A conceited person
forgets God's place in his or her life. Read
Proverbs 16:2; 25:27; 26:12; 27:2; 28:11,13.

□ LIFE QUESTIONS:
Which of these responses tempts you most?
Why?

---

*ᵃ*21 The meaning of the Hebrew for this word is uncertain.   *ᵃ*1 Or *Jakeh of Massa*   *ᵇ*1 Masoretic Text; with a different word division of the Hebrew
declared, "I am weary, O God; / I am weary, O God, and faint.

nor have I knowledge of the Holy One.
4Who has gone up to heaven and come down?
Who has gathered up the wind in the hollow
of his hands?
Who has wrapped up the waters in his cloak?
Who has established all the ends of the
earth?
What is his name, and the name of his son?
Tell me if you know!

5"Every word of God is flawless;
he is a shield to those who take refuge in
him.
6Do not add to his words,
or he will rebuke you and prove you a liar.

7"Two things I ask of you, O LORD;
do not refuse me before I die:
8Keep falsehood and lies far from me;
give me neither poverty nor riches,
but give me only my daily bread.
9Otherwise, I may have too much and disown
you
and say, 'Who is the LORD?'
Or I may become poor and steal,
and so dishonour the name of my God.

10"Do not slander a servant to his master,
or he will curse you, and you will pay for it.

11"There are those who curse their fathers
and do not bless their mothers;
12those who are pure in their own eyes
and yet are not cleansed of their filth;
13those whose eyes are ever so haughty,
whose glances are so disdainful;
14those whose teeth are swords
and whose jaws are set with knives
to devour the poor from the earth,
the needy from among mankind.

15"The leech has two daughters.
'Give! Give!' they cry.

"There are three things that are never satisfied,
four that never say, 'Enough!':
16the grave,c the barren womb,
land, which is never satisfied with water,
and fire, which never says, 'Enough!'

17"The eye that mocks a father,
that scorns obedience to a mother,
will be pecked out by the ravens of the valley,
will be eaten by the vultures.

18"There are three things that are too amazing for
me,
four that I do not understand:
19the way of an eagle in the sky,
the way of a snake on a rock,
the way of a ship on the high seas,
and the way of a man with a maiden.

20"This is the way of an adulteress:
She eats and wipes her mouth
and says, 'I've done nothing wrong.'

21"Under three things the earth trembles,
under four it cannot bear up:

22a servant who becomes king,
a fool who is full of food,
23an unloved woman who is married,
and a maidservant who displaces her
mistress.

24"Four things on earth are small,
yet they are extremely wise:
25Ants are creatures of little strength,
yet they store up their food in the summer;
26coniesd are creatures of little power,
yet they make their home in the crags;
27locusts have no king,
yet they advance together in ranks;
28a lizard can be caught with the hand,
yet it is found in kings' palaces.

29"There are three things that are stately in their
stride,
four that move with stately bearing:
30a lion, mighty among beasts,
who retreats before nothing;
31a strutting cock, a he-goat,
and a king with his army around him.e

32"If you have played the fool and exalted
yourself,
or if you have planned evil,
clap your hand over your mouth!
33For as churning the milk produces butter,
and as twisting the nose produces blood,
so stirring up anger produces strife."

■ SAYINGS OF KING LEMUEL

31 The sayings of King Lemuel—an oraclea his
mother taught him:

2"O my son, O son of my womb,
O son of my vows,b
3do not spend your strength on women,
your vigour on those who ruin kings.

4"It is not for kings, O Lemuel—
not for kings to drink wine,
not for rulers to crave beer,
5lest they drink and forget what the law decrees,
and deprive all the oppressed of their rights.
6Give beer to those who are perishing,
wine to those who are in anguish;
7let them drink and forget their poverty
and remember their misery no more.

8"Speak up for those who cannot speak for
themselves,
for the rights of all who are destitute.
9Speak up and judge fairly;
defend the rights of the poor and needy."

31:8 ■ FOR THE VOICELESS
The German pastor Dietrich Bonhoeffer frequently
quoted this verse in the years before World War II.
He was urging his fellow Christians to speak up
for Hitler's victims, particularly Jews who had been
stripped of their civil rights.

---

c16 Hebrew Sheol   d26 That is, the hyrax or rock badger   e31 Or king secure against revolt.   a1 Or of Lemuel king of Massa, which   b2 Or I
the answer to my prayers

■ EPILOGUE: THE WIFE OF NOBLE CHARACTER

[10c]A wife of noble character who can find?
    She is worth far more than rubies.
[11]Her husband has full confidence in her
    and lacks nothing of value.
[12]She brings him good, not harm,
    all the days of her life.
[13]She selects wool and flax
    and works with eager hands.
[14]She is like the merchant ships,
    bringing her food from afar.
[15]She gets up while it is still dark;
    she provides food for her family
    and portions for her servant girls.
[16]She considers a field and buys it;
    out of her earnings she plants a
    vineyard.
[17]She sets about her work vigorously;
    her arms are strong for her tasks.
[18]She sees that her trading is profitable,
    and her lamp does not go out at night.
[19]In her hand she holds the distaff
    and grasps the spindle with her fingers.
[20]She opens her arms to the poor
    and extends her hands to the needy.

[21]When it snows, she has no fear for her
    household;
    for all of them are clothed in scarlet.
[22]She makes coverings for her bed;
    she is clothed in fine linen and purple.
[23]Her husband is respected at the city gate,
    where he takes his seat among the elders of
    the land.
[24]She makes linen garments and sells them,
    and supplies the merchants with sashes.
[25]She is clothed with strength and dignity;
    she can laugh at the days to come.
[26]She speaks with wisdom,
    and faithful instruction is on her tongue.
[27]She watches over the affairs of her household
    and does not eat the bread of idleness.
[28]Her children arise and call her blessed;
    her husband also, and he praises her:
[29]"Many women do noble things,
    but you surpass them all."
[30]Charm is deceptive, and beauty is fleeting;
    but a woman who fears the LORD is to be
    praised.
[31]Give her the reward she has earned,
    and let her works bring her praise at the city
    gate.

---

c10 Verses 10–31 are an acrostic, each verse beginning with a successive letter of the Hebrew alphabet.

ECCLESIASTES

■ WHEN LIFE SEEMS SENSELESS

A BOOK FOR OUR TIME

"MEANINGLESS! MEANINGLESS!" SAYS THE TEACHER. "UTTERLY MEANINGLESS!
EVERYTHING IS MEANINGLESS." ■ 1:2

"In this world there are only two tragedies", said
Irish writer Oscar Wilde. "One is not getting what
one wants, and the other is getting it." This
paradoxical proverb has often proved true.
Consider a larger-than-life character from the 20th
century, a man named Howard Hughes.

■ WORLD'S RICHEST MAN
At age 45 Hughes was one of the most glamorous
men in America. He courted actresses, piloted
exotic test aircraft, and worked on top-secret CIA
contracts. He owned a string of hotels around the
world, and even an airline – TWA – to carry him on
global jaunts.

Twenty years later, at 65, Howard
Hughes still had plenty of money – $2.3 billion,
to be exact. But the world's richest man had
become one of its most pathetic. He lived in
small, dark rooms atop his hotels, without sun
and without joy. He was unkempt: a scraggly
beard had grown waist-length, his hair fell well
down his back, and his fingernails were two
inches long. His once-powerful 6' 4" frame had
shrunk to about 100 pounds.

This famous man spent most of his time
watching movies over and over again, with the
same movie showing as many as 150 times. He
lay naked in bed, deathly afraid of germs. Life
held no meaning for him. Finally, emaciated and
hooked on drugs, he died at 67, for lack of a
medical device his own company had helped to
develop.

■ A KING'S CHARMED LIFE
Howard Hughes is an extreme example of a
syndrome that can afflict the rich and famous. His
attitude towards life closely followed the thoughts
of another successful man, a great king who ruled
Israel long ago. This book, Ecclesiastes, records
what happened to that man who had everything.

The author of Ecclesiastes had tasted
just about everything life has to offer. Wealth?

No-one could exceed his luxurious lifestyle
(2:4–9). Wisdom? His was world-renowned
(1:13–18). Fame? He was king, the most famous
man of his time (1:12). Systematically, he
sampled all of life's powers and pleasures, yet
all ultimately disappointed him. All proved
meaningless.

What is the point of life? he asked. You
work hard, and someone else gets all the credit.
You struggle to be good, and evil people take
advantage of you. You accumulate money, and it
just goes to spoiled heirs. You seek pleasure,
and it turns sour on you. And everyone – rich or
poor, good or evil – meets the same end. We all
die. There is only one word to describe this life:
meaningless!

■ LIFE UNDER THE SUN
Ecclesiastes strikes a responsive chord in our age.
Its words show up in folk songs and at important
political events. No century has seen such
progress, and yet such despair. What is the
purpose of life anyway? Is there any ultimate
meaning? "Is that all there is?" asked one
songwriter after listing life's pleasures.

A key phrase in this book, "under the
sun", describes the world lived on one level,
apart from God and without any belief in the
after-life. If you live on that level, you may well
conclude that life is meaningless.

Ecclesiastes gives some words of hope,
including the final summary: "Fear God and keep
his commandments, for this is the whole duty
of man" (12:13). That's the positive message,
the "lesson" of Ecclesiastes. But such positive
words are almost overwhelmed by the author's
powerful negative example. You could
summarise his whole life in Jesus' one
statement, "What good will it be for a man if he
gains the whole world, yet forfeits his soul?"
(Matthew 16:26).

■ HOW TO READ ECCLESIASTES

Ecclesiastes attracts extreme reactions. For several hundred years, Jewish scholars fiercely debated whether the book should even be included in the Old Testament. Yet American novelist Thomas Wolfe said of it, "Ecclesiastes is the greatest single piece of writing I have ever known, and the wisdom expressed in it the most lasting and profound".

Because of the book's unique nature, it is important to keep certain principles in mind while reading it. Consider Ecclesiastes as a whole. The Teacher was exploring various philosophies of life. During his search, he tried different approaches, including hedonism, the unrestrained pursuit of pleasure. The book honestly records the author's search without endorsing it.

At times the author concludes with despairing statements that directly contradict other parts of the Bible (for example, the recurring phrase, "Everything is meaningless!"). Read such individual statements in their context. Just as the book of Job contains arguments that God directly refuted later, so Ecclesiastes contains many isolated statements that contradict its final conclusion.

Ecclesiastes performs two very valuable functions. First, it should stimulate compassion for those who are trapped in despair and live in a meaningless world, alone, without God. The author brilliantly captures the futility and meaninglessness of that world, expressing a philosophy of life widespread in the 20th century.

But the book includes more than despair. It also blends in proverbs about how life should be lived, pungent observations that can be easily overlooked. Look for these nuggets of wisdom, especially towards the end of the book. (You may also find it helpful to balance out Ecclesiastes with the more confident advice of Proverbs.)

By asking questions, the author of Ecclesiastes helped prepare for the answers God ultimately provided. The Teacher concluded, "Everything is meaningless!" under the sun, but when Jesus Christ came, he promised life "to the full" (John 10:10).

■ 3-TRACK READING PLAN

For an explanation and complete listing of the 3-track reading plan, turn to page x.

■ TRACK 1:
Two-Week Courses on the Bible
See page x for information on these courses.

■ TRACK 2:
An Overview of Ecclesiastes in 1 Day
□ Day 1. Read the Introduction to Ecclesiastes and then chapter 3, perhaps the most enduring portion of the book's poetry. Folksinger Pete Seeger used the first part verbatim in a famous song, and former United States President John F. Kennedy had these words read at his inauguration.
Now turn to page xi for your next Track 2 reading project.

■ TRACK 3:
All of Ecclesiastes in 12 Days
After you have read through Ecclesiastes, turn to pages xii–xiii for your next Track 3 reading project.

□ 1   □ 2   □ 3   □ 4
□ 5   □ 6   □ 7   □ 8
□ 9   □ 10   □ 11   □ 12

■ Everything Is Meaningless

1 The words of the Teacher,*a* son of David, king of Jerusalem:

2"Meaningless! Meaningless!"
　　says the Teacher.
"Utterly meaningless!
　　Everything is meaningless."

3What does man gain from all his labour
　　at which he toils under the sun?
4Generations come and generations go,
　　but the earth remains for ever.
5The sun rises and the sun sets,
　　and hurries back to where it rises.
6The wind blows to the south
　　and turns to the north;
round and round it goes,
　　ever returning on its course.

7All streams flow into the sea,
　　yet the sea is never full.
To the place the streams come from,
　　there they return again.
8All things are wearisome,
　　more than one can say.
The eye never has enough of seeing,
　　nor the ear its fill of hearing.
9What has been will be again,
　　what has been done will be done again;
　　there is nothing new under the sun.
10Is there anything of which one can say,
　　"Look! This is something new"?
It was here already, long ago;
　　it was here before our time.
11There is no remembrance of men of old,
　　and even those who are yet to come
will not be remembered
　　by those who follow.

a 1 Or *leader of the assembly*; also in verses 2 and 12

■ Wisdom Is Meaningless

¹²I, the Teacher, was king over Israel in Jerusalem. ¹³I devoted myself to study and to explore by wisdom all that is done under heaven. What a heavy burden God has laid on men! ¹⁴I have seen all the things that are done under the sun; all of them are meaningless, a chasing after the wind.

¹⁵What is twisted cannot be straightened;
    what is lacking cannot be counted.

¹⁶I thought to myself, "Look, I have grown and increased in wisdom more than anyone who has ruled over Jerusalem before me; I have experienced much of wisdom and knowledge." ¹⁷Then I applied myself to the understanding of wisdom, and also of madness and folly, but I learned that this, too, is a chasing after the wind.

¹⁸For with much wisdom comes much sorrow;
    the more knowledge, the more grief.

■ Pleasures Are Meaningless

2 I thought in my heart, "Come now, I will test you with pleasure to find out what is good." But that also proved to be meaningless. ²"Laughter," I said, "is foolish. And what does pleasure accomplish?" ³I tried cheering myself with wine, and embracing folly—my mind still guiding me with wisdom. I wanted to see what was worth while for men to do under heaven during the few days of their lives.

2:1 ■ OUTSIDE THE PALACE

The first two chapters of Ecclesiastes tell of "the Teacher's" own experience of despair and meaninglessness. The life described in this autobiographical section resembles that of King Solomon. In the rest of the book, the Teacher examines the world around him to see if others have found answers to life "under the sun". To his disappointment, he finds the same pattern repeated over and over again.

---

⁴I undertook great projects: I built houses for myself and planted vineyards. ⁵I made gardens and parks and planted all kinds of fruit trees in them. ⁶I made reservoirs to water groves of flourishing trees. ⁷I bought male and female slaves and had other slaves who were born in my house. I also owned more herds and flocks than anyone in Jerusalem before me. ⁸I amassed silver and gold for myself, and the treasure of kings and provinces. I acquired men and women singers, and a harem*ᵃ* as well—the delights of the heart of man. ⁹I became greater by far than anyone in Jerusalem before me. In all this my wisdom stayed with me.

¹⁰I denied myself nothing my eyes desired;
    I refused my heart no pleasure.
My heart took delight in all my work,
    and this was the reward for all my labour.
¹¹Yet when I surveyed all that my hands had
    done
    and what I had toiled to achieve,

everything was meaningless, a chasing after the
    wind;
    nothing was gained under the sun.

■ Wisdom and Folly Are Meaningless

¹²Then I turned my thoughts to consider
    wisdom,
    and also madness and folly.
What more can the king's successor do
    than what has already been done?
¹³I saw that wisdom is better than folly,
    just as light is better than darkness.
¹⁴The wise man has eyes in his head,
    while the fool walks in the darkness;
but I came to realise
    that the same fate overtakes them both.

¹⁵Then I thought in my heart,

"The fate of the fool will overtake me also.
    What then do I gain by being wise?"
I said in my heart,
    "This too is meaningless."
¹⁶For the wise man, like the fool, will not be long
    remembered;
    in days to come both will be forgotten.
Like the fool, the wise man too must die!

■ Toil Is Meaningless

¹⁷So I hated life, because the work that is done under the sun was grievous to me. All of it is meaningless, a chasing after the wind. ¹⁸I hated all the things I had toiled for under the sun, because I must leave them to the one who comes after me. ¹⁹And who knows whether he will be a wise man or a fool? Yet he will have control over all the work into which I have poured my effort and skill under the sun. This too is meaningless. ²⁰So my heart began to despair over all my toilsome labour under the sun. ²¹For a man may do his work with wisdom, knowledge and skill, and then he must leave all he owns to someone who has not worked for it. This too is meaningless and a great misfortune. ²²What does a man get for all the toil and anxious striving with which he labours under the sun? ²³All his days his work is pain and grief; even at night his mind does not rest. This too is meaningless.

²⁴A man can do nothing better than to eat and drink and find satisfaction in his work. This too, I see, is from the hand of God, ²⁵for without him, who can eat or find enjoyment? ²⁶To the man who pleases him, God gives wisdom, knowledge and happiness, but to the sinner he gives the task of gathering and storing up wealth to hand it over to the one who pleases God. This too is meaningless, a chasing after the wind.

■ A Time for Everything

3 There is a time for everything,
    and a season for every activity under
    heaven:

²   a time to be born and a time to die,
    a time to plant and a time to uproot,
³   a time to kill and a time to heal,
    a time to tear down and a time to build,

ᵃ8 The meaning of the Hebrew for this phrase is uncertain.

⁴ a time to weep and a time to laugh,
   a time to mourn and a time to dance,
⁵ a time to scatter stones and a time to gather
      them,
   a time to embrace and a time to refrain,
⁶ a time to search and a time to give up,
   a time to keep and a time to throw away,
⁷ a time to tear and a time to mend,
   a time to be silent and a time to speak,
⁸ a time to love and a time to hate,
   a time for war and a time for peace.

3:4 ■ CHANGE OR NO CHANGE?

At first the Teacher complained that nothing ever changes (1:10–14). Now in this passage – made famous by a popular song in the 1960s – he indicates that life is full of changes. The French proverb, "The more things change, the more they stay the same", expresses this same paradox. For someone in despair who can see no meaning in life, everything that happens seems like an endless, repetitive cycle of futility.

⁹What does the worker gain from his toil? ¹⁰I have seen the burden God has laid on men. ¹¹He has made everything beautiful in its time. He has also set eternity in the hearts of men; yet they cannot fathom what God has done from beginning to end. ¹²I know that there is nothing better for men than to be happy and do good while they live. ¹³That everyone may eat and drink, and find satisfaction in all his toil – this is the gift of God. ¹⁴I know that everything God does will endure for ever; nothing can be added to it and nothing taken from it. God does it so that men will revere him.

¹⁵Whatever is has already been,
   and what will be has been before;
   and God will call the past to account.ᵃ

¹⁶And I saw something else under the sun:

In the place of judgment – wickedness was
      there,
   in the place of justice – wickedness was
   there.

¹⁷I thought in my heart,

"God will bring to judgment
   both the righteous and the wicked,
for there will be a time for every activity,
   a time for every deed."

¹⁸I also thought, "As for men, God tests them so that they may see that they are like the animals. ¹⁹Man's fate is like that of the animals; the same fate awaits them both: As one dies, so dies the other. All have the same breath;ᵇ man has no advantage over the animal. Everything is meaningless. ²⁰All go to the same place; all come from dust, and to dust all return. ²¹Who knows if the spirit of man rises upward and if the spirit of the animalᶜ goes down into the earth?"

²²So I saw that there is nothing better for a man than to enjoy his work, because that is his lot. For who can bring him to see what will happen after him?

3:20 ■ IS THERE AN AFTER-LIFE?

Old Testament writers said very little about the after-life. Not until Jesus' coming did God reveal details about heaven and hell. In this passage, the author wonders aloud whether death will be the end of everything. Yet he also adds some intriguing hints about the future. God "has also set eternity in the hearts of men", he declares (verse 11). He also refers to a time of future judgment (verse 17).

■ Oppression, Toil, Friendlessness

4 Again I looked and saw all the oppression that was taking place under the sun:

I saw the tears of the oppressed –
   and they have no comforter;
   power was on the side of their oppressors –
   and they have no comforter.
²And I declared that the dead,
   who had already died,
are happier than the living,
   who are still alive.
³But better than both
   is he who has not yet been,
who has not seen the evil
   that is done under the sun.

⁴And I saw that all labour and all achievement spring from man's envy of his neighbour. This too is meaningless, a chasing after the wind.

⁵The fool folds his hands
   and ruins himself.
⁶Better one handful with tranquillity
   than two handfuls with toil
   and chasing after the wind.

⁷Again I saw something meaningless under the sun:

⁸There was a man all alone;
   he had neither son nor brother.
There was no end to his toil,
   yet his eyes were not content with his
      wealth.
"For whom am I toiling," he asked,
   "and why am I depriving myself of
      enjoyment?"
This too is meaningless –
   a miserable business!

⁹Two are better than one,
   because they have a good return for their
      work:
¹⁰If one falls down,
   his friend can help him up.
But pity the man who falls
   and has no-one to help him up!
¹¹Also, if two lie down together, they will keep
      warm.
   But how can one keep warm alone?
¹²Though one may be overpowered,

ᵃ 15 Or God calls back the past   ᵇ 19 Or spirit   ᶜ 21 Or Who knows the spirit of man, which rises upward, or the spirit of the animal, which

two can defend themselves.
A cord of three strands is not quickly broken.

■ Advancement Is Meaningless

13Better a poor but wise youth than an old but foolish king who no longer knows how to take warning. 14The youth may have come from prison to the kingship, or he may have been born in poverty within his kingdom. 15I saw that all who lived and walked under the sun followed the youth, the king's successor. 16There was no end to all the people who were before them. But those who came later were not pleased with the successor. This too is meaningless, a chasing after the wind.

■ Stand in Awe of God

5 Guard your steps when you go to the house of God. Go near to listen rather than to offer the sacrifice of fools, who do not know that they do wrong.

2Do not be quick with your mouth,
    do not be hasty in your heart
    to utter anything before God.
  God is in heaven
    and you are on earth,
    so let your words be few.
3As a dream comes when there are many cares,
    so the speech of a fool when there are many
        words.

4When you make a vow to God, do not delay in fulfilling it. He has no pleasure in fools; fulfil your vow. 5It is better not to vow than to make a vow and not fulfil it. 6Do not let your mouth lead you into sin. And do not protest to the ⌊temple⌋ messenger, "My vow was a mistake." Why should God be angry at what you say and destroy the work of your hands? 7Much dreaming and many words are meaningless. Therefore stand in awe of God.

■ Riches Are Meaningless

8If you see the poor oppressed in a district, and justice and rights denied, do not be surprised at such things; for one official is eyed by a higher one, and over them both are others higher still. 9The increase from the land is taken by all; the king himself profits from the fields.

10Whoever loves money never has money
        enough;
    whoever loves wealth is never satisfied with
        his income.
    This too is meaningless.

5:10 ■ NEVER ENOUGH

Someone asked John D. Rockefeller, the richest man of his time, how much money is enough. He replied with a perfect definition of greed: "Just a little bit more." A real estate tycoon said something similar: "I don't want all the land in the world, just whatever touches mine."

11As goods increase,
    so do those who consume them.

And what benefit are they to the owner
    except to feast his eyes on them?

12The sleep of a labourer is sweet,
    whether he eats little or much,
but the abundance of a rich man
    permits him no sleep.

13I have seen a grievous evil under the sun:

wealth hoarded to the harm of its owner,
14   or wealth lost through some misfortune,
so that when he has a son
    there is nothing left for him.
15Naked a man comes from his mother's womb,
    and as he comes, so he departs.
He takes nothing from his labour
    that he can carry in his hand.

16This too is a grievous evil:

As a man comes, so he departs,
    and what does he gain,
    since he toils for the wind?
17All his days he eats in darkness,
    with great frustration, affliction and anger.

18Then I realised that it is good and proper for a man to eat and drink, and to find satisfaction in his toilsome labour under the sun during the few days of life God has given him—for this is his lot. 19Moreover, when God gives any man wealth and possessions, and enables him to enjoy them, to accept his lot and be happy in his work—this is a gift of God. 20He seldom reflects on the days of his life, because God keeps him occupied with gladness of heart.

5:18 ■ GOOD FOR SOMETHING

As he tasted various attractions in life—work, food, drink, success—the Teacher decided that all are "meaningless". None gave ultimate satisfaction. But in passages like this one, he admits that such good things are gifts from God and have a temporary value. Some possessions are better than none, wisdom is better than ignorance, life is better than death.

6 I have seen another evil under the sun, and it weighs heavily on men: 2God gives a man wealth, possessions and honour, so that he lacks nothing his heart desires, but God does not enable him to enjoy them, and a stranger enjoys them instead. This is meaningless, a grievous evil.

3A man may have a hundred children and live many years; yet no matter how long he lives, if he cannot enjoy his prosperity and does not receive proper burial, I say that a stillborn child is better off than he. 4It comes without meaning, it departs in darkness, and in darkness its name is shrouded. 5Though it never saw the sun or knew anything, it has more rest than does that man—6even if he lives a thousand years twice over but fails to enjoy his prosperity. Do not all go to the same place?

7All man's efforts are for his mouth,
    yet his appetite is never satisfied.
8What advantage has a wise man

over a fool?
What does a poor man gain
  by knowing how to conduct himself before
    others?
⁹Better what the eye sees
  than the roving of the appetite.
This too is meaningless,
  a chasing after the wind.

¹⁰Whatever exists has already been named,
  and what man is has been known;
no man can contend
  with one who is stronger than he.
¹¹The more the words,
  the less the meaning,
  and how does that profit anyone?

¹²For who knows what is good for a man in life,
during the few and meaningless days he passes
through like a shadow? Who can tell him what will
happen under the sun after he is gone?

■ Wisdom

7 A good name is better than fine perfume,
  and the day of death better than the day
    of birth.
²It is better to go to a house of mourning
  than to go to a house of feasting,
for death is the destiny of every man;
  the living should take this to heart.
³Sorrow is better than laughter,
  because a sad face is good for the heart.
⁴The heart of the wise is in the house of
    mourning,
  but the heart of fools is in the house of
    pleasure.
⁵It is better to heed a wise man's rebuke
  than to listen to the song of fools.
⁶Like the crackling of thorns under the pot,
  so is the laughter of fools.
This too is meaningless.

⁷Extortion turns a wise man into a fool,
  and a bribe corrupts the heart.
⁸The end of a matter is better than its beginning,
  and patience is better than pride.
⁹Do not be quickly provoked in your spirit,
  for anger resides in the lap of fools.

¹⁰Do not say, "Why were the old days better than
    these?"
  For it is not wise to ask such questions.

¹¹Wisdom, like an inheritance, is a good thing
  and benefits those who see the sun.
¹²Wisdom is a shelter
  as money is a shelter,
but the advantage of knowledge is this:
  that wisdom preserves the life of its
    possessor.

¹³Consider what God has done:

Who can straighten
  what he has made crooked?
¹⁴When times are good, be happy;
  but when times are bad, consider:
God has made the one

as well as the other.
Therefore, a man cannot discover
  anything about his future.

¹⁵In this meaningless life of mine I have seen both
of these:

a righteous man perishing in his righteousness,
  and a wicked man living long in his
    wickedness.
¹⁶Do not be over-righteous,
  neither be overwise—
  why destroy yourself?
¹⁷Do not be overwicked,
  and do not be a fool—
  why die before your time?
¹⁸It is good to grasp the one
  and not let go of the other.
The man who fears God will avoid all
  ⌐extremes⌐.ᵃ

7:15 ■ COMPANION BOOK

Passages in Ecclesiastes sound eerily like the
book of Job. Both books are "philosophical",
asking the hardest questions about life. Both
authors battled against despair, but for opposite
reasons: Job was overwhelmed by tragedy and
pain while the Teacher was jaded by luxury and
success. No matter what their status in life,
everyone has to face the same basic issues: Is
there a God? Is life unfair? Does it have meaning?

---

¹⁹Wisdom makes one wise man more powerful
  than ten rulers in a city.

²⁰There is not a righteous man on earth
  who does what is right and never sins.

²¹Do not pay attention to every word people say,
  or you may hear your servant cursing you—
²²for you know in your heart
  that many times you yourself have cursed
    others.

²³All this I tested by wisdom and I said,

"I am determined to be wise"—
  but this was beyond me.
²⁴Whatever wisdom may be,
  it is far off and most profound—
  who can discover it?
²⁵So I turned my mind to understand,
  to investigate and to search out wisdom and
    the scheme of things
and to understand the stupidity of wickedness
  and the madness of folly.

²⁶I find more bitter than death
  the woman who is a snare,
whose heart is a trap
  and whose hands are chains.
The man who pleases God will escape her,
  but the sinner she will ensnare.

²⁷"Look," says the Teacher,ᵇ "this is what I have
discovered:

ᵃ 18 Or will follow them both   ᵇ 27 Or leader of the assembly

"Adding one thing to another to discover the
scheme of things —
28 while I was still searching
but not finding —
I found one ⌊upright⌋ man among a thousand,
but not one ⌊upright⌋ woman among them all.
29This only have I found:
God made mankind upright,
but men have gone in search of many
schemes."

8 Who is like the wise man?
Who knows the explanation of things?
Wisdom brightens a man's face
and changes its hard appearance.

■ Obey the King

2Obey the king's command, I say, because you
took an oath before God. 3Do not be in a hurry to
leave the king's presence. Do not stand up for a bad
cause, for he will do whatever he pleases. 4Since a
king's word is supreme, who can say to him, "What
are you doing?"

5Whoever obeys his command will come to no
harm,
and the wise heart will know the proper
time and procedure.
6For there is a proper time and procedure for
every matter,
though a man's misery weighs heavily upon
him.

7Since no man knows the future,
who can tell him what is to come?
8No man has power over the wind to contain
it;[a]
so no-one has power over the day of his
death.
As no-one is discharged in time of war,
so wickedness will not release those who
practise it.

9All this I saw, as I applied my mind to everything
done under the sun. There is a time when a man
lords it over others to his own[b] hurt. 10Then too,
I saw the wicked buried — those who used to come
and go from the holy place and receive praise[c] in
the city where they did this. This too is meaningless.
11When the sentence for a crime is not quickly
carried out, the hearts of the people are filled with
schemes to do wrong. 12Although a wicked man
commits a hundred crimes and still lives a long
time, I know that it will go better with God-fearing
men, who are reverent before God. 13Yet because
the wicked do not fear God, it will not go well with
them, and their days will not lengthen like a
shadow.
14There is something else meaningless that occurs on earth: righteous men who get what the
wicked deserve, and wicked men who get what the
righteous deserve. This too, I say, is meaningless.
15So I commend the enjoyment of life, because
nothing is better for a man under the sun than to eat
and drink and be glad. Then joy will accompany him

in his work all the days of the life God has given him
under the sun.
16When I applied my mind to know wisdom and
to observe man's labour on earth — his eyes not seeing sleep day or night — 17then I saw all that God has
done. No-one can comprehend what goes on under
the sun. Despite all his efforts to search it out, man
cannot discover its meaning. Even if a wise man
claims he knows, he cannot really comprehend it.

8:17 ■ GOD'S FAULT?
Despite their similarities, Job and Ecclesiastes
reveal important differences. As this verse shows,
the Teacher never really expected to solve life's
riddles; his attitude of resignation contrasts with
Job's combativeness. Also, in his anguish, Job
sometimes questioned the character of God
himself, demanding a personal explanation. At no
time did the Teacher blame God for the unfairness
and meaninglessness he saw around him. "God
made mankind upright", he concludes, "but men
have gone in search of many schemes" (7:29).

■ A Common Destiny for All

9 So I reflected on all this and concluded that the
righteous and the wise and what they do are in
God's hands, but no man knows whether love or
hate awaits him. 2All share a common destiny — the
righteous and the wicked, the good and the bad,[a]
the clean and the unclean, those who offer sacrifices
and those who do not.

As it is with the good man,
so with the sinner;
as it is with those who take oaths,
so with those who are afraid to take them.

3This is the evil in everything that happens under
the sun: The same destiny overtakes all. The hearts
of men, moreover, are full of evil and there is madness in their hearts while they live, and afterwards
they join the dead. 4Anyone who is among the living
has hope[b] — even a live dog is better off than a dead
lion!

5For the living know that they will die,
but the dead know nothing;
they have no further reward,
and even the memory of them is forgotten.
6Their love, their hate
and their jealousy have long since vanished;
never again will they have a part
in anything that happens under the sun.

7Go, eat your food with gladness, and drink your
wine with a joyful heart, for it is now that God
favours what you do. 8Always be clothed in white,
and always anoint your head with oil. 9Enjoy life
with your wife, whom you love, all the days of this
meaningless life that God has given you under the
sun — all your meaningless days. For this is your lot
in life and in your toilsome labour under the sun.
10Whatever your hand finds to do, do it with all your
might, for in the grave,[c] where you are going, there

---

*a8 Or over his spirit to retain it   b9 Or to their   c10 Some Hebrew manuscripts and Septuagint (Aquila); most Hebrew manuscripts and are forgotten
a2 Septuagint (Aquila), Vulgate and Syriac; Hebrew does not have and the bad.   b4 Or What then is to be chosen? With all who live, there is hope
c10 Hebrew Sheol*

is neither working nor planning nor knowledge nor wisdom.

[11]I have seen something else under the sun:

The race is not to the swift
or the battle to the strong,
nor does food come to the wise
or wealth to the brilliant
or favour to the learned;
but time and chance happen to them all.

9:11 ■ LIFE IS UNFAIR

Chapters 8 and 9 eloquently voice the unfairness of life. People don't get what they deserve, claims the Teacher. Good people suffer while wicked people prosper. Everything seems determined only by time and chance. The Teacher's doubts about the after-life (see 3:20) affected all his thinking, because he saw the utter unfairness of life around him. In contrast, New Testament authors, with a solid belief in the after-life, showed confidence that God would ultimately judge all people with fairness.

[12]Moreover, no man knows when his hour will come:

As fish are caught in a cruel net,
or birds are taken in a snare,
so men are trapped by evil times
that fall unexpectedly upon them.

■ Wisdom Better Than Folly

[13]I also saw under the sun this example of wisdom that greatly impressed me: [14]There was once a small city with only a few people in it. And a powerful king came against it, surrounded it and built huge siegeworks against it. [15]Now there lived in that city a man poor but wise, and he saved the city by his wisdom. But nobody remembered that poor man. [16]So I said, "Wisdom is better than strength." But the poor man's wisdom is despised, and his words are no longer heeded.

[17]The quiet words of the wise are more to be heeded
than the shouts of a ruler of fools.
[18]Wisdom is better than weapons of war,
but one sinner destroys much good.

10 As dead flies give perfume a bad smell,
so a little folly outweighs wisdom and honour.
[2]The heart of the wise inclines to the right,
but the heart of the fool to the left.
[3]Even as he walks along the road,
the fool lacks sense
and shows everyone how stupid he is.
[4]If a ruler's anger rises against you,
do not leave your post;
calmness can lay great errors to rest.

[5]There is an evil I have seen under the sun,
the sort of error that arises from a ruler:
[6]Fools are put in many high positions,

while the rich occupy the low ones.
[7]I have seen slaves on horseback,
while princes go on foot like slaves.

[8]Whoever digs a pit may fall into it;
whoever breaks through a wall may be bitten
by a snake.
[9]Whoever quarries stones may be injured by them;
whoever splits logs may be endangered by them.

[10]If the axe is dull
and its edge unsharpened,
more strength is needed
but skill will bring success.

[11]If a snake bites before it is charmed,
there is no profit for the charmer.

[12]Words from a wise man's mouth are gracious,
but a fool is consumed by his own lips.
[13]At the beginning his words are folly;
at the end they are wicked madness —
[14]   and the fool multiplies words.

No-one knows what is coming —
who can tell him what will happen after him?

[15]A fool's work wearies him;
he does not know the way to town.

[16]Woe to you, O land whose king was a servant[a]
and whose princes feast in the morning.
[17]Blessed are you, O land whose king is of noble
birth
and whose princes eat at a proper time —
for strength and not for drunkenness.

[18]If a man is lazy, the rafters sag;
if his hands are idle, the house leaks.

[19]A feast is made for laughter,
and wine makes life merry,
but money is the answer for everything.

[20]Do not revile the king even in your thoughts,
or curse the rich in your bedroom,
because a bird of the air may carry your words,
and a bird on the wing may report what you
say.

■ Bread Upon the Waters

11 Cast your bread upon the waters,
for after many days you will find it again.
[2]Give portions to seven, yes to eight,
for you do not know what disaster may come
upon the land.

[3]If clouds are full of water,
they pour rain upon the earth.
Whether a tree falls to the south or to the
north,
in the place where it falls, there will it lie.
[4]Whoever watches the wind will not plant;
whoever looks at the clouds will not reap.

[5]As you do not know the path of the wind,
or how the body is formed[a] in a mother's
womb,

---

a 16 Or king is a child   a 5 Or know how life (or the spirit) / enters the body being formed

so you cannot understand the work of God,
　　the Maker of all things.

11:5 ■ BEYOND UNDERSTANDING

Even the Teacher, a man who possessed brilliant
powers of wisdom and observation, had to
conclude some things are beyond understanding.
Failing in his attempt to "figure out" life, he fell
back on simple advice: fear God and obey him, no
matter how things seem to you. In essence, he
concluded in favour of a life of faith. For him, an
old man, much of life had already passed; in
eloquent poetry he describes the decay that was
already at work in his body (12:1–7). Thus he
stressed, "Remember your Creator in the days of
your youth" (12:1).

6Sow your seed in the morning,
　　and at evening let not your hands be idle,
for you do not know which will succeed,
　　whether this or that,
　　or whether both will do equally well.

■ Remember Your Creator While Young

7Light is sweet,
　　and it pleases the eyes to see the sun.
8However many years a man may live,
　　let him enjoy them all.
But let him remember the days of darkness,
　　for they will be many.
Everything to come is meaningless.

9Be happy, young man, while you are young,
　　and let your heart give you joy in the days of
　　　　your youth.
Follow the ways of your heart
　　and whatever your eyes see,
but know that for all these things
　　God will bring you to judgment.
10So then, banish anxiety from your heart
　　and cast off the troubles of your body,
　　for youth and vigour are meaningless.

12 Remember your Creator
　　in the days of your youth,
before the days of trouble come
　　and the years approach when you will say,
　　"I find no pleasure in them"—
2before the sun and the light
　　and the moon and the stars grow dark,
　　and the clouds return after the rain;
3when the keepers of the house tremble,
　　and the strong men stoop,
when the grinders cease because they are few,
　　and those looking through the windows
　　　　grow dim;
4when the doors to the street are closed
　　and the sound of grinding fades;

when men rise up at the sound of birds,
　　but all their songs grow faint;
5when men are afraid of heights
　　and of dangers in the streets;
when the almond tree blossoms
　　and the grasshopper drags himself along
　　and desire no longer is stirred.
Then man goes to his eternal home
　　and mourners go about the streets.

6Remember him—before the silver cord is
　　　　severed,
　　or the golden bowl is broken;
before the pitcher is shattered at the spring,
　　or the wheel broken at the well,
7and the dust returns to the ground it came
　　　　from,
　　and the spirit returns to God who gave it.

8"Meaningless! Meaningless!" says the Teacher.*a*
　　"Everything is meaningless!"

■ The Conclusion of the Matter

9Not only was the Teacher wise, but also he imparted knowledge to the people. He pondered and
searched out and set in order many proverbs. 10The
Teacher searched to find just the right words, and
what he wrote was upright and true.

11The words of the wise are like goads, their collected sayings like firmly embedded nails—given by
one Shepherd. 12Be warned, my son, of anything in
addition to them.

Of making many books there is no end, and much
study wearies the body.

13Now all has been heard;
　　here is the conclusion of the matter:
Fear God and keep his commandments,
　　for this is the whole ⌊duty⌋ of man.
14For God will bring every deed into judgment,
　　including every hidden thing,
　　whether it is good or evil.

12:13 ■ THE GAMBLE

Having tried everything life has to offer, the
Teacher circles back to this uncomplicated
formula for making sense of our time on earth.
Although Ecclesiastes displays little of the
confidence of the book of Proverbs preceding it,
both arrive at exactly the same conclusion (see
Proverbs 1:7).

The 17th-century mathematician and
philosopher Blaise Pascal, who also struggled with
issues of meaninglessness, concluded that faith
sometimes resembles a wager. He told his friends,
"If I believe in God and life after death and you do
not, and if there is no God, we both lose when we
die. However, if there is a God, you still lose and I
gain everything."

a8 Or the leader of the assembly; also in verses 9 and 10

SONG OF SONGS

INTRODUCTION

■ AN INTOXICATING LOVE

A POEM ABOUT LOVE THE WAY IT'S MEANT TO BE

MANY WATERS CANNOT QUENCH LOVE; RIVERS CANNOT WASH IT AWAY. ■ 8:7

Flick the radio on, switch to any station, and what are you likely to hear? Love songs. Songs of new love, songs of disappointed love, songs of grateful love, songs of crazy love. Times change, but through history the flow of love songs is a constant.

Plenty of people are shocked to find an explicit love song in the Bible – complete with erotic lyrics. But Song of Songs is exactly that. It shows no embarrassment about lovers enjoying each other's bodies, and talking about it. Consequently, intermittent attempts have been made to rule Song of Songs out of the Bible or to make it for "Adults Only". In 16th-century Spain, for instance, professor Fray Luis de Leon was dragged out of his classroom and imprisoned for four years. His crime? He translated Song of Songs into Spanish.

■ ALLEGORICAL INTERPRETATION
More often, Song of Songs has been read as though it had nothing to do with lovers at all. Many have interpreted it as an allegory of love between God and his people. Some of these interpretations identify every poetic detail with some corresponding facet of our relationship to God. For instance, the bride's hair may be interpreted as non-Jewish nations who come to Christ. The famous 12th-century monk Saint Bernard of Clairvaux, using this allegorical approach, wrote 86 sermons on the first two chapters of Song of Songs.

Nowadays, few follow that kind of interpretation. Most scholars believe that the poem was intended to celebrate love between a newly married couple. God values love between a man and a woman. That's why he placed this song in his holy Bible. It may have been sung first at a wedding.

■ NAKED AND UNASHAMED
These lovers love to look at each other. They love to tell each other what they feel. They revel in the sensuous: the beauty of nature, the scent of perfumes and spices. They are openly erotic.

Their intoxication with love sounds quite up-to-date, not so different from what you hear on the radio. Yet Song of Songs conveys a very different atmosphere from most modern love songs. The explicit lyrics never become even slightly dirty. This love comes from the Garden of Eden, when both man and woman were naked and unashamed. It is tender, filled with delight, natural. You sense no shame or guilt; you feel that God is with the two as they love.

The lovers act as equals. Both woman and man take the initiative in praising each other. They don't flirt or play games: they say what they mean.

Yet they show caution and dignity in their love. While at the peak of joy, the lovers repeatedly warn others not to stir up love prematurely (2:7; 3:5; 8:4). They recognise the dangerously explosive side of love. "For love is as strong as death, its jealousy unyielding as the grave. It burns like blazing fire, like a mighty flame" (8:6).

■ HOW TO READ SONG OF SONGS

Since love songs are always popular, many people approach Song of Songs with great expectations. However, readers often find the book different from what they had expected.

Two main problems may hinder today's reader. One is the poetic imagery. No modern lover would say, "Your hair is like a flock of goats" (4:1), or, "Your nose is like the tower of Lebanon" (7:4). While some images in Song of Songs appeal – "His banner over me is love" (2:4) or "Love is as strong as death" (8:6) – the majority of the book's metaphors sound strange to our ears.

Most of the comparisons aren't visual, but emotional. For instance, when the lover tells his beloved that "your two breasts are like two fawns" (4:5), he isn't saying that her breasts look like deer. He is saying that they bring out the same tender feelings baby deer do. When you read strange-sounding metaphors in Song of Songs, don't ask, "What did these things (pomegranates, myrrh, a flock of sheep) look like?" but ask, "What were the lovers' emotions when they thought of them?"

A second problem: Song of Songs is hard to follow. One part doesn't seem connected to the next. Think of it as a series of snapshots of a couple in love – snapshots not necessarily in order. Put together in one photo album, they show the profound feelings of newly married lovers.

Though Song of Songs is primarily about love on the human level, many Christians and Jews have read it as a book about God's love. This was probably not the author's original intent, but it is a legitimate and inspiring way to look at the book. After all, God made human love, and other parts of the Bible suggest its similarity to God's love. (See Hosea 1–3 and Ephesians 5:22–33.) Song of Songs never makes this connection, but it does present a love so rich, so full, so unashamed that it's natural to think of God and his love for us.

■ 3-TRACK READING PLAN

For an explanation and complete listing of the 3-track reading plan, turn to page x.

■ TRACK 1:
Two-Week Courses on the Bible
See page x for information on these courses.

■ TRACK 2:
An Overview of Song of Songs

in 1 Day
☐ Day 1. Read the Introduction to Song of Songs and chapter 2, a beautiful love poem.
Now turn to page xi for your next Track 2 reading project.

■ TRACK 3:
All of Song of Songs in 8 Days
After you have read through Song of Songs, turn to pages xii–xiii for your next Track 3 reading project.

☐ 1   ☐ 2   ☐ 3   ☐ 4
☐ 5   ☐ 6   ☐ 7   ☐ 8

1 Solomon's Song of Songs.

■ Beloved*a*
²Let him kiss me with the kisses of his mouth –
for your love is more delightful than wine.
³Pleasing is the fragrance of your perfumes;
your name is like perfume poured out.
No wonder the maidens love you!
⁴Take me away with you – let us hurry!
Let the king bring me into his chambers.

■ Friends
We rejoice and delight in you;*b*
we will praise your love more than wine.

■ Beloved
How right they are to adore you!

⁵Dark am I, yet lovely,
O daughters of Jerusalem,
dark like the tents of Kedar,
like the tent curtains of Solomon.*c*
⁶Do not stare at me because I am dark,
because I am darkened by the sun.
My mother's sons were angry with me
and made me take care of the vineyards;
my own vineyard I have neglected.
⁷Tell me, you whom I love, where you graze
your flock
and where you rest your sheep at midday.
Why should I be like a veiled woman
beside the flocks of your friends?

■ Friends
⁸If you do not know, most beautiful of women,
follow the tracks of the sheep
and graze your young goats
by the tents of the shepherds.

1:6 ■ TAN LINES
Modern Britons, who lavish millions of pounds on suntan creams and foreign holidays, consider a suntan desirable, despite its health risks. Not so in Victorian times – or in Solomon's time. Soft white skin marked a more refined person who had not been required to work outdoors.

■ Lover
⁹I liken you, my darling, to a mare
harnessed to one of the chariots of Pharaoh.
¹⁰Your cheeks are beautiful with ear-rings,
your neck with strings of jewels.
¹¹We will make you ear-rings of gold,
studded with silver.

■ Beloved
¹²While the king was at his table,
my perfume spread its fragrance.
¹³My lover is to me a sachet of myrrh
resting between my breasts.
¹⁴My lover is to me a cluster of henna blossoms
from the vineyards of En Gedi.

*a*2 Primarily on the basis of the gender of the Hebrew pronouns used, male and female speakers are indicated in the margins by the captions *Lover* and *Beloved* respectively. The words of others are marked *Friends*. In some instances the divisions and their captions are debatable.   *b*4 The Hebrew is masculine singular.   *c*5 Or *Salma*

■ Lover
¹⁵How beautiful you are, my darling!
  Oh, how beautiful!
  Your eyes are doves.

■ Beloved
¹⁶How handsome you are, my lover!
  Oh, how charming!
  And our bed is verdant.

■ Lover
¹⁷The beams of our house are cedars;
  our rafters are firs.

■ Beloved*a*
2 I am a rose*b* of Sharon,
      a lily of the valleys.

■ Lover
²Like a lily among thorns
    is my darling among the maidens.

■ Beloved
³Like an apple tree among the trees of the forest
    is my lover among the young men.
  I delight to sit in his shade,
    and his fruit is sweet to my taste.
⁴He has taken me to the banquet hall,
    and his banner over me is love.
⁵Strengthen me with raisins,
    refresh me with apples,
    for I am faint with love.
⁶His left arm is under my head,
    and his right arm embraces me.
⁷Daughters of Jerusalem, I charge you
    by the gazelles and by the does of the field:
  Do not arouse or awaken love
    until it so desires.

2:4 ■ HIS BANNER OVER ME

A "banner" was a large military flag that held a fighting unit together in battle. In the noise and dust of the fight, soldiers needed a visible sign to keep them orientated. For these lovers, a public and visible declaration of love forms a "banner", keeping them together.

⁸Listen! My lover!
    Look! Here he comes,
  leaping across the mountains,
    bounding over the hills.
⁹My lover is like a gazelle or a young stag.
    Look! There he stands behind our wall,
  gazing through the windows,
    peering through the lattice.
¹⁰My lover spoke and said to me,
    "Arise, my darling,
    my beautiful one, and come with me.
¹¹See! The winter is past;
    the rains are over and gone.
¹²Flowers appear on the earth;
    the season of singing has come,
    the cooing of doves

is heard in our land.
¹³The fig-tree forms its early fruit;
    the blossoming vines spread their fragrance.
  Arise, come, my darling;
    my beautiful one, come with me."

■ Lover
¹⁴My dove in the clefts of the rock,
    in the hiding-places on the mountainside,
  show me your face,
    let me hear your voice;
  for your voice is sweet,
    and your face is lovely.
¹⁵Catch for us the foxes,
    the little foxes
  that ruin the vineyards,
    our vineyards that are in bloom.

■ Beloved
¹⁶My lover is mine and I am his;
    he browses among the lilies.
¹⁷Until the day breaks
    and the shadows flee,
  turn, my lover,
    and be like a gazelle
  or like a young stag
    on the rugged hills.*c*

3 All night long on my bed
    I looked for the one my heart loves;
  I looked for him but did not find him.
²I will get up now and go about the city,
    through its streets and squares;
  I will search for the one my heart loves.
  So I looked for him but did not find him.
³The watchmen found me
    as they made their rounds in the city.
  "Have you seen the one my heart loves?"
⁴Scarcely had I passed them
    when I found the one my heart loves.
  I held him and would not let him go
    till I had brought him to my mother's house,
    to the room of the one who conceived me.
⁵Daughters of Jerusalem, I charge you
    by the gazelles and by the does of the field:
  Do not arouse or awaken love
    until it so desires.

3:5 ■ LET LOVE SLEEP

If love is so wonderful, as this poem beautifully sings, shouldn't people pursue it recklessly? Yet the beloved warns them not to. Three times she urges others not to force love, but to let it develop at its own rate. Love should wait for its proper time.

⁶Who is this coming up from the desert
    like a column of smoke,
  perfumed with myrrh and incense
    made from all the spices of the merchant?
⁷Look! It is Solomon's carriage,
    escorted by sixty warriors,
    the noblest of Israel,
⁸all of them wearing the sword,

---

a1 Or Lover   *b1 Possibly a member of the crocus family*   *c17 Or the hills of Bether*

all experienced in battle,
each with his sword at his side,
    prepared for the terrors of the night.
⁹King Solomon made for himself the carriage;
    he made it of wood from Lebanon.
¹⁰Its posts he made of silver,
    its base of gold.
Its seat was upholstered with purple,
    its interior lovingly inlaid
    by*ᵃ* the daughters of Jerusalem.
¹¹Come out, you daughters of Zion,
    and look at King Solomon wearing the
        crown,
    the crown with which his mother crowned
        him
on the day of his wedding,
    the day his heart rejoiced.

■ Lover

4 How beautiful you are, my darling!
    Oh, how beautiful!
    Your eyes behind your veil are doves.
    Your hair is like a flock of goats
    descending from Mount Gilead.
²Your teeth are like a flock of sheep just shorn,
    coming up from the washing.
Each has its twin;
    not one of them is alone.
³Your lips are like a scarlet ribbon;
    your mouth is lovely.
Your temples behind your veil
    are like the halves of a pomegranate.
⁴Your neck is like the tower of David,
    built with elegance;*ᵃ*
on it hang a thousand shields,
    all of them shields of warriors.
⁵Your two breasts are like two fawns,
    like twin fawns of a gazelle
    that browse among the lilies.
⁶Until the day breaks
    and the shadows flee,
I will go to the mountain of myrrh
    and to the hill of incense.
⁷All beautiful you are, my darling;
    there is no flaw in you.

⁸Come with me from Lebanon, my bride,
    come with me from Lebanon.
Descend from the crest of Amana,
    from the top of Senir, the summit of Hermon,
from the lions' dens
    and the mountain haunts of the leopards.
⁹You have stolen my heart, my sister, my bride;
    you have stolen my heart
with one glance of your eyes,
    with one jewel of your necklace.
¹⁰How delightful is your love, my sister,
    my bride!
How much more pleasing is your love
    than wine,
and the fragrance of your perfume
    than any spice!
¹¹Your lips drop sweetness as the honeycomb,
    my bride;
milk and honey are under your tongue.

The fragrance of your garments is like that of
    Lebanon.
¹²You are a garden locked up, my sister, my
    bride;
you are a spring enclosed, a sealed fountain.
¹³Your plants are an orchard of pomegranates
    with choice fruits,
    with henna and nard,
¹⁴   nard and saffron,
    calamus and cinnamon,
    with every kind of incense tree,
    with myrrh and aloes
    and all the finest spices.
¹⁵You are*ᵇ* a garden fountain,
    a well of flowing water
    streaming down from Lebanon.

■ Beloved

¹⁶Awake, north wind,
    and come, south wind!
Blow on my garden,
    that its fragrance may spread abroad.
Let my lover come into his garden
    and taste its choice fruits.

■ Lover

5 I have come into my garden, my sister, my
    bride;
    I have gathered my myrrh with my spice.
I have eaten my honeycomb and my honey;
    I have drunk my wine and my milk.

■ Friends

Eat, O friends, and drink;
    drink your fill, O lovers.

■ Beloved

²I slept but my heart was awake.
    Listen! My lover is knocking:
"Open to me, my sister, my darling,
    my dove, my flawless one.
My head is drenched with dew,
    my hair with the dampness of the night."
³I have taken off my robe—
    must I put it on again?
I have washed my feet—
    must I soil them again?
⁴My lover thrust his hand through the
        latch-opening;
    my heart began to pound for him.
⁵I arose to open for my lover,
    and my hands dripped with myrrh,
my fingers with flowing myrrh,
    on the handles of the lock.
⁶I opened for my lover,
    but my lover had left; he was gone.
    My heart sank at his departure.*ᵃ*
I looked for him but did not find him.
    I called him but he did not answer.
⁷The watchmen found me
    as they made their rounds in the city.
They beat me, they bruised me;
    they took away my cloak,
    those watchmen of the walls!
⁸O daughters of Jerusalem, I charge you—

ᵃ 10 Or *its inlaid interior a gift of love / from*   *ᵃ* 4 The meaning of the Hebrew for this word is uncertain.   *ᵇ* 15 Or *I am* (spoken by the *Beloved)*
ᵃ 6 Or *heart had gone out to him when he spoke*

if you find my lover,
what will you tell him?
  Tell him I am faint with love.

5:2–8 ■ A NIGHTMARE

This short passage and the first five verses of
chapter 3 are strange and troubling interludes.
Many scholars think they are dream sequences,
nightmares showing that the beauty of love also
brings an increased vulnerability to pain and fear.
Here, the beloved is slow to get out of bed to
welcome her lover. As a result, he is gone when
she reaches the door.

■ Friends

⁹How is your beloved better than others,
  most beautiful of women?
How is your beloved better than others,
  that you charge us so?

■ Beloved

¹⁰My lover is radiant and ruddy,
  outstanding among ten thousand.
¹¹His head is purest gold;
  his hair is wavy
  and black as a raven.
¹²His eyes are like doves
  by the water streams,
washed in milk,
  mounted like jewels.
¹³His cheeks are like beds of spice
  yielding perfume.
His lips are like lilies
  dripping with myrrh.
¹⁴His arms are rods of gold
  set with chrysolite.
His body is like polished ivory
  decorated with sapphires.ᵇ
¹⁵His legs are pillars of marble
  set on bases of pure gold.
His appearance is like Lebanon,
  choice as its cedars.
¹⁶His mouth is sweetness itself;
  he is altogether lovely.
This is my lover, this my friend,
  O daughters of Jerusalem.

■ Friends

6 Where has your lover gone,
    most beautiful of women?
Which way did your lover turn,
  that we may look for him with you?

■ Beloved

²My lover has gone down to his garden,
  to the beds of spices,
to browse in the gardens
  and to gather lilies.
³I am my lover's and my lover is mine;
  he browses among the lilies.

■ Lover

⁴You are beautiful, my darling, as Tirzah,
  lovely as Jerusalem,
  majestic as troops with banners.
⁵Turn your eyes from me;
  they overwhelm me.
Your hair is like a flock of goats
  descending from Gilead.
⁶Your teeth are like a flock of sheep
  coming up from the washing.
Each has its twin,
  not one of them is alone.
⁷Your temples behind your veil
  are like the halves of a pomegranate.
⁸Sixty queens there may be,
  and eighty concubines,
  and virgins beyond number;
⁹but my dove, my perfect one, is unique,
  the only daughter of her mother,
  the favourite of the one who bore her.
The maidens saw her and called her blessed;
  the queens and concubines praised her.

■ Friends

¹⁰Who is this that appears like the dawn,
  fair as the moon, bright as the sun,
  majestic as the stars in procession?

■ Lover

¹¹I went down to the grove of nut trees
  to look at the new growth in the valley,
to see if the vines had budded
  or the pomegranates were in bloom.
¹²Before I realised it,
  my desire set me among the royal chariots of
    my people.ᵃ

■ Friends

¹³Come back, come back, O Shulammite;
  come back, come back, that we may gaze on
    you!

■ Lover

Why would you gaze on the Shulammite
  as on the dance of Mahanaim?

7 How beautiful your sandalled feet,
    O prince's daughter!
Your graceful legs are like jewels,
  the work of a craftsman's hands.
²Your navel is a rounded goblet
  that never lacks blended wine.
Your waist is a mound of wheat
  encircled by lilies.
³Your breasts are like two fawns,
  twins of a gazelle.
⁴Your neck is like an ivory tower.
Your eyes are the pools of Heshbon
  by the gate of Bath Rabbim.
Your nose is like the tower of Lebanon
  looking towards Damascus.
⁵Your head crowns you like Mount Carmel.
  Your hair is like royal tapestry;
  the king is held captive by its tresses.
⁶How beautiful you are and how pleasing,

ᵇ 14 Or lapis lazuli   ᵃ 12 Or among the chariots of Amminadab; or among the chariots of the people of the prince

O love, with your delights!
7Your stature is like that of the palm,
    and your breasts like clusters of fruit.
8I said, "I will climb the palm tree;
    I will take hold of its fruit."
May your breasts be like the clusters of the
      vine,
    the fragrance of your breath like apples,
9 and your mouth like the best wine.

■ Beloved
May the wine go straight to my lover,
    flowing gently over lips and teeth.*a*
10I belong to my lover,
    and his desire is for me.
11Come, my lover, let us go to the countryside,
    let us spend the night in the villages.*b*
12Let us go early to the vineyards
    to see if the vines have budded,
if their blossoms have opened,
    and if the pomegranates are in bloom —
there I will give you my love.
13The mandrakes send out their fragrance,
    and at our door is every delicacy,
both new and old,
    that I have stored up for you, my lover.

8 If only you were to me like a brother,
     who was nursed at my mother's breasts!
Then, if I found you outside,
    I would kiss you,
    and no-one would despise me.
2I would lead you
    and bring you to my mother's house —
    she who has taught me.
I would give you spiced wine to drink,
    the nectar of my pomegranates.
3His left arm is under my head
    and his right arm embraces me.
4Daughters of Jerusalem, I charge you:
    Do not arouse or awaken love
    until it so desires.

8:1 ■ A BROTHERLY KISS
In oriental culture, even a married couple could
not express their love publicly. Only a brother and
sister could openly kiss. The beloved is wishing
she had the right to show their love to the world.

■ Friends
5Who is this coming up from the desert
    leaning on her lover?

■ Beloved
Under the apple tree I roused you;
    there your mother conceived you,

there she who was in labour gave you birth.
6Place me like a seal over your heart,
    like a seal on your arm;
for love is as strong as death,
    its jealousy*a* unyielding as the grave.*b*
It burns like blazing fire,
    like a mighty flame.*c*
7Many waters cannot quench love;
    rivers cannot wash it away.
If one were to give
    all the wealth of his house for love,
    it*d* would be utterly scorned.

8:6 ■ LOVE AND DEATH
Death sweeps everything away. It yields to
no-one, and once you are in its power you cannot
escape. So with love: it takes control of your life,
and like a gigantic fire, it cannot be doused. Love
must be treated with the greatest caution and
respect.

■ Friends
8We have a young sister,
    and her breasts are not yet grown.
What shall we do for our sister
    for the day she is spoken for?
9If she is a wall,
    we will build towers of silver on her.
If she is a door,
    we will enclose her with panels of cedar.

■ Beloved
10I am a wall,
    and my breasts are like towers.
Thus I have become in his eyes
    like one bringing contentment.
11Solomon had a vineyard in Baal Hamon;
    he let out his vineyard to tenants.
Each was to bring for its fruit
    a thousand shekels*e* of silver.
12But my own vineyard is mine to give;
    the thousand shekels are for you, O Solomon,
    and two hundred*f* are for those who tend
      its fruit.

■ Lover
13You who dwell in the gardens
    with friends in attendance,
    let me hear your voice!

■ Beloved
14Come away, my lover,
    and be like a gazelle
or like a young stag
    on the spice-laden mountains.

---

*a*9 Septuagint, Aquila, Vulgate and Syriac; Hebrew *lips of sleepers*   *b*11 Or *henna bushes*   *a*6 Or *ardour*   *b*6 Hebrew *Sheol*   *c*6 Or / *like the very flame of the LORD*   *d*7 Or *he*   *e*11 That is, about 25 pounds (about 11.5 kilograms); also in verse 12   *f*12 That is, about 5 pounds (about 2.3 kilograms)

ISAIAH

INTRODUCTION

■ PROPHET, POET, AND POLITICIAN

HIS NATION AT A CROSSROADS, ISAIAH ROSE TO MEET THE CHALLENGE

AND HE LOOKED FOR JUSTICE, BUT SAW BLOODSHED; FOR RIGHTEOUSNESS, BUT HEARD CRIES OF DISTRESS. ■ 5:7

The prophet Isaiah was a giant of Jewish history. He was the Shakespeare of Hebrew literature, and the New Testament quotes him more than all the other prophets combined. No other biblical author can match his rich vocabulary and use of imagery.

And yet Isaiah spent his days not in an ivory tower, but in the corridors of power. He served as adviser to the kings of Judah and helped set the course of his nation.

■ DAYS OF CRISIS

Isaiah lived at a crucial time, midway between the founding of the kingdom under Saul and David and its eventual destruction. A civil war had split the Israelites into North (Israel) and South (Judah), and Isaiah lived in the more pious Southern Kingdom.

When Isaiah began his work, the nation seemed strong and wealthy. But Isaiah saw signs of grave danger. People were using their power to harass the poor. Men went around drunk; women cared more about their clothes than about their neighbours' hunger. People gave lip service to God and kept up the outward appearance of religion but did little more.

Outside dangers loomed even larger. The armies of neighbouring Israel were rattling swords and spears at the border. On all sides, monster empires were growing, especially Egypt

and Assyria. Judah was caught in a pincer's grip. Should the nation choose one of the empires as an ally?

■ HARSH WORDS FROM AN UNCOMPROMISING PROPHET

The nation of Judah, said Isaiah, stood at a crossroads: it could either regain its footing or begin a dangerous slide downwards. The prophet did not temper his message for the sake of popular opinion. He had harsh and unyielding words about what changes must take place.

Although he moved in royal circles, Isaiah was hardly a yes-man in politics. Sometimes he stood alone against a tide of optimism. His very name meant "The LORD saves", and he warned kings that relying on military power or wealth or any force other than God would lead to disaster.

Isaiah outlasted four kings, but he finally offended one beyond repair. King Manasseh (notorious for practising infant sacrifice) found Isaiah's strong words too much to bear. Tradition records that he had Isaiah killed by fastening him between two planks of wood and sawing his body in half.

Manasseh has long since disappeared into obscurity. But Isaiah, through this book, endures as one of the great authors of all time. Sometimes the pen *is* mightier than the sword.

■ HOW TO READ ISAIAH

In the eighth century B.C., about the time Homer was writing *The Iliad* and *The Odyssey*, Isaiah wrote the book that bears his name. It is arguably the most eloquent book in the Old Testament, and you will probably recognise many verses and phrases.

Isaiah is full of profound insights into the nature of God and his plan for the earth. Due to its length and its peculiar organisation, however, the book may seem hard to grasp.

Remember that Isaiah consists of a collection of many messages on various topics,

pulled together into groupings. To understand Isaiah, it helps to think of "road signs" that set off the major groupings. Here is a summary of them:

Isaiah 1–12: Isaiah's call and messages of warning to Judah during the prosperous days of the kingdom. (These came mostly in the reigns of Jotham and Ahaz: see "A Line-up of Rulers", pages 260–268.)

Isaiah 13 – 23: Isaiah's messages to all the nations around Judah – including enemies and close allies.

Isaiah 24 – 35: A view of the earth's future (24 – 27) and specific messages to the people of Judah as they faced Assyria's imminent invasion.

Isaiah 36 – 39: An interlude telling of great crises faced by King Hezekiah. The focus of the book moves from Assyria to Babylon.

Isaiah 40 – 48: Prophecies addressed to a very different situation, 200 years into the future. Now Babylon, not Assyria, is the great enemy.

Isaiah 49 – 55: A word of hope about final deliverance through the "suffering servant".

Isaiah 56–66: General warnings to Judah, and a view of the future.

■ 3-TRACK READING PLAN

For an explanation and complete listing of the 3-track reading plan, turn to page x.

■ TRACK 1:
Two-Week Courses on the Bible
The Track 1 reading programme on the Old Testament includes one chapter from Isaiah. See page x for a complete listing of this course.

■ TRACK 2:
An Overview of Isaiah in 6 Days
☐ Day 1. Read the Introduction to Isaiah and also chapter 6. This chapter describes Isaiah's dramatic call.
☐ Day 2. Read chapter 25, a song of praise.

☐ Day 3. Read chapter 40, a great description of God and his power over the whole earth.
☐ Day 4. Read chapter 52, which gives detailed descriptions of God's ultimate plan.
☐ Day 5. Read chapter 53, a remarkable prophecy quoted at least ten times in the New Testament.
☐ Day 6. Read chapter 55, a word of great comfort from God.
Now turn to page xi for your next Track 2 reading project.

■ TRACK 3:
All of Isaiah in 63 Days
After you have read through

Isaiah, turn to pages xii–xiii for your next Track 3 reading project.

☐ 1	☐ 2	☐ 3	☐ 4–5
☐ 6	☐ 7	☐ 8	☐ 9
☐ 10	☐ 11	☐ 12	☐ 13
☐ 14	☐ 15	☐ 16	☐ 17
☐ 18	☐ 19–20		☐ 21
☐ 22	☐ 23	☐ 24	☐ 25
☐ 26	☐ 27	☐ 28	☐ 29
☐ 30	☐ 31	☐ 32	☐ 33
☐ 34	☐ 35	☐ 36	☐ 37
☐ 38–39		☐ 40	☐ 41
☐ 42	☐ 43	☐ 44	☐ 45
☐ 46	☐ 47	☐ 48	☐ 49
☐ 50	☐ 51	☐ 52	☐ 53
☐ 54	☐ 55	☐ 56	☐ 57
☐ 58	☐ 59	☐ 60	☐ 61
☐ 62	☐ 63	☐ 64	☐ 65
☐ 66			

1 The vision concerning Judah and Jerusalem that Isaiah son of Amoz saw during the reigns of Uzziah, Jotham, Ahaz and Hezekiah, kings of Judah.

■ A Rebellious Nation
²Hear, O heavens! Listen, O earth!
For the LORD has spoken:
"I reared children and brought them up,
but they have rebelled against me.
³The ox knows his master
the donkey his owner's manger,
but Israel does not know,
my people do not understand."

⁴Ah, sinful nation,
a people loaded with guilt,
a brood of evildoers,
children given to corruption!
They have forsaken the LORD;
they have spurned the Holy One of Israel
and turned their backs on him.

⁵Why should you be beaten any more?
Why do you persist in rebellion?
Your whole head is injured,
your whole heart afflicted.
⁶From the sole of your foot to the top of your head
there is no soundness—
only wounds and bruises

and open sores,
not cleansed or bandaged
or soothed with oil.

⁷Your country is desolate,
your cities burned with fire;
your fields are being stripped by foreigners
right before you,
laid waste as when overthrown by strangers.
⁸The Daughter of Zion is left
like a shelter in a vineyard,
like a hut in a field of melons,
like a city under siege.
⁹Unless the LORD Almighty
had left us some survivors,
we would have become like Sodom,
we would have been like Gomorrah.

¹⁰Hear the word of the LORD,
you rulers of Sodom;
listen to the law of our God,
you people of Gomorrah!
¹¹"The multitude of your sacrifices—
what are they to me?" says the LORD.
"I have more than enough of burnt offerings,
of rams and the fat of fattened animals;
I have no pleasure
in the blood of bulls and lambs and goats.
¹²When you come to appear before me,
who has asked this of you,

this trampling of my courts?
¹³Stop bringing meaningless offerings!
Your incense is detestable to me.
New Moons, Sabbaths and convocations—
I cannot bear your evil assemblies.
¹⁴Your New Moon festivals and your appointed
feasts
my soul hates.
They have become a burden to me;
I am weary of bearing them.
¹⁵When you spread out your hands in prayer,
I will hide my eyes from you;
even if you offer many prayers,
I will not listen.
Your hands are full of blood;
¹⁶   wash and make yourselves clean.
Take your evil deeds
out of my sight!
Stop doing wrong,
¹⁷   learn to do right!
Seek justice,
encourage the oppressed.ᵃ
Defend the cause of the fatherless,
plead the case of the widow.

1:14 ■ THE NEW SODOM

Is God finished with Israel? He denounces them
as "Sodom and Gomorrah" (verse 10), judging
their worship worthless, and their prayers an
insult. But just when his tirade reaches its peak,
God invites the Israelites to "come . . . reason"
with him. Sins "like scarlet" shall be "as white as
snow" (verse 18). God judges his people not to
destroy them, but to bring them to repentance,
forgiveness, and redemption.

¹⁸"Come now, let us reason together,"
says the LORD.
"Though your sins are like scarlet,
they shall be as white as snow;
though they are red as crimson,
they shall be like wool.
¹⁹If you are willing and obedient,
you will eat the best from the land;
²⁰but if you resist and rebel,
you will be devoured by the sword."
For the mouth of the LORD has spoken.

²¹See how the faithful city
has become a harlot!
She once was full of justice;
righteousness used to dwell in her—
but now murderers!
²²Your silver has become dross,
your choice wine is diluted with water.
²³Your rulers are rebels,
companions of thieves;
they all love bribes
and chase after gifts.
They do not defend the cause of the fatherless;
the widow's case does not come before
them.
²⁴Therefore the Lord, the LORD Almighty,
the Mighty One of Israel, declares:

"Ah, I will get relief from my foes
and avenge myself on my enemies.
²⁵I will turn my hand against you;
I will thoroughly purge away your dross
and remove all your impurities.
²⁶I will restore your judges as in days of old,
your counsellors as at the beginning.
Afterwards you will be called
the City of Righteousness,
the Faithful City."

1:23 ■ JUSTICE, NOT RELIGION

Isaiah 1 paints a striking picture of conditions in
Judah. Descriptions of luxury indicate that the
nation was prospering economically. There was no
shortage of offerings, prayers, and religious
celebrations (verses 11–17). But Isaiah
condemned Judah for not putting religion into
practice by defending weak people, such as
widows and the fatherless. The country's
prosperity had come at the poor's expense.

²⁷Zion will be redeemed with justice,
her penitent ones with righteousness.
²⁸But rebels and sinners will both be broken,
and those who forsake the LORD will perish.

²⁹"You will be ashamed because of the sacred
oaks
in which you have delighted;
you will be disgraced because of the gardens
that you have chosen.
³⁰You will be like an oak with fading leaves,
like a garden without water.
³¹The mighty man will become tinder
and his work a spark;
both will burn together,
with no-one to quench the fire."

■ The Mountain of the LORD

2 This is what Isaiah son of Amoz saw concerning
Judah and Jerusalem:

²In the last days

the mountain of the LORD's temple will be
established
as chief among the mountains;
it will be raised above the hills,
and all nations will stream to it.

³Many peoples will come and say,

"Come, let us go up to the mountain of the
LORD,
to the house of the God of Jacob.
He will teach us his ways,
so that we may walk in his paths."
The law will go out from Zion,
the word of the LORD from Jerusalem.
⁴He will judge between the nations
and will settle disputes for many peoples.
They will beat their swords into ploughshares
and their spears into pruning hooks.
Nation will not take up sword against nation,
nor will they train for war any more.

ᵃ 17 Or / rebuke the oppressor

⁵Come, O house of Jacob,
  let us walk in the light of the LORD.

■ The Day of the LORD
⁶You have abandoned your people,
  the house of Jacob.
They are full of superstitions from the East;
  they practise divination like the Philistines
  and clasp hands with pagans.
⁷Their land is full of silver and gold;
  there is no end to their treasures.
Their land is full of horses;
  there is no end to the chariots.
⁸Their land is full of idols;
  they bow down to the work of their hands,
  to what their fingers have made.
⁹So man will be brought low
  and mankind humbled—
  do not forgive them.ᵃ

¹⁰Go into the rocks,
  hide in the ground
from dread of the LORD
  and the splendour of his majesty!
¹¹The eyes of the arrogant man will be humbled
  and the pride of men brought low;
the LORD alone will be exalted in that day.

¹²The LORD Almighty has a day in store
  for all the proud and lofty,
  for all that is exalted
  (and they will be humbled),
¹³for all the cedars of Lebanon, tall and lofty,
  and all the oaks of Bashan,
¹⁴for all the towering mountains
  and all the high hills,
¹⁵for every lofty tower
  and every fortified wall,
¹⁶for every trading shipᵇ
  and every stately vessel.
¹⁷The arrogance of man will be brought low
  and the pride of men humbled;
the LORD alone will be exalted in that day,
¹⁸ and the idols will totally disappear.

¹⁹Men will flee to caves in the rocks
  and to holes in the ground
from the dread of the LORD
  and the splendour of his majesty,
  when he rises to shake the earth.
²⁰In that day men will throw away
  to the rodents and bats
their idols of silver and idols of gold,
  which they made to worship.
²¹They will flee to caverns in the rocks
  and to the overhanging crags
from dread of the LORD
  and the splendour of his majesty,
  when he rises to shake the earth.

²²Stop trusting in man,
  who has but a breath in his nostrils.
Of what account is he?

ᵃ9 Or not raise them up   ᵇ16 Hebrew every ship of Tarshish

■ Judgment on Jerusalem and Judah
3 See now, the Lord,
   the LORD Almighty,
is about to take from Jerusalem and Judah
  both supply and support:
all supplies of food and all supplies of water,
²   the hero and warrior,
the judge and prophet,
  the soothsayer and elder,
³the captain of fifty and man of rank,
  the counsellor, skilled craftsman and clever
  enchanter.

⁴I will make boys their officials;
  mere children will govern them.
⁵People will oppress each other—
  man against man, neighbour against
  neighbour.
The young will rise up against the old,
  the base against the honourable.

⁶A man will seize one of his brothers
  at his father's home, and say,
"You have a cloak, you be our leader;
  take charge of this heap of ruins!"
⁷But in that day he will cry out,
  "I have no remedy.
I have no food or clothing in my house;
  do not make me the leader of the people."

3:6 ■ TOTAL ANARCHY
Isaiah foresees a time of judgment on Judah,
when total anarchy will prevail. Leaders will be
chosen at random, and the nation's supply of
young men will be decimated by war (verse 25).
The vivid passage on the haughty women of Zion
(3:16–4:1) shows why this book is admired for its
writing style.

⁸Jerusalem staggers,
  Judah is falling;
their words and deeds are against the LORD,
  defying his glorious presence.
⁹The look on their faces testifies against them;
  they parade their sin like Sodom;
  they do not hide it.
Woe to them!
  They have brought disaster upon themselves.

¹⁰Tell the righteous it will be well with them,
  for they will enjoy the fruit of their deeds.
¹¹Woe to the wicked! Disaster is upon them!
  They will be paid back for what their hands
  have done.

¹²Youths oppress my people,
  women rule over them.
O my people, your guides lead you astray;
  they turn you from the path.

¹³The LORD takes his place in court;
  he rises to judge the people.
¹⁴The LORD enters into judgment
  against the elders and leaders of his people:
"It is you who have ruined my vineyard;
  the plunder from the poor is in your houses.

¹⁵What do you mean by crushing my people
   and grinding the faces of the poor?"
      declares the Lord, the LORD Almighty.

¹⁶The LORD says,
   "The women of Zion are haughty,
walking along with outstretched necks,
   flirting with their eyes,
tripping along with mincing steps,
   with ornaments jingling on their ankles.
¹⁷Therefore the Lord will bring sores on the
   heads of the women of Zion;
   the LORD will make their scalps bald."

¹⁸In that day the Lord will snatch away their
finery: the bangles and headbands and crescent
necklaces, ¹⁹the ear-rings and bracelets and veils,
²⁰the head-dresses and ankle chains and sashes, the
perfume bottles and charms, ²¹the signet rings and
nose rings, ²²the fine robes and the capes and
cloaks, the purses ²³and mirrors, and the linen garments and tiaras and shawls.

²⁴Instead of fragrance there will be a stench;
   instead of a sash, a rope;
   instead of well-dressed hair, baldness;
   instead of fine clothing, sackcloth;
   instead of beauty, branding.
²⁵Your men will fall by the sword,
   your warriors in battle.
²⁶The gates of Zion will lament and mourn;
   destitute, she will sit on the ground.

4 In that day seven women
    will take hold of one man
and say, "We will eat our own food
   and provide our own clothes;
only let us be called by your name.
   Take away our disgrace!"

■ The Branch of the LORD
   ²In that day the Branch of the LORD will be beautiful and glorious, and the fruit of the land will be the
pride and glory of the survivors in Israel. ³Those
who are left in Zion, who remain in Jerusalem, will
be called holy, all who are recorded among the living in Jerusalem. ⁴The Lord will wash away the filth
of the women of Zion; he will cleanse the blood-
stains from Jerusalem by a spirit*a* of judgment and
a spirit*a* of fire. ⁵Then the LORD will create over all
of Mount Zion and over those who assemble there
a cloud of smoke by day and a glow of flaming fire
by night; over all the glory will be a canopy. ⁶It will
be a shelter and shade from the heat of the day, and
a refuge and hiding-place from the storm and rain.

■ The Song of the Vineyard
5 I will sing for the one I love
    a song about his vineyard:
My loved one had a vineyard
   on a fertile hillside.
²He dug it up and cleared it of stones
   and planted it with the choicest vines.
He built a watchtower in it
   and cut out a winepress as well.
Then he looked for a crop of good grapes,

but it yielded only bad fruit.

³"Now you dwellers in Jerusalem and men of
   Judah,
   judge between me and my vineyard.
⁴What more could have been done for my
   vineyard
   than I have done for it?
When I looked for good grapes,
   why did it yield only bad?
⁵Now I will tell you
   what I am going to do to my vineyard:
I will take away its hedge,
   and it will be destroyed;
I will break down its wall,
   and it will be trampled.
⁶I will make it a wasteland,
   neither pruned nor cultivated,
   and briers and thorns will grow there.
I will command the clouds
   not to rain on it."

5:4 ■ WHAT CAN GOD DO?
The "Song of the Vineyard" beautifully summarises
God's message to Judah. Although he had done
everything possible to care for the nation, his
"vineyard" – the house of Israel – had produced
only wild grapes. What else could he do but allow
it to grow wild and uncultivated? Jesus used a
related analogy in some of his parables (Matthew
20:1–16; 21:33–46; Mark 12:1–12; Luke 13:6–9;
20:9–19).

---

⁷The vineyard of the LORD Almighty
   is the house of Israel,
and the men of Judah
   are the garden of his delight.
And he looked for justice, but saw bloodshed;
   for righteousness, but heard cries of distress.

■ Woes and Judgments
⁸Woe to you who add house to house
   and join field to field
till no space is left
   and you live alone in the land.

⁹The LORD Almighty has declared in my hearing:

"Surely the great houses will become desolate,
   the fine mansions left without occupants.
¹⁰A ten-acre*a* vineyard will produce only a
   bath*b* of wine,
   a homer*c* of seed only an ephah*d* of grain."

¹¹Woe to those who rise early in the morning
   to run after their drinks,
who stay up late at night
   till they are inflamed with wine.
¹²They have harps and lyres at their banquets,
   tambourines and flutes and wine,
but they have no regard for the deeds of the
   LORD,
   no respect for the work of his hands.
¹³Therefore my people will go into exile
   for lack of understanding;

---

a 4 Or *the Spirit*   *a 10* Hebrew *ten-yoke,* that is, the land ploughed by 10 yoke of oxen in one day   *b 10* That is, probably about 5 gallons (about 22 litres)
c 10 That is, probably about 6 bushels (about 220 litres)   *d 10* That is, probably about ⅗ bushel (about 22 litres)

their men of rank will die of hunger
and their masses will be parched with thirst.
14Therefore the grave*e* enlarges its appetite
and opens its mouth without limit;
into it will descend their nobles and masses
with all their brawlers and revellers.
15So man will be brought low
and mankind humbled,
the eyes of the arrogant humbled.
16But the LORD Almighty will be exalted by his
justice,
and the holy God will show himself holy by
his righteousness.
17Then sheep will graze as in their own pasture;
lambs will feed*f* among the ruins of the
rich.

18Woe to those who draw sin along with cords of
deceit,
and wickedness as with cart ropes,
19to those who say, "Let God hurry,
let him hasten his work
so that we may see it.
Let it approach,
let the plan of the Holy One of Israel come,
so that we may know it."

20Woe to those who call evil good
and good evil,
who put darkness for light
and light for darkness,
who put bitter for sweet
and sweet for bitter.

21Woe to those who are wise in their own eyes
and clever in their own sight.

22Woe to those who are heroes at drinking wine
and champions at mixing drinks,
23who acquit the guilty for a bribe,
but deny justice to the innocent.
24Therefore, as tongues of fire lick up straw
and as dry grass sinks down in the flames,
so their roots will decay
and their flowers blow away like dust;
for they have rejected the law of the LORD
Almighty
and spurned the word of the Holy One of
Israel.
25Therefore the LORD's anger burns against his
people;
his hand is raised and he strikes them down.
The mountains shake,
and the dead bodies are like refuse in the
streets.

Yet for all this, his anger is not turned away,
his hand is still upraised.

26He lifts up a banner for the distant nations,
he whistles for those at the ends of the earth.
Here they come,
swiftly and speedily!
27Not one of them grows tired or stumbles,
not one slumbers or sleeps;
not a belt is loosened at the waist,
not a sandal thong is broken.
28Their arrows are sharp,

all their bows are strung;
their horses' hoofs seem like flint,
their chariot wheels like a whirlwind.
29Their roar is like that of the lion,
they roar like young lions;
they growl as they seize their prey
and carry it off with no-one to rescue.
30In that day they will roar over it
like the roaring of the sea.
And if one looks at the land,
he will see darkness and distress;
even the light will be darkened by the
clouds.

■ Isaiah's Commission

6 In the year that King Uzziah died, I saw the Lord
seated on a throne, high and exalted, and the
train of his robe filled the temple. 2Above him were
seraphs, each with six wings: With two wings they
covered their faces, with two they covered their
feet, and with two they were flying. 3And they were
calling to one another:

"Holy, holy, holy is the LORD Almighty;
the whole earth is full of his glory."

4At the sound of their voices the doorposts and
thresholds shook and the temple was filled with
smoke.

6:2 ■ A MESSAGE FROM GOD
Isaiah experienced a dramatic call from God to
become a prophet. The message was personally
delivered by *seraphs*, a term that appears only
here and means "something burning and
dazzling". Evidently, seraphs were angels who
acted as spokesmen for God.

5"Woe to me!" I cried. "I am ruined! For I am a
man of unclean lips, and I live among a people of
unclean lips, and my eyes have seen the King, the
LORD Almighty."
6Then one of the seraphs flew to me with a live
coal in his hand, which he had taken with tongs
from the altar. 7With it he touched my mouth and
said, "See, this has touched your lips; your guilt is
taken away and your sin atoned for."
8Then I heard the voice of the Lord saying,
"Whom shall I send? And who will go for us?"
And I said, "Here am I. Send me!"
9He said, "Go and tell this people:

" 'Be ever hearing, but never understanding;
be ever seeing, but never perceiving.'
10Make the heart of this people calloused;
make their ears dull
and close their eyes.*a*
Otherwise they might see with their eyes,
hear with their ears,
understand with their hearts,
and turn and be healed."

11Then I said, "For how long, O Lord?"
And he answered:

"Until the cities lie ruined

---

e 14 Hebrew *Sheol*   *f* 17 Septuagint; Hebrew / *strangers will eat*   *a* 9, 10 Hebrew; Septuagint *'You will be ever hearing, but never understanding; / you
will be ever seeing, but never perceiving.' / 10 This people's heart has become calloused; / they hardly hear with their ears, / and they have closed their eyes*

and without inhabitant,
until the houses are left deserted
    and the fields ruined and ravaged,
¹²until the LORD has sent everyone far away
    and the land is utterly forsaken.
¹³And though a tenth remains in the land,
    it will again be laid waste.
But as the terebinth and oak
    leave stumps when they are cut down,
    so the holy seed will be the stump in the
        land."

■ The Sign of Immanuel

7 When Ahaz son of Jotham, the son of Uzziah,
    was king of Judah, King Rezin of Aram and
Pekah son of Remaliah king of Israel marched up to
fight against Jerusalem, but they could not overpower it.

²Now the house of David was told, "Aram has allied itself with*a* Ephraim"; so the hearts of Ahaz and
his people were shaken, as the trees of the forest are
shaken by the wind.

³Then the LORD said to Isaiah, "Go out, you and
your son Shear-Jashub,*b* to meet Ahaz at the end of
the aqueduct of the Upper Pool, on the road to the
Washerman's Field. ⁴Say to him, 'Be careful, keep
calm and don't be afraid. Do not lose heart because
of these two smouldering stubs of firewood—because of the fierce anger of Rezin and Aram and of
the son of Remaliah. ⁵Aram, Ephraim and Remaliah's
son have plotted your ruin, saying, ⁶"Let us invade
Judah; let us tear it apart and divide it among ourselves, and make the son of Tabeel king over it."
⁷Yet this is what the Sovereign LORD says:

" 'It will not take place,
    it will not happen,
⁸for the head of Aram is Damascus,
    and the head of Damascus is only Rezin.
Within sixty-five years
    Ephraim will be too shattered to be a people.
⁹The head of Ephraim is Samaria,
    and the head of Samaria is only Remaliah's
        son.
If you do not stand firm in your faith,
    you will not stand at all.' "

¹⁰Again the LORD spoke to Ahaz, ¹¹"Ask the LORD
your God for a sign, whether in the deepest depths
or in the highest heights."

¹²But Ahaz said, "I will not ask; I will not put the
LORD to the test."

¹³Then Isaiah said, "Hear now, you house of
David! Is it not enough to try the patience of men?
Will you try the patience of my God also? ¹⁴Therefore the Lord himself will give you*c* a sign: The virgin will be with child and will give birth to a son,
and*d* will call him Immanuel.*e* ¹⁵He will eat curds
and honey when he knows enough to reject the
wrong and choose the right. ¹⁶But before the boy
knows enough to reject the wrong and choose the
right, the land of the two kings you dread will be
laid waste. ¹⁷The LORD will bring on you and on
your people and on the house of your father a time

unlike any since Ephraim broke away from Judah—
he will bring the king of Assyria."

¹⁸In that day the LORD will whistle for flies from
the distant streams of Egypt and for bees from the
land of Assyria. ¹⁹They will all come and settle in the
steep ravines and in the crevices in the rocks, on all
the thornbushes and at all the water holes. ²⁰In that
day the Lord will use a razor hired from beyond the
River*f*—the king of Assyria—to shave your head
and the hair of your legs, and to take off your beards
also. ²¹In that day, a man will keep alive a young
cow and two goats. ²²And because of the abundance
of the milk they give, he will have curds to eat. All
who remain in the land will eat curds and honey.
²³In that day, in every place where there were a
thousand vines worth a thousand silver shekels,*g*
there will be only briers and thorns. ²⁴Men will go
there with bow and arrow, for the land will be covered with briers and thorns. ²⁵As for all the hills
once cultivated by the hoe, you will no longer go
there for fear of the briers and thorns; they will become places where cattle are turned loose and
where sheep run.

7:14 ■ A FAMOUS SIGN
Like so many prophecies, this one probably had
two meanings: one for Isaiah's time and another
much later. Isaiah urged King Ahaz to seek a sign
from God about Judah's safety from its
neighbours. Ahaz, notoriously stubborn and
ungodly, refused.
    Isaiah told of the sign anyway: a young boy
would be born, and before he grew out of
childhood Judah's feared enemies would be
destroyed. Only 12 years after this prediction, the
Northern Kingdom of Israel fell. The New
Testament sees a further meaning in this
prophecy, applying it to the birth of Jesus Christ
(Matthew 1:23).

■ Assyria, the LORD's Instrument

8 The LORD said to me, "Take a large scroll and
    write on it with an ordinary pen: Maher-Shalal-
Hash-Baz.*a* ²And I will call in Uriah the priest and
Zechariah son of Jeberekiah as reliable witnesses
for me."

³Then I went to the prophetess, and she conceived and gave birth to a son. And the LORD said to
me, "Name him Maher-Shalal-Hash-Baz. ⁴Before the
boy knows how to say 'My father' or 'My mother',
the wealth of Damascus and the plunder of Samaria
will be carried off by the king of Assyria."

⁵The LORD spoke to me again:

⁶"Because this people has rejected
    the gently flowing waters of Shiloah
and rejoices over Rezin
    and the son of Remaliah,
⁷therefore the Lord is about to bring against
        them
    the mighty floodwaters of the River*b*—
    the king of Assyria with all his pomp.
It will overflow all its channels,

---

a 2 Or *has set up camp in*   *b* 3 *Shear-Jashub means a remnant will return.*   *c* 14 The Hebrew is plural.   *d* 14 Masoretic Text; Dead Sea Scrolls *and*
he or and they   *e* 14 *Immanuel means God with us.*   *f* 20 That is, the Euphrates   *g* 23 That is, about 25 pounds (about 11.5 kilograms)
a 1 *Maher-Shalal-Hash-Baz means quick to the plunder, swift to the spoil*; also in verse 3.   *b* 7 That is, the Euphrates

run over all its banks
⁸and sweep on into Judah, swirling over it,
    passing through it and reaching up to the
    neck.
Its outspread wings will cover the breadth of
    your land,
    O Immanuel!"ᶜ

⁹Raise the war cry,ᵈ you nations, and be
    shattered!
Listen, all you distant lands.
Prepare for battle, and be shattered!
Prepare for battle, and be shattered!
¹⁰Devise your strategy, but it will be thwarted;
    propose your plan, but it will not stand,
    for God is with us.ᵉ

■ Fear God
¹¹The LORD spoke to me with his strong hand
upon me, warning me not to follow the way of this
people. He said:

¹²"Do not call conspiracy
    everything that these people call
        conspiracy;ᶠ
    do not fear what they fear,
    and do not dread it.
¹³The LORD Almighty is the one you are to regard
        as holy,
    he is the one you are to fear,
    he is the one you are to dread,
¹⁴and he will be a sanctuary;
    but for both houses of Israel he will be
a stone that causes men to stumble
    and a rock that makes them fall.
And for the people of Jerusalem he will be
    a trap and a snare.
¹⁵Many of them will stumble;
    they will fall and be broken,
    they will be snared and captured."

¹⁶Bind up the testimony
    and seal up the law among my disciples.
¹⁷I will wait for the LORD,
    who is hiding his face from the house of
        Jacob.
    I will put my trust in him.

¹⁸Here am I, and the children the LORD has given
me. We are signs and symbols in Israel from the
LORD Almighty, who dwells on Mount Zion.
¹⁹When men tell you to consult mediums and
spiritists, who whisper and mutter, should not a
people enquire of their God? Why consult the dead
on behalf of the living? ²⁰To the law and to the testimony! If they do not speak according to this word,
they have no light of dawn. ²¹Distressed and hungry,
they will roam through the land; when they are famished, they will become enraged and, looking upward, will curse their king and their God. ²²Then
they will look towards the earth and see only distress and darkness and fearful gloom, and they will
be thrust into utter darkness.

■ To Us a Child Is Born
9 Nevertheless, there will be no more gloom for
    those who were in distress. In the past he hum-
bled the land of Zebulun and the land of Naphtali,
but in the future he will honour Galilee of the Gentiles, by the way of the sea, along the Jordan—

8:20 ■ WHOM TO BELIEVE?
King Ahaz and his people sought guidance from
every source but the right one. They consulted
mediums, spiritists, even the dead. Isaiah
suggests ironically that they try God. "To the law
and to the testimony!" he says—that is, to the
Scriptures, which give God's commandments and
the testimony of what great things he has done.

²The people walking in darkness
    have seen a great light;
on those living in the land of the shadow of
        deathᵃ
    a light has dawned.
³You have enlarged the nation
    and increased their joy;
they rejoice before you
    as people rejoice at the harvest,
as men rejoice
    when dividing the plunder.
⁴For as in the day of Midian's defeat,
    you have shattered
the yoke that burdens them,
    the bar across their shoulders,
    the rod of their oppressor.
⁵Every warrior's boot used in battle
    and every garment rolled in blood
will be destined for burning,
    will be fuel for the fire.
⁶For to us a child is born,
    to us a son is given,
    and the government will be on his shoulders.
And he will be called
    Wonderful Counsellor,ᵇ Mighty God,
    Everlasting Father, Prince of Peace.
⁷Of the increase of his government and peace
    there will be no end.
He will reign on David's throne
    and over his kingdom,
establishing and upholding it
    with justice and righteousness
    from that time on and for ever.
The zeal of the LORD Almighty
    will accomplish this.

9:6 ■ A CHILD IS BORN
Isaiah includes many direct predictions of the
coming Messiah, including this passage, which
established that the Messiah will come from
Galilee (verse 1). The lands Isaiah mentions as
"humbled" in verse 1 are the very regions
devastated by Assyria's armies (2 Kings 15:29).
Thus Isaiah offers a word of distant hope for those
parts of his nation most affected by war.

ᶜ8 Immanuel means God with us.   ᵈ9 Or Do your worst   ᵉ10 Hebrew Immanuel   ᶠ12 Or Do not call for a treaty / every time these people call for a
treaty   ᵃ2 Or land of darkness   ᵇ6 Or Wonderful, Counsellor

■ The LORD's Anger Against Israel

⁸The Lord has sent a message against Jacob;
    it will fall on Israel.
⁹All the people will know it—
    Ephraim and the inhabitants of Samaria—
who say with pride
    and arrogance of heart,
¹⁰"The bricks have fallen down,
    but we will rebuild with dressed stone;
the fig-trees have been felled,
    but we will replace them with cedars."
¹¹But the LORD has strengthened Rezin's foes
        against them
    and has spurred their enemies on.
¹²Arameans from the east and Philistines from the
        west
    have devoured Israel with open mouth.

Yet for all this, his anger is not turned away,
    his hand is still upraised.

¹³But the people have not returned to him who
        struck them,
    nor have they sought the LORD Almighty.
¹⁴So the LORD will cut off from Israel both head
        and tail,
    both palm branch and reed in a single day;
¹⁵the elders and prominent men are the head,
    the prophets who teach lies are the tail.
¹⁶Those who guide this people mislead them,
    and those who are guided are led astray.
¹⁷Therefore the Lord will take no pleasure in the
        young men,
    nor will he pity the fatherless and widows,
for everyone is ungodly and wicked,
    every mouth speaks vileness.

Yet for all this, his anger is not turned away,
    his hand is still upraised.

¹⁸Surely wickedness burns like a fire;
    it consumes briers and thorns,
it sets the forest thickets ablaze,
    so that it rolls upward in a column of smoke.
¹⁹By the wrath of the LORD Almighty
    the land will be scorched
and the people will be fuel for the fire;
    no-one will spare his brother.
²⁰On the right they will devour,
    but still be hungry;
on the left they will eat,
    but not be satisfied.
Each will feed on the flesh of his own
    offspring:ᶜ
²¹ Manasseh will feed on Ephraim, and Ephraim
        on Manasseh;
    together they will turn against Judah.

Yet for all this, his anger is not turned away,
    his hand is still upraised.

10 Woe to those who make unjust laws,
    to those who issue oppressive decrees,
²to deprive the poor of their rights
    and withhold justice from the oppressed of
        my people,
making widows their prey

and robbing the fatherless.
³What will you do on the day of reckoning,
    when disaster comes from afar?
To whom will you run for help?
    Where will you leave your riches?
⁴Nothing will remain but to cringe among the
        captives
    or fall among the slain.

Yet for all this, his anger is not turned away,
    his hand is still upraised.

■ God's Judgment on Assyria

⁵"Woe to the Assyrian, the rod of my anger,
    in whose hand is the club of my wrath!
⁶I send him against a godless nation,
    I dispatch him against a people who anger
        me,
to seize loot and snatch plunder,
    and to trample them down like mud in the
        streets.
⁷But this is not what he intends,
    this is not what he has in mind;
his purpose is to destroy,
    to put an end to many nations.
⁸'Are not my commanders all kings?' he says.
⁹ 'Has not Calno fared like Carchemish?
Is not Hamath like Arpad,
    and Samaria like Damascus?
¹⁰As my hand seized the kingdoms of the idols,
    kingdoms whose images excelled those of
        Jerusalem and Samaria—
¹¹shall I not deal with Jerusalem and her images
    as I dealt with Samaria and her idols?' "

10:7 ■ GOD'S HAND IN HISTORY
In this comment, God reveals how he works
through history in hidden, indirect ways. The
pagan empire Assyria had no idea that it was
being used by the true God—it dealt with
Jerusalem just as it dealt with any nation and its
idols (verse 11). Nevertheless, Assyria would serve
God's purpose, and would one day be punished
for its own pride and greed (verse 12).

¹²When the Lord has finished all his work against
Mount Zion and Jerusalem, he will say, "I will punish the king of Assyria for the wilful pride of his
heart and the haughty look in his eyes. ¹³For he says:

" 'By the strength of my hand I have done this,
    and by my wisdom, because I have
        understanding.
I removed the boundaries of nations,
    I plundered their treasures;
like a mighty one I subduedᵃ their kings.
¹⁴As one reaches into a nest,
    so my hand reached for the wealth of the
        nations;
as men gather abandoned eggs,
    so I gathered all the countries;
not one flapped a wing,
    or opened its mouth to chirp.' "

ᶜ20 Or arm   ᵃ13 Or / I subdued the mighty,

15Does the axe raise itself above him who swings
  it,
  or the saw boast against him who uses it?
As if a rod were to wield him who lifts it up,
  or a club brandish him who is not wood!
16Therefore, the Lord, the LORD Almighty,
  will send a wasting disease upon his sturdy
  warriors;
under his pomp a fire will be kindled
  like a blazing flame.
17The Light of Israel will become a fire,
  their Holy One a flame;
in a single day it will burn and consume
  his thorns and his briers.
18The splendour of his forests and fertile fields
  it will completely destroy,
  as when a sick man wastes away.
19And the remaining trees of his forests will be so
  few
  that a child could write them down.

■ The Remnant of Israel
20In that day the remnant of Israel,
  the survivors of the house of Jacob,
will no longer rely on him
  who struck them down
but will truly rely on the LORD,
  the Holy One of Israel.
21A remnant will return,b a remnant of Jacob
  will return to the Mighty God.
22Though your people, O Israel, be like the sand
  by the sea,
  only a remnant will return.
Destruction has been decreed,
  overwhelming and righteous.
23The Lord, the LORD Almighty, will carry out
  the destruction decreed upon the whole
  land.

24Therefore, this is what the Lord, the LORD
Almighty, says:

"O my people who live in Zion,
  do not be afraid of the Assyrians,
who beat you with a rod
  and lift up a club against you, as Egypt did.
25Very soon my anger against you will end
  and my wrath will be directed to their
  destruction."

26The LORD Almighty will lash them with a whip,
  as when he struck down Midian at the rock
  of Oreb;
and he will raise his staff over the waters,
  as he did in Egypt.
27In that day their burden will be lifted from
  your shoulders,
  their yoke from your neck;
the yoke will be broken
  because you have grown so fat.c

28They enter Aiath;
  they pass through Migron;
  they store supplies at Michmash.
29They go over the pass, and say,
  "We will camp overnight at Geba."
Ramah trembles;

Gibeah of Saul flees.
30Cry out, O Daughter of Gallim!
  Listen, O Laishah!
  Poor Anathoth!
31Madmenah is in flight;
  the people of Gebim take cover.
32This day they will halt at Nob;
  they will shake their fist
at the mount of the Daughter of Zion,
  at the hill of Jerusalem.

33See, the Lord, the LORD Almighty,
  will lop off the boughs with great power.
The lofty trees will be felled,
  the tall ones will be brought low.
34He will cut down the forest thickets with an
  axe;
Lebanon will fall before the Mighty One.

■ The Branch From Jesse

11 A shoot will come up from the stump of
  Jesse;
  from his roots a Branch will bear fruit.
2The Spirit of the LORD will rest on him—
  the Spirit of wisdom and of understanding,
  the Spirit of counsel and of power,
  the Spirit of knowledge and of the fear of the
  LORD—
3and he will delight in the fear of the LORD.

He will not judge by what he sees with his
  eyes,
  or decide by what he hears with his ears;

11:1 ■ THE GOOD OLD DAYS
To express his message of hope to the Israelite
people, Isaiah appealed to their fondest memories.
This chapter borrows images from three of the
greatest events from the past: the prosperous
dynasty of David when Israel was united (verse 1);
the Garden of Eden (verses 6–9); and the miracles
of the exodus from Egypt (verse 15). Whatever the
state of "the good old days", the future time of
peace will exceed it.

4but with righteousness he will judge the needy,
  with justice he will give decisions for the
  poor of the earth.
He will strike the earth with the rod of his
  mouth;
with the breath of his lips he will slay the
  wicked.
5Righteousness will be his belt
  and faithfulness the sash round his waist.

6The wolf will live with the lamb,
  the leopard will lie down with the goat,
the calf and the lion and the yearlinga
  together;
  and a little child will lead them.
7The cow will feed with the bear,
  their young will lie down together,
  and the lion will eat straw like the ox.
8The infant will play near the hole of the cobra,

---

b21 Hebrew shear-jashub; also in verse 22   c27 Hebrew; Septuagint broken / from your shoulders   a6 Hebrew; Septuagint lion will feed

and the young child put his hand into the
viper's nest.
⁹They will neither harm nor destroy
on all my holy mountain,
for the earth will be full of the knowledge of
the LORD
as the waters cover the sea.

¹⁰In that day the Root of Jesse will stand as a banner for the peoples; the nations will rally to him, and
his place of rest will be glorious. ¹¹In that day the
Lord will reach out his hand a second time to reclaim the remnant that is left of his people from Assyria, from Lower Egypt, from Upper Egypt,ᵇ from
Cush,ᶜ from Elam, from Babylonia,ᵈ from Hamath
and from the islands of the sea.

¹²He will raise a banner for the nations
and gather the exiles of Israel;
he will assemble the scattered people of Judah
from the four quarters of the earth.
¹³Ephraim's jealousy will vanish,
and Judah's enemiesᵉ will be cut off;
Ephraim will not be jealous of Judah,
nor Judah hostile towards Ephraim.
¹⁴They will swoop down on the slopes of
Philistia to the west;
together they will plunder the people to the
east.
They will lay hands on Edom and Moab,
and the Ammonites will be subject to them.
¹⁵The LORD will dry up
the gulf of the Egyptian sea;
with a scorching wind he will sweep his hand
over the Euphrates River.ᶠ
He will break it up into seven streams
so that men can cross over in sandals.
¹⁶There will be a highway for the remnant of his
people
that is left from Assyria,
as there was for Israel
when they came up from Egypt.

■ Songs of Praise

12 In that day you will say:

"I will praise you, O LORD.
Although you were angry with me,
your anger has turned away
and you have comforted me.
²Surely God is my salvation;
I will trust and not be afraid.
The LORD, the LORD, is my strength and my
song;
he has become my salvation."
³With joy you will draw water
from the wells of salvation.

⁴In that day you will say:

"Give thanks to the LORD, call on his name;
make known among the nations what he has
done,
and proclaim that his name is exalted.
⁵Sing to the LORD, for he has done glorious
things;
let this be known to all the world.

⁶Shout aloud and sing for joy, people of Zion,
for great is the Holy One of Israel among
you."

12:6 ■ A KEY PHRASE
The first 12 chapters contain specific messages to
Judah. But now Isaiah shifts his focus to
surrounding nations. He ends the first section with
a reference to the "Holy One of Israel", a key
phrase that hints at the special relationship
between God and his covenant nation. The phrase
appears only five times in the rest of the Old
Testament, but 26 times in Isaiah.

■ A Prophecy Against Babylon

13 An oracle concerning Babylon that Isaiah son
of Amoz saw:

²Raise a banner on a bare hilltop,
shout to them;
beckon to them
to enter the gates of the nobles.
³I have commanded my holy ones;
I have summoned my warriors to carry out
my wrath—
those who rejoice in my triumph.

⁴Listen, a noise on the mountains,
like that of a great multitude!
Listen, an uproar among the kingdoms,
like nations massing together!
The LORD Almighty is mustering
an army for war.
⁵They come from faraway lands,
from the ends of the heavens—
the LORD and the weapons of his wrath—
to destroy the whole country.

⁶Wail, for the day of the LORD is near;
it will come like destruction from the
Almighty.ᵃ
⁷Because of this, all hands will go limp,
every man's heart will melt.
⁸Terror will seize them,
pain and anguish will grip them;
they will writhe like a woman in labour.
They will look aghast at each other,
their faces aflame.

⁹See, the day of the LORD is coming—
a cruel day, with wrath and fierce anger—
to make the land desolate
and destroy the sinners within it.
¹⁰The stars of heaven and their constellations
will not show their light.
The rising sun will be darkened
and the moon will not give its light.
¹¹I will punish the world for its evil,
the wicked for their sins.
I will put an end to the arrogance of the
haughty
and will humble the pride of the ruthless.
¹²I will make man scarcer than pure gold,
more rare than the gold of Ophir.
¹³Therefore I will make the heavens tremble;

ᵇ11 Hebrew from Pathros   ᶜ11 That is, the upper Nile region   ᵈ11 Hebrew Shinar   ᵉ13 Or hostility   ᶠ15 Hebrew the River   ᵃ6 Hebrew
Shaddai

and the earth will shake from its place
at the wrath of the LORD Almighty,
in the day of his burning anger.

¹⁴Like a hunted gazelle,
like sheep without a shepherd,
each will return to his own people,
each will flee to his native land.

¹⁵Whoever is captured will be thrust through;
all who are caught will fall by the sword.

¹⁶Their infants will be dashed to pieces before
their eyes;
their houses will be looted and their wives
ravished.

¹⁷See, I will stir up against them the Medes,
who do not care for silver
and have no delight in gold.

¹⁸Their bows will strike down the young men;
they will have no mercy on infants
nor will they look with compassion on
children.

¹⁹Babylon, the jewel of kingdoms,
the glory of the Babylonians'ᵇ pride,
will be overthrown by God
like Sodom and Gomorrah.

²⁰She will never be inhabited
or lived in through all generations;
no Arab will pitch his tent there,
no shepherd will rest his flocks there.

²¹But desert creatures will lie there,
jackals will fill her houses;
there the owls will dwell,
and there the wild goats will leap about.

²²Hyenas will howl in her strongholds,
jackals in her luxurious palaces.
Her time is at hand,
and her days will not be prolonged.

14 The LORD will have compassion on Jacob;
once again he will choose Israel
and will settle them in their own land.
Aliens will join them
and unite with the house of Jacob.

²Nations will take them
and bring them to their own place.
And the house of Israel will possess the nations
as menservants and maidservants in the
LORD's land.
They will make captives of their captors
and rule over their oppressors.

³On the day the LORD gives you relief from suffering and turmoil and cruel bondage, ⁴you will take
up this taunt against the king of Babylon:

How the oppressor has come to an end!
How his furyᵃ has ended!

⁵The LORD has broken the rod of the wicked,
the sceptre of the rulers,

⁶which in anger struck down peoples
with unceasing blows,
and in fury subdued nations
with relentless aggression.

⁷All the lands are at rest and at peace;
they break into singing.

⁸Even the pine trees and the cedars of Lebanon

exult over you and say,
"Now that you have been laid low,
no woodsman comes to cut us down."

⁹The graveᵇ below is all astir
to meet you at your coming;
it rouses the spirits of the departed to greet
you—
all those who were leaders in the world;
it makes them rise from their thrones—
all those who were kings over the nations.

¹⁰They will all respond,
they will say to you,
"You also have become weak, as we are;
you have become like us."

¹¹All your pomp has been brought down to the
grave,
along with the noise of your harps;
maggots are spread out beneath you
and worms cover you.

¹²How you have fallen from heaven,
O morning star, son of the dawn!
You have been cast down to the earth,
you who once laid low the nations!

¹³You said in your heart,
"I will ascend to heaven;
I will raise my throne
above the stars of God;
I will sit enthroned on the mount of assembly,
on the utmost heights of the sacred
mountain.ᶜ

¹⁴I will ascend above the tops of the clouds;
I will make myself like the Most High."

¹⁵But you are brought down to the grave,
to the depths of the pit.

14:12 ■ FALL OF THE MORNING STAR

A name used of Satan—"Lucifer", or "morning
star"—comes from this verse. The word *Lucifer*
refers to Venus, one of the brightest objects in the
sky. Yet, when the sun rises, the light of even the
brightest morning star is totally eclipsed.

In context, Isaiah was describing the cruelly
oppressive king of Babylon, who swelled with
pride but would be brought down to defeat.
However, Isaiah may be hinting at a force behind
the human king: Satan himself. Isaiah's metaphor
of the faded morning star aptly describes the
eclipse of the haughty king of Babylon—and of
Satan.

¹⁶Those who see you stare at you,
they ponder your fate:
"Is this the man who shook the earth
and made kingdoms tremble,

¹⁷the man who made the world a desert,
who overthrew its cities
and would not let his captives go home?"

¹⁸All the kings of the nations lie in state,
each in his own tomb.

¹⁹But you are cast out of your tomb
like a rejected branch;
you are covered with the slain,

ᵇ 19 Or *Chaldeans'*
in verses 11 and 15   ᵃ 4 Dead Sea Scrolls, Septuagint and Syriac; the meaning of the word in the Masoretic Text is uncertain.   ᵇ 9 Hebrew *Sheol*; also
ᶜ 13 Or *the north*; Hebrew *Zaphon*

with those pierced by the sword,
those who descend to the stones of the pit.
Like a corpse trampled underfoot,
20   you will not join them in burial,
for you have destroyed your land
and killed your people.

The offspring of the wicked
will never be mentioned again.
21Prepare a place to slaughter his sons
for the sins of their forefathers;
they are not to rise to inherit the land
and cover the earth with their cities.

22"I will rise up against them,"
declares the LORD Almighty.
"I will cut off from Babylon her name and
survivors,
her offspring and descendants,"
                                    declares the LORD.
23"I will turn her into a place for owls
and into swampland;
I will sweep her with the broom of
destruction,"
declares the LORD Almighty.

■ A Prophecy Against Assyria
24The LORD Almighty has sworn,

"Surely, as I have planned, so it will be,
and as I have purposed, so it will stand.
25I will crush the Assyrian in my land;
on my mountains I will trample him down.
His yoke will be taken from my people,
and his burden removed from their
shoulders."

26This is the plan determined for the whole
world;
this is the hand stretched out over all
nations.
27For the LORD Almighty has purposed, and who
can thwart him?
His hand is stretched out, and who can turn
it back?

■ A Prophecy Against the Philistines
28This oracle came in the year King Ahaz died:

29Do not rejoice, all you Philistines,
that the rod that struck you is broken;
from the root of that snake will spring up a
viper,
its fruit will be a darting, venomous serpent.
30The poorest of the poor will find pasture,
and the needy will lie down in safety.
But your root I will destroy by famine;
it will slay your survivors.

31Wail, O gate! Howl, O city!
Melt away, all you Philistines!
A cloud of smoke comes from the north,
and there is not a straggler in its ranks.
32What answer shall be given
to the envoys of that nation?
"The LORD has established Zion,

and in her his afflicted people will find
refuge."

■ A Prophecy Against Moab

15 An oracle concerning Moab:

Ar in Moab is ruined,
destroyed in a night!
Kir in Moab is ruined,
destroyed in a night!
2Dibon goes up to its temple,
to its high places to weep;
Moab wails over Nebo and Medeba.
Every head is shaved
and every beard cut off.
3In the streets they wear sackcloth;
on the roofs and in the public squares
they all wail,
prostrate with weeping.
4Heshbon and Elealeh cry out,
their voices are heard all the way to Jahaz.
Therefore the armed men of Moab cry out,
and their hearts are faint.

5My heart cries out over Moab;
her fugitives flee as far as Zoar,
as far as Eglath Shelishiyah.
They go up the way to Luhith,
weeping as they go;
on the road to Horonaim
they lament their destruction.
6The waters of Nimrim are dried up
and the grass is withered;
the vegetation is gone
and nothing green is left.
7So the wealth they have acquired and stored up
they carry away over the Ravine of the
Poplars.
8Their outcry echoes along the border of Moab;
their wailing reaches as far as Eglaim,
their lamentation as far as Beer Elim.
9Dimon's*a* waters are full of blood,
but I will bring still more upon Dimon*a* —
a lion upon the fugitives of Moab
and upon those who remain in the land.

16 Send lambs as tribute
to the ruler of the land,
from Sela, across the desert,
to the mount of the Daughter of Zion.
2Like fluttering birds
pushed from the nest,
so are the women of Moab
at the fords of the Arnon.

3"Give us counsel,
render a decision.
Make your shadow like night—
at high noon.
Hide the fugitives,
do not betray the refugees.
4Let the Moabite fugitives stay with you;
be their shelter from the destroyer."

The oppressor will come to an end,
and destruction will cease;

---

a9 Masoretic Text; Dead Sea Scrolls, some Septuagint manuscripts and Vulgate Dibon

the aggressor will vanish from the land.
⁵In love a throne will be established;
  in faithfulness a man will sit on it—
  one from the house*a* of David—
one who in judging seeks justice
  and speeds the cause of righteousness.

⁶We have heard of Moab's pride—
  her overweening pride and conceit,
her pride and her insolence—
  but her boasts are empty.
⁷Therefore the Moabites wail,
  they wail together for Moab.

Lament and grieve
  for the men*b* of Kir Haraseth.
⁸The fields of Heshbon wither,
  the vines of Sibmah also.
The rulers of the nations
  have trampled down the choicest vines,
which once reached Jazer
  and spread towards the desert.
Their shoots spread out
  and went as far as the sea.
⁹So I weep, as Jazer weeps,
  for the vines of Sibmah.
O Heshbon, O Elealeh,

■ FAITH IN GOD OR THE MILITARY? INSIGHT
WHERE DOES A WEAK NATION TURN FOR HELP?

THIS IS THE PLAN DETERMINED FOR THE
WHOLE WORLD; THIS IS THE HAND
STRETCHED OUT OVER ALL NATIONS.
■ 14:26

In 1944, wild cheering greeted the Russian
tanks that rolled into Poland. The Russians were
freeing Poland from the Nazis, and grateful
Poles showered the liberating soldiers with fresh
flowers.
    But 45 years later, Russian troops had
worn out their welcome, and the Polish
government asked them to leave. The Polish
experience offers living proof of a painful lesson
of history: military help from great powers
usually comes with strings attached.

■ A SMALL NATION SEEKS HELP
What can a small nation do when facing a
military giant? Judah found itself in that
predicament early in Isaiah's career. When two
neighbouring nations invaded, the tiny kingdom
suffered heavy losses. King Ahaz and the people
of Judah were shaken, "as the trees of the
forest are shaken by the wind" (7:2). Panicked,
Ahaz sought Isaiah's advice.
    Isaiah had received a "call" to ministry
as dramatic as any recorded in the Bible
(chapter 6). King Ahaz knew that Isaiah would
deliver a message straight from God, no matter
how unpopular. Still, Ahaz was hardly prepared
for what Isaiah said: Stay calm, don't worry,
simply trust God.
    The attacking kings were mere
"smouldering stubs of firewood", Isaiah declared
(7:4). Whatever happens, don't seek help from
an empire like Assyria; if you do, you will invite
in the very army that will one day destroy you.

■ THE LONG SLIDE BEGINS
But Ahaz, reeling from the invasion, wanted
quick relief. Ignoring Isaiah's warnings, he
negotiated a treaty with mighty Assyria, using as
a bribe the treasury of the temple in Jerusalem.

    In the short term, Ahaz's decision
brought results. No army of that day could
match the Assyrian war machine, and all
Judah's enemies fell to the onslaught. Israel, to
the north, was wiped off the map. At last
Judah had peace. But at what cost?
    Perhaps as part of the treaty with
Assyria, Ahaz began corrupting Judah's
religion. He first closed the doors of the temple
to worship, and later replaced the sacred altar
to God with a foreign one. He officially adopted
Assyria's state religion, going so far as to
make a human sacrifice of his sons in a fire. In
every way King Ahaz became a puppet king,
under the thumb of Assyria. Foreign armies
stayed in Judah. Indeed, Assyria's help had
come with strings attached.

■ MESSAGES FOR THEN AND NOW
The prophet Isaiah was furious. He had grown
up in a boom time in Judah, under a good
king. Suddenly he saw his country become a
mere pawn of Assyria, trading away even its
great religious heritage.
    Chapters 7–19 record his passionate
words, not only against Judah, but against her
neighbours also. He told of a reckoning day,
when each nation would be punished for its sin
and rebellion. The immediate future looked
very bleak, and Isaiah minced no words in
describing it.
    But Isaiah did not stop there. He went
on to project far into the future, in familiar
words that still stir up hope and longing. This
section begins with a question from a king
about where to turn for help. It ends with a
grand sweep of all of history.

□ LIFE QUESTIONS:
What do you think Isaiah would say if he were
writing today about such super-power
countries as the United States and the Soviet
Union?

---

a 5 Hebrew *tent*   *b* 7 Or "*raisin cakes*," a word play

I drench you with tears!
The shouts of joy over your ripened fruit
and over your harvests have been stilled.
¹⁰Joy and gladness are taken away from the
orchards;
no-one sings or shouts in the vineyards;
no-one treads out wine at the presses,
for I have put an end to the shouting.
¹¹My heart laments for Moab like a harp,
my inmost being for Kir Haraseth.
¹²When Moab appears at her high place,
she only wears herself out;
when she goes to her shrine to pray,
it is to no avail.

16:9 ■ A PROPHET'S PAIN
Although Isaiah often delivered bad news to the
nations around him, he never took pleasure in it.
Remarkably, he often deeply identified with the
pain of other, non-Israelite nations such as Moab
(see 15:5). Chapters 15–16 were probably used
as sources for Jeremiah 48. (Jeremiah was
another prophet who suffered greatly.)

¹³This is the word the LORD has already spoken
concerning Moab. ¹⁴But now the LORD says: "Within
three years, as a servant bound by contract would
count them, Moab's splendour and all her many
people will be despised, and her survivors will be
very few and feeble."

■ An Oracle Against Damascus
17 An oracle concerning Damascus:

"See, Damascus will no longer be a city
but will become a heap of ruins.
²The cities of Aroer will be deserted
and left to flocks, which will lie down,
with no-one to make them afraid.
³The fortified city will disappear from Ephraim,
and royal power from Damascus;
the remnant of Aram will be
like the glory of the Israelites,"
declares the LORD Almighty.

⁴"In that day the glory of Jacob will fade;
the fat of his body will waste away.
⁵It will be as when a reaper gathers the standing
corn
and harvests the corn with his arm—
as when a man gleans ears of corn
in the Valley of Rephaim.
⁶Yet some gleanings will remain,
as when an olive tree is beaten,
leaving two or three olives on the topmost
branches,
four or five on the fruitful boughs,"
declares the LORD,
the God of Israel.

⁷In that day men will look to their Maker
and turn their eyes to the Holy One of Israel.
⁸They will not look to the altars,
the work of their hands,

and they will have no regard for the Asherah
polesᵃ
and the incense altars their fingers have
made.

⁹In that day their strong cities, which they left because of the Israelites, will be like places abandoned
to thickets and undergrowth. And all will be desolation.

¹⁰You have forgotten God your Saviour;
you have not remembered the Rock, your
fortress.
Therefore, though you set out the finest plants
and plant imported vines,
¹¹though on the day you set them out, you make
them grow,
and on the morning when you plant them,
you bring them to bud,
yet the harvest will be as nothing
in the day of disease and incurable pain.

¹²Oh, the raging of many nations—
they rage like the raging sea!
Oh, the uproar of the peoples—
they roar like the roaring of great waters!
¹³Although the peoples roar like the roar of
surging waters,
when he rebukes them they flee far away,
driven before the wind like chaff on the hills,
like tumble-weed before a gale.
¹⁴In the evening, sudden terror!
Before the morning, they are gone!
This is the portion of those who loot us,
the lot of those who plunder us.

■ A Prophecy Against Cush
18 Woe to the land of whirring wingsᵃ
along the rivers of Cush,ᵇ
²which sends envoys by sea
in papyrus boats over the water.

Go, swift messengers,
to a people tall and smooth-skinned,
to a people feared far and wide,
an aggressive nation of strange speech,
whose land is divided by rivers.

³All you people of the world,
you who live on the earth,
when a banner is raised on the mountains,
you will see it,
and when a trumpet sounds,
you will hear it.
⁴This is what the LORD says to me:
"I will remain quiet and will look on from
my dwelling-place,
like shimmering heat in the sunshine,
like a cloud of dew in the heat of harvest."
⁵For, before the harvest, when the blossom is
gone
and the flower becomes a ripening grape,
he will cut off the shoots with pruning knives,
and cut down and take away the spreading
branches.
⁶They will all be left to the mountain birds of
prey

ᵃ8 That is, symbols of the goddess Asherah   ᵃ1 Or of locusts   ᵇ1 That is, the upper Nile region

and to the wild animals;
the birds will feed on them all summer,
the wild animals all winter.

⁷At that time gifts will be brought to the LORD Almighty

from a people tall and smooth-skinned,
from a people feared far and wide,
an aggressive nation of strange speech,
whose land is divided by rivers—

the gifts will be brought to Mount Zion, the place of the Name of the LORD Almighty.

■ A Prophecy About Egypt

19 An oracle concerning Egypt:

See, the LORD rides on a swift cloud
and is coming to Egypt.
The idols of Egypt tremble before him,
and the hearts of the Egyptians melt within
them.

²"I will stir up Egyptian against Egyptian—
brother will fight against brother,
neighbour against neighbour,
city against city,
kingdom against kingdom.
³The Egyptians will lose heart,
and I will bring their plans to nothing;
they will consult the idols and the spirits of the
dead,
the mediums and the spiritists.
⁴I will hand the Egyptians over
to the power of a cruel master,
and a fierce king will rule over them,"
declares the Lord, the LORD Almighty.

⁵The waters of the river will dry up,
and the river bed will be parched and dry.
⁶The canals will stink;
the streams of Egypt will dwindle and dry
up.
The reeds and rushes will wither,
⁷　also the plants along the Nile,
at the mouth of the river.
Every sown field along the Nile
will become parched, will blow away and be
no more.
⁸The fishermen will groan and lament,
all who cast hooks into the Nile;
those who throw nets on the water
will pine away.
⁹Those who work with combed flax will despair,

the weavers of fine linen will lose hope.
¹⁰The workers in cloth will be dejected,
and all the wage earners will be sick at heart.

¹¹The officials of Zoan are nothing but fools;
the wise counsellors of Pharaoh give
senseless advice.
How can you say to Pharaoh,
"I am one of the wise men,
a disciple of the ancient kings"?

¹²Where are your wise men now?
Let them show you and make known
what the LORD Almighty
has planned against Egypt.
¹³The officials of Zoan have become fools,
the leaders of Memphis*ᵃ* are deceived;
the cornerstones of her peoples
have led Egypt astray.
¹⁴The LORD has poured into them
a spirit of dizziness;
they make Egypt stagger in all that she does,
as a drunkard staggers around in his vomit.
¹⁵There is nothing Egypt can do—
head or tail, palm branch or reed.

¹⁶In that day the Egyptians will be like women. They will shudder with fear at the uplifted hand that the LORD Almighty raises against them. ¹⁷And the land of Judah will bring terror to the Egyptians; everyone to whom Judah is mentioned will be terrified, because of what the LORD Almighty is planning against them.

¹⁸In that day five cities in Egypt will speak the language of Canaan and swear allegiance to the LORD Almighty. One of them will be called the City of Destruction.*ᵇ*

¹⁹In that day there will be an altar to the LORD in the heart of Egypt, and a monument to the LORD at its border. ²⁰It will be a sign and witness to the LORD Almighty in the land of Egypt. When they cry out to the LORD because of their oppressors, he will send them a saviour and defender, and he will rescue them. ²¹So the LORD will make himself known to the Egyptians, and in that day they will acknowledge the LORD. They will worship with sacrifices and grain offerings; they will make vows to the LORD and keep them. ²²The LORD will strike Egypt with a plague; he will strike them and heal them. They will turn to the LORD, and he will respond to their pleas and heal them.

²³In that day there will be a highway from Egypt to Assyria. The Assyrians will go to Egypt and the Egyptians to Assyria. The Egyptians and Assyrians will worship together. ²⁴In that day Israel will be the third, along with Egypt and Assyria, a blessing on the earth. ²⁵The LORD Almighty will bless them, saying, "Blessed be Egypt my people, Assyria my handiwork, and Israel my inheritance."

■ A Prophecy Against Egypt and Cush

20 In the year that the supreme commander, sent by Sargon king of Assyria, came to Ashdod and attacked and captured it—²at that time the LORD spoke through Isaiah son of Amoz. He said to him, "Take off the sackcloth from your body and the

a 13 Hebrew *Noph*
(that is, Heliopolis)　　*b 18* Most manuscripts of the Masoretic Text; some manuscripts of the Masoretic Text, Dead Sea Scrolls and Vulgate *City of the Sun*

sandals from your feet." And he did so, going around stripped and barefoot.

20:2 ■ A DRAMATIC OBJECT LESSON
Isaiah was an educated and urbane prophet, at home in the corridors of power. His reputation must have made this object lesson very shocking: for three years he walked around stripped and barefoot, in the guise of a slave, to protest against a planned alliance with Egypt and Cush. He had originally opposed an alliance with Assyria. Now he opposed a treaty with other nations as well.

³Then the LORD said, "Just as my servant Isaiah has gone stripped and barefoot for three years, as a sign and portent against Egypt and Cush,ᵃ ⁴so the king of Assyria will lead away stripped and barefoot the Egyptian captives and Cushite exiles, young and old, with buttocks bared—to Egypt's shame. ⁵Those who trusted in Cush and boasted in Egypt will be afraid and put to shame. ⁶In that day the people who live on this coast will say, 'See what has happened to those we relied on, those we fled to for help and deliverance from the king of Assyria! How then can we escape?' "

■ A Prophecy Against Babylon

21 An oracle concerning the Desert by the Sea:

Like whirlwinds sweeping through the
    southland,
an invader comes from the desert,
    from a land of terror.

²A dire vision has been shown to me:
    The traitor betrays, the looter takes loot.
Elam, attack! Media, lay siege!
    I will bring to an end all the groaning she
    caused.

³At this my body is racked with pain,
    pangs seize me, like those of a woman in
    labour;
I am staggered by what I hear,
    I am bewildered by what I see.
⁴My heart falters,
    fear makes me tremble;

■ CATASTROPHES THROUGH GOD'S EYES
AN ENDLESS CYCLE OF WAR AND DEATH—WHAT DID IT MEAN?

AT THIS MY BODY IS RACKED WITH PAIN, PANGS SEIZE ME, LIKE THOSE OF A WOMAN IN LABOUR; I AM STAGGERED BY WHAT I HEAR, I AM BEWILDERED BY WHAT I SEE. ■ 21:3

There is one easy way to picture the Middle East of Isaiah's day: simply follow today's newspaper headlines and project backwards in time. Then, as now, one nation would invade its neighbour, levelling cities and devastating the land and its people. The prophet Isaiah longed for an end to the cycle, much as modern-day residents of Lebanon, Israel or Kuwait do today.

Isaiah looked at the world with a kind of split vision. Around him, he saw spiritual decay and the dreary cycle of war and death. Yet God had given him a clear vision of what his nation could one day become: a pure people, faithful to God, living in peace with "war no more".

■ A KINGDOM FOR A PURPOSE
With God's view of the future shining brightly before him, Isaiah went about reinterpreting history. Others in Judah looked upon military invasions as terrible catastrophes. In contrast, Isaiah—though he felt anguish over the events—saw glimpses of a higher purpose.

Isaiah said that Judah had to endure pain and suffering in order to be purified. He counselled against making political alliances to forestall the punishment. God's people had to go through the fire, and from the trials a

remnant—a small remaining number of persons—would emerge that God could then use to accomplish his work. Isaiah went so far as to name his own son "a remnant will return" as a walking object lesson of his message to Judah (see Isaiah 7:3 and footnote).

Why had the Jews been called by God in the first place? They were to be a "light for the Gentiles", Isaiah said, a nation used by God to bring his truth to other nations. And out of the land of Judah God would raise up a great Prince who would rule over all the earth.

■ WHO IS IN CHARGE?
In short, God had not discarded his people, no matter how bleak things looked. The Israelites would ultimately become a missionary nation, pointing others to God.

Above all messages, Isaiah stressed this one: God is in charge of history. To Judah—surrounded by enemies, staggering from invasion, weary of bloodshed—God seemed far away and distant. Isaiah assured them that the great powers of earth were mere tools in God's hands; he would use them and fling them aside.

□ LIFE QUESTIONS:
Isaiah described people who felt afraid and abandoned by God. Have you ever felt like that? How does Isaiah's message offer hope for us today?

ᵃ3 That is, the upper Nile region; also in verse 5

the twilight I longed for
    has become a horror to me.

⁵They set the tables,
    they spread the rugs,
    they eat, they drink!
Get up, you officers,
    oil the shields!

⁶This is what the Lord says to me:

"Go, post a lookout
    and have him report what he sees.
⁷When he sees chariots
    with teams of horses,
riders on donkeys
    or riders on camels,
let him be alert,
    fully alert."

⁸And the lookout[a] shouted,

"Day after day, my lord, I stand on the
    watchtower;
every night I stay at my post.
⁹Look, here comes a man in a chariot
    with a team of horses.
And he gives back the answer:
    'Babylon has fallen, has fallen!
All the images of its gods
    lie shattered on the ground!' "

¹⁰O my people, crushed on the threshing-floor,
    I tell you what I have heard
from the LORD Almighty,
    from the God of Israel.

■ A Prophecy Against Edom
    ¹¹An oracle concerning Dumah:[b]

Someone calls to me from Seir,
    "Watchman, what is left of the night?
    Watchman, what is left of the night?"
¹²The watchman replies,
    "Morning is coming, but also the night.
If you would ask, then ask;
    and come back yet again."

■ A Prophecy Against Arabia
    ¹³An oracle concerning Arabia:

You caravans of Dedanites,
    who camp in the thickets of Arabia,
¹⁴ bring water for the thirsty;
you who live in Tema,
    bring food for the fugitives.
¹⁵They flee from the sword,
    from the drawn sword,
from the bent bow
    and from the heat of battle.

¹⁶This is what the Lord says to me: "Within one
year, as a servant bound by contract would count it,
all the pomp of Kedar will come to an end. ¹⁷The
survivors of the bowmen, the warriors of Kedar, will
be few." The LORD, the God of Israel, has spoken.

■ A Prophecy About Jerusalem
22 An oracle concerning the Valley of Vision:

    What troubles you now,
    that you have all gone up on the roofs,
²O town full of commotion,
    O city of tumult and revelry?
Your slain were not killed by the sword,
    nor did they die in battle.
³All your leaders have fled together;
    they have been captured without using the
        bow.
All you who were caught were taken prisoner
    together,
having fled while the enemy was still far
    away.
⁴Therefore I said, "Turn away from me;
    let me weep bitterly.
Do not try to console me
    over the destruction of my people."

⁵The Lord, the LORD Almighty, has a day
    of tumult and trampling and terror
    in the Valley of Vision,
a day of battering down walls
    and of crying out to the mountains.
⁶Elam takes up the quiver,
    with her charioteers and horses;
    Kir uncovers the shield.
⁷Your choicest valleys are full of chariots,
    and horsemen are posted at the city gates;
⁸ the defences of Judah are stripped away.

And you looked in that day
    to the weapons in the Palace of the Forest;
⁹you saw that the City of David
    had many breaches in its defences;
you stored up water
    in the Lower Pool.
¹⁰You counted the buildings in Jerusalem
    and tore down houses to strengthen the wall.
¹¹You built a reservoir between the two walls
    for the water of the Old Pool,
but you did not look to the One who made it,
    or have regard for the One who planned it
        long ago.

¹²The Lord, the LORD Almighty,
    called you on that day
to weep and to wail,
    to tear out your hair and put on sackcloth.
¹³But see, there is joy and revelry,
    slaughtering of cattle and killing of sheep,
    eating of meat and drinking of wine!
"Let us eat and drink," you say,
    "for tomorrow we die!"

¹⁴The LORD Almighty has revealed this in my
hearing: "Till your dying day this sin will not be
atoned for," says the Lord, the LORD Almighty.

¹⁵This is what the Lord, the LORD Almighty, says:

"Go, say to this steward,
    to Shebna, who is in charge of the palace:
¹⁶What are you doing here and who gave you
    permission
    to cut out a grave for yourself here,

---

a 8 Dead Sea Scrolls and Syriac; Masoretic Text *A lion*   *b 11 Dumah* means *silence* or *stillness*, a word play on *Edom.*

hewing your grave on the height
    and chiselling your resting place in the rock?

22:12 ■ SMILES INSTEAD OF TEARS

This chapter may refer to Jerusalem's deliverance
recorded in Isaiah 36–37. Isaiah was distressed
because, although great devastation was
prophesied, Jerusalem was celebrating, not
mourning. People had reinforced walls and built
water reservoirs to prepare for war, but had not
turned to God for help (verse 11). Israelites at that
time had a certain arrogance about the city of
Jerusalem, believing that God would never allow it
to fall into enemy hands.

¹⁷"Beware, the LORD is about to take firm hold of
    you
    and hurl you away, O you mighty man.
¹⁸He will roll you up tightly like a ball
    and throw you into a large country.
There you will die
    and there your splendid chariots will
        remain—
    you disgrace to your master's house!
¹⁹I will depose you from your office,
    and you will be ousted from your position.

²⁰"In that day I will summon my servant, Eliakim
son of Hilkiah. ²¹I will clothe him with your robe
and fasten your sash around him and hand your
authority over to him. He will be a father to those
who live in Jerusalem and to the house of Judah. ²²I
will place on his shoulder the key to the house of
David; what he opens no-one can shut, and what he
shuts no-one can open. ²³I will drive him like a peg
into a firm place; he will be a seat^a of honour for
the house of his father. ²⁴All the glory of his family
will hang on him: its offspring and offshoots—all its
lesser vessels, from the bowls to all the jars.

²⁵"In that day," declares the LORD Almighty, "the
peg driven into the firm place will give way; it will
be sheared off and will fall, and the load hanging on
it will be cut down." The LORD has spoken.

■ A Prophecy About Tyre

23

An oracle concerning Tyre:

Wail, O ships of Tarshish!
    For Tyre is destroyed
    and left without house or harbour.
From the land of Cyprus^a
    word has come to them.

²Be silent, you people of the island
    and you merchants of Sidon,
    whom the seafarers have enriched.
³On the great waters
    came the grain of the Shihor;
the harvest of the Nile^b was the revenue of
        Tyre,
    and she became the market-place of the
        nations.

⁴Be ashamed, O Sidon, and you, O fortress of the
    sea,
for the sea has spoken:
"I have neither been in labour nor given birth;
    I have neither reared sons nor brought up
        daughters."
⁵When word comes to Egypt,
    they will be in anguish at the report from
        Tyre.

23:1 ■ THE DECLINE OF TYRE

In Isaiah's day the city of Tyre was a major power,
dominating the sea trade in the eastern
Mediterranean. Her many colonies included the
island of Cyprus, and her merchants travelled as
far as the Indian Ocean and the English Channel.
But not long after this prophecy Assyria
conquered the city, and Tyre's king fled to
Cyprus.

⁶Cross over to Tarshish;
    wail, you people of the island.
⁷Is this your city of revelry,
    the old, old city,
whose feet have taken her
    to settle in far-off lands?
⁸Who planned this against Tyre,
    the bestower of crowns,
whose merchants are princes,
    whose traders are renowned in the earth?
⁹The LORD Almighty planned it,
    to bring low the pride of all glory
    and to humble all who are renowned on the
        earth.

¹⁰Till^c your land as along the Nile,
    O Daughter of Tarshish,
    for you no longer have a harbour.
¹¹The LORD has stretched out his hand over the
        sea
    and made its kingdoms tremble.
He has given an order concerning Phoenicia^d
    that her fortresses be destroyed.
¹²He said, "No more of your revelling,
    O Virgin Daughter of Sidon, now crushed!

"Up, cross over to Cyprus;^e
    even there you will find no rest."
¹³Look at the land of the Babylonians,^f
    this people that is now of no account!
The Assyrians have made it
    a place for desert creatures;
they raised up their siege towers,
    they stripped its fortresses bare
    and turned it into a ruin.

¹⁴Wail, you ships of Tarshish;
    your fortress is destroyed!

¹⁵At that time Tyre will be forgotten for seventy
years, the span of a king's life. But at the end of these
seventy years, it will happen to Tyre as in the song
of the prostitute:

^a23 Or throne   ^a1 Hebrew Kittim   ^b2, 3 Masoretic Text; one Dead Sea Scroll Sidon, / who cross over the sea; / your envoys ³are on the great waters.
/ The grain of the Shihor, / the harvest of the Nile,   ^c10 Dead Sea Scrolls and some Septuagint manuscripts; Masoretic Text Go through   ^d11 Hebrew
Canaan   ^e12 Hebrew Kittim   ^f13 Or Chaldeans

16"Take up a harp, walk through the city,
O prostitute forgotten;
play the harp well, sing many a song,
so that you will be remembered."

17At the end of seventy years, the LORD will deal
with Tyre. She will return to her hire as a prostitute
and will ply her trade with all the kingdoms on the
face of the earth. 18Yet her profit and her earnings
will be set apart for the LORD; they will not be stored
up or hoarded. Her profits will go to those who live
before the LORD, for abundant food and fine clothes.

■ The LORD's Devastation of the Earth

24 See, the LORD is going to lay waste the
earth
and devastate it;
he will ruin its face
and scatter its inhabitants—
2it will be the same
for priest as for people,
for master as for servant,
for mistress as for maid,
for seller as for buyer,
for borrower as for lender,
for debtor as for creditor.
3The earth will be completely laid waste
and totally plundered.

The LORD has spoken
this word.

4The earth dries up and withers,
the world languishes and withers,
the exalted of the earth languish.
5The earth is defiled by its people;
they have disobeyed the laws,
violated the statutes
and broken the everlasting covenant.
6Therefore a curse consumes the earth;
its people must bear their guilt.
Therefore earth's inhabitants are burned up,
and very few are left.
7The new wine dries up and the vine withers;
all the merrymakers groan.
8The gaiety of the tambourines is stilled,
the noise of the revellers has stopped,
the joyful harp is silent.
9No longer do they drink wine with a song;
the beer is bitter to its drinkers.
10The ruined city lies desolate;
the entrance to every house is barred.
11In the streets they cry out for wine;
all joy turns to gloom,
all gaiety is banished from the earth.
12The city is left in ruins,
its gate is battered to pieces.
13So will it be on the earth
and among the nations,
as when an olive tree is beaten,
or as when gleanings are left after the grape
harvest.
14They raise their voices, they shout for joy;
from the west they acclaim the LORD's
majesty.
15Therefore in the east give glory to the LORD;

exalt the name of the LORD, the God of Israel,
in the islands of the sea.
16From the ends of the earth we hear singing:
"Glory to the Righteous One."

But I said, "I waste away, I waste away!
Woe to me!
The treacherous betray!
With treachery the treacherous betray!"
17Terror and pit and snare await you,
O people of the earth.
18Whoever flees at the sound of terror
will fall into a pit;
whoever climbs out of the pit
will be caught in a snare.

The floodgates of the heavens are opened,
the foundations of the earth shake.
19The earth is broken up,
the earth is split asunder,
the earth is thoroughly shaken.
20The earth reels like a drunkard,
it sways like a hut in the wind;
so heavy upon it is the guilt of its rebellion
that it falls—never to rise again.

21In that day the LORD will punish
the powers in the heavens above
and the kings on the earth below.
22They will be herded together
like prisoners bound in a dungeon;
they will be shut up in prison
and be punished*a* after many days.
23The moon will be abashed, the sun ashamed;
for the LORD Almighty will reign
on Mount Zion and in Jerusalem,
and before its elders, gloriously.

■ Praise to the LORD

25 O LORD, you are my God;
I will exalt you and praise your name,
for in perfect faithfulness
you have done marvellous things,
things planned long ago.
2You have made the city a heap of rubble,
the fortified town a ruin,
the foreigners' stronghold a city no more;
it will never be rebuilt.
3Therefore strong peoples will honour you;
cities of ruthless nations will revere you.
4You have been a refuge for the poor,
a refuge for the needy in his distress,
a shelter from the storm
and a shade from the heat.
For the breath of the ruthless
is like a storm driving against a wall
5 and like the heat of the desert.
You silence the uproar of foreigners;
as heat is reduced by the shadow of a cloud,
so the song of the ruthless is stilled.

6On this mountain the LORD Almighty will
prepare
a feast of rich food for all peoples,
a banquet of aged wine—
the best of meats and the finest of wines.
7On this mountain he will destroy

a 22 Or released

the shroud that enfolds all peoples,
the sheet that covers all nations;
⁸ he will swallow up death for ever.
The Sovereign LORD will wipe away the tears
from all faces;
he will remove the disgrace of his people
from all the earth.
                    The LORD has spoken.

⁹In that day they will say,

"Surely this is our God;
we trusted in him, and he saved us.
This is the LORD, we trusted in him;
let us rejoice and be glad in his salvation."

25:6 ■ A PROMISE OF ETERNAL LIFE

The Old Testament includes only a few hints about resurrection and the after-life, and this is one of the strongest. Isaiah follows a devastating chapter on God's judgment of the whole earth (chapter 24) with a bright promise of a future life. Then, death and pain will be abolished (see verses 7–8 and 26:19), and God will reign with perfect justice.

¹⁰The hand of the LORD will rest on this
mountain;
but Moab will be trampled under him
as straw is trampled down in the manure.
¹¹They will spread out their hands in it,
as a swimmer spreads out his hands to swim.
God will bring down their pride
despite the cleverness^a of their hands.
¹²He will bring down your high fortified walls
and lay them low;
he will bring them down to the ground,
to the very dust.

■ A Song of Praise

26 In that day this song will be sung in the land of Judah:

We have a strong city;
God makes salvation
its walls and ramparts.
²Open the gates
that the righteous nation may enter,
the nation that keeps faith.
³You will keep in perfect peace
him whose mind is steadfast,
because he trusts in you.
⁴Trust in the LORD for ever,
for the LORD, the LORD, is the Rock eternal.
⁵He humbles those who dwell on high,
he lays the lofty city low;
he levels it to the ground
and casts it down to the dust.
⁶Feet trample it down—
the feet of the oppressed,
the footsteps of the poor.

⁷The path of the righteous is level;
O upright One, you make the way of the
righteous smooth.
⁸Yes, LORD, walking in the way of your laws,^a

we wait for you;
your name and renown
are the desire of our hearts.

26:3 ■ PERFECT PEACE

Isaiah, who lived in a time of tremendous turmoil, predicted more of the same. Godly people would suffer along with everybody else, he said. How should believers cope? Isaiah urged them to focus on a reality greater than their current troubles: to keep their minds steady on God, who never loses control over events.

⁹My soul yearns for you in the night;
in the morning my spirit longs for you.
When your judgments come upon the earth,
the people of the world learn righteousness.
¹⁰Though grace is shown to the wicked,
they do not learn righteousness;
even in a land of uprightness they go on doing
evil
and regard not the majesty of the LORD.
¹¹O LORD, your hand is lifted high,
but they do not see it.
Let them see your zeal for your people and be
put to shame;
let the fire reserved for your enemies
consume them.

¹²LORD, you establish peace for us;
all that we have accomplished you have done
for us.
¹³O LORD, our God, other lords besides you have
ruled over us,
but your name alone do we honour.
¹⁴They are now dead, they live no more;
those departed spirits do not rise.
You punished them and brought them to ruin;
you wiped out all memory of them.
¹⁵You have enlarged the nation, O LORD;
you have enlarged the nation.
You have gained glory for yourself;
you have extended all the borders of the
land.

¹⁶LORD, they came to you in their distress;
when you disciplined them,
they could barely whisper a prayer.^b
¹⁷As a woman with child and about to give birth
writhes and cries out in her pain,
so were we in your presence, O LORD.
¹⁸We were with child, we writhed in pain,
but we gave birth to wind.
We have not brought salvation to the earth;
we have not given birth to people of the
world.

¹⁹But your dead will live;
their bodies will rise.
You who dwell in the dust,
wake up and shout for joy.
Your dew is like the dew of the morning;
the earth will give birth to her dead.

²⁰Go, my people, enter your rooms

^a11 The meaning of the Hebrew for this word is uncertain.   ^a8 Or judgments   ^b16 The meaning of the Hebrew for this clause is uncertain.

and shut the doors behind you;
hide yourselves for a little while
    until his wrath has passed by.
21See, the LORD is coming out of his dwelling
    to punish the people of the earth for their
       sins.
The earth will disclose the blood shed upon
    her;
    she will conceal her slain no longer.

■ Deliverance of Israel

27 In that day,

the LORD will punish with his sword,
    his fierce, great and powerful sword,
Leviathan the gliding serpent,
    Leviathan the coiling serpent;
he will slay the monster of the sea.

27:1 ■ A PROPHECY FOR THE WORLD
Most of Isaiah 1–39 concerns specific nations in
the prophet's own time. But chapters 24 to 27
form a unit that seems to sum up all world history.
Those chapters contain some of Isaiah's strongest
imagery.

2In that day—

"Sing about a fruitful vineyard:
3 I, the LORD, watch over it;
    I water it continually.
I guard it day and night
    so that no-one may harm it.
4 I am not angry.
If only there were briers and thorns
       confronting me!
I would march against them in battle;
    I would set them all on fire.
5Or else let them come to me for refuge;
    let them make peace with me,
    yes, let them make peace with me."

6In days to come Jacob will take root,
    Israel will bud and blossom
    and fill all the world with fruit.

7Has ⌊the LORD⌋ struck her
    as he struck down those who struck her?
Has she been killed
    as those were killed who killed her?
8By warfare*a* and exile you contend with her—
    with his fierce blast he drives her out,
    as on a day the east wind blows.
9By this, then, will Jacob's guilt be atoned for,
    and this will be the full fruitage of the
       removal of his sin:
When he makes all the altar stones
    to be like chalk stones crushed to pieces,
no Asherah poles*b* or incense altars
    will be left standing.
10The fortified city stands desolate,
    an abandoned settlement, forsaken like the
       desert;
there the calves graze,
    there they lie down;

they strip its branches bare.
11When its twigs are dry, they are broken off
    and women come and make fires with them.
For this is a people without understanding;
    so their Maker has no compassion on them,
    and their Creator shows them no favour.

12In that day the LORD will thresh from the flowing Euphrates*c* to the Wadi of Egypt, and you, O
Israelites, will be gathered up one by one. 13And in
that day a great trumpet will sound. Those who
were perishing in Assyria and those who were exiled in Egypt will come and worship the LORD on the
holy mountain in Jerusalem.

■ Woe to Ephraim

28 Woe to that wreath, the pride of Ephraim's
    drunkards,
to the fading flower, his glorious beauty,
set on the head of a fertile valley—
    to that city, the pride of those laid low by
       wine!
2See, the Lord has one who is powerful and
       strong.
Like a hailstorm and a destructive wind,
like a driving rain and a flooding downpour,
    he will throw it forcefully to the ground.
3That wreath, the pride of Ephraim's drunkards,
    will be trampled underfoot.
4That fading flower, his glorious beauty,
    set on the head of a fertile valley,
will be like a fig ripe before harvest—
    as soon as someone sees it and takes it in his
       hand,
    he swallows it.

5In that day the LORD Almighty
    will be a glorious crown,
a beautiful wreath
    for the remnant of his people.
6He will be a spirit of justice
    to him who sits in judgment,
a source of strength
    to those who turn back the battle at the gate.

7And these also stagger from wine
    and reel from beer:
Priests and prophets stagger from beer
    and are befuddled with wine;
they reel from beer,
    they stagger when seeing visions,
    they stumble when rendering decisions.
8All the tables are covered with vomit
    and there is not a spot without filth.

9"Who is it he is trying to teach?
    To whom is he explaining his message?
To children weaned from their milk,
    to those just taken from the breast?
10For it is:
Do and do, do and do,
    rule on rule, rule on rule;*a*
    a little here, a little there."

11Very well then, with foreign lips and strange
       tongues
God will speak to this people,

---

a8 See Septuagint; the meaning of the Hebrew for this word is uncertain.   *b9* That is, symbols of the goddess Asherah   *c12* Hebrew *River*
a10 Hebrew / *sav lasav sav lasav / kav lakav kav lakav* (possibly meaningless sounds; perhaps a mimicking of the prophet's words); also in verse 13

¹²to whom he said,
 "This is the resting-place, let the weary rest";
 and, "This is the place of repose"—
 but they would not listen.
¹³So then, the word of the LORD to them will
  become:
 Do and do, do and do,
 rule on rule, rule on rule;
 a little here, a little there—
 so that they will go and fall backwards,
 be injured and snared and captured.

¹⁴Therefore hear the word of the LORD, you
  scoffers
 who rule this people in Jerusalem.
¹⁵You boast, "We have entered into a covenant
  with death,
 with the grave[b] we have made an
  agreement.
 When an overwhelming scourge sweeps by,
 it cannot touch us,
 for we have made a lie our refuge
 and falsehood[c] our hiding-place."

¹⁶So this is what the Sovereign LORD says:

 "See, I lay a stone in Zion,
 a tested stone,
 a precious cornerstone for a sure foundation;
 the one who trusts will never be dismayed.
¹⁷I will make justice the measuring line
 and righteousness the plumb-line;
 hail will sweep away your refuge, the lie,
 and water will overflow your hiding-place.
¹⁸Your covenant with death will be annulled;
 your agreement with the grave will not
  stand.
 When the overwhelming scourge sweeps by,
 you will be beaten down by it.
¹⁹As often as it comes it will carry you away;
 morning after morning, by day and by night,
 it will sweep through."

 The understanding of this message
 will bring sheer terror.
²⁰The bed is too short to stretch out on,
 the blanket too narrow to wrap around you.
²¹The LORD will rise up as he did at Mount
  Perazim,
 he will rouse himself as in the Valley of
  Gibeon—
 to do his work, his strange work,
 and perform his task, his alien task.
²²Now stop your mocking,
 or your chains will become heavier;
 the Lord, the LORD Almighty, has told me
 of the destruction decreed against the whole
  land.

²³Listen and hear my voice;
 pay attention and hear what I say.
²⁴When a farmer ploughs for planting, does he
  plough continually?
 Does he keep on breaking up and harrowing
  the soil?
²⁵When he has levelled the surface,

does he not sow caraway and scatter
  cummin?
Does he not plant wheat in its place,[d]
 barley in its plot,[d]
 and spelt in its field?
²⁶His God instructs him
 and teaches him the right way.

28:24 ■ LIKE A WISE FARMER
Drawing an analogy from farming, Isaiah shows
that God varies his treatment of nations,
depending on conditions. Just as different crops—
grain, barley, caraway, cummin—require different
farming techniques, so each nation requires
individual treatment. Those who readily repent
need only light punishment, while stubborn nations
need further discipline.

---

²⁷Caraway is not threshed with a sledge,
 nor is a cartwheel rolled over cummin;
 caraway is beaten out with a rod,
 and cummin with a stick.
²⁸Grain must be ground to make bread;
 so one does not go on threshing it for ever.
 Though he drives the wheels of his
  threshing-cart over it,
 his horses do not grind it.
²⁹All this also comes from the LORD Almighty,
 wonderful in counsel and magnificent in
  wisdom.

■ Woe to David's City

29 Woe to you, Ariel, Ariel,
    the city where David settled!
 Add year to year
 and let your cycle of festivals go on.
²Yet I will besiege Ariel;
 she will mourn and lament,
 she will be to me like an altar hearth.[a]
³I will encamp against you all around;
 I will encircle you with towers
 and set up my siege works against you.
⁴Brought low, you will speak from the ground;
 your speech will mumble out of the dust.
 Your voice will come ghostlike from the earth;
 out of the dust your speech will whisper.

⁵But your many enemies will become like fine
  dust,
 the ruthless hordes like blown chaff.
 Suddenly, in an instant,
⁶ the LORD Almighty will come
 with thunder and earthquake and great noise,
 with windstorm and tempest and flames of a
  devouring fire.
⁷Then the hordes of all the nations that fight
  against Ariel,
 that attack her and her fortress and besiege
  her,
 will be as it is with a dream,
 with a vision in the night—
⁸as when a hungry man dreams that he is eating,
 but he awakens, and his hunger remains;

---

[b] 15 Hebrew *Sheol*; also in verse 18   [c] 15 Or *false gods*   [d] 25 The meaning of the Hebrew for this word is uncertain.   [a] 2 The Hebrew for *altar hearth* sounds like the Hebrew for *Ariel*.

as when a thirsty man dreams that he is
 drinking,
but he awakens faint, with his thirst
 unquenched.
So will it be with the hordes of all the nations
 that fight against Mount Zion.

9Be stunned and amazed,
 blind yourselves and be sightless;
be drunk, but not from wine,
 stagger, but not from beer.
10The LORD has brought over you a deep sleep:
 He has sealed your eyes (the prophets);
 he has covered your heads (the seers).

11For you this whole vision is nothing but words
sealed in a scroll. And if you give the scroll to someone who can read, and say to him, "Read this,
please," he will answer, "I can't; it is sealed." 12Or if
you give the scroll to someone who cannot read,
and say, "Read this, please," he will answer, "I don't
know how to read."

13The Lord says:

"These people come near to me with their
 mouth
 and honour me with their lips,
 but their hearts are far from me.
Their worship of me
 is made up only of rules taught by men.b
14Therefore once more I will astound these
 people
 with wonder upon wonder;
the wisdom of the wise will perish,
 the intelligence of the intelligent will vanish."
15Woe to those who go to great depths
 to hide their plans from the LORD,
who do their work in darkness and think,
 "Who sees us? Who will know?"
16You turn things upside down,
 as if the potter were thought to be like the
 clay!
Shall what is formed say to him who formed it,
 "He did not make me"?
Can the pot say of the potter,
 "He knows nothing"?

17In a very short time, will not Lebanon be
 turned into a fertile field
 and the fertile field seem like a forest?
18In that day the deaf will hear the words of the
 scroll,
 and out of gloom and darkness
 the eyes of the blind will see.
19Once more the humble will rejoice in the LORD;
 the needy will rejoice in the Holy One of
 Israel.

20The ruthless will vanish,
 the mockers will disappear,
 and all who have an eye for evil will be cut
 down—
21those who with a word make a man out to be
 guilty,
 who ensnare the defender in court
 and with false testimony deprive the
 innocent of justice.

22Therefore this is what the LORD, who redeemed
Abraham, says to the house of Jacob:

"No longer will Jacob be ashamed;
 no longer will their faces grow pale.
23When they see among them their children,
 the work of my hands,
they will keep my name holy;
 they will acknowledge the holiness of the
 Holy One of Jacob,
 and will stand in awe of the God of Israel.
24Those who are wayward in spirit will gain
 understanding;
 those who complain will accept instruction."

■ Woe to the Obstinate Nation

30 "Woe to the obstinate children,"
 declares the LORD,
"to those who carry out plans that are not
 mine,
 forming an alliance, but not by my Spirit,
 heaping sin upon sin;
2who go down to Egypt
 without consulting me;
who look for help to Pharaoh's protection,
 to Egypt's shade for refuge.
3But Pharaoh's protection will be to your shame,
 Egypt's shade will bring you disgrace.
4Though they have officials in Zoan
 and their envoys have arrived in Hanes,
5everyone will be put to shame
 because of a people useless to them,
who bring neither help nor advantage,
 but only shame and disgrace."

6An oracle concerning the animals of the Negev:

Through a land of hardship and distress,
 of lions and lionesses,
 of adders and darting snakes,

b 13 Hebrew; Septuagint They worship me in vain; / their teachings are but rules taught by men

the envoys carry their riches on donkeys'
    backs,
  their treasures on the humps of camels,
to that unprofitable nation,
7   to Egypt, whose help is utterly useless.
  Therefore I call her
    Rahab the Do-Nothing.

8Go now, write it on a tablet for them,
  inscribe it on a scroll,
that for the days to come
  it may be an everlasting witness.
9These are rebellious people, deceitful children,
  children unwilling to listen to the LORD's
    instruction.
10They say to the seers,
  "See no more visions!"
and to the prophets,
  "Give us no more visions of what is right!
Tell us pleasant things,
  prophesy illusions.
11Leave this way,
  get off this path,
and stop confronting us
  with the Holy One of Israel!"

12Therefore, this is what the Holy One of Israel
says:

"Because you have rejected this message,
  relied on oppression
  and depended on deceit,
13this sin will become for you
  like a high wall, cracked and bulging,
  that collapses suddenly, in an instant.
14It will break in pieces like pottery,
  shattered so mercilessly
that among its pieces not a fragment will be
    found
  for taking coals from a hearth
  or scooping water out of a cistern."

15This is what the Sovereign LORD, the Holy One
of Israel, says:

"In repentance and rest is your salvation,
  in quietness and trust is your strength,
  but you would have none of it.
16You said, 'No, we will flee on horses.'
  Therefore you will flee!
You said, 'We will ride off on swift horses.'
  Therefore your pursuers will be swift!
17A thousand will flee
  at the threat of one;
at the threat of five
  you will all flee away,
till you are left
  like a flagstaff on a mountaintop,
  like a banner on a hill."

18Yet the LORD longs to be gracious to you;
  he rises to show you compassion.
For the LORD is a God of justice.
  Blessed are all who wait for him!

19O people of Zion, who live in Jerusalem, you
will weep no more. How gracious he will be when
you cry for help! As soon as he hears, he will answer

you. 20Although the Lord gives you the bread of adversity and the water of affliction, your teachers will
be hidden no more; with your own eyes you will see
them. 21Whether you turn to the right or to the left,
your ears will hear a voice behind you, saying, "This
is the way; walk in it." 22Then you will defile your
idols overlaid with silver and your images covered
with gold; you will throw them away like a men-
strual cloth and say to them, "Away with you!"

23He will also send you rain for the seed you sow
in the ground, and the food that comes from the
land will be rich and plentiful. In that day your cattle
will graze in broad meadows. 24The oxen and donkeys that work the soil will eat fodder and mash,
spread out with fork and shovel. 25In the day of
great slaughter, when the towers fall, streams of
water will flow on every high mountain and every
lofty hill. 26The moon will shine like the sun, and the
sunlight will be seven times brighter, like the light
of seven full days, when the LORD binds up the
bruises of his people and heals the wounds he inflicted.

27See, the Name of the LORD comes from afar,
  with burning anger and dense clouds of
    smoke;
his lips are full of wrath,
  and his tongue is a consuming fire.
28His breath is like a rushing torrent,
  rising up to the neck.
He shakes the nations in the sieve of
    destruction;
  he places in the jaws of the peoples
  a bit that leads them astray.
29And you will sing
  as on the night you celebrate a holy festival;
your hearts will rejoice
  as when people go up with flutes
to the mountain of the LORD,
  to the Rock of Israel.
30The LORD will cause men to hear his majestic
    voice
  and will make them see his arm coming
    down
with raging anger and consuming fire,
  with cloudburst, thunderstorm and hail.
31The voice of the LORD will shatter Assyria;
  with his sceptre he will strike them down.
32Every stroke the LORD lays on them
  with his punishing rod
will be to the music of tambourines and harps,
  as he fights them in battle with the blows of
    his arm.
33Topheth has long been prepared;
  it has been made ready for the king.
Its fire pit has been made deep and wide,
  with an abundance of fire and wood;
the breath of the LORD,
  like a stream of burning sulphur,
  sets it ablaze.

■ Woe to Those Who Rely on Egypt

31 Woe to those who go down to Egypt for
    help,
  who rely on horses,

who trust in the multitude of their chariots
  and in the great strength of their horsemen,

30:27 ■ AN END TO PUNISHMENT

Isaiah minces no words in his fierce descriptions of the punishment awaiting Judah. But as this chapter shows, the punishment will reach an end, and then God will turn on the surrounding evil nations. The fire of judgment will culminate in Topheth (verse 33), a valley near Jerusalem where human sacrifices were offered to the god Molech.

---

but do not look to the Holy One of Israel,
  or seek help from the LORD.
²Yet he too is wise and can bring disaster;

he does not take back his words.
He will rise up against the house of the wicked,
  against those who help evildoers.
³But the Egyptians are men and not God;
  their horses are flesh and not spirit.
When the LORD stretches out his hand,
  he who helps will stumble,
  he who is helped will fall;
  both will perish together.

⁴This is what the LORD says to me:

"As a lion growls,
  a great lion over his prey—
and though a whole band of shepherds
  is called together against him,
he is not frightened by their shouts

■ A TIME OF CRISIS
DEFEAT SEEMED CERTAIN TO EVERYONE BUT ISAIAH

INSIGHT

"ASSYRIA WILL FALL BY A SWORD THAT IS NOT OF MAN." ■ 31:8

After two dismal decades under King Ahaz, Judah finally saw a ray of hope when Hezekiah ascended the throne. 2 Kings summarises his reign in this way: "There was no-one like him among all the kings of Judah, either before him or after him" (2 Kings 18:5).

    Isaiah reached the peak of his ministry under King Hezekiah, who often sought his advice. The king needed Isaiah's help; he had inherited a kingdom in mortal danger from Assyria.

■ PROTESTING A FOOLISH REBELLION

How could Judah break free from Assyrian domination? Like other kings before him, Hezekiah thought of joining with other countries. Both Egypt and a rising Babylon seemed eager to court Judah as an ally.

    Isaiah, however, said no. He urged Hezekiah to trust only in God. To dramatise his point, the court prophet did a shocking thing: he stalked around stripped and barefoot for three years as a protest against the pro-Egypt lobby (20:1–6). This protest forms the background for some of the strongest speeches in Isaiah's book (chapters 18–20; 30–31).

    Isaiah's protest failed, however. Not even Hezekiah could resist the temptation to oppose Assyria. First, he shored up the defences of Jerusalem and built up the city's water supplies. Then, he formed an alliance of small kingdoms and led an outright rebellion against Assyria.

■ REVENGE OF AN EMPIRE

Assyria lowered the boom. Its armies smashed into Judah, levelling 46 walled cities and carrying away 200,150 captives. The Assyrian king demanded huge sums of money from Hezekiah, whom he mockingly described as "a bird in a cage".

    Hezekiah, cowering under siege in Jerusalem, once more turned to Isaiah for advice. Should he surrender? Assyrian soldiers were already pressing in around the walls, hurling insults at the demoralised citizens inside.

    Isaiah avoided an "I told you so" attitude. Against all odds, he again recommended prayer and reliance on the power of God. Have faith, he said; don't surrender, don't fear. Assyria will return home, wounded (37:5–7).

    Isaiah's deep courage and optimism raised the morale of all Jerusalem. And in a spectacular way (37:36; also 2 Kings 19), God took care of the Assyrian army.

■ AN AUTHENTIC HERO

Chapters 18–35 contain Isaiah's messages from this period, including many of the very words that stirred a desperate nation to faith. Without his inspiring example, Jerusalem might have surrendered.

    Many of the prophets of Israel and Judah were loners, voices "crying in the desert". Isaiah was an exception. He had the king's ear at a critical moment in Judah's history. Because of his effectiveness, Isaiah went down in history as a great statesman and hero.

□ LIFE QUESTIONS:

In your life, what experience has called for the most courage and faith? How did you respond at the time?

or disturbed by their clamour—
so the LORD Almighty will come down
   to do battle on Mount Zion and on its
      heights.
⁵Like birds hovering overhead,
   the LORD Almighty will shield Jerusalem;
he will shield it and deliver it,
   he will 'pass over' it and will rescue it."

⁶Return to him you have so greatly revolted
against, O Israelites. ⁷For in that day every one of
you will reject the idols of silver and gold your sinful hands have made.

⁸"Assyria will fall by a sword that is not of man;
   a sword, not of mortals, will devour them.
They will flee before the sword
   and their young men will be put to forced
      labour.
⁹Their stronghold will fall because of terror;
   at sight of the battle standard their
      commanders will panic,"
declares the LORD,
   whose fire is in Zion,
   whose furnace is in Jerusalem.

■ The Kingdom of Righteousness

32 See, a king will reign in righteousness
   and rulers will rule with justice.
²Each man will be like a shelter from the wind
   and a refuge from the storm,
like streams of water in the desert
   and the shadow of a great rock in a thirsty
      land.

32:1 ■ SHIFTING STANCE IN TIME
Isaiah's writings often shift confusingly, describing
the present surroundings and then moving on to
predict the future. At times Isaiah even projects
himself into the future, writing in the past tense
about events that have not yet happened. Note
the shifting time sequence in this chapter.

³Then the eyes of those who see will no longer
      be closed,
   and the ears of those who hear will listen.
⁴The mind of the rash will know and
      understand,
   and the stammering tongue will be fluent
      and clear.
⁵No longer will the fool be called noble
   nor the scoundrel be highly respected.
⁶For the fool speaks folly,
   his mind is busy with evil:
He practises ungodliness
   and spreads error concerning the LORD;
the hungry he leaves empty
   and from the thirsty he withholds water.
⁷The scoundrel's methods are wicked,
   he makes up evil schemes
to destroy the poor with lies,
   even when the plea of the needy is just.
⁸But the noble man makes noble plans,
   and by noble deeds he stands.

■ The Women of Jerusalem
⁹You women who are so complacent,
   rise up and listen to me;
you daughters who feel secure,
   hear what I have to say!
¹⁰In little more than a year
   you who feel secure will tremble;
the grape harvest will fail,
   and the harvest of fruit will not come.
¹¹Tremble, you complacent women;
   shudder, you daughters who feel secure!
Strip off your clothes,
   put sackcloth round your waists.
¹²Beat your breasts for the pleasant fields,
   for the fruitful vines
¹³and for the land of my people,
   a land overgrown with thorns and briers—
yes, mourn for all houses of merriment
   and for this city of revelry.
¹⁴The fortress will be abandoned,
   the noisy city deserted;
citadel and watchtower will become a
      wasteland for ever,
   the delight of donkeys, a pasture for flocks,
¹⁵till the Spirit is poured upon us from on high,
   and the desert becomes a fertile field,
   and the fertile field seems like a forest.
¹⁶Justice will dwell in the desert
   and righteousness live in the fertile field.
¹⁷The fruit of righteousness will be peace;
   the effect of righteousness will be quietness
      and confidence for ever.
¹⁸My people will live in peaceful dwelling-places,
   in secure homes,
   in undisturbed places of rest.
¹⁹Though hail flattens the forest
   and the city is levelled completely,
²⁰how blessed you will be,
   sowing your seed by every stream,
   and letting your cattle and donkeys range
      free.

■ Distress and Help

33 Woe to you, O destroyer,
   you who have not been destroyed!
Woe to you, O traitor,
   you who have not been betrayed!
When you stop destroying,
   you will be destroyed;
when you stop betraying,
   you will be betrayed.

²O LORD, be gracious to us;
   we long for you.
Be our strength every morning,
   our salvation in time of distress.
³At the thunder of your voice, the peoples flee;
   when you rise up, the nations scatter.
⁴Your plunder, O nations, is harvested as by
      young locusts;
   like a swarm of locusts men pounce on it.

⁵The LORD is exalted, for he dwells on high;
   he will fill Zion with justice and
      righteousness.
⁶He will be the sure foundation for your times,

a rich store of salvation and wisdom and
knowledge;
the fear of the LORD is the key to this
treasure.*

7Look, their brave men cry aloud in the streets;
the envoys of peace weep bitterly.
8The highways are deserted,
no travellers are on the roads.
The treaty is broken,
its witnesses[b] are despised,
no-one is respected.
9The land mourns[c] and wastes away,
Lebanon is ashamed and withers;
Sharon is like the Arabah,
and Bashan and Carmel drop their leaves.

10"Now will I arise," says the LORD.
"Now will I be exalted;
now will I be lifted up.
11You conceive chaff,
you give birth to straw;
your breath is a fire that consumes you.
12The peoples will be burned as if to lime;
like cut thornbushes they will be set ablaze."

13You who are far away, hear what I have done;
you who are near, acknowledge my power!
14The sinners in Zion are terrified;
trembling grips the godless:
"Who of us can dwell with the consuming fire?
Who of us can dwell with everlasting
burning?"
15He who walks righteously
and speaks what is right,
who rejects gain from extortion
and keeps his hand from accepting bribes,
who stops his ears against plots of murder
and shuts his eyes against contemplating
evil—
16this is the man who will dwell on the heights,
whose refuge will be the mountain fortress.
His bread will be supplied,
and water will not fail him.

17Your eyes will see the king in his beauty
and view a land that stretches afar.
18In your thoughts you will ponder the former
terror:
"Where is that chief officer?
Where is the one who took the revenue?
Where is the officer in charge of the towers?"
19You will see those arrogant people no more,
those people of an obscure speech,
with their strange, incomprehensible tongue.

20Look upon Zion, the city of our festivals;
your eyes will see Jerusalem,
a peaceful abode, a tent that will not be
moved;
its stakes will never be pulled up,
nor any of its ropes broken.
21There the LORD will be our Mighty One.
It will be like a place of broad rivers and
streams.
No galley with oars will ride them,
no mighty ship will sail them.

22For the LORD is our judge,
the LORD is our lawgiver,
the LORD is our king;
it is he who will save us.

23Your rigging hangs loose:
The mast is not held secure,
the sail is not spread.
Then an abundance of spoils will be divided
and even the lame will carry off plunder.
24No-one living in Zion will say, "I am ill";
and the sins of those who dwell there will be
forgiven.

■ Judgment Against the Nations

34 Come near, you nations, and listen;
pay attention, you peoples!
Let the earth hear, and all that is in it,
the world, and all that comes out of it!
2The LORD is angry with all nations;
his wrath is upon all their armies.
He will totally destroy[a] them,
he will give them over to slaughter.
3Their slain will be thrown out,
their dead bodies will send up a stench;
the mountains will be soaked with their
blood.
4All the stars of the heavens will be dissolved
and the sky rolled up like a scroll;
all the starry host will fall
like withered leaves from the vine,
like shrivelled figs from the fig-tree.

34:1 ■ ISAIAH THE HISTORIAN

Isaiah's book includes many references to nations
and leaders of his day. Perhaps more than any
other prophet, Isaiah had a deep sense of history.
In fact, he wrote an account of the life of King
Uzziah and a record of the rulers of Israel and
Judah (see 2 Chronicles 26:22; 32:32). Although
neither of these books has survived, the one that
bears his name gives a blow-by-blow analysis of
all the nations of his time.

5My sword has drunk its fill in the heavens;
see, it descends in judgment on Edom,
the people I have totally destroyed.
6The sword of the LORD is bathed in blood,
it is covered with fat—
the blood of lambs and goats,
fat from the kidneys of rams.
For the LORD has a sacrifice in Bozrah
and a great slaughter in Edom.
7And the wild oxen will fall with them,
the bull calves and the great bulls.
Their land will be drenched with blood,
and the dust will be soaked with fat.

8For the LORD has a day of vengeance,
a year of retribution, to uphold Zion's cause.
9Edom's streams will be turned into pitch,
her dust into burning sulphur;
her land will become blazing pitch!
10It will not be quenched night and day;

---

*a*6 Or *is a treasure from him*   *b*8 Dead Sea Scrolls; Masoretic Text / *the cities*   *c*9 Or *dries up*   *a*2 The Hebrew term refers to the irrevocable giving
over of things or persons to the LORD, often by totally destroying them; also in verse 5.

its smoke will rise for ever.
From generation to generation it will lie
   desolate;
no-one will ever pass through it again.
[11]The desert owl[b] and screech owl[b] will
      possess it;
   the great owl[b] and the raven will nest there.
God will stretch out over Edom
   the measuring line of chaos
   and the plumb-line of desolation.
[12]Her nobles will have nothing there to be called
      a kingdom,
   all her princes will vanish away.
[13]Thorns will overrun her citadels,
   nettles and brambles her strongholds.
She will become a haunt for jackals,
   a home for owls.
[14]Desert creatures will meet with hyenas,
   and wild goats will bleat to each other;
there the night creatures will also repose
   and find for themselves places of rest.
[15]The owl will nest there and lay eggs,
   she will hatch them, and care for her young
      under the shadow of her wings;
there also the falcons will gather,
   each with its mate.

[16]Look in the scroll of the LORD and read:

None of these will be missing,
   not one will lack her mate.
For it is his mouth that has given the order,
   and his Spirit will gather them together.
[17]He allots their portions;
   his hand distributes them by measure.
They will possess it for ever
   and dwell there from generation to
      generation.

■ Joy of the Redeemed

35 The desert and the parched land will be
      glad;
   the wilderness will rejoice and blossom.
Like the crocus, [2]it will burst into bloom;
   it will rejoice greatly and shout for joy.
The glory of Lebanon will be given to it,
   the splendour of Carmel and Sharon;
they will see the glory of the LORD,
   the splendour of our God.

[3]Strengthen the feeble hands,
   steady the knees that give way;
[4]say to those with fearful hearts,
   "Be strong, do not fear;
your God will come,
   he will come with vengeance;
with divine retribution
   he will come to save you."

[5]Then will the eyes of the blind be opened
   and the ears of the deaf unstopped.
[6]Then will the lame leap like a deer,
   and the mute tongue shout for joy.
Water will gush forth in the wilderness
   and streams in the desert.

[7]The burning sand will become a pool,
   the thirsty ground bubbling springs.
In the haunts where jackals once lay,
   grass and reeds and papyrus will grow.

[8]And a highway will be there;
   it will be called the Way of Holiness.
The unclean will not journey on it;
   it will be for those who walk in that Way;
   wicked fools will not go about on it.[a]
[9]No lion will be there,
   nor will any ferocious beast get up on it;
   they will not be found there.
But only the redeemed will walk there,
[10]   and the ransomed of the LORD will return.
They will enter Zion with singing;
   everlasting joy will crown their heads.
Gladness and joy will overtake them,
   and sorrow and sighing will flee away.

■ Sennacherib Threatens Jerusalem

36 In the fourteenth year of King Hezekiah's
      reign, Sennacherib king of Assyria attacked
all the fortified cities of Judah and captured them.
[2]Then the king of Assyria sent his field commander
with a large army from Lachish to King Hezekiah at
Jerusalem. When the commander stopped at the
aqueduct of the Upper Pool, on the road to the
Washerman's Field, [3]Eliakim son of Hilkiah the palace administrator, Shebna the secretary, and Joah
son of Asaph the recorder went out to him.

> **36:1** ■ BRIDGE CHAPTERS
> After a beautiful poem describing the renewed
> world God will make, Isaiah plunges into a
> historical account of Judah's troubles with the
> superpower Assyria. These next four historical
> chapters (which closely follow 2 Kings
> 18:13 – 20:19) form a bridge between problems
> with Assyria (chapters 1–35) and those with
> Babylon (chapters 40–66). They record some of
> the greatest crises in Isaiah's and King Hezekiah's
> lives, beginning with Assyria's final assault on
> Jerusalem and ending with Hezekiah's biggest
> blunder. That blunder led to Isaiah's prediction
> that Babylon would someday destroy Judah.

[4]The field commander said to them, "Tell Hezekiah,

   " 'This is what the great king, the king of Assyria, says: On what are you basing this confidence of yours? [5]You say you have strategy and
military strength—but you speak only empty
words. On whom are you depending, that you
rebel against me? [6]Look now, you are depending on Egypt, that splintered reed of a staff,
which pierces a man's hand and wounds him if
he leans on it! Such is Pharaoh king of Egypt to
all who depend on him. [7]And if you say to me,
"We are depending on the LORD our God"—
isn't he the one whose high places and altars
Hezekiah removed, saying to Judah and Jerusalem, "You must worship before this altar"?

---

b 11 The precise identification of these birds is uncertain.   a 8 Or / the simple will not stray from it

8" 'Come now, make a bargain with my master, the king of Assyria: I will give you two thousand horses—if you can put riders on them! 9How then can you repulse one officer of the least of my master's officials, even though you are depending on Egypt for chariots and horsemen? 10Furthermore, have I come to attack and destroy this land without the LORD? The LORD himself told me to march against this country and destroy it.' "

11Then Eliakim, Shebna and Joah said to the field commander, "Please speak to your servants in Aramaic, since we understand it. Don't speak to us in Hebrew in the hearing of the people on the wall."

36:11 ■ FEAR IN THE CITY
The Assyrian commander showed great skill in demoralising the besieged residents of Jerusalem. King Hezekiah's own officials were terrified (36:22–37:4). Only Isaiah stood firm in believing that God could save the city. Earlier (see 22:15–25), God had expressed through Isaiah utter contempt for these very officials of Hezekiah.

12But the commander replied, "Was it only to your master and you that my master sent me to say these things, and not to the men sitting on the wall—who, like you, will have to eat their own filth and drink their own urine?"

13Then the commander stood and called out in Hebrew, "Hear the words of the great king, the king of Assyria! 14This is what the king says: Do not let Hezekiah deceive you. He cannot deliver you! 15Do not let Hezekiah persuade you to trust in the LORD when he says, 'The LORD will surely deliver us; this city will not be given into the hand of the king of Assyria.'

16"Do not listen to Hezekiah. This is what the king of Assyria says: Make peace with me and come out to me. Then every one of you will eat from his own vine and fig-tree and drink water from his own cistern, 17until I come and take you to a land like your own—a land of corn and new wine, a land of bread and vineyards.

18"Do not let Hezekiah mislead you when he says, 'The LORD will deliver us.' Has the god of any nation ever delivered his land from the hand of the king of Assyria? 19Where are the gods of Hamath and Arpad? Where are the gods of Sepharvaim? Have they rescued Samaria from my hand? 20Who of all the gods of these countries has been able to save his land from me? How then can the LORD deliver Jerusalem from my hand?"

21But the people remained silent and said nothing in reply, because the king had commanded, "Do not answer him."

22Then Eliakim son of Hilkiah the palace administrator, Shebna the secretary, and Joah son of Asaph the recorder went to Hezekiah, with their clothes torn, and told him what the field commander had said.

■ Jerusalem's Deliverance Foretold
37 When King Hezekiah heard this, he tore his clothes and put on sackcloth and went into the temple of the LORD. 2He sent Eliakim the palace administrator, Shebna the secretary, and the leading priests, all wearing sackcloth, to the prophet Isaiah son of Amoz. 3They told him, "This is what Hezekiah says: This day is a day of distress and rebuke and disgrace, as when children come to the point of birth and there is no strength to deliver them. 4It may be that the LORD your God will hear the words of the field commander, whom his master, the king of Assyria, has sent to ridicule the living God, and that he will rebuke him for the words the LORD your God has heard. Therefore pray for the remnant that still survives."

5When King Hezekiah's officials came to Isaiah, 6Isaiah said to them, "Tell your master, 'This is what the LORD says: Do not be afraid of what you have heard—those words with which the underlings of the king of Assyria have blasphemed me. 7Listen! I am going to put a spirit in him so that when he hears a certain report, he will return to his own country, and there I will have him cut down with the sword.' "

8When the field commander heard that the king of Assyria had left Lachish, he withdrew and found the king fighting against Libnah.

9Now Sennacherib received a report that Tirhakah, the Cushite[a] king ⌊of Egypt⌋, was marching out to fight against him. When he heard it, he sent messengers to Hezekiah with this word: 10"Say to Hezekiah king of Judah: Do not let the god you depend on deceive you when he says, 'Jerusalem will not be handed over to the king of Assyria.' 11Surely you have heard what the kings of Assyria have done to all the countries, destroying them completely. And will you be delivered? 12Did the gods of the nations that were destroyed by my forefathers deliver them—the gods of Gozan, Haran, Rezeph and the people of Eden who were in Tel Assar? 13Where is the king of Hamath, the king of Arpad, the king of the city of Sepharvaim, or of Hena or Ivvah?"

■ Hezekiah's Prayer
14Hezekiah received the letter from the messengers and read it. Then he went up to the temple of the LORD and spread it out before the LORD. 15And Hezekiah prayed to the LORD: 16"O LORD Almighty, God of Israel, enthroned between the cherubim, you alone are God over all the kingdoms of the earth. You have made heaven and earth. 17Give ear, O LORD, and hear; open your eyes, O LORD, and see; listen to all the words Sennacherib has sent to insult the living God.

18"It is true, O LORD, that the Assyrian kings have laid waste all these peoples and their lands. 19They have thrown their gods into the fire and destroyed them, for they were not gods but only wood and stone, fashioned by human hands. 20Now, O LORD our God, deliver us from his hand, so that all kingdoms on earth may know that you alone, O LORD, are God."[b]

a9 That is, from the upper Nile region   b20 Dead Sea Scrolls (see also 2 Kings 19:19); Masoretic Text alone are the LORD

■ Sennacherib's Fall

21Then Isaiah son of Amoz sent a message to Hezekiah: "This is what the LORD, the God of Israel, says: Because you have prayed to me concerning Sennacherib king of Assyria, 22this is the word the LORD has spoken against him:

"The Virgin Daughter of Zion
  despises and mocks you.
The Daughter of Jerusalem
  tosses her head as you flee.
23Who is it you have insulted and blasphemed?
  Against whom have you raised your voice
and lifted your eyes in pride?
  Against the Holy One of Israel!
24By your messengers
  you have heaped insults on the Lord.
And you have said,
  'With my many chariots
I have ascended the heights of the mountains,
  the utmost heights of Lebanon.
I have cut down its tallest cedars,
  the choicest of its pines.
I have reached its remotest heights,
  the finest of its forests.
25I have dug wells in foreign lands*c*
  and drunk the water there.
With the soles of my feet
  I have dried up all the streams of Egypt.'

26"Have you not heard?
  Long ago I ordained it.
In days of old I planned it;
  now I have brought it to pass,
that you have turned fortified cities
  into piles of stone.
27Their people, drained of power,
  are dismayed and put to shame.
They are like plants in the field,
  like tender green shoots,
like grass sprouting on the roof,
  scorched*d* before it grows up.

28"But I know where you stay
  and when you come and go
  and how you rage against me.
29Because you rage against me
  and because your insolence has reached my
    ears,
I will put my hook in your nose
  and my bit in your mouth,
and I will make you return
  by the way you came.

30"This will be the sign for you, O Hezekiah:

"This year you will eat what grows by itself,
  and the second year what springs from that.
But in the third year sow and reap,
  plant vineyards and eat their fruit.
31Once more a remnant of the house of Judah
  will take root below and bear fruit above.
32For out of Jerusalem will come a remnant,
  and out of Mount Zion a band of survivors.
The zeal of the LORD Almighty
  will accomplish this.

33"Therefore this is what the LORD says concerning the king of Assyria:

"He will not enter this city
  or shoot an arrow here.
He will not come before it with shield
  or build a siege ramp against it.
34By the way that he came he will return;
  he will not enter this city,"
                                              declares the LORD.
35"I will defend this city and save it,
  for my sake and for the sake of David my
    servant!"

36Then the angel of the LORD went out and put to death a hundred and eighty-five thousand men in the Assyrian camp. When the people got up the next morning—there were all the dead bodies! 37So Sennacherib king of Assyria broke camp and withdrew. He returned to Nineveh and stayed there.

38One day, while he was worshipping in the temple of his god Nisroch, his sons Adrammelech and Sharezer cut him down with the sword, and they escaped to the land of Ararat. And Esarhaddon his son succeeded him as king.

■ Hezekiah's Illness

38 In those days Hezekiah became ill and was at the point of death. The prophet Isaiah son of Amoz went to him and said, "This is what the LORD says: Put your house in order, because you are going to die; you will not recover."

> **38:1 ■ FIFTEEN MORE YEARS**
> When the doctor solemnly pronounces a disease terminal, who doesn't crave a second chance? After Isaiah announced to Hezekiah that his disease would be fatal, Hezekiah did not give up. He wept bitterly and asked God to remember his devotion. In response, God sent Isaiah back with an amazing message: he had granted Hezekiah fifteen additional years. Here, as so often in the Bible, God changes events because of prayer.

2Hezekiah turned his face to the wall and prayed to the LORD, 3"Remember, O LORD, how I have walked before you faithfully and with wholehearted devotion and have done what is good in your eyes." And Hezekiah wept bitterly.

4Then the word of the LORD came to Isaiah: 5"Go and tell Hezekiah, 'This is what the LORD, the God of your father David, says: I have heard your prayer and seen your tears; I will add fifteen years to your life. 6And I will deliver you and this city from the hand of the king of Assyria. I will defend this city.

7" 'This is the LORD's sign to you that the LORD will do what he has promised: 8I will make the shadow cast by the sun go back the ten steps it has gone down on the stairway of Ahaz.' " So the sunlight went back the ten steps it had gone down.

9A writing of Hezekiah king of Judah after his illness and recovery:

10I said, "In the prime of my life

---

c 25 Dead Sea Scrolls (see also 2 Kings 19:24); Masoretic Text does not have *in foreign lands*.   *d 27* Some manuscripts of the Masoretic Text, Dead Sea Scrolls and some Septuagint manuscripts (see also 2 Kings 19:26); most manuscripts of the Masoretic Text *roof / and terraced fields*

must I go through the gates of death[a]
  and be robbed of the rest of my years?"
[11]I said, "I will not again see the LORD,
  the LORD, in the land of the living;
no longer will I look on mankind,
  or be with those who now dwell in this
    world.[b]
[12]Like a shepherd's tent my house
  has been pulled down and taken from me.
Like a weaver I have rolled up my life,
  and he has cut me off from the loom;
  day and night you made an end of me.
[13]I waited patiently till dawn,
  but like a lion he broke all my bones;
  day and night you made an end of me.
[14]I cried like a swift or thrush,
  I moaned like a mourning dove.
My eyes grew weak as I looked to the heavens.
  I am troubled; O Lord, come to my aid!"

[15]But what can I say?
  He has spoken to me, and he himself has
    done this.
I will walk humbly all my years
  because of this anguish of my soul.
[16]Lord, by such things men live;
  and my spirit finds life in them too.
You restored me to health
  and let me live.
[17]Surely it was for my benefit
  that I suffered such anguish.
In your love you kept me
  from the pit of destruction;
you have put all my sins
  behind your back.
[18]For the grave[c] cannot praise you,
  death cannot sing your praise;
those who go down to the pit
  cannot hope for your faithfulness.
[19]The living, the living—they praise you,
  as I am doing today;
fathers tell their children
  about your faithfulness.

[20]The LORD will save me,
  and we will sing with stringed instruments
all the days of our lives
  in the temple of the LORD.

[21]Isaiah had said, "Prepare a poultice of figs and apply it to the boil, and he will recover." [22]Hezekiah had asked, "What will be the sign that I will go up to the temple of the LORD?"

■ Envoys From Babylon

39 At that time Merodach-Baladan son of Baladan king of Babylon sent Hezekiah letters and a gift, because he had heard of his illness and recovery. [2]Hezekiah received the envoys gladly and showed them what was in his storehouses—the silver, the gold, the spices, the fine oil, his entire armoury and everything found among his treasures. There was nothing in his palace or in all his kingdom that Hezekiah did not show them.

[3]Then Isaiah the prophet went to King Hezekiah

and asked, "What did those men say, and where did they come from?"

"From a distant land," Hezekiah replied. "They came to me from Babylon."

[4]The prophet asked, "What did they see in your palace?"

"They saw everything in my palace," Hezekiah said. "There is nothing among my treasures that I did not show them."

[5]Then Isaiah said to Hezekiah, "Hear the word of the LORD Almighty: [6]The time will surely come when everything in your palace, and all that your fathers have stored up until this day, will be carried off to Babylon. Nothing will be left, says the LORD. [7]And some of your descendants, your own flesh and blood who will be born to you, will be taken away, and they will become eunuchs in the palace of the king of Babylon."

[8]"The word of the LORD you have spoken is good," Hezekiah replied. For he thought, "There will be peace and security in my lifetime."

■ Comfort for God's People

40 Comfort, comfort my people,
  says your God.
[2]Speak tenderly to Jerusalem,
  and proclaim to her
that her hard service has been completed,
  that her sin has been paid for,
that she has received from the LORD's hand
  double for all her sins.

[3]A voice of one calling:
"In the desert prepare
  the way for the LORD;[a]
make straight in the wilderness
  a highway for our God.[b]
[4]Every valley shall be raised up,
  every mountain and hill made low;
the rough ground shall become level,
  the rugged places a plain.
[5]And the glory of the LORD will be revealed,
  and all mankind together will see it.
    For the mouth of the LORD has spoken."

40:3 ■ VOICE IN THE WILDERNESS
Beginning here, Isaiah's emphasis shifts away from judgment and towards comfort. The comfort will ultimately come through God's glorious arrival, which God's people should prepare for by building a "highway" for God to travel on. In the New Testament, John the Baptist identified himself as the "voice" calling for this preparation (John 1:23). The "earthmoving" he demanded was repentance from sin, a preparation for Jesus' arrival.

[6]A voice says, "Cry out."
  And I said, "What shall I cry?"

"All men are like grass,
  and all their glory is like the flowers of the
    field.
[7]The grass withers and the flowers fall,

because the breath of the LORD blows on
them.
Surely the people are grass.
8The grass withers and the flowers fall,
but the word of our God stands for ever."

9You who bring good tidings to Zion,
go up on a high mountain.
You who bring good tidings to Jerusalem,c
lift up your voice with a shout,
lift it up, do not be afraid;
say to the towns of Judah,
"Here is your God!"
10See, the Sovereign LORD comes with power,
and his arm rules for him.
See, his reward is with him,
and his recompense accompanies him.
11He tends his flock like a shepherd:
He gathers the lambs in his arms
and carries them close to his heart;
he gently leads those that have young.

12Who has measured the waters in the hollow of
his hand,
or with the breadth of his hand marked off
the heavens?
Who has held the dust of the earth in a basket,
or weighed the mountains on the scales
and the hills in a balance?
13Who has understood the mindd of the LORD,
or instructed him as his counsellor?
14Whom did the LORD consult to enlighten him,
and who taught him the right way?
Who was it that taught him knowledge
or showed him the path of understanding?

15Surely the nations are like a drop in a bucket;
they are regarded as dust on the scales;
he weighs the islands as though they were
fine dust.
16Lebanon is not sufficient for altar fires,
nor its animals enough for burnt offerings.
17Before him all the nations are as nothing;
they are regarded by him as worthless
and less than nothing.

18To whom, then, will you compare God?
What image will you compare him to?
19As for an idol, a craftsman casts it,
and a goldsmith overlays it with gold
and fashions silver chains for it.
20A man too poor to present such an offering
selects wood that will not rot.
He looks for a skilled craftsman
to set up an idol that will not topple.

21Do you not know?
Have you not heard?
Has it not been told you from the beginning?
Have you not understood since the earth was
founded?
22He sits enthroned above the circle of the earth,
and its people are like grasshoppers.
He stretches out the heavens like a canopy,
and spreads them out like a tent to live in.
23He brings princes to naught

and reduces the rulers of this world to
nothing.
24No sooner are they planted,
no sooner are they sown,
no sooner do they take root in the ground,
than he blows on them and they wither,
and a whirlwind sweeps them away like
chaff.

25"To whom will you compare me?
Or who is my equal?" says the Holy One.
26Lift your eyes and look to the heavens:
Who created all these?
He who brings out the starry host one by one,
and calls them each by name.
Because of his great power and mighty
strength,
not one of them is missing.

27Why do you say, O Jacob,
and complain, O Israel,
"My way is hidden from the LORD;
my cause is disregarded by my God"?
28Do you not know?
Have you not heard?
The LORD is the everlasting God,
the Creator of the ends of the earth.
He will not grow tired or weary,
and his understanding no-one can fathom.
29He gives strength to the weary
and increases the power of the weak.
30Even youths grow tired and weary,
and young men stumble and fall;
31but those who hope in the LORD
will renew their strength.
They will soar on wings like eagles;
they will run and not grow weary,
they will walk and not be faint.

■ The Helper of Israel
41 "Be silent before me, you islands!
Let the nations renew their strength!
Let them come forward and speak;
let us meet together at the place of
judgment.

2"Who has stirred up one from the east,
calling him in righteousness to his service?a
He hands nations over to him
and subdues kings before him.
He turns them to dust with his sword,
to wind-blown chaff with his bow.
3He pursues them and moves on unscathed,
by a path his feet have not travelled before.
4Who has done this and carried it through,
calling forth the generations from the
beginning?
I, the LORD—with the first of them
and with the last—I am he."

5The islands have seen it and fear;
the ends of the earth tremble.
They approach and come forward;
6   each helps the other
and says to his brother, "Be strong!"
7The craftsman encourages the goldsmith,
and he who smooths with the hammer

c9 Or O Zion, bringer of good tidings, / go up on a high mountain. / O Jerusalem, bringer of good tidings   d13 Or Spirit; or spirit   a2 Or / whom
victory meets at every step

A NEW SONG
A DRAMATIC CHANGE IN TONE: COMFORT AND HOPE FOR THE WORST OF TIMES

THOSE WHO HOPE IN THE LORD WILL RENEW THEIR STRENGTH. THEY WILL SOAR ON WINGS LIKE EAGLES; THEY WILL RUN AND NOT GROW WEARY, THEY WILL WALK AND NOT BE FAINT. ■ 40:31

You can sense the change in the very first words of chapter 40. "Comfort, comfort my people, says your God. Speak tenderly to Jerusalem, and proclaim to her that her hard service has been completed." Soft, reassuring words replace the harsh warnings of Isaiah's earlier chapters.

During much of Isaiah's life, Judah was confident and strong. But the prophecies beginning in chapter 40 project forwards to a radically different scene. The land of Judah has been devastated, and the Jews have been taken captive. Jerusalem lies in ruins. Some 200 years separate what is described in the first part of Isaiah from the latter part. (Many scholars believe these later prophecies were given by another prophet.)

■ WHAT HAPPENED IN THE MEANTIME

To understand the rest of the book of Isaiah, you need to understand what happened in those 200 years. The confident nation Isaiah once knew slid further and further downwards. At the same time a new empire, Babylon, gained strength. This new enemy invaded Judah.

The armies of Babylon did something no army had accomplished since King David's time: they conquered Jerusalem itself. Siege engines breached the walls. Judah's king was led out of Jerusalem, blinded. Their homes destroyed, most of the city's inhabitants followed their king in chains. The dark period of Babylonian captivity began.

Prophets of this period, and those who prophesied in advance about the coming catastrophes, faced huge questions. Was God abandoning his "eternal" throne of David? How could he watch in silence as his own nation — his own temple — was ripped to shreds by pagan armies?

■ THREE GREAT HOPES

Reflecting the change in circumstances, Isaiah 40–66 shifts into a new key. Gone are the bleak predictions of judgment on the Jews. Instead, a majestic message of hope and joy and light breaks in, beginning with the opening words of comfort. The prophet sets out to re-establish faith in God.

What happened to Judah, Isaiah teaches, was not God's defeat. God had in mind a new thing, a plan far more grand than anything seen before.

The author of Isaiah expresses the plan as a series of wonderful reasons for hope. First, he says, will come deliverance from the Babylonian captivity. A new star, a ruler named Cyrus, will arise in the east and set the Jews free. He will allow them to return to Jerusalem to begin the long task of rebuilding a city and a nation. Chapters 40–48 detail God's confident predictions about Cyrus and the relief he would give captive Jews.

Indeed, just such a ruler did ascend to the throne in ancient Persia (present-day Iran). Cyrus smashed Babylon's armies in one decisive battle. As recorded in Ezra 1:1–4, he granted the Jews permission to return to their city and rebuild.

In words that have become very familiar, the book of Isaiah tells of two further hopes for the future. A mysterious figure called "the servant" appears in chapter 49. That servant, through his suffering, would provide a way to rescue the entire world. Finally, in conclusion, the prophet turns to a faraway time, when God will usher in peace for all in a new heaven and new earth. "The Holy One of Israel" (one of Isaiah's favourite names for God) will rule as the God of the whole earth.

■ SURVIVING TOUGH TIMES

Isaiah 40–66 had immense practical value for the people who first heard it. The Jews, facing a series of great crises, needed the prophet's message of hope: forgiveness was on the way; the Jews, though scattered, would one day be gathered "one by one".

Further, Isaiah teaches that no matter how difficult the circumstances, God can use them for our benefit. Again and again in the Israelites' history, good times led to decadence. In contrast, times of suffering tested and refined the true people of God. Ultimately, suffering would lead to the salvation of all the world.

□ LIFE QUESTIONS:

Try to put yourself in the place of the Jews back then. Would you have found the prophet's words comforting?

spurs on him who strikes the anvil.
He says of the welding, "It is good."
He nails down the idol so that it will not
topple.

41:4 ■ HOW TO UNDERSTAND GOD

Chapters 40–46 echo the majestic chapters at the end of Job. God shows himself as master of the universe. Before him, nations are like a drop in a bucket (40:15) and people are like grasshoppers (40:22). He taunts all other so-called "gods": such idols are carved of the same tree used to cook supper! (44:12–20). The true God, the God of the Israelites, is the One who created the universe (45:12,18), who called Abraham (41:8), who rescued the Israelites from slavery in Egypt. For the dispirited Jewish survivors of Babylon's invasion, this exalted view of God was a reminder that God had neither vanished nor rejected them.

8"But you, O Israel, my servant,
  Jacob, whom I have chosen,
  you descendants of Abraham my friend,
9I took you from the ends of the earth,
  from its farthest corners I called you.
I said, 'You are my servant';
  I have chosen you and have not rejected
  you.
10So do not fear, for I am with you;
  do not be dismayed, for I am your God.
I will strengthen you and help you;
  I will uphold you with my righteous right
  hand.

11"All who rage against you
  will surely be ashamed and disgraced;
those who oppose you
  will be as nothing and perish.
12Though you search for your enemies,
  you will not find them.
Those who wage war against you
  will be as nothing at all.
13For I am the LORD, your God,
  who takes hold of your right hand
and says to you, Do not fear;
  I will help you.
14Do not be afraid, O worm Jacob,
  O little Israel,
for I myself will help you," declares the LORD,
  your Redeemer, the Holy One of Israel.
15"See, I will make you into a threshing-sledge,
  new and sharp, with many teeth.
You will thresh the mountains and crush them,
  and reduce the hills to chaff.
16You will winnow them, the wind will pick
  them up,
  and a gale will blow them away.
But you will rejoice in the LORD
  and glory in the Holy One of Israel.

17"The poor and needy search for water,
  but there is none;
  their tongues are parched with thirst.
But I the LORD will answer them;

I, the God of Israel, will not forsake them.
18I will make rivers flow on barren heights,
  and springs within the valleys.
I will turn the desert into pools of water,
  and the parched ground into springs.
19I will put in the desert
  the cedar and the acacia, the myrtle and the
  olive.
I will set pines in the wasteland,
  the fir and the cypress together,
20so that people may see and know,
  may consider and understand,
that the hand of the LORD has done this,
  that the Holy One of Israel has created it.

21"Present your case," says the LORD.
  "Set forth your arguments," says Jacob's King.
22"Bring in ⌞ your idols⌟ to tell us
  what is going to happen.
Tell us what the former things were,
  so that we may consider them
  and know their final outcome.
Or declare to us the things to come,
23   tell us what the future holds,
  so that we may know you are gods.
Do something, whether good or bad,
  so that we will be dismayed and filled with
  fear.
24But you are less than nothing
  and your works are utterly worthless;
  he who chooses you is detestable.

25"I have stirred up one from the north, and he
  comes—
  one from the rising sun who calls on my
  name.
He treads on rulers as if they were mortar,
  as if he were a potter treading the clay.
26Who told of this from the beginning, so that we
  could know,
  or beforehand, so that we could say, 'He was
  right'?
No-one told of this,
  no-one foretold it,
  no-one heard any words from you.
27I was the first to tell Zion, 'Look, here they
  are!'
  I gave to Jerusalem a messenger of good
  tidings.
28I look but there is no-one—
  no-one among them to give counsel,
  no-one to give answer when I ask them.
29See, they are all false!
  Their deeds amount to nothing;
  their images are but wind and confusion.

■ The Servant of the LORD

42 "Here is my servant, whom I uphold,
  my chosen one in whom I delight;
I will put my Spirit on him
  and he will bring justice to the nations.
2He will not shout or cry out,
  or raise his voice in the streets.
3A bruised reed he will not break,
  and a smouldering wick he will not snuff out.
In faithfulness he will bring forth justice;

4 he will not falter or be discouraged
  till he establishes justice on earth.
  In his law the islands will put their hope."

42:1 ■ THE SOLUTION

Having described shocking injustice, Isaiah now gives the solution: God's servant, who in a quiet, gentle, steady way will bring justice not only to Israel but to "the nations" — that is, the entire earth. Matthew 12:18–21, quoting this passage, identifies the servant as Jesus.

5This is what God the LORD says—
  he who created the heavens and stretched
    them out,
  who spread out the earth and all that comes
    out of it,
who gives breath to its people,
  and life to those who walk on it:
6"I, the LORD, have called you in righteousness;
  I will take hold of your hand.
I will keep you and will make you
  to be a covenant for the people
  and a light for the Gentiles,
7to open eyes that are blind,
  to free captives from prison
  and to release from the dungeon those who
    sit in darkness.

8"I am the LORD; that is my name!
  I will not give my glory to another
  or my praise to idols.
9See, the former things have taken place,
  and new things I declare;
before they spring into being
  I announce them to you."

■ Song of Praise to the LORD
10Sing to the LORD a new song,
  his praise from the ends of the earth,
you who go down to the sea, and all that is in
    it,
  you islands, and all who live in them.
11Let the desert and its towns raise their voices;
  let the settlements where Kedar lives rejoice.
Let the people of Sela sing for joy;
  let them shout from the mountaintops.
12Let them give glory to the LORD
  and proclaim his praise in the islands.
13The LORD will march out like a mighty man,
  like a warrior he will stir up his zeal;
with a shout he will raise the battle cry
  and will triumph over his enemies.

14"For a long time I have kept silent,
  I have been quiet and held myself back.
But now, like a woman in childbirth,
  I cry out, I gasp and pant.
15I will lay waste the mountains and hills
  and dry up all their vegetation;
I will turn rivers into islands
  and dry up the pools.
16I will lead the blind by ways they have not
    known,

along unfamiliar paths I will guide them;
I will turn the darkness into light before them
  and make the rough places smooth.
These are the things I will do;
  I will not forsake them.

42:14 ■ DOES GOD CARE?

After telling of his power, God goes on to describe the depth of his feelings for his people. He uses tender and sometimes shocking language, especially in this comparison of his pain to that of childbirth.

17But those who trust in idols,
  who say to images, 'You are our gods,'
  will be turned back in utter shame.

■ Israel Blind and Deaf
18"Hear, you deaf;
  look, you blind, and see!
19Who is blind but my servant,
  and deaf like the messenger I send?
Who is blind like the one committed to me,
  blind like the servant of the LORD?
20You have seen many things, but have paid no
    attention;
  your ears are open, but you hear nothing."
21It pleased the LORD
  for the sake of his righteousness
  to make his law great and glorious.
22But this is a people plundered and looted,
  all of them trapped in pits
  or hidden away in prisons.
They have become plunder,
  with no-one to rescue them;
they have been made loot,
  with no-one to say, "Send them back."

23Which of you will listen to this
  or pay close attention in time to come?
24Who handed Jacob over to become loot,
  and Israel to the plunderers?
Was it not the LORD,
  against whom we have sinned?
For they would not follow his ways;
  they did not obey his law.
25So he poured out on them his burning anger,
  the violence of war.
It enveloped them in flames, yet they did not
    understand;
  it consumed them, but they did not take it to
    heart.

■ Israel's Only Saviour
43 But now, this is what the LORD says—
  he who created you, O Jacob,
  he who formed you, O Israel:
"Fear not, for I have redeemed you;
  I have summoned you by name; you are
    mine.
2When you pass through the waters,
  I will be with you;
and when you pass through the rivers,
  they will not sweep over you.

When you walk through the fire,
    you will not be burned;
    the flames will not set you ablaze.
³For I am the LORD, your God,
    the Holy One of Israel, your Saviour;
I give Egypt for your ransom,
    Cush*a* and Seba in your stead.
⁴Since you are precious and honoured in my
        sight,
    and because I love you,
I will give men in exchange for you,
    and people in exchange for your life.
⁵Do not be afraid, for I am with you;
    I will bring your children from the east
    and gather you from the west.
⁶I will say to the north, 'Give them up!'
    and to the south, 'Do not hold them back.'
Bring my sons from afar
    and my daughters from the ends of the
        earth—
⁷everyone who is called by my name,
    whom I created for my glory,
    whom I formed and made."

43:3 ■ RANSOM FOR THE CAPTIVES

God speaks of providing the nations of Egypt,
Cush, and Seba as a ransom or reward for
allowing the Jews to return to their land.
Historically, Cyrus of Persia permitted the Jews to
resettle in the sixth century B.C. Shortly after that,
Persia conquered the territories mentioned here.

⁸Lead out those who have eyes but are blind,
    who have ears but are deaf.
⁹All the nations gather together
    and the peoples assemble.
Which of them foretold this
    and proclaimed to us the former things?
Let them bring in their witnesses to prove they
        were right,
    so that others may hear and say, "It is true."
¹⁰"You are my witnesses," declares the LORD,
    "and my servant whom I have chosen,
so that you may know and believe me
    and understand that I am he.
Before me no god was formed,
    nor will there be one after me.
¹¹I, even I, am the LORD,
    and apart from me there is no saviour.
¹²I have revealed and saved and proclaimed—
    I, and not some foreign god among you.
You are my witnesses," declares the LORD, "that
        I am God.
¹³   Yes, and from ancient days I am he.
No-one can deliver out of my hand.
    When I act, who can reverse it?"

■ God's Mercy and Israel's Unfaithfulness
¹⁴This is what the LORD says—
    your Redeemer, the Holy One of Israel:
    "For your sake I will send to Babylon
    and bring down as fugitives all the
        Babylonians,*b*

in the ships in which they took pride.
¹⁵I am the LORD, your Holy One,
    Israel's Creator, your King."

43:10 ■ COURTROOM DRAMA

Isaiah pictures a court-like drama, in which the
world assembles to decide who is really God. As
each would-be god calls witnesses in turn, the
God of Israel calls his people to witness for him.
They had heard God's prediction that he would
bring back his people, scattered all over the
Middle East, to re-establish their nation. As his
witnesses, they need only testify that he has done
what he promised.

¹⁶This is what the LORD says—
    he who made a way through the sea,
    a path through the mighty waters,
¹⁷who drew out the chariots and horses,
    the army and reinforcements together,
and they lay there, never to rise again,
    extinguished, snuffed out like a wick:
¹⁸"Forget the former things;
    do not dwell on the past.
¹⁹See, I am doing a new thing!
    Now it springs up; do you not perceive it?
I am making a way in the desert
    and streams in the wasteland.
²⁰The wild animals honour me,
    the jackals and the owls,
because I provide water in the desert
    and streams in the wasteland,
to give drink to my people, my chosen,
²¹   the people I formed for myself
    that they may proclaim my praise.

²²"Yet you have not called upon me, O Jacob,
    you have not wearied yourselves for me,
        O Israel.
²³You have not brought me sheep for burnt
        offerings,
    nor honoured me with your sacrifices.
I have not burdened you with grain offerings
    nor wearied you with demands for incense.
²⁴You have not bought any fragrant calamus for
        me,
    or lavished on me the fat of your sacrifices.
But you have burdened me with your sins
    and wearied me with your offences.

²⁵"I, even I, am he who blots out
    your transgressions, for my own sake,
    and remembers your sins no more.
²⁶Review the past for me,
    let us argue the matter together;
    state the case for your innocence.
²⁷Your first father sinned;
    your spokesmen rebelled against me.
²⁸So I will disgrace the dignitaries of your
        temple,
    and I will consign Jacob to destruction*c*
    and Israel to scorn.

a 3 That is, the upper Nile region   *b 14* Or *Chaldeans*   *c 28* The Hebrew term refers to the irrevocable giving over of things or persons to the LORD, often
by totally destroying them.

■ Israel the Chosen

44 "But now listen, O Jacob, my servant,
Israel, whom I have chosen.
²This is what the LORD says—
he who made you, who formed you in the
womb,
and who will help you:
Do not be afraid, O Jacob, my servant,
Jeshurun, whom I have chosen.
³For I will pour water on the thirsty land,
and streams on the dry ground;
I will pour out my Spirit on your offspring,
and my blessing on your descendants.
⁴They will spring up like grass in a meadow,
like poplar trees by flowing streams.
⁵One will say, 'I belong to the LORD';
another will call himself by the name of
Jacob;
still another will write on his hand, 'The
LORD's',
and will take the name Israel.

■ The LORD, Not Idols

⁶"This is what the LORD says—
Israel's King and Redeemer, the LORD
Almighty:
I am the first and I am the last;
apart from me there is no God.
⁷Who then is like me? Let him proclaim it.
Let him declare and lay out before me
what has happened since I established my
ancient people,
and what is yet to come—
yes, let him foretell what will come.
⁸Do not tremble, do not be afraid.
Did I not proclaim this and foretell it long
ago?
You are my witnesses. Is there any God besides
me?
No, there is no other Rock; I know not one."

⁹All who make idols are nothing,
and the things they treasure are worthless.
Those who would speak up for them are blind;
they are ignorant, to their own shame.
¹⁰Who shapes a god and casts an idol,
which can profit him nothing?
¹¹He and his kind will be put to shame;
craftsmen are nothing but men.
Let them all come together and take their
stand;
they will be brought down to terror and
infamy.

¹²The blacksmith takes a tool
and works with it in the coals;
he shapes an idol with hammers,
he forges it with the might of his arm.
He gets hungry and loses his strength;
he drinks no water and grows faint.
¹³The carpenter measures with a line
and makes an outline with a marker;
he roughs it out with chisels
and marks it with compasses.
He shapes it in the form of man,
of man in all his glory,

that it may dwell in a shrine.
¹⁴He cut down cedars,
or perhaps took a cypress or oak.
He let it grow among the trees of the forest,
or planted a pine, and the rain made it grow.
¹⁵It is man's fuel for burning;
some of it he takes and warms himself,
he kindles a fire and bakes bread.
But he also fashions a god and worships it;
he makes an idol and bows down to it.
¹⁶Half of the wood he burns in the fire;
over it he prepares his meal,
he roasts his meat and eats his fill.
He also warms himself and says,
"Ah! I am warm; I see the fire."
¹⁷From the rest he makes a god, his idol;
he bows down to it and worships.
He prays to it and says,
"Save me; you are my god."
¹⁸They know nothing, they understand nothing;
their eyes are plastered over so that they
cannot see,
and their minds closed so that they cannot
understand.
¹⁹No-one stops to think,
no-one has the knowledge or understanding
to say,
"Half of it I used for fuel;
I even baked bread over its coals,
I roasted meat and I ate.
Shall I make a detestable thing from what is
left?
Shall I bow down to a block of wood?"
²⁰He feeds on ashes, a deluded heart misleads
him;
he cannot save himself, or say,
"Is not this thing in my right hand a lie?"

²¹"Remember these things, O Jacob,
for you are my servant, O Israel.
I have made you, you are my servant;
O Israel, I will not forget you.
²²I have swept away your offences like a cloud,
your sins like the morning mist.
Return to me,
for I have redeemed you."

²³Sing for joy, O heavens, for the LORD has done
this;
shout aloud, O earth beneath.
Burst into song, you mountains,
you forests and all your trees,
for the LORD has redeemed Jacob,
he displays his glory in Israel.

■ Jerusalem to Be Inhabited

²⁴"This is what the LORD says—
your Redeemer, who formed you in the
womb:

I am the LORD,
who has made all things,
who alone stretched out the heavens,
who spread out the earth by myself,

²⁵who foils the signs of false prophets
and makes fools of diviners,

who overthrows the learning of the wise
  and turns it into nonsense,
26who carries out the words of his servants
  and fulfils the predictions of his messengers,

who says of Jerusalem, 'It shall be inhabited,'
  of the towns of Judah, 'They shall be built,'
  and of their ruins, 'I will restore them,'
27who says to the watery deep, 'Be dry,
  and I will dry up your streams,'
28who says of Cyrus, 'He is my shepherd
  and will accomplish all that I please;
  he will say of Jerusalem, "Let it be rebuilt,"
  and of the temple, "Let its foundations be
    laid." '

44:28 ■ CYRUS THE SHEPHERD

God demonstrated his control over human history
by using a foreigner, the emperor of a new
Medo-Persian empire, to accomplish his will. "I
summon you by name and bestow on you a title
of honour," said God, "though you do not
acknowledge me" (45:4). As predicted in this
verse, Cyrus freed the Jewish captives in Babylon
and allowed them to return to Jerusalem to rebuild
the temple.

45 "This is what the LORD says to his
      anointed,
  to Cyrus, whose right hand I take hold of
to subdue nations before him
  and to strip kings of their armour,
to open doors before him
  so that gates will not be shut:
2I will go before you
  and will level the mountains;a
I will break down gates of bronze
  and cut through bars of iron.
3I will give you the treasures of darkness,
  riches stored in secret places,
so that you may know that I am the LORD,
  the God of Israel, who summons you by
    name.
4For the sake of Jacob my servant,
  of Israel my chosen,
I summon you by name
  and bestow on you a title of honour,
  though you do not acknowledge me.
5I am the LORD, and there is no other;
  apart from me there is no God.
I will strengthen you,
  though you have not acknowledged me,
6so that from the rising of the sun
  to the place of its setting
men may know there is none besides me.
  I am the LORD, and there is no other.
7I form the light and create darkness,
  I bring prosperity and create disaster;
I, the LORD, do all these things.

8"You heavens above, rain down righteousness;
  let the clouds shower it down.
Let the earth open wide,
  let salvation spring up,

let righteousness grow with it;
  I, the LORD, have created it.

9"Woe to him who quarrels with his Maker,
  to him who is but a potsherd among the
    potsherds on the ground.
Does the clay say to the potter,
  'What are you making?'
Does your work say,
  'He has no hands'?
10Woe to him who says to his father,
  'What have you begotten?'
or to his mother,
  'What have you brought to birth?'

45:9 ■ QUARRELS WITH GOD

Quarrelling with your Maker goes far beyond the
spirited dialogue that Moses, Job, and Jeremiah
engaged in. Isaiah is describing an insolent assault
on God's competence. Not only is it wrong, it is
ridiculous — as ridiculous as a pot complaining
about the shape the potter gives it. In Romans
9:20, Paul applies this analogy to complaints that
God had treated the Jews unfairly.

11"This is what the LORD says—
  the Holy One of Israel, and its Maker:
Concerning things to come,
  do you question me about my children,
  or give me orders about the work of my
    hands?
12It is I who made the earth
  and created mankind upon it.
My own hands stretched out the heavens;
  I marshalled their starry hosts.
13I will raise up Cyrusb in my righteousness:
  I will make all his ways straight.
He will rebuild my city
  and set my exiles free,
but not for a price or reward,
  says the LORD Almighty."

14This is what the LORD says:

"The products of Egypt and the merchandise of
    Cush,c
  and those tall Sabeans—
they will come over to you
  and will be yours;
they will trudge behind you,
  coming over to you in chains.
They will bow down before you
  and plead with you, saying,
'Surely God is with you, and there is no other;
  there is no other god.' "

15Truly you are a God who hides himself,
  O God and Saviour of Israel.
16All the makers of idols will be put to shame
    and disgraced;
  they will go off into disgrace together.
17But Israel will be saved by the LORD
  with an everlasting salvation;
you will never be put to shame or disgraced,
  to ages everlasting.

a 2 Dead Sea Scrolls and Septuagint; the meaning of the word in the Masoretic Text is uncertain.   b 13 Hebrew him   c 14 That is, the upper Nile region

¹⁸For this is what the LORD says—
  he who created the heavens,
    he is God;
  he who fashioned and made the earth,
    he founded it;
  he did not create it to be empty,
    but formed it to be inhabited—
  he says:
  "I am the LORD,
    and there is no other.
¹⁹I have not spoken in secret,
    from somewhere in a land of darkness;
  I have not said to Jacob's descendants,
    'Seek me in vain.'
  I, the LORD, speak the truth;
    I declare what is right.

²⁰"Gather together and come;
    assemble, you fugitives from the nations.
  Ignorant are those who carry about idols of
    wood,
    who pray to gods that cannot save.
²¹Declare what is to be, present it—
    let them take counsel together.
  Who foretold this long ago,
    who declared it from the distant past?
  Was it not I, the LORD?
    And there is no God apart from me,
  a righteous God and a Saviour;
    there is none but me.

45:21 ■ FORETELLING THE FUTURE
Isaiah contains many predictions of future events.
These chapters tell of Cyrus' rise from the east.
Elsewhere, the prophet gives specific predictions
about the coming Messiah and about events near
the end of time. God uses these predictions as
proof of his power and knowledge, challenging the
pagan gods to foretell anything (41:23).

²²"Turn to me and be saved,
    all you ends of the earth;
    for I am God, and there is no other.
²³By myself I have sworn,
    my mouth has uttered in all integrity
    a word that will not be revoked:
  Before me every knee will bow;
    by me every tongue will swear.
²⁴They will say of me, 'In the LORD alone
    are righteousness and strength.'"
  All who have raged against him
    will come to him and be put to shame.
²⁵But in the LORD all the descendants of Israel
    will be found righteous and will exult.

■ Gods of Babylon
46 Bel bows down, Nebo stoops low;
    their idols are borne by beasts of
    burden.ᵃ
  The images that are carried about are
    burdensome,
    a burden for the weary.
²They stoop and bow down together;
    unable to rescue the burden,

  they themselves go off into captivity.

³"Listen to me, O house of Jacob,
    all you who remain of the house of Israel,
  you whom I have upheld since you were
    conceived,
    and have carried since your birth.
⁴Even to your old age and grey hairs
    I am he, I am he who will sustain you.
  I have made you and I will carry you;
    I will sustain you and I will rescue you.

46:4 ■ I CARRIED YOU
Is religion a burden? For idol worshippers,
certainly, in the most literal sense: their helpless
gods had to be carried around on carts (verse 1).
In contrast, God carries his people, and has done
so from the time of their conception and birth. He
won't stop; he will sustain and rescue them in
their old age.

⁵"To whom will you compare me or count me
    equal?
  To whom will you liken me that we may be
    compared?
⁶Some pour out gold from their bags
    and weigh out silver on the scales;
  they hire a goldsmith to make it into a god,
    and they bow down and worship it.
⁷They lift it to their shoulders and carry it;
    they set it up in its place, and there it stands.
    From that spot it cannot move.
  Though one cries out to it, it does not answer;
    it cannot save him from his troubles.

⁸"Remember this, fix it in mind,
    take it to heart, you rebels.
⁹Remember the former things, those of long ago;
    I am God, and there is no other;
    I am God, and there is none like me.
¹⁰I make known the end from the beginning,
    from ancient times, what is still to come.
  I say: My purpose will stand,
    and I will do all that I please.
¹¹From the east I summon a bird of prey;
    from a far-off land, a man to fulfil my
    purpose.
  What I have said, that will I bring about;
    what I have planned, that will I do.
¹²Listen to me, you stubborn-hearted,
    you who are far from righteousness.
¹³I am bringing my righteousness near,
    it is not far away;
    and my salvation will not be delayed.
  I will grant salvation to Zion,
    my splendour to Israel.

■ The Fall of Babylon
47 "Go down, sit in the dust,
    Virgin Daughter of Babylon;
  sit on the ground without a throne,
    Daughter of the Babylonians.ᵃ
  No more will you be called
    tender or delicate.

ᵃ1 Or are but beasts and cattle   ᵃ1 Or Chaldeans; also in verse 5

²Take millstones and grind flour;
    take off your veil.
Lift up your skirts, bare your legs,
    and wade through the streams.
³Your nakedness will be exposed
    and your shame uncovered.
I will take vengeance;
    I will spare no-one."

47:1 ■ AN EVIL QUEEN

Over the centuries, Babylon became a byword for evil among the Jews, for she was the nation that had destroyed Jerusalem and its temple. Psalm 137, composed by captive Jews in Babylon, expresses their anguish. But in this chapter God predicts that the great queen will become a prostitute, surprised by a sudden catastrophe. The same theme is echoed in the book of Revelation, which applies the symbolism of "Babylon the Great" to another evil empire (Revelation 18).

⁴Our Redeemer—the LORD Almighty is his
        name—
    is the Holy One of Israel.

⁵"Sit in silence, go into darkness,
    Daughter of the Babylonians;
no more will you be called
    queen of kingdoms.
⁶I was angry with my people
    and desecrated my inheritance;
I gave them into your hand,
    and you showed them no mercy.
Even on the aged
    you laid a very heavy yoke.
⁷You said, 'I will continue for ever—
    the eternal queen!'
But you did not consider these things
    or reflect on what might happen.

⁸"Now then, listen, you wanton creature,
    lounging in your security
and saying to yourself,
    'I am, and there is none besides me.
I will never be a widow
    or suffer the loss of children.'
⁹Both of these will overtake you
    in a moment, on a single day:
loss of children and widowhood.
They will come upon you in full measure,
    in spite of your many sorceries
    and all your potent spells.
¹⁰You have trusted in your wickedness
    and have said, 'No-one sees me.'
Your wisdom and knowledge mislead you
    when you say to yourself,
    'I am, and there is none besides me.'
¹¹Disaster will come upon you,
    and you will not know how to conjure it
        away.
A calamity will fall upon you
    that you cannot ward off with a ransom;
a catastrophe you cannot foresee
    will suddenly come upon you.

¹²"Keep on, then, with your magic spells
    and with your many sorceries,
    which you have laboured at since childhood.
Perhaps you will succeed,
    perhaps you will cause terror.
¹³All the counsel you have received has only
        worn you out!
Let your astrologers come forward,
    those stargazers who make predictions month
        by month,
    let them save you from what is coming upon
        you.
¹⁴Surely they are like stubble;
    the fire will burn them up.
They cannot even save themselves
    from the power of the flame.
Here are no coals to warm anyone;
    here is no fire to sit by.
¹⁵That is all they can do for you—
    these you have laboured with
    and trafficked with since childhood.
Each of them goes on in his error;
    there is not one that can save you.

■ Stubborn Israel

48 "Listen to this, O house of Jacob,
    you who are called by the name of Israel
    and come from the line of Judah,
you who take oaths in the name of the LORD
    and invoke the God of Israel—
    but not in truth or righteousness—
²you who call yourselves citizens of the holy
        city
    and rely on the God of Israel—
    the LORD Almighty is his name:
³I foretold the former things long ago,
    my mouth announced them and I made them
        known;
    then suddenly I acted, and they came to pass.
⁴For I knew how stubborn you were;
    the sinews of your neck were iron,
    your forehead was bronze.
⁵Therefore I told you these things long ago;
    before they happened I announced them to
        you
so that you could not say,
    'My idols did them;
    my wooden image and metal god ordained
        them.'
⁶You have heard these things; look at them all.
    Will you not admit them?

"From now on I will tell you of new things,
    of hidden things unknown to you.
⁷They are created now, and not long ago;
    you have not heard of them before today.
So you cannot say,
    'Yes, I knew of them.'
⁸You have neither heard nor understood;
    from of old your ear has not been open.
Well do I know how treacherous you are;
    you were called a rebel from birth.
⁹For my own name's sake I delay my wrath;
    for the sake of my praise I hold it back from
        you,

so as not to cut you off.
¹⁰See, I have refined you, though not as silver;
   I have tested you in the furnace of affliction.
¹¹For my own sake, for my own sake, I do this.
   How can I let myself be defamed?
   I will not yield my glory to another.

■ Israel Freed

¹²"Listen to me, O Jacob,
   Israel, whom I have called:
I am he;
   I am the first and I am the last.
¹³My own hand laid the foundations of the earth,
   and my right hand spread out the heavens;
when I summon them,
   they all stand up together.

¹⁴"Come together, all of you, and listen:
   Which of ˪the idols˩ has foretold these things?
The LORD's chosen ally
   will carry out his purpose against Babylon;
   his arm will be against the Babylonians.ᵃ
¹⁵I, even I, have spoken;
   yes, I have called him.
I will bring him,
   and he will succeed in his mission.

¹⁶"Come near me and listen to this:

"From the first announcement I have not
      spoken in secret;
   at the time it happens, I am there."

And now the Sovereign LORD has sent me,
   with his Spirit.

¹⁷This is what the LORD says—
   your Redeemer, the Holy One of Israel:
"I am the LORD your God,
   who teaches you what is best for you,
   who directs you in the way you should go.
¹⁸If only you had paid attention to my
      commands,
   your peace would have been like a river,
   your righteousness like the waves of the sea.
¹⁹Your descendants would have been like the
      sand,
   your children like its numberless grains;
their name would never be cut off
   nor destroyed from before me."

²⁰Leave Babylon,
   flee from the Babylonians!
Announce this with shouts of joy
   and proclaim it.
Send it out to the ends of the earth;
   say, "The LORD has redeemed his servant
      Jacob."
²¹They did not thirst when he led them through
      the deserts;
   he made water flow for them from the rock;
he split the rock
   and water gushed out.

²²"There is no peace," says the LORD, "for the
      wicked."

■ The Servant of the LORD

49 Listen to me, you islands;
      hear this, you distant nations:
Before I was born the LORD called me;
   from my birth he has made mention of my
      name.
²He made my mouth like a sharpened sword,
   in the shadow of his hand he hid me;
he made me into a polished arrow
   and concealed me in his quiver.
³He said to me, "You are my servant,
   Israel, in whom I will display my splendour."
⁴But I said, "I have laboured to no purpose;
   I have spent my strength in vain and for
      nothing.
Yet what is due to me is in the LORD's hand,
   and my reward is with my God."

⁵And now the LORD says—
   he who formed me in the womb to be his
      servant
to bring Jacob back to him
   and gather Israel to himself,
for I am honoured in the eyes of the LORD
   and my God has been my strength—
⁶he says:
"It is too small a thing for you to be my servant
   to restore the tribes of Jacob
   and bring back those of Israel I have kept.
I will also make you a light for the Gentiles,
   that you may bring my salvation to the ends
      of the earth."

49:6 ■ ISRAEL'S FINAL DESTINY
The book of Isaiah spells out Israel's ultimate
destiny: to be a light for the Gentiles and to bring
salvation to the ends of the earth. Isaiah is not
introducing a brand-new thought—God had made
clear his intentions in the original covenant
(Genesis 22:18). But, along the way, Israel and
Judah's desire for political greatness had
obscured their original calling.

---

⁷This is what the LORD says—
   the Redeemer and Holy One of Israel—
to him who was despised and abhorred by the
      nation,
   to the servant of rulers:
"Kings will see you and rise up,
   princes will see and bow down,
because of the LORD, who is faithful,
   the Holy One of Israel, who has chosen you."

■ Restoration of Israel

⁸This is what the LORD says:

"In the time of my favour I will answer you,
   and in the day of salvation I will help you;
I will keep you and will make you
   to be a covenant for the people,
to restore the land
   and to reassign its desolate inheritances,
⁹to say to the captives, 'Come out,'
   and to those in darkness, 'Be free!'

ᵃ 14 Or Chaldeans; also in verse 20

"They will feed beside the roads
and find pasture on every barren hill.
¹⁰They will neither hunger nor thirst,
nor will the desert heat or the sun beat upon
them.
He who has compassion on them will guide
them
and lead them beside springs of water.
¹¹I will turn all my mountains into roads,
and my highways will be raised up.
¹²See, they will come from afar—
some from the north, some from the west,
some from the region of Aswan."ᵃ

¹³Shout for joy, O heavens;
rejoice, O earth;
burst into song, O mountains!
For the LORD comforts his people
and will have compassion on his afflicted
ones.

¹⁴But Zion said, "The LORD has forsaken me,
the Lord has forgotten me."

¹⁵"Can a mother forget the baby at her breast
and have no compassion on the child she has
borne?
Though she may forget,
I will not forget you!
¹⁶See, I have engraved you on the palms of my
hands;
your walls are ever before me.
¹⁷Your sons hasten back,
and those who laid you waste depart from
you.
¹⁸Lift up your eyes and look around;
all your sons gather and come to you.
As surely as I live," declares the LORD,
"you will wear them all as ornaments;
you will put them on, like a bride.

¹⁹"Though you were ruined and made desolate
and your land laid waste,
now you will be too small for your people,
and those who devoured you will be far
away.
²⁰The children born during your bereavement
will yet say in your hearing,
'This place is too small for us;
give us more space to live in.'
²¹Then you will say in your heart,
'Who bore me these?
I was bereaved and barren;
I was exiled and rejected.
Who brought these up?
I was left all alone,
but these—where have they come from?' "

²²This is what the Sovereign LORD says:

"See, I will beckon to the Gentiles,
I will lift up my banner to the peoples;
they will bring your sons in their arms
and carry your daughters on their shoulders.
²³Kings will be your foster fathers,
and their queens your nursing mothers.

They will bow down before you with their
faces to the ground;
they will lick the dust at your feet.
Then you will know that I am the LORD;
those who hope in me will not be
disappointed."

²⁴Can plunder be taken from warriors,
or captives rescued from the fierce?ᵇ

²⁵But this is what the LORD says:

"Yes, captives will be taken from warriors,
and plunder retrieved from the fierce;
I will contend with those who contend with
you,
and your children I will save.
²⁶I will make your oppressors eat their own flesh;
they will be drunk on their own blood, as
with wine.
Then all mankind will know
that I, the LORD, am your Saviour,
your Redeemer, the Mighty One of Jacob."

■ Israel's Sin and the Servant's Obedience

50

This is what the LORD says:

"Where is your mother's certificate of divorce
with which I sent her away?
Or to which of my creditors
did I sell you?
Because of your sins you were sold;
because of your transgressions your mother
was sent away.
²When I came, why was there no-one?
When I called, why was there no-one to
answer?
Was my arm too short to ransom you?
Do I lack the strength to rescue you?
By a mere rebuke I dry up the sea,
I turn rivers into a desert;
their fish rot for lack of water
and die of thirst.
³I clothe the sky with darkness
and make sackcloth its covering."

⁴The Sovereign LORD has given me an instructed
tongue,
to know the word that sustains the weary.
He wakens me morning by morning,
wakens my ear to listen like one being
taught.
⁵The Sovereign LORD has opened my ears,
and I have not been rebellious;
I have not drawn back.
⁶I offered my back to those who beat me,
my cheeks to those who pulled out my
beard;
I did not hide my face
from mocking and spitting.
⁷Because the Sovereign LORD helps me,
I will not be disgraced.
Therefore have I set my face like flint,
and I know I will not be put to shame.
⁸He who vindicates me is near.
Who then will bring charges against me?
Let us face each other!

Who is my accuser?
Let him confront me!
⁹It is the Sovereign LORD who helps me.
Who is he who will condemn me?
They will all wear out like a garment;
the moths will eat them up.

¹⁰Who among you fears the LORD
and obeys the word of his servant?
Let him who walks in the dark,
who has no light,
trust in the name of the LORD
and rely on his God.
¹¹But now, all you who light fires
and provide yourselves with flaming torches,
go, walk in the light of your fires
and of the torches you have set ablaze.
This is what you shall receive from my hand:
You will lie down in torment.

■ Everlasting Salvation for Zion

51 "Listen to me, you who pursue righteousness
and who seek the LORD:
Look to the rock from which you were cut
and to the quarry from which you were hewn;
²look to Abraham, your father,
and to Sarah, who gave you birth.
When I called him he was but one,
and I blessed him and made him many.
³The LORD will surely comfort Zion
and will look with compassion on all her ruins;
he will make her deserts like Eden,
her wastelands like the garden of the LORD.
Joy and gladness will be found in her,
thanksgiving and the sound of singing.

⁴"Listen to me, my people;
hear me, my nation:
The law will go out from me;
my justice will become a light to the nations.
⁵My righteousness draws near speedily,
my salvation is on the way,
and my arm will bring justice to the nations.
The islands will look to me
and wait in hope for my arm.
⁶Lift up your eyes to the heavens,
look at the earth beneath;
the heavens will vanish like smoke,
the earth will wear out like a garment
and its inhabitants die like flies.
But my salvation will last for ever,
my righteousness will never fail.

⁷"Hear me, you who know what is right,
you people who have my law in your hearts:
Do not fear the reproach of men
or be terrified by their insults.
⁸For the moth will eat them up like a garment;
the worm will devour them like wool.
But my righteousness will last for ever,
my salvation through all generations."

⁹Awake, awake! Clothe yourself with strength,
O arm of the LORD;

awake, as in days gone by,
as in generations of old.
Was it not you who cut Rahab to pieces,
who pierced that monster through?

51:9 ■ RAHAB THE MONSTER
The Rahab in Isaiah (here and in 30:7) should not be confused with the Rahab who helped Joshua's spies in Jericho (Joshua 2). Rather, the word refers to a sea-monster that appears in much Middle Eastern mythology. Because the mythological monster lived in the Nile River region, *Rahab* can stand for the nation of Egypt, as it does here.

¹⁰Was it not you who dried up the sea,
the waters of the great deep,
who made a road in the depths of the sea
so that the redeemed might cross over?
¹¹The ransomed of the LORD will return.
They will enter Zion with singing;
everlasting joy will crown their heads.
Gladness and joy will overtake them,
and sorrow and sighing will flee away.

¹²"I, even I, am he who comforts you.
Who are you that you fear mortal men,
the sons of men, who are but grass,
¹³that you forget the LORD your Maker,
who stretched out the heavens
and laid the foundations of the earth,
that you live in constant terror every day
because of the wrath of the oppressor,
who is bent on destruction?
For where is the wrath of the oppressor?
¹⁴ The cowering prisoners will soon be set free;
they will not die in their dungeon,
nor will they lack bread.
¹⁵For I am the LORD your God,
who churns up the sea so that its waves roar—
the LORD Almighty is his name.
¹⁶I have put my words in your mouth
and covered you with the shadow of my hand—
I who set the heavens in place,
who laid the foundations of the earth,
and who say to Zion, 'You are my people.' "

■ The Cup of the LORD's Wrath
¹⁷Awake, awake!
Rise up, O Jerusalem,
you who have drunk from the hand of the LORD
the cup of his wrath,
you who have drained to its dregs
the goblet that makes men stagger.
¹⁸Of all the sons she bore
there was none to guide her;
of all the sons she brought up
there was none to take her by the hand.
¹⁹These double calamities have come upon you—

who can comfort you?—
ruin and destruction, famine and sword—

who can*a* console you?
²⁰Your sons have fainted;
  they lie at the head of every street,
  like antelope caught in a net.
They are filled with the wrath of the LORD
  and the rebuke of your God.

²¹Therefore hear this, you afflicted one,
  made drunk, but not with wine.
²²This is what your Sovereign LORD says,
  your God, who defends his people:
"See, I have taken out of your hand
  the cup that made you stagger;
from that cup, the goblet of my wrath,
  you will never drink again.
²³I will put it into the hands of your tormentors,
  who said to you,
'Fall prostrate that we may walk over you.'
And you made your back like the ground,
  like a street to be walked over."

52 Awake, awake, O Zion,
  clothe yourself with strength.
Put on your garments of splendour,
  O Jerusalem, the holy city.
The uncircumcised and defiled
  will not enter you again.
²Shake off your dust;
  rise up, sit enthroned, O Jerusalem.
Free yourself from the chains on your neck,
  O captive Daughter of Zion.

³For this is what the LORD says:

"You were sold for nothing,
  and without money you will be redeemed."

⁴For this is what the Sovereign LORD says:

"At first my people went down to Egypt to live;
  lately, Assyria has oppressed them.

⁵"And now what do I have here?" declares the
LORD.

"For my people have been taken away for
    nothing,
  and those who rule them mock,"*a*
                     declares the LORD.
"And all day long
  my name is constantly blasphemed.
⁶Therefore my people will know my name;
  therefore in that day they will know
that it is I who foretold it.
  Yes, it is I."

⁷How beautiful on the mountains
  are the feet of those who bring good news,
who proclaim peace,
  who bring good tidings,
  who proclaim salvation,
who say to Zion,
  "Your God reigns!"
⁸Listen! Your watchmen lift up their voices;
  together they shout for joy.
When the LORD returns to Zion,
  they will see it with their own eyes.
⁹Burst into songs of joy together,
  you ruins of Jerusalem,

for the LORD has comforted his people,
  he has redeemed Jerusalem.

52:7 ■ BEAUTIFUL FEET
Isaiah portrays the joy of carrying good news to
those desperately hoping for it – perhaps a city
waiting for news of a battle in which all their
young men were at risk. But Isaiah's news is not
of war; it is of God's people returning from exile,
with the Lord himself leading the way. In Romans
10:15, Paul applied this joyful cheer to the
messengers who, like himself, bore the good news
of Jesus Christ.

---

¹⁰The LORD will lay bare his holy arm
  in the sight of all the nations,
and all the ends of the earth will see
  the salvation of our God.

¹¹Depart, depart, go out from there!
  Touch no unclean thing!
Come out from it and be pure,
  you who carry the vessels of the LORD.
¹²But you will not leave in haste
  or go in flight;
for the LORD will go before you,
  the God of Israel will be your rear guard.

■ The Suffering and Glory of the Servant
¹³See, my servant will act wisely;*b*
  he will be raised and lifted up and highly
    exalted.
¹⁴Just as there were many who were appalled at
    him*c* –
  his appearance was so disfigured beyond that
    of any man
  and his form marred beyond human
    likeness –
¹⁵so will he sprinkle many nations,*d*
  and kings will shut their mouths because of
    him.
For what they were not told, they will see,
  and what they have not heard, they will
    understand.

53 Who has believed our message
  and to whom has the arm of the LORD
    been revealed?
²He grew up before him like a tender shoot,
  and like a root out of dry ground.
He had no beauty or majesty to attract us to
    him,
  nothing in his appearance that we should
    desire him.
³He was despised and rejected by men,
  a man of sorrows, and familiar with suffering.
Like one from whom men hide their faces
  he was despised, and we esteemed him not.

⁴Surely he took up our infirmities
  and carried our sorrows,
yet we considered him stricken by God,
  smitten by him, and afflicted.
⁵But he was pierced for our transgressions,
  he was crushed for our iniquities;

---

a 19 Dead Sea Scrolls, Septuagint, Vulgate and Syriac; Masoretic Text / *how can I
prosper*   *c 14* Hebrew *you*   *d 15* Hebrew; Septuagint *so will many nations marvel at him*   *a 5* Dead Sea Scrolls and Vulgate; Masoretic Text *wail*   *b 13* Or *will*

the punishment that brought us peace was
      upon him,
  and by his wounds we are healed.
⁶We all, like sheep, have gone astray,
   each of us has turned to his own way;
 and the LORD has laid on him
   the iniquity of us all.

⁷He was oppressed and afflicted,
   yet he did not open his mouth;
 he was led like a lamb to the slaughter,
   and as a sheep before her shearers is silent,
   so he did not open his mouth.

⁸By oppression*a* and judgment he was taken
   away.

53:5 ■ HEALING WOUNDS
Throughout the New Testament, the Suffering
Servant described here is understood to be Jesus.
This astounding verse claims that his wounds heal
us. Peter explained it this way: when Jesus died
on the cross, his suffering and death "healed" us
of our sins, enabling us to live for righteousness
(1 Peter 2:24).

■ THE SUFFERING SERVANT
A GREAT VICTORY LOOKED AT FIRST LIKE DEFEAT

INSIGHT

HE WAS DESPISED AND REJECTED BY
MEN, A MAN OF SORROWS, AND
FAMILIAR WITH SUFFERING. ■ 53:3

Chapters 49–55 of Isaiah tell of a "suffering
servant" who will come from Israel to bring light
to all nations. Who is this suffering servant?
    Jewish scholars puzzled over these
passages for centuries. Many considered them
the most significant part of the entire Old
Testament, and yet they could not agree on
exactly what the prophet meant. (Four passages
especially are called the "servant songs":
42:1–9; 49:1–13; 50:4–9; 52:13–53:12).

■ A NATION OR A PERSON?
Sometimes the verses speak about the nation of
Israel as a whole: "You are my servant, Israel, in
whom I will display my splendour" (49:3). But in
other places the servant seems to refer to a
specific individual, a great leader who suffers
terribly.
    Isaiah presents the servant as the
deliverer of all humankind. And yet it portrays
him more as a tragic figure than as a hero:
"He had no beauty or majesty to attract us to
him. . . . He was oppressed and afflicted, yet he
did not open his mouth; he was led like a lamb
to the slaughter" (53:2,7).
    Some Jewish scholars guessed the
prophet was describing himself or another
prophet, such as Jeremiah. Still others focused
their hopes on a Messiah to come. They
expected a king from very humble origins,
whose power would depend not on swords, but
on the spirits of people committed to him.

■ AN ANSWER FROM THE NEW TESTAMENT
The idea of the suffering servant did not really
catch on among the Jewish nation. They longed
for a victorious Messiah, not a suffering one.
The image of the suffering servant went

underground, as it were, lying dormant for
centuries.
    Then, in a very dramatic scene early in
his ministry, Jesus quoted from one of the
servant passages in Isaiah (Luke 4:18–19).
"Then he rolled up the scroll, gave it back to
the attendant and sat down. The eyes of
everyone in the synagogue were fastened on
him, and he began by saying to them, 'Today
this scripture is fulfilled in your hearing' " (Luke
4:20–21).
    Following his example, the New
Testament writers named Jesus as the servant,
at least ten times. In one instance, Philip
corrected an Ethiopian official who had
wondered if the suffering servant referred to an
ancient prophet (Acts 8:26–35).

■ THE FINAL SACRIFICE
Isaiah 49–55 includes vivid scenes of the
servant's sufferings, predictions that found
their fulfilment in Jesus' death on the cross.
Written like an eyewitness account, they were
actually composed centuries before Christ's
death.
    According to Isaiah, the servant died
for a very specific purpose: "He was pierced
for our transgressions" (53:5). Through his
wounds, the suffering servant won a great
victory. His death made possible a future when
all that is wrong on earth will be set right.
Significantly, the book of Isaiah does not end
with the suffering servant image. It goes on to
describe a wonderful life in a new heaven and
new earth made possible by the servant's
death.

□ LIFE QUESTIONS:
If you had been a Jew in Jesus' day, would
you have been disappointed in the Messiah?
Why did Jesus choose to come as a suffering
servant rather than, say, a triumphant army
general?

---

a 8 Or From arrest

And who can speak of his descendants?
For he was cut off from the land of the living;
    for the transgression of my people he was
        stricken.*b*
⁹He was assigned a grave with the wicked,
    and with the rich in his death,
though he had done no violence,
    nor was any deceit in his mouth.

¹⁰Yet it was the LORD's will to crush him and
        cause him to suffer,
    and though the LORD makes*c* his life a guilt
        offering,
he will see his offspring and prolong his days,
    and the will of the LORD will prosper in his
        hand.
¹¹After the suffering of his soul,
    he will see the light ⌊of life⌋*d* and be
        satisfied;*e*
by his knowledge*f* my righteous servant will
        justify many,
    and he will bear their iniquities.
¹²Therefore I will give him a portion among the
        great,*g*
    and he will divide the spoils with the
        strong,*b*
because he poured out his life unto death,
    and was numbered with the transgressors.
For he bore the sin of many,
    and made intercession for the transgressors.

■ The Future Glory of Zion

54

"Sing, O barren woman,
    you who never bore a child;
burst into song, shout for joy,
    you who were never in labour;
because more are the children of the desolate
        woman
    than of her who has a husband,"
                                        says the LORD.
²"Enlarge the place of your tent,
    stretch your tent curtains wide,
        do not hold back;
lengthen your cords,
    strengthen your stakes.
³For you will spread out to the right and to the
        left;
    your descendants will dispossess nations
    and settle in their desolate cities.

⁴"Do not be afraid; you will not suffer shame.
    Do not fear disgrace; you will not be
        humiliated.
You will forget the shame of your youth
    and remember no more the reproach of your
        widowhood.
⁵For your Maker is your husband —
    the LORD Almighty is his name —
the Holy One of Israel is your Redeemer;
    he is called the God of all the earth.
⁶The LORD will call you back
    as if you were a wife deserted and distressed
        in spirit —
a wife who married young,

only to be rejected," says your God.
⁷"For a brief moment I abandoned you,
    but with deep compassion I will bring you
        back.
⁸In a surge of anger
    I hid my face from you for a moment,
but with everlasting kindness
    I will have compassion on you,"
        says the LORD your Redeemer.

54:6 ■ JERUSALEM'S FUTURE
The book of Isaiah insists that God will not
permanently divorce the nation of Israel. It
foretells a time when the ruined capital city will
be rebuilt and achieve a greatness it has never
known. Yet the description in these chapters
goes far beyond what has ever been realised in
Jerusalem. It merges into a vision of the future,
when sin and sorrow will be no more and people
will live in final peace with God.

⁹"To me this is like the days of Noah,
    when I swore that the waters of Noah would
        never again cover the earth.
So now I have sworn not to be angry with you,
    never to rebuke you again.
¹⁰Though the mountains be shaken
    and the hills be removed,
yet my unfailing love for you will not be
        shaken
    nor my covenant of peace be removed,"
    says the LORD, who has compassion on you.

¹¹"O afflicted city, lashed by storms and not
        comforted,
    I will build you with stones of turquoise,*a*
    your foundations with sapphires.*b*
¹²I will make your battlements of rubies,
    your gates of sparkling jewels,
    and all your walls of precious stones.
¹³All your sons will be taught by the LORD,
    and great will be your children's peace.
¹⁴In righteousness you will be established:
Tyranny will be far from you;
    you will have nothing to fear.
Terror will be far removed;
    it will not come near you.
¹⁵If anyone does attack you, it will not be my
        doing;
    whoever attacks you will surrender to you.

¹⁶"See, it is I who created the blacksmith
    who fans the coals into flame
    and forges a weapon fit for its work.
And it is I who have created the destroyer to
        work havoc;
¹⁷   no weapon forged against you will prevail,
    and you will refute every tongue that accuses
        you.
This is the heritage of the servants of the LORD,
    and this is their vindication from me,"
                                        declares the LORD.

---

b 8 Or away. / Yet who of his generation considered / that he was cut off from the land of the living / for the transgression of my people, / to whom the blow was due?   *c* 10 Hebrew *though you make*   *d* 11 Dead Sea Scrolls (see also Septuagint); Masoretic Text does not have *the light ⌊of life⌋*.   *e* 11 Or (with Masoretic Text) 11*He will see the result of the suffering of his soul / and be satisfied*   *f* 11 Or *by knowledge of him*   *g* 12 Or *many*   *b* 12 Or *numerous*   *a* 11 The meaning of the Hebrew for this word is uncertain.   *b* 11 Or *lapis lazuli*

■ Invitation to the Thirsty

55 "Come, all you who are thirsty,
come to the waters;
and you who have no money,
come, buy and eat!
Come, buy wine and milk
without money and without cost.
²Why spend money on what is not bread,
and your labour on what does not satisfy?
Listen, listen to me, and eat what is good,
and your soul will delight in the richest of
fare.
³Give ear and come to me;
hear me, that your soul may live.
I will make an everlasting covenant with you,
my faithful love promised to David.
⁴See, I have made him a witness to the peoples,
a leader and commander of the peoples.
⁵Surely you will summon nations you know not,
and nations that do not know you will hasten
to you,
because of the LORD your God,
the Holy One of Israel,
for he has endowed you with splendour."

55:1 ■ WHO CAN BE SAVED?
God, through Isaiah, issues an open invitation to
"all . . . who are thirsty". Anyone can eat and drink
this meal, free of charge. The only requirement is
that they come. In verse 6 Isaiah urges everyone
to take this opportunity for forgiveness while it is
so freely available.

⁶Seek the LORD while he may be found;
call on him while he is near.
⁷Let the wicked forsake his way
and the evil man his thoughts.
Let him turn to the LORD, and he will have
mercy on him,
and to our God, for he will freely pardon.

⁸"For my thoughts are not your thoughts,
neither are your ways my ways,"
declares the LORD.
⁹"As the heavens are higher than the earth,
so are my ways higher than your ways
and my thoughts than your thoughts.
¹⁰As the rain and the snow
come down from heaven,
and do not return to it
without watering the earth
and making it bud and flourish,
so that it yields seed for the sower and bread
for the eater,
¹¹so is my word that goes out from my mouth:
It will not return to me empty,
but will accomplish what I desire
and achieve the purpose for which I sent it.
¹²You will go out in joy
and be led forth in peace;
the mountains and hills
will burst into song before you,
and all the trees of the field
will clap their hands.

¹³Instead of the thornbush will grow the pine
tree,
and instead of briers the myrtle will grow.
This will be for the LORD's renown,
for an everlasting sign,
which will not be destroyed."

■ Salvation for Others

56 This is what the LORD says:

"Maintain justice
and do what is right,
for my salvation is close at hand
and my righteousness will soon be revealed.
²Blessed is the man who does this,
the man who holds it fast,
who keeps the Sabbath without desecrating it,
and keeps his hand from doing any evil."

³Let no foreigner who has bound himself to the
LORD say,
"The LORD will surely exclude me from his
people."
And let not any eunuch complain,
"I am only a dry tree."

⁴For this is what the LORD says:

"To the eunuchs who keep my Sabbaths,
who choose what pleases me
and hold fast to my covenant—
⁵to them I will give within my temple and its
walls
a memorial and a name
better than sons and daughters;
I will give them an everlasting name
that will not be cut off.
⁶And foreigners who bind themselves to the
LORD
to serve him,
to love the name of the LORD,
and to worship him,
all who keep the Sabbath without desecrating it
and who hold fast to my covenant—
⁷these I will bring to my holy mountain
and give them joy in my house of prayer.
Their burnt offerings and sacrifices
will be accepted on my altar;
for my house will be called
a house of prayer for all nations."
⁸The Sovereign LORD declares—
he who gathers the exiles of Israel:
"I will gather still others to them
besides those already gathered."

■ God's Accusation Against the Wicked
⁹Come, all you beasts of the field,
come and devour, all you beasts of the
forest!
¹⁰Israel's watchmen are blind,
they all lack knowledge;
they are all mute dogs,
they cannot bark;
they lie around and dream,
they love to sleep.
¹¹They are dogs with mighty appetites;

they never have enough.
They are shepherds who lack understanding;
they all turn to their own way,
each seeks his own gain.

56:7 ■ HOUSE OF PRAYER

Traditionally, foreigners and eunuchs were excluded from worshipping God (see Exodus 12:43; Deuteronomy 23:1,3,7–8). But now God promises to welcome all those once excluded. The New Testament church welcomed foreigners and eunuchs into God's family; in contrast, the temple in Jerusalem never made non-Jews welcome. Jesus complained that rather than creating a "house of prayer for all nations", merchants had turned it into a "den of robbers" (Mark 11:17).

56:10 ■ DOG-LIKE PROPHETS

This passage gives one of the most scathing denunciations of Israel's corrupt spiritual leaders in the entire Bible.

12"Come," each one cries, "let me get wine!
Let us drink our fill of beer!
And tomorrow will be like today,
or even far better."

57 The righteous perish,
and no-one ponders it in his heart;
devout men are taken away,
and no-one understands
that the righteous are taken away
to be spared from evil.
2Those who walk uprightly
enter into peace;
they find rest as they lie in death.

3"But you—come here, you sons of a sorceress,
you offspring of adulterers and prostitutes!
4Whom are you mocking?
At whom do you sneer
and stick out your tongue?
Are you not a brood of rebels,
the offspring of liars?
5You burn with lust among the oaks
and under every spreading tree;
you sacrifice your children in the ravines
and under the overhanging crags.
6⌊The idols⌋ among the smooth stones of the ravines are your portion;
they, they are your lot.
Yes, to them you have poured out drink offerings
and offered grain offerings.
In the light of these things, should I relent?
7You have made your bed on a high and lofty hill;
there you went up to offer your sacrifices.
8Behind your doors and your doorposts
you have put your pagan symbols.
Forsaking me, you uncovered your bed,
you climbed into it and opened it wide;

you made a pact with those whose beds you love,
and you looked on their nakedness.
9You went to Molech*a* with olive oil
and increased your perfumes.
You sent your ambassadors*b* far away;
you descended to the grave*c* itself!
10You were wearied by all your ways,
but you would not say, 'It is hopeless.'
You found renewal of your strength,
and so you did not faint.

11"Whom have you so dreaded and feared
that you have been false to me,
and have neither remembered me
nor pondered this in your hearts?
Is it not because I have long been silent
that you do not fear me?
12I will expose your righteousness and your works,
and they will not benefit you.
13When you cry out for help,
let your collection ⌊of idols⌋ save you!
The wind will carry all of them off,
a mere breath will blow them away.
But the man who makes me his refuge
will inherit the land
and possess my holy mountain."

■ Comfort for the Contrite
14And it will be said:

"Build up, build up, prepare the road!
Remove the obstacles out of the way of my people."
15For this is what the high and lofty One says—
he who lives for ever, whose name is holy:
"I live in a high and holy place,
but also with him who is contrite and lowly in spirit,
to revive the spirit of the lowly
and to revive the heart of the contrite.
16I will not accuse for ever,
nor will I always be angry,
for then the spirit of man would grow faint before me—
the breath of man that I have created.
17I was enraged by his sinful greed;
I punished him, and hid my face in anger,
yet he kept on in his wilful ways.
18I have seen his ways, but I will heal him;
I will guide him and restore comfort to him,
19   creating praise on the lips of the mourners in Israel.
Peace, peace, to those far and near,"
says the LORD. "And I will heal them."
20But the wicked are like the tossing sea,
which cannot rest,
whose waves cast up mire and mud.
21"There is no peace," says my God, "for the wicked."

■ True Fasting
58 "Shout it aloud, do not hold back.
Raise your voice like a trumpet.
Declare to my people their rebellion

a9 Or to the king   b9 Or idols   c9 Hebrew Sheol

and to the house of Jacob their sins.
²For day after day they seek me out;
    they seem eager to know my ways,
as if they were a nation that does what is right
    and has not forsaken the commands of its
        God.
They ask me for just decisions
    and seem eager for God to come near them.
³'Why have we fasted,' they say,
    'and you have not seen it?
Why have we humbled ourselves,
    and you have not noticed?'

"Yet on the day of your fasting, you do as you
        please
    and exploit all your workers.
⁴Your fasting ends in quarrelling and strife,
    and in striking each other with wicked fists.
You cannot fast as you do today
    and expect your voice to be heard on high.
⁵Is this the kind of fast I have chosen,
    only a day for a man to humble himself?
Is it only for bowing one's head like a reed
    and for lying on sackcloth and ashes?
Is that what you call a fast,
    a day acceptable to the LORD?

⁶"Is not this the kind of fasting I have chosen:
to loose the chains of injustice
    and untie the cords of the yoke,
to set the oppressed free
    and break every yoke?
⁷Is it not to share your food with the hungry
    and to provide the poor wanderer with
        shelter —
when you see the naked, to clothe him,
    and not to turn away from your own flesh
        and blood?
⁸Then your light will break forth like the dawn,
    and your healing will quickly appear;
then your righteousness*a* will go before you,
    and the glory of the LORD will be your rear
        guard.
⁹Then you will call, and the LORD will answer;
    you will cry for help, and he will say: Here
        am I.

"If you do away with the yoke of oppression,
    with the pointing finger and malicious talk,
¹⁰and if you spend yourselves on behalf of the
        hungry
    and satisfy the needs of the oppressed,
then your light will rise in the darkness,
    and your night will become like the
        noonday.

58:6 ■ RELIGION AT ITS BEST
The book of Isaiah begins in chapter 1 by
exposing false religion that had the right form and
ritual, but no true sincerity. This chapter gives the
other side: the spiritual work God prefers. The
book of James includes a similar perspective
(1:27).

---

¹¹The LORD will guide you always;

a 8 Or your righteous One

he will satisfy your needs in a sun-scorched
        land
    and will strengthen your frame.
You will be like a well-watered garden,
    like a spring whose waters never fail.
¹²Your people will rebuild the ancient ruins
    and will raise up the age-old foundations;
you will be called Repairer of Broken Walls,
    Restorer of Streets with Dwellings.

¹³"If you keep your feet from breaking the
        Sabbath
    and from doing as you please on my holy
        day,
if you call the Sabbath a delight
    and the LORD's holy day honourable,
and if you honour it by not going your own
        way
    and not doing as you please or speaking idle
        words,
¹⁴then you will find your joy in the LORD,
    and I will cause you to ride on the heights of
        the land
    and to feast on the inheritance of your father
        Jacob."
        The mouth of the LORD has spoken.

■ Sin, Confession and Redemption
59 Surely the arm of the LORD is not too short
        to save,
    nor his ear too dull to hear.
²But your iniquities have separated
    you from your God;
your sins have hidden his face from you,
    so that he will not hear.
³For your hands are stained with blood,
    your fingers with guilt.
Your lips have spoken lies,
    and your tongue mutters wicked things.
⁴No-one calls for justice;
    no-one pleads his case with integrity.
They rely on empty arguments and speak lies;
    they conceive trouble and give birth to evil.
⁵They hatch the eggs of vipers
    and spin a spider's web.
Whoever eats their eggs will die,
    and when one is broken, an adder is hatched.
⁶Their cobwebs are useless for clothing;
    they cannot cover themselves with what they
        make.
Their deeds are evil deeds,
    and acts of violence are in their hands.
⁷Their feet rush into sin;
    they are swift to shed innocent blood.
Their thoughts are evil thoughts;
    ruin and destruction mark their ways.
⁸The way of peace they do not know;
    there is no justice in their paths.
They have turned them into crooked roads;
    no-one who walks in them will know peace.

⁹So justice is far from us,
    and righteousness does not reach us.
We look for light, but all is darkness;
    for brightness, but we walk in deep shadows.
¹⁰Like the blind we grope along the wall,

feeling our way like men without eyes.
At midday we stumble as if it were twilight;
    among the strong, we are like the dead.
11We all growl like bears;
    we moan mournfully like doves.
We look for justice, but find none;
    for deliverance, but it is far away.

12For our offences are many in your sight,
    and our sins testify against us.
Our offences are ever with us,
    and we acknowledge our iniquities:
13rebellion and treachery against the LORD,
    turning our backs on our God,
fomenting oppression and revolt,
    uttering lies our hearts have conceived.
14So justice is driven back,
    and righteousness stands at a distance;
truth has stumbled in the streets,
    honesty cannot enter.
15Truth is nowhere to be found,
    and whoever shuns evil becomes a prey.

The LORD looked and was displeased
    that there was no justice.
16He saw that there was no-one,
    he was appalled that there was no-one to
        intervene;
so his own arm worked salvation for him,
    and his own righteousness sustained him.
17He put on righteousness as his breastplate,
    and the helmet of salvation on his head;
he put on the garments of vengeance
    and wrapped himself in zeal as in a cloak.
18According to what they have done,
    so will he repay
wrath to his enemies
    and retribution to his foes;
he will repay the islands their due.
19From the west, men will fear the name of the
        LORD,
    and from the rising of the sun, they will
        revere his glory.
For he will come like a pent-up flood
    that the breath of the LORD drives along.ᵃ

20"The Redeemer will come to Zion,
    to those in Jacob who repent of their sins,"
                        declares the LORD.

21"As for me, this is my covenant with them," says
the LORD. "My Spirit, who is on you, and my words
that I have put in your mouth will not depart from
your mouth, or from the mouths of your children,
or from the mouths of their descendants from this
time on and for ever," says the LORD.

■ The Glory of Zion

60 "Arise, shine, for your light has come,
    and the glory of the LORD rises upon you.
2See, darkness covers the earth
    and thick darkness is over the peoples,
but the LORD rises upon you
    and his glory appears over you.
3Nations will come to your light,
    and kings to the brightness of your dawn.

4"Lift up your eyes and look about you:
    All assemble and come to you;
your sons come from afar,
    and your daughters are carried on the arm.
5Then you will look and be radiant,
    your heart will throb and swell with joy;
the wealth on the seas will be brought to you,
    to you the riches of the nations will come.
6Herds of camels will cover your land,
    young camels of Midian and Ephah.
And all from Sheba will come,
    bearing gold and incense
    and proclaiming the praise of the LORD.
7All Kedar's flocks will be gathered to you,
    the rams of Nebaioth will serve you;
they will be accepted as offerings on my altar,
    and I will adorn my glorious temple.

8"Who are these that fly along like clouds,
    like doves to their nests?
9Surely the islands look to me;
    in the lead are the ships of Tarshish,ᵃ
bringing your sons from afar,
    with their silver and gold,
to the honour of the LORD your God,
    the Holy One of Israel,
    for he has endowed you with splendour.

10"Foreigners will rebuild your walls,
    and their kings will serve you.
Though in anger I struck you,
    in favour I will show you compassion.
11Your gates will always stand open,
    they will never be shut, day or night,
so that men may bring you the wealth of the
        nations—
    their kings led in triumphal procession.
12For the nation or kingdom that will not serve
        you will perish;
    it will be utterly ruined.

13"The glory of Lebanon will come to you,
    the pine, the fir and the cypress together,
to adorn the place of my sanctuary;
    and I will glorify the place of my feet.
14The sons of your oppressors will come bowing
        before you;
    all who despise you will bow down at your
        feet
and will call you the City of the LORD,
    Zion of the Holy One of Israel.

15"Although you have been forsaken and hated,
    with no-one travelling through,
I will make you the everlasting pride
    and the joy of all generations.
16You will drink the milk of nations
    and be nursed at royal breasts.
Then you will know that I, the LORD, am your
        Saviour,
    your Redeemer, the Mighty One of Jacob.
17Instead of bronze I will bring you gold,
    and silver in place of iron.
Instead of wood I will bring you bronze,
    and iron in place of stones.
I will make peace your governor

ᵃ19 Or When the enemy comes in like a flood, / the Spirit of the LORD will put him to flight   ᵃ9 Or the trading ships

and righteousness your ruler.
¹⁸No longer will violence be heard in your land,
    nor ruin or destruction within your borders,
but you will call your walls Salvation
    and your gates Praise.
¹⁹The sun will no more be your light by day,
    nor will the brightness of the moon shine on
        you,
for the LORD will be your everlasting light,
    and your God will be your glory.
²⁰Your sun will never set again,
    and your moon will wane no more;
the LORD will be your everlasting light,
    and your days of sorrow will end.
²¹Then will all your people be righteous
    and they will possess the land for ever.
They are the shoot I have planted,
    the work of my hands,
    for the display of my splendour.
²²The least of you will become a thousand,
    the smallest a mighty nation.
I am the LORD;
    in its time I will do this swiftly.'

■ The Year of the LORD's Favour

61 The Spirit of the Sovereign LORD is on me,
    because the LORD has anointed me
to preach good news to the poor.
He has sent me to bind up the broken-hearted,
    to proclaim freedom for the captives
    and release from darkness for the
        prisoners,*ᵃ*
²to proclaim the year of the LORD's favour
    and the day of vengeance of our God,
to comfort all who mourn,
³   and provide for those who grieve in Zion—
to bestow on them a crown of beauty
        instead of ashes,
the oil of gladness
        instead of mourning,
and a garment of praise
        instead of a spirit of despair.
They will be called oaks of righteousness,
    a planting of the LORD
    for the display of his splendour.

61:1 ■ JESUS BEGAN HERE
When Jesus was ready to announce himself and
his mission, he began with a dramatic quotation of
this passage (Luke 4:18–19). Notably, he stopped
in mid-sentence, before he reached the phrase
"the day of vengeance of our God". Jesus taught
that this day of vengeance would indeed take
place, but at the time of his second coming, not
his first.

⁴They will rebuild the ancient ruins
    and restore the places long devastated;
they will renew the ruined cities
    that have been devastated for generations.
⁵Aliens will shepherd your flocks;
    foreigners will work your fields and
        vineyards.

⁶And you will be called priests of the LORD,
    you will be named ministers of our God.
You will feed on the wealth of nations,
    and in their riches you will boast.

⁷Instead of their shame
    my people will receive a double portion,
and instead of disgrace
    they will rejoice in their inheritance;
and so they will inherit a double portion in
        their land,
    and everlasting joy will be theirs.

⁸"For I, the LORD, love justice;
    I hate robbery and iniquity.
In my faithfulness I will reward them
    and make an everlasting covenant with them.
⁹Their descendants will be known among the
        nations
    and their offspring among the peoples.
All who see them will acknowledge
    that they are a people the LORD has blessed."

¹⁰I delight greatly in the LORD;
    my soul rejoices in my God.
For he has clothed me with garments of
        salvation
    and arrayed me in a robe of righteousness,
as a bridegroom adorns his head like a priest,
    and as a bride adorns herself with her jewels.
¹¹For as the soil makes the young plant come up
    and a garden causes seeds to grow,
so the Sovereign LORD will make righteousness
        and praise
    spring up before all nations.

■ Zion's New Name

62 For Zion's sake I will not keep silent,
    for Jerusalem's sake I will not remain
        quiet,
till her righteousness shines out like the dawn,
    her salvation like a blazing torch.
²The nations will see your righteousness,
    and all kings your glory;
you will be called by a new name
    that the mouth of the LORD will bestow.
³You will be a crown of splendour in the LORD's
        hand,
    a royal diadem in the hand of your God.
⁴No longer will they call you Deserted,
    or name your land Desolate.
But you will be called Hephzibah,*ᵃ*
    and your land Beulah;*ᵇ*
for the LORD will take delight in you,
    and your land will be married.
⁵As a young man marries a maiden,
    so will your sons*ᶜ* marry you;
as a bridegroom rejoices over his bride,
    so will your God rejoice over you.

⁶I have posted watchmen on your walls,
    O Jerusalem;
they will never be silent day or night.
You who call on the LORD,
    give yourselves no rest,
⁷and give him no rest till he establishes
        Jerusalem

---

*ᵃ*1 Hebrew; Septuagint *the blind*   *ᵃ*4 Hephzibah means *my delight is in her.*   *ᵇ*4 Beulah means *married.*   *ᶜ*5 Or *Builder* and makes her the praise of the earth.

⁸The LORD has sworn by his right hand
    and by his mighty arm:
"Never again will I give your grain
    as food for your enemies,
and never again will foreigners drink the new
        wine
    for which you have toiled;
⁹but those who harvest it will eat it
    and praise the LORD,
and those who gather the grapes will drink it
    in the courts of my sanctuary."

¹⁰Pass through, pass through the gates!
    Prepare the way for the people.
Build up, build up the highway!
    Remove the stones.
Raise a banner for the nations.

¹¹The LORD has made proclamation
    to the ends of the earth:
"Say to the Daughter of Zion,
    'See, your Saviour comes!
See, his reward is with him,
    and his recompense accompanies him.' "
¹²They will be called the Holy People,
    the Redeemed of the LORD;
and you will be called Sought After,
    the City No Longer Deserted.

■ God's Day of Vengeance and Redemption

63 Who is this coming from Edom,
    from Bozrah, with his garments stained
    crimson?
Who is this, robed in splendour,
    striding forward in the greatness of his
        strength?

"It is I, speaking in righteousness,
    mighty to save."

²Why are your garments red,
    like those of one treading the winepress?

³"I have trodden the winepress alone;
    from the nations no-one was with me.
I trampled them in my anger
    and trod them down in my wrath;
their blood spattered my garments,
    and I stained all my clothing.
⁴For the day of vengeance was in my heart,
    and the year of my redemption has come.
⁵I looked, but there was no-one to help,
    I was appalled that no-one gave support;
so my own arm worked salvation for me,
    and my own wrath sustained me.
⁶I trampled the nations in my anger;
    in my wrath I made them drunk
    and poured their blood on the ground."

■ Praise and Prayer

⁷I will tell of the kindnesses of the LORD,
    the deeds for which he is to be praised,
    according to all the LORD has done for us—
yes, the many good things he has done
    for the house of Israel,

according to his compassion and many
        kindnesses.
⁸He said, "Surely they are my people,
    sons who will not be false to me";
    and so he became their Saviour.
⁹In all their distress he too was distressed,
    and the angel of his presence saved them.
In his love and mercy he redeemed them;
    he lifted them up and carried them
    all the days of old.
¹⁰Yet they rebelled
    and grieved his Holy Spirit.
So he turned and became their enemy
    and he himself fought against them.

63:9 ■ A LESSON FROM HISTORY
The Babylonian captivity brought a grave crisis to
the Israelites. To them, God's own integrity was at
stake. They had a treaty, or covenant, with him.
Had he abandoned them? In this chapter, the
prophet reviews all the good things God has done
for the Israelites and says that, even in the worst
times, "in all their distress he too was distressed."
If God had been with them in the past, then he
would be with them in the future. Then he turns to
God directly and makes an impassioned appeal
for help: "Oh, that you would rend the heavens
and come down" (64:1).

---

¹¹Then his people recalled*ᵃ* the days of old,
    the days of Moses and his people—
where is he who brought them through the sea,
    with the shepherd of his flock?
Where is he who set
    his Holy Spirit among them,
¹²who sent his glorious arm of power
    to be at Moses' right hand,
who divided the waters before them,
    to gain for himself everlasting renown,
¹³who led them through the depths?
Like a horse in open country,
    they did not stumble;
¹⁴like cattle that go down to the plain,
    they were given rest by the Spirit of the
        LORD.
This is how you guided your people
    to make for yourself a glorious name.

¹⁵Look down from heaven and see
    from your lofty throne, holy and glorious.
Where are your zeal and your might?
    Your tenderness and compassion are
        withheld from us.
¹⁶But you are our Father,
    though Abraham does not know us
    or Israel acknowledge us;
you, O LORD, are our Father,
    our Redeemer from of old is your name.
¹⁷Why, O LORD, do you make us wander from
        your ways
    and harden our hearts so we do not revere
        you?
Return for the sake of your servants,
    the tribes that are your inheritance.

ᵃ 11 Or But may he recall

¹⁸For a little while your people possessed your
        holy place,
   but now our enemies have trampled down
        your sanctuary.
¹⁹We are yours from of old;
   but you have not ruled over them,
   they have not been called by your name.*b*

64 Oh, that you would rend the heavens and
    come down,
   that the mountains would tremble before
        you!
²As when fire sets twigs ablaze
    and causes water to boil,
come down to make your name known to your
        enemies
   and cause the nations to quake before you!
³For when you did awesome things that we did
        not expect,
   you came down, and the mountains trembled
        before you.
⁴Since ancient times no-one has heard,
   no ear has perceived,
no eye has seen any God besides you,
   who acts on behalf of those who wait for
        him.

⁵You come to the help of those who gladly do
        right,
   who remember your ways.
But when we continued to sin against them,
   you were angry.
   How then can we be saved?
⁶All of us have become like one who is unclean,
   and all our righteous acts are like filthy rags;
we all shrivel up like a leaf,
   and like the wind our sins sweep us away.
⁷No-one calls on your name
   or strives to lay hold of you;
for you have hidden your face from us
   and made us waste away because of our sins.

⁸Yet, O LORD, you are our Father.
   We are the clay, you are the potter;
   we are all the work of your hand.
⁹Do not be angry beyond measure, O LORD;
   do not remember our sins for ever.
   Oh, look upon us we pray,
   for we are all your people.
¹⁰Your sacred cities have become a desert;
   even Zion is a desert, Jerusalem a desolation.
¹¹Our holy and glorious temple, where our
        fathers praised you,
   has been burned with fire,

■ A GLIMPSE OF THINGS TO COME   INSIGHT
WHEN ALL OUR BEST DREAMS WILL COME TRUE

"BEHOLD, I WILL CREATE NEW HEAVENS
AND A NEW EARTH. THE FORMER
THINGS WILL NOT BE REMEMBERED,
NOR WILL THEY COME TO MIND." ■ 65:17

Everybody wants a glimpse into the future, and
the last part of Isaiah gives just that. It tells what
will happen at the end of our age on earth. The
account is not easy to decipher, however,
because the prophet shifts back and forth
between his own time and the final events on
earth.

■ A MISSIONARY BOOK
To the original audience of Israelites, Isaiah
makes one thing clear: God would not
permanently divorce Israel. "For a brief moment I
abandoned you," says God, "but with deep
compassion I will bring you back" (54:7). There
is a future for his chosen people.
   Isaiah declares that Israel's future
involves other nations. Foreigners will flock to
Jerusalem: "My house will be called a house of
prayer for all nations" (56:7). Word about God
will go out to nations nearby and far away, and
to distant islands that have never heard of him
(66:18–21).
   Thus the last part of Isaiah, addressed
to a people facing deep despair, opens the door
for the Jews to become a gift to all people. This

prophecy saw fulfilment in Jesus, who
recruited disciples to take his message to
everyone. Through his life and death, the
suffering servant indeed introduced the gospel
to the entire world.

■ WHAT ISAIAH SAYS TO US
The book of Isaiah goes on to describe a new
beginning, a time of final triumph and peace. In
that day, there will be no need for tears. Wild
animals will tamely lie down together. The sun
and moon will fade, overwhelmed by the
brightness of God's glory.
   In chapters 60 and 65, the prophet
describes the future with such eloquence that
New Testament books like Revelation could not
improve on the language; they merely quoted
Isaiah. Even today some of these
phrases – "beat their swords into
ploughshares", for example – surface in
popular language, expressing our deepest
longings for peace.
   We dream of a time of peace, without
pain or fear or disease or death. Isaiah assures
us that one day those dreams will come true.

□ LIFE QUESTIONS:
What would you most like to see changed
about your world? Does Isaiah speak to that
change?

---

b 19 Or We are like those you have never ruled, / like those never called by your name

and all that we treasured lies in ruins.
¹²After all this, O LORD, will you hold yourself
   back?
   Will you keep silent and punish us beyond
   measure?

■ Judgment and Salvation

65 "I revealed myself to those who did not
   ask for me;
   I was found by those who did not seek me.
To a nation that did not call on my name,
   I said, 'Here am I, here am I.'
²All day long I have held out my hands
   to an obstinate people,
who walk in ways not good,
   pursuing their own imaginations—
³a people who continually provoke me
   to my very face,
offering sacrifices in gardens
   and burning incense on altars of brick;

65:3 ■ PROVOKING GOD

In this speech, God is directly attacking the most
repulsive practices of Judah, notably its idolatry.
"Gardens" refers to the gardens that usually
surrounded pagan shrines. Verse 4 mentions the
superstitious practice of sitting in cemeteries to
seek help from the dead. And the "flesh of pigs"
was eaten in a sacrificial meal for a pagan god—
faithful Jews did not eat pork.

⁴who sit among the graves
   and spend their nights keeping secret vigil;
who eat the flesh of pigs,
   and whose pots hold broth of unclean meat;
⁵who say, 'Keep away; don't come near me,
   for I am too sacred for you!'
Such people are smoke in my nostrils,
   a fire that keeps burning all day.

⁶"See, it stands written before me;
   I will not keep silent but will pay back in
      full;
   I will pay it back into their laps—
⁷both your sins and the sins of your fathers,"
   says the LORD.
"Because they burned sacrifices on the
      mountains
   and defied me on the hills,
I will measure into their laps
   the full payment for their former deeds."

⁸This is what the LORD says:

"As when juice is still found in a cluster of
      grapes
   and men say, 'Don't destroy it,
      there is yet some good in it,'
so will I do on behalf of my servants;
   I will not destroy them all.
⁹I will bring forth descendants from Jacob,
   and from Judah those who will possess my
      mountains;
my chosen people will inherit them,
   and there will my servants live.

¹⁰Sharon will become a pasture for flocks,
   and the Valley of Achor a resting place for
      herds,
   for my people who seek me.

¹¹"But as for you who forsake the LORD
   and forget my holy mountain,
who spread a table for Fortune
   and fill bowls of mixed wine for Destiny,
¹²I will destine you for the sword,
   and you will all bend down for the slaughter;
for I called but you did not answer,
   I spoke but you did not listen.
You did evil in my sight
   and chose what displeases me."

¹³Therefore this is what the Sovereign LORD says:

"My servants will eat,
   but you will go hungry;
my servants will drink,
   but you will go thirsty;
my servants will rejoice,
   but you will be put to shame.
¹⁴My servants will sing
   out of the joy of their hearts,
but you will cry out
   from anguish of heart
   and wail in brokenness of spirit.
¹⁵You will leave your name
   to my chosen ones as a curse;
the Sovereign LORD will put you to death,
   but to his servants he will give another
      name.
¹⁶Whoever invokes a blessing in the land
   will do so by the God of truth;
he who takes an oath in the land
   will swear by the God of truth.
For the past troubles will be forgotten
   and hidden from my eyes.

■ New Heavens and a New Earth

¹⁷"Behold, I will create
   new heavens and a new earth.
The former things will not be remembered,
   nor will they come to mind.
¹⁸But be glad and rejoice for ever
   in what I will create,
for I will create Jerusalem to be a delight
   and its people a joy.
¹⁹I will rejoice over Jerusalem
   and take delight in my people;
the sound of weeping and of crying
   will be heard in it no more.

²⁰"Never again will there be in it
   an infant who lives but a few days,
   or an old man who does not live out his
      years;
he who dies at a hundred
   will be thought a mere youth;
he who fails to reachᵃ a hundred
   will be considered accursed.
²¹They will build houses and dwell in them;
   they will plant vineyards and eat their fruit.
²²No longer will they build houses and others
      live in them,

ᵃ 20 Or / the sinner who reaches

or plant and others eat.
For as the days of a tree,
    so will be the days of my people;
my chosen ones will long enjoy
    the works of their hands.

65:17 ■ NEW EARTH

Human beings have always longed for a Utopia.
Isaiah repeatedly promises just that, here and in
chapters 11 and 35. He has in mind a whole new
earth, in which people will build and farm, work
and raise children – but without frustration. The
violence and sadness that mark our earth will
vanish. The key to that new era will be an intimate
relationship with God. "Before they call I will
answer; while they are still speaking I will hear"
(verse 24).

23They will not toil in vain
    or bear children doomed to misfortune;
for they will be a people blessed by the LORD,
    they and their descendants with them.
24Before they call I will answer;
    while they are still speaking I will hear.
25The wolf and the lamb will feed together,
    and the lion will eat straw like the ox,
    but dust will be the serpent's food.
They will neither harm nor destroy
    on all my holy mountain,"
                says the LORD.

■ Judgment and Hope

66 This is what the LORD says:

"Heaven is my throne,
    and the earth is my footstool.
Where is the house you will build for me?
    Where will my resting place be?
2Has not my hand made all these things,
    and so they came into being?"
            declares the LORD.

"This is the one I esteem:
    he who is humble and contrite in spirit,
    and trembles at my word.
3But whoever sacrifices a bull
    is like one who kills a man,
and whoever offers a lamb,
    like one who breaks a dog's neck;
whoever makes a grain offering
    is like one who presents pig's blood,
and whoever burns memorial incense,
    like one who worships an idol.
They have chosen their own ways,
    and their souls delight in their abominations;
4so I also will choose harsh treatment for them
    and will bring upon them what they dread.
For when I called, no-one answered,
    when I spoke, no-one listened.
They did evil in my sight
    and chose what displeases me."

5Hear the word of the LORD,
    you who tremble at his word;

"Your brothers who hate you,
    and exclude you because of my name, have
      said,
'Let the LORD be glorified,
    that we may see your joy!'
    Yet they will be put to shame.
6Hear that uproar from the city,
    hear that noise from the temple!
It is the sound of the LORD
    repaying his enemies all they deserve.

7"Before she goes into labour,
    she gives birth;
before the pains come upon her,
    she delivers a son.
8Who has ever heard of such a thing?
    Who has ever seen such things?
Can a country be born in a day
    or a nation be brought forth in a moment?
Yet no sooner is Zion in labour
    than she gives birth to her children.
9Do I bring to the moment of birth
    and not give delivery?" says the LORD.
"Do I close up the womb
    when I bring to delivery?" says your God.
10"Rejoice with Jerusalem and be glad for her,
    all you who love her;
rejoice greatly with her,
    all you who mourn over her.
11For you will nurse and be satisfied
    at her comforting breasts;
you will drink deeply
    and delight in her overflowing abundance."

12For this is what the LORD says:

"I will extend peace to her like a river,
    and the wealth of nations like a flooding
      stream;
you will nurse and be carried on her arm
    and dandled on her knees.
13As a mother comforts her child,
    so will I comfort you;
    and you will be comforted over Jerusalem."

66:9 ■ PAIN WITH A PURPOSE

Nowhere does the book of Isaiah minimise the
pain Israel went through; the prophet shared the
nation's agony. But God makes clear that the pain
was not arbitrary and purposeless. Like childbirth,
this pain will lead to something happy and good.
"As a mother comforts her child, so will I comfort
you" (verse 13). In one last word of triumph, God
reaffirms that the suffering of the Israelites will one
day lead to a great missionary outreach among all
humanity (verses 19,23).

14When you see this, your heart will rejoice
    and you will flourish like grass;
the hand of the LORD will be made known to
      his servants,
    but his fury will be shown to his foes.
15See, the LORD is coming with fire,
    and his chariots are like a whirlwind;
he will bring down his anger with fury,

and his rebuke with flames of fire.
[16]For with fire and with his sword
    the LORD will execute judgment upon all
        men,
    and many will be those slain by the LORD.

[17]"Those who consecrate and purify themselves
to go into the gardens, following the one in the
midst of[a] those who eat the flesh of pigs and rats
and other abominable things—they will meet their
end together," declares the LORD.

[18]"And I, because of their actions and their imaginations, am about to come[b] and gather all nations and tongues, and they will come and see my
glory.

[19]"I will set a sign among them, and I will send
some of those who survive to the nations—to Tarshish, to the Libyans[c] and Lydians (famous as
archers), to Tubal and Greece, and to the distant
islands that have not heard of my fame or seen my
glory. They will proclaim my glory among the nations. [20]And they will bring all your brothers, from
all the nations, to my holy mountain in Jerusalem as
an offering to the LORD—on horses, in chariots and
wagons, and on mules and camels," says the LORD.
"They will bring them, as the Israelites bring their
grain offerings, to the temple of the LORD in ceremonially clean vessels. [21]And I will select some of them
also to be priests and Levites," says the LORD.

[22]"As the new heavens and the new earth that I
make will endure before me," declares the LORD, "so
will your name and descendants endure. [23]From
one New Moon to another and from one Sabbath to
another, all mankind will come and bow down before me," says the LORD. [24]"And they will go out and
look upon the dead bodies of those who rebelled
against me; their worm will not die, nor will their
fire be quenched, and they will be loathsome to all
mankind."

---

[a]17 Or gardens behind one of your temples, and   [b]18 The meaning of the Hebrew for this clause is uncertain.   [c]19 Some Septuagint manuscripts Put
(Libyans); Hebrew Pul

JEREMIAH

■ GOD'S RELUCTANT MESSENGER

JEREMIAH FELT FRIGHTENED AND INSECURE – BUT HE BURNED WITH A MESSAGE

"DO NOT BE AFRAID OF THEM, FOR I AM WITH YOU AND WILL RESCUE YOU," DECLARES THE LORD. ■ 1:8

Jeremiah lived one of the most dramatic lives in the Bible, and that is saying something. But he never learned to like his role. Through all the excitement he remained reluctant, insecure, and often unhappy.

God chose him to be "over nations and kingdoms to uproot and tear down, to destroy and overthrow, to build and to plant" (1:10). To accomplish that, Jeremiah had only one resource – his mouth. How did he respond to such an awesome challenge? "Ah, Sovereign LORD," he said, "I do not know how to speak; I am only a child" (1:6). He didn't stride forward; he barely hung on. He wanted out of the job.

His only encouragement was God's promise: "Today I have made you a fortified city, an iron pillar and a bronze wall to stand against the whole land" (1:18). For 40 years Jeremiah gave top officials a warning they hated to hear and refused to heed. Several times they arrested and imprisoned him; they nearly killed him.

His message? With God's approval, the savage Babylonians would sweep down into Judah. Clever alliances with other powers like Egypt would not help, said Jeremiah. Neither would Judah's half-hearted religion. Judah's only hope lay in renewing an alliance with the living God.

■ A DISTURBING GLIMPSE OF JEREMIAH'S MIND
The book of Jeremiah stands out not for beautiful poetry or great ideas. Its power comes from its disturbing glimpse of Jeremiah's mind. Jeremiah talked like a man who has awakened from a nightmare, convinced that the nightmare is coming true. His words were sledgehammer blows

designed to crack the hardest, most indifferent skull. Though he wished to keep quiet, he found that God's "word is in my heart like a fire, a fire shut up in my bones" (20:9).

No prophet exposed his feelings more than Jeremiah. His relationship with God was streaked with quarrels, reproaches, and outbursts. He told God he wished he were dead (20:14 – 18). He accused God of being unreliable (15:18). But God offered no sympathy. Rather, he promised more of the same, reminding Jeremiah of his promise to stand by him (12:5–6; 15:19–20). Their relationship, doubts and all, forms one of the best examples in the Bible of what it means to follow God in spite of everything.

■ REASON TO FEAR
Jeremiah frankly feared death. He wearied of ridicule. He hated standing alone against the crowd. He told God how he felt. Yet he obeyed God, and in the end his message proved true. He stands as a far greater man than the kings in their luxurious palaces who imprisoned him and burned his writings.

He spoke a gloomy message in a gloomy time, and as a result his words are not always pleasant to read. He reminds us, in an era of artificial cheer and television smiles, that God's message is not always comforting and encouraging. People who disregard God will have reason to fear. For a world that defies him, he plans judgment. And no-one, not even his chosen messengers, will escape suffering. God's presence will make them strong enough to face it.

■ HOW TO READ JEREMIAH

Suppose you find, in an old trunk, a thick bundle of letters written by your great uncle. You soon realise that they are all out of order. One he wrote from the trenches of France during World War I.

The next also refers to a war, but from the references to the British Prime Minister Winston Churchill you soon recognise it as World War II, over 20 years later.

Those letters might contain the whole of your uncle's life, but to get his story straight, you'd have to read the whole bundle. A reader of Jeremiah finds a very similar situation. The book is an anthology of prophecies given at different times. They jump forwards and backwards in history, and if you imagine that the book is in chronological order, you will become very confused. Fortunately, it is not hard to reconstruct the order of the main events of Jeremiah's life.

Jeremiah spoke to a nation about to be destroyed by war. Three hundred years before him, the Israelites had split into two countries, Israel in the North and Judah in the South. About 100 years before Jeremiah, Assyria had conquered the Northern Kingdom. This disaster was "World War I" in Old Testament history.

Now, during Jeremiah's life, World War II threatened. Another fierce kingdom, Babylon, assembled troops against the remaining Southern Kingdom. Would God save his chosen people? Jeremiah loudly insisted for more than 20 years that God would punish Judah just as he had Israel, by letting Babylon take them into captivity. He lived to see his predictions come true.

Many passages in Jeremiah refer to the five kings he knew. When you see their names, use them as a reference point in figuring out the order of events:

Josiah (17 years)
Jehoahaz (3 months)
Jehoiakim (12 years)
Jehoiachin (3 months)
Zedekiah (11 years)

Second Kings 23–25 or 2 Chronicles 34–36 gives an overall historical summary of their reigns. You can read a brief synopsis in "A Line-up of Rulers", pages 260–268. The better you grasp the historical situation Jeremiah lived in, the more insight you will have into his words.

To capture the full emotion of Jeremiah, you may want to read the first few chapters out loud.

■ 3-TRACK READING PLAN

For an explanation and complete listing of the 3-track reading plan, turn to page x.

■ TRACK 1:
Two-Week Courses on the Bible
See page x for information on these courses.

■ TRACK 2:
An Overview of Jeremiah in 4 Days
☐ Day 1. Read the Introduction to Jeremiah and chapter 2, for God's passionate indictment of his people.
☐ Day 2. Read chapter 15, part of an emotional dialogue between Jeremiah and God.
☐ Day 3. Read chapter 31, God's promise of restoration and a new covenant.
☐ Day 4. Read chapter 38, for Jeremiah's dramatic skirmishes with death in the last days of Jerusalem.
Now turn to page xi for your next Track 2 reading project.

■ TRACK 3:
All of Jeremiah in 51 Days
After you have read through Jeremiah, turn to pages xii–xiii

for your next Track 3 reading project.

1 The words of Jeremiah son of Hilkiah, one of the priests at Anathoth in the territory of Benjamin. ²The word of the LORD came to him in the thirteenth year of the reign of Josiah son of Amon king of Judah, ³and through the reign of Jehoiakim son of Josiah king of Judah, down to the fifth month of the eleventh year of Zedekiah son of Josiah king of Judah, when the people of Jerusalem went into exile.

■ The Call of Jeremiah
⁴The word of the LORD came to me, saying,

⁵"Before I formed you in the womb I knew*a* you,
before you were born I set you apart;
I appointed you as a prophet to the nations."

⁶"Ah, Sovereign LORD," I said, "I do not know how to speak; I am only a child."

⁷But the LORD said to me, "Do not say, 'I am only a child.' You must go to everyone I send you to and say whatever I command you. ⁸Do not be afraid of them, for I am with you and will rescue you," declares the LORD.

⁹Then the LORD reached out his hand and touched my mouth and said to me, "Now, I have put my words in your mouth. ¹⁰See, today I appoint you over nations and kingdoms to uproot and tear down, to destroy and overthrow, to build and to plant."

¹¹The word of the LORD came to me: "What do you see, Jeremiah?"

"I see the branch of an almond tree," I replied.

¹²The LORD said to me, "You have seen correctly, for I am watching*b* to see that my word is fulfilled."

¹³The word of the LORD came to me again: "What do you see?"

a 5 Or *chose*   *b 12* The Hebrew for *watching* sounds like the Hebrew for *almond tree*.

"I see a boiling pot, tilting away from the north," I answered.

[14]The LORD said to me, "From the north disaster will be poured out on all who live in the land. [15]I am about to summon all the peoples of the northern kingdoms," declares the LORD.

"Their kings will come and set up their thrones
    in the entrance of the gates of Jerusalem;
they will come against all her surrounding walls
    and against all the towns of Judah.
[16]I will pronounce my judgments on my people
    because of their wickedness in forsaking me,
in burning incense to other gods
    and in worshipping what their hands have
        made.

[17]"Get yourself ready! Stand up and say to them whatever I command you. Do not be terrified by them, or I will terrify you before them. [18]Today I have made you a fortified city, an iron pillar and a bronze wall to stand against the whole land — against the kings of Judah, its officials, its priests and the people of the land. [19]They will fight against you but will not overcome you, for I am with you and will rescue you," declares the LORD.

1:18 ■ TOO YOUNG?

Like Moses before him, Jeremiah responded reluctantly to God's call. "I am only a child", he protested, feeling too inexperienced to carry such responsibility (verse 6). But God contradicted him. Age and experience did not matter; God's presence did (verse 8). In the face of powerful opposition, God would make Jeremiah as strong as iron.

■ Israel Forsakes God

2 The word of the LORD came to me: [2]"Go and proclaim in the hearing of Jerusalem:

" 'I remember the devotion of your youth,
    how as a bride you loved me
and followed me through the desert,
    through a land not sown.
[3]Israel was holy to the LORD,
    the firstfruits of his harvest;
all who devoured her were held guilty,
    and disaster overtook them,' "
                        declares the LORD.

[4]Hear the word of the LORD, O house of Jacob,
    all you clans of the house of Israel.

[5]This is what the LORD says:

"What fault did your fathers find in me,
    that they strayed so far from me?
They followed worthless idols
    and became worthless themselves.
[6]They did not ask, 'Where is the LORD,
    who brought us up out of Egypt
and led us through the barren wilderness,
    through a land of deserts and rifts,
a land of drought and darkness,[a]

a land where no-one travels and no-one
    lives?'
[7]I brought you into a fertile land
    to eat its fruit and rich produce.
But you came and defiled my land
    and made my inheritance detestable.
[8]The priests did not ask,
    'Where is the LORD?'
Those who deal with the law did not know me;
    the leaders rebelled against me.
The prophets prophesied by Baal,
    following worthless idols.

[9]"Therefore I bring charges against you again,"
                        declares the LORD.
    "And I will bring charges against your
        children's children.
[10]Cross over to the coasts of Kittim[b] and look,
    send to Kedar[c] and observe closely;
    see if there has ever been anything like this:
[11]Has a nation ever changed its gods?
    (Yet they are not gods at all.)
But my people have exchanged their[d] Glory
    for worthless idols.
[12]Be appalled at this, O heavens,
    and shudder with great horror,"
                        declares the LORD.
[13]"My people have committed two sins:
They have forsaken me,
    the spring of living water,
and have dug their own cisterns,
    broken cisterns that cannot hold water.

2:13 ■ AN ASTOUNDING TRADE

Jeremiah piles image on top of image, searching for a way to express the astounding fact that Israelites had traded the living God for the idols of their neighbours. Here he compares the deed to exchanging a spring of living water for a leaky cistern. In verse 20 he graphically compares idolatry to sexual promiscuity. In an interesting twist, Jesus offered "living water" to a sexually promiscuous Samaritan woman in John 4:10.

[14]Is Israel a servant, a slave by birth?
    Why then has he become plunder?
[15]Lions have roared;
    they have growled at him.
They have laid waste his land;
    his towns are burned and deserted.
[16]Also, the men of Memphis[e] and Tahpanhes
    have shaved the crown of your head.[f]
[17]Have you not brought this on yourselves
    by forsaking the LORD your God
    when he led you in the way?
[18]Now why go to Egypt
    to drink water from the Shihor?[g]
And why go to Assyria
    to drink water from the River?[h]
[19]Your wickedness will punish you;
    your backsliding will rebuke you.
Consider then and realise
    how evil and bitter it is for you

a 6 Or and the shadow of death   b 10 That is, Cyprus and western coastlands   c 10 The home of Bedouin tribes in the Syro-Arabian desert
d 11 Masoretic Text; an ancient Hebrew scribal tradition my   e 16 Hebrew Noph   f 16 Or have cracked your skull   g 18 That is, a branch of the Nile
b 18 That is, the Euphrates

when you forsake the LORD your God
  and have no awe of me,"
                    declares the Lord,
                          the LORD Almighty.

20"Long ago you broke off your yoke
  and tore off your bonds;
  you said, 'I will not serve you!'
Indeed, on every high hill
  and under every spreading tree
  you lay down as a prostitute.
21I had planted you like a choice vine
  of sound and reliable stock.
How then did you turn against me
  into a corrupt, wild vine?
22Although you wash yourself with soda
  and use an abundance of soap,
  the stain of your guilt is still before me,"
            declares the Sovereign LORD.
23"How can you say, 'I am not defiled;
  I have not run after the Baals'?
See how you behaved in the valley;
  consider what you have done.
You are a swift she-camel
  running here and there,
24a wild donkey accustomed to the desert,
  sniffing the wind in her craving—
  in her heat who can restrain her?
Any males that pursue her need not tire
      themselves;
  at mating time they will find her.
25Do not run until your feet are bare
  and your throat is dry.
But you said, 'It's no use!
  I love foreign gods,
  and I must go after them.'

26"As a thief is disgraced when he is caught,
  so the house of Israel is disgraced—
they, their kings and their officials,
  their priests and their prophets.
27They say to wood, 'You are my father,'
  and to stone, 'You gave me birth.'
They have turned their backs to me
  and not their faces;
yet when they are in trouble, they say,
  'Come and save us!'
28Where then are the gods you made for
      yourselves?
  Let them come if they can save you
  when you are in trouble!
For you have as many gods
  as you have towns, O Judah.

29"Why do you bring charges against me?
  You have all rebelled against me,"
                    declares the LORD.
30"In vain I punished your people;
  they did not respond to correction.
Your sword has devoured your prophets
  like a ravening lion.

31"You of this generation, consider the word of
the LORD:

"Have I been a desert to Israel
  or a land of great darkness?

Why do my people say, 'We are free to roam;
  we will come to you no more'?
32Does a maiden forget her jewellery,
  a bride her wedding ornaments?
Yet my people have forgotten me,
  days without number.
33How skilled you are at pursuing love!
  Even the worst of women can learn from
      your ways.
34On your clothes men find
  the lifeblood of the innocent poor,
  though you did not catch them breaking in.
Yet in spite of all this
35 you say, 'I am innocent;
  he is not angry with me.'
But I will pass judgment on you
  because you say, 'I have not sinned.'
36Why do you go about so much,
  changing your ways?
You will be disappointed by Egypt
  as you were by Assyria.
37You will also leave that place
  with your hands on your head,
for the LORD has rejected those you trust;
  you will not be helped by them.

3 "If a man divorces his wife
    and she leaves him and marries another
    man,
should he return to her again?
  Would not the land be completely defiled?
But you have lived as a prostitute with many
      lovers—
  would you now return to me?"
                          declares the LORD.
2"Look up to the barren heights and see.
  Is there any place where you have not been
      ravished?
By the roadside you sat waiting for lovers,
  sat like a nomad*a* in the desert.
You have defiled the land
  with your prostitution and wickedness.
3Therefore the showers have been withheld,
  and no spring rains have fallen.
Yet you have the brazen look of a prostitute;
  you refuse to blush with shame.
4Have you not just called to me:

3:2 ■ RITUAL SEX

Today, the news that a minister or priest has
committed adultery sends shock waves through
the community. But Israel's neighbours in ancient
times actually incorporated adultery into their
religious rites. Pagans worshipped their gods
through cultic prostitution, believing sex would put
them in tune with divine power. This ritual sex
went on at religious shrines located on the "high
places" (hilltops). When Israel joined in their
neighbours' worship, God quite rightly called it
adultery—both physical and spiritual. Israel was
going out with every god in town.

---

a2 Or an Arab

'My Father, my friend from my youth,
⁵will you always be angry?
    Will your wrath continue for ever?'
This is how you talk,
    but you do all the evil you can."

■ Unfaithful Israel

⁶During the reign of King Josiah, the LORD said to me, "Have you seen what faithless Israel has done? She has gone up on every high hill and under every spreading tree and has committed adultery there. ⁷I thought that after she had done all this she would return to me but she did not, and her unfaithful sister Judah saw it. ⁸I gave faithless Israel her certificate of divorce and sent her away because of all her adulteries. Yet I saw that her unfaithful sister Judah had no fear; she also went out and committed adultery. ⁹Because Israel's immorality mattered so little

to her, she defiled the land and committed adultery with stone and wood. ¹⁰In spite of all this, her unfaithful sister Judah did not return to me with all her heart, but only in pretence," declares the LORD.

¹¹The LORD said to me, "Faithless Israel is more righteous than unfaithful Judah. ¹²Go, proclaim this message towards the north:

" 'Return, faithless Israel,' declares the LORD,
    'I will frown on you no longer,
for I am merciful,' declares the LORD,
    'I will not be angry for ever.
¹³Only acknowledge your guilt—
    you have rebelled against the LORD your God,
you have scattered your favours to foreign gods
    under every spreading tree,
    and have not obeyed me,' "

                                    declares the LORD.

■ A LOVER'S QUARREL
THE VIOLENT EMOTIONS OF A SCORNED LOVER

INSIGHT

"YOU HAVE LIVED AS A PROSTITUTE WITH MANY LOVERS—WOULD YOU NOW RETURN TO ME?" DECLARES THE LORD.
■ 3:1

The call comes late, after midnight, to a policeman who grimaces and shakes his head. Then, siren screaming, he races towards the house. Neighbours heard a woman's cries. Someone saw a man threatening her with a knife. As the policeman pulls up to the house, he hears her high-pitched shrieks. She is begging for mercy—from her husband.

Such cases are called "domestic disturbances". They happen nearly every night, and particularly at weekends. The police usually dislike getting called in. Both husband and wife can turn on the person who is "interfering".

Lovers' quarrels may seem silly to outsiders, but they are deadly serious to those involved. Some turn violent, even murderous. The most precious, desired gift anyone can offer has been abused. Love has been betrayed. Lovers react to that with violent emotions.

■ WORDS THAT TEAR HIS HEART
It is a lovers' quarrel that Jeremiah exposes in chapters 2 and 3 and the emotions are violent and helpless. Again and again God makes his charge against Judah. Of all the nations, he had picked her; he had tenderly offered his protection and care. But she keeps sleeping with other men. He warns her again and again, but she ignores him. She saw how he divorced her sister Israel. Doesn't she know he will do the same to her?

God's words bleed pain. He accuses as though he cannot help himself, although his words tear his own heart. First, he is tender,

full of memories: "I remember . . . how as a bride you loved me and followed me through the desert" (2:2). But then you "tore off your bonds; you said, 'I will not serve you!' Indeed, on every high hill and under every spreading tree you lay down as a prostitute" (2:20). In disgust God compares Judah to a donkey in heat, "sniffing the wind in her craving. . . . Any males that pursue her need not tire themselves" (2:24). But the comparison hurts him more than her. His love, not hers, is scorned.

■ MARRIED TO A WHORE
The prophet Hosea was the first to draw the picture of God married to a prostitute. Jeremiah amplifies it. The comparison cries out both the passionate love God feels for his people and the terrible, wounded pain he feels at their betrayal. Jeremiah's imagery is violent and dark, but underneath it, something wonderful shines out: the tender and personal love of God for his people.

The "adultery" Jeremiah wrote about focuses on the worship of idols. Most modern people find it hard to understand why Israelites felt any impulse to kneel before wooden or metal statues, or why their doing so made God furious. But when Jeremiah refers to it as adultery, God's hatred of idolatry becomes understandable. God meant his people to have only one true love in their lives—God himself. God the lover will not take second place; he refuses to share his bride.

☐ LIFE QUESTIONS:
Have you ever fought with God? What issues were you fighting about?

14"Return, faithless people," declares the LORD,
"for I am your husband. I will choose you—one
from a town and two from a clan—and bring you to
Zion. 15Then I will give you shepherds after my own
heart, who will lead you with knowledge and understanding. 16In those days, when your numbers have
increased greatly in the land," declares the LORD,
"men will no longer say, 'The ark of the covenant of
the LORD.' It will never enter their minds or be remembered; it will not be missed, nor will another
one be made. 17At that time they will call Jerusalem
The Throne of the LORD, and all nations will gather
in Jerusalem to honour the name of the LORD. No
longer will they follow the stubbornness of their
evil hearts. 18In those days the house of Judah will
join the house of Israel, and together they will come
from a northern land to the land I gave your forefathers as an inheritance.

3:10 ■ A SUPERFICIAL CHANGE
King Josiah, one of the few good kings in Judah's
history, led a massive religious reform (see 2 Kings
22 and 23). While Josiah was unquestionably
sincere, Jeremiah saw that the nation's return to
God wasn't. Jeremiah's accusation was borne out
after King Josiah's death: Judah returned quickly
to her former ways.

19"I myself said,

" 'How gladly would I treat you like sons
    and give you a desirable land,
    the most beautiful inheritance of any nation.'
I thought you would call me 'Father'
    and not turn away from following me.
20But like a woman unfaithful to her husband,
    so you have been unfaithful to me, O house
        of Israel,"
                                        declares the LORD.

21A cry is heard on the barren heights,
    the weeping and pleading of the people of
        Israel,
because they have perverted their ways
    and have forgotten the LORD their God.

22"Return, faithless people;
    I will cure you of backsliding."

"Yes, we will come to you,
    for you are the LORD our God.
23Surely the ⌐idolatrous⌐ commotion on the hills
    and mountains is a deception;
surely in the LORD our God
    is the salvation of Israel.
24From our youth shameful gods have consumed
    the fruits of our fathers' labour—
their flocks and herds,
    their sons and daughters.
25Let us lie down in our shame,
    and let our disgrace cover us.
We have sinned against the LORD our God,
    both we and our fathers;
from our youth till this day
    we have not obeyed the LORD our God."

4 "If you will return, O Israel,
    return to me,"
                                        declares the LORD.
"If you put your detestable idols out of my
        sight
    and no longer go astray,
2and if in a truthful, just and righteous way
    you swear, 'As surely as the LORD lives,'
then the nations will be blessed by him
    and in him they will glory."

3This is what the LORD says to the men of Judah
and to Jerusalem:

"Break up your unploughed ground
    and do not sow among thorns.
4Circumcise yourselves to the LORD,
    circumcise your hearts,
    you men of Judah and people of Jerusalem,
or my wrath will break out and burn like fire
    because of the evil you have done—
    burn with no-one to quench it.

4:4 ■ CIRCUMCISED HEARTS
All male Jewish babies underwent circumcision, a
sign of their "set-apartness" as God's chosen
people. Often, though, circumcision became just a
ritual, not reflecting any real difference in the way
people lived. Jeremiah used a startling
metaphor—"circumcise your hearts"—to remind
the Israelites that membership in God's family
should make a difference inside, not just on the
surface. The apostle Paul wrote that Christ brings
about this inner circumcision (Colossians 2:11).

■ Disaster From the North
5"Announce in Judah and proclaim in Jerusalem
        and say:
    'Sound the trumpet throughout the land!'
Cry aloud and say:
    'Gather together!
    Let us flee to the fortified cities!'
6Raise the signal to go to Zion!
    Flee for safety without delay!
For I am bringing disaster from the north,
    even terrible destruction."

7A lion has come out of his lair;
    a destroyer of nations has set out.
He has left his place
    to lay waste your land.
Your towns will lie in ruins
    without inhabitant.
8So put on sackcloth,
    lament and wail,
for the fierce anger of the LORD
    has not turned away from us.

9"In that day," declares the LORD,
    "the king and the officials will lose heart,
the priests will be horrified,
    and the prophets will be appalled."

10Then I said, "Ah, Sovereign LORD, how completely you have deceived this people and Jeru-

salem by saying, 'You will have peace,' when the sword is at our throats."

¹¹At that time this people and Jerusalem will be told, "A scorching wind from the barren heights in the desert blows towards my people, but not to winnow or cleanse; ¹²a wind too strong for that comes from me.ᵃ Now I pronounce my judgments against them."

¹³Look! He advances like the clouds,
    his chariots come like a whirlwind,
his horses are swifter than eagles.
    Woe to us! We are ruined!
¹⁴O Jerusalem, wash the evil from your heart and
    be saved.
    How long will you harbour wicked thoughts?
¹⁵A voice is announcing from Dan,
    proclaiming disaster from the hills of
        Ephraim.
¹⁶"Tell this to the nations,
    proclaim it to Jerusalem:
'A besieging army is coming from a distant land,
    raising a war cry against the cities of Judah.
¹⁷They surround her like men guarding a field,
    because she has rebelled against me,' "
                    declares the LORD.
¹⁸"Your own conduct and actions
    have brought this upon you.
This is your punishment.
    How bitter it is!
    How it pierces to the heart!"

¹⁹Oh, my anguish, my anguish!
    I writhe in pain.
Oh, the agony of my heart!
    My heart pounds within me,
    I cannot keep silent.
For I have heard the sound of the trumpet;
    I have heard the battle cry.
²⁰Disaster follows disaster;
    the whole land lies in ruins.
In an instant my tents are destroyed,
    my shelter in a moment.
²¹How long must I see the battle standard
    and hear the sound of the trumpet?

²²"My people are fools;
    they do not know me.
They are senseless children;
    they have no understanding.
They are skilled in doing evil;
    they know not how to do good."

²³I looked at the earth,
    and it was formless and empty;
and at the heavens,
    and their light was gone.

4:23 ■ RETURN TO THE VOID
Jeremiah used words from Genesis 1:2 to describe the effect of the Israelites' sin. It was as though the Israelites were carrying the earth back to the chaos before creation, destroying all the beauty and order God had made.

²⁴I looked at the mountains,
    and they were quaking;
all the hills were swaying.
²⁵I looked, and there were no people;
    every bird in the sky had flown away.
²⁶I looked, and the fruitful land was a desert;
    all its towns lay in ruins
before the LORD, before his fierce anger.

²⁷This is what the LORD says:

"The whole land will be ruined,
    though I will not destroy it completely.
²⁸Therefore the earth will mourn
    and the heavens above grow dark,
because I have spoken and will not relent,
    I have decided and will not turn back."

²⁹At the sound of horsemen and archers
    every town takes to flight.
Some go into the thickets;
    some climb up among the rocks.
All the towns are deserted;
    no-one lives in them.

³⁰What are you doing, O devastated one?
    Why dress yourself in scarlet
    and put on jewels of gold?
Why shade your eyes with paint?
    You adorn yourself in vain.
Your lovers despise you;
    they seek your life.

³¹I hear a cry as of a woman in labour,
    a groan as of one bearing her first child—
the cry of the Daughter of Zion gasping for
        breath,
    stretching out her hands and saying,
"Alas! I am fainting;
    my life is given over to murderers."

■ Not One Is Upright
5 "Go up and down the streets of Jerusalem,
    look around and consider,
    search through her squares.
If you can find but one person
    who deals honestly and seeks the truth,
    I will forgive this city.

5:1 ■ SEARCH FOR AN HONEST PERSON
In Genesis 18:22–33, Abraham tried to convince God not to destroy Sodom and Gomorrah if as many as ten righteous people could be found. God agreed, but evidently the ten did not exist. Here, God offers to forgive Jerusalem if a *single* honest person can be found. God's people had sunk to Sodom's level (23:14).

²Although they say, 'As surely as the LORD lives,'
    still they are swearing falsely."

³O LORD, do not your eyes look for truth?
    You struck them, but they felt no pain;
    you crushed them but they refused
        correction.

ᵃ 12 Or comes at my command

They made their faces harder than stone
   and refused to repent.
4I thought, "These are only the poor;
   they are foolish,
for they do not know the way of the LORD,
   the requirements of their God.
5So I will go to the leaders
   and speak to them;
surely they know the way of the LORD,
   the requirements of their God."
But with one accord they too had broken off
      the yoke
   and torn off the bonds.
6Therefore a lion from the forest will attack
      them,
   a wolf from the desert will ravage them,
a leopard will lie in wait near their towns
   to tear to pieces any who venture out,
for their rebellion is great
   and their backslidings many.

7"Why should I forgive you?
   Your children have forsaken me
   and sworn by gods that are not gods.
I supplied all their needs,
   yet they committed adultery
   and thronged to the houses of prostitutes.
8They are well-fed, lusty stallions,
   each neighing for another man's wife.
9Should I not punish them for this?"
   declares the LORD.
"Should I not avenge myself
   on such a nation as this?

10"Go through her vineyards and ravage them,
   but do not destroy them completely.
Strip off her branches,
   for these people do not belong to the LORD.
11The house of Israel and the house of Judah
   have been utterly unfaithful to me,"
                           declares the LORD.

12They have lied about the LORD;
   they said, "He will do nothing!
No harm will come to us;
   we will never see sword or famine.
13The prophets are but wind
   and the word is not in them;
   so let what they say be done to them."

5:12 ■ DON'T WORRY, BE HAPPY
Nobody likes bad news, and if you can find a way
to shrug it off, you probably will. So the people of
Judah treated Jeremiah's gloomy prophecies as
so much hot air. To protect their comfortable
lifestyles, they pictured a God who was
uninvolved, either unable or unwilling to interfere.

14Therefore this is what the LORD God Almighty
says:

"Because the people have spoken these words,
   I will make my words in your mouth a fire
   and these people the wood it consumes.
15O house of Israel," declares the LORD,

"I am bringing a distant nation against you—
   an ancient and enduring nation,
a people whose language you do not know,
   whose speech you do not understand.
16Their quivers are like an open grave;
   all of them are mighty warriors.
17They will devour your harvests and food,
   devour your sons and daughters;
they will devour your flocks and herds,
   devour your vines and fig-trees.
With the sword they will destroy
   the fortified cities in which you trust.

18"Yet even in those days," declares the LORD, "I
will not destroy you completely. 19And when the
people ask, 'Why has the LORD our God done all this
to us?' you will tell them, 'As you have forsaken me
and served foreign gods in your own land, so now
you will serve foreigners in a land not your own.'

20"Announce this to the house of Jacob
   and proclaim it in Judah:
21Hear this, you foolish and senseless people,
   who have eyes but do not see,
   who have ears but do not hear:
22Should you not fear me?" declares the LORD.
   "Should you not tremble in my presence?
I made the sand a boundary for the sea,
   an everlasting barrier it cannot cross.
The waves may roll, but they cannot prevail;
   they may roar, but they cannot cross it.
23But these people have stubborn and rebellious
      hearts;
   they have turned aside and gone away.
24They do not say to themselves,
   'Let us fear the LORD our God,
who gives autumn and spring rains in season,
   who assures us of the regular weeks of
      harvest.'
25Your wrongdoings have kept these away;
   your sins have deprived you of good.

26"Among my people are wicked men
   who lie in wait like men who snare birds
   and like those who set traps to catch men.
27Like cages full of birds,
   their houses are full of deceit;
they have become rich and powerful
28   and have grown fat and sleek.
Their evil deeds have no limit;
   they do not plead the case of the fatherless
      to win it,
   they do not defend the rights of the poor.
29Should I not punish them for this?"
   declares the LORD.
"Should I not avenge myself
   on such a nation as this?

30"A horrible and shocking thing
   has happened in the land:
31The prophets prophesy lies,
   the priests rule by their own authority,
and my people love it this way.
   But what will you do in the end?

■ Jerusalem Under Siege

6 "Flee for safety, people of Benjamin!
  Flee from Jerusalem!
Sound the trumpet in Tekoa!
  Raise the signal over Beth Hakkerem!
For disaster looms out of the north,
  even terrible destruction.
²I will destroy the Daughter of Zion,
  so beautiful and delicate.
³Shepherds with their flocks will come against
  her;
  they will pitch their tents round her,
  each tending his own portion."

⁴"Prepare for battle against her!
  Arise, let us attack at noon!
But, alas, the daylight is fading,
  and the shadows of evening grow long.
⁵So arise, let us attack at night
  and destroy her fortresses!"

⁶This is what the LORD Almighty says:

"Cut down the trees
  and build siege ramps against Jerusalem.
This city must be punished;
  it is filled with oppression.
⁷As a well pours out its water,
  so she pours out her wickedness.
Violence and destruction resound in her;
  her sickness and wounds are ever before me.
⁸Take warning, O Jerusalem,
  or I will turn away from you
and make your land desolate
  so that no-one can live in it."

⁹This is what the LORD Almighty says:

"Let them glean the remnant of Israel
  as thoroughly as a vine;
pass your hand over the branches again,
  like one gathering grapes."

¹⁰To whom can I speak and give warning?
  Who will listen to me?
Their ears are closedᵃ
  so that they cannot hear.
The word of the LORD is offensive to them;
  they find no pleasure in it.
¹¹But I am full of the wrath of the LORD,
  and I cannot hold it in.

"Pour it out on the children in the street
  and on the young men gathered together;
both husband and wife will be caught in it,
  and the old, those weighed down with years.
¹²Their houses will be turned over to others,
  together with their fields and their wives,
when I stretch out my hand
  against those who live in the land,"
                          declares the LORD.
¹³"From the least to the greatest,
  all are greedy for gain;
prophets and priests alike,
  all practise deceit.
¹⁴They dress the wound of my people
  as though it were not serious.
'Peace, peace,' they say,

  when there is no peace.

6:14 ■ GREEDY DOCTORS
A good doctor sometimes has to convey bad
tidings, delivering a diagnosis of cancer, for
example. But in Judah the spiritual "doctors"
(prophets and priests) only gave out good news.
They covered up serious wounds with a Band-Aid.

¹⁵Are they ashamed of their loathsome conduct?
  No, they have no shame at all;
  they do not even know how to blush.
So they will fall among the fallen;
  they will be brought down when I punish
  them,"
                          says the LORD.

¹⁶This is what the LORD says:

"Stand at the crossroads and look;
  ask for the ancient paths,
ask where the good way is, and walk in it,
  and you will find rest for your souls.
But you said, 'We will not walk in it.'
¹⁷I appointed watchmen over you and said,
  'Listen to the sound of the trumpet!'
But you said, 'We will not listen.'
¹⁸Therefore hear, O nations;
  observe, O witnesses,
  what will happen to them.
¹⁹Hear, O earth:
I am bringing disaster on this people,
  the fruit of their schemes,
because they have not listened to my words
  and have rejected my law.
²⁰What do I care about incense from Sheba
  or sweet calamus from a distant land?
Your burnt offerings are not acceptable;
  your sacrifices do not please me."

²¹Therefore this is what the LORD says:

"I will put obstacles before this people.
  Fathers and sons alike will stumble over
  them;
neighbours and friends will perish."

²²This is what the LORD says:

"Look, an army is coming
  from the land of the north;
a great nation is being stirred up
  from the ends of the earth.
²³They are armed with bow and spear;
  they are cruel and show no mercy.
They sound like the roaring sea
  as they ride on their horses;
they come like men in battle formation
  to attack you, O Daughter of Zion."

²⁴We have heard reports about them,
  and our hands hang limp.
Anguish has gripped us,
  pain like that of a woman in labour.
²⁵Do not go out to the fields
  or walk on the roads,
for the enemy has a sword,

and there is terror on every side.
²⁶O my people, put on sackcloth
  and roll in ashes;
mourn with bitter wailing
  as for an only son,
for suddenly the destroyer
  will come upon us.

²⁷"I have made you a tester of metals
  and my people the ore,
that you may observe
  and test their ways.
²⁸They are all hardened rebels,
  going about to slander.
They are bronze and iron;
  they all act corruptly.
²⁹The bellows blow fiercely
  to burn away the lead with fire,
but the refining goes on in vain;
  the wicked are not purged out.
³⁰They are called rejected silver,
  because the LORD has rejected them."

■ False Religion Worthless

7 This is the word that came to Jeremiah from the
LORD: ²"Stand at the gate of the LORD's house and
there proclaim this message:
  " 'Hear the word of the LORD, all you people of
Judah who come through these gates to worship the
LORD. ³This is what the LORD Almighty, the God of
Israel, says: Reform your ways and your actions, and
I will let you live in this place. ⁴Do not trust in de-
ceptive words and say, "This is the temple of the
LORD, the temple of the LORD, the temple of the
LORD!" ⁵If you really change your ways and your actions and deal with each other justly, ⁶if you do not
oppress the alien, the fatherless or the widow and
do not shed innocent blood in this place, and if you
do not follow other gods to your own harm, ⁷then
I will let you live in this place, in the land I gave to
your forefathers for ever and ever. ⁸But look, you
are trusting in deceptive words that are worthless.
  ⁹" 'Will you steal and murder, commit adultery
and perjury,*a* burn incense to Baal and follow other
gods you have not known, ¹⁰and then come and
stand before me in this house, which bears my
Name, and say, "We are safe"—safe to do all these
detestable things? ¹¹Has this house, which bears my
Name, become a den of robbers to you? But I have
been watching! declares the LORD.

7:11 ■ A DEN OF ROBBERS

Israelites of Jeremiah's time felt that they were
safe from invasion as long as they had the temple.
After all, they thought, God would not let his home
be destroyed (verse 4). But the Lord, through
Jeremiah, said that the temple had become "a
den of robbers" and would be demolished. In
Jeremiah's lifetime this prediction came true.
Jesus quoted the reference to a den of robbers
when driving out money-changers from the rebuilt
temple (Mark 11:17).

---

¹²" 'Go now to the place in Shiloh where I first

made a dwelling for my Name, and see what I did to
it because of the wickedness of my people Israel.
¹³While you were doing all these things, declares
the LORD, I spoke to you again and again, but you did
not listen; I called you, but you did not answer.
¹⁴Therefore, what I did to Shiloh I will now do to
the house that bears my Name, the temple you trust
in, the place I gave to you and your fathers. ¹⁵I will
thrust you from my presence, just as I did all your
brothers, the people of Ephraim.'
  ¹⁶"So do not pray for this people nor offer any
plea or petition for them; do not plead with me, for
I will not listen to you. ¹⁷Do you not see what they
are doing in the towns of Judah and in the streets of
Jerusalem? ¹⁸The children gather wood, the fathers
light the fire, and the women knead the dough and
make cakes of bread for the Queen of Heaven. They
pour out drink offerings to other gods to provoke
me to anger. ¹⁹But am I the one they are provoking?
declares the LORD. Are they not rather harming
themselves, to their own shame?
  ²⁰" 'Therefore this is what the Sovereign LORD
says: My anger and my wrath will be poured out on
this place, on man and beast, on the trees of the field
and on the fruit of the ground, and it will burn and
not be quenched.
  ²¹" 'This is what the LORD Almighty, the God of
Israel, says: Go ahead, add your burnt offerings to
your other sacrifices and eat the meat yourselves!
²²For when I brought your forefathers out of Egypt
and spoke to them, I did not just give them commands about burnt offerings and sacrifices, ²³but I
gave them this command: Obey me, and I will be
your God and you will be my people. Walk in all the
ways I command you, that it may go well with you.
²⁴But they did not listen or pay attention; instead,
they followed the stubborn inclinations of their evil
hearts. They went backward and not forward.
²⁵From the time your forefathers left Egypt until
now, day after day, again and again I sent you my
servants the prophets. ²⁶But they did not listen to
me or pay attention. They were stiff-necked and did
more evil than their forefathers.'
  ²⁷"When you tell them all this, they will not listen
to you; when you call to them, they will not answer.
²⁸Therefore say to them, 'This is the nation that has
not obeyed the LORD its God or responded to correction. Truth has perished; it has vanished from
their lips. ²⁹Cut off your hair and throw it away; take
up a lament on the barren heights, for the LORD has
rejected and abandoned this generation that is under his wrath.

■ The Valley of Slaughter

  ³⁰" 'The people of Judah have done evil in my
eyes, declares the LORD. They have set up their detestable idols in the house that bears my Name and
have defiled it. ³¹They have built the high places of
Topheth in the Valley of Ben Hinnom to burn their
sons and daughters in the fire—something I did not
command, nor did it enter my mind. ³²So beware,
the days are coming, declares the LORD, when people will no longer call it Topheth or the Valley of
Ben Hinnom, but the Valley of Slaughter, for they
will bury the dead in Topheth until there is no more

---

a 9 Or and swear by false gods

room. ³³Then the carcasses of this people will become food for the birds of the air and the beasts of the earth, and there will be no-one to frighten them away. ³⁴I will bring an end to the sounds of joy and gladness and to the voices of bride and bridegroom in the towns of Judah and the streets of Jerusalem, for the land will become desolate.

8 "'At that time, declares the LORD, the bones of the kings and officials of Judah, the bones of the priests and prophets, and the bones of the people of Jerusalem will be removed from their graves. ²They will be exposed to the sun and the moon and all the stars of the heavens, which they have loved and served and which they have followed and consulted and worshipped. They will not be gathered up or buried, but will be like refuse lying on the ground. ³Wherever I banish them, all the survivors of this evil nation will prefer death to life, declares the LORD Almighty.'

■ Sin and Punishment
⁴"Say to them, 'This is what the LORD says:

"'When men fall down, do they not get up?
    When a man turns away, does he not return?
⁵Why then have these people turned away?
    Why does Jerusalem always turn away?
They cling to deceit;
    they refuse to return.
⁶I have listened attentively,
    but they do not say what is right.
No-one repents of his wickedness,
    saying, "What have I done?"
Each pursues his own course
    like a horse charging into battle.
⁷Even the stork in the sky
    knows her appointed seasons,
and the dove, the swift and the thrush
    observe the time of their migration.
But my people do not know
    the requirements of the LORD.

⁸"'How can you say, "We are wise,
    for we have the law of the LORD,"
when actually the lying pen of the scribes
    has handled it falsely?
⁹The wise will be put to shame;
    they will be dismayed and trapped.
Since they have rejected the word of the LORD,
    what kind of wisdom do they have?
¹⁰Therefore I will give their wives to other men
    and their fields to new owners.
From the least to the greatest,
    all are greedy for gain;
prophets and priests alike,
    all practise deceit.
¹¹They dress the wound of my people
    as though it were not serious.
"Peace, peace," they say,
    when there is no peace.
¹²Are they ashamed of their loathsome conduct?
    No, they have no shame at all;
    they do not even know how to blush.
So they will fall among the fallen;

they will be brought down when they are punished,
                        says the LORD.

¹³"'I will take away their harvest,
                        declares the LORD.
There will be no grapes on the vine.
There will be no figs on the tree,
    and their leaves will wither.
What I have given them
    will be taken from them.'"ᵃ

¹⁴"Why are we sitting here?
    Gather together!
Let us flee to the fortified cities
    and perish there!
For the LORD our God has doomed us to perish
    and given us poisoned water to drink,
    because we have sinned against him.
¹⁵We hoped for peace
    but no good has come,
for a time of healing
    but there was only terror.
¹⁶The snorting of the enemy's horses
    is heard from Dan;
at the neighing of their stallions
    the whole land trembles.
They have come to devour
    the land and everything in it,
    the city and all who live there."

¹⁷"See, I will send venomous snakes among you,
    vipers that cannot be charmed,
    and they will bite you,"
                        declares the LORD.

¹⁸O my Comforterᵇ in sorrow,
    my heart is faint within me.
¹⁹Listen to the cry of my people
    from a land far away:
"Is the LORD not in Zion?
    Is her King no longer there?"

"Why have they provoked me to anger with
        their images,
    with their worthless foreign idols?"

²⁰"The harvest is past,
    the summer has ended,
    and we are not saved."

²¹Since my people are crushed, I am crushed;
    I mourn, and horror grips me.
²²Is there no balm in Gilead?
    Is there no physician there?
Why then is there no healing
    for the wound of my people?

9 ¹Oh, that my head were a spring of water
    and my eyes a fountain of tears!
I would weep day and night
    for the slain of my people.
²Oh, that I had in the desert
    a lodging place for travellers,
so that I might leave my people
    and go away from them;
for they are all adulterers,
    a crowd of unfaithful people.

³"They make ready their tongue
    like a bow, to shoot lies;

ᵃ 13 The meaning of the Hebrew for this sentence is uncertain.   ᵇ 18 The meaning of the Hebrew for this word is uncertain.

it is not by truth
   that they triumph*a* in the land.

9:1 ■ A FOUNTAIN OF TEARS

Jeremiah never stood aside like a stern moralist, enjoying others' well-deserved sufferings. He felt the bitterness of the judgment he announced. "Since my people are crushed, I am crushed; I mourn, and horror grips me" (8:21). In the end, Jeremiah swallowed the bitter medicine of exile like the others.

Jeremiah reminds us of another "man of sorrows". Like Jesus, Jeremiah wept over Jerusalem. Like Jesus, he was rejected by his own home town (11:18–23). Jeremiah even compared himself to a lamb led to the slaughter (11:19), language that would later be applied to Jesus' sacrifice for our sins.

They go from one sin to another;
   they do not acknowledge me,"
                        declares the LORD.
4"Beware of your friends;
   do not trust your brothers.
For every brother is a deceiver,*b*
   and every friend a slanderer.
5Friend deceives friend,
   and no-one speaks the truth.
They have taught their tongues to lie;
   they weary themselves with sinning.
6You*c* live in the midst of deception;
   in their deceit they refuse to acknowledge
     me,"
                        declares the LORD.

7Therefore this is what the LORD Almighty says:

"See, I will refine and test them,
   for what else can I do
   because of the sin of my people?
8Their tongue is a deadly arrow;
   it speaks with deceit.
With his mouth each speaks cordially to his
     neighbour,
   but in his heart he sets a trap for him.
9Should I not punish them for this?"
   declares the LORD.
"Should I not avenge myself
   on such a nation as this?"

10I will weep and wail for the mountains
   and take up a lament concerning the desert
     pastures.
They are desolate and untravelled,
   and the lowing of cattle is not heard.
The birds of the air have fled
   and the animals are gone.

11"I will make Jerusalem a heap of ruins,
   a haunt of jackals;
and I will lay waste the towns of Judah
   so that no-one can live there."

12What man is wise enough to understand this? Who has been instructed by the LORD and can explain it? Why has the land been ruined and laid waste like a desert that no-one can cross?

13The LORD said, "It is because they have forsaken my law, which I set before them; they have not obeyed me or followed my law. 14Instead, they have followed the stubbornness of their hearts; they have followed the Baals, as their fathers taught them." 15Therefore, this is what the LORD Almighty, the God of Israel, says: "See, I will make this people eat bitter food and drink poisoned water. 16I will scatter them among nations that neither they nor their fathers have known, and I will pursue them with the sword until I have destroyed them."

17This is what the LORD Almighty says:

"Consider now! Call for the wailing women to
     come;
   send for the most skilful of them.
18Let them come quickly
   and wail over us
till our eyes overflow with tears
   and water streams from our eyelids.
19The sound of wailing is heard from Zion:
   'How ruined we are!
How great is our shame!
We must leave our land
   because our houses are in ruins.' "

20Now, O women, hear the word of the LORD;
   open your ears to the words of his mouth.
Teach your daughters how to wail;
   teach one another a lament.
21Death has climbed in through our windows
   and has entered our fortresses;
it has cut off the children from the streets
   and the young men from the public squares.

22Say, "This is what the LORD declares:

" 'The dead bodies of men will lie
   like refuse on the open field,
like cut corn behind the reaper,
   with no-one to gather them.' "

23This is what the LORD says:

"Let not the wise man boast of his wisdom
   or the strong man boast of his strength
   or the rich man boast of his riches,
24but let him who boasts boast about this:
   that he understands and knows me,
that I am the LORD, who exercises kindness,
   justice and righteousness on earth,
   for in these I delight,"
                        declares the LORD.

9:24 ■ CONFIDENT IN GOD

In dire circumstances like those Jeremiah predicts, what has value? Wisdom? Strength? Money? In the midst of a devastating invasion, these will get you nothing. Only one thing will count: a living, confident relationship with God. If you have that, it's worth boasting about. Paul quoted this verse in writing to the Corinthians (1 Corinthians 1:31); he said that God seems to prefer to work through the weak and poor, who have little else to boast about.

a3 Or lies; / they are not valiant for truth   *b4 Or a deceiving Jacob*   *c6 That is, Jeremiah (the Hebrew is singular)*

²⁵"The days are coming," declares the LORD, "when I will punish all who are circumcised only in the flesh—²⁶Egypt, Judah, Edom, Ammon, Moab and all who live in the desert in distant places.*d* For all these nations are really uncircumcised, and even the whole house of Israel is uncircumcised in heart."

■ God and Idols

10 Hear what the LORD says to you, O house of Israel. ²This is what the LORD says:

"Do not learn the ways of the nations
    or be terrified by signs in the sky,
    though the nations are terrified by them.
³For the customs of the peoples are worthless;
    they cut a tree out of the forest,
    and a craftsman shapes it with his chisel.
⁴They adorn it with silver and gold;
    they fasten it with hammer and nails
    so that it will not totter.
⁵Like a scarecrow in a melon patch,
    their idols cannot speak;
they must be carried
    because they cannot walk.
Do not fear them;
    they can do no harm
    nor can they do any good."

⁶No-one is like you, O LORD;
    you are great,
    and your name is mighty in power.
⁷Who should not revere you,
    O King of the nations?
This is your due.
Among all the wise men of the nations
    and in all their kingdoms,
    there is no-one like you.
⁸They are all senseless and foolish;
    they are taught by worthless wooden idols.
⁹Hammered silver is brought from Tarshish
    and gold from Uphaz.
What the craftsman and goldsmith have made
    is then dressed in blue and purple—
    all made by skilled workers.
¹⁰But the LORD is the true God;
    he is the living God, the eternal King.
When he is angry, the earth trembles;
    the nations cannot endure his wrath.

¹¹"Tell them this: 'These gods, who did not make the heavens and the earth, will perish from the earth and from under the heavens.' "*a*

¹²But God made the earth by his power;
    he founded the world by his wisdom
    and stretched out the heavens by his
        understanding.
¹³When he thunders, the waters in the heavens
        roar;
    he makes clouds rise from the ends of the
        earth.
He sends lightning with the rain
    and brings out the wind from his
        storehouses.
¹⁴Everyone is senseless and without knowledge;

every goldsmith is shamed by his idols.
His images are a fraud;
    they have no breath in them.
¹⁵They are worthless, the objects of mockery;
    when their judgment comes, they will perish.
¹⁶He who is the Portion of Jacob is not like
        these,
    for he is the Maker of all things,
including Israel, the tribe of his inheritance—
    the LORD Almighty is his name.

■ Coming Destruction

¹⁷Gather up your belongings to leave the land,
    you who live under siege.
¹⁸For this is what the LORD says:
"At this time I will hurl out
    those who live in this land;
I will bring distress on them
    so that they may be captured."

¹⁹Woe to me because of my injury!
    My wound is incurable!
Yet I said to myself,
    "This is my sickness, and I must endure it."
²⁰My tent is destroyed;
    all its ropes are snapped.
My sons are gone from me and are no more;
    no-one is left now to pitch my tent
    or to set up my shelter.
²¹The shepherds are senseless
    and do not enquire of the LORD;
so they do not prosper
    and all their flock is scattered.
²²Listen! The report is coming—
    a great commotion from the land of the
        north!
It will make the towns of Judah desolate,
    a haunt of jackals.

■ Jeremiah's Prayer

²³I know, O LORD, that a man's life is not his own;
    it is not for man to direct his steps.
²⁴Correct me, LORD, but only with justice—
    not in your anger,
    lest you reduce me to nothing.
²⁵Pour out your wrath on the nations
    that do not acknowledge you,
    on the peoples who do not call on your
        name.
For they have devoured Jacob;
    they have devoured him completely
    and destroyed his homeland.

■ The Covenant Is Broken

11 This is the word that came to Jeremiah from the LORD: ²"Listen to the terms of this covenant and tell them to the people of Judah and to those who live in Jerusalem. ³Tell them that this is what the LORD, the God of Israel, says: 'Cursed is the man who does not obey the terms of this covenant—⁴the terms I commanded your forefathers when I brought them out of Egypt, out of the iron-smelting furnace.' I said, 'Obey me and do everything I command you, and you will be my people, and I will be your God. ⁵Then I will fulfil the oath

d 26 Or desert and who clip the hair by their foreheads   *a 11 The text of this verse is in Aramaic.*

I swore to your forefathers, to give them a land flowing with milk and honey'—the land you possess today."

I answered, "Amen, LORD."

⁶The LORD said to me, "Proclaim all these words in the towns of Judah and in the streets of Jerusalem: 'Listen to the terms of this covenant and follow them. ⁷From the time I brought your forefathers up from Egypt until today, I warned them again and again, saying, "Obey me." ⁸But they did not listen or pay attention; instead, they followed the stubbornness of their evil hearts. So I brought on them all the curses of the covenant I had commanded them to follow but that they did not keep.' "

11:8 ■ DAY OF RECKONING

If you sign a note to buy a house, you have to follow through. Miss too many payments, and the bank will evict you. So it was with Israel. Hundreds of years before Jeremiah's time, God had made a "covenant" with them—a treaty binding him to be their God, in exchange for their obedience (see "The Covenant", page 68). This was formally ratified, along with a series of "blessings" and "curses"—good consequences for obedience, bad consequences for disobedience—as recorded in Deuteronomy 28. Now, God announces, because the covenant has been broken, severe punishment must follow.

⁹Then the LORD said to me, "There is a conspiracy among the people of Judah and those who live in Jerusalem. ¹⁰They have returned to the sins of their forefathers, who refused to listen to my words. They have followed other gods to serve them. Both the house of Israel and the house of Judah have broken the covenant I made with their forefathers. ¹¹Therefore this is what the LORD says: 'I will bring on them a disaster they cannot escape. Although they cry out to me, I will not listen to them. ¹²The towns of Judah and the people of Jerusalem will go and cry out to the gods to whom they burn incense, but they will not help them at all when disaster strikes. ¹³You have as many gods as you have towns, O Judah; and the altars you have set up to burn incense to that shameful god Baal are as many as the streets of Jerusalem.'

¹⁴"Do not pray for this people nor offer any plea or petition for them, because I will not listen when they call to me in the time of their distress.

¹⁵"What is my beloved doing in my temple
    as she works out her evil schemes with
        many?
    Can consecrated meat avert ⌐your
        punishment⌐?
When you engage in your wickedness,
    then you rejoice."ᵃ

¹⁶The LORD called you a thriving olive tree
    with fruit beautiful in form.
But with the roar of a mighty storm
    he will set it on fire,
    and its branches will be broken.

¹⁷The LORD Almighty, who planted you, has decreed disaster for you, because the house of Israel and the house of Judah have done evil and provoked me to anger by burning incense to Baal.

■ Plot Against Jeremiah

¹⁸Because the LORD revealed their plot to me, I knew it, for at that time he showed me what they were doing. ¹⁹I had been like a gentle lamb led to the slaughter; I did not realise that they had plotted against me, saying,

"Let us destroy the tree and its fruit;
    let us cut him off from the land of the living,
    that his name be remembered no more."
²⁰But, O LORD Almighty, you who judge
        righteously
    and test the heart and mind,
let me see your vengeance upon them,
    for to you I have committed my cause.

²¹"Therefore this is what the LORD says about the men of Anathoth who are seeking your life and saying, 'Do not prophesy in the name of the LORD or you will die by our hands'—²²therefore this is what the LORD Almighty says: 'I will punish them. Their young men will die by the sword, their sons and daughters by famine. ²³Not even a remnant will be left to them, because I will bring disaster on the men of Anathoth in the year of their punishment.' "

11:23 ■ HOME TOWN ENEMIES

Jeremiah's life was endangered several times because of his message. On this occasion, men from his home town were plotting against him. Though Jeremiah was completely unprepared for their attack, God protected him. Other prophets, however, had been killed (2:30).

■ Jeremiah's Complaint

12 You are always righteous, O LORD,
    when I bring a case before you.
Yet I would speak with you about your justice:
    Why does the way of the wicked prosper?
    Why do all the faithless live at ease?
²You have planted them, and they have taken
        root;
    they grow and bear fruit.
You are always on their lips
    but far from their hearts.
³Yet you know me, O LORD;
    you see me and test my thoughts about you.
Drag them off like sheep to be butchered!
    Set them apart for the day of slaughter!
⁴How long will the land lie parchedᵃ
    and the grass in every field be withered?
Because those who live in it are wicked,
    the animals and birds have perished.
Moreover, the people are saying,
    "He will not see what happens to us."

■ God's Answer

⁵"If you have raced with men on foot
    and they have worn you out,

ᵃ15 Or Could consecrated meat avert your punishment? / Then you would rejoice   ᵃ4 Or land mourn

how can you compete with horses?
If you stumble in safe country,[b]
  how will you manage in the thickets by[c]
    the Jordan?
6Your brothers, your own family—
  even they have betrayed you;
  they have raised a loud cry against you.
Do not trust them,
  though they speak well of you.

7"I will forsake my house,
  abandon my inheritance;
I will give the one I love
  into the hands of her enemies.
8My inheritance has become to me
  like a lion in the forest.
She roars at me;
  therefore I hate her.
9Has not my inheritance become to me
  like a speckled bird of prey
  that other birds of prey surround and
    attack?
Go and gather all the wild beasts;
  bring them to devour.
10Many shepherds will ruin my vineyard
  and trample down my field;
they will turn my pleasant field
  into a desolate wasteland.
11It will be made a wasteland,
  parched and desolate before me;
the whole land will be laid waste
  because there is no-one who cares.
12Over all the barren heights in the desert
  destroyers will swarm,
for the sword of the LORD will devour
  from one end of the land to the other;
  no-one will be safe.
13They will sow wheat but reap thorns;
  they will wear themselves out but gain
    nothing.
So bear the shame of your harvest
  because of the LORD's fierce anger."

14This is what the LORD says: "As for all my wicked neighbours who seize the inheritance I gave to my people Israel, I will uproot them from their lands and I will uproot the house of Judah from among them. 15But after I uproot them, I will again have compassion and will bring each of them back to his own inheritance and his own country. 16And if they learn well the ways of my people and swear by my name, saying, 'As surely as the LORD lives'—even as they once taught my people to swear by Baal—then they will be established among my people. 17But if any nation does not listen, I will completely uproot and destroy it," declares the LORD.

12:16 ■ HOPE FOR THE GENTILES
Through most of the Old Testament, Israel's Gentile neighbours seem to have no part in God's plan. Here, though, God clearly promises them his salvation.

■ A Linen Belt

13 This is what the LORD said to me: "Go and buy a linen belt and put it round your waist, but do not let it touch water." 2So I bought a belt, as the LORD directed, and put it round my waist.

3Then the word of the LORD came to me a second time: 4"Take the belt you bought and are wearing round your waist, and go now to Perath[a] and hide it there in a crevice in the rocks." 5So I went and hid it at Perath, as the LORD told me.

6Many days later the LORD said to me, "Go now to Perath and get the belt I told you to hide there." 7So I went to Perath and dug up the belt and took it from the place where I had hidden it, but now it was ruined and completely useless.

8Then the word of the LORD came to me: 9"This is what the LORD says: 'In the same way I will ruin the pride of Judah and the great pride of Jerusalem. 10These wicked people, who refuse to listen to my words, who follow the stubbornness of their hearts and go after other gods to serve and worship them, will be like this belt—completely useless! 11For as a belt is bound round a man's waist, so I bound the whole house of Israel and the whole house of Judah to me,' declares the LORD, 'to be my people for my renown and praise and honour. But they have not listened.'

■ Wineskins

12"Say to them: 'This is what the LORD, the God of Israel, says: Every wineskin should be filled with wine.' And if they say to you, 'Don't we know that every wineskin should be filled with wine?' 13then tell them, 'This is what the LORD says: I am going to fill with drunkenness all who live in this land, including the kings who sit on David's throne, the priests, the prophets and all those living in Jerusalem. 14I will smash them one against the other, fathers and sons alike, declares the LORD. I will allow no pity or mercy or compassion to keep me from destroying them.' "

■ Threat of Captivity

15Hear and pay attention,
  do not be arrogant,
  for the LORD has spoken.
16Give glory to the LORD your God
  before he brings the darkness,
before your feet stumble
  on the darkening hills.
You hope for light,
  but he will turn it to thick darkness
  and change it to deep gloom.
17But if you do not listen,
  I will weep in secret
  because of your pride;
my eyes will weep bitterly,
  overflowing with tears,
  because the LORD's flock will be taken
    captive.

18Say to the king and to the queen mother,
  "Come down from your thrones,
for your glorious crowns
  will fall from your heads."

---

b 5 Or If you put your trust in a land of safety   c 5 Or the flooding of   a 4 Or possibly the Euphrates; also in verses 5–7

¹⁹The cities in the Negev will be shut up,
  and there will be no-one to open them.
All Judah will be carried into exile,
  carried completely away.

²⁰Lift up your eyes and see
  those who are coming from the north.
Where is the flock that was entrusted to you,
  the sheep of which you boasted?
²¹What will you say when ⌊the LORD⌋ sets over
  you
  those you cultivated as your special allies?
Will not pain grip you
  like that of a woman in labour?
²²And if you ask yourself,
  "Why has this happened to me?" —
it is because of your many sins
  that your skirts have been torn off
  and your body ill-treated.
²³Can the Ethiopian[b] change his skin
  or the leopard its spots?
Neither can you do good
  who are accustomed to doing evil.

²⁴"I will scatter you like chaff
  driven by the desert wind.
²⁵This is your lot,
  the portion I have decreed for you,"
                        declares the LORD,
"because you have forgotten me
  and trusted in false gods.
²⁶I will pull up your skirts over your face
  that your shame may be seen —
²⁷your adulteries and lustful neighings,
  your shameless prostitution!
I have seen your detestable acts
  on the hills and in the fields.
Woe to you, O Jerusalem!
  How long will you be unclean?"

■ Drought, Famine, Sword

14 This is the word of the LORD to Jeremiah concerning the drought:

²"Judah mourns,
  her cities languish;
they wail for the land,
  and a cry goes up from Jerusalem.
³The nobles send their servants for water;
  they go to the cisterns
  but find no water.
They return with their jars unfilled;
  dismayed and despairing,
  they cover their heads.
⁴The ground is cracked
  because there is no rain in the land;
the farmers are dismayed
  and cover their heads.
⁵Even the doe in the field
  deserts her newborn fawn
  because there is no grass.
⁶Wild donkeys stand on the barren heights
  and pant like jackals;
their eyesight fails
  for lack of pasture."

⁷Although our sins testify against us,
  O LORD, do something for the sake of your
  name.
For our backsliding is great;
  we have sinned against you.
⁸O Hope of Israel,
  its Saviour in times of distress,
why are you like a stranger in the land,
  like a traveller who stays only a night?
⁹Why are you like a man taken by surprise,
  like a warrior powerless to save?
You are among us, O LORD,
  and we bear your name;
  do not forsake us!

¹⁰This is what the LORD says about this people:

"They greatly love to wander;
  they do not restrain their feet.
So the LORD does not accept them;
  he will now remember their wickedness
  and punish them for their sins."

¹¹Then the LORD said to me, "Do not pray for the
well-being of this people. ¹²Although they fast, I will
not listen to their cry; though they offer burnt offerings and grain offerings, I will not accept them. Instead, I will destroy them with the sword, famine
and plague."

14:11 ■ GOD'S PATIENCE EXHAUSTED

God gave Jeremiah these dreaded instructions,
repeated nowhere else in the Bible: "Do not pray
for this people . . . because I will not listen"
(11:14). He repeated that message twice (7:16;
14:11). He told Jeremiah, "Even if Moses and
Samuel were to stand before me, my heart would
not go out to this people. Send them away from
my presence!" (15:1).

¹³But I said, "Ah, Sovereign LORD, the prophets
keep telling them, 'You will not see the sword or
suffer famine. Indeed, I will give you lasting peace
in this place.'"
¹⁴Then the LORD said to me, "The prophets are
prophesying lies in my name. I have not sent them
or appointed them or spoken to them. They are
prophesying to you false visions, divinations, idolatries[a] and the delusions of their own minds.
¹⁵Therefore, this is what the LORD says about the
prophets who are prophesying in my name: I did
not send them, yet they are saying, 'No sword or
famine will touch this land.' Those same prophets
will perish by sword and famine. ¹⁶And the people
they are prophesying to will be thrown out into the
streets of Jerusalem because of the famine and
sword. There will be no-one to bury them or their
wives, their sons or their daughters. I will pour out
on them the calamity they deserve.

¹⁷"Speak this word to them:

" 'Let my eyes overflow with tears
  night and day without ceasing;
for my virgin daughter — my people —

ᵇ23 Hebrew *Cushite* (probably a person from the upper Nile region)   ᵃ14 Or *visions, worthless divinations*

has suffered a grievous wound,
  a crushing blow.
18If I go into the country,
  I see those slain by the sword;
if I go into the city,
  I see the ravages of famine.
Both prophet and priest
  have gone to a land they know not.' "

19Have you rejected Judah completely?
  Do you despise Zion?
Why have you afflicted us
  so that we cannot be healed?
We hoped for peace
  but no good has come,
for a time of healing
  but there is only terror.
20O LORD, we acknowledge our wickedness
  and the guilt of our fathers;
we have indeed sinned against you.
21For the sake of your name do not despise us;
  do not dishonour your glorious throne.
Remember your covenant with us
  and do not break it.
22Do any of the worthless idols of the nations
    bring rain?
Do the skies themselves send down showers?
No, it is you, O LORD our God.
Therefore our hope is in you,
  for you are the one who does all this.

15 Then the LORD said to me: "Even if Moses and Samuel were to stand before me, my heart would not go out to this people. Send them away from my presence! Let them go! 2And if they ask you, 'Where shall we go?' tell them, 'This is what the LORD says:

" 'Those destined for death, to death;
those for the sword, to the sword;
those for starvation, to starvation;
those for captivity, to captivity.'

3"I will send four kinds of destroyers against them," declares the LORD, "the sword to kill and the dogs to drag away and the birds of the air and the beasts of the earth to devour and destroy. 4I will make them abhorrent to all the kingdoms of the earth because of what Manasseh son of Hezekiah king of Judah did in Jerusalem.

5"Who will have pity on you, O Jerusalem?
  Who will mourn for you?
  Who will stop to ask how you are?
6You have rejected me," declares the LORD.
  "You keep on backsliding.
So I will lay hands on you and destroy you;
  I can no longer show compassion.
7I will winnow them with a winnowing fork
  at the city gates of the land.
I will bring bereavement and destruction on
    my people,
  for they have not changed their ways.
8I will make their widows more numerous
  than the sand of the sea.
At midday I will bring a destroyer
  against the mothers of their young men;

suddenly I will bring down on them
  anguish and terror.
9The mother of seven will grow faint
  and breathe her last.
Her sun will set while it is still day;
  she will be disgraced and humiliated.
I will put the survivors to the sword
  before their enemies,"
                   declares the LORD.

10Alas, my mother, that you gave me birth,
  a man with whom the whole land strives and
    contends!
I have neither lent nor borrowed,
  yet everyone curses me.

11The LORD said,

"Surely I will deliver you for a good purpose;
  surely I will make your enemies plead with
    you
in times of disaster and times of distress.

12"Can a man break iron—
  iron from the north—or bronze?
13Your wealth and your treasures
  I will give as plunder, without charge,
because of all your sins
  throughout your country.
14I will enslave you to your enemies
  in*a* a land you do not know,
for my anger will kindle a fire
  that will burn against you."

15You understand, O LORD;
  remember me and care for me.
Avenge me on my persecutors.
You are long-suffering—do not take me away;
  think of how I suffer reproach for your sake.
16When your words came, I ate them;
  they were my joy and my heart's delight,
for I bear your name,
  O LORD God Almighty.
17I never sat in the company of revellers,
  never made merry with them;
I sat alone because your hand was on me
  and you had filled me with indignation.
18Why is my pain unending
  and my wound grievous and incurable?
Will you be to me like a deceptive brook,
  like a spring that fails?

19Therefore this is what the LORD says:

"If you repent, I will restore you
  that you may serve me;
if you utter worthy, not worthless, words,
  you will be my spokesman.
Let this people turn to you,
  but you must not turn to them.
20I will make you a wall to this people,
  a fortified wall of bronze;
they will fight against you
  but will not overcome you,
for I am with you
  to rescue and save you,"
                   declares the LORD.

a 14 Some Hebrew manuscripts, Septuagint and Syriac (see also Jer. 17:4); most Hebrew manuscripts *I will cause your enemies to bring you / into*

21"I will save you from the hands of the wicked
and redeem you from the grasp of the cruel."

■ Day of Disaster

16 Then the word of the LORD came to me: 2"You must not marry and have sons or daughters in this place." 3For this is what the LORD says about the sons and daughters born in this land and about the women who are their mothers and the men who are their fathers: 4"They will die of deadly diseases. They will not be mourned or buried but will be like refuse lying on the ground. They will perish by sword and famine, and their dead bodies will become food for the birds of the air and the beasts of the earth."

5For this is what the LORD says: "Do not enter a house where there is a funeral meal; do not go to mourn or show sympathy, because I have withdrawn my blessing, my love and my pity from this people," declares the LORD. 6"Both high and low will die in this land. They will not be buried or mourned, and no-one will cut himself or shave his head for them. 7No-one will offer food to comfort those who mourn for the dead—not even for a father or a mother—nor will anyone give them a drink to console them.

8"And do not enter a house where there is feasting and sit down to eat and drink. 9For this is what the LORD Almighty, the God of Israel, says: Before your eyes and in your days I will bring an end to the sounds of joy and gladness and to the voices of bride and bridegroom in this place.

16:8 ■ NO SOCIAL LIFE

Jeremiah was a man swallowed up in his work. He had no family and little social life, because God told him never to marry and not to attend weddings, funerals, or any other ceremonial feasts (verses 1–9). God's message through him was so negative that a tale of woe or complaint came to be known as a "jeremiad". Other prophets kept predicting peace (14:13), but Jeremiah couldn't say what people wanted to hear. He told the truth, and the truth was bleak. Nevertheless, Jeremiah experienced the joy and delight of receiving God's word, and bearing God's name (15:16).

10"When you tell these people all this and they ask you, 'Why has the LORD decreed such a great disaster against us? What wrong have we done? What sin have we committed against the LORD our God?' 11then say to them, 'It is because your fathers forsook me,' declares the LORD, 'and followed other gods and served and worshipped them. They forsook me and did not keep my law. 12But you have behaved more wickedly than your fathers. See how each of you is following the stubbornness of his evil heart instead of obeying me. 13So I will throw you out of this land into a land neither you nor your fathers have known, and there you will serve other gods day and night, for I will show you no favour.'

14"However, the days are coming," declares the LORD, "when men will no longer say, 'As surely as the LORD lives, who brought the Israelites up out of Egypt,' 15but they will say, 'As surely as the LORD lives, who brought the Israelites up out of the land of the north and out of all the countries where he had banished them.' For I will restore them to the land I gave to their forefathers.

16"But now I will send for many fishermen," declares the LORD, "and they will catch them. After that I will send for many hunters, and they will hunt them down on every mountain and hill and from the crevices of the rocks. 17My eyes are on all their ways; they are not hidden from me, nor is their sin concealed from my eyes. 18I will repay them double for their wickedness and their sin, because they have defiled my land with the lifeless forms of their vile images and have filled my inheritance with their detestable idols."

19O LORD, my strength and my fortress,
my refuge in time of distress,
to you the nations will come
from the ends of the earth and say,
"Our fathers possessed nothing but false gods,
worthless idols that did them no good.
20Do men make their own gods?
Yes, but they are not gods!"

21"Therefore I will teach them—
this time I will teach them
my power and might.
Then they will know
that my name is the LORD.

17 "Judah's sin is engraved with an iron tool,
inscribed with a flint point,
on the tablets of their hearts
and on the horns of their altars.
2Even their children remember
their altars and Asherah poles[a]
beside the spreading trees
and on the high hills.
3My mountain in the land
and your[b] wealth and all your treasures
I will give away as plunder,
together with your high places,
because of sin throughout your country.
4Through your own fault you will lose
the inheritance I gave you.
I will enslave you to your enemies
in a land you do not know,
for you have kindled my anger,
and it will burn for ever."

5This is what the LORD says:

"Cursed is the one who trusts in man,
who depends on flesh for his strength
and whose heart turns away from the LORD.
6He will be like a bush in the wastelands;
he will not see prosperity when it comes.
He will dwell in the parched places of the
desert,
in a salt land where no-one lives.

7"But blessed is the man who trusts in the LORD,
whose confidence is in him.
8He will be like a tree planted by the water
that sends out its roots by the stream.

a2 That is, symbols of the goddess Asherah   b2, 3 Or hills / 3and the mountains of the land. / Your

It does not fear when heat comes;
    its leaves are always green.
It has no worries in a year of drought
    and never fails to bear fruit."

17:6 ■ WHOM TO TRUST?

Buy two identical plants in a nursery. Plant one in a desert, and one by a river. For a few days they'll look alike, but what happens after a few weeks? That's the image Jeremiah uses. The person who trusts in human beings will end up like a shrivelled bush (verse 6), while the person who trusts God will be like a tree that has its roots sunk deep beside a stream (verse 8).

9The heart is deceitful above all things
    and beyond cure.
    Who can understand it?

10"I the LORD search the heart
    and examine the mind,
to reward a man according to his conduct,
    according to what his deeds deserve."

11Like a partridge that hatches eggs it did not lay
    is the man who gains riches by unjust means.
When his life is half gone, they will desert him,
    and in the end he will prove to be a fool.

12A glorious throne, exalted from the beginning,
    is the place of our sanctuary.
13O LORD, the hope of Israel,
    all who forsake you will be put to shame.
Those who turn away from you will be written
      in the dust
because they have forsaken the LORD,
    the spring of living water.

14Heal me, O LORD, and I shall be healed;
    save me and I shall be saved,
    for you are the one I praise.
15They keep saying to me,
    "Where is the word of the LORD?
    Let it now be fulfilled!"
16I have not run away from being your shepherd;
    you know I have not desired the day of
      despair.
    What passes my lips is open before you.
17Do not be a terror to me;
    you are my refuge in the day of disaster.
18Let my persecutors be put to shame,
    but keep me from shame;
let them be terrified,
    but keep me from terror.
Bring on them the day of disaster;
    destroy them with double destruction.

■ Keeping the Sabbath Holy

19This is what the LORD said to me: "Go and stand at the gate of the people, through which the kings of Judah go in and out; stand also at all the other gates of Jerusalem. 20Say to them, 'Hear the word of the LORD, O kings of Judah and all people of Judah and everyone living in Jerusalem who come through these gates. 21This is what the LORD says: Be careful not to carry a load on the Sabbath day or bring it through the gates of Jerusalem. 22Do not bring a load out of your houses or do any work on the Sabbath, but keep the Sabbath day holy, as I commanded your forefathers. 23Yet they did not listen or pay attention; they were stiff-necked and would not listen or respond to discipline. 24But if you are careful to obey me, declares the LORD, and bring no load through the gates of this city on the Sabbath, but keep the Sabbath day holy by not doing any work on it, 25then kings who sit on David's throne will come through the gates of this city with their officials. They and their officials will come riding in chariots and on horses, accompanied by the men of Judah and those living in Jerusalem, and this city will be inhabited for ever. 26People will come from the towns of Judah and the villages around Jerusalem, from the territory of Benjamin and the western foothills, from the hill country and the Negev, bringing burnt offerings and sacrifices, grain offerings, incense and thank-offerings to the house of the LORD. 27But if you do not obey me to keep the Sabbath day holy by not carrying any load as you come through the gates of Jerusalem on the Sabbath day, then I will kindle an unquenchable fire in the gates of Jerusalem that will consume her fortresses.'"

■ At the Potter's House

18 This is the word that came to Jeremiah from the LORD: 2"Go down to the potter's house, and there I will give you my message." 3So I went down to the potter's house, and I saw him working at the wheel. 4But the pot he was shaping from the clay was marred in his hands; so the potter formed it into another pot, shaping it as seemed best to him.

5Then the word of the LORD came to me: 6"O house of Israel, can I not do with you as this potter does?" declares the LORD. "Like clay in the hand of the potter, so are you in my hand, O house of Israel. 7If at any time I announce that a nation or kingdom is to be uprooted, torn down and destroyed, 8and if that nation I warned repents of its evil, then I will relent and not inflict on it the disaster I had planned. 9And if at another time I announce that a nation or kingdom is to be built up and planted, 10and if it does evil in my sight and does not obey me, then I will reconsider the good I had intended to do for it.

18:6 ■ THE POTTER AND THE CLAY

God is in control – a message vividly portrayed to Jeremiah as he watched a potter begin again on a pot that did not take the shape he wanted it to take. Israelites had gradually come to think that God, because he had chosen them as his people, was obliged to protect them. But their unnatural behaviour towards him had brought God to the point of "starting again". In Romans 9:21, Paul returned to this metaphor to answer people who were claiming that God was unjust.

11"Now therefore say to the people of Judah and those living in Jerusalem, 'This is what the LORD says:

Look! I am preparing a disaster for you and devising a plan against you. So turn from your evil ways, each one of you, and reform your ways and your actions.' ¹²But they will reply, 'It's no use. We will continue with our own plans; each of us will follow the stubbornness of his evil heart.' "

¹³Therefore this is what the LORD says:

"Enquire among the nations:
    Who has ever heard anything like this?
A most horrible thing has been done
    by Virgin Israel.
¹⁴Does the snow of Lebanon
    ever vanish from its rocky slopes?
Do its cool waters from distant sources
    ever cease to flow?ᵃ
¹⁵Yet my people have forgotten me;
    they burn incense to worthless idols,
which made them stumble in their ways
    and in the ancient paths.
They made them walk in bypaths
    and on roads not built up.
¹⁶Their land will be laid waste,
    an object of lasting scorn;
all who pass by will be appalled
    and will shake their heads.
¹⁷Like a wind from the east,
    I will scatter them before their enemies;
I will show them my back and not my face
    in the day of their disaster."

¹⁸They said, "Come, let's make plans against Jeremiah; for the teaching of the law by the priest will not be lost, nor will counsel from the wise, nor the word from the prophets. So come, let's attack him with our tongues and pay no attention to anything he says."

¹⁹Listen to me, O LORD;
    hear what my accusers are saying!
²⁰Should good be repaid with evil?
    Yet they have dug a pit for me.
Remember that I stood before you
    and spoke on their behalf
    to turn your wrath away from them.
²¹So give their children over to famine;
    hand them over to the power of the sword.
Let their wives be made childless and widows;
    let their men be put to death,
    their young men slain by the sword in battle.
²²Let a cry be heard from their houses
    when you suddenly bring invaders against them,
for they have dug a pit to capture me
    and have hidden snares for my feet.
²³But you know, O LORD,
    all their plots to kill me.
Do not forgive their crimes
    or blot out their sins from your sight.
Let them be overthrown before you;
    deal with them in the time of your anger.

19 This is what the LORD says: "Go and buy a clay jar from a potter. Take along some of the elders of the people and of the priests ²and go out to the Valley of Ben Hinnom, near the entrance of the Potsherd Gate. There proclaim the words I tell you, ³and say, 'Hear the word of the LORD, O kings of Judah and people of Jerusalem. This is what the LORD Almighty, the God of Israel, says: Listen! I am going to bring a disaster on this place that will make the ears of everyone who hears of it tingle. ⁴For they have forsaken me and made this a place of foreign gods; they have burned sacrifices in it to gods that neither they nor their fathers nor the kings of Judah ever knew, and they have filled this place with the blood of the innocent. ⁵They have built the high places of Baal to burn their sons in the fire as offerings to Baal—something I did not command or mention, nor did it enter my mind. ⁶So beware, the days are coming, declares the LORD, when people will no longer call this place Topheth or the Valley of Ben Hinnom, but the Valley of Slaughter.

⁷" 'In this place I will ruinᵃ the plans of Judah and Jerusalem. I will make them fall by the sword before their enemies, at the hands of those who seek their lives, and I will give their carcasses as food to the birds of the air and the beasts of the earth. ⁸I will devastate this city and make it an object of scorn; all who pass by will be appalled and will scoff because of all its wounds. ⁹I will make them eat the flesh of their sons and daughters, and they will eat one another's flesh during the stress of the siege imposed on them by the enemies who seek their lives.'

¹⁰"Then break the jar while those who go with you are watching, ¹¹and say to them, 'This is what the LORD Almighty says: I will smash this nation and this city just as this potter's jar is smashed and cannot be repaired. They will bury the dead in Topheth until there is no more room. ¹²This is what I will do to this place and to those who live here, declares the LORD. I will make this city like Topheth. ¹³The houses in Jerusalem and those of the kings of Judah will be defiled like this place, Topheth—all the houses where they burned incense on the roofs to all the starry hosts and poured out drink offerings to other gods.' "

¹⁴Jeremiah then returned from Topheth, where the LORD had sent him to prophesy, and stood in the court of the LORD's temple and said to all the people, ¹⁵"This is what the LORD Almighty, the God of Israel, says: 'Listen! I am going to bring on this city and the villages around it every disaster I pronounced against them, because they were stiff-necked and would not listen to my words.' "

■ Jeremiah and Pashhur

20 When the priest Pashhur son of Immer, the chief officer in the temple of the LORD, heard Jeremiah prophesying these things, ²he had Jeremiah the prophet beaten and put in the stocks at the Upper Gate of Benjamin at the LORD's temple. ³The next day, when Pashhur released him from the stocks, Jeremiah said to him, "The LORD's name for you is not Pashhur, but Magor-Missabib.ᵃ ⁴For this is what the LORD says: 'I will make you a terror to yourself and to all your friends; with your own eyes you will see them fall by the sword of their enemies. I will hand all Judah over to the king of Babylon, who will carry them away to Babylon or put them to the sword. ⁵I will hand over to their enemies all

---

ᵃ14 The meaning of the Hebrew for this sentence is uncertain.   ᵃ7 The Hebrew for *ruin* sounds like the Hebrew for *jar* (see verses 1 and 10).
ᵃ3 *Magor-Missabib* means *terror on every side*.

the wealth of this city—all its products, all its valuables and all the treasures of the kings of Judah. They will take it away as plunder and carry it off to Babylon. ⁶And you, Pashhur, and all who live in your house will go into exile to Babylon. There you will die and be buried, you and all your friends to whom you have prophesied lies.' "

■ Jeremiah's Complaint

⁷O LORD, you deceived*b* me, and I was
    deceived;*b*

you overpowered me and prevailed.
I am ridiculed all day long;
    everyone mocks me.
⁸Whenever I speak, I cry out
    proclaiming violence and destruction.
So the word of the LORD has brought me
    insult and reproach all day long.
⁹But if I say, "I will not mention him
    or speak any more in his name,"
his word is in my heart like a fire,
    a fire shut up in my bones.

■ IDOLATRY
IT STILL FLOURISHES, EVEN WITHOUT STATUES

INSIGHT

"THEY HAVE FORSAKEN ME AND MADE THIS A PLACE OF FOREIGN GODS."
■ 19:4

Suppose you found a friend carving a small statue out of a piece of wood. "What are you going to do with that?" you ask. "I'm going to worship it," he says. "I've got a nice spot in my bedroom where I can kneel down and ask it for things."

Or imagine people on a suburban street pooling their wedding rings and other jewellery to make a statue they can put in the park. They plan to kill animals and leave the meat out in front of the statue.

To modern society, idolatry is as weird as cannibalism; we're not tempted to try it. But since a great part of the Old Testament is concerned with idolatry, we need to get some idea of what people saw in it—and why God condemned it.

■ MIXING RELIGIONS
In Jeremiah's day, practically everybody practised idolatry. Israelites had a hard time seeing that a few statues interfered with their relationship with the one true God. They worshipped the God of Abraham, but mixed in the gods of countries surrounding them. They had idols right in the Jerusalem temple (7:30). They could go to worship God right after burning incense to Baal (7:9–10).

They had built shrines on top of many hills—the "high places"—and under the tallest trees so that worship could be carried out conveniently, without a trip to Jerusalem. They ignored the prophets' warnings that God hated this "mixed" religion.

Judah's neighbours believed in many gods, each having its sphere of influence. The Jews themselves had begun to wonder: why should their God be so different? Why should he want to knock out all competition? If idols were a fraud, mere carvings (10:4), why should God worry about them?

■ THE EVILS IDOLS STOOD FOR
Idols were far from innocent, however. They stood for vile, angry gods who could hurt you unless you bartered for peace. The highest sacrifice? Slaughter your own son. The Israelites had adopted this practice (19:5).

According to these idol-worshipping religions, success came through the fertile power of nature and the gods. You could tune in to such power by having sex with temple prostitutes, either male or female. The Israelites also borrowed this (2 Kings 23:7). These ideas disgusted the God of Israel. By mixing such practices with their devotion to him, God's people were becoming confused about his true character. (For more on idolatry, see "Why All the Fuss about Idols?" page 340.)

■ IDOLATRY TODAY
The New Testament broadens the definition of idolatry so that it applies to us, even though we worship no statues. Paul said that greed is idolatry (Ephesians 5:5; Colossians 3:5). The things people get greedy for—money, sex, power, even food—can function as little gods. When we feel depressed, we turn to them for comfort. When we're happy, we give them the credit. We gradually become their slaves. But this is exactly the place for God in our lives, and God alone. If something else takes his place, we are as guilty of idolatry as the people Jeremiah spoke to. God cannot share us. He is either the only God, or he is not God at all.

Jealousy is an ugly emotion, but in some situations it is the only appropriate response. A father is jealous of his children; he will fight never to give them up to another family. A husband is jealous of his wife; he will not share her most intimate love with anyone else. So God feels about his people. They belong to him, and to him alone.

□ LIFE QUESTIONS:
Where do you turn when you're troubled? Do money, success, popularity, or other factors serve as substitutes for God?

*b*7 Or persuaded

20:9 ■ FIRE IN...

When Jeremiah spoke ... complained angrily about th... him. Here he claimed that God... into carrying a message that people ridiculed (verse 7). Jeremiah cursed his own birth, wishing he had been still-born (verses 14–18). Just how did God "overpower" Jeremiah? God's message was like fire in his bones, so powerful that he could not resist telling it. The "force" God used on Jeremiah was the power of truth.

10I hear many whispering,
    "Terror on every side!
    Report him! Let's report him!"
All my friends
    are waiting for me to slip, saying,
"Perhaps he will be deceived;
    then we will prevail over him
    and take our revenge on him."

11But the LORD is with me like a mighty warrior;
    so my persecutors will stumble and not
      prevail.
They will fail and be thoroughly disgraced;
    their dishonour will never be forgotten.
12O LORD Almighty, you who examine the
      righteous
    and probe the heart and mind,
let me see your vengeance upon them,
    for to you I have committed my cause.

13Sing to the LORD!
    Give praise to the LORD!
He rescues the life of the needy
    from the hands of the wicked.

14Cursed be the day I was born!
    May the day my mother bore me not be
      blessed!
15Cursed be the man who brought my father the
      news,
    who made him very glad, saying,
    "A child is born to you—a son!"
16May that man be like the towns
    the LORD overthrew without pity.
May he hear wailing in the morning,
    a battle cry at noon.
17For he did not kill me in the womb,
    with my mother as my grave,
    her womb enlarged for ever.
18Why did I ever come out of the womb
    to see trouble and sorrow
    and to end my days in shame?

■ God Rejects Zedekiah's Request

21 The word came to Jeremiah from the LORD when King Zedekiah sent to him Pashhur son of Malkijah and the priest Zephaniah son of Maaseiah. They said: 2"Enquire now of the LORD for us because Nebuchadnezzara king of Babylon is attacking us. Perhaps the LORD will perform wonders

inside this city... ...ered them, "Tell Zede... ...God of Israel, says: I a... an outstretched hand and a mighty arm in anger and fury and great wrath. 6I will strike down those who live in this city—both men and animals—and they will die of a terrible plague. 7After that, declares the LORD, I will hand over Zedekiah king of Judah, his officials and the people in this city who survive the plague, sword and famine, to Nebuchadnezzar king of Babylon and to their enemies who seek their lives. He will put them to the sword; he will show them no mercy or pity or compassion.'

21:7 ■ GOD'S ANSWER: NO

Prayer changes things, but the results depend on who's asking and what their motives are. Faced with a crisis, King Zedekiah asked Jeremiah to pray to God on his behalf. He hoped for a miracle, but the answer Jeremiah received was anything but good news. Not only would God not help, he would fight against Zedekiah and his people. Why was God's response so negative? Because nobody had paid attention to his warnings. Judah wanted to be rescued—not to alter its behaviour.

8"Furthermore, tell the people, 'This is what the LORD says: See, I am setting before you the way of life and the way of death. 9Whoever stays in this city will die by the sword, famine or plague. But whoever goes out and surrenders to the Babylonians who are besieging you will live; he will escape with his life. 10I have determined to do this city harm and not good, declares the LORD. It will be given into the hands of the king of Babylon, and he will destroy it with fire.'

11"Moreover, say to the royal house of Judah, 'Hear the word of the LORD; 12O house of David, this is what the LORD says:

" 'Administer justice every morning;
    rescue from the hand of his oppressor
    the one who has been robbed,
or my wrath will break out and burn like fire
    because of the evil you have done—
    burn with no-one to quench it.
13I am against you, ⌐Jerusalem,⌐
    you who live above this valley
    on the rocky plateau,

                declares the LORD—
you who say, "Who can come against us?
    Who can enter our refuge?"
14I will punish you as your deeds deserve,
                declares the LORD.
I will kindle a fire in your forests
    that will consume everything around you.' "

a2 Hebrew Nebuchadrezzar, of which Nebuchadnezzar is a variant; here and often in Jeremiah and Ezekiel   b4 Or Chaldeans; also in verse 9

■ Judgment Against Evil

22 This is wh... ...ou, your
message ... ...me through these
palace ... LORD says: Do what is just
of Judah. ... the from the hand of his oppressor the
offic... ...ho has been robbed. Do no wrong or violence
to the alien, the fatherless or the widow, and do not
shed innocent blood in this place. 4For if you are
careful to carry out these commands, then kings
who sit on David's throne will come through the
gates of this palace, riding in chariots and on horses,
accompanied by their officials and their people.
5But if you do not obey these commands, declares
the LORD, I swear by myself that this palace will become a ruin.' "

6For this is what the LORD says about the palace
of the king of Judah:

"Though you are like Gilead to me,
    like the summit of Lebanon,
I will surely make you like a desert,
    like towns not inhabited.
7I will send destroyers against you,
    each man with his weapons,
and they will cut up your fine cedar beams
    and throw them into the fire.

8"People from many nations will pass by this city
and will ask one another, 'Why has the LORD done
such a thing to this great city?' 9And the answer will
be: 'Because they have forsaken the covenant of the
LORD their God and have worshipped and served
other gods.' "

10Do not weep for the dead ˻king˼ or mourn his
    loss;
    rather, weep bitterly for him who is exiled,
because he will never return
    nor see his native land again.

11For this is what the LORD says about Shalluma son
of Josiah, who succeeded his father as king of Judah
but has gone from this place: "He will never return.
12He will die in the place where they have led him
captive; he will not see this land again."

13"Woe to him who builds his palace by
        unrighteousness,
    his upper rooms by injustice,
making his countrymen work for nothing,
    not paying them for their labour.
14He says, 'I will build myself a great palace
    with spacious upper rooms.'
So he makes large windows in it,
    panels it with cedar
    and decorates it in red.

15"Does it make you a king
    to have more and more cedar?
Did not your father have food and drink?
    He did what was right and just,
    so all went well with him.
16He defended the cause of the poor and needy,
    and so all went well.
Is that not what it means to know me?"

eyes and your heart
    are set only on dishonest gain,
on shedding innocent blood
    and on oppression and extortion."

18Therefore this is what the LORD says about Jehoiakim son of Josiah king of Judah:

"They will not mourn for him:
    'Alas, my brother! Alas, my sister!'
They will not mourn for him:
    'Alas, my master! Alas, his splendour!'
19He will have the burial of a donkey—
    dragged away and thrown
    outside the gates of Jerusalem."

20"Go up to Lebanon and cry out,
    let your voice be heard in Bashan,
cry out from Abarim,
    for all your allies are crushed.
21I warned you when you felt secure,
    but you said, 'I will not listen!'
This has been your way from your youth;
    you have not obeyed me.
22The wind will drive all your shepherds away,
    and your allies will go into exile.
Then you will be ashamed and disgraced
    because of all your wickedness.
23You who live in 'Lebanon',b
    who are nestled in cedar buildings,
how you will groan when pangs come upon
        you,
    pain like that of a woman in labour!

24"As surely as I live," declares the LORD, "even if
you, Jehoiachinc son of Jehoiakim king of Judah,
were a signet ring on my right hand, I would still
pull you off. 25I will hand you over to those who
seek your life, those you fear—to Nebuchadnezzar
king of Babylon and to the Babylonians.d 26I will
hurl you and the mother who gave you birth into
another country, where neither of you was born,
and there you both will die. 27You will never come
back to the land you long to return to."

28Is this man Jehoiachin a despised, broken pot,
    an object no-one wants?
Why will he and his children be hurled out,
    cast into a land they do not know?
29O land, land, land,
    hear the word of the LORD!
30This is what the LORD says:
"Record this man as if childless,
    a man who will not prosper in his lifetime,
for none of his offspring will prosper,
    none will sit on the throne of David
    or rule any more in Judah."

■ The Righteous Branch

23 "Woe to the shepherds who are destroying
    and scattering the sheep of my pasture!" de-
clares the LORD. 2Therefore this is what the LORD,
the God of Israel, says to the shepherds who tend
my people: "Because you have scattered my flock
and driven them away and have not bestowed care
on them, I will bestow punishment on you for the

---

a 11 Also called *Jehoahaz*   b 23 That is, the palace in Jerusalem (see 1 Kings 7:2)   c 24 Hebrew *Coniah*, a variant of *Jehoiachin*; also in verse 28
d 25 Or *Chaldeans*

evil yo...
will gather...
countries where...
them back to their p...
ful and increase in numb...
over them who will tend th...
longer be afraid or terrified, nor...
ing," declares the LORD.

5"The days are coming," declares the LORD,
    "when I will raise up to David*a* a righteous
        Branch,
a King who will reign wisely
    and do what is just and right in the land.
6In his days Judah will be saved
    and Israel will live in safety.
This is the name by which he will be called:
    The LORD Our Righteousness.

23:6 ■ THE MESSIANIC PROMISE
Long before, God had promised David that his
descendants would always rule Israel. But the
kings who followed David had been more like
wolves than shepherds of God's people. Jeremiah
predicted that the kings of his day would either be
killed or carried into captivity—which in fact
occurred. He also predicted that a good king
would replace them—the Messiah.

7"So then, the days are coming," declares the LORD,
"when people will no longer say, 'As surely as the
LORD lives, who brought the Israelites up out of
Egypt,' 8but they will say, 'As surely as the LORD
lives, who brought the descendants of Israel up out
of the land of the north and out of all the countries
where he had banished them.' Then they will live in
their own land."

■ Lying Prophets
9Concerning the prophets:

My heart is broken within me;
    all my bones tremble.
I am like a drunken man,
    like a man overcome by wine,
because of the LORD
    and his holy words.
10The land is full of adulterers;
    because of the curse*b* the land lies
        parched*c*
    and the pastures in the desert are withered.
The ⌊prophets⌋ follow an evil course
    and use their power unjustly.

11"Both prophet and priest are godless;
    even in my temple I find their wickedness,"
                declares the LORD.

12"Therefore their path will become slippery;
    they will be banished to darkness
    and there they will fall.
I will bring disaster on them
    in the year they are punished,"
                declares the LORD.

13"Among the prophets of Samaria

... repulsive thing:
...Baal...Israel astray.
the people of Jerusalem...of Jerusalem...ble...lie...

15Therefore, this is what the LORD Almighty says
concerning the prophets:

"I will make them eat bitter food
    and drink poisoned water,
because from the prophets of Jerusalem
    ungodliness has spread throughout the land."

16This is what the LORD Almighty says:

"Do not listen to what the prophets are
        prophesying to you;
    they fill you with false hopes.
They speak visions from their own minds,
    not from the mouth of the LORD.
17They keep saying to those who despise me,
    'The LORD says: You will have peace.'
And to all who follow the stubbornness of their
        hearts
    they say, 'No harm will come to you.'
18But which of them has stood in the council of
        the LORD
    to see or to hear his word?
    Who has listened and heard his word?
19See, the storm of the LORD
    will burst out in wrath,
a whirlwind swirling down
    on the heads of the wicked.
20The anger of the LORD will not turn back
    until he fully accomplishes
    the purposes of his heart.
In days to come
    you will understand it clearly.
21I did not send these prophets,
    yet they have run with their message;
I did not speak to them,
    yet they have prophesied.
22But if they had stood in my council,
    they would have proclaimed my words to
        my people
and would have turned them from their evil
        ways
    and from their evil deeds.

23"Am I only a God nearby,"
                declares the LORD,
    "and not a God far away?
24Can anyone hide in secret places
    so that I cannot see him?"
                declares the LORD.
"Do not I fill heaven and earth?"
                declares the LORD.

25"I have heard what the prophets say who
prophesy lies in my name. They say, 'I had a dream!
I had a dream!' 26How long will this continue in the
hearts of these lying prophets, who prophesy the

---

*a*5 Or up from David's line   *b*10 Or because of these things   *c*10 Or land mourns

delusions of their ... who has my
dreams they tell ...at has straw to do
forget my na... the LORD. 29"Is not my word
through ... res the LORD, "and like a hammer that
dream ... a rock in pieces?

30"Therefore," declares the LORD, "I am against the prophets who steal from one another words supposedly from me. 31Yes," declares the LORD, "I am against the prophets who wag their own tongues and yet declare, 'The LORD declares.' 32Indeed, I am against those who prophesy false dreams," declares the LORD. "They tell them and lead my people astray with their reckless lies, yet I did not send or appoint them. They do not benefit these people in the least," declares the LORD.

> ### 23:25 ■ QUESTIONABLE DREAMS
> For the casual observer, it must have been difficult to tell real prophets from false prophets in Jeremiah's day. Jeremiah was outnumbered by optimists who claimed that God gave them dreams and messages. In reality, their dreams had nothing to do with God's word, and anyone who compared their message with Scripture could have seen the difference. They predicted peace when God had promised severe punishment for his people's sins.

■ False Oracles and False Prophets

33"When these people, or a prophet or a priest, ask you, 'What is the oracle*d* of the LORD?' say to them, 'What oracle?*e* I will forsake you, declares the LORD.' 34If a prophet or a priest or anyone else claims, 'This is the oracle of the LORD,' I will punish that man and his household. 35This is what each of you keeps on saying to his friend or relative: 'What is the LORD's answer?' or 'What has the LORD spoken?' 36But you must not mention 'the oracle of the LORD' again, because every man's own word becomes his oracle and so you distort the words of the living God, the LORD Almighty, our God. 37This is what you keep saying to a prophet: 'What is the LORD's answer to you?' or 'What has the LORD spoken?' 38Although you claim, 'This is the oracle of the LORD,' this is what the LORD says: You used the words, 'This is the oracle of the LORD,' even though I told you that you must not claim, 'This is the oracle of the LORD.' 39Therefore, I will surely forget you and cast you out of my presence along with the city I gave to you and your fathers. 40I will bring upon you everlasting disgrace — everlasting shame that will not be forgotten."

■ Two Baskets of Figs

24 After Jehoiachin*a* son of Jehoiakim king of Judah and the officials, the craftsmen and the artisans of Judah were carried into exile from Jerusalem to Babylon by Nebuchadnezzar king of Bab-

...wed me two baskets of figs placed ... of the temple of the LORD. 2One basket had very good figs, like those that ripen early; the other basket had very poor figs, so bad that they could not be eaten.

3Then the LORD asked me, "What do you see, Jeremiah?"

"Figs," I answered. "The good ones are very good, but the poor ones are so bad that they cannot be eaten."

4Then the word of the LORD came to me: 5"This is what the LORD, the God of Israel, says: 'Like these good figs, I regard as good the exiles from Judah, whom I sent away from this place to the land of the Babylonians.*b* 6My eyes will watch over them for their good, and I will bring them back to this land. I will build them up and not tear them down; I will plant them and not uproot them. 7I will give them a heart to know me, that I am the LORD. They will be my people, and I will be their God, for they will return to me with all their heart.

8" 'But like the poor figs, which are so bad that they cannot be eaten,' says the LORD, 'so will I deal with Zedekiah king of Judah, his officials and the survivors from Jerusalem, whether they remain in this land or live in Egypt. 9I will make them abhorrent and an offence to all the kingdoms of the earth, a reproach and a byword, an object of ridicule and cursing, wherever I banish them. 10I will send the sword, famine and plague against them until they are destroyed from the land I gave to them and their fathers.' "

■ Seventy Years of Captivity

25 The word came to Jeremiah concerning all the people of Judah in the fourth year of Jehoiakim son of Josiah king of Judah, which was the first year of Nebuchadnezzar king of Babylon. 2So Jeremiah the prophet said to all the people of Judah and to all those living in Jerusalem: 3For twenty-three years—from the thirteenth year of Josiah son of Amon king of Judah until this very day—the word of the LORD has come to me and I have spoken to you again and again, but you have not listened.

4And though the LORD has sent all his servants the prophets to you again and again, you have not listened or paid any attention. 5They said, "Turn now, each of you, from your evil ways and your evil practices, and you can stay in the land the LORD gave to you and your fathers for ever and ever. 6Do not follow other gods to serve and worship them; do not provoke me to anger with what your hands have made. Then I will not harm you."

7"But you did not listen to me," declares the LORD, "and you have provoked me with what your hands have made, and you have brought harm to yourselves."

8Therefore the LORD Almighty says this: "Because you have not listened to my words, 9I will summon all the peoples of the north and my servant Nebuchadnezzar king of Babylon," declares the LORD, "and I will bring them against this land and its inhabitants and against all the surrounding nations. I will completely destroy*a* them and make them an

d 33 Or burden (see Septuagint and Vulgate)   *e 33* Hebrew; Septuagint and Vulgate 'You are the burden'; the Hebrew for oracle and burden is the same.
a 1 Hebrew Jeconiah, a variant of Jehoiachin   *b 5* Or Chaldeans   *a 9* The Hebrew term refers to the irrevocable giving over of things or persons to the LORD, often by totally destroying them.

object ...
10I will ban...
ness, the voices
of millstones and t...
country will become
these nations will serve the...
enty years.

body thrown into...
people.

JEREM...

25:11 ■ GONE, BUT NOT FOR EVER
Seventy years of captivity, God predicted. This probably represents a rounded-up number; the precise length of the captivity can be calculated in different ways, since several waves of captives were taken away and several waves of exiles returned. The number 70 has a deeper significance, though: it says that the punishment, though long and severe (at least two generations would die far from home) would not last for ever. Unlike other nations taken into captivity, Israel will return. God's judgment is limited, but his mercy is for ever.

12"But when the seventy years are fulfilled, I will punish the king of Babylon and his nation, the land of the Babylonians,*b* for their guilt," declares the LORD, "and will make it desolate for ever. 13I will bring upon that land all the things I have spoken against it, all that are written in this book and prophesied by Jeremiah against all the nations. 14They themselves will be enslaved by many nations and great kings; I will repay them according to their deeds and the work of their hands."

■ The Cup of God's Wrath
15This is what the LORD, the God of Israel, said to me: "Take from my hand this cup filled with the wine of my wrath and make all the nations to whom I send you drink it. 16When they drink it, they will stagger and go mad because of the sword I will send among them."

17So I took the cup from the LORD's hand and made all the nations to whom he sent me drink it: 18Jerusalem and the towns of Judah, its kings and officials, to make them a ruin and an object of horror and scorn and cursing, as they are today; 19Pharaoh king of Egypt, his attendants, his officials and all his people, 20and all the foreign people there; all the kings of Uz; all the kings of the Philistines (those of Ashkelon, Gaza, Ekron, and the people left at Ashdod); 21Edom, Moab and Ammon; 22all the kings of Tyre and Sidon; the kings of the coastlands across the sea; 23Dedan, Tema, Buz and all who are in distant places;*c* 24all the kings of Arabia and all the kings of the foreign people who live in the desert; 25all the kings of Zimri, Elam and Media; 26and all the kings of the north, near and far, one after the other — all the kingdoms on the face of the earth. And after all of them, the king of Sheshach*d* will drink it too.

27"Then tell them, 'This is what the LORD Almighty, the God of Israel, says: Drink, get drunk and vomit, and fall to rise no more because of the sword I will send among you.' 28But if they refuse

... from your hand and drink, ...
... LORD Almighty says: You mus...
... to bring disaster on th...
... ill you indeed go unp...
... ed, for I am calling...
... the earth, de...
... them

" 'The LORD will roar from on high;
he will thunder from his holy dwelling
and roar mightily against his land.
He will shout like those who tread the grapes,
shout against all who live on the earth.
31The tumult will resound to the ends of the earth,
for the LORD will bring charges against the nations;
he will bring judgment on all mankind
and put the wicked to the sword,' "
declares the LORD.

32This is what the LORD Almighty says:

"Look! Disaster is spreading
from nation to nation;
a mighty storm is rising
from the ends of the earth."

33At that time those slain by the LORD will be everywhere — from one end of the earth to the other. They will not be mourned or gathered up or buried, but will be like refuse lying on the ground.

34Weep and wail, you shepherds;
roll in the dust, you leaders of the flock.
For your time to be slaughtered has come;
you will fall and be shattered like fine pottery.
35The shepherds will have nowhere to flee,
the leaders of the flock no place to escape.
36Hear the cry of the shepherds,
the wailing of the leaders of the flock,
for the LORD is destroying their pasture.
37The peaceful meadows will be laid waste
because of the fierce anger of the LORD.
38Like a lion he will leave his lair,
and their land will become desolate
because of the sword*e* of the oppressor
and because of the LORD's fierce anger.

■ Jeremiah Threatened With Death
26 Early in the reign of Jehoiakim son of Josiah king of Judah, this word came from the LORD: 2"This is what the LORD says: Stand in the courtyard of the LORD's house and speak to all the people of the towns of Judah who come to worship in the house of the LORD. Tell them everything I command you; do not omit a word. 3Perhaps they will listen and each will turn from his evil way. Then I will relent and not bring on them the disaster I was planning because of the evil they have done. 4Say to them, 'This is what the LORD says: If you do not listen to me and follow my law, which I have set before you, 5and if you do not listen to the words of my servants the prophets, whom I have sent to you again and

b 12 Or *Chaldeans*   *c 23* Or *who clip the hair by their foreheads*   *d 26 Sheshach* is a cryptogram for Babylon.   *e 38* Some Hebrew manuscripts and Septuagint (see also Jer. 46:16 and 50:16); most Hebrew manuscripts *anger* again (though you ... make this house ... of cursing am... The priests, the prophets and all the people ... house of ... finished telling all the LORD had commanded ... him and said, "You must die! 9Why do you prophesy in the LORD's name that this house will be like Shiloh and this city will be desolate and deserted?" And all the people crowded around Jeremiah in the house of the LORD.

10When the officials of Judah heard about these things, they went up from the royal palace to the house of the LORD and took their places at the entrance of the New Gate of the LORD's house. 11Then the priests and the prophets said to the officials and all the people, "This man should be sentenced to death because he has prophesied against this city. You have heard it with your own ears!"

12Then Jeremiah said to all the officials and all the people: "The LORD sent me to prophesy against this house and this city all the things you have heard. 13Now reform your ways and your actions and obey the LORD your God. Then the LORD will relent and not bring the disaster he has pronounced against you. 14As for me, I am in your hands; do with me whatever you think is good and right. 15Be assured, however, that if you put me to death, you will bring the guilt of innocent blood on yourselves and on this city and on those who live in it, for in truth the LORD has sent me to you to speak all these words in your hearing."

16Then the officials and all the people said to the priests and the prophets, "This man should not be sentenced to death! He has spoken to us in the name of the LORD our God."

17Some of the elders of the land stepped forward and said to the entire assembly of people, 18"Micah of Moresheth prophesied in the days of Hezekiah king of Judah. He told all the people of Judah, 'This is what the LORD Almighty says:

" 'Zion will be ploughed like a field,
Jerusalem will become a heap of rubble,
the temple hill a mound overgrown with
thickets.'a

19"Did Hezekiah king of Judah or anyone else in Judah put him to death? Did not Hezekiah fear the LORD and seek his favour? And did not the LORD relent, so that he did not bring the disaster he pronounced against them? We are about to bring a terrible disaster on ourselves!"

20(Now Uriah son of Shemaiah from Kiriath Jearim was another man who prophesied in the name of the LORD; he prophesied the same things against this city and this land as Jeremiah did. 21When King Jehoiakim and all his officers and officials heard his words, the king sought to put him to death. But Uriah heard of it and fled in fear to Egypt. 22King Jehoiakim, however, sent Elnathan son of Acbor to Egypt, along with some other men. 23They brought Uriah out of Egypt and took him to King Jehoiakim, who had him struck down with a sword and his

---

the burial place of the common

26:19 ■ SCRIPTURE SAVES A LIFE
Jeremiah's scorn for the temple was considered sacrilege and might have cost him his life. (Another prophet, Uriah, was assassinated for the same message—see verses 20–23.) But some of the elders remembered the treatment given Micah years before. Hezekiah—a good king—had listened to Micah. Based on this precedent, Jeremiah was allowed to live.

24Furthermore, Ahikam son of Shaphan supported Jeremiah, and so he was not handed over to the people to be put to death.

■ Judah to Serve Nebuchadnezzar

27 Early in the reign of Zedekiaha son of Josiah king of Judah, this word came to Jeremiah from the LORD: 2This is what the LORD said to me: "Make a yoke out of straps and crossbars and put it on your neck. 3Then send word to the kings of Edom, Moab, Ammon, Tyre and Sidon through the envoys who have come to Jerusalem to Zedekiah king of Judah. 4Give them a message for their masters and say, 'This is what the LORD Almighty, the God of Israel, says: "Tell this to your masters: 5With my great power and outstretched arm I made the earth and its people and the animals that are on it, and I give it to anyone I please. 6Now I will hand all your countries over to my servant Nebuchadnezzar king of Babylon; I will make even the wild animals subject to him. 7All nations will serve him and his son and his grandson until the time for his land comes; then many nations and great kings will subjugate him.

8" 'If, however, any nation or kingdom will not serve Nebuchadnezzar king of Babylon or bow its neck under his yoke, I will punish that nation with the sword, famine and plague, declares the LORD, until I destroy it by his hand. 9So do not listen to your prophets, your diviners, your interpreters of dreams, your mediums or your sorcerers who tell you, 'You will not serve the king of Babylon.' 10They prophesy lies to you that will only serve to remove you far from your lands; I will banish you and you will perish. 11But if any nation will bow its neck under the yoke of the king of Babylon and serve him, I will let that nation remain in its own land to till it and to live there, declares the LORD.' " '

12I gave the same message to Zedekiah king of Judah. I said, "Bow your neck under the yoke of the king of Babylon; serve him and his people, and you will live. 13Why will you and your people die by the sword, famine and plague with which the LORD has threatened any nation that will not serve the king of Babylon? 14Do not listen to the words of the prophets who say to you, 'You will not serve the king of Babylon,' for they are prophesying lies to you. 15I have not sent them,' declares the LORD. 'They are prophesying lies in my name. Therefore, I will

---

a 18 Micah 3:12   *a 1* A few Hebrew manuscripts and Syriac (see also Jer. 27:3, 12 and 28:1); most Hebrew manuscripts *Jehoiakim* (most Septuagint manuscripts do not have this verse.)

27:12 ■ COUNSE...

By the time Zedekiah too... surrendered to Babylon. Two ... had already been exiled, including ... King Jehoiachin. The desire for independence ... not die easily, however. Zedekiah, who had been put into office as a puppet king, soon began scheming for revolution. Jeremiah persistently counselled submission to Babylon—unpopular advice that nearly cost him his life when he was accused of treason.

...m Babylon. [7]Nevertheless, ...in your hearing and in the ... early times the pro... have prophesied ... countries and ... prophesies ...by the

the neck of the prophet Jeremiah and ...

he said before all the people, "This is what the LORD says: 'In the same way will I break the yoke of Nebuchadnezzar king of Babylon off the neck of all the nations within two years.' " At this, the prophet Jeremiah went on his way.

[12]Shortly after the prophet Hananiah had broken the yoke off the neck of the prophet Jeremiah, the word of the LORD came to Jeremiah: [13]"Go and tell Hananiah, 'This is what the LORD says: You have broken a wooden yoke, but in its place you will get a yoke of iron. [14]This is what the LORD Almighty, the God of Israel, says: I will put an iron yoke on the necks of all these nations to make them serve Nebuchadnezzar king of Babylon, and they will serve him. I will even give him control over the wild animals.' "

[15]Then the prophet Jeremiah said to Hananiah the prophet, "Listen, Hananiah! The LORD has not sent you, yet you have persuaded this nation to trust in lies. [16]Therefore, this is what the LORD says: 'I am about to remove you from the face of the earth. This very year you are going to die, because you have preached rebellion against the LORD.' "

[17]In the seventh month of that same year, Hananiah the prophet died.

■ A Letter to the Exiles

29 This is the text of the letter that the prophet Jeremiah sent from Jerusalem to the surviving elders among the exiles and to the priests, the prophets and all the other people Nebuchadnezzar had carried into exile from Jerusalem to Babylon. [2](This was after King Jehoiachin and the queen mother, the court officials and the leaders of Judah and Jerusalem, the craftsmen and the artisans had gone into exile from Jerusalem.) [3]He entrusted the letter to Elasah son of Shaphan and to Gemariah son of Hilkiah, whom Zedekiah king of Judah sent to King Nebuchadnezzar in Babylon. It said:

[4]This is what the LORD Almighty, the God of Israel, says to all those I carried into exile from Jerusalem to Babylon: [5]"Build houses and settle down; plant gardens and eat what they produce. [6]Marry and have sons and daughters; find wives for your sons and give your daughters in marriage, so that they too may have sons and daughters. Increase in number there; do not decrease. [7]Also, seek the peace and prosperity of the city to which I have carried you into exile. Pray to the LORD for it, because if it prospers, you too will prosper. [8]Yes, this is what the LORD Almighty, the God of Israel, says: "Do not let the prophets and diviners among you deceive you. Do not listen to the dreams you encourage them to have. [9]They

[16]Then I said to the priests and all these people, "This is what the LORD says: Do not listen to the prophets who say, 'Very soon now the articles from the LORD's house will be brought back from Babylon.' They are prophesying lies to you. [17]Do not listen to them. Serve the king of Babylon, and you will live. Why should this city become a ruin? [18]If they are prophets and have the word of the LORD, let them plead with the LORD Almighty that the furnishings remaining in the house of the LORD and in the palace of the king of Judah and in Jerusalem not be taken to Babylon. [19]For this is what the LORD Almighty says about the pillars, the Sea, the movable stands and the other furnishings that are left in this city, [20]which Nebuchadnezzar king of Babylon did not take away when he carried Jehoiachin[b] son of Jehoiakim king of Judah into exile from Jerusalem to Babylon, along with all the nobles of Judah and Jerusalem—[21]yes, this is what the LORD Almighty, the God of Israel, says about the things that are left in the house of the LORD and in the palace of the king of Judah and in Jerusalem: [22]They will be taken to Babylon and there they will remain until the day I come for them,' declares the LORD. 'Then I will bring them back and restore them to this place.' "

■ The False Prophet Hananiah

28 In the fifth month of that same year, the fourth year, early in the reign of Zedekiah king of Judah, the prophet Hananiah son of Azzur, who was from Gibeon, said to me in the house of the LORD in the presence of the priests and all the people: [2]"This is what the LORD Almighty, the God of Israel, says: 'I will break the yoke of the king of Babylon. [3]Within two years I will bring back to this place all the articles of the LORD's house that Nebuchadnezzar king of Babylon removed from here and took to Babylon. [4]I will also bring back to this place Jehoiachin son of Jehoiakim king of Judah and all the other exiles from Judah who went to Babylon,' declares the LORD, 'for I will break the yoke of the king of Babylon.' "

[5]Then the prophet Jeremiah replied to the prophet Hananiah before the priests and all the people who were standing in the house of the LORD. [6]He said, "Amen! May the LORD do so! May the LORD fulfil the words you have prophesied by bringing the articles of the LORD's house and all the exiles back to

b 20 Hebrew *Jeconiah*, a variant of *Jehoiachin*; also in 28:4 and 29:2

are prophesying...
not sent them...

29:1 ... work, a sizable
During ... already living in Babylon.
co... Daniel, a young man who
...to tremendous power in court, and the
prophet Ezekiel. Ezekiel was preaching at the
same time as Jeremiah, and their messages are
similar in many ways. Since neither one mentions
the other, however, we can't be sure whether they
were acquainted.

¹⁰This is what the LORD says: "When seventy
years are completed for Babylon, I will come
to you and fulfil my gracious promise to bring
you back to this place. ¹¹For I know the plans
I have for you," declares the LORD, "plans to
prosper you and not to harm you, plans to give
you hope and a future. ¹²Then you will call
upon me and come and pray to me, and I will
listen to you. ¹³You will seek me and find me
when you seek me with all your heart. ¹⁴I will
be found by you," declares the LORD, "and will
bring you back from captivity.ᵃ I will gather
you from all the nations and places where I
have banished you," declares the LORD, "and
will bring you back to the place from which I
carried you into exile."

¹⁵You may say, "The LORD has raised up
prophets for us in Babylon," ¹⁶but this is what
the LORD says about the king who sits on
David's throne and all the people who remain
in this city, your countrymen who did not go
with you into exile—¹⁷yes, this is what the
LORD Almighty says: "I will send the sword,
famine and plague against them and I will make
them like poor figs that are so bad they cannot
be eaten. ¹⁸I will pursue them with the sword,
famine and plague and will make them abhorrent to all the kingdoms of the earth and an
object of cursing and horror, of scorn and
reproach, among all the nations where I drive
them. ¹⁹For they have not listened to my
words," declares the LORD, "words that I sent to
them again and again by my servants the
prophets. And you exiles have not listened
either," declares the LORD.

²⁰Therefore, hear the word of the LORD, all
you exiles whom I have sent away from Jerusalem to Babylon. ²¹This is what the LORD
Almighty, the God of Israel, says about Ahab
son of Kolaiah and Zedekiah son of Maaseiah,
who are prophesying lies to you in my name:
"I will hand them over to Nebuchadnezzar king
of Babylon, and he will put them to death before your very eyes. ²²Because of them, all the
exiles from Judah who are in Babylon will use
this curse: 'The LORD treat you like Zedekiah
and Ahab, whom the king of Babylon burned in
the fire.' ²³For they have done outrageous
things in Israel; they have committed adultery

...ours' wives and in my name
...oken lies, which I did not tell them to
do. I know it and am a witness to it," declares
the LORD.

■ Message to Shemaiah
²⁴Tell Shemaiah the Nehelamite, ²⁵"This is what
the LORD Almighty, the God of Israel, says: You sent
letters in your own name to all the people in Jerusalem, to Zephaniah son of Maaseiah the priest, and
to all the other priests. You said to Zephaniah,
²⁶'The LORD has appointed you priest in place of Jehoiada to be in charge of the house of the LORD; you
should put any madman who acts like a prophet into
the stocks and neck-irons. ²⁷So why have you not
reprimanded Jeremiah from Anathoth, who poses as
a prophet among you? ²⁸He has sent this message to
us in Babylon: It will be a long time. Therefore build
houses and settle down; plant gardens and eat what
they produce.' "

²⁹Zephaniah the priest, however, read the letter
to Jeremiah the prophet. ³⁰Then the word of the
LORD came to Jeremiah: ³¹"Send this message to all
the exiles: 'This is what the LORD says about Shemaiah the Nehelamite: Because Shemaiah has
prophesied to you, even though I did not send him,
and has led you to believe a lie, ³²this is what the
LORD says: I will surely punish Shemaiah the Nehelamite and his descendants. He will have no-one left
among this people, nor will he see the good things
I will do for my people, declares the LORD, because
he has preached rebellion against me.' "

■ Restoration of Israel
30 This is the word that came to Jeremiah from
the LORD: ²"This is what the LORD, the God of
Israel, says: 'Write in a book all the words I have spoken to you. ³The days are coming,' declares the
LORD, 'when I will bring my people Israel and Judah
back from captivityᵃ and restore them to the land
I gave to their forefathers to possess,' says the LORD."

⁴These are the words the LORD spoke concerning
Israel and Judah: ⁵"This is what the LORD says:

" 'Cries of fear are heard—
        terror, not peace.
⁶Ask and see:
        Can a man bear children?
Then why do I see every strong man
        with his hands on his stomach like a woman
            in labour,
        every face turned deathly pale?
⁷How awful that day will be!
        None will be like it.
It will be a time of trouble for Jacob,
        but he will be saved out of it.

⁸" 'In that day,' declares the LORD Almighty,
        'I will break the yoke off their necks
and will tear off their bonds;
        no longer will foreigners enslave them.
⁹Instead, they will serve the LORD their God
        and David their king,
            whom I will raise up for them.

¹⁰" 'So do not fear, O Jacob my servant;

ᵃ 14 Or will restore your fortunes   ᵃ 3 Or will restore the fortunes of my people Israel and Judah

THE PEOPLE WHO REFUSE TO DIE
THEIR POWERFUL NEIGHBOURS HAVE DISAPPEARED – BUT THE JEWS LIVE ON

INSIGHT

"I WILL SURELY SAVE YOU OUT OF A DISTANT PLACE, YOUR DESCENDANTS FROM THE LAND OF THEIR EXILE. JACOB WILL AGAIN HAVE PEACE AND SECURITY, AND NO-ONE WILL MAKE HIM AFRAID."
■ 30:10

If you get lost in North London, and wander into the Bethnal Green area, prepare to be surprised. Boys playing football look odd: long, uncut curls of hair trail from above their ears down past their shoulders. Men dressed in black, with long, untrimmed beards, coach from the sidelines. All the women you see wear wigs because they've shaved their heads completely. Is this a new cult from the Far East? The latest fashion from Covent Garden?

You've stumbled into a community of Hasidic Jews. They live, not by the latest craze, but by ancient rules based on Old Testament laws. They follow complicated dietary regulations. They keep one set of bowls for meat, and another for dairy products. Young men devote long hours of study to the Hebrew Old Testament. Though they are English and live in London, their cultural compass points to Mount Sinai, where God gave Moses the Law.

■ JEWS OUTLIVED THEIR ENEMIES
The Jewish people have survived, astonishingly. Who in Jeremiah's time could have predicted their persistence, when they were hemmed in and threatened with total destruction? The Babylonians conquered and carried them into exile. But where are the Babylonians today? They have vanished. Desert sand covers their capital.

The story of the Jews is a long chronicle of discrimination, exile, punishment and slaughter. Against no other people have such destructive measures been taken. Yet they have survived, and thrived. Their language endures. Their book, the Old Testament, is part of the great best-seller of all time. They have rebuilt their nation.

Even more remarkably, this durability was predicted in writing 2,500 years ago. God promised in the clearest terms that he would never reject his people.

■ THE NEW COVENANT
Jeremiah, known for his stinging denunciations and repeated predictions of savage destruction, also brought word of God's eternal faithfulness and of a new covenant replacing the old, broken one. The new covenant would improve generously on the old one, Jeremiah said. God would no longer simply list rules for his people to obey. He would plant those rules in their hearts, so they would want to obey (31:33). Each individual would know the Lord personally. God would offer forgiveness for sins.

Jeremiah promised more than that. He said a new king from David's line would come to rule. He would be called "The LORD Our Righteousness" (23:5–8). Israel would return from exile to their land. They would farm there again. They would rebuild Jerusalem and again worship God there. Jeremiah wrote these rosy words in the face of Israel's worst catastrophe.

Jeremiah didn't just deliver these messages. He acted them out. He made what was either one of the stupidest financial investments of all time, or a remarkable act of faith. He bought property from a relative at the height of the Babylonian siege (chapter 32). God had promised Jeremiah that someday the property would be worth money again, to his children or grandchildren. He believed and invested in that distant prospect. He bet on the survival of Israel.

■ THE FULFILMENT OF PROPHECY
Christians agree that the new king Jeremiah predicted was Jesus. They agree that Jesus brought the new covenant, which puts the law into people's hearts and enables them to know God. But on the restoration of Israel Christians hold different opinions. Some feel that the modern nation of Israel is, at least partly, the reincarnated nation Jeremiah wrote about. Others feel that the New Testament teaches that Christians of all races form Jeremiah's "new nation" of God's people, and that the promises apply allegorically to them.

All agree, though, that what Jesus set out to do is not yet finished. Someday he will destroy the forces of evil and fully establish his new kingdom.

□ LIFE QUESTIONS:
Jeremiah bought a field as a sign of his faith in the future of Israel. By what "investments" can you demonstrate practical faith in God's kingdom?

do not be dismayed, O Israel,'
>   declares the LORD.
'I will surely save you out of a distant place,
    your descendants from the land of their
        exile.
Jacob will again have peace and security,
    and no-one will make him afraid.
¹¹I am with you and will save you,'
    declares the LORD.
'Though I completely destroy all the nations
    among which I scatter you,
    I will not completely destroy you.
I will discipline you but only with justice;
    I will not let you go entirely unpunished.'

30:11 ■ FREE AGAIN

Though Jeremiah spoke mainly of God's
judgment, he also offered hope beyond judgment.
Someday, Israel would be free again. The
prophecy of this verse has been fulfilled: not one
of the powerful cultures surrounding Israel has
endured, but the Jews have survived with their
language, customs, and religion intact.

¹²"This is what the LORD says:

" 'Your wound is incurable,
    your injury beyond healing.
¹³There is no-one to plead your cause,
    no remedy for your sore,
    no healing for you.
¹⁴All your allies have forgotten you;
    they care nothing for you.
I have struck you as an enemy would
    and punished you as would the cruel,
because your guilt is so great
    and your sins so many.
¹⁵Why do you cry out over your wound,
    your pain that has no cure?
Because of your great guilt and many sins
    I have done these things to you.

¹⁶" 'But all who devour you will be devoured;
    all your enemies will go into exile.
Those who plunder you will be plundered;
    all who make spoil of you I will despoil.
¹⁷But I will restore you to health
    and heal your wounds,'
>   declares the LORD,
'because you are called an outcast,
    Zion for whom no-one cares.'

¹⁸"This is what the LORD says:

" 'I will restore the fortunes of Jacob's tents
    and have compassion on his dwellings;
the city will be rebuilt on her ruins,
    and the palace will stand in its proper place.
¹⁹From them will come songs of thanksgiving
    and the sound of rejoicing.
I will add to their numbers,
    and they will not be decreased;
I will bring them honour,
    and they will not be disdained.
²⁰Their children will be as in days of old,

and their community will be established
    before me;
I will punish all who oppress them.
²¹Their leader will be one of their own;
    their ruler will arise from among them.
I will bring him near and he will come close to
        me,
    for who is he who will devote himself
    to be close to me?'
>   declares the LORD.
²²" 'So you will be my people,
    and I will be your God.' "

²³See, the storm of the LORD
    will burst out in wrath,
a driving wind swirling down
    on the heads of the wicked.
²⁴The fierce anger of the LORD will not turn back
    until he fully accomplishes
    the purposes of his heart.
In days to come
    you will understand this.

31 "At that time," declares the LORD, "I will be
the God of all the clans of Israel, and they
will be my people."
²This is what the LORD says:

"The people who survive the sword
    will find favour in the desert;
    I will come to give rest to Israel."

³The LORD appeared to us in the past,[a] saying:

"I have loved you with an everlasting love;
    I have drawn you with loving-kindness.
⁴I will build you up again
    and you will be rebuilt, O Virgin Israel.
Again you will take up your tambourines
    and go out to dance with the joyful.
⁵Again you will plant vineyards
    on the hills of Samaria;
the farmers will plant them
    and enjoy their fruit.
⁶There will be a day when watchmen cry out
    on the hills of Ephraim,
'Come, let us go up to Zion,
    to the LORD our God.' "

⁷This is what the LORD says:

"Sing with joy for Jacob;
    shout for the foremost of the nations.
Make your praises heard, and say,
    'O LORD, save your people,
    the remnant of Israel.'
⁸See, I will bring them from the land of the
        north
    and gather them from the ends of the earth.
Among them will be the blind and the lame,
    expectant mothers and women in labour;
    a great throng will return.
⁹They will come with weeping;
    they will pray as I bring them back.
I will lead them beside streams of water
    on a level path where they will not stumble,
because I am Israel's father,

^a3 Or LORD has appeared to us from afar

and Ephraim is my firstborn son.

10"Hear the word of the LORD, O nations;
    proclaim it in distant coastlands:
'He who scattered Israel will gather them
    and will watch over his flock like a
        shepherd.'
11For the LORD will ransom Jacob
    and redeem them from the hand of those
        stronger than they.
12They will come and shout for joy on the
        heights of Zion;
    they will rejoice in the bounty of the LORD—
the grain, the new wine and the oil,
    the young of the flocks and herds.
They will be like a well-watered garden,
    and they will sorrow no more.
13Then maidens will dance and be glad,
    young men and old as well.
I will turn their mourning into gladness;
    I will give them comfort and joy instead of
        sorrow.
14I will satisfy the priests with abundance,
    and my people will be filled with my
        bounty,"
                    declares the LORD.

15This is what the LORD says:

"A voice is heard in Ramah,
    mourning and great weeping,
Rachel weeping for her children
    and refusing to be comforted,
    because her children are no more."

31:15 ■ PAIN IN REDEMPTION

The Babylonians used Ramah, a town north of Jerusalem, as a collection point for the captives they were about to exile. Rachel, the "mother of Israel", was buried near there, and she is portrayed as weeping over the exiles. But the Lord's voice answers hers, offering hope for their return. Matthew related this verse to King Herod's slaughter of all baby boys in the vicinity of Bethlehem (Matthew 2:18). In deepest grief, God is not absent: he is planning redemption.

16This is what the LORD says:

"Restrain your voice from weeping
    and your eyes from tears,
for your work will be rewarded,"
                    declares the LORD.
"They will return from the land of the
        enemy.
17So there is hope for your future,"
                    declares the LORD.
"Your children will return to their own land.

18"I have surely heard Ephraim's moaning:
'You disciplined me like an unruly calf,
    and I have been disciplined.
Restore me, and I will return,
    because you are the LORD my God.
19After I strayed,
    I repented;

after I came to understand,
    I beat my breast.
I was ashamed and humiliated
    because I bore the disgrace of my youth.'
20Is not Ephraim my dear son,
    the child in whom I delight?
Though I often speak against him,
    I still remember him.
Therefore my heart yearns for him;
    I have great compassion for him,"
                    declares the LORD.

21"Set up road signs;
    put up guideposts.
Take note of the highway,
    the road that you take.
Return, O Virgin Israel,
    return to your towns.
22How long will you wander,
    O unfaithful daughter?
The LORD will create a new thing on earth—
    a woman will surround[b] a man."

23This is what the LORD Almighty, the God of Israel, says: "When I bring them back from captivity,[c]
the people in the land of Judah and in its towns will
once again use these words: 'The LORD bless you, O
righteous dwelling, O sacred mountain.' 24People
will live together in Judah and all its towns—farmers and those who move about with their flocks. 25I
will refresh the weary and satisfy the faint."

26At this I awoke and looked around. My sleep
had been pleasant to me.

27"The days are coming," declares the LORD,
"when I will plant the house of Israel and the house
of Judah with the offspring of men and of animals.
28Just as I watched over them to uproot and tear
down, and to overthrow, destroy and bring disaster,
so I will watch over them to build and to plant," declares the LORD. 29"In those days people will no
longer say,

'The fathers have eaten sour grapes,
    and the children's teeth are set on edge.'

30Instead, everyone will die for his own sin; whoever eats sour grapes—his own teeth will be set on
edge.

31"The time is coming," declares the LORD,
    "when I will make a new covenant
with the house of Israel
    and with the house of Judah.
32It will not be like the covenant
    I made with their forefathers
when I took them by the hand
    to lead them out of Egypt,
because they broke my covenant,
    though I was a husband to[d] them,"[e]
                    declares the LORD.
33"This is the covenant that I will make with the
        house of Israel
    after that time," declares the LORD.
"I will put my law in their minds
    and write it on their hearts.
I will be their God,
    and they will be my people.

b22 Or will go about ⸤seeking⸥; or will protect   c23 Or I restore their fortunes   d32 Hebrew; Septuagint and Syriac covenant, / and I turned away from
e32 Or was their master

³⁴No longer will a man teach his neighbour,
   or a man his brother, saying, 'Know the
      LORD,'
because they will all know me,
   from the least of them to the greatest,"
                              declares the LORD.
"For I will forgive their wickedness
   and will remember their sins no more."

31:33 ■ LAW IN THEIR HEARTS
The book of Hebrews quotes this passage
(Hebrews 8:8–12) in explaining why Christians no
longer live by Old Testament regulations. The
written law was useful, and God-given. But as the
history of Israel proved, it didn't have the power to
transform people's inner attitudes. Something
more was needed. God would have to change his
people from the inside out, putting his law into
their hearts through his Holy Spirit.

³⁵This is what the LORD says,

he who appoints the sun
   to shine by day,
who decrees the moon and stars
   to shine by night,
who stirs up the sea
   so that its waves roar —
   the LORD Almighty is his name:
³⁶"Only if these decrees vanish from my sight,"
   declares the LORD,
"will the descendants of Israel ever cease
   to be a nation before me."

³⁷This is what the LORD says:

"Only if the heavens above can be measured
   and the foundations of the earth below be
      searched out
will I reject all the descendants of Israel
   because of all they have done,"
                              declares the LORD.

³⁸"The days are coming," declares the LORD,
"when this city will be rebuilt for me from the
Tower of Hananel to the Corner Gate. ³⁹The measuring line will stretch from there straight to the hill
of Gareb and then turn to Goah. ⁴⁰The whole valley
where dead bodies and ashes are thrown, and all the
terraces out to the Kidron Valley on the east as far
as the corner of the Horse Gate, will be holy to the
LORD. The city will never again be uprooted or demolished."

■ Jeremiah Buys a Field

32 This is the word that came to Jeremiah from
the LORD in the tenth year of Zedekiah king
of Judah, which was the eighteenth year of Nebuchadnezzar. ²The army of the king of Babylon was
then besieging Jerusalem, and Jeremiah the prophet
was confined in the courtyard of the guard in the
royal palace of Judah.
³Now Zedekiah king of Judah had imprisoned
him there, saying, "Why do you prophesy as you do?
You say, 'This is what the LORD says: I am about to

hand this city over to the king of Babylon, and he
will capture it. ⁴Zedekiah king of Judah will not escape out of the hands of the Babyloniansᵃ but will
certainly be handed over to the king of Babylon, and
will speak with him face to face and see him with his
own eyes. ⁵He will take Zedekiah to Babylon, where
he will remain until I deal with him, declares the
LORD. If you fight against the Babylonians, you will
not succeed.' "

⁶Jeremiah said, "The word of the LORD came to
me: ⁷Hanamel son of Shallum your uncle is going to
come to you and say, 'Buy my field at Anathoth, because as nearest relative it is your right and duty to
buy it.'

32:7 ■ BARGAIN HUNTING
Jerusalem, under siege from the most powerful
army in the world, hardly looked like a prime
market for real estate. Nevertheless, God told
Jeremiah to buy up family property that was
presently occupied by Babylonians. Though
worthless in the short run, it would grow valuable
when Jeremiah's heirs returned from exile.
Through his outrageous investment, Jeremiah put
his money where his mouth was. He showed
practical faith that God would bring his people
back.

⁸"Then, just as the LORD had said, my cousin Hanamel came to me in the courtyard of the guard and
said, 'Buy my field at Anathoth in the territory of
Benjamin. Since it is your right to redeem it and possess it, buy it for yourself.'
"I knew that this was the word of the LORD; ⁹so I
bought the field at Anathoth from my cousin Hanamel and weighed out for him seventeen shekelsᵇ of
silver. ¹⁰I signed and sealed the deed, had it witnessed, and weighed out the silver on the scales. ¹¹I
took the deed of purchase — the sealed copy containing the terms and conditions, as well as the unsealed copy — ¹²and I gave this deed to Baruch son
of Neriah, the son of Mahseiah, in the presence of
my cousin Hanamel and of the witnesses who had
signed the deed and of all the Jews sitting in the
courtyard of the guard.
¹³"In their presence I gave Baruch these instructions: ¹⁴'This is what the LORD Almighty, the God of
Israel, says: Take these documents, both the sealed
and unsealed copies of the deed of purchase, and
put them in a clay jar so that they will last a long
time. ¹⁵For this is what the LORD Almighty, the God
of Israel, says: Houses, fields and vineyards will again
be bought in this land.'
¹⁶"After I had given the deed of purchase to Baruch son of Neriah, I prayed to the LORD:
¹⁷"Ah, Sovereign LORD, you have made the
heavens and the earth by your great power and
outstretched arm. Nothing is too hard for you.
¹⁸You show love to thousands but bring the
punishment for the fathers' sins into the laps of
their children after them. O great and powerful
God, whose name is the LORD Almighty, ¹⁹great
are your purposes and mighty are your deeds.

ᵃ4 Or *Chaldeans*; also in verses 5, 24, 25, 28, 29 and 43   ᵇ9 That is, about 7 ounces (about 200 grams)

Your eyes are open to all the ways of men; you reward everyone according to his conduct and as his deeds deserve. 20You performed miraculous signs and wonders in Egypt and have continued them to this day, both in Israel and among all mankind, and have gained the renown that is still yours. 21You brought your people Israel out of Egypt with signs and wonders, by a mighty hand and an outstretched arm and with great terror. 22You gave them this land you had sworn to give to their forefathers, a land flowing with milk and honey. 23They came in and took possession of it, but they did not obey you or follow your law; they did not do what you commanded them to do. So you brought all this disaster upon them.

24"See how the siege ramps are built up to take the city. Because of the sword, famine and plague, the city will be handed over to the Babylonians who are attacking it. What you said has happened, as you now see. 25And though the city will be handed over to the Babylonians, you, O Sovereign LORD, say to me, 'Buy the field with silver and have the transaction witnessed.' "

26Then the word of the LORD came to Jeremiah: 27"I am the LORD, the God of all mankind. Is anything too hard for me? 28Therefore, this is what the LORD says: I am about to hand this city over to the Babylonians and to Nebuchadnezzar king of Babylon, who will capture it. 29The Babylonians who are attacking this city will come in and set it on fire; they will burn it down, along with the houses where the people provoked me to anger by burning incense on the roofs to Baal and by pouring out drink offerings to other gods.

30"The people of Israel and Judah have done nothing but evil in my sight from their youth; indeed, the people of Israel have done nothing but provoke me with what their hands have made, declares the LORD. 31From the day it was built until now, this city has so aroused my anger and wrath that I must remove it from my sight. 32The people of Israel and Judah have provoked me by all the evil they have done—they, their kings and officials, their priests and prophets, the men of Judah and the people of Jerusalem. 33They turned their backs to me and not their faces; though I taught them again and again, they would not listen or respond to discipline. 34They set up their abominable idols in the house that bears my Name and defiled it. 35They built high places for Baal in the Valley of Ben Hinnom to sacrifice their sons and daughtersc to Molech, though I never commanded, nor did it enter my mind, that they should do such a detestable thing and so make Judah sin.

36"You are saying about this city, 'By the sword, famine and plague it will be handed over to the king of Babylon'; but this is what the LORD, the God of Israel, says: 37I will surely gather them from all the lands where I banish them in my furious anger and great wrath; I will bring them back to this place and let them live in safety. 38They will be my people, and I will be their God. 39I will give them singleness

of heart and action, so that they will always fear me for their own good and the good of their children after them. 40I will make an everlasting covenant with them: I will never stop doing good to them, and I will inspire them to fear me, so that they will never turn away from me. 41I will rejoice in doing them good and will assuredly plant them in this land with all my heart and soul.

32:40 ■ A NEW COVENANT
The foundation of Israel was its covenant with God. It bound both sides together on the basis of clear-cut expectations (see "The Covenant", page 68). Israel had never really lived up to the covenant, however. Here (and in 31:31–34) God promised a new covenant, far better than the old one. It would change the people's thinking. Paul amplified the contrast in 2 Corinthians 2:12 – 3:18. The new covenant came in Christ.

42"This is what the LORD says: As I have brought all this great calamity on this people, so I will give them all the prosperity I have promised them. 43Once more fields will be bought in this land of which you say, 'It is a desolate waste, without men or animals, for it has been handed over to the Babylonians.' 44Fields will be bought for silver, and deeds will be signed, sealed and witnessed in the territory of Benjamin, in the villages around Jerusalem, in the towns of Judah and in the towns of the hill country, of the western foothills and of the Negev, because I will restore their fortunes,d declares the LORD."

■ Promise of Restoration

33 While Jeremiah was still confined in the courtyard of the guard, the word of the LORD came to him a second time: 2"This is what the LORD says, he who made the earth, the LORD who formed it and established it—the LORD is his name: 3'Call to me and I will answer you and tell you great and unsearchable things you do not know.' 4For this is what the LORD, the God of Israel, says about the houses in this city and the royal palaces of Judah that have been torn down to be used against the siege ramps and the sword 5in the fight with the Babylonians:a 'They will be filled with the dead bodies of the men I will slay in my anger and wrath. I will hide my face from this city because of all its wickedness.

6" 'Nevertheless, I will bring health and healing to it; I will heal my people and will let them enjoy abundant peace and security. 7I will bring Judah and Israel back from captivityb and will rebuild them as they were before. 8I will cleanse them from all the sin they have committed against me and will forgive all their sins of rebellion against me. 9Then this city will bring me renown, joy, praise and honour before all nations on earth that hear of all the good things I do for it; and they will be in awe and will tremble at the abundant prosperity and peace I provide for it.'

10"This is what the LORD says: 'You say about this

c 35 Or to make their sons and daughters pass through ⌊the fire⌋   d 44 Or will bring them back from captivity   a 5 Or Chaldeans   b 7 Or will restore the fortunes of Judah and Israel place, "It is a desolate waste, without men or animals." Yet in the towns of Judah and the streets of Jerusalem that are deserted, inhabited by neither men nor animals, there will be heard once more [11]the sounds of joy and gladness, the voices of bride and bridegroom, and the voices of those who bring thank-offerings to the house of the LORD, saying,

"Give thanks to the LORD Almighty,
   for the LORD is good;
his love endures for ever."

For I will restore the fortunes of the land as they were before,' says the LORD.

[12]"This is what the LORD Almighty says: 'In this place, desolate and without men or animals—in all its towns there will again be pastures for shepherds to rest their flocks. [13]In the towns of the hill country, of the western foothills and of the Negev, in the territory of Benjamin, in the villages around Jerusalem and in the towns of Judah, flocks will again pass under the hand of the one who counts them,' says the LORD.

[14]" 'The days are coming,' declares the LORD, 'when I will fulfil the gracious promise I made to the house of Israel and to the house of Judah.

[15]" 'In those days and at that time
I will make a righteous Branch sprout from
   David's line;
he will do what is just and right in the land.
[16]In those days Judah will be saved
   and Jerusalem will live in safety.
This is the name by which it[c] will be called:
   The LORD Our Righteousness.'

[17]For this is what the LORD says: 'David will never fail to have a man to sit on the throne of the house of Israel, [18]nor will the priests, who are Levites, ever fail to have a man to stand before me continually to offer burnt offerings, to burn grain offerings and to present sacrifices.' "

33:18 ■ UNCHANGED PROMISES

Jerusalem lay in rubble, and survivors must surely have wondered whether God's covenants had been irrevocably broken. In this message through Jeremiah, God says that his promises still stand. Israel will always have an heir of David to provide leadership, and priests to lead in worship. The New Testament, and particularly the book of Hebrews, teaches that these promises are fulfilled for ever in Jesus, who is both priest and king.

[19]The word of the LORD came to Jeremiah: [20]"This is what the LORD says: 'If you can break my covenant with the day and my covenant with the night, so that day and night no longer come at their appointed time, [21]then my covenant with David my servant—and my covenant with the Levites who are priests ministering before me—can be broken and David will no longer have a descendant to reign on his throne. [22]I will make the descendants of David my servant and the Levites who minister before me as

countless as the stars of the sky and as measureless as the sand on the seashore.' "

[23]The word of the LORD came to Jeremiah: [24]"Have you not noticed that these people are saying, 'The LORD has rejected the two kingdoms[d] he chose'? So they despise my people and no longer regard them as a nation. [25]This is what the LORD says: 'If I have not established my covenant with day and night and the fixed laws of heaven and earth, [26]then I will reject the descendants of Jacob and David my servant and will not choose one of his sons to rule over the descendants of Abraham, Isaac and Jacob. For I will restore their fortunes[e] and have compassion on them.' "

■ Warning to Zedekiah

34 While Nebuchadnezzar king of Babylon and all his army and all the kingdoms and peoples in the empire he ruled were fighting against Jerusalem and all its surrounding towns, this word came to Jeremiah from the LORD: [2]"This is what the LORD, the God of Israel, says: Go to Zedekiah king of Judah and tell him, 'This is what the LORD says: I am about to hand this city over to the king of Babylon, and he will burn it down. [3]You will not escape from his grasp but will surely be captured and handed over to him. You will see the king of Babylon with your own eyes, and he will speak with you face to face. And you will go to Babylon.

[4]" 'Yet hear the promise of the LORD, O Zedekiah king of Judah. This is what the LORD says concerning you: You will not die by the sword; [5]you will die peacefully. As people made a funeral fire in honour of your fathers, the former kings who preceded you, so they will make a fire in your honour and lament, "Alas, O master!" I myself make this promise, declares the LORD.' "

[6]Then Jeremiah the prophet told all this to Zedekiah king of Judah, in Jerusalem, [7]while the army of the king of Babylon was fighting against Jerusalem and the other cities of Judah that were still holding out—Lachish and Azekah. These were the only fortified cities left in Judah.

■ Freedom for Slaves

[8]The word came to Jeremiah from the LORD after King Zedekiah had made a covenant with all the people in Jerusalem to proclaim freedom for the slaves. [9]Everyone was to free his Hebrew slaves, both male and female; no-one was to hold a fellow Jew in bondage. [10]So all the officials and people who entered into this covenant agreed that they would free their male and female slaves and no longer hold them in bondage. They agreed, and set them free. [11]But afterwards they changed their minds and took back the slaves they had freed and enslaved them again.

[12]Then the word of the LORD came to Jeremiah: [13]"This is what the LORD, the God of Israel, says: I made a covenant with your forefathers when I brought them out of Egypt, out of the land of slavery. I said, [14]'Every seventh year each of you must free any fellow Hebrew who has sold himself to you. After he has served you for six years, you must let him go free.'[a] Your fathers, however, did not listen

---

to me or pay attention to me. [15]Recently you repented and did what is right in my sight: Each of you proclaimed freedom to his countrymen. You even made a covenant before me in the house that bears my Name. [16]But now you have turned round and profaned my name; each of you has taken back the male and female slaves you had set free to go where they wished. You have forced them to become your slaves again.

[17]"Therefore, this is what the LORD says: You have not obeyed me; you have not proclaimed freedom for your fellow countrymen. So I now proclaim 'freedom' for you, declares the LORD — 'freedom' to fall by the sword, plague and famine. I will make you abhorrent to all the kingdoms of the earth. [18]The men who have violated my covenant and have not fulfilled the terms of the covenant they made before me, I will treat like the calf they cut in two and then walked between its pieces. [19]The leaders of Judah and Jerusalem, the court officials, the priests and all the people of the land who walked between the pieces of the calf, [20]I will hand over to their enemies who seek their lives. Their dead bodies will become food for the birds of the air and the beasts of the earth.

[21]"I will hand Zedekiah king of Judah and his officials over to their enemies who seek their lives, to the army of the king of Babylon, which has withdrawn from you. [22]I am going to give the order, declares the LORD, and I will bring them back to this city. They will fight against it, take it and burn it down. And I will lay waste the towns of Judah so that no-one can live there."

■ The Recabites

35 This is the word that came to Jeremiah from the LORD during the reign of Jehoiakim son of Josiah king of Judah: [2]"Go to the Recabite family and invite them to come to one of the side rooms of the house of the LORD and give them wine to drink."

[3]So I went to get Jaazaniah son of Jeremiah, the son of Habazziniah, and his brothers and all his sons — the whole family of the Recabites. [4]I brought them into the house of the LORD, into the room of the sons of Hanan son of Igdaliah the man of God. It was next to the room of the officials, which was over that of Maaseiah son of Shallum the doorkeeper. [5]Then I set bowls full of wine and some cups before the men of the Recabite family and said to them, "Drink some wine."

[6]But they replied, "We do not drink wine, because our forefather Jonadab son of Recab gave us this command: 'Neither you nor your descendants must ever drink wine. [7]Also you must never build houses, sow seed or plant vineyards; you must never have any of these things, but must always live in tents. Then you will live a long time in the land where you are nomads.' [8]We have obeyed everything our forefather Jonadab son of Recab commanded us. Neither we nor our wives nor our sons and daughters have ever drunk wine [9]or built houses to live in or had vineyards, fields or crops. [10]We have lived in tents and have fully obeyed everything our forefather Jonadab commanded us. [11]But when Nebuchadnezzar king of Babylon

invaded this land, we said, 'Come, we must go to Jerusalem to escape the Babylonian[a] and Aramean armies.' So we have remained in Jerusalem."

[12]Then the word of the LORD came to Jeremiah, saying: [13]"This is what the LORD Almighty, the God of Israel, says: Go and tell the men of Judah and the people of Jerusalem, 'Will you not learn a lesson and obey my words?' declares the LORD. [14]'Jonadab son of Recab ordered his sons not to drink wine and this command has been kept. To this day they do not drink wine, because they obey their forefather's command. But I have spoken to you again and again, yet you have not obeyed me. [15]Again and again I sent all my servants the prophets to you. They said, "Each of you must turn from your wicked ways and reform your actions; do not follow other gods to serve them. Then you shall live in the land I have given to you and your fathers." But you have not paid attention or listened to me. [16]The descendants of Jonadab son of Recab have carried out the command their forefather gave them, but these people have not obeyed me.'

35:14 ■ TEETOTALLERS
The Recabites had a family tradition of not drinking, and nothing Jeremiah said or did could budge them from it. He made their tenacity the basis of a sermon. If family traditions are carried on for generations, why not *God's* traditions?

[17]"Therefore, this is what the LORD God Almighty, the God of Israel, says: 'Listen! I am going to bring on Judah and on everyone living in Jerusalem every disaster I pronounced against them. I spoke to them, but they did not listen; I called to them, but they did not answer.' "

[18]Then Jeremiah said to the family of the Recabites, "This is what the LORD Almighty, the God of Israel, says: 'You have obeyed the command of your forefather Jonadab and have followed all his instructions and have done everything he ordered.' [19]Therefore, this is what the LORD Almighty, the God of Israel, says: 'Jonadab son of Recab shall never fail to have a man to serve me.' "

■ Jehoiakim Burns Jeremiah's Scroll

36 In the fourth year of Jehoiakim son of Josiah king of Judah, this word came to Jeremiah from the LORD: [2]"Take a scroll and write on it all the words I have spoken to you concerning Israel, Judah and all the other nations from the time I began speaking to you in the reign of Josiah till now. [3]Perhaps when the people of Judah hear about every disaster I plan to inflict on them, each of them will turn from his wicked way; then I will forgive their wickedness and their sin."

[4]So Jeremiah called Baruch son of Neriah, and while Jeremiah dictated all the words the LORD had spoken to him, Baruch wrote them on the scroll. [5]Then Jeremiah told Baruch, "I am restricted; I cannot go to the LORD's temple. [6]So you go to the house of the LORD on a day of fasting and read to the people from the scroll the words of the LORD that you wrote

as I dictated. Read them to all the people of Judah who come in from their towns. 7Perhaps they will bring their petition before the LORD, and each will turn from his wicked ways, for the anger and wrath pronounced against this people by the LORD are great."

8Baruch son of Neriah did everything Jeremiah the prophet told him to do; at the LORD's temple he read the words of the LORD from the scroll. 9In the ninth month of the fifth year of Jehoiakim son of Josiah king of Judah, a time of fasting before the LORD was proclaimed for all the people in Jerusalem and those who had come from the towns of Judah. 10From the room of Gemariah son of Shaphan the secretary, which was in the upper courtyard at the entrance of the New Gate of the temple, Baruch read to all the people at the LORD's temple the words of Jeremiah from the scroll.

11When Micaiah son of Gemariah, the son of Shaphan, heard all the words of the LORD from the scroll, 12he went down to the secretary's room in the royal palace, where all the officials were sitting: Elishama the secretary, Delaiah son of Shemaiah, Elnathan son of Acbor, Gemariah son of Shaphan, Zedekiah son of Hananiah, and all the other officials.

13After Micaiah told them everything he had heard Baruch read to the people from the scroll, 14all the officials sent Jehudi son of Nethaniah, the son of Shelemiah, the son of Cushi, to say to Baruch, "Bring the scroll from which you have read to the people and come." So Baruch son of Neriah went to them with the scroll in his hand. 15They said to him, "Sit down, please, and read it to us."

So Baruch read it to them. 16When they heard all these words, they looked at each other in fear and said to Baruch, "We must report all these words to the king." 17Then they asked Baruch, "Tell us, how did you come to write all this? Did Jeremiah dictate it?"

18"Yes," Baruch replied, "he dictated all these words to me, and I wrote them in ink on the scroll."

19Then the officials said to Baruch, "You and Jeremiah, go and hide. Don't let anyone know where you are."

20After they put the scroll in the room of Elishama the secretary, they went to the king in the courtyard and reported everything to him. 21The king sent Jehudi to get the scroll, and Jehudi brought it from the room of Elishama the secretary and read it to the king and all the officials standing

■ LIVING PARABLES
JEREMIAH'S BIZARRE PROTESTS

INSIGHT

"YOU HAVE NOT PAID ATTENTION OR LISTENED TO ME." ■ 35:15

Occasionally the evening news brings us word of someone's bizarre protest. Animal rights liberators fire-bomb shops. Poll tax demonstraters set themselves on fire. Environmental activists chain themselves to trees to protest logging. Marchers block the entrance to a nuclear power station. Such protests leave many people feeling uneasy. We can't easily imagine a serious political figure, or a respectable pastor, acting that way.

But Jeremiah's life was full of such protests, at the express command of God. He made an ox yoke and wore it everywhere until the false prophet Hananiah took it off and broke it in the temple one day. (Jeremiah prophesied Hananiah's death, and within two months he was gone.) Jeremiah's point? He wanted to emphasise the yoke of captivity the king of Babylon would put on Judah's shoulders. The story is in chapters 27–28.

On another occasion (chapter 35) Jeremiah invited a group of well-known non-drinkers into a room in the temple and offered them wine. They refused, and that made another sermon. If they could remember their vows not to drink, then why couldn't the people of Judah and Jerusalem remember the words of the living God?

■ NOTHING WAS TOO UNDIGNIFIED

Jeremiah bought a beautiful linen sash and buried it in a hole until it was ruined (chapter 13). He invited the rulers of Jerusalem to take a trip outside the city, and in the midst of a sermon about God's anger smashed a pot to smithereens (chapter 19). And in his most famous "enacted parable", Jeremiah bought a farm while the Babylonian army was knocking at Jerusalem's door (chapter 32). He might as well have been a Jew buying property within a German concentration camp during World War II, for all the hope he had of using it. But his action demonstrated bold hope. Someday his family would farm there again.

Why such weird activity? It says less about Jeremiah than it does about the God who gave the orders. God would not let go of his people until he had done all in his power to turn them round. Nothing was too undignified; no carnival ploy was too corny. So long as he had the slightest hope of breaking through to them, he would keep shouting.

□ LIFE QUESTIONS:

How does God get through to you? Does he use dramatic means like Jeremiah's or quieter methods?

beside him. ²²It was the ninth month and the king was sitting in the winter apartment, with a fire burning in the brazier in front of him. ²³Whenever Jehudi had read three or four columns of the scroll, the king cut them off with a scribe's knife and threw them into the brazier, until the entire scroll was burned in the fire. ²⁴The king and all his attendants who heard all these words showed no fear, nor did they tear their clothes. ²⁵Even though Elnathan, Delaiah and Gemariah urged the king not to burn the scroll, he would not listen to them. ²⁶Instead, the king commanded Jerahmeel, a son of the king, Seraiah son of Azriel and Shelemiah son of Abdeel to arrest Baruch the scribe and Jeremiah the prophet. But the LORD had hidden them.

²⁷After the king burned the scroll containing the words that Baruch had written at Jeremiah's dictation, the word of the LORD came to Jeremiah: ²⁸"Take another scroll and write on it all the words that were on the first scroll, which Jehoiakim king of Judah burned up. ²⁹Also tell Jehoiakim king of Judah, 'This is what the LORD says: You burned that scroll and said, "Why did you write on it that the king of Babylon would certainly come and destroy this land and cut off both men and animals from it?" ³⁰Therefore, this is what the LORD says about Jehoiakim king of Judah: He will have no-one to sit on the throne of David; his body will be thrown out and exposed to the heat by day and the frost by night. ³¹I will punish him and his children and his attendants for their wickedness; I will bring on them and those living in Jerusalem and the people of Judah every disaster I pronounced against them, because they have not listened.' "

³²So Jeremiah took another scroll and gave it to the scribe Baruch son of Neriah, and as Jeremiah dictated, Baruch wrote on it all the words of the scroll that Jehoiakim king of Judah had burned in the fire. And many similar words were added to them.

■ Jeremiah in Prison

37 Zedekiah son of Josiah was made king of Judah by Nebuchadnezzar king of Babylon; he reigned in place of Jehoiachin*ᵃ* son of Jehoiakim. ²Neither he nor his attendants nor the people of the land paid any attention to the words the LORD had spoken through Jeremiah the prophet.

³King Zedekiah, however, sent Jehucal son of Shelemiah with the priest Zephaniah son of Maaseiah to Jeremiah the prophet with this message: "Please pray to the LORD our God for us."

⁴Now Jeremiah was free to come and go among the people, for he had not yet been put in prison. ⁵Pharaoh's army had marched out of Egypt, and when the Babylonsᵇ who were besieging Jerusalem heard the report about them, they withdrew from Jerusalem.

⁶Then the word of the LORD came to Jeremiah the prophet: ⁷"This is what the LORD, the God of Israel, says: Tell the king of Judah, who sent you to enquire of me, 'Pharaoh's army, which has marched out to support you, will go back to its own land, to Egypt. ⁸Then the Babylonians will return and attack this city; they will capture it and burn it down.'

⁹"This is what the LORD says: Do not deceive yourselves, thinking, 'The Babylonians will surely leave us.' They will not! ¹⁰Even if you were to defeat the entire Babylonianᶜ army that is attacking you and only wounded men were left in their tents, they would come out and burn this city down."

37:5 ■ THE SIEGE LIFTED
Israel was a small nation, hemmed in by bigger powers such as Egypt and Babylon. Israelite kings often attempted to keep their independence by playing off the big powers against each other. King Zedekiah tried to get Egypt to intervene against Babylon, and during this brief period it seemed he had succeeded. Because the Egyptian army marched out, Nebuchadnezzar lifted his siege of Jerusalem. Jeremiah, who had warned that this foreign policy must ultimately fail, was arrested for treason.

¹¹After the Babylonian army had withdrawn from Jerusalem because of Pharaoh's army, ¹²Jeremiah started to leave the city to go to the territory of Benjamin to get his share of the property among the people there. ¹³But when he reached the Benjamin Gate, the captain of the guard, whose name was Irijah son of Shelemiah, the son of Hananiah, arrested him and said, "You are deserting to the Babylonians!"

¹⁴"That's not true!" Jeremiah said. "I am not deserting to the Babylonians." But Irijah would not listen to him; instead, he arrested Jeremiah and brought him to the officials. ¹⁵They were angry with Jeremiah and had him beaten and imprisoned in the house of Jonathan the secretary, which they had made into a prison.

¹⁶Jeremiah was put into a vaulted cell in a dungeon, where he remained a long time. ¹⁷Then King Zedekiah sent for him and had him brought to the palace, where he asked him privately, "Is there any word from the LORD?"

"Yes," Jeremiah replied, "you will be handed over to the king of Babylon."

¹⁸Then Jeremiah said to King Zedekiah, "What crime have I committed against you or your officials or this people, that you have put me in prison? ¹⁹Where are your prophets who prophesied to you, 'The king of Babylon will not attack you or this land'? ²⁰But now, my lord the king, please listen. Let me bring my petition before you: Do not send me back to the house of Jonathan the secretary, or I shall die there."

²¹King Zedekiah then gave orders for Jeremiah to be placed in the courtyard of the guard and given bread from the street of the bakers each day until all the bread in the city was gone. So Jeremiah remained in the courtyard of the guard.

■ Jeremiah Thrown Into a Cistern

38 Shephatiah son of Mattan, Gedaliah son of Pashhur, Jehucal*ᵃ* son of Shelemiah, and Pashhur son of Malkijah heard what Jeremiah was telling all the people when he said, ²"This is what

---

ᵃ 1 Hebrew *Coniah*, a variant of *Jehoiachin*   *ᵇ 5* Or *Chaldeans*; also in verses 8, 9, 13 and 14   *ᶜ 10* Or *Chaldean*; also in verse 11   *ᵃ 1* Hebrew *Jucal*, a variant of *Jehucal* the LORD says: 'Whoever stays in this city will die by the sword, famine or plague, but whoever goes over to the Babylonians[b] will live. He will escape with his life; he will live.' [3]And this is what the LORD says: 'This city will certainly be handed over to the army of the king of Babylon, who will capture it.' "

[4]Then the officials said to the king, "This man should be put to death. He is discouraging the soldiers who are left in this city, as well as all the people, by the things he is saying to them. This man is not seeking the good of these people but their ruin."

[5]"He is in your hands," King Zedekiah answered. "The king can do nothing to oppose you."

[6]So they took Jeremiah and put him into the cistern of Malkijah, the king's son, which was in the courtyard of the guard. They lowered Jeremiah by ropes into the cistern; it had no water in it, only mud, and Jeremiah sank down into the mud.

[7]But Ebed-Melech, a Cushite,[c] an official[d] in the royal palace, heard that they had put Jeremiah into the cistern. While the king was sitting in the Benjamin Gate, [8]Ebed-Melech went out of the palace and said to him, [9]"My lord the king, these men have acted wickedly in all they have done to Jeremiah the prophet. They have thrown him into a cistern, where he will starve to death when there is no longer any bread in the city."

38:9 ■ CLOSE TO DEATH

Jeremiah was arrested during the long, final siege of Jerusalem – a time when food became so short that some Israelites resorted to cannibalism. Imprisoned at the bottom of an empty cistern, the prophet could easily have starved to death. Interestingly, only a foreigner cared enough to go to the king and convince him to let Jeremiah out. For this, Ebed-Melech received a special message from God (39:15–18).

[10]Then the king commanded Ebed-Melech the Cushite, "Take thirty men from here with you and lift Jeremiah the prophet out of the cistern before he dies."

[11]So Ebed-Melech took the men with him and went to a room under the treasury in the palace. He took some old rags and worn-out clothes from there and let them down with ropes to Jeremiah in the cistern. [12]Ebed-Melech the Cushite said to Jeremiah, "Put these old rags and worn-out clothes under your arms to pad the ropes." Jeremiah did so, [13]and they pulled him up with the ropes and lifted him out of the cistern. And Jeremiah remained in the courtyard of the guard.

■ Zedekiah Questions Jeremiah Again

[14]Then King Zedekiah sent for Jeremiah the prophet and had him brought to the third entrance to the temple of the LORD. "I am going to ask you something," the king said to Jeremiah. "Do not hide anything from me."

[15]Jeremiah said to Zedekiah, "If I give you an answer, will you not kill me? Even if I did give you counsel, you would not listen to me."

[16]But King Zedekiah swore this oath secretly to Jeremiah: "As surely as the LORD lives, who has given us breath, I will neither kill you nor hand you over to those who are seeking your life."

[17]Then Jeremiah said to Zedekiah, "This is what the LORD God Almighty, the God of Israel, says: 'If you surrender to the officers of the king of Babylon, your life will be spared and this city will not be burned down; you and your family will live. [18]But if you will not surrender to the officers of the king of Babylon, this city will be handed over to the Babylonians and they will burn it down; you yourself will not escape from their hands.' "

[19]King Zedekiah said to Jeremiah, "I am afraid of the Jews who have gone over to the Babylonians, for the Babylonians may hand me over to them and they will ill-treat me."

[20]"They will not hand you over," Jeremiah replied. "Obey the LORD by doing what I tell you. Then it will go well with you, and your life will be spared. [21]But if you refuse to surrender, this is what the LORD has revealed to me: [22]All the women left in the palace of the king of Judah will be brought out to the officials of the king of Babylon. Those women will say to you:

" 'They misled you and overcame you—
    those trusted friends of yours.
Your feet are sunk in the mud;
    your friends have deserted you.'

[23]"All your wives and children will be brought out to the Babylonians. You yourself will not escape from their hands but will be captured by the king of Babylon; and this city will[e] be burned down."

[24]Then Zedekiah said to Jeremiah, "Do not let anyone know about this conversation, or you may die. [25]If the officials hear that I talked with you, and they come to you and say, 'Tell us what you said to the king and what the king said to you; do not hide it from us or we will kill you,' [26]then tell them, 'I was pleading with the king not to send me back to Jonathan's house to die there.' "

[27]All the officials did come to Jeremiah and question him, and he told them everything the king had ordered him to say. So they said no more to him, for no-one had heard his conversation with the king.

[28]And Jeremiah remained in the courtyard of the guard until the day Jerusalem was captured.

■ The Fall of Jerusalem

39 This is how Jerusalem was taken: [1]In the ninth year of Zedekiah king of Judah, in the tenth month, Nebuchadnezzar king of Babylon marched against Jerusalem with his whole army and laid siege to it. [2]And on the ninth day of the fourth month of Zedekiah's eleventh year, the city wall was broken through. [3]Then all the officials of the king of Babylon came and took seats in the Middle Gate: Nergal-Sharezer of Samgar, Nebo-Sarsekim[a] a chief officer, Nergal-Sharezer a high official and all the other officials of the king of Babylon. [4]When Zedekiah king of Judah and all the soldiers saw them, they fled; they left the city at night by way of the king's garden, through the gate between the two walls, and headed towards the Arabah.[b]

[5]But the Babylonian[c] army pursued them and overtook Zedekiah in the plains of Jericho. They captured him and took him to Nebuchadnezzar king of Babylon at Riblah in the land of Hamath, where he pronounced sentence on him. [6]There at Riblah the king of Babylon slaughtered the sons of Zedekiah before his eyes and also killed all the nobles of Judah. [7]Then he put out Zedekiah's eyes and bound him with bronze shackles to take him to Babylon.

[8]The Babylonians[d] set fire to the royal palace and the houses of the people and broke down the walls of Jerusalem. [9]Nebuzaradan commander of the imperial guard carried into exile to Babylon the people who remained in the city, along with those who had gone over to him, and the rest of the people. [10]But Nebuzaradan the commander of the guard left behind in the land of Judah some of the poor people, who owned nothing; and at that time he gave them vineyards and fields.

[11]Now Nebuchadnezzar king of Babylon had given these orders about Jeremiah through Nebuzaradan commander of the imperial guard: [12]"Take him and look after him; don't harm him but do for him whatever he asks." [13]So Nebuzaradan the commander of the guard, Nebushazban a chief officer, Nergal-Sharezer a high official and all the other officers of the king of Babylon [14]sent and had Jeremiah taken out of the courtyard of the guard. They handed him over to Gedaliah son of Ahikam, the son of Shaphan, to take him back to his home. So he remained among his own people.

39:12 ■ INFLUENTIAL PRISONER
Jeremiah's message of doom made him unpopular in Jerusalem but evidently impressed the conquering Babylonians. The highest officials knew about the prophet and gave explicit instructions to see that he was not hurt. Later they offered him his freedom (40:4).

---

[15]While Jeremiah had been confined in the courtyard of the guard, the word of the LORD came to him: [16]"Go and tell Ebed-Melech the Cushite, 'This is what the LORD Almighty, the God of Israel, says: I am about to fulfil my words against this city through disaster, not prosperity. At that time they will be fulfilled before your eyes. [17]But I will rescue you on that day, declares the LORD; you will not be handed over to those you fear. [18]I will save you; you will not fall by the sword but will escape with your life, because you trust in me, declares the LORD.'"

■ Jeremiah Freed

40 The word came to Jeremiah from the LORD after Nebuzaradan commander of the imperial guard had released him at Ramah. He had found Jeremiah bound in chains among all the captives from Jerusalem and Judah who were being carried into exile to Babylon. [2]When the commander of the guard found Jeremiah, he said to him, "The LORD your God decreed this disaster for this place. [3]And now the LORD has brought it about; he has done just as he said he would. All this happened because you people sinned against the LORD and did not obey him. [4]But today I am freeing you from the chains on your wrists. Come with me to Babylon, if you like, and I will look after you; but if you do not want to, then don't come. Look, the whole country lies before you; go wherever you please." [5]However, before Jeremiah turned to go,[a] Nebuzaradan added, "Go back to Gedaliah son of Ahikam, the son of Shaphan, whom the king of Babylon had appointed over the towns of Judah, and live with him among the people, or go anywhere else you please."

Then the commander gave him provisions and a present and let him go. [6]So Jeremiah went to Gedaliah son of Ahikam at Mizpah and stayed with him among the people who were left behind in the land.

■ Gedaliah Assassinated

[7]When all the army officers and their men who were still in the open country heard that the king of Babylon had appointed Gedaliah son of Ahikam as governor over the land and had put him in charge of the men, women and children who were the poorest in the land and who had not been carried into exile to Babylon, [8]they came to Gedaliah at Mizpah—Ishmael son of Nethaniah, Johanan and Jonathan the sons of Kareah, Seraiah son of Tanhumeth, the sons of Ephai the Netophathite, and Jaazaniah[b] the son of the Maacathite, and their men. [9]Gedaliah son of Ahikam, the son of Shaphan, took an oath to reassure them and their men. "Do not be afraid to serve the Babylonians,"[c] he said. "Settle down in the land and serve the king of Babylon, and it will go well with you. [10]I myself will stay in Mizpah to represent you before the Babylonians who come to us, but you are to harvest the wine, summer fruit and oil, and put them in your storage jars, and live in the towns you have taken over."

[11]When all the Jews in Moab, Ammon, Edom and all the other countries heard that the king of Babylon had left a remnant in Judah and had appointed Gedaliah son of Ahikam, the son of Shaphan, as governor over them, [12]they all came back to the land of Judah, to Gedaliah at Mizpah, from all the countries where they had been scattered. And they harvested an abundance of wine and summer fruit.

40:12 ■ FALSE HOPES
The Babylonians, once they had captured rebel Jerusalem, left some of the common people behind under a governor. When other Jews scattered in the region heard news of this, they came home and gathered an excellent harvest — undoubtedly from fields the exiles had left behind. But even this small nucleus of Jews was to be scattered — this time due to local political infighting.

---

[13]Johanan son of Kareah and all the army officers still in the open country came to Gedaliah at Mizpah [14]and said to him, "Don't you know that Baalis king of the Ammonites has sent Ishmael son of Nethaniah to take your life?" But Gedaliah son of Ahikam did not believe them.

---

[c]5 Or Chaldean   [d]8 Or Chaldeans   [a]5 Or Jeremiah answered   [b]8 Hebrew Jezaniah, a variant of Jaazaniah   [c]9 Or Chaldeans; also in verse 10

¹⁵Then Johanan son of Kareah said privately to Gedaliah in Mizpah, "Let me go and kill Ishmael son of Nethaniah, and no-one will know it. Why should he take your life and cause all the Jews who are gathered around you to be scattered and the remnant of Judah to perish?"

¹⁶But Gedaliah son of Ahikam said to Johanan son of Kareah, "Don't do such a thing! What you are saying about Ishmael is not true."

41 In the seventh month Ishmael son of Nethaniah, the son of Elishama, who was of royal blood and had been one of the king's officers, came with ten men to Gedaliah son of Ahikam at Mizpah. While they were eating together there, ²Ishmael son of Nethaniah and the ten men who were with him got up and struck down Gedaliah son of Ahikam, the son of Shaphan, with the sword, killing the one whom the king of Babylon had appointed as governor over the land. ³Ishmael also killed all the Jews who were with Gedaliah at Mizpah, as well as the Babylonianᵃ soldiers who were there.

⁴The day after Gedaliah's assassination, before anyone knew about it, ⁵eighty men who had shaved off their beards, torn their clothes and cut themselves came from Shechem, Shiloh and Samaria, bringing grain offerings and incense with them to the house of the LORD. ⁶Ishmael son of Nethaniah went out from Mizpah to meet them, weeping as he went. When he met them, he said, "Come to Gedaliah son of Ahikam." ⁷When they went into the city, Ishmael son of Nethaniah and the men who were with him slaughtered them and threw them into a cistern. ⁸But ten of them said to Ishmael, "Don't kill us! We have wheat and barley, oil and honey, hidden in a field." So he let them alone and did not kill them with the others. ⁹Now the cistern where he threw all the bodies of the men he had killed along with Gedaliah was the one King Asa had made as part of his defence against Baasha king of Israel. Ishmael son of Nethaniah filled it with the dead.

¹⁰Ishmael made captives of all the rest of the people who were in Mizpah—the king's daughters along with all the others who were left there, over whom Nebuzaradan commander of the imperial guard had appointed Gedaliah son of Ahikam. Ishmael son of Nethaniah took them captive and set out to cross over to the Ammonites.

¹¹When Johanan son of Kareah and all the army officers who were with him heard about all the crimes Ishmael son of Nethaniah had committed, ¹²they took all their men and went to fight Ishmael son of Nethaniah. They caught up with him near the great pool in Gibeon. ¹³When all the people Ishmael had with him saw Johanan son of Kareah and the army officers who were with him, they were glad. ¹⁴All the people Ishmael had taken captive at Mizpah turned and went over to Johanan son of Kareah. ¹⁵But Ishmael son of Nethaniah and eight of his men escaped from Johanan and fled to the Ammonites.

■ Flight to Egypt

¹⁶Then Johanan son of Kareah and all the army officers who were with him led away all the survivors from Mizpah whom he had recovered from Ishmael son of Nethaniah after he had assassinated

Gedaliah son of Ahikam: the soldiers, women, children and court officials he had brought from Gibeon. ¹⁷And they went on, stopping at Geruth Kimham near Bethlehem on their way to Egypt ¹⁸to escape the Babylonians.ᵇ They were afraid of them because Ishmael son of Nethaniah had killed Gedaliah son of Ahikam, whom the king of Babylon had appointed as governor over the land.

42 Then all the army officers, including Johanan son of Kareah and Jezaniahᵃ son of Hoshaiah, and all the people from the least to the greatest approached ²Jeremiah the prophet and said to him, "Please hear our petition and pray to the LORD your God for this entire remnant. For as you now see, though we were once many, now only a few are left. ³Pray that the LORD your God will tell us where we should go and what we should do."

⁴"I have heard you," replied Jeremiah the prophet. "I will certainly pray to the LORD your God as you have requested; I will tell you everything the LORD says and will keep nothing back from you."

⁵Then they said to Jeremiah, "May the LORD be a true and faithful witness against us if we do not act in accordance with everything the LORD your God sends you to tell us. ⁶Whether it is favourable or unfavourable, we will obey the LORD our God, to whom we are sending you, so that it will go well with us, for we will obey the LORD our God."

⁷Ten days later the word of the LORD came to Jeremiah. ⁸So he called together Johanan son of Kareah and all the army officers who were with him and all the people from the least to the greatest. ⁹He said to them, "This is what the LORD, the God of Israel, to whom you sent me to present your petition, says: ¹⁰'If you stay in this land, I will build you up and not tear you down; I will plant you and not uproot you, for I am grieved over the disaster I have inflicted on you. ¹¹Do not be afraid of the king of Babylon, whom you now fear. Do not be afraid of him, declares the LORD, for I am with you and will save you and deliver you from his hands. ¹²I will show you compassion so that he will have compassion on you and restore you to your land.'

¹³"However, if you say, 'We will not stay in this land,' and so disobey the LORD your God, ¹⁴and if you say, 'No, we will go and live in Egypt, where we will not see war or hear the trumpet or be hungry for bread,' ¹⁵then hear the word of the LORD, O remnant of Judah. This is what the LORD Almighty, the God of Israel, says: 'If you are determined to go to Egypt and you do go to settle there, ¹⁶then the sword you fear will overtake you there, and the famine you dread will follow you into Egypt, and there you will die. ¹⁷Indeed, all who are determined to go to Egypt to settle there will die by the sword, famine and plague; not one of them will survive or escape the disaster I will bring on them.' ¹⁸This is what the LORD Almighty, the God of Israel, says: 'As my anger and wrath have been poured out on those who lived in Jerusalem, so will my wrath be poured out on you when you go to Egypt. You will be an object of cursing and horror, of condemnation and reproach; you will never see this place again.'

¹⁹"O remnant of Judah, the LORD has told you, 'Do not go to Egypt.' Be sure of this: I warn you today

ᵃ3 Or Chaldean   ᵇ18 Or Chaldeans   ᵃ1 Hebrew; Septuagint (see also 43:2) Azariah

²⁰that you made a fatal mistake*b* when you sent me to the LORD your God and said, 'Pray to the LORD our God for us; tell us everything he says and we will do it.' ²¹I have told you today, but you still have not obeyed the LORD your God in all he sent me to tell you. ²²So now, be sure of this: You will die by the sword, famine and plague in the place where you want to go to settle."

43 When Jeremiah finished telling the people all the words of the LORD their God—everything the LORD had sent him to tell them—²Azariah son of Hoshaiah and Johanan son of Kareah and all the arrogant men said to Jeremiah, "You are lying! The LORD our God has not sent you to say, 'You must not go to Egypt to settle there.' ³But Baruch son of Neriah is inciting us against us to hand us over to the Babylonians,*a* so that they may kill us or carry us into exile to Babylon."

43:3 ■ CLOSED MINDS
Jeremiah was kidnapped by the few Israelites remaining in Jerusalem. Fearful that the Babylonians would blame them for the governor's murder, they took Jeremiah with them as they headed for Egypt. They stopped near Bethlehem to ask Jeremiah if they were doing the right thing. When he told them God wanted them to go back, they called him a liar. Jeremiah was disbelieved from the beginning to the end of his ministry, even by those who had seen some of his predictions come true.

---

⁴So Johanan son of Kareah and all the army officers and all the people disobeyed the LORD's command to stay in the land of Judah. ⁵Instead, Johanan son of Kareah and all the army officers led away all the remnant of Judah who had come back to live in the land of Judah from all the nations where they had been scattered. ⁶They also led away all the men, women and children and the king's daughters whom Nebuzaradan commander of the imperial guard had left with Gedaliah son of Ahikam, the son of Shaphan, and Jeremiah the prophet and Baruch son of Neriah. ⁷So they entered Egypt in disobedience to the LORD and went as far as Tahpanhes.

⁸In Tahpanhes the word of the LORD came to Jeremiah: ⁹"While the Jews are watching, take some large stones with you and bury them in clay in the brick pavement at the entrance to Pharaoh's palace in Tahpanhes. ¹⁰Then say to them, 'This is what the LORD Almighty, the God of Israel, says: I will send for my servant Nebuchadnezzar king of Babylon, and I will set his throne over these stones I have buried here; he will spread his royal canopy above them. ¹¹He will come and attack Egypt, bringing death to those destined for death, captivity to those destined for captivity, and the sword to those destined for the sword. ¹²He*b* will set fire to the temples of the gods of Egypt; he will burn their temples and take their gods captive. As a shepherd wraps his garment round him, so will he wrap Egypt round himself and depart from there unscathed. ¹³There in the temple of the sun*c* in Egypt he will demolish the sacred

pillars and will burn down the temples of the gods of Egypt.' "

■ **Disaster Because of Idolatry**

44 This word came to Jeremiah concerning all the Jews living in Lower Egypt—in Migdol, Tahpanhes and Memphis*a*—and in Upper Egypt:*b* ²"This is what the LORD Almighty, the God of Israel, says: You saw the great disaster I brought on Jerusalem and on all the towns of Judah. Today they lie deserted and in ruins ³because of the evil they have done. They provoked me to anger by burning incense and by worshipping other gods that neither they nor you nor your fathers ever knew. ⁴Again and again I sent my servants the prophets, who said, 'Do not do this detestable thing that I hate!' ⁵But they did not listen or pay attention; they did not turn from their wickedness or stop burning incense to other gods. ⁶Therefore, my fierce anger was poured out; it raged against the towns of Judah and the streets of Jerusalem and made them the desolate ruins they are today.

⁷"Now this is what the LORD God Almighty, the God of Israel, says: Why bring such great disaster on yourselves by cutting off from Judah the men and women, the children and infants, and so leave yourselves without a remnant? ⁸Why provoke me to anger with what your hands have made, burning incense to other gods in Egypt, where you have come to live? You will destroy yourselves and make yourselves an object of cursing and reproach among all the nations on earth. ⁹Have you forgotten the wickedness committed by your fathers and by the kings and queens of Judah and the wickedness committed by you and your wives in the land of Judah and the streets of Jerusalem? ¹⁰To this day they have not humbled themselves or shown reverence, nor have they followed my law and the decrees I set before you and your fathers.

¹¹"Therefore, this is what the LORD Almighty, the God of Israel, says: I am determined to bring disaster on you and to destroy all Judah. ¹²I will take away the remnant of Judah who were determined to go to Egypt to settle there. They will all perish in Egypt; they will fall by the sword or die from famine. From the least to the greatest, they will die by sword or famine. They will become an object of cursing and horror, of condemnation and reproach. ¹³I will punish those who live in Egypt with the sword, famine and plague, as I punished Jerusalem. ¹⁴None of the remnant of Judah who have gone to live in Egypt will escape or survive to return to the land of Judah, to which they long to return and live; none will return except a few fugitives."

¹⁵Then all the men who knew that their wives were burning incense to other gods, along with all the women who were present—a large assembly—and all the people living in Lower and Upper Egypt,*c* said to Jeremiah, ¹⁶"We will not listen to the message you have spoken to us in the name of the LORD! ¹⁷We will certainly do everything we said we would: We will burn incense to the Queen of Heaven and will pour out drink offerings to her just as we and our fathers, our kings and our officials did in the towns of Judah and in the streets of Jerusalem.

---

b20 Or you erred in your hearts   a3 Or Chaldeans   b12 Or I   c13 Or in Heliopolis   a1 Hebrew Noph   b1 Hebrew in Pathros
c15 Hebrew in Egypt and Pathros

At that time we had plenty of food and were well off and suffered no harm. [18]But ever since we stopped burning incense to the Queen of Heaven and pouring out drink offerings to her, we have had nothing and have been perishing by sword and famine."

44:18 ■ QUEEN OF HEAVEN
"Queen of Heaven" was a title for Ishtar, a Babylonian goddess of fertility. Israelites – women especially – had worshipped her for a very long time, until the revival sparked by King Josiah put a stop to the practice (2 Kings 22). Now, about 35 years after Josiah's campaign, Israelites blamed their downfall on his reform. Jeremiah tried to set the record straight: it was *persistence* in pagan worship that had led to their destruction.

---

[19]The women added, "When we burned incense to the Queen of Heaven and poured out drink offerings to her, did not our husbands know that we were making cakes like her image and pouring out drink offerings to her?"

[20]Then Jeremiah said to all the people, both men and women, who were answering him, [21]"Did not the LORD remember and think about the incense burned in the towns of Judah and the streets of Jerusalem by you and your fathers, your kings and your officials and the people of the land? [22]When the LORD could no longer endure your wicked actions and the detestable things you did, your land became an object of cursing and a desolate waste without inhabitants, as it is today. [23]Because you have burned incense and have sinned against the LORD and have not obeyed him or followed his law or his decrees or his stipulations, this disaster has come upon you, as you now see."

[24]Then Jeremiah said to all the people, including the women, "Hear the word of the LORD, all you people of Judah in Egypt. [25]This is what the LORD Almighty, the God of Israel, says: You and your wives have shown by your actions what you promised when you said, 'We will certainly carry out the vows we made to burn incense and pour out drink offerings to the Queen of Heaven.'

"Go ahead then, do what you promised! Keep your vows! [26]But hear the word of the LORD, all Jews living in Egypt: 'I swear by my great name,' says the LORD, 'that no-one from Judah living anywhere in Egypt shall ever again invoke my name or swear, "As surely as the Sovereign LORD lives." [27]For I am watching over them for harm, not for good; the Jews in Egypt will perish by sword and famine until they are all destroyed. [28]Those who escape the sword and return to the land of Judah from Egypt will be very few. Then the whole remnant of Judah who came to live in Egypt will know whose word will stand – mine or theirs.

[29]" 'This will be the sign to you that I will punish you in this place,' declares the LORD, 'so that you will know that my threats of harm against you will surely stand.' [30]This is what the LORD says: 'I am going to hand Pharaoh Hophra king of Egypt over to his enemies who seek his life, just as I handed Zedekiah king of Judah over to Nebuchadnezzar king of Babylon, the enemy who was seeking his life.' "

■ A Message to Baruch

45 This is what Jeremiah the prophet told Baruch son of Neriah in the fourth year of Jehoiakim son of Josiah king of Judah, after Baruch had written on a scroll the words Jeremiah was then dictating: [2]"This is what the LORD, the God of Israel, says to you, Baruch: [3]You said, 'Woe to me! The LORD has added sorrow to my pain; I am worn out with groaning and find no rest.' "

[4]⌞The LORD said,⌟ "Say this to him: 'This is what the LORD says: I will overthrow what I have built and uproot what I have planted, throughout the land. [5]Should you then seek great things for yourself? Seek them not. For I will bring disaster on all people, declares the LORD, but wherever you go I will let you escape with your life.' "

■ A Message About Egypt

46 This is the word of the LORD that came to Jeremiah the prophet concerning the nations:

[2]Concerning Egypt:

This is the message against the army of Pharaoh Neco king of Egypt, which was defeated at Carchemish on the Euphrates River by Nebuchadnezzar king of Babylon in the fourth year of Jehoiakim son of Josiah king of Judah:

[3]"Prepare your shields, both large and small,
    and march out for battle!
[4]Harness the horses,
    mount the steeds!
Take your positions
    with helmets on!
Polish your spears,
    put on your armour!
[5]What do I see?
    They are terrified,
they are retreating,
    their warriors are defeated.
They flee in haste
    without looking back,
    and there is terror on every side,"
                            declares the LORD.
[6]"The swift cannot flee
    nor the strong escape.
In the north by the River Euphrates
    they stumble and fall.

[7]"Who is this that rises like the Nile,
    like rivers of surging waters?
[8]Egypt rises like the Nile,
    like rivers of surging waters.
She says, 'I will rise and cover the earth;
    I will destroy cities and their people.'
[9]Charge, O horses!
    Drive furiously, O charioteers!
March on, O warriors –
    men of Cush[a] and Put who carry shields,
    men of Lydia who draw the bow.

¹⁰But that day belongs to the Lord, the LORD
      Almighty—
   a day of vengeance, for vengeance on his
      foes.
The sword will devour till it is satisfied,
   till it has quenched its thirst with blood.
For the Lord, the LORD Almighty, will offer
      sacrifice
   in the land of the north by the River
      Euphrates.

¹¹"Go up to Gilead and get balm,
   O Virgin Daughter of Egypt.
But you multiply remedies in vain;
   there is no healing for you.
¹²The nations will hear of your shame;
   your cries will fill the earth.
One warrior will stumble over another;
   both will fall down together."

¹³This is the message the LORD spoke to Jeremiah
the prophet about the coming of Nebuchadnezzar
king of Babylon to attack Egypt:

¹⁴"Announce this in Egypt, and proclaim it in
      Migdol;
   proclaim it also in Memphis*b* and
      Tahpanhes:
'Take your positions and get ready,
   for the sword devours those around you.'

¹⁵Why will your warriors be laid low?
   They cannot stand, for the LORD will push
      them down.
¹⁶They will stumble repeatedly;
   they will fall over each other.
They will say, 'Get up, let us go back
   to our own people and our native lands,
   away from the sword of the oppressor.'
¹⁷There they will exclaim,
   'Pharaoh king of Egypt is only a loud noise;
   he has missed his opportunity.'

¹⁸"As surely as I live," declares the King,
   whose name is the LORD Almighty,
"one will come who is like Tabor among the
      mountains,
   like Carmel by the sea.
¹⁹Pack your belongings for exile,
   you who live in Egypt,
for Memphis will be laid waste
   and lie in ruins without inhabitant.

²⁰"Egypt is a beautiful heifer,
   but a gadfly is coming
   against her from the north.
²¹The mercenaries in her ranks
   are like fattened calves.
They too will turn and flee together,
   they will not stand their ground,

WORLD AT WAR
WHILE NATIONS BATTLE, GOD IS IN CONTROL

INSIGHT

"THE SWORD WILL DEVOUR TILL IT IS
SATISFIED, TILL IT HAS QUENCHED ITS
THIRST WITH BLOOD." ■ 46:10

Turn on the TV news. Scenes from round the
world flash across the screen. In the Middle
East, a bomb explodes and a building collapses.
Bodies lie in the gutter. Women howl with
anguish over their dead.
      Seconds later you are in Africa.
Revolutionaries, rifles brandished over their
heads, march through captured streets. The
camera zeroes in on the crumpled body of their
former president.
      The scene shifts to a Central American
capital. Sirens scream round a burning
restaurant while stretcher-bearers carry out the
moaning victims of a drug-lord attack. Next, in
Africa again, starving children grimace at you,
too far gone to beg for food. Then you see
snatches of violence in United States ghettoes,
scenes of ethnic unrest in Europe and political
protests in Tibet and India. The world is whirling
out of control. Your mind cannot take it in; one
disaster muddles with another.

■ GOD IS IN CONTROL
In chapters 46 to 50, Jeremiah gives a similar

portrait of the world. We flash by imagination
from one country to the next. We smell the
rotting bodies; we hear the exultant cries of
conquerors. Jeremiah shows, in vivid colour, a
world as frightening as ours.
      But there is a difference. TV news
leaves viewers with a dizzy feeling that chaos
reigns. But Jeremiah's vision shows,
paradoxically, that God is in control. Through
these disasters God punishes those who have
opposed his will. As Israel's neighbours are
destroyed, exiled Jews are freed to return to
their land. History is not just "one thing after
another". God gives it a sense of direction.
      Jeremiah delivered his longest and
most biting message to Babylon, Judah's
conqueror. Their sheer arrogance, their
assumption that they could do whatever they
liked, drew God's fury. To a lesser degree,
other countries followed the same pattern.
God did not judge them by his law, because
they never knew it. He judged them for their
pride. They ought to have shown humility
before God.

□ LIFE QUESTIONS:
Can you discern any pattern or purpose to the
violence in the world today?

b 14 Hebrew Noph; also in verse 19

for the day of disaster is coming upon them,
    the time for them to be punished.
22Egypt will hiss like a fleeing serpent
    as the enemy advances in force;
they will come against her with axes,
    like men who cut down trees.
23They will chop down her forest,"
               declares the LORD,
    "dense though it be.
They are more numerous than locusts,
    they cannot be counted.
24The Daughter of Egypt will be put to shame,
    handed over to the people of the north."

25The LORD Almighty, the God of Israel, says: "I am about to bring punishment on Amon god of Thebes,c on Pharaoh, on Egypt and her gods and her kings, and on those who rely on Pharaoh. 26I will hand them over to those who seek their lives, to Nebuchadnezzar king of Babylon and his officers. Later, however, Egypt will be inhabited as in times past," declares the LORD.

27"Do not fear, O Jacob my servant;
    do not be dismayed, O Israel.
I will surely save you out of a distant place,
    and your descendants from the land of their
        exile.
Jacob will again have peace and security,
    and no-one will make him afraid.
28Do not fear, O Jacob my servant,
    for I am with you," declares the LORD.
"Though I completely destroy all the nations
    among which I scatter you,
I will not completely destroy you.
I will discipline you but only with justice;
    I will not let you go entirely unpunished."

■ A Message About the Philistines

47 This is the word of the LORD that came to Jeremiah the prophet concerning the Philistines before Pharaoh attacked Gaza:

2This is what the LORD says:

"See how the waters are rising in the north;
    they will become an overflowing torrent.
They will overflow the land and everything in
      it,
    the towns and those who live in them.
The people will cry out;
    all who dwell in the land will wail
3at the sound of the hoofs of galloping steeds,
    at the noise of enemy chariots
    and the rumble of their wheels.
Fathers will not turn to help their children;
    their hands will hang limp.
4For the day has come
    to destroy all the Philistines
and to cut off all survivors
    who could help Tyre and Sidon.
The LORD is about to destroy the Philistines,
    the remnant from the coasts of Caphtor.a
5Gaza will shave her head in mourning;
    Ashkelon will be silenced.

O remnant on the plain,
    how long will you cut yourselves?

6" 'Ah, sword of the LORD,' ⌐you cry,⌐
    'how long till you rest?
Return to your scabbard;
    cease and be still.'
7But how can it rest
    when the LORD has commanded it,
when he has ordered it
    to attack Ashkelon and the coast?"

■ A Message About Moab

48 Concerning Moab:

This is what the LORD Almighty, the God of Israel, says:

"Woe to Nebo, for it will be ruined.
    Kiriathaim will be disgraced and captured;
    the strongholda will be disgraced and
        shattered.
2Moab will be praised no more;
    in Heshbonb men will plot her downfall:
    'Come, let us put an end to that nation.'
You too, O Madmen,c will be silenced;
    the sword will pursue you.
3Listen to the cries from Horonaim,
    cries of great havoc and destruction.
4Moab will be broken;
    her little ones will cry out.d
5They go up the way to Luhith,
    weeping bitterly as they go;
on the road down to Horonaim
    anguished cries over the destruction are
        heard.
6Flee! Run for your lives;
    become like a bushe in the desert.
7Since you trust in your deeds and riches,
    you too will be taken captive,
and Chemosh will go into exile,
    together with his priests and officials.
8The destroyer will come against every town,
    and not a town will escape.
The valley will be ruined
    and the plateau destroyed,
because the LORD has spoken.
9Put salt on Moab,
    for she will be laid waste;f
her towns will become desolate,
    with no-one to live in them.

48:7 ■ **AN EXILED GOD**
The gods of the Middle East tended to occupy a certain territory – thus each city had its own god. Chemosh, the chief god of Moab, was worshipped through child sacrifice (2 Kings 3:27). Here Jeremiah predicts that not only would the Moabites go into exile – their god would too. These gods were powerless before the God of Israel.

10"A curse on him who is lax in doing the LORD's
    work!

---

c25 Hebrew No   a4 That is, Crete   a1 Or / Misgab   b2 The Hebrew for Heshbon sounds like the Hebrew for plot.   c2 The name of the Moabite town Madmen sounds like the Hebrew for be silenced.   d4 Hebrew; Septuagint / proclaim it to Zoar   e6 Or like Aroer   f9 Or Give wings to Moab, / for she will fly away

A curse on him who keeps his sword from
  bloodshed!

¹¹"Moab has been at rest from youth,
  like wine left on its dregs,
not poured from one jar to another—
  she has not gone into exile.
So she tastes as she did,
  and her aroma is unchanged.
¹²But days are coming,"
  declares the LORD,
"when I will send men who pour from jars,
  and they will pour her out;
they will empty her jars
  and smash her jugs.
¹³Then Moab will be ashamed of Chemosh,
  as the house of Israel was ashamed
  when they trusted in Bethel.

¹⁴"How can you say, 'We are warriors,
  men valiant in battle'?
¹⁵Moab will be destroyed and her towns invaded;
  her finest young men will go down in the
    slaughter,"
  declares the King, whose name is the LORD
    Almighty.
¹⁶"The fall of Moab is at hand;
  her calamity will come quickly.
¹⁷Mourn for her, all who live around her,
  all who know her fame;
say, 'How broken is the mighty sceptre,
  how broken the glorious staff!'

¹⁸"Come down from your glory
  and sit on the parched ground,
  O inhabitants of the Daughter of Dibon,
for he who destroys Moab
  will come up against you
  and ruin your fortified cities.
¹⁹Stand by the road and watch,
  you who live in Aroer.
Ask the man fleeing and the woman escaping,
  ask them, 'What has happened?'
²⁰Moab is disgraced, for she is shattered.
  Wail and cry out!
Announce by the Arnon
  that Moab is destroyed.
²¹Judgment has come to the plateau—
  to Holon, Jahzah and Mephaath,
²² to Dibon, Nebo and Beth Diblathaim,
²³ to Kiriathaim, Beth Gamul and Beth Meon,
²⁴ to Kerioth and Bozrah—
  to all the towns of Moab, far and near.
²⁵Moab's horn ^{g} is cut off;
  her arm is broken,"
            declares the LORD.

²⁶"Make her drunk,
  for she has defied the LORD.
Let Moab wallow in her vomit;
  let her be an object of ridicule.
²⁷Was not Israel the object of your ridicule?
  Was she caught among thieves,
that you shake your head in scorn
  whenever you speak of her?
²⁸Abandon your towns and dwell among the
  rocks,

you who live in Moab.
Be like a dove that makes its nest
  at the mouth of a cave.

²⁹"We have heard of Moab's pride—
  her overweening pride and conceit,
  her pride and arrogance
  and the haughtiness of her heart.
³⁰I know her insolence but it is futile,"
            declares the LORD,
  "and her boasts accomplish nothing.
³¹Therefore I wail over Moab,
  for all Moab I cry out,
  I moan for the men of Kir Hareseth.
³²I weep for you, as Jazer weeps,
  O vines of Sibmah.
Your branches spread as far as the sea;
  they reached as far as the sea of Jazer.
The destroyer has fallen
  on your ripened fruit and grapes.
³³Joy and gladness are gone
  from the orchards and fields of Moab.
I have stopped the flow of wine from the
    presses;
  no-one treads them with shouts of joy.
Although there are shouts,
  they are not shouts of joy.

³⁴"The sound of their cry rises
  from Heshbon to Elealeh and Jahaz,
  from Zoar as far as Horonaim and Eglath
    Shelishiyah,
for even the waters of Nimrim are dried up.
³⁵In Moab I will put an end
  to those who make offerings on the high
    places
  and burn incense to their gods,"
            declares the LORD.
³⁶"So my heart laments for Moab like a flute;
  it laments like a flute for the men of Kir
    Hareseth.
The wealth they acquired is gone.
³⁷Every head is shaved
  and every beard cut off;
every hand is slashed
  and every waist is covered with sackcloth.
³⁸On all the roofs in Moab
  and in the public squares
there is nothing but mourning,
  for I have broken Moab
  like a jar that no-one wants,"
            declares the LORD.
³⁹"How shattered she is! How they wail!
  How Moab turns her back in shame!
Moab has become an object of ridicule,
  an object of horror to all those around her."

⁴⁰This is what the LORD says:

"Look! An eagle is swooping down,
  spreading its wings over Moab.
⁴¹Kerioth ^{b} will be captured
  and the strongholds taken.
In that day the hearts of Moab's warriors
  will be like the heart of a woman in labour.
⁴²Moab will be destroyed as a nation
  because she defied the LORD.

^{g}25 Horn here symbolises strength. ^{b}41 Or The cities

43Terror and pit and snare await you,
   O people of Moab,"
                              declares the LORD.
44"Whoever flees from the terror
   will fall into a pit,
whoever climbs out of the pit
   will be caught in a snare;
for I will bring upon Moab
   the year of her punishment,"
                              declares the LORD.

45"In the shadow of Heshbon
   the fugitives stand helpless,
for a fire has gone out from Heshbon,
   a blaze from the midst of Sihon;
it burns the foreheads of Moab,
   the skulls of the noisy boasters.

48:43 ■ WELL-TURNED PHRASE
Some of Jeremiah's language eludes translation,
especially when, as here, he chooses Hebrew
words for the sake of sound. "Terror, pit, snare"
are translations of "pahad, pahat, pah". Isaiah (or
some poet before him) had already minted the
phrase, generations before Jeremiah (see Isaiah
24:17).

46Woe to you, O Moab!
   The people of Chemosh are destroyed;
your sons are taken into exile
   and your daughters into captivity.

47"Yet I will restore the fortunes of Moab
   in days to come,"
                              declares the LORD.

Here ends the judgment on Moab.

■ A Message About Ammon

49 Concerning the Ammonites:

   This is what the LORD says:

"Has Israel no sons?
   Has she no heirs?
Why then has Molech*a* taken possession of
      Gad?
   Why do his people live in its towns?
2But the days are coming,"
   declares the LORD,
"when I will sound the battle cry
   against Rabbah of the Ammonites;
it will become a mound of ruins,
   and its surrounding villages will be set on
      fire.
Then Israel will drive out
   those who drove her out,"
                              says the LORD.
3"Wail, O Heshbon, for Ai is destroyed!
   Cry out, O inhabitants of Rabbah!
Put on sackcloth and mourn;
   rush here and there inside the walls,
for Molech will go into exile,
   together with his priests and officials.
4Why do you boast of your valleys,

boast of your valleys so fruitful?
O unfaithful daughter,
   you trust in your riches and say,
   'Who will attack me?'
5I will bring terror on you
   from all those around you,"
                              declares the Lord,
                                    the LORD Almighty.
"Every one of you will be driven away,
   and no-one will gather the fugitives.

6"Yet afterwards, I will restore the fortunes of
      the Ammonites,"
                              declares the LORD.

■ A Message About Edom
7Concerning Edom:

   This is what the LORD Almighty says:

"Is there no longer wisdom in Teman?
   Has counsel perished from the prudent?
   Has their wisdom decayed?
8Turn and flee, hide in deep caves,
   you who live in Dedan,
for I will bring disaster on Esau
   at the time I punish him.
9If grape-pickers came to you,
   would they not leave a few grapes?
If thieves came during the night,
   would they not steal only as much as they
      wanted?
10But I will strip Esau bare;
   I will uncover his hiding-places,
   so that he cannot conceal himself.
His children, relatives and neighbours will
      perish,
   and he will be no more.
11Leave your orphans; I will protect their lives.
   Your widows too can trust in me."

12This is what the LORD says: "If those who do not
deserve to drink the cup must drink it, why should
you go unpunished? You will not go unpunished,
but must drink it. 13I swear by myself," declares the
LORD, "that Bozrah will become a ruin and an object
of horror, of reproach and of cursing; and all its
towns will be in ruins for ever."

14I have heard a message from the LORD:
   An envoy was sent to the nations to say,
   "Assemble yourselves to attack it!
   Rise up for battle!"

15"Now I will make you small among the nations,
   despised among men.
16The terror you inspire
   and the pride of your heart have deceived
      you,
you who live in the clefts of the rocks,
   who occupy the heights of the hill.
Though you build your nest as high as the
      eagle's,
   from there I will bring you down,"
                              declares the LORD.
17"Edom will become an object of horror;
   all who pass by will be appalled and will
      scoff

---

a 1 *Or their king;* Hebrew *malcam;* also in verse 3

because of all its wounds.
¹⁸As Sodom and Gomorrah were overthrown,
    along with their neighbouring towns,"
                                    says the LORD,
"so no-one will live there;
    no man will dwell in it.

¹⁹"Like a lion coming up from Jordan's thickets
    to a rich pasture-land,
I will chase Edom from its land in an instant.
    Who is the chosen one I will appoint for
        this?
Who is like me and who can challenge me?
    And what shepherd can stand against me?"
²⁰Therefore, hear what the LORD has planned
    against Edom,
    what he has purposed against those who live
        in Teman:
The young of the flock will be dragged away;
    he will completely destroy their pasture
        because of them.
²¹At the sound of their fall the earth will tremble;
    their cry will resound to the Red Sea.^b
²²Look! An eagle will soar and swoop down,
    spreading its wings over Bozrah.
In that day the hearts of Edom's warriors
    will be like the heart of a woman in labour.

■ A Message About Damascus
    ²³Concerning Damascus:

"Hamath and Arpad are dismayed,
    for they have heard bad news.
They are disheartened,
    troubled like^c the restless sea.
²⁴Damascus has become feeble,
    she has turned to flee
    and panic has gripped her;
anguish and pain have seized her,
    pain like that of a woman in labour.
²⁵Why has the city of renown not been
        abandoned,
    the town in which I delight?
²⁶Surely, her young men will fall in the streets;
    all her soldiers will be silenced in that day,"
                        declares the LORD Almighty.
²⁷"I will set fire to the walls of Damascus;
    it will consume the fortresses of Ben-Hadad."

■ A Message About Kedar and Hazor
    ²⁸Concerning Kedar and the kingdoms of Hazor,
which Nebuchadnezzar king of Babylon attacked:

This is what the LORD says:

"Arise, and attack Kedar
    and destroy the people of the East.
²⁹Their tents and their flocks will be taken;
    their shelters will be carried off
    with all their goods and camels.
Men will shout to them,
    'Terror on every side!'

³⁰"Flee quickly away!
    Stay in deep caves, you who live in Hazor,"
                            declares the LORD.

"Nebuchadnezzar king of Babylon has plotted
        against you;
    he has devised a plan against you.

³¹"Arise and attack a nation at ease,
    which lives in confidence,"
                        declares the LORD,
"a nation that has neither gates nor bars;
    its people live alone.
³²Their camels will become plunder,
    and their large herds will be booty.
I will scatter to the winds those who are in
        distant places^d
    and will bring disaster on them from every
        side,"
                        declares the LORD.
³³"Hazor will become a haunt of jackals,
    a desolate place for ever.
No-one will live there;
    no man will dwell in it."

■ A Message About Elam
    ³⁴This is the word of the LORD that came to Jere-
miah the prophet concerning Elam, early in the
reign of Zedekiah king of Judah:

³⁵This is what the LORD Almighty says:

"See, I will break the bow of Elam,
    the mainstay of their might.
³⁶I will bring against Elam the four winds
    from the four quarters of the heavens;
I will scatter them to the four winds,
    and there will not be a nation
    where Elam's exiles do not go.
³⁷I will shatter Elam before their foes,
    before those who seek their lives;
I will bring disaster upon them,
    even my fierce anger,"
                        declares the LORD.
"I will pursue them with the sword
    until I have made an end of them.
³⁸I will set my throne in Elam
    and destroy her king and officials,"
                        declares the LORD.

³⁹"Yet I will restore the fortunes of Elam
    in days to come,"
                        declares the LORD.

■ A Message About Babylon
50 This is the word the LORD spoke through
    Jeremiah the prophet concerning Babylon
and the land of the Babylonians:^a

²"Announce and proclaim among the nations,
    lift up a banner and proclaim it;
    keep nothing back, but say,
'Babylon will be captured;
    Bel will be put to shame,
    Marduk filled with terror.
Her images will be put to shame
    and her idols filled with terror.'
³A nation from the north will attack her
    and lay waste her land.
No-one will live in it;
    both men and animals will flee away.

^b21 Hebrew *Yam Suph*; that is, Sea of Reeds   ^c23 Hebrew *on* or *by*   ^d32 Or *who clip the hair by their foreheads*   ^a1 Or *Chaldeans*; also in
verses 8, 25, 35 and 45

4"In those days, at that time,"
   declares the LORD,
"the people of Israel and the people of Judah
   together
   will go in tears to seek the LORD their God.

50:1 ■ NONE ESCAPE

Chapters 46–50 record a virtual catalogue of Israel's enemies. Jeremiah begins with Egypt, goes on to Israel's immediate (small) neighbours, and ends with arch-enemy Babylon. No nation is exempt from God's justice.

5They will ask the way to Zion
   and turn their faces towards it.
They will come and bind themselves to the
   LORD
   in an everlasting covenant
   that will not be forgotten.

6"My people have been lost sheep;
   their shepherds have led them astray
   and caused them to roam on the mountains.
They wandered over mountain and hill
   and forgot their own resting place.
7Whoever found them devoured them;
   their enemies said, 'We are not guilty,
for they sinned against the LORD, their true
   pasture,
   the LORD, the hope of their fathers.'

8"Flee out of Babylon;
   leave the land of the Babylonians,
   and be like the goats that lead the flock.
9For I will stir up and bring against Babylon
   an alliance of great nations from the land of
   the north.
They will take up their positions against her,
   and from the north she will be captured.
Their arrows will be like skilled warriors
   who do not return empty-handed.
10So Babylonia[b] will be plundered;
   all who plunder her will have their fill,"
                        declares the LORD.

11"Because you rejoice and are glad,
   you who pillage my inheritance,
because you frolic like a heifer threshing corn
   and neigh like stallions,
12your mother will be greatly ashamed;
   she who gave you birth will be disgraced.
She will be the least of the nations—
   a wilderness, a dry land, a desert.
13Because of the LORD's anger she will not be
   inhabited
   but will be completely desolate.
All who pass Babylon will be horrified and scoff
   because of all her wounds.

14"Take up your positions round Babylon,
   all you who draw the bow.
Shoot at her! Spare no arrows,
   for she has sinned against the LORD.
15Shout against her on every side!
   She surrenders, her towers fall,

her walls are torn down.
Since this is the vengeance of the LORD,
   take vengeance on her;
   do to her as she has done to others.
16Cut off from Babylon the sower,
   and the reaper with his sickle at harvest.
Because of the sword of the oppressor
   let everyone return to his own people,
   let everyone flee to his own land.

17"Israel is a scattered flock
   that lions have chased away.
The first to devour him
   was the king of Assyria;
the last to crush his bones
   was Nebuchadnezzar king of Babylon."

18Therefore this is what the LORD Almighty, the
God of Israel, says:

"I will punish the king of Babylon and his land
   as I punished the king of Assyria.
19But I will bring Israel back to his own pasture
   and he will graze on Carmel and Bashan;
his appetite will be satisfied
   on the hills of Ephraim and Gilead.
20In those days, at that time,"
   declares the LORD,
"search will be made for Israel's guilt,
   but there will be none,
and for the sins of Judah,
   but none will be found,
   for I will forgive the remnant I spare.

50:20 ■ AN END TO GUILT

For 50 chapters the book of Jeremiah hammers away at Israel's guilt. Because of it, punishment was bound to come. Yet the forgiveness to come from God will be as absolute as the guilt: a search for Israel's sins will not uncover a single one.

21"Attack the land of Merathaim
   and those who live in Pekod.
Pursue, kill and completely destroy[c] them,"
                        declares the LORD.
   "Do everything I have commanded you.
22The noise of battle is in the land,
   the noise of great destruction!
23How broken and shattered
   is the hammer of the whole earth!
How desolate is Babylon
   among the nations!
24I set a trap for you, O Babylon,
   and you were caught before you knew it;
you were found and captured
   because you opposed the LORD.
25The LORD has opened his arsenal
   and brought out the weapons of his wrath,
for the Sovereign LORD Almighty has work to do
   in the land of the Babylonians.
26Come against her from afar.
   Break open her granaries;
   pile her up like heaps of grain.
Completely destroy her
   and leave her no remnant.

b 10 Or Chaldea   c 21 The Hebrew term refers to the irrevocable giving over of things or persons to the LORD, often by totally destroying them; also in verse 26.

27Kill all her young bulls;
    let them go down to the slaughter!
Woe to them! For their day has come,
    the time for them to be punished.
28Listen to the fugitives and refugees from
    Babylon
    declaring in Zion
how the LORD our God has taken vengeance,
    vengeance for his temple.

29"Summon archers against Babylon,
    all those who draw the bow.
Encamp all round her;
    let no-one escape.
Repay her for her deeds;
    do to her as she has done.
For she defied the LORD,
    the Holy One of Israel.
30Therefore, her young men will fall in the
    streets;
    all her soldiers will be silenced in that day,"
                    declares the LORD.
31"See, I am against you, O arrogant one,"
    declares the Lord, the LORD Almighty,
"for your day has come,
    the time for you to be punished.
32The arrogant one will stumble and fall
    and no-one will help her up;
I will kindle a fire in her towns
    that will consume all who are around her."

33This is what the LORD Almighty says:

"The people of Israel are oppressed,
    and the people of Judah as well.
All their captors hold them fast,
    refusing to let them go.
34Yet their Redeemer is strong;
    the LORD Almighty is his name.
He will vigorously defend their cause
    so that he may bring rest to their land,
    but unrest to those who live in Babylon.

35"A sword against the Babylonians!"
    declares the LORD —
"against those who live in Babylon
    and against her officials and wise men!
36A sword against her false prophets!
    They will become fools.
A sword against her warriors!
    They will be filled with terror.
37A sword against her horses and chariots
    and all the foreigners in her ranks!
    They will become women.
A sword against her treasures!
    They will be plundered.
38A drought on*d* her waters!
    They will dry up.
For it is a land of idols,
    idols that will go mad with terror.

39"So desert creatures and hyenas will live there,
    and there the owl will dwell.
It will never again be inhabited
    or lived in from generation to generation.
40As God overthrew Sodom and Gomorrah

along with their neighbouring towns,"
                    declares the LORD,
"so no-one will live there;
    no man will dwell in it.

41"Look! An army is coming from the north;
    a great nation and many kings
    are being stirred up from the ends of the
    earth.
42They are armed with bows and spears;
    they are cruel and without mercy.
They sound like the roaring sea
    as they ride on their horses;
they come like men in battle formation
    to attack you, O Daughter of Babylon.
43The king of Babylon has heard reports about
    them,
    and his hands hang limp.
Anguish has gripped him,
    pain like that of a woman in labour.
44Like a lion coming up from Jordan's thickets
    to a rich pasture-land,
I will chase Babylon from its land in an instant.
    Who is the chosen one I will appoint for this?
Who is like me and who can challenge me?
    And what shepherd can stand against me?"
45Therefore, hear what the LORD has planned
    against Babylon,
    what he has purposed against the land of the
    Babylonians:
The young of the flock will be dragged away;
    he will completely destroy their pasture
    because of them.
46At the sound of Babylon's capture the earth will
    tremble;
    its cry will resound among the nations.

51

This is what the LORD says:

"See, I will stir up the spirit of a destroyer
    against Babylon and the people of Leb
    Kamai.*a*
2I will send foreigners to Babylon
    to winnow her and to devastate her land;
they will oppose her on every side
    in the day of her disaster.
3Let not the archer string his bow,
    nor let him put on his armour.
Do not spare her young men;
    completely destroy*b* her army.
4They will fall down slain in Babylon,*c*
    fatally wounded in her streets.
5For Israel and Judah have not been forsaken
    by their God, the LORD Almighty,
though their land*d* is full of guilt
    before the Holy One of Israel.

6"Flee from Babylon!
    Run for your lives!
    Do not be destroyed because of her sins.
It is time for the LORD's vengeance;
    he will pay her what she deserves.
7Babylon was a gold cup in the LORD's hand;
    she made the whole earth drunk.
The nations drank her wine;
    therefore they have now gone mad.

---

*d*38 Or *A sword against*   *a*1 *Leb Kamai* is a cryptogram for Chaldea, that is, Babylonia.   *b*3 The Hebrew term refers to the irrevocable giving over of
things or persons to the LORD, often by totally destroying them.   *c*4 Or *Chaldea*   *d*5 Or *I and the land ˌof the Babyloniansˌ*

8Babylon will suddenly fall and be broken.
  Wail over her!
Get balm for her pain;
  perhaps she can be healed.

9" 'We would have healed Babylon,
  but she cannot be healed;
let us leave her and each go to his own land,
  for her judgment reaches to the skies,
  it rises as high as the clouds.'

10" 'The LORD has vindicated us;
  come, let us tell in Zion
  what the LORD our God has done.'

11"Sharpen the arrows,
  take up the shields!
The LORD has stirred up the kings of the Medes,
  because his purpose is to destroy Babylon.
The LORD will take vengeance,
  vengeance for his temple.
12Lift up a banner against the walls of Babylon!
  Reinforce the guard,
station the watchmen,
  prepare an ambush!
The LORD will carry out his purpose,
  his decree against the people of Babylon.
13You who live by many waters
  and are rich in treasures,
your end has come,
  the time for you to be cut off.

51:13 ■ WATERS OF BABYLON

Water has always been precious in the Middle
East, and Babylon's mighty Euphrates River,
complemented by a magnificent system of
irrigation canals, was a major source of wealth
and security in times of drought. The modern-day
nations of Iraq, Iran, and Turkey still argue — and
sometimes fight — over this resource.

14The LORD Almighty has sworn by himself:
  I will surely fill you with men, as with a
    swarm of locusts,
  and they will shout in triumph over you.

15"He made the earth by his power;
  he founded the world by his wisdom
  and stretched out the heavens by his
    understanding.
16When he thunders, the waters in the heavens
    roar;
  he makes clouds rise from the ends of the
    earth.
He sends lightning with the rain
  and brings out the wind from his
    storehouses.

17"Every man is senseless and without knowledge;
  every goldsmith is shamed by his idols.
His images are a fraud;
  they have no breath in them.
18They are worthless, the objects of mockery;
  when their judgment comes, they will perish.
19He who is the Portion of Jacob is not like
    these,

for he is the Maker of all things,
  including the tribe of his inheritance —
  the LORD Almighty is his name.

20"You are my war club,
  my weapon for battle —
with you I shatter nations,
  with you I destroy kingdoms,
21with you I shatter horse and rider,
  with you I shatter chariot and driver,
22with you I shatter man and woman,
  with you I shatter old man and youth,
  with you I shatter young man and maiden,
23with you I shatter shepherd and flock,
  with you I shatter farmer and oxen,
  with you I shatter governors and officials.

24"Before your eyes I will repay Babylon and all
who live in Babyloniae for all the wrong they have
done in Zion," declares the LORD.

25"I am against you, O destroying mountain,
  you who destroy the whole earth,"
                              declares the LORD.
"I will stretch out my hand against you,
  roll you off the cliffs,
  and make you a burnt-out mountain.
26No rock will be taken from you for a
    cornerstone,
  nor any stone for a foundation,
  for you will be desolate for ever,"
                              declares the LORD.

27"Lift up a banner in the land!
  Blow the trumpet among the nations!
Prepare the nations for battle against her;
  summon against her these kingdoms:
  Ararat, Minni and Ashkenaz.
Appoint a commander against her;
  send up horses like a swarm of locusts.
28Prepare the nations for battle against her —
  the kings of the Medes,
their governors and all their officials,
  and all the countries they rule.
29The land trembles and writhes,
  for the LORD's purposes against Babylon
    stand —
to lay waste the land of Babylon
  so that no-one will live there.
30Babylon's warriors have stopped fighting;
  they remain in their strongholds.
Their strength is exhausted;
  they have become like women.
Her dwellings are set on fire;
  the bars of her gates are broken.
31One courier follows another
  and messenger follows messenger
to announce to the king of Babylon
  that his entire city is captured,
32the river crossings seized,
  the marshes set on fire,
  and the soldiers terrified."

33This is what the LORD Almighty, the God of Israel, says:

"The Daughter of Babylon is like a
    threshing-floor

e 24 Or *Chaldea*; also in verse 35

at the time it is trampled;
the time to harvest her will soon come."

34"Nebuchadnezzar king of Babylon has devoured
us,
he has thrown us into confusion,
he has made us an empty jar.
Like a serpent he has swallowed us
and filled his stomach with our delicacies,
and then has spewed us out.
35May the violence done to our flesh*f* be upon
Babylon,"
say the inhabitants of Zion.
"May our blood be on those who live in
Babylonia,"
says Jerusalem.

36Therefore, this is what the LORD says:

"See, I will defend your cause
and avenge you;
I will dry up her sea
and make her springs dry.
37Babylon will be a heap of ruins,
a haunt of jackals,
an object of horror and scorn,
a place where no-one lives.
38Her people all roar like young lions,
they growl like lion cubs.
39But while they are aroused,
I will set out a feast for them
and make them drunk,
so that they shout with laughter—
then sleep for ever and not awake,"
declares the LORD.
40"I will bring them down
like lambs to the slaughter,
like rams and goats.

41"How Sheshach*g* will be captured,
the boast of the whole earth seized!
What a horror Babylon will be
among the nations!
42The sea will rise over Babylon;
its roaring waves will cover her.
43Her towns will be desolate,
a dry and desert land,
a land where no-one lives,
through which no man travels.
44I will punish Bel in Babylon
and make him spew out what he has
swallowed.
The nations will no longer stream to him.
And the wall of Babylon will fall.

45"Come out of her, my people!
Run for your lives!
Run from the fierce anger of the LORD.
46Do not lose heart or be afraid
when rumours are heard in the land;
one rumour comes this year, another the next,
rumours of violence in the land
and of ruler against ruler.
47For the time will surely come
when I will punish the idols of Babylon;
her whole land will be disgraced
and her slain will all lie fallen within her.

48Then heaven and earth and all that is in them
will shout for joy over Babylon,
for out of the north
destroyers will attack her,"
declares the LORD.

49"Babylon must fall because of Israel's slain,
just as the slain in all the earth
have fallen because of Babylon.
50You who have escaped the sword,
leave and do not linger!
Remember the LORD in a distant land,
and think on Jerusalem."

51"We are disgraced,
for we have been insulted
and shame covers our faces,
because foreigners have entered
the holy places of the LORD's house."

52"But days are coming," declares the LORD,
"when I will punish her idols,
and throughout her land
the wounded will groan.
53Even if Babylon reaches the sky
and fortifies her lofty stronghold,
I will send destroyers against her,"
declares the LORD.

51:53 ■ APOCALYPTIC ARROGANCE

The arrogance of Babylon—her sense of absolute,
untouchable power—became an emblem of the
forces God will ultimately destroy. Jeremiah was
probably thinking only of Babylon's towering
ziggurat (or temple) and double wall defences. But
Babylon's "reaching for the sky" suggested an
image of a nation trying to compete with God.
Revelation 18—written long after Jeremiah's
Babylon had been destroyed—described the fall
of another proud and wealthy "Babylon" at the
end of the age.

54"The sound of a cry comes from Babylon,
the sound of great destruction
from the land of the Babylonians.*b*
55The LORD will destroy Babylon;
he will silence her noisy din.
Waves ⌐of enemies⌐ will rage like great waters;
the roar of their voices will resound.
56A destroyer will come against Babylon;
her warriors will be captured,
and their bows will be broken.
For the LORD is a God of retribution;
he will repay in full.
57I will make her officials and wise men drunk,
her governors, officers and warriors as well;
they will sleep for ever and not awake,"
declares the King, whose name is the LORD
Almighty.

58This is what the LORD Almighty says:

"Babylon's thick wall will be levelled
and her high gates set on fire;
the peoples exhaust themselves for nothing,

---

f35 Or done to us and to our children   g41 Sheshach is a cryptogram for Babylon.   b54 Or Chaldeans the nations' labour is only fuel for the flames."

59This is the message Jeremiah gave to the staff officer Seraiah son of Neriah, the son of Mahseiah, when he went to Babylon with Zedekiah king of Judah in the fourth year of his reign. 60Jeremiah had written on a scroll about all the disasters that would come upon Babylon—all that had been recorded concerning Babylon. 61He said to Seraiah, "When you get to Babylon, see that you read all these words aloud. 62Then say, 'O LORD, you have said you will destroy this place, so that neither man nor animal will live in it; it will be desolate for ever.' 63When you finish reading this scroll, tie a stone to it and throw it into the Euphrates. 64Then say, 'So will Babylon sink to rise no more because of the disaster I will bring upon her. And her people will fall.' "

The words of Jeremiah end here.

■ The Fall of Jerusalem

52 Zedekiah was twenty-one years old when he became king, and he reigned in Jerusalem for eleven years. His mother's name was Hamutal daughter of Jeremiah; she was from Libnah. 2He did evil in the eyes of the LORD, just as Jehoiakim had done. 3It was because of the LORD's anger that all this happened to Jerusalem and Judah, and in the end he thrust them from his presence.

Now Zedekiah rebelled against the king of Babylon.

4So in the ninth year of Zedekiah's reign, on the tenth day of the tenth month, Nebuchadnezzar king of Babylon marched against Jerusalem with his whole army. They camped outside the city and built siege works all around it. 5The city was kept under siege until the eleventh year of King Zedekiah.

6By the ninth day of the fourth month the famine in the city had become so severe that there was no food for the people to eat. 7Then the city wall was broken through, and the whole army fled. They left the city at night through the gate between the two walls near the king's garden, though the Babylonians*a* were surrounding the city. They fled towards the Arabah,*b* 8but the Babylonian*c* army pursued King Zedekiah and overtook him in the plains of Jericho. All his soldiers were separated from him and scattered, 9and he was captured.

He was taken to the king of Babylon at Riblah in the land of Hamath, where he pronounced sentence on him. 10There at Riblah the king of Babylon slaughtered the sons of Zedekiah before his eyes; he also killed all the officials of Judah. 11Then he put out Zedekiah's eyes, bound him with bronze shackles and took him to Babylon, where he put him in prison till the day of his death.

12On the tenth day of the fifth month, in the nineteenth year of Nebuchadnezzar king of Babylon, Nebuzaradan commander of the imperial guard, who served the king of Babylon, came to Jerusalem. 13He set fire to the temple of the LORD, the royal palace and all the houses of Jerusalem. Every important building he burned down. 14The whole Babylonian army under the commander of the imperial guard broke down all the walls around Jerusalem.

15Nebuzaradan the commander of the guard carried into exile some of the poorest people and those who remained in the city, along with the rest of the craftsmen*d* and those who had gone over to the king of Babylon. 16But Nebuzaradan left behind the rest of the poorest people of the land to work the vineyards and fields.

52:13 ■ TOTAL DESTRUCTION

A small but subtle change telegraphs a huge turnaround. Verse 4 gives the date in terms of (Israelite) King Zedekiah's reign; verse 12 gives it in terms of (Babylonian) King Nebuchadnezzar. From this point on in history, Israel survived only on the periphery of other nations' empires. Instead of reckoning years in terms of their own leaders' time in office, Israel would base their calendar on the empires that ruled them.

17The Babylonians broke up the bronze pillars, the movable stands and the bronze Sea that were at the temple of the LORD and they carried all the bronze to Babylon. 18They also took away the pots, shovels, wick trimmers, sprinkling bowls, dishes and all the bronze articles used in the temple service. 19The commander of the imperial guard took away the basins, censers, sprinkling bowls, pots, lampstands, dishes and bowls used for drink offerings—all that were made of pure gold or silver.

20The bronze from the two pillars, the Sea and the twelve bronze bulls under it, and the movable stands, which King Solomon had made for the temple of the LORD, was more than could be weighed. 21Each of the pillars was eighteen cubits high and twelve cubits in circumference;*e* each was four fingers thick, and hollow. 22The bronze capital on the top of the one pillar was five cubits*f* high and was decorated with a network and pomegranates of bronze all around. The other pillar, with its pomegranates, was similar. 23There were ninety-six pomegranates on the sides; the total number of pomegranates above the surrounding network was a hundred.

24The commander of the guard took as prisoners Seraiah the chief priest, Zephaniah the priest next in rank and the three doorkeepers. 25Of those still in the city, he took the officer in charge of the fighting men, and seven royal advisers. He also took the secretary who was chief officer in charge of conscripting the people of the land and sixty of his men who were found in the city. 26Nebuzaradan the commander took them all and brought them to the king of Babylon at Riblah. 27There at Riblah, in the land of Hamath, the king had them executed.

So Judah went into captivity, away from her land. 28This is the number of the people Nebuchadnezzar carried into exile:

in the seventh year, 3,023 Jews;
29in Nebuchadnezzar's eighteenth year,
   832 people from Jerusalem;
30in his twenty-third year,
   745 Jews taken into exile by Nebuzaradan

*a*7 Or Chaldeans; also in verse 17   *b*7 Or the Jordan Valley   *c*8 Or Chaldean; also in verse 14   *d*15 Or populace   *e*21 That is, about 27 feet (about 8.1 metres) high and 18 feet (about 5.5 metres) in circumference   *f*22 That is, about 7½ feet (about 2.3 metres) the commander of the imperial guard. There were 4,600 people in all.

■ Jehoiachin Released

³¹In the thirty-seventh year of the exile of Jehoiachin king of Judah, in the year Evil-Merodach^g became king of Babylon, he released Jehoiachin king of Judah and freed him from prison on the twenty-fifth day of the twelfth month. ³²He spoke kindly to him and gave him a seat of honour higher than those of the other kings who were with him in Babylon. ³³So Jehoiachin put aside his prison clothes and for the rest of his life ate regularly at the king's table. ³⁴Day by day the king of Babylon gave Jehoiachin a regular allowance as long as he lived, till the day of his death.

LAMENTATIONS

■ A CITY IN RUINS

THERE WAS NOTHING LEFT TO DO BUT WEEP

"IS IT NOTHING TO YOU, ALL YOU WHO PASS BY?" ■ 1:12

Every year the world pauses to remember one awful day in Hiroshima, Japan, when the power of the atom came out of the sky. Opinions vary over whether an atom bomb was necessary to end World War II. Necessary or not, however, Hiroshima was a horrible tragedy. Though the survivors have gone on with their lives, they cannot forget. Nor can the rest of the world. Hiroshima's shadow stretches down to our time.

■ FIVE POEMS OF GRIEF

Lamentations offers five poems written from a state of dazed grief worthy of Hiroshima. A whole city has been destroyed. Brothers, sisters, children, friends are all gone. Men the town admired wander the body-littered streets, their skins shrivelled and their faces barely recognisable. Starvation has even compelled women to cook their own children (4:10).

And so the author mourns. He carefully reviews everything he has seen and felt, his pain darkening every line. He writes the first four poems in an acrostic style, following the Hebrew alphabet, one letter for each stanza. Perhaps this system helps him to pursue the subject thoroughly and not to break down in spasms of emotion. When he thinks of the starving children, he nearly does (2:11).

■ GOD CAUSED THE CARNAGE

The author of Lamentations — tradition ascribes it to Jeremiah — evidently had seen the siege and destruction of Jerusalem in 586 B.C., when the Babylonian army burned and destroyed all the principal buildings and carried most of the surviving inhabitants into exile. Lamentations conducts a kind of post-mortem on the death of Jerusalem, examining the body in clinical detail.

Like a doctor, Lamentations' author seeks to know the cause of death. He has no final doubt: though the Babylonians did the work, ultimately God was responsible. But could God willingly create such misery? The author seems stunned that God has actually destroyed his own people, though he admits they richly deserved the punishment. "The Lord is like an enemy," he cries in astonishment (2:5). "Even when I call out or cry for help, he shuts out my prayer" (3:8). "He dragged me from the path and mangled me and left me without help" (3:11). "He has broken my teeth with gravel" (3:16).

But, though astonished and grief-stricken, the author never doubts God's justice. Jerusalem's destruction came as a result of sin (1:5). This fact prompts quiet hope, based on the character of God. "Though he brings grief, he will show compassion, so great is his unfailing love. For he does not willingly bring affliction or grief to the children of men" (3:32–33). When sin is eliminated, the Lord acts quickly to forgive and heal.

■ LOOKING FOR RECOVERY

Though the grief of Lamentations is as deep and heavy as any ever written, hope lies at the bottom. The author does not say "Cheer up!" to himself or anyone else. He mourns passionately and fully. But in mourning he looks to recovery. Lamentations ends with a prayer to God, asking him to restore his people, "unless you have utterly rejected us and are angry with us beyond measure" (5:22). Behind that "unless" lies confidence. God can never be angry without limits.

The author of Lamentations doesn't soften his words to God for fear of offending him. He expresses the full and dreadful horror of what he has seen, and he gives God full responsibility. But, remembering that the Lord is a loving God, he counts on God to heal Israel's wounds. This time of mourning will be followed by another time, a time to dance.

■ HOW TO READ LAMENTATIONS

Lamentations is poetry, one poem per chapter. Its main purpose is not to describe events, nor to teach lessons, though it does both. Its intent is to express grief, to pour out before God the horror and bitterness of what has happened to Jerusalem. These five poems can help you to understand what it meant for Jews to see Jerusalem destroyed. They can also help you learn to deal appropriately with grief, your own or others'. Read them expressively,

preferably out loud, so that you catch the deep emotion. Note that the author does not rush to express his hope in God, but fully grieves for the tragedy he was involved in.

Lamentations is not difficult to understand, though some of the poetical allusions may become clearer if you use a Bible dictionary or a commentary. For a summary of the destruction that inspired Lamentations, read 2 Kings 25.

■ 3-TRACK READING PLAN

For an explanation and complete listing of the 3-track reading plan, turn to page x.

■ TRACK 1:
Two-Week Courses on the Bible
See page x for information on these courses.

■ TRACK 2:
An Overview of Lamentations in 1 Day

☐ Day 1. Read the Introduction to Lamentations and chapter 3, which contains both bitter grief and quiet hope.
Now turn to page xi for your next Track 2 reading project.

■ TRACK 3:
All of Lamentations in 5 Days
After you have read through Lamentations, turn to pages xii–xiii for your next Track 3 reading project.

☐ 1   ☐ 2   ☐ 3   ☐ 4
☐ 5

1 *a* How deserted lies the city,
    once so full of people!
How like a widow is she,
    who once was great among the nations!
She who was queen among the provinces
    has now become a slave.

²Bitterly she weeps at night,
    tears are upon her cheeks.
Among all her lovers
    there is none to comfort her.
All her friends have betrayed her;
    they have become her enemies.

³After affliction and harsh labour,
    Judah has gone into exile.
She dwells among the nations;
    she finds no resting place.
All who pursue her have overtaken her
    in the midst of her distress.

⁴The roads to Zion mourn,
    for no-one comes to her appointed feasts.
All her gateways are desolate,
    her priests groan,
her maidens grieve,
    and she is in bitter anguish.

⁵Her foes have become her masters;
    her enemies are at ease.
The LORD has brought her grief
    because of her many sins.
Her children have gone into exile,
    captive before the foe.

⁶All the splendour has departed
    from the Daughter of Zion.
Her princes are like deer
    that find no pasture;

in weakness they have fled
    before the pursuer.

⁷In the days of her affliction and wandering
    Jerusalem remembers all the treasures
    that were hers in days of old.
When her people fell into enemy hands,
    there was no-one to help her.
Her enemies looked at her
    and laughed at her destruction.

1:4 ■ STRUCTURED PASSION

Middle Easterners often commemorated catastrophes in poetry and song, as a kind of dirge in memory of the event. (See Psalm 137 for another example.) Lamentations, a response to the destruction of Jerusalem, contains as much passion as any book in the Bible. Yet, remarkably, the author has poured his passion into a highly structured form of poetry. Note that each chapter contains exactly 22 verses, or "stanzas", except for chapter 3, which has 66 verses (3 times 22). There were 22 letters in the Hebrew alphabet, and all but one of these poems follow an acrostic form, with each stanza beginning with a different letter of the alphabet.

⁸Jerusalem has sinned greatly
    and so has become unclean.
All who honoured her despise her,
    for they have seen her nakedness;
she herself groans
    and turns away.

⁹Her filthiness clung to her skirts;

a This chapter is an acrostic poem, the verses of which begin with the successive letters of the Hebrew alphabet.

she did not consider her future.
Her fall was astounding;
   there was none to comfort her.
"Look, O LORD, on my affliction,
   for the enemy has triumphed."

¹⁰The enemy laid hands
   on all her treasures;
she saw pagan nations
   enter her sanctuary—
those you had forbidden
   to enter your assembly.

1:10 ■ THE TEMPLE DESTROYED

Non-Jews were barred from the holy places of the temple. But when the Babylonians conquered Jerusalem, they not only entered the temple; they looted and burned it. This shook devout Jews deeply; more than anything else it showed that God had given them up. Even today Orthodox Jews observe the anniversary of the temple's destruction by reading the book of Lamentations aloud, and pilgrims daily recite its prayers at the Wailing Wall in Jerusalem.

¹¹All her people groan
   as they search for bread;
they barter their treasures for food
   to keep themselves alive.
"Look, O LORD, and consider,
   for I am despised."

¹²"Is it nothing to you, all you who pass by?
   Look around and see.
Is any suffering like my suffering
   that was inflicted on me,
that the LORD brought on me
   in the day of his fierce anger?

¹³"From on high he sent fire,
   sent it down into my bones.
He spread a net for my feet
   and turned me back.
He made me desolate,
   faint all the day long.

¹⁴"My sins have been bound into a yoke;ᵇ
   by his hands they were woven together.
They have come upon my neck
   and the Lord has sapped my strength.
He has handed me over
   to those I cannot withstand.

¹⁵"The Lord has rejected
   all the warriors in my midst;
he has summoned an army against me
   toᶜ crush my young men.
In his winepress the Lord has trampled
   the Virgin Daughter of Judah.

¹⁶"This is why I weep
   and my eyes overflow with tears.
No-one is near to comfort me,
   no-one to restore my spirit.
My children are destitute

   because the enemy has prevailed."

¹⁷Zion stretches out her hands,
   but there is no-one to comfort her.
The LORD has decreed for Jacob
   that his neighbours become his foes;
Jerusalem has become
   an unclean thing among them.

¹⁸"The LORD is righteous,
   yet I rebelled against his command.
Listen, all you peoples;
   look upon my suffering.
My young men and maidens
   have gone into exile.

¹⁹"I called to my allies
   but they betrayed me.
My priests and my elders
   perished in the city
while they searched for food
   to keep themselves alive.

²⁰"See, O LORD, how distressed I am!
   I am in torment within,
and in my heart I am disturbed,
   for I have been most rebellious.
Outside, the sword bereaves;
   inside, there is only death.

²¹"People have heard my groaning,
   but there is no-one to comfort me.
All my enemies have heard of my distress;
   they rejoice at what you have done.
May you bring the day you have announced
   so that they may become like me.

²²"Let all their wickedness come before you;
   deal with them
as you have dealt with me
   because of all my sins.
My groans are many
   and my heart is faint."

2ᵃ How the Lord has covered the Daughter of Zion
   with the cloud of his anger!ᵇ
He has hurled down the splendour of Israel
   from heaven to earth;
he has not remembered his footstool
   in the day of his anger.

²Without pity the Lord has swallowed up
   all the dwellings of Jacob;
in his wrath he has torn down
   the strongholds of the Daughter of Judah.
He has brought her kingdom and its princes
   down to the ground in dishonour.

³In fierce anger he has cut off
   every hornᶜ of Israel.
He has withdrawn his right hand
   at the approach of the enemy.
He has burned in Jacob like a flaming fire
   that consumes everything around it.

⁴Like an enemy he has strung his bow;
   his right hand is ready.

ᵇ14 Most Hebrew manuscripts; Septuagint *He kept watch over my sins*   ᶜ15 Or *has set a time for me / when he will*   ᵃThis chapter is an acrostic poem, the verses of which begin with the successive letters of the Hebrew alphabet.   ᵇ1 Or *How the LORD in his anger / has treated the Daughter of Zion with contempt!*   ᶜ3 Or / *all the strength*; or *every king*; *horn here symbolises strength.*

Like a foe he has slain
   all who were pleasing to the eye;
he has poured out his wrath like fire
   on the tent of the Daughter of Zion.

⁵The Lord is like an enemy;
   he has swallowed up Israel.
He has swallowed up all her palaces
   and destroyed her strongholds.
He has multiplied mourning and lamentation
   for the Daughter of Judah.

⁶He has laid waste his dwelling like a garden;
   he has destroyed his place of meeting.
The LORD has made Zion forget
   her appointed feasts and her Sabbaths;
in his fierce anger he has spurned
   both king and priest.

⁷The Lord has rejected his altar
   and abandoned his sanctuary.
He has handed over to the enemy
   the walls of her palaces;
they have raised a shout in the house of the
      LORD
   as on the day of an appointed feast.

⁸The LORD determined to tear down
   the wall around the Daughter of Zion.
He stretched out a measuring line
   and did not withhold his hand from
      destroying.
He made ramparts and walls lament;
   together they wasted away.

⁹Her gates have sunk into the ground;
   their bars he has broken and destroyed.
Her king and her princes are exiled among the
      nations,
   the law is no more,
and her prophets no longer find
   visions from the LORD.

¹⁰The elders of the Daughter of Zion
   sit on the ground in silence;
they have sprinkled dust on their heads
   and put on sackcloth.
The young women of Jerusalem
   have bowed their heads to the ground.

¹¹My eyes fail from weeping,
   I am in torment within,
my heart is poured out on the ground
   because my people are destroyed,
because children and infants faint
   in the streets of the city.

¹²They say to their mothers,
   "Where is bread and wine?"
as they faint like wounded men
   in the streets of the city,
as their lives ebb away
   in their mothers' arms.

¹³What can I say for you?
   With what can I compare you,
   O Daughter of Jerusalem?
To what can I liken you,
   that I may comfort you,

O Virgin Daughter of Zion?
Your wound is as deep as the sea.
   Who can heal you?

2:12 ■ PITY THE CHILDREN

Everyone suffered in the destruction of Jerusalem, rich and poor, young and old, male and female. Lamentations grieves for them all, but especially for the children, who were dying of hunger. During the long siege, hunger grew so fierce that mothers ate their own children (2:20; 4:10). Compassion for children had disappeared (4:3–4).

¹⁴The visions of your prophets
   were false and worthless;
they did not expose your sin
   to ward off your captivity.
The oracles they gave you
   were false and misleading.

¹⁵All who pass your way
   clap their hands at you;
they scoff and shake their heads
   at the Daughter of Jerusalem:
"Is this the city that was called
   the perfection of beauty,
   the joy of the whole earth?"

¹⁶All your enemies open their mouths
   wide against you;
they scoff and gnash their teeth
   and say, "We have swallowed her up.
This is the day we have waited for;
   we have lived to see it."

¹⁷The LORD has done what he planned;
   he has fulfilled his word,
   which he decreed long ago.
He has overthrown you without pity,
   he has let the enemy gloat over you,
   he has exalted the horn*ᵈ* of your foes.

¹⁸The hearts of the people
   cry out to the Lord.
O wall of the Daughter of Zion,
   let your tears flow like a river
   day and night;
give yourself no relief,
   your eyes no rest.

¹⁹Arise, cry out in the night,
   as the watches of the night begin;
pour out your heart like water
   in the presence of the Lord.
Lift up your hands to him
   for the lives of your children,
who faint from hunger
   at the head of every street.

²⁰"Look, O LORD, and consider:
   Whom have you ever treated like this?
Should women eat their offspring,
   the children they have cared for?
Should priest and prophet be killed
   in the sanctuary of the Lord?

ᵈ 17 Horn here symbolises strength.

21"Young and old lie together
in the dust of the streets;
my young men and maidens
have fallen by the sword.
You have slain them in the day of your anger;
you have slaughtered them without pity.

22"As you summon to a feast day,
so you summoned against me terrors on
every side.
In the day of the LORD's anger
no-one escaped or survived;
those I cared for and reared,
my enemy has destroyed."

3 ᵃ I am the man who has seen affliction
by the rod of his wrath.
²He has driven me away and made me walk
in darkness rather than light;
³indeed, he has turned his hand against me
again and again, all day long.

3:1 ■ AUTOBIOGRAPHY OF PAIN

Ancient traditions say that Jeremiah wrote the
book of Lamentations, and if so, this chapter
records that doleful prophet's autobiography of
pain. He was persecuted by enemies, thrown in a
well, dragged captive, and jailed. Jeremiah knew,
of course, that the people who did those things
were God's enemies too, and he had delivered
strong pronouncements against them. Yet to a
person in pain – like Job, like Jeremiah – it often
feels as if God himself has turned his back.

⁴He has made my skin and my flesh grow old
and has broken my bones.
⁵He has besieged me and surrounded me
with bitterness and hardship.
⁶He has made me dwell in darkness
like those long dead.

⁷He has walled me in so that I cannot escape;
he has weighed me down with chains.
⁸Even when I call out or cry for help,
he shuts out my prayer.
⁹He has barred my way with blocks of stone;
he has made my paths crooked.

¹⁰Like a bear lying in wait,
like a lion in hiding,
¹¹he dragged me from the path and mangled me
and left me without help.
¹²He drew his bow
and made me the target for his arrows.

¹³He pierced my heart
with arrows from his quiver.
¹⁴I became the laughing-stock of all my people;
they mock me in song all day long.
¹⁵He has filled me with bitter herbs
and sated me with gall.

¹⁶He has broken my teeth with gravel;
he has trampled me in the dust.
¹⁷I have been deprived of peace;
I have forgotten what prosperity is.

¹⁸So I say, "My splendour is gone
and all that I had hoped from the LORD."

¹⁹I remember my affliction and my wandering,
the bitterness and the gall.
²⁰I well remember them,
and my soul is downcast within me.
²¹Yet this I call to mind
and therefore I have hope:

²²Because of the LORD's great love we are not
consumed,
for his compassions never fail.
²³They are new every morning;
great is your faithfulness.
²⁴I say to myself, "The LORD is my portion;
therefore I will wait for him."

²⁵The LORD is good to those whose hope is in
him,
to the one who seeks him;
²⁶it is good to wait quietly
for the salvation of the LORD.
²⁷It is good for a man to bear the yoke
while he is young.

²⁸Let him sit alone in silence,
for the LORD has laid it on him.
²⁹Let him bury his face in the dust –
there may yet be hope.
³⁰Let him offer his cheek to one who would
strike him,
and let him be filled with disgrace.

³¹For men are not cast off
by the Lord for ever.
³²Though he brings grief, he will show
compassion,
so great is his unfailing love.
³³For he does not willingly bring affliction
or grief to the children of men.

3:33 ■ HOPE FOR THE GRIEVING

Lamentations bares the full horror of suffering, yet
offers hope based on the character of God. He
has let some survive (verse 22), and he is not a
God to be angry with them for ever. Their duty is
to accept fully their grief, and quietly meditate on
its meaning while waiting for the Lord.

³⁴To crush underfoot
all prisoners in the land,
³⁵to deny a man his rights
before the Most High,
³⁶to deprive a man of justice –
would not the Lord see such things?

³⁷Who can speak and have it happen
if the Lord has not decreed it?
³⁸Is it not from the mouth of the Most High
that both calamities and good things come?
³⁹Why should any living man complain
when punished for his sins?

⁴⁰Let us examine our ways and test them,
and let us return to the LORD.
⁴¹Let us lift up our hearts and our hands

ᵃThis chapter is an acrostic poem; the verses of each stanza begin with the successive letters of the Hebrew alphabet, and the verses within each stanza
begin with the same letter.

to God in heaven, and say:
42"We have sinned and rebelled
and you have not forgiven.

43"You have covered yourself with anger and
pursued us;
you have slain without pity.
44You have covered yourself with a cloud
so that no prayer can get through.
45You have made us scum and refuse
among the nations.

46"All our enemies have opened their mouths
wide against us.
47We have suffered terror and pitfalls,
ruin and destruction."
48Streams of tears flow from my eyes
because my people are destroyed.

49My eyes will flow unceasingly,
without relief,
50until the LORD looks down
from heaven and sees.
51What I see brings grief to my soul
because of all the women of my city.

52Those who were my enemies without cause
hunted me like a bird.
53They tried to end my life in a pit
and threw stones at me;
54the waters closed over my head,
and I thought I was about to be cut off.

55I called on your name, O LORD,
from the depths of the pit.
56You heard my plea: "Do not close your ears
to my cry for relief."
57You came near when I called you,
and you said, "Do not fear."

58O Lord, you took up my case;
you redeemed my life.
59You have seen, O LORD, the wrong done to me.
Uphold my cause!
60You have seen the depth of their vengeance,
all their plots against me.

61O LORD, you have heard their insults,
all their plots against me—
62what my enemies whisper and mutter
against me all day long.
63Look at them! Sitting or standing,
they mock me in their songs.

64Pay them back what they deserve, O LORD,
for what their hands have done.
65Put a veil over their hearts,
and may your curse be on them!
66Pursue them in anger and destroy them
from under the heavens of the LORD.

4 *a* How the gold has lost its lustre,
the fine gold become dull!
The sacred gems are scattered
at the head of every street.

2How the precious sons of Zion,
once worth their weight in gold,

are now considered as pots of clay,
the work of a potter's hands!

3Even jackals offer their breasts
to nurse their young,
but my people have become heartless
like ostriches in the desert.

4Because of thirst the infant's tongue
sticks to the roof of its mouth;
the children beg for bread,
but no-one gives it to them.

4:4 ■ STARVING TO DEATH

Horrible scenes of starvation, like those shown in documentaries of African famines in recent times, were seen in the streets of Jerusalem during the Babylonian invasion. Foreign armies encircled the city for two years, cutting off all sources of food. The residents of this once-proud city resorted to eating their own children (verse 10) just to stay alive.

5Those who once ate delicacies
are destitute in the streets.
Those nurtured in purple
now lie on ash heaps.

6The punishment of my people
is greater than that of Sodom,
which was overthrown in a moment
without a hand turned to help her.

7Their princes were brighter than snow
and whiter than milk,
their bodies more ruddy than rubies,
their appearance like sapphires.*b*

8But now they are blacker than soot;
they are not recognised in the streets.
Their skin has shrivelled on their bones;
it has become as dry as a stick.

9Those killed by the sword are better off
than those who die of famine;
racked with hunger, they waste away
for lack of food from the field.

10With their own hands compassionate women
have cooked their own children,
who became their food
when my people were destroyed.

11The LORD has given full vent to his wrath;
he has poured out his fierce anger.
He kindled a fire in Zion
that consumed her foundations.

12The kings of the earth did not believe,
nor did any of the world's people,
that enemies and foes could enter
the gates of Jerusalem.

13But it happened because of the sins of her
prophets
and the iniquities of her priests,
who shed within her
the blood of the righteous.

---

*a*This chapter is an acrostic poem, the verses of which begin with the successive letters of the Hebrew alphabet.   *b* 7 Or *lapis lazuli*

14Now they grope through the streets
　　like men who are blind.
They are so defiled with blood
　　that no-one dares to touch their garments.

15"Go away! You are unclean!" men cry to them.
　　"Away! Away! Don't touch us!"
When they flee and wander about,
　　people among the nations say,
　　"They can stay here no longer."

16The LORD himself has scattered them;
　　he no longer watches over them.
The priests are shown no honour,
　　the elders no favour.

17Moreover, our eyes failed,
　　looking in vain for help;
from our towers we watched
　　for a nation that could not save us.

4:17 ■ FALSE HOPE

In the last decades before Jerusalem was conquered, Judah's kings frequently tried to play Egypt, another superpower, against Babylon. Right to the end they expected Egypt's armies to rescue them. But as Jeremiah had warned, Egypt proved to be an unreliable ally (Jeremiah 2:36–37; 37:5–8).

18Men stalked us at every step,
　　so we could not walk in our streets.
Our end was near, our days were numbered,
　　for our end had come.

19Our pursuers were swifter
　　than eagles in the sky;
they chased us over the mountains
　　and lay in wait for us in the desert.

20The LORD's anointed, our very life breath,
　　was caught in their traps.
We thought that under his shadow
　　we would live among the nations.

21Rejoice and be glad, O Daughter of Edom,
　　you who live in the land of Uz.
But to you also the cup will be passed;
　　you will be drunk and stripped naked.

22O Daughter of Zion, your punishment will end;
　　he will not prolong your exile.

But, O Daughter of Edom, he will punish your
　　sin
and expose your wickedness.

5 Remember, O LORD, what has happened to us;
　　look, and see our disgrace.
2Our inheritance has been turned over to aliens,
　　our homes to foreigners.
3We have become orphans and fatherless,
　　our mothers like widows.
4We must buy the water we drink;
　　our wood can be had only at a price.
5Those who pursue us are at our heels;
　　we are weary and find no rest.
6We submitted to Egypt and Assyria
　　to get enough bread.
7Our fathers sinned and are no more,
　　and we bear their punishment.
8Slaves rule over us,
　　and there is none to free us from their
　　hands.
9We get our bread at the risk of our lives
　　because of the sword in the desert.
10Our skin is hot as an oven,
　　feverish from hunger.
11Women have been ravished in Zion,
　　and virgins in the towns of Judah.
12Princes have been hung up by their hands;
　　elders are shown no respect.
13Young men toil at the millstones;
　　boys stagger under loads of wood.
14The elders are gone from the city gate;
　　the young men have stopped their music.
15Joy is gone from our hearts;
　　our dancing has turned to mourning.
16The crown has fallen from our head.
　　Woe to us, for we have sinned!
17Because of this our hearts are faint;
　　because of these things our eyes grow dim
18for Mount Zion, which lies desolate,
　　with jackals prowling over it.

19You, O LORD, reign for ever;
　　your throne endures from generation to
　　generation.
20Why do you always forget us?
　　Why do you forsake us so long?
21Restore us to yourself, O LORD, that we may
　　return;
　　renew our days as of old
22unless you have utterly rejected us
　　and are angry with us beyond measure.

EZEKIEL

■ SEEING THE UNSEEN GOD

GOD SHOWED HIMSELF TO EZEKIEL IN UNEARTHLY RADIANCE

LIKE THE APPEARANCE OF A RAINBOW IN THE CLOUDS ON A RAINY DAY, SO WAS THE RADIANCE AROUND HIM. . . . WHEN I SAW IT, I FELL FACE DOWN. ■ 1:28

Ezekiel begins with a description so unearthly that some have suggested the prophet saw a UFO. Indeed, there are similarities: glowing lights, quick movements, inhuman figures shrouded with fire. But at least one critical difference sets Ezekiel's story apart. UFOs typically appear in remote places and then mysteriously zoom off, never to be heard from again. The majestic being Ezekiel described was not rushing off to disappear. He wanted to be known — by everyone.

For Ezekiel was quite sure that he had seen and heard the God of the Bible. While few have been privileged to see him as Ezekiel did, this God had been speaking plainly for generations. His words were on record.

Before such splendour Ezekiel felt utterly weak and inadequate, just as Isaiah had during a similar vision (Isaiah 6). He fell on his face, repeatedly. But God raised Ezekiel to his feet and gave him a message to deliver.

■ A STUNNING PORTRAIT OF GOD

In describing his call by God, Ezekiel groped for words. He portrayed a God of stunning grandeur, above and beyond our world. Yet this supernatural God was inescapably near and real. He demanded complete obedience. Surprisingly, he appeared to Ezekiel in Babylon — the last place an Israelite expected to see him. This God could not be locked in by national or geographical boxes. He ruled the earth.

Ezekiel repeated this classic message over 60 times: "Then they will know that I am the LORD". God said it when promising the destruction of Jerusalem in the first 24 chapters. He said it when predicting the downfall of Israel's neighbours in chapters 25 to 32. And, after Jerusalem had fallen, God said it when promising a great future in the last 16 chapters. God did not want to remain vague or far off. He wanted his people to know him. More, Ezekiel's God wanted to live with his people. He wanted to make his home in the centre of their city.

■ A STRANGE BOOK

Ezekiel has a reputation for strangeness, partly because of the unearthly visions with which his book begins and ends, and partly because Ezekiel acted out God's messages through some bizarre behaviour. (For instance, for months at a time he lay in public on his side, bound by ropes, facing a clay model of Jerusalem.) Strange? When a car is speeding down a road unaware that the bridge is impassable, you may take strange measures to get the driver's attention. You may scream and gesture so wildly that people think you are mad. So it was with Ezekiel. His message came in the most vivid form possible, meant to force people to pay attention.

Ezekiel lived in perhaps the most tragic period of his people's existence. They had been tempting fate for generations, ignoring God's messengers (prophets like Micah, Amos, Isaiah) who warned that if they didn't listen to God, they would be destroyed. Finally, Babylonian armies swept through Judah, deporting large groups of citizens.

Ezekiel had gone into exile in one of the first groups, as had Daniel. Ezekiel became God's messenger as a captive in Babylon. His voice blended in stereo with Jeremiah's, still in Jerusalem. Both prophets warned their people (who kept plotting ways to break free of Babylon) that the captives were going to be in Babylon for a long time. They predicted that Babylon's oppression would grow heavier: Jerusalem and the temple would be destroyed. Since Judah had ignored God's repeated warnings, God would use another means to get their attention: suffering.

■ A NEW JERUSALEM

Yet even while punishing them, God's aim remained the same: to make himself known. God had warned Ezekiel that the Israelites were unlikely to listen (3:7), even from captivity. They preferred idols to the living God. Yet Ezekiel's messages and dramas and visions continued to come, year after year. It's as though God were saying through him, "Some way, some day, I will get through to them. If the message doesn't reach their hearts one way, I'll try another".

Ezekiel ends with hope. The final chapters show a new Jerusalem rising from the ruins of the old. The renewed city would never die, for it would be built on an unshifting reality: "They will know that I am the LORD". The burning vision of God that Ezekiel had seen would become accessible to all. God would make himself at home there for ever. Ezekiel's last verse says it all: "And the name of the city from that time on will be: THE LORD IS THERE".

■ HOW TO READ EZEKIEL

The special difficulty in reading Ezekiel is the dizzying variety of forms he used to get his message across. The book is like a multimedia package – a mix of visions, messages, dramas, poems. But three remarkable visions of God bracket the package, beginning, middle, and end (1:1–3:15; 8:1–6 and 11:16–25; 40:1–4 and 43:1–9). And throughout, one line is repeated: "Then they will know that I am the LORD". All God's messages are meant to shock his people into restoring a living relationship with him.

As you read Ezekiel, note down when each prophecy was made and its dominant image – Jerusalem as a prostitute, as a spreading grapevine, as a shaved head, etc. (For insight into why Ezekiel sometimes acted out his message in bizarre fashion, read "Living Parables", page 678.) Don't skip ahead too fast as you read – take time to think about the message in each section. Remember that the book of Ezekiel compresses messages God gave over 22 years. Try to imagine the impact of each message on the people who first heard or saw it.

Most of what Ezekiel said in Babylonia concerned a dramatic military situation hundreds of miles away in Jerusalem. His message changed from doom to hope in chapter 33; the turning point came with news of Jerusalem's fall. You can get to know the historical situation by reading 2 Kings 23:36–25:12. "A Line-up of Rulers", pages 260–268, can help you place Ezekiel in Israel's history.

A fascinating though difficult study is the design of the renewed temple, which Ezekiel described in chapters 40–43. A commentary on Ezekiel or a Bible dictionary (under "Ezekiel" or "temple") can help immensely in understanding these visions.

■ 3-TRACK READING PLAN

For an explanation and complete listing of the 3-track reading plan, turn to page x.

■ TRACK 1:
Two-Week Courses on the Bible
See page x for information on these courses.

■ TRACK 2:
An Overview of Ezekiel in 4 Days
☐ Day 1. Read the Introduction to Ezekiel and chapter 1, the majestic vision of a living God who appeared to Ezekiel.
☐ Day 2. Read chapters 2–3, which tell how God called Ezekiel to deliver a difficult message.
☐ Day 3. Read chapter 4, one of the most dramatic of the "enacted parables" Ezekiel performed.
☐ Day 4. Read chapter 37, a message of hope and resurrection for a defeated people.
Now turn to page xi for your next Track 2 reading project.

■ TRACK 3:
All of Ezekiel in 47 Days
After you have read through Ezekiel, turn to pages xii–xiii for your next Track 3 reading project.

☐ 1	☐ 2–3	☐ 4	☐ 5
☐ 6	☐ 7	☐ 8	☐ 9
☐ 10	☐ 11	☐ 12	☐ 13
☐ 14	☐ 15	☐ 16	☐ 17
☐ 18	☐ 19	☐ 20	☐ 21
☐ 22	☐ 23	☐ 24	☐ 25
☐ 26	☐ 27	☐ 28	☐ 29
☐ 30	☐ 31	☐ 32	☐ 33
☐ 34	☐ 35	☐ 36	☐ 37
☐ 38	☐ 39	☐ 40	☐ 41
☐ 42	☐ 43	☐ 44	☐ 45
☐ 46	☐ 47	☐ 48	

■ The Living Creatures and the Glory of the LORD

1 In the*a* thirtieth year, in the fourth month on the fifth day, while I was among the exiles by the Kebar River, the heavens were opened and I saw visions of God.

²On the fifth of the month—it was the fifth year of the exile of King Jehoiachin—³the word of the LORD came to Ezekiel the priest, the son of Buzi,*b* by the Kebar River in the land of the Babylonians.*c* There the hand of the LORD was upon him.

1:3 ■ FOREIGN APPEARANCE

Most ancient religions worshipped tribal gods, whose rule extended only within the tribal territory. As an exile, Ezekiel may have wondered whether the God of Israel would still speak so far from home. But it was in Babylon that God appeared. The terrifying vision in a windstorm revealed a God who ruled over the entire world, awesome, magnificent, exalted, far more powerful than the Babylonian armies.

⁴I looked, and I saw a windstorm coming out of the north—an immense cloud with flashing lightning and surrounded by brilliant light. The centre of the fire looked like glowing metal, ⁵and in the fire was what looked like four living creatures. In appearance their form was that of a man, ⁶but each of them had four faces and four wings. ⁷Their legs were straight; their feet were like those of a calf and gleamed like burnished bronze. ⁸Under their wings on their four sides they had the hands of a man. All four of them had faces and wings, ⁹and their wings touched one another. Each one went straight ahead; they did not turn as they moved.

¹⁰Their faces looked like this: Each of the four had the face of a man, and on the right side each had the face of a lion, and on the left the face of an ox; each also had the face of an eagle. ¹¹Such were their faces. Their wings were spread out upwards; each had two wings, one touching the wing of another creature on either side, and two wings covering its body. ¹²Each one went straight ahead. Wherever the spirit would go, they would go, without turning as they went. ¹³The appearance of the living creatures was like burning coals of fire or like torches. Fire moved back and forth among the creatures; it was bright, and lightning flashed out of it. ¹⁴The creatures sped back and forth like flashes of lightning.

¹⁵As I looked at the living creatures, I saw a wheel on the ground beside each creature with its four faces. ¹⁶This was the appearance and structure of the wheels: They sparkled like chrysolite, and all four looked alike. Each appeared to be made like a wheel intersecting a wheel. ¹⁷As they moved, they would go in any one of the four directions the creatures faced; the wheels did not turn about*d* as the creatures went. ¹⁸Their rims were high and awesome, and all four rims were full of eyes all around.

¹⁹When the living creatures moved, the wheels beside them moved; and when the living creatures rose from the ground, the wheels also rose. ²⁰Wherever the spirit would go, they would go, and the wheels would rise along with them, because the spirit of the living creatures was in the wheels. ²¹When the creatures moved, they also moved; when the creatures stood still, they also stood still; and when the creatures rose from the ground, the wheels rose along with them, because the spirit of the living creatures was in the wheels.

²²Spread out above the heads of the living creatures was what looked like an expanse, sparkling like ice, and awesome. ²³Under the expanse their wings were stretched out one towards the other, and each had two wings covering its body. ²⁴When the creatures moved, I heard the sound of their wings, like the roar of rushing waters, like the voice of the Almighty,*e* like the tumult of an army. When they stood still, they lowered their wings.

²⁵Then there came a voice from above the expanse over their heads as they stood with lowered wings. ²⁶Above the expanse over their heads was what looked like a throne of sapphire,*f* and high above on the throne was a figure like that of a man. ²⁷I saw that from what appeared to be his waist up he looked like glowing metal, as if full of fire, and that from there down he looked like fire; and brilliant light surrounded him. ²⁸Like the appearance of a rainbow in the clouds on a rainy day, so was the radiance around him.

This was the appearance of the likeness of the glory of the LORD. When I saw it, I fell face down, and I heard the voice of one speaking.

■ Ezekiel's Call

2 He said to me, "Son of man, stand up on your feet and I will speak to you." ²As he spoke, the Spirit came into me and raised me to my feet, and I heard him speaking to me.

³He said: "Son of man, I am sending you to the Israelites, to a rebellious nation that has rebelled against me; they and their fathers have been in revolt against me to this very day. ⁴The people to whom I am sending you are obstinate and stubborn. Say to them, 'This is what the Sovereign LORD says.' ⁵And whether they listen or fail to listen—for they are a rebellious house—they will know that a prophet has been among them. ⁶And you, son of man, do not be afraid of them or their words. Do not be afraid, though briers and thorns are all around you and you live among scorpions. Do not be afraid of what they say or terrified by them, though they are a rebellious house. ⁷You must speak my words to them, whether they listen or fail to listen, for they are rebellious. ⁸But you, son of man, listen to what I say to you. Do not rebel like that rebellious house; open your mouth and eat what I give you."

⁹Then I looked, and I saw a hand stretched out to me. In it was a scroll, ¹⁰which he unrolled before me. On both sides of it were written words of lament and mourning and woe.

3 And he said to me, "Son of man, eat what is before you, eat this scroll; then go and speak to the house of Israel." ²So I opened my mouth, and he gave me the scroll to eat.

³Then he said to me, "Son of man, eat this scroll I am giving you and fill your stomach with it." So I ate it, and it tasted as sweet as honey in my mouth.

---

a 1 Or ‚my‚   *b* 3 Or Ezekiel son of Buzi the priest   *c* 3 Or Chaldeans   *d* 17 Or aside   *e* 24 Hebrew Shaddai   *f* 26 Or lapis lazuli

⁴He then said to me: "Son of man, go now to the house of Israel and speak my words to them. ⁵You are not being sent to a people of obscure speech and difficult language, but to the house of Israel—⁶not to many peoples of obscure speech and difficult language, whose words you cannot understand. Surely if I had sent you to them, they would have listened to you. ⁷But the house of Israel is not willing to listen to you because they are not willing to listen to me, for the whole house of Israel is hardened and obstinate. ⁸But I will make you as unyielding and hardened as they are. ⁹I will make your forehead like the hardest stone, harder than flint. Do not be afraid of them or terrified by them, though they are a rebellious house."

3:3 ■ EAT THE SCROLL
The scroll with words of woe looked inedible, but tasted sweet as honey to Ezekiel. Most of God's prophets gave bitter messages of warning, but God's word sustained and strengthened them as they served him. (See also Jeremiah's experience, in Jeremiah 15:16.) Similarly, the book of Revelation tells of a scroll being eaten (Revelation 10:9–11). Many of Ezekiel's images are paralleled in that book.

¹⁰And he said to me, "Son of man, listen carefully and take to heart all the words I speak to you. ¹¹Go now to your countrymen in exile and speak to them. Say to them, 'This is what the Sovereign LORD says,' whether they listen or fail to listen."

¹²Then the Spirit lifted me up, and I heard behind me a loud rumbling sound—May the glory of the LORD be praised in his dwelling-place!—¹³the sound of the wings of the living creatures brushing against each other and the sound of the wheels beside them, a loud rumbling sound. ¹⁴The Spirit then lifted me up and took me away, and I went in bitterness and in the anger of my spirit, with the strong hand of the LORD upon me. ¹⁵I came to the exiles who lived at Tel Abib near the Kebar River. And there, where they were living, I sat among them for seven days—overwhelmed.

■ Warning to Israel

¹⁶At the end of seven days the word of the LORD came to me: ¹⁷"Son of man, I have made you a watchman for the house of Israel; so hear the word I speak and give them warning from me. ¹⁸When I say to a wicked man, 'You will surely die,' and you do not warn him or speak out to dissuade him from his evil ways in order to save his life, that wicked man will die for*a* his sin, and I will hold you accountable for his blood. ¹⁹But if you do warn the wicked man and he does not turn from his wickedness or from his evil ways, he will die for his sin; but you will have saved yourself.

²⁰"Again, when a righteous man turns from his righteousness and does evil, and I put a stumbling-block before him, he will die. Since you did not warn him, he will die for his sin. The righteous things he did will not be remembered, and I will

hold you accountable for his blood. ²¹But if you do warn the righteous man not to sin and he does not sin, he will surely live because he took warning, and you will have saved yourself."

²²The hand of the LORD was upon me there, and he said to me, "Get up and go out to the plain, and there I will speak to you." ²³So I got up and went out to the plain. And the glory of the LORD was standing there, like the glory I had seen by the Kebar River, and I fell face down.

²⁴Then the Spirit came into me and raised me to my feet. He spoke to me and said: "Go, shut yourself inside your house. ²⁵And you, son of man, they will tie with ropes; you will be bound so that you cannot go out among the people. ²⁶I will make your tongue stick to the roof of your mouth so that you will be silent and unable to rebuke them, though they are a rebellious house. ²⁷But when I speak to you, I will open your mouth and you shall say to them, 'This is what the Sovereign LORD says.' Whoever will listen let him listen, and whoever will refuse let him refuse; for they are a rebellious house.

■ Siege of Jerusalem Symbolised

4 "Now, son of man, take a clay tablet, put it in front of you and draw the city of Jerusalem on it. ²Then lay siege to it: Erect siege works against it, build a ramp up to it, set up camps against it and put battering-rams around it. ³Then take an iron pan, place it as an iron wall between you and the city and turn your face towards it. It will be under siege, and you shall besiege it. This will be a sign to the house of Israel.

⁴"Then lie on your left side and put the sin of the house of Israel upon yourself.*a* You are to bear their sin for the number of days you lie on your side. ⁵I have assigned you the same number of days as the years of their sin. So for 390 days you will bear the sin of the house of Israel.

⁶"After you have finished this, lie down again, this time on your right side, and bear the sin of the house of Judah. I have assigned you 40 days, a day for each year. ⁷Turn your face towards the siege of Jerusalem and with bared arm prophesy against her. ⁸I will tie you up with ropes so that you cannot turn from one side to the other until you have finished the days of your siege.

⁹"Take wheat and barley, beans and lentils, millet and spelt; put them in a storage jar and use them to make bread for yourself. You are to eat it during the 390 days you lie on your side. ¹⁰Weigh out twenty shekels*b* of food to eat each day and eat it at set times. ¹¹Also measure out a sixth of a hin*c* of water and drink it at set times. ¹²Eat the food as you would a barley cake; bake it in the sight of the people, using human excrement for fuel." ¹³The LORD said, "In this way the people of Israel will eat defiled food among the nations where I will drive them."

¹⁴Then I said, "Not so, Sovereign LORD! I have never defiled myself. From my youth until now I have never eaten anything found dead or torn by wild animals. No unclean meat has ever entered my mouth."

¹⁵"Very well," he said, "I will let you bake your

a 18 Or *in*; also in verses 19 and 20   *a 4* Or *your side*   *b 10* That is, about 8 ounces (about 0.2 kilogram)   *c 11* That is, about 1 pint (about 0.6 litre) bread over cow manure instead of human excrement."

¹⁶He then said to me: "Son of man, I will cut off the supply of food in Jerusalem. The people will eat rationed food in anxiety and drink rationed water in despair, ¹⁷for food and water will be scarce. They will be appalled at the sight of each other and will waste away because of*d* their sin.

5 "Now, son of man, take a sharp sword and use it as a barber's razor to shave your head and your beard. Then take a set of scales and divide up the hair. ²When the days of your siege come to an end, burn a third of the hair with fire inside the city. Take a third and strike it with the sword all around the city. And scatter a third to the wind. For I will pursue them with drawn sword. ³But take a few strands of hair and tuck them away in the folds of your garment. ⁴Again, take a few of these and throw them into the fire and burn them up. A fire will spread from there to the whole house of Israel.

⁵"This is what the Sovereign LORD says: This is Jerusalem, which I have set in the centre of the nations, with countries all around her. ⁶Yet in her wickedness she has rebelled against my laws and decrees more than the nations and countries around her. She has rejected my laws and has not followed my decrees.

5:5 ■ NAVEL OF THE UNIVERSE

Maps dating from the Middle Ages often showed Jerusalem and Israel as the centre of a flat world. The practice probably stemmed from several verses like this one, referring to Jerusalem as "the centre of the nations". Geography was not what God had in mind, however. Jerusalem was at the centre of his love. A lover might say something similar: "You're the centre of my universe."

---

⁷"Therefore this is what the Sovereign LORD says: You have been more unruly than the nations around you and have not followed my decrees or kept my laws. You have not even*a* conformed to the standards of the nations around you.

⁸"Therefore this is what the Sovereign LORD says: I myself am against you, Jerusalem, and I will inflict punishment on you in the sight of the nations. ⁹Because of all your detestable idols, I will do to you what I have never done before and will never do again. ¹⁰Therefore in your midst fathers will eat their children, and children will eat their fathers. I will inflict punishment on you and will scatter all your survivors to the winds. ¹¹Therefore as surely as I live, declares the Sovereign LORD, because you have defiled my sanctuary with all your vile images and detestable practices, I myself will withdraw my favour; I will not look on you with pity or spare you. ¹²A third of your people will die of the plague or perish by famine inside you; a third will fall by the sword outside your walls; and a third I will scatter to the winds and pursue with drawn sword.

¹³"Then my anger will cease and my wrath against them will subside, and I will be avenged. And when I have spent my wrath upon them, they will know that I the LORD have spoken in my zeal.

¹⁴"I will make you a ruin and a reproach among the nations around you, in the sight of all who pass by. ¹⁵You will be a reproach and a taunt, a warning and an object of horror to the nations around you when I inflict punishment on you in anger and in wrath and with stinging rebuke. I the LORD have spoken. ¹⁶When I shoot at you with my deadly and destructive arrows of famine, I will shoot to destroy you. I will bring more and more famine upon you and cut off your supply of food. ¹⁷I will send famine and wild beasts against you, and they will leave you childless. Plague and bloodshed will sweep through you, and I will bring the sword against you. I the LORD have spoken."

■ A Prophecy Against the Mountains of Israel

6 The word of the LORD came to me: ²"Son of man, set your face against the mountains of Israel; prophesy against them ³and say: 'O mountains of Israel, hear the word of the Sovereign LORD. This is what the Sovereign LORD says to the mountains and hills, to the ravines and valleys: I am about to bring a sword against you, and I will destroy your high places. ⁴Your altars will be demolished and your incense altars will be smashed; and I will slay your people in front of your idols. ⁵I will lay the dead bodies of the Israelites in front of their idols, and I will scatter your bones around your altars. ⁶Wherever you live, the towns will be laid waste and the high places demolished, so that your altars will be laid waste and devastated, your idols smashed and ruined, your incense altars broken down, and what you have made wiped out. ⁷Your people will fall slain among you, and you will know that I am the LORD.

⁸"'But I will spare some, for some of you will escape the sword when you are scattered among the lands and nations. ⁹Then in the nations where they have been carried captive, those who escape will remember me—how I have been grieved by their adulterous hearts, which have turned away from me, and by their eyes, which have lusted after their idols. They will loathe themselves for the evil they have done and for all their detestable practices. ¹⁰And they will know that I am the LORD; I did not threaten in vain to bring this calamity on them.

6:9 ■ A DIM VIEW OF IDOLATRY

Ezekiel said little about exploitation and injustice. He concentrated on Israel's rejection of a relationship with the living God; they preferred idols instead. The Hebrew word translated "idols" here is used 38 times in Ezekiel, nine in the rest of the Old Testament. Some scholars believe the word is derived from "pellet of dung", indicating Ezekiel's scorn.

---

¹¹"'This is what the Sovereign LORD says: Strike your hands together and stamp your feet and cry out "Alas!" because of all the wicked and detestable practices of the house of Israel, for they will fall by the sword, famine and plague. ¹²He that is far away

---

will die of the plague, and he that is near will fall by the sword, and he that survives and is spared will die of famine. So will I spend my wrath upon them. [13]And they will know that I am the LORD, when their people lie slain among their idols around their altars, on every high hill and on all the mountaintops, under every spreading tree and every leafy oak — places where they offered fragrant incense to all their idols. [14]And I will stretch out my hand against them and make the land a desolate waste from the desert to Diblah[a] — wherever they live. Then they will know that I am the LORD.' "

■ The End Has Come

7 The word of the LORD came to me: [2]"Son of man, this is what the Sovereign LORD says to the land of Israel: The end! The end has come upon the four corners of the land. [3]The end is now upon you and I will unleash my anger against you. I will judge you according to your conduct and repay you for all your detestable practices. [4]I will not look on you with pity or spare you; I will surely repay you for your conduct and the detestable practices among you. Then you will know that I am the LORD.

[5]"This is what the Sovereign LORD says: Disaster! An unheard-of[a] disaster is coming. [6]The end has come! The end has come! It has roused itself against you. It has come! [7]Doom has come upon you — you who dwell in the land. The time has come, the day is near; there is panic, not joy, upon the mountains. [8]I am about to pour out my wrath on you and spend my anger against you; I will judge you according to your conduct and repay you for all your detestable practices. [9]I will not look on you with pity or spare you; I will repay you in accordance with your conduct and the detestable practices among you. Then you will know that it is I the LORD who strikes the blow.

[10]"The day is here! It has come! Doom has burst forth, the rod has budded, arrogance has blossomed! [11]Violence has grown into[b] a rod to punish wickedness; none of the people will be left, none of that crowd — no wealth, nothing of value. [12]The time has come, the day has arrived. Let not the buyer rejoice nor the seller grieve, for wrath is upon the whole crowd. [13]The seller will not recover the land he has sold as long as both of them live, for the vision concerning the whole crowd will not be reversed. Because of their sins, not one of them will preserve his life. [14]Though they blow the trumpet and get everything ready, no-one will go into battle, for my wrath is upon the whole crowd.

[15]"Outside is the sword, inside are plague and famine; those in the country will die by the sword, and those in the city will be devoured by famine and plague. [16]All who survive and escape will be in the mountains, moaning like doves of the valleys, each because of his sins. [17]Every hand will go limp, and every knee will become as weak as water. [18]They will put on sackcloth and be clothed with terror. Their faces will be covered with shame and their heads will be shaved. [19]They will throw their silver into the streets, and their gold will be an unclean thing. Their silver and gold will not be able to save them in the day of the LORD's wrath. They will not

satisfy their hunger or fill their stomachs with it, for it has made them stumble into sin. [20]They were proud of their beautiful jewellery and used it to make their detestable idols and vile images. Therefore I will turn these into an unclean thing for them. [21]I will hand it all over as plunder to foreigners and as loot to the wicked of the earth, and they will defile it. [22]I will turn my face away from them, and they will desecrate my treasured place; robbers will enter it and desecrate it.

[23]"Prepare chains, because the land is full of bloodshed and the city is full of violence. [24]I will bring the most wicked of the nations to take possession of their houses; I will put an end to the pride of the mighty, and their sanctuaries will be desecrated. [25]When terror comes, they will seek peace, but there will be none. [26]Calamity upon calamity will come, and rumour upon rumour. They will try to get a vision from the prophet; the teaching of the law by the priest will be lost, as will the counsel of the elders. [27]The king will mourn, the prince will be clothed with despair, and the hands of the people of the land will tremble. I will deal with them according to their conduct, and by their own standards I will judge them. Then they will know that I am the LORD."

■ Idolatry in the Temple

8 In the sixth year, in the sixth month on the fifth day, while I was sitting in my house and the elders of Judah were sitting before me, the hand of the Sovereign LORD came upon me there. [2]I looked, and I saw a figure like that of a man.[a] From what appeared to be his waist down he was like fire, and from there up his appearance was as bright as glowing metal. [3]He stretched out what looked like a hand and took me by the hair of my head. The Spirit lifted me up between earth and heaven and in visions of God he took me to Jerusalem, to the entrance to the north gate of the inner court, where the idol that provokes to jealousy stood. [4]And there before me was the glory of the God of Israel, as in the vision I had seen in the plain.

[5]Then he said to me, "Son of man, look towards the north." So I looked, and in the entrance north of the gate of the altar I saw this idol of jealousy.

[6]And he said to me, "Son of man, do you see what they are doing — the utterly detestable things the house of Israel is doing here, things that will drive me far from my sanctuary? But you will see things that are even more detestable."

8:6 ■ DETESTABLE THINGS

Ezekiel, a priest, had a special concern about the abuses going on in the temple. Here, in a vision, he sees painful details of these practices, notably idol worship (verses 5,10) and sun worship (verse 16). The leaders of Israel had lost faith in their God, and were desperately trying alternatives. Here and elsewhere Ezekiel accuses leaders by name; his original audience would have known them well.

---

a 14 Most Hebrew manuscripts; a few Hebrew manuscripts *Riblah*
b 11 Or *The violent one has become*   *a 2* Or *saw a fiery figure*   *a 5* Most Hebrew manuscripts; some Hebrew manuscripts and Syriac *Disaster after*

7Then he brought me to the entrance to the court. I looked, and I saw a hole in the wall. 8He said to me, "Son of man, now dig into the wall." So I dug into the wall and saw a doorway there.

9And he said to me, "Go in and see the wicked and detestable things they are doing here." 10So I went in and looked, and I saw portrayed all over the walls all kinds of crawling things and detestable animals and all the idols of the house of Israel. 11In front of them stood seventy elders of the house of Israel, and Jaazaniah son of Shaphan was standing among them. Each had a censer in his hand, and a fragrant cloud of incense was rising.

12He said to me, "Son of man, have you seen what the elders of the house of Israel are doing in the darkness, each at the shrine of his own idol? They say, 'The LORD does not see us; the LORD has forsaken the land.' " 13Again, he said, "You will see them doing things that are even more detestable."

14Then he brought me to the entrance to the north gate of the house of the LORD, and I saw women sitting there, mourning for Tammuz. 15He said to me, "Do you see this, son of man? You will see things that are even more detestable than this."

16He then brought me into the inner court of the house of the LORD, and there at the entrance to the temple, between the portico and the altar, were about twenty-five men. With their backs towards the temple of the LORD and their faces towards the east, they were bowing down to the sun in the east.

17He said to me, "Have you seen this, son of man? Is it a trivial matter for the house of Judah to do the detestable things they are doing here? Must they also fill the land with violence and continually provoke me to anger? Look at them putting the branch to their nose! 18Therefore I will deal with them in anger; I will not look on them with pity or spare them. Although they shout in my ears, I will not listen to them."

■ Idolaters Killed

9 Then I heard him call out in a loud voice, "Bring the guards of the city here, each with a weapon in his hand." 2And I saw six men coming from the direction of the upper gate, which faces north, each with a deadly weapon in his hand. With them was a man clothed in linen who had a writing kit at his side. They came in and stood beside the bronze altar.

3Now the glory of the God of Israel went up from above the cherubim, where it had been, and moved to the threshold of the temple. Then the LORD called to the man clothed in linen who had the writing kit at his side 4and said to him, "Go throughout the city of Jerusalem and put a mark on the foreheads of those who grieve and lament over all the detestable things that are done in it."

5As I listened, he said to the others, "Follow him through the city and kill, without showing pity or compassion. 6Slaughter old men, young men and maidens, women and children, but do not touch anyone who has the mark. Begin at my sanctuary." So they began with the elders who were in front of the temple.

7Then he said to them, "Defile the temple and fill the courts with the slain. Go!" So they went out and began killing throughout the city. 8While they were killing and I was left alone, I fell face down, crying out, "Ah, Sovereign LORD! Are you going to destroy the entire remnant of Israel in this outpouring of your wrath on Jerusalem?"

9:4 ■ THE SAVING MARK
The man in linen marked those to be saved with a *taw,* the final letter in the Hebrew alphabet, written in the oldest script as "x" – a cross, as Christians have noted.

9He answered me, "The sin of the house of Israel and Judah is exceedingly great; the land is full of bloodshed and the city is full of injustice. They say, 'The LORD has forsaken the land; the LORD does not see.' 10So I will not look on them with pity or spare them, but I will bring down on their own heads what they have done."

11Then the man in linen with the writing kit at his side brought back word, saying, "I have done as you commanded."

■ The Glory Departs From the Temple

10 I looked, and I saw the likeness of a throne of sapphire[a] above the expanse that was over the heads of the cherubim. 2The LORD said to the man clothed in linen, "Go in among the wheels beneath the cherubim. Fill your hands with burning coals from among the cherubim and scatter them over the city." And as I watched, he went in.

3Now the cherubim were standing on the south side of the temple when the man went in, and a cloud filled the inner court. 4Then the glory of the LORD rose from above the cherubim and moved to the threshold of the temple. The cloud filled the temple, and the court was full of the radiance of the glory of the LORD. 5The sound of the wings of the cherubim could be heard as far away as the outer court, like the voice of God Almighty[b] when he speaks.

6When the LORD commanded the man in linen, "Take fire from among the wheels, from among the cherubim," the man went in and stood beside a wheel. 7Then one of the cherubim reached out his hand to the fire that was among them. He took up some of it and put it into the hands of the man in linen, who took it and went out. 8(Under the wings of the cherubim could be seen what looked like the hands of a man.)

9I looked, and I saw beside the cherubim four wheels, one beside each of the cherubim; the wheels sparkled like chrysolite. 10As for their appearance, the four of them looked alike; each was like a wheel intersecting a wheel. 11As they moved, they would go in any one of the four directions the cherubim faced; the wheels did not turn about[c] as the cherubim went. The cherubim went in whatever direction the head faced, without turning as they went. 12Their entire bodies, including their backs, their hands and their wings, were completely full of eyes, as were their four wheels. 13I heard the wheels being called "the whirling wheels". [14]Each of the cherubim had four faces: One face was that of a cherub, the second the face of a man, the third the face of a lion, and the fourth the face of an eagle.

[15]Then the cherubim rose upwards. These were the living creatures I had seen by the Kebar River. [16]When the cherubim moved, the wheels beside them moved; and when the cherubim spread their wings to rise from the ground, the wheels did not leave their side. [17]When the cherubim stood still, they also stood still; and when the cherubim rose, they rose with them, because the spirit of the living creatures was in them.

[18]Then the glory of the LORD departed from over the threshold of the temple and stopped above the cherubim. [19]While I watched, the cherubim spread their wings and rose from the ground, and as they went, the wheels went with them. They stopped at the entrance to the east gate of the LORD's house, and the glory of the God of Israel was above them.

10:18 ■ GOOD-BYE, GOD

What would it mean if the Queen became so disgusted with the state of the country that she abdicated and just faded from the public eye? Such news would be incredible, with far-reaching results. Ezekiel's vision indicates even bigger problems for the Israelites. God—the same powerful God who appeared to Ezekiel in Babylon (chapter 1)—leaves the temple. Sick of his people's corruption, he simply moves out.

[20]These were the living creatures I had seen beneath the God of Israel by the Kebar River, and I realised that they were cherubim. [21]Each had four faces and four wings, and under their wings was what looked like the hands of a man. [22]Their faces had the same appearance as those I had seen by the Kebar River. Each one went straight ahead.

■ Judgment on Israel's Leaders

11 Then the Spirit lifted me up and brought me to the gate of the house of the LORD that faces east. There at the entrance to the gate were twenty-five men, and I saw among them Jaazaniah son of Azzur and Pelatiah son of Benaiah, leaders of the people. [2]The LORD said to me, "Son of man, these are the men who are plotting evil and giving wicked advice in this city. [3]They say, 'Will it not soon be time to build houses?[a] This city is a cooking pot, and we are the meat.' [4]Therefore prophesy against them; prophesy, son of man."

[5]Then the Spirit of the LORD came upon me, and he told me to say: "This is what the LORD says: That is what you are saying, O house of Israel, but I know what is going through your mind. [6]You have killed many people in this city and filled its streets with the dead.

[7]"Therefore this is what the Sovereign LORD says: The bodies you have thrown there are the meat and this city is the pot, but I will drive you out of it. [8]You fear the sword, and the sword is what I will bring against you, declares the Sovereign LORD. [9]I will

drive you out of the city and hand you over to foreigners and inflict punishment on you. [10]You will fall by the sword, and I will execute judgment on you at the borders of Israel. Then you will know that I am the LORD. [11]This city will not be a pot for you, nor will you be the meat in it; I will execute judgment on you at the borders of Israel. [12]And you will know that I am the LORD, for you have not followed my decrees or kept my laws but have conformed to the standards of the nations around you."

[13]Now as I was prophesying, Pelatiah son of Benaiah died. Then I fell face down and cried out in a loud voice, "Ah, Sovereign LORD! Will you completely destroy the remnant of Israel?"

[14]The word of the LORD came to me: [15]"Son of man, your brothers—your brothers who are your blood-relatives[b] and the whole house of Israel—are those of whom the people of Jerusalem have said, 'They are[c] far away from the LORD; this land was given to us as our possession.'

■ Promised Return of Israel

[16]"Therefore say: 'This is what the Sovereign LORD says: Although I sent them far away among the nations and scattered them among the countries, yet for a little while I have been a sanctuary for them in the countries where they have gone.'

[17]"Therefore say: 'This is what the Sovereign LORD says: I will gather you from the nations and bring you back from the countries where you have been scattered, and I will give you back the land of Israel again.'

[18]"They will return to it and remove all its vile images and detestable idols. [19]I will give them an undivided heart and put a new spirit in them; I will remove from them their heart of stone and give them a heart of flesh. [20]Then they will follow my decrees and be careful to keep my laws. They will be my people, and I will be their God. [21]But as for those whose hearts are devoted to their vile images and detestable idols, I will bring down on their own heads what they have done, declares the Sovereign LORD."

[22]Then the cherubim, with the wheels beside them, spread their wings, and the glory of the God of Israel was above them. [23]The glory of the LORD went up from within the city and stopped above the mountain east of it. [24]The Spirit lifted me up and brought me to the exiles in Babylonia[d] in the vision given by the Spirit of God.

Then the vision I had seen went up from me, [25]and I told the exiles everything the LORD had shown me.

■ The Exile Symbolised

12 The word of the LORD came to me: [2]"Son of man, you are living among a rebellious people. They have eyes to see but do not see and ears to hear but do not hear, for they are a rebellious people.

[3]"Therefore, son of man, pack your belongings for exile and in the daytime, as they watch, set out and go from where you are to another place. Perhaps they will understand, though they are a rebellious house. [4]During the daytime, while they watch,

bring out your belongings packed for exile. Then in the evening, while they are watching, go out like those who go into exile. [5]While they watch, dig through the wall and take your belongings out through it. [6]Put them on your shoulder as they are watching and carry them out at dusk. Cover your face so that you cannot see the land, for I have made you a sign to the house of Israel."

[7]So I did as I was commanded. During the day I brought out my things packed for exile. Then in the evening I dug through the wall with my hands. I took my belongings out at dusk, carrying them on my shoulders while they watched.

[8]In the morning the word of the LORD came to me: [9]"Son of man, did not that rebellious house of Israel ask you, 'What are you doing?'

[10]"Say to them, 'This is what the Sovereign LORD says: This oracle concerns the prince in Jerusalem and the whole house of Israel who are there.' [11]Say to them, 'I am a sign to you.'

"As I have done, so it will be done to them. They will go into exile as captives.

[12]"The prince among them will put his things on his shoulder at dusk and leave, and a hole will be dug in the wall for him to go through. He will cover his face so that he cannot see the land. [13]I will spread my net for him, and he will be caught in my snare; I will bring him to Babylonia, the land of the Chaldeans, but he will not see it, and there he will die. [14]I will scatter to the winds all those around him — his staff and all his troops — and I will pursue them with drawn sword.

12:12 ■ OUT THROUGH THE HOLE
Ezekiel's prediction of Jerusalem's leader leaving through a hole in the wall was literally fulfilled. You can read about it in 2 Kings 25:4–7 or Jeremiah 39:4–7.

[15]"They will know that I am the LORD, when I disperse them among the nations and scatter them through the countries. [16]But I will spare a few of them from the sword, famine and plague, so that in the nations where they go they may acknowledge all their detestable practices. Then they will know that I am the LORD."

[17]The word of the LORD came to me: [18]"Son of man, tremble as you eat your food, and shudder in fear as you drink your water. [19]Say to the people of the land: 'This is what the Sovereign LORD says about those living in Jerusalem and in the land of Israel: They will eat their food in anxiety and drink their water in despair, for their land will be stripped of everything in it because of the violence of all who live there. [20]The inhabited towns will be laid waste and the land will be desolate. Then you will know that I am the LORD.' "

[21]The word of the LORD came to me: [22]"Son of man, what is this proverb you have in the land of Israel: 'The days go by and every vision comes to nothing'? [23]Say to them, 'This is what the Sovereign LORD says: I am going to put an end to this proverb, and they will no longer quote it in Israel.' Say to

them, 'The days are near when every vision will be fulfilled. [24]For there will be no more false visions or flattering divinations among the people of Israel. [25]But I the LORD will speak what I will, and it shall be fulfilled without delay. For in your days, you rebellious house, I will fulfil whatever I say, declares the Sovereign LORD.' "

[26]The word of the LORD came to me: [27]"Son of man, the house of Israel is saying, 'The vision he sees is for many years from now, and he prophesies about the distant future.'

[28]"Therefore say to them, 'This is what the Sovereign LORD says: None of my words will be delayed any longer; whatever I say will be fulfilled, declares the Sovereign LORD.' "

■ False Prophets Condemned

13 The word of the LORD came to me: [2]"Son of man, prophesy against the prophets of Israel who are now prophesying. Say to those who prophesy out of their own imagination: 'Hear the word of the LORD! [3]This is what the Sovereign LORD says: Woe to the foolish[a] prophets who follow their own spirit and have seen nothing! [4]Your prophets, O Israel, are like jackals among ruins. [5]You have not gone up to the breaks in the wall to repair it for the house of Israel so that it will stand firm in the battle on the day of the LORD. [6]Their visions are false and their divinations a lie. They say, "The LORD declares", when the LORD has not sent them; yet they expect their words to be fulfilled. [7]Have you not seen false visions and uttered lying divinations when you say, "The LORD declares", though I have not spoken?

[8]" 'Therefore this is what the Sovereign LORD says: Because of your false words and lying visions, I am against you, declares the Sovereign LORD. [9]My hand will be against the prophets who see false visions and utter lying divinations. They will not belong to the council of my people or be listed in the records of the house of Israel, nor will they enter the land of Israel. Then you will know that I am the Sovereign LORD.

[10]" 'Because they lead my people astray, saying, "Peace", when there is no peace, and because, when a flimsy wall is built, they cover it with whitewash, [11]therefore tell those who cover it with whitewash that it is going to fall. Rain will come in torrents, and I will send hailstones hurtling down, and violent winds will burst forth. [12]When the wall collapses, will people not ask you, "Where is the whitewash you covered it with?"

[13]" 'Therefore this is what the Sovereign LORD says: In my wrath I will unleash a violent wind, and in my anger hailstones and torrents of rain will fall with destructive fury. [14]I will tear down the wall you have covered with whitewash and will level it to the ground so that its foundation will be laid bare. When it[b] falls, you will be destroyed in it; and you will know that I am the LORD. [15]So I will spend my wrath against the wall and against those who covered it with whitewash. I will say to you, "The wall is gone and so are those who whitewashed it, [16]those prophets of Israel who prophesied to

Jerusalem and saw visions of peace for her when there was no peace, declares the Sovereign LORD." '

13:10 ■ WHITEWASH

The Hebrew word translated "whitewash" means "to plaster over". The picture is of a poorly constructed wall that is carefully plastered so that it looks well built. False prophets, wanting everyone to be happy, spoke cheerfully about the future. But they were only covering up the surface of fundamental problems. A storm, God warns, will strip off their coat of whitewash, and the flawed wall will collapse. In contrast, real prophets were unafraid of exposing the truth, however bad, for only then could problems be remedied.

Ezekiel 13:6–9 asserts that the false prophets thought up messages, then attributed them to God. Ezekiel, on the other hand, was repeatedly seized by a supernatural power. See, for examples, Ezekiel 8:1–5; 10:1–2; 24:1–2; and 33:21–22.

17"Now, son of man, set your face against the daughters of your people who prophesy out of their own imagination. Prophesy against them 18and say, 'This is what the Sovereign LORD says: Woe to the women who sew magic charms on all their wrists and make veils of various lengths for their heads in order to ensnare people. Will you ensnare the lives of my people but preserve your own? 19You have profaned me among my people for a few handfuls of barley and scraps of bread. By lying to my people, who listen to lies, you have killed those who should not have died and have spared those who should not live.

20" 'Therefore this is what the Sovereign LORD says: I am against your magic charms with which you ensnare people like birds and I will tear them from your arms; I will set free the people that you ensnare like birds. 21I will tear off your veils and save my people from your hands, and they will no longer fall prey to your power. Then you will know that I am the LORD. 22Because you disheartened the righteous with your lies, when I had brought them no grief, and because you encouraged the wicked not to turn from their evil ways and so save their lives, 23therefore you will no longer see false visions or practise divination. I will save my people from your hands. And then you will know that I am the LORD.' "

■ Idolaters Condemned

14 Some of the elders of Israel came to me and sat down in front of me. 2Then the word of the LORD came to me: 3"Son of man, these men have set up idols in their hearts and put wicked stumbling-blocks before their faces. Should I let them enquire of me at all? 4Therefore speak to them and tell them, 'This is what the Sovereign LORD says: When any Israelite sets up idols in his heart and puts a wicked stumbling-block before his face and then goes to a prophet, I the LORD will answer him myself in keeping with his great idolatry. 5I will do this to recapture the hearts of the people of Israel, who have all deserted me for their idols.'

6"Therefore say to the house of Israel, 'This is what the Sovereign LORD says: Repent! Turn from your idols and renounce all your detestable practices!

7" 'When any Israelite or any alien living in Israel separates himself from me and sets up idols in his heart and puts a wicked stumbling-block before his face and then goes to a prophet to enquire of me, I the LORD will answer him myself. 8I will set my face against that man and make him an example and a byword. I will cut him off from my people. Then you will know that I am the LORD.

9" 'And if the prophet is enticed to utter a prophecy, I the LORD have enticed that prophet, and I will stretch out my hand against him and destroy him from among my people Israel. 10They will bear their guilt—the prophet will be as guilty as the one who consults him. 11Then the people of Israel will no longer stray from me, nor will they defile themselves any more with all their sins. They will be my people, and I will be their God, declares the Sovereign LORD.' "

■ Judgment Inescapable

12The word of the LORD came to me: 13"Son of man, if a country sins against me by being unfaithful and I stretch out my hand against it to cut off its food supply and send famine upon it and kill its men and their animals, 14even if these three men—Noah, Daniel[a] and Job—were in it, they could save only themselves by their righteousness, declares the Sovereign LORD.

15"Or if I send wild beasts through that country and they leave it childless and it becomes desolate so that no-one can pass through it because of the beasts, 16as surely as I live, declares the Sovereign LORD, even if these three men were in it, they could not save their own sons or daughters. They alone would be saved, but the land would be desolate.

17"Or if I bring a sword against that country and say, 'Let the sword pass throughout the land,' and I kill its men and their animals, 18as surely as I live, declares the Sovereign LORD, even if these three men were in it, they could not save their own sons or daughters. They alone would be saved.

19"Or if I send a plague into that land and pour out my wrath upon it through bloodshed, killing its men and their animals, 20as surely as I live, declares the Sovereign LORD, even if Noah, Daniel and Job were in it, they could save neither son nor daughter. They would save only themselves by their righteousness.

21"For this is what the Sovereign LORD says: How much worse will it be when I send against Jerusalem my four dreadful judgments—sword and famine and wild beasts and plague—to kill its men and their animals! 22Yet there will be some survivors—sons and daughters who will be brought out of it. They will come to you, and when you see their conduct and their actions, you will be consoled regarding the disaster I have brought upon Jerusalem—every disaster I have brought upon it. 23You will be consoled when you see their conduct

---

a 14 Or Danel; the Hebrew spelling may suggest a person other than the prophet Daniel; also in verse 20.

and their actions, for you will know that I have done nothing in it without cause, declares the Sovereign LORD."

Jerusalem, a Useless Vine

15 The word of the LORD came to me: 2"Son of man, how is the wood of a vine better than that of a branch on any of the trees in the forest? 3Is wood ever taken from it to make anything useful? Do they make pegs from it to hang things on? 4And after it is thrown on the fire as fuel and the fire burns both ends and chars the middle, is it then useful for anything? 5If it was not useful for anything when it was whole, how much less can it be made into something useful when the fire has burned it and it is charred?

6"Therefore this is what the Sovereign LORD says: As I have given the wood of the vine among the trees of the forest as fuel for the fire, so will I treat the people living in Jerusalem. 7I will set my face against them. Although they have come out of the fire, the fire will yet consume them. And when I set my face against them, you will know that I am the LORD. 8I will make the land desolate because they have been unfaithful, declares the Sovereign LORD."

An Allegory of Unfaithful Jerusalem

16 The word of the LORD came to me: 2"Son of man, confront Jerusalem with her detestable practices 3and say, 'This is what the Sovereign LORD says to Jerusalem: Your ancestry and birth were in the land of the Canaanites; your father was an Amorite and your mother a Hittite. 4On the day you were born your cord was not cut, nor were you washed with water to make you clean, nor were you rubbed with salt or wrapped in cloths. 5No-one looked on you with pity or had compassion enough to do any of these things for you. Rather, you were thrown out into the open field, for on the day you were born you were despised.

6" 'Then I passed by and saw you kicking about in your blood, and as you lay there in your blood I said to you, "Live!"ᵃ 7I made you grow like a plant of the field. You grew up and developed and became the most beautiful of jewels.ᵇ Your breasts were formed and your hair grew, you who were naked and bare.

8" 'Later I passed by, and when I looked at you and saw that you were old enough for love, I spread the corner of my garment over you and covered your nakedness. I gave you my solemn oath and entered into a covenant with you, declares the Sovereign LORD, and you became mine.

9" 'I bathedᶜ you with water and washed the blood from you and put ointments on you. 10I clothed you with an embroidered dress and put leather sandals on you. I dressed you in fine linen and covered you with costly garments. 11I adorned you with jewellery: I put bracelets on your arms and a necklace around your neck, 12and I put a ring on your nose, ear-rings on your ears and a beautiful crown on your head. 13So you were adorned with gold and silver; your clothes were of fine linen and costly fabric and embroidered cloth. Your food was fine flour, honey and olive oil. You became very beautiful and rose to be a queen. 14And your fame spread among the nations on account of your beauty, because the splendour I had given you made your beauty perfect, declares the Sovereign LORD.

15" 'But you trusted in your beauty and used your fame to become a prostitute. You lavished your favours on anyone who passed by and your beauty became his.ᵈ 16You took some of your garments to make gaudy high places, where you carried on your prostitution. Such things should not happen, nor should they ever occur. 17You also took the fine jewellery I gave you, the jewellery made of my gold and silver, and you made for yourself male idols and engaged in prostitution with them. 18And you took your embroidered clothes to put on them, and you offered my oil and incense before them. 19Also the food I provided for you — the fine flour, olive oil and honey I gave you to eat — you offered as fragrant incense before them. That is what happened, declares the Sovereign LORD.

20" 'And you took your sons and daughters whom you bore to me and sacrificed them as food to the idols. Was your prostitution not enough? 21You slaughtered my children and sacrificed themᵉ to the idols. 22In all your detestable practices and your prostitution you did not remember the days of your youth, when you were naked and bare, kicking about in your blood.

23" 'Woe! Woe to you, declares the Sovereign LORD. In addition to all your other wickedness, 24you built a mound for yourself and made a lofty shrine in every public square. 25At the head of every street you built your lofty shrines and degraded your beauty, offering your body with increasing promiscuity to anyone who passed by. 26You engaged in prostitution with the Egyptians, your lustful neighbours, and provoked me to anger with your increasing promiscuity. 27So I stretched out my hand against you and reduced your territory; I gave you over to the greed of your enemies, the daughters of the Philistines, who were shocked by your lewd conduct. 28You engaged in prostitution with the Assyrians too, because you were insatiable; and even after that, you still were not satisfied. 29Then you increased your promiscuity to include Babylonia,ᶠ a land of merchants, but even with this you were not satisfied.

30" 'How weak-willed you are, declares the

16:26 ■ WORSE THAN A WHORE
In this graphic allegory, Ezekiel compares Jerusalem to an abandoned baby whom God rescues and raises with great tenderness. (Female children, often unwanted, were sometimes left to die.) Yet she rebels, preferring life on the wild side. She becomes a prostitute, then sinks even lower. Rather than being paid for her services, she actually *pays* for sex (verse 34). Ezekiel is depicting Israel's eagerness to adopt the religious practices of her neighbours.

ᵃ6 A few Hebrew manuscripts, Septuagint and Syriac; most Hebrew manuscripts *"Live!" And as you lay there in your blood I said to you, "Live!"* ᵇ7 Or *became mature* ᶜ9 Or *I had bathed* ᵈ15 Most Hebrew manuscripts; one Hebrew manuscript (see some Septuagint manuscripts) *by. Such a thing should not happen* ᵉ21 Or *and made them pass through ⸤the fire⸥* ᶠ29 Or *Chaldea*

Sovereign LORD, when you do all these things, acting like a brazen prostitute! 31When you built your mounds at the head of every street and made your lofty shrines in every public square, you were unlike a prostitute, because you scorned payment.

32" 'You adulterous wife! You prefer strangers to your own husband! 33Every prostitute receives a fee, but you give gifts to all your lovers, bribing them to come to you from everywhere for your illicit favours. 34So in your prostitution you are the opposite of others; no-one runs after you for your favours. You are the very opposite, for you give payment and none is given to you.

35" 'Therefore, you prostitute, hear the word of the LORD! 36This is what the Sovereign LORD says: Because you poured out your wealth*g* and exposed your nakedness in your promiscuity with your lovers, and because of all your detestable idols, and because you gave them your children's blood, 37therefore I am going to gather all your lovers, with whom you found pleasure, those you loved as well as those you hated. I will gather them against you from all around and will strip you in front of them, and they will see all your nakedness. 38I will sentence you to the punishment of women who commit adultery and who shed blood; I will bring upon you the blood vengeance of my wrath and jealous anger. 39Then I will hand you over to your lovers, and they will tear down your mounds and destroy your lofty shrines. They will strip you of your clothes and take your fine jewellery and leave you naked and bare. 40They will bring a mob against you, who will stone you and hack you to pieces with their swords. 41They will burn down your houses and inflict punishment on you in the sight of many women. I will put a stop to your prostitution, and you will no longer pay your lovers. 42Then my wrath against you will subside and my jealous anger will turn away from you; I will be calm and no longer angry.

43" 'Because you did not remember the days of your youth but enraged me with all these things, I will surely bring down on your head what you have done, declares the Sovereign LORD. Did you not add lewdness to all your other detestable practices?

44" 'Everyone who quotes proverbs will quote this proverb about you: "Like mother, like daughter." 45You are a true daughter of your mother, who despised her husband and her children; and you are a true sister of your sisters, who despised their husbands and their children. Your mother was a Hittite and your father an Amorite. 46Your older sister was Samaria, who lived to the north of you with her daughters; and your younger sister, who lived to the south of you with her daughters, was Sodom. 47You not only walked in their ways and copied their detestable practices, but in all your ways you soon became more depraved than they. 48As surely as I live, declares the Sovereign LORD, your sister Sodom and her daughters never did what you and your daughters have done.

49" 'Now this was the sin of your sister Sodom: She and her daughters were arrogant, overfed and unconcerned; they did not help the poor and needy. 50They were haughty and did detestable things

before me. Therefore I did away with them as you have seen. 51Samaria did not commit half the sins you did. You have done more detestable things than they, and have made your sisters seem righteous by all these things you have done. 52Bear your disgrace, for you have furnished some justification for your sisters. Because your sins were more vile than theirs, they appear more righteous than you. So then, be ashamed and bear your disgrace, for you have made your sisters appear righteous.

16:49 ■ THE SIN OF SODOM
Why had God destroyed Sodom and Gomorrah? The Genesis 19 account suggests sexual perversion and violence as the cause. Ezekiel here adds an interesting aspect: arrogant, uncaring wealth. The attempt at homosexual gang rape, chronicled in Genesis, was only part of a bigger problem.

53" 'However, I will restore the fortunes of Sodom and her daughters and of Samaria and her daughters, and your fortunes along with them, 54so that you may bear your disgrace and be ashamed of all you have done in giving them comfort. 55And your sisters, Sodom with her daughters and Samaria with her daughters, will return to what they were before; and you and your daughters will return to what you were before. 56You would not even mention your sister Sodom in the day of your pride, 57before your wickedness was uncovered. Even so, you are now scorned by the daughters of Edom*b* and all her neighbours and the daughters of the Philistines—all those around you who despise you. 58You will bear the consequences of your lewdness and your detestable practices, declares the LORD.

59" 'This is what the Sovereign LORD says: I will deal with you as you deserve, because you have despised my oath by breaking the covenant. 60Yet I will remember the covenant I made with you in the days of your youth, and I will establish an everlasting covenant with you. 61Then you will remember your ways and be ashamed when you receive your sisters, both those who are older than you and those who are younger. I will give them to you as daughters, but not on the basis of my covenant with you. 62So I will establish my covenant with you, and you will know that I am the LORD. 63Then, when I make atonement for you for all you have done, you will remember and be ashamed and never again open your mouth because of your humiliation, declares the Sovereign LORD.' "

■ Two Eagles and a Vine

17 The word of the LORD came to me: 2"Son of man, set forth an allegory and tell the house of Israel a parable. 3Say to them, 'This is what the Sovereign LORD says: A great eagle with powerful wings, long feathers and full plumage of varied colours came to Lebanon. Taking hold of the top of a cedar, 4he broke off its topmost shoot and carried it away to a land of merchants, where he planted it in a city of traders.

---

*g*36 Or *lust*   *b*57 Many Hebrew manuscripts and Syriac; most Hebrew manuscripts, Septuagint and Vulgate *Aram*

5" 'He took some of the seed of your land and put it in fertile soil. He planted it like a willow by abundant water, ⁶and it sprouted and became a low, spreading vine. Its branches turned towards him, but its roots remained under it. So it became a vine and produced branches and put out leafy boughs.

7" 'But there was another great eagle with powerful wings and full plumage. The vine now sent out its roots towards him from the plot where it was planted and stretched out its branches to him for water. ⁸It had been planted in good soil by abundant water so that it would produce branches, bear fruit and become a splendid vine.'

9"Say to them, 'This is what the Sovereign LORD says: Will it thrive? Will it not be uprooted and stripped of its fruit so that it withers? All its new growth will wither. It will not take a strong arm or many people to pull it up by the roots. ¹⁰Even if it is transplanted, will it thrive? Will it not wither completely when the east wind strikes it — wither away in the plot where it grew?' "

11Then the word of the LORD came to me: ¹²"Say to this rebellious house, 'Do you not know what these things mean?' Say to them: 'The king of Babylon went to Jerusalem and carried off her king and her nobles, bringing them back with him to Babylon. ¹³Then he took a member of the royal family and made a treaty with him, putting him under oath. He also carried away the leading men of the land, ¹⁴so that the kingdom would be brought low, unable to rise again, surviving only by keeping his treaty. ¹⁵But the king rebelled against him by sending his envoys to Egypt to get horses and a large army. Will he succeed? Will he who does such things escape? Will he break the treaty and yet escape?

16" 'As surely as I live, declares the Sovereign LORD, he shall die in Babylon, in the land of the king who put him on the throne, whose oath he despised and whose treaty he broke. ¹⁷Pharaoh with his mighty army and great horde will be of no help to him in war, when ramps are built and siege works erected to destroy many lives. ¹⁸He despised the oath by breaking the covenant. Because he had given his hand in pledge and yet did all these things, he shall not escape.

19" 'Therefore this is what the Sovereign LORD says: As surely as I live, I will bring down on his head my oath that he despised and my covenant that he broke. ²⁰I will spread my net for him, and he will be caught in my snare. I will bring him to Babylon and execute judgment upon him there because he was unfaithful to me. ²¹All his fleeing troops will fall by the sword, and the survivors will be scattered to the winds. Then you will know that I the LORD have spoken.

22" 'This is what the Sovereign LORD says: I myself will take a shoot from the very top of a cedar and plant it; I will break off a tender sprig from its topmost shoots and plant it on a high and lofty mountain. ²³On the mountain heights of Israel I will plant it; it will produce branches and bear fruit and become a splendid cedar. Birds of every kind will nest in it; they will find shelter in the shade of its branches. ²⁴All the trees of the field will know that I the LORD bring down the tall tree and make the low tree grow tall. I dry up the green tree and make the dry tree flourish.

" 'I the LORD have spoken, and I will do it.' "

■ The Soul Who Sins Will Die

18 The word of the LORD came to me: ²"What do you people mean by quoting this proverb about the land of Israel:

" 'The fathers eat sour grapes,
and the children's teeth are set on edge'?

18:2 ■ JEREMIAH AND EZEKIEL
This proverb, which suggests the way children pay for their parents' sins, was also quoted by Jeremiah (Jeremiah 31:29). While Ezekiel did his work in Babylon, Jeremiah carried out a parallel work in Jerusalem. Neither mentions the other, but their messages carry many similarities. Note particularly Jeremiah 1:14–19; 3:6–13; 6:27–30; 8:10–11; 15:1–2; 16:5–8; 23:16–40; 24; 29; 31:27–34; 39 — all passages that have close parallels in Ezekiel.

3"As surely as I live, declares the Sovereign LORD, you will no longer quote this proverb in Israel. ⁴For every living soul belongs to me, the father as well as the son — both alike belong to me. The soul who sins is the one who will die.

5"Suppose there is a righteous man
who does what is just and right.
⁶He does not eat at the mountain shrines
or look to the idols of the house of Israel.
He does not defile his neighbour's wife
or lie with a woman during her period.
⁷He does not oppress anyone,
but returns what he took in pledge for a
loan.
He does not commit robbery,
but gives his food to the hungry
and provides clothing for the naked.
⁸He does not lend at usury
or take excessive interest.ᵃ
He withholds his hand from doing wrong
and judges fairly between man and man.
⁹He follows my decrees
and faithfully keeps my laws.
That man is righteous;
he will surely live,
declares the Sovereign LORD.

10"Suppose he has a violent son, who sheds blood or does any of these other thingsᵇ ¹¹(though the father has done none of them):

"He eats at the mountain shrines.
He defiles his neighbour's wife.
¹²He oppresses the poor and needy.
He commits robbery.
He does not return what he took in pledge.
He looks to the idols.
He does detestable things.
¹³He lends at usury and takes excessive interest.

ᵃ8 Or take interest; similarly in verses 13 and 17   ᵇ10 Or things to a brother

Will such a man live? He will not! Because he has done all these detestable things, he will surely be put to death and his blood will be on his own head.

14"But suppose this son has a son who sees all the sins his father commits, and though he sees them, he does not do such things:

15"He does not eat at the mountain shrines
  or look to the idols of the house of Israel.
He does not defile his neighbour's wife.
16He does not oppress anyone
  or require a pledge for a loan.
He does not commit robbery,
  but gives his food to the hungry
  and provides clothing for the naked.
17He withholds his hand from sin^c
  and takes no usury or excessive interest.
He keeps my laws and follows my decrees.

He will not die for his father's sin; he will surely live. 18But his father will die for his own sin, because he practised extortion, robbed his brother and did what was wrong among his people.

19"Yet you ask, 'Why does the son not share the guilt of his father?' Since the son has done what is just and right and has been careful to keep all my decrees, he will surely live. 20The soul who sins is the one who will die. The son will not share the guilt of the father, nor will the father share the guilt of the son. The righteousness of the righteous man will be credited to him, and the wickedness of the wicked will be charged against him.

21"But if a wicked man turns away from all the sins he has committed and keeps all my decrees and does what is just and right, he will surely live; he will not die. 22None of the offences he has committed will be remembered against him. Because of the righteous things he has done, he will live. 23Do I take any pleasure in the death of the wicked? declares the Sovereign LORD. Rather, am I not pleased when they turn from their ways and live?

24"But if a righteous man turns from his righteousness and commits sin and does the same detestable things the wicked man does, will he live? None of the righteous things he has done will be remembered. Because of the unfaithfulness he is guilty of and because of the sins he has committed, he will die.

25"Yet you say, 'The way of the Lord is not just.' Hear, O house of Israel: Is my way unjust? Is it not your ways that are unjust? 26If a righteous man turns from his righteousness and commits sin, he will die for it; because of the sin he has committed he will die. 27But if a wicked man turns away from the wickedness he has committed and does what is just and right, he will save his life. 28Because he considers all the offences he has committed and turns away from them, he will surely live; he will not die. 29Yet the house of Israel says, 'The way of the Lord is not just.' Are my ways unjust, O house of Israel? Is it not your ways that are unjust?

30"Therefore, O house of Israel, I will judge you, each one according to his ways, declares the Sovereign LORD. Repent! Turn away from all your offences; then sin will not be your downfall. 31Rid yourselves of all the offences you have committed,

and get a new heart and a new spirit. Why will you die, O house of Israel? 32For I take no pleasure in the death of anyone, declares the Sovereign LORD. Repent and live!

18:25 ■ GOD IS UNFAIR?

"The way of the Lord is not just" was probably less of a complaint than a fatalistic sigh, much like our saying, "Life isn't fair." People had lost any sense that they were suffering because of their sins. They were saying that it made no difference how they acted. Determined to break down this attitude, God guaranteed forgiveness for those who turn away from their sins.

■ A Lament for Israel's Princes

19 "Take up a lament concerning the princes of Israel 2and say:

" 'What a lioness was your mother
    among the lions!
She lay down among the young lions
  and reared her cubs.
3She brought up one of her cubs,
  and he became a strong lion.
He learned to tear the prey
  and he devoured men.
4The nations heard about him,
  and he was trapped in their pit.
They led him with hooks
  to the land of Egypt.

5" 'When she saw her hope unfulfilled,
    her expectation gone,
she took another of her cubs
  and made him a strong lion.
6He prowled among the lions,
  for he was now a strong lion.
He learned to tear the prey
  and he devoured men.
7He broke down^a their strongholds
  and devastated their towns.
The land and all who were in it
  were terrified by his roaring.
8Then the nations came against him,
  those from regions round about.
They spread their net for him,
  and he was trapped in their pit.
9With hooks they pulled him into a cage
  and brought him to the king of Babylon.
They put him in prison,
  so his roar was heard no longer
  on the mountains of Israel.

10" 'Your mother was like a vine in your
    vineyard^b
  planted by the water;
it was fruitful and full of branches
  because of abundant water.
11Its branches were strong,
  fit for a ruler's sceptre.
It towered high
  above the thick foliage,
conspicuous for its height

---

^c 17 Septuagint (see also verse 8); Hebrew *from the poor*   ^a 7 Targum (see Septuagint); Hebrew *He knew*   ^b 10 Two Hebrew manuscripts; most Hebrew manuscripts *your blood*

and for its many branches.
¹²But it was uprooted in fury
    and thrown to the ground.
The east wind made it shrivel,
    it was stripped of its fruit;
its strong branches withered
    and fire consumed them.
¹³Now it is planted in the desert,
    in a dry and thirsty land.
¹⁴Fire spread from one of its main*c* branches
    and consumed its fruit.
No strong branch is left on it
    fit for a ruler's sceptre.'

This is a lament and is to be used as a lament."

■ Rebellious Israel

20 In the seventh year, in the fifth month on the tenth day, some of the elders of Israel came to enquire of the LORD, and they sat down in front of me.

²Then the word of the LORD came to me: ³"Son of man, speak to the elders of Israel and say to them, 'This is what the Sovereign LORD says: Have you come to enquire of me? As surely as I live, I will not let you enquire of me, declares the Sovereign LORD.'

20:3 ■ DON'T ASK GOD

Does God always want people to pray? According to this passage, time sometimes runs out on prayer. When elders came to Ezekiel to ask God for direction, God said: Don't bother. What is the use, when he has told them over and over what the problem is? He has nothing more to say.

⁴"Will you judge them? Will you judge them, son of man? Then confront them with the detestable practices of their fathers ⁵and say to them: 'This is what the Sovereign LORD says: On the day I chose Israel, I swore with uplifted hand to the descendants of the house of Jacob and revealed myself to them in Egypt. With uplifted hand I said to them, "I am the LORD your God." ⁶On that day I swore to them that I would bring them out of Egypt into a land I had searched out for them, a land flowing with milk and honey, the most beautiful of all lands. ⁷And I said to them, "Each of you, get rid of the vile images you have set your eyes on, and do not defile yourselves with the idols of Egypt. I am the LORD your God."

⁸" 'But they rebelled against me and would not listen to me; they did not get rid of the vile images they had set their eyes on, nor did they forsake the idols of Egypt. So I said I would pour out my wrath on them and spend my anger against them in Egypt. ⁹But for the sake of my name I did what would keep it from being profaned in the eyes of the nations they lived among and in whose sight I had revealed myself to the Israelites by bringing them out of Egypt. ¹⁰Therefore I led them out of Egypt and brought them into the desert. ¹¹I gave them my decrees and made known to them my laws, for the man who obeys them will live by them. ¹²Also I gave them my Sabbaths as a sign between us, so they would know that I the LORD made them holy.

¹³" 'Yet the people of Israel rebelled against me in the desert. They did not follow my decrees but rejected my laws — although the man who obeys them will live by them — and they utterly desecrated my Sabbaths. So I said I would pour out my wrath on them and destroy them in the desert. ¹⁴But for the sake of my name I did what would keep it from being profaned in the eyes of the nations in whose sight I had brought them out. ¹⁵Also with uplifted hand I swore to them in the desert that I would not bring them into the land I had given them — a land flowing with milk and honey, most beautiful of all lands — ¹⁶because they rejected my laws and did not follow my decrees and desecrated my Sabbaths. For their hearts were devoted to their idols. ¹⁷Yet I looked on them with pity and did not destroy them or put an end to them in the desert. ¹⁸I said to their children in the desert, "Do not follow the statutes of your fathers or keep their laws or defile yourselves with their idols. ¹⁹I am the LORD your God; follow my decrees and be careful to keep my laws. ²⁰Keep my Sabbaths holy, that they may be a sign between us. Then you will know that I am the LORD your God."

²¹" 'But the children rebelled against me: They did not follow my decrees, they were not careful to keep my laws — although the man who obeys them will live by them — and they desecrated my Sabbaths. So I said I would pour out my wrath on them and spend my anger against them in the desert. ²²But I withheld my hand, and for the sake of my name I did what would keep it from being profaned in the eyes of the nations in whose sight I had brought them out. ²³Also with uplifted hand I swore to them in the desert that I would disperse them among the nations and scatter them through the countries, ²⁴because they had not obeyed my laws but had rejected my decrees and desecrated my Sabbaths, and their eyes ⌞lusted⌟ after their fathers' idols. ²⁵I also gave them over to statutes that were not good and laws they could not live by; ²⁶I let them become defiled through their gifts — the sacrifice of every firstborn*a* — that I might fill them with horror so that they would know that I am the LORD.'

²⁷"Therefore, son of man, speak to the people of Israel and say to them, 'This is what the Sovereign LORD says: In this also your fathers blasphemed me by forsaking me: ²⁸When I brought them into the land I had sworn to give them and they saw any high hill or any leafy tree, there they offered their sacrifices, made offerings that provoked me to anger, presented their fragrant incense and poured out their drink offerings. ²⁹Then I said to them: What is this high place you go to?' " (It is called Bamah*b* to this day.)

■ Judgment and Restoration

³⁰"Therefore say to the house of Israel: 'This is what the Sovereign LORD says: Will you defile yourselves the way your fathers did and lust after their vile images? ³¹When you offer your gifts — the sacrifice of your sons in*c* the fire — you continue to defile yourselves with all your idols to this day. Am I to let you enquire of me, O house of Israel? As

---

*c*14 Or from under its   *a*26 Or — making every firstborn pass through ⌞the fire⌟   *b*29 Bamah means high place.   *c*31 Or — making your sons pass
through

surely as I live, declares the Sovereign LORD, I will not let you enquire of me.

32" 'You say, "We want to be like the nations, like the peoples of the world, who serve wood and stone." But what you have in mind will never happen. 33As surely as I live, declares the Sovereign LORD, I will rule over you with a mighty hand and an outstretched arm and with outpoured wrath. 34I will bring you from the nations and gather you from the countries where you have been scattered—with a mighty hand and an outstretched arm and with outpoured wrath. 35I will bring you into the desert of the nations and there, face to face, I will execute judgment upon you. 36As I judged your fathers in the desert of the land of Egypt, so I will judge you, declares the Sovereign LORD. 37I will take note of you as you pass under my rod, and I will bring you into the bond of the covenant. 38I will purge you of those who revolt and rebel against me. Although I will bring them out of the land where they are living, yet they will not enter the land of Israel. Then you will know that I am the LORD.

20:32 ■ LIKE EVERYBODY ELSE

"Everybody does it!" children sometimes whine to their parents. Good parents aren't swayed, however. They want their children to live up to their own potential, not mimic everybody else.

Like those children, Israelites grew tired of their calling. They wanted to relax and live like other nations. But God swears he will never let it happen. He will remain strict, even putting them through another desert experience to purify them, but he absolutely refuses to let them conform.

39" 'As for you, O house of Israel, this is what the Sovereign LORD says: Go and serve your idols, every one of you! But afterwards you will surely listen to me and no longer profane my holy name with your gifts and idols. 40For on my holy mountain, the high mountain of Israel, declares the Sovereign LORD, there in the land the entire house of Israel will serve me, and there I will accept them. There I will require your offerings and your choice gifts,*d* along with all your holy sacrifices. 41I will accept you as fragrant incense when I bring you out from the nations and gather you from the countries where you have been scattered, and I will show myself holy among you in the sight of the nations. 42Then you will know that I am the LORD, when I bring you into the land of Israel, the land I had sworn with uplifted hand to give to your fathers. 43There you will remember your conduct and all the actions by which you have defiled yourselves, and you will loathe yourselves for all the evil you have done. 44You will know that I am the LORD, when I deal with you for my name's sake and not according to your evil ways and your corrupt practices, O house of Israel, declares the Sovereign LORD.' "

■ Prophecy Against the South

45The word of the LORD came to me: 46"Son of man, set your face towards the south; preach against the south and prophesy against the forest of the southland. 47Say to the southern forest: 'Hear the word of the LORD. This is what the Sovereign LORD says: I am about to set fire to you, and it will consume all your trees, both green and dry. The blazing flame will not be quenched, and every face from south to north will be scorched by it. 48Everyone will see that I the LORD have kindled it; it will not be quenched.' "

49Then I said, "Ah, Sovereign LORD! They are saying of me, 'Isn't he just telling parables?' "

■ Babylon, God's Sword of Judgment

21 The word of the LORD came to me: 2"Son of man, set your face against Jerusalem and preach against the sanctuary. Prophesy against the land of Israel 3and say to her: 'This is what the LORD says: I am against you. I will draw my sword from its scabbard and cut off from you both the righteous and the wicked. 4Because I am going to cut off the righteous and the wicked, my sword will be unsheathed against everyone from south to north. 5Then all people will know that I the LORD have drawn my sword from its scabbard; it will not return again.'

6"Therefore groan, son of man! Groan before them with broken heart and bitter grief. 7And when they ask you, 'Why are you groaning?' you shall say, 'Because of the news that is coming. Every heart will melt and every hand go limp; every spirit will become faint and every knee become as weak as water.' It is coming! It will surely take place, declares the Sovereign LORD."

8The word of the LORD came to me: 9"Son of man, prophesy and say, 'This is what the Lord says:

" 'A sword, a sword,
    sharpened and polished—
10sharpened for the slaughter,
    polished to flash like lightning!

" 'Shall we rejoice in the sceptre of my son ⌊Judah⌋? The sword despises every such stick.

11" 'The sword is appointed to be polished,
    to be grasped with the hand;
it is sharpened and polished,
    made ready for the hand of the slayer.
12Cry out and wail, son of man,
    for it is against my people;
    it is against all the princes of Israel.
They are thrown to the sword
    along with my people.
Therefore beat your breast.

13" 'Testing will surely come. And what if the sceptre ⌊of Judah⌋, which the sword despises, does not continue? declares the Sovereign LORD.'

14"So then, son of man, prophesy
    and strike your hands together.
Let the sword strike twice,
    even three times.
It is a sword for slaughter—
    a sword for great slaughter,
    closing in on them from every side.
15So that hearts may melt

d40 Or and the gifts of your firstfruits

and the fallen be many,
I have stationed the sword for slaughter[a]
    at all their gates.
Oh! It is made to flash like lightning,
    it is grasped for slaughter.
16O sword, slash to the right,
    then to the left,
    wherever your blade is turned.
17I too will strike my hands together,
    and my wrath will subside.
I the LORD have spoken.' "

18The word of the LORD came to me: 19"Son of man, mark out two roads for the sword of the king of Babylon to take, both starting from the same country. Make a signpost where the road branches off to the city. 20Mark out one road for the sword to come against Rabbah of the Ammonites and another against Judah and fortified Jerusalem. 21For the king of Babylon will stop at the fork in the road, at the junction of the two roads, to seek an omen: He will cast lots with arrows, he will consult his idols, he will examine the liver. 22Into his right hand will come the lot for Jerusalem, where he is to set up battering-rams, to give the command to slaughter, to sound the battle cry, to set battering-rams against the gates, to build a ramp and to erect siege works. 23It will seem like a false omen to those who have sworn allegiance to him, but he will remind them of their guilt and take them captive.

21:21 ■ LIVER-GAZING
This verse shows how an ancient Babylonian king might seek direction from his gods. Casting lots with arrows apparently meant marking arrows with various alternatives, putting them in a quiver, and drawing one out. Consulting idols would mean praying to them, perhaps hoping for a dream or an omen. The livers of animals, like tea leaves today, were often studied in ancient times; their shape or colour was supposed to tell the future.

24"Therefore this is what the Sovereign LORD says: 'Because you people have brought to mind your guilt by your open rebellion, revealing your sins in all that you do — because you have done this, you will be taken captive.

25" 'O profane and wicked prince of Israel, whose day has come, whose time of punishment has reached its climax, 26this is what the Sovereign LORD says: Take off the turban, remove the crown. It will not be as it was: The lowly will be exalted and the exalted will be brought low. 27A ruin! A ruin! I will make it a ruin! It will not be restored until he comes to whom it rightfully belongs; to him I will give it.'

28"And you, son of man, prophesy and say, 'This is what the Sovereign LORD says about the Ammonites and their insults:

" 'A sword, a sword,
    drawn for the slaughter,
    polished to consume
    and to flash like lightning!
29Despite false visions concerning you

and lying divinations about you,
    it will be laid on the necks
    of the wicked who are to be slain,
whose day has come,
    whose time of punishment has reached its
        climax.
30Return the sword to its scabbard.
    In the place where you were created,
    in the land of your ancestry,
    I will judge you.
31I will pour out my wrath upon you
    and breathe out my fiery anger against you;
I will hand you over to brutal men,
    men skilled in destruction.
32You will be fuel for the fire,
    your blood will be shed in your land,
you will be remembered no more;
    for I the LORD have spoken.' "

■ Jerusalem's Sins

22 The word of the LORD came to me: 2"Son of man, will you judge her? Will you judge this city of bloodshed? Then confront her with all her detestable practices 3and say: 'This is what the Sovereign LORD says: O city that brings on herself doom by shedding blood in her midst and defiles herself by making idols, 4you have become guilty because of the blood you have shed and have become defiled by the idols you have made. You have brought your days to a close, and the end of your years has come. Therefore I will make you an object of scorn to the nations and a laughing-stock to all the countries. 5Those who are near and those who are far away will mock you, O infamous city, full of turmoil.

6" 'See how each of the princes of Israel who are in you uses his power to shed blood. 7In you they have treated father and mother with contempt; in you they have oppressed the alien and ill-treated the fatherless and the widow. 8You have despised my holy things and desecrated my Sabbaths. 9In you are slanderous men bent on shedding blood; in you are those who eat at the mountain shrines and commit lewd acts. 10In you are those who dishonour their fathers' bed; in you are those who violate women during their period, when they are ceremonially unclean. 11In you one man commits a detestable offence with his neighbour's wife, another shamefully defiles his daughter-in-law, and another violates his sister, his own father's daughter. 12In you men accept bribes to shed blood; you take usury and excessive interest[a] and make unjust gain from your neighbours by extortion. And you have forgotten me, declares the Sovereign LORD.

13" 'I will surely strike my hands together at the unjust gain you have made and at the blood you have shed in your midst. 14Will your courage endure or your hands be strong in the day I deal with you? I the LORD have spoken, and I will do it. 15I will disperse you among the nations and scatter you through the countries; and I will put an end to your uncleanness. 16When you have been defiled[b] in the eyes of the nations, you will know that I am the LORD.' "

17Then the word of the LORD came to me: 18"Son of man, the house of Israel has become dross to me;

all of them are the copper, tin, iron and lead left inside a furnace. They are but the dross of silver. [19]Therefore this is what the Sovereign LORD says: 'Because you have all become dross, I will gather you into Jerusalem. [20]As men gather silver, copper, iron, lead and tin into a furnace to melt it with a fiery blast, so will I gather you in my anger and my wrath and put you inside the city and melt you. [21]I will gather you and I will blow on you with my fiery wrath, and you will be melted inside her. [22]As silver is melted in a furnace, so you will be melted inside her, and you will know that I the LORD have poured out my wrath upon you.'"

[23]Again the word of the LORD came to me: [24]"Son of man, say to the land, 'You are a land that has had no rain or showers[c] in the day of wrath.' [25]There is a conspiracy of her princes[d] within her like a roaring lion tearing its prey; they devour people, take treasures and precious things and make many widows within her. [26]Her priests do violence to my law and profane my holy things; they do not distinguish between the holy and the common; they teach that there is no difference between the unclean and the clean; and they shut their eyes to the keeping of my Sabbaths, so that I am profaned among them. [27]Her officials within her are like wolves tearing their prey; they shed blood and kill people to make unjust gain. [28]Her prophets whitewash these deeds for them by false visions and lying divinations. They say, 'This is what the Sovereign LORD says'—when the LORD has not spoken. [29]The people of the land practise extortion and commit robbery; they oppress the poor and needy and ill-treat the alien, denying them justice.

[30]"I looked for a man among them who would build up the wall and stand before me in the gap on behalf of the land so that I would not have to destroy it, but I found none. [31]So I will pour out my wrath on them and consume them with my fiery anger, bringing down on their own heads all they have done, declares the Sovereign LORD."

■ Two Adulterous Sisters

23 The word of the LORD came to me: [2]"Son of man, there were two women, daughters of the same mother. [3]They became prostitutes in Egypt, engaging in prostitution from their youth. In that land their breasts were fondled and their virgin bosoms caressed. [4]The older was named Oholah, and her sister was Oholibah. They were mine and gave birth to sons and daughters. Oholah is Samaria, and Oholibah is Jerusalem.

[5]"Oholah engaged in prostitution while she was still mine; and she lusted after her lovers, the Assyrians—warriors [6]clothed in blue, governors and commanders, all of them handsome young men, and mounted horsemen. [7]She gave herself as a prostitute to all the elite of the Assyrians and defiled herself with all the idols of everyone she lusted after. [8]She did not give up the prostitution she began in Egypt, when during her youth men slept with her, caressed her virgin bosom and poured out their lust upon her.

[9]"Therefore I handed her over to her lovers, the Assyrians, for whom she lusted. [10]They stripped her naked, took away her sons and daughters and killed her with the sword. She became a byword among women, and punishment was inflicted on her.

[11]"Her sister Oholibah saw this, yet in her lust and prostitution she was more depraved than her sister. [12]She too lusted after the Assyrians—governors and commanders, warriors in full dress, mounted horsemen, all handsome young men. [13]I saw that she too defiled herself; both of them went the same way.

[14]"But she carried her prostitution still further. She saw men portrayed on a wall, figures of Chaldeans[a] portrayed in red, [15]with belts round their waists and flowing turbans on their heads; all of them looked like Babylonian chariot officers, natives of Chaldea.[b] [16]As soon as she saw them, she lusted after them and sent messengers to them in Chaldea. [17]Then the Babylonians came to her, to the bed of love, and in their lust they defiled her. After she had been defiled by them, she turned away from them in disgust. [18]When she carried on her prostitution openly and exposed her nakedness, I turned away from her in disgust, just as I had turned away from her sister. [19]Yet she became more and more promiscuous as she recalled the days of her youth, when she was a prostitute in Egypt. [20]There she lusted after her lovers, whose genitals were like those of donkeys and whose emission was like that of horses. [21]So you longed for the lewdness of your youth, when in Egypt your bosom was caressed and your young breasts fondled.[c]

[22]"Therefore, Oholibah, this is what the Sovereign LORD says: I will stir up your lovers against you, those you turned away from in disgust, and I will bring them against you from every side—[23]the Babylonians and all the Chaldeans, the men of Pekod and Shoa and Koa, and all the Assyrians with them, handsome young men, all of them governors and commanders, chariot officers and men of high rank, all mounted on horses. [24]They will come against you with weapons,[d] chariots and wagons and with a throng of people; they will take up positions against you on every side with large and small shields and with helmets. I will turn you over to them for punishment, and they will punish you according to their standards. [25]I will direct my jealous anger against you, and they will deal with you in fury. They will cut off your noses and your ears, and those of you who are left will fall by the sword. They will take away your sons and daughters, and those of you who are left will be consumed by fire. [26]They will also strip you of your clothes and take your fine jewellery. [27]So I will put a stop to the lewdness and prostitution you began in Egypt. You will not look on these things with longing or remember Egypt any more.

[28]"For this is what the Sovereign LORD says: I am about to hand you over to those you hate, to those you turned away from in disgust. [29]They will deal with you in hatred and take away everything you have worked for. They will leave you naked and bare, and the shame of your prostitution will be exposed. Your lewdness and promiscuity [30]have brought this upon you, because you lusted after the nations and defiled yourself with their idols. [31]You

c 24 Septuagint; Hebrew *has not been cleansed or rained on*　　d 25 Septuagint; Hebrew *prophets*　　a 14 Or *Babylonians*　　b 15 Or *Babylonia*; also in verse 16　　c 21 Syriac (see also verse 3); Hebrew *caressed because of your young breasts*　　d 24 The meaning of the Hebrew for this word is uncertain.

have gone the way of your sister; so I will put her cup into your hand.

³²"This is what the Sovereign LORD says:

"You will drink your sister's cup,
    a cup large and deep;
it will bring scorn and derision,
    for it holds so much.
³³You will be filled with drunkenness and
        sorrow,
    the cup of ruin and desolation,
    the cup of your sister Samaria.
³⁴You will drink it and drain it dry;
    you will dash it to pieces
    and tear your breasts.

I have spoken, declares the Sovereign LORD.

³⁵"Therefore this is what the Sovereign LORD says: Since you have forgotten me and thrust me behind your back, you must bear the consequences of your lewdness and prostitution."

³⁶The LORD said to me: "Son of man, will you judge Oholah and Oholibah? Then confront them with their detestable practices, ³⁷for they have committed adultery and blood is on their hands. They committed adultery with their idols; they even sacrificed their children, whom they bore to me,ᵉ as food for them. ³⁸They have also done this to me: At that same time they defiled my sanctuary and desecrated my Sabbaths. ³⁹On the very day they sacrificed their children to their idols, they entered my sanctuary and desecrated it. That is what they did in my house.

⁴⁰"They even sent messengers for men who came from far away, and when they arrived you bathed yourself for them, painted your eyes and put on your jewellery. ⁴¹You sat on an elegant couch, with a table spread before it on which you had placed the incense and oil that belonged to me.

⁴²"The noise of a carefree crowd was around her; Sabeansᶠ were brought from the desert along with men from the rabble, and they put bracelets on the arms of the woman and her sister and beautiful crowns on their heads. ⁴³Then I said about the one worn out by adultery, 'Now let them use her as a prostitute, for that is all she is.' ⁴⁴And they slept with her. As men sleep with a prostitute, so they slept with those lewd women, Oholah and Oholibah. ⁴⁵But righteous men will sentence them to the punishment of women who commit adultery and shed blood, because they are adulterous and blood is on their hands.

⁴⁶"This is what the Sovereign LORD says: Bring a

■ THE RUNAWAYS
A STORY MEANT TO MAKE YOU SICK

INSIGHT

"NOW LET THEM USE HER AS A PROSTITUTE, FOR THAT IS ALL SHE IS."
■ 23:43

This story, which uses sexually explicit language, turns you off, not on. It tells of two sisters who choose promiscuous sex. Once they are involved, nothing satisfies them. They go from one man to the next. God calls them prostitutes, but they don't do it for the money. They do it because they like to live perversely.

　　Finally, in grief and frustration, God turns them over to their chosen lovers, who treat them like dirt. God seems to take angry satisfaction in this. Love makes him angry – angry enough to weep.

■ AN ALLEGORY OF LOVE
Ezekiel doesn't pretend that these two sisters are real people. From the beginning he identifies them with the capitals of the two halves of Israel – Samaria in the North, which the Assyrians had wiped out over 100 years before, and Jerusalem in the South. Samaria was properly rewarded for her prostitution, Ezekiel says, and Jerusalem will be too. The story of the two sisters is, in a sense, one more graphic way of saying that God has been patient with Jerusalem long enough. (A similar story is told in Ezekiel 16.)

■ A DRASTIC DOSE OF REALITY
God had promised the Israelites everything their hearts desired if they would stick by him. But they were always getting friendly with other nations whose prosperity and power they envied. In those days, a little nation like Israel couldn't just sign a friendship pact with a big power. Political alliances meant accepting the big power's religion and worshipping its gods alongside your own. God warned Israel against this repeatedly, but they ignored the warning. Therefore, Ezekiel says, they will get their wish. They will experience first-hand the care and concern of their Babylonian "lovers".

　　God responds like a father who has finally given up trying to regulate his daughter's bad habits. He tells her, "Get out! Find out for yourself what life is like on the street!" God says, "You will drink your sister's cup, a cup large and deep; it will bring scorn and derision, for it holds so much. . . . You will drink it and drain it dry; you will dash it to pieces and tear your breasts" (23:32–34). He says it in anger, but also in hope that such bitter grief will awaken Israel to the disastrous choices she made in rejecting God's care.

□ LIFE QUESTIONS:
Have you ever loved someone who didn't love you back? What emotions did you feel?

ᵉ 37 Or even made the children they bore to me pass through ⌐the fire⌐   ᶠ 42 Or drunkards mob against them and give them over to terror and plunder. [47]The mob will stone them and cut them down with their swords; they will kill their sons and daughters and burn down their houses.

[48]"So I will put an end to lewdness in the land, that all women may take warning and not imitate you. [49]You will suffer the penalty for your lewdness and bear the consequences of your sins of idolatry. Then you will know that I am the Sovereign LORD."

■ The Cooking Pot

24 In the ninth year, in the tenth month on the tenth day, the word of the LORD came to me: [2]"Son of man, record this date, this very date, because the king of Babylon has laid siege to Jerusalem this very day. [3]Tell this rebellious house a parable and say to them: 'This is what the Sovereign LORD says:

" 'Put on the cooking pot; put it on
and pour water into it.
[4]Put into it the pieces of meat,
all the choice pieces—the leg and the
shoulder.
Fill it with the best of these bones;
[5] take the pick of the flock.
Pile wood beneath it for the bones;
bring it to the boil
and cook the bones in it.

24:2 ■ PROPHET'S PROOF

With Ezekiel living in Babylon, news from Israel took months to reach him. By recording the date when God told him the final siege of Jerusalem had begun, Ezekiel would have evidence that he was genuinely a prophet of God.

[6]" 'For this is what the Sovereign LORD says:

" 'Woe to the city of bloodshed,
to the pot now encrusted,
whose deposit will not go away!
Empty it piece by piece
without casting lots for them.

[7]" 'For the blood she shed is in her midst:
She poured it on the bare rock;
she did not pour it on the ground,
where the dust would cover it.
[8]To stir up wrath and take revenge
I put her blood on the bare rock,
so that it would not be covered.

[9]" 'Therefore this is what the Sovereign LORD says:

" 'Woe to the city of bloodshed!
I, too, will pile the wood high.
[10]So heap on the wood
and kindle the fire.
Cook the meat well,
mixing in the spices;
and let the bones be charred.
[11]Then set the empty pot on the coals
till it becomes hot and its copper glows
so its impurities may be melted
and its deposit burned away.

[12]It has frustrated all efforts;
its heavy deposit has not been removed,
not even by fire.

[13]" 'Now your impurity is lewdness. Because I tried to cleanse you but you would not be cleansed from your impurity, you will not be clean again until my wrath against you has subsided.

[14]" 'I the LORD have spoken. The time has come for me to act. I will not hold back; I will not have pity, nor will I relent. You will be judged according to your conduct and your actions, declares the Sovereign LORD.' "

■ Ezekiel's Wife Dies

[15]The word of the LORD came to me: [16]"Son of man, with one blow I am about to take away from you the delight of your eyes. Yet do not lament or weep or shed any tears. [17]Groan quietly; do not mourn for the dead. Keep your turban fastened and your sandals on your feet; do not cover the lower part of your face or eat the customary food ⌊of mourners⌋."

[18]So I spoke to the people in the morning, and in the evening my wife died. The next morning I did as I had been commanded.

[19]Then the people asked me, "Won't you tell us what these things have to do with us?"

[20]So I said to them, "The word of the LORD came to me: [21]Say to the house of Israel, 'This is what the Sovereign LORD says: I am about to desecrate my sanctuary—the stronghold in which you take pride, the delight of your eyes, the object of your affection. The sons and daughters you left behind will fall by the sword. [22]And you will do as I have done. You will not cover the lower part of your face or eat the customary food ⌊of mourners⌋. [23]You will keep your turbans on your heads and your sandals on your feet. You will not mourn or weep but will waste away because of[a] your sins and groan among yourselves. [24]Ezekiel will be a sign to you; you will do just as he has done. When this happens, you will know that I am the Sovereign LORD.'

[25]"And you, son of man, on the day I take away their stronghold, their joy and glory, the delight of their eyes, their heart's desire, and their sons and daughters as well—[26]on that day a fugitive will come to tell you the news. [27]At that time your mouth will be opened; you will speak with him and will no longer be silent. So you will be a sign to them, and they will know that I am the LORD."

■ A Prophecy Against Ammon

25 The word of the LORD came to me: [2]"Son of man, set your face against the Ammonites and prophesy against them. [3]Say to them, 'Hear the word of the Sovereign LORD. This is what the Sovereign LORD says: Because you said "Aha!" over my sanctuary when it was desecrated and over the land of Israel when it was laid waste and over the people of Judah when they went into exile, [4]therefore I am going to give you to the people of the East as a possession. They will set up their camps and pitch their

[a]23 Or away in

tents among you; they will eat your fruit and drink your milk. ⁵I will turn Rabbah into a pasture for camels and Ammon into a resting place for sheep. Then you will know that I am the LORD. ⁶For this is what the Sovereign LORD says: Because you have clapped your hands and stamped your feet, rejoicing with all the malice of your heart against the land of Israel, ⁷therefore I will stretch out my hand against you and give you as plunder to the nations. I will cut you off from the nations and exterminate you from the countries. I will destroy you, and you will know that I am the LORD.' "

■ A Prophecy Against Moab

⁸"This is what the Sovereign LORD says: 'Because Moab and Seir said, "Look, the house of Judah has become like all the other nations," ⁹therefore I will expose the flank of Moab, beginning at its frontier towns—Beth Jeshimoth, Baal Meon and Kiriathaim—the glory of that land. ¹⁰I will give Moab along with the Ammonites to the people of the East as a possession, so that the Ammonites will not be remembered among the nations; ¹¹and I will inflict punishment on Moab. Then they will know that I am the LORD.' "

JUST WHAT THEY DESERVED
GOD WILL JUDGE EVERY NATION IN THE WORLD

INSIGHT

"I WILL CARRY OUT GREAT VENGEANCE ON THEM AND PUNISH THEM IN MY WRATH. THEN THEY WILL KNOW THAT I AM THE LORD." ■ 25:17

World War II ended in Europe with the surrender of the German army. People danced in the streets.

But the victorious allies could not simply pack and go home. They had captured thousands of Nazis. Among them were some of the most brutal murderers the world has ever known — monsters, really, who had enriched themselves with the gold and jewellery of the millions of Jews they had exterminated.

A question came up: under what law could the Nazis be tried? American, British or French law didn't apply in Germany. Faced with this dilemma, the Allies invented something new: the Nuremberg trials for war crimes. Judgments were based on a belief in a higher law — an international code of right and wrong that applies to every person, regardless of country. Under this unwritten law many Nazi leaders were condemned to death.

■ NATIONS ON TRIAL
Ezekiel introduces a similar concept of justice, beginning in chapter 25. In the first 24 chapters he had spoken harsh words to the Israelites, who had repeatedly broken the law God had given them. But now Ezekiel's vision expands to nations who never had that law. Ezekiel marches through Ammon, Moab, Edom, Philistia — four nations that, on the small scale of Palestinian geography, could be seen with the naked eye from Jerusalem.

Each nation has its moment in court, and each is condemned for its inhumane malice against Israel. (The sentences Ezekiel gave were soon carried out historically. The nations listed vanished from the face of the earth, victims of the same violence they had used against Israel.)

Ezekiel goes on to Tyre, 100 miles up the coast. Tyre's soul was profit; its merchants controlled trade for the whole Mediterranean. Because of their wealth and success, they considered themselves virtual gods (28:2,6). They had callously rejoiced in Jerusalem's downfall, seeing it as a chance for increased trade (26:2). For such unfeeling arrogance, God would sentence them. Nebuchadnezzar began this punishment in Ezekiel's era, and centuries later Alexander the Great finished it off by razing the city to the ground. Tyre became, as Ezekiel had predicted, "a bare rock, and . . . a place to spread fishing nets" (26:14).

■ A COMIC CONDEMNATION
Pausing briefly to give a judgment against Sidon, Ezekiel travels on to Egypt. His words might have seemed comic. Who does he think he is, passing judgment on one of the great powers of his day? Ezekiel, a captive from a two-bit country about to be overrun, sounds rather like a refugee from Haiti shaking his fist at the United States. Yet Ezekiel confidently asserts that Egypt can start mourning now. As it happened, Egypt, a great power for many centuries, lost its dominance and has never regained it (29:15).

Perhaps, in taking up these nations' fates, Ezekiel intended to build suspense for the climactic tragedy of Jerusalem's fall. But certainly this trial of the nations demonstrated that Jerusalem had not been singled out for justice. Every nation would be judged by the standard of right and wrong that they knew. If God was harder on Judah, it was only because Judah knew so much more about God and his expectations.

□ LIFE QUESTIONS:
Do you believe in universal standards of right and wrong? What "code of conduct" applies to everybody, regardless of their upbringing?

■ A Prophecy Against Edom

12"This is what the Sovereign LORD says: 'Because Edom took revenge on the house of Judah and became very guilty by doing so, 13therefore this is what the Sovereign LORD says: I will stretch out my hand against Edom and kill its men and their animals. I will lay it waste, and from Teman to Dedan they will fall by the sword. 14I will take vengeance on Edom by the hand of my people Israel, and they will deal with Edom in accordance with my anger and my wrath; they will know my vengeance, declares the Sovereign LORD.' "

■ A Prophecy Against Philistia

15"This is what the Sovereign LORD says: 'Because the Philistines acted in vengeance and took revenge with malice in their hearts, and with ancient hostility sought to destroy Judah, 16therefore this is what the Sovereign LORD says: I am about to stretch out my hand against the Philistines, and I will cut off the Kerethites and destroy those remaining along the coast. 17I will carry out great vengeance on them and punish them in my wrath. Then they will know that I am the LORD, when I take vengeance on them.' "

■ A Prophecy Against Tyre

26 In the eleventh year, on the first day of the month, the word of the LORD came to me: 2"Son of man, because Tyre has said of Jerusalem, 'Aha! The gate to the nations is broken, and its doors have swung open to me; now that she lies in ruins I will prosper,' 3therefore this is what the Sovereign LORD says: I am against you, O Tyre, and I will bring many nations against you, like the sea casting up its waves. 4They will destroy the walls of Tyre and pull down her towers; I will scrape away her rubble and make her a bare rock. 5Out in the sea she will become a place to spread fishing nets, for I have spoken, declares the Sovereign LORD. She will become plunder for the nations, 6and her settlements on the mainland will be ravaged by the sword. Then they will know that I am the LORD.

7"For this is what the Sovereign LORD says: From the north I am going to bring against Tyre Nebuchadnezzar*a* king of Babylon, king of kings, with horses and chariots, with horsemen and a great army. 8He will ravage your settlements on the mainland with the sword; he will set up siege works against you, build a ramp up to your walls and raise his shields against you. 9He will direct the blows of his battering-rams against your walls and demolish your towers with his weapons. 10His horses will be so many that they will cover you with dust. Your walls will tremble at the noise of the war horses, wagons and chariots when he enters your gates as men enter a city whose walls have been broken through. 11The hoofs of his horses will trample all your streets; he will kill your people with the sword, and your strong pillars will fall to the ground. 12They will plunder your wealth and loot your merchandise; they will break down your walls and demolish your fine houses and throw your stones, timber and rubble into the sea. 13I will put an end to your noisy songs, and the music of your harps will be heard no more. 14I will make you a bare rock, and you will become a place to spread fishing nets. You will never be rebuilt, for I the LORD have spoken, declares the Sovereign LORD.

> 26:14 ■ ALEXANDER THE GREAT
> Tyre, a city on the Mediterranean coast, included two rocky offshore islands. Nebuchadnezzar captured the mainland city in 572 B.C., just 12 years after the fall of Jerusalem. But the islands were not taken until Alexander the Great destroyed them two centuries later. True to this prophecy, the city has never been rebuilt.

15"This is what the Sovereign LORD says to Tyre: Will not the coastlands tremble at the sound of your fall, when the wounded groan and the slaughter takes place in you? 16Then all the princes of the coast will step down from their thrones and lay aside their robes and take off their embroidered garments. Clothed with terror, they will sit on the ground, trembling every moment, appalled at you. 17Then they will take up a lament concerning you and say to you:

" 'How you are destroyed, O city of renown,
        peopled by men of the sea!
You were a power on the seas,
        you and your citizens;
you put your terror
        on all who lived there.
18Now the coastlands tremble
        on the day of your fall;
the islands in the sea
        are terrified at your collapse.'

19"This is what the Sovereign LORD says: When I make you a desolate city, like cities no longer inhabited, and when I bring the ocean depths over you and its vast waters cover you, 20then I will bring you down with those who go down to the pit, to the people of long ago. I will make you dwell in the earth below, as in ancient ruins, with those who go down to the pit, and you will not return or take your place*b* in the land of the living. 21I will bring you to a horrible end and you will be no more. You will be sought, but you will never again be found, declares the Sovereign LORD."

■ A Lament for Tyre

27 The word of the LORD came to me: 2"Son of man, take up a lament concerning Tyre. 3Say to Tyre, situated at the gateway to the sea, merchant of peoples on many coasts, 'This is what the Sovereign LORD says:

" 'You say, O Tyre,
        "I am perfect in beauty."
4Your domain was on the high seas;
        your builders brought your beauty to
            perfection.
5They made all your timbers
        of pine trees from Senir;*a*
they took a cedar from Lebanon
        to make a mast for you.

---

*a 7 Hebrew *Nebuchadrezzar*, of which *Nebuchadnezzar* is a variant; here and often in Ezekiel and Jeremiah   *b 20 Septuagint; Hebrew *return, and I will give glory*   *a 5 That is, Hermon

⁶Of oaks from Bashan
    they made your oars;
of cypress wood*b* from the coasts of Cyprus*c*
    they made your deck, inlaid with ivory.
⁷Fine embroidered linen from Egypt was your
    sail
    and served as your banner;
your awnings were of blue and purple
    from the coasts of Elishah.
⁸Men of Sidon and Arvad were your oarsmen;
    your skilled men, O Tyre, were aboard as
        your seamen.
⁹Veteran craftsmen of Gebal*d* were on board
    as shipwrights to caulk your seams.
All the ships of the sea and their sailors
    came alongside to trade for your wares.

¹⁰" 'Men of Persia, Lydia and Put
    served as soldiers in your army.
They hung their shields and helmets on your
    walls,
    bringing you splendour.
¹¹Men of Arvad and Helech
    manned your walls on every side;
men of Gammad
    were in your towers.
They hung their shields around your walls;
    they brought your beauty to perfection.

¹²" 'Tarshish did business with you because of
your great wealth of goods; they exchanged silver,
iron, tin and lead for your merchandise.
¹³" 'Greece, Tubal and Meshech traded with you;
they exchanged slaves and articles of bronze for
your wares.
¹⁴" 'Men of Beth Togarmah exchanged work
horses, war horses and mules for your merchandise.
¹⁵" 'The men of Rhodes*e* traded with you, and
many coastlands were your customers; they paid
you with ivory tusks and ebony.
¹⁶" 'Aram*f* did business with you because of
your many products; they exchanged turquoise,
purple fabric, embroidered work, fine linen, coral
and rubies for your merchandise.
¹⁷" 'Judah and Israel traded with you; they exchanged wheat from Minnith and confections,*g*
honey, oil and balm for your wares.
¹⁸" 'Damascus, because of your many products
and great wealth of goods, did business with you in
wine from Helbon and wool from Zahar.
¹⁹" 'Danites and Greeks from Uzal bought your
merchandise; they exchanged wrought iron, cassia
and calamus for your wares.
²⁰" 'Dedan traded in saddle blankets with you.
²¹" 'Arabia and all the princes of Kedar were your
customers; they did business with you in lambs,
rams and goats.
²²" 'The merchants of Sheba and Raamah traded
with you; for your merchandise they exchanged the
finest of all kinds of spices and precious stones, and
gold.
²³" 'Haran, Canneh and Eden and merchants of
Sheba, Asshur and Kilmad traded with you. ²⁴In
your market-place they traded with you beautiful
garments, blue fabric, embroidered work and

multicoloured rugs with cords twisted and tightly
knotted.

²⁵" 'The ships of Tarshish serve
    as carriers for your wares.
You are filled with heavy cargo
    in the heart of the sea.
²⁶Your oarsmen take you
    out to the high seas.
But the east wind will break you to pieces
    in the heart of the sea.
²⁷Your wealth, merchandise and wares,
    your mariners, seamen and shipwrights,
your merchants and all your soldiers,
    and everyone else on board
will sink into the heart of the sea
    on the day of your shipwreck.
²⁸The shorelands will quake
    when your seamen cry out.
²⁹All who handle the oars
    will abandon their ships;
the mariners and all the seamen
    will stand on the shore.
³⁰They will raise their voice
    and cry bitterly over you;
they will sprinkle dust on their heads
    and roll in ashes.
³¹They will shave their heads because of you
    and will put on sackcloth.
They will weep over you with anguish of soul
    and with bitter mourning.
³²As they wail and mourn over you,
    they will take up a lament concerning you:
"Who was ever silenced like Tyre,
    surrounded by the sea?"
³³When your merchandise went out on the seas,
    you satisfied many nations;
with your great wealth and your wares
    you enriched the kings of the earth.
³⁴Now you are shattered by the sea
    in the depths of the waters;
your wares and all your company
    have gone down with you.
³⁵All who live in the coastlands
    are appalled at you;
their kings shudder with horror
    and their faces are distorted with fear.
³⁶The merchants among the nations hiss at you;
    you have come to a horrible end
    and will be no more.' "

■ A Prophecy Against the King of Tyre

28 The word of the LORD came to me: ²"Son of
man, say to the ruler of Tyre, 'This is what
the Sovereign LORD says:

" 'In the pride of your heart
    you say, "I am a god;
I sit on the throne of a god
    in the heart of the seas."
But you are a man and not a god,
    though you think you are as wise as a god.
³Are you wiser than Daniel?*a*
    Is no secret hidden from you?
⁴By your wisdom and understanding

---

b 6 Targum; the Masoretic Text has a different division of the consonants.   *c 6* Hebrew *Kittim*   *d 9* That is, Byblos   *e 15* Septuagint; Hebrew *Dedan*
f 16 Most Hebrew manuscripts; some Hebrew manuscripts and Syriac *Edom*   *g 17* The meaning of the Hebrew for this word is uncertain.   *a 3* Or *Danel;*
the Hebrew spelling may suggest a person other than the prophet Daniel.

you have gained wealth for yourself
and amassed gold and silver
in your treasuries.
⁵By your great skill in trading
you have increased your wealth,
and because of your wealth
your heart has grown proud.

28:3 ■ DIFFERENT DANIEL

This Daniel, also mentioned in 14:14, is probably
not the prophet Daniel, but an earlier patriarch
revered for his wisdom. The prophet Daniel,
Ezekiel's fellow exile in Babylon, would probably
not have gained such renown so soon. Also, his
name is spelled slightly differently in Hebrew.

⁶" 'Therefore this is what the Sovereign LORD says:

" 'Because you think you are wise,
as wise as a god,
⁷I am going to bring foreigners against you,
the most ruthless of nations;
they will draw their swords against your beauty
and wisdom
and pierce your shining splendour.
⁸They will bring you down to the pit,
and you will die a violent death
in the heart of the seas.
⁹Will you then say, "I am a god,"
in the presence of those who kill you?
You will be but a man, not a god,
in the hands of those who slay you.
¹⁰You will die the death of the uncircumcised
at the hands of foreigners.

I have spoken, declares the Sovereign LORD.' "

¹¹The word of the LORD came to me: ¹²"Son of
man, take up a lament concerning the king of Tyre
and say to him: 'This is what the Sovereign LORD
says:

" 'You were the model of perfection,
full of wisdom and perfect in beauty.
¹³You were in Eden,
the garden of God;
every precious stone adorned you:
ruby, topaz and emerald,
chrysolite, onyx and jasper,
sapphire,ᵇ turquoise and beryl.ᶜ
Your settings and mountingsᵈ were made of
gold;
on the day you were created they were
prepared.
¹⁴You were anointed as a guardian cherub,
for so I ordained you.
You were on the holy mount of God;
you walked among the fiery stones.
¹⁵You were blameless in your ways
from the day you were created
till wickedness was found in you.
¹⁶Through your widespread trade
you were filled with violence,
and you sinned.

So I drove you in disgrace from the mount of
God,
and I expelled you, O guardian cherub,
from among the fiery stones.
¹⁷Your heart became proud
on account of your beauty,
and you corrupted your wisdom
because of your splendour.
So I threw you to the earth;
I made a spectacle of you before kings.
¹⁸By your many sins and dishonest trade
you have desecrated your sanctuaries.
So I made a fire come out from you,
and it consumed you,
and I reduced you to ashes on the ground
in the sight of all who were watching.
¹⁹All the nations who knew you
are appalled at you;
you have come to a horrible end
and will be no more.' "

■ A Prophecy Against Sidon

²⁰The word of the LORD came to me: ²¹"Son of
man, set your face against Sidon; prophesy against
her ²²and say: 'This is what the Sovereign LORD says:

" 'I am against you, O Sidon,
and I will gain glory within you.
They will know that I am the LORD,
when I inflict punishment on her
and show myself holy within her.
²³I will send a plague upon her
and make blood flow in her streets.
The slain will fall within her,
with the sword against her on every side.
Then they will know that I am the LORD.

²⁴" 'No longer will the people of Israel have malicious neighbours who are painful briers and sharp
thorns. Then they will know that I am the Sovereign
LORD.

²⁵" 'This is what the Sovereign LORD says: When I
gather the people of Israel from the nations where
they have been scattered, I will show myself holy
among them in the sight of the nations. Then they
will live in their own land, which I gave to my servant Jacob. ²⁶They will live there in safety and will
build houses and plant vineyards; they will live in
safety when I inflict punishment on all their neighbours who maligned them. Then they will know
that I am the LORD their God.' "

■ A Prophecy Against Egypt

29 In the tenth year, in the tenth month on the
twelfth day, the word of the LORD came to
me: ²"Son of man, set your face against Pharaoh king
of Egypt and prophesy against him and against all
Egypt. ³Speak to him and say: 'This is what the Sovereign LORD says:

" 'I am against you, Pharaoh king of Egypt,
you great monster lying among your streams.
You say, "The Nile is mine;
I made it for myself."
⁴But I will put hooks in your jaws

ᵇ 13 Or lapis lazuli   ᶜ 13 The precise identification of some of these precious stones is uncertain.   ᵈ 13 The meaning of the Hebrew for this phrase is
uncertain.

and make the fish of your streams stick to
    your scales.
I will pull you out from among your streams,
    with all the fish sticking to your scales.
[5]I will leave you in the desert,
    you and all the fish of your streams.
You will fall on the open field
    and not be gathered or picked up.
I will give you as food
    to the beasts of the earth and the birds of
      the air.

[6]Then all who live in Egypt will know that I am the
LORD.

  " 'You have been a staff of reed for the house of
Israel. [7]When they grasped you with their hands,
you splintered and you tore open their shoulders;
when they leaned on you, you broke and their backs
were wrenched.[a]

29:7 ■ UNRELIABLE EGYPT
When threatened by another superpower (Babylon
or Assyria), Israel often turned to Egypt for help.
Each time that nation let Israel down. Right up
until the final destruction of Jerusalem, the
Israelites expected Egypt to come to their rescue,
but its mighty armies never appeared.

[8]" 'Therefore this is what the Sovereign LORD says:
I will bring a sword against you and kill your men
and their animals. [9]Egypt will become a desolate
wasteland. Then they will know that I am the LORD.
  " 'Because you said, "The Nile is mine; I made it,"
[10]therefore I am against you and against your
streams, and I will make the land of Egypt a ruin and
a desolate waste from Migdol to Aswan, as far as the
border of Cush.[b] [11]No foot of man or animal will
pass through it; no-one will live there for forty years.
[12]I will make the land of Egypt desolate among devastated lands, and her cities will lie desolate for forty
years among ruined cities. And I will disperse the
Egyptians among the nations and scatter them
through the countries.
  [13]" 'Yet this is what the Sovereign LORD says: At
the end of forty years I will gather the Egyptians
from the nations where they were scattered. [14]I will
bring them back from captivity and return them to
Upper Egypt,[c] the land of their ancestry. There
they will be a lowly kingdom. [15]It will be the lowliest of kingdoms and will never again exalt itself
above the other nations. I will make it so weak that
it will never again rule over the nations. [16]Egypt will
no longer be a source of confidence for the people
of Israel but will be a reminder of their sin in turning
to her for help. Then they will know that I am the
Sovereign LORD.' "

  [17]In the twenty-seventh year, in the first month
on the first day, the word of the LORD came to me:
[18]"Son of man, Nebuchadnezzar king of Babylon
drove his army in a hard campaign against Tyre;
every head was rubbed bare and every shoulder
made raw. Yet he and his army got no reward from
the campaign he led against Tyre. [19]Therefore this

is what the Sovereign LORD says: I am going to give
Egypt to Nebuchadnezzar king of Babylon, and he
will carry off its wealth. He will loot and plunder the
land as pay for his army. [20]I have given him Egypt
as a reward for his efforts because he and his army
did it for me, declares the Sovereign LORD.
  [21]"On that day I will make a horn[d] grow for the
house of Israel, and I will open your mouth among
them. Then they will know that I am the LORD."

■ A Lament for Egypt

30
The word of the LORD came to me: [2]"Son of
man, prophesy and say: 'This is what the Sovereign LORD says:

" 'Wail and say,
  "Alas for that day!"
[3]For the day is near,
  the day of the LORD is near—
a day of clouds,
  a time of doom for the nations.
[4]A sword will come against Egypt,
  and anguish will come upon Cush.[a]
When the slain fall in Egypt,
  her wealth will be carried away
  and her foundations torn down.

[5]Cush and Put, Lydia and all Arabia, Libya[b] and the
people of the covenant land will fall by the sword
along with Egypt.
  [6]" 'This is what the LORD says:

" 'The allies of Egypt will fall
  and her proud strength will fail.
From Migdol to Aswan
  they will fall by the sword within her,
             declares the Sovereign LORD.
[7]" 'They will be desolate
  among desolate lands,
and their cities will lie
  among ruined cities.
[8]Then they will know that I am the LORD,
  when I set fire to Egypt
  and all her helpers are crushed.

  [9]" 'On that day messengers will go out from me
in ships to frighten Cush out of her complacency.
Anguish will take hold of them on the day of Egypt's
doom, for it is sure to come.

  [10]" 'This is what the Sovereign LORD says:

" 'I will put an end to the hordes of Egypt
  by the hand of Nebuchadnezzar king of
    Babylon.
[11]He and his army—the most ruthless of
    nations—
will be brought in to destroy the land.
They will draw their swords against Egypt
  and fill the land with the slain.
[12]I will dry up the streams of the Nile
  and sell the land to evil men;
by the hand of foreigners
  I will lay waste the land and everything in it.

I the LORD have spoken.

---

[a]7 Syriac (see also Septuagint and Vulgate); Hebrew *and you caused their backs to stand*   [b]10 That is, the upper Nile region   [c]14 Hebrew *to Pathros*
[d]21 *Horn* here symbolises strength.   [a]4 That is, the upper Nile region; also in verses 5 and 9   [b]5 Hebrew *Cub*

13" 'This is what the Sovereign LORD says:
" 'I will destroy the idols
    and put an end to the images in Memphis.^{c}
No longer will there be a prince in Egypt,
    and I will spread fear throughout the land.

30:11 ■ MOST RUTHLESS

Babylonians had a well-deserved reputation for cruelty. When they finally took Jerusalem at the end of a two-and-a-half-year siege, they executed all of King Zedekiah's sons while he watched. Then they put out his eyes and carted him off to Babylon (see 2 Kings 25:7).

14I will lay waste Upper Egypt,^{d}
    set fire to Zoan
    and inflict punishment on Thebes.^{e}
15I will pour out my wrath on Pelusium,^{f}
    the stronghold of Egypt,
    and cut off the hordes of Thebes.
16I will set fire to Egypt;
    Pelusium will writhe in agony.
Thebes will be taken by storm;
    Memphis will be in constant distress.
17The young men of Heliopolis^g and Bubastis^h
    will fall by the sword,
    and the cities themselves will go into
        captivity.
18Dark will be the day at Tahpanhes
    when I break the yoke of Egypt;
    there her proud strength will come to an
        end.
She will be covered with clouds,
    and her villages will go into captivity.
19So I will inflict punishment on Egypt,
    and they will know that I am the LORD.' "

20In the eleventh year, in the first month on the seventh day, the word of the LORD came to me: 21"Son of man, I have broken the arm of Pharaoh king of Egypt. It has not been bound up for healing or put in a splint so as to become strong enough to hold a sword. 22Therefore this is what the Sovereign LORD says: I am against Pharaoh king of Egypt. I will break both his arms, the good arm as well as the broken one, and make the sword fall from his hand. 23I will disperse the Egyptians among the nations and scatter them through the countries. 24I will strengthen the arms of the king of Babylon and put my sword in his hand, but I will break the arms of Pharaoh, and he will groan before him like a mortally wounded man. 25I will strengthen the arms of the king of Babylon, but the arms of Pharaoh will fall limp. Then they will know that I am the LORD, when I put my sword into the hand of the king of Babylon and he brandishes it against Egypt. 26I will disperse the Egyptians among the nations and scatter them through the countries. Then they will know that I am the LORD."

■ A Cedar in Lebanon

31 In the eleventh year, in the third month on the first day, the word of the LORD came to me: 2"Son of man, say to Pharaoh king of Egypt and to his hordes:

" 'Who can be compared with you in majesty?
3Consider Assyria, once a cedar in Lebanon,
    with beautiful branches overshadowing the
        forest;
it towered on high,
    its top above the thick foliage.
4The waters nourished it,
    deep springs made it grow tall;
their streams flowed
    all around its base
and sent their channels
    to all the trees of the field.
5So it towered higher
    than all the trees of the field;
its boughs increased
    and its branches grew long,
    spreading because of abundant waters.
6All the birds of the air
    nested in its boughs,
all the beasts of the field
    gave birth under its branches;
all the great nations
    lived in its shade.
7It was majestic in beauty,
    with its spreading boughs,
for its roots went down
    to abundant waters.
8The cedars in the garden of God
    could not rival it,
nor could the pine trees
    equal its boughs,
nor could the plane trees
    compare with its branches—
no tree in the garden of God
    could match its beauty.
9I made it beautiful
    with abundant branches,
the envy of all the trees of Eden
    in the garden of God.

10" 'Therefore this is what the Sovereign LORD says: Because it towered on high, lifting its top above the thick foliage, and because it was proud of its height, 11I handed it over to the ruler of the nations, for him to deal with according to its wickedness. I cast it aside, 12and the most ruthless of foreign nations cut it down and left it. Its boughs fell on the mountains and in all the valleys; its branches lay broken in all the ravines of the land. All the nations of the earth came out from under its shade and left it. 13All the birds of the air settled on the fallen tree, and all the beasts of the field were among its branches. 14Therefore no other trees by the waters are ever to tower proudly on high, lifting their tops above the thick foliage. No other trees so well-watered are ever to reach such a height; they are all destined for death, for the earth below, among mortal men, with those who go down to the pit.

15" 'This is what the Sovereign LORD says: On the day it was brought down to the grave^a I covered the deep springs with mourning for it; I held back its streams, and its abundant waters were restrained. Because of it I clothed Lebanon with gloom, and all the trees of the field withered away. 16I made the nations tremble at the sound of its fall when I

^{c}13 Hebrew Noph; also in verse 16 ^{d}14 Hebrew waste Pathros ^{e}14 Hebrew No; also in verses 15 and 16 ^{f}15 Hebrew Sin; also in verse 16
^{g}17 Hebrew Awen (or On) ^{h}17 Hebrew Pi Beseth ^{a}15 Hebrew Sheol; also in verses 16 and 17

brought it down to the grave with those who go down to the pit. Then all the trees of Eden, the choicest and best of Lebanon, all the trees that were well-watered, were consoled in the earth below. ¹⁷Those who lived in its shade, its allies among the nations, had also gone down to the grave with it, joining those killed by the sword.

¹⁸ 'Which of the trees of Eden can be compared with you in splendour and majesty? Yet you, too, will be brought down with the trees of Eden to the earth below; you will lie among the uncircumcised, with those killed by the sword.

" 'This is Pharaoh and all his hordes, declares the Sovereign LORD.' "

■ A Lament for Pharaoh

32 In the twelfth year, in the twelfth month on the first day, the word of the LORD came to me: ²"Son of man, take up a lament concerning Pharaoh king of Egypt and say to him:

" 'You are like a lion among the nations;
   you are like a monster in the seas
thrashing about in your streams,
   churning the water with your feet
   and muddying the streams.

³" 'This is what the Sovereign LORD says:

" 'With a great throng of people
   I will cast my net over you,
   and they will haul you up in my net.
⁴I will throw you on the land
   and hurl you on the open field.
I will let all the birds of the air settle on you
   and all the beasts of the earth gorge
      themselves on you.
⁵I will spread your flesh on the mountains
   and fill the valleys with your remains.
⁶I will drench the land with your flowing blood
   all the way to the mountains,
   and the ravines will be filled with your flesh.
⁷When I snuff you out, I will cover the heavens
   and darken their stars;
I will cover the sun with a cloud,
   and the moon will not give its light.
⁸All the shining lights in the heavens
   I will darken over you;
I will bring darkness over your land,
               declares the Sovereign LORD.
⁹I will trouble the hearts of many peoples
   when I bring about your destruction among
      the nations,
   among[a] lands you have not known.
¹⁰I will cause many peoples to be appalled at
      you,
   and their kings will shudder with horror
      because of you
   when I brandish my sword before them.
On the day of your downfall
   each of them will tremble
   every moment for his life.

¹¹" 'For this is what the Sovereign LORD says:

" 'The sword of the king of Babylon
   will come against you.

¹²I will cause your hordes to fall
   by the swords of mighty men —
   the most ruthless of all nations.
They will shatter the pride of Egypt,
   and all her hordes will be overthrown.
¹³I will destroy all her cattle
   from beside abundant waters
no longer to be stirred by the foot of man
   or muddied by the hoofs of cattle.
¹⁴Then I will let her waters settle
   and make her streams flow like oil,
               declares the Sovereign LORD.
¹⁵When I make Egypt desolate
   and strip the land of everything in it,
   when I strike down all who live there,
   then they will know that I am the LORD.'

¹⁶"This is the lament they will chant for her. The daughters of the nations will chant it; for Egypt and all her hordes they will chant it, declares the Sovereign LORD."

¹⁷In the twelfth year, on the fifteenth day of the month, the word of the LORD came to me: ¹⁸"Son of man, wail for the hordes of Egypt and consign to the earth below both her and the daughters of mighty nations, with those who go down to the pit. ¹⁹Say to them, 'Are you more favoured than others? Go down and be laid among the uncircumcised.' ²⁰They will fall among those killed by the sword. The sword is drawn; let her be dragged off with all her hordes. ²¹From within the grave[b] the mighty leaders will say of Egypt and her allies, 'They have come down and they lie with the uncircumcised, with those killed by the sword.'

32:21 ■ THE AFTER-LIFE

Though eternal life shines through a few Old Testament passages (see "Life after Death", page 474), life after death was extremely vague in most of the Old Testament. The grave was represented by a place called "Sheol". The fate of the nations described here as "within the grave" gives a vivid, eerie sense of death.

²²"Assyria is there with her whole army; she is surrounded by the graves of all her slain, all who have fallen by the sword. ²³Their graves are in the depths of the pit and her army lies around her grave. All who had spread terror in the land of the living are slain, fallen by the sword.

²⁴"Elam is there, with all her hordes around her grave. All of them are slain, fallen by the sword. All who had spread terror in the land of the living went down uncircumcised to the earth below. They bear their shame with those who go down to the pit. ²⁵A bed is made for her among the slain, with all her hordes around her grave. All of them are uncircumcised, killed by the sword. Because their terror had spread in the land of the living, they bear their shame with those who go down to the pit; they are laid among the slain.

²⁶"Meshech and Tubal are there, with all their hordes around their graves. All of them are

a 9 Hebrew; Septuagint bring you into captivity among the nations, / to   b 21 Hebrew Sheol; also in verse 27 uncircumcised, killed by the sword because they spread their terror in the land of the living. 27Do they not lie with the other uncircumcised warriors who have fallen, who went down to the grave with their weapons of war, whose swords were placed under their heads? The punishment for their sins rested on their bones, though the terror of these warriors had stalked through the land of the living.

28"You too, O Pharaoh, will be broken and will lie among the uncircumcised, with those killed by the sword.

29"Edom is there, her kings and all her princes; despite their power, they are laid with those killed by the sword. They lie with the uncircumcised, with those who go down to the pit.

30"All the princes of the north and all the Sidonians are there; they went down with the slain in disgrace despite the terror caused by their power. They lie uncircumcised with those killed by the sword and bear their shame with those who go down to the pit.

31"Pharaoh—he and all his army—will see them and he will be consoled for all his hordes that were killed by the sword, declares the Sovereign LORD. 32Although I had him spread terror in the land of the living, Pharaoh and all his hordes will be laid among the uncircumcised, with those killed by the sword, declares the Sovereign LORD."

■ Ezekiel a Watchman

33 The word of the LORD came to me: 2"Son of man, speak to your countrymen and say to them: 'When I bring the sword against a land, and the people of the land choose one of their men and make him their watchman, 3and he sees the sword coming against the land and blows the trumpet to warn the people, 4then if anyone hears the trumpet but does not take warning and the sword comes and takes his life, his blood will be on his own head. 5Since he heard the sound of the trumpet but did not take warning, his blood will be on his own head. If he had taken warning, he would have saved himself. 6But if the watchman sees the sword coming and does not blow the trumpet to warn the people and the sword comes and takes the life of one of them, that man will be taken away because of his sin, but I will hold the watchman accountable for his blood.'

7"Son of man, I have made you a watchman for the house of Israel; so hear the word I speak and give them warning from me. 8When I say to the wicked, 'O wicked man, you will surely die,' and you do not speak out to dissuade him from his ways, that wicked man will die for[a] his sin, and I will hold you accountable for his blood. 9But if you do warn the wicked man to turn from his ways and he does not do so, he will die for his sin, but you will be saved yourself.

10"Son of man, say to the house of Israel, 'This is what you are saying: "Our offences and sins weigh us down, and we are wasting away because of[b] them. How then can we live?"' 11Say to them, 'As surely as I live, declares the Sovereign LORD, I take no pleasure in the death of the wicked, but rather that they turn from their ways and live. Turn! Turn from your evil ways! Why will you die, O house of Israel?'

12"Therefore, son of man, say to your countrymen, 'The righteousness of the righteous man will not save him when he disobeys, and the wickedness of the wicked man will not cause him to fall when he turns from it. The righteous man, if he sins, will not be allowed to live because of his former righteousness.' 13If I tell the righteous man that he will surely live, but then he trusts in his righteousness and does evil, none of the righteous things he has done will be remembered; he will die for the evil he has done. 14And if I say to the wicked man, 'You will surely die,' but he then turns away from his sin and does what is just and right—15if he gives back what he took in pledge for a loan, returns what he has stolen, follows the decrees that give life, and does no evil, he will surely live; he will not die. 16None of the sins he has committed will be remembered against him. He has done what is just and right; he will surely live.

17"Yet your countrymen say, 'The way of the Lord is not just.' But it is their way that is not just. 18If a righteous man turns from his righteousness and does evil, he will die for it. 19And if a wicked man turns away from his wickedness and does what is just and right, he will live by doing so. 20Yet, O house of Israel, you say, 'The way of the Lord is not just.' But I will judge each of you according to his own ways."

■ Jerusalem's Fall Explained

21In the twelfth year of our exile, in the tenth month on the fifth day, a man who had escaped from Jerusalem came to me and said, "The city has fallen!" 22Now the evening before the man arrived, the hand of the LORD was upon me, and he opened my mouth before the man came to me in the morning. So my mouth was opened and I was no longer silent.

23Then the word of the LORD came to me: 24"Son of man, the people living in those ruins in the land of Israel are saying, 'Abraham was only one man, yet he possessed the land. But we are many; surely the land has been given to us as our possession.' 25Therefore say to them, 'This is what the Sovereign LORD says: Since you eat meat with the blood still in it and look to your idols and shed blood, should you then possess the land? 26You rely on your sword, you do detestable things, and each of you defiles his

a 8 Or in; also in verse 9   b 10 Or away in

neighbour's wife. Should you then possess the land?'

33:22 ■ END OF THE SILENCE
For nearly eight years, since the beginning of his ministry, Ezekiel had been silent except when giving God's words. Now, an exile arrived in Babylon with bad news from Jerusalem: the temple had been burned, the city destroyed. Ezekiel's long silence ended, by God's permission. His message of doom ended too, for his prediction of punishment had come true. From this point on, Ezekiel's prophecies take up a more hopeful theme, of rebuilding a broken people.

27"Say this to them: 'This is what the Sovereign LORD says: As surely as I live, those who are left in the ruins will fall by the sword, those out in the country I will give to the wild animals to be devoured, and those in strongholds and caves will die of a plague. 28I will make the land a desolate waste, and her proud strength will come to an end, and the mountains of Israel will become desolate so that no-one will cross them. 29Then they will know that I am the LORD, when I have made the land a desolate waste because of all the detestable things they have done.'

30"As for you, son of man, your countrymen are talking together about you by the walls and at the doors of the houses, saying to each other, 'Come

■ THE TURNING POINT
FROM HERE FORWARD, EZEKIEL OFFERS GOOD NEWS

INSIGHT

IN THE TWELFTH YEAR OF OUR EXILE . . . A MAN WHO HAD ESCAPED FROM JERUSALEM CAME TO ME AND SAID, "THE CITY HAS FALLEN!" ■ 33:21

To their children parents can seem frighteningly inconsistent. One minute a father is gripping his son's wrist, shouting about something. The next moment, punishment over, he is talking about going camping together next summer. How can he change so drastically? Why so angry one minute and so loving the next?

The sudden change makes sense only if you grasp that most parents hate the role of disciplinarian. They punish in order to correct something they see as harmful. Afterwards, they put punishment behind them as quickly as possible, because they dream of better times in the future.

■ A HAPPIER LIFE FOR EZEKIEL
Ezekiel portrays just such a drastic change between God and Israel. Until chapter 33 he had offered mostly anger and threats. Suddenly, in verse 21, the news of Jerusalem's fall reached Ezekiel. The punishment, long threatened, had come. From this point on, Ezekiel's message from God became dominated by dreams of the future — happy dreams. Ezekiel's life became happier too. After seven years of virtual silence (3:26–27 — he spoke only what God told him to), he opened his mouth freely again.

God, speaking through Ezekiel, began to paint the future with the same vivid colours he had used to promise punishment. He spoke of Israel as a flock of sheep and himself as their loving shepherd (chapter 34). He previewed the mountains of Israel as they will look under his full blessing (chapter 36) — very different from the prediction given those same mountains in chapter 6.

God showed Ezekiel a valley of dry bones rising up and taking life (chapter 37), a vision that has inspired musicians and preachers ever since. He forecast a fantastic battle with evil forces from the north, Gog and Magog, in which God's people would triumph magnificently (chapters 38–39). Then, in his final vision, God showed Ezekiel the nation of Israel restored, with its boundaries extended far into hostile territory, its temple rebuilt in new splendour (chapters 40–48). The Lord would come back to his home, to live with his people.

■ THE TEMPLE'S SIGNIFICANCE
The temple, to Israel, was a sign of God's love. By taking up a home there, he committed himself to be with them permanently — not to come and go but to be available at any and all times to his people. When he left the temple (10:18) and let it be razed to the ground by the Babylonians (2 Kings 25:9), he communicated clearly that Israel had forfeited any right to his care.

So Ezekiel's vision of a rebuilt temple, with God's glory filling it, was a promise of new hope. The temple has never been rebuilt according to the precise description Ezekiel gave (chapters 40–43), and many scholars understand his portrayal as symbolic. But the central beauty of the temple is this: "THE LORD IS THERE". The glorious, astonishing God whom Ezekiel first saw in the Babylonian desert will make his home in the centre of the land. He will not always be angry. He has great plans for the happiness of his people.

☐ LIFE QUESTIONS:
In your relationship with God, are you more concerned with past failures? Or with hopes for the future?

and hear the message that has come from the LORD.'
³¹My people come to you, as they usually do, and sit
before you to listen to your words, but they do not
put them into practice. With their mouths they express devotion, but their hearts are greedy for unjust gain. ³²Indeed, to them you are nothing more
than one who sings love songs with a beautiful voice
and plays an instrument well, for they hear your
words but do not put them into practice.

³³"When all this comes true — and it surely will —
then they will know that a prophet has been among
them."

■ Shepherds and Sheep

34 The word of the LORD came to me: ²"Son of
man, prophesy against the shepherds of

Israel; prophesy and say to them: 'This is what the
Sovereign LORD says: Woe to the shepherds of
Israel who only take care of themselves! Should not
shepherds take care of the flock? ³You eat the curds,
clothe yourselves with the wool and slaughter the
choice animals, but you do not take care of the
flock. ⁴You have not strengthened the weak or
healed the sick or bound up the injured. You have
not brought back the strays or searched for the lost.
You have ruled them harshly and brutally. ⁵So they
were scattered because there was no shepherd, and
when they were scattered they became food for all
the wild animals. ⁶My sheep wandered over all the
mountains and on every high hill. They were scattered over the whole earth, and no-one searched or
looked for them.

⁷" 'Therefore, you shepherds, hear the word of

■ THE SAD TRUTH
EZEKIEL BECAME POPULAR OVERNIGHT – BUT THE PRAISE WAS EMPTY

INSIGHT

"MY PEOPLE COME TO YOU . . . AND SIT
BEFORE YOU TO LISTEN TO YOUR
WORDS, BUT THEY DO NOT PUT THEM
INTO PRACTICE." ■ 33:31

God warned Ezekiel it would be a terrible job.
Nobody would listen to his message. He would
find his own people "hardened and obstinate"
(3:7). And how would God help him? "I will
make you as unyielding and hardened as they
are" (3:8).
        As a result Ezekiel lived a lonely life.
Those few who believed his prophecies
expected nothing to happen in their lifetime
(12:27). People thought of Ezekiel as someone
just telling stories (20:49). They couldn't believe
that God would let Jerusalem fall, as Ezekiel
was stubbornly predicting.
        Then, after years of prophecy, news
came that Babylon had conquered Jerusalem
(33:21). Suddenly Ezekiel was popular. People
talked about him, flocked to hear his words,
expressed devotion. But they listened to Ezekiel
without changing their hearts. He was just
someone "who sings love songs with a beautiful
voice" (33:32). The people heard his words but
did not put them into practice.

■ A DREADFUL MESSAGE
In some ways Ezekiel could sympathise with the
people's negative attitude. He did not like his
message either; sometimes it horrified him.
Twice, seeing God's judgment, he fell face
down in horror, crying out (9:8; 11:13). When
God told him to cook food over human
excrement, a symbol of defilement, he was too
shocked to agree (4:14). When his wife, "the
delight of his eyes", died, he was not even
allowed to weep (24:15–24).

Ezekiel had to subordinate ordinary
human emotions to the unpleasant task God
had given him: to tell the truth, the whole truth,
and nothing but the truth, and to tell it in a
way that the Israelites could not ignore. "As
surely as I live, declares the Sovereign LORD, I
take no pleasure in the death of the wicked,
but rather that they turn from their ways and
live. Turn! Turn from your evil ways! Why will
you die, O house of Israel?" (33:11).

■ FALSE OPTIMISM
The false prophets, by contrast, tended to be
optimists. They overlooked their nation's
corruption and predicted that everything would
work out. Chapter 13 records Ezekiel's words
against them. "Woe to the foolish prophets
who follow their own spirit and have seen
nothing!" he said (13:3). They would
"whitewash" a bad situation with claims that
God could never let Jerusalem be destroyed
(13:10–16).
        In the end Ezekiel got to deliver
genuine good news: the promise of restored
life. He saw a vision that still lives in song:
scattered, bleached bones coming to life
(37:1–14). In another vision, he saw God return
to live in Jerusalem (43:1–5). Ezekiel didn't live
to see these hopeful predictions fulfilled. But
you can be sure he enjoyed making them far
more than he enjoyed his predictions of
disaster.

☐ LIFE QUESTIONS:
Is there any place today for "bad news" of the
kind Ezekiel proclaimed?

the LORD: [8]As surely as I live, declares the Sovereign LORD, because my flock lacks a shepherd and so has been plundered and has become food for all the wild animals, and because my shepherds did not search for my flock but cared for themselves rather than for my flock, [9]therefore, O shepherds, hear the word of the LORD: [10]This is what the Sovereign LORD says: I am against the shepherds and will hold them accountable for my flock. I will remove them from tending the flock so that the shepherds can no longer feed themselves. I will rescue my flock from their mouths, and it will no longer be food for them.

33:32 ■ PROPHETIC ENTERTAINMENT
Ezekiel's popularity soared after Jerusalem's fall, for his warnings had all come true. Even so, his audience listened just for entertainment, as they would to music. God reminds Ezekiel that the true purpose of prophecy is to change people's lives, not to draw a crowd.

---

[11]" 'For this is what the Sovereign LORD says: I myself will search for my sheep and look after them. [12]As a shepherd looks after his scattered flock when he is with them, so will I look after my sheep. I will rescue them from all the places where they were scattered on a day of clouds and darkness. [13]I will bring them out from the nations and gather them from the countries, and I will bring them into their own land. I will pasture them on the mountains of Israel, in the ravines and in all the settlements in the land. [14]I will tend them in a good pasture, and the mountain heights of Israel will be their grazing land. There they will lie down in good grazing land, and there they will feed in a rich pasture on the mountains of Israel. [15]I myself will tend my sheep and make them lie down, declares the Sovereign LORD. [16]I will search for the lost and bring back the strays. I will bind up the injured and strengthen the weak, but the sleek and the strong I will destroy. I will shepherd the flock with justice.

34:11 ■ THE GOOD SHEPHERD
Ezekiel, who used strong imagery throughout his writing, developed the image of God as a shepherd with more detail than any other author in the Bible. To people who herded sheep for a living, the simile had tremendous impact.

The same comparison is used repeatedly throughout the Bible. One much-loved passage is Psalm 23, which begins, "The LORD is my shepherd." Jesus called himself "the good shepherd" (John 10:11–16) and had compassion on crowds because they were like "sheep without a shepherd" (Mark 6:34). The image of God as a shepherd begins with Jacob (Genesis 48:15) and ends with Revelation 7:17.

---

[17]" 'As for you, my flock, this is what the Sovereign LORD says: I will judge between one sheep and another, and between rams and goats. [18]Is it not enough for you to feed on the good pasture? Must you also trample the rest of your pasture with your feet? Is it not enough for you to drink clear water? Must you also muddy the rest with your feet? [19]Must my flock feed on what you have trampled and drink what you have muddied with your feet?

[20]" 'Therefore this is what the Sovereign LORD says to them: See, I myself will judge between the fat sheep and the lean sheep. [21]Because you shove with flank and shoulder, butting all the weak sheep with your horns until you have driven them away, [22]I will save my flock, and they will no longer be plundered. I will judge between one sheep and another. [23]I will place over them one shepherd, my servant David, and he will tend them; he will tend them and be their shepherd. [24]I the LORD will be their God, and my servant David will be prince among them. I the LORD have spoken.

[25]" 'I will make a covenant of peace with them and rid the land of wild beasts so that they may live in the desert and sleep in the forests in safety. [26]I will bless them and the places surrounding my hill.[a] I will send down showers in season; there will be showers of blessing. [27]The trees of the field will yield their fruit and the ground will yield its crops; the people will be secure in their land. They will know that I am the LORD, when I break the bars of their yoke and rescue them from the hands of those who enslaved them. [28]They will no longer be plundered by the nations, nor will wild animals devour them. They will live in safety, and no-one will make them afraid. [29]I will provide for them a land renowned for its crops, and they will no longer be victims of famine in the land or bear the scorn of the nations. [30]Then they will know that I, the LORD their God, am with them and that they, the house of Israel, are my people, declares the Sovereign LORD. [31]You my sheep, the sheep of my pasture, are people, and I am your God, declares the Sovereign LORD.' "

■ A Prophecy Against Edom

35 The word of the LORD came to me: [2]"Son of man, set your face against Mount Seir; prophesy against it [3]and say: 'This is what the Sovereign LORD says: I am against you, Mount Seir, and I will stretch out my hand against you and make you a desolate waste. [4]I will turn your towns into ruins and you will be desolate. Then you will know that I am the LORD.

[5]" 'Because you harboured an ancient hostility and delivered the Israelites over to the sword at the time of their calamity, the time their punishment reached its climax, [6]therefore as surely as I live, declares the Sovereign LORD, I will give you over to bloodshed and it will pursue you. Since you did not hate bloodshed, bloodshed will pursue you. [7]I will make Mount Seir a desolate waste and cut off from it all who come and go. [8]I will fill your mountains with the slain; those killed by the sword will fall on your hills and in your valleys and in all your ravines. [9]I will make you desolate for ever; your towns will not be inhabited. Then you will know that I am the LORD.

[10]" 'Because you have said, "These two nations and countries will be ours and we will take

[a] 26 Or I will make them and the places surrounding my hill a blessing

possession of them," even though I the LORD was there, [11]therefore as surely as I live, declares the Sovereign LORD, I will treat you in accordance with the anger and jealousy you showed in your hatred of them and I will make myself known among them when I judge you. [12]Then you will know that I the LORD have heard all the contemptible things you have said against the mountains of Israel. You said, "They have been laid waste and have been given over to us to devour." [13]You boasted against me and spoke against me without restraint, and I heard it. [14]This is what the Sovereign LORD says: While the whole earth rejoices, I will make you desolate. [15]Because you rejoiced when the inheritance of the house of Israel became desolate, that is how I will treat you. You will be desolate, O Mount Seir, you and all of Edom. Then they will know that I am the LORD.' "

35:5 ■ BAD BLOOD

Ill will between two clans dated from the beginning, when Jacob cheated his brother Esau out of the family inheritance. Over the centuries Esau's descendants became the nation of Edom, and Jacob's became Israel. Bad feelings persisted. To Israelites, however, this incident was the ultimate offence: when Babylon burned down Jerusalem, the Edomites looted the city and egged on the Babylonians.

■ A Prophecy to the Mountains of Israel

36 "Son of man, prophesy to the mountains of Israel and say, 'O mountains of Israel, hear the word of the LORD. [2]This is what the Sovereign LORD says: The enemy said of you, "Aha! The ancient heights have become our possession." ' [3]Therefore prophesy and say, 'This is what the Sovereign LORD says: Because they ravaged and hounded you from every side so that you became the possession of the rest of the nations and the object of people's malicious talk and slander, [4]therefore, O mountains of Israel, hear the word of the Sovereign LORD: This is what the Sovereign LORD says to the mountains and hills, to the ravines and valleys, to the desolate ruins and the deserted towns that have been plundered and ridiculed by the rest of the nations around you — [5]this is what the Sovereign LORD says: In my burning zeal I have spoken against the rest of the nations, and against Edom, for with glee and with malice in their hearts they made my land their own possession so that they might plunder its pastureland.' [6]Therefore prophesy concerning the land of Israel and say to the mountains and hills, to the ravines and valleys: 'This is what the Sovereign LORD says: I speak in my jealous wrath because you have suffered the scorn of the nations. [7]Therefore this is what the Sovereign LORD says: I swear with uplifted hand that the nations around you will also suffer scorn.

[8]" 'But you, O mountains of Israel, will produce branches and fruit for my people Israel, for they will soon come home. [9]I am concerned for you and will look on you with favour; you will be ploughed and sown, [10]and I will multiply the number of people

upon you, even the whole house of Israel. The towns will be inhabited and the ruins rebuilt. [11]I will increase the number of men and animals upon you, and they will be fruitful and become numerous. I will settle people on you as in the past and will make you prosper more than before. Then you will know that I am the LORD. [12]I will cause people, my people Israel, to walk upon you. They will possess you, and you will be their inheritance; you will never again deprive them of their children.

[13]" 'This is what the Sovereign LORD says: Because people say to you, "You devour men and deprive your nation of its children," [14]therefore you will no longer devour men or make your nation childless, declares the Sovereign LORD. [15]No longer will I make you hear the taunts of the nations, and no longer will you suffer the scorn of the peoples or cause your nation to fall, declares the Sovereign LORD.' "

[16]Again the word of the LORD came to me: [17]"Son of man, when the people of Israel were living in their own land, they defiled it by their conduct and their actions. Their conduct was like a woman's monthly uncleanness in my sight. [18]So I poured out my wrath on them because they had shed blood in the land and because they had defiled it with their idols. [19]I dispersed them among the nations, and they were scattered through the countries; I judged them according to their conduct and their actions. [20]And wherever they went among the nations they profaned my holy name, for it was said of them, 'These are the LORD's people, and yet they had to leave his land.' [21]I had concern for my holy name, which the house of Israel profaned among the nations where they had gone.

[22]"Therefore say to the house of Israel, 'This is what the Sovereign LORD says: It is not for your sake, O house of Israel, that I am going to do these things, but for the sake of my holy name, which you have profaned among the nations where you have gone. [23]I will show the holiness of my great name, which has been profaned among the nations, the name you have profaned among them. Then the nations will know that I am the LORD, declares the Sovereign LORD, when I show myself holy through you before their eyes.

[24]" 'For I will take you out of the nations; I will gather you from all the countries and bring you back into your own land. [25]I will sprinkle clean water on you, and you will be clean; I will cleanse you from all your impurities and from all your idols. [26]I will give you a new heart and put a new spirit in you; I will remove from you your heart of stone and give you a heart of flesh. [27]And I will put my Spirit in you and move you to follow my decrees and be careful to keep my laws. [28]You will live in the land I gave your forefathers; you will be my people, and I will be your God. [29]I will save you from all your uncleanness. I will call for the corn and make it plentiful and will not bring famine upon you. [30]I will increase the fruit of the trees and the crops of the field, so that you will no longer suffer disgrace among the nations because of famine. [31]Then you will remember your evil ways and wicked deeds, and you will loathe yourselves for your sins and

detestable practices. [32]I want you to know that I am not doing this for your sake, declares the Sovereign LORD. Be ashamed and disgraced for your conduct, O house of Israel!

36:27 ■ A NEW SPIRIT

Like Jeremiah, Ezekiel realised that Israel needed more than a fresh start. To avoid making the same mistakes all over again, they needed new motivation and orientation. God must work radical surgery on them, to implant a new heart and a new spirit. Jesus' followers believed that this began when the Holy Spirit came at Pentecost (Acts 2:17–21).

[33]" 'This is what the Sovereign LORD says: On the day I cleanse you from all your sins, I will resettle your towns, and the ruins will be rebuilt. [34]The desolate land will be cultivated instead of lying desolate in the sight of all who pass through it. [35]They will say, "This land that was laid waste has become like the garden of Eden; the cities that were lying in ruins, desolate and destroyed, are now fortified and inhabited." [36]Then the nations around you that remain will know that I the LORD have rebuilt what was destroyed and have replanted what was desolate. I the LORD have spoken, and I will do it.'

[37]"This is what the Sovereign LORD says: Once again I will yield to the plea of the house of Israel and do this for them: I will make their people as numerous as sheep, [38]as numerous as the flocks for offerings at Jerusalem during her appointed feasts. So will the ruined cities be filled with flocks of people. Then they will know that I am the LORD."

■ The Valley of Dry Bones

37 The hand of the LORD was upon me, and he brought me out by the Spirit of the LORD and set me in the middle of a valley; it was full of bones. [2]He led me to and fro among them, and I saw a great many bones on the floor of the valley, bones that were very dry. [3]He asked me, "Son of man, can these bones live?"

I said, "O Sovereign LORD, you alone know."

[4]Then he said to me, "Prophesy to these bones and say to them, 'Dry bones, hear the word of the LORD! [5]This is what the Sovereign LORD says to these bones: I will make breath[a] enter you, and you will come to life. [6]I will attach tendons to you and make flesh come upon you and cover you with skin; I will put breath in you, and you will come to life. Then you will know that I am the LORD.' "

[7]So I prophesied as I was commanded. And as I was prophesying, there was a noise, a rattling sound, and the bones came together, bone to bone. [8]I looked, and tendons and flesh appeared on them and skin covered them, but there was no breath in them.

[9]Then he said to me, "Prophesy to the breath; prophesy, son of man, and say to it, 'This is what the Sovereign LORD says: Come from the four winds, O breath, and breathe into these slain, that they may live.' " [10]So I prophesied as he commanded me, and

breath entered them; they came to life and stood up on their feet—a vast army.

37:9 ■ DRY BONES

This marvellous vision, celebrated in a famous song, begins with a collection of bones littering a valley floor. Before Ezekiel's eyes, the bones come together, assembling into skeletons and growing flesh and skin. The bodies stay dead, however, until in a dramatic moment God puts breath into them. The Hebrew for "breath" also means Spirit, and the vision would have reminded any Jew of Genesis 2:7, where God breathed life into the first man.

God is reminding Ezekiel that it would take a miracle to bring the remnants of Israel back together from the many locations where they were scattered. But to be truly alive, Israel will need a greater miracle: a new Spirit, breathed by God. Only a new creation can resurrect Israel or anyone else.

[11]Then he said to me: "Son of man, these bones are the whole house of Israel. They say, 'Our bones are dried up and our hope is gone; we are cut off.' [12]Therefore prophesy and say to them: 'This is what the Sovereign LORD says: O my people, I am going to open your graves and bring you up from them; I will bring you back to the land of Israel. [13]Then you, my people, will know that I am the LORD, when I open your graves and bring you up from them. [14]I will put my Spirit in you and you will live, and I will settle you in your own land. Then you will know that I the LORD have spoken, and I have done it, declares the LORD.' "

■ One Nation Under One King

[15]The word of the LORD came to me: [16]"Son of man, take a stick of wood and write on it, 'Belonging to Judah and the Israelites associated with him.' Then take another stick of wood, and write on it, 'Ephraim's stick, belonging to Joseph and all the house of Israel associated with him.' [17]Join them together into one stick so that they will become one in your hand.

[18]"When your countrymen ask you, 'Won't you tell us what you mean by this?' [19]say to them, 'This is what the Sovereign LORD says: I am going to take the stick of Joseph—which is in Ephraim's hand—and of the Israelite tribes associated with him, and join it to Judah's stick, making them a single stick of wood, and they will become one in my hand.' [20]Hold before their eyes the sticks you have written on [21]and say to them, 'This is what the Sovereign LORD says: I will take the Israelites out of the nations where they have gone. I will gather them from all around and bring them back into their own land. [22]I will make them one nation in the land, on the mountains of Israel. There will be one king over all of them and they will never again be two nations or be divided into two kingdoms. [23]They will no longer defile themselves with their idols and vile images or with any of their offences, for I will save them from

---

[a]5 The Hebrew for this word can also mean *wind* or *spirit* (see verses 6–14).

all their sinful backsliding,[b] and I will cleanse them. They will be my people, and I will be their God.

37:22 ■ NORTH AND SOUTH REUNITED

Israel longed to be reunited. The Jews had been split into two nations (sometimes at war) since the days of Solomon, over 300 years before. Yet, like East and West Germany, now united again, and North and South Korea today, they had not forgotten their common origin. God promised to reunite the two — even though one had been in exile, scattered among other nations, for over 100 years.

24" 'My servant David will be king over them, and they will all have one shepherd. They will follow my laws and be careful to keep my decrees. 25They will live in the land I gave to my servant Jacob, the land where your fathers lived. They and their children and their children's children will live there for ever, and David my servant will be their prince for ever. 26I will make a covenant of peace with them; it will be an everlasting covenant. I will establish them and increase their numbers, and I will put my sanctuary among them for ever. 27My dwelling-place will be with them; I will be their God, and they will be my people. 28Then the nations will know that I the LORD make Israel holy, when my sanctuary is among them for ever.' "

■ A Prophecy Against Gog

38 The word of the LORD came to me: 2"Son of man, set your face against Gog, of the land of Magog, the chief prince of[a] Meshech and Tubal; prophesy against him 3and say: 'This is what the Sovereign LORD says: I am against you, O Gog, chief prince of[b] Meshech and Tubal. 4I will turn you around, put hooks in your jaws and bring you out with your whole army—your horses, your horsemen fully armed, and a great horde with large and small shields, all of them brandishing their swords. 5Persia, Cush[c] and Put will be with them, all with shields and helmets, 6also Gomer with all its troops, and Beth Togarmah from the far north with all its troops—the many nations with you.

7" 'Get ready; be prepared, you and all the hordes gathered about you, and take command of them. 8After many days you will be called to arms. In future years you will invade a land that has recovered from war, whose people were gathered from many nations to the mountains of Israel, which had long been desolate. They had been brought out from the nations, and now all of them live in safety. 9You and all your troops and the many nations with you will go up, advancing like a storm; you will be like a cloud covering the land.

10" 'This is what the Sovereign LORD says: On that day thoughts will come into your mind and you will devise an evil scheme. 11You will say, "I will invade a land of unwalled villages; I will attack a peaceful and unsuspecting people—all of them living without walls and without gates and bars. 12I will

plunder and loot and turn my hand against the resettled ruins and the people gathered from the nations, rich in livestock and goods, living at the centre of the land." 13Sheba and Dedan and the merchants of Tarshish and all her villages[d] will say to you, "Have you come to plunder? Have you gathered your hordes to loot, to carry off silver and gold, to take away livestock and goods and to seize much plunder?" '

14"Therefore, son of man, prophesy and say to Gog: 'This is what the Sovereign LORD says: In that day, when my people Israel are living in safety, will you not take notice of it? 15You will come from your place in the far north, you and many nations with you, all of them riding on horses, a great horde, a mighty army. 16You will advance against my people Israel like a cloud that covers the land. In days to come, O Gog, I will bring you against my land, so that the nations may know me when I show myself holy through you before their eyes.

17" 'This is what the Sovereign LORD says: Are you not the one I spoke of in former days by my servants the prophets of Israel? At that time they prophesied for years that I would bring you against them. 18This is what will happen in that day: When Gog attacks the land of Israel, my hot anger will be aroused, declares the Sovereign LORD. 19In my zeal and fiery wrath I declare that at that time there shall be a great earthquake in the land of Israel. 20The fish of the sea, the birds of the air, the beasts of the field, every creature that moves along the ground, and all the people on the face of the earth will tremble at my presence. The mountains will be overturned, the cliffs will crumble and every wall will fall to the ground. 21I will summon a sword against Gog on all my mountains, declares the Sovereign LORD. Every man's sword will be against his brother. 22I will execute judgment upon him with plague and bloodshed; I will pour down torrents of rain, hailstones and burning sulphur on him and on his troops and on the many nations with him. 23And so I will show my greatness and my holiness, and I will make myself known in the sight of many nations. Then they will know that I am the LORD.'

39 "Son of man, prophesy against Gog and say: 'This is what the Sovereign LORD says: I am against you, O Gog, chief prince of[a] Meshech and Tubal. 2I will turn you around and drag you along. I will bring you from the far north and send you against the mountains of Israel. 3Then I will strike your bow from your left hand and make your arrows drop from your right hand. 4On the mountains of Israel you will fall, you and all your troops and the nations with you. I will give you as food to all kinds of carrion birds and to the wild animals. 5You will fall in the open field, for I have spoken, declares the Sovereign LORD. 6I will send fire on Magog and on those who live in safety in the coastlands, and they will know that I am the LORD.

7" 'I will make known my holy name among my people Israel. I will no longer let my holy name be profaned, and the nations will know that I the LORD am the Holy One in Israel. 8It is coming! It will surely take place, declares the Sovereign LORD. This is the day I have spoken of.

---

[b] 23 Many Hebrew manuscripts (see also Septuagint); most Hebrew manuscripts all their dwelling-places where they sinned   [a] 2 Or the prince of Rosh,
[b] 3 Or Gog, prince of Rosh,   [c] 5 That is, the upper Nile region   [d] 13 Or her strong lions   [a] 1 Or Gog, prince of Rosh,

9" 'Then those who live in the towns of Israel will go out and use the weapons for fuel and burn them up — the small and large shields, the bows and arrows, the war clubs and spears. For seven years they will use them for fuel. 10They will not need to gather wood from the fields or cut it from the forests, because they will use the weapons for fuel. And they will plunder those who plundered them and loot those who looted them, declares the Sovereign LORD.

11" 'On that day I will give Gog a burial place in Israel, in the valley of those who travel east towards[b] the Sea.[c] It will block the way of travellers, because Gog and all his hordes will be buried there. So it will be called the Valley of Hamon Gog.[d]

12" 'For seven months the house of Israel will be burying them in order to cleanse the land. 13All the people of the land will bury them, and the day I am glorified will be a memorable day for them, declares the Sovereign LORD.

14" 'Men will be regularly employed to cleanse the land. Some will go throughout the land and, in addition to them, others will bury those that remain on the ground. At the end of the seven months they will begin their search. 15As they go through the land and one of them sees a human bone, he will set up a marker beside it until the gravediggers have buried it in the Valley of Hamon Gog. 16(Also a town called Hamonah[e] will be there.) And so they will cleanse the land.'

17"Son of man, this is what the Sovereign LORD says: Call out to every kind of bird and all the wild animals: 'Assemble and come together from all around to the sacrifice I am preparing for you, the great sacrifice on the mountains of Israel. There you will eat flesh and drink blood. 18You will eat the flesh of mighty men and drink the blood of the princes of the earth as if they were rams and lambs, goats and bulls — all of them fattened animals from Bashan. 19At the sacrifice I am preparing for you, you will eat fat till you are glutted and drink blood till you are drunk. 20At my table you will eat your fill of horses and riders, mighty men and soldiers of every kind,' declares the Sovereign LORD.

21"I will display my glory among the nations, and all the nations will see the punishment I inflict and the hand I lay upon them. 22From that day forward the house of Israel will know that I am the LORD their God. 23And the nations will know that the people of Israel went into exile for their sin, because

they were unfaithful to me. So I hid my face from them and handed them over to their enemies, and they all fell by the sword. 24I dealt with them according to their uncleanness and their offences, and I hid my face from them.

25"Therefore this is what the Sovereign LORD says: I will now bring Jacob back from captivity[f] and will have compassion on all the people of Israel, and I will be zealous for my holy name. 26They will forget their shame and all the unfaithfulness they showed towards me when they lived in safety in their land with no-one to make them afraid. 27When I have brought them back from the nations and have gathered them from the countries of their enemies, I will show myself holy through them in the sight of many nations. 28Then they will know that I am the LORD their God, for though I sent them into exile among the nations, I will gather them to their own land, not leaving any behind. 29I will no longer hide my face from them, for I will pour out my Spirit on the house of Israel, declares the Sovereign LORD."

■ The New Temple Area

40 In the twenty-fifth year of our exile, at the beginning of the year, on the tenth of the month, in the fourteenth year after the fall of the city — on that very day the hand of the LORD was upon me and he took me there. 2In visions of God he took me to the land of Israel and set me on a very high mountain, on whose south side were some buildings that looked like a city. 3He took me there, and I saw a man whose appearance was like bronze; he was standing in the gateway with a linen cord and a measuring rod in his hand. 4The man said to me, "Son of man, look with your eyes and hear with your ears and pay attention to everything I am going to show you, for that is why you have been brought here. Tell the house of Israel everything you see."

■ The East Gate to the Outer Court

5I saw a wall completely surrounding the temple area. The length of the measuring rod in the man's hand was six long cubits, each of which was a cubit[a] and a handbreadth.[b] He measured the wall; it was one measuring rod thick and one rod high.

6Then he went to the gate facing east. He climbed its steps and measured the threshold of the gate; it was one rod deep.[c] 7The alcoves for the guards were one rod long and one rod wide, and the

---

b11 Or of   c11 That is, the Dead Sea   d11 Hamon Gog means hordes of Gog.   e16 Hamonah means horde.   f25 Or now restore the fortunes of Jacob   a5 The common cubit was about 1½ feet (about 0.5 metre).   b5 That is, about 3 inches (about 8 centimetres)   c6 Septuagint; Hebrew deep, the first threshold, one rod deep projecting walls between the alcoves were five cubits thick. And the threshold of the gate next to the portico facing the temple was one rod deep.

8Then he measured the portico of the gateway; 9it*d* was eight cubits deep and its jambs were two cubits thick. The portico of the gateway faced the temple.

10Inside the east gate were three alcoves on each side; the three had the same measurements, and the faces of the projecting walls on each side had the same measurements. 11Then he measured the width of the entrance to the gateway; it was ten cubits and its length was thirteen cubits. 12In front of each alcove was a wall one cubit high, and the alcoves were six cubits square. 13Then he measured the gateway from the top of the rear wall of one alcove to the top of the opposite one; the distance was twenty-five cubits from one parapet opening to the opposite one. 14He measured along the faces of the projecting walls all around the inside of the gateway—sixty cubits. The measurement was up to the portico*e* facing the courtyard.*f* 15The distance from the entrance of the gateway to the far end of its portico was fifty cubits. 16The alcoves and the projecting walls inside the gateway were surmounted by narrow parapet openings all round, as was the portico; the openings all round faced inward. The faces of the projecting walls were decorated with palm trees.

■ The Outer Court

17Then he brought me into the outer court. There I saw some rooms and a pavement that had been constructed all round the court; there were thirty rooms along the pavement. 18It abutted the sides of the gateways and was as wide as they were long; this was the lower pavement. 19Then he measured the distance from the inside of the lower gateway to the outside of the inner court; it was a hundred cubits on the east side as well as on the north.

■ The North Gate

20Then he measured the length and width of the gate facing north, leading into the outer court. 21Its alcoves—three on each side—its projecting walls and its portico had the same measurements as those of the first gateway. It was fifty cubits long and twenty-five cubits wide. 22Its openings, its portico and its palm tree decorations had the same measurements as those of the gate facing east. Seven steps led up to it, with its portico opposite them. 23There was a gate to the inner court facing the north gate, just as there was on the east. He measured from one gate to the opposite one; it was a hundred cubits.

■ The South Gate

24Then he led me to the south side and I saw a gate facing south. He measured its jambs and its portico, and they had the same measurements as the others. 25The gateway and its portico had narrow openings all round, like the openings of the others. It was fifty cubits long and twenty-five cubits wide. 26Seven steps led up to it, with its portico opposite

them; it had palm tree decorations on the faces of the projecting walls on each side. 27The inner court also had a gate facing south, and he measured from this gate to the outer gate on the south side; it was a hundred cubits.

■ Gates to the Inner Court

28Then he brought me into the inner court through the south gate, and he measured the south gate; it had the same measurements as the others. 29Its alcoves, its projecting walls and its portico had the same measurements as the others. The gateway and its portico had openings all round. It was fifty cubits long and twenty-five cubits wide. 30(The porticoes of the gateways around the inner court were twenty-five cubits wide and five cubits deep.) 31Its portico faced the outer court; palm trees decorated its jambs, and eight steps led up to it.

32Then he brought me to the inner court on the east side, and he measured the gateway; it had the same measurements as the others. 33Its alcoves, its projecting walls and its portico had the same measurements as the others. The gateway and its portico had openings all round. It was fifty cubits long and twenty-five cubits wide. 34Its portico faced the outer court; palm trees decorated the jambs on either side, and eight steps led up to it.

35Then he brought me to the north gate and measured it. It had the same measurements as the others, 36as did its alcoves, its projecting walls and its portico, and it had openings all round. It was fifty cubits long and twenty-five cubits wide. 37Its portico*g* faced the outer court; palm trees decorated the jambs on either side, and eight steps led up to it.

■ The Rooms for Preparing Sacrifices

38A room with a doorway was by the portico in each of the inner gateways, where the burnt offerings were washed. 39In the portico of the gateway were two tables on each side, on which the burnt offerings, sin offerings and guilt offerings were slaughtered. 40By the outside wall of the portico of the gateway, near the steps at the entrance to the north gateway were two tables, and on the other side of the steps were two tables. 41So there were four tables on one side of the gateway and four on the other—eight tables in all—on which the sacrifices were slaughtered. 42There were also four tables of dressed stone for the burnt offerings, each a cubit and a half long, a cubit and a half wide and a cubit high. On them were placed the utensils for slaughtering the burnt offerings and the other sacrifices. 43And double-pronged hooks, each a handbreadth long, were attached to the wall all around. The tables were for the flesh of the offerings.

■ Rooms for the Priests

44Outside the inner gate, within the inner court, were two rooms, one*b* at the side of the north gate and facing south, and another at the side of the south*i* gate and facing north. 45He said to me, "The room facing south is for the priests who have charge of the temple, 46and the room facing north is for the priests who have charge of the altar. These are the

*d*8, 9 Many Hebrew manuscripts, Septuagint, Vulgate and Syriac; most Hebrew manuscripts *gateway facing the temple; it was one rod deep.* 9*Then he measured the portico of the gateway; it* *e*14 Septuagint; Hebrew *projecting wall* *f*14 The meaning of the Hebrew for this verse is uncertain. *g*37 Septuagint (see also verses 31 and 34); Hebrew *jambs* *h*44 Septuagint; Hebrew *were rooms for singers, which were* *i*44 Septuagint; Hebrew *east* sons of Zadok, who are the only Levites who may draw near to the LORD to minister before him."

⁴⁷Then he measured the court: It was square—a hundred cubits long and a hundred cubits wide. And the altar was in front of the temple.

■ The Temple

⁴⁸He brought me to the portico of the temple and measured the jambs of the portico; they were five cubits wide on either side. The width of the entrance was fourteen cubits and its projecting walls were ʲ three cubits wide on either side. ⁴⁹The portico was twenty cubits wide, and twelveᵏ cubits from front to back. It was reached by a flight of stairs,ˡ and there were pillars on each side of the jambs.

41 Then the man brought me to the outer sanctuary and measured the jambs; the width of the jambs was six cubitsᵃ on each side.ᵇ ²The entrance was ten cubits wide, and the projecting walls on each side of it were five cubits wide. He also measured the outer sanctuary; it was forty cubits long and twenty cubits wide.

41:2 ■ SEEING THE NEW TEMPLE

You'll find it easier to visualise Ezekiel's temple if you look at a sketch from a Bible dictionary. (Look under "Temple" or "Ezekiel".) Ezekiel's description reveals fascinating insights. For instance, the number of steps up towards the Holy Place grows greater at each stage, so that a worshipper mounts increasingly higher. But the doorways grow narrower (40:48; 41:2–3)—suggesting that the nearer to God's presence one climbs, the narrower the path he or she must follow.

---

³Then he went into the inner sanctuary and measured the jambs of the entrance; each was two cubits wide. The entrance was six cubits wide, and the projecting walls on each side of it were seven cubits wide. ⁴And he measured the length of the inner sanctuary; it was twenty cubits, and its width was twenty cubits across the end of the outer sanctuary. He said to me, "This is the Most Holy Place."

⁵Then he measured the wall of the temple; it was six cubits thick, and each side room round the temple was four cubits wide. ⁶The side rooms were on three levels, one above another, thirty on each level. There were ledges all round the wall of the temple to serve as supports for the side rooms, so that the supports were not inserted into the wall of the temple. ⁷The side rooms all round the temple were wider at each successive level. The structure surrounding the temple was built in ascending stages, so that the rooms widened as one went upward. A stairway went up from the lowest floor to the top floor through the middle floor.

⁸I saw that the temple had a raised base all round it, forming the foundation of the side rooms. It was the length of the rod, six long cubits. ⁹The outer wall of the side rooms was five cubits thick. The open area between the side rooms of the temple

¹⁰and the ⌐priests'¬ rooms was twenty cubits wide all round the temple. ¹¹There were entrances to the side rooms from the open area, one on the north and another on the south; and the base adjoining the open area was five cubits wide all round.

¹²The building facing the temple courtyard on the west side was seventy cubits wide. The wall of the building was five cubits thick all round, and its length was ninety cubits.

¹³Then he measured the temple; it was a hundred cubits long, and the temple courtyard and the building with its walls were also a hundred cubits long. ¹⁴The width of the temple courtyard on the east, including the front of the temple, was a hundred cubits.

¹⁵Then he measured the length of the building facing the courtyard at the rear of the temple, including its galleries on each side; it was a hundred cubits.

The outer sanctuary, the inner sanctuary and the portico facing the court, ¹⁶as well as the thresholds and the narrow windows and galleries round the three of them—everything beyond and including the threshold was covered with wood. The floor, the wall up to the windows, and the windows were covered. ¹⁷In the space above the outside of the entrance to the inner sanctuary and on the walls at regular intervals all round the inner and outer sanctuary ¹⁸were carved cherubim and palm trees. Palm trees alternated with cherubim. Each cherub had two faces: ¹⁹the face of a man towards the palm tree on one side and the face of a lion towards the palm tree on the other. They were carved all round the whole temple. ²⁰From the floor to the area above the entrance, cherubim and palm trees were carved on the wall of the outer sanctuary.

²¹The outer sanctuary had a rectangular doorframe, and the one at the front of the Most Holy Place was similar. ²²There was a wooden altar three cubits high and two cubits square;ᶜ its corners, its baseᵈ and its sides were of wood. The man said to me, "This is the table that is before the LORD." ²³Both the outer sanctuary and the Most Holy Place had double doors. ²⁴Each door had two leaves—two hinged leaves for each door. ²⁵And on the doors of the outer sanctuary were carved cherubim and palm trees like those carved on the walls, and there was a wooden overhang on the front of the portico. ²⁶On the side walls of the portico were narrow windows with palm trees carved on each side. The side rooms of the temple also had overhangs.

■ Rooms for the Priests

42 Then the man led me northward into the outer court and brought me to the rooms opposite the temple courtyard and opposite the outer wall on the north side. ²The building whose door faced north was a hundred cubitsᵃ long and fifty cubits wide. ³Both in the section twenty cubits from the inner court and in the section opposite the pavement of the outer court, gallery faced gallery at the three levels. ⁴In front of the rooms was an inner passageway ten cubits wide and a hundred cubitsᵇ

ʲ48 Septuagint; Hebrew *entrance was*   ᵏ49 Septuagint; Hebrew *eleven*   ˡ49 Hebrew; Septuagint *Ten steps led up to it*   ᵃ1 The common cubit was about 1½ feet (about 0.5 metre).   ᵇ1 One Hebrew manuscript and Septuagint; most Hebrew manuscripts *side, the width of the tent*   ᶜ22 Septuagint; Hebrew *long*   ᵈ22 Septuagint; Hebrew *length*   ᵃ2 The common cubit was about 1½ feet (about 0.5 metre).   ᵇ4 Septuagint and Syriac; Hebrew *and one cubit* long. Their doors were on the north. ⁵Now the upper rooms were narrower, for the galleries took more space from them than from the rooms on the lower and middle floors of the building. ⁶The rooms on the third floor had no pillars, as the courts had; so they were smaller in floor space than those on the lower and middle floors. ⁷There was an outer wall parallel to the rooms and the outer court; it extended in front of the rooms for fifty cubits. ⁸While the row of rooms on the side next to the outer court was fifty cubits long, the row on the side nearest the sanctuary was a hundred cubits long. ⁹The lower rooms had an entrance on the east side as one enters them from the outer court.

¹⁰On the south side*ᶜ* along the length of the wall of the outer court, adjoining the temple courtyard and opposite the outer wall, were rooms ¹¹with a passageway in front of them. These were like the rooms on the north; they had the same length and width, with similar exits and dimensions. Similar to the doorways on the north ¹²were the doorways of the rooms on the south. There was a doorway at the beginning of the passageway that was parallel to the corresponding wall extending eastward, by which one enters the rooms.

¹³Then he said to me, "The north and south rooms facing the temple courtyard are the priests' rooms, where the priests who approach the LORD will eat the most holy offerings. There they will put the most holy offerings — the grain offerings, the sin offerings and the guilt offerings — for the place is holy. ¹⁴Once the priests enter the holy precincts, they are not to go into the outer court until they leave behind the garments in which they minister, for these are holy. They are to put on other clothes before they go near the places that are for the people."

¹⁵When he had finished measuring what was inside the temple area, he led me out by the east gate and measured the area all around: ¹⁶He measured the east side with the measuring rod; it was five hundred cubits.*ᵈ* ¹⁷He measured the north side; it was five hundred cubits*ᵉ* by the measuring rod. ¹⁸He measured the south side; it was five hundred cubits by the measuring rod. ¹⁹Then he turned to the west side and measured; it was five hundred cubits by the measuring rod. ²⁰So he measured the area on all four sides. It had a wall round it, five hundred cubits long and five hundred cubits wide, to separate the holy from the common.

■ The Glory Returns to the Temple

43 Then the man brought me to the gate facing east, ²and I saw the glory of the God of Israel coming from the east. His voice was like the roar of rushing waters, and the land was radiant with his glory. ³The vision I saw was like the vision I had seen when he*ᵃ* came to destroy the city and like the visions I had seen by the Kebar River, and I fell face down. ⁴The glory of the LORD entered the temple through the gate facing east. ⁵Then the Spirit lifted me up and brought me into the inner court, and the glory of the LORD filled the temple.

⁶While the man was standing beside me, I heard someone speaking to me from inside the temple. ⁷He said: "Son of man, this is the place of my throne and the place for the soles of my feet. This is where I will live among the Israelites for ever. The house of Israel will never again defile my holy name — neither they nor their kings — by their prostitution*ᵇ* and the lifeless idols*ᶜ* of their kings at their high places. ⁸When they placed their threshold next to my threshold and their doorposts beside my doorposts, with only a wall between me and them, they defiled my holy name by their detestable practices. So I destroyed them in my anger. ⁹Now let them put away from me their prostitution and the lifeless idols of their kings, and I will live among them for ever.

43:4 ■ THE GLORY RETURNS

Nineteen years had passed since Ezekiel saw the glory of the Lord leave the temple (11:22–23). That temple was now dust and ashes and broken stones: the conquering Babylonians had burnt and destroyed it. The new temple Ezekiel saw in this vision symbolised that God would again live with his renewed people.

---

¹⁰"Son of man, describe the temple to the people of Israel, that they may be ashamed of their sins. Let them consider the plan, ¹¹and if they are ashamed of all they have done, make known to them the design of the temple — its arrangement, its exits and entrances — its whole design and all its regulations*ᵈ* and laws. Write these down before them so that they may be faithful to its design and follow all its regulations.

¹²"This is the law of the temple: All the surrounding area on top of the mountain will be most holy. Such is the law of the temple.

■ The Altar

¹³"These are the measurements of the altar in long cubits, that cubit being a cubit*ᵉ* and a handbreadth:*ᶠ* Its gutter is a cubit deep and a cubit wide, with a rim of one span*ᵍ* around the edge. And this is the height of the altar: ¹⁴From the gutter on the ground up to the lower ledge it is two cubits high and a cubit wide, and from the smaller ledge up to the larger ledge it is four cubits high and a cubit wide. ¹⁵The altar hearth is four cubits high, and four horns project upward from the hearth. ¹⁶The altar hearth is square, twelve cubits long and twelve cubits wide. ¹⁷The upper ledge also is square, fourteen cubits long and fourteen cubits wide, with a rim of half a cubit and a gutter of a cubit all round. The steps of the altar face east."

¹⁸Then he said to me, "Son of man, this is what the Sovereign LORD says: These will be the regulations for sacrificing burnt offerings and sprinkling blood upon the altar when it is built: ¹⁹You are to give a young bull as a sin offering to the priests, who are Levites, of the family of Zadok, who come near to minister before me, declares the Sovereign LORD.

---

*ᶜ*10 Septuagint; Hebrew *Eastward*   *ᵈ*16 See Septuagint of verse 17; Hebrew *rods*; also in verses 18 and 19.   *ᵉ*17 Septuagint; Hebrew *rods*
*ᵃ*3 Some Hebrew manuscripts and Vulgate; most Hebrew manuscripts *I*   *ᵇ*7 Or *their spiritual adultery*; also in verse 9   *ᶜ*7 Or *the corpses*; also in verse 9   *ᵈ*11 Some Hebrew manuscripts and Septuagint; most Hebrew manuscripts *regulations and its whole design*   *ᵉ*13 The common cubit was about 1½ feet (about 0.5 metre).   *ᶠ*13 That is, about 3 inches (about 8 centimetres).   *ᵍ*13 That is, about 9 inches (about 23 centimetres)

²⁰You are to take some of its blood and put it on the four horns of the altar and on the four corners of the upper ledge and all round the rim, and so purify the altar and make atonement for it. ²¹You are to take the bull for the sin offering and burn it in the designated part of the temple area outside the sanctuary.

²²"On the second day you are to offer a male goat without defect for a sin offering, and the altar is to be purified as it was purified with the bull. ²³When you have finished purifying it, you are to offer a young bull and a ram from the flock, both without defect. ²⁴You are to offer them before the LORD, and the priests are to sprinkle salt on them and sacrifice them as a burnt offering to the LORD.

²⁵"For seven days you are to provide a male goat daily for a sin offering; you are also to provide a young bull and a ram from the flock, both without defect. ²⁶For seven days they are to make atonement for the altar and cleanse it; thus they will dedicate it. ²⁷At the end of these days, from the eighth day on, the priests are to present your burnt offerings and fellowship offerings*b* on the altar. Then I will accept you, declares the Sovereign LORD."

■ The Prince, the Levites, the Priests

44 Then the man brought me back to the outer gate of the sanctuary, the one facing east, and it was shut. ²The LORD said to me, "This gate is to remain shut. It must not be opened; no-one may enter through it. It is to remain shut because the LORD, the God of Israel, has entered through it. ³The prince himself is the only one who may sit inside the gateway to eat in the presence of the LORD. He is to enter by way of the portico of the gateway and go out the same way."

⁴Then the man brought me by way of the north gate to the front of the temple. I looked and saw the glory of the LORD filling the temple of the LORD, and I fell face down.

⁵The LORD said to me, "Son of man, look carefully, listen closely and give attention to everything I tell you concerning all the regulations regarding the temple of the LORD. Give attention to the entrance of the temple and all the exits of the sanctuary. ⁶Say to the rebellious house of Israel, 'This is what the Sovereign LORD says: Enough of your detestable practices, O house of Israel! ⁷In addition to all your other detestable practices, you brought foreigners uncircumcised in heart and flesh into my sanctuary, desecrating my temple while you offered me food, fat and blood, and you broke my covenant. ⁸Instead of carrying out your duty in regard to my holy things, you put others in charge of my sanctuary. ⁹This is what the Sovereign LORD says: No foreigner uncircumcised in heart and flesh is to enter my sanctuary, not even the foreigners who live among the Israelites.

¹⁰" 'The Levites who went far from me when Israel went astray and who wandered from me after their idols must bear the consequences of their sin. ¹¹They may serve in my sanctuary, having charge of the gates of the temple and serving in it; they may slaughter the burnt offerings and sacrifices for the people and stand before the people and serve them. ¹²But because they served them in the presence of their idols and made the house of Israel fall into sin, therefore I have sworn with uplifted hand that they must bear the consequences of their sin, declares the Sovereign LORD. ¹³They are not to come near to serve me as priests or come near any of my holy things or my most holy offerings; they must bear the shame of their detestable practices. ¹⁴Yet I will put them in charge of the duties of the temple and all the work that is to be done in it.

¹⁵" 'But the priests, who are Levites and descendants of Zadok and who faithfully carried out the duties of my sanctuary when the Israelites went astray from me, are to come near to minister before me; they are to stand before me to offer sacrifices of fat and blood, declares the Sovereign LORD. ¹⁶They alone are to enter my sanctuary; they alone are to come near my table to minister before me and perform my service.

¹⁷" 'When they enter the gates of the inner court, they are to wear linen clothes; they must not wear any woollen garment while ministering at the gates of the inner court or inside the temple. ¹⁸They are to wear linen turbans on their heads and linen undergarments round their waists. They must not wear anything that makes them perspire. ¹⁹When they go out into the outer court where the people are, they are to take off the clothes they have been ministering in and leave them in the sacred rooms, and put on other clothes, so that they do not consecrate the people by means of their garments.

²⁰" 'They must not shave their heads or let their hair grow long, but they are to keep the hair of their heads trimmed. ²¹No priest is to drink wine when he enters the inner court. ²²They must not marry widows or divorced women; they may marry only virgins of Israelite descent or widows of priests. ²³They are to teach my people the difference between the holy and the common and show them how to distinguish between the unclean and the clean.

²⁴" 'In any dispute, the priests are to serve as judges and decide it according to my ordinances. They are to keep my laws and my decrees for all my appointed feasts, and they are to keep my Sabbaths holy.

²⁵" 'A priest must not defile himself by going near a dead person; however, if the dead person was his father or mother, son or daughter, brother or unmarried sister, then he may defile himself. ²⁶After he is cleansed, he must wait seven days. ²⁷On the day he goes into the inner court of the sanctuary to minister in the sanctuary, he is to offer a sin offering for himself, declares the Sovereign LORD.

²⁸" 'I am to be the only inheritance the priests have. You are to give them no possession in Israel; I will be their possession. ²⁹They will eat the grain offerings, the sin offerings and the guilt offerings; and everything in Israel devoted*a* to the LORD will belong to them. ³⁰The best of all the firstfruits and of all your special gifts will belong to the priests. You are to give them the first portion of your ground meal so that a blessing may rest on your household. ³¹The priests must not eat anything, bird or animal, found dead or torn by wild animals.

b 27 Traditionally *peace offerings*   *a 29* The Hebrew term refers to the irrevocable giving over of things or persons to the LORD.

■ Division of the Land

45 " 'When you allot the land as an inheritance, you are to present to the LORD a portion of the land as a sacred district, 25,000 cubits long and 20,000ª cubits wide; the entire area will be holy. ²Of this, a section 500 cubits square is to be for the sanctuary, with 50 cubits around it for open land. ³In the sacred district, measure off a section 25,000 cubitsᵇ long and 10,000 cubitsᶜ wide. In it will be the sanctuary, the Most Holy Place. ⁴It will be the sacred portion of the land for the priests, who minister in the sanctuary and who draw near to minister before the LORD. It will be a place for their houses as well as a holy place for the sanctuary. ⁵An area 25,000 cubits long and 10,000 cubits wide will belong to the Levites, who serve in the temple, as their possession for towns to live in.ᵈ

⁶" 'You are to give the city as its property an area 5,000 cubits wide and 25,000 cubits long, adjoining the sacred portion; it will belong to the whole house of Israel.

⁷" 'The prince will have the land bordering each side of the area formed by the sacred district and the property of the city. It will extend westward from the west side and eastward from the east side, running lengthwise from the western to the eastern border parallel to one of the tribal portions. ⁸This land will be his possession in Israel. And my princes will no longer oppress my people but will allow the house of Israel to possess the land according to their tribes.

⁹" 'This is what the Sovereign LORD says: You have gone far enough, O princes of Israel! Give up your violence and oppression and do what is just and right. Stop dispossessing my people, declares the Sovereign LORD. ¹⁰You are to use accurate scales, an accurate ephahᵉ and an accurate bath.ᶠ ¹¹The ephah and the bath are to be the same size, the bath containing a tenth of a homerᵍ and the ephah a tenth of a homer; the homer is to be the standard measure for both. ¹²The shekelʰ is to consist of twenty gerahs. Twenty shekels plus twenty-five shekels plus fifteen shekels equal one mina.ⁱ

45:10 ■ HONEST WEIGHT
The Bible, always practical, doesn't bother to define honesty in philosophic terms. It merely says, "Don't cheat on your measures." Such cheating was a common problem in Judah (see, for instance, Micah 6:10–12). Archaeologists have found many weights once used in Hebrew market-places, but very few have weighed exactly the weight inscribed on them.

■ Offerings and Holy Days

¹³" 'This is the special gift you are to offer: a sixth of an ephah from each homer of wheat and a sixth of an ephah from each homer of barley. ¹⁴The prescribed portion of oil, measured by the bath, is a tenth of a bath from each cor (which consists of ten

baths or one homer, for ten baths are equivalent to a homer). ¹⁵Also one sheep is to be taken from every flock of two hundred from the well-watered pastures of Israel. These will be used for the grain offerings, burnt offerings and fellowship offeringsʲ to make atonement for the people, declares the Sovereign LORD. ¹⁶All the people of the land will participate in this special gift for the use of the prince in Israel. ¹⁷It will be the duty of the prince to provide the burnt offerings, grain offerings and drink offerings at the festivals, the New Moons and the Sabbaths—at all the appointed feasts of the house of Israel. He will provide the sin offerings, grain offerings, burnt offerings and fellowship offerings to make atonement for the house of Israel.

¹⁸" 'This is what the Sovereign LORD says: In the first month on the first day you are to take a young bull without defect and purify the sanctuary. ¹⁹The priest is to take some of the blood of the sin offering and put it on the doorposts of the temple, on the four corners of the upper ledge of the altar and on the gateposts of the inner court. ²⁰You are to do the same on the seventh day of the month for anyone who sins unintentionally or through ignorance; so you are to make atonement for the temple.

²¹" 'In the first month on the fourteenth day you are to observe the Passover, a feast lasting seven days, during which you shall eat bread made without yeast. ²²On that day the prince is to provide a bull as a sin offering for himself and for all the people of the land. ²³Every day during the seven days of the Feast he is to provide seven bulls and seven rams without defect as a burnt offering to the LORD, and a male goat for a sin offering. ²⁴He is to provide as a grain offering an ephah for each bull and an ephah for each ram, along with a hinᵏ of oil for each ephah.

²⁵" 'During the seven days of the Feast, which begins in the seventh month on the fifteenth day, he is to make the same provision for sin offerings, burnt offerings, grain offerings and oil.

46 " 'This is what the Sovereign LORD says: The gate of the inner court facing east is to be shut on the six working days, but on the Sabbath day and on the day of the New Moon it is to be opened. ²The prince is to enter from the outside through the portico of the gateway and stand by the gatepost. The priests are to sacrifice his burnt offering and his fellowship offerings.ª He is to worship at the threshold of the gateway and then go out, but the gate will not be shut until evening. ³On the Sabbaths and New Moons the people of the land are to worship in the presence of the LORD at the entrance to that gateway. ⁴The burnt offering the prince brings to the LORD on the Sabbath day is to be six male lambs and a ram, all without defect. ⁵The grain offering given with the ram is to be an ephah,ᵇ and the grain offering with the lambs is to be as much as he pleases, along with a hinᶜ of oil for each ephah. ⁶On the day of the New Moon he is to offer a young bull, six lambs and a ram, all without defect. ⁷He is to provide as a grain offering one ephah with the bull,

ª1 Septuagint (see also verses 3 and 5 and 48:9); Hebrew 10,000   ᵇ3 That is, about 7 miles (about 11 kilometres)   ᶜ3 That is, about 3 miles (about 5 kilometres)   ᵈ5 Septuagint; Hebrew temple; they will have as their possession 20 rooms   ᵉ10 An ephah was a dry measure.   ᶠ10 A bath was a liquid measure.   ᵍ11 A homer was a dry measure.   ᵇ12 A shekel weighed about ⅖ ounce (about 11.5 grams).   ⁱ12 That is, 60 shekels; the common mina was 50 shekels.   ʲ15 Traditionally peace offerings; also in verse 17   ᵏ24 That is, probably about 6 pints (about 4 litres)   ª2 Traditionally peace offerings; also in verse 12   ᵇ5 That is, probably about ⅗ bushel (about 22 litres)   ᶜ5 That is, probably about 6 pints (about 4 litres) one ephah with the ram, and with the lambs as much as he wants to give, along with a hin of oil with each ephah. [8]When the prince enters, he is to go in through the portico of the gateway, and he is to come out the same way.

[9]" 'When the people of the land come before the LORD at the appointed feasts, whoever enters by the north gate to worship is to go out by the south gate; and whoever enters by the south gate is to go out by the north gate. No-one is to return through the gate by which he entered, but each is to go out by the opposite gate. [10]The prince is to be among them, going in when they go in and going out when they go out.

[11]" 'At the festivals and the appointed feasts, the grain offering is to be an ephah with a bull, an ephah with a ram, and with the lambs as much as one pleases, along with a hin of oil for each ephah. [12]When the prince provides a freewill offering to the LORD—whether a burnt offering or fellowship offerings—the gate facing east is to be opened for him. He shall offer his burnt offering or his fellowship offerings as he does on the Sabbath day. Then he shall go out, and after he has gone out, the gate will be shut.

[13]" 'Every day you are to provide a year-old lamb without defect for a burnt offering to the LORD; morning by morning you shall provide it. [14]You are also to provide with it morning by morning a grain offering, consisting of a sixth of an ephah with a third of a hin of oil to moisten the flour. The presenting of this grain offering to the LORD is a lasting ordinance. [15]So the lamb and the grain offering and the oil shall be provided morning by morning for a regular burnt offering.

[16]" 'This is what the Sovereign LORD says: If the prince makes a gift from his inheritance to one of his sons, it will also belong to his descendants; it is to be their property by inheritance. [17]If, however, he makes a gift from his inheritance to one of his servants, the servant may keep it until the year of freedom; then it will revert to the prince. His inheritance belongs to his sons only; it is theirs. [18]The prince must not take any of the inheritance of the people, driving them off their property. He is to give his sons their inheritance out of his own property, so that none of my people will be separated from his property.' "

[19]Then the man brought me through the entrance at the side of the gate to the sacred rooms facing north, which belonged to the priests, and showed me a place at the western end. [20]He said to me, "This is the place where the priests will cook the guilt offering and the sin offering and bake the grain offering, to avoid bringing them into the outer court and consecrating the people."

[21]He then brought me to the outer court and led me round to its four corners, and I saw in each corner another court. [22]In the four corners of the outer court were enclosed[d] courts, forty cubits long and thirty cubits wide; each of the courts in the four corners was the same size. [23]Around the inside of each of the four courts was a ledge of stone, with places for fire built all round under the ledge. [24]He said to me, "These are the kitchens where those who

minister at the temple will cook the sacrifices of the people."

■ The River From the Temple

47 The man brought me back to the entrance of the temple, and I saw water coming out from under the threshold of the temple towards the east (for the temple faced east). The water was coming down from under the south side of the temple, south of the altar. [2]He then brought me out through the north gate and led me round the outside to the outer gate facing east, and the water was flowing from the south side.

[3]As the man went eastward with a measuring line in his hand, he measured off a thousand cubits[a] and then led me through water that was ankle-deep. [4]He measured off another thousand cubits and led me through water that was knee-deep. He measured off another thousand and led me through water that was up to the waist. [5]He measured off another thousand, but now it was a river that I could not cross, because the water had risen and was deep enough to swim in—a river that no-one could cross. [6]He asked me, "Son of man, do you see this?"

Then he led me back to the bank of the river. [7]When I arrived there, I saw a great number of trees on each side of the river. [8]He said to me, "This water flows towards the eastern region and goes down into the Arabah,[b] where it enters the Sea.[c] When it empties into the Sea,[c] the water there becomes fresh. [9]Swarms of living creatures will live wherever the river flows. There will be large numbers of fish, because this water flows there and makes the salt water fresh; so where the river flows everything will live. [10]Fishermen will stand along the shore; from En Gedi to En Eglaim there will be places for spreading nets. The fish will be of many kinds—like the fish of the Great Sea.[d] [11]But the swamps and marshes will not become fresh; they will be left for salt. [12]Fruit trees of all kinds will grow on both banks of the river. Their leaves will not wither, nor will their fruit fail. Every month they will bear, because the water from the sanctuary flows to them. Their fruit will serve for food and their leaves for healing."

47:12 ■ RIVER FROM THE TEMPLE
This river, flowing from the temple, had miraculous properties: it reversed the deadly saltiness of the Dead Sea and produced healing fruit on its banks. The early Christians used similar symbolism; in John's vision of a new Jerusalem (Revelation 22), he saw a river of life flowing from the throne of God.

■ The Boundaries of the Land

[13]This is what the Sovereign LORD says: "These are the boundaries by which you are to divide the land for an inheritance among the twelve tribes of Israel, with two portions for Joseph. [14]You are to divide it equally among them. Because I swore with uplifted hand to give it to your forefathers, this land will become your inheritance.

---

[d]22 The meaning of the Hebrew for this word is uncertain.   [a]3 That is, about 1,500 feet (about 460 metres)   [b]8 Or the Jordan Valley   [c]8 That is, the Dead Sea   [d]10 That is, the Mediterranean; also in verses 15, 19 and 20

¹⁵"This is to be the boundary of the land:

"On the north side it will run from the Great Sea by the Hethlon road past Lebo*ᵉ* Hamath to Zedad, ¹⁶Berothah*ᶠ* and Sibraim (which lies on the border between Damascus and Hamath), as far as Hazer Hatticon, which is on the border of Hauran. ¹⁷The boundary will extend from the sea to Hazar Enan,*ᵍ* along the northern border of Damascus, with the border of Hamath to the north. This will be the north boundary.

¹⁸"On the east side the boundary will run between Hauran and Damascus, along the Jordan between Gilead and the land of Israel, to the eastern sea and as far as Tamar.*ᵇ* This will be the east boundary.

¹⁹"On the south side it will run from Tamar as far as the waters of Meribah Kadesh, then along the Wadi ˻of Egypt˼ to the Great Sea. This will be the south boundary.

²⁰"On the west side, the Great Sea will be the boundary to a point opposite Lebo*ⁱ* Hamath. This will be the west boundary.

²¹"You are to distribute this land among yourselves according to the tribes of Israel. ²²You are to allot it as an inheritance for yourselves and for the aliens who have settled among you and who have children. You are to consider them as native-born Israelites; along with you they are to be allotted an inheritance among the tribes of Israel. ²³In whatever tribe the alien settles, there you are to give him his inheritance," declares the Sovereign LORD.

■ The Division of the Land

48 "These are the tribes, listed by name: At the northern frontier, Dan will have one portion; it will follow the Hethlon road to Lebo*ᵃ* Hamath; Hazar Enan and the northern border of Damascus next to Hamath will be part of its border from the east side to the west side.

²"Asher will have one portion; it will border the territory of Dan from east to west.

³"Naphtali will have one portion; it will border the territory of Asher from east to west.

⁴"Manasseh will have one portion; it will border the territory of Naphtali from east to west.

⁵"Ephraim will have one portion; it will border the territory of Manasseh from east to west.

⁶"Reuben will have one portion; it will border the territory of Ephraim from east to west.

⁷"Judah will have one portion; it will border the territory of Reuben from east to west.

⁸"Bordering the territory of Judah from east to west will be the portion you are to present as a special gift. It will be 25,000 cubits*ᵇ* wide, and its length from east to west will equal one of the tribal portions; the sanctuary will be in the centre of it.

⁹"The special portion you are to offer to the LORD will be 25,000 cubits long and 10,000 cubits*ᶜ* wide. ¹⁰This will be the sacred portion for the priests. It will be 25,000 cubits long on the north side, 10,000 cubits wide on the west side, 10,000

cubits wide on the east side and 25,000 cubits long on the south side. In the centre of it will be the sanctuary of the LORD. ¹¹This will be for the consecrated priests, the Zadokites, who were faithful in serving me and did not go astray as the Levites did when the Israelites went astray. ¹²It will be a special gift to them from the sacred portion of the land, a most holy portion, bordering the territory of the Levites.

¹³"Alongside the territory of the priests, the Levites will have an allotment 25,000 cubits long and 10,000 cubits wide. Its total length will be 25,000 cubits and its width 10,000 cubits. ¹⁴They must not sell or exchange any of it. This is the best of the land and must not pass into other hands, because it is holy to the LORD.

¹⁵"The remaining area, 5,000 cubits wide and 25,000 cubits long, will be for the common use of the city, for houses and for pasture-land. The city will be in the centre of it ¹⁶and will have these measurements: the north side 4,500 cubits, the south side 4,500 cubits, the east side 4,500 cubits, and the west side 4,500 cubits. ¹⁷The pasture-land for the city will be 250 cubits on the north, 250 cubits on the south, 250 cubits on the east, and 250 cubits on the west. ¹⁸What remains of the area, bordering on the sacred portion and running the length of it, will be 10,000 cubits on the east side and 10,000 cubits on the west side. Its produce will supply food for the workers of the city. ¹⁹The workers from the city who farm it will come from all the tribes of Israel. ²⁰The entire portion will be a square, 25,000 cubits on each side. As a special gift you will set aside the sacred portion, along with the property of the city.

²¹"What remains on both sides of the area formed by the sacred portion and the city property will belong to the prince. It will extend eastward from the 25,000 cubits of the sacred portion to the eastern border, and westward from the 25,000 cubits to the western border. Both these areas running the length of the tribal portions will belong to the prince, and the sacred portion with the temple sanctuary will be in the centre of them. ²²So the property of the Levites and the property of the city will lie in the centre of the area that belongs to the prince. The area belonging to the prince will lie between the border of Judah and the border of Benjamin.

²³"As for the rest of the tribes: Benjamin will have one portion; it will extend from the east side to the west side.

²⁴"Simeon will have one portion; it will border the territory of Benjamin from east to west.

²⁵"Issachar will have one portion; it will border the territory of Simeon from east to west.

²⁶"Zebulun will have one portion; it will border the territory of Issachar from east to west.

²⁷"Gad will have one portion; it will border the territory of Zebulun from east to west.

²⁸"The southern boundary of Gad will run south from Tamar to the waters of Meribah Kadesh, then along the Wadi ˻of Egypt˼ to the Great Sea.*ᵈ*

²⁹"This is the land you are to allot as an inheritance to the tribes of Israel, and these will be their portions," declares the Sovereign LORD.

ᵉ15 Or past the entrance to　ᶠ15, 16 See Septuagint and Ezekiel 48:1; Hebrew road to go into Zedad, ¹⁶Hamath, Berothah　ᵍ17 Hebrew Enon, a variant of Enan　ᵇ18 Septuagint and Syriac; Hebrew Israel. You will measure to the eastern sea　ⁱ20 Or opposite the entrance to　ᵃ1 Or to the entrance to　ᵇ8 That is, about 7 miles (about 11 kilometres)　ᶜ9 That is, about 3 miles (about 5 kilometres)　ᵈ28 That is, the Mediterranean

■ The Gates of the City

³⁰"These will be the exits of the city: Beginning on the north side, which is 4,500 cubits long, ³¹the gates of the city will be named after the tribes of Israel. The three gates on the north side will be the gate of Reuben, the gate of Judah and the gate of Levi.

³²"On the east side, which is 4,500 cubits long, will be three gates: the gate of Joseph, the gate of Benjamin and the gate of Dan.

³³"On the south side, which measures 4,500 cubits, will be three gates: the gate of Simeon, the gate of Issachar and the gate of Zebulun.

³⁴"On the west side, which is 4,500 cubits long, will be three gates: the gate of Gad, the gate of Asher and the gate of Naphtali.

³⁵"The distance all around will be 18,000 cubits.

"And the name of the city from that time on will be:

THE LORD IS THERE."

48:30 ■ GATES TO THE CITY
These twelve gates, named after the twelve tribes of Israel, are also described in the new Jerusalem (Revelation 21:12). Other details of Ezekiel's vision are echoed in Revelation 21–22: for example, the view from a high mountain (Ezekiel 40:2), the angel guide (40:3), and the healing river (47:12). The most important similarity is reflected in the name of Ezekiel's city: "THE LORD IS THERE" (48:35). As Revelation expresses it, "Now the dwelling of God is with men, and he will live with them" (Revelation 21:3).

DANIEL

■ "KIDNAPPED"

EVEN AS PRIME MINISTER, DANIEL REMAINED A LONELY OUTSIDER

DANIEL RESOLVED NOT TO DEFILE HIMSELF WITH THE ROYAL FOOD AND WINE, AND HE
ASKED THE CHIEF OFFICIAL FOR PERMISSION NOT TO DEFILE HIMSELF IN THIS WAY.
■ 1:8

As a young man, Daniel could have anticipated an outstanding future in Jerusalem. He came from a prominent family, and he had a first-rate mind (1:4). But, when the Babylonian army dragged him captive to a faraway country, they didn't ask about his plans and dreams.

True, the Babylonians recognised Daniel's potential and put him into a top civil service training programme. But even the study material was distasteful to a Jew: it covered sorcery, magic, and a pagan, multigod religion. After graduation Daniel was put to work for the Babylonian king, who continued to war against Daniel's people for nearly 20 more years.

Anyone far from home feels lonely. But Daniel was one of those whose lives get lost in the shuffle of history — refugees, captives. He was destined to spend his life as an alien in Babylon. We have no record that he ever married or had family members nearby.

■ GREAT PERSONAL COURAGE

Through his ability and God's blessing he rose to the post of prime minister of Babylon. Yet he remained an outsider. The higher he rose, the more prominent a target he became. Babylonians resented his foreign background and his political success. Their plots put him under pressure to compromise his faith, to fit in, to bend his principles. His life was often at risk.

Daniel's career near the top lasted at least 66 years, so that by the time he was thrown into the lions' den (chapter 6), he must have been in his 80s. Throughout these years he laboured with great effectiveness for Babylon. He was respectful and diligent, even though working for pagan kings. Yet he never compromised his faith. He would not bend, even when threatened with death. The Bible gives no better model of how to live with and serve those who don't share or respect your beliefs.

■ THE SHAPE OF THE FUTURE

Near the end of Daniel's life God gave him a series of visions, described in chapters 7–12. In graphic images God showed Daniel the pattern of future history. Daniel's people would duplicate his own experience, but on a world stage.

The Jews, Daniel's visions showed, would be caught in a political storm, battered about by a series of world empires. Daniel foresaw nations raging in battle against each other. He foresaw God's people thrown in between these nations, suffering through no fault of their own. They would be helpless until God himself rescued them from their troubles. Daniel foresaw, in the end, all people falling down to worship "one like a son of man" (7:13). This was the title Jesus applied to himself when he came, nearly six centuries after Daniel, to bring the good news of salvation for all people.

■ SPREADING THE WORD

Daniel's people had thought of God in terms of their own small community, their own capital city and the temple there. Not only were the Jews God's chosen people, but (they tended to think) they held exclusive rights to him.

But God had never intended his blessings to stop with the Jews. He had the world in mind. At the time he called Abraham, he had promised that through Abraham's offspring he would bless the whole earth (Genesis 12:3).

The Jews had found it difficult enough to keep their own faith, let alone spread it to others. Only while captives in Babylon, unwillingly dragged far from home, did they begin to convince others that their God deserved honour. The proclamations Nebuchadnezzar and Darius made because of Daniel (4:2–3; 6:26–27) honoured God more than anything a king of Judah had done in years.

■ HOW TO READ DANIEL

Daniel breaks into two parts, each quite different from the other. The first six chapters tell the "famous" Daniel stories – including the stories of three men thrown into a fiery furnace and Daniel in the lions' den. Any of these chapters would make a script for a thriller. As you read them, reflect on the principles Daniel lived by, far from home and in dangerous circumstances. Ask yourself what Daniel can teach you about faithfulness to God in similarly "alien" circumstances.

Most people find chapters 7–12 far more difficult: they record Daniel's visions about the future of world history. Such symbolism was a familiar mode of expression in the ancient world, but it reads very strangely now – almost like science fiction. Look for broad impressions of how God's people can live, caught in the jaws of brutal world politics. Let the visual symbols engage your emotions and imagination.

If you seek a more detailed understanding of these visions, a commentary on Daniel will be a great help. In some passages, background information on ancient world history is essential. A good commentary can offer this, along with an interpretation of difficult symbols.

You can place Daniel's message in the context of Israelite history by looking at "A Line-up of Rulers", pages 260–268.

■ 3-TRACK READING PLAN

For an explanation and complete listing of the 3-track reading plan, turn to page x.

■ TRACK 1:
Two-Week Courses on the Bible
The Track 1 reading programme on the Old Testament includes one chapter from Daniel. See page x for a complete listing of this course.

■ TRACK 2:
An Overview of Daniel in 4 Days
□ Day 1. Read the

Introduction to Daniel and chapter 1, which describes Daniel's courage in rejecting compromise. He set a lifelong pattern.
□ Day 2. Read chapter 3, the famous story of three men thrown into a fiery furnace.
□ Day 3. Read chapter 5, the "handwriting on the wall" that announced the destruction of a great empire.
□ Day 4. Read chapter 6, Daniel in the lions' den.

Now turn to page xi for your next Track 2 reading project.

■ TRACK 3:
All of Daniel in 12 Days
After you have read through Daniel, turn to pages xii–xiii for your next Track 3 reading project.

□ 1   □ 2   □ 3   □ 4
□ 5   □ 6   □ 7   □ 8
□ 9   □ 10 □ 11 □ 12

■ Daniel's Training in Babylon

1 In the third year of the reign of Jehoiakim king of Judah, Nebuchadnezzar king of Babylon came to Jerusalem and besieged it. ²And the Lord delivered Jehoiakim king of Judah into his hand, along with some of the articles from the temple of God. These he carried off to the temple of his god in Babylonia*a* and put in the treasure-house of his god.

³Then the king ordered Ashpenaz, chief of his court officials, to bring in some of the Israelites from the royal family and the nobility – ⁴young men without any physical defect, handsome, showing aptitude for every kind of learning, well informed, quick to understand, and qualified to serve in the king's palace. He was to teach them the language and literature of the Babylonians.*b* ⁵The king assigned them a daily amount of food and wine from the king's table. They were to be trained for three years, and after that they were to enter the king's service.

⁶Among these were some from Judah: Daniel, Hananiah, Mishael and Azariah. ⁷The chief official gave them new names: to Daniel, the name Belteshazzar; to Hananiah, Shadrach; to Mishael, Meshach; and to Azariah, Abednego.

⁸But Daniel resolved not to defile himself with the royal food and wine, and he asked the chief official for permission not to defile himself in this way. ⁹Now God had caused the official to show favour and sympathy to Daniel, ¹⁰but the official told Daniel, "I am afraid of my lord the king, who has assigned your*c* food and drink. Why should he see you looking worse than the other young men of your age? The king would then have my head because of you."

¹¹Daniel then said to the guard whom the chief official had appointed over Daniel, Hananiah, Mishael and Azariah, ¹²"Please test your servants for ten days: Give us nothing but vegetables to eat and water to drink. ¹³Then compare our appearance with that of the young men who eat the royal food, and treat your servants in accordance with what you see." ¹⁴So he agreed to this and tested them for ten days.

¹⁵At the end of the ten days they looked healthier and better nourished than any of the young men who ate the royal food. ¹⁶So the guard took away their choice food and the wine they were to drink and gave them vegetables instead.

¹⁷To these four young men God gave knowledge and understanding of all kinds of literature and

a 2 Hebrew Shinar   b 4 Or Chaldeans   c 10 The Hebrew for your and you in this verse is plural.

learning. And Daniel could understand visions and dreams of all kinds.

18At the end of the time set by the king to bring them in, the chief official presented them to Nebuchadnezzar. 19The king talked with them, and he found none equal to Daniel, Hananiah, Mishael and Azariah; so they entered the king's service. 20In every matter of wisdom and understanding about which the king questioned them, he found them ten times better than all the magicians and enchanters in his whole kingdom.

21And Daniel remained there until the first year of King Cyrus.

■ Nebuchadnezzar's Dream

2 In the second year of his reign, Nebuchadnezzar had dreams; his mind was troubled and he could not sleep. 2So the king summoned the magicians, enchanters, sorcerers and astrologers*a* to tell him what he had dreamed. When they came in and stood before the king, 3he said to them, "I have had a dream that troubles me and I want to know what it means."*b*

4Then the astrologers answered the king in Aramaic,*c* "O king, live for ever! Tell your servants the dream, and we will interpret it."

2:4 ■ A CHANGE IN LANGUAGE

The astrologers spoke in Aramaic, the most common language of the Middle East during this period. From this point to the end of chapter 7, Daniel was written in Aramaic, instead of Hebrew. Only the book of Ezra is similarly split into two languages. Some theorise that these chapters would have been of general interest throughout the Middle East and so were put in a language that everyone could understand.

5The king replied to the astrologers, "This is what I have firmly decided: If you do not tell me what my dream was and interpret it, I will have you cut into pieces and your houses turned into piles of rubble. 6But if you tell me the dream and explain it, you will receive from me gifts and rewards and great honour. So tell me the dream and interpret it for me."

7Once more they replied, "Let the king tell his servants the dream, and we will interpret it."

8Then the king answered, "I am certain that you are trying to gain time, because you realise that this is what I have firmly decided: 9If you do not tell me the dream, there is just one penalty for you. You have conspired to tell me misleading and wicked things, hoping the situation will change. So then, tell me the dream, and I will know that you can interpret it for me."

10The astrologers answered the king, "There is not a man on earth who can do what the king asks! No king, however great and mighty, has ever asked such a thing of any magician or enchanter or astrologer. 11What the king asks is too difficult. No-one can reveal it to the king except the gods, and they do not live among men."

12This made the king so angry and furious that he ordered the execution of all the wise men of Babylon. 13So the decree was issued to put the wise men to death, and men were sent to look for Daniel and his friends to put them to death.

14When Arioch, the commander of the king's guard, had gone out to put to death the wise men of Babylon, Daniel spoke to him with wisdom and tact. 15He asked the king's officer, "Why did the king issue such a harsh decree?" Arioch then explained the matter to Daniel. 16At this, Daniel went in to the king and asked for time, so that he might interpret the dream for him.

17Then Daniel returned to his house and explained the matter to his friends Hananiah, Mishael and Azariah. 18He urged them to plead for mercy from the God of heaven concerning this mystery, so that he and his friends might not be executed with the rest of the wise men of Babylon. 19During the night the mystery was revealed to Daniel in a vision. Then Daniel praised the God of heaven 20and said:

"Praise be to the name of God for ever and
    ever;
  wisdom and power are his.
21He changes times and seasons;
  he sets up kings and deposes them.
He gives wisdom to the wise
  and knowledge to the discerning.
22He reveals deep and hidden things;
  he knows what lies in darkness,
  and light dwells with him.
23I thank and praise you, O God of my fathers:
  You have given me wisdom and power,
  you have made known to me what we asked of
    you,
  you have made known to us the dream of
    the king."

2:20 ■ REVEALING PRAYER

This brief "psalm" gives insight into Daniel's spiritual life. It begins by expressing absolute confidence in God's control over the world: Daniel clung to such faith even while living in an enemy nation that had just destroyed God's temple in Jerusalem. Also, the prayer shows Daniel's spirit of humility and praise in the midst of crisis: he paused to give God credit before rushing to the king to interpret his dream.

■ Daniel Interprets the Dream

24Then Daniel went to Arioch, whom the king had appointed to execute the wise men of Babylon, and said to him, "Do not execute the wise men of Babylon. Take me to the king, and I will interpret his dream for him."

25Arioch took Daniel to the king at once and said, "I have found a man among the exiles from Judah who can tell the king what his dream means."

26The king asked Daniel (also called Belteshazzar), "Are you able to tell me what I saw in my dream and interpret it?"

27Daniel replied, "No wise man, enchanter, magician or diviner can explain to the king the mystery

*a2 Or Chaldeans; also in verses 4, 5 and 10   b3 Or was   c4 The text from here through chapter 7 is in Aramaic.

he has asked about, 28but there is a God in heaven who reveals mysteries. He has shown King Nebuchadnezzar what will happen in days to come. Your dream and the visions that passed through your mind as you lay on your bed are these:

29"As you were lying there, O king, your mind turned to things to come, and the revealer of mysteries showed you what is going to happen. 30As for me, this mystery has been revealed to me, not because I have greater wisdom than other living men, but so that you, O king, may know the interpretation and that you may understand what went through your mind.

31"You looked, O king, and there before you stood a large statue—an enormous, dazzling statue, awesome in appearance. 32The head of the statue was made of pure gold, its chest and arms of silver, its belly and thighs of bronze, 33its legs of iron, its feet partly of iron and partly of baked clay. 34While you were watching, a rock was cut out, but not by human hands. It struck the statue on its feet of iron and clay and smashed them. 35Then the iron, the clay, the bronze, the silver and the gold were broken to pieces at the same time and became like chaff on a threshing-floor in the summer. The wind swept them away without leaving a trace. But the rock that struck the statue became a huge mountain and filled the whole earth.

36"This was the dream, and now we will interpret it to the king. 37You, O king, are the king of kings. The God of heaven has given you dominion and power and might and glory; 38in your hands he has placed mankind and the beasts of the field and the birds of the air. Wherever they live, he has made you ruler over them all. You are that head of gold.

39"After you, another kingdom will rise, inferior to yours. Next, a third kingdom, one of bronze, will rule over the whole earth. 40Finally, there will be a fourth kingdom, strong as iron—for iron breaks and smashes everything—and as iron breaks things to pieces, so it will crush and break all the others. 41Just as you saw that the feet and toes were partly of baked clay and partly of iron, so this will be a divided kingdom; yet it will have some of the strength of iron in it, even as you saw iron mixed with clay. 42As the toes were partly iron and partly clay, so this kingdom will be partly strong and partly brittle. 43And just as you saw the iron mixed with baked clay, so the people will be a mixture and will not remain united, any more than iron mixes with clay.

44"In the time of those kings, the God of heaven will set up a kingdom that will never be destroyed, nor will it be left to another people. It will crush all those kingdoms and bring them to an end, but it will itself endure for ever. 45This is the meaning of the vision of the rock cut out of a mountain, but not by human hands—a rock that broke the iron, the bronze, the clay, the silver and the gold to pieces.

"The great God has shown the king what will take place in the future. The dream is true and the interpretation is trustworthy."

46Then King Nebuchadnezzar fell prostrate before Daniel and paid him honour and ordered that an offering and incense be presented to him. 47The king said to Daniel, "Surely your God is the God of gods and the Lord of kings and a revealer of mysteries, for you were able to reveal this mystery."

48Then the king placed Daniel in a high position and lavished many gifts on him. He made him ruler over the entire province of Babylon and placed him in charge of all its wise men. 49Moreover, at Daniel's request the king appointed Shadrach, Meshach and Abednego administrators over the province of Babylon, while Daniel himself remained at the royal court.

2:48 ■ A NATION OF DREAMERS

The Babylonians highly valued dream interpretation, for they believed the gods spoke to them through dreams. "If a man cannot remember the dream he saw, his personal god is angry with him", says one Babylonian proverb. That proverb helps explain Nebuchadnezzar's panic over forgetting his dream—and his lavish reward to Daniel for recalling and interpreting it.

■ The Image of Gold and the Fiery Furnace

3 King Nebuchadnezzar made an image of gold, ninety feet high and nine feet*a* wide, and set it up on the plain of Dura in the province of Babylon. 2He then summoned the satraps, prefects, governors, advisers, treasurers, judges, magistrates and all the other provincial officials to come to the dedication of the image he had set up. 3So the satraps, prefects, governors, advisers, treasurers, judges, magistrates and all the other provincial officials assembled for the dedication of the image that King Nebuchadnezzar had set up, and they stood before it.

4Then the herald loudly proclaimed, "This is what you are commanded to do, O peoples, nations and men of every language: 5As soon as you hear the sound of the horn, flute, zither, lyre, harp, pipes and all kinds of music, you must fall down and worship the image of gold that King Nebuchadnezzar has set up. 6Whoever does not fall down and worship will immediately be thrown into a blazing furnace."

7Therefore, as soon as they heard the sound of the horn, flute, zither, lyre, harp and all kinds of music, all the peoples, nations and men of every language fell down and worshipped the image of gold that King Nebuchadnezzar had set up.

8At this time some astrologers*b* came forward and denounced the Jews. 9They said to King Nebuchadnezzar, "O king, live for ever! 10You have issued a decree, O king, that everyone who hears the sound of the horn, flute, zither, lyre, harp, pipes and all kinds of music must fall down and worship the image of gold, 11and that whoever does not fall down and worship will be thrown into a blazing furnace. 12But there are some Jews whom you have set over the affairs of the province of Babylon—Shadrach, Meshach and Abednego—who pay no attention to you, O king. They neither serve your gods nor worship the image of gold you have set up."

13Furious with rage, Nebuchadnezzar summoned Shadrach, Meshach and Abednego. So these men were brought before the king, 14and Nebuchadnez-

a 1 Aramaic sixty cubits high and six cubits wide *(about 27 metres high and 2.7 metres wide)* *b 8 Or* Chaldeans zar said to them, "Is it true, Shadrach, Meshach and Abednego, that you do not serve my gods or worship the image of gold I have set up? ¹⁵Now when you hear the sound of the horn, flute, zither, lyre, harp, pipes and all kinds of music, if you are ready to fall down and worship the image I made, very good. But if you do not worship it, you will be thrown immediately into a blazing furnace. Then what god will be able to rescue you from my hand?"

¹⁶Shadrach, Meshach and Abednego replied to the king, "O Nebuchadnezzar, we do not need to defend ourselves before you in this matter. ¹⁷If we are thrown into the blazing furnace, the God we serve is able to save us from it, and he will rescue us from your hand, O king. ¹⁸But even if he does not, we want you to know, O king, that we will not serve your gods or worship the image of gold you have set up."

3:18 ■ WHETHER RESCUED OR NOT

Daniel's three friends illustrated perfectly the quality of faith that is later commended in Hebrews 11. When allegiance to God led them to commit an act of civil disobedience, they were willing to face the consequences *whether or not* God rescued them. Daniel himself faced a severe test of faith, with a similarly happy ending (see chapter 6). Along with Elijah and Elisha, he was one of the few Old Testament prophets whose ministry was marked by miracles.

¹⁹Then Nebuchadnezzar was furious with Shadrach, Meshach and Abednego, and his attitude towards them changed. He ordered the furnace to be heated seven times hotter than usual ²⁰and commanded some of the strongest soldiers in his army to tie up Shadrach, Meshach and Abednego and throw them into the blazing furnace. ²¹So these men, wearing their robes, trousers, turbans and other clothes, were bound and thrown into the blazing furnace. ²²The king's command was so urgent and the furnace so hot that the flames of the fire killed the soldiers who took up Shadrach, Meshach and Abednego, ²³and these three men, firmly tied, fell into the blazing furnace.

²⁴Then King Nebuchadnezzar leaped to his feet in amazement and asked his advisers, "Weren't there three men that we tied up and threw into the fire?"

They replied, "Certainly, O king."

²⁵He said, "Look! I see four men walking around in the fire, unbound and unharmed, and the fourth looks like a son of the gods."

²⁶Nebuchadnezzar then approached the opening of the blazing furnace and shouted, "Shadrach, Meshach and Abednego, servants of the Most High God, come out! Come here!"

So Shadrach, Meshach and Abednego came out of the fire, ²⁷and the satraps, prefects, governors and royal advisers crowded around them. They saw that the fire had not harmed their bodies, nor was a hair of their heads singed; their robes were not scorched, and there was no smell of fire on them.

²⁸Then Nebuchadnezzar said, "Praise be to the God of Shadrach, Meshach and Abednego, who has sent his angel and rescued his servants! They trusted in him and defied the king's command and were willing to give up their lives rather than serve or worship any god except their own God. ²⁹Therefore I decree that the people of any nation or language who say anything against the God of Shadrach, Meshach and Abednego be cut into pieces and their houses be turned into piles of rubble, for no other god can save in this way."

³⁰Then the king promoted Shadrach, Meshach and Abednego in the province of Babylon.

■ Nebuchadnezzar's Dream of a Tree

4 King Nebuchadnezzar,

To the peoples, nations and men of every language, who live in all the world:

May you prosper greatly!

²It is my pleasure to tell you about the miraculous signs and wonders that the Most High God has performed for me.

³How great are his signs,
   how mighty his wonders!
His kingdom is an eternal kingdom;
   his dominion endures from generation
   to generation.

⁴I, Nebuchadnezzar, was at home in my palace, contented and prosperous. ⁵I had a dream that made me afraid. As I was lying in my bed, the images and visions that passed through my mind terrified me. ⁶So I commanded that all the wise men of Babylon be brought before me to interpret the dream for me. ⁷When the magicians, enchanters, astrologers[a] and diviners came, I told them the dream, but they could not interpret it for me. ⁸Finally, Daniel came into my presence and I told him the dream. (He is called Belteshazzar, after the name of my god, and the spirit of the holy gods is in him.)

4:8 ■ THE NAME OF A GOD

Names were extremely important in biblical times, for they conveyed something of a person's identity. Thus God sometimes gave a person a new name to indicate a changed life. However, the name the Babylonians presented to Daniel, Belteshazzar, was no gift from God. It was taken from "Bel", a title for the Babylonian god Marduk. Daniel was surrounded by an alien culture and could not avoid every aspect of it.

⁹I said, "Belteshazzar, chief of the magicians, I know that the spirit of the holy gods is in you, and no mystery is too difficult for you. Here is my dream; interpret it for me. ¹⁰These are the visions I saw while lying in my bed: I looked, and there before me stood a tree in the middle of the land. Its height was enormous. ¹¹The tree grew large and strong and its top touched the sky; it was visible to the ends of the earth.

ᵃ7 Or *Chaldeans*

¹²Its leaves were beautiful, its fruit abundant, and on it was food for all. Under it the beasts of the field found shelter, and the birds of the air lived in its branches; from it every creature was fed.

¹³"In the visions I saw while lying in my bed, I looked, and there before me was a messenger,ᵇ a holy one, coming down from heaven. ¹⁴He called in a loud voice: 'Cut down the tree and trim off its branches; strip off its leaves and scatter its fruit. Let the animals flee from under it and the birds from its branches. ¹⁵But let the stump and its roots, bound with iron and bronze, remain in the ground, in the grass of the field.

" 'Let him be drenched with the dew of heaven, and let him live with the animals among the plants of the earth. ¹⁶Let his mind be changed from that of a man and let him be given the mind of an animal, till seven timesᶜ pass by for him.

¹⁷" 'The decision is announced by messengers, the holy ones declare the verdict, so that the living may know that the Most High is sovereign over the kingdoms of men and gives them to anyone he wishes and sets over them the lowliest of men.'

¹⁸"This is the dream that I, King Nebuchadnezzar, had. Now, Belteshazzar, tell me what it means, for none of the wise men in my kingdom can interpret it for me. But you can, because the spirit of the holy gods is in you."

■ Daniel Interprets the Dream

¹⁹Then Daniel (also called Belteshazzar) was greatly perplexed for a time, and his thoughts terrified him. So the king said, "Belteshazzar, do not let the dream or its meaning alarm you."

Belteshazzar answered, "My lord, if only the dream applied to your enemies and its meaning to your adversaries! ²⁰The tree you saw, which grew large and strong, with its top touching the sky, visible to the whole earth, ²¹with beautiful leaves and abundant fruit, providing food for all, giving shelter to the beasts of the field, and having nesting places in its branches for the birds of the air—²²you, O king, are that tree! You have become great and strong; your greatness has grown until it reaches the sky, and your dominion extends to distant parts of the earth.

²³"You, O king, saw a messenger, a holy one, coming down from heaven and saying, 'Cut down the tree and destroy it, but leave the stump, bound with iron and bronze, in the grass of the field, while its roots remain in the ground. Let him be drenched with the dew of heaven; let him live like the wild animals, until seven times pass by for him.'

²⁴"This is the interpretation, O king, and this is the decree the Most High has issued against my lord the king: ²⁵You will be driven away from people and will live with the wild animals; you will eat grass like cattle and be drenched with the dew of heaven. Seven times will pass by for you until you acknowledge that the Most High is sovereign over the kingdoms of men and gives them to anyone he wishes. ²⁶The command to leave the stump of the tree with its roots means that your kingdom will be restored to you when you acknowledge that Heaven rules. ²⁷Therefore, O king, be pleased to accept my advice: Renounce your sins by doing what is right, and your wickedness by being kind to the oppressed. It may be that then your prosperity will continue."

■ The Dream Is Fulfilled

²⁸All this happened to King Nebuchadnezzar. ²⁹Twelve months later, as the king was walking on the roof of the royal palace of Babylon, ³⁰he said, "Is not this the great Babylon I have built as the royal residence, by my mighty power and for the glory of my majesty?"

³¹The words were still on his lips when a voice came from heaven, "This is what is decreed for you, King Nebuchadnezzar: Your royal authority has been taken from you. ³²You will be driven away from people and will live with the wild animals; you will eat grass like cattle. Seven times will pass by for you until you acknowledge that the Most High is sovereign over the kingdoms of men and gives them to anyone he wishes."

³³Immediately what had been said about Nebuchadnezzar was fulfilled. He was driven away from people and ate grass like cattle. His body was drenched with the dew of heaven until his hair grew like the feathers of an eagle and his nails like the claws of a bird.

³⁴At the end of that time, I, Nebuchadnezzar, raised my eyes towards heaven, and my sanity was restored. Then I praised the Most High; I honoured and glorified him who lives for ever.

His dominion is an eternal dominion;
   his kingdom endures from generation
      to generation.
³⁵All the peoples of the earth
   are regarded as nothing.
He does as he pleases
   with the powers of heaven
   and the peoples of the earth.
No-one can hold back his hand
   or say to him: "What have you done?"

³⁶At the same time that my sanity was restored, my honour and splendour were returned to me for the glory of my kingdom. My advisers and nobles sought me out, and I was restored to my throne and became even greater than before. ³⁷Now I, Nebuchadnezzar, praise and exalt and glorify the King of heaven, because everything he does is right and all his ways are just. And those who walk in pride he is able to humble.

ᵇ13 Or watchman; also in verses 17 and 23   ᶜ16 Or years; also in verses 23, 25 and 32

■ The Writing on the Wall

5 King Belshazzar gave a great banquet for a thousand of his nobles and drank wine with them. ²While Belshazzar was drinking his wine, he gave orders to bring in the gold and silver goblets that Nebuchadnezzar his father*a* had taken from the temple in Jerusalem, so that the king and his nobles, his wives and his concubines might drink from them. ³So they brought in the gold goblets that had been taken from the temple of God in Jerusalem, and the king and his nobles, his wives and his concubines drank from them. ⁴As they drank the wine, they praised the gods of gold and silver, of bronze, iron, wood and stone.

5:1 ■ THE THRONE ROOM
Modern archaeological excavation has found, in the Babylonian palace, a large room (about 150 feet by 50 feet — almost one quarter the size of a football field) that has become known as the Throne Room. One wall had a design of blue enamelled bricks, but the other three were covered in white plaster (see verse 5).

---

⁵Suddenly the fingers of a human hand appeared and wrote on the plaster of the wall, near the lampstand in the royal palace. The king watched the hand as it wrote. ⁶His face turned pale and he was so frightened that his knees knocked together and his legs gave way.

⁷The king called out for the enchanters, astrologers*b* and diviners to be brought and said to these wise men of Babylon, "Whoever reads this writing and tells me what it means will be clothed in purple and have a gold chain placed around his neck, and he will be made the third highest ruler in the kingdom."

⁸Then all the king's wise men came in, but they could not read the writing or tell the king what it meant. ⁹So King Belshazzar became even more terrified and his face grew more pale. His nobles were baffled.

¹⁰The queen,*c* hearing the voices of the king and his nobles, came into the banquet hall. "O king, live for ever!" she said. "Don't be alarmed! Don't look so pale! ¹¹There is a man in your kingdom who has the spirit of the holy gods in him. In the time of your father he was found to have insight and intelligence and wisdom like that of the gods. King Nebuchadnezzar your father — your father the king, I say — appointed him chief of the magicians, enchanters, astrologers and diviners. ¹²This man Daniel, whom the king called Belteshazzar, was found to have a keen mind and knowledge and understanding, and also the ability to interpret dreams, explain riddles and solve difficult problems. Call for Daniel, and he will tell you what the writing means."

¹³So Daniel was brought before the king, and the king said to him, "Are you Daniel, one of the exiles my father the king brought from Judah? ¹⁴I have heard that the spirit of the gods is in you and that you have insight, intelligence and outstanding wisdom. ¹⁵The wise men and enchanters were brought before me to read this writing and tell me what it means, but they could not explain it. ¹⁶Now I have heard that you are able to give interpretations and to solve difficult problems. If you can read this writing and tell me what it means, you will be clothed in purple and have a gold chain placed around your neck, and you will be made the third highest ruler in the kingdom."

¹⁷Then Daniel answered the king, "You may keep your gifts for yourself and give your rewards to someone else. Nevertheless, I will read the writing for the king and tell him what it means.

¹⁸"O king, the Most High God gave your father Nebuchadnezzar sovereignty and greatness and glory and splendour. ¹⁹Because of the high position he gave him, all the peoples and nations and men of every language dreaded and feared him. Those the king wanted to put to death, he put to death; those he wanted to spare, he spared; those he wanted to promote, he promoted; and those he wanted to humble, he humbled. ²⁰But when his heart became arrogant and hardened with pride, he was deposed from his royal throne and stripped of his glory. ²¹He was driven away from people and given the mind of an animal; he lived with the wild donkeys and ate grass like cattle; and his body was drenched with the dew of heaven, until he acknowledged that the Most High God is sovereign over the kingdoms of men and sets over them anyone he wishes.

²²"But you his son,*d* O Belshazzar, have not humbled yourself, though you knew all this. ²³Instead, you have set yourself up against the Lord of heaven. You had the goblets from his temple brought to you, and you and your nobles, your wives and your concubines drank wine from them. You praised the gods of silver and gold, of bronze, iron, wood and stone, which cannot see or hear or understand. But you did not honour the God who holds in his hand your life and all your ways. ²⁴Therefore he sent the hand that wrote the inscription.

²⁵"This is the inscription that was written:

MENE, MENE, TEKEL, PARSIN*e*

²⁶"This is what these words mean:

*Mene*ᶠ: God has numbered the days of your reign and brought it to an end.
²⁷*Tekel*ᵍ: You have been weighed on the scales and found wanting.
²⁸*Peres*ʰ: Your kingdom is divided and given to the Medes and Persians."

²⁹Then at Belshazzar's command, Daniel was clothed in purple, a gold chain was placed around his neck, and he was proclaimed the third highest ruler in the kingdom.

³⁰That very night Belshazzar, king of the Babylonians,*i* was slain, ³¹and Darius the Mede took over the kingdom, at the age of sixty-two.

---

a 2 Or *ancestor*; or *predecessor*; also in verses 11, 13 and 18 *b* 7 Or *Chaldeans*; also in verse 11 *c* 10 Or *queen mother* *d* 22 Or *descendant*; or *successor* *e* 25 Aramaic *UPARSIN* (that is, *AND PARSIN*) *f* 26 *Mene* can mean *numbered* or *mina* (a unit of money). *g* 27 *Tekel* can mean *weighed* or *shekel*. *b* 28 *Peres* (the singular of *Parsin*) can mean *divided* or *Persia* or *a half mina* or *a half shekel*. *i* 30 Or *Chaldeans*

■ Daniel in the Den of Lions

6 It pleased Darius to appoint 120 satraps to rule throughout the kingdom, ²with three administrators over them, one of whom was Daniel. The satraps were made accountable to them so that the king might not suffer loss. ³Now Daniel so distinguished himself among the administrators and the satraps by his exceptional qualities that the king planned to set him over the whole kingdom. ⁴At this, the administrators and the satraps tried to find grounds for charges against Daniel in his conduct of government affairs, but they were unable to do so. They could find no corruption in him, because he was trustworthy and neither corrupt nor negligent. ⁵Finally these men said, "We will never find any basis for charges against this man Daniel unless it has something to do with the law of his God."

5:30 ■ SNEAK ATTACK
Two empires, the Medes and the Persians, joined forces to overthrow Babylon, the dominant power of the day. Invading armies diverted the river Euphrates to another channel, then marched along the dry river bed underneath the city walls. The site of ancient Babylon lies about fifty miles from modern-day Baghdad, Iraq.

⁶So the administrators and the satraps went as a group to the king and said: "O King Darius, live for ever! ⁷The royal administrators, prefects, satraps, advisers and governors have all agreed that the king should issue an edict and enforce the decree that anyone who prays to any god or man during the next thirty days, except to you, O king, shall be thrown into the lions' den. ⁸Now, O king, issue the decree and put it in writing so that it cannot be altered—in accordance with the laws of the Medes and Persians, which cannot be repealed." ⁹So King Darius put the decree in writing.

¹⁰Now when Daniel learned that the decree had been published, he went home to his upstairs room where the windows opened towards Jerusalem. Three times a day he got down on his knees and prayed, giving thanks to his God, just as he had done before. ¹¹Then these men went as a group and found Daniel praying and asking God for help. ¹²So they went to the king and spoke to him about his royal decree: "Did you not publish a decree that during the next thirty days anyone who prays to any god or man except to you, O king, would be thrown into the lions' den?"

The king answered, "The decree stands—in accordance with the laws of the Medes and Persians, which cannot be repealed."

¹³Then they said to the king, "Daniel, who is one of the exiles from Judah, pays no attention to you, O king, or to the decree you put in writing. He still prays three times a day." ¹⁴When the king heard this, he was greatly distressed; he was determined to rescue Daniel and made every effort until sundown to save him.

¹⁵Then the men went as a group to the king and said to him, "Remember, O king, that according to the law of the Medes and Persians no decree or edict that the king issues can be changed."

6:10 ■ A JEWISH ORIENTATION
Daniel had lost much of his Jewish heritage— even his name had been changed to a Babylonian one (1:7). Certainly he could not worship God in the way God's law commanded, through sacrifices at the temple in Jerusalem. He did, however, point himself towards the promised land three times a day in prayer. Not even the threat of death could make him vary this practice. By this time Daniel had been in Babylon over 60 years; he was probably in his 80s.

¹⁶So the king gave the order, and they brought Daniel and threw him into the lions' den. The king said to Daniel, "May your God, whom you serve continually, rescue you!"

¹⁷A stone was brought and placed over the mouth of the den, and the king sealed it with his own signet ring and with the rings of his nobles, so that Daniel's situation might not be changed. ¹⁸Then the king returned to his palace and spent the night without eating and without any entertainment being brought to him. And he could not sleep.

¹⁹At the first light of dawn, the king got up and hurried to the lions' den. ²⁰When he came near the den, he called to Daniel in an anguished voice, "Daniel, servant of the living God, has your God, whom you serve continually, been able to rescue you from the lions?"

²¹Daniel answered, "O king, live for ever! ²²My God sent his angel, and he shut the mouths of the lions. They have not hurt me, because I was found innocent in his sight. Nor have I ever done any wrong before you, O king."

²³The king was overjoyed and gave orders to lift Daniel out of the den. And when Daniel was lifted from the den, no wound was found on him, because he had trusted in his God.

²⁴At the king's command, the men who had falsely accused Daniel were brought in and thrown into the lions' den, along with their wives and children. And before they reached the floor of the den, the lions overpowered them and crushed all their bones.

²⁵Then King Darius wrote to all the peoples, nations and men of every language throughout the land:

"May you prosper greatly!

²⁶"I issue a decree that in every part of my kingdom people must fear and reverence the God of Daniel.

"For he is the living God
        and he endures for ever;
his kingdom will not be destroyed,
        his dominion will never end.
²⁷He rescues and he saves;
        he performs signs and wonders
        in the heavens and on the earth.

He has rescued Daniel
from the power of the lions."

²⁸So Daniel prospered during the reign of Darius and the reign of Cyrus*ᵃ* the Persian.

■ Daniel's Dream of Four Beasts

7 In the first year of Belshazzar king of Babylon, Daniel had a dream, and visions passed through his mind as he was lying on his bed. He wrote down the substance of his dream.

²Daniel said: "In my vision at night I looked, and there before me were the four winds of heaven churning up the great sea. ³Four great beasts, each different from the others, came up out of the sea.

⁴"The first was like a lion, and it had the wings of an eagle. I watched until its wings were torn off and it was lifted from the ground so that it stood on two feet like a man, and the heart of a man was given to it.

⁵"And there before me was a second beast, which looked like a bear. It was raised up on one of its sides, and it had three ribs in its mouth between its teeth. It was told, 'Get up and eat your fill of flesh!'

⁶"After that, I looked, and there before me was another beast, one that looked like a leopard. And on its back it had four wings like those of a bird. This beast had four heads, and it was given authority to rule.

⁷"After that, in my vision at night I looked, and there before me was a fourth beast—terrifying and

frightening and very powerful. It had large iron teeth; it crushed and devoured its victims and trampled underfoot whatever was left. It was different from all the former beasts, and it had ten horns.

⁸"While I was thinking about the horns, there before me was another horn, a little one, which came up among them; and three of the first horns were uprooted before it. This horn had eyes like the eyes of a man and a mouth that spoke boastfully.

⁹"As I looked,

"thrones were set in place,
and the Ancient of Days took his seat.
His clothing was as white as snow;
the hair of his head was white like wool.
His throne was flaming with fire,
and its wheels were all ablaze.
¹⁰A river of fire was flowing,
coming out from before him.
Thousands upon thousands attended him;
ten thousand times ten thousand stood
before him.
The court was seated,
and the books were opened.

¹¹"Then I continued to watch because of the boastful words the horn was speaking. I kept looking until the beast was slain and its body destroyed and thrown into the blazing fire. ¹²(The other beasts had been stripped of their authority, but were allowed to live for a period of time.)

¹³"In my vision at night I looked, and there before

■ SYMBOLS OF POWER
THE BIGGER THE TYRANT, THE MORE STATUES LITTER THE LANDSCAPE

INSIGHT

"IN MY VISION AT NIGHT I LOOKED, AND THERE BEFORE ME WAS A FOURTH BEAST—TERRIFYING AND FRIGHTENING AND VERY POWERFUL. IT HAD LARGE IRON TEETH; IT CRUSHED AND DEVOURED ITS VICTIMS." ■ 7:7

It's no surprise that Nebuchadnezzar erected a gold image for people to worship (chapter 3). Kings and rulers love to display statues or gigantic photos as symbols of their power. The

bigger the tyrants, the more of their statues litter the landscape.

It seems reasonable, then, that Daniel's visions depict political realms through statues and symbolic animals. But since each of the visions uses a different set of symbols, you can easily lose track of what the symbols stand for. This chart may help you to coordinate Daniel's view of four great empires —and the almighty God who overwhelms their power in the end:

	Babylon	Medo-Persia	Greece	Rome	Kingdom of God
Chapter 2	gold	silver	bronze	iron	supernatural rock
Chapter 7	lion	bear	leopard	beast with horns	Ancient of Days, Son of Man
Chapter 8	—	ram	goat	—	—
Chapter 11	—	—	king of North	—	—

□ LIFE QUESTIONS:
What images "litter the landscape" in our time?

Are they symbols of power? If so, how does that power affect you?

---

*ᵃ*28 Or Darius, that is, the reign of Cyrus

me was one like a son of man, coming with the clouds of heaven. He approached the Ancient of Days and was led into his presence. [14]He was given authority, glory and sovereign power; all peoples, nations and men of every language worshipped him. His dominion is an everlasting dominion that will not pass away, and his kingdom is one that will never be destroyed.

7:13 ■ A SON OF MAN

God's power is given to one "like a son of man" rather than to those like beasts. The contrast suggests God's kingdom has power that is humane, not savage or bestial. Jesus adopted this term for himself.

■ The Interpretation of the Dream

[15]"I, Daniel, was troubled in spirit, and the visions that passed through my mind disturbed me. [16]I approached one of those standing there and asked him the true meaning of all this.

"So he told me and gave me the interpretation of these things: [17]'The four great beasts are four kingdoms that will rise from the earth. [18]But the saints of the Most High will receive the kingdom and will possess it for ever—yes, for ever and ever.'

[19]"Then I wanted to know the true meaning of the fourth beast, which was different from all the others and most terrifying, with its iron teeth and bronze claws—the beast that crushed and devoured its victims and trampled underfoot whatever was left. [20]I also wanted to know about the ten horns on its head and about the other horn that came up, before which three of them fell—the horn that looked more imposing than the others and that had eyes and a mouth that spoke boastfully. [21]As I watched, this horn was waging war against the saints and defeating them, [22]until the Ancient of Days came and pronounced judgment in favour of the saints of the Most High, and the time came when they possessed the kingdom.

[23]"He gave me this explanation: 'The fourth beast is a fourth kingdom that will appear on earth. It will be different from all the other kingdoms and will devour the whole earth, trampling it down and crushing it. [24]The ten horns are ten kings who will come from this kingdom. After them another king will arise, different from the earlier ones; he will subdue three kings. [25]He will speak against the Most High and oppress his saints and try to change the set times and the laws. The saints will be handed over to him for a time, times and half a time.[a]

[26]"But the court will sit, and his power will be taken away and completely destroyed for ever. [27]Then the sovereignty, power and greatness of the kingdoms under the whole heaven will be handed over to the saints, the people of the Most High. His kingdom will be an everlasting kingdom, and all rulers will worship and obey him.'

[28]"This is the end of the matter. I, Daniel, was deeply troubled by my thoughts, and my face turned pale, but I kept the matter to myself."

■ Daniel's Vision of a Ram and a Goat

8 In the third year of King Belshazzar's reign, I, Daniel, had a vision, after the one that had already appeared to me. [2]In my vision I saw myself in the citadel of Susa in the province of Elam; in the vision I was beside the Ulai Canal. [3]I looked up, and there before me was a ram with two horns, standing beside the canal, and the horns were long. One of the horns was longer than the other but grew up later. [4]I watched the ram as he charged towards the west and the north and the south. No animal could stand against him, and none could rescue from his power. He did as he pleased and became great.

[5]As I was thinking about this, suddenly a goat with a prominent horn between his eyes came from the west, crossing the whole earth without touching the ground. [6]He came towards the two-horned ram I had seen standing beside the canal and charged at him in great rage. [7]I saw him attack the ram furiously, striking the ram and shattering his two horns. The ram was powerless to stand against him; the goat knocked him to the ground and trampled on him, and none could rescue the ram from his power. [8]The goat became very great, but at the height of his power his large horn was broken off, and in its place four prominent horns grew up towards the four winds of heaven.

[9]Out of one of them came another horn, which started small but grew in power to the south and to the east and towards the Beautiful Land. [10]It grew until it reached the host of the heavens, and it threw some of the starry host down to the earth and trampled on them. [11]It set itself up to be as great as the Prince of the host; it took away the daily sacrifice from him, and the place of his sanctuary was brought low. [12]Because of rebellion, the host ⌊of the saints⌋[a] and the daily sacrifice were given over to it. It prospered in everything it did, and truth was thrown to the ground.

[13]Then I heard a holy one speaking, and another holy one said to him, "How long will it take for the vision to be fulfilled—the vision concerning the daily sacrifice, the rebellion that causes desolation, and the surrender of the sanctuary and of the host that will be trampled underfoot?"

[14]He said to me, "It will take 2,300 evenings and mornings; then the sanctuary will be reconsecrated."

■ The Interpretation of the Vision

[15]While I, Daniel, was watching the vision and trying to understand it, there before me stood one who looked like a man. [16]And I heard a man's voice from the Ulai calling, "Gabriel, tell this man the meaning of the vision."

[17]As he came near the place where I was standing, I was terrified and fell prostrate. "Son of man," he said to me, "understand that the vision concerns the time of the end."

[18]While he was speaking to me, I was in a deep sleep, with my face to the ground. Then he touched me and raised me to my feet. [19]He said: "I am going to tell you what will happen later in the time of wrath, because the vision concerns the appointed time of the end.[b] [20]The

---

a 25 Or for a year, two years and half a year   *a 12 Or rebellion, the armies*   *b 19 Or because the end will be at the appointed time* two-horned ram that you saw represents the kings of Media and Persia. ²¹The shaggy goat is the king of Greece, and the large horn between his eyes is the first king. ²²The four horns that replaced the one that was broken off represent four kingdoms that will emerge from his nation but will not have the same power.

²³"In the latter part of their reign, when rebels have become completely wicked, a stern-faced king, a master of intrigue, will arise. ²⁴He will become very strong, but not by his own power. He will cause astounding devastation and will succeed in whatever he does. He will destroy the mighty men and the holy people. ²⁵He will cause deceit to prosper, and he will consider himself superior. When they feel secure, he will destroy many and take his stand against the Prince of princes. Yet he will be destroyed, but not by human power.

²⁶"The vision of the evenings and mornings that has been given you is true, but seal up the vision, for it concerns the distant future."

8:26 ■ LONG DELAY

Twice (here and 12:4) the angel tells Daniel to seal up the vision because it concerns the distant future. Pointedly, in Revelation, the last book of the Bible, an angel tells John, "Do not seal up the words of the prophecy of this book, because the time is near" (Revelation 22:10). Daniel and Revelation, written hundreds of years apart, arrive at the same conclusion: no matter how bad things look, God is in control of history and will one day reclaim the earth.

²⁷I, Daniel, was exhausted and lay ill for several days. Then I got up and went about the king's business. I was appalled by the vision; it was beyond understanding.

■ Daniel's Prayer

9 In the first year of Darius son of Xerxes[a] (a Mede by descent), who was made ruler over the Babylonian[b] kingdom — ²in the first year of his reign, I, Daniel, understood from the Scriptures, according to the word of the LORD given to Jeremiah the prophet, that the desolation of Jerusalem would last seventy years. ³So I turned to the Lord God and pleaded with him in prayer and petition, in fasting, and in sackcloth and ashes.

9:2 ■ FAVOURED BY GOD AND KINGS

This chapter gives a rare glimpse of one prophet, Daniel, being comforted by the words of another, Jeremiah. Daniel's response shows that, despite his government service to two enemy empires (Babylon and Persia), loyalty to his homeland never faltered. The remarkable prayer that follows expresses well his intimate relationship with God.

⁴I prayed to the LORD my God and confessed:

"O Lord, the great and awesome God, who keeps his covenant of love with all who love him and obey his commands, ⁵we have sinned and done wrong. We have been wicked and have rebelled; we have turned away from your commands and laws. ⁶We have not listened to your servants the prophets, who spoke in your name to our kings, our princes and our fathers, and to all the people of the land.

⁷"Lord, you are righteous, but this day we are covered with shame — the men of Judah and people of Jerusalem and all Israel, both near and far, in all the countries where you have scattered us because of our unfaithfulness to you. ⁸O LORD, we and our kings, our princes and our fathers are covered with shame because we have sinned against you. ⁹The Lord our God is merciful and forgiving, even though we have rebelled against him; ¹⁰we have not obeyed the LORD our God or kept the laws he gave us through his servants the prophets. ¹¹All Israel has transgressed your law and turned away, refusing to obey you.

"Therefore the curses and sworn judgments written in the Law of Moses, the servant of God, have been poured out on us, because we have sinned against you. ¹²You have fulfilled the words spoken against us and against our rulers by bringing upon us great disaster. Under the whole heaven nothing has ever been done like what has been done to Jerusalem. ¹³Just as it is written in the Law of Moses, all this disaster has come upon us, yet we have not sought the favour of the LORD our God by turning from our sins and giving attention to your truth. ¹⁴The LORD did not hesitate to bring the disaster upon us, for the LORD our God is righteous in everything he does; yet we have not obeyed him.

¹⁵"Now, O Lord our God, who brought your people out of Egypt with a mighty hand and who made for yourself a name that endures to this day, we have sinned, we have done wrong. ¹⁶O Lord, in keeping with all your righteous acts, turn away your anger and your wrath from Jerusalem, your city, your holy hill. Our sins and the iniquities of our fathers have made Jerusalem and your people an object of scorn to all those around us.

¹⁷"Now, our God, hear the prayers and petitions of your servant. For your sake, O Lord, look with favour on your desolate sanctuary. ¹⁸Give ear, O God, and hear; open your eyes and see the desolation of the city that bears your Name. We do not make requests of you because we are righteous, but because of your great mercy. ¹⁹O Lord, listen! O Lord, forgive! O Lord, hear and act! For your sake, O my God, do not delay, because your city and your people bear your Name."

■ The Seventy "Sevens"

²⁰While I was speaking and praying, confessing my sin and the sin of my people Israel and making my request to the LORD my God for his holy hill — ²¹while I was still in prayer, Gabriel, the man I had

a 1 Hebrew Ahasuerus   b 1 Or Chaldean

seen in the earlier vision, came to me in swift flight about the time of the evening sacrifice. [22]He instructed me and said to me, "Daniel, I have now come to give you insight and understanding. [23]As soon as you began to pray, an answer was given, which I have come to tell you, for you are highly esteemed. Therefore, consider the message and understand the vision:

[24]"Seventy 'sevens'[c] are decreed for your people and your holy city to finish[d] transgression, to put an end to sin, to atone for wickedness, to bring in everlasting righteousness, to seal up vision and prophecy and to anoint the most holy.[e]

[25]"Know and understand this: From the issuing of the decree[f] to restore and rebuild Jerusalem until the Anointed One,[g] the ruler, comes, there will be seven 'sevens', and sixty-two 'sevens'. It will be rebuilt with streets and a trench, but in times of trouble. [26]After the sixty-two 'sevens', the Anointed One will be cut off and will have nothing.[b] The people of the ruler who will come will destroy the city and the sanctuary. The end will come like a flood: War will continue until the end, and desolations have been decreed. [27]He will confirm a covenant with many for one 'seven'.[i] In the middle of the 'seven'[i] he will put an end to sacrifice and offering. And on a wing ₍of the temple₎ he will set up an abomination that causes desolation, until the end that is decreed is poured out on him.[j]"[k]

■ Daniel's Vision of a Man

10 In the third year of Cyrus king of Persia, a revelation was given to Daniel (who was called Belteshazzar). Its message was true and it concerned a great war.[a] The understanding of the message came to him in a vision.

[2]At that time I, Daniel, mourned for three weeks. [3]I ate no choice food; no meat or wine touched my lips; and I used no lotions at all until the three weeks were over.

[4]On the twenty-fourth day of the first month, as I was standing on the bank of the great river, the Tigris, [5]I looked up and there before me was a man dressed in linen, with a belt of the finest gold round his waist. [6]His body was like chrysolite, his face like lightning, his eyes like flaming torches, his arms and legs like the gleam of burnished bronze, and his voice like the sound of a multitude.

[7]I, Daniel, was the only one who saw the vision; the men with me did not see it, but such terror overwhelmed them that they fled and hid themselves. [8]So I was left alone, gazing at this great vision; I had no strength left, my face turned deathly pale and I was helpless. [9]Then I heard him speaking, and as I listened to him, I fell into a deep sleep, my face to the ground.

[10]A hand touched me and set me trembling on my hands and knees. [11]He said, "Daniel, you who are highly esteemed, consider carefully the words I am about to speak to you, and stand up, for I have now been sent to you." And when he said this to me, I stood up trembling.

[12]Then he continued, "Do not be afraid, Daniel.

Since the first day that you set your mind to gain understanding and to humble yourself before your God, your words were heard, and I have come in response to them. [13]But the prince of the Persian kingdom resisted me twenty-one days. Then Michael, one of the chief princes, came to help me, because I was detained there with the king of Persia. [14]Now I have come to explain to you what will happen to your people in the future, for the vision concerns a time yet to come."

[15]While he was saying this to me, I bowed with my face towards the ground and was speechless. [16]Then one who looked like a man[b] touched my lips, and I opened my mouth and began to speak. I said to the one standing before me, "I am overcome with anguish because of the vision, my lord, and I am helpless. [17]How can I, your servant, talk with you, my lord? My strength is gone and I can hardly breathe."

[18]Again the one who looked like a man touched me and gave me strength. [19]"Do not be afraid, O man highly esteemed," he said. "Peace! Be strong now; be strong."

When he spoke to me, I was strengthened and said, "Speak, my lord, since you have given me strength."

[20]So he said, "Do you know why I have come to you? Soon I will return to fight against the prince of Persia, and when I go, the prince of Greece will come; [21]but first I will tell you what is written in the Book of Truth. (No-one supports me against them

11 except Michael, your prince. [1]And in the first year of Darius the Mede, I took my stand to support and protect him.)

> **10:20 ■ SLOW TO ANSWER PRAYER**
> These comments come from what seems to be an angelic messenger. They hint at heavenly warfare human beings know little about. When prayers go unanswered for long periods, more may be involved than we ever dream.

■ The Kings of the South and the North

[2]"Now then, I tell you the truth: Three more kings will appear in Persia, and then a fourth, who will be far richer than all the others. When he has gained power by his wealth, he will stir up everyone against the kingdom of Greece. [3]Then a mighty king will appear, who will rule with great power and do as he pleases. [4]After he has appeared, his empire will be broken up and parcelled out towards the four winds of heaven. It will not go to his descendants, nor will it have the power he exercised, because his empire will be uprooted and given to others.

[5]"The king of the South will become strong, but one of his commanders will become even stronger than he and will rule his own kingdom with great power. [6]After some years, they will become allies. The daughter of the king of the South will go to the king of the North to make an alliance, but she will not retain her power, and he and his power[a] will

c 24 Or 'weeks'; also in verses 25 and 26   d 24 Or restrain   e 24 Or Most Holy Place; or most holy One   f 25 Or word   g 25 Or an anointed one; also in verse 26   b 26 Or off and will have no-one; or off, but not for himself   i 27 Or 'week'   j 27 Or it   k 27 Or And one who causes desolation will come upon the pinnacle of the abominable ₍temple₎, until the end that is decreed is poured out on the desolated ₍city₎   a 1 Or true and burdensome   b 16 Most manuscripts of the Masoretic Text; one manuscript of the Masoretic Text, Dead Sea Scrolls and Septuagint Then something that looked like a man's hand   a 6 Or offspring not last. In those days she will be handed over, together with her royal escort and her father[b] and the one who supported her.

7"One from her family line will arise to take her place. He will attack the forces of the king of the North and enter his fortress; he will fight against them and be victorious. 8He will also seize their gods, their metal images and their valuable articles of silver and gold and carry them off to Egypt. For some years he will leave the king of the North alone. 9Then the king of the North will invade the realm of the king of the South but will retreat to his own country. 10His sons will prepare for war and assemble a great army, which will sweep on like an irresistible flood and carry the battle as far as his fortress.

11"Then the king of the South will march out in a rage and fight against the king of the North, who will raise a large army, but it will be defeated. 12When the army is carried off, the king of the South will be filled with pride and will slaughter many thousands, yet he will not remain triumphant. 13For the king of the North will muster another army, larger than the first; and after several years, he will advance with a huge army fully equipped.

14"In those times many will rise against the king of the South. The violent men among your own people will rebel in fulfilment of the vision, but without success. 15Then the king of the North will come and build up siege ramps and will capture a fortified city. The forces of the South will be powerless to resist; even their best troops will not have the strength to stand. 16The invader will do as he pleases; no-one will be able to stand against him. He will establish himself in the Beautiful Land and will have the power to destroy it. 17He will determine to come with the might of his entire kingdom and will make an alliance with the king of the South. And he will give him a daughter in marriage in order to overthrow the kingdom, but his plans[c] will not succeed or help him. 18Then he will turn his attention to the coastlands and will take many of them, but a commander will put an end to his insolence and will turn his insolence back upon him. 19After this, he will turn back towards the fortresses of his own country but will stumble and fall, to be seen no more.

20"His successor will send out a tax collector to maintain the royal splendour. In a few years, however, he will be destroyed, yet not in anger or in battle.

21"He will be succeeded by a contemptible person who has not been given the honour of royalty. He will invade the kingdom when its people feel secure, and he will seize it through intrigue. 22Then an overwhelming army will be swept away before him; both it and a prince of the covenant will be destroyed. 23After coming to an agreement with him, he will act deceitfully, and with only a few people he will rise to power. 24When the richest provinces feel secure, he will invade them and will achieve what neither his fathers nor his forefathers did. He will distribute plunder, loot and wealth among his followers. He will plot the overthrow of fortresses—but only for a time.

25"With a large army he will stir up his strength and courage against the king of the South. The king of the South will wage war with a large and very powerful army, but he will not be able to stand because of the plots devised against him. 26Those who eat from the king's provisions will try to destroy him; his army will be swept away, and many will fall in battle. 27The two kings, with their hearts bent on evil, will sit at the same table and lie to each other, but to no avail, because an end will still come at the appointed time. 28The king of the North will return to his own country with great wealth, but his heart will be set against the holy covenant. He will take action against it and then return to his own country.

29"At the appointed time he will invade the South again, but this time the outcome will be different from what it was before. 30Ships of the western coastlands[d] will oppose him, and he will lose heart. Then he will turn back and vent his fury against the holy covenant. He will return and show favour to those who forsake the holy covenant.

31"His armed forces will rise up to desecrate the temple fortress and will abolish the daily sacrifice. Then they will set up the abomination that causes desolation. 32With flattery he will corrupt those who have violated the covenant, but the people who know their God will firmly resist him.

33"Those who are wise will instruct many, though for a time they will fall by the sword or be burned or captured or plundered. 34When they fall, they will receive a little help, and many who are not sincere will join them. 35Some of the wise will stumble, so that they may be refined, purified and made spotless until the time of the end, for it will still come at the appointed time.

■ The King Who Exalts Himself

36"The king will do as he pleases. He will exalt and magnify himself above every god and will say unheard-of things against the God of gods. He will be successful until the time of wrath is completed, for what has been determined must take place. 37He will show no regard for the gods of his fathers or for the one desired by women, nor will he regard any god, but will exalt himself above them all. 38Instead of them, he will honour a god of fortresses; a god unknown to his fathers he will honour with gold and silver, with precious stones and costly gifts. 39He will attack the mightiest fortresses with the help of a foreign god and will greatly honour those who acknowledge him. He will make them rulers over many people and will distribute the land at a price.[e]

40"At the time of the end the king of the South will engage him in battle, and the king of the North will storm out against him with chariots and cavalry and a great fleet of ships. He will invade many countries and sweep through them like a flood. 41He will also invade the Beautiful Land. Many countries will fall, but Edom, Moab and the leaders of Ammon will be delivered from his hand. 42He will extend his power over many countries; Egypt will not escape. 43He will gain control of the treasures of gold and silver and all the riches of Egypt, with the Libyans and Nubians in submission. 44But reports from the

b6 Or child (see Vulgate and Syriac)   c17 Or but she   d30 Hebrew of Kittim   e39 Or land for a reward

11:37 ■ EXALTED ABOVE THE GODS

The tyrant Antiochus IV, whom most commentators believe is described here, minted many coins showing his portrait. The early coins were merely stamped, "King Antiochus". But, as he grew more obsessed with his own importance, he added features to his portrait that made him look like the Greek gods Apollo or Zeus, and to his given name he appended the title "Epiphanes" — "God Manifest". Such behaviour earned him the nickname "Antiochus Epimanes" — "crazy Antiochus".

east and the north will alarm him, and he will set out in a great rage to destroy and annihilate many. ⁴⁵He will pitch his royal tents between the seas at *ᶠ* the beautiful holy mountain. Yet he will come to his end, and no-one will help him.

■ The End Times

12 "At that time Michael, the great prince who protects your people, will arise. There will be a time of distress such as has not happened from the beginning of nations until then. But at that time your people — everyone whose name is found written in the book — will be delivered. ²Multitudes who sleep in the dust of the earth will awake: some to everlasting life, others to shame and everlasting

■ IN THE HANDS OF TYRANTS
DANIEL'S VISIONS PORTRAY HISTORY AS ONE BESTIAL EMPIRE AFTER ANOTHER

INSIGHT

"THE KING WILL DO AS HE PLEASES. HE WILL EXALT AND MAGNIFY HIMSELF ABOVE EVERY GOD AND WILL SAY UNHEARD-OF THINGS AGAINST THE GOD OF GODS." ■ 11:36

Josef Stalin, head of the Soviet Union from 1924 to 1953, murdered millions. His supporters knew that the slightest slip would lead them to the executioner. Of 1,966 delegates to one Party Congress, Stalin had 1,108 — all Stalin supporters — arrested and killed. Of the 139 Central Committee members, 98 were shot.

In spite of this, the nation virtually worshipped Stalin. He had made himself a god. Every public park displayed his statue. Every newspaper published lavish tributes daily. For one of his birthdays, an entire museum in Moscow was stripped so it could be filled with his birthday presents. He was called Father of the Peoples, the Greatest Genius in History, the Shining Sun of Humanity, the Life-giving Force of Socialism.

He was not the first, nor the last, of his kind. Increasingly, it seems, totalitarian leaders promise everything — and demand everything. They brutally dispose of anyone who opposes them. Hitler, Stalin, Idi Amin, Chairman Mao, the Ayatollah Khomeini, Saddam Hussein . . . the list grows longer.

■ A SINGLE, CRUEL KING

Daniel's visions predicted such tyrants. History, in these visions, is one terrible empire after another. Each is stronger but more bestial than the last.

The focus narrows (in 8:23–25 and 11:21–45) to a single, cruel king. Most scholars agree the description matches Antiochus IV of Syria. An obscure tyrant who ruled a century and a half before Jesus, he was the Jews' worst enemy in history, until Hitler.

Antiochus, never totally victorious against arch-enemy Egypt, took out his frustrations on little Jerusalem. He determined to make that city Greek rather than Jewish by rooting out its religion. He sold the high priest's position to an opportunist and transformed the temple into an altar for the Greek god Zeus. This desecration sparked one of history's earliest guerrilla wars, the Maccabean revolt that began in 168 B.C. Antiochus conquered Jerusalem twice, slaughtering thousands. He outlawed Judaism and proclaimed himself to be God incarnate.

■ THE END OF THE TYRANT

And yet, for all his power and terror, Antiochus died raving from insanity, and his mark on history has virtually disappeared. Ironically, the religion he sought to destroy has endured and touched the whole world. This is just what you could expect from reading Daniel. Terrible rulers rise up one after another, but they disappear just as quickly. We can expect political terror. But we can count on God.

The New Testament suggests that Antiochus' brutal pattern will culminate someday in the anti-christ, an arrogant leader who will dominate the world and persecute God's people as never before. Many scholars believe that the last part of Daniel's final vision refers to this character. Yet despite the anti-christ's power, he too will fall in the end. God's justice will rule the earth. Those who believe in such an outcome have reason to be as brave as Daniel.

□ LIFE QUESTIONS:

How does Daniel's view of history affect your perspective on world politics? How should a Christian regard the human "powers-that-be"?

contempt. ³Those who are wise*a* will shine like the brightness of the heavens, and those who lead many to righteousness, like the stars for ever and ever. ⁴But you, Daniel, close up and seal the words of the scroll until the time of the end. Many will go here and there to increase knowledge."

12:2 ■ RESURRECTION

While eternal life is usually portrayed cloudily in the Old Testament, this verse clearly predicts that we will live for ever.

⁵Then I, Daniel, looked, and there before me stood two others, one on this bank of the river and one on the opposite bank. ⁶One of them said to the man clothed in linen, who was above the waters of the river, "How long will it be before these astonishing things are fulfilled?"

⁷The man clothed in linen, who was above the waters of the river, lifted his right hand and his left hand towards heaven, and I heard him swear by him who lives for ever, saying, "It will be for a time, times and half a time.*b* When the power of the holy people has been finally broken, all these things will be completed."

⁸I heard, but I did not understand. So I asked, "My lord, what will the outcome of all this be?"

⁹He replied, "Go your way, Daniel, because the words are closed up and sealed until the time of the end. ¹⁰Many will be purified, made spotless and refined, but the wicked will continue to be wicked. None of the wicked will understand, but those who are wise will understand.

¹¹"From the time that the daily sacrifice is abolished and the abomination that causes desolation is set up, there will be 1,290 days. ¹²Blessed is the one who waits for and reaches the end of the 1,335 days.

¹³"As for you, go your way till the end. You will rest, and then at the end of the days you will rise to receive your allotted inheritance."

---

a 3 Or *who impart wisdom*   *b 7* Or *a year, two years and half a year*

HOSEA

INTRODUCTION

■ TEARING GOD'S HEART
WHY WOULD HE LOVE SUCH A WOMAN?

"SHE DECKED HERSELF WITH RINGS AND JEWELLERY, AND WENT AFTER HER LOVERS,
BUT ME SHE FORGOT," DECLARES THE LORD. ■ 2:13

Hosea begins with a love story – a painful,
personal love story, the prophet's very own.
Hosea had married a woman who acted like a
prostitute. Yet the more she hurt him, the more
Hosea loved her. He gave her everything a good
wife deserved: his love, his home, his name, his
reputation. She responded by sleeping around
with other men. He warned her, he pleaded with
her, he punished her. She humiliated him until he
wanted to cry, yet still he clung to her.

Why did Hosea begin with his personal
life? Because God had expressly told him to
relate it to another, more tragic love story: the
painful love of God for his people. God could
have simply declared, "Israel is like a wife to
me – an adulterous wife". Instead, he used
Hosea to act out the treachery in real life – and
to show in living colour God's fury, his jealousy,
and above all else, his love for his people.

■ WINDING DOWN TO A BITTER END
Virtually every chapter of Hosea talks about the
"prostitution" or "adultery" of God's people (1:2;
2:2,4; 3:1; 4:2,10–15,18; 5:3–4; 6:10; 7:4; 8:9;
9:1). Underlying some hard words is a remarkably
tender revelation: God doesn't want to be only
"master" to his people. He wants to be a husband,
giving all of himself in intimate love.

Hosea spoke and acted these messages
to the northern part of God's divided country –
Israel or "Ephraim", as Hosea sometimes called
it. King Jeroboam II's reign was a time of
prosperity; the prophet Amos blasted the rich for

their greedy injustices towards the poor. But
soon after Jeroboam's death the national fabric
began to unravel. In just over 20 years six kings
took the throne – four of them by murdering the
previous king. Hosea probably lived to see the
massive Assyrian armies storm the capital and
deport all the Israelite citizens to other lands.
God's "wife" was carried off, just as he had
warned.

■ GOD IS A LOVER
When most people must have been preoccupied
with politics and military matters, Hosea kept his
message aimed at idol worship, which he referred
to as adultery. He saw that as the root of Israel's
problems.

Israel tended to mix religions freely – to
think that everybody's religion had a little truth in
it, and the more religion you got, the better off
you would be. Many prophets attacked Israel's
idol worship. Hosea shows that God's concern
about idolatry is no fussy, religious matter. It is
terribly personal. God, the lover, will not share
his bride with anyone else.

God's anger and jealousy, expressed so
often throughout the Old Testament, reflect his
powerful love. Sin does not merely break God's
law, it breaks his heart. He punishes to get his
lover's attention. Yet even when she turns her
back on him, he sticks with her. He is willing to
suffer, in the hope that some day she will
change. Hosea shows that God longs not to
punish, but to love.

■ HOW TO READ HOSEA

Hosea is one of the most emotional books in the
Bible, an outpouring of suffering love from God's
heart. This shows in the writing, which jumps
impulsively from one thought to the next. Read a
chapter dramatically aloud, and you will get this
sense. It is almost like listening in on a husband-
and-wife fight.

The book divides into two parts. In the
first three chapters, the prophet Hosea briefly
describes his marriage to an adulterous woman
and makes the connection to Israel's
unfaithfulness to God. From chapter 4 onwards
this dramatic, personal beginning is not
mentioned again. But it has set the stage. God's

deep love, his disappointment and anger, and his determination to persevere with his unfaithful wife pour out in a series of vivid speeches.

For a historical perspective on Hosea's times, read from 2 Kings 14:23 to 17:41, noting that some sections describe Judah, the southern nation, while the rest relate to the deteriorating Israel Hosea knew. This history is summarised in "A Line-up of Rulers", pages 260–268. The prophet Amos spoke to the North at about the same time as Hosea, but from a noticeably different point of view. Amos concentrated on law and justice, with special concern for the poor, while Hosea concentrated on the broken relationship with God that led to this injustice. Together, these two prophets provide a three-dimensional view of Israel's problems.

Because Hosea is so emotional, he doesn't stop to explain a large number of images or biblical references. A Bible dictionary will help you understand the names and places you aren't familiar with.

■ 3-TRACK READING PLAN

For an explanation and complete listing of the 3-track reading plan, turn to page x.

■ TRACK 1:
Two-Week Courses on the Bible
See page x for information on these courses.

■ TRACK 2:
An Overview of Hosea in 2 Days
□ Day 1. Read the

Introduction to Hosea and chapters 2 and 3, which compare Hosea's marriage to Israel's relationship with God.
□ Day 2. Read chapter 11, which shows God's powerful, competing emotions as he thinks of Israel.
Now turn to page xi for your next Track 2 reading project.

■ TRACK 3:
All of Hosea in 10 Days
After you have read through Hosea, turn to pages xii–xiii for your next Track 3 reading project.

□ 1 □ 2–3 □ 4   □ 5
□ 6–7 □ 8 □ 9   □ 10
□ 11–12 □ 13–14

1 The word of the LORD that came to Hosea son of Beeri during the reigns of Uzziah, Jotham, Ahaz and Hezekiah, kings of Judah, and during the reign of Jeroboam son of Joash king of Israel:

■ Hosea's Wife and Children

2When the LORD began to speak through Hosea, the LORD said to him, "Go, take to yourself an adulterous wife and children of unfaithfulness, because the land is guilty of the vilest adultery in departing from the LORD." 3So he married Gomer daughter of Diblaim, and she conceived and bore him a son.

4Then the LORD said to Hosea, "Call him Jezreel, because I will soon punish the house of Jehu for the massacre at Jezreel, and I will put an end to the kingdom of Israel. 5In that day I will break Israel's bow in the Valley of Jezreel."

6Gomer conceived again and gave birth to a daughter. Then the LORD said to Hosea, "Call her Lo-Ruhamah,*a* for I will no longer show love to the house of Israel, that I should at all forgive them. 7Yet I will show love to the house of Judah; and I will save them—not by bow, sword or battle, or by horses and horsemen, but by the LORD their God."

8After she had weaned Lo-Ruhamah, Gomer had another son. 9Then the LORD said, "Call him Lo-Ammi,*b* for you are not my people, and I am not your God.

10"Yet the Israelites will be like the sand on the seashore, which cannot be measured or counted. In the place where it was said to them, 'You are not my people', they will be called 'sons of the living God'. 11The people of Judah and the people of Israel will be reunited, and they will appoint one leader and will come up out of the land, for great will be the day of Jezreel.

2 "Say of your brothers, 'My people', and of your sisters, 'My loved one'.

■ Israel Punished and Restored

2"Rebuke your mother, rebuke her,
   for she is not my wife,
   and I am not her husband.
Let her remove the adulterous look from her face
   and the unfaithfulness from between her breasts.

1:4 ■ CHILDREN'S STRANGE NAMES
At God's direction, Hosea named his three children in a way that symbolised God's anger. Their names show God's increasing judgment against Israel's adultery: first comes punishment, then a loss of love, finally total divorce. The first name, Jezreel, refers to a historical incident from 2 Kings 9–10. Jezreel was the place where King Jehu slaughtered a wicked king and all his associates (2 Kings 10:11). Hosea lived to see his prediction of punishment on Jehu's house fulfilled, when the last king in Jehu's line was murdered (2 Kings 15:8–12).

Punishment, however, was not the last word. *Jezreel* has a double meaning—both to "scatter" and to "sow". In verse 11 and in verses 22–23 of chapter 2, *Jezreel* takes on the hopeful sense of planting new life. Hosea's other two children's names are similarly turned from curses to blessings. God's anger leads to new life.

3Otherwise I will strip her naked
   and make her as bare as on the day she was born;

a6 Lo-Ruhamah means not loved.   *b9 Lo-Ammi means not my people.*

I will make her like a desert,
    turn her into a parched land,
    and slay her with thirst.
⁴I will not show my love to her children,
    because they are the children of adultery.
⁵Their mother has been unfaithful
    and has conceived them in disgrace.
She said, 'I will go after my lovers,
    who give me my food and my water,
    my wool and my linen, my oil and my drink.'
⁶Therefore I will block her path with
        thornbushes;
    I will wall her in so that she cannot find her
        way.
⁷She will chase after her lovers but not catch
        them;
    she will look for them but not find them.
Then she will say,
    'I will go back to my husband as at first,
    for then I was better off than now.'
⁸She has not acknowledged that I was the one
    who gave her the grain, the new wine and
        oil,
    who lavished on her the silver and gold—
    which they used for Baal.

⁹"Therefore I will take away my grain when it
        ripens,
    and my new wine when it is ready.
I will take back my wool and my linen,
    intended to cover her nakedness.
¹⁰So now I will expose her lewdness
    before the eyes of her lovers;
    no-one will take her out of my hands.
¹¹I will stop all her celebrations:
    her yearly festivals, her New Moons,
    her Sabbath days—all her appointed feasts.
¹²I will ruin her vines and her fig-trees,
    which she said were her pay from her lovers;
    I will make them a thicket,
    and wild animals will devour them.
¹³I will punish her for the days
    she burned incense to the Baals;
    she decked herself with rings and jewellery,
    and went after her lovers,
    but me she forgot,"
                                            declares the LORD.

¹⁴"Therefore I am now going to allure her;
    I will lead her into the desert
    and speak tenderly to her.
¹⁵There I will give her back her vineyards,
    and will make the Valley of Achor*ᵃ* a door
        of hope.
There she will sing*ᵇ* as in the days of her
        youth,
    as in the day she came up out of Egypt.

¹⁶"In that day," declares the LORD,
    "you will call me 'my husband';
    you will no longer call me 'my master'.*ᶜ*
¹⁷I will remove the names of the Baals from her
        lips;

no longer will their names be invoked.
¹⁸In that day I will make a covenant for them
    with the beasts of the field and the birds of
        the air
    and the creatures that move along the
        ground.
Bow and sword and battle
    I will abolish from the land,
    so that all may lie down in safety.
¹⁹I will betroth you to me for ever;
    I will betroth you in*ᵈ* righteousness and
        justice,
    in*ᵉ* love and compassion.
²⁰I will betroth you in faithfulness,
    and you will acknowledge the LORD.

²¹"In that day I will respond,"
    declares the LORD—
    "I will respond to the skies,
    and they will respond to the earth;
²²and the earth will respond to the grain,
    the new wine and oil,
    and they will respond to Jezreel.*ᶠ*
²³I will plant her for myself in the land;
    I will show my love to the one I called 'Not
        my loved one'.*ᵍ*
I will say to those called 'Not my people',*ʰ*
    'You are my people';
    and they will say, 'You are my God.'"

■ Hosea's Reconciliation With His Wife

3 The LORD said to me, "Go, show your love to
    your wife again, though she is loved by another
and is an adulteress. Love her as the LORD loves the
Israelites, though they turn to other gods and love
the sacred raisin cakes."

3:1 ■ PARABLE OF LOVE

No other prophet lived out an object lesson with
quite the same emotional force as Hosea did.
Gomer had sunk so low as to sell herself into
slavery, but Hosea purchased her back and
reclaimed her as his wife. That remarkable deed,
certainly the subject of his countrymen's gossip,
symbolised God's undying love for his people.
Though they had dragged his name in the mud,
still he welcomed them back.

---

²So I bought her for fifteen shekels*ᵃ* of silver and
about a homer and a lethek*ᵇ* of barley. ³Then I told
her, "You are to live with*ᶜ* me for many days; you
must not be a prostitute or be intimate with any
man, and I will live with*ᶜ* you."
⁴For the Israelites will live for many days without
king or prince, without sacrifice or sacred stones,
without ephod or idol. ⁵Afterwards the Israelites
will return and seek the LORD their God and David
their king. They will come trembling to the LORD
and to his blessings in the last days.

ᵃ 15 Achor means *trouble*.   ᵇ 15 Or *respond*   ᶜ 16 Hebrew *baal*   ᵈ 19 Or *with; also in verse 20*   ᵉ 19 Or *with*   ᶠ 22 Jezreel means *God plants*.
ᵍ 23 Hebrew *Lo-Ruhamah*   ʰ 23 Hebrew *Lo-Ammi*   ᵃ 2 That is, about 6 ounces (about 170 grams)   ᵇ 2 That is, probably about 9 bushels (about
330 litres)   ᶜ 3 Or *wait for*

■ The Charge Against Israel

4 Hear the word of the LORD, you Israelites,
because the LORD has a charge to bring
against you who live in the land:
"There is no faithfulness, no love,
no acknowledgment of God in the land.
²There is only cursing,ᵃ lying and murder,
stealing and adultery;
they break all bounds,
and bloodshed follows bloodshed.
³Because of this the land mourns,ᵇ
and all who live in it waste away;
the beasts of the field and the birds of the air
and the fish of the sea are dying.

⁴"But let no man bring a charge,
let no man accuse another,
for your people are like those
who bring charges against a priest.
⁵You stumble day and night,
and the prophets stumble with you.
So I will destroy your mother—
⁶ my people are destroyed from lack of
knowledge.

"Because you have rejected knowledge,
I also reject you as my priests;
because you have ignored the law of your God,
I also will ignore your children.
⁷The more the priests increased,
the more they sinned against me;
they exchangedᶜ theirᵈ Glory for
something disgraceful.

4:7 ■ POOR TRADE

Early in its history, the Northern Kingdom of Israel began appointing its own priests from ineligible tribes (1 Kings 12:31). These priests led the people in the worship of golden calves—idols— instead of in the worship of the God of Abraham and Moses. This verse has an echo in Romans 1:23, where Paul blasts pagans who exchange the glory of immortal God for mere statues of birds, animals, and reptiles.

⁸They feed on the sins of my people
and relish their wickedness.
⁹And it will be: Like people, like priests.
I will punish both of them for their ways
and repay them for their deeds.

¹⁰"They will eat but not have enough;
they will engage in prostitution but not
increase,
because they have deserted the LORD
to give themselves ¹¹to prostitution,
to old wine and new,
which take away the understanding ¹²of my
people.
They consult a wooden idol
and are answered by a stick of wood.
A spirit of prostitution leads them astray;
they are unfaithful to their God.
¹³They sacrifice on the mountaintops
and burn offerings on the hills,

under oak, poplar and terebinth,
where the shade is pleasant.
Therefore your daughters turn to prostitution
and your daughters-in-law to adultery.

¹⁴"I will not punish your daughters
when they turn to prostitution,
nor your daughters-in-law
when they commit adultery,
because the men themselves consort with
harlots
and sacrifice with shrine-prostitutes—
a people without understanding will come to
ruin!

4:13 ■ REAL PROSTITUTION

In each of the first nine chapters of his book, Hosea describes Israel's sin as prostitution or adultery. This is primarily symbolism meant to emphasise God's deep, personal love for Israel and his pain when the Israelites desert him to go after other gods.

But *prostitution* has a literal meaning also. The religions Israel pursued taught that human sexuality was tied to agricultural fertility. To encourage good crops, believers in these religions practised their human fertility. This meant organised prostitution, done as part of their worship experience.

¹⁵"Though you commit adultery, O Israel,
let not Judah become guilty.

"Do not go to Gilgal;
do not go up to Beth Aven.ᵉ
And do not swear, 'As surely as the LORD
lives!'
¹⁶The Israelites are stubborn,
like a stubborn heifer.
How then can the LORD pasture them
like lambs in a meadow?
¹⁷Ephraim is joined to idols;
leave him alone!
¹⁸Even when their drinks are gone,
they continue their prostitution;
their rulers dearly love shameful ways.
¹⁹A whirlwind will sweep them away,
and their sacrifices will bring them shame.

■ Judgment Against Israel

5 "Hear this, you priests!
Pay attention, you Israelites!
Listen, O royal house!
This judgment is against you:
You have been a snare at Mizpah,
a net spread out on Tabor.
²The rebels are deep in slaughter.
I will discipline all of them.
³I know all about Ephraim;
Israel is not hidden from me.
Ephraim, you have now turned to prostitution;
Israel is corrupt.

⁴"Their deeds do not permit them
to return to their God.

ᵃ2 That is, to pronounce a curse upon   ᵇ3 Or *dries up*   ᶜ7 Syriac and an ancient Hebrew scribal tradition; Masoretic Text *I will exchange*
ᵈ7 Masoretic Text; an ancient Hebrew scribal tradition *my*   ᵉ15 *Beth Aven* means *house of wickedness* (a name for Bethel, which means *house of God*).

A spirit of prostitution is in their heart;
  they do not acknowledge the LORD.
⁵Israel's arrogance testifies against them;
  the Israelites, even Ephraim, stumble in their
    sin;
  Judah also stumbles with them.
⁶When they go with their flocks and herds
  to seek the LORD,
they will not find him;
  he has withdrawn himself from them.
⁷They are unfaithful to the LORD;
  they give birth to illegitimate children.
Now their New Moon festivals
  will devour them and their fields.

⁸"Sound the trumpet in Gibeah,
  the horn in Ramah.
Raise the battle cry in Beth Aven;ᵃ
  lead on, O Benjamin.
⁹Ephraim will be laid waste
  on the day of reckoning.
Among the tribes of Israel
  I proclaim what is certain.
¹⁰Judah's leaders are like those
  who move boundary stones.
I will pour out my wrath on them
  like a flood of water.
¹¹Ephraim is oppressed,
  trampled in judgment,
  intent on pursuing idols.ᵇ
¹²I am like a moth to Ephraim,
  like rot to the people of Judah.

¹³"When Ephraim saw his sickness,
  and Judah his sores,
then Ephraim turned to Assyria,
  and sent to the great king for help.
But he is not able to cure you,
  not able to heal your sores.
¹⁴For I will be like a lion to Ephraim,
  like a great lion to Judah.
I will tear them to pieces and go away;
  I will carry them off, with no-one to rescue
    them.
¹⁵Then I will go back to my place
  until they admit their guilt.
And they will seek my face;
  in their misery they will earnestly seek me."

■ Israel Unrepentant
6 "Come, let us return to the LORD.
He has torn us to pieces
  but he will heal us;
he has injured us
  but he will bind up our wounds.
²After two days he will revive us;
  on the third day he will restore us,
  that we may live in his presence.
³Let us acknowledge the LORD;
  let us press on to acknowledge him.
As surely as the sun rises,
  he will appear;
he will come to us like the winter rains,
  like the spring rains that water the earth."

⁴"What can I do with you, Ephraim?
  What can I do with you, Judah?
Your love is like the morning mist,
  like the early dew that disappears.
⁵Therefore I cut you in pieces with my
    prophets,
  I killed you with the words of my mouth;
  my judgments flashed like lightning upon
    you.
⁶For I desire mercy, not sacrifice,
  and acknowledgment of God rather than
    burnt offerings.
⁷Like Adam,ᵃ they have broken the covenant—
  they were unfaithful to me there.
⁸Gilead is a city of wicked men,
  stained with footprints of blood.
⁹As marauders lie in ambush for a man,
  so do bands of priests;
they murder on the road to Shechem,
  committing shameful crimes.
¹⁰I have seen a horrible thing
  in the house of Israel.
There Ephraim is given to prostitution
  and Israel is defiled.

¹¹"Also for you, Judah,
  a harvest is appointed.

"Whenever I would restore the fortunes of my
    people,
7 ¹whenever I would heal Israel,
  the sins of Ephraim are exposed
  and the crimes of Samaria revealed.
They practise deceit,
  thieves break into houses,
  bandits rob in the streets;
²but they do not realise
  that I remember all their evil deeds.
Their sins engulf them;
  they are always before me.

³"They delight the king with their wickedness,
  the princes with their lies.
⁴They are all adulterers,
  burning like an oven
whose fire the baker need not stir
  from the kneading of the dough till it rises.
⁵On the day of the festival of our king
  the princes become inflamed with wine,
  and he joins hands with the mockers.
⁶Their hearts are like an oven;
  they approach him with intrigue.
Their passion smoulders all night;
  in the morning it blazes like a flaming fire.
⁷All of them are hot as an oven;
  they devour their rulers.
All their kings fall,
  and none of them calls on me.

⁸"Ephraim mixes with the nations;
  Ephraim is a flat cake not turned over.
⁹Foreigners sap his strength,
  but he does not realise it.
His hair is sprinkled with grey,
  but he does not notice.
¹⁰Israel's arrogance testifies against him,
  but despite all this

ᵃ8 Beth Aven means *house of wickedness* (a name for Bethel, which means *house of God*).   ᵇ11 The meaning of the Hebrew for this word is uncertain.
ᵃ7 Or *As at Adam;* or *Like men*

he does not return to the LORD his God
or search for him.

7:4 ■ SMOULDERING PASSION

In parts of the Middle East, ovens are made of
clay and shaped like a large cone or beehive. The
baker builds a fire inside and tends it until the clay
gets very hot. Then, fire and wood ash can be
pulled out and the fresh dough placed inside. It
rises due to the heat contained inside the oven,
which stays hot long after the fire has been
removed. Such was Israel's lust for other gods: it
kept on smouldering, like a self-fuelling oven
(verse 6).

11"Ephraim is like a dove,
　easily deceived and senseless—
now calling to Egypt,
　now turning to Assyria.
12When they go, I will throw my net over them;
　I will pull them down like birds of the air.
When I hear them flocking together,
　I will catch them.
13Woe to them,
　because they have strayed from me!
Destruction to them,
　because they have rebelled against me!
I long to redeem them
　but they speak lies against me.
14They do not cry out to me from their hearts
　but wail upon their beds.
They gather together*a* for grain and new wine
　but turn away from me.
15I trained them and strengthened them,
　but they plot evil against me.
16They do not turn to the Most High;
　they are like a faulty bow.
Their leaders will fall by the sword
　because of their insolent words.
For this they will be ridiculed
　in the land of Egypt.

■ Israel to Reap the Whirlwind

8 "Put the trumpet to your lips!
An eagle is over the house of the LORD
because the people have broken my covenant
　and rebelled against my law.
2Israel cries out to me,
　'O our God, we acknowledge you!'
3But Israel has rejected what is good;
　an enemy will pursue him.
4They set up kings without my consent;
　they choose princes without my approval.
With their silver and gold
　they make idols for themselves
　to their own destruction.
5Throw out your calf-idol, O Samaria!
　My anger burns against them.
How long will they be incapable of purity?
6 They are from Israel!
This calf—a craftsman has made it;
　it is not God.

It will be broken in pieces,
　that calf of Samaria.
7"They sow the wind
　and reap the whirlwind.
The stalk has no head;
　it will produce no flour.
Were it to yield grain,
　foreigners would swallow it up.
8Israel is swallowed up;
　now she is among the nations
　like a worthless thing.
9For they have gone up to Assyria
　like a wild donkey wandering alone.
Ephraim has sold herself to lovers.
10Although they have sold themselves among the
　nations,
　I will now gather them together.
They will begin to waste away
　under the oppression of the mighty king.

11"Though Ephraim built many altars for sin
　offerings,
　these have become altars for sinning.
12I wrote for them the many things of my law,
　but they regarded them as something alien.
13They offer sacrifices given to me
　and they eat the meat,
　but the LORD is not pleased with them.
Now he will remember their wickedness
　and punish their sins:
They will return to Egypt.
14Israel has forgotten his Maker
　and built palaces;
Judah has fortified many towns.
But I will send fire upon their cities
　that will consume their fortresses."

8:11 ■ HOW TO BE RELIGIOUS WITHOUT PLEASING GOD

The Israelites didn't think they were rejecting God.
In fact, they became increasingly pious. (See
6:1–3; 8:2,11,13; and 10:1 for their expressions of
faith.) But they wanted to worship on their terms,
not God's. While their sacrifices to God increased,
they kept on worshipping idols as well.

■ Punishment for Israel

9 Do not rejoice, O Israel;
do not be jubilant like the other nations.
For you have been unfaithful to your God;
　you love the wages of a prostitute
　at every threshing-floor.
2Threshing-floors and winepresses will not feed
　the people;
　the new wine will fail them.
3They will not remain in the LORD's land;
　Ephraim will return to Egypt
　and eat unclean*a* food in Assyria.
4They will not pour out wine offerings to the
　LORD,
　nor will their sacrifices please him.
Such sacrifices will be to them like the bread of
　mourners;
　all who eat them will be unclean.

a14 Most Hebrew manuscripts; some Hebrew manuscripts and Septuagint *They slash themselves*　　*a3* That is, ceremonially unclean

This food will be for themselves;
  it will not come into the temple of the LORD.

5What will you do on the day of your appointed
      feasts,
    on the festival days of the LORD?
6Even if they escape from destruction,
    Egypt will gather them,
    and Memphis will bury them.
  Their treasures of silver will be taken over by
      briers,
    and thorns will overrun their tents.
7The days of punishment are coming,
    the days of reckoning are at hand.
    Let Israel know this.
  Because your sins are so many
    and your hostility so great,
  the prophet is considered a fool,
    the inspired man a maniac.
8The prophet, along with my God,
    is the watchman over Ephraim,b
  yet snares await him on all his paths,
    and hostility in the house of his God.
9They have sunk deep into corruption,
    as in the days of Gibeah.
  God will remember their wickedness
    and punish them for their sins.

9:9 ■ TWO INSTANCES OF EVIL
The "days of Gibeah" evidently refers to the
vicious murder of a woman, told in Judges 19–21.
This horrifying incident was a version of Sodom
and Gomorrah right in Israel. Another incident
(verse 10), equally bad in its own way, occurred at
Baal Peor (see Numbers 25:1–3). Israelite men
en route to the promised land slept with Moabite
women and worshipped their gods. From both
these incidents, Hosea proves that sin is nothing
new to Israel.

10"When I found Israel,
    it was like finding grapes in the desert;
  when I saw your fathers,
    it was like seeing the early fruit on the
        fig-tree.
  But when they came to Baal Peor,
    they consecrated themselves to that shameful
        idol
  and became as vile as the thing they loved.
11Ephraim's glory will fly away like a bird—
    no birth, no pregnancy, no conception.
12Even if they bring up children,
    I will bereave them of every one.
  Woe to them
    when I turn away from them!
13I have seen Ephraim, like Tyre,
    planted in a pleasant place.
  But Ephraim will bring out
    their children to the slayer."

14Give them, O LORD—
    what will you give them?
  Give them wombs that miscarry
    and breasts that are dry.

15"Because of all their wickedness in Gilgal,
    I hated them there.
  Because of their sinful deeds,
    I will drive them out of my house.
  I will no longer love them;
    all their leaders are rebellious.
16Ephraim is blighted,
    their root is withered,
    they yield no fruit.
  Even if they bear children,
    I will slay their cherished offspring."

17My God will reject them
    because they have not obeyed him;
  they will be wanderers among the nations.

10 Israel was a spreading vine;
    he brought forth fruit for himself.
  As his fruit increased,
    he built more altars;
  as his land prospered,
    he adorned his sacred stones.
2Their heart is deceitful,
    and now they must bear their guilt.
  The LORD will demolish their altars
    and destroy their sacred stones.

3Then they will say, "We have no king
    because we did not revere the LORD.
  But even if we had a king,
    what could he do for us?"
4They make many promises,
    take false oaths
    and make agreements;
  therefore lawsuits spring up
    like poisonous weeds in a ploughed field.
5The people who live in Samaria fear
    for the calf-idol of Beth Aven.a
  Its people will mourn over it,
    and so will its idolatrous priests,
  those who had rejoiced over its splendour,
    because it is taken from them into exile.
6It will be carried to Assyria
    as tribute for the great king.
  Ephraim will be disgraced;
    Israel will be ashamed of its wooden idols.b
7Samaria and its king will float away
    like a twig on the surface of the waters.
8The high places of wickednessc will be
        destroyed—
    it is the sin of Israel.
  Thorns and thistles will grow up
    and cover their altars.
  Then they will say to the mountains, "Cover
        us!"
    and to the hills, "Fall on us!"

9"Since the days of Gibeah, you have sinned,
        O Israel,
    and there you have remained.d
  Did not war overtake
    the evildoers in Gibeah?
10When I please, I will punish them;
    nations will be gathered against them
  to put them in bonds for their double sin.
11Ephraim is a trained heifer
    that loves to thresh;

---

b8 Or The prophet is the watchman over Ephraim, / the people of my God   a5 Beth Aven means house of wickedness (a name for Bethel, which means
house of God).   b6 Or its counsel   c8 Hebrew aven, a reference to Beth Aven (a derogatory name for Bethel)   d9 Or there a stand was taken

so I will put a yoke
    on her fair neck.
I will drive Ephraim,
    Judah must plough,
    and Jacob must break up the ground.

10:5 ■ THE NEW GOLDEN CALF

Beth Aven ("house of wickedness") is a sarcastic reference to Bethel ("house of God"), which is mentioned more times in the Bible than any other city except Jerusalem. When Israel split into North and South, the northern king, Jeroboam I, made Bethel the chief religious sanctuary, to replace Jerusalem. There he put up a golden calf for people to worship (1 Kings 12:26–30). Mixing worship of the one true God with the idol worship of Baal was, according to Hosea, the root of Israel's trouble.

¹²Sow for yourselves righteousness,
    reap the fruit of unfailing love,
and break up your unploughed ground;
    for it is time to seek the LORD,
until he comes
    and showers righteousness on you.
¹³But you have planted wickedness,
    you have reaped evil,
    you have eaten the fruit of deception.
Because you have depended on your own
        strength
    and on your many warriors,
¹⁴the roar of battle will rise against your people,
    so that all your fortresses will be
        devastated—
    as Shalman devastated Beth Arbel on the day of
        battle,
    when mothers were dashed to the ground
        with their children.
¹⁵Thus will it happen to you, O Bethel,
    because your wickedness is great.
When that day dawns,
    the king of Israel will be completely
        destroyed.

■ God's Love for Israel

11 "When Israel was a child, I loved him,
        and out of Egypt I called my son.
²But the more I*a* called Israel,
    the further they went from me.*b*
They sacrificed to the Baals
    and they burned incense to images.
³It was I who taught Ephraim to walk,
    taking them by the arms;
but they did not realise
    it was I who healed them.
⁴I led them with cords of human kindness,
    with ties of love;
I lifted the yoke from their neck
    and bent down to feed them.

⁵"Will they not return to Egypt
    and will not Assyria rule over them
    because they refuse to repent?
⁶Swords will flash in their cities,

will destroy the bars of their gates
    and put an end to their plans.

11:1 ■ REBEL SON

God has already illustrated his unquenchable love for Israel through the real-life parable of Hosea and his unfaithful wife. Now he introduces yet another picture: a rebellious son. According to the laws of Deuteronomy, a rebel son could be sentenced to death by stoning (Deuteronomy 21:18–21). But God cannot make himself carry out that sentence (verses 8–9). He gives his people one more chance.

⁷My people are determined to turn from me.
    Even if they call to the Most High,
    he will by no means exalt them.

⁸"How can I give you up, Ephraim?
    How can I hand you over, Israel?
How can I treat you like Admah?
    How can I make you like Zeboiim?
My heart is changed within me;
    all my compassion is aroused.
⁹I will not carry out my fierce anger,
    nor will I turn and devastate Ephraim.
For I am God, and not man—
    the Holy One among you.
I will not come in wrath.*c*
¹⁰They will follow the LORD;
    he will roar like a lion.
When he roars,
    his children will come trembling from the
        west.
¹¹They will come trembling
    like birds from Egypt,
    like doves from Assyria.
I will settle them in their homes,"
    declares the LORD.

■ Israel's Sin

¹²Ephraim has surrounded me with lies,
    the house of Israel with deceit.
And Judah is unruly against God,
    even against the faithful Holy One.

12 ¹Ephraim feeds on the wind;
        he pursues the east wind all day
    and multiplies lies and violence.
He makes a treaty with Assyria
    and sends olive oil to Egypt.
²The LORD has a charge to bring against Judah;
    he will punish Jacob*a* according to his ways
    and repay him according to his deeds.
³In the womb he grasped his brother's heel;
    as a man he struggled with God.
⁴He struggled with the angel and overcame him;
    he wept and begged for his favour.
He found him at Bethel
    and talked with him there—
⁵the LORD God Almighty,
    the LORD is his name of renown!
⁶But you must return to your God;
    maintain love and justice,
    and wait for your God always.

---

*a*2 Some Septuagint manuscripts; Hebrew *they* (figuratively, *he deceives*).   *b*2 Septuagint; Hebrew *them*   *c*9 Or *come against any city*   *a*2 *Jacob* means *he grasps the heel*

⁷The merchant uses dishonest scales;
  he loves to defraud.
⁸Ephraim boasts,
  "I am very rich; I have become wealthy.
With all my wealth they will not find in me
  any iniquity or sin."

12:2 ■ JACOB, A MAN AND A COUNTRY

"Israel" was a nation named after a man — a man also known as Jacob, whose story is told principally in Genesis 25–35. He was greedy and grasping, and he went into exile for it. Yet he had another side: an eagerness to meet God and be blessed by him, culminating in his night-time "wrestling with God" (Genesis 32). Though Jacob went into exile, as would Israel, he came back with God's blessing on his future. So, Hosea suggests, could the nation that carried his name.

⁹"I am the LORD your God,
  ⌊who brought you⌋ out of^b Egypt;
I will make you live in tents again,
  as in the days of your appointed feasts.
¹⁰I spoke to the prophets,
  gave them many visions
  and told parables through them."

¹¹Is Gilead wicked?
  Its people are worthless!
Do they sacrifice bulls in Gilgal?
  Their altars will be like piles of stones
  on a ploughed field.
¹²Jacob fled to the country of Aram;^{c}
  Israel served to get a wife,
  and to pay for her he tended sheep.
¹³The LORD used a prophet to bring Israel up
  from Egypt,
  by a prophet he cared for him.
¹⁴But Ephraim has bitterly provoked him to
  anger;
  his Lord will leave upon him the guilt of his
  bloodshed
  and will repay him for his contempt.

■ The LORD's Anger Against Israel

13 When Ephraim spoke, men trembled;
  he was exalted in Israel.
  But he became guilty of Baal worship and
  died.
²Now they sin more and more;
  they make idols for themselves from their
  silver,
cleverly fashioned images,
  all of them the work of craftsmen.
It is said of these people,
  "They offer human sacrifice
  and kiss^a the calf-idols."
³Therefore they will be like the morning mist,
  like the early dew that disappears,
  like chaff swirling from a threshing-floor,
  like smoke escaping through a window.

⁴"But I am the LORD your God,

⌊who brought you⌋ out of^b Egypt.
You shall acknowledge no God but me,
  no Saviour except me.

13:3 ■ AS RELIABLE AS THE WIND

The fruitlessness of Israel's deeds is beautifully expressed in the metaphor of wind: they feed on it, they pursue it all day (12:1), they sow it, and they reap the whirlwind (8:7). Their love is like the morning mist, or dew (6:4), and their lives will be as lasting as the early dew or as chaff or as smoke escaping out a window (13:3).

⁵I cared for you in the desert,
  in the land of burning heat.
⁶When I fed them, they were satisfied;
  when they were satisfied, they became
  proud;
  then they forgot me.
⁷So I will come upon them like a lion,
  like a leopard I will lurk by the path.
⁸Like a bear robbed of her cubs,
  I will attack them and rip them open.
Like a lion I will devour them;
  a wild animal will tear them apart.

⁹"You are destroyed, O Israel,
  because you are against me, against your
  helper.
¹⁰Where is your king, that he may save you?
  Where are your rulers in all your towns,
  of whom you said,
  'Give me a king and princes'?
¹¹So in my anger I gave you a king,
  and in my wrath I took him away.
¹²The guilt of Ephraim is stored up,
  his sins are kept on record.
¹³Pains as of a woman in childbirth come to him,
  but he is a child without wisdom;
when the time arrives,
  he does not come to the opening of the
  womb.

¹⁴"I will ransom them from the power of the
  grave;^{c}
  I will redeem them from death.
Where, O death, are your plagues?
  Where, O grave,^{c} is your destruction?

"I will have no compassion,
15 even though he thrives among his brothers.
An east wind from the LORD will come,
  blowing in from the desert;
his spring will fail
  and his well dry up.
His storehouse will be plundered
  of all its treasures.
¹⁶The people of Samaria must bear their guilt,
  because they have rebelled against their God.
They will fall by the sword;
  their little ones will be dashed to the ground,
  their pregnant women ripped open."

---

^{b}9 Or God / ever since you were in ^{c}12 That is, North-west Mesopotamia ^{a}2 Or "Men who sacrifice / kiss ^{b}4 Or God / ever since you were in
^{c}14 Hebrew Sheol

■ Repentance to Bring Blessing

14 Return, O Israel, to the LORD your God.
Your sins have been your downfall!
²Take words with you
and return to the LORD.
Say to him:
"Forgive all our sins
and receive us graciously,
that we may offer the fruit of our lips.ᵃ
³Assyria cannot save us;
we will not mount war-horses.
We will never again say 'Our gods'
to what our own hands have made,
for in you the fatherless find compassion."

⁴"I will heal their waywardness
and love them freely,
for my anger has turned away from them.
⁵I will be like the dew to Israel;
he will blossom like a lily.
Like a cedar of Lebanon
he will send down his roots;
⁶ his young shoots will grow.
His splendour will be like an olive tree,
his fragrance like a cedar of Lebanon.
⁷Men will dwell again in his shade.
He will flourish like the corn.

He will blossom like a vine,
and his fame will be like the wine from
Lebanon.
⁸O Ephraim, what more have Iᵇ to do with
idols?
I will answer him and care for him.
I am like a green pine tree;
your fruitfulness comes from me."

14:5 ■ NEW HOPE
In its conclusion the book of Hosea, so full of
torment, dissolves into a series of serene images
of what Israel can become. God compares the
nation to a lily (beauty), a cedar (strength), an olive
tree (value), a fragrant tree (delight), grain
(abundance), a grapevine (fruitfulness). Thus a
book dominated by images of unfaithfulness – an
adulteress wife, a rebellious son – ends with the
firm promise of restoration.

⁹Who is wise? He will realise these things.
Who is discerning? He will understand them.
The ways of the LORD are right;
the righteous walk in them,
but the rebellious stumble in them.

ᵃ2 Or offer our lips as sacrifices of bulls   ᵇ8 Or What more has Ephraim

JOEL

■ THE MEANING OF A NATURAL DISASTER

WHAT'S BEHIND A DEVASTATING LOCUST PLAGUE?

BEFORE THEM THE EARTH SHAKES, THE SKY TREMBLES, THE SUN AND MOON ARE DARKENED, AND THE STARS NO LONGER SHINE. ■ 2:10

"Their number was astounding; the whole face of the mountain was black with them. On they came like a living deluge. We dug trenches, and kindled fires, and beat and burned to death 'heaps upon heaps'; but the effort was utterly useless. Wave after wave rolled up the mountainside and poured over rocks, walls, ditches and hedges – those behind covering up and bridging over the masses already killed. It was perfectly appalling to watch this animated river as it flowed up the road and ascended the hill above my house. For four days they continued to pass on towards the east. . . ."

Eye-witness W. M. Thomson is describing a locust plague. Descriptions of the aftermath sound just as awful. When locusts have passed, the terrain looks as though it has been swept by a scorching fire.

■ WHY HAVE I LIVED?

Many awestruck observers have written accounts of locust swarms, but none more graphically than the prophet Joel. In striking, polished imagery he described the devastation. His people faced starvation. Joel drew a verbal portrait of grief and fear.

Natural disasters provoke questions. Why did God allow this disaster to happen? Why have I lived and others died? Is there a lesson here? For Joel, a plague of locusts led to deep insights into God's universal plan.

Joel had no doubt that God was behind the plague. In fact, he pictured God leading the locusts like an army into battle (2:11). They represented "the day of the LORD", a judgment on Israel. Unlike many of the other prophets, Joel did not devote time to an analysis of Israel's failings. He concentrated, instead, on a cure.

Joel urged the priests to call a nationwide day of prayer and fasting to lead the people back to God. Then God would roll back the damage done by the locusts, and more: "You will have plenty to eat, until you are full, and you will praise the name of the LORD your God, who has worked wonders for you" (2:26). They would emerge from the experience with new, durable confidence in God's love. So it has often proved for God's people: a disaster has pressed them to a deeper relationship with him.

■ GOD'S BIGGER PLANS

Though the locust plague was by far the worst Joel had ever heard of (1:2–3), no historical record of this particular invasion has endured, other than the one Joel left us. The truth is, even the worst natural disasters fade from memory. Joel wanted the disaster to turn people's attention towards something more lasting – towards an eternal God.

Joel wanted God's people to believe that God controlled the locusts, and, even more important, that God shaped the entire course of history to his plan. As terribly as the locusts had destroyed, and as wonderfully as God had rolled back their destruction, these events only foreshadowed far more terrible and wonderful things. Joel saw that God's Spirit would transform his people into those who love him constantly, not just when a disaster catches their attention. After a time of terrible judgment, God would create a renewed, secure city for his people, in which he himself would live.

■ HOW TO READ JOEL

Joel breaks naturally into two parts. Up to 2:28, it talks about a locust invasion and the response of God's people to such a natural disaster. From that verse on, however, Joel's view rises above the local situation and deals with the far-off future.

Joel rarely refers to unfamiliar people, places, or events, so you can read it fairly easily without using any outside reference like a Bible dictionary. The challenge is to connect his understanding of a natural disaster – a locust plague – with his vision of the future.

The Bible often refers to "the day of the LORD" as the time when God will completely take charge of our world. But Joel seems to see "the day of the LORD" partly revealed in the disasters of his day. As you read, try to see the similarities Joel draws between the locust invasion and the final consummation of history. Ask yourself: how do I respond to disaster? How would Joel want me to respond?

■ 3-TRACK READING PLAN

For an explanation and complete listing of the 3-track reading plan, turn to page x.

■ TRACK 1:
Two-Week Courses on the Bible
See page x for information on these courses.

■ TRACK 2:
An Overview of Joel in 1 Day

□ Day 1. Read the Introduction to Joel and chapter 2, which describes the locust plague and its effect on the people's relationship with God.
Now turn to page xi for your next Track 2 reading project.

■ TRACK 3:
All of Joel in 3 Days
After you have read through Joel, turn to pages xii–xiii for your next Track 3 reading project.

□ 1   □ 2   □ 3

1 The word of the LORD that came to Joel son of Pethuel.

■ An Invasion of Locusts

²Hear this, you elders;
    listen, all who live in the land.
Has anything like this ever happened in your days
    or in the days of your forefathers?
³Tell it to your children,
    and let your children tell it to their children,
    and their children to the next generation.
⁴What the locust swarm has left
    the great locusts have eaten;
what the great locusts have left
    the young locusts have eaten;
what the young locusts have left
    other locusts*a* have eaten.

1:4 ■ DOOMSDAY

Nowadays we tend to think of doomsday in terms of nuclear holocaust. But until recent times the most powerful weapons in the world belonged to nature. Earthquakes, floods, and plagues of illness caused far more destruction than arrows, spears, and swords. Natural disasters were frightening and unpredictable: a plague of locusts, for example, could wipe out an entire food supply overnight.

⁵Wake up, you drunkards, and weep!
    Wail, all you drinkers of wine;
wail because of the new wine,
    for it has been snatched from your lips.
⁶A nation has invaded my land,
    powerful and without number;

it has the teeth of a lion,
    the fangs of a lioness.
⁷It has laid waste my vines
    and ruined my fig-trees.
It has stripped off their bark
    and thrown it away,
    leaving their branches white.

⁸Mourn like a virgin*b* in sackcloth
    grieving for the husband*c* of her youth.
⁹Grain offerings and drink offerings
    are cut off from the house of the LORD.
The priests are in mourning,
    those who minister before the LORD.
¹⁰The fields are ruined,
    the ground is dried up;*d*
the grain is destroyed,
    the new wine is dried up,
    the oil fails.
¹¹Despair, you farmers,
    wail, you vine growers;
grieve for the wheat and the barley,
    because the harvest of the field is destroyed.
¹²The vine is dried up
    and the fig-tree is withered;
the pomegranate, the palm and the apple tree —
    all the trees of the field — are dried up.
Surely the joy of mankind
    is withered away.

■ A Call to Repentance

¹³Put on sackcloth, O priests, and mourn;
    wail, you who minister before the altar.
Come, spend the night in sackcloth,
    you who minister before my God;
for the grain offerings and drink offerings

---

*a*4 The precise meaning of the four Hebrew words used here for locusts is uncertain.   *b*8 Or *young woman*   *c*8 Or *betrothed*   *d*10 Or *ground mourns*

are withheld from the house of your God.
¹⁴Declare a holy fast;
    call a sacred assembly.
Summon the elders
    and all who live in the land
to the house of the LORD your God,
    and cry out to the LORD.

¹⁵Alas for that day!
    For the day of the LORD is near;
    it will come like destruction from the
        Almighty.ᵉ

¹⁶Has not the food been cut off
    before our very eyes—
joy and gladness
    from the house of our God?
¹⁷The seeds are shrivelled
    beneath the clods.ᶠ
The storehouses are in ruins,
    the granaries have been broken down,
    for the grain has dried up.
¹⁸How the cattle moan!
    The herds mill about
because they have no pasture;
    even the flocks of sheep are suffering.

1:18 ■ TOTAL DEVASTATION
No wine for the drunkards, no husbands for young brides, no crops for the farmers, no offerings for the priests—the disaster was affecting every part of society. Cattle moaned, sheep wandered in starvation. People had nowhere to turn but to God, concluded Joel. So why didn't they?

¹⁹To you, O LORD, I call,
    for fire has devoured the open pastures
    and flames have burned up all the trees of
        the field.
²⁰Even the wild animals pant for you;
    the streams of water have dried up
    and fire has devoured the open pastures.

■ An Army of Locusts
2 Blow the trumpet in Zion;
    sound the alarm on my holy hill.
Let all who live in the land tremble,
    for the day of the LORD is coming.
It is close at hand—
²   a day of darkness and gloom,
    a day of clouds and blackness.
Like dawn spreading across the mountains
    a large and mighty army comes,
such as never was of old
    nor ever will be in ages to come.

³Before them fire devours,
    behind them a flame blazes.
Before them the land is like the garden of Eden,
    behind them, a desert waste—
    nothing escapes them.
⁴They have the appearance of horses;
    they gallop along like cavalry.
⁵With a noise like that of chariots
    they leap over the mountaintops,

like a crackling fire consuming stubble,
    like a mighty army drawn up for battle.

⁶At the sight of them, nations are in anguish;
    every face turns pale.
⁷They charge like warriors;
    they scale walls like soldiers.
They all march in line,
    not swerving from their course.
⁸They do not jostle each other;
    each marches straight ahead.
They plunge through defences
    without breaking ranks.
⁹They rush upon the city;
    they run along the wall.
They climb into the houses;
    like thieves they enter through the windows.

¹⁰Before them the earth shakes,
    the sky trembles,
the sun and moon are darkened,
    and the stars no longer shine.
¹¹The LORD thunders
    at the head of his army;
his forces are beyond number,
    and mighty are those who obey his
        command.
The day of the LORD is great;
    it is dreadful.
    Who can endure it?

■ Rend Your Heart
¹²"Even now," declares the LORD,
    "return to me with all your heart,
    with fasting and weeping and mourning."

¹³Rend your heart
    and not your garments.
Return to the LORD your God,
    for he is gracious and compassionate,
slow to anger and abounding in love,
    and he relents from sending calamity.
¹⁴Who knows? He may turn and have pity
    and leave behind a blessing—
grain offerings and drink offerings
    for the LORD your God.

2:13 ■ TORN HEARTS
In the Old Testament, men and women tore their robes as a sign of sorrow and mourning. (Middle Easterners do so still.) Jacob, Moses, Joshua, Elijah, David, and Job all tore their clothes as an expression of grief or anguish. In Joel's day, however, God looked for change on the inside, not just another outward show of remorse. He sought broken hearts, not torn garments.

¹⁵Blow the trumpet in Zion,
    declare a holy fast,
    call a sacred assembly.
¹⁶Gather the people,
    consecrate the assembly;
bring together the elders,
    gather the children,
    those nursing at the breast.

ᵉ 15 Hebrew *Shaddai*   ᶠ 17 The meaning of the Hebrew for this word is uncertain.

Let the bridegroom leave his room
  and the bride her chamber.
[17]Let the priests, who minister before the LORD,
  weep between the temple porch and the
  altar.
Let them say, "Spare your people, O LORD.
  Do not make your inheritance an object of
  scorn,
  a byword among the nations.
Why should they say among the peoples,
  'Where is their God?'"

■ The LORD's Answer
[18]Then the LORD will be jealous for his land
  and take pity on his people.

[19]The LORD will reply[a] to them:

"I am sending you grain, new wine and oil,
  enough to satisfy you fully;
never again will I make you
  an object of scorn to the nations.

[20]"I will drive the northern army far from you,
  pushing it into a parched and barren land,
with its front columns going into the eastern
  sea[b]
and those in the rear into the western sea.[c]
And its stench will go up;
  its smell will rise."

Surely he has done great things.[d]
[21] Be not afraid, O land;
  be glad and rejoice.
Surely the LORD has done great things.
[22] Be not afraid, O wild animals,
  for the open pastures are becoming green.
The trees are bearing their fruit;
  the fig-tree and the vine yield their riches.
[23]Be glad, O people of Zion,
  rejoice in the LORD your God,
for he has given you
  the autumn rains in righteousness.[e]
He sends you abundant showers,
  both autumn and spring rains, as before.
[24]The threshing-floors will be filled with grain;
  the vats will overflow with new wine and oil.

[25]"I will repay you for the years the locusts have
  eaten—
  the great locust and the young locust,
  the other locusts and the locust swarm[f]—
my great army that I sent among you.
[26]You will have plenty to eat, until you are full,
  and you will praise the name of the LORD
  your God,
who has worked wonders for you;
  never again will my people be shamed.
[27]Then you will know that I am in Israel,
  that I am the LORD your God,
  and that there is no other;
never again will my people be shamed.

■ The Day of the LORD
[28]"And afterwards,
  I will pour out my Spirit on all people.

Your sons and daughters will prophesy,
  your old men will dream dreams,
  your young men will see visions.
[29]Even on my servants, both men and women,
  I will pour out my Spirit in those days.

2:29 ■ THE SPIRIT POURED OUT
This prophecy was quoted by Peter on the day of
Pentecost (Acts 2:17–21). He said it had been
fulfilled when the Holy Spirit came on Jesus'
disciples. Paul also quoted verse 32 in Romans
10:12–13, making the point that God would
respond to Jews and non-Jews without
distinction.

---

[30]I will show wonders in the heavens
  and on the earth,
  blood and fire and billows of smoke.
[31]The sun will be turned to darkness
  and the moon to blood
  before the coming of the great and dreadful
  day of the LORD.
[32]And everyone who calls
  on the name of the LORD will be saved;
for on Mount Zion and in Jerusalem
  there will be deliverance,
  as the LORD has said,
among the survivors
  whom the LORD calls.

■ The Nations Judged
3 "In those days and at that time,
  when I restore the fortunes of Judah and
  Jerusalem,
[2]I will gather all nations
  and bring them down to the Valley of
  Jehoshaphat.[a]
There I will enter into judgment against them
  concerning my inheritance, my people Israel,
for they scattered my people among the nations
  and divided up my land.
[3]They cast lots for my people
  and traded boys for prostitutes;
they sold girls for wine
  that they might drink.

3:3 ■ GAMBLING PRIZES
The Babylonians who invaded Judah fulfilled this
prophecy literally: they seized captives as part of
the spoils of war, divided them up by casting lots,
then traded them for prostitutes and wine. In this
section, God promises vengeance on such war
crimes.

---

[4]"Now what have you against me, O Tyre and Sidon and all you regions of Philistia? Are you repaying me for something I have done? If you are paying
me back, I will swiftly and speedily return on your
own heads what you have done. [5]For you took my
silver and my gold and carried off my finest treasures to your temples. [6]You sold the people of Judah

---

[a]18, 19 Or LORD was jealous . . . / and took pity . . . / [19]The LORD replied
/ Surely it has done great things." [e]23 Or / the teacher for righteousness;
uncertain. [a]2 Jehoshaphat means the LORD judges; also in verse 12.   [b]20 That is, the Dead Sea   [c]20 That is, the Mediterranean   [d]20 Or rise.
[f]25 The precise meaning of the four Hebrew words used here for locusts is

and Jerusalem to the Greeks, that you might send them far from their homeland.

⁷"See, I am going to rouse them out of the places to which you sold them, and I will return on your own heads what you have done. ⁸I will sell your sons and daughters to the people of Judah, and they will sell them to the Sabeans, a nation far away." The LORD has spoken.

⁹Proclaim this among the nations:
    Prepare for war!
Rouse the warriors!
    Let all the fighting men draw near and attack.
¹⁰Beat your ploughshares into swords
    and your pruning hooks into spears.
Let the weakling say,
    "I am strong!"
¹¹Come quickly, all you nations from every side,
    and assemble there.

Bring down your warriors, O LORD!

¹²"Let the nations be roused;
    let them advance into the Valley of
        Jehoshaphat,
for there I will sit
    to judge all the nations on every side.
¹³Swing the sickle,
    for the harvest is ripe.
Come, trample the grapes,
    for the winepress is full
    and the vats overflow—
so great is their wickedness!"

¹⁴Multitudes, multitudes
in the valley of decision!
For the day of the LORD is near
    in the valley of decision.
¹⁵The sun and moon will be darkened,
    and the stars no longer shine.
¹⁶The LORD will roar from Zion
    and thunder from Jerusalem;
    the earth and the sky will tremble.
But the LORD will be a refuge for his people,
    a stronghold for the people of Israel.

■ Blessings for God's People

¹⁷"Then you will know that I, the LORD your God,
    dwell in Zion, my holy hill.
Jerusalem will be holy;
    never again will foreigners invade her.

¹⁸"In that day the mountains will drip new wine,
    and the hills will flow with milk;
    all the ravines of Judah will run with water.
A fountain will flow out of the LORD's house
    and will water the valley of acacias.ᵇ
¹⁹But Egypt will be desolate,
    Edom a desert waste,
because of violence done to the people of
        Judah,
    in whose land they shed innocent blood.
²⁰Judah will be inhabited for ever
    and Jerusalem through all generations.
²¹Their bloodguilt, which I have not pardoned,
    I will pardon."

The LORD dwells in Zion!

AMOS

INTRODUCTION

■ JUSTICE!

A SIMPLE FARMER TAKES ON A MATERIALISTIC NATION

"LET JUSTICE ROLL ON LIKE A RIVER, RIGHTEOUSNESS LIKE A NEVER-FAILING STREAM!"
■ 5:24

Business had never been better. For the first time in generations, Israel faced no military threat. Since they controlled the crucial trade routes, merchants piled up big profits. Luxuries became readily available – new stone houses, ivory-inlaid furniture, top-grade meat and fine wine, the best body lotions.

Amid such peace and prosperity, one lone voice scraped like fingernails on a blackboard. Amos spoke bluntly with a farmer's vocabulary, calling the city socialites "cows" (4:1). A mere shepherd – among the poorest of all professions – he treated luxury with scorn. Worst of all, Amos was a foreigner from the South – from Tekoa, a small town in Judah. Since Israel had split from the South about 170 years before, Israelite leaders did not take kindly to criticism from a southerner.

But to Amos, social acceptance didn't matter. He was no professional prophet, making his living talking smoothly about God (7:14). God had called him to leave his job and carry a message. God had said go, and Amos had obeyed.

■ GOD'S VIEW OF "RELIGION"

The people Amos addressed had plenty of "religion". They went regularly to shrines for worship. They looked forward to "the day of the LORD", when God would fulfil all their expectations for their country. But Amos brought unexpected

bad news from God: "I hate, I despise your religious feasts" (5:21). God didn't want sacrifice or singing. He demanded justice.

Amos listed all Israel's neighbours, announcing God's judgment for their crimes against humanity. Israelites liked this kind of talk; they felt superior to all these nations. But having caught the Israelites' attention, Amos circled dramatically home. God would judge Israel too. The people, their beautiful homes, their sacred altars – all would be destroyed.

■ THE CHARACTER OF GOD

More than any other book in the Bible, Amos concentrates on injustice. Israel had plenty of other faults he might have blasted. Their religious system, for instance, centred on two calf-idols. But Amos wasted little breath on that. He focused on the facts that met his eyes and ears in every market-place: oppression of the poor, dishonest business, bribery in court, privilege bought with money.

The wealthy Israelites were getting their luxuries at the expense of the poor. They congratulated themselves on their devotion to God with no sense that they had cut the heart out of their relationship to him. They wanted God to fit conveniently into life as an additive. God showed himself through Amos as lordly, absolute, inescapable. He must be master over all of life, including business affairs.

■ HOW TO READ AMOS

Perhaps because he was a farmer, Amos used a plain writing style, filled with strong country language. The organisation of his book is clear too: chapters 1–2 line up the Middle Eastern nations for trial, chapters 3–6 give a series of messages from God (usually beginning with "Hear this word"), and the last three chapters convey God's judgment through five graphic visions.

Throughout, Amos sticks close to his main concern: cruelty and inhumanity between people. The injustices Amos condemns often sound familiar today. As you read, ask yourself, "What would Amos say about me and about my people?"

It is a good idea to read Amos and Hosea together, for they give two views of the same situation. A visitor from the South, Amos was shocked by the injustices he saw in every market-place. Hosea emphasised the inner dimension, an abused relationship to a loving God.

Amos predicted that Israel would be punished, and his prediction proved right. After King Jeroboam, the government deteriorated. Five kings took the throne in the next 13 years; four were assassinated. In 30 years Israel was permanently dismantled by Assyrian armies. For historical background, read 2 Kings 14:23–17:41, noting that the kings of both Israel and Judah are interspersed. For a briefer account, read the summaries of their reigns in "A Line-up of Rulers", pages 260–268.

■ 3-TRACK READING PLAN

For an explanation and complete listing of the 3-track reading plan, turn to page x.

■ **TRACK 1:**
Two-Week Courses on the Bible
The Track 1 reading programme on the Old Testament includes one chapter from Amos. See page x for a complete listing of this course.

■ **TRACK 2:**
An Overview of Amos in 1 Day
☐ Day 1. Read the Introduction to Amos and chapter 4, which sums up God's majestic anger against his people.
Now turn to page xi for your next Track 2 reading project.

■ **TRACK 3:**
All of Amos in 9 Days
After you have read through Amos, turn to pages xii–xiii for your next Track 3 reading project.

☐ 1   ☐ 2   ☐ 3   ☐ 4
☐ 5   ☐ 6   ☐ 7   ☐ 8
☐ 9

1 The words of Amos, one of the shepherds of Tekoa—what he saw concerning Israel two years before the earthquake, when Uzziah was king of Judah and Jeroboam son of Jehoash*a* was king of Israel. ²He said:

"The LORD roars from Zion
    and thunders from Jerusalem;
the pastures of the shepherds dry up,*b*
    and the top of Carmel withers."

■ Judgment on Israel's Neighbours
³This is what the LORD says:

"For three sins of Damascus,
    even for four, I will not turn back ˌmy
        wrathˌ.
Because she threshed Gilead
    with sledges having iron teeth,
⁴I will send fire upon the house of Hazael
    that will consume the fortresses of
        Ben-Hadad.
⁵I will break down the gate of Damascus;
    I will destroy the king who is in*c* the Valley
        of Aven*d*
and the one who holds the sceptre in Beth
    Eden.
The people of Aram will go into exile to
    Kir,"
                                        says the LORD.

⁶This is what the LORD says:

"For three sins of Gaza,
    even for four, I will not turn back ˌmy
        wrathˌ.
Because she took captive whole communities
    and sold them to Edom,
⁷I will send fire upon the walls of Gaza
    that will consume her fortresses.
⁸I will destroy the king*e* of Ashdod

and the one who holds the sceptre in
    Ashkelon.
I will turn my hand against Ekron,
    till the last of the Philistines is dead,"
                                        says the Sovereign LORD.

⁹This is what the LORD says:

"For three sins of Tyre,
    even for four, I will not turn back ˌmy
        wrathˌ.
Because she sold whole communities of
    captives to Edom,
    disregarding a treaty of brotherhood,
¹⁰I will send fire upon the walls of Tyre
    that will consume her fortresses."

1:9 ■ ATROCITIES

Amos began with thundering pronouncements against the enemies of Israel and Judah. His local audience must have cheered as he called down judgment on the blatant misdeeds of their neighbours: selling slaves, breaking treaties, ripping open pregnant women, desecrating the dead. But then Amos turned his attention to his own countrymen (2:4–16). God held his people to a far higher standard of morality. Israelites failed by breaking God's law; their neighbours were judged guilty of "crimes against humanity", for breaking laws of common decency.

¹¹This is what the LORD says:

"For three sins of Edom,
    even for four, I will not turn back ˌmy
        wrathˌ.
Because he pursued his brother with a sword,
    stifling all compassion,*f*
because his anger raged continually
    and his fury flamed unchecked,
¹²I will send fire upon Teman

*a*1 Hebrew *Joash*, a variant of *Jehoash*   *b*2 Or *shepherds mourn*   *c*5 Or *the inhabitants of*   *d*5 *Aven* means *wickedness*.   *e*8 Or *inhabitants*
*f*11 Or *sword / and destroyed his allies*

that will consume the fortresses of Bozrah."

¹³This is what the LORD says:

"For three sins of Ammon,
    even for four, I will not turn back ⌐my
        wrath⌐.
Because he ripped open the pregnant women
        of Gilead
    in order to extend his borders,
¹⁴I will set fire to the walls of Rabbah
    that will consume her fortresses
amid war cries on the day of battle,
    amid violent winds on a stormy day.
¹⁵Her king ⁸ will go into exile,
    he and his officials together,"
                                    says the LORD.

2 This is what the LORD says:

"For three sins of Moab,
    even for four, I will not turn back ⌐my
        wrath⌐.
Because he burned, as if to lime,
    the bones of Edom's king,
²I will send fire upon Moab
    that will consume the fortresses of Kerioth.ᵃ
Moab will go down in great tumult
    amid war cries and the blast of the trumpet.
³I will destroy her ruler
    and kill all her officials with him,"
                                    says the LORD.

⁴This is what the LORD says:

"For three sins of Judah,
    even for four, I will not turn back ⌐my
        wrath⌐.
Because they have rejected the law of the LORD
    and have not kept his decrees,
because they have been led astray by false
        gods,ᵇ
    the godsᶜ their ancestors followed,
⁵I will send fire upon Judah
    that will consume the fortresses of
        Jerusalem."

■ Judgment on Israel
⁶This is what the LORD says:

"For three sins of Israel,
    even for four, I will not turn back ⌐my
        wrath⌐.
They sell the righteous for silver,
    and the needy for a pair of sandals.
⁷They trample on the heads of the poor
    as upon the dust of the ground
    and deny justice to the oppressed.
Father and son use the same girl
    and so profane my holy name.
⁸They lie down beside every altar
    on garments taken in pledge.
In the house of their god
    they drink wine taken as fines.

⁹"I destroyed the Amorite before them,
    though he was tall as the cedars
    and strong as the oaks.

I destroyed his fruit above
    and his roots below.

2:8 ■ RUTHLESS DEBT COLLECTORS
Bankers making loans usually want collateral to
back up the promise to repay. In Amos' day poor
people resorted to pledging the very clothes on
their backs as collateral. Debt collectors who took
a debtor's garments flagrantly violated God's law
(Exodus 22:25–27). Worse, they were using the
clothes as bedding when they went to their
shrines to worship God.

---

¹⁰"I brought you up out of Egypt,
    and I led you for forty years in the desert
    to give you the land of the Amorites.
¹¹I also raised up prophets from among your sons
    and Nazirites from among your young men.
Is this not true, people of Israel?"
                                    declares the LORD.
¹²"But you made the Nazirites drink wine
    and commanded the prophets not to
        prophesy.

¹³"Now then, I will crush you
    as a cart crushes when loaded with grain.
¹⁴The swift will not escape,
    the strong will not muster their strength,
    and the warrior will not save his life.
¹⁵The archer will not stand his ground,
    the fleet-footed soldier will not get away,
    and the horseman will not save his life.
¹⁶Even the bravest warriors
    will flee naked on that day,"
                                    declares the LORD.

■ Witnesses Summoned Against Israel
3 Hear this word the LORD has spoken against you,
    O people of Israel — against the whole family I
brought up out of Egypt:

²"You only have I chosen
    of all the families of the earth;
therefore I will punish you
    for all your sins."

³Do two walk together
    unless they have agreed to do so?
⁴Does a lion roar in the thicket
    when he has no prey?
Does he growl in his den
    when he has caught nothing?
⁵Does a bird fall into a trap on the ground
    where no snare has been set?
Does a trap spring up from the earth
    when there is nothing to catch?
⁶When a trumpet sounds in a city,
    do not the people tremble?
When disaster comes to a city,
    has not the LORD caused it?

⁷Surely the Sovereign LORD does nothing
    without revealing his plan
    to his servants the prophets.

ᵍ 15 Or / Molech; Hebrew malcam   ᵃ 2 Or of her cities   ᵇ 4 Or by lies   ᶜ 4 Or lies

8The lion has roared—
   who will not fear?
The Sovereign LORD has spoken—
   who can but prophesy?

9Proclaim to the fortresses of Ashdod
   and to the fortresses of Egypt:
"Assemble yourselves on the mountains of
   Samaria;
   see the great unrest within her
   and the oppression among her people."

10"They do not know how to do right," declares
   the LORD,
   "who hoard plunder and loot in their
   fortresses."

11Therefore this is what the Sovereign LORD says:

"An enemy will overrun the land;
   he will pull down your strongholds
   and plunder your fortresses."

12This is what the LORD says:

"As a shepherd saves from the lion's mouth
   only two leg bones or a piece of an ear,
so will the Israelites be saved,
those who sit in Samaria
   on the edge of their beds
   and in Damascus on their couches."*a*

13"Hear this and testify against the house of
Jacob," declares the Lord, the LORD God Almighty.

14"On the day I punish Israel for her sins,
   I will destroy the altars of Bethel;
the horns of the altar will be cut off
   and fall to the ground.
15I will tear down the winter house
   along with the summer house;
the houses adorned with ivory will be
   destroyed
   and the mansions will be demolished,"
                        declares the LORD.

■ Israel Has Not Returned to God

4 Hear this word, you cows of Bashan on
   Mount Samaria,
   you women who oppress the poor and crush
      the needy
·   and say to your husbands, "Bring us some
      drinks!"
2The Sovereign LORD has sworn by his holiness:
   "The time will surely come
   when you will be taken away with hooks,
      the last of you with fish-hooks.
3You will each go straight out
      through breaks in the wall,
   and you will be cast out towards Harmon,"*a*
                        declares the LORD.
4"Go to Bethel and sin;
   go to Gilgal and sin yet more.
Bring your sacrifices every morning,
   your tithes every three years.*b*
5Burn leavened bread as a thank-offering
   and brag about your freewill offerings—
boast about them, you Israelites,
   for this is what you love to do,"
                        declares the Sovereign LORD.

6"I gave you empty stomachs*c* in every city
   and lack of bread in every town,
   yet you have not returned to me,"
                        declares the LORD.

4:1 ■ PRIZE COWS
With searing scornfulness, Amos paints a picture
of women living in sheer luxury. These "cows"
thought only of their pleasure, not of the
oppressed poor who made their life of luxury
possible. Amos paints their punishment just as
vividly. The brutal Assyrian armies, who later
captured Israel and took its people into exile, left
monuments portraying their captives being
dragged off with hooks in their mouths.

7"I also withheld rain from you
   when the harvest was still three months
      away.
I sent rain on one town,
   but withheld it from another.
One field had rain;
   another had none and dried up.
8People staggered from town to town for water
   but did not get enough to drink,
   yet you have not returned to me,"
                        declares the LORD.

9"Many times I struck your gardens and
      vineyards,
   I struck them with blight and mildew.
Locusts devoured your fig and olive trees,
   yet you have not returned to me,"
                        declares the LORD.

10"I sent plagues among you
   as I did to Egypt.
I killed your young men with the sword,
   along with your captured horses.
I filled your nostrils with the stench of your
      camps,
   yet you have not returned to me,"
                        declares the LORD.

11"I overthrew some of you
   as I*d* overthrew Sodom and Gomorrah.
You were like a burning stick snatched from
      the fire,
   yet you have not returned to me,"
                        declares the LORD.

12"Therefore this is what I will do to you, Israel,
   and because I will do this to you,
   prepare to meet your God, O Israel."

13He who forms the mountains,
   creates the wind,
   and reveals his thoughts to man,
he who turns dawn to darkness,
   and treads the high places of the earth—
   the LORD God Almighty is his name.

---

a 12 The meaning of the Hebrew for this line is uncertain.   *a 3* Masoretic Text; with a different word division of the Hebrew (see Septuagint) *out, O mountain
of oppression*   *b 4* Or *tithes on the third day*   *c 6* Hebrew *you cleanness of teeth*   *d 11* Hebrew *God*

■ A Lament and Call to Repentance

5 Hear this word, O house of Israel, this lament I take up concerning you:

2"Fallen is Virgin Israel,
    never to rise again,
deserted in her own land,
    with no-one to lift her up."

4:12 ■ BEFORE IT'S TOO LATE

This is the most famous verse in Amos, thanks to graffiti artists who write "Prepare to meet thy God!" in unlikely places. Amos has just reviewed a series of natural disasters — famine, drought, blight, plagues, war — any of which should have been enough to turn the nation to God. But Israel did not respond, and now Amos is holding out one last chance for repentance.

3This is what the Sovereign LORD says:

"The city that marches out a thousand strong
        for Israel
    will have only a hundred left;
the town that marches out a hundred strong
    will have only ten left."

4This is what the LORD says to the house of Israel:

"Seek me and live;
5   do not seek Bethel,
do not go to Gilgal,
    do not journey to Beersheba.
For Gilgal will surely go into exile,
    and Bethel will be reduced to nothing."[a]
6Seek the LORD and live,
    or he will sweep through the house of
        Joseph like a fire;
it will devour,
    and Bethel will have no-one to quench it.

7You who turn justice into bitterness
    and cast righteousness to the ground
8(he who made the Pleiades and Orion,
    who turns blackness into dawn
    and darkens day into night,
who calls for the waters of the sea
    and pours them out over the face of the
        land —
    the LORD is his name —
9he flashes destruction on the stronghold
    and brings the fortified city to ruin),
10you hate the one who reproves in court
    and despise him who tells the truth.

11You trample on the poor
    and force him to give you grain.
Therefore, though you have built stone
        mansions,
    you will not live in them;
though you have planted lush vineyards,
    you will not drink their wine.
12For I know how many are your offences
    and how great your sins.

You oppress the righteous and take bribes

and you deprive the poor of justice in the
        courts.
13Therefore the prudent man keeps quiet in such
        times,
    for the times are evil.

14Seek good, not evil,
    that you may live.
Then the LORD God Almighty will be with you,
    just as you say he is.
15Hate evil, love good;
    maintain justice in the courts.
Perhaps the LORD God Almighty will have
        mercy
    on the remnant of Joseph.

16Therefore this is what the Lord, the LORD God Almighty, says:

"There will be wailing in all the streets
    and cries of anguish in every public square.
The farmers will be summoned to weep
    and the mourners to wail.
17There will be wailing in all the vineyards,
    for I will pass through your midst,"
                                    says the LORD.

■ The Day of the LORD
18Woe to you who long
    for the day of the LORD!
Why do you long for the day of the LORD?
    That day will be darkness, not light.
19It will be as though a man fled from a lion
    only to meet a bear,
as though he entered his house
    and rested his hand on the wall
    only to have a snake bite him.
20Will not the day of the LORD be darkness, not
        light —
    pitch-dark, without a ray of brightness?

5:20 ■ THE DAY OF THE LORD

In Amos' day as today, some religious people looked forward to "the day of the LORD", when God will intervene personally in history and save his people. Israelites, assuming that "God is on our side", thought it would be a great day for them. But Amos contradicted their expectations. In a few words he depicted "the day of the LORD" as a nightmare.

21"I hate, I despise your religious feasts;
    I cannot stand your assemblies.
22Even though you bring me burnt offerings and
        grain offerings,
    I will not accept them.
Though you bring choice fellowship offerings,[b]
    I will have no regard for them.
23Away with the noise of your songs!
    I will not listen to the music of your harps.
24But let justice roll on like a river,
    righteousness like a never-failing stream!

25"Did you bring me sacrifices and offerings

---

a5 Or grief; or wickedness; Hebrew aven, a reference to Beth Aven (a derogatory name for Bethel)   b22 Traditionally peace offerings

for forty years in the desert, O house of
Israel?
²⁶You have lifted up the shrine of your king,
the pedestal of your idols,
the star of your god— c
which you made for yourselves.
²⁷Therefore I will send you into exile beyond
Damascus,"
says the LORD, whose name is God Almighty.

■ Woe to the Complacent

6 Woe to you who are complacent in Zion,
and to you who feel secure on Mount
Samaria,
you notable men of the foremost nation,
to whom the people of Israel come!
²Go to Calneh and look at it;
go from there to great Hamath,
and then go down to Gath in Philistia.
Are they better off than your two kingdoms?
Is their land larger than yours?
³You put off the evil day
and bring near a reign of terror.
⁴You lie on beds inlaid with ivory
and lounge on your couches.
You dine on choice lambs
and fattened calves.
⁵You strum away on your harps like David
and improvise on musical instruments.
⁶You drink wine by the bowlful
and use the finest lotions,
but you do not grieve over the ruin of
Joseph.
⁷Therefore you will be among the first to go
into exile;
your feasting and lounging will end.

6:1 ■ SOFT AND FAT

Amos is at his sarcastic best in this message to
"the notable men of the foremost nation".
Consistently, Israel proved much better at handling
hardship than success. In prosperous times like
Amos' they grew addicted to luxury and power,
forgetting all about God. Hundreds of years
before, Moses had warned against this very
syndrome (Deuteronomy 8:10–20).

■ The LORD Abhors the Pride of Israel

⁸The Sovereign LORD has sworn by himself— the
LORD God Almighty declares:

"I abhor the pride of Jacob
and detest his fortresses;
I will deliver up the city
and everything in it."

⁹If ten men are left in one house, they too will die.
¹⁰And if a relative who is to burn the bodies comes
to carry them out of the house and asks anyone still
hiding there, "Is anyone with you?" and he says,
"No," then he will say, "Hush! We must not mention
the name of the LORD."

¹¹For the LORD has given the command,

and he will smash the great house into
pieces
and the small house into bits.

¹²Do horses run on the rocky crags?
Does one plough there with oxen?
But you have turned justice into poison
and the fruit of righteousness into
bitterness—
¹³you who rejoice in the conquest of Lo Debarᵃ
and say, "Did we not take Karnaimᵇ by our
own strength?"

¹⁴For the LORD God Almighty declares,
"I will stir up a nation against you, O house
of Israel,
that will oppress you all the way
from Leboᶜ Hamath to the valley of the
Arabah."

■ Locusts, Fire and a Plumb-Line

7 This is what the Sovereign LORD showed me: He
was preparing swarms of locusts after the king's
share had been harvested and just as the second
crop was coming up. ²When they had stripped the
land clean, I cried out, "Sovereign LORD, forgive!
How can Jacob survive? He is so small!"

³So the LORD relented.

"This will not happen," the LORD said.

⁴This is what the Sovereign LORD showed me: The
Sovereign LORD was calling for judgment by fire; it
dried up the great deep and devoured the land.
⁵Then I cried out, "Sovereign LORD, I beg you, stop!
How can Jacob survive? He is so small!"

⁶So the LORD relented.

"This will not happen either," the Sovereign LORD
said.

⁷This is what he showed me: the Lord was standing by a wall that had been built true to plumb, with
a plumb-line in his hand. ⁸And the LORD asked me,
"What do you see, Amos?"

"A plumb-line," I replied.

Then the Lord said, "Look, I am setting a plumb-
line among my people Israel; I will spare them no
longer.

7:8 ■ A PLUMB LINE

A plumb line is a weight on the end of a string;
builders use it to make certain that their walls
stand straight. A wall may look right, but if it
doesn't match a plumb line, it is out of kilter.
Similarly God will use a plumb line to judge
whether Israel is "straight" by his standards.

⁹"The high places of Isaac will be destroyed
and the sanctuaries of Israel will be ruined;
with my sword I will rise against the house
of Jeroboam."

■ Amos and Amaziah

¹⁰Then Amaziah the priest of Bethel sent a message to Jeroboam king of Israel: "Amos is raising a
conspiracy against you in the very heart of Israel.

ᶜ 26 Or lifted up Sakkuth your king / and Kaiwan your idols, / your star-gods; Septuagint lifted up the shrine of Molech / and the star of your god Rephan, /
their idols   ᵃ 13 Lo Debar means nothing.   ᵇ 13 Karnaim means horns; horn here symbolises strength.   ᶜ 14 Or from the entrance to

The land cannot bear all his words. [11]For this is what Amos is saying:

" 'Jeroboam will die by the sword,
and Israel will surely go into exile,
away from their native land.' "

[12]Then Amaziah said to Amos, "Get out, you seer! Go back to the land of Judah. Earn your bread there and do your prophesying there. [13]Don't prophesy any more at Bethel, because this is the king's sanctuary and the temple of the kingdom."

[14]Amos answered Amaziah, "I was neither a prophet nor a prophet's son, but I was a shepherd, and I also took care of sycamore-fig trees. [15]But the LORD took me from tending the flock and said to me, 'Go, prophesy to my people Israel.' [16]Now then, hear the word of the LORD. You say,

" 'Do not prophesy against Israel,
and stop preaching against the house of
Isaac.'

[17]"Therefore this is what the LORD says:

" 'Your wife will become a prostitute in the
city,
and your sons and daughters will fall by the
sword.
Your land will be measured and divided up,
and you yourself will die in a pagan[a]
country.
And Israel will certainly go into exile,
away from their native land.' "

■ A Basket of Ripe Fruit

8 This is what the Sovereign LORD showed me: a basket of ripe fruit. [2]"What do you see, Amos?" he asked.

"A basket of ripe fruit," I answered.

Then the LORD said to me, "The time is ripe for my people Israel; I will spare them no longer.

[3]"In that day," declares the Sovereign LORD, "the songs in the temple will turn to wailing.[a] Many, many bodies—flung everywhere! Silence!"

[4]Hear this, you who trample the needy
and do away with the poor of the land,

[5]saying,

"When will the New Moon be over
that we may sell grain,
and the Sabbath be ended
that we may market wheat?"—
skimping the measure,
boosting the price
and cheating with dishonest scales,
[6]buying the poor with silver
and the needy for a pair of sandals,
selling even the sweepings with the wheat.

[7]The LORD has sworn by the Pride of Jacob: "I will never forget anything they have done.

[8]"Will not the land tremble for this,
and all who live in it mourn?
The whole land will rise like the Nile;
it will be stirred up and then sink
like the river of Egypt.

[9]"In that day," declares the Sovereign LORD,

"I will make the sun go down at noon
and darken the earth in broad daylight.
[10]I will turn your religious feasts into mourning
and all your singing into weeping.
I will make all of you wear sackcloth
and shave your heads.
I will make that time like mourning for an only
son
and the end of it like a bitter day.

[11]"The days are coming," declares the Sovereign
LORD,
"when I will send a famine through the
land—
not a famine of food or a thirst for water,
but a famine of hearing the words of the
LORD.
[12]Men will stagger from sea to sea
and wander from north to east,
searching for the word of the LORD,
but they will not find it.

8:11 ■ WORST OF ALL FAMINES

In this chapter, God describes devastations that will fall upon Israel if they do not repent. One judgment, however stands out above all others: the nation will experience the silence of God, a famine of the words of the Lord. A few more prophets succeeded Amos, but after Malachi no prophet appeared in Israel for four centuries, until John the Baptist came to announce Jesus.

[13]"In that day

"the lovely young women and strong young
men
will faint because of thirst.
[14]They who swear by the shame[b] of Samaria,
or say, 'As surely as your god lives, O Dan',
or, 'As surely as the god[c] of Beersheba
lives'—
they will fall,
never to rise again."

■ Israel to Be Destroyed

9 I saw the Lord standing by the altar, and he said:

"Strike the tops of the pillars
so that the thresholds shake.
Bring them down on the heads of all the
people;
those who are left I will kill with the sword.
Not one will get away,
none will escape.
[2]Though they dig down to the depths of the
grave,[a]
from there my hand will take them.
Though they climb up to the heavens,
from there I will bring them down.
[3]Though they hide themselves on the top of
Carmel,
there I will hunt them down and seize them.

---

[a] 17 Hebrew an unclean   [a] 3 Or "the temple singers will wail   [b] 14 Or by Ashima; or by the idol   [c] 14 Or power   [a] 2 Hebrew to Sheol

Though they hide from me at the bottom of the
    sea,
  there I will command the serpent to bite
    them.
4Though they are driven into exile by their
    enemies,
  there I will command the sword to slay
    them.
I will fix my eyes upon them
  for evil and not for good."

9:4 ■ AN INESCAPABLE GOD

The beautiful verses of Psalm 139:7–12 describe
God's inescapable presence as a comfort. Here,
in similar poetry, Amos gives the opposite side of
that truth. Those whom God opposes can find no
refuge. They may hide on top of Mount Carmel, or
even at the very bottom of the sea, but God's eye
will follow them.

5The Lord, the LORD Almighty,
  he who touches the earth and it melts,
  and all who live in it mourn—
the whole land rises like the Nile,
  then sinks like the river of Egypt—
6he who builds his lofty palace*b* in the heavens
  and sets its foundation*c* on the earth,
who calls for the waters of the sea
  and pours them out over the face of the
    land—
  the LORD is his name.

7"Are not you Israelites
  the same to me as the Cushites?"*d*
                          declares the LORD.
"Did I not bring Israel up from Egypt,
  the Philistines from Caphtor*e*
  and the Arameans from Kir?

8"Surely the eyes of the Sovereign LORD
  are on the sinful kingdom.

I will destroy it
  from the face of the earth—
yet I will not totally destroy
  the house of Jacob,"
                          declares the LORD.
9"For I will give the command,
  and I will shake the house of Israel
  among all the nations
as grain is shaken in a sieve,
  and not a pebble will reach the ground.
10All the sinners among my people
  will die by the sword,
all those who say,
  'Disaster will not overtake or meet us.'

■ Israel's Restoration

11"In that day I will restore
  David's fallen tent.
I will repair its broken places,
  restore its ruins,
  and build it as it used to be,
12so that they may possess the remnant of Edom
  and all the nations that bear my name,"*f*
                          declares the LORD,
                          who will do these things.

13"The days are coming," declares the LORD,

"when the reaper will be overtaken by the
    ploughman
  and the planter by the one treading grapes.
New wine will drip from the mountains
  and flow from all the hills.
14I will bring back my exiled*g* people Israel;
  they will rebuild the ruined cities and live in
    them.
They will plant vineyards and drink their wine;
  they will make gardens and eat their fruit.
15I will plant Israel in their own land,
  never again to be uprooted
  from the land I have given them,"

                          says the LORD your God.

---

b6 The meaning of the Hebrew for this phrase is uncertain.   *c6* The meaning of the Hebrew for this word is uncertain.   *d7* That is, people from the
upper Nile region   *e7* That is, Crete   *f12* Hebrew; Septuagint *so that the remnant of men / and all the nations that bear my name may seek ‗the Lord‗*
g14 Or *will restore the fortunes of my*

OBADIAH

■ POETIC JUSTICE

OBADIAH GAVE THE FINAL WORD ON A BLOOD FEUD

"AS YOU HAVE DONE, IT WILL BE DONE TO YOU." ■ 15

The feud began with twin brothers, Jacob and Esau. Esau, the older by minutes, would have inherited family leadership, but in a moment of hunger he traded it for a meal (Genesis 25:19–34). Jacob went on to become the founding father of the nation of Israel. Esau, a born hunter, moved south-east to desolate mountain country. He founded the nation of Edom.

Their descendants continued the quarrel. Over hundreds of years the two nations battled repeatedly but inconclusively. The Edomites' capital, Sela, sat on a high plateau above a sheer cliff; the only access was by a deep ravine. From that well-protected enclave, the Edomites raided Israel.

Though the Israelites had been commanded, "Do not abhor an Edomite, for he is your brother" (Deuteronomy 23:7), they grew to regard the Edomites as cruel and heartless. Repeatedly the prophets predicted Edom's punishment by God. The final straw came when Babylon dismembered Jerusalem and took its citizens into exile. The Edomites egged on the conquering army, preyed on fleeing Israelites, and helped plunder Jerusalem. Psalm 137, one of the saddest passages in the Bible, records the Israelite's bitterness over this. As Esau had cared more for a meal than for the family name,

so his descendants cared more for the profit they could get from plunder than for the compassion they owed a brother.

■ FAIR RETURN FOR CRUELTY
Obadiah predicts poetic justice for proud Edom: their treachery towards Judah (verses 11–12) repaid with treachery from their own allies (7), their robbery (13) repaid with robbery (5–6), their violence (10) with violence (9), their love of destruction (12–14) repaid with utter destruction (10,18). Obadiah predicts that down-trodden Israel will rise again, while Edom will disappear from the face of the earth.

This prediction came precisely true. Edom was destroyed, not by Israel but by a series of foreign invaders. The last remnant of Edomites were destroyed in the Roman siege of Jerusalem in A.D. 70. Ironically, the nation that had tormented Jews in Jerusalem later died defending that city.

Why does this blood feud earn a place in Scripture? It demonstrates God's ongoing protection of his people from their enemies. It also shows that God's standards extend beyond his chosen people. Every nation will be judged, like Edom, by their own standard: "As you have done, it will be done to you" (15).

■ HOW TO READ OBADIAH

The shortest book in the Old Testament, Obadiah can easily be read and understood in one sitting. Many readers, however, have a hard time seeing the importance of this ongoing border feud between blood relatives.

A Bible dictionary can summarise the centuries of violence. Look under "Edom".

Perhaps, though, you can only fully appreciate Israel's feelings by reflecting on your own when a close relative treats you cruelly. A family betrayal is uniquely offensive to God and humanity. Obadiah reminds us that justice will be done.

■ 3-TRACK READING PLAN

For an explanation and complete listing of the 3-track reading plan, turn to page x.

■ TRACK 1:
Two-Week Courses on the
Bible
See page x for information on
these courses.

■ TRACK 2:
An Overview of Obadiah in
1 Day

☐ Day 1. Read the
Introduction to Obadiah and
all of Obadiah.
Now turn to page xi for your
next Track 2 reading project.

■ TRACK 3:
All of Obadiah in 1 Day
After you have read through
Obadiah, turn to pages xii–xiii
for your next Track 3 reading
project.

☐ Obadiah

¹The vision of Obadiah.

This is what the Sovereign LORD says about
Edom—

We have heard a message from the LORD:
    An envoy was sent to the nations to say,
    "Rise, and let us go against her for battle"—

²"See, I will make you small among the nations;
    you will be utterly despised.
³The pride of your heart has deceived you,
    you who live in the clefts of the rocks*a*
    and make your home on the heights,
you who say to yourself,
    'Who can bring me down to the ground?'
⁴Though you soar like the eagle
    and make your nest among the stars,
    from there I will bring you down,"
                    declares the LORD.
⁵"If thieves came to you,
    if robbers in the night—
Oh, what a disaster awaits you—
    would they not steal only as much as they
        wanted?
If grape pickers came to you,
    would they not leave a few grapes?
⁶But how Esau will be ransacked,
    his hidden treasures pillaged!
⁷All your allies will force you to the border;
    your friends will deceive and overpower you;
those who eat your bread will set a trap for
        you,*b*
    but you will not detect it.

⁸"In that day," declares the LORD,
    "will I not destroy the wise men of Edom,
    men of understanding in the mountains of
        Esau?
⁹Your warriors, O Teman, will be terrified,
    and everyone in Esau's mountains
    will be cut down in the slaughter.
¹⁰Because of the violence against your brother
        Jacob,
    you will be covered with shame;
    you will be destroyed for ever.
¹¹On the day you stood aloof
    while strangers carried off his wealth

and foreigners entered his gates
    and cast lots for Jerusalem,
    you were like one of them.
¹²You should not look down on your brother
    in the day of his misfortune,
nor rejoice over the people of Judah
    in the day of their destruction,
nor boast so much
    in the day of their trouble.
¹³You should not march through the gates of my
        people
    in the day of their disaster,
nor look down on them in their calamity
    in the day of their disaster,
nor seize their wealth
    in the day of their disaster.
¹⁴You should not wait at the crossroads
    to cut down their fugitives,
nor hand over their survivors
    in the day of their trouble.

¹⁵"The day of the LORD is near
    for all nations.
As you have done, it will be done to you;
    your deeds will return upon your own head.
¹⁶Just as you drank on my holy hill,
    so all the nations will drink continually;
they will drink and drink
    and be as if they had never been.
¹⁷But on Mount Zion will be deliverance;
    it will be holy,
and the house of Jacob
    will possess its inheritance.
¹⁸The house of Jacob will be a fire
    and the house of Joseph a flame;
the house of Esau will be stubble,
    and they will set it on fire and consume it.
There will be no survivors
    from the house of Esau."
                    The LORD has spoken.

¹⁹People from the Negev will occupy
    the mountains of Esau,
and people from the foothills will possess
    the land of the Philistines.
They will occupy the fields of Ephraim and
        Samaria,
    and Benjamin will possess Gilead.

---

a 3 Or *of Sela*   *b 7* The meaning of the Hebrew for this clause is uncertain.

²⁰This company of Israelite exiles who are in
    Canaan
will possess ⌊the land⌋ as far as Zarephath;
    the exiles from Jerusalem who are in Sepharad

will possess the towns of the Negev.
²¹Deliverers will go up onᶜ Mount Zion
    to govern the mountains of Esau.
And the kingdom will be the LORD's.

ᶜ21 Or from

JONAH

INTRODUCTION

■ GOOD NEWS FOR THE ENEMY?

JONAH BALKED AT LOVING THE CRUEL ASSYRIANS

"NINEVEH HAS MORE THAN A HUNDRED AND TWENTY THOUSAND PEOPLE. . . . SHOULD I
NOT BE CONCERNED ABOUT THAT GREAT CITY?" ■ 4:11

Jesus told his followers, "Love your enemies and
pray for those who persecute you" (Matthew 5:44).
While everyone talks admiringly about that
command, loving your enemies is no easy thing.
Many people doubt whether it is even right.
Should we forgive the Nazis? Should we make a
point to be kind to the Ku Klux Klan? Should we
have compassion on dictators like Saddam
Hussein?

The book of Jonah tells the story of a
man whom God instructed to love his enemies in
Nineveh. True to life, the prophet Jonah did just
the opposite of what God commanded. He
refused to go to the people he hated. Instead,
he tried to run away from the Lord.

Nineveh was a large, important city in
Assyria, situated on the river Tigris. It posed a
grave military threat to tiny Israel. God sent
Jonah there, and he responded without
hesitation: in Joppa he caught a boat going in
the opposite direction. Obviously, Jonah didn't
want to warn Nineveh's citizens that they were
about to be destroyed. He suspected they would
repent and God would forgive them.

■ WHY JONAH DIDN'T WANT TO GO
We can't be sure why Jonah hated Assyria, but
another short Old Testament book, Nahum, gives
a clue. This book, also completely dedicated to
Nineveh, describes a ruthless, bloodthirsty people.
The Assyrians themselves left monuments to their
cruelty — long, boastful inscriptions describing their

torture and slaughter of people who opposed
them.

Israelites had reasons to hate and fear
Nineveh. But God *loved* Nineveh. He wanted to
save the city, not destroy it. He knew Nineveh
was ripe for change. When Jonah finally
preached there, the entire city believed his
message and repented. Though cruel and
hardened, Nineveh was ready to believe God.
Israel had never responded to a prophet like
these Assyrians did.

■ AN ATTITUDE LIKE GOD'S
Since God repeatedly warned the Israelites not to
intermarry with people of other religions, and even
ordered them to drive other nations out of the
promised land, some readers conclude that the
Old Testament is racially narrow-minded. They say
the New Testament gives the first indication that
God cares for non-Jewish people.

The book of Jonah contradicts that view.
It shows, instead, that God wanted to use
Israelites like Jonah as agents of his concern.
They would preach doom but always with the
hope that the warning would lead to repentance.

Jonah needed to develop an attitude like
God's towards his enemies. Insistently, God led
Jonah to this understanding of his own mind and
heart. The book of Jonah is a story of a
miraculous change in Nineveh, but even more a
story of miraculous change in Jonah.

■ HOW TO READ JONAH

Like Esther and Ruth, Jonah is a delightful short
narrative by a master writer. Its spiritual
implications are powerful and obvious. You can
easily read it at one sitting.

As you read Jonah, notice the changes
that the city of Nineveh goes through. Try also
to trace the changes that occur in Jonah, and
observe how God pushes him to make these
changes. Then ask yourself: What did this book

say to its original Jewish readers? What does it
say to me?

You may also be interested in following
Nineveh's entire history. Though the Ninevites
repented in Jonah's time, they later returned to
old patterns. Later prophets (Nahum and
Zephaniah) predicted Nineveh's downfall for
"endless cruelty" (Nahum 3:19), and in 612 B.C.
that city was destroyed, never to be inhabited

again. A Bible dictionary can summarise Nineveh's long history as a world power; look under "Assyria". To place Jonah in Israelite history, see "A Line-up of Rulers", pages 260–268.

Is Jonah a "fish story"? Interpreters differ over whether it should be read as a parable (not necessarily factual) or as historical fact. At least one reliable account exists of a man swallowed by a sperm whale and later found, alive, in the whale's stomach. Jonah's historical basis cannot be dismissed simply because of the "great fish".

More to the point, Jesus compared himself to Jonah, and the people of his time to the Ninevites (Matthew 12:39–41; Luke 11:29–32). He predicted that "the men of Nineveh will stand up at the judgment with this generation and condemn it; for they repented at the preaching of Jonah, and now one greater than Jonah is here". It is hard to see how fictional characters could stand up at an event Jesus evidently believed would be historical.

■ 3-TRACK READING PLAN

For an explanation and complete listing of the 3-track reading plan, turn to page x.

■ TRACK 1:
Two-Week Courses on the Bible
See page x for information on these courses.

■ TRACK 2:
An Overview of Jonah in 1 Day
☐ Day 1. Read the

Introduction to Jonah and chapters 3 and 4. These two short chapters tell the less familiar part of the story: how Jonah got to Nineveh and became more bitter than before.
Now turn to page xi for your next Track 2 reading project.

■ TRACK 3:
All of Jonah in 2 Days
After you have read through Jonah, turn to pages xii–xiii for your next Track 3 reading project.

☐ 1–2 ☐ 3–4

■ Jonah Flees From the LORD

1 The word of the LORD came to Jonah son of Amittai: ²"Go to the great city of Nineveh and preach against it, because its wickedness has come up before me."

³But Jonah ran away from the LORD and headed for Tarshish. He went down to Joppa, where he found a ship bound for that port. After paying the fare, he went aboard and sailed for Tarshish to flee from the LORD.

⁴Then the LORD sent a great wind on the sea, and such a violent storm arose that the ship threatened to break up. ⁵All the sailors were afraid and each cried out to his own god. And they threw the cargo into the sea to lighten the ship.

But Jonah had gone below deck, where he lay down and fell into a deep sleep. ⁶The captain went to him and said, "How can you sleep? Get up and call on your god! Maybe he will take notice of us, and we will not perish."

⁷Then the sailors said to each other, "Come, let us cast lots to find out who is responsible for this calamity." They cast lots and the lot fell on Jonah.

⁸So they asked him, "Tell us, who is responsible for making all this trouble for us? What do you do? Where do you come from? What is your country? From what people are you?"

⁹He answered, "I am a Hebrew and I worship the LORD, the God of heaven, who made the sea and the land."

¹⁰This terrified them and they asked, "What have you done?" (They knew he was running away from the LORD, because he had already told them so.)

¹¹The sea was getting rougher and rougher. So they asked him, "What should we do to you to make the sea calm down for us?"

¹²"Pick me up and throw me into the sea," he replied, "and it will become calm. I know that it is my fault that this great storm has come upon you."

¹³Instead, the men did their best to row back to land. But they could not, for the sea grew even wilder than before. ¹⁴Then they cried to the LORD, "O LORD, please do not let us die for taking this man's life. Do not hold us accountable for killing an innocent man, for you, O LORD, have done as you pleased." ¹⁵Then they took Jonah and threw him overboard, and the raging sea grew calm. ¹⁶At this the men greatly feared the LORD, and they offered a sacrifice to the LORD and made vows to him.

¹⁷But the LORD provided a great fish to swallow Jonah, and Jonah was inside the fish three days and three nights.

■ Jonah's Prayer

2 From inside the fish Jonah prayed to the LORD his God. ²He said:

"In my distress I called to the LORD,
    and he answered me.
From the depths of the grave^a I called for help,
    and you listened to my cry.
³You hurled me into the deep,
    into the very heart of the seas,
    and the currents swirled about me;
all your waves and breakers
    swept over me.
⁴I said, 'I have been banished
    from your sight;
yet I will look again
    towards your holy temple.'
⁵The engulfing waters threatened me,^{b}
    the deep surrounded me;
    seaweed was wrapped around my head.

^{a}2 Hebrew *Sheol* ^{b}5 Or *waters were at my throat*

⁶To the roots of the mountains I sank down;
  the earth beneath barred me in for ever.
But you brought my life up from the pit,
  O LORD my God.

⁷"When my life was ebbing away,
  I remembered you, LORD,
and my prayer rose to you,
  to your holy temple.

⁸"Those who cling to worthless idols
  forfeit the grace that could be theirs.
⁹But I, with a song of thanksgiving,
  will sacrifice to you.
What I have vowed I will make good.
  Salvation comes from the LORD."

¹⁰And the LORD commanded the fish, and it vomited Jonah onto dry land.

■ Jonah Goes to Nineveh

3 Then the word of the LORD came to Jonah a
  second time: ²"Go to the great city of Nineveh
and proclaim to it the message I give you."
  ³Jonah obeyed the word of the LORD and went to
Nineveh. Now Nineveh was a very important city—
a visit required three days. ⁴On the first day, Jonah
started into the city. He proclaimed: "Forty more
days and Nineveh will be overturned." ⁵The Ninevites believed God. They declared a fast, and all of
them, from the greatest to the least, put on sackcloth.

3:3 ■ HOW BIG A CITY?
Archaeologists who have dug up Nineveh report
that at its peak its walls were 7¾ miles in
circumference. Since it would not take three days
to go around a city of that size, most probably the
"three days" refers to the administrative district of
which Nineveh was the capital. This comprised
four cities with a circumference of about 60 miles.
Another possibility: perhaps it took Jonah three
days to go to every neighbourhood, market-place,
and city gate with his message.

⁶When the news reached the king of Nineveh, he
rose from his throne, took off his royal robes, covered himself with sackcloth and sat down in the
dust. ⁷Then he issued a proclamation in Nineveh:

"By the decree of the king and his nobles:

Do not let any man or beast, herd or flock,
taste anything; do not let them eat or drink.
⁸But let man and beast be covered with sackcloth. Let everyone call urgently on God. Let
them give up their evil ways and their

violence. ⁹Who knows? God may yet relent
and with compassion turn from his fierce anger so that we will not perish."

¹⁰When God saw what they did and how they
turned from their evil ways, he had compassion and
did not bring upon them the destruction he had
threatened.

■ Jonah's Anger at the LORD's Compassion

4 But Jonah was greatly displeased and became
  angry. ²He prayed to the LORD, "O LORD, is this
not what I said when I was still at home? That is why
I was so quick to flee to Tarshish. I knew that you
are a gracious and compassionate God, slow to
anger and abounding in love, a God who relents
from sending calamity. ³Now, O LORD, take away my
life, for it is better for me to die than to live."

4:2 ■ TOO MERCIFUL A GOD?
The poet Robert Frost said, "After Jonah, you
could never trust God not to be merciful again."
Frustrated, the prophet discloses why he ran away
from God in the first place: he was afraid God
would forgive his arch-enemies. In fact, God did
just that, after Nineveh repented with an
eagerness that the Jews themselves often lacked
(see Matthew 12:41). Pointedly, the book of Jonah
ends with a question. Can anyone put limits on
God's mercy and forgiveness?

⁴But the LORD replied, "Have you any right to be
angry?"
  ⁵Jonah went out and sat down at a place east of
the city. There he made himself a shelter, sat in its
shade and waited to see what would happen to the
city. ⁶Then the LORD God provided a vine and made
it grow up over Jonah to give shade for his head to
ease his discomfort, and Jonah was very happy
about the vine. ⁷But at dawn the next day God provided a worm, which chewed the vine so that it
withered. ⁸When the sun rose, God provided a
scorching east wind, and the sun blazed on Jonah's
head so that he grew faint. He wanted to die, and
said, "It would be better for me to die than to live."
  ⁹But God said to Jonah, "Do you have a right to
be angry about the vine?"
  "I do," he said. "I am angry enough to die."
  ¹⁰But the LORD said, "You have been concerned
about this vine, though you did not tend it or make
it grow. It sprang up overnight and died overnight.
¹¹But Nineveh has more than a hundred and twenty
thousand people who cannot tell their right hand
from their left, and many cattle as well. Should I not
be concerned about that great city?"

MICAH

■ LIGHT IN A DARK TIME

EVIL AND VIOLENCE WERE CREEPING SOUTH TOWARDS JERUSALEM

AND WHAT DOES THE LORD REQUIRE OF YOU? TO ACT JUSTLY AND TO LOVE MERCY AND TO WALK HUMBLY WITH YOUR GOD. ■ 6:8

Country boys often lose perspective in the big city. They gawp at the tall buildings, the fancy clothes, and the showy symbols of power. Micah was a country boy from Moresheth, a small village in the no-man's-land south-west of Jerusalem. While his contemporary, Isaiah, moved in and out of the king's palace, Micah shows no sign of travelling in such circles.

Yet this country boy kept his sense of perspective. The blood and violence of his day did not overwhelm him, nor was he intimidated by powerful and wealthy people. He spoke like a person who had seen the world through God's eyes.

Micah lived in one of the darkest times in Israel's history, a time of brutal warfare. The country had long been split into North and South. Micah saw war break out between these sides, with 120,000 deaths on the southern side alone (2 Chronicles 28:6). Then Assyria, the brutal chief power of the day, smashed the Northern Kingdom after a three-year siege of its capital, Samaria. Only a miracle kept those same Assyrian armies out of Jerusalem (2 Chronicles 32). But for how long would the South remain free?

■ THE SIN OF THE SOUTH

Micah had no doubt about how to interpret these chaotic events. God had punished the northern nation of Israel for sins summarised in 2 Kings 17:16–17: idolatry, Baal worship, child sacrifice, magic and sorcery. Now these same activities were creeping south into Judah – so much so that Micah referred in disgust to Jerusalem as a "high

place", the traditional setting for pagan idol worship (1:5). The same judgment the North had suffered would come to Judah if people continued to disobey God.

Other historical accounts give more details of the South's sins. They describe how King Ahaz set up a foreign altar in God's temple, altering the temple construction "in deference to the king of Assyria" (2 Kings 16:18). He gave his own children in human sacrifice and shut the Lord's temple, substituting altars on every street corner (2 Chronicles 28:3,24–25). Along with this religious corruption came every other kind of sin: dishonesty (Micah 6:10–11), bribery (3:11), injustice (2:2), and distrust that destroyed families (7:5–6).

■ BEYOND THE DARKNESS

Yet Micah saw light ahead. He perceived a majestic God over all events, who punished his people only to purify and restore them. Along with making some of the Bible's frankest predictions of destruction, Micah gave some of the clearest predictions of the Messiah, the leader who would come to save Israel. Micah's perspective encompassed not only the events of his time but events far into the future, when the nations "will beat their swords into ploughshares" (4:3).

Micah looked straight at the darkness of his time and at the darkness yet to come. But his perspective – God's perspective – enabled him to see beyond darkness. "Do not gloat over me, my enemy! Though I have fallen, I will rise. Though I sit in darkness, the LORD will be my light" (7:8).

■ HOW TO READ MICAH

Micah had the big view of history, and thus he covered a lot of ground. His book, only seven chapters, is loaded with pronouncements on the events of several thousand years. Because so

much is jammed into so short a space, reading Micah can be confusing. A fragment may deal with the Messiah, for instance, and without warning the next few verses shift to the battle against Assyria.

To grasp Micah's message, think of his book as a collection of short speeches. One speech doesn't necessarily lead into the next. Instead of reading quickly from start to finish, pause after each short section to see whether you understand what it says. Try to understand who is speaking. Sometimes God speaks, sometimes Micah, sometimes the rebellious people.

In general, Micah follows this outline: chapters 1–3 indict both Northern and Southern Kingdoms, with their leaders; chapters 4 and 5 turn to the wonderful future God is planning; the last two chapters give the trial, punishment, and hope of the guilty nations.

It's very helpful to understand Micah's historical situation. Micah 1:1 names the kings of Judah he worked under. You can read about these kings, and their northern counterparts, in 2 Kings 15:27–20:21 and 2 Chronicles 27–32. For a brief summary, see "A Line-up of Rulers", pages 260–268.

■ 3-TRACK READING PLAN

For an explanation and complete listing of the 3-track reading plan, turn to page x.

■ TRACK 1:
Two-Week Courses on the Bible
See page x for information on these courses.

■ TRACK 2:
An Overview of Micah in 1 Day
☐ Day 1. Read the

Introduction to Micah and chapter 6, which includes one of the most succinct statements in the Old Testament of what God wants our lives to be.
Now turn to page xi for your next Track 2 reading project.

■ TRACK 3:
All of Micah in 7 Days
After you have read through Micah, turn to pages xii–xiii for your next Track 3 reading project.

☐ 1   ☐ 2   ☐ 3   ☐ 4
☐ 5   ☐ 6   ☐ 7

1 The word of the LORD that came to Micah of Moresheth during the reigns of Jotham, Ahaz and Hezekiah, kings of Judah—the vision he saw concerning Samaria and Jerusalem.

²Hear, O peoples, all of you,
    listen, O earth and all who are in it,
that the Sovereign LORD may witness against
        you,
    the Lord from his holy temple.

■ Judgment Against Samaria and Jerusalem
³Look! The LORD is coming from his
        dwelling-place;
    he comes down and treads the high places of
        the earth.
⁴The mountains melt beneath him
    and the valleys split apart,
like wax before the fire,
    like water rushing down a slope.
⁵All this is because of Jacob's transgression,
    because of the sins of the house of Israel.
What is Jacob's transgression?
    Is it not Samaria?
What is Judah's high place?
    Is it not Jerusalem?

⁶"Therefore I will make Samaria a heap of
        rubble,
    a place for planting vineyards.
I will pour her stones into the valley
    and lay bare her foundations.
⁷All her idols will be broken to pieces;
    all her temple gifts will be burned with fire;
    I will destroy all her images.
Since she gathered her gifts from the wages of
        prostitutes,

as the wages of prostitutes they will again be
        used."

■ Weeping and Mourning
⁸Because of this I will weep and wail;
    I will go about barefoot and naked.
I will howl like a jackal
    and moan like an owl.
⁹For her wound is incurable;
    it has come to Judah.
Itᵃ has reached the very gate of my people,
    even to Jerusalem itself.
¹⁰Tell it not in Gath;ᵇ
    weep not at all.ᶜ
In Beth Ophrahᵈ
    roll in the dust.

1:10 ■ A PASSION FOR PUNNING
Puns stump even the best translators. In verses 10–15 Micah plays on the names of a series of Israelite towns — probably marking the path Assyrian invaders followed. The puns were not meant to be funny. They extracted grief from the place-names of the invasion. NIV footnotes explain Micah's Hebrew puns, which are virtually untranslatable.

---

¹¹Pass on in nakedness and shame,
    you who live in Shaphir.ᵉ
Those who live in Zaananᶠ
    will not come out.
Beth Ezel is in mourning;
    its protection is taken from you.
¹²Those who live in Marothᵍ writhe in pain,
    waiting for relief,

ᵃ9 Or He   ᵇ10 Gath sounds like the Hebrew for tell.   ᶜ10 Hebrew; Septuagint may suggest not in Acco. The Hebrew for in Acco sounds like the Hebrew for weep.   ᵈ10 Beth Ophrah means house of dust.   ᵉ11 Shaphir means pleasant.   ᶠ11 Zaanan sounds like the Hebrew for come out.
ᵍ12 Maroth sounds like the Hebrew for bitter.

because disaster has come from the LORD,
even to the gate of Jerusalem.
¹³You who live in Lachish,ᵇ
harness the team to the chariot.
You were the beginning of sin
to the Daughter of Zion,
for the transgressions of Israel
were found in you.
¹⁴Therefore you will give parting gifts
to Moresheth Gath.
The town of Aczibⁱ will prove deceptive
to the kings of Israel.
¹⁵I will bring a conqueror against you
who live in Mareshah.ʲ
He who is the glory of Israel
will come to Adullam.
¹⁶Shave your heads in mourning
for the children in whom you delight;
make yourselves as bald as the vulture,
for they will go from you into exile.

■ Man's Plans and God's

2 Woe to those who plan iniquity,
to those who plot evil on their beds!
At morning's light they carry it out
because it is in their power to do it.
²They covet fields and seize them,
and houses, and take them.
They defraud a man of his home,
a fellow-man of his inheritance.

³Therefore, the LORD says:

"I am planning disaster against this people,
from which you cannot save yourselves.
You will no longer walk proudly,
for it will be a time of calamity.
⁴In that day men will ridicule you;
they will taunt you with this mournful song:
'We are utterly ruined;
my people's possession is divided up.
He takes it from me!
He assigns our fields to traitors.' "

⁵Therefore you will have no-one in the assembly
of the LORD
to divide the land by lot.

■ False Prophets

⁶"Do not prophesy," their prophets say.
"Do not prophesy about these things;
disgrace will not overtake us."
⁷Should it be said, O house of Jacob:
"Is the Spirit of the LORD angry?
Does he do such things?"

"Do not my words do good
to him whose ways are upright?
⁸Lately my people have risen up
like an enemy.
You strip off the rich robe
from those who pass by without a care,
like men returning from battle.
⁹You drive the women of my people
from their pleasant homes.

You take away my blessing
from their children for ever.
¹⁰Get up, go away!
For this is not your resting place,
because it is defiled,
it is ruined, beyond all remedy.
¹¹If a liar and deceiver comes and says,
'I will prophesy for you plenty of wine and
beer,'
he would be just the prophet for this people!

2:11 ■ PLENTY OF BEER
Modern politicians are filled with dread by the
newspaper shout-line "interest rates must rise".
They love to be popular, and hate to bring bad
news. Prophets in Micah's time were just the
same. They insisted that Micah stop predicting
bad news (2:6; 3:5) and join their peace
bandwagon. In fact, says Micah sarcastically, the
ideal prophet for feel-good Israel would predict
plenty of wine and beer.

■ Deliverance Promised

¹²"I will surely gather all of you, O Jacob;
I will surely bring together the remnant of
Israel.
I will bring them together like sheep in a pen,
like a flock in its pasture;
the place will throng with people.
¹³One who breaks open the way will go up
before them;
they will break through the gate and go out.
Their king will pass through before them,
the LORD at their head."

■ Leaders and Prophets Rebuked

3 Then I said,

"Listen, you leaders of Jacob,
you rulers of the house of Israel.
Should you not know justice,
² you who hate good and love evil;
who tear the skin from my people
and the flesh from their bones;
³who eat my people's flesh,
strip off their skin
and break their bones in pieces;
who chop them up like meat for the pan,
like flesh for the pot."

⁴Then they will cry out to the LORD,
but he will not answer them.
At that time he will hide his face from them
because of the evil they have done.

⁵This is what the LORD says:

"As for the prophets
who lead my people astray,
if one feeds them,
they proclaim 'peace';

ᵇ13 Lachish sounds like the Hebrew for team.   ⁱ14 Aczib means deception.   ʲ15 Mareshah sounds like the Hebrew for conqueror.

if he does not,
   they prepare to wage war against him.
⁶Therefore night will come over you, without
   visions,
   and darkness, without divination.
The sun will set for the prophets,
   and the day will go dark for them.
⁷The seers will be ashamed
   and the diviners disgraced.
They will all cover their faces
   because there is no answer from God."

⁸But as for me, I am filled with power,
   with the Spirit of the LORD,
   and with justice and might,
to declare to Jacob his transgression,
   to Israel his sin.
⁹Hear this, you leaders of the house of
   Jacob,
   you rulers of the house of Israel,
who despise justice
   and distort all that is right;
¹⁰who build Zion with bloodshed,
   and Jerusalem with wickedness.
¹¹Her leaders judge for a bribe,
   her priests teach for a price,
   and her prophets tell fortunes for money.
Yet they lean upon the LORD and say,
   "Is not the LORD among us?
   No disaster will come upon us."
¹²Therefore because of you,
   Zion will be ploughed like a field,
Jerusalem will become a heap of rubble,
   the temple hill a mound overgrown with
   thickets.

■ The Mountain of the LORD

4 In the last days

the mountain of the LORD's temple will be
   established
   as chief among the mountains;
it will be raised above the hills,
   and peoples will stream to it.

3:12 ■ LIFE-SAVING PROPHECY

One hundred years after this clear prophecy of its destruction, Jerusalem still stood. By that time Jeremiah was making similar predictions, which led to his arrest for treason. Some of the city leaders, however, quoted Micah's "ancient" prophecy, pointing out that since Micah had not been put to death, neither should Jeremiah be (Jeremiah 26:18–19). Their memory probably saved Jeremiah's life.

Within another 20 years, both Micah's and Jeremiah's predictions came true and Jerusalem was reduced to rubble.

²Many nations will come and say,

"Come, let us go up to the mountain of the
   LORD,
   to the house of the God of Jacob.
He will teach us his ways,
   so that we may walk in his paths."
The law will go out from Zion,
   the word of the LORD from Jerusalem.
³He will judge between many peoples

■ SEEING IN TWO DIMENSIONS
LITTLE DISTINCTION BETWEEN NEXT WEEK AND THE NEXT THOUSAND YEARS

THEY WILL BEAT THEIR SWORDS INTO PLOUGHSHARES AND THEIR SPEARS INTO PRUNING HOOKS. ■ 4:3

When you see a mountain range from a distance, it's very difficult to tell which peak is the highest. A smaller mountain may loom largest simply because it is closer to you than a higher peak.

Micah, and many of the other Old Testament prophets, saw the future like that. They made little distinction between events coming next week and events that would come a thousand years later. They seemed to see the future with limited "depth perception".

In the space of one verse, for instance, Micah shifts from a prediction (3:12) that Jerusalem will become a mound of rubble – a prophecy fulfilled about 100 years later – to a prophecy (4:1) that the same mountain will be

lifted up as "chief among the mountains" – something that has yet to be fulfilled today. In 5:2 comes a prediction that Matthew 2:6 records as fulfilled by Jesus' birth in Bethlehem 700 years later.

In Micah, the thousands of years between these fulfilments are unclear. They all seem to be about the same distance into the future. Almost certainly, Micah himself saw them unclearly. 1 Peter 1:10–11 comments that "the prophets . . . searched intently and with the greatest care, trying to find out the time and circumstances to which the Spirit of Christ in them was pointing when he predicted the sufferings of Christ and the glories that would follow."

☐ LIFE QUESTIONS:

What emotions do you feel knowing that some prophecies have not yet been fulfilled?

and will settle disputes for strong nations far
and wide.
They will beat their swords into ploughshares
and their spears into pruning hooks.
Nation will not take up sword against nation,
nor will they train for war any more.

4:3 ■ PARALLEL WITH ISAIAH

Micah 4:1–3, which describes the wonderful future
in store for the world, has an almost exact parallel
in Isaiah 2:2–4. Isaiah must have quoted Micah, or
vice versa, or perhaps both quoted a third,
unknown prophet. Both prophets spoke in
Jerusalem at about the same time.

⁴Every man will sit under his own vine
and under his own fig-tree,
and no-one will make them afraid,
for the LORD Almighty has spoken.
⁵All the nations may walk
in the name of their gods;
we will walk in the name of the LORD
our God for ever and ever.

■ The LORD's Plan
⁶"In that day," declares the LORD,

"I will gather the lame;
I will assemble the exiles
and those I have brought to grief.
⁷I will make the lame a remnant,
those driven away a strong nation.
The LORD will rule over them in Mount Zion
from that day and for ever.
⁸As for you, O watchtower of the flock,
O stronghold*ᵃ* of the Daughter of Zion,
the former dominion will be restored to you;
kingship will come to the Daughter of
Jerusalem."

⁹Why do you now cry aloud—
have you no king?
Has your counsellor perished,
that pain seizes you like that of a woman in
labour?
¹⁰Writhe in agony, O Daughter of Zion,
like a woman in labour,
for now you must leave the city
to camp in the open field.
You will go to Babylon;
there you will be rescued.
There the LORD will redeem you
out of the hand of your enemies.

¹¹But now many nations
are gathered against you.
They say, "Let her be defiled,
let our eyes gloat over Zion!"
¹²But they do not know
the thoughts of the LORD;
they do not understand his plan,
he who gathers them like sheaves to the
threshing-floor.
¹³"Rise and thresh, O Daughter of Zion,

for I will give you horns of iron;
I will give you hoofs of bronze
and you will break to pieces many nations."

You will devote their ill-gotten gains to the
LORD,
their wealth to the Lord of all the earth.

■ A Promised Ruler From Bethlehem
5 Marshal your troops, O city of troops,*ᵃ*
for a siege is laid against us.
They will strike Israel's ruler
on the cheek with a rod.

²"But you, Bethlehem Ephrathah,
though you are small among the clans*ᵇ* of
Judah,
out of you will come for me
one who will be ruler over Israel,
whose origins*ᶜ* are from of old,
from ancient times."*ᵈ*

5:2 ■ MESSIAH'S BIRTHPLACE

When the Magi came looking for a newborn "king
of the Jews", King Herod asked the biblical
scholars where to search. They referred him to
this passage (see Matthew 2:6), which predicted
that the Messiah would come from the small town
of Bethlehem. Micah also describes Christ as a
shepherd who will not merely bring peace, but *be*
Israel's peace.

³Therefore Israel will be abandoned
until the time when she who is in labour
gives birth
and the rest of his brothers return
to join the Israelites.

⁴He will stand and shepherd his flock
in the strength of the LORD,
in the majesty of the name of the LORD his
God.
And they will live securely, for then his
greatness
will reach to the ends of the earth.
⁵ And he will be their peace.

■ Deliverance and Destruction
When the Assyrian invades our land
and marches through our fortresses,
we will raise against him seven shepherds,
even eight leaders of men.
⁶They will rule*ᵉ* the land of Assyria with the
sword,
the land of Nimrod with drawn sword.*ᶠ*
He will deliver us from the Assyrian
when he invades our land
and marches into our borders.

⁷The remnant of Jacob will be
in the midst of many peoples
like dew from the LORD,
like showers on the grass,
which do not wait for man
or linger for mankind.

ᵃ8 Or hill   *ᵃ1* Or Strengthen your walls, O walled city   *ᵇ2* Or rulers   *ᶜ2* Hebrew *goings out*   *ᵈ2* Or from days of eternity   *ᵉ6* Or crush
ᶠ6 Or Nimrod in its gates

8The remnant of Jacob will be among the
      nations,
   in the midst of many peoples,
like a lion among the beasts of the forest,
   like a young lion among flocks of sheep,
which mauls and mangles as it goes,
   and no-one can rescue.
9Your hand will be lifted up in triumph over
      your enemies,
   and all your foes will be destroyed.

10"In that day," declares the LORD,

"I will destroy your horses from among you
   and demolish your chariots.
11I will destroy the cities of your land
   and tear down all your strongholds.
12I will destroy your witchcraft
   and you will no longer cast spells.
13I will destroy your carved images
   and your sacred stones from among you;
you will no longer bow down
   to the work of your hands.
14I will uproot from among you your Asherah
      poles g
   and demolish your cities.
15I will take vengeance in anger and wrath
   upon the nations that have not obeyed me."

■ The LORD's Case Against Israel
6 Listen to what the LORD says:

"Stand up, plead your case before the
      mountains;
   let the hills hear what you have to say.
2Hear, O mountains, the LORD's accusation;
   listen, you everlasting foundations of the
      earth.
For the LORD has a case against his people;
   he is lodging a charge against Israel.

3"My people, what have I done to you?
   How have I burdened you? Answer me.
4I brought you up out of Egypt
   and redeemed you from the land of slavery.
I sent Moses to lead you,
   also Aaron and Miriam.
5My people, remember
   what Balak king of Moab counselled
   and what Balaam son of Beor answered.
Remember ⌐your journey⌐ from Shittim to
      Gilgal,
   that you may know the righteous acts of the
      LORD."

6With what shall I come before the LORD
   and bow down before the exalted God?
Shall I come before him with burnt offerings,
   with calves a year old?
7Will the LORD be pleased with thousands of
      rams,
   with ten thousand rivers of oil?
Shall I offer my firstborn for my transgression,
   the fruit of my body for the sin of my soul?
8He has showed you, O man, what is good.
   And what does the LORD require of you?

To act justly and to love mercy
   and to walk humbly with your God.

6:5 ■ NAMES WITH MEANING

Speaking to people who knew their own history
well, Micah needed only to mention names like
Balaam and Balak to recall God's goodness and
humankind's disobedience. Numbers 22–24 tells
the story of Balaam, in which Balak tried to get
Balaam to curse Israel. Balaam gave this famous
reply: "How can I curse those whom God has not
cursed?" (Numbers 23:8). The trip from Shittim to
Gilgal apparently refers to Israel's miraculous
crossing of the Jordan River (Joshua 3:1;
4:19–20), the final stage in their journey from
slavery in Egypt to freedom in the promised land.
These events, which had occurred about 500
years before, were as real to the Israelites as
yesterday.

Verse 16 offers a different kind of memory: "the
statutes of Omri and all the practices of Ahab's
house". Omri and his son Ahab were two of the
most notoriously wicked kings in Israelite history
(1 Kings 16:21–33). Ahab went so far as to marry
Jezebel, a Phoenician princess, and set up a
temple for her god, Baal, in the new capital of
Samaria. He sponsored her massacre of genuine
prophets.

6:8 ■ WHAT GOD WANTS

Micah's most famous pronouncement summarises
the qualities that matter to God. Jesus spoke in
similar terms to the Pharisees about their religious
hypocrisy: they gave a tenth of even their spices
to God, yet they neglected justice, mercy, and
faithfulness (Matthew 23:23).

■ Israel's Guilt and Punishment
   9Listen! The LORD is calling to the city —
      and to fear your name is wisdom —
   "Heed the rod and the One who appointed
      it.a
10Am I still to forget, O wicked house,
   your ill-gotten treasures
   and the short ephah,b which is accursed?
11Shall I acquit a man with dishonest scales,
   with a bag of false weights?
12Her rich men are violent;
   her people are liars
   and their tongues speak deceitfully.
13Therefore, I have begun to destroy you,
   to ruin you because of your sins.
14You will eat but not be satisfied;
   your stomach will still be empty.c
You will store up but save nothing,
   because what you save I will give to the
      sword.
15You will plant but not harvest;
   you will press olives but not use the oil on
      yourselves,
   you will crush grapes but not drink the wine.

---

g 14 That is, symbols of the goddess Asherah   a 9 The meaning of the Hebrew for this line is uncertain.   b 10 An ephah was a dry measure.
c 14 The meaning of the Hebrew for this word is uncertain.

16You have observed the statutes of Omri
    and all the practices of Ahab's house,
    and you have followed their traditions.
Therefore I will give you over to ruin
    and your people to derision;
    you will bear the scorn of the nations."*d*

■ Israel's Misery

7 What misery is mine!
I am like one who gathers summer fruit
    at the gleaning of the vineyard;
there is no cluster of grapes to eat,
    none of the early figs that I crave.
2The godly have been swept from the land;
    not one upright man remains.
All men lie in wait to shed blood;
    each hunts his brother with a net.
3Both hands are skilled in doing evil;
    the ruler demands gifts,
the judge accepts bribes,
    the powerful dictate what they desire—
they all conspire together.
4The best of them is like a brier,
    the most upright worse than a thorn hedge.
The day of your watchmen has come,
    the day God visits you.
Now is the time of their confusion.
5Do not trust a neighbour;
    put no confidence in a friend.
Even with her who lies in your embrace
    be careful of your words.
6For a son dishonours his father,
    a daughter rises up against her mother,
a daughter-in-law against her mother-in-law—
    a man's enemies are the members of his own
        household.

7But as for me, I watch in hope for the LORD,
I wait for God my Saviour;
    my God will hear me.

■ Israel Will Rise

8Do not gloat over me, my enemy!
    Though I have fallen, I will rise.
Though I sit in darkness,
    the LORD will be my light.
9Because I have sinned against him,
    I will bear the LORD's wrath,
until he pleads my case
    and establishes my right.
He will bring me out into the light;
    I will see his righteousness.
10Then my enemy will see it
    and will be covered with shame,
she who said to me,
    "Where is the LORD your God?"
My eyes will see her downfall;

even now she will be trampled underfoot
    like mire in the streets.

11The day for building your walls will come,
    the day for extending your boundaries.
12In that day people will come to you
    from Assyria and the cities of Egypt,
even from Egypt to the Euphrates
    and from sea to sea
    and from mountain to mountain.
13The earth will become desolate because of its
        inhabitants,
    as the result of their deeds.

■ Prayer and Praise

14Shepherd your people with your staff,
    the flock of your inheritance,
which lives by itself in a forest,
    in fertile pasture-lands.*a*
Let them feed in Bashan and Gilead
    as in days long ago.

15"As in the days when you came out of Egypt,
    I will show them my wonders."

16Nations will see and be ashamed,
    deprived of all their power.
They will lay their hands on their mouths
    and their ears will become deaf.
17They will lick dust like a snake,
    like creatures that crawl on the ground.
They will come trembling out of their dens;
    they will turn in fear to the LORD our God
    and will be afraid of you.
18Who is a God like you,
    who pardons sin and forgives the
        transgression
of the remnant of his inheritance?
You do not stay angry for ever
    but delight to show mercy.
19You will again have compassion on us;
    you will tread our sins underfoot
and hurl all our iniquities into the depths of
        the sea.
20You will be true to Jacob,
    and show mercy to Abraham,
as you pledged on oath to our fathers
    in days long ago.

7:18 ■ NOBODY LIKE GOD
Theologians use big words to describe God's
unique qualities: transcendence, omnipotence,
omnipresence. Micah marvelled even more over
this: God's *forgiveness*. Unlike the angry gods of
other nations, Israel's God delighted to show
mercy.

---

d 16 Septuagint; Hebrew *scorn due to my people*   *a 14* Or *in the middle of Carmel*

NAHUM

■ GOD'S ANSWER TO INJUSTICE

A POWER ABOVE THE POWERS

WHO CAN WITHSTAND HIS INDIGNATION? WHO CAN ENDURE HIS FIERCE ANGER? ■ 1:6

Is life fair? It rarely seems so, especially in international politics. The most vicious dictators thrive, and raw power is the key ingredient in a successful foreign policy. Weak people get trampled on.

As a citizen of Judah, the prophet Nahum felt the force of such injustice. His message from God concerned the greatest city of the time, Nineveh. This city, the capital of Assyria, represented raw, brutal power – "endless cruelty", as Nahum put it (3:19). Though Nineveh was hundreds of miles north-east of Judah, her power dominated the Middle East. In contrast, Judah was a small, fragile state barely clinging to independence.

■ NAHUM'S NERVE

Judah's sister nation to the north, Israel, had already been defeated by Assyria and carried into exile. Only God's miraculous intervention had saved Judah on that occasion. And now, in Nahum's time, the Assyrians had returned. They dragged off Manasseh, the king, with a hook in his nose (2 Chronicles 33:11). Judah was forced to pay tribute as a vassal state.

Few people can stare into the face of such raw power and come away unimpressed. Nahum did so only because he had seen a far greater power – the power of a God whose wrath could shatter rocks. If God was angry,

how could Nineveh stand? Nahum's absolute confidence in God is underlined throughout this book.

It took nerve to stand up and predict the downfall of the most powerful nation in the world. Yet, in this book, Nahum sounds unintimidated, almost lordly. He spoke with confidence because he knew God's character: "the LORD will not leave the guilty unpunished" (1:3).

■ DECLINE AND FALL OF NINEVEH

Within a few years, Nahum's predictions came true. Nineveh did fall, never to rise again. The greatest city in the world became a pile of rubble overgrown with grass. Both Alexander the Great and Napoleon camped near it but had no idea a city had ever been there. The site became known as "the mound of many sheep".

The name *Nahum* means "comfort". Though Nahum describes God's anger, his message offers comfort to those who live with injustice and evil. "The LORD is good," said Nahum, "a refuge in times of trouble. He cares for those who trust in him, but with an overwhelming flood . . . he will pursue his foes into darkness" (1:7–8). Nineveh is gone, but Nahum's testimony lives on, reminding us that though God's justice may seem slow, nothing can ultimately escape it.

■ HOW TO READ NAHUM

Nahum stands out from the other short prophetic books in two ways. He addressed a foreign city – Nineveh – instead of his own home nation, and he used unusually vivid language.

You can read more background on Judah and its relationship to Nineveh in the following historical accounts: 2 Kings 17–19 and 2 Chronicles 32–33:13. The background will help you understand why God was so angry at Nineveh.

As you read Nahum, pay special attention to the vivid imagery. Some of the best examples are the following:

Descriptions of warfare: 2:3–7; 3:1–3

Nineveh like a pool with its water draining out: 2:8

Nineveh like a lions' den, full of bones: 2:11–12

Nineveh like a prostitute shamed in the streets: 3:5–6

Nineveh's fortresses like fig trees, with fruit shaken into the mouth of their attacker: 3:12

Nineveh's numerous citizens like grasshoppers: prolific, voracious, and quickly disappearing: 3:15–17

■ 3-TRACK READING PLAN

For an explanation and complete listing of the 3-track reading plan, turn to page x.

■ TRACK 1:
Two-Week Courses on the Bible
See page x for information on these courses.

■ TRACK 2:
An Overview of Nahum in

1 Day
☐ Day 1. Read the Introduction to Nahum and chapter 1, which portrays God's anger against Nineveh's injustice.
Now turn to page xi for your next Track 2 reading project.

■ TRACK 3:
All of Nahum in 3 Days
After you have read through Nahum, turn to pages xii–xiii for your next Track 3 reading project.

☐ 1   ☐ 2   ☐ 3

1 An oracle concerning Nineveh. The book of the vision of Nahum the Elkoshite.

■ The LORD's Anger Against Nineveh

2The LORD is a jealous and avenging God;
the LORD takes vengeance and is filled with wrath.
The LORD takes vengeance on his foes
and maintains his wrath against his enemies.
3The LORD is slow to anger and great in power;
the LORD will not leave the guilty unpunished.
His way is in the whirlwind and the storm,
and clouds are the dust of his feet.

1:3 ■ GOD IS SLOW TO ANGER

God's anger against Nineveh had not appeared overnight. Assyria had been the dominant world power for at least 300 years. Once before, Jonah had carried a message of condemnation to its chief city, Nineveh. As was always true with God's prophets, Jonah's condemnation sounded absolute. Actually, it included an escape clause. In Jeremiah 18:7–10, God spelled it out: "If at any time I announce that a nation or kingdom is to be uprooted, torn down and destroyed, and if that nation I warned repents of its evil, then I will relent." Hearing Jonah, the Ninevites had repented, and God had spared their city.

The repentance had not lasted, however. By Nahum's time, Nineveh had returned to her evil ways. God's anger, while slow to develop, was sure.

4He rebukes the sea and dries it up;
he makes all the rivers run dry.
Bashan and Carmel wither
and the blossoms of Lebanon fade.
5The mountains quake before him
and the hills melt away.
The earth trembles at his presence,
the world and all who live in it.
6Who can withstand his indignation?
Who can endure his fierce anger?

His wrath is poured out like fire;
the rocks are shattered before him.
7The LORD is good,
a refuge in times of trouble.
He cares for those who trust in him,
8 but with an overwhelming flood
he will make an end of ⌊Nineveh⌋;
he will pursue his foes into darkness.
9Whatever they plot against the LORD
he a will bring to an end;
trouble will not come a second time.
10They will be entangled among thorns
and drunk from their wine;
they will be consumed like dry stubble. b
11From you, ⌊O Nineveh,⌋ has one come forth
who plots evil against the LORD
and counsels wickedness.

12This is what the LORD says:

"Although they have allies and are numerous,
they will be cut off and pass away.
Although I have afflicted you, ⌊O Judah,⌋
I will afflict you no more.
13Now I will break their yoke from your neck
and tear your shackles away."

14The LORD has given a command concerning you, ⌊Nineveh⌋:
"You will have no descendants to bear your name.
I will destroy the carved images and cast idols
that are in the temple of your gods.
I will prepare your grave,
for you are vile."

15Look, there on the mountains,
the feet of one who brings good news,
who proclaims peace!
Celebrate your festivals, O Judah,
and fulfil your vows.
No more will the wicked invade you;
they will be completely destroyed.

■ Nineveh to Fall

2 An attacker advances against you, ⌊Nineveh⌋.
Guard the fortress,
watch the road,

a9 Or What do you foes plot against the LORD? / He   b10 The meaning of the Hebrew for this verse is uncertain.

brace yourselves,
marshal all your strength!

2The LORD will restore the splendour of Jacob
 like the splendour of Israel,
though destroyers have laid them waste
 and have ruined their vines.

3The shields of his soldiers are red;
 the warriors are clad in scarlet.
The metal on the chariots flashes
 on the day they are made ready;
 the spears of pine are brandished.*a*
4The chariots storm through the streets,
 rushing back and forth through the squares.
They look like flaming torches;
 they dart about like lightning.

5He summons his picked troops,
 yet they stumble on their way.
They dash to the city wall;
 the protective shield is put in place.

2:5 ■ BATTLE TACTICS

To most people, mighty Nineveh seemed
impregnable. A thick protective wall eight miles
long encircled the city, and just to reach the wall
attackers had to cross a moat 150 feet wide.
Behind those fortifications waited the Assyrian
troops, renowned for their cruelty. One Assyrian
king boasted of erecting a pyramid of chopped-off
heads in front of an enemy's city. Even so, Nahum
predicted Nineveh's complete downfall.

6The river gates are thrown open
 and the palace collapses.
7It is decreed*b* that ⌊the city⌋
 be exiled and carried away.
Its slave girls moan like doves
 and beat upon their breasts.
8Nineveh is like a pool,
 and its water is draining away.
"Stop! Stop!" they cry,
 but no-one turns back.
9Plunder the silver!
 Plunder the gold!
The supply is endless,
 the wealth from all its treasures!
10She is pillaged, plundered, stripped!
 Hearts melt, knees give way,
 bodies tremble, every face grows pale.

11Where now is the lions' den,
 the place where they fed their young,
where the lion and lioness went,
 and the cubs, with nothing to fear?
12The lion killed enough for his cubs
 and strangled the prey for his mate,
filling his lairs with the kill
 and his dens with the prey.
13"I am against you,"
 declares the LORD Almighty.
"I will burn up your chariots in smoke,
 and the sword will devour your young lions.
I will leave you no prey on the earth.

The voices of your messengers
 will no longer be heard."

■ Woe to Nineveh

3 Woe to the city of blood,
 full of lies,
full of plunder,
 never without victims!
2The crack of whips,
 the clatter of wheels,
galloping horses
 and jolting chariots!
3Charging cavalry,
 flashing swords
 and glittering spears!
Many casualties,
 piles of dead,
bodies without number,
 people stumbling over the corpses—
4all because of the wanton lust of a harlot,
 alluring, the mistress of sorceries,
who enslaved nations by her prostitution
 and peoples by her witchcraft.

5"I am against you," declares the LORD Almighty.
 "I will lift your skirts over your face.
I will show the nations your nakedness
 and the kingdoms your shame.
6I will pelt you with filth,
 I will treat you with contempt
 and make you a spectacle.
7All who see you will flee from you and say,
 'Nineveh is in ruins—who will mourn for
  her?'
 Where can I find anyone to comfort you?"

8Are you better than Thebes,*a*
 situated on the Nile,
 with water around her?
The river was her defence,
 the waters her wall.

3:8 ■ ANOTHER POWERFUL CITY

In approximately 663 B.C. Assyria overwhelmed
Thebes, the ancient, wealthy capital of Upper
Egypt. This victory seemed to symbolise Assyria's
absolute power. To Nahum, however, the battle
told a different tale. If Thebes was vulnerable, so
was proud Nineveh. About 50 years after
capturing Thebes, Nineveh fell to the Babylonians.
The mention of Thebes' downfall enables us to
date Nahum's message within that 50-year period.

9Cush*b* and Egypt were her boundless strength;
 Put and Libya were among her allies.
10Yet she was taken captive
 and went into exile.
Her infants were dashed to pieces
 at the head of every street.
Lots were cast for her nobles,
 and all her great men were put in chains.
11You too will become drunk;
 you will go into hiding
 and seek refuge from the enemy.

a3 Hebrew; Septuagint and Syriac / the horsemen rush to and fro   *b7 The meaning of the Hebrew for this word is uncertain.*   *a8 Hebrew No Amon*
b9 That is, the upper Nile region

¹²All your fortresses are like fig-trees
    with their first ripe fruit;
when they are shaken,
    the figs fall into the mouth of the eater.
¹³Look at your troops —
    they are all women!
The gates of your land
    are wide open to your enemies;
    fire has consumed their bars.

¹⁴Draw water for the siege,
    strengthen your defences!
Work the clay,
    tread the mortar,
    repair the brickwork!
¹⁵There the fire will devour you;
    the sword will cut you down
    and, like grasshoppers, consume you.
Multiply like grasshoppers,
    multiply like locusts!
¹⁶You have increased the number of your
    merchants

till they are more than the stars of the sky,
but like locusts they strip the land
    and then fly away.
¹⁷Your guards are like locusts,
    your officials like swarms of locusts
    that settle in the walls on a cold day —
but when the sun appears they fly away,
    and no-one knows where.

¹⁸O king of Assyria, your shepherds[c] slumber;
    your nobles lie down to rest.
Your people are scattered on the mountains
    with no-one to gather them.
¹⁹Nothing can heal your wound;
    your injury is fatal.
Everyone who hears the news about you
    claps his hands at your fall,
for who has not felt
    your endless cruelty?

HABAKKUK

■ THE PROBLEM OF EVIL

HABAKKUK'S QUESTION: "WHY IS GOD SILENT WHILE THE WICKED SUCCEED?"

"THE RIGHTEOUS WILL LIVE BY HIS FAITH." ■ 2:4

The book of Habakkuk begins with a complaint. The prophet saw injustice, violence, and evil in his own country, yet God remained silent and invisible. Why didn't God intervene? Why did he give no answer when Habakkuk called out for help? Habakkuk took these questions directly to God, in prayer.

God answered him, but hardly in the way Habakkuk had anticipated. God said he was sending the Babylonians to punish Judah. God's words described a ruthless, savage army that would tear Israel apart.

So Habakkuk complained again. Could this be justice – punishing Judah through an even more evil nation? Deeply perplexed, Habakkuk waited to see what answer God would give to his second complaint.

How long he had to wait, we do not know. But God did reply, and his answer is perhaps the best explanation we have of God's attitude towards evil. It satisfied Habakkuk, so that his book, which begins with a complaint, ends with one of the most beautiful songs in the Bible.

■ TWO CERTAINTIES TO LIVE BY

God pointed out two certainties to Habakkuk. First, the violent, proud Babylonians would be paid back with the very weapons they had used on others. Just as they destroyed nations, they would be destroyed. "Has not the LORD Almighty determined . . . that nations exhaust themselves for nothing?" (2:13). Evil may dominate the earth, but it always wears itself out.

The second certainty was God's character. He may be silent for a time, but not for ever. "The earth will be filled with the knowledge of the glory of the LORD, as the waters cover the sea" (2:14). In chapter 3, Habakkuk "saw" this powerful glory, and his heart pounded. It changed his attitude from one of complaint to one of joy.

Because the future belongs to God, a believer can cling to the truth embodied in 2:4: "The righteous will live by his faith." Habakkuk beautifully expressed this attitude of faith in the last three verses of his book: no matter how hard life might become, he would rejoice and find strength in the Lord.

■ LIVING BY FAITH

Did Habakkuk explain why God allows evil? Not precisely. He did affirm that God has not lost control. Evil is moving towards its own logical end of self-destruction, and God's glory will someday fill the earth. Habakkuk offers no proof of this, merely the record of God's communication to him. A believer can find hope and joy through faith in God, regardless of circumstances. Habakkuk's capsule of faith was quoted at three crucial points in the New Testament: Romans 1:17; Galatians 3:11; and Hebrews 10:38.

Though Habakkuk probably did not live to see it, the Babylonians were destroyed. Today they are merely a memory. Yet we, like Habakkuk, must still wait in faith to see the earth "filled with the knowledge of the glory of the LORD".

■ HOW TO READ HABAKKUK

Other prophets carried messages from God to humankind; Habakkuk addressed God alone. He pondered deep riddles of life while wrestling with two terrible realities: the degeneration of his own nation and the certainty that it was about to be overrun by another, worse nation. How can a just God allow, even use, such evil? To fully delve into Habakkuk's questions, you may want to read the book of Job and Psalm 73, which explore related issues.

The first two chapters of Habakkuk tell of two "complaints" and two answers. As you read, try to imagine the emotional changes Habakkuk experienced as he talked with God. Then read the joyful psalm of chapter 3 (set to music, either by Habakkuk or someone else) and ask yourself: where did this joyful confidence come from?

■ 3-TRACK READING PLAN

For an explanation and complete listing of the 3-track reading plan, turn to page x.

■ TRACK 1:
Two-Week Courses on the Bible
See page x for information on these courses.

■ TRACK 2:
An Overview of Habakkuk in 1 Day

□ Day 1. Read the Introduction to Habakkuk and chapter 1, which gives you a flavour of the dialogue between God and the prophet.
Now turn to page xi for your next Track 2 reading project.

■ TRACK 3:
All of Habakkuk in 3 Days
After you have read through Habakkuk, turn to pages xii–xiii for your next Track 3 reading project.

□ 1   □ 2   □ 3

1 The oracle that Habakkuk the prophet received.

■ Habakkuk's Complaint
²How long, O LORD, must I call for help,
    but you do not listen?
Or cry out to you, "Violence!"
    but you do not save?
³Why do you make me look at injustice?
    Why do you tolerate wrong?
Destruction and violence are before me;
    there is strife, and conflict abounds.
⁴Therefore the law is paralysed,
    and justice never prevails.
The wicked hem in the righteous,
    so that justice is perverted.

■ The LORD's Answer
⁵"Look at the nations and watch—
    and be utterly amazed.
For I am going to do something in your days
    that you would not believe,
    even if you were told.

1:5 ■ UNBELIEVABLE!
To Habakkuk and his fellow Israelites, it seemed unbelievable. How could God hand his own people over to the cruel and arrogant Babylonians? But incredible reversals can happen to people who think they have an automatic entitlement with God. Hundreds of years later the apostle Paul quoted this verse to a synagogue congregation (Acts 13:41), urging them not to let complacency keep them from accepting Jesus.

⁶I am raising up the Babylonians,ᵃ
    that ruthless and impetuous people,
who sweep across the whole earth
    to seize dwelling-places not their own.
⁷They are a feared and dreaded people;
    they are a law to themselves
    and promote their own honour.
⁸Their horses are swifter than leopards,
    fiercer than wolves at dusk.
Their cavalry gallops headlong;

their horsemen come from afar.
They fly like a vulture swooping to devour;
⁹   they all come bent on violence.
Their hordesᵇ advance like a desert wind
    and gather prisoners like sand.
¹⁰They deride kings
    and scoff at rulers.
They laugh at all fortified cities;
    they build earthen ramps and capture them.
¹¹Then they sweep past like the wind and go on—
    guilty men, whose own strength is their god."

■ Habakkuk's Second Complaint
¹²O LORD, are you not from everlasting?
    My God, my Holy One, we will not die.
O LORD, you have appointed them to execute judgment;
    O Rock, you have ordained them to punish.
¹³Your eyes are too pure to look on evil;
    you cannot tolerate wrong.
Why then do you tolerate the treacherous?
    Why are you silent while the wicked
    swallow up those more righteous than themselves?
¹⁴You have made men like fish in the sea,
    like sea creatures that have no ruler.
¹⁵The wicked foe pulls all of them up with hooks,
    he catches them in his net,
he gathers them up in his drag-net;
    and so he rejoices and is glad.
¹⁶Therefore he sacrifices to his net
    and burns incense to his drag-net,
for by his net he lives in luxury
    and enjoys the choicest food.
¹⁷Is he to keep on emptying his net,
    destroying nations without mercy?

1:16 ■ WORSHIPPING THE MILITARY
The Babylonians had their own gods, but Habakkuk claimed that they really worshipped their "net", that is, their military might. God described them as "guilty men, whose own strength is their god" (verse 11).

ᵃ6 Or Chaldeans   ᵇ9 The meaning of the Hebrew for this word is uncertain.

2 I will stand at my watch
and station myself on the ramparts;
I will look to see what he will say to me,
and what answer I am to give to this
complaint.*a*

■ The LORD's Answer
²Then the LORD replied:

"Write down the revelation
and make it plain on tablets
so that a herald*b* may run with it.
³For the revelation awaits an appointed time;
it speaks of the end
and will not prove false.
Though it linger, wait for it;
it*c* will certainly come and will not delay.

⁴"See, he is puffed up;
his desires are not upright—
but the righteous will live by his faith*d*—

2:4 ■ RIGHTEOUS BY FAITH

Has any brief slogan made a bigger impact than
this one? For Habakkuk, "the righteous will live by
his faith" meant that righteous people must
patiently trust God in a difficult time. The New
Testament quoted Habakkuk in a wider context
(Romans 1:17; Galatians 3:11; Hebrews
10:38–39), saying not only that believers must live
by faith, but that they are *saved* by grace through
faith. When Martin Luther read that quote in
Romans, it changed his life, and "righteousness by
faith" became a rallying cry of the Protestant
Reformation.

---

⁵indeed, wine betrays him;
he is arrogant and never at rest.
Because he is as greedy as the grave*e*
and like death is never satisfied,
he gathers to himself all the nations
and takes captive all the peoples.

⁶"Will not all of them taunt him with ridicule and
scorn, saying,

" 'Woe to him who piles up stolen goods
and makes himself wealthy by extortion!
How long must this go on?'
⁷Will not your debtors*f* suddenly arise?
Will they not wake up and make you
tremble?
Then you will become their victim.
⁸Because you have plundered many nations,
the peoples who are left will plunder you.
For you have shed man's blood;
you have destroyed lands and cities and
everyone in them.

⁹"Woe to him who builds his realm by unjust
gain

to set his nest on high,
to escape the clutches of ruin!
¹⁰You have plotted the ruin of many peoples,
shaming your own house and forfeiting your
life.
¹¹The stones of the wall will cry out,
and the beams of the woodwork will echo it.
¹²"Woe to him who builds a city with bloodshed
and establishes a town by crime!
¹³Has not the LORD Almighty determined
that the people's labour is only fuel for the
fire,
that the nations exhaust themselves for
nothing?
¹⁴For the earth will be filled with the knowledge
of the glory of the LORD,
as the waters cover the sea.

¹⁵"Woe to him who gives drink to his
neighbours,
pouring it from the wineskin till they are
drunk,
so that he can gaze on their naked bodies.
¹⁶You will be filled with shame instead of glory.
Now it is your turn! Drink and be
exposed!*g*
The cup from the LORD's right hand is coming
round to you,
and disgrace will cover your glory.
¹⁷The violence you have done to Lebanon will
overwhelm you,
and your destruction of animals will terrify
you.
For you have shed man's blood;
you have destroyed lands and cities and
everyone in them.

¹⁸"Of what value is an idol, since a man has
carved it?
Or an image that teaches lies?
For he who makes it trusts in his own creation;
he makes idols that cannot speak.
¹⁹Woe to him who says to wood, 'Come to life!'
Or to lifeless stone, 'Wake up!'
Can it give guidance?
It is covered with gold and silver;
there is no breath in it.
²⁰But the LORD is in his holy temple;
let all the earth be silent before him."

■ Habakkuk's Prayer
3 A prayer of Habakkuk the prophet. On
*shigionoth.*a

²LORD, I have heard of your fame;
I stand in awe of your deeds, O LORD.
Renew them in our day,
in our time make them known;
in wrath remember mercy.

³God came from Teman,
the Holy One from Mount Paran.　　*Selah*b
His glory covered the heavens
and his praise filled the earth.
⁴His splendour was like the sunrise;
rays flashed from his hand,

---

*a*1 Or *and what to answer when I am rebuked*　*b*2 Or *so that whoever reads it*　*c*3 Or *Though he linger, wait for him; / he*　*d*4 Or *faithfulness*
*e*5 Hebrew *Sheol*　*f*7 Or *creditors*　*g*16 Masoretic Text; Dead Sea Scrolls, Aquila, Vulgate and Syriac (see also Septuagint) *and stagger*
*a*1 Probably a literary or musical term　*b*3 A word of uncertain meaning; possibly a musical term; also in verses 9 and 13

where his power was hidden.
5Plague went before him;
    pestilence followed his steps.
6He stood, and shook the earth;
    he looked, and made the nations tremble.
The ancient mountains crumbled
    and the age-old hills collapsed.
    His ways are eternal.
7I saw the tents of Cushan in distress,
0the dwellings of Midian in anguish.

8Were you angry with the rivers, O LORD?
    Was your wrath against the streams?
Did you rage against the sea
    when you rode with your horses
    and your victorious chariots?
9You uncovered your bow,
    you called for many arrows.   *Selah*
You split the earth with rivers;
10 the mountains saw you and writhed.
Torrents of water swept by;
    the deep roared
    and lifted its waves on high.

11Sun and moon stood still in the heavens
    at the glint of your flying arrows,
    at the lightning of your flashing spear.
12In wrath you strode through the earth
    and in anger you threshed the nations.
13You came out to deliver your people,
    to save your anointed one.
You crushed the leader of the land of
    wickedness,
    you stripped him from head to foot.   *Selah*
14With his own spear you pierced his head
    when his warriors stormed out to scatter us,
    gloating as though about to devour
    the wretched who were in hiding.

15You trampled the sea with your horses,
    churning the great waters.
16I heard and my heart pounded,
    my lips quivered at the sound;
decay crept into my bones,
    and my legs trembled.
Yet I will wait patiently for the day of calamity
    to come on the nation invading us.
17Though the fig-tree does not bud
    and there are no grapes on the vines,
though the olive crop fails
    and the fields produce no food,
though there are no sheep in the pen
    and no cattle in the stalls,
18yet I will rejoice in the LORD,
    I will be joyful in God my Saviour.

19The Sovereign LORD is my strength;
    he makes my feet like the feet of a deer,
    he enables me to go on the heights.

For the director of music. On my stringed
    instruments.

3:14 ■ GOD AT WORK

"With his own spear you pierced his head" is how
Habakkuk sees God overcoming the leader of evil.
Earlier (2:6–7), Habakkuk had demonstrated how
this would work out: the Babylonians' own
enemies would treat them just as they had treated
others. Violence turns back on the violent. On the
surface, God's power is not always visible, but the
person of faith knows that God is behind it all.

ZEPHANIAH

INTRODUCTION

■ BEYOND DARKNESS

A WORLDWIDE CATASTROPHE AND A SHINING LIGHT

"THE LORD . . . WILL QUIET YOU WITH HIS LOVE, HE WILL REJOICE OVER YOU WITH
SINGING." ■ 3:17

Zephaniah wrote not long after Manasseh had
ended his 50-year reign in Judah. One of the
worst kings on record, Manasseh had made idol
worship and child sacrifice common practice. He
had built altars for star worshippers in God's
temple and had encouraged male prostitution as
part of the religious ritual. He had also "shed so
much innocent blood that he filled Jerusalem from
end to end" (2 Kings 21:16). His son Amon carried
on in the same way during his short reign.

Then came King Josiah, who took the
throne at the age of eight, after his father's
assassination. The Bible says there was never a
king like Josiah (2 Kings 23:25). He led a reform,
destroying all the pagan idols and restoring the
temple. He organised the first Passover
celebration in generations.

Zephaniah, who was probably related to
the king through his great-great-grandfather King
Hezekiah, apparently spoke just before these big
changes. The nation's future hung in the
balance, and Zephaniah's words may well have
helped tip it towards renewal of faith in God.

■ FROM GLOOM TO EXULTATION
Zephaniah's book begins in deep gloom. Like
other prophets, he condemned the sins of his
nation and predicted judgment from God. But he
went one big step further. He talked repeatedly
about "the day of the LORD" and saw that it would
be a supernatural event sweeping clean the whole
planet. Zephaniah offered no hope that it could be
avoided. The Lord had warned and pleaded, but
to no avail (3:6–7). Zephaniah saw hope for a
minority only. A faithful, humble remnant could be
sheltered from disaster if they would seek God.

Beyond the judgment fires Zephaniah
saw something remarkably bright. He predicted
that a purified remnant of God's people, truthful
and humble, would trust in God. He foresaw a
remade world learning to worship God.

Therefore this short book, which starts
with such gloom, ends with an ecstatic song of
joy: an anticipation of the kingdom to come after
the judgment. God's blessing will flow freely as
every nation worships him. Zephaniah's words
may have been influential in encouraging
Josiah's reforms, but his vision extended far
beyond. The New Testament speaks often, like
Zephaniah, of the worldwide judgment and a
renewed world to come.

■ HOW TO READ ZEPHANIAH

Zephaniah will seem more interesting if you grasp
the historical situation in which he wrote. For the
decadence that led to King Josiah's reforms, read
2 Kings 21. Josiah's history is told in chapters 22
and 23. Second Chronicles 33–35 tells the same
story with slightly different details. You can find a
brief summary of these reigns in "A Line-up of
Rulers", pages 260–268.

Zephaniah is easily understood. It has a
clear and symmetrical structure, opening (after a
brief introduction) with a warning of judgment for
Judah and its capital of Jerusalem, then
extending the judgment to Judah's neighbours,
and closing in chapter 3 with good news about
Jerusalem.

■ 3-TRACK READING PLAN

For an explanation and complete listing of the 3-track reading plan, turn to page x.

■ TRACK 1:
Two-Week Courses on the Bible
See page x for information on these courses.

■ TRACK 2:
An Overview of Zephaniah in

1 Day
□ Day 1: Read the Introduction to Zephaniah and chapter 3, with its hopeful portrait of Jerusalem after the judgment.
Now turn to page xi for your next Track 2 reading project.

■ TRACK 3:
All of Zephaniah in 3 Days
After you have read through Zephaniah, turn to pages xii–xiii for your next Track 3 reading project.

□ 1   □ 2   □ 3

---

1 The word of the LORD that came to Zephaniah son of Cushi, the son of Gedaliah, the son of Amariah, the son of Hezekiah, during the reign of Josiah son of Amon king of Judah:

1:1 ■ ROYAL BLOOD

Prophets had to be hand-picked by God. Education or family background didn't qualify them for the job. Zephaniah, however, came from an impressive family. His great-great-grandfather was King Hezekiah. Despite his royal blood, Zephaniah was blunt and uncompromising; he took no kid-glove approach to prophecy.

■ Warning of Coming Destruction
²"I will sweep away everything
from the face of the earth,"
                        declares the LORD.
³"I will sweep away both men and animals;
I will sweep away the birds of the air
and the fish of the sea.
The wicked will have only heaps of rubble[a]
when I cut off man from the face of the
earth,"
                        declares the LORD.

■ Against Judah
⁴"I will stretch out my hand against Judah
and against all who live in Jerusalem.
I will cut off from this place every remnant of
Baal,
the names of the pagan and the idolatrous
priests—
⁵those who bow down on the roofs
to worship the starry host,
those who bow down and swear by the LORD
and who also swear by Molech,[b]
⁶those who turn back from following the LORD
and neither seek the LORD nor enquire of
him.
⁷Be silent before the Sovereign LORD,
for the day of the LORD is near.
The LORD has prepared a sacrifice;
he has consecrated those he has invited.
⁸On the day of the LORD's sacrifice
I will punish the princes
and the king's sons
and all those clad

in foreign clothes.
⁹On that day I will punish
all who avoid stepping on the threshold,[c]
who fill the temple of their gods
with violence and deceit.

¹⁰"On that day," declares the LORD,
"a cry will go up from the Fish Gate,
wailing from the New Quarter,
and a loud crash from the hills.
¹¹Wail, you who live in the market district;[d]
all your merchants will be wiped out,
all who trade with[e] silver will be ruined.
¹²At that time I will search Jerusalem with lamps
and punish those who are complacent,
who are like wine left on its dregs,
who think, 'The LORD will do nothing,
either good or bad.'

1:12 ■ PRACTICAL ATHEISM

The people of Judah did terrible things, such as worshipping Molech (verse 5), the Ammonite god who sometimes required child sacrifice. Zephaniah singled out another sin, however, that was just as damaging: complacency. They weren't formal atheists, but they acted like it.

---

¹³Their wealth will be plundered,
their houses demolished.
They will build houses
but not live in them;
they will plant vineyards
but not drink the wine.

■ The Great Day of the LORD
¹⁴"The great day of the LORD is near—
near and coming quickly.
Listen! The cry on the day of the LORD will be
bitter,
the shouting of the warrior there.
¹⁵That day will be a day of wrath,
a day of distress and anguish,
a day of trouble and ruin,
a day of darkness and gloom,
a day of clouds and blackness,
¹⁶a day of trumpet and battle cry
against the fortified cities
and against the corner towers.
¹⁷I will bring distress on the people

---

a 3 The meaning of the Hebrew for this line is uncertain.   *b 5* Hebrew *Malcam*, that is, Milcom   *c 9* See 1 Samuel 5:5.   *d 11* Or *the Mortar*
e 11 Or *in*

and they will walk like blind men,
because they have sinned against the LORD.
Their blood will be poured out like dust
and their entrails like filth.
18Neither their silver nor their gold
will be able to save them
on the day of the LORD's wrath.
In the fire of his jealousy
the whole world will be consumed,
for he will make a sudden end
of all who live in the earth."

2 Gather together, gather together,
O shameful nation,
2before the appointed time arrives
and that day sweeps on like chaff,
before the fierce anger of the LORD comes upon
you,
before the day of the LORD's wrath comes
upon you.
3Seek the LORD, all you humble of the land,
you who do what he commands.
Seek righteousness, seek humility;
perhaps you will be sheltered
on the day of the LORD's anger.

■ Against Philistia
4Gaza will be abandoned
and Ashkelon left in ruins.
At midday Ashdod will be emptied
and Ekron uprooted.
5Woe to you who live by the sea,
O Kerethite people;
the word of the LORD is against you,
O Canaan, land of the Philistines.

"I will destroy you,
and none will be left."

6The land by the sea, where the Kerethites*a*
dwell,
will be a place for shepherds and sheep pens.
7It will belong to the remnant of the house of
Judah;
there they will find pasture.
In the evening they will lie down
in the houses of Ashkelon.
The LORD their God will care for them;
he will restore their fortunes.*b*

■ Against Moab and Ammon
8"I have heard the insults of Moab
and the taunts of the Ammonites,
who insulted my people
and made threats against their land.
9Therefore, as surely as I live,"
declares the LORD Almighty, the God of
Israel,
"surely Moab will become like Sodom,
the Ammonites like Gomorrah—
a place of weeds and salt pits,
a wasteland for ever.
The remnant of my people will plunder them;
the survivors of my nation will inherit their
land."

10This is what they will get in return for their
pride,
for insulting and mocking the people of the
LORD Almighty.
11The LORD will be awesome to them
when he destroys all the gods of the land.
The nations on every shore will worship him,
every one in its own land.

■ Against Cush
12"You too, O Cushites,*c*
will be slain by my sword."

■ Against Assyria
13He will stretch out his hand against the north
and destroy Assyria,
leaving Nineveh utterly desolate
and dry as the desert.
14Flocks and herds will lie down there,
creatures of every kind.
The desert owl and the screech owl
will roost on her columns.
Their calls will echo through the windows,
rubble will be in the doorways,
the beams of cedar will be exposed.
15This is the carefree city
that lived in safety.
She said to herself,
"I am, and there is none besides me."
What a ruin she has become,
a lair for wild beasts!
All who pass by her scoff
and shake their fists.

■ The Future of Jerusalem
3 Woe to the city of oppressors,
rebellious and defiled!
2She obeys no-one,
she accepts no correction.
She does not trust in the LORD,
she does not draw near to her God.
3Her officials are roaring lions,
her rulers are evening wolves,
who leave nothing for the morning.
4Her prophets are arrogant;
they are treacherous men.
Her priests profane the sanctuary
and do violence to the law.
5The LORD within her is righteous;
he does no wrong.
Morning by morning he dispenses his justice,
and every new day he does not fail,
yet the unrighteous know no shame.

6"I have cut off nations;
their strongholds are demolished.
I have left their streets deserted,
with no-one passing through.
Their cities are destroyed;
no-one will be left—no-one at all.
7I said to the city,
'Surely you will fear me
and accept correction!'
Then her dwelling would not be cut off,
nor all my punishments come upon her.

a 6 The meaning of the Hebrew for this word is uncertain.   *b 7 Or will bring back their captives*   *c 12* That is, people from the upper Nile region

But they were still eager
    to act corruptly in all they did.
8Therefore wait for me," declares the LORD,
    "for the day I will stand up to testify.*
I have decided to assemble the nations,
    to gather the kingdoms
and to pour out my wrath on them—
    all my fierce anger.
The whole world will be consumed
    by the fire of my jealous anger.

9"Then will I purify the lips of the peoples,
    that all of them may call on the name of the
        LORD
    and serve him shoulder to shoulder.
10From beyond the rivers of Cush*
    my worshippers, my scattered people,
    will bring me offerings.
11On that day you will not be put to shame
    for all the wrongs you have done to me,
because I will remove from this city
    those who rejoice in their pride.
Never again will you be haughty
    on my holy hill.
12But I will leave within you

3:12 ■ MEEK WILL INHERIT

As on Wall Street, as in the streets of many cities,
"survival of the fittest" might have been
Jerusalem's motto. Its officials were like wolves,
devouring everything in sight (verse 3). Could only
the ruthless survive? Zephaniah said no. In fact,
he claimed, only the meek and the humble, those
who trust God and simply tell the truth, would live
in security. Jesus said something similar: "Blessed
are the meek, for they will inherit the earth"
(Matthew 5:5).

---

the meek and humble,
    who trust in the name of the LORD.
13The remnant of Israel will do no wrong;
    they will speak no lies,
    nor will deceit be found in their mouths.
They will eat and lie down
    and no-one will make them afraid."

14Sing, O Daughter of Zion;
    shout aloud, O Israel!
Be glad and rejoice with all your heart,
    O Daughter of Jerusalem!
15The LORD has taken away your punishment,
    he has turned back your enemy.
The LORD, the King of Israel, is with you;
    never again will you fear any harm.
16On that day they will say to Jerusalem,
    "Do not fear, O Zion;
    do not let your hands hang limp.
17The LORD your God is with you,
    he is mighty to save.
He will take great delight in you,
    he will quiet you with his love,
    he will rejoice over you with singing."

18"The sorrows for the appointed feasts
    I will remove from you;
    they are a burden and a reproach to you.*
19At that time I will deal
    with all who oppressed you;
I will rescue the lame
    and gather those who have been scattered.
I will give them praise and honour
    in every land where they were put to shame.
20At that time I will gather you;
    at that time I will bring you home.
I will give you honour and praise
    among all the peoples of the earth
when I restore your fortunes*
    before your very eyes,"
                              says the LORD.

---

*8 Septuagint and Syriac; Hebrew will rise up to plunder   *10 That is, the upper Nile region   *18 Or "I will gather you who mourn for the appointed
feasts; / your reproach is a burden to you   *20 Or I bring back your captives

HAGGAI

INTRODUCTION

■ THE PROPHET WHO GOT RESULTS

FOR ONCE, GOD'S PEOPLE LISTENED

THE WHOLE REMNANT OF THE PEOPLE OBEYED THE VOICE OF THE LORD THEIR GOD AND THE MESSAGE OF THE PROPHET HAGGAI, BECAUSE THE LORD THEIR GOD HAD SENT HIM.
■ 1:12

Sometimes, at crucial moments, a single voice can stir a directionless mass of people to action. Prime Minister Winston Churchill's inspiring oratory may have saved Britain in World War II. American clergyman and civil rights leader Martin Luther King's sermons and speeches captured America's conscience in the 1950s and 60s.

Haggai's words, similarly, rang clear in a time of confusion. The Jews had come back from their exile in Babylon nearly 20 years before. But they seemed to have forgotten the point of returning. After one false start on the temple, the returned exiles had devoted their energy to building their own houses. The ruins of Solomon's temple stood as a nagging reminder that they had neglected God.

Now Haggai urged these pioneers to "give careful thought" to their situation. He did not rage like Jeremiah or produce eloquent poems like Isaiah. He put it simply and logically. They had worked hard, but what had it earned them? Their crops were unsuccessful. Their money disappeared as soon as they earned it. Why? Haggai asked. Because they had mistaken their priorities. They needed to put God first. They needed to rebuild his temple.

■ A RESPONSE FROM THE HEART
People responded to Haggai immediately. Prophets before him, such as Amos, Isaiah, and Jeremiah, had spoken for decades without seeing such a heartfelt reaction. Haggai's messages span a mere four months, but he accomplished everything he set out to do. In four years the temple was complete.

What made the temple so important? After all, the proper sacrifices and rituals could be carried out on a makeshift altar. But God's reputation was at stake. He could not be properly honoured so long as the house he called home lay in ruins. The temple symbolised God's presence, and Israel's priorities.

Would rebuilding the temple change Israel's financial situation? Haggai's first words promised nothing. He simply said, "Give careful thought to your ways," and pointed out that Israel's lack of prosperity was God's doing. They had worked hard, but God had withheld the rain their crops needed. A month later (2:1–9) Haggai said that God had glorious plans for Israel, plans that would shake the whole earth. But he referred to God's presence with them, not to good crops.

Only on the last day accounted for in this brief book did Haggai get back to the subject of harvests. He said that God wanted his people to "give careful thought" again – this time to the dramatic difference they would see in their harvests now that they had put God first. "From this day on I will bless you", God said through Haggai (2:18–19).

■ HOW TO READ HAGGAI

One of the shortest books in the Bible, Haggai can easily be read at a sitting. Haggai's words came at a critical time in the life of the nation of Israel. They mark one of the few times in all history when God spoke and his people quickly and unquestioningly obeyed. For the historical background, read Ezra 1–6. Haggai's crucial message is mentioned in Ezra 5:1–2. "A Line-up of Rulers", pages 260–268, can help you place Haggai in Israelite history.

There is a progression to God's warnings and his promises through Haggai. Study each of Haggai's messages, and note down what encouragement, what warning, and what hope God offered Israel. How did God motivate them to obey him?

■ 3-TRACK READING PLAN

For an explanation and complete listing of the 3-track reading plan, turn to page x.

■ TRACK 1:
Two-Week Courses on the
Bible
See page x for information on
these courses.

■ TRACK 2:
An Overview of Haggai in

1 Day
☐ Day 1. Read the
Introduction to Haggai and
chapter 1, which tells how
Haggai's message changed
Israel's direction.
Now turn to page xi for your
next Track 2 reading project.

■ TRACK 3:
All of Haggai in 2 Days
After you have read through
Haggai, turn to pages xii–xiii
for your next Track 3 reading
project.

☐ 1   ☐ 2

■ A Call to Build the House of the LORD

1 In the second year of King Darius, on the first day of the sixth month, the word of the LORD came through the prophet Haggai to Zerubbabel son of Shealtiel, governor of Judah, and to Joshua*a* son of Jehozadak, the high priest:

²This is what the LORD Almighty says: "These people say, 'The time has not yet come for the LORD's house to be built.' "

³Then the word of the LORD came through the prophet Haggai: ⁴"Is it a time for you yourselves to be living in your panelled houses, while this house remains a ruin?"

⁵Now this is what the LORD Almighty says: "Give careful thought to your ways. ⁶You have planted much, but have harvested little. You eat, but never have enough. You drink, but never have your fill. You put on clothes, but are not warm. You earn wages, only to put them in a purse with holes in it."

⁷This is what the LORD Almighty says: "Give careful thought to your ways. ⁸Go up into the mountains and bring down timber and build the house, so that I may take pleasure in it and be honoured," says the LORD. ⁹"You expected much, but see, it turned out to be little. What you brought home, I blew away. Why?" declares the LORD Almighty. "Because of my house, which remains a ruin, while each of you is busy with his own house. ¹⁰Therefore, because of you the heavens have withheld their dew and the earth its crops. ¹¹I called for a drought on the fields and the mountains, on the grain, the new wine, the oil and whatever the ground produces, on men and cattle, and on the labour of your hands."

¹²Then Zerubbabel son of Shealtiel, Joshua son of Jehozadak, the high priest, and the whole remnant of the people obeyed the voice of the LORD their God and the message of the prophet Haggai, because the LORD their God had sent him. And the people feared the LORD.

¹³Then Haggai, the LORD's messenger, gave this message of the LORD to the people: "I am with you," declares the LORD. ¹⁴So the LORD stirred up the spirit of Zerubbabel son of Shealtiel, governor of Judah, and the spirit of Joshua son of Jehozadak, the high priest, and the spirit of the whole remnant of the people. They came and began work on the house of the LORD Almighty, their God, ¹⁵on the twenty-fourth day of the sixth month in the second year of King Darius.

a 1 A variant of Jeshua; here and elsewhere in Haggai

■ The Promised Glory of the New House

2 On the twenty-first day of the seventh month, the word of the LORD came through the prophet Haggai: ²"Speak to Zerubbabel son of Shealtiel, governor of Judah, to Joshua son of Jehozadak, the high priest, and to the remnant of the people. Ask them, ³'Who of you is left who saw this house in its former glory? How does it look to you now? Does it not seem to you like nothing? ⁴But now be strong, O Zerubbabel,' declares the LORD. 'Be strong, O Joshua son of Jehozadak, the high priest. Be strong, all you people of the land,' declares the LORD, 'and work. For I am with you,' declares the LORD Almighty. ⁵'This is what I covenanted with you when you came out of Egypt. And my Spirit remains among you. Do not fear.'

> ### 1:13 ■ CHANGE OF TONE
> For two decades the Israelites had ignored God's strong desire for them to rebuild the temple. When they finally responded and got to work, however, God's sternness melted immediately. "I am with you," he told them. And although the new temple going up seemed a sad imitation of Solomon's masterpiece, God still spoke with gentleness and kindness (2:2–5). Haggai, one of the last prophets, indicates God's eagerness to respond with mercy.

⁶"This is what the LORD Almighty says: 'In a little while I will once more shake the heavens and the earth, the sea and the dry land. ⁷I will shake all nations, and the desired of all nations will come, and I will fill this house with glory,' says the LORD Almighty. ⁸'The silver is mine and the gold is mine,' declares the LORD Almighty. ⁹'The glory of this present house will be greater than the glory of the former house,' says the LORD Almighty. 'And in this place I will grant peace,' declares the LORD Almighty."

■ Blessings for a Defiled People

¹⁰On the twenty-fourth day of the ninth month, in the second year of Darius, the word of the LORD came to the prophet Haggai: ¹¹"This is what the LORD Almighty says: 'Ask the priests what the law says: ¹²If a person carries consecrated meat in the fold of his garment, and that fold touches some

bread or stew, some wine, oil or other food, does it become consecrated?' "

The priests answered, "No."

2:12 ■ ONE-WAY CONTAMINATION

"One bad apple spoils the barrel", the saying goes; but one good apple doesn't clean up the rotten ones. In a similar vein, Haggai asked, "Which is contagious, good or evil?" In the Old Testament law, he found that consecrated meat — set aside to be used in sacrificial worship — did not "spread" its holiness. But a person who became "unclean" did spread his or her defilement. Under the Old Testament law, evil spread, but goodness did not. The Israelites' failure to rebuild the temple had defiled everything they touched — even their good deeds.

¹³Then Haggai said, "If a person defiled by contact with a dead body touches one of these things, does it become defiled?"

"Yes," the priests replied, "it becomes defiled."

¹⁴Then Haggai said, " 'So it is with this people and this nation in my sight,' declares the LORD. 'Whatever they do and whatever they offer there is defiled.

¹⁵" 'Now give careful thought to this from this day on*a* — consider how things were before one stone was laid on another in the LORD's temple. ¹⁶When anyone came to a heap of twenty measures, there were only ten. When anyone went to a wine vat to draw fifty measures, there were only twenty. ¹⁷I struck all the work of your hands with blight, mildew and hail, yet you did not turn to me,' declares the LORD. ¹⁸'From this day on, from this twenty-fourth day of the ninth month, give careful

thought to the day when the foundation of the LORD's temple was laid. Give careful thought: ¹⁹Is there yet any seed left in the barn? Until now, the vine and the fig-tree, the pomegranate and the olive tree have not borne fruit.

" 'From this day on I will bless you.' "

2:23 ■ THE IMPRINT OF THE MASTER

Some 78 years before, King Jehoiachin had been captured and taken to Babylon. God had rejected him: "Even if you, Jehoiachin . . . , were a signet ring on my right hand, I would still pull you off." (Jeremiah 22:24).

But now his grandson Zerubbabel had come back to Jerusalem, chosen again as the Lord's "signet ring". Such a ring was used in place of a signature, to impress the king's seal on important documents. God had accepted men from the royal line of David as his chosen leaders again. The complete fulfilment of this prophecy would have to wait for Zerubbabel's descendant Jesus, a son of David who fully printed God's image on humanity.

■ Zerubbabel the LORD's Signet Ring

²⁰The word of the LORD came to Haggai a second time on the twenty-fourth day of the month: ²¹"Tell Zerubbabel governor of Judah that I will shake the heavens and the earth. ²²I will overturn royal thrones and shatter the power of the foreign kingdoms. I will overthrow chariots and their drivers; horses and their riders will fall, each by the sword of his brother.

²³" 'On that day,' declares the LORD Almighty, 'I will take you, my servant Zerubbabel son of Shealtiel,' declares the LORD, 'and I will make you like my signet ring, for I have chosen you,' declares the LORD Almighty."

---

a 15 Or to the days past

ZECHARIAH

■ STARTING AGAIN

HOW COULD THEY REBUILD WITH BROKEN PIECES?

"THE LORD SAYS: 'I WILL RETURN TO JERUSALEM WITH MERCY, AND THERE MY HOUSE WILL BE REBUILT.' " ■ 1:16

When the Jews reviewed their history, it looked like a long slide downhill. Consistently, they had responded to God's love by grumbling against him, by disobeying his law, by worshipping idols. Finally, after centuries of warning, punishment had come. Jerusalem was flattened. The survivors marched off in chains towards the other end of the world.

They had not merely lost a battle. They had lost, seemingly, their place in God's heart and their future as his special people.

But hope for a new start came in exile. When Persian emperor Cyrus took power, he offered the Jews a chance to return to their land and rebuild their temple. Some jumped at the chance. They took the long journey to a homeland most of them had never seen (you can read about the trip in the first chapters of Ezra). They wanted not merely to rebuild; they hoped somehow to escape the downward, anti-God trend that had plagued their nation from its beginnings.

■ HOPE BEGINS TO FADE

They found a disheartening scene. Their once-beautiful city was a ghost town. Everything of value had been destroyed. Fertile fields were overgrown. The region was almost empty of people.

The small band of returned exiles built an altar on the grounds of the ruined temple. But soon they grew discouraged about actual rebuilding. They had enough trouble finding shelter and eking out a living from the land.

When their non-Jewish neighbours fought against rebuilding the temple, the former exiles gave up. Their hopes of a glorious "new beginning" began to fade.

The temple stayed in a state of disrepair for nearly 20 years, until the prophets Haggai and Zechariah stirred up renewed interest. These prophets saw that as long as the temple lay in ruins, Israel's distinctive character as a people of God was ruined, too. At their urging, the Jews organised to build again.

The book of Zechariah is a record from that critical period of rebuilding. Its first recorded message dates from approximately two months after the temple foundation was laid. The temple was completed four years later, at least partly due to Zechariah's encouraging words.

■ NEEDED: A CHANGE OF HEART

Zechariah wasn't mainly interested in a building, however. More important was the relationship with God that the temple symbolised. In his first recorded words Zechariah warned his people not to be like their ancestors. What good had a temple done them? A really new beginning required a change of heart. " 'Return to me,' declares the LORD Almighty, 'and I will return to you' "(1:3).

The last half of Zechariah widens its view to the whole world. The small refugee community of Jews, Zechariah says, holds the world's future. Their new beginning would become the hope of the world.

■ HOW TO READ ZECHARIAH

Most people find Zechariah difficult to understand. Throughout the book you will find references to people and to events that are hard to interpret. A commentary can be a great help, clarifying the meaning of these details. For historical background on Zechariah's times, read Ezra 1–6. Zechariah is mentioned by name in Ezra 5:1.

The book of Zechariah breaks into three parts. The first six chapters offer eight symbolic visions, which were meant to encourage the builders of the temple. They are not too difficult to understand if you take them one at a time and don't rush through them. Their main emphasis: God is at work again. He plans to live with his people in Jerusalem. He will protect them from their enemies, cleanse them from their sins, banish evil. He is making a new beginning for them.

Chapters 7–8 address the quality of life God wants his renewed people to enjoy. These words contain many encouraging promises to Israel.

The last six chapters are packed with puzzling references to the struggles Israel must endure in becoming what God wants. You will find predictions of terrible suffering and absolute victory. These chapters, as complex as they are, helped the Gospel writers understand Jesus' suffering, death, and resurrection. The writers quoted these chapters as they wrote of Jesus' final days. The book of Revelation, telling of the final goal of history, also drew on Zechariah's predictions.

■ 3-TRACK READING PLAN

For an explanation and complete listing of the 3-track reading plan, turn to page x.

■ TRACK 1:
Two-Week Courses on the Bible
See page x for information on these courses.

■ TRACK 2:
An Overview of Zechariah in 1 Day

☐ Day 1. Read the Introduction to Zechariah and chapter 8, which describes the future God has in mind for his people.
Now turn to page xi for your next Track 2 reading project.

■ TRACK 3:
All of Zechariah in 11 Days
After you have read through Zechariah, turn to pages xii–xiii for your next Track 3 reading project.

☐ 1   ☐ 2–3 ☐ 4–5 ☐ 6
☐ 7   ☐ 8   ☐ 9   ☐ 10
☐ 11 ☐ 12–13   ☐ 14

■ A Call to Return to the LORD

1 In the eighth month of the second year of Darius, the word of the LORD came to the prophet Zechariah son of Berekiah, the son of Iddo.

2"The LORD was very angry with your forefathers. 3Therefore tell the people: This is what the LORD Almighty says: 'Return to me,' declares the LORD Almighty, 'and I will return to you,' says the LORD Almighty. 4Do not be like your forefathers, to whom the earlier prophets proclaimed: This is what the LORD Almighty says: 'Turn from your evil ways and your evil practices.' But they would not listen or pay attention to me, declares the LORD. 5Where are your forefathers now? And the prophets, do they live for ever? 6But did not my words and my decrees, which I commanded my servants the prophets, overtake your forefathers?

"Then they repented and said, 'The LORD Almighty has done to us what our ways and practices deserve, just as he determined to do.' "

■ The Man Among the Myrtle Trees

7On the twenty-fourth day of the eleventh month, the month of Shebat, in the second year of Darius, the word of the LORD came to the prophet Zechariah son of Berekiah, the son of Iddo.

8During the night I had a vision—and there before me was a man riding a red horse! He was standing among the myrtle trees in a ravine. Behind him were red, brown and white horses.

9I asked, "What are these, my lord?"

The angel who was talking with me answered, "I will show you what they are."

10Then the man standing among the myrtle trees explained, "They are the ones the LORD has sent to go throughout the earth."

11And they reported to the angel of the LORD, who was standing among the myrtle trees, "We have gone throughout the earth and found the whole world at rest and in peace."

12Then the angel of the LORD said, "LORD Almighty, how long will you withhold mercy from Jerusalem and from the towns of Judah, which you have been angry with these seventy years?" 13So the LORD spoke kind and comforting words to the angel who talked with me.

14Then the angel who was speaking to me said, "Proclaim this word: This is what the LORD Almighty says: 'I am very jealous for Jerusalem and Zion, 15but I am very angry with the nations that feel secure. I was only a little angry, but they added to the calamity.'

16"Therefore, this is what the LORD says: 'I will return to Jerusalem with mercy, and there my house will be rebuilt. And the measuring line will be stretched out over Jerusalem,' declares the LORD Almighty.

17"Proclaim further: This is what the LORD Almighty says: 'My towns will again overflow with prosperity, and the LORD will again comfort Zion and choose Jerusalem.' "

■ Four Horns and Four Craftsmen

18Then I looked up—and there before me were four horns! 19I asked the angel who was speaking to me, "What are these?"

He answered me, "These are the horns that scattered Judah, Israel and Jerusalem."

20Then the LORD showed me four craftsmen. 21I asked, "What are these coming to do?"

He answered, "These are the horns that scattered Judah so that no-one could raise his head, but the craftsmen have come to terrify them and throw down these horns of the nations who lifted up their horns against the land of Judah to scatter its people."

■ A Man With a Measuring Line

2 Then I looked up—and there before me was a man with a measuring line in his hand! ²I asked, "Where are you going?"

He answered me, "To measure Jerusalem, to find out how wide and how long it is."

1:18 ■ BRUTE POWER
In an agricultural society that does its ploughing with oxen, nothing is stronger than a bull. Probably because of this, horns are frequently used as symbols of power in the Old Testament. In our day we might say "bulldozer".

³Then the angel who was speaking to me left, and another angel came to meet him ⁴and said to him: "Run, tell that young man, 'Jerusalem will be a city without walls because of the great number of men and livestock in it. ⁵And I myself will be a wall of fire around it,' declares the LORD, 'and I will be its glory within.'

⁶"Come! Come! Flee from the land of the north," declares the LORD, "for I have scattered you to the four winds of heaven," declares the LORD.

⁷"Come, O Zion! Escape, you who live in the Daughter of Babylon!" ⁸For this is what the LORD Almighty says: "After he has honoured me and has sent me against the nations that have plundered you—for whoever touches you touches the apple of his eye—⁹I will surely raise my hand against them so that their slaves will plunder them.ᵃ Then you will know that the LORD Almighty has sent me.

¹⁰"Shout and be glad, O Daughter of Zion. For I am coming, and I will live among you," declares the LORD. ¹¹"Many nations will be joined with the LORD in that day and will become my people. I will live among you and you will know that the LORD Almighty has sent me to you. ¹²The LORD will inherit Judah as his portion in the holy land and will again choose Jerusalem. ¹³Be still before the LORD, all mankind, because he has roused himself from his holy dwelling."

■ Clean Garments for the High Priest

3 Then he showed me Joshuaᵃ the high priest standing before the angel of the LORD, and Satanᵇ standing at his right side to accuse him. ²The LORD said to Satan, "The LORD rebuke you, Satan! The LORD, who has chosen Jerusalem, rebuke you! Is not this man a burning stick snatched from the fire?"

³Now Joshua was dressed in filthy clothes as he stood before the angel. ⁴The angel said to those who were standing before him, "Take off his filthy clothes."

Then he said to Joshua, "See, I have taken away your sin, and I will put rich garments on you."

⁵Then I said, "Put a clean turban on his head." So they put a clean turban on his head and clothed him, while the angel of the LORD stood by.

⁶The angel of the LORD gave this charge to Joshua: ⁷"This is what the LORD Almighty says: 'If you will walk in my ways and keep my requirements, then

you will govern my house and have charge of my courts, and I will give you a place among these standing here.

3:1 ■ BAD NEWS, GOOD NEWS
References to the high priest Joshua also appear throughout Haggai. Whereas Zechariah uses him as a symbol of the rebellious nation, Haggai tells of Joshua's later transformation and obedience to God. Although Haggai and Zechariah cover the same time period, they show radically different styles. Haggai emphasises the positive and gives a very straightforward message; Zechariah warns of danger and conveys his message in visions and symbols.

⁸" 'Listen, O high priest Joshua and your associates seated before you, who are men symbolic of things to come: I am going to bring my servant, the Branch. ⁹See, the stone I have set in front of Joshua! There are seven eyesᶜ on that one stone, and I will engrave an inscription on it,' says the LORD Almighty, 'and I will remove the sin of this land in a single day.

¹⁰" 'In that day each of you will invite his neighbour to sit under his vine and fig-tree,' declares the LORD Almighty."

■ The Gold Lampstand and the Two Olive Trees

4 Then the angel who talked with me returned and wakened me, as a man is wakened from his sleep. ²He asked me, "What do you see?"

I answered, "I see a solid gold lampstand with a bowl at the top and seven lights on it, with seven channels to the lights. ³Also there are two olive trees by it, one on the right of the bowl and the other on its left."

⁴I asked the angel who talked with me, "What are these, my lord?"

⁵He answered, "Do you not know what these are?"

"No, my lord," I replied.

⁶So he said to me, "This is the word of the LORD to Zerubbabel: 'Not by might nor by power, but by my Spirit,' says the LORD Almighty.

⁷"Whatᵃ are you, O mighty mountain? Before Zerubbabel you will become level ground. Then he will bring out the capstone to shouts of 'God bless it! God bless it!' "

⁸Then the word of the LORD came to me: ⁹"The hands of Zerubbabel have laid the foundation of this temple; his hands will also complete it. Then you will know that the LORD Almighty has sent me to you.

¹⁰"Who despises the day of small things? Men will rejoice when they see the plumb-line in the hand of Zerubbabel.

"(These seven are the eyes of the LORD, which range throughout the earth.)"

¹¹Then I asked the angel, "What are these two olive trees on the right and the left of the lampstand?"

¹²Again I asked him, "What are these two olive

branches beside the two gold pipes that pour out golden oil?"

¹³He replied, "Do you not know what these are?"

"No, my lord," I said.

¹⁴So he said, "These are the two who are anointed toᵇ serve the Lord of all the earth."

■ The Flying Scroll

5 I looked again — and there before me was a flying scroll!

²He asked me, "What do you see?"

I answered, "I see a flying scroll, thirty feet long and fifteen feet wide."ᵃ

5:1 ■ A MESSAGE FOR EVERYONE

The flying scroll probably symbolises God's law, which condemns sin. It is unrolled and flying like a banner for all to read — not rolled up for only priests to read.

³And he said to me, "This is the curse that is going out over the whole land; for according to what it says on one side, every thief will be banished, and according to what it says on the other, everyone who swears falsely will be banished. ⁴The LORD Almighty declares, 'I will send it out, and it will enter the house of the thief and the house of him who swears falsely by my name. It will remain in his house and destroy it, both its timbers and its stones.' "

■ The Woman in a Basket

⁵Then the angel who was speaking to me came forward and said to me, "Look up and see what this is that is appearing."

⁶I asked, "What is it?"

He replied, "It is a measuring basket."ᵇ And he added, "This is the iniquityᶜ of the people throughout the land."

⁷Then the cover of lead was raised, and there in the basket sat a woman! ⁸He said, "This is wickedness," and he pushed her back into the basket and pushed the lead cover down over its mouth.

⁹Then I looked up — and there before me were two women, with the wind in their wings! They had wings like those of a stork, and they lifted up the basket between heaven and earth.

¹⁰"Where are they taking the basket?" I asked the angel who was speaking to me.

¹¹He replied, "To the country of Babyloniaᵈ to build a house for it. When it is ready, the basket will be set there in its place."

■ Four Chariots

6 I looked up again — and there before me were four chariots coming out from between two mountains — mountains of bronze! ²The first chariot had red horses, the second black, ³the third white, and the fourth dappled — all of them powerful. ⁴I asked the angel who was speaking to me, "What are these, my lord?"

⁵The angel answered me, "These are the four spiritsᵃ of heaven, going out from standing in the presence of the Lord of the whole world. ⁶The one with the black horses is going towards the north country, the one with the white horses towards the west,ᵇ and the one with the dappled horses towards the south."

⁷When the powerful horses went out, they were straining to go throughout the earth. And he said, "Go throughout the earth!" So they went throughout the earth.

⁸Then he called to me, "Look, those going towards the north country have given my Spiritᶜ rest in the land of the north."

■ A Crown for Joshua

⁹The word of the LORD came to me: ¹⁰"Take ₍silver and gold₎ from the exiles Heldai, Tobijah and Jedaiah, who have arrived from Babylon. Go the same day to the house of Josiah son of Zephaniah. ¹¹Take the silver and gold and make a crown, and set it on the head of the high priest, Joshua son of Jehozadak. ¹²Tell him this is what the LORD Almighty says: 'Here is the man whose name is the Branch, and he will branch out from his place and build the temple of the LORD. ¹³It is he who will build the temple of the LORD, and he will be clothed with majesty and will sit and rule on his throne. And he will be a priest on his throne. And there will be harmony between the two.' ¹⁴The crown will be given to Heldai,ᵈ Tobijah, Jedaiah and Henᵉ son of Zephaniah as a memorial in the temple of the LORD. ¹⁵Those who are far away will come and help to build the temple of the LORD, and you will know that the LORD Almighty has sent me to you. This will happen if you diligently obey the LORD your God."

■ Justice and Mercy, Not Fasting

7 In the fourth year of King Darius, the word of the LORD came to Zechariah on the fourth day of the ninth month, the month of Kislev. ²The people of Bethel had sent Sharezer and Regem-Melech, together with their men, to entreat the LORD ³by asking the priests of the house of the LORD Almighty and the prophets, "Should I mourn and fast in the fifth month, as I have done for so many years?"

7:3 ■ REPENT FOR HOW LONG?

While in exile, Jews had fasted and mourned on certain days in memory of the siege and overthrow of Jerusalem. Now that they had returned to Jerusalem they wanted to know: should we keep fasting? Zechariah's answer came in 8:19: fasting should now be replaced with feasting. But Zechariah warned that all religious ceremonies, however proper, were meaningless unless people's lives were controlled by God.

⁴Then the word of the LORD Almighty came to me: ⁵"Ask all the people of the land and the priests, 'When you fasted and mourned in the fifth and seventh months for the past seventy years, was it really for me that you fasted? ⁶And when you were eating

ᵇ14 Or two who bring oil and   ᵃ2 Hebrew twenty cubits long and ten cubits wide (about 9 metres long and 4.5 metres wide)   ᵇ6 Hebrew an ephah; also in verses 7–11   ᶜ6 Or appearance   ᵈ11 Hebrew Shinar   ᵃ5 Or winds   ᵇ6 Or horses after them   ᶜ8 Or spirit   ᵈ14 Syriac; Hebrew Helem   ᵉ14 Or and the gracious one, the and drinking, were you not just feasting for yourselves? [7]Are these not the words the LORD proclaimed through the earlier prophets when Jerusalem and its surrounding towns were at rest and prosperous, and the Negev and the western foothills were settled?' "

[8]And the word of the LORD came again to Zechariah: [9]"This is what the LORD Almighty says: 'Administer true justice; show mercy and compassion to one another. [10]Do not oppress the widow or the fatherless, the alien or the poor. In your hearts do not think evil of each other.'

[11]"But they refused to pay attention; stubbornly they turned their backs and stopped up their ears. [12]They made their hearts as hard as flint and would not listen to the law or to the words that the LORD Almighty had sent by his Spirit through the earlier prophets. So the LORD Almighty was very angry.

[13]" 'When I called, they did not listen; so when they called, I would not listen,' says the LORD Almighty. [14]'I scattered them with a whirlwind among all the nations, where they were strangers. The land was left so desolate behind them that no-one could come or go. This is how they made the pleasant land desolate.' "

■ The LORD Promises to Bless Jerusalem

8 Again the word of the LORD Almighty came to me. [2]This is what the LORD Almighty says: "I am very jealous for Zion; I am burning with jealousy for her."

[3]This is what the LORD says: "I will return to Zion and dwell in Jerusalem. Then Jerusalem will be called the City of Truth, and the mountain of the LORD Almighty will be called the Holy Mountain."

[4]This is what the LORD Almighty says: "Once again men and women of ripe old age will sit in the streets of Jerusalem, each with cane in hand because of his age. [5]The city streets will be filled with boys and girls playing there."

8:4 ■ SAFE STREETS

To refugees inhabiting a city overrun by conquerors, the promise of streets safe for senior citizens and playful children seemed almost too much to ask. But God assured them that Jerusalem would once again become stable and secure. "Will it seem marvellous to me?" he asks, with a touch of irony (verse 6).

[6]This is what the LORD Almighty says: "It may seem marvellous to the remnant of this people at that time, but will it seem marvellous to me?" declares the LORD Almighty.

[7]This is what the LORD Almighty says: "I will save my people from the countries of the east and the west. [8]I will bring them back to live in Jerusalem; they will be my people, and I will be faithful and righteous to them as their God."

[9]This is what the LORD Almighty says: "You who now hear these words spoken by the prophets who were there when the foundation was laid for the house of the LORD Almighty, let your hands be strong so that the temple may be built. [10]Before that time there were no wages for man or beast. No-one could go about his business safely because of his enemy, for I had turned every man against his neighbour. [11]But now I will not deal with the remnant of this people as I did in the past," declares the LORD Almighty.

[12]"The seed will grow well, the vine will yield its fruit, the ground will produce its crops, and the heavens will drop their dew. I will give all these things as an inheritance to the remnant of this people. [13]As you have been an object of cursing among the nations, O Judah and Israel, so will I save you, and you will be a blessing. Do not be afraid, but let your hands be strong."

[14]This is what the LORD Almighty says: "Just as I had determined to bring disaster upon you and showed no pity when your fathers angered me," says the LORD Almighty, [15]"so now I have determined to do good again to Jerusalem and Judah. Do not be afraid. [16]These are the things you are to do: Speak the truth to each other, and render true and sound judgment in your courts; [17]do not plot evil against your neighbour, and do not love to swear falsely. I hate all this," declares the LORD.

[18]Again the word of the LORD Almighty came to me. [19]This is what the LORD Almighty says: "The fasts of the fourth, fifth, seventh and tenth months will become joyful and glad occasions and happy festivals for Judah. Therefore love truth and peace."

[20]This is what the LORD Almighty says: "Many peoples and the inhabitants of many cities will yet come, [21]and the inhabitants of one city will go to another and say, 'Let us go at once to entreat the LORD and seek the LORD Almighty. I myself am going.' [22]And many peoples and powerful nations will come to Jerusalem to seek the LORD Almighty and to entreat him."

[23]This is what the LORD Almighty says: "In those days ten men from all languages and nations will take firm hold of one Jew by the hem of his robe and say, 'Let us go with you, because we have heard that God is with you.' "

■ Judgment on Israel's Enemies
An Oracle

9 The word of the LORD is against the land of Hadrach
and will rest upon Damascus—
for the eyes of men and all the tribes of Israel
are on the LORD—[a]
[2]and upon Hamath too, which borders on it,
and upon Tyre and Sidon, though they are
very skilful.
[3]Tyre has built herself a stronghold;
she has heaped up silver like dust,
and gold like the dirt of the streets.
[4]But the Lord will take away her possessions
and destroy her power on the sea,
and she will be consumed by fire.
[5]Ashkelon will see it and fear;
Gaza will writhe in agony,
and Ekron too, for her hope will wither.
Gaza will lose her king

[a] 1 Or Damascus. / For the eye of the LORD is on all mankind, / as well as on the tribes of Israel.

and Ashkelon will be deserted.
⁶Foreigners will occupy Ashdod,
    and I will cut off the pride of the Philistines.
⁷I will take the blood from their mouths,
    the forbidden food from between their teeth.
Those who are left will belong to our God
    and become leaders in Judah,
    and Ekron will be like the Jebusites.
⁸But I will defend my house
    against marauding forces.
Never again will an oppressor overrun my
        people,
    for now I am keeping watch.

■ The Coming of Zion's King
⁹Rejoice greatly, O Daughter of Zion!
    Shout, Daughter of Jerusalem!
See, your king*ᵇ* comes to you,
    righteous and having salvation,
    gentle and riding on a donkey,
    on a colt, the foal of a donkey.
¹⁰I will take away the chariots from Ephraim
    and the war-horses from Jerusalem,
    and the battle-bow will be broken.
He will proclaim peace to the nations.
    His rule will extend from sea to sea
    and from the River*ᶜ* to the ends of the
        earth.*ᵈ*

¹¹As for you, because of the blood of my
        covenant with you,
    I will free your prisoners from the waterless
        pit.

9:9 ■ DONKEY OF PEACE
The Gospel writers refer back to this verse in connection with Jesus' triumphal entry into Jerusalem (Matthew 21:5; John 12:15). More warlike leaders normally rode on stallions, but Zechariah pointedly notes that the coming king will ban chariots and war-horses (verse 10). Jesus scrupulously followed the pattern of a king described here – often disappointing his followers, who sought a more militaristic leader.

¹²Return to your fortress, O prisoners of hope;
    even now I announce that I will restore
        twice as much to you.
¹³I will bend Judah as I bend my bow
    and fill it with Ephraim.
I will rouse your sons, O Zion,
    against your sons, O Greece,
    and make you like a warrior's sword.

■ The LORD Will Appear
¹⁴Then the LORD will appear over them;
    his arrow will flash like lightning.

■ NEW KING, NEW KINGDOM
THE PARADOX OF LEADERSHIP THAT TRIUMPHS THROUGH SUFFERING

INSIGHT

YOUR KING COMES TO YOU, RIGHTEOUS AND HAVING SALVATION, GENTLE AND RIDING ON A DONKEY. ■ 9:9

The book of Zechariah takes a radical turn at chapter 9. A series of messages from God, expressed in fragmented images, tells the future of the world – and the role of God's people in it.

These chapters are difficult to understand, even in our day. The ultimate future is clearly good, however: instead of remaining a small, subject nation, God's people will shake the world. The nations will worship at Jerusalem. "The LORD will be king over the whole earth" (14:9).

How could it be? Even for the Israelites this dream sounded far-fetched. In Zechariah's day they needed clearance from the far-off Persian government just to rebuild their temple. Persia was the centre of their world. Jerusalem hardly mattered. How could Israel become a great nation?

■ A REJECTED LEADER
These chapters of Zechariah show Israel's greatness emerging through struggle and suffering. No-one who reads these words could

have a glib idea that God makes things easy. Evil and misery virtually triumph before God's final intervention.

The key to Israel's future is an expected leader – a very unusual leader. People naturally expected the Messiah to be a triumphant warrior, especially since many Old Testament prophecies spoke of him that way. But this king would come on a donkey instead of a war-horse (9:9). Zechariah speaks of a shepherd – a term for "leader" – who would be rejected by the nation (11:4–17). It describes a nation in mourning for "the one they have pierced" (12:10).

All these predictions of an expected leader were quoted in the New Testament as applying to Jesus: a king without an army, whose crown was made of thorns. In all the Old Testament, only Isaiah (especially in chapter 53) captures so fully the paradox of Jesus' life: gentle leadership that triumphs through suffering.

□ LIFE QUESTIONS:
Who is the "greatest" person you've known very well? Did some kind of suffering contribute to his or her greatness?

ᵇ9 Or King   *ᶜ10* That is, the Euphrates   *ᵈ10* Or the end of the land

The Sovereign LORD will sound the trumpet;
   he will march in the storms of the south,
15 and the LORD Almighty will shield them.
They will destroy
   and overcome with slingstones.
They will drink and roar as with wine;
   they will be full like a bowl
   used for sprinkling*e* the corners of the altar.
16The LORD their God will save them on that day
   as the flock of his people.
They will sparkle in his land
   like jewels in a crown.
17How attractive and beautiful they will be!
   Grain will make the young men thrive,
   and new wine the young women.

■ The LORD Will Care for Judah

10 Ask the LORD for rain in the springtime;
   it is the LORD who makes the storm
   clouds.
He gives showers of rain to men,
   and plants of the field to everyone.
2The idols speak deceit,
   diviners see visions that lie;
they tell dreams that are false,
   they give comfort in vain.
Therefore the people wander like sheep
   oppressed for lack of a shepherd.

3"My anger burns against the shepherds,
   and I will punish the leaders;
for the LORD Almighty will care
   for his flock, the house of Judah,
   and make them like a proud horse in battle.
4From Judah will come the cornerstone,
   from him the tent peg,
   from him the battle-bow,
   from him every ruler.
5Together they*a* will be like mighty men
   trampling the muddy streets in battle.
Because the LORD is with them,
   they will fight and overthrow the horsemen.

6"I will strengthen the house of Judah
   and save the house of Joseph.
I will restore them
   because I have compassion on them.
They will be as though
   I had not rejected them,
for I am the LORD their God
   and I will answer them.
7The Ephraimites will become like mighty men,
   and their hearts will be glad as with wine.
Their children will see it and be joyful;
   their hearts will rejoice in the LORD.
8I will signal for them
   and gather them in.
Surely I will redeem them;
   they will be as numerous as before.
9Though I scatter them among the peoples,
   yet in distant lands they will remember me.
They and their children will survive,
   and they will return.
10I will bring them back from Egypt
   and gather them from Assyria.
I will bring them to Gilead and Lebanon,

and there will not be room enough for them.
11They will pass through the sea of trouble;
   the surging sea will be subdued
   and all the depths of the Nile will dry up.
Assyria's pride will be brought down
   and Egypt's sceptre will pass away.
12I will strengthen them in the LORD
   and in his name they will walk,"
               declares the LORD.

11 Open your doors, O Lebanon,
   so that fire may devour your cedars!
2Wail, O pine tree, for the cedar has fallen;
   the stately trees are ruined!
Wail, oaks of Bashan;
   the dense forest has been cut down!
3Listen to the wail of the shepherds:
   their rich pastures are destroyed!
Listen to the roar of the lions;
   the lush thicket of the Jordan is ruined!

■ Two Shepherds

4This is what the LORD my God says: "Pasture the flock marked for slaughter. 5Their buyers slaughter them and go unpunished. Those who sell them say, 'Praise the LORD, I am rich!' Their own shepherds do not spare them. 6For I will no longer have pity on the people of the land," declares the LORD. "I will hand everyone over to his neighbour and his king. They will oppress the land, and I will not rescue them from their hands."

7So I pastured the flock marked for slaughter, particularly the oppressed of the flock. Then I took two staffs and called one Favour and the other Union, and I pastured the flock. 8In one month I got rid of the three shepherds.

The flock detested me, and I grew weary of them 9and said, "I will not be your shepherd. Let the dying die, and the perishing perish. Let those who are left eat one another's flesh."

11:7 ■ WHO ARE THE SHEPHERDS?

The prophets' messages often had a double meaning: one for the people who first heard them, and another, deeper meaning for future times. In this passage, Zechariah plays the role of the good shepherd who is rejected, an image that Jesus later applied to himself. Similarly, the Jews in Zechariah's day had many "foolish shepherd" leaders, but this description (verses 15–17) may also foreshadow the New Testament's "antichrist".

10Then I took my staff called Favour and broke it, revoking the covenant I had made with all the nations. 11It was revoked on that day, and so the afflicted of the flock who were watching me knew it was the word of the LORD.

12I told them, "If you think it best, give me my pay; but if not, keep it." So they paid me thirty pieces of silver.

13And the LORD said to me, "Throw it to the potter"—the handsome price at which they priced me! So I took the thirty pieces of silver and threw them into the house of the LORD to the potter.

---

e 15 Or bowl, / like   *a* 4, 5 Or ruler, all of them together. / 5 They

14Then I broke my second staff called Union, breaking the brotherhood between Judah and Israel.

15Then the LORD said to me, "Take again the equipment of a foolish shepherd. 16For I am going to raise up a shepherd over the land who will not care for the lost, or seek the young, or heal the injured, or feed the healthy, but will eat the meat of the choice sheep, tearing off their hoofs.

17"Woe to the worthless shepherd,
 who deserts the flock!
May the sword strike his arm and his right eye!
 May his arm be completely withered,
 his right eye totally blinded!"

■ Jerusalem's Enemies to Be Destroyed
An Oracle

12 This is the word of the LORD concerning Israel. The LORD, who stretches out the heavens, who lays the foundation of the earth, and who forms the spirit of man within him, declares: 2"I am going to make Jerusalem a cup that sends all the surrounding peoples reeling. Judah will be besieged as well as Jerusalem. 3On that day, when all the nations of the earth are gathered against her, I will make Jerusalem an immovable rock for all the nations. All who try to move it will injure themselves. 4On that day I will strike every horse with panic and its rider with madness," declares the LORD. "I will keep a watchful eye over the house of Judah, but I will blind all the horses of the nations. 5Then the leaders of Judah will say in their hearts, 'The people of Jerusalem are strong, because the LORD Almighty is their God.'

6"On that day I will make the leaders of Judah like a brazier in a woodpile, like a flaming torch among sheaves. They will consume right and left all the surrounding peoples, but Jerusalem will remain intact in her place.

7"The LORD will save the dwellings of Judah first, so that the honour of the house of David and of Jerusalem's inhabitants may not be greater than that of Judah. 8On that day the LORD will shield those who live in Jerusalem, so that the feeblest among them will be like David, and the house of David will be like God, like the Angel of the LORD going before them. 9On that day I will set out to destroy all the nations that attack Jerusalem.

■ Mourning for the One They Pierced
10"And I will pour out on the house of David and the inhabitants of Jerusalem a spirit*a* of grace and supplication. They will look on*b* me, the one they have pierced, and they will mourn for him as one mourns for an only child, and grieve bitterly for him as one grieves for a firstborn son. 11On that day the weeping in Jerusalem will be great, like the weeping of Hadad Rimmon in the plain of Megiddo. 12The land will mourn, each clan by itself, with their wives by themselves: the clan of the house of David and their wives, the clan of the house of Nathan and their wives, 13the clan of the house of Levi and their wives, the clan of Shimei and their wives, 14and all the rest of the clans and their wives.

■ Cleansing From Sin

13 "On that day a fountain will be opened to the house of David and the inhabitants of Jerusalem, to cleanse them from sin and impurity.

2"On that day, I will banish the names of the idols from the land, and they will be remembered no more," declares the LORD Almighty. "I will remove both the prophets and the spirit of impurity from the land. 3And if anyone still prophesies, his father and mother, to whom he was born, will say to him, 'You must die, because you have told lies in the LORD's name.' When he prophesies, his own parents will stab him.

4"On that day every prophet will be ashamed of his prophetic vision. He will not put on a prophet's garment of hair in order to deceive. 5He will say, 'I am not a prophet. I am a farmer; the land has been my livelihood since my youth.'*a* 6If someone asks him, 'What are these wounds on your body?'*b* he will answer, 'The wounds I was given at the house of my friends.'

■ The Shepherd Struck, the Sheep Scattered
7"Awake, O sword, against my shepherd,
 against the man who is close to me!"
 declares the LORD Almighty.
"Strike the shepherd,
 and the sheep will be scattered,
 and I will turn my hand against the little
 ones.

> **13:7 ■ A PROPHECY OF JESUS**
> Jesus applied this verse to himself just before he died (Matthew 26:31). Some commentators believe that his words about the shepherd who "lays down his life for the sheep" (John 10:11) also drew on this passage. Zechariah's prophecies were on the minds of the Gospel writers: 9:9 is quoted in Matthew 21:5; 12:10 in John 19:37; and 11:12–13 in Matthew 27:9.

8In the whole land," declares the LORD,
 "two-thirds will be struck down and perish;
 yet one-third will be left in it.
9This third I will bring into the fire;
 I will refine them like silver
 and test them like gold.
They will call on my name
 and I will answer them;
I will say, 'They are my people,'
 and they will say, 'The LORD is our God.' "

■ The LORD Comes and Reigns

14 A day of the LORD is coming when your plunder will be divided among you.

2I will gather all the nations to Jerusalem to fight against it; the city will be captured, the houses ransacked, and the women raped. Half of the city will go into exile, but the rest of the people will not be taken from the city. 3Then the LORD will go out and fight against those nations, as he fights in the day of battle. 4On that day his feet will stand on the Mount of Olives, east of

---

a 10 Or the Spirit   b 10 Or to   a 5 Or farmer; a man sold me in my youth   b 6 Or wounds between your hands

Jerusalem, and the Mount of Olives will be split in two from east to west, forming a great valley, with half of the mountain moving north and half moving south. ⁵You will flee by my mountain valley, for it will extend to Azel. You will flee as you fled from the earthquake*ᵃ* in the days of Uzziah king of Judah. Then the LORD my God will come, and all the holy ones with him.

⁶On that day there will be no light, no cold or frost. ⁷It will be a unique day, without daytime or night-time—a day known to the LORD. When evening comes, there will be light.

⁸On that day living water will flow out from Jerusalem, half to the eastern sea*ᵇ* and half to the western sea,*ᶜ* in summer and in winter.

⁹The LORD will be king over the whole earth. On that day there will be one LORD, and his name the only name.

14:9 ■ CATASTROPHES TO COME?

Biblical scholars disagree on how to understand the images in this chapter. To some, the catastrophes portrayed—a mountain splitting in two, a day without light or cold, people rotting on their feet (verses 4,6,12)—take on added significance in an era of nuclear weapons and a possible greenhouse effect. Others interpret these images in more symbolic ways. Regardless, Zechariah makes it clear that the end result of the earth's turmoil will be good news for all followers of God.

¹⁰The whole land, from Geba to Rimmon, south of Jerusalem, will become like the Arabah. But Jerusalem will be raised up and remain in its place, from the Benjamin Gate to the site of the First Gate, to the Corner Gate, and from the Tower of Hananel to the royal winepresses. ¹¹It will be inhabited; never again will it be destroyed. Jerusalem will be secure.

¹²This is the plague with which the LORD will strike all the nations that fought against Jerusalem: Their flesh will rot while they are still standing on

their feet, their eyes will rot in their sockets, and their tongues will rot in their mouths. ¹³On that day men will be stricken by the LORD with great panic. Each man will seize the hand of another, and they will attack each other. ¹⁴Judah too will fight at Jerusalem. The wealth of all the surrounding nations will be collected—great quantities of gold and silver and clothing. ¹⁵A similar plague will strike the horses and mules, the camels and donkeys, and all the animals in those camps.

¹⁶Then the survivors from all the nations that have attacked Jerusalem will go up year after year to worship the King, the LORD Almighty, and to celebrate the Feast of Tabernacles. ¹⁷If any of the peoples of the earth do not go up to Jerusalem to worship the King, the LORD Almighty, they will have no rain. ¹⁸If the Egyptian people do not go up and take part, they will have no rain. The LORD*ᵈ* will bring on them the plague he inflicts on the nations that do not go up to celebrate the Feast of Tabernacles. ¹⁹This will be the punishment of Egypt and the punishment of all the nations that do not go up to celebrate the Feast of Tabernacles.

²⁰On that day HOLY TO THE LORD will be inscribed on the bells of the horses, and the cooking pots in the LORD's house will be like the sacred bowls in front of the altar. ²¹Every pot in Jerusalem and Judah will be holy to the LORD Almighty, and all who come to sacrifice will take some of the pots and cook in them. And on that day there will no longer be a Canaanite*ᵉ* in the house of the LORD Almighty.

14:21 ■ NO MORE SEPARATION

The priests and the temple had always been separate and more holy than the rest of Israel. HOLY TO THE LORD had been inscribed on the priests' turbans (Exodus 28:36) as a symbol of this. But, Zechariah predicted, in the future such words would decorate even horses. Ordinary kitchen pots would become as sacred as the holy sacramental vessels. There would no longer be a distinction between the sacred and secular, for everything would be sacred.

ᵃ5 Or *⁵My mountain valley will be blocked and will extend to Azel. It will be blocked as it was blocked because of the earthquake*   *ᵇ8* That is, the Dead Sea   *ᶜ8* That is, the Mediterranean   *ᵈ18* Or part, then the LORD   *ᵉ21* Or merchant

MALACHI

INTRODUCTION

■ WHEN FAITH GROWS WEARY
MALACHI SPOKE TO PEOPLE "GOING THROUGH THE MOTIONS"

"A SON HONOURS HIS FATHER, AND A SERVANT HIS MASTER. IF I AM A FATHER, WHERE IS THE HONOUR DUE ME?" ■ 1:6

Success has dangers of its own. When you reach the top, you may tend to slacken off. Spiritual life can gradually deteriorate too.

Malachi, in this short book, tried to awaken Israel from laziness in relating to God. Years before, they had optimistically returned to Jerusalem after a long exile. Their faith had grown deeper through difficulties. Despite fierce opposition they had rebuilt the temple, the symbol of their hope in God. They had expected God to supernaturally fill it with his glory and make their nation the centre of the world.

By Malachi's time Israel's hope had faded. In fact, life seemed to have passed the Israelites by. They could not see that God loved them (1:2), and they felt that serving God brought no reward (2:17; 3:14).

■ NO BIG SINNERS

The people of Jerusalem had become lukewarm. Their complaints showed it, and so did their actions. They were not "big" sinners like the people before the exile, who had practised child sacrifice and brought idols into the temple. Malachi's people had kept their religion, but they had lost contact with the God whom the religion was all about.

While Malachi mentioned the same injustices and evils earlier prophets had blasted (3:5), he concentrated most of his energy on problems that may seem petty in comparison: mixed marriages, divorce, and apathetic worship (shown in their second-rate offerings). Through Malachi's eyes, we see the Israelites going through the motions of their faith, doing the bare minimum.

How do you heat up a lukewarm faith? Malachi used several tactics. He began with God's love. To his audience, it was not apparent. But if they would compare their situation with neighbouring Edom's, they would see that God had been caring for them all along.

■ CURING A CARELESS ATTITUDE

Malachi then challenged the Jews to take obedience seriously. They were bringing injured or sick animals to God for offerings. "Try offering them to your governor!" Malachi said. "Would he be pleased with you?" (1:8). Malachi urged them to bring the perfect animals God's law demands and his honour requires. Malachi further demanded that they stop marrying women of other religions, a practice that inevitably introduced religious compromise. They must also put an end to divorce. And finally, they must bring a full tenth — the "tithe" — of their income to God at the temple. Their skimping amounted to robbery — robbery from God.

Malachi didn't demand these changes just because they were in the rulebook. They were actions meant to symbolise an inner attitude. The people must practise their faith seriously. " 'Test me in this,' says the LORD Almighty, 'and see if I will not throw open the floodgates of heaven and pour out so much blessing that you will not have room enough for it' " (3:10).

■ THE LAST VOICE

Malachi's was the last Old Testament voice. It reverberated through 400 or more years of biblical silence. During those years at least some of Malachi's message took hold. Led by the Pharisees, Jews became increasingly devoted to keeping the Old Testament law. Unfortunately, many of them lost Malachi's main point. They forgot that the law was not an end in itself. It was a means by which to give God the honour he deserves.

■ HOW TO READ MALACHI

God's voice dominates Malachi, the voice of a loving father pleading with his children. The people's response is given in the form of seven questions or complaints. The result is a kind of dialogue — almost an argument — which lets you see into the personal attitudes of God and the people he is speaking to.

As in most arguments, a variety of issues are raised, but they are all rooted in a few basic attitudes. As you read through Malachi, try to see what attitudes lay behind the questions, complaints, and problems of God's people. Also note what attitudes lay behind God's words and promises to them.

You can place Malachi's message in the context of Israelite history by looking up "A Line-up of Rulers", pages 260–268.

■ 3-TRACK READING PLAN

For an explanation and complete listing of the 3-track reading plan, turn to page x.

■ TRACK 1:
Two-Week Courses on the Bible
See page x for information on these courses.

■ TRACK 2:
An Overview of Malachi in 1

Day
☐ Day 1. Read the Introduction to Malachi and chapter 3, which lays out some of God's promises and expectations for his people. Now turn to page xi for your next Track 2 reading project.

■ TRACK 3:
All of Malachi in 3 Days
After you have read through Malachi, turn to pages xii–xiii for your next Track 3 reading project.

☐ 1   ☐ 2   ☐ 3–4

1 An oracle: The word of the LORD to Israel through Malachi.*

■ Jacob Loved, Esau Hated

²"I have loved you," says the LORD.

"But you ask, 'How have you loved us?'

"Was not Esau Jacob's brother?" the LORD says. "Yet I have loved Jacob, ³but Esau I have hated, and I have turned his mountains into a wasteland and left his inheritance to the desert jackals."

1:2 ■ SPURNED

Lovers remember when they first fell for someone. They also remember how that person responded, especially if their love met rejection.

In Malachi, God starts the conversation: "I have loved you." Then he traces all of Israel's sins back to their underlying contempt for that love. They have not honoured him as a father (verse 6) or worshipped him as the great King he is (verse 11). Instead, they have shown contempt, bringing second-rate offerings (verse 8), saying, "What a burden!" and sniffing contemptuously at his table (verse 13).

---

⁴Edom may say, "Though we have been crushed, we will rebuild the ruins."

But this is what the LORD Almighty says: "They may build, but I will demolish. They will be called the Wicked Land, a people always under the wrath of the LORD. ⁵You will see it with your own eyes and say, 'Great is the LORD — even beyond the borders of Israel!'

■ Blemished Sacrifices

⁶"A son honours his father, and a servant his master. If I am a father, where is the honour due to me? If I am a master, where is the respect due to me?" says the LORD Almighty. "It is you, O priests, who show contempt for my name.

"But you ask, 'How have we shown contempt for your name?'

⁷"You place defiled food on my altar.

"But you ask, 'How have we defiled you?'

"By saying that the LORD's table is contemptible. ⁸When you bring blind animals for sacrifice, is that not wrong? When you sacrifice crippled or diseased animals, is that not wrong? Try offering them to your governor! Would he be pleased with you? Would he accept you?" says the LORD Almighty.

⁹"Now implore God to be gracious to us. With such offerings from your hands, will he accept you?" — says the LORD Almighty.

¹⁰"Oh, that one of you would shut the temple doors, so that you would not light useless fires on my altar! I am not pleased with you," says the LORD Almighty, "and I will accept no offering from your hands. ¹¹My name will be great among the nations, from the rising to the setting of the sun. In every place incense and pure offerings will be brought to my name, because my name will be great among the nations," says the LORD Almighty.

¹²"But you profane it by saying of the Lord's table, 'It is defiled', and of its food, 'It is contemptible.' ¹³And you say, 'What a burden!' and you sniff at it contemptuously," says the LORD Almighty.

"When you bring injured, crippled or diseased animals and offer them as sacrifices, should I accept them from your hands?" says the LORD. ¹⁴"Cursed is

---

1 Malachi means my messenger.

the cheat who has an acceptable male in his flock and vows to give it, but then sacrifices a blemished animal to the Lord. For I am a great king," says the LORD Almighty, "and my name is to be feared among the nations.

■ **Admonition for the Priests**

2 "And now this admonition is for you, O priests. ²If you do not listen, and if you do not set your heart to honour my name," says the LORD Almighty, "I will send a curse upon you, and I will curse your blessings. Yes, I have already cursed them, because you have not set your heart to honour me.

³"Because of you I will rebuke*a* your descendants;*b* I will spread on your faces the offal from your festival sacrifices, and you will be carried off with it. ⁴And you will know that I have sent you this admonition so that my covenant with Levi may continue," says the LORD Almighty. ⁵"My covenant was with him, a covenant of life and peace, and I gave them to him; this called for reverence and he revered me and stood in awe of my name. ⁶True instruction was in his mouth and nothing false was found on his lips. He walked with me in peace and uprightness, and turned many from sin.

⁷"For the lips of a priest ought to preserve knowledge, and from his mouth men should seek instruction—because he is the messenger of the LORD Almighty. ⁸But you have turned from the way and by your teaching have caused many to stumble; you have violated the covenant with Levi," says the LORD Almighty. ⁹"So I have caused you to be despised and humiliated before all the people, because you have not followed my ways but have shown partiality in matters of the law."

■ **Judah Unfaithful**

¹⁰Have we not all one Father?*c* Did not one God create us? Why do we profane the covenant of our fathers by breaking faith with one another?

¹¹Judah has broken faith. A detestable thing has been committed in Israel and in Jerusalem: Judah has desecrated the sanctuary the LORD loves, by marrying the daughter of a foreign god. ¹²As for the man who does this, whoever he may be, may the LORD cut him off*d* from the tents of Jacob*d*—even though he brings offerings to the LORD Almighty.

¹³Another thing you do: You flood the LORD's altar with tears. You weep and wail because he no longer pays attention to your offerings or accepts them with pleasure from your hands. ¹⁴You ask, "Why?" It is because the LORD is acting as the witness between you and the wife of your youth, because you have broken faith with her, though she is your partner, the wife of your marriage covenant.

¹⁵Has not ⌊the LORD⌋ made them one? In flesh and spirit they are his. And why one? Because he was seeking godly offspring.*e* So guard yourself in your spirit, and do not break faith with the wife of your youth.

¹⁶"I hate divorce," says the LORD God of Israel, "and I hate a man's covering himself*f* with violence as well as with his garment," says the LORD Almighty.

So guard yourself in your spirit, and do not break faith.

■ **The Day of Judgment**

¹⁷You have wearied the LORD with your words. "How have we wearied him?" you ask.

> **2:16 ■ I HATE DIVORCE**
> Divorce was legal in Israel (see Deuteronomy 24:1–4), so perhaps people made no connection between their troubles and the divorce statistics. Malachi straightens them out. God *hates* divorce, legal or not. The marriage covenant between a man and woman should be kept faithfully. Jesus said much the same thing in Matthew 19:1–9.

By saying, "All who do evil are good in the eyes of the LORD, and he is pleased with them" or "Where is the God of justice?"

> **2:17 ■ WHY SERVE GOD?**
> Here and in 3:14 people harshly complained that they could see no point in serving God, when you got no special reward. In responding, God did not try to convince them that the righteous were, in fact, better off. He told them that he keeps a "scroll of remembrance" (3:16), on which he records those who fear him, and that sometime in the future he will come as judge, destroying the wicked and preserving those who fear him. The value of serving him will be obvious someday, even if it is not today.

3 "See, I will send my messenger, who will prepare the way before me. Then suddenly the Lord you are seeking will come to his temple; the messenger of the covenant, whom you desire, will come," says the LORD Almighty.

²But who can endure the day of his coming? Who can stand when he appears? For he will be like a refiner's fire or a launderer's soap. ³He will sit as a refiner and purifier of silver; he will purify the Levites and refine them like gold and silver. Then the LORD will have men who will bring offerings in righteousness, ⁴and the offerings of Judah and Jerusalem will be acceptable to the LORD, as in days gone by, as in former years.

⁵"So I will come near to you for judgment. I will be quick to testify against sorcerers, adulterers and perjurers, against those who defraud labourers of their wages, who oppress the widows and the fatherless, and deprive aliens of justice, but do not fear me," says the LORD Almighty.

■ **Robbing God**

⁶"I the LORD do not change. So you, O descendants of Jacob, are not destroyed. ⁷Ever since the time of your forefathers you have turned away from my decrees and have not kept them. Return to me, and I will return to you," says the LORD Almighty.

a 3 Or cut off (see Septuagint)   b 3 Or will blight your corn   c 10 Or father   d 12 Or 12May the LORD cut off from the tents of Jacob anyone who gives testimony on behalf of the man who does this   e 15 Or 15But the one ⌊who is our father⌋ did not do this, not as long as life remained in him. And what was he seeking? An offspring from God   f 16 Or his wife

"But you ask, 'How are we to return?'
8"Will a man rob God? Yet you rob me.
"But you ask, 'How do we rob you?'
"In tithes and offerings. 9You are under a curse—
the whole nation of you—because you are robbing
me. 10Bring the whole tithe into the storehouse,
that there may be food in my house. Test me in this,"
says the LORD Almighty, "and see if I will not throw
open the floodgates of heaven and pour out so
much blessing that you will not have room enough
for it. 11I will prevent pests from devouring your
crops, and the vines in your fields will not cast their
fruit," says the LORD Almighty. 12"Then all the nations will call you blessed, for yours will be a delightful land," says the LORD Almighty.

3:10 ■ TESTING THE TITHE
Like a salesman offering a free sample, God urges
the Israelites to test him out. If they bring their
tithes to the temple, they will see how God
blesses them, opening the "floodgates of heaven"
to pour out an abundance. The "tithe" was at least
a tenth of their income, used to feed the priests,
pay temple expenses, and help the poor.

13"You have said harsh things against me," says
the LORD.
"Yet you ask, 'What have we said against you?'
14"You have said, 'It is futile to serve God. What
did we gain by carrying out his requirements and
going about like mourners before the LORD
Almighty? 15But now we call the arrogant blessed.
Certainly the evildoers prosper, and even those who
challenge God escape.' "
16Then those who feared the LORD talked with
each other, and the LORD listened and heard. A scroll

of remembrance was written in his presence concerning those who feared the LORD and honoured
his name.

4:5 ■ THE SECOND ELIJAH
The prophet Elijah, Malachi predicted, would
precede the Lord. This prophecy was carefully
noted in the New Testament. Jesus identified John
the Baptist as the one predicted (Matthew 11:14;
17:9–13).

17"They will be mine," says the LORD Almighty, "in
the day when I make up my treasured possession.*
I will spare them, just as in compassion a man spares
his son who serves him. 18And you will again see the
distinction between the righteous and the wicked,
between those who serve God and those who do
not.

■ The Day of the LORD
4 "Surely the day is coming; it will burn like a furnace. All the arrogant and every evildoer will be
stubble, and that day that is coming will set them on
fire," says the LORD Almighty. "Not a root or a branch
will be left to them. 2But for you who revere my
name, the sun of righteousness will rise with healing
in its wings. And you will go out and leap like calves
released from the stall. 3Then you will trample
down the wicked; they will be ashes under the soles
of your feet on the day when I do these things," says
the LORD Almighty.
4"Remember the law of my servant Moses, the decrees and laws I gave him at Horeb for all Israel.
5"See, I will send you the prophet Elijah before
that great and dreadful day of the LORD comes. 6He
will turn the hearts of the fathers to their children,
and the hearts of the children to their fathers; or else
I will come and strike the land with a curse."

a 17 Or Almighty, "my treasured possession, in the day when I act

OUTLINE OF OLD TESTAMENT HISTORY

This outline emphasises broad historical periods rather than specific events.
Dates, which often depend on scholarly interpretation, are approximate.

2000 B.C.

1500

THE
JUDGES

ADAM
AND EVE

ABRAHAM

ISAAC

JACOB

JOSEPH

MOSES

JOSHUA

PATRIARCHAL
AGE

CONQUEST
OF CANAAN

EXODUS

SOJOURN
IN EGYPT

GENESIS

EXODUS
TO JUDGES

1000   500   0 A.D.

SAMUEL
SAUL
DAVID
SOLOMON

ISRAEL

EXILE TO
ASSYRIA

JESUS

DIVIDED
KINGDOM

JUDAH

PERIOD OF
THE JUDGES

UNITED
KINGDOM

EXILES
RETURN

EXILE TO
BABYLON

1 & 2 KINGS
2 CHRONICLES
AND MOST PROPHETS

EZRA
NEHEMIAH
ESTHER

1 & 2 SAMUEL
1 CHRONICLES

EZEKIEL
DANIEL

THE NEW TESTAMENT

MATTHEW

■ A BRIDGE FROM OLD TO NEW

WHY START WITH A LIST OF NAMES?

"SHE WILL GIVE BIRTH TO A SON, AND YOU ARE TO GIVE HIM THE NAME JESUS, BECAUSE HE WILL SAVE HIS PEOPLE FROM THEIR SINS." ■ 1:21

For four hundred years, nothing new was added to the Bible. The prophets fell silent. During this time, Middle Eastern empires rose and fell, and the tiny nation of Israel suffered under the domination of greater powers like Greece and Rome.

And then something momentous happened. A baby was born – a baby unlike any who had ever come before. By introducing this baby who grew into the man Jesus, the book of Matthew opens a whole new section of the Bible – the New Testament.

Matthew makes his intentions clear from the very first sentence: he connects Jesus' arrival with the Old Testament story line. Jesus was a Jew, he says, the son of Abraham. And also a king, the son of David. Matthew then sets out to prove an audacious claim: this Jesus, from the humble town of Nazareth, is the very "Messiah", the deliverer promised earlier in the Old Testament. (*Christ* is a Greek translation of the word *Messiah*.)

■ JESUS' FAMILY TREE

People all over the world, especially Jews, had been eagerly awaiting the Messiah. His coming would change the entire history of the world, they believed. Could this carpenter's son be the long-expected king? To answer that question, Matthew starts with a genealogy.

Genealogies – long lists of names – rarely prove interesting to anyone but the people directly involved. To those people, however, the lists are anything but boring.

Listen to one modern author describe what it was like to hear an ancient genealogy: "There is an expression, 'the peak experience', a moment which emotionally can never again be equalled in your life. I had mine, that first day in the village of Juffure, in black west Africa . . . Goose bumps came out on me the size of marbles." With those words, Alex Haley, author of *Roots*, recalls the day he first heard, from the lips of an aged story-teller, the account of young Kunta Kinte being taken captive by slave traders in 1752.

■ THE IMPORTANCE OF ROOTS

Haley's ancestors in Tennessee and Virginia had descended directly from a native African captured in a tiny village in Gambia. The day he listened to the gentle African elder recite, "And so-and-so took as a wife so-and-so, and begat so-and-so", the final link in Haley's family chain snapped into place. *Roots* tells the story of this connection.

In a similar way, the book of Matthew doesn't begin with Jesus' birth, but reaches back further to establish his roots. If indeed Jesus is the Messiah, his ancestors must match up to that claim. As any student of history knows, kings don't merely declare themselves; they must belong to a royal line. Matthew traces Jesus' lineage to the father of the Jewish race, Abraham – who first received the promise of the Messiah – then to the great Jewish king David.

■ LINKS TO THE OLD TESTAMENT

After recording Jesus' bloodline, Matthew narrates the story of Jesus' life on earth. He relies heavily on the Old Testament, quoting it more frequently than does any other New Testament author. (Note such phrases as "So was fulfilled what was said through the prophets.")

The first book in the New Testament, then, stands as the Gospel that pulls things together, the link between the old and the new. Matthew starts with Jesus' roots, but he also contrasts Jesus with the traditional Jewish picture of the Messiah. Jesus, a king, ended thousands of years of eager waiting. But he came to establish a wholly new kind of kingdom – a kingdom different from what anyone expected.

■ HOW TO READ MATTHEW

Anybody who has looked over an Inland Revenue form knows what tax collectors like: neat, orderly rows of figures, with all expenses and income classified by type and source. Fittingly, the Gospel attributed to former tax collector Matthew reflects systematic, ledger-sheet thinking. He doesn't tell Jesus' story chronologically; he groups facts topically.

Matthew collects Jesus' sayings in five main places. First comes the famous Sermon on the Mount in chapters 5–7. Chapter 10 records Jesus' instructions to his disciples about their mission; chapter 13, a series of parables on the kingdom; chapter 18, Christ's words on the church as a community; and chapters 23–25, Jesus' thoughts on religious hypocrisy and his predictions of the future. Sandwiched in among these five great discourses you'll find connected scenes of Jesus in action.

The skillful blending of Jesus' action and teaching has helped earn this Gospel an esteemed place in literature. Artists are often drawn to it as a summary of Jesus' ministry: witness J.S. Bach's greatest choral work, *Saint Matthew's Passion,* the joyous play *Godspell,* and Italian film maker Pasolini's film *The Gospel according to Saint Matthew.* The French sceptic Renan praised Matthew as "the most important book of Christendom – the most important book that has ever been written".

Two approaches will help in a detailed study of Matthew. First, consider how it differs from the other three Gospels; this will give you some idea of Matthew's distinctive purpose. Then, you will find it enlightening to look up many of Matthew's references to the Old Testament. Most are cited in the NIV footnotes.

■ 3-TRACK READING PLAN

For an explanation and complete listing of the 3-track reading plan, turn to page x.

■ TRACK 1:
Two-Week Courses on the Bible
The Track 1 reading programme on the Life and Teachings of Jesus includes four chapters from Matthew. See page x for a complete listing of this course.

■ TRACK 2:
An Overview of Matthew in 7 Days
☐ Day 1. Read the Introduction to Matthew. Then turn to Matthew 5 and begin the Sermon on the Mount.
☐ Day 2. Read chapter 6, a continuation of Jesus' longest single speech, perhaps the most familiar passage in the entire Bible.
☐ Day 3. Matthew 13 records

some of Jesus' parables – concise stories with a powerful meaning behind them. Read these parables about the "kingdom of heaven", referring to "What Should a Leader Look Like?" page 845, for help in understanding.
☐ Day 4. As a former tax collector, Matthew was especially sensitive to what Jesus had to say about money. Read his comments on this and other topics in chapter 19.
☐ Day 5. The last three chapters of Matthew give a complete, factual account of Jesus' death. Read chapter 26, the story of the arrest and trial.
☐ Day 6. Continue the

crucifixion story with chapter 27.
☐ Day 7. Read chapter 28, which tells of Jesus' resurrection.
Now turn to page xi for your next Track 2 reading project.

■ TRACK 3:
All of Matthew in 28 Days
After you have read through Matthew a chapter a day, turn to pages xii–xiii for your next Track 3 reading project.

☐ 1	☐ 2	☐ 3	☐ 4
☐ 5	☐ 6	☐ 7	☐ 8
☐ 9	☐ 10	☐ 11	☐ 12
☐ 13	☐ 14	☐ 15	☐ 16
☐ 17	☐ 18	☐ 19	☐ 20
☐ 21	☐ 22	☐ 23	☐ 24
☐ 25	☐ 26	☐ 27	☐ 28

■ The Genealogy of Jesus
☐ See Ruth 4:18–22; 1 Chronicles 3:10–17; Luke 3:23–38

1 A record of the genealogy of Jesus Christ the son of David, the son of Abraham:

2Abraham was the father of Isaac,
    Isaac the father of Jacob,
    Jacob the father of Judah and his brothers,
3Judah the father of Perez and Zerah, whose
    mother was Tamar,
    Perez the father of Hezron,
    Hezron the father of Ram,
4Ram the father of Amminadab,
    Amminadab the father of Nahshon,
    Nahshon the father of Salmon,
5Salmon the father of Boaz, whose mother
    was Rahab,
    Boaz the father of Obed, whose mother was
    Ruth,
    Obed the father of Jesse,
6and Jesse the father of King David.

David was the father of Solomon, whose
    mother had been Uriah's wife,

1:6 ■ SHADY ANCESTORS

Matthew's list differs from many Jewish genealogies by including women, and a surprising selection of women at that. Tamar, a Gentile, tricked and seduced her father-in-law, then bore illegitimate twins (Genesis 38); Rahab, another Gentile, once worked as a prostitute (Joshua 2; 6); Ruth also grew up as a pagan Gentile (Ruth 1–4); and Uriah's wife Bathsheba committed adultery with King David (2 Samuel 11–12). Many of the men listed had unsavoury pasts as well; taken together, these ancestors of Jesus vividly demonstrate God's ability to work with all sorts of people.

7Solomon the father of Rehoboam,
    Rehoboam the father of Abijah,
    Abijah the father of Asa,
8Asa the father of Jehoshaphat,
    Jehoshaphat the father of Jehoram,
    Jehoram the father of Uzziah,
9Uzziah the father of Jotham,
    Jotham the father of Ahaz,
    Ahaz the father of Hezekiah,
10Hezekiah the father of Manasseh,
    Manasseh the father of Amon,
    Amon the father of Josiah,
11and Josiah the father of Jeconiah a and his
    brothers at the time of the exile to
    Babylon.

12After the exile to Babylon:
    Jeconiah was the father of Shealtiel,
    Shealtiel the father of Zerubbabel,
13Zerubbabel the father of Abiud,
    Abiud the father of Eliakim,
    Eliakim the father of Azor,
14Azor the father of Zadok,
    Zadok the father of Akim,
    Akim the father of Eliud,

15Eliud the father of Eleazar,
    Eleazar the father of Matthan,
    Matthan the father of Jacob,
16and Jacob the father of Joseph, the husband
    of Mary, of whom was born Jesus, who is
    called Christ.

17Thus there were fourteen generations in all from Abraham to David, fourteen from David to the exile to Babylon, and fourteen from the exile to the Christ. b

■ The Birth of Jesus Christ
18This is how the birth of Jesus Christ came about: His mother Mary was pledged to be married to Joseph, but before they came together, she was found to be with child through the Holy Spirit. 19Because Joseph her husband was a righteous man and did not want to expose her to public disgrace, he had in mind to divorce her quietly.

1:18 ■ MORE THAN ENGAGED

Jewish custom in Joseph and Mary's day recognised a state called "betrothal" that fell somewhere between our modern commitments of engagement and marriage. A betrothal was more binding than an engagement: it could only be broken with an act of divorce. And if a betrothed woman became pregnant, she was regarded as an adulteress.

20But after he had considered this, an angel of the Lord appeared to him in a dream and said, "Joseph son of David, do not be afraid to take Mary home as your wife, because what is conceived in her is from the Holy Spirit. 21She will give birth to a son, and you are to give him the name Jesus, c because he will save his people from their sins."

22All this took place to fulfil what the Lord had said through the prophet: 23"The virgin will be with child and will give birth to a son, and they will call him Immanuel" d — which means, "God with us."

24When Joseph woke up, he did what the angel of the Lord had commanded him and took Mary home as his wife. 25But he had no union with her until she gave birth to a son. And he gave him the name Jesus.

■ The Visit of the Magi

2 After Jesus was born in Bethlehem in Judea, during the time of King Herod, Magi a from the east came to Jerusalem 2and asked, "Where is the one who has been born king of the Jews? We saw his star in the east b and have come to worship him."

3When King Herod heard this he was disturbed, and all Jerusalem with him. 4When he had called together all the people's chief priests and teachers of the law, he asked them where the Christ c was to be born. 5"In Bethlehem in Judea," they replied, "for this is what the prophet has written:

6" 'But you, Bethlehem, in the land of Judah,
    are by no means least among the rulers of
    Judah;
    for out of you will come a ruler

a 11 That is, Jehoiachin; also in verse 12   b 17 Or Messiah. "The Christ" (Greek) and "the Messiah" (Hebrew) both mean "the Anointed One".   c 21 Jesus is the Greek form of Joshua, which means the LORD saves.   d 23 Isaiah 7:14   a 1 Traditionally Wise Men   b 2 Or star when it rose   c 4 Or Messiah who will be the shepherd of my people Israel.'*d*"

7Then Herod called the Magi secretly and found out from them the exact time the star had appeared. 8He sent them to Bethlehem and said, "Go and make a careful search for the child. As soon as you find him, report to me, so that I too may go and worship him."

9After they had heard the king, they went on their way, and the star they had seen in the east*e* went ahead of them until it stopped over the place where the child was. 10When they saw the star, they were overjoyed. 11On coming to the house, they saw the child with his mother Mary, and they bowed down and worshipped him. Then they opened their treasures and presented him with gifts of gold and of incense and of myrrh. 12And having been warned in a dream not to go back to Herod, they returned to their country by another route.

2:11 ■ THE WISE MEN
Of the four Gospels, Matthew alone tells of the visit of the Magi, or Wise Men. This incident shows that people from other parts of the world, not just from Israel, were anticipating the Messiah. The Magi's visit points out that Jesus came for all people, not just the Jews. The last words of this Gospel spell out that mission very clearly.

■ The Escape to Egypt
13When they had gone, an angel of the Lord appeared to Joseph in a dream. "Get up," he said, "take the child and his mother and escape to Egypt. Stay there until I tell you, for Herod is going to search for the child to kill him."

14So he got up, took the child and his mother during the night and left for Egypt, 15where he stayed until the death of Herod. And so was fulfilled what the Lord had said through the prophet: "Out of Egypt I called my son."*f*

16When Herod realised that he had been outwitted by the Magi, he was furious, and he gave orders to kill all the boys in Bethlehem and its vicinity who were two years old and under, in accordance with the time he had learned from the Magi. 17Then what was said through the prophet Jeremiah was fulfilled:

18"A voice is heard in Ramah,
weeping and great mourning,
Rachel weeping for her children
and refusing to be comforted,
because they are no more."*g*

■ The Return to Nazareth
19After Herod died, an angel of the Lord appeared in a dream to Joseph in Egypt 20and said, "Get up, take the child and his mother and go to the land of Israel, for those who were trying to take the child's life are dead."

21So he got up, took the child and his mother and went to the land of Israel. 22But when he heard that Archelaus was reigning in Judea in place of his father Herod, he was afraid to go there. Having been warned in a dream, he withdrew to the district of Galilee, 23and he went and lived in a town called Nazareth. So was fulfilled what was said through the prophets: "He will be called a Nazarene."

■ John the Baptist Prepares the Way
□ See Mark 1:3–8; Luke 3:2–17

3 In those days John the Baptist came, preaching in the Desert of Judea 2and saying, "Repent, for the kingdom of heaven is near." 3This is he who was spoken of through the prophet Isaiah:

"A voice of one calling in the desert,
'Prepare the way for the Lord,
make straight paths for him.' "*a*

4John's clothes were made of camel's hair, and he had a leather belt round his waist. His food was locusts and wild honey. 5People went out to him from Jerusalem and all Judea and the whole region of the Jordan. 6Confessing their sins, they were baptised by him in the Jordan River.

7But when he saw many of the Pharisees and Sadducees coming to where he was baptising, he said to them: "You brood of vipers! Who warned you to flee from the coming wrath? 8Produce fruit in keeping with repentance. 9And do not think you can say to yourselves, 'We have Abraham as our father.' I tell you that out of these stones God can raise up children for Abraham. 10The axe is already at the root of the trees, and every tree that does not produce good fruit will be cut down and thrown into the fire.

11"I baptise you with*b* water for repentance. But after me will come one who is more powerful than I, whose sandals I am not fit to carry. He will baptise you with the Holy Spirit and with fire. 12His winnowing fork is in his hand, and he will clear his threshing-floor, gathering his wheat into the barn and burning up the chaff with unquenchable fire."

■ The Baptism of Jesus
□ See Mark 1:9–11; Luke 3:21–22; John 1:31–34

13Then Jesus came from Galilee to the Jordan to be baptised by John. 14But John tried to deter him, saying, "I need to be baptised by you, and do you come to me?"

15Jesus replied, "Let it be so now; it is proper for us to do this to fulfil all righteousness." Then John consented.

16As soon as Jesus was baptised, he went up out of the water. At that moment heaven was opened, and he saw the Spirit of God descending like a dove and lighting on him. 17And a voice from heaven said, "This is my Son, whom I love; with him I am well pleased."

■ The Temptation of Jesus
□ See Mark 1:12–13; Luke 4:1–13

4 Then Jesus was led by the Spirit into the desert to be tempted by the devil. 2After fasting for forty days and forty nights, he was hungry. 3The tempter came to him and said, "If you are the Son of God, tell these stones to become bread."

4Jesus answered, "It is written: 'Man does not live on bread alone, but on every word that comes from the mouth of God.'*a*"

*d*6 Micah 5:2   *e*9 Or *seen when it rose*   *f*15 Hosea 11:1   *g*18 Jer. 31:15   *a*3 Isaiah 40:3   *b*11 Or *in*   *a*4 Deut. 8:3

5Then the devil took him to the holy city and had him stand on the highest point of the temple. 6"If you are the Son of God," he said, "throw yourself down. For it is written:

" 'He will command his angels concerning you,
    and they will lift you up in their hands,
so that you will not strike your foot against a
    stone.'b"

7Jesus answered him, "It is also written: 'Do not put the Lord your God to the test.'c"

8Again, the devil took him to a very high mountain and showed him all the kingdoms of the world and their splendour. 9"All this I will give you," he said, "if you will bow down and worship me."

10Jesus said to him, "Away from me, Satan! For it is written: 'Worship the Lord your God, and serve him only.'d"

11Then the devil left him, and angels came and attended him.

■ Jesus Begins to Preach

12When Jesus heard that John had been put in prison, he returned to Galilee. 13Leaving Nazareth, he went and lived in Capernaum, which was by the lake in the area of Zebulun and Naphtali—14to fulfil what was said through the prophet Isaiah:

15"Land of Zebulun and land of Naphtali,
    the way to the sea, along the Jordan,
    Galilee of the Gentiles—
16the people living in darkness
    have seen a great light;
on those living in the land of the shadow of
    death
    a light has dawned."e

17From that time on Jesus began to preach, "Repent, for the kingdom of heaven is near."

4:17 ■ WORDS FOR JEWISH READERS
Matthew wrote for a primarily Jewish audience. Starting with his opening chapter, he affirms that Jesus is the Messiah, backing up that claim by constant reference to the Old Testament. Often Matthew leaves Jewish phrases and customs unexplained, assuming that his readers are familiar with them. And, where other Gospel writers say, "kingdom of God", he uses the phrase "kingdom of heaven", out of respect for Jews, who never wrote out the word God.

■ The Calling of the First Disciples
□ See Mark 1:16–20; Luke 5:2–11; John 1:35–42

18As Jesus was walking beside the Sea of Galilee, he saw two brothers, Simon called Peter and his brother Andrew. They were casting a net into the lake, for they were fishermen. 19"Come, follow me," Jesus said, "and I will make you fishers of men." 20At once they left their nets and followed him.

21Going on from there, he saw two other brothers, James son of Zebedee and his brother John. They were in a boat with their father Zebedee, preparing their nets. Jesus called them, 22and immediately they left the boat and their father and followed him.

■ Jesus Heals the Sick

23Jesus went throughout Galilee, teaching in their synagogues, preaching the good news of the kingdom, and healing every disease and sickness among the people. 24News about him spread all over Syria, and people brought to him all who were ill with various diseases, those suffering severe pain, the demon-possessed, those having seizures, and the paralysed, and he healed them. 25Large crowds from Galilee, the Decapolis,f Jerusalem, Judea and the region across the Jordan followed him.

■ The Beatitudes
□ See Luke 6:20–23

5 Now when he saw the crowds, he went up on a mountainside and sat down. His disciples came to him, 2and he began to teach them, saying:

3"Blessed are the poor in spirit,
    for theirs is the kingdom of heaven.
4Blessed are those who mourn,
    for they will be comforted.
5Blessed are the meek,
    for they will inherit the earth.
6Blessed are those who hunger and thirst for
    righteousness,
    for they will be filled.
7Blessed are the merciful,
    for they will be shown mercy.
8Blessed are the pure in heart,
    for they will see God.
9Blessed are the peacemakers,
    for they will be called sons of God.
10Blessed are those who are persecuted because
    of righteousness,
    for theirs is the kingdom of heaven.

11"Blessed are you when people insult you, persecute you and falsely say all kinds of evil against you because of me. 12Rejoice and be glad, because great is your reward in heaven, for in the same way they persecuted the prophets who were before you.

■ Salt and Light

13"You are the salt of the earth. But if the salt loses its saltiness, how can it be made salty again? It is no longer good for anything, except to be thrown out and trampled by men.

14"You are the light of the world. A city on a hill cannot be hidden. 15Neither do people light a lamp and put it under a bowl. Instead they put it on its stand, and it gives light to everyone in the house. 16In the same way, let your light shine before men, that they may see your good deeds and praise your Father in heaven.

■ The Fulfilment of the Law

17"Do not think that I have come to abolish the Law or the Prophets; I have not come to abolish them but to fulfil them. 18I tell you the truth, until heaven and earth disappear, not the smallest letter, not the least stroke of a pen, will by any means disappear from the Law until everything is

---

b6 Psalm 91:11,12   c7 Deut. 6:16   d10 Deut. 6:13   e16 Isaiah 9:1,2   f25 That is, the Ten Cities accomplished. 19Anyone who breaks one of the least of these commandments and teaches others to do the same will be called least in the kingdom of heaven, but whoever practises and teaches these commands will be called great in the kingdom of heaven. 20For I tell you that unless your righteousness surpasses that of the Pharisees and the teachers of the law, you will certainly not enter the kingdom of heaven.

5:17 ■ JESUS AND MOSES' LAW
In this statement, Jesus clarifies his relationship to the Law of Moses. The next verses get more specific, contrasting Jesus' teaching with many common interpretations of that Law. "You have heard that it was said . . . ", he begins, and then concludes, "But I tell you . . ." Jesus revealed the true intent of the Old Testament law, rather than its legalistic interpretations.

■ Murder
21"You have heard that it was said to the people long ago, 'Do not murder,^{a} and anyone who murders will be subject to judgment.' 22But I tell you that anyone who is angry with his brother^b will be subject to judgment. Again, anyone who says to his brother, 'Raca,'^{c} is answerable to the Sanhedrin. But anyone who says, 'You fool!' will be in danger of the fire of hell.

23"Therefore, if you are offering your gift at the altar and there remember that your brother has something against you, 24leave your gift there in front of the altar. First go and be reconciled to your brother; then come and offer your gift.

25"Settle matters quickly with your adversary who is taking you to court. Do it while you are still with him on the way, or he may hand you over to the judge, and the judge may hand you over to the officer, and you may be thrown into prison. 26I tell you the truth, you will not get out until you have paid the last penny.^{d}

■ Adultery
27"You have heard that it was said, 'Do not commit adultery.'^{e} 28But I tell you that anyone who looks at a woman lustfully has already committed adultery with her in his heart. 29If your right eye causes you to sin, gouge it out and throw it away. It is better for you to lose one part of your body than for your whole body to be thrown into hell. 30And if your right hand causes you to sin, cut it off and throw it away. It is better for you to lose one part of your body than for your whole body to go into hell.

■ Divorce
31"It has been said, 'Anyone who divorces his wife must give her a certificate of divorce.'^{f} 32But I tell you that anyone who divorces his wife, except for marital unfaithfulness, causes her to become an adulteress, and anyone who marries the divorced woman commits adultery.

■ Oaths
33"Again, you have heard that it was said to the people long ago, 'Do not break your oath, but keep the oaths you have made to the Lord.' 34But I tell you, Do not swear at all: either by heaven, for it is God's throne; 35or by the earth, for it is his footstool; or by Jerusalem, for it is the city of the Great King. 36And do not swear by your head, for you cannot make even one hair white or black. 37Simply let your 'Yes' be 'Yes', and your 'No', 'No'; anything beyond this comes from the evil one.

■ An Eye for an Eye
38"You have heard that it was said, 'Eye for eye, and tooth for tooth.'^{g} 39But I tell you, Do not resist an evil person. If someone strikes you on the right cheek, turn to him the other also. 40And if someone wants to sue you and take your tunic, let him have your cloak as well. 41If someone forces you to go one mile, go with him two miles. 42Give to the one who asks you, and do not turn away from the one who wants to borrow from you.

■ Love for Enemies
43"You have heard that it was said, 'Love your neighbour^b and hate your enemy.' 44But I tell you: Love your enemies^i and pray for those who persecute you, 45that you may be sons of your Father in heaven. He causes his sun to rise on the evil and the good, and sends rain on the righteous and the unrighteous. 46If you love those who love you, what reward will you get? Are not even the tax collectors doing that? 47And if you greet only your brothers, what are you doing more than others? Do not even pagans do that? 48Be perfect, therefore, as your heavenly Father is perfect.

5:44 ■ PRAYING FOR PERSECUTORS
Jesus got a chance to live out these words when, nailed to a cross, he prayed for his persecutors (Luke 23:34). The example of Stephen, the first Christian martyr (Acts 7:60), shows that some followers also put Jesus' command into practice – a fact that surely impressed one persecutor named Saul.

■ Giving to the Needy
6 "Be careful not to do your 'acts of righteousness' before men, to be seen by them. If you do, you will have no reward from your Father in heaven.

2"So when you give to the needy, do not announce it with trumpets, as the hypocrites do in the synagogues and on the streets, to be honoured by men. I tell you the truth, they have received their reward in full. 3But when you give to the needy, do not let your left hand know what your right hand is doing, 4so that your giving may be in secret. Then your Father, who sees what is done in secret, will reward you.

---

^{a}21 Exodus 20:13 ^{b}22 Some manuscripts brother without cause ^{c}22 An Aramaic term of contempt ^{d}26 Greek kodrantes ^{e}27 Exodus 20:14
^{f}31 Deut. 24:1 ^{g}38 Exodus 21:24; Lev. 24:20 and Deut. 19:21 ^{b}43 Lev. 19:18 ^{i}44 Some late manuscripts enemies, bless those who curse you, do good to those who hate you

■ Prayer
□ See Luke 11:2–4

5"And when you pray, do not be like the hypocrites, for they love to pray standing in the synagogues and on the street corners to be seen by men. I tell you the truth, they have received their reward in full. 6But when you pray, go into your room, close the door and pray to your Father, who is unseen. Then your Father, who sees what is done in secret, will reward you. 7And when you pray, do not keep on babbling like pagans, for they think they will be heard because of their many words. 8Do not be like them, for your Father knows what you need before you ask him.

9"This, then, is how you should pray:

" 'Our Father in heaven,
hallowed be your name,
10your kingdom come,
your will be done
on earth as it is in heaven.
11Give us today our daily bread.
12Forgive us our debts,

as we also have forgiven our debtors.
13And lead us not into temptation,
but deliver us from the evil one.'ᵃ

14For if you forgive men when they sin against you, your heavenly Father will also forgive you. 15But if you do not forgive men their sins, your Father will not forgive your sins.

■ Fasting

16"When you fast, do not look sombre as the hypocrites do, for they disfigure their faces to show men they are fasting. I tell you the truth, they have received their reward in full. 17But when you fast, put oil on your head and wash your face, 18so that it will not be obvious to men that you are fasting, but only to your Father, who is unseen; and your Father, who sees what is done in secret, will reward you.

■ Treasures in Heaven

19"Do not store up for yourselves treasures on earth, where moth and rust destroy, and where

■ LETTING THE INSIDE MATCH THE OUTSIDE
IS EVERYONE A HYPOCRITE?

"YOUR FATHER, WHO SEES WHAT IS
DONE IN SECRET, WILL REWARD YOU."
■ 6:4

Almost all of us live two lives: what people see outside and what is really going on inside. In school we learn what outward signs of attention will please the teacher. At a job we learn to "put up a good front" whenever the boss happens to stroll by. As if donning masks, we style our hair, choose our clothes, and use body language to impress those round us. Over time, we learn to excel at hiding truly serious problems.

People tend to judge by outward appearances and so can easily be fooled. Acquaintances are often shocked when a mass-murderer is arrested. "He seemed like such a nice man!" they insist. The outside appearance did not match the inside reality.

■ A BLAST AT HYPOCRITES
Chapters 5–7 announce that the time has come for us to change not just the outside, but the inside. In Jesus' day, religious people tried to impress each other with showy outward behaviour. They wore gaunt and hungry looks during a brief fast, prayed grandiosely if people were watching, and went so far as to wear Bible verses strapped to their foreheads and left arms.

In his famous Sermon on the Mount, Jesus blasts the hypocrisy behind such seemingly harmless practices. God is not fooled by appearances. We cannot fake behaviour to

impress him. He knows that inside the best of us lurk dark thoughts of hatred, pride, and lust – internal problems only he can deal with. Jesus goes on to present a truly radical way of life, free of pretence.

■ FAMILIAR YET STARTLING WORDS
These three chapters, among the most analysed in the entire Bible, present a fresh view of the world. You will probably recognise many familiar sections, including the Golden Rule and the Lord's Prayer.

In one sense, Jesus says, the truths presented here are not new: they fulfil, rather than abolish, the Old Testament law. In another sense the way of life described is more radical than anything before or since. Jesus' words turn many normal assumptions upside down. With statements like, "Blessed are the poor in spirit . . . those who mourn . . . the meek . . . the peacemakers . . . those who are persecuted", Jesus attacks those who strive to build a good image by appearing powerful, successful and assertive.

Perhaps most radical of all, The Sermon on the Mount introduces the possibility of living solely for God and not for appearances. At last we can bring our inner and outer lives together.

□ LIFE QUESTIONS:
Do other people see what you're really like inside? How do your friends try to impress each other?

ᵃ13 Or from evil; some late manuscripts one, / for yours is the kingdom and the power and the glory for ever. Amen.

thieves break in and steal. 20But store up for yourselves treasures in heaven, where moth and rust do not destroy, and where thieves do not break in and steal. 21For where your treasure is, there your heart will be also.

22"The eye is the lamp of the body. If your eyes are good, your whole body will be full of light. 23But if your eyes are bad, your whole body will be full of darkness. If then the light within you is darkness, how great is that darkness!

24"No-one can serve two masters. Either he will hate the one and love the other, or he will be devoted to the one and despise the other. You cannot serve both God and Money.

■ Do Not Worry
☐ See Luke 12:22–31

25"Therefore I tell you, do not worry about your life, what you will eat or drink; or about your body, what you will wear. Is not life more important than food, and the body more important than clothes? 26Look at the birds of the air; they do not sow or reap or store away in barns, and yet your heavenly Father feeds them. Are you not much more valuable than they? 27Who of you by worrying can add a single hour to his life?*b*

28"And why do you worry about clothes? See how the lilies of the field grow. They do not labour or spin. 29Yet I tell you that not even Solomon in all his splendour was dressed like one of these. 30If that is how God clothes the grass of the field, which is here today and tomorrow is thrown into the fire, will he not much more clothe you, O you of little faith? 31So do not worry, saying, 'What shall we eat?' or 'What shall we drink?' or 'What shall we wear?' 32For the pagans run after all these things, and your heavenly Father knows that you need them. 33But seek first his kingdom and his righteousness, and all these things will be given to you as well. 34Therefore do not worry about tomorrow, for tomorrow will worry about itself. Each day has enough trouble of its own.

■ Judging Others
☐ See Luke 6:41–42

7 "Do not judge, or you too will be judged. 2For in the same way as you judge others, you will be judged, and with the measure you use, it will be measured to you.

3"Why do you look at the speck of sawdust in your brother's eye and pay no attention to the plank in your own eye? 4How can you say to your brother, 'Let me take the speck out of your eye,' when all the time there is a plank in your own eye? 5You hypocrite, first take the plank out of your own eye, and then you will see clearly to remove the speck from your brother's eye.

6"Do not give dogs what is sacred; do not throw your pearls to pigs. If you do, they may trample them under their feet, and then turn and tear you to pieces.

b 27 Or *single cubit to his height*

■ Ask, Seek, Knock
☐ See Luke 11:9–13

7"Ask and it will be given to you; seek and you will find; knock and the door will be opened to you. 8For everyone who asks receives; he who seeks finds; and to him who knocks, the door will be opened.

9"Which of you, if his son asks for bread, will give him a stone? 10Or if he asks for a fish, will give him a snake? 11If you, then, though you are evil, know how to give good gifts to your children, how much more will your Father in heaven give good gifts to those who ask him! 12So in everything, do to others what you would have them do to you, for this sums up the Law and the Prophets.

7:12 ■ GOLDEN RULE
Other religions (Judaism, Hinduism, Buddhism, Confucianism) had some form of this saying, but most were stated negatively: "Don't do to others what you wouldn't want them to do to you". Jesus' version is far more open-ended and challenging.

■ The Narrow and Wide Gates

13"Enter through the narrow gate. For wide is the gate and broad is the road that leads to destruction, and many enter through it. 14But small is the gate and narrow the road that leads to life, and only a few find it.

■ A Tree and Its Fruit

15"Watch out for false prophets. They come to you in sheep's clothing, but inwardly they are ferocious wolves. 16By their fruit you will recognise them. Do people pick grapes from thornbushes, or figs from thistles? 17Likewise every good tree bears good fruit, but a bad tree bears bad fruit. 18A good tree cannot bear bad fruit, and a bad tree cannot bear good fruit. 19Every tree that does not bear good fruit is cut down and thrown into the fire. 20Thus, by their fruit you will recognise them.

21"Not everyone who says to me, 'Lord, Lord,' will enter the kingdom of heaven, but only he who does the will of my Father who is in heaven. 22Many will say to me on that day, 'Lord, Lord, did we not prophesy in your name, and in your name drive out demons and perform many miracles?' 23Then I will tell them plainly, 'I never knew you. Away from me, you evildoers!'

■ The Wise and Foolish Builders
☐ See Luke 6:47–49

24"Therefore everyone who hears these words of mine and puts them into practice is like a wise man who built his house on the rock. 25The rain came down, the streams rose, and the winds blew and beat against that house; yet it did not fall, because it had its foundation on the rock. 26But everyone who hears these words of mine and does not put them into practice is like a foolish man who built his house on sand. 27The rain came down, the streams rose, and the winds blew and beat against that house, and it fell with a great crash."

²⁸When Jesus had finished saying these things, the crowds were amazed at his teaching, ²⁹because he taught as one who had authority, and not as their teachers of the law.

■ The Man With Leprosy
□ See Mark 1:40–44; Luke 5:12–14

8 When he came down from the mountainside, large crowds followed him. ²A man with leprosy*ᵃ* came and knelt before him and said, "Lord, if you are willing, you can make me clean."

³Jesus reached out his hand and touched the man. "I am willing," he said. "Be clean!" Immediately he was cured*ᵇ* of his leprosy. ⁴Then Jesus said to him, "See that you don't tell anyone. But go, show yourself to the priest and offer the gift Moses commanded, as a testimony to them."

■ The Faith of the Centurion
□ See Luke 7:1–10

⁵When Jesus had entered Capernaum, a centurion came to him, asking for help. ⁶"Lord," he said, "my servant lies at home paralysed and in terrible suffering."

⁷Jesus said to him, "I will go and heal him."

⁸The centurion replied, "Lord, I do not deserve to have you come under my roof. But just say the word, and my servant will be healed. ⁹For I myself am a man under authority, with soldiers under me. I tell this one, 'Go,' and he goes; and that one, 'Come,' and he comes. I say to my servant, 'Do this,' and he does it."

¹⁰When Jesus heard this, he was astonished and said to those following him, "I tell you the truth, I have not found anyone in Israel with such great faith. ¹¹I say to you that many will come from the east and the west, and will take their places at the feast with Abraham, Isaac and Jacob in the kingdom of heaven. ¹²But the subjects of the kingdom will be thrown outside, into the darkness, where there will be weeping and gnashing of teeth."

¹³Then Jesus said to the centurion, "Go! It will be done just as you believed it would." And his servant was healed at that very hour.

■ Jesus Heals Many
□ See Mark 1:29–34; Luke 4:38–41

¹⁴When Jesus came into Peter's house, he saw Peter's mother-in-law lying in bed with a fever. ¹⁵He touched her hand and the fever left her, and she got up and began to wait on him.

¹⁶When evening came, many who were demon-possessed were brought to him, and he drove out the spirits with a word and healed all the sick. ¹⁷This was to fulfil what was spoken through the prophet Isaiah:

"He took up our infirmities
and carried our diseases."*ᶜ*

■ The Cost of Following Jesus
□ See Luke 9:57–60

¹⁸When Jesus saw the crowd around him, he gave orders to cross to the other side of the lake. ¹⁹Then a teacher of the law came to him and said, "Teacher, I will follow you wherever you go."

8:14 ■ ACTIONS FOLLOW WORDS
Typically, Matthew blends together Jesus' words and actions. Chapters 5–7 contain Jesus' longest recorded speech, the Sermon on the Mount – a speech that greatly impressed the audience. The next few chapters mention ten miracles performed by Jesus, which further established his authority. Those who benefited – a despised leprosy victim, a Roman officer, a housewife, two violent demoniacs, a quadriplegic, a synagogue ruler – demonstrate the "wideness in God's mercy" Jesus had just described.

²⁰Jesus replied, "Foxes have holes and birds of the air have nests, but the Son of Man has nowhere to lay his head."

²¹Another disciple said to him, "Lord, first let me go and bury my father."

²²But Jesus told him, "Follow me, and let the dead bury their own dead."

■ Jesus Calms the Storm
□ See Mark 4:36–41; Luke 8:22–25

²³Then he got into the boat and his disciples followed him. ²⁴Without warning, a furious storm came up on the lake, so that the waves swept over the boat. But Jesus was sleeping. ²⁵The disciples went and woke him, saying, "Lord, save us! We're going to drown!"

²⁶He replied, "You of little faith, why are you so afraid?" Then he got up and rebuked the winds and the waves, and it was completely calm.

²⁷The men were amazed and asked, "What kind of man is this? Even the winds and the waves obey him!"

■ The Healing of Two Demon-possessed Men
□ See Mark 5:1–17; Luke 8:26–37

²⁸When he arrived at the other side in the region of the Gadarenes,*ᵈ* two demon-possessed men coming from the tombs met him. They were so violent that no-one could pass that way. ²⁹"What do you want with us, Son of God?" they shouted. "Have you come here to torture us before the appointed time?"

³⁰Some distance from them a large herd of pigs was feeding. ³¹The demons begged Jesus, "If you drive us out, send us into the herd of pigs."

³²He said to them, "Go!" So they came out and went into the pigs, and the whole herd rushed down the steep bank into the lake and died in the water. ³³Those tending the pigs ran off, went into the town and reported all this, including what had happened to the demon-possessed men. ³⁴Then the whole town went out to meet Jesus. And when they saw him, they pleaded with him to leave their region.

*ᵃ*2 The Greek word was used for various diseases affecting the skin – not necessarily leprosy.   *ᵇ*3 Greek *made clean*   *ᶜ*17 Isaiah 53:4   *ᵈ*28 Some manuscripts *Gergesenes*; others *Gerasenes*

■ Jesus Heals a Paralytic
☐ See Mark 2:3–12; Luke 5:18–26

9 Jesus stepped into a boat, crossed over and came to his own town. ²Some men brought to him a paralytic, lying on a mat. When Jesus saw their faith, he said to the paralytic, "Take heart, son; your sins are forgiven."

³At this, some of the teachers of the law said to themselves, "This fellow is blaspheming!"

⁴Knowing their thoughts, Jesus said, "Why do you entertain evil thoughts in your hearts? ⁵Which is easier: to say, 'Your sins are forgiven,' or to say, 'Get up and walk'? ⁶But so that you may know that the Son of Man has authority on earth to forgive sins. . . ." Then he said to the paralytic, "Get up, take your mat and go home." ⁷And the man got up and went home. ⁸When the crowd saw this, they were filled with awe; and they praised God, who had given such authority to men.

■ The Calling of Matthew
☐ See Mark 2:14–17; Luke 5:27–32

⁹As Jesus went on from there, he saw a man named Matthew sitting at the tax collector's booth. "Follow me," he told him, and Matthew got up and followed him.

9:9 ■ UNPOPULAR PROFESSION

Tax collectors like Matthew were even less popular in Jesus' day than now. Many Jews viewed them as traitors serving the hated Roman empire. To make things worse, they worked on a commission basis, allowing them to set their own rates, which often led to extortion.

In this poignant scene, the Gospel tells how Jesus first called Matthew and then came to his house to mingle freely with "tax collectors and 'sinners' ". By following Jesus, Matthew turned his back on a lucrative government job. He was gradually transformed into a loyal disciple who applied his orderly mind to organise this account of Jesus' life.

¹⁰While Jesus was having dinner at Matthew's house, many tax collectors and "sinners" came and ate with him and his disciples. ¹¹When the Pharisees saw this, they asked his disciples, "Why does your teacher eat with tax collectors and 'sinners'?"

¹²On hearing this, Jesus said, "It is not the healthy who need a doctor, but the sick. ¹³But go and learn what this means: 'I desire mercy, not sacrifice.'ᵃ For I have not come to call the righteous, but sinners."

■ Jesus Questioned About Fasting
☐ See Mark 2:18–22; Luke 5:33–39

¹⁴Then John's disciples came and asked him, "How is it that we and the Pharisees fast, but your disciples do not fast?"

¹⁵Jesus answered, "How can the guests of the bridegroom mourn while he is with them? The time will come when the bridegroom will be taken from them; then they will fast.

ᵃ13 Hosea 6:6

¹⁶"No-one sews a patch of unshrunk cloth on an old garment, for the patch will pull away from the garment, making the tear worse. ¹⁷Neither do men pour new wine into old wineskins. If they do, the skins will burst, the wine will run out and the wineskins will be ruined. No, they pour new wine into new wineskins, and both are preserved."

■ A Dead Girl and a Sick Woman
☐ See Mark 5:22–43; Luke 8:41–56

¹⁸While he was saying this, a ruler came and knelt before him and said, "My daughter has just died. But come and put your hand on her, and she will live." ¹⁹Jesus got up and went with him, and so did his disciples.

²⁰Just then a woman who had been subject to bleeding for twelve years came up behind him and touched the edge of his cloak. ²¹She said to herself, "If I only touch his cloak, I will be healed."

²²Jesus turned and saw her. "Take heart, daughter," he said, "your faith has healed you." And the woman was healed from that moment.

²³When Jesus entered the ruler's house and saw the flute players and the noisy crowd, ²⁴he said, "Go away. The girl is not dead but asleep." But they laughed at him. ²⁵After the crowd had been put outside, he went in and took the girl by the hand, and she got up. ²⁶News of this spread through all that region.

■ Jesus Heals the Blind and Mute

²⁷As Jesus went on from there, two blind men followed him, calling out, "Have mercy on us, Son of David!"

²⁸When he had gone indoors, the blind men came to him, and he asked them, "Do you believe that I am able to do this?"

"Yes, Lord," they replied.

²⁹Then he touched their eyes and said, "According to your faith will it be done to you"; ³⁰and their sight was restored. Jesus warned them sternly, "See that no-one knows about this." ³¹But they went out and spread the news about him all over that region.

³²While they were going out, a man who was demon-possessed and could not talk was brought to Jesus. ³³And when the demon was driven out, the man who had been mute spoke. The crowd was amazed and said, "Nothing like this has ever been seen in Israel."

³⁴But the Pharisees said, "It is by the prince of demons that he drives out demons."

■ The Workers Are Few

³⁵Jesus went through all the towns and villages, teaching in their synagogues, preaching the good news of the kingdom and healing every disease and sickness. ³⁶When he saw the crowds, he had compassion on them, because they were harassed and helpless, like sheep without a shepherd. ³⁷Then he said to his disciples, "The harvest is plentiful but the workers are few. ³⁸Ask the Lord of the harvest, therefore, to send out workers into his harvest field."

■ Jesus Sends Out the Twelve
☐ See Mark 6:8–11; Luke 9:3–5; 10:4–12

10 He called his twelve disciples to him and gave them authority to drive out evil*a* spirits and to heal every disease and sickness.

²These are the names of the twelve apostles: first, Simon (who is called Peter) and his brother Andrew; James son of Zebedee, and his brother John; ³Philip and Bartholomew; Thomas and Matthew the tax collector; James son of Alphaeus, and Thaddaeus; ⁴Simon the Zealot and Judas Iscariot, who betrayed him.

⁵These twelve Jesus sent out with the following instructions: "Do not go among the Gentiles or enter any town of the Samaritans. ⁶Go rather to the lost sheep of Israel. ⁷As you go, preach this message: 'The kingdom of heaven is near.' ⁸Heal the sick, raise the dead, cleanse those who have leprosy,*b* drive out demons. Freely you have received, freely give. ⁹Do not take along any gold or silver or copper in your belts; ¹⁰take no bag for the journey, or extra tunic, or sandals or a staff; for the worker is worth his keep.

¹¹"Whatever town or village you enter, search for some worthy person there and stay at his house until you leave. ¹²As you enter the home, give it your greeting. ¹³If the home is deserving, let your peace rest on it; if it is not, let your peace return to you. ¹⁴If anyone will not welcome you or listen to your words, shake the dust off your feet when you leave that home or town. ¹⁵I tell you the truth, it will be more bearable for Sodom and Gomorrah on the day of judgment than for that town. ¹⁶I am sending you out like sheep among wolves. Therefore be as shrewd as snakes and as innocent as doves.

¹⁷"Be on your guard against men; they will hand you over to the local councils and flog you in their synagogues. ¹⁸On my account you will be brought before governors and kings as witnesses to them and to the Gentiles. ¹⁹But when they arrest you, do not worry about what to say or how to say it. At that time you will be given what to say, ²⁰for it will not be you speaking, but the Spirit of your Father speaking through you.

²¹"Brother will betray brother to death, and a father his child; children will rebel against their parents and have them put to death. ²²All men will hate you because of me, but he who stands firm to the end will be saved. ²³When you are persecuted in one place, flee to another. I tell you the truth, you will not finish going through the cities of Israel before the Son of Man comes.

²⁴"A student is not above his teacher, nor a servant above his master. ²⁵It is enough for the student to be like his teacher, and the servant like his master. If the head of the house has been called Beelzebub,*c* how much more the members of his household!

²⁶"So do not be afraid of them. There is nothing concealed that will not be disclosed, or hidden that will not be made known. ²⁷What I tell you in the dark, speak in the daylight; what is whispered in your ear, proclaim from the roofs. ²⁸Do not be afraid of those who kill the body but cannot kill the soul. Rather, be afraid of the One who can destroy both

soul and body in hell. ²⁹Are not two sparrows sold for a penny?*d* Yet not one of them will fall to the ground apart from the will of your Father. ³⁰And even the very hairs of your head are all numbered. ³¹So don't be afraid; you are worth more than many sparrows.

³²"Whoever acknowledges me before men, I will also acknowledge him before my Father in heaven. ³³But whoever disowns me before men, I will disown him before my Father in heaven.

³⁴"Do not suppose that I have come to bring peace to the earth. I did not come to bring peace, but a sword. ³⁵For I have come to turn

" 'a man against his father,
   a daughter against her mother,
a daughter-in-law against her mother-in-law—
³⁶   a man's enemies will be the members of his
       own household.'*e*

³⁷"Anyone who loves his father or mother more than me is not worthy of me; anyone who loves his son or daughter more than me is not worthy of me; ³⁸and anyone who does not take his cross and follow me is not worthy of me. ³⁹Whoever finds his life will lose it, and whoever loses his life for my sake will find it.

⁴⁰"He who receives you receives me, and he who receives me receives the one who sent me. ⁴¹Anyone who receives a prophet because he is a prophet will receive a prophet's reward, and anyone who receives a righteous man because he is a righteous man will receive a righteous man's reward. ⁴²And if anyone gives even a cup of cold water to one of these little ones because he is my disciple, I tell you the truth, he will certainly not lose his reward."

■ Jesus and John the Baptist
☐ See Luke 7:18–35

11 After Jesus had finished instructing his twelve disciples, he went on from there to teach and preach in the towns of Galilee.*a*

²When John heard in prison what Christ was doing, he sent his disciples ³to ask him, "Are you the one who was to come, or should we expect someone else?"

11:2 ■ THE ONE TO COME?
John's question here may reflect confusion over the Messiah's role. If, like many Jews, John was expecting a political Messiah who would overthrow the Romans, his imprisonment may have caused him to wonder why Jesus wasn't taking action. Jesus responded by clarifying the kind of kingdom he came to establish: a kingdom that brought healing, liberation, and good news—but not necessarily political power.

---

⁴Jesus replied, "Go back and report to John what you hear and see: ⁵The blind receive sight, the lame walk, those who have leprosy*b* are cured, the deaf hear, the dead are raised, and the good news is preached to the poor. ⁶Blessed is the man who does not fall away on account of me."

a 1 Greek *unclean*   *b* 8 The Greek word was used for various diseases affecting the skin—not necessarily leprosy.   *c* 25 Greek *Beezeboul* or *Beelzeboul*
d 29 Greek *an assarion*   *e* 36 Micah 7:6   *a* 1 Greek *in their towns*   *b* 5 The Greek word was used for various diseases affecting the skin—not necessarily leprosy.

7As John's disciples were leaving, Jesus began to speak to the crowd about John: "What did you go out into the desert to see? A reed swayed by the wind? 8If not, what did you go out to see? A man dressed in fine clothes? No, those who wear fine clothes are in kings' palaces. 9Then what did you go out to see? A prophet? Yes, I tell you, and more than a prophet. 10This is the one about whom it is written:

" 'I will send my messenger ahead of you,
who will prepare your way before you.'c

11I tell you the truth: Among those born of women there has not risen anyone greater than John the Baptist; yet he who is least in the kingdom of heaven is greater than he. 12From the days of John the Baptist until now, the kingdom of heaven has been forcefully advancing, and forceful men lay hold of it. 13For all the Prophets and the Law prophesied until John. 14And if you are willing to accept it, he is the Elijah who was to come. 15He who has ears, let him hear.

16"To what can I compare this generation? They are like children sitting in the market-places and calling out to others:

17" 'We played the flute for you,
and you did not dance;
we sang a dirge,
and you did not mourn.'

18For John came neither eating nor drinking, and they say, 'He has a demon.' 19The Son of Man came eating and drinking, and they say, 'Here is a glutton and a drunkard, a friend of tax collectors and "sinners".' But wisdom is proved right by her actions."

■ Woe on Unrepentant Cities
□ See Luke 10:13–15

20Then Jesus began to denounce the cities in which most of his miracles had been performed, because they did not repent. 21"Woe to you, Korazin! Woe to you, Bethsaida! If the miracles that were performed in you had been performed in Tyre and Sidon, they would have repented long ago in sackcloth and ashes. 22But I tell you, it will be more bearable for Tyre and Sidon on the day of judgment than for you. 23And you, Capernaum, will you be lifted up to the skies? No, you will go down to the depths.d If the miracles that were performed in you had been performed in Sodom, it would have remained to this day. 24But I tell you that it will be more bearable for Sodom on the day of judgment than for you."

■ Rest for the Weary
□ See Luke 10:21–22

25At that time Jesus said, "I praise you, Father, Lord of heaven and earth, because you have hidden these things from the wise and learned, and revealed them to little children. 26Yes, Father, for this was your good pleasure.

27"All things have been committed to me by my Father. No-one knows the Son except the Father, and no-one knows the Father except the Son and those to whom the Son chooses to reveal him.

28"Come to me, all you who are weary and burdened, and I will give you rest. 29Take my yoke upon you and learn from me, for I am gentle and humble in heart, and you will find rest for your souls. 30For my yoke is easy and my burden is light."

11:20 ■ MIRACLES AREN'T ENOUGH
Surprisingly, seeing supernatural miracles didn't lead people to repent and follow Jesus' teaching. Throughout his ministry, Jesus showed annoyance with crowds who flocked to see a popular leader do something supernatural. He wanted from them not applause, but commitment. Gradually, he relied more and more on parables, which, in private, he would explain to his disciples (see 13:11–17).

■ Lord of the Sabbath
□ See Mark 2:23 – 3:6; Luke 6:1–11

12 At that time Jesus went through the cornfields on the Sabbath. His disciples were hungry and began to pick some ears of corn and eat them. 2When the Pharisees saw this, they said to him, "Look! Your disciples are doing what is unlawful on the Sabbath."

3He answered, "Haven't you read what David did when he and his companions were hungry? 4He entered the house of God, and he and his companions ate the consecrated bread—which was not lawful for them to do, but only for the priests. 5Or haven't you read in the Law that on the Sabbath the priests in the temple desecrate the day and yet are innocent? 6I tell you that onea greater than the temple is here. 7If you had known what these words mean, 'I desire mercy, not sacrifice,'b you would not have condemned the innocent. 8For the Son of Man is Lord of the Sabbath."

9Going on from that place, he went into their synagogue, 10and a man with a shrivelled hand was there. Looking for a reason to accuse Jesus, they asked him, "Is it lawful to heal on the Sabbath?"

11He said to them, "If any of you has a sheep and it falls into a pit on the Sabbath, will you not take hold of it and lift it out? 12How much more valuable is a man than a sheep! Therefore it is lawful to do good on the Sabbath."

12:12 ■ PHARISEES TAKE OFFENCE
Chapter 12 gives insight into why the Pharisees were offended by Jesus. First, his disciples picked grain on the Sabbath (verses 1–7), something forbidden by the Pharisees. A provocative healing on the Sabbath followed. Jesus accused the Pharisees of caring more for the letter of the law than the spirit, so much so that they showed more concern for animal life than human.

13Then he said to the man, "Stretch out your hand." So he stretched it out and it was completely restored, just as sound as the other. 14But the

c 10 Mal. 3:1   d 23 Greek Hades   a 6 Or something; also in verses 41 and 42   b 7 Hosea 6:6

Pharisees went out and plotted how they might kill Jesus.

God's Chosen Servant

15Aware of this, Jesus withdrew from that place. Many followed him, and he healed all their sick, 16warning them not to tell who he was. 17This was to fulfil what was spoken through the prophet Isaiah:

18"Here is my servant whom I have chosen,
  the one I love, in whom I delight;
I will put my Spirit on him,
  and he will proclaim justice to the nations.
19He will not quarrel or cry out;
  no-one will hear his voice in the streets.
20A bruised reed he will not break,
  and a smouldering wick he will not snuff out,
  till he leads justice to victory.
21 In his name the nations will put their
    hope."c

Jesus and Beelzebub
☐ See Mark 3:23–27; Luke 11:17–22

22Then they brought him a demon-possessed man who was blind and mute, and Jesus healed him, so that he could both talk and see. 23All the people were astonished and said, "Could this be the Son of David?"

24But when the Pharisees heard this, they said, "It is only by Beelzebub,d the prince of demons, that this fellow drives out demons."

25Jesus knew their thoughts and said to them, "Every kingdom divided against itself will be ruined, and every city or household divided against itself will not stand. 26If Satan drives out Satan, he is divided against himself. How then can his kingdom stand? 27And if I drive out demons by Beelzebub, by whom do your people drive them out? So then, they will be your judges. 28But if I drive out demons by the Spirit of God, then the kingdom of God has come upon you.

29"Or again, how can anyone enter a strong man's house and carry off his possessions unless he first ties up the strong man? Then he can rob his house. 30"He who is not with me is against me, and he who does not gather with me scatters. 31And so I tell you, every sin and blasphemy will be forgiven men, but the blasphemy against the Spirit will not be forgiven. 32Anyone who speaks a word against the Son of Man will be forgiven, but anyone who speaks against the Holy Spirit will not be forgiven, either in this age or in the age to come.

33"Make a tree good and its fruit will be good, or make a tree bad and its fruit will be bad, for a tree is recognised by its fruit. 34You brood of vipers, how can you who are evil say anything good? For out of the overflow of the heart the mouth speaks. 35The good man brings good things out of the good stored up in him, and the evil man brings evil things out of the evil stored up in him. 36But I tell you that men will have to give account on the day of judgment for every careless word they have spoken. 37For by your words you will be acquitted, and by your words you will be condemned."

The Sign of Jonah
☐ See Luke 11:29–32

38Then some of the Pharisees and teachers of the law said to him, "Teacher, we want to see a miraculous sign from you."

39He answered, "A wicked and adulterous generation asks for a miraculous sign! But none will be given it except the sign of the prophet Jonah. 40For as Jonah was three days and three nights in the belly of a huge fish, so the Son of Man will be three days and three nights in the heart of the earth. 41The men of Nineveh will stand up at the judgment with this generation and condemn it; for they repented at the preaching of Jonah, and now onee greater than Jonah is here. 42The Queen of the South will rise at the judgment with this generation and condemn it; for she came from the ends of the earth to listen to Solomon's wisdom, and now one greater than Solomon is here.

43"When an evilf spirit comes out of a man, it goes through arid places seeking rest and does not find it. 44Then it says, 'I will return to the house I left.' When it arrives, it finds the house unoccupied, swept clean and put in order. 45Then it goes and takes with it seven other spirits more wicked than itself, and they go in and live there. And the final condition of that man is worse than the first. That is how it will be with this wicked generation."

Jesus' Mother and Brothers
☐ See Mark 3:31–35; Luke 8:19–21

46While Jesus was still talking to the crowd, his mother and brothers stood outside, wanting to speak to him. 47Someone told him, "Your mother and brothers are standing outside, wanting to speak to you."g

48He replied to him, "Who is my mother, and who are my brothers?" 49Pointing to his disciples, he said, "Here are my mother and my brothers. 50For whoever does the will of my Father in heaven is my brother and sister and mother."

The Parable of the Sower
☐ See Mark 4:1–20; Luke 8:4–15

13 That same day Jesus went out of the house and sat by the lake. 2Such large crowds gathered round him that he got into a boat and sat in it, while all the people stood on the shore. 3Then he told them many things in parables, saying: "A farmer went out to sow his seed. 4As he was scattering the seed, some fell along the path, and the birds came and ate it up. 5Some fell on rocky places, where it did not have much soil. It sprang up quickly, because the soil was shallow. 6But when the sun came up, the plants were scorched, and they withered because they had no root. 7Other seed fell among thorns, which grew up and choked the plants. 8Still other seed fell on good soil, where it produced a crop — a hundred, sixty or thirty times what was sown. 9He who has ears, let him hear."

10The disciples came to him and asked, "Why do you speak to the people in parables?"

11He replied, "The knowledge of the secrets of the kingdom of heaven has been given to you, but not to them. 12Whoever has will be given more, and

c21 Isaiah 42:1–4   d24 Greek Beezeboul or Beelzeboul; also in verse 27   e41 Or something; also in verse 42   f43 Greek unclean   g47 Some manuscripts do not have verse 47.

he will have an abundance. Whoever does not have, even what he has will be taken from him. [13]This is why I speak to them in parables:

"Though seeing, they do not see;
   though hearing, they do not hear or
     understand.

[14]In them is fulfilled the prophecy of Isaiah:

" 'You will be ever hearing but never
   understanding;
   you will be ever seeing but never perceiving.
[15]For this people's heart has become calloused;
   they hardly hear with their ears,
   and they have closed their eyes.
Otherwise they might see with their eyes,
   hear with their ears,
   understand with their hearts
and turn, and I would heal them.'[a]

[16]"But blessed are your eyes because they see, and your ears because they hear. [17]For I tell you the truth, many prophets and righteous men longed to see what you see but did not see it, and to hear what you hear but did not hear it.

[18]"Listen then to what the parable of the sower means: [19]When anyone hears the message about the kingdom and does not understand it, the evil one comes and snatches away what was sown in his heart. This is the seed sown along the path. [20]The one who received the seed that fell on rocky places is the man who hears the word and at once receives it with joy. [21]But since he has no root, he lasts only a short time. When trouble or persecution comes because of the word, he quickly falls away. [22]The one who received the seed that fell among the thorns is the man who hears the word, but the worries of this life and the deceitfulness of wealth choke it, making it unfruitful. [23]But the one who received the seed that fell on good soil is the man who hears the word and understands it. He produces a crop, yielding a hundred, sixty or thirty times what was sown."

■ The Parable of the Weeds

[24]Jesus told them another parable: "The kingdom of heaven is like a man who sowed good seed in his field. [25]But while everyone was sleeping, his enemy came and sowed weeds among the wheat, and went away. [26]When the wheat sprouted and formed ears, then the weeds also appeared.

[27]"The owner's servants came to him and said,

'Sir, didn't you sow good seed in your field? Where then did the weeds come from?'

[28]" 'An enemy did this,' he replied.

"The servants asked him, 'Do you want us to go and pull them up?'

[29]" 'No,' he answered, 'because while you are pulling the weeds, you may root up the wheat with them. [30]Let both grow together until the harvest. At that time I will tell the harvesters: First collect the weeds and tie them in bundles to be burned; then gather the wheat and bring it into my barn.' "

■ The Parables of the Mustard Seed and the Yeast
☐ See Mark 4:30–32; Luke 13:18–21

[31]He told them another parable: "The kingdom of heaven is like a mustard seed, which a man took and planted in his field. [32]Though it is the smallest of all your seeds, yet when it grows, it is the largest of garden plants and becomes a tree, so that the birds of the air come and perch in its branches."

[33]He told them still another parable: "The kingdom of heaven is like yeast that a woman took and mixed into a large amount[b] of flour until it worked all through the dough."

[34]Jesus spoke all these things to the crowd in parables; he did not say anything to them without using a parable. [35]So was fulfilled what was spoken through the prophet:

"I will open my mouth in parables,
   I will utter things hidden since the creation
     of the world."[c]

■ The Parable of the Weeds Explained

[36]Then he left the crowd and went into the house. His disciples came to him and said, "Explain to us the parable of the weeds in the field."

[37]He answered, "The one who sowed the good seed is the Son of Man. [38]The field is the world, and the good seed stands for the sons of the kingdom. The weeds are the sons of the evil one, [39]and the enemy who sows them is the devil. The harvest is the end of the age, and the harvesters are angels.

[40]"As the weeds are pulled up and burned in the fire, so it will be at the end of the age. [41]The Son of Man will send out his angels, and they will weed out of his kingdom everything that causes sin and all who do evil. [42]They will throw them into the fiery furnace, where there will be weeping and gnashing of teeth. [43]Then the righteous will shine like the sun in the kingdom of their Father. He who has ears, let him hear.

■ The Parables of the Hidden Treasure and the Pearl

[44]"The kingdom of heaven is like treasure hidden in a field. When a man found it, he hid it again, and then in his joy went and sold all he had and bought that field.

[45]"Again, the kingdom of heaven is like a merchant looking for fine pearls. [46]When he found one of great value, he went away and sold everything he had and bought it.

---

[a] 15 Isaiah 6:9,10   [b] 33 Greek three satas (probably about ⅗ bushel or 22 litres)   [c] 35 Psalm 78:2

■ The Parable of the Net

47"Once again, the kingdom of heaven is like a net that was let down into the lake and caught all kinds of fish. 48When it was full, the fishermen pulled it up on the shore. Then they sat down and collected the good fish in baskets, but threw the bad away. 49This is how it will be at the end of the age. The angels will come and separate the wicked from the righteous 50and throw them into the fiery furnace, where there will be weeping and gnashing of teeth.

51"Have you understood all these things?" Jesus asked.

"Yes," they replied.

52He said to them, "Therefore every teacher of the law who has been instructed about the kingdom of heaven is like the owner of a house who brings out of his storeroom new treasures as well as old."

■ A Prophet Without Honour
☐ See Mark 6:1–6

53When Jesus had finished these parables, he moved on from there. 54Coming to his home town, he began teaching the people in their synagogue, and they were amazed. "Where did this man get this

■ WHAT SHOULD A LEADER LOOK LIKE?
NOT EVERYONE WANTED JESUS' KIND OF KINGDOM

INSIGHT

"WHERE DID THIS MAN GET THIS WISDOM AND THESE MIRACULOUS POWERS?" THEY ASKED. "ISN'T THIS THE CARPENTER'S SON?" ■ 13:54–55

Important leaders, such as presidents and prime ministers, work hard to convey an impression of confidence and power. A leader, they assume, should look like a leader, and many of them hire an "image consultant" to train them and to dress them. Wherever they go, press agents, bodyguards, loyal assistants and throngs of eager admirers follow in their wake.

Matthew depicts Jesus as a true leader – a king, in fact – but one who broke stereotypes. Jesus had undeniable power. He could quiet an angry storm and even walk on the surface of a lake. Yet he used that power compassionately, for the sake of others: to feed the hungry and heal the sick. He wasn't concerned about a powerful image.

■ A NEW KIND OF KINGDOM
First-century Jews, who hated the Roman empire, would have rallied eagerly around a militant Jewish king. They rebelled often until a vengeful Roman general flattened Jerusalem in A.D. 70. The kingdom Jesus presented, however, didn't meet their expectations.

At the beginning of his ministry, Jesus turned down a tempting offer of glory and territory (4:8–11), and he consistently resisted the pressures of the crowd. Although he was the most powerful leader ever, he spent his time telling stories, not raising an army. As a true Messiah, he sought not to satisfy people's false image of him, but to please God.

In chapter 13, Matthew collects several of the stories Jesus told to describe his "kingdom of heaven" – a phrase used 32 times in Matthew. Although Jesus never concisely defined the phrase, he gave many clues about the nature of his kingdom. The kingdom is so important, he said, that belonging to it is worth selling everything a person owns.

Jesus said his kingdom doesn't have geographical boundaries. Unlike, say, Greece or China or Spain, it can't be charted on a map. Its followers live right among their enemies, not separated from them by a moat or a wall. Yet Jesus predicted that his kingdom would show remarkable growth even in an evil environment bent on its destruction.

■ THE DISCIPLES FAIL TO UNDERSTAND
The "kingdom of heaven" consists of the rule of God in the world. It's made up of people of all races and from all nations who loyally follow God's will on earth. Jesus stressed that this new kingdom was a major advance in God's plan: its least member, he said, is even greater than John the Baptist (11:11).

The disciples, accustomed to more traditional images of power and leadership, couldn't quite grasp Jesus' concept of the kingdom. They kept asking him to explain his parables even as they jockeyed vainly for status.

As the days passed, the disciples became convinced that Jesus was "the Christ, the Son of the living God!" – Peter won warm praise for that assertion (16:17). But he received Jesus' strongest rebuke in the next scene when he recoiled from the idea that his leader might soon suffer and die.

The paradoxes of Jesus' style of leadership deepened as he neared Jerusalem, the capital city. He allowed one moment of public triumph, on the day we call Palm Sunday. Yet, even then he rode not a chariot or a stallion, but a donkey. And a few days later he left his followers an enduring emblem: not a royal banner or a sceptre, but an executioner's cross.

☐ LIFE QUESTIONS:
Could Jesus run for political office in the United Kingdom? What kind of leader do people want today?

wisdom and these miraculous powers?" they asked. [55]"Isn't this the carpenter's son? Isn't his mother's name Mary, and aren't his brothers James, Joseph, Simon and Judas? [56]Aren't all his sisters with us? Where then did this man get all these things?" [57]And they took offence at him.

But Jesus said to them, "Only in his home town and in his own house is a prophet without honour."

13:57 ■ NO RESPECT AT HOME

Jesus had opened his ministry at home in a synagogue, an occasion marked by a near-riot. When he returned later, he aroused great curiosity but little belief. The townsfolk couldn't fathom that one who'd been raised in their midst by a carpenter was now teaching like a rabbi and performing miracles. Jesus declined to display his supernatural power for them, and quietly withdrew.

---

[58]And he did not do many miracles there because of their lack of faith.

■ John the Baptist Beheaded
□ See Mark 6:14–29

14 At that time Herod the tetrarch heard the reports about Jesus, [2]and he said to his attendants, "This is John the Baptist; he has risen from the dead! That is why miraculous powers are at work in him."

[3]Now Herod had arrested John and bound him and put him in prison because of Herodias, his brother Philip's wife, [4]for John had been saying to him: "It is not lawful for you to have her." [5]Herod wanted to kill John, but he was afraid of the people, because they considered him a prophet.

14:5 ■ A WIFE'S REVENGE

John the Baptist offended King Herod with his blunt accusations, but Mark 6 points out that most of the venom came from Herod's wife (whom the king had stolen from his brother Philip). Herod had mixed feelings about John. He liked to listen to the prophet and had a respectful fear of him and his stern message. After falling into a trap set by his wife and stepdaughter, however, he succumbed to peer pressure and ordered John's execution.

---

[6]On Herod's birthday the daughter of Herodias danced for them and pleased Herod so much [7]that he promised with an oath to give her whatever she asked. [8]Prompted by her mother, she said, "Give me here on a platter the head of John the Baptist." [9]The king was distressed, but because of his oaths and his dinner guests, he ordered that her request be granted [10]and had John beheaded in the prison. [11]His head was brought in on a platter and given to the girl, who carried it to her mother. [12]John's

disciples came and took his body and buried it. Then they went and told Jesus.

■ Jesus Feeds the Five Thousand
□ See Mark 6:32–44; Luke 9:10–17; John 6:1–13

[13]When Jesus heard what had happened, he withdrew by boat privately to a solitary place. Hearing of this, the crowds followed him on foot from the towns. [14]When Jesus landed and saw a large crowd, he had compassion on them and healed their sick.

[15]As evening approached, the disciples came to him and said, "This is a remote place, and it's already getting late. Send the crowds away, so that they can go to the villages and buy themselves some food."

[16]Jesus replied, "They do not need to go away. You give them something to eat."

[17]"We have here only five loaves of bread and two fish," they answered.

[18]"Bring them here to me," he said. [19]And he directed the people to sit down on the grass. Taking the five loaves and the two fish and looking up to heaven, he gave thanks and broke the loaves. Then he gave them to the disciples, and the disciples gave them to the people. [20]They all ate and were satisfied, and the disciples picked up twelve basketfuls of broken pieces that were left over. [21]The number of those who ate was about five thousand men, besides women and children.

■ Jesus Walks on the Water
□ See Mark 6:45–51; John 6:15–21

[22]Immediately Jesus made the disciples get into the boat and go on ahead of him to the other side, while he dismissed the crowd. [23]After he had dismissed them, he went up on a mountainside by himself to pray. When evening came, he was there alone, [24]but the boat was already a considerable distance[a] from land, buffeted by the waves because the wind was against it.

[25]During the fourth watch of the night Jesus went out to them, walking on the lake. [26]When the disciples saw him walking on the lake, they were terrified. "It's a ghost," they said, and cried out in fear.

[27]But Jesus immediately said to them: "Take courage! It is I. Don't be afraid."

[28]"Lord, if it's you," Peter replied, "tell me to come to you on the water."

[29]"Come," he said.

Then Peter got down out of the boat, walked on the water and came towards Jesus. [30]But when he saw the wind, he was afraid and, beginning to sink, cried out, "Lord, save me!"

[31]Immediately Jesus reached out his hand and caught him. "You of little faith," he said, "why did you doubt?"

[32]And when they climbed into the boat, the wind died down. [33]Then those who were in the boat worshipped him, saying, "Truly you are the Son of God."

[34]When they had crossed over, they landed at Gennesaret. [35]And when the men of that place recognised Jesus, they sent word to all the surrounding country. People brought all their sick to him [36]and begged him to let the sick just touch the edge of his cloak, and all who touched him were healed.

a 24 Greek many stadia

■ Clean and Unclean
☐ See Mark 7:1–23

15 Then some Pharisees and teachers of the law came to Jesus from Jerusalem and asked, [2]"Why do your disciples break the tradition of the elders? They don't wash their hands before they eat!"

15:1 ■ ATTACKING LEGALISM
The Pharisees and teachers of the law considered their own strict traditions as binding as Old Testament law. In this passage, Jesus points out glaring inconsistencies in those traditions.

[3]Jesus replied, "And why do you break the command of God for the sake of your tradition? [4]For God said, 'Honour your father and mother'[a] and 'Anyone who curses his father or mother must be put to death.'[b] [5]But you say that if a man says to his father or mother, 'Whatever help you might otherwise have received from me is a gift devoted to God,' [6]he is not to 'honour his father'[c] with it. Thus you nullify the word of God for the sake of your tradition. [7]You hypocrites! Isaiah was right when he prophesied about you:

[8]" 'These people honour me with their lips,
     but their hearts are far from me.
[9]They worship me in vain;
     their teachings are but rules taught by
         men.'[d]"

[10]Jesus called the crowd to him and said, "Listen and understand. [11]What goes into a man's mouth does not make him 'unclean', but what comes out of his mouth, that is what makes him 'unclean'."

[12]Then the disciples came to him and asked, "Do you know that the Pharisees were offended when they heard this?"

[13]He replied, "Every plant that my heavenly Father has not planted will be pulled up by the roots. [14]Leave them; they are blind guides.[e] If a blind man leads a blind man, both will fall into a pit."

[15]Peter said, "Explain the parable to us."

[16]"Are you still so dull?" Jesus asked them. [17]"Don't you see that whatever enters the mouth goes into the stomach and then out of the body? [18]But the things that come out of the mouth come from the heart, and these make a man 'unclean'. [19]For out of the heart come evil thoughts, murder, adultery, sexual immorality, theft, false testimony, slander. [20]These are what make a man 'unclean'; but eating with unwashed hands does not make him 'unclean'."

■ The Faith of the Canaanite Woman
☐ See Mark 7:24–30

[21]Leaving that place, Jesus withdrew to the region of Tyre and Sidon. [22]A Canaanite woman from that vicinity came to him, crying out, "Lord, Son of David, have mercy on me! My daughter is suffering terribly from demon-possession."

[23]Jesus did not answer a word. So his disciples came to him and urged him, "Send her away, for she keeps crying out after us."

[24]He answered, "I was sent only to the lost sheep of Israel."

[25]The woman came and knelt before him. "Lord, help me!" she said.

[26]He replied, "It is not right to take the children's bread and toss it to their dogs."

[27]"Yes, Lord," she said, "but even the dogs eat the crumbs that fall from their masters' table."

[28]Then Jesus answered, "Woman, you have great faith! Your request is granted." And her daughter was healed from that very hour.

■ Jesus Feeds the Four Thousand
☐ See Mark 8:1–10

[29]Jesus left there and went along the Sea of Galilee. Then he went up on a mountainside and sat down. [30]Great crowds came to him, bringing the lame, the blind, the crippled, the mute and many others, and laid them at his feet; and he healed them. [31]The people were amazed when they saw the mute speaking, the crippled made well, the lame walking and the blind seeing. And they praised the God of Israel.

[32]Jesus called his disciples to him and said, "I have compassion for these people; they have already been with me three days and have nothing to eat. I do not want to send them away hungry, or they may collapse on the way."

15:32 ■ TWO FEEDINGS
In back-to-back chapters, Matthew reports on two incidents that can be easily confused. The feeding of the 5,000 (chapter 14) came at the height of Jesus' popularity and made a huge impression: all four Gospels report on it. Only Matthew and Mark, however, record this separate miracle performed for a slightly smaller crowd. In Mark's account (Mark 8:1–10), Jesus seems amazed that his disciples, having seen the first miracle, doubt his ability to supply a crowd's needs this second time.

[33]His disciples answered, "Where could we get enough bread in this remote place to feed such a crowd?"

[34]"How many loaves do you have?" Jesus asked.

"Seven," they replied, "and a few small fish."

[35]He told the crowd to sit down on the ground. [36]Then he took the seven loaves and the fish, and when he had given thanks, he broke them and gave them to the disciples, and they in turn to the people. [37]They all ate and were satisfied. Afterwards the disciples picked up seven basketfuls of broken pieces that were left over. [38]The number of those who ate was four thousand, besides women and children. [39]After Jesus had sent the crowd away, he got into the boat and went to the vicinity of Magadan.

a4 Exodus 20:12; Deut. 5:16   b4 Exodus 21:17; Lev. 20:9   c6 Some manuscripts *father or his mother*   d9 Isaiah 29:13   e14 Some manuscripts *guides of the blind*

■ The Demand for a Sign
☐ See Mark 8:11–21

16 The Pharisees and Sadducees came to Jesus and tested him by asking him to show them a sign from heaven.

[2]He replied,[a] "When evening comes, you say, 'It will be fair weather, for the sky is red,' [3]and in the morning, 'Today it will be stormy, for the sky is red and overcast.' You know how to interpret the appearance of the sky, but you cannot interpret the signs of the times. [4]A wicked and adulterous generation looks for a miraculous sign, but none will be given it except the sign of Jonah." Jesus then left them and went away.

■ The Yeast of the Pharisees and Sadducees
[5]When they went across the lake, the disciples forgot to take bread. [6]"Be careful," Jesus said to them. "Be on your guard against the yeast of the Pharisees and Sadducees."

[7]They discussed this among themselves and said, "It is because we didn't bring any bread."

[8]Aware of their discussion, Jesus asked, "You of little faith, why are you talking among yourselves about having no bread? [9]Do you still not understand? Don't you remember the five loaves for the five thousand, and how many basketfuls you gathered? [10]Or the seven loaves for the four thousand, and how many basketfuls you gathered? [11]How is it you don't understand that I was not talking to you about bread? But be on your guard against the yeast of the Pharisees and Sadducees." [12]Then they understood that he was not telling them to guard against the yeast used in bread, but against the teaching of the Pharisees and Sadducees.

■ Peter's Confession of Christ
☐ See Mark 8:27–29; Luke 9:18–20

[13]When Jesus came to the region of Caesarea Philippi, he asked his disciples, "Who do people say the Son of Man is?"

16:13 ■ PETER'S HIGHS AND LOWS
The disciple Peter earned a reputation for impulsiveness, and this chapter shows him at his very best and very worst. He won highest praise for discerning Jesus' true identity, but in the very next paragraph he made one of his biggest blunders. He wanted Jesus to avoid pain, not understanding that the pain of the cross would bring salvation to the whole world.

[14]They replied, "Some say John the Baptist; others say Elijah; and still others, Jeremiah or one of the prophets."

[15]"But what about you?" he asked. "Who do you say I am?"

[16]Simon Peter answered, "You are the Christ,[b] the Son of the living God."

[17]Jesus replied, "Blessed are you, Simon son of Jonah, for this was not revealed to you by man, but by my Father in heaven. [18]And I tell you that you are

Peter,[c] and on this rock I will build my church, and the gates of Hades[d] will not overcome it.[e] [19]I will give you the keys of the kingdom of heaven; whatever you bind on earth will be[f] bound in heaven, and whatever you loose on earth will be[f] loosed in heaven." [20]Then he warned his disciples not to tell anyone that he was the Christ.

■ Jesus Predicts His Death
☐ See Mark 8:31 – 9:1; Luke 9:22–27

[21]From that time on Jesus began to explain to his disciples that he must go to Jerusalem and suffer many things at the hands of the elders, chief priests and teachers of the law, and that he must be killed and on the third day be raised to life.

[22]Peter took him aside and began to rebuke him. "Never, Lord!" he said. "This shall never happen to you!"

[23]Jesus turned and said to Peter, "Get behind me, Satan! You are a stumbling-block to me; you do not have in mind the things of God, but the things of men."

[24]Then Jesus said to his disciples, "If anyone would come after me, he must deny himself and take up his cross and follow me. [25]For whoever wants to save his life[g] will lose it, but whoever loses his life for me will find it. [26]What good will it be for a man if he gains the whole world, yet forfeits his soul? Or what can a man give in exchange for his soul? [27]For the Son of Man is going to come in his Father's glory with his angels, and then he will reward each person according to what he has done. [28]I tell you the truth, some who are standing here will not taste death before they see the Son of Man coming in his kingdom."

■ The Transfiguration
☐ See Mark 9:2–13; Luke 9:28–36

17 After six days Jesus took with him Peter, James and John the brother of James, and led them up a high mountain by themselves. [2]There he was transfigured before them. His face shone like the sun, and his clothes became as white as the light. [3]Just then there appeared before them Moses and Elijah, talking with Jesus.

[4]Peter said to Jesus, "Lord, it is good for us to be here. If you wish, I will put up three shelters — one for you, one for Moses and one for Elijah."

[5]While he was still speaking, a bright cloud enveloped them, and a voice from the cloud said, "This is my Son, whom I love; with him I am well pleased. Listen to him!"

17:5 ■ UNFORGETTABLE MOMENT
Three of Jesus' disciples had the opportunity to observe this dramatic scene of God's approving of his Son Jesus. Moses, the first great lawgiver, and Elijah, the first great prophet, appeared with Jesus, and God spoke from heaven. The apostle Peter described the impact of this experience in 2 Peter 1:16–18.

---

[a]2 Some early manuscripts do not have the rest of verse 2 and all of verse 3.   [b]16 Or *Messiah*; also in verse 20   [c]18 *Peter* means *rock*.   [d]18 Or *hell*   [e]18 Or *not prove stronger than it*   [f]19 Or *have been*   [g]25 The Greek word means either *life* or *soul*; also in verse 26.

6When the disciples heard this, they fell face down to the ground, terrified. 7But Jesus came and touched them. "Get up," he said. "Don't be afraid." 8When they looked up, they saw no-one except Jesus.

9As they were coming down the mountain, Jesus instructed them, "Don't tell anyone what you have seen, until the Son of Man has been raised from the dead."

10The disciples asked him, "Why then do the teachers of the law say that Elijah must come first?"

11Jesus replied, "To be sure, Elijah comes and will restore all things. 12But I tell you, Elijah has already come, and they did not recognise him, but have done to him everything they wished. In the same way the Son of Man is going to suffer at their hands." 13Then the disciples understood that he was talking to them about John the Baptist.

■ The Healing of a Boy With a Demon
□ See Mark 9:14–28; Luke 9:37–42

14When they came to the crowd, a man approached Jesus and knelt before him. 15"Lord, have mercy on my son," he said. "He has seizures and is suffering greatly. He often falls into the fire or into the water. 16I brought him to your disciples, but they could not heal him."

17"O unbelieving and perverse generation," Jesus replied, "how long shall I stay with you? How long shall I put up with you? Bring the boy here to me." 18Jesus rebuked the demon, and it came out of the boy, and he was healed from that moment.

19Then the disciples came to Jesus in private and asked, "Why couldn't we drive it out?"

20He replied, "Because you have so little faith. I tell you the truth, if you have faith as small as a mustard seed, you can say to this mountain, 'Move from here to there' and it will move. Nothing will be impossible for you."a

22When they came together in Galilee, he said to them, "The Son of Man is going to be betrayed into the hands of men. 23They will kill him, and on the third day he will be raised to life." And the disciples were filled with grief.

■ The Temple Tax
24After Jesus and his disciples arrived in Capernaum, the collectors of the two-drachma tax came to Peter and asked, "Doesn't your teacher pay the temple tax?"b

25"Yes, he does," he replied.

When Peter came into the house, Jesus was the first to speak. "What do you think, Simon?" he asked. "From whom do the kings of the earth collect duty and taxes—from their own sons or from others?"

26"From others," Peter answered.

"Then the sons are exempt," Jesus said to him. 27"But so that we may not offend them, go to the lake and throw out your line. Take the first fish you catch; open its mouth and you will find a four-drachma coin. Take it and give it to them for my tax and yours."

■ The Greatest in the Kingdom of Heaven
□ See Mark 9:33–37; Luke 9:46–48

18 At that time the disciples came to Jesus and asked, "Who is the greatest in the kingdom of heaven?"

2He called a little child and had him stand among them. 3And he said: "I tell you the truth, unless you change and become like little children, you will never enter the kingdom of heaven. 4Therefore, whoever humbles himself like this child is the greatest in the kingdom of heaven.

5"And whoever welcomes a little child like this in my name welcomes me. 6But if anyone causes one of these little ones who believe in me to sin, it would be better for him to have a large millstone hung around his neck and to be drowned in the depths of the sea.

7"Woe to the world because of the things that cause people to sin! Such things must come, but woe to the man through whom they come! 8If your hand or your foot causes you to sin, cut it off and throw it away. It is better for you to enter life maimed or crippled than to have two hands or two feet and be thrown into eternal fire. 9And if your eye causes you to sin, gouge it out and throw it away. It is better for you to enter life with one eye than to have two eyes and be thrown into the fire of hell.

■ The Parable of the Lost Sheep
□ See Luke 15:4–7

10"See that you do not look down on one of these little ones. For I tell you that their angels in heaven always see the face of my Father in heaven.a

12"What do you think? If a man owns a hundred sheep, and one of them wanders away, will he not leave the ninety-nine on the hills and go to look for the one that wandered off? 13And if he finds it, I tell you the truth, he is happier about that one sheep than about the ninety-nine that did not wander off. 14In the same way your Father in heaven is not willing that any of these little ones should be lost.

■ A Brother Who Sins Against You
15"If your brother sins against you,b go and show him his fault, just between the two of you. If he listens to you, you have won your brother over. 16But if he will not listen, take one or two others along, so that 'every matter may be established by the testimony of two or three witnesses.'c 17If he refuses to listen to them, tell it to the church; and if he refuses to listen even to the church, treat him as you would a pagan or a tax collector.

18"I tell you the truth, whatever you bind on earth will bed bound in heaven, and whatever you loose on earth will bed loosed in heaven.

19"Again, I tell you that if two of you on earth agree about anything you ask for, it will be done for you by my Father in heaven. 20For where two or three come together in my name, there am I with them."

■ The Parable of the Unmerciful Servant
21Then Peter came to Jesus and asked, "Lord, how many times shall I forgive my brother when he sins against me? Up to seven times?"

a 20 Some manuscripts you. 21 But this kind does not go out except by prayer and fasting.   b 24 Greek the two drachmas   a 10 Some manuscripts heaven. 11 The Son of Man came to save what was lost.   b 15 Some manuscripts do not have against you.   c 16 Deut. 19:15   d 18 Or have been

22Jesus answered, "I tell you, not seven times, but seventy-seven times.*e*

23"Therefore, the kingdom of heaven is like a king who wanted to settle accounts with his servants. 24As he began the settlement, a man who owed him ten thousand talents*f* was brought to him. 25Since he was not able to pay, the master ordered that he and his wife and his children and all that he had be sold to repay the debt.

18:23 ■ MATTHEW AND MONEY

Just as Luke, a doctor, gives more descriptive accounts of physical healings, Matthew, a former tax collector, highlights stories about money. This story in chapter 18, as well as others in chapters 20 and 25, appears only in Matthew's Gospel. Significantly, the former tax collector records Jesus' strongest words on treatment of the poor and needy.

26"The servant fell on his knees before him. 'Be patient with me,' he begged, 'and I will pay back everything.' 27The servant's master took pity on him, cancelled the debt and let him go.

28"But when that servant went out, he found one of his fellow-servants who owed him a hundred denarii.*g* He grabbed him and began to choke him. 'Pay back what you owe me!' he demanded.

29"His fellow-servant fell to his knees and begged him, 'Be patient with me, and I will pay you back.'

30"But he refused. Instead, he went off and had the man thrown into prison until he could pay the debt. 31When the other servants saw what had happened, they were greatly distressed and went and told their master everything that had happened.

32"Then the master called the servant in. 'You wicked servant,' he said, 'I cancelled all that debt of yours because you begged me to. 33Shouldn't you have had mercy on your fellow-servant just as I had on you?' 34In anger his master turned him over to the jailers to be tortured, until he should pay back all he owed.

35"This is how my heavenly Father will treat each of you unless you forgive your brother from your heart."

■ Divorce
☐ See Mark 10:1–12

19 When Jesus had finished saying these things, he left Galilee and went into the region of Judea to the other side of the Jordan. 2Large crowds followed him, and he healed them there.

3Some Pharisees came to him to test him. They asked, "Is it lawful for a man to divorce his wife for any and every reason?"

4"Haven't you read," he replied, "that at the beginning the Creator 'made them male and female',*a* 5and said, 'For this reason a man will leave his father and mother and be united to his wife, and the two will become one flesh'*b*? 6So they are no longer two, but one. Therefore what God has joined together, let man not separate."

7"Why then," they asked, "did Moses command

that a man give his wife a certificate of divorce and send her away?"

8Jesus replied, "Moses permitted you to divorce your wives because your hearts were hard. But it was not this way from the beginning. 9I tell you that anyone who divorces his wife, except for marital unfaithfulness, and marries another woman commits adultery."

19:9 ■ NO-FAULT DIVORCE?

In Jesus' day Pharisees debated how to interpret Old Testament rules concerning divorce. As usual, they tried to pull Jesus into the dispute. A famous rabbi named Hillel taught that a man could divorce his wife if she did anything at all to displease him, such as burning his food. A stricter school headed by Shammai limited grounds for divorce to marital infidelity. Jesus clearly sided with Shammai but pointed much deeper, beyond the technicalities of divorce to God's original design for marriage.

10The disciples said to him, "If this is the situation between a husband and wife, it is better not to marry."

11Jesus replied, "Not everyone can accept this word, but only those to whom it has been given. 12For some are eunuchs because they were born that way; others were made that way by men; and others have renounced marriage*c* because of the kingdom of heaven. The one who can accept this should accept it."

■ The Little Children and Jesus
☐ See Mark 10:13–16; Luke 18:15–17

13Then little children were brought to Jesus for him to place his hands on them and pray for them. But the disciples rebuked those who brought them.

14Jesus said, "Let the little children come to me, and do not hinder them, for the kingdom of heaven belongs to such as these." 15When he had placed his hands on them, he went on from there.

■ The Rich Young Man
☐ See Mark 10:17–30; Luke 18:18–30

16Now a man came up to Jesus and asked, "Teacher, what good thing must I do to get eternal life?"

17"Why do you ask me about what is good?" Jesus replied. "There is only One who is good. If you want to enter life, obey the commandments."

18"Which ones?" the man enquired.

Jesus replied, " 'Do not murder, do not commit adultery, do not steal, do not give false testimony, 19honour your father and mother,'*d* and 'love your neighbour as yourself.'*e*"

20"All these I have kept," the young man said. "What do I still lack?"

21Jesus answered, "If you want to be perfect, go, sell your possessions and give to the poor, and you will have treasure in heaven. Then come, follow me."

22When the young man heard this, he went away sad, because he had great wealth.

---

e22 Or seventy times seven   *f24 That is, millions of pounds*   *g28 That is, a few pounds*   *a4 Gen. 1:27*   *b5 Gen. 2:24*   *c12 Or have made themselves eunuchs*   *d19 Exodus 20:12–16; Deut. 5:16–20*   *e19 Lev. 19:18*

²³Then Jesus said to his disciples, "I tell you the truth, it is hard for a rich man to enter the kingdom of heaven. ²⁴Again I tell you, it is easier for a camel to go through the eye of a needle than for a rich man to enter the kingdom of God."

²⁵When the disciples heard this, they were greatly astonished and asked, "Who then can be saved?"

²⁶Jesus looked at them and said, "With man this is impossible, but with God all things are possible."

²⁷Peter answered him, "We have left everything to follow you! What then will there be for us?"

²⁸Jesus said to them, "I tell you the truth, at the renewal of all things, when the Son of Man sits on his glorious throne, you who have followed me will also sit on twelve thrones, judging the twelve tribes of Israel. ²⁹And everyone who has left houses or brothers or sisters or father or mother/ or children or fields for my sake will receive a hundred times as much and will inherit eternal life. ³⁰But many who are first will be last, and many who are last will be first.

■ The Parable of the Workers in the Vineyard

20 "For the kingdom of heaven is like a landowner who went out early in the morning to hire men to work in his vineyard. ²He agreed to pay them a denarius for the day and sent them into his vineyard.

20:1 ■ UNFAIR PAY

Jesus' story makes little economic sense, which was his point exactly. He is giving a parable about grace, and you can't calculate the grace of God like you can a day's wages. We receive it as a gift from God, not as something we work hard to earn. The person who comes to God at the end of life – like the robber on the cross – enjoys the same ultimate benefits as someone who follows God from early childhood. Jealousy of another's "unfair" rewards can take the joy from your own.

---

³"About the third hour he went out and saw others standing in the market-place doing nothing. ⁴He told them, 'You also go and work in my vineyard, and I will pay you whatever is right.' ⁵So they went.

"He went out again about the sixth hour and the ninth hour and did the same thing. ⁶About the eleventh hour he went out and found still others standing around. He asked them, 'Why have you been standing here all day long doing nothing?'

⁷" 'Because no-one has hired us,' they answered.

"He said to them, 'You also go and work in my vineyard.'

⁸"When evening came, the owner of the vineyard said to his foreman, 'Call the workers and pay them their wages, beginning with the last ones hired and going on to the first.'

⁹"The workers who were hired about the eleventh hour came and each received a denarius. ¹⁰So when those came who were hired first, they expected to receive more. But each one of them also received a denarius. ¹¹When they received it, they began to grumble against the landowner. ¹²'These men who were hired last worked only one hour,' they said, 'and you have made them equal to us who have borne the burden of the work and the heat of the day.'

¹³"But he answered one of them, 'Friend, I am not being unfair to you. Didn't you agree to work for a denarius? ¹⁴Take your pay and go. I want to give the man who was hired last the same as I gave you. ¹⁵Don't I have the right to do what I want with my own money? Or are you envious because I am generous?'

¹⁶"So the last will be first, and the first will be last."

■ Jesus Again Predicts His Death
☐ See Mark 10:32–34; Luke 18:31–33

¹⁷Now as Jesus was going up to Jerusalem, he took the twelve disciples aside and said to them, ¹⁸"We are going up to Jerusalem, and the Son of Man will be betrayed to the chief priests and the teachers of the law. They will condemn him to death ¹⁹and will turn him over to the Gentiles to be mocked and flogged and crucified. On the third day he will be raised to life!"

■ A Mother's Request
☐ See Mark 10:35–45

²⁰Then the mother of Zebedee's sons came to Jesus with her sons and, kneeling down, asked a favour of him.

²¹"What is it you want?" he asked.

She said, "Grant that one of these two sons of mine may sit at your right and the other at your left in your kingdom."

²²"You don't know what you are asking," Jesus said to them. "Can you drink the cup I am going to drink?"

"We can," they answered.

²³Jesus said to them, "You will indeed drink from my cup, but to sit at my right or left is not for me to grant. These places belong to those for whom they have been prepared by my Father."

²⁴When the ten heard about this, they were indignant with the two brothers. ²⁵Jesus called them together and said, "You know that the rulers of the Gentiles lord it over them, and their high officials exercise authority over them. ²⁶Not so with you. Instead, whoever wants to become great among you must be your servant, ²⁷and whoever wants to be first must be your slave – ²⁸just as the Son of Man did not come to be served, but to serve, and to give his life as a ransom for many."

■ Two Blind Men Receive Sight
☐ See Mark 10:46–52; Luke 18:35–43

²⁹As Jesus and his disciples were leaving Jericho, a large crowd followed him. ³⁰Two blind men were sitting by the roadside, and when they heard that Jesus was going by, they shouted, "Lord, Son of David, have mercy on us!"

³¹The crowd rebuked them and told them to be quiet, but they shouted all the louder, "Lord, Son of David, have mercy on us!"

f29 Some manuscripts *mother or wife*

³²Jesus stopped and called them. "What do you want me to do for you?" he asked.

³³"Lord," they answered, "we want our sight."

³⁴Jesus had compassion on them and touched their eyes. Immediately they received their sight and followed him.

■ The Triumphal Entry
☐ See Mark 11:1–10; Luke 19:29–38; John 12:12–15

21 As they approached Jerusalem and came to Bethphage on the Mount of Olives, Jesus sent two disciples, ²saying to them, "Go to the village ahead of you, and at once you will find a donkey tied there, with her colt by her. Untie them and bring them to me. ³If anyone says anything to you, tell him that the Lord needs them, and he will send them right away."

⁴This took place to fulfil what was spoken through the prophet:

⁵"Say to the Daughter of Zion,
'See, your king comes to you,
gentle and riding on a donkey,
on a colt, the foal of a donkey.' "ᵃ

⁶The disciples went and did as Jesus had instructed them. ⁷They brought the donkey and the colt, placed their cloaks on them, and Jesus sat on them. ⁸A very large crowd spread their cloaks on the road, while others cut branches from the trees and spread them on the road. ⁹The crowds that went ahead of him and those that followed shouted,

"Hosannaᵇ to the Son of David!"

"Blessed is he who comes in the name of the Lord!"ᶜ

"Hosannaᵇ in the highest!"

¹⁰When Jesus entered Jerusalem, the whole city was stirred and asked, "Who is this?"

¹¹The crowds answered, "This is Jesus, the prophet from Nazareth in Galilee."

■ Jesus at the Temple
☐ See Mark 11:15–18; Luke 19:45–47

¹²Jesus entered the temple area and drove out all who were buying and selling there. He overturned the tables of the money-changers and the benches of those selling doves. ¹³"It is written," he said to them, " 'My house will be called a house of prayer,'ᵈ but you are making it a 'den of robbers'.ᵉ"

21:12 ■ DRASTIC ACTION

In Jesus' day, activities at the temple, supposedly the centre for worship of God, had taken on a commercial cast. Merchants sold sacrificial animals to pilgrims and foreigners at inflated prices. The system was designed more for profit than for true worship. Jesus responded first by aggressively turning out these "robbers", and then by turning his attention to the people with real needs, the blind and the lame.

---

¹⁴The blind and the lame came to him at the temple, and he healed them. ¹⁵But when the chief priests and the teachers of the law saw the wonderful things he did and the children shouting in the temple area, "Hosanna to the Son of David," they were indignant.

¹⁶"Do you hear what these children are saying?" they asked him.

"Yes," replied Jesus, "have you never read,

" 'From the lips of children and infants
you have ordained praise'ᶠ?"

¹⁷And he left them and went out of the city to Bethany, where he spent the night.

■ The Fig-Tree Withers
☐ See Mark 11:12–14,20–24

¹⁸Early in the morning, as he was on his way back to the city, he was hungry. ¹⁹Seeing a fig-tree by the road, he went up to it but found nothing on it except leaves. Then he said to it, "May you never bear fruit again!" Immediately the tree withered.

²⁰When the disciples saw this, they were amazed. "How did the fig-tree wither so quickly?" they asked.

²¹Jesus replied, "I tell you the truth, if you have faith and do not doubt, not only can you do what was done to the fig-tree, but also you can say to this mountain, 'Go, throw yourself into the sea,' and it will be done. ²²If you believe, you will receive whatever you ask for in prayer."

■ The Authority of Jesus Questioned
☐ See Mark 11:27–33; Luke 20:1–8

²³Jesus entered the temple courts, and, while he was teaching, the chief priests and the elders of the people came to him. "By what authority are you doing these things?" they asked. "And who gave you this authority?"

²⁴Jesus replied, "I will also ask you one question. If you answer me, I will tell you by what authority I am doing these things. ²⁵John's baptism—where did it come from? Was it from heaven, or from men?"

They discussed it among themselves and said, "If we say, 'From heaven', he will ask, 'Then why didn't you believe him?' ²⁶But if we say, 'From men'—we are afraid of the people, for they all hold that John was a prophet."

²⁷So they answered Jesus, "We don't know."

Then he said, "Neither will I tell you by what authority I am doing these things.

■ The Parable of the Two Sons

²⁸"What do you think? There was a man who had two sons. He went to the first and said, 'Son, go and work today in the vineyard.'

²⁹" 'I will not,' he answered, but later he changed his mind and went.

³⁰"Then the father went to the other son and said the same thing. He answered, 'I will, sir,' but he did not go.

³¹"Which of the two did what his father wanted?"

"The first," they answered.

Jesus said to them, "I tell you the truth, the tax

ᵃ5 Zech. 9:9   ᵇ9 A Hebrew expression meaning "Save!" which became an exclamation of praise; also in verse 15   ᶜ9 Psalm 118:26   ᵈ13 Isaiah 56:7   ᵉ13 Jer. 7:11   ᶠ16 Psalm 8:2

collectors and the prostitutes are entering the kingdom of God ahead of you. [32]For John came to you to show you the way of righteousness, and you did not believe him, but the tax collectors and the prostitutes did. And even after you saw this, you did not repent and believe him.

■ The Parable of the Tenants
☐ See Mark 12:1–12; Luke 20:9–19
[33]"Listen to another parable: There was a landowner who planted a vineyard. He put a wall around it, dug a winepress in it and built a watchtower.

Then he rented the vineyard to some farmers and went away on a journey. [34]When the harvest time approached, he sent his servants to the tenants to collect his fruit.

[35]"The tenants seized his servants; they beat one, killed another, and stoned a third. [36]Then he sent other servants to them, more than the first time, and the tenants treated them in the same way. [37]Last of all, he sent his son to them. 'They will respect my son,' he said.

[38]"But when the tenants saw the son, they said to each other, 'This is the heir. Come, let's kill him and

■ OUT TO GET JESUS
JESUS CONFRONTS HIS ENEMIES

INSIGHT

WHEN THE CHIEF PRIESTS AND THE PHARISEES HEARD JESUS' PARABLES, THEY KNEW HE WAS TALKING ABOUT THEM. THEY LOOKED FOR A WAY TO ARREST HIM, BUT THEY WERE AFRAID OF THE CROWD. ■ 21:45–46

The mere birth of Jesus had threatened King Herod so much that he had ordered a bloody slaughter of boy babies. The pattern of opposition continued. Early on, Jesus openly predicted his own death.

Beginning in chapter 19, Matthew explains some of the escalating tensions between Jesus and the groups who resisted him. Enemies followed him from town to town, setting traps. Even so, Jesus neither tempered his words nor tried to hide. Instead, he used the occasions of conflict to warn his disciples and the watching crowds against those enemies, whose fury only increased.

Chapter 22 shows Jesus confronting three different groups of enemies on the same day: two religious sects, the Pharisees and the Sadducees, as well as the political Herodians. Jesus easily avoided their carefully devised verbal traps. In fact, he succeeded so brilliantly that Matthew concludes, "From that day on no-one dared to ask him any more questions" (22:46).

■WHAT DID JESUS HAVE AGAINST THE PHARISEES?
Students of history have often puzzled over why Jesus lashed out so strongly at one Jewish sect, the Pharisees – a group the New Testament mentions 100 times. At first glance, they seem like people Jesus should have liked. They were the most religious people of the day. More than any other group, they strove to follow the letter of the Old Testament law. Their very name, meaning "separatists", hinted at their desire to rise above normal behaviour.

Pharisees were legalists: besides unduly focusing on minute details of the law, they embellished it with their own strict traditions. For example, a person could ride a donkey without breaking the Sabbath rules, but if he carried a switch to speed up the animal, he would be guilty of laying a burden on it.

A Pharisee could give to a beggar on the Sabbath only if the beggar stuck his hand inside the home of the Pharisee so that the Pharisee needn't reach outside. A woman couldn't look in the mirror on the Sabbath – she might see a grey hair and be tempted to pull it out.

Matthew 23 records Jesus' eloquent verdict on the Pharisees. He scored them for being proud and cliquish and petty, and for refusing to admit their wrongs. External, showy forms of legalism, he said, tend to divert attention away from a person's inner attitude towards God and other people.

■ARE THERE PHARISEES NOW?
As he entered into the last weeks of his life on earth, Jesus polarised people. He boldly contrasted his own teaching with that of his opponents. In addition, he warned his followers about what to expect after his death. Opposition from enemies like the Pharisees wouldn't fade away when he departed. Rather, it would crescendo until the day of final judgment.

Jesus singled out the Pharisees as an example of legalism carried to an extreme. But he wasn't talking merely against an ancient Jewish sect. His words describe persistent tendencies of human beings, then and now. The errors he mentioned have characterised the church throughout its history. Christians still battle against pride and intolerance and a religion based on deeds.

☐LIFE QUESTIONS:
Jesus describes characteristics of Pharisees in the first century. But what about our own time? What Pharisee-like qualities exist in your church? In you?

take his inheritance.' ³⁹So they took him and threw him out of the vineyard and killed him.

⁴⁰"Therefore, when the owner of the vineyard comes, what will he do to those tenants?"

⁴¹"He will bring those wretches to a wretched end," they replied, "and he will rent the vineyard to other tenants, who will give him his share of the crop at harvest time."

⁴²Jesus said to them, "Have you never read in the Scriptures:

" 'The stone the builders rejected
has become the capstone;ᵍ
the Lord has done this,
and it is marvellous in our eyes'ᵇ?

⁴³"Therefore I tell you that the kingdom of God will be taken away from you and given to a people who will produce its fruit. ⁴⁴He who falls on this stone will be broken to pieces, but he on whom it falls will be crushed."ⁱ

⁴⁵When the chief priests and the Pharisees heard Jesus' parables, they knew he was talking about them. ⁴⁶They looked for a way to arrest him, but they were afraid of the crowd because the people held that he was a prophet.

■ The Parable of the Wedding Banquet

22 Jesus spoke to them again in parables, saying: ²"The kingdom of heaven is like a king who prepared a wedding banquet for his son. ³He sent his servants to those who had been invited to the banquet to tell them to come, but they refused to come.

⁴"Then he sent some more servants and said, 'Tell those who have been invited that I have prepared my dinner: My oxen and fattened cattle have been slaughtered, and everything is ready. Come to the wedding banquet.'

⁵"But they paid no attention and went off—one to his field, another to his business. ⁶The rest seized his servants, ill-treated them and killed them. ⁷The king was enraged. He sent his army and destroyed those murderers and burned their city.

⁸"Then he said to his servants, 'The wedding banquet is ready, but those I invited did not deserve to come. ⁹Go to the street corners and invite to the banquet anyone you find.' ¹⁰So the servants went out into the streets and gathered all the people they could find, both good and bad, and the wedding hall was filled with guests.

¹¹"But when the king came in to see the guests, he noticed a man there who was not wearing wedding clothes. ¹²'Friend,' he asked, 'how did you get in here without wedding clothes?' The man was speechless.

¹³"Then the king told the attendants, 'Tie him hand and foot, and throw him outside, into the darkness, where there will be weeping and gnashing of teeth.'

¹⁴"For many are invited, but few are chosen."

■ Paying Taxes to Caesar
□ See Mark 12:13–17; Luke 20:20–26

¹⁵Then the Pharisees went out and laid plans to trap him in his words. ¹⁶They sent their disciples to him along with the Herodians. "Teacher," they said, "we know you are a man of integrity and that you teach the way of God in accordance with the truth. You aren't swayed by men, because you pay no attention to who they are. ¹⁷Tell us then, what is your opinion? Is it right to pay taxes to Caesar or not?"

22:17 ■ A NO-WIN SITUATION
The Pharisees, allied with a party following King Herod, posed a question designed to trap Jesus regardless of his answer. If Jesus said, Pay the taxes, he would lose the support of the independent-minded Jews; if he said, Don't pay, he could be turned in to Rome for breaking the law.

¹⁸But Jesus, knowing their evil intent, said, "You hypocrites, why are you trying to trap me? ¹⁹Show me the coin used for paying the tax." They brought him a denarius, ²⁰and he asked them, "Whose portrait is this? And whose inscription?"

²¹"Caesar's," they replied.

Then he said to them, "Give to Caesar what is Caesar's, and to God what is God's."

²²When they heard this, they were amazed. So they left him and went away.

■ Marriage at the Resurrection
□ See Mark 12:18–27; Luke 20:27–40

²³That same day the Sadducees, who say there is no resurrection, came to him with a question. ²⁴"Teacher," they said, "Moses told us that if a man dies without having children, his brother must marry the widow and have children for him. ²⁵Now there were seven brothers among us. The first one married and died, and since he had no children, he left his wife to his brother. ²⁶The same thing happened to the second and third brother, right on down to the seventh. ²⁷Finally, the woman died. ²⁸Now then, at the resurrection, whose wife will she be of the seven, since all of them were married to her?"

²⁹Jesus replied, "You are in error because you do not know the Scriptures or the power of God. ³⁰At the resurrection people will neither marry nor be given in marriage; they will be like the angels in heaven. ³¹But about the resurrection of the dead— have you not read what God said to you, ³²'I am the God of Abraham, the God of Isaac, and the God of Jacob'ᵃ? He is not the God of the dead but of the living."

³³When the crowds heard this, they were astonished at his teaching.

■ The Greatest Commandment
□ See Mark 12:28–31

³⁴Hearing that Jesus had silenced the Sadducees, the Pharisees got together. ³⁵One of them, an expert in the law, tested him with this question: ³⁶"Teacher, which is the greatest commandment in the Law?"

³⁷Jesus replied: " 'Love the Lord your God with all your heart and with all your soul and with all your

---

ᵍ42 Or cornerstone   ᵇ42 Psalm 118:22,23   ⁱ44 Some manuscripts do not have verse 44.   ᵃ32 Exodus 3:6

mind.'*b* ³⁸This is the first and greatest commandment. ³⁹And the second is like it: 'Love your neighbour as yourself.'*c* ⁴⁰All the Law and the Prophets
hang on these two commandments."

■ Whose Son Is the Christ?
☐ See Mark 12:35–37; Luke 20:41–44

⁴¹While the Pharisees were gathered together,
Jesus asked them, ⁴²"What do you think about the
Christ?*d* Whose son is he?"

"The son of David," they replied.

⁴³He said to them, "How is it then that David,
speaking by the Spirit, calls him 'Lord'? For he says,

⁴⁴" 'The Lord said to my Lord:
"Sit at my right hand
until I put your enemies
under your feet." '*e*

⁴⁵If then David calls him 'Lord', how can he be his
son?" ⁴⁶No-one could say a word in reply, and from
that day on no-one dared to ask him any more questions.

■ Seven Woes
☐ See Mark 12:38–39; Luke 20:45–46

23 Then Jesus said to the crowds and to his disciples: ²"The teachers of the law and the
Pharisees sit in Moses' seat. ³So you must obey them
and do everything they tell you. But do not do what
they do, for they do not practise what they preach.
⁴They tie up heavy loads and put them on men's
shoulders, but they themselves are not willing to lift
a finger to move them.

⁵"Everything they do is done for men to see: They
make their phylacteries*a* wide and the tassels on
their garments long; ⁶they love the place of honour
at banquets and the most important seats in the
synagogues; ⁷they love to be greeted in the market-
places and to have men call them 'Rabbi'.

⁸"But you are not to be called 'Rabbi', for you
have only one Master and you are all brothers. ⁹And
do not call anyone on earth 'father', for you have
one Father, and he is in heaven. ¹⁰Nor are you to be
called 'teacher', for you have one Teacher, the
Christ.*b* ¹¹The greatest among you will be your servant. ¹²For whoever exalts himself will be humbled,
and whoever humbles himself will be exalted.

¹³"Woe to you, teachers of the law and Pharisees,
you hypocrites! You shut the kingdom of heaven in
men's faces. You yourselves do not enter, nor will
you let those enter who are trying to.*c*

¹⁵"Woe to you, teachers of the law and Pharisees,
you hypocrites! You travel over land and sea to win
a single convert, and when he becomes one, you
make him twice as much a son of hell as you are.

¹⁶"Woe to you, blind guides! You say, 'If anyone
swears by the temple, it means nothing; but if anyone swears by the gold of the temple, he is bound
by his oath.' ¹⁷You blind fools! Which is greater: the
gold, or the temple that makes the gold sacred?
¹⁸You also say, 'If anyone swears by the altar, it
means nothing; but if anyone swears by the gift on
it, he is bound by his oath.' ¹⁹You blind men! Which
is greater: the gift, or the altar that makes the gift

sacred? ²⁰Therefore, he who swears by the altar
swears by it and by everything on it. ²¹And he who
swears by the temple swears by it and by the one
who dwells in it. ²²And he who swears by heaven
swears by God's throne and by the one who sits
on it.

²³"Woe to you, teachers of the law and Pharisees,
you hypocrites! You give a tenth of your spices—
mint, dill and cummin. But you have neglected the
more important matters of the law—justice, mercy
and faithfulness. You should have practised the latter, without neglecting the former. ²⁴You blind
guides! You strain out a gnat but swallow a camel.

23:24 ■ STRAINING AT GNATS
The Pharisees, who literally strained water through
a cloth to filter out unclean gnats, could hardly
miss the point of Jesus' biting humour. Jesus was
not attacking them for being strict *per se*, but
rather for focusing on trivial matters while ignoring
more important issues: justice, mercy, faithfulness.
He blasted their smug, hypocritical sense of
superiority.

---

²⁵"Woe to you, teachers of the law and Pharisees,
you hypocrites! You clean the outside of the cup
and dish, but inside they are full of greed and self-
indulgence. ²⁶Blind Pharisee! First clean the inside
of the cup and dish, and then the outside also will
be clean.

²⁷"Woe to you, teachers of the law and Pharisees,
you hypocrites! You are like whitewashed tombs,
which look beautiful on the outside but on the inside are full of dead men's bones and everything unclean. ²⁸In the same way, on the outside you appear
to people as righteous but on the inside you are full
of hypocrisy and wickedness.

²⁹"Woe to you, teachers of the law and Pharisees,
you hypocrites! You build tombs for the prophets
and decorate the graves of the righteous. ³⁰And you
say, 'If we had lived in the days of our forefathers,
we would not have taken part with them in shedding the blood of the prophets.' ³¹So you testify
against yourselves that you are the descendants of
those who murdered the prophets. ³²Fill up, then,
the measure of the sin of your forefathers!

³³"You snakes! You brood of vipers! How will you
escape being condemned to hell? ³⁴Therefore I am
sending you prophets and wise men and teachers.
Some of them you will kill and crucify; others you
will flog in your synagogues and pursue from town
to town. ³⁵And so upon you will come all the righteous blood that has been shed on earth, from the
blood of righteous Abel to the blood of Zechariah
son of Barakiah, whom you murdered between the
temple and the altar. ³⁶I tell you the truth, all this
will come upon this generation.

³⁷"O Jerusalem, Jerusalem, you who kill the
prophets and stone those sent to you, how often I
have longed to gather your children together, as a
hen gathers her chicks under her wings, but you
were not willing. ³⁸Look, your house is left to you

---

*b*37 Deut. 6:5   *c*39 Lev. 19:18   *d*42 Or *Messiah*   *e*44 Psalm 110:1   *a*5 That is, boxes containing Scripture verses, worn on forehead and arm
*b*10 Or *Messiah*   *c*13 Some manuscripts *to.* 14*Woe to you, teachers of the law and Pharisees, you hypocrites! You devour widows' houses and for a
show make lengthy prayers. Therefore you will be punished more severely.*

desolate. 39For I tell you, you will not see me again until you say, 'Blessed is he who comes in the name of the Lord.'*d*"

■ Signs of the End of the Age
□ See Mark 13:1–37; Luke 21:5–36

24 Jesus left the temple and was walking away when his disciples came up to him to call his attention to its buildings. 2"Do you see all these things?" he asked. "I tell you the truth, not one stone here will be left on another; every one will be thrown down."

24:2 ■ STONES OVERTURNED
Jesus' prediction came true four decades after his death, in A.D. 70, when the Roman army crushed a Jewish rebellion in Jerusalem. Soldiers knocked down the massive stones of the temple in search of the melted gold that had run down between the stones as the temple burned. The largest stones weighed over 400 tons, but General Titus' soldiers levelled them all.

3As Jesus was sitting on the Mount of Olives, the disciples came to him privately. "Tell us," they said, "when will this happen, and what will be the sign of your coming and of the end of the age?"

4Jesus answered: "Watch out that no-one deceives you. 5For many will come in my name, claiming, 'I am the Christ,'*a* and will deceive many. 6You will hear of wars and rumours of wars, but see to it that you are not alarmed. Such things must happen, but the end is still to come. 7Nation will rise against nation, and kingdom against kingdom. There will be famines and earthquakes in various places. 8All these are the beginning of birth-pains.

9"Then you will be handed over to be persecuted and put to death, and you will be hated by all nations because of me. 10At that time many will turn away from the faith and will betray and hate each other, 11and many false prophets will appear and deceive many people. 12Because of the increase of wickedness, the love of most will grow cold, 13but he who stands firm to the end will be saved. 14And this gospel of the kingdom will be preached in the whole world as a testimony to all nations, and then the end will come.

15"So when you see standing in the holy place 'the abomination that causes desolation',*b* spoken of through the prophet Daniel—let the reader understand—16then let those who are in Judea flee to the mountains. 17Let no-one on the roof of his house go down to take anything out of the house. 18Let no-one in the field go back to get his cloak. 19How dreadful it will be in those days for pregnant women and nursing mothers! 20Pray that your flight will not take place in winter or on the Sabbath. 21For then there will be great distress, unequalled from the beginning of the world until now—and never to be equalled again. 22If those days had not been cut short, no-one would survive, but for the sake of the elect those days will be shortened. 23At that time if anyone says to you, 'Look, here is the Christ!' or,

'There he is!' do not believe it. 24For false Christs and false prophets will appear and perform great signs and miracles to deceive even the elect—if that were possible. 25See, I have told you ahead of time.

26"So if anyone tells you, 'There he is, out in the desert,' do not go out; or, 'Here he is, in the inner rooms,' do not believe it. 27For as lightning that comes from the east is visible even in the west, so will be the coming of the Son of Man. 28Wherever there is a carcass, there the vultures will gather.

29"Immediately after the distress of those days

" 'the sun will be darkened,
    and the moon will not give its light;
the stars will fall from the sky,
    and the heavenly bodies will be shaken.'*c*

30"At that time the sign of the Son of Man will appear in the sky, and all the nations of the earth will mourn. They will see the Son of Man coming on the clouds of the sky, with power and great glory. 31And he will send his angels with a loud trumpet call, and they will gather his elect from the four winds, from one end of the heavens to the other.

32"Now learn this lesson from the fig-tree: As soon as its twigs get tender and its leaves come out, you know that summer is near. 33Even so, when you see all these things, you know that it*d* is near, right at the door. 34I tell you the truth, this generation*e* will certainly not pass away until all these things have happened. 35Heaven and earth will pass away, but my words will never pass away.

■ The Day and Hour Unknown
□ See Luke 12:42–46; 17:26–27

36"No-one knows about that day or hour, not even the angels in heaven, nor the Son,*f* but only the Father. 37As it was in the days of Noah, so it will be at the coming of the Son of Man. 38For in the days before the flood, people were eating and drinking, marrying and giving in marriage, up to the day Noah entered the ark; 39and they knew nothing about what would happen until the flood came and took them all away. That is how it will be at the coming of the Son of Man. 40Two men will be in the field; one will be taken and the other left. 41Two women will be grinding with a hand mill; one will be taken and the other left.

24:36 ■ WHEN WILL JESUS RETURN?
Matthew 24 records one of Jesus' longest statements about the future. Jesus gives direct clues to events that will precede his second coming. But, notably, almost half the chapter consists of warnings that no-one can predict the precise time of his coming.

42"Therefore keep watch, because you do not know on what day your Lord will come. 43But understand this: If the owner of the house had known at what time of night the thief was coming, he would have kept watch and would not have let his house be broken into. 44So you also must be

d 39 Psalm 118:26   *a 5* Or *Messiah;* also in verse 23   *b 15* Daniel 9:27; 11:31; 12:11   *c 29* Isaiah 13:10; 34:4   *d 33* Or *he*   *e 34* Or *race*
f 36 Some manuscripts do not have *nor the Son.*

ready, because the Son of Man will come at an hour when you do not expect him.

⁴⁵"Who then is the faithful and wise servant, whom the master has put in charge of the servants in his household to give them their food at the proper time? ⁴⁶It will be good for that servant whose master finds him doing so when he returns. ⁴⁷I tell you the truth, he will put him in charge of all his possessions. ⁴⁸But suppose that servant is wicked and says to himself, 'My master is staying away a long time,' ⁴⁹and he then begins to beat his fellow-servants and to eat and drink with drunkards. ⁵⁰The master of that servant will come on a day when he does not expect him and at an hour he is not aware of. ⁵¹He will cut him to pieces and assign him a place with the hypocrites, where there will be weeping and gnashing of teeth.

■ The Parable of the Ten Virgins

25 "At that time the kingdom of heaven will be like ten virgins who took their lamps and went out to meet the bridegroom. ²Five of them were foolish and five were wise. ³The foolish ones took their lamps but did not take any oil with them. ⁴The wise, however, took oil in jars along with their lamps. ⁵The bridegroom was a long time in coming, and they all became drowsy and fell asleep.

⁶"At midnight the cry rang out: 'Here's the bridegroom! Come out to meet him!'

⁷"Then all the virgins woke up and trimmed their lamps. ⁸The foolish ones said to the wise, 'Give us some of your oil; our lamps are going out.'

⁹" 'No,' they replied, 'there may not be enough for both us and you. Instead, go to those who sell oil and buy some for yourselves.'

¹⁰"But while they were on their way to buy the oil, the bridegroom arrived. The virgins who were ready went in with him to the wedding banquet. And the door was shut.

¹¹"Later the others also came. 'Sir! Sir!' they said. 'Open the door for us!'

¹²"But he replied, 'I tell you the truth, I don't know you.'

¹³"Therefore keep watch, because you do not know the day or the hour.

■ The Parable of the Talents

¹⁴"Again, it will be like a man going on a journey, who called his servants and entrusted his property to them. ¹⁵To one he gave five talents*a* of money, to another two talents, and to another one talent, each according to his ability. Then he went on his journey. ¹⁶The man who had received the five talents went at once and put his money to work and gained five more. ¹⁷So also, the one with the two talents gained two more. ¹⁸But the man who had received the one talent went off, dug a hole in the ground and hid his master's money.

¹⁹"After a long time the master of those servants returned and settled accounts with them. ²⁰The man who had received the five talents brought the other five. 'Master,' he said, 'you entrusted me with five talents. See, I have gained five more.'

²¹"His master replied, 'Well done, good and faithful servant! You have been faithful with a few things;

I will put you in charge of many things. Come and share your master's happiness!'

> **25:15 ■ ORIGINAL TALENT**
> Today when we speak of a "talented" musician or athlete, we are actually harking back to this parable. A talent in Jesus' time was a valuable sum of money worth about two years' wages. Because of this parable, the word acquired a different meaning. Each person in the kingdom of heaven is given a certain number of gifts and opportunities ("talents") to serve God. We can either waste those opportunities or invest them in a way that furthers the kingdom.

²²"The man with the two talents also came. 'Master,' he said, 'you entrusted me with two talents; see, I have gained two more.'

²³"His master replied, 'Well done, good and faithful servant! You have been faithful with a few things; I will put you in charge of many things. Come and share your master's happiness!'

²⁴"Then the man who had received the one talent came. 'Master,' he said, 'I knew that you are a hard man, harvesting where you have not sown and gathering where you have not scattered seed. ²⁵So I was afraid and went out and hid your talent in the ground. See, here is what belongs to you.'

²⁶"His master replied, 'You wicked, lazy servant! So you knew that I harvest where I have not sown and gather where I have not scattered seed? ²⁷Well then, you should have put my money on deposit with the bankers, so that when I returned I would have received it back with interest.

²⁸" 'Take the talent from him and give it to the one who has the ten talents. ²⁹For everyone who has will be given more, and he will have an abundance. Whoever does not have, even what he has will be taken from him. ³⁰And throw that worthless servant outside, into the darkness, where there will be weeping and gnashing of teeth.'

■ The Sheep and the Goats

³¹"When the Son of Man comes in his glory, and all the angels with him, he will sit on his throne in heavenly glory. ³²All the nations will be gathered before him, and he will separate the people one from another as a shepherd separates the sheep from the goats. ³³He will put the sheep on his right and the goats on his left.

³⁴"Then the King will say to those on his right, 'Come, you who are blessed by my Father; take your inheritance, the kingdom prepared for you since the creation of the world. ³⁵For I was hungry and you gave me something to eat, I was thirsty and you gave me something to drink, I was a stranger and you invited me in, ³⁶I needed clothes and you clothed me, I was sick and you looked after me, I was in prison and you came to visit me.'

³⁷"Then the righteous will answer him, 'Lord, when did we see you hungry and feed you, or thirsty and give you something to drink? ³⁸When did we see you a stranger and invite you in, or needing

---

a 15 A talent was worth several hundred pounds.

clothes and clothe you? ³⁹When did we see you sick or in prison and go to visit you?'

⁴⁰"The King will reply, 'I tell you the truth, whatever you did for one of the least of these brothers of mine, you did for me.'

⁴¹"Then he will say to those on his left, 'Depart from me, you who are cursed, into the eternal fire prepared for the devil and his angels. ⁴²For I was hungry and you gave me nothing to eat, I was thirsty and you gave me nothing to drink, ⁴³I was a stranger and you did not invite me in, I needed clothes and you did not clothe me, I was sick and in prison and you did not look after me.'

⁴⁴"They also will answer, 'Lord, when did we see you hungry or thirsty or a stranger or needing clothes or sick or in prison, and did not help you?'

⁴⁵"He will reply, 'I tell you the truth, whatever you did not do for one of the least of these, you did not do for me.'

⁴⁶"Then they will go away to eternal punishment, but the righteous to eternal life."

■ The Plot Against Jesus
□ See Mark 14:1–2; Luke 22:1–2

26 When Jesus had finished saying all these things, he said to his disciples, ²"As you know, the Passover is two days away—and the Son of Man will be handed over to be crucified."

³Then the chief priests and the elders of the people assembled in the palace of the high priest, whose name was Caiaphas, ⁴and they plotted to arrest Jesus in some sly way and kill him. ⁵"But not during the Feast," they said, "or there may be a riot among the people."

26:4 ■ "SOME SLY WAY"
The religious leaders failed in their plan to dispose of Jesus quietly. He was killed during a national holiday while Jerusalem swarmed with pilgrims. Yet his death sparked no riots, and in the end even his devoted followers abandoned him. The chief priests and elders might have congratulated themselves on a successful mission—except for what happened on Easter Sunday.

■ Jesus Anointed at Bethany
□ See Mark 14:3–9

⁶While Jesus was in Bethany in the home of a man known as Simon the Leper, ⁷a woman came to him with an alabaster jar of very expensive perfume, which she poured on his head as he was reclining at the table.

⁸When the disciples saw this, they were indignant. "Why this waste?" they asked. ⁹"This perfume could have been sold at a high price and the money given to the poor."

¹⁰Aware of this, Jesus said to them, "Why are you bothering this woman? She has done a beautiful thing to me. ¹¹The poor you will always have with you, but you will not always have me. ¹²When she poured this perfume on my body, she did it to prepare me for burial. ¹³I tell you the truth, wherever this gospel is preached throughout the world, what she has done will also be told, in memory of her."

■ Judas Agrees to Betray Jesus
□ See Mark 14:10–11; Luke 22:3–6

¹⁴Then one of the Twelve—the one called Judas Iscariot—went to the chief priests ¹⁵and asked, "What are you willing to give me if I hand him over to you?" So they counted out for him thirty silver coins. ¹⁶From then on Judas watched for an opportunity to hand him over.

■ The Lord's Supper
□ See Mark 14:12–25; Luke 22:7–13

¹⁷On the first day of the Feast of Unleavened Bread, the disciples came to Jesus and asked, "Where do you want us to make preparations for you to eat the Passover?"

¹⁸He replied, "Go into the city to a certain man and tell him, 'The Teacher says: My appointed time is near. I am going to celebrate the Passover with my disciples at your house.' " ¹⁹So the disciples did as Jesus had directed them and prepared the Passover.

²⁰When evening came, Jesus was reclining at the table with the Twelve. ²¹And while they were eating, he said, "I tell you the truth, one of you will betray me."

²²They were very sad and began to say to him one after the other, "Surely not I, Lord?"

²³Jesus replied, "The one who has dipped his hand into the bowl with me will betray me. ²⁴The Son of Man will go just as it is written about him. But woe to that man who betrays the Son of Man! It would be better for him if he had not been born."

²⁵Then Judas, the one who would betray him, said, "Surely not I, Rabbi?"

Jesus answered, "Yes, it is you."ᵃ

²⁶While they were eating, Jesus took bread, gave thanks and broke it, and gave it to his disciples, saying, "Take and eat; this is my body."

²⁷Then he took the cup, gave thanks and offered it to them, saying, "Drink from it, all of you. ²⁸This is my blood of theᵇ covenant, which is poured out for many for the forgiveness of sins. ²⁹I tell you, I will not drink of this fruit of the vine from now on until that day when I drink it anew with you in my Father's kingdom."

³⁰When they had sung a hymn, they went out to the Mount of Olives.

■ Jesus Predicts Peter's Denial
□ See Mark 14:27–31; Luke 22:31–34

³¹Then Jesus told them, "This very night you will all fall away on account of me, for it is written:

" 'I will strike the shepherd,
    and the sheep of the flock will be
        scattered.'ᶜ

³²But after I have risen, I will go ahead of you into Galilee."

³³Peter replied, "Even if all fall away on account of you, I never will."

³⁴"I tell you the truth," Jesus answered, "this very night, before the cock crows, you will disown me three times."

ᵃ25 Or "You yourself have said it"   ᵇ28 Some manuscripts the new   ᶜ31 Zech. 13:7

35But Peter declared, "Even if I have to die with you, I will never disown you." And all the other disciples said the same.

■ Gethsemane
☐ See Mark 14:32–42; Luke 22:40–46

36Then Jesus went with his disciples to a place called Gethsemane, and he said to them, "Sit here while I go over there and pray." 37He took Peter and the two sons of Zebedee along with him, and he began to be sorrowful and troubled. 38Then he said to them, "My soul is overwhelmed with sorrow to the point of death. Stay here and keep watch with me."

39Going a little farther, he fell with his face to the ground and prayed, "My Father, if it is possible, may this cup be taken from me. Yet not as I will, but as you will."

40Then he returned to his disciples and found them sleeping. "Could you men not keep watch with me for one hour?" he asked Peter. 41"Watch and pray so that you will not fall into temptation. The spirit is willing, but the body is weak."

42He went away a second time and prayed, "My Father, if it is not possible for this cup to be taken away unless I drink it, may your will be done."

43When he came back, he again found them sleeping, because their eyes were heavy. 44So he left them and went away once more and prayed the third time, saying the same thing.

45Then he returned to the disciples and said to them, "Are you still sleeping and resting? Look, the hour is near, and the Son of Man is betrayed into the hands of sinners. 46Rise, let us go! Here comes my betrayer!"

■ Jesus Arrested
☐ See Mark 14:43–50; Luke 22:47–53

47While he was still speaking, Judas, one of the Twelve, arrived. With him was a large crowd armed with swords and clubs, sent from the chief priests and the elders of the people. 48Now the betrayer had arranged a signal with them: "The one I kiss is the man; arrest him." 49Going at once to Jesus, Judas said, "Greetings, Rabbi!" and kissed him.

26:47 ■ A NAME DISGRACED

Judas (like Jesus) was a common name for Jewish men in those days; it is the Greek form of Judah. He came from a region called Judea, whereas all the other disciples came from Galilee. Yet he gained enough trust to be named the disciples' treasurer. The Bible gives few details on Judas' motive for betraying Jesus. He may have become disillusioned when Jesus didn't fulfil his expectations of a powerful king and Messiah.

50Jesus replied, "Friend, do what you came for."d Then the men stepped forward, seized Jesus and arrested him. 51With that, one of Jesus' companions reached for his sword, drew it out and struck the servant of the high priest, cutting off his ear.

52"Put your sword back in its place," Jesus said to him, "for all who draw the sword will die by the sword. 53Do you think I cannot call on my Father, and he will at once put at my disposal more than twelve legions of angels? 54But how then would the Scriptures be fulfilled that say it must happen in this way?"

55At that time Jesus said to the crowd, "Am I leading a rebellion, that you have come out with swords and clubs to capture me? Every day I sat in the temple courts teaching, and you did not arrest me. 56But this has all taken place that the writings of the prophets might be fulfilled." Then all the disciples deserted him and fled.

■ Before the Sanhedrin
☐ See Mark 14:53–65; John 18:12–13,19–24

57Those who had arrested Jesus took him to Caiaphas, the high priest, where the teachers of the law and the elders had assembled. 58But Peter followed him at a distance, right up to the courtyard of the high priest. He entered and sat down with the guards to see the outcome.

59The chief priests and the whole Sanhedrin were looking for false evidence against Jesus so that they could put him to death. 60But they did not find any, though many false witnesses came forward.

Finally two came forward 61and declared, "This fellow said, 'I am able to destroy the temple of God and rebuild it in three days.' "

62Then the high priest stood up and said to Jesus, "Are you not going to answer? What is this testimony that these men are bringing against you?" 63But Jesus remained silent.

The high priest said to him, "I charge you under oath by the living God: Tell us if you are the Christ,e the Son of God."

64"Yes, it is as you say," Jesus replied. "But I say to all of you: In the future you will see the Son of Man sitting at the right hand of the Mighty One and coming on the clouds of heaven."

65Then the high priest tore his clothes and said, "He has spoken blasphemy! Why do we need any more witnesses? Look, now you have heard the blasphemy. 66What do you think?"

"He is worthy of death," they answered.

67Then they spat in his face and struck him with their fists. Others slapped him 68and said, "Prophesy to us, Christ. Who hit you?"

■ Peter Disowns Jesus
☐ See Mark 14:66–72; Luke 22:52–62; John 18:16–18,25–27

69Now Peter was sitting out in the courtyard, and a servant girl came to him. "You also were with Jesus of Galilee," she said.

70But he denied it before them all. "I don't know what you're talking about," he said.

71Then he went out to the gateway, where another girl saw him and said to the people there, "This fellow was with Jesus of Nazareth."

72He denied it again, with an oath: "I don't know the man!"

73After a little while, those standing there went up to Peter and said, "Surely you are one of them, for your accent gives you away."

d 50 Or "Friend, why have you come?"   e 63 Or Messiah; also in verse 68

74Then he began to call down curses on himself and he swore to them, "I don't know the man!"

26:73 ■ TELL-TALE ACCENT
Revolutionaries and troublemakers in Palestine usually operated in the rugged countryside. In Jerusalem, a city alive with rumours, Peter's Galilean accent made him suspect, for it marked him as a non-local. Jesus, also from Galilee, had already been arrested.

Immediately a cock crowed. 75Then Peter remembered the word Jesus had spoken: "Before the cock crows, you will disown me three times." And he went outside and wept bitterly.

■ Judas Hangs Himself

27 Early in the morning, all the chief priests and the elders of the people came to the decision to put Jesus to death. 2They bound him, led him away and handed him over to Pilate, the governor.

3When Judas, who had betrayed him, saw that Jesus was condemned, he was seized with remorse and returned the thirty silver coins to the chief priests and the elders. 4"I have sinned," he said, "for I have betrayed innocent blood."

"What is that to us?" they replied. "That's your responsibility."

5So Judas threw the money into the temple and left. Then he went away and hanged himself.

6The chief priests picked up the coins and said, "It is against the law to put this into the treasury, since it is blood money." 7So they decided to use the money to buy the potter's field as a burial place for foreigners. 8That is why it has been called the Field of Blood to this day. 9Then what was spoken by Jeremiah the prophet was fulfilled: "They took the thirty silver coins, the price set on him by the people of Israel, 10and they used them to buy the potter's field, as the Lord commanded me."a

■ Jesus Before Pilate
☐ See Mark 15:2–15; Luke 23:2–3,18–25; John 18:29 – 19:16

11Meanwhile Jesus stood before the governor, and the governor asked him, "Are you the king of the Jews?"

"Yes, it is as you say," Jesus replied.

12When he was accused by the chief priests and the elders, he gave no answer. 13Then Pilate asked him, "Don't you hear the testimony they are bringing against you?" 14But Jesus made no reply, not even to a single charge — to the great amazement of the governor.

15Now it was the governor's custom at the Feast to release a prisoner chosen by the crowd. 16At that time they had a notorious prisoner, called Barabbas. 17So when the crowd had gathered, Pilate asked them, "Which one do you want me to release to you: Barabbas, or Jesus who is called Christ?" 18For he

■ THE KILLING OF A KING
ARREST, TRIAL, AND EXECUTION

INSIGHT

"WHAT SHALL I DO, THEN, WITH JESUS WHO IS CALLED CHRIST?" PILATE ASKED. THEY ALL ANSWERED, "CRUCIFY HIM!" ■ 27:22

In spare, unadorned language the last three chapters of Matthew draw together the deep ironies of Jesus' life. From the first sentence, Matthew has stressed that Jesus is the Messiah, a true king. This Gospel is sometimes called the "royal" Gospel because it refers so many times to kingship.

But at the end of his life, the man whom wise men had crossed a continent to worship was sold, like a slave, for thirty pieces of silver. Jesus got a royal robe and crown at last – but as a cruel, mocking joke. Blood from the wounds on his back clotted on the robe, and the crown of thorns streaked his face with more blood.

A short time before, he had blistered the religious leaders with accusations. But when they put him on the stand and accused him, his strong voice stayed mostly silent.

■ JESUS' SELF-DEFENCE
Jesus' enemies asked him two chief questions: "Are you the king of the Jews?" and "Are you the Messiah?" He answered with a simple "Yes, it is as you say" (27:11), confirming the major themes woven throughout Matthew's book. Finally he was executed, with his "crime" – being a king – posted above his sagging body.

Jesus was indeed a king, but not the kind of king people expected. Even his disciples, who had known Jesus intimately for three years, slipped away in doubt.

The story, however, doesn't end with the death scene in chapter 27. Good Friday would never have been called "good" without the miracle described next. The king came back! And the writer who opened his book by tracing Jesus' Jewish roots ends it with Jesus' stirring call to take the good news to all nations.

☐ LIFE QUESTIONS:
The people who crucified Jesus – what did they hate in him? Is it the same today?

a 10 See Zech. 11:12,13; Jer. 19:1–13; 32:6–9.

knew it was out of envy that they had handed Jesus over to him.

[19]While Pilate was sitting on the judge's seat, his wife sent him this message: "Don't have anything to do with that innocent man, for I have suffered a great deal today in a dream because of him."

[20]But the chief priests and the elders persuaded the crowd to ask for Barabbas and to have Jesus executed.

[21]"Which of the two do you want me to release to you?" asked the governor.

"Barabbas," they answered.

[22]"What shall I do, then, with Jesus who is called Christ?" Pilate asked.

They all answered, "Crucify him!"

[23]"Why? What crime has he committed?" asked Pilate.

But they shouted all the louder, "Crucify him!"

[24]When Pilate saw that he was getting nowhere, but that instead an uproar was starting, he took water and washed his hands in front of the crowd. "I am innocent of this man's blood," he said. "It is your responsibility!"

[25]All the people answered, "Let his blood be on us and on our children!"

[26]Then he released Barabbas to them. But he had Jesus flogged, and handed him over to be crucified.

■ The Soldiers Mock Jesus
☐ See Mark 15:16-20

[27]Then the governor's soldiers took Jesus into the Praetorium and gathered the whole company of soldiers round him. [28]They stripped him and put a scarlet robe on him, [29]and then twisted together a crown of thorns and set it on his head. They put a staff in his right hand and knelt in front of him and mocked him. "Hail, king of the Jews!" they said. [30]They spat on him, and took the staff and struck him on the head again and again. [31]After they had mocked him, they took off the robe and put his own clothes on him. Then they led him away to crucify him.

■ The Crucifixion
☐ See Mark 15:22-32; Luke 23:33-43; John 19:17-24

[32]As they were going out, they met a man from Cyrene, named Simon, and they forced him to carry the cross. [33]They came to a place called Golgotha (which means The Place of the Skull). [34]There they offered Jesus wine to drink, mixed with gall; but after tasting it, he refused to drink it. [35]When they had crucified him, they divided up his clothes by casting lots.[b] [36]And sitting down, they kept watch over him there. [37]Above his head they placed the written charge against him: THIS IS JESUS, THE KING OF THE JEWS. [38]Two robbers were crucified with him, one on his right and one on his left. [39]Those who passed by hurled insults at him, shaking their heads [40]and saying, "You who are going to destroy the temple and build it in three days, save yourself! Come down from the cross, if you are the Son of God!"

[41]In the same way the chief priests, the teachers of the law and the elders mocked him. [42]"He saved others," they said, "but he can't save himself! He's

the King of Israel! Let him come down now from the cross, and we will believe in him. [43]He trusts in God. Let God rescue him now if he wants him, for he said, 'I am the Son of God.' " [44]In the same way the robbers who were crucified with him also heaped insults on him.

■ The Death of Jesus
☐ See Mark 15:33-41; Luke 23:44-49

[45]From the sixth hour until the ninth hour darkness came over all the land. [46]About the ninth hour Jesus cried out in a loud voice, "*Eloi, Eloi,[c] lama sabachthani?*"—which means, "My God, my God, why have you forsaken me?"[d]

[47]When some of those standing there heard this, they said, "He's calling Elijah."

[48]Immediately one of them ran and got a sponge. He filled it with wine vinegar, put it on a stick, and offered it to Jesus to drink. [49]The rest said, "Now leave him alone. Let's see if Elijah comes to save him."

[50]And when Jesus had cried out again in a loud voice, he gave up his spirit.

[51]At that moment the curtain of the temple was torn in two from top to bottom. The earth shook and the rocks split. [52]The tombs broke open and the bodies of many holy people who had died were raised to life. [53]They came out of the tombs, and after Jesus' resurrection they went into the holy city and appeared to many people.

27:51 ■ A CURTAIN IS TORN

At Jesus' death, the massive, thick curtain in the temple in Jerusalem ripped in two. This curtain sealed off the Most Holy Place. No-one except the high priest was allowed into the presence of God in that Most Holy Place. And the high priest was permitted in only once a year, on a special day. The author of Hebrews looked on the miraculously torn curtain as symbolic: it signified the immediate access to God made possible by Jesus' death (Hebrews 10:19-20).

---

[54]When the centurion and those with him who were guarding Jesus saw the earthquake and all that had happened, they were terrified, and exclaimed, "Surely he was the Son[e] of God!"

[55]Many women were there, watching from a distance. They had followed Jesus from Galilee to care for his needs. [56]Among them were Mary Magdalene, Mary the mother of James and Joses, and the mother of Zebedee's sons.

■ The Burial of Jesus
☐ See Mark 15:42-47; Luke 23:50-56; John 19:38-42

[57]As evening approached, there came a rich man from Arimathea, named Joseph, who had himself become a disciple of Jesus. [58]Going to Pilate, he asked for Jesus' body, and Pilate ordered that it be given to him. [59]Joseph took the body, wrapped it in a clean linen cloth, [60]and placed it in his own new tomb that he had cut out of the rock. He rolled a big stone in front of the entrance to the tomb and went

---

[b]35 A few late manuscripts *lots that the word spoken by the prophet might be fulfilled: "They divided my garments among themselves and cast lots for my clothing."* (Psalm 22:18)   [c]46 Some manuscripts *Eli, Eli*   [d]46 Psalm 22:1   [e]54 Or *a son*

away. 61Mary Magdalene and the other Mary were sitting there opposite the tomb.

The Guard at the Tomb

62The next day, the one after Preparation Day, the chief priests and the Pharisees went to Pilate. 63"Sir," they said, "we remember that while he was still alive that deceiver said, 'After three days I will rise again.' 64So give the order for the tomb to be made secure until the third day. Otherwise, his disciples may come and steal the body and tell the people that he has been raised from the dead. This last deception will be worse than the first."

65"Take a guard," Pilate answered. "Go, make the tomb as secure as you know how." 66So they went and made the tomb secure by putting a seal on the stone and posting the guard.

The Resurrection

☐ See Mark 16:1–8; Luke 24:1–10

28 After the Sabbath, at dawn on the first day of the week, Mary Magdalene and the other Mary went to look at the tomb.

2There was a violent earthquake, for an angel of the Lord came down from heaven and, going to the tomb, rolled back the stone and sat on it. 3His appearance was like lightning, and his clothes were white as snow. 4The guards were so afraid of him that they shook and became like dead men.

28:4 ■ COVER-UP

Throughout Jesus' extraordinary life, people found all sorts of reasons to doubt him, even in the face of unexplainable events. These guards, for instance, were virtual eye-witnesses of the greatest miracle of all time, Jesus' resurrection. Yet a few hours later they made a deal with the chief priests to cover up the story (verses 11–15). Then, as now, people who choose not to believe can always find a rationale.

5The angel said to the women, "Do not be afraid, for I know that you are looking for Jesus, who was crucified. 6He is not here; he has risen, just as he said. Come and see the place where he lay. 7Then go quickly and tell his disciples: 'He has risen from the dead and is going ahead of you into Galilee. There you will see him.' Now I have told you."

8So the women hurried away from the tomb, afraid yet filled with joy, and ran to tell his disciples. 9Suddenly Jesus met them. "Greetings," he said. They came to him, clasped his feet and worshipped him. 10Then Jesus said to them, "Do not be afraid. Go and tell my brothers to go to Galilee; there they will see me."

The Guards' Report

11While the women were on their way, some of the guards went into the city and reported to the chief priests everything that had happened. 12When the chief priests had met with the elders and devised a plan, they gave the soldiers a large sum of money, 13telling them, "You are to say, 'His disciples came during the night and stole him away while we were asleep.' 14If this report gets to the governor, we will satisfy him and keep you out of trouble." 15So the soldiers took the money and did as they were instructed. And this story has been widely circulated among the Jews to this very day.

The Great Commission

16Then the eleven disciples went to Galilee, to the mountain where Jesus had told them to go. 17When they saw him, they worshipped him; but some doubted. 18Then Jesus came to them and said, "All authority in heaven and on earth has been given to me. 19Therefore go and make disciples of all nations, baptising them in*a* the name of the Father and of the Son and of the Holy Spirit, 20and teaching them to obey everything I have commanded you. And surely I am with you always, to the very end of the age."

---

a 19 Or *into*; see Acts 8:16; 19:5; Rom. 6:3; 1 Cor. 1:13; 10:2 and Gal. 3:27.

MARK

■ THE FAST-PACED GOSPEL

MARK READS LIKE THE SCRIPT FOR AN ACTION MOVIE

NEWS ABOUT HIM SPREAD QUICKLY OVER THE WHOLE REGION OF GALILEE. ■ 1:28

Brief introductory credits flash on the screen. Then the camera pans across an expanse of bleached sand, inhabited mostly by scorpions, lizards, and tarantulas. At last, through the shimmering heat, a lone figure appears: an eccentric wearing camel's hair and crying something in the thin desert air. So begins Mark.

It helps to imagine the book of Mark as a concisely edited documentary film. Unlike the other Gospels, this one has little tolerance for dialogue and personal reflection. The author is writing to a restless, impatient audience – people more like movie-goers than readers.

Mark deftly controls camera angles, alternately panning across large crowds and zooming in on individual people. He leaves no doubt about the main character. After the opening shot of John the Baptist, he moves Jesus to centre stage and the camera follows him everywhere.

■ AN EMPHASIS ON ACTION

Those who look for an outline in Mark come away baffled: all the spliced-together scenes defy structure. One author observed that Mark shows Jesus "scattering miracles like rice at a wedding". Matthew and Luke each give four chapters of historical warm-up before recording a miracle by Jesus; Mark covers three miracles and a group event in the first chapter alone.

In contrast to all its action scenes, the book includes only a sampling of Jesus' parables. It focuses on events, not speeches or editorial comments. Mark shows concert-hall-size crowds pressing around Jesus so tightly that he launches a boat to escape them. Wherever he goes, the crowds follow, buzzing about his remarkable life. "Is he the Holy One of God?" "Is he mad?" "Isn't this the carpenter's boy?"

■ A BREATHLESS PACE

By dispensing with all but bare-bones action, Mark manages to achieve more drama than perhaps any other biblical writer. Action guarantees an attentive audience, and Mark jams sequences together breathlessly. *At once* the Spirit sends Jesus into the desert; *at once* the disciples respond to Jesus' call to follow him; Jesus' touch *immediately* heals a man with leprosy – 42 times this book uses the Greek 'hurry-up' adverb translated several different ways into English.

Characters rush from place to place, jostle among crowds, are astonished at mighty works. Mark is a Gospel of exclamation points, full of words like *amazed, overwhelmed, terrified*. A phenomenon is loose on the earth, and the author is determined to capture its impact for future generations.

■ HOW TO READ MARK

About 90 per cent of Mark's content appears in the other three Gospels, but the book makes an ideal starting place for someone who knows little about Jesus. Its style – simple sentences, without complicated transitions or long speeches – makes understanding easier. In fact, Mark was probably written as a missionary book to people who knew next to nothing about the new Christian faith.

Except where he cites Jesus' own quotations, Mark quotes the Old Testament directly in only one place (1:2–3). In addition, Mark doesn't refer to the Old Testament Law, a

striking difference from the other Gospels. Such facts indicate that his book was written to a non-Jewish audience, probably the Romans.

You'll need no special instructions on reading Mark. This book's breezy style makes it as understandable as a newspaper. Because it loosely follows the chronology of Jesus' life, Mark offers an excellent introduction to the life of Jesus. As you read, stop and ponder the events Mark records. Why did Mark select these facts? What meaning did they have for the people in Jesus' day? What about for you?

■ 3-TRACK READING PLAN

For an explanation and complete listing of the 3-track reading plan, turn to page x.

■ TRACK 1:
Two-Week Courses on the
Bible
The Track 1 reading
programme on the Life and
Teachings of Jesus includes
two chapters from Mark. See
page x for a complete listing
of this course.

■ TRACK 2:
An Overview of Mark in 15
Days
Reading Mark will give you a
quick summary of Jesus' acts
on this earth. For this reason,
plan to spend two weeks
reading all 16 chapters of
Mark.
□ Day 1. Read the
Introduction to Mark, then
chapter 1.
□ Day 2. Read chapter 2's
record of scenes from Jesus'
life during a period of popular
acclaim.
□ Day 3. Read chapter 3,
which shows Jesus calling his
12 disciples.
□ Day 4. Read the brief

parables and the account of
the calming of a storm in
chapter 4.
□ Day 5. Mark 5 tells of three
miracles of healing; note the
different crowd reaction to
each one.
□ Day 6. Read chapter 6,
which includes several famous
miracles and also the story of
John the Baptist's beheading.
□ Day 7. Read chapter 7,
which shows the Pharisees'
opposition to Jesus beginning
to mount.
□ Day 8. As you read chapter
8, notice, on the one hand,
Jesus' increasing popularity
and, on the other, the growing
tension that will eventually
culminate in his death.
□ Day 9. Read the account of
Jesus' transfiguration and the
other events recorded in
chapter 9.
□ Day 10. Mark 10 records
Jesus' teaching on divorce,
humility, and wealth.
□ Day 11. Read chapter 11's
account of Jesus' entry into

Jerusalem for the last week of
his life.
□ Day 12. Read chapter 12,
which includes Jesus'
teaching on a variety of
topics.
□ Day 13. Read chapter 13
for Jesus' predictions of the
end of the world.
□ Day 14. Mark 14 records
the events leading up to
Jesus' arrest, as well as his
trial before a Jewish court.
□ Day 15. Read chapters 15
and 16, which report the last
events in Jesus' life on earth.
Now turn to page xi for your
next Track 2 reading project.

■ TRACK 3:
All of Mark in 15 Days
After you have read through
Mark, turn to pages xii–xiii for
your next Track 3 reading
project.

□ 1	□ 2	□ 3	□ 4
□ 5	□ 6	□ 7	□ 8
□ 9	□ 10	□ 11	□ 12
□ 13	□ 14	□ 15–16	

■ John the Baptist Prepares the Way
□ See Matthew 3:1–11; Luke 3:2–16

1 The beginning of the gospel about Jesus Christ,
the Son of God.*a*

²It is written in Isaiah the prophet:

"I will send my messenger ahead of you,
    who will prepare your way"*b* —
³"a voice of one calling in the desert,
'Prepare the way for the Lord,
    make straight paths for him.' "*c*

⁴And so John came, baptising in the desert region
and preaching a baptism of repentance for the forgiveness of sins. ⁵The whole Judean countryside and
all the people of Jerusalem went out to him. Confessing their sins, they were baptised by him in the
Jordan River. ⁶John wore clothing made of camel's
hair, with a leather belt round his waist, and he ate
locusts and wild honey. ⁷And this was his message:
"After me will come one more powerful than I, the
thongs of whose sandals I am not worthy to stoop
down and untie. ⁸I baptise you with*d* water, but he
will baptise you with the Holy Spirit."

■ The Baptism and Temptation of Jesus
□ See Matthew 3:13–17; 4:1–11; Luke 3:21–22; 4:1–13
⁹At that time Jesus came from Nazareth in Galilee

and was baptised by John in the Jordan. ¹⁰As Jesus
was coming up out of the water, he saw heaven being torn open and the Spirit descending on him like
a dove. ¹¹And a voice came from heaven: "You
are my Son, whom I love; with you I am well
pleased."

¹²At once the Spirit sent him out into the desert,
¹³and he was in the desert for forty days, being
tempted by Satan. He was with the wild animals, and
angels attended him.

■ The Calling of the First Disciples
□ See Matthew 4:18–22; Luke 5:2–11; John 1:35–42
¹⁴After John was put in prison, Jesus went into
Galilee, proclaiming the good news of God. ¹⁵"The
time has come," he said. "The kingdom of God is
near. Repent and believe the good news!"

¹⁶As Jesus walked beside the Sea of Galilee, he
saw Simon and his brother Andrew casting a net
into the lake, for they were fishermen. ¹⁷"Come, follow me," Jesus said, "and I will make you fishers of
men." ¹⁸At once they left their nets and followed
him.

¹⁹When he had gone a little farther, he saw James
son of Zebedee and his brother John in a boat, preparing their nets. ²⁰Without delay he called them,
and they left their father Zebedee in the boat with
the hired men and followed him.

a1 Some manuscripts do not have *the Son of God*.   *b2* Mal. 3:1   *c3* Isaiah 40:3   *d8* Or *in*

■ Jesus Drives Out an Evil Spirit
☐ See Luke 4:31–37

²¹They went to Capernaum, and when the Sabbath came, Jesus went into the synagogue and began to teach. ²²The people were amazed at his teaching, because he taught them as one who had authority, not as the teachers of the law. ²³Just then a man in their synagogue who was possessed by an evil*e* spirit cried out, ²⁴"What do you want with us, Jesus of Nazareth? Have you come to destroy us? I know who you are—the Holy One of God!"

1:14 ■ INTO THE COUNTRYSIDE
Possibly, Jesus withdrew to Galilee in order to escape the political turmoil spawned by John's arrest. He went on to spend almost two-thirds of his working life in this rather remote northern region, the lushest and most picturesque part of Palestine. Except for festival times when he travelled to Jerusalem, Jesus showed a marked preference for rural and small-town areas.

²⁵"Be quiet!" said Jesus sternly. "Come out of him!" ²⁶The evil spirit shook the man violently and came out of him with a shriek.

²⁷The people were all so amazed that they asked each other, "What is this? A new teaching—and with authority! He even gives orders to evil spirits and they obey him." ²⁸News about him spread quickly over the whole region of Galilee.

■ Jesus Heals Many
☐ See Matthew 8:14–17; Luke 4:38–41

²⁹As soon as they left the synagogue, they went with James and John to the home of Simon and Andrew. ³⁰Simon's mother-in-law was in bed with a fever, and they told Jesus about her. ³¹So he went to her, took her hand and helped her up. The fever left her and she began to wait on them.

³²That evening after sunset the people brought to Jesus all the sick and demon-possessed. ³³The whole town gathered at the door, ³⁴and Jesus healed many who had various diseases. He also drove out many demons, but he would not let the demons speak because they knew who he was.

■ Jesus Prays in a Solitary Place
☐ See Luke 4:42–43

³⁵Very early in the morning, while it was still dark, Jesus got up, left the house and went off to a solitary place, where he prayed. ³⁶Simon and his companions went to look for him, ³⁷and when they found him, they exclaimed: "Everyone is looking for you!"

³⁸Jesus replied, "Let us go somewhere else—to the nearby villages—so that I can preach there also. That is why I have come." ³⁹So he travelled throughout Galilee, preaching in their synagogues and driving out demons.

■ A Man With Leprosy
☐ See Matthew 8:2–4; Luke 5:12–14

⁴⁰A man with leprosy*f* came to him and begged him on his knees, "If you are willing, you can make me clean."

⁴¹Filled with compassion, Jesus reached out his hand and touched the man. "I am willing," he said. "Be clean!" ⁴²Immediately the leprosy left him and he was cured.

⁴³Jesus sent him away at once with a strong warning: ⁴⁴"See that you don't tell this to anyone. But go, show yourself to the priest and offer the sacrifices that Moses commanded for your cleansing, as a testimony to them." ⁴⁵Instead he went out and began to talk freely, spreading the news. As a result, Jesus could no longer enter a town openly but stayed outside in lonely places. Yet the people still came to him from everywhere.

■ Jesus Heals a Paralytic
☐ See Matthew 9:2–8; Luke 5:18–26

2 A few days later, when Jesus again entered Capernaum, the people heard that he had come home. ²So many gathered that there was no room left, not even outside the door, and he preached the word to them. ³Some men came, bringing to him a paralytic, carried by four of them. ⁴Since they could not get him to Jesus because of the crowd, they made an opening in the roof above Jesus and, after digging through it, lowered the mat the paralysed man was lying on. ⁵When Jesus saw their faith, he said to the paralytic, "Son, your sins are forgiven."

2:4 ■ BARRIERS TO THE DISABLED
One disabled person has pointed out this story's relevance to the modern controversy over accessibility. "Any disabled person can supply lots of stories like this one—entering a church through the sacristy (or, worse, having to be carried up the front steps like a child), coming into a lecture hall by means of a goods lift and then through the kitchen or utility room before being able to join the 'normal' people who come in the front door." The paralytic's friends found a rather drastic solution to the problem, and Jesus, impressed, honoured their (plural) faith.

⁶Now some teachers of the law were sitting there, thinking to themselves, ⁷"Why does this fellow talk like that? He's blaspheming! Who can forgive sins but God alone?"

⁸Immediately Jesus knew in his spirit that this was what they were thinking in their hearts, and he said to them, "Why are you thinking these things? ⁹Which is easier: to say to the paralytic, 'Your sins are forgiven,' or to say, 'Get up, take your mat and walk'? ¹⁰But that you may know that the Son of Man has authority on earth to forgive sins . . . ." He said to the paralytic, ¹¹"I tell you, get up, take your mat and go home." ¹²He got up, took his mat and walked out in full view of them all. This amazed everyone and they praised God, saying, "We have never seen anything like this!"

---

e 23 Greek *unclean*; also in verses 26 and 27   *f 40* The Greek word was used for various diseases affecting the skin—not necessarily leprosy.

■ The Calling of Levi
☐ See Matthew 9:9–13; Luke 5:27–32

¹³Once again Jesus went out beside the lake. A large crowd came to him, and he began to teach them. ¹⁴As he walked along, he saw Levi son of Alphaeus sitting at the tax collector's booth. "Follow me," Jesus told him, and Levi got up and followed him.

¹⁵While Jesus was having dinner at Levi's house, many tax collectors and "sinners" were eating with him and his disciples, for there were many who followed him. ¹⁶When the teachers of the law who were Pharisees saw him eating with the "sinners" and tax collectors, they asked his disciples: "Why does he eat with tax collectors and 'sinners'?"

¹⁷On hearing this, Jesus said to them, "It is not the healthy who need a doctor, but the sick. I have not come to call the righteous, but sinners."

■ Jesus Questioned About Fasting
☐ See Matthew 9:14–17; Luke 5:33–38

¹⁸Now John's disciples and the Pharisees were fasting. Some people came and asked Jesus, "How is it that John's disciples and the disciples of the Pharisees are fasting, but yours are not?"

¹⁹Jesus answered, "How can the guests of the bridegroom fast while he is with them? They cannot, so long as they have him with them. ²⁰But the time will come when the bridegroom will be taken from them, and on that day they will fast.

²¹"No-one sews a patch of unshrunk cloth on an old garment. If he does, the new piece will pull away from the old, making the tear worse. ²²And no-one pours new wine into old wineskins. If he does, the wine will burst the skins, and both the wine and the wineskins will be ruined. No, he pours new wine into new wineskins."

■ Lord of the Sabbath
☐ See Matthew 12:1–14; Luke 6:1–11

²³One Sabbath Jesus was going through the cornfields, and as his disciples walked along, they began to pick some ears of corn. ²⁴The Pharisees said to him, "Look, why are they doing what is unlawful on the Sabbath?"

²⁵He answered, "Have you never read what David did when he and his companions were hungry and in need? ²⁶In the days of Abiathar the high priest, he entered the house of God and ate the consecrated bread, which is lawful only for priests to eat. And he also gave some to his companions."

²⁷Then he said to them, "The Sabbath was made for man, not man for the Sabbath. ²⁸So the Son of Man is Lord even of the Sabbath."

3 Another time he went into the synagogue, and a man with a shrivelled hand was there. ²Some of them were looking for a reason to accuse Jesus, so they watched him closely to see if he would heal him on the Sabbath. ³Jesus said to the man with the shrivelled hand, "Stand up in front of everyone."

⁴Then Jesus asked them, "Which is lawful on the Sabbath: to do good or to do evil, to save life or to kill?" But they remained silent.

⁵He looked round at them in anger and, deeply distressed at their stubborn hearts, said to the man,

"Stretch out your hand." He stretched it out, and his hand was completely restored. ⁶Then the Pharisees went out and began to plot with the Herodians how they might kill Jesus.

■ Crowds Follow Jesus
☐ See Matthew 12:15–16; Luke 6:17–19

⁷Jesus withdrew with his disciples to the lake, and a large crowd from Galilee followed. ⁸When they heard all he was doing, many people came to him from Judea, Jerusalem, Idumea, and the regions across the Jordan and around Tyre and Sidon. ⁹Because of the crowd he told his disciples to have a small boat ready for him, to keep the people from crowding him. ¹⁰For he had healed many, so that those with diseases were pushing forward to touch him. ¹¹Whenever the evilᵃ spirits saw him, they fell down before him and cried out, "You are the Son of God." ¹²But he gave them strict orders not to tell who he was.

■ The Appointing of the Twelve Apostles

¹³Jesus went up on a mountainside and called to him those he wanted, and they came to him. ¹⁴He appointed twelve—designating them apostlesᵇ—that they might be with him and that he might send them out to preach ¹⁵and to have authority to drive out demons. ¹⁶These are the twelve he appointed: Simon (to whom he gave the name Peter); ¹⁷James son of Zebedee and his brother John (to them he gave the name Boanerges, which means Sons of Thunder); ¹⁸Andrew, Philip, Bartholomew, Matthew, Thomas, James son of Alphaeus, Thaddaeus, Simon the Zealot ¹⁹and Judas Iscariot, who betrayed him.

■ Jesus and Beelzebub
☐ See Matthew 12:25–29; Luke 11:17–22

²⁰Then Jesus entered a house, and again a crowd gathered, so that he and his disciples were not even able to eat. ²¹When his family heard about this, they went to take charge of him, for they said, "He is out of his mind."

²²And the teachers of the law who came down from Jerusalem said, "He is possessed by Beelzebub!ᶜ By the prince of demons he is driving out demons."

²³So Jesus called them and spoke to them in parables: "How can Satan drive out Satan? ²⁴If a kingdom is divided against itself, that kingdom cannot stand. ²⁵If a house is divided against itself, that house cannot stand. ²⁶And if Satan opposes himself and is divided, he cannot stand; his end has come. ²⁷In fact, no-one can enter a strong man's house and carry off his possessions unless he first ties up the strong man. Then he can rob his house. ²⁸I tell you the truth, all the sins and blasphemies of men will be forgiven them. ²⁹But whoever blasphemes against the Holy Spirit will never be forgiven; he is guilty of an eternal sin."

³⁰He said this because they were saying, "He has an evil spirit."

ᵃ 11 Greek *unclean*; also in verse 30   ᵇ 14 Some manuscripts do not have *designating them apostles*.   ᶜ 22 Greek *Beezeboul* or *Beelzeboul*

■ Jesus' Mother and Brothers
□ See Matthew 12:46–50; Luke 8:19–21

³¹Then Jesus' mother and brothers arrived. Standing outside, they sent someone in to call him. ³²A crowd was sitting around him, and they told him, "Your mother and brothers are outside looking for you."

3:30 ■ OUT OF HIS MIND?

Jesus provoked a strong reaction in just about everyone. In this instance, Jesus' own family members questioned his sanity, and teachers of the law wondered about demon-possession. He aroused the fiercest opposition among his own neighbours and among the religious "professionals" of his day. But, as Mark shows, throngs of other people were amazed by his authoritative teaching and his miraculous powers. Personal contact with Jesus left virtually no-one unmoved.

³³"Who are my mother and my brothers?" he asked.

³⁴Then he looked at those seated in a circle around him and said, "Here are my mother and my brothers! ³⁵Whoever does God's will is my brother and sister and mother."

■ The Parable of the Sower
□ See Matthew 13:1–15,18–23; Luke 8:4–15

4 Again Jesus began to teach by the lake. The crowd that gathered round him was so large that he got into a boat and sat in it out on the lake, while all the people were along the shore at the water's edge. ²He taught them many things by parables, and in his teaching said: ³"Listen! A farmer went out to sow his seed. ⁴As he was scattering the seed, some fell along the path, and the birds came and ate it up. ⁵Some fell on rocky places, where it did not have much soil. It sprang up quickly, because the soil was shallow. ⁶But when the sun came up, the plants were scorched, and they withered because they had no root. ⁷Other seed fell among thorns, which grew up and choked the plants, so that they did not bear grain. ⁸Still other seed fell on good soil. It came up, grew and produced a crop, multiplying thirty, sixty, or even a hundred times."

⁹Then Jesus said, "He who has ears to hear, let him hear."

¹⁰When he was alone, the Twelve and the others around him asked him about the parables. ¹¹He told them, "The secret of the kingdom of God has been given to you. But to those on the outside everything is said in parables ¹²so that,

" 'they may be ever seeing but never
        perceiving,
   and ever hearing but never understanding;
otherwise they might turn and be forgiven!'ᵃ"

¹³Then Jesus said to them, "Don't you understand this parable? How then will you understand any parable? ¹⁴The farmer sows the word. ¹⁵Some people are like seed along the path, where the word is

sown. As soon as they hear it, Satan comes and takes away the word that was sown in them. ¹⁶Others, like seed sown on rocky places, hear the word and at once receive it with joy. ¹⁷But since they have no root, they last only a short time. When trouble or persecution comes because of the word, they quickly fall away. ¹⁸Still others, like seed sown among thorns, hear the word; ¹⁹but the worries of this life, the deceitfulness of wealth and the desires for other things come in and choke the word, making it unfruitful. ²⁰Others, like seed sown on good soil, hear the word, accept it, and produce a crop—thirty, sixty or even a hundred times what was sown."

■ A Lamp on a Stand

²¹He said to them, "Do you bring in a lamp to put it under a bowl or a bed? Instead, don't you put it on its stand? ²²For whatever is hidden is meant to be disclosed, and whatever is concealed is meant to be brought out into the open. ²³If anyone has ears to hear, let him hear."

²⁴"Consider carefully what you hear," he continued. "With the measure you use, it will be measured to you—and even more. ²⁵Whoever has will be given more; whoever does not have, even what he has will be taken from him."

■ The Parable of the Growing Seed

²⁶He also said, "This is what the kingdom of God is like. A man scatters seed on the ground. ²⁷Night and day, whether he sleeps or gets up, the seed sprouts and grows, though he does not know how. ²⁸All by itself the soil produces corn—first the stalk, then the ear, then the full grain in the ear. ²⁹As soon as the grain is ripe, he puts the sickle to it, because the harvest has come."

■ The Parable of the Mustard Seed
□ See Matthew 13:31–32; Luke 13:18–19

³⁰Again he said, "What shall we say the kingdom of God is like, or what parable shall we use to describe it? ³¹It is like a mustard seed, which is the smallest seed you plant in the ground. ³²Yet when planted, it grows and becomes the largest of all garden plants, with such big branches that the birds of the air can perch in its shade."

4:30 ■ SCARCE PARABLES

Unlike Matthew and Luke, Mark devotes little space to parables, the unique form of teaching Jesus often relied on. Yet Mark includes as many miracles as does any Gospel. Clearly, this book emphasises action over words.

³³With many similar parables Jesus spoke the word to them, as much as they could understand. ³⁴He did not say anything to them without using a parable. But when he was alone with his own disciples, he explained everything.

ᵃ12 Isaiah 6:9,10

■ Jesus Calms the Storm
☐ See Matthew 8:18,23–27; Luke 8:22–25

³⁵That day when evening came, he said to his disciples, "Let us go over to the other side." ³⁶Leaving the crowd behind, they took him along, just as he was, in the boat. There were also other boats with him. ³⁷A furious squall came up, and the waves broke over the boat, so that it was nearly swamped. ³⁸Jesus was in the stern, sleeping on a cushion. The disciples woke him and said to him, "Teacher, don't you care if we drown?"

³⁹He got up, rebuked the wind and said to the waves, "Quiet! Be still!" Then the wind died down and it was completely calm.

⁴⁰He said to his disciples, "Why are you so afraid? Do you still have no faith?"

⁴¹They were terrified and asked each other, "Who is this? Even the wind and the waves obey him!"

INSIGHT

WHY COME TO EARTH?
THE ONLY WAY GOD COULD GET THROUGH

THEY WERE TERRIFIED AND ASKED EACH OTHER, "WHO IS THIS? EVEN THE WIND AND THE WAVES OBEY HIM!" ■ 4:41

American radio broadcaster Paul Harvey once told a modern parable about a religious sceptic who worked as a farmer. One raw winter night the man heard an irregular thumping sound against the kitchen door. He went to a window and watched as tiny, shivering sparrows, attracted to the evident warmth inside, beat in vain against the glass.

Touched, the farmer bundled himself up and trudged through fresh snow to open the barn door for the struggling birds. He turned on the lights and tossed some hay in a corner. But the sparrows, which had scattered in all directions when he emerged from the house, hid in the darkness, afraid.

The man tried various tactics to get them into the barn. He laid down a trail of cheese biscuit crumbs to direct them. He tried circling behind the birds to drive them towards the barn. Nothing worked. He, a huge, alien creature, had terrified them; the birds couldn't comprehend that he actually desired to help.

The farmer withdrew to his house and watched the doomed sparrows through a window. As he stared, a thought hit him like lightning from a clear blue sky: *If only I could become a bird – one of them – just for a moment. Then I wouldn't frighten them so. I could show them the way to warmth and safety.*

At the same moment, another thought dawned on him. He had grasped the reason Jesus was born.

■ WHEN GOD CAME TO EARTH
A man becoming a bird is nothing compared to God becoming a man. The concept of a sovereign eternal being who created the universe, confining himself to a human body was – and is – too much for some people to believe. But how else could God truly communicate with us?

We don't know what God looked like as a man; no Gospel writer described the physical appearance of Jesus. But, in other ways, Mark painted a full picture of his humanity. Jesus, who claimed to be God, didn't have a supernatural "glow" about him. His own neighbours and family marvelled that he seemed so, well, normal.

Mark does not diminish Jesus. He shows the power of a man who healed the blind with a simple touch (8:25), and the authority of a teacher so captivating that people sat three days in a row, with empty stomachs, just to hear him (8:2). Even after Jesus hushed them, people wouldn't stop talking about his miracles.

But Mark also reveals the full range of Jesus' emotions: a surge of compassion for a person with leprosy (1:41), a deep sigh in response to nagging Pharisees (8:12), a look of anger and distress at cold-hearted legalists (3:5), and then an awful cry on the cross, "My God, my God, why have you forsaken me?" (15:34). Jesus was sometimes witty, and he sometimes cried. He got tired: five times, Mark records, he sought a quiet place for rest away from the crowds.

■ LIKE NO ONE ELSE
Jesus was like no other person who ever lived. Twelve men left their jobs and families at a single command to follow him. Yet Jesus was also fully "one of us". He needed food and friends. He got lonely and tired. He showed anger and disappointment. Because Jesus experienced all we experience as human beings, he can understand us completely, and share in our joys and sorrows.

Mark portrays both sides of Jesus – the divine and the human. The disciples needed to see both dimensions to give their lives to him.

☐ LIFE QUESTIONS:
Suppose that Jesus had never come, that God had merely sent an elaborate love letter. What difference would that make?

■ The Healing of a Demon-possessed Man
□ See Matthew 8:28–34; Luke 8:26–39

5 They went across the lake to the region of the Gerasenes.*a* 2When Jesus got out of the boat, a man with an evil*b* spirit came from the tombs to meet him. 3This man lived in the tombs, and no-one could bind him any more, not even with a chain. 4For he had often been chained hand and foot, but he tore the chains apart and broke the irons on his feet. No-one was strong enough to subdue him. 5Night and day among the tombs and in the hills he would cry out and cut himself with stones.

6When he saw Jesus from a distance, he ran and fell on his knees in front of him. 7He shouted at the top of his voice, "What do you want with me, Jesus, Son of the Most High God? Swear to God that you won't torture me!" 8For Jesus had said to him, "Come out of this man, you evil spirit!"

9Then Jesus asked him, "What is your name?"

"My name is Legion," he replied, "for we are many." 10And he begged Jesus again and again not to send them out of the area.

11A large herd of pigs was feeding on the nearby hillside. 12The demons begged Jesus, "Send us among the pigs; allow us to go into them." 13He gave them permission, and the evil spirits came out and went into the pigs. The herd, about two thousand in number, rushed down the steep bank into the lake and were drowned.

14Those tending the pigs ran off and reported this in the town and countryside, and the people went out to see what had happened. 15When they came to Jesus, they saw the man who had been possessed by the legion of demons, sitting there, dressed and in his right mind; and they were afraid. 16Those who had seen it told the people what had happened to the demon-possessed man — and told about the pigs as well. 17Then the people began to plead with Jesus to leave their region.

18As Jesus was getting into the boat, the man who had been demon-possessed begged to go with him. 19Jesus did not let him, but said, "Go home to your family and tell them how much the Lord has done for you, and how he has had mercy on you." 20So the man went away and began to tell in the Decapolis*c* how much Jesus had done for him. And all the people were amazed.

■ A Dead Girl and a Sick Woman
□ See Matthew 9:18–26; Luke 8:41–56

21When Jesus had again crossed over by boat to the other side of the lake, a large crowd gathered round him while he was by the lake. 22Then one of the synagogue rulers, named Jairus, came there. Seeing Jesus, he fell at his feet 23and pleaded earnestly with him, "My little daughter is dying. Please come and put your hands on her so that she will be healed and live." 24So Jesus went with him.

A large crowd followed and pressed around him. 25And a woman was there who had been subject to bleeding for twelve years. 26She had suffered a great deal under the care of many doctors and had spent all she had, yet instead of getting better she grew worse. 27When she heard about Jesus, she came up behind him in the crowd and touched his cloak, 28because she thought, "If I just touch his clothes, I will be healed." 29Immediately her bleeding stopped and she felt in her body that she was freed from her suffering.

30At once Jesus realised that power had gone out from him. He turned around in the crowd and asked, "Who touched my clothes?"

31"You see the people crowding against you," his disciples answered, "and yet you can ask, 'Who touched me?' "

32But Jesus kept looking around to see who had done it. 33Then the woman, knowing what had happened to her, came and fell at his feet and, trembling with fear, told him the whole truth. 34He said to her, "Daughter, your faith has healed you. Go in peace and be freed from your suffering."

35While Jesus was still speaking, some men came from the house of Jairus, the synagogue ruler. "Your daughter is dead," they said. "Why bother the teacher any more?"

36Ignoring what they said, Jesus told the synagogue ruler, "Don't be afraid; just believe."

37He did not let anyone follow him except Peter, James and John the brother of James. 38When they came to the home of the synagogue ruler, Jesus saw a commotion, with people crying and wailing loudly. 39He went in and said to them, "Why all this commotion and wailing? The child is not dead but asleep." 40But they laughed at him.

After he put them all out, he took the child's father and mother and the disciples who were with him, and went in where the child was. 41He took her by the hand and said to her, *"Talitha koum!"* (which means, "Little girl, I say to you, get up!"). 42Immediately the girl stood up and walked around (she was twelve years old). At this they were completely astonished. 43He gave strict orders not to let anyone know about this, and told them to give her something to eat.

5:43 ■ DON'T TELL
Seven times in Mark, Jesus asked people who had seen a miracle not to tell anyone. He was protecting himself from the crush of crowds that flocked to him when word of his miracles spread — as it usually did, despite his orders — and from the opposition forces who were already tailing him. Jesus soon recognised that the kind of excitement generated by miracles did not automatically convert into the life-changing faith he sought to arouse.

■ A Prophet Without Honour
□ See Matthew 13:54–58

6 Jesus left there and went to his home town, accompanied by his disciples. 2When the Sabbath came, he began to teach in the synagogue, and many who heard him were amazed.

"Where did this man get these things?" they asked. "What's this wisdom that has been given him,

---

a 1 Some manuscripts *Gadarenes*; other manuscripts *Gergesenes*   *b 2* Greek *unclean*; also in verses 8 and 13   *c 20* That is, the Ten Cities that he even does miracles! ³Isn't this the carpenter? Isn't this Mary's son and the brother of James, Joseph,ᵃ Judas and Simon? Aren't his sisters here with us?" And they took offence at him.

⁴Jesus said to them, "Only in his home town, among his relatives and in his own house is a prophet without honour." ⁵He could not do any miracles there, except lay his hands on a few sick people and heal them. ⁶And he was amazed at their lack of faith.

■ Jesus Sends Out the Twelve
☐ See Matthew 10:1,9–14; Luke 9:1,3–5

Then Jesus went round teaching from village to village. ⁷Calling the Twelve to him, he sent them out two by two and gave them authority over evilᵇ spirits.

⁸These were his instructions: "Take nothing for the journey except a staff—no bread, no bag, no money in your belts. ⁹Wear sandals but not an extra tunic. ¹⁰Whenever you enter a house, stay there until you leave that town. ¹¹And if any place will not welcome you or listen to you, shake the dust off your feet when you leave, as a testimony against them."

¹²They went out and preached that people should repent. ¹³They drove out many demons and anointed many sick people with oil and healed them.

■ John the Baptist Beheaded
☐ See Matthew 14:1–12

¹⁴King Herod heard about this, for Jesus' name had become well known. Some were saying,ᶜ "John the Baptist has been raised from the dead, and that is why miraculous powers are at work in him."

¹⁵Others said, "He is Elijah."

And still others claimed, "He is a prophet, like one of the prophets of long ago."

¹⁶But when Herod heard this, he said, "John, the man I beheaded, has been raised from the dead!"

¹⁷For Herod himself had given orders to have John arrested, and he had him bound and put in prison. He did this because of Herodias, his brother Philip's wife, whom he had married. ¹⁸For John had been saying to Herod, "It is not lawful for you to have your brother's wife." ¹⁹So Herodias nursed a grudge against John and wanted to kill him. But she was not able to, ²⁰because Herod feared John and protected him, knowing him to be a righteous and

■ EYEWITNESS REPORTS
WHERE DID MARK GET HIS FACTS?

INSIGHT

HE DID NOT LET ANYONE FOLLOW HIM EXCEPT PETER, JAMES AND JOHN THE BROTHER OF JAMES. ■ 5:37

When people translate the Bible into a new language, they have a lot of explaining to do. How do you convey Christianity to someone who has never heard of Abraham or Moses or the apostles Peter and Paul? Where do you start?

More often than not, translators begin with the book of Mark. Its simple sentences and brief, action-filled scenes allow for easier translation. It reads like a newspaper. And the book seems written for a foreign culture (perhaps the Romans) in the first place: common Jewish customs are explained in parentheses.

■ THE PETER CONNECTION
Perhaps the most compelling feature of Mark to an unfamiliar reader, though, is its vividness. It has the feel of an eyewitness account. Those who study such things have concluded that Mark probably got his facts from Peter, one of Jesus' intimate disciples. Peter, or someone like him, provided believable, close-up details.

Jesus spent his time in the desert "with the wild animals" (1:13). When he went to pray, he got up "very early in the morning, while it was still dark" (1:35)—a memorable detail to Jesus' disciples, sometimes known for their

untimely sleeping habits. In the midst of a furious squall Jesus lay in a boat "sleeping on a cushion" (4:38).

Whoever told Mark about the scene on the Mount of Transfiguration described Jesus' clothes as "dazzling white, whiter than anyone in the world could bleach them" (9:3). And only Mark tells us that Peter sat with the guards during Jesus' trial, warming himself by the fire.

■ WHY DETAILS MATTER
You can say these details don't matter, and it's true that Matthew and Luke recounted the same events without them. But as any good writer knows, details like these make a story come alive. Vivid images that stuck in the eyewitness' memory will probably stick with the reader as well.

For example, Mark could have matter-of-factly told of people being healed, but it just didn't happen that way. A blind man, "throwing his cloak aside . . . jumped to his feet and came to Jesus" (10:50). And after the paralytic stood up, "This amazed everyone and they praised God, saying, 'We have never seen anything like this!' " (2:12).

☐ LIFE QUESTIONS:
As you read Mark, what "eyewitness details" stand out to you?

ᵃ3 Greek *Joses*, a variant of *Joseph*   ᵇ7 Greek *unclean*   ᶜ14 Some early manuscripts *He was saying* holy man. When Herod heard John, he was greatly puzzled;*d* yet he liked to listen to him.

21Finally the opportune time came. On his birthday Herod gave a banquet for his high officials and military commanders and the leading men of Galilee. 22When the daughter of Herodias came in and danced, she pleased Herod and his dinner guests.

The king said to the girl, "Ask me for anything you want, and I'll give it to you." 23And he promised her with an oath, "Whatever you ask I will give you, up to half my kingdom."

24She went out and said to her mother, "What shall I ask for?"

"The head of John the Baptist," she answered.

25At once the girl hurried in to the king with the request: "I want you to give me right now the head of John the Baptist on a platter."

26The king was greatly distressed, but because of his oaths and his dinner guests, he did not want to refuse her. 27So he immediately sent an executioner with orders to bring John's head. The man went, beheaded John in the prison, 28and brought back his head on a platter. He presented it to the girl, and she gave it to her mother. 29On hearing of this, John's disciples came and took his body and laid it in a tomb.

6:29 ■ NEW RECRUITS
Jesus got some of his original disciples from John the Baptist (see John 1:35,40), and after John's execution even more of them joined up with Jesus. But as Acts 19:1–5 makes clear, some of John's disciples never heard the word about Jesus. Two decades after John's death, Paul stumbled across a group of loyal followers in Ephesus, hundreds of miles away.

■ Jesus Feeds the Five Thousand
□ See Matthew 14:13–21; Luke 9:10–17; John 6:5–13

30The apostles gathered round Jesus and reported to him all they had done and taught. 31Then, because so many people were coming and going that they did not even have a chance to eat, he said to them, "Come with me by yourselves to a quiet place and get some rest."

6:31 ■ THE NEED TO GET AWAY
Mark graphically shows the press of the crowds around Jesus. Wherever he went, people followed, bringing him the sick to heal and challenging him with questions. In five separate places (3:7–9; 6:31; 6:45; 7:24; 9:30) Mark records that Jesus took his disciples aside to some quiet place, to escape the crush of the crowd.

32So they went away by themselves in a boat to a solitary place. 33But many who saw them leaving recognised them and ran on foot from all the towns and got there ahead of them. 34When Jesus landed and saw a large crowd, he had compassion on them,

because they were like sheep without a shepherd. So he began teaching them many things.

35By this time it was late in the day, so his disciples came to him. "This is a remote place," they said, "and it's already very late. 36Send the people away so that they can go to the surrounding countryside and villages and buy themselves something to eat."

37But he answered, "You give them something to eat."

They said to him, "That would take eight months of a man's wages!*e* Are we to go and spend that much on bread and give it to them to eat?"

38"How many loaves do you have?" he asked. "Go and see."

When they found out, they said, "Five—and two fish."

39Then Jesus directed them to have all the people sit down in groups on the green grass. 40So they sat down in groups of hundreds and fifties. 41Taking the five loaves and the two fish and looking up to heaven, he gave thanks and broke the loaves. Then he gave them to his disciples to set before the people. He also divided the two fish among them all. 42They all ate and were satisfied, 43and the disciples picked up twelve basketfuls of broken pieces of bread and fish. 44The number of the men who had eaten was five thousand.

■ Jesus Walks on the Water
□ See Matthew 14:22–32; John 6:15–21

45Immediately Jesus made his disciples get into the boat and go on ahead of him to Bethsaida, while he dismissed the crowd. 46After leaving them, he went up on a mountainside to pray.

47When evening came, the boat was in the middle of the lake, and he was alone on land. 48He saw the disciples straining at the oars, because the wind was against them. About the fourth watch of the night he went out to them, walking on the lake. He was about to pass by them, 49but when they saw him walking on the lake, they thought he was a ghost. They cried out, 50because they all saw him and were terrified.

Immediately he spoke to them and said, "Take courage! It is I. Don't be afraid." 51Then he climbed into the boat with them, and the wind died down. They were completely amazed, 52for they had not understood about the loaves; their hearts were hardened.

53When they had crossed over, they landed at Gennesaret and anchored there. 54As soon as they got out of the boat, people recognised Jesus. 55They ran throughout that whole region and carried the sick on mats to wherever they heard he was. 56And wherever he went—into villages, towns or countryside—they placed the sick in the market-places. They begged him to let them touch even the edge of his cloak, and all who touched him were healed.

■ Clean and Unclean
□ See Matthew 15:1–20

7 The Pharisees and some of the teachers of the law who had come from Jerusalem gathered round Jesus and 2saw some of his disciples eating

---

d 20 Some early manuscripts he did many things   e 37 Greek take two hundred denarii food with hands that were "unclean", that is, un-washed. ³(The Pharisees and all the Jews do not eat unless they give their hands a ceremonial washing, holding to the tradition of the elders. ⁴When they come from the market-place they do not eat unless they wash. And they observe many other traditions, such as the washing of cups, pitchers and kettles.ᵃ)

7:3 ■ EXPLAINING JEWISH CUSTOMS
The parenthetical remark in verses 3–4 explains a common Jewish custom of ceremonial hand-washing. Such remarks as these indicate that Mark was writing to a non-Jewish audience who needed background explanations.

⁵So the Pharisees and teachers of the law asked Jesus, "Why don't your disciples live according to the tradition of the elders instead of eating their food with 'unclean' hands?"

⁶He replied, "Isaiah was right when he proph-esied about you hypocrites; as it is written:

" 'These people honour me with their lips,
    but their hearts are far from me.
⁷They worship me in vain;
    their teachings are but rules taught by
        men.'ᵇ

⁸You have let go of the commands of God and are holding on to the traditions of men."

⁹And he said to them: "You have a fine way of set-ting aside the commands of God in order to ob-serveᶜ your own traditions! ¹⁰For Moses said, 'Honour your father and your mother,'ᵈ and, 'Any-one who curses his father or mother must be put to death.'ᵉ ¹¹But you say that if a man says to his father or mother: 'Whatever help you might other-wise have received from me is Corban' (that is, a gift devoted to God), ¹²then you no longer let him do anything for his father or mother. ¹³Thus you nullify the word of God by your tradition that you have handed down. And you do many things like that."

¹⁴Again Jesus called the crowd to him and said, "Listen to me, everyone, and understand this. ¹⁵Nothing outside a man can make him 'unclean' by going into him. Rather, it is what comes out of a man that makes him 'unclean'."ᶠ

¹⁷After he had left the crowd and entered the house, his disciples asked him about this parable. ¹⁸"Are you so dull?" he asked. "Don't you see that nothing that enters a man from the outside can make him 'unclean'? ¹⁹For it doesn't go into his heart but into his stomach, and then out of his body." (In saying this, Jesus declared all foods "clean".)

²⁰He went on: "What comes out of a man is what makes him 'unclean'. ²¹For from within, out of men's hearts, come evil thoughts, sexual immoral-ity, theft, murder, adultery, ²²greed, malice, deceit, lewdness, envy, slander, arrogance and folly. ²³All these evils come from inside and make a man 'un-clean'."

■ The Faith of a Syro-Phoenician Woman
□ See Matthew 15:21–28

²⁴Jesus left that place and went to the vicinity of Tyre.ᵍ He entered a house and did not want any-one to know it; yet he could not keep his presence secret. ²⁵In fact, as soon as she heard about him, a woman whose little daughter was possessed by an evilᵇ spirit came and fell at his feet. ²⁶The woman was a Greek, born in Syrian Phoenicia. She begged Jesus to drive the demon out of her daughter.

²⁷"First let the children eat all they want," he told her, "for it is not right to take the children's bread and toss it to their dogs."

²⁸"Yes, Lord," she replied, "but even the dogs un-der the table eat the children's crumbs."

²⁹Then he told her, "For such a reply, you may go; the demon has left your daughter."

³⁰She went home and found her child lying on the bed, and the demon gone.

■ The Healing of a Deaf and Mute Man
□ See Matthew 15:29–31

³¹Then Jesus left the vicinity of Tyre and went through Sidon, down to the Sea of Galilee and into the region of the Decapolis.ⁱ ³²There some people brought to him a man who was deaf and could hardly talk, and they begged him to place his hand on the man.

³³After he took him aside, away from the crowd, Jesus put his fingers into the man's ears. Then he spat and touched the man's tongue. ³⁴He looked up to heaven and with a deep sigh said to him, "*Eph-phatha!*" (which means, "Be opened!"). ³⁵At this, the man's ears were opened, his tongue was loos-ened and he began to speak plainly.

³⁶Jesus commanded them not to tell anyone. But the more he did so, the more they kept talking about it. ³⁷People were overwhelmed with amazement. "He has done everything well," they said. "He even makes the deaf hear and the mute speak."

■ Jesus Feeds the Four Thousand
□ See Matthew 15:32–39

8 During those days another large crowd gath-ered. Since they had nothing to eat, Jesus called his disciples to him and said, ²"I have compassion for these people; they have already been with me three days and have nothing to eat. ³If I send them home hungry, they will collapse on the way, be-cause some of them have come a long distance."

⁴His disciples answered, "But where in this re-mote place can anyone get enough bread to feed them?"

⁵"How many loaves do you have?" Jesus asked. "Seven," they replied.

⁶He told the crowd to sit down on the ground. When he had taken the seven loaves and given thanks, he broke them and gave them to his dis-ciples to set before the people, and they did so. ⁷They had a few small fish as well; he gave thanks for them also and told the disciples to distribute them. ⁸The people ate and were satisfied. Afterwards the disciples picked up seven basketfuls of broken pieces that were left over. ⁹About four thousand

ᵃ4 Some early manuscripts *pitchers, kettles and dining couches*   ᵇ6,7 Isaiah 29:13   ᶜ9 Some manuscripts *set up*   ᵈ10 Exodus 20:12; Deut. 5:16
ᵉ10 Exodus 21:17; Lev. 20:9   ᶠ15 Some early manuscripts *'unclean'.* ¹⁶*If anyone has ears to hear, let him hear."*   ᵍ24 Many early manuscripts *Tyre and Sidon*   ᵇ25 Greek *unclean*   ⁱ31 That is, the Ten Cities

men were present. And having sent them away, [10]he got into the boat with his disciples and went to the region of Dalmanutha.

8:8 ■ LOST IN TRANSLATION

Often details get lost when a book is translated from one language to another. For example, the Greek word for the "baskets" used in the feeding of the 5,000 (6:43) is used for small, lunchbox-size baskets. In the feeding of the 4,000, leftovers filled seven *large* baskets; the same word describes the basket the apostle Paul would hide in to escape from Damascus (Acts 9:25).

---

[11]The Pharisees came and began to question Jesus. To test him, they asked him for a sign from heaven. [12]He sighed deeply and said, "Why does this generation ask for a miraculous sign? I tell you the truth, no sign will be given to it." [13]Then he left them, got back into the boat and crossed to the other side.

■ The Yeast of the Pharisees and Herod

[14]The disciples had forgotten to bring bread, except for one loaf they had with them in the boat. [15]"Be careful," Jesus warned them. "Watch out for the yeast of the Pharisees and that of Herod."

[16]They discussed this with one another and said, "It is because we have no bread."

[17]Aware of their discussion, Jesus asked them: "Why are you talking about having no bread? Do you still not see or understand? Are your hearts hardened? [18]Do you have eyes but fail to see, and ears but fail to hear? And don't you remember? [19]When I broke the five loaves for the five thousand, how many basketfuls of pieces did you pick up?"

"Twelve," they replied.

[20]"And when I broke the seven loaves for the four thousand, how many basketfuls of pieces did you pick up?"

They answered, "Seven."

[21]He said to them, "Do you still not understand?"

■ TRAINING THE 12 DISCIPLES
A MOST UNPROMISING GROUP OF RECRUITS

INSIGHT

"DO YOU HAVE EYES BUT FAIL TO SEE, AND EARS BUT FAIL TO HEAR?" ■ 8:18

A skilled dramatist, Mark describes the crowd reactions to Jesus all through his account. He shows people astonished, confused, and upset by Jesus' actions. Always, twelve people, the disciples, linger in the background, working out the logistics of Jesus' ministry.

At first, the disciples did not distinguish themselves – to put it mildly. Their most obvious trait was denseness: "Are you so dull?" Jesus asked (7:18), and again, "How long shall I put up with you?" (9:19).

■ DENSE DISCIPLES

About halfway through the book of Mark (chapter 8), the focus shifts away from the crowds and on to the disciples. In spite of their erratic performance, Jesus devoted much of his time to them. Outsiders still gathered to watch and listen, but Jesus concentrated on training the Twelve, preparing them to carry on his work after his departure.

How did the disciples handle the increased attention? If anything, they proved even more inept. When Jesus referred to his coming death, they either missed the point or foolishly protested his plans. Sometimes they squabbled about who deserved the most favoured position. They obviously didn't understand the dazzling events going on around them. In short, the disciples amply

demonstrated the mixture of good and bad present in all of us.

Near the end of Mark, as events moved towards Jesus' death, the disciples grew more anxious and assertive. Jesus singled out two followers in particular, John and Peter, for his strongest reprimands. Ultimately, despite vigorous pronouncements of loyalty, each one of the Twelve sneaked quietly and ashamedly away from Jesus in his moment of deepest need.

■ A DECISIVE CHANGE

One event, however, dramatically altered them. Something passed through their lives like a flame: Jesus' resurrection from death. After that, Jesus' patient hours of training seemed to bear fruit at last.

The disciples' change in behaviour is astonishing. Of the proofs for the resurrection of Jesus, one of the most compelling is simply to compare these cowering disciples as portrayed in a Gospel like Mark with the bold, confident figures in the book of Acts. There, in a remarkable irony, we see the incredible advance of the early church being led by the two disciples with the thickest heads of all: John and Peter.

□ LIFE QUESTIONS:

Sometimes we think of the disciples as saints or heroes, but Mark shows their weak spots. What weak spots keep you from following Jesus as you might?

■ The Healing of a Blind Man at Bethsaida

²²They came to Bethsaida, and some people brought a blind man and begged Jesus to touch him. ²³He took the blind man by the hand and led him outside the village. When he had spat on the man's eyes and put his hands on him, Jesus asked, "Do you see anything?"

²⁴He looked up and said, "I see people; they look like trees walking around."

²⁵Once more Jesus put his hands on the man's eyes. Then his eyes were opened, his sight was restored, and he saw everything clearly. ²⁶Jesus sent him home, saying, "Don't go into the village."ᵃ

■ Peter's Confession of Christ
☐ See Matthew 16:13–16; Luke 9:18–20

²⁷Jesus and his disciples went on to the villages around Caesarea Philippi. On the way he asked them, "Who do people say I am?"

²⁸They replied, "Some say John the Baptist; others say Elijah; and still others, one of the prophets."

²⁹"But what about you?" he asked. "Who do you say I am?"

Peter answered, "You are the Christ."ᵇ

8:29 ■ PETER LEARNS HUMILITY

Most scholars believe that Mark got his eye-witness details from the disciple Peter. If so, the book reveals something about how Peter changed. Mark tells of three separate instances when Jesus rebuked Peter (see, for example, verse 33), but omits several compliments paid him. For example, compare this passage to a parallel account in Matthew 16:13–20, where Jesus commended Peter highly. Evidently, brash Peter learned a few lessons about humility along the way.

³⁰Jesus warned them not to tell anyone about him.

■ Jesus Predicts His Death
☐ See Matthew 16:21–28; Luke 9:22–27

³¹He then began to teach them that the Son of Man must suffer many things and be rejected by the elders, chief priests and teachers of the law, and that he must be killed and after three days rise again. ³²He spoke plainly about this, and Peter took him aside and began to rebuke him.

³³But when Jesus turned and looked at his disciples, he rebuked Peter. "Get behind me, Satan!" he said. "You do not have in mind the things of God, but the things of men."

³⁴Then he called the crowd to him along with his disciples and said: "If anyone would come after me, he must deny himself and take up his cross and follow me. ³⁵For whoever wants to save his lifeᶜ will lose it, but whoever loses his life for me and for the gospel will save it. ³⁶What good is it for a man to gain the whole world, yet forfeit his soul? ³⁷Or what can a man give in exchange for his soul? ³⁸If anyone is ashamed of me and my words in this adulterous

and sinful generation, the Son of Man will be ashamed of him when he comes in his Father's glory with the holy angels."

9 And he said to them, "I tell you the truth, some who are standing here will not taste death before they see the kingdom of God come with power."

■ The Transfiguration
☐ See Matthew 17:1–13; Luke 9:28–36

²After six days Jesus took Peter, James and John with him and led them up a high mountain, where they were all alone. There he was transfigured before them. ³His clothes became dazzling white, whiter than anyone in the world could bleach them. ⁴And there appeared before them Elijah and Moses, who were talking with Jesus.

⁵Peter said to Jesus, "Rabbi, it is good for us to be here. Let us put up three shelters—one for you, one for Moses and one for Elijah." ⁶(He did not know what to say, they were so frightened.)

⁷Then a cloud appeared and enveloped them, and a voice came from the cloud: "This is my Son, whom I love. Listen to him!"

⁸Suddenly, when they looked round, they no longer saw anyone with them except Jesus.

⁹As they were coming down the mountain, Jesus gave them orders not to tell anyone what they had seen until the Son of Man had risen from the dead. ¹⁰They kept the matter to themselves, discussing what "rising from the dead" meant.

¹¹And they asked him, "Why do the teachers of the law say that Elijah must come first?"

¹²Jesus replied, "To be sure, Elijah does come first, and restores all things. Why then is it written that the Son of Man must suffer much and be rejected? ¹³But I tell you, Elijah has come, and they have done to him everything they wished, just as it is written about him."

■ The Healing of a Boy With an Evil Spirit
☐ See Matthew 17:14–19,22–23; Luke 9:37–45

¹⁴When they came to the other disciples, they saw a large crowd around them and the teachers of the law arguing with them. ¹⁵As soon as all the people saw Jesus, they were overwhelmed with wonder and ran to greet him.

¹⁶"What are you arguing with them about?" he asked.

¹⁷A man in the crowd answered, "Teacher, I brought you my son, who is possessed by a spirit that has robbed him of speech. ¹⁸Whenever it seizes him, it throws him to the ground. He foams at the mouth, gnashes his teeth and becomes rigid. I asked your disciples to drive out the spirit, but they could not."

¹⁹"O unbelieving generation," Jesus replied, "how long shall I stay with you? How long shall I put up with you? Bring the boy to me."

²⁰So they brought him. When the spirit saw Jesus, it immediately threw the boy into a convulsion. He fell to the ground and rolled around, foaming at the mouth.

²¹Jesus asked the boy's father, "How long has he been like this?"

ᵃ26 Some manuscripts Don't go and tell anyone in the village   ᵇ29 Or Messiah. "The Christ" (Greek) and "the Messiah" (Hebrew) both mean "the Anointed One".   ᶜ35 The Greek word means either life or soul; also in verse 36.

"From childhood," he answered. 22"It has often thrown him into fire or water to kill him. But if you can do anything, take pity on us and help us."

23" 'If you can'?" said Jesus. "Everything is possible for him who believes."

24Immediately the boy's father exclaimed, "I do believe; help me overcome my unbelief!"

25When Jesus saw that a crowd was running to the scene, he rebuked the evil*a* spirit. "You deaf and mute spirit," he said, "I command you, come out of him and never enter him again."

26The spirit shrieked, convulsed him violently and came out. The boy looked so much like a corpse that many said, "He's dead." 27But Jesus took him by the hand and lifted him to his feet, and he stood up.

28After Jesus had gone indoors, his disciples asked him privately, "Why couldn't we drive it out?"

29He replied, "This kind can come out only by prayer."*b*

30They left that place and passed through Galilee. Jesus did not want anyone to know where they were, 31because he was teaching his disciples. He said to them, "The Son of Man is going to be betrayed into the hands of men. They will kill him, and after three days he will rise." 32But they did not understand what he meant and were afraid to ask him about it.

9:31 ■ BAFFLING THOUGHTS

At the height of his popularity, as throngs of people were following him, Jesus began to talk about his suffering and death. Such talk baffled his disciples, whose image of a Messiah included no such dark notions. (When reality finally hit, they would all desert him and flee [14:50].) Although Jesus made a point of mentioning his resurrection whenever he talked about his death, the disciples grasped neither concept — until he had died and then come back.

■ Who Is the Greatest?
□ See Matthew 18:1–5; Luke 9:46–48

33They came to Capernaum. When he was in the house, he asked them, "What were you arguing about on the road?" 34But they kept quiet because on the way they had argued about who was the greatest.

35Sitting down, Jesus called the Twelve and said, "If anyone wants to be first, he must be the very last, and the servant of all."

36He took a little child and had him stand among them. Taking him in his arms, he said to them, 37"Whoever welcomes one of these little children in my name welcomes me; and whoever welcomes me does not welcome me but the one who sent me."

■ Whoever Is Not Against Us Is for Us
□ See Luke 9:49–50

38"Teacher," said John, "we saw a man driving out demons in your name and we told him to stop, because he was not one of us."

39"Do not stop him," Jesus said. "No-one who

does a miracle in my name can in the next moment say anything bad about me, 40for whoever is not against us is for us. 41I tell you the truth, anyone who gives you a cup of water in my name because you belong to Christ will certainly not lose his reward.

■ Causing to Sin

42"And if anyone causes one of these little ones who believe in me to sin, it would be better for him to be thrown into the sea with a large millstone tied around his neck. 43If your hand causes you to sin, cut it off. It is better for you to enter life maimed than with two hands to go into hell, where the fire never goes out.*c* 45And if your foot causes you to sin, cut it off. It is better for you to enter life crippled than to have two feet and be thrown into hell.*d* 47And if your eye causes you to sin, pluck it out. It is better for you to enter the kingdom of God with one eye than to have two eyes and be thrown into hell, 48where

" 'their worm does not die,
    and the fire is not quenched.'*e*

49Everyone will be salted with fire.

50"Salt is good, but if it loses its saltiness, how can you make it salty again? Have salt in yourselves, and be at peace with each other."

■ Divorce
□ See Matthew 19:1–9

10 Jesus then left that place and went into the region of Judea and across the Jordan. Again crowds of people came to him, and as was his custom, he taught them.

2Some Pharisees came and tested him by asking, "Is it lawful for a man to divorce his wife?"

10:2 ■ TEACHING ON DIVORCE

The Pharisees tested Jesus with questions about common practices of divorce and remarriage. Jesus responded by pointing back to the origin of marriage at creation. His disciples were surprised by his strict views on divorce, and questioned him further in private. For other passages on this topic, see Matthew 19:1–12 and 1 Corinthians 7:1–16.

3"What did Moses command you?" he replied.

4They said, "Moses permitted a man to write a certificate of divorce and send her away."

5"It was because your hearts were hard that Moses wrote you this law," Jesus replied. 6"But at the beginning of creation God 'made them male and female'.*a* 7For this reason a man will leave his father and mother and be united to his wife,*b* 8and the two will become one flesh.'*c* So they are no longer two, but one. 9Therefore what God has joined together, let man not separate."

10When they were in the house again, the disciples asked Jesus about this. 11He answered, "Anyone who divorces his wife and marries another woman commits adultery against her. 12And if she

---

a 25 Greek *unclean*   *b 29* Some manuscripts *prayer and fasting*   *c 43* Some manuscripts *out*, 44*where / " 'their worm does not die, / and the fire is not quenched.'*   *d 45* Some manuscripts *hell,* 46*where / " 'their worm does not die, / and the fire is not quenched.'*   *e 48* Isaiah 66:24   *a 6* Gen. 1:27
b 7 Some early manuscripts *do not have and be united to his wife.*   *c 8* Gen. 2:24

divorces her husband and marries another man, she commits adultery."

■ The Little Children and Jesus
☐ See Matthew 19:13–15; Luke 18:15–17

13People were bringing little children to Jesus to have him touch them, but the disciples rebuked them. 14When Jesus saw this, he was indignant. He said to them, "Let the little children come to me, and do not hinder them, for the kingdom of God belongs to such as these. 15I tell you the truth, anyone who will not receive the kingdom of God like a little child will never enter it." 16And he took the children in his arms, put his hands on them and blessed them.

■ The Rich Young Man
☐ See Matthew 19:16–30; Luke 18:18–30

17As Jesus started on his way, a man ran up to him and fell on his knees before him. "Good teacher," he asked, "what must I do to inherit eternal life?"

18"Why do you call me good?" Jesus answered. "No-one is good—except God alone. 19You know the commandments: 'Do not murder, do not commit adultery, do not steal, do not give false testimony, do not defraud, honour your father and mother.'d"

20"Teacher," he declared, "all these I have kept since I was a boy."

21Jesus looked at him and loved him. "One thing you lack," he said. "Go, sell everything you have and give to the poor, and you will have treasure in heaven. Then come, follow me."

22At this the man's face fell. He went away sad, because he had great wealth.

23Jesus looked around and said to his disciples, "How hard it is for the rich to enter the kingdom of God!"

24The disciples were amazed at his words. But Jesus said again, "Children, how hard it ise to enter the kingdom of God! 25It is easier for a camel to go through the eye of a needle than for a rich man to enter the kingdom of God."

26The disciples were even more amazed, and said to each other, "Who then can be saved?"

10:26 ■ THE WEALTH BARRIER
Religious teachers of that time saw wealth as a positive sign of God's approval, which explains the disciples' bewilderment. Jesus contradicted such ideas by teaching that wealth can actually be a barrier keeping people out of the kingdom of God.

27Jesus looked at them and said, "With man this is impossible, but not with God; all things are possible with God."

28Peter said to him, "We have left everything to follow you!"

29"I tell you the truth," Jesus replied, "no-one who has left home or brothers or sisters or mother or father or children or fields for me and the gospel 30will fail to receive a hundred times as much in this present age (homes, brothers, sisters, mothers,

children and fields—and with them, persecutions) and in the age to come, eternal life. 31But many who are first will be last, and the last first."

■ Jesus Again Predicts His Death
☐ See Matthew 20:17–19; Luke 18:31–33

32They were on their way up to Jerusalem, with Jesus leading the way, and the disciples were astonished, while those who followed were afraid. Again he took the Twelve aside and told them what was going to happen to him. 33"We are going up to Jerusalem," he said, "and the Son of Man will be betrayed to the chief priests and teachers of the law. They will condemn him to death and will hand him over to the Gentiles, 34who will mock him and spit on him, flog him and kill him. Three days later he will rise."

■ The Request of James and John
☐ See Matthew 20:20–28

35Then James and John, the sons of Zebedee, came to him. "Teacher," they said, "we want you to do for us whatever we ask."

36"What do you want me to do for you?" he asked.

37They replied, "Let one of us sit at your right and the other at your left in your glory."

38"You don't know what you are asking," Jesus said. "Can you drink the cup I drink or be baptised with the baptism I am baptised with?"

39"We can," they answered.

Jesus said to them, "You will drink the cup I drink and be baptised with the baptism I am baptised with, 40but to sit at my right or left is not for me to grant. These places belong to those for whom they have been prepared."

41When the ten heard about this, they became indignant with James and John. 42Jesus called them together and said, "You know that those who are regarded as rulers of the Gentiles lord it over them, and their high officials exercise authority over them. 43Not so with you. Instead, whoever wants to become great among you must be your servant, 44and whoever wants to be first must be slave of all. 45For even the Son of Man did not come to be served, but to serve, and to give his life as a ransom for many."

■ Blind Bartimaeus Receives His Sight
☐ See Matthew 20:29–34; Luke 18:35–43

46Then they came to Jericho. As Jesus and his disciples, together with a large crowd, were leaving the city, a blind man, Bartimaeus (that is, the Son of Timaeus), was sitting by the roadside begging. 47When he heard that it was Jesus of Nazareth, he began to shout, "Jesus, Son of David, have mercy on me!"

48Many rebuked him and told him to be quiet, but he shouted all the more, "Son of David, have mercy on me!"

49Jesus stopped and said, "Call him."

So they called to the blind man, "Cheer up! On your feet! He's calling you." 50Throwing his cloak aside, he jumped to his feet and came to Jesus.

51"What do you want me to do for you?" Jesus asked him.

d19 Exodus 20:12–16; Deut. 5:16–20   e24 Some manuscripts is for those who trust in riches

The blind man said, "Rabbi, I want to see."
52"Go," said Jesus, "your faith has healed you." Immediately he received his sight and followed Jesus along the road.

■ The Triumphal Entry
□ See Matthew 21:1–9; Luke 19:29–38; John 12:12–15

11 As they approached Jerusalem and came to Bethphage and Bethany at the Mount of Olives, Jesus sent two of his disciples, 2saying to them, "Go to the village ahead of you, and just as you enter it, you will find a colt tied there, which no-one has ever ridden. Untie it and bring it here. 3If anyone asks you, 'Why are you doing this?' tell him, 'The Lord needs it and will send it back here shortly.' "

4They went and found a colt outside in the street, tied at a doorway. As they untied it, 5some people standing there asked, "What are you doing, untying that colt?" 6They answered as Jesus had told them to, and the people let them go. 7When they brought the colt to Jesus and threw their cloaks over it, he sat on it. 8Many people spread their cloaks on the road, while others spread branches they had cut in the fields. 9Those who went ahead and those who followed shouted,

"Hosanna!"a

"Blessed is he who comes in the name of the Lord!"b

10"Blessed is the coming kingdom of our father David!"

"Hosanna in the highest!"

11:9 ■ SHORT-LIVED ACCEPTANCE
During much of his ministry, Jesus hushed up news about his miraculous power and his identity as the true Messiah. But in this rare scene, large crowds clearly recognised him as the Messiah and honoured him as such. The next few chapters, however, demonstrate how tragically short-lived public acceptance proved to be.

11Jesus entered Jerusalem and went to the temple. He looked around at everything, but since it was already late, he went out to Bethany with the Twelve.

■ Jesus Clears the Temple
□ See Matthew 21:12–16; Luke 19:45–47; John 2:13–16

12The next day as they were leaving Bethany, Jesus was hungry. 13Seeing in the distance a fig-tree in leaf, he went to find out if it had any fruit. When he reached it, he found nothing but leaves, because it was not the season for figs. 14Then he said to the tree, "May no-one ever eat fruit from you again." And his disciples heard him say it.

15On reaching Jerusalem, Jesus entered the temple area and began driving out those who were buying and selling there. He overturned the tables of the money-changers and the benches of those selling doves, 16and would not allow anyone to carry merchandise through the temple courts. 17And as he taught them, he said, "Is it not written:

" 'My house will be called
    a house of prayer for all nations'c?

But you have made it 'a den of robbers'.d"

11:16 ■ BIG BUSINESS
The outer court of the temple, accessible to non-Jews, encompassed a huge area about the size of ten football pitches. Some business there was legitimate: out-of-town pilgrims needed a way to obtain sacrificial animals and to change money into local currency. Apparently, though, the business had fallen into the hands of people more interested in profit than in worship.

18The chief priests and the teachers of the law heard this and began looking for a way to kill him, for they feared him, because the whole crowd was amazed at his teaching.

19When evening came, theye went out of the city.

■ The Withered Fig-Tree
□ See Matthew 21:19–22

20In the morning, as they went along, they saw the fig-tree withered from the roots. 21Peter remembered and said to Jesus, "Rabbi, look! The fig-tree you cursed has withered!"

22"Havef faith in God," Jesus answered. 23"I tell you the truth, if anyone says to this mountain, 'Go, throw yourself into the sea,' and does not doubt in his heart but believes that what he says will happen, it will be done for him. 24Therefore I tell you, whatever you ask for in prayer, believe that you have received it, and it will be yours. 25And when you stand praying, if you hold anything against anyone, forgive him, so that your Father in heaven may forgive you your sins."g

■ The Authority of Jesus Questioned
□ See Matthew 21:23–27; Luke 20:1–8

27They arrived again in Jerusalem, and while Jesus was walking in the temple courts, the chief priests, the teachers of the law and the elders came to him. 28"By what authority are you doing these things?" they asked. "And who gave you authority to do this?"

29Jesus replied, "I will ask you one question. Answer me, and I will tell you by what authority I am doing these things. 30John's baptism—was it from heaven, or from men? Tell me!"

31They discussed it among themselves and said, "If we say, 'From heaven', he will ask, 'Then why didn't you believe him?' 32But if we say, 'From men' ...." (They feared the people, for everyone held that John really was a prophet.)

33So they answered Jesus, "We don't know."

Jesus said, "Neither will I tell you by what authority I am doing these things."

---

a9 A Hebrew expression meaning "Save!" which became an exclamation of praise; also in verse 10.   b9 Psalm 118:25,26   c17 Isaiah 56:7   d17 Jer. 7:11   e19 Some early manuscripts he   f22 Some early manuscripts If you have   g25 Some manuscripts sins. 26But if you do not forgive, neither will your Father who is in heaven forgive your sins.

■ The Parable of the Tenants
☐ See Matthew 21:33–46; Luke 20:9–19

12 He then began to speak to them in parables: "A man planted a vineyard. He put a wall around it, dug a pit for the winepress and built a watchtower. Then he rented the vineyard to some farmers and went away on a journey. 2At harvest time he sent a servant to the tenants to collect from them some of the fruit of the vineyard. 3But they seized him, beat him and sent him away empty-handed. 4Then he sent another servant to them; they struck this man on the head and treated him shamefully. 5He sent still another, and that one they killed. He sent many others; some of them they beat, others they killed.

6"He had one left to send, a son, whom he loved. He sent him last of all, saying, 'They will respect my son.'

7"But the tenants said to one another, 'This is the heir. Come, let's kill him, and the inheritance will be ours.' 8So they took him and killed him, and threw him out of the vineyard.

9"What then will the owner of the vineyard do? He will come and kill those tenants and give the vineyard to others. 10Haven't you read this scripture:

" 'The stone the builders rejected
    has become the capstone;*a*
11the Lord has done this,
    and it is marvellous in our eyes'*b*?"

12Then they looked for a way to arrest him because they knew he had spoken the parable against them. But they were afraid of the crowd; so they left him and went away.

■ Paying Taxes to Caesar
☐ See Matthew 22:15–22; Luke 20:20–26

13Later they sent some of the Pharisees and Herodians to Jesus to catch him in his words. 14They came to him and said, "Teacher, we know you are a man of integrity. You aren't swayed by men, because you pay no attention to who they are; but you teach the way of God in accordance with the truth. Is it right to pay taxes to Caesar or not? 15Should we pay or shouldn't we?"

But Jesus knew their hypocrisy. "Why are you trying to trap me?" he asked. "Bring me a denarius and let me look at it." 16They brought the coin, and he asked them, "Whose portrait is this? And whose inscription?"

"Caesar's," they replied.

17Then Jesus said to them, "Give to Caesar what is Caesar's and to God what is God's."

And they were amazed at him.

■ Marriage at the Resurrection
☐ See Matthew 22:23–33; Luke 20:27–38

18Then the Sadducees, who say there is no resurrection, came to him with a question. 19"Teacher," they said, "Moses wrote for us that if a man's brother dies and leaves a wife but no children, the man must marry the widow and have children for his brother. 20Now there were seven brothers. The first one married and died without leaving any children.

21The second one married the widow, but he also died, leaving no child. It was the same with the third. 22In fact, none of the seven left any children. Last of all, the woman died too. 23At the resurrection*c* whose wife will she be, since the seven were married to her?"

12:13 ■ OPPOSITION HEATS UP
While in Jerusalem, Jesus was surrounded by hostile groups. Mark 12 records a series of attempts to bait him: by the Pharisees and Sadducees, by the political Herodians, and by the teachers of the law. Each group challenged Jesus with a situation designed to trap him and anger the crowd.

24Jesus replied, "Are you not in error because you do not know the Scriptures or the power of God? 25When the dead rise, they will neither marry nor be given in marriage; they will be like the angels in heaven. 26Now about the dead rising—have you not read in the book of Moses, in the account of the bush, how God said to him, 'I am the God of Abraham, the God of Isaac, and the God of Jacob'*d*? 27He is not the God of the dead, but of the living. You are badly mistaken!"

■ The Greatest Commandment
☐ See Matthew 22:34–40

28One of the teachers of the law came and heard them debating. Noticing that Jesus had given them a good answer, he asked him, "Of all the commandments, which is the most important?"

29"The most important one," answered Jesus, "is this: 'Hear, O Israel, the Lord our God, the Lord is one.*e* 30Love the Lord your God with all your heart and with all your soul and with all your mind and with all your strength.'*f* 31The second is this: 'Love your neighbour as yourself.'*g* There is no commandment greater than these."

32"Well said, teacher," the man replied. "You are right in saying that God is one and there is no other but him. 33To love him with all your heart, with all your understanding and with all your strength, and to love your neighbour as yourself is more important than all burnt offerings and sacrifices."

34When Jesus saw that he had answered wisely, he said to him, "You are not far from the kingdom of God." And from then on no-one dared ask him any more questions.

■ Whose Son Is the Christ?
☐ See Matthew 22:41–46; Luke 20:41–44

35While Jesus was teaching in the temple courts, he asked, "How is it that the teachers of the law say that the Christ*b* is the son of David? 36David himself, speaking by the Holy Spirit, declared:

" 'The Lord said to my Lord:
    "Sit at my right hand
until I put your enemies
    under your feet." '*i*

---

*a*10 Or *cornerstone*   *b*11 Psalm 118:22,23   *c*23 Some manuscripts *resurrection, when men rise from the dead,*   *d*26 Exodus 3:6   *e*29 Or the *Lord our God is one Lord*   *f*30 Deut. 6:4,5   *g*31 Lev. 19:18   *b*35 Or *Messiah*   *i*36 Psalm 110:1

37David himself calls him 'Lord'. How then can he be his son?"

The large crowd listened to him with delight.

38As he taught, Jesus said, "Watch out for the teachers of the law. They like to walk around in flowing robes and be greeted in the market-places, 39and have the most important seats in the synagogues and the places of honour at banquets. 40They devour widows' houses and for a show make lengthy prayers. Such men will be punished most severely."

■ The Widow's Offering
☐ See Luke 21:1–4

41Jesus sat down opposite the place where the offerings were put and watched the crowd putting their money into the temple treasury. Many rich people threw in large amounts. 42But a poor widow came and put in two very small copper coins,*j* worth only a fraction of a penny.*k*

12:42 ■ EXPLOITING WIDOWS
The simple act of faithfulness by an impoverished widow made a stark contrast to others' pompous public displays. Some teachers "devour widows' houses", Jesus had said (verse 40). Teachers of the law lived off the gifts of supporters, and, then as now, the gullible poor made a tempting target.

43Calling his disciples to him, Jesus said, "I tell you the truth, this poor widow has put more into the treasury than all the others. 44They all gave out of their wealth; but she, out of her poverty, put in everything—all she had to live on."

■ Signs of the End of the Age
☐ See Matthew 24:1–51; Luke 21:5–36

13 As he was leaving the temple, one of his disciples said to him, "Look, Teacher! What massive stones! What magnificent buildings!"

2"Do you see all these great buildings?" replied Jesus. "Not one stone here will be left on another; every one will be thrown down."

3As Jesus was sitting on the Mount of Olives opposite the temple, Peter, James, John and Andrew asked him privately, 4"Tell us, when will these things happen? And what will be the sign that they are all about to be fulfilled?"

5Jesus said to them: "Watch out that no-one deceives you. 6Many will come in my name, claiming, 'I am he,' and will deceive many. 7When you hear of wars and rumours of wars, do not be alarmed. Such things must happen, but the end is still to come. 8Nation will rise against nation, and kingdom against kingdom. There will be earthquakes in various places, and famines. These are the beginning of birth-pains.

9"You must be on your guard. You will be handed over to the local councils and flogged in the synagogues. On account of me you will stand before governors and kings as witnesses to them. 10And the gospel must first be preached to all nations. 11Whenever you are arrested and brought to trial,

do not worry beforehand about what to say. Just say whatever is given you at the time, for it is not you speaking, but the Holy Spirit.

13:10 ■ TO ALL NATIONS
Preaching the gospel to all nations was probably a new thought to the disciples, who still thought in terms of a Messiah for the Jews. But some of them would spend the remainder of their lives making this prophecy come true.

12"Brother will betray brother to death, and a father his child. Children will rebel against their parents and have them put to death. 13All men will hate you because of me, but he who stands firm to the end will be saved.

14"When you see 'the abomination that causes desolation'*a* standing where it*b* does not belong—let the reader understand—then let those who are in Judea flee to the mountains. 15Let no-one on the roof of his house go down or enter the house to take anything out. 16Let no-one in the field go back to get his cloak. 17How dreadful it will be in those days for pregnant women and nursing mothers! 18Pray that this will not take place in winter, 19because those will be days of distress unequalled from the beginning, when God created the world, until now—and never to be equalled again. 20If the Lord had not cut short those days, no-one would survive. But for the sake of the elect, whom he has chosen, he has shortened them. 21At that time if anyone says to you, 'Look, here is the Christ!'*c* or, 'Look, there he is!' do not believe it. 22For false Christs and false prophets will appear and perform signs and miracles to deceive the elect—if that were possible. 23So be on your guard; I have told you everything ahead of time.

24"But in those days, following that distress,

" 'the sun will be darkened,
    and the moon will not give its light;
25the stars will fall from the sky,
    and the heavenly bodies will be shaken.'*d*

26"At that time men will see the Son of Man coming in clouds with great power and glory. 27And he will send his angels and gather his elect from the four winds, from the ends of the earth to the ends of the heavens.

28"Now learn this lesson from the fig-tree: As soon as its twigs get tender and its leaves come out, you know that summer is near. 29Even so, when you see these things happening, you know that it is near, right at the door. 30I tell you the truth, this generation*e* will certainly not pass away until all these things have happened. 31Heaven and earth will pass away, but my words will never pass away.

■ The Day and Hour Unknown
32"No-one knows about that day or hour, not even the angels in heaven, nor the Son, but only the Father. 33Be on guard! Be alert!*f* You do not know when that time will come. 34It's like a man going away: He leaves his house and puts his servants in

---

*j 42 Greek two lepta   k 42 Greek kodrantes   a 14 Daniel 9:27; 11:31; 12:11
34:4   e 30 Or race   f 33 Some manuscripts alert and pray   b 14 Or he; also in verse 29   c 21 Or Messiah   d 25 Isaiah 13:10;*

charge, each with his assigned task, and tells the one at the door to keep watch.

35"Therefore keep watch because you do not know when the owner of the house will come back—whether in the evening, or at midnight, or when the cock crows, or at dawn. 36If he comes suddenly, do not let him find you sleeping. 37What I say to you, I say to everyone: 'Watch!' "

■ Jesus Anointed at Bethany
☐ See Matthew 26:2–16; Luke 22:1–6

14 Now the Passover and the Feast of Unleavened Bread were only two days away, and the chief priests and the teachers of the law were looking for some sly way to arrest Jesus and kill him. 2"But not during the Feast," they said, "or the people may riot."

14:1 ■ FESTIVAL TIME IN JERUSALEM
The Passover, celebrating the Jews' deliverance from Egypt, was one of the high points of the Jewish calendar. All males older than twelve went to Jerusalem for the holiday. Thus the city was filled with hundreds of thousands of pilgrims at the time of Jesus' death.

3While he was in Bethany, reclining at the table in the home of a man known as Simon the Leper, a woman came with an alabaster jar of very expensive perfume, made of pure nard. She broke the jar and poured the perfume on his head.

4Some of those present were saying indignantly to one another, "Why this waste of perfume? 5It could have been sold for more than a year's wages*a* and the money given to the poor." And they rebuked her harshly.

6"Leave her alone," said Jesus. "Why are you bothering her? She has done a beautiful thing to me. 7The poor you will always have with you, and you can help them any time you want. But you will not always have me. 8She did what she could. She poured perfume on my body beforehand to prepare for my burial. 9I tell you the truth, wherever the gospel is preached throughout the world, what she has done will also be told, in memory of her."

10Then Judas Iscariot, one of the Twelve, went to the chief priests to betray Jesus to them. 11They were delighted to hear this and promised to give him money. So he watched for an opportunity to hand him over.

■ The Lord's Supper
☐ See Matthew 26:17–30; Luke 22:7–23

12On the first day of the Feast of Unleavened Bread, when it was customary to sacrifice the Passover lamb, Jesus' disciples asked him, "Where do you want us to go and make preparations for you to eat the Passover?"

13So he sent two of his disciples, telling them, "Go into the city, and a man carrying a jar of water will meet you. Follow him. 14Say to the owner of the house he enters, 'The Teacher asks: Where is my guest room, where I may eat the Passover with my disciples?' 15He will show you a large upper room, furnished and ready. Make preparations for us there."

16The disciples left, went into the city and found things just as Jesus had told them. So they prepared the Passover.

17When evening came, Jesus arrived with the Twelve. 18While they were reclining at the table eating, he said, "I tell you the truth, one of you will betray me—one who is eating with me."

19They were saddened, and one by one they said to him, "Surely not I?"

20"It is one of the Twelve," he replied, "one who dips bread into the bowl with me. 21The Son of Man will go just as it is written about him. But woe to that man who betrays the Son of Man! It would be better for him if he had not been born."

22While they were eating, Jesus took bread, gave thanks and broke it, and gave it to his disciples, saying, "Take it; this is my body."

14:22 ■ ORIGINAL LORD'S SUPPER
Virtually all Christian churches celebrate the practice of Communion (Mass, Eucharist, or Lord's Supper) in some form. Matthew, Mark, and Luke each record the original Passover meal when Jesus instituted the practice.

23Then he took the cup, gave thanks and offered it to them, and they all drank from it.

24"This is my blood of the*b* covenant, which is poured out for many," he said to them. 25"I tell you the truth, I will not drink again of the fruit of the vine until that day when I drink it anew in the kingdom of God."

26When they had sung a hymn, they went out to the Mount of Olives.

■ Jesus Predicts Peter's Denial
☐ See Matthew 26:31–35

27"You will all fall away," Jesus told them, "for it is written:

" 'I will strike the shepherd,
    and the sheep will be scattered.'*c*

28But after I have risen, I will go ahead of you into Galilee."

29Peter declared, "Even if all fall away, I will not."

30"I tell you the truth," Jesus answered, "today—yes, tonight—before the cock crows twice*d* you yourself will disown me three times."

31But Peter insisted emphatically, "Even if I have to die with you, I will never disown you." And all the others said the same.

■ Gethsemane
☐ See Matthew 26:36–46; Luke 22:40–46

32They went to a place called Gethsemane, and Jesus said to his disciples, "Sit here while I pray." 33He took Peter, James and John along with him,

---

a 5 Greek *than three hundred denarii*   *b 24* Some manuscripts *the new*   *c 27* Zech. 13:7   *d 30* Some early manuscripts do not have *twice*.

and he began to be deeply distressed and troubled. ³⁴"My soul is overwhelmed with sorrow to the point of death," he said to them. "Stay here and keep watch."

³⁵Going a little farther, he fell to the ground and prayed that if possible the hour might pass from him. ³⁶"Abba,ᵉ Father," he said, "everything is possible for you. Take this cup from me. Yet not what I will, but what you will."

³⁷Then he returned to his disciples and found them sleeping. "Simon," he said to Peter, "are you asleep? Could you not keep watch for one hour? ³⁸Watch and pray so that you will not fall into temptation. The spirit is willing, but the body is weak."

³⁹Once more he went away and prayed the same thing. ⁴⁰When he came back, he again found them sleeping, because their eyes were heavy. They did not know what to say to him.

⁴¹Returning the third time, he said to them, "Are you still sleeping and resting? Enough! The hour has come. Look, the Son of Man is betrayed into the hands of sinners. ⁴²Rise! Let us go! Here comes my betrayer!"

■ Jesus Arrested
☐ See Matthew 26:47–56; Luke 22:47–50; John 18:3–11

⁴³Just as he was speaking, Judas, one of the Twelve, appeared. With him was a crowd armed with swords and clubs, sent from the chief priests, the teachers of the law, and the elders.

⁴⁴Now the betrayer had arranged a signal with them: "The one I kiss is the man; arrest him and lead him away under guard." ⁴⁵Going at once to Jesus, Judas said, "Rabbi!" and kissed him. ⁴⁶The men seized Jesus and arrested him. ⁴⁷Then one of those standing near drew his sword and struck the servant of the high priest, cutting off his ear.

⁴⁸"Am I leading a rebellion," said Jesus, "that you have come out with swords and clubs to capture me? ⁴⁹Every day I was with you, teaching in the temple courts, and you did not arrest me. But the Scriptures must be fulfilled." ⁵⁰Then everyone deserted him and fled.

⁵¹A young man, wearing nothing but a linen garment, was following Jesus. When they seized him, ⁵²he fled naked, leaving his garment behind.

■ Before the Sanhedrin
☐ See Matthew 26:57–68; John 18:12–13,19–24

⁵³They took Jesus to the high priest, and all the chief priests, elders and teachers of the law came together. ⁵⁴Peter followed him at a distance, right into the courtyard of the high priest. There he sat with the guards and warmed himself at the fire.

⁵⁵The chief priests and the whole Sanhedrin were looking for evidence against Jesus so that they could put him to death, but they did not find any. ⁵⁶Many testified falsely against him, but their statements did not agree.

⁵⁷Then some stood up and gave this false testimony against him: ⁵⁸"We heard him say, 'I will destroy this man-made temple and in three days will build another, not made by man.' " ⁵⁹Yet even then their testimony did not agree.

⁶⁰Then the high priest stood up before them and asked Jesus, "Are you not going to answer? What is this testimony that these men are bringing against you?" ⁶¹But Jesus remained silent and gave no answer.

Again the high priest asked him, "Are you the Christ,ᶠ the Son of the Blessed One?"

⁶²"I am," said Jesus. "And you will see the Son of Man sitting at the right hand of the Mighty One and coming on the clouds of heaven."

⁶³The high priest tore his clothes. "Why do we need any more witnesses?" he asked. ⁶⁴"You have heard the blasphemy. What do you think?"

They all condemned him as worthy of death. ⁶⁵Then some began to spit at him; they blindfolded him, struck him with their fists, and said, "Prophesy!" And the guards took him and beat him.

■ Peter Disowns Jesus
☐ See Matthew 26:69–75; Luke 22:56–62; John 18:16–18,25–27

⁶⁶While Peter was below in the courtyard, one of the servant girls of the high priest came by. ⁶⁷When she saw Peter warming himself, she looked closely at him.

"You also were with that Nazarene, Jesus," she said.

⁶⁸But he denied it. "I don't know or understand what you're talking about," he said, and went out into the entrance.ᵍ

⁶⁹When the servant girl saw him there, she said again to those standing around, "This fellow is one of them." ⁷⁰Again he denied it.

After a little while, those standing near said to Peter, "Surely you are one of them, for you are a Galilean."

⁷¹He began to call down curses on himself, and he swore to them, "I don't know this man you're talking about."

⁷²Immediately the cock crowed the second time.ᵇ Then Peter remembered the word Jesus had spoken to him: "Before the cock crows twiceⁱ you will disown me three times." And he broke down and wept.

ᵉ36 Aramaic for *Father*   ᶠ61 Or *Messiah*   ᵍ68 Some early manuscripts *entrance and the cock crowed*   ᵇ72 Some early manuscripts do not have the second time.   ⁱ72 Some early manuscripts do not have *twice*.

■ Jesus Before Pilate
☐ See Matthew 27:11–26; Luke 23:2–3,18–25; John
18:29 – 19:16

15 Very early in the morning, the chief priests, with the elders, the teachers of the law and the whole Sanhedrin, reached a decision. They bound Jesus, led him away and turned him over to Pilate.

15:1 ■ APPEAL FOR A DEATH PENALTY
Roman law granted the Jews many freedoms, including the right to their Jewish court system, a council called the Sanhedrin. However, the Sanhedrin had no authority to order the death penalty. Seeking that sentence, Jesus' opponents sent him to Pilate, the Roman governor.

2"Are you the king of the Jews?" asked Pilate.

"Yes, it is as you say," Jesus replied.

3The chief priests accused him of many things. 4So again Pilate asked him, "Aren't you going to answer? See how many things they are accusing you of."

5But Jesus still made no reply, and Pilate was amazed.

6Now it was the custom at the Feast to release a prisoner whom the people requested. 7A man called Barabbas was in prison with the insurrectionists who had committed murder in the uprising. 8The crowd came up and asked Pilate to do for them what he usually did.

9"Do you want me to release to you the king of the Jews?" asked Pilate, 10knowing it was out of envy that the chief priests had handed Jesus over to him. 11But the chief priests stirred up the crowd to have Pilate release Barabbas instead.

12"What shall I do, then, with the one you call the king of the Jews?" Pilate asked them.

13"Crucify him!" they shouted.

14"Why? What crime has he committed?" asked Pilate.

But they shouted all the louder, "Crucify him!"

15Wanting to satisfy the crowd, Pilate released Barabbas to them. He had Jesus flogged, and handed him over to be crucified.

■ The Soldiers Mock Jesus
☐ See Matthew 27:27–31

16The soldiers led Jesus away into the palace (that is, the Praetorium) and called together the whole company of soldiers. 17They put a purple robe on him, then twisted together a crown of thorns and set it on him. 18And they began to call out to him, "Hail, king of the Jews!" 19Again and again they struck him on the head with a staff and spat on him. Falling on their knees, they paid homage to him. 20And when they had mocked him, they took off the purple robe and put his own clothes on him. Then they led him out to crucify him.

■ The Crucifixion
☐ See Matthew 27:33–44; Luke 23:33–43; John 19:17–24

21A certain man from Cyrene, Simon, the father of Alexander and Rufus, was passing by on his way in from the country, and they forced him to carry the cross. 22They brought Jesus to the place called Golgotha (which means The Place of the Skull). 23Then they offered him wine mixed with myrrh, but he did not take it. 24And they crucified him. Dividing up his clothes, they cast lots to see what each would get.

25It was the third hour when they crucified him. 26The written notice of the charge against him read: THE KING OF THE JEWS. 27They crucified two robbers with him, one on his right and one on his left.*a* 29Those who passed by hurled insults at him, shaking their heads and saying, "So! You who are going to destroy the temple and build it in three days, 30come down from the cross and save yourself!"

31In the same way the chief priests and the teachers of the law mocked him among themselves. "He saved others," they said, "but he can't save himself! 32Let this Christ,*b* this King of Israel, come down now from the cross, that we may see and believe." Those crucified with him also heaped insults on him.

15:25 ■ DEATH WITHOUT DIGNITY
Romans reserved their most cruel form of execution – crucifixion – for slaves and the worst criminals. Skeletons of crucifixion victims show that thick nails were pounded through the wrist and heel bones. Death (from asphyxiation) usually took many hours or even several days.

■ The Death of Jesus
☐ See Matthew 27:45–56; Luke 23:44–49

33At the sixth hour darkness came over the whole land until the ninth hour. 34And at the ninth hour Jesus cried out in a loud voice, *"Eloi, Eloi, lama sabachthani?"* – which means, "My God, my God, why have you forsaken me?"*c*

35When some of those standing near heard this, they said, "Listen, he's calling Elijah."

36One man ran, filled a sponge with wine vinegar, put it on a stick, and offered it to Jesus to drink. "Now leave him alone. Let's see if Elijah comes to take him down," he said.

37With a loud cry, Jesus breathed his last.

38The curtain of the temple was torn in two from top to bottom. 39And when the centurion, who stood there in front of Jesus, heard his cry and*d* saw how he died, he said, "Surely this man was the Son*e* of God!"

40Some women were watching from a distance. Among them were Mary Magdalene, Mary the mother of James the younger and of Joses, and Salome. 41In Galilee these women had followed him and cared for his needs. Many other women who had come up with him to Jerusalem were also there.

---

a27 Some manuscripts left, 28and the scripture was fulfilled which says, "He was counted with the lawless ones" (Isaiah 53:12)   b32 Or Messiah
c34 Psalm 22:1   d39 Some manuscripts do not have heard his cry and.   e39 Or a son

■ The Burial of Jesus
☐ See Matthew 27:57–61; Luke 23:50–56; John 19:38–42

[42]It was Preparation Day (that is, the day before the Sabbath). So as evening approached, [43]Joseph of Arimathea, a prominent member of the Council, who was himself waiting for the kingdom of God, went boldly to Pilate and asked for Jesus' body. [44]Pilate was surprised to hear that he was already dead. Summoning the centurion, he asked him if Jesus had already died. [45]When he learned from the centurion that it was so, he gave the body to Joseph. [46]So Joseph bought some linen cloth, took down the body, wrapped it in the linen, and placed it in a tomb cut out of rock. Then he rolled a stone against the entrance of the tomb. [47]Mary Magdalene and Mary the mother of Joses saw where he was laid.

■ The Resurrection
☐ See Matthew 28:1–8; Luke 24:1–10

16 When the Sabbath was over, Mary Magdalene, Mary the mother of James, and Salome bought spices so that they might go to anoint Jesus' body. [2]Very early on the first day of the week, just after sunrise, they were on their way to the tomb [3]and they asked each other, "Who will roll the stone away from the entrance of the tomb?"

[4]But when they looked up, they saw that the

THE DAY OF EXECUTION
THE DISCIPLES WERE TOTALLY UNPREPARED

INSIGHT

AND WHEN THE CENTURION, WHO STOOD THERE IN FRONT OF JESUS, HEARD HIS CRY AND SAW HOW HE DIED, HE SAID, "SURELY THIS MAN WAS THE SON OF GOD!" ■ 15:39

Events in Jesus' life – the birth in a manger, the death on a cross – can become so familiar that we miss the point. They're too close to us. In thinking about them, it sometimes helps to let the mind wander and search out whole new images.

A Bible study group was asked to suggest word images that might apply to Jesus. Common ones surfaced first: a shepherd, a lamb, a door. Then out of nowhere came a wildly different metaphor: "fireworks in reverse". Everyone turned, puzzled, to the middle-aged woman who had spoken.

"Think about it," she said. "Fireworks explode with brilliant, dazzling colours and loud noises . . . yet they start out in an ordinary-looking paper package. When God became a man, the opposite happened. The Creator of everything in the universe confined himself to an unimpressive human package."

■ WHEN THE IMPOSSIBLE HAPPENED
No event in the life of Jesus fits the woman's metaphor better than his execution in Jerusalem. The idea was inconceivable, even to Jesus' closest followers. The Son of God die? How could this be?

Could the Creator of all things succumb to his creation? Disciples who had slogged through every other confrontation by his side now forsook him. It made no sense for Jesus, the Messiah, to die.

Not until later would other thoughts click into place: memories of Old Testament customs that hauntingly pointed to a cross, prophecies of a Messiah who was King but also a Suffering Servant (see Isaiah 53). To die was, after all, the central reason Jesus came to earth; he had insisted on that from the beginning.

■ THE MOST IMPORTANT WEEK
Jesus' last week so impressed the disciples that the four chroniclers of his life, including Mark, devoted one-third of their space to that final week in Jerusalem. By the time they wrote it down, of course, they could see his death in a new light: as a mournful prelude to the greatest miracle of all, his resurrection.

Even so, nothing could erase the impact of those fear-filled, final days. When the eerie darkness had lifted and Jesus had breathed his last, the disciples had learned something profound about God, and about love.

Dorothy Sayers put it this way: "Whatever game He is playing with His creation, He has kept His own rules and played fair. He can exact nothing from man that He has not exacted from Himself. He has Himself gone through the whole of human experience, from the trivial irritations of family life and the cramping restriction of hard work and lack of money to the worst horrors of pain and humiliation, defeat, despair, and death. When He was a man, He played the man. He was born in poverty and died in disgrace and thought it well worthwhile" (from *Christian Letters to a Post-Christian World*).

At no other point in history did the fireworks appear so powerless as the day Jesus died. They had not yet been lit.

☐ LIFE QUESTIONS:
Put yourself in the disciples' place. How would you have responded to news of Jesus' death? Would you have believed in him still?

stone, which was very large, had been rolled away. ⁵As they entered the tomb, they saw a young man dressed in a white robe sitting on the right side, and they were alarmed.

16:1 ■ A LATE ANOINTING
Jewish rules forbade handling dead bodies during the Sabbath. Because Jesus died during the Sabbath celebration, his friends and relatives couldn't properly embalm and prepare his body. They returned to the tomb later for this purpose, only to find the greatest surprise of their lives.

⁶"Don't be alarmed," he said. "You are looking for Jesus the Nazarene, who was crucified. He has risen! He is not here. See the place where they laid him. ⁷But go, tell his disciples and Peter, 'He is going ahead of you into Galilee. There you will see him, just as he told you.' "

16:7 ■ ... AND PETER
The messenger who informed the women about Jesus' resurrection pointedly asked them to tell "his disciples and Peter", singling out the disciple who had vehemently denied Jesus. John 21 records a further, moving scene in which Jesus specifically reinstated Peter.

⁸Trembling and bewildered, the women went out and fled from the tomb. They said nothing to anyone, because they were afraid.

[The most reliable early manuscripts and other ancient witnesses do not have Mark 16:9–20.]

⁹When Jesus rose early on the first day of the week, he appeared first to Mary Magdalene, out of whom he had driven seven demons. ¹⁰She went and told those who had been with him and who were mourning and weeping. ¹¹When they heard that Jesus was alive and that she had seen him, they did not believe it.

¹²Afterwards Jesus appeared in a different form to two of them while they were walking in the country. ¹³These returned and reported it to the rest; but they did not believe them either.

¹⁴Later Jesus appeared to the Eleven as they were eating; he rebuked them for their lack of faith and their stubborn refusal to believe those who had seen him after he had risen.

¹⁵He said to them, "Go into all the world and preach the good news to all creation. ¹⁶Whoever believes and is baptised will be saved, but whoever does not believe will be condemned. ¹⁷And these signs will accompany those who believe: In my name they will drive out demons; they will speak in new tongues; ¹⁸they will pick up snakes with their hands; and when they drink deadly poison, it will not hurt them at all; they will place their hands on sick people, and they will get well."

¹⁹After the Lord Jesus had spoken to them, he was taken up into heaven and he sat at the right hand of God. ²⁰Then the disciples went out and preached everywhere, and the Lord worked with them and confirmed his word by the signs that accompanied it.

LUKE

INTRODUCTION

■ LIKE A JOY-FILLED MUSICAL
SOMETHING WAS BREWING ON PLANET EARTH

BUT THE ANGEL SAID TO THEM, "DO NOT BE AFRAID. I BRING YOU GOOD NEWS OF
GREAT JOY THAT WILL BE FOR ALL THE PEOPLE." ■ 2:10

Although Luke covers the same basic territory as
Matthew and Mark, he gives away his own slant in
the very first chapters. Matthew begins with a
formal family genealogy; Mark opens with a
bleached desert scene. In contrast, Luke
describes a hearty celebration.

The way Luke tells it, events surrounding
Jesus' birth resembled a joy-filled musical.
Characters crowded into the scene: a white-
haired great-uncle, an astonished virgin, a
tottery old prophetess. They all smiled broadly
and, as likely as not, burst into song.

Once Mary had recovered from the
shock of seeing an angel, she let rip with a
beautiful hymn. The old priest Zechariah broke
nine months of muteness with a rousing poem,
and even the unborn John the Baptist kicked for
joy inside his mother's womb (1:44). When Jesus
finally made an entrance, in an inconspicuous
stable, the sky filled with singing angels. Clearly,
something was brewing on planet Earth.

■ HISTORY SPLIT IN TWO
You get the feeling when you read his account that
Luke wanted to capture in words the spirit of

"great joy" that the angel predicted (2:10). Among
dreary, defeated villagers in a remote corner of the
Roman empire, something climactically good was
bursting out.

The author tells us (1:1–4) that he
researched many accounts of Jesus' life.
Intimate details in these first two chapters show
that he relied heavily on eye-witnesses, for no
other Gospel writer picked up so many facts.
Careful attention to detail and an underlying tone
of joy characterise Luke's book.

Jesus' birth literally split history into two
parts; we commemorate the event whenever we
write a date. The book of Luke takes us back to
the world before there was an A.D. or B.C., when
Jesus' life was just beginning.

Even now, almost 2,000 years later, the
commemoration of Jesus' birth still gives cause
for joy. We eat better during the Christmas
season, buy gifts for others, donate to charity,
and sing more often. Our feelings of celebration
are gentle after-effects, reminders of the
remarkable moment when God became a man
and lived on earth.

■ HOW TO READ LUKE

Luke probably did not know Jesus personally. But
as a dedicated convert in the early church, he
accompanied the apostle Paul on missionary trips.
In three of his letters, Paul refers to Luke with
great affection.

As he mentions in his introduction, Luke
eventually saw the need to draw up a carefully
researched account of the life of Christ. Many
accounts of varying quality existed then, but
Luke set out to interview eye-witnesses and
compose a thoughtful summary. His book shows
thoroughness and detail. It starts before Jesus'
birth, and ends with his ascension into heaven.

You should find Luke a very appealing
book to read. Luke was a gifted writer, and the

stories he records have won their place among
the classics of literature: the Good Samaritan,
the Lost Son, the Rich Man and Lazarus. If Mark
is a Gospel of action, Luke is a Gospel of
relationships. It contains very good character
descriptions.

Look for the many different ethnic,
religious, economic, and social groups in Luke.
Think of the diverse groups in a country like the
United Kingdom today. How do you think each
of them would respond to Jesus in the flesh?

Note especially two large sections of
Luke that present material found nowhere else:
chapters 1–2 and chapters 10–19.

■ 3-TRACK READING PLAN

For an explanation and complete listing of the 3-track reading plan, turn to page x.

■ **TRACK 1:**
Two-Week Courses on the Bible
The Track 1 reading programme on the Life and Teachings of Jesus includes four chapters from Luke. See page x for a complete listing of this course.

■ **TRACK 2:**
An Overview of Luke in 8 Days
Over the next eight days, read from the material that's found in no other Gospel but Luke's.
□ Day 1. Read the Introduction to Luke and then Luke's account in chapter 1 of the events preceding Jesus' birth.

□ Day 2. Read the familiar Christmas passage, chapter 2.
□ Day 3. Read chapter 10, which includes the parable of the Good Samaritan.
□ Day 4. Read chapter 12, in which Jesus draws a strong contrast between those who trust him, no matter how poor, and haughty rich people.
□ Day 5. Read the famous parables, or short stories, that Jesus tells in chapter 15.
□ Day 6. Read chapter 16's two familiar stories: the shrewd manager and the rich man and Lazarus.
□ Day 7. Read chapter 18.
□ Day 8. How did Jesus'

disciples react to his resurrection? Read a good description in chapter 24. Now turn to page xi for your next Track 2 reading project.

■ **TRACK 3:**
All of Luke in 24 Days
After you have read through Luke, turn to pages xii–xiii for your next Track 3 reading project.

□ 1	□ 2	□ 3	□ 4
□ 5	□ 6	□ 7	□ 8
□ 9	□ 10	□ 11	□ 12
□ 13	□ 14	□ 15	□ 16
□ 17	□ 18	□ 19	□ 20
□ 21	□ 22	□ 23	□ 24

■ Introduction

1 Many have undertaken to draw up an account of the things that have been fulfilled[a] among us, ²just as they were handed down to us by those who from the first were eye-witnesses and servants of the word. ³Therefore, since I myself have carefully investigated everything from the beginning, it seemed good also to me to write an orderly account for you, most excellent Theophilus, ⁴so that you may know the certainty of the things you have been taught.

1:3 ■ LUKE THE HISTORIAN
A historian looks for original sources of information – people who were personally involved in the events being described. Luke doesn't claim to be an eye-witness himself, but he had carefully interviewed many who were. As the apostle Paul's travelling companion, Luke must have met many such sources. The Gospel of Luke is the first of a two-part work; the book of Acts continues the story.

■ The Birth of John the Baptist Foretold

⁵In the time of Herod king of Judea there was a priest named Zechariah, who belonged to the priestly division of Abijah; his wife Elizabeth was also a descendant of Aaron. ⁶Both of them were upright in the sight of God, observing all the Lord's commandments and regulations blamelessly. ⁷But they had no children, because Elizabeth was barren; and they were both well on in years.

⁸Once when Zechariah's division was on duty and he was serving as priest before God, ⁹he was chosen by lot, according to the custom of the priesthood, to go into the temple of the Lord and burn

incense. ¹⁰And when the time for the burning of incense came, all the assembled worshippers were praying outside.

¹¹Then an angel of the Lord appeared to him, standing at the right side of the altar of incense. ¹²When Zechariah saw him, he was startled and was gripped with fear. ¹³But the angel said to him: "Do not be afraid, Zechariah; your prayer has been heard. Your wife Elizabeth will bear you a son, and you are to give him the name John. ¹⁴He will be a joy and delight to you, and many will rejoice because of his birth, ¹⁵for he will be great in the sight of the Lord. He is never to take wine or other fermented drink, and he will be filled with the Holy Spirit even from birth.[b] ¹⁶Many of the people of Israel will he bring back to the Lord their God. ¹⁷And he will go on before the Lord, in the spirit and power of Elijah, to turn the hearts of the fathers to their children and the disobedient to the wisdom of the righteous—to make ready a people prepared for the Lord."

¹⁸Zechariah asked the angel, "How can I be sure of this? I am an old man and my wife is well on in years."

¹⁹The angel answered, "I am Gabriel. I stand in the presence of God, and I have been sent to speak to you and to tell you this good news. ²⁰And now you will be silent and not able to speak until the day this happens, because you did not believe my words, which will come true at their proper time."

²¹Meanwhile, the people were waiting for Zechariah and wondering why he stayed so long in the temple. ²²When he came out, he could not speak to them. They realised he had seen a vision in the temple, for he kept making signs to them but remained unable to speak.

²³When his time of service was completed, he returned home. ²⁴After this his wife Elizabeth became

a 1 Or been surely believed   b 15 Or from his mother's womb pregnant and for five months remained in seclusion. 25"The Lord has done this for me," she said. "In these days he has shown his favour and taken away my disgrace among the people."

The Birth of Jesus Foretold

26In the sixth month, God sent the angel Gabriel to Nazareth, a town in Galilee, 27to a virgin pledged to be married to a man named Joseph, a descendant of David. The virgin's name was Mary. 28The angel went to her and said, "Greetings, you who are highly favoured! The Lord is with you."

29Mary was greatly troubled at his words and wondered what kind of greeting this might be. 30But the angel said to her, "Do not be afraid, Mary, you have found favour with God. 31You will be with child and give birth to a son, and you are to give him the name Jesus. 32He will be great and will be called the Son of the Most High. The Lord God will give him the throne of his father David, 33and he will reign over the house of Jacob for ever; his kingdom will never end."

34"How will this be," Mary asked the angel, "since I am a virgin?"

35The angel answered, "The Holy Spirit will come upon you, and the power of the Most High will overshadow you. So the holy one to be born will be called^c the Son of God. 36Even Elizabeth your relative is going to have a child in her old age, and she who was said to be barren is in her sixth month. 37For nothing is impossible with God."

38"I am the Lord's servant," Mary answered. "May it be to me as you have said." Then the angel left her.

Mary Visits Elizabeth

39At that time Mary got ready and hurried to a town in the hill country of Judea, 40where she entered Zechariah's home and greeted Elizabeth. 41When Elizabeth heard Mary's greeting, the baby leaped in her womb, and Elizabeth was filled with the Holy Spirit. 42In a loud voice she exclaimed: "Blessed are you among women, and blessed is the child you will bear! 43But why am I so favoured, that the mother of my Lord should come to me? 44As soon as the sound of your greeting reached my ears, the baby in my womb leaped for joy. 45Blessed is she who has believed that what the Lord has said to her will be accomplished!"

Mary's Song

☐ See 1 Samuel 2:1–10

46And Mary said:

"My soul glorifies the Lord
47 and my spirit rejoices in God my Saviour,
48for he has been mindful
    of the humble state of his servant.
From now on all generations will call me
    blessed,
49 for the Mighty One has done great things for
    me —
    holy is his name.
50His mercy extends to those who fear him,
    from generation to generation.
51He has performed mighty deeds with his arm;

he has scattered those who are proud in
    their inmost thoughts.
52He has brought down rulers from their thrones
    but has lifted up the humble.
53He has filled the hungry with good things
    but has sent the rich away empty.
54He has helped his servant Israel,
    remembering to be merciful
55to Abraham and his descendants for ever,
    even as he said to our fathers."

56Mary stayed with Elizabeth for about three months and then returned home.

The Birth of John the Baptist

57When it was time for Elizabeth to have her baby, she gave birth to a son. 58Her neighbours and relatives heard that the Lord had shown her great mercy, and they shared her joy.

59On the eighth day they came to circumcise the child, and they were going to name him after his father Zechariah, 60but his mother spoke up and said, "No! He is to be called John."

61They said to her, "There is no-one among your relatives who has that name."

62Then they made signs to his father, to find out what he would like to name the child. 63He asked for a writing tablet, and to everyone's astonishment he wrote, "His name is John." 64Immediately his mouth was opened and his tongue was loosed, and he began to speak, praising God. 65The neighbours were all filled with awe, and throughout the hill country of Judea people were talking about all these things. 66Everyone who heard this wondered about it, asking, "What then is this child going to be?" For the Lord's hand was with him.

Zechariah's Song

67His father Zechariah was filled with the Holy Spirit and prophesied:

68"Praise be to the Lord, the God of Israel,
    because he has come and has redeemed his
        people.
69He has raised up a horn^d of salvation for us
    in the house of his servant David
70(as he said through his holy prophets of long
        ago),
71salvation from our enemies
    and from the hand of all who hate us —
72to show mercy to our fathers
    and to remember his holy covenant,
73 the oath he swore to our father Abraham:
74to rescue us from the hand of our enemies,
    and to enable us to serve him without fear
75 in holiness and righteousness before him all
        our days.

76And you, my child, will be called a prophet of
        the Most High;
    for you will go on before the Lord to
        prepare the way for him,
77to give his people the knowledge of salvation
    through the forgiveness of their sins,
78because of the tender mercy of our God,

---

^{c}35 Or So the child to be born will be called holy, ^{d}69 Horn here symbolises strength.

by which the rising sun will come to us from
heaven
79to shine on those living in darkness
and in the shadow of death,
to guide our feet into the path of peace."

80And the child grew and became strong in spirit;
and he lived in the desert until he appeared publicly
to Israel.

■ The Birth of Jesus

2 In those days Caesar Augustus issued a decree
that a census should be taken of the entire Roman world. (2This was the first census that took
place while Quirinius was governor of Syria.) 3And
everyone went to his own town to register.

2:1 ■ DATING BY EMPERORS

Among biblical writers, only Luke dated the events
he wrote about by referring to Roman emperors.
He had determined (1:1–4) to write a thorough,
factual account of Jesus' life, which included
setting the events in historical context. Because of
the Roman census mentioned here, Mary had to
travel from her home town in a very advanced
state of pregnancy. As a result, the Messiah was
born in Bethlehem, fulfilling an ancient prophecy.

4So Joseph also went up from the town of Nazareth in Galilee to Judea, to Bethlehem the town of
David, because he belonged to the house and line of
David. 5He went there to register with Mary, who
was pledged to be married to him and was expecting a child. 6While they were there, the time came
for the baby to be born, 7and she gave birth to her
firstborn, a son. She wrapped him in cloths and
placed him in a manger, because there was no room
for them in the inn.

■ The Shepherds and the Angels

8And there were shepherds living out in the fields
near by, keeping watch over their flocks at night.
9An angel of the Lord appeared to them, and the
glory of the Lord shone around them, and they were
terrified. 10But the angel said to them, "Do not be
afraid. I bring you good news of great joy that will
be for all the people. 11Today in the town of David
a Saviour has been born to you; he is Christ[a] the
Lord. 12This will be a sign to you: You will find a
baby wrapped in cloths and lying in a manger."

13Suddenly a great company of the heavenly host
appeared with the angel, praising God and saying,

14"Glory to God in the highest,
and on earth peace to men on whom his
favour rests."

15When the angels had left them and gone into
heaven, the shepherds said to one another, "Let's go
to Bethlehem and see this thing that has happened,
which the Lord has told us about."

16So they hurried off and found Mary and Joseph,
and the baby, who was lying in the manger. 17When
they had seen him, they spread the word concerning what had been told them about this child, 18and

all who heard it were amazed at what the shepherds
said to them. 19But Mary treasured up all these
things and pondered them in her heart. 20The shepherds returned, glorifying and praising God for all
the things they had heard and seen, which were just
as they had been told.

2:8 ■ CAST OF CHARACTERS

If a public relations firm planned the introduction
of God's Son on earth, whom would they invite?
Certainly not the group Luke introduces. No
Roman emperor or Greek philosopher attended.
Instead, Luke tells of an obscure priest and his
wife, a carpenter and his young fiancée, a group
of shepherds, and two elderly people. Jesus never
had much to do with the high and mighty, except
during his trial and execution. He would change
the world through the lives of ordinary people.

■ Jesus Presented in the Temple

21On the eighth day, when it was time to circumcise him, he was named Jesus, the name the angel
had given him before he had been conceived.

22When the time of their purification according
to the Law of Moses had been completed, Joseph
and Mary took him to Jerusalem to present him to
the Lord 23(as it is written in the Law of the Lord,
"Every firstborn male is to be consecrated to the
Lord"[b]), 24and to offer a sacrifice in keeping with
what is said in the Law of the Lord: "a pair of doves
or two young pigeons".[c]

25Now there was a man in Jerusalem called Simeon, who was righteous and devout. He was waiting
for the consolation of Israel, and the Holy Spirit was
upon him. 26It had been revealed to him by the Holy
Spirit that he would not die before he had seen the
Lord's Christ. 27Moved by the Spirit, he went into
the temple courts. When the parents brought in the
child Jesus to do for him what the custom of the Law
required, 28Simeon took him in his arms and praised
God, saying:

29"Sovereign Lord, as you have promised,
you now dismiss[d] your servant in peace.
30For my eyes have seen your salvation,
31   which you have prepared in the sight of all
people,
32a light for revelation to the Gentiles
and for glory to your people Israel."

33The child's father and mother marvelled at
what was said about him. 34Then Simeon blessed
them and said to Mary, his mother: "This child is
destined to cause the falling and rising of many in
Israel, and to be a sign that will be spoken against,
35so that the thoughts of many hearts will be revealed. And a sword will pierce your own soul too."

36There was also a prophetess, Anna, the daughter of Phanuel, of the tribe of Asher. She was very
old; she had lived with her husband seven years
after her marriage, 37and then was a widow until she
was eighty-four.[e] She never left the temple but
worshipped night and day, fasting and praying.
38Coming up to them at that very moment, she gave

---

a 11 Or Messiah. "The Christ" (Greek) and "the Messiah" (Hebrew) both mean "the Anointed One"; also in verse 26.   b 23 Exodus 13:2,12   c 24 Lev. 12:8
d 29 Or promised, / now dismiss   e 37 Or widow for eighty-four years

thanks to God and spoke about the child to all who were looking forward to the redemption of Jerusalem.

39When Joseph and Mary had done everything required by the Law of the Lord, they returned to Galilee to their own town of Nazareth. 40And the child grew and became strong; he was filled with wisdom, and the grace of God was upon him.

■ The Boy Jesus at the Temple
41Every year his parents went to Jerusalem for the Feast of the Passover. 42When he was twelve years old, they went up to the Feast, according to the custom. 43After the Feast was over, while his parents were returning home, the boy Jesus stayed behind in Jerusalem, but they were unaware of it. 44Thinking he was in their company, they travelled on for a day. Then they began looking for him among their relatives and friends. 45When they did not find him, they went back to Jerusalem to look for him. 46After three days they found him in the temple courts, sitting among the teachers, listening to them and asking them questions. 47Everyone who heard him was amazed at his understanding and his answers. 48When his parents saw him, they were astonished. His mother said to him, "Son, why have you treated us like this? Your father and I have been anxiously searching for you."

2:41 ■ JESUS' CHILDHOOD
Most Christmas pageants rely heavily on Luke because of his thoroughness in reporting the facts of Jesus' birth. And only Luke recorded the brief glimpses of Jesus' early years given in this chapter. For this reason, many scholars believe that Luke must have interviewed Mary, mother of Jesus, during his investigations into Jesus' life.

49"Why were you searching for me?" he asked. "Didn't you know I had to be in my Father's house?" 50But they did not understand what he was saying to them.

51Then he went down to Nazareth with them and was obedient to them. But his mother treasured all these things in her heart. 52And Jesus grew in wisdom and stature, and in favour with God and men.

■ John the Baptist Prepares the Way
☐ See Matthew 3:1–10; Mark 1:3–5
3 In the fifteenth year of the reign of Tiberius Caesar—when Pontius Pilate was governor of Judea, Herod tetrarch of Galilee, his brother Philip tetrarch of Iturea and Traconitis, and Lysanias tetrarch of Abilene—2during the high priesthood of Annas and Caiaphas, the word of God came to John son of Zechariah in the desert. 3He went into all the country around the Jordan, preaching a baptism of repentance for the forgiveness of sins. 4As is written in the book of the words of Isaiah the prophet:

"A voice of one calling in the desert,
'Prepare the way for the Lord,
    make straight paths for him.
5Every valley shall be filled in,

every mountain and hill made low.
The crooked roads shall become straight,
    the rough ways smooth.
6And all mankind will see God's salvation.' "a

7John said to the crowds coming out to be baptised by him, "You brood of vipers! Who warned you to flee from the coming wrath? 8Produce fruit in keeping with repentance. And do not begin to say to yourselves, 'We have Abraham as our father.' For I tell you that out of these stones God can raise up children for Abraham. 9The axe is already at the root of the trees, and every tree that does not produce good fruit will be cut down and thrown into the fire."

10"What should we do then?" the crowd asked.
11John answered, "The man with two tunics should share with him who has none, and the one who has food should do the same."

12Tax collectors also came to be baptised. "Teacher," they asked, "what should we do?"

13"Don't collect any more than you are required to," he told them.

14Then some soldiers asked him, "And what should we do?"

He replied, "Don't extort money and don't accuse people falsely—be content with your pay."

15The people were waiting expectantly and were all wondering in their hearts if John might possibly be the Christ.b 16John answered them all, "I baptise you withc water. But one more powerful than I will come, the thongs of whose sandals I am not worthy to untie. He will baptise you with the Holy Spirit and with fire. 17His winnowing fork is in his hand to clear his threshing-floor and to gather the wheat into his barn, but he will burn up the chaff with unquenchable fire." 18And with many other words John exhorted the people and preached the good news to them.

19But when John rebuked Herod the tetrarch because of Herodias, his brother's wife, and all the other evil things he had done, 20Herod added this to them all: He locked John up in prison.

■ The Baptism and Genealogy of Jesus
☐ See Matthew 1:1–17; 3:13–17; Mark 1:9–11
21When all the people were being baptised, Jesus was baptised too. And as he was praying, heaven was opened 22and the Holy Spirit descended on him in bodily form like a dove. And a voice came from heaven: "You are my Son, whom I love; with you I am well pleased."

23Now Jesus himself was about thirty years old when he began his ministry. He was the son, so it was thought, of Joseph,

the son of Heli, 24the son of Matthat,
    the son of Levi, the son of Melki,
    the son of Jannai, the son of Joseph,
25the son of Mattathias, the son of Amos,
    the son of Nahum, the son of Esli,
    the son of Naggai, 26the son of Maath,
    the son of Mattathias, the son of Semein,
    the son of Josech, the son of Joda,
27the son of Joanan, the son of Rhesa,
    the son of Zerubbabel, the son of Shealtiel,

a6 Isaiah 40:3–5   b15 Or Messiah   c16 Or in

the son of Neri, [28]the son of Melki,
the son of Addi, the son of Cosam,
the son of Elmadam, the son of Er,
[29]the son of Joshua, the son of Eliezer,
the son of Jorim, the son of Matthat,
the son of Levi, [30]the son of Simeon,
the son of Judah, the son of Joseph,
the son of Jonam, the son of Eliakim,
[31]the son of Melea, the son of Menna,
the son of Mattatha, the son of Nathan,
the son of David, [32]the son of Jesse,
the son of Obed, the son of Boaz,
the son of Salmon,[d] the son of Nahshon,
[33]the son of Amminadab, the son of Ram,[e]
the son of Hezron, the son of Perez,
the son of Judah, [34]the son of Jacob,
the son of Isaac, the son of Abraham,
the son of Terah, the son of Nahor,
[35]the son of Serug, the son of Reu,
the son of Peleg, the son of Eber,
the son of Shelah, [36]the son of Cainan,
the son of Arphaxad, the son of Shem,
the son of Noah, the son of Lamech,
[37]the son of Methuselah, the son of Enoch,
the son of Jared, the son of Mahalalel,
the son of Kenan, [38]the son of Enosh,
the son of Seth, the son of Adam,
the son of God.

3:38 ■ A GOSPEL FOR THE GENTILES
Matthew's Gospel traced Jesus' roots back to
Abraham, father of the Jewish race. But Luke,
probably the only Gentile writer of the New
Testament, emphasised that Jesus' good news
was for all people, not just the Jews. In keeping
with that purpose, he carried Jesus' lineage all the
way back to the first man, Adam.

■ The Temptation of Jesus
□ See Matthew 4:1–11; Mark 1:12–13

4 Jesus, full of the Holy Spirit, returned from the
Jordan and was led by the Spirit in the desert,
[2]where for forty days he was tempted by the devil.
He ate nothing during those days, and at the end of
them he was hungry.

[3]The devil said to him, "If you are the Son of God,
tell this stone to become bread."

[4]Jesus answered, "It is written: 'Man does not live
on bread alone.'[a]"

[5]The devil led him up to a high place and showed
him in an instant all the kingdoms of the world.
[6]And he said to him, "I will give you all their authority and splendour, for it has been given to me, and
I can give it to anyone I want to. [7]So if you worship
me, it will all be yours."

[8]Jesus answered, "It is written: 'Worship the Lord
your God and serve him only.'[b]"

[9]The devil led him to Jerusalem and had him
stand on the highest point of the temple. "If you are
the Son of God," he said, "throw yourself down from
here. [10]For it is written:

" 'He will command his angels concerning you

to guard you carefully;
[11]they will lift you up in their hands,
so that you will not strike your foot against a
stone.'[c]"

[12]Jesus answered, "It says: 'Do not put the Lord
your God to the test.'[d]"

[13]When the devil had finished all this tempting,
he left him until an opportune time.

■ Jesus Rejected at Nazareth

[14]Jesus returned to Galilee in the power of the
Spirit, and news about him spread through the
whole countryside. [15]He taught in their synagogues,
and everyone praised him.

[16]He went to Nazareth, where he had been
brought up, and on the Sabbath day he went into the
synagogue, as was his custom. And he stood up to
read. [17]The scroll of the prophet Isaiah was handed
to him. Unrolling it, he found the place where it is
written:

[18]"The Spirit of the Lord is on me,
because he has anointed me
to preach good news to the poor.
He has sent me to proclaim freedom for the
prisoners
and recovery of sight for the blind,
to release the oppressed,
[19]   to proclaim the year of the Lord's favour."[e]

[20]Then he rolled up the scroll, gave it back to the
attendant and sat down. The eyes of everyone in the
synagogue were fastened on him, [21]and he began by
saying to them, "Today this scripture is fulfilled in
your hearing."

[22]All spoke well of him and were amazed at the
gracious words that came from his lips. "Isn't this
Joseph's son?" they asked.

[23]Jesus said to them, "Surely you will quote this
proverb to me: 'Physician, heal yourself! Do here in
your home town what we have heard that you did
in Capernaum.' "

[24]"I tell you the truth," he continued, "no prophet
is accepted in his home town. [25]I assure you that
there were many widows in Israel in Elijah's time,
when the sky was shut for three and a half years and
there was a severe famine throughout the land.
[26]Yet Elijah was not sent to any of them, but to a
widow in Zarephath in the region of Sidon. [27]And
there were many in Israel with leprosy[f] in the time
of Elisha the prophet, yet not one of them was
cleansed — only Naaman the Syrian."

[28]All the people in the synagogue were furious
when they heard this. [29]They got up, drove him out
of the town, and took him to the brow of the hill on
which the town was built, in order to throw him
down the cliff. [30]But he walked right through the
crowd and went on his way.

■ Jesus Drives Out an Evil Spirit

[31]Then he went down to Capernaum, a town in
Galilee, and on the Sabbath began to teach the people. [32]They were amazed at his teaching, because
his message had authority.

---

[d] 32 Some early manuscripts *Sala*   [e] 33 Some manuscripts *Amminadab, the son of Admin, the son of Arni*; other manuscripts vary widely.
[a] 4 Deut. 8:3   [b] 8 Deut. 6:13   [c] 11 Psalm 91:11,12   [d] 12 Deut. 6:16   [e] 19 Isaiah 61:1,2   [f] 27 The Greek word was used for various diseases affecting the skin — not necessarily leprosy.

33In the synagogue there was a man possessed by a demon, an evil[g] spirit. He cried out at the top of his voice, 34"Ha! What do you want with us, Jesus of Nazareth? Have you come to destroy us? I know who you are—the Holy One of God!"

4:26 ■ HARD WORDS FOR THE JEWS
Luke's book stresses the universal appeal of the gospel. In both of these Old Testament stories (the Zarephath widow and Naaman), God sent a prophet to perform a miracle for foreigners (non-Jews). Such an emphasis scandalised the Jews, who saw themselves as God's uniquely chosen people. Jesus' words proved so inflammatory that a mob attempted to kill him. As far as is known, Jesus never returned to his home territory of Nazareth.

35"Be quiet!" Jesus said sternly. "Come out of him!" Then the demon threw the man down before them all and came out without injuring him.

36All the people were amazed and said to each other, "What is this teaching? With authority and power he gives orders to evil spirits and they come out!" 37And the news about him spread throughout the surrounding area.

■ Jesus Heals Many
□ See Matthew 8:14–17; Mark 1:29–38
38Jesus left the synagogue and went to the home of Simon. Now Simon's mother-in-law was suffering from a high fever, and they asked Jesus to help her. 39So he bent over her and rebuked the fever, and it left her. She got up at once and began to wait on them.

40When the sun was setting, the people brought to Jesus all who had various kinds of sickness, and laying his hands on each one, he healed them. 41Moreover, demons came out of many people, shouting, "You are the Son of God!" But he rebuked them and would not allow them to speak, because they knew he was the Christ.[b]

42At daybreak Jesus went out to a solitary place. The people were looking for him and when they came to where he was, they tried to keep him from leaving them. 43But he said, "I must preach the good news of the kingdom of God to the other towns also, because that is why I was sent." 44And he kept on preaching in the synagogues of Judea.[i]

■ The Calling of the First Disciples
□ See Matthew 4:18–22; Mark 1:16–20; John 1:40–42
5 One day as Jesus was standing by the Lake of Gennesaret,[a] with the people crowding round him and listening to the word of God, 2he saw at the water's edge two boats, left there by the fishermen, who were washing their nets. 3He got into one of the boats, the one belonging to Simon, and asked him to put out a little from shore. Then he sat down and taught the people from the boat.

4When he had finished speaking, he said to Simon, "Put out into deep water, and let down[b] the nets for a catch."

5Simon answered, "Master, we've worked hard all night and haven't caught anything. But because you say so, I will let down the nets."

6When they had done so, they caught such a large number of fish that their nets began to break. 7So they signalled to their partners in the other boat to come and help them, and they came and filled both boats so full that they began to sink.

8When Simon Peter saw this, he fell at Jesus' knees and said, "Go away from me, Lord; I am a sinful man!" 9For he and all his companions were astonished at the catch of fish they had taken, 10and so were James and John, the sons of Zebedee, Simon's partners.

Then Jesus said to Simon, "Don't be afraid; from now on you will catch men." 11So they pulled their boats up on shore, left everything and followed him.

■ The Man With Leprosy
□ See Matthew 8:2–4; Mark 1:40–44
12While Jesus was in one of the towns, a man came along who was covered with leprosy.[c] When he saw Jesus, he fell with his face to the ground and begged him, "Lord, if you are willing, you can make me clean."

13Jesus reached out his hand and touched the man. "I am willing," he said. "Be clean!" And immediately the leprosy left him.

14Then Jesus ordered him, "Don't tell anyone, but go, show yourself to the priest and offer the sacrifices that Moses commanded for your cleansing, as a testimony to them."

15Yet the news about him spread all the more, so that crowds of people came to hear him and to be healed of their sicknesses. 16But Jesus often withdrew to lonely places and prayed.

■ Jesus Heals a Paralytic
□ See Matthew 9:2–8; Mark 2:3–12
17One day as he was teaching, Pharisees and teachers of the law, who had come from every village of Galilee and from Judea and Jerusalem, were sitting there. And the power of the Lord was present for him to heal the sick. 18Some men came carrying a paralytic on a mat and tried to take him into the house to lay him before Jesus. 19When they could not find a way to do this because of the crowd, they went up on the roof and lowered him on his mat through the tiles into the middle of the crowd, right in front of Jesus.

20When Jesus saw their faith, he said, "Friend, your sins are forgiven."

5:20 ■ GROUP FAITH
The paralytic's friends showed remarkable determination to get him to Jesus. Luke writes that *their* faith—the man's and his friends'—moved Jesus to forgive and to heal. Jesus recognised that a helpless man needed help to come to him. Often an individual comes to Christ only with the persistent encouragement of friends and family.

---

g 33 Greek *unclean*; also in verse 36   b 41 Or *Messiah*   i 44 Or *the land of the Jews*; some manuscripts *Galilee*   a 1 That is, Sea of Galilee
b 4 The Greek verb is plural.   c 12 The Greek word was used for various diseases affecting the skin—not necessarily leprosy.

²¹The Pharisees and the teachers of the law began thinking to themselves, "Who is this fellow who speaks blasphemy? Who can forgive sins but God alone?"

²²Jesus knew what they were thinking and asked, "Why are you thinking these things in your hearts? ²³Which is easier: to say, 'Your sins are forgiven,' or to say, 'Get up and walk'? ²⁴But that you may know that the Son of Man has authority on earth to forgive sins...." He said to the paralysed man, "I tell you, get up, take your mat and go home." ²⁵Immediately he stood up in front of them, took what he had been lying on and went home praising God. ²⁶Everyone was amazed and gave praise to God. They were filled with awe and said, "We have seen remarkable things today."

■ The Calling of Levi
☐ See Matthew 9:9–13; Mark 2:14–17

²⁷After this, Jesus went out and saw a tax collector by the name of Levi sitting at his tax booth. "Follow me," Jesus said to him, ²⁸and Levi got up, left everything and followed him.

²⁹Then Levi held a great banquet for Jesus at his house, and a large crowd of tax collectors and others were eating with them. ³⁰But the Pharisees and the teachers of the law who belonged to their sect complained to his disciples, "Why do you eat and drink with tax collectors and 'sinners'?"

³¹Jesus answered them, "It is not the healthy who need a doctor, but the sick. ³²I have not come to call the righteous, but sinners to repentance."

■ A PHYSICIAN LOOKS AT THE POOR
THE SURPRISING EMPHASIS OF AN UPPER-CLASS WRITER

"IT IS NOT THE HEALTHY WHO NEED A DOCTOR, BUT THE SICK." ■ 5:31

A great doctor once compared his professional duties to working at the complaint desk of a large department store. "All through medical school I studied the body's wonderful engineering. A healthy body is perfect – absolutely beautiful to observe. But in practice I spend my time treating people whose bodies don't work right. I hear only complaints. After a while, it's easy to lose perspective."

Luke, a physician, knew first-hand about sick and suffering people; he, too, heard their daily complaints. Yet somehow he never became callous. In fact, his Gospel focuses on Jesus' ministry to society's "complaint desk": the poor, the sick, and the neglected.

■ JESUS ANNOUNCES HIS MISSION
In Luke, even Mary's opening song strikes a chord for the poor and hungry (1:46–55). Using his favourite title for Jesus ("Son of Man") 80 times, Luke reveals him as a true servant of all humanity.

Luke 4 shows Jesus boldly declaring why he came to earth. He had just resisted temptations of wealth and power, and returned from the desert to his home town. There Jesus, a local village boy, announced his unique mission from God: to preach good news to the poor, to free prisoners, heal the blind and release the oppressed (4:18–19).

With little editorial comment, Luke follows Jesus from town to town. Jesus avoided such fashionable places as the resort town of Tiberias. He stayed near the farming

communities and fishing villages clustered round the Sea of Galilee, serving the needs of humble people.

Reaction to Jesus varied. Naturally, the sick clamoured for his attention, begging for healing. Even a few powerful people believed in him, including a respected Roman centurion and a synagogue ruler. But the religious leaders constantly challenged his actions, and his own neighbours angrily chased him out of town.

■ AN UNLIKELY FRIEND OF THE POOR
Luke skilfully brings his characters to life in vignettes. Learned and sophisticated, he uses the finest Greek of any Gospel writer; but, ironically, he focuses mainly on the poor and the outcast. Women, largely ignored by ancient historians, play a large role: Luke introduces 13 women mentioned in no other Gospel. He also shows a delight and appreciation for children.

It may seem strange that Luke, by education and profession a member of the upper class, emerged as a champion of the poor and the oppressed. Evidently Jesus' message had affected him deeply. As Jesus said, "It is not the healthy who need a doctor, but the sick. I have not come to call the righteous, but sinners to repentance" (5:31–32).

☐ LIFE QUESTIONS:
As Luke tells it, Jesus threatened the rich and powerful, but appealed to the poor and outcast. If Jesus came today, how would those two groups in our society respond to him?

■ Jesus Questioned About Fasting
□ See Matthew 9:14–17; Mark 2:18–22

33They said to him, "John's disciples often fast and pray, and so do the disciples of the Pharisees, but yours go on eating and drinking."

34Jesus answered, "Can you make the guests of the bridegroom fast while he is with them? 35But the time will come when the bridegroom will be taken from them; in those days they will fast."

36He told them this parable: "No-one tears a patch from a new garment and sews it on an old one. If he does, he will have torn the new garment, and the patch from the new will not match the old. 37And no-one pours new wine into old wineskins. If he does, the new wine will burst the skins, the wine will run out and the wineskins will be ruined. 38No, new wine must be poured into new wineskins. 39And no-one after drinking old wine wants the new, for he says, 'The old is better.' "

■ Lord of the Sabbath
□ See Matthew 12:1–14; Mark 2:23–3:6

6 One Sabbath Jesus was going through the corn-fields, and his disciples began to pick some ears of corn, rub them in their hands and eat the grain. 2Some of the Pharisees asked, "Why are you doing what is unlawful on the Sabbath?"

3Jesus answered them, "Have you never read what David did when he and his companions were hungry? 4He entered the house of God, and taking the consecrated bread, he ate what is lawful only for priests to eat. And he also gave some to his companions." 5Then Jesus said to them, "The Son of Man is Lord of the Sabbath."

6On another Sabbath he went into the synagogue and was teaching, and a man was there whose right hand was shrivelled. 7The Pharisees and the teachers of the law were looking for a reason to accuse Jesus, so they watched him closely to see if he would heal on the Sabbath. 8But Jesus knew what they were thinking and said to the man with the shrivelled hand, "Get up and stand in front of everyone." So he got up and stood there.

9Then Jesus said to them, "I ask you, which is lawful on the Sabbath: to do good or to do evil, to save life or to destroy it?"

6:9 ■ RULES WITHOUT LOVE
Luke's vignettes on Jesus and the Sabbath (see also 13:10–17) demonstrate the legalism Jesus opposed. Jews of his day observed very strict rules governing what could be done on the Sabbath. Religious leaders became furious at Jesus for "breaking" the traditions. His crime? Healing people on the Sabbath. Jesus refused to let traditions interfere with compassion for needy people.

10He looked round at them all, and then said to the man, "Stretch out your hand." He did so, and his hand was completely restored. 11But they were furious and began to discuss with one another what they might do to Jesus.

■ The Twelve Apostles
□ See Matthew 10:2–4; Mark 3:16–19; Acts 1:13

12One of those days Jesus went out to a mountainside to pray, and spent the night praying to God. 13When morning came, he called his disciples to him and chose twelve of them, whom he also designated apostles: 14Simon (whom he named Peter), his brother Andrew, James, John, Philip, Bartholomew, 15Matthew, Thomas, James son of Alphaeus, Simon who was called the Zealot, 16Judas son of James, and Judas Iscariot, who became a traitor.

■ Blessings and Woes
□ See Matthew 5:3–12

17He went down with them and stood on a level place. A large crowd of his disciples was there and a great number of people from all over Judea, from Jerusalem, and from the coast of Tyre and Sidon, 18who had come to hear him and to be healed of their diseases. Those troubled by evil*a* spirits were cured, 19and the people all tried to touch him, because power was coming from him and healing them all.

20Looking at his disciples, he said:

"Blessed are you who are poor,
    for yours is the kingdom of God.
21Blessed are you who hunger now,
    for you will be satisfied.
Blessed are you who weep now,
    for you will laugh.
22Blessed are you when men hate you,
    when they exclude you and insult you
    and reject your name as evil,
    because of the Son of Man.

23"Rejoice in that day and leap for joy, because great is your reward in heaven. For that is how their fathers treated the prophets.

24"But woe to you who are rich,
    for you have already received your comfort.
25Woe to you who are well fed now,
    for you will go hungry.
Woe to you who laugh now,
    for you will mourn and weep.
26Woe to you when all men speak well of you,
    for that is how their fathers treated the false
    prophets.

■ Love for Enemies

27"But I tell you who hear me: Love your enemies, do good to those who hate you, 28bless those who curse you, pray for those who ill-treat you. 29If someone strikes you on one cheek, turn to him the other also. If someone takes your cloak, do not stop him from taking your tunic. 30Give to everyone who asks you, and if anyone takes what belongs to you, do not demand it back. 31Do to others as you would have them do to you.

32"If you love those who love you, what credit is that to you? Even 'sinners' love those who love them. 33And if you do good to those who are good to you, what credit is that to you? Even 'sinners' do that. 34And if you lend to those from whom you expect repayment, what credit is that to you? Even

a 18 Greek unclean

'sinners' lend to 'sinners', expecting to be repaid in full. 35But love your enemies, do good to them, and lend to them without expecting to get anything back. Then your reward will be great, and you will be sons of the Most High, because he is kind to the ungrateful and wicked. 36Be merciful, just as your Father is merciful.

■ Judging Others
□ See Matthew 7:1–5
37"Do not judge, and you will not be judged. Do not condemn, and you will not be condemned. Forgive, and you will be forgiven. 38Give, and it will be given to you. A good measure, pressed down, shaken together and running over, will be poured into your lap. For with the measure you use, it will be measured to you."

39He also told them this parable: "Can a blind man lead a blind man? Will they not both fall into a pit? 40A student is not above his teacher, but everyone who is fully trained will be like his teacher.

41"Why do you look at the speck of sawdust in your brother's eye and pay no attention to the plank in your own eye? 42How can you say to your brother, 'Brother, let me take the speck out of your eye,' when you yourself fail to see the plank in your own eye? You hypocrite, first take the plank out of your eye, and then you will see clearly to remove the speck from your brother's eye.

■ A Tree and Its Fruit
□ See Matthew 7:16,18,20
43"No good tree bears bad fruit, nor does a bad tree bear good fruit. 44Each tree is recognised by its own fruit. People do not pick figs from thornbushes, or grapes from briers. 45The good man brings good things out of the good stored up in his heart, and the evil man brings evil things out of the evil stored up in his heart. For out of the overflow of his heart his mouth speaks.

■ The Wise and Foolish Builders
□ See Matthew 7:24–27
46"Why do you call me, 'Lord, Lord,' and do not do what I say? 47I will show you what he is like who comes to me and hears my words and puts them into practice. 48He is like a man building a house, who dug down deep and laid the foundation on rock. When the flood came, the torrent struck that house but could not shake it, because it was well built. 49But the one who hears my words and does not put them into practice is like a man who built a house on the ground without a foundation. The moment the torrent struck that house, it collapsed and its destruction was complete."

■ The Faith of the Centurion
□ See Matthew 8:5–13
7 When Jesus had finished saying all this in the hearing of the people, he entered Capernaum. 2There a centurion's servant, whom his master valued highly, was sick and about to die. 3The centurion heard of Jesus and sent some elders of the Jews to him, asking him to come and heal his servant. 4When they came to Jesus, they pleaded earnestly

with him, "This man deserves to have you do this, 5because he loves our nation and has built our synagogue." 6So Jesus went with them.

He was not far from the house when the centurion sent friends to say to him: "Lord, don't trouble yourself, for I do not deserve to have you come under my roof. 7That is why I did not even consider myself worthy to come to you. But say the word, and my servant will be healed. 8For I myself am a man under authority, with soldiers under me. I tell this one, 'Go', and he goes; and that one, 'Come', and he comes. I say to my servant, 'Do this', and he does it."

9When Jesus heard this, he was amazed at him, and turning to the crowd following him, he said, "I tell you, I have not found such great faith even in Israel." 10Then the men who had been sent returned to the house and found the servant well.

■ Jesus Raises a Widow's Son
11Soon afterwards, Jesus went to a town called Nain, and his disciples and a large crowd went along with him. 12As he approached the town gate, a dead person was being carried out—the only son of his mother, and she was a widow. And a large crowd from the town was with her. 13When the Lord saw her, his heart went out to her and he said, "Don't cry."

14Then he went up and touched the coffin, and those carrying it stood still. He said, "Young man, I say to you, get up!" 15The dead man sat up and began to talk, and Jesus gave him back to his mother.

16They were all filled with awe and praised God. "A great prophet has appeared among us," they said. "God has come to help his people." 17This news about Jesus spread throughout Judea[a] and the surrounding country.

■ Jesus and John the Baptist
□ See Matthew 11:2–19
18John's disciples told him about all these things. Calling two of them, 19he sent them to the Lord to ask, "Are you the one who was to come, or should we expect someone else?"

7:19 ■ EVEN JOHN QUESTIONED
The crowds Jesus attracted wavered between enthusiastic support and outright rejection of him. Evidently, some of the controversy even affected John the Baptist, who had baptised Jesus and pronounced him the Son of God (see John 1:34). John, then in prison, sent his disciples to confirm whether Jesus was the true Messiah. Jesus reassured him with a direct reference to the prophecies of Isaiah 61 (see also Luke 4:18–21).

20When the men came to Jesus, they said, "John the Baptist sent us to you to ask, 'Are you the one who was to come, or should we expect someone else?'"

21At that very time Jesus cured many who had diseases, sicknesses and evil spirits, and gave sight to many who were blind. 22So he replied to the

---

a 17 Or the land of the Jews

messengers, "Go back and report to John what you have seen and heard: The blind receive sight, the lame walk, those who have leprosy[b] are cured, the deaf hear, the dead are raised, and the good news is preached to the poor. [23]Blessed is the man who does not fall away on account of me."

[24]After John's messengers left, Jesus began to speak to the crowd about John: "What did you go out into the desert to see? A reed swayed by the wind? [25]If not, what did you go out to see? A man dressed in fine clothes? No, those who wear expensive clothes and indulge in luxury are in palaces. [26]But what did you go out to see? A prophet? Yes, I tell you, and more than a prophet. [27]This is the one about whom it is written:

" 'I will send my messenger ahead of you,
     who will prepare your way before you.'[c]

[28]I tell you, among those born of women there is no-one greater than John; yet the one who is least in the kingdom of God is greater than he."

([29]All the people, even the tax collectors, when they heard Jesus' words, acknowledged that God's way was right, because they had been baptised by John. [30]But the Pharisees and experts in the law rejected God's purpose for themselves, because they had not been baptised by John.)

[31]"To what, then, can I compare the people of this generation? What are they like? [32]They are like children sitting in the market-place and calling out to each other:

" 'We played the flute for you,
     and you did not dance;
   we sang a dirge,
     and you did not cry.'

[33]For John the Baptist came neither eating bread nor drinking wine, and you say, 'He has a demon.' [34]The Son of Man came eating and drinking, and you say, 'Here is a glutton and a drunkard, a friend of tax collectors and "sinners". ' [35]But wisdom is proved right by all her children."

■ Jesus Anointed by a Sinful Woman

[36]Now one of the Pharisees invited Jesus to have dinner with him, so he went to the Pharisee's house and reclined at the table. [37]When a woman who had lived a sinful life in that town learned that Jesus was eating at the Pharisee's house, she brought an alabaster jar of perfume, [38]and as she stood behind him at his feet weeping, she began to wet his feet with her tears. Then she wiped them with her hair, kissed them and poured perfume on them.

[39]When the Pharisee who had invited him saw this, he said to himself, "If this man were a prophet, he would know who is touching him and what kind of woman she is—that she is a sinner."

[40]Jesus answered him, "Simon, I have something to tell you."

"Tell me, teacher," he said.

[41]"Two men owed money to a certain money-lender. One owed him five hundred denarii,[d] and the other fifty. [42]Neither of them had the money to pay him back, so he cancelled the debts of both. Now which of them will love him more?"

[43]Simon replied, "I suppose the one who had the bigger debt cancelled."

"You have judged correctly," Jesus said.

[44]Then he turned towards the woman and said to Simon, "Do you see this woman? I came into your house. You did not give me any water for my feet, but she wet my feet with her tears and wiped them with her hair. [45]You did not give me a kiss, but this woman, from the time I entered, has not stopped kissing my feet. [46]You did not put oil on my head, but she has poured perfume on my feet. [47]Therefore, I tell you, her many sins have been forgiven— for she loved much. But he who has been forgiven little loves little."

[48]Then Jesus said to her, "Your sins are forgiven."

[49]The other guests began to say among themselves, "Who is this who even forgives sins?"

[50]Jesus said to the woman, "Your faith has saved you; go in peace."

■ The Parable of the Sower
□ See Matthew 13:2–23; Mark 4:1–20

8 After this, Jesus travelled about from one town and village to another, proclaiming the good news of the kingdom of God. The Twelve were with him, [2]and also some women who had been cured of evil spirits and diseases: Mary (called Magdalene) from whom seven demons had come out; [3]Joanna the wife of Chuza, the manager of Herod's household; Susanna; and many others. These women were helping to support them out of their own means.

8:3 ■ JESUS' SUPPORT
In the Middle East of that day, teachers travelled from town to town, accepting the gifts of appreciative listeners. Luke points out that certain women who had been healed by Jesus helped to provide for him. In all, Luke introduces 13 women who do not appear in the other Gospels.

[1]While a large crowd was gathering and people were coming to Jesus from town after town, he told this parable: [5]"A farmer went out to sow his seed. As he was scattering the seed, some fell along the path; it was trampled on, and the birds of the air ate it up. [6]Some fell on rock, and when it came up, the plants withered because they had no moisture. [7]Other seed fell among thorns, which grew up with it and choked the plants. [8]Still other seed fell on good soil. It came up and yielded a crop, a hundred times more than was sown."

When he said this, he called out, "He who has ears to hear, let him hear."

[9]His disciples asked him what this parable meant. [10]He said, "The knowledge of the secrets of the kingdom of God has been given to you, but to others I speak in parables, so that,

" 'though seeing, they may not see;
     though hearing, they may not understand.'[a]

[11]"This is the meaning of the parable: The seed is the word of God. [12]Those along the path are the ones who hear, and then the devil comes and takes

b 22 The Greek word was used for various diseases affecting the skin—not necessarily leprosy.   c 27 Mal. 3:1   d 41 A denarius was a coin worth about a day's wages.   a 10 Isaiah 6:9

away the word from their hearts, so that they may not believe and be saved. ¹³Those on the rock are the ones who receive the word with joy when they hear it, but they have no root. They believe for a while, but in the time of testing they fall away. ¹⁴The seed that fell among thorns stands for those who hear, but as they go on their way they are choked by life's worries, riches and pleasures, and they do not mature. ¹⁵But the seed on good soil stands for those with a noble and good heart, who hear the word, retain it, and by persevering produce a crop.

■ A Lamp on a Stand

¹⁶"No-one lights a lamp and hides it in a jar or puts it under a bed. Instead, he puts it on a stand, so that those who come in can see the light. ¹⁷For there is nothing hidden that will not be disclosed, and nothing concealed that will not be known or brought out into the open. ¹⁸Therefore consider carefully how you listen. Whoever has will be given more; whoever does not have, even what he thinks he has will be taken from him."

■ Jesus' Mother and Brothers
☐ See Matthew 12:46–50; Mark 3:31–35

¹⁹Now Jesus' mother and brothers came to see him, but they were not able to get near him because of the crowd. ²⁰Someone told him, "Your mother and brothers are standing outside, wanting to see you."

²¹He replied, "My mother and brothers are those who hear God's word and put it into practice."

■ Jesus Calms the Storm
☐ See Matthew 8:23–27; Mark 4:36–41

²²One day Jesus said to his disciples, "Let's go over to the other side of the lake." So they got into a boat and set out. ²³As they sailed, he fell asleep. A squall came down on the lake, so that the boat was being swamped, and they were in great danger.

²⁴The disciples went and woke him, saying, "Master, Master, we're going to drown!"

He got up and rebuked the wind and the raging waters; the storm subsided, and all was calm. ²⁵"Where is your faith?" he asked his disciples.

In fear and amazement they asked one another, "Who is this? He commands even the winds and the water, and they obey him."

■ The Healing of a Demon-possessed Man
☐ See Matthew 8:28–34; Mark 5:1–20

²⁶They sailed to the region of the Gerasenes,ᵇ which is across the lake from Galilee. ²⁷When Jesus stepped ashore, he was met by a demon-possessed man from the town. For a long time this man had not worn clothes or lived in a house, but had lived in the tombs. ²⁸When he saw Jesus, he cried out and fell at his feet, shouting at the top of his voice, "What do you want with me, Jesus, Son of the Most High God? I beg you, don't torture me!" ²⁹For Jesus had commanded the evilᶜ spirit to come out of the man. Many times it had seized him, and though he was chained hand and foot and kept under guard, he had broken his chains and had been driven by the demon into solitary places.

³⁰Jesus asked him, "What is your name?"

"Legion," he replied, because many demons had gone into him. ³¹And they begged him repeatedly not to order them to go into the Abyss.

8:27 ■ HOMELESS

Much as mentally troubled people live under bridges today, this disturbed man had fled society to live in the tombs. Cemeteries in the ancient world were located far from town, because people feared the spirits of the dead. The man was violent and uncontrollable, and he greeted Jesus with bizarre behaviour. Jesus, rather than avoiding him, went straight to the heart of his problem.

³²A large herd of pigs was feeding there on the hillside. The demons begged Jesus to let them go into them, and he gave them permission. ³³When the demons came out of the man, they went into the pigs, and the herd rushed down the steep bank into the lake and was drowned.

³⁴When those tending the pigs saw what had happened, they ran off and reported this in the town and countryside, ³⁵and the people went out to see what had happened. When they came to Jesus, they found the man from whom the demons had gone out, sitting at Jesus' feet, dressed and in his right mind; and they were afraid. ³⁶Those who had seen it told the people how the demon-possessed man had been cured. ³⁷Then all the people of the region of the Gerasenes asked Jesus to leave them, because they were overcome with fear. So he got into the boat and left.

³⁸The man from whom the demons had gone out begged to go with him, but Jesus sent him away, saying, ³⁹"Return home and tell how much God has done for you." So the man went away and told all over the town how much Jesus had done for him.

■ A Dead Girl and a Sick Woman
☐ See Matthew 9:18–26; Mark 5:22–43

⁴⁰Now when Jesus returned, a crowd welcomed him, for they were all expecting him. ⁴¹Then a man named Jairus, a ruler of the synagogue, came and fell at Jesus' feet, pleading with him to come to his house ⁴²because his only daughter, a girl of about twelve, was dying.

As Jesus was on his way, the crowds almost crushed him. ⁴³And a woman was there who had been subject to bleeding for twelve years,ᵈ but no-one could heal her. ⁴⁴She came up behind him and touched the edge of his cloak, and immediately her bleeding stopped.

⁴⁵"Who touched me?" Jesus asked.

When they all denied it, Peter said, "Master, the people are crowding and pressing against you."

⁴⁶But Jesus said, "Someone touched me; I know that power has gone out from me."

⁴⁷Then the woman, seeing that she could not go unnoticed, came trembling and fell at his feet. In the presence of all the people, she told why she had touched him and how she had been instantly

---

ᵇ 26 Some manuscripts Gadarenes; other manuscripts Gergesenes; also in verse 37　　ᶜ 29 Greek unclean　　ᵈ 43 Many manuscripts years, and she had
spent all she had on doctors

healed. 48Then he said to her, "Daughter, your faith has healed you. Go in peace."

49While Jesus was still speaking, someone came from the house of Jairus, the synagogue ruler. "Your daughter is dead," he said. "Don't bother the teacher any more."

50Hearing this, Jesus said to Jairus, "Don't be afraid; just believe, and she will be healed."

51When he arrived at the house of Jairus, he did not let anyone go in with him except Peter, John and James, and the child's father and mother. 52Meanwhile, all the people were wailing and mourning for her. "Stop wailing," Jesus said. "She is not dead but asleep."

53They laughed at him, knowing that she was dead. 54But he took her by the hand and said, "My child, get up!" 55Her spirit returned, and at once she stood up. Then Jesus told them to give her something to eat. 56Her parents were astonished, but he ordered them not to tell anyone what had happened.

■ Jesus Sends Out the Twelve
☐ See Matthew 10:9–15; Mark 6:8–11

9 When Jesus had called the Twelve together, he gave them power and authority to drive out all demons and to cure diseases, 2and he sent them out to preach the kingdom of God and to heal the sick. 3He told them: "Take nothing for the journey—no staff, no bag, no bread, no money, no extra tunic. 4Whatever house you enter, stay there until you leave that town. 5If people do not welcome you, shake the dust off your feet when you leave their town, as a testimony against them." 6So they set out and went from village to village, preaching the gospel and healing people everywhere.

7Now Herod the tetrarch heard about all that was going on. And he was perplexed, because some were saying that John had been raised from the dead, 8others that Elijah had appeared, and still others that one of the prophets of long ago had come back to life. 9But Herod said, "I beheaded John. Who, then, is this I hear such things about?" And he tried to see him.

■ Jesus Feeds the Five Thousand
☐ See Matthew 14:13–21; Mark 6:32–44; John 6:5–13

10When the apostles returned, they reported to Jesus what they had done. Then he took them with him and they withdrew by themselves to a town called Bethsaida, 11but the crowds learned about it and followed him. He welcomed them and spoke to them about the kingdom of God, and healed those who needed healing.

12Late in the afternoon the Twelve came to him and said, "Send the crowd away so they can go to the surrounding villages and countryside and find food and lodging, because we are in a remote place here."

13He replied, "You give them something to eat."

They answered, "We have only five loaves of bread and two fish—unless we go and buy food for all this crowd." 14(About five thousand men were there.)

But he said to his disciples, "Make them sit down in groups of about fifty each." 15The disciples did so, and everybody sat down. 16Taking the five loaves and the two fish and looking up to heaven, he gave thanks and broke them. Then he gave them to the disciples to set before the people. 17They all ate and were satisfied, and the disciples picked up twelve basketfuls of broken pieces that were left over.

■ Peter's Confession of Christ
☐ See Matthew 16:13–16; Mark 8:27–29

18Once when Jesus was praying in private and his disciples were with him, he asked them, "Who do the crowds say I am?"

19They replied, "Some say John the Baptist; others say Elijah; and still others, that one of the prophets of long ago has come back to life."

20"But what about you?" he asked. "Who do you say I am?"

Peter answered, "The Christa of God."

21Jesus strictly warned them not to tell this to anyone. 22And he said, "The Son of Man must suffer many things and be rejected by the elders, chief priests and teachers of the law, and he must be killed and on the third day be raised to life."

23Then he said to them all: "If anyone would come after me, he must deny himself and take up his cross daily and follow me. 24For whoever wants to save his life will lose it, but whoever loses his life for me will save it. 25What good is it for a man to gain the whole world, and yet lose or forfeit his very self? 26If anyone is ashamed of me and my words, the Son of Man will be ashamed of him when he comes in his glory and in the glory of the Father and of the holy angels. 27I tell you the truth, some who are standing here will not taste death before they see the kingdom of God."

9:27 ■ SEEING THE KINGDOM
Jesus predicted that some of his disciples would "see the kingdom of God" before tasting death. Eight days later, three of them witnessed Jesus gleaming like a flash of lightning and talking with the long-dead Moses and Elijah (verses 29–30). Many scholars think the Transfiguration fulfilled Jesus' "seeing the kingdom" prediction. Apart from this moment, Jesus looked like any other man during his years on earth. He had none of the brilliant glory associated with God in the Old Testament (see, for example, Exodus 40:34).

■ The Transfiguration
☐ See Matthew 17:1–8; Mark 9:2–8

28About eight days after Jesus said this, he took Peter, John and James with him and went up onto a mountain to pray. 29As he was praying, the appearance of his face changed, and his clothes became as bright as a flash of lightning. 30Two men, Moses and Elijah, 31appeared in glorious splendour, talking with Jesus. They spoke about his departure, which he was about to bring to fulfilment at Jerusalem. 32Peter and his companions were very sleepy, but when they became fully awake, they saw his glory and the two men standing with him. 33As the men

a20 Or Messiah

were leaving Jesus, Peter said to him, "Master, it is good for us to be here. Let us put up three shelters—one for you, one for Moses and one for Elijah." (He did not know what he was saying.)

34While he was speaking, a cloud appeared and enveloped them, and they were afraid as they entered the cloud. 35A voice came from the cloud, saying, "This is my Son, whom I have chosen; listen to him." 36When the voice had spoken, they found that Jesus was alone. The disciples kept this to themselves, and told no-one at that time what they had seen.

■ The Healing of a Boy With an Evil Spirit
☐ See Matthew 17:14–18,22–23; Mark 9:14–27,30–32

37The next day, when they came down from the mountain, a large crowd met him. 38A man in the crowd called out, "Teacher, I beg you to look at my son, for he is my only child. 39A spirit seizes him and he suddenly screams; it throws him into convulsions so that he foams at the mouth. It scarcely ever leaves him and is destroying him. 40I begged your disciples to drive it out, but they could not."

41"O unbelieving and perverse generation," Jesus replied, "how long shall I stay with you and put up with you? Bring your son here."

42Even while the boy was coming, the demon threw him to the ground in a convulsion. But Jesus rebuked the evilᵇ spirit, healed the boy and gave him back to his father. 43And they were all amazed at the greatness of God.

While everyone was marvelling at all that Jesus did, he said to his disciples, 44"Listen carefully to what I am about to tell you: The Son of Man is going to be betrayed into the hands of men." 45But they did not understand what this meant. It was hidden from them, so that they did not grasp it, and they were afraid to ask him about it.

■ Who Will Be the Greatest?
☐ See Matthew 18:1–5; Mark 9:33–40

46An argument started among the disciples as to which of them would be the greatest. 47Jesus, knowing their thoughts, took a little child and made him stand beside him. 48Then he said to them, "Whoever welcomes this little child in my name welcomes me; and whoever welcomes me welcomes the one who sent me. For he who is least among you all—he is the greatest."

49"Master," said John, "we saw a man driving out demons in your name and we tried to stop him, because he is not one of us."

50"Do not stop him," Jesus said, "for whoever is not against you is for you."

■ Samaritan Opposition

51As the time approached for him to be taken up to heaven, Jesus resolutely set out for Jerusalem. 52And he sent messengers on ahead, who went into a Samaritan village to get things ready for him; 53but the people there did not welcome him, because he was heading for Jerusalem. 54When the disciples

James and John saw this, they asked, "Lord, do you want us to call fire down from heaven to destroy them?"ᶜ 55But Jesus turned and rebuked them, 56andᵈ they went to another village.

■ The Cost of Following Jesus
☐ See Matthew 8:19–22

57As they were walking along the road, a man said to him, "I will follow you wherever you go."

58Jesus replied, "Foxes have holes and birds of the air have nests, but the Son of Man has nowhere to lay his head."

59He said to another man, "Follow me."

But the man replied, "Lord, first let me go and bury my father."

9:59 ■ BURYING HIS FATHER
The man's request to "let me go and bury my father" didn't necessarily mean that the man's father had just died. Possibly the expression was a figure of speech, a way of saying, "Let me wait until my father has died". Jesus instead stressed the urgency of his mission.

60Jesus said to him, "Let the dead bury their own dead, but you go and proclaim the kingdom of God." 61Still another said, "I will follow you, Lord; but first let me go back and say good-bye to my family."

62Jesus replied, "No-one who puts his hand to the plough and looks back is fit for service in the kingdom of God."

■ Jesus Sends Out the Seventy-two
☐ See Luke 9:3–5

10 After this the Lord appointed seventy-twoᵃ others and sent them two by two ahead of him to every town and place where he was about to go. 2He told them, "The harvest is plentiful, but the workers are few. Ask the Lord of the harvest, therefore, to send out workers into his harvest field. 3Go! I am sending you out like lambs among wolves. 4Do not take a purse or bag or sandals; and do not greet anyone on the road.

5"When you enter a house, first say, 'Peace to this house.' 6If a man of peace is there, your peace will rest on him; if not, it will return to you. 7Stay in that house, eating and drinking whatever they give you, for the worker deserves his wages. Do not move around from house to house.

8"When you enter a town and are welcomed, eat what is set before you. 9Heal the sick who are there and tell them, 'The kingdom of God is near you.' 10But when you enter a town and are not welcomed, go into its streets and say, 11'Even the dust of your town that sticks to our feet we wipe off against you. Yet be sure of this: The kingdom of God is near.' 12I tell you, it will be more bearable on that day for Sodom than for that town.

13"Woe to you, Korazin! Woe to you, Bethsaida! For if the miracles that were performed in you had

ᵇ42 Greek unclean   ᶜ54 Some manuscripts them, even as Elijah did   ᵈ55,56 Some manuscripts them. And he said, "You do not know what kind of spirit you are of, for the Son of Man did not come to destroy men's lives, but to save them." 56And   ᵃ1 Some manuscripts seventy; also in verse 17 been performed in Tyre and Sidon, they would have repented long ago, sitting in sackcloth and ashes. [14]But it will be more bearable for Tyre and Sidon at the judgment than for you. [15]And you, Capernaum, will you be lifted up to the skies? No, you will go down to the depths.[b]

[16]"He who listens to you listens to me; he who rejects you rejects me; but he who rejects me rejects him who sent me."

[17]The seventy-two returned with joy and said, "Lord, even the demons submit to us in your name."

[18]He replied, "I saw Satan fall like lightning from heaven. [19]I have given you authority to trample on snakes and scorpions and to overcome all the power of the enemy; nothing will harm you. [20]However, do not rejoice that the spirits submit to you, but rejoice that your names are written in heaven."

[21]At that time Jesus, full of joy through the Holy Spirit, said, "I praise you, Father, Lord of heaven and earth, because you have hidden these things from the wise and learned, and revealed them to little children. Yes, Father, for this was your good pleasure.

[22]"All things have been committed to me by my Father. No-one knows who the Son is except the Father, and no-one knows who the Father is except

■ THE POWER OF A NAME
JESUS' TIME ON EARTH WAS RUNNING OUT

INSIGHT

HE WHO LISTENS TO YOU LISTENS TO ME; HE WHO REJECTS YOU REJECTS ME. ■ 10:16

Christians speak "in the name of Jesus". But that familiar phrase may have lost meaning for some of us. Consider:
  College second-year Tom Bowers took a summer job as an apprentice on the governor of Michigan's staff. He spent the first few weeks turning out memos, returning mundane phone calls and straightening files. But one day a harried manager asked Tom to write a public statement on the state's new law enforcement programme. Tom composed a brief announcement and took it to the governor.
  The next day, as he rounded the corner by a newsagent, his eyes opened wide. Headlined across the front page of the *Detroit News* was the announcement he had composed. It dawned on him that, all over the city, people would be reading his very own words as the governor's.
  Throughout that summer, Tom discovered the power of the governor's name. If he sent a letter to a mayor under his own signature, it would probably be filed under "Ignore". Who was Tom Bowers? If, however, the governor put his name at the bottom, the letter got instant attention anywhere in the state. That summer Tom worked "in the name of the governor" — he represented the governor.

■ JESUS' CRASH TRAINING COURSE
It is one thing to represent the governor of Michigan; it is quite another to represent God and use his name. Yet Jesus had exactly that plan in mind for his followers. He hand-selected simple folk like James and Andrew to bear his name and represent him to the world. In the same way that a governor or prime minister delegates authority to people acting on his behalf, Jesus gave his followers his own authority and power.

Jesus' time on earth was running out. Luke 9:51 records that he "resolutely set out for Jerusalem", on his way to die. Only a few weeks remained for him to train those people who would be left behind to carry his name: "Christ-ians". Jesus used the time as a crash training course for his followers.
  Chapters 9—19 contain many of Jesus' events and sayings found nowhere else in the Bible. First he sent out the Twelve, then 72 others, to announce his message to all who would listen. These chapters convey Jesus' last detailed instructions to his loyal followers.

■ FINAL INSTRUCTIONS
Everything about Jesus' life increased in intensity along the treacherous road to Jerusalem. As he taught his small group of disciples, gawping crowds shoved in from all sides, sometimes even trampling each other underfoot. From those crowds, Pharisees tossed out loaded questions, seeking to trap Jesus.
  Jesus did not soften his words in the face of danger. Instead, he emphasised the severe cost of following him. Frequently he talked about prayer, the church's life-giving connection to the Father.
  Later, the apostle Paul would say that we, the church, actually form Christ's body in the world. By coming to earth, and then leaving, Jesus ushered in a completely new chapter in history. And, as he prepared for departure, he called on his people — the disciples, and us — to represent him. In every sense, we bear his name.

□ LIFE QUESTIONS:
What does it mean to pray "in Jesus' name"? How can your life have the power and authority of Jesus behind it?

the Son and those to whom the Son chooses to reveal him."

23Then he turned to his disciples and said privately, "Blessed are the eyes that see what you see. 24For I tell you that many prophets and kings wanted to see what you see but did not see it, and to hear what you hear but did not hear it."

■ The Parable of the Good Samaritan
☐ See Matthew 22:34–40; Mark 12:28–31

25On one occasion an expert in the law stood up to test Jesus. "Teacher," he asked, "what must I do to inherit eternal life?"

26"What is written in the Law?" he replied. "How do you read it?"

27He answered: " 'Love the Lord your God with all your heart and with all your soul and with all your strength and with all your mind';*c* and, 'Love your neighbour as yourself.'*d*"

28"You have answered correctly," Jesus replied. "Do this and you will live."

29But he wanted to justify himself, so he asked Jesus, "And who is my neighbour?"

30In reply Jesus said: "A man was going down from Jerusalem to Jericho, when he fell into the hands of robbers. They stripped him of his clothes, beat him and went away, leaving him half-dead. 31A priest happened to be going down the same road, and when he saw the man, he passed by on the other side. 32So too, a Levite, when he came to the place and saw him, passed by on the other side. 33But a Samaritan, as he travelled, came where the man was; and when he saw him, he took pity on him. 34He went to him and bandaged his wounds, pouring on oil and wine. Then he put the man on his own donkey, brought him to an inn and took care of him. 35The next day he took out two silver coins*e* and gave them to the innkeeper. 'Look after him,' he said, 'and when I return, I will reimburse you for any extra expense you may have.'

36"Which of these three do you think was a neighbour to the man who fell into the hands of robbers?"

37The expert in the law replied, "The one who had mercy on him."

Jesus told him, "Go and do likewise."

■ At the Home of Martha and Mary

38As Jesus and his disciples were on their way, he came to a village where a woman named Martha opened her home to him. 39She had a sister called Mary, who sat at the Lord's feet listening to what he said. 40But Martha was distracted by all the preparations that had to be made. She came to him and asked, "Lord, don't you care that my sister has left me to do the work by myself? Tell her to help me!"

41"Martha, Martha," the Lord answered, "you are worried and upset about many things, 42but only one thing is needed.*f* Mary has chosen what is better, and it will not be taken away from her."

■ Jesus' Teaching on Prayer
☐ See Matthew 6:9–13; 7:7–11

11 One day Jesus was praying in a certain place. When he finished, one of his disciples said to him, "Lord, teach us to pray, just as John taught his disciples."

2He said to them, "When you pray, say:

" 'Father,*a*
hallowed be your name,
　your kingdom come.*b*
3Give us each day our daily bread.
4Forgive us our sins,
　for we also forgive everyone who sins against
　　us.*c*
And lead us not into temptation.' "*d*

5Then he said to them, "Suppose one of you has a friend, and he goes to him at midnight and says, 'Friend, lend me three loaves of bread, 6because a friend of mine on a journey has come to me, and I have nothing to set before him.'

7"Then the one inside answers, 'Don't bother me. The door is already locked, and my children are with me in bed. I can't get up and give you anything.' 8I tell you, though he will not get up and give him the bread because he is his friend, yet because of the man's boldness*e* he will get up and give him as much as he needs.

9"So I say to you: Ask and it will be given to you; seek and you will find; knock and the door will be opened to you. 10For everyone who asks receives; he who seeks finds; and to him who knocks, the door will be opened.

11"Which of you fathers, if your son asks for*f* a fish, will give him a snake instead? 12Or if he asks for an egg, will give him a scorpion? 13If you then, though you are evil, know how to give good gifts to

c27 Deut. 6:5　*d27* Lev. 19:18　*e35* Greek *two denarii*　*f42* Some manuscripts *but few things are needed — or only one*　*a2* Some manuscripts *Our Father in heaven*　*b2* Some manuscripts *come. May your will be done on earth as it is in heaven.*　*c4* Greek *everyone who is indebted to us*　*d4* Some manuscripts *temptation but deliver us from the evil one*　*e8* Or *persistence*　*f11* Some manuscripts *for bread, will give him a stone; or if he asks for* your children, how much more will your Father in heaven give the Holy Spirit to those who ask him!"

■ Jesus and Beelzebub
☐ See Matthew 12:22,24–29,43–45; Mark 3:23–27

14Jesus was driving out a demon that was mute. When the demon left, the man who had been mute spoke, and the crowd was amazed. 15But some of them said, "By Beelzebub,*g* the prince of demons, he is driving out demons." 16Others tested him by asking for a sign from heaven.

17Jesus knew their thoughts and said to them: "Any kingdom divided against itself will be ruined, and a house divided against itself will fall. 18If Satan is divided against himself, how can his kingdom stand? I say this because you claim that I drive out demons by Beelzebub. 19Now if I drive out demons by Beelzebub, by whom do your followers drive them out? So then, they will be your judges. 20But if I drive out demons by the finger of God, then the kingdom of God has come to you.

11:17 ■ JESUS OR LINCOLN?
Abraham Lincoln is often credited with saying, "A house divided against itself cannot stand". Actually, Lincoln quoted Jesus, who was refuting a frivolous accusation that his power came from Satan (Beelzebub). Jesus suggested that if Satan used his power against his own cause, Satan's kingdom would soon fall. Lincoln applied this principle to the not-so-United States just before the Civil War: a nation divided over such a fundamental issue as slavery could not endure.

21"When a strong man, fully armed, guards his own house, his possessions are safe. 22But when someone stronger attacks and overpowers him, he takes away the armour in which the man trusted and divides up the spoils.

23"He who is not with me is against me, and he who does not gather with me, scatters.

24"When an evil*b* spirit comes out of a man, it goes through arid places seeking rest and does not find it. Then it says, 'I will return to the house I left.' 25When it arrives, it finds the house swept clean and put in order. 26Then it goes and takes seven other spirits more wicked than itself, and they go in and live there. And the final condition of that man is worse than the first."

27As Jesus was saying these things, a woman in the crowd called out, "Blessed is the mother who gave you birth and nursed you."

28He replied, "Blessed rather are those who hear the word of God and obey it."

■ The Sign of Jonah
☐ See Matthew 12:39–42

29As the crowds increased, Jesus said, "This is a wicked generation. It asks for a miraculous sign, but none will be given it except the sign of Jonah. 30For as Jonah was a sign to the Ninevites, so also will the Son of Man be to this generation. 31The Queen of the South will rise at the judgment with the men of this generation and condemn them; for she came from the ends of the earth to listen to Solomon's wisdom, and now one*i* greater than Solomon is here. 32The men of Nineveh will stand up at the judgment with this generation and condemn it; for they repented at the preaching of Jonah, and now one greater than Jonah is here.

11:29 ■ SENSATION-SEEKERS
Jesus had no tolerance for people who begged for miraculous signs. Here and elsewhere he declared that no amount of proof would convince those who stubbornly refused to believe in him. In contrast, certain Old Testament Gentiles believed even though they had far less evidence.

■ The Lamp of the Body
☐ See Matthew 6:22–23

33"No-one lights a lamp and puts it in a place where it will be hidden, or under a bowl. Instead he puts it on its stand, so that those who come in may see the light. 34Your eye is the lamp of your body. When your eyes are good, your whole body also is full of light. But when they are bad, your body also is full of darkness. 35See to it, then, that the light within you is not darkness. 36Therefore, if your whole body is full of light, and no part of it dark, it will be completely lighted, as when the light of a lamp shines on you."

■ Six Woes

37When Jesus had finished speaking, a Pharisee invited him to eat with him; so he went in and reclined at the table. 38But the Pharisee, noticing that Jesus did not first wash before the meal, was surprised.

39Then the Lord said to him, "Now then, you Pharisees clean the outside of the cup and dish, but inside you are full of greed and wickedness. 40You foolish people! Did not the one who made the outside make the inside also? 41But give what is inside ˌthe dishˌ*j* to the poor, and everything will be clean for you.

42"Woe to you Pharisees, because you give God a tenth of your mint, rue and all other kinds of garden herbs, but you neglect justice and the love of God. You should have practised the latter without leaving the former undone.

43"Woe to you Pharisees, because you love the most important seats in the synagogues and greetings in the market-places.

44"Woe to you, because you are like unmarked graves, which men walk over without knowing it."

45One of the experts in the law answered him, "Teacher, when you say these things, you insult us also."

46Jesus replied, "And you experts in the law, woe to you, because you load people down with burdens they can hardly carry, and you yourselves will not lift one finger to help them.

47"Woe to you, because you build tombs for the prophets, and it was your forefathers who killed them. 48So you testify that you approve of what your

g 15 Greek Beezeboul or Beelzeboul; also in verses 18 and 19   b 24 Greek unclean   i 31 Or something; also in verse 32   j 41 Or what you have forefathers did; they killed the prophets, and you build their tombs. [49]Because of this, God in his wisdom said, 'I will send them prophets and apostles, some of whom they will kill and others they will persecute.' [50]Therefore this generation will be held responsible for the blood of all the prophets that has been shed since the beginning of the world, [51]from the blood of Abel to the blood of Zechariah, who was killed between the altar and the sanctuary. Yes, I tell you, this generation will be held responsible for it all.

[52]"Woe to you experts in the law, because you have taken away the key to knowledge. You yourselves have not entered, and you have hindered those who were entering."

[53]When Jesus left there, the Pharisees and the teachers of the law began to oppose him fiercely and to besiege him with questions, [54]waiting to catch him in something he might say.

■ Warnings and Encouragements
□ See Matthew 10:26–33

12 Meanwhile, when a crowd of many thousands had gathered, so that they were trampling on one another, Jesus began to speak first to his disciples, saying: "Be on your guard against the yeast of the Pharisees, which is hypocrisy. [2]There is nothing concealed that will not be disclosed, or hidden that will not be made known. [3]What you have said in the dark will be heard in the daylight, and what you have whispered in the ear in the inner rooms will be proclaimed from the roofs.

[4]"I tell you, my friends, do not be afraid of those who kill the body and after that can do no more. [5]But I will show you whom you should fear: Fear him who, after the killing of the body, has power to throw you into hell. Yes, I tell you, fear him. [6]Are not five sparrows sold for two pennies?[a] Yet not one of them is forgotten by God. [7]Indeed, the very hairs of your head are all numbered. Don't be afraid; you are worth more than many sparrows.

[8]"I tell you, whoever acknowledges me before men, the Son of Man will also acknowledge him before the angels of God. [9]But he who disowns me before men will be disowned before the angels of God. [10]And everyone who speaks a word against the Son of Man will be forgiven, but anyone who blasphemes against the Holy Spirit will not be forgiven.

[11]"When you are brought before synagogues, rulers and authorities, do not worry about how you will defend yourselves or what you will say, [12]for the Holy Spirit will teach you at that time what you should say."

■ The Parable of the Rich Fool
[13]Someone in the crowd said to him, "Teacher, tell my brother to divide the inheritance with me."

[14]Jesus replied, "Man, who appointed me a judge or an arbiter between you?" [15]Then he said to them, "Watch out! Be on your guard against all kinds of greed; a man's life does not consist in the abundance of his possessions."

[16]And he told them this parable: "The ground of a certain rich man produced a good crop. [17]He

thought to himself, 'What shall I do? I have no place to store my crops.'

12:15 ■ WHEN MONEY IS USELESS

Jesus refused to get involved in a family dispute about money. In this statement, he neatly summarised his usual approach to money. He did not condemn the possession of it. But he did warn against putting faith in money to secure the future. The rich man's money did him absolutely no good the night of his death. To emphasise his point, Jesus referred back to King Solomon, the richest man in the Old Testament (verse 27). The lesson: trust in God and his kingdom, and free yourself of worry about money and possessions.

---

[18]"Then he said, 'This is what I'll do. I will tear down my barns and build bigger ones, and there I will store all my grain and my goods. [19]And I'll say to myself, "You have plenty of good things laid up for many years. Take life easy; eat, drink and be merry." '

[20]"But God said to him, 'You fool! This very night your life will be demanded from you. Then who will get what you have prepared for yourself?'

[21]"This is how it will be with anyone who stores up things for himself but is not rich towards God."

■ Do Not Worry
□ See Matthew 6:25–33

[22]Then Jesus said to his disciples: "Therefore I tell you, do not worry about your life, what you will eat; or about your body, what you will wear. [23]Life is more than food, and the body more than clothes. [24]Consider the ravens: They do not sow or reap, they have no storeroom or barn; yet God feeds them. And how much more valuable you are than birds! [25]Who of you by worrying can add a single hour to his life?[b] [26]Since you cannot do this very little thing, why do you worry about the rest?

[27]"Consider how the lilies grow. They do not labour or spin. Yet I tell you, not even Solomon in all his splendour was dressed like one of these. [28]If that is how God clothes the grass of the field, which is here today, and tomorrow is thrown into the fire, how much more will he clothe you, O you of little faith! [29]And do not set your heart on what you will eat or drink; do not worry about it. [30]For the pagan world runs after all such things, and your Father knows that you need them. [31]But seek his kingdom, and these things will be given to you as well.

[32]"Do not be afraid, little flock, for your Father has been pleased to give you the kingdom. [33]Sell your possessions and give to the poor. Provide purses for yourselves that will not wear out, a treasure in heaven that will not be exhausted, where no thief comes near and no moth destroys. [34]For where your treasure is, there your heart will be also.

■ Watchfulness
□ See Matthew 24:43–51; Mark 13:33–37

[35]"Be dressed ready for service and keep your lamps burning, [36]like men waiting for their master

---

a 6 Greek two assaria   b 25 Or single cubit to his height to return from a wedding banquet, so that when he comes and knocks they can immediately open the door for him. 37It will be good for those servants whose master finds them watching when he comes. I tell you the truth, he will dress himself to serve, will have them recline at the table and will come and wait on them. 38It will be good for those servants whose master finds them ready, even if he comes in the second or third watch of the night. 39But understand this: If the owner of the house had known at what hour the thief was coming, he would not have let his house be broken into. 40You also must be ready, because the Son of Man will come at an hour when you do not expect him."

41Peter asked, "Lord, are you telling this parable to us, or to everyone?"

42The Lord answered, "Who then is the faithful and wise manager, whom the master puts in charge of his servants to give them their food allowance at the proper time? 43It will be good for that servant whom the master finds doing so when he returns. 44I tell you the truth, he will put him in charge of all his possessions. 45But suppose the servant says to himself, 'My master is taking a long time in coming,' and he then begins to beat the menservants and maidservants and to eat and drink and get drunk. 46The master of that servant will come on a day when he does not expect him and at an hour he is not aware of. He will cut him to pieces and assign him a place with the unbelievers.

47"That servant who knows his master's will and does not get ready or does not do what his master wants will be beaten with many blows. 48But the one who does not know and does things deserving punishment will be beaten with few blows. From everyone who has been given much, much will be demanded; and from the one who has been entrusted with much, much more will be asked.

■ Not Peace but Division
☐ See Matthew 10:34–36
49"I have come to bring fire on the earth, and how I wish it were already kindled! 50But I have a baptism to undergo, and how distressed I am until it is completed! 51Do you think I came to bring peace on earth? No, I tell you, but division. 52From now on there will be five in one family divided against each other, three against two and two against three. 53They will be divided, father against son and son against father, mother against daughter and daughter against mother, mother-in-law against daughter-in-law and daughter-in-law against mother-in-law."

■ Interpreting the Times
54He said to the crowd: "When you see a cloud rising in the west, immediately you say, 'It's going to rain,' and it does. 55And when the south wind blows, you say, 'It's going to be hot,' and it is. 56Hypocrites! You know how to interpret the appearance of the earth and the sky. How is it that you don't know how to interpret this present time?

57"Why don't you judge for yourselves what is right? 58As you are going with your adversary to the magistrate, try hard to be reconciled to him on the way, or he may drag you off to the judge, and the judge turn you over to the officer, and the officer throw you into prison. 59I tell you, you will not get out until you have paid the last penny."c

■ Repent or Perish
13 Now there were some present at that time who told Jesus about the Galileans whose blood Pilate had mixed with their sacrifices. 2Jesus answered, "Do you think that these Galileans were worse sinners than all the other Galileans because they suffered this way? 3I tell you, no! But unless you repent, you too will all perish. 4Or those eighteen who died when the tower in Siloam fell on them—do you think they were more guilty than all the others living in Jerusalem? 5I tell you, no! But unless you repent, you too will all perish."

6Then he told this parable: "A man had a fig-tree, planted in his vineyard, and he went to look for fruit on it, but did not find any. 7So he said to the man who took care of the vineyard, 'For three years now I've been coming to look for fruit on this fig-tree and haven't found any. Cut it down! Why should it use up the soil?'

8" 'Sir,' the man replied, 'leave it alone for one more year, and I'll dig round it and fertilise it. 9If it bears fruit next year, fine! If not, then cut it down.' "

■ A Crippled Woman Healed on the Sabbath
10On a Sabbath Jesus was teaching in one of the synagogues, 11and a woman was there who had been crippled by a spirit for eighteen years. She was bent over and could not straighten up at all. 12When Jesus saw her, he called her forward and said to her, "Woman, you are set free from your infirmity." 13Then he put his hands on her, and immediately she straightened up and praised God.

14Indignant because Jesus had healed on the Sabbath, the synagogue ruler said to the people, "There are six days for work. So come and be healed on those days, not on the Sabbath."

15The Lord answered him, "You hypocrites! Doesn't each of you on the Sabbath untie his ox or donkey from the stall and lead it out to give it water? 16Then should not this woman, a daughter of Abraham, whom Satan has kept bound for eighteen long years, be set free on the Sabbath day from what bound her?"

17When he said this, all his opponents were humiliated, but the people were delighted with all the wonderful things he was doing.

■ The Parables of the Mustard Seed and the Yeast
☐ See Matthew 13:31–33; Mark 4:30–32
18Then Jesus asked, "What is the kingdom of God like? What shall I compare it to? 19It is like a mustard seed, which a man took and planted in his garden. It grew and became a tree, and the birds of the air perched in its branches."

20Again he asked, "What shall I compare the kingdom of God to? 21It is like yeast that a woman took and mixed into a large amounta of flour until it worked all through the dough."

c 59 Greek lepton   a 21 Greek three satas (probably about ⅗ bushel or 22 litres)

■ The Narrow Door

22Then Jesus went through the towns and villages, teaching as he made his way to Jerusalem. 23Someone asked him, "Lord, are only a few people going to be saved?"

He said to them, 24"Make every effort to enter through the narrow door, because many, I tell you, will try to enter and will not be able to. 25Once the owner of the house gets up and closes the door, you will stand outside knocking and pleading, 'Sir, open the door for us.'

"But he will answer, 'I don't know you or where you come from.'

26"Then you will say, 'We ate and drank with you, and you taught in our streets.'

27"But he will reply, 'I don't know you or where you come from. Away from me, all you evildoers!'

28"There will be weeping there, and gnashing of teeth, when you see Abraham, Isaac and Jacob and all the prophets in the kingdom of God, but you yourselves thrown out. 29People will come from east and west and north and south, and will take their places at the feast in the kingdom of God. 30Indeed there are those who are last who will be first, and first who will be last."

■ Jesus' Sorrow for Jerusalem
☐ See Matthew 23:37–39

31At that time some Pharisees came to Jesus and said to him, "Leave this place and go somewhere else. Herod wants to kill you."

32He replied, "Go tell that fox, 'I will drive out demons and heal people today and tomorrow, and on the third day I will reach my goal.' 33In any case, I must keep going today and tomorrow and the next day—for surely no prophet can die outside Jerusalem!

13:32 ■ WHO HAD REAL POWER?
Jesus was executed by powerful political authorities, among them the Roman official Herod. But this statement, spoken before his arrest, reveals who had the real power. Jesus dismissed Herod as "that fox", a Jewish expression for a worthless or insignificant person. Jesus' death on a cross came as no surprise to him; in fact, here he calls it his "goal".

34"O Jerusalem, Jerusalem, you who kill the prophets and stone those sent to you, how often I have longed to gather your children together, as a hen gathers her chicks under her wings, but you were not willing! 35Look, your house is left to you desolate. I tell you, you will not see me again until you say, 'Blessed is he who comes in the name of the Lord.'*b*"

■ Jesus at a Pharisee's House

14 One Sabbath, when Jesus went to eat in the house of a prominent Pharisee, he was being carefully watched. 2There in front of him was a man suffering from dropsy. 3Jesus asked the Pharisees and experts in the law, "Is it lawful to heal on the Sabbath or not?" 4But they remained silent. So taking hold of the man, he healed him and sent him away.

5Then he asked them, "If one of you has a son*a* or an ox that falls into a well on the Sabbath day, will you not immediately pull him out?" 6And they had nothing to say.

7When he noticed how the guests picked the places of honour at the table, he told them this parable: 8"When someone invites you to a wedding feast, do not take the place of honour, for a person more distinguished than you may have been invited. 9If so, the host who invited both of you will come and say to you, 'Give this man your seat.' Then, humiliated, you will have to take the least important place. 10But when you are invited, take the lowest place, so that when your host comes, he will say to you, 'Friend, move up to a better place.' Then you will be honoured in the presence of all your fellow guests. 11For everyone who exalts himself will be humbled, and he who humbles himself will be exalted."

12Then Jesus said to his host, "When you give a luncheon or dinner, do not invite your friends, your brothers or relatives, or your rich neighbours; if you do, they may invite you back and so you will be repaid. 13But when you give a banquet, invite the poor, the crippled, the lame, the blind, 14and you will be blessed. Although they cannot repay you, you will be repaid at the resurrection of the righteous."

■ The Parable of the Great Banquet

15When one of those at the table with him heard this, he said to Jesus, "Blessed is the man who will eat at the feast in the kingdom of God."

16Jesus replied: "A certain man was preparing a great banquet and invited many guests. 17At the time of the banquet he sent his servant to tell those who had been invited, 'Come, for everything is now ready.'

18"But they all alike began to make excuses. The first said, 'I have just bought a field, and I must go and see it. Please excuse me.'

19"Another said, 'I have just bought five yoke of oxen, and I'm on my way to try them out. Please excuse me.'

20"Still another said, 'I have just got married, so I can't come.'

21"The servant came back and reported this to his master. Then the owner of the house became angry and ordered his servant, 'Go out quickly into the streets and alleys of the town and bring in the poor, the crippled, the blind and the lame.'

22"'Sir,' the servant said, 'what you ordered has been done, but there is still room.'

23"Then the master told his servant, 'Go out to the roads and country lanes and make them come in, so that my house will be full. 24I tell you, not one of those men who were invited will get a taste of my banquet.'"

■ The Cost of Being a Disciple

25Large crowds were travelling with Jesus, and turning to them he said: 26"If anyone comes to me

---

*b*35 Psalm 118:26   *a*5 Some manuscripts *donkey*

and does not hate his father and mother, his wife and children, his brothers and sisters — yes, even his own life — he cannot be my disciple. 27And anyone who does not carry his cross and follow me cannot be my disciple.

28"Suppose one of you wants to build a tower. Will he not first sit down and estimate the cost to see if he has enough money to complete it? 29For if he lays the foundation and is not able to finish it, everyone who sees it will ridicule him, 30saying, 'This fellow began to build and was not able to finish.'

31"Or suppose a king is about to go to war against another king. Will he not first sit down and consider whether he is able with ten thousand men to oppose the one coming against him with twenty thousand? 32If he is not able, he will send a delegation while the other is still a long way off and will ask for terms of peace. 33In the same way, any of you who does not give up everything he has cannot be my disciple.

34"Salt is good, but if it loses its saltiness, how can it be made salty again? 35It is fit neither for the soil nor for the manure heap; it is thrown out.

"He who has ears to hear, let him hear."

■ The Parable of the Lost Sheep
☐ See Matthew 18:12–14

15 Now the tax collectors and "sinners" were all gathering round to hear him. 2But the Pharisees and the teachers of the law muttered, "This man welcomes sinners, and eats with them."

3Then Jesus told them this parable: 4"Suppose one of you has a hundred sheep and loses one of them. Does he not leave the ninety-nine in the open country and go after the lost sheep until he finds it? 5And when he finds it, he joyfully puts it on his shoulders 6and goes home. Then he calls his friends and neighbours together and says, 'Rejoice with me; I have found my lost sheep.' 7I tell you that in the same way there will be more rejoicing in heaven over one sinner who repents than over ninety-nine righteous persons who do not need to repent.

15:3 ■ SEVERE AND GENTLE STORIES
The collection of stories in chapters 14 and 15, found only in Luke's Gospel, shows the two-edged thrust of Jesus' message. The stern warnings in chapter 14 are directed to the proud, who either see no need for God or refuse to pay the cost of following him. The three stories in the next chapter progressively show the limitless love of God for those in real need. He stands ready to forgive all who turn to him.

■ The Parable of the Lost Coin
8"Or suppose a woman has ten silver coins*a* and loses one. Does she not light a lamp, sweep the house and search carefully until she finds it? 9And when she finds it, she calls her friends and neighbours together and says, 'Rejoice with me; I have found my lost coin.' 10In the same way, I tell you,

there is rejoicing in the presence of the angels of God over one sinner who repents."

■ The Parable of the Lost Son
11Jesus continued: "There was a man who had two sons. 12The younger one said to his father, 'Father, give me my share of the estate.' So he divided his property between them.

13"Not long after that, the younger son got together all he had, set off for a distant country and there squandered his wealth in wild living. 14After he had spent everything, there was a severe famine in that whole country, and he began to be in need. 15So he went and hired himself out to a citizen of that country, who sent him to his fields to feed pigs. 16He longed to fill his stomach with the pods that the pigs were eating, but no-one gave him anything.

17"When he came to his senses, he said, 'How many of my father's hired men have food to spare, and here I am starving to death! 18I will set out and go back to my father and say to him: Father, I have sinned against heaven and against you. 19I am no longer worthy to be called your son; make me like one of your hired men.' 20So he got up and went to his father.

"But while he was still a long way off, his father saw him and was filled with compassion for him; he ran to his son, threw his arms around him and kissed him.

21"The son said to him, 'Father, I have sinned against heaven and against you. I am no longer worthy to be called your son.'*b*

22"But the father said to his servants, 'Quick! Bring the best robe and put it on him. Put a ring on his finger and sandals on his feet. 23Bring the fattened calf and kill it. Let's have a feast and celebrate. 24For this son of mine was dead and is alive again; he was lost and is found.' So they began to celebrate.

25"Meanwhile, the older son was in the field. When he came near the house, he heard music and dancing. 26So he called one of the servants and asked him what was going on. 27'Your brother has come,' he replied, 'and your father has killed the fattened calf because he has him back safe and sound.'

28"The older brother became angry and refused to go in. So his father went out and pleaded with him. 29But he answered his father, 'Look! All these years I've been slaving for you and never disobeyed your orders. Yet you never gave me even a young goat so I could celebrate with my friends. 30But when this son of yours who has squandered your property with prostitutes comes home, you kill the fattened calf for him!'

15:28 ■ TWO LOST BROTHERS?
The parable of the Lost Son actually tells of two sons, one irresponsible, the other hardworking. One wastes his life and comes home humbled; the other proudly refuses to celebrate his brother's home-coming. The story ends with one son in a joyful family celebration, and his brother outside, bitterly unwilling to forgive. Which son is really lost?

---

*a*8 Greek ten *drachmas*, each worth about a day's wages   *b*21 Some early manuscripts son. *Make me like one of your hired men.*

31" 'My son,' the father said, 'you are always with me, and everything I have is yours. 32But we had to celebrate and be glad, because this brother of yours was dead and is alive again; he was lost and is found.' "

■ The Parable of the Shrewd Manager

16 Jesus told his disciples: "There was a rich man whose manager was accused of wasting his possessions. 2So he called him in and asked him, 'What is this I hear about you? Give an account of your management, because you cannot be manager any longer.'

3"The manager said to himself, 'What shall I do now? My master is taking away my job. I'm not strong enough to dig, and I'm ashamed to beg—4I know what I'll do so that, when I lose my job here, people will welcome me into their houses.'

5"So he called in each one of his master's debtors. He asked the first, 'How much do you owe my master?'

6" 'Eight hundred gallons*a* of olive oil,' he replied.

"The manager told him, 'Take your bill, sit down quickly, and make it four hundred.'

7"Then he asked the second, 'And how much do you owe?'

" 'A thousand bushels*b* of wheat,' he replied.

"He told him, 'Take your bill and make it eight hundred.'

8"The master commended the dishonest manager because he had acted shrewdly. For the people of this world are more shrewd in dealing with their own kind than are the people of the light. 9I tell you, use worldly wealth to gain friends for yourselves, so that when it is gone, you will be welcomed into eternal dwellings.

10"Whoever can be trusted with very little can also be trusted with much, and whoever is dishonest with very little will also be dishonest with much. 11So if you have not been trustworthy in handling worldly wealth, who will trust you with true riches? 12And if you have not been trustworthy with someone else's property, who will give you property of your own?

13"No servant can serve two masters. Either he will hate the one and love the other, or he will be devoted to the one and despise the other. You cannot serve both God and Money."

14The Pharisees, who loved money, heard all this and were sneering at Jesus. 15He said to them, "You are the ones who justify yourselves in the eyes of men, but God knows your hearts. What is highly valued among men is detestable in God's sight.

■ Additional Teachings

16"The Law and the Prophets were proclaimed until John. Since that time, the good news of the kingdom of God is being preached, and everyone is forcing his way into it. 17It is easier for heaven and earth to disappear than for the least stroke of a pen to drop out of the Law.

18"Anyone who divorces his wife and marries another woman commits adultery, and the man who marries a divorced woman commits adultery.

■ The Rich Man and Lazarus

19"There was a rich man who was dressed in purple and fine linen and lived in luxury every day. 20At his gate was laid a beggar named Lazarus, covered with sores 21and longing to eat what fell from the rich man's table. Even the dogs came and licked his sores.

22"The time came when the beggar died and the angels carried him to Abraham's side. The rich man also died and was buried. 23In hell,*c* where he was in torment, he looked up and saw Abraham far away, with Lazarus by his side. 24So he called to him, 'Father Abraham, have pity on me and send Lazarus to dip the tip of his finger in water and cool my tongue, because I am in agony in this fire.'

25"But Abraham replied, 'Son, remember that in your lifetime you received your good things, while Lazarus received bad things, but now he is comforted here and you are in agony. 26And besides all this, between us and you a great chasm has been fixed, so that those who want to go from here to you cannot, nor can anyone cross over from there to us.'

27"He answered, 'Then I beg you, father, send Lazarus to my father's house, 28for I have five brothers. Let him warn them, so that they will not also come to this place of torment.'

29"Abraham replied, 'They have Moses and the Prophets; let them listen to them.'

30" 'No, father Abraham,' he said, 'but if someone from the dead goes to them, they will repent.'

31"He said to him, 'If they do not listen to Moses and the Prophets, they will not be convinced even if someone rises from the dead.' "

16:31 ■ STUBBORNLY UNCONVINCED
With the concluding statement in this famous story of Lazarus, Jesus made a poignant prophecy, although his listeners at the time probably missed the point. Many of them, especially the Pharisees, refused to believe him even after he rose from the dead.

■ Sin, Faith, Duty

17 Jesus said to his disciples: "Things that cause people to sin are bound to come, but woe to that person through whom they come. 2It would be better for him to be thrown into the sea with a millstone tied round his neck than for him to cause one of these little ones to sin. 3So watch yourselves.

"If your brother sins, rebuke him, and if he repents, forgive him. 4If he sins against you seven times in a day, and seven times comes back to you and says, 'I repent,' forgive him."

5The apostles said to the Lord, "Increase our faith!"

6He replied, "If you have faith as small as a mustard seed, you can say to this mulberry tree, 'Be uprooted and planted in the sea,' and it will obey you.

7"Suppose one of you had a servant ploughing or looking after the sheep. Would he say to the servant when he comes in from the field, 'Come along now and sit down to eat'? 8Would he not rather say, 'Prepare my supper, get yourself ready and wait on me

---

a6 Greek *one hundred batous* (probably about 3 kilolitres)   *b7* Greek *one hundred korous* (probably about 35 kilolitres)   *c23* Greek *Hades* while I eat and drink; after that you may eat and drink'? 9Would he thank the servant because he did what he was told to do? 10So you also, when you have done everything you were told to do, should say, 'We are unworthy servants; we have only done our duty.' "

■ Ten Healed of Leprosy

11Now on his way to Jerusalem, Jesus travelled along the border between Samaria and Galilee. 12As he was going into a village, ten men who had leprosy*a* met him. They stood at a distance 13and called out in a loud voice, "Jesus, Master, have pity on us!"

14When he saw them, he said, "Go, show yourselves to the priests." And as they went, they were cleansed.

15One of them, when he saw he was healed, came back, praising God in a loud voice. 16He threw himself at Jesus' feet and thanked him—and he was a Samaritan.

17Jesus asked, "Were not all ten cleansed? Where are the other nine? 18Was no-one found to return and give praise to God except this foreigner?" 19Then he said to him, "Rise and go; your faith has made you well."

■ The Coming of the Kingdom of God

20Once, having been asked by the Pharisees when the kingdom of God would come, Jesus replied, "The kingdom of God does not come with your careful observation, 21nor will people say, 'Here it is,' or 'There it is,' because the kingdom of God is within*b* you."

22Then he said to his disciples, "The time is coming when you will long to see one of the days of the Son of Man, but you will not see it. 23Men will tell you, 'There he is!' or 'Here he is!' Do not go running off after them. 24For the Son of Man in his day*c* will be like the lightning, which flashes and lights up the sky from one end to the other. 25But first he must suffer many things and be rejected by this generation.

26"Just as it was in the days of Noah, so also will it be in the days of the Son of Man. 27People were eating, drinking, marrying and being given in marriage up to the day Noah entered the ark. Then the flood came and destroyed them all.

28"It was the same in the days of Lot. People were eating and drinking, buying and selling, planting and building. 29But the day Lot left Sodom, fire and sulphur rained down from heaven and destroyed them all.

30"It will be just like this on the day the Son of Man is revealed. 31On that day no-one who is on the roof of his house, with his goods inside, should go down to get them. Likewise, no-one in the field should go back for anything. 32Remember Lot's wife! 33Whoever tries to keep his life will lose it, and whoever loses his life will preserve it. 34I tell you, on that night two people will be in one bed; one will be taken and the other left. 35Two women will be grinding grain together; one will be taken and the other left."*d*

37"Where, Lord?" they asked.

He replied, "Where there is a dead body, there the vultures will gather."

■ The Parable of the Persistent Widow

18 Then Jesus told his disciples a parable to show them that they should always pray and not give up. 2He said: "In a certain town there was a judge who neither feared God nor cared about men. 3And there was a widow in that town who kept coming to him with the plea, 'Grant me justice against my adversary.'

4"For some time he refused. But finally he said to himself, 'Even though I don't fear God or care about men, 5yet because this widow keeps bothering me, I will see that she gets justice, so that she won't eventually wear me out with her coming!' "

6And the Lord said, "Listen to what the unjust judge says. 7And will not God bring about justice for his chosen ones, who cry out to him day and night? Will he keep putting them off? 8I tell you, he will see that they get justice, and quickly. However, when the Son of Man comes, will he find faith on the earth?"

■ The Parable of the Pharisee and the Tax Collector

9To some who were confident of their own righteousness and looked down on everybody else, Jesus told this parable: 10"Two men went up to the temple to pray, one a Pharisee and the other a tax collector. 11The Pharisee stood up and prayed about*a* himself: 'God, I thank you that I am not like other men—robbers, evildoers, adulterers—or even like this tax collector. 12I fast twice a week and give a tenth of all I get.'

18:9 ■ LUKE AND THE UNDERDOG
Luke's concern for the humble comes through clearly in the stories he selected, especially in chapters 18 and 19. The parable of the Pharisee and the tax collector, for example, draws a sharp contrast between the proud and the humble. Stories that follow also feature the humble: little children, a blind beggar, another tax collector.

13"But the tax collector stood at a distance. He would not even look up to heaven, but beat his breast and said, 'God, have mercy on me, a sinner.'

14"I tell you that this man, rather than the other, went home justified before God. For everyone who exalts himself will be humbled, and he who humbles himself will be exalted."

■ The Little Children and Jesus
□ See Matthew 19:13–15; Mark 10:13–16

15People were also bringing babies to Jesus to have him touch them. When the disciples saw this, they rebuked them. 16But Jesus called the children to him and said, "Let the little children come to me, and do not hinder them, for the kingdom of God belongs to such as these. 17I tell you the truth, anyone who will not receive the kingdom of God like a little child will never enter it."

---

a12 The Greek word was used for various diseases affecting the skin—not necessarily leprosy.   *b21* Or *among*   *c24* Some manuscripts do not have *in his day.*   *d35* Some manuscripts *left.* 36*Two men will be in the field; one will be taken and the other left.*   *a11* Or *to*

The Rich Ruler

☐ See Matthew 19:16–29; Mark 10:17–30

¹⁸A certain ruler asked him, "Good teacher, what must I do to inherit eternal life?"

¹⁹"Why do you call me good?" Jesus answered. "No-one is good — except God alone. ²⁰You know the commandments: 'Do not commit adultery, do not murder, do not steal, do not give false testimony, honour your father and mother.'^b"

²¹"All these I have kept since I was a boy," he said.

²²When Jesus heard this, he said to him, "You still lack one thing. Sell everything you have and give to the poor, and you will have treasure in heaven. Then come, follow me."

²³When he heard this, he became very sad, because he was a man of great wealth. ²⁴Jesus looked at him and said, "How hard it is for the rich to enter the kingdom of God! ²⁵Indeed, it is easier for a camel to go through the eye of a needle than for a rich man to enter the kingdom of God."

²⁶Those who heard this asked, "Who then can be saved?"

²⁷Jesus replied, "What is impossible with men is possible with God."

²⁸Peter said to him, "We have left all we had to follow you!"

²⁹"I tell you the truth," Jesus said to them, "no-one who has left home or wife or brothers or parents or children for the sake of the kingdom of God ³⁰will fail to receive many times as much in this age and, in the age to come, eternal life."

Jesus Again Predicts His Death

☐ See Matthew 20:17–19; Mark 10:32–34

³¹Jesus took the Twelve aside and told them, "We are going up to Jerusalem, and everything that is written by the prophets about the Son of Man will be fulfilled. ³²He will be turned over to the Gentiles. They will mock him, insult him, spit on him, flog him and kill him. ³³On the third day he will rise again."

³⁴The disciples did not understand any of this. Its meaning was hidden from them, and they did not know what he was talking about.

A Blind Beggar Receives His Sight

☐ See Matthew 20:29–34; Mark 10:46–52

³⁵As Jesus approached Jericho, a blind man was sitting by the roadside begging. ³⁶When he heard the crowd going by, he asked what was happening. ³⁷They told him, "Jesus of Nazareth is passing by."

³⁸He called out, "Jesus, Son of David, have mercy on me!"

³⁹Those who led the way rebuked him and told him to be quiet, but he shouted all the more, "Son of David, have mercy on me!"

⁴⁰Jesus stopped and ordered the man to be brought to him. When he came near, Jesus asked him, ⁴¹"What do you want me to do for you?"

"Lord, I want to see," he replied.

⁴²Jesus said to him, "Receive your sight; your faith has healed you." ⁴³Immediately he received his sight and followed Jesus, praising God. When all the people saw it, they also praised God.

Zacchaeus the Tax Collector

19 Jesus entered Jericho and was passing through. ²A man was there by the name of Zacchaeus; he was a chief tax collector and was wealthy. ³He wanted to see who Jesus was, but being a short man he could not, because of the crowd. ⁴So he ran ahead and climbed a sycamore-fig tree to see him, since Jesus was coming that way.

⁵When Jesus reached the spot, he looked up and said to him, "Zacchaeus, come down immediately. I must stay at your house today." ⁶So he came down at once and welcomed him gladly.

⁷All the people saw this and began to mutter, "He has gone to be the guest of a 'sinner'."

⁸But Zacchaeus stood up and said to the Lord, "Look, Lord! Here and now I give half of my possessions to the poor, and if I have cheated anybody out of anything, I will pay back four times the amount."

⁹Jesus said to him, "Today salvation has come to this house, because this man, too, is a son of Abraham. ¹⁰For the Son of Man came to seek and to save what was lost."

19:10 ■ SEEK AND SAVE

A Jew who had sided with the hated Roman oppressors, Zacchaeus still had enough religious sensitivity to be curious about Jesus. Seeing his interest, Jesus took the initiative. He stopped the procession and called out to Zacchaeus, inviting himself to a meal at Zacchaeus' home. Though befriending Zacchaeus upset the crowd, Jesus proclaimed it as typical of his ministry: to seek and to save the lost.

The Parable of the Ten Minas

¹¹While they were listening to this, he went on to tell them a parable, because he was near Jerusalem and the people thought that the kingdom of God was going to appear at once. ¹²He said: "A man of noble birth went to a distant country to have himself appointed king and then to return. ¹³So he called ten of his servants and gave them ten minas.^a 'Put this money to work,' he said, 'until I come back.'

¹⁴"But his subjects hated him and sent a delegation after him to say, 'We don't want this man to be our king.'

¹⁵"He was made king, however, and returned home. Then he sent for the servants to whom he had given the money, in order to find out what they had gained with it.

¹⁶"The first one came and said, 'Sir, your mina has earned ten more.'

¹⁷" 'Well done, my good servant!' his master replied. 'Because you have been trustworthy in a very small matter, take charge of ten cities.'

¹⁸"The second came and said, 'Sir, your mina has earned five more.'

¹⁹"His master answered, 'You take charge of five cities.'

²⁰"Then another servant came and said, 'Sir, here is your mina; I have kept it laid away in a piece of

^b20 Exodus 20:12–16; Deut. 5:16–20   ^a13 A mina was about three months' wages.

cloth. 21I was afraid of you, because you are a hard man. You take out what you did not put in and reap what you did not sow.'

22"His master replied, 'I will judge you by your own words, you wicked servant! You knew, did you, that I am a hard man, taking out what I did not put in, and reaping what I did not sow? 23Why then didn't you put my money on deposit, so that when I came back, I could have collected it with interest?'

24"Then he said to those standing by, 'Take his mina away from him and give it to the one who has ten minas.'

25" 'Sir,' they said, 'he already has ten!'

26"He replied, 'I tell you that to everyone who has, more will be given, but as for the one who has nothing, even what he has will be taken away. 27But those enemies of mine who did not want me to be a king over them – bring them here and kill them in front of me.' "

■ The Triumphal Entry
☐ See Matthew 21:1–9; Mark 11:1–10; John 12:12–15

28After Jesus had said this, he went on ahead, going up to Jerusalem. 29As he approached Bethphage and Bethany at the hill called the Mount of Olives, he sent two of his disciples, saying to them, 30"Go to the village ahead of you, and as you enter it, you

HANDLING TOUGH QUESTIONS
WHY SO MANY STORIES?

THE CHIEF PRIESTS, THE TEACHERS OF THE LAW AND THE LEADERS AMONG THE PEOPLE WERE TRYING TO KILL HIM. YET THEY COULD NOT FIND ANY WAY TO DO IT, BECAUSE ALL THE PEOPLE HUNG ON HIS WORDS. ■ 19:47–48

Suffering strikes like an earthquake, without warning, causing sudden devastation. Twenty-nine teenagers die when a school bus plunges off a bridge. A hurricane smashes into Mexico. An epidemic of cholera breaks out in South America.

Psychological tremors follow, often in the form of questions. "Why did God let this happen? Did we do something wrong? Why does God permit such suffering?"

In Jesus' day, rumours buzzed about two catastrophes: Pontius Pilate's slaughter of Galileans and the collapse of a tower (13:1–4). Naturally, people round Jesus questioned him about these events, but his answers puzzled them. He refused to be drawn into a discussion of the age-old problem of pain. He merely dismissed the common opinion that tragedies happen to people who deserve them and deflected the issue back to the questioners as a general warning (13:4–5; see also "What Job Teaches about Suffering", page 460).

■ THE HEART OF THE QUESTION
Jesus' response to the questions on suffering illustrate how he dealt with difficult issues. Religious leaders and philosophical types were constantly trying to stop him with an arsenal of tough questions. Usually their tactics backfired as Jesus expertly turned their questions back on them.

Conscious of the listening crowds, Jesus avoided long arguments, instead emphasising the need for people to change behaviour. His answers cut to the heart of the question, and to the hearts of his listeners.

When teaching, Jesus often relied on a parable – a compact short story with a moral. Speaking in parables allowed him to continue training his disciples "privately", despite the throngs of onlookers (8:10). He could explain the meaning to the disciples later on when they were alone together. Parables also helped preserve his message: years later, as people reflected on what Jesus taught, his parables came to mind in vivid detail.

■ SIMPLE STORIES WITH A PROFOUND POINT
Luke, a master story-teller, collected 18 parables that appear nowhere else, and he also retold some of the most familiar. While Matthew emphasises parables of the kingdom, Luke adds those that focus on people: the good Samaritan, a persistent widow, the lost son. His parables speak to heavy subjects, but in an unexpectedly disarming way.

Jesus' style of handling tough questions contrasts sharply with Paul's. The apostle Paul wrapped concepts in theological words and gave formal explanations. In careful prose he patiently probed such complex words as *forgiveness* and *justification*.

Jesus, speaking to a restless crowd of thousands, communicated the same message in three progressive stories – the Lost Sheep, the Lost Coin and the Lost Son (15:1–32). Scottish Christians like to call that last story "The Wonderful Father". It expresses the heart of Jesus' message about as well as any ten-volume theological work.

☐ LIFE QUESTIONS:
What one question would you most like to ask Jesus in person? Given how he handled tough questions in Luke, can you imagine how he might respond to yours?

will find a colt tied there, which no-one has ever ridden. Untie it and bring it here. ³¹If anyone asks you, 'Why are you untying it?' tell him, 'The Lord needs it.' "

³²Those who were sent ahead went and found it just as he had told them. ³³As they were untying the colt, its owners asked them, "Why are you untying the colt?"

³⁴They replied, "The Lord needs it."

³⁵They brought it to Jesus, threw their cloaks on the colt and put Jesus on it. ³⁶As he went along, people spread their cloaks on the road.

³⁷When he came near the place where the road goes down the Mount of Olives, the whole crowd of disciples began joyfully to praise God in loud voices for all the miracles they had seen:

³⁸"Blessed is the king who comes in the name of
　　the Lord!"^b

"Peace in heaven and glory in the highest!"

³⁹Some of the Pharisees in the crowd said to Jesus, "Teacher, rebuke your disciples!"

⁴⁰"I tell you," he replied, "if they keep quiet, the stones will cry out."

⁴¹As he approached Jerusalem and saw the city, he wept over it ⁴²and said, "If you, even you, had only known on this day what would bring you peace — but now it is hidden from your eyes. ⁴³The days will come upon you when your enemies will build an embankment against you and encircle you and hem you in on every side. ⁴⁴They will dash you to the ground, you and the children within your walls. They will not leave one stone on another, because you did not recognise the time of God's coming to you."

19:44 ■ WAILING WALL
Jesus' tearful prediction of total destruction was fulfilled in A.D. 70, when the Romans crushed a Jewish revolt by razing the city. In modern Jerusalem, the Wailing Wall is one of the few places where some of the original stonework of Jerusalem can still be seen.

■ Jesus at the Temple
□ See Matthew 21:12–16; Mark 11:15–18; John 2:13–16

⁴⁵Then he entered the temple area and began driving out those who were selling. ⁴⁶"It is written," he said to them, " 'My house will be a house of prayer';^c but you have made it 'a den of robbers'.^d "

⁴⁷Every day he was teaching at the temple. But the chief priests, the teachers of the law and the leaders among the people were trying to kill him. ⁴⁸Yet they could not find any way to do it, because all the people hung on his words.

■ The Authority of Jesus Questioned
□ See Matthew 21:23–27; Mark 11:27–33

20 One day as he was teaching the people in the temple courts and preaching the gospel, the chief priests and the teachers of the law, together with the elders, came up to him. ²"Tell us by what authority you are doing these things," they said. "Who gave you this authority?"

³He replied, "I will also ask you a question. Tell me, ⁴John's baptism — was it from heaven, or from men?"

⁵They discussed it among themselves and said, "If we say, 'From heaven', he will ask, 'Why didn't you believe him?' ⁶But if we say, 'From men', all the people will stone us, because they are persuaded that John was a prophet."

⁷So they answered, "We don't know where it was from."

⁸Jesus said, "Neither will I tell you by what authority I am doing these things."

■ The Parable of the Tenants
□ See Matthew 21:33–46; Mark 12:1–12

⁹He went on to tell the people this parable: "A man planted a vineyard, rented it to some farmers and went away for a long time. ¹⁰At harvest time he sent a servant to the tenants so they would give him some of the fruit of the vineyard. But the tenants beat him and sent him away empty-handed. ¹¹He sent another servant, but that one also they beat and treated shamefully and sent away empty-handed. ¹²He sent still a third, and they wounded him and threw him out.

¹³"Then the owner of the vineyard said, 'What shall I do? I will send my son, whom I love; perhaps they will respect him.'

¹⁴"But when the tenants saw him, they talked the matter over. 'This is the heir,' they said. 'Let's kill him, and the inheritance will be ours.' ¹⁵So they threw him out of the vineyard and killed him.

"What then will the owner of the vineyard do to them? ¹⁶He will come and kill those tenants and give the vineyard to others."

When the people heard this, they said, "May this never be!"

¹⁷Jesus looked directly at them and asked, "Then what is the meaning of that which is written:

" 'The stone the builders rejected
　　has become the capstone'^{a, b}?

¹⁸Everyone who falls on that stone will be broken to pieces, but he on whom it falls will be crushed."

¹⁹The teachers of the law and the chief priests looked for a way to arrest him immediately, because they knew he had spoken this parable against them. But they were afraid of the people.

■ Paying Taxes to Caesar
□ See Matthew 22:15–22; Mark 12:13–17

²⁰Keeping a close watch on him, they sent spies, who pretended to be honest. They hoped to catch Jesus in something he said so that they might hand him over to the power and authority of the governor. ²¹So the spies questioned him: "Teacher, we know that you speak and teach what is right, and that you do not show partiality but teach the way of God in accordance with the truth. ²²Is it right for us to pay taxes to Caesar or not?"

²³He saw through their duplicity and said to

---

b 38 Psalm 118:26　　*c 46* Isaiah 56:7　　*d 46* Jer. 7:11　　*a 17* Or *cornerstone*　　*b 17* Psalm 118:22

them, 24"Show me a denarius. Whose portrait and inscription are on it?"

25"Caesar's," they replied.

He said to them, "Then give to Caesar what is Caesar's, and to God what is God's."

26They were unable to trap him in what he had said there in public. And astonished by his answer, they became silent.

■ The Resurrection and Marriage
□ See Matthew 22:23–33; Mark 12:18–27

27Some of the Sadducees, who say there is no resurrection, came to Jesus with a question. 28"Teacher," they said, "Moses wrote for us that if a man's brother dies and leaves a wife but no children, the man must marry the widow and have children for his brother. 29Now there were seven brothers. The first one married a woman and died childless. 30The second 31and then the third married her, and in the same way the seven died, leaving no children. 32Finally, the woman died too. 33Now then, at the resurrection whose wife will she be, since the seven were married to her?"

34Jesus replied, "The people of this age marry and are given in marriage. 35But those who are considered worthy of taking part in that age and in the resurrection from the dead will neither marry nor be given in marriage, 36and they can no longer die; for they are like the angels. They are God's children, since they are children of the resurrection. 37But in the account of the bush, even Moses showed that the dead rise, for he calls the Lord 'the God of Abraham, and the God of Isaac, and the God of Jacob'.c 38He is not the God of the dead, but of the living, for to him all are alive."

39Some of the teachers of the law responded, "Well said, teacher!" 40And no-one dared to ask him any more questions.

■ Whose Son Is the Christ?
□ See Matthew 22:41 – 23:7; Mark 12:35–40

41Then Jesus said to them, "How is it that they say the Christd is the Son of David? 42David himself declares in the Book of Psalms:

" 'The Lord said to my Lord:
    "Sit at my right hand
43until I make your enemies
    a footstool for your feet." 'e

44David calls him 'Lord'. How then can he be his son?"

45While all the people were listening, Jesus said to his disciples, 46"Beware of the teachers of the law. They like to walk around in flowing robes and love to be greeted in the market-places and have the most important seats in the synagogues and the places of honour at banquets. 47They devour widows' houses and for a show make lengthy prayers. Such men will be punished most severely."

■ The Widow's Offering
□ See Mark 12:41–44

21 As he looked up, Jesus saw the rich putting their gifts into the temple treasury. 2He also saw a poor widow put in two very small copper coins.a 3"I tell you the truth," he said, "this poor widow has put in more than all the others. 4All these people gave their gifts out of their wealth; but she out of her poverty put in all she had to live on."

20:44 ■ JESUS ASKS A QUESTION
In the midst of many questions thrown at him, Jesus offers one back. The passage, quoting Psalm 110:1, is difficult to understand, but Jesus may have been trying to clear up a misunderstanding about the Messiah. Nationalistic Jews of that day were expecting a Messiah, or a "Son of David", out of the same mould as the great Jewish king who defeated Israel's enemies. But Jesus shows that David himself acknowledged the Messiah to come as "Lord", or One far greater than a mere earthly king.

■ Signs of the End of the Age
□ See Matthew 24; Mark 13

5Some of his disciples were remarking about how the temple was adorned with beautiful stones and with gifts dedicated to God. But Jesus said, 6"As for what you see here, the time will come when not one stone will be left on another; every one of them will be thrown down."

7"Teacher," they asked, "when will these things happen? And what will be the sign that they are about to take place?"

8He replied: "Watch out that you are not deceived. For many will come in my name, claiming, 'I am he,' and 'The time is near.' Do not follow them. 9When you hear of wars and revolutions, do not be frightened. These things must happen first, but the end will not come right away."

10Then he said to them: "Nation will rise against nation, and kingdom against kingdom. 11There will be great earthquakes, famines and pestilences in various places, and fearful events and great signs from heaven.

12"But before all this, they will lay hands on you and persecute you. They will deliver you to synagogues and prisons, and you will be brought before kings and governors, and all on account of my name. 13This will result in your being witnesses to them. 14But make up your mind not to worry beforehand how you will defend yourselves. 15For I will give you words and wisdom that none of your adversaries will be able to resist or contradict. 16You will be betrayed even by parents, brothers, relatives and friends, and they will put some of you to death. 17All men will hate you because of me. 18But not a hair of your head will perish. 19By standing firm you will gain life.

20"When you see Jerusalem being surrounded by armies, you will know that its desolation is near. 21Then let those who are in Judea flee to the mountains, let those in the city get out, and let those in the country not enter the city. 22For this is the time of punishment in fulfilment of all that has been written. 23How dreadful it will be in those days for pregnant women and nursing mothers! There will be great distress in the land and wrath against this people. 24They will fall by the sword and will be taken as prisoners to all the nations. Jerusalem will be trampled on by the Gentiles until the times of the Gentiles are fulfilled.

25"There will be signs in the sun, moon and stars. On the earth, nations will be in anguish and perplexity at the roaring and tossing of the sea. 26Men will faint from terror, apprehensive of what is coming on the world, for the heavenly bodies will be shaken. 27At that time they will see the Son of Man coming in a cloud with power and great glory. 28When these things begin to take place, stand up and lift up your heads, because your redemption is drawing near."

29He told them this parable: "Look at the fig-tree and all the trees. 30When they sprout leaves, you can see for yourselves and know that summer is near. 31Even so, when you see these things happening, you know that the kingdom of God is near.

32"I tell you the truth, this generation*b* will certainly not pass away until all these things have happened. 33Heaven and earth will pass away, but my words will never pass away.

34"Be careful, or your hearts will be weighed down with dissipation, drunkenness and the anxieties of life, and that day will close on you unexpectedly like a trap. 35For it will come upon all those who live on the face of the whole earth. 36Be always on the watch, and pray that you may be able to escape all that is about to happen, and that you may be able to stand before the Son of Man."

37Each day Jesus was teaching at the temple, and each evening he went out to spend the night on the hill called the Mount of Olives, 38and all the people came early in the morning to hear him at the temple.

■ Judas Agrees to Betray Jesus
□ See Matthew 26:2–5; Mark 14:1–2,10–11

22 Now the Feast of Unleavened Bread, called the Passover, was approaching, 2and the chief priests and the teachers of the law were looking for some way to get rid of Jesus, for they were afraid of the people. 3Then Satan entered Judas, called Iscariot, one of the Twelve. 4And Judas went to the chief priests and the officers of the temple guard and discussed with them how he might betray Jesus. 5They were delighted and agreed to give him money. 6He consented, and watched for an opportunity to hand Jesus over to them when no crowd was present.

■ The Last Supper
□ See Matthew 26:17–19,26–29; Mark 14:12–16,22–25

7Then came the day of Unleavened Bread on which the Passover lamb had to be sacrificed. 8Jesus sent Peter and John, saying, "Go and make preparations for us to eat the Passover."

9"Where do you want us to prepare for it?" they asked.

10He replied, "As you enter the city, a man carrying a jar of water will meet you. Follow him to the house that he enters, 11and say to the owner of the house, 'The Teacher asks: Where is the guest room, where I may eat the Passover with my disciples?'

12He will show you a large upper room, all furnished. Make preparations there."

13They left and found things just as Jesus had told them. So they prepared the Passover.

14When the hour came, Jesus and his apostles reclined at the table. 15And he said to them, "I have eagerly desired to eat this Passover with you before I suffer. 16For I tell you, I will not eat it again until it finds fulfilment in the kingdom of God."

17After taking the cup, he gave thanks and said, "Take this and divide it among you. 18For I tell you I will not drink again of the fruit of the vine until the kingdom of God comes."

19And he took bread, gave thanks and broke it, and gave it to them, saying, "This is my body given for you; do this in remembrance of me."

20In the same way, after the supper he took the cup, saying, "This cup is the new covenant in my blood, which is poured out for you. 21But the hand of him who is going to betray me is with mine on the table. 22The Son of Man will go as it has been decreed, but woe to that man who betrays him." 23They began to question among themselves which of them it might be who would do this.

24Also a dispute arose among them as to which of them was considered to be greatest. 25Jesus said to them, "The kings of the Gentiles lord it over them; and those who exercise authority over them call themselves Benefactors. 26But you are not to be like that. Instead, the greatest among you should be like the youngest, and the one who rules like the one who serves. 27For who is greater, the one who is at the table or the one who serves? Is it not the one who is at the table? But I am among you as one who serves. 28You are those who have stood by me in my trials. 29And I confer on you a kingdom, just as my Father conferred one on me, 30so that you may eat and drink at my table in my kingdom and sit on thrones, judging the twelve tribes of Israel.

22:24 ■ STATUS-CONSCIOUS DISCIPLES
Even at the emotional Last Supper scene described here, the disciples fell into their habit of worrying about rank and status. Not until after Jesus had died and returned did they understand the true nature of the kingdom he was setting into motion. It is a kingdom primarily of spiritual, not political, power. And in it, the greatest is the one who serves others.

31"Simon, Simon, Satan has asked to sift you*a* as wheat. 32But I have prayed for you, Simon, that your faith may not fail. And when you have turned back, strengthen your brothers."

33But he replied, "Lord, I am ready to go with you to prison and to death."

34Jesus answered, "I tell you, Peter, before the cock crows today, you will deny three times that you know me."

35Then Jesus asked them, "When I sent you without purse, bag or sandals, did you lack anything?"

"Nothing," they answered.

b 32 Or race   a 31 The Greek is plural.

36He said to them, "But now if you have a purse, take it, and also a bag; and if you don't have a sword, sell your cloak and buy one. 37It is written: 'And he was numbered with the transgressors';b and I tell you that this must be fulfilled in me. Yes, what is written about me is reaching its fulfilment."

38The disciples said, "See, Lord, here are two swords."

"That is enough," he replied.

■ Jesus Prays on the Mount of Olives
☐ See Matthew 26:36–46; Mark 14:32–42

39Jesus went out as usual to the Mount of Olives, and his disciples followed him. 40On reaching the place, he said to them, "Pray that you will not fall into temptation." 41He withdrew about a stone's throw beyond them, knelt down and prayed, 42"Father, if you are willing, take this cup from me; yet not my will, but yours be done." 43An angel from heaven appeared to him and strengthened him. 44And being in anguish, he prayed more earnestly, and his sweat was like drops of blood falling to the ground.c

45When he rose from prayer and went back to the disciples, he found them asleep, exhausted from sorrow. 46"Why are you sleeping?" he asked them. "Get up and pray so that you will not fall into temptation."

■ Jesus Arrested
☐ See Matthew 26:47–56; Mark 14:43–50; John 18:3–11

47While he was still speaking a crowd came up, and the man who was called Judas, one of the Twelve, was leading them. He approached Jesus to kiss him, 48but Jesus asked him, "Judas, are you betraying the Son of Man with a kiss?"

49When Jesus' followers saw what was going to happen, they said, "Lord, should we strike with our swords?" 50And one of them struck the servant of the high priest, cutting off his right ear.

51But Jesus answered, "No more of this!" And he touched the man's ear and healed him.

52Then Jesus said to the chief priests, the officers of the temple guard, and the elders, who had come for him, "Am I leading a rebellion, that you have come with swords and clubs? 53Every day I was with you in the temple courts, and you did not lay a hand on me. But this is your hour—when darkness reigns."

■ Peter Disowns Jesus
☐ See Matthew 26:69–75; Mark 14:66–72; John 18:16–18,25–27

54Then seizing him, they led him away and took him into the house of the high priest. Peter followed at a distance. 55But when they had kindled a fire in the middle of the courtyard and had sat down together, Peter sat down with them. 56A servant girl saw him seated there in the firelight. She looked closely at him and said, "This man was with him."

57But he denied it. "Woman, I don't know him," he said.

58A little later someone else saw him and said, "You also are one of them."

"Man, I am not!" Peter replied.

59About an hour later another asserted, "Certainly this fellow was with him, for he is a Galilean."

22:58 ■ DESERTED BY HIS FRIENDS
Peter showed courage by following Jesus, rather than going into hiding. Perhaps trying to gain information, he even went into the high priest's courtyard. But there he was recognised, partly because of his Galilean accent (see Matthew 26:73). After denying that he knew Jesus, Peter remembered with pain his boast that he would be willing to die with Jesus (verse 33). Jesus had accurately predicted that even Peter would desert him.

60Peter replied, "Man, I don't know what you're talking about!" Just as he was speaking, the cock crowed. 61The Lord turned and looked straight at Peter. Then Peter remembered the word the Lord had spoken to him: "Before the cock crows today, you will disown me three times." 62And he went outside and wept bitterly.

■ The Guards Mock Jesus
☐ See Matthew 26:67–68; Mark 14:65; John 18:22–23

63The men who were guarding Jesus began mocking and beating him. 64They blindfolded him and demanded, "Prophesy! Who hit you?" 65And they said many other insulting things to him.

■ Jesus Before Pilate and Herod
☐ See Matthew 26:63–66; Mark 14:61–63; John 18:19–21

66At daybreak the council of the elders of the people, both the chief priests and teachers of the law, met together, and Jesus was led before them. 67"If you are the Christ,"d they said, "tell us."

Jesus answered, "If I tell you, you will not believe me, 68and if I asked you, you would not answer. 69But from now on, the Son of Man will be seated at the right hand of the mighty God."

70They all asked, "Are you then the Son of God?"

He replied, "You are right in saying I am."

71Then they said, "Why do we need any more testimony? We have heard it from his own lips."

23 Then the whole assembly rose and led him off to Pilate. 2And they began to accuse him, saying, "We have found this man subverting our nation. He opposes payment of taxes to Caesar and claims to be Christ,a a king."

3So Pilate asked Jesus, "Are you the king of the Jews?"

"Yes, it is as you say," Jesus replied.

4Then Pilate announced to the chief priests and the crowd, "I find no basis for a charge against this man."

5But they insisted, "He stirs up the people all over Judeab by his teaching. He started in Galilee and has come all the way here."

6On hearing this, Pilate asked if the man was a Galilean. 7When he learned that Jesus was under Herod's jurisdiction, he sent him to Herod, who was also in Jerusalem at that time.

8When Herod saw Jesus, he was greatly pleased,

b 37 Isaiah 53:12   c 44 Some early manuscripts do not have verses 43 and 44.   d 67 Or Messiah   a 2 Or Messiah; also in verses 35 and 39
b 5 Or over the land of the Jews

because for a long time he had been wanting to see him. From what he had heard about him, he hoped to see him perform some miracle. [9]He plied him with many questions, but Jesus gave him no answer. [10]The chief priests and the teachers of the law were standing there, vehemently accusing him. [11]Then Herod and his soldiers ridiculed and mocked him. Dressing him in an elegant robe, they sent him back to Pilate. [12]That day Herod and Pilate became friends—before this they had been enemies.

[13]Pilate called together the chief priests, the rulers and the people, [14]and said to them, "You brought me this man as one who was inciting the people to rebellion. I have examined him in your presence and have found no basis for your charges against him. [15]Neither has Herod, for he sent him back to us; as you can see, he has done nothing to deserve death. [16]Therefore, I will punish him and then release him."[c]

[18]With one voice they cried out, "Away with this man! Release Barabbas to us!" ([19]Barabbas had been thrown into prison for an insurrection in the city, and for murder.)

[20]Wanting to release Jesus, Pilate appealed to them again. [21]But they kept shouting, "Crucify him! Crucify him!"

[22]For the third time he spoke to them: "Why? What crime has this man committed? I have found in him no grounds for the death penalty. Therefore I will have him punished and then release him."

[23]But with loud shouts they insistently demanded that he be crucified, and their shouts prevailed. [24]So Pilate decided to grant their demand. [25]He released the man who had been thrown into prison for insurrection and murder, the one they asked for, and surrendered Jesus to their will.

23:25 ■ WHO SHOULD TRY JESUS?

The Gospels record a "pass-the-buck" sequence in Jesus' encounter with Roman justice. The Jewish court, or Sanhedrin, judged Jesus guilty of blasphemy, but it had no authority to carry out a death sentence. Therefore, the religious leaders took Jesus to Pilate, the Roman governor of Judea. Along the way, they changed the religious charge against Jesus to a political one, which alone would call for Roman punishment.

Pilate showed cowardice. First, he deferred the case to Herod, who had jurisdiction over Jesus' home region. Herod taunted and mocked Jesus, and then sent him back. Three times Pilate tried to get the Jewish leaders to release Jesus, but finally he yielded to the demands for capital punishment.

■ The Crucifixion

☐ See Matthew 27:33–44; Mark 15:22–32; John 19:17–24

[26]As they led him away, they seized Simon from Cyrene, who was on his way in from the country, and put the cross on him and made him carry it behind Jesus. [27]A large number of people followed him, including women who mourned and wailed for him. [28]Jesus turned and said to them, "Daughters of Jerusalem, do not weep for me; weep for yourselves

and for your children. [29]For the time will come when you will say, 'Blessed are the barren women, the wombs that never bore and the breasts that never nursed!' [30]Then

> " 'they will say to the mountains, "Fall on us!"
> and to the hills "Cover us!" '[d]

[31]For if men do these things when the tree is green, what will happen when it is dry?"

[32]Two other men, both criminals, were also led out with him to be executed. [33]When they came to the place called the Skull, there they crucified him, along with the criminals—one on his right, the other on his left. [34]Jesus said, "Father, forgive them, for they do not know what they are doing."[e] And they divided up his clothes by casting lots.

[35]The people stood watching, and the rulers even sneered at him. They said, "He saved others; let him save himself if he is the Christ of God, the Chosen One."

[36]The soldiers also came up and mocked him. They offered him wine vinegar [37]and said, "If you are the king of the Jews, save yourself."

[38]There was a written notice above him, which read: THIS IS THE KING OF THE JEWS.

[39]One of the criminals who hung there hurled insults at him: "Aren't you the Christ? Save yourself and us!"

[40]But the other criminal rebuked him. "Don't you fear God," he said, "since you are under the same sentence? [41]We are punished justly, for we are getting what our deeds deserve. But this man has done nothing wrong."

[42]Then he said, "Jesus, remember me when you come into your kingdom.[f]"

[43]Jesus answered him, "I tell you the truth, today you will be with me in paradise."

■ Jesus' Death

☐ See Matthew 27:45–56; Mark 15:33–41

[44]It was now about the sixth hour, and darkness came over the whole land until the ninth hour, [45]for the sun stopped shining. And the curtain of the temple was torn in two. [46]Jesus called out with a loud voice, "Father, into your hands I commit my spirit." When he had said this, he breathed his last.

[47]The centurion, seeing what had happened, praised God and said, "Surely this was a righteous man." [48]When all the people who had gathered to witness this sight saw what took place, they beat their breasts and went away. [49]But all those who knew him, including the women who had followed him from Galilee, stood at a distance, watching these things.

■ Jesus' Burial

☐ See Matthew 27:57–61; Mark 15:42–47; John 19:38–42

[50]Now there was a man named Joseph, a member of the Council, a good and upright man, [51]who had not consented to their decision and action. He came from the Judean town of Arimathea and he was waiting for the kingdom of God. [52]Going to Pilate, he asked for Jesus' body. [53]Then he took it down, wrapped it in linen cloth and placed it in a tomb cut in the rock, one in which no-one had yet been laid.

---

c 16 Some manuscripts him." 17 Now he was obliged to release one man to them at the Feast. *d 30 Hosea 10:8* *e 34 Some early manuscripts do not have this sentence.* *f 42 Some manuscripts come with your kingly power*

⁵⁴It was Preparation Day, and the Sabbath was about to begin.

⁵⁵The women who had come with Jesus from Galilee followed Joseph and saw the tomb and how his body was laid in it. ⁵⁶Then they went home and prepared spices and perfumes. But they rested on the Sabbath in obedience to the commandment.

■ The Resurrection

☐ See Matthew 28:1–8; Mark 16:1–8; John 20:1–8

24 On the first day of the week, very early in the morning, the women took the spices they had prepared and went to the tomb. ²They found the stone rolled away from the tomb, ³but when they entered, they did not find the body of the Lord Jesus. ⁴While they were wondering about this, suddenly two men in clothes that gleamed like lightning stood beside them. ⁵In their fright the women bowed down with their faces to the ground, but the men said to them, "Why do you look for the living among the dead? ⁶He is not here; he has risen! Remember how he told you, while he was still with you in Galilee: ⁷'The Son of Man must be delivered into the hands of sinful men, be crucified and on the third day be raised again.' " ⁸Then they remembered his words.

⁹When they came back from the tomb, they told all these things to the Eleven and to all the others. ¹⁰It was Mary Magdalene, Joanna, Mary the mother

■ FINAL GLIMPSES OF JESUS
THE MOST IMPORTANT WEEK IN HISTORY

INSIGHT

> BUT WITH LOUD SHOUTS THEY INSISTENTLY DEMANDED THAT HE BE CRUCIFIED, AND THEIR SHOUTS PREVAILED. ■ 23:23

Everything about Jesus seemed to come together during his last few days on earth, and surely those days offer a key to understanding him. As if on a roller-coaster, people's reactions to him plunged from heady exhilaration to murderous rejection overnight.

Those last days included one scene of triumph, a grand entry into Jerusalem. Pilgrims were filling the streets in holiday celebration. In a gallant gesture for Jesus, they laid their coats before him, and they roared their approval as he approached. But against that tumultuous background, Jesus sat weeping, painfully aware that their praise was hollow.

Even as Jesus' popularity with the masses was soaring, spies joined the ranks of onlookers, assailing him with questions and verbal traps. Jesus knew he wasn't safe anywhere, even in an intimate gathering with his disciples. During this and his disciples' last meal together, one of the Twelve rose and left the room to bargain for Jesus' life.

■ THE DARKEST DAY AND THE BRIGHTEST
At Jesus' arrest, the religious and political power-brokers had a look at him at last. They had heard many intriguing rumours, and hoped that he would perform for them like a magician (23:8). Jesus declined. He had never sought their kind of power, and would not then, even with his life at stake.

Outside, the crowd that previously had shouted, "Blessed is the king!" took up a very different chant: "Crucify him!" Jesus' life was doomed. The one who had come to save the world was about to be destroyed by it.

In two back-to-back closing chapters Luke records the darkest day in history . . . and the brightest. No-one was more surprised than Jesus' disciples to hear reports that the man they had seen die on Friday was walking around on Sunday. It seemed like hysterical nonsense at first – until he did appear, and they could deny it no longer.

■ ORDINARY PEOPLE, AN EXTRAORDINARY DISCOVERY
Luke adds one scene that captures the terrible confusion of those final days. Two of Jesus' disciples were walking away from Jerusalem, downhearted. Their dream was over; all the mounting hopes of the last few years had died with Jesus on the cross.

A strange man appeared beside the two forlorn disciples. Bizarrely, he seemed the only man alive who hadn't heard about the incredible week in Jerusalem. He talked with them, tracing the whole story of the gospel, beginning with Moses and the prophets.

The stranger intrigued them, and they asked him to stay longer. At mealtime the last link snapped into place. It was Jesus! No-one else. Without a doubt, he was alive.

Ordinary people, with more than a touch of cowardice, had followed Jesus, listened to him, and watched him die (from a distance, to keep themselves safe). But seeing Jesus alive changed all that. Luke's story began with joy, and it ends that way: "Then they worshipped him and returned to Jerusalem with great joy" (24:52). Before long they were out telling the world about it.

☐ LIFE QUESTIONS:
Suppose you had been in the room to hear the first news of Jesus' resurrection. Would you have believed it? What makes you believe it now?

of James, and the others with them who told this to the apostles. ¹¹But they did not believe the women, because their words seemed to them like nonsense. ¹²Peter, however, got up and ran to the tomb. Bending over, he saw the strips of linen lying by themselves, and he went away, wondering to himself what had happened.

■ On the Road to Emmaus

¹³Now that same day two of them were going to a village called Emmaus, about seven miles*a* from Jerusalem. ¹⁴They were talking with each other about everything that had happened. ¹⁵As they talked and discussed these things with each other, Jesus himself came up and walked along with them; ¹⁶but they were kept from recognising him.

¹⁷He asked them, "What are you discussing together as you walk along?"

They stood still, their faces downcast. ¹⁸One of them, named Cleopas, asked him, "Are you only a visitor to Jerusalem and do not know the things that have happened there in these days?"

¹⁹"What things?" he asked.

"About Jesus of Nazareth," they replied. "He was a prophet, powerful in word and deed before God and all the people. ²⁰The chief priests and our rulers handed him over to be sentenced to death, and they crucified him; ²¹but we had hoped that he was the one who was going to redeem Israel. And what is more, it is the third day since all this took place. ²²In addition, some of our women amazed us. They went to the tomb early this morning ²³but didn't find his body. They came and told us that they had seen a vision of angels, who said he was alive. ²⁴Then some of our companions went to the tomb and found it just as the women had said, but him they did not see."

²⁵He said to them, "How foolish you are, and how slow of heart to believe all that the prophets have spoken! ²⁶Did not the Christ*b* have to suffer these things and then enter his glory?" ²⁷And beginning with Moses and all the Prophets, he explained to them what was said in all the Scriptures concerning himself.

24:27 ■ OLD TESTAMENT 101
When the disciples first began to tell about Jesus' resurrection, they quoted Old Testament scriptures and explained how Jesus fulfilled their predictions. (See, for example, Peter's sermons in Acts 2 and 3.) They were probably following what Jesus had taught on the road to Emmaus. Jesus went through the entire Old Testament, explaining how his life crowned centuries of God's work.

---

²⁸As they approached the village to which they were going, Jesus acted as if he were going further. ²⁹But they urged him strongly, "Stay with us, for it is nearly evening; the day is almost over." So he went in to stay with them.

³⁰When he was at the table with them, he took bread, gave thanks, broke it and began to give it to them. ³¹Then their eyes were opened and they recognised him, and he disappeared from their sight. ³²They asked each other, "Were not our hearts burning within us while he talked with us on the road and opened the Scriptures to us?"

³³They got up and returned at once to Jerusalem. There they found the Eleven and those with them, assembled together ³⁴and saying, "It is true! The Lord has risen and has appeared to Simon." ³⁵Then the two told what had happened on the way, and how Jesus was recognised by them when he broke the bread.

■ Jesus Appears to the Disciples

³⁶While they were still talking about this, Jesus himself stood among them and said to them, "Peace be with you."

³⁷They were startled and frightened, thinking they saw a ghost. ³⁸He said to them, "Why are you troubled, and why do doubts rise in your minds? ³⁹Look at my hands and my feet. It is I myself! Touch me and see; a ghost does not have flesh and bones, as you see I have."

⁴⁰When he had said this, he showed them his hands and feet. ⁴¹And while they still did not believe it because of joy and amazement, he asked them, "Do you have anything here to eat?" ⁴²They gave him a piece of broiled fish, ⁴³and he took it and ate it in their presence.

⁴⁴He said to them, "This is what I told you while I was still with you: Everything must be fulfilled that is written about me in the Law of Moses, the Prophets and the Psalms."

⁴⁵Then he opened their minds so they could understand the Scriptures. ⁴⁶He told them, "This is what is written: The Christ will suffer and rise from the dead on the third day, ⁴⁷and repentance and forgiveness of sins will be preached in his name to all nations, beginning at Jerusalem. ⁴⁸You are witnesses of these things. ⁴⁹I am going to send you what my Father has promised; but stay in the city until you have been clothed with power from on high."

■ The Ascension

⁵⁰When he had led them out to the vicinity of Bethany, he lifted up his hands and blessed them. ⁵¹While he was blessing them, he left them and was taken up into heaven. ⁵²Then they worshipped him and returned to Jerusalem with great joy. ⁵³And they stayed continually at the temple, praising God.

---

a 13 Greek *sixty stadia* (about 11 kilometres)   *b* 26 Or *Messiah*; also in verse 46

JOHN

■ GOD BREAKS THE SILENCE

HE SPOKE IN THE ONLY WAY WE COULD TRULY UNDERSTAND

THE WORD BECAME FLESH AND MADE HIS DWELLING AMONG US. ■ 1:14

Unless a person communicates to you, in speech or gestures or even facial expressions, you can't get to know him or her. What goes on behind the mask of skin will always remain a mystery.

God, too, was a mystery until he broke his silence. He spoke once, and all creation sprang to life – quasars, oceans, whales, giraffes, orchids, and beetles. He spoke again, says John, and this time the Word took the form of a man, Jesus Christ. John's book tells the story of that Word who became flesh.

■ DIFFERENT FROM OTHER GOSPELS

It's clear from the first few paragraphs that John departed sharply from the style of Matthew, Mark, and Luke. The other Gospel writers focused on events, following Jesus through the bustling market-places and villages.

Unlike them, John assumed readers knew the basic facts about Jesus. Instead of focusing on facts, he mulled over the profound meaning of what Jesus had said and done. The book of John reads as if it were written under a great, shady tree by an author who had lots of time for reflection.

In his first sentence, John highlights Christ's nature. There are no Christmas scenes here: no stables, shepherds, or wise men. John tells nothing of Jesus' birth and youth. He introduces him as the adult Son of God. After an eloquent prologue, the book shows John the Baptist humbly pointing to Jesus, "the thongs of whose sandals I am not worthy to untie" (1:27).

■ JESUS SENT WITH A MISSION

John selected vignettes from no more than 20 days in Jesus' life, and arranged them so that they present a Messiah who knows "where I came from and where I am going" (8:14). Jesus was not simply a "man who fell to earth", but God's Son, sent to do the work of the Father. His repeated references to the One "who sent me" give a cadence to the book.

According to John, Christ participated in the original creation act. But later he was sent to earth as the Word, the sum of all that God wanted to say. God spoke in the only way we could truly understand: by becoming one of us.

■ HOW TO READ JOHN

New Christians often turn to the book of John because it spells out so clearly the basics of the faith. Jesus proves who he is, diagnoses humanity's problems, and bluntly describes what is necessary for conversion. You will probably recognise familiar verses and phrases in this remarkable book (such as Jesus' "I am" sayings).

John selected seven "signs" or miracles (five of which aren't reported elsewhere) and built a story around them. As you read John,

note how the author weaves together his story and its meaning.

It's best to read John in units. Don't just read a paragraph or a chapter. Follow the sectional headings and read a complete section, both the action and the commentary on it. John does not primarily relate events; he interprets those events.

Look carefully for the audiences Jesus addresses. Is he talking to his disciples? To his opponents? To the large crowds? He treats each audience differently.

■ 3-TRACK READING PLAN

For an explanation and complete listing of the 3-track reading plan, turn to page x.

■ TRACK 1:
Two-Week Courses on the Bible
The Track 1 reading programme on the Life and Teachings of Jesus includes four chapters from John. See page x for a complete listing of this course.

■ TRACK 2:
An Overview of John in 8 Days
□ Day 1. Read the Introduction to John and then turn to John 3, which contains perhaps the best-known verse in the entire Bible (verse 16). Read Jesus' conversation with Nicodemus.
□ Day 2. John 5 and 6 contain Jesus' blunt teaching about who he was and why he

came to earth. Read chapter 6, noting how John weaves together a miracle, the crowd's reaction to it, then Jesus' comments on it.
□ Day 3. Read chapter 10, another familiar passage.
□ Day 4. The next four readings are taken from John's report of the Last Supper. Begin with chapter 14.
□ Day 5. Read chapter 15, where Jesus explains the image of a vine and its branches.
□ Day 6. Read chapter 16, noting especially what Jesus says about the Holy Spirit. John contains more teaching about the Holy Spirit than any other Gospel.

□ Day 7. Read chapter 17, a farewell prayer Jesus prayed for his disciples.
□ Day 8. Read John's account of Jesus' resurrection, chapter 20. Now turn to page xi for your next Track 2 reading project.

■ TRACK 3:
All of John in 21 Days
After you have read through John, turn to pages xii–xiii for your next Track 3 reading project.

□ 1 □ 2 □ 3 □ 4
□ 5 □ 6 □ 7 □ 8
□ 9 □ 10 □ 11 □ 12
□ 13 □ 14 □ 15 □ 16
□ 17 □ 18 □ 19 □ 20
□ 21

■ The Word Became Flesh

1 In the beginning was the Word, and the Word was with God, and the Word was God. ²He was with God in the beginning.
³Through him all things were made; without him nothing was made that has been made. ⁴In him was life, and that life was the light of men. ⁵The light shines in the darkness, but the darkness has not understood*a* it.
⁶There came a man who was sent from God; his name was John. ⁷He came as a witness to testify concerning that light, so that through him all men might believe. ⁸He himself was not the light; he came only as a witness to the light. ⁹The true light that gives light to every man was coming into the world.*b*
¹⁰He was in the world, and though the world was made through him, the world did not recognise him. ¹¹He came to that which was his own, but his own did not receive him. ¹²Yet to all who received him, to those who believed in his name, he gave the right to become children of God—¹³children born not of natural descent,*c* nor of human decision or a husband's will, but born of God.
¹⁴The Word became flesh and made his dwelling among us. We have seen his glory, the glory of the One and Only,*d* who came from the Father, full of grace and truth. ¹⁵John testifies concerning him. He cries out, saying, "This was he of whom I said, 'He who comes after me has surpassed me because he was before me.'" ¹⁶From the fulness of his grace we have all received one blessing after another. ¹⁷For the law was given through Moses; grace and truth came through Jesus Christ. ¹⁸No-one has ever seen

God, but God the One and Only,*e,f* who is at the Father's side, has made him known.

■ John the Baptist Denies Being the Christ
¹⁹Now this was John's testimony when the Jews of Jerusalem sent priests and Levites to ask him who he was. ²⁰He did not fail to confess, but confessed freely, "I am not the Christ."*g*

> **1:14 ■ JESUS THE WORD**
> John used language with special meaning for both Greek and Jewish readers. In Greek philosophy, "word" (*logos*) was a key term, often referring to the power of reason undergirding all creation. For Jews, too, "word" had great significance, for God spoke his word to create the world and to transform his people. Yet John's meaning passed beyond the Greek and Jewish ideas. An eight-year-old girl expressed it well. When asked why Jesus was called the Word, she said, "Because Jesus is all God wanted to say to us".

²¹They asked him, "Then who are you? Are you Elijah?"
He said, "I am not."
"Are you the Prophet?"
He answered, "No."
²²Finally they said, "Who are you? Give us an answer to take back to those who sent us. What do you say about yourself?"
²³John replied in the words of Isaiah the prophet, "I am the voice of one calling in the desert, 'Make straight the way for the Lord.'*b*"
²⁴Now some Pharisees who had been sent

---

a 5 Or darkness, and the darkness has not overcome   *b 9 Or This was the true light that gives light to every man who comes into the world*   *c 13 Greek of bloods*   *d 14 Or the Only Begotten*   *e 18 Or the Only Begotten*   *f 18 Some manuscripts but the only (or only begotten) Son*   *g 20 Or Messiah. "The Christ" (Greek) and "the Messiah" (Hebrew) both mean "the Anointed One"; also in verse 25.*   *b 23 Isaiah 40:3*

25questioned him, "Why then do you baptise if you are not the Christ, nor Elijah, nor the Prophet?"

26"I baptise with*i* water," John replied, "but among you stands one you do not know. 27He is the one who comes after me, the thongs of whose sandals I am not worthy to untie."

28This all happened at Bethany on the other side of the Jordan, where John was baptising.

■ Jesus the Lamb of God

29The next day John saw Jesus coming towards him and said, "Look, the Lamb of God, who takes away the sin of the world! 30This is the one I meant when I said, 'A man who comes after me has surpassed me because he was before me.' 31I myself did not know him, but the reason I came baptising with water was that he might be revealed to Israel."

32Then John gave this testimony: "I saw the Spirit come down from heaven as a dove and remain on him. 33I would not have known him, except that the one who sent me to baptise with water told me, 'The man on whom you see the Spirit come down and remain is he who will baptise with the Holy Spirit.' 34I have seen and I testify that this is the Son of God."

■ Jesus' First Disciples

35The next day John was there again with two of his disciples. 36When he saw Jesus passing by, he said, "Look, the Lamb of God!"

37When the two disciples heard him say this, they followed Jesus. 38Turning round, Jesus saw them following and asked, "What do you want?"

They said, "Rabbi" (which means Teacher), "where are you staying?"

39"Come," he replied, "and you will see."

So they went and saw where he was staying, and spent that day with him. It was about the tenth hour.

1:39 ■ GRADUAL DISCIPLES
Other Gospels show the disciples dropping their nets and following Jesus instantly. John describes a more gradual process. When two of John the Baptist's disciples grew curious, Jesus invited them to come and spend a day with him. Soon, they were ready to tell others what they had seen and heard.

40Andrew, Simon Peter's brother, was one of the two who heard what John had said and who had followed Jesus. 41The first thing Andrew did was to find his brother Simon and tell him, "We have found the Messiah" (that is, the Christ). 42And he brought him to Jesus.

Jesus looked at him and said, "You are Simon son of John. You will be called Cephas" (which, when translated, is Peter*j*).

■ Jesus Calls Philip and Nathanael

43The next day Jesus decided to leave for Galilee. Finding Philip, he said to him, "Follow me."

44Philip, like Andrew and Peter, was from the town of Bethsaida. 45Philip found Nathanael and told him, "We have found the one Moses wrote about in the Law, and about whom the prophets also wrote—Jesus of Nazareth, the son of Joseph."

46"Nazareth! Can anything good come from there?" Nathanael asked.

"Come and see," said Philip.

47When Jesus saw Nathanael approaching, he said of him, "Here is a true Israelite, in whom there is nothing false."

48"How do you know me?" Nathanael asked.

Jesus answered, "I saw you while you were still under the fig-tree before Philip called you."

49Then Nathanael declared, "Rabbi, you are the Son of God; you are the King of Israel."

50Jesus said, "You believe*k* because I told you I saw you under the fig-tree. You shall see greater things than that." 51He then added, "I tell you*l* the truth, you*l* shall see heaven open, and the angels of God ascending and descending on the Son of Man."

■ Jesus Changes Water to Wine

2 On the third day a wedding took place at Cana in Galilee. Jesus' mother was there, 2and Jesus and his disciples had also been invited to the wedding. 3When the wine was gone, Jesus' mother said to him, "They have no more wine."

4"Dear woman, why do you involve me?" Jesus replied. "My time has not yet come."

5His mother said to the servants, "Do whatever he tells you."

6Nearby stood six stone water jars, the kind used by the Jews for ceremonial washing, each holding from twenty to thirty gallons.*a*

2:6 ■ EYE-WITNESS DETAILS
Numerous specific details show that an eye-witness wrote the book of John. Here, the author describes stone water jars; elsewhere, he records the exact number of fish caught (21:11).

7Jesus said to the servants, "Fill the jars with water"; so they filled them to the brim.

8Then he told them, "Now draw some out and take it to the master of the banquet."

They did so, 9and the master of the banquet tasted the water that had been turned into wine. He did not realise where it had come from, though the servants who had drawn the water knew. Then he called the bridegroom aside 10and said, "Everyone brings out the choice wine first and then the cheaper wine after the guests have had too much to drink; but you have saved the best till now."

11This, the first of his miraculous signs, Jesus performed at Cana in Galilee. He thus revealed his glory, and his disciples put their faith in him.

■ Jesus Clears the Temple
□ See Matthew 21:12–13; Mark 11:15–17; Luke 19:45–46

12After this he went down to Capernaum with his mother and brothers and his disciples. There they stayed for a few days.

13When it was almost time for the Jewish

Passover, Jesus went up to Jerusalem. ¹⁴In the temple courts he found men selling cattle, sheep and doves, and others sitting at tables exchanging money. ¹⁵So he made a whip out of cords, and drove all from the temple area, both sheep and cattle; he scattered the coins of the money-changers and overturned their tables. ¹⁶To those who sold doves he said, "Get these out of here! How dare you turn my Father's house into a market!"

¹⁷His disciples remembered that it is written: "Zeal for your house will consume me."*b*

¹⁸Then the Jews demanded of him, "What miraculous sign can you show us to prove your authority to do all this?"

¹⁹Jesus answered them, "Destroy this temple, and I will raise it again in three days."

²⁰The Jews replied, "It has taken forty-six years to build this temple, and you are going to raise it in three days?" ²¹But the temple he had spoken of was his body. ²²After he was raised from the dead, his disciples recalled what he had said. Then they believed the Scripture and the words that Jesus had spoken.

²³Now while he was in Jerusalem at the Passover Feast, many people saw the miraculous signs he was doing and believed in his name.*c* ²⁴But Jesus would not entrust himself to them, for he knew all men. ²⁵He did not need man's testimony about man, for he knew what was in a man.

■ Jesus Teaches Nicodemus

3 Now there was a man of the Pharisees named Nicodemus, a member of the Jewish ruling council. ²He came to Jesus at night and said, "Rabbi, we know you are a teacher who has come from God. For no-one could perform the miraculous signs you are doing if God were not with him."

⁵Jesus answered, "I tell you the truth, no-one can enter the kingdom of God unless he is born of water and the Spirit. ⁶Flesh gives birth to flesh, but the Spirit*b* gives birth to spirit. ⁷You should not be surprised at my saying, 'You*c* must be born again.' ⁸The wind blows wherever it pleases. You hear its sound, but you cannot tell where it comes from or where it is going. So it is with everyone born of the Spirit."

⁹"How can this be?" Nicodemus asked.

¹⁰"You are Israel's teacher," said Jesus, "and do you not understand these things? ¹¹I tell you the truth, we speak of what we know, and we testify to what we have seen, but still you people do not accept our testimony. ¹²I have spoken to you of earthly things and you do not believe; how then will you believe if I speak of heavenly things? ¹³No-one has ever gone into heaven except the one who came from heaven—the Son of Man.*d* ¹⁴Just as Moses lifted up the snake in the desert, so the Son of Man must be lifted up, ¹⁵that everyone who believes in him may have eternal life.*e*

¹⁶"For God so loved the world that he gave his one and only Son,*f* that whoever believes in him shall not perish but have eternal life. ¹⁷For God did not send his Son into the world to condemn the world, but to save the world through him. ¹⁸Whoever believes in him is not condemned, but whoever does not believe stands condemned already because he has not believed in the name of God's one and only Son.*g* ¹⁹This is the verdict: Light has come into the world, but men loved darkness instead of light because their deeds were evil. ²⁰Everyone who does evil hates the light, and will not come into the light for fear that his deeds will be exposed. ²¹But whoever lives by the truth comes into the light, so that it may be seen plainly that what he has done has been done through God."*b*

3:2 ■ A REASON FOR SECRECY

This meeting took place at night, in secret. Nicodemus was a ruling member of the Pharisees, a group that violently opposed Jesus. He probably risked danger by meeting with Jesus. Two other references to Nicodemus indicate that Jesus must have had a strong effect on him. He stood up for Jesus at the Jewish ruling council (7:50) and helped prepare Jesus' body for burial (19:39).

Jesus' meeting with the Samaritan woman (4:4–42) probably had some of the same tension, although it occurred in daylight. Conversations between a Jew and a Samaritan, let alone between a religious teacher and an adulterer, were taboo.

3:16 ■ THE GOSPEL IN A NUTSHELL

This verse has probably been memorised more than any other in the Bible. In a few words it tells the story of salvation: God's love for the world, God's gift of his Son, and the opportunity for anyone who believes to be saved.

■ John the Baptist's Testimony About Jesus

²²After this, Jesus and his disciples went out into the Judean countryside, where he spent some time with them, and baptised. ²³Now John also was baptising at Aenon near Salim, because there was plenty of water, and people were constantly coming to be baptised. ²⁴(This was before John was put in prison.) ²⁵An argument developed between some of John's disciples and a certain Jew*i* over the matter of ceremonial washing. ²⁶They came to John and said to him, "Rabbi, that man who was with you on the other side of the Jordan—the one you testified about—well, he is baptising, and everyone is going to him."

³In reply Jesus declared, "I tell you the truth, no-one can see the kingdom of God unless he is born again."*a*

⁴"How can a man be born when he is old?" Nicodemus asked. "Surely he cannot enter a second time into his mother's womb to be born!"

b 17 Psalm 69:9   *c 23* Or *and believed in him*   *a 3* Or *born from above; also in verse 7*   *b 6* Or *but spirit*   *c 7* The Greek is plural.   *d 13* Some manuscripts *Man, who is in heaven*   *e 15* Or *believes may have eternal life in him*   *f 16* Or *his only begotten Son*   *g 18* Or *God's only begotten Son*   *b 21* Some interpreters end the quotation after verse 15.   *i 25* Some manuscripts *and certain Jews*

27To this John replied, "A man can receive only what is given him from heaven. 28You yourselves can testify that I said, 'I am not the Christ*j* but am sent ahead of him.' 29The bride belongs to the bridegroom. The friend who attends the bridegroom waits and listens for him, and is full of joy when he hears the bridegroom's voice. That joy is mine, and it is now complete. 30He must become greater; I must become less.

31"The one who comes from above is above all; the one who is from the earth belongs to the earth, and speaks as one from the earth. The one who comes from heaven is above all. 32He testifies to what he has seen and heard, but no-one accepts his testimony. 33The man who has accepted it has certified that God is truthful. 34For the one whom God has sent speaks the words of God, for God*k* gives the Spirit without limit. 35The Father loves the Son and has placed everything in his hands. 36Whoever believes in the Son has eternal life, but whoever rejects the Son will not see life, for God's wrath remains on him."*l*

■ Jesus Talks With a Samaritan Woman

4 The Pharisees heard that Jesus was gaining and baptising more disciples than John, 2although in fact it was not Jesus who baptised, but his disciples. 3When the Lord learned of this, he left Judea and went back once more to Galilee.

4Now he had to go through Samaria. 5So he came to a town in Samaria called Sychar, near the plot of ground Jacob had given to his son Joseph. 6Jacob's well was there, and Jesus, tired as he was from the journey, sat down by the well. It was about the sixth hour.

7When a Samaritan woman came to draw water,

■ CONVERSATIONS WITH JESUS
HOW DID JESUS TALK TO ORDINARY PEOPLE?

INSIGHT

THE WOMAN SAID, "I KNOW THAT MESSIAH (CALLED CHRIST) IS COMING. WHEN HE COMES, HE WILL EXPLAIN EVERYTHING TO US." THEN JESUS DECLARED, "I WHO SPEAK TO YOU AM HE." ■ 4:25–26

Water. Where it's plentiful, we tend to take it for granted, like air. We run a deep bath, wash the car, even let a sprinkler spurt for hours to keep the grass green.

Not so in the desert, where even plants hoard water with bristly defenses. There, water takes on a mythical aura. Taunting visions of pools and streams dance in the heat waves. A craving for water crowds out all other thoughts, and one spoonful, on a parched tongue, is worth gold.

To a woman in a dry land who spent part of each day hauling clay jugs to and from a well, water was the most powerful symbol imaginable. Little wonder that when Jesus offered "living water" that would never run dry (4:10,14), the Samaritan woman paid attention.

■ PROFOUNDLY SIMPLE WORDS
A simple word or phrase with a profound meaning: that is the style of Jesus' teaching as presented in John. No biblical author used simpler, more commonplace words: *water, world, light, life, birth, love, truth.* Yet John used them with such depth that hundreds of authors since have tried to plumb their meaning.

Reading John is like sitting in a canoe in the middle of a deep, pristine lake. The clarity of the water reveals everything under the surface – you think. Yet, as you gaze deeper, you can never see the bottom. Something always remains hidden.

Those who look for a neat scheme of organisation in John usually fail. John's Gospel omits many of the events recorded in Mark, most of the long public speeches of Matthew and all of the parables of Luke. Its teaching emerges mainly through Jesus' intimate encounters with diverse people.

■ LISTENING IN ON PRIVATE CONVERSATIONS
Jesus uttered some of his most memorable sayings in the midst of very ordinary conversations. The book of John rarely shows him speaking to large crowds. Instead, we see Jesus meeting secretly with a nervous religious leader (3:1–21), or talking with a promiscuous woman (4:5–26) beside a well. Both visitors carried away simple-yet-profound images (a second birth, living water), and today we recall those words as among the most familiar in all the Bible.

John paints close-ups of individuals who responded to Jesus on earth. Some followed him courageously, others remained sceptical, and still others reacted with hostility. Often, John reports, people simply "did not understand", despite Jesus' use of visual images. In short, response to the Son of God on earth nearly 2,000 years ago bears a striking resemblance to the world's response to him now.

□ LIFE QUESTIONS:
Imagine yourself in a private conversation with Jesus, much like the Samaritan woman's. What would you want to talk about?

j28 Or Messiah *k34* Greek he *l36* Some interpreters end the quotation after verse 30.

Jesus said to her, "Will you give me a drink?" [8](His disciples had gone into the town to buy food.)

[9]The Samaritan woman said to him, "You are a Jew and I am a Samaritan woman. How can you ask me for a drink?" (For Jews do not associate with Samaritans.[a])

4:9 ■ BRIDGING DIFFERENCES

When one church brands another a cult, it usually creates long-standing bitterness. The Samaritans and the Jews felt that way about each other. Samaritan religion closely resembled Judaism, but on key issues its followers had gone their own way. They accepted only the first five books of the Old Testament, and insisted that Mount Gerizim, not Jerusalem, was the proper place to worship God. Though Jews and Samaritans usually avoided each other, Jesus reached across these barriers.

[10]Jesus answered her, "If you knew the gift of God and who it is that asks you for a drink, you would have asked him and he would have given you living water."

[11]"Sir," the woman said, "you have nothing to draw with and the well is deep. Where can you get this living water? [12]Are you greater than our father Jacob, who gave us the well and drank from it himself, as did also his sons and his flocks and herds?"

[13]Jesus answered, "Everyone who drinks this water will be thirsty again, [14]but whoever drinks the water I give him will never thirst. Indeed, the water I give him will become in him a spring of water welling up to eternal life."

[15]The woman said to him, "Sir, give me this water so that I won't get thirsty and have to keep coming here to draw water."

[16]He told her, "Go, call your husband and come back."

[17]"I have no husband," she replied.

Jesus said to her, "You are right when you say you have no husband. [18]The fact is, you have had five husbands, and the man you now have is not your husband. What you have just said is quite true."

[19]"Sir," the woman said, "I can see that you are a prophet. [20]Our fathers worshipped on this mountain, but you Jews claim that the place where we must worship is in Jerusalem."

[21]Jesus declared, "Believe me, woman, a time is coming when you will worship the Father neither on this mountain nor in Jerusalem. [22]You Samaritans worship what you do not know; we worship what we do know, for salvation is from the Jews. [23]Yet a time is coming and has now come when the true worshippers will worship the Father in spirit and truth, for they are the kind of worshippers the Father seeks. [24]God is spirit, and his worshippers must worship in spirit and in truth."

[25]The woman said, "I know that Messiah" (called Christ) "is coming. When he comes, he will explain everything to us."

[26]Then Jesus declared, "I who speak to you am he."

■ The Disciples Rejoin Jesus

[27]Just then his disciples returned and were surprised to find him talking with a woman. But no-one asked, "What do you want?" or "Why are you talking with her?"

[28]Then, leaving her water jar, the woman went back to the town and said to the people, [29]"Come, see a man who told me everything I ever did. Could this be the Christ?"[b] [30]They came out of the town and made their way towards him.

[31]Meanwhile his disciples urged him, "Rabbi, eat something."

[32]But he said to them, "I have food to eat that you know nothing about."

[33]Then his disciples said to each other, "Could someone have brought him food?"

[34]"My food," said Jesus, "is to do the will of him who sent me and to finish his work. [35]Do you not say, 'Four months more and then the harvest'? I tell you, open your eyes and look at the fields! They are ripe for harvest. [36]Even now the reaper draws his wages, even now he harvests the crop for eternal life, so that the sower and the reaper may be glad together. [37]Thus the saying 'One sows and another reaps' is true. [38]I sent you to reap what you have not worked for. Others have done the hard work, and you have reaped the benefits of their labour."

■ Many Samaritans Believe

[39]Many of the Samaritans from that town believed in him because of the woman's testimony, "He told me everything I ever did." [40]So when the Samaritans came to him, they urged him to stay with them, and he stayed two days. [41]And because of his words many more became believers.

[42]They said to the woman, "We no longer believe just because of what you said; now we have heard for ourselves, and we know that this man really is the Saviour of the world."

■ Jesus Heals the Official's Son

[43]After the two days he left for Galilee. [44](Now Jesus himself had pointed out that a prophet has no honour in his own country.) [45]When he arrived in Galilee, the Galileans welcomed him. They had seen all that he had done in Jerusalem at the Passover Feast, for they also had been there.

[46]Once more he visited Cana in Galilee, where he had turned the water into wine. And there was a certain royal official whose son lay sick at Capernaum. [47]When this man heard that Jesus had arrived in Galilee from Judea, he went to him and begged him to come and heal his son, who was close to death.

[48]"Unless you people see miraculous signs and wonders," Jesus told him, "you will never believe."

[49]The royal official said, "Sir, come down before my child dies."

[50]Jesus replied, "You may go. Your son will live."

The man took Jesus at his word and departed. [51]While he was still on the way, his servants met him with the news that his boy was living. [52]When he enquired as to the time when his son got better, they said to him, "The fever left him yesterday at the seventh hour."

[a]9 Or do not use dishes Samaritans have used   [b]29 Or Messiah

⁵³Then the father realised that this was the exact time at which Jesus had said to him, "Your son will live." So he and all his household believed.

4:50 ■ A LONG-DISTANCE MIRACLE
This miracle has certain similarities to another performed at the request of a Roman centurion (Luke 7:2–10; Matthew 8:5–13). Of Jesus' two dozen recorded miracles of healing, only these occurred over a distance.

⁵⁴This was the second miraculous sign that Jesus performed, having come from Judea to Galilee.

■ The Healing at the Pool

5 Some time later, Jesus went up to Jerusalem for a feast of the Jews. ²Now there is in Jerusalem near the Sheep Gate a pool, which in Aramaic is called Bethesda^a and which is surrounded by five covered colonnades. ³Here a great number of disabled people used to lie — the blind, the lame, the paralysed.^b ⁵One who was there had been an invalid for thirty-eight years. ⁶When Jesus saw him lying there and learned that he had been in this condition for a long time, he asked him, "Do you want to get well?"

⁷"Sir," the invalid replied, "I have no-one to help me into the pool when the water is stirred. While I am trying to get in, someone else goes down ahead of me."

⁸Then Jesus said to him, "Get up! Pick up your mat and walk." ⁹At once the man was cured; he picked up his mat and walked.

The day on which this took place was a Sabbath, ¹⁰and so the Jews said to the man who had been healed, "It is the Sabbath; the law forbids you to carry your mat."

¹¹But he replied, "The man who made me well said to me, 'Pick up your mat and walk.' "

¹²So they asked him, "Who is this fellow who told you to pick it up and walk?"

¹³The man who was healed had no idea who it was, for Jesus had slipped away into the crowd that was there.

¹⁴Later Jesus found him at the temple and said to him, "See, you are well again. Stop sinning or something worse may happen to you." ¹⁵The man went away and told the Jews that it was Jesus who had made him well.

■ Life Through the Son

¹⁶So, because Jesus was doing these things on the Sabbath, the Jews persecuted him. ¹⁷Jesus said to them, "My Father is always at his work to this very day, and I, too, am working." ¹⁸For this reason the Jews tried all the harder to kill him; not only was he breaking the Sabbath, but he was even calling God his own Father, making himself equal with God.

¹⁹Jesus gave them this answer: "I tell you the truth, the Son can do nothing by himself; he can do only what he sees his Father doing, because whatever the Father does the Son also does. ²⁰For the Father loves the Son and shows him all he does. Yes, to your amazement he will show him even greater things than these. ²¹For just as the Father raises the dead and gives them life, even so the Son gives life to whom he is pleased to give it. ²²Moreover, the Father judges no-one, but has entrusted all judgment to the Son, ²³that all may honour the Son just as they honour the Father. He who does not honour the Son does not honour the Father, who sent him.

²⁴"I tell you the truth, whoever hears my word and believes him who sent me has eternal life and will not be condemned; he has crossed over from death to life. ²⁵I tell you the truth, a time is coming and has now come when the dead will hear the voice of the Son of God and those who hear will live. ²⁶For as the Father has life in himself, so he has granted the Son to have life in himself. ²⁷And he has given him authority to judge because he is the Son of Man.

²⁸"Do not be amazed at this, for a time is coming when all who are in their graves will hear his voice ²⁹and come out — those who have done good will rise to live, and those who have done evil will rise to be condemned. ³⁰By myself I can do nothing; I judge only as I hear, and my judgment is just, for I seek not to please myself but him who sent me.

■ Testimonies About Jesus

³¹"If I testify about myself, my testimony is not valid. ³²There is another who testifies in my favour, and I know that his testimony about me is valid.

³³"You have sent to John and he has testified to the truth. ³⁴Not that I accept human testimony; but I mention it that you may be saved. ³⁵John was a lamp that burned and gave light, and you chose for a time to enjoy his light.

³⁶"I have testimony weightier than that of John. For the very work that the Father has given me to finish, and which I am doing, testifies that the Father has sent me. ³⁷And the Father who sent me has himself testified concerning me. You have never heard his voice nor seen his form, ³⁸nor does his word dwell in you, for you do not believe the one he sent. ³⁹You diligently study^c the Scriptures because you think that by them you possess eternal life. These are the Scriptures that testify about me, ⁴⁰yet you refuse to come to me to have life.

⁴¹"I do not accept praise from men, ⁴²but I know you. I know that you do not have the love of God in your hearts. ⁴³I have come in my Father's name, and you do not accept me; but if someone else comes in his own name, you will accept him. ⁴⁴How can you believe if you accept praise from one another, yet make no effort to obtain the praise that comes from the only God?^d

⁴⁵"But do not think I will accuse you before the Father. Your accuser is Moses, on whom your hopes are set. ⁴⁶If you believed Moses, you would believe me, for he wrote about me. ⁴⁷But since you do not believe what he wrote, how are you going to believe what I say?"

---

^a2 Some manuscripts *Bethzatha*; other manuscripts *Bethsaida*   ^b3 Some less important manuscripts *paralysed — and they waited for the moving of the waters.* ⁴*From time to time an angel of the Lord would come down and stir up the waters. The first one into the pool after each such disturbance would be cured of whatever disease he had.*   ^c39 Or *Study diligently* (the imperative)   ^d44 Some early manuscripts *the Only One*

■ Jesus Feeds the Five Thousand
☐ See Matthew 14:13–21; Mark 6:32–44; Luke 9:10–17

6 Some time after this, Jesus crossed to the far shore of the Sea of Galilee (that is, the Sea of Tiberias), ²and a great crowd of people followed him because they saw the miraculous signs he had performed on the sick. ³Then Jesus went up on a mountainside and sat down with his disciples. ⁴The Jewish Passover Feast was near.

⁵When Jesus looked up and saw a great crowd coming towards him, he said to Philip, "Where shall we buy bread for these people to eat?" ⁶He asked this only to test him, for he already had in mind what he was going to do.

⁷Philip answered him, "Eight months' wages[a] would not buy enough bread for each one to have a bite!"

⁸Another of his disciples, Andrew, Simon Peter's brother, spoke up, ⁹"Here is a boy with five small barley loaves and two small fish, but how far will they go among so many?"

6:9 ■ BETTER BREAD
The feeding of the five thousand is the only miracle (except Jesus' resurrection) that all four Gospels record. It shows Jesus meeting the most basic human need, using barley loaves, the least expensive kind of bread. Many Jews believed that the Messiah would renew the miraculous manna that their ancestors had eaten under Moses. Jesus pointed to a better, life-changing meal — himself. As the bread of life (verse 35), he would nourish his people far better than any miraculous meal.

¹⁰Jesus said, "Make the people sit down." There was plenty of grass in that place, and the men sat down, about five thousand of them. ¹¹Jesus then took the loaves, gave thanks, and distributed to those who were seated as much as they wanted. He did the same with the fish.

¹²When they had all had enough to eat, he said to his disciples, "Gather the pieces that are left over. Let nothing be wasted." ¹³So they gathered them and filled twelve baskets with the pieces of the five barley loaves left over by those who had eaten.

¹⁴After the people saw the miraculous sign that Jesus did, they began to say, "Surely this is the Prophet who is to come into the world." ¹⁵Jesus, knowing that they intended to come and make him king by force, withdrew again to a mountain by himself.

■ Jesus Walks on the Water
☐ See Matthew 14:22–33; Mark 6:47–51

¹⁶When evening came, his disciples went down to the lake, ¹⁷where they got into a boat and set off across the lake for Capernaum. By now it was dark, and Jesus had not yet joined them. ¹⁸A strong wind was blowing and the waters grew rough. ¹⁹When they had rowed three or three and a half miles,[b] they saw Jesus approaching the boat, walking on the water; and they were terrified. ²⁰But he said to

them, "It is I; don't be afraid." ²¹Then they were willing to take him into the boat, and immediately the boat reached the shore where they were heading.

²²The next day the crowd that had stayed on the opposite shore of the lake realised that only one boat had been there, and that Jesus had not entered it with his disciples, but that they had gone away alone. ²³Then some boats from Tiberias landed near the place where the people had eaten the bread after the Lord had given thanks. ²⁴Once the crowd realised that neither Jesus nor his disciples were there, they got into the boats and went to Capernaum in search of Jesus.

■ Jesus the Bread of Life
²⁵When they found him on the other side of the lake, they asked him, "Rabbi, when did you get here?"

²⁶Jesus answered, "I tell you the truth, you are looking for me, not because you saw miraculous signs but because you ate the loaves and had your fill. ²⁷Do not work for food that spoils, but for food that endures to eternal life, which the Son of Man will give you. On him God the Father has placed his seal of approval."

²⁸Then they asked him, "What must we do to do the works God requires?"

²⁹Jesus answered, "The work of God is this: to believe in the one he has sent."

³⁰So they asked him, "What miraculous sign then will you give that we may see it and believe you? What will you do? ³¹Our forefathers ate the manna in the desert; as it is written: 'He gave them bread from heaven to eat.'[c]"

³²Jesus said to them, "I tell you the truth, it is not Moses who has given you the bread from heaven, but it is my Father who gives you the true bread from heaven. ³³For the bread of God is he who comes down from heaven and gives life to the world."

³⁴"Sir," they said, "from now on give us this bread."

³⁵Then Jesus declared, "I am the bread of life. He who comes to me will never go hungry, and he who believes in me will never be thirsty. ³⁶But as I told you, you have seen me and still you do not believe. ³⁷All that the Father gives me will come to me, and whoever comes to me I will never drive away. ³⁸For I have come down from heaven not to do my will but to do the will of him who sent me. ³⁹And this is the will of him who sent me, that I shall lose none of all that he has given me, but raise them up at the last day. ⁴⁰For my Father's will is that everyone who looks to the Son and believes in him shall have eternal life, and I will raise him up at the last day."

⁴¹At this the Jews began to grumble about him because he said, "I am the bread that came down from heaven." ⁴²They said, "Is this not Jesus, the son of Joseph, whose father and mother we know? How can he now say, 'I came down from heaven'?"

⁴³"Stop grumbling among yourselves," Jesus answered. ⁴⁴"No-one can come to me unless the Father who sent me draws him, and I will raise him up at the last day. ⁴⁵It is written in the Prophets: 'They will all be taught by God.'[d] Everyone who

---

a 7 Greek two hundred denarii   b 19 Greek rowed twenty-five or thirty stadia (about 5 or 6 kilometres)   c 31 Exodus 16:4; Neh. 9:15; Psalm 78:24,25
d 45 Isaiah 54:13

listens to the Father and learns from him comes to me. ⁴⁶No-one has seen the Father except the one who is from God; only he has seen the Father. ⁴⁷I tell you the truth, he who believes has everlasting life. ⁴⁸I am the bread of life. ⁴⁹Your forefathers ate the manna in the desert, yet they died. ⁵⁰But here is the bread that comes down from heaven, which a man may eat and not die. ⁵¹I am the living bread that came down from heaven. If anyone eats of this bread, he will live for ever. This bread is my flesh, which I will give for the life of the world."

⁵²Then the Jews began to argue sharply among themselves, "How can this man give us his flesh to eat?"

⁵³Jesus said to them, "I tell you the truth, unless you eat the flesh of the Son of Man and drink his blood, you have no life in you. ⁵⁴Whoever eats my flesh and drinks my blood has eternal life, and I will raise him up at the last day. ⁵⁵For my flesh is real food and my blood is real drink. ⁵⁶Whoever eats my flesh and drinks my blood remains in me, and I in him. ⁵⁷Just as the living Father sent me and I live because of the Father, so the one who feeds on me will live because of me. ⁵⁸This is the bread that came down from heaven. Your forefathers ate manna and died, but he who feeds on this bread will live for ever." ⁵⁹He said this while teaching in the synagogue in Capernaum.

■ Many Disciples Desert Jesus

⁶⁰On hearing it, many of his disciples said, "This is a hard teaching. Who can accept it?"

6:60 ■ TOO HARD TO SWALLOW

Chapter 6 shows the full cycle of people's response to Jesus. At first, excited by his miracle of feeding the 5,000, folk tried to make him king. But Jesus escaped. The next day he rebuked them for having an interest only in physical concerns, not in spiritual truth (verse 26). He used the miracle of the feeding to give an important lesson on the bread of life, using words that were later applied to the Lord's Supper, or the Eucharist. These words, however, so disappointed the sensation-seeking crowd that many turned away from him.

⁶¹Aware that his disciples were grumbling about this, Jesus said to them, "Does this offend you? ⁶²What if you see the Son of Man ascend to where he was before! ⁶³The Spirit gives life; the flesh counts for nothing. The words I have spoken to you are spirit[e] and they are life. ⁶⁴Yet there are some of you who do not believe." For Jesus had known from the beginning which of them did not believe and who would betray him. ⁶⁵He went on to say, "This is why I told you that no-one can come to me unless the Father has enabled him."

⁶⁶From this time many of his disciples turned back and no longer followed him.

⁶⁷"You do not want to leave too, do you?" Jesus asked the Twelve.

⁶⁸Simon Peter answered him, "Lord, to whom shall we go? You have the words of eternal life. ⁶⁹We believe and know that you are the Holy One of God."

⁷⁰Then Jesus replied, "Have I not chosen you, the Twelve? Yet one of you is a devil!" ⁷¹(He meant Judas, the son of Simon Iscariot, who, though one of the Twelve, was later to betray him.)

■ Jesus Goes to the Feast of Tabernacles

7 After this, Jesus went around in Galilee, purposely staying away from Judea because the Jews there were waiting to take his life. ²But when the Jewish Feast of Tabernacles was near, ³Jesus' brothers said to him, "You ought to leave here and go to Judea, so that your disciples may see the miracles you do. ⁴No-one who wants to become a public figure acts in secret. Since you are doing these things, show yourself to the world." ⁵For even his own brothers did not believe in him.

⁶Therefore Jesus told them, "The right time for me has not yet come; for you any time is right. ⁷The world cannot hate you, but it hates me because I testify that what it does is evil. ⁸You go to the Feast. I am not yet[a] going up to this Feast, because for me the right time has not yet come." ⁹Having said this, he stayed in Galilee.

¹⁰However, after his brothers had left for the Feast, he went also, not publicly, but in secret. ¹¹Now at the Feast the Jews were watching for him and asking, "Where is that man?"

¹²Among the crowds there was widespread whispering about him. Some said, "He is a good man."

Others replied, "No, he deceives the people."

7:12 ■ PUBLIC OPINION

At one time a musician who wanted a national reputation had to play at the Royal Albert Hall, in the nation's cultural capital. Similarly, Jesus' brothers wanted him to appear in Jerusalem, Israel's political and religious centre. But Jesus had less faith than they in public opinion, and John shows why. The crowds that came to Jerusalem were curious but sceptical. Some thought Jesus a good man, some considered him a con artist. They were amazed at his knowledge of Scripture, but attributed his ideas to demon-possession (verse 20). They couldn't agree whether he was the Messiah (verse 43).

¹³But no-one would say anything publicly about him for fear of the Jews.

■ Jesus Teaches at the Feast

¹⁴Not until halfway through the Feast did Jesus go up to the temple courts and begin to teach. ¹⁵The Jews were amazed and asked, "How did this man get such learning without having studied?"

¹⁶Jesus answered, "My teaching is not my own. It comes from him who sent me. ¹⁷If anyone chooses to do God's will, he will find out whether my teaching comes from God or whether I speak on my own. ¹⁸He who speaks on his own does so to gain honour for himself, but he who works for the honour of the

---

e 63 Or *Spirit*   *a 8* Some early manuscripts do not have *yet.*

one who sent him is a man of truth; there is nothing false about him. [19]Has not Moses given you the law? Yet not one of you keeps the law. Why are you trying to kill me?"

[20]"You are demon-possessed," the crowd answered. "Who is trying to kill you?"

[21]Jesus said to them, "I did one miracle, and you are all astonished. [22]Yet, because Moses gave you circumcision (though actually it did not come from Moses, but from the patriarchs), you circumcise a child on the Sabbath. [23]Now if a child can be circumcised on the Sabbath so that the law of Moses may not be broken, why are you angry with me for healing the whole man on the Sabbath? [24]Stop judging by mere appearances, and make a right judgment."

■ Is Jesus the Christ?

[25]At that point some of the people of Jerusalem began to ask, "Isn't this the man they are trying to kill? [26]Here he is, speaking publicly, and they are not saying a word to him. Have the authorities really concluded that he is the Christ?[b] [27]But we know where this man is from; when the Christ comes, no-one will know where he is from."

[28]Then Jesus, still teaching in the temple courts, cried out, "Yes, you know me, and you know where I am from. I am not here on my own, but he who sent me is true. You do not know him, [29]but I know him because I am from him and he sent me."

[30]At this they tried to seize him, but no-one laid a hand on him, because his time had not yet come. [31]Still, many in the crowd put their faith in him. They said, "When the Christ comes, will he do more miraculous signs than this man?"

[32]The Pharisees heard the crowd whispering such things about him. Then the chief priests and the Pharisees sent temple guards to arrest him.

[33]Jesus said, "I am with you for only a short time, and then I go to the one who sent me. [34]You will look for me, but you will not find me; and where I am, you cannot come."

[35]The Jews said to one another, "Where does this man intend to go that we cannot find him? Will he go where our people live scattered among the Greeks, and teach the Greeks? [36]What did he mean when he said, 'You will look for me, but you will not find me,' and 'Where I am, you cannot come'?"

[37]On the last and greatest day of the Feast, Jesus stood and said in a loud voice, "If anyone is thirsty, let him come to me and drink. [38]Whoever believes in me, as[c] the Scripture has said, streams of living water will flow from within him." [39]By this he meant the Spirit, whom those who believed in him were later to receive. Up to that time the Spirit had not been given, since Jesus had not yet been glorified.

[40]On hearing his words, some of the people said, "Surely this man is the Prophet."

[41]Others said, "He is the Christ."

Still others asked, "How can the Christ come from Galilee? [42]Does not the Scripture say that the Christ will come from David's family[d] and from Bethlehem, the town where David lived?" [43]Thus the people were divided because of Jesus. [44]Some wanted to seize him, but no-one laid a hand on him.

■ Unbelief of the Jewish Leaders

[45]Finally the temple guards went back to the chief priests and Pharisees, who asked them, "Why didn't you bring him in?"

[46]"No-one ever spoke the way this man does," the guards declared.

[47]"You mean he has deceived you also?" the Pharisees retorted. [48]"Has any of the rulers or of the Pharisees believed in him? [49]No! But this mob that knows nothing of the law—there is a curse on them."

[50]Nicodemus, who had gone to Jesus earlier and who was one of their own number, asked, [51]"Does our law condemn a man without first hearing him to find out what he is doing?"

[52]They replied, "Are you from Galilee, too? Look into it, and you will find that a prophet[e] does not come out of Galilee."

_____

[The earliest and most reliable manuscripts and other ancient witnesses do not have John 7:53–8:11.]

[53]Then each went to his own home.

8 But Jesus went to the Mount of Olives. [2]At dawn he appeared again in the temple courts, where all the people gathered round him, and he sat down to teach them. [3]The teachers of the law and the Pharisees brought in a woman caught in adultery. They made her stand before the group [4]and said to Jesus, "Teacher, this woman was caught in the act of adultery. [5]In the Law Moses commanded us to stone such women. Now what do you say?" [6]They were using this question as a trap, in order to have a basis for accusing him.

But Jesus bent down and started to write on the ground with his finger. [7]When they kept on questioning him, he straightened up and said to them, "If any one of you is without sin, let him be the first to throw a stone at her." [8]Again he stooped down and wrote on the ground.

8:6 ■ BELONG IN THE BIBLE?

Because most ancient manuscripts don't include this story about the woman caught in adultery, many scholars question whether it was added later or perhaps originally fell at a different place in the Gospel. According to the story, the Pharisees weren't following Moses' law, which required the woman's partner in crime to appear also. Interestingly, verse 6 records the only scene of Jesus writing.

[9]At this, those who heard began to go away one at a time, the older ones first, until only Jesus was left, with the woman still standing there. [10]Jesus straightened up and asked her, "Woman, where are they? Has no-one condemned you?"

[11]"No-one, sir," she said.

b 26 Or Messiah; also in verses 27, 31, 41 and 42   c 37, 38 Or If anyone is thirsty, let him come to me. / And let him drink, 38 who believes in me. / As   d 42 Greek seed   e 52 Two early manuscripts the Prophet

"Then neither do I condemn you," Jesus declared. "Go now and leave your life of sin."

■ The Validity of Jesus' Testimony

12When Jesus spoke again to the people, he said, "I am the light of the world. Whoever follows me will never walk in darkness, but will have the light of life."

13The Pharisees challenged him, "Here you are, appearing as your own witness; your testimony is not valid."

14Jesus answered, "Even if I testify on my own behalf, my testimony is valid, for I know where I came from and where I am going. But you have no idea where I come from or where I am going. 15You judge by human standards; I pass judgment on no-one. 16But if I do judge, my decisions are right, because I am not alone. I stand with the Father, who sent me. 17In your own Law it is written that the testimony of two men is valid. 18I am one who testifies for myself; my other witness is the Father, who sent me."

19Then they asked him, "Where is your father?"

"You do not know me or my Father," Jesus replied. "If you knew me, you would know my Father also." 20He spoke these words while teaching in the temple area near the place where the offerings were put. Yet no-one seized him, because his time had not yet come.

21Once more Jesus said to them, "I am going away, and you will look for me, and you will die in your sin. Where I go, you cannot come."

22This made the Jews ask, "Will he kill himself? Is that why he says, 'Where I go, you cannot come'?"

23But he continued, "You are from below; I am from above. You are of this world; I am not of this world. 24I told you that you would die in your sins; if you do not believe that I am ˌthe one I claim to beˌ,*a* you will indeed die in your sins."

25"Who are you?" they asked.

"Just what I have been claiming all along," Jesus replied. 26"I have much to say in judgment of you. But he who sent me is reliable, and what I have heard from him I tell the world."

27They did not understand that he was telling them about his Father. 28So Jesus said, "When you have lifted up the Son of Man, then you will know that I am ˌthe one I claim to beˌ, and that I do nothing on my own but speak just what the Father has taught me. 29The one who sent me is with me; he has not left me alone, for I always do what pleases him." 30Even as he spoke, many put their faith in him.

■ The Children of Abraham

31To the Jews who had believed him, Jesus said, "If you hold to my teaching, you are really my disciples. 32Then you will know the truth, and the truth will set you free."

33They answered him, "We are Abraham's descendants*b* and have never been slaves of anyone. How can you say that we shall be set free?"

34Jesus replied, "I tell you the truth, everyone who sins is a slave to sin. 35Now a slave has no

permanent place in the family, but a son belongs to it for ever. 36So if the Son sets you free, you will be free indeed. 37I know you are Abraham's descendants. Yet you are ready to kill me, because you have no room for my word. 38I am telling you what I have seen in the Father's presence, and you do what you have heard from your father."*c*

39"Abraham is our father," they answered.

"If you were Abraham's children," said Jesus, "then you would*d* do the things Abraham did. 40As it is, you are determined to kill me, a man who has told you the truth that I heard from God. Abraham did not do such things. 41You are doing the things your own father does."

"We are not illegitimate children," they protested. "The only Father we have is God himself."

■ The Children of the Devil

42Jesus said to them, "If God were your Father, you would love me, for I came from God and now am here. I have not come on my own; but he sent me. 43Why is my language not clear to you? Because you are unable to hear what I say. 44You belong to your father, the devil, and you want to carry out your father's desire. He was a murderer from the beginning, not holding to the truth, for there is no truth in him. When he lies, he speaks his native language, for he is a liar and the father of lies. 45Yet because I tell the truth, you do not believe me! 46Can any of you prove me guilty of sin? If I am telling the truth, why don't you believe me? 47He who belongs to God hears what God says. The reason you do not hear is that you do not belong to God."

■ The Claims of Jesus About Himself

48The Jews answered him, "Aren't we right in saying that you are a Samaritan and demon-possessed?"

49"I am not possessed by a demon," said Jesus, "but I honour my Father and you dishonour me. 50I am not seeking glory for myself; but there is one who seeks it, and he is the judge. 51I tell you the truth, if anyone keeps my word, he will never see death."

52At this the Jews exclaimed, "Now we know that you are demon-possessed! Abraham died and so did the prophets, yet you say that if anyone keeps your word, he will never taste death. 53Are you greater than our father Abraham? He died, and so did the prophets. Who do you think you are?"

54Jesus replied, "If I glorify myself, my glory means nothing. My Father, whom you claim as your God, is the one who glorifies me. 55Though you do not know him, I know him. If I said I did not, I would be a liar like you, but I do know him and keep his word. 56Your father Abraham rejoiced at the thought of seeing my day; he saw it and was glad."

57"You are not yet fifty years old," the Jews said to him, "and you have seen Abraham!"

58"I tell you the truth," Jesus answered, "before Abraham was born, I am!" 59At this, they picked up stones to stone him, but Jesus hid himself, slipping away from the temple grounds.

---

a 24 Or *I am he*; also in verse 28   *b 33* Greek *seed*; also in verse 37   *c 38* Or *presence. Therefore do what you have heard from the Father.*
d 39 Some early manuscripts *"If you are Abraham's children," said Jesus, "then*

■ Jesus Heals a Man Born Blind

9 As he went along, he saw a man blind from birth. ²His disciples asked him, "Rabbi, who sinned, this man or his parents, that he was born blind?"

9:2 ■ SUFFERING AND SIN
In this story, Jesus corrects a commonly held notion that suffering comes because of sin. The healed man became a loyal spokesman for Jesus. His testimony, however, failed to convince the Pharisees, who also rejected Jesus' teaching about why the man had been born blind (verse 34). In typical style, John wove together the incident with Jesus' comments on a different kind of blindness.

³"Neither this man nor his parents sinned," said Jesus, "but this happened so that the work of God might be displayed in his life. ⁴As long as it is day, we must do the work of him who sent me. Night is coming, when no-one can work. ⁵While I am in the world, I am the light of the world."

⁶Having said this, he spat on the ground, made some mud with the saliva, and put it on the man's eyes. ⁷"Go," he told him, "wash in the Pool of Siloam" (this word means Sent). So the man went and washed, and came home seeing.

⁸His neighbours and those who had formerly seen him begging asked, "Isn't this the same man who used to sit and beg?" ⁹Some claimed that he was.

Others said, "No, he only looks like him."

But he himself insisted, "I am the man."

¹⁰"How then were your eyes opened?" they demanded.

¹¹He replied, "The man they call Jesus made some mud and put it on my eyes. He told me to go to Siloam and wash. So I went and washed, and then I could see."

¹²"Where is this man?" they asked him.

"I don't know," he said.

■ The Pharisees Investigate the Healing

¹³They brought to the Pharisees the man who had been blind. ¹⁴Now the day on which Jesus had made the mud and opened the man's eyes was a Sabbath. ¹⁵Therefore the Pharisees also asked him how he had received his sight. "He put mud on my eyes," the man replied, "and I washed, and now I see."

¹⁶Some of the Pharisees said, "This man is not from God, for he does not keep the Sabbath." But others asked, "How can a sinner do such miraculous signs?" So they were divided.

¹⁷Finally they turned again to the blind man, "What have you to say about him? It was your eyes he opened."

The man replied, "He is a prophet."

¹⁸The Jews still did not believe that he had been blind and had received his sight until they sent for the man's parents. ¹⁹"Is this your son?" they asked. "Is this the one you say was born blind? How is it that now he can see?"

²⁰"We know he is our son," the parents answered, "and we know he was born blind. ²¹But how he can see now, or who opened his eyes, we don't know. Ask him. He is of age; he will speak for himself." ²²His parents said this because they were afraid of the Jews, for already the Jews had decided that anyone who acknowledged that Jesus was the Christ[a] would be put out of the synagogue. ²³That was why his parents said, "He is of age; ask him."

²⁴A second time they summoned the man who had been blind. "Give glory to God,"[b] they said. "We know this man is a sinner."

²⁵He replied, "Whether he is a sinner or not, I don't know. One thing I do know. I was blind but now I see!"

²⁶Then they asked him, "What did he do to you? How did he open your eyes?"

²⁷He answered, "I have told you already and you did not listen. Why do you want to hear it again? Do you want to become his disciples, too?"

²⁸Then they hurled insults at him and said, "You are this fellow's disciple! We are disciples of Moses! ²⁹We know that God spoke to Moses, but as for this fellow, we don't even know where he comes from."

³⁰The man answered, "Now that is remarkable! You don't know where he comes from, yet he opened my eyes. ³¹We know that God does not listen to sinners. He listens to the godly man who does his will. ³²Nobody has ever heard of opening the eyes of a man born blind. ³³If this man were not from God, he could do nothing."

³⁴To this they replied, "You were steeped in sin at birth; how dare you lecture us!" And they threw him out.

■ Spiritual Blindness

³⁵Jesus heard that they had thrown him out, and when he found him, he said, "Do you believe in the Son of Man?"

³⁶"Who is he, sir?" the man asked. "Tell me so that I may believe in him."

³⁷Jesus said, "You have now seen him; in fact, he is the one speaking with you."

³⁸Then the man said, "Lord, I believe," and he worshipped him.

³⁹Jesus said, "For judgment I have come into this world, so that the blind will see and those who see will become blind."

⁴⁰Some Pharisees who were with him heard him say this and asked, "What? Are we blind too?"

⁴¹Jesus said, "If you were blind, you would not be guilty of sin; but now that you claim you can see, your guilt remains."

■ The Shepherd and His Flock

10 "I tell you the truth, the man who does not enter the sheep pen by the gate, but climbs in by some other way, is a thief and a robber. ²The man who enters by the gate is the shepherd of his sheep. ³The watchman opens the gate for him, and the sheep listen to his voice. He calls his own sheep by name and leads them out. ⁴When he has brought out all his own, he goes on ahead of them, and his sheep follow him because they know his voice. ⁵But they will never follow a stranger; in fact, they will

a 22 Or Messiah   b 24 A solemn charge to tell the truth (see Joshua 7:19) run away from him because they do not recognise a stranger's voice." [6]Jesus used this figure of speech, but they did not understand what he was telling them.

10:4 ■ GOOD SHEPHERD
Unlike modern-day shepherds, who use dogs to drive their flocks, Palestinian shepherds walked ahead, calling the sheep to follow. Only a familiar voice would make them come. In the Old Testament, God was called the "Shepherd of Israel" (Psalm 80:1), and God's appointed leaders were often referred to as shepherds. In claiming to be the good shepherd, Jesus was asserting his leadership over a flock he was willing to die for.

[7]Therefore Jesus said again, "I tell you the truth, I am the gate for the sheep. [8]All who ever came before me were thieves and robbers, but the sheep did not listen to them. [9]I am the gate; whoever enters through me will be saved.[a] He will come in and go out, and find pasture. [10]The thief comes only to steal and kill and destroy; I have come that they may have life, and have it to the full.

[11]"I am the good shepherd. The good shepherd lays down his life for the sheep. [12]The hired hand is not the shepherd who owns the sheep. So when he sees the wolf coming, he abandons the sheep and runs away. Then the wolf attacks the flock and scatters it. [13]The man runs away because he is a hired hand and cares nothing for the sheep.

[14]"I am the good shepherd; I know my sheep and my sheep know me — [15]just as the Father knows me and I know the Father — and I lay down my life for the sheep. [16]I have other sheep that are not of this sheep pen. I must bring them also. They too will listen to my voice, and there shall be one flock and one shepherd. [17]The reason my Father loves me is that I lay down my life — only to take it up again. [18]No-one takes it from me, but I lay it down of my own accord. I have authority to lay it down and authority to take it up again. This command I received from my Father."

[19]At these words the Jews were again divided. [20]Many of them said, "He is demon-possessed and raving mad. Why listen to him?"

[21]But others said, "These are not the sayings of a man possessed by a demon. Can a demon open the eyes of the blind?"

■ The Unbelief of the Jews
[22]Then came the Feast of Dedication[b] at Jerusalem. It was winter, [23]and Jesus was in the temple area walking in Solomon's Colonnade. [24]The Jews gathered round him, saying, "How long will you keep us in suspense? If you are the Christ,[c] tell us plainly."

[25]Jesus answered, "I did tell you, but you do not believe. The miracles I do in my Father's name speak for me, [26]but you do not believe because you are not my sheep. [27]My sheep listen to my voice; I know them, and they follow me. [28]I give them eternal life, and they shall never perish; no-one can

snatch them out of my hand. [29]My Father, who has given them to me, is greater than all;[d] no-one can snatch them out of my Father's hand. [30]I and the Father are one."

[31]Again the Jews picked up stones to stone him, [32]but Jesus said to them, "I have shown you many great miracles from the Father. For which of these do you stone me?"

[33]"We are not stoning you for any of these," replied the Jews, "but for blasphemy, because you, a mere man, claim to be God."

[34]Jesus answered them, "Is it not written in your Law, 'I have said you are gods'[e]? [35]If he called them 'gods', to whom the word of God came — and the Scripture cannot be broken — [36]what about the one whom the Father set apart as his very own and sent into the world? Why then do you accuse me of blasphemy because I said, 'I am God's Son'? [37]Do not believe me unless I do what my Father does. [38]But if I do it, even though you do not believe me, believe the miracles, that you may know and understand that the Father is in me, and I in the Father." [39]Again they tried to seize him, but he escaped their grasp.

[40]Then Jesus went back across the Jordan to the place where John had been baptising in the early days. Here he stayed [41]and many people came to him. They said, "Though John never performed a miraculous sign, all that John said about this man was true." [42]And in that place many believed in Jesus.

■ The Death of Lazarus
11 Now a man named Lazarus was sick. He was from Bethany, the village of Mary and her sister Martha. [2]This Mary, whose brother Lazarus now lay sick, was the same one who poured perfume on the Lord and wiped his feet with her hair. [3]So the sisters sent word to Jesus, "Lord, the one you love is sick."

[4]When he heard this, Jesus said, "This sickness will not end in death. No, it is for God's glory so that God's Son may be glorified through it." [5]Jesus loved Martha and her sister and Lazarus. [6]Yet when he heard that Lazarus was sick, he stayed where he was two more days.

[7]Then he said to his disciples, "Let us go back to Judea."

[8]"But Rabbi," they said, "a short while ago the Jews tried to stone you, and yet you are going back there?"

[9]Jesus answered, "Are there not twelve hours of daylight? A man who walks by day will not stumble, for he sees by this world's light. [10]It is when he walks by night that he stumbles, for he has no light."

[11]After he had said this, he went on to tell them, "Our friend Lazarus has fallen asleep; but I am going there to wake him up."

[12]His disciples replied, "Lord, if he sleeps, he will get better." [13]Jesus had been speaking of his death, but his disciples thought he meant natural sleep.

[14]So then he told them plainly, "Lazarus is dead, [15]and for your sake I am glad I was not there, so that you may believe. But let us go to him."

[16]Then Thomas (called Didymus) said to the rest

a9 Or kept safe   b22 That is, Hanukkah   c24 Or Messiah   d29 Many early manuscripts What my Father has given me is greater than all
e34 Psalm 82:6

of the disciples, "Let us also go, that we may die with him."

■ Jesus Comforts the Sisters

¹⁷On his arrival, Jesus found that Lazarus had already been in the tomb for four days. ¹⁸Bethany was less than two miles*a* from Jerusalem, ¹⁹and many Jews had come to Martha and Mary to comfort them in the loss of their brother. ²⁰When Martha heard that Jesus was coming, she went out to meet him, but Mary stayed at home.

²¹"Lord," Martha said to Jesus, "if you had been here, my brother would not have died. ²²But I know that even now God will give you whatever you ask." ²³Jesus said to her, "Your brother will rise again." ²⁴Martha answered, "I know he will rise again in the resurrection at the last day."

²⁵Jesus said to her, "I am the resurrection and the life. He who believes in me will live, even though he dies; ²⁶and whoever lives and believes in me will never die. Do you believe this?"

²⁷"Yes, Lord," she told him, "I believe that you are the Christ,*b* the Son of God, who was to come into the world."

²⁸And after she had said this, she went back and called her sister Mary aside. "The Teacher is here,"

■ A MODERN SHEPHERD
WHAT A "GOOD SHEPHERD" WOULD LOOK LIKE TODAY

INSIGHT

"I HAVE COME THAT THEY MAY HAVE LIFE, AND HAVE IT TO THE FULL." ■ 10:10

Some of the Bible's rural illustrations simply do not transfer easily into modern life. What is a "good shepherd" like? What did Jesus mean by the term?

A small drama that took place on the slopes of Washington's Mount Rainier may shed light on the meaning of the "good shepherd". One Memorial Day weekend a Christian dentist named James Reddick was teaching his 12-year-old daughter and 11-year-old son the joy of mountain hiking. A sudden storm came up, battering them with hurricane-force winds and thick, wet sheets of snow. A blinding "whiteout" made it impossible to see or move on the steep slopes.

■ WILLING TO DIE

Reddick laboriously dug an oblong trench with an aluminum mess kit, then tucked his children into sleeping bags away from the entrance. He covered the opening with tarpaulin, but it kept blowing away, exposing the trench to the swirling snow outside. Reddick found he had to lie directly across the opening, using his own weight to hold down the edges of the tarpaulin. His body protected his son and daughter from the howling wind.

Two days passed before searchers finally noticed the corner of a rucksack protruding from deep snow. They rushed to the site, hoping the snow-covered mound would contain the three missing hikers. Inside, they found Sharon and David Reddick, very much alive. But the stiff body of their father lay against one wall of the snow cave. He had "taken the cold spot", in one searcher's words, by using his own back as the outer wall.

An image something like that must have filled the minds of Jesus' listeners as he described a good shepherd who "lays down his life" for his sheep (10:11). Nothing — not ravaging cold, thieves or wolves — would come between the good shepherd and his sheep. He would die for their protection.

■ POPULARITY, FOR A WHILE

As Jesus headed towards final tragedy in Jerusalem, the theme of death, *his* death, kept surfacing in his parables and direct statements. Ironically, his followers were growing in numbers. His popularity had reached a peak with the feeding of 5,000 people on a handful of morsels, a miracle mentioned by all four Gospel writers.

The groundswell of support to make Jesus king deeply impressed his followers; Jesus, however, escaped into the hills (6:15). He would not be a king on the crowd's terms. He continued on his lonely mission, stirring up controversy and hatred by healing people on the Sabbath and by proclaiming himself equal with God.

■ IGNORING AN IMPRESSIVE MIRACLE

Many Jews came over to Jesus after one of his most impressive signs: bringing Lazarus back to life. But, simultaneously, religious leaders concluded callously that it was best for one man (Jesus) to die rather than upset the whole world (11:50). Four separate times they tried to seize him.

Jesus came to offer "life" — one of those one-syllable words, swollen with meaning, that John threaded through his narrative. Lazarus received that life in an astonishingly literal way, providing yet another sign of Jesus' ultimate power. Jesus, though, made preparations to give up his own life, making the ultimate sacrifice of the good shepherd.

□ LIFE QUESTIONS:

What have you sacrificed for the sake of another person?

---

a 18 Greek *fifteen stadia* (about 3 kilometres)   *b* 27 Or *Messiah* she said, "and is asking for you." [29]When Mary heard this, she got up quickly and went to him. [30]Now Jesus had not yet entered the village, but was still at the place where Martha had met him. [31]When the Jews who had been with Mary in the house, comforting her, noticed how quickly she got up and went out, they followed her, supposing she was going to the tomb to mourn there.

11:21 ■ IF ONLY . . .

Mary and Martha had very different personalities, but the same response to pain. Both sisters, meeting Jesus, said the same thing: "If you had been here, my brother would not have died" (verses 21,32). They had asked Jesus to come, and for reasons they could not understand, he had delayed. The healing they longed for had not occurred. Jesus gave the sisters no explanation of his timing, but showed he had a reason: to demonstrate his power over death.

[32]When Mary reached the place where Jesus was and saw him, she fell at his feet and said, "Lord, if you had been here, my brother would not have died."

[33]When Jesus saw her weeping, and the Jews who had come along with her also weeping, he was deeply moved in spirit and troubled. [34]"Where have you laid him?" he asked.

"Come and see, Lord," they replied.

[35]Jesus wept.

[36]Then the Jews said, "See how he loved him!" [37]But some of them said, "Could not he who opened the eyes of the blind man have kept this man from dying?"

■ Jesus Raises Lazarus From the Dead

[38]Jesus, once more deeply moved, came to the tomb. It was a cave with a stone laid across the entrance. [39]"Take away the stone," he said.

"But, Lord," said Martha, the sister of the dead man, "by this time there is a bad odour, for he has been there four days."

[40]Then Jesus said, "Did I not tell you that if you believed, you would see the glory of God?"

[41]So they took away the stone. Then Jesus looked up and said, "Father, I thank you that you have heard me. [42]I knew that you always hear me, but I said this for the benefit of the people standing here, that they may believe that you sent me."

[43]When he had said this, Jesus called in a loud voice, "Lazarus, come out!" [44]The dead man came out, his hands and feet wrapped with strips of linen, and a cloth around his face.

Jesus said to them, "Take off the grave clothes and let him go."

■ The Plot to Kill Jesus

[45]Therefore many of the Jews who had come to visit Mary, and had seen what Jesus did, put their faith in him. [46]But some of them went to the Pharisees and told them what Jesus had done. [47]Then the chief priests and the Pharisees called a meeting of the Sanhedrin.

"What are we accomplishing?" they asked. "Here is this man performing many miraculous signs. [48]If we let him go on like this, everyone will believe in him, and then the Romans will come and take away both our place[c] and our nation."

[49]Then one of them, named Caiaphas, who was high priest that year, spoke up, "You know nothing at all! [50]You do not realise that it is better for you that one man die for the people than that the whole nation perish."

[51]He did not say this on his own, but as high priest that year he prophesied that Jesus would die for the Jewish nation, [52]and not only for that nation but also for the scattered children of God, to bring them together and make them one. [53]So from that day on they plotted to take his life.

11:53 ■ CLIMAX OF THE DRAMA

John wrote his book with a great sense of drama. The first six chapters reveal the identity of Jesus. The next six chapters (7–12) show the increasingly divided opinions about Jesus. On the one hand, his disciples were won over, and Jesus gained a loyal following among the people. On the other hand, his enemies rejected all the evidence about him. Their opposition culminated in this plot, which finally brought about Jesus' death.

[54]Therefore Jesus no longer moved about publicly among the Jews. Instead he withdrew to a region near the desert, to a village called Ephraim, where he stayed with his disciples.

[55]When it was almost time for the Jewish Passover, many went up from the country to Jerusalem for their ceremonial cleansing before the Passover. [56]They kept looking for Jesus, and as they stood in the temple area they asked one another, "What do you think? Isn't he coming to the Feast at all?" [57]But the chief priests and Pharisees had given orders that if anyone found out where Jesus was, he should report it so that they might arrest him.

■ Jesus Anointed at Bethany

12 Six days before the Passover, Jesus arrived at Bethany, where Lazarus lived, whom Jesus had raised from the dead. [2]Here a dinner was given in Jesus' honour. Martha served, while Lazarus was among those reclining at the table with him. [3]Then Mary took about a pint[a] of pure nard, an expensive perfume; she poured it on Jesus' feet and wiped his feet with her hair. And the house was filled with the fragrance of the perfume.

[4]But one of his disciples, Judas Iscariot, who was later to betray him, objected, [5]"Why wasn't this perfume sold and the money given to the poor? It was worth a year's wages."[b] [6]He did not say this because he cared about the poor but because he was a thief; as keeper of the money bag, he used to help himself to what was put into it.

[7]"Leave her alone," Jesus replied. "⌜It was intended⌝ that she should save this perfume for the

---

c 48 Or temple   a 3 Greek a litra (probably about 0.5 litre)   b 5 Greek three hundred denarii day of my burial. ⁸You will always have the poor among you, but you will not always have me."

⁹Meanwhile a large crowd of Jews found out that Jesus was there and came, not only because of him but also to see Lazarus, whom he had raised from the dead. ¹⁰So the chief priests made plans to kill Lazarus as well, ¹¹for on account of him many of the Jews were going over to Jesus and putting their faith in him.

■ The Triumphal Entry
☐ See Matthew 21:4–9; Mark 11:7–10; Luke 19:35–38

¹²The next day the great crowd that had come for the Feast heard that Jesus was on his way to Jerusalem. ¹³They took palm branches and went out to meet him, shouting,

"Hosanna!"ᶜ

"Blessed is he who comes in the name of the Lord!"ᵈ

"Blessed is the King of Israel!"

¹⁴Jesus found a young donkey and sat upon it, as it is written,

¹⁵"Do not be afraid, O Daughter of Zion;
    see, your king is coming,
    seated on a donkey's colt."ᵉ

¹⁶At first his disciples did not understand all this. Only after Jesus was glorified did they realise that these things had been written about him and that they had done these things to him.

¹⁷Now the crowd that was with him when he called Lazarus from the tomb and raised him from the dead continued to spread the word. ¹⁸Many people, because they had heard that he had given this miraculous sign, went out to meet him. ¹⁹So the Pharisees said to one another, "See, this is getting us nowhere. Look how the whole world has gone after him!"

■ Jesus Predicts His Death

²⁰Now there were some Greeks among those who went up to worship at the Feast. ²¹They came to Philip, who was from Bethsaida in Galilee, with a request. "Sir," they said, "we would like to see Jesus." ²²Philip went to tell Andrew; Andrew and Philip in turn told Jesus.

²³Jesus replied, "The hour has come for the Son of Man to be glorified. ²⁴I tell you the truth, unless a grain of wheat falls to the ground and dies, it remains only a single seed. But if it dies, it produces many seeds. ²⁵The man who loves his life will lose it, while the man who hates his life in this world will keep it for eternal life. ²⁶Whoever serves me must follow me; and where I am, my servant also will be. My Father will honour the one who serves me.

²⁷"Now my heart is troubled, and what shall I say? 'Father, save me from this hour'? No, it was for this very reason I came to this hour. ²⁸Father, glorify your name!"

Then a voice came from heaven, "I have glorified it, and will glorify it again." ²⁹The crowd that was there and heard it said it had thundered; others said an angel had spoken to him.

³⁰Jesus said, "This voice was for your benefit, not mine. ³¹Now is the time for judgment on this world; now the prince of this world will be driven out. ³²But I, when I am lifted up from the earth, will draw all men to myself." ³³He said this to show the kind of death he was going to die.

³⁴The crowd spoke up, "We have heard from the Law that the Christᶠ will remain for ever, so how can you say, 'The Son of Man must be lifted up'? Who is this 'Son of Man'?"

³⁵Then Jesus told them, "You are going to have the light just a little while longer. Walk while you have the light, before darkness overtakes you. The man who walks in the dark does not know where he is going. ³⁶Put your trust in the light while you have it, so that you may become sons of light." When he had finished speaking, Jesus left and hid himself from them.

■ The Jews Continue in Their Unbelief

³⁷Even after Jesus had done all these miraculous signs in their presence, they still would not believe in him. ³⁸This was to fulfil the word of Isaiah the prophet:

"Lord, who has believed our message
    and to whom has the arm of the Lord been
        revealed?"ᵍ

³⁹For this reason they could not believe, because, as Isaiah says elsewhere:

⁴⁰"He has blinded their eyes
    and deadened their hearts,
so they can neither see with their eyes,
    nor understand with their hearts,
    nor turn—and I would heal them."ᵇ

⁴¹Isaiah said this because he saw Jesus' glory and spoke about him.

⁴²Yet at the same time many even among the leaders believed in him. But because of the Pharisees they would not confess their faith for fear they would be put out of the synagogue; ⁴³for they loved praise from men more than praise from God.

⁴⁴Then Jesus cried out, "When a man believes in me, he does not believe in me only, but in the one who sent me. ⁴⁵When he looks at me, he sees the one who sent me. ⁴⁶I have come into the world as a light, so that no-one who believes in me should stay in darkness.

⁴⁷"As for the person who hears my words but does not keep them, I do not judge him. For I did not come to judge the world, but to save it. ⁴⁸There is a judge for the one who rejects me and does not accept my words; that very word which I spoke will condemn him at the last day. ⁴⁹For I did not speak of my own accord, but the Father who sent me commanded me what to say and how to say it. ⁵⁰I know that his command leads to eternal life. So whatever I say is just what the Father has told me to say."

■ Jesus Washes His Disciples' Feet

13 It was just before the Passover Feast. Jesus knew that the time had come for him to leave this world and go to the Father. Having loved his

---

ᶜ13 A Hebrew expression meaning "Save!" which became an exclamation of praise   ᵈ13 Psalm 118:25,26   ᵉ15 Zech. 9:9   ᶠ34 Or Messiah   ᵍ38 Isaiah 53:1   ᵇ40 Isaiah 6:10

own who were in the world, he now showed them the full extent of his love.*a*

²The evening meal was being served, and the devil had already prompted Judas Iscariot, son of Simon, to betray Jesus. ³Jesus knew that the Father had put all things under his power, and that he had come from God and was returning to God; ⁴so he got up from the meal, took off his outer clothing, and wrapped a towel round his waist. ⁵After that, he poured water into a basin and began to wash his disciples' feet, drying them with the towel that was wrapped round him.

13:4 ■ THE ROLE OF A SERVANT

Before beginning an intimate meal with his disciples, Jesus gave them a lesson about humility. Normally, slaves performed the act of washing the feet of dinner guests. Here Jesus, the guest of honour, dressed himself like a slave, with a towel around his waist, and insisted on washing the feet of his disciples. Paul comments on Jesus' servanthood in Philippians 2:5–11.

⁶He came to Simon Peter, who said to him, "Lord, are you going to wash my feet?"

⁷Jesus replied, "You do not realise now what I am doing, but later you will understand."

⁸"No," said Peter, "you shall never wash my feet." Jesus answered, "Unless I wash you, you have no part with me."

⁹"Then, Lord," Simon Peter replied, "not just my feet but my hands and my head as well!"

¹⁰Jesus answered, "A person who has had a bath needs only to wash his feet; his whole body is clean. And you are clean, though not every one of you." ¹¹For he knew who was going to betray him, and that was why he said not every one was clean.

¹²When he had finished washing their feet, he put on his clothes and returned to his place. "Do you understand what I have done for you?" he asked them. ¹³"You call me 'Teacher' and 'Lord', and rightly so, for that is what I am. ¹⁴Now that I, your Lord and Teacher, have washed your feet, you also should wash one another's feet. ¹⁵I have set you an example that you should do as I have done for you. ¹⁶I tell you the truth, no servant is greater than his master, nor is a messenger greater than the one who sent him. ¹⁷Now that you know these things, you will be blessed if you do them.

■ Jesus Predicts His Betrayal

¹⁸"I am not referring to all of you; I know those I have chosen. But this is to fulfil the scripture: 'He who shares my bread has lifted up his heel against me.'*b*

¹⁹"I am telling you now before it happens, so that when it does happen you will believe that I am He. ²⁰I tell you the truth, whoever accepts anyone I send accepts me; and whoever accepts me accepts the one who sent me."

²¹After he had said this, Jesus was troubled in spirit and testified, "I tell you the truth, one of you is going to betray me."

²²His disciples stared at one another, at a loss to know which of them he meant. ²³One of them, the disciple whom Jesus loved, was reclining next to him. ²⁴Simon Peter motioned to this disciple and said, "Ask him which one he means."

²⁵Leaning back against Jesus, he asked him, "Lord, who is it?"

²⁶Jesus answered, "It is the one to whom I will give this piece of bread when I have dipped it in the dish." Then, dipping the piece of bread, he gave it to Judas Iscariot, son of Simon. ²⁷As soon as Judas took the bread, Satan entered into him.

"What you are about to do, do quickly," Jesus told him, ²⁸but no-one at the meal understood why Jesus said this to him. ²⁹Since Judas had charge of the money, some thought Jesus was telling him to buy what was needed for the Feast, or to give something to the poor. ³⁰As soon as Judas had taken the bread, he went out. And it was night.

■ Jesus Predicts Peter's Denial
☐ See Matthew 26:33–35; Mark 14:29–31; Luke 22:33–34

³¹When he was gone, Jesus said, "Now is the Son of Man glorified and God is glorified in him. ³²If God is glorified in him,*c* God will glorify the Son in himself, and will glorify him at once.

³³"My children, I will be with you only a little longer. You will look for me, and just as I told the Jews, so I tell you now: Where I am going, you cannot come.

³⁴"A new command I give you: Love one another. As I have loved you, so you must love one another. ³⁵By this all men will know that you are my disciples, if you love one another."

³⁶Simon Peter asked him, "Lord, where are you going?"

Jesus replied, "Where I am going, you cannot follow now, but you will follow later."

³⁷Peter asked, "Lord, why can't I follow you now? I will lay down my life for you."

³⁸Then Jesus answered, "Will you really lay down your life for me? I tell you the truth, before the cock crows, you will disown me three times!

■ Jesus Comforts His Disciples

14 "Do not let your hearts be troubled. Trust in God;*a* trust also in me. ²In my Father's house are many rooms; if it were not so, I would have told you. I am going there to prepare a place for you. ³And if I go and prepare a place for you, I will come back and take you to be with me that you also may be where I am. ⁴You know the way to the place where I am going."

■ Jesus the Way to the Father

⁵Thomas said to him, "Lord, we don't know where you are going, so how can we know the way?"

⁶Jesus answered, "I am the way and the truth and the life. No-one comes to the Father except through me. ⁷If you really knew me, you would know*b* my Father as well. From now on, you do know him and have seen him."

⁸Philip said, "Lord, show us the Father and that will be enough for us."

---

*a*1 Or *he loved them to the last*   *b*18 Psalm 41:9   *c*32 Many early manuscripts do not have *If God is glorified in him.*   *a*1 Or *You trust in God*
*b*7 Some early manuscripts *If you really have known me, you will know*

9Jesus answered: "Don't you know me, Philip, even after I have been among you such a long time? Anyone who has seen me has seen the Father. How can you say, 'Show us the Father'? 10Don't you believe that I am in the Father, and that the Father is in me? The words I say to you are not just my own. Rather, it is the Father, living in me, who is doing his work. 11Believe me when I say that I am in the Father and the Father is in me; or at least believe on the evidence of the miracles themselves. 12I tell you the truth, anyone who has faith in me will do what I have been doing. He will do even greater things than these, because I am going to the Father. 13And I will do whatever you ask in my name, so that the Son may bring glory to the Father. 14You may ask me for anything in my name, and I will do it.

■ Jesus Promises the Holy Spirit

15"If you love me, you will obey what I command. 16And I will ask the Father, and he will give you another Counsellor to be with you for ever — 17the Spirit of truth. The world cannot accept him, because it neither sees him nor knows him. But you

■ JOHN'S REASON FOR WRITING INSIGHT
HANDPICKED INCIDENTS THAT PROVE A POINT

"BELIEVE ME WHEN I SAY THAT I AM IN THE FATHER AND THE FATHER IS IN ME; OR AT LEAST BELIEVE ON THE EVIDENCE OF THE MIRACLES THEMSELVES."
■ 14:11

As the first British woman Prime Minister, Margaret Thatcher is an historic figure that future generations will want to read about. In time, many biographies will be written about her. Some will explore her personal and family life, some her role in the Falklands war, some her relationships with other heads of state. Imagine, though, a biography written about only one aspect of the Prime Minister: Thatcher the orator.

Stories from her Lincolnshire childhood or about her own children would probably not be included in such a book. Instead, details would be given about her training as she listened to tape recordings of her voice and practised lowering her pitch and delivering her words more slowly. Extracts of some of her speeches in the House of Commons might be included as examples of her skill, but details about her foreign policy or the monetarism of the Conservative Party would not warrant an inclusion in this biography.

Such an incomplete biography would serve one purpose: to establish Margaret Thatcher's abilities as a public orator.

■ EVERYTHING FOR A PURPOSE
Like such a biographer, John wrote his book about Jesus for a similarly limited purpose, which he states very clearly: "These are written that you may believe that Jesus is the Christ, the Son of God, and that by believing you may have life in his name" (20:31). The book is not so much a biography as an argument. Its author has hand-picked incidents to demonstrate that Jesus is unlike any man who has ever lived; he is the Son of God.

This purpose shows up, for example, in how John treats Jesus' miracles. Although Matthew, Mark and Luke all record miracles, John goes one step further and calls them "signs". A sign points to something. In John, supernatural acts are one more proof of Jesus' unique nature. Jesus refused to perform miracles as magic to dazzle the crowds but used them instead as object lessons to teach about himself.

After feeding 5,000 people from one packed lunch, Jesus described himself as the bread of life (6:1–59). Just before restoring sight to a blind man, he called himself the light of the world (9:1–7). Nothing "just happens" in John; everything underscores the author's overall theme.

■ MERELY A GREAT MAN?
Because Jesus is so clear in describing his own nature, a statement like "I'm ready to accept Jesus as a great moral teacher, but I don't accept his claim to be God" doesn't hold up. As C.S. Lewis has said, "That is the one thing we must not say. A man who was merely a man and said the sort of things Jesus said would not be a great moral teacher. He would either be a lunatic — on a level with the man who says he is a poached egg — or else he would be the Devil of Hell. You must make your choice. Either this man was, and is, the Son of God: or else a madman or something worse."

According to John, not everyone believed Jesus was divine: "Who do you think you are?" some indignantly demanded (8:53). Doubters had him killed for making such an audacious claim. But it is hardly possible to read John without being convinced that Jesus himself claimed to be God.

□ LIFE QUESTIONS:
Despite what C.S. Lewis says, many people do think of Jesus as "merely a great man". How do they rationalise it?

know him, for he lives with you and will be^c in you. ^{18}I will not leave you as orphans; I will come to you. ^{19}Before long, the world will not see me any more, but you will see me. Because I live, you also will live. ^{20}On that day you will realise that I am in my Father, and you are in me, and I am in you. ^{21}Whoever has my commands and obeys them, he is the one who loves me. He who loves me will be loved by my Father, and I too will love him and show myself to him."

^{22}Then Judas (not Judas Iscariot) said, "But, Lord, why do you intend to show yourself to us and not to the world?"

^{23}Jesus replied, "If anyone loves me, he will obey my teaching. My Father will love him, and we will come to him and make our home with him. ^{24}He who does not love me will not obey my teaching. These words you hear are not my own; they belong to the Father who sent me.

^{25}"All this I have spoken while still with you. ^{26}But the Counsellor, the Holy Spirit, whom the Father will send in my name, will teach you all things and will remind you of everything I have said to you. ^{27}Peace I leave with you; my peace I give you. I do not give to you as the world gives. Do not let your hearts be troubled and do not be afraid.

^{28}"You heard me say, 'I am going away and I am coming back to you.' If you loved me, you would be glad that I am going to the Father, for the Father is greater than I. ^{29}I have told you now before it happens, so that when it does happen you will believe. ^{30}I will not speak with you much longer, for the prince of this world is coming. He has no hold on me, ^{31}but the world must learn that I love the Father and that I do exactly what my Father has commanded me.

"Come now; let us leave.

■ The Vine and the Branches

15 "I am the true vine, and my Father is the gardener. ^{2}He cuts off every branch in me that bears no fruit, while every branch that does bear fruit he prunes^a so that it will be even more fruitful. ^{3}You are already clean because of the word I have spoken to you. ^{4}Remain in me, and I will remain in you. No branch can bear fruit by itself; it must remain in the vine. Neither can you bear fruit unless you remain in me.

^{5}"I am the vine; you are the branches. If a man remains in me and I in him, he will bear much fruit; apart from me you can do nothing. ^{6}If anyone does not remain in me, he is like a branch that is thrown away and withers; such branches are picked up, thrown into the fire and burned. ^{7}If you remain in me and my words remain in you, ask whatever you wish, and it will be given you. ^{8}This is to my Father's glory, that you bear much fruit, showing yourselves to be my disciples.

^{9}"As the Father has loved me, so have I loved me. Now remain in my love. ^{10}If you obey my commands, you will remain in my love, just as I have obeyed my Father's commands and remain in his love. ^{11}I have told you this so that my joy may be in

you and that your joy may be complete. ^{12}My command is this: Love each other as I have loved you. ^{13}Greater love has no-one than this, that he lay down his life for his friends. ^{14}You are my friends if you do what I command. ^{15}I no longer call you servants, because a servant does not know his master's business. Instead, I have called you friends, for everything that I learned from my Father I have made known to you. ^{16}You did not choose me, but I chose you and appointed you to go and bear fruit—fruit that will last. Then the Father will give you whatever you ask in my name. ^{17}This is my command: Love each other.

15:1 ■ JESUS AS THE VINE

Old Testament prophets referred to the Israelites as God's "vine", or "vineyard". But as Jesus often pointed out, the Jews had failed to bear fruit. Here he claims the image for himself, "I am the vine".

John frequently records Jesus' use of the words *I am*: "I am the bread of life", "I am the way and the truth and the life". The phrase stood out sharply to Jewish leaders, because God had been known as the great I AM to the Jews (Exodus 3:14). Jewish unbelievers, recognising that Jesus was claiming to be God, reacted with shock and outrage.

■ The World Hates the Disciples

^{18}"If the world hates you, keep in mind that it hated me first. ^{19}If you belonged to the world, it would love you as its own. As it is, you do not belong to the world, but I have chosen you out of the world. That is why the world hates you. ^{20}Remember the words I spoke to you: 'No servant is greater than his master.'^{b} If they persecuted me, they will persecute you also. If they obeyed my teaching, they will obey yours also. ^{21}They will treat you this way because of my name, for they do not know the One who sent me. ^{22}If I had not come and spoken to them, they would not be guilty of sin. Now, however, they have no excuse for their sin. ^{23}He who hates me hates my Father as well. ^{24}If I had not done among them what no-one else did, they would not be guilty of sin. But now they have seen these miracles, and yet they have hated both me and my Father. ^{25}But this is to fulfil what is written in their Law: 'They hated me without reason.'^{c}

^{26}"When the Counsellor comes, whom I will send to you from the Father, the Spirit of truth who goes out from the Father, he will testify about me. ^{27}And you also must testify, for you have been with me from the beginning.

16 "All this I have told you so that you will not go astray. ^{2}They will put you out of the synagogue; in fact, a time is coming when anyone who kills you will think he is offering a service to God. ^{3}They will do such things because they have not known the Father or me. ^{4}I have told you this, so that when the time comes you will remember that I warned you. I did not tell you this at first because I was with you.

---

^{c}17 Some early manuscripts *and is* ^{a}2 The Greek for *prunes* also means *cleans*. ^{b}20 John 13:16 ^{c}25 Psalms 35:19; 69:4

■ The Work of the Holy Spirit

5"Now I am going to him who sent me, yet none of you asks me, 'Where are you going?' 6Because I have said these things, you are filled with grief. 7But I tell you the truth: It is for your good that I am going away. Unless I go away, the Counsellor will not come to you; but if I go, I will send him to you. 8When he comes, he will convict the world of guilt*a* in regard to sin and righteousness and judgment: 9in regard to sin, because men do not believe in me; 10in regard to righteousness, because I am going to the Father, where you can see me no longer; 11and in regard to judgment, because the prince of this world now stands condemned.

16:6 ■ FILLED WITH GRIEF

Good-byes are always sad, and for the disciples this farewell speech was especially so. They had staked their lives on Jesus, and without him they could see no future. Jesus, however, promised that he was leaving for their own good. He would send the Holy Spirit to guide them into "all truth" (verse 13). In fact, as Acts shows, only after Jesus' departure did these confused disciples fully grasp the meaning of his death and resurrection and begin to proclaim it joyfully to everyone around them.

12"I have much more to say to you, more than you can now bear. 13But when he, the Spirit of truth, comes, he will guide you into all truth. He will not speak on his own; he will speak only what he hears, and he will tell you what is yet to come. 14He will bring glory to me by taking from what is mine and making it known to you. 15All that belongs to the Father is mine. That is why I said the Spirit will take from what is mine and make it known to you.

16"In a little while you will see me no more, and then after a little while you will see me."

■ The Disciples' Grief Will Turn to Joy

17Some of his disciples said to one another, "What does he mean by saying, 'In a little while you will see me no more, and then after a little while you will see me,' and 'Because I am going to the Father'?" 18They kept asking, "What does he mean by 'a little while'? We don't understand what he is saying."

19Jesus saw that they wanted to ask him about this, so he said to them, "Are you asking one another what I meant when I said, 'In a little while you will see me no more, and then after a little while you will see me'? 20I tell you the truth, you will weep and mourn while the world rejoices. You will grieve, but your grief will turn to joy. 21A woman giving birth to a child has pain because her time has come; but when her baby is born she forgets the anguish because of her joy that a child is born into the world. 22So with you: Now is your time of grief, but I will see you again and you will rejoice, and no-one will take away your joy. 23In that day you will no longer ask me anything. I tell you the truth, my Father will give you whatever you ask in my name. 24Until now you have not asked for anything in my name. Ask and you will receive, and your joy will be complete.

25"Though I have been speaking figuratively, a time is coming when I will no longer use this kind of language but will tell you plainly about my Father. 26In that day you will ask in my name. I am not saying that I will ask the Father on your behalf. 27No, the Father himself loves you because you have loved me and have believed that I came from God. 28I came from the Father and entered the world; now I am leaving the world and going back to the Father."

29Then Jesus' disciples said, "Now you are speaking clearly and without figures of speech. 30Now we can see that you know all things and that you do not even need to have anyone ask you questions. This makes us believe that you came from God."

31"You believe at last!"*b* Jesus answered. 32"But a time is coming, and has come, when you will be scattered, each to his own home. You will leave me all alone. Yet I am not alone, for my Father is with me.

33"I have told you these things, so that in me you may have peace. In this world you will have trouble. But take heart! I have overcome the world."

■ Jesus Prays for Himself

17 After Jesus said this, he looked towards heaven and prayed:

"Father, the time has come. Glorify your Son, that your Son may glorify you. 2For you granted him authority over all people that he might give eternal life to all those you have given him. 3Now this is eternal life: that they may know you, the only true God, and Jesus Christ, whom you have sent. 4I have brought you glory on earth by completing the work you gave me to do. 5And now, Father, glorify me in your presence with the glory I had with you before the world began.

■ Jesus Prays for His Disciples

6"I have revealed you*a* to those whom you gave me out of the world. They were yours; you gave them to me and they have obeyed your word. 7Now they know that everything you have given me comes from you. 8For I gave them the words you gave me and they accepted them. They knew with certainty that I came from you, and they believed that you sent me. 9I pray for them. I am not praying for the world, but for those you have given me, for they are yours. 10All I have is yours, and all you have is mine. And glory has come to me through them. 11I will remain in the world no longer, but they are still in the world, and I am coming to you. Holy Father, protect them by the power of your name—the name you gave me—so that they may be one as we are one. 12While I was with them, I protected them and kept them safe by that name you gave me. None has been lost except the one doomed to destruction so that Scripture would be fulfilled.

---

a 8 Or *will expose the guilt of the world*   *b* 31 Or *"Do you now believe?"*   *a* 6 Greek *your name*; also in verse 26

¹³"I am coming to you now, but I say these things while I am still in the world, so that they may have the full measure of my joy within them. ¹⁴I have given them your word and the world has hated them, for they are not of the world any more than I am of the world. ¹⁵My prayer is not that you take them out of the world but that you protect them from the evil one. ¹⁶They are not of the world, even as I am not of it. ¹⁷Sanctify[b] them by the truth; your word is truth. ¹⁸As you sent me into the world, I have sent them into the world. ¹⁹For them I sanctify myself, that they too may be truly sanctified.

■ Jesus Prays for All Believers

²⁰"My prayer is not for them alone. I pray also for those who will believe in me through their message, ²¹that all of them may be one, Father, just as you are in me and I am in you.

May they also be in us so that the world may believe that you have sent me. ²²I have given them the glory that you gave me, that they may be one as we are one: ²³I in them and you in me. May they be brought to complete unity to let the world know that you sent me and have loved them even as you have loved me.

17:21 ■ JESUS' LONGEST PRAYER
The famous prayer recorded here concludes a kind of commissioning or graduation. In it, Jesus turns over his mission to the disciples and, by extension, to all believers who would follow.

---

²⁴"Father, I want those you have given me to be with me where I am, and to see my glory, the glory you have given me because you loved me before the creation of the world. ²⁵"Righteous Father, though the world does

---

■ THE LAST MEAL TOGETHER
THE LONGEST, MOST EMOTIONAL NIGHT OF JESUS' LIFE

INSIGHT

"YOU WILL GRIEVE, BUT YOUR GRIEF WILL TURN TO JOY." ■ 16:20

John devoted one-third of his book to the last 24-hour period Jesus spent on earth. Five chapters (13–17) describe one of the scenes from that period, and nothing like these chapters exists elsewhere in the Bible. In their slow-motion, realistic detail, they provide an intimate memoir of Jesus' most anguished evening.

Leonardo da Vinci immortalised the setting in his famous painting *The Last Supper,* with the participants arranged on one side of the table as if posing for the artist. But John gives few physical details; instead, he focuses on a whirlpool of emotional currents.

John holds a light to the disciples' faces, and you can almost see the awareness flickering in their eyes. All that Jesus had told them was slowly sinking in. As for Jesus, "having loved his own who were in the world, he now showed them the full extent of his love" (13:1).

■ JESUS PREPARES TO LEAVE
Never before had Jesus been so direct with them. Around the table he avoided parables and painstakingly answered the disciples' redundant questions. Never was he more "theological". He alone fully recognised the significance of this last evening before his death. The world was about to undergo a convulsive trauma, and the 11 fearful men with him were his hope for that world.

"It is for your good that I am going away," Jesus said (16:7), but the disciples were too busy discussing the meaning of "going away" to comprehend the good that would follow.

Nevertheless, Jesus kept explaining until at last the disciples showed signs of understanding. God's Son had entered the world to reside in one body. He was leaving earth to return to the Father. But the Spirit would come and reside in many bodies. Jesus seemed aware that much of what they nodded their heads at now would not sink in until later.

■ PAIN BEFORE JOY
Jesus concluded his words with a ringing declaration, "Take heart! I have overcome the world" (16:33). How hollow this statement would seem the next evening, when his pale, abused body hung on an executioner's cross. The disciples' emotions — and faith — would rise and plummet in one unforgettable day. Jesus predicted this, too, likening the pain to the spasms of childbirth before great joy breaks through (16:21–22).

In his longest recorded prayer, Jesus summed up his feelings and his plans for the tight circle of friends gathered around him. He prayed, too, for the others who would follow them, stretching in an unbroken chain throughout history. And then he led the little band to his appointment with death.

□ LIFE QUESTIONS:
Have you ever been around someone facing death? How did he or she act? What does his response to impending death reveal about why Jesus came to earth?

---

b 17 Greek *hagiazo* (*set apart for sacred use* or *make holy*); also in verse 19 not know you, I know you, and they know that you have sent me. 26I have made you known to them, and will continue to make you known in order that the love you have for me may be in them and that I myself may be in them."

■ Jesus Arrested

☐ See Matthew 26:47–56; Mark 14:43–50; Luke 22:47–53

18 When he had finished praying, Jesus left with his disciples and crossed the Kidron Valley. On the other side there was an olive grove, and he and his disciples went into it.

2Now Judas, who betrayed him, knew the place, because Jesus had often met there with his disciples. 3So Judas came to the grove, guiding a detachment of soldiers and some officials from the chief priests and Pharisees. They were carrying torches, lanterns and weapons.

4Jesus, knowing all that was going to happen to him, went out and asked them, "Who is it you want?"

5"Jesus of Nazareth," they replied.

"I am he," Jesus said. (And Judas the traitor was standing there with them.) 6When Jesus said, "I am he," they drew back and fell to the ground.

7Again he asked them, "Who is it you want?" And they said, "Jesus of Nazareth."

8"I told you that I am he," Jesus answered. "If you are looking for me, then let these men go." 9This happened so that the words he had spoken would be fulfilled: "I have not lost one of those you gave me."*a*

10Then Simon Peter, who had a sword, drew it and struck the high priest's servant, cutting off his right ear. (The servant's name was Malchus.)

11Jesus commanded Peter, "Put your sword away! Shall I not drink the cup the Father has given me?"

■ Jesus Taken to Annas

☐ See Matthew 26:57

12Then the detachment of soldiers with its commander and the Jewish officials arrested Jesus. They bound him 13and brought him first to Annas, who was the father-in-law of Caiaphas, the high priest that year. 14Caiaphas was the one who had advised the Jews that it would be good if one man died for the people.

■ Peter's First Denial

☐ See Matthew 26:69–70; Mark 14:66–68; Luke 22:55–57

15Simon Peter and another disciple were following Jesus. Because this disciple was known to the high priest, he went with Jesus into the high priest's courtyard, 16but Peter had to wait outside at the door. The other disciple, who was known to the high priest, came back, spoke to the girl on duty there and brought Peter in.

17"You are not one of his disciples, are you?" the girl at the door asked Peter.

He replied, "I am not."

18It was cold, and the servants and officials stood round a fire they had made to keep warm. Peter also was standing with them, warming himself.

■ The High Priest Questions Jesus

☐ See Matthew 26:59–68; Mark 14:55–65; Luke 22:63–71

19Meanwhile, the high priest questioned Jesus about his disciples and his teaching.

20"I have spoken openly to the world," Jesus replied. "I always taught in synagogues or at the temple, where all the Jews come together. I said nothing in secret. 21Why question me? Ask those who heard me. Surely they know what I said."

22When Jesus said this, one of the officials near by struck him in the face. "Is this the way you answer the high priest?" he demanded.

23"If I said something wrong," Jesus replied, "testify as to what is wrong. But if I spoke the truth, why did you strike me?" 24Then Annas sent him, still bound, to Caiaphas the high priest.*b*

■ Peter's Second and Third Denials

☐ See Matthew 26:71–75; Mark 14:69–72; Luke 22:58–62

25As Simon Peter stood warming himself, he was asked, "You are not one of his disciples, are you?" He denied it, saying, "I am not."

26One of the high priest's servants, a relative of the man whose ear Peter had cut off, challenged him, "Didn't I see you with him in the olive grove?" 27Again Peter denied it, and at that moment a cock began to crow.

■ Jesus Before Pilate

☐ See Matthew 27:11–18,20–23; Mark 15:2–15; Luke 23:2–3,18–25

28Then the Jews led Jesus from Caiaphas to the palace of the Roman governor. By now it was early morning, and to avoid ceremonial uncleanness the Jews did not enter the palace; they wanted to be able to eat the Passover. 29So Pilate came out to them and asked, "What charges are you bringing against this man?"

30"If he were not a criminal," they replied, "we would not have handed him over to you."

31Pilate said, "Take him yourselves and judge him by your own law."

"But we have no right to execute anyone," the Jews objected. 32This happened so that the words Jesus had spoken indicating the kind of death he was going to die would be fulfilled.

33Pilate then went back inside the palace, summoned Jesus and asked him, "Are you the king of the Jews?"

34"Is that your own idea," Jesus asked, "or did others talk to you about me?"

35"Am I a Jew?" Pilate replied. "It was your people and your chief priests who handed you over to me. What is it you have done?"

36Jesus said, "My kingdom is not of this world. If it were, my servants would fight to prevent my arrest by the Jews. But now my kingdom is from another place."

37"You are a king, then!" said Pilate.

Jesus answered, "You are right in saying I am a king. In fact, for this reason I was born, and for this I came into the world, to testify to the truth. Everyone on the side of truth listens to me."

38"What is truth?" Pilate asked. With this he went out again to the Jews and said, "I find no basis for a

a 9 John 6:39   b 24 Or (Now Annas had sent him, still bound, to Caiaphas the high priest.)

charge against him. [39]But it is your custom for me to release to you one prisoner at the time of the Passover. Do you want me to release 'the king of the Jews'?"

[40]They shouted back, "No, not him! Give us Barabbas!" Now Barabbas had taken part in a rebellion.

■ Jesus Sentenced to be Crucified
☐ See Matthew 27:27–31; Mark 15:16–20

19 Then Pilate took Jesus and had him flogged. [2]The soldiers twisted together a crown of thorns and put it on his head. They clothed him in a purple robe [3]and went up to him again and again, saying, "Hail, king of the Jews!" And they struck him in the face.

[4]Once more Pilate came out and said to the Jews, "Look, I am bringing him out to you to let you know that I find no basis for a charge against him." [5]When Jesus came out wearing the crown of thorns and the purple robe, Pilate said to them, "Here is the man!"

[6]As soon as the chief priests and their officials saw him, they shouted, "Crucify! Crucify!"

But Pilate answered, "You take him and crucify him. As for me, I find no basis for a charge against him."

[7]The Jews insisted, "We have a law, and according to that law he must die, because he claimed to be the Son of God."

[8]When Pilate heard this, he was even more afraid, [9]and he went back inside the palace. "Where do you come from?" he asked Jesus, but Jesus gave him no answer. [10]"Do you refuse to speak to me?" Pilate said. "Don't you realise I have power either to free you or to crucify you?"

[11]Jesus answered, "You would have no power over me if it were not given to you from above. Therefore the one who handed me over to you is guilty of a greater sin."

[12]From then on, Pilate tried to set Jesus free, but the Jews kept shouting, "If you let this man go, you are no friend of Caesar. Anyone who claims to be a king opposes Caesar."

[13]When Pilate heard this, he brought Jesus out and sat down on the judge's seat at a place known as the Stone Pavement (which in Aramaic is Gabbatha). [14]It was the day of Preparation of Passover Week, about the sixth hour.

"Here is your king," Pilate said to the Jews.

[15]But they shouted, "Take him away! Take him away! Crucify him!"

"Shall I crucify your king?" Pilate asked.

"We have no king but Caesar," the chief priests answered.

[16]Finally Pilate handed him over to them to be crucified.

■ The Crucifixion
☐ See Matthew 27:33–44; Mark 15:22–32; Luke 23:33–43

So the soldiers took charge of Jesus. [17]Carrying his own cross, he went out to the place of the Skull (which in Aramaic is called Golgotha). [18]Here they crucified him, and with him two others — one on each side and Jesus in the middle.

[19]Pilate had a notice prepared and fastened to the cross. It read: JESUS OF NAZARETH, THE KING OF THE JEWS. [20]Many of the Jews read this sign, for the place where Jesus was crucified was near the city, and the sign was written in Aramaic, Latin and Greek. [21]The chief priests of the Jews protested to Pilate, "Do not write 'The King of the Jews', but that this man claimed to be king of the Jews."

[22]Pilate answered, "What I have written, I have written."

[23]When the soldiers crucified Jesus, they took his clothes, dividing them into four shares, one for each of them, with the undergarment remaining. This garment was seamless, woven in one piece from top to bottom.

[24]"Let's not tear it," they said to one another. "Let's decide by lot who will get it."

This happened that the scripture might be fulfilled which said,

"They divided my garments among them
    and cast lots for my clothing."[a]

So this is what the soldiers did.

[25]Near the cross of Jesus stood his mother, his mother's sister, Mary the wife of Clopas, and Mary Magdalene. [26]When Jesus saw his mother there, and the disciple whom he loved standing near by, he said to his mother, "Dear woman, here is your son," [27]and to the disciple, "Here is your mother." From that time on, this disciple took her into his home.

■ The Death of Jesus
☐ See Matthew 27:48,50; Mark 15:36–37; Luke 23:36

[28]Later, knowing that all was now completed, and so that the Scripture would be fulfilled, Jesus said, "I am thirsty." [29]A jar of wine vinegar was there, so they soaked a sponge in it, put the sponge on a stalk of the hyssop plant, and lifted it to Jesus' lips. [30]When he had received the drink, Jesus said, "It is finished." With that, he bowed his head and gave up his spirit.

[31]Now it was the day of Preparation, and the next day was to be a special Sabbath. Because the Jews did not want the bodies left on the crosses during the Sabbath, they asked Pilate to have the legs broken and the bodies taken down. [32]The soldiers therefore came and broke the legs of the first man who had been crucified with Jesus, and then those of the other. [33]But when they came to Jesus and found that he was already dead, they did not break his legs. [34]Instead, one of the soldiers pierced Jesus' side with a spear, bringing a sudden flow of blood and water. [35]The man who saw it has given testimony, and his testimony is true. He knows that he tells the truth, and he testifies so that you also may believe. [36]These things happened so that the scripture would be fulfilled: "Not one of his bones will be broken,"[b] [37]and, as another scripture says, "They will look on the one they have pierced."[c]

■ The Burial of Jesus
☐ See Matthew 27:57–61; Mark 15:42–47; Luke 23:50–56

[38]Later, Joseph of Arimathea asked Pilate for the body of Jesus. Now Joseph was a disciple of Jesus, but secretly because he feared the Jews. With Pilate's permission, he came and took the body away.

[a]24 Psalm 22:18   [b]36 Exodus 12:46; Num. 9:12; Psalm 34:20   [c]37 Zech. 12:10

39He was accompanied by Nicodemus, the man who earlier had visited Jesus at night. Nicodemus brought a mixture of myrrh and aloes, about seventy-five pounds.d 40Taking Jesus' body, the two of them wrapped it, with the spices, in strips of linen. This was in accordance with Jewish burial customs. 41At the place where Jesus was crucified, there was a garden, and in the garden a new tomb, in which no-one had ever been laid. 42Because it was the Jewish day of Preparation and since the tomb was near by, they laid Jesus there.

19:31 ■ SPEEDING UP DEATH

Soldiers broke the bones of crucified men to speed up their dying, here so the bodies could be removed before the holy day that followed. Jesus had already died, so his bones were left intact. This fulfilled Old Testament promises that the Messiah's bones would not be broken and that his side would be pierced with a spear (Exodus 12:46; Zechariah 12:10).

■ The Empty Tomb
□ See Matthew 28:1–8; Mark 16:1–8; Luke 24:1–10

20 Early on the first day of the week, while it was still dark, Mary Magdalene went to the tomb and saw that the stone had been removed from the entrance. 2So she came running to Simon Peter and the other disciple, the one Jesus loved, and said, "They have taken the Lord out of the tomb, and we don't know where they have put him!"

3So Peter and the other disciple started for the tomb. 4Both were running, but the other disciple outran Peter and reached the tomb first. 5He bent over and looked in at the strips of linen lying there but did not go in. 6Then Simon Peter, who was behind him, arrived and went into the tomb. He saw the strips of linen lying there, 7as well as the burial cloth that had been around Jesus' head. The cloth was folded up by itself, separate from the linen. 8Finally the other disciple, who had reached the tomb first, also went inside. He saw and believed. 9(They still did not understand from Scripture that Jesus had to rise from the dead.)

■ Jesus Appears to Mary Magdalene
10Then the disciples went back to their homes, 11but Mary stood outside the tomb crying. As she wept, she bent over to look into the tomb 12and saw two angels in white, seated where Jesus' body had been, one at the head and the other at the foot.

13They asked her, "Woman, why are you crying?"

"They have taken my Lord away," she said, "and I don't know where they have put him." 14At this, she turned round and saw Jesus standing there, but she did not realise that it was Jesus.

15"Woman," he said, "why are you crying? Who is it you are looking for?"

Thinking he was the gardener, she said, "Sir, if you have carried him away, tell me where you have put him, and I will get him."

16Jesus said to her, "Mary."

She turned towards him and cried out in Aramaic, "Rabboni!" (which means Teacher).

17Jesus said, "Do not hold on to me, for I have not yet returned to the Father. Go instead to my brothers and tell them, 'I am returning to my Father and your Father, to my God and your God.'"

18Mary Magdalene went to the disciples with the news: "I have seen the Lord!" And she told them that he had said these things to her.

■ Jesus Appears to His Disciples
19On the evening of that first day of the week, when the disciples were together, with the doors locked for fear of the Jews, Jesus came and stood among them and said, "Peace be with you!" 20After he said this, he showed them his hands and side. The disciples were overjoyed when they saw the Lord.

21Again Jesus said, "Peace be with you! As the Father has sent me, I am sending you." 22And with that he breathed on them and said, "Receive the Holy Spirit. 23If you forgive anyone his sins, they are forgiven; if you do not forgive them, they are not forgiven."

■ Jesus Appears to Thomas
24Now Thomas (called Didymus), one of the Twelve, was not with the disciples when Jesus came. 25So the other disciples told him, "We have seen the Lord!"

But he said to them, "Unless I see the nail marks in his hands and put my finger where the nails were, and put my hand into his side, I will not believe it."

20:25 ■ DOUBTING THOMAS

The sceptical Thomas is sometimes singled out, as though he had unusual doubts. In reality, none of the disciples believed in Jesus' resurrection until they saw him for themselves. Thomas had been absent, though, when Jesus first appeared to the others. He stayed sceptical until Jesus appeared again, and summoned Thomas to touch him. Seeing was believing for all the disciples, but Jesus specially commended those who believed without such first-hand evidence.

26A week later his disciples were in the house again, and Thomas was with them. Though the doors were locked, Jesus came and stood among them and said, "Peace be with you!" 27Then he said to Thomas, "Put your finger here; see my hands. Reach out your hand and put it into my side. Stop doubting and believe."

28Thomas said to him, "My Lord and my God!"

29Then Jesus told him, "Because you have seen me, you have believed; blessed are those who have not seen and yet have believed."

30Jesus did many other miraculous signs in the presence of his disciples, which are not recorded in this book. 31But these are written that you maya believe that Jesus is the Christ, the Son of God, and that by believing you may have life in his name.

d39 Greek a hundred litrai (about 34 kilograms)   a31 Some manuscripts may continue to

■ Jesus and the Miraculous Catch of Fish

21 Afterwards Jesus appeared again to his disciples, by the Sea of Tiberias.*a* It happened this way: ²Simon Peter, Thomas (called Didymus), Nathanael from Cana in Galilee, the sons of Zebedee, and two other disciples were together. ³"I'm going out to fish," Simon Peter told them, and they said, "We'll go with you." So they went out and got into the boat, but that night they caught nothing.

⁴Early in the morning, Jesus stood on the shore, but the disciples did not realise that it was Jesus.

⁵He called out to them, "Friends, haven't you any fish?"

"No," they answered.

⁶He said, "Throw your net on the right side of the boat and you will find some." When they did, they were unable to haul the net in because of the large number of fish.

⁷Then the disciple whom Jesus loved said to Peter, "It is the Lord!" As soon as Simon Peter heard him say, "It is the Lord," he wrapped his outer garment around him (for he had taken it off) and jumped into the water. ⁸The other disciples followed in the boat, towing the net full of fish, for they were not far from shore, about a hundred yards.*b* ⁹When they landed, they saw a fire of burning coals there with fish on it, and some bread.

¹⁰Jesus said to them, "Bring some of the fish you have just caught."

¹¹Simon Peter climbed aboard and dragged the net ashore. It was full of large fish, 153, but even with so many the net was not torn. ¹²Jesus said to them, "Come and have breakfast." None of the disciples dared ask him, "Who are you?" They knew it was the Lord. ¹³Jesus came, took the bread and gave it to them, and did the same with the fish. ¹⁴This was now the third time Jesus appeared to his disciples after he was raised from the dead.

■ Jesus Reinstates Peter

¹⁵When they had finished eating, Jesus said to Simon Peter, "Simon son of John, do you truly love me more than these?"

"Yes, Lord," he said, "you know that I love you."

Jesus said, "Feed my lambs."

21:15 ■ DO YOU LOVE ME?
John ends his book with a moving scene in which Jesus spoke to Peter and "the disciple whom Jesus loved", presumably John himself. Jesus asked Peter the same question three times, a painful reminder of Peter's three denials of him. But this reinstatement helped embolden Peter to become one of the early church's most fearless spokesmen.

---

¹⁶Again Jesus said, "Simon son of John, do you truly love me?"

He answered, "Yes, Lord, you know that I love you."

■ A CHANGE OF HEART AND MIND
WHATEVER HAPPENED TO THE "SON OF THUNDER"?

INSIGHT

THIS IS THE DISCIPLE WHO TESTIFIES TO THESE THINGS AND WHO WROTE THEM DOWN. WE KNOW THAT HIS TESTIMONY IS TRUE. ■ 21:24

The disciple John had been favoured to share private moments with Jesus. As part of an inner circle of three, he saw Jesus transfigured, watched him bring Jairus' daughter back to life, and waited for him in the Garden of Gethsemane.

After Jesus was arrested, John witnessed the sequence of his trials. He was the only disciple mentioned as being near the cross at Jesus' death and one of the very first to learn of Christ's resurrection. Somehow, this process changed John.

■ FROM THUNDER TO LOVE
John wore an amusing nickname, "Son of Thunder" (Mark 3:17), and several incidents in the Gospels hint that this name reflected his stormy personality. John jealously resented competition from rival miracle workers (Mark 9:38), and he insisted on the best seat in the kingdom of heaven for himself. Once, he wanted to call fire down from heaven to destroy a hostile town (Luke 9:54).

Somewhere in his life, the thunder clouds broke apart. Eventually he got a new nickname: "the apostle of love". John's books – this Gospel and the letters John wrote later – are marked by a recurring emphasis on love.

Naturally, the spiritual pilgrimage of John influenced his written record of Jesus' life. His changed personality may provide a clue to his unique style of telling Jesus' story through a handful of poignant episodes. Perhaps these few scenes are the memories of Jesus that finally convinced John himself that Jesus was, indeed, the Son of God.

□ LIFE QUESTIONS:
Getting to know Jesus changes a person. How have you been changed?

---

a 1 That is, Sea of Galilee   *b 8* Greek *about two hundred cubits* (about 90 metres)

Jesus said, "Take care of my sheep."

[17]The third time he said to him, "Simon son of John, do you love me?"

Peter was hurt because Jesus asked him the third time, "Do you love me?" He said, "Lord, you know all things; you know that I love you."

Jesus said, "Feed my sheep. [18]I tell you the truth, when you were younger you dressed yourself and went where you wanted; but when you are old you will stretch out your hands, and someone else will dress you and lead you where you do not want to go." [19]Jesus said this to indicate the kind of death by which Peter would glorify God. Then he said to him, "Follow me!"

[20]Peter turned and saw that the disciple whom Jesus loved was following them. (This was the one who had leaned back against Jesus at the supper and had said, "Lord, who is going to betray you?") [21]When Peter saw him, he asked, "Lord, what about him?"

[22]Jesus answered, "If I want him to remain alive until I return, what is that to you? You must follow me." [23]Because of this, the rumour spread among the brothers that this disciple would not die. But Jesus did not say that he would not die; he only said, "If I want him to remain alive until I return, what is that to you?"

[24]This is the disciple who testifies to these things and who wrote them down. We know that his testimony is true.

[25]Jesus did many other things as well. If every one of them were written down, I suppose that even the whole world would not have room for the books that would be written.

ACTS

INTRODUCTION

■ THE LINKING BOOK

IMAGINE A BIBLE WITHOUT THE BOOK OF ACTS

"YOU WILL RECEIVE POWER WHEN THE HOLY SPIRIT COMES ON YOU; AND YOU WILL BE MY WITNESSES." ■ 1:8

The New Testament divides neatly into two nearly equal sections. The first consists of four Gospels that tell about Jesus' life on earth. The second section, beginning with Romans, concerns churches that sprang up after Jesus left. In between stands the book of Acts.

The best way to appreciate Acts is to imagine a Bible without it. You have just read the life of Jesus, highlighted by four different authors, and you turn to Romans: "Paul, a servant of Christ Jesus . . . to all in Rome who are loved by God and called to be saints". Rome? How did the story get there from Jerusalem?

Next you'd find two books, also from Paul (who's he?), addressed to "the church of God in Corinth". Another book follows, written to the church in Galatia, then one to Ephesus, and so on with more letters to other exotic locales. Obviously, something is missing. Without Acts, the New Testament leaps from an orderly history of one man, Jesus, to a collection of unexplained personal correspondence.

■ A PLAN REVEALED BY JESUS

With Acts, everything fits into place. This book provides a transition from the life of Christ to the new church. It introduces Paul and explains how a minority religion crossed the sea to Rome, the capital of the empire. A reader of Acts visits key cities sprinkled around the Mediterranean, meets the principal leaders of the new movement, and gets a strong scent of the problems that will occupy Paul's letters.

Luke, a physician, had written the third Gospel as an account of "all that Jesus began to do and to teach" (Acts 1:1). The book of Acts resumes the story, hinting that this history, too, will show Jesus at work, but in a quite different form. "I will build my church," Jesus had promised (Matthew 16:18), and Acts graphically shows how that process began.

Jesus himself had laid out the plot in his last recorded words on earth: "You will be my witnesses in Jerusalem, and in all Judea and Samaria, and to the ends of the earth" (1:8). Acts faithfully follows that outline: the first seven chapters show the church in Jerusalem, the next five focus on Judea and Samaria, and the rest of the book follows the spread of the gospel to the outposts of Roman civilisation.

■ BOISTEROUS BEGINNINGS

The book opens in Jerusalem, during the Pentecost holiday. Over a million pilgrims were milling about the city when suddenly a group of 120 believers came alive. Jesus' followers hit the streets with a bold new style, and 3,000 joined up on the first day alone. Starting with that boisterous scene, Luke spins a historical adventure tale.

Due to Luke's writing skill, Acts reads like a novel, skipping from one exhilarating scene to the next. Wherever the apostles went, action swirled, riots erupted, and a small church took root. In an era when new religions were ten a penny, the Christian faith became a worldwide phenomenon. Acts tells how.

■ HOW TO READ ACTS

Acts reads like well-written history. It follows a logical plan, includes fascinating details, and focuses on the most dramatic events. In that sense, it is self-explanatory.

The first twelve chapters concentrate mainly on the apostle Peter. The rest of Acts features Paul (also called Saul), and the book

explains how he became accepted as the first and foremost Christian missionary. Paul made three extensive trips in Acts, then a final voyage in chains to Rome (see map 9, "The World of the New Testament", at the back of this Bible).

Acts records the early history of relations between the church and the Roman empire. It also gives important background information on such cities as Corinth, Ephesus, and Philippi — cities Paul later wrote letters to. The material in Acts will help you understand what Paul is writing about in 1 and 2 Corinthians, Ephesians, Philippians, and the other letters.

Acts also summarises 18 different speeches by Paul, Peter, and a few others.

These speeches make a fascinating study in themselves: the apostles were beginning to interpret the facts of Jesus' life in the light of their spiritual significance. As you read them, note how the speakers chose their words and content with the audience in mind, and then note the audience's reaction.

■ 3-TRACK READING PLAN

For an explanation and complete listing of the 3-track reading plan, turn to page x.

■ TRACK 1:
Two-Week Courses on the Bible
The Track 1 reading programme on the Life and Teachings of Paul includes six chapters from Acts. See page x for a complete listing of this course.

■ TRACK 2:
An Overview of Acts in 9 Days
☐ Day 1. Read the Introduction to Acts and then Acts 1, which describes Jesus' last appearance to the disciples.
☐ Day 2. Read about the remarkable events of Pentecost in chapter 2.
☐ Day 3. Chapter 5 gives a glimpse of life in the early

Christian church — some good parts and also a tragic scene of failure.
☐ Day 4. Read Acts 9 to learn the details of Saul's conversion.
☐ Day 5. Chapter 16 tells of Paul's dramatic experiences in Philippi, a city that produced one of Paul's favourite churches.
☐ Day 6. Chapter 17 shows Paul on some of the most difficult assignments of his missionary journeys.
☐ Day 7. Read chapter 26, Paul's recounting of his personal story to a king.
☐ Day 8. Read chapter 27, which tells of Paul's shipwreck on the way to Rome.
☐ Day 9. Read chapter 28,

which describes Paul's last setting, under house arrest in Rome, where he probably wrote some of his New Testament letters.
Now turn to page xi for your next Track 2 reading project.

■ TRACK 3:
All of Acts in 28 Days
After you have read through Acts, turn to pages xii–xiii for your next Track 3 reading project.

☐ 1	☐ 2	☐ 3	☐ 4
☐ 5	☐ 6	☐ 7	☐ 8
☐ 9	☐ 10	☐ 11	☐ 12
☐ 13	☐ 14	☐ 15	☐ 16
☐ 17	☐ 18	☐ 19	☐ 20
☐ 21	☐ 22	☐ 23	☐ 24
☐ 25	☐ 26	☐ 27	☐ 28

■ Jesus Taken Up Into Heaven

1 In my former book, Theophilus, I wrote about all that Jesus began to do and to teach ²until the day he was taken up to heaven, after giving instructions through the Holy Spirit to the apostles he had chosen. ³After his suffering, he showed himself to these men and gave many convincing proofs that he was alive. He appeared to them over a period of forty days and spoke about the kingdom of God. ⁴On one occasion, while he was eating with them, he gave them this command: "Do not leave Jerusalem, but wait for the gift my Father promised, which you have heard me speak about. ⁵For John baptised with*a* water, but in a few days you will be baptised with the Holy Spirit."

⁶So when they met together, they asked him, "Lord, are you at this time going to restore the kingdom to Israel?"

⁷He said to them: "It is not for you to know the times or dates the Father has set by his own authority. ⁸But you will receive power when the Holy Spirit comes on you; and you will be my witnesses in Jerusalem, and in all Judea and Samaria, and to the ends of the earth."

⁹After he said this, he was taken up before their very eyes, and a cloud hid him from their sight.

¹⁰They were looking intently up into the sky as he was going, when suddenly two men dressed in white stood beside them. ¹¹"Men of Galilee," they said, "why do you stand here looking into the sky? This same Jesus, who has been taken from you into heaven, will come back in the same way you have seen him go into heaven."

■ Matthias Chosen to Replace Judas

¹²Then they returned to Jerusalem from the hill called the Mount of Olives, a Sabbath day's walk*b* from the city. ¹³When they arrived, they went upstairs to the room where they were staying. Those present were Peter, John, James and Andrew; Philip and Thomas, Bartholomew and Matthew; James son of Alphaeus and Simon the Zealot, and Judas son of James. ¹⁴They all joined together constantly in prayer, along with the women and Mary the mother of Jesus, and with his brothers.

¹⁵In those days Peter stood up among the believers*c* (a group numbering about a hundred and twenty) ¹⁶and said, "Brothers, the Scripture had to be fulfilled which the Holy Spirit spoke long ago through the mouth of David concerning Judas, who served as guide for those who arrested Jesus — ¹⁷he was one of our number and shared in this ministry."

¹⁸(With the reward he got for his wickedness, Judas bought a field; there he fell headlong, his body burst open and all his intestines spilled out. ¹⁹Everyone in Jerusalem heard about this, so they called

a 5 Or in   *b 12 That is, about ¾ of a mile (about 1,100 metres)*   *c 15 Greek brothers* that field in their language Akeldama, that is, Field of Blood.)

²⁰"For," said Peter, "it is written in the Book of Psalms,

" 'May his place be deserted;
let there be no-one to dwell in it,'ᵈ

and,

" 'May another take his place of leadership.'ᵉ

²¹Therefore it is necessary to choose one of the men who have been with us the whole time the Lord Jesus went in and out among us, ²²beginning from John's baptism to the time when Jesus was taken up from us. For one of these must become a witness with us of his resurrection."

1:21 ■ INNER CIRCLE
The group of Jesus' closest disciples known as the Twelve became "the Eleven" after Judas' death. In choosing a replacement for the betrayer, the disciples favoured an old-timer who had been with Jesus from the very beginning. Evidently several people qualified, and the group cast lots between two to make the final choice. This is the Bible's last mention of casting lots, a method used in the Old Testament to discern God's will; after Pentecost the disciples relied directly on the Holy Spirit for guidance.

²³So they proposed two men: Joseph called Barsabbas (also known as Justus) and Matthias. ²⁴Then they prayed, "Lord, you know everyone's heart. Show us which of these two you have chosen ²⁵to take over this apostolic ministry, which Judas left to go where he belongs." ²⁶Then they cast lots, and the lot fell to Matthias; so he was added to the eleven apostles.

■ The Holy Spirit Comes at Pentecost

2 When the day of Pentecost came, they were all together in one place. ²Suddenly a sound like the blowing of a violent wind came from heaven and filled the whole house where they were sitting. ³They saw what seemed to be tongues of fire that separated and came to rest on each of them. ⁴All of them were filled with the Holy Spirit and began to speak in other tonguesᵃ as the Spirit enabled them.

⁵Now there were staying in Jerusalem God-fearing Jews from every nation under heaven. ⁶When they heard this sound, a crowd came together in bewilderment, because each one heard them speaking in his own language. ⁷Utterly amazed, they asked: "Are not all these men who are speaking Galileans? ⁸Then how is it that each of us hears them in his own native language? ⁹Parthians, Medes and Elamites; residents of Mesopotamia, Judea and Cappadocia, Pontus and Asia, ¹⁰Phrygia and Pamphylia, Egypt and the parts of Libya near Cyrene; visitors from Rome ¹¹(both Jews and converts to Judaism); Cretans and Arabs—we hear them declaring the wonders of God in our own tongues!"

¹²Amazed and perplexed, they asked one another, "What does this mean?"

¹³Some, however, made fun of them and said, "They have had too much wine."ᵇ

■ Peter Addresses the Crowd

¹⁴Then Peter stood up with the Eleven, raised his voice and addressed the crowd: "Fellow Jews and all of you who live in Jerusalem, let me explain this to you; listen carefully to what I say. ¹⁵These men are not drunk, as you suppose. It's only nine in the morning! ¹⁶No, this is what was spoken by the prophet Joel:

¹⁷" 'In the last days, God says,
I will pour out my Spirit on all people.
Your sons and daughters will prophesy,
your young men will see visions,
your old men will dream dreams.
¹⁸Even on my servants, both men and women,
I will pour out my Spirit in those days,
and they will prophesy.
¹⁹I will show wonders in the heaven above
and signs on the earth below,
blood and fire and billows of smoke.
²⁰The sun will be turned to darkness
and the moon to blood
before the coming of the great and glorious
day of the Lord.
²¹And everyone who calls
on the name of the Lord will be saved.'ᶜ

²²"Men of Israel, listen to this: Jesus of Nazareth was a man accredited by God to you by miracles, wonders and signs, which God did among you through him, as you yourselves know. ²³This man was handed over to you by God's set purpose and foreknowledge; and you, with the help of wicked men,ᵈ put him to death by nailing him to the cross. ²⁴But God raised him from the dead, freeing him from the agony of death, because it was impossible for death to keep its hold on him. ²⁵David said about him:

" 'I saw the Lord always before me.
Because he is at my right hand,
I will not be shaken.
²⁶Therefore my heart is glad and my tongue
rejoices;
my body also will live in hope,
²⁷because you will not abandon me to the grave,
nor will you let your Holy One see decay.
²⁸You have made known to me the paths of life;
you will fill me with joy in your presence.'ᵉ

²⁹"Brothers, I can tell you confidently that the patriarch David died and was buried, and his tomb is here to this day. ³⁰But he was a prophet and knew that God had promised him on oath that he would place one of his descendants on his throne. ³¹Seeing what was ahead, he spoke of the resurrection of the Christ,ᶠ that he was not abandoned to the grave, nor did his body see decay. ³²God has raised this Jesus to life, and we are all witnesses of the fact. ³³Exalted to the right hand of God, he has received from the Father the promised Holy Spirit and has

ᵈ20 Psalm 69:25   ᵉ20 Psalm 109:8   ᵃ4 Or languages; also in verse 11   ᵇ13 Or sweet wine   ᶜ21 Joel 2:28–32   ᵈ23 Or of those not having the law (that is, Gentiles)   ᵉ28 Psalm 16:8–11   ᶠ31 Or Messiah. "The Christ" (Greek) and "the Messiah" (Hebrew) both mean "the Anointed One"; also in verse 36.

poured out what you now see and hear. ³⁴For David did not ascend to heaven, and yet he said,

" 'The Lord said to my Lord:
    "Sit at my right hand
³⁵until I make your enemies
    a footstool for your feet." ' ᵍ

³⁶"Therefore let all Israel be assured of this: God has made this Jesus, whom you crucified, both Lord and Christ."

³⁷When the people heard this, they were cut to the heart and said to Peter and the other apostles, "Brothers, what shall we do?"

³⁸Peter replied, "Repent and be baptised, every one of you, in the name of Jesus Christ for the forgiveness of your sins. And you will receive the gift of the Holy Spirit. ³⁹The promise is for you and your children and for all who are far off—for all whom the Lord our God will call."

⁴⁰With many other words he warned them; and he pleaded with them, "Save yourselves from this corrupt generation." ⁴¹Those who accepted his message were baptised, and about three thousand were added to their number that day.

■ The Fellowship of the Believers

⁴²They devoted themselves to the apostles' teaching and to the fellowship, to the breaking of bread and to prayer. ⁴³Everyone was filled with awe, and many wonders and miraculous signs were done by the apostles. ⁴⁴All the believers were together and had everything in common. ⁴⁵Selling their possessions and goods, they gave to anyone as he had need. ⁴⁶Every day they continued to meet together in the temple courts. They broke bread in their homes and ate together with glad and sincere hearts, ⁴⁷praising God and enjoying the favour of all the people. And the Lord added to their number daily those who were being saved.

2:42 ■ INFANT CHURCH

Acts records a series of stages through which the Christian church became a separate movement. At this point, the followers of Jesus were still keeping the pattern of traditional Jewish worship: prayers in the temple at 9 a.m., 3 p.m., and sunset (3:1). Yet this paragraph shows them also developing a new form of "house churches" based on communal sharing and fellowship.

■ Peter Heals the Crippled Beggar

3 One day Peter and John were going up to the temple at the time of prayer—at three in the afternoon. ²Now a man crippled from birth was being carried to the temple gate called Beautiful, where he was put every day to beg from those going into the temple courts. ³When he saw Peter and John about to enter, he asked them for money. ⁴Peter looked straight at him, as did John. Then Peter said, "Look at us!" ⁵So the man gave them his attention, expecting to get something from them.

⁶Then Peter said, "Silver or gold I do not have, but what I have I give you. In the name of Jesus

Christ of Nazareth, walk." ⁷Taking him by the right hand, he helped him up, and instantly the man's feet and ankles became strong. ⁸He jumped to his feet and began to walk. Then he went with them into the temple courts, walking and jumping, and praising God. ⁹When all the people saw him walking and praising God, ¹⁰they recognised him as the same man who used to sit begging at the temple gate called Beautiful, and they were filled with wonder and amazement at what had happened to him.

■ Peter Speaks to the Onlookers

¹¹While the beggar held on to Peter and John, all the people were astonished and came running to them in the place called Solomon's Colonnade. ¹²When Peter saw this, he said to them: "Men of Israel, why does this surprise you? Why do you stare at us as if by our own power or godliness we had made this man walk? ¹³The God of Abraham, Isaac and Jacob, the God of our fathers, has glorified his servant Jesus. You handed him over to be killed, and you disowned him before Pilate, though he had decided to let him go. ¹⁴You disowned the Holy and Righteous One and asked that a murderer be released to you. ¹⁵You killed the author of life, but God raised him from the dead. We are witnesses of this. ¹⁶By faith in the name of Jesus, this man whom you see and know was made strong. It is Jesus' name and the faith that comes through him that has given this complete healing to him, as you can all see.

3:12 ■ KNOWING THE AUDIENCE

Peter's speeches in chapters 2 and 3 offer excellent examples of adapting the gospel message to a particular audience. Preaching to Jews gathered in Jerusalem to celebrate Pentecost, he relied heavily on quotations from the Old Testament. Although his main intent was to tell them about Jesus, he referred to Joel, David, Abraham, Isaac, Jacob, Moses, and Samuel. His words proved so effective that 3,000 people were converted the first day. Jewish leaders soon arrested Peter and John.

¹⁷"Now, brothers, I know that you acted in ignorance, as did your leaders. ¹⁸But this is how God fulfilled what he had foretold through all the prophets, saying that his Christᵃ would suffer. ¹⁹Repent, then, and turn to God, so that your sins may be wiped out, that times of refreshing may come from the Lord, ²⁰and that he may send the Christ, who has been appointed for you—even Jesus. ²¹He must remain in heaven until the time comes for God to restore everything, as he promised long ago through his holy prophets. ²²For Moses said, 'The Lord your God will raise up for you a prophet like me from among your own people; you must listen to everything he tells you. ²³Anyone who does not listen to him will be completely cut off from among his people.'ᵇ

²⁴"Indeed, all the prophets from Samuel on, as many as have spoken, have foretold these days. ²⁵And you are heirs of the prophets and of the

ᵍ 35 Psalm 110:1   ᵃ 18 Or Messiah; also in verse 20   ᵇ 23 Deut. 18:15,18,19 covenant God made with your fathers. He said to Abraham, 'Through your offspring all peoples on earth will be blessed.'[c] 26When God raised up his servant, he sent him first to you to bless you by turning each of you from your wicked ways."

■ Peter and John Before the Sanhedrin

4 The priests and the captain of the temple guard and the Sadducees came up to Peter and John while they were speaking to the people. 2They were greatly disturbed because the apostles were teaching the people and proclaiming in Jesus the resurrection of the dead. 3They seized Peter and John, and because it was evening, they put them in jail until the next day. 4But many who heard the message believed, and the number of men grew to about five thousand.

5The next day the rulers, elders and teachers of the law met in Jerusalem. 6Annas the high priest was there, and so were Caiaphas, John, Alexander and the other men of the high priest's family. 7They had Peter and John brought before them and began to question them: "By what power or what name did you do this?"

8Then Peter, filled with the Holy Spirit, said to them: "Rulers and elders of the people! 9If we are being called to account today for an act of kindness shown to a cripple and are asked how he was healed, 10then know this, you and all the people of Israel: It is by the name of Jesus Christ of Nazareth, whom you crucified but whom God raised from the dead, that this man stands before you healed. 11He is

■ MORE THAN A GHOST
THE BEST PROOF THAT JESUS IS ALIVE

INSIGHT

"YOU KILLED THE AUTHOR OF LIFE, BUT GOD RAISED HIM FROM THE DEAD. WE ARE WITNESSES OF THIS." ■ 3:15

"He looks as if he's seen a ghost!" What image comes to mind when you hear that? A face drained of blood, a trembling jaw, pasty skin and thin lips, a look of terror.

Seeing a ghost doesn't make a person stronger and more confident. The witness is usually reluctant to talk about the experience. Self-doubt attacks in waves: *Was it real? Maybe I was hallucinating . . . it was so dark and eerie.*

■ A CONVINCING CHANGE
When Jesus showed up after his death, his disciples went through a did-we-see-a-ghost? phase, complete with terror, disbelief and wild rumours. But it didn't last long. In 40 days Jesus made enough undeniable appearances to convince each of his disciples — even sceptical Thomas — that he had indeed overthrown death.

As Acts shows, the disciples began acting the opposite of people who think they've seen a ghost. Rather, they acted like people who had just witnessed the most astounding event in all history. They couldn't wait to tell the world about it.

Exuberance, not fear, lit up the disciples' faces. In the streets of Jerusalem and in the temple, to anyone who would listen, they cried out the news that couldn't be true, but was. "Jesus is alive! The man who died has come back — he's the Messiah we've been waiting for!"

If you're ever tempted to doubt Jesus' resurrection, take a sober look at his changed followers in Acts. Consider Peter, for instance. He had cowered in the shadows at the trial scene, trying to look inconspicuous. Out of fear of arrest, he had even cursed and denied knowing Jesus. Could this be the same man, standing before the most distinguished religious leaders in the land, blasting them as murderers (chapter 3)? Something ignited Peter that would not easily be snuffed out.

■ RESPONSE TO A NEW MESSAGE
When Jesus was on earth he mostly preached "the kingdom", sometimes even warning his followers not to mention that he was the Messiah. In Acts, the word is out. Jesus is the theme of every speech, whether delivered in the temple square or in the luxurious setting of a royal palace, to working-class pagans or cultured Greek philosophers. Reports of his resurrection resound throughout Acts.

To those who heard, the message sounded like the first note of music to people born deaf. Five thousand men believed (4:4), as did many priests (6:7) and many thousands of Jews (21:20). The scanty band of followers Jesus had left behind was soon organising and electing officers to handle the needs of a growing church.

Acts follows the core of leaders from place to place, as a remarkable drama unfolds. A few men, mostly unlearned, were setting into motion a world-wide outreach that would ultimately reshape civilisation. A revolution was underway, but not one with weapons. This one was powered by the work of God in simple men who had seen a miracle. As Peter said, "We cannot help speaking about what we have seen and heard" (4:20).

□ LIFE QUESTIONS:
The disciples led mass conversions to Christ. What made them such effective spokesmen?

[c]25 Gen. 22:18; 26:4

" 'the stone you builders rejected,
which has become the capstone.'*a, b*

4:1 ■ ALARMED SADDUCEES

The coalition arrayed against the disciples resembled the group that had arrested Jesus in Gethsemane. The priests were working hand in hand with Roman rulers, who allowed them to maintain a police force (or "temple guard") to keep order in the temple. Reports of Jesus' resurrection from the dead especially alarmed the Sadducees, a party of priests who denied there would ever be a resurrection from the dead (see also 5:17 and 23:6–8).

12Salvation is found in no-one else, for there is no other name under heaven given to men by which we must be saved."

13When they saw the courage of Peter and John and realised that they were unschooled, ordinary men, they were astonished and they took note that these men had been with Jesus. 14But since they could see the man who had been healed standing there with them, there was nothing they could say. 15So they ordered them to withdraw from the Sanhedrin and then conferred together. 16"What are we going to do with these men?" they asked. "Everybody living in Jerusalem knows they have done an outstanding miracle, and we cannot deny it. 17But to stop this thing from spreading any further among the people, we must warn these men to speak no longer to anyone in this name."

18Then they called them in again and commanded them not to speak or teach at all in the name of Jesus. 19But Peter and John replied, "Judge for yourselves whether it is right in God's sight to obey you rather than God. 20For we cannot help speaking about what we have seen and heard."

21After further threats they let them go. They could not decide how to punish them, because all the people were praising God for what had happened. 22For the man who was miraculously healed was over forty years old.

■ The Believers' Prayer

23On their release, Peter and John went back to their own people and reported all that the chief priests and elders had said to them. 24When they heard this, they raised their voices together in prayer to God. "Sovereign Lord," they said, "you made the heaven and the earth and the sea, and everything in them. 25You spoke by the Holy Spirit through the mouth of your servant, our father David:

" 'Why do the nations rage
and the peoples plot in vain?
26The kings of the earth take their stand
and the rulers gather together
against the Lord
and against his Anointed One.'*c, d*

27Indeed Herod and Pontius Pilate met together with the Gentiles and the people*e* of Israel in this city to conspire against your holy servant Jesus, whom you anointed. 28They did what your power and will had decided beforehand should happen. 29Now, Lord, consider their threats and enable your servants to speak your word with great boldness. 30Stretch out your hand to heal and perform miraculous signs and wonders through the name of your holy servant Jesus."

31After they prayed, the place where they were meeting was shaken. And they were all filled with the Holy Spirit and spoke the word of God boldly.

■ The Believers Share Their Possessions

32All the believers were one in heart and mind. No-one claimed that any of his possessions was his own, but they shared everything they had. 33With great power the apostles continued to testify to the resurrection of the Lord Jesus, and much grace was upon them all. 34There were no needy persons among them. For from time to time those who owned lands or houses sold them, brought the money from the sales 35and put it at the apostles' feet, and it was distributed to anyone as he had need.

36Joseph, a Levite from Cyprus, whom the apostles called Barnabas (which means Son of Encouragement), 37sold a field he owned and brought the money and put it at the apostles' feet.

■ Ananias and Sapphira

5 Now a man named Ananias, together with his wife Sapphira, also sold a piece of property. 2With his wife's full knowledge he kept back part of the money for himself, but brought the rest and put it at the apostles' feet.

3Then Peter said, "Ananias, how is it that Satan has so filled your heart that you have lied to the Holy Spirit and have kept for yourself some of the money you received for the land? 4Didn't it belong to you before it was sold? And after it was sold, wasn't the money at your disposal? What made you think of doing such a thing? You have not lied to men but to God."

5:4 ■ DEADLY DECEIT

As Peter makes clear, Ananias and Sapphira were punished not for holding back money but for lying about it. They were misrepresenting themselves spiritually, trying to appear especially pious and generous. At the very beginning of the church (the word first appears in Acts in verse 11), God set a stern standard of absolute honesty and integrity.

5When Ananias heard this, he fell down and died. And great fear seized all who heard what had happened. 6Then the young men came forward, wrapped up his body, and carried him out and buried him.

7About three hours later his wife came in, not knowing what had happened. 8Peter asked her, "Tell me, is this the price you and Ananias got for the land?"

"Yes," she said, "that is the price."

⁹Peter said to her, "How could you agree to test the Spirit of the Lord? Look! The feet of the men who buried your husband are at the door, and they will carry you out also."

¹⁰At that moment she fell down at his feet and died. Then the young men came in and, finding her dead, carried her out and buried her beside her husband. ¹¹Great fear seized the whole church and all who heard about these events.

■ The Apostles Heal Many

¹²The apostles performed many miraculous signs and wonders among the people. And all the believers used to meet together in Solomon's Colonnade. ¹³No-one else dared join them, even though they were highly regarded by the people. ¹⁴Nevertheless, more and more men and women believed in the Lord and were added to their number. ¹⁵As a result, people brought the sick into the streets and laid them on beds and mats so that at least Peter's shadow might fall on some of them as he passed by. ¹⁶Crowds gathered also from the towns around Jerusalem, bringing their sick and those tormented by evilᵃ spirits, and all of them were healed.

■ The Apostles Persecuted

¹⁷Then the high priest and all his associates, who were members of the party of the Sadducees, were filled with jealousy. ¹⁸They arrested the apostles and put them in the public jail. ¹⁹But during the night an angel of the Lord opened the doors of the jail and brought them out. ²⁰"Go, stand in the temple courts," he said, "and tell the people the full message of this new life."

²¹At daybreak they entered the temple courts, as they had been told, and began to teach the people.

When the high priest and his associates arrived, they called together the Sanhedrin—the full assembly of the elders of Israel—and sent to the jail for the apostles. ²²But on arriving at the jail, the officers did not find them there. So they went back and reported, ²³"We found the jail securely locked, with the guards standing at the doors; but when we opened them, we found no-one inside." ²⁴On hearing this report, the captain of the temple guard and the chief priests were puzzled, wondering what would come of this.

²⁵Then someone came and said, "Look! The men you put in jail are standing in the temple courts teaching the people." ²⁶At that, the captain went with his officers and brought the apostles. They did not use force, because they feared that the people would stone them.

²⁷Having brought the apostles, they made them appear before the Sanhedrin to be questioned by the high priest. ²⁸"We gave you strict orders not to teach in this name," he said. "Yet you have filled Jerusalem with your teaching and are determined to make us guilty of this man's blood."

²⁹Peter and the other apostles replied: "We must obey God rather than men! ³⁰The God of our fathers raised Jesus from the dead—whom you had killed by hanging him on a tree. ³¹God exalted him to his own right hand as Prince and Saviour that he might give repentance and forgiveness of sins to Israel.

³²We are witnesses of these things, and so is the Holy Spirit, whom God has given to those who obey him."

³³When they heard this, they were furious and wanted to put them to death. ³⁴But a Pharisee named Gamaliel, a teacher of the law, who was honoured by all the people, stood up in the Sanhedrin and ordered that the men be put outside for a little while. ³⁵Then he addressed them: "Men of Israel, consider carefully what you intend to do to these men. ³⁶Some time ago Theudas appeared, claiming to be somebody, and about four hundred men rallied to him. He was killed, all his followers were dispersed, and it all came to nothing. ³⁷After him, Judas the Galilean appeared in the days of the census and led a band of people in revolt. He too was killed, and all his followers were scattered. ³⁸Therefore, in the present case I advise you: Leave these men alone! Let them go! For if their purpose or activity is of human origin, it will fail. ³⁹But if it is from God, you will not be able to stop these men; you will only find yourselves fighting against God."

5:34 ■ ANCIENT TERRORISM

Terrorist acts have had a long history in the Middle East, as Gamaliel's speech shows. During the years surrounding Jesus' life, several revolutionaries had led armed uprisings, two of whom Gamaliel refers to here. Several decades later, the apostle Paul was mistaken for an Egyptian who had staged a terrorist revolt in the desert (21:38).

Gamaliel, who urged a cautious approach on the issue, was a revered and wise rabbi in his day. He followed the progressive branch of Judaism that originated with the rabbi Hillel, and Saul (who became the apostle Paul) was one of his pupils (22:3).

⁴⁰His speech persuaded them. They called the apostles in and had them flogged. Then they ordered them not to speak in the name of Jesus, and let them go.

⁴¹The apostles left the Sanhedrin, rejoicing because they had been counted worthy of suffering disgrace for the Name. ⁴²Day after day, in the temple courts and from house to house, they never stopped teaching and proclaiming the good news that Jesus is the Christ.ᵇ

■ The Choosing of the Seven

6 In those days when the number of disciples was increasing, the Grecian Jews among them complained against the Hebraic Jews because their widows were being overlooked in the daily distribution of food. ²So the Twelve gathered all the disciples together and said, "It would not be right for us to neglect the ministry of the word of God in order to wait on tables. ³Brothers, choose seven men from among you who are known to be full of the Spirit and wisdom. We will turn this responsibility over to them ⁴and will give our attention to prayer and the ministry of the word."

ᵃ 16 Greek unclean   ᵇ 42 Or Messiah

⁵This proposal pleased the whole group. They chose Stephen, a man full of faith and of the Holy Spirit; also Philip, Procorus, Nicanor, Timon, Parmenas, and Nicolas from Antioch, a convert to Judaism. ⁶They presented these men to the apostles, who prayed and laid their hands on them.

6:5 ■ A CURE FOR DISCRIMINATION

From the start, the church ran into complaints from a neglected minority, the Grecian Jews, or Hellenists. This branch of Jews retained many Greek customs and chose to speak Greek rather than Hebrew. The disciples' response in creating a new church office shows considerable diplomacy. The names of the seven appointees indicate they were all Grecian Jews. In other words, the disciples entrusted the minority with full authority to solve their own problems. The first Christian martyr, Stephen, came out of that group of seven.

⁷So the word of God spread. The number of disciples in Jerusalem increased rapidly, and a large number of priests became obedient to the faith.

■ Stephen Seized

⁸Now Stephen, a man full of God's grace and power, did great wonders and miraculous signs among the people. ⁹Opposition arose, however, from members of the Synagogue of the Freedmen (as it was called)—Jews of Cyrene and Alexandria as well as the provinces of Cilicia and Asia. These men began to argue with Stephen, ¹⁰but they could not stand up against his wisdom or the Spirit by whom he spoke.

¹¹Then they secretly persuaded some men to say, "We have heard Stephen speak words of blasphemy against Moses and against God."

¹²So they stirred up the people and the elders and the teachers of the law. They seized Stephen and brought him before the Sanhedrin. ¹³They produced false witnesses, who testified, "This fellow never stops speaking against this holy place and against the law. ¹⁴For we have heard him say that this Jesus of Nazareth will destroy this place and change the customs Moses handed down to us."

¹⁵All who were sitting in the Sanhedrin looked intently at Stephen, and they saw that his face was like the face of an angel.

■ THE SECRET BEHIND THE EARLY CHURCH
THE REAL POWER AT WORK IN ACTS

"LEAVE THESE MEN ALONE! LET THEM GO! FOR IF THEIR PURPOSE OR ACTIVITY IS OF HUMAN ORIGIN, IT WILL FAIL. BUT IF IT IS FROM GOD, YOU WILL NOT BE ABLE TO STOP THESE MEN; YOU WILL ONLY FIND YOURSELVES FIGHTING AGAINST GOD." ■ 5:38–39

Author J.B. Phillips, after spending 14 years translating the New Testament, sat back and reflected on his most lasting impressions. He kept returning to the book of Acts and its portrait of an infant church. "The sick are not merely prayed about," said Phillips, "they are healed, often suddenly and dramatically. . . . Human nature is changed. The fresh air of Heaven blows gustily through these pages.

"The early church lived dangerously, but never before has such a handful of people exerted such widespread influence. . . . To put it shortly, the lasting excitement which follows the reading of the book is this: *the thing works!*"

■ WHO WAS BEHIND THE SUCCESS?
Why did it work? Acts points decisively to the power of God, through his Holy Spirit. Luke carefully notes that every major decision of the young church was made under the Spirit's guidance. Indeed, some have suggested Acts should really be titled *Acts of the Holy Spirit* because of his dominant role. Luke mentions the Holy Spirit 57 times in Acts.

The disciples waited for the Spirit in Jerusalem before beginning to preach (2:4). According to Luke, the Holy Spirit fell on each new group of believers: on Jews (4:31), then on Samaritans (8:17), then Gentiles (10:44), and finally John the Baptist's disciples (19:6).

■ FOR THEIR GOOD
As the church grew, the disciples gradually began to understand what Jesus had meant when he said, "It is for your good that I am going away. Unless I go away, the Counsellor will not come to you; but if I go, I will send him to you" (John 16:7). Although Jesus himself departed, God became present in each one of them, making his activity in the world more widespread than ever before.

The Spirit personally directed each major advance of the church. He sent Philip into the desert to meet an Ethiopian (8:29), set apart missionaries in Antioch (13:2), guided the first big church council (15:1–28), and helped plan Paul's itinerary (13:4; 16:6). As presented in Acts, the Spirit was no vague mist but a living person, who spoke, guided in decisions and fuelled the church with the energy of faith.

□ LIFE QUESTIONS:
How is the Holy Spirit active in your life?

■ **Stephen's Speech to the Sanhedrin**

7 Then the high priest asked him, "Are these charges true?"

[2]To this he replied: "Brothers and fathers, listen to me! The God of glory appeared to our father Abraham while he was still in Mesopotamia, before he lived in Haran. [3]'Leave your country and your people,' God said, 'and go to the land I will show you.'[a]

[4]"So he left the land of the Chaldeans and settled in Haran. After the death of his father, God sent him to this land where you are now living. [5]He gave him no inheritance here, not even a foot of ground. But God promised him that he and his descendants after him would possess the land, even though at that time Abraham had no child. [6]God spoke to him in this way: 'Your descendants will be strangers in a country not their own, and they will be enslaved and ill-treated for four hundred years. [7]But I will punish the nation they serve as slaves,' God said, 'and afterwards they will come out of that country and worship me in this place.'[b] [8]Then he gave Abraham the covenant of circumcision. And Abraham became the father of Isaac and circumcised him eight days after his birth. Later Isaac became the father of Jacob, and Jacob became the father of the twelve patriarchs.

[9]"Because the patriarchs were jealous of Joseph, they sold him as a slave into Egypt. But God was with him [10]and rescued him from all his troubles. He gave Joseph wisdom and enabled him to gain the goodwill of Pharaoh king of Egypt; so he made him ruler over Egypt and all his palace.

[11]"Then a famine struck all Egypt and Canaan, bringing great suffering, and our fathers could not find food. [12]When Jacob heard that there was grain in Egypt, he sent our fathers on their first visit. [13]On their second visit, Joseph told his brothers who he was, and Pharaoh learned about Joseph's family. [14]After this, Joseph sent for his father Jacob and his whole family, seventy-five in all. [15]Then Jacob went down to Egypt, where he and our fathers died. [16]Their bodies were brought back to Shechem and placed in the tomb that Abraham had bought from the sons of Hamor at Shechem for a certain sum of money.

[17]"As the time drew near for God to fulfil his promise to Abraham, the number of our people in Egypt greatly increased. [18]Then another king, who knew nothing about Joseph, became ruler of Egypt. [19]He dealt treacherously with our people and oppressed our forefathers by forcing them to throw out their newborn babies so that they would die.

[20]"At that time Moses was born, and he was no ordinary child.[c] For three months he was cared for in his father's house. [21]When he was placed outside, Pharaoh's daughter took him and brought him up as her own son. [22]Moses was educated in all the wisdom of the Egyptians and was powerful in speech and action.

[23]"When Moses was forty years old, he decided to visit his fellow Israelites. [24]He saw one of them being ill-treated by an Egyptian, so he went to his defence and avenged him by killing the Egyptian. [25]Moses thought that his own people would realise that God was using him to rescue them, but they did not. [26]The next day Moses came upon two Israelites who were fighting. He tried to reconcile them by saying, 'Men, you are brothers; why do you want to hurt each other?'

[27]"But the man who was ill-treating the other pushed Moses aside and said, 'Who made you ruler and judge over us? [28]Do you want to kill me as you killed the Egyptian yesterday?'[d] [29]When Moses heard this, he fled to Midian, where he settled as a foreigner and had two sons.

[30]"After forty years had passed, an angel appeared to Moses in the flames of a burning bush in the desert near Mount Sinai. [31]When he saw this, he was amazed at the sight. As he went over to look more closely, he heard the Lord's voice: [32]'I am the God of your fathers, the God of Abraham, Isaac and Jacob.'[e] Moses trembled with fear and did not dare to look.

[33]"Then the Lord said to him, 'Take off your sandals; the place where you are standing is holy ground. [34]I have indeed seen the oppression of my people in Egypt. I have heard their groaning and have come down to set them free. Now come, I will send you back to Egypt.'[f]

[35]"This is the same Moses whom they had rejected with the words, 'Who made you ruler and judge?' He was sent to be their ruler and deliverer by God himself, through the angel who appeared to him in the bush. [36]He led them out of Egypt and did wonders and miraculous signs in Egypt, at the Red Sea[g] and for forty years in the desert.

7:35 ■ PROVOCATIVE WORDS

The early part of Stephen's speech must have pleased his Jewish audience. He was, in effect, giving a brief overview of history from the Jewish point of view, featuring such famous ancestors as Abraham, Joseph, Moses, and David. But then Stephen turned the tables, directly attacking the Jewish establishment.

He compared their treatment of Jesus with earlier Jewish rejection of God's messengers. He also called into question Jewish temple worship, claiming that "the Most High does not live in houses made by men" (verse 48). He ended the speech by calling them traitors and murderers. Stephen's death and the resulting persecution in Jerusalem scattered the disciples, helping to fulfil what Jesus had predicted just before leaving the earth (1:8).

---

[37]"This is that Moses who told the Israelites, 'God will send you a prophet like me from your own people.'[b] [38]He was in the assembly in the desert, with the angel who spoke to him on Mount Sinai, and with our fathers; and he received living words to pass on to us.

[39]"But our fathers refused to obey him. Instead, they rejected him and in their hearts turned back to Egypt. [40]They told Aaron, 'Make us gods who will go before us. As for this fellow Moses who led us out

of Egypt—we don't know what has happened to him!'[i] [41]That was the time they made an idol in the form of a calf. They brought sacrifices to it and held a celebration in honour of what their hands had made. [42]But God turned away and gave them over to the worship of the heavenly bodies. This agrees with what is written in the book of the prophets:

" 'Did you bring me sacrifices and offerings
    for forty years in the desert, O house of
    Israel?
[43]You have lifted up the shrine of Molech
    and the star of your god Rephan,
    the idols you made to worship.
Therefore I will send you into exile'[j] beyond
    Babylon.

[44]"Our forefathers had the tabernacle of the Testimony with them in the desert. It had been made as God directed Moses, according to the pattern he had seen. [45]Having received the tabernacle, our fathers under Joshua brought it with them when they took the land from the nations God drove out before them. It remained in the land until the time of David, [46]who enjoyed God's favour and asked that he might provide a dwelling-place for the God of Jacob.[k] [47]But it was Solomon who built the house for him.

[48]"However, the Most High does not live in houses made by men. As the prophet says:

[49]" 'Heaven is my throne,
    and the earth is my footstool.
What kind of house will you build for me?
                              says the Lord.
Or where will my resting place be?
[50]Has not my hand made all these things?'[l]

[51]"You stiff-necked people, with uncircumcised hearts and ears! You are just like your fathers: You always resist the Holy Spirit! [52]Was there ever a prophet your fathers did not persecute? They even killed those who predicted the coming of the Righteous One. And now you have betrayed and murdered him— [53]you who have received the law that was put into effect through angels but have not obeyed it."

■ The Stoning of Stephen
[54]When they heard this, they were furious and gnashed their teeth at him. [55]But Stephen, full of the Holy Spirit, looked up to heaven and saw the glory of God, and Jesus standing at the right hand of God. [56]"Look," he said, "I see heaven open and the Son of Man standing at the right hand of God."

[57]At this they covered their ears and, yelling at the top of their voices, they all rushed at him, [58]dragged him out of the city and began to stone him. Meanwhile, the witnesses laid their clothes at the feet of a young man named Saul. [59]While they were stoning him, Stephen prayed, "Lord Jesus, receive my spirit." [60]Then he fell on his knees and cried out, "Lord, do not hold this sin

against them." When he had said this, he fell asleep.

8 And Saul was there, giving approval to his death.

■ The Church Persecuted and Scattered
On that day a great persecution broke out against the church at Jerusalem, and all except the apostles were scattered throughout Judea and Samaria. [2]Godly men buried Stephen and mourned deeply for him. [3]But Saul began to destroy the church. Going from house to house, he dragged off men and women and put them in prison.

■ Philip in Samaria
[4]Those who had been scattered preached the word wherever they went. [5]Philip went down to a city in Samaria and proclaimed the Christ[a] there. [6]When the crowds heard Philip and saw the miraculous signs he did, they all paid close attention to what he said. [7]With shrieks, evil[b] spirits came out of many, and many paralytics and cripples were healed. [8]So there was great joy in that city.

8:5 ■ CROSSING RACIAL BARRIERS
Philip's visit to Samaria was quite remarkable in its day. Jewish people had little to do with the Samaritans, whom they looked down on for racial and religious reasons. Later, Philip met with an Ethiopian official on a mission that crossed racial barriers. The modern Christian church in Ethiopia claims an uninterrupted descent from the conversion described in chapter 8.

■ Simon the Sorcerer
[9]Now for some time a man named Simon had practised sorcery in the city and amazed all the people of Samaria. He boasted that he was someone great, [10]and all the people, both high and low, gave him their attention and exclaimed, "This man is the divine power known as the Great Power." [11]They followed him because he had amazed them for a long time with his magic. [12]But when they believed Philip as he preached the good news of the kingdom of God and the name of Jesus Christ, they were baptised, both men and women. [13]Simon himself believed and was baptised. And he followed Philip everywhere, astonished by the great signs and miracles he saw.

[14]When the apostles in Jerusalem heard that Samaria had accepted the word of God, they sent Peter and John to them. [15]When they arrived, they prayed for them that they might receive the Holy Spirit, [16]because the Holy Spirit had not yet come upon any of them; they had simply been baptised into[c] the name of the Lord Jesus. [17]Then Peter and John placed their hands on them, and they received the Holy Spirit.

[18]When Simon saw that the Spirit was given at the laying on of the apostles' hands, he offered them money [19]and said, "Give me also this ability so that everyone on whom I lay my hands may receive the Holy Spirit."

[20]Peter answered: "May your money perish with you, because you thought you could buy the gift of

[i]40 Exodus 32:1   [j]43 Amos 5:25–27   [k]46 Some early manuscripts the house of Jacob   [l]50 Isaiah 66:1,2   [a]5 Or Messiah   [b]7 Greek unclean   [c]16 Or in

God with money! [21]You have no part or share in this ministry, because your heart is not right before God. [22]Repent of this wickedness and pray to the Lord. Perhaps he will forgive you for having such a thought in your heart. [23]For I see that you are full of bitterness and captive to sin."

8:20 ■ GOSPEL GREED

The tendency to exploit spiritual power for material profit did not originate with the television age. Simon, a local magician, saw the gospel as a way to increase his own fame. The disciples had no more tolerance for his attitude than they had for the lies of Ananias and Sapphira (Acts 5).

[24]Then Simon answered, "Pray to the Lord for me so that nothing you have said may happen to me."

[25]When they had testified and proclaimed the word of the Lord, Peter and John returned to Jerusalem, preaching the gospel in many Samaritan villages.

■ Philip and the Ethiopian

[26]Now an angel of the Lord said to Philip, "Go south to the road—the desert road—that goes down from Jerusalem to Gaza." [27]So he started out, and on his way he met an Ethiopian[d] eunuch, an important official in charge of all the treasury of Candace, queen of the Ethiopians. This man had gone to Jerusalem to worship, [28]and on his way home was sitting in his chariot reading the book of Isaiah the prophet. [29]The Spirit told Philip, "Go to that chariot and stay near it."

[30]Then Philip ran up to the chariot and heard the man reading Isaiah the prophet. "Do you understand what you are reading?" Philip asked.

[31]"How can I," he said, "unless someone explains it to me?" So he invited Philip to come up and sit with him.

■ THE DANGER IN BEING A CHRISTIAN
IT BEGAN AS A JEWISH SECT; FIERCE PERSECUTION ONLY HELPED IT SPREAD

ON THAT DAY A GREAT PERSECUTION BROKE OUT AGAINST THE CHURCH AT JERUSALEM, AND ALL EXCEPT THE APOSTLES WERE SCATTERED THROUGHOUT JUDEA AND SAMARIA.
■ 8:1

In some countries, a person who becomes a Christian forfeits a good education and job. And in a few countries, a person who converts risks his or her life. One church historian estimates more Christians have been martyred in this century than in all preceding centuries put together.

Yet, strangely, more often than not, intense persecution of Christians leads to a spurt of growth in the church. An ancient saying expresses this phenomenon, "The blood of martyrs is the seed of the church."

■ THE FIRST BIG ADVANCE

For a while, the new faith enjoyed popular favour. But very soon it involved grave risk. In the book of Acts, the persecution that produced the first Christian martyr, Stephen, ironically brought about the advance of Christianity outside its Jewish base. Forced out of stormy Jerusalem, the scattering Jewish Christians turned to other races and ethnic groups. Philip preached first to the despised Samaritans, and then crossed racial barriers by helping to convert an official from Ethiopia.

Acts documents a dramatic change in the faith. What had been viewed as an offshoot of the Jewish religion, a "sect of the Nazarenes", began to encompass people from other religions, races, and cultures. Before long, the centre of church activity moved from Jerusalem to the city of Antioch. There, people coined the word Christian, indicating how separate the new faith had become. Never again would it be considered "just a Jewish thing".

■ BREAKING THE JEWISH MOULD

As Luke tells it, the transition to other ethnic groups required some adjustments. Jewish disciples balked at letting go of their centuries-old traditions and allowing the church to be flooded with non-Jews.

Peter, one of the most loyal Jews, explained his dilemma this way, "Who was I to think that I could oppose God?" (11:17). A direct, unmistakable vision from God (10:9–23) overcame Peter's resistance to accepting non-Jews, and later a decisive church council settled on a policy towards them (15:1–21).

As the pages of Acts turn, whole provinces and cultures open up to the gospel. The faith that had been guarded by a small knot of intimates, all Jews who knew Jesus personally, broke out into a rough world of soldiers, sorcerers, merchants and antagonists from other religions. This process was not without its bloody and frightening moments.

□ LIFE QUESTIONS:

If severe persecution came to the church in your region today, what would happen to your faith?

---

d 27 That is, from the upper Nile region

³²The eunuch was reading this passage of Scripture:

"He was led like a sheep to the slaughter,
and as a lamb before the shearer is silent,
so he did not open his mouth.
³³In his humiliation he was deprived of justice.
Who can speak of his descendants?
For his life was taken from the earth."ᵉ

³⁴The eunuch asked Philip, "Tell me, please, who is the prophet talking about, himself or someone else?" ³⁵Then Philip began with that very passage of Scripture and told him the good news about Jesus.
³⁶As they travelled along the road, they came to some water and the eunuch said, "Look, here is water. Why shouldn't I be baptised?"ᶠ ³⁸And he gave orders to stop the chariot. Then both Philip and the eunuch went down into the water and Philip baptised him. ³⁹When they came up out of the water, the Spirit of the Lord suddenly took Philip away, and the eunuch did not see him again, but went on his way rejoicing. ⁴⁰Philip, however, appeared at Azotus and travelled about, preaching the gospel in all the towns until he reached Caesarea.

■ Saul's Conversion

9 Meanwhile, Saul was still breathing out murderous threats against the Lord's disciples. He went to the high priest ²and asked him for letters to the synagogues in Damascus, so that if he found any there who belonged to the Way, whether men or women, he might take them as prisoners to Jerusalem. ³As he neared Damascus on his journey, suddenly a light from heaven flashed around him. ⁴He fell to the ground and heard a voice say to him, "Saul, Saul, why do you persecute me?"

9:2 ■ NAMING THE NEW RELIGION
In the early days of the church, its believers were given a variety of labels. Here, they are called members of "the Way"; elsewhere, "the brothers" (9:30), "all the believers" (2:44), and "the Nazarene sect" (24:5). Luke reports (11:26) that in the city of Antioch they were first called "Christians", a name that stuck. Roman writers often used the word *Christian* in a derisive sense, reflecting the hostility that greeted the first believers.

⁵"Who are you, Lord?" Saul asked.
"I am Jesus, whom you are persecuting," he replied. ⁶"Now get up and go into the city, and you will be told what you must do."
⁷The men travelling with Saul stood there speechless; they heard the sound but did not see anyone. ⁸Saul got up from the ground, but when he opened his eyes he could see nothing. So they led him by the hand into Damascus. ⁹For three days he was blind, and did not eat or drink anything.
¹⁰In Damascus there was a disciple named Ananias. The Lord called to him in a vision, "Ananias!"
"Yes, Lord," he answered.
¹¹The Lord told him, "Go to the house of Judas on

Straight Street and ask for a man from Tarsus named Saul, for he is praying. ¹²In a vision he has seen a man named Ananias come and place his hands on him to restore his sight."
¹³"Lord," Ananias answered, "I have heard many reports about this man and all the harm he has done to your saints in Jerusalem. ¹⁴And he has come here with authority from the chief priests to arrest all who call on your name."
¹⁵But the Lord said to Ananias, "Go! This man is my chosen instrument to carry my name before the Gentiles and their kings and before the people of Israel. ¹⁶I will show him how much he must suffer for my name."
¹⁷Then Ananias went to the house and entered it. Placing his hands on Saul, he said, "Brother Saul, the Lord—Jesus, who appeared to you on the road as you were coming here—has sent me so that you may see again and be filled with the Holy Spirit." ¹⁸Immediately, something like scales fell from Saul's eyes, and he could see again. He got up and was baptised, ¹⁹and after taking some food, he regained his strength.

■ Saul in Damascus and Jerusalem
Saul spent several days with the disciples in Damascus. ²⁰At once he began to preach in the synagogues that Jesus is the Son of God. ²¹All those who heard him were astonished and asked, "Isn't he the man who caused havoc in Jerusalem among those who call on this name? And hasn't he come here to take them as prisoners to the chief priests?" ²²Yet Saul grew more and more powerful and baffled the Jews living in Damascus by proving that Jesus is the Christ.ᵃ

9:21 ■ ALTERED MISSION
Damascus, said to be the oldest continually occupied city in the world, is now capital of present-day Syria. Saul undertook the 150-mile journey from Jerusalem in order to persecute Christians there, but on the "Damascus Road" he had an encounter that changed his life for ever. In the end, Paul had to flee the Jewish zealots he had originally come to aid.
Although Luke does not mention it, some time during this period Paul withdrew to Arabia, where he had an extended time to think through his new faith and mission (Galatians 1:17).

²³After many days had gone by, the Jews conspired to kill him, ²⁴but Saul learned of their plan. Day and night they kept close watch on the city gates in order to kill him. ²⁵But his followers took him by night and lowered him in a basket through an opening in the wall.
²⁶When he came to Jerusalem, he tried to join the disciples, but they were all afraid of him, not believing that he really was a disciple. ²⁷But Barnabas took him and brought him to the apostles. He told them how Saul on his journey had seen the Lord and that the Lord had spoken to him, and how in Damascus he had preached fearlessly in the name of Jesus. ²⁸So

ᵉ33 Isaiah 53:7,8   ᶠ36 Some late manuscripts *baptised?*" ³⁷Philip said, "If you believe with all your heart, you may." The eunuch answered, "I believe that Jesus Christ is the Son of God."   ᵃ22 Or *Messiah*

RECURITING FROM THE OPPOSITION
A FORMER BOUNTY HUNTER BREAKS THROUGH TO THE GENTILES

ALL THOSE WHO HEARD HIM [SAUL] WERE ASTONISHED AND ASKED, "ISN'T HE THE MAN WHO RAISED HAVOC IN JERUSALEM AMONG THOSE WHO CALL ON THIS NAME?" ■ 9:21

With a touch of theatrics, the Indianapolis judge shook his head very slowly back and forth as his clerk read John Erwin's offences from a red record book. He had skipped school too many times to count. He had stolen petty items, like torch batteries, only to discard them. He had stolen bicycles, ridden them to the scrapyard, and destroyed them.

Most recently, twelve-year-old John had joined a gang of young toughs and threatened his foster parents with a .22 rifle. The judge leaned forward and announced, "Young man, I don't know how any one boy can be as mean as they say you are. But I'm convinced you'll never change. I'm going to send you to a Manual Labour Institute for correction, and I predict you'll spend most of your life in institutions."

■ VOLUNTARY LIFE IMPRISONMENT

Three decades later the judge's prophecy has been partially fulfilled: in all, John Erwin has spent over 25 years in a large, notorious institution – Chicago's Cook County jail. But not as an inmate. The judge was mostly wrong: John did change. Remarkably.

During a stint in the army, Erwin met a family who adopted him, determined to show him the same love they had shown their own children. The defences he had built up in a childhood of violence and sexual abuse slowly melted. He experienced God's love and forgiveness, and he became a new person.

As a free man determined to help set others free, he founded and led the PACE Institute, one of America's most successful prison rehabilitation programmes. Then he went on to join the staff of Charles Colson's Prison Fellowship.

When asked why he has been so effective in the failure-ridden field of prison work, Erwin replies, "Maybe it's because I've been behind bars, like these prisoners. Most of them came from miserable homes also, and were abused by their parents. I understand what makes life so hard for them – and my story gives them hope. I don't give up on people. If God can change me, he can change them too."

■ A COMPLETE TURNAROUND

Converts like John Erwin often make the best crusaders. Former alcoholics can convince others of drinking's dangers. Exiles from Communist countries, such as Alexander Solzhenitsyn, often become the most vehement anti-Communists. And when the book of Acts introduces the most effective Christian missionary of all time, he turns out to be a former bounty hunter of Christians.

How did a Jewish sect become the largest Gentile religion? How did an Asian faith become associated with European civilisation? The answers can be traced back to the remarkable career of Paul, apostle to the Gentiles.

Paul (formerly called Saul) made his first appearance in Acts (8:1), assisting at the brutal stoning of Stephen. Later, he led a gang of persecutors on a violent campaign against Christian believers. But then came a miraculous turnabout on the road to Damascus (9:1–19).

■ A COURAGEOUS CAREER

Acts is constructed like a drama that delays introducing the hero until the stage is finally set. Beginning in chapter 13, the spotlight in Acts moves from Peter to Paul and follows him throughout the rest of the book. Other Christians, knowing Paul's old reputation, were initially sceptical about his conversion. But he soon proved to be as fiery and intense in preaching Christ as he had been in working against him.

Paul spearheaded the campaign to grant Gentiles full acceptance without subjecting them to Jewish law. He had himself been liberated from bondage to confining laws, and he insisted on a life based on God's free forgiveness, not legalism.

During his journeys, Paul wrote half the New Testament books, and in them he laid the groundwork for much of Christian theology. All the while, he carried on a courageous career despite jailings, beatings and riots. He was perhaps the most thoroughly converted man who ever lived.

□ LIFE QUESTIONS:

Has your life changed quickly and dramatically, as Paul's did, or slowly and gradually?

Saul stayed with them and moved about freely in Jerusalem, speaking boldly in the name of the Lord. [29]He talked and debated with the Grecian Jews, but they tried to kill him. [30]When the brothers learned of this, they took him down to Caesarea and sent him off to Tarsus.

[31]Then the church throughout Judea, Galilee and Samaria enjoyed a time of peace. It was strengthened; and encouraged by the Holy Spirit, it grew in numbers, living in the fear of the Lord.

■ Aeneas and Dorcas

[32]As Peter travelled about the country, he went to visit the saints in Lydda. [33]There he found a man named Aeneas, a paralytic who had been bedridden for eight years. [34]"Aeneas," Peter said to him, "Jesus Christ heals you. Get up and tidy up your mat." Immediately Aeneas got up. [35]All those who lived in Lydda and Sharon saw him and turned to the Lord.

[36]In Joppa there was a disciple named Tabitha (which, when translated, is Dorcas[b]), who was always doing good and helping the poor. [37]About that time she became sick and died, and her body was washed and placed in an upstairs room. [38]Lydda was near Joppa; so when the disciples heard that Peter was in Lydda, they sent two men to him and urged him, "Please come at once!"

[39]Peter went with them, and when he arrived he was taken upstairs to the room. All the widows stood around him, crying and showing him the robes and other clothing that Dorcas had made while she was still with them.

[40]Peter sent them all out of the room; then he got down on his knees and prayed. Turning towards the dead woman, he said, "Tabitha, get up." She opened her eyes, and seeing Peter she sat up. [41]He took her by the hand and helped her to her feet. Then he called the believers and the widows and presented her to them alive. [42]This became known all over Joppa, and many people believed in the Lord. [43]Peter stayed in Joppa for some time with a tanner named Simon.

■ Cornelius Calls for Peter

10 At Caesarea there was a man named Cornelius, a centurion in what was known as the Italian Regiment. [2]He and all his family were devout and God-fearing; he gave generously to those in need and prayed to God regularly. [3]One day at about three in the afternoon he had a vision. He distinctly saw an angel of God, who came to him and said, "Cornelius!"

[4]Cornelius stared at him in fear. "What is it, Lord?" he asked.

The angel answered, "Your prayers and gifts to the poor have come up as a memorial offering before God. [5]Now send men to Joppa to bring back a man named Simon who is called Peter. [6]He is staying with Simon the tanner, whose house is by the sea."

[7]When the angel who spoke to him had gone, Cornelius called two of his servants and a devout soldier who was one of his attendants. [8]He told them everything that had happened and sent them to Joppa.

■ Peter's Vision

[9]About noon the following day as they were on their journey and approaching the city, Peter went up on the roof to pray. [10]He became hungry and wanted something to eat, and while the meal was being prepared, he fell into a trance. [11]He saw heaven opened and something like a large sheet being let down to earth by its four corners. [12]It contained all kinds of four-footed animals, as well as reptiles of the earth and birds of the air. [13]Then a voice told him, "Get up, Peter. Kill and eat."

> **10:9 ■ A SHIFT FROM PETER TO PAUL**
> The first part of Acts, especially chapters 9–12, concentrates on the life of Peter. He represented the conservative Jewish contingent, and Acts reports that God gave him direct revelation to understand his plan of outreach to the Gentiles. But a man named Saul had been converted, and beginning with chapter 13, Acts follows his story almost exclusively.

[14]"Surely not, Lord!" Peter replied. "I have never eaten anything impure or unclean."

[15]The voice spoke to him a second time, "Do not call anything impure that God has made clean."

[16]This happened three times, and immediately the sheet was taken back to heaven.

[17]While Peter was wondering about the meaning of the vision, the men sent by Cornelius found out where Simon's house was and stopped at the gate. [18]They called out, asking if Simon who was known as Peter was staying there.

[19]While Peter was still thinking about the vision, the Spirit said to him, "Simon, three[a] men are looking for you. [20]So get up and go downstairs. Do not hesitate to go with them, for I have sent them."

[21]Peter went down and said to the men, "I'm the one you're looking for. Why have you come?"

[22]The men replied, "We have come from Cornelius the centurion. He is a righteous and God-fearing man, who is respected by all the Jewish people. A holy angel told him to have you come to his house so that he could hear what you have to say." [23]Then Peter invited the men into the house to be his guests.

■ Peter at Cornelius' House

The next day Peter started out with them, and some of the brothers from Joppa went along. [24]The following day he arrived in Caesarea. Cornelius was expecting them and had called together his relatives and close friends. [25]As Peter entered the house, Cornelius met him and fell at his feet in reverence. [26]But Peter made him get up. "Stand up," he said, "I am only a man myself." [27]Talking with him, Peter went inside and found a large gathering of people. [28]He said to them: "You are well aware that it is against our law for a Jew to associate with a Gentile or visit him. But God has shown me that I should not call any man impure or unclean. [29]So when I was sent for, I came without

[b]36 Both Tabitha (Aramaic) and Dorcas (Greek) mean gazelle.   [a]19 One early manuscript two; other manuscripts do not have the number.

raising any objection. May I ask why you sent for me?"

30Cornelius answered: "Four days ago I was in my house praying at this hour, at three in the afternoon. Suddenly a man in shining clothes stood before me 31and said, 'Cornelius, God has heard your prayer and remembered your gifts to the poor. 32Send to Joppa for Simon who is called Peter. He is a guest in the home of Simon the tanner, who lives by the sea.' 33So I sent for you immediately, and it was good of you to come. Now we are all here in the presence of God to listen to everything the Lord has commanded you to tell us."

34Then Peter began to speak: "I now realise how true it is that God does not show favouritism 35but accepts men from every nation who fear him and do what is right. 36You know the message God sent to the people of Israel, telling the good news of peace through Jesus Christ, who is Lord of all. 37You know what has happened throughout Judea, beginning in Galilee after the baptism that John preached— 38how God anointed Jesus of Nazareth with the Holy Spirit and power, and how he went around doing good and healing all who were under the power of the devil, because God was with him.

39"We are witnesses of everything he did in the country of the Jews and in Jerusalem. They killed him by hanging him on a tree, 40but God raised him from the dead on the third day and caused him to be seen. 41He was not seen by all the people, but by witnesses whom God had already chosen—by us who ate and drank with him after he rose from the dead. 42He commanded us to preach to the people and to testify that he is the one whom God appointed as judge of the living and the dead. 43All the prophets testify about him that everyone who believes in him receives forgiveness of sins through his name."

44While Peter was still speaking these words, the Holy Spirit came on all who heard the message. 45The circumcised believers who had come with Peter were astonished that the gift of the Holy Spirit had been poured out even on the Gentiles. 46For they heard them speaking in tongues*b* and praising God.

Then Peter said, 47"Can anyone keep these people from being baptised with water? They have received the Holy Spirit just as we have." 48So he ordered that they be baptised in the name of Jesus Christ. Then they asked Peter to stay with them for a few days.

■ Peter Explains His Actions

11 The apostles and the brothers throughout Judea heard that the Gentiles also had received the word of God. 2So when Peter went up to Jerusalem, the circumcised believers criticised him 3and said, "You went into the house of uncircumcised men and ate with them."

4Peter began and explained everything to them precisely as it had happened: 5"I was in the city of Joppa praying, and in a trance I saw a vision. I saw something like a large sheet being let down from heaven by its four corners, and it came down to where I was. 6I looked into it and saw four-footed

animals of the earth, wild beasts, reptiles, and birds of the air. 7Then I heard a voice telling me, 'Get up, Peter. Kill and eat.'

11:1 ■ EARTHSHAKING CHANGE

Nearly 2,000 years later, the decision to accept Gentiles into the church on equal footing with Jews may seem minor, but at the time it was a hotly debated issue of enormous consequence. Antioch, the first church with a large number of Gentile members, sparked a major controversy with the Jewish-dominated church in Jerusalem (see Acts 15). The third largest city in the Roman empire, Antioch was a crossroads between the Mediterranean and the eastern world, and from here the first missionaries went out to other nations and cultures.

8"I replied, 'Surely not, Lord! Nothing impure or unclean has ever entered my mouth.'

9"The voice spoke from heaven a second time, 'Do not call anything impure that God has made clean.' 10This happened three times, and then it was pulled up to heaven again.

11"Right then three men who had been sent to me from Caesarea stopped at the house where I was staying. 12The Spirit told me to have no hesitation about going with them. These six brothers also went with me, and we entered the man's house. 13He told us how he had seen an angel appear in his house and say, 'Send to Joppa for Simon who is called Peter. 14He will bring you a message through which you and all your household will be saved.'

15"As I began to speak, the Holy Spirit came on them as he had come on us at the beginning. 16Then I remembered what the Lord had said: 'John baptised with*a* water, but you will be baptised with the Holy Spirit.' 17So if God gave them the same gift as he gave us, who believed in the Lord Jesus Christ, who was I to think that I could oppose God?"

18When they heard this, they had no further objections and praised God, saying, "So then, God has granted even the Gentiles repentance unto life."

■ The Church in Antioch

19Now those who had been scattered by the persecution in connection with Stephen travelled as far as Phoenicia, Cyprus and Antioch, telling the message only to Jews. 20Some of them, however, men from Cyprus and Cyrene, went to Antioch and began to speak to Greeks also, telling them the good news about the Lord Jesus. 21The Lord's hand was with them, and a great number of people believed and turned to the Lord.

22News of this reached the ears of the church at Jerusalem, and they sent Barnabas to Antioch. 23When he arrived and saw the evidence of the grace of God, he was glad and encouraged them all to remain true to the Lord with all their hearts. 24He was a good man, full of the Holy Spirit and faith, and a great number of people were brought to the Lord.

25Then Barnabas went to Tarsus to look for Saul, 26and when he found him, he brought him to

---

b 46 Or other languages   *a* 16 Or in

Antioch. So for a whole year Barnabas and Saul met with the church and taught great numbers of people. The disciples were called Christians first at Antioch.

27During this time some prophets came down from Jerusalem to Antioch. 28One of them, named Agabus, stood up and through the Spirit predicted that a severe famine would spread over the entire Roman world. (This happened during the reign of Claudius.) 29The disciples, each according to his ability, decided to provide help for the brothers living in Judea. 30This they did, sending their gift to the elders by Barnabas and Saul.

11:28 ■ DURING THE REIGN OF . . .
The historian Luke is the only New Testament author who dates his books by referring to Roman emperors. He refers to Claudius three times in Acts; the events in Luke's Gospel occur during the reigns of Tiberius and Augustus.

■ Peter's Miraculous Escape From Prison

12 It was about this time that King Herod arrested some who belonged to the church, intending to persecute them. 2He had James, the brother of John, put to death with the sword. 3When he saw that this pleased the Jews, he proceeded to seize Peter also. This happened during the Feast of Unleavened Bread. 4After arresting him, he put him in prison, handing him over to be guarded by four squads of four soldiers each. Herod intended to bring him out for public trial after the Passover.

5So Peter was kept in prison, but the church was earnestly praying to God for him.

6The night before Herod was to bring him to trial, Peter was sleeping between two soldiers, bound with two chains, and sentries stood guard at the entrance. 7Suddenly an angel of the Lord appeared and a light shone in the cell. He struck Peter on the side and woke him up. "Quick, get up!" he said, and the chains fell off Peter's wrists.

8Then the angel said to him, "Put on your clothes and sandals." And Peter did so. "Wrap your cloak around you and follow me," the angel told him. 9Peter followed him out of the prison, but he had no idea that what the angel was doing was really happening; he thought he was seeing a vision. 10They passed the first and second guards and came to the iron gate leading to the city. It opened for them by itself, and they went through it. When they had walked the length of one street, suddenly the angel left him.

11Then Peter came to himself and said, "Now I know without a doubt that the Lord sent his angel and rescued me from Herod's clutches and from everything the Jewish people were anticipating."

12When this had dawned on him, he went to the house of Mary the mother of John, also called Mark, where many people had gathered and were praying. 13Peter knocked at the outer entrance, and a servant girl named Rhoda came to answer the door. 14When she recognised Peter's voice, she was so overjoyed she ran back without opening it and exclaimed, "Peter is at the door!"

15"You're out of your mind," they told her. When she kept insisting that it was so, they said, "It must be his angel."

16But Peter kept on knocking, and when they opened the door and saw him, they were astonished. 17Peter motioned with his hand for them to be quiet and described how the Lord had brought him out of prison. "Tell James and the brothers about this," he said, and then he left for another place.

18In the morning, there was no small commotion among the soldiers as to what had become of Peter. 19After Herod had a thorough search made for him and did not find him, he cross-examined the guards and ordered that they be executed.

12:19 ■ GUARDS WITHOUT ALLIES
The soldiers who had unsuccessfully guarded Jesus' tomb were protected by a conspiracy hatched by the Jewish establishment (Matthew 28:12–15). This passage sheds light on their eagerness to agree to a cover-up plan: Rome dealt harshly with guards who did not perform their duty. In contrast, the guards who had been on duty when Peter "escaped" (he was set free by an angel) had no-one to plead for them. Herod ordered their execution.

■ Herod's Death

Then Herod went from Judea to Caesarea and stayed there a while. 20He had been quarrelling with the people of Tyre and Sidon; they now joined together and sought an audience with him. Having secured the support of Blastus, a trusted personal servant of the king, they asked for peace, because they depended on the king's country for their food supply.

21On the appointed day Herod, wearing his royal robes, sat on his throne and delivered a public address to the people. 22They shouted, "This is the voice of a god, not of a man." 23Immediately, because Herod did not give praise to God, an angel of the Lord struck him down, and he was eaten by worms and died.

24But the word of God continued to increase and spread.

25When Barnabas and Saul had finished their mission, they returned from*a* Jerusalem, taking with them John, also called Mark.

■ Barnabas and Saul Sent Off

13 In the church at Antioch there were prophets and teachers: Barnabas, Simeon called Niger, Lucius of Cyrene, Manaen (who had been brought up with Herod the tetrarch) and Saul. 2While they were worshipping the Lord and fasting, the Holy Spirit said, "Set apart for me Barnabas and Saul for the work to which I have called them." 3So after they had fasted and prayed, they placed their hands on them and sent them off.

■ On Cyprus

4The two of them, sent on their way by the Holy Spirit, went down to Seleucia and sailed from there to Cyprus. 5When they arrived at Salamis, they proclaimed the word of God in the Jewish synagogues. John was with them as their helper.

6They travelled through the whole island until they came to Paphos. There they met a Jewish sorcerer and false prophet named Bar-Jesus, 7who was an attendant of the proconsul, Sergius Paulus. The proconsul, an intelligent man, sent for Barnabas and Saul because he wanted to hear the word of God. 8But Elymas the sorcerer (for that is what his name means) opposed them and tried to turn the proconsul from the faith. 9Then Saul, who was also called Paul, filled with the Holy Spirit, looked straight at Elymas and said, 10"You are a child of the devil and an enemy of everything that is right! You are full of all kinds of deceit and trickery. Will you never stop perverting the right ways of the Lord? 11Now the hand of the Lord is against you. You are going to be blind, and for a time you will be unable to see the light of the sun."

Immediately mist and darkness came over him, and he groped about, seeking someone to lead him by the hand. 12When the proconsul saw what had happened, he believed, for he was amazed at the teaching about the Lord.

■ In Pisidian Antioch

13From Paphos, Paul and his companions sailed to Perga in Pamphylia, where John left them to return to Jerusalem. 14From Perga they went on to Pisidian Antioch. On the Sabbath they entered the synagogue and sat down. 15After the reading from the Law and the Prophets, the synagogue rulers sent word to them, saying, "Brothers, if you have a message of encouragement for the people, please speak."

13:15 ■ VISITING SPEAKER

Synagogue rulers customarily invited a visiting rabbi to address the congregation, and in this case the apostle Paul responded by delivering his longest-recorded sermon. The rulers got more than they bargained for: the next week virtually the whole city turned out to hear him, resulting in a near-riot (verses 44–45).

16Standing up, Paul motioned with his hand and said: "Men of Israel and you Gentiles who worship God, listen to me! 17The God of the people of Israel chose our fathers; he made the people prosper during their stay in Egypt, with mighty power he led them out of that country, 18he endured their conduct[a] for about forty years in the desert, 19he overthrew seven nations in Canaan and gave their land to his people as their inheritance. 20All this took about 450 years.

"After this, God gave them judges until the time of Samuel the prophet. 21Then the people asked for a king, and he gave them Saul son of Kish, of the tribe of Benjamin, who ruled for forty years. 22After removing Saul, he made David their king. He testified concerning him: 'I have found David son of Jesse a man after my own heart; he will do everything I want him to do.'

23"From this man's descendants God has brought to Israel the Saviour Jesus, as he promised. 24Before the coming of Jesus, John preached repentance and baptism to all the people of Israel. 25As John was completing his work, he said: 'Who do you think I am? I am not that one. No, but he is coming after me, whose sandals I am not worthy to untie.'

26"Brothers, children of Abraham, and you God-fearing Gentiles, it is to us that this message of salvation has been sent. 27The people of Jerusalem and their rulers did not recognise Jesus, yet in condemning him they fulfilled the words of the prophets that are read every Sabbath. 28Though they found no proper ground for a death sentence, they asked Pilate to have him executed. 29When they had carried out all that was written about him, they took him down from the tree and laid him in a tomb. 30But God raised him from the dead, 31and for many days he was seen by those who had travelled with him from Galilee to Jerusalem. They are now his witnesses to our people.

32"We tell you the good news: What God promised our fathers 33he has fulfilled for us, their children, by raising up Jesus. As it is written in the second Psalm:

" 'You are my Son;
    today I have become your Father.'[b, c]

34The fact that God raised him from the dead, never to decay, is stated in these words:

" 'I will give you the holy and sure blessings
    promised to David.'[d]

35So it is stated elsewhere:

" 'You will not let your Holy One see decay.'[e]

36"For when David had served God's purpose in his own generation, he fell asleep; he was buried with his fathers and his body decayed. 37But the one whom God raised from the dead did not see decay.

38"Therefore, my brothers, I want you to know that through Jesus the forgiveness of sins is proclaimed to you. 39Through him everyone who believes is justified from everything you could not be justified from by the law of Moses. 40Take care that what the prophets have said does not happen to you:

41" 'Look, you scoffers,
    wonder and perish,
for I am going to do something in your days
    that you would never believe,
    even if someone told you.'[f]"

42As Paul and Barnabas were leaving the synagogue, the people invited them to speak further about these things on the next Sabbath. 43When the congregation was dismissed, many of the Jews and devout converts to Judaism followed Paul and Barnabas, who talked with them and urged them to continue in the grace of God.

44On the next Sabbath almost the whole city

a 18 Some manuscripts and cared for them   b 33 Or have begotten you   c 33 Psalm 2:7   d 34 Isaiah 55:3   e 35 Psalm 16:10   f 41 Hab. 1:5 gathered to hear the word of the Lord. ⁴⁵When the Jews saw the crowds, they were filled with jealousy and talked abusively against what Paul was saying. ⁴⁶Then Paul and Barnabas answered them boldly: "We had to speak the word of God to you first. Since you reject it and do not consider yourselves worthy of eternal life, we now turn to the Gentiles. ⁴⁷For this is what the Lord has commanded us:

" 'I have made youᵍ a light for the Gentiles,
    that youᵍ may bring salvation to the ends of
    the earth.'ᵇ"

13:46 ■ APOSTLE TO THE GENTILES
This incident is the first of several occasions in Acts showing Paul turning away from the Jews (see 18:6; 19:9). When the Jews rejected his message, he went to the Gentiles. Eventually he became known as the "apostle to the Gentiles", even though he maintained a deep love for his own people (see Romans 9:1–5).

⁴⁸When the Gentiles heard this, they were glad and honoured the word of the Lord; and all who were appointed for eternal life believed.

⁴⁹The word of the Lord spread through the whole region. ⁵⁰But the Jews incited the God-fearing women of high standing and the leading men of the city. They stirred up persecution against Paul and Barnabas, and expelled them from their region. ⁵¹So they shook the dust from their feet in protest against them and went to Iconium. ⁵²And the disciples were filled with joy and with the Holy Spirit.

■ In Iconium

14 At Iconium Paul and Barnabas went as usual into the Jewish synagogue. There they spoke so effectively that a great number of Jews and Gentiles believed. ²But the Jews who refused to believe stirred up the Gentiles and poisoned their minds against the brothers. ³So Paul and Barnabas spent considerable time there, speaking boldly for the Lord, who confirmed the message of his grace by enabling them to do miraculous signs and wonders. ⁴The people of the city were divided; some sided with the Jews, others with the apostles. ⁵There was a plot afoot among the Gentiles and Jews, together with their leaders, to ill-treat them and stone them. ⁶But they found out about it and fled to the Lycaonian cities of Lystra and Derbe and to the surrounding country, ⁷where they continued to preach the good news.

■ In Lystra and Derbe

⁸In Lystra there sat a man crippled in his feet, who was lame from birth and had never walked. ⁹He listened to Paul as he was speaking. Paul looked directly at him, saw that he had faith to be healed ¹⁰and called out, "Stand up on your feet!" At that, the man jumped up and began to walk.

¹¹When the crowd saw what Paul had done, they shouted in the Lycaonian language, "The gods have come down to us in human form!" ¹²Barnabas they

called Zeus, and Paul they called Hermes because he was the chief speaker. ¹³The priest of Zeus, whose temple was just outside the city, brought bulls and wreaths to the city gates because he and the crowd wanted to offer sacrifices to them.

¹⁴But when the apostles Barnabas and Paul heard of this, they tore their clothes and rushed out into the crowd, shouting: ¹⁵"Men, why are you doing this? We too are only men, human like you. We are bringing you good news, telling you to turn from these worthless things to the living God, who made heaven and earth and sea and everything in them. ¹⁶In the past, he let all nations go their own way. ¹⁷Yet he has not left himself without testimony: He has shown kindness by giving you rain from heaven and crops in their seasons; he provides you with plenty of food and fills your hearts with joy." ¹⁸Even with these words, they had difficulty keeping the crowd from sacrificing to them.

¹⁹Then some Jews came from Antioch and Iconium and won the crowd over. They stoned Paul and dragged him outside the city, thinking he was dead. ²⁰But after the disciples had gathered round him, he got up and went back into the city. The next day he and Barnabas left for Derbe.

■ The Return to Antioch in Syria

²¹They preached the good news in that city and won a large number of disciples. Then they returned to Lystra, Iconium and Antioch, ²²strengthening the disciples and encouraging them to remain true to the faith. "We must go through many hardships to enter the kingdom of God," they said. ²³Paul and Barnabas appointed eldersᵃ for them in each church and, with prayer and fasting, committed them to the Lord, in whom they had put their trust. ²⁴After going through Pisidia, they came into Pamphylia, ²⁵and when they had preached the word in Perga, they went down to Attalia. ²⁶From Attalia they sailed back to Antioch, where they had been committed to the grace of God for the work they had now completed. ²⁷On arriving there, they gathered the church together and reported all that God had done through them and how he had opened the door of faith to the Gentiles. ²⁸And they stayed there a long time with the disciples.

■ The Council at Jerusalem

15 Some men came down from Judea to Antioch and were teaching the brothers: "Unless you are circumcised, according to the custom taught by Moses, you cannot be saved." ²This brought Paul and Barnabas into sharp dispute and debate with them. So Paul and Barnabas were appointed, along with some other believers, to go up to Jerusalem to see the apostles and elders about this question. ³The church sent them on their way, and as they travelled through Phoenicia and Samaria, they told how the Gentiles had been converted. This news made all the brothers very glad. ⁴When they came to Jerusalem, they were welcomed by the church and the apostles and elders, to whom they reported everything God had done through them.

⁵Then some of the believers who belonged to the

ᵍ47 The Greek is singular.   ᵇ47 Isaiah 49:6   ᵃ23 Or Barnabas ordained elders; or Barnabas had elders elected party of the Pharisees stood up and said, "The Gentiles must be circumcised and required to obey the law of Moses."

6The apostles and elders met to consider this question. 7After much discussion, Peter got up and addressed them: "Brothers, you know that some time ago God made a choice among you that the Gentiles might hear from my lips the message of the gospel and believe. 8God, who knows the heart, showed that he accepted them by giving the Holy Spirit to them, just as he did to us. 9He made no distinction between us and them, for he purified their hearts by faith. 10Now then, why do you try to test God by putting on the necks of the disciples a yoke that neither we nor our fathers have been able to bear? 11No! We believe it is through the grace of our Lord Jesus that we are saved, just as they are."

15:7 ■ THE FIRST CHURCH COUNCIL
Chapter 15 gives a fascinating glimpse into Jewish/Gentile politics in the early church, recounting a debate between such leaders as Peter, Paul, and James. "Some time ago", Peter began his speech — about ten years had passed since his startling experience with Gentiles recorded in Acts 10. By now Gentiles probably outnumbered Jewish believers worldwide.

The leaders agreed on a compromise position that removed some of the barriers between the two groups. They issued a formal position paper, reproduced here, in which Jewish Christians asked the Gentiles to honour four of their practices, two moral issues and two cultural. The two on food relate to a "kosher" method of food preparation designed to keep people from ingesting any animal blood.

12The whole assembly became silent as they listened to Barnabas and Paul telling about the miraculous signs and wonders God had done among the Gentiles through them. 13When they finished, James spoke up: "Brothers, listen to me. 14Simon[a] has described to us how God at first showed his concern by taking from the Gentiles a people for himself. 15The words of the prophets are in agreement with this, as it is written:

16" 'After this I will return
    and rebuild David's fallen tent.
  Its ruins I will rebuild,
    and I will restore it,
17that the remnant of men may seek the Lord,
    and all the Gentiles who bear my name,
  says the Lord, who does these things'[b]
18   that have been known for ages.[c]

19"It is my judgment, therefore, that we should not make it difficult for the Gentiles who are turning to God. 20Instead we should write to them, telling them to abstain from food polluted by idols, from sexual immorality, from the meat of strangled animals and from blood. 21For Moses has been preached in every city from the earliest times and is read in the synagogues on every Sabbath."

■ The Council's Letter to Gentile Believers
22Then the apostles and elders, with the whole church, decided to choose some of their own men and send them to Antioch with Paul and Barnabas. They chose Judas (called Barsabbas) and Silas, two men who were leaders among the brothers. 23With them they sent the following letter:

The apostles and elders, your brothers,

To the Gentile believers in Antioch, Syria and Cilicia:

Greetings.

24We have heard that some went out from us without our authorisation and disturbed you, troubling your minds by what they said. 25So we all agreed to choose some men and send them to you with our dear friends Barnabas and Paul — 26men who have risked their lives for the name of our Lord Jesus Christ. 27Therefore we are sending Judas and Silas to confirm by word of mouth what we are writing. 28It seemed good to the Holy Spirit and to us not to burden you with anything beyond the following requirements: 29You are to abstain from food sacrificed to idols, from blood, from the meat of strangled animals and from sexual immorality. You will do well to avoid these things.

Farewell.

30The men were sent off and went down to Antioch, where they gathered the church together and delivered the letter. 31The people read it and were glad for its encouraging message. 32Judas and Silas, who themselves were prophets, said much to encourage and strengthen the brothers. 33After spending some time there, they were sent off by the brothers with the blessing of peace to return to those who had sent them.[d] 35But Paul and Barnabas remained in Antioch, where they and many others taught and preached the word of the Lord.

■ Disagreement Between Paul and Barnabas
36Some time later Paul said to Barnabas, "Let us go back and visit the brothers in all the towns where we preached the word of the Lord and see how they are doing." 37Barnabas wanted to take John, also called Mark, with them, 38but Paul did not think it wise to take him, because he had deserted them in Pamphylia and had not continued with them in the work. 39They had such a sharp disagreement that they parted company. Barnabas took Mark and sailed for Cyprus, 40but Paul chose Silas and left, commended by the brothers to the grace of the Lord. 41He went through Syria and Cilicia, strengthening the churches.

■ Timothy Joins Paul and Silas
16 He came to Derbe and then to Lystra, where a disciple named Timothy lived, whose mother was a Jewess and a believer, but whose father was a Greek. 2The brothers at Lystra and Iconium spoke well of him. 3Paul wanted to take him

a 14 Greek Simeon, a variant of Simon; that is, Peter   b 17 Amos 9:11,12   c 17,18 Some manuscripts things'– / 18known to the Lord for ages is his
work   d 33 Some manuscripts them, 34but Silas decided to remain there

along on the journey, so he circumcised him because of the Jews who lived in that area, for they all knew that his father was a Greek. [4]As they travelled from town to town, they delivered the decisions reached by the apostles and elders in Jerusalem for the people to obey. [5]So the churches were strengthened in the faith and grew daily in numbers.

■ Paul's Vision of the Man of Macedonia
[6]Paul and his companions travelled throughout the region of Phrygia and Galatia, having been kept by the Holy Spirit from preaching the word in the province of Asia. [7]When they came to the border of Mysia, they tried to enter Bithynia, but the Spirit of Jesus would not allow them to. [8]So they passed by Mysia and went down to Troas. [9]During the night Paul had a vision of a man of Macedonia standing and begging him, "Come over to Macedonia and help us." [10]After Paul had seen the vision, we got ready at once to leave for Macedonia, concluding that God had called us to preach the gospel to them.

16:10 ■ FIRST-HAND REPORT
In Acts 16, 21, and 28, Luke uses "we" in writing, for he accompanied the apostle Paul on some of his trips. His close association with Paul meant he had immediate access to the central character in Acts 13–28.

■ Lydia's Conversion in Philippi
[11]From Troas we put out to sea and sailed straight for Samothrace, and the next day on to Neapolis. [12]From there we travelled to Philippi, a Roman colony and the leading city of that district of Macedonia. And we stayed there several days.
[13]On the Sabbath we went outside the city gate to the river, where we expected to find a place of prayer. We sat down and began to speak to the women who had gathered there. [14]One of those listening was a woman named Lydia, a dealer in purple cloth from the city of Thyatira, who was a worshipper of God. The Lord opened her heart to respond to Paul's message. [15]When she and the members of her household were baptised, she invited us to her home. "If you consider me a believer in the Lord," she said, "come and stay at my house." And she persuaded us.

■ Paul and Silas in Prison
[16]Once when we were going to the place of prayer, we were met by a slave girl who had a spirit by which she predicted the future. She earned a great deal of money for her owners by fortune-telling. [17]This girl followed Paul and the rest of us, shouting, "These men are servants of the Most High God, who are telling you the way to be saved." [18]She kept this up for many days. Finally Paul became so troubled that he turned round and said to the spirit, "In the name of Jesus Christ I command you to come out of her!" At that moment the spirit left her.
[19]When the owners of the slave girl realised that their hope of making money was gone, they seized Paul and Silas and dragged them into the market-place to face the authorities. [20]They brought them before the magistrates and said, "These men are Jews, and are throwing our city into an uproar [21]by advocating customs unlawful for us Romans to accept or practise."
[22]The crowd joined in the attack against Paul and Silas, and the magistrates ordered them to be stripped and beaten. [23]After they had been severely flogged, they were thrown into prison, and the jailer was commanded to guard them carefully. [24]Upon receiving such orders, he put them in the inner cell and fastened their feet in the stocks.
[25]About midnight Paul and Silas were praying and singing hymns to God, and the other prisoners were listening to them. [26]Suddenly there was such a violent earthquake that the foundations of the prison were shaken. At once all the prison doors flew open, and everybody's chains came loose. [27]The jailer woke up, and when he saw the prison doors open, he drew his sword and was about to kill himself because he thought the prisoners had escaped. [28]But Paul shouted, "Don't harm yourself! We are all here!"
[29]The jailer called for lights, rushed in and fell trembling before Paul and Silas. [30]He then brought them out and asked, "Sirs, what must I do to be saved?"
[31]They replied, "Believe in the Lord Jesus, and you will be saved—you and your household." [32]Then they spoke the word of the Lord to him and to all the others in his house. [33]At that hour of the night the jailer took them and washed their wounds; then immediately he and all his family were baptised. [34]The jailer brought them into his house and set a meal before them; he was filled with joy because he had come to believe in God—he and his whole family.
[35]When it was daylight, the magistrates sent their officers to the jailer with the order: "Release those men." [36]The jailer told Paul, "The magistrates have ordered that you and Silas be released. Now you can leave. Go in peace."
[37]But Paul said to the officers: "They beat us publicly without a trial, even though we are Roman citizens, and threw us into prison. And now do they want to get rid of us quietly? No! Let them come themselves and escort us out."
[38]The officers reported this to the magistrates, and when they heard that Paul and Silas were Roman citizens, they were alarmed. [39]They came to appease them and escorted them from the prison, requesting them to leave the city. [40]After Paul and Silas came out of the prison, they went to Lydia's house, where they met with the brothers and encouraged them. Then they left.

■ In Thessalonica
17 When they had passed through Amphipolis and Apollonia, they came to Thessalonica, where there was a Jewish synagogue. [2]As his custom was, Paul went into the synagogue, and on three Sabbath days he reasoned with them from the Scriptures, [3]explaining and proving that the Christ[a] had to suffer and rise from the dead. "This Jesus I am proclaiming to you is the Christ,"[a] he said. [4]Some

[a] 3 Or Messiah

of the Jews were persuaded and joined Paul and Silas, as did a large number of God-fearing Greeks and not a few prominent women.

5But the Jews were jealous; so they rounded up some bad characters from the market-place, formed a mob and started a riot in the city. They rushed to Jason's house in search of Paul and Silas in order to bring them out to the crowd.*b* 6But when they did not find them, they dragged Jason and some other brothers before the city officials, shouting: "These men who have caused trouble all over the world have now come here, 7and Jason has welcomed them into his house. They are all defying Caesar's decrees, saying that there is another king, one called Jesus." 8When they heard this, the crowd and the city officials were thrown into turmoil. 9Then they put Jason and the others on bail and let them go.

■ In Berea
10As soon as it was night, the brothers sent Paul and Silas away to Berea. On arriving there, they went to the Jewish synagogue. 11Now the Bereans were of more noble character than the Thessalonians, for they received the message with great eagerness and examined the Scriptures every day to see if what Paul said was true. 12Many of the Jews believed, as did also a number of prominent Greek women and many Greek men.

13When the Jews in Thessalonica learned that Paul was preaching the word of God at Berea, they went there too, agitating the crowds and stirring them up. 14The brothers immediately sent Paul to the coast, but Silas and Timothy stayed at Berea. 15The men who escorted Paul brought him to Athens and then left with instructions for Silas and Timothy to join him as soon as possible.

■ In Athens
16While Paul was waiting for them in Athens, he was greatly distressed to see that the city was full of idols. 17So he reasoned in the synagogue with the Jews and the God-fearing Greeks, as well as in the market-place day by day with those who happened to be there. 18A group of Epicurean and Stoic philosophers began to dispute with him. Some of them asked, "What is this babbler trying to say?" Others remarked, "He seems to be advocating foreign gods." They said this because Paul was preaching the good news about Jesus and the resurrection. 19Then they took him and brought him to a meeting of the Areopagus, where they said to him, "May we know what this new teaching is that you are presenting? 20You are bringing some strange ideas to our ears, and we want to know what they mean." 21(All the Athenians and the foreigners who lived there spent their time doing nothing but talking about and listening to the latest ideas.)

22Paul then stood up in the meeting of the Areopagus and said: "Men of Athens! I see that in every way you are very religious. 23For as I walked around and looked carefully at your objects of worship, I even found an altar with this inscription: TO AN UNKNOWN GOD. Now what you worship as something unknown I am going to proclaim to you.

24"The God who made the world and everything in it is the Lord of heaven and earth and does not live in temples built by hands. 25And he is not served by human hands, as if he needed anything, because he himself gives all men life and breath and everything else. 26From one man he made every nation of men, that they should inhabit the whole earth; and he determined the times set for them and the exact places where they should live. 27God did this so that men would seek him and perhaps reach out for him and find him, though he is not far from each one of us. 28'For in him we live and move and have our being.' As some of your own poets have said, 'We are his offspring.'

17:16 ■ FLEXIBLE APPROACH
In places like Thessalonica and Berea, Paul went first to the synagogues, where he tried to convince fellow Jews that Jesus Christ was the Messiah promised in the Old Testament. In Athens he initially took that same approach, but few Athenians had the Old Testament background to understand his argument. Paul soon began comparing his God to the many gods they worshipped. The ancients used to say, "It is easier to find a god than a man in Athens."

29"Therefore since we are God's offspring, we should not think that the divine being is like gold or silver or stone — an image made by man's design and skill. 30In the past God overlooked such ignorance, but now he commands all people everywhere to repent. 31For he has set a day when he will judge the world with justice by the man he has appointed. He has given proof of this to all men by raising him from the dead."

32When they heard about the resurrection of the dead, some of them sneered, but others said, "We want to hear you again on this subject." 33At that, Paul left the Council. 34A few men became followers of Paul and believed. Among them was Dionysius, a member of the Areopagus, also a woman named Damaris, and a number of others.

17:32 ■ A TOUGH AUDIENCE
Paul gave a remarkable speech to a gathering of philosophers and thinkers in the sophisticated university city of Athens. It appears he met with little success, and the results may have troubled him greatly. Acts 18:5 hints at a shift in his approach. Some scholars believe that the first four chapters of 1 Corinthians, reflecting on this period of time, may describe the strong impact of his experience in Athens.

■ In Corinth
18 After this, Paul left Athens and went to Corinth. 2There he met a Jew named Aquila, a native of Pontus, who had recently come from Italy with his wife Priscilla, because Claudius had ordered all the Jews to leave Rome. Paul went to see them, 3and because he was a tentmaker as they

---

b 5 Or *the assembly of the people*

were, he stayed and worked with them. ⁴Every Sabbath he reasoned in the synagogue, trying to persuade Jews and Greeks.

⁵When Silas and Timothy came from Macedonia, Paul devoted himself exclusively to preaching, testifying to the Jews that Jesus was the Christ.ᵃ ⁶But when the Jews opposed Paul and became abusive, he shook out his clothes in protest and said to them, "Your blood be on your own heads! I am clear of my responsibility. From now on I will go to the Gentiles."

⁷Then Paul left the synagogue and went next door to the house of Titius Justus, a worshipper of God. ⁸Crispus, the synagogue ruler, and his entire household believed in the Lord; and many of the Corinthians who heard him believed and were baptised.

⁹One night the Lord spoke to Paul in a vision: "Do not be afraid; keep on speaking, do not be silent. ¹⁰For I am with you, and no-one is going to attack and harm you, because I have many people in this city." ¹¹So Paul stayed for a year and a half, teaching them the word of God.

¹²While Gallio was proconsul of Achaia, the Jews made a united attack on Paul and brought him into court. ¹³"This man," they charged, "is persuading the people to worship God in ways contrary to the law."

¹⁴Just as Paul was about to speak, Gallio said to the Jews, "If you Jews were making a complaint about some misdemeanour or serious crime, it would be reasonable for me to listen to you. ¹⁵But since it involves questions about words and names and your own law—settle the matter yourselves. I

ON THE ROAD WITH THE APOSTLE PAUL
PAUL, BOTH JEWISH AND ROMAN, TOOK THE GOSPEL INTO THE MELTING POT

BUT WHEN THE JEWS OPPOSED PAUL AND BECAME ABUSIVE, HE SHOOK OUT HIS CLOTHES IN PROTEST AND SAID TO THEM, "YOUR BLOOD BE ON YOUR OWN HEADS! I AM CLEAR OF MY RESPONSIBILITY. FROM NOW ON I WILL GO TO THE GENTILES." ■ 18:6

The book of Acts follows Paul on three distinct missionary journeys along the north-eastern shores of the Mediterranean Sea. Normally in the ancient world, travel posed great hazards, with pirates, barbarian armies and hostile border guards clogging up the roads. But by Paul's lifetime, Rome had established absolute mastery over a vast territory. Empire-wide peace, the famous *Pax Romana* – a condition that existed only twice in 700 years – prevailed.

Roman engineers had criss-crossed the empire with a network of roads (built so well that many still survive), and as a Roman citizen Paul had a passport to any destination. Language, too, was unified. The Greek tongue, as well as the Greek style of thinking, crossed ethnic barriers.

■ PAUL'S STRATEGY
In his missionary ventures, Paul focused primarily on chief trade towns, capital cities and Roman colonies. Like modern cities today, these comprised a melting pot of diverse cultures. From these places, the gospel message would be carried across the globe.

Usually, Paul began with a visit to a local synagogue, establishing contact with fellow Jews. If they rejected his message, as often happened, he quickly turned to a non-Jewish audience.

When a promising church was established, Paul stayed on, sometimes as long

as three years, to teach and to direct its spiritual growth. His letters glow with affection for the friends he developed in this way. (Acts 20 gives a glimpse of the intimacy he shared with one such group.) On his second and third journeys Paul revisited many of the churches he had founded.

■ UNUSUAL QUALIFICATIONS, IMPRESSIVE RESULTS
Paul's background uniquely qualified him for his adventures. A Pharisee who had studied with the famous teacher Gamaliel, he fully understood the Jewish mind. Roman citizenship gave him the status and respect he needed to gain official recognition and to survive threatening legal scrapes.

Paul's mastery of languages helped him also. He used Aramaic to relate to the early church leaders in Jerusalem, and fluency in Greek made possible a speech before philosophers in Athens.

Sometimes Paul was used by God to work miracles. In one tragi-comic episode, a sleepy listener succumbed to Paul's all-night sermon and fell out of a third-storey window (20:7–12); Paul raised him from the dead.

By the end of his eventful life, Paul had left a ring of burgeoning churches around the eastern Mediterranean. To make sure his work would go on, he trained such leaders as Silas, Titus, Timothy and the man who recorded much of what we know about Paul's life – Luke himself.

□ LIFE QUESTIONS:
Why did God choose Paul to lead the early church? What special qualifications do you have that God could use?

ᵃ 5 Or *Messiah*; also in verse 28

will not be a judge of such things." 16So he had them ejected from the court. 17Then they all turned on Sosthenes the synagogue ruler and beat him in front of the court. But Gallio showed no concern whatever.

18:15 ■ A SECULAR VIEW
Like many Roman officials, Gallio showed little interest in religious matters. However, his decision not to hear charges against Paul had far-reaching consequences. Gallio was an important ruler — brother of the philosopher Seneca and in line for a high office in Rome. By treating Christianity as a part of Judaism he was granting it a form of official protection, for Judaism had already been formally recognised as a religion.

Ironically, when Gallio eventually returned to Rome, he was killed on the orders of Nero — one of the first emperors to begin persecuting Christians.

■ Priscilla, Aquila and Apollos

18Paul stayed on in Corinth for some time. Then he left the brothers and sailed for Syria, accompanied by Priscilla and Aquila. Before he sailed, he had his hair cut off at Cenchrea because of a vow he had taken. 19They arrived at Ephesus, where Paul left Priscilla and Aquila. He himself went into the synagogue and reasoned with the Jews. 20When they asked him to spend more time with them, he declined. 21But as he left, he promised, "I will come back if it is God's will." Then he set sail from Ephesus. 22When he landed at Caesarea, he went up and greeted the church and then went down to Antioch.

23After spending some time in Antioch, Paul set out from there and travelled from place to place throughout the region of Galatia and Phrygia, strengthening all the disciples.

24Meanwhile a Jew named Apollos, a native of Alexandria, came to Ephesus. He was a learned man, with a thorough knowledge of the Scriptures. 25He had been instructed in the way of the Lord, and he spoke with great fervour[b] and taught about Jesus accurately, though he knew only the baptism of John. 26He began to speak boldly in the synagogue. When Priscilla and Aquila heard him, they invited him to their home and explained to him the way of God more adequately.

27When Apollos wanted to go to Achaia, the brothers encouraged him and wrote to the disciples there to welcome him. On arriving, he was a great help to those who by grace had believed. 28For he vigorously refuted the Jews in public debate, proving from the Scriptures that Jesus was the Christ.

■ Paul in Ephesus

19 While Apollos was at Corinth, Paul took the road through the interior and arrived at Ephesus. There he found some disciples 2and asked them, "Did you receive the Holy Spirit when[a] you believed?"

They answered, "No, we have not even heard that there is a Holy Spirit."

3So Paul asked, "Then what baptism did you receive?"

"John's baptism," they replied.

4Paul said, "John's baptism was a baptism of repentance. He told the people to believe in the one coming after him, that is, in Jesus." 5On hearing this, they were baptised into[b] the name of the Lord Jesus. 6When Paul placed his hands on them, the Holy Spirit came on them, and they spoke in tongues[c] and prophesied. 7There were about twelve men in all.

8Paul entered the synagogue and spoke boldly there for three months, arguing persuasively about the kingdom of God. 9But some of them became obstinate; they refused to believe and publicly maligned the Way. So Paul left them. He took the disciples with him and had discussions daily in the lecture hall of Tyrannus. 10This went on for two years, so that all the Jews and Greeks who lived in the province of Asia heard the word of the Lord.

19:9 ■ SPORTS AND EDUCATION
Greek lecture halls or gymnasiums, such as this one at Tyrannus, often were built as training rooms for Olympic athletes and later converted to educational purposes. (The word "gymnasium" comes from a Greek word that means, literally, "to train in the nude".) Modern Americans use this ancient word for athletic facilities; Europeans, especially Germans, use it in referring to secondary schools.

11God did extraordinary miracles through Paul, 12so that even handkerchiefs and aprons that had touched him were taken to the sick, and their illnesses were cured and the evil spirits left them.

13Some Jews who went around driving out evil spirits tried to invoke the name of the Lord Jesus over those who were demon-possessed. They would say, "In the name of Jesus, whom Paul preaches, I command you to come out." 14Seven sons of Sceva, a Jewish chief priest, were doing this. 15⌊One day⌋ the evil spirit answered them, "Jesus I know, and I know about Paul, but who are you?" 16Then the man who had the evil spirit jumped on them and overpowered them all. He gave them such a beating that they ran out of the house naked and bleeding.

17When this became known to the Jews and Greeks living in Ephesus, they were all seized with fear, and the name of the Lord Jesus was held in high honour. 18Many of those who believed now came and openly confessed their evil deeds. 19A number who had practised sorcery brought their scrolls together and burned them publicly. When they calculated the value of the scrolls, the total came to fifty thousand drachmas.[d] 20In this way the word of the Lord spread widely and grew in power.

21After all this had happened, Paul decided to go to Jerusalem, passing through Macedonia and Achaia. "After I have been there," he said, "I must visit Rome also." 22He sent two of his helpers,

---

b25 Or with fervour in the Spirit   a2 Or after   b5 Or in   c6 Or other languages   d19 A drachma was a silver coin worth about a day's wages.

Timothy and Erastus, to Macedonia, while he stayed in the province of Asia a little longer.

■ The Riot in Ephesus

23About that time there arose a great disturbance about the Way. 24A silversmith named Demetrius, who made silver shrines of Artemis, brought in no little business for the craftsmen. 25He called them together, along with the workmen in related trades, and said: "Men, you know we receive a good income from this business. 26And you see and hear how this fellow Paul has convinced and led astray large numbers of people here in Ephesus and in practically the whole province of Asia. He says that man-made gods are no gods at all. 27There is danger not only that our trade will lose its good name, but also that the temple of the great goddess Artemis will be discredited, and the goddess herself, who is worshipped throughout the province of Asia and the world, will be robbed of her divine majesty."

19:24 ■ COMMERCIALISED RELIGION
Ephesus was devoted to idolatry and to profit, and Paul's message threatened both. The citizens took great pride in their temple, one of the seven wonders of the ancient world, and were outraged at anyone who might interfere with their profitable businesses dependent on religious pilgrims. The story presents a clear case of mob psychology. Paul started a riot, but he also founded one of his strongest churches, a community that later inspired the book of Ephesians.

28When they heard this, they were furious and began shouting: "Great is Artemis of the Ephesians!" 29Soon the whole city was in an uproar. The people seized Gaius and Aristarchus, Paul's travelling companions from Macedonia, and rushed as one man into the theatre. 30Paul wanted to appear before the crowd, but the disciples would not let him. 31Even some of the officials of the province, friends of Paul, sent him a message begging him not to venture into the theatre.

32The assembly was in confusion: Some were shouting one thing, some another. Most of the people did not even know why they were there. 33The Jews pushed Alexander to the front, and some of the crowd shouted instructions to him. He motioned for silence in order to make a defence before the people. 34But when they realised he was a Jew, they all shouted in unison for about two hours: "Great is Artemis of the Ephesians!"

35The city clerk quietened the crowd and said: "Men of Ephesus, doesn't all the world know that the city of Ephesus is the guardian of the temple of the great Artemis and of her image, which fell from heaven? 36Therefore, since these facts are undeniable, you ought to be quiet and not do anything rash. 37You have brought these men here, though they have neither robbed temples nor blasphemed our goddess. 38If, then, Demetrius and his fellow craftsmen have a grievance against anybody, the courts are open and there are proconsuls. They can

press charges. 39If there is anything further you want to bring up, it must be settled in a legal assembly. 40As it is, we are in danger of being charged with rioting because of today's events. In that case we would not be able to account for this commotion, since there is no reason for it." 41After he had said this, he dismissed the assembly.

■ Through Macedonia and Greece

20 When the uproar had ended, Paul sent for the disciples and, after encouraging them, said good-bye and set out for Macedonia. 2He travelled through that area, speaking many words of encouragement to the people, and finally arrived in Greece, 3where he stayed three months. Because the Jews made a plot against him just as he was about to sail for Syria, he decided to go back through Macedonia. 4He was accompanied by Sopater son of Pyrrhus from Berea, Aristarchus and Secundus from Thessalonica, Gaius from Derbe, Timothy also, and Tychicus and Trophimus from the province of Asia. 5These men went on ahead and waited for us at Troas. 6But we sailed from Philippi after the Feast of Unleavened Bread, and five days later joined the others at Troas, where we stayed seven days.

20:4 ■ NO CHEATING
In the days before electronic banking, money had to be carried in person. Thus Paul's plan to transfer the famine relief funds collected in Greece and Asia to the churches in Judea (see 24:17) posed some problems. Eager to avoid suspicion, Paul invited representatives from the donating churches to accompany him. That way he could assure everyone the money was used as promised, and not for personal gain. Second Corinthians 8 gives more details about this offering.

■ Eutychus Raised From the Dead at Troas

7On the first day of the week we came together to break bread. Paul spoke to the people and, because he intended to leave the next day, kept on talking until midnight. 8There were many lamps in the upstairs room where we were meeting. 9Seated in a window was a young man named Eutychus, who was sinking into a deep sleep as Paul talked on and on. When he was sound asleep, he fell to the ground from the third storey and was picked up dead. 10Paul went down, threw himself on the young man and put his arms around him. "Don't be alarmed," he said. "He's alive!" 11Then he went upstairs again and broke bread and ate. After talking until daylight, he left. 12The people took the young man home alive and were greatly comforted.

■ Paul's Farewell to the Ephesian Elders

13We went on ahead to the ship and sailed for Assos, where we were going to take Paul aboard. He had made this arrangement because he was going there on foot. 14When he met us at Assos, we took him aboard and went on to Mitylene. 15The next day we set sail from there and arrived off Kios. The day after that we crossed over to Samos, and on the following day arrived at Miletus. [16]Paul had decided to sail past Ephesus to avoid spending time in the province of Asia, for he was in a hurry to reach Jerusalem, if possible, by the day of Pentecost.

[17]From Miletus, Paul sent to Ephesus for the elders of the church. [18]When they arrived, he said to them: "You know how I lived the whole time I was with you, from the first day I came into the province of Asia. [19]I served the Lord with great humility and with tears, although I was severely tested by the plots of the Jews. [20]You know that I have not hesitated to preach anything that would be helpful to you but have taught you publicly and from house to house. [21]I have declared to both Jews and Greeks that they must turn to God in repentance and have faith in our Lord Jesus.

[22]"And now, compelled by the Spirit, I am going to Jerusalem, not knowing what will happen to me there. [23]I only know that in every city the Holy Spirit warns me that prison and hardships are facing me. [24]However, I consider my life worth nothing to me, if only I may finish the race and complete the task the Lord Jesus has given me — the task of testifying to the gospel of God's grace.

[25]"Now I know that none of you among whom I have gone about preaching the kingdom will ever see me again. [26]Therefore, I declare to you today that I am innocent of the blood of all men. [27]For I have not hesitated to proclaim to you the whole will of God. [28]Keep watch over yourselves and all the flock of which the Holy Spirit has made you overseers.[a] Be shepherds of the church of God,[b] which he bought with his own blood. [29]I know that after I leave, savage wolves will come in among you and will not spare the flock. [30]Even from your own number men will arise and distort the truth in order

PAUL'S LEGAL BATTLES
470 ROMAN SOLDIERS PROTECTED HIM FROM A LYNCH MOB

INSIGHT

"AND NOW, COMPELLED BY THE SPIRIT, I AM GOING TO JERUSALEM, NOT KNOWING WHAT WILL HAPPEN TO ME THERE. I ONLY KNOW THAT IN EVERY CITY THE HOLY SPIRIT WARNS ME THAT PRISON AND HARDSHIPS ARE FACING ME." ■ 20:22–23

The drumbeat starts with the last verse in chapter 20: "What grieved them most was his statement that they would never see his face again". After this, wherever he went, Paul's friends begged him not to go to Jerusalem. One of them bound his own hands and feet with Paul's belt, publicly role-playing what was in store for Paul (21:10–11).

But Paul had survived shipwrecks, a stoning, beatings and long nights in jail, and fear had never stopped him. Besides, he knew that God wanted him to take his word to Rome, and no disaster in Jerusalem could prevent that.

■ A DANGEROUS REVOLUTIONARY?
Thus, against all advice Paul went to Jerusalem. His reputation as a Christian missionary had spread, to such an extent that it took a brigade of 470 Roman soldiers to protect him from a Jewish lynch mob.

Luke details the process of Roman justice so thoroughly that some have speculated he wrote Acts as a legal brief for Paul's defence. Was Paul a violent terrorist intent on inciting revolt? Luke meticulously records that, no, Paul had no political ambitions and consistently worked within Roman law.

Most of the time, Roman law found Paul innocent. An official in Corinth dismissed

charges against him (18:15), as did the town clerk at Ephesus (19:35–41). In Judea Governor Festus and King Agrippa both concluded Paul might have been freed outright had he not appealed to Caesar (26:32).

■ THE BEGINNING OF THE END
Paul's last days of freedom summarise his turbulent life. His friends' fears regarding Jerusalem proved well-founded. A murderous mob there assailed him with trumped-up charges, and he had to be rescued bodily by soldiers.

In typical brazen style, Paul asked to address the unruly crowd, using the chance to confront them with his life's testimony. The crowd listened until he got to the part about a mission to the Gentiles; then it erupted.

In his speech (22:3–21), Paul referred back to the day he stood on the sidelines cheering as Stephen, the first Christian martyr, was killed. That violent scene was for ever etched in Paul's mind as a reminder of his former life. But another memory was even more powerful: the blinding light on the road to Damascus. Ever after that event in Damascus, Paul seemed determined to stun the human race as he had been stunned on that desert road. No matter how many nights in jail it cost him.

□ LIFE QUESTIONS:
Acts 20 shows Paul's closeness to other Christians. What produced such intense feelings? What could increase your closeness with others?

a 28 Traditionally *bishops*   b 28 Many manuscripts *of the Lord* to draw away disciples after them. ³¹So be on your guard! Remember that for three years I never stopped warning each of you night and day with tears.

³²"Now I commit you to God and to the word of his grace, which can build you up and give you an inheritance among all those who are sanctified. ³³I have not coveted anyone's silver or gold or clothing. ³⁴You yourselves know that these hands of mine have supplied my own needs and the needs of my companions. ³⁵In everything I did, I showed you that by this kind of hard work we must help the weak, remembering the words the Lord Jesus himself said: 'It is more blessed to give than to receive.' "

20:35 ■ EMOTIONAL FAREWELL

Paul had worked in Ephesus for longer than in any other city. Before leaving on his fateful trip to Jerusalem, he called the elders to Miletus for a final farewell (verse 17). In his speech, he quotes a saying from Jesus – the only New Testament quotation from Jesus not found in the Gospels.

³⁶When he had said this, he knelt down with all of them and prayed. ³⁷They all wept as they embraced him and kissed him. ³⁸What grieved them most was his statement that they would never see his face again. Then they accompanied him to the ship.

■ On to Jerusalem

21

After we had torn ourselves away from them, we put out to sea and sailed straight to Cos. The next day we went to Rhodes and from there to Patara. ²We found a ship crossing over to Phoenicia, went on board and set sail. ³After sighting Cyprus and passing to the south of it, we sailed on to Syria. We landed at Tyre, where our ship was to unload its cargo. ⁴Finding the disciples there, we stayed with them seven days. Through the Spirit they urged Paul not to go on to Jerusalem. ⁵But when our time was up, we left and continued on our way. All the disciples and their wives and children accompanied us out of the city, and there on the beach we knelt to pray. ⁶After saying good-bye to each other, we went aboard the ship, and they returned home.

⁷We continued our voyage from Tyre and landed at Ptolemais, where we greeted the brothers and stayed with them for a day. ⁸Leaving the next day, we reached Caesarea and stayed at the house of Philip the evangelist, one of the Seven. ⁹He had four unmarried daughters who prophesied.

¹⁰After we had been there a number of days, a prophet named Agabus came down from Judea. ¹¹Coming over to us, he took Paul's belt, tied his own hands and feet with it and said, "The Holy Spirit says, 'In this way the Jews of Jerusalem will bind the owner of this belt and will hand him over to the Gentiles.' "

¹²When we heard this, we and the people there pleaded with Paul not to go up to Jerusalem. ¹³Then Paul answered, "Why are you weeping and breaking my heart? I am ready not only to be bound, but also to die in Jerusalem for the name of the Lord Jesus." ¹⁴When he would not be dissuaded, we gave up and said, "The Lord's will be done."

¹⁵After this, we got ready and went up to Jerusalem. ¹⁶Some of the disciples from Caesarea accompanied us and brought us to the home of Mnason, where we were to stay. He was a man from Cyprus and one of the early disciples.

■ Paul's Arrival at Jerusalem

¹⁷When we arrived at Jerusalem, the brothers received us warmly. ¹⁸The next day Paul and the rest of us went to see James, and all the elders were present. ¹⁹Paul greeted them and reported in detail what God had done among the Gentiles through his ministry.

²⁰When they heard this, they praised God. Then they said to Paul: "You see, brother, how many thousands of Jews have believed, and all of them are zealous for the law. ²¹They have been informed that you teach all the Jews who live among the Gentiles to turn away from Moses, telling them not to circumcise their children or live according to our customs. ²²What shall we do? They will certainly hear that you have come, ²³so do what we tell you. There are four men with us who have made a vow. ²⁴Take these men, join in their purification rites and pay their expenses, so that they can have their heads shaved. Then everybody will know there is no truth in these reports about you, but that you yourself are living in obedience to the law. ²⁵As for the Gentile believers, we have written to them our decision that they should abstain from food sacrificed to idols, from blood, from the meat of strangled animals and from sexual immorality."

²⁶The next day Paul took the men and purified himself along with them. Then he went to the temple to give notice of the date when the days of purification would end and the offering would be made for each of them.

■ Paul Arrested

²⁷When the seven days were nearly over, some Jews from the province of Asia saw Paul at the temple. They stirred up the whole crowd and seized him, ²⁸shouting, "Men of Israel, help us! This is the man who teaches all men everywhere against our people and our law and this place. And besides, he has brought Greeks into the temple area and defiled this holy place." ²⁹(They had previously seen Trophimus the Ephesian in the city with Paul and assumed that Paul had brought him into the temple area.)

³⁰The whole city was aroused, and the people came running from all directions. Seizing Paul, they dragged him from the temple, and immediately the gates were shut. ³¹While they were trying to kill him, news reached the commander of the Roman troops that the whole city of Jerusalem was in an uproar. ³²He at once took some officers and soldiers and ran down to the crowd. When the rioters saw the commander and his soldiers, they stopped beating Paul.

³³The commander came up and arrested him and ordered him to be bound with two chains. Then he

asked who he was and what he had done. ³⁴Some in the crowd shouted one thing and some another, and since the commander could not get at the truth because of the uproar, he ordered that Paul be taken into the barracks. ³⁵When Paul reached the steps, the violence of the mob was so great he had to be carried by the soldiers. ³⁶The crowd that followed kept shouting, "Away with him!"

21:28 ■ A TRUMPED-UP CHARGE

Ironically, the arrest that led to Paul's final imprisonment came about because of a misunderstanding. He was actually trying to reassure the Jerusalem church of his loyalty by agreeing to take Jewish vows. But a rumour spread that Paul had illegally taken an "unclean" Gentile into a forbidden part of the temple, and a mob scene ensued. The remainder of Acts reports on various stages of Paul's legal appeals.

■ Paul Speaks to the Crowd

³⁷As the soldiers were about to take Paul into the barracks, he asked the commander, "May I say something to you?"

"Do you speak Greek?" he replied. ³⁸"Aren't you the Egyptian who started a revolt and led four thousand terrorists out into the desert some time ago?"

³⁹Paul answered, "I am a Jew, from Tarsus in Cilicia, a citizen of no ordinary city. Please let me speak to the people."

⁴⁰Having received the commander's permission, Paul stood on the steps and motioned to the crowd. When they were all silent, he said to them in Aramaic*ᵃ*: ¹"Brothers and fathers, listen now to my defence."

22 ²When they heard him speak to them in Aramaic, they became very quiet.

Then Paul said: ³"I am a Jew, born in Tarsus of Cilicia, but brought up in this city. Under Gamaliel I was thoroughly trained in the law of our fathers and was just as zealous for God as any of you are today. ⁴I persecuted the followers of this Way to their death, arresting both men and women and throwing them into prison, ⁵as also the high priest and all the Council can testify. I even obtained letters from them to their brothers in Damascus, and went there to bring these people as prisoners to Jerusalem to be punished.

⁶"About noon as I came near Damascus, suddenly a bright light from heaven flashed around me. ⁷I fell to the ground and heard a voice say to me, 'Saul! Saul! Why do you persecute me?'

⁸" 'Who are you, Lord?' I asked.

" 'I am Jesus of Nazareth, whom you are persecuting,' he replied. ⁹My companions saw the light, but they did not understand the voice of him who was speaking to me.

¹⁰" 'What shall I do, Lord?' I asked.

" 'Get up,' the Lord said, 'and go into Damascus. There you will be told all that you have been assigned to do.' ¹¹My companions led me by the hand into Damascus, because the brilliance of the light had blinded me.

¹²"A man named Ananias came to see me. He was a devout observer of the law and highly respected by all the Jews living there. ¹³He stood beside me and said, 'Brother Saul, receive your sight!' And at that very moment I was able to see him.

22:6 ■ THREE VERSIONS

Paul's change from persecutor to Christian missionary makes for one of the most dramatic conversion stories in the New Testament. Acts gives three versions: Luke's historical report in chapter 9; Paul's self-defence here before a Jewish mob; and his formal testimony before Agrippa (chapter 26), a descendant of the ruler who tried to kill the infant Jesus in Bethlehem. Each version adds new details custom-tailored to the specific audience.

¹⁴"Then he said: 'The God of our fathers has chosen you to know his will and to see the Righteous One and to hear words from his mouth. ¹⁵You will be his witness to all men of what you have seen and heard. ¹⁶And now what are you waiting for? Get up, be baptised and wash your sins away, calling on his name.'

¹⁷"When I returned to Jerusalem and was praying at the temple, I fell into a trance ¹⁸and saw the Lord speaking. 'Quick!' he said to me. 'Leave Jerusalem immediately, because they will not accept your testimony about me.'

¹⁹" 'Lord,' I replied, 'these men know that I went from one synagogue to another to imprison and beat those who believe in you. ²⁰And when the blood of your martyr*ᵃ* Stephen was shed, I stood there giving my approval and guarding the clothes of those who were killing him.'

²¹"Then the Lord said to me, 'Go; I will send you far away to the Gentiles.' "

■ Paul the Roman Citizen

²²The crowd listened to Paul until he said this. Then they raised their voices and shouted, "Rid the earth of him! He's not fit to live!"

²³As they were shouting and throwing off their cloaks and flinging dust into the air, ²⁴the commander ordered Paul to be taken into the barracks. He directed that he be flogged and questioned in order to find out why the people were shouting at him like this. ²⁵As they stretched him out to flog him, Paul said to the centurion standing there, "Is it legal for you to flog a Roman citizen who hasn't even been found guilty?"

²⁶When the centurion heard this, he went to the commander and reported it. "What are you going to do?" he asked. "This man is a Roman citizen."

²⁷The commander went to Paul and asked, "Tell me, are you a Roman citizen?"

"Yes, I am," he answered.

²⁸Then the commander said, "I had to pay a big price for my citizenship."

"But I was born a citizen," Paul replied.

²⁹Those who were about to question him withdrew immediately. The commander himself was

ᵃ40 Or possibly *Hebrew*; also in 22:2   *ᵃ20* Or *witness* alarmed when he realised that he had put Paul, a Roman citizen, in chains.

■ Before the Sanhedrin

30The next day, since the commander wanted to find out exactly why Paul was being accused by the Jews, he released him and ordered the chief priests and all the Sanhedrin to assemble. Then he brought Paul and had him stand before them.

23 Paul looked straight at the Sanhedrin and said, "My brothers, I have fulfilled my duty to God in all good conscience to this day." 2At this the high priest Ananias ordered those standing near Paul to strike him on the mouth. 3Then Paul said to him, "God will strike you, you whitewashed wall! You sit there to judge me according to the law, yet you yourself violate the law by commanding that I be struck!"

4Those who were standing near Paul said, "You dare to insult God's high priest?"

5Paul replied, "Brothers, I did not realise that he was the high priest; for it is written: 'Do not speak evil about the ruler of your people.'a"

6Then Paul, knowing that some of them were Sadducees and the others Pharisees, called out in the Sanhedrin, "My brothers, I am a Pharisee, the son of a Pharisee. I stand on trial because of my hope in the resurrection of the dead." 7When he said this, a dispute broke out between the Pharisees and the Sadducees, and the assembly was divided. 8(The Sadducees say that there is no resurrection, and that there are neither angels nor spirits, but the Pharisees acknowledge them all.)

23:6 ■ PAUL UNDER ATTACK

Under pressure, Paul proved to be a formidable opponent. In this scene, he spoke back to a priest who struck him on the mouth. Using great skill, Paul divided his accusers by exploiting the differences between two Jewish sects, the Pharisees and Sadducees (see note on 4:1). Paul managed to arouse such intense opposition that a group of 40 conspirators vowed not to eat or drink until they had killed him.

9There was a great uproar, and some of the teachers of the law who were Pharisees stood up and argued vigorously. "We find nothing wrong with this man," they said. "What if a spirit or an angel has spoken to him?" 10The dispute became so violent that the commander was afraid Paul would be torn to pieces by them. He ordered the troops to go down and take him away from them by force and bring him into the barracks.

11The following night the Lord stood near Paul and said, "Take courage! As you have testified about me in Jerusalem, so you must also testify in Rome."

■ The Plot to Kill Paul

12The next morning the Jews formed a conspiracy and bound themselves with an oath not to eat or drink until they had killed Paul. 13More than forty men were involved in this plot. 14They went to the chief priests and elders and said, "We have taken a solemn oath not to eat anything until we have killed Paul. 15Now then, you and the Sanhedrin petition the commander to bring him before you on the pretext of wanting more accurate information about his case. We are ready to kill him before he gets here."

16But when the son of Paul's sister heard of this plot, he went into the barracks and told Paul.

23:16 ■ PAUL'S FAMILY

This mention of Paul's nephew is the only reference to Paul's family. Born a Roman citizen in Tarsus (22:28), Paul probably came from a rather prominent family. Only a minority of people in the Roman empire held citizenship, especially in occupied lands. Citizenship could be purchased at a great price or awarded by Roman authorities, but Paul specifies that his came through inheritance.

17Then Paul called one of the centurions and said, "Take this young man to the commander; he has something to tell him." 18So he took him to the commander.

The centurion said, "Paul, the prisoner, sent for me and asked me to bring this young man to you because he has something to tell you."

19The commander took the young man by the hand, drew him aside and asked, "What is it you want to tell me?"

20He said: "The Jews have agreed to ask you to bring Paul before the Sanhedrin tomorrow on the pretext of wanting more accurate information about him. 21Don't give in to them, because more than forty of them are waiting in ambush for him. They have taken an oath not to eat or drink until they have killed him. They are ready now, waiting for your consent to their request."

22The commander dismissed the young man and cautioned him, "Don't tell anyone that you have reported this to me."

■ Paul Transferred to Caesarea

23Then he called two of his centurions and ordered them, "Get ready a detachment of two hundred soldiers, seventy horsemen and two hundred spearmenb to go to Caesarea at nine tonight. 24Provide mounts for Paul so that he may be taken safely to Governor Felix."

25He wrote a letter as follows:

26Claudius Lysias,

To His Excellency, Governor Felix:

Greetings.

27This man was seized by the Jews and they were about to kill him, but I came with my troops and rescued him, for I had learned that he is a Roman citizen. 28I wanted to know why they were accusing him, so I brought him to their Sanhedrin. 29I found that the accusation

a5 Exodus 22:28   b23 The meaning of the Greek for this word is uncertain.

had to do with questions about their law, but there was no charge against him that deserved death or imprisonment. [30]When I was informed of a plot to be carried out against the man, I sent him to you at once. I also ordered his accusers to present to you their case against him.

[31]So the soldiers, carrying out their orders, took Paul with them during the night and brought him as far as Antipatris. [32]The next day they let the cavalry go on with him, while they returned to the barracks. [33]When the cavalry arrived in Caesarea, they delivered the letter to the governor and handed Paul over to him. [34]The governor read the letter and asked what province he was from. Learning that he was from Cilicia, [35]he said, "I will hear your case when your accusers get here." Then he ordered that Paul be kept under guard in Herod's palace.

■ The Trial Before Felix

24 Five days later the high priest Ananias went down to Caesarea with some of the elders and a lawyer named Tertullus, and they brought their charges against Paul before the governor. [2]When Paul was called in, Tertullus presented his case before Felix: "We have enjoyed a long period of peace under you, and your foresight has brought about reforms in this nation. [3]Everywhere and in every way, most excellent Felix, we acknowledge this with profound gratitude. [4]But in order not to weary you further, I would request that you be kind enough to hear us briefly.

[5]"We have found this man to be a troublemaker, stirring up riots among the Jews all over the world. He is a ringleader of the Nazarene sect [6]and even tried to desecrate the temple; so we seized him. [8]By[a] examining him yourself you will be able to learn the truth about all these charges we are bringing against him."

[9]The Jews joined in the accusation, asserting that these things were true.

[10]When the governor motioned for him to speak, Paul replied: "I know that for a number of years you have been a judge over this nation; so I gladly make my defence. [11]You can easily verify that no more than twelve days ago I went up to Jerusalem to worship. [12]My accusers did not find me arguing with anyone at the temple, or stirring up a crowd in the synagogues or anywhere else in the city. [13]And they cannot prove to you the charges they are now making against me. [14]However, I admit that I worship the God of our fathers as a follower of the Way, which they call a sect. I believe everything that agrees with the Law and that is written in the Prophets, [15]and I have the same hope in God as these men, that there will be a resurrection of both the righteous and the wicked. [16]So I strive always to keep my conscience clear before God and man.

[17]"After an absence of several years, I came to Jerusalem to bring my people gifts for the poor and to present offerings. [18]I was ceremonially clean when they found me in the temple courts doing this. There was no crowd with me, nor was I involved in any disturbance. [19]But there are some Jews from the province of Asia, who ought to be here before you and bring charges if they have anything against me. [20]Or these who are here should state what crime they found in me when I stood before the Sanhedrin — [21]unless it was this one thing I shouted as I stood in their presence: 'It is concerning the resurrection of the dead that I am on trial before you today.' "

[22]Then Felix, who was well acquainted with the Way, adjourned the proceedings. "When Lysias the commander comes," he said, "I will decide your case." [23]He ordered the centurion to keep Paul under guard but to give him some freedom and permit his friends to take care of his needs.

[24]Several days later Felix came with his wife Drusilla, who was a Jewess. He sent for Paul and listened to him as he spoke about faith in Christ Jesus. [25]As Paul discoursed on righteousness, self-control and the judgment to come, Felix was afraid and said, "That's enough for now! You may leave. When I find it convenient, I will send for you." [26]At the same time he was hoping that Paul would offer him a bribe, so he sent for him frequently and talked with him.

[27]When two years had passed, Felix was succeeded by Porcius Festus, but because Felix wanted to grant a favour to the Jews, he left Paul in prison.

24:27 ■ LEFT IN CHAINS

Felix was unpopular with the Jews of Palestine. The brief report in Acts shows him to be shrewd and even corrupt (verse 26). Recalled by Rome because of his troubles with the Jews, Felix left Paul in chains for a period of two years. When the new Roman ruler arrived, the controversy over Paul hadn't died down. Jewish leaders immediately confronted Festus with their charges against Paul.

■ The Trial Before Festus

25 Three days after arriving in the province, Festus went up from Caesarea to Jerusalem, [2]where the chief priests and Jewish leaders appeared before him and presented the charges against Paul. [3]They urgently requested Festus, as a favour to them, to have Paul transferred to Jerusalem, for they were preparing an ambush to kill him along the way. [4]Festus answered, "Paul is being held at Caesarea, and I myself am going there soon. [5]Let some of your leaders come with me and press charges against the man there, if he has done anything wrong."

[6]After spending eight or ten days with them, he went down to Caesarea, and the next day he convened the court and ordered that Paul be brought before him. [7]When Paul appeared, the Jews who had come down from Jerusalem stood around him, bringing many serious charges against him, which they could not prove.

[8]Then Paul made his defence: "I have done nothing wrong against the law of the Jews or against the temple or against Caesar."

[9]Festus, wishing to do the Jews a favour, said to

---

[a] 6–8 Some manuscripts him and wanted to judge him according to our law. [7]But the commander, Lysias, came and with the use of much force snatched him from our hands [8]and ordered his accusers to come before you. By

Paul, "Are you willing to go up to Jerusalem and stand trial before me there on these charges?"

10Paul answered: "I am now standing before Caesar's court, where I ought to be tried. I have not done any wrong to the Jews, as you yourself know very well. 11If, however, I am guilty of doing anything deserving death, I do not refuse to die. But if the charges brought against me by these Jews are not true, no-one has the right to hand me over to them. I appeal to Caesar!"

12After Festus had conferred with his council, he declared: "You have appealed to Caesar. To Caesar you will go!"

■ Festus Consults King Agrippa

13A few days later King Agrippa and Bernice arrived at Caesarea to pay their respects to Festus. 14Since they were spending many days there, Festus discussed Paul's case with the king. He said: "There is a man here whom Felix left as a prisoner. 15When I went to Jerusalem, the chief priests and elders of the Jews brought charges against him and asked that he be condemned.

25:13 ■ TWO RULERS

In Jesus' day Rome ruled Palestine through local rulers (the Herods) and their overseer Pilate, a governor who reported directly to Rome. Now, around A.D. 59 or 60, their counterparts were the Roman governor Festus and the last of the Herods, Agrippa II. Festus, a responsible leader, dealt with Paul's case promptly, whereas his predecessor Felix had stalled for two years, leaving Paul in prison. Festus used the visit of Herod Agrippa to schedule this special inquiry into Paul's case.

16"I told them that it is not the Roman custom to hand over any man before he has faced his accusers and has had an opportunity to defend himself against their charges. 17When they came here with me, I did not delay the case, but convened the court the next day and ordered the man to be brought in. 18When his accusers got up to speak, they did not charge him with any of the crimes I had expected. 19Instead, they had some points of dispute with him about their own religion and about a dead man named Jesus whom Paul claimed was alive. 20I was at a loss how to investigate such matters; so I asked if he would be willing to go to Jerusalem and stand trial there on these charges. 21When Paul made his appeal to be held over for the Emperor's decision, I ordered him to be held until I could send him to Caesar."

22Then Agrippa said to Festus, "I would like to hear this man myself."

He replied, "Tomorrow you will hear him."

■ Paul Before Agrippa

23The next day Agrippa and Bernice came with great pomp and entered the audience room with the high ranking officers and the leading men of the city. At the command of Festus, Paul was brought in. 24Festus said: "King Agrippa, and all who are present

with us, you see this man! The whole Jewish community has petitioned me about him in Jerusalem and here in Caesarea, shouting that he ought not to live any longer. 25I found he had done nothing deserving of death, but because he made his appeal to the Emperor I decided to send him to Rome. 26But I have nothing definite to write to His Majesty about him. Therefore I have brought him before all of you, and especially before you, King Agrippa, so that as a result of this investigation I may have something to write. 27For I think it is unreasonable to send on a prisoner without specifying the charges against him."

26 Then Agrippa said to Paul, "You have permission to speak for yourself."

So Paul motioned with his hand and began his defence: 2"King Agrippa, I consider myself fortunate to stand before you today as I make my defence against all the accusations of the Jews, 3and especially so because you are well acquainted with all the Jewish customs and controversies. Therefore, I beg you to listen to me patiently.

4"The Jews all know the way I have lived ever since I was a child, from the beginning of my life in my own country, and also in Jerusalem. 5They have known me for a long time and can testify, if they are willing, that according to the strictest sect of our religion, I lived as a Pharisee. 6And now it is because of my hope in what God has promised our fathers that I am on trial today. 7This is the promise our twelve tribes are hoping to see fulfilled as they earnestly serve God day and night. O King, it is because of this hope that the Jews are accusing me. 8Why should any of you consider it incredible that God raises the dead?

9"I too was convinced that I ought to do all that was possible to oppose the name of Jesus of Nazareth. 10And that is just what I did in Jerusalem. On the authority of the chief priests I put many of the saints in prison, and when they were put to death, I cast my vote against them. 11Many a time I went from one synagogue to another to have them punished, and I tried to force them to blaspheme. In my obsession against them, I even went to foreign cities to persecute them.

12"On one of these journeys I was going to Damascus with the authority and commission of the chief priests. 13About noon, O King, as I was on the road, I saw a light from heaven, brighter than the sun, blazing around me and my companions. 14We all fell to the ground, and I heard a voice saying to me in Aramaic,ᵃ 'Saul, Saul, why do you persecute me? It is hard for you to kick against the goads.'

26:14 ■ KICKING THE OX-GOADS

The proverb comes from a sharp "goad" farmers used to control their oxen hitched to a plough. It means something like, "You are only hurting yourself."

15"Then I asked, 'Who are you, Lord?'

" 'I am Jesus, whom you are persecuting,' the

ᵃ14 Or Hebrew

Lord replied. [16]'Now get up and stand on your feet. I have appeared to you to appoint you as a servant and as a witness of what you have seen of me and what I will show you. [17]I will rescue you from your own people and from the Gentiles. I am sending you to them [18]to open their eyes and turn them from darkness to light, and from the power of Satan to God, so that they may receive forgiveness of sins and a place among those who are sanctified by faith in me.'

[19]"So then, King Agrippa, I was not disobedient to the vision from heaven. [20]First to those in Damascus, then to those in Jerusalem and in all Judea, and to the Gentiles also, I preached that they should repent and turn to God and prove their repentance by their deeds. [21]That is why the Jews seized me in the temple courts and tried to kill me. [22]But I have had God's help to this very day, and so I stand here and testify to small and great alike. I am saying nothing beyond what the prophets and Moses said would happen — [23]that the Christ[b] would suffer and, as the first to rise from the dead, would proclaim light to his own people and to the Gentiles."

[24]At this point Festus interrupted Paul's defence. "You are out of your mind, Paul!" he shouted. "Your great learning is driving you insane."

[25]"I am not insane, most excellent Festus," Paul replied. "What I am saying is true and reasonable. [26]The king is familiar with these things, and I can speak freely to him. I am convinced that none of this has escaped his notice, because it was not done in a corner. [27]King Agrippa, do you believe the prophets? I know you do."

[28]Then Agrippa said to Paul, "Do you think that in such a short time you can persuade me to be a Christian?"

[29]Paul replied, "Short time or long — I pray God that not only you but all who are listening to me today may become what I am, except for these chains."

[30]The king rose, and with him the governor and Bernice and those sitting with them. [31]They left the room, and while talking with one another, they said, "This man is not doing anything that deserves death or imprisonment."

[32]Agrippa said to Festus, "This man could have been set free if he had not appealed to Caesar."

■ Paul Sails for Rome

27 When it was decided that we would sail for Italy, Paul and some other prisoners were handed over to a centurion named Julius, who belonged to the Imperial Regiment. [2]We boarded a ship from Adramyttium about to sail for ports along the coast of the province of Asia, and we put out to sea. Aristarchus, a Macedonian from Thessalonica, was with us.

[3]The next day we landed at Sidon; and Julius, in kindness to Paul, allowed him to go to his friends so they might provide for his needs. [4]From there we put out to sea again and passed to the lee of Cyprus because the winds were against us. [5]When we had sailed across the open sea off the coast of Cilicia and Pamphylia, we landed at Myra in Lycia. [6]There the centurion found an Alexandrian ship sailing for Italy

and put us on board. [7]We made slow headway for many days and had difficulty arriving off Cnidus. When the wind did not allow us to hold our course, we sailed to the lee of Crete, opposite Salmone. [8]We moved along the coast with difficulty and came to a place called Fair Havens, near the town of Lasea.

[9]Much time had been lost, and sailing had already become dangerous because by now it was after the Fast.[a] So Paul warned them, [10]"Men, I can see that our voyage is going to be disastrous and bring great loss to ship and cargo, and to our own lives also." [11]But the centurion, instead of listening to what Paul said, followed the advice of the pilot and of the owner of the ship. [12]Since the harbour was unsuitable to winter in, the majority decided that we should sail on, hoping to reach Phoenix and winter there. This was a harbour in Crete, facing both south-west and north-west.

■ The Storm

[13]When a gentle south wind began to blow, they thought they had obtained what they wanted; so they weighed anchor and sailed along the shore of Crete. [14]Before very long, a wind of hurricane force, called the "north-easter", swept down from the island. [15]The ship was caught by the storm and could not head into the wind; so we gave way to it and were driven along. [16]As we passed to the lee of a small island called Cauda, we were hardly able to make the lifeboat secure. [17]When the men had hoisted it aboard, they passed ropes under the ship itself to hold it together. Fearing that they would run aground on the sand-bars of Syrtis, they lowered the sea anchor and let the ship be driven along. [18]We took such a violent battering from the storm that the next day they began to throw the cargo overboard. [19]On the third day, they threw the ship's tackle overboard with their own hands. [20]When neither sun nor stars appeared for many days and the storm continued raging, we finally gave up all hope of being saved.

27:13 ■ SAILING LOG
Luke was no sailor, but he portrays an authentically detailed account of the trip and storm. For example, sailors can sense that they are "approaching land" (verse 27) long before they see it, both by an acutely developed sense of smell and also by the sound of breaking waves, which carries far out to sea. In the eastern Mediterranean, autumn winds blow from the west, which made westward sailing difficult for ships of that day.

[21]After the men had gone a long time without food, Paul stood up before them and said: "Men, you should have taken my advice not to sail from Crete; then you would have spared yourselves this damage and loss. [22]But now I urge you to keep up your courage, because not one of you will be lost; only the ship will be destroyed. [23]Last night an angel of the God whose I am and whom I serve stood beside me [24]and said, 'Do not be afraid, Paul. You must stand

b 23 Or Messiah   a 9 That is, the Day of Atonement (Yom Kippur) trial before Caesar; and God has graciously given you the lives of all who sail with you.' 25So keep up your courage, men, for I have faith in God that it will happen just as he told me. 26Nevertheless, we must run aground on some island."

■ The Shipwreck

27On the fourteenth night we were still being driven across the Adriatic*b* Sea, when about midnight the sailors sensed they were approaching land. 28They took soundings and found that the water was one hundred and twenty feet*c* deep. A short time later they took soundings again and found it was ninety feet*d* deep. 29Fearing that we would be dashed against the rocks, they dropped four anchors from the stern and prayed for daylight. 30In an attempt to escape from the ship, the sailors let the lifeboat down into the sea, pretending they were going to lower some anchors from the bow. 31Then Paul said to the centurion and the soldiers, "Unless these men stay with the ship, you cannot be saved." 32So the soldiers cut the ropes that held the lifeboat and let it fall away.

33Just before dawn Paul urged them all to eat. "For the last fourteen days," he said, "you have been in constant suspense and have gone without food — you haven't eaten anything. 34Now I urge you to take some food. You need it to survive. Not one of you will lose a single hair from his head." 35After he said this, he took some bread and gave thanks to God in front of them all. Then he broke it and began to eat. 36They were all encouraged and ate some food themselves. 37Altogether there were 276 of us on board. 38When they had eaten as much as they wanted, they lightened the ship by throwing the grain into the sea.

39When daylight came, they did not recognise the land, but they saw a bay with a sandy beach, where they decided to run the ship aground if they could. 40Cutting loose the anchors, they left them in the sea and at the same time untied the ropes that held the rudders. Then they hoisted the foresail to the wind and made for the beach. 41But the ship struck a sand-bar and ran aground. The bow stuck fast and would not move, and the stern was broken to pieces by the pounding of the surf.

42The soldiers planned to kill the prisoners to prevent any of them from swimming away and escaping. 43But the centurion wanted to spare Paul's life and kept them from carrying out their plan. He ordered those who could swim to jump overboard first and get to land. 44The rest were to get there on planks or on pieces of the ship. In this way everyone reached land in safety.

■ Ashore on Malta

28 Once safely on shore, we found out that the island was called Malta. 2The islanders showed us unusual kindness. They built a fire and welcomed us all because it was raining and cold. 3Paul gathered a pile of brushwood and, as he put it on the fire, a viper, driven out by the heat, fastened itself on his hand. 4When the islanders saw the snake

hanging from his hand, they said to each other, "This man must be a murderer; for though he escaped from the sea, Justice has not allowed him to live." 5But Paul shook the snake off into the fire and suffered no ill effects. 6The people expected him to swell up or suddenly fall dead, but after waiting a long time and seeing nothing unusual happen to him, they changed their minds and said he was a god.

7There was an estate near by that belonged to Publius, the chief official of the island. He welcomed us to his home and for three days entertained us hospitably. 8His father was sick in bed, suffering from fever and dysentery. Paul went in to see him and, after prayer, placed his hands on him and healed him. 9When this had happened, the rest of the sick on the island came and were cured. 10They honoured us in many ways and when we were ready to sail, they furnished us with the supplies we needed.

■ Arrival at Rome

11After three months we put out to sea in a ship that had wintered in the island. It was an Alexandrian ship with the figurehead of the twin gods Castor and Pollux. 12We put in at Syracuse and stayed there three days. 13From there we set sail and arrived at Rhegium. The next day the south wind came up, and on the following day we reached Puteoli. 14There we found some brothers who invited us to spend a week with them. And so we came to Rome. 15The brothers there had heard that we were coming, and they travelled as far as the Forum of Appius and the Three Taverns to meet us. At the sight of these men Paul thanked God and was encouraged. 16When we got to Rome, Paul was allowed to live by himself, with a soldier to guard him.

28:16 ■ TIME ON HIS HANDS
Luke reports that controversy about the Christian "sect" had preceded Paul to Rome (verse 22). The apostle put his time of house arrest to good use, evangelising all who came to see him and writing to the churches he had founded along the way. Such New Testament books as Philippians, Colossians, Ephesians, and Philemon came out of this period of protective custody, which may have lasted four years.

■ Paul Preaches at Rome Under Guard

17Three days later he called together the leaders of the Jews. When they had assembled, Paul said to them: "My brothers, although I have done nothing against our people or against the customs of our ancestors, I was arrested in Jerusalem and handed over to the Romans. 18They examined me and wanted to release me, because I was not guilty of any crime deserving death. 19But when the Jews objected, I was compelled to appeal to Caesar — not that I had any charge to bring against my own people. 20For this reason I have asked to see you and talk with

---

b 27 In ancient times the name referred to an area extending well south of Italy. (about 27 metres)   *c 28* Greek *twenty orguias* (about 37 metres)   *d 28* Greek *fifteen orguias* you. It is because of the hope of Israel that I am bound with this chain."

21 They replied, "We have not received any letters from Judea concerning you, and none of the brothers who have come from there has reported or said anything bad about you. 22 But we want to hear what your views are, for we know that people everywhere are talking against this sect."

23 They arranged to meet Paul on a certain day, and came in even larger numbers to the place where he was staying. From morning till evening he explained and declared to them the kingdom of God and tried to convince them about Jesus from the Law of Moses and from the Prophets. 24 Some were convinced by what he said, but others would not believe. 25 They disagreed among themselves and began to leave after Paul had made this final statement: "The Holy Spirit spoke the truth to your forefathers when he said through Isaiah the prophet:

26 " 'Go to this people and say,
"You will be ever hearing but never
      understanding;
   you will be ever seeing but never
      perceiving."
27 For this people's heart has become calloused;
   they hardly hear with their ears,
   and they have closed their eyes.
Otherwise they might see with their eyes,
   hear with their ears,
   understand with their hearts
and turn, and I would heal them.'a

28 "Therefore I want you to know that God's salvation has been sent to the Gentiles, and they will listen!"b

30 For two whole years Paul stayed there in his own rented house and welcomed all who came to see him. 31 Boldly and without hindrance he preached the kingdom of God and taught about the Lord Jesus Christ.

■ ROME AT LAST
PAUL FINALLY MADE IT TO THE CAPITAL – IN CHAINS

INSIGHT

FROM MORNING TILL EVENING HE EXPLAINED AND DECLARED TO THEM THE KINGDOM OF GOD AND TRIED TO CONVINCE THEM ABOUT JESUS FROM THE LAW OF MOSES AND FROM THE PROPHETS. ■ 28:23

Acts records 18 speeches in all, the last three of which were delivered before a very select audience. Roman officials, intrigued by the most talked-about prisoner in their corner of the empire, brought Paul out and asked him to perform, like a trained bear. As a result of their inquisition, he got his long-awaited trip to Rome.

It is hard for us today to realise how completely the city of Rome then dominated the world. "All roads lead to Rome" was more than a figure of speech. Like a centre of gravity, the city attracted all the roads and commerce, all the leaders and thinkers and fortune-seekers of the empire. Political and military power fanned out from Rome. It was the indisputable capital of the world. If Christianity was to gain a foothold anywhere, it had to be in Rome.

■ A MISSIONARY IN CHAINS
Ironically, Paul, the greatest spokesman for the Christian faith, arrived in Rome as a prisoner. He was exhausted, having just survived a harrowing shipwreck. In Rome, Paul got hours of quiet solitude to work on fond letters to the churches he had left behind.b

In one sense, Acts ends anticlimactically, for Luke leaves Paul's life dangling. Most scholars believe Paul was released from this imprisonment and expanded his ministry into new frontiers. Luke records nothing of this period, and nothing about the trial of Paul or his eventual fate. He ends with a single memory, frozen in time: Paul, confined to his house, welcoming and preaching to all who come.

Paul could no longer choose his audience; they had to seek him. But boldly, in the heart of mighty Rome, he talked of a new kingdom and a new king. Christianity had made the journey, and the transition, from Jerusalem to Rome.

□ LIFE QUESTIONS:
Is it better for Christianity to be popular or unpopular?

a 27 Isaiah 6:9,10   b 28 Some manuscripts listen!" 29 After he said this, the Jews left, arguing vigorously among themselves.

ROMANS

■ A MOST DEMANDING AUDIENCE

IF YOU WERE STRANDED ON A DESERTED ISLAND, WHAT BOOK
WOULD YOU WANT ALONG?

I THANK MY GOD THROUGH JESUS CHRIST FOR ALL OF YOU, BECAUSE YOUR FAITH IS
BEING REPORTED ALL OVER THE WORLD. ■ 1:8

Imagine yourself on a college speech course. Your assignment: a brief speech on "the meaning of life". Over late-night cups of coffee, you outline the Christian faith and what it means to you. You devote a lot of time to this assignment — after all, this speech may be the only clear expression of faith your classmates will ever hear.

But what if you were asked to write up the speech for your local paper? Instead of a few dozen listeners, you would have thousands of readers. Undoubtedly, you would devote even more time and care to preparation.

■ LETTER TO THE CENTRE OF THE WORLD

Let your imagination run even further. How would you react if you were asked to adapt this same speech for a front-page story in the *Guardian* or the *Daily Telegraph*? These newspapers have sophisticated, demanding readers. In writing for them, you would meticulously pore over every word, polishing phrases and making sure your thoughts were complete and well-expressed.

You can see a similar process at work in the apostle Paul's various letters. Some of his letters were, like a college speech, addressed to a small cluster of people he knew by name. Often they consisted of warm, personal words of advice or even fatherly scolding.

But, *Romans* . . . the very title of this book conjures up images of the powerful empire that ruled the western world. To people of Paul's

day, Rome was the centre of the world in every way: law, culture, power, and learning. A letter to this sophisticated audience had to be impressive indeed.

In Romans, Paul brilliantly set down the whole scope of Christian doctrine, which, at that time, was still being passed along orally from town to town. Paul wanted to convince those demanding readers that Christ held the answers to all of life's important questions.

■ ONE-VOLUME SUMMARY

Literary types are often asked questions like this: "What one book would you most want along if you were stranded on a deserted island?" (author G.K. Chesterton gave a classic reply: *"Thomas' Guide to Practical Shipbuilding"*!) If asked the same question about a single book of the Bible, many Christians would choose Romans. Compact enough to fit on one spread of a modern newspaper, Romans still manages to encompass all essentials of the Christian faith.

Despite its thoroughness, however, Romans does not read like a dry book of theology. Great revivals in church history have been spawned by a study of this book. Augustine, Martin Luther, and John Wesley all trace their spiritual renewals to a reading of Romans. It gives the apostle Paul's final answer to questions about the "meaning of life".

■ HOW TO READ ROMANS

Romans is a book to savour, slowly and carefully. Paul is developing an argument, and his logic unfolds thought by thought from the very first chapter. You may recognise many well-known verses in Romans; note these in their context as a part of Paul's overall presentation.

Romans divides into a clear outline. Chapters 1–3 introduce the book and give the need for the good news of the gospel. The end

of chapter 3, called the "central theological passage in the Bible", compresses the core message in a brief paragraph. Chapters 4 and 5 expand on that message.

Romans 6–8 discuss the working out of the gospel in a Christian's life. Paul then pauses for three chapters (9–11) to link his argument to the Old Testament history of the Jews. From there, he proceeds to give practical advice on specific problems (12–16).

It will require time and concentration to grasp fully the teachings of Romans; few people would claim to have "mastered" this book. But it has no equal as a concise, reasonable statement of the Christian faith.

■ 3-TRACK READING PLAN

For an explanation and complete listing of the 3-track reading plan, turn to page x.

■ TRACK 1:
Two-Week Courses on the Bible
The Track 1 reading programme on the Life and Teachings of Paul includes three chapters from Romans. See page x for a complete listing of this course.

■ TRACK 2:
An Overview of Romans in 4 Days
□ Day 1. Read the Introduction to Romans and

then read chapter 3 as a summary of the whole book. Take your time as you read the end, verses 21–31.
□ Day 2. Read of Paul's struggles against sin in chapter 7.
□ Day 3. Paul concludes this great section on the Christian life with the triumphant message of chapter 8.
□ Day 4. Paul gets practical towards the end of the book. Read his direct instructions on how to live in chapter 12.

Now turn to page xi for your next Track 2 reading project.

■ TRACK 3:
All of Romans in 14 Days
After you have read through Romans, turn to pages xii–xiii for your next Track 3 reading project.

□ 1   □ 2   □ 3   □ 4
□ 5   □ 6   □ 7   □ 8
□ 9.   □ 10   □ 11
□ 12–13   □ 14
□ 15–16

1 Paul, a servant of Christ Jesus, called to be an apostle and set apart for the gospel of God— ²the gospel he promised beforehand through his prophets in the Holy Scriptures ³regarding his Son, who as to his human nature was a descendant of David, ⁴and who through the Spirit*a* of holiness was declared with power to be the Son of God,*b* by his resurrection from the dead: Jesus Christ our Lord. ⁵Through him and for his name's sake, we received grace and apostleship to call people from among all the Gentiles to the obedience that comes from faith. ⁶And you also are among those who are called to belong to Jesus Christ.

⁷To all in Rome who are loved by God and called to be saints:

Grace and peace to you from God our Father and from the Lord Jesus Christ.

■ Paul's Longing to Visit Rome
⁸First, I thank my God through Jesus Christ for all of you, because your faith is being reported all over the world. ⁹God, whom I serve with my whole heart in preaching the gospel of his Son, is my witness how constantly I remember you ¹⁰in my prayers at all times; and I pray that now at last by God's will the way may be opened for me to come to you. ¹¹I long to see you so that I may impart to you some spiritual gift to make you strong—¹²that is, that you and I may be mutually encouraged by each other's faith. ¹³I do not want you to be unaware, brothers, that I planned many times to come to you (but have been prevented from doing so until now) in order that I might have a harvest among you, just as I have had among the other Gentiles. ¹⁴I am bound both to Greeks and non-Greeks, both to the wise and the foolish. ¹⁵That is why I am so eager to preach the gospel also to you who are at Rome.

¹⁶I am not ashamed of the gospel, because it is the power of God for the salvation of everyone who believes: first for the Jew, then for the Gentile. ¹⁷For in the gospel a righteousness from God is revealed, a righteousness that is by faith from first to last,*c* just as it is written: "The righteous will live by faith."*d*

1:17 ■ LUTHER'S GATEWAY
Verses 16–17, which contain a summary of Paul's message to the Romans, changed Martin Luther for ever. After he finally understood the phrase "righteousness from God", Luther said, "I felt myself to be reborn and to have gone through open doors into paradise. The whole of Scripture took on a new meaning . . . . This passage of Paul became to me a gateway to heaven."

■ God's Wrath Against Mankind
¹⁸The wrath of God is being revealed from heaven against all the godlessness and wickedness of men who suppress the truth by their wickedness, ¹⁹since what may be known about God is plain to them, because God has made it plain to them. ²⁰For since the creation of the world God's invisible qualities—his eternal power and divine nature—have been clearly seen, being understood from what has been made, so that men are without excuse.

²¹For although they knew God, they neither glorified him as God nor gave thanks to him, but their thinking became futile and their foolish hearts were darkened. ²²Although they claimed to be wise, they became fools ²³and exchanged the glory of the immortal God for images made to look like mortal man and birds and animals and reptiles.

²⁴Therefore God gave them over in the sinful desires of their hearts to sexual impurity for the

*a*4 Or who as to his spirit   *b*4 Or was appointed to be the Son of God with power   *c*17 Or is from faith to faith   *d*17 Hab. 2:4

degrading of their bodies with one another. 25They exchanged the truth of God for a lie, and worshipped and served created things rather than the Creator—who is for ever praised. Amen.

1:20 ■ NO EXCUSES

From Adam and Eve onwards, people have tended to blame others, not themselves, for what goes wrong. Romans 1-3 sets forth an important principle that has been widely recognised by recovery groups such as Alcoholics Anonymous: unless you first accept responsibility for wrong behaviour and stop blaming others, you'll never get well.

26Because of this, God gave them over to shameful lusts. Even their women exchanged natural relations for unnatural ones. 27In the same way the men also abandoned natural relations with women and were inflamed with lust for one another. Men committed indecent acts with other men, and received in themselves the due penalty for their perversion. 28Furthermore, since they did not think it worth while to retain the knowledge of God, he gave them over to a depraved mind, to do what ought not to be done. 29They have become filled with every kind of wickedness, evil, greed and depravity. They are full of envy, murder, strife, deceit and malice. They are gossips, 30slanderers, God-haters, insolent, arrogant and boastful; they invent ways of doing evil; they disobey their parents; 31they are senseless, faithless, heartless, ruthless. 32Although they know God's righteous decree that those who do such things deserve death, they not only continue to do these very things but also approve of those who practise them.

■ God's Righteous Judgment

2 You, therefore, have no excuse, you who pass judgment on someone else, for at whatever point you judge the other, you are condemning yourself, because you who pass judgment do the same things. 2Now we know that God's judgment against those who do such things is based on truth. 3So when you, a mere man, pass judgment on them and yet do the same things, do you think you will escape God's judgment? 4Or do you show contempt for the riches of his kindness, tolerance and patience, not realising that God's kindness leads you towards repentance?

2:1 ■ UNSETTLING PROVERBS

"It takes one to know one." "The pot calls the kettle black." Or, as the Spanish say, "The donkey calls the pig 'long ears'." All these proverbs echo Paul's point: we often criticise in others the very thing we ourselves say or do.

5But because of your stubbornness and your unrepentant heart, you are storing up wrath against yourself for the day of God's wrath, when his righteous judgment will be revealed. 6God "will give to each person according to what he has done".a 7To those who by persistence in doing good seek glory, honour and immortality, he will give eternal life. 8But for those who are self-seeking and who reject the truth and follow evil, there will be wrath and anger. 9There will be trouble and distress for every human being who does evil: first for the Jew, then for the Gentile; 10but glory, honour and peace for everyone who does good: first for the Jew, then for the Gentile. 11For God does not show favouritism.

12All who sin apart from the law will also perish apart from the law, and all who sin under the law will be judged by the law. 13For it is not those who hear the law who are righteous in God's sight, but it is those who obey the law who will be declared righteous. 14(Indeed, when Gentiles, who do not have the law, do by nature things required by the law, they are a law for themselves, even though they do not have the law, 15since they show that the requirements of the law are written on their hearts, their consciences also bearing witness, and their thoughts now accusing, now even defending them.) 16This will take place on the day when God will judge men's secrets through Jesus Christ, as my gospel declares.

■ The Jews and the Law

17Now you, if you call yourself a Jew; if you rely on the law and brag about your relationship to God; 18if you know his will and approve of what is superior because you are instructed by the law; 19if you are convinced that you are a guide for the blind, a light for those who are in the dark, 20an instructor of the foolish, a teacher of infants, because you have in the law the embodiment of knowledge and truth—21you, then, who teach others, do you not teach yourself? You who preach against stealing, do you steal? 22You who say that people should not commit adultery, do you commit adultery? You who abhor idols, do you rob temples? 23You who brag about the law, do you dishonour God by breaking the law? 24As it is written: "God's name is blasphemed among the Gentiles because of you."b

25Circumcision has value if you observe the law, but if you break the law, you have become as though you had not been circumcised. 26If those who are not circumcised keep the law's requirements, will they not be regarded as though they were circumcised? 27The one who is not circumcised physically and yet obeys the law will condemn you who, even though you have thec written code and circumcision, are a law-breaker.

28A man is not a Jew if he is only one outwardly, nor is circumcision merely outward and physical. 29No, a man is a Jew if he is one inwardly; and circumcision is circumcision of the heart, by the Spirit, not by the written code. Such a man's praise is not from men, but from God.

■ God's Faithfulness

3 What advantage, then, is there in being a Jew, or what value is there in circumcision? 2Much in every way! First of all, they have been entrusted with the very words of God.

3What if some did not have faith? Will their lack

---

a6 Psalm 62:12; Prov. 24:12   b24 Isaiah 52:5; Ezek. 36:22   c27 Or who, by means of a of faith nullify God's faithfulness? [4]Not at all! Let God be true, and every man a liar. As it is written:

"So that you may be proved right when you speak
and prevail when you judge."[a]

[5]But if our unrighteousness brings out God's righteousness more clearly, what shall we say? That God is unjust in bringing his wrath on us? (I am using a human argument.) [6]Certainly not! If that were so, how could God judge the world? [7]Someone might argue, "If my falsehood enhances God's truthfulness and so increases his glory, why am I still condemned as a sinner?" [8]Why not say — as we are being slanderously reported as saying and as some claim that we say — "Let us do evil that good may result"? Their condemnation is deserved.

■ No-one Is Righteous
[9]What shall we conclude then? Are we any better?[b] Not at all! We have already made the charge that Jews and Gentiles alike are all under sin. [10]As it is written:

"There is no-one righteous, not even one;
[11]   there is no-one who understands,
        no-one who seeks God.
[12]All have turned away,
        they have together become worthless;
there is no-one who does good,
        not even one."[c]
[13]"Their throats are open graves;
        their tongues practise deceit."[d]
"The poison of vipers is on their lips."[e]
[14]   "Their mouths are full of cursing and
        bitterness."[f]
[15]"Their feet are swift to shed blood;
[16]   ruin and misery mark their ways,
[17]and the way of peace they do not know."[g]
[18]   "There is no fear of God before their eyes."[b]

3:10 ■ NEED FOR A CURE
If a doctor suddenly appeared on a television news programme announcing, in an excited voice, a cure for the Paraguayan flu, who would notice? For his discovery to impress us so deeply that we would seek vaccination, he would first need to prove the terrible danger of the unknown virus.

Paul's message in Romans is the great news about God's amazing grace: a complete cure is available to all. But people won't seek a cure until they know they are ill. Thus, Romans begins with one of the darkest descriptions in the Bible. Paul concludes, "There is no-one righteous, not even one". The entire world is doomed to spiritual death unless a cure can be found.

[19]Now we know that whatever the law says, it says to those who are under the law, so that every mouth may be silenced and the whole world held accountable to God. [20]Therefore no-one will be declared righteous in his sight by observing the law; rather, through the law we become conscious of sin.

■ Righteousness Through Faith
[21]But now a righteousness from God, apart from law, has been made known, to which the Law and the Prophets testify. [22]This righteousness from God comes through faith in Jesus Christ to all who believe. There is no difference, [23]for all have sinned and fall short of the glory of God, [24]and are justified freely by his grace through the redemption that came by Christ Jesus. [25]God presented him as a sacrifice of atonement,[i] through faith in his blood. He did this to demonstrate his justice, because in his forbearance he had left the sins committed beforehand unpunished [26] — he did it to demonstrate his justice at the present time, so as to be just and the one who justifies those who have faith in Jesus.

[27]Where, then, is boasting? It is excluded. On what principle? On that of observing the law? No, but on that of faith. [28]For we maintain that a man is justified by faith apart from observing the law. [29]Is God the God of Jews only? Is he not the God of Gentiles too? Yes, of Gentiles too, [30]since there is only one God, who will justify the circumcised by faith and the uncircumcised through that same faith. [31]Do we, then, nullify the law by this faith? Not at all! Rather, we uphold the law.

■ Abraham Justified by Faith
4 What then shall we say that Abraham, our forefather, discovered in this matter? [2]If, in fact, Abraham was justified by works, he had something to boast about — but not before God. [3]What does the Scripture say? "Abraham believed God, and it was credited to him as righteousness."[a]

[4]Now when a man works, his wages are not credited to him as a gift, but as an obligation. [5]However, to the man who does not work but trusts God who justifies the wicked, his faith is credited as righteousness. [6]David says the same thing when he speaks of the blessedness of the man to whom God credits righteousness apart from works:

[7]"Blessed are they
        whose transgressions are forgiven,
        whose sins are covered.
[8]Blessed is the man
        whose sin the Lord will never count against
        him."[b]

[9]Is this blessedness only for the circumcised, or also for the uncircumcised? We have been saying that Abraham's faith was credited to him as righteousness. [10]Under what circumstances was it credited? Was it after he was circumcised, or before? It was not after, but before! [11]And he received the sign of circumcision, a seal of the righteousness that he had by faith while he was still uncircumcised. So then, he is the father of all who believe but have not been circumcised, in order that righteousness might be credited to them. [12]And he is also the father of the circumcised who not only are circumcised but who also walk in the footsteps of the faith that our father Abraham had before he was circumcised.

[13]It was not through law that Abraham and his offspring received the promise that he would be

a 4 Psalm 51:4   b 9 Or worse   c 12 Psalms 14:1–3; 53:1–3; Eccles. 7:20   d 13 Psalm 5:9   e 13 Psalm 140:3   f 14 Psalm 10:7
g 17 Isaiah 59:7,8   b 18 Psalm 36:1   i 25 Or as the one who would turn aside his wrath, taking away sin   a 3 Gen. 15:6; also in verse 22
b 8 Psalm 32:1,2

heir of the world, but through the righteousness that comes by faith. [14]For if those who live by law are heirs, faith has no value and the promise is worthless, [15]because law brings wrath. And where there is no law there is no transgression.

4:13 ■ HOW TO PLEASE GOD

Paul goes to great lengths in chapter 4 to make a theological point. He traces the Jewish heritage back to Abraham, who lived hundreds of years before Moses and the Old Testament law. Abraham, says Paul, pleased God exactly as we do: through faith. The Old Testament law was never meant to bridge the gap between God and people. Only Jesus Christ could do that. Paul stresses that the law was given not to bring about redemption, but to point out the need for it (5:20).

[16]Therefore, the promise comes by faith, so that it may be by grace and may be guaranteed to all Abraham's offspring—not only to those who are of the law but also to those who are of the faith of Abraham. He is the father of us all. [17]As it is written: "I have made you a father of many nations."[c] He is our father in the sight of God, in whom he believed—the God who gives life to the dead and calls things that are not as though they were.

[18]Against all hope, Abraham in hope believed and so became the father of many nations, just as it had been said to him, "So shall your offspring be."[d] [19]Without weakening in his faith, he faced the fact that his body was as good as dead—since he was about a hundred years old—and that Sarah's womb was also dead. [20]Yet he did not waver through unbelief regarding the promise of God, but was strengthened in his faith and gave glory to God, [21]being fully persuaded that God had power to do what he had promised. [22]This is why "it was credited to him as righteousness." [23]The words "it was credited to him" were written not for him alone, [24]but also for us, to whom God will credit righteousness—for us who believe in him who raised Jesus our Lord from the dead. [25]He was delivered over to death for our sins and was raised to life for our justification.

■ Peace and Joy

5 Therefore, since we have been justified through faith, we[a] have peace with God through our Lord Jesus Christ, [2]through whom we have gained access by faith into this grace in which we now stand. And we[a] rejoice in the hope of the glory of God. [3]Not only so, but we[a] also rejoice in our sufferings, because we know that suffering produces perseverance; [4]perseverance, character; and character, hope. [5]And hope does not disappoint us, because God has poured out his love into our hearts by the Holy Spirit, whom he has given us.

[6]You see, at just the right time, when we were still powerless, Christ died for the ungodly. [7]Very rarely will anyone die for a righteous man, though for a good man someone might possibly dare to die. [8]But God demonstrates his own love for us in this: While we were still sinners, Christ died for us.

[9]Since we have now been justified by his blood, how much more shall we be saved from God's wrath through him! [10]For if, when we were God's enemies, we were reconciled to him through the death of his Son, how much more, having been reconciled, shall we be saved through his life! [11]Not only is this so, but we also rejoice in God through our Lord Jesus Christ, through whom we have now received reconciliation.

5:1 ■ WHAT IT'S THERE FOR

In Romans, Paul constructs a step-by-step argument much like a legal brief, as shown by his frequent use of the legal term "therefore" (20 times in all). Step one: no-one is righteous and we all need help (3:20); Step two: God has provided that help in the form of his Son, making peace with us (5:11); Step three: therefore God no longer condemns those who are in Christ (8:1).

■ Death Through Adam, Life Through Christ

[12]Therefore, just as sin entered the world through one man, and death through sin, and in this way death came to all men, because all sinned— [13]for before the law was given, sin was in the world. But sin is not taken into account when there is no law. [14]Nevertheless, death reigned from the time of Adam to the time of Moses, even over those who did not sin by breaking a command, as did Adam, who was a pattern of the one to come.

[15]But the gift is not like the trespass. For if the many died by the trespass of the one man, how much more did God's grace and the gift that came by the grace of the one man, Jesus Christ, overflow to the many! [16]Again, the gift of God is not like the result of the one man's sin: The judgment followed one sin and brought condemnation, but the gift followed many trespasses and brought justification. [17]For if, by the trespass of the one man, death reigned through that one man, how much more will those who receive God's abundant provision of grace and of the gift of righteousness reign in life through the one man, Jesus Christ.

[18]Consequently, just as the result of one trespass was condemnation for all men, so also the result of one act of righteousness was justification that brings life for all men. [19]For just as through the disobedience of the one man the many were made sinners, so also through the obedience of the one man the many will be made righteous.

[20]The law was added so that the trespass might increase. But where sin increased, grace increased all the more, [21]so that, just as sin reigned in death, so also grace might reign through righteousness to bring eternal life through Jesus Christ our Lord.

■ Dead to Sin, Alive in Christ

6 What shall we say, then? Shall we go on sinning, so that grace may increase? [2]By no means! We died to sin; how can we live in it any longer? [3]Or don't you know that all of us who were baptised into Christ Jesus were baptised into his death? [4]We were therefore buried with him through baptism into

[c]17 Gen. 17:5   [d]18 Gen. 15:5   [a]1,2,3 Or let us

A MODERN PEACE CHILD
GOD SPANS THE GULF

INSIGHT

VERY RARELY WILL ANYONE DIE FOR A RIGHTEOUS MAN, THOUGH FOR A GOOD MAN SOMEONE MIGHT POSSIBLY DARE TO DIE. BUT GOD DEMONSTRATES HIS OWN LOVE FOR US IN THIS: WHILE WE WERE STILL SINNERS, CHRIST DIED FOR US. ■ 5:7–8

Don Richardson spent several frustrating years among the Sawi tribe in New Guinea. He had come from America as an anthropologist/ missionary, hoping to bring the Christian message to a nearly stone-age tribe. But his message kept colliding with the tribe's unusual beliefs.

Christian values of love and forgiveness had no appeal to the Sawi, for they held up deceit as the highest virtue. They saw no reason to change their patterns of cruelty and cannibalism. In fact, when Richardson told them the story of Jesus, only one incident sparked their interest: the story of Judas' betrayal! To the Sawi, Judas was a genuine hero; he had shrewdly penetrated the trusted inner circle of disciples before turning against Jesus.

■ A MYSTERIOUS CEREMONY

Every time Richardson tried to share Christ with the Sawi, the attempt miscarried. Finally, after watching the fourteenth bloody battle fought outside his home, Richardson reached the end of his patience. How could he ever break through to such violent people? He decided to leave New Guinea, despite the Sawi's pleas that he stay.

Just before Richardson left, the Sawi and their deadly enemies, the Haenam tribe, staged an elaborate ceremony in front of his home. It was their final effort to convince the missionary to stay.

The entire village gathered to watch the event. All were silent except the Sawi chief's wife. She screamed loudly as the chief seized their six-month-old baby from her arms and held him high in the air. The chief then carried his son to the enemy chief and gave him to his enemies. A member of the tribe explained to Richardson that the Haenam tribe would rename the baby and rear him as one of its own.

■ BREAKTHROUGH

Richardson knew that no Sawi could be fully trusted, since any action might be part of an elaborate deception. But that memorable day he learned of the one great exception: the peace child. A chief's giving his own son to his enemies – that profound, painful act would overcome all suspicion. By mutual agreement, as long as the peace child lived, no wars could be fought between the two tribes.

Something clicked in Don Richardson's mind as he watched the spectacle. At last he had found an analogy – a parallel story – built into the Sawi's culture that could convey the message of a forgiving God. He gathered members of the tribe round him and, with a pounding heart and dry throat, told them of God's peace child. God had sent his own Son, Jesus, to live among enemies, to make peace with humankind.

■ A KEY PASSAGE

Perhaps Paul felt that same pounding heart and dry throat as he presented in 11 concise verses, Romans 3:21–31, the meaning of God's offering of his peace child Jesus. The first part of Romans spelled out the vast gulf between God and people. Now Paul describes how God spanned this gulf. Some have called this section "the central theological passage in the Bible".

After stating the facts, Paul backs them up with historical proofs in chapters 4 and 5. American politicians often defend their positions by appealing to founding fathers, men like George Washington and Abraham Lincoln. Similarly, Paul keeps his Jewish audience in mind. He supports his concepts by citing Abraham, Moses and even Adam.

Christ's death, says Paul, was not a new idea, an addition to the Old Testament law. Rather, it was the completion of the law, what the Old Testament implied and foreshadowed. Like the Sawi, the Jewish culture had its own "redemptive analogies"; and they all found true fulfilment in Jesus Christ.

□ LIFE QUESTIONS:

Have you ever felt far from God? Does Romans 3–5 say anything that might help during those times?

death in order that, just as Christ was raised from the dead through the glory of the Father, we too may live a new life.

6:1 ■ MORE SIN, MORE FORGIVENESS?

Paul often uses this writing technique: he pauses in the middle of an argument to answer objections or questions that may be occurring to the reader. Some people have actually reached the conclusion that horrifies Paul in this passage. The Russian monk Rasputin, for example, concluded, "I'll sin more to earn more forgiveness." He lived a bizarre life of immorality.

[5]If we have been united with him like this in his death, we will certainly also be united with him in his resurrection. [6]For we know that our old self was crucified with him so that the body of sin might be done away with,[a] that we should no longer be slaves to sin—[7]because anyone who has died has been freed from sin.

[8]Now if we died with Christ, we believe that we will also live with him. [9]For we know that since Christ was raised from the dead, he cannot die again; death no longer has mastery over him. [10]The death he died, he died to sin once for all; but the life he lives, he lives to God.

[11]In the same way, count yourselves dead to sin but alive to God in Christ Jesus. [12]Therefore do not let sin reign in your mortal body so that you obey its evil desires. [13]Do not offer the parts of your body to sin, as instruments of wickedness, but rather offer yourselves to God, as those who have been brought from death to life; and offer the parts of your body to him as instruments of righteousness. [14]For sin shall not be your master, because you are not under law, but under grace.

■ Slaves to Righteousness

[15]What then? Shall we sin because we are not under law but under grace? By no means! [16]Don't you know that when you offer yourselves to someone to obey him as slaves, you are slaves to the one whom you obey—whether you are slaves to sin, which leads to death, or to obedience, which leads to righteousness? [17]But thanks be to God that, though you used to be slaves to sin, you wholeheartedly obeyed the form of teaching to which you were entrusted. [18]You have been set free from sin and have become slaves to righteousness.

[19]I put this in human terms because you are weak in your natural selves. Just as you used to offer the parts of your body in slavery to impurity and to ever-increasing wickedness, so now offer them in slavery to righteousness leading to holiness. [20]When you were slaves to sin, you were free from the control of righteousness. [21]What benefit did you reap at that time from the things you are now ashamed of? Those things result in death! [22]But now that you have been set free from sin and have become slaves to God, the benefit you reap leads to

holiness, and the result is eternal life. [23]For the wages of sin is death, but the gift of God is eternal life in[b] Christ Jesus our Lord.

■ An Illustration From Marriage

7 Do you not know, brothers—for I am speaking to men who know the law—that the law has authority over a man only as long as he lives? [2]For example, by law a married woman is bound to her husband as long as he is alive, but if her husband dies, she is released from the law of marriage. [3]So then, if she marries another man while her husband is still alive, she is called an adulteress. But if her husband dies, she is released from that law and is not an adulteress, even though she marries another man.

[4]So, my brothers, you also died to the law through the body of Christ, that you might belong to another, to him who was raised from the dead, in order that we might bear fruit to God. [5]For when we were controlled by the sinful nature,[a] the sinful passions aroused by the law were at work in our bodies, so that we bore fruit for death. [6]But now, by dying to what once bound us, we have been released from the law so that we serve in the new way of the Spirit, and not in the old way of the written code.

■ Struggling With Sin

[7]What shall we say, then? Is the law sin? Certainly not! Indeed I would not have known what sin was except through the law. For I would not have known what coveting really was if the law had not said, "Do not covet."[b] [8]But sin, seizing the opportunity afforded by the commandment, produced in me every kind of covetous desire. For apart from law, sin is dead. [9]Once I was alive apart from law; but when the commandment came, sin sprang to life and I died. [10]I found that the very commandment that was intended to bring life actually brought death. [11]For sin, seizing the opportunity afforded by the commandment, deceived me, and through the commandment put me to death. [12]So then, the law is holy, and the commandment is holy, righteous and good.

7:7 ■ HIDDEN DANGERS

A strict disciplinarian like Paul had little trouble keeping most of the Ten Commandments. Outward actions such as swearing, murder, adultery, stealing, and lying could be measured and controlled. But the internal, invisible sin of coveting proved far more bedevilling. As Jesus made clear in the Sermon on the Mount, invisible sins like coveting, lust, and anger can have the same toxic effects as the more outward manifestations of stealing, adultery, and murder.

[13]Did that which is good, then, become death to me? By no means! But in order that sin might be recognised as sin, it produced death in me through what was good, so that through the commandment sin might become utterly sinful.

14We know that the law is spiritual; but I am unspiritual, sold as a slave to sin. 15I do not understand what I do. For what I want to do I do not do, but what I hate I do. 16And if I do what I do not want to do, I agree that the law is good. 17As it is, it is no longer I myself who do it, but it is sin living in me. 18I know that nothing good lives in me, that is, in my sinful nature.c For I have the desire to do what is good, but I cannot carry it out. 19For what I do is not the good I want to do; no, the evil I do not want to do—this I keep on doing. 20Now if I do what I do not want to do, it is no longer I who do it, but it is sin living in me that does it.

21So I find this law at work: When I want to do good, evil is right there with me. 22For in my inner being I delight in God's law; 23but I see another law at work in the members of my body, waging war against the law of my mind and making me a prisoner of the law of sin at work within my members. 24What a wretched man I am! Who will rescue me from this body of death? 25Thanks be to God— through Jesus Christ our Lord!

So then, I myself in my mind am a slave to God's law, but in the sinful nature a slave to the law of sin.

■ Life Through the Spirit

8 Therefore, there is now no condemnation for those who are in Christ Jesus,a 2because through Christ Jesus the law of the Spirit of life set me free from the law of sin and death. 3For what the law was powerless to do in that it was weakened by the sinful nature,b God did by sending his own Son in the likeness of sinful man to be a sin offering.c And so he condemned sin in sinful man,d 4in order that the righteous requirements of the law might be fully met in us, who do not live according to the sinful nature but according to the Spirit.

5Those who live according to the sinful nature have their minds set on what that nature desires; but those who live in accordance with the Spirit have their minds set on what the Spirit desires. 6The mind of sinful mane is death, but the mind controlled by the Spirit is life and peace; 7the sinful mindf is hostile to God. It does not submit to God's law, nor can it do so. 8Those controlled by the sinful nature cannot please God.

9You, however, are controlled not by the sinful nature but by the Spirit, if the Spirit of God lives in you. And if anyone does not have the Spirit of Christ,

■ INNER STRUGGLES
A BATTLE, AND A VICTORY

INSIGHT

SO I FIND THIS LAW AT WORK: WHEN I WANT TO DO GOOD, EVIL IS RIGHT THERE WITH ME. ■ 7:21

The first part of Romans paints a grand picture of God's grace and forgiveness, so grand that Paul opens himself up to some tricky questions. "I think I like what I'm hearing," a devious person may exclaim as he or she finishes the first part of Romans. "The more I sin, the more opportunity God has to forgive me, right? Then I can live any way I want!"

In chapter 6, Paul reacts to the "Now I have an excuse to sin" line of thinking with shock and outrage. And then he turns to practical issues in the Christian life. Why is it that sin is so hard to overcome? Does God forgive every sin, no matter how bad? What really happens when we become Christians? Do we change or don't we?

■ ILLUSTRATIONS FROM LIFE

When Paul was trying to be a good person (by keeping all the law) in his own strength, he was ultimately defeated by the sin problem. Although his intentions were good, he was attempting to win the battle over sin by his own plan and ability. There is only one solution to that kind of struggle. Paul concludes at the end, "What a wretched man I am! Who will rescue me from this body of death? Thanks be to God—through Jesus Christ our Lord!" (7:24–25a).

The very best proof of the Christian faith is a believer with a changed life. Paul calls Christians to "count yourselves dead to sin but alive to God in Christ Jesus" (6:11), and he wrote as if this were really possible!

■ A FINAL ANSWER

Then, like a gust of fresh air, chapter 8 follows with one of the most hopeful passages in the Bible. The Holy Spirit is its theme, and Paul defines the Spirit's role in our lives. The Spirit works alongside us as we relate to God, even praying for us when we don't know what to ask (8:26). Mainly, the Spirit teaches us the benefits of being a child of God.

Conflict won't disappear completely yet, says Paul, for we are part of a "groaning", imperfect creation (8:18–25). But with God working for us, we can be *more than* conquerors, and one day God will make all of creation perfect again. That promise should assure us that nothing can separate us from God's love (8:38–39).

□ LIFE QUESTIONS:

Which person do you identify with—the one who is struggling to please God on personal strength alone, or the one who is trusting in Christ for victory over sin?

---

c18 Or my flesh   a1 Some later manuscripts Jesus, who do not live according to the sinful nature but according to the Spirit,   b3 Or the flesh; also in verses 4, 5, 8, 9, 12 and 13   c3 Or man, for sin   d3 Or in the flesh   e6 Or mind set on the flesh   f7 Or the mind set on the flesh he does not belong to Christ. [10]But if Christ is in you, your body is dead because of sin, yet your spirit is alive because of righteousness. [11]And if the Spirit of him who raised Jesus from the dead is living in you, he who raised Christ from the dead will also give life to your mortal bodies through his Spirit, who lives in you.

[12]Therefore, brothers, we have an obligation — but it is not to the sinful nature, to live according to it. [13]For if you live according to the sinful nature, you will die; but if by the Spirit you put to death the misdeeds of the body, you will live, [14]because those who are led by the Spirit of God are sons of God. [15]For you did not receive a spirit that makes you a slave again to fear, but you received the Spirit of sonship.[g] And by him we cry, "Abba,[b] Father." [16]The Spirit himself testifies with our spirit that we are God's children. [17]Now if we are children, then we are heirs — heirs of God and co-heirs with Christ, if indeed we share in his sufferings in order that we may also share in his glory.

■ Future Glory

[18]I consider that our present sufferings are not worth comparing with the glory that will be revealed in us. [19]The creation waits in eager expectation for the sons of God to be revealed. [20]For the creation was subjected to frustration, not by its own choice, but by the will of the one who subjected it, in hope [21]that[i] the creation itself will be liberated from its bondage to decay and brought into the glorious freedom of the children of God.

> ## 8:18 ■ WORTH THE STRUGGLE
> Paul never minimises suffering; after all, his own life included beatings, imprisonment, shipwrecks, assassination attempts, and chronic illness. But he insists with absolute conviction that future rewards will outweigh all present sufferings.
>
> Olympic athletes endure years of eight-hour practice sessions and much discipline and pain for the goal of winning a gold medal. Similarly, the Christian's life on earth may involve many difficulties (verses 22–23), but the end result will make them seem worthwhile.

[22]We know that the whole creation has been groaning as in the pains of childbirth right up to the present time. [23]Not only so, but we ourselves, who have the firstfruits of the Spirit, groan inwardly as we wait eagerly for our adoption as sons, the redemption of our bodies. [24]For in this hope we were saved. But hope that is seen is no hope at all. Who hopes for what he already has? [25]But if we hope for what we do not yet have, we wait for it patiently.

[26]In the same way, the Spirit helps us in our weakness. We do not know what we ought to pray for, but the Spirit himself intercedes for us with groans that words cannot express. [27]And he who searches our hearts knows the mind of the Spirit, because the Spirit intercedes for the saints in accordance with God's will.

■ More Than Conquerors

[28]And we know that in all things God works for the good of those who love him,[j] who[k] have been called according to his purpose. [29]For those God foreknew he also predestined to be conformed to the likeness of his Son, that he might be the firstborn among many brothers. [30]And those he predestined, he also called; those he called, he also justified; those he justified, he also glorified.

> ## 8:28 ■ ONLY GOOD THINGS?
> This famous verse is often misquoted or stretched to mean more than it says. It should be read together with the next two paragraphs. Paul doesn't promise that only good, or pleasurable, things will come to the Christian. What he does say is that even the difficult experiences described in verses 35–39 can be used in God's overall plan for good. And nothing can separate us from the love of God.

[31]What, then, shall we say in response to this? If God is for us, who can be against us? [32]He who did not spare his own Son, but gave him up for us all — how will he not also, along with him, graciously give us all things? [33]Who will bring any charge against those whom God has chosen? It is God who justifies. [34]Who is he that condemns? Christ Jesus, who died — more than that, who was raised to life — is at the right hand of God and is also interceding for us. [35]Who shall separate us from the love of Christ? Shall trouble or hardship or persecution or famine or nakedness or danger or sword? [36]As it is written:

> "For your sake we face death all day long;
>   we are considered as sheep to be
>   slaughtered."[l]

[37]No, in all these things we are more than conquerors through him who loved us. [38]For I am convinced that neither death nor life, neither angels nor demons,[m] neither the present nor the future, nor any powers, [39]neither height nor depth, nor anything else in all creation, will be able to separate us from the love of God that is in Christ Jesus our Lord.

■ God's Sovereign Choice

9 I speak the truth in Christ — I am not lying, my conscience confirms it in the Holy Spirit — [2]I have great sorrow and unceasing anguish in my heart. [3]For I could wish that I myself were cursed and cut off from Christ for the sake of my brothers, those of my own race, [4]the people of Israel. Theirs is the adoption as sons; theirs the divine glory, the covenants, the receiving of the law, the temple worship and the promises. [5]Theirs are the patriarchs, and from them is traced the human ancestry of Christ, who is God over all, for ever praised![a] Amen.

[6]It is not as though God's word had failed. For not all who are descended from Israel are Israel. [7]Nor because they are his descendants are they all Abraham's children. On the contrary, "It is through Isaac

---

g 15 Or adoption   b 15 Aramaic for Father   i 20,21 Or subjected it in hope. 21 For   j 28 Some manuscripts And we know that all things work together for good to those who love God   k 28 Or works together with those who love him to bring about what is good – with those who   l 36 Psalm 44:22   m 38 Or nor heavenly rulers   a 5 Or Christ, who is over all. God be for ever praised! Or Christ. God who is over all be for ever praised!

that your offspring will be reckoned."*b* *8*In other words, it is not the natural children who are God's children, but it is the children of the promise who are regarded as Abraham's offspring. *9*For this was how the promise was stated: "At the appointed time I will return, and Sarah will have a son."*c*

*10*Not only that, but Rebekah's children had one and the same father, our father Isaac. *11*Yet, before the twins were born or had done anything good or bad—in order that God's purpose in election might stand: *12*not by works but by him who calls—she was told, "The older will serve the younger."*d* *13*Just as it is written: "Jacob I loved, but Esau I hated."*e*

*14*What then shall we say? Is God unjust? Not at all! *15*For he says to Moses,

"I will have mercy on whom I have mercy,
    and I will have compassion on whom I have
        compassion."*f*

*16*It does not, therefore, depend on man's desire or effort, but on God's mercy. *17*For the Scripture says to Pharaoh: "I raised you up for this very purpose, that I might display my power in you and that my name might be proclaimed in all the earth."*g* *18*Therefore God has mercy on whom he wants to have mercy, and he hardens whom he wants to harden.

*19*One of you will say to me: "Then why does God still blame us? For who resists his will?" *20*But who are you, O man, to talk back to God? "Shall what is formed say to him who formed it, 'Why did you make me like this?' "*b* *21*Does not the potter have the right to make out of the same lump of clay some pottery for noble purposes and some for common use?

9:19 ■ QUESTIONS, ANYONE?
Frequently Paul interrupts his writing with a question or series of questions. In doing so, he is imitating the style he learned from rabbis in his earlier training. The story is told of one student who asked, "Why do you rabbis so often put your teaching in the form of a question?" The reply: "So what's wrong with a question?"

---

*22*What if God, choosing to show his wrath and make his power known, bore with great patience the objects of his wrath—prepared for destruction? *23*What if he did this to make the riches of his glory known to the objects of his mercy, whom he prepared in advance for glory—*24*even us, whom he also called, not only from the Jews but also from the Gentiles? *25*As he says in Hosea:

"I will call them 'my people' who are not my
        people;
    and I will call her 'my loved one' who is not
        my loved one,"*i*

*26*and,

■ **A CRUSHING BLOW TO PAUL**
DOES GOD BREAK HIS PROMISES?

INSIGHT

I HAVE GREAT SORROW AND
UNCEASING ANGUISH IN MY HEART.
■ 9:2

Does anything bring more pain to a new Christian than family rejection? A teenager converts to Christianity. Her parents overreact, assuming their daughter has fallen for some weird cult. They slap away all her attempts to present the appealing facts of the gospel. What is good news for her is seen as bad news by the family.

    Some new Christians can melt down the walls of suspicion and hostility. But others are treated like diseased persons by other family members and forced to live in a state of emotional quarantine.

    Anyone who has lived through such an experience can understand the agonising dilemma Paul faced. Members of his own race, the Jews, were rejecting the gospel he had committed his life to.

■ CAN GOD BE TRUSTED?
Rejection by the Jews was a crushing blow to Paul, and he interrupted his letter to the Romans to consider the dilemma. These three chapters (9–11) contain some of his strongest words ever, including an offer to forfeit his own relationship with Christ for the sake of his race (9:3).

    The issues discussed here apply to non-Jews as well, for they raise basic questions about God. Had he given up on the Jewish people, ignoring the promises he made to them in Old Testament times? If so, couldn't he also break promises made to us today?

    For Paul, a Jew who called himself an apostle to the Gentiles, no other issue was so important to resolve. He couldn't rest until he linked the brilliant theology set forth in Romans to God's past, present and future activity among the Jews.

□ LIFE QUESTIONS:
Romans 9–11 explains how God worked with people disappointed in him: the Jews. Have you ever been deeply disappointed in God? What does Paul say that might help answer your questions?

---

b 7 Gen. 21:12   *c* 9 Gen. 18:10,14   *d* 12 Gen. 25:23   *e* 13 Mal. 1:2,3   *f* 15 Exodus 33:19   *g* 17 Exodus 9:16   *b* 20 Isaiah 29:16; 45:9
i 25 Hosea 2:23

"It will happen that in the very place where it
was said to them,
'You are not my people,'
they will be called 'sons of the living God'."*j*

27Isaiah cries out concerning Israel:

"Though the number of the Israelites be like
the sand by the sea,
only the remnant will be saved.
28For the Lord will carry out
his sentence on earth with speed and
finality."*k*

29It is just as Isaiah said previously:

"Unless the Lord Almighty
had left us descendants,
we would have become like Sodom,
we would have been like Gomorrah."*l*

■ Israel's Unbelief
30What then shall we say? That the Gentiles, who
did not pursue righteousness, have obtained it, a
righteousness that is by faith; 31but Israel, who pursued a law of righteousness, has not attained it.
32Why not? Because they pursued it not by faith but
as if it were by works. They stumbled over the
"stumbling-stone". 33As it is written:

"See, I lay in Zion a stone that causes men to
stumble
and a rock that makes them fall,
and the one who trusts in him will never be
put to shame."*m*

10 Brothers, my heart's desire and prayer to
God for the Israelites is that they may be
saved. 2For I can testify about them that they are
zealous for God, but their zeal is not based on
knowledge. 3Since they did not know the righteousness that comes from God and sought to establish
their own, they did not submit to God's righteousness. 4Christ is the end of the law so that there may
be righteousness for everyone who believes.

5Moses describes in this way the righteousness
that is by the law: "The man who does these things
will live by them."*a* 6But the righteousness that is
by faith says: "Do not say in your heart, 'Who will
ascend into heaven?'*b*" (that is, to bring Christ
down) 7"or 'Who will descend into the deep?'*c*"
(that is, to bring Christ up from the dead). 8But
what does it say? "The word is near you; it is in your
mouth and in your heart,"*d* that is, the word of faith
we are proclaiming: 9That if you confess with your
mouth, "Jesus is Lord," and believe in your heart
that God raised him from the dead, you will be
saved. 10For it is with your heart that you believe
and are justified, and it is with your mouth that you
confess and are saved. 11As the Scripture says, "Anyone who trusts in him will never be put to
shame."*e* 12For there is no difference between Jew
and Gentile — the same Lord is Lord of all and richly
blesses all who call on him, 13for, "Everyone who
calls on the name of the Lord will be saved."*f*
14How, then, can they call on the one they have

not believed in? And how can they believe in the
one of whom they have not heard? And how can
they hear without someone preaching to them?
15And how can they preach unless they are sent? As
it is written, "How beautiful are the feet of those
who bring good news!"*g*

16But not all the Israelites accepted the good
news. For Isaiah says, "Lord, who has believed our
message?"*b* 17Consequently, faith comes from
hearing the message, and the message is heard
through the word of Christ. 18But I ask: Did they not
hear? Of course they did:

"Their voice has gone out into all the earth,
their words to the ends of the world."*i*

19Again I ask: Did Israel not understand? First, Moses
says,

"I will make you envious by those who are not
a nation;
I will make you angry by a nation that has no
understanding."*j*

20And Isaiah boldly says,

"I was found by those who did not seek me;
I revealed myself to those who did not ask
for me."*k*

21But concerning Israel he says,

"All day long I have held out my hands
to a disobedient and obstinate people."*l*

■ The Remnant of Israel
11 I ask then: Did God reject his people? By no
means! I am an Israelite myself, a descendant
of Abraham, from the tribe of Benjamin. 2God did
not reject his people, whom he foreknew. Don't you
know what the Scripture says in the passage about
Elijah — how he appealed to God against Israel:
3"Lord, they have killed your prophets and torn
down your altars; I am the only one left, and they are
trying to kill me"*a*? 4And what was God's answer to
him? "I have reserved for myself seven thousand
who have not bowed the knee to Baal."*b* 5So too,
at the present time there is a remnant chosen by
grace. 6And if by grace, then it is no longer by
works; if it were, grace would no longer be grace.*c*

7What then? What Israel sought so earnestly it did
not obtain, but the elect did. The others were hardened, 8as it is written:

"God gave them a spirit of stupor,
eyes so that they could not see
and ears so that they could not hear,
to this very day."*d*

9And David says:

"May their table become a snare and a trap,
a stumbling-block and a retribution for them.
10May their eyes be darkened so they cannot see,
and their backs be bent for ever."*e*

j26 Hosea 1:10   *k28* Isaiah 10:22,23   *l29* Isaiah 1:9   *m33* Isaiah 8:14; 28:16   *a5* Lev. 18:5   *b6* Deut. 30:12   *c7* Deut. 30:13
d8 Deut. 30:14   *e11* Isaiah 28:16   *f13* Joel 2:32   *g15* Isaiah 52:7   *b16* Isaiah 53:1   *i18* Psalm 19:4   *j19* Deut. 32:21   *k20* Isaiah 65:1
l21 Isaiah 65:2   *a3* 1 Kings 19:10,14   *b4* 1 Kings 19:18   *c6* Some manuscripts *by grace. But if by works, then it is no longer grace; if it were, work
would no longer be work.*   *d8* Deut. 29:4; Isaiah 29:10   *e10* Psalm 69:22,23

■ Ingrafted Branches

11Again I ask: Did they stumble so as to fall beyond recovery? Not at all! Rather, because of their transgression, salvation has come to the Gentiles to make Israel envious. 12But if their transgression means riches for the world, and their loss means riches for the Gentiles, how much greater riches will their fulness bring!

11:11 ■ THE FUTURE OF THE JEWS

In chapters 9 and 10, Paul painfully admits that, on the whole, the Jews did not believe in Christ. Despite all the advantages of Old Testament history, they "stumbled over the 'stumbling stone' " (9:32). In chapter 11, Paul goes back over that history and asks whether it was futile. Will the Jews come to believe in Christ one day? Did their tragic experience produce any advantage for the rest of the world? This chapter clearly shows God's eternal love for his chosen people. Paul concludes with a poetic outburst, celebrating God's mysterious ways of working on earth.

13I am talking to you Gentiles. Inasmuch as I am the apostle to the Gentiles, I make much of my ministry 14in the hope that I may somehow arouse my own people to envy and save some of them. 15For if their rejection is the reconciliation of the world, what will their acceptance be but life from the dead? 16If the part of the dough offered as firstfruits is holy, then the whole batch is holy; if the root is holy, so are the branches.

17If some of the branches have been broken off, and you, though a wild olive shoot, have been grafted in among the others and now share in the nourishing sap from the olive root, 18do not boast over those branches. If you do, consider this: You do not support the root, but the root supports you. 19You will say then, "Branches were broken off so that I could be grafted in." 20Granted. But they were broken off because of unbelief, and you stand by faith. Do not be arrogant, but be afraid. 21For if God did not spare the natural branches, he will not spare you either.

22Consider therefore the kindness and sternness of God: sternness to those who fell, but kindness to you, provided that you continue in his kindness. Otherwise, you also will be cut off. 23And if they do not persist in unbelief, they will be grafted in, for God is able to graft them in again. 24After all, if you were cut out of an olive tree that is wild by nature, and contrary to nature were grafted into a cultivated olive tree, how much more readily will these, the natural branches, be grafted into their own olive tree!

■ All Israel Will Be Saved

25I do not want you to be ignorant of this mystery, brothers, so that you may not be conceited: Israel has experienced a hardening in part until the full number of the Gentiles has come in. 26And so all Israel will be saved, as it is written:

"The deliverer will come from Zion;
    he will turn godlessness away from Jacob.
27And this is*f* my covenant with them
    when I take away their sins."*g*

11:24 ■ UNNATURAL BOTANY

Botanists and orchard growers commonly use grafting to improve their stock of flowers and fruit. Usually they graft a weaker, cultivated branch onto a wild but sturdy root stock. Paul admits that "contrary to nature" God has grafted the wild branches (Gentiles) onto the cultivated roots (Jews) — a reverse technique sometimes used to reinvigorate an olive tree.

28As far as the gospel is concerned, they are enemies on your account; but as far as election is concerned, they are loved on account of the patriarchs, 29for God's gifts and his call are irrevocable. 30Just as you who were at one time disobedient to God have now received mercy as a result of their disobedience, 31so they too have now become disobedient in order that they too may now*b* receive mercy as a result of God's mercy to you. 32For God has bound all men over to disobedience so that he may have mercy on them all.

■ Doxology

33Oh, the depth of the riches of the wisdom
    and*i* knowledge of God!
    How unsearchable his judgments,
    and his paths beyond tracing out!
34"Who has known the mind of the Lord?
    Or who has been his counsellor?"*j*
35"Who has ever given to God,
    that God should repay him?"*k*
36For from him and through him and to him are
    all things.
    To him be the glory for ever! Amen.

■ Living Sacrifices

12 Therefore, I urge you, brothers, in view of God's mercy, to offer your bodies as living sacrifices, holy and pleasing to God — this is your spiritual*a* act of worship. 2Do not conform any longer to the pattern of this world, but be transformed by the renewing of your mind. Then you will be able to test and approve what God's will is — his good, pleasing and perfect will.

3For by the grace given me I say to every one of you: Do not think of yourself more highly than you ought, but rather think of yourself with sober judgment, in accordance with the measure of faith God has given you. 4Just as each of us has one body with many members, and these members do not all have the same function, 5so in Christ we who are many form one body, and each member belongs to all the others. 6We have different gifts, according to the grace given us. If a man's gift is prophesying, let him use it in proportion to his*b* faith. 7If it is serving, let him serve; if it is teaching, let him teach; 8if it is

---

*f*27 Or will be   *g*27 Isaiah 59:20,21; 27:9; Jer. 31:33,34   *b*31 Some manuscripts do not have *now*.   *i*33 Or *riches and the wisdom and the*
*j*34 Isaiah 40:13   *k*35 Job 41:11   *a*1 Or *reasonable*   *b*6 Or *in agreement with the*

encouraging, let him encourage; if it is contributing to the needs of others, let him give generously; if it is leadership, let him govern diligently; if it is showing mercy, let him do it cheerfully.

■ Love

⁹Love must be sincere. Hate what is evil; cling to what is good. ¹⁰Be devoted to one another in brotherly love. Honour one another above yourselves. ¹¹Never be lacking in zeal, but keep your spiritual fervour, serving the Lord. ¹²Be joyful in hope, patient in affliction, faithful in prayer. ¹³Share with God's people who are in need. Practise hospitality.

¹⁴Bless those who persecute you; bless and do not curse. ¹⁵Rejoice with those who rejoice; mourn with those who mourn. ¹⁶Live in harmony with one another. Do not be proud, but be willing to associate with people of low position.ᶜ Do not be conceited.

¹⁷Do not repay anyone evil for evil. Be careful to do what is right in the eyes of everybody. ¹⁸If it is possible, as far as it depends on you, live at peace with everyone. ¹⁹Do not take revenge, my friends, but leave room for God's wrath, for it is written: "It is mine to avenge; I will repay,"ᵈ says the Lord. ²⁰On the contrary:

"If your enemy is hungry, feed him;
    if he is thirsty, give him something to drink.
In doing this, you will heap burning coals on
    his head."ᵉ

²¹Do not be overcome by evil, but overcome evil with good.

■ Submission to the Authorities

13 Everyone must submit himself to the governing authorities, for there is no authority except that which God has established. The authorities that exist have been established by God. ²Consequently, he who rebels against the authority is rebelling against what God has instituted, and those who do so will bring judgment on themselves. ³For rulers hold no terror for those who do right, but for those who do wrong. Do you want to be free from fear of the one in authority? Then do what is right and he will commend you. ⁴For he is God's servant to do you good. But if you do wrong, be afraid, for he does not bear the sword for nothing. He is God's servant, an agent of wrath to bring punishment on the wrongdoer. ⁵Therefore, it is necessary to submit to the authorities, not only because of possible punishment but also because of conscience.

13:1 ■ CHRISTIANS AND THE EMPIRE

For most of his ministry, Paul benefited from the legal protection of the Roman empire. The first generation of Christians received the same freedom of worship and legal protection as did the Jews. But soon emperors such as Nero vengefully turned on Christians, torturing and murdering thousands of them, probably including Paul himself. History shows that most of them followed Paul's difficult advice in this passage, refusing to revolt against the government no matter how hostile it became.

■ DOWN-TO-EARTH PROBLEMS
WHEN CHRISTIANS DISAGREE ABOUT WHAT'S RIGHT AND WRONG

INSIGHT

HATE WHAT IS EVIL; CLING TO WHAT IS GOOD. ■ 12:9

Too often theology is viewed as stuff for hermits and marooned shipwreck victims. When there's nothing else to do, *then* is the time to ask abstract questions about God.

Such a notion would surely have exasperated the apostle Paul. To him, theology *was* worthless unless it made a difference in how people lived. Therefore, he concluded the most concise theological book in the Bible with a down-to-earth discussion of contemporary problems.

■ REVOLUTIONARIES AND WEAKER BROTHERS

The issue of politics surfaces in Romans (13:1–7). How should a Christian relate to government? In Paul's day, when Christians were living under Nero's tyrannical regime, that question was hotly debated, as it still is in our revolution-oriented era.

Christians in Rome were also disagreeing on what was proper behaviour for a Christian (14:1 – 15:4). One person was sure another was sinning; but that "offender" was convinced his accuser was hopelessly narrow-minded. Who was right? The specific issues change with each culture, but Paul's guidelines on the proper attitudes apply to all.

Paul did not live as an intellectual recluse. He applied his theology to life, practising what he preached. In fact, the lofty book of Romans was written while he was out raising money for famine victims in Jerusalem (15:25–27).

☐ LIFE QUESTIONS:

Christians in Paul's day hotly debated such issues as eating meat, celebrating holidays and drinking wine. What issues do Christians debate today? What attitude should we have towards Christians we differ with?

ᶜ 16 Or *willing to do menial work*   ᵈ 19 Deut. 32:35   ᵉ 20 Prov. 25:21,22

6This is also why you pay taxes, for the authorities are God's servants, who give their full time to governing. 7Give everyone what you owe him: If you owe taxes, pay taxes; if revenue, then revenue; if respect, then respect; if honour, then honour.

■ Love, for the Day Is Near

8Let no debt remain outstanding, except the continuing debt to love one another, for he who loves his fellow-man has fulfilled the law. 9The commandments, "Do not commit adultery," "Do not murder," "Do not steal," "Do not covet,"*a* and whatever other commandment there may be, are summed up in this one rule: "Love your neighbour as yourself."*b* 10Love does no harm to its neighbour. Therefore love is the fulfilment of the law.

11And do this, understanding the present time. The hour has come for you to wake up from your slumber, because our salvation is nearer now than when we first believed. 12The night is nearly over; the day is almost here. So let us put aside the deeds of darkness and put on the armour of light. 13Let us behave decently, as in the daytime, not in orgies and drunkenness, not in sexual immorality and debauchery, not in dissension and jealousy. 14Rather, clothe yourselves with the Lord Jesus Christ, and do not think about how to gratify the desires of the sinful nature.*c*

■ The Weak and the Strong

14 Accept him whose faith is weak, without passing judgment on disputable matters. 2One man's faith allows him to eat everything, but another man, whose faith is weak, eats only vegetables. 3The man who eats everything must not look down on him who does not, and the man who does not eat everything must not condemn the man who does, for God has accepted him. 4Who are you to judge someone else's servant? To his own master he stands or falls. And he will stand, for the Lord is able to make him stand.

14:2 ■ WEAK OR STRONG?

According to Paul, a weaker brother is a new believer who needs many rules and regulations. Christians in Paul's day debated such issues as vegetarianism, eating meat sacrificed to idols, and celebrating pagan festival days. Paul's advice to both weak and strong Christians of his day applies to people in all cultures who debate questionable issues. Elsewhere, Paul speaks to legalists: "strong" Christians who nevertheless insist on many rules and regulations (see Colossians 2:16–23).

5One man considers one day more sacred than another; another man considers every day alike. Each one should be fully convinced in his own mind. 6He who regards one day as special, does so to the Lord. He who eats meat, eats to the Lord, for he gives thanks to God; and he who abstains, does so to the Lord and gives thanks to God. 7For none of us lives to himself alone and none of us dies to himself alone. 8If we live, we live to the Lord; and if we die, we die to the Lord. So, whether we live or die, we belong to the Lord.

9For this very reason, Christ died and returned to life so that he might be the Lord of both the dead and the living. 10You, then, why do you judge your brother? Or why do you look down on your brother? For we will all stand before God's judgment seat. 11It is written:

" 'As surely as I live,' says the Lord,
'Every knee will bow before me;
     every tongue will confess to God.' "*a*

12So then, each of us will give an account of himself to God.

13Therefore let us stop passing judgment on one another. Instead, make up your mind not to put any stumbling-block or obstacle in your brother's way. 14As one who is in the Lord Jesus, I am fully convinced that no food*b* is unclean in itself. But if anyone regards something as unclean, then for him it is unclean. 15If your brother is distressed because of what you eat, you are no longer acting in love. Do not by your eating destroy your brother for whom Christ died. 16Do not allow what you consider good to be spoken of as evil. 17For the kingdom of God is not a matter of eating and drinking, but of righteousness, peace and joy in the Holy Spirit, 18because anyone who serves Christ in this way is pleasing to God and approved by men.

19Let us therefore make every effort to do what leads to peace and to mutual edification. 20Do not destroy the work of God for the sake of food. All food is clean, but it is wrong for a man to eat anything that causes someone else to stumble. 21It is better not to eat meat or drink wine or to do anything else that will cause your brother to fall.

22So whatever you believe about these things keep between yourself and God. Blessed is the man who does not condemn himself by what he approves. 23But the man who has doubts is condemned if he eats, because his eating is not from faith; and everything that does not come from faith is sin.

15 We who are strong ought to bear with the failings of the weak and not to please ourselves. 2Each of us should please his neighbour for his good, to build him up. 3For even Christ did not please himself but, as it is written: "The insults of those who insult you have fallen on me."*a* 4For everything that was written in the past was written to teach us, so that through endurance and the encouragement of the Scriptures we might have hope.

5May the God who gives endurance and encouragement give you a spirit of unity among yourselves as you follow Christ Jesus, 6so that with one heart and mouth you may glorify the God and Father of our Lord Jesus Christ.

7Accept one another, then, just as Christ accepted you, in order to bring praise to God. 8For I tell you that Christ has become a servant of the Jews*b* on behalf of God's truth, to confirm the promises made to the patriarchs 9so that the Gentiles may glorify God for his mercy, as it is written:

a9 Exodus 20:13–15,17; Deut. 5:17–19,21   *b9* Lev. 19:18   *c14* Or *the flesh*   *a11* Isaiah 45:23   *b14* Or *that nothing*   *a3* Psalm 69:9
b8 Greek *circumcision*

"Therefore I will praise you among the
    Gentiles;
  I will sing hymns to your name."*c*

10Again, it says,

"Rejoice, O Gentiles, with his people."*d*

11And again,

"Praise the Lord, all you Gentiles,
  and sing praises to him, all you peoples."*e*

12And again, Isaiah says,

"The Root of Jesse will spring up,
  one who will arise to rule over the nations;
the Gentiles will hope in him."*f*

13May the God of hope fill you with all joy and
peace as you trust in him, so that you may overflow
with hope by the power of the Holy Spirit.

■ Paul the Minister to the Gentiles
    14I myself am convinced, my brothers, that you
yourselves are full of goodness, complete in knowledge and competent to instruct one another. 15I
have written to you quite boldly on some points, as
if to remind you of them again, because of the grace
God gave me 16to be a minister of Christ Jesus to the
Gentiles with the priestly duty of proclaiming the
gospel of God, so that the Gentiles might become an
offering acceptable to God, sanctified by the Holy
Spirit.
    17Therefore I glory in Christ Jesus in my service
to God. 18I will not venture to speak of anything except what Christ has accomplished through me in
leading the Gentiles to obey God by what I have said
and done—19by the power of signs and miracles,
through the power of the Spirit. So from Jerusalem
all the way round to Illyricum, I have fully proclaimed the gospel of Christ. 20It has always been
my ambition to preach the gospel where Christ was
not known, so that I would not be building on someone else's foundation. 21Rather, as it is written:

"Those who were not told about him will see,
  and those who have not heard will
    understand."*g*

22This is why I have often been hindered from coming to you.

■ Paul's Plan to Visit Rome
    23But now that there is no more place for me to
work in these regions, and since I have been longing
for many years to see you, 24I plan to do so when I
go to Spain. I hope to visit you while passing
through and to have you assist me on my journey
there, after I have enjoyed your company for a
while. 25Now, however, I am on my way to Jerusalem in the service of the saints there. 26For Macedonia and Achaia were pleased to make a
contribution for the poor among the saints in Jerusalem. 27They were pleased to do it, and indeed
they owe it to them. For if the Gentiles have shared
in the Jews' spiritual blessings, they owe it to the
Jews to share with them their material blessings.

28So after I have completed this task and have made
sure that they have received this fruit, I will go to
Spain and visit you on the way. 29I know that when
I come to you, I will come in the full measure of the
blessing of Christ.

15:26 ■ PAUL THE FUND-RAISER
Paul wrote Romans while travelling to raise funds
for famine relief. Another letter (2 Corinthians 8)
gives more details on this mercy mission on behalf
of the Jews in Jerusalem. Paul's actions set an
example of unity for a church composed of both
Jews and Gentiles—unity sorely needed by
groups racked by the divisions described in
chapter 14.

30I urge you, brothers, by our Lord Jesus Christ
and by the love of the Spirit, to join me in my struggle by praying to God for me. 31Pray that I may be
rescued from the unbelievers in Judea and that my
service in Jerusalem may be acceptable to the saints
there, 32so that by God's will I may come to you
with joy and together with you be refreshed. 33The
God of peace be with you all. Amen.

■ Personal Greetings
16 I commend to you our sister Phoebe, a servant*a* of the church in Cenchrea. 2I ask you
to receive her in the Lord in a way worthy of the
saints and to give her any help she may need from
you, for she has been a great help to many people,
including me.

3Greet Priscilla*b* and Aquila, my fellow-workers in
    Christ Jesus. 4They risked their lives for me. Not
    only I but all the churches of the Gentiles are
    grateful to them.
5Greet also the church that meets at their house.
  Greet my dear friend Epenetus, who was the first
    convert to Christ in the province of Asia.
6Greet Mary, who worked very hard for you.
7Greet Andronicus and Junias, my relatives who
    have been in prison with me. They are outstand-
    ing among the apostles, and they were in Christ
    before I was.
8Greet Ampliatus, whom I love in the Lord.
9Greet Urbanus, our fellow-worker in Christ, and
    my dear friend Stachys.
10Greet Apelles, tested and approved in Christ.
  Greet those who belong to the household of Aris-
    tobulus.
11Greet Herodion, my relative.
  Greet those in the household of Narcissus who
    are in the Lord.
12Greet Tryphena and Tryphosa, those women who
    work hard in the Lord.
  Greet my dear friend Persis, another woman who
    has worked very hard in the Lord.
13Greet Rufus, chosen in the Lord, and his mother,
    who has been a mother to me, too.
14Greet Asyncritus, Phlegon, Hermes, Patrobas,
    Hermas and the brothers with them.

c9 2 Samuel 22:50; Psalm 18:49   *d10* Deut. 32:43   *e11* Psalm 117:1   *f12* Isaiah 11:10   *g21* Isaiah 52:15   *a1* Or *deaconess*   *b3* Greek
Prisca, a variant of *Priscilla*

¹⁵Greet Philologus, Julia, Nereus and his sister, and Olympas and all the saints with them. ¹⁶Greet one another with a holy kiss.

All the churches of Christ send greetings.

¹⁷I urge you, brothers, to watch out for those who cause divisions and put obstacles in your way that are contrary to the teaching you have learned. Keep away from them. ¹⁸For such people are not serving our Lord Christ, but their own appetites. By smooth talk and flattery they deceive the minds of naïve people. ¹⁹Everyone has heard about your obedience, so I am full of joy over you; but I want you to be wise about what is good, and innocent about what is evil.

²⁰The God of peace will soon crush Satan under your feet.

The grace of our Lord Jesus be with you.

²¹Timothy, my fellow-worker, sends his greetings to you, as do Lucius, Jason and Sosipater, my relatives.

²²I, Tertius, who wrote down this letter, greet you in the Lord.

²³Gaius, whose hospitality I and the whole church here enjoy, sends you his greetings.

Erastus, who is the city's director of public works, and our brother Quartus send you their greetings.ᶜ

²⁵Now to him who is able to establish you by my gospel and the proclamation of Jesus Christ, according to the revelation of the mystery hidden for long ages past, ²⁶but now revealed and made known through the prophetic writings by the command of the eternal God, so that all nations might believe and obey him — ²⁷to the only wise God be glory for ever through Jesus Christ! Amen.

16:23 ■ PAUL'S FRIENDS

This chapter contains a fascinating list of Paul's friends and co-workers, many of whom would be unknown apart from their mention here. Although Paul himself had not yet visited Rome, a Christian community had taken root in the imperial capital. The list includes prominent women in the church (Phoebe, Priscilla, Junias, Tryphena, Tryphosa, Persis), common slave names (Ampliatus, Urbanus, Stachys, Apelles), and possible royalty (the household of Aristobulus — probably the grandson of Herod the Great).

Paul was writing from Corinth, where his friends included the city's director of public works. At Corinth archaeologists have dug up a block of stone that may refer to this man: it bears the Latin inscription "Erastus, commissioner of public works, bore the expense of this pavement."

1 CORINTHIANS

■ THE LAST PLACE TO START A CHURCH

NO-ONE EXPECTED MUCH FROM CRAZY CORINTH

BROTHERS, THINK OF WHAT YOU WERE WHEN YOU WERE CALLED. NOT MANY OF YOU WERE WISE BY HUMAN STANDARDS; NOT MANY WERE INFLUENTIAL; NOT MANY WERE OF NOBLE BIRTH. BUT GOD CHOSE THE FOOLISH THINGS OF THE WORLD TO SHAME THE WISE; GOD CHOSE THE WEAK THINGS OF THE WORLD TO SHAME THE STRONG.
■ 1:26–27

Every large city has one pocket where prostitutes, strippers, gamblers, and drug dealers hang out. Tourists stroll by to gawp at the sights. In London, it's Soho; in Leeds, Chapeltown; in New Orleans, Bourbon Street; and in Las Vegas, it's virtually anywhere.

In the ancient world, the whole city of Corinth was known for that kind of lifestyle. Romans made the Corinthians the butt of dirty jokes, and playwrights consistently portrayed them as drunken brawlers. The Greek verb "to Corinthianize" meant to live shamelessly and immorally.

■ A WIDE-OPEN CITY

Everyone knew what the Corinthians worshipped: money and the kinky things it could buy. Money flowed freely, for Corinth straddled one of the Roman empire's most vital trade routes. When a ship was wrecked nearby, salvage companies housed the hapless sailors at inflated prices while they scrambled to auction off the ship's cargo. The city was a sprawling open-air market, filled with slaves, Orientals, Jews, Greeks, Egyptians, sailors, athletes, gamblers, and charioteers.

Yet Corinth was no blue-collar town. It had a population of 700,000, second only to Rome's, and as the capital of a large province, the city hosted a parade of Roman diplomats and dignitaries. Its clever citizens made a showcase of new "Corinthian" architecture and prided themselves on having a cosmopolitan outlook.

For their religious ideal, the fun-loving Corinthians adopted Venus, the goddess of love.

A temple built in her honour employed more than 1,000 prostitutes.

■ PAUL TAKES ON THE CORINTHIANS

Due to all these influences, Corinth loomed as the one city "least likely to convert" to the Christian faith. What crazy cults and new religions did spring up there quickly gave in to the prevailing good-time atmosphere.

The mighty Paul, reeling from one of his most difficult missionary assignments in Athens, came to Corinth "in weakness and fear, and with much trembling" (2:3). He knew its strategic importance: if the gospel could take root there, it could transplant anywhere – and probably would, considering Corinth's crossroads location.

Paul worked in Corinth for 18 months. To everyone's surprise, the church he founded became one of the largest in the first century. But several years later he heard reports that the church, true to its city's heritage, had broken out in a series of spiritual ills. The distressing news prompted the letter known as 1 Corinthians.

The tone of this letter differs drastically from the one that precedes it. If Romans was stylistically carved in stone, 1 Corinthians was dashed off in tears and anger. One of Paul's longest letters, it covers the greatest variety of topics, partly because the Corinthians added bizarre new twists to ethical issues. In it, Paul gives practical advice on a series of church problems as well as a fascinating glimpse into the personal lives of early Christians.

■ HOW TO READ 1 CORINTHIANS

To fully appreciate Paul's letters, keep in mind that they are personal correspondence. We are actually reading someone else's mail.

In 1 Corinthians a riled apostle gives direct, forthright advice to a troubled local church. Paul saw alarming trends at work, and he used his full literary powers to set its members on the right course. He tried sarcasm, emotional pleas, autobiography, poetry, and lengthy arguments.

First, you will encounter the problems that had been reported to Paul: divisions in the church, a case of incest, court cases, the abuse of Christian freedom, chaos in the worship services. Paul lunges into these problems early

in the book. Then, beginning with chapter 7, he takes up some other problems the Corinthians had written to him about: marriage and the single life, pagan festivals, behaviour of women, spiritual gifts, and the resurrection of the dead.

This first letter to the Corinthians presents a foundation for practical Christian ethics. Use the sectional headings throughout the book to locate those issues that especially trouble you. Not all the problems discussed will apply directly to modern situations. But the general principles underlying Paul's advice do apply. As you read, look for those principles behind Paul's arguments.

■ 3-TRACK READING PLAN

For an explanation and complete listing of the 3-track reading plan, turn to page x.

■ TRACK 1:
Two-Week Courses on the Bible
The Track 1 reading programme on the Life and Teachings of Paul includes two chapters from 1 Corinthians. See page x for a complete listing of this course.

■ TRACK 2:
An Overview of 1 Corinthians in 2 Days
The emotional tone of 1 Corinthians makes for

exciting reading throughout, but two chapters especially can't be missed.
□ Day 1. Read the Introduction to 1 Corinthians, then chapter 13. Paul is at the top of his literary form as he defines love in one of the most famous passages in all of literature.
□ Day 2. Read chapter 15, a crucial passage on life after death and resurrection from the dead.

Now turn to page xi for your next Track 2 reading project.

■ TRACK 3:
All of 1 Corinthians in 14 Days
After you have read through 1 Corinthians, turn to pages xii–xiii for your next Track 3 reading project.

□ 1	□ 2	□ 3	□ 4–5
□ 6	□ 7	□ 8–9	□ 10
□ 11	□ 12	□ 13	□ 14
□ 15	□ 16		

1 Paul, called to be an apostle of Christ Jesus by the will of God, and our brother Sosthenes,

²To the church of God in Corinth, to those sanctified in Christ Jesus and called to be holy, together with all those everywhere who call on the name of our Lord Jesus Christ — their Lord and ours:

³Grace and peace to you from God our Father and the Lord Jesus Christ.

■ Thanksgiving
⁴I always thank God for you because of his grace given you in Christ Jesus. ⁵For in him you have been enriched in every way — in all your speaking and in all your knowledge — ⁶because our testimony about Christ was confirmed in you. ⁷Therefore you do not lack any spiritual gift as you eagerly wait for our Lord Jesus Christ to be revealed. ⁸He will keep you strong to the end, so that you will be blameless on the day of our Lord Jesus Christ. ⁹God, who has called you into fellowship with his Son Jesus Christ our Lord, is faithful.

■ Divisions in the Church
¹⁰I appeal to you, brothers, in the name of our Lord Jesus Christ, that all of you agree with one another so that there may be no divisions among you and that you may be perfectly united in mind and thought. ¹¹My brothers, some from Chloe's household have informed me that there are quarrels among you. ¹²What I mean is this: One of you says, "I follow Paul"; another, "I follow Apollos"; another, "I follow Cephas";ᵃ still another, "I follow Christ."

¹³Is Christ divided? Was Paul crucified for you? Were you baptised intoᵇ the name of Paul? ¹⁴I am thankful that I did not baptise any of you except Crispus and Gaius, ¹⁵so no-one can say that you were baptised into my name. (¹⁶Yes, I also baptised the household of Stephanas; beyond that, I don't remember if I baptised anyone else.) ¹⁷For Christ did not send me to baptise, but to preach the gospel — not with words of human wisdom, lest the cross of Christ be emptied of its power.

■ Christ the Wisdom and Power of God
¹⁸For the message of the cross is foolishness to those who are perishing, but to us who are being saved it is the power of God. ¹⁹For it is written:

ᵃ 12 That is, Peter   ᵇ 13 Or in; also in verse 15

"I will destroy the wisdom of the wise;
   the intelligence of the intelligent I will
    frustrate."*c*

20Where is the wise man? Where is the scholar? Where is the philosopher of this age? Has not God made foolish the wisdom of the world? 21For since in the wisdom of God the world through its wisdom did not know him, God was pleased through the foolishness of what was preached to save those who believe. 22Jews demand miraculous signs and Greeks look for wisdom, 23but we preach Christ crucified: a stumbling-block to Jews and foolishness to Gentiles, 24but to those whom God has called, both Jews and Greeks, Christ the power of God and the wisdom of God. 25For the foolishness of God is wiser than man's wisdom, and the weakness of God is stronger than man's strength.

26Brothers, think of what you were when you were called. Not many of you were wise by human standards; not many were influential; not many were of noble birth. 27But God chose the foolish things of the world to shame the wise; God chose the weak things of the world to shame the strong. 28He chose the lowly things of this world and the despised things—and the things that are not—to nullify the things that are, 29so that no-one may boast before him. 30It is because of him that you are in Christ Jesus, who has become for us wisdom from God—that is, our righteousness, holiness and redemption. 31Therefore, as it is written: "Let him who boasts boast in the Lord."*d*

2 When I came to you, brothers, I did not come with eloquence or superior wisdom as I proclaimed to you the testimony about God.*a* 2For I resolved to know nothing while I was with you except Jesus Christ and him crucified. 3I came to you in weakness and fear, and with much trembling. 4My message and my preaching were not with wise and persuasive words, but with a demonstration of the Spirit's power, 5so that your faith might not rest on men's wisdom, but on God's power.

2:3 ■ PAUL AT A CROSSROADS
This brief paragraph hints at a grave personal crisis in the apostle Paul's ministry, and Acts 16–18 gives important background. In three cities Paul saw a promising beginning crushed by fanatical Jews. Then in Athens he met little success in communicating to the intelligentsia. Many scholars believe that he reached Corinth shaken and discouraged and that he resolved to make Christ the sole subject of his teaching and preaching while there.

■ Wisdom From the Spirit
6We do, however, speak a message of wisdom among the mature, but not the wisdom of this age or of the rulers of this age, who are coming to nothing. 7No, we speak of God's secret wisdom, a wisdom that has been hidden and that God destined for our glory before time began. 8None of the rulers of this age understood it, for if they had, they would

not have crucified the Lord of glory. 9However, as it is written:

"No eye has seen,
   no ear has heard,
no mind has conceived
   what God has prepared for those who love
    him"*b*—

10but God has revealed it to us by his Spirit.

The Spirit searches all things, even the deep things of God. 11For who among men knows the thoughts of a man except the man's spirit within him? In the same way no-one knows the thoughts of God except the Spirit of God. 12We have not received the spirit of the world but the Spirit who is from God, that we may understand what God has freely given us. 13This is what we speak, not in words taught us by human wisdom but in words taught by the Spirit, expressing spiritual truths in spiritual words.*c* 14The man without the Spirit does not accept the things that come from the Spirit of God, for they are foolishness to him, and he cannot understand them, because they are spiritually discerned. 15The spiritual man makes judgments about all things, but he himself is not subject to any man's judgment:

16"For who has known the mind of the Lord
   that he may instruct him?"*d*

But we have the mind of Christ.

■ On Divisions in the Church
3 Brothers, I could not address you as spiritual but as worldly—mere infants in Christ. 2I gave you milk, not solid food, for you were not yet ready for it. Indeed, you are still not ready. 3You are still worldly. For since there is jealousy and quarrelling among you, are you not worldly? Are you not acting like mere men? 4For when one says, "I follow Paul," and another, "I follow Apollos," are you not mere men?

5What, after all, is Apollos? And what is Paul? Only servants, through whom you came to believe—as the Lord has assigned to each his task. 6I planted the seed, Apollos watered it, but God made it grow. 7So neither he who plants nor he who waters is anything, but only God, who makes things grow. 8The man who plants and the man who waters have one purpose, and each will be rewarded according to his own labour. 9For we are God's fellow-workers; you are God's field, God's building.

3:5 ■ PERSONALITY CULTS
In this chapter, Paul expands on a theme first introduced in 1:12. Converts were lining up behind various church leaders: Peter, who had walked and talked with Christ on earth; Apollos, with his sophisticated, cultivated style; Paul, the famous missionary; and Christ himself. Paul had no tolerance for that kind of hero worship. He stressed vigorously that the Corinthians belonged only to God, not to any human worker.

---

c 19 Isaiah 29:14   *d* 31 Jer. 9:24   *a* 1 Some manuscripts *as I proclaimed to you God's mystery*   *b* 9 Isaiah 64:4   *c* 13 Or *Spirit, interpreting spiritual truths to spiritual men*   *d* 16 Isaiah 40:13

10By the grace God has given me, I laid a foundation as an expert builder, and someone else is building on it. But each one should be careful how he builds. 11For no-one can lay any foundation other than the one already laid, which is Jesus Christ. 12If any man builds on this foundation using gold, silver, costly stones, wood, hay or straw, 13his work will be shown for what it is, because the Day will bring it to light. It will be revealed with fire, and the fire will test the quality of each man's work. 14If what he has built survives, he will receive his reward. 15If it is burned up, he will suffer loss; he himself will be saved, but only as one escaping through the flames.

16Don't you know that you yourselves are God's temple and that God's Spirit lives in you? 17If anyone destroys God's temple, God will destroy him; for God's temple is sacred, and you are that temple.

18Do not deceive yourselves. If any one of you thinks he is wise by the standards of this age, he should become a "fool" so that he may become wise. 19For the wisdom of this world is foolishness in God's sight. As it is written: "He catches the wise in their craftiness";*a* 20and again, "The Lord knows that the thoughts of the wise are futile."*b* 21So then, no more boasting about men! All things are yours, 22whether Paul or Apollos or Cephas*c* or the world or life or death or the present or the future—all are yours, 23and you are of Christ, and Christ is of God.

■ Apostles of Christ

4 So then, men ought to regard us as servants of Christ and as those entrusted with the secret things of God. 2Now it is required that those who have been given a trust must prove faithful. 3I care very little if I am judged by you or by any human court; indeed, I do not even judge myself. 4My conscience is clear, but that does not make me innocent. It is the Lord who judges me. 5Therefore judge nothing before the appointed time; wait till the Lord comes. He will bring to light what is hidden in darkness and will expose the motives of men's hearts. At that time each will receive his praise from God.

6Now, brothers, I have applied these things to myself and Apollos for your benefit, so that you may learn from us the meaning of the saying, "Do not go beyond what is written." Then you will not take pride in one man over against another. 7For who makes you different from anyone else? What do you have that you did not receive? And if you did receive it, why do you boast as though you did not?

8Already you have all you want! Already you have become rich! You have become kings—and that without us! How I wish that you really had become kings so that we might be kings with you! 9For it seems to me that God has put us apostles on display at the end of the procession, like men condemned to die in the arena. We have been made a spectacle

■ LIKE AN ANGRY LETTER FROM HOME
A WELL-DESERVED SCOLDING FROM A GRIEVING "PARENT"

I AM NOT WRITING THIS TO SHAME YOU, BUT TO WARN YOU, AS MY DEAR CHILDREN. ■ 4:14

Imagine a college fresher, standing in a corridor amid a swirl of chattering students. In two minutes the next lecture will begin. But, for her, time has stopped. She has just opened a tear-stained, 12-page letter from her parents.

The tone of the letter takes her by surprise. Her parents are normally reserved, not given to emotional outbursts. Their letters are warm and friendly. Not this time. Somehow they have heard about her recent behaviour on campus, and they are very hurt. In a torrent of words, they pour out their feelings for her and their equally deep disappointment.

1 Corinthians reflects the same tone: it is an intimate, well-deserved scolding from a grieved parent. "I am not writing this to shame you," says Paul, "but to warn you, as my dear children" (4:14).

■ PAUL'S SHIFTING MOODS
No other letter in the New Testament reveals such a wide range of Paul's emotions. At his own financial expense, he had invested 18 risk-filled months in Corinth. But afterwards his

rebellious "children" had launched personal attacks against him. Paul reacted like any parent first informed of his child's shocking behaviour. His moods in 1 Corinthians bounce from anger to shame, from sorrow to indignation.

Chapter 3, for example, begins with a stern lecture to "mere infants in Christ". This leads to biting sarcasm (4:8), which melts into the tender pleas of a spiritual father. Six times in chapter 6 Paul asks, "Do you not know . . . ?" Finally, in chapter 7, he gets to the practical questions that had prompted his letter in the first place.

The apostle Paul was a superbly educated logician who could skilfully weave together history and philosophy. But he also brooded over his missionary churches like a parent. He asked the Corinthians pointedly, "Shall I come to you with a whip, or in love and with a gentle spirit?" (4:21). In this letter, we see a little of both.

□ LIFE QUESTIONS:
How do you react when someone—a parent, teacher, boss, pastor—tries to straighten you out?

a 19 Job 5:13   *b 20* Psalm 94:11   *c 22* That is, Peter to the whole universe, to angels as well as to men. ¹⁰We are fools for Christ, but you are so wise in Christ! We are weak, but you are strong! You are honoured, we are dishonoured! ¹¹To this very hour we go hungry and thirsty, we are in rags, we are brutally treated, we are homeless. ¹²We work hard with our own hands. When we are cursed, we bless; when we are persecuted, we endure it; ¹³when we are slandered, we answer kindly. Up to this moment we have become the scum of the earth, the refuse of the world.

4:8 ■ A HINT OF TRIALS TO COME
Paul's intense feelings come to the surface in this paragraph, as sharply worded as any in the New Testament. He alludes (verse 9) to the Roman practice of parading the gladiators condemned to death – a poignant reference in view of the martyr's fate that awaited him and other apostles.

¹⁴I am not writing this to shame you, but to warn you, as my dear children. ¹⁵Even though you have ten thousand guardians in Christ, you do not have many fathers, for in Christ Jesus I became your father through the gospel. ¹⁶Therefore I urge you to imitate me. ¹⁷For this reason I am sending to you Timothy, my son whom I love, who is faithful in the Lord. He will remind you of my way of life in Christ Jesus, which agrees with what I teach everywhere in every church.

¹⁸Some of you have become arrogant, as if I were not coming to you. ¹⁹But I will come to you very soon, if the Lord is willing, and then I will find out not only how these arrogant people are talking, but what power they have. ²⁰For the kingdom of God is not a matter of talk but of power. ²¹What do you prefer? Shall I come to you with a whip, or in love and with a gentle spirit?

■ Expel the Immoral Brother!
5 It is actually reported that there is sexual immorality among you, and of a kind that does not occur even among pagans: A man has his father's wife. ²And you are proud! Shouldn't you rather have been filled with grief and have put out of your fellowship the man who did this? ³Even though I am not physically present, I am with you in spirit. And I have already passed judgment on the one who did this, just as if I were present. ⁴When you are assembled in the name of our Lord Jesus and I am with you in spirit, and the power of our Lord Jesus is present, ⁵hand this man over to Satan, so that the sinful nature[a] may be destroyed and his spirit saved on the day of the Lord.

⁶Your boasting is not good. Don't you know that a little yeast works through the whole batch of dough? ⁷Get rid of the old yeast that you may be a new batch without yeast – as you really are. For Christ, our Passover lamb, has been sacrificed. ⁸Therefore let us keep the Festival, not with the old yeast, the yeast of malice and wickedness, but with bread without yeast, the bread of sincerity and truth.

⁹I have written to you in my letter not to associate with sexually immoral people – ¹⁰not at all meaning the people of this world who are immoral, or the greedy and swindlers, or idolaters. In that case you would have to leave this world. ¹¹But now I am writing to you that you must not associate with anyone who calls himself a brother but is sexually immoral or greedy, an idolater or a slanderer, a drunkard or a swindler. With such a man do not even eat.

5:5 ■ HANDED OVER TO SATAN
The strong phrase used in this verse has a biblical parallel in 1 Timothy 1:20. To Paul, expelling someone from the church and Christian privileges meant pushing them out into the world ruled by Satan. In both references, however, Paul stresses that the action was designed to teach the offender a lesson.

¹²What business is it of mine to judge those outside the church? Are you not to judge those inside? ¹³God will judge those outside. "Expel the wicked man from among you."[b]

■ Lawsuits Among Believers
6 If any of you has a dispute with another, dare he take it before the ungodly for judgment instead of before the saints? ²Do you not know that the saints will judge the world? And if you are to judge the world, are you not competent to judge trivial cases? ³Do you not know that we will judge angels? How much more the things of this life! ⁴Therefore, if you have disputes about such matters, appoint as judges even men of little account in the church![a] ⁵I say this to shame you. Is it possible that there is nobody among you wise enough to judge a dispute between believers? ⁶But instead, one brother goes to law against another – and this in front of unbelievers!

⁷The very fact that you have lawsuits among you means you have been completely defeated already. Why not rather be wronged? Why not rather be cheated? ⁸Instead, you yourselves cheat and do wrong, and you do this to your brothers.

⁹Do you not know that the wicked will not inherit the kingdom of God? Do not be deceived: Neither the sexually immoral nor idolaters nor adulterers nor male prostitutes nor homosexual offenders ¹⁰nor thieves nor the greedy nor drunkards nor slanderers nor swindlers will inherit the kingdom of God. ¹¹And that is what some of you were. But you were washed, you were sanctified, you were justified in the name of the Lord Jesus Christ and by the Spirit of our God.

■ Sexual Immorality
¹²"Everything is permissible for me" – but not everything is beneficial. "Everything is permissible for me" – but I will not be mastered by anything.

---

[a]5 Or that his body; or that the flesh   [b]13 Deut. 17:7; 19:19; 21:21; 22:21,24; 24:7   [a]4 Or matters, do you appoint as judges men of little account in the church?

¹³"Food for the stomach and the stomach for food"—but God will destroy them both. The body is not meant for sexual immorality, but for the Lord, and the Lord for the body. ¹⁴By his power God raised the Lord from the dead, and he will raise us also. ¹⁵Do you not know that your bodies are members of Christ himself? Shall I then take the members of Christ and unite them with a prostitute? Never! ¹⁶Do you not know that he who unites himself with a prostitute is one with her in body? For it is said, "The two will become one flesh."*b* ¹⁷But he who unites himself with the Lord is one with him in spirit.

6:12 ■ CORINTHIAN SLOGANS

The phrases given here in quotes ("Everything is permissible for me"; "Food for the stomach and the stomach for food") appear to be slogans the Corinthians had used in justifying their loose behaviour. Paul doesn't refute their ideas outright, but rather points to the ultimate effect of their excesses.

---

¹⁸Flee from sexual immorality. All other sins a man commits are outside his body, but he who sins sexually sins against his own body. ¹⁹Do you not know that your body is a temple of the Holy Spirit, who is in you, whom you have received from God? You are not your own; ²⁰you were bought at a price. Therefore honour God with your body.

■ Marriage

7 Now for the matters you wrote about: It is good for a man not to marry.*a* ²But since there is so much immorality, each man should have his own wife, and each woman her own husband. ³The husband should fulfil his marital duty to his wife, and likewise the wife to her husband. ⁴The wife's body does not belong to her alone but also to her husband. In the same way, the husband's body does not belong to him alone but also to his wife. ⁵Do not deprive each other except by mutual consent and for a time, so that you may devote yourselves to prayer. Then come together again so that Satan will not tempt you because of your lack of self-control. ⁶I say this as a concession, not as a command. ⁷I wish that all men were as I am. But each man has his own gift from God; one has this gift, another has that.

⁸Now to the unmarried and the widows I say: It is good for them to stay unmarried, as I am. ⁹But if they cannot control themselves, they should marry, for it is better to marry than to burn with passion.

¹⁰To the married I give this command (not I, but the Lord): A wife must not separate from her husband. ¹¹But if she does, she must remain unmarried or else be reconciled to her husband. And a husband must not divorce his wife.

¹²To the rest I say this (I, not the Lord): If any brother has a wife who is not a believer and she is willing to live with him, he must not divorce her. ¹³And if a woman has a husband who is not a

---

■ WHEN EVERYTHING GOES WRONG
A CHURCH OF FORMER IDOLATERS, ADULTERERS, THIEVES, AND DRUNKARDS

NOW FOR THE MATTERS YOU WROTE
ABOUT . . . ■ 7:1

If anything can go wrong, it will." This tongue-in-cheek principle, known as Murphy's Law, is cited by economists, sports team owners and big-city mayors. Human nature somehow guarantees that nothing turns out quite the way it's supposed to. And the church at Corinth provides a darkly shining example of Murphy's Law.

To be sure, Corinthian Christians started out with the odds stacked against them. Imagine a church composed of converted idolaters, adulterers, male prostitutes, thieves, drunkards and swindlers (6:9–11). The church made up of people from such backgrounds soon encountered a multitude of problems. Paul faced a huge challenge: for one thing, he had to convince these people of the immorality of sexual activities that had been a part of everyday worship under their old religion.

■ LOCAL AND UNIVERSAL ISSUES
1 Corinthians is Paul's careful response to that multitude of problems, some of which had been posed to him as questions in a letter (7:1). Many of his answers relate directly to Corinth's local situation. In that culture, as in Muslim countries today, whether or not to wear a veil was a major issue for women (11:3–10). Eating meat sacrificed to pagan idols also disturbed some new Christians (10:18–33).

But other problems discussed here turn up in every culture: divisions in the church, lawsuits, immorality, the single life, the extent of Christian freedoms, differing views of worship and the place of tongue-speaking and other spiritual gifts. Not every breakdown in Corinth will recur in churches today, but Paul's principles apply to our own unpredictable experiences with Murphy's Law.

☐ LIFE QUESTIONS:
Think of the most "Corinthian" television show you know. Then imagine: if the lead characters became Christians, what problems would they encounter?

---

b 16 Gen. 2:24   *a* 1 Or "It is good for a man not to have sexual relations with a woman."

believer and he is willing to live with her, she must not divorce him. 14For the unbelieving husband has been sanctified through his wife, and the unbelieving wife has been sanctified through her believing husband. Otherwise your children would be unclean, but as it is, they are holy.

15But if the unbeliever leaves, let him do so. A believing man or woman is not bound in such circumstances; God has called us to live in peace. 16How do you know, wife, whether you will save your husband? Or, how do you know, husband, whether you will save your wife?

17Nevertheless, each one should retain the place in life that the Lord assigned to him and to which God has called him. This is the rule I lay down in all the churches. 18Was a man already circumcised when he was called? He should not become uncircumcised. Was a man uncircumcised when he was called? He should not be circumcised. 19Circumcision is nothing and uncircumcision is nothing. Keeping God's commands is what counts. 20Each one should remain in the situation which he was in when God called him. 21Were you a slave when you were called? Don't let it trouble you—although if you can gain your freedom, do so. 22For he who was a slave when he was called by the Lord is the Lord's freedman; similarly, he who was a free man when he was called is Christ's slave. 23You were bought at a price; do not become slaves of men. 24Brothers, each man, as responsible to God, should remain in the situation God called him to.

25Now about virgins: I have no command from the Lord, but I give a judgment as one who by the Lord's mercy is trustworthy. 26Because of the present crisis, I think that it is good for you to remain as you are. 27Are you married? Do not seek a divorce. Are you unmarried? Do not look for a wife. 28But if you do marry, you have not sinned; and if a virgin marries, she has not sinned. But those who marry will face many troubles in this life, and I want to spare you this.

7:25 ■ PAUL'S PERSONAL OPINIONS

In discussing the thorny issue of singleness and marriage, Paul carefully distinguishes what is his personal opinion and what is a clear revelation from God. He explains in verse 29 why he reached these conclusions.

29What I mean, brothers, is that the time is short. From now on those who have wives should live as if they had none; 30those who mourn, as if they did not; those who are happy, as if they were not; those who buy something, as if it were not theirs to keep; 31those who use the things of the world, as if not engrossed in them. For this world in its present form is passing away.

32I would like you to be free from concern. An unmarried man is concerned about the Lord's affairs—how he can please the Lord. 33But a married man is concerned about the affairs of this world—how he can please his wife—34and his interests are divided. An unmarried woman or virgin is concerned about the Lord's affairs: Her aim is to be devoted to the Lord in both body and spirit. But a married woman is concerned about the affairs of this world—how she can please her husband. 35I am saying this for your own good, not to restrict you, but that you may live in a right way in undivided devotion to the Lord.

36If anyone thinks he is acting improperly towards the virgin he is engaged to, and if she is getting on in years and he feels he ought to marry, he should do as he wants. He is not sinning. They should get married. 37But the man who has settled the matter in his own mind, who is under no compulsion but has control over his own will, and who has made up his mind not to marry the virgin—this man also does the right thing. 38So then, he who marries the virgin does right, but he who does not marry her does even better.b

39A woman is bound to her husband as long as he lives. But if her husband dies, she is free to marry anyone she wishes, but he must belong to the Lord. 40In my judgment, she is happier if she stays as she is—and I think that I too have the Spirit of God.

■ Food Sacrificed to Idols

8 Now about food sacrificed to idols: We know that we all possess knowledge.a Knowledge puffs up, but love builds up. 2The man who thinks he knows something does not yet know as he ought to know. 3But the man who loves God is known by God.

4So then, about eating food sacrificed to idols: We know that an idol is nothing at all in the world and that there is no God but one. 5For even if there are so-called gods, whether in heaven or on earth (as indeed there are many "gods" and many "lords"), 6yet for us there is but one God, the Father, from whom all things came and for whom we live; and there is but one Lord, Jesus Christ, through whom all things came and through whom we live.

7But not everyone knows this. Some people are still so accustomed to idols that when they eat such food they think of it as having been sacrificed to an idol, and since their conscience is weak, it is defiled. 8But food does not bring us near to God; we are no worse if we do not eat, and no better if we do.

9Be careful, however, that the exercise of your freedom does not become a stumbling-block to the weak. 10For if anyone with a weak conscience sees you who have this knowledge eating in an idol's temple, won't he be emboldened to eat what has been sacrificed to idols? 11So this weak brother, for whom Christ died, is destroyed by your knowledge. 12When you sin against your brothers in this way and wound their weak conscience, you sin against Christ. 13Therefore, if what I eat causes my brother to fall into sin, I will never eat meat again, so that I will not cause him to fall.

b 36-38 Or 36If anyone thinks he is not treating his daughter properly, and if she is getting on in years, and he feels she ought to marry, he should do as he wants. He is not sinning. He should let her get married. 37But the man who has settled the matter in his own mind, who is under no compulsion but has control over his own will, and who has made up his mind to keep the virgin unmarried—this man also does the right thing. 38So then, he who gives his virgin in marriage does right, but he who does not give her in marriage does even better.   a 1 Or "We all possess knowledge," as you say

■ The Rights of an Apostle

9 Am I not free? Am I not an apostle? Have I not seen Jesus our Lord? Are you not the result of my work in the Lord? [2]Even though I may not be an apostle to others, surely I am to you! For you are the seal of my apostleship in the Lord.

[3]This is my defence to those who sit in judgment on me. [4]Don't we have the right to food and drink? [5]Don't we have the right to take a believing wife along with us, as do the other apostles and the Lord's brothers and Cephas?[a] [6]Or is it only I and Barnabas who must work for a living?

[7]Who serves as a soldier at his own expense? Who plants a vineyard and does not eat of its grapes? Who tends a flock and does not drink of the milk? [8]Do I say this merely from a human point of view? Doesn't the Law say the same thing? [9]For it is written in the Law of Moses: "Do not muzzle an ox while it is treading out the grain."[b] Is it about oxen that God is concerned? [10]Surely he says this for us, doesn't he? Yes, this was written for us, because when the ploughman ploughs and the thresher threshes, they ought to do so in the hope of sharing in the harvest. [11]If we have sown spiritual seed among you, is it too much if we reap a material harvest from you? [12]If others have this right of support from you, shouldn't we have it all the more?

But we did not use this right. On the contrary, we put up with anything rather than hinder the gospel of Christ. [13]Don't you know that those who work in the temple get their food from the temple, and those who serve at the altar share in what is offered on the altar? [14]In the same way, the Lord has commanded that those who preach the gospel should receive their living from the gospel.

[15]But I have not used any of these rights. And I am not writing this in the hope that you will do such things for me. I would rather die than have anyone deprive me of this boast. [16]Yet when I preach the gospel, I cannot boast, for I am compelled to preach. Woe to me if I do not preach the gospel! [17]If I preach voluntarily, I have a reward; if not voluntarily, I am simply discharging the trust committed to me. [18]What then is my reward? Just this: that in preaching the gospel I may offer it free of charge, and so not make use of my rights in preaching it.

[19]Though I am free and belong to no man, I make myself a slave to everyone, to win as many as possible. [20]To the Jews I became like a Jew, to win the Jews. To those under the law I became like one under the law (though I myself am not under the law), so as to win those under the law. [21]To those not having the law I became like one not having the law (though I am not free from God's law but am under Christ's law), so as to win those not having the law. [22]To the weak I became weak, to win the weak. I have become all things to all men so that by all possible means I might save some. [23]I do all this for the sake of the gospel, that I may share in its blessings.

[24]Do you not know that in a race all the runners run, but only one gets the prize? Run in such a way as to get the prize. [25]Everyone who competes in the games goes into strict training. They do it to get a crown that will not last; but we do it to get a crown that will last for ever. [26]Therefore I do not run like a man running aimlessly; I do not fight like a man beating the air. [27]No, I beat my body and make it my slave so that after I have preached to others, I myself will not be disqualified for the prize.

9:22 ■ A POSITIVE AND A NEGATIVE
After discussing the specific questions that had surfaced in the church at Corinth, Paul gives two examples from life. The first, a positive one, points to the actions of the apostles. Although they had certain "rights" and freedoms, they didn't insist on them. Rather, they adapted to the practices of people around them to win them over. In contrast, the ancient Israelites (chapter 10) had consistently given in to their own weaknesses. Paul urges the Corinthians to follow his example, not that of the Israelites (11:1).

■ Warnings From Israel's History

10 For I do not want you to be ignorant of the fact, brothers, that our forefathers were all under the cloud and that they all passed through the sea. [2]They were all baptised into Moses in the cloud and in the sea. [3]They all ate the same spiritual food [4]and drank the same spiritual drink; for they drank from the spiritual rock that accompanied them, and that rock was Christ. [5]Nevertheless, God was not pleased with most of them; their bodies were scattered over the desert.

[6]Now these things occurred as examples[a] to keep us from setting our hearts on evil things as they did. [7]Do not be idolaters, as some of them were; as it is written: "The people sat down to eat and drink and got up to indulge in pagan revelry."[b] [8]We should not commit sexual immorality, as some of them did — and in one day twenty-three thousand of them died. [9]We should not test the Lord, as some of them did — and were killed by snakes. [10]And do not grumble, as some of them did — and were killed by the destroying angel.

[11]These things happened to them as examples and were written down as warnings for us, on whom the fulfilment of the ages has come. [12]So, if you think you are standing firm, be careful that you don't fall! [13]No temptation has seized you except what is common to man. And God is faithful; he will not let you be tempted beyond what you can bear. But when you are tempted, he will also provide a way out so that you can stand up under it.

■ Idol Feasts and the Lord's Supper

[14]Therefore, my dear friends, flee from idolatry. [15]I speak to sensible people; judge for yourselves what I say. [16]Is not the cup of thanksgiving for which we give thanks a participation in the blood of Christ? And is not the bread that we break a participation in the body of Christ? [17]Because there is one loaf, we, who are many, are one body, for we all partake of the one loaf.

[18]Consider the people of Israel: Do not those who eat the sacrifices participate in the altar? [19]Do I mean then that a sacrifice offered to an idol is anything, or that an idol is anything? [20]No, but the

---

sacrifices of pagans are offered to demons, not to God, and I do not want you to be participants with demons. 21You cannot drink the cup of the Lord and the cup of demons too; you cannot have a part in both the Lord's table and the table of demons. 22Are we trying to arouse the Lord's jealousy? Are we stronger than he?

■ The Believer's Freedom

23"Everything is permissible"—but not everything is beneficial. "Everything is permissible"—but not everything is constructive. 24Nobody should seek his own good, but the good of others.

25Eat anything sold in the meat market without raising questions of conscience, 26for, "The earth is the Lord's, and everything in it."c

27If some unbeliever invites you to a meal and you want to go, eat whatever is put before you without raising questions of conscience. 28But if anyone says to you, "This has been offered in sacrifice," then do not eat it, both for the sake of the man who told you and for conscience' saked—29the other man's conscience, I mean, not yours. For why should my freedom be judged by another's conscience? 30If I take part in the meal with thankfulness, why am I denounced because of something I thank God for?

31So whether you eat or drink or whatever you do, do it all for the glory of God. 32Do not cause anyone to stumble, whether Jews, Greeks or the church of God—33even as I try to please everybody in every way. For I am not seeking my own good but the good of many, so that they may be saved. 11 1Follow my example, as I follow the example of Christ.

■ Propriety in Worship

2I praise you for remembering me in everything and for holding to the teachings,a just as I passed them on to you.

3Now I want you to realise that the head of every man is Christ, and the head of the woman is man, and the head of Christ is God. 4Every man who prays or prophesies with his head covered dishonours his head. 5And every woman who prays or prophesies with her head uncovered dishonours her head—it is just as though her head were shaved. 6If a woman does not cover her head, she should have her hair cut off; and if it is a disgrace for a woman to have her hair cut or shaved off, she should cover her head. 7A man ought not to cover his head,b since he is the image and glory of God; but the woman is the glory of man. 8For man did not come from woman, but woman from man; 9neither was man created for woman, but woman for man. 10For this reason, and because of the angels, the woman ought to have a sign of authority on her head.

11In the Lord, however, woman is not independent of man, nor is man independent of woman. 12For as woman came from man, so also man is born of woman. But everything comes from God. 13Judge for yourselves: Is it proper for a woman to pray to God with her head uncovered? 14Does not the very nature of things teach you that if a man has long hair,

it is a disgrace to him, 15but that if a woman has long hair, it is her glory? For long hair is given to her as a covering. 16If anyone wants to be contentious about this, we have no other practice—nor do the churches of God.

11:5 ■ WOMEN IN CORINTH
In the Middle East, a woman who appeared in public barefaced, without a veil, showed loose morals. Some Muslim countries today still retain that custom. Paul's advice applied directly to the cultural situation in Corinth, where unruly women were disrupting the worship services.

■ The Lord's Supper

17In the following directives I have no praise for you, for your meetings do more harm than good. 18In the first place, I hear that when you come together as a church, there are divisions among you, and to some extent I believe it. 19No doubt there have to be differences among you to show which of you have God's approval. 20When you come together, it is not the Lord's Supper you eat, 21for as you eat, each of you goes ahead without waiting for anybody else. One remains hungry, another gets drunk. 22Don't you have homes to eat and drink in? Or do you despise the church of God and humiliate those who have nothing? What shall I say to you? Shall I praise you for this? Certainly not!

23For I received from the Lord what I also passed on to you: The Lord Jesus, on the night he was betrayed, took bread, 24and when he had given thanks, he broke it and said, "This is my body, which is for you; do this in remembrance of me." 25In the same way, after supper he took the cup, saying, "This cup is the new covenant in my blood; do this, whenever you drink it, in remembrance of me." 26For whenever you eat this bread and drink this cup, you proclaim the Lord's death until he comes.

27Therefore, whoever eats the bread or drinks the cup of the Lord in an unworthy manner will be guilty of sinning against the body and blood of the Lord. 28A man ought to examine himself before he eats of the bread and drinks of the cup. 29For anyone who eats and drinks without recognising the body of the Lord eats and drinks judgment on himself. 30That is why many among you are weak and sick, and a number of you have fallen asleep. 31But if we judged ourselves, we would not come under judgment. 32When we are judged by the Lord, we are being disciplined so that we will not be condemned with the world.

33So then, my brothers, when you come together to eat, wait for each other. 34If anyone is hungry, he should eat at home, so that when you meet together it may not result in judgment.

And when I come I will give further directions.

■ Spiritual Gifts

12 Now about spiritual gifts, brothers, I do not want you to be ignorant. 2You know that when you were pagans, somehow or other you

c26 Psalm 24:1   d28 Some manuscripts conscience' sake, for "the earth is the Lord's and everything in it"   a2 Or traditions   b4–7 Or 4Every man who prays or prophesies with long hair dishonours his head. 5And every woman who prays or prophesies with no covering .of hair, on her head dishonours her head—she is just like one of the "shorn women". 6If a woman has no covering, let her be for now with short hair, but since it is a disgrace for a woman to have her hair shorn or shaved again, she should grow it again. 7A man ought not to have long hair were influenced and led astray to mute idols. ³Therefore I tell you that no-one who is speaking by the Spirit of God says, "Jesus be cursed," and no-one can say, "Jesus is Lord," except by the Holy Spirit.

⁴There are different kinds of gifts, but the same Spirit. ⁵There are different kinds of service, but the same Lord. ⁶There are different kinds of working, but the same God works all of them in all men.

⁷Now to each one the manifestation of the Spirit is given for the common good. ⁸To one there is given through the Spirit the message of wisdom, to another the message of knowledge by means of the same Spirit, ⁹to another faith by the same Spirit, to another gifts of healing by that one Spirit, ¹⁰to another miraculous powers, to another prophecy, to another distinguishing between spirits, to another speaking in different kinds of tongues,ᵃ and to still another the interpretation of tongues.ᵃ ¹¹All these are the work of one and the same Spirit, and he gives them to each one, just as he determines.

■ One Body, Many Parts

¹²The body is a unit, though it is made up of many parts; and though all its parts are many, they form one body. So it is with Christ. ¹³For we were all baptised byᵇ one Spirit into one body—whether Jews or Greeks, slave or free—and we were all given the one Spirit to drink.

¹⁴Now the body is not made up of one part but of many. ¹⁵If the foot should say, "Because I am not a hand, I do not belong to the body," it would not for that reason cease to be part of the body. ¹⁶And if the ear should say, "Because I am not an eye, I do not belong to the body," it would not for that reason cease to be part of the body. ¹⁷If the whole body were an eye, where would the sense of hearing be? If the whole body were an ear, where would the sense of smell be? ¹⁸But in fact God has arranged the parts in the body, every one of them, just as he wanted them to be. ¹⁹If they were all one part, where would the body be? ²⁰As it is, there are many parts, but one body.

²¹The eye cannot say to the hand, "I don't need you!" And the head cannot say to the feet, "I don't

■ LESSONS FROM THE HUMAN BODY
THE BODY NEEDS AN EYE, AND THE EYE NEEDS A BODY

THE BODY IS A UNIT, THOUGH IT IS MADE UP OF MANY PARTS; AND THOUGH ALL ITS PARTS ARE MANY, THEY FORM ONE BODY. SO IT IS WITH CHRIST. ■ 12:12

Can you get along in life without eyes? Of course, but you must make adjustments. You must rely more on other senses and depend on friends, or perhaps a guide dog, for extra help. Regardless of what adjustments you make, however, your body will remain incomplete without eyes. You will miss out on colour and design and all the visual delights this world offers.

An eyeless body can cope, but a bodyless eye is unimaginable. The most beautiful eyes in the world, when detached from a body, are lifeless and worthless. Eyes need a body that will bring them blood and receive their nerve impulses.

■ MANY PARTS, ALL WORKING TOGETHER

In chapter 12 Paul gives a clever anatomy lesson, with a purpose. By comparing members of the church of Christ to parts of a human body, he neatly explains two complementary truths the Corinthians had failed to comprehend. Any part of a body, he says—such as an eye or a foot—makes a valuable contribution to the whole body. Whenever a single member is missing, the entire body suffers.

And, he continues, no member can survive if isolated from the rest. Alone, an eye is useless. All parts must co-operate to form a single, unified body.

Paul relied on body images to explain both the diversity and unity of God's followers. The body analogy fitted so well that he referred to it two dozen times in his various letters. It became his favourite way of portraying the church.

■ AN EMPHASIS ON UNITY

A church as diverse as Corinth knew about the differences among various members, so Paul's letter to them stressed the unity part of the analogy. How can diverse people work together in a spiritual body? He answered that question with the famous lyrical description of love in chapter 13. After that eloquent statement, he went on to discuss the Corinthians' various spiritual gifts.

Chapters 12–14 address issues that troubled the patchwork Corinthian church and that still disturb the church today. The solution, in our time as well as Paul's, is for each person to respect other members of the body and to take direction from Jesus Christ, the head.

□ LIFE QUESTIONS:
Of Paul's list of spiritual gifts, which are prominent in your church? Are any overlooked? How do you fit in?

ᵃ 10 Or languages; also in verse 28   ᵇ 13 Or with; or in

need you!" 22On the contrary, those parts of the body that seem to be weaker are indispensable, 23and the parts that we think are less honourable we treat with special honour. And the parts that are unpresentable are treated with special modesty, 24while our presentable parts need no special treatment. But God has combined the members of the body and has given greater honour to the parts that lacked it, 25so that there should be no division in the body, but that its parts should have equal concern for each other. 26If one part suffers, every part suffers with it; if one part is honoured, every part rejoices with it.

27Now you are the body of Christ, and each one of you is a part of it. 28And in the church God has appointed first of all apostles, second prophets, third teachers, then workers of miracles, also those having gifts of healing, those able to help others, those with gifts of administration, and those speaking in different kinds of tongues. 29Are all apostles? Are all prophets? Are all teachers? Do all work miracles? 30Do all have gifts of healing? Do all speak in tongues?*c* Do all interpret? 31But eagerly desire*d* the greater gifts.

■ Love

And now I will show you the most excellent way.

13 If I speak in the tongues*a* of men and of angels, but have not love, I am only a resounding gong or a clanging cymbal. 2If I have the gift of prophecy and can fathom all mysteries and all knowledge, and if I have a faith that can move mountains, but have not love, I am nothing. 3If I give all I possess to the poor and surrender my body to the flames,*b* but have not love, I gain nothing.

4Love is patient, love is kind. It does not envy, it does not boast, it is not proud. 5It is not rude, it is not self-seeking, it is not easily angered, it keeps no record of wrongs. 6Love does not delight in evil but rejoices with the truth. 7It always protects, always trusts, always hopes, always perseveres.

8Love never fails. But where there are prophecies, they will cease; where there are tongues, they will be stilled; where there is knowledge, it will pass away. 9For we know in part and we prophesy in part, 10but when perfection comes, the imperfect disappears. 11When I was a child, I talked like a child, I thought like a child, I reasoned like a child. When I became a man, I put childish ways behind me. 12Now we see but a poor reflection as in a mirror; then we shall see face to face. Now I know in part; then I shall know fully, even as I am fully known.

13And now these three remain: faith, hope and love. But the greatest of these is love.

■ Gifts of Prophecy and Tongues

14 Follow the way of love and eagerly desire spiritual gifts, especially the gift of prophecy. 2For anyone who speaks in a tongue*a* does not speak to men but to God. Indeed, no-one understands him; he utters mysteries with his spirit.*b* 3But everyone who prophesies speaks to men for their strengthening, encouragement and comfort.

4He who speaks in a tongue edifies himself, but he who prophesies edifies the church. 5I would like every one of you to speak in tongues,*c* but I would rather have you prophesy. He who prophesies is greater than one who speaks in tongues,*c* unless he interprets, so that the church may be edified.

14:2 ■ SPEAKING IN TONGUES

1 Corinthians 12–14 gives the New Testament's most complete teaching on supernatural gifts such as healing and speaking in tongues. Paul stresses two concerns: (1) "Sensational" gifts must not be given higher rank than they deserve (chapter 13 stresses the superiority of simple love); (2) These gifts should contribute to orderly and proper worship, not confusion. The Corinthians seemed to take everything to excess – whether practising immorality, celebrating the Lord's Supper, or exercising spiritual gifts.

6Now, brothers, if I come to you and speak in tongues, what good will I be to you, unless I bring you some revelation or knowledge or prophecy or word of instruction? 7Even in the case of lifeless things that make sounds, such as the flute or harp, how will anyone know what tune is being played unless there is a distinction in the notes? 8Again, if the trumpet does not sound a clear call, who will get ready for battle? 9So it is with you. Unless you speak intelligible words with your tongue, how will anyone know what you are saying? You will just be speaking into the air. 10Undoubtedly there are all sorts of languages in the world, yet none of them is without meaning. 11If then I do not grasp the meaning of what someone is saying, I am a foreigner to the speaker, and he is a foreigner to me. 12So it is with you. Since you are eager to have spiritual gifts, try to excel in gifts that build up the church.

13For this reason anyone who speaks in a tongue should pray that he may interpret what he says. 14For if I pray in a tongue, my spirit prays, but my mind is unfruitful. 15So what shall I do? I will pray with my spirit, but I will also pray with my mind; I will sing with my spirit, but I will also sing with my mind. 16If you are praising God with your spirit, how can one who finds himself among those who do not understand*d* say "Amen" to your thanksgiving, since he does not know what you are saying? 17You may be giving thanks well enough, but the other man is not edified.

18I thank God that I speak in tongues more than all of you. 19But in the church I would rather speak five intelligible words to instruct others than ten thousand words in a tongue.

20Brothers, stop thinking like children. In regard to evil be infants, but in your thinking be adults. 21In the Law it is written:

"Through men of strange tongues
    and through the lips of foreigners
I will speak to this people,
    but even then they will not listen to me,"*e*
says the Lord.

---

c30 Or other languages   d31 Or But you are eagerly desiring   a1 Or languages   b3 Some early manuscripts body that I may boast
a2 Or another language; also in verses 4, 13, 14, 19, 26 and 27   b2 Or by the Spirit   c5 Or other languages; also in verses 6, 18, 22, 23 and 39
d16 Or among the enquirers   e21 Isaiah 28:11,12

22Tongues, then, are a sign, not for believers but for unbelievers; prophecy, however, is for believers, not for unbelievers. 23So if the whole church comes together and everyone speaks in tongues, and some who do not understand*f* or some unbelievers come in, will they not say that you are out of your mind? 24But if an unbeliever or someone who does not understand*g* comes in while everybody is prophesying, he will be convinced by all that he is a sinner and will be judged by all, 25and the secrets of his heart will be laid bare. So he will fall down and worship God, exclaiming, "God is really among you!"

■ Orderly Worship
26What then shall we say, brothers? When you come together, everyone has a hymn, or a word of instruction, a revelation, a tongue or an interpretation. All of these must be done for the strengthening of the church. 27If anyone speaks in a tongue, two — or at the most three — should speak, one at a time, and someone must interpret. 28If there is no interpreter, the speaker should keep quiet in the church and speak to himself and God.

29Two or three prophets should speak, and the others should weigh carefully what is said. 30And if a revelation comes to someone who is sitting down, the first speaker should stop. 31For you can all prophesy in turn so that everyone may be instructed and encouraged. 32The spirits of prophets are subject to the control of prophets. 33For God is not a God of disorder but of peace.

As in all the congregations of the saints, 34women should remain silent in the churches. They are not allowed to speak, but must be in submission, as the Law says. 35If they want to enquire about something, they should ask their own husbands at home; for it is disgraceful for a woman to speak in the church.

36Did the word of God originate with you? Or are you the only people it has reached? 37If anybody thinks he is a prophet or spiritually gifted, let him acknowledge that what I am writing to you is the Lord's command. 38If he ignores this, he himself will be ignored.*b*

39Therefore, my brothers, be eager to prophesy, and do not forbid speaking in tongues. 40But everything should be done in a fitting and orderly way.

■ The Resurrection of Christ
15 Now, brothers, I want to remind you of the gospel I preached to you, which you received and on which you have taken your stand. 2By this gospel you are saved, if you hold firmly to the word I preached to you. Otherwise, you have believed in vain.

3For what I received I passed on to you as of first importance:*a* that Christ died for our sins according to the Scriptures, 4that he was buried, that he was raised on the third day according to the Scriptures, 5and that he appeared to Peter,*b* and then to the Twelve. 6After that, he appeared to more than five hundred of the brothers at the same time, most of whom are still living, though some have fallen asleep. 7Then he appeared to James, then to all the

apostles, 8and last of all he appeared to me also, as to one abnormally born.

15:8 ■ BASIC CHRISTIANITY
Paul stresses the basics every Christian must believe: that Christ died for our sins, that he was buried (really dead), and that he rose again. Listing some of the many people who saw Jesus after his resurrection, Paul includes himself, last of all. He is referring to his encounter with Christ on the road to Damascus (see Acts 9).

9For I am the least of the apostles and do not even deserve to be called an apostle, because I persecuted the church of God. 10But by the grace of God I am what I am, and his grace to me was not without effect. No, I worked harder than all of them — yet not I, but the grace of God that was with me. 11Whether, then, it was I or they, this is what we preach, and this is what you believed.

■ The Resurrection of the Dead
12But if it is preached that Christ has been raised from the dead, how can some of you say that there is no resurrection of the dead? 13If there is no resurrection of the dead, then not even Christ has been raised. 14And if Christ has not been raised, our preaching is useless and so is your faith. 15More than that, we are then found to be false witnesses about God, for we have testified about God that he raised Christ from the dead. But he did not raise him if in fact the dead are not raised. 16For if the dead are not raised, then Christ has not been raised either. 17And if Christ has not been raised, your faith is futile; you are still in your sins. 18Then those also who have fallen asleep in Christ are lost. 19If only for this life we have hope in Christ, we are to be pitied more than all men.

20But Christ has indeed been raised from the dead, the firstfruits of those who have fallen asleep. 21For since death came through a man, the resurrection of the dead comes also through a man. 22For as in Adam all die, so in Christ all will be made alive. 23But each in his own turn: Christ, the firstfruits; then, when he comes, those who belong to him. 24Then the end will come, when he hands over the kingdom to God the Father after he has destroyed all dominion, authority and power. 25For he must reign until he has put all his enemies under his feet. 26The last enemy to be destroyed is death. 27For he "has put everything under his feet".*c* Now when it says that "everything" has been put under him, it is clear that this does not include God himself, who put everything under Christ. 28When he has done this, then the Son himself will be made subject to him who put everything under him, so that God may be all in all.

29Now if there is no resurrection, what will those do who are baptised for the dead? If the dead are not raised at all, why are people baptised for them? 30And as for us, why do we endanger ourselves every hour? 31I die every day — I mean that, brothers — just as surely as I glory over you in Christ

---

f 23 Or some enquirers   *g 24* Or or some enquirer   *b 38* Some manuscripts *If he is ignorant of this, let him be ignorant*   *a 3* Or you at the first
b 5 Greek *Cephas*   *c 27* Psalm 8:6

Jesus our Lord. 32If I fought wild beasts in Ephesus for merely human reasons, what have I gained? If the dead are not raised,

"Let us eat and drink,
    for tomorrow we die."d

33Do not be misled: "Bad company corrupts good character." 34Come back to your senses as you ought, and stop sinning; for there are some who are ignorant of God—I say this to your shame.

■ The Resurrection Body

35But someone may ask, "How are the dead raised? With what kind of body will they come?" 36How foolish! What you sow does not come to life unless it dies. 37When you sow, you do not plant the body that will be, but just a seed, perhaps of wheat or of something else. 38But God gives it a body as he has determined, and to each kind of seed he gives its own body. 39All flesh is not the same: Men have one kind of flesh, animals have another, birds another and fish another. 40There are also heavenly bodies and there are earthly bodies; but the splendour of the heavenly bodies is one kind, and the splendour of the earthly bodies is another. 41The sun has one kind of splendour, the moon another and the stars another; and star differs from star in splendour.

42So will it be with the resurrection of the dead. The body that is sown is perishable, it is raised imperishable; 43it is sown in dishonour, it is raised in glory; it is sown in weakness, it is raised in power; 44it is sown a natural body, it is raised a spiritual body.

If there is a natural body, there is also a spiritual body. 45So it is written: "The first man Adam became a living being";e the last Adam, a life-giving spirit. 46The spiritual did not come first, but the natural, and after that the spiritual. 47The first man was of the dust of the earth, the second man from heaven. 48As was the earthly man, so are those who are of the earth; and as is the man from heaven, so also are those who are of heaven. 49And just as we have borne the likeness of the earthly man, so shall wef bear the likeness of the man from heaven.

50I declare to you, brothers, that flesh and blood cannot inherit the kingdom of God, nor does the perishable inherit the imperishable. 51Listen, I tell you a mystery: We will not all sleep, but we will all be changed—52in a flash, in the twinkling of an eye, at the last trumpet. For the trumpet will sound, the dead will be raised imperishable, and we will be changed. 53For the perishable must clothe itself with the imperishable, and the mortal with immortality. 54When the perishable has been clothed with the imperishable, and the mortal with immortality, then the saying that is written will come true: "Death has been swallowed up in victory."g

55"Where, O death, is your victory?
    Where, O death, is your sting?"b

56The sting of death is sin, and the power of sin is the law. 57But thanks be to God! He gives us the victory through our Lord Jesus Christ.

58Therefore, my dear brothers, stand firm. Let nothing move you. Always give yourselves fully to the work of the Lord, because you know that your labour in the Lord is not in vain.

■ THE WORST DANGER OF ALL   INSIGHT
WHY BELIEVE IN LIFE AFTER DEATH?

IF THERE IS NO RESURRECTION OF THE DEAD, THEN NOT EVEN CHRIST HAS BEEN RAISED. AND IF CHRIST HAS NOT BEEN RAISED, OUR PREACHING IS USELESS AND SO IS YOUR FAITH.
■ 15:13–14

Most of the problems raised by the church at Corinth concerned personal behaviour. After tackling each of those problems, Paul turned to one last question, a matter of doctrine. Some people in the church were challenging the Christian belief in an afterlife. Death, they said, is the end.

    Many people have questioned the afterlife. In Jesus' day, a Jewish sect called Sadducees denied the resurrection from the dead. Doubters persist today (among them: many Black Muslims, Buddhists and Marxists and most atheists). But Paul saw the matter of life after death as the most explosive issue in the Corinthian church.

■ PITIABLE CHRISTIANS
If there's no future life, he thundered, the entire Christian message would be a lie. He, Paul, would have no reason to continue as a minister; Christ's death would have merely wasted blood; and Christians would be the most pitiable of all people.

    Chapter 15 weaves together the threads of Christian belief about death. It shows how death is finally conquered and becomes, not an end, but a beginning. Cheered by such a triumphant note, the apostle Paul sums up his counsel to the Corinthians with a ringing challenge to "stand firm".

☐ LIFE QUESTIONS:
Which of Paul's arguments in chapter 15 do you find most convincing? How does belief in an afterlife affect you?

d 32 Isaiah 22:13   e 45 Gen. 2:7   f 49 Some early manuscripts so let us   g 54 Isaiah 25:8   b 55 Hosea 13:14

■ The Collection for God's People

16 Now about the collection for God's people: Do what I told the Galatian churches to do. ²On the first day of every week, each one of you should set aside a sum of money in keeping with his income, saving it up, so that when I come no collections will have to be made. ³Then, when I arrive, I will give letters of introduction to the men you approve and send them with your gift to Jerusalem. ⁴If it seems advisable for me to go also, they will accompany me.

16:1 ■ REMEMBERING THE POOR
Paul's deep concern for the poor in Jerusalem comes up often in the New Testament. He mentions taking a collection here, as well as in Romans and 2 Corinthians. He knew that widespread concern for the mother church in Jerusalem would do much to further unity between Jewish and Gentile Christians.

■ Personal Requests

⁵After I go through Macedonia, I will come to you—for I will be going through Macedonia. ⁶Perhaps I will stay with you awhile, or even spend the winter, so that you can help me on my journey, wherever I go. ⁷I do not want to see you now and make only a passing visit; I hope to spend some time with you, if the Lord permits. ⁸But I will stay on at Ephesus until Pentecost, ⁹because a great door for effective work has opened to me, and there are many who oppose me.

¹⁰If Timothy comes, see to it that he has nothing to fear while he is with you, for he is carrying on the work of the Lord, just as I am. ¹¹No-one, then, should refuse to accept him. Send him on his way in peace so that he may return to me. I am expecting him along with the brothers.

¹²Now about our brother Apollos: I strongly urged him to go to you with the brothers. He was quite unwilling to go now, but he will go when he has the opportunity.

¹³Be on your guard; stand firm in the faith; be men of courage; be strong. ¹⁴Do everything in love.

¹⁵You know that the household of Stephanas were the first converts in Achaia, and they have devoted themselves to the service of the saints. I urge you, brothers, ¹⁶to submit to such as these and to everyone who joins in the work, and labours at it. ¹⁷I was glad when Stephanas, Fortunatus and Achaicus arrived, because they have supplied what was lacking from you. ¹⁸For they refreshed my spirit and yours also. Such men deserve recognition.

■ Final Greetings

¹⁹The churches in the province of Asia send you greetings. Aquila and Priscilla*a* greet you warmly in the Lord, and so does the church that meets at their house. ²⁰All the brothers here send you greetings. Greet one another with a holy kiss.

²¹I, Paul, write this greeting in my own hand.

²²If anyone does not love the Lord—a curse be on him. Come, O Lord!*b*

²³The grace of the Lord Jesus be with you.

²⁴My love to all of you in Christ Jesus. Amen.*c*

---

a 19 Greek *Prisca*, a variant of *Priscilla*   *b 22* In Aramaic the expression *Come, O Lord* is *Marana tha*.   *c 24* Some manuscripts do not have *Amen*.

2 CORINTHIANS

■ A BOOK OF JOY AND SADNESS

WHY ISN'T PAUL CELEBRATING HIS VICTORY?

INDEED, IN OUR HEARTS WE FELT THE SENTENCE OF DEATH. BUT THIS HAPPENED THAT
WE MIGHT NOT RELY ON OURSELVES BUT ON GOD, WHO RAISES THE DEAD. ■ 1:9

Athletes sometimes have a strange reaction to a
great victory. Some call it "morning-after
sickness". An Olympic gymnast who has trained
for 15 years wakes up the day after her gold
medal performance feeling oddly depressed.
Paradoxically, the sweet taste of victory can take
on a bitter edge.

An even more pungent feeling may hit
those who prevail in personal disputes. The man
who wins a crucial court case is stabbed by
sympathy for those he defeated. The politician
who waves jubilantly to a cheering crowd on
election night winces inwardly at the bruises she
suffered – and inflicted – during the campaign.
The husband who insisted on a divorce leaves
the final settlement feeling sad and burdened.

■ LINGERING PAIN

Something like that bittersweet state must have
plagued the apostle Paul when he wrote
2 Corinthians. He had just won a great victory in
convincing the Corinthians to come over to his
side. His spirit had surged upon hearing Titus'
news of their wave of support for him (7:6–16). His
previous letter, a personal risk, had paid off.
Reflecting Paul's triumph, this letter spontaneously
breaks out in jubilant praise and thanksgiving.

And yet, in no other letter does Paul so
openly admit his frustrations. Immediately after a
spare greeting he mentions hardships so severe
that "we despaired even of life" (1:8). Numerous

references crop up regarding the tense relations
he and the Corinthians have had. Paul wonders
aloud if he has been too hard on them; he
acknowledges his own lingering pain.

■ A DIARY FOR TWO AUDIENCES

Second Corinthians, full of allusions and personal
references, reads more like a diary than a public
document. If 1 Corinthians analyses the problems
of the Corinthian church, this sequel reveals the
problems Paul himself experienced.

He doesn't gloat over his victory in
getting the Corinthians' support. Rather, he
makes himself vulnerable and opens a window
into his inner self. He summarises his state as
"hard pressed on every side, but not crushed;
perplexed, but not in despair; persecuted, but
not abandoned; struck down, but not destroyed"
(4:8–9).

Although random selections from
2 Corinthians demonstrate the author's
seesawing moods, the book as a whole reveals
a tenacious man on the rebound. Paul expresses
relief that the Corinthians' problems are being
resolved, even as he points out new danger
signs in the church. Always he keeps in mind a
dual readership: the majority who support him,
for whom he has warm, loving words, and the
minority of dissenters who pose a grave threat
to church unity.

■ HOW TO READ 2 CORINTHIANS

Of all Paul's letters, 2 Corinthians reads most like
a personal letter and least like a public document.
He wrote it when an intense struggle with the
Corinthian church was coming to a head. As a
result, it reveals much about Paul's troubled state.
He half-apologised for speaking so freely, for
appearing to be boasting, and for spending time
on "foolishness".

Read 2 Corinthians like you would read
any personal letter. Try to visualise the mood of

the apostle Paul as he was writing, and look
between the lines for clues that would help
explain his relationship with the church at
Corinth. What were his enemies accusing him
of? Watch especially for Paul's spirited reply to
criticism, especially in the last four chapters. He
tells about certain events in his life that are
recorded nowhere else.

You will probably notice that Paul is tying
up loose ends in this letter: for example, he is

preparing for a third visit to Corinth and asking them to get a collection ready. Yet amid these practical matters he pauses to write profound words on such topics as suffering, giving, and personal ministry.

■ 3-TRACK READING PLAN

For an explanation and complete listing of the 3-track reading plan, turn to page x.

■ TRACK 1:
Two-Week Courses on the Bible
See page x for information on these courses.

■ TRACK 2:
An Overview of 2 Corinthians in 2 Days
□ Day 1. Read the Introduction to 2 Corinthians,

then chapter 4. It helps explain how Paul kept going despite all his hardships.
□ Day 2. Read chapter 12, which includes a brief description of Paul's "out-of-the-body" experience and his mysterious "thorn in the flesh".
Now turn to page xi for your next Track 2 reading project.

■ TRACK 3:
All of 2 Corinthians in 10 Days
After you have read through 2 Corinthians, turn to pages xii–xiii for your next Track 3 reading project.

□ 1　□ 2–3　□ 4　□ 5
□ 6　□ 7　□ 8–9　□ 10
□ 11　□ 12–13

1 Paul, an apostle of Christ Jesus by the will of God, and Timothy our brother,

To the church of God in Corinth, together with all the saints throughout Achaia:

²Grace and peace to you from God our Father and the Lord Jesus Christ.

■ The God of All Comfort
³Praise be to the God and Father of our Lord Jesus Christ, the Father of compassion and the God of all comfort, ⁴who comforts us in all our troubles, so that we can comfort those in any trouble with the comfort we ourselves have received from God. ⁵For just as the sufferings of Christ flow over into our lives, so also through Christ our comfort overflows. ⁶If we are distressed, it is for your comfort and salvation; if we are comforted, it is for your comfort, which produces in you patient endurance of the same sufferings we suffer. ⁷And our hope for you is firm, because we know that just as you share in our sufferings, so also you share in our comfort.

⁸We do not want you to be uninformed, brothers, about the hardships we suffered in the province of Asia. We were under great pressure, far beyond our ability to endure, so that we despaired even of life. ⁹Indeed, in our hearts we felt the sentence of death. But this happened that we might not rely on ourselves but on God, who raises the dead. ¹⁰He has delivered us from such a deadly peril, and he will deliver us. On him we have set our hope that he will continue to deliver us, ¹¹as you help us by your prayers. Then many will give thanks on ourᵃ behalf for the gracious favour granted us in answer to the prayers of many.

■ Paul's Change of Plans
¹²Now this is our boast: Our conscience testifies that we have conducted ourselves in the world, and especially in our relations with you, in the holiness and sincerity that are from God. We have done so not according to worldly wisdom but according to God's grace. ¹³For we do not write to you anything you cannot read or understand. And I hope that, ¹⁴as

you have understood us in part, you will come to understand fully that you can boast of us just as we will boast of you in the day of the Lord Jesus.

1:8 ■ ON THE REBOUND
Paul does not tell what specific hardships he had faced in Asia; they were probably known to the original audience. But in four separate places in this letter (chapters 4,6,11,12) he spells out an accumulation of hardships that plagued his ministry. Such life-threatening trials had recently driven him into a deep state of despair. He survived, though, and was now using his new-found vitality to comfort and reassure concerned friends in Corinth.

¹⁵Because I was confident of this, I planned to visit you first so that you might benefit twice. ¹⁶I planned to visit you on my way to Macedonia and to come back to you from Macedonia, and then to have you send me on my way to Judea. ¹⁷When I planned this, did I do it lightly? Or do I make my plans in a worldly manner so that in the same breath I say, "Yes, yes" and "No, no"?

¹⁸But as surely as God is faithful, our message to you is not "Yes" and "No". ¹⁹For the Son of God, Jesus Christ, who was preached among you by me and Silasᵇ and Timothy, was not "Yes" and "No", but in him it has always been "Yes." ²⁰For no matter how many promises God has made, they are "Yes" in Christ. And so through him the "Amen" is spoken by us to the glory of God. ²¹Now it is God who makes both us and you stand firm in Christ. He anointed us, ²²set his seal of ownership on us, and put his Spirit in our hearts as a deposit, guaranteeing what is to come.

²³I call God as my witness that it was in order to spare you that I did not return to Corinth. ²⁴Not that we lord it over your faith, but we work with you for

2 your joy, because it is by faith you stand firm. ¹So I made up my mind that I would not make another painful visit to you. ²For if I grieve you, who

ᵃ 11 Many manuscripts your　ᵇ 19 Greek Silvanus, a variant of Silas is left to make me glad but you whom I have grieved? ³I wrote as I did so that when I came I should not be distressed by those who ought to make me rejoice. I had confidence in all of you, that you would all share my joy. ⁴For I wrote to you out of great distress and anguish of heart and with many tears, not to grieve you but to let you know the depth of my love for you.

■ Forgiveness for the Sinner

⁵If anyone has caused grief, he has not so much grieved me as he has grieved all of you, to some extent—not to put it too severely. ⁶The punishment inflicted on him by the majority is sufficient for him. ⁷Now instead, you ought to forgive and comfort him, so that he will not be overwhelmed by excessive sorrow. ⁸I urge you, therefore, to reaffirm your love for him. ⁹The reason I wrote to you was to see if you would stand the test and be obedient in everything. ¹⁰If you forgive anyone, I also forgive him. And what I have forgiven—if there was anything to forgive—I have forgiven in the sight of Christ for your sake, ¹¹in order that Satan might not outwit us. For we are not unaware of his schemes.

■ Ministers of the New Covenant

¹²Now when I went to Troas to preach the gospel of Christ and found that the Lord had opened a door for me, ¹³I still had no peace of mind, because I did not find my brother Titus there. So I said good-bye to them and went on to Macedonia.

¹⁴But thanks be to God, who always leads us in triumphal procession in Christ and through us spreads everywhere the fragrance of the knowledge of him. ¹⁵For we are to God the aroma of Christ among those who are being saved and those who are perishing. ¹⁶To the one we are the smell of death; to the other, the fragrance of life. And who is equal to such a task? ¹⁷Unlike so many, we do not peddle the word of God for profit. On the contrary, in Christ we speak before God with sincerity, like men sent from God.

3 Are we beginning to commend ourselves again? Or do we need, like some people, letters of recommendation to you or from you? ²You yourselves are our letter, written on our hearts, known and read by everybody. ³You show that you are a letter from Christ, the result of our ministry, written not with ink but with the Spirit of the living God, not on tablets of stone but on tablets of human hearts.

■ A MYSTERIOUS VISIT
PAUL'S BREAK WITH THE CORINTHIANS

INSIGHT

SO I MADE UP MY MIND THAT I WOULD NOT MAKE ANOTHER PAINFUL VISIT TO YOU. ■ 2:1

Those who try to piece together Paul's life story from fragments in the two Corinthian letters and the book of Acts usually come away puzzled. Paul, addressing friends who knew that history intimately, saw no need to review every stage of their relationship. Yet for us, reading centuries later, some chronology would help explain his allusions and his emotional state.

Many scholars believe two events occurred to which Paul refers only in passing: the "painful visit" and the letter written "out of great distress".

■ A CHANGE IN PLANS

In the first two chapters Paul explains a change of plans whereby he decided not to visit Corinth because he didn't want to make "another painful visit" (2:1). What visit was he referring to?

During his first visit to Corinth, spanning 18 months, the church took shape (Acts 18:11). Paul probably would not have described that time as a "painful visit", for his relationship with them at that time was basically positive. Evidently he made a second visit to Corinth, not recorded in Acts, that included a painful confrontation.

Paul planned a third visit to Corinth, but postponed it because he didn't want to stir up the conflict. Later, he wondered about rescheduling that third visit (12:14; 13:1).

■ THE LONGED-FOR RECONCILIATION

2 Corinthians also mentions a letter written out of great distress and with many tears (2:4; 7:8). This letter, coming after Paul's unsettling second visit, contained such strong wording that he feared the Corinthians' response. He fleetingly regretted having written the letter. Had it ruptured their relationship? While he preached in the seaport town of Troas, Paul anxiously awaited some report of their reaction, through Titus.

One can imagine Paul rushing to the dock as ships from Macedonia came to unload, fervently scanning the vessels for some sign of Titus. Finally, unable to find peace of mind, he left his ministry in Troas to seek out Titus in Macedonia.

News from Titus at last calmed Paul. The Corinthians had indeed repented (7:7–9) and now wanted to restore ties with him. Feeling encouraged, Paul contemplated a third visit as he wrote 2 Corinthians. He used the letter to rebuild his relationship with them and to spell out his reasons for coming.

□ LIFE QUESTIONS:

Have you ever experienced a tear in a relationship like the one described here? How have you found healing?

2:14 ■ VICTORY PARTY

On their return from battle, Roman generals were honoured with a triumphal procession, much like the ticker-tape parades given for modern heroes. As the victorious army paraded their loot and conquered captives, the streets would be filled with fragrance from burning incense and the smells of the victory feast being prepared.

3:2 ■ A HUMAN LETTER

Chapters 3–5 form one of the Bible's great passages on professional ministry: what is involved in representing Christ on earth. Responding to attacks, Paul defends his "style" of ministry. He discusses the ultimate goal of ministry and the grace of God in using mere "jars of clay" (4:7) to accomplish his work. But the final proof of effectiveness, he says, is people's lives. In this way, the Corinthians themselves are his best letter of recommendation, for he brought them the gospel in the first place.

4Such confidence as this is ours through Christ before God. 5Not that we are competent in ourselves to claim anything for ourselves, but our competence comes from God. 6He has made us competent as ministers of a new covenant—not of the letter but of the Spirit; for the letter kills, but the Spirit gives life.

■ The Glory of the New Covenant

7Now if the ministry that brought death, which was engraved in letters on stone, came with glory, so that the Israelites could not look steadily at the face of Moses because of its glory, fading though it was, 8will not the ministry of the Spirit be even more glorious? 9If the ministry that condemns men is glorious, how much more glorious is the ministry that brings righteousness! 10For what was glorious has no glory now in comparison with the surpassing glory. 11And if what was fading away came with glory, how much greater is the glory of that which lasts!

12Therefore, since we have such a hope, we are very bold. 13We are not like Moses, who would put a veil over his face to keep the Israelites from gazing at it while the radiance was fading away. 14But their minds were made dull, for to this day the same veil remains when the old covenant is read. It has not been removed, because only in Christ is it taken away. 15Even to this day when Moses is read, a veil covers their hearts. 16But whenever anyone turns to the Lord, the veil is taken away. 17Now the Lord is the Spirit, and where the Spirit of the Lord is, there is freedom. 18And we, who with unveiled faces all reflect*a* the Lord's glory, are being transformed into his likeness with ever-increasing glory, which comes from the Lord, who is the Spirit.

■ Treasures in Jars of Clay

4 Therefore, since through God's mercy we have this ministry, we do not lose heart. 2Rather, we have renounced secret and shameful ways; we do not use deception, nor do we distort the word of God. On the contrary, by setting forth the truth plainly we commend ourselves to every man's conscience in the sight of God. 3And even if our gospel is veiled, it is veiled to those who are perishing. 4The god of this age has blinded the minds of unbelievers, so that they cannot see the light of the gospel of the glory of Christ, who is the image of God. 5For we do not preach ourselves, but Jesus Christ as Lord, and ourselves as your servants for Jesus' sake. 6For God, who said, "Let light shine out of darkness,"*a* made his light shine in our hearts to give us the light of the knowledge of the glory of God in the face of Christ.

7But we have this treasure in jars of clay to show that this all-surpassing power is from God and not from us. 8We are hard pressed on every side, but not crushed; perplexed, but not in despair; 9persecuted, but not abandoned; struck down, but not destroyed. 10We always carry around in our body the death of Jesus, so that the life of Jesus may also be revealed in our body. 11For we who are alive are always being given over to death for Jesus' sake, so that his life may be revealed in our mortal body. 12So then, death is at work in us, but life is at work in you.

4:7 ■ A PICTURE OF WEAKNESS

Where would you keep expensive jewellery? You would want a safe, secure place. You wouldn't stash valuables in, say, a tattered cardboard box. Yet this image comes close to the one Paul used to describe his ministry: "jars of clay". In his day jars were about as common — and as safe — as cardboard boxes are today.

The treasure Paul refers to is the incredible message of the gospel: God's good news of forgiveness and the promise of life for ever. Yet, amazingly, God chose to enclose that treasure in people who are like "jars of clay". Clay jars are ordinary and highly breakable, and Paul tells us he is both. An immortal God chooses mere humans as his personal representatives. "And who is equal to such a task?" Paul asks (2:16). He determines to draw attention to the treasure inside him, not to himself.

13It is written: "I believed; therefore I have spoken."*b* With that same spirit of faith we also believe and therefore speak, 14because we know that the one who raised the Lord Jesus from the dead will also raise us with Jesus and present us with you in his presence. 15All this is for your benefit, so that the grace that is reaching more and more people may cause thanksgiving to overflow to the glory of God.

16Therefore we do not lose heart. Though outwardly we are wasting away, yet inwardly we are being renewed day by day. 17For our light and momentary troubles are achieving for us an eternal glory that far outweighs them all. 18So we fix our

a 18 Or *contemplate*   a 6 Gen. 1:3   b 13 Psalm 116:10

eyes not on what is seen, but on what is unseen. For what is seen is temporary, but what is unseen is eternal.

■ Our Heavenly Dwelling

5 Now we know that if the earthly tent we live in is destroyed, we have a building from God, an eternal house in heaven, not built by human hands. [2]Meanwhile we groan, longing to be clothed with our heavenly dwelling, [3]because when we are clothed, we will not be found naked. [4]For while we are in this tent, we groan and are burdened, because we do not wish to be unclothed but to be clothed with our heavenly dwelling, so that what is mortal may be swallowed up by life. [5]Now it is God who has made us for this very purpose and has given us the Spirit as a deposit, guaranteeing what is to come.

5:1 ■ THE BODY AS A TENT

Paul often refers to his frail and abused body in this letter. But in this passage he looks past life on earth to a future life when, he says, we will have new bodies "not built by human hands". The contrast between tent and house shows the temporary nature of a body in this life compared to what is to come.

[6]Therefore we are always confident and know that as long as we are at home in the body we are away from the Lord. [7]We live by faith, not by sight. [8]We are confident, I say, and would prefer to be away from the body and at home with the Lord. [9]So we make it our goal to please him, whether we are at home in the body or away from it. [10]For we must all appear before the judgment seat of Christ, that each one may receive what is due to him for the things done while in the body, whether good or bad.

■ The Ministry of Reconciliation

[11]Since, then, we know what it is to fear the Lord, we try to persuade men. What we are is plain to God, and I hope it is also plain to your conscience. [12]We are not trying to commend ourselves to you again, but are giving you an opportunity to take pride in us, so that you can answer those who take pride in what is seen rather than in what is in the heart. [13]If we are out of our mind, it is for the sake of God; if we are in our right mind, it is for you. [14]For Christ's love compels us, because we are convinced that one died for all, and therefore all died. [15]And he died for all, that those who live should no longer live for themselves but for him who died for them and was raised again.

[16]So from now on we regard no-one from a worldly point of view. Though we once regarded Christ in this way, we do so no longer. [17]Therefore, if anyone is in Christ, he is a new creation; the old has gone, the new has come! [18]All this is from God, who reconciled us to himself through Christ and gave us the ministry of reconciliation: [19]that God was reconciling the world to himself in Christ, not counting men's sins against them. And he has committed to us the message of reconciliation. [20]We are therefore Christ's ambassadors, as though God were making his appeal through us. We implore you on Christ's behalf: Be reconciled to God. [21]God made him who had no sin to be sin[a] for us, so that in him we might become the righteousness of God.

6 As God's fellow-workers we urge you not to receive God's grace in vain. [2]For he says,

"In the time of my favour I heard you,
    and in the day of salvation I helped you."[a]

I tell you, now is the time of God's favour, now is the day of salvation.

■ Paul's Hardships

[3]We put no stumbling-block in anyone's path, so that our ministry will not be discredited. [4]Rather, as servants of God we commend ourselves in every way: in great endurance; in troubles, hardships and distresses; [5]in beatings, imprisonments and riots; in hard work, sleepless nights and hunger; [6]in purity, understanding, patience and kindness; in the Holy Spirit and in sincere love; [7]in truthful speech and in the power of God; with weapons of righteousness in the right hand and in the left; [8]through glory and dishonour, bad report and good report; genuine, yet regarded as impostors; [9]known, yet regarded as unknown; dying, and yet we live on; beaten, and yet not killed; [10]sorrowful, yet always rejoicing; poor, yet making many rich; having nothing, and yet possessing everything.

[11]We have spoken freely to you, Corinthians, and opened wide our hearts to you. [12]We are not withholding our affection from you, but you are withholding yours from us. [13]As a fair exchange — I speak as to my children — open wide your hearts also.

■ Do Not Be Yoked With Unbelievers

[14]Do not be yoked together with unbelievers. For what do righteousness and wickedness have in common? Or what fellowship can light have with darkness? [15]What harmony is there between Christ and Belial?[b] What does a believer have in common with an unbeliever? [16]What agreement is there between the temple of God and idols? For we are the temple of the living God. As God has said: "I will live with them and walk among them, and I will be their God, and they will be my people."[c]

6:14 ■ UNEQUAL YOKES

A yoke is a curved wooden bar that fits across the necks of two animals used to pull a plough or wagon. Yoke together a short, speedy calf with a tall, sluggish ox, and you're asking for trouble. Paul probably had in mind the false teachers who so often bedevilled the Corinthians, but his wise principle applies to many other alliances between believers and unbelievers.

[17]"Therefore come out from them
    and be separate,
                                   says the Lord.

---

a 21 Or be a sin offering   a 2 Isaiah 49:8   b 15 Greek Beliar, a variant of Belial   c 16 Lev. 26:12; Jer. 32:38; Ezek. 37:27

Touch no unclean thing,
and I will receive you."*d*
18"I will be a Father to you,
and you will be my sons and daughters,
says the Lord Almighty."*e*

7 Since we have these promises, dear friends, let us purify ourselves from everything that contaminates body and spirit, perfecting holiness out of reverence for God.

■ Paul's Joy

2Make room for us in your hearts. We have wronged no-one, we have corrupted no-one, we have exploited no-one. 3I do not say this to condemn you; I have said before that you have such a place in our hearts that we would live or die with you. 4I have great confidence in you; I take great pride in you. I am greatly encouraged; in all our troubles my joy knows no bounds.

5For when we came into Macedonia, this body of ours had no rest, but we were harassed at every turn — conflicts on the outside, fears within. 6But God, who comforts the downcast, comforted us by the coming of Titus, 7and not only by his coming but also by the comfort you had given him. He told us about your longing for me, your deep sorrow, your ardent concern for me, so that my joy was greater than ever.

8Even if I caused you sorrow by my letter, I do not regret it. Though I did regret it — I see that my letter hurt you, but only for a little while — 9yet now I am happy, not because you were made sorry, but because your sorrow led you to repentance. For you became sorrowful as God intended and so were not harmed in any way by us. 10Godly sorrow brings repentance that leads to salvation and leaves no regret, but worldly sorrow brings death. 11See what this godly sorrow has produced in you: what earnestness, what eagerness to clear yourselves, what indignation, what alarm, what longing, what concern, what readiness to see justice done. At every point you have proved yourselves to be innocent in this matter. 12So even though I wrote to you, it was not on account of the one who did the wrong or of the injured party, but rather that before God you could see for yourselves how devoted to us you are. 13By all this we are encouraged.

In addition to our own encouragement, we were especially delighted to see how happy Titus was, be-

---

7:11 ■ WHAT SUFFERING PRODUCES
When he wrote about suffering, Paul concentrated not merely on the pain itself, but on what qualities it produced in those who had faith. In this case, he cites the emotional suffering the Corinthians had experienced because of his letter. Although the suffering was unpleasant, it produced something of great value: an abrupt change in their attitudes.

---

cause his spirit has been refreshed by all of you. 14I had boasted to him about you, and you have not embarrassed me. But just as everything we said to you

was true, so our boasting about you to Titus has proved to be true as well. 15And his affection for you is all the greater when he remembers that you were all obedient, receiving him with fear and trembling. 16I am glad I can have complete confidence in you.

■ Generosity Encouraged

8 And now, brothers, we want you to know about the grace that God has given the Macedonian churches. 2Out of the most severe trial, their overflowing joy and their extreme poverty welled up in rich generosity. 3For I testify that they gave as much as they were able, and even beyond their ability. Entirely on their own, 4they urgently pleaded with us for the privilege of sharing in this service to the saints. 5And they did not do as we expected, but they gave themselves first to the Lord and then to us in keeping with God's will. 6So we urged Titus, since he had earlier made a beginning, to bring also to completion this act of grace on your part. 7But just as you excel in everything — in faith, in speech, in knowledge, in complete earnestness and in your love for us*a* — see that you also excel in this grace of giving.

8I am not commanding you, but I want to test the sincerity of your love by comparing it with the earnestness of others. 9For you know the grace of our Lord Jesus Christ, that though he was rich, yet for your sakes he became poor, so that you through his poverty might become rich.

10And here is my advice about what is best for you in this matter: Last year you were the first not only to give but also to have the desire to do so. 11Now finish the work, so that your eager willingness to do it may be matched by your completion of it, according to your means. 12For if the willingness is there, the gift is acceptable according to what one has, not according to what he does not have.

13Our desire is not that others might be relieved while you are hard pressed, but that there might be equality. 14At the present time your plenty will supply what they need, so that in turn their plenty will supply what you need. Then there will be equality, 15as it is written: "He who gathered much did not have too much, and he who gathered little did not have too little."*b*

■ Titus Sent to Corinth

16I thank God, who put into the heart of Titus the same concern I have for you. 17For Titus not only welcomed our appeal, but he is coming to you with much enthusiasm and on his own initiative. 18And we are sending along with him the brother who is praised by all the churches for his service to the gospel. 19What is more, he was chosen by the churches to accompany us as we carry the offering, which we administer in order to honour the Lord himself and to show our eagerness to help. 20We want to avoid any criticism of the way we administer this liberal gift. 21For we are taking pains to do what is right, not only in the eyes of the Lord but also in the eyes of men.

22In addition, we are sending with them our brother who has often proved to us in many ways

---

d 17 Isaiah 52:11; Ezek. 20:34,41   *e 18* 2 Samuel 7:14; 7:8   *a 7* Some manuscripts *in our love for you*   *b 15* Exodus 16:18

that he is zealous, and now even more so because of his great confidence in you. 23As for Titus, he is my partner and fellow-worker among you; as for our brothers, they are representatives of the churches and an honour to Christ. 24Therefore show these men the proof of your love and the reason for our pride in you, so that the churches can see it.

9 There is no need for me to write to you about this service to the saints. 2For I know your eagerness to help, and I have been boasting about it to the Macedonians, telling them that since last year you in Achaia were ready to give; and your enthusiasm has stirred most of them to action. 3But I am sending the brothers in order that our boasting about you in this matter should not prove hollow, but that you may be ready, as I said you would be. 4For if any Macedonians come with me and find you unprepared, we — not to say anything about you — would be ashamed of having been so confident. 5So I thought it necessary to urge the brothers to visit you in advance and finish the arrangements for the generous gift you had promised. Then it will be ready as a generous gift, not as one grudgingly given.

■ Sowing Generously

6Remember this: Whoever sows sparingly will also reap sparingly, and whoever sows generously will also reap generously. 7Each man should give what he has decided in his heart to give, not reluctantly or under compulsion, for God loves a cheerful giver. 8And God is able to make all grace abound to you, so that in all things at all times, having all that you need, you will abound in every good work. 9As it is written:

"He has scattered abroad his gifts to the poor;
his righteousness endures for ever."*a*

10Now he who supplies seed to the sower and bread for food will also supply and increase your store of seed and will enlarge the harvest of your righteous-

9:6 ■ BONUSES OF GIVING

In taking his collection for poor people, Paul mainly appealed to the Christian responsibility to help those in need. But in this passage he details generosity's side effects. Giving actually enriches and benefits the giver, he says. Also, a gift can serve as an act of worship to God and can inspire other people's faith and thanksgiving.

ness. 11You will be made rich in every way so that you can be generous on every occasion, and through us your generosity will result in thanksgiving to God.

12This service that you perform is not only supplying the needs of God's people but is also overflowing in many expressions of thanks to God. 13Because of the service by which you have proved yourselves, men will praise God for the obedience that accompanies your confession of the gospel of

■ DON'T FORGET THE POOR
A FUND-RAISING LETTER FROM PAUL HIMSELF

INSIGHT

EACH MAN SHOULD GIVE WHAT HE HAS DECIDED IN HIS HEART TO GIVE, NOT RELUCTANTLY OR UNDER COMPULSION, FOR GOD LOVES A CHEERFUL GIVER.
■ 9:7

Giving to charity has become almost a national pastime, and Christian Aid envelopes however crucial seem to be the unglamorous "poor relations" as the nation sits glued to the TV waiting to be excited by the London Marathon; entertained by the Save the Children fund-raising; and educated by the Live Aid programmes.

The apostle Paul certainly couldn't engineer anything on this scale — the media resources were just not available to him. But 2 Corinthians does present a direct appeal for funds [similar to that of the national Christian Aid week in the UK] (chapters 8–9). Jewish Christians near Jerusalem were reportedly on the edge of starvation. Paul seized on the crisis as a perfect chance for Gentile Christians to reach out in compassion and demonstrate their spiritual unity with Jewish Christians.

■ PRACTISING WHAT HE PREACHED
In these two chapters, Paul outlines a philosophy of Christian giving, holding up Jesus Christ as a model. He explains the goal of such giving and the proper attitude of the givers. He even applies a little pressure by citing examples of Christians less well-heeled than the Corinthians (8:1–6; 9:1–5).

This brief passage on giving shows Paul's holistic concerns. While still recuperating from personal trauma, he had agreed to head up a major fund-raising drive on behalf of the needy in Jerusalem. Later, working on that very project, he paused to write the profoundly theological book of Romans (Romans 15:25–26). His scholarship didn't dampen a zeal for practical Christian love; his concern for souls didn't crowd out concern for their hungry bodies.

□ LIFE QUESTIONS:
Compare Paul's appeal for funds with those you see in the mail and in the media. Is there a different emphasis?

*a*9 Psalm 112:9

Christ, and for your generosity in sharing with them and with everyone else. [14]And in their prayers for you their hearts will go out to you, because of the surpassing grace God has given you. [15]Thanks be to God for his indescribable gift!

■ Paul's Defence of His Ministry

10 By the meekness and gentleness of Christ, I appeal to you—I, Paul, who am "timid" when face to face with you, but "bold" when away! [2]I beg you that when I come I may not have to be as bold as I expect to be towards some people who think that we live by the standards of this world. [3]For though we live in the world, we do not wage war as the world does. [4]The weapons we fight with are not the weapons of the world. On the contrary, they have divine power to demolish strongholds. [5]We demolish arguments and every pretension that sets itself up against the knowledge of God, and we take captive every thought to make it obedient to Christ. [6]And we will be ready to punish every act of disobedience, once your obedience is complete.

[7]You are looking only on the surface of things.[a] If anyone is confident that he belongs to Christ, he should consider again that we belong to Christ just as much as he. [8]For even if I boast somewhat freely about the authority the Lord gave us for building you up rather than pulling you down, I will not be ashamed of it. [9]I do not want to seem to be trying to frighten you with my letters. [10]For some say, "His letters are weighty and forceful, but in person he is unimpressive and his speaking amounts to nothing." [11]Such people should realise that what we are in our letters when we are absent, we will be in our actions when we are present.

10:7 ■ STYLE OR SUBSTANCE?

Paul had an image problem, and his enemies were taking advantage of it by ridiculing his unimpressive personal style. Though a powerful, direct, and engaging speaker, Paul was spurned by those who preferred a more golden-tongued style, with lots of rhetorical flourish (verse 10). Such orators may have attracted applause and money, but Paul was looking for results in the form of changed lives, not profit or fame.

In the next two chapters, Paul reviews his qualifications, but he also ironically "boasts" of his weaknesses. Judge a messenger by the substance of the gospel he or she preaches, Paul seems to say—not by fancy words or a flashy style.

[12]We do not dare to classify or compare ourselves with some who commend themselves. When they measure themselves by themselves and compare themselves with themselves, they are not wise. [13]We, however, will not boast beyond proper limits, but will confine our boasting to the field God has assigned to us, a field that reaches even to you. [14]We are not going too far in our boasting, as would be the case if we had not come to you, for we did get

as far as you with the gospel of Christ. [15]Neither do we go beyond our limits by boasting of work done by others.[b] Our hope is that, as your faith continues to grow, our area of activity among you will greatly expand, [16]so that we can preach the gospel in the regions beyond you. For we do not want to boast about work already done in another man's territory. [17]But, "Let him who boasts boast in the Lord."[c] [18]For it is not the one who commends himself who is approved, but the one whom the Lord commends.

■ Paul and the False Apostles

11 I hope you will put up with a little of my foolishness; but you are already doing that. [2]I am jealous for you with a godly jealousy. I promised you to one husband, to Christ, so that I might present you as a pure virgin to him. [3]But I am afraid that just as Eve was deceived by the serpent's cunning, your minds may somehow be led astray from your sincere and pure devotion to Christ. [4]For if someone comes to you and preaches a Jesus other than the Jesus we preached, or if you receive a different spirit from the one you received, or a different gospel from the one you accepted, you put up with it easily enough. [5]But I do not think I am in the least inferior to those "super-apostles". [6]I may not be a trained speaker, but I do have knowledge. We have made this perfectly clear to you in every way.

[7]Was it a sin for me to lower myself in order to elevate you by preaching the gospel of God to you free of charge? [8]I robbed other churches by receiving support from them so as to serve you. [9]And when I was with you and needed something, I was not a burden to anyone, for the brothers who came from Macedonia supplied what I needed. I have kept myself from being a burden to you in any way, and will continue to do so. [10]As surely as the truth of Christ is in me, nobody in the regions of Achaia will stop this boasting of mine. [11]Why? Because I do not love you? God knows I do! [12]And I will keep on doing what I am doing in order to cut the ground from under those who want an opportunity to be considered equal with us in the things they boast about.

[13]For such men are false apostles, deceitful workmen, masquerading as apostles of Christ. [14]And no wonder, for Satan himself masquerades as an angel of light. [15]It is not surprising, then, if his servants masquerade as servants of righteousness. Their end will be what their actions deserve.

■ Paul Boasts About His Sufferings

[16]I repeat: Let no-one take me for a fool. But if you do, then receive me just as you would a fool, so that I may do a little boasting. [17]In this self-confident boasting I am not talking as the Lord would, but as a fool. [18]Since many are boasting in the way the world does, I too will boast. [19]You gladly put up with fools since you are so wise! [20]In fact, you even put up with anyone who enslaves you or exploits you or takes advantage of you or pushes himself forward or slaps you in the face. [21]To my shame I admit that we were too weak for that!

What anyone else dares to boast about—I am

---

a 7 Or *Look at the obvious facts*   *b* 13–15 Or 13*We, however, will not boast about things that cannot be measured, but we will boast according to the standard of measurement that the God of measure has assigned us—a measurement that relates even to you.* 14 . . . 15*Neither do we boast about things that cannot be measured in regard to the work done by others.*   *c* 17 Jer. 9:24

speaking as a fool—I also dare to boast about. ²²Are they Hebrews? So am I. Are they Israelites? So am I. Are they Abraham's descendants? So am I. ²³Are they servants of Christ? (I am out of my mind to talk like this.) I am more. I have worked much harder, been in prison more frequently, been flogged more severely, and been exposed to death again and again. ²⁴Five times I received from the Jews the forty lashes minus one. ²⁵Three times I was beaten with rods, once I was stoned, three times I was shipwrecked, I spent a night and a day in the open sea, ²⁶I have been constantly on the move. I have been in danger from rivers, in danger from bandits, in danger from my own countrymen, in danger from Gentiles; in danger in the city, in danger in the country, in danger at sea; and in danger from false brothers. ²⁷I have laboured and toiled and have often gone without sleep; I have known hunger and thirst and have often gone without food; I have been cold and naked. ²⁸Besides everything else, I face daily the pressure of my concern for all the churches. ²⁹Who is weak, and I do not feel weak? Who is led into sin, and I do not inwardly burn?

³⁰If I must boast, I will boast of the things that show my weakness. ³¹The God and Father of the Lord Jesus, who is to be praised for ever, knows that I am not lying. ³²In Damascus the governor under King Aretas had the city of the Damascenes guarded in order to arrest me. ³³But I was lowered in a basket from a window in the wall and slipped through his hands.

11:24 ■ PAUL'S MANY TRIALS

Acts records many of the apostle Paul's adventures and trials, but this passage shows that other disasters occurred as well. "Forty lashes minus one" was the maximum punishment allowed under Jewish law—five times Paul had been judged and sentenced by the Jews for his activities as a Christian. In addition, he was often imprisoned under Roman law and sometimes beaten with rods (an illegal punishment for a Roman citizen such as Paul).

■ Paul's Vision and His Thorn

12 I must go on boasting. Although there is nothing to be gained, I will go on to visions and revelations from the Lord. ²I know a man in Christ who fourteen years ago was caught up to the third heaven. Whether it was in the body or out of the body I do not know—God knows. ³And I know that this man—whether in the body or apart from the body I do not know, but God knows—⁴was caught up to paradise. He heard inexpressible things, things that man is not permitted to tell. ⁵I will boast about a man like that, but I will not boast

■ PAUL HAS HAD ENOUGH
ANSWERING HIS CRITICS

INSIGHT

I REPEAT: LET NO-ONE TAKE ME FOR A FOOL. ■ 11:16

Verse 1 of chapter 10 introduces a dramatic shift in tone. The first nine chapters mainly show Paul's relief at seeing encouraging signs in Corinth. But these last four chapters make clear that hostility was still raging. In fact, some have guessed this section was taken from the painful letter Paul referred to earlier (2:4). Here at the end of 2 Corinthians, Paul boldly confronts his critics.

Who were his antagonists? A picture of them emerges if you compile all the accusations Paul answers throughout the letter. Basically, they were carping troublemakers. In their eyes, Paul could do nothing right.

Paul's enemies in Corinth had blasted him for not visiting them as promised; yet when he did visit they gossiped, "In person he is unimpressive and his speaking amounts to nothing" (10:10). They had criticised him for not taking a salary and then hinted he was misusing funds (8:20; 11:7–9). To these "super-apostles" (11:5), Paul somehow appeared simultaneously unimpressive and yet crafty; overly strict and yet worldly. Some even hinted he was out of his mind (5:13).

■ A RINGING SELF-DEFENCE

You can almost sense Paul declaring "I've had it!" and then rolling up his sleeves to refute the charges. He insists that the future of the Corinthian church, not just his own reputation, is at stake. What does he feel? Something like the burning jealousy of a father who watches his virgin daughter being seduced away from her true lover (11:2–3).

These four remarkable chapters show Paul's passionate nature. Frustrated by having to defend himself, he almost stammers in print. He is determined to convince the Corinthians that he is motivated by a desire to serve God, not by any schemes of profit or power. Along the way, he lists an amazing catalogue of his physical sufferings and reveals intimate details of his spiritual life, including one incident still shrouded in mystery (12:1–6).

Judge for yourself, Paul seems to say, to the Corinthians and to all of us. Look at my life and decide, Whose fool am I?

☐ LIFE QUESTIONS:

Have you ever been wrongly accused of something? How did you react to your accusers?

about myself, except about my weaknesses. [6]Even if I should choose to boast, I would not be a fool, because I would be speaking the truth. But I refrain, so no-one will think more of me than is warranted by what I do or say.

[7]To keep me from becoming conceited because of these surpassingly great revelations, there was given me a thorn in my flesh, a messenger of Satan, to torment me. [8]Three times I pleaded with the Lord to take it away from me. [9]But he said to me, "My grace is sufficient for you, for my power is made perfect in weakness." Therefore I will boast all the more gladly about my weaknesses, so that Christ's power may rest on me. [10]That is why, for Christ's sake, I delight in weaknesses, in insults, in hardships, in persecutions, in difficulties. For when I am weak, then I am strong.

12:7 ■ THE THORN IN PAUL'S FLESH

Bible scholars don't agree on the precise nature of Paul's "thorn". Some suggest a physical ailment, such as an eye disease, malaria, or epilepsy. Others interpret it as a spiritual temptation, or a sequence of failures in his ministry. The Bible gives no clear evidence on the precise nature of this affliction. Regardless, Paul stresses that God permitted the thorn to continue, despite his prayers for relief, to teach him an important lesson about grace and dependence. This conclusion echoes Paul's thoughts on the Corinthians' suffering in chapter 7.

■ Paul's Concern for the Corinthians

[11]I have made a fool of myself, but you drove me to it. I ought to have been commended by you, for I am not in the least inferior to the "super-apostles", even though I am nothing. [12]The things that mark an apostle — signs, wonders and miracles — were done among you with great perseverance. [13]How were you inferior to the other churches, except that I was never a burden to you? Forgive me this wrong!

[14]Now I am ready to visit you for the third time, and I will not be a burden to you, because what I want is not your possessions but you. After all, children should not have to save up for their parents, but parents for their children. [15]So I will very gladly spend for you everything I have and expend myself as well. If I love you more, will you love me less? [16]Be that as it may, I have not been a burden to you. Yet, crafty fellow that I am, I caught you by trickery! [17]Did I exploit you through any of the men I sent you? [18]I urged Titus to go to you and I sent our brother with him. Titus did not exploit you, did he?

Did we not act in the same spirit and follow the same course?

[19]Have you been thinking all along that we have been defending ourselves to you? We have been speaking in the sight of God as those in Christ; and everything we do, dear friends, is for your strengthening. [20]For I am afraid that when I come I may not find you as I want you to be, and you may not find me as you want me to be. I fear that there may be quarrelling, jealousy, outbursts of anger, factions, slander, gossip, arrogance and disorder. [21]I am afraid that when I come again my God will humble me before you, and I will be grieved over many who have sinned earlier and have not repented of the impurity, sexual sin and debauchery in which they have indulged.

■ Final Warnings

13 This will be my third visit to you. "Every matter must be established by the testimony of two or three witnesses."[a] [2]I already gave you a warning when I was with you the second time. I now repeat it while absent: On my return I will not spare those who sinned earlier or any of the others, [3]since you are demanding proof that Christ is speaking through me. He is not weak in dealing with you, but is powerful among you. [4]For to be sure, he was crucified in weakness, yet he lives by God's power. Likewise, we are weak in him, yet by God's power we will live with him to serve you.

[5]Examine yourselves to see whether you are in the faith; test yourselves. Do you not realise that Christ Jesus is in you — unless, of course, you fail the test? [6]And I trust that you will discover that we have not failed the test. [7]Now we pray to God that you will not do anything wrong. Not that people will see that we have stood the test but that you will do what is right even though we may seem to have failed. [8]For we cannot do anything against the truth, but only for the truth. [9]We are glad whenever we are weak but you are strong; and our prayer is for your perfection. [10]This is why I write these things when I am absent, that when I come I may not have to be harsh in my use of authority — the authority the Lord gave me for building you up, not for tearing you down.

■ Final Greetings

[11]Finally, brothers, good-bye. Aim for perfection, listen to my appeal, be of one mind, live in peace. And the God of love and peace will be with you.

[12]Greet one another with a holy kiss. [13]All the saints send their greetings.

[14]May the grace of the Lord Jesus Christ, and the love of God, and the fellowship of the Holy Spirit be with you all.

a 1 Deut. 19:15

GALATIANS

■ NO SECOND-CLASS CHRISTIANS

A PROTEST AGAINST TREASON

BUT EVEN IF WE OR AN ANGEL FROM HEAVEN SHOULD PREACH A GOSPEL OTHER THAN THE ONE WE PREACHED TO YOU, LET HIM BE ETERNALLY CONDEMNED! ■ 1:8

Paul is angry. You can almost see his face: flushed red, with lines of tension working in his jaw. Typically, he greets his readers briefly and then launches into warm praise of them. But in this letter shock and dismay replace the usual warmth. A crisis threatens the Galatians, and Paul opens with a withering blast against the people responsible.

■ WHAT'S THE PROBLEM?

Yet, when you read a few chapters, you may wonder why the apostle is so upset. Galatia seems innocent of the kinkiness of Corinth; Paul describes no incest or idolatry here. Instead, he brings up common, everyday Jewish affairs such as the observance of festival days and the practice of ancient traditions, especially circumcision. Where is the big crisis?

Paul could foresee the outcome of the Galatians' thinking: by unduly stressing their Jewish heritage, the Galatians would soon devalue what Christ had done. They would start trusting in their own human effort (their keeping of "the law") to gain acceptance by God (3:1–5).

If the Galatians continued their policies, the bedrock of the gospel would crumble. Faith in Christ would become just one of many steps in salvation, not the only one. The gospel itself would be perverted (1:6–9).

■ A DANGEROUS CLASS STRUCTURE

Paul saw other ominous dangers ahead for the fledgling Christian church. As a Jewish Roman citizen who spoke Greek, he knew well the innate human tendency to look down on people. Roman citizens snubbed non-Romans; Greeks looked down their noses at Romans; and Jews, with their exalted history and highly developed religion, felt superior to other cultures.

The Galatians' insistence on strict Jewish rules would bring side effects. Subtle distinctions between Christians would inevitably creep in: *faith in Christ is fine, but a circumcised person who keeps the Jewish law . . . that's far better.* Already, such thoughts had infected two esteemed apostles, Peter and Barnabas. Circumcised Christians were snubbing uncircumcised ones as second-class citizens.

The letter to the Galatians, then, is protesting against treason. It lashes out against subtle dangers that can ultimately pervert the gospel and divide the church. Paul insists that Jesus Christ came to tear down walls between people, not to build them up. In him there is neither Jew nor Greek, slave nor free, male nor female (3:28). Faith in him, not anyone's set of laws (2:16), opens the door to acceptance by God.

■ HOW TO READ GALATIANS

Galatians reads like a dramatic court trial. On one side of the courtroom stand Paul's accusers. Persuasive and powerful, these "Judaisers" have followed Paul from town to town, spreading rumours and contradicting his version of the Christian faith.

On the other side sits the jury, the Galatian Christians. They have enjoyed warm friendship with Paul in the past, but some of the charges against him are serious. Did he invent parts of the gospel he preached to them? Has God really given him a special insight? Is it true that his message of "freedom" will lead to a weak, immoral church? Should they turn their backs on their Jewish heritage?

Paul, acting in his own self-defence, paces the courtroom. He uses a variety of debating styles: tight logic, historical reviews, and personal outrage. His integrity, and ultimately Jesus Christ's integrity, is at stake.

In topical content, Galatians covers much the same ground as Romans. But in style, it crackles with a fighting spirit. As you read it, try to visualise that courtroom scene, and judge for yourself Paul's effectiveness as a defendant.

■ 3-TRACK READING PLAN

For an explanation and complete listing of the 3-track reading plan, turn to page x.

■ **TRACK 1:**
Two-Week Courses on the Bible
The Track 1 reading programme on the Life and Teachings of Paul includes one chapter from Galatians. See page x for a complete listing of this course.

■ **TRACK 2:**
An Overview of Galatians in

1 Day
□ Day 1. Read the Introduction to Galatians, then chapter 3. You'll have to concentrate to follow all the arguments. But this chapter gives an essential interpretation of the Old Testament. Study it as a sample of Paul's defence in Galatians.

Now turn to page xi for your next Track 2 reading project.

■ **TRACK 3:**
All of Galatians in 5 Days
After you have read through Galatians, turn to pages xii–xiii for your next Track 3 reading project.

□ 1   □ 2   □ 3   □ 4
□ 5–6

1 Paul, an apostle—sent not from men nor by man, but by Jesus Christ and God the Father, who raised him from the dead—²and all the brothers with me,

To the churches in Galatia:

³Grace and peace to you from God our Father and the Lord Jesus Christ, ⁴who gave himself for our sins to rescue us from the present evil age, according to the will of our God and Father, ⁵to whom be glory for ever and ever. Amen.

■ **No Other Gospel**
⁶I am astonished that you are so quickly deserting the one who called you by the grace of Christ and are turning to a different gospel—⁷which is really no gospel at all. Evidently some people are throwing you into confusion and are trying to pervert the gospel of Christ. ⁸But even if we or an angel from heaven should preach a gospel other than the one we preached to you, let him be eternally condemned! ⁹As we have already said, so now I say again: If anybody is preaching to you a gospel other than what you accepted, let him be eternally condemned!

¹⁰Am I now trying to win the approval of men, or of God? Or am I trying to please men? If I were still trying to please men, I would not be a servant of Christ.

■ **Paul Called by God**
¹¹I want you to know, brothers, that the gospel I preached is not something that man made up. ¹²I did not receive it from any man, nor was I taught it; rather, I received it by revelation from Jesus Christ.

¹³For you have heard of my previous way of life in Judaism, how intensely I persecuted the church of God and tried to destroy it. ¹⁴I was advancing in Judaism beyond many Jews of my own age and was extremely zealous for the traditions of my fathers. ¹⁵But when God, who set me apart from birth*ᵃ* and called me by his grace, was pleased ¹⁶to reveal his Son in me so that I might preach him among the Gentiles, I did not consult any man, ¹⁷nor did I go up to Jerusalem to see those who were apostles

before I was, but I went immediately into Arabia and later returned to Damascus.

¹⁸Then after three years, I went up to Jerusalem to get acquainted with Peter*ᵇ* and stayed with him fifteen days. ¹⁹I saw none of the other apostles—only James, the Lord's brother. ²⁰I assure you before God that what I am writing to you is no lie. ²¹Later I went to Syria and Cilicia. ²²I was personally unknown to the churches of Judea that are in Christ. ²³They only heard the report: "The man who formerly persecuted us is now preaching the faith he once tried to destroy." ²⁴And they praised God because of me.

■ **Paul Accepted by the Apostles**
2 Fourteen years later I went up again to Jerusalem, this time with Barnabas. I took Titus along also. ²I went in response to a revelation and set before them the gospel that I preach among the Gentiles. But I did this privately to those who seemed to be leaders, for fear that I was running or had run my race in vain. ³Yet not even Titus, who was with me, was compelled to be circumcised, even though he was a Greek. ⁴This matter arose⌐ because some false brothers had infiltrated our ranks to spy on the freedom we have in Christ Jesus and to make us slaves. ⁵We did not give in to them for a moment, so that the truth of the gospel might remain with you.

⁶As for those who seemed to be important—whatever they were makes no difference to me; God does not judge by external appearance—those men added nothing to my message. ⁷On the contrary, they saw that I had been entrusted with the task of preaching the gospel to the Gentiles,*ᵃ* just as Peter had been to the Jews.*ᵇ* ⁸For God, who was at work in the ministry of Peter as an apostle to the Jews, was also at work in my ministry as an apostle to the Gentiles. ⁹James, Peter*ᶜ* and John, those reputed to be pillars, gave me and Barnabas the right hand of fellowship when they recognised the grace given to me. They agreed that we should go to the Gentiles, and they to the Jews. ¹⁰All they asked was that we should continue to remember the poor, the very thing I was eager to do.

ᵃ 15 Or *from my mother's womb*   *ᵇ 18* Greek *Cephas*   *ᵃ 7* Greek *uncircumcised*   *ᵇ 7* Greek *circumcised*; also in verses 8 and 9   *ᶜ 9* Greek *Cephas*; also in verses 11 and 14

■ Paul Opposes Peter

11When Peter came to Antioch, I opposed him to his face, because he was clearly in the wrong. 12Before certain men came from James, he used to eat with the Gentiles. But when they arrived, he began to draw back and separate himself from the Gentiles because he was afraid of those who belonged to the circumcision group. 13The other Jews joined him in his hypocrisy, so that by their hypocrisy even Barnabas was led astray.

2:11 ■ FORCING A CONFRONTATION

Galatians 2 gives a fascinating behind-the-scenes account of how the Jewish/Gentile question was splitting the early church. Peter and James, sympathetic to Jewish Christians, acted hypocritically in their treatment of Gentiles until Paul confronted them publicly. Acts 15 gives a more detailed account of the official disagreements and how they were finally resolved.

14When I saw that they were not acting in line with the truth of the gospel, I said to Peter in front of them all, "You are a Jew, yet you live like a Gentile and not like a Jew. How is it, then, that you force Gentiles to follow Jewish customs?

15"We who are Jews by birth and not 'Gentile sinners' 16know that a man is not justified by observing the law, but by faith in Jesus Christ. So we, too, have put our faith in Christ Jesus that we may be justified by faith in Christ and not by observing the law, because by observing the law no-one will be justified.

17"If, while we seek to be justified in Christ, it becomes evident that we ourselves are sinners, does that mean that Christ promotes sin? Absolutely not! 18If I rebuild what I destroyed, I prove that I am a law-breaker. 19For through the law I died to the law so that I might live for God. 20I have been crucified with Christ and I no longer live, but Christ lives in me. The life I live in the body, I live by faith in the Son of God, who loved me and gave himself for me. 21I do not set aside the grace of God, for if righteousness could be gained through the law, Christ died for nothing!"d

■ Faith or Observance of the Law

3 You foolish Galatians! Who has bewitched you? Before your very eyes Jesus Christ was clearly portrayed as crucified. 2I would like to learn just one thing from you: Did you receive the Spirit by observing the law, or by believing what you heard? 3Are you so foolish? After beginning with the Spirit, are you now trying to attain your goal by human effort? 4Have you suffered so much for nothing—if it really was for nothing? 5Does God give you his Spirit and work miracles among you because you observe the law, or because you believe what you heard?

6Consider Abraham: "He believed God, and it was credited to him as righteousness."a 7Understand, then, that those who believe are children of Abraham. 8The Scripture foresaw that God would justify the Gentiles by faith, and announced the gospel in advance to Abraham: "All nations will be blessed through you."b 9So those who have faith are blessed along with Abraham, the man of faith.

10All who rely on observing the law are under a curse, for it is written: "Cursed is everyone who does not continue to do everything written in the Book of the Law."c 11Clearly no-one is justified before God by the law, because, "The righteous will live by faith."d 12The law is not based on faith; on the contrary, "The man who does these things will live by them."e 13Christ redeemed us from the curse of the law by becoming a curse for us, for it is written: "Cursed is everyone who is hung on a tree."f 14He redeemed us in order that the blessing given to Abraham might come to the Gentiles through Christ Jesus, so that by faith we might receive the promise of the Spirit.

■ The Law and the Promise

15Brothers, let me take an example from everyday life. Just as no-one can set aside or add to a human covenant that has been duly established, so it is in this case. 16The promises were spoken to Abraham and to his seed. The Scripture does not say "and to seeds", meaning many people, but "and to your seed",g meaning one person, who is Christ. 17What I mean is this: The law, introduced 430 years later, does not set aside the covenant previously established by God and thus do away with the promise. 18For if the inheritance depends on the law, then it no longer depends on a promise; but God in his grace gave it to Abraham through a promise.

3:17 ■ THE 430-YEAR GAP

In chapter 3, Paul uses clever arguments to put the entire Old Testament law in a new perspective. The law was never intended to make possible a way to God, he says (verses 11,21). Rather, the law was given to "lead us to Christ" (verse 24) by convincing us of the impossibility of gaining God's acceptance on our own. To prove his point, Paul mentions a 430-year gap between Abraham and Moses. God gave his promises to Abraham, who lived long before Moses ever received the law; therefore, Abraham couldn't possibly have depended on the law. God's promise reached final fulfilment in Jesus, whom Paul calls Abraham's "seed" (verse 16).

19What, then, was the purpose of the law? It was added because of transgressions until the Seed to whom the promise referred had come. The law was put into effect through angels by a mediator. 20A mediator, however, does not represent just one party; but God is one.

21Is the law, therefore, opposed to the promises of God? Absolutely not! For if a law had been given that could impart life, then righteousness would certainly have come by the law. 22But the Scripture declares that the whole world is a prisoner of sin, so that what was promised, being given through faith in Jesus Christ, might be given to those who believe.

23Before this faith came, we were held prisoners

d21 Some interpreters end the quotation after verse 14.   a6 Gen. 15:6   b8 Gen. 12:3; 18:18; 22:18   c10 Deut. 27:26   d11 Hab. 2:4
e12 Lev. 18:5   f13 Deut. 21:23   g16 Gen. 12:7; 13:15; 24:7

by the law, locked up until faith should be revealed. [24]So the law was put in charge to lead us to Christ[b] that we might be justified by faith. [25]Now that faith has come, we are no longer under the supervision of the law.

■ Sons of God

[26]You are all sons of God through faith in Christ Jesus, [27]for all of you who were baptised into Christ have clothed yourselves with Christ. [28]There is neither Jew nor Greek, slave nor free, male nor female, for you are all one in Christ Jesus. [29]If you belong to Christ, then you are Abraham's seed, and heirs according to the promise.

4 What I am saying is that as long as the heir is a child, he is no different from a slave, although he owns the whole estate. [2]He is subject to guardians and trustees until the time set by his father. [3]So also, when we were children, we were in slavery under the basic principles of the world. [4]But when the time had fully come, God sent his Son, born of a woman, born under law, [5]to redeem those under law, that we might receive the full rights of sons. [6]Because you are sons, God sent the Spirit of his Son into our hearts, the Spirit who calls out, "Abba,[a] Father." [7]So you are no longer a slave, but a son; and since you are a son, God has made you also an heir.

■ Paul's Concern for the Galatians

[8]Formerly, when you did not know God, you were slaves to those who by nature are not gods. [9]But now that you know God — or rather are known by God — how is it that you are turning back to those weak and miserable principles? Do you wish to be enslaved by them all over again? [10]You are observing special days and months and seasons and years! [11]I fear for you, that somehow I have wasted my efforts on you.

[12]I plead with you, brothers, become like me, for I became like you. You have done me no wrong. [13]As you know, it was because of an illness that I first preached the gospel to you. [14]Even though my illness was a trial to you, you did not treat me with contempt or scorn. Instead, you welcomed me as if I were an angel of God, as if I were Christ Jesus himself. [15]What has happened to all your joy? I can testify that, if you could have done so, you would have torn out your eyes and given them to me. [16]Have I now become your enemy by telling you the truth?

4:15 ■ PAUL'S ANGUISH

Paul's letter wavers between abstract reasoning and intensely emotional pleading. As this paragraph shows, Paul had once enjoyed intimate closeness with the people of Galatia. He feels anguish and personal rejection because they now seem to be turning their backs on the faith he had carefully taught them. He is in the pains of childbirth, he says, waiting anxiously for them to grow out of their false ideas (verse 19).

■ **LEGALISM**
CAN WE DO ANYTHING TO MAKE GOD LOVE US MORE?

INSIGHT

BUT NOW THAT YOU KNOW GOD — OR RATHER ARE KNOWN BY GOD — HOW IS IT THAT YOU ARE TURNING BACK TO THOSE WEAK AND MISERABLE PRINCIPLES? ■ 4:9

Before his conversion, Paul was one of the best legalists who ever lived. A loyal Jew, he tortured Christians who stepped outside Jewish tradition to follow Christ. If a person could reach God by obeying the law, then he, the strict Pharisee, would have done it.

But in Galatians, he blasts the idea that God's love is conditioned by how many rules we obey. Legalism is like a cage: it can only condemn people and lock them behind bars. As Paul points out, no-one has kept all of God's laws perfectly, and all who try ultimately fail (3:10–11).

■ NO STRINGS ATTACHED

Chapters 3–4 draw sharp contrasts: a prisoner and a free man, a sheltered child and an adult. Don't act like a slave or a child, Paul says. Act like a privileged son, an heir to a great fortune!

Galatians has been called the "Magna Charta of Christian liberty". "It is for freedom that Christ has set us free," Paul declares (5:1). Galatians teaches that there is nothing we can do to make God love us more – or love us less. We don't have to "earn" God's love by slavishly following rules.

Martin Luther said Galatians was "my own little epistle. I have betrothed myself to it; it is my Katie von Bora [Luther's wife]." This slim book proclaims that God has given his love freely, with no strings attached. We should never get over the awesome implications of that truth, Galatians says. Evidently, Paul didn't.

☐ LIFE QUESTIONS:

The early Christians went in two directions. Some, like the people in Galatia, became obsessed with legalism. Others took their Christian freedom too far: they refused to follow anyone's rules. Which is the greater danger in your circle?

---

b24 Or charge until Christ came   a6 Aramaic for Father

[17]Those people are zealous to win you over, but for no good. What they want is to alienate you ͺfrom usͺ, so that you may be zealous for them. [18]It is fine to be zealous, provided the purpose is good, and to be so always and not just when I am with you. [19]My dear children, for whom I am again in the pains of childbirth until Christ is formed in you, [20]how I wish I could be with you now and change my tone, because I am perplexed about you!

■ Hagar and Sarah
[21]Tell me, you who want to be under the law, are you not aware of what the law says? [22]For it is written that Abraham had two sons, one by the slave woman and the other by the free woman. [23]His son by the slave woman was born in the ordinary way; but his son by the free woman was born as the result of a promise.

[24]These things may be taken figuratively, for the women represent two covenants. One covenant is from Mount Sinai and bears children who are to be slaves: This is Hagar. [25]Now Hagar stands for Mount Sinai in Arabia and corresponds to the present city of Jerusalem, because she is in slavery with her children. [26]But the Jerusalem that is above is free, and she is our mother. [27]For it is written:

"Be glad, O barren woman,
    who bears no children;
break forth and cry aloud,
    you who have no labour pains;

because more are the children of the desolate
    woman
    than of her who has a husband."[b]

[28]Now you, brothers, like Isaac, are children of promise. [29]At that time the son born in the ordinary way persecuted the son born by the power of the Spirit. It is the same now. [30]But what does the Scripture say? "Get rid of the slave woman and her son, for the slave woman's son will never share in the inheritance with the free woman's son."[c] [31]Therefore, brothers, we are not children of the slave woman, but of the free woman.

■ Freedom in Christ
5 It is for freedom that Christ has set us free. Stand firm, then, and do not let yourselves be burdened again by a yoke of slavery.

[2]Mark my words! I, Paul, tell you that if you let yourselves be circumcised, Christ will be of no value to you at all. [3]Again I declare to every man who lets himself be circumcised that he is required to obey the whole law. [4]You who are trying to be justified by law have been alienated from Christ; you have fallen away from grace. [5]But by faith we eagerly await through the Spirit the righteousness for which we hope. [6]For in Christ Jesus neither circumcision nor uncircumcision has any value. The only thing that counts is faith expressing itself through love.

[7]You were running a good race. Who cut in on you and kept you from obeying the truth? [8]That

---

■ **PAUL FIGHTS BACK**
WHEN FREEDOM GETS DANGEROUS

INSIGHT

THE ONLY THING THAT COUNTS IS FAITH EXPRESSING ITSELF THROUGH LOVE.
■ 5:6

Over the years Paul caught on to his opponents' crafty ways of undermining him. Galatians provides a textbook case of his response to critics.

First, Paul answered their personal attacks. Some had questioned his right to be called an apostle. In chapters 1 and 2, Paul insists that he received the gospel directly from God. In addition, he has met every criterion of an apostle.

Chapters 3 and 4 deal with Paul's ideas. Had he strayed too far from Old Testament law and customs? Some hinted that Paul was preaching an incomplete gospel. He answered those objections with a carefully reasoned look at the Old Testament, focusing on Abraham, the father of the Jewish race.

■ WHAT TO DO WITH FREEDOM
Then Paul turned to more practical matters. Stressing freedom, not rules, left him open to

criticism. Did his strong emphasis on freedom lead to loose morals? To answer this question, he ended Galatians, a letter devoted to Christian liberty, with a warning.

"Why did Christ set us free?" Paul asks. To make possible a life of orgies, drunkenness and witchcraft? Obviously no. Christ freed us from worrying about whether we are "doing enough" to please God and from uselessly following external forms. But we should use that freedom to serve one another in love and to live a Spirit-filled life.

His arguments and emotions exhausted, Paul concludes, "Neither circumcision nor uncircumcision means anything; what counts is a new creation" (6:15). A released prisoner, a freed slave, the bountiful fruit of a living tree – all the images in Galatians convey *life*, an abundant life in the Spirit of God, readily available to every Christian.

□ LIFE QUESTIONS:
Read over the qualities of life in the Spirit listed in 5:22–23. Do these characterise your life?

---

kind of persuasion does not come from the one who calls you. 9"A little yeast works through the whole batch of dough." 10I am confident in the Lord that you will take no other view. The one who is throwing you into confusion will pay the penalty, whoever he may be. 11Brothers, if I am still preaching circumcision, why am I still being persecuted? In that case the offence of the cross has been abolished. 12As for those agitators, I wish they would go the whole way and emasculate themselves!

13You, my brothers, were called to be free. But do not use your freedom to indulge the sinful nature;*a* rather, serve one another in love. 14The entire law is summed up in a single command: "Love your neighbour as yourself."*b* 15If you keep on biting and devouring each other, watch out or you will be destroyed by each other.

■ Life by the Spirit

16So I say, live by the Spirit, and you will not gratify the desires of the sinful nature. 17For the sinful nature desires what is contrary to the Spirit, and the Spirit what is contrary to the sinful nature. They are in conflict with each other, so that you do not do what you want. 18But if you are led by the Spirit, you are not under law.

19The acts of the sinful nature are obvious: sexual immorality, impurity and debauchery; 20idolatry and witchcraft; hatred, discord, jealousy, fits of rage, selfish ambition, dissensions, factions 21and envy; drunkenness, orgies, and the like. I warn you, as I did before, that those who live like this will not inherit the kingdom of God.

22But the fruit of the Spirit is love, joy, peace, patience, kindness, goodness, faithfulness, 23gentleness and self-control. Against such things there is no law. 24Those who belong to Christ Jesus have crucified the sinful nature with its passions and desires. 25Since we live by the Spirit, let us keep in step with the Spirit. 26Let us not become conceited, provoking and envying each other.

■ Doing Good to All

6 Brothers, if someone is caught in a sin, you who are spiritual should restore him gently. But watch yourself, or you also may be tempted. 2Carry each other's burdens, and in this way you will fulfil the law of Christ. 3If anyone thinks he is something when he is nothing, he deceives himself. 4Each one should test his own actions. Then he can take pride in himself, without comparing himself to somebody else, 5for each one should carry his own load.

6Anyone who receives instruction in the word must share all good things with his instructor.

7Do not be deceived: God cannot be mocked. A man reaps what he sows. 8The one who sows to please his sinful nature, from that nature*a* will reap destruction; the one who sows to please the Spirit, from the Spirit will reap eternal life. 9Let us not become weary in doing good, for at the proper time we will reap a harvest if we do not give up. 10Therefore, as we have opportunity, let us do good to all people, especially to those who belong to the family of believers.

■ Not Circumcision but a New Creation

11See what large letters I use as I write to you with my own hand!

6:2 ■ MIXING GENTLENESS WITH HARSHNESS

Galatians contains some of Paul's harshest language, for he sensed a danger that could destroy the church's faith. But the book also includes some of Paul's most familiar and comforting words. Chapter 6 describes a spirit of tolerance and forgiveness towards those who fail. It also offers encouragement for people who grow tired of doing good when it appears justice is not winning through.

12Those who want to make a good impression outwardly are trying to compel you to be circumcised. The only reason they do this is to avoid being persecuted for the cross of Christ. 13Not even those who are circumcised obey the law, yet they want you to be circumcised that they may boast about your flesh. 14May I never boast except in the cross of our Lord Jesus Christ, through which*b* the world has been crucified to me, and I to the world. 15Neither circumcision nor uncircumcision means anything; what counts is a new creation. 16Peace and mercy to all who follow this rule, even to the Israel of God.

17Finally, let no-one cause me trouble, for I bear on my body the marks of Jesus.

18The grace of our Lord Jesus Christ be with your spirit, brothers. Amen.

---

a 13 Or the flesh; also in verses 16, 17, 19 and 24   *b* 14 Lev. 19:18   *a* 8 Or his flesh, from the flesh   *b* 14 Or whom

EPHESIANS

■ FOR THE DISCOURAGED

GOOD NEWS FOR THOSE WHO FEEL ABANDONED AND UNLOVED

YOU ARE NO LONGER FOREIGNERS AND ALIENS, BUT FELLOW CITIZENS WITH GOD'S PEOPLE AND MEMBERS OF GOD'S HOUSEHOLD. ■ 2:19

Imagine yourself a child, abandoned on the streets of New York. Your immigrant parents died on the ship on the way to America. You have no money and no relatives. You can't speak English. And you are left to fend for yourself.

As many as 30,000 orphans found themselves in exactly that predicament in 1850. They slept in alleys, huddling for warmth in boxes or metal drums. To survive, the boys mostly stole, caught rats to eat, or rummaged in rubbish bins. Girls sometimes worked as "panel thieves" for prostitutes, slipping their tiny hands through camouflaged openings in the walls to lift a watch or wallet from a preoccupied customer.

Immigrants were flooding New York City then, and no-one had the time or money to look after the orphans—no-one, that is, except Charles Loring Brace, a 26-year-old minister. Horrified by their plight, he organised a unique solution, the Orphan Train. The idea was simple: pack hundreds of orphans on a train heading west and announce to towns along the way that anyone could claim a new son or daughter when the Orphan Train chugged through.

■ ADOPTED INTO A NEW LIFE

By the time the last Orphan Train steamed west in 1929, 100,000 children had found new homes and new lives. Two orphans from such trains became governors, one served as a United States congressman, and still another was a U.S. Supreme Court justice.

The Orphan Train provides a vivid parable of the message of Ephesians. To capture Paul's enthusiasm in this book, imagine one more stage in your life as a street urchin in New York.

You have learned to survive and fight off starvation. But one day, someone takes you and puts you on a smoke-belching train jammed with hundreds of other foreign-speaking youngsters. Three days later you are selected by a kindly middle-aged couple in Michigan who introduce themselves as Mr. and Mrs. Henry Ford. You are driven (in a car) to the largest house you have ever seen, and they quietly explain that you are now part of their family. Everything they have is yours to use and enjoy. At long last, by some miracle, you have a family and a home—and what a home!

■ WELCOME TO THE FAMILY

Paul conveys a feeling something like that in Ephesians, a rich book that expands the message of Jesus' parable of the Lost Son (Luke 15). A big "Welcome Home!" banner is stretched across the lawn, confetti swirls in the air, balloons lunge skyward, and a band plays. Christians have been adopted directly into the family of God. This is a good news book, to put it mildly.

If you feel discouraged or wonder if God really cares or question whether the Christian life is worth the effort, read Ephesians. You will no longer feel like an orphan. Paul describes the "riches of Christ" available to all and points to us, God's adopted children, as his sparkling "Exhibit A" in all the universe (3:10).

Ephesians contains staggering thoughts. Paul wants his readers to grasp "how wide and long and high and deep is the love of Christ" (3:18). He cranks up the volume to express that love, and not one low, mournful note sneaks in.

■ HOW TO READ EPHESIANS

In many ways, Ephesians is Paul's "summing-up" book. The same subjects appear in greater detail in books like Romans, 1 Corinthians, and 1 Thessalonians. But in Ephesians, Paul gives an overall view of the grand scheme of the gospel. Only now, Paul says, has God's hidden plan for all of history come to light.

Because it compresses such large thoughts into such a short space, Ephesians deserves very careful study. Read the first three chapters slowly, digesting one paragraph at a time. Such study will prove rewarding: Ephesians gives exuberant good news about the nature of the universe and God's plan for believers.

Like other letters from Paul, Ephesians divides fairly neatly between doctrine (chapters 1–3) and practical advice (4–6). The last half details how our lives should change as a result of the great things described in the first part.

■ 3-TRACK READING PLAN

For an explanation and complete listing of the 3-track reading programme, turn to page x.

■ TRACK 1:
Two-Week Courses on the Bible
The Track 1 reading programme on the Life and Teachings of Paul includes one chapter from Ephesians. See page x for a complete listing of this course.

■ TRACK 2:
An Overview of Ephesians in 2 Days
☐ Day 1. Read the Introduction to Ephesians, then chapter 2.
☐ Day 2. Read chapter 3. You may also want to look at the famous "armour" passage (6:10–18).
Now turn to page xi for your next Track 2 reading project.

■ TRACK 3:
All of Ephesians in 6 Days
After you have read through Ephesians, turn to pages xii–xiii for your next Track 3 reading project.

☐ 1   ☐ 2   ☐ 3   ☐ 4
☐ 5   ☐ 6

1 Paul, an apostle of Christ Jesus by the will of God,

To the saints in Ephesus,^{a} the faithful^b in Christ Jesus:

^{2}Grace and peace to you from God our Father and the Lord Jesus Christ.

■ Spiritual Blessings in Christ
^{3}Praise be to the God and Father of our Lord Jesus Christ, who has blessed us in the heavenly realms with every spiritual blessing in Christ. ^{4}For he chose us in him before the creation of the world to be holy and blameless in his sight. In love ^{5}he^c predestined us to be adopted as his sons through Jesus Christ, in accordance with his pleasure and will — ^{6}to the praise of his glorious grace, which he has freely given us in the One he loves. ^{7}In him we have redemption through his blood, the forgiveness of sins, in accordance with the riches of God's grace ^{8}that he lavished on us with all wisdom and understanding. ^{9}And he^d made known to us the mystery of his will according to his good pleasure, which he purposed in Christ, ^{10}to be put into effect when the times will have reached their fulfilment — to bring all things in heaven and on earth together under one head, even Christ.

^{11}In him we were also chosen,^{e} having been predestined according to the plan of him who works out everything in conformity with the purpose of his will, ^{12}in order that we, who were the first to hope in Christ, might be for the praise of his glory. ^{13}And you also were included in Christ when you heard the word of truth, the gospel of your salvation. Having believed, you were marked in him with a seal, the promised Holy Spirit, ^{14}who is a deposit guaranteeing our inheritance until the redemption of those who are God's possession — to the praise of his glory.

■ Thanksgiving and Prayer
^{15}For this reason, ever since I heard about your faith in the Lord Jesus and your love for all the saints, ^{16}I have not stopped giving thanks for you, remembering you in my prayers. ^{17}I keep asking that the God of our Lord Jesus Christ, the glorious Father, may give you the Spirit^f of wisdom and revelation, so that you may know him better. ^{18}I pray also that the eyes of your heart may be enlightened in order that you may know the hope to which he has called you, the riches of his glorious inheritance in the saints, ^{19}and his incomparably great power for us who believe. That power is like the working of his mighty strength, ^{20}which he exerted in Christ when he raised him from the dead and seated him at his right hand in the heavenly realms, ^{21}far above all rule and authority, power and dominion, and every title that can be given, not only in the present age but also in the one to come. ^{22}And God placed all things under his feet and appointed him to be head over everything for the church, ^{23}which is his body, the fulness of him who fills everything in every way.

1:13 ■ BRANDED
Cattle ranchers brand their cattle, loggers carve a symbol on a tree, dignitaries seal their important papers with wax — all these are marks of ownership. According to Paul, the Holy Spirit is God's proof of ownership for Christians. More, he is a "deposit" guaranteeing a great inheritance.

■ Made Alive in Christ
2 As for you, you were dead in your transgressions and sins, ^{2}in which you used to live when you followed the ways of this world and of the ruler of the kingdom of the air, the spirit who is now at work in those who are disobedient. ^{3}All of us also

---

^{a}1 Some early manuscripts do not have in Ephesus. ^{b}1 Or believers who are understanding, ^{9}he ^{e}11 Or were made heirs ^{f}17 Or a spirit ^{c}4,5 Or sight in love. ^{5}He ^{d}8, 9 Or us. With all wisdom and lived among them at one time, gratifying the cravings of our sinful nature[a] and following its desires and thoughts. Like the rest, we were by nature objects of wrath. [4]But because of his great love for us, God, who is rich in mercy, [5]made us alive with Christ even when we were dead in transgressions — it is by grace you have been saved. [6]And God raised us up with Christ and seated us with him in the heavenly realms in Christ Jesus, [7]in order that in the coming ages he might show the incomparable riches of his grace, expressed in his kindness to us in Christ Jesus. [8]For it is by grace you have been saved, through faith — and this not from yourselves, it is the gift of God — [9]not by works, so that no-one can boast. [10]For we are God's workmanship, created in Christ Jesus to do good works, which God prepared in advance for us to do.

1:19 ■ PROVEN POWER
Throughout the Old Testament, God cites the liberation of slaves from Egypt as evidence of his power (over the most powerful nation of the time). "I am the God who brought you out of Egypt," he says. The New Testament holds up an even greater proof: God's ability to give life to the dead. That same life-giving power is available to the individual believer, Paul proclaims.

2:8 ■ GIVEN, NOT EARNED
As a converted legalist, Paul insisted on one fact of the gospel: eternal life comes not by any ritual of rule-keeping (which he calls "works"), but by the grace of God. Yet in this paragraph he notes that God intends us to "do good works". Paul makes a clear distinction: Good works do nothing to help us obtain God's favour, but they follow naturally as we experience the love of Christ.

■ One in Christ
[11]Therefore, remember that formerly you who are Gentiles by birth and called "uncircumcised" by those who call themselves "the circumcision" (that done in the body by the hands of men) — [12]remember that at that time you were separate from Christ, excluded from citizenship in Israel and foreigners to the covenants of the promise, without hope and without God in the world. [13]But now in Christ Jesus you who once were far away have been brought near through the blood of Christ.

[14]For he himself is our peace, who has made the two one and has destroyed the barrier, the dividing wall of hostility, [15]by abolishing in his flesh the law with its commandments and regulations. His purpose was to create in himself one new man out of the two, thus making peace, [16]and in this one body to reconcile both of them to God through the cross, by which he put to death their hostility. [17]He came and preached peace to you who were far away and peace to those who were near. [18]For through him we both have access to the Father by one Spirit.

[19]Consequently, you are no longer foreigners and aliens, but fellow-citizens with God's people and members of God's household, [20]built on the foundation of the apostles and prophets, with Christ Jesus himself as the chief cornerstone. [21]In him the whole building is joined together and rises to become a holy temple in the Lord. [22]And in him you too are being built together to become a dwelling in which God lives by his Spirit.

2:14 ■ DESTROYING THE BARRIERS
A Jewish missionary to the Gentiles, Paul wrote and talked constantly about tearing down the barriers between Jews and Gentiles. Jews kept themselves separate from Gentiles by many cultural and religious barriers. Perhaps the most vivid symbol of separation was an actual wall in the temple. Non-Jews could never enter the temple courts beyond that wall, and a further wall separated Jewish men from Jewish women. Here Paul describes how Christ utterly destroyed the "wall of hostility". (See also Galatians 3:28.)

■ Paul the Preacher to the Gentiles
3 For this reason I, Paul, the prisoner of Christ Jesus for the sake of you Gentiles—
[2]Surely you have heard about the administration of God's grace that was given to me for you, [3]that is, the mystery made known to me by revelation, as I have already written briefly. [4]In reading this, then, you will be able to understand my insight into the mystery of Christ, [5]which was not made known to men in other generations as it has now been revealed by the Spirit to God's holy apostles and prophets. [6]This mystery is that through the gospel the Gentiles are heirs together with Israel, members together of one body, and sharers together in the promise in Christ Jesus.

[7]I became a servant of this gospel by the gift of God's grace given me through the working of his power. [8]Although I am less than the least of all God's people, this grace was given me: to preach to the Gentiles the unsearchable riches of Christ, [9]and to make plain to everyone the administration of this mystery, which for ages past was kept hidden in God, who created all things. [10]His intent was that now, through the church, the manifold wisdom of God should be made known to the rulers and authorities in the heavenly realms, [11]according to his eternal purpose which he accomplished in Christ Jesus our Lord. [12]In him and through faith in him we may approach God with freedom and confidence. [13]I ask you, therefore, not to be discouraged because of my sufferings for you, which are your glory.

■ A Prayer for the Ephesians
[14]For this reason I kneel before the Father, [15]from whom his whole family[a] in heaven and on earth derives its name. [16]I pray that out of his glorious riches he may strengthen you with power through his Spirit in your inner being, [17]so that Christ may dwell in your hearts through faith. And I pray that you, being rooted and established in love, [18]may have power, together with all the saints, to grasp

[a]3 Or our flesh   [a]15 Or whom all fatherhood

how wide and long and high and deep is the love of Christ, [19]and to know this love that surpasses knowledge — that you may be filled to the measure of all the fulness of God.

3:16 ■ READING BETWEEN THE LINES
Paul's prayers often give some of the best insights into the local situation. This prayer (verses 14–21) and the one in chapter 1 (verses 15–23) indicate the church at Ephesus was well-grounded. In Ephesians Paul does not dwell on any urgent problems; instead, he tries to raise the sights of young Christians who have not fully grasped the extent of God's love and grace.

---

[20]Now to him who is able to do immeasurably more than all we ask or imagine, according to his power that is at work within us, [21]to him be glory in the church and in Christ Jesus throughout all generations, for ever and ever! Amen.

■ Unity in the Body of Christ

4 As a prisoner for the Lord, then, I urge you to live a life worthy of the calling you have received. [2]Be completely humble and gentle; be patient, bearing with one another in love. [3]Make every effort to keep the unity of the Spirit through the bond of peace. [4]There is one body and one Spirit — just as you were called to one hope when you were called — [5]one Lord, one faith, one baptism; [6]one God and Father of all, who is over all and through all and in all.

[7]But to each one of us grace has been given as Christ apportioned it. [8]This is why it[a] says:

"When he ascended on high,
he led captives in his train
and gave gifts to men."[b]

[9](What does "he ascended" mean except that he also descended to the lower, earthly regions?[c] [10]He who descended is the very one who ascended higher than all the heavens, in order to fill the whole universe.) [11]It was he who gave some to be apostles, some to be prophets, some to be evangelists, and some to be pastors and teachers, [12]to prepare God's people for works of service, so that the body of Christ may be built up [13]until we all reach unity in the faith and in the knowledge of the Son of God and become mature, attaining to the whole measure of the fulness of Christ.

[14]Then we will no longer be infants, tossed back and forth by the waves, and blown here and there by every wind of teaching and by the cunning and craftiness of men in their deceitful scheming. [15]Instead, speaking the truth in love, we will in all things grow up into him who is the Head, that is, Christ. [16]From him the whole body, joined and held together by every supporting ligament, grows and builds itself up in love, as each part does its work.

■ Living as Children of Light

[17]So I tell you this, and insist on it in the Lord, that you must no longer live as the Gentiles do, in the futility of their thinking. [18]They are darkened in their understanding and separated from the life of God because of the ignorance that is in them due to the hardening of their hearts. [19]Having lost all sensitivity, they have given themselves over to sensuality so as to indulge in every kind of impurity, with a continual lust for more.

4:19 ■ LOSS OF SENSITIVITY
Medical conditions that destroy nerves — leprosy, spinal cord injury, diabetes — are among the most difficult to treat. Without a sense of touch or pain, the patient can get a bedsore by lying in the same position too long, or a footsore by wearing too-tight shoes. The body no longer warns of danger. According to Paul, people can also develop a kind of moral insensitivity, silencing their consciences and hardening their hearts. That condition can prove fatal.

---

[20]You, however, did not come to know Christ that way. [21]Surely you heard of him and were taught in him in accordance with the truth that is in Jesus. [22]You were taught, with regard to your former way of life, to put off your old self, which is being corrupted by its deceitful desires; [23]to be made new in the attitude of your minds; [24]and to put on the new self, created to be like God in true righteousness and holiness.

[25]Therefore each of you must put off falsehood and speak truthfully to his neighbour, for we are all members of one body. [26]"In your anger do not sin"[d]: Do not let the sun go down while you are still angry, [27]and do not give the devil a foothold. [28]He who has been stealing must steal no longer, but must work, doing something useful with his own hands, that he may have something to share with those in need.

[29]Do not let any unwholesome talk come out of your mouths, but only what is helpful for building others up according to their needs, that it may benefit those who listen. [30]And do not grieve the Holy Spirit of God, with whom you were sealed for the day of redemption. [31]Get rid of all bitterness, rage and anger, brawling and slander, along with every form of malice. [32]Be kind and compassionate to one another, forgiving each other, just as in Christ God forgave you.

5 Be imitators of God, therefore, as dearly loved children [2]and live a life of love, just as Christ loved us and gave himself up for us as a fragrant offering and sacrifice to God.

[3]But among you there must not be even a hint of sexual immorality, or of any kind of impurity, or of greed, because these are improper for God's holy people. [4]Nor should there be obscenity, foolish talk or coarse joking, which are out of place, but rather thanksgiving. [5]For of this you can be sure: No immoral, impure or greedy person — such a man is an idolater — has any inheritance in the kingdom of Christ and of God.[a] [6]Let no-one deceive you with empty words, for because of such things God's

---

*a*8 Or *God*   *b*8 Psalm 68:18   *c*9 Or *the depths of the earth*   *d*26 Psalm 4:4   *a*5 Or *kingdom of the Christ and God* wrath comes on those who are disobedient. [7]Therefore do not be partners with them.

[8]For you were once darkness, but now you are light in the Lord. Live as children of light [9](for the fruit of the light consists in all goodness, righteousness and truth) [10]and find out what pleases the Lord. [11]Have nothing to do with the fruitless deeds of darkness, but rather expose them. [12]For it is shameful even to mention what the disobedient do in secret. [13]But everything exposed by the light becomes visible, [14]for it is light that makes everything visible. This is why it is said:

"Wake up, O sleeper,
    rise from the dead,
and Christ will shine on you."

[15]Be very careful, then, how you live — not as unwise but as wise, [16]making the most of every opportunity, because the days are evil. [17]Therefore do not be foolish, but understand what the Lord's will is. [18]Do not get drunk on wine, which leads to debauchery. Instead, be filled with the Spirit. [19]Speak to one another with psalms, hymns and spiritual songs. Sing and make music in your heart to the Lord, [20]always giving thanks to God the Father for everything, in the name of our Lord Jesus Christ.

[21]Submit to one another out of reverence for Christ.

5:21 ■ THE KEY TO SUBMISSION

Many readers have struggled with the advice Paul gives in the next few paragraphs. This simple sentence sets the tone for all that follows: we are to submit to others because of our reverence for Christ. In other words, in any human relationship — husband and wife, child and parent, slave and master — a third party is involved, Christ himself. Paul urges us to conduct those relationships in the light of Christ's own spirit.

■ Wives and Husbands

[22]Wives, submit to your husbands as to the Lord. [23]For the husband is the head of the wife as Christ is the head of the church, his body, of which he is the Saviour. [24]Now as the church submits to Christ,

■ LETTERS FROM PRISON
TIME AT LAST TO TACKLE THE GRANDEST QUESTION OF ALL

INSIGHT

I AM AN AMBASSADOR IN CHAINS. PRAY THAT I MAY DECLARE IT [THE GOSPEL] FEARLESSLY, AS I SHOULD. ■ 6:20

To stimulate creativity, many authors seek out a scenic setting. Yet some of the world's most famous literature originated in, of all places, a prison cell. John Bunyan wrote his *Pilgrim's Progress* there. Russian novelist Alexander Solzhenitsyn's vast output had its conception behind barbed wire, as did his compatriot Dostoevski's.

Parts of the Bible were written in prison as well. Ephesians represents one of Paul's "prison letters" (together with Philippians, Colossians and Philemon).

■ TIME ON HIS HANDS

Prison offers authors one precious commodity: time to think and reflect. When Paul wrote his prison letters, he was no longer journeying from town to town, stamping out fires set by his enemies. Settled into passably comfortable surroundings (probably confined to a house), he could slip off his sandals and devote attention to lofty concepts.

Unlike Paul's other letters, Ephesians does not address any urgent problems. With a sigh of relief, the apostle turned to the grandest question of all: "What is God's overall purpose for this world?" Paul answers the question this way: "To bring all things in heaven and on earth together under one head, even Christ" (1:10).

■ A POSITIVE APPROACH

The apostle Paul often borrowed from the language of athletics to press home a crucial point, and Ephesians ends with a well-composed pep talk. In keeping with this letter's uplifting style, Paul does not scold or warn; rather, he begins, "I urge you to live a life worthy of the calling you have received" (4:1).

Already Paul has taught that Christ lives in each Christian — we are his body. Now he exhorts his readers to think through what it means to represent Christ in the world. When people look at Christians, do they see the qualities of Christ on display?

The last half of Ephesians spells out practical steps towards Christian maturity. Paul blends each new thought into his overall theme, urging us to love *as Christ loved*, to forgive *as Christ forgave*, to submit *as you would to Christ* (5:2; 4:32; 5:21).

Ironically, it took a stint in prison to loosen up Paul for this endeavour. The book of Ephesians can hardly introduce a new thought without bursting into a song or a prayer. It is no wonder the English poet Samuel Taylor Coleridge called the book "the divinest composition of man".

□ LIFE QUESTIONS:

Suppose you were put in prison. What kind of letters would you write?

so also wives should submit to their husbands in everything.

²⁵Husbands, love your wives, just as Christ loved the church and gave himself up for her ²⁶to make her holy, cleansing*b* her by the washing with water through the word, ²⁷and to present her to himself as a radiant church, without stain or wrinkle or any other blemish, but holy and blameless. ²⁸In this same way, husbands ought to love their wives as their own bodies. He who loves his wife loves himself. ²⁹After all, no-one ever hated his own body, but he feeds and cares for it, just as Christ does the church—³⁰for we are members of his body. ³¹"For this reason a man will leave his father and mother and be united to his wife, and the two will become one flesh."*c* ³²This is a profound mystery—but I am talking about Christ and the church. ³³However, each one of you also must love his wife as he loves himself, and the wife must respect her husband.

■ Children and Parents

6 Children, obey your parents in the Lord, for this is right. ²"Honour your father and mother"—which is the first commandment with a promise—³"that it may go well with you and that you may enjoy long life on the earth."*a*

⁴Fathers, do not exasperate your children; instead, bring them up in the training and instruction of the Lord.

■ Slaves and Masters

⁵Slaves, obey your earthly masters with respect and fear, and with sincerity of heart, just as you would obey Christ. ⁶Obey them not only to win their favour when their eye is on you, but like slaves of Christ, doing the will of God from your heart. ⁷Serve wholeheartedly, as if you were serving the Lord, not men, ⁸because you know that the Lord will reward everyone for whatever good he does, whether he is slave or free.

⁹And masters, treat your slaves in the same way. Do not threaten them, since you know that he who is both their Master and yours is in heaven, and there is no favouritism with him.

■ The Armour of God

¹⁰Finally, be strong in the Lord and in his mighty power. ¹¹Put on the full armour of God so that you can take your stand against the devil's schemes. ¹²For our struggle is not against flesh and blood, but against the rulers, against the authorities, against the powers of this dark world and against the spiritual forces of evil in the heavenly realms. ¹³Therefore put on the full armour of God, so that when the day of evil comes, you may be able to stand your ground, and after you have done everything, to stand. ¹⁴Stand firm then, with the belt of truth buckled round your waist, with the breastplate of righteousness in place, ¹⁵and with your feet fitted with the readiness that comes from the gospel of peace. ¹⁶In addition to all this, take up the shield of faith, with which you can extinguish all the flaming arrows of the evil one. ¹⁷Take the helmet of salvation and the sword of the Spirit, which is the word of God. ¹⁸And pray in the Spirit on all occasions with all kinds of prayers and requests. With this in mind, be alert and always keep on praying for all the saints.

6:11 ■ THE ARMOUR OF GOD

Ephesians concludes with a concise analogy, perhaps inspired by a glimpse of a Roman soldier, outfitted in armour, patrolling the grounds of Paul's prison. Paul viewed the Christian life as a kind of warfare, and he wanted his readers to prepare for combat with a dangerous opponent. Bible scholars often note two details: 1) Only the "sword of the Spirit" is an offensive weapon; all the rest were used for defence; 2) No armour protects the back and rear; Paul made no provision for running away from a spiritual battle.

¹⁹Pray also for me, that whenever I open my mouth, words may be given me so that I will fearlessly make known the mystery of the gospel, ²⁰for which I am an ambassador in chains. Pray that I may declare it fearlessly, as I should.

■ Final Greetings

²¹Tychicus, the dear brother and faithful servant in the Lord, will tell you everything, so that you also may know how I am and what I am doing. ²²I am sending him to you for this very purpose, that you may know how we are, and that he may encourage you.

²³Peace to the brothers, and love with faith from God the Father and the Lord Jesus Christ. ²⁴Grace to all who love our Lord Jesus Christ with an undying love.

---

b 26 Or having cleansed   *c 31 Gen. 2:24*   *a 3 Deut. 5:16*

PHILIPPIANS

INTRODUCTION

■ CHEERFUL SOUNDS FROM A JAIL CELL
JOY WHEN IT'S LEAST EXPECTED

FINALLY, MY BROTHERS, REJOICE IN THE LORD! ■ 3:1

Joy. The word has a quick, poignant ring to it. Yet it, like other words, has been drained of meaning over the years, even used as a name for a dishwashing detergent in America. Nowadays *joy* is used most commonly for a sensation like *thrill*.

We think of joy as something you save up for months to experience and then splurge on in a moment of exhilaration: a trip to Disney World, a free-fall dive, a heart-stopping ride on the world's largest roller coaster, a hot-air balloon trip. Paul had a different understanding of the word, as this letter reveals.

■ WHEN YOU FEEL LIKE DESPAIRING
Philippians uses the word *joy* or *rejoice* every few paragraphs, but the joy it describes doesn't vanish after your heart starts beating normally again. Rejoice, says Paul, when someone selfishly tries to steal the limelight from you. And when you meet persecution for your faith. And when you are facing death.

In fact, the most joyous book in the Bible comes from the pen of an author chained to a Roman guard. Many scholars believe that Paul wrote Philippians in Rome just about the time Nero began tossing Christians to ravenous lions and burning them as torches to illuminate his banquets. How could a rational man devote a letter to the topic of joy while his survival was in serious jeopardy? In such an environment, how could joy possibly thrive?

■ TURNING EVIL INTO GOOD
Paul hints at an answer in a burst of eloquence in chapter 2 (verses 5–11). This pithy, metrical

paragraph may have been a hymn familiar to the early church. In it, Paul discusses Christ's perspective in coming to earth.

During the Christmas season we celebrate that special night when God visited earth as a baby. But to the rest of the universe the event looked like an astounding humiliation. God, the Creator of all, took on the unimpressive body of a human being to endure a confining life and grisly death on planet Earth.

Paul points to this death to show that God can take even the darkest moment in history and turn it into good. The cross, and Jesus' not staying dead, proves that nothing is powerful enough to stamp out a reason for joy — joy "in the Lord", as Paul says.

■ VICTORY IN JAIL
Thus even the normally depressing state of imprisonment didn't bother Paul. As he wrote Philippians, he must have recalled his first visit to Philippi. Then, a most unusual jail-break occurred: the jail broke, but the prisoners didn't (Acts 16:22–28).

Even when Paul stayed in jail for long periods, God used the experience to advance the gospel. As he wrote Philippians, conversions were occurring among the Roman palace soldiers, forced by guard duty to overhear Paul's daily ministry.

Paul summarised his life philosophy in a famous "to be or not to be" soliloquy, concluding that "to live is Christ and to die is gain" (1:21). God is even stronger than death, and that makes a Christian's joy indestructible.

■ HOW TO READ PHILIPPIANS

Philippians is simple and straightforward. It's not a formal treatise, but a warm letter to friends. Read it as you would read any personal letter. From the clues Paul gives, try to imagine the relationship between him and the Philippians.

What did he like about them? Why were they so important to him?

The Introduction refers to the common use of the words *joy* and *rejoice*. Check out each of these, noticing how Paul can find joy in any circumstance. Use Philippians like a devotional book, first reflecting on what it says, then applying it to your own life.

■ 3-TRACK READING PLAN

For an explanation and complete listing of the 3-track reading plan, turn to page x.

■ TRACK 1:
Two-Week Courses on the Bible
The Track 1 reading programme on the Life and Teachings of Paul includes one chapter from Philippians. See page x for a complete listing of this course.

■ TRACK 2:
An Overview of Philippians in 1 Day
□ Day 1. Read the Introduction to Philippians, then chapter 2, noticing especially the central passage set off in poetic form (verses 5–11).
Now turn to page xi for your next Track 2 reading project.

■ TRACK 3:
All of Philippians in 4 Days
After you have read through Philippians, turn to pages xii–xiii for your next Track 3 reading project.

□ 1   □ 2   □ 3   □ 4

1 Paul and Timothy, servants of Christ Jesus,

To all the saints in Christ Jesus at Philippi, together with the overseers*a* and deacons:

²Grace and peace to you from God our Father and the Lord Jesus Christ.

■ Thanksgiving and Prayer
³I thank my God every time I remember you. ⁴In all my prayers for all of you, I always pray with joy ⁵because of your partnership in the gospel from the first day until now, ⁶being confident of this, that he who began a good work in you will carry it on to completion until the day of Christ Jesus.

⁷It is right for me to feel this way about all of you, since I have you in my heart; for whether I am in chains or defending and confirming the gospel, all of you share in God's grace with me. ⁸God can testify how I long for all of you with the affection of Christ Jesus.

> ## 1:7 ■ PAUL'S PARTNERS
> Strong-minded though he was, Paul never worked alone. The warmth in this book comes partly from his confidence that the Philippian Christians were his partners (verse 5), sharing in God's grace. He counted on their prayers (verse 19). At the end of this letter, Paul returns to this theme of partnership, rejoicing in the Philippians' love and thoughtfulness (4:10–19).

⁹And this is my prayer: that your love may abound more and more in knowledge and depth of insight, ¹⁰so that you may be able to discern what is best and may be pure and blameless until the day of Christ, ¹¹filled with the fruit of righteousness that comes through Jesus Christ—to the glory and praise of God.

■ Paul's Chains Advance the Gospel
¹²Now I want you to know, brothers, that what has happened to me has really served to advance the gospel. ¹³As a result, it has become clear throughout the whole palace guard*b* and to everyone else that I am in chains for Christ. ¹⁴Because of my chains, most of the brothers in the Lord have been encouraged to speak the word of God more courageously and fearlessly.

¹⁵It is true that some preach Christ out of envy and rivalry, but others out of goodwill. ¹⁶The latter do so in love, knowing that I am put here for the defence of the gospel. ¹⁷The former preach Christ out of selfish ambition, not sincerely, supposing that they can stir up trouble for me while I am in chains.*c* ¹⁸But what does it matter? The important thing is that in every way, whether from false motives or true, Christ is preached. And because of this I rejoice.

Yes, and I will continue to rejoice, ¹⁹for I know that through your prayers and the help given by the Spirit of Jesus Christ, what has happened to me will turn out for my deliverance.*d* ²⁰I eagerly expect and hope that I will in no way be ashamed, but will have sufficient courage so that now as always Christ will be exalted in my body, whether by life or by death. ²¹For to me, to live is Christ and to die is gain. ²²If I am to go on living in the body, this will mean fruitful labour for me. Yet what shall I choose? I do not know! ²³I am torn between the two: I desire to depart and be with Christ, which is better by far; ²⁴but it is more necessary for you that I remain in the body. ²⁵Convinced of this, I know that I will remain, and I will continue with all of you for your progress and joy in the faith, ²⁶so that through my being with you again your joy in Christ Jesus will overflow on account of me.

²⁷Whatever happens, conduct yourselves in a manner worthy of the gospel of Christ. Then, whether I come and see you or only hear about you in my absence, I will know that you stand firm in one spirit, contending as one man for the faith of the gospel ²⁸without being frightened in any way by those who oppose you. This is a sign to them that they will be destroyed, but that you will be saved—and that by God. ²⁹For it has been granted to you on behalf of Christ not only to believe on him, but also to suffer for him, ³⁰since you are going through the

---

a 1 Traditionally *bishops*   *b 13* Or *whole palace*   *c 16,17* Some late manuscripts have verses 16 and 17 in reverse order.   *d 19* Or *salvation* same struggle you saw I had, and now hear that I still have.

■ Imitating Christ's Humility

2 If you have any encouragement from being united with Christ, if any comfort from his love, if any fellowship with the Spirit, if any tenderness and compassion, ²then make my joy complete by being like-minded, having the same love, being one in spirit and purpose. ³Do nothing out of selfish ambition or vain conceit, but in humility consider others better than yourselves. ⁴Each of you should look not only to your own interests, but also to the interests of others.

⁵Your attitude should be the same as that of Christ Jesus:

⁶Who, being in very nature*a* God,
　　did not consider equality with God
　　　something to be grasped,
⁷but made himself nothing,
　　taking the very nature*b* of a servant,
　　being made in human likeness.
⁸And being found in appearance as a man,
　　he humbled himself
　　and became obedient to death—even death
　　　on a cross!
⁹Therefore God exalted him to the highest place

and gave him the name that is above every
　　name,
¹⁰that at the name of Jesus every knee should
　　bow,
　　in heaven and on earth and under the earth,
¹¹and every tongue confess that Jesus Christ is
　　Lord,
　　to the glory of God the Father.

■ Shining as Stars

¹²Therefore, my dear friends, as you have always obeyed—not only in my presence, but now much more in my absence—continue to work out your salvation with fear and trembling, ¹³for it is God who works in you to will and to act according to his good purpose.

> **2:12-13 ■ WORKING WITH GOD**
> Philippians, a practical book, presents theology simply and without elaboration. These verses describe both the human and divine element in our faith: we "work out" our salvation, and yet God "works" in us to accomplish it. Philippians 3:16 expresses a similar paradox: Paul urges that we "live up to what we have already attained".

¹⁴Do everything without complaining or arguing,

■ PAUL'S FAVOURITE CHURCH
WHEN OTHERS FAILED, THESE FRIENDS DIDN'T

INSIGHT

I THANK MY GOD EVERY TIME I REMEMBER YOU. ■ 1:3

The Christian church hasn't had a perfect record throughout history. If you take a random sample of adjectives people use to describe the church, the list will probably include such labels as *racist, judgmental, narrow, divided, pompous.*
　　The church of Jesus Christ has fallen far short of the ideals entrusted to it — so far short that we may sometimes forget what the church is supposed to look like. Problems existed from the beginning: Paul's letters to Galatia, Corinth and Colosse flame with indignation against defects in the early church.
　　Occasionally, however, a church came along that worked, against all odds. Philippi was one of those rare congregations.

■LOYAL FRIENDS

From its birth, the church in Philippi had two strikes against it. Its first recorded converts were an Asiatic Jewish merchant, a Greek slave girl employed as a sideshow fortune-teller and a gruff Roman jailer (Acts 16). Yet more than a decade later, when Paul wrote to the church, he could hardly find words warm enough to express his pride and affection.

Paul turned down money gifts from other churches, out of fear that his enemies might twist the facts and accuse him of being a crook. But he trusted the Philippians. At least four separate times they sacrificed to meet his needs. And they also sent Epaphroditus on an arduous journey to care for Paul in prison.
　　Paul wrote Philippians, in fact, mainly as a thank-you for all that his friends had done. Its bright, happy tone reflects the fondness he felt for his favourite church.
　　Nevertheless, Paul couldn't resist an opportunity to give some fatherly advice. In a fireside-chat tone, he warned of encroaching dangers: divisions, a strain of perfectionism and inroads by those who wished to turn Christians back to the Jewish faith. Always, though, he returned to his underlying theme of joy, an emotion that seemed to come easily when Paul remembered the Philippians.

□LIFE QUESTIONS:

What does Paul single out for praise in the Philippian church? How are those qualities present in your church?

[15]so that you may become blameless and pure, children of God without fault in a crooked and depraved generation, in which you shine like stars in the universe [16]as you hold out[c] the word of life — in order that I may boast on the day of Christ that I did not run or labour for nothing. [17]But even if I am being poured out like a drink offering on the sacrifice and service coming from your faith, I am glad and rejoice with all of you. [18]So you too should be glad and rejoice with me.

Timothy and Epaphroditus

[19]I hope in the Lord Jesus to send Timothy to you soon, that I also may be cheered when I receive news about you. [20]I have no-one else like him, who takes a genuine interest in your welfare. [21]For everyone looks out for his own interests, not those of Jesus Christ. [22]But you know that Timothy has proved himself, because as a son with his father he has served with me in the work of the gospel. [23]I hope, therefore, to send him as soon as I see how things go with me. [24]And I am confident in the Lord that I myself will come soon.

[25]But I think it is necessary to send back to you Epaphroditus, my brother, fellow-worker and fellow-soldier, who is also your messenger, whom you sent to take care of my needs. [26]For he longs for all of you and is distressed because you heard he was ill. [27]Indeed he was ill, and almost died. But God had mercy on him, and not on him only but also on me, to spare me sorrow upon sorrow. [28]Therefore I am all the more eager to send him, so that when you see him again you may be glad and I may have less anxiety. [29]Welcome him in the Lord with great joy, and honour men like him, [30]because he almost died for the work of Christ, risking his life to make up for the help you could not give me.

2:25 ■ A HELPER FOR PAUL
The paragraph on Epaphroditus reveals the warm feelings between Paul and the church at Philippi. If Paul was imprisoned at Rome, as many scholars believe, then Epaphroditus travelled more than 700 miles to be with him. He fell sick while visiting Paul and was now returning to Philippi, probably carrying this letter to hand-deliver.

No Confidence in the Flesh

3 Finally, my brothers, rejoice in the Lord! It is no trouble for me to write the same things to you again, and it is a safeguard for you.

[2]Watch out for those dogs, those men who do evil, those mutilators of the flesh. [3]For it is we who are the circumcision, we who worship by the Spirit of God, who glory in Christ Jesus, and who put no confidence in the flesh — [4]though I myself have reasons for such confidence.

If anyone else thinks he has reasons to put confidence in the flesh, I have more: [5]circumcised on the eighth day, of the people of Israel, of the tribe of Benjamin, a Hebrew of Hebrews; in regard to the law, a Pharisee; [6]as for zeal, persecuting the church; as for legalistic righteousness, faultless.

[7]But whatever was to my profit I now consider loss for the sake of Christ. [8]What is more, I consider everything a loss compared to the surpassing greatness of knowing Christ Jesus my Lord, for whose sake I have lost all things. I consider them rubbish, that I may gain Christ [9]and be found in him, not having a righteousness of my own that comes from the law, but that which is through faith in Christ — the righteousness that comes from God and is by faith. [10]I want to know Christ and the power of his resurrection and the fellowship of sharing in his sufferings, becoming like him in his death, [11]and so, somehow, to attain to the resurrection from the dead.

Pressing on Towards the Goal

[12]Not that I have already obtained all this, or have already been made perfect, but I press on to take hold of that for which Christ Jesus took hold of me. [13]Brothers, I do not consider myself yet to have taken hold of it. But one thing I do: Forgetting what is behind and straining towards what is ahead, [14]I press on towards the goal to win the prize for which God has called me heavenwards in Christ Jesus.

[15]All of us who are mature should take such a view of things. And if on some point you think differently, that too God will make clear to you. [16]Only let us live up to what we have already attained.

[17]Join with others in following my example, brothers, and take note of those who live according to the pattern we gave you. [18]For, as I have often told you before and now say again even with tears, many live as enemies of the cross of Christ. [19]Their destiny is destruction, their god is their stomach, and their glory is in their shame. Their mind is on earthly things. [20]But our citizenship is in heaven. And we eagerly await a Saviour from there, the Lord Jesus Christ, [21]who, by the power that enables him to bring everything under his control, will transform our lowly bodies so that they will be like his glorious body.

4 Therefore, my brothers, you whom I love and long for, my joy and crown, that is how you should stand firm in the Lord, dear friends!

Exhortations

[2]I plead with Euodia and I plead with Syntyche to agree with each other in the Lord. [3]Yes, and I ask you, loyal yokefellow,[a] help these women who have contended at my side in the cause of the gospel, along with Clement and the rest of my fellow-workers, whose names are in the book of life.

4:2 ■ WOMEN IN THE CHURCH
Although these two women were stirring up trouble in Philippi, women played a positive role in that church. In fact, Paul's first convert in Europe was Lydia, a businesswoman. Paul met with her and a group of women by a river, and later stayed in her house (see Acts 16).

---

[4]Rejoice in the Lord always. I will say it again: Rejoice! [5]Let your gentleness be evident to all. The

---

c 16 Or hold on to   a 3 Or loyal Syzygus

Lord is near. [6]Do not be anxious about anything, but in everything, by prayer and petition, with thanksgiving, present your requests to God. [7]And the peace of God, which transcends all understanding, will guard your hearts and your minds in Christ Jesus.

[8]Finally, brothers, whatever is true, whatever is noble, whatever is right, whatever is pure, whatever is lovely, whatever is admirable — if anything is excellent or praiseworthy — think about such things. [9]Whatever you have learned or received or heard from me, or seen in me — put it into practice. And the God of peace will be with you.

■ Thanks for Their Gifts

[10]I rejoice greatly in the Lord that at last you have renewed your concern for me. Indeed, you have been concerned, but you had no opportunity to show it. [11]I am not saying this because I am in need, for I have learned to be content whatever the circumstances. [12]I know what it is to be in need, and I know what it is to have plenty. I have learned the secret of being content in any and every situation, whether well fed or hungry, whether living in plenty or in want. [13]I can do everything through him who gives me strength.

[14]Yet it was good of you to share in my troubles. [15]Moreover, as you Philippians know, in the early days of your acquaintance with the gospel, when I set out from Macedonia, not one church shared with me in the matter of giving and receiving, ex-

cept you only; [16]for even when I was in Thessalonica, you sent me aid again and again when I was in need. [17]Not that I am looking for a gift, but I am looking for what may be credited to your account. [18]I have received full payment and even more; I am amply supplied, now that I have received from Epaphroditus the gifts you sent. They are a fragrant offering, an acceptable sacrifice, pleasing to God. [19]And my God will meet all your needs according to his glorious riches in Christ Jesus.

[20]To our God and Father be glory for ever and ever. Amen.

4:13 ■ PAUL'S SECRET

Shipwrecked, beaten, imprisoned, Paul had seen the down side of life. He had also known prosperity. Both, he suggests, offer temptations. But Paul had discovered a secret for contentment in all situations: his deeply personal sense of living in Christ. In this he found the strength to handle anything.

■ Final Greetings

[21]Greet all the saints in Christ Jesus. The brothers who are with me send greetings. [22]All the saints send you greetings, especially those who belong to Caesar's household.

[23]The grace of the Lord Jesus Christ be with your spirit. Amen.[b]

[b]23 Some manuscripts do not have *Amen*.

COLOSSIANS

■ BATTLING THE CULTS
FOR EVERYTHING WORTHWHILE, THERE EXISTS A COUNTERFEIT

SEE TO IT THAT NO-ONE TAKES YOU CAPTIVE THROUGH HOLLOW AND DECEPTIVE
PHILOSOPHY. ■ 2:8

You see them in strange outfits on street corners,
chanting phrases with too many vowels and
punctuating the chants with a noisy tambourine.
Or in airports, thrusting books or flowers into your
face. Or in California, all over California. You think
of them as crazy cults, populated by misfits. Then
one day you hear about a friend of yours.

She seemed normal until suddenly,
without warning, she snapped. Her parents
searched desperately, even hiring private
detectives to help get her back. They found her
surrounded by allies, with a new name, a new
hairstyle, and, so it seemed, a new brain. She
stared at them with clear eyes and told them
they were missing out on the most wonderful
experience of life. She had joined a cult.

Cults come in all varieties, some recent
spin-offs from the New Age movement, others
sporting exotic names like Hare Krishna or the
Church of Scientology. They demand much from
their members: a lifetime of discipline and
absolute loyalty. And they also promise much in
return: the pathway to a secret, hidden
knowledge available only to those who follow
them.

■ A BREEDING GROUND
The first-century town of Colosse was a perfect
breeding ground for cults. Situated on a major
trade route from the East, Colosse entertained a
steady stream of Oriental traders with mysterious
religious ideas. Even Jews in that area worshipped
angels and river spirits.

Early Christian converts soon confronted
new variations of the gospel. Then, as now,
many cults didn't reject Jesus Christ outright;
they merely worked him into a more elaborate
scheme. Christ and simple forms of worship,
they taught, were fine for beginners, but for the
"deep things of God", well, some further steps
would be required.

■ THE BEST DEFENCE
Paul doesn't give a complete glossary of the
"hollow and deceptive philosophy" the Colossians
were sorting through. From his arguments, we can
gather that the philosophy must have included
strains of Jewish legalism mixed in with angel
worship, Greek philosophy, and strict self-denial.

The best defence is a good offence.
Rather than attacking each peculiar belief point
by point, Paul countered with a positive
theology. The principles he outlines in this book
can be used today to judge new cults.

"Christ is enough," Paul declares. He is
God, the fulness of God, the One who made the
world, the reason that everything exists. All the
mystery and treasure and wisdom you could ask
for are found in the person of Jesus Christ; there
is no need to look elsewhere.

■ APPROACH GOD DIRECTLY
Because Jesus bridged the chasm between God
and us, we don't have to approach God indirectly,
through a ladder of angels or other gods. We have
no need to prove our worth through superior
behaviour. We can come to God directly and
boldly because of Christ.

As for Jewish practices, they were mere
shadows, made obsolete by Christ's coming.
Why not concentrate on the actual image that
God sent to earth?

Before Christ, Paul grants, a mystery was
kept hidden for many centuries (1:26). But with
Christ, everything broke out into the open. The
fulness of God lived, died, and came back from
death in broad daylight. Why settle for
counterfeits?

■ HOW TO READ COLOSSIANS

Although this letter was written to counter specific problems in the church at Colosse, it includes some of Paul's most eloquent writing about Jesus Christ. Chapter 1 contains a soaring paragraph (1:15–20) that may have been used as a hymn by the early church. Note in this book how Paul concludes all his arguments by referring to Christ.

Chapters 2 and 3 deal with dangerous tendencies in Colosse. Paul argues against a "mystery" religion by firmly asserting that Christ is the complete expression of the mystery of God. As you read these two chapters, try to imagine what kind of behaviour at Colosse troubled Paul.

■ 3-TRACK READING PLAN

For an explanation and complete listing of the 3-track reading plan, turn to page x.

■ TRACK 1:
Two-Week Courses on the Bible
See page x for information on these courses.

■ TRACK 2:
An Overview of Colossians in 1 Day

☐ Day 1. Read the Introduction to Colossians, then chapter 1, noting especially Paul's prayer, which precedes the hymnlike paragraph (verses 15–20). Now turn to page xi for your next Track 2 reading project.

■ TRACK 3:
All of Colossians in 4 Days
After you have read through Colossians, turn to pages xii–xiii for your next Track 3 reading project.

☐ 1   ☐ 2   ☐ 3   ☐ 4

1 Paul, an apostle of Christ Jesus by the will of God, and Timothy our brother,

²To the holy and faithful*a* brothers in Christ at Colosse:

Grace and peace to you from God our Father.*b*

■ Thanksgiving and Prayer

³We always thank God, the Father of our Lord Jesus Christ, when we pray for you, ⁴because we have heard of your faith in Christ Jesus and of the love you have for all the saints — ⁵the faith and love that spring from the hope that is stored up for you in heaven and that you have already heard about in the word of truth, the gospel ⁶that has come to you. All over the world this gospel is bearing fruit and growing, just as it has been doing among you since the day you heard it and understood God's grace in all its truth. ⁷You learned it from Epaphras, our dear fellow-servant, who is a faithful minister of Christ on our*c* behalf, ⁸and who also told us of your love in the Spirit.

⁹For this reason, since the day we heard about you, we have not stopped praying for you and asking God to fill you with the knowledge of his will through all spiritual wisdom and understanding. ¹⁰And we pray this in order that you may live a life worthy of the Lord and may please him in every way: bearing fruit in every good work, growing in the knowledge of God, ¹¹being strengthened with all power according to his glorious might so that you may have great endurance and patience, and joyfully ¹²giving thanks to the Father, who has qualified you*d* to share in the inheritance of the saints in the kingdom of light. ¹³For he has rescued us from the dominion of darkness and brought us into the kingdom of the Son he loves, ¹⁴in whom we have redemption,*e* the forgiveness of sins.

■ The Supremacy of Christ

¹⁵He is the image of the invisible God, the first-born over all creation. ¹⁶For by him all things were created: things in heaven and on earth, visible and invisible, whether thrones or powers or rulers or authorities; all things were created by him and for him. ¹⁷He is before all things, and in him all things hold together. ¹⁸And he is the head of the body, the church; he is the beginning and the firstborn from among the dead, so that in everything he might have the supremacy. ¹⁹For God was pleased to have all his fulness dwell in him, ²⁰and through him to reconcile to himself all things, whether things on earth or things in heaven, by making peace through his blood, shed on the cross.

²¹Once you were alienated from God and were enemies in your minds because of*f* your evil behaviour. ²²But now he has reconciled you by Christ's physical body through death to present you holy in his sight, without blemish and free from accusation — ²³if you continue in your faith, established and firm, not moved from the hope held out in the gospel. This is the gospel that you heard and that has been proclaimed to every creature under heaven, and of which I, Paul, have become a servant.

1:21 ■ GETTING PRACTICAL

Although Paul's letters often launch out into theologically deep water, they always lead back to practical issues: What difference does theology make to daily life? The preceding paragraph (verses 15–20) contains a compressed summary of the absolute supremacy of Christ. Now Paul turns to the practical: Christ's supreme power does not distance us from but rather brings us closer to God. He alone has the ability to span the vast gap between God and humanity.

---

*a*2 Or *believing*   *b*2 Some manuscripts *Father and the Lord Jesus Christ*   *c*7 Some manuscripts *your*   *d*12 Some manuscripts *us*   *e*14 A few late manuscripts *redemption through his blood*   *f*21 Or *minds, as shown by*

■ Paul's Labour for the Church

²⁴Now I rejoice in what was suffered for you, and I fill up in my flesh what is still lacking in regard to Christ's afflictions, for the sake of his body, which is the church. ²⁵I have become its servant by the commission God gave me to present to you the word of God in its fulness — ²⁶the mystery that has been kept hidden for ages and generations, but is now disclosed to the saints. ²⁷To them God has chosen to make known among the Gentiles the glorious riches of this mystery, which is Christ in you, the hope of glory.

²⁸We proclaim him, admonishing and teaching everyone with all wisdom, so that we may present everyone perfect in Christ. ²⁹To this end I labour, struggling with all his energy, which so powerfully works in me.

2 I want you to know how much I am struggling for you and for those at Laodicea, and for all who have not met me personally. ²My purpose is that they may be encouraged in heart and united in love, so that they may have the full riches of complete understanding, in order that they may know the mystery of God, namely, Christ, ³in whom are hidden all the treasures of wisdom and knowledge. ⁴I tell you this so that no-one may deceive you by fine-sounding arguments. ⁵For though I am absent from you in body, I am present with you in spirit and delight to see how orderly you are and how firm your faith in Christ is.

■ Freedom From Human Regulations Through Life With Christ

⁶So then, just as you received Christ Jesus as Lord, continue to live in him, ⁷rooted and built up in him, strengthened in the faith as you were taught, and overflowing with thankfulness.

⁸See to it that no-one takes you captive through hollow and deceptive philosophy, which depends on human tradition and the basic principles of this world rather than on Christ.

⁹For in Christ all the fulness of the Deity lives in bodily form, ¹⁰and you have been given fulness in Christ, who is the Head over every power and authority. ¹¹In him you were also circumcised, in the putting off of the sinful nature,ᵃ not with a circumcision done by the hands of men but with the circumcision done by Christ, ¹²having been buried with him in baptism and raised with him through your faith in the power of God, who raised him from the dead.

¹³When you were dead in your sins and in the uncircumcision of your sinful nature,ᵇ God made youᶜ alive with Christ. He forgave us all our sins, ¹⁴having cancelled the written code, with its regulations, that was against us and that stood opposed to us; he took it away, nailing it to the cross. ¹⁵And having disarmed the powers and authorities, he made a public spectacle of them, triumphing over them by the cross.ᵈ

¹⁶Therefore do not let anyone judge you by what you eat or drink, or with regard to a religious festival, a New Moon celebration or a Sabbath day. ¹⁷These are a shadow of the things that were to come; the reality, however, is found in Christ. ¹⁸Do not let anyone who delights in false humility and the worship of angels disqualify you for the prize. Such a person goes into great detail about what he has seen, and his unspiritual mind puffs him up with idle notions. ¹⁹He has lost connection with the Head, from whom the whole body, supported and held together by its ligaments and sinews, grows as God causes it to grow.

2:16 ■ THE SEARCH FOR WHOLENESS

Legalism in Paul's day concerned such issues as diet, festival days, and religious ceremony. In these two paragraphs, Paul tells why such rules that appear 'spiritual' can actually lead a person away from God. Then, in chapter 3, he details what holy living *should* look like.

In his letter, Paul portrays the Christian life very optimistically. The Christians in Colosse were searching for "fullness" in the same way that modern people work to become "holistic" or "self-actualised". After first affirming that Jesus contains all the fullness of God, Paul asserts that true fullness is found only in Christ (verse 10).

²⁰Since you died with Christ to the basic principles of this world, why, as though you still belonged to it, do you submit to its rules: ²¹"Do not handle! Do not taste! Do not touch!"? ²²These are all destined to perish with use, because they are based on human commands and teachings. ²³Such regulations indeed have an appearance of wisdom, with their self-imposed worship, their false humility and their harsh treatment of the body, but they lack any value in restraining sensual indulgence.

■ Rules for Holy Living

3 Since, then, you have been raised with Christ, set your hearts on things above, where Christ is seated at the right hand of God. ²Set your minds on things above, not on earthly things. ³For you died, and your life is now hidden with Christ in God. ⁴When Christ, who is yourᵃ life, appears, then you also will appear with him in glory.

3:1 ■ FAMILIAR WORDS

If Colossians strikes you as vaguely familiar, don't be surprised. Paul's letters tend to follow a pattern: a greeting, a prayer, some doctrine, and a practical application of how we should live. Colossians sounds especially familiar because many of its verses have close parallels in Ephesians. In fact, of Ephesians' 155 verses, 78 appear in some form in Colossians.

⁵Put to death, therefore, whatever belongs to your earthly nature: sexual immorality, impurity, lust, evil desires and greed, which is idolatry. ⁶Because of these, the wrath of God is coming.ᵇ ⁷You used to walk in these ways, in the life you once lived. ⁸But now you must rid yourselves of all such things as these: anger, rage, malice, slander and

---

ᵃ11 Or the flesh   ᵇ13 Or your flesh   ᶜ13 Some manuscripts us   ᵈ15 Or them in him   ᵃ4 Some manuscripts our   ᵇ6 Some early manuscripts coming on those who are disobedient filthy language from your lips. ⁹Do not lie to each other, since you have taken off your old self with its practices ¹⁰and have put on the new self, which is being renewed in knowledge in the image of its Creator. ¹¹Here there is no Greek or Jew, circumcised or uncircumcised, barbarian, Scythian, slave or free, but Christ is all, and is in all.

3:11 ■ THE ORIGINAL BARBARIANS

The word "barbarians" meant those who did not speak Greek. To civilised people of that day, their languages sounded like a stammering repetition of the same syllables – barbarbarbar – hence the word barbarian. Scythians were likewise considered uncivilised and brutish. By mentioning such people, Paul was underlining the all-encompassing breadth of God's grace.

---

¹²Therefore, as God's chosen people, holy and dearly loved, clothe yourselves with compassion, kindness, humility, gentleness and patience. ¹³Bear with each other and forgive whatever grievances you may have against one another. Forgive as the Lord forgave you. ¹⁴And over all these virtues put on love, which binds them all together in perfect unity.

¹⁵Let the peace of Christ rule in your hearts, since as members of one body you were called to peace. And be thankful. ¹⁶Let the word of Christ dwell in you richly as you teach and admonish one another with all wisdom, and as you sing psalms, hymns and spiritual songs with gratitude in your hearts to God. ¹⁷And whatever you do, whether in word or deed, do it all in the name of the Lord Jesus, giving thanks to God the Father through him.

■ Rules for Christian Households

¹⁸Wives, submit to your husbands, as is fitting in the Lord.

¹⁹Husbands, love your wives and do not be harsh with them.

²⁰Children, obey your parents in everything, for this pleases the Lord.

²¹Fathers, do not embitter your children, or they will become discouraged.

²²Slaves, obey your earthly masters in everything; and do it, not only when their eye is on you and to win their favour, but with sincerity of heart and reverence for the Lord. ²³Whatever you do, work at it with all your heart, as working for the Lord, not for men, ²⁴since you know that you will receive an inheritance from the Lord as a reward. It is the Lord Christ you are serving. ²⁵Anyone who does wrong will be repaid for his wrong, and there is no favouritism.

4 Masters, provide your slaves with what is right and fair, because you know that you also have a Master in heaven.

■ Further Instructions

²Devote yourselves to prayer, being watchful and thankful. ³And pray for us, too, that God may open a door for our message, so that we may proclaim the mystery of Christ, for which I am in chains. ⁴Pray that I may proclaim it clearly, as I should. ⁵Be wise in the way you act towards outsiders; make the most of every opportunity. ⁶Let your conversation be always full of grace, seasoned with salt, so that you may know how to answer everyone.

■ Final Greetings

⁷Tychicus will tell you all the news about me. He is a dear brother, a faithful minister and fellow-servant in the Lord. ⁸I am sending him to you for the express purpose that you may know about our[a] circumstances and that he may encourage your hearts. ⁹He is coming with Onesimus, our faithful and dear brother, who is one of you. They will tell you everything that is happening here.

¹⁰My fellow-prisoner Aristarchus sends you his greetings, as does Mark, the cousin of Barnabas. (You have received instructions about him; if he comes to you, welcome him.) ¹¹Jesus, who is called Justus, also sends greetings. These are the only Jews among my fellow-workers for the kingdom of God, and they have proved a comfort to me. ¹²Epaphras, who is one of you and a servant of Christ Jesus, sends greetings. He is always wrestling in prayer for you, that you may stand firm in all the will of God, mature and fully assured. ¹³I vouch for him that he is working hard for you and for those at Laodicea and Hierapolis. ¹⁴Our dear friend Luke, the doctor, and Demas send greetings. ¹⁵Give my greetings to the brothers at Laodicea, and to Nympha and the church in her house.

4:12 ■ PROMINENT NAMES

Characteristically, Paul ended his letters with personal messages. Epaphras, who is mentioned twice in Colossians (1:7; 4:12), served with Paul and may have founded the church there. The short book of Philemon (verse 23) mentions him as a fellow prisoner with Paul. The main characters in that book, Philemon and his slave Onesimus, also came from Colosse, and Paul refers to a hoped-for visit to Colosse in his letter to Philemon (verse 22).

---

¹⁶After this letter has been read to you, see that it is also read in the church of the Laodiceans and that you in turn read the letter from Laodicea.

¹⁷Tell Archippus: "See to it that you complete the work you have received in the Lord."

¹⁸I, Paul, write this greeting in my own hand. Remember my chains. Grace be with you.

---

a 8 Some manuscripts that he may know about your

1 THESSALONIANS

INTRODUCTION

■ WHAT MADE PAUL SUCCESSFUL?

THE APOSTLE FUSSES OVER THE CITY THAT ONCE CHASED HIM AWAY

HOW CAN WE THANK GOD ENOUGH FOR YOU IN RETURN FOR ALL THE JOY WE HAVE IN THE PRESENCE OF OUR GOD BECAUSE OF YOU? ■ 3:9

A modern-day evangelist lamented, "Whenever the apostle Paul visited a city, the residents started a riot; when I visit one, they serve tea." The church in Thessalonica, like many of Paul's churches, was born amid violent upheaval. An angry mob took offence at Paul's work and chased him out of town, accusing him of causing "trouble all over the world" (Acts 17:6).

Generally, people do not start riots without a good reason, and in Paul's case they had one. Almost everywhere he visited, an enthusiastic church came to life, provoking the jealousy of the Jewish and Roman establishments.

■ A CONCERNED PARENT

This letter, 1 Thessalonians, gives important clues into what made Paul so effective at founding churches. Accepted as one of the earliest of Paul's letters, it probably dates from A.D. 50 or 51 and provides a first-hand account of Paul's relationship with a missionary church barely 20 years after Jesus' departure.

Someone once asked John and Charles Wesley's mother which of her ten surviving children she loved the most. She replied, "The one who is sick until he's well, and the one who's away from home until he's back." If someone had asked Paul which church concerned him most, he probably would have

answered, "The one with the most problems until it's healthy, the one I've been separated from longest until I return."

When Paul lived with the Thessalonians, he was gentle and loving, "like a mother caring for her little children" (2:7). Later, absent from them, he wrote as if he had only them on his mind all day. In 1 Thessalonians, he praised their strengths, fussed over reports of their weaknesses, and continually thanked God for their spiritual progress.

■ QUESTIONING PAUL'S MOTIVES

Some people in the church had questioned Paul's motives, so he opened the letter with a careful review of his work among them. In those days free-lance teachers of religion and philosophy sought a profit; Paul reminded the Thessalonians that he had worked night and day to avoid becoming a financial burden. He also painstakingly explained his unavoidable absence from them.

First Thessalonians stands out from the four books that precede it because, unlike them, this letter doesn't major in theology. Rather, it reveals the gratitude, disappointment, and joy of a beloved missionary who can't stop thinking about the church he left behind. Surely one reason for Paul's success centres on his churches' having made as big an impression on Paul as he made on them.

■ HOW TO READ 1 THESSALONIANS

This book provides a touching glimpse of Paul as a pastor. Paul visited Thessalonica at a troubled time in his ministry, while enemies were tailing him from town to town (see Acts 16–17). After he left, the church continued to meet hostility.

First Thessalonians is our earliest record of the life of a Christian community. Paul wrote this letter after receiving a mostly positive report (from Timothy) on the Thessalonians' spiritual

health. He rejoiced at the good news, but also showed concern over the church's problems.

As you read 1 Thessalonians, notice the issues that Paul addresses: Christians were raising questions about Jesus' return to earth and were disagreeing on matters of morality. But mainly, look for signs of Paul's relationship to the church at Thessalonica.

■ 3-TRACK READING PLAN

For an explanation and complete listing of the 3-track reading plan, turn to page x.

■ **TRACK 1:**
Two-Week Courses on the Bible
See page x for information on these courses.

■ **TRACK 2:**
An Overview of 1 Thessalonians in 1 Day

☐ **Day 1.** Read the Introduction to 1 Thessalonians, then chapters 3 and 4. The chapters are very short, so you can easily read two together.
Now turn to page xi for your next Track 2 reading project.

■ **TRACK 3:**
All of 1 Thessalonians in 3 Days
After you have read through 1 Thessalonians, turn to pages xii–xiii for your next Track 3 reading project.

☐ 1–2 ☐ 3–4 ☐ 5

1 Paul, Silas*a* and Timothy,

To the church of the Thessalonians in God the Father and the Lord Jesus Christ:

Grace and peace to you.*b*

■ **Thanksgiving for the Thessalonians' Faith**
²We always thank God for all of you, mentioning you in our prayers. ³We continually remember before our God and Father your work produced by faith, your labour prompted by love, and your endurance inspired by hope in our Lord Jesus Christ.

⁴For we know, brothers loved by God, that he has chosen you, ⁵because our gospel came to you not simply with words, but also with power, with the Holy Spirit and with deep conviction. You know how we lived among you for your sake. ⁶You became imitators of us and of the Lord; in spite of severe suffering, you welcomed the message with the joy given by the Holy Spirit. ⁷And so you became a model to all the believers in Macedonia and Achaia. ⁸The Lord's message rang out from you not only in Macedonia and Achaia—your faith in God has become known everywhere. Therefore we do not need to say anything about it, ⁹for they themselves report what kind of reception you gave us. They tell how you turned to God from idols to serve the living and true God, ¹⁰and to wait for his Son from heaven, whom he raised from the dead—Jesus, who rescues us from the coming wrath.

■ **Paul's Ministry in Thessalonica**
2 You know, brothers, that our visit to you was not a failure. ²We had previously suffered and been insulted in Philippi, as you know, but with the help of our God we dared to tell you his gospel in spite of strong opposition. ³For the appeal we make does not spring from error or impure motives, nor are we trying to trick you. ⁴On the contrary, we speak as men approved by God to be entrusted with the gospel. We are not trying to please men but God, who tests our hearts. ⁵You know we never used flattery, nor did we put on a mask to cover up greed—God is our witness. ⁶We were not looking for praise from men, not from you or anyone else.

As apostles of Christ we could have been a burden to you, ⁷but we were gentle among you, like a mother caring for her little children. ⁸We loved you so much that we were delighted to share with you not only the gospel of God but our lives as well, because you had become so dear to us. ⁹Surely you remember, brothers, our toil and hardship; we worked night and day in order not to be a burden to anyone while we preached the gospel of God to you.

2:9 ■ WORKING FOR A LIVING
Paul supported his own ministry with a trade (tent-making) rather than take funds from others. He did this to avoid suspicion that he was profiting financially from his spiritual work. With the Thessalonians, his hard work gave another advantage: it set a good example for those who were quitting their jobs in anticipation of Christ's return to earth.

¹⁰You are witnesses, and so is God, of how holy, righteous and blameless we were among you who believed. ¹¹For you know that we dealt with each of you as a father deals with his own children, ¹²encouraging, comforting and urging you to live lives worthy of God, who calls you into his kingdom and glory.

¹³And we also thank God continually because, when you received the word of God, which you heard from us, you accepted it not as the word of men, but as it actually is, the word of God, which is at work in you who believe. ¹⁴For you, brothers, became imitators of God's churches in Judea, which are in Christ Jesus: You suffered from your own countrymen the same things those churches suffered from the Jews, ¹⁵who killed the Lord Jesus and the prophets and also drove us out. They displease God and are hostile to all men ¹⁶in their effort to keep us from speaking to the Gentiles so that they may be saved. In this way they always heap up their sins to the limit. The wrath of God has come upon them at last.*a*

■ **Paul's Longing to See the Thessalonians**
¹⁷But, brothers, when we were torn away from you for a short time (in person, not in thought), out of our intense longing we made every effort to see you. ¹⁸For we wanted to come to you—certainly I, Paul, did, again and again—but Satan stopped us.

---

a 1 Greek *Silvanus*, a variant of *Silas*   *b* 1 Some early manuscripts *you from God our Father and the Lord Jesus Christ*   *a* 16 Or *them fully*

19For what is our hope, our joy, or the crown in which we will glory in the presence of our Lord Jesus when he comes? Is it not you? 20Indeed, you are our glory and joy.

3 So when we could stand it no longer, we thought it best to be left by ourselves in Athens. 2We sent Timothy, who is our brother and God's fellow-worker*a* in spreading the gospel of Christ, to strengthen and encourage you in your faith, 3so that no-one would be unsettled by these trials. You know quite well that we were destined for them. 4In fact, when we were with you, we kept telling you that we would be persecuted. And it turned out that way, as you well know. 5For this reason, when I could stand it no longer, I sent to find out about your faith. I was afraid that in some way the tempter might have tempted you and our efforts might have been useless.

3:4 ■ PAUL DEFENDS HIS ACTIONS
First Thessalonians indicates some people had questioned Paul's true motives regarding their church. Throughout his ministry, Paul endured constant criticism and personal attacks. Here he replies by reviewing his history with the church. This section (2:17–3:10) details Paul's foiled attempts at a personal visit and then his sending Timothy as a messenger.

■ Timothy's Encouraging Report
6But Timothy has just now come to us from you and has brought good news about your faith and love. He has told us that you always have pleasant memories of us and that you long to see us, just as we also long to see you. 7Therefore, brothers, in all our distress and persecution we were encouraged about you because of your faith. 8For now we really live, since you are standing firm in the Lord. 9How can we thank God enough for you in return for all the joy we have in the presence of our God because of you? 10Night and day we pray most earnestly that we may see you again and supply what is lacking in your faith.

11Now may our God and Father himself and our Lord Jesus clear the way for us to come to you. 12May the Lord make your love increase and overflow for each other and for everyone else, just as ours does for you. 13May he strengthen your hearts so that you will be blameless and holy in the presence of our God and Father when our Lord Jesus comes with all his holy ones.

■ Living to Please God
4 Finally, brothers, we instructed you how to live in order to please God, as in fact you are living. Now we ask you and urge you in the Lord Jesus to do this more and more. 2For you know what instructions we gave you by the authority of the Lord Jesus. 3It is God's will that you should be sanctified: that you should avoid sexual immorality; 4that each of you should learn to control his own body*a* in a way that is holy and honourable, 5not in passionate lust like the heathen, who do not know God; 6and that

in this matter no-one should wrong his brother or take advantage of him. The Lord will punish men for all such sins, as we have already told you and warned you. 7For God did not call us to be impure, but to live a holy life. 8Therefore, he who rejects this instruction does not reject man but God, who gives you his Holy Spirit.

9Now about brotherly love we do not need to write to you, for you yourselves have been taught by God to love each other. 10And in fact, you do love all the brothers throughout Macedonia. Yet we urge you, brothers, to do so more and more.

11Make it your ambition to lead a quiet life, to mind your own business and to work with your hands, just as we told you, 12so that your daily life may win the respect of outsiders and so that you will not be dependent on anybody.

■ The Coming of the Lord
13Brothers, we do not want you to be ignorant about those who fall asleep, or to grieve like the rest of men, who have no hope. 14We believe that Jesus died and rose again and so we believe that God will bring with Jesus those who have fallen asleep in him. 15According to the Lord's own word, we tell you that we who are still alive, who are left till the coming of the Lord, will certainly not precede those who have fallen asleep. 16For the Lord himself will come down from heaven, with a loud command, with the voice of the archangel and with the trumpet call of God, and the dead in Christ will rise first. 17After that, we who are still alive and are left will be caught up together with them in the clouds to meet the Lord in the air. And so we will be with the Lord for ever. 18Therefore encourage each other with these words.

4:13 ■ THE SLEEP OF DEATH
The Bible sometimes uses the word *asleep* to describe people who have died. In this context, Paul was answering a question the Thessalonians had asked. What of people who died before Christ's second coming – would they be left behind? Paul assures them that all people in Christ would have an after-life with him – not just those still alive when he returned.

---

5 Now, brothers, about times and dates we do not need to write to you, 2for you know very well that the day of the Lord will come like a thief in the night. 3While people are saying, "Peace and safety", destruction will come on them suddenly, as labour pains on a pregnant woman, and they will not escape.

4But you, brothers, are not in darkness so that this day should surprise you like a thief. 5You are all sons of the light and sons of the day. We do not belong to the night or to the darkness. 6So then, let us not be like others, who are asleep, but let us be alert and self-controlled. 7For those who sleep, sleep at night, and those who get drunk, get drunk at night. 8But since we belong to the day, let us be self-controlled,

---

a2 Some manuscripts brother and fellow-worker; other manuscripts brother and God's servant   a4 Or learn to live with his own wife; or learn to acquire a wife putting on faith and love as a breastplate, and the hope of salvation as a helmet. 9For God did not appoint us to suffer wrath but to receive salvation through our Lord Jesus Christ. 10He died for us so that, whether we are awake or asleep, we may live together with him. 11Therefore encourage one another and build each other up, just as in fact you are doing.

■ Final Instructions
12Now we ask you, brothers, to respect those who work hard among you, who are over you in the Lord and who admonish you. 13Hold them in the highest regard in love because of their work. Live in peace with each other. 14And we urge you, brothers, warn those who are idle, encourage the timid, help the weak, be patient with everyone. 15Make sure that nobody pays back wrong for wrong, but always try to be kind to each other and to everyone else.

16Be joyful always; 17pray continually; 18give thanks in all circumstances, for this is God's will for you in Christ Jesus.

19Do not put out the Spirit's fire; 20do not treat prophecies with contempt. 21Test everything. Hold on to the good. 22Avoid every kind of evil.

23May God himself, the God of peace, sanctify you through and through. May your whole spirit, soul and body be kept blameless at the coming of our Lord Jesus Christ. 24The one who calls you is faithful and he will do it.

25Brothers, pray for us. 26Greet all the brothers with a holy kiss. 27I charge you before the Lord to have this letter read to all the brothers.

28The grace of our Lord Jesus Christ be with you.

■ PREPARING FOR THE END
OBSESSED WITH JESUS' SECOND COMING

INSIGHT

NOW, BROTHERS, ABOUT TIMES AND DATES WE DO NOT NEED TO WRITE TO YOU. ■ 5:1

You see them occasionally on the street corners of modern cities: strange, bearded men with hand-lettered wooden signs draped over their bodies. "Jesus is coming again!" they proclaim. "Prepare to meet thy doom!" Similar messages are scrawled on rocks or on motorway bridges. And every few years a new prophet comes along suggesting a new, revised date for Jesus' return.

Archaeologists have yet to unearth Thessalonican graffiti, but this letter makes it clear that 19 centuries ago people were already awaiting Jesus' promised return to earth. In fact, they were worried. What about people who died before Jesus returned? they wondered. Would they somehow miss out on life after death? Paul gives a direct and encouraging answer.

■ A MIXTURE OF FEAR AND HOPE
The Thessalonians had good reason to concern themselves with the future: they lived in constant danger of persecution by the authorities. On any night a knock on the door or the scrape of footsteps outside could mean imprisonment or death. Understandably, the young church looked to Jesus' second coming with longing and hope.

Paul assured them that hope in the future was well-founded, whether or not they lived to see Jesus' return. But he warned against an undue fixation on the future. He urged the Thessalonians to get back to work, indicating that some enthusiasts had quit their jobs to prepare for Jesus' return. Lead a quiet life and mind your own business, Paul advised (4:11).

■ WAITING FOR JESUS' RETURN
The Thessalonians were merely the first in a long line of Christians obsessed with future events. Whole generations since have been caught up in frenzied speculations on the exact time and place of the second coming, only to watch their predictions misfire. Paul shrugs off such speculation (5:1–2). He presents the right way and the wrong way to prepare for Jesus' return.

Paul does not show undue alarm. The mild tone of his rebukes indicates his confidence in the Thessalonians. He asks that they follow God "more and more", as in fact they are already doing (4:1,10; 5:11).

History records that the first readers of this letter responded well. Despite lurking problems (4:3–12), the church in Thessalonica continued to show vigour and health for many years. Christians there stayed so faithful throughout persecutions that their city became known as "The City of Orthodoxy".

□ LIFE QUESTIONS:
How should Jesus' second coming affect us and how can we prepare for it? What extremes does Paul warn against?

2 THESSALONIANS

INTRODUCTION

■ A PATIENT WHO DIDN'T FOLLOW ORDERS

WHEN GOOD ADVICE GOES IGNORED

AND AS FOR YOU, BROTHERS, NEVER TIRE OF DOING WHAT IS RIGHT. ■ 3:13

His light humour and casual manner are gone now. When he was setting the bone, the doctor joked about the benefits of your wearing your arm in a sling every day: instant sympathy from your friends, an opportunity for wild stories on how you got hurt, an easy alibi to avoid heavy work.

But now, three weeks later, lines of concern crease his forehead as he studies the X-rays and notes the slow progress of healing. "I told you to take it easy! Are you giving that arm any rest at all? You can't expect new bone to grow overnight, you know."

When you describe the throbbing pain of the last few days, he grimaces, shakes his head, and scribbles something on a prescription pad. "You shouldn't be feeling pain at this stage", he grumbles. "If you had followed my advice from the beginning you wouldn't need these pills." He then repeats all the instructions he gave you on the first visit, using stronger, less friendly words.

■ SAME ADVICE, STERNER WORDS

The book of 2 Thessalonians resembles such a follow-up visit to a family doctor. If you list the topics Paul covers, you will find an uncanny similarity to the subjects of his first letter: Jesus' second coming, spiritual growth, idleness among certain nonworkers. However, a sterner, more formal approach replaces the warm tenderness of the first letter.

Obviously, the Thessalonians failed to listen well the first time. Paul wrote this second letter just a few months later, summarising his message this way: "So then, brothers, stand firm and hold to the teachings we passed on to you, whether by word of mouth or by letter" (2:15). Instead of coaxing, Paul now commands.

■ STAMPING OUT A RUMOUR

One topic, Jesus' return, dominates 2 Thessalonians more than any other. Church members were stirred up by a false report, allegedly from Paul, claiming that the last days had already arrived (2:2). Paul denies the report and outlines several events that must occur before the day of the Lord arrives.

Here, as elsewhere, the Bible does not focus on the last days in an abstract, theoretical way. Rather, it draws a practical application to how we should live. Paul cautions his readers to be patient and steady. He asks them to trust that Jesus' return will finally bring justice to the earth, urges them to live worthily for that day, and commands them not to tolerate idleness — a prescription for health that has equal potency today.

■ HOW TO READ 2 THESSALONIANS

Second Thessalonians has many parallels to its companion letter. The Christians in Thessalonica were still struggling with major problems, and each of the three chapters of this book concerns one of them.

Chapter 1 gives encouragement to Christians who were undergoing persecution for their faith. Chapter 2 attacks head-on the false teaching about the day of the Lord. Rumours about the day of the Lord had caused great excitement and speculation, leading to the practical errors Paul addresses in chapter 3.

Paul's specific words about what must happen before the day of the Lord make this letter a key part of New Testament prophecy. The prophecy passages aren't self-explanatory, and may require a Bible reference book for understanding.

Although 2 Thessalonians is Paul's shortest letter to a church, it contains four of his prayers. Note especially his concern for the Thessalonians as expressed in the prayers.

■ 3-TRACK READING PLAN

For an explanation and complete listing of the 3-track reading plan, turn to page x.

■ TRACK 1:
Two-Week Courses on the
Bible
See page x for information on
these courses.

■ TRACK 2:
An Overview of
2 Thessalonians in 1 Day

□ Day 1. Read the
Introduction to
2 Thessalonians, then chapter
2, the key chapter predicting
what events will precede
Jesus' return.
Now turn to page xi for your
next Track 2 reading project.

■ TRACK 3:
All of 2 Thessalonians in
2 Days
After you have read through
2 Thessalonians, turn to pages
xii–xiii for your next Track 3
reading project.

□ 1–2 □ 3

1 Paul, Silas*a* and Timothy,

To the church of the Thessalonians in God our
Father and the Lord Jesus Christ:

²Grace and peace to you from God the Father and
the Lord Jesus Christ.

■ Thanksgiving and Prayer
³We ought always to thank God for you, brothers,
and rightly so, because your faith is growing more
and more, and the love every one of you has for
each other is increasing. ⁴Therefore, among God's
churches we boast about your perseverance and
faith in all the persecutions and trials you are enduring.
⁵All this is evidence that God's judgment is right,
and as a result you will be counted worthy of the
kingdom of God, for which you are suffering. ⁶God
is just: He will pay back trouble to those who trouble you ⁷and give relief to you who are troubled,
and to us as well. This will happen when the Lord
Jesus is revealed from heaven in blazing fire with his
powerful angels. ⁸He will punish those who do not
know God and do not obey the gospel of our Lord
Jesus. ⁹They will be punished with everlasting destruction and shut out from the presence of the
Lord and from the majesty of his power ¹⁰on the day
he comes to be glorified in his holy people and to
be marvelled at among all those who have believed.
This includes you, because you believed our testimony to you.

1:6 ■ IS LIFE UNFAIR?
This question bothers nearly everyone who gets
persecuted or who sees someone profit from
wrong-doing. Paul's answer would probably be,
"Yes, but only temporarily". He had the firm
conviction that one day God would indeed turn
the tables on the unfairness of life.

¹¹With this in mind, we constantly pray for you,
that our God may count you worthy of his calling,
and that by his power he may fulfil every good purpose of yours and every act prompted by your faith.
¹²We pray this so that the name of our Lord Jesus
may be glorified in you, and you in him, according
to the grace of our God and the Lord Jesus Christ.*b*

■ The Man of Lawlessness
2 Concerning the coming of our Lord Jesus Christ
and our being gathered to him, we ask you,
brothers, ²not to become easily unsettled or
alarmed by some prophecy, report or letter supposed to have come from us, saying that the day of
the Lord has already come. ³Don't let anyone deceive you in any way, for ⌐that day will not come⌐
until the rebellion occurs and the man of lawlessness*a* is revealed, the man doomed to destruction.
⁴He will oppose and will exalt himself over everything that is called God or is worshipped, so that he
sets himself up in God's temple, proclaiming himself
to be God.
⁵Don't you remember that when I was with you
I used to tell you these things? ⁶And now you know
what is holding him back, so that he may be revealed at the proper time. ⁷For the secret power of
lawlessness is already at work; but the one who now
holds it back will continue to do so till he is taken
out of the way. ⁸And then the lawless one will be
revealed, whom the Lord Jesus will overthrow with
the breath of his mouth and destroy by the splendour of his coming. ⁹The coming of the lawless one
will be in accordance with the work of Satan displayed in all kinds of counterfeit miracles, signs and
wonders, ¹⁰and in every sort of evil that deceives
those who are perishing. They perish because they
refused to love the truth and so be saved. ¹¹For this
reason God sends them a powerful delusion so that
they will believe the lie ¹²and so that all will be condemned who have not believed the truth but have
delighted in wickedness.

2:7 ■ EXACTLY WHAT WILL HAPPEN?
Nearly every age has come up with a different
interpretation of this passage. No-one is certain
about the "secret power of lawlessness" or "the
one who now holds it back". A British writer, Tom
Davies, quite sincerely, proposes television as the
lawless one, since it has made violence so
popular. This passage is obscure because Paul
refers to further information he had taught the
Thessalonians in person. (Even another New
Testament author admitted that Paul's letters
contain "some things that are hard to understand"
[2 Peter 3:16].)

*a*1 Greek Silvanus, a variant of Silas   *b*12 Or God and Lord, Jesus Christ   *a*3 Some manuscripts sin

■ Stand Firm

[13]But we ought always to thank God for you, brothers loved by the Lord, because from the beginning God chose you[b] to be saved through the sanctifying work of the Spirit and through belief in the truth. [14]He called you to this through our gospel, that you might share in the glory of our Lord Jesus Christ. [15]So then, brothers, stand firm and hold to the teachings[c] we passed on to you, whether by word of mouth or by letter.

[16]May our Lord Jesus Christ himself and God our Father, who loved us and by his grace gave us eternal encouragement and good hope, [17]encourage your hearts and strengthen you in every good deed and word.

■ Request for Prayer

3 Finally, brothers, pray for us that the message of the Lord may spread rapidly and be honoured, just as it was with you. [2]And pray that we may be delivered from wicked and evil men, for not everyone has faith. [3]But the Lord is faithful, and he will strengthen and protect you from the evil one. [4]We have confidence in the Lord that you are doing and will continue to do the things we command. [5]May the Lord direct your hearts into God's love and Christ's perseverance.

■ Warning Against Idleness

[6]In the name of the Lord Jesus Christ, we command you, brothers, to keep away from every brother who is idle and does not live according to the teaching[a] you received from us. [7]For you yourselves know how you ought to follow our example. We were not idle when we were with you, [8]nor did we eat anyone's food without paying for it. On the contrary, we worked night and day, labouring and toiling so that we would not be a burden to any of you. [9]We did this, not because we do not have the right to such help, but in order to make ourselves a model for you to follow. [10]For even when we were with you, we gave you this rule: "If a man will not work, he shall not eat."

3:10 ■ NO WORK, NO EAT

Paul's first letter to the Thessalonians had affirmed that Jesus could return at any time, unexpectedly. Evidently, this anticipation had prompted some to quit their jobs and do nothing but wait for the second coming. (Dozens of times religious sects have followed the same pattern by heading for remote areas to await Christ's return.) To correct the imbalance, in this second letter Paul stresses that certain events must happen before Christ's return. He also warns strongly against idleness.

[11]We hear that some among you are idle. They are not busy; they are busybodies. [12]Such people we command and urge in the Lord Jesus Christ to settle down and earn the bread they eat. [13]And as for you, brothers, never tire of doing what is right.

[14]If anyone does not obey our instruction in this letter, take special note of him. Do not associate with him, in order that he may feel ashamed. [15]Yet do not regard him as an enemy, but warn him as a brother.

■ Final Greetings

[16]Now may the Lord of peace himself give you peace at all times and in every way. The Lord be with all of you.

[17]I, Paul, write this greeting in my own hand, which is the distinguishing mark in all my letters. This is how I write.

[18]The grace of our Lord Jesus Christ be with you all.

---

[b] 13 Some manuscripts *because God chose you as his firstfruits*　　　[c] 15 Or *traditions*　　　[a] 6 Or *tradition*

1 TIMOTHY

■ THE HARDEST JOB

TIMOTHY STEPS INTO A HORNET'S NEST

DON'T LET ANYONE LOOK DOWN ON YOU BECAUSE YOU ARE YOUNG, BUT SET AN EXAMPLE FOR THE BELIEVERS. ■ 4:12

Who has the most difficult job? A brain surgeon? A trapeze artist who risks death with every leap? A nuclear engineer? Or perhaps an air traffic controller, who determines the safety of thousands of passengers. A number of professions might be nominated as the most difficult of all.

But if the apostle Paul were alive today, to that question he would very probably reply, "Without doubt – a pastor's job is the hardest." In contrast to professionals who specialise, a pastor must call upon wide-ranging skills. In a given week a pastor may act as a psychologist, priest, social worker, hospital chaplain, administrator, personnel supervisor, philosopher, and communicator.

Paul was acutely aware of the vital nature of such a job. Churches sprouted up wherever he visited, but whether they survived or failed depended largely on what kind of local leadership developed.

■ FINAL WORDS TO A YOUNG FRIEND

To assure that his work would continue, Paul turned more and more to a few loyal friends, especially Timothy and Titus. He wrote them explicit instructions in the three letters that follow, known collectively as "The Pastoral Letters".

Paul wrote 1 Timothy near the end of his life. Rugged years of ministry had passed, years marked by stonings, beatings, jailings, and riots. Paul knew that his age, his enemies, or the increasingly brutal Roman empire would soon catch up with him.

Timothy, a young man, ranked high in Paul's esteem. Converted during Paul's first missionary journey, he had over the years gained the apostle's complete trust. When a volcano of discontent rumbled in some distant church like Corinth or Thessalonica, Paul quickly dispatched Timothy to try and prevent an eruption.

"I have no-one else like him," Paul once wrote of Timothy. "As a son with his father he has served with me in the work of the gospel" (Philippians 2:20,22). Through a swarm of controversies, into prison, on the road – wherever Paul went – Timothy loyally followed. Six of Paul's letters begin with the news that Timothy is at his side.

■ TIMOTHY BECOMES A PASTOR

Timothy took on, at Paul's request, that difficult job of heading a local church. The congregation at Ephesus, loose and informal, needed order and a more defined structure. To muddle the scene further, certain members of the church had embraced false doctrines. In this letter, Paul advises his understudy on such matters as worship procedures, the control of unruly women, leadership standards, and policies regarding widows, slaves, and rich people.

Although this book addresses a historical situation from the first century, many problems in the early church – underpaid staff members, a generation gap, an integrity shortage, abuse of social aid, love of money – persist today. A pastor's job description hasn't changed much, or grown any easier, over the centuries.

■ HOW TO READ 1 TIMOTHY

Despite a weak stomach and timid disposition, Timothy had proved his mettle to Paul in many ways, and Paul wrote this letter to challenge him to a difficult task.

Paul doesn't give many details on the false doctrines Timothy had to combat. These letters, however, include vague hints about

super-spiritual living, Jewish genealogies, myths, and fables. Look for the problems Paul alludes to and ask yourself whether they have any modern equivalents.

In his instructions, Paul counselled Timothy to combat heresy not by being forceful and argumentative, but by living an exemplary life and by bringing order to the church. Paul's challenge to live a model life applies directly to us; it remains a powerful prescription for the Christian life.

■ 3-TRACK READING PLAN

For an explanation and complete listing of the 3-track reading plan, turn to page x.

■ TRACK 1:
Two-Week Courses on the Bible
See page x for information on these courses.

■ TRACK 2:
An Overview of 1 Timothy in

1 Day
☐ Day 1. Read the Introduction to 1 Timothy, then chapter 1, which serves as a good introduction to Paul's "Pastoral Letters".
Now turn to page xi for your next Track 2 reading project.

■ TRACK 3:
All of 1 Timothy in 4 Days
After you have read through 1 Timothy, turn to pages xii–xiii for your next Track 3 reading project.

☐ 1–2 ☐ 3–4 ☐ 5   ☐ 6

1 Paul, an apostle of Christ Jesus by the command of God our Saviour and of Christ Jesus our hope,

[2]To Timothy my true son in the faith:

Grace, mercy and peace from God the Father and Christ Jesus our Lord.

■ Warning Against False Teachers of the Law
[3]As I urged you when I went into Macedonia, stay there in Ephesus so that you may command certain men not to teach false doctrines any longer [4]nor to devote themselves to myths and endless genealogies. These promote controversies rather than God's work—which is by faith. [5]The goal of this command is love, which comes from a pure heart and a good conscience and a sincere faith. [6]Some have wandered away from these and turned to meaningless talk. [7]They want to be teachers of the law, but they do not know what they are talking about or what they so confidently affirm.

■ The Lord's Grace to Paul
[12]I thank Christ Jesus our Lord, who has given me strength, that he considered me faithful, appointing me to his service. [13]Even though I was once a blasphemer and a persecutor and a violent man, I was shown mercy because I acted in ignorance and unbelief. [14]The grace of our Lord was poured out on me abundantly, along with the faith and love that are in Christ Jesus.

[15]Here is a trustworthy saying that deserves full acceptance: Christ Jesus came into the world to save sinners—of whom I am the worst. [16]But for that very reason I was shown mercy so that in me, the worst of sinners, Christ Jesus might display his unlimited patience as an example for those who would believe on him and receive eternal life. [17]Now to the King eternal, immortal, invisible, the only God, be honour and glory for ever and ever. Amen.

[18]Timothy, my son, I give you this instruction in keeping with the prophecies once made about you, so that by following them you may fight the good

---

1:3 ■ STRATEGIC PLACE
The city of Ephesus crops up throughout the New Testament, which indicates its strategic importance as gateway to Asia. Paul's first visit there resulted in a major riot (Acts 19). He nevertheless stayed on three years, instructing believers and establishing a powerful church. As this letter was written, Paul's trusted associate Timothy was serving as pastor in Ephesus. Revelation 2 indicates that Timothy had mixed success in combating the problems identified in this letter.

1:18 ■ TIMOTHY'S CALLING
In three separate places in his letters to Timothy, Paul refers to his associate's special calling to the ministry. This passage alludes to prophecies made about him. 1 Timothy 4:14 mentions a special ceremony when the church elders "laid their hands" on him. And in 2 Timothy (1:6) Paul specifies that he, too, had been part of such a ceremony. Timothy came from a Christian household; both his grandmother and mother were believers (2 Timothy 1:5).

---

[8]We know that the law is good if one uses it properly. [9]We also know that law[a] is made not for the righteous but for lawbreakers and rebels, the ungodly and sinful, the unholy and irreligious; for those who kill their fathers or mothers, for murderers, [10]for adulterers and perverts, for slave traders and liars and perjurers—and for whatever else is contrary to the sound doctrine [11]that conforms to the glorious gospel of the blessed God, which he entrusted to me.

fight, [19]holding on to faith and a good conscience. Some have rejected these and so have shipwrecked their faith. [20]Among them are Hymenaeus and Alexander, whom I have handed over to Satan to be taught not to blaspheme.

■ Instructions on Worship
2 I urge, then, first of all, that requests, prayers, intercession and thanksgiving be made for everyone—[2]for kings and all those in authority, that we may live peaceful and quiet lives in all godliness

[a]9 Or that the law

and holiness. ³This is good, and pleases God our Saviour, ⁴who wants all men to be saved and to come to a knowledge of the truth. ⁵For there is one God and one mediator between God and men, the man Christ Jesus, ⁶who gave himself as a ransom for all men—the testimony given in its proper time. ⁷And for this purpose I was appointed a herald and an apostle—I am telling the truth, I am not lying—and a teacher of the true faith to the Gentiles.

2:1 ■ TIME TO GET ORGANISED

Chapters 2 and 3 give detailed instructions concerning worship and church organisation. When Paul wrote this letter, near the end of his life, churches such as Ephesus had been established for many years. The time had come for a more formal organisation and for instructions governing appropriate and inappropriate behaviour in church.

⁸I want men everywhere to lift up holy hands in prayer, without anger or disputing.

⁹I also want women to dress modestly, with decency and propriety, not with braided hair or gold or pearls or expensive clothes, ¹⁰but with good deeds, appropriate for women who profess to worship God.

¹¹A woman should learn in quietness and full submission. ¹²I do not permit a woman to teach or to have authority over a man; she must be silent. ¹³For Adam was formed first, then Eve. ¹⁴And Adam was not the one deceived; it was the woman who was deceived and became a sinner. ¹⁵But women*a* will be saved*b* through childbearing—if they continue in faith, love and holiness with propriety.

■ Overseers and Deacons

3 Here is a trustworthy saying: If anyone sets his heart on being an overseer,*a* he desires a noble task. ²Now the overseer must be above reproach, the husband of but one wife, temperate, self-controlled, respectable, hospitable, able to teach, ³not given to drunkenness, not violent but gentle, not quarrelsome, not a lover of money. ⁴He must manage his own family well and see that his children obey him with proper respect. ⁵(If anyone does not know how to manage his own family, how can he take care of God's church?) ⁶He must not be a recent convert, or he may become conceited and fall under the same judgment as the devil. ⁷He must also have a good reputation with outsiders, so that he will not fall into disgrace and into the devil's trap.

⁸Deacons, likewise, are to be men worthy of respect, sincere, not indulging in much wine, and not pursuing dishonest gain. ⁹They must keep hold of the deep truths of the faith with a clear conscience. ¹⁰They must first be tested; and then if there is nothing against them, let them serve as deacons.

¹¹In the same way, their wives*b* are to be women worthy of respect, not malicious talkers but temperate and trustworthy in everything.

¹²A deacon must be the husband of but one wife and must manage his children and his household

well. ¹³Those who have served well gain an excellent standing and great assurance in their faith in Christ Jesus.

3:10 ■ TOO YOUNG FOR THE JOB?

Few people succeed in athletics or professional careers without practice, time, and effort. Paul looked for some of those same qualities in choosing experienced leaders for churches. Ironically, however, Timothy himself was only in his thirties. His upbringing had prepared him early for spiritual leadership, and in his case Paul urged boldness and confidence (4:12).

¹⁴Although I hope to come to you soon, I am writing you these instructions so that, ¹⁵if I am delayed, you will know how people ought to conduct themselves in God's household, which is the church of the living God, the pillar and foundation of the truth. ¹⁶Beyond all question, the mystery of godliness is great:

He*c* appeared in a body,*d*
   was vindicated by the Spirit,
was seen by angels,
   was preached among the nations,
was believed on in the world,
   was taken up in glory.

■ Instructions to Timothy

4 The Spirit clearly says that in later times some will abandon the faith and follow deceiving spirits and things taught by demons. ²Such teachings come through hypocritical liars, whose consciences have been seared as with a hot iron. ³They forbid people to marry and order them to abstain from certain foods, which God created to be received with thanksgiving by those who believe and who know the truth. ⁴For everything God created is good, and nothing is to be rejected if it is received with thanksgiving, ⁵because it is consecrated by the word of God and prayer.

⁶If you point these things out to the brothers, you will be a good minister of Christ Jesus, brought up in the truths of the faith and of the good teaching that you have followed. ⁷Have nothing to do with godless myths and old wives' tales; rather, train yourself to be godly. ⁸For physical training is of some value, but godliness has value for all things, holding promise for both the present life and the life to come.

⁹This is a trustworthy saying that deserves full acceptance ¹⁰(and for this we labour and strive), that we have put our hope in the living God, who is the Saviour of all men, and especially of those who believe.

¹¹Command and teach these things. ¹²Don't let anyone look down on you because you are young, but set an example for the believers in speech, in life, in love, in faith and in purity. ¹³Until I come, devote yourself to the public reading of Scripture, to preaching and to teaching. ¹⁴Do not neglect your

---

a 15 Greek *she*   *b* 15 Or *restored*   *a* 1 Traditionally *bishop*; also in verse 2   *b* 11 Or *way, deaconesses*   *c* 16 Some manuscripts *God*
d 16 Or *in the flesh*

gift, which was given you through a prophetic message when the body of elders laid their hands on you.

¹⁵Be diligent in these matters; give yourself wholly to them, so that everyone may see your progress. ¹⁶Watch your life and doctrine closely. Persevere in them, because if you do, you will save both yourself and your hearers.

■ Advice About Widows, Elders and Slaves

5 Do not rebuke an older man harshly, but exhort him as if he were your father. Treat younger men as brothers, ²older women as mothers, and younger women as sisters, with absolute purity.

³Give proper recognition to those widows who are really in need. ⁴But if a widow has children or grandchildren, these should learn first of all to put

■ ATHLETE IN TRAINING
OVERCOMING PERSONAL DISABILITIES

INSIGHT

TRAIN YOURSELF TO BE GODLY. FOR PHYSICAL TRAINING IS OF SOME VALUE, BUT GODLINESS HAS VALUE FOR ALL THINGS, HOLDING PROMISE FOR BOTH THE PRESENT LIFE AND THE LIFE TO COME. ■ 4:7–8

Bob Champion was a fit and successful 31-year-old. He had won more than 350 steeplechase races in only 12 years. Then they told him that he had only 8 more months to live. His feelings of good health were an illusion often associated with his particular form of illness – he had cancer.

During the Spring he'd raced at Stratford, fallen and been kicked by his horse. The pain was incredible but his instincts as a jockey forced him back into the saddle and he had carried on not knowing that serious damage had been done. It wasn't until he returned from a holiday and mentioned the persistent lump to one of the vets at the stables that he realised there was a problem.

The doctors told the jockey that he had a 75 per cent chance of full recovery if he underwent a drastic new cancer treatment. With those odds, he agreed to the treatment and went through months of the most devastating side effects: terrible sickness; agonising constipation; loss of hair; loss of weight; weakness and muscle wastage; numbness in his hands and feet; lung damage; and in the long term, sterility. The whole time, his worst fear was that he would go through all this and not be able to ride again. A professional sportsman had not been in his situation before and none of the doctors seemed very confident that he would ride again.

■ AGAINST ALL ODDS
Bob was determined never to give in and give up racing. He persisted in attending race meetings in between treatments and when he was finally released from hospital, it took him only 7 months to get his old job back as a stable jockey. It was an uphill struggle though and he had to adjust to many things: he went to a warmer climate to train; he had to put on weight; he played tennis and ran in bare feet to get the feeling back; he raced on the flat; he

was "jocked off" or replaced by other jockeys in races he was due to run. He even enjoyed falling off, as getting back on instantly proved that he'd not lost his nerve.

Finally, his dream came true and he proved to himself, to a crowd of 60,000 and to a TV audience of 750 million that he was still one of the very best despite his long illness, when he won the Grand National on Aldaniti (one of the nation's favourite horses).

Bob Champion had lived up to his name. Through single-minded determination he had set himself a goal and by his 100% effort every day he had achieved it. Not only had he returned to peak physical condition, but he had won one of the hardest and most prestigious races in the country.

■ A LESSON FROM ATHLETICS
Paul uses the analogy of physical training in his letter to Timothy, urging him to train himself for godliness the same way disciplined athletes train for competition. Bob Champion had to overcome physical barriers; Timothy faced personality barriers. Several times Paul refers to Timothy's reserved, timid disposition, which probably contributed to his chronic stomach trouble.

Given his shyness and his half-Jewish, half-Gentile ancestry, Timothy did not seem the ideal choice to fight heresy in a turbulent church. But Paul was convinced he could do the job. He encouraged Timothy with such motivating phrases as "I charge you" and "I urge you". He also reminded Timothy of his ordination, a commitment he had made long before.

Harassed Christians need a model, an example of how they should live, perhaps even more than they need words of wisdom. In 1 Timothy, Paul urges his loyal friend to become that model by accepting the discipline and hard work required.

□ LIFE QUESTIONS:
Do you have any personality traits that make Christian service seem difficult? What specific "training instructions" did Paul give Timothy that might also apply to you?

their religion into practice by caring for their own family and so repaying their parents and grand-parents, for this is pleasing to God. 5The widow who is really in need and left all alone puts her hope in God and continues night and day to pray and to ask God for help. 6But the widow who lives for pleasure is dead even while she lives. 7Give the people these instructions, too, so that no-one may be open to blame. 8If anyone does not provide for his relatives, and especially for his immediate family, he has de-nied the faith and is worse than an unbeliever.

9No widow may be put on the list of widows un-less she is over sixty, has been faithful to her hus-band,ᵃ 10and is well known for her good deeds, such as bringing up children, showing hospitality, washing the feet of the saints, helping those in trou-ble and devoting herself to all kinds of good deeds.

5:9 ■ WELFARE MENTALITY

Chapter 5 gives fascinating insight into early church problems that have parallels in today's social programmes. Evidently, some members of the Ephesus congregation had been taking advantage of others' charity. Young widows were using the church's resources when they should have been looking for other means of support. Paul outlines a form of "enrolment" to establish who was truly needy.

11As for younger widows, do not put them on such a list. For when their sensual desires overcome their dedication to Christ, they want to marry. 12Thus they bring judgment on themselves, because they have broken their first pledge. 13Besides, they get into the habit of being idle and going about from house to house. And not only do they become idlers, but also gossips and busybodies, saying things they ought not to. 14So I counsel younger widows to marry, to have children, to manage their homes and to give the enemy no opportunity for slander. 15Some have in fact already turned away to follow Satan.

16If any woman who is a believer has widows in her family, she should help them and not let the church be burdened with them, so that the church can help those widows who are really in need.

17The elders who direct the affairs of the church well are worthy of double honour, especially those whose work is preaching and teaching. 18For the Scripture says, "Do not muzzle the ox while it is treading out the grain,"ᵇ and "The worker deserves his wages."ᶜ 19Do not entertain an accusation against an elder unless it is brought by two or three witnesses. 20Those who sin are to be rebuked pub-licly, so that the others may take warning.

21I charge you, in the sight of God and Christ Jesus and the elect angels, to keep these instructions without partiality, and to do nothing out of favourit-ism.

22Do not be hasty in the laying on of hands, and do not share in the sins of others. Keep yourself pure.

23Stop drinking only water, and use a little wine because of your stomach and your frequent ill-nesses.

24The sins of some men are obvious, reaching the place of judgment ahead of them; the sins of others trail behind them. 25In the same way, good deeds are obvious, and even those that are not cannot be hidden.

6 All who are under the yoke of slavery should consider their masters worthy of full respect, so that God's name and our teaching may not be slan-dered. 2Those who have believing masters are not to show less respect for them because they are brothers. Instead, they are to serve them even bet-ter, because those who benefit from their service are believers, and dear to them. These are the things you are to teach and urge on them.

■ Love of Money

3If anyone teaches false doctrines and does not agree to the sound instruction of our Lord Jesus Christ and to godly teaching, 4he is conceited and understands nothing. He has an unhealthy interest in controversies and quarrels about words that re-sult in envy, strife, malicious talk, evil suspicions 5and constant friction between men of corrupt mind, who have been robbed of the truth and who think that godliness is a means to financial gain.

6But godliness with contentment is great gain. 7For we brought nothing into the world, and we can take nothing out of it. 8But if we have food and clothing, we will be content with that. 9People who want to get rich fall into temptation and a trap and into many foolish and harmful desires that plunge men into ruin and destruction. 10For the love of money is a root of all kinds of evil. Some people, eager for money, have wandered from the faith and pierced themselves with many griefs.

6:7 ■ TWO FAMILIAR QUOTES

Paul's parting advice to Timothy includes two sayings that have become familiar quotations. Verse 7 is usually quoted accurately. But verse 10, also familiar, is often misquoted as "money is the root of all evil". An established church had already developed a professional class of Christian workers, and Paul warned against the motive of profit-seeking.

■ Paul's Charge to Timothy

11But you, man of God, flee from all this, and pur-sue righteousness, godliness, faith, love, endurance and gentleness. 12Fight the good fight of the faith. Take hold of the eternal life to which you were called when you made your good confession in the presence of many witnesses. 13In the sight of God, who gives life to everything, and of Christ Jesus, who while testifying before Pontius Pilate made the good confession, I charge you 14to keep this com-mand without spot or blame until the appearing of our Lord Jesus Christ, 15which God will bring about in his own time—God, the blessed and only Ruler, the King of kings and Lord of lords, 16who alone is immortal and who lives in unapproachable light,

ᵃ9 Or has had but one husband   ᵇ18 Deut. 25:4   ᶜ18 Luke 10:7

whom no-one has seen or can see. To him be honour and might for ever. Amen.

[17]Command those who are rich in this present world not to be arrogant nor to put their hope in wealth, which is so uncertain, but to put their hope in God, who richly provides us with everything for our enjoyment. [18]Command them to do good, to be rich in good deeds, and to be generous and willing to share. [19]In this way they will lay up treasure for themselves as a firm foundation for the coming age, so that they may take hold of the life that is truly life.

[20]Timothy, guard what has been entrusted to your care. Turn away from godless chatter and the opposing ideas of what is falsely called knowledge, [21]which some have professed and in so doing have wandered from the faith.

Grace be with you.

2 TIMOTHY

■ PASSING THE TORCH

THE APOSTLE PAUL'S LAST KNOWN WORDS

AND THE THINGS YOU HAVE HEARD ME SAY IN THE PRESENCE OF MANY WITNESSES
ENTRUST TO RELIABLE MEN WHO WILL ALSO BE QUALIFIED TO TEACH OTHERS. ■ 2:2

Every four years the world watches an ancient ritual unfold: the passing of the Olympic torch. The spectacular pageantry of the opening ceremonies cannot begin until the final carrier of the torch arrives in the stadium. The torch symbolically links the modern Olympic Games to their 2,700-year history.

"Passing the torch" has become a familiar phrase, used when the Chairman of ICI introduces his successor to the public, or when an esteemed orchestra conductor hands over his baton, or a great sports figure tutors her replacement. Often the retiring person delivers an emotional farewell speech. He or she has finished the work; the time has come to pass the torch to another.

■ CHOOSING TIMOTHY
As the weary apostle Paul neared certain death, with imprisonment preventing him from travelling, he, too, began to think of a successor. It was time to pass the torch, and he decided on the young man Timothy.

At first glance, shy Timothy hardly seemed an adequate replacement, but Paul had few options. "Everyone in the province of Asia has deserted me," he lamented (1:15). This letter, 2 Timothy, reveals his deep reliance on Timothy's loyal friendship. Life was closing in on

the apostle, and he felt a sombre sense of abandonment.

At times in this letter, Paul lectures Timothy like a master sergeant, calling on him to stand firm, overcome shame, and hold to the faith. Elsewhere, his tone softens into the fond affirmation of a grateful father. Throughout, the bonds of deep friendship are evident: from Paul recalling Timothy's family heritage (1:5) to his urging Timothy to bring him a heavy coat before winter (4:13,21).

■ AN EMOTIONAL MOMENT
Paul's moods alternate between sadness and confidence, nostalgia and grave concern. As he wrote this letter, he contemplated the disquieting months ahead and the prospect of young, divided churches left without his guidance. In these, his last known written words, he sought to prepare Timothy for the inevitable day when the message of God would depend on him and other reliable workers (2:2).

Despite his circumstances, Paul's farewell message from behind bars is gracious, even triumphant. The spreading of the gospel is far too big a task to be limited to any one man. "I am . . . chained like a criminal," Paul declares, "but God's word is not chained" (2:9).

■ HOW TO READ 2 TIMOTHY

Second Timothy has proved encouraging to Christian workers throughout history. Paul, facing death, did not wallow in self-pity, but instead used this last communication to inspire and challenge his associate Timothy.

This letter reveals much about Paul's emotional state and physical circumstances. As you read it, look for glimpses into Paul's loneliness and suffering. The apostle tells where he turned for strength when he faced personal trials.

In addition, 2 Timothy gives much valuable counsel to those of us who, like Timothy, have inherited the task of representing Christ on earth. Paul stresses the importance of relying on Scripture and of living a life of discipline. As you read this letter, put yourself in Timothy's place; imagine receiving one last personal letter from your great mentor. What final words of advice does he give?

■ 3-TRACK READING PLAN

For an explanation and complete listing of the 3-track reading plan, turn to page x.

■ TRACK 1:
Two-Week Courses on the
Bible
See page x for information on
these courses.

■ TRACK 2:
An Overview of 2 Timothy in
1 Day

☐ Day 1. Read the
Introduction to 2 Timothy and
then chapter 2, which
contains a summary of Paul's
challenge to Timothy.
Now turn to page xi for your
next Track 2 reading project.

■ TRACK 3:
All of 2 Timothy in 4 Days
After you have read through
2 Timothy, turn to pages
xii–xiii for your next Track 3
reading project.

☐ 1   ☐ 2   ☐ 3   ☐ 4

1 Paul, an apostle of Christ Jesus by the will of
God, according to the promise of life that is in
Christ Jesus,

2To Timothy, my dear son:

Grace, mercy and peace from God the Father and
Christ Jesus our Lord.

■ Encouragement to Be Faithful

3I thank God, whom I serve, as my forefathers did,
with a clear conscience, as night and day I constantly remember you in my prayers. 4Recalling
your tears, I long to see you, so that I may be filled
with joy. 5I have been reminded of your sincere
faith, which first lived in your grandmother Lois and
in your mother Eunice and, I am persuaded, now
lives in you also. 6For this reason I remind you to fan
into flame the gift of God, which is in you through
the laying on of my hands. 7For God did not give us
a spirit of timidity, but a spirit of power, of love and
of self-discipline.

8So do not be ashamed to testify about our Lord,
or ashamed of me his prisoner. But join with me in
suffering for the gospel, by the power of God, 9who
has saved us and called us to a holy life—not because of anything we have done but because of his
own purpose and grace. This grace was given us in
Christ Jesus before the beginning of time, 10but it
has now been revealed through the appearing of our
Saviour, Christ Jesus, who has destroyed death and
has brought life and immortality to light through the
gospel. 11And of this gospel I was appointed a herald
and an apostle and a teacher. 12That is why I am suffering as I am. Yet I am not ashamed, because I know
whom I have believed, and am convinced that he is
able to guard what I have entrusted to him for that
day. 13What you heard from me, keep as the pattern of
sound teaching, with faith and love in Christ Jesus.
14Guard the good deposit that was entrusted to
you—guard it with the help of the Holy Spirit who
lives in us.

15You know that everyone in the province of Asia
has deserted me, including Phygelus and Hermoge-
nes. 16May the Lord show mercy to the household of
Onesiphorus, because he often refreshed me and

was not ashamed of my chains. 17On the contrary,
when he was in Rome, he searched hard for me until
he found me. 18May the Lord grant that he will find
mercy from the Lord on that day! You know very
well in how many ways he helped me in Ephesus.

2 You then, my son, be strong in the grace that is
in Christ Jesus. 2And the things you have heard
me say in the presence of many witnesses entrust to
reliable men who will also be qualified to teach
others. 3Endure hardship with us like a good soldier
of Christ Jesus. 4No-one serving as a soldier gets involved in civilian affairs—he wants to please his
commanding officer. 5Similarly, if anyone competes
as an athlete, he does not receive the victor's crown
unless he competes according to the rules. 6The
hardworking farmer should be the first to receive a
share of the crops. 7Reflect on what I am saying, for
the Lord will give you insight into all this.

> **2:4 ■ SOLDIER, ATHLETE, FARMER**
> Writing to a friend who knew him well, Paul saw
> no need to expand on the three analogies in this
> paragraph; he simply mentions them and tells
> Timothy to reflect on them. Paul was fully
> conscious of the threats and dangers facing his
> own life, and he wanted Timothy to train himself in
> preparation for any hardships that he might have
> to face.

8Remember Jesus Christ, raised from the dead,
descended from David. This is my gospel, 9for
which I am suffering even to the point of being
chained like a criminal. But God's word is not
chained. 10Therefore I endure everything for the
sake of the elect, that they too may obtain the salvation that is in Christ Jesus, with eternal glory.
11Here is a trustworthy saying:

If we died with him,
    we will also live with him;
12if we endure,
    we will also reign with him.
If we disown him,
    he will also disown us;
13if we are faithless,
    he will remain faithful,
    for he cannot disown himself.

■ A Workman Approved by God

14Keep reminding them of these things. Warn them before God against quarrelling about words; it is of no value, and only ruins those who listen. 15Do your best to present yourself to God as one approved, a workman who does not need to be ashamed and who correctly handles the word of truth. 16Avoid godless chatter, because those who indulge in it will become more and more ungodly. 17Their teaching will spread like gangrene. Among them are Hymenaeus and Philetus, 18who have wandered away from the truth. They say that the resurrection has already taken place, and they destroy the faith of some. 19Nevertheless, God's solid foundation stands firm, sealed with this inscription: "The Lord knows those who are his,"*a* and, "Everyone who confesses the name of the Lord must turn away from wickedness."

20In a large house there are articles not only of gold and silver, but also of wood and clay; some are for noble purposes and some for ignoble. 21If a man cleanses himself from the latter, he will be an instrument for noble purposes, made holy, useful to the Master and prepared to do any good work.

22Flee the evil desires of youth, and pursue righteousness, faith, love and peace, along with those who call on the Lord out of a pure heart. 23Don't have anything to do with foolish and stupid arguments, because you know they produce quarrels. 24And the Lord's servant must not quarrel; instead, he must be kind to everyone, able to teach, not resentful. 25Those who oppose him he must gently instruct, in the hope that God will grant them repentance leading them to a knowledge of the truth, 26and that they will come to their senses and escape from the trap of the devil, who has taken them captive to do his will.

■ Godlessness in the Last Days

3 But mark this: There will be terrible times in the last days. 2People will be lovers of themselves, lovers of money, boastful, proud, abusive, disobedient to their parents, ungrateful, unholy, 3without love, unforgiving, slanderous, without self-control, brutal, not lovers of the good, 4treacherous, rash, conceited, lovers of pleasure rather than lovers of God — 5having a form of godliness but denying its power. Have nothing to do with them.

6They are the kind who worm their way into homes and gain control over weak-willed women, who are loaded down with sins and are swayed by all kinds of evil desires, 7always learning but never able to acknowledge the truth. 8Just as Jannes and Jambres opposed Moses, so also these men oppose the truth — men of depraved minds, who, as far as the faith is concerned, are rejected. 9But they will not get very far because, as in the case of those men, their folly will be clear to everyone.

■ Paul's Charge to Timothy

10You, however, know all about my teaching, my way of life, my purpose, faith, patience, love, endurance, 11persecutions, sufferings — what kinds of things happened to me in Antioch, Iconium and Lystra, the persecutions I endured. Yet the Lord rescued me from all of them. 12In fact, everyone who wants to live a godly life in Christ Jesus will be persecuted, 13while evil men and impostors will go from bad to worse, deceiving and being deceived. 14But as for you, continue in what you have learned and have become convinced of, because you know those from whom you learned it, 15and how from infancy you have known the holy Scriptures, which are able to make you wise for salvation through faith in Christ Jesus. 16All Scripture is God-breathed and is useful for teaching, rebuking, correcting and training in righteousness, 17so that the man of God may be thoroughly equipped for every good work.

3:8 ■ WHO WERE JANNES AND JAMBRES?

These names, not mentioned in the Old Testament, were handed down in Jewish tradition as the names of the Egyptian magicians who opposed Moses during the ten plagues against Egypt (Exodus 7:11; 9:11).

3:16 ■ SCRIPTURE IS GOD-BREATHED

This important verse gives the origin of the term *inspiration*, which literally means "God-breathed". Although the Bible doesn't spell out the mechanics of how God inspired the writers, it makes clear that the ultimate source was God himself.

4 In the presence of God and of Christ Jesus, who will judge the living and the dead, and in view of his appearing and his kingdom, I give you this charge: 2Preach the Word; be prepared in season and out of season; correct, rebuke and encourage — with great patience and careful instruction. 3For the time will come when men will not put up with sound doctrine. Instead, to suit their own desires, they will gather around them a great number of teachers to say what their itching ears want to hear. 4They will turn their ears away from the truth and turn aside to myths. 5But you, keep your head in all situations, endure hardship, do the work of an evangelist, discharge all the duties of your ministry.

6For I am already being poured out like a drink offering, and the time has come for my departure. 7I have fought the good fight, I have finished the race, I have kept the faith. 8Now there is in store for me the crown of righteousness, which the Lord, the righteous Judge, will award to me on that day — and not only to me, but also to all who have longed for his appearing.

■ Personal Remarks

9Do your best to come to me quickly, 10for Demas, because he loved this world, has deserted me and has gone to Thessalonica. Crescens has gone to Galatia, and Titus to Dalmatia. 11Only Luke is with me. Get Mark and bring him with you, because he is helpful to me in my ministry. 12I sent Tychicus to

Ephesus. [13]When you come, bring the cloak that I left with Carpus at Troas, and my scrolls, especially the parchments.

4:17 ■ SECOND IMPRISONMENT IN ROME
Acts 28 describes a period when Paul was held under house arrest in Rome, but the conditions hinted at in this letter are quite different. Paul wrote 2 Timothy much later, after the Roman empire had turned against Christians, and the tone of this letter (verses 6–9) implies that he had little hope of freedom. His request for a cloak and parchments (verse 13) indicates that he was arrested suddenly, without warning.

[14]Alexander the metalworker did me a great deal of harm. The Lord will repay him for what he has done. [15]You too should be on your guard against him, because he strongly opposed our message.

[16]At my first defence, no-one came to my support, but everyone deserted me. May it not be held against them. [17]But the Lord stood at my side and gave me strength, so that through me the message might be fully proclaimed and all the Gentiles might hear it. And I was delivered from the lion's mouth. [18]The Lord will rescue me from every evil attack and will bring me safely to his heavenly kingdom. To him be glory for ever and ever. Amen.

■ Final Greetings
[19]Greet Priscilla[a] and Aquila and the household of Onesiphorus. [20]Erastus stayed in Corinth, and I left Trophimus sick in Miletus. [21]Do your best to get here before winter. Eubulus greets you, and so do Pudens, Linus, Claudia and all the brothers.
[22]The Lord be with your spirit. Grace be with you.

■ A LETTER FROM DEATH ROW
PAUL SEES THE END

INSIGHT

I AM ALREADY BEING POURED OUT LIKE A DRINK OFFERING, AND THE TIME HAS COME FOR MY DEPARTURE. ■ 4:6

Occasionally, writings surface from death row, the earnest scratchings of prisoners who know each word may be their last. Whole books, for example, were discovered amid the ruins of Nazi death camps. Understandably, these writings don't usually dwell on abstract, philosophical themes. They chronicle the day-to-day reality of the struggle to survive.

Quite naturally, Paul did not devote much space to doctrine in his death row letter. He stuck to personal advice on vital issues such as courage and personal integrity.

■ PAUL'S GRIM FUTURE
Although Paul does not elaborate on his present circumstances in 2 Timothy, he mentions that at his first trial not a single witness came forward to defend him (4:16). Through supernatural strength he successfully defended himself, but his prospects in a new trial appeared grim (4:6).

Paul's arrest probably occurred in the wave of anti-Christian persecutions begun by Nero in A.D. 64. That crazed emperor tortured Christians by crucifying them, by wrapping them in animal skins and turning his hunting dogs loose on them, and by burning them alive, as human torches, to illuminate the games in his garden. Is it any wonder that Paul, imprisoned in that era, exhorted Timothy on the need for boldness and the likelihood of suffering for Christ?

■ THE COMING CONFLICT
Towards the end of his life, Paul viewed the future as a growing struggle. Immorality and false teaching would "spread like gangrene" (2:17); he urged Christians to counteract those forces with personal purity. The battle between good and evil would only intensify, he said.

After making some predictions about "the last days", Paul composed a formal charge to Timothy — a last will and testament to his spiritual son (4:1–8). He concluded, "I have fought the good fight, I have finished the race, I have kept the faith" (4:7). Tradition teaches that Paul was killed by Rome for his faith. But because of his life and the legacy he passed on, the world would never be the same.

☐ LIFE QUESTIONS:
If you drafted a spiritual "last will and testament" for your friends, what would you say?

TITUS

INTRODUCTION

■ DIVERSE PEOPLE, DIVERSE PROBLEMS
AN ISLAND OF LIARS, BRUTES, AND GLUTTONS

THESE, THEN, ARE THE THINGS YOU SHOULD TEACH. ■ 2:15

Modern people reading about the past can blur people together into a uniform, faceless crowd of strangers. It's hard to visualise individual people you read about.

Actually, the people Paul addressed were as diverse as those you might meet on the streets of London or Bradford today. Consider Crete, an island populated by five fiercely independent ethnic groups. Its main knowledge of the outside world came through pirates and coarse sailors. Add to that mixture a large community of straight-laced Jews, and you can see why the Cretan church was born amid conflict.

■ TITUS THE TROUBLESHOOTER
When problems erupted in this stormy congregation, Paul dispatched Titus, his trusted associate of 15 years. The book of Galatians (2:1–5) introduced Titus as proof that a non-Jew could become a fully acceptable Christian.

When Titus' name occurs in the New Testament, he is usually seen serving as Paul's troubleshooter, the one called on to deal with local crises. Twice he was sent on a diplomatic mission to the rowdy church at Corinth. This letter indicates he faced an equally challenging task on Crete. Paul wrote the book of Titus as a set of personal instructions on how to handle a difficult assignment.

Because he was writing to people who knew the local circumstances well, Paul rarely bothered to give background for us years-later

"over-the-shoulder" readers. But we can gain insights into the conditions by reading between the lines. For example, when Paul tells Titus to search for a leader "not quick-tempered, not given to drunkenness, not violent, not pursuing dishonest gain" (1:7), that description implies something about the average Cretan. One of the island's own poets described Cretans as "always liars, evil brutes, lazy gluttons" (1:12), and the Greeks had even coined a special verb for lying: "to Cretize".

■ PRACTICAL THEOLOGY
Titus 2 lists some of the diverse groups in the church: older men, older women, younger women, young men, slaves. Each presented a set of problems that needed attention, and Paul gave Titus specific counsel on each group. Although he was mainly emphasising the need for good living, Paul also dropped in a few concise restatements of the gospel message. His theology was never distantly theoretical; he applied it to real-life human problems.

Taken as a group, the three pastoral letters (1 and 2 Timothy plus Titus) show Paul, an old man now, learning to rely more and more on capable assistants to carry on his work. The Cretans needed a hard-hitting, practical reminder of "sound doctrine" based on a God "who does not lie" (1:2). The instructions in Titus give the man for whom the book was named – and us – the needed jolt.

■ HOW TO READ TITUS

Like 1 and 2 Timothy, Titus was written to an individual, not a church. This letter has similarities to 1 Timothy, but is less personal and more official. The book of Acts doesn't mention Titus, but 14 references to him in Paul's letters indicate that he was one of Paul's most trusted helpers.

In some letters, such as Galatians, Paul fought valiantly against legalism. But the church in Crete, full of immature Christians, needed basic lessons in morality, and Paul spelled them out for Titus. Using a very straightforward style, he told his associate what he would prescribe in such circumstances.

Because it is written in such a direct style – almost like a training manual – Titus needs little explanation. Paul's meaning comes through clearly. Note particularly how Paul adapts his overall principles to specific groups in chapter 2. And give careful study to the "nuggets" of theology in these passages: 1:1–4, 2:11–14, and 3:4–7.

■ 3-TRACK READING PLAN

For an explanation and complete listing of the 3-track reading plan, turn to page x.

■ TRACK 1:
Two-Week Courses on the Bible
See page x for information on these courses.

■ TRACK 2:
An Overview of Titus in 1 Day

□ Day 1. Read the Introduction to Titus, then chapter 2, which contains Paul's practical advice for the diverse groups in the Cretan church.
Now turn to page xi for your next Track 2 reading project.

■ TRACK 3:
All of Titus in 2 Days
After you have read through Titus, turn to pages xii–xiii for your next Track 3 reading project.

□ 1   □ 2–3

1 Paul, a servant of God and an apostle of Jesus Christ for the faith of God's elect and the knowledge of the truth that leads to godliness – ²a faith and knowledge resting on the hope of eternal life, which God, who does not lie, promised before the beginning of time, ³and at his appointed season he brought his word to light through the preaching entrusted to me by the command of God our Saviour,

---

1:2 ■ NO LIES

Right away Paul characterises God as the One who does not lie. God's truthfulness made a sharp contrast to the Cretans themselves (verse 12) as well as to many gods of that era. The Romans exalted their emperors, worshipping them as divine despite the flaws and weaknesses that everyone knew about. Paul contrasts the message about Jesus as the eternal "word" of truth.

---

⁴To Titus, my true son in our common faith:

Grace and peace from God the Father and Christ Jesus our Saviour.

■ Titus' Task in Crete

⁵The reason I left you in Crete was that you might straighten out what was left unfinished and appoint*ᵃ* elders in every town, as I directed you. ⁶An elder must be blameless, the husband of but one wife, a man whose children believe and are not open to the charge of being wild and disobedient. ⁷Since an overseer*ᵇ* is entrusted with God's work, he must be blameless – not overbearing, not quick-tempered, not given to drunkenness, not violent, not pursuing dishonest gain. ⁸Rather he must be hospitable, one who loves what is good, who is self-controlled, upright, holy and disciplined. ⁹He must hold firmly to the trustworthy message as it has been taught, so that he can encourage others by sound doctrine and refute those who oppose it.

¹⁰For there are many rebellious people, mere talkers and deceivers, especially those of the circumcision group. ¹¹They must be silenced, because they are ruining whole households by teaching things they ought not to teach – and that for the sake of dishonest gain. ¹²Even one of their own prophets has said, "Cretans are always liars, evil brutes, lazy gluttons." ¹³This testimony is true. Therefore, rebuke them sharply, so that they will be sound in the faith ¹⁴and will pay no attention to Jewish myths or to the commands of those who reject the truth. ¹⁵To the pure, all things are pure, but to those who are corrupted and do not believe, nothing is pure. In fact, both their minds and consciences are corrupted. ¹⁶They claim to know God, but by their actions they deny him. They are detestable, disobedient and unfit for doing anything good.

■ What Must Be Taught to Various Groups

2 You must teach what is in accord with sound doctrine. ²Teach the older men to be temperate, worthy of respect, self-controlled, and sound in faith, in love and in endurance.

³Likewise, teach the older women to be reverent in the way they live, not to be slanderers or addicted to much wine, but to teach what is good. ⁴Then they can train the younger women to love their husbands and children, ⁵to be self-controlled and pure, to be busy at home, to be kind, and to be subject to their husbands, so that no-one will malign the word of God.

⁶Similarly, encourage the young men to be self-controlled. ⁷In everything set them an example by doing what is good. In your teaching show integrity, seriousness ⁸and soundness of speech that cannot be condemned, so that those who oppose you may be ashamed because they have nothing bad to say about us.

⁹Teach slaves to be subject to their masters in everything, to try to please them, not to talk back to them, ¹⁰and not to steal from them, but to show that they can be fully trusted, so that in every way they will make the teaching about God our Saviour attractive.

¹¹For the grace of God that brings salvation has appeared to all men. ¹²It teaches us to say "No" to ungodliness and worldly passions, and to live self-controlled, upright and godly lives in this present age, ¹³while we wait for the blessed hope – the glorious appearing of our great God and Saviour, Jesus Christ, ¹⁴who gave himself for us to redeem us from

---

ᵃ5 Or ordain   ᵇ7 Traditionally bishop

all wickedness and to purify for himself a people that are his very own, eager to do what is good.

15These, then, are the things you should teach. Encourage and rebuke with all authority. Do not let anyone despise you.

these are unprofitable and useless. 10Warn a divisive person once, and then warn him a second time. After that, have nothing to do with him. 11You may be sure that such a man is warped and sinful; he is self-condemned.

2:15 ■ FOOLISH QUESTIONS

In addition to the problems hinted at in chapter 2, the Cretan church struggled with issues its Jewish members introduced. These trends towards myths and "foolish controversies and genealogies and arguments and quarrels about the law" (3:9) resemble the heresies Paul had warned against in the book of Colossians. Titus had to be prepared to deal with problems both of doctrine and of righteous living.

3:5 ■ NUGGETS OF THEOLOGY

Despite its practical, instructive tone, Titus contains three outstanding passages of Paul's theology. They appear in 1:1–4, 2:11–14, and 3:4–7. This last passage balances Paul's stress on clean living in Titus. Verse 5 makes clear that "righteous things" do not earn us acceptance by God. Rather, they are a natural response from people who have experienced God's forgiveness and love.

■ Doing What Is Good

3 Remind the people to be subject to rulers and authorities, to be obedient, to be ready to do whatever is good, 2to slander no-one, to be peaceable and considerate, and to show true humility towards all men.

3At one time we too were foolish, disobedient, deceived and enslaved by all kinds of passions and pleasures. We lived in malice and envy, being hated and hating one another. 4But when the kindness and love of God our Saviour appeared, 5he saved us, not because of righteous things we had done, but because of his mercy. He saved us through the washing of rebirth and renewal by the Holy Spirit, 6whom he poured out on us generously through Jesus Christ our Saviour, 7so that, having been justified by his grace, we might become heirs having the hope of eternal life. 8This is a trustworthy saying. And I want you to stress these things, so that those who have trusted in God may be careful to devote themselves to doing what is good. These things are excellent and profitable for everyone.

9But avoid foolish controversies and genealogies and arguments and quarrels about the law, because

■ Final Remarks

12As soon as I send Artemas or Tychicus to you, do your best to come to me at Nicopolis, because I have decided to winter there. 13Do everything you can to help Zenas the lawyer and Apollos on their way and see that they have everything they need. 14Our people must learn to devote themselves to doing what is good, in order that they may provide for daily necessities and not live unproductive lives.

3:12 ■ MAIL CARRIERS

In Roman times, the most reliable postal system was to give a letter to a trusted friend. Paul used Tychicus to carry letters both to Ephesus and to Colosse. Tychicus also accompanied Paul on his trip to distribute gifts to the poor of Jerusalem (Acts 20:4).

15Everyone with me sends you greetings. Greet those who love us in the faith.

Grace be with you all.

PHILEMON

■ LETTER TO A SLAVE OWNER

A SLAVE'S LIFE HANGS IN THE BALANCE

ALTHOUGH IN CHRIST I COULD BE BOLD AND ORDER YOU TO DO WHAT YOU OUGHT TO
DO, YET I APPEAL TO YOU ON THE BASIS OF LOVE. ■ 8–9

Onesimus was a runaway slave, a hunted fugitive whose life was in constant danger. He had two options. He could spend his days hiding in the dark, grimy alleys of a Roman city, dodging soldiers and bounty hunters. Or, he could do the unthinkable and return to his master.

The laws of the empire were harsh. If Onesimus did return, his master Philemon had the legal power to sentence him to immediate execution. If Philemon mercifully decided to let him live, Onesimus would have the letter *F* (for *Fugitivus*) seared on his forehead with a branding iron, marking him for life.

■ PAUL DEFENDS A RUNAWAY

His conversion to Christ through Paul's ministry greatly complicated the decision of the runaway slave. Onesimus knew he couldn't keep running all his life. He had wronged his legal owner, and, painful as it seemed, he needed to make amends.

The apostle Paul, sympathetic to the slave's cause, agreed to use his full influence on Philemon. Onesimus' life hung in the balance. This 468-word letter to the slave owner masterfully brings together Paul's skills of persuasion and diplomacy.

Every phrase in Philemon is crafted to produce the best possible effect. Paul appeals to Philemon's friendship, his status as a Christian leader, his sense of love and compassion. He doesn't order Philemon outright to consent, yet he applies blatant pressure, reminding Philemon that "you owe me your very self" (verse 19). Addressing the letter to Philemon's church (verse 2) increases the pressure, as does Paul's promise of a personal visit (verse 22).

■ CHRISTIANITY AND SLAVERY

Slavery existed for 1,800 years after this letter was written, and it took the full moral force of Christianity to ban it from the globe. But the tiny book of Philemon shows that the faith had a profound impact on slavery long before abolition.

Christ can revolutionise any social relationship. Onesimus, a runaway, decided to turn himself in. In Philemon, Paul asks for a second miracle. He pleads with the owner to "welcome him as you would welcome me" (verse 17). Such an attitude, in that culture, was social dynamite.

■ HOW TO READ PHILEMON

Obviously, Paul had a close relationship with both the slave Onesimus and his owner Philemon. Some scholars believe that Onesimus first heard about Christ when he shared a jail cell with the apostle (see verses 9–10). As you read Philemon, look for clues into Paul's relationship with each person.

Philemon gives us a model of Christian diplomacy. As you read it, think of awkward social situations you know about: two estranged friends or a parent-child conflict, for example. Notice the kind of persuasion used by Paul, and try to apply it to your own circumstances.

■ 3-TRACK READING PLAN

For an explanation and complete listing of the 3-track reading plan, turn to page x.

■ TRACK 1:
Two-Week Courses on the
Bible
See page x for information on
these courses.

■ TRACK 2:
Philemon in 1 Day
☐ Day 1. Just one chapter
long, Philemon will take only
a few minutes to read.
Now turn to page xi for your
next Track 2 reading project.

■ TRACK 3:
All of Philemon in 1 Day
After you have read through
Philemon, turn to pages xii–xiii
for your next Track 3 reading
project.

☐ Philemon

¹Paul, a prisoner of Christ Jesus, and Timothy our brother,

To Philemon our dear friend and fellow-worker, ²to Apphia our sister, to Archippus our fellow-soldier and to the church that meets in your home:

³Grace to you and peace from God our Father and the Lord Jesus Christ.

■ Thanksgiving and Prayer

⁴I always thank my God as I remember you in my prayers, ⁵because I hear about your faith in the Lord Jesus and your love for all the saints. ⁶I pray that you may be active in sharing your faith, so that you will have a full understanding of every good thing we have in Christ. ⁷Your love has given me great joy and encouragement, because you, brother, have refreshed the hearts of the saints.

■ Paul's Plea for Onesimus

⁸Therefore, although in Christ I could be bold and order you to do what you ought to do, ⁹yet I appeal to you on the basis of love. I then, as Paul— an old man and now also a prisoner of Christ Jesus— ¹⁰I appeal to you for my son Onesimus,ᵃ who became my son while I was in chains. ¹¹Formerly he was useless to you, but now he has become useful both to you and to me.

¹²I am sending him—who is my very heart— back to you. ¹³I would have liked to keep him with me so that he could take your place in helping me while I am in chains for the gospel. ¹⁴But I did not want to do anything without your consent, so that any favour you do will be spontaneous and not forced. ¹⁵Perhaps the reason he was separated from you for a little while was that you might have him back for good—¹⁶no longer as a slave, but better than a slave, as a dear brother. He is very dear to me but even dearer to you, both as a man and as a brother in the Lord.

¹⁷So if you consider me a partner, welcome him as you would welcome me. ¹⁸If he has done you any wrong or owes you anything, charge it to me. ¹⁹I, Paul, am writing this with my own hand. I will pay it back—not to mention that you owe me your very self. ²⁰I do wish, brother, that I may have some benefit from you in the Lord; refresh my heart in Christ. ²¹Confident of your obedience, I write to you, knowing that you will do even more than I ask.

²²And one thing more: Prepare a guest room for me, because I hope to be restored to you in answer to your prayers.

11 ■ NO LONGER USELESS

Onesimus in Greek means "useful", and Paul playfully makes a pun from the name. A runaway slave was useless; a converted former slave could prove very useful—provided Philemon receives him in the right spirit. Accept him back, urges Paul, "no longer as a slave, but . . . as a dear brother" (verse 16).

²³Epaphras, my fellow-prisoner in Christ Jesus, sends you greetings. ²⁴And so do Mark, Aristarchus, Demas and Luke, my fellow-workers.

²⁵The grace of the Lord Jesus Christ be with your spirit.

ᵃ10 *Onesimus* means *useful.*

HEBREWS

■ TIME TO DECIDE

DOES IT MATTER WHAT YOU BELIEVE AS LONG AS YOU'RE SINCERE?

HOW SHALL WE ESCAPE IF WE IGNORE SUCH A GREAT SALVATION? ■ 2:3

You can go through much of life deliberately avoiding hard decisions. But sometimes you have no choice; the situation forces you to make a decision. Consider an example from the sport of rock-climbing.

Sooner or later, every rock-climber faces a dreaded section of slick granite that offers no ledges or cracks to grasp. When you come to such a wall, you can abandon the climb. Or, you can risk a move like "the pendulum".

■ THE PENDULUM
The pendulum works the way it sounds: as high above you as you can reach, you fasten a loop with a metal nut and slide the rope through the loop. Then you climb down a few feet, dangle on the end of the rope, and try to swing across the sheer section. It takes nerve. You must lean out against the rope into empty space and, with a well-timed push, vault across the face of the cliff. If your lunge towards a safer spot fails, you swing helplessly back and try again.

After your entire party has swung the pendulum, you pull the rope all the way through the loop. From then on, there's no turning back. You have crossed a section of cliff that requires a rope to swing on and a loop to attach it to. The loop is now out of your reach, and the rope coiled at your feet. There is only one way to go: up.

■ WORTH THE RISK?
The author of Hebrews wrote to people who faced just such a climactic, can't-turn-back decision. It involved not a rock climb, but their entire future. Should they stick with the familiar routine of the Jewish religion? After all, it enjoyed Rome's official protection and had traditions going back thousands of years. Or should they take a risk and join the growing body of people who called themselves Christians? Those readers needed some compelling reasons to choose Christianity. At that time new converts were being thrown out of Jewish temples, tossed into jail, and even tortured. Was faith in Christ worth the risk?

The tug of the old and the fear of the new kept many interested people, especially Jews, teetering on the edge of Christianity. And the book of Hebrews seems designed to push such people towards a decisive commitment, in one direction or the other. Point by point, the author shows how Christ improved on the Jewish way. Hebrews is a no-holds-barred argument on why Christianity is *better* (a key word in Hebrews) than Judaism. The new faith is worth any risk.

■ DRAWING ON THE OLD TESTAMENT
For the sake of Jewish readers, the author painstakingly cites Old Testament passages, more than 80 times in all. He develops the case for Christ like a lawyer, but with the charged emotions befitting the life-and-death issues involved.

Although Hebrews mainly focuses on the Jewish religion, comparing it to Christianity, the book also speaks to our time. Today people ask, "Are religions all that different? Isn't the most important thing to be sincere?" Hebrews insists that there are decisive reasons to choose Christ. The author urges his readers to leap forward to a new experience with God through Jesus.

■ HOW TO READ HEBREWS

Who wrote Hebrews? Did the author have a particular group of readers in mind? Scholars have debated these questions for centuries without reaching agreement. The truth is, no-one knows for certain either the author or the intended audience of Hebrews.

Nevertheless, the book does give some information about its first readers. They had heard the gospel through contemporaries of Jesus (2:3), and their conversion had brought on physical persecution (10:32–34). One fact leaps out: their spiritual state greatly distressed the unidentified author. Five times in the book of Hebrews he interrupts a careful line of reasoning to fire off a warning (2:1; 3:7; 5:11; 10:26; 12:25).

Hebrews is actually a commentary on the Old Testament. It examines many Jewish customs and shows how Jesus brought about a "better covenant" to replace many of those laws. (*Covenant* means the same thing as *Testament:* a firm agreement between God and humanity.) Therefore, to fully appreciate Hebrews, you

should have some familiarity with such books as Exodus, Leviticus, and Numbers.

As you read, look at the bottom of each page for NIV footnotes referring to the Old Testament. If you can't figure out what a text in Hebrews means, try looking back to the original passage.

To follow the logic in Hebrews, note each use of the word *better* and *superior*. The author compares Jesus Christ to the angels, to Moses, to the priests Aaron and Melchizedek, and to Abraham.

■ 3-TRACK READING PLAN

For an explanation and complete listing of the 3-track reading plan, turn to page x.

■ TRACK 1:
Two-Week Courses on the Bible
See page x for information on these courses.

■ TRACK 2:
An Overview of Hebrews in 3 Days
☐ Day 1. Read the Introduction to Hebrews, then chapter 2. There you will learn about God's decision to send his Son to earth and why it

was so important that Jesus come as a fully *human* being, not as some kind of alien.
☐ Day 2. Hebrews 11 lists many Old Testament heroes, with a capsular description of how each one demonstrated faith. Read this famous chapter.
☐ Day 3. Read Hebrews 12, which combines a pep talk with a brief summary of the entire book.

Now turn to page xi for your next Track 2 reading project.

■ TRACK 3:
All of Hebrews in 11 Days
After you have read through Hebrews, turn to pages xii–xiii for your next Track 3 reading project.

☐ 1   ☐ 2   ☐ 3–4 ☐ 5–6
☐ 7   ☐ 8   ☐ 9   ☐ 10
☐ 11 ☐ 12 ☐ 13

■ The Son Superior to Angels

1 In the past God spoke to our forefathers through the prophets at many times and in various ways, ²but in these last days he has spoken to us by his Son, whom he appointed heir of all things, and through whom he made the universe. ³The Son is the radiance of God's glory and the exact representation of his being, sustaining all things by his powerful word. After he had provided purification for sins, he sat down at the right hand of the Majesty in heaven. ⁴So he became as much superior to the angels as the name he has inherited is superior to theirs.

⁵For to which of the angels did God ever say,

"You are my Son;
today I have become your Father"*a,b*?

Or again,

"I will be his Father,
and he will be my Son"*c*?

⁶And again, when God brings his firstborn into the world, he says,

"Let all God's angels worship him."*d*

⁷In speaking of the angels he says,

"He makes his angels winds,
his servants flames of fire."*e*

⁸But about the Son he says,

"Your throne, O God, will last for ever and ever,
and righteousness will be the sceptre of your kingdom.
⁹You have loved righteousness and hated wickedness;
therefore God, your God, has set you above your companions
by anointing you with the oil of joy."*f*

¹⁰He also says,

"In the beginning, O Lord, you laid the foundations of the earth,
and the heavens are the work of your hands.

1:10 ■ NOT BY CHANCE
Quotations from the Old Testament fill the book of Hebrews from the second paragraph onwards. The author is making the point that God's plan, unfolding from the beginning of time, has now culminated in the visit of his Son to earth.

¹¹They will perish, but you remain;
they will all wear out like a garment.
¹²You will roll them up like a robe;
like a garment they will be changed.
But you remain the same,
and your years will never end."*g*

¹³To which of the angels did God ever say,

*a5 Or have begotten you   b5 Psalm 2:7   c5 2 Samuel 7:14; 1 Chron. 17:13   d6 Deut. 32:43 (see Dead Sea Scrolls and Septuagint)
e7 Psalm 104:4   f9 Psalm 45:6,7   g12 Psalm 102:25–27*

"Sit at my right hand
  until I make your enemies
    a footstool for your feet"*h*?

¹⁴Are not all angels ministering spirits sent to serve those who will inherit salvation?

1:14 ■ RESPECT FOR ANGELS

In earlier times, people freely accepted the existence of angels and accorded them honour and respect. Jewish people retold stories of how angels had assisted Abraham, Moses, Elijah, Balaam, and Daniel. (In fact, several New Testament letters warn Jewish Christians against the common practice of worshipping angels.) To prove its argument about Christ being superior, Hebrews must show that angels served his purposes, not vice versa.

■ Warning to Pay Attention

2 We must pay more careful attention, therefore, to what we have heard, so that we do not drift away. ²For if the message spoken by angels was binding, and every violation and disobedience received its just punishment, ³how shall we escape if we ignore such a great salvation? This salvation, which was first announced by the Lord, was confirmed to us by those who heard him. ⁴God also testified to it by signs, wonders and various miracles, and gifts of the Holy Spirit distributed according to his will.

■ Jesus Made Like His Brothers

⁵It is not to angels that he has subjected the world to come, about which we are speaking. ⁶But there is a place where someone has testified:

"What is man that you are mindful of him,
  the son of man that you care for him?
⁷You made him a little*a* lower than the angels;
  you crowned him with glory and honour
⁸   and put everything under his feet."*b*

In putting everything under him, God left nothing that is not subject to him. Yet at present we do not see everything subject to him. ⁹But we see Jesus, who was made a little lower than the angels, now crowned with glory and honour because he suffered death, so that by the grace of God he might taste death for everyone. ¹⁰In bringing many sons to glory, it was fitting that God, for whom and through whom everything exists, should make the author of their salvation perfect through suffering. ¹¹Both the one who makes men holy and those who are made holy are of the same family. So Jesus is not ashamed to call them brothers. ¹²He says,

"I will declare your name to my brothers;
  in the presence of the congregation I will
    sing your praises."*c*

¹³And again,

"I will put my trust in him."*d*

And again he says,

"Here am I, and the children God has given
    me."*e*

¹⁴Since the children have flesh and blood, he too shared in their humanity so that by his death he might destroy him who holds the power of death — that is, the devil — ¹⁵and free those who all their lives were held in slavery by their fear of death. ¹⁶For surely it is not angels he helps, but Abraham's descendants. ¹⁷For this reason he had to be made like his brothers in every way, in order that he might become a merciful and faithful high priest in service to God, and that he might make atonement for*f* the sins of the people. ¹⁸Because he himself suffered when he was tempted, he is able to help those who are being tempted.

2:17 ■ LIKE US IN EVERY WAY

Hebrews goes further than any other New Testament book in explaining Jesus' human nature. Why was it so important that Jesus share our humanity? Hebrews stresses three reasons: (1) so that, in dying, he could free us from the power of death (verses 14–15); (2) so that, by becoming the final sacrifice for sin, he could reconcile us to God (5:8–9); and (3) so that, in experiencing temptation, he can better help us with our own temptations (verse 18).

■ Jesus Greater Than Moses

3 Therefore, holy brothers, who share in the heavenly calling, fix your thoughts on Jesus, the apostle and high priest whom we confess. ²He was faithful to the one who appointed him, just as Moses was faithful in all God's house. ³Jesus has been found worthy of greater honour than Moses, just as the builder of a house has greater honour than the house itself. ⁴For every house is built by someone, but God is the builder of everything. ⁵Moses was faithful as a servant in all God's house, testifying to what would be said in the future. ⁶But Christ is faithful as a son over God's house. And we are his house, if we hold on to our courage and the hope of which we boast.

■ Warning Against Unbelief

⁷So, as the Holy Spirit says:

"Today, if you hear his voice,
⁸   do not harden your hearts
  as you did in the rebellion,
    during the time of testing in the desert,
⁹where your fathers tested and tried me
  and for forty years saw what I did.
¹⁰That is why I was angry with that generation,
  and I said, 'Their hearts are always going
    astray,
  and they have not known my ways.'
¹¹So I declared on oath in my anger,
  'They shall never enter my rest.' "*a*

¹²See to it, brothers, that none of you has a sinful, unbelieving heart that turns away from the living

---

b 13 Psalm 110:1   *a 7* Or *him for a little while;* also in verse 9   *b 8* Psalm 8:4–6   *c 12* Psalm 22:22   *d 13* Isaiah 8:17   *e 13* Isaiah 8:18
f 17 Or *and that he might turn aside God's wrath, taking away*   *a 11* Psalm 95:7–11

God. ¹³But encourage one another daily, as long as it is called Today, so that none of you may be hardened by sin's deceitfulness. ¹⁴We have come to share in Christ if we hold firmly till the end the confidence we had at first. ¹⁵As has just been said:

"Today, if you hear his voice,
  do not harden your hearts
  as you did in the rebellion."*b*

¹⁶Who were they who heard and rebelled? Were they not all those Moses led out of Egypt? ¹⁷And with whom was he angry for forty years? Was it not with those who sinned, whose bodies fell in the desert? ¹⁸And to whom did God swear that they would never enter his rest if not to those who disobeyed?*c* ¹⁹So we see that they were not able to enter, because of their unbelief.

■ A Sabbath-rest for the People of God

4 Therefore, since the promise of entering his rest still stands, let us be careful that none of you be found to have fallen short of it. ²For we also have had the gospel preached to us, just as they did; but the message they heard was of no value to them, because those who heard did not combine it with faith.*a* ³Now we who have believed enter that rest, just as God has said,

"So I declared on oath in my anger,
  'They shall never enter my rest.' "*b*

And yet his work has been finished since the creation of the world. ⁴For somewhere he has spoken about the seventh day in these words: "And on the seventh day God rested from all his work."*c* ⁵And again in the passage above he says, "They shall never enter my rest."

⁶It still remains that some will enter that rest, and those who formerly had the gospel preached to them did not go in, because of their disobedience. ⁷Therefore God again set a certain day, calling it Today, when a long time later he spoke through David, as was said before:

"Today, if you hear his voice,
  do not harden your hearts."*d*

⁸For if Joshua had given them rest, God would not have spoken later about another day. ⁹There remains, then, a Sabbath-rest for the people of God;

■ IS CHRIST BETTER?
THE UNIQUENESS OF JESUS

INSIGHT

JESUS HAS BEEN FOUND WORTHY OF GREATER HONOUR THAN MOSES, JUST AS THE BUILDER OF A HOUSE HAS GREATER HONOUR THAN THE HOUSE ITSELF. ■ 3:3

In time, a work of art by a great artist gains enormous value because of its creator's reputation. Even a musty notebook full of scratchings, if found to be Leonardo da Vinci's, would suddenly be worth millions of pounds. Similarly, houses designed by English architect John Nash retain high value simply because of his name.

To dramatise his argument that Christ is superior to any religious system, the author of Hebrews uses an analogy: Which has greater honour, the builder of a house or the house itself? Obviously, the builder has more honour; the house is just one expression of his genius.

■ IN A CATEGORY BY HIMSELF
Likewise, Hebrews says, Christ has more honour than anyone else on earth. As Creator of the universe, he actually designed and made all people (1:2). That puts him in a different category of greatness, far above Moses, Aaron and other Jewish heroes.

"Therefore," Hebrews urges, "fix your thoughts on Jesus" (3:1). He deserves all respect and allegiance. By becoming human, Jesus learned first-hand the temptations and sufferings that people undergo, so that he can now represent us sympathetically to God (4:14–15). The author goes on to prove that Jesus fulfilled all the Old Testament requirements. He was the one priest who could permanently bring together God and the human race (7:23–27). And, as God, he had the power through his death to remove the final barrier of sin between God and humankind (9:11–15).

■ FREE ACCESS TO GOD
Over time, the author argues, God chose various ways to reveal himself: creation, the prophets, and the Old Testament Scriptures. But the final, complete self-expression culminated in his Son. Jesus is the one worthy of honour.

Because of Jesus, we no longer have to approach God through a priest, as the Israelites did. Christ's work makes God available to all who have faith in him. And God no longer dwells in an elaborately designed temple; *we* have become his house (3:6), his work of art.

☐ LIFE QUESTIONS:
People sometimes say about Jesus, "I don't believe he was God, but he was a very fine man—like Gandhi or Buddha." What arguments does the author of Hebrews use to contradict this?

---

*b*15 Psalm 95:7,8   *c*18 Or *disbelieved*   *a*2 Many manuscripts *because they did not share in the faith of those who obeyed*   *b*3 Psalm 95:11; also in verse 5   *c*4 Gen. 2:2   *d*7 Psalm 95:7,8

10for anyone who enters God's rest also rests from his own work, just as God did from his. 11Let us, therefore, make every effort to enter that rest, so that no-one will fall by following their example of disobedience.

12For the word of God is living and active. Sharper than any double-edged sword, it penetrates even to dividing soul and spirit, joints and marrow; it judges the thoughts and attitudes of the heart. 13Nothing in all creation is hidden from God's sight. Everything is uncovered and laid bare before the eyes of him to whom we must give account.

4:13 ■ MIND READER

Advances in technology – MRI tests, x-ray machines, CAT scans – make it possible for doctors to peer inside the human body and judge what goes on there. But no-one has yet devised a machine that can peer inside the brain to detect thoughts and attitudes. God has such ability; why try to hide?

■ Jesus the Great High Priest

14Therefore, since we have a great high priest who has gone through the heavens,e Jesus the Son of God, let us hold firmly to the faith we profess. 15For we do not have a high priest who is unable to sympathise with our weaknesses, but we have one who has been tempted in every way, just as we are – yet was without sin. 16Let us then approach the throne of grace with confidence, so that we may receive mercy and find grace to help us in our time of need.

5 Every high priest is selected from among men and is appointed to represent them in matters related to God, to offer gifts and sacrifices for sins. 2He is able to deal gently with those who are ignorant and are going astray, since he himself is subject to weakness. 3This is why he has to offer sacrifices for his own sins, as well as for the sins of the people. 4No-one takes this honour upon himself; he must be called by God, just as Aaron was. 5So Christ also did not take upon himself the glory of becoming a high priest. But God said to him,

"You are my Son;
    today I have become your Father."a, b

6And he says in another place,

"You are a priest for ever,
    in the order of Melchizedek."c

7During the days of Jesus' life on earth, he offered up prayers and petitions with loud cries and tears to the one who could save him from death, and he was heard because of his reverent submission. 8Although he was a son, he learned obedience from what he suffered 9and, once made perfect, he became the source of eternal salvation for all who obey him 10and was designated by God to be high priest in the order of Melchizedek.

■ Warning Against Falling Away

11We have much to say about this, but it is hard to explain because you are slow to learn. 12In fact, though by this time you ought to be teachers, you need someone to teach you the elementary truths of God's word all over again. You need milk, not solid food! 13Anyone who lives on milk, being still an infant, is not acquainted with the teaching about righteousness. 14But solid food is for the mature, who by constant use have trained themselves to distinguish good from evil.

6 Therefore let us leave the elementary teachings about Christ and go on to maturity, not laying again the foundation of repentance from acts that lead to death,a and of faith in God, 2instruction about baptisms, the laying on of hands, the resurrection of the dead, and eternal judgment. 3And God permitting, we will do so.

4It is impossible for those who have once been enlightened, who have tasted the heavenly gift, who have shared in the Holy Spirit, 5who have tasted the goodness of the word of God and the powers of the coming age, 6if they fall away, to be brought back to repentance, becauseb to their loss they are crucifying the Son of God all over again and subjecting him to public disgrace.

6:4 ■ CAN A BELIEVER FALL AWAY?

This passage has caused interpreters great difficulty. People who don't believe in "eternal security" think the passage refers to Christians who fall away from the faith. Others, such as John Calvin, insist that the author of Hebrews must be referring to people who never fully became Christians, because other verses seem to teach the eternal security of those in Christ (see John 5:24; 6:37; Romans 8:1; Hebrews 8:12). Regardless, the author is writing about a hypothetical situation. He is not describing what happened, but only what could happen: if such a falling away ever did occur, it would be impossible to rescue such people again. A somewhat similar argument appears at the end of chapter 10.

7Land that drinks in the rain often falling on it and that produces a crop useful to those for whom it is farmed receives the blessing of God. 8But land that produces thorns and thistles is worthless and is in danger of being cursed. In the end it will be burned.

9Even though we speak like this, dear friends, we are confident of better things in your case – things that accompany salvation. 10God is not unjust; he will not forget your work and the love you have shown him as you have helped his people and continue to help them. 11We want each of you to show this same diligence to the very end, in order to make your hope sure. 12We do not want you to become lazy, but to imitate those who through faith and patience inherit what has been promised.

■ The Certainty of God's Promise

13When God made his promise to Abraham, since there was no-one greater for him to swear by, he swore by himself, [14]saying, "I will surely bless you and give you many descendants."[c] [15]And so after waiting patiently, Abraham received what was promised.

[16]Men swear by someone greater than themselves, and the oath confirms what is said and puts an end to all argument. [17]Because God wanted to make the unchanging nature of his purpose very clear to the heirs of what was promised, he confirmed it with an oath. [18]God did this so that, by two unchangeable things in which it is impossible for God to lie, we who have fled to take hold of the hope offered to us may be greatly encouraged. [19]We have this hope as an anchor for the soul, firm and secure. It enters the inner sanctuary behind the curtain, [20]where Jesus, who went before us, has entered on our behalf. He has become a high priest forever, in the order of Melchizedek.

■ Melchizedek the Priest

7 This Melchizedek was king of Salem and priest of God Most High. He met Abraham returning from the defeat of the kings and blessed him, [2]and Abraham gave him a tenth of everything. First, his name means "king of righteousness"; then also, "king of Salem" means "king of peace". [3]Without father or mother, without genealogy, without beginning of days or end of life, like the Son of God he remains a priest for ever.

7:1 ■ WHO IS MELCHIZEDEK?

This mysterious person appears in only two places in the Old Testament: Genesis 14 and Psalm 110. Although a Gentile, Melchizedek worshipped the true God. In addition to being a priest, he was also a king. (The Jews would never have permitted such dual office-holding.) Hebrews demonstrates that the priesthood of Melchizedek was superior to that of Aaron; but both of them were exceeded by the great high priest, Jesus himself. Because he is both priest and king, Jesus is "in the order of" Melchizedek. (See "Out of Nowhere", page 524, for more details.)

[4]Just think how great he was: Even the patriarch Abraham gave him a tenth of the plunder! [5]Now the law requires the descendants of Levi who become priests to collect a tenth from the people — that is, their brothers — even though their brothers are descended from Abraham. [6]This man, however, did not trace his descent from Levi, yet he collected a tenth from Abraham and blessed him who had the promises. [7]And without doubt the lesser person is blessed by the greater. [8]In the one case, the tenth is collected by men who die; but in the other case, by him who is declared to be living. [9]One might even say that Levi, who collects the tenth, paid the tenth through Abraham, [10]because when Melchizedek met Abraham, Levi was still in the body of his ancestor.

■ Jesus Like Melchizedek

[11]If perfection could have been attained through the Levitical priesthood (for on the basis of it the law was given to the people), why was there still need for another priest to come — one in the order of Melchizedek, not in the order of Aaron? [12]For when there is a change of the priesthood, there must also be a change of the law. [13]He of whom these things are said belonged to a different tribe, and no-one from that tribe has ever served at the altar. [14]For it is clear that our Lord descended from Judah, and in regard to that tribe Moses said nothing about priests. [15]And what we have said is even more clear if another priest like Melchizedek appears, [16]one who has become a priest not on the basis of a regulation as to his ancestry but on the basis of the power of an indestructible life. [17]For it is declared:

"You are a priest for ever,
   in the order of Melchizedek."[a]

[18]The former regulation is set aside because it was weak and useless [19](for the law made nothing perfect), and a better hope is introduced, by which we draw near to God.

7:19 ■ DRAWING NEAR

The original Jewish readers of Hebrews were still following the "old covenant" law, and this book was written to show them how things had changed for their benefit. In Old Testament times only the high priest could "draw near" to God, and then only once a year when he entered the curtained-off Most Holy Place. As Hebrews points out, Jesus entered that inner room on our behalf (6:20). When he died, the curtain ripped in two; now any of us can draw near without fear.

[20]And it was not without an oath! Others became priests without any oath, [21]but he became a priest with an oath when God said to him:

"The Lord has sworn
   and will not change his mind:
'You are a priest for ever.' "[b]

[22]Because of this oath, Jesus has become the guarantee of a better covenant.

[23]Now there have been many of those priests, since death prevented them from continuing in office; [24]but because Jesus lives for ever, he has a permanent priesthood. [25]Therefore he is able to save completely[c] those who come to God through him, because he always lives to intercede for them.

[26]Such a high priest meets our need — one who is holy, blameless, pure, set apart from sinners, exalted above the heavens. [27]Unlike the other high priests, he does not need to offer sacrifices day after day, first for his own sins, and then for the sins of the people. He sacrificed for their sins once for all when he offered himself. [28]For the law appoints as high priests men who are weak; but the oath, which came after the law, appointed the Son, who has been made perfect for ever.

[c]14 Gen. 22:17   [a]17 Psalm 110:4   [b]21 Psalm 110:4   [c]25 Or for ever

■ The High Priest of a New Covenant

8 The point of what we are saying is this: We do have such a high priest, who sat down at the right hand of the throne of the Majesty in heaven, [2]and who serves in the sanctuary, the true tabernacle set up by the Lord, not by man.

[3]Every high priest is appointed to offer both gifts and sacrifices, and so it was necessary for this one also to have something to offer. [4]If he were on earth, he would not be a priest, for there are already men who offer the gifts prescribed by the law. [5]They serve at a sanctuary that is a copy and shadow of what is in heaven. This is why Moses was warned when he was about to build the tabernacle: "See to it that you make everything according to the pattern shown you on the mountain."[a] [6]But the ministry Jesus has received is as superior to theirs as the covenant of which he is mediator is superior to the old one, and it is founded on better promises.

[7]For if there had been nothing wrong with that first covenant, no place would have been sought for another. [8]But God found fault with the people and said:[b]

"The time is coming, declares the Lord,
   when I will make a new covenant
with the house of Israel
   and with the house of Judah.
[9]It will not be like the covenant
   I made with their forefathers

NEW LIGHT ON THE OLD TESTAMENT
THE ADVANTAGES OF LIVING NOW

FOR IF THERE HAD BEEN NOTHING WRONG WITH THAT FIRST COVENANT, NO PLACE WOULD HAVE BEEN SOUGHT FOR ANOTHER. ■ 8:7

To understand the difference between an original and a copy, consider trying to photograph the largest animal, a whale. Roy Chapman Andrews describes it:

"Once in Alaska we raised a humpback's spout and ran up close before the animal submerged. Ten minutes later, without warning, the floor of the ocean seemed to rise and a mountainous black body, dripping with foam, heaved upward, almost over our heads. It paused an instant, then fell sidewise to be swallowed up by a vortex of green water. With the camera ready in my hands I stared at the thing. The whale had dropped back scarcely twenty feet away; if it had fallen the other way, the vessel would have been crushed beneath its forty tons."

How can you adequately communicate the impact of something that immense? Photographers have recorded humpback whales bursting from the water, or "lobtailing" (standing on their heads and waving their mighty flukes high in the air). But no photograph can capture the sheer bigness of such an animal. A baby blue whale gains a tonne of weight a month. An adult blue whale's heart weighs 1,000 pounds. How can any two-dimensional photograph convey such gargantuan size?

■ COMPARING THE COPY TO THE ORIGINAL
Even the best photograph is just a copy, a representation of its subject's reality. No 8x10 rectangle can contain a whale. No photo sequence of the Grand Canyon is as grand as the canyon itself. The photograph preserves a mere two-dimensional copy of reality.

Hebrews uses that word *copy* to describe the images and rituals of the Old Testament: Passover feasts, sacrifices and other priestly duties. They were mere shadows, expressing the reality to come in Jesus Christ. No ceremony alone, however elaborate, can adequately express the experience of God himself, any more than a photograph of a whale or a mountain can adequately represent a whale or a mountain.

According to Hebrews, the Old Testament rituals were a copy, but Christ is the original. The author pulls up time-hallowed images from the Jewish tradition – sacrifices, laws, blood, the tabernacle, the priest, the Day of Atonement – and explains how Christ revealed once and for all the meaning these images only hinted at. The incomplete, shadowy copy contrasts with the perfect, genuine reality.

■ WHICH IS BETTER?
As always, Hebrews stresses the advantages of living now, rather than in the Old Testament ("the first covenant"). Because of Christ, sacrifices are no longer necessary (10:11–12), and God's laws are now written in our minds and on our hearts, not in a formal code (8:10). "It is finished," Christ cried out from the cross (John 19:30); the author of Hebrews describes how.

Copies have some value. A photograph of a whale, for example, conveys much to those who will never encounter one. But, as the author of Hebrews asks, who would prefer a copy to the real thing?

□ LIFE QUESTIONS:
What practical help does Hebrews give on how to read the Old Testament? Of what value are the Old Testament laws and religious rituals?

---

a 5 Exodus 25:40   *b* 8 Some manuscripts may be translated *fault and said to the people.*

when I took them by the hand
  to lead them out of Egypt,
because they did not remain faithful to my
      covenant,
  and I turned away from them,
                            declares the Lord.
[10]This is the covenant I will make with the house
    of Israel
  after that time, declares the Lord.
I will put my laws in their minds
  and write them on their hearts.
I will be their God,
  and they will be my people.
[11]No longer will a man teach his neighbour,
  or a man his brother, saying, 'Know the
      Lord,'
because they will all know me,
  from the least of them to the greatest.
[12]For I will forgive their wickedness
  and will remember their sins no more."[c]

[13]By calling this covenant "new", he has made the
first one obsolete; and what is obsolete and ageing
will soon disappear.

■ Worship in the Earthly Tabernacle

9 Now the first covenant had regulations for worship and also an earthly sanctuary. [2]A tabernacle was set up. In its first room were the lampstand,
the table and the consecrated bread; this was called
the Holy Place. [3]Behind the second curtain was a
room called the Most Holy Place, [4]which had the
golden altar of incense and the gold-covered ark of
the covenant. This ark contained the gold jar of
manna, Aaron's staff that had budded, and the stone
tablets of the covenant. [5]Above the ark were the
cherubim of the Glory, overshadowing the atonement cover.[a] But we cannot discuss these things in
detail now.

[6]When everything had been arranged like this,
the priests entered regularly into the outer room to
carry on their ministry. [7]But only the high priest entered the inner room, and that only once a year, and
never without blood, which he offered for himself
and for the sins the people had committed in ignorance. [8]The Holy Spirit was showing by this that the
way into the Most Holy Place had not yet been disclosed as long as the first tabernacle was still standing. [9]This is an illustration for the present time,
indicating that the gifts and sacrifices being offered
were not able to clear the conscience of the worshipper. [10]They are only a matter of food and drink
and various ceremonial washings — external regulations applying until the time of the new order.

■ The Blood of Christ

[11]When Christ came as high priest of the good
things that are already here,[b] he went through the
greater and more perfect tabernacle that is not man-
made, that is to say, not a part of this creation. [12]He
did not enter by means of the blood of goats and
calves; but he entered the Most Holy Place once for
all by his own blood, having obtained eternal redemption. [13]The blood of goats and bulls and the
ashes of a heifer sprinkled on those who are

ceremonially unclean sanctify them so that they
are outwardly clean. [14]How much more, then, will
the blood of Christ, who through the eternal Spirit
offered himself unblemished to God, cleanse our
consciences from acts that lead to death,[c] so
that we may serve the living God!

9:11 ■ MORE PERFECT
Descriptions of the tabernacle and offerings take
up much of Exodus, Leviticus, Numbers, and
Deuteronomy, leading some scholars to judge it
the largest single subject covered in the Bible. Yet
Hebrews, concerned to prove the superiority of a
new covenant, devotes a mere 10 verses to the
tabernacle (verses 1–10). The great high priest,
Christ himself, has made the old system obsolete.

[15]For this reason Christ is the mediator of a new
covenant, that those who are called may receive the
promised eternal inheritance — now that he has
died as a ransom to set them free from the sins committed under the first covenant.

[16]In the case of a will,[d] it is necessary to prove
the death of the one who made it, [17]because a will
is in force only when somebody has died; it never
takes effect while the one who made it is living.
[18]This is why even the first covenant was not put
into effect without blood. [19]When Moses had proclaimed every commandment of the law to all the
people, he took the blood of calves, together with
water, scarlet wool and branches of hyssop, and
sprinkled the scroll and all the people. [20]He said,
"This is the blood of the covenant, which God has
commanded you to keep."[e] [21]In the same way, he
sprinkled with the blood both the tabernacle and
everything used in its ceremonies. [22]In fact, the law
requires that nearly everything be cleansed with
blood, and without the shedding of blood there is
no forgiveness.

[23]It was necessary, then, for the copies of the
heavenly things to be purified with these sacrifices,
but the heavenly things themselves with better sacrifices than these. [24]For Christ did not enter a man-
made sanctuary that was only a copy of the true one;
he entered heaven itself, now to appear for us in
God's presence. [25]Nor did he enter heaven to offer
himself again and again, the way the high priest enters the Most Holy Place every year with blood that
is not his own. [26]Then Christ would have had to suffer many times since the creation of the world. But
now he has appeared once for all at the end of the
ages to do away with sin by the sacrifice of himself.
[27]Just as man is destined to die once, and after that
to face judgment, [28]so Christ was sacrificed once to
take away the sins of many people; and he will appear a second time, not to bear sin, but to bring salvation to those who are waiting for him.

■ Christ's Sacrifice Once for All

10 The law is only a shadow of the good things
that are coming — not the realities themselves. For this reason it can never, by the same sacrifices repeated endlessly year after year, make

c 12 Jer. 31:31–34   a 5 Traditionally *the mercy seat*   b 11 Some early manuscripts *are to come*   c 14 Or *from useless rituals*   d 16 Same Greek
word as *covenant*; also in verse 17   e 20 Exodus 24:8

perfect those who draw near to worship. ²If it could, would they not have stopped being offered? For the worshippers would have been cleansed once for all, and would no longer have felt guilty for their sins. ³But those sacrifices are an annual reminder of sins, ⁴because it is impossible for the blood of bulls and goats to take away sins.

9:26 ■ A ONCE-FOR-ALL SACRIFICE

Jewish readers of Hebrews were very familiar with the religious rituals described in this chapter (see Leviticus 9 and 16 for the original instructions). Step by step, the author shows how Christ's new covenant improves on the old one. Instead of many sacrifices, he made only one, himself, thus gaining free and complete forgiveness for us. The chapter uses an analogy to explain why Christ's death was necessary (verse 17). It compares God's grace to a will. Wealth is only passed down when a death occurs; Christ's death freed the inheritance for us.

⁵Therefore, when Christ came into the world, he said:

"Sacrifice and offering you did not desire,
 but a body you prepared for me;
⁶with burnt offerings and sin offerings
 you were not pleased.
⁷Then I said, 'Here I am — it is written about me
 in the scroll —
 I have come to do your will, O God.' "ᵃ

⁸First he said, "Sacrifices and offerings, burnt offerings and sin offerings you did not desire, nor were you pleased with them" (although the law required them to be made). ⁹Then he said, "Here I am, I have come to do your will." He sets aside the first to establish the second. ¹⁰And by that will, we have been made holy through the sacrifice of the body of Jesus Christ once for all.

¹¹Day after day every priest stands and performs his religious duties; again and again he offers the same sacrifices, which can never take away sins. ¹²But when this priest had offered for all time one sacrifice for sins, he sat down at the right hand of God. ¹³Since that time he waits for his enemies to be made his footstool, ¹⁴because by one sacrifice he has made perfect for ever those who are being made holy.

10:12 ■ WHY CHRIST SAT DOWN

Hebrews makes special mention that Christ "sat down" after finishing his priestly duties. Jewish priests never sat down; the tabernacle and the temple did not have seats. They did their work standing up as a symbol that it was never finished. Having finished the work of a priest once for all, Christ "sat down".

¹⁵The Holy Spirit also testifies to us about this. First he says:

¹⁶"This is the covenant I will make with them
 after that time, says the Lord.
 I will put my laws in their hearts,
 and I will write them on their minds."ᵇ

¹⁷Then he adds:

"Their sins and lawless acts
 I will remember no more."ᶜ

¹⁸And where these have been forgiven, there is no longer any sacrifice for sin.

■ A Call to Persevere

¹⁹Therefore, brothers, since we have confidence to enter the Most Holy Place by the blood of Jesus, ²⁰by a new and living way opened for us through the curtain, that is, his body, ²¹and since we have a great priest over the house of God, ²²let us draw near to God with a sincere heart in full assurance of faith, having our hearts sprinkled to cleanse us from a guilty conscience and having our bodies washed with pure water. ²³Let us hold unswervingly to the hope we profess, for he who promised is faithful. ²⁴And let us consider how we may spur one another on towards love and good deeds. ²⁵Let us not give up meeting together, as some are in the habit of doing, but let us encourage one another — and all the more as you see the Day approaching.

²⁶If we deliberately keep on sinning after we have received the knowledge of the truth, no sacrifice for sins is left, ²⁷but only a fearful expectation of judgment and of raging fire that will consume the enemies of God. ²⁸Anyone who rejected the law of Moses died without mercy on the testimony of two or three witnesses. ²⁹How much more severely do you think a man deserves to be punished who has trampled the Son of God under foot, who has treated as an unholy thing the blood of the covenant that sanctified him, and who has insulted the Spirit of grace? ³⁰For we know him who said, "It is mine to avenge; I will repay,"ᵈ and again, "The Lord will judge his people."ᵉ ³¹It is a dreadful thing to fall into the hands of the living God.

³²Remember those earlier days after you had received the light, when you stood your ground in a great contest in the face of suffering. ³³Sometimes you were publicly exposed to insult and persecution; at other times you stood side by side with those who were so treated. ³⁴You sympathised with those in prison and joyfully accepted the confiscation of your property, because you knew that you yourselves had better and lasting possessions.

³⁵So do not throw away your confidence; it will be richly rewarded. ³⁶You need to persevere so that when you have done the will of God, you will receive what he has promised. ³⁷For in just a very little while,

"He who is coming will come and will not
 delay.
³⁸ But my righteous oneᶠ will live by faith.
 And if he shrinks back,
 I will not be pleased with him."ᵍ

³⁹But we are not of those who shrink back and are destroyed, but of those who believe and are saved.

ᵃ7 Psalm 40:6–8 (see Septuagint)   ᵇ16 Jer. 31:33   ᶜ17 Jer. 31:34   ᵈ30 Deut. 32:35   ᵉ30 Deut. 32:36; Psalm 135:14   ᶠ38 One early manuscript *But the righteous*   ᵍ38 Hab. 2:3,4

■ By Faith

11 Now faith is being sure of what we hope for and certain of what we do not see. ²This is what the ancients were commended for.

³By faith we understand that the universe was formed at God's command, so that what is seen was not made out of what was visible.

⁴By faith Abel offered God a better sacrifice than Cain did. By faith he was commended as a righteous man, when God spoke well of his offerings. And by faith he still speaks, even though he is dead.

⁵By faith Enoch was taken from this life, so that he did not experience death; he could not be found, because God had taken him away. For before he was taken, he was commended as one who pleased God. ⁶And without faith it is impossible to please God, because anyone who comes to him must believe that he exists and that he rewards those who earnestly seek him.

⁷By faith Noah, when warned about things not yet seen, in holy fear built an ark to save his family. By his faith he condemned the world and became heir of the righteousness that comes by faith.

⁸By faith Abraham, when called to go to a place he would later receive as his inheritance, obeyed and went, even though he did not know where he was going. ⁹By faith he made his home in the promised land like a stranger in a foreign country; he lived in tents, as did Isaac and Jacob, who were heirs with him of the same promise. ¹⁰For he was looking forward to the city with foundations, whose architect and builder is God.

¹¹By faith Abraham, even though he was past age — and Sarah herself was barren — was enabled to become a father because he*a* considered him faithful who had made the promise. ¹²And so from this one man, and he as good as dead, came descendants as numerous as the stars in the sky and as countless as the sand on the seashore.

¹³All these people were still living by faith when they died. They did not receive the things promised; they only saw them and welcomed them from a distance. And they admitted that they were aliens and strangers on earth. ¹⁴People who say such things show that they are looking for a country of their own. ¹⁵If they had been thinking of the country they had left, they would have had opportunity to return. ¹⁶Instead, they were longing for a better country — a heavenly one. Therefore God is not ashamed to be called their God, for he has prepared a city for them.

■ WHAT IS TRUE FAITH?
NOT EVEN GIANTS OF FAITH GET EXACTLY WHAT THEY WANT

INSIGHT

THESE WERE ALL COMMENDED FOR THEIR FAITH, YET NONE OF THEM RECEIVED WHAT HAD BEEN PROMISED.
■ 11:39

What is faith? And how can you be sure you've got it? Some Christians think of faith as an almost magical force: if you muster up enough of it, you'll get rich, stay healthy and live a contented life, they say. Yet how does one "muster up" faith? What are signs of true faith?

The author of Hebrews launches into a detailed description of faith, complete with references to several dozen biographical models. (Some have dubbed Hebrews 11 the "Faith Hall of Fame".) "Without faith," Hebrews says bluntly, "it is impossible to please God"(11:6).

■ NOT WHAT YOU'D EXPECT
But the picture of faith emerging from these chapters contains some surprises. The author uses words and phrases like "persevere", "endure", "do not lose heart". In many instances, the heroes cited did not receive the promise they hoped for; some ended up flogged and destitute, hiding out in goatskins (11:36–38). Many died — horrible deaths.

Faith, concludes the author, most resembles a difficult race. The runner has his or her eyes on the winner's prize, and, despite nagging temptations to slacken the pace, refuses to let up until he or she crosses the finish line. "Throw off everything that hinders," Hebrews coaches (12:1). "Strengthen your feeble arms and weak knees" (12:12).

■ IS IT WORTH THE STRUGGLE?
Why do people punish their bodies to run a gruelling marathon race? Most runners name two reasons: the sense of personal reward they get and the physical benefits of the exercise. The same two rewards apply in the spiritual realm: great prizes await those who persevere, and the very process of living by faith builds strong character. In this race, no-one loses. If you finish, you get the reward.

Here, as elsewhere, Hebrews holds up Jesus, who endured great suffering for our sakes (12:2–3), as the ultimate example. The faith described in Hebrews is not sugar-coated; God does not guarantee a life of luxury and ease. It is tough faith: a constant commitment to hang on and believe God against all odds, no matter what.

□ LIFE QUESTIONS:
Hebrews 11 mentions some people who prospered and some who suffered, yet all had faith. Taking into account what this passage says, try to come up with your own definition of faith.

---

a 11 Or By faith even Sarah, who was past age, was enabled to bear children because she

¹⁷By faith Abraham, when God tested him, offered Isaac as a sacrifice. He who had received the promises was about to sacrifice his one and only son, ¹⁸even though God had said to him, "It is through Isaac that your offspring^b will be reckoned."^c ¹⁹Abraham reasoned that God could raise the dead, and figuratively speaking, he did receive Isaac back from death.

11:16 ■ NOT ASHAMED

The list of God's favourites in Hebrews 11 includes blemished characters such as Samson and Rahab, triumphant winners such as David and Barak, and then a whole list of anonymous "failures" who faced torture and persecution. Yet at some point all of these displayed the kind of faith that pleases God.

²⁰By faith Isaac blessed Jacob and Esau in regard to their future.

²¹By faith Jacob, when he was dying, blessed each of Joseph's sons, and worshipped as he leaned on the top of his staff.

²²By faith Joseph, when his end was near, spoke about the exodus of the Israelites from Egypt and gave instructions about his bones.

²³By faith Moses' parents hid him for three months after he was born, because they saw he was no ordinary child, and they were not afraid of the king's edict.

²⁴By faith Moses, when he had grown up, refused to be known as the son of Pharaoh's daughter. ²⁵He chose to be ill-treated along with the people of God rather than to enjoy the pleasures of sin for a short time. ²⁶He regarded disgrace for the sake of Christ as of greater value than the treasures of Egypt, because he was looking ahead to his reward. ²⁷By faith he left Egypt, not fearing the king's anger; he persevered because he saw him who is invisible. ²⁸By faith he kept the Passover and the sprinkling of blood, so that the destroyer of the firstborn would not touch the firstborn of Israel.

²⁹By faith the people passed through the Red Sea^d as on dry land; but when the Egyptians tried to do so, they were drowned.

³⁰By faith the walls of Jericho fell, after the people had marched around them for seven days.

³¹By faith the prostitute Rahab, because she welcomed the spies, was not killed with those who were disobedient.^e

³²And what more shall I say? I do not have time to tell about Gideon, Barak, Samson, Jephthah, David, Samuel and the prophets, ³³who through faith conquered kingdoms, administered justice, and gained what was promised; who shut the mouths of lions, ³⁴quenched the fury of the flames, and escaped the edge of the sword; whose weakness was turned to strength; and who became powerful in battle and routed foreign armies. ³⁵Women received back their dead, raised to life again. Others were tortured and refused to be released, so that they might gain a better resurrection. ³⁶Some faced jeers and flogging, while still others were chained

and put in prison. ³⁷They were stoned;^f they were sawn in two; they were put to death by the sword. They went about in sheepskins and goatskins, destitute, persecuted and ill-treated — ³⁸the world was not worthy of them. They wandered in deserts and mountains, and in caves and holes in the ground.

³⁹These were all commended for their faith, yet none of them received what had been promised. ⁴⁰God had planned something better for us so that only together with us would they be made perfect.

■ God Disciplines His Sons

12 Therefore, since we are surrounded by such a great cloud of witnesses, let us throw off everything that hinders and the sin that so easily entangles, and let us run with perseverance the race marked out for us. ²Let us fix our eyes on Jesus, the author and perfecter of our faith, who for the joy set before him endured the cross, scorning its shame, and sat down at the right hand of the throne of God. ³Consider him who endured such opposition from sinful men, so that you will not grow weary and lose heart.

12:1 ■ PEP TALK

Chapter 12 makes clear why Hebrews 11 devoted such attention to martyrs from the past. The early Christians who first read this book were facing persecution, and their faith was bending under the pressure. Think of the "great cloud of witnesses" who have gone before, Hebrews urges, and fix your eyes on Jesus, who volunteered to die on your behalf. With its imagery borrowed from athletics, this portion of Hebrews sounds like a coach's half-time speech delivered to competitors in danger of giving up.

⁴In your struggle against sin, you have not yet resisted to the point of shedding your blood. ⁵And you have forgotten that word of encouragement that addresses you as sons:

"My son, do not make light of the Lord's
        discipline,
    and do not lose heart when he rebukes you,
⁶because the Lord disciplines those he loves,
    and he punishes everyone he accepts as a
        son."^a

⁷Endure hardship as discipline; God is treating you as sons. For what son is not disciplined by his father? ⁸If you are not disciplined (and everyone undergoes discipline), then you are illegitimate children and not true sons. ⁹Moreover, we have all had human fathers who disciplined us and we respected them for it. How much more should we submit to the Father of our spirits and live! ¹⁰Our fathers disciplined us for a little while as they thought best; but God disciplines us for our good, that we may share in his holiness. ¹¹No discipline seems pleasant at the time, but painful. Later on, however, it produces a harvest of righteousness and peace for those who have been trained by it.

^b18 Greek seed   ^c18 Gen. 21:12   ^d29 That is, Sea of Reeds   ^e31 Or unbelieving   ^f37 Some early manuscripts stoned; they were put to the test;   ^a6 Prov. 3:11,12

12Therefore, strengthen your feeble arms and weak knees! 13"Make level paths for your feet,"[b] so that the lame may not be disabled, but rather healed.

■ Warning Against Refusing God

14Make every effort to live in peace with all men and to be holy; without holiness no-one will see the Lord. 15See to it that no-one misses the grace of God and that no bitter root grows up to cause trouble and defile many. 16See that no-one is sexually immoral, or is godless like Esau, who for a single meal sold his inheritance rights as the oldest son. 17Afterwards, as you know, when he wanted to inherit this blessing, he was rejected. He could bring about no change of mind, though he sought the blessing with tears.

18You have not come to a mountain that can be touched and that is burning with fire; to darkness, gloom and storm; 19to a trumpet blast or to such a voice speaking words that those who heard it begged that no further word be spoken to them, 20because they could not bear what was commanded: "If even an animal touches the mountain, it must be stoned."[c] 21The sight was so terrifying that Moses said, "I am trembling with fear."[d]

12:18 ■ A VIVID CONTRAST

The author of Hebrews has been arguing that Christ's new covenant is far better than the old one between God and the Jews. This one section (verses 18–28) uses powerful images to summarise the great difference between encountering God in the way Moses did in the Old Testament and encountering him through Jesus. It also predicts that even greater things are in store: a new kingdom and new creation.

22But you have come to Mount Zion, to the heavenly Jerusalem, the city of the living God. You have come to thousands upon thousands of angels in joyful assembly, 23to the church of the firstborn, whose names are written in heaven. You have come to God, the judge of all men, to the spirits of righteous men made perfect, 24to Jesus the mediator of a new covenant, and to the sprinkled blood that speaks a better word than the blood of Abel.

25See to it that you do not refuse him who speaks. If they did not escape when they refused him who warned them on earth, how much less will we, if we turn away from him who warns us from heaven? 26At that time his voice shook the earth, but now he has promised, "Once more I will shake not only the earth but also the heavens."[e] 27The words "once more" indicate the removing of what can be shaken — that is, created things — so that what cannot be shaken may remain.

28Therefore, since we are receiving a kingdom that cannot be shaken, let us be thankful, and so worship God acceptably with reverence and awe, 29for our "God is a consuming fire."[f]

■ Concluding Exhortations

13 Keep on loving each other as brothers. 2Do not forget to entertain strangers, for by so doing some people have entertained angels without knowing it. 3Remember those in prison as if you were their fellow-prisoners, and those who are illtreated as if you yourselves were suffering.

4Marriage should be honoured by all, and the marriage bed kept pure, for God will judge the adulterer and all the sexually immoral. 5Keep your lives free from the love of money and be content with what you have, because God has said,

"Never will I leave you;
    never will I forsake you."[a]

6So we say with confidence,

"The Lord is my helper; I will not be afraid.
    What can man do to me?"[b]

7Remember your leaders, who spoke the word of God to you. Consider the outcome of their way of life and imitate their faith. 8Jesus Christ is the same yesterday and today and for ever. 9Do not be carried away by all kinds of strange teachings. It is good for our hearts to be strengthened by grace, not by ceremonial foods, which are of no value to those who eat them. 10We have an altar from which those who minister at the tabernacle have no right to eat. 11The high priest carries the blood of animals into the Most Holy Place as a sin offering, but the bodies are burned outside the camp. 12And so Jesus also suffered outside the city gate to make the people holy through his own blood. 13Let us, then, go to him outside the camp, bearing the disgrace he bore. 14For here we do not have an enduring city, but we are looking for the city that is to come. 15Through Jesus, therefore, let us continually offer to God a sacrifice of praise — the fruit of lips that confess his name. 16And do not forget to do good and to share with others, for with such sacrifices God is pleased.

13:15 ■ SACRIFICE OF PRAISE

In form, Hebrews is more theological than practical. But in the last chapter the author adds a list of specific commands and suggestions. Even here, however, he makes one last reference to sacrifice. Now, we have only a "sacrifice of praise" to offer, because Christ accomplished all that was needed.

17Obey your leaders and submit to their authority. They keep watch over you as men who must give an account. Obey them so that their work will be a joy, not a burden, for that would be of no advantage to you.

18Pray for us. We are sure that we have a clear conscience and desire to live honourably in every way. 19I particularly urge you to pray so that I may be restored to you soon.

20May the God of peace, who through the blood

---

b13 Prov. 4:26   c20 Exodus 19:12,13   d21 Deut. 9:19   e26 Haggai 2:6   f29 Deut. 4:24   a5 Deut. 31:6   b6 Psalm 118:6,7 of the eternal covenant brought back from the dead our Lord Jesus, that great Shepherd of the sheep, [21]equip you with everything good for doing his will, and may he work in us what is pleasing to him, through Jesus Christ, to whom be glory for ever and ever. Amen.

[22]Brothers, I urge you to bear with my word of exhortation, for I have written you only a short letter.

[23]I want you to know that our brother Timothy has been released. If he arrives soon, I will come with him to see you.

[24]Greet all your leaders and all God's people. Those from Italy send you their greetings.

[25]Grace be with you all.

JAMES

■ WORDS ARE NOT ENOUGH

YOU CAN BELIEVE ALL THE RIGHT THINGS, YET STILL BE COMPLETELY WRONG

DO NOT MERELY LISTEN TO THE WORD, AND SO DECEIVE YOURSELVES. DO WHAT IT SAYS. ■ 1:22

Where there is life, there is motion. Some antelopes, as well as the cheetah, can sprint faster than the legal speed limit for cars. Rutting stags, charging one another head first, collide with such force that the sound echoes like a gunshot through forest glades. Canada geese, fanned out across the sky in an orderly V, battle winds for 1,000 miles, nonstop, before dropping back to earth.

Sometimes we keep relics of life: a prize salmon in a glass jar hanging above a fireplace, a fragile, perfect seashell, an exotic butterfly mounted on a pin. But these are mere mementos: life has gone from them, and with it motion.

■ A SURE SIGN OF LIFE

Authors of the Bible often look to nature for analogies to express spiritual truth. And the book of James, controversial because of its emphasis on "good works", is perhaps best understood through the analogy of motion. In the spiritual realm also, where there's life there will be motion.

When a person becomes a Christian, new life begins, and inevitably that life must express itself through "spiritual motion", or good deeds. In James' words, "What good is it . . . if a man claims to have faith but has no deeds?" (2:14).

Movement does not cause life, but it does invariably follow life. It's a sure sign that life is present. Similarly, genuine faith in Christ should always result in actions that demonstrate the faith.

■ DOES JAMES CONTRADICT PAUL?

James is not writing about how to become a Christian, but rather how to act like one. Having all the correct beliefs about God will hardly suffice:

even demons believe in God. Real, life-giving faith should produce motion, and James minces no words in describing the specific spiritual actions expected of Christians.

Christian thinkers, notably Martin Luther, have struggled to reconcile the message of James with that of Paul, who so firmly warned against slavish legalism. But Paul never belittled holy living. When he wrote to carousers, such as in his letters to the Corinthians, he railed against immorality as strongly as James.

Evidently, James' readers were not even flirting with legalism. They lived at the other extreme, ignoring those laws God had clearly revealed. James had a simple remedy: "Do not merely listen to the word. . . . Do what it says" (1:22).

■ STRAIGHT TO THE POINT

Unlike the apostle Paul, James was no urbane man of letters. He was a simple, homespun preacher, perturbed at people who were not living as they should. His letter covers a wide range of topics, applying the Christian faith to specific problems and commanding readers to live out their beliefs.

Be humble! James orders. *Submit to God! Stop sinning!* James is as forthright as an Old Testament prophet; it's hard to miss his point.

Modern readers of James face the same dilemma as the first recipients of this unsettling letter. His words are easy enough to understand, but are we doing what he says? What kind of motion characterises our spiritual lives? As Luther himself said, "You are saved by faith alone, but if faith is alone it is not faith."

■ HOW TO READ JAMES

Few New Testament writers achieve the clarity or the "punch" of James. He doesn't spend time expanding subpoints or worrying about literary structure. As a result, the book of James reads like a collection of pithy proverbs. (It's sometimes called the "Proverbs of the New Testament".) As you read, it may help to group the material by subject; James tends to return to themes repeatedly.

As leader of the headquarters church in Jerusalem, James knew how to speak with authority. You don't have to look for hidden meanings in this book. James tells you clearly how you should act, in 54 direct commands. Note that many of these have parallels to Jesus' Sermon on the Mount. As you read, keep in mind the diverse audience he was addressing, which included the rich and the poor. Note his "asides" to specific groups.

■ 3-TRACK READING PLAN

For an explanation and complete listing of the 3-track reading plan, turn to page x.

■ TRACK 1:
Two-Week Courses on the Bible
See page x for information on these courses.

■ TRACK 2:
An Overview of James in

1 Day
☐ Day 1. Read the Introduction to James, then chapter 1, on how the Christian should respond to tough times, or "trials".
Now turn to page xi for your next Track 2 reading project.

■ TRACK 3:
All of James in 4 Days
After you have read through James, turn to pages xii–xiii for your next Track 3 reading project.

☐ 1   ☐ 2   ☐ 3–4 ☐ 5

1 James, a servant of God and of the Lord Jesus Christ,

To the twelve tribes scattered among the nations:

Greetings.

■ Trials and Temptations
²Consider it pure joy, my brothers, whenever you face trials of many kinds, ³because you know that the testing of your faith develops perseverance. ⁴Perseverance must finish its work so that you may be mature and complete, not lacking anything. ⁵If any of you lacks wisdom, he should ask God, who gives generously to all without finding fault, and it will be given to him. ⁶But when he asks, he must believe and not doubt, because he who doubts is like a wave of the sea, blown and tossed by the wind. ⁷That man should not think he will receive anything from the Lord; ⁸he is a double-minded man, unstable in all he does.

1:3 ■ PRODUCTIVE PAIN
James' call for joy in the face of trials may seem shocking or even insensitive at first. A close reading, though, makes clear that James finds joy in the *results* of the trials, not in the trials themselves. Even difficult times can produce good qualities, such as perseverance. This positive, or "redemptive", approach to suffering surfaces throughout the New Testament (see Romans 5:1–5; 1 Peter 1:3–9).

⁹The brother in humble circumstances ought to take pride in his high position. ¹⁰But the one who is rich should take pride in his low position, because he will pass away like a wild flower. ¹¹For the sun rises with scorching heat and withers the plant; its blossom falls and its beauty is destroyed. In the same way, the rich man will fade away even while he goes about his business.

¹²Blessed is the man who perseveres under trial, because when he has stood the test, he will receive the crown of life that God has promised to those who love him.

¹³When tempted, no-one should say, "God is tempting me." For God cannot be tempted by evil, nor does he tempt anyone; ¹⁴but each one is tempted when, by his own evil desire, he is dragged away and enticed. ¹⁵Then, after desire has conceived, it gives birth to sin; and sin, when it is full-grown, gives birth to death.

¹⁶Don't be deceived, my dear brothers. ¹⁷Every good and perfect gift is from above, coming down from the Father of the heavenly lights, who does not change like shifting shadows. ¹⁸He chose to give us birth through the word of truth, that we might be a kind of firstfruits of all he created.

■ Listening and Doing
¹⁹My dear brothers, take note of this: Everyone should be quick to listen, slow to speak and slow to become angry, ²⁰for man's anger does not bring about the righteous life that God desires. ²¹Therefore, get rid of all moral filth and the evil that is so prevalent, and humbly accept the word planted in you, which can save you.

²²Do not merely listen to the word, and so deceive yourselves. Do what it says. ²³Anyone who listens to the word but does not do what it says is like a man who looks at his face in a mirror ²⁴and, after looking at himself, goes away and immediately forgets what he looks like. ²⁵But the man who looks intently into the perfect law that gives freedom, and

continues to do this, not forgetting what he has heard, but doing it—he will be blessed in what he does.

²⁶If anyone considers himself religious and yet does not keep a tight rein on his tongue, he deceives himself and his religion is worthless. ²⁷Religion that God our Father accepts as pure and faultless is this: to look after orphans and widows in their distress and to keep oneself from being polluted by the world.

■ Favouritism Forbidden

2 My brothers, as believers in our glorious Lord Jesus Christ, don't show favouritism. ²Suppose a man comes into your meeting wearing a gold ring and fine clothes, and a poor man in shabby clothes also comes in. ³If you show special attention to the man wearing fine clothes and say, "Here's a good seat for you," but say to the poor man, "You stand there" or "Sit on the floor by my feet," ⁴have you not discriminated among yourselves and become judges with evil thoughts?

2:1 ■ PLAY NO FAVOURITES

James 1 tells Christians to act out their faith. James 2 gives a very pointed example of church members deferring to the wealthy and powerful. This direct application, hitting close to home, characterises James. He leaves no room for ambiguity.

⁵Listen, my dear brothers: Has not God chosen those who are poor in the eyes of the world to be rich in faith and to inherit the kingdom he promised those who love him? ⁶But you have insulted the poor. Is it not the rich who are exploiting you? Are they not the ones who are dragging you into court? ⁷Are they not the ones who are slandering the noble name of him to whom you belong?

⁸If you really keep the royal law found in Scripture, "Love your neighbour as yourself,"ᵃ you are doing right. ⁹But if you show favouritism, you sin and are convicted by the law as law-breakers. ¹⁰For whoever keeps the whole law and yet stumbles at just one point is guilty of breaking all of it. ¹¹For he who said, "Do not commit adultery,"ᵇ also said, "Do not murder."ᶜ If you do not commit adultery but do commit murder, you have become a law-breaker.

¹²Speak and act as those who are going to be judged by the law that gives freedom, ¹³because judgment without mercy will be shown to anyone who has not been merciful. Mercy triumphs over judgment!

■ Faith and Deeds

¹⁴What good is it, my brothers, if a man claims to have faith but has no deeds? Can such faith save him? ¹⁵Suppose a brother or sister is without clothes and daily food. ¹⁶If one of you says to him, "Go, I wish you well; keep warm and well fed," but does nothing about his physical needs, what good is it? ¹⁷In

the same way, faith by itself, if it is not accompanied by action, is dead.

¹⁸But someone will say, "You have faith; I have deeds."

Show me your faith without deeds, and I will show you my faith by what I do. ¹⁹You believe that there is one God. Good! Even the demons believe that—and shudder.

²⁰You foolish man, do you want evidence that faith without deeds is useless?ᵈ ²¹Was not our ancestor Abraham considered righteous for what he did when he offered his son Isaac on the altar? ²²You see that his faith and his actions were working together, and his faith was made complete by what he did. ²³And the scripture was fulfilled that says, "Abraham believed God, and it was credited to him as righteousness,"ᵉ and he was called God's friend. ²⁴You see that a person is justified by what he does and not by faith alone.

²⁵In the same way, was not even Rahab the prostitute considered righteous for what she did when she gave lodging to the spies and sent them off in a different direction? ²⁶As the body without the spirit is dead, so faith without deeds is dead.

■ Taming the Tongue

3 Not many of you should presume to be teachers, my brothers, because you know that we who teach will be judged more strictly. ²We all stumble in many ways. If anyone is never at fault in what he says, he is a perfect man, able to keep his whole body in check.

³When we put bits into the mouths of horses to make them obey us, we can turn the whole animal. ⁴Or take ships as an example. Although they are so large and are driven by strong winds, they are steered by a very small rudder wherever the pilot wants to go. ⁵Likewise the tongue is a small part of the body, but it makes great boasts. Consider what a great forest is set on fire by a small spark. ⁶The tongue also is a fire, a world of evil among the parts of the body. It corrupts the whole person, sets the whole course of his life on fire, and is itself set on fire by hell.

3:3 ■ COLOURFUL LANGUAGE

Vivid, homely pictures from nature give a visual character to James' words, almost as if each thought were a photograph. He refers to sea froth, wilted flowers, a forest fire, a horse's bit, the morning mist, a hungry moth, the farmer's spring rains, a giant ship, and a salt-water spring. Paul, a more educated writer, alluded to culture and athletics and human relationships. But James felt most comfortable borrowing simple images from nature.

⁷All kinds of animals, birds, reptiles and creatures of the sea are being tamed and have been tamed by man, ⁸but no man can tame the tongue. It is a restless evil, full of deadly poison.

⁹With the tongue we praise our Lord and Father, and with it we curse men, who have been made in

ᵃ8 Lev. 19:18   ᵇ11 Exodus 20:14; Deut. 5:18   ᶜ11 Exodus 20:13; Deut. 5:17   ᵈ20 Some early manuscripts dead   ᵉ23 Gen. 15:6

God's likeness. ¹⁰Out of the same mouth come praise and cursing. My brothers, this should not be. ¹¹Can both fresh water and salt*a* water flow from the same spring? ¹²My brothers, can a fig-tree bear olives, or a grapevine bear figs? Neither can a salt spring produce fresh water.

■ Two Kinds of Wisdom

¹³Who is wise and understanding among you? Let him show it by his good life, by deeds done in the humility that comes from wisdom. ¹⁴But if you harbour bitter envy and selfish ambition in your hearts, do not boast about it or deny the truth. ¹⁵Such "wisdom" does not come down from heaven but is earthly, unspiritual, of the devil. ¹⁶For where you have envy and selfish ambition, there you find disorder and every evil practice.

¹⁷But the wisdom that comes from heaven is first of all pure; then peace-loving, considerate, submissive, full of mercy and good fruit, impartial and sincere. ¹⁸Peacemakers who sow in peace raise a harvest of righteousness.

■ Submit Yourselves to God

4 What causes fights and quarrels among you? Don't they come from your desires that battle within you? ²You want something but don't get it. You kill and covet, but you cannot have what you want. You quarrel and fight. You do not have, because you do not ask God. ³When you ask, you do not receive, because you ask with wrong motives, that you may spend what you get on your pleasures.

4:1 ■ THE NEED FOR SELF-CONTROL

If you had to distil the message of James into one word, it might be *self-control*. Chapters 4 and 5, which contain some of James' most striking imagery, show how simple greed and desire can corrode the church and destroy unity. And, indeed, many of the Jewish Christians he was writing to soon experienced an abrupt turn of fortune. They lost their wealth and suffered severe persecution.

⁴You adulterous people, don't you know that friendship with the world is hatred towards God? Anyone who chooses to be a friend of the world becomes an enemy of God. ⁵Or do you think Scripture says without reason that the spirit he caused to live in us envies intensely?*a* ⁶But he gives us more grace. That is why Scripture says:

"God opposes the proud
    but gives grace to the humble."*b*

⁷Submit yourselves, then, to God. Resist the devil,

■ CONFLICTS OF RICH AND POOR
A DIFFERENT KIND OF CLASS STRUGGLE

INSIGHT

GOD OPPOSES THE PROUD BUT GIVES GRACE TO THE HUMBLE. ■ 4:6

Our society tends to divide the rich and the poor. The two groups have little daily contact, and you would have a very hard time communicating a single message to both the very rich and the very poor.

Yet it seems James' original readers included both those groups. In one paragraph James addresses the haughty, privileged people of wealth, and in the next paragraph he turns to poor people undergoing severe trials. (Note the shift between 5:1 and 5:7.)

The two groups had different problems. The wealthy were selfish. They showed insensitivity and snobbishness to the poor. For their part, the poor responded with envy and grumbling. They blamed God for their poverty.

■ WHO IS DOUBLE-MINDED?

James gave advice on the specific problems of each group, but he also implied they have much in common. For both rich and poor the most important struggle is not outside – the conditions we live in – but rather inside. All of us experience the inner conflict of being pulled by powerful, contrary forces. Will we move towards Christ and the life he taught, or in the opposite direction? Will we trust God or reject him?

James coined a new word to describe this inner conflict: he called it being "double-minded" (4:8). For rich and poor, this conflict may express itself in different ways, as James went on to explain. But double-mindedness is a tug-of-war between divided loyalties. The essential struggle to obey God is no different for either group.

As he discussed the rich and the poor, James relied on many of the actual phrases Jesus had used, especially in the Sermon on the Mount. (This is quite understandable if the author was James the brother of Jesus, as many scholars believe.) He applied what Jesus taught in a fresh, new way, calling on all of us – rich and poor – to be single-minded in our commitment to follow that way.

□ LIFE QUESTIONS:

James 2 warns against favouritism based on social class. Does such favouritism happen among Christians today? Is there any difference between the way rich and poor people think about following Jesus?

*a*11 Greek *bitter* (see also verse 14)   *a*5 Or *that God jealously longs for the spirit that he made to live in us*; or *that the Spirit he caused to live in us longs*
jealously   *b*6 Prov. 3:34

and he will flee from you. ⁸Come near to God and he will come near to you. Wash your hands, you sinners, and purify your hearts, you double-minded. ⁹Grieve, mourn and wail. Change your laughter to mourning and your joy to gloom. ¹⁰Humble yourselves before the Lord, and he will lift you up.

¹¹Brothers, do not slander one another. Anyone who speaks against his brother or judges him speaks against the law and judges it. When you judge the law, you are not keeping it, but sitting in judgment on it. ¹²There is only one Lawgiver and Judge, the one who is able to save and destroy. But you—who are you to judge your neighbour?

■ Boasting About Tomorrow
¹³Now listen, you who say, "Today or tomorrow we will go to this or that city, spend a year there, carry on business and make money." ¹⁴Why, you do not even know what will happen tomorrow. What is your life? You are a mist that appears for a little while and then vanishes. ¹⁵Instead, you ought to say, "If it is the Lord's will, we will live and do this or that." ¹⁶As it is, you boast and brag. All such boasting is evil. ¹⁷Anyone, then, who knows the good he ought to do and doesn't do it, sins.

■ Warning to Rich Oppressors
5 Now listen, you rich people, weep and wail because of the misery that is coming upon you. ²Your wealth has rotted, and moths have eaten your clothes. ³Your gold and silver are corroded. Their corrosion will testify against you and eat your flesh like fire. You have hoarded wealth in the last days. ⁴Look! The wages you failed to pay the workmen who mowed your fields are crying out against you. The cries of the harvesters have reached the ears of the Lord Almighty. ⁵You have lived on earth in luxury and self-indulgence. You have fattened yourselves in the day of slaughter.ᵃ ⁶You have condemned and murdered innocent men, who were not opposing you.

■ Patience in Suffering
⁷Be patient, then, brothers, until the Lord's coming. See how the farmer waits for the land to yield its valuable crop and how patient he is for the autumn and spring rains. ⁸You too, be patient and stand firm, because the Lord's coming is near. ⁹Don't grumble against each other, brothers, or you

will be judged. The Judge is standing at the door!
¹⁰Brothers, as an example of patience in the face of suffering, take the prophets who spoke in the name of the Lord. ¹¹As you know, we consider blessed those who have persevered. You have heard of Job's perseverance and have seen what the Lord finally brought about. The Lord is full of compassion and mercy.

¹²Above all, my brothers, do not swear—not by heaven or by earth or by anything else. Let your "Yes" be yes, and your "No", no, or you will be condemned.

■ The Prayer of Faith
¹³Is any one of you in trouble? He should pray. Is anyone happy? Let him sing songs of praise. ¹⁴Is any one of you sick? He should call the elders of the church to pray over him and anoint him with oil in the name of the Lord. ¹⁵And the prayer offered in faith will make the sick person well; the Lord will raise him up. If he has sinned, he will be forgiven. ¹⁶Therefore confess your sins to each other and pray for each other so that you may be healed. The prayer of a righteous man is powerful and effective.

5:10 ■ WAITING IT OUT
In this section, James expands on the idea (1:2–4) that God can use suffering for our benefit. He realistically concedes that the rejoicing in the face of trials may not come right away. To develop such an attitude will take patience and perseverance. James mentions two sources of support for someone trying to cope with suffering: 1) the past example of people like the prophets and Job; 2) the church's ministry of healing and prayer.

¹⁷Elijah was a man just like us. He prayed earnestly that it would not rain, and it did not rain on the land for three and a half years. ¹⁸Again he prayed, and the heavens gave rain, and the earth produced its crops.

¹⁹My brothers, if one of you should wander from the truth and someone should bring him back, ²⁰remember this: Whoever turns a sinner from the error of his way will save him from death and cover over a multitude of sins.

ᵃ5 Or yourselves as in a day of feasting

1 PETER

■ A WORD TO THE SUFFERING
WHAT TO DO WHEN TROUBLE COMES

DEAR FRIENDS, DO NOT BE SURPRISED AT THE PAINFUL TRIAL YOU ARE SUFFERING, AS
THOUGH SOMETHING STRANGE WERE HAPPENING TO YOU. ■ 4:12

A distant, swirling cloud of dust signalled the
approach of Turkish death squads. But who could
escape? The villages of Armenia sat exposed and
defenceless on a rocky plain. Doomed Christians
clung together on the floors of their homes,
praying, singing, and shivering with fear.

This scene was repeated often during
World War I, and it usually ended in a massacre.
The Turkish assault against Armenian Christians
was one of history's worst religion-inspired
bloodbaths: over one million people died. But,
sadly, the Armenian tragedy was but one of
many attacks against 20th-century Christians.

More people have died for their religious
faith in this century than in all the rest of history
combined. Thousands of Christians died in East
Africa, first in the Mau Mau uprising and then
during Ugandan dictator Idi Amin's reign of
terror. Millions more suffered under Soviet and
Chinese governments. And the oppression goes
on: even today some countries imprison and
torture converts to Christianity. This fact alone
makes the book of 1 Peter starkly relevant for
modern readers.

■ HOW TO RESPOND TO PERSECUTION
What advice would you give Christians about to
undergo persecution? The apostle Peter took up
that challenge just as ominous rumblings from
Rome were striking fear into every Christian
community. Half-crazed Nero had seized on
believers as scapegoats for the ills of his empire.

Should the persecuted Christians flee or
resist? Should they tone down their outward
signs of faith? Give up? Peter's readers, their
lives in danger, needed clear advice on suffering.

They also wanted explanations of the
meaning of suffering. Why does God allow it?
Can good result? Does God care? In short, they

were asking the questions that occur to any
Christian who goes through great trial.

According to Peter, suffering should not
catch a Christian off guard. We are "strangers"
(1:17) in a hostile world, and where Christians
thrive, storm clouds may gather. Suffering is an
expected part of a life of sincere faith.

■ PETER'S OWN EXPERIENCE
On the subject of suffering, Peter makes an ideal
counsellor for readers then and now. He had been
flogged and imprisoned for his own faith, once
even expecting execution (Acts 12). Also, Peter
had personally watched Jesus endure suffering,
and in this letter he points to him as an example
of how to respond.

Peter encourages his readers to "live
such good lives among the pagans that, though
they accuse you of doing wrong, they may see
your good deeds and glorify God" (2:12).
Suffering can refine believers and give us an
opportunity to prove our faith, the result thus
working out for our benefit.

This book emphasises a further point
also: suffering is temporary, to be endured only
for "a little while" (1:6; 5:10). Those who suffer
with Christ will also glory with him in a life for
ever free of pain. Sceptics have criticised the
church for stressing a future life rather than
working to improve this one. "You promise pie in
the sky by and by," they taunt. But to Peter's
readers — wary of enemies on the prowl, unsure
of surviving another day — that message was as
tangible and nourishing as food.

According to 1 Peter, our hope that
suffering will one day cease is not a mirage but
a "living hope" (1:3) in the One who has
conquered death.

■ HOW TO READ 1 PETER

At first Christianity enjoyed official toleration by the Roman empire, but gradually the government turned against it. Rome resented the Christians' talk about another kingdom and their objections to idolatry and decadence.

Although 1 Peter was originally written to people in severe danger, its lessons apply to all of us, for we all experience pain of some kind. Why don't things work out the way we want? Is God trying to tell us something? Peter gives authoritative answers. As you read, try to apply what he says to your own situation.

Peter's writing style reveals his simple fisherman background: he uses pithy peasant expressions and awkwardly shifts back and forth between doctrine and advice. Chapter 2 (verses 18–25) shows an excellent example. Peter gives

a deep insight into what it meant for Christ to suffer on our behalf, but he includes it in a practical section on slaves and governments. Thus, he blends doctrine (what to believe) with practice (how to behave).

More a preacher than a writer, Peter structured his book like a rambling sermon. Look for the 34 direct commands included. Peter's reliance on common figures of speech – a cornerstone, a lamb, a shepherd – makes the book very quotable.

But Peter was not simply giving homespun advice; he was well-grounded in the teachings of Jesus and the prophets. Proportionately, he quotes from the Old Testament more than any other New Testament author.

■ 3-TRACK READING PLAN

For an explanation and complete listing of the 3-track reading plan, turn to page x.

■ TRACK 1:
Two-Week Courses on the Bible
See page x for information on these courses.

■ TRACK 2:
An Overview of 1 Peter in

1 Day
□ Day 1. Read the Introduction to 1 Peter, then chapter 1 for a capsular summary of the letter's style and message.
Now turn to page xi for your next Track 2 reading project.

■ TRACK 3:
All of 1 Peter in 4 Days
After you have read through 1 Peter, turn to pages xii–xiii for your next Track 3 reading project.

□ 1   □ 2   □ 3   □ 4–5

1 Peter, an apostle of Jesus Christ,

To God's elect, strangers in the world, scattered throughout Pontus, Galatia, Cappadocia, Asia and Bithynia, ²who have been chosen according to the foreknowledge of God the Father, through the sanctifying work of the Spirit, for obedience to Jesus Christ and sprinkling by his blood:

Grace and peace be yours in abundance.

■ Praise to God for a Living Hope
³Praise be to the God and Father of our Lord Jesus Christ! In his great mercy he has given us new birth into a living hope through the resurrection of Jesus Christ from the dead, ⁴and into an inheritance that can never perish, spoil or fade – kept in heaven for you, ⁵who through faith are shielded by God's power until the coming of the salvation that is ready to be revealed in the last time. ⁶In this you greatly rejoice, though now for a little while you may have had to suffer grief in all kinds of trials. ⁷These have come so that your faith – of greater worth than gold, which perishes even though refined by fire – may be proved genuine and may result in praise, glory and honour when Jesus Christ is revealed. ⁸Though you have not seen him, you love him; and even though you do not see him now, you believe in him and are filled with an inexpressible and glorious joy, ⁹for you are receiving the goal of your faith, the salvation of your souls.

¹⁰Concerning this salvation, the prophets, who spoke of the grace that was to come to you, searched intently and with the greatest care, ¹¹trying to find out the time and circumstances to which the Spirit of Christ in them was pointing when he predicted the sufferings of Christ and the glories that would follow. ¹²It was revealed to them that they were not serving themselves but you, when they spoke of the things that have now been told you by those who have preached the gospel to you by the Holy Spirit sent from heaven. Even angels long to look into these things.

1:7 ■ REFINER'S FIRE
A prospector who discovers gold-bearing rock sends it to an assayer for evaluation. Testing by fire will melt off most impurities, and the true gold will emerge purified. Suffering acts in much the same way, says Peter: it exposes and refines true faith. In addition, faith in the midst of such trials will earn future rewards.

■ Be Holy
¹³Therefore, prepare your minds for action; be self-controlled; set your hope fully on the grace to be given you when Jesus Christ is revealed. ¹⁴As obedient children, do not conform to the evil desires you had when you lived in ignorance. ¹⁵But just as he who called you is holy, so be holy in all

you do; [16]for it is written: "Be holy, because I am holy."[a]

[17]Since you call on a Father who judges each man's work impartially, live your lives as strangers here in reverent fear. [18]For you know that it was not with perishable things such as silver or gold that you were redeemed from the empty way of life handed down to you from your forefathers, [19]but with the precious blood of Christ, a lamb without blemish or defect. [20]He was chosen before the creation of the world, but was revealed in these last times for your sake. [21]Through him you believe in God, who raised him from the dead and glorified him, and so your faith and hope are in God.

[22]Now that you have purified yourselves by obeying the truth so that you have sincere love for your brothers, love one another deeply, from the heart.[b] [23]For you have been born again, not of perishable seed, but of imperishable, through the living and enduring word of God. [24]For,

"All men are like grass,
    and all their glory is like the flowers of the field;
the grass withers and the flowers fall,
[25]   but the word of the Lord stands for ever."[c]

And this is the word that was preached to you.

2 Therefore, rid yourselves of all malice and all deceit, hypocrisy, envy, and slander of every kind. [2]Like newborn babies, crave pure spiritual milk, so that by it you may grow up in your salvation, [3]now that you have tasted that the Lord is good.

■ The Living Stone and a Chosen People

[4]As you come to him, the living Stone — rejected by men but chosen by God and precious to him — [5]you also, like living stones, are being built into a spiritual house to be a holy priesthood, offering spiritual sacrifices acceptable to God through Jesus Christ. [6]For in Scripture it says:

"See, I lay a stone in Zion,
    a chosen and precious cornerstone,
and the one who trusts in him
    will never be put to shame."[a]

[7]Now to you who believe, this stone is precious. But to those who do not believe,

"The stone the builders rejected
    has become the capstone,"[b, c]

[8]and,

"A stone that causes men to stumble
    and a rock that makes them fall."[d]

They stumble because they disobey the message — which is also what they were destined for.

[9]But you are a chosen people, a royal priesthood, a holy nation, a people belonging to God, that you may declare the praises of him who called you out of darkness into his wonderful light. [10]Once you were not a people, but now you are the people of God; once you had not received mercy, but now you have received mercy.

[11]Dear friends, I urge you, as aliens and strangers in the world, to abstain from sinful desires, which war against your soul. [12]Live such good lives among the pagans that, though they accuse you of doing wrong, they may see your good deeds and glorify God on the day he visits us.

2:4 ■ A PLAY ON WORDS
In verses 4–9, Peter constructs a detailed metaphor out of a very common object: a stone. He refers to Christ as a stone rejected by builders, the kind of useless rock someone trips over. Yet this stone, Jesus, becomes the corner-stone of a new building composed of Christians ("living stones"). This metaphor has much in common with Paul's references to the "body of Christ", but Peter (nicknamed the "rock") uses architectural rather than biological terms.

2:11 ■ ENDANGERED STRANGERS
At first Christians had enjoyed the official protection of the Roman empire. Under Nero (A.D. 54–68) all that changed, and the apostles Peter and Paul were probably martyred during Nero's regime. Peter addressed this letter to "strangers in the world" (1:1), an indication that Christians were now viewed as a separate, persecuted minority without legal rights.

■ Submission to Rulers and Masters

[13]Submit yourselves for the Lord's sake to every authority instituted among men: whether to the king, as the supreme authority, [14]or to governors, who are sent by him to punish those who do wrong and to commend those who do right. [15]For it is God's will that by doing good you should silence the ignorant talk of foolish men. [16]Live as free men, but do not use your freedom as a cover-up for evil; live as servants of God. [17]Show proper respect to everyone: Love the brotherhood of believers, fear God, honour the king.

[18]Slaves, submit yourselves to your masters with all respect, not only to those who are good and considerate, but also to those who are harsh. [19]For it is commendable if a man bears up under the pain of unjust suffering because he is conscious of God. [20]But how is it to your credit if you receive a beating for doing wrong and endure it? But if you suffer for doing good and you endure it, this is commendable before God. [21]To this you were called, because Christ suffered for you, leaving you an example, that you should follow in his steps.

[22]"He committed no sin,
    and no deceit was found in his mouth."[e]

[23]When they hurled their insults at him, he did not retaliate; when he suffered, he made no threats. Instead, he entrusted himself to him who judges justly. [24]He himself bore our sins in his body on the tree, so that we might die to sins and live for righteousness; by his wounds you have been healed.

a16 Lev. 11:44,45; 19:2; 20:7   *b22* Some early manuscripts *from a pure heart*   *c25* Isaiah 40:6–8   *a6* Isaiah 28:16   *b7* Or *cornerstone*
c7 Psalm 118:22   *d8* Isaiah 8:14   *e22* Isaiah 53:9

²⁵For you were like sheep going astray, but now you have returned to the Shepherd and Overseer of your souls.

■ Wives and Husbands

3 Wives, in the same way be submissive to your husbands so that, if any of them do not believe the word, they may be won over without words by the behaviour of their wives, ²when they see the purity and reverence of your lives. ³Your beauty should not come from outward adornment, such as braided hair and the wearing of gold jewellery and fine clothes. ⁴Instead, it should be that of your inner self, the unfading beauty of a gentle and quiet spirit, which is of great worth in God's sight. ⁵For this is the way the holy women of the past who put their hope in God used to make themselves beautiful. They were submissive to their own husbands, ⁶like Sarah, who obeyed Abraham and called him her master. You are her daughters if you do what is right and do not give way to fear.

⁷Husbands, in the same way be considerate as you live with your wives, and treat them with respect as the weaker partner and as heirs with you of the gracious gift of life, so that nothing will hinder your prayers.

■ Suffering for Doing Good

⁸Finally, all of you, live in harmony with one another; be sympathetic, love as brothers, be compassionate and humble. ⁹Do not repay evil with evil or insult with insult, but with blessing, because to this

■ A MAN NAMED "THE ROCK"
PETER SLOWLY LEARNED HOW TO LIVE UP TO HIS NICKNAME

INSIGHT

HUMBLE YOURSELVES, THEREFORE, UNDER GOD'S MIGHTY HAND, THAT HE MAY LIFT YOU UP IN DUE TIME. ■ 5:6

You can't miss Peter in the four Gospels. He stands out like a country bumpkin, pushing to the head of the queue and coming out with loud, outrageous assertions. Every list of the disciples names him first, and Peter is often seen elbowing his way to centre stage.

He was likeable enough, with a big heart and unlimited enthusiasm. He just had too many rough edges. He swung like a pendulum, bold and courageous at one moment, yet cowardly when it really counted.

■ SIGNS OF MELLOWING
But by the time Peter sat down to write this letter, late in his life, a lot had changed. You can sense the change in the very words he chooses: words like *humble* and *submit*. This book contains nothing of the brash, aggressive style evident in the Gospels. He is heeding Jesus' last command to him: "Feed my sheep" (John 21:17). Gruff Peter has become a tender shepherd.

To get the full impact of Peter's transformation, you must read about him in the Gospels (especially in Mark), and then turn directly to this letter. Blustery, loud-mouthed Peter now counsels wives to have "the unfading beauty of a gentle and quiet spirit" (3:4) and husbands to treat their wives with consideration and respect (3:7). The man who sliced off an ear in Jesus' defence (John 18:10) now advises submission to every government authority (2:13). Peter once vigorously protested Jesus' prediction of death (Mark 8:32); now he solemnly commends Christ's suffering as an ideal (2:21–24).

It's easy to believe Peter is describing himself when he writes such statements as "Once you were not a people, but now you are the people of God" (2:10) and "You were like sheep going astray, but now you have returned to the Shepherd and Overseer of your souls" (2:25). Over time the shifting sand of Peter's personality solidified into granite.

■ NEVER TOO LATE
Peter finally earned the nickname that Jesus gave him long before: the "rock" (Matthew 16:18). And when he instructs his readers to stand fast in the true grace of God (5:12), you get the feeling Peter has learned through hard experience the lessons he is now passing on to others.

If Paul is the apostle of faith, Peter is the apostle of hope. God does not give up on people, as Peter's life amply demonstrates. We have reason to hope, whatever our circumstances — even when facing suffering or death.

Tradition reports that Peter was crucified head down on a Roman cross; he thought himself unworthy to die right side up like Jesus. Peter died still believing his promise of a happy ending: "And the God of all grace, who called you to his eternal glory in Christ, after you have suffered a little while, will himself restore you and make you strong, firm and steadfast" (5:10). He wrote like a man who knew.

□ LIFE QUESTIONS:
If Jesus were to give you a nickname, what would it be? Has your personality undergone major changes? What still needs work?

you were called so that you may inherit a blessing. [10]For,

"Whoever would love life
    and see good days
must keep his tongue from evil
    and his lips from deceitful speech.
[11]He must turn from evil and do good;
    he must seek peace and pursue it.
[12]For the eyes of the Lord are on the righteous
    and his ears are attentive to their prayer,
but the face of the Lord is against those who
    do evil."[a]

[13]Who is going to harm you if you are eager to do good? [14]But even if you should suffer for what is right, you are blessed. "Do not fear what they fear;[b] do not be frightened."[c] [15]But in your hearts set apart Christ as Lord. Always be prepared to give an answer to everyone who asks you to give the reason for the hope that you have. But do this with gentleness and respect, [16]keeping a clear conscience, so that those who speak maliciously against your good behaviour in Christ may be ashamed of their slander. [17]It is better, if it is God's will, to suffer for doing good than for doing evil. [18]For Christ died for sins once for all, the righteous for the unrighteous, to bring you to God. He was put to death in the body but made alive by the Spirit, [19]through whom[d] also he went and preached to the spirits in prison [20]who disobeyed long ago when God waited patiently in the days of Noah while the ark was being built. In it only a few people, eight in all, were saved through water, [21]and this water symbolises baptism that now saves you also — not the removal of dirt from the body but the pledge[e] of a good conscience towards God. It saves you by the resurrection of Jesus Christ, [22]who has gone into heaven and is at God's right hand — with angels, authorities and powers in submission to him.

3:19 ■ THE SPIRITS IN PRISON
At least 18 major theories have been proposed to explain Peter's meaning in verses 18–22. Primarily, scholars differ over what the phrase "spirits in prison" refers to. Were "the spirits" people in some intermediate state of death, or the fallen angels alluded to in Genesis 6:1–4? No-one knows for sure. Peter uses the obscure reference to make a point about the ultimate good that came from the suffering Jesus endured.

■ Living for God
4 Therefore, since Christ suffered in his body, arm yourselves also with the same attitude, because he who has suffered in his body is done with sin. [2]As a result, he does not live the rest of his earthly life for evil human desires, but rather for the will of God. [3]For you have spent enough time in the past doing what pagans choose to do — living in debauchery, lust, drunkenness, orgies, carousing and detestable idolatry. [4]They think it strange that you do not plunge with them into the same flood of dissipation, and they heap abuse on you. [5]But they will

have to give account to him who is ready to judge the living and the dead. [6]For this is the reason the gospel was preached even to those who are now dead, so that they might be judged according to men in regard to the body, but live according to God in regard to the spirit.

[7]The end of all things is near. Therefore be clear minded and self-controlled so that you can pray. [8]Above all, love each other deeply, because love covers over a multitude of sins. [9]Offer hospitality to one another without grumbling. [10]Each one should use whatever gift he has received to serve others, faithfully administering God's grace in its various forms. [11]If anyone speaks, he should do it as one speaking the very words of God. If anyone serves, he should do it with the strength God provides, so that in all things God may be praised through Jesus Christ. To him be the glory and the power for ever and ever. Amen.

■ Suffering for Being a Christian
[12]Dear friends, do not be surprised at the painful trial you are suffering, as though something strange were happening to you. [13]But rejoice that you participate in the sufferings of Christ, so that you may be overjoyed when his glory is revealed. [14]If you are insulted because of the name of Christ, you are blessed, for the Spirit of glory and of God rests on you. [15]If you suffer, it should not be as a murderer or thief or any other kind of criminal, or even as a meddler. [16]However, if you suffer as a Christian, do not be ashamed, but praise God that you bear that name. [17]For it is time for judgment to begin with the family of God; and if it begins with us, what will the outcome be for those who do not obey the gospel of God? [18]And,

"If it is hard for the righteous to be saved,
    what will become of the ungodly and the
        sinner?"[a]

4:13 ■ RADICAL SHIFT
This one verse, above all others, shows how much Peter had changed. He received Jesus' strongest rebuke (Mark 8:33) for objecting to the suggestion that Jesus would suffer. But now he presents suffering for Christ as a privilege, a way to participate in Christ's glory.

---

[19]So then, those who suffer according to God's will should commit themselves to their faithful Creator and continue to do good.

■ To Elders and Young Men
5 To the elders among you, I appeal as a fellow-elder, a witness of Christ's sufferings and one who also will share in the glory to be revealed: [2]Be shepherds of God's flock that is under your care, serving as overseers — not because you must, but because you are willing, as God wants you to be; not greedy for money, but eager to serve; [3]not lording

---

a 12 Psalm 34:12–16   *b 14* Or *not fear their threats*   *c 14* Isaiah 8:12   *d 18,19* Or *alive in the spirit,* 19*through which*   *e 21* Or *response*
a 18 Prov. 11:31

it over those entrusted to you, but being examples to the flock. [4]And when the Chief Shepherd appears, you will receive the crown of glory that will never fade away.

[5]Young men, in the same way be submissive to those who are older. All of you, clothe yourselves with humility towards one another, because,

"God opposes the proud
but gives grace to the humble."[a]

[6]Humble yourselves, therefore, under God's mighty hand, that he may lift you up in due time. [7]Cast all your anxiety on him because he cares for you.

[8]Be self-controlled and alert. Your enemy the devil prowls around like a roaring lion looking for someone to devour. [9]Resist him, standing firm in the faith, because you know that your brothers

throughout the world are undergoing the same kind of sufferings.

[10]And the God of all grace, who called you to his eternal glory in Christ, after you have suffered a little while, will himself restore you and make you strong, firm and steadfast. [11]To him be the power for ever and ever. Amen.

■ Final Greetings

[12]With the help of Silas,[b] whom I regard as a faithful brother, I have written to you briefly, encouraging you and testifying that this is the true grace of God. Stand fast in it.

[13]She who is in Babylon, chosen together with you, sends you her greetings, and so does my son Mark. [14]Greet one another with a kiss of love.

Peace to all of you who are in Christ.

a 5 Prov. 3:34   b 12 Greek *Silvanus*, a variant of *Silas*

2 PETER

■ A THREAT FROM WITHIN

THE WORST DANGERS AREN'T ALWAYS WELL MARKED

DEAR FRIENDS, THIS IS NOW MY SECOND LETTER TO YOU. I HAVE WRITTEN BOTH OF THEM AS REMINDERS TO STIMULATE YOU TO WHOLESOME THINKING. ■ 3:1

First-century apostles must have felt like pioneers in a mosquito-infested swamp. A pest attacked them. *Slap!* They'd kill it, and instantly another would land. Wherever they went new dangers swarmed up.

One group denied Jesus was God; then another declared him God but not fully man. The apostles denounced legalism, only to encounter 'free spirits' who assumed that "anything goes". Members of one church quit work and huddled together to await Jesus' return; those of another gave up on his returning at all.

Second Peter was written in response to a young church's jumpy tendencies. Whereas 1 Peter centred on fearsome dangers from outside, this letter speaks to dangers from within. False teachers were stirring up dissent, questioning basic doctrines, and leading Christians into immorality.

■ WARNING SIGNS

In its advice to the various squabbling groups,

2 Peter calls for a return to the true gospel. "I will always remind you of these things," the author says (1:12) and proceeds to go over some basic facts of how Christians should believe and behave. The book doesn't introduce many new insights; rather, it erects a giant warning sign against common pitfalls that endanger the church.

A key word, *knowledge*, echoes throughout this letter: 2 Peter refreshes readers' memories regarding the proper knowledge that makes possible "everything we need for life and godliness" (1:3). The author carefully grounds his knowledge in Old Testament prophets and eye-witness accounts of Jesus' life, not in "cleverly invented stories" (1:16). And he urges his readers to resist dangers by living blamelessly.

The answer to false knowledge, the author bluntly insists, is true knowledge; the answer to immoral living is moral living. As he prepares to die (1:14), the author of 2 Peter gets in one last appeal for truth.

■ HOW TO READ 2 PETER

Although 1 and 2 Peter claim the same author, they have many differences in style and approach. Second Peter is unrefined in writing style, more shrill and less gentle than the first letter. (Many scholars question whether the apostle Peter actually wrote the whole letter, but the letter does claim his authorship and shows some signs of his influence.)

Perhaps the difference in audiences explains the two approaches. The Bible views suffering – persecution from outside – as a purifying influence that often results in an even stronger church. Thus 1 Peter has an encouraging and devotional tone. But the real danger to a church comes from the inside, from immoral behaviour and false teaching. Second Peter, in strong words, addresses those "inside" dangers.

As you read it, try to put yourself in the place of the original audience. What dangers does the author warn against? Are there parallels today? Chapters 1 and 3 can be universally applied. Chapter 2 concerns itself more directly with the particular false teachers plaguing the first-century church.

In tone and actual content, 2 Peter resembles the tiny book of Jude. Both deal with the same problems and propose the same solutions.

When reading 2 Peter, look for the key word *knowledge*, and related words like *thinking, reminders/remind, and remember*. The author appeals to true knowledge that can correct many of the young church's errors.

■ 3-TRACK READING PLAN

For an explanation and complete listing of the 3-track reading plan, turn to page x.

■ TRACK 1:
Two-Week Courses on the
Bible
See page x for information on
these courses.

■ TRACK 2:
An Overview of 2 Peter in

1 Day
☐ Day 1. Read the
Introduction to 2 Peter, then
chapter 1.
Now turn to page xi for your
next Track 2 reading project.

■ TRACK 3:
All of 2 Peter in 3 Days
After you have read through
2 Peter, turn to pages xii–xiii
for your next Track 3 reading
project.

☐ 1   ☐ 2   ☐ 3

1 Simon Peter, a servant and apostle of Jesus Christ,

To those who through the righteousness of our God and Saviour Jesus Christ have received a faith as precious as ours:

²Grace and peace be yours in abundance through the knowledge of God and of Jesus our Lord.

■ Making One's Calling and Election Sure

³His divine power has given us everything we need for life and godliness through our knowledge of him who called us by his own glory and goodness. ⁴Through these he has given us his very great and precious promises, so that through them you may participate in the divine nature and escape the corruption in the world caused by evil desires. ⁵For this very reason, make every effort to add to your faith goodness; and to goodness, knowledge; ⁶and to knowledge, self-control; and to self-control, perseverance; and to perseverance, godliness; ⁷and to godliness, brotherly kindness; and to brotherly kindness, love. ⁸For if you possess these qualities in increasing measure, they will keep you from being ineffective and unproductive in your knowledge of our Lord Jesus Christ. ⁹But if anyone does not have them, he is short-sighted and blind, and has forgotten that he has been cleansed from his past sins. ¹⁰Therefore, my brothers, be all the more eager to make your calling and election sure. For if you do these things, you will never fall, ¹¹and you will receive a rich welcome into the eternal kingdom of our Lord and Saviour Jesus Christ.

■ Prophecy of Scripture

¹²So I will always remind you of these things, even though you know them and are firmly established in the truth you now have. ¹³I think it is right to refresh your memory as long as I live in the tent of this body, ¹⁴because I know that I will soon put it aside, as our Lord Jesus Christ has made clear to me. ¹⁵And I will make every effort to see that after my departure you will always be able to remember these things.

¹⁶We did not follow cleverly invented stories when we told you about the power and coming of our Lord Jesus Christ, but we were eye-witnesses of his majesty. ¹⁷For he received honour and glory from God the Father when the voice came to him from the Majestic Glory, saying, "This is my Son, whom I love; with him I am well pleased."ᵃ ¹⁸We ourselves heard this voice that came from heaven when we were with him on the sacred mountain.

1:14 ■ APPROACHING DEATH

The person writing these words was nearing death, a fact that may partially explain the book's forceful tone. An eye-witness (verse 16) of Jesus on earth was watching a young church stray from Christ's clear teaching. This letter may offer the last chance to oppose the deterioration.

¹⁹And we have the word of the prophets made more certain, and you will do well to pay attention to it, as to a light shining in a dark place, until the day dawns and the morning star rises in your hearts. ²⁰Above all, you must understand that no prophecy of Scripture came about by the prophet's own interpretation. ²¹For prophecy never had its origin in the will of man, but men spoke from God as they were carried along by the Holy Spirit.

■ False Teachers and Their Destruction

2 But there were also false prophets among the people, just as there will be false teachers among you. They will secretly introduce destructive heresies, even denying the sovereign Lord who bought them—bringing swift destruction on themselves. ²Many will follow their shameful ways and will bring the way of truth into disrepute. ³In their greed these teachers will exploit you with stories they have made up. Their condemnation has long been hanging over them, and their destruction has not been sleeping.

⁴For if God did not spare angels when they sinned, but sent them to hell,ᵃ putting them into gloomy dungeonsᵇ to be held for judgment; ⁵if he did not spare the ancient world when he brought the flood on its ungodly people, but protected Noah, a preacher of righteousness, and seven others; ⁶if he condemned the cities of Sodom and Gomorrah by burning them to ashes, and made them an example of what is going to happen to the ungodly; ⁷and if he rescued Lot, a righteous man, who was distressed by the filthy lives of lawless men ⁸(for that righteous man, living among them day after day,

---

ᵃ17 Matt. 17:5; Mark 9:7; Luke 9:35   ᵃ4 Greek Tartarus   ᵇ4 Some manuscripts into chains of darkness was tormented in his righteous soul by the lawless deeds he saw and heard)—⁹if this is so, then the Lord knows how to rescue godly men from trials and to hold the unrighteous for the day of judgment, while continuing their punishment.ᶜ ¹⁰This is especially true of those who follow the corrupt desire of the sinful natureᵈ and despise authority.

Bold and arrogant, these men are not afraid to slander celestial beings; ¹¹yet even angels, although they are stronger and more powerful, do not bring slanderous accusations against such beings in the presence of the Lord. ¹²But these men blaspheme in matters they do not understand. They are like brute beasts, creatures of instinct, born only to be caught and destroyed, and like beasts they too will perish.

2:5 ■ THREE WORLDS

Second Peter refers to three great ages of the earth. The first, the ancient world, was destroyed by the flood in Noah's day. The present time, in which we are now living, will be destroyed by fire (3:10). But the author points with hope to an age that has not yet come: a new heaven and a new earth (3:13).

¹³They will be paid back with harm for the harm they have done. Their idea of pleasure is to carouse in broad daylight. They are blots and blemishes, revelling in their pleasures while they feast with you.ᵉ ¹⁴With eyes full of adultery, they never stop sinning; they seduce the unstable; they are experts in greed—an accursed brood! ¹⁵They have left the straight way and wandered off to follow the way of Balaam son of Beor, who loved the wages of wickedness. ¹⁶But he was rebuked for his wrongdoing by a donkey—a beast without speech—who spoke with a man's voice and restrained the prophet's madness.

¹⁷These men are springs without water and mists driven by a storm. Blackest darkness is reserved for them. ¹⁸For they mouth empty, boastful words and, by appealing to the lustful desires of sinful human nature, they entice people who are just escaping from those who live in error. ¹⁹They promise them freedom, while they themselves are slaves of depravity—for a man is a slave to whatever has mastered him. ²⁰If they have escaped the corruption of the world by knowing our Lord and Saviour Jesus Christ and are again entangled in it and overcome, they are worse off at the end than they were at the beginning. ²¹It would have been better for them not to have known the way of righteousness, than to have known it and then to turn their backs on the sacred command that was passed on to them. ²²Of them the proverbs are true: "A dog returns to its vomit,"ᶠ and, "A sow that is washed goes back to her wallowing in the mud."

■ The Day of the Lord

3 Dear friends, this is now my second letter to you. I have written both of them as reminders to stimulate you to wholesome thinking. ²I want you to recall the words spoken in the past by the holy prophets and the command given by our Lord and Saviour through your apostles.

³First of all, you must understand that in the last days scoffers will come, scoffing and following their own evil desires. ⁴They will say, "Where is this 'coming' he promised? Ever since our fathers died, everything goes on as it has since the beginning of creation." ⁵But they deliberately forget that long ago by God's word the heavens existed and the earth was formed out of water and by water. ⁶By these waters also the world of that time was deluged and destroyed. ⁷By the same word the present heavens and earth are reserved for fire, being kept for the day of judgment and destruction of ungodly men.

⁸But do not forget this one thing, dear friends: With the Lord a day is like a thousand years, and a thousand years are like a day. ⁹The Lord is not slow in keeping his promise, as some understand slowness. He is patient with you, not wanting anyone to perish, but everyone to come to repentance.

¹⁰But the day of the Lord will come like a thief. The heavens will disappear with a roar; the elements will be destroyed by fire, and the earth and everything in it will be laid bare.ᵃ

3:10 ■ THE FATE OF THE EARTH

The time of global destruction described here was a common theme in letters to the early churches. Talk of a coming judgment and the overthrow of the existing world threatened and alarmed Rome, the chief power in the existing world then. Such doomsday prophecies aroused Roman hostility against Christians.

¹¹Since everything will be destroyed in this way, what kind of people ought you to be? You ought to live holy and godly lives ¹²as you look forward to the day of God and speed its coming.ᵇ That day will bring about the destruction of the heavens by fire, and the elements will melt in the heat. ¹³But in keeping with his promise we are looking forward to a new heaven and a new earth, the home of righteousness.

3:15 ■ A FELLOW AUTHOR

This comment is one of the rare instances in which a New Testament author refers directly to another New Testament book. Evidently, 2 Peter was written late enough that a group of Paul's letters already existed. Scholars use clues like this one to date books of the Bible.

¹⁴So then, dear friends, since you are looking forward to this, make every effort to be found spotless, blameless and at peace with him. ¹⁵Bear in mind that our Lord's patience means salvation, just as our dear brother Paul also wrote to you with the wisdom that God gave him. ¹⁶He writes the same way in all his letters, speaking in them of these matters.

ᶜ9 Or unrighteous for punishment until the day of judgment   ᵈ10 Or the flesh   ᵉ13 Some manuscripts in their love feasts   ᶠ22 Prov. 26:11
ᵃ10 Some manuscripts be burned up   ᵇ12 Or as you wait eagerly for the day of God to come

His letters contain some things that are hard to understand, which ignorant and unstable people distort, as they do the other Scriptures, to their own destruction.

[17]Therefore, dear friends, since you already know this, be on your guard so that you may not be carried away by the error of lawless men and fall from your secure position. [18]But grow in the grace and knowledge of our Lord and Saviour Jesus Christ. To him be glory both now and for ever! Amen.

1 JOHN

■ WORDS THAT GET POLLUTED
A PROBLEM WITH THE NEW GENERATION

LET US NOT LOVE WITH WORDS OR TONGUE BUT WITH ACTIONS AND IN TRUTH. ■ 3:18

Over time, common phrases can be stripped of meaning and applied to something else entirely. Take "born again", for example. First coined by Jesus, this phrase was resurrected in the sixties during the Jesus Movement. Soon it was snatched up as an advertising slogan to describe such things as a used car and even a football player making a comeback.

Christianity has been around so long that people borrow its words for quite different meanings. *Jesus,* the centre of our faith, is also a common curse word.

■ SAME WORDS, DIFFERENT MEANINGS
This tendency to pollute language is not new. Even at the close of the first century, words were being twisted and drained of their original meanings. When the apostle John wrote his letters, the Christian faith was perhaps 50 or 60 years old. A generation had grown up in Christian homes, and a distinct subculture was already developing.

Some people were using familiar phrases such as "knowing God", "walk in the light", and "born of God", but with new, distorted meanings. The apostle responded with fire. He knew that a confused, subtle distortion of truth is harder to resist than an outright denial.

In this book, John chooses key words (*light, sin, Christ, love, faith,* etc.), "disinfects"

them, and then restores their original meanings. He points back to the truths behind the words. Repeatedly, he begins with the phrase "If we claim . . . ." and proceeds to show what actions must result if we claim to live in the true light and to know God.

■ A STEP FURTHER
John wrote his Gospel account of Jesus' life in order to bring readers to a belief in Christ (John 20:31). He directed this letter to people who were already Christians, outlining how that faith should affect a person's life. God is light, he says; so walk in the light. He is spirit; so worship him in the proper spirit. He is love; so demonstrate that love to others.

At times John shows the tender concern of a pastor, calling his readers "my dear children" (2:1) and urging them to "love one another" (3:11). But in other places his stern language hints at why he once wore the nickname "Son of Thunder".

John was probably the last surviving apostle when he wrote this book. He lived almost to the end of the first century. But he was not too old to fight vigorously against whatever might corrupt the faith that had inspired him for so many years.

■ HOW TO READ 1 JOHN

First John is constructed like a piece of music. Its author states a few simple themes — light, truth, life, love — then builds variations on them. Relying on simple words and a rhythmic style, John writes in universal terms that apply to any time period.

Yet the book is understood far better if you know something about the environment in which John was writing. Therefore, begin your

reading with "Who Were the Gnostics?" on page 1090.

As you read John, note the pattern. He defines a word, such as *light,* discusses its opposite, *darkness,* and then describes what a life in the light should look like. In every case, he shows God as the source of power in the Christian life.

■ 3-TRACK READING PLAN

For an explanation and complete listing of the 3-track reading plan, turn to page x.

■ TRACK 1:
Two-Week Courses on the
Bible
See page x for information on
these courses.

■ TRACK 2:
An Overview of 1 John in
1 Day

☐ Day 1. Read the
Introduction to 1 John, then
chapter 3, a great summary of
the love of God and how it
should affect our lives.
Now turn to page xi for your
next Track 2 reading project.

■ TRACK 3:
All of 1 John in 4 Days
After you have read through
1 John, turn to pages xii–xiii
for your next Track 3 reading
project.

☐ 1–2 ☐ 3   ☐ 4   ☐ 5

■ The Word of Life

1 That which was from the beginning, which we
have heard, which we have seen with our eyes,
which we have looked at and our hands have
touched—this we proclaim concerning the Word of
life. ²The life appeared; we have seen it and testify
to it, and we proclaim to you the eternal life, which
was with the Father and has appeared to us. ³We
proclaim to you what we have seen and heard, so
that you also may have fellowship with us. And our
fellowship is with the Father and with his Son,
Jesus Christ. ⁴We write this to make our*a* joy
complete.

> ## 1:4 ■ EYE-WITNESS
> In contrast to most New Testament letters, this
> one does not identify its author. Certain hints and
> distinctive patterns of style, though, make it very
> likely that the apostle John wrote it in advanced
> age. Simply compare the first paragraph of this
> letter with the first few paragraphs of the Gospel
> of John to see the similarities. The author also
> emphasises that he was a close eye-witness of
> Jesus' life, a fact consistent with the "disciple
> whom Jesus loved".

■ Walking in the Light

⁵This is the message we have heard from him and
declare to you: God is light; in him there is no darkness at all. ⁶If we claim to have fellowship with him
yet walk in the darkness, we lie and do not live by
the truth. ⁷But if we walk in the light, as he is in the
light, we have fellowship with one another, and the
blood of Jesus, his Son, purifies us from all*b* sin.

⁸If we claim to be without sin, we deceive ourselves and the truth is not in us. ⁹If we confess our
sins, he is faithful and just and will forgive us our
sins and purify us from all unrighteousness. ¹⁰If we
claim we have not sinned, we make him out to be
a liar and his word has no place in our lives.

2 My dear children, I write this to you so that you
will not sin. But if anybody does sin, we have
one who speaks to the Father in our defence—Jesus
Christ, the Righteous One. ²He is the atoning sacrifice for our sins, and not only for ours but also for*a*
the sins of the whole world.

³We know that we have come to know him if we
obey his commands. ⁴The man who says, "I know
him," but does not do what he commands is a liar,
and the truth is not in him. ⁵But if anyone obeys his
word, God's love*b* is truly made complete in him.
This is how we know we are in him: ⁶Whoever
claims to live in him must walk as Jesus did.

⁷Dear friends, I am not writing you a new command but an old one, which you have had since the
beginning. This old command is the message you
have heard. ⁸Yet I am writing you a new command;
its truth is seen in him and you, because the
darkness is passing and the true light is already
shining.

⁹Anyone who claims to be in the light but hates
his brother is still in the darkness. ¹⁰Whoever loves
his brother lives in the light, and there is nothing in
him*c* to make him stumble. ¹¹But whoever hates
his brother is in the darkness and walks around in
the darkness; he does not know where he is going,
because the darkness has blinded him.

¹²I write to you, dear children,
  because your sins have been forgiven on
    account of his name.
¹³I write to you, fathers,
  because you have known him who is from
    the beginning.
I write to you, young men,
  because you have overcome the evil one.
I write to you, dear children,
  because you have known the Father.
¹⁴I write to you, fathers,
  because you have known him who is from
    the beginning.
I write to you, young men,
  because you are strong,
  and the word of God lives in you,
  and you have overcome the evil one.

> ## 2:12 ■ A FRIENDLY INTERRUPTION
> John begins his book with a stern warning against
> false ideas. But this lyrical section interrupts the
> flow with a warm greeting to true believers in the
> church. Many commentators believe that John
> intended the three categories (dear children,
> young men, fathers) to represent three different
> stages in his readers' spiritual lives.

---

*a*4 Some manuscripts your   *b*7 Or every   *a*2 Or He is the one who turns aside God's wrath, taking away our sins, and not only ours but also
*b*5 Or word, love for God   *c*10 Or it

■ Do Not Love the World

¹⁵Do not love the world or anything in the world. If anyone loves the world, the love of the Father is not in him. ¹⁶For everything in the world — the cravings of sinful man, the lust of his eyes and the boasting of what he has and does — comes not from the Father but from the world. ¹⁷The world and its desires pass away, but the man who does the will of God lives for ever.

■ Warning Against Antichrists

¹⁸Dear children, this is the last hour; and as you have heard that the antichrist is coming, even now many antichrists have come. This is how we know it is the last hour. ¹⁹They went out from us, but they did not really belong to us. For if they had belonged to us, they would have remained with us; but their going showed that none of them belonged to us. ²⁰But you have an anointing from the Holy One, and all of you know the truth.ᵈ ²¹I do not write to you because you do not know the truth, but because you do know it and because no lie comes from the truth. ²²Who is the liar? It is the man who denies that Jesus is the Christ. Such a man is the antichrist — he denies the Father and the Son. ²³No-one who denies the Son has the Father; whoever acknowledges the Son has the Father also.

2:22 ■ TOUGH LOVE
John had two nicknames. "The apostle of love" uses the word *love* 35 times in this brief letter alone. But the letter also hints at why he earned his original nickname, "Son of Thunder" (Mark 3:17). As one of Jesus' disciples, John had wanted to call fire down from heaven on unresponsive villages (Luke 9:54). Jesus rebuked such a notion, and John mellowed considerably over the years. Still, he reserves some choice words for enemies of the gospel: he brands them antichrists (2:18), liars (2:22), and children of the devil (3:10).

²⁴See that what you have heard from the beginning remains in you. If it does, you also will remain in the Son and in the Father. ²⁵And this is what he promised us — even eternal life.
²⁶I am writing these things to you about those who are trying to lead you astray. ²⁷As for you, the anointing you received from him remains in you, and you do not need anyone to teach you. But as his anointing teaches you about all things and as that anointing is real, not counterfeit — just as it has taught you, remain in him.

■ Children of God

²⁸And now, dear children, continue in him, so that when he appears we may be confident and unashamed before him at his coming.
²⁹If you know that he is righteous, you know that everyone who does what is right has been born of him.

3 How great is the love the Father has lavished on us, that we should be called children of God! And that is what we are! The reason the world does not know us is that it did not know him. ²Dear friends, now we are children of God, and what we will be has not yet been made known. But we know that when he appears,ᵃ we shall be like him, for we shall see him as he is. ³Everyone who has this hope in him purifies himself, just as he is pure.
⁴Everyone who sins breaks the law; in fact, sin is lawlessness. ⁵But you know that he appeared so that he might take away our sins. And in him is no sin. ⁶No-one who lives in him keeps on sinning. No-one who continues to sin has either seen him or known him.
⁷Dear children, do not let anyone lead you astray. He who does what is right is righteous, just as he is righteous. ⁸He who does what is sinful is of the devil, because the devil has been sinning from the beginning. The reason the Son of God appeared was to destroy the devil's work. ⁹No-one who is born of God will continue to sin, because God's seed remains in him; he cannot go on sinning, because he has been born of God. ¹⁰This is how we know who the children of God are and who the children of the devil are: Anyone who does not do what is right is not a child of God; nor is anyone who does not love his brother.

■ Love One Another

¹¹This is the message you heard from the beginning: We should love one another. ¹²Do not be like Cain, who belonged to the evil one and murdered his brother. And why did he murder him? Because his own actions were evil and his brother's were righteous. ¹³Do not be surprised, my brothers, if the world hates you. ¹⁴We know that we have passed from death to life, because we love our brothers. Anyone who does not love remains in death. ¹⁵Anyone who hates his brother is a murderer, and you know that no murderer has eternal life in him.

3:11 ■ LOVE VERSUS HATE
Very often John defines words in relation to their opposites: light versus darkness, truth versus falsehood, life versus death. In this paragraph, he begins with a command to "love one another", then goes on to illustrate the life of hate before coming back to define love. Many of 1 John's themes are developed in this "circular" method.

¹⁶This is how we know what love is: Jesus Christ laid down his life for us. And we ought to lay down our lives for our brothers. ¹⁷If anyone has material possessions and sees his brother in need but has no pity on him, how can the love of God be in him? ¹⁸Dear children, let us not love with words or tongue but with actions and in truth. ¹⁹This then is how we know that we belong to the truth, and how we set our hearts at rest in his presence ²⁰whenever our hearts condemn us. For God is greater than our hearts, and he knows everything.
²¹Dear friends, if our hearts do not condemn us,

ᵈ20 Some manuscripts *and you know all things*   ᵃ2 Or *when it is made known* we have confidence before God ²²and receive from him anything we ask, because we obey his commands and do what pleases him. ²³And this is his command: to believe in the name of his Son, Jesus Christ, and to love one another as he commanded us. ²⁴Those who obey his commands live in him, and he in them. And this is how we know that he lives in us: We know it by the Spirit he gave us.

■ Test the Spirits

4 Dear friends, do not believe every spirit, but test the spirits to see whether they are from God, because many false prophets have gone out into the world. ²This is how you can recognise the Spirit of God: Every spirit that acknowledges that Jesus Christ has come in the flesh is from God, ³but every spirit that does not acknowledge Jesus is not from God. This is the spirit of the antichrist, which you have heard is coming and even now is already in the world.

⁴You, dear children, are from God and have overcome them, because the one who is in you is greater than the one who is in the world. ⁵They are from the world and therefore speak from the viewpoint of the world, and the world listens to them. ⁶We are from God, and whoever knows God listens to us; but whoever is not from God does not listen to us. This is how we recognise the Spirit*ᵃ* of truth and the spirit of falsehood.

■ God's Love and Ours

⁷Dear friends, let us love one another, for love comes from God. Everyone who loves has been born of God and knows God. ⁸Whoever does not love does not know God, because God is love. ⁹This is how God showed his love among us: He sent his one and only Son*ᵇ* into the world that we might live through him. ¹⁰This is love: not that we loved God, but that he loved us and sent his Son as an atoning sacrifice for*ᶜ* our sins. ¹¹Dear friends, since God so loved us, we also ought to love one another. ¹²No-one has ever seen God; but if we love one another, God lives in us and his love is made complete in us.

■ WHO WERE THE GNOSTICS?
A DANGEROUS CULT THAT PROVED FATALLY ATTRACTIVE

INSIGHT

THIS IS HOW YOU CAN RECOGNISE THE SPIRIT OF GOD: EVERY SPIRIT THAT ACKNOWLEDGES THAT JESUS CHRIST HAS COME IN THE FLESH IS FROM GOD.
■ 4:2

As Christianity spread across the Mediterranean, it came into contact with other religions. Greeks and Romans tried to absorb the faith into their own philosophies, just as some Jews had initially.

Intellectual centres of the Mediterranean raised questions about Jesus: Who was he? If he was God, how could he die? And a popular new cult called Gnosticism (from the Greek word for knowledge, *gnosis*) gained ground in an attempt to explain these things. The cult thrived especially among the intellectual elite.

■ COULD GOD HAVE A BODY?
Gnostics stumbled on the Christian concept of God's becoming human. Because they believed a physical body was intrinsically evil, they denied that a pure God could take on a body. Some dealt with the problem by claiming that Jesus was never a real human being, but a phantom, a temporary appearance of God who only looked human. Others proposed that God had "descended" on Jesus at his baptism, but left him before his death.

The apostle John debated in person with Gnostics of his day, and he had Gnostic thinking in mind when he wrote this letter. The very first sentence expressly states that the author has

seen, heard and touched Jesus – implying he could not have been a phantom, or pure spirit. Throughout the letter, and especially in 4:2–3, the author lambastes those who deny that Jesus came in the flesh.

■ LIVE AS YOU PLEASE
To Gnostics, all matter was evil. Only the spirit was pure, and Gnostics sought to rise to a higher, more spiritual plane. This teaching often produced a side effect: people who strove to rise above matter didn't care about personal ethics. Their pure spirits could not be tainted by "earthly" sin. Thus, they could act any way they wanted.

Ageing John roared out against the twin dangers of Gnosticism: immoral living and doubts that Christ became a man. Beliefs must be judged by the actions they produce, and John stresses the theme of brotherly love. He primarily refutes errors by presenting a wholesome picture of the Christian life as it is supposed to be lived.

True fellowship is not a secret initiation into a New Age-type elite, but a relationship with the Father through Christ. And that also entails responsibilities to others in God's family.

□ LIFE QUESTIONS:
Gnosticism showed itself in several ways: the belief that matter was evil, a desire for "super-spirituality", a tendency towards loose morals. How can we counter those same trends among Christians today?

13We know that we live in him and he in us, because he has given us of his Spirit. 14And we have seen and testify that the Father has sent his Son to be the Saviour of the world. 15If anyone acknowledges that Jesus is the Son of God, God lives in him and he in God. 16And so we know and rely on the love God has for us.

God is love. Whoever lives in love lives in God, and God in him. 17In this way, love is made complete among us so that we will have confidence on the day of judgment, because in this world we are like him. 18There is no fear in love. But perfect love drives out fear, because fear has to do with punishment. The one who fears is not made perfect in love.

19We love because he first loved us. 20If anyone says, "I love God," yet hates his brother, he is a liar. For anyone who does not love his brother, whom he has seen, cannot love God, whom he has not seen. 21And he has given us this command: Whoever loves God must also love his brother.

■ Faith in the Son of God

5 Everyone who believes that Jesus is the Christ is born of God, and everyone who loves the father loves his child as well. 2This is how we know that we love the children of God: by loving God and carrying out his commands. 3This is love for God: to obey his commands. And his commands are not burdensome, 4for everyone born of God overcomes the world. This is the victory that has overcome the world, even our faith. 5Who is it that overcomes the world? Only he who believes that Jesus is the Son of God.

6This is the one who came by water and blood — Jesus Christ. He did not come by water only, but by water and blood. And it is the Spirit who testifies, because the Spirit is the truth. 7For there are three that testify: 8thea Spirit, the water and the blood; and the three are in agreement. 9We accept man's testimony, but God's testimony is greater because it is the testimony of God, which he has given about his Son. 10Anyone who believes in the Son of God has this testimony in his heart. Anyone who does not believe God has made him out to be a liar, be-

cause he has not believed the testimony God has given about his Son. 11And this is the testimony: God has given us eternal life, and this life is in his Son. 12He who has the Son has life; he who does not have the Son of God does not have life.

> **5:8 ■ WATER, BLOOD, AND SPIRIT**
> The apostle John relied heavily on symbolic language in his Gospel account of Jesus' life. Here, too, he uses symbols in giving proofs of Jesus. Water may refer to Jesus' baptism, blood to his death on the cross, and the Spirit to the Holy Spirit who descended on Jesus. John refers to these three as a "testimony" from God about his Son.

■ Concluding Remarks

13I write these things to you who believe in the name of the Son of God so that you may know that you have eternal life. 14This is the confidence we have in approaching God: that if we ask anything according to his will, he hears us. 15And if we know that he hears us — whatever we ask — we know that we have what we asked of him.

16If anyone sees his brother commit a sin that does not lead to death, he should pray and God will give him life. I refer to those whose sin does not lead to death. There is a sin that leads to death. I am not saying that he should pray about that. 17All wrongdoing is sin, and there is sin that does not lead to death.

18We know that anyone born of God does not continue to sin; the one who was born of God keeps him safe, and the evil one cannot harm him. 19We know that we are children of God, and that the whole world is under the control of the evil one. 20We know also that the Son of God has come and has given us understanding, so that we may know him who is true. And we are in him who is true — even in his Son Jesus Christ. He is the true God and eternal life.

21Dear children, keep yourselves from idols.

---

a 7,8 Late manuscripts of the Vulgate *testify in heaven: the Father, the Word and the Holy Spirit, and these three are one.* 8*And there are three that testify on earth: the* (not found in any Greek manuscript before the sixteenth century)

2 JOHN

■ UNDESIRABLE GUESTS

WHEN A "WELCOME" SIGN IS INAPPROPRIATE

WATCH OUT THAT YOU DO NOT LOSE WHAT YOU HAVE WORKED FOR. ■ 8

Roman roads made first-century travel safer and easier than ever before, but Holiday Inns were still centuries away. Therefore, when teachers of the Christian faith travelled the empire, they relied on local Christians for food and lodging.

Before long, false teachers (such as Gnostics) also hit the circuit, joined by religious racketeers attracted primarily to the free food and lodging. The two letters, 2 John and 3 John, the shortest books in the entire Bible, concern themselves with the mounting problems of hospitality for the "circuit-rider" teachers.

■ SHOW DISCRETION, BUT ALSO LOVE
Heresies had already sprung up in many local churches, and 2 John urges true Christians to us discretion in testing a visitor's message and motive. The author cautions against entertaining visitors who do not teach the truth about Christ.

True to his nickname, the apostle of love repeats his motto, "Love one another", even in this letter of warning. The ancient writer Jerome (A.D. 374–419) tells of the frail apostle John, in extreme old age, being carried into his congregation mumbling only, "Love one another." When asked why he talked of nothing else, John replied, "Because it is the Lord's command, and if this only is done, it is enough."

■ HOW TO READ 2 AND 3 JOHN

These two books are best read together, since each gives one side of a problem facing a young church. Try to imagine the setting back then, when Christianity was still new and many teachers came along claiming special insights. Do you see any parallels among Christians today? Look for the specific advice John gave in those circumstances.

■ 3-TRACK READING PLAN

For an explanation and complete listing of the 3-track reading plan, turn to page x.

■ TRACK 1:
Two-Week Courses on the Bible
See page x for information on these courses.

■ TRACK 2:
Read 2 and 3 John Together

in 1 Day
□ Day 1. These books are only one short chapter each, so you can easily read the two together.
Now turn to page xi for your next Track 2 reading project.

■ TRACK 3:
All of 2 and 3 John in 1 Day
Read both books in one day. After you have finished, turn to pages xii–xiii for your next Track 3 reading project.

□ 2 John, 3 John

[1]The elder,

To the chosen lady and her children, whom I love in the truth—and not I only, but also all who know the truth—[2]because of the truth, which lives in us and will be with us for ever:

[3]Grace, mercy and peace from God the Father and from Jesus Christ, the Father's Son, will be with us in truth and love.

[4]It has given me great joy to find some of your children walking in the truth, just as the Father commanded us. [5]And now, dear lady, I am not writing you a new command but one we have had from the beginning. I ask that we love one another. [6]And this is love: that we walk in obedience to his commands. As you have heard from the beginning, his command is that you walk in love.

[7]Many deceivers, who do not acknowledge Jesus Christ as coming in the flesh, have gone out into the world. Any such person is the deceiver and the antichrist. [8]Watch out that you do not lose what you have worked for, but that you may be rewarded fully. [9]Anyone who runs ahead and does not continue in the teaching of Christ does not have God; whoever continues in the teaching has both the Father and the Son. [10]If anyone comes to you and does not bring this teaching, do not take him into your house or welcome him. [11]Anyone who welcomes him shares in his wicked work.

7 ■ ANNOYING DECEIVERS

This paragraph shows that the enemies warned about in 1 John were still roaming about, stirring up trouble in the churches. The description of their beliefs—"who do not acknowledge Jesus Christ as coming in the flesh"—brings to mind the teaching of the Gnostics (see "Who Were the Gnostics?" page 1090), one of the main targets of that first letter.

[12]I have much to write to you, but I do not want to use paper and ink. Instead, I hope to visit you and talk with you face to face, so that our joy may be complete.

[13]The children of your chosen sister send their greetings.

3 JOHN

INTRODUCTION

■ GUIDELINES FOR HOSPITALITY

THE SAME QUESTIONS CROP UP IN EVERY AGE, IN EVERY PLACE

I HAVE NO GREATER JOY THAN TO HEAR THAT MY CHILDREN ARE WALKING IN THE TRUTH. ■ 4

Taken together, this letter and its companion give a balanced view of proper Christian hospitality. Second John warned against entertaining false teachers. But 3 John praises a man named Gaius for warmly welcoming genuine Christian teachers. His actions had been opposed by Diotrephes, a cantankerous church dictator, who was also gossiping against John.

In a very condensed form, John's two letters deal with heresy and church splits, two problems that have plagued the church in every age, in every place. To defend against those dangers, John urges love and discernment. Believers must know whom to accept and support, and whom to resist.

■ HOW TO READ 3 JOHN

See How to Read 2 and 3 John, page 1092.

¹The elder,

To my dear friend Gaius, whom I love in the truth.

²Dear friend, I pray that you may enjoy good health and that all may go well with you, even as your soul is getting along well. ³It gave me great joy to have some brothers come and tell about your faithfulness to the truth and how you continue to walk in the truth. ⁴I have no greater joy than to hear that my children are walking in the truth.

4 ■ NO GREATER JOY
Scholars estimate that the apostle John was between 80 and 90 years old when he wrote the letters bearing his name. He identifies himself as "the elder" (which may also refer to his office in a local church) and writes fondly of "my children". The letters carry the tone of an old man dispensing his last words of advice and taking grandfatherly pride in the progress of his spiritual heirs.

⁵Dear friend, you are faithful in what you are doing for the brothers, even though they are strangers to you. ⁶They have told the church about your love. You will do well to send them on their way in a manner worthy of God. ⁷It was for the sake of the Name that they went out, receiving no help from the pagans. ⁸We ought therefore to show hospitality to such men so that we may work together for the truth.

⁹I wrote to the church, but Diotrephes, who loves to be first, will have nothing to do with us. ¹⁰So if I come, I will call attention to what he is doing, gossiping maliciously about us. Not satisfied with that, he refuses to welcome the brothers. He also stops those who want to do so and puts them out of the church.

¹¹Dear friend, do not imitate what is evil but what is good. Anyone who does what is good is from God. Anyone who does what is evil has not seen God. ¹²Demetrius is well spoken of by everyone—and even by the truth itself. We also speak well of him, and you know that our testimony is true.

¹³I have much to write to you, but I do not want to do so with pen and ink. ¹⁴I hope to see you soon, and we will talk face to face.

Peace to you. The friends here send their greetings. Greet the friends there by name.

JUDE

■ WATCH OUT!

SOUNDING AN ALARM

I FELT I HAD TO WRITE AND URGE YOU TO CONTEND FOR THE FAITH. ■ 3

In some countries, if you sign up for a driver's training course, you'll begin with several hours of classroom lectures on "Rules of the Road". The instructor will drill you on the shapes and colours of warning signs — signs that announce danger on the roads.

Driving seems all very academic, until you slide behind the wheel. There, a missed stop sign won't just lower a test score; it could cost you your life. Your instructor, rather than calmly correcting you, will shout, "Look out!"

Jude writes in the style of a teacher who is watching a freight train bear down on his learner driver. Bells ring out, crossing gates go down, red lights flash. He admits this kind of letter isn't his preference; he intended a more high-minded treatise on salvation (verse 3). But the church was facing mortal dangers, and so Jude dashed off a vehement warning.

■ WHO WERE THE TROUBLEMAKERS?

Jude doesn't elaborate on what the troublemakers

(verse 4) were teaching — perhaps he didn't want to honour their ideas by discussing them. Their behaviour, however, is fair game: he fires away at their hypocrisy, divisiveness, and loose morals. He calls them spies and urges believers to fight for the true faith. At his poetic best, he borrows vivid images from nature to describe these people (12–13).

Short and vigorous, the book of Jude brings to mind a message from one of the fiery Old Testament prophets. Yet Jude holds out hope for his readers. Sincere believers can keep themselves in God's love, and some wavering souls can still be snatched "from the fire" (21–23). (Even when battling heretics, Jude does not hint at persecuting the offenders — no burnings at the stake here.)

Jude closes with a familiar and joy-filled doxology, the one part of his letter still quoted widely in modern churches.

■ HOW TO READ JUDE

In tone, Jude reads a lot like James and 2 Peter: it is simple, hard-hitting, and stern. In fact, it seems to copy entire sections of 2 Peter.

You can read through Jude in a few minutes, to get the force of his argument. But to truly appreciate his letter, you should reflect on (and look up) his various Old Testament references. Jude supports his arguments with

extensive illustrations from history, and he even quotes from two Jewish books not accepted as part of the Bible, *The Assumption of Moses* (verse 9) and the book of *Enoch* (verse 14).

All these citations support Jude's main thrust, which he summarises eloquently in the last few paragraphs.

■ 3-TRACK READING PLAN

For an explanation and complete listing of the 3-track reading plan, turn to page x.

■ TRACK 1:
Two-Week Courses on the Bible
See page x for information on these courses.

■ TRACK 2:
Read Jude in 1 Day
☐ Day 1. Just one chapter long, Jude will take only a few minutes to read.
Now turn to page xi for your next Track 2 reading project.

■ TRACK 3:
All of Jude in 1 Day
After you have read Jude, turn to pages xii–xiii for your next Track 3 reading project.

☐ Jude

¹Jude, a servant of Jesus Christ and a brother of James,

To those who have been called, who are loved by God the Father and kept by*a* Jesus Christ:

²Mercy, peace and love be yours in abundance.

■ The Sin and Doom of Godless Men

³Dear friends, although I was very eager to write to you about the salvation we share, I felt I had to write and urge you to contend for the faith that was once for all entrusted to the saints. ⁴For certain men whose condemnation was written about*b* long ago have secretly slipped in among you. They are godless men, who change the grace of our God into a licence for immorality and deny Jesus Christ our only Sovereign and Lord.

⁵Though you already know all this, I want to remind you that the Lord*c* delivered his people out of Egypt, but later destroyed those who did not believe. ⁶And the angels who did not keep their positions of authority but abandoned their own home—these he has kept in darkness, bound with everlasting chains for judgment on the great Day. ⁷In a similar way, Sodom and Gomorrah and the surrounding towns gave themselves up to sexual immorality and perversion. They serve as an example of those who suffer the punishment of eternal fire.

⁸In the very same way, these dreamers pollute their own bodies, reject authority and slander celestial beings. ⁹But even the archangel Michael, when he was disputing with the devil about the body of Moses, did not dare to bring a slanderous accusation against him, but said, "The Lord rebuke you!" ¹⁰Yet these men speak abusively against whatever they do not understand; and what things they do understand by instinct, like unreasoning animals—these are the very things that destroy them.

¹¹Woe to them! They have taken the way of Cain; they have rushed for profit into Balaam's error; they have been destroyed in Korah's rebellion.

¹²These men are blemishes at your love feasts, eating with you without the slightest qualm—shepherds who feed only themselves. They are clouds without rain, blown along by the wind; autumn trees, without fruit and uprooted—twice dead. ¹³They are wild waves of the sea, foaming up their shame; wandering stars, for whom blackest darkness has been reserved for ever.

11 ■ BAD MODELS

Jude mentions three Old Testament characters as powerful illustrations of qualities to avoid: the selfishness of Cain, the greed of Balaam, the rebelliousness of Korah. (Their stories can be found in Genesis 4, Numbers 22, and Numbers 16.) After filling his letter with such negative examples, however, Jude concludes triumphantly that God "is able to keep you from falling" (verse 24).

¹⁴Enoch, the seventh from Adam, prophesied about these men: "See, the Lord is coming with thousands upon thousands of his holy ones ¹⁵to judge everyone, and to convict all the ungodly of all the ungodly acts they have done in the ungodly way, and of all the harsh words ungodly sinners have spoken against him." ¹⁶These men are grumblers and fault-finders; they follow their own evil desires; they boast about themselves and flatter others for their own advantage.

■ A Call to Persevere

¹⁷But, dear friends, remember what the apostles of our Lord Jesus Christ foretold. ¹⁸They said to you, "In the last times there will be scoffers who will follow their own ungodly desires." ¹⁹These are the men who divide you, who follow mere natural instincts and do not have the Spirit.

²⁰But you, dear friends, build yourselves up in your most holy faith and pray in the Holy Spirit. ²¹Keep yourselves in God's love as you wait for the mercy of our Lord Jesus Christ to bring you to eternal life.

²²Be merciful to those who doubt; ²³snatch others from the fire and save them; to others show mercy, mixed with fear—hating even the clothing stained by corrupted flesh.

■ Doxology

²⁴To him who is able to keep you from falling and to present you before his glorious presence without fault and with great joy—²⁵to the only God our Saviour be glory, majesty, power and authority, through Jesus Christ our Lord, before all ages, now and for evermore! Amen.

---

*a*1 Or for; or in   *b*4 Or men who were marked out for condemnation   *c*5 Some early manuscripts Jesus

REVELATION

■ A BOOK FULL OF MYSTERIES

WHY REVELATION IS HARD TO UNDERSTAND

BLESSED IS THE ONE WHO READS THE WORDS OF THIS PROPHECY, AND BLESSED ARE THOSE WHO HEAR IT AND TAKE TO HEART WHAT IS WRITTEN IN IT, BECAUSE THE TIME IS NEAR. ■ 1:3

The Roman empire had its own version of Alcatraz: a rocky island called Patmos. Prisoners banished to that hard-labour colony usually wasted away and died. In that desolate setting a man named John had a series of visions he wrote down as Revelation, the strangest book in the New Testament.

John probably wrote this book about 60 years after Jesus left the earth. Questions were troubling the church. Was Jesus coming back as he had promised? Where did he go? To do what? Why didn't he return immediately? Revelation addresses those issues.

■ WRITING IN CODE

No other New Testament book resembles Revelation in style. Yet during its time similar Jewish "apocalyptic" books (books that symbolically picture the ultimate destruction of evil and the triumph of good) flourished. Authors, writing to persecuted Christians anxious about their future, predicted what would take place. Often, they used coded language to protect themselves; for example, they substituted a word like Babylon when criticising Rome, just in case their writings fell into the wrong hands.

The codes in Revelation are effective — so effective that few people today agree on exactly what they mean. Some people think many of the predictions in Revelation have not yet been fulfiled; perhaps John was writing about events that will come to pass in our own generation, they say. A best-selling book, Hal Lindsey's The Late Great Planet Earth, interprets Revelation that way.

Others explain Revelation in terms of the first century, concluding that many of the events prophesied in code took place during the Roman empire. Still others find clues to John's meaning spread out over 2,000 years of church history, or surmise that he employed symbols merely to describe an idealised battle of good and evil.

■ TWO DANGERS

Because of all the conflicting theories about Revelation, readers are tempted to respond in one of two ways. Some judge the book so perplexingly weird that they can find no reason to read it at all. How can anyone be sure of its meaning?

Others fall prey to the opposite danger. They pore over Revelation and conclude they have discovered the secret explanation of each obscure detail. To the latter group, it may be humbling to learn that every generation since the first century has come up with different interpretations of the prophecies.

■ WHY READ REVELATION?

Why read this strange book? John gives a good clue in the first phrase, which introduces this book as "the revelation of Jesus Christ". Revelation gives a unique picture of Jesus Christ, and the New Testament would be incomplete without it. The Gospels describe Jesus' life on earth from four different viewpoints. The letters discuss the deep significance of the resurrected Christ and what he accomplished. But Revelation shows Jesus Christ from a new perspective: as the mighty ruler of the cosmic forces of good. When John saw him in this exalted state, he fell at Jesus' feet as though dead (1:17).

Although Revelation does not remove the mystery surrounding Jesus' return and the end of the world, it does throw light on those events. It cannot be reduced to a mere timetable of events; it speaks lasting truths to every generation of readers. Revelation tells of Christ's future triumph over all the evil in the universe. This crucial message of final hope was needed by its original readers in the first century and is still needed by us today.

■ HOW TO READ REVELATION

Revelation is probably the most intimidating book in the Bible. It packs in so many symbols and obscure details that most readers find themselves plagued by the sensation that they are missing something.

All new forms of writing seem intimidating at first: for example, consider your very first science fiction book, filled with weird names and unearthly creatures, and governed by its own rules of writing. Science fiction seems very strange until you learn the techniques used by virtually all science fiction writers. Once you understand the form, it makes more sense. The same applies to Revelation. It will probably seem strange at first, because it uses techniques of symbolism and visions not commonly used elsewhere in the New Testament.

It is best to read Revelation one vision at a time, rather than all at once. The seven main visions give a view of similar events from different angles.

1. The church on earth (1–3)
2. The Lamb and the seven seals (4–7)
3. Seven angels with trumpets (8–11)
4. The church persecuted by Satan and the beast (12–14)

5. The seven bowls of God's wrath (15–16)
6. Judgment of Babylon (17–19:10).
7. Final judgment and final victory (19:11 to end).

Try to read completely through a vision, following the sectional headings marked in the Bible text.

As you read, look behind the visual symbols for the meaning they point to. Ask yourself, What does this tell me about Christ, about God, about the real meaning of history? Don't try to analyse details at first; just follow the main flow of thought.

Keep in mind also the condition of the persecuted Christians who first received this book. They needed not a precise calendar of future events, but rather a word of encouragement and hope. They needed faith that, no matter how things looked, God was in charge of history and good would ultimately triumph. Revelation provides this hope, for them and for us.

Finally, a good Bible dictionary or commentary will clear up much of the confusion about Revelation.

■ 3-TRACK READING PLAN

For an explanation and complete listing of the 3-track reading plan, turn to page x.

■ TRACK 1:
Two-Week Courses on the Bible
See page x for information on these courses.

■ TRACK 2:
An Overview of Revelation in 3 Days
☐ Day 1. Read the Introduction to Revelation,

then chapter 1, to see how John introduces this book.
☐ Day 2. Read chapter 12 as a sample of the writing contained in this book of visions.
☐ Day 3. Read chapter 21 for a glimpse of the final end of the universe.
Now turn to page xi for your next Track 2 reading project.

■ TRACK 3:
All of Revelation in 19 Days
After you have read through Revelation, turn to pages xii–xiii for your next Track 3 reading project.

☐ 1   ☐ 2   ☐ 3   ☐ 4–5
☐ 6   ☐ 7   ☐ 8   ☐ 9
☐ 10–11   ☐ 12   ☐ 13
☐ 14   ☐ 15–16   ☐ 17
☐ 18   ☐ 19   ☐ 20   ☐ 21
☐ 22

■ Prologue

1 The revelation of Jesus Christ, which God gave him to show his servants what must soon take place. He made it known by sending his angel to his servant John, ²who testifies to everything he saw — that is, the word of God and the testimony of Jesus Christ. ³Blessed is the one who reads the words of this prophecy, and blessed are those who hear it and take to heart what is written in it, because the time is near.

■ Greetings and Doxology

⁴John,

To the seven churches in the province of Asia:

Grace and peace to you from him who is, and who was, and who is to come, and from the seven spirits ᵃ before his throne, ⁵and from Jesus Christ, who is the faithful witness, the firstborn from the dead, and the ruler of the kings of the earth.

To him who loves us and has freed us from our sins by his blood, ⁶and has made us to be a kingdom and priests to serve his God and Father — to him be glory and power for ever and ever! Amen.

⁷Look, he is coming with the clouds,
    and every eye will see him,
even those who pierced him;
    and all the peoples of the earth will mourn
        because of him.
                                So shall it be! Amen.

⁸"I am the Alpha and the Omega," says the Lord God, "who is, and who was, and who is to come, the Almighty."

■ One Like a Son of Man

⁹I, John, your brother and companion in the suffering and kingdom and patient endurance that are ours in Jesus, was on the island of Patmos because of the word of God and the testimony of Jesus. ¹⁰On the Lord's Day I was in the Spirit, and I heard behind me a loud voice like a trumpet, ¹¹which said: "Write on a scroll what you see and send it to the seven churches: to Ephesus, Smyrna, Pergamum, Thyatira, Sardis, Philadelphia and Laodicea."

¹²I turned round to see the voice that was speaking to me. And when I turned I saw seven golden lampstands, ¹³and among the lampstands was someone "like a son of man", ᵇ dressed in a robe reaching down to his feet and with a golden sash round his chest. ¹⁴His head and hair were white like wool, as white as snow, and his eyes were like blazing fire. ¹⁵His feet were like bronze glowing in a furnace, and his voice was like the sound of rushing waters. ¹⁶In his right hand he held seven stars, and out of his mouth came a sharp double-edged sword. His face was like the sun shining in all its brilliance.

¹⁷When I saw him, I fell at his feet as though dead. Then he placed his right hand on me and said: "Do not be afraid. I am the First and the Last. ¹⁸I am the Living One; I was dead, and behold I am alive for ever and ever! And I hold the keys of death and Hades.

¹⁹"Write, therefore, what you have seen, what is now and what will take place later. ²⁰The mystery of the seven stars that you saw in my right hand and of the seven golden lampstands is this: The seven stars are the angels ᶜ of the seven churches, and the seven lampstands are the seven churches.

■ To the Church in Ephesus

2 "To the angel ᵃ of the church in Ephesus write:

These are the words of him who holds the seven stars in his right hand and walks among the seven golden lampstands: ²I know your deeds, your hard work and your perseverance. I know that you cannot tolerate wicked men, that you have tested those who claim to be apostles but are not, and have found them false. ³You have persevered and have endured hardships for my name, and have not grown weary.

⁴Yet I hold this against you: You have forsaken your first love. ⁵Remember the height from which you have fallen! Repent and do the things you did at first. If you do not repent, I will come to you and remove your lampstand from its place. ⁶But you have this in your favour: You hate the practices of the Nicolaitans, which I also hate.

⁷He who has an ear, let him hear what the Spirit says to the churches. To him who overcomes, I will give the right to eat from the tree of life, which is in the paradise of God.

■ To the Church in Smyrna

⁸"To the angel of the church in Smyrna write:

These are the words of him who is the First and the Last, who died and came to life again. ⁹I know your afflictions and your poverty — yet you are rich! I know the slander of those who say they are Jews and are not, but are a synagogue of Satan. ¹⁰Do not be afraid of what you are about to suffer. I tell you, the devil will put some of you in prison to test you, and you will suffer persecution for ten days. Be faithful, even to the point of death, and I will give you the crown of life.

¹¹He who has an ear, let him hear what the Spirit says to the churches. He who overcomes will not be hurt at all by the second death.

■ To the Church in Pergamum

¹²"To the angel of the church in Pergamum write:

These are the words of him who has the sharp, double-edged sword. ¹³I know where you live — where Satan has his throne. Yet you remain true to my name. You did not renounce your faith in me, even in the days of Antipas, my faithful witness, who was put to death in your city—where Satan lives.

14Nevertheless, I have a few things against you: You have people there who hold to the teaching of Balaam, who taught Balak to entice the Israelites to sin by eating food sacrificed to idols and by committing sexual immorality. 15Likewise you also have those who hold to the teaching of the Nicolaitans. 16Repent therefore! Otherwise, I will soon come to you and will fight against them with the sword of my mouth.

17He who has an ear, let him hear what the Spirit says to the churches. To him who overcomes, I will give some of the hidden manna. I will also give him a white stone with a new name written on it, known only to him who receives it.

■ To the Church in Thyatira
18"To the angel of the church in Thyatira write:

These are the words of the Son of God, whose eyes are like blazing fire and whose feet are like burnished bronze. 19I know your deeds, your love and faith, your service and perseverance, and that you are now doing more than you did at first.

20Nevertheless, I have this against you: You tolerate that woman Jezebel, who calls herself a prophetess. By her teaching she misleads my servants into sexual immorality and the eating of food sacrificed to idols. 21I have given her time to repent of her immorality, but she is unwilling. 22So I will cast her on a bed of suffering, and I will make those who commit adultery with her suffer intensely, unless they repent of her ways. 23I will strike her children dead. Then all the churches will know that I am he who searches hearts and minds, and I will repay each of you according to your deeds. 24Now I say to the rest of you in Thyatira, to you who do not hold to her teaching and have not learned Satan's so-called deep secrets (I will not impose any other burden on you): 25Only hold on to what you have until I come. 26To him who overcomes and does my will to the end, I will give authority over the nations—

27'He will rule them with an iron sceptre;
   he will dash them to pieces like
      pottery'b—

just as I have received authority from my Father. 28I will also give him the morning star. 29He who has an ear, let him hear what the Spirit says to the churches.

■ To the Church in Sardis
3 "To the angela of the church in Sardis write:

These are the words of him who holds the seven spiritsb of God and the seven stars. I know your deeds; you have a reputation of being alive, but you are dead. 2Wake up! Strengthen what remains and is about to die, for I have not found your deeds complete in the sight of my God. 3Remember, therefore, what you have received and heard; obey it, and repent. But if you do not wake up, I will come like a thief, and you will not know at what time I will come to you.

4Yet you have a few people in Sardis who have not soiled their clothes. They will walk with me, dressed in white, for they are worthy. 5He who overcomes will, like them, be dressed in white. I will never blot out his name from the book of life, but will acknowledge his name before my Father and his angels. 6He who has an ear, let him hear what the Spirit says to the churches.

■ To the Church in Philadelphia

7"To the angel of the church in Philadelphia write:

These are the words of him who is holy and true, who holds the key of David. What he opens no-one can shut, and what he shuts no-one can open. 8I know your deeds. See, I have placed before you an open door that no-one can shut. I know that you have little strength, yet you have kept my word and have not denied my name. 9I will make those who are of the synagogue of Satan, who claim to be Jews though they are not, but are liars—I will make them come and fall down at your feet and acknowledge that I have loved you. 10Since you have kept my command to endure patiently, I will also keep you from the hour of trial that is going to come upon the whole world to test those who live on the earth.

¹¹I am coming soon. Hold on to what you have, so that no-one will take your crown. ¹²Him who overcomes I will make a pillar in the temple of my God. Never again will he leave it. I will write on him the name of my God and the name of the city of my God, the new Jerusalem, which is coming down out of heaven from my God; and I will also write on him my new name. ¹³He who has an ear, let him hear what the Spirit says to the churches.

■ To the Church in Laodicea

¹⁴"To the angel of the church in Laodicea write:

These are the words of the Amen, the faithful and true witness, the ruler of God's creation. ¹⁵I know your deeds, that you are neither cold nor hot. I wish you were either one or the other! ¹⁶So, because you are lukewarm—neither hot nor cold—I am about to spit you out of my mouth. ¹⁷You say, 'I am rich; I have acquired wealth and do not need a thing.' But you do not realise that you are wretched, pitiful, poor, blind and naked. ¹⁸I counsel you to buy from me gold refined in the fire, so that you can become rich; and white clothes to wear, so that you can cover your shameful nakedness; and salve to put on your eyes, so that you can see.

¹⁹Those whom I love I rebuke and discipline. So be earnest, and repent. ²⁰Here I am! I stand at the door and knock. If anyone hears my voice and opens the door, I will come in and eat with him, and he with me.

²¹To him who overcomes, I will give the right to sit with me on my throne, just as I overcame and sat down with my Father on his throne. ²²He who has an ear, let him hear what the Spirit says to the churches."

■ The Throne in Heaven

4 After this I looked, and there before me was a door standing open in heaven. And the voice I had first heard speaking to me like a trumpet said, "Come up here, and I will show you what must take place after this." ²At once I was in the Spirit, and there before me was a throne in heaven with someone sitting on it. ³And the one who sat there had the appearance of jasper and carnelian. A rainbow, resembling an emerald, encircled the throne. ⁴Surrounding the throne were twenty-four other thrones, and seated on them were twenty-four elders. They were dressed in white and had crowns of gold on their heads. ⁵From the throne came flashes of lightning, rumblings and peals of thunder. Before the throne, seven lamps were blazing. These are the seven spirits[a] of God. ⁶Also before the throne there was what looked like a sea of glass, clear as crystal.

In the centre, around the throne, were four living creatures, and they were covered with eyes, in front and behind. ⁷The first living creature was like a lion, the second was like an ox, the third had a face like a man, the fourth was like a flying eagle. ⁸Each of the four living creatures had six wings and was covered with eyes all around, even under his wings. Day and night they never stop saying:

"Holy, holy, holy
is the Lord God Almighty,
who was, and is, and is to come."

⁹Whenever the living creatures give glory, honour and thanks to him who sits on the throne and who lives for ever and ever, ¹⁰the twenty-four elders fall down before him who sits on the throne, and worship him who lives for ever and ever. They lay their crowns before the throne and say:

¹¹"You are worthy, our Lord and God,
to receive glory and honour and power,
for you created all things,
and by your will they were created
and have their being."

4:7 ■ STRANGE CREATURES

The Old Testament prophet Ezekiel had a somewhat similar vision (Ezekiel 1:9–10). In his version, however, each individual creature had four faces: human, lion, ox, and eagle. These symbols held special meaning for people of that day, much as the American eagle or British lion does today. For more information see "A Startling Image of Jesus", page 1102.

■ The Scroll and the Lamb

5 Then I saw in the right hand of him who sat on the throne a scroll with writing on both sides and sealed with seven seals. ²And I saw a mighty angel proclaiming in a loud voice, "Who is worthy to break the seals and open the scroll?" ³But no-one in heaven or on earth or under the earth could open the scroll or even look inside it. ⁴I wept and wept because no-one was found who was worthy to open the scroll or look inside. ⁵Then one of the elders said to me, "Do not weep! See, the Lion of the tribe of Judah, the Root of David, has triumphed. He is able to open the scroll and its seven seals."

5:1 ■ SEALS AND SCROLLS

Certain words and phrases used in Revelation had a clearer meaning to ancient readers familiar with the objects. For example, important documents were sent written on a papyrus scroll sealed with several wax seals. Only the proper person, in the presence of witnesses, could open the document. Thus in this vision, only the "worthy" creature is able to break the seal.

⁶Then I saw a Lamb, looking as if it had been slain, standing in the centre of the throne, encircled by the four living creatures and the elders. He had seven horns and seven eyes, which are the seven spirits[a] of God sent out into all the earth. ⁷He came and took the scroll from the right hand of him who sat on the throne. ⁸And when he had taken it, the four living creatures and the twenty-four elders fell

[a]5 Or the sevenfold Spirit   [a]6 Or the sevenfold Spirit

down before the Lamb. Each one had a harp and they were holding golden bowls full of incense, which are the prayers of the saints. ⁹And they sang a new song:

"You are worthy to take the scroll
　　and to open its seals,
because you were slain,
　　and with your blood you purchased men for
　　　　God
　　from every tribe and language and people
　　　　and nation.
¹⁰You have made them to be a kingdom and
　　　　priests to serve our God,
　　and they will reign on the earth."

¹¹Then I looked and heard the voice of many angels, numbering thousands upon thousands, and ten thousand times ten thousand. They encircled the throne and the living creatures and the elders. ¹²In a loud voice they sang:

"Worthy is the Lamb, who was slain,

to receive power and wealth and wisdom and
　　　　strength
and honour and glory and praise!"

¹³Then I heard every creature in heaven and on earth and under the earth and on the sea, and all that is in them, singing:

"To him who sits on the throne and to the
　　　　Lamb
be praise and honour and glory and power,
　　　　for ever and ever!"

¹⁴The four living creatures said, "Amen", and the elders fell down and worshipped.

■ The Seals

6 I watched as the Lamb opened the first of the seven seals. Then I heard one of the four living creatures say in a voice like thunder, "Come!" ²I looked, and there before me was a white horse! Its rider held a bow, and he was given a crown, and he rode out as a conqueror bent on conquest.

³When the Lamb opened the second seal, I heard

■ A STARTLING IMAGE OF JESUS　INSIGHT
A HELPLESS LAMB – THE MIGHTIEST OF ALL CREATURES

I WEPT AND WEPT BECAUSE NO-ONE WAS FOUND WHO WAS WORTHY TO OPEN THE SCROLL OR LOOK INSIDE.
■ 5:4

Images of Jesus abound in Revelation, and one way to study the book is to follow a single image through the entire book. After his luminous appearance in the first chapter, Jesus is presented as a king, a warrior on a horse, the Lord of the whole earth, the husband of a bride. Of all the images, however, none is so startling and unlikely as the one in John's second vision. Yet it takes hold and appears repeatedly throughout the book.

To set the stage for this vision, the book of Revelation uses more visual drama than a science fiction film. Lightning flashes, the sky growls and awesome creatures encircle a lofty throne. Four of the creatures (4:6) seem to symbolise the most impressive examples of all creation, for a common saying in those days went,

The mightiest among the birds is the eagle.
The mightiest among the domestic animals is the bull.
The mightiest among the wild beasts is the lion.
And the mightiest of all is man.

■ONLY ONE WORTHY
A question resounds in the heavens, "Who is

worthy to break the seals and open the scroll?" (5:2). In other words, who is worthy to unloose the next phase of history? No-one can answer, much to John's dismay. Not one of the four impressive creatures qualifies.

But suddenly John sees another creature, a "Lamb, looking as if it had been slain" (5:6). The image contains a great paradox. None of the majestic angels or elders or living creatures has the right to break the seals. Only a Lamb does – a helpless, slaughtered Lamb.

John records a song of celebration ("You are worthy to take the scroll and to open its seals, because you were slain, and with your blood you purchased men for God" [5:9]), a song later set to earthly music in Handel's *Messiah*. And elsewhere in Revelation true believers are identified as being recorded in the "Lamb's book of life" (21:27).

This powerful image resurfaces often in Revelation, a book of warfare between good and evil. Christ the King is also the Lamb, the one who died for us. His death on the cross, seemingly a great defeat, actually ushered in a decisive victory, for him and for us. Good was not destroyed; it triumphed.

□LIFE QUESTIONS:
What meaning does the image of Jesus as a slain Lamb have for you? What are your favourite "pictures" or images of Jesus?

the second living creature say, "Come!" [4]Then an-other horse came out, a fiery red one. Its rider was given power to take peace from the earth and to make men slay each other. To him was given a large sword.

[5]When the Lamb opened the third seal, I heard the third living creature say, "Come!" I looked, and there before me was a black horse! Its rider was holding a pair of scales in his hand. [6]Then I heard what sounded like a voice among the four living creatures, saying, "A quart[a] of wheat for a day's wages,[b] and three quarts of barley for a day's wages,[b] and do not damage the oil and the wine!"

[7]When the Lamb opened the fourth seal, I heard the voice of the fourth living creature say, "Come!" [8]I looked, and there before me was a pale horse! Its rider was named Death, and Hades was following close behind him. They were given power over a fourth of the earth to kill by sword, famine and plague, and by the wild beasts of the earth.

[9]When he opened the fifth seal, I saw under the altar the souls of those who had been slain because of the word of God and the testimony they had maintained. [10]They called out in a loud voice, "How long, Sovereign Lord, holy and true, until you judge the inhabitants of the earth and avenge our blood?" [11]Then each of them was given a white robe, and they were told to wait a little longer, until the num-ber of their fellow-servants and brothers who were to be killed as they had been was completed.

[12]I watched as he opened the sixth seal. There was a great earthquake. The sun turned black like sackcloth made of goat hair, the whole moon turned blood red, [13]and the stars in the sky fell to earth, as late figs drop from a fig-tree when shaken by a strong wind. [14]The sky receded like a scroll, rolling up, and every mountain and island was removed from its place.

[15]Then the kings of the earth, the princes, the generals, the rich, the mighty, and every slave and every free man hid in caves and among the rocks of the mountains. [16]They called to the mountains and the rocks, "Fall on us and hide us from the face of him who sits on the throne and from the wrath of the Lamb! [17]For the great day of their wrath has come, and who can stand?"

■ 144,000 Sealed

7 After this I saw four angels standing at the four corners of the earth, holding back the four winds of the earth to prevent any wind from blow-ing on the land or on the sea or on any tree. [2]Then I saw another angel coming up from the east, having the seal of the living God. He called out in a loud voice to the four angels who had been given power to harm the land and the sea: [3]"Do not harm the land or the sea or the trees until we put a seal on the foreheads of the servants of our God." [4]Then I heard the number of those who were sealed: 144,000 from all the tribes of Israel.

[5]From the tribe of Judah 12,000 were sealed,
  from the tribe of Reuben 12,000,
  from the tribe of Gad 12,000,
  [6]from the tribe of Asher 12,000,

from the tribe of Naphtali 12,000,
  from the tribe of Manasseh 12,000,
  [7]from the tribe of Simeon 12,000,
  from the tribe of Levi 12,000,
  from the tribe of Issachar 12,000,
  [8]from the tribe of Zebulun 12,000,
  from the tribe of Joseph 12,000,
  from the tribe of Benjamin 12,000.

7:1 ■ SIGNIFICANT NUMBERS

Numbers had a great symbolic significance in the Bible, and especially to the writer of Revelation. This concept is foreign to most modern readers; a rough parallel might be the "unlucky" significance some attach to the number 13. The most obviously symbolic numbers in Revelation are 4, 7, 12, and their multiples.

The number 4 seems to stand for the created universe (four points of the compass, four winds of the earth), and thus the four living creatures (4:6) represent all creation. In the Bible, the number 7 denotes perfection or completion, probably because the Genesis creation account covers seven days. The 12 tribes of Israel in the Old Testament and 12 apostles in the New indicate that the number 12 stands for the church, or God's redeemed people from both covenants.

A number multiplied by 10s, such as 144,000 (12x12x10x10x10), suggests an indefinite but very large figure. Therefore, 144,000 may stand for the entire church throughout history.

■ The Great Multitude in White Robes

[9]After this I looked and there before me was a great multitude that no-one could count, from every nation, tribe, people and language, standing before the throne and in front of the Lamb. They were wearing white robes and were holding palm branches in their hands. [10]And they cried out in a loud voice:

"Salvation belongs to our God,
who sits on the throne,
and to the Lamb."

[11]All the angels were standing round the throne and around the elders and the four living creatures. They fell down on their faces before the throne and worshipped God, [12]saying:

"Amen!
Praise and glory
and wisdom and thanks and honour
and power and strength
be to our God for ever and ever.
Amen!"

[13]Then one of the elders asked me, "These in white robes—who are they, and where did they come from?"

[14]I answered, "Sir, you know."

And he said, "These are they who have come out of the great tribulation; they have washed their robes and made them white in the blood of the Lamb. [15]Therefore,

a 6 Greek a choinix (probably about a litre)   b 6 Greek a denarius

"they are before the throne of God
　　and serve him day and night in his temple;
　　and he who sits on the throne will spread his
　　　tent over them.
16Never again will they hunger;
　　never again will they thirst.
The sun will not beat upon them,
　　nor any scorching heat.
17For the Lamb at the centre of the throne will
　　be their shepherd;
　　he will lead them to springs of living water.
And God will wipe away every tear from their
　　eyes."

■ The Seventh Seal and the Golden Censer

8 When he opened the seventh seal, there was silence in heaven for about half an hour.
　2And I saw the seven angels who stand before
God, and to them were given seven trumpets.

　3Another angel, who had a golden censer, came
and stood at the altar. He was given much incense
to offer, with the prayers of all the saints, on the
golden altar before the throne. 4The smoke of the
incense, together with the prayers of the saints,
went up before God from the angel's hand. 5Then
the angel took the censer, filled it with fire from the
altar, and hurled it on the earth; and there came
peals of thunder, rumblings, flashes of lightning and
an earthquake.

■ The Trumpets
　6Then the seven angels who had the seven trumpets prepared to sound them.
　7The first angel sounded his trumpet, and there

came hail and fire mixed with blood, and it was
hurled down upon the earth. A third of the earth
was burned up, a third of the trees were burned up,
and all the green grass was burned up.
　8The second angel sounded his trumpet, and
something like a huge mountain, all ablaze, was
thrown into the sea. A third of the sea turned into
blood, 9a third of the living creatures in the sea died,
and a third of the ships were destroyed.
　10The third angel sounded his trumpet, and a
great star, blazing like a torch, fell from the sky on
a third of the rivers and on the springs of water —
11the name of the star is Wormwood.ᵃ A third of
the waters turned bitter, and many people died
from the waters that had become bitter.
　12The fourth angel sounded his trumpet, and a
third of the sun was struck, a third of the moon, and
a third of the stars, so that a third of them turned
dark. A third of the day was without light, and also
a third of the night.
　13As I watched, I heard an eagle that was flying in
mid-air call out in a loud voice: "Woe! Woe! Woe to
the inhabitants of the earth, because of the trumpet
blasts about to be sounded by the other three
angels!"

9 The fifth angel sounded his trumpet, and I saw
a star that had fallen from the sky to the earth.
The star was given the key to the shaft of the Abyss.
2When he opened the Abyss, smoke rose from it like
the smoke from a gigantic furnace. The sun and sky
were darkened by the smoke from the Abyss. 3And
out of the smoke locusts came down upon the earth
and were given power like that of scorpions of the
earth. 4They were told not to harm the grass of the
earth or any plant or tree, but only those people
who did not have the seal of God on their foreheads.
5They were not given power to kill them, but only
to torture them for five months. And the agony they
suffered was like that of the sting of a scorpion when
it strikes a man. 6During those days men will seek
death, but will not find it; they will long to die, but
death will elude them.
　7The locusts looked like horses prepared for
battle. On their heads they wore something like
crowns of gold, and their faces resembled human
faces. 8Their hair was like women's hair, and their
teeth were like lions' teeth. 9They had breastplates
like breastplates of iron, and the sound of their
wings was like the thundering of many horses and
chariots rushing into battle. 10They had tails and
stings like scorpions, and in their tails they had
power to torment people for five months. 11They
had as king over them the angel of the Abyss, whose
name in Hebrew is Abaddon, and in Greek, Apol-
lyon.ᵃ
　12The first woe is past; two other woes are yet to
come.
　13The sixth angel sounded his trumpet, and I
heard a voice coming from the hornsᵇ of the
golden altar that is before God. 14It said to the sixth
angel who had the trumpet, "Release the four angels
who are bound at the great river Euphrates." 15And
the four angels who had been kept ready for this
very hour and day and month and year were

ᵃ 11 That is, Bitterness　　ᵃ 11 Abaddon and Apollyon mean Destroyer.　　ᵇ 13 That is, projections released to kill a third of mankind. [16]The number of the mounted troops was two hundred million. I heard their number.

[17]The horses and riders I saw in my vision looked like this: Their breastplates were fiery red, dark blue, and yellow as sulphur. The heads of the horses resembled the heads of lions, and out of their mouths came fire, smoke and sulphur. [18]A third of mankind was killed by the three plagues of fire, smoke and sulphur that came out of their mouths.

[19]The power of the horses was in their mouths and in their tails; for their tails were like snakes, having heads with which they inflict injury.

[20]The rest of mankind that were not killed by these plagues still did not repent of the work of their hands; they did not stop worshipping demons, and idols of gold, silver, bronze, stone and wood—idols that cannot see or hear or walk. [21]Nor did they repent of their murders, their magic arts, their sexual immorality or their thefts.

■ REVELATION'S USE OF SYMBOLS   INSIGHT
WHY ARE THERE SO MANY THEORIES EXPLAINING REVELATION?

THE LOCUSTS LOOKED LIKE HORSES PREPARED FOR BATTLE. ON THEIR HEADS THEY WORE SOMETHING LIKE CROWNS OF GOLD, AND THEIR FACES RESEMBLED HUMAN FACES. ■ 9:7

"There never has been a book provoking more delirium, foolishness, and irrational movements, without any relationship to Jesus Christ," concluded Jacques Ellul, author of a commentary on Revelation. Readers tend to fixate wildly on details, mainly because John relied so heavily on symbols to express his meaning in this book.

Creatures covered with eyes and sprouting horns, eagles wheeling in the sky, molten mountains hurtling into the ocean—such rich imagery excites frenzied attempts to explain every word. John interprets some symbols for us—"The seven stars are the angels of the seven churches" (1:20)—and hints broadly at the meaning of others, such as the four horsemen in chapter 6. But many questions remain unanswered. For example, do the major visions describe consecutive periods of history, or do they foretell the same events from different angles?

■ LOOK AT THE BROAD PICTURE
Artists find that symbols communicate with special power. When Spanish artist Pablo Picasso painted his massive *Guernica*, he attempted to express what had happened in war-ravaged Spain on April 28, 1937. He created a work of art, not a photographic record. The painting does communicate the tragedy at Guernica, but artfully, symbolically.

In a similar way, John poetically renders human events so strange and climactic as to be otherwise inexpressible. If he had wanted to, God could have revealed a precise timetable of future events, but instead Jesus warned specifically against such speculation about the future. In keeping with that approach, Revelation does not so much outline future events as hint at the cosmic significance that goes on *behind* history.

Readers new to Revelation should start by viewing scenes as a whole, looking for an overall meaning. The visions are like Jesus' parables: each has a main thrust, and some of the details may serve merely to dramatise or add literary fullness to the scene. No-one can find the precise meaning behind every detail in John's visions. Those who seek to explain each symbol too quickly may easily miss the meaning of the symbol as well as the grand emotional sweep of the book.

■ SEARCHING FOR A SYSTEM
Revelation will always attract scholars who search for the meaning behind each symbol. It is no easy undertaking: over 300 allusions to the Old Testament and an elaborate system of symbolic numbers must be counted into any explanation. History has been proved thousands of explainers wrong. People from every generation—especially in the hectic days around A.D. 1000 and in the 14th and 19th centuries, as well as in contemporary times dominated by Middle East tensions—have insisted the end of the world was just around the corner.

Today, some believe that Revelation's symbols—statues that talk, fire coming from heaven, totalitarian economic control, massive changes in the earth and sea—come hauntingly close to 20th-century phenomena. The wholesale devastation of earth prophesied in the middle chapters seems eerily up-to-date.

Yet, calamities merely provide a backdrop to John's main thrust: followers of Christ will be made safe at last. "God will wipe away every tear from their eyes," he says (7:17). Much of Revelation remains shrouded in mystery, but the final results shine out clearly.

□ LIFE QUESTIONS:
Two potential dangers in reading Revelation (see Introduction) are avoiding it entirely or getting obsessed with its details. Which danger are you most familiar with? Why do we need the message of Revelation today?

■ The Angel and the Little Scroll

10 Then I saw another mighty angel coming down from heaven. He was robed in a cloud, with a rainbow above his head; his face was like the sun, and his legs were like fiery pillars. [2]He was holding a little scroll, which lay open in his hand. He planted his right foot on the sea and his left foot on the land, [3]and he gave a loud shout like the roar of a lion. When he shouted, the voices of the seven thunders spoke. [4]And when the seven thunders spoke, I was about to write; but I heard a voice from heaven say, "Seal up what the seven thunders have said and do not write it down."

9:20 ■ JUDGMENTS FOR A PURPOSE

Revelation records a number of severe judgments, in chapters 6, 9, and 16. It carefully mentions the purpose of these judgments: to convince humankind that its rebellion is futile and encourage it to repent. In this way, the judgments are similar to the 10 plagues against Egypt. Like the 10 plagues, these judgments do not ultimately work. The failure of people to repent makes necessary the final judgment against the source of all evil.

[5]Then the angel I had seen standing on the sea and on the land raised his right hand to heaven. [6]And he swore by him who lives for ever and ever, who created the heavens and all that is in them, the earth and all that is in it, and the sea and all that is in it, and said, "There will be no more delay! [7]But in the days when the seventh angel is about to sound his trumpet, the mystery of God will be accomplished, just as he announced to his servants the prophets."

[8]Then the voice that I had heard from heaven spoke to me once more: "Go, take the scroll that lies open in the hand of the angel who is standing on the sea and on the land."

[9]So I went to the angel and asked him to give me the little scroll. He said to me, "Take it and eat it. It will turn your stomach sour, but in your mouth it will be as sweet as honey." [10]I took the little scroll from the angel's hand and ate it. It tasted as sweet as honey in my mouth, but when I had eaten it, my stomach turned sour. [11]Then I was told, "You must prophesy again about many peoples, nations, languages and kings."

■ The Two Witnesses

11 I was given a reed like a measuring rod and was told, "Go and measure the temple of God and the altar, and count the worshippers there. [2]But exclude the outer court; do not measure it, because it has been given to the Gentiles. They will trample on the holy city for 42 months. [3]And I will give power to my two witnesses, and they will prophesy for 1,260 days, clothed in sackcloth." [4]These are the two olive trees and the two lampstands that stand before the Lord of the earth. [5]If anyone tries to harm them, fire comes from their mouths and devours their enemies. This is how anyone who wants to harm them must die. [6]These men have power to shut up the sky so that it will not rain during the time they are prophesying; and they have power to turn the waters into blood and to strike the earth with every kind of plague as often as they want.

11:1 ■ OLD TESTAMENT ECHOES

A full understanding of Revelation requires detailed study of such Old Testament prophets as Ezekiel and Daniel. John frequently borrows images from those books. For example, the passage here on the temple of God parallels Ezekiel 40. Similarly, many passages referring to kings and political empires are reminiscent of Daniel's visions.

[7]Now when they have finished their testimony, the beast that comes up from the Abyss will attack them, and overpower and kill them. [8]Their bodies will lie in the street of the great city, which is figuratively called Sodom and Egypt, where also their Lord was crucified. [9]For three and a half days men from every people, tribe, language and nation will gaze on their bodies and refuse them burial. [10]The inhabitants of the earth will gloat over them and will celebrate by sending each other gifts, because these two prophets had tormented those who live on earth.

[11]But after the three and a half days a breath of life from God entered them, and they stood on their feet, and terror struck those who saw them. [12]Then they heard a loud voice from heaven saying to them, "Come up here." And they went up to heaven in a cloud, while their enemies looked on.

[13]At that very hour there was a severe earthquake and a tenth of the city collapsed. Seven thousand people were killed in the earthquake, and the survivors were terrified and gave glory to the God of heaven.

[14]The second woe has passed; the third woe is coming soon.

■ The Seventh Trumpet

[15]The seventh angel sounded his trumpet, and there were loud voices in heaven, which said:

"The kingdom of the world has become the
    kingdom of our Lord and of his Christ,
and he will reign for ever and ever."

[16]And the twenty-four elders, who were seated on their thrones before God, fell on their faces and worshipped God, [17]saying:

"We give thanks to you, Lord God Almighty,
    the One who is and who was,
because you have taken your great power
    and have begun to reign.
[18]The nations were angry;
    and your wrath has come.
The time has come for judging the dead,
    and for rewarding your servants the prophets
and your saints and those who reverence your
        name,
    both small and great—
and for destroying those who destroy the
        earth."

¹⁹Then God's temple in heaven was opened, and within his temple was seen the ark of his covenant. And there came flashes of lightning, rumblings, peals of thunder, an earthquake and a great hailstorm.

The Woman and the Dragon

12 A great and wondrous sign appeared in heaven: a woman clothed with the sun, with the moon under her feet and a crown of twelve stars on her head. ²She was pregnant and cried out in pain as she was about to give birth. ³Then another sign appeared in heaven: an enormous red dragon with seven heads and ten horns and seven crowns on his heads. ⁴His tail swept a third of the stars out of the sky and flung them to the earth. The dragon stood in front of the woman who was about to give birth, so that he might devour her child the moment it was born. ⁵She gave birth to a son, a male child, who will rule all the nations with an iron sceptre.

And her child was snatched up to God and to his throne. ⁶The woman fled into the desert to a place prepared for her by God, where she might be taken care of for 1,260 days.

⁷And there was war in heaven. Michael and his angels fought against the dragon, and the dragon and his angels fought back. ⁸But he was not strong enough, and they lost their place in heaven. ⁹The great dragon was hurled down—that ancient serpent called the devil, or Satan, who leads the whole world astray. He was hurled to the earth, and his angels with him.

¹⁰Then I heard a loud voice in heaven say:

"Now have come the salvation and the power
    and the kingdom of our God,
  and the authority of his Christ.
For the accuser of our brothers,
    who accuses them before our God day and
      night,
  has been hurled down.

■ A LOOK BEHIND THE SCENES   INSIGHT
CHRISTMAS FROM HEAVEN'S PERSPECTIVE

THE DRAGON STOOD IN FRONT OF THE WOMAN WHO WAS ABOUT TO GIVE BIRTH, SO THAT HE MIGHT DEVOUR HER CHILD THE MOMENT IT WAS BORN.
■ 12:4

Christmas Day. We celebrate it with a sudden splurge of money and gifts and an attempt to rediscover the joy of the first Christmas. Manger displays in town squares recreate the scene in Bethlehem on that day long ago.

As many interpret it, chapter 12 describes Christmas day also, but its point of view differs radically from that of the Gospels. Revelation does not tell of shepherds, a crazed king bent on infanticide, and a stable; rather, it pictures a murderous dragon leading a ferocious struggle in heaven. His attack when Christ was born launches a series of bloody rebellions against the forces of good.

■ TWO HISTORIES AT ONCE
The view of Christ's birth in Revelation 12 gives a glimpse into the pattern of the entire book. John is fusing things seen with things normally not seen. In daily life, two parallel histories occur simultaneously: one on earth and one in heaven. Revelation, however, views them together. It parts the curtain, allowing a quick look behind the scenes at the cosmic impact of what happens on earth.

Every inch of this planet is claimed by God and counter-claimed by Satan. We normally experience only the visible, everyday effects of this struggle. We feel it, for example, when we make a choice between what we know is wrong and what is right. But, as we are living out our lives on earth, the supernatural universe is simultaneously at war. Revelation draws the contrasts sharply: good versus evil, the Lamb versus the dragon, Jerusalem versus Babylon, the bride versus the prostitute.

■ IS GOD IN CONTROL OF HISTORY?
Sometimes the "war in heaven" can break out into actual violence on earth, as it did when Jesus came. Revelation was originally written to people who were facing extreme persecution from the Roman empire. Revelation establishes that a war is being waged on this planet between good and evil, a war that reflects a larger struggle in the whole universe. But, no matter how it looks, God is in firm control of history. To first-century Christians, Rome was the arch-villain, and allusions to that empire crop up in these chapters. John asserts that Jesus Christ, and not an emperor, determines the flow of history.

Events are marching on to a definite climax; history has meaning. Ultimately, even the despots of history will end up fulfilling the plan mapped out for them by God. Pontius Pilate and his Roman soldiers demonstrated that truth starkly. They thought they were getting rid of Jesus by crucifying him. Instead, they made possible the salvation of the world.

□ LIFE QUESTIONS:
As Revelation tells it, events that appear tragic can work great good. Have you ever experienced that in your life?

11They overcame him
    by the blood of the Lamb
    and by the word of their testimony;
they did not love their lives so much
    as to shrink from death.
12Therefore rejoice, you heavens
    and you who dwell in them!
But woe to the earth and the sea,
    because the devil has gone down to you!
He is filled with fury,
    because he knows that his time is short."

13When the dragon saw that he had been hurled
to the earth, he pursued the woman who had given
birth to the male child. 14The woman was given the
two wings of a great eagle, so that she might fly to
the place prepared for her in the desert, where she
would be taken care of for a time, times and half a
time, out of the serpent's reach. 15Then from his
mouth the serpent spewed water like a river, to
overtake the woman and sweep her away with the
torrent. 16But the earth helped the woman by opening its mouth and swallowing the river that the
dragon had spewed out of his mouth. 17Then the
dragon was enraged at the woman and went off
to make war against the rest of her offspring—
those who obey God's commandments and hold to

13 the testimony of Jesus. 1And the dragon*a*
stood on the shore of the sea.

■ The Beast out of the Sea
    And I saw a beast coming out of the sea. He had
ten horns and seven heads, with ten crowns on his
horns, and on each head a blasphemous name. 2The
beast I saw resembled a leopard, but had feet like
those of a bear and a mouth like that of a lion. The
dragon gave the beast his power and his throne and
great authority. 3One of the heads of the beast
seemed to have had a fatal wound, but the fatal
wound had been healed. The whole world was astonished and followed the beast. 4Men worshipped
the dragon because he had given authority to the
beast, and they also worshipped the beast and asked,
"Who is like the beast? Who can make war against
him?"
    5The beast was given a mouth to utter proud
words and blasphemies and to exercise his authority for forty-two months. 6He opened his mouth
to blaspheme God, and to slander his name and his
dwelling-place and those who live in heaven. 7He
was given power to make war against the saints and
to conquer them. And he was given authority over
every tribe, people, language and nation. 8All inhabitants of the earth will worship the beast—all whose
names have not been written in the book of life belonging to the Lamb that was slain from the creation
of the world.*b*
    9He who has an ear, let him hear.

10If anyone is to go into captivity,
    into captivity he will go.
If anyone is to be killed*c* with the sword,
    with the sword he will be killed.

This calls for patient endurance and faithfulness on
the part of the saints.

■ The Beast out of the Earth
    11Then I saw another beast, coming out of the
earth. He had two horns like a lamb, but he spoke
like a dragon. 12He exercised all the authority of the
first beast on his behalf, and made the earth and its
inhabitants worship the first beast, whose fatal
wound had been healed. 13And he performed great
and miraculous signs, even causing fire to come
down from heaven to earth in full view of men.
14Because of the signs he was given power to do on
behalf of the first beast, he deceived the inhabitants
of the earth. He ordered them to set up an image in
honour of the beast who was wounded by the
sword and yet lived. 15He was given power to give
breath to the image of the first beast, so that it could
speak and cause all who refused to worship the image to be killed. 16He also forced everyone, small
and great, rich and poor, free and slave, to receive
a mark on his right hand or on his forehead, 17so that
no-one could buy or sell unless he had the mark,
which is the name of the beast or the number of his
name.

**13:5 ■ FORTY-TWO MONTHS OF
TRIALS**
This mysterious number has prompted much
speculation. Literally it means "a time, times and
half a time" (see 12:14), that is, one year plus two
years plus half a year, or three and a half years. It
occurs several places in Revelation. Could it
simply be half the perfect number 7, thus
representing the age of the new covenant (the
time between the first and second coming of
Christ)? Or does it refer to literal months: a brief
but intense three-and-one-half year period of great
persecution against the church? If so, did these
42 months already take place during the Roman
persecutions of Christians? Or are they still in the
future?
    Those who believe the 42 months are in the
future frequently speak of the period as "the great
tribulation" and call the beast the antichrist, a
name used elsewhere in the Bible. Several schools
of thought have developed around the tribulation.
Pre-tribulationists believe that Jesus will come to
remove the church from earth just before the great
tribulation. Post-tribulationists believe the church
will go through a time of trials before Jesus
returns. Mid-tribulationists believe the church will
be taken away during the tribulation.

18This calls for wisdom. If anyone has insight, let
him calculate the number of the beast, for it is man's
number. His number is 666.

■ The Lamb and the 144,000
14 Then I looked, and there before me was the
Lamb, standing on Mount Zion, and with him
144,000 who had his name and his Father's name
written on their foreheads. 2And I heard a sound
from heaven like the roar of rushing waters and like
a loud peal of thunder. The sound I heard was like
that of harpists playing their harps. 3And they sang

---

a 1 Some late manuscripts And I   *b 8 Or written from the creation of the world in the book of life belonging to the Lamb that was slain*   *c 10 Some*
manuscripts *anyone kills*

a new song before the throne and before the four living creatures and the elders. No-one could learn the song except the 144,000 who had been redeemed from the earth. [4]These are those who did not defile themselves with women, for they kept themselves pure. They follow the Lamb wherever he goes. They were purchased from among men and offered as firstfruits to God and the Lamb. [5]No lie was found in their mouths; they are blameless.

14:1 ■ GOOD NEWS WITH BAD

According to Revelation, human history will end not with a whimper but with a series of loud bangs. And yet John frequently reminds his readers that the spasms of violence will lead to a time of eternal peace, with God ruling over a restored heaven and earth. The peaceful scene of a heavenly choir in this chapter is sandwiched between two accounts of tribulation and judgment. John drops in such scenes like orchestral interludes in the midst of a tumultuous opera: they reassure us of a future in which all creation performs together in harmony.

■ The Three Angels

[6]Then I saw another angel flying in mid-air, and he had the eternal gospel to proclaim to those who live on the earth — to every nation, tribe, language and people. [7]He said in a loud voice, "Fear God and give him glory, because the hour of his judgment has come. Worship him who made the heavens, the earth, the sea and the springs of water."

[8]A second angel followed and said, "Fallen! Fallen is Babylon the Great, which made all the nations drink the maddening wine of her adulteries."

[9]A third angel followed them and said in a loud voice: "If anyone worships the beast and his image and receives his mark on the forehead or on the hand, [10]he, too, will drink of the wine of God's fury, which has been poured full strength into the cup of his wrath. He will be tormented with burning sulphur in the presence of the holy angels and of the Lamb. [11]And the smoke of their torment rises for ever and ever. There is no rest day or night for those who worship the beast and his image, or for anyone who receives the mark of his name." [12]This calls for patient endurance on the part of the saints who obey God's commandments and remain faithful to Jesus.

[13]Then I heard a voice from heaven say, "Write: Blessed are the dead who die in the Lord from now on."

"Yes," says the Spirit, "they will rest from their labour, for their deeds will follow them."

■ The Harvest of the Earth

[14]I looked, and there before me was a white cloud, and seated on the cloud was one "like a son of man"[a] with a crown of gold on his head and a sharp sickle in his hand. [15]Then another angel came out of the temple and called in a loud voice to him who was sitting on the cloud, "Take your sickle and reap, because the time to reap has come, for the harvest of the earth is ripe." [16]So he who was seated on the cloud swung his sickle over the earth, and the earth was harvested.

[17]Another angel came out of the temple in heaven, and he too had a sharp sickle. [18]Still another angel, who had charge of the fire, came from the altar and called in a loud voice to him who had the sharp sickle, "Take your sharp sickle and gather the clusters of grapes from the earth's vine, because its grapes are ripe." [19]The angel swung his sickle on the earth, gathered its grapes and threw them into the great winepress of God's wrath. [20]They were trampled in the winepress outside the city, and blood flowed out of the press, rising as high as the horses' bridles for a distance of 1,600 stadia.[b]

■ Seven Angels With Seven Plagues

15 I saw in heaven another great and marvellous sign: seven angels with the seven last plagues — last, because with them God's wrath is completed. [2]And I saw what looked like a sea of glass mixed with fire and, standing beside the sea, those who had been victorious over the beast and his image and over the number of his name. They held harps given them by God [3]and sang the song of Moses the servant of God and the song of the Lamb:

"Great and marvellous are your deeds,
    Lord God Almighty.
Just and true are your ways,
    King of the ages.
[4]Who will not fear you, O Lord,
    and bring glory to your name?
For you alone are holy.
All nations will come
    and worship before you,
for your righteous acts have been revealed."

[5]After this I looked and in heaven the temple, that is, the tabernacle of the Testimony, was opened. [6]Out of the temple came the seven angels with the seven plagues. They were dressed in clean, shining linen and wore golden sashes round their chests. [7]Then one of the four living creatures gave to the seven angels seven golden bowls filled with the wrath of God, who lives for ever and ever. [8]And the temple was filled with smoke from the glory of God and from his power, and no-one could enter the temple until the seven plagues of the seven angels were completed.

■ The Seven Bowls of God's Wrath

16 Then I heard a loud voice from the temple saying to the seven angels, "Go, pour out the seven bowls of God's wrath on the earth."

[2]The first angel went and poured out his bowl on the land, and ugly and painful sores broke out on the people who had the mark of the beast and worshipped his image.

[3]The second angel poured out his bowl on the sea, and it turned into blood like that of a dead man, and every living thing in the sea died.

[4]The third angel poured out his bowl on the rivers and springs of water, and they became blood. [5]Then I heard the angel in charge of the waters say:

a 14 Daniel 7:13   b 20 That is, about 180 miles (about 300 kilometres)

"You are just in these judgments,
  you who are and who were, the Holy One,
  because you have so judged;
[6]for they have shed the blood of your saints and
    prophets,
  and you have given them blood to drink as
    they deserve."

[7]And I heard the altar respond:

"Yes, Lord God Almighty,
  true and just are your judgments."

[8]The fourth angel poured out his bowl on the
sun, and the sun was given power to scorch people
with fire. [9]They were seared by the intense heat and
they cursed the name of God, who had control over
these plagues, but they refused to repent and glorify
him.

[10]The fifth angel poured out his bowl on the
throne of the beast, and his kingdom was plunged
into darkness. Men gnawed their tongues in agony
[11]and cursed the God of heaven because of their
pains and their sores, but they refused to repent of
what they had done.

[12]The sixth angel poured out his bowl on the
great river Euphrates, and its water was dried up to
prepare the way for the kings from the East. [13]Then
I saw three evil[a] spirits that looked like frogs; they
came out of the mouth of the dragon, out of the
mouth of the beast and out of the mouth of the false
prophet. [14]They are spirits of demons performing
miraculous signs, and they go out to the kings of the
whole world, to gather them for the battle on the
great day of God Almighty.

[15]"Behold, I come like a thief! Blessed is he who
stays awake and keeps his clothes with him, so that
he may not go naked and be shamefully exposed."

[16]Then they gathered the kings together to the
place that in Hebrew is called Armageddon.

16:16 ■ THE BATTLE OF ARMAGEDDON

Armageddon has been the site of many military
struggles in Israel's history. Some historians
estimate that more wars have been fought here
than any other location in the world. It is an
appropriate setting (or symbol) for the final
struggle between good and evil.

[17]The seventh angel poured out his bowl into the
air, and out of the temple came a loud voice from
the throne, saying, "It is done!" [18]Then there came
flashes of lightning, rumblings, peals of thunder and
a severe earthquake. No earthquake like it has ever
occurred since man has been on earth, so tremendous was the quake. [19]The great city split into three
parts, and the cities of the nations collapsed. God
remembered Babylon the Great and gave her the
cup filled with the wine of the fury of his wrath.
[20]Every island fled away and the mountains could
not be found. [21]From the sky huge hailstones of
about a hundred pounds each fell upon men. And
they cursed God on account of the plague of hail,
because the plague was so terrible.

■ The Woman on the Beast

17 One of the seven angels who had the seven
bowls came and said to me, "Come, I will
show you the punishment of the great prostitute,
who sits on many waters. [2]With her the kings of the
earth committed adultery and the inhabitants of the
earth were intoxicated with the wine of her adulteries."

[3]Then the angel carried me away in the Spirit into
a desert. There I saw a woman sitting on a scarlet
beast that was covered with blasphemous names
and had seven heads and ten horns. [4]The woman
was dressed in purple and scarlet, and was glittering
with gold, precious stones and pearls. She held a
golden cup in her hand, filled with abominable
things and the filth of her adulteries. [5]This title was
written on her forehead:

MYSTERY
BABYLON THE GREAT
THE MOTHER OF PROSTITUTES
AND OF THE ABOMINATIONS OF THE EARTH.

[6]I saw that the woman was drunk with the blood of
the saints, the blood of those who bore testimony to
Jesus.

When I saw her, I was greatly astonished. [7]Then
the angel said to me: "Why are you astonished? I will
explain to you the mystery of the woman and of the
beast she rides, which has the seven heads and ten
horns. [8]The beast, which you saw, once was, now is
not, and will come up out of the Abyss and go to his
destruction. The inhabitants of the earth whose
names have not been written in the book of life from
the creation of the world will be astonished when
they see the beast, because he once was, now is not,
and yet will come.

[9]"This calls for a mind with wisdom. The seven
heads are seven hills on which the woman sits.
[10]They are also seven kings. Five have fallen, one is,
the other has not yet come; but when he does come,
he must remain for a little while. [11]The beast who
once was, and now is not, is an eighth king. He belongs to the seven and is going to his destruction.

[12]"The ten horns you saw are ten kings who have
not yet received a kingdom, but who for one hour
will receive authority as kings along with the beast.
[13]They have one purpose and will give their power
and authority to the beast. [14]They will make war
against the Lamb, but the Lamb will overcome them
because he is Lord of lords and King of kings—and
with him will be his called, chosen and faithful followers."

[15]Then the angel said to me, "The waters you saw,
where the prostitute sits, are peoples, multitudes,
nations and languages. [16]The beast and the ten
horns you saw will hate the prostitute. They will
bring her to ruin and leave her naked; they will eat
her flesh and burn her with fire. [17]For God has put
it into their hearts to accomplish his purpose by
agreeing to give the beast their power to rule, until
God's words are fulfilled. [18]The woman you saw is
the great city that rules over the kings of the earth."

a 13 Greek unclean

■ The Fall of Babylon

18 After this I saw another angel coming down from heaven. He had great authority, and the earth was illuminated by his splendour. ²With a mighty voice he shouted:

"Fallen! Fallen is Babylon the Great!
    She has become a home for demons
and a haunt for every evil*a* spirit,
    a haunt for every unclean and detestable
        bird.
³For all the nations have drunk
    the maddening wine of her adulteries.
The kings of the earth committed adultery with
        her,
    and the merchants of the earth grew rich
        from her excessive luxuries."

18:2 ■ WHAT IS BABYLON?
Many people believe Babylon was a coded substitute for Rome, the city set on seven hills (17:9). Revelation was almost surely written to Christians undergoing great persecution from harsh Roman emperors. Scholars who see Babylon as Rome sometimes try to identify the kings mentioned here as specific Roman rulers.

However, not all interpreters agree. Some suggest that Babylon stands for Jerusalem, and others believe we cannot clearly identify Babylon. Rather, they say, it can represent all powerful world systems that kill faithful Christians and seduce people away from God. Regardless, chapter 18 reveals that the great enemy, Babylon, will disappear for ever (verse 21).

---

⁴Then I heard another voice from heaven say:

"Come out of her, my people,
    so that you will not share in her sins,
    so that you will not receive any of her
        plagues;
⁵for her sins are piled up to heaven,
    and God has remembered her crimes.
⁶Give back to her as she has given;
    pay her back double for what she has done.
    Mix her a double portion from her own cup.
⁷Give her as much torture and grief
    as the glory and luxury she gave herself.
In her heart she boasts,
    'I sit as queen; I am not a widow,
    and I will never mourn.'
⁸Therefore in one day her plagues will overtake
        her:
    death, mourning and famine.
She will be consumed by fire,
    for mighty is the Lord God who judges her.

⁹"When the kings of the earth who committed adultery with her and shared her luxury see the smoke of her burning, they will weep and mourn over her. ¹⁰Terrified at her torment, they will stand far off and cry:

" 'Woe! Woe, O great city,
    O Babylon, city of power!

a2 Greek unclean

In one hour your doom has come!'

¹¹"The merchants of the earth will weep and mourn over her because no-one buys their cargoes any more—¹²cargoes of gold, silver, precious stones and pearls; fine linen, purple, silk and scarlet cloth; every sort of citron wood, and articles of every kind made of ivory, costly wood, bronze, iron and marble; ¹³cargoes of cinnamon and spice, of incense, myrrh and frankincense, of wine and olive oil, of fine flour and wheat; cattle and sheep; horses and carriages; and bodies and souls of men.
¹⁴"They will say, 'The fruit you longed for is gone from you. All your riches and splendour have vanished, never to be recovered.' ¹⁵The merchants who sold these things and gained their wealth from her will stand far off, terrified at her torment. They will weep and mourn ¹⁶and cry out:

" 'Woe! Woe, O great city,
    dressed in fine linen, purple and scarlet,
    and glittering with gold, precious stones and
        pearls!
¹⁷In one hour such great wealth has been
        brought to ruin!'

"Every sea captain, and all who travel by ship, the sailors, and all who earn their living from the sea, will stand far off. ¹⁸When they see the smoke of her burning, they will exclaim, 'Was there ever a city like this great city?' ¹⁹They will throw dust on their heads, and with weeping and mourning cry out:

" 'Woe! Woe, O great city,
    where all who had ships on the sea
        became rich through her wealth!
In one hour she has been brought to ruin!
²⁰Rejoice over her, O heaven!
    Rejoice, saints and apostles and prophets!
God has judged her for the way she treated
        you.' "

²¹Then a mighty angel picked up a boulder the size of a large millstone and threw it into the sea, and said:

"With such violence
    the great city of Babylon will be thrown
        down,
    never to be found again.
²²The music of harpists and musicians, flute
        players and trumpeters,
    will never be heard in you again.
No workman of any trade
    will ever be found in you again.
The sound of a millstone
    will never be heard in you again.
²³The light of a lamp
    will never shine in you again.
The voice of bridegroom and bride
    will never be heard in you again.
Your merchants were the world's great men.
    By your magic spell all the nations were led
        astray.
²⁴In her was found the blood of prophets and of
        the saints,
    and of all who have been killed on the
        earth."

■ Hallelujah!

19 After this I heard what sounded like the roar of a great multitude in heaven shouting:

"Hallelujah!
Salvation and glory and power belong to our
    God,
2 for true and just are his judgments.
He has condemned the great prostitute
    who corrupted the earth by her adulteries.
He has avenged on her the blood of his
    servants."

18:21 ■ NEWSPAPER PROPHECY
The fact that Baghdad, Iraq, sits just 50 miles from the historical site of Babylon led some commentators to predict that the Gulf War of 1991 would escalate into the battle of Armageddon. Instead, the "mother of all battles" on the ground lasted just 100 hours.
    Revelation has defied many such prognosticators. A man who claimed to have cracked the biblical code wrote the bestselling book *88 Reasons Why the Rapture Will Be in 1988*. And not long before that a well-known television evangelist predicted the Soviet Union would invade Israel in 1982. Revelation contains a code intriguing enough to hold the interest of every generation, but obscure enough to have kept the best scholars guessing for almost 2,000 years. That may have been John's intent: to have each new wave of readers grapple with its meaning in their own historical context.

3And again they shouted:

"Hallelujah!
The smoke from her goes up for ever and
    ever."

4The twenty-four elders and the four living creatures fell down and worshipped God, who was seated on the throne. And they cried:

"Amen, Hallelujah!"

5Then a voice came from the throne, saying:

"Praise our God,
    all you his servants,
you who fear him,
    both small and great!"

6Then I heard what sounded like a great multitude, like the roar of rushing waters and like loud peals of thunder, shouting:

"Hallelujah!
For our Lord God Almighty reigns.
7Let us rejoice and be glad
    and give him glory!
For the wedding of the Lamb has come,
    and his bride has made herself ready.
8Fine linen, bright and clean,
    was given her to wear."

(Fine linen stands for the righteous acts of the saints.)

9Then the angel said to me, "Write: 'Blessed are those who are invited to the wedding supper of the Lamb!' " And he added, "These are the true words of God."

10At this I fell at his feet to worship him. But he said to me, "Do not do it! I am a fellow-servant with you and with your brothers who hold to the testimony of Jesus. Worship God! For the testimony of Jesus is the spirit of prophecy."

■ The Rider on the White Horse
11I saw heaven standing open and there before me was a white horse, whose rider is called Faithful and True. With justice he judges and makes war. 12His eyes are like blazing fire, and on his head are many crowns. He has a name written on him that no-one knows but he himself. 13He is dressed in a robe dipped in blood, and his name is the Word of God. 14The armies of heaven were following him, riding on white horses and dressed in fine linen, white and clean. 15Out of his mouth comes a sharp sword with which to strike down the nations. "He will rule them with an iron sceptre."[a] He treads the winepress of the fury of the wrath of God Almighty. 16On his robe and on his thigh he has this name written:

KING OF KINGS AND LORD OF LORDS.

17And I saw an angel standing in the sun, who cried in a loud voice to all the birds flying in mid-air, "Come, gather together for the great supper of God, 18so that you may eat the flesh of kings, generals, and mighty men, of horses and their riders, and the flesh of all people, free and slave, small and great."

19Then I saw the beast and the kings of the earth and their armies gathered together to make war against the rider on the horse and his army. 20But the beast was captured, and with him the false prophet who had performed the miraculous signs on his behalf. With these signs he had deluded those who had received the mark of the beast and worshipped his image. The two of them were thrown alive into the fiery lake of burning sulphur. 21The rest of them were killed with the sword that came out of the mouth of the rider on the horse, and all the birds gorged themselves on their flesh.

■ The Thousand Years
20 And I saw an angel coming down out of heaven, having the key to the Abyss and holding in his hand a great chain. 2He seized the dragon, that ancient serpent, who is the devil, or Satan, and bound him for a thousand years. 3He threw him into the Abyss, and locked and sealed it over him, to keep him from deceiving the nations any more until the thousand years were ended. After that, he must be set free for a short time.

4I saw thrones on which were seated those who had been given authority to judge. And I saw the souls of those who had been beheaded because of their testimony for Jesus and because of the word of God. They had not worshipped the beast or his image and had not received his mark on their foreheads or their hands. They came to life and reigned with Christ for a thousand years. 5(The rest of the dead did not come to life until the thousand years were ended.) This is the first resurrection. 6Blessed and holy are those who have part in the first resurrection. The second death has no power over them, but they will be priests of God and of Christ and will reign with him for a thousand years.

20:3 ■ THE MILLENNIUM

Christians interpret the thousand-year reign referred to here in a variety of ways:

1. Postmillennialism believes that the church itself will, through its expanding influence, bring about a time of peace and prosperity in preparation for the return of Christ. This view was far more popular in the 19th century, when people were optimistic about progress and the future.

2. Premillennialism believes that Christ will return to earth and reign here in person, ushering in a period of great peace. During this period, Satan will be bound up, but will lead a final revolt at the end of the thousand years.

3. Amillennialism interprets this passage much less literally. Some amillennialists hold that the millennium has already been going on, but that the reign of Christ is taking place in heaven, not on earth. Others believe the church is establishing the kingdom of Christ now, between Jesus' first and second coming.

Because so little information is given on the millennium, no-one can be completely sure. The "thousand year" period itself may be symbolic, standing for a very long period of time. Regardless, all positions agree that ultimately this world will end with Jesus' establishment of an eternal kingdom.

■ Satan's Doom

7When the thousand years are over, Satan will be released from his prison 8and will go out to deceive the nations in the four corners of the earth — Gog and Magog — to gather them for battle. In number they are like the sand on the seashore. 9They marched across the breadth of the earth and surrounded the camp of God's people, the city he loves. But fire came down from heaven and devoured them. 10And the devil, who deceived them, was thrown into the lake of burning sulphur, where the beast and the false prophet had been thrown. They will be tormented day and night for ever and ever.

■ The Dead Are Judged

11Then I saw a great white throne and him who was seated on it. Earth and sky fled from his presence, and there was no place for them. 12And I saw the dead, great and small, standing before the throne, and books were opened. Another book was opened, which is the book of life. The dead were judged according to what they had done as recorded in the books. 13The sea gave up the dead that were in it, and death and Hades gave up the dead that were in them, and each person was judged according to what he had done. 14Then death and Ha-

des were thrown into the lake of fire. The lake of fire is the second death. 15If anyone's name was not found written in the book of life, he was thrown into the lake of fire.

■ The New Jerusalem

21 Then I saw a new heaven and a new earth, for the first heaven and the first earth had passed away, and there was no longer any sea. 2I saw the Holy City, the new Jerusalem, coming down out of heaven from God, prepared as a bride beautifully dressed for her husband. 3And I heard a loud voice from the throne saying, "Now the dwelling of God is with men, and he will live with them. They will be his people, and God himself will be with them and be their God. 4He will wipe every tear from their eyes. There will be no more death or mourning or crying or pain, for the old order of things has passed away."

5He who was seated on the throne said, "I am making everything new!" Then he said, "Write this down, for these words are trustworthy and true."

6He said to me: "It is done. I am the Alpha and the Omega, the Beginning and the End. To him who is thirsty I will give to drink without cost from the spring of the water of life. 7He who overcomes will inherit all this, and I will be his God and he will be my son. 8But the cowardly, the unbelieving, the vile, the murderers, the sexually immoral, those who practise magic arts, the idolaters and all liars — their place will be in the fiery lake of burning sulphur. This is the second death."

9One of the seven angels who had the seven bowls full of the seven last plagues came and said to me, "Come, I will show you the bride, the wife of the Lamb." 10And he carried me away in the Spirit to a mountain great and high, and showed me the Holy City, Jerusalem, coming down out of heaven from God. 11It shone with the glory of God, and its brilliance was like that of a very precious jewel, like a jasper, clear as crystal. 12It had a great, high wall with twelve gates, and with twelve angels at the gates. On the gates were written the names of the twelve tribes of Israel. 13There were three gates on the east, three on the north, three on the south and three on the west. 14The wall of the city had twelve foundations, and on them were the names of the twelve apostles of the Lamb.

15The angel who talked with me had a measuring rod of gold to measure the city, its gates and its walls. 16The city was laid out like a square, as long as it was wide. He measured the city with the rod and found it to be 12,000 stadia*a* in length, and as wide and high as it is long. 17He measured its wall and it was 144 cubits*b* thick,*c* by man's measurement, which the angel was using. 18The wall was made of jasper, and the city of pure gold, as pure as glass. 19The foundations of the city walls were decorated with every kind of precious stone. The first foundation was jasper, the second sapphire, the third chalcedony, the fourth emerald, 20the fifth sardonyx, the sixth carnelian, the seventh chrysolite, the eighth beryl, the ninth topaz, the tenth chrysoprase, the eleventh jacinth, and the twelfth amethyst.*d* 21The twelve gates were twelve pearls,

---

a 16 That is, about 1,400 miles (about 2,200 kilometres)   *b 17* That is, about 200 feet (about 65 metres)   *c 17* Or *high*   *d 20* The precise identification of some of these precious stones is uncertain.

each gate made of a single pearl. The great street of the city was of pure gold, like transparent glass.

²²I did not see a temple in the city, because the Lord God Almighty and the Lamb are its temple. ²³The city does not need the sun or the moon to shine on it, for the glory of God gives it light, and the Lamb is its lamp. ²⁴The nations will walk by its light, and the kings of the earth will bring their splendour into it. ²⁵On no day will its gates ever be shut, for there will be no night there. ²⁶The glory and honour of the nations will be brought into it. ²⁷Nothing impure will ever enter it, nor will anyone who does what is shameful or deceitful, but only those whose names are written in the Lamb's book of life.

■ The River of Life

22 Then the angel showed me the river of the water of life, as clear as crystal, flowing from the throne of God and of the Lamb ²down the middle of the great street of the city. On each side of the river stood the tree of life, bearing twelve crops of fruit, yielding its fruit every month. And the leaves of the tree are for the healing of the nations. ³No longer will there be any curse. The throne of God and of the Lamb will be in the city, and his servants will serve him. ⁴They will see his face, and his name will be on their foreheads. ⁵There will be no more night. They will not need the light of a lamp or the light of the sun, for the Lord God will give them light. And they will reign for ever and ever.

⁶The angel said to me, "These words are trustworthy and true. The Lord, the God of the spirits of the prophets, sent his angel to show his servants the things that must soon take place."

22:1 ■ EDEN REGAINED

The last two chapters of Revelation contain numerous parallels to the description of the Garden of Eden in the first three chapters of Genesis. Revelation describes a new creation that excludes all the things that spoiled Eden. There will be no night and no death. Satan will disappear for ever, and nothing impure will enter the new city. People will walk with God again, just as they did in Eden. There will be no crying or pain. Once again humankind will rule over creation, this time with open access to the tree of life. Everything put wrong by human rebellion in Eden will be set right. In Eden, Adam and Eve were driven from the garden; in the new earth, they will see God's face.

■ Jesus Is Coming

⁷"Behold, I am coming soon! Blessed is he who keeps the words of the prophecy in this book."

⁸I, John, am the one who heard and saw these things. And when I had heard and seen them, I fell down to worship at the feet of the angel who had been showing them to me. ⁹But he said to me, "Do not do it! I am a fellow-servant with you and with your brothers the prophets and of all who keep the words of this book. Worship God!"

■ A HAPPY ENDING AFTER ALL
THE LAST WORD IS THE BEST NEWS OF ALL

INSIGHT

THEN I SAW A NEW HEAVEN AND A NEW EARTH. ■ 21:1

We sense it at rare moments. The first real day of spring, when the air is heavy with the scent of blooms and new life sprouts everywhere. Or even in winter, when an unexpected snowstorm clothes a grey, dingy city in pure white. Or when we watch a baby animal at play in the zoo. Or remember the first sudden twinge of romantic love.

This world may be full of pollution, war, crime and hate. But inside us, all of us, linger remnants that remind us of what the world could be like – of what *we* could be like. The Old Testament prophets dreamed of "that day" when creation would be made new. And those sensations, following a dismal monotone of predicted catastrophes, burst out of the last few chapters of Revelation. That perfect world is not merely a dream; it will come true.

■ A NEW WORLD AT LAST

There will be no more tears then, nor pain. Wild animals will frolic, not kill. Once again creation will work the way God intended. Peace will reign not only between God and individuals, but between him and all creation. The kingdom comes out into the open. The City of God flings wide its gates.

Revelation ends on a note of great triumph. Somehow, out of all the bad news augured here, good news emerges – spectacular Good News. To those who believe, Revelation becomes a book not of fear, but of hope. God will prevail. All will be made new.

The Bible began, back in Genesis, with a tragic defeat, when humanity, made in the image of God, rebelled. It ends with a reunion – a marriage, Revelation calls it. There is a happy ending after all.

□ LIFE QUESTIONS:
If you could design a perfect world, what would it look like?

¹⁰Then he told me, "Do not seal up the words of the prophecy of this book, because the time is near. ¹¹Let him who does wrong continue to do wrong; let him who is vile continue to be vile; let him who does right continue to do right; and let him who is holy continue to be holy."

¹²"Behold, I am coming soon! My reward is with me, and I will give to everyone according to what he has done. ¹³I am the Alpha and the Omega, the First and the Last, the Beginning and the End.

¹⁴"Blessed are those who wash their robes, that they may have the right to the tree of life and may go through the gates into the city. ¹⁵Outside are the dogs, those who practise magic arts, the sexually immoral, the murderers, the idolaters and everyone who loves and practises falsehood.

¹⁶"I, Jesus, have sent my angel to give you^a this testimony for the churches. I am the Root and the Offspring of David, and the bright Morning Star."

¹⁷The Spirit and the bride say, "Come!" And let him who hears say, "Come!" Whoever is thirsty, let him come; and whoever wishes, let him take the free gift of the water of life.

¹⁸I warn everyone who hears the words of the prophecy of this book: If anyone adds anything to them, God will add to him the plagues described in this book. ¹⁹And if anyone takes words away from this book of prophecy, God will take away from him his share in the tree of life and in the holy city, which are described in this book.

²⁰He who testifies to these things says, "Yes, I am coming soon."

Amen. Come, Lord Jesus.

²¹The grace of the Lord Jesus be with God's people. Amen.

---

a 16 The Greek is plural.

■ TABLE OF WEIGHTS AND MEASURES

BIBLICAL UNIT		APPROXIMATE IMPERIAL UNIT	METRIC EQUIVALENT
■ WEIGHTS			
talent	(60 minas)	75 pounds	34 kilograms
mina	(50 shekels)	1 ¼ pounds	0.6 kilogram
shekel	(2 bekas)	⅖ ounce	11.5 grams
pim	(⅔ shekel)	⅓ ounce	7.6 grams
beka	(10 gerahs)	⅕ ounce	5.5 grams
gerah		1/50 ounce	0.6 gram
■ LENGTH			
cubit		18 inches	0.5 metre
span		9 inches	23 centimetres
handbreadth		3 inches	8 centimetres
■ CAPACITY			
☐ DRY MEASURE			
cor [homer]	(10 ephahs)	6 bushels	220 litres
lethek	(5 ephahs)	3 bushels	110 litres
ephah	(10 omers)	⅗ bushel	22 litres
seah	(⅓ ephah)	13 pints	7.3 litres
omer	(1/10 ephah)	4 pints	2 litres
cab	(1/18 ephah)	2 pints	1 litre
☐ LIQUID MEASURE			
bath	(1 ephah)	5 gallons	22 litres
hin	(⅙ bath)	7 pints	4 litres
log	(1/72 bath)	½ pint	0.3 litre

The figures of the table are calculated on the basis of a shekel equalling 11.5 grams, a cubit equalling 18 inches and an ephah equalling 22 litres. It is based upon the best available information, but it is not intended to be mathematically precise; like the measurement equivalents in the footnotes, it merely gives approximate amounts and distances. Weights and measures differed somewhat at various times and places in the ancient world. There is uncertainty particularly about the ephah and the bath; further discoveries may give more light on these units of capacity.

■ SUBJECT GUIDE

The Subject Guide is not a "concordance" that shows where the Bible uses a certain word. Rather, it lists major subjects that may be of interest, along with the Bible *passages* (not single verses, usually) that speak to these subjects. Topics of pressing interest or major significance have been highlighted within the list. Although we have tried to be comprehensive, any list of subjects must necessarily be restrictive. The italicised titles in quotes refer to Highlights, Insights, or Introductions on the subject. Page numbers are given in boldface type.

■ A

AARON – brother of and spokesman for Moses; became the first high priest
with Moses, Exodus 4:10–12:50–**p. 54**
made priest, Exodus 28–29 **p. 75**; *"The First High Priest"* – **p. 93**
his role with golden calf, Exodus 32–**p. 78**
budding of his staff, Numbers 17–**p. 131**
his death, Numbers 20:23–29–**p. 134**

ABEL – Adam's second son; murdered by his brother Cain
his life, Genesis 4:1–9–**p. 7**
example of faith, Hebrews 11:1–4–**p. 1068**
relationship to Christ, Hebrews 12:22–24–**p. 1070**

ABORTION – death of a foetus through a medical procedure
penalty for harming foetus, Exodus 21:22–25–**p. 70**
unborn life important to God, Psalm 139–**p. 535**

ABRAHAM – founder of the Jewish nation
called by God, Genesis 11:26–12:20–**p. 12**
his life, Genesis 11:26–25:11–**p. 12**
and Melchizedek, Genesis 14:18–24–**p. 15**
covenant with, Genesis 15;17–**p. 15**
and Hagar, Genesis 16–**p. 15**
prayed for Sodom and Gomorrah, Genesis 18:16–33–**p. 17**
asked to sacrifice his son, Genesis 22–**p. 20**
his death, Genesis 25:1–11–**p. 24**
his true offspring are believers, Romans 4–**p. 979**; Galatians 3:6–29–**p. 1018**
faith demonstrated by deeds, James 2:20–24–**p. 1074**

ABSALOM – third son of David, by Maacah
his revenge on Amnon, 2 Samuel 13–14–**p. 280**
in hiding, *"A Refuge with His Family"* – **p. 281**
rebellion against David, 2 Samuel 15:1–19:8–**p. 282**; *"No Way Back"* – **p. 283**

ADAM – the first man
his creation and life, Genesis 1:26–5:5–**p. 5**
his fall into sin, Genesis 3–**p. 7**
Jesus and the line of Adam, Luke 3:23–38–**p. 889**
Jesus as second Adam, Romans 5:12–21–**p. 981**;
1 Corinthians 15:21–22,42–57–**p. 1003**

ADOPTION – becoming a child of one who is not your biological parent
Abraham and adoption of an heir, Genesis 15:1–6–**p. 15**; Genesis 16–**p. 15**
Israel as God's adopted son, Exodus 4:21–23–**p. 54**; Jeremiah 31:9, 16–20–**p. 672**
Believers as God's adopted children, John 1:12–13–**p. 918**; Romans 8:12–25–**p. 984**; Galatians 3:26–4:7–**p. 1019**; Ephesians 1:3–8–**p. 1023**

ADULTERY – sexual unfaithfulness of a married person
laws against, Numbers 5:12–31–**p. 120**
David and Bathsheba, 2 Samuel 11–12–**p. 277**

warnings against, Proverbs 5–**p. 546**; Proverbs 6:20–35–**p. 547**
avoiding, *"A Safeguard Against Lust"* – **p. 130**
Jesus' views on, Matthew 5:27–32–**p. 836**
effect on the church, 1 Corinthians 5–**p. 996**

AFTER-LIFE – *see* ETERNAL LIFE, HEAVEN, HELL, RESURRECTION

AHAB – Israel's most wicked king
ascended throne, 1 Kings 16:29–33–**p. 313**
contest with Elijah, 1 Kings 18–**p. 314**
and Naboth's vineyard, 1 Kings 21–**p. 318**
his death, 1 Kings 22:34–38–**p. 322**

ALCOHOL – *see* DRINKING ALCOHOL, WINE

AMBITION – strong desire for success, honour, or power (*see also* PRIDE, SERVANTHOOD)

competing with God, *"Human Ambition"* – **p. 12**
at the tower of Babel, Genesis 11:1–11–**p. 12**
results of, Matthew 16:21–27–**p. 848**
of disciples, Mark 9:33–37; 10:35–45–**p. 875**
the antichrist, 2 Thessalonians 2:1–4–**p. 1042**

ANGELS – heavenly beings created by God
assist people, Genesis 24–**p. 22**
protect people, Psalm 91:11–13–**p. 513**
execute judgment, Matthew 13:24–50–**p. 844**
deliver messages, *"A Message from God"* – **p. 590**; Luke 1:26–38–**p. 887**; 2:8–15–**p. 887**
execute judgment, Matthew 13:24–50–**p. 844**; Revelation 14:17–16:21–**p. 1109**
purpose of, *"Respect for Angels"* – **p. 1061**
Christ greater than, Hebrews 1:5–14–**p. 1060**
serve in heaven, Revelation 8–9–**p. 1104**
spiritual warriors, Revelation 12:7–12–**p. 1107**

ANGER
of God:
towards sin, Numbers 11:1–35–**p. 126**; *"God Is Slow to Anger"* – **p. 798**; Romans 1:18–32–**p. 977**
tempered with mercy, Psalm 103–**p. 517**; Hosea 11:8–11–**p. 517**
averted through Christ, Romans 5–**p. 981**
of human beings:
Cain's, *"Improper Offerings"* – **p. 8**
Moses', Exodus 32:15–35–**p. 79**
David's, *"Cool Head"* – **p. 255**
Jonah's, Jonah 3–4–**p. 790**
dealing with, *"Angry Inside"* – **p. 470**
"In your anger do not sin", Ephesians 4:26–**p. 1025**
be slow to anger, James 1:19–20–**p. 1073**

ANIMALS
purpose of, *"Just for Fun"* – **p. 518**
God's love for, *"The Wildness of Animals"* – **p. 463**
showing God's power, *"Behemoth and Leviathan?"* – **p. 465**

ANTICHRIST – an evil person or power; a false Christ, expected
in the end times
    prophesied by Daniel, Daniel 11:36–45 – **p. 758**
    Jesus' teaching on, Mark 13:1–37 – **p. 879**
    will be destroyed, 2 Thessalonians 2:1–12 – **p. 1042**
    qualities of, 1 John 2:18–23 – **p. 1089**; 4:1–6 – **p. 1089**
    visions of, Revelation 11–13 – **p. 1106**
    destruction of, Revelation 19:19–21 – **p. 1112**

ANXIETY
    overcome by trust in God, Matthew 6:25–34 – **p. 838**; Luke
      12:22–34 – **p. 902**
    subdued through prayer, Philippians 4:4–9 – **p. 1031**

APOLLOS – an Alexandrian Jew who preached in Corinth
    with Priscilla and Aquila, Acts 18:24–28 – **p. 965**
    followers of, 1 Corinthians 3:1–9 – **p. 994**
    partners with Paul, 1 Corinthians 4:1–7 – **p. 995**

APOSTLES – title given to the followers of Christ who founded the
early church, especially the 12 disciples and Paul
    commissioned, Matthew 28:16–20 – **p. 863**
    disciples called, Luke 5:1–11 – **p. 891**; 6:12–16 – **p. 891**
    replacement for Judas, Acts 1:12–26 – **p. 944**
    received Holy Spirit, Acts 2 – **p. 945**
    Paul as, 1 Corinthians 9 – **p. 998**; Galatians 1:1–2:10 – **p. 1017**
    foundation of the church, Ephesians 2:19–22 – **p. 1024**;
      Revelation 21:14 – **p. 1113**

ARK OF THE COVENANT – the Israelites' sacred chest
containing the tablets of the law
    description of, Exodus 25:10–22 – **p. 72**
    and crossing the Jordan, Joshua 3 – **p. 184**
    contents of, *"What's In the Ark"* – **p. 132**
    represented God's power, 1 Samuel 4–5 – **p. 235**
    David returns it to Jerusalem, 2 Samuel 6:1–15 – **p. 274**;
      1 Chronicles 13:1–14 – **p. 361**; 15:1–16:6 – **p. 361**
    reverence for, *"Why Did Uzzah Die?"* – **p. 361**
    lost, *"Proof of the Covenant"* – **p. 379**

ARMAGEDDON
    in the valley of Megiddo, *"A Bloody Battlefield"* – **p. 402**
    final role, *"The Battle of Armageddon"* – **p. 1110**

ART – creative expression such as music, dance, painting,
sculpture, writing, architecture
    ordained by God, Exodus 31:1–11 – **p. 78**; 35:30–36:2 – **p. 78**
    excellence needed, Psalm 33:1–3 – **p. 482**

ASCENSION – Christ's rising into heaven after the resurrection
    prophesied, Psalm 27 – **p. 480**
    described, Luke 24:36–53 – **p. 917**; Acts 1:1–11 – **p. 944**
    related to Pentecost, John 16:5–16 – **p. 936**; Ephesians
      4:7–13 – **p. 1025**

ASSURANCE OF SALVATION – certainty of God's forgiveness
and love

    built on trust, Psalm 37 – **p. 485**
    through Christ, Romans 8 – **p. 983**
    produced by faith, 2 Timothy 1:8–12 – **p. 1051**
    achieved by obeying God, 1 John 2:28–3:24 – **p. 1089**
    achieved by believing God's word, 1 John 5:9–13 – **p. 1092**

ASTROLOGY – seeking information about human events from the
stars (*see also* WITCHCRAFT)
    powerless, Isaiah 47:12–15 – **p. 625**
    Daniel discredits, Daniel 2 – **p. 748**

ATHENS
    Paul preaching in, *"Flexible Approach"* – **p. 963**

ATHLETICS
    Christianity compared to running, 1 Corinthians
      9:24–27 – **p. 999**; Hebrews 12:1–2 – **p. 1069**
    Christianity compared to wrestling, Ephesians 6:10–18 – **p. 1028**
    competing according to rules, 2 Timothy 2:5 – **p. 1051**
    training for, *"Athlete in Training"* – **p. 1047**; *"Soldier, Athlete,
      Farmer"* – **p. 1051**
    in Ephesus, *"Sports and Education"* – **p. 965**

ATONEMENT – payment for sin; associated with the Israelites'
Day of Atonement, when a blood sacrifice was made for the sins
of the nation (*see also* JUSTIFICATION, SALVATION)
    by sacrifice, *"The Reason for Sacrifice"* – **p. 91**
    Hebrew ritual of, Leviticus 16 – **p. 101**
    Christ as our, Romans 3:21–26 – **p. 979**; 2 Corinthians
      5:14–21 – **p. 1010**; Hebrews 9 – **p. 1066**; 1 Peter
      2:22–25 – **p. 1079**; 1 John 1:8–2:2 – **p. 1088**

B

BAAL – god of the Phoenicians and Canaanites
    worshipped in Israel, 1 Kings 16:29–34 – **p. 313**; 2 Kings
      17:7–23 – **p. 338**; 21:1–9 – **p. 338**
    defeated by Elijah, 1 Kings 18 – **p. 314**; *"Elijah Rubs It
      In"* – **p. 316**

BABYLON
    as symbol of evil, *"An Evil Queen"* – **p. 625**; *"Apocalyptic
      Arrogance"* – **p. 693**; *"What Is Babylon?"* – **p. 1111**
    and archaeology, *"The Throne Room"* – **p. 752**
    fall of, *"Sneak Attack"* – **p. 753**
    cruelty of, *"Gambling Prizes"* – **p. 774**
    prophecies against, Isaiah 13:1–14:23 – **p. 595**;
      21:1–10 – **p. 595**; 47:1–15 – **p. 595**; Jeremiah
      50:1–51:58 – **p. 689**

BACKSLIDING – departure from a life of faith in and obedience to
God
    displeases God, Psalm 78 – **p. 505**
    a serious sin, Hebrews 6:4–6 – **p. 1063**; 10:26–31 – **p. 1063**
    forgiveness for, Revelation 2:4–5 – **p. 1099**;
      3:2–3,15–21 – **p. 1099**
    examples of:
      Israel at Mount Sinai, Exodus 32 – **p. 78**
      Solomon, 1 Kings 11 – **p. 306**
      Hymenaeus and Alexander, 1 Timothy 1:19–20 – **p. 1045**
    in the end times, 2 Timothy 3:1–10 – **p. 1052**

BALAAM – man employed by the Moabites to curse the Israelites
    his loyalty, *"Whose Side Is Balaam On?"* – **p. 137**
    stopped by God, Numbers 22–24 – **p. 135**
    prophecy fulfilled, *"Balaam's Prophecy"* – **p. 138**
    death of, Numbers 31:1–24 – **p. 143**

BAPTISM – a water ritual, used as a spiritual symbol (*see also*
HOLY SPIRIT, JOHN THE BAPTIST)
    Jesus' baptism, Matthew 3:13–15 – **p. 834**
    as sign of repentance, Matthew 3:1–12 – **p. 834**
    as sign of conversion, Matthew 28:16–20 – **p. 863**
    in the early church, Acts 2:37–41 – **p. 946**; 8:26–39 – **p. 946**
    and the believer's death and resurrection in Christ, Romans
      6 – **p. 981**; Colossians 2:11–12 – **p. 1035**
    of the Holy Spirit, Acts 1:1–8 – **p. 944**; 1 Corinthians
      12:12–13 – **p. 1001**

BARABBAS – criminal released by Pilate instead of Jesus
    set free, Matthew 27:11–26 – **p. 860**

BARGAINING
    in the middle East, *"Let's Make a Deal"* – **p. 22**; *"Oriental
      Bargaining"* – **p. 58**

BATHSHEBA – committed adultery with David and later married
him (*see also* DAVID, SOLOMON)
    life of, 2 Samuel 11:1–12:25 – **p. 277**
    helped Solomon become king, 1 Kings 1:11–31 – **p. 296**

BEAUTY

    inner, 1 Samuel 16:1–13 – **p. 246**; *"Skin-Deep Beauty"* – **p. 551**;
      1 Timothy 2:9 – **p. 1046**; 1 Peter 3:1–7 – **p. 1080**
    of Bathsheba, 2 Samuel 11 – **p. 277**
    of Esther, Esther 2:1–18 – **p. 431**
    changing standards of, *"Tan Lines"* – **p. 580**

BEGGARS – *see* POOR

BETRAYAL
by a friend, *"Betrayed by a Friend"* – **p. 495**
of Jesus by Judas, Matthew 26:14–16,47–49 – **p. 858**

BIBLE
as history, *"Selective History"* – **p. 52**; *"Three Kinds of Brick"* – **p. 54**; *"Unfair Credit?"* – **p. 336**; *"The Ring of Truth"* – **p. 409**; *"Away at War"* – **p. 431**; *"Is Esther Accurate?"* – **p. 436**; *"Bridge Chapters"* – **p. 613**; *"Dating by Emperors"* – **p. 888**; *"The Linking Book"* – **p. 943**; *"During the Reign of . . ."* – **p. 958**; ; *"Sailing Log"* – **p. 973**
compilation of, *"Out of Print"* – **p. 135**; *"Using Other Sources"* – **p. 308**; *"The Five Books"* – **p. 502** *"Belong in the Bible?"* – **p. 926**; *"Sound Familiar?"* – **p. 494**
in praise of, Psalm 19:7–11 – **p. 476**; 119:1–176 – **p. 476**
used by Satan, *"Satan and the Bible"* – **p. 513**
languages, *"A Change in Language"* – **p. 748**
literary devices in, *"Well-Turned Phrase"* – **p. 688**; *"Structured Passion"* – **p. 697**; *"A Passion for Punning"* – **p. 791**
translation of, *"Lost in Translation"* – **p. 873**
importance of, 2 Timothy 3:14–17 – **p. 1052**
inspired by God, *"Scripture is God-Breathed"* – **p. 1052**; 2 Peter 1:19–21 – **p. 1084**
act on, James 1:19–27 – **p. 1073**
interpreting, *"A Book Full of Mysteries"* – **p. 1097**; *"Seals and Scrolls"* – **p. 1101**; *"Old Testament Echoes"* – **p. 1106**

BITTERNESS – lingering resentment or anger
avoid, Ephesians 4:29–32 – **p. 1025**
as sin, James 3:13–18 – **p. 1075**

BLASPHEMY – bringing reproach against God and his name
a sin against God, Exodus 20:7 – **p. 67**; Leviticus 24:13–23 – **p. 110**
Jesus charged with, Matthew 9:1–8 – **p. 840**; Matthew 26:57–67 – **p. 859**
against the Holy Spirit, Mark 3:20–30 – **p. 866**

BLESSINGS
material blessings, Deuteronomy 7:12–16 – **p. 157**; Psalm 67 – **p. 499**
spiritual blessings, Psalm 32 – **p. 482**; John 1:14–17 – **p. 918**; Ephesians 1:3–14 – **p. 1023**
showers of blessings, Ezekiel 34:26–30 – **p. 733**
the Beatitudes, Matthew 5:1–11 – **p. 835**; Luke 6:20–22 – **p. 893**

BLOOD – used to represent the life of a creature, often in sacrifices or rituals of cleansing
instructions to Noah about shedding, Genesis 9:1–6 – **p. 10**
role in the covenant, *"Covenant Blood"* – **p. 72**
for purification of priests, Exodus 29 – **p. 76**
in offerings to God, especially for sin, Leviticus 1,3,4 – **p. 87**
the Day of Atonement, Leviticus 16 – **p. 101**

BLOOD OF CHRIST – shed on the cross as Jesus died
wine as sign of, in the Lord's Supper, Matthew 26:27–29 – **p. 858**; 1 Corinthians 11:23–32 – **p. 1000**
as payment for sin, Hebrews 9:11–28 – **p. 1066**
redemption through, Ephesians 1:7–8 – **p. 1023**; 1 Peter 1:18–19 – **p. 1079**
reconciliation through, Ephesians 2:11–18 – **p. 1024**
cleansing through, 1 John 1:7–10 – **p. 1088**

BOASTING
about God, *"Confident in God"* – **p. 653**

BODY OF CHRIST
signified by bread in the Lord's Supper, Mark 14:22–24 – **p. 880**
as metaphor for church, Romans 12:3–8 – **p. 987**; 1 Corinthians 12:12–31 – **p. 1001**; *"Lessons from the Human Body"* – **p. 1001**
Jesus as the head, Ephesians 1:22–23 – **p. 1023**; Colossians 1:18–24 – **p. 1034**
completely human, Hebrews 2:14–18 – **p. 1061**
now a glorious body, 1 Corinthians 15:35–49 – **p. 1004**; Philippians 3:20–21 – **p. 1031**

BORN AGAIN – spiritual rebirth or conversion (*see also* CONVERSION, SALVATION)
necessity of, John 3:1–21 – **p. 920**

---

marked by holiness, Titus 3:4–8 – **p. 1057**; 1 Peter 1:13–23 – **p. 1078**

C

CAIN – first son of Adam and Eve; murdered his brother Abel
life of, Genesis 4:1–26 – **p. 7**
a warning to believers, 1 John 3:11–13 – **p. 1089**

CALEB – one of 12 spies sent by Moses into promised land
report of, Numbers 13:1–14:38 – **p. 127**
receives Hebron, Joshua 14:1–15 – **p. 195**

CALVARY – *see* GOLGOTHA

CANAAN – land God promised to the Israelites; later called Palestine
trade routes in, *"On the Road"* – **p. 14**
promised to Abraham, Genesis 13:14–17 – **p. 14**; Genesis 15:12–21 – **p. 15**
promised to Isaac, Genesis 26:1–6 – **p. 24**
promised to Jacob, Genesis 28:10–22 – **p. 27**
Moses can't go in, Deuteronomy 34:1–12 – **p. 180**
Joshua conquers, Joshua 1–12 – **p. 182**; *"Two Accounts of Warfare"* – **p. 194**
inhabitants punished, *"Is a War Ever Holy?"* – **p. 192**
inhabitants not eliminated, *"Hints of Failure"* – **p. 196**; *"Missing an Opportunity"* – **p. 198**

CELIBACY – abstaining from marriage
calling to, Matthew 19:4–12 – **p. 850**
advantages of, 1 Corinthians 7:32–40 – **p. 998**
not required, 1 Timothy 4:1–5 – **p. 1046**

CHARACTER
revealed, *"Deeper Meanings"* – **p. 552**

CHEATING
by Laban, *"Jacob Meets His Match"* – **p. 30**
by Jacob, *"Misplaced Faith"* – **p. 31**
forbidden, *"Honest Weight"* – **p. 742**

CHILDREN
should honour parents, Exodus 20:12 – **p. 67**; Ephesians 6:1–4 – **p. 1028**
praising God, *"Children's Power"* – **p. 471**
a gift from God, Psalm 127 – **p. 532**
formed by God in the womb, Psalm 139:13–16 – **p. 536**
should listen to instruction, Proverbs 1 – **p. 542**
suffering of, *"Pity the Children"* – **p. 699**
punishment of, *"Rebel Son"* – **p. 768**
used as an example of humility, Matthew 18:1–4 – **p. 849**
blessed by Jesus, Mark 10:13–16 – **p. 876**
of God through Christ, John 1:12–13 – **p. 918**; Romans 8:12–17 – **p. 984**; Galatians 3:26–4:7 – **p. 1019**

CHOIR – David's, *"Bad Father, Good Children"* – **p. 511**; *"And Now, the Choir . . ."* – **p. 355**
used by Ezra and Nehemiah, *"Victory Party"* – **p. 427**
heavenly, *"Good News with Bad"* – **p. 1109**

CHRIST – *see* MESSIAH

CHRISTIANS – name given to followers of Christ
first called, Acts 11:26 – **p. 957**; *"Naming the New Religion"* – **p. 954**
how to become, Romans 10:9–13 – **p. 986**
marks of, Galatians 5:22–26 – **p. 1022**

CHRISTIAN LIVING
over a lifetime, *"A View from Old Age"* – **p. 502**
struggles, *"Inner Struggles"* – **p. 983**; *"A Positive and a Negative"* – **p. 999**
questions about, *"Down-to-earth Problems"* – **p. 988**; *"Weak or Strong?"* – **p. 989**; *"When Everything Goes Wrong"* – **p. 997**
and theology, *"Getting Practical"* – **p. 1034**
well-rounded, *"The Search for Wholeness"* – **p. 1035**; *"Words Are Not Enough"* – **p. 1072**

not being idle, *"No Work, No Eat"* – p. 1043
training for, *"Athlete in Training"* – p. 1047; *"Soldier, Athlete, Farmer"* – p. 1051; *"What Is True Faith?"* – p. 1068
leaving, *"Can a Believer Fall Away?"* – p. 1063
problems with money, *"Conflicts of Rich and Poor"* – p. 1075
stages in, *"A Friendly Interruption"* – p. 1088

CHURCH – both the local assemblies of Christians and the worldwide community of believers
promised by Christ, Matthew 16:13–20 – p. 848
beginnings of, *"Infant Church"* – p. 946
growth of, *"The Linking Book"* – p. 943; *"The Secret Behind the Early Church"* – p. 950; *"Crossing Racial Barriers"* – p. 952; *"The Danger in Being a Christian"* – p. 953; *"On the Road with the Apostle Paul"* – p. 964
organisation of, *"A Cure for Discrimination"* – p. 950; *"The First Church Council"* – p. 961; *"The Hardest Job"* – p. 1044; *"Time to Get Organised"* – p. 1046
unity of, Romans 12:3–8 – p. 987; Ephesians 4:1–14 – p. 1025
founded on Christ and the apostles, 1 Corinthians 3:1–15 – p. 994; Ephesians 2:19–22 – p. 1024
as body of Christ, 1 Corinthians 12:12–28 – p. 1001
problems in early, *"When Everything Goes Wrong"* – p. 997; *"Diverse People, Diverse Problems"* – p. 1054
locations of early, *"Cities on a Mail Route"* – p. 1100
Christ's relationship to, Ephesians 4:7–16 – p. 1025
Christ's message to seven churches, Revelation 2–3 – p. 1099

CIRCUMCISION – removal of the foreskin in males; established by God to signify his relationship with the Israelites
sign of covenant, Genesis 17:9–14 – p. 16
symbolic, *"Uncircumcised Hearts"* – p. 112; *"Circumcised Hearts"* – p. 647
no longer necessary, Romans 4:4–12 – p. 979; Galatians 5:1–12 – p. 1020
linked with baptism, Colossians 2:11–12 – p. 1035

CITIES OF REFUGE
purpose of, *"Controlling Blood Feuds"* – p. 147; *"Cities of Refuge"* – p. 199

CLEANNESS
laws of clean and unclean, Leviticus 11–15 – p. 95
cleansing from sin, Psalm 51:1–9 – p. 492; Hebrews 10:19–22 – p. 1067; 1 John 1:5–10 – p. 1088

COLOSSE – city in Asia to which Paul wrote the letter "Colossians"
Paul's friends in, *"Prominent Names"* – p. 1036

COMFORT

through silent sharing, *"Keeping Quiet"* – p. 439
in grief, Job 2:11–13 – p. 439; Psalm 23 – p. 478
in trouble, Psalm 46 – p. 490; Romans 8:18–39 – p. 984
when we sin, Psalm 103 – p. 517
when afraid, Isaiah 41:8–20 – p. 619
from God, Isaiah 40:1–11 – p. 616
from Holy Spirit, John 14:1–4,15–27 – p. 933
share with others, 2 Corinthians 1:3–7 – p. 1007; *"Mixing Gentleness with Harshness"* – p. 1021

COMMUNION – *see* LORD'S SUPPER

COMPASSION – to have pity for and show kindness to another
of God, Exodus 34:4–7 – p. 80; Psalm 103:8–12 – p. 517; Jonah 3 – p. 790
commanded by God, Micah 6:6–8 – p. 795; Galatians 6:1–10 – p. 1022
of Jesus, Matthew 9:35–38 – p. 840; 14:13–14 – p. 840; 15:29–39 – p. 840; John 11:17–44 – p. 930
sign of faith, 1 John 3:11–24 – p. 1089

COMPLAINING
not condemned by God, *"A Shocking Lack of Piety"* – p. 447

CONFESSION – an acknowledgment of the truth
of Christ:
  Peter's, Matthew 16:13–20 – p. 848
  Thomas's, John 20:24–31 – p. 940

as Lord, Romans 10:9–13 – p. 986; Philippians 2:9–11 – p. 1030
as Son of God, 1 John 4:2–3,13–16 – p. 1090
of sin:
  Ezra's, Ezra 9 – p. 412
  David's, Psalm 51 – p. 492
  Isaiah's, Isaiah 6 – p. 590
  Daniel's, Daniel 9 – p. 756
  lost son's, Luke 15:11–32 – p. 905
  tax collector's, Luke 18:9–14 – p. 907
  to one another, James 5:16 – p. 1077
  to God, 1 John 1:5–2:2 – p. 1088

CONFORMITY – to adopt the values and practices of a group
to evil-doers, Proverbs 4:10–19 – p. 545
to the world, James 4:1–10,17 – p. 1075

CONSCIENCE – awareness of one's actions as either right or wrong (*see also* CONFESSION, FORGIVENESS)
guilty, Psalm 38 – p. 486
accuses us of sin, Romans 2:12–16 – p. 978
be sensitive to others', Romans 14 – p. 989; 1 Corinthians 8 – p. 998; 10:23–11:1 – p. 998
silencing of, *"Loss of Sensitivity"* – p. 1025
cleansed by Christ, Hebrews 10:19–22 – p. 1067

CONVERSION – to turn away from sin and to God through repentance and faith (*see also* BORN AGAIN, PAUL, SALVATION)

result of God's love, Jeremiah 31:3–14 – p. 672
of Samaritan woman, John 4:1–30,39–42 – p. 921
of an Ethiopian eunuch, Acts 8:26–40 – p. 953
of Paul, Acts 9:1–25 – p. 955; *"Recruiting from the Opposition"* – p. 955
of Lydia, Acts 16:11–15 – p. 962
of a jailer, Acts 16:22–34 – p. 962
become new through, 2 Corinthians 5:17–19 – p. 1010
by grace, Ephesians 2:1–10 – p. 1023

CORINTH
church started, Acts 18:1–17 – p. 963
life in, *"The Last Place to Start a Church"* – p. 992; *"Corinthian Slogans"* – p. 997
and Paul, *"A Book of Joy and Sadness"* – p. 1006; *"A Mysterious Visit"* – p. 1008; *"Paul Has Had Enough"* – p. 1014

COURAGE
the call to be courageous, Joshua 1 – p. 182
David's, 1 Samuel 17:26–50 – p. 247
shown by kings of Judah, *"The Great Reformers"* – p. 388
Esther's, *"A Profile of Courage"* – p. 429
Daniel's, *"Kidnapped"* – p. 746
Daniel's three friends, Daniel 3 – p. 749
the apostles', Acts 4 – p. 947; 5:17–42 – p. 947

COVENANT – an agreement between two parties; a solemn promise or vow, especially between God and people
with Noah, Genesis 9:1–17 – p. 10
with Abraham, Genesis 15; 17:1–14 – p. 15; *"Promises, Promises"* – p. 21
with Israelites in Old Testament, *"Book of the Covenant"* – p. 67; *"The Covenant"* – p. 68; Exodus 19:3–8,24 – p. 66; *"A Personal Plea"* – p. 149; Deuteronomy 29 – p. 174
benefits of keeping, *"Healthier, Wealthier, and Wiser"* – p. 158
illustrated by Joshua, *"Blessings and Curses"* – p. 189
with David, 2 Samuel 7:1–17 – p. 275
punishment for breaking, *"Day of Reckoning"* – p. 655
new, *"A New Covenant"* – p. 675; 2 Corinthians 2:12–3:18 – p. 1008; Hebrews 8:7–13 – p. 1065; 10:1–18 – p. 1065; *"More Perfect"* – p. 842; *"A Vivid Contrast"* – p. 1070
with Israelites in New Testament, *"A Crushing Blow to Paul"* – p. 985

COVETING – envious desire for something that belongs to another (*see also* ENVY, GREED)
commandment on, Exodus 20:17 – p. 67
Achan's, Joshua 7 – p. 187

D

make them of all nations, Matthew 28:6–20 – **p. 863**
called Christians, Acts 11:26 – **p. 957**
DISCIPLESHIP – the act of following and learning from a teacher,
especially Jesus
not waiting, *"Burying His Father"* – **p. 898**
cost of, Luke 14:25–34 – **p. 904**
evidence of, John 15:1–17 – **p. 935**
result of love, John 21:15–19 – **p. 941**
DISCIPLINE – training that moulds, instructs, corrects
by parents, Proverbs 23:13–23 – **p. 562**; *"How to Raise
Children"* – **p. 561**
by God, *"Like Everybody Else"* – **p. 718**; Hebrews
12:1–13 – **p. 1069**
by the church, 1 Corinthians 5 – **p. 996**
by God's Word, 2 Timothy 3:14–17 – **p. 1052**
DISCOURAGEMENT (*see also* COMFORT)
overcoming, Joshua 1:1–9 – **p. 183**; Psalm 42 – **p. 488**; Psalm
77:1–15 – **p. 504**; John 14:1–27 – **p. 933**; 2 Corinthians
4:7–12,16–18 – **p. 1009**; *"For the Discouraged"* – **p. 1022**
of Job, *"Why Keep on Living?"* – **p. 441**
in life, *"Companion Book"* – **p. 575**
DISCRIMINATION (*see also* RACISM)
against the Israelites, *"New Tyrant in Town"* – **p. 52**
on basis of wealth, *"Play No Favourites"* – **p. 1074**
eliminated in Christ, *"The Original Barbarians"* – **p. 1036**;
Ephesians 2:11–18 – **p. 1024**
DISEASE (*see also* HEALING)
cleansing from, *"A Bird Set Free"* – **p. 99**
treatment of, *"Bad Medical Advice"* – **p. 386**
DISOBEDIENCE (*see also* OBEDIENCE)
Israel's in entering Canaan, *"Imperfect Timing"* – **p. 129**
warnings against, *"Final Warnings"* – **p. 146**; *"A Scent of
Doom"* – **p. 174**
DIVORCE
Mosaic law on, Deuteronomy 24:1–4 – **p. 170**
God's view of, *"I Hate Divorce"* – **p. 823**
Jesus' teaching on, Matthew 19:1–12 – **p. 850**; Mark
10:2–12 – **p. 875**; *"Teaching on Divorce"* – **p. 875**
a pardonable sin, John 4:4–42 – **p. 921**
Paul's teaching on, 1 Corinthians 7:10–16 – **p. 997**

DOUBT (*see also* FAITH)

of Abraham, Genesis 12:10–20 – **p. 13**
of Sarah, Genesis 18:1–15 – **p. 17**
of Moses, Exodus 4:1–17 – **p. 53**
of Gideon, Judges 6 – **p. 210**
of Peter, Matthew 14:22–32 – **p. 846**
overcoming, Mark 9:14–29 – **p. 874**; 11:22–25 – **p. 874**;
James 1:2–7 – **p. 1073**
of John the Baptist, Luke 7:18–23 – **p. 894**
of Thomas, John 20:24–31 – **p. 940**

DREAMS (*see also* VISIONS)
of Jacob, Genesis 28:10–22 – **p. 27**
interpreted by Joseph, Genesis 37 – **p. 36**; 41 – **p. 36**
meaning of, *"A Nightmare"* – **p. 583**; *"A Nation of
Dreamers"* – **p. 749**
false prophecy through, Jeremiah 23:25–32 – **p. 665**; Ezekiel
13:1–9 – **p. 711**
interpreted by Daniel, Daniel 2 – **p. 748**; 4 – **p. 748**
at the birth of Jesus, Matthew 2 – **p. 833**
of Pilate's wife, Matthew 27:19 – **p. 861**
in the last days, Acts 2:14–21 – **p. 945**
DRINKING ALCOHOL (*see also* WINE)
warnings about, Proverbs 20:1 – **p. 558**; 23:29–35 – **p. 558**;
Isaiah 5:11–12 – **p. 589**; *"The Dangers of Wine"* – **p. 562**;
Ephesians 5:18 – **p. 1026**
vow against, *"Teetotallers"* – **p. 677**
examples of overindulgence
of Noah, Genesis 9:20 – **p. 11**
of Lot, Genesis 19:32–35 – **p. 19**
of Xerxes, Esther 1:10 – **p. 430**

at the Lord's Supper, 1 Corinthians 11:21 – **p. 1000**

 E

EARTH (*see also* ECOLOGY)
created by God, Genesis 1:1–25 – **p. 5**; *"Ecology Plus"* – **p. 518**
care for, Genesis 1:26–31 – **p. 5**
exhibits God's love, Psalm 33:1–11 – **p. 482**
not eternal, *"Outlasting the Universe"* – **p. 517**
ages of, *"Three Worlds"* – **p. 1085**
waits for redemption, Romans 8:18–25 – **p. 984**
destruction of, *"The Fate of the Earth"* – **p. 1085**
new, *"New Earth"* – **p. 640**; 2 Peter 3:3–13 – **p. 1085**; Revelation
21:1–22:5 – **p. 1113**; *"Eden Regained"* – **p. 1114**
ECOLOGY – keeping a proper balance in nature
God's concern for, *"Respect for Nature"* – **p. 168**
appreciation of, *"Ecology Plus"* – **p. 518**
EDOM – *see* Esau
EGYPT
Joseph taken there, Genesis 37 – **p. 36**
Israelites moved there, Genesis 39–50 – **p. 38**
exodus from, Exodus 1–13 – **p. 51**
judgment of, Isaiah 19 – **p. 600**; Jeremiah 42 – **p. 682**; Ezekiel
29–30 – **p. 726**
Jesus taken there, Matthew 2:13–20 – **p. 834**
ELDER – a designated leader of the Jewish people and of the
church
leaders of the Jewish council, Acts 5:17–42 – **p. 949**
leaders appointed in churches, Acts 14:21–25 – **p. 960**; Titus
1:5–9 – **p. 1055**
Paul's farewell speech to, Acts 20:13–38 – **p. 966**
qualifications for, 1 Timothy 3:1–7 – **p. 1046**
ELECTION – God's choosing a people for himself
of Abraham, Genesis 12:1–9 – **p. 13**
of Israel, Exodus 19:1–6 – **p. 66**; Deuteronomy
10:12–22 – **p. 160**; Isaiah 41:8–16 – **p. 619**
of Jesus' disciples, John 15:9–17 – **p. 935**
of Jacob, Romans 9:6–13 – **p. 984**
of the church, Ephesians 1:3–14 – **p. 1023**; 1 Peter
2:1–10 – **p. 1079**
make it sure, 2 Peter 1:3–10 – **p. 1084**
ELI – a priest and judge of Israel
life of, 1 Samuel 1–4 – **p. 231**
ELIJAH – Israelite prophet well known for his confrontation with
the priests of Baal (*see also* BAAL, ELISHA)
life of, 1 Kings 17–19 – **p. 313**; 21 – **p. 313**
and Baal, 1 Kings 18:16–46 – **p. 314**; *"The Contest"* – **p. 315**
death of, 2 Kings 2 – **p. 323**; *"An Obscure Compliment"* – **p. 323**
second coming, *"The Second Elijah"* – **p. 824**
at transfiguration, Luke 9:28–36 – **p. 897**
ELISHA – prophet who succeeded Elijah
chosen by Elijah, 1 Kings 19:16–21 – **p. 317**
life of, 2 Kings 2–13 – **p. 323**; *"Replacing a Legend"* – **p. 324**
mocked, *"Background on the Bears"* – **p. 325**
heals Naaman, 2 Kings 5:1–27 – **p. 327**; *"Harder on the
Rich"* – **p. 327**
ENEMY
cursing, *"What about Curses?"* – **p. 536**; *"Tough Love"* – **p. 1089**
treat with kindness, Proverbs 25:21–22 – **p. 564**; Romans
12:19–21 – **p. 988**
love for, *"Good News for the Enemy?"* – **p. 787**; Luke
6:27–36 – **p. 893**
ENOCH
his faith, *"The Man Who Did Not Die"* – **p. 9**
ENVY (*see also* JEALOUSY, GREED)
of Joseph by brothers, Genesis 37 – **p. 36**
comes from inside, Mark 7:20–23 – **p. 872**
trouble from, James 3:13–4:10 – **p. 1075**

EPHESUS
religion in, *"Commercialised Religion"* – p. 966
Paul preaching in, *"Sports and Education"* – p. 965
Paul's farewell to, Acts 20:13–38 – p. 966
church in, *"Strategic Place"* – p. 1045

ESAU
– son of Isaac and Rebekah; older brother of Jacob
despised his birthright, *"No Sympathy for Esau"* – p. 24
cheated by Jacob, Genesis 25:19–34 – p. 24; Genesis
27:1–28:9 – p. 25
forgives Jacob, Genesis 33 – p. 33
descendants of, *"Blood Feud"* – p. 134; *"Bad Blood"* – p. 734;
"Poetic Justice" – p. 784

ESTHER
made queen, Esther 2 – p. 431
her wisdom, *"Subtle Approach"* – p. 434

ETERNAL LIFE
– life everlasting with God, which begins at
conversion (*see also* BORN AGAIN, CONVERSION, SALVATION,
HEAVEN)

in Psalms, *"Life after Death"* – p. 474
hints of in Old Testament, *"Is There an After-life?"* – p. 573
to inherit, Matthew 19:16–30 – p. 850
through rebirth, John 3:1–21 – p. 920
gift of God, Romans 6:15–23 – p. 982
assurance of, 1 John 5:1–15 – p. 1092

EVANGELISM
– telling and living the good news of Christ's
salvation (*see also* MISSIONS)
by lifestyle, *"Old Testament Evangelism"* – p. 154
call to, Matthew 28:16–20 – p. 863; Luke 24:45–52 – p. 917;
Acts 1:1–11 – p. 944
gift of, Ephesians 4:1–16 – p. 1025; 2 Timothy 4:1–5 – p. 1052

EVE
– the first woman
life of, Genesis 1:26 – 5:2 – p. 5
temptation of, Genesis 3 – p. 7
mentioned in the New Testament, 1 Corinthians
11:2–16 – p. 1000; 1 Timothy 2:8–15 – p. 1046

EVIL (*see also* SATAN, SIN)
introduction of, Genesis 3:1–24 – p. 7
used by God, *"You Intended Evil"* – p. 49; *"Evil Spirit"* – p. 215
people, *"Blowing in the Wind"* – p. 469
repent of, Jeremiah 18:1–12 – p. 660
problem of, Job 1 – 42 – p. 437; *"The Song of the
Cross"* – p. 478; *"God's Fault?"* – p. 576; *"The Problem of
Evil"* – p. 801
spreads, *"One-way Contamination"* – p. 811; *"Evil
Everywhere"* – p. 470
battle with good, *"A Look Behind the Scenes"* – p. 1107

EVOLUTION
– theory of the development of species (*see also*
CREATION)
controversy over, *"How the World Began"* – p. 6

EXCOMMUNICATION
for purpose of teaching, *"Handed Over to Satan"* – p. 996;
1 Corinthians 5 – p. 996; 1 Timothy 1:20 – p. 1045

EXAMPLE
Christ as, John 13:1–17 – p. 932; Philippians 2:1–11 – p. 1030
Old Testament stories as, 1 Corinthians 10:1–13 – p. 999;
Hebrews 11:4–40 – p. 1068
Christians as, Philippians 2:14–15 – p. 1030; 1 Thessalonians
1 – p. 1037; 1 Peter 2:11–12 – p. 1079
Job, of patience, James 5:10–11 – p. 1077
Elijah, of prayer, James 5:16–18 – p. 1077

EXILE
northern kingdom to Assyria, 2 Kings 17 – p. 338
southern kingdom to Babylon, 2 Kings 25 – p. 346; 2 Chronicles
36 – p. 402
return from, *"After the Exile"* – p. 358; *"Beginning
Again"* – p. 404; *"Starting Again"* – p. 812
Jews' enemies after, *"A Flash Forward"* – p. 408; *"Powerful
Opponents"* – p. 417
won't last forever, *"Gone, But Not For Ever"* – p. 667

EYE-WITNESSES
of Jesus' ministry, *"Eye-witness Reports"* – p. 870; *"Like a Joy-
filled Musical"* – p. 885; *"Eye-witness Details"* – p. 919; *"Eye-
witness"* – p. 1088
of Jesus' resurrection, *"Cover-up"* – p. 862; *"More Than a
Ghost"* – p. 947; *"Basic Christianity"* – p. 1003
of Paul's ministry, *"First-hand Report"* – p. 962

EZEKIEL
life of, *"Seeing the Unseen God"* – p. 703
burden of, *"The Sad Truth"* – p. 732
proof of his message, *"Prophet's Proof"* – p. 722
as a watchman, *"Watch Out"* – p. 730

EZRA
– a leader of the Jews who returned from exile
life of, Ezra 7 – 10 – p. 410; Nehemiah 8 – p. 421; 12 – p. 421
concern about intermarriage, *"Ezra, a Man of the Heart"* – p. 410

F

FAITH
– trust in and reliance on God
of Abraham, *"Abraham"* – p. 13; Genesis 15:6 – p. 15
Abraham's lack of, *"A Substitute Wife"* – p. 16
simple, *"Keep It Simple"* – p. 176
shown by widow of Zarephath, *"Down to the Last Meal"* – p. 314
shown by Ezra, *"Risk of Faith"* – p. 412
during suffering, *"When Bad Things Happened to a Good
Person"* – p. 437; *"Seeing in the Dark"* – p. 466; *"Refiner's
Fire"* – p. 1078
living by, *"Beyond Understanding"* – p. 578; *"Whom to
Trust?"* – p. 660; Matthew 6:25–34 – p. 838; *"Time to
Decide"* – p. 1059;
during crisis, *"A Time of Crisis"* – p. 610
lukewarm, *"When Faith Grows Weary"* – p. 821
necessary for salvation, Romans 3:21 – 5:11 – p. 979; Galatians
2 – 3 – p. 1017; Ephesians 2:1–10 – p. 1023
our part in, *"Working with God"* – p. 1030
heroes of, Hebrews 11 – p. 1067; *"What Is True
Faith?"* – p. 1068
shown by deeds, *"Bargain Hunting"* – p. 674; James
2:14–26 – p. 1074; *"Words Are Not Enough"* – p. 1072

FAITHFULNESS
of God, Psalm 78 – p. 505; Psalm 111 – p. 523; Lamentations
3:22–32 – p. 700
an aspect of the Spirit's fruit, Galatians 5:16–26 – p. 1022
of Moses, Hebrews 3 – p. 1061
expected of Christians, Revelation 2:8–11 – p. 1099

FALSE PROPHETS
used by God, *"Whose Side Is Balaam On?"* – p. 137
tests for, *"Testing Prophets"* – p. 162
denounced, *"Dog-like Prophets"* – p. 633
predicting good, *"Greedy Doctors"* – p. 650;
"Whitewash" – p. 712; *"Plenty of Beer"* – p. 792
use of dreams, *"Questionable Dreams"* – p. 666

FALSE TEACHERS
avoiding, *"Unequal Yokes"* – p. 1010
recognising, *"Battling the Cults"* – p. 1033; *"Foolish
Questions"* – p. 1056; *"A Threat from Within"* – p. 1083; *"Who
Were the Gnostics?"* – p. 1090; *"Undesirable
Guests"* – p. 1092; *"Watch Out"* – p. 1095
distorting the truth, *"Words That Get Polluted"* – p. 1087
Gnostics, *"Annoying Deceivers"* – p. 1093
emperor worship, *"Satan's Throne"* – p. 1100

FAME
transience of, Isaiah 14:9–20 – p. 596
unreliability of, Ezekiel 33:30–32 – p. 731
unimportant, 1 Corinthians 3:1–23 – p. 994

FAMILY

established in Garden of Eden, Genesis 2:18–24 – **p. 6**
obligations to, *"A Brother's Duty"* – **p. 37**
quarrels within, *"Family Battles"* – **p. 38**; *"Family Jealousy"* – **p. 127**
built by God, Psalm 127–128 – **p. 532**
of God, *"For the Discouraged"* – **p. 1022**; Ephesians 2:19–22 – **p. 1024**
family relations, Ephesians 5:21–6:4 – **p. 1026**; Colossians 3:18–21 – **p. 1037**

FAMINE

in Egypt and Palestine, *"An Unusual Famine"* – **p. 41**
in Israel, Ruth 1:1 – **p. 228**; 1 Kings 17 – **p. 313**; 2 Kings 6:25–8:2 – **p. 329**

FASTING – abstinence from food or drink for a period of time, especially for spiritual reasons

at a time of national crisis, 2 Chronicles 20:1–13 – **p. 388**; Esther 4 – **p. 432**; Joel 2:15–17 – **p. 773**
true, Isaiah 58 – **p. 633**
proper time for, *"Repent for How Long?"* – **p. 815**
Jesus' teaching on, Matthew 6:16–18 – **p. 837**
disciples', Acts 13:1–3 – **p. 958**; 14:23 – **p. 958**

FEAR – reverence and awe for God

commanded, Deuteronomy 6:10–25 – **p. 156**; Ecclesiastes 12:8–14 – **p. 579**
good, Psalm 33 – **p. 482**
guide to living, *"The Fear of the Lord"* – **p. 548**
the beginning of wisdom, Proverbs 9:10–12 – **p. 549**

FEAR – fright or alarm

combating, Psalm 23 – **p. 478**; 56 – **p. 478**; 91 – **p. 478**; Jeremiah 1:4–19 – **p. 643**; Luke 12:4–12 – **p. 902**
comfort in, John 14 – **p. 933**

FELLOWSHIP

expressed in sharing, Acts 2:42–47 – **p. 946**; 4:24–35 – **p. 946**
with the Holy Spirit, 2 Corinthians 13:14 – **p. 1016**
in church, Ephesians 4:17–5:21 – **p. 1025**
with God, 1 John 1 – **p. 1087**

FESTIVALS – see JEWISH HOLY DAYS

FLATTERY

deceives, *"Flattering Advice"* – **p. 284**; *"Dangerous Flattery"* – **p. 567**
displeases God, Psalm 12 – **p. 472**

FOOD

provided by God, *"No More Free Lunch"* – **p. 186**
provided by Christ, Matthew 14:13–21 – **p. 846**; John 6 – **p. 923**
glorify God through, 1 Corinthians 10:23–11:1 – **p. 1000**
as god, Philippians 3:19 – **p. 1031**

FOOL (see also WISDOM)

in biblical terms, *"The Making of a Fool"* – **p. 565**

FOREIGN NATIONS

opposing Judah and Israel, *"Troublesome Neighbours"* – **p. 335**
Israel's alliances with, *"Ahaz's Fateful Decisions"* – **p. 337**; *"The Siege Lifted"* – **p. 679**; *"False Hope"* – **p. 594**; *"The Runaways"* – **p. 721**; *"Unreliable Egypt"* – **p. 727**
praising God, *"Who are God's People?"* – **p. 491**; *"House of Prayer"* – **p. 633**
loved by God, *"God Reaches Out"* – **p. 498**
loss of power of, *"The Decline of Tyre"* – **p. 603**
used by God, *"Cyrus the Shepherd"* – **p. 623**
cruelty of, *"Most Ruthless"* – **p. 728**
preaching gospel to, *"To All Nations"* – **p. 879**
entering the church, *"Earthshaking Change"* – **p. 957**
salvation of, *"Hope for the Gentiles"* – **p. 656**; *"The Wise Men"* – **p. 834**
judged by God, *"Just What They Deserved"* – **p. 723**

FORGIVENESS

human, Genesis 33 – **p. 33**; 50:15–21 – **p. 33**; Luke 15:17–24 – **p. 905**; Acts 7:60 – **p. 952**
God's, Exodus 34:4–7 – **p. 80**; Psalm 103:8–12 – **p. 517**; Micah 7:18–20 – **p. 797**; *"Nobody Like God"* – **p. 796**
absolute, *"An End to Guilt"* – **p. 690**

for sins, Psalm 130 – **p. 533**
how often, Matthew 18:21–35 – **p. 849**
through Christ, Mark 2:1–11 – **p. 865**; Colossians 2:6–15 – **p. 1035**; *"A Modern Peace Child"* – **p. 981**
in the church, 2 Corinthians 2:5–11 – **p. 1008**

FREE WILL

Pharaoh's, *"Pharaoh's Hard Heart"* – **p. 57**
Israel's, *"Free Choice"* – **p. 202**
David's, *"Satan or the Lord?"* – **p. 292**

FREEDOM

through obeying, *"Free At Last"* – **p. 50**
in Christ, John 8:31–36 – **p. 927**; Galatians 4:21–5:26 – **p. 1020**; *"Legalism"* – **p. 1019**; *"Paul Fights Back"* – **p. 1020**
from sin and our human nature, Romans 6 – **p. 981**
from law, Romans 8:1–17 – **p. 983**; Galatians 3:8–25 – **p. 1018**

FRIENDSHIP

acts of, *"Loyal Friends in Death"* – **p. 259**; *"How to be a Good Friend"* – **p. 557**
faithfulness in, Proverbs 27:6,10,17 – **p. 565**
giving advice in, *"A Mixture of True and False"* – **p. 443**; *"What Not to Say to a Hurting Person"* – **p. 442**; *"A Wrong Time for Cheer"* – **p. 449**; *"Battle of Words"* – **p. 449**; *"A Silent Friend Decides to Speak Up"* – **p. 457**; *"Kinder, Gentler Friend"* – **p. 458**
importance of, Ecclesiastes 4:7–12 – **p. 573**
of David and Jonathan, 1 Samuel 20 – **p. 249**; *"Final Farewell"* – **p. 252**; *"The Survival of a Family"* – **p. 253**
of Jesus with Mary, Martha, and Lazarus, John 11:1–44 – **p. 929**
of Ruth and Naomi, *"A Rare Bond of Love"* – **p. 227**
with the world, James 4 – **p. 1075**
with the wrong people, *"Unholy Alliance"* – **p. 319**

FRUIT OF THE SPIRIT

described, Galatians 5:16–26 – **p. 1022**

FUTURE (see also SECOND COMING)

seeking omens of, *"The Witch of Endor"* – **p. 257**; *"Liver-Gazing"* – **p. 719**
revealed by God, *"Foretelling the Future"* – **p. 624**; *"A Glimpse of Things to Come"* – **p. 638**
of the earth, *"Catastrophes to Come?"* – **p. 820**
preoccupation with, Matthew 6:25–34 – **p. 838**; Luke 12:13–48 – **p. 902**; *"Preparing for the End"* – **p. 1040**
Jesus' statements about, *"When Will Jesus Return?"* – **p. 856**
uncertain, James 4:13–17 – **p. 1077**
of God's kingdom, *"A Happy Ending After All"* – **p. 1114**

 G

GABRIEL – an angel who carried messages from God

with Daniel, Daniel 8, 9 – **p. 755**
with Zechariah, Luke 1:5–25 – **p. 886**
with Mary, Luke 1:26–38 – **p. 887**

GALILEE – region in northern Palestine

towns given to Hiram, *"Good-for-nothing Towns"* – **p. 305**
Jesus' ministry there predicted, Isaiah 9:1–7 – **p. 592**; Matthew 4:12–17 – **p. 835**
Jesus' ministry in, *"Into the Countryside"* – **p. 865**
home of Mary and Joseph, Luke 1:26 – **p. 887**; Luke 2:39 – **p. 889**

GARDEN OF EDEN

God created, Genesis 2:8–17 – **p. 6**
expulsion from, Genesis 3 – **p. 7**

GENEALOGY

shows God's care, *"Compressed History"* – **p. 349**
importance to the Israelites, *"A Family Record"* – **p. 348**; *"Key People"* – **p. 354**; *"The Source of Genealogies"* – **p. 357**; *"A People Preserved"* – **p. 406**; *"Remembering our Past"* – **p. 420**
of Jesus, *"A Bridge from Old to New"* – **p. 831**; *"A Gospel for the Gentiles"* – **p. 890**

GENTILES – see FOREIGN NATIONS

H

obeying with your, *"Law of the Heart"* – **p. 171**
God knows, 1 Samuel 16:1–13 – **p. 246**
cleansing of, Psalm 51 – **p. 492**
undivided, *"Heart Surgery"* – **p. 510**
life flows from, Proverbs 4:23 – **p. 546**
deceitful, Jeremiah 17:9–10 – **p. 660**
leads to action, Matthew 12:33–37 – **p. 843**

HEAVEN – a place of perfect happiness and eternal communion
with God

hints of in Old Testament, *"Life after Death"* – **p. 474**
God rules from, Psalm 99 – **p. 515**; Isaiah 66:1–2 – **p. 640**
new, Isaiah 65:17–25 – **p. 639**; Revelation 21 – 22 – **p. 1113**
treasures in, Matthew 6:19–24 – **p. 837**
for righteous, Matthew 25:31–46 – **p. 857**
citizenship in, Philippians 3:12 – 4:1 – **p. 1031**
inhabitants of, Hebrews 11 – **p. 1067**
visions of, Revelation 4 – 5 – **p. 1101**; Revelation 7 – **p. 1103**

HELL – a place of eternal punishment and sorrow
hints of in Old Testament, Job 24:21–26 – **p. 453**; Psalm
49:10–15 – **p. 491**; Daniel 12 – **p. 759**
to avoid, Matthew 5:21–30 – **p. 836**; Romans 8:1–16 – **p. 983**
for evil-doers, Matthew 13:24–30,36–43 – **p. 844**
punishment in, 2 Thessalonians 1:3–12 – **p. 1042**; Jude
5–13 – **p. 1098**; Revelation 20:11–14 – **p. 1113**
keep others from, Jude 17–23 – **p. 1098**

HERESIES – *see* FALSE TEACHERS

HEROD – name of a line of rulers of Palestine
the Great, Matthew 2 – **p. 833**
Antipas, Matthew 14:1–12 – **p. 846**; *"Guards Without
Allies"* – **p. 958**
Agrippa I, Acts 12:1–23 – **p. 958**

HEZEKIAH – king of Judah for 29 years; reopened the temple his
father had closed
life of, 2 Kings 18 – 20 – **p. 339**; *"King of
Contradictions"* – **p. 340**
restores worship, 2 Chronicles 29 – 31 – **p. 395**
crisis with Isaiah, Isaiah 36 – 39 – **p. 613**

HISTORY
God working in, *"God's Hand in History"* – **p. 593**; *"Catastrophes
Through God's Eyes"* – **p. 601**; *"Like a Wise
Farmer"* – **p. 607**; *"A New Song"* – **p. 618**; *"Ransom for the
Captives"* – **p. 621**; *"World at War"* – **p. 685**;
"Kidnapped" – **p. 746**; *"In the Hands of Tyrants"* – **p. 759**;
"The Meaning of a Natural Disaster" – **p. 771**; *"Light in a Dark
Time"* – **p. 790**; *"A Look Behind the Scenes"* – **p. 1107**
as encouragement, *"Why the Clean Up?"* – **p. 352**
interpreting, *"Moral of the Story"* – **p. 359**
prophesied, *"A Prophecy for the World"* – **p. 606**; *"Foretelling the
Future"* – **p. 624**; *"New King, New Kingdom"* – **p. 817**

HOLOCAUST
original meaning of, *"Original Holocaust"* – **p. 88**

HOLY – separated or set apart for God
called to be, Exodus 19:1–5 – **p. 66**; Leviticus 11:44–45 – **p. 96**;
1 Peter 1:13–16 – **p. 1078**; 2:9–10 – **p. 1078**
lifestyle, *"National Reminders"* – **p. 124**
God's character, Psalm 99 – **p. 515**; Isaiah 6 – **p. 590**
One of Israel, *"A Key Phrase"* – **p. 595**
all things becoming, *"No More Separation"* – **p. 820**
imitate God's holiness, Ephesians 4:17 – 5:21 – **p. 1025**

HOLY SPIRIT – the third person of the Trinity; also known as the
Counsellor who is active in the lives of believers (*see also* FRUIT
OF THE SPIRIT)

in the Old Testament, *"The Spirit and Samson"* – **p. 220**; Psalm
51:11 – **p. 493**; Isaiah 11:1–5 – **p. 594**; 61:1–3 – **p. 594**
his coming prophesied, *"A New Spirit"* – **p. 735**; *"The Spirit
Poured Out"* – **p. 774**

anointed Jesus, Luke 3:21–22 – **p. 889**; 4:1–27 – **p. 889**
comfort from, John 14:15–31 – **p. 934**
work of, John 16:5–16 – **p. 936**; *"Branded"* – **p. 1023**
coming to the disciples, Acts 2 – **p. 945**
in the early church, *"The Secret Behind the Early
Church"* – **p. 950**
directs the church, Acts 13:1–4 – **p. 958**; 16:6–7 – **p. 958**
filled with, Acts 19:1–7 – **p. 965**; Ephesians 5:18 – **p. 1026**
life through, Romans 8:1–17 – **p. 983**
in Christians, 1 Corinthians 2:6–16 – **p. 994**; 3:16–17 – **p. 994**

HOMOSEXUALITY
result of sin, Romans 1:18–32 – **p. 977**
listed as sin, 1 Corinthians 6:9–11 – **p. 996**; 1 Timothy
1:9–11 – **p. 1045**

HONESTY
Samuel's, *"Accuse Me!"* – **p. 240**
God desires, Psalm 15 – **p. 473**

HOPE
for the Israelites, *"Hope in a Time of Sorrow"* – **p. 365**; *"Free
Again"* – **p. 672**; *"The Turning Point"* – **p. 731**; *"New
Hope"* – **p. 770**
in the Lord, Psalm 42 – 43 – **p. 488**; 1 Timothy
6:17–19 – **p. 1049**
while waiting for God, *"A Desperate Hope"* – **p. 446**; *"An
Outburst of Hope"* – **p. 450**; *"A New Song"* – **p. 618**; *"Hope
for the Grieving"* – **p. 700**
because of the past, *"A Time for Hope"* – **p. 375**; *"Remembering
Back"* – **p. 505**
for total redemption, *"A Glimpse of Things to Come"* – **p. 638**; *"A
Happy Ending After All"* – **p. 1114**
does not disappoint, Romans 5:1–11 – **p. 981**
for resurrection, 1 Corinthians 15 – **p. 1003**
in Christ, Colossians 1:3–27 – **p. 1034**; 1 Peter
1:13–16 – **p. 1078**

HOSPITALITY
expected, *"A Breach of Hospitality"* – **p. 224**
Jesus' words on, Luke 14:12–14 – **p. 904**
responsibility of, Romans 12:13 – **p. 988**; 1 Peter 4:9 – **p. 1081**;
"Guidelines for Hospitality" – **p. 1094**
entertaining angels, Hebrews 13:1–3 – **p. 1070**
when not to extend, *"Undesirable Guests"* – **p. 1092**

HUMAN BEINGS
created in God's image, Genesis 1:26–31 – **p. 5**
made by God, *"How the World Began"* – **p. 6**
glory of, Psalm 8 – **p. 471**
intricately made, Psalm 139:13–16 – **p. 536**
apart from God, *"Three Problem People"* – **p. 544**; *"Outside the
Palace"* – **p. 572**

HUMILITY
of David, *"Rare Trait"* – **p. 364**
living in, Micah 6:6–8 – **p. 795**; Colossians 3:12–17 – **p. 1037**;
1 Peter 5:5–7 – **p. 1082**
like children, Matthew 18:1–4 – **p. 849**
encouraged, *"Luke and the Underdog"* – **p. 907**; *"The Role of a
Servant"* – **p. 933**; Romans 12:1–21 – **p. 987**; 1 Peter
5:5–7 – **p. 1082**
of Christ, 2 Corinthians 8:8–9 – **p. 1011**; Philippians
2:1–11 – **p. 1030**

HUSBAND
duty to wife, 1 Corinthians 7:1–5 – **p. 997**
love for wife, Ephesians 5:25–33 – **p. 1027**; Colossians
3:19 – **p. 1037**

HYPOCRISY
in worshipping God, *"Hypocrites"* – **p. 608**; *"Letting the Inside
Match the Outside"* – **p. 837**
avoid, Matthew 6:1–24 – **p. 836**
described, Matthew 23 – **p. 855**
condemned, James 1:19–2:13 – **p. 1073**; 1 John
3:17–19 – **p. 1089**

IDOLATRY — the worship of idols; putting something before God
commandment against, Exodus 20:3–6 – **p. 67**
Canaanite, *"Detestable Ways"* – **p. 166**
during time of the judges, *"Sad Commentary"* – **p. 223**
attraction of, *"Why All the Fuss about Idols?"* – **p. 340**
Judah's lust for, *"Provoking God"* – **p. 639**
Israel's lust for, *"Smouldering Passion"* – **p. 766**
as adultery, *"Ritual Sex"* – **p. 647**; *"A Lover's Quarrel"* – **p. 646**;
    "Worse than a Whore" – **p. 713**; *"The Runaways"* – **p. 721**;
    "Tearing God's Heart" – **p. 761**
emptiness of, *"Idolatry"* – **p. 662**; Isaiah 44:6–23 – **p. 622**
greed is, Colossians 3:5 – **p. 1035**

IDOLS
of Laban, *"Household Gods"* – **p. 32**
of Egypt, *"Attack on False Gods"* – **p. 59**
golden calf, *"Recent Discovery"* – **p. 78**
Israel defending its, *"Topsy-turvy"* – **p. 211**
of Judah, *"Notorious Asherah Poles"* – **p. 310**; *"Queen of
    Heaven"* – **p. 684**
worthless, *"An Exiled God"* – **p. 686**; *"A Dim View of
    Idolatry"* – **p. 707**

IMAGE OF GOD — (see HUMAN BEING)

INCARNATION — God taking human flesh; birth of Jesus
taught, Matthew 1:18–25 – **p. 833**; Luke 1–2 – **p. 885**; John
    1:1–18 – **p. 918**
reason for, *"Contempt, not Sympathy"* – **p. 446**; *"Why Come to
    Earth?"* – **p. 868**
heresies denying, *"Who Were the Gnostics?"* – **p. 1090**

INCEST — sexual relations with a family member
Lot and his daughters, *"Family Quarrels"* – **p. 19**
Reuben's, *"A Sin that Lies Sleeping"* – **p. 35**
forbidden, Leviticus 18:1–18 – **p. 103**

INFERTILITY
Sarah's, Genesis 18:1–15 – **p. 17**
Hannah's prayer concerning, 1 Samuel 1:1–2:11 – **p. 232**
Elizabeth's, Luke 1:7–25 – **p. 886**

INSPIRATION — the Bible as inspired by the Holy Spirit (see
BIBLE)

INTERCESSION — the prayer of one person for another
examples of, Genesis 18:23–32 – **p. 17**; 1 Kings
    8:33–51 – **p. 304**; Ezra 9:5–15 – **p. 412**; Daniel
    9:3–19 – **p. 756**
of Jesus for us, John 17 – **p. 936**; Romans 8:31–34 – **p. 984**;
    Hebrews 7:24–25 – **p. 1064**; 1 John 2:1 – **p. 1088**
of the Holy Spirit, Romans 8:26–27 – **p. 984**
commanded, 1 Timothy 2:1–2 – **p. 1045**; James 5:16 – **p. 1077**;

ISAAC — only son of Abraham by Sarah; born miraculously in their
old age
birth predicted, Genesis 18:1–15 – **p. 17**
as sacrifice, Genesis 22:1–19 – **p. 20**
marries Rebekah, Genesis 24 – **p. 22**
blesses sons, Genesis 27 – **p. 25**; *"Sense of Smell"* – **p. 26**
death of, Genesis 35:16–29 – **p. 34**
chosen by God, Romans 9:6–9 – **p. 984**; Galatians
    4:21–31 – **p. 1020**

ISAIAH
as an author, *"Prophet, Poet, and Politician"* – **p. 585**
his call as prophet, Isaiah 6 – **p. 590**
his reaction to his message, *"A Prophet's Pain"* – **p. 599**
his political involvement, *"Foreign Policy"* – **p. 600**; *"A Time of
    Crisis"* – **p. 610**
as historian, *"Isaiah the Historian"* – **p. 612**

ISRAEL — name God gave to Jacob, the father of the Israelite
nation (see also JACOB)
given name, Genesis 32:22–32 – **p. 33**
twelve sons of, Genesis 49 – **p. 47**

ISRAEL — nation of God's chosen people, composed of 12 tribes;
its history makes up much of the Old Testament (see also
JUDAH)
tribes of, *"The Younger Brother"* – **p. 47**; *"Two for One"* – **p. 116**

and Egypt, *"Final Escape"* – **p. 63**
in the desert, *"A Place for Everyone"* – **p. 116**
census of, *"How Many Israelites?"* – **p. 117**; *"Recount"* – **p. 140**;
    "Act of Pride" – **p. 367**
dividing Canaan, *"Trouble Ahead"* – **p. 145**; *"Dividing Up the
    Land"* – **p. 194**
relationships between tribes, *"Explosive Quarrel"* – **p. 201**; *"A
    Soft Answer"* – **p. 217**; *"A State of Anarchy"* – **p. 222**;
    "Hanging by a Thread" – **p. 222**; *"Unified Front"* – **p. 383**;
    "North Versus South" – **p. 288**; *"Joseph's Heirs"* – **p. 356**
size of the kingdom, *"How Large Was Israel?"* – **p. 300**
enemies of, *"Troublesome Neighbours"* – **p. 335**; *"None
    Escape"* – **p. 690**
God's presence in, *"Red-letter Day"* – **p. 362**
relationship to God, *"Experience Teaches"* – **p. 155**; *"A Lesson
    from History"* – **p. 637**; *"God's Patience Exhausted"* – **p. 657**;
    "The Future of the Jews" – **p. 987**
splitting into two nations, *"The Nation Splits Apart"* – **p. 311**
governed by judges, *"The Bad Old Days"* – **p. 507**
promise of being reunited, *"North and South Reunited"* – **p. 736**
images of restoration of, *"New Hope"* – **p. 770**
in prosperity, *"Soft and Fat"* – **p. 781**

ISRAEL — Northern Kingdom; the nation of the northern 10 tribes
after rebelling against Rehoboam
ruled by Omri, *"A Strong, Weak King"* – **p. 313**
fall of, *"The Great Wars of Israel"* – **p. 321**
rulers of, *"A Line-up of Rulers"* – **p. 260**
places of worship, *"Northern Visitors"* – **p. 385**
warnings to, *"Tearing God's Heart"* – **p. 761**; *"Justice!"* – **p. 776**

JACOB — son of Isaac and Rebekah; younger brother of Esau (see
also ISRAEL)
life of, Genesis 25–49 – **p. 24**
steals birthright, Genesis 25:19–34 – **p. 24**
steals blessing, Genesis 27 – **p. 25**; *"Con Man in God's
    Family?"* – **p. 27**; *"Surface Reconciliation"* – **p. 33**
dream of, Genesis 28:10–22 – **p. 27**
his marriages, Genesis 29–30 – **p. 29**
wrestles with God, Genesis 32 – **p. 32**
symbolising the nation Israel, *"Jacob, a Man and a
    Country"* – **p. 769**

JAMES — son of Zebedee; an apostle and brother of apostle John
call of, Matthew 4:18–22 – **p. 835**
at transfiguration, Matthew 17:1–13 – **p. 848**
sought top place in kingdom, Mark 10:35–45 – **p. 876**
death of, Acts 12:1–2 – **p. 958**

JANNES AND JAMBRES
possible identification of, *"Who Were Jannes and
    Jambres?"* – **p. 1052**

JEALOUSY
of God, Exodus 34:14 – **p. 80**; Deuteronomy 32:15–22 – **p. 178**;
    "Idolatry" – **p. 662**
command against, Romans 13:13 – **p. 989**; 2 Corinthians
    12:19–21 – **p. 1016**
between people, 1 Corinthians 3:1–23 – **p. 994**

JEHOSHAPHAT — king of Judah
life of, 1 Kings 22 – **p. 319**; 2 Chronicles 17–22 – **p. 386**

JEPHTHAH — judge of Israel, known for his foolish vow
character of, *"A Man Like David"* – **p. 216**

JEREMIAH
as an author, *"Jeremiah's Influence"* – **p. 346**; *"God's Reluctant
    Messenger"* – **p. 642**
reluctant, *"Too Young?"* – **p. 644**
warnings ignored, *"Don't Worry, Be Happy"* – **p. 649**
faithful, *"No Social Life"* – **p. 659**
motivation, *"Fire in His Bones"* – **p. 663**
protected by Babylonians, *"Influential Prisoner"* – **p. 681**
kidnapped, *"Closed Minds"* – **p. 683**

through servanthood, John 13:1–17 – **p. 932**
an aspect of the Spirit's fruit, Galatians 5:16–26 – **p. 1022**
always, Philippians 4:4–9 – **p. 1031**
in all circumstances, *"Paul's Secret"* – **p. 1032**
in suffering, Colossians 1:24 – **p. 1035**; James 1:2–18; 1 Peter
    4:12–19; *"Like a Joy-filled Musical"* – **p. 885**; *"Cheerful
    Sounds from a Jail Cell"* – **p. 1028**

JUDAH – Southern Kingdom; nation of the southern tribes of
Benjamin and Judah that remained loyal to Rehoboam
loyalty of, *"The Nation Splits Apart"* – **p. 311**
invaded by Sennacherib, *"Invasion"* – **p. 399**
fall of, *"The Great Wars of Israel"* – **p. 321**; *"A Kingdom
    Disappears"* – **p. 347**; *"Total Destruction"* – **p. 694**
fighting with Israel, *"Ahaz's Fateful Decisions"* – **p. 337**
reform in, *"Too Little Too Late"* – **p. 346**
rulers of, *"A Line-up of Rulers"* – **p. 260**; *"A Brighter
    Outlook"* – **p. 384**; *"The Great Reformers"* – **p. 388**
extent of its sin, *"Search for an Honest Person"* – **p. 648**; *"Light
    in a Dark Time"* – **p. 790**
complacency of, *"Practical Atheism"* – **p. 806**

JUDAS ISCARIOT – the disciple who betrayed Jesus
as betrayer, *"A Name Disgraced"* – **p. 859**; Matthew
    26:47–56 – **p. 859**
death of, Matthew 27:1–10 – **p. 860**; Acts 1:18–19 – **p. 944**
as treasurer, John 12:1–8 – **p. 931**

JUDGING OTHERS
unfairly, *"Unfair Accusation"* – **p. 445**
not to be done, Romans 14:1–13 – **p. 989**; James
    4:9–12 – **p. 1077**
Jesus' words on, Matthew 7:1–5 – **p. 838**
with mercy, James 2:1–13 – **p. 1074**

JUDGMENT
God as judge, Psalm 94 – **p. 513**
Jesus as judge, Acts 10:34–43 – **p. 957**
God's standards for, *"A Higher Standard"* – **p. 338**
final, Matthew 24:36 – 25:46 – **p. 856**; 2 Thessalonians
    1–2 – **p. 1041**; Revelation 18–20 – **p. 1110**

JUSTICE
through law, *"A National Law Library"* – **p. 106**
cry for, *"Self-Righteous?"* – **p. 480**; *"Rough Words"* – **p. 496**;
    "What About Curses?" – **p. 536**
God executes, Psalm 146 – **p. 539**; *"Just What They
    Deserved"* – **p. 723**; *"God's Answer to Injustice"* – **p. 797**;
    "God at Work" – **p. 3**
for the oppressed, *"For the Voiceless"* – **p. 568**
through God's servant, *"The Solution"* – **p. 620**
as true worship, Isaiah 58 – **p. 633**
injustice condemned, Amos 5 – **p. 779**; Micah 6 – **p. 795**
God's standards of, *"Justice!"* – **p. 776**; *"A Plumb Line"* – **p. 781**;
    "Poetic Justice" – **p. 784**

JUSTIFICATION – to be freed from guilt or blame
by faith, Romans 3:21–31 – **p. 979**; 4:1 – 5:11 – **p. 979**; Galatians
    2:15–21 – **p. 1018**

 K

KINDNESS – a hospitable, friendly attitude towards others (*see*
HOSPITALITY)
an aspect of the Spirit's fruit, Galatians 5:16–26 – **p. 1022**

KING
God's requirements for, *"Prescription for a King"* – **p. 166**
Israel asks for, 1 Samuel 8 – **p. 237**
Samuel's comments on, 1 Samuel 12 – **p. 241**
as God's servant, *"The First King"* – **p. 241**
limits to power of, *"No King"* – **p. 214**; *"Limits on the
    King"* – **p. 239**
abuse of power of, *"A King of Excess"* – **p. 306**; *"A Stolen
    Vineyard"* – **p. 318**; *"Solomon's Forced Labour"* – **p. 377**;
    "The Messianic Promise" – **p. 665**
confusing names of, *"Two Kings, One Name"* – **p. 330**
rejected from tribe of Benjamin, *"Dynasty Rejected"* – **p. 357**

people's view of, *"A Wedding Fit for a King"* – **p. 490**
God as, Psalm 47 – **p. 491**; 99 – **p. 491**; 1 Timothy
    1:15–17 – **p. 1045**
Jesus as, *"The Killing of a King"* – **p. 860**
Jesus on David's throne, Luke 1:26–38 – **p. 887**
Jesus now ruling at God's right hand, Ephesians
    1:15–34 – **p. 1023**; Hebrews 1:1–12 – **p. 1060**

KINGDOM OF GOD (*or* KINGDOM OF HEAVEN) – wherever God
is reigning; also, the people experiencing God's reign
parables of, Matthew 13:1–52 – **p. 843**;
    18:10–14,21–35 – **p. 843**; 20:1–16 – **p. 851**;
    21:28–46 – **p. 852**; 22:1–14 – **p. 854**; 25:1–46 – **p. 857**
has come in Jesus, Mark 1:14–15 – **p. 864**; Luke
    7:18–22 – **p. 894**; 11:14–20 – **p. 894**
nature of, *"What Should a Leader Look Like?"* – **p. 845**; *"Status-
    conscious Disciples"* – **p. 912**
to be handed over to God, 1 Corinthians 15:20–28 – **p. 1003**

 L

LAMB OF GOD – a title John the Baptist gave to Jesus
removes sin, John 1:29–42 – **p. 919**
receives praise, Revelation 5 – **p. 1101**
worthy, *"A Startling Image of Jesus"* – **p. 1102**

LAUGHTER
of Sarah, Genesis 18:1–15 – **p. 17**; 21:1–7 – **p. 17**
God's, Psalm 2 – **p. 469**
time for, Ecclesiastes 3:1–8 – **p. 572**

LAW – a set of commandments given by God
concerning the firstborn, *"The Firstborn Principle"* – **p. 62**
given to Moses, Exodus 19:1 – 24:8 – **p. 66**; *"Long-lasting
    Laws"* – **p. 68**; *"The Covenant"* – **p. 68**
of purification, *"An Invisible Danger"* – **p. 98**
distinctive features, *"A National Law Library"* – **p. 106**
reviewed, *"Interruptions of the Story"* – **p. 142**
motive for obeying, *"The Bottom Line"* – **p. 105**; *"Who Needs
    Laws?"* – **p. 163**
rediscovered by Josiah, *"Historic Discovery"* – **p. 161**; *"Dramatic
    Discovery"* – **p. 344**
after exile, *"A People of the Book"* – **p. 422**
love for, *"A Love Poem to God's Law"* – **p. 528**
flying scroll a symbol of, *"A Message for Everyone"* – **p. 815**
fulfillment of, Matthew 5:17–48 – **p. 835**; *"New Light on the Old
    Testament"* – **p. 1065**
in hearts, Jeremiah 31:33 – **p. 673**; *"Law in Their
    Hearts"* – **p. 674**; Hebrews 8 – **p. 1064**
not enough for salvation, *"How to Please God"* – **p. 980**; *"No
    Second-Class Christians"* – **p. 1016**; *"The 430-Year
    Gap"* – **p. 1018**
legalism, *"Do Not Add"* – **p. 153**; *"Jesus and Moses'
    Law"* – **p. 836**; *"Attacking Legalism"* – **p. 847**; *"Straining at
    Gnats"* – **p. 855**; *"Rules Without Love"* – **p. 893**;
    "Legalism" – **p. 1019**

LAZARUS – brother of Mary and Martha; close friend of Jesus
Jesus raises from the dead, John 11:1–44 – **p. 929**

LAZARUS – character in story Jesus told
carried to Abraham's side, Luke 16:19–31 – **p. 906**

LAZINESS
results of, *"The Problem with Laziness"* – **p. 563**; *"The Excuses
    of a Lazy Man"* – **p. 564**
warnings against, 2 Thessalonians 3:6–15 – **p. 1044**

LEADERSHIP
God's help for, *"Who, Me?"* – **p. 53**; *"Unlikely Leaders"* – **p. 212**;
    "A Donkey Hunt" – **p. 238**
rivalry in, *"Burdens of Leadership"* – **p. 127**; *"A Sense of God's
    Timing"* – **p. 254**; *"Potential Rivals"* – **p. 271**
Joshua's, *"Filling Moses' Shoes"* – **p. 203**
Israel's need for, *"What Leadership Requires"* – **p. 231**
failures of, *"Why Saul Was Rejected"* – **p. 245**; *"The Man Who
    had Everything"* – **p. 294**
by David, *"The Life of King David"* – **p. 269**

by Ezra, *"Ezra, a Man of the Heart"* – **p. 410**
by Nehemiah, *"A Man of Action"* – **p. 415**
through suffering, *"New King, New Kingdom"* – **p. 817**
Jesus', *"What Should a Leader Look Like?"* – **p. 845**; *"Good Shepherd"* – **p. 929**
following, Hebrews 13:7–17 – **p. 1070**
qualities of, 1 Timothy 3:1–10 – **p. 1046**

LEGALISM – *see* LAW

LEPROSY (*see also* DISEASE)
wrong diagnosis of, *"Misidentification"* – **p. 97**

LEVITE – a descendant of Levi who served God and worked in the temple. (Priests were Levites, but not all Levites were priests; some had lesser duties.)
as representatives, *"Designated Firstborn"* – **p. 118**
duties established for, Numbers 3 – **p. 117**; 1 Chronicles 23–24 – **p. 368**; *"Keeping the Temple"* – **p. 368**
received cities, Numbers 35 – **p. 147**
support of, *"No Land for Levites"* – **p. 132**

LIFE (*see also* ETERNAL LIFE)
shortness of, Psalm 39 – **p. 486**
a wise, *"God and 'How-to-Succeed' "* – **p. 549**; *"A Matter of Life and Death"* – **p. 554**
purpose of, *"When Life Seems Senseless"* – **p. 570**
cycles in, *"Change or No Change?"* – **p. 573**
good things in, *"Good for Something"* – **p. 574**
making sense of, *"The Gamble"* – **p. 578**
unfairness of, *"Life Is Unfair"* – **p. 577**; *"Is Life Unfair?"* – **p. 1042**
saving your, Matthew 16:24–28 – **p. 848**
eternal, John 3:16–21 – **p. 920**; John 6:25–69 – **p. 924**; *"The Worst Danger of All"* – **p. 1004**; Colossians 3:1–4 – **p. 1035**
living water, John 4:1–26 – **p. 921**
sacrifice of, *"A Modern Shepherd"* – **p. 930**
Jesus brings it to the full, John 10:1–18 – **p. 928**
a gift of God, Acts 17:24–28 – **p. 963**

LIGHT
created first by God, Genesis 1:1–5 – **p. 5**
seeing by God's, *"Light Makes Light"* – **p. 485**
God's Word as, Psalm 119:105 – **p. 529**
of the world, Matthew 5:14–16 – **p. 835**
Jesus as, John 1:1–18 – **p. 918**; 8:12 – **p. 918**
believers as children of, Ephesians 5:8–14 – **p. 1026**; 1 John 1 – **p. 1087**

LION
killed by Samson, Judges 14 – **p. 218**
killed by David, 1 Samuel 17:34–35 – **p. 247**
and lamb together, Isaiah 11:6–9 – **p. 594**; 65:25 – **p. 594**
Daniel in den of, Daniel 6 – **p. 752**
Christ as, Revelation 5:1–5 – **p. 1101**

LISTENING
becoming wise by, *"The Supreme Gift of Wisdom"* – **p. 553**

LITERACY – ability to read and write
Moses', *"First Writing"* – **p. 66**
in ancient times, *"Early Literacy"* – **p. 214**

LONELINESS
cry of, Psalm 22 – **p. 477**
Jesus', Matthew 26:36–46 – **p. 859**
Paul's, 2 Timothy 4:16–18 – **p. 1054**

LORD
revealed to Moses, Exodus 3 – **p. 53**
of lords, Deuteronomy 10:17 – **p. 160**; 1 Timothy 6:13–16 – **p. 1048**; Revelation 19:13–16 – **p. 1112**
Jesus as, Acts 2:14–36 – **p. 945**; Romans 10:9–10 – **p. 986**; Philippians 2:5–11 – **p. 1030**

LORD'S PRAYER
taught, Matthew 6:5–15 – **p. 837**

LORD'S SUPPER – a ritual sharing bread and wine; also called Communion and Eucharist
Jesus began, *"Original Lord's Supper"* – **p. 880**; Luke 22:7–23 – **p. 912**
instructions concerning, 1 Corinthians 11:17–34 – **p. 1000**

LOT – nephew of Abraham who settled in the land near Sodom
separates from Abram, Genesis 13 – **p. 14**
in Sodom, Genesis 18:16–19:38 – **p. 17**

LOVE
shown to an enemy, *"A Captive's Compassion"* – **p. 327**; Romans 12:18–21 – **p. 988**
responding to God's, *"God's Great Concern"* – **p. 540**; *"Spurned"* – **p. 822**
between man and woman, *"Whom Should You Marry?"* – **p. 560**; *"An Intoxicating Love"* – **p. 579**; *"Let Love Sleep"* – **p. 581**
proverbs about, *"Love is the Greatest"* – **p. 550**
symbols of, *"His Banner over Me"* – **p. 581**; *"Parable of Love"* – **p. 763**
power of, *"Love and Death"* – **p. 584**
expressions of, *"A Brotherly Kiss"* – **p. 584**
of God for his people, *"Does God Care?"* – **p. 620**; *"A Lover's Quarrel"* – **p. 646**; Jeremiah 31:1–6 – **p. 672**
of God for non-Jews, *"Good News for the Enemy?"* – **p. 787**
commanded, Mark 12:28–34 – **p. 878**; *"More Than a Feeling"* – **p. 160**; John 13:34–35 – **p. 933**; Romans 12:9–21 – **p. 988**
described, 1 Corinthians 13 – **p. 1002**
an aspect of the Spirit's fruit, Galatians 5:13–26 – **p. 1022**
of the world, 1 John 2:15–17 – **p. 1089**
God is, 1 John 4:7–21 – **p. 1090**

LUKE – author of the third Gospel; physician who travelled with Paul
sources, *"Luke the Historian"* – **p. 886**; *"Jesus' Childhood"* – **p. 889**
emphasis of, *"A Physician Looks at the Poor"* – **p. 892**; *"Severe and Gentle Stories"* – **p. 905**
travel companion of Paul, Acts 16:10–17 – **p. 962**; 20:5–21:18 – **p. 962**; 27:1–28:16 – **p. 962**

LUST – intense desire (*see* SEX)

LYING
by Abraham, *"Abraham's Half-Truth"* – **p. 14**
law against, Exodus 20:16 – **p. 67**
penalty for, Leviticus 6:1–7 – **p. 91**
by the Gibeonites, *"Tricked!"* – **p. 189**
by David, *"Disobeying the Law"* – **p. 250**; *"David's Double Game"* – **p. 256**
to David, *"The 'Traitor's' Story"* – **p. 287**
by Peter, Matthew 26:69–74 – **p. 859**
Satan the father of, John 8:44 – **p. 927**
by Ananias and Sapphira, *"Deadly Deceit"* – **p. 948**
mark of old nature, Ephesians 4:17–5:21 – **p. 1025**

 M

MAGIC – *see* ASTROLOGY, WITCHCRAFT

MARK – author of the second Gospel and missionary helper to Paul and Barnabas
as author, *"The Anonymous Author"* – **p. 881**

MARRIAGE (*see also* DIVORCE, HUSBAND, LOVE, WIFE)
God ordained, Genesis 2:18–25 – **p. 6**; *"The First Marriage"* – **p. 7**
with unbelievers, *"Marrying Foreigners"* – **p. 22**; *"Intermarriage"* – **p. 208**; *"The First Sign of Trouble"* – **p. 218**; *"Inconsistent Ethics"* – **p. 381**; *"Corrupt Leaders"* – **p. 413**
for political reasons, *"Political Marriages"* – **p. 331**
importance of, *"Whom Should You Marry?"* – **p. 560**; Matthew 19:1–12 – **p. 850**
joys of, *"An Intoxicating Love"* – **p. 579**
Jewish customs about, *"More Than Engaged"* – **p. 833**
Jesus' teaching on, *"No-Fault Divorce?"* – **p. 850**
relationship, Ephesians 5:22–33 – **p. 1026**; Colossians 3:18–19 – **p. 1037**; 1 Peter 3:1–7 – **p. 1080**
Paul's advice on, 1 Corinthians 7 – **p. 997**

MARTHA AND MARY – sisters of Lazarus; friends of Jesus
Jesus at home of, Luke 10:38–42 – **p. 900**
at Lazarus's death, John 11 – **p. 929**
washed Jesus' feet, John 12:1–8 – **p. 931**

MARTYR – one who gives up life for the faith
Stephen as, Acts 7 – p. 950
Paul as, "A Hint of Trials to Come" – p. 996; "A Letter fro... Death Row" – p. 1053
by Nero, "Endangered Strangers" – p. 1079
many examples of, Hebrews 11:35–40 – p. 1069; Revelation 6:9–11 – p. 1103

MARY – mother of Jesus; wife of Joseph
Jesus born to, Matthew 1:18 – 2:23 – p. 833; Luke 1:26–56 – p. 887; Luke 2 – p. 888
concerned for Jesus, Mark 3:20–35 – p. 866; Luke 2:41–52 – p. 889
requests Jesus' first miracle, John 2:1–11 – p. 919
at crucifixion, John 19:16–27 – p. 939

MARY MAGDALENE – a close friend of Jesus
present at crucifixion, Mark 15:33–41 – p. 882
had been demon-possessed, Luke 8:1–3 – p. 895
first one at empty tomb, John 20:1–18 – p. 940

MATTHEW – author of the first Gospel; left his work to follow Jesus; also called Levi
transformed, "Unpopular Profession" – p. 840
hosted a dinner for Jesus, Mark 2:13–17 – p. 866

MEDIATOR – someone who helps bring harmony between two parties
Jesus as, 1 Timothy 2:1–6 – p. 1045; Hebrews 9:11–28 – p. 1066

MEDITATION – see QUIET TIME

MELCHIZEDEK – priest and king
blessed Abram, Genesis 14:17–20 – p. 15
pointed to Christ, Psalm 110 – p. 523; Hebrews 5:1–10 – p. 1063; Hebrews 7 – p. 1064; "Who is Melchizedek?" – p. 1064
as example of leader, "Out of Nowhere" – p. 524

MEMORIALS
created for future generations, "Monuments" – p. 204

MEMORIES
giving hope, "Fond Memories" – p. 445; "Remembering Back" – p. 505; "The Good Old Days" – p. 455

MERCY
pleading for, Psalm 4 – p. 469; Luke 18:9–14 – p. 907
of God, Psalm 108:8–12 – p. 522; Psalm 123 – p. 531; "Too Merciful a God?" – p. 789; Luke 1:46–79 – p. 887; Romans 9:15–18 – p. 985
for the merciful, "A Key Characteristic" – p. 488; James 2:12–13 – p. 1074

MESSENGERS
in Persia, "Pony Express" – p. 432
of good news, "Beautiful Feet" – p. 629
Paul's, "Mail Carriers" – p. 1056

MESSIAH – a king and deliverer expected by the Jewish people; Christ
precedent for, "Mystery Man" – p. 15
promised by God, "God's Great Promise" – p. 275; "Promise to David" – p. 534
meaning of, "The Messiah in the Psalms" – p. 469
prophecies concerning, Psalm 2 – p. 469; 110 – p. 469; "The Song of the Cross" – p. 478; "A Wedding Fit for a King" – p. 490; "The Suffering Servant" – p. 630; Isaiah 9:1–7 – p. 592; 11:1–12 – p. 592; 53:1–12 – p. 592; 61:1–3 – p. 636; Daniel 7:13–14 – p. 754; "Jesus Asks a Question" – p. 911
as a leader, "Out of Nowhere" – p. 524
David's son as, "A Bridge from Old to New" – p. 831
Jesus as, Matthew 11:1–6 – p. 841; "The Killing of a King" – p. 860; "Short-lived Acceptance" – p. 877; "The Day of Execution" – p. 883; Luke 4:14–21 – p. 890

MICHAEL – the archangel appointed to guard the Jewish people
with Daniel, Daniel 10 – p. 757; 12:1–13 – p. 757
and war in heaven, Revelation 12 – p. 1107

MILITARY (see also WAR)
serving in, "Uncommon Military Rules" – p. 167
trusting in, "Lessons from the Battlefield" – p. 399; "Faith in God or the Military?" – p. 598; "Worshipping the Military" – p. 802

MILLENNIUM – Latin word for "thousand years"; used in connection with a period in the last days
described, Revelation 20:1–15 – p. 1112
views of, "The Millennium" – p. 1113

MINISTER – see PASTOR

MINISTRY
Paul's style of, "A Human Letter" – p. 1009
self-supporting, "Working for a Living" – p. 1038

MIRACLES – extraordinary events done through God's power
ten plagues, "Day of the Locusts" – p. 56
limited effect of, "When God Was Obvious" – p. 73; "Miracles Aren't Enough" – p. 842; "Don't Tell" – p. 869; "Sensation-Seekers" – p. 901
of Elisha, "Elisha's Miracles" – p. 326
after Sermon on the Mount, "Actions Follow Words" – p. 839
feeding crowds, "Two Feedings" – p. 847; "Better Bread" – p. 924
not done in Nazareth, "No Respect at Home" – p. 846
done at a distance, "A Long-distance Miracle" – p. 923
lead to belief, John 4:43–54 – p. 922; 20:30–31 – p. 922; "John's Reason for Writing" – p. 934
done to glorify God, John 11:1–44 – p. 929

MIRIAM – prophetess, sister of Moses and Aaron
led singing/dancing, Exodus 15:19–21 – p. 64
disagreed with Moses, Numbers 12 – p. 127

MISSIONS (see also EVANGELISM)
Israel's role in, "Catastrophes Through God's Eyes" – p. 601; "Israel's Final Destiny" – p. 626
highly praised, Isaiah 52:7–10 – p. 629; Romans 10:14–15 – p. 986
command to, Matthew 28:16–20 – p. 863; Luke 24:45–52 – p. 917; Acts 1:1–11 – p. 944
responsibility of every Christian, Acts 8:1–6 – p. 952; 1 Peter 3:15–16 – p. 1081
Barnabas and Saul (Paul) sent, Acts 13:1–3 – p. 958
Paul's journeys, Acts 13 – 28 – p. 958

MONEY
God owns everything, Deuteronomy 8 – p. 157; Psalm 24 – p. 479
rules about loans, "Respect People, Not Money" – p. 170
serving, Matthew 6:19–34 – p. 837
stories about, "Matthew and Money" – p. 850
trusting, "When Money is Useless" – p. 902; Psalm 62:10 – p. 497
love of, 1 Timothy 6:3–19 – p. 1048; "Two Familiar Quotes" – p. 1048; James 5:1–5 – p. 1077

MOSES – used by God to deliver Israelites from slavery in Egypt; God gave him the Ten Commandments
life of, Exodus 2 – 40 – p. 52; Numbers 1 – 36 – p. 114; Deuteronomy 1 – 34 – p. 150
birth of, Exodus 2 – p. 52
called by God, Exodus 3 – 4 – p. 53
leads Israelites out of Egypt, Exodus 5 – 15 – p. 54; "Free at Last" – p. 529
received law, Exodus 19 – 31 – p. 66
wilderness wanderings, Numbers 13 – 36 – p. 127
his communication with God, "The Lord to Moses" – p. 123
punished by God, "Moses' Sin" – p. 134; "Moses Stayed Out" – p. 141
final message to Israel, "A Personal Plea" – p. 149; "Dying Words" – p. 179
blames Israelites, "Distributing Blame" – p. 151
foresees Israel's future, "A Scent of Doom" – p. 174; "Moses Gets a Preview" – p. 180
death of, Deuteronomy 34 – p. 180

N

 O

 P

PHARISEES – a strict Jewish sect; careful observers of the law, known for their piety
offended, *"Pharisees Take Offence"* – p. 842
Jesus confronting, Matthew 23 – p. 855; Mark 7:1–23 – p. 871; Luke 11:37–54 – p. 901
opposing Jesus, *"Out to Get Jesus"* – p. 853; *"A No-win Situation"* – p. 854; Matthew 16:1–4 – p. 848; 22:15–45 – p. 848
parable concerning, Luke 18:9–14 – p. 907
Paul's history with, Acts 23:6–11 – p. 970; Philippians 3:2–7 – p. 1031

PHILIP – an evangelist of the early church
with eunuch, Acts 8:26–40 – p. 953
four daughters, Acts 21:9 – p. 968

PHILIPPI
church started by Paul, Acts 16:11–40 – p. 962
relationship with Paul, *"A Helper for Paul"* – p. 1031; *"Paul's Favourite Church"* – p. 1030

PHILISTINES – people who migrated to and lived in an area of Canaan during Old Testament times; they frequently warred with the Israelites
Samson fights, Judges 13:1 – 16:31 – p. 218
power of, *"Military Dominance"* – p. 242
Jonathan fights, 1 Samuel 13 – 14 – p. 241
David fights, 1 Samuel 17:1–58 – p. 246; 2 Samuel 5:17–25 – p. 274; 1 Chronicles 14:8–17 – p. 362
prophecies against, Isaiah 14:28–32 – p. 597; Jeremiah 47:1–7 – p. 686; Ezekiel 25:15–17 – p. 724; Amos 1:6–8 – p. 777

PILATE – a Roman ruler in Palestine during Jesus' lifetime
authorised Jesus' crucifixion, Matthew 27:11–26 – p. 860
with Jesus, John 18:28 – 19:22 – p. 938

PLAGUES
sent by God, *"Day of the Locusts"* – p. 56
ten, Exodus 7:14 – 12:29 – p. 56

PLEASURE
eternal, Psalm 16 – p. 473
God's, Psalm 147:10–11 – p. 540
earthly, Ecclesiastes 2:1–16 – p. 572

POETRY
in the Psalms, *"The Right Words"* – p. 533
in Proverbs, *"Hebrew Poetry"* – p. 549

POLITICS – *see* GOVERNMENT

POOR
God's care for, Deuteronomy 10:17–19 – p. 160; 24:19–22 – p. 160; Luke 1:39–56 – p. 887
responsibility to, Deuteronomy 15:1–11 – p. 164; 24:10–22 – p. 164
reasons for being, *"What Makes People Poor?"* – p. 550
oppression of, *"Justice, Not Religion"* – p. 587; *"Justice for the Poor"* – p. 537; *"Lucky Rich"* – p. 554; Amos 2:6–16 – p. 778
punishment for oppressing, *"Prize Cows"* – p. 779
Jesus' identification with, Matthew 25:31–46 – p. 857
Luke's identification with, *"A Physician Looks at the Poor"* – p. 892
Paul's concern for, *"Remembering the Poor"* – p. 1005; *"Don't Forget the Poor"* – p. 170
equal treatment of, James 2:1–13 – p. 1074

POPULARITY
not to be sought, Philippians 2:1–11 – p. 1030
judging by, James 2:1–13 – p. 1074

POWER (*see also* MIRACLES)
of kings, *"Adultery and Murder"* – p. 279
of God, 1 Chronicles 29:10–13 – p. 373; *"Chariots of Fire"* – p. 328; *"God Pulls Out the Stops"* – p. 462; *"God's Answer to Injustice"* – p. 797
temporary, *"Another Powerful City"* – p. 799
symbols of, *"Brute Power"* – p. 814
Jesus' perspective on, *"Taste of Power"* – p. 900
in this world, *"Who Had Real Power?"* – p. 904
of the gospel, Romans 1:16–17 – p. 977
not to be sought, Philippians 2:1–11 – p. 1030

PRAISE
God worthy of, Psalm 18 – p. 475; Revelation 4 – 5 – p. 1101
commanded, Psalm 145 – 150 – p. 539
public, *"Going Public"* – p. 476
for Christ and salvation, Ephesians 1:3–14 – p. 1023

PRAYER – communication with God (*see also* INTERCESSION)
of Moses, *"Famous Prayers"* – p. 126
of Jehoshaphat, *"A Model Prayer"* – p. 389
toward Jerusalem, *"Where God Dwells"* – p. 304; *"A Jewish Orientation"* – p. 753
of Nehemiah, *"The 'Arrow Prayer' "* – p. 416
and action, *"Praise the Lord and Fight"* – p. 418
recalling God's providence, *"Stained-Glass Prayer"* – p. 423
answered, Psalm 34 – p. 483
for healing, *"Fifteen More Years"* – p. 615
answered negatively, *"God's Answer: No"* – p. 663; *"Don't Ask God"* – p. 717
of Daniel, *"Revealing Prayer"* – p. 748
waiting for answers to, *"Slow to Answer Prayer"* – p. 757
for enemies, *"Praying for Persecutors"* – p. 836
Jesus' teaching on, Matthew 6:5–15 – p. 837; 7:7–12 – p. 837; Luke 18:1–14 – p. 907
submission in, Matthew 26:36–46 – p. 859
Jesus' habit of, *"Seeking Privacy"* – p. 881
confidence in, John 15:1–8 – p. 935
Jesus', for his disciples, John 17 – p. 936; *"Jesus' Longest Prayer"* – p. 937
Paul's, Romans 1:8–12 – p. 977; Ephesians 1:15–19 – p. 1023; 3:14–18 – p. 1023; Colossians 1:9–14 – p. 1034
when suffering, Romans 8:18–27 – p. 984
when answer differs from request, 2 Corinthians 12:7–10 – p. 1016
for wisdom, James 1:5–7 – p. 1073

PREDESTINATION – doctrine that God has predetermined that all believers are saved through Christ (*see also* ELECTION, FREE WILL)
Jacob chosen, *"Con Man in God's Family?"* – p. 27
Jews chosen, *"Why the Israelites?"* – p. 79
Eli's sons rejected, *"God in Charge"* – p. 234
God's foreknowledge, Romans 8:28–30 – p. 984
in love, Ephesians 1:3–14 – p. 1023

PRIDE (*see also* HUMILITY)
of Joseph, *"Big Mouth"* – p. 36
warnings against, Proverbs 8:13 – p. 548; 16:5,14 – p. 548; 21:4,24 – p. 548
God humbles, Isaiah 2:10–22 – p. 588
of Jews in Jerusalem, *"Smiles Instead of Tears"* – p. 603
of Antiochus, *"Exalted Above the Gods"* – p. 760
of the complacent, *"Unbelievable!"* – p. 802
avoid, Romans 12 – p. 987
God opposes, James 4:4–6 – p. 1075

PRIEST – one designated to perform sacred rites and act as an intermediary between people and God (*see also* AARON, MELCHIZEDEK)
Old Testament, Exodus 28 – 29 – p. 75; 39:1–31 – p. 75; Leviticus 8 – 10 – p. 93
purification of, *"The Whole Body"* – p. 76
regulations for, *"Priestly Privileges"* – p. 93
punished for disobedience, *"Fatal Error"* – p. 95
in politics, *"The Priests Take Up Arms"* – p. 391
false, *"Poor Trade"* – p. 764
Jesus as, Hebrews 4:14 – 5:10 – p. 1063; Hebrews 7:1 – 10:18 – p. 1064
Christians as, 1 Peter 2:4–12 – p. 1079; Revelation 1:6 – p. 1099

PRISON
Joseph in, Genesis 39 – 40 – p. 38
visit those in, Matthew 25:31–46 – p. 857
Peter's release from, Acts 12:1–19 – p. 958

Q

R

1:13–14 – p. **1034**; Hebrews 9:11–14 – p. **1066**; "*A Modern Peace Child*" – p. **981**; 1 Peter 1:17–21 – p. **1079**

REHOBOAM – son of Solomon; first king of Judah
life of, 1 Kings 12 – p. **308**; 1 Kings 14 – p. **310**

RELIGION
true, "*Religion at Its Best*" – p. **634**; "*What God Wants*" – p. **795**; "*Which One Showed Love?*" – p. **900**
mixed, "*How to be Religious Without Pleasing God*" – p. **766**; "*The New Golden Calf*" – p. **768**
Paul on Greek religion, Acts 17:22–31 – p. **963**
combating false, "*Battling the Cults*" – p. **1033**
pure, James 1:26–27 – p. **1074**

RESPONSIBILITY
for sin, Ezekiel 18 – p. **715**
accepting, "*No Excuses*" – p. **978**
to love others, 1 John 3:11–24 – p. **1089**

REST
day of, Genesis 2:1–3 – p. **5**; Exodus 20:8 – p. **67**
for the land, "*Revenge of the Land*" – p. **112**
year of, "*A Year of Freedom*" – p. **425**
in God, Psalm 23 – p. **478**; 62 – p. **478**
for weary, Matthew 11:25–30 – p. **842**

RESURRECTION
hinted in Old Testament, "*A Promise of Eternal Life*" – p. **605**; "*Resurrection!*" – p. **474**; Job 19:23–27 – p. **449**; Ezekiel 37:1–14 – p. **735**; Daniel 12:1–2 – p. **759**
foretold, "*Resurrection!*" – p. **474**; "*Stubbornly Unconvinced*" – p. **906**
of Jesus, Matthew 27:57 – 28:20 – p. **861**; "*Final Glimpses of Jesus*" – p. **915**; "*More Than a Ghost*" – p. **947**
Jesus predicts his own, Mark 8:31 – p. **874**; 9:31 – p. **874**; 10:33–34 – p. **874**
of the dead, 1 Corinthians 15 – p. **1003**; "*The Worst Danger of All*" – p. **1004**; 1 Thessalonians 4:13–18 – p. **1039**
of the body, "*The Body as a Tent*" – p. **1010**
as proof of God's power, "*Proven Power*" – p. **1024**; Ephesians 1:15–23 – p. **1023**
spiritual in Christ, Romans 6:1–14 – p. **981**; Colossians 2:9–15 – p. **1035**; 3:1–17 – p. **1035**

REVENGE (*see also* CITIES OF REFUGE)
Joseph not taking, "*Weeping and Terror*" – p. **44**
of David, "*Paying Back Joab*" – p. **297**
belongs to God, "*God's Vengeance*" – p. **179**
on enemies, "*Jehu's Slaughters*" – p. **332** do not take, Matthew 5:38–47 – p. **836**; Romans 12:17–21 – p. **988**

REVERENCE (*see also* FEAR)
for God, "*Living With Fire*" – p. **87**; "*Touch and Die*" – p. **119**; "*Is God Frightening?*" – p. **484**

REVELATION – God's disclosure of himself and his truth
in nature, Psalm 19:1–6 – p. **476**; Acts 14:14–17 – p. **960**; Romans 1:18–23 – p. **977**
in Jesus Christ, John 1:1–18 – p. **918**; Hebrews 1 – p. **1059**
in the Bible, 2 Timothy 3:14–17 – p. **1052**; 2 Peter 1:19–21 – p. **1084**

REWARD
everyone according to deeds, Leviticus 26 – p. **111**; Psalm 62:11–12 – p. **497**; Jeremiah 17:10 – p. **660**; 2 Corinthians 5:1–10 – p. **1010**
for evil, "*Short-Run Rewards*" – p. **503**
for serving God, "*Why Serve God?*" – p. **823**
in heaven, Matthew 5:3–12 – p. **835**; Mark 10:29–31 – p. **876**; 1 Corinthians 3:10–15 – p. **995**

RICHES – *see* MONEY, POOR, WEALTH

RIGHTEOUSNESS – the state of being perfect, without sin
attribute of God, Psalm 7 – p. **470**; Jeremiah 23:1–6 – p. **664**
rewarded by God, "*Never Abandoned*" – p. **486**
from God, "*Luther's Gateway*" – p. **977**
by faith, "*What God Looks For*" – p. **15**; "*The Benefits of Faith*" – p. **482**; "*Righteous by Faith*" – p. **803**; Romans 4:6–8 – p. **979**; Galatians 2:15–21 – p. **1018**; Philippians 3:7–11 – p. **1031**
goal of Christian life, Matthew 6:25–34 – p. **838**; 1 Timothy 6:11–16 – p. **1048**; 1 Peter 2:24–25 – p. **1079**

ROCK
God as, Deuteronomy 32:1–4 – p. **177**; Psalm 18 – p. **475**; Isaiah 26 – p. **605**
Peter as, Matthew 16:16–20 – p. **848**; John 1:35–42 – p. **919**
Christ as, 1 Corinthians 10:1–4 – p. **999**; 1 Peter 2:1–10 – p. **1079**

ROME – capital of the Roman empire; ruled Palestine during the time of Christ; a church was started here
Paul travels to, "*Rome at Last*" – p. **975**; Acts 27:1 – 28:31 – p. **973**
letter (Romans) to church in, "*A Most Demanding Audience*" – p. **976**
treatment of Christians in, "*Christians and the Empire*" – p. **988**

RUTH – Moabite woman who married Boaz and became an ancestor of Jesus
ethnic background, "*The Worst of Times*" – p. **228**
friendship with her mother-in-law, "*A Rare Bond of Love*" – p. **227**
in Jesus' genealogy, Matthew 1:5 – p. **833**

 # S

SABBATH – a day of worship and rest; traditionally Saturday for Jews
to be kept holy, Exodus 20:8–11 – p. **67**; Ezekiel 20:1–29 – p. **717**
laws concerning, Exodus 31:14–15 – p. **78**; Leviticus 23:1–3 – p. **108**
made for people, Mark 2:23 – 3:6 – p. **866**
symbol of eternal rest, Hebrews 4:1–11 – p. **1062**

SACRIFICE – offering of something valuable to God
Cain's and Abel's, Genesis 4:1–5 – p. **7**
Noah's, Genesis 8:20–22 – p. **10**
Abraham's, Genesis 12:1–11 – p. **13**; 22:1–19 – p. **13**
prescribed, Leviticus 1 – 7 – p. **87**
offered as representative, "*The One for the Many*" – p. **89**
types of, "*The Reason for Sacrifice*" – p. **91**
choice of, "*The Very Best for God*" – p. **107**
Christ as, Isaiah 53 – p. **629**; Hebrews 10 – p. **1066**
our lives as, Romans 12:1–2 – p. **987**; "*A Better Sacrifice*" – p. **487**
of praise, "*Sacrifice of Praise*" – p. **1070**

SADDUCEES – a small but powerful Jewish sect in Christ's time; denied life after death
Jesus warns against, Matthew 16:1–12 – p. **848**
Jesus confronts, Mark 12:18–23 – p. **878**
opposed early church, Acts 4:1–22 – p. **947**; Acts 5:17–42 – p. **949**
opposed Paul, Acts 23:1–11 – p. **970**

SALVATION – deliverance from danger or evil; especially deliverance from all that separates people from God (*see also* CONVERSION, JUSTIFICATION, REPENTANCE)

SICKNESS – *see* DISEASE, HEALING, PRAYER

SIN (*see also* CONFESSION, EVIL, FORGIVENESS, GUILT)
Adam's and Eve's, Genesis 3 – **p. 7**
unintentional, *"Ignorance Isn't Bliss"* – **p. 90**
against another person, *"Double Jeopardy"* – **p. 92**
far-reaching results, *"Sin As a Cancer"* – **p. 286**
present in everyone, *"Who Seeks God?"* – **p. 473**
confession of, Psalm 32 – **p. 482**; Psalm 51 – **p. 492**
symbolised, *"Return to the Void"* – **p. 648**
sexual, *"Two Instances of Evil"* – **p. 767**
God's anger with, Romans 1:18–32 – **p. 977**; *"More Sin, More Forgiveness?"* – **p. 982**
dead to, Romans 5:12–6:23 – **p. 981**
conflict with, Romans 7 – **p. 982**; *"Inner Struggles"* – **p. 983**; *"Hidden Dangers"* – **p. 982**
forgiveness of, 1 John 1:5–2:14 – **p. 1088**

SINAI – name of the mountain where God talked with Moses; also called Mount Horeb
God appeared to Moses at, Exodus 3 – **p. 53**
law given at, Exodus 19 – **p. 66**
worshipping golden calf at, Exodus 32 – **p. 78**
Elijah at, 1 Kings 19:8–18 – **p. 316**

SINGING (*see also* MUSIC, SONGS)
to the Lord, Ephesians 5:19–21 – **p. 1026**; Colossians 3:16 – **p. 1037**

SLAVERY
in Egypt, *"Oppressed by Egypt"* – **p. 55**
Israel's laws on, *"Slave Rights"* – **p. 70**
freedom from, Leviticus 25:35–55 – **p. 111**; Jeremiah 34:8–22 – **p. 676**
to sin, Romans 6:15–23 – **p. 982**; Galatians 4 – **p. 1019**
Paul's advice to slaves, Ephesians 6:5–8 – **p. 1028**; Colossians 3:22–25 – **p. 1037**; 1 Timothy 6:1–2 – **p. 1048**
Paul's advice to slave owner, Ephesians 6:19 – **p. 1028**; Colossians 4:1 – **p. 1037**; *"Letter to a Slave Owner"* – **p. 1057**
Peter's advice on, 1 Peter 2:18–25 – **p. 1079**

SLEEP
peaceful, Psalm 3:5 – **p. 469**
unable to, *"Sleepless Nights"* – **p. 504**; *"Lying in Bed"* – **p. 527**

SODOM AND GOMORRAH – cities that God destroyed because of wickedness
Lot saved in, Genesis 18:16–19:29 – **p. 17**; *"A Catastrophe Sent from God"* – **p. 18**
sin of, Ezekiel 16:44–52 – **p. 714**

SOLOMON – third and last king of united Israel; son of David and Bathsheba
becomes king, 1 Kings 1:1–4:34 – **p. 296**; *"A Second Coronation"* – **p. 374**
builds temple, 1 Kings 5:1–9:9 – **p. 300**
wisdom of, 1 Kings 3:1–28 – **p. 298**; 4:29–34 – **p. 298**
his wealth, *"The Man Who Had Everything"* – **p. 294**; *"Prosperity under Solomon"* – **p. 301**
his personality, *"Wise Yet Ruthless"* – **p. 298**
God's anger with, 1 Kings 11:1–43 – **p. 306**
and his wives, *"So Many Women"* – **p. 307**
his failures, *"Solomon's Peak"* – **p. 379**
and the Queen of Sheba, *"An Unfounded Rumour"* – **p. 382**

SON OF GOD
prophesied, *"The Son of God"* – **p. 523**
Christ as, Matthew 14:22–36 – **p. 846**
Peter's confession, Matthew 16:13–20 – **p. 848**

SON OF MAN
in Daniel's vision, *"A Son of Man"* – **p. 755**
Jesus as, *"Familiar Title"* – **p. 1099**

SONGS
of Moses, Exodus 15:1–18 – **p. 63**; *"A Story for All Time"* – **p. 63**
given to Moses, Deuteronomy 31:19–32:43 – **p. 177**; *"Mixed Emotions"* – **p. 178**
of David, *"David's Psalms"* – **p. 290**
addressed to God, *"Cries from the Heart"* – **p. 467**
at the Passover, *"Psalms of the Last Supper"* – **p. 524**
in the New Testament church, Ephesians 5:18–20 – **p. 1026**; Colossians 3:15–17 – **p. 1037**

SONS OF GOD
in heaven, Revelation 5–6 – **p. 1101**

SONS OF GOD
in the Old Testament, *"The Sons of God"* – **p. 9**; Psalm 82:6 – **p. 509**; *"Among the Gods"* – **p. 508**

SORROW (*see also* COMFORT, DISCOURAGEMENT, GRIEF)
God responds to, Exodus 3:1–9 – **p. 53**
symbol of, *"Torn Hearts"* – **p. 773**
Jesus experiences, Matthew 26:36–46 – **p. 859**

SOUL – the non-physical element in humans (sometimes called "spirit")
in context of death, Ecclesiastes 12:7 – **p. 579**; Revelation 6:9–10 – **p. 1103**
distinguished from spirit, 1 Thessalonians 5:23 – **p. 1041**; Hebrews 4:12 – **p. 1063**
activities of, Deuteronomy 6:1–5 – **p. 156**; Psalm 42 – **p. 488**; 103 – **p. 488**; 130 – **p. 488**

SPEECH
power of, *"Who Owns Your Lips?"* – **p. 472**; *"Verbal Dynamite"* – **p. 556**
control of, James 3:1–12 – **p. 1074**

SPIRIT – *see* DEMONS, FRUIT OF THE SPIRIT, HOLY SPIRIT

STARVATION
in Jerusalem, *"Starving to Death"* – **p. 701**

STEALING
command against, Exodus 20:15 – **p. 67**; Ephesians 4:28 – **p. 1025**
laws about, Exodus 22:1–15 – **p. 70**; Leviticus 19:11–13 – **p. 104**
robbing God, Malachi 3:8–10 – **p. 824**

STEPHEN – the first Christian martyr
chosen as deacon, Acts 6:1–7 – **p. 949**
tried and executed, Acts 6:8–8:3 – **p. 950**

STEWARDSHIP – management and accountability for something that belongs to someone else; especially human stewardship of God's gifts
parable concerning, Matthew 25:14–30 – **p. 857**
faithful, Luke 12:35–48 – **p. 902**; 16:10–12 – **p. 902**
of time, Ephesians 5:15–16 – **p. 1026**

SUBMISSION
because of love for Christ, *"The Key to Submission"* – **p. 1026**
of Christians to each other, Ephesians 5:21 – **p. 1026**
to government, Romans 13:1–7 – **p. 988**; 1 Peter 2:13–17 – **p. 1079**

SUCCESS

Lot's in Sodom, *"A Man of Substance"* – **p. 18**
basis for real, *"Secret of Success"* – **p. 183**
from God, Proverbs 3 – **p. 544**
true, Matthew 5:1–12 – **p. 835**; *"God and How-to-Succeed"* – **p. 549**
parable concerning, Luke 12:13–21 – **p. 902**
without love, 1 Corinthians 13 – **p. 1002**
from God's perspective, *"Not Ashamed"* – **p. 1069**

SUFFERING – to endure physical or emotional loss and pain (*see also* COMFORT, DISCOURAGEMENT, PAIN)
the problem of, Job 1–42 – **p. 437**; *"When Bad Things Happened to a Good Person"* – **p. 437**; *"What Not to Say to a Hurting Person"* – **p. 442**; *"When God Seems Angry"* – **p. 448**; *"What Job Teaches about Suffering"* – **p. 460**; *"A Silent Friend Decides to Speak Up"* – **p. 457**; *"Suffering and Sin"* – **p. 928**
God knows our, Psalm 69 – **p. 500**
God's presence in, Psalm 73 – **p. 502**; *"Pain in Redemption"* – **p. 673**; *"Only Good Things?"* – **p. 984**
without God, *"Total Devastation"* – **p. 773**
with Christ, Romans 8:12–17 – **p. 984**; 2 Corinthians 1:5 – **p. 1007**; 1 Peter 4:12–19 – **p. 1081**
compared to eternal glory, *"Worth the Struggle"* – **p. 984**; 2 Corinthians 4:16–18 – **p. 1009**
for Christ, Colossians 1:24 – **p. 1035**; Hebrews 10:32–39 – **p. 1067**; Revelation 1 – **p. 1098**

benefits of, *"Waiting It Out"* – p. 1076; *"A Word to the Suffering"* – p. 1077; **"Radical Shift"** – p. 1081
Christ's, 1 Peter 2:13–25 – p. 1079; *"The Spirits in Prison"* – p. 1081
for doing right, 1 Peter 3:8–22 – p. 1080; 4:12–19 – p. 1080

SUICIDE (*see also* JUDAS ISCARIOT, SAUL)
jailer saved from, Acts 16:22–36 – p. 962

SWEARING – taking an oath, making a solemn promise (*see also* PROFANITY)
Jesus' teaching on, Matthew 5:33–37 – p. 836
of God by himself, Hebrews 6:13–15 – p. 1063
James's teaching on, James 5:12 – p. 1077

SYMBOL
of peace, *"Peace Symbol"* – p. 10
of Christ, *"Bronze Snake"* – p. 135; *"Last-place Winner"* – p. 526; *"Jesus as the Vine"* – p. 935; *"Water, Blood, and Spirit"* – p. 1091
of victory, *"Scalps"* – p. 248
of humiliation, *"Act of Humiliation"* – p. 190; *"Thumbs and Big Toes"* – p. 206; *"David's Bad Conscience"* – p. 253
of importance, *"The Apple of Your Eye"* – p. 547
of evil, *"Gog and Magog"* – p. 737
of ineffectiveness, *"Kicking the Ox-goads"* – p. 972
vine and kingdom of God, Psalm 80:8–18 – p. 508; Isaiah 5:1–7 – p. 589; John 15:1–17 – p. 935
of believers, *"A Play on Words"* – p. 1079
in Revelation, *"Strange Creatures"* – p. 1101; *"Revelation's Use of Symbols"* – p. 1105

 T

TABERNACLE – place of worship for Israelites from the time of the desert experience to the completion of the temple when Solomon was king
building instructions, Exodus 25–26 – p. 72; *"Following Orders"* – p. 85;
where God dwells, *"A Portable Cathedral"* – p. 82
furnishings of, *"Sacred Furniture"* – p. 83
during David's reign, *"Two Tabernacles"* – p. 364
spiritual, Hebrews 9 – p. 1066

TALENTS – *see* GIFTS, STEWARDSHIP

TAXES
Jesus' response to, Matthew 22:15–22 – p. 854
Paul's words on, Romans 13:1–7 – p. 988

TEMPLE – the Israelite place of worship; the first and most magnificent was built by Solomon
curtain in, *"A Torn Curtain"* – p. 74; *"A Temporary Separation"* – p. 378; *"A Curtain is Torn"* – p. 861
through many years, *"History of the Temple"* – p. 301; *"Between the Temples"* – p. 403
limited access, *"Off-limits for People"* – p. 303; *"The Temple Destroyed"* – p. 698
Solomon's, 1 Kings 5–8 – p. 300; *"A Man of Blood"* – p. 368
God's home, *"Home-coming"* – p. 509
opposition to rebuilding, *"Ironic Outcome"* – p. 409
rebuilt, Ezra 1–6 – p. 404; *"The Prophet Who Got Results"* – p. 809; *"Starting Again"* – p. 812; *"Change of Tone"* – p. 810
abuse of, *"A Den of Robbers"* – p. 651; *"Detestable Things"* – p. 708; *"Drastic Action"* – p. 852; *"Big Business"* – p. 877; John 2:12–25 – p. 919
abandoned by God, *"Good-bye, God"* – p. 710
Ezekiel's vision of, Ezekiel 40–43 – p. 737; *"The Turning Point"* – p. 731; *"Seeing the New Temple"* – p. 739; *"The Glory Returns"* – p. 740; *"Taking Measurements"* – p. 737
Jesus' body as, John 2:12–22 – p. 919
church as, 1 Corinthians 3:16–17 – p. 995; 2 Corinthians 6:16 – p. 1010; Ephesians 2:18–22 – p. 1024
heavenly, Hebrews 8:1–12 – p. 1065; Revelation 21:22 – p. 1114

TEMPTATION – something that tests a person's righteousness and strength of character
of Adam and Eve, Genesis 3 – p. 7
prayer about, Matthew 6:13 – p. 837
of Jesus, Luke 4:1–13 – p. 890; *"Words for the Devil"* – p. 157
a way out, 1 Corinthians 10:12–13 – p. 999; Hebrews 2:17–18 – p. 1061; 4:15–16 – p. 1061
resist, Ephesians 6:10–20 – p. 1028; *"Bad Models"* – p. 1096
origin of, James 1:13–18 – p. 1073

TEN COMMANDMENTS – the moral laws given to Moses by God
Moses receives, Exodus 19–20 – p. 66
Moses repeats, Deuteronomy 5 – p. 155
Jesus enlarges, Matthew 5–7 – p. 835
summary of, Matthew 22:37–40 – p. 854; Romans 13:8–10 – p. 989

THANKFULNESS
for God's care, Psalm 30 – p. 481; 136 – p. 481
Paul's, Ephesians 1:15–23 – p. 1023; Philippians 1:3–8 – p. 1029; 4:10–20 – p. 1029; Colossians 1:3–7 – p. 1034
express, Psalm 100 – p. 515; Colossians 3:15–17 – p. 1037; 1 Thessalonians 5:18 – p. 1041

THESSALONICA
Paul's ministry to, *"What Made Paul Successful?"* – p. 1037; *"A Patient Who Didn't Follow Orders"* – p. 1041

THOMAS – one of the 12 disciples, often called "Doubting Thomas"
courage of, John 11:1–16 – p. 929
doubt of, John 20:19–31 – p. 940

TIME
God's use of, *"God Takes Time"* – p. 5
our use of, Ephesians 5:15 – p. 1026; Colossians 4:5 – p. 1037
for everything, Ecclesiastes 3:1–8 – p. 572

TIMOTHY – Paul's helper on missionary journeys; while still a young man he took on the responsibilities of guiding the church in Ephesus
with Paul, Acts 16:1–5 – p. 961; 20:1–4 – p. 961; Philippians 2:19–24 – p. 1031; *"The Hardest Job"* – p. 1044
sent to Corinth, 1 Corinthians 4:14–17 – p. 996
letters to, 1 and 2 Timothy – p. 1044
his calling, *"Timothy's Calling"* – p. 1045
successor to Paul, *"Passing the Torch"* – p. 1050

TITHE – a tenth of one's income that is given to God
Abraham's, Genesis 14:20 – p. 15; Hebrews 7:1–10 – p. 1064
Old Testament command, Leviticus 27:30–33 – p. 114; Deuteronomy 12:6–7 – p. 161
refusing to give, Nehemiah 13:10–12 – p. 427; Malachi 3:8–10 – p. 824
blessed by God, *"Testing the Tithe"* – p. 824
not enough, Luke 11:42 – p. 901; 18:9–14 – p. 901

TITUS
sent to Corinth, 2 Corinthians 7 – p. 1011; 2 Corinthians 8:16–24 – p. 1011
and Paul, *"Diverse People, Diverse Problems"* – p. 1054
not circumcised, Galatians 1:1–10 – p. 1017
letter to, Titus 1–3 – p. 1054

TONGUE – *see* SPEECH

TONGUES – God-given gift of praise in other languages
in early church, Acts 2:1–13 – p. 945; Acts 10:44–48 – p. 957; Acts 19:1–7 – p. 965
orderly use of, 1 Corinthians 12–14 – p. 1000

TRADITION – teachings and religious observances passed down from generation to generation
by parents to children, Deuteronomy 6:6–9 – p. 156; Psalm 78 – p. 505
dangers of, Mark 7 – p. 871; Philippians 3:2–11 – p. 1031
by apostles to believers, 1 Corinthians 15:1–11 – p. 1003; 2 Thessalonians 2:15 – p. 1044

TRANSFIGURATION
observed by disciples, *"Unforgettable Moment"* – p. 848
predicted, *"Seeing the Kingdom"* – p. 897

TRIALS – tests or ordeals that people go through
  to teach obedience, Deuteronomy 8:1–5 – **p. 157**
  for adultery, *"Test for Adultery"* – **p. 120**
  perseverance through, James 1:2–18 – **p. 1073**; Revelation
    3:7–13 – **p. 1100**
  refine faith, James 1:1–7 – **p. 1073**; 1 Peter 1:3–9 – **p. 1078**

TRIBULATION – trouble in one's life; often associated with the
  Great Tribulation, a period of suffering sent by God in the end
  times
  prophesied, Daniel 12:1–4 – **p. 759**
  Jesus' teaching on, Matthew 24 – **p. 856**
  survivors of, Revelation 7:9–17 – **p. 1103**
  views of, *"Forty-two Months of Trials"* – **p. 1108**

TRINITY – the Christian doctrine of God as Father, Son, and Holy
  Spirit, three-in-one
  in name of, Matthew 28:16–20 – **p. 863**
  blessing of, 2 Corinthians 13:14 – **p. 1016**
  in salvation, Titus 3:3–8 – **p. 1057**; Jude 20–21 – **p. 1098**

TRUST – *see* FAITH

TRUTH
  worship in, John 4:19–26 – **p. 922**
  God's Word as, John 7:13–19 – **p. 925**
  sets us free, John 8:31–38 – **p. 927**
  Jesus is, John 14:5–14 – **p. 933**; *"No Lies"* – **p. 1055**
  knowing and walking in, 2 Timothy 2:8–26 – **p. 1051**;
    2 John – **p. 1092**; 3 John – **p. 1094**

 U

UNBELIEF (*see also* FAITH)
  Abraham's, *"Laughing at God"* – **p. 16**
  Israelites', *"Forty Years of Misery"* – **p. 114**

UNCLEANNESS
  reason for rules of, *"Of Ravens and Rabbits"* – **p. 96**
  law concerning, *"An Invisible Danger"* – **p. 98**; *"Types of
    Uncleanness"* – **p. 121**

UNITY

  Israel's need for, *"Hanging by a Thread"* – **p. 222**; *"The First
    King"* – **p. 241**; *"Accent on Unity"* – **p. 360**
  goodness of, Psalm 133 – **p. 533**
  Jesus' prayer for, John 17 – **p. 936**
  of early church, Acts 2:42–47 – **p. 946**; *"Paul the Fund-
    raiser"* – **p. 990**; *"Personality Cults"* – **p. 994**; *"Lessons from
    the Human Body"* – **p. 1001**; *"No Second-Class
    Christians"* – **p. 1016**
  absent in Corinth, 1 Corinthians 1–4 – **p. 992**
  symbolised in Lord's Supper, 1 Corinthians 10:16–17 – **p. 999**;
    11:17–34 – **p. 999**
  in Christ, Galatians 3:26–28 – **p. 1019**; Ephesians
    4:1–16 – **p. 1025**

URIM AND THUMMIM
  God's instruction concerning, Exodus 28:30 – **p. 75**
  given to Aaron and descendants, Leviticus 8:8 – **p. 93**;
    Deuteronomy 33:8–11 – **p. 179**
  after the exile, *"The Need for Guidance"* – **p. 407**

 V

VIRGIN BIRTH – the birth of Jesus Christ while his mother Mary
  was a virgin
  predicted, Isaiah 7:1–14 – **p. 591**
  described, Matthew 1:18–25 – **p. 833**; Luke 1:26–38 – **p. 887**

VISIONS – revelations; things seen through something other than
  ordinary sight
  as guidance, *"Appealing to a Vision"* – **p. 440**

Isaiah's, Isaiah 6 – **p. 590**
Ezekiel's, Ezekiel 1–3 – **p. 704**; 37:1–14 – **p. 704**; *"Dry
  Bones"* – **p. 735**
Daniel's, *"Kidnapped"* – **p. 746**; *"Symbols of Power"* – **p. 754**
in last days, Joel 2:28–32 – **p. 774**
Peter's, Acts 10:1–11:18 – **p. 956**
Paul's, Acts 18:9–10 – **p. 964**; 2 Corinthians 12:1–10 – **p. 1014**
John's, Revelation 1–22 – **p. 1098**

 W

WAR (*see also* PEACE)
  reasons for, *"Acts of War"* – **p. 144**; *"Reasons for
    Warfare"* – **p. 158**; *"Is a War Ever Holy?"* – **p. 192**; *"Old
    Enemies"* – **p. 244**; **"Comedy of Errors** *"* – **p. 366**
  strategy in, *"War Strategy"* – **p. 189**; *"Battle Strategy"* – **p. 257**
  methods of, *"Camel Power"* – **p. 211**; *"Military
    Setbacks"* – **p. 207**; *"Everyone Watched Goliath"* – **p. 246**;
    "Not Ready for Chariots" – **p. 276**
  weapons of, *"Advanced Weaponry"* – **p. 191**; *"Deadly
    Rocks"* – **p. 247**
  preparing for, *"A Military Hero"* – **p. 278**
  hired soldiers in, *"Mercenaries"* – **p. 282**
  necessary limits of, *"Limits of a Just War"* – **p. 395**
  God's hand in, Psalm 79 – **p. 507**; *"World at War"* – **p. 685**
  will end, Isaiah 2:1–5 – **p. 587**
  images from, *"Victory Party"* – **p. 427**
  spiritual, Ephesians 6:10–20 – **p. 1028**; Revelation 12 – **p. 1107**

WARNINGS
  to Judah, *"Prophet, Poet, and Politician"* – **p. 585**; *"Isaiah in His
    Prime"* – **p. 608**
  to Christians, *"Like an Angry Letter from Home"* – **p. 995**; *"Watch
    Out"* – **p. 730**

WATER
  as symbol, *"An Astounding Trade"* – **p. 644**; *"River from the
    Temple"* – **p. 743**; John 4:10–14 – **p. 922**; John
    7:37–38 – **p. 926**; Revelation 22:1–2 – **p. 1114**
  importance of, *"Waters of Babylon"* – **p. 692**

WEALTH (*see also* MONEY, POOR)
  distribution of, *"Property Rights"* – **p. 111**
  God's hand in, 1 Samuel 2:1–10 – **p. 233**
  Solomon's, *"The Man Who Had Everything"* – **p. 294**
  of the wicked, *"Wicked People Prosper"* – **p. 451**; *"Money Can't
    Buy Life"* – **p. 492**
  arrogance in, Amos 6:1–7 – **p. 781**; 1 Timothy 6:3–19 – **p. 1048**
  Jesus' teaching on, Matthew 19:16–30 – **p. 850**; *"The Wealth
    Barrier"* – **p. 876**
  no favoritism toward those with, James 2:1–13 – **p. 1074**
  because of obedience, *"Healthier, Wealthier, and Wiser"* – **p. 158**
  reasons for, *"What Makes People Poor?"* – **p. 550**
  doesn't bring happiness, *"When Life Seems Senseless"* – **p. 570**

WEAPONS – *see* WAR

WEEPING
  of Joseph, *"Joseph in Tears"* – **p. 42**
  of David, 2 Samuel 1 – **p. 269**; 18:19–19:8 – **p. 269**
  doesn't last, *"One-night Guest"* – **p. 481**
  of a woman with Jesus, Luke 7:36–50 – **p. 895**
  of Jesus, Luke 19:41–44 – **p. 910**; John 11:1–43 – **p. 929**

WELFARE (*see also* POOR)
  God's programmes of, *"A Form of Welfare"* – **p. 104**; *"Tithe to
    the Poor"* – **p. 164**; *"Don't Forget the Poor"* – **p. 170**; *"Caring
    for the Poor"* – **p. 229**
  in the early church, *"Welfare Mentality"* – **p. 1048**

WIDOW – a woman whose husband is dead; in ancient Israel a
  husband's death usually brought poverty and powerlessness
  special to God, Exodus 22:22–24 – **p. 71**; Deuteronomy
    24:17–22 – **p. 170**; *"Poor and Helpless"* – **p. 555**
  praised by Jesus, *"Exploiting Widows"* – **p. 879**
  in the church, 1 Corinthians 7:8–9 – **p. 997**; 1 Timothy
    5:3–16 – **p. 1047**

WIFE (*see also* HUSBAND, MARRIAGE)
  virtuous, Proverbs 31:10–31–**p. 569**
  relationship to husband, Ephesians 5:21–33–**p. 1026**;
    Colossians 3:18–19–**p. 1037**; 1 Peter 3:1–7–**p. 1080**
WILDERNESS – *see* DESERT

WILL OF GOD

  in suffering, "*What Job Teaches about Suffering*"–**p. 460**;
    1 Peter 4:12–19–**p. 1081**
  submission to, "*The Potter and the Clay*"–**p. 660**; "*Counselling
    Surrender*"–**p. 669**; Matthew 26:36–46–**p. 859**; James
    4:13–15–**p. 1077**
  Jesus came to do, John 4:34–**p. 922**; 6:38–**p. 922**; Philippians
    2:5–11–**p. 1030**
  discovering, Romans 12:1–8–**p. 987**; 1 Thessalonians
    4:1–8–**p. 1039**
  everything done in accordance with, Ephesians 1:3–14–**p. 1023**

WINE (*see also* DRINKING ALCOHOL)
  used in Persia, "*The Influence of Wine*"–**p. 430**
  drunkenness from, Proverbs 23:29–35–**p. 562**
  in the Lord's Supper, Matthew 26:17–30–**p. 858**
  water into, John 2:1–11–**p. 919**
  for health, 1 Timothy 5:23–**p. 1048**
WISDOM – practical insight; the skill of living successfully
  Solomon's, "*Solomon's Wish*"–**p. 299**
  comes from God, "*A Poem on Wisdom*"–**p. 454**
  begins with fear of the Lord, Psalm 111–**p. 523**; Proverbs
    1:1–7–**p. 543**
  in understanding life, "*Uncommon Sense*"–**p. 542**
  praise of, Proverbs 1:20–4:27–**p. 544**; 8:1–9:18–**p. 544**
  love of, "*A Lifelong Quest*"–**p. 545**
  in making choices, "*Be Careful*"–**p. 553**
  through listening, "*The Supreme Gift of Wisdom*"–**p. 553**
  spiritual, 1 Corinthians 2:6–16–**p. 994**; James 1:5–8–**p. 1073**
WITCHCRAFT
  displeases God, Leviticus 20:6–7–**p. 105**; Deuteronomy
    18:10–12–**p. 166**; Isaiah 47:10–14–**p. 625**; Galatians
    5:19–21–**p. 1022**
  Saul's consulting of, 1 Samuel 28–**p. 256**
  inadequacy of, Isaiah 8:19–22–**p. 592**
  rejected by early church, Acts 8:9–24–**p. 952**;
    13:6–12–**p. 952**; 19:13–19–**p. 952**
WITNESSING (*see also* EYE-WITNESSES)
  to God's faithfulness, "*Courtroom Drama*"–**p. 621**
  persistent, "*Group Faith*"–**p. 891**
  entrusted by God to believers, "*A Picture of
    Weakness*"–**p. 1009**; Acts 1:1–11–**p. 944**;
    10:34–43–**p. 944**
WOMEN
  creation of, Genesis 1:26–31–**p. 5**; 2:18–24–**p. 5**
  with the patriarchs, "*The Women of Genesis*"–**p. 29**
  offerings by, "*For Poor People*"–**p. 96**
  rights of, "*Daughters' Rights*"–**p. 197**
  as a judge, "*Honour to a Woman*"–**p. 209**
  power of, "*Sexist Attitudes*"–**p. 216**
  as political symbols, "*Women in Politics*"–**p. 272**; "*No Way
    Back*"–**p. 283**; "*After More Than a Wife?*"–**p. 297**
  as prophets, 2 Kings 22:14–20–**p. 344**; Acts 21:8–9–**p. 968**;
    1 Corinthians 11:2–16–**p. 1000**
  value of, "*Whom Should You Marry?*"–**p. 560**
  helping Jesus, "*Jesus' Support*"–**p. 895**
  involved in church work, Romans 16:1–2–**p. 990**; Philippians
    4:2–3–**p. 1031**
  customs concerning, "*Women in Corinth*"–**p. 1000**
  in Christ no male or female, Galatians 3:16–29–**p. 1018**
WORD OF GOD (*see also* BIBLE)
  as power of creation, Genesis 1–**p. 4**; Psalm 33:6–9–**p. 482**;
    Hebrews 11:1–3–**p. 1068**
  not given for 400 years, "*Worst of All Famines*"–**p. 782**
  our tool against Satan, Matthew 4:1–11–**p. 834**; Ephesians
    6:10–17–**p. 1028**

Jesus as, John 1:1–18–**p. 918**; "*Jesus the Word*"–**p. 918**;
  Revelation 19:13–16–**p. 1112**
sharper than a sword, Hebrews 4:12–13–**p. 1063**
as power to regenerate, James 1:18–**p. 1073**; 1 Peter
  1:22–25–**p. 1079**

WORK (*see also* REST, SABBATH)

  God's, Genesis 1:1–2:1–**p. 5**; "*God at Work*"–**p. 3**; Psalm
    46–**p. 490**; 104:24–32–**p. 490**; John 5:16–30–**p. 923**
  Adam's, Genesis 2:15–20–**p. 6**; Genesis 3:17–19–**p. 7**
  value of menial, "*Little People*"–**p. 369**
  satisfaction in, Ecclesiastes 2:17–26–**p. 572**; Isaiah
    28:23–29–**p. 607**
  importance of, 2 Thessalonians 3:6–15–**p. 1044**

WORKS – *see* DEEDS
WORLD – values, ideas, practices, and relationships of the
  culture-at-large, especially those that are not God-directed
  proclaiming gospel to, Matthew 28:16–20–**p. 863**
  Jesus came to save, John 3:1–21–**p. 920**; 2 Corinthians
    5:16–21–**p. 1010**
  conforming to, Romans 12:1–8–**p. 987**; 1 John
    2:15–17–**p. 1089**
  friendship with, James 4:1–12–**p. 1075**
  overcoming, 1 John 5:1–5–**p. 1092**
WORRY – *see* ANXIETY
WORSHIP – giving reverence and honour to God (*see also*
  PRAISE, PRAYER)
  only God, Exodus 20:4–5–**p. 67**; Matthew 4:10–**p. 835**
  and the tabernacle, "*Tabernacle Layout*"–**p. 84**
  joyful, "*Seven Days of Rejoicing*"–**p. 109**; Psalm 100–**p. 515**
  commanded, Deuteronomy 6:13–17–**p. 156**; Matthew
    4:10–**p. 835**
  costly, "*The Cost of True Worship*"–**p. 293**
  dishes used in Israel's, "*Gold and Silver Dishes*"–**p. 123**
  foundations of Israel's, "*Hope in a Time of Sorrow*"–**p. 365**;
    "*The Way They Worshipped*"–**p. 500**
  David's preparation for, "*Major Enterprise*"–**p. 371**
  through songs, "*Cries from the Heart*"–**p. 467**; "*Lyrics for the
    Living God*"–**p. 483**
  true, Amos 5:18–27–**p. 780**
  apathetic, "*When Faith Grows Weary*"–**p. 821**
  in spirit and truth, John 4:20–24–**p. 922**
  instructions concerning, 1 Corinthians 11–14–**p. 1000**
  in heaven, Revelation 5–**p. 1101**; 7–**p. 1101**

 X

XERXES – king of Persian empire and husband of Esther
  character of, "*Xerxes: A Wild Man*"–**p. 433**

 Y

YOUTH (*see also* CHILDREN)
  remember God in, Ecclesiastes 11:7–12:7–**p. 579**
  will see visions, Joel 2:28–32–**p. 774**; Acts 2:13–36–**p. 945**
  not unqualified for leadership, "*Too Young for the
    Job?*"–**p. 1046**
  set an example in, 1 Timothy 4:11–16–**p. 1046**

 Z

ZACCHAEUS – a tax collector from Jericho
  meets Jesus, Luke 19:1–10–**p. 908**

ZERUBBABEL – leader of first group of exiles to return to
Jerusalem
led Jews back, Ezra 2 – **p. 406**
reinstituted worship of God, Ezra 3 – **p. 407**
helped rebuild the temple, Ezra 4:1–5 – **p. 407**; 5 – **p. 407**;
    Haggai 1:1–12 – **p. 810**; Zechariah 4:1–9 – **p. 814**

ZION – one of the hills on which Jerusalem stood; also used to
refer to all Jerusalem, to the Jewish people, or to heaven (see
also HEAVEN, JERUSALEM)
David captures, 2 Samuel 5:6–16 – **p. 274**
as heaven, Psalm 9 – **p. 471**; Hebrews 12:22–29 – **p. 1070**
the whole city of Jerusalem, Psalm 48 – **p. 491**

■ WHERE TO FIND IT

■ WELL-KNOWN EVENTS
(in approximate order of occurrence)

Creation, Genesis 1–2
The first sin, or fall, Genesis 3
Cain kills Abel, Genesis 4
Noah and the ark, Genesis 6–9
Sodom and Gomorrah, Genesis 18–19
Abraham sacrifices Isaac, Genesis 22
Jacob's ladder, Genesis 28:10–22
Joseph and the coat, Genesis 37
Moses' birth, Exodus 2
Moses and the burning bush, Exodus 3
Plagues on Egypt, Exodus 7–11
The exodus, Exodus 12–13
The Ten Commandments, Exodus 20
The battle of Jericho, Joshua 6
Gideon and the fleece, Judges 6–7
Samson and Delilah, Judges 13–16
God calls the boy Samuel, 1 Samuel 1–3
David and Goliath, 1 Samuel 17
David and Bathsheba, 2 Samuel 11
Elijah versus the priests of Baal, 1 Kings 18
The miracles of Elisha, 2 Kings 4–5
Ezekiel and the dry bones, Ezekiel 37
Daniel in the lions' den, Daniel 6

Jonah and the fish, Jonah 1
Hosea and his adulterous wife, Hosea 1–3
Birth of Jesus, Luke 1–2
Baptism of Jesus, Mark 1:9–11
Temptation of Jesus, Luke 4:1–13
Jesus clears the temple, John 2:12–25
The transfiguration of Jesus, Matthew 17:1–13
Jesus raises Lazarus from the dead, John 11:1–46
Jesus' triumphal entry into Jerusalem, Mark 11:1–11
Jesus and the widow's offering, Mark 12:41–44
The Last Supper, Luke 22:7–38
Jesus washes his disciples' feet, John 13:1–17
Jesus at Gethsemane, Matthew 26:36–56
Judas betrays Jesus, Luke 22:1–53
Peter denies Christ, Luke 22:54–62
The crucifixion, Matthew 26:57–27:66
Resurrection and ascension, Luke 24
Holy Spirit at Pentecost, Acts 2
Stephen stoned, Acts 6–7
Paul's conversion, Acts 9:1–31
Peter's escape from prison, Acts 12:1–19
Paul and Silas in prison, Acts 16:16–40

■ MIRACLES OF JESUS
(in biblical order)

■ HEALING OF INDIVIDUALS
Man with leprosy, Matthew 8:1–4; Mark 1:40–44; Luke 5:12–14
Roman centurion's servant, Matthew 8:5–13; Luke 7:1–10
Peter's mother-in-law, Matthew 8:14–17; Mark 1:29–31; Luke 4:38–39
Two demon-possessed men from Gadara, Matthew 8:28–34
Paralysed man, Matthew 9:1–8; Mark 2:1–12; Luke 5:17–26
Two blind men, Matthew 9:27–31
Man mute and possessed, Matthew 9:32–33
Man blind, mute, and possessed, Matthew 12:22
Canaanite woman's daughter, Matthew 15:21–28
Boy with epilepsy, Matthew 17:14–18
Two blind men, Matthew 20:29–34
Man with a shrivelled hand, Matthew 12:9–13; Mark 3:1–5; Luke 6:6–11
Man with an evil spirit, Mark 1:23–26; Luke 4:33–36
Deaf mute, Mark 7:31–37
Blind man, Mark 8:22–26
Bartimaeus, or one blind man, Mark 10:46–52; Luke 18:35–43
Woman with bleeding, Luke 8:43–48
Crippled woman, Luke 13:11–13
Man with dropsy, Luke 14:1–4

Ten men with leprosy, Luke 17:11–19
The high priest's servant, Luke 22:50–51
Royal official's son, John 4:46–54
Man at the pool of Bethesda, John 5:1–9

■ CONTROL OF NATURE
Calming of storm, Matthew 8:22–27; Mark 4:35–41; Luke 8:22–25
Feeding of 5,000, Matthew 14:1–21; Mark 6:35–44; Luke 9:12–17; John 6:5–15
Walking on water, Matthew 14:22–23; Mark 6:45–52; John 6:16–21
Feeding of 4,000, Matthew 15:29–39; Mark 8:1–9
Fish with coin, Matthew 17:24–27
Fig tree withers, Matthew 21:18–22; Mark 11:12–14,20–25
Huge catch of fish, Luke 5:1–11; John 21:1–11
Water into wine, John 2:1–11

■ RAISING THE DEAD
Jairus's daughter, Mark 5:22–42
Widow at Nain's son, Luke 7:11–15
Lazarus, John 11:1–44

■ PARABLES OF JESUS
(in alphabetical order)

Cancelled debts, Luke 7:41–43
Cost of discipleship, Luke 14:28–33
Faithful servant, Luke 12:42–48
Fig tree, Matthew 24:32–35; Mark 13:28–29; Luke 21:29–31
Good Samaritan, Luke 10:30–37
The great banquet, Luke 14:16–24
Growing seed, Mark 4:26–29
Hidden treasure and pearl, Matthew 13:44–46
Honour at a banquet, Luke 14:7–14
Light of the world, Matthew 5:14–15
Lost coin, Luke 15:8–10
Lost sheep, Matthew 18:12–14; Luke 15:3–7
Mustard seed, Matthew 13:31–32
New wine in old wineskins, Matthew 9:16–17; Mark 2:21–22; Luke 5:36–39
Net, Matthew 13:47–50
Obedient servants, Luke 17:7–10
Persistent friend, Luke 11:5–8
Persistent widow, Luke 18:2–8
Pharisee and the tax collector, Luke 18:10–14

Prodigal (or lost) son, Luke 15:11–32
Rich fool, Luke 12:16–21
Rich man and Lazarus, Luke 16:19–31
Sheep and the goats, Matthew 25:31–46
Shrewd manager, Luke 16:1–8
Sower, Matthew 13:1–8,18–23; Mark 4:3–8,14–20; Luke 8:5–8,11–15
Talents, Matthew 25:14–30
Tenants, Matthew 21:33–44; Mark 12:1–12; Luke 20:9–18
Ten minas, Luke 19:11–27
Ten virgins, Matthew 25:1–13
Two sons, Matthew 21:28–31
Unfruitful fig tree, Luke 13:6–9
Unmerciful servant, Matthew 18:23–34
Watchful servants, Luke 12:35–40
Wedding banquet, Matthew 22:2–40
Weeds, Matthew 13:24–30, 36–43
Wise and foolish builders, Matthew 7:24–27; Luke 6:47–49
Workers in the vineyard, Matthew 20:1–16
Yeast, Matthew 13:33; Luke 13:20–21

■ TEACHINGS OF JESUS
(in approximate order of occurrence)

Beatitudes, Matthew 5:1–12
Bread of life, John 6:25–59
Born again, John 3:1–21
Discipleship, Luke 14:25–35
Give to Caesar, Mark 12:13–17
Good shepherd, John 10:1–21
Golden Rule, Luke 6:31
Greatest commandment, Matthew 22:34–40

Living water, John 4:1–26
Lord's prayer, Matthew 6:5–15
Sending out the Twelve, Matthew 10
Sermon on the Mount, Matthew 5–7
Vine and branches, John 15:1–17
The way and the truth and the life, John 14:5–14
Wealth, Matthew 19:16–30
Worry, Luke 12:22–34

■ GLOSSARY OF NON-BIBLICAL PEOPLE AND PLACES

This glossary lists the names and gives brief descriptions of most of the non-biblical people and places cited in Introductions, Insights, and Highlights. We have made every effort to be accurate and comprehensive, while acknowledging the limitations of such a list.

Alcatraz — an island in the San Francisco Bay, former site of a famous U.S. prison (reference can be found on page 1097).

Idi Amin — (1925–) at one time the cruel dictator of the East African nation of Uganda, known for his persecution of Christians (references can be found on pages 759 and 1077).

Roy Chapman Andrews — (1884–1960) U.S. naturalist and explorer, best known for books on his central Asiatic field trips (reference can be found on page 1065).

Armenia — a region and ancient kingdom in south-western Asia, usually regarded as comprising the north-eastern part of Turkey and the Armenian Soviet Socialist Republic (reference can be found on page 1077).

Augustine — (354–430) bishop of Hippo in Roman Africa who was in his day the dominant personality of the Western church (reference can be found on page 976).

Joseph Bayly — American author, educator, and long-time columnist for *Eternity* magazine, known for books such as *The View From a Hearse* and *Psalms of My Life* (reference can be found on page 445).

Bernard of Clairvaux — (1090–1153) the abbot of Clairvaux in France, a mystic and reformer known as a writer of sermons and treatises (reference can be found on page 579).

William Booth — (1829–1912) founder of the Salvation Army, deeply committed to evangelistic and social justice activities (reference can be found on page 483).

Dietrich Bonhoeffer — (1906–1945) German theologian who resisted the Nazi regime and was executed for treason; known for such books as *The Cost of Discipleship* (reference can be found on page 568).

Charles Loring Brace — (1826–1890) U.S. reformer and pioneer social welfare worker, founder and director of the Children's Aid Society of New York City (reference can be found on page 1022).

Buddha — (563–483 B.C.) Indian philosopher, founder of Buddhism (reference can be found on page 1062).

Frederick Buechner — (1926–) ordained Presbyterian minister, called by the *New York Times* the leading clergyman/writer in the U.S., the widely read author of 11 novels and 10 works of non fiction (reference can be found on page 464).

Corrie ten Boom — (1892–1983) well-known writer and speaker, known especially for her book *The Hiding Place*, which tells how her family hid Jews from the Gestapo during the Nazi occupation of Holland (reference can be found on page 388).

John Bunyan — (1628–1688) English Puritan minister, considered to be the greatest literary genius to come out of the Puritan movement (reference can be found on page 1026).

John Calvin — (1509–1564) French-born Genevan theologian and reformer, a leader in the Protestant Reformation of the 16th century (reference can be found on page 1063).

Rachel Carson — (1907–1964) U.S. scientist and writer, a pioneer in the environmentalist movement, especially in her warnings about the effects of pesticides on the environment (reference can be found on page 518).

Bob Champion — famous steeplechase jockey and winner of the Grand National known for his battle against cancer (reference can be found on page 1047).

Chartres — a city in north-western France, site of the great cathedral of Notre Dame (reference can be found on page 82).

G.K. Chesterton — (1874–1936) English journalist and author, outstanding as critic, polemicist, and rhetorical poet (reference can be found on page 976).

Winston Churchill — (1874–1965) British statesman and orator, the great national leader during World War II (references can be found on pages 493, 642, and 809).

Samuel Taylor Coleridge — (1772–1834) English poet, lecturer, journalist, and critic of literature, theology, philosophy, and society (reference can be found on page 1026).

Charles Colson — U.S. government official during Richard Nixon's presidency, convicted for his role in the Watergate scandal; now active as an evangelical Christian author and the founder and leader of a prison ministry (reference can be found on page 955).

Leonardo da Vinci — (1452–1519) Florentine artist and scientist, known for such works as *The Last Supper* and the *Mona Lisa* (references can be found on pages 937 and 1062).

Fedor Mikhailovich Dostoevski — (1821–1881) Russian novelist of international reputation, generally acknowledged as one of the profoundest creative artists of the 19th century, known for such works as *The Brothers Karamazov* (reference can be found on page 1026).

Albert Einstein — (1879–1955) German-born physicist, who emigrated to the United States; creator of the theory of relativity (reference can be found on page 464).

Jacques Ellul — (1912–) French historian and sociologist known for works such as *The Meaning of the City* and *The Technological Society* (reference can be found on page 1105).

Henry Ford — (1863–1947) U.S. industrialist known as the creator of modern mass production, most notably in the assembly-line method of automobile production (reference can be found on page 1022).

Robert Frost — (1874–1963) American poet who used symbols from common life to express the values of rural New England, four-time winner of the Pulitzer Prize (reference can be found on page 789).

Mohandas Karamchand Gandhi — (1869–1948) architect of India's freedom through a non-violent revolution (references can be found on pages 50 and 1062).

Grand Canyon — an immense gorge cut by the Colorado River into the high plateaus of the northern part of Arizona (reference can be found on page 1065).

Alex Haley — African–American author best known for his book *Roots*, the basis of a made-for-television miniseries (reference can be found on page 831).

Georg Friedrich Handel — (1685–1759) German-born composer who spent the majority of his life in England; the greatest English composer of the late baroque era, best known for his oratorio *The Messiah* (reference can be found on page 1102).

Hare Krishna — a religious sect of Hindu character, founded by an Indian holy man; its followers are characterised by rhythmic chanting of the "Hare Krsna" (reference can be found on page 1033).

Paul Harvey — an American radio newscaster known for his unique intonation and special interest stories (reference can be found on page 868).

Herodotus — (5th century B.C.) Greek author of a history of the Persian Wars (references can be found on pages 343, 430, and 432).

Hindus — adherents of Hinduism, a religious system whose precepts govern a vast range of human activity outside the scope of most modern religions; the Republic of India is home to more than 95 percent of all Hindus (reference can be found on page 340).

Hiroshima — a seaport city in south-western Japan, the first city on which the U.S. air force dropped an atomic bomb in 1945 (reference can be found on page 696).

Adolf Hitler — (1889–1945) Austrian-born politician, leader of the Nazi party, who became dictator of Germany in 1933 and led the nation into World War II (references can be found on pages 52, 321, 429, and 759).

Homer — Greek epic poet, regarded as the author of many narrative poems, and according to later tradition, author of the *Iliad and Odyssey* (reference can be found on page 585).

Howard Hughes — (1905–1976) an eccentric American businessman who amassed a fortune but died a miserable recluse (reference can be found on page 570).

Samuel Huntington — (1731–1796) signer of the Declaration of Independence, president of the continental congress (1779–81) and governor of Connecticut (reference can be found on page 241).

Saddam Hussein — (1937–) the cruel president of Iraq, who led his nation into the Persian Gulf War (1991) as a result of Iraq's invasion of Kuwait (references can be found on pages 52, 759, and 787).

Kali — Hindu goddess, usually represented as black with bloody hands, eyes, teeth, and tongue, whose worship appears to be an extension of the widespread mother-goddess cult (reference can be found on page 340).

Ruholla Mussavi Khomeini — (1900–1989) one-time religious leader of Iran, served as the leader of the Shi'ite Muslims, who comprise about 90 percent of Iran's population (reference can be found on page 759).

Derek Kidner — former warden of Tyndale House, Cambridge, and author of numerous Old Testament commentaries and expositions (reference can be found on page 29).

Martin Luther King — (1929–1968) U.S. African-American clergyman who received the 1964 Nobel Peace Prize for his leadership in the non-violent struggle for racial equality in the U.S. (reference can be found on page 809).

Ku Klux Klan — a secret, masked organisation that, after the American Civil War, became the chief instrument of the white underground resistance movement in the south against northerners and African-Americans (reference can be found on page 787).

C.S. Lewis — (1898–1963) Irish-born author who achieved worldwide fame for books on Christian apologetics and other subjects; known for books such as

The Screwtape Letters, *Mere Christianity*, and *The Chronicles of Narnia* (reference can be found on page 934).

Abraham Lincoln — (1809–1865) 16th president of the U.S., led the nation during the Civil War; the issuer of the Emancipation Proclamation, which directly or indirectly led to freedom for hundreds of thousands of slaves (references can be found on pages 50, 901, and 981).

Martin Luther — (1483–1546) German religious leader who began the Protestant Reformation (references can be found on pages 803, 976, 977, 1019, and 1072).

Mao Tse Tung — (1893–1976) Chinese revolutionist and statesman, Communist Party leader and founder of the Chinese communist state (reference can be found on page 759).

Mau Mau — a nativistic cult among the Kikuya tribe in Kenya responsible for a 1950 rebellion directed against the presence of Europeans in Kenya and their ownership of land (reference can be found on page 1077).

Michelangelo — (1475–1564) a native Italian, he is considered to be the greatest painter of the Renaissance and the most famous of all sculptors since the time of the Greeks, best known for his statue of "David" and his four-year painting project in the Sistine Chapel in Rome (reference can be found on page 3).

Bill Miner — (1847–1913) notorious outlaw who terrorised stagecoach runs in the western U.S. (reference can be found on page 174).

John Nash — (1752–1835) architect known for his design of Regent's Street, Regent's Park and Brighton Pavilion (reference can be found on page 1062).

Nazis — followers of the National Socialist party in Germany, a party headed by Adolf Hitler, who took control of the country in 1933 (reference can be found on pages 388 and 787).

John Newton — (1725–1807) one of the leaders of the Evangelical revival in England, a former seafarer who after his conversion to Christianity wrote hymns (most notably *Amazing Grace*) and devotional letters (reference can be found on page 439).

Blaise Pascal — (1623–1662) French mathematician and philosopher, author of a comprehensive treatise on Christian apologetics (reference can be found on page 578).

Louis Pasteur — (1822–1895) French chemist and microbiologist who developed a vaccine for rabies and the method of heat pasteurisation for liquid foods and beverages (reference can be found on page 98).

J.B. Phillips — British pastor who devoted much of his life to writing a fresh translation of the New Testament, publishing the entire New Testament in 1958 and revising it in 1972 (reference can be found on page 950).

Pablo Picasso — (1881–1973) Spanish painter, sculptor, and engraver, the most influential independent artist of the 20th century (reference can be found on page 1105).

Grigori Efimovich Rasputin — (1872–1916) Russian peasant and mystic notorious for his phenomenal sexual appetite and his impact as the voice of the peasantry (reference can be found on page 982).

John D. Rockefeller — (1874–1960) American oil magnate and philanthropist (reference can be found on page 574).

Franklin Delano Roosevelt — (1882–1945) the U.S.'s 32nd president and only president to be re-elected three times, he served during the New Deal era and World War II (reference can be found on page 149).

Dorothy Sayers — (1893–1957) noted English writer of mystery novels, featuring the sleuth Lord Peter Wimsey (reference can be found on page 883).

Scientology, Church of — a quasi-scientific and religious discipline founded by American Ron Hubbard, it formally became the Church of Scientology in 1955 (reference can be found on page 1033).

Ignaz Philipp Semmelweis — (1818–1865) Hungarian physician who had a dramatic influence on the development of knowledge and control of infection, notably through his work in the control of puerperal (childbirth) fever (reference can be found on page 98).

William Shakespeare — (1564–1616) Elizabethan Englishman generally acknowledged as not only England's, but the world's, greatest poet and playwright (references can be found on pages 38, 528, and 585).

Sistine Chapel — the pope's private chapel, built under commission from Sixtus IV; Julius II commissioned Michelangelo to paint its ceiling (reference can be found on page 3).

Aleksandr Solzhenitsyn — (1918–) noted Russian author known for such works as *One Day in the Life of Ivan Denisovich* and *The Gulag Archipelago* (references can be found on pages 446, 955, and 1026).

Josef Stalin — (1879–1953) leader of the Communist party of the Soviet Union, generalissimo and dictator of the USSR and one of the most powerful, complex, and controversial figures in world history (reference can be found on page 759).

Margaret Thatcher — (1925–) first British woman Prime Minister, serving as leader of the Conservative Party 1979–1990 (reference can be found on page 934).

J.R. Tolkien — (1892–1973) English author best known for his imaginative works such as *Lord of the Rings* (reference can be found on page 315).

Katie von Bora — a former nun, she married Protestant Reformer Martin Luther in 1525 (reference can be found on page 1019).

Lech Walesa — champion of the working class in Poland who rallied the nation to independence from Russian influence (reference can be found on page 50).

George Washington — (1732–1799) commander in chief, statesman, and first president of the U.S. (references can be found on pages 50, 241, 254, 981, and 1009).

Charles Wesley — (1707–1788) English clergyman, poet, and hymnwriter who, together with his brother John, started the Methodist movement in the Church of England (reference can be found on page 1037).

John Wesley — (1703–1791) English clergyman and founder of Methodism (references can be found on pages 976 and 1037).

Oscar Wilde — (1854–1900) Irish poet and dramatist, author of such works as *The Importance of Being Earnest* and *The Picture of Dorian Gray* (reference can be found on page 570).

Thomas Wolfe — (1900–1938) American novelist, known for such works as *Look Homeward, Angel* (reference can be found on page 571).

NOTES

NOTES

NOTES

NOTES

NOTES

NOTES

INDEX TO MAPS

Many places in the Bible were known by different names at different times or in different languages. Alternative names are given in brackets after the main entries. Place names for which the geographical locations are uncertain are followed by a question mark.

Each place name in the index is followed by a map number and a letter. On the map referred to, the letter can be found at the top of the map frame. The place can be found vertically below the letter.

Map 1   The World of the Bible

© Hodder & Stoughton

| a | b | c | d | e | f | g | h | i | j | k | l | m | n | o | p | q |

45°N

15°E

30°E

45°E

60°E

45°N

(Aral Sea)

(Caspian Sea)

Ashkenaz (Scythians?)

Gomer
(Cimmerians?)

(Black Sea)

MEDIA

Ecbatana

Zagros Mountains

Lake
Urmia

PERSIA

Persepolis

Persian Gulf

Lake Van

ASSYRIA

Nineveh

Tigris

Elam

Halys

HITTITE EMPIRE

(Anatolia) Mountains

Taurus Mountains

MITANNI

Haran

Mesopotamia

Euphrates

Mari

BABYLONIA

Babylon

Ebla

Damascus

Aram

Ugarit

Lebanon

Jerusalem

Canaan

Dead Sea

Cyprus

Troy

Greece

Athens

Sparta

Crete

MACEDONIA

Mediterranean Sea (The Great Sea)

Libya

Sinai?

Memphis

(Lower)

EGYPT

(Upper)

Nile

Pathros

Thebes
(No)

Svene

Cush
(Ethiopia)

A r a b i a

Red   Sea

Ophir?

Joktan

Ophir?

Sheba?

Uzal

Timna

Hazarmaveth

Eden

Italy

Rome

Sardinia

Sicily

Tropic of Cancer

30°N

30°N

15°N

15°N

30°E

60°E

Scale

0   200   400   600 miles

0   200   400   600   800 kilometres

Martha's Vineyard,
USA – same scale

Isle of Wight, UK –
same scale

Map 2   The World of the Old Testament

a	b	c	d	e	f	g	h	i	j	k

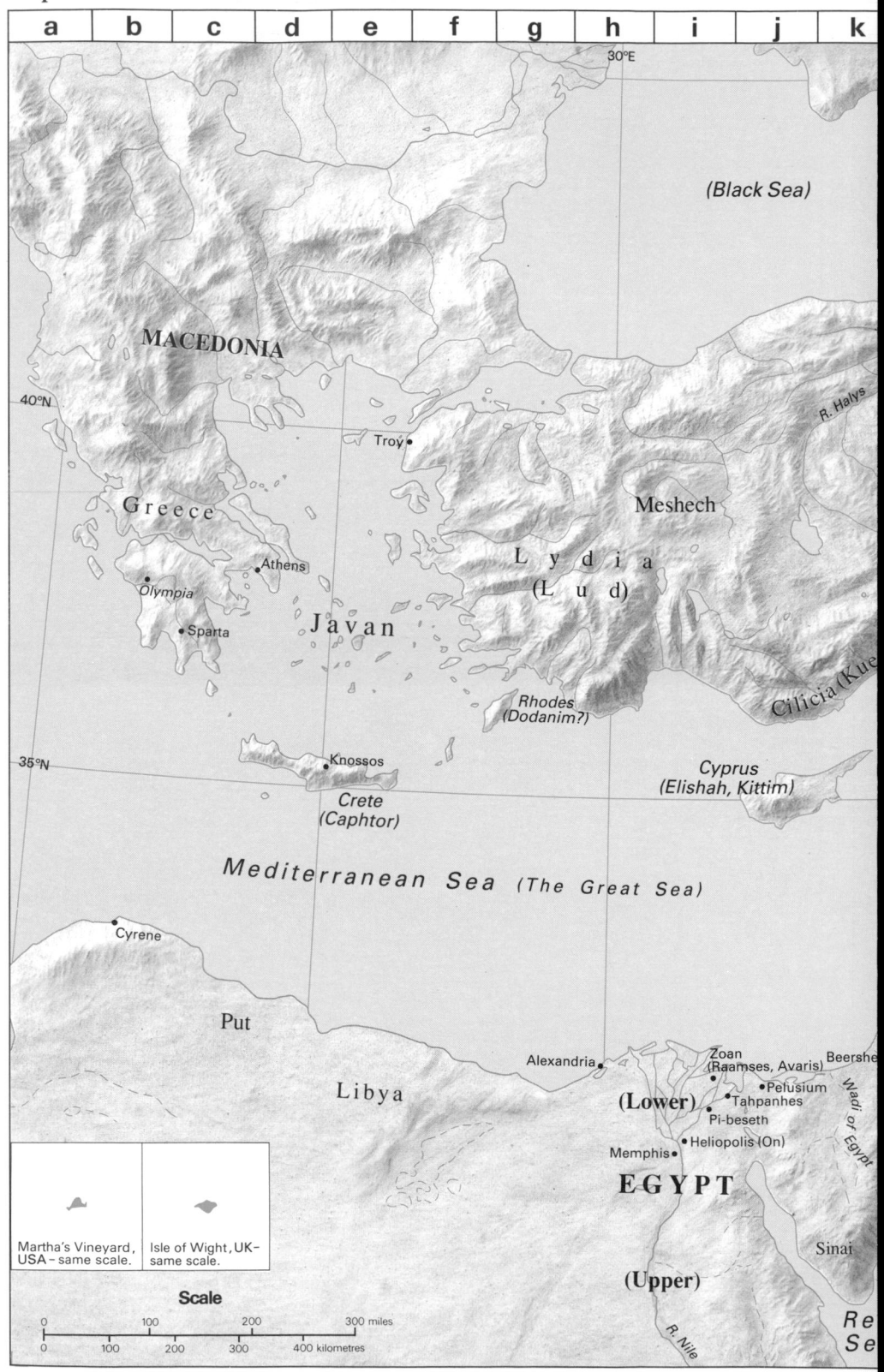

30°E

(Black Sea)

MACEDONIA

40°N

Troy •

G r e e c e

Athens •

• Olympia

• Sparta

Meshech

L y d i a
(L u d)

J a v a n

Rhodes
(Dodanim?)

35°N

Knossos •

Cyprus
(Elishah, Kittim)

Crete
(Caphtor)

Cilicia (Kue

R. Halys

M e d i t e r r a n e a n   S e a   *(The Great Sea)*

• Cyrene

Put

Alexandria •

Zoan
(Raamses, Avaris)   Beershe

• Pelusium

L i b y a

(Lower) • • Tahpanhes

Pi-beseth •

• Heliopolis (On)

Memphis •

Wadi of Egypt

E G Y P T

Sinai

(Upper)

Re
Se

R. Nile

Martha's Vineyard, USA – same scale.	Isle of Wight, UK – same scale.

Scale

0	100	200	300 miles

0	100	200	300	400 kilometres

l　m　n　o　p　q　r　s　t　u　v

Ashkenaz

50°E

Gomer

40°N

Ararat

ubal

Musri

•Togarmah

Minni

Greater Zab

MEDIA
(Madai)

Issus

•Haran

Carchemish

•Gozan

Nineveh•　Calah
(Nimrud)

Calno
•Arpad

Paddan Aram

ASSYRIA

alakh

Beth-eden

R. Orontes

Tiphsah

R. Euphrates

Asshur•　Lesser Zab

•Nuzi

•Ecbatana

Syria

Rezeph

R. Tigris

arit
s Shamra)

•Hamath

rvad
polis

•Kadesh

•Tadmor
(Palmyra)

•Mari

blos

•Riblah

ARAM (Syria)

Akkad

Pekod

Elam

on

•Damascus

Babylon•

BABYLONIA

Sumer
(Shinar)

Susa
•

re

•Dan

Nippur •

Hauran

lerusalem

(Erech) Uruk •
Larsa (Ellasar)　•Ur

30°N

Nebaioth

Kedar

ra

Edom (Seir)

•Bozrah

•Dumah

•Teman?

Buz

Ephah

A　r　a　b　i　a

•Tema

•Dedan

© Hodder & Stoughton

ion Geber

Map 3 Abraham to Joseph

| a | b | c | d | e | f | g | h | i | j | k |

36°30'E · 36°E · El Paran · Midian 35°30'E · 35°E · Kadesh 34°30'E
Beer Lahai Roi

Edom
(Seir)

To Egypt

31°N

↓ N

North on this map
is at the bottom to
reflect the direction
of Abraham's approach.

Hazezon-tamar? · The Negev

Zoar · Possible sites of
Valley of Siddim,
Sodom, Gomorrah,
Admah, Zeboiim

Not covered
with water in
ancient times.

Moab

Beersheba

R. Arnon

Gerar?

Shaveh/Kiriathaim

Salt
Sea

31°30'N

Hebron
Mamre

Hill Country of Judah

The Shephelah

Plain of Philistia

Bethlehem

Jerusalem

32°N

Ai · Bethel (Luz)

Hill Country

of Ephraim

The Great Sea

The Arabah

Mahanaim · R. Jabbok
Penuel

Shechem

Ammon

The Desert

Gilead

River Jordan

Dothan

32°30'N

Ham

The Great Plain

Carmel

R. Yarmuk

Lower
Galilee

Ashtaroth
Karnaim

Sea of
Chinnereth

Upper
Galilee

33°N

Hazor

Lake Huleh

Abraham's Journeys

Scale

0 · 10 · 20 · 30 miles
0 · 10 · 20 · 30 · 40 kilometres

Dan

Tyre

Mt Hermon

Aram

Martha's Vineyard, USA–
same scale.

Isle of Wight, UK–
same scale.

33°30'N

Damascus

Sidon

Paddan
Aram · Haran

© Hodder & Stoughton

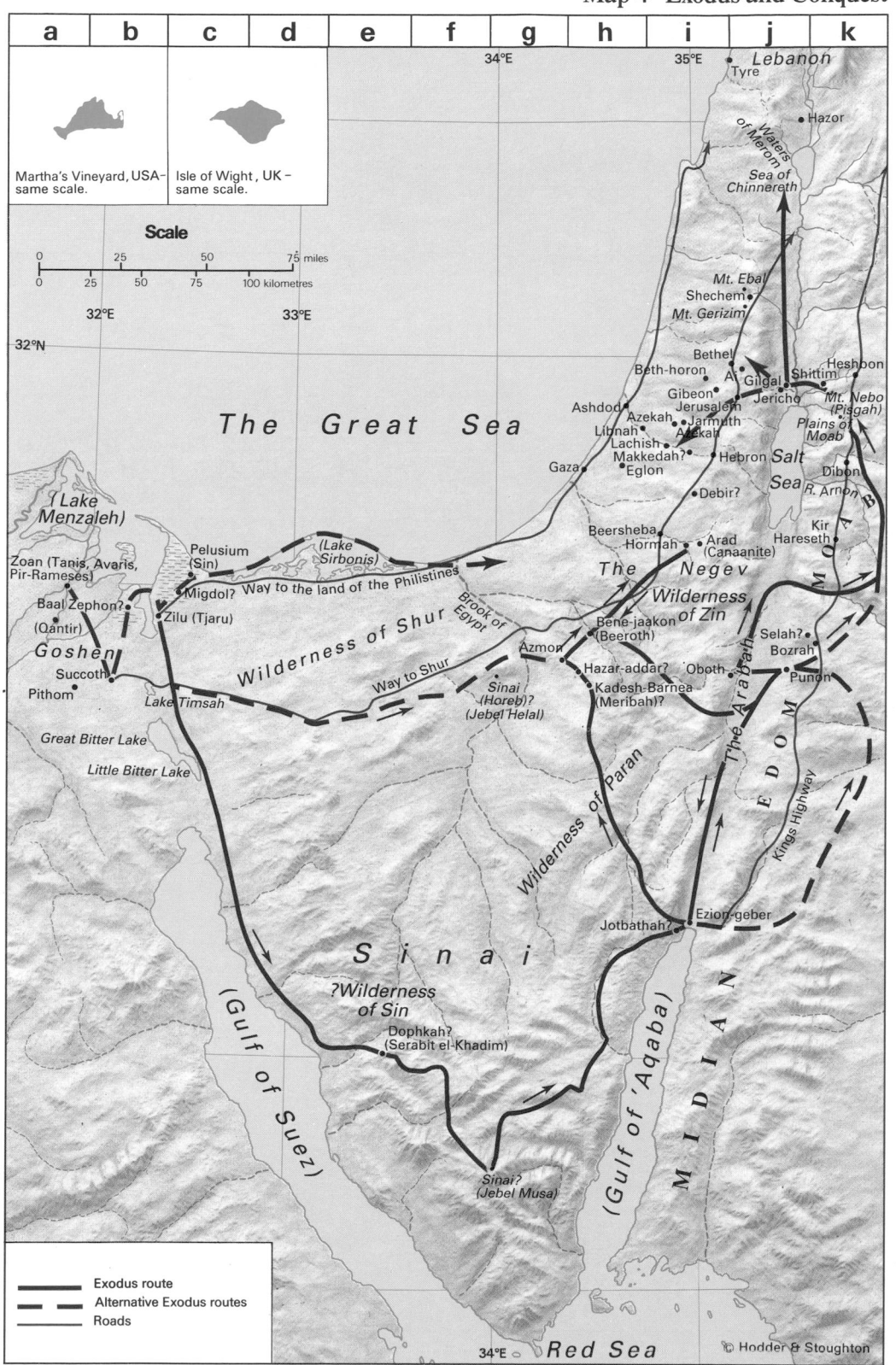

Map 4 Exodus and Conquest

Map 5　Palestine before the Monarchy

Damascus

Mt. Hermon

Mt. Lebanon

Argob

Geshur

Dan (Laish)

DAN

Kedesh

Hazor

Merom

Sea of
Galilee
(Chinnereth)

R. Yarmuk

NAPHTALI

Havvoth-jair

M
A
N
A
S
S
E
H

Kamon

Tob

Ramoth Gilead

Abel-meholah?

Jabesh-gilead

Tabbath?

Sidon

R. Leontes

Ahlab

Tyre

ASHER

Rehob

Aphek

Bethlehem

ZEBULUN

R. Kishon

Harosheth
ha-goiim

Achzib
(Helbah)

Acco

Mt. Tabor

ISSACHAR

Beth-shan

Megiddo

Taanach

Mt.
Gilboa

Ibleam

Thebez

MANASSEH

Dor

33°30'N

33°N

32°30'N

The

Scale

0   10   20   30 miles

0   10   20   30   40 kilometres

Martha's Vineyard, USA –
same scale.

Isle of Wight, UK –
same scale.

a b c d e f g h i j k l m n o p q

Great
Sea

The Desert

Succoth?
Penuel
R. Jabbok
GAD
Jogbebah
Rabbah

Heshbon
Jahaz
REUBEN
Dibon
Aroer
R. Arnon

Brook Zered

Edom

Salt Sea

Gilgal
Jericho

Pirathon
Mt. Gerizim
Arumah?
Hill Country
Lebonah
Shiloh
EPHRAIM
of Ephraim
Ophrah?
Bethel (Luz)
Beth-horon Mizpah Michmash
Timnah- B E N J A M I N
serah Ramah Geba
Shaalbim Gibeah
Aphek Ramathaim- Gezer Aijalon Kiriath-jearim (Baalah)
zophim Jerusalem
(D A N) Zorah Eshtaol
Valley of Sorek V. Timnah Beth-shemesh Bethlehem
Ekron Azekah JUDAH
Ashdod of Elah Socoh
Gath? Hebron

Arad

Debir?

Ashkelon
Debir?
SIMEON
Beersheba Hormah?
Gaza Aroer

Philistine

Tamar
(City of Palms?)

Edom

The Negev

32°N

31°30N

31°N

34°30E   35°E   35°30E   36°E   36°30E

© Hodder & Stoughton

Map 6   The Kingdoms of Israel and Judah

Zobah
ARAM
• Damascus
R. Pharpar
R. Abana
Mt. Hermon
Lebo Hamath
Beth Rehob
Ijon
Sidon
Lebanon
Zarephath
Tyre
Aphek
R. Kishon
Great Plain
Mt. Carmel
Jokn(m)eam
Abel
beth-maacah
Dan
Maacah
Janoah
Kedesh
Hazor
Sea of
Chinnereth
Galilee
Mt. Tabor
Endor
Shunem
Jezreel
Mt. Gilboa
Megiddo
Taanach
Dothan
Ibleam
Samaria
Tirzah
Geshur
Bashan
Argob
Karnaim
Helam?
Tob
Ramoth-gilead
Arbel (Irbid)
Rogelim
Abel-meholah
Brook
Cherith
Jabesh-
gilead
Tishbe
Lo-debar
Beth-shan
R. Yarmuk
River Jordan
ISRAEL
Judah
The

33°30′N
33°N
32°30′N

Scale

0   10   20   30 miles
0   10   20   30   40 kilometres

Martha's Vineyard, USA–
same scale.

Isle of Wight, UK –
same scale.

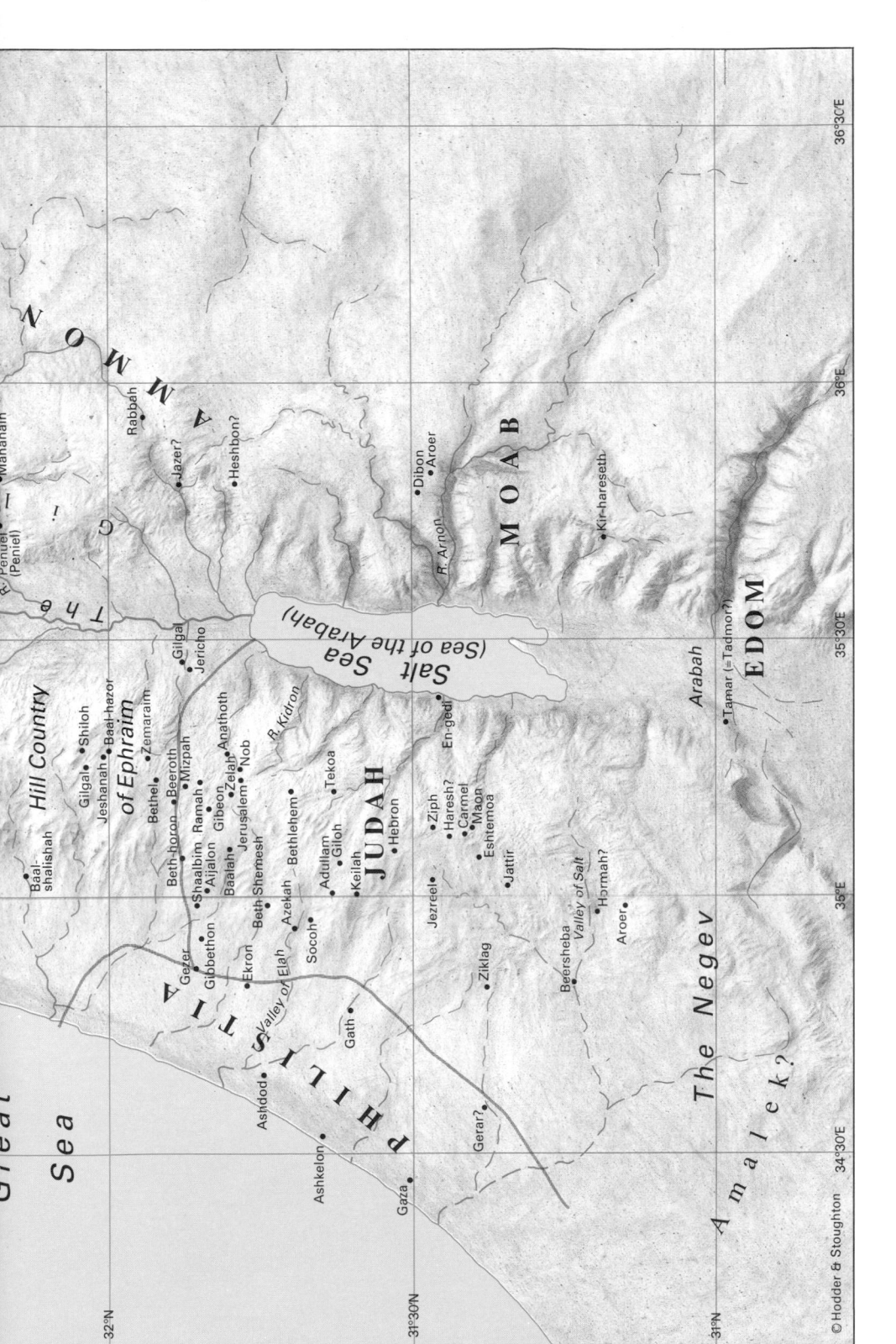

Great Sea

Ashkelon

Gaza

PHILISTIA

Ashdod

Gerar?

Gath

Ekron

Gibbethon

Gezer

Valley of Elah

Socoh

Azekah

Beth Shemesh

Baalah

Beth-horon

Shaalbim
Ramah

Aijalon

Gibeon
Zelah
Jerusalem

Mizpah

Beeroth

Bethel

Baal-hazor

Zemaraim

Shiloh

Jeshanah

Gilgal

Baal-shalishah

Hill Country
of Ephraim

Gilgal

Jericho

R. Kidron

Anathoth

Nob

Adullam

Bethlehem

Giloh

Keilah

Tekoa

Hebron

JUDAH

Ziph

Haresh?
Carmel
Maon
Eshtemoa

Jattir

En-gedi

Salt Sea
(Sea of the Arabah)

Ziklag

Beersheba
Valley of Salt

Hormah?

Aroer

Jezreel?

The Negev

A m a l e k ?

Arabah

Tamar (= Tadmor?)

EDOM

Dibon
Aroer

R. Arnon

M O A B

Kir-hareseth

Heshbon?

Jazer?

Rabbah

A M M O N

G i l e a d

The

Penuel (Peniel)

Mahanaim

31°N
31°30N
32°N

34°30E
35°E
35°30E
36°E
36°30E

© Hodder & Stoughton

Map 7 Judah before and after the Exile

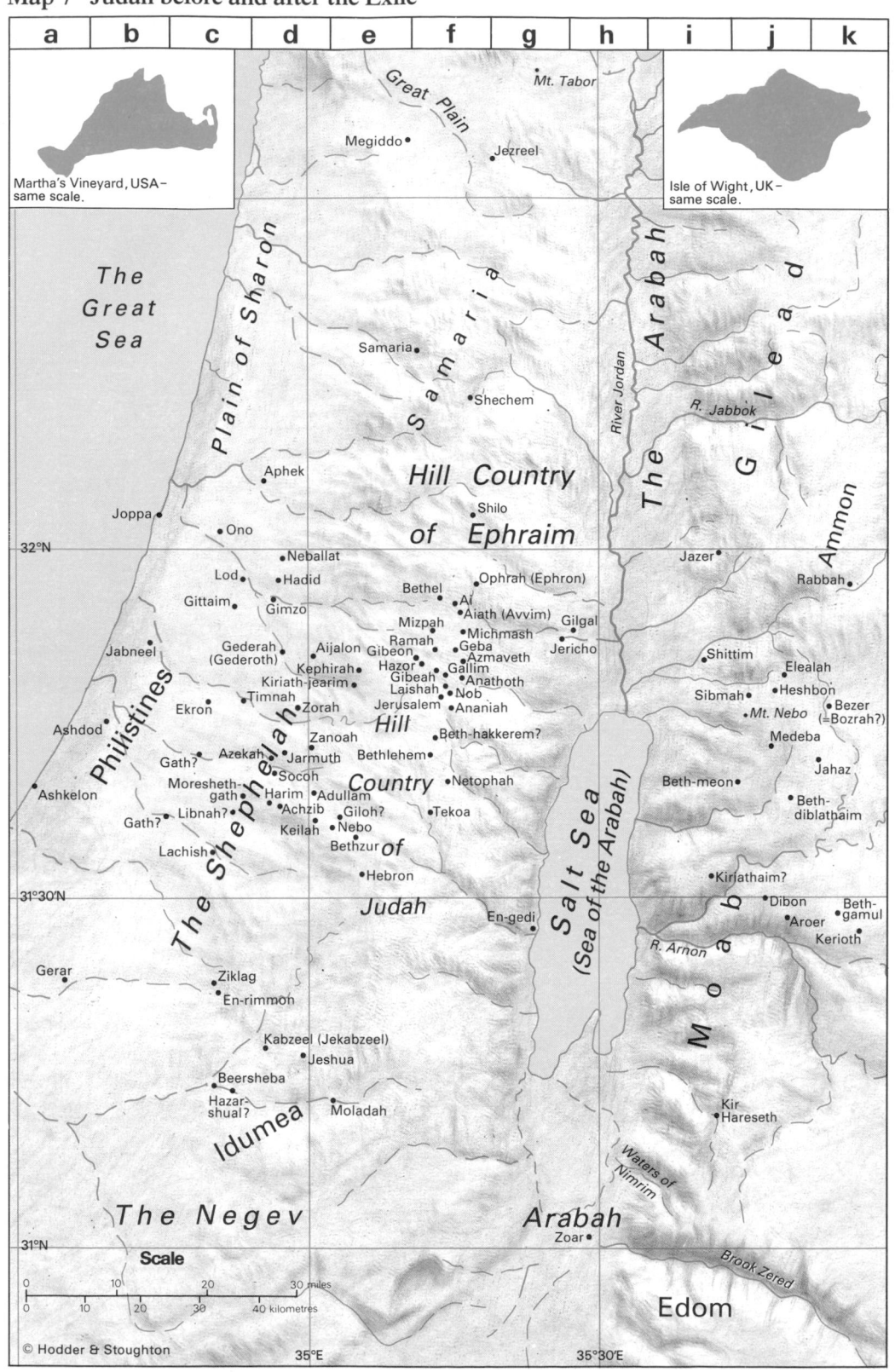

| a | b | c | d | e | f | g | h | i | j | k |

Martha's Vineyard, USA – same scale.

Isle of Wight, UK – same scale.

Great Plain

Mt. Tabor

Megiddo

Jezreel

The Great Sea

Plain of Sharon

Samaria

Samaria

Shechem

River Jordan

The Arabah

R. Jabbok

The Gilead

Ammon

Aphek

Hill Country

Shilo

of Ephraim

Joppa

Ono

32°N

Neballat

Lod

Hadid

Bethel

Ophrah (Ephron)

Jazer

Rabbah

Gittaim

Gimzo

Ai

Aiath (Avvim)

Mizpah

Michmash

Gilgal

Jabneel

Gederah (Gederoth)

Aijalon

Gibeon

Ramah

Geba

Azmaveth

Jericho

Shittim

Elealah

Kephirah

Hazor

Gibeah

Gallim

Anathoth

Sibmah

Heshbon

Kiriath-jearim

Laishah

Nob

Mt. Nebo

Bezer (=Bozrah?)

Ekron

Timnah

Zorah

Jerusalem

Ananiah

Medeba

Ashdod

Hill

Zanoah

Beth-hakkerem?

Gath?

Azekah

Jarmuth

Bethlehem

Country

Netophah

Beth-meon

Jahaz

Ashkelon

Moresheth-gath

Harim

Adullam

Giloh?

Tekoa

Beth-diblathaim

Gath?

Libnah?

Achzib

of

Keilah

Nebo

Lachish

Bethzur

Judah

Kiriathaim?

Hebron

Dibon

Beth-gamul

31°30′N

Aroer

Kerioth

En-gedi

R. Arnon

Moab

Gerar

Ziklag

Salt Sea (Sea of the Arabah)

En-rimmon

Kabzeel (Jekabzeel)

Jeshua

Beersheba

Hazar-shual?

Moladah

Idumea

Kir Hareseth

The Negev

Arabah

Waters of Nimrim

Zoar

31°N

Scale

| 0 | 10 | 20 | 30 miles |

| 0 | 10 | 20 | 30 | 40 kilometres |

© Hodder & Stoughton

35°E

35°30′E

Brook Zered

Edom

Philistines

The Shephelah

Map 8 Jerusalem in Old Testament Times

| a | b | c | d | e | f | g | h | i | j | k |

Scale

0   100   200   300 m
0   100   200   300 yds

Present area of Haram es Sharif
(Dome of the Rock)

Buildings

City of David

Walls of Solomon and later

Old Gate?

Tower of
the Hundred?

Sheep Gate?

Fish Gate?

Tower of Hananel?

Temple

8th century
walls

=?=

Tower of
the Ovens?

Palace

Solomon's
additions?

Nehemiah's Wall

8th century
walls

Hezekiah's Tunnel

Gihon Spring

City
of
David
(Ophel)
Zion

Old Conduit

K
i
d
r
o
n

V
a
l
l
e
y

(Tyropoeon) Cheesemaker valley

8th century (?)
and later walls

H
i
n
n
o
m

v
a
l
l
e
y

(T o p h e t h ?)

Upper pool

Dung
gate?

Fountain Gate?

8th century walls(?)

Lower pool

Dung Gate?/Valley Gate?

Dung gate?

En Rogel
Spring

Metres

—760

—700

—640

© Hodder & Stoughton

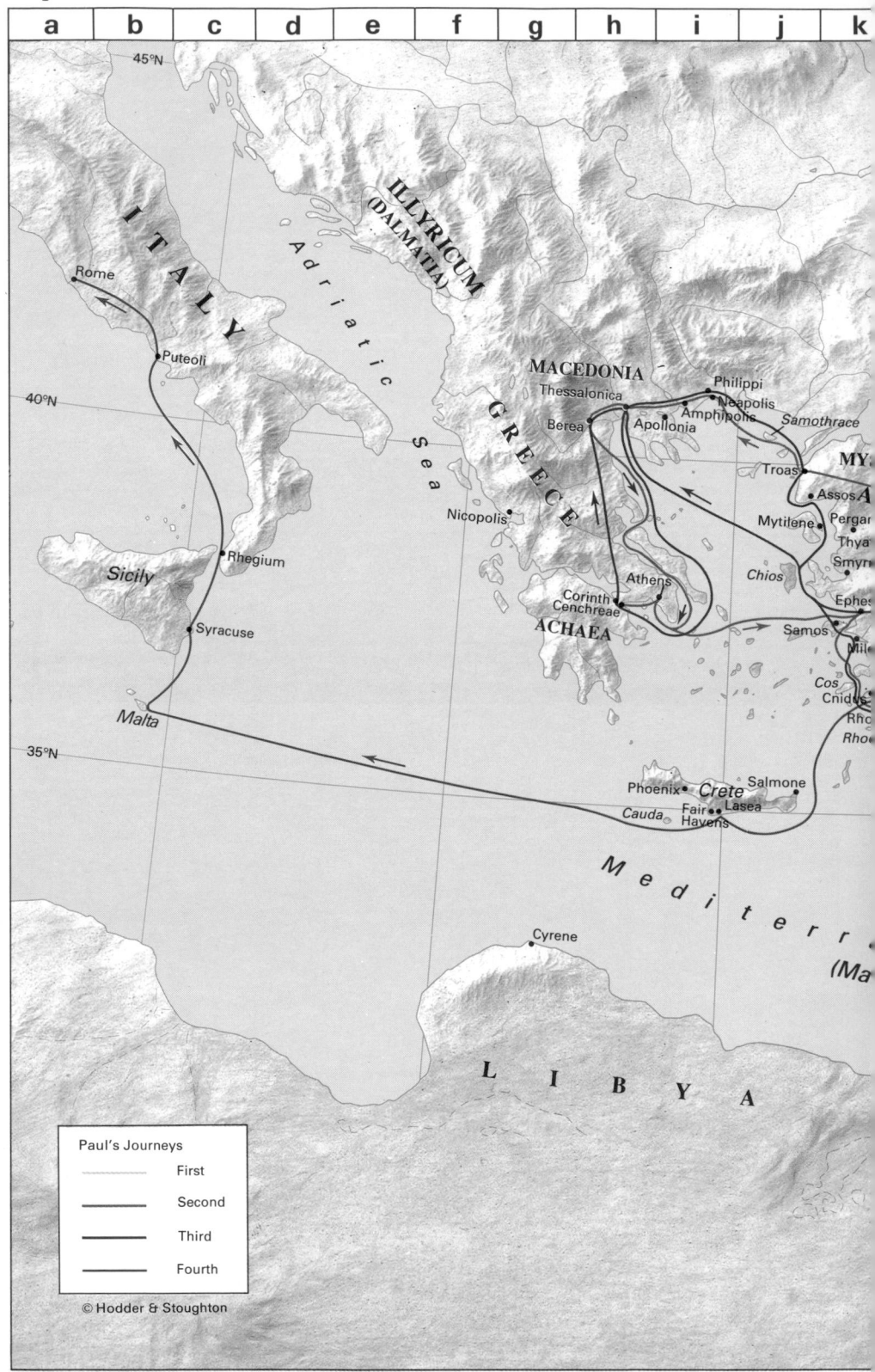

Map 9 The World of the New Testament

| a | b | c | d | e | f | g | h | i | j | k |

45°N

ITALY

ILLYRICUM
(DALMATIA)

Adriatic Sea

Rome

Puteoli

40°N

MACEDONIA
Thessalonica
Berea

Philippi
Neapolis
Amphipolis
Apollonia

Samothrace

GREECE

Troas

MY

Assos

A

Nicopolis

Mytilene

Pergar

Thya

Rhegium

Sicily

Chios

Smyr

Athens

Ephes

Syracuse

Corinth
Cenchreae

ACHAEA

Samos

Mile

Malta

Cos
Cnidus

Rho

Rho

35°N

Salmone

Phoenix
Cauda

Crete
Fair
Havens

Lasea

Mediterr

(Ma

Cyrene

L I B Y A

Paul's Journeys

....	First
———	Second
———	Third
———	Fourth

© Hodder & Stoughton

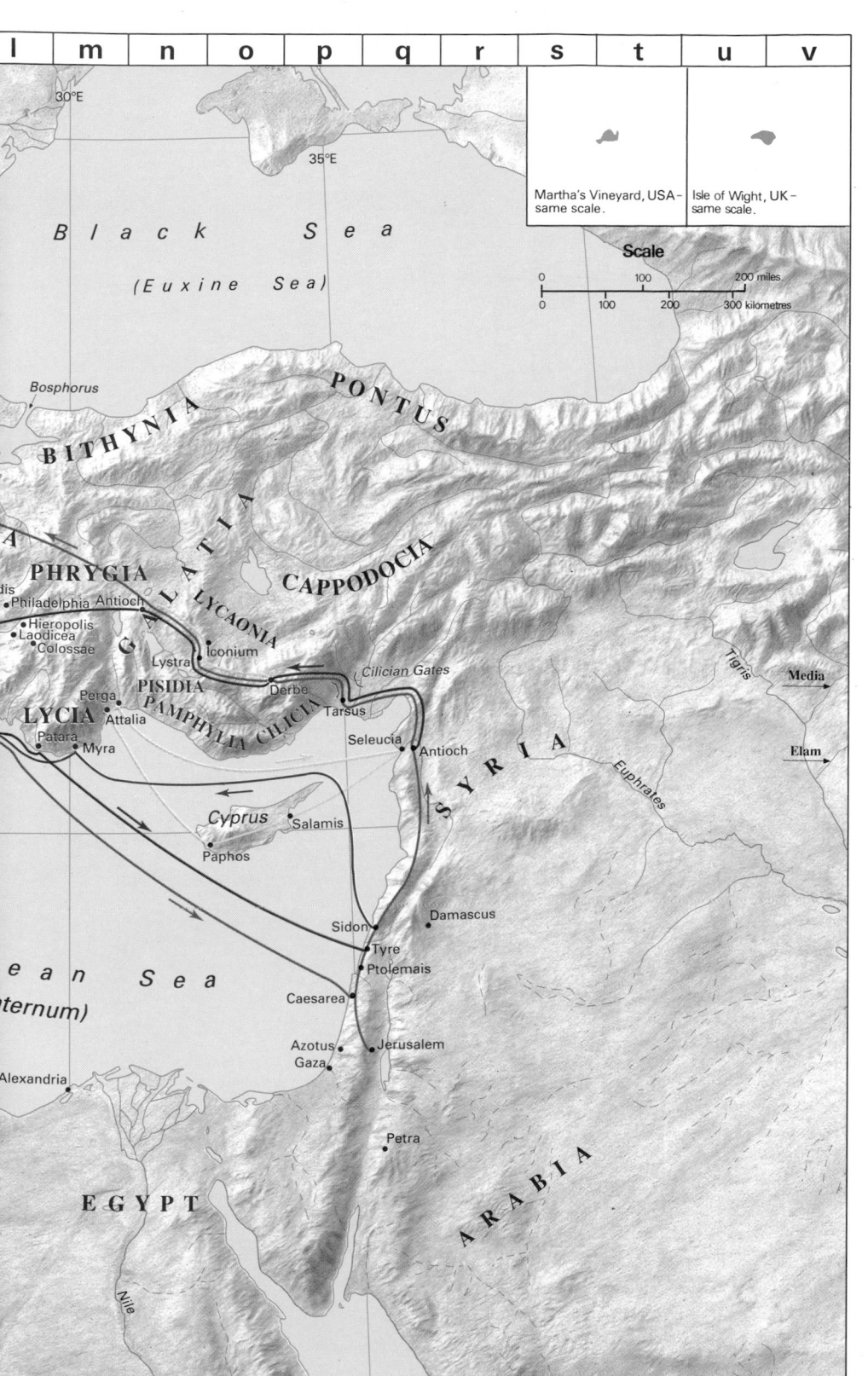

30°E

35°E

Martha's Vineyard, USA –
same scale.

Isle of Wight, UK –
same scale.

Scale

| 0 | | 100 | | 200 miles |

| 0 | 100 | 200 | 300 kilometres |

B l a c k   S e a

(E u x i n e   S e a)

Bosphorus

BITHYNIA

PONTUS

GALATIA

PHRYGIA

LYCAONIA

CAPPODOCIA

dis

Philadelphia

Antioch

Hieropolis

Laodicea

Colossae

Lystra

Iconium

Cilician Gates

Derbe

PISIDIA

Perga

PAMPHYLIA

CILICIA

Tarsus

LYCIA

Attalia

Seleucia

Patara

Myra

Antioch

S Y R I A

Tigris

Media

Elam

Euphrates

Cyprus

Salamis

Paphos

Damascus

e a n   S e a

Sidon

Tyre

(nternum)

Ptolemais

Caesarea

Azotus

Jerusalem

Gaza

Alexandria

Petra

A R A B I A

E G Y P T

Nile

Map 10   Palestine in New Testament Times

Scale

	0		10		20		30 miles
0		10		20		30	40 kilometres

Martha's Vineyard, USA – same scale.

Isle of Wight, UK – same scale.

33°30'N

33'N

32°30'N

Damascus

Abilene

Mt. Hermon

PROVINCE OF SYRIA

Caesarea Philippi (Paneas)

Iturea

Sidon

Phoenicia

Zarephath

Tyre

TETRARCHY OF PHILIP

Trachonitis

Batanaea

Gaulanitis

L. Huleh (Semechonitis)

Chorazin

Bethsaida

Capernaum

Gennesaret

Sea of Galilee (Genneserat, Tiberias)

Gergesa?

Hippos

Tiberias

Taricheae (Magadan)

Cana?

Nazareth

Mt. Tabor

Nain?

R. Yarmuk

R. Gadara

DECAPOLIS

Gerasa

Scythopolis

Pella

Salim?

Aenon?

AN

GALILEE

Galilee

Cana?

Sepphoris

The Great Plain (Esdraelon)

R. Kishon

Mt. Carmel

Ptolemais

Caesarea

Samaria

The